Cadillac
America's Luxury Car
Robert C. Ackerson

TAB TAB BOOKS Inc.
Blue Ridge Summit, PA

Dedication

This book is dedicated to my brother, Wallace Ackerson, in appreciation for his many years of encouragement and support of my love of American automobiles.

FIRST EDITION
FIRST PRINTING

Copyright © 1988 by TAB BOOKS Inc.
Printed in the United States of America

Library of Congress Cataloging in Publication Data

Ackerson, Robert C.
    Cadillac—America's luxury car.

    Includes index.
    1. Cadillac automobile—History. I. Title.
TL215.C27A25   1988   629.2'222   88-2128
ISBN 0-8306-9120-0

TAB BOOKS Inc. offers software for
sale. For information and a catalog,
please contact TAB Software Department,
Blue Ridge Summit, PA 17294-0850.

Questions regarding the content of this book
should be addressed to:

Reader Inquiry Branch
TAB BOOKS Inc.
Blue Ridge Summit, PA 17294-0214

Edited by Lonnie Dalrymple.
Designed by Suzanne L. Cheatle.

Contents

Preface

AS WORK ON THIS HISTORY of Cadillac was completed, Cadillac was embarking on one of its most important projects; the launching of the Allante. As historic as that event is, it might, in the future, be less important than the restructuring of Cadillac within the General Motors organization. In essence, Cadillac in early 1987 was regaining control over many aspects of engineering and manufacturing that it had lost in 1984. At that time, it seemed to make sense to increase the efficiency of those activities by centralizing them under the Buick-Oldsmobile-Cadillac and Chevrolet-Pontiac-Canada umbrellas.

Three years later, however, the need for Cadillac to underscore its status as not only America's finest automobile, but also its most distinctive, mandated a step back to an era when Cadillac, in a very intimate way, was in charge of its own destiny.

For Cadillac historians, this move is the right one at the right time. Cadillac's history, unequaled among American cars, is one filled with dramatic steps forward, both in terms of styling and design, that set the pace for the entire industry. That heritage will now set the pace for Cadillacs in the remaining years of the twentieth century and beyond.

Acknowledgments

I'VE LONG SUSPECTED that a measurement of the quality of an automobile can be determined by the caliber of the men and women who collect, restore, and staff those lonely ramparts reserved for car-club officers. Like the car that binds them together, members of the Albany, New York, Cadillac-La Salle Club, who gave so willingly of their talents and time to this book, are the "Standard of the World." In particular, heartfelt appreciation goes to Jackie and Dan O'Roucke, Ellis and Bev Gershen, and Chris and Mary Jo Clausen.

For their assistance in providing photographs and valuable information, I wish to thank John Gunnell, editor of *Old Cars Weekly*; Floyd Joliet of the General Motors design staff; and members of Cadillac's public relations department, including its director, Sherie Perelli; Norb Barthos; and especially Don Hederich, who extended many courtesies.

For their help in giving me access to the library resources of the State University of New York, special thanks goes to Dr. Clifford Craven, president of the State University College at Oneonta, New York; his secretary, Bonnie Wood; and David Lasher, vice-president for College Relations and Development.

Patiently processing my many requests for information were Andrea Gerberg of the Milne Library staff and Gladys Smith, librarian of the Schenevus Community Library. Equally helpful was Louis Haverson, curator of the automotive section at the Free Library of Philadelphia.

Providing more help then he ever imagined was my close friend and fellow car enthusiast, Dick Wood. To my wife, Grace, and daughters, Cindy, Lynn, and Susan is extended a sincere thanks for their help and encouragement during this book's development.

All of these people gave willingly of their time and talent and, while not responsible for any shortcomings of this book, most certainly share in its strengths. May their tribe increase.

Introduction

THIS BOOK depicts the history of one of America's most distinguished marques: a car recognized internationally as America's "Standard For The World."

Cadillac entered the postwar era with a reputation for performance, engineering, and quality based on nearly a half-century of achievements in those areas. In 1908, Cadillac startled the motoring world when, after three of its cars were completely dismantled and their parts mixed, three "new" cars were assembled from the resulting conglomeration of parts at England's famous Brooklands track. On the heel of this demonstration of Cadillac manufacturing expertise came two more examples that Cadillacs were also durable, reliable, and fast automobiles. After the cars were reassembled, they completed a 500-mile run at full throttle around the Brooklands track at 34 mph. Subsequently, one of the trio competed in the 2,000-mile Royal Automobile Club trial where it won a silver cup.

As a result of the standardization demonstration, Cadillac was presented the Dewar Trophy, England's most prestigious award for technical achievement. In 1913, Cadillac became the first car to receive a second Dewar Trophy. This time it was for the self starter whose principal designer was Charles Kettering. This master engineer, one of the prime architects of General Motors' rise to industrial power, would have a great influence over Cadillac history for many years.

Cadillac's next great leap forward was the introduction of its first V-8 engine in 1914. Then came what is regarded as one of the most important events of the classic era, the introduction of the V-16 engine in 1930. Although the aura of this engine, as well as that of its V-12 derivative, was dimmed by the consequences of the Great Depression, it was one of the greatest examples of Cadillac's ability to design and produce an engine equal to or better than Europe's best at a far lower price. This point was made very clear by comparison tests conducted by Rolls-Royce between the Cadillac V-16 and the contemporary Rolls-Royce Phantom II.

When production resumed in late 1945, Cadillac, like other manufacturers, was confined to an abbreviated product line. But these constraints were soon left behind; and in 1948 and 1949, Cadillac startled its opposition with back-to-back styling and engineering achievements.

Sad to say, most Cadillac histories, while detailing in great depth Cadillac's postwar achievements and glories, seem to dismiss the decades since the war as of little importance. This oversight creates the false impression— buoyed by many critics who seem intent on distorting, rather than reporting, Cadillac history—that contemporary Cadillacs are somehow less worthy of analysis than earlier examples. Furthermore, this approach implies that much of automotive history since 1945 lacks the appeal of earlier years. All of this is patently false. Automotive history is, if anything, more exciting than ever and at its center are cars such as the modern Cadillacs. There's no doubt that this view will become prevalent as the current level of intense international competition, stimulating new directions of design and engineering, continues to be manifested in the form of new models and technical innovations.

By focusing exclusively on the years since 1946, this volume brings, both for the general reader and the inveterate Cadillac enthusiast, that time span into perspective. Since it also provides the reader with an overview of Cadillac's competitors, a clear picture emerges both of Cadillac's response to moves by other luxury-car makers and the impact of its achievements.

Cadillac has not been, as we've noted, without its critics. Indeed in recent years, it has become a sine qua non of many automotive journalists to approach any examination of Cadillac with an ingrained prejudice. This may well be "The Penalty of Leadership" for Cadillac. But let the point be clearly made: Cadillac's record of innovation, whether it be measured by technical, marketing, or styling, ranks among the world's best. Those achievements are the reason for this book.

Prologue

Prewar Positioning and Postwar Stratagems

THE FIRST POSTWAR CADILLAC, a Series Sixty-One four-door sedan, left the assembly line at East Grand Boulevard on October 17, 1945. Its departure set in motion four decades of automotive production that would redefine and underscore Cadillac's venerable "Standard of the World" slogan. Between that date and February 4, 1942, when its final 1942 model had been built, Cadillac, like the rest of the American automobile industry, had committed its plant facilities to the production of war material. In Cadillac's case, this meant the manufacture of M-5 and M-24 light tanks, powered by two Cadillac V-8 engines and utilizing a Hydra-Matic transmission; the M-8 howitzer carriage; and the M-19 anti-aircraft weapon. In addition, Cadillac also contributed to the design and production of Allison aircraft engines.

Well before the final M-24 tank was completed on August 24, 1945, General Motors made public plans for a major expansion of its industrial base as soon as the war came to a close. For example, General Motors President Charles E. Wilson told the House Committee on Postwar Planning that GM wanted to add 10 more plants to the 102 it currently had at a cost of $5 million. The role that Cadillac would play in GM's plans to extend its share of the automobile market was outlined by Cadillac general manager Nicholas Dreystadt on September 22, 1945, when announcing the 1946 model, he stated: "The Cadillac division of General Motors will aim at the production and sale of 100,000 passenger cars in the first full year of production." Less than two weeks later at a New York City meeting with Cadillac distributors, he revealed that the production goal for 1947 had been set at 125,000 units.

That Cadillac did not reach the first goal until the 1950 calendar year, when 110,535 cars were built, nor the latter until 1955, doesn't detract from the significance of Dreystadt's comments, for among America's prestige automobiles, Cadillac was in the strongest position to capture the major share of the expanding market for high-priced automobiles. The

base of this strength, while deeply rooted in Cadillac history, had become apparent in the immediate prewar years.

The Great Depression decimated the ranks of American luxury-car manufacturers, leaving the survivors searching for new means to continue. Packard, while by no means abandoning its expensive senior series, introduced the One-Twenty series in 1935 with a starting price for the Business Coupe of $980. For the 1937 model year, Packard moved further afield from its traditional market with the Packard Six models whose prices began at $795. The result on Packard sales was spectacular. In 1937, the senior series Packard output was just 7,093, while respective production figures of the Packard Six and Packard One-Twenty were 65,400 and 50,100.

Lincoln followed a similar, but certainly not identical pattern of survival by unveiling the Lincoln-Zephyr in 1936. The Zephyr was immediately regarded as a styling triumph, representing a dramatic dash into the future, while the new Packards remained true to previous Packard appearances. Moreover, the Lincoln-Zephyr was not inexpensive. Only two models, a two-door and a four-door sedan, were initially offered at $1,275 and $1,320 respectively. But sales of the Zephyr were 14,944 in its first model year in comparison with the K-series Lincolns' 1,515.

Chrysler's participation in luxury-car production didn't begin until 1926, a time when Cadillac, Lincoln, and Packard were all well established and recognized for technical prowess and custom coach work. Chrysler was not to be underrated however. Its corporate behavior was as dynamic as its namesake's personality. Walter Chrysler's achievements in successfully challenging Ford and Chevrolet with the Plymouth made any move by his company an action to be reckoned with. Yet, Chrysler had been in production only since 1923, and its entrance into the fine-car field seemed almost presumptuous. This view seemed to gain more validity by Chrysler's use of a six-cylinder engine for the 1926 Chrysler Imperial 80. Just three years earlier, in 1923, Packard's new straight-eight engine's debut coincided with that of the Type 51 Cadillac V-8, with its 90° compensated crankshaft. The age of the luxury car powered by a large six-cylinder engine was obviously on the wane, but Chrysler took it out in style, promoting its 1928 L-80 Imperial with its 112-horsepower, 309-cubic-inch engine as "America's Most Powerful Motorcar." The arrival of the Duesenberg J with 265 horsepower rendered this claim obsolete; but in that year, the most powerful Packard peaked at 109 horsepower with Cadillac's engine developing a maximum of 90 horsepower.

On July 1, 1930, the first of the eight-cylinder Chrysler Imperials, whose engine's 384.8-cubic-inch displacement matched that of the Packard eight, was introduced. Just seven months earlier, Cadillac had stunned the automotive industry with the announcement of its V-16 engine. Nonetheless, the consensus of most contemporary automotive historians is that Chrysler's top model was worthy of being regarded as a competitor to both Packard and Cadillac.

Chrysler broke with the rest of the industry in 1934 with its Airflow models, which were offered in three Imperial variations ranging in wheelbase from 128 to 146.5 inches with engines of 130 to 150 horsepower. These were design landmark cars capable of outstanding performance. In 1934, a 130-horsepower, CV Chrysler Airflow Imperial set numerous records for American closed stock cars in Class B (5 to 8 liters).

But the Airflow design was just too advanced and controversial to succeed in the 1930s either as a medium-priced or luxury automobile. By 1937 when production ceased, a mere 9,124 Airflow Imperials had been assembled. Abandoning the Airflow was one matter, dropping the Imperial was quite another; and for the rest of the decade, Chrysler offered both Imperial and Crown Imperial models.

For the most part, however, their prices brought them into only limited competition with Cadillac. Also setting them further away from any direct comparison with Cadillac was their conservative styling. This was improved in 1939, but it remained bulbous, uninspiring, and not very applicable to automobiles intended for affluent customers. In effect, Chrysler was in the least desirable position of the companies that would at war's end be regarded as Cadillac's competitors.

Cadillac was in a somewhat different position vis-a-vis these competitors, since from 1927, it had as a "companion car," the La Salle. Although its fate was in doubt at times during the thirties, the existence of the La Salle enabled Cadillac to capture a respectable, if not dominant, share of the market for cars with a price ranging from just under $1,000 to approximately $1,500. However, while Packard and Lincoln were rearranging their marketing strategies to cope with the new reality, Cadillac was not standing pat. In October 1935, it introduced the Series Sixty, which, although manufactured only through the 1938 model year, enabled Cadillac to exploit an important segment of the market for prestige automobiles that was untouched by both Lincoln and Packard. The Series Sixty coupe, at

$1,695, was approximately $500 more expensive than a comparable La Salle, and $420 more than a Lincoln-Zephyr coupe. In the Cadillac lineup, the model closest in price to the Series Sixty was the $2,595 Series Seventy coupe.

The Series Sixty was a small Cadillac with a 121-inch wheelbase (compared with the Series Seventy's 131-inch wheelbase), and it shared General Motors' "B" body with some Buick and Oldsmobile models; but it was a Cadillac through and through. In its debut year, it featured hydraulic brakes and a 332-cubic-inch version of Cadillac's new V-8 engine. The result was a boost in Cadillac sales to 12,880 from the previous year's level of 3,636. More importantly than this encouraging upturn was the maintenance of the Cadillac name as one that was not attached to a truly low-priced automobile.

Moreover, Cadillac, just two years later, in 1938, offered two more compelling reasons for it to be regarded as America's premier luxury automobile—a new V-16 engine and the dramatically styled Series Sixty Special sedan. Both were indications of Cadillac expertise and were hailed by the general public and critics as major accomplishments. Cadillac received acclaim for the Sixty Special's low-slung looks and the modern design of the new 135-degree lightweight V-16. At 1,050 pounds, it weighed less than the 1,165-pound V-12 and the 1,294-pound V-16 engine it replaced and weighed only 120 pounds more than the much smaller 346-cid V-8 engine.

As the thirties came to an end, Cadillac was not alone among American luxury cars with both new styling and engines. In 1940, Packard introduced a 356-cubic-inch, straight-eight, which with 160 horsepower was the most powerful eight-cylinder motor available in an American automobile. Although it trailed Cadillac's Series Sixty Special to the market by nearly three years, the Packard Clipper, introduced in April 1941, was a stunning illustration that it too could offer a superbly styled automobile at a price competitive with the Sixty Special. In its first model year, the Packard Clipper's production totaled 16,600. The following year, the Clipper style was extended to the 127-inch wheelbase, One-Sixty club sedan and touring sedan models.

Closer in time to the Series Sixty's introduction was the production of the first Lincoln Continental (which for the 1940 model year was identified as the Lincoln-Zephyr-Continental) on October 3, 1939. The Continental was acclaimed as a styling tour-de-force but production was extremely limited, totaling only 404. The next year's output was also modest, consisting of 1,250 cars. Meanwhile, the Lincoln-Zephyr, which was totally restyled in 1940, was unable to match the popularity of either Packard's One-Twenty or Cadillac's La Salle. The former's 1940 production was 28,128, which, along with 62,300 Packard Six models and 7,562 Senior models, gave Packard its second-best prewar production year.

But the following year, the fundamental strength of Cadillac's position in the luxury-car field relative to its competitors became obvious. The La Salle was discontinued, replaced, in effect, by the Series Sixty-One line; Hydra-Matic and air conditioning became options; all series used the same 346-cubic-inch V-8; and all cars had new styling.

Where did all this leave Cadillac? With a total output of 60,130 cars, a widely accepted appearance that, compared with Lincoln's and Packard's, was perceived as new and fresh, and most importantly, with an image totally unsullied by forays into lower price fields.

Much has been written about the role of the Packard Six and One-Twenty in Packard's history and the importance of the Lincoln-Continental as a classic design. In both cases, these have not been unworthy exercises. The two Packard lines were pure and simple, Packard's salvation. The Continental was a design of timeless appeal. But when postwar production resumed, it was Cadillac that emerged in the position of greatest strength. Its leadership was committed to Cadillac's stature as the highest point in General Motors' automotive hierarchy and wasn't distracted by any lesser carryovers from the era of survival.

Packard, on the other hand, waited too long to attempt to regain its once prominent position. As late as 1953, for example, Packard ads spoke of its "return to the fine car field." Lincoln, to its credit, returned the Continental into production, but its output remained limited and relatively unsignificant. Not until the 1949 model year would a new body style for the Lincoln appear. Up to that time, it used the old prewar Zephyr body. Even at that point, Lincoln had to share body dies with Mercury. For the Cosmopolitan models, a 125-inch-wheelbase body style was offered, but its appearance paled beside that of contemporary Cadillacs. Furthermore, the Lincoln's "new" engine was, in contrast with Cadillac's trend-setting, overhead-valve V-8, of an already dated L-head design. Also placing the Lincoln at a disadvantage to Cadillac was the lack of an automatic transmission option. When one was offered in mid-1949, it was General Motors' Hydra-Matic!

1946

Cadillac: Improved Even More in War Than in Peace

CADILLAC GENERAL MANAGER Nicholas Dreystadt introduced the first postwar Cadillacs on September 22, 1945. Although these 1946 model-year cars were based on the 1942 models, Dreystadt could claim they contained 63 improvements. Not the least of these were found under the hood. Cadillac's 346-cubic-inch V-8 looked similar to its prewar version, but it was in many ways a more refined powerplant.

Cadillac was rightly proud of its role in the nation's defense during World War II and reported that many improvements made for 1946 were directly traceable to the use of the Cadillac V-8 in various types of military vehicles.

CHANGES AND IMPROVEMENTS

Primary changes included use of longer lasting Morraine Durxe 300-type main and connecting-rod bearings. These had steel-backed shells with a copper-nickel alloy matrix covered by a thin high-quality babbit overlay. The new pistons were of a three-, rather than a two-ring design as used before the war. The rings were mounted lower on the piston to provide increased resistance to scuffing. Both improved oil control and economy was provided by the larger slots of the oil rings. Changes to the valve guides consisted of a ferrox treatment that Cadillac said resulted in both quieter operation and longer valve guide and stem life. The valve guide's dimensions were increased for added resistance to valve sticking. The carburetor, supplied by both Carter and Stromberg, was redesigned to resist gumming of the choke and throttle shafts.

Drawing on its wartime experiences with synthetic rubber parts, which had proven to be more durable than prewar natural rubber versions, Cadillac equipped its 1946 models with fan and generator belts of a heat and oil-resisting synthetic rubber.

Additional refinements included a new inertia oil fitting, resulting in cleaner oil delivered to the valve lifters, a redesigned choke mechanism intended to lessen any tendency to stick due to gum deposits, and

changes to the choke design that resulted in more uniform operation. An improved accelerator pump provided a more positive action for better acceleration. Rounding out changes made in the Cadillac's external engine linkage system were new throttle controls for cars with Hydra-Matic, enabling more precise adjustments to be made with less difficulty. All Cadillacs had a common accelerator and linkage that was less susceptible to sticking and made the car's operation smoother.

Cadillac had not been the first General Motors' automotive division to offer Hydra-Matic as an option. That distinction when to Oldsmobile with its 1940 models. During the war, Cadillac produced in excess of 73,000 Hydra-Matics for the M-5 and M-2F tanks; the M-8, M-37, and T-64 howitzer motor carriages; the M-19 gun carrier; an amphibious tank, the LVT-111; and even a snowmobile identified as the BFT-2. T-17 armored cars powered by two Chevrolet, six-cylinder engines also used Hydra-Matic transmissions.

The operation of these vehicles in combat gave General Motors a tremendous opportunity to improve the Hydra-Matic for civilian use. Customers who had owned prewar models were quick to note the absence of the whirring sound heard when the Hydra-Matic Cadillacs were first started. This was due to changes in the torus-fin spacing.

An even more welcome change was the addition of a hydraulic blocking valve to the transmission, which prevented the reverse anchor from engaging when the reverse gear was turning. Both the front and rear bands were larger for greater strength and were ground to a more precise shape. A new oil pump of simpler design and with greater capacity maintained a more consistent oil flow. Whereas older Hydra-Matics used six pistons of 1.5-inch diameter in each clutch, the new model was fitted with a single, 6-inch diameter, hydraulically operated unit. The clutch drive plates now used a nonmetallic facing that offered longer life and smoother shifting.

These improvements coincided with widespread

1

acceptance of Hydra-Matic by new Cadillac owners. Thirty percent of all 1941 Cadillacs were fitted with Hydra-Matic. The short 1942 model year saw acceptance double to 62 percent. In the 1946 model run, 87 percent of the Cadillacs built were equipped with Hydra-Matic even though it was a $176 option. In 1947 and 1948, the level of acceptance rose to 92 and 97 percent, respectively. Beginning in 1950, Hydra-Matic was standard equipment for the Series Sixty Special and Series Sixty-Two models. The last Cadillac available with a manual transmission was the 1954 Series Seventy-Five Fleetwoods.

Aside from these developments and the use of larger rivets attaching the ring gear to the differential and the installation of heavy-duty rear-wheel bearings on the commercial chassis, no other changes were made in the Cadillac's mechanical specifications.

Cadillac's egg-crate grille format had been introduced in 1941 and further refined the following year. At that point, its basic design themes were firmly established. The vertical bars maintained a link with the classic era, while the four horizontal units emphasized the width and low build destined to be key evolutionary factors in Cadillac's future styling.

In this perspective, the placement and form of the bumper guards and fog and parking lights merit attention. In 1941, the rectangular parking lights were positioned within the grille assembly, while the optional, circular-shaped fog lights (or a circular casting with a four-pointed star and concentric circles surrounding a V emblem) were placed directly below the headlights.

This began a design format, consisting of periodic rearranging and resizing of the auxiliary lights and bumpers, that wouldn't end until 1958. For example, in 1942, the parking lights became circular; the fog lights, now incorporated in the grille network, were rectangular; and the inboard-positioned bumper guards were larger and bullet-shaped.

Also strengthening the image-making role of Cadillac's head-on appearance was the increased wraparound bumper. Another design feature found on the 1941 model that would serve Cadillac for many years was the placement of the gas cap under the hinged driver-side tail lamp.

In 1946, both Cadillac's parking and optional fog lamps were rectangular. The basic grille format was left unchanged, although the horizontal bars were extended slightly to create the impression of a lowered height. Also evident was the addition of Cadillac block lettering on the front fenders and a less flamboyant, more conservative hood ornament. The bumpers now had more of a wraparound design. In addition, they were of three-piece construction which made possible the separate replacement of the ends or the center section.

Since it had been registered as a trademark in August 1906, Cadillac's crest had been prominently displayed on its automobiles. It wasn't until the 1946 models that the crest was linked to a V. In time these two forms would be indelibly linked in the public's view. All 1946 Cadillacs carried them on the hood and rear deck; and when Cadillac introduced its overhead-valve

V-8 in 1949, this union would assume a far greater significance.

All trim molding was once again either stainless-steel or chrome-plated die castings. All of the latter were of increased thickness for added durability. Certainly appreciated by Cadillac's customers were changes intended to extend body life and reduce service requirements. All interior sheet metal surfaces below the body belt line were painted to combat rusting. Ventilating louvers were added to such places as the rocker sills and door bottoms that were likely to collect moisture. Additional antirust and corrosion measures introduced with the latest Cadillacs included larger water-drain slots, sealing of joints where water or road salt tended to collect with caulking compound and use of thicker rear-body panels.

DIFFERENCES AMONG MODELS

Most manufacturers resuming production with prewar designs reduced the number of models in their lineup. In Cadillac's case, this meant the elimination of the Series Sixty-Three and Sixty-Seven, leaving the Series Sixty-One as Cadillac's lowest priced line. Two models—the $2,052 Club Coupe and the $2,175 four-door Sedan—were offered. In both models, plain-paneled seats were standard. Customers could select either a Heatherstone broadcloth or two-tone cord interior. Color choices were limited to blue-gray or tan.

The two Series Sixty-Two closed models, of which the four-door version was the most popular Cadillac of 1946 with a production of 14,900 units, were offered with the same interior fabric and color choices available for the Series Sixty-One. Setting them apart from these less-expensive models was their upholstery, consisting of plain-paneled cushions and semipleated seat backs. Production of the $2,284 Club Sedan reached 2,323.

Less common (1,342 were produced) and certainly more sporting was the Series Sixty-Two Convertible Coupe. Its interior combined leather in black, tan, green, blue or red with Bedford cord.

The Series Sixty Special with its quilted door panels and elegant Fleetwood appointments was priced at $3,054. Production for the 1946 model run was 5,700. Its 133-inch wheelbase provided rear seat occupants with considerably more leg room than did the less expensive sedans. External identification of a Series Sixty Special, in addition to its greater length as compared with a Series Sixty-Two four-door sedan, were its chrome, rather than black rubber, rear-fender gravel guards, Fleetwood rear-deck script, five chrome louvers positioned on the rear roof pillar, 2-inch wider doors, and individual door drip moldings.

Unlike the Series Sixty-One, Sixty-Two, and Sixty Special Cadillacs, which shared their body shells with other General Motors' automobiles, the Series Seventy-Five body was an exclusive Cadillac offering. Five body styles were available, and their output was very limited. Setting the 1946 Series Seventy-Five models apart from previous versions were their stainless-steel running boards.

1946 Series Seventy-Five 7-Passenger Touring Sedan.

1946 Series Sixty Special.

1946 Series Sixty-Two Convertible Coupe.

1946 Series Sixty-One 5-Passenger Touring Sedan.

CADILLAC VITAL STATISTICS: 1946

Series	Model	Body Type	Factory Price ($)	Weight (lbs.)	Production (#)
61	6109	4 dr Sedan	2146	4145	2200
	6107	2 dr Club Coupe	2022	4065	800
62	6269	4 dr Sedan	2324	4240	14,900
	6207	2 dr Club Coupe	2249	4100	2323
	6267	2 dr Convertible	2521	4462	1342
60	6069	4 dr Sedan	3054	4348	5700
75	7519	4 dr Sedan	4238	4848	150
	7523	4 dr Sedan 7p	4415	4865	225
	7533	4 dr Imp Sedan	4609	4926	17
	7523L	4 dr Bus Sedan 9p	4093	4840	22
	7533L	4 dr Bus Imp Sedan	4286	4850	17

CADILLAC'S DOMESTIC COMPETITION

Since Packard had sold the tooling for its prewar senior series to the Soviet Union during the war, all 1946 Packards used Clipper bodies. In price and status, they were ranked from bottom to top as Clipper Six, Clipper Standard and DeLuxe Eight, Super Clipper, and Custom Super Clipper Eight. Of these, only the last three could be regarded as alternatives to the purchase of a Cadillac.

Changes in the 1946 Packard were minor, consisting of details such as a new center grille and license-plate brackets plus the removal of the outer ridge on the wheel covers.

Powering both the Super Clipper and Custom Clipper was Packard's 356-cubic-inch straight-eight with nine main bearings, which had first been used for the 1940 models. With a 6.85:1 compression ratio, hydraulic valve lifters, and a two-barrel carburetor, it was rated at 165 horsepower at 3,600 rpm.

Packard's 1946 calendar-year output of 30,883 cars narrowly exceeded Cadillac's 29,144. Of Packard's total, 15,892 were Clipper Six Series models. Nonetheless, when Packard and Cadillac output in the prestige-car price range were compared, Packard still had several areas of strength. For example, Packard's DeLuxe Clipper out-produced Cadillac's Series Sixty-One 5,714 to 3,001. At the upper end of the spectrum, Cadillac assembled 1,921 units in the Series Seventy-Five Fleetwood line. Packard's Custom Super Clipper Eight on a 148-inch wheelbase was competitive at 1,291 units.

However, output of 18,566 Series Sixty-Two Cadillacs overwhelmed the Super Clipper's production of 4,923 by nearly four to one. Furthermore, the 127-inch wheelbase Custom Super Clipper's production total of 1,472 was far less than the Series Sixty Special's production of 5,700.

The association with a less expensive automobile and a gradual lessening of its impact in the luxury-car field, which loomed over the Packard name, also affected Lincoln in the early postwar years. All of its models, as noted earlier, were based on the 125-inch wheelbase Zephyr chassis of 1942. The Zephyr name, however, was not continued.

The 1946 Lincolns were not unattractive and, to the credit of their designers, were easily distinguishable from their 1942 counterparts. For example, a new grille combining both horizontal and vertical bars, larger bumpers (with twin vertical bars highly suggestive of Cadillac's), plus a new hood ornament and hubcaps with a raised hexagonal center made it easy to identify the latest model.

However, this strength was offset by several serious shortcomings. In form, the Lincoln was dated. The last time the Zephyr has been restyled was in 1940. In effect, this placed the postwar Lincoln closer to the thirties than either Packard or Cadillac. In 1940, it might have been wise to closely link new Zephyrs with their 1939 versions. But in 1946, it gave new Lincolns an old look. Also hampering Lincoln's initial postwar image was its V-12 engine, which had been introduced on the original 1936 Zephyr. Throughout the thirties, it had developed a reputation for oil consumption and poor performance. By 1946, most of these troubles were

behind the V-12; but when compared with the solid reputation of the Cadillac V-8 and the Packard straight-eight, the Lincoln engine was perceived as less than their equal.

For 1946, the Lincoln's bore was reduced from 2.9375 to 2.7875 inches, lowering its displacement from 306 to 292 cubic inches. During the model run, a new, greater capacity oil pump was adopted. Peak horsepower of the V-12 was 130 at 3,600 rpm.

The three Lincoln models—a sedan, convertible coupe, and club coupe of which 16,645 were built—compared in price to the Series Sixty-One and Sixty-Two Cadillacs. Cadillac did not have, in terms of concept, a direct counterpart to the Lincoln Continental Convertible and Club Coupe, whose respective prices were $4,474 and $4,392. In price, the only comparable Cadillacs were the Series Seventy-Five Fleetwoods. Production of these Lincolns was very low, consisting of 201 Convertibles and 265 Club Coupes.

Chrysler's 1946 models were less ornate than the 1942 versions, with most of the trim found on the latter cars eliminated. But with only two models, the eight-passenger, $3,825, Crown Imperial Limousine and Sedan on a 145.5-inch wheelbase, Chrysler wasn't strongly represented in the upper-price class. Furthermore, the Crown Imperial attached little interest as indicated by the output of only 650 eight-passenger Sedans and 750 Limousines in the 1946-1948 time span. A very small number of Derham-bodied versions were also produced during that time.

Powering the Crown Imperial was the L-head Spitfire Eight, displacing 323.5 cubic inches and developing 135 horsepower at 3,800 rpm.

Positioned at the top end of the New Yorker series were the $2,718 Town & Country Sedan and $2,718 Convertible Coupe. These had a collective production of 8,475 units from 1946 through 1948. While the Town & Country models would later assume collectible status, their presence in the Chrysler line had minimal impact on Chrysler's status relative to Cadillac.

At this time with the wide-open seller's market unfolding, Chrysler's reliance, like Packard's, on lower priced models seemed to matter little. But in just a few years, Cadillac's strong base of strength would yield tremendous dividends. Chrysler, in contrast, would be forced to begin at almost ground zero to establish the Imperial as a viable alternative to Cadillac.

SPECIFICATIONS

Engine

Type: V-type, L-head, eight cylinders
Bore × stroke: 3.5 × 4.5 inches
Displacement: 346 cubic inches
Horsepower: 150 @ 3,400 rpm
Torque: 274 lb-ft @ 1,600 rpm
Compression ratio: 7.25:1
Fuel system: Carter or Stromberg two-barrel carburetor
Gas tank capacity: 20 gallons

Chassis/Drivetrain

Front suspension: Independent with A-arms, coil springs, hydraulic shock absorbers, stabilizer bar

Rear suspension: Semielliptical leaf springs, semi-floating rear axle with 3.77:1 ratio, hydraulic shock absorbers

Steering: Saginaw recirculating ball, 21.3:1 overall ratio

Electrical system: 6-volt

Transmission: 3-speed manual, column-mounted shift

Frame: Channel-section with X-member junction and reinforced side members

Tires: 4-ply, 7.00 × 15

    Series 75: 7.50 × 16

Brakes: Hydraulic, 12-inch drums, total braking area: 208 square inch

Dimensions

Wheelbase:
    Series 61: 215 inches
    Series 62: 129 inches
    Series 60 Special: 133 inches
    Series 75: 136 inches

Width: 80.75 inches

Overall length:
    Series 61: 215 inches
    Series 62: 220 inches
    Series 60 Special: 224 inches
    Series 75: 227 inches

Front/rear tread: 59/63 inches

Popular Options

Hydra-Matic: $176.47

Full-size wheel discs: $18.89

Wheel-trim rings: $8.84

Fog lamps: $29.14

Radio

Heater and defroster: $39.32

Automatic underseat heater:
    Series 61, 62, 60 Special: $70.07
    Series 75: $76.24

Backup light: $13.03

Special steering wheel: $17.74

License plate frames: $3.39

Glareproof mirror: $5.04

Windshield washer: $10.11

1947

A New Standard of the World

CADILLAC PRODUCTION improved considerably in 1947. Model-year output totaled 61,926, with that for the calendar year reaching 59,436. Once again the prewar body was mildly restyled to distinguish it from the previous year's.

CHANGES AND IMPROVEMENTS

Most noticeable was the reduction of horizontal grille bars from six to five and the concurrent wider spacing between the remaining bars. Also evident was the greater width of these bars, which, except for the top header bar, were stamped units. Small extensions were also added to the uppermost bar. Initially the vertical bars were of stainless steel; but after approximately 2,000 cars, a switch was made to stainless-steel construction.

Eliminated from the grille were the small, rectangular parking/directional lights. Instead, circular units mounted in a die-cast panel directly below the headlights were used. If fog lights were ordered, combination fog, parking, and directionals were installed in the same location.

All models used stainless-steel, chrome-plated rear fender shields. The Cadillac name on the front fenders was now in script rather than block letters. Yet another small, but easily detected change was the filling of space between the hood-mounted V and crest by a field of horizontal bands. On the rear deck, the V and crest found on non-Fleetwood models in 1946 were replaced by a winged Cadillac crest similar to that last used in 1941. Curiously, the Series Seventy-Five models also used this identification on their trunk lids, while the Sixty Specials retained Fleetwood lettering.

Capturing the attention of many owners of lesser cars were Cadillacs outfitted with the new, optional "Sombrero," full-size wheel discs. Along with wide, white sidewall tires, they became two building blocks of America's early postwar automotive culture.

As in 1946, the latest Cadillacs used two separate dash arrangements. This duality originated in 1942 when the Series Sixty-Two and Sixty Special bowed in with an all-new dash with two circular instrument dials mounted to the speedometer's left, combining oil pressure and engine temperature in one unit and fuel level and ammeter in the second. The larger speedometer and equal-sized clock were separated by a larger "waterfall" panel. The remaining Cadillacs used the 1941 dash panel, which placed the clock and speedometer higher in the panel and positioned the engine temperature, ammeter, fuel level, and oil pressure dials in a horizontal panel adjacent to the speedometer.

Beginning with the Series Sixty Special, and expanding to all other Cadillacs shortly after 1947 model production began, was a new carpeting arrangement using small round grommets, edged with chrome moldings to surround the steering column, clutch, and brake pedals.

Cadillac's technical specifications were all but left unchanged for 1947. The use of hydraulic valve lifters with hardened ball seats, a feature found on some late-1946 cars, was continued. For 1947, the shape of the ball seat was changed. Among the minor detail refinements phased in on the 1947 Cadillacs was an improved emergency brake conduit with a new synthetic rubber tube, which Cadillac said eliminated any possibility of water entering the cable, and a reshaped oil filler tube, which lessened the sharp bend of the oil-level indicator.

DIFFERENCES AMONG MODELS

No changes were made in Cadillac's model lineup. Both the Sixty-One Touring Sedan and Club Coupe retained their fastback styling as did the Series Sixty-Two Club Coupe. The Series Sixty-Two Touring Sedan contained a notch-back profile.

While Cadillac described the Series Sixty-One models as "designed to bring Cadillac's incomparable standards of quality to the widest possible owner group," the Series Sixty-Two Cadillacs were regarded

1947 Series Sixty-One 5-Passenger Touring Sedan.

1947 Series Sixty-Two 5-Passenger Club Coupe.

1947 Series Seventy-Five 5-Passenger Touring Sedan.

8   *Cadillac—America's Luxury Car*

as the ultimate example of the Fisher-bodied Cadillacs. "In all Cadillac history," it was claimed, "there has never been such a perfect blending of quality and practicality as is offered in the 1947 Cadillac Series Sixty-Two."

But even these superlatives paled before Cadillac's portrayal of the Sixty Special. "From the day," noted Cadillac, "some ten years ago when it first startled the automotive world with its smartness and performance—and inaugurated an entirely new approach to automotive design—the Cadillac Sixty Special has paced the progression in the motor car field." For 1947, Cadillac called attention to the Sixty Special's oriental walnut interior trim paneling, Bedford cord or striped broadcloth upholstery, individually wrapped Marshall seat springs, front-seat-back-mounted ashtray, electric clock, and "All-Weather" ventilation system.

Almost as if it had already dismissed the top-ranked Lincoln, Packard, and Imperial models as meaningful competition, Cadillac explained: "The dominance of the great Cadillac-Fleetwood Seventy-Five is so pronounced that even the most casual inspection reveals its

1947 Series Sixty-Two 5-Passenger Touring Sedan.

CADILLAC VITAL STATISTICS: 1947

Series	Model	Body Type	Factory Price ($)	Weight (lbs.)	Production (#)
61	6109	4 dr Sedan	2324	4138	5160
	6107	2 dr Club Coupe	2200	4082	3395
62	6269	4 dr Sedan	2523	4201	25,834
	6207	2 dr Club Coupe	2446	7245	
	6267	2 dr Convertible	2902	4450	6755
60	6069	4 dr Sedan	3195	4351	8500
75	7519	4 dr Sedan	4471	4836	300
	7523	4 dr Sedan 7p	4686	4861	890
	7533	4 dr Imp Sedan 7p	4887	4939	80
	7523L	4 dr Bus Sedan 9p	4368	4762	135
	7533L	4 dr Bus Imp Sedan 9p	4560	4822	80

superiority." Emphasizing its limited production status, Cadillac added that its "Fleetwood coachcraft reveals the artistry of the one remaining builder who works exclusively to custom standards." Adding the final touch of class was Cadillac's suggestion to prospective Series Seventy-Five owners of "a personal conference with your dealer so you may express your individual preference concerning the many options available to the purchase of this incomparable car."

CADILLAC'S DOMESTIC COMPETITION

Packard, Lincoln and Chrysler had made no changes of any consequence. The latest Packard Clippers were unaltered except for a revised two-tone, exterior-color arrangement in which the trunk lids and window frames on four-door models were no longer painted the same color as the top part of the body.

Both Packard's calendar-year and model-year production was respectable. The former was 55,477, the latter 35,336.

The changes found in the 1947 Lincoln and Continental models consisted of revamped hood ornaments and hubcaps. All Lincoln models had a "Lincoln" script on the hood where a trim piece had been located on the 1946 models. Also adopted by Lincoln were conventional exterior door handles. Total Lincoln and Continental production was 21,460.

The weak sister of American luxury cars, the Chrysler Crown Imperial, was similarly changed only in minute details. For example, red taillight buttons were used rather than the white units of 1946, and the high beam headlight indicator was relocated to the speedometer face.

Chrysler was still years away from making the Imperial a true competitor to Cadillac. But in the meantime, it, along with Packard and Lincoln, were about to receive a lesson in styling leadership from Cadillac, which would make it very apparent that Cadillac was the master and they mere apprentices.

SPECIFICATIONS

Unchanged from 1946

Popular Options

Hydra-Matic: $186.34
Full-size wheel discs: $25.08
Wheel-trim rings: $9.38
Fog lights: $30.12
Radio: $87.19
Rear-compartment radio (Series 75 only): $151.93
Vacuum Aerial: $13.54
Heater and defroster: $43.28
Automatic underseat heater:
    Series 61, 62, 60 Special: $76.15
    Series 75: $85.40
Backup light: $11.50
License plate frames: $3.63
Glareproof mirror: $5.00
Windshield washer: $10.96
Special steering wheel (Series 61 and 62 only): $19.54
Fleetwood Robe: $55.00 (lined)
    $85.00 (double broadcloth)
    $5.50 extra for Monogram
Spotlight: $21.60
Outside rear-view mirror: $6.50
Seat covers: $27.00
Gas-tank cap lock: $2.75

1948

America's Most Distinguished Motor Car

DURING WORLD WAR II, Americans who had to make do with automobiles of varying vintage and condition, were served up visions the form postwar cars would take by numerous publications. The more fanciful of these predictions foresaw cars with bubble tops and exotic power plants. Other forecasts, more down to earth and a bit more austere, prophesied automobiles reduced both in size and opulence to accommodate a world of inflation, limited fuel supplies, and diminishing sources of natural resources.

CHANGES AND IMPROVEMENTS

Within the Cadillac organization, there was some sentiment for a new product reflecting this mentality that would, among other details, have a dechromed grille. Fortunately this outlook never took hold. Soon it was cast completely into the background by the aftermath of an event having far-reaching consequences. This was the well-known and fabled viewing in 1939 by Harley Earl (who was to be appointed vice-president in charge of GM styling in 1940) and key members of his staff of a P-38 Lockheed Lightning interceptor at Selfridge Field near Detroit. The impact of this encounter on not only Cadillac, but other GM products as well, was profound. For Cadillac, the single most important result was the rear fender of its 1948 models.

It's important to appreciate (in the context of the controversy surrounding the introduction of the tail fins) just how clearly Cadillac was reading public sentiment in those years. Prior to World War II, Harley Earl was aware that at least some Cadillac customers wanted their cars to be more distinctive. In 1949, he acknowledged receiving complaints from important businessmen that they could buy an Oldsmobile instead of a Cadillac and most of their acquaintances wouldn't even notice. That point is open to challenge; but with the 1948 models, it was left without any support.

After careful examination of the P-38 from a respectful distance, Earl's staff didn't need to be told

what to do next. Before the year ended, they had designed scale models that became the basis for the prototype, appropriately named the "Interception," of the 1948 Cadillac.

Consider other styling features of those ⅜-scale models inspired by the P-38 that found their way into production. Following the adoption of the rear fender fins in 1948 came the hardtop coupe in 1949. Four years later, the wraparound windshield arrived, evolving into its ultimate complex-curved configuration in 1959. Yet, Cadillac never went for the pronounced bullet-shaped nose as did Studebaker and (to a lesser degree) Ford. After all, the age of the prop plane, as a leading edge of technology, was long past by the late forties. Cadillac was living in the here-and-now of the jet age and not interested in adopting obsolete symbols of power. Also never seen on a production Cadillac were the skirted front fenders of the scale models. Nash went this route starting with the 1949 models; and although it hung on stubbornly until 1956, this styling feature was never a marketing success. It's even plausible to argue that that sort of unpopular styling played a role in the demise of Nash after 1957.

When the 1948 models first appeared, public acceptance of the new Cadillac rear fender line was less than overwhelming. To some observers, perhaps attuned to change on a more gradual scale, it was too much, too soon. Reports from GM auto shows indicated nearly half of the spectators didn't like them. This lukewarm response was not the first time that the fins were in trouble. In the 1945-1946 time span, both Harley Earl and Cadillac general manager Nicholas Dreystadt had wavered in their commitment to fins before giving the final go-ahead for production. But the more the public saw of the fins, the more they liked them; and by the end of the model year, they were firmly established as a symbol of Cadillac's styling leadership.

Tail fins weren't by any means the sole reason for the 1948 Cadillac's popularity. These cars were a near-perfect example of Cadillac's ability to blend together old and new design elements, accentuated by Earl's sense of timing that told him when the public could embrace a radical new idea.

The Cadillac body, like the other first-generation, postwar GM cars, retained a distinct rear-fender outline that gave drama and character to Cadillac's appearance even without the fins. The bumpers, with their outer extremities wrapping around and upward into the rear fenders, were more integrated into the overall body form than previously. Replacing the winged trunk emblem of 1947 was a Cadillac crest and V. Not scheduled for removal was Cadillac's hidden gas filler cap. Nestled under the left fender's taillight assembly, it was well on its way to becoming one of the most memorable (and copied) design features of the postwar era.

Up front, what else was to be expected but an egg-crate grille, maintaining identity with previous models. Yet, with just two horizontal bars and seven vertical fins, it was unmistakably new. In similar fashion, Cadillac's use of curved glass for the two-piece windshield beckoned to the future while not foresaking appearance continuity. Completing Cadillac's new front end were chromed headlight rings.

The interior of the new Cadillac was highlighted by a unique "rainbow" speedometer gauge layout used only for 1948. Various reasons have been given for its short life span, ranging from high cost to its dislike by GM president Charles Wilson. All the instruments were gathered in a semicircle cluster facing the driver. The speedometer, shaped in the form of a half-moon, occupied the upper portion, while gauges for the ammeter, fuel level, temperature, and oil pressure were located in the bottom section. The cluster face had a blue gunmetal finish. All gauge pointers, gradations, and figures were white.

Beneath the 1948 Cadillac's glamour and glitter were mechanical components familiar to the owners of older models. The frame was constructed of channel-section steel with a center X-member. The independent front suspension, consisting of A-arms and coil springs, had its geometry slightly altered to provide zero caster and camber. Also changed were the shock-absorber valves and springs. Except for the Series Seventy-Five models, all the new Cadillacs were equipped with larger (8.20 × 15 in place of 7.00 × 15), low-pressure (24 instead of 28 pounds), four-ply tires. Carried over from 1948 were Cadillac's 12-inch Bendix hydraulic brakes with a total swept area of 208 square inches.

Revisions to the 346-cid, L-head V-8 consisted of a new thermostat, which provided a quicker warm-up while being more resistant to leaks, and a new moisture-proof, hermetically sealed, oil-filled coil. Changes in the Hydra-Matic transmission involved the reduction of rotating weight by use of die-cast aluminum, front and rear clutch pistons. Not the most earth-shaking news for 1948, but certainly appreciated whenever a 1948 Cadillac was driven in the rain, was the announcement that a more powerful windshield-wiper motor was standard.

For Cadillac enthusiasts who delighted in pointing out changes made from year to year that most owners seldom noticed, there were two additional revisions for 1948. The first was the repositioning of the Owner Identification Card from the cowl kickpad to the underhood, radiator air deflector. The second concerned changes made in the form of the standard wheel disc. The 1947 version had a single drain hole, and the height of the inner ring measured 2.25 inches. The 1948 models had wheel discs with two drain holes and a quarter-inch higher inner ring.

Compared with corresponding 1947 models, the 1948 Cadillacs (with the exception of the Series Seventy-Five) were marginally lighter and thus performed on a par or slightly better than their predecessors. General Motors Proving Ground reports of a Series Sixty-One Sedan with Hydra-Matic and four passengers showed a 0 to 60 mph time of 16.3 seconds and a top speed of 93.3 mph. Other acceleration times were 10 to 25 mph, 2.5 seconds; 25 to 45 mph, 5.7 seconds; 45 to 60 mph, 6.9 seconds; and 60 to 75 mph, 11.5 seconds.

DIFFERENCES AMONG MODELS

The Series Sixty-One (and Series Sixty-Two) two-door Coupes took the fastback styling format to what is generally regarded as one of its finest forms. A year later, the arrival of the Coupe de Ville would signal that the end was near for this venerable body form; but in 1948, these cars were elegant examples of Cadillac's ability to blend an established form into a new era of styling.

Once again the entry-level Cadillacs were not strong sellers. Even the $2,728 Coupe's styling failed to stir its popularity, as evident by an output of 3,521. The $2,866 Series Sixty-One Sedan's production totaled 5,081, which was less than in 1947. This was in spite of Cadillac's declaration that "a car of genuine distinction, the Series Sixty-One Sedan features, for the first time, the clear-cut deck treatment previously reserved only for the more expensive Cadillac series."

Series Sixty-One interiors were conservative. No seat-back bolsters were used, and the single-color fabric seats were fitted with darker piping. Both the door panels and kickpads were of a plain design. All Cadillacs used Di-Noc transfers for their moldings, which on the Series Sixty-One were of a brown-leather-grain pattern.

It was easy to distinguish a Series Sixty-Two from a Series Sixty-One Cadillac. The higher priced models had three horizontal, chrome stripes mounted just below the taillights, a lower body sill molding between the front and rear-wheel cutouts, and a front-fender stone guard.

Series Sixty-Two Sedan interiors featured two-toned fabrics, a ribbed kickpad, and horizontal dividers for the door panels. The Series Sixty-One Convertible seats were upholstered in leather with cloth-trimmed seatbacks. The door panels were also cloth covered. Five colors were offered for the leather, while the trim was available in two colors. As standard equipment, the Convertible's front and rear windows, top, and front seat were hydraulically operated.

The Series Sixty-Two Cadillacs were popular with the public The $2,996 Sedan was, with a production total of 23,997, Cadillac's best-selling model by a wide margin. As in 1947, the other Series Sixty-Two models,

1948 Series Sixty Special.

1948 Series Sixty-One Sedan.

CADILLAC VITAL STATISTICS: 1948

Series	Model	Body Type	Factory Price ($)	Weight (lbs.)	Production (#)
61	6169	4 dr Sedan	2833	4145	5081
	6107	2 dr Club Coupe	2728	4070	3521
62	6269	4 dr Sedan	2996	4180	23,997
	6207	2 dr Club Coupe	2912	4125	4764
	6267	2 dr Convertible Coupe	3442	4450	5450
60 Special	6069	4 dr Sedan	3820	4370	11,399
75	7519	4 dr Sedan 5p	4779	4865	220
	7523	4 dr Sedan 7p	4999	4910	595
	7533	4 dr Imp Sedan 7p	5199	4930	626
	7523L	4 dr Bus Sedan 9p	4679	4925	35
	7533L	4 dr Bus Imp Sedan 9p	4868	4930	25

the $2,912 Club Coupe, and $3,442 Convertible remained far behind the Sedan's output level, with respective production marks of 4,764 and 5,450.

Of all the 1948 Cadillacs, the most exquisitely tailored was the Series Sixty Special. Truly worthy of being regarded as a modern classic, it represents one of Cadillac's outstanding postwar styling achievements. With a 133-inch wheelbase and 226-inch overall length, it was noticeably longer than the Series Sixty-One and Sixty-Two Cadillacs. Moreover, it retained key elements of the traditional Series Sixty Special identification, such as elongated doors, unique door trim, and the roof-pillar-mounted chrome slashes. All of these were blended into the new body without appearing intrusive or dated.

Then there was the matter of the Sixty Special's side-body trim. Only a "Cadillac" script was mounted on the front fender. Unlike the Series Sixty-One and Sixty-Two models, no side chrome spears were used. Added was a rear-fender extension to the rocker-panel trim, accentuating the Sixty Special's length without adding any sense of exaggeration or excess. The Sixty Special's rear-fender stone guard (a definition based more on symbolism than function) was not found on other models. Like the 1948 Cadillac's "rudder-type"

rear fender fins, this feature was directly traceable to the P-38. In its Sixty Special form, the shield, etched with extremely fine horizontal bars, flowed downward to become an integral part of the lower fender, body-trim line. As in previous years, Fleetwood script was mounted on the Sixty Special's rear-deck lid. Here too, the Sixty Special was set apart from other Cadillacs because of a more squared-off trunk profile.

The expectations aroused by the Sixty Special's exterior were fully met by its interior appointments. Six choices of shadow broadcloth and Bedford cord, as well as combinations of leather and cloth, were offered. Trim moldings were in a black leather-grained Di-Noc transfer.

The rear seat cushions were 3.25 inches wider than those in the Series Sixty-One and Sixty-Two Sedans. "Hydro-Lectric" hydraulic controls for the windows and front seat were standard. Production of the $3,820 Sixty Special totaled 6,561 cars.

While still handsome automobiles, the Series Seventy-Five models were clearly the dowager queens of the 1948 Cadillacs. Cadillac, for a time, considered abandoning this segment of the luxury-car field to Packard, but wisely chose to remain active in what was a highly visible, albeit limited, market. Essentially un-

1948 Series Sixty-One Coupe.

1948 Series Seventy-Five Limousine.

14   *Cadillac—America's Luxury Car*

changed from 1947 except for the new Cadillac dash (which had a burled walnut rather than the leather-grain finish used on other Cadillacs), the use of Cadillac script rather than lettering on the front fenders and a new background for the hood emblem, the Series Seventy-Five Cadillacs would not receive new styling until 1950.

CADILLAC'S DOMESTIC COMPETITION

To declare that Cadillac's competitors were caught off guard by its 1948 models is to understate the situation. In fairness to both Lincoln and Chrysler, they had their new models ready early in 1949. Yet neither was nearly as spectacular as the 1948 Cadillacs. Furthermore, Cadillac still remained in the limelight in 1949 with its new ohv V-8 (Chapter 4).

This left Cadillac's great rival, Packard, as the only American luxury automobile to directly challenge its new styling in 1948. The merits of the Twenty-Second Series Packards, which in convertible form, were first introduced in July 1948, have long been debated by both Packard's critics and proponents. Those in favor regard their appearance as a masterful blend of key elements of Packard's classic era with the best features of modern, envelope-body styling. The opposition, which has never been modest about expressing its views, sees it as uninspired, dull, bulbous, and, in the worst cut of them all, as "the Bathtub Packards."

Like Cadillac, Packard carefully maintained styling continuity through a front-grille arrangement that made possible an advertisement headlined, "One Guess What Name It Bears!," to not contain the Packard name. But was this the key to sales success? Unlike Cadillac, Packard, even in a time of newness, seemed overly concerned with the past, a bit too conservative for the dawning of an age of affluence with a marked propensity toward fresh approaches and new ideas. Admittedly, the bulk of this analysis benefits from the unwaveringly accurate perspective of hindsight.

In 1948, Packard received plenty of acclamations about its styling. The Fashion Academy of New York, for example, presented it with a gold medal for being the "Fashion Car of the Year." Judging from Packard's production figures for 1948, it had little to fear from its critics. A calendar-year output of 98,897 cars was second only to 1937's total of 109,518 units, and a model-year total of 95,495 was equally impressive. In comparison, Cadillac's calendar-year figure was 66,209, with model-year assemblies totaling 52,706.

Furthermore, Packard, a bit belatedly, realigned its model lineup to more effectively challenge Cadillac in key sectors of the luxury car market. Use of six-cylinder engines, for example, was limited to taxicab and export model production. Equally important to the Packard image was the expansion of the Custom Eight line to include a convertible model, the Convertible Victoria, which was not offered by Cadillac in its Fleetwood Seventy-Five series, and a commercial chassis. At the same time, Packard emphasized the Custom Eight's top status in the Packard lineup by its unique egg-crate grille, standard cormorant hood ornament, twin chrome side-body trim strips, and rear-deck insert. Interior appointments were impressive, including large pearwood door panels, leather seat bolsters with Bedford cord upholstery and cut-pile carpeting with foam backing. Six interior courtesy lights were fitted as was a woolen headliner with front-to-rear stitching.

Matched against these impressive automobiles with their ultra-smooth, nine main-bearing, 356-cubic-inch, 160-hp, straight-eight engines, the Seventy-Five Fleetwoods with their prewar bodies were clearly dated. Whereas Custom Eight Packard output was a surprisingly strong 7,271 cars, that of the Series Seventy-Five Fleetwoods was only 1,260 units, plus two commercial chasses. The bulk of Packard's output was found in its Eight and DeLuxe Eight lines, which were its counterparts to Cadillac's Series Sixty-One cars. Their production totaled 60,589 units.

As noted earlier, output of Series Sixty-One Cadillacs totaled just 8,603 units, including one commercial chassis. Quite a different situation existed in the contest between Packard's Super Eight and Cadillac's Series Sixty-Two. Packard's entry in this part of the market reached a production level of 22,450 cars. Cadillac's output of 34,213 was divided among 23,997 four-door Sedans, 4,764 two-door Club Coupes, 5,450 Convertibles, and two commercial chasses. This comparison is blurred somewhat by the inclusion of 1,766 Super Eights on the long, 141-inch wheelbase. Cadillac did not offer any models of this nature.

With Chrysler and Lincoln offering their first new postwar models plus Packard's introduction of Ultramatic automatic transmission for its golden anniversary models (it was also Chrysler's silver anniversary), 1949 shaped up as a wide-open year in the luxury-car market. But while those cars would soon become part of history, it was Cadillac that was about to make history.

SPECIFICATIONS

Engine

Type: V-type, L-head, eight cylinders
Bore × stroke: 3.50 × 4.5 inches
Displacement: 346 cubic inches
Horsepower: 150 @ 3,400 rpm
Torque: 283 lb-ft @ 1,600 rpm
Compression ratio: 7.25:1
Fuel System: Carter or Stromberg, two-barrel carburetor

Chassis/Drivetrain

Front suspension: Independent with A-arms, helical-coil springs, hydraulic-lever shock absorbers, torsion bar, stabilizer bar
Rear suspension: Semielliptical leaf springs, hydraulic-lever shock absorbers, cross-link stabilizer bar
Springs measure 54.5 × 2 inches on all except 75, which has 56.5- × -2-inch springs
Steering: Saginaw recirculating ball, 25.6:1 overall ratio

Electrical system: 6-volt battery, Delco Remy peak-
    load, current-controlled generator
Transmission: 3-speed manual, column-mounted
    shift, 10.5-inch diameter clutch
    (Series 75:   11-inch diameter)
Frame: Channel-section steel with X-center member
    and reinforced side members
Tires: 4-ply, 8.20 × 15
    Series 75:   7.5 × 16
Brakes: Hydraulic, 12-inch diameter
    Total braking area 208 square inches

Dimensions

Wheelbase:
    Series 61 and 62:   126 inches
    Series 60 Special: 133 inches
    Series 75:   136 inches
Width: 79 inches
Overall length:
    Series 61 and 62:   214 inches
    Series 60 Special: 226 inches
    Series 75:   226 inches

Front/rear tread: 59/63 inches
    Series 75:   58.5/62.5 inches

Popular Options

Hydra-Matic: $186
Radio: $85.50
    Series 75, rear compartment: $147
Vacuum antenna: $13.60
    Series 75: $15
Heater: $90
    Series 75: $123.50
Ventilating defroster heater: $60
Hydraulic windows (standard Series 62 convertible, 60
    Special, Series 75): $121.65
Spotlight
Rear-window defroster
Fog lights: $38
Wheel discs: $25
Wheel-trim rings: $9.50
Special steering wheel: $19.50
Glareproof mirror: $5
Windshield washer: $11
Backup light: $11

1949

The World's Most Distinguished Motor Car

FOR GOOD REASON, the years from 1948 through 1970 or 1971 have been labeled the "Golden Age of the American Automobile" by automotive historians. The availability of inexpensive gasoline, an expanding highway system, higher levels of expendable income, plus an eagerness on the public's part for exciting new cars with increasingly flamboyant styling and ever more powerful engines was all that Detroit needed to give full rein to its collective imagination. The final products came in for their fair share of criticism—all too often superficial and failing to recognize the important engineering milestones of the postwar years.

V-8 ENGINE

Certainly if the 1948 Cadillac established the styling theme for the age, then the new ohv V-8 engine introduced just a year later established its pace. With this engine, Cadillac not only moved ahead of its direct competition in an all-important area where customer awareness was very high, but became an industry pace-setter.

Cadillac announced this engine with boldness and audacity. "Mechanically," it reported, "the 1949 Cadillac offers one of the greatest engineering advancements in 45 years of fine car building. This year Cadillac introduces the Cadillac Valve-In-Head V-8 engine, a bold step forward because it completely displaces the finest performing engine ever to power a motor car. Now at the height of its success, Cadillac offers an entirely new engine—smoother, quieter, better performing, more economical to operate and maintain—one of the greatest engineering advancements in Cadillac's entire history." The introduction of the 135-horsepower 303-cid, ohv V-8 Oldsmobile engine just a few months later, and its availability in the lightweight 88 model gave Oldsmobile a popular-priced performance machine. But this did not take the luster away from Cadillac's achievement.

The engine Cadillac used for its 1949 models was destined for a long and full life, eventually displacing

429 cubic inches and benefiting from a steady stream of refinements, earning an enviable reputation for smooth operation, reliability, and power. For the 1964 model year, the Cadillac V-8 was redesigned to take full advantage of technologic and technical advances and in this form remained in production until 1968.

In the light of the 1970 Cadillac Eldorado's V-8, which with 500 cubic inches was the world's largest production engine, it's interesting to recall that early in its preproduction period, the ohv V-8 displaced just 289 cubic inches. By April 1947, this had been increased to 309 cubic inches. The decision to go one step further to 331 cubic inches was prompted by Oldsmobile's plan to market its V-8 with a displacement of 303 cubic inches.

Cadillac's use of a single engine for all its models began in 1941 and wasn't abandoned until 1975 when the Seville was introduced. The studies by Boss Kettering into the development of engines with high compression ratios and overhead valves, as well as Cadillac's engineering prowess, made it almost a certainty that when Cadillac replaced its 346-cid, L-head V-8, it would be with an engine of advanced design. But it's not likely that anyone, at least outside Cadillac, expected an engine that would provide one of the key themes for the earlier mentioned "Golden Age" and make Cadillac a performance automobile.

When Cadillac was attracting a great deal of attention in 1936 with the new Series Sixty models, its engine design engineers were involved in preliminary work on the next generation Cadillac V-8. When the product of their efforts, the 331-cid, ohv V-8 was introduced, Cadillac noted that "as early as 1936 Cadillac engineers foresaw the directions which automotive power should take—toward lighter, more powerful, high compression engines." From that point until production of war goods became Cadillac's number one priority, numerous V-type engine configurations were evaluated, including an all-aluminum V-12; but it was the V-8 arrangement that eventually prevailed.

While some critics might regard a decade-plus time span (even when the intervening war years are considered) as an inordinately long concept-to-production scale, Cadillac saw it quite differently. "It is typical of Cadillac," it explained, "that its new valve-in-head engine was not offered to Cadillac owners until more than 12 years after it was first conceived. In the intervening years, every idea that seemed to promise greater performance, longer life, greater power, smoother, quieter operation was tried, many theories were discarded altogether, many others were modified."

Cadillac always provided General Motors with individuals who, within its relatively small environs, learned their trade extremely well, and the new V-8 engine project yielded a bumper crop of individuals who later assumed positions of great responsibility at GM. In announcing the replacement of General Manager Nicholas Dreystadt (who became Chevrolet's general manager) by John Gordon, Cadillac described him as "a man who in twenty-three years has worked his way up from a 60-cent-an-hour laboratory assistant to manager of his Division." Joining Cadillac in 1923 he was, by 1929, foreman of its Experimental Laboratory, four years becoming its Motor Design Engineer. In 1940, he was appointed the assistant to the chief engineer in charge of engines at General Motors' Allison Division. Three years later, he was back at Cadillac as its chief engineer.

One of his first actions as Cadillac's general manager was to appoint Ed Cole as his successor in that pivotal position. Cole, at age 37, was already an "engineer's engineer." In 1932, after completing engineering work at the General Motors Institute, he became a Cadillac laboratory assistant. Less than six years later, he was a research engineer. During World War II, Cole's talent propelled his career forward. In 1943, he became chief design engineer and a year later assistant chief engineer.

Rounding out the talented triumvirate whose handiwork would make Cadillac synonymous with the V-8 was Harry Barr. In their paper dealing with the new Cadillac V-8, published in the May 1949 SAE Journal, Ed Cole and Harry Barr cited seven major design objectives that had been attained by its development: a higher compression ratio, reduced engine size and weight, a cleaner external design, improved serviceability, smooth performance, increased power, and greater durability. The 346-cid, L-head V-8, in its 1948 form, had a compression ratio of 7.25:1, its successor, at 7.50:1, wasn't much higher, but it would eventually peak at 10.5:1.

In his SAE paper, "Fuel and Engines for Higher Power and Greater Efficiency," published in the June 1945 SAE Journal, Charles Kettering, GM technical chief, noted that he regarded the two most important elements in engine history as the development of better fuels and the design of higher compression engines. These two factors had to develop concurrently since the use of a higher octane fuel in a low compression engine was nothing more than a prime example of the law of diminishing returns.

Not to be ignored was the limitations the L-head engine imposed upon compression ratio levels.

Experimental L-head engines with compression ratios as high as 8.6:1 were studied by Cadillac; but at that point, the engine's capacity to "breathe" was impeded and a fair amount of combustion roughness was experienced. In contrast to this dismal performance was the success of the Kettering team, which in 1945-1946, was working on an engine that could structurally handle the rigor of an ultrahigh (approximately 12:1 compression ratio). The Kettering engine, which was installed in a standard Oldsmobile and road tested in 1946, was an inline-six with equal bore and stroke and a displacement of 180 cubic inches. This engine and the insight into future design it represented was, since he retired in June 1947, Kettering's final contribution to the industry he had served so long and so well.

Production engines never quite reached the compression levels Kettering envisioned, but the ohv V-8, which encompassed a relatively high compression philosophy, owed much to Kettering's pioneering efforts. The second design objective, an engine with reduced size and weight, was achieved in a most dramatic fashion. Whereas the old engine's ready-to-run weight was 992.4 pounds, the new V-8's comparative weight was 771.7 pounds, or a reduction of 220.7 pounds. When divided into component weights, the overhead valve V-8's superiority was equally impressive:

Engine Weight (lbs)

Components	1948	1949
Block, crankcase	303.2	191.7
Clutch, flywheel housing	39.4	30.7
Crankshaft	92.4	61.6
Flywheel	50.3	33.4
Connecting rods	19	13
Intake, exhaust manifolds	64.4	52.2
Radiator core, tank	40	25.6
Coolant	52	38

Equally impressive were the new engine's more compact external measurements. Its length was 4.1 inches shorter, while its height was reduced by 3.7 inches.

Cadillac was justifiably proud of the new V-8's more functional exterior design, noting that "all components are located for good service accessibility. For example, the fuel pump is centrally located away from the exhaust manifold heat. Carburetor bowl and fuel pump temperatures are 30 degrees Fahrenheit lower than in the 1948 engine, improving resistance to vapor lock."

In the areas of improved performance and power, the new Cadillac V-8 easily exceeded the 346-cubic-inch L-head in all important categories. With a bore and stroke of 3.8125 cubic inches and 3.625 inches, respectively, it had, at 331 cubic inches, a smaller displacement. Yet its maximum net horsepower output of 135 at 2500 rpm was superior to the 1948 engine's 125 hp at 3200 rpm. Respective gross horsepower ratings of the two engines were 160 at 3,800 rpm and 150 at 3,400 rpm. Their maximum torque outputs were 312 lb.-ft. at 1,800 rpm and 283 lb.-ft. at 1,600 rpm.

As expected, the horsepower and torque of the new engine made the 1949 Cadillac substantially superior in performance to its predecessor. General Motors conducted tests of 1948 and 1949 model Series Sixty-One Sedans equipped with Hydra-Matic transmission and carrying four passengers. Without exception, the 1949 Series Sixty-One was the superior performer. Whereas the 1948 model needed 16.3 seconds to accelerate from 0 to 60 mph, the newer model required just 13.4. In top speed, GM credited the ohv V-8 with a maximum of 99.6 mph, substantially superior to the 1948 Cadillac's peak speed of 93.3 mph. As expected of an automobile capable of reaching 80 mph from a standing start in under 30 seconds, the 1949 Cadillac possessed excellent passing-range performance. To increase speed from 45 to 60 mph needed only 5.2 seconds (the 1948's best time was 6.9 seconds), and to reach 75 mph from 60 mph required 8.7 seconds, which was far superior to the 11.5 second mark of the 1948 V-8.

Against the backdrop of these performance figures, Cadillac claims for its new V-8 seemed boastful only to the uninformed. "We know," Cadillac told its prospective customers, "that when all is said and done, the greatest proof of Cadillac's great new engine will be on the road—with the owner himself at the wheel. It is then—in day-by-day driving—that the full story of Cadillac's magnificent performance will be revealed . . . You will find its response to acceleration amazingly fast and sparkling . . . It is unlikely that you will ever extend the Cadillac engine to its limits of power or speed, but it is certain that you will experience an entirely new motoring sensation because Cadillac has built into its new engine performance standards which were never known before."

Cadillac, as expected of a company that in 1949 described its products as "always the standard of the world," went to great lengths to ensure that its new V-8 was thoroughly tested before reaching market. There were two problems, however, that needed correction. It was important to keep the manifold heat-control valve loose to avoid premature valve burning and not until engine number 56,108 (August 1949) was a problem with oil leakage around the valve covers resolved. Overall though, this was a wonderfully trouble-free engine whose durable operation reflected the extensive testing that had been a key part of its development.

"It is doubtful," explained Cadillac, "if any engine has ever had a more thorough testing—in the laboratories and on the roads—than the new Cadillac powerplant." Backing up this assertion was a long list of evaluation hurdles the V-8 had passed in outstanding fashion. In its final production form, the V-8 had completed over 1 million test miles and over 25 engines built between 1946 and 1948 served as subjects for numerous stress tests.

Cadillac was particularly proud of the performance of a production model V-8 in the "Laboratory Endurance Test." This consisted of a run exceeding 100 hours duration at an engine speed of 4,250 rpm, which was equivalent to a speed above 108 mph. At the end, Cadillac reported "there was no appreciable wear on engine parts—there had been no mechanical breakdowns."

The attention Cadillac's new V-8 received created the incorrect impression that little else of consequence was changed for 1949. Cadillac historically had improved its products incrementally as well as by leaps and bounds, and 1949 was no exception. Cadillac servicemen welcomed the installation of a new type of flanged rear-axle shaft when such jobs as removing the rear brake drums had to be undertaken. Anyone who used the Cadillac's 160-horsepower engine to its fullest appreciated the installation of brake linings, shoes, and drums that were a ½-inch wider. Overall, the Hydra-Matic transmission was left unaltered. But here too were changes, minor in nature, that were appreciated by Cadillac drivers. For example, relatively simple internal modifications resulted in reduced "creeping" at stop lights and more consistent shift points.

CHANGES AND IMPROVEMENTS

Cadillac was the only American luxury-car manufacturer to introduce its 1949 models during calendar-year 1948. As expected, the lion's share of media attention was captured by the new V-8 engine. Yet Cadillac, in typical fashion, had made certain that the new models would be easily distinguishable from the old ones, whether or not they were in motion. Almost instant identification of the 1949 version was made possible by its grille format, which was much wider than the 1949's, while still using a combination of five vertical and two horizontal bars, but rearranging them to take advantage of the lowered profile of the V-8 engine-radiator. A key evolutionary development to be observed on the 1949 models was the extension of the grille work onto the front-fender wraparound by the use of grooved extension panels. Eliminated from the Series Sixty-Two models were the triple chrome stripes found below the taillights on the 1948's. On all Cadillacs but the Series Seventy-Five, another band of chrome was added to fully include the red reflector button into the light design. Creating the impression of increased overall length was the relocation of the Goddess hood ornament further forward. This suggestion was reinforced by a longer hood line.

Eliminated from the lower hood surface was the raised bead found on the 1948 models. Sedans in both Series Sixty-One and Sixty-Two now had a crease line extending across the back from rear door to rear door. Used on all bodies were new "snap-on" clips for the reveal moldings. During the model year, yet another change, a square trunk lid, was adopted, providing additional luggage space. The highly regarded dash layout of 1948, with its rainbow speedometer, central mounted glove box, and fully curved surface, was replaced by a more conservative version, with the glove box moved to the passenger's side and an oblong-shaped speedometer-gauge insert. Mounted in the center was a winged Cadillac emblem similar to both the 1940 Cadillac radiator badge and the trunk-lid identification plate used in 1947.

DIFFERENCES AMONG MODELS

The Series Sixty-One Sedan and Club Coupe models continued to lack the front-fender stone shields found on the Series Sixty-Two. Series Sixty-One customers could select a dual-tone cloth upholstery in either tan or gray. Door panels were finished in a plain fabric. The dash panel was covered with a cameo-grain Di Noc transfer with lighter-toned inserts.

The Series Sixty-Two sedan, priced at $3,050, was Cadillac's top-volume model, as confirmed by its 37,617 production total. Along with the $2,966 Club Coupe, whose 1949 model output was 7,505, the Sedan's interior featured seat and seat-back inserts of either broadcloth or Bedford cord in gray or brown. Both the seat-back bolsters and armrests were covered in a darker, harmonizing broadcloth.

An all-leather interior, offered in five colors, was standard fare for the $3,497 Series Sixty-Two Convertible, whose output reached an even 8,000 units.

Its top was available in either tan or black. The dash panel was painted.

The elegantly styled exterior of the Sixty Special was joined by an interior of either all cloth or a leather-and-cloth combination. Available with blue or green shadow-stripe broadcloth or Bedford cord were black leather seat bolsters. If tan leather bolsters were selected, they were combined with a tan shadow-stripe cloth. Regardless of the upholstery selected, all seats and interior panels had a block pattern, given a tailored touch by the installation of buttons. Output of the Series Sixty Special Sedan, priced at $3,829, was 11,399.

While the Cadillac ohv V-8 marked the start of a new era of power and performance for Cadillac, the production of the Series Seventy-Five model for 1949 symbolized the final curtain call for that prewar body style. The grand dame left the scene in style, though, powered by the new ohv V-8, sporting the new form dash, and produced in respectable numbers.

1949 Series Sixty Special.

1949 Series Sixty-Two Touring Sedan.

CADILLAC VITAL STATISTICS: 1949

Series	Model	Body Type	Factory Price ($)	Weight (lbs.)	Production (#)
61	6169	4 dr Sedan	2893	3910	15,738
	6107	2 dr Club Coupe	2788	3835	6409
62	6269	4 dr Sedan	3050	3951	37,617*
	6207	2 dr Club Coupe	2966	3857	7515
	6237	2 dr Coupe de Ville	3497	4272	2150
	6267	2 dr Convertible	3497	4213	8000
60	6069	4 dr Sedan	3828	4124	11,399
75	7519	4 dr Sedan	4750	4580	220
	7523	4 dr Sedan 7p	4970	4621	595
	7533	4 dr Imp Sedan 7p	5770	4643	626
	7523L	4 dr Bus Sedan 9p	4650	4491	35
	7533L	4 dr Imp Bus Sedan 9p	4839	4542	25

*360 Sedans were also exported in completely knocked-down form (CKD)

1949 Series Sixty-Two Convertible Coupe.

1949 Series Sixty-Two Coupe de Ville.

CADILLAC'S DOMESTIC COMPETITION

Cadillac began the 1949 model run with 114,000 unfilled orders on hand and with a production goal of 72,500. Earlier in 1948, some concerns had been expressed by *Business Week* that the days when demand for luxury cars exceeded supply was part of the past. On the eve of the presidential election between Harry S. Truman and challenger Thomas E. Dewey, Cadillac General Manager Don E. Ahrens released a statement expressing his views on that matter as well as several other issues. "Those who have sufficient cash," he said, "would buy cars regardless of who won the election and according to the backlog of our orders there are many thousands who have the money." As far as the future was concerned, Ahrens said, "I do not look for a buyer's market in the higher price bracket for more than a year."

His optimism was obviously shared by his counterparts at Lincoln, Chrysler, and Packard, who were eager to increase their market share at Cadillac's expense.

Packard was still years away from having an ohv V-8 ready for the assembly line and didn't offer its 1949, Twenty-Third Series until May 1949. Styling variations were of a minor nature. On all models except for the station sedan and commercial vehicles, oval-, instead of rectangular-shaped taillights were used. In addition, Packard nameplates were installed on the front fenders. Chrome side spears, cast in the traditional Packard form, were also used.

In a surprising move, Packard downgraded slightly the Custom Series' competitive status vis-a-vis the Cadillac Series Seventy-Five Fleetwoods. Its interior was somewhat less luxurious, and the 148-inch wheelbase sedan and limousines were dropped. At the same time, Packard realigned the Super Eight to make it more competitive with the Series Sixty-Two Cadillacs. Two new models with pseudo-Custom grilles, the Super De-Luxe four-door sedan and club sedan with prices respectively of $2,919 and $2,894, were offered. With the exception of the seven-passenger sedan and limousine models, which continued their 120-inch wheelbases of 1948, all Super Eights had the 127-inch wheelbase previously reserved for use on Custom Packards.

This type of model lineup fine tuning wasn't easily deciphered by the general public, who regarded Packard's new Ultramatic automatic transmission of much more importance. This two-speed torque converter with the advanced feature of a direct-drive clutch was standard on Custom models and a $225 option for other Packards. It arrived not a moment too soon as Cadillac reported that 98 percent of its 1948 models were sold with Hydra-Matic.

Prior to the introduction of Chrysler's 1949 (Silver Anniversary) models, there was a good deal of speculation about which path Chrysler had followed in their styling. *Fortune* magazine, for example, mused as to whether Chrysler had sensation models ready to sell or was rather attempting to cover up its lack of fresh new ideas. In February, when Dodge, the first of Chrysler's new models, debuted, the answer was

obvious: Chrysler was going to be more conservative than Ford or General Motors. The new Chryslers were spacious, well built, and functional. In terms of their mechanical structure, they were as familiar and as exciting as yesterday's news.

In spite of some praiseworthy features as safety-rim wheels and bonded brake linings, Chrysler was woefully outclassed by the technical impact of Cadillac's new engine. No major changes were made in the L-head, 135-horsepower, eight-cylinder engine, powering those Chryslers in the New Yorker, Town and Country, Imperial, and Crown Imperial models that were comparable to models offered by Cadillac.

Like Chrysler, Lincoln spread its product offerings to reach not only the luxury-car field but the upper, middle-priced class as well. For 1949, this strategy involved two distinct Lincoln series. Competing with such cars as the Buick Roadmaster and Chrysler New Yorker were 120-inch wheelbase Lincolns, sharing their body shells with Mercury. Priced between the Series Sixty-Two and Fleetwood Sixty Special Cadillacs were four Lincoln Cosmopolitan models (a four-door sedan, two-door coupe, convertible, and a four-door town sedan) with a 125-inch wheelbase and 220.5-inch overall length.

On paper, these Cosmopolitans seemed to be formidable challengers to Cadillac. In addition to their new styling, they also were powered by the first V-8 used by Lincoln since 1932. Unlike Chrysler, Lincoln did not opt for a conservative approach to postwar automotive fashion, and the Cosmopolitan retained little, if any, relationship with earlier Lincolns. What they lacked was a distinctive styling element that would capture the imagination of car buyers. They appeared ponderous; had awkward-looking recessed headlight shells; and suffered from their large slab sides, emphasizing bulk rather than creating any impression of fleetness.

Lincoln also erred in the design of its new V-8 engine. While Cadillac associated itself with advanced automotive developments, Lincoln opted to stay with the dated, L-head format. The result was not inspiring, exciting, or particularly memorable. With a bore and stroke of 3.5 inches and 4.375 inches, the Lincoln V-8 displaced 336.7 cubic inches and was rated at 152 horsepower. Extremely heavy, it outweighed Cadillac's V-8 by some 200 pounds.

Although Cadillac's engine had some "shakedown" problems, the most serious being leaky rocker covers on early models, the Lincoln V-8 was afflicted with a pronounced oil burning tendency, which wasn't really resolved until late in the 1950 model year, and an inferior engine alloy composition causing cracked blocks on some early cars. Lincoln's quality also suffered from Ford Motor Company's corporate restructuring, which resulted in their being designed and built under a rigid time frame that left many minor details unattended. For example, a minimum of 118 changes were incorporated in the Cosmopolitan's design during the 1949 model run. Already mentioned, but worth repeating, is the fact that the Cosmopolitans didn't have automatic transmissions until Hydra-Matic became optional late in the model run.

As expected, the somewhat out-of-step strategy of Cadillac's competitors put them at a disadvantage to a company that had a clear vision of what it wanted to achieve. And yet, Cadillac showed it had one more card to play before the model year came to an end with the July introduction of its Coupe de Ville, two-door hardtop coupe in the Series Sixty-Two line. Production of these cars was extremely limited at 2,150, but their presence underscored Cadillac's ability to reach important milestones in automotive design far sooner than its opposition. In typical understated fashion, Cadillac described the Coupe de Ville as a car "designed for those who seek the low-swept lines and open-airness of a convertible—combined with the comfort, convenience and safety of a closed car. It is a classic example of modernity and practicality—one of the most desirable and most useful models ever to issue from the boards of Cadillac designers." The status of the Coupe de Ville was highlighted by its distinction as being not only the final 1949 model Cadillac built on November 25, 1949, but also the one millionth Cadillac of all time!

Almost from day one of the model year, it was apparent that 1949 would be another sensational year for Cadillac. By August, Cadillac General Manager John Gordon could announce that the production of 51,560 Cadillacs during the first seven months of the year had established a new Cadillac record for that time span. "This new high-production level," he announced, "exceeds by more than 5,000 units the previous mark for a similar period set in 1946 and is more than 16,000 units ahead of the highest figure for any similar period since the war."

At model year's end, Cadillac's output, at 92,554, was tantalizingly close to the-then magical 100,000 mark. The total for Packard's model year, which didn't begin until May 1949, was 63,817. In virtually every category, Cadillac was clearly out front of its old rival. The vintage-styled Sedan Seventy-Five Fleetwoods reached an output of 1,861 units, ahead of the Custom Packard's production level of 1,201 cars. The bulk of Packard's output (53,168) was of its Eight and Eight DeLuxe models, none of which had counterparts in the Cadillac line.

Chrysler, which admittedly wasn't making a serious effort to challenge Cadillac, produced 24,491 cars in its New Yorker series (in contract with 22,148 Cadillac Series Sixty-Ones) and another 1,000 Town & Country convertibles (priced at $3,970). Any contest between Imperial and Crown Imperial Chryslers with Cadillac's Seventy-Five Fleetwoods was strictly a figment of wishful thinking at Chrysler since only 50 Imperials and 85 Crown Imperials were produced.

Lincoln's efforts with its Cosmopolitans yielded a total output of 35,123 cars. The most popular model, the $3,238 Sport Sedan accounted for 18,906 units.

To their credit, both Lincoln and Chrysler had V-8s under development that would erase Cadillac's margin of superiority in that all-important category; but looking forward to 1950, they could do little but bide their time and hope for better days ahead. Cadillac also envisioned a future that was equally rosy; and not only was launching freshly restyled cars in 1950, but via a group of enthusiastic American sportsmen, it was going to the races—and not as a spectator's car!

SPECIFICATIONS

Except for the following, specifications were unchanged from 1948

Engine

Type: V-type, ohv, eight cylinders
Bore × stroke: 3.8125 × 3.625 inches
Displacement: 331.0 cubic inches
Horsepower: 160 @ 3,800 rpm
Torque: 312 lb-ft @ 1,800 rpm
Compression ratio: 7.50:1
Fuel system: Carter WCD, two-barrel carburetor

Dimensions

Overall length:
    Series 61 and 62: 215.1 inches

1950

In Its 48th Year as Standard of the World

THE RESULTS of *Fortune* magazine's annual survey of reader's attitudes in 1950 provided precious little comfort for executives of Cadillac's competitors, since it indicated that nearly half of all automobile owners in the United States would select a Cadillac if given their choice of any new automobile. Cadillac was voted, by a five-to-one margin, America's favorite automobile, even though, as Cadillac later explained, "only a small percentage of American motorists have ever owned or driven a Cadillac—or, for that matter, so much as enjoyed a ride in one."

That percentage moved up a few notches during 1950 as, for the first time, both Cadillac's model- and calendar-year outputs exceeded 100,000 units. Their respective levels were 103,857 and 110,535. By any measurement, it was a spectacular year. Cadillac's prediction that it would be one "destined to see Cadillac's measure of leadership lengthened and strengthened in every respect" was uncannily accurate.

The list of Cadillac's achievements was a long one. At year's start, a round of significant price reductions were harbingers of good things to come. The old-style Series Seventy-Five Fleetwoods were retired, making way for a new generation of sharp-looking limousines and nine-passenger sedans; all Cadillacs had a new appearance; a stunning success was scored in the 1950 Mobilgas Economy Run; praiseworthy performances were also achieved in two of the premier auto sports events of that era, Mexico's PanAmerican Road Race and the 24-hour Le Mans Endurance Race in France.

CHANGES AND IMPROVEMENTS

Heading Cadillac's extensive restyling was a one-piece curved windshield, longer rear decks, and a new fender line that saw the distinct outline of the rear fender give way to a simulated rear air intake, accentuating Cadillac's extended length. The front grille was more massive and now incorporated the parking light. On those models ordered with the optional fog lights, a larger lamp unit without the standard concentric rings was installed.

In addition to producing 716 Sedans and 743 Limousines in Series Seventy-Five form, Cadillac also supplied 2,052 commercial chasses, which had a 157-inch wheelbase. Previous units had used a 163-inch wheelbase.

Not receiving much publicity in 1950 was Cadillac's new frame and suspension system. Through 1949, Cadillac frame and suspension design was basically that found on prewar models. No revolutionary changes were made, but the 1950 setup was both lighter and stronger. Helical-coil front springs were used in conjunction with semielliptic rear leafs measuring 2 × 54 ½ inches. Those installed on the Series Seventy-Five were 2 inches longer. The frame was of central X-member design with reinforced side members.

In its second year of production, Cadillac's ohv V-8 was equipped with a new oil-bath air cleaner with increased intake capacity and a redesigned intake manifold that was claimed to eliminate any possibility of icing.

The four-speed Hydra-Matic was also improved by the addition of a modulated, line-pressure control, which regulated the line pressure according to the throttle opening. This, said Cadillac, eliminated any noticeable downshift in gear ratio when the transmission went from second to first gear.

The introduction of Cadillac's new V-8 engine occurred at a time when Americans were rediscovering the sports car; refining the form of the hot rod; and, in general, reaffirming, to the dismay of social planners, their long-term love affair with the automobile. As a result, Cadillacs and Cadillac engines suddenly began to appear in the most unlikely places. The reason, of course, was the V-8's potency. Tom McCahill, whose road tests in *Mechanix Illustrated* magazine were read religiously by car buffs for three decades, declared in his test of a Series Sixty-One hardtop Coupe (*Mechanix Illustrated*, October 1950) that for general use the 1950 Cadillac was the best yet from Detroit. He also considered the Cadillac V-8 the world's number one production engine.

DIFFERENCES AMONG MODELS

Unlike 1949 when they used the same 126-inch wheelbase as the more expensive Series Sixty-Two models, the 1950 Series Sixty-One Cadillacs had a 122-inch wheelbase chassis not used elsewhere in the Cadillac line. Series Sixty-One four-door models were easily distinguished from other four-door Cadillacs by their unique rear-window wraparound, which extended across the width of the car, and absence of rear-door window ventpanes.

The Sedan's interior was tailored in two-tone gray of either broadcloth or corded cloth. The seats and seat backs were in the lighter tone and were finished with French seams. The door panels were trimmed in a darker tone and were fitted with six buttons. Seat and door kick panels of imitation leather were separated from the rest of the upholstery by a narrow, stainless steel strip. Door trim panels and window moldings were in Morocco brown. In the rear, gray pile carpeting was installed with matching rubber carpets used at the front. Both a center folddown and side armrests were provided for rear-seat occupants.

No fastback/sedanette body styles were offered by Cadillac for 1950. Filling this void in the Sixty-One line was a two-door hardtop, rather unimaginatively identified as the Coupe model. The seats and seat backs on the Coupe were upholstered in a light-toned fabric with the door panels and seat cushions finished in a darker material. Window moldings and trim panels were Morocco brown. Matching the color of the dark-tone upholstery were the rubber floor carpets. All interior hardware was bright chrome and the door handles and window controls were set in a Morocco grain panel with a gray insert. Large, box-type armrests with built-in ashtrays were placed at the extreme ends of the rear seat. Both models' overall length of 211⅛ inches was 4 inches shorter than that of the 1949 versions. The rear deck line of the Coupe was considerably longer than that of the Sedan. The respective factory prices of the Sedan and Coupe were $2,866 and $2,761. While output of Series Sixty-One four-door Sedans declined slightly from 15,738 in 1949 to 14,619 in 1950, the hardtop Coupe proved far more popular, with an output of 11,839, than had the old Club Coupe whose final year's production had totaled 6,409.

In presenting its Series Sixty-Two models, Cadillac explained that "there is a body type offered in this series to meet practically every taste and requirement." As had been the case since production resumed after the war, the only convertible offered by Cadillac was a Sixty-Two version. Along with other Sixty-Two models, its wheelbase measured 126 inches, with overall length reaching 215.875 inches. The lower body edge on these Cadillacs was fitted with full-length chrome panels, unlike the Sixty-One models which used chrome trim only on the lower-fender-skirt edge and the trailing edge of the rear-fender character line.

All Series Sixty-Two Cadillacs had Fleetwood interiors, which on the Convertible consisted of leather trim offered in five solid colors or two-tone options of green or blue. A light-toned insert extending into the front door panel from the dashboard contained the hydraulic controls for the Convertible's standard power-window lifts. It was framed in molding painted to match the body color. Each door panel also carried a chrome V. Fine-pile carpeting, colored to match the dark-toned leather, was installed front and rear.

Power windows were also standard for the Coupe de Ville model, which was offered in a less expensive ($3,150 to $3,523) base-price form as the Sixty-Two Coupe. Both cars had nearly identical exteriors; but on closer examination, the Coupe de Ville's chrome dripmolding was noted. Absent from the 1950 model's exterior trim was the Coupe de Ville script found on the 1949 version. Much more apparent were the differences found in the two cars' interiors. The Coupe's featured two-tone gray broadcloth with either plain, pattern, or Bedford cloth. Rear armrests with ashtrays were used, and the side panels were trimmed in a horizontal pleat motif trimmed by narrow chrome-trim moldings. Fine-pile carpeting harmonizing with the dark-toned upholstery was standard. The rear parcel shelf was covered with an artificial-grain leather.

The Coupe de Ville's interior, in Cadillac's view, "features a deluxe handling throughout." A two-tone leather and broadcloth combination of either gray leather with dark blue cloth or tan leather with tan broadcloth was offered. The seat bolsters and upper-door panels were finished in the leather trim, which was divided into 3-inch wide sections. The cloth upholstery was used for the seat cushions, seat backs, and lower-door panels.

An imitation-leather headliner divided by chrome-top bows gave the Coupe de Ville's interior added distinction. Other points of interest included chrome window and trim moldings, painted door moldings, and individual robe cords mounted on the front seat backs. A dark-toned carpeting was used. Standard equipment on the Coupe de Ville included hydraulic operation of the windows and front seat.

The four-door Sedan Cadillac offered in Series Sixty-Two form had a more conservative Fleetwood interior, consisting of two-tone gray combinations of broadcloth, striped cloth, or Bedford cord with French seams. The seats and seat backs were light colored, while the bolsters and seat cushion sides were dark. Primary features of the two-tone door panels included long armrests, chrome moldings, and French-seamed horizontal pleats for the lower, dark-toned section. The front-door hardware, except for the manual window control, was gathered in a panel insert of pearl beige. Dark-finish, imitation leather, harmonizing with the dark-toned upholstery, was used for the door and seat kick panels. Matching dark-wool-pile carpeting covered the front and rear compartment floors. Power windows were optional.

1950 Series Sixty-Two Coupe.

1950 Series Sixty-Two Sedan.

CADILLAC VITAL STATISTICS: 1950

Series	Model	Body Type	Factory Price ($)	Weight (lbs.)	Production (#)
61	6169	4 dr Coupe	2866	3822	14,619
	6107	2 dr Club Coupe	2761	3829	11,839
62	6219	4 dr Sedan	3234	4012	41,890
	6237	2 dr Club Coupe	3150	3993	6434
	6237D	2 dr Coupe de Ville	3523	4074	4507
	6267	2 dr Convertible	3654	4316	6986
60	6019	4 dr Sedan	3797	4136	
75	7523	4 dr Sedan 7p	4737	4555	716
	7533	4 dr Imp Sedan 7p	4959	4586	743

1950 Series Sixty-Two Convertible.

Although the Series Sixty-Two Sedan used the same rear deck and rear fenders as the Series Sixty-One Sedan, its longer, 126-inch wheelbase, and a different roof line, featuring a narrow, rear corner pillar and ventpane, made it easy to distinguish between the two cars.

These traditional production leaders continued to be Cadillac's pacemakers in 1950. The Series Sixty-Two Sedan was by far Cadillac's most popular model, as indicated by its production level of 41,897. Closely grouped were the Club Coupe's and Convertible's respective outputs of 6,434 and 6,986 cars. Coupe de Villes were still uncommon sights on American roads, measured by the assembly of only 4,507 units.

"There is only one Cadillac-Fleetwood Sixty Special Model," Cadillac told prospective customers, "a beautiful four-door Sedan, whose extra length and graceful full-flowing line distinguish it as the aristocrat of the highways." With a 130-inch wheelbase plus longer and higher rear deck and rear fenders, the Sixty Special's overall length was 224.875 inches, which made it a considerably larger automobile than the Series Sixty-One and Sixty-Two Sedans. Unique to the Sixty Special were the eight, vertical chrome louvers on its rear fender. As expected, the interior of the Sixty Special (whose New York City delivered price was reduced for 1950 from $4,131 to $3,920) was, in Cadillac's words, "a charming expression of advanced coach work by Fleetwood featuring superb taste, roominess and consummate comfort." Owners could select their upholstery from four different colors—green, tan, blue, or gray—in either plain or patterned materials.

These upholstery material and color choices were available in combinations of pattern or cord seats and seat backs or in a plain cloth. All seats and seat backs were divided into square "biscuits" trimmed with cloth buttons. The same pattern was used for the center door panel, which was bracketed by plain cloth on its top and bottom. Both front- and rear-door kickpads were of bright chrome as were all window frames. The driver's door contained hydraulic controls for all windows. Along with the door handles, they were set in a panel with a pattern insert framed with molding painted to blend with the upholstery's color. Mounted in the recessed, heavily padded seat back was an ashtray, cigarette lighter, and a cloth-covered robe cord.

Wool-pile carpeting was used, colored to match the upholstery and trim. An artificial-leather heel pad was placed under the driver's foot controls.

Standard equipment included Hydra-Matic (which was also standard on Series Sixty-Two models and optional at $174 on all other Cadillacs) and hydraulically operated window lifts and front-seat adjustments. Output of the Series Sixty Special totaled 13,755 cars.

With its 1950 model Series Seventy-Five (as in earlier years both "75" and "Seventy-Five" identification was used) seven-passenger Sedan and Limousine (with a dividing front partition), Cadillac removed the last link with its prewar body design. Perhaps just a bit self-conscious about having kept the Series Seventy-Five with its old-style exposed running boards and appearance in production for so many years, Cadillac described its successor as "new throughout. Long and low, its modern exterior appearance strikes a completely new note in cars of this exclusive type and character." Its 146-inch wheelbase was 10 inches longer than that of the previous model. Overall length was 236.575 inches. Appearance of the new Series Seventy-Five followed the general form of the other Cadillacs.

From the rear, a smaller back light identified the Series Seventy-Five. Both the rear fenders and deck of the Seventy-Five were identical to those used on the Series Sixty-Two Sedan. Unlike the Series Sixty Special, which carried a Fleetwood script on its trunk lid, the Seventy Five was fitted with a Cadillac wreath and crest.

The Seventy-Five's commodious interior provided two jump seats for occasional use and a regal environment for the rear-seat occupants. The seat cushion and seat back had a tufted center section with wide plain bolsters. Either Bedford cord or broadcloth upholstery was optional in a choice of tan or gray. The garnish moldings, door panels, and floor carpets were in harmonizing colors. On Limousine models the front seats and door panels were trimmed in black leather. The seat and seat backs had 2.5-inch pipings. Black imitation leather was used for the headliner. Under foot was floor carpeting of mottled black leather. Also having a black finish were the steering column and instrument panel.

The Limousine divider featured a stationary upper portion, which eliminated the upholstered liner used on previous models. Set into the divided brown-burl, walnut-grain molding was an electric clock. Fitting into two assist handles at either side of the divider was a cloth-covered robe cord. On Limousine versions, the front seat was stationary; on the Sedan, it was adjustable.

Although the standard transmission for the Seventy-Five was a three-speed manual, the list of features included in its price ($4,770 for the seven-passenger Sedan, $4,959 for the Limousine) was lengthy, including power windows, a rear-compartment clock, center armrest, and robe cord. Also fitted for passenger convenience were cigarette lighters and ashtrays in the front-seat back and side armrests.

CADILLAC'S ENTRY INTO RACING

At this time, a British sports car maker, Sydney Allard, had been enjoying the sights and sounds of his cars, powered by Cadillac V-8's, matching and more often beating such formidable marques as Ferrari, Maserati, and Jaguar in both American and European sports car competition. Even more significant was the decision of Briggs S. Cunningham, a respected and talented American sportsman, to enter a team of Cadillacs in the 1950 24-hour Le Mans race. This was not the first time an American car had competed at Le Mans. As early as 1925, American cars, driven by Europeans, had made a good account of themselves at Le Mans. In 1925, two Chryslers competed and one finished sixth overall, averaging 56.2 mph. The following year, one of three entries by Willys-Overland completed the race in seventh place. In 1928, the Chryslers arrived and came away with second, third, and fourth places. In the years following this outstanding achievement, other American manufacturers, such as Stutz and Duesenberg, raced at Le Mans; but after 1935, no American cars entered until the Cunningham Cadillacs made their appearance in 1950.

Cunningham had originally planned to enter a team of Cadillac-powered Fords for the first Carrera PanAmerican and Le Mans. These Fordillacs were hybrid speedsters produced in small quantities by Frick-Tappet Motors, owned jointly by Bill Frick and Phil Walters, both of whom were to play important roles in Cunningham's racing efforts. Unfortunately, neither the Mexican nor French race officials were convinced the Fordallic was a true production car. In truth, there were other cars competing at Le Mans that were even further removed from the world of assembly-line-built cars than the Fordallic, but what was OK for a French car wasn't for a Yankee V-8.

During this time span, entries for Le Mans were by "invitation only"; and through the efforts of his close friend Luigi Chinetti, who also shared Cunningham's enthusiasm for Ferraris, Cunningham received two invitations for the race, provided his entries were production models.

Certainly meeting this criterion were the two Series Sixty-One hardtop Cadillacs Cunningham selected for his first Le Mans venture. The idea of Cadillacs competing in the world's premier sports car event was incongruous to some enthusiasts who perceived the Cadillac as a sedate car for the wealthy, incapable of anything approaching sports car performance. The Cadillac wasn't, of course, a sports car, but it was a durable, powerful automobile that, as its second place finish in the 1950 Carrera PanAmerican indicated, was a force to be reckoned with in any long-distance race.

As prepared for Le Mans, one of the Cunningham Cadillacs received a somewhat ungainly but, given the state-of-the-art in 1950, a fairly aerodynamic body designed by Grumman Aircraft engineers. Its engine was modified via the use of five down-draft carburetors mounted on a special intake manifold. The second Cadillac retained its stock body but was equipped with a two-carburetor setup. Additional changes included the use of stiffer, French-built shock absorbers and the installation of an additional, 35-gallon, fuel tank in the trunk and air scoops welded on the brake drums to direct additional air to the linings.

During practice sessions, the two Cadillacs turned in impressive lap times. The Coupe was clocked at 117 mph, while the open two-seater's top speed was nearly 130 mph. In the race, the Cunningham team had its fair share of problems. On the second lap, Briggs Cunningham, then driving the two-seater, lost precious time digging his car out of the notorious Mulsanne sand bank. Eventually the Cadillac lost both first and second gears and was reduced to lapping the entire course in high gear.

During the race, both Cadillacs gradually moved up in the standings. After one hour of racing, the Coupe was in 19th position with the roadster well back in 35th place. But at midnight, with the race one third completed, their respective places were 17th and 15th. After the roadster's gear box became unglued, the Coupe moved ahead to finish 10th overall with the roadster next in the standings. Their average speeds for 26 hours were 81.51 mph and 81.33 mph. The winning car, a thinly disguised Talbot Grand Prix car, had maintained an average of 89.72 mph, barely 8 mph faster than the Cadillac's. Cunningham soon switched to Chrysler's V-8 in his sports cars and in 1953 achieved a third-place finish at Le Mans.

Back in the United States, Cunningham's achievement attracted relatively limited attention, in sharp contrast to the publicity Cadillac's Debutante model received. As part of the 38-car General Motors show held at the Waldorf-Astoria in early February 1950, this special tawny-yellow convertible was viewed by over 300,000 people. Touted as a $35,000 automobile, the Debutante was upholstered in Silver satin and "Somaliland" leopard skin (with a leopard tail serving as a robe cord). All interior hardware was gold-plated. The attractive female model who explained this car's features to showgoers wore a coat with the same pattern as the Debutante's interior. Both were supplied by the same furrier. After looking over the Debutante, comedian Peter Lind Hayes quipped, "A beautiful car, who shot it!"

CADILLAC'S DOMESTIC COMPETITION

In stark contrast to Cadillac's record-setting performance on all fronts in 1950, the news from Packard was most noted for its lack of newness. In anticipation of the rebodied models scheduled for 1951, the Twenty-Third Series Packards were carried over into 1950 almost unchanged. In contrast to Cadillac's list of numerous styling and engineering improvements, the big news for Packard fans was limited to such running changes as rear-seat draft deflectors for Sedans, woodgrained tissue dispensers, and accelerator-peddle wear pads. Packard's calendar sales were down only slightly to 106,457, but of this only 42,640 were credited to the 1950 models.

Chrysler, for 1950, continued to match obsolete straight-eights with conservative styling that was generally regarded as improved over 1949's. Unfortunately, the new grille work for the Imperials and Crown Imperials too closely followed Cadillac's lead to be regarded as an original design. In addition, the two-door hardtop model added to the Town and Country and New Yorker series was entering a segment of the market where Cadillac had been active for a year.

Both Chrysler Division and Chrysler Corporation were doing extremely well in 1950 and were planning moves that would make the upper-line Chryslers far more competitive with Cadillac. But in 1950, the production of only 10,650 Imperials and 414 Crown Imperials were vivid illustrations of just how difficult it would be to overcome Cadillac's substantial lead over its competitors.

Lincoln's 1950 model-year sales dropped to 17,439 Lincolns and 10,741 Cosmopolitans. The Cosmopolitans were restyled to eliminate the awkward "droop look" of the 1949s, but their appeal was hampered not only by the reputation of the 1949s for mechanical troubles but by an absence of both convertible and hardtop models. An attractive two-door Cosmopolitan Capri Coupe was offered, but its

description as "the ultimate in fine-car styling" was presumptuous.

SPECIFICATIONS

Engine

Type: V-type, ohv, eight cylinders
Bore × stroke: 3.8125 × 3.625 inches
Displacement: 331 cubic inches
Horsepower: 160 @ 3,800 rpm
Torque: 312 lb-ft @ 1,800 rpm
Compression ratio: 7.5:1
Fuel system: Carter WCD, two-barrel, down-draft carburetor
Electrical system: 6-volt

Chassis/Drivetrain

Transmission: 3-speed manual, synchromesh on second and third gears, semicentrifugal, single-plate torbend disc, 10.5-inch diameter, Series 75: 11 inch
Frame: Rigid X-type, reinforced side members with deep X-member junction
Rear axle: Hypoid, semifloating
  ratio with standard transmission: 3.77:1, Series 75: 4.27:1
  ratio with Hydra-Matic: 3.36:1, Series 75: 3.77:1
Front suspension: Independent, helical coil
Rear suspension: Semielliptic leaf springs, 54.5 inches × 2 inches
  Series 75: 56.5 × 2 inches
Steering: Recirculating ball-type, overall ratio: 25.47:1
Tires: Low-pressure 4-ply, 8.00 × 15
  Series 75: 6-ply, 8.22 × 15

Dimensions

Wheelbase:
  Series 61: 122 inches
  Series 62: 126 inches
  Series 60 Special: 130 inches
  Series 75: 146.75 inches
Width: 80.125 inches
Front/rear tread: 59/63 inches
Overall length:
  Series 61: 211.875 inches
  Series 62: 215.875
  Series 60 Special: 224.875 inches
  Series 75: 235.575 inches

Popular Options

Hyrda-Matic (standard on Series 62, and 60 Special): $174
Power windows (standard on Series 62 Convertible, Coupe De Ville, 60 Special)
Power seat (standard on Series 62 Convertible, Coupe De Ville, 60 Special)
Standard heater and defroster
Automatic heating system

Automatic push-button radio
All-weather ventilating system
Syncro-matic radio and rear speaker
Full-size wheelcovers
Windshield washer
Fog lights (includes parking and direction lights)
White sidewall tires
Exterior rear-view mirror

License-plate frames
Spotlight
Fleetwood robe
Seat covers
Vanity mirror
External sun visor
Full wheelcovers
Wheel-trim rings

1951

In Its 49th Year as Standard of the World

AMIDST REPORTS claiming that restrictions and material shortages caused by the Korean War would limit passenger-car output to between four and five million units (compared with 1950's record output of 6,672,200 cars), the 1951 Cadillacs were introduced on December 17, 1950.

CHANGES AND IMPROVEMENTS

The most important styling changes consisted of small egg-crate inserts for the outer grille panels; much larger front bumper guards, now virtually an integral part of the bumper; and "cadet-visor" headlight bezels. Also revised was the Hydra-Matic quadrant (now enclosed by the steering column cover). Previously it had been labeled N, DR, LR, R. It now read N, D, L, R. Additional interior detail changes included blunt rather than bullet-shaped handles for the directional and shift levers.

The limited popularity of the Series Sixty-One line continued to be disappointing. Cadillac was clearly correct in spirit, if not in fact, by describing the Sixty-One Series as "particularly popular with those motorists who are taking their first step up to Cadillac." Cadillac also regarded them as "most remarkable" since "they offered every detail of Cadillac's thorough-going goodness, at a price actually competitive with numerous other makes of cars." This assertion stood up under the scrutiny of comparison shopping. The Coupe and Sedan models were priced respectively at $2,831 and $2,940. The six-cylinder Hudson Hornet, making its debut in 1951, was priced at $2,568 (four-door Sedan) and $2,869 (Hollywood Hardtop). The 1951 Nash Ambassador Custom four-door Sedan, powered by an ohv six-cylinder engine cost $2,501. Most industry observers would concur that none of these products provided owners with the same status as did ownership of a Cadillac.

Compared with contemporary Packard and Chrysler models, the Series Sixty-One was priced very competitively. The least expensive Chrysler Saratoga, two-door Club Coupe cost $2,989. Packard's 200 Series were several hundred dollars less expensive than the Series Sixty-One Cadillacs, but it's debatable that they were direct competitors. In midyear, Packard introduced two, 250 Series models, a two-door hardtop Coupe and a Convertible with respective prices of $3,234 and $3,391. It's not inappropriate to regard these Packards as alternatives to the Series Sixty-One Cadillacs.

European interest in the Cadillac, piqued by its fine showing at Le Mans, remained high. *The Autocar*, which tested a Series Sixty-Two four-door Sedan in its November 9, 1951, issue, praised its performance as outstanding and lauded Cadillac's handling, which it considered as having a minimal amount of roll in turns while providing the driver with excellent feel. Like their American counterparts, *The Autocar* testers complained of the tendency for Cadillac's brakes to quickly fade under strenuous use. But overall, the Cadillac received good grades from a select group of drivers with a very broad background of testing experiences.

The American position, at least from the perspective of Griff Borgeson who tested an identical Series Sixty-Two for *Motor Trend* (November, 1951), praised Cadillac's extraordinary fuel economy. At a constant 45 mph, the Cadillac with Hydra-Matic and a 3.36:1 rear axle delivered 24.0 mpg. At 60 mph, this declined to a still impressive 18.1 mpg. However, it was less than satisfied with its handling qualities. Singled out for criticism were the tendency of the Cadillac's rear end to skip about at speeds of 70 mph or above, the limited steering control in sharp turns, and the high level of tire squeal when pushed hard in the corners.

DIFFERENCES AMONG MODELS

Series Sixty-One interior appointments featured bolstered seat cushions and backs in two-tone combinations of either gray or tan. The upholstery combined a plain broadcloth with either a figured pattern or striped cord material. The two-tone panels featured upper quarters in broadcloth risers while the lower portion was covered in either the figured or striped cord material. Window moldings and trim panels were in a harmonizing painted finish. The headliner was in a light-toned material. Wool-pile carpeting complemented the interior color. The Sedan model now carried a V medallion in its rear C-pillar.

Series Sixty-One production was discontinued midway through the model year after 2,300 sedans and 2,400 Coupes had been built. In sharp contrast were the production levels attained by the Series Sixty-Two models. Their volume leader was the $3,528 Sedan of which 54,596 were sold. This made it Cadillac's most popular model of 1951. Both the Series Sixty-Two Sedan and $3,436 Coupe, whose production reached 12,132, had two-tone interiors of either a patterned cord or plain cloth in gray or tan. The seat backs and seats had 6-inch wide pleats with alternating dark and light shades in the side and door panels. All molding and trim panels were painted to harmonize with the upholstery color. Somewhat more chrome trim was found in the Sixty-Two interior than was used for the Sixty-One models.

The Coupe de Ville, in Cadillac's words, carried "the sports motif to its fullest expression." A dark broadcloth upholstery with harmonizing leather trim was available in three color combinations—blue and gray, tan and buff, and two-tone green. The wool-pile carpeting matched the upholstery color, while the headliner's color was the same as the leather trim. As in 1950, exposed chrome-top bows were intended to simulate a convertible roof design. A new external feature of the Coupe de Ville was the gold-colored "Coupe de Ville" script mounted on the roof pillar. Both the Coupe de Ville and Series Sixty-Two convertible had as standard equipment hydraulically operated windows with both individual controls and a master control switch located in the left front-door panel.

The $3,987 convertible was a rare sight even as a new automobile, only 6,117 were assembled. Three single colors as well as two-tone combinations of green or blue were offered for its all-leather interior. The seat cushions, seat backs, and the top and bottom of the door and side panels were pleated with dark-toned leather. If a two-tone combination was selected, a plain, lighter-toned leather was installed in the door and side panels, as well as across the top of the seat backs. The instrument and trim panels were painted to match the exterior color, while the carpeting color was that of the dark-tone leather. In addition to its windows, the Convertible's top and seat adjustment were hydraulically operated. No doubt arousing the interests of some sports car enthusiasts was Cadillac's description of the Convertible as "a fine sports car."

As in 1950, the Series Sixty-Two models had a longer, 126-inch to 122-inch, wheelbase than the Series Sixty-One Cadillac. They continued to have full-length, lower-body trim not found on the Series Sixty-One. The Sedan model was also distinguished from its Series Sixty-One counterpart by its rear-vent panels and the less extensive wraparound of the rear back light.

As in previous years, the Series Sixty Special was the focal point of Cadillac's effective promotion of its status as America's most prestigious automobile. It was "magnificent . . . a car so distinguished that it knows no rival for the affections of the motoring public . . . a model which has played a major role in building Cadillac's reputation as the 'Standard of the World'."

External identification of the Series Sixty was identical to that applied to the 1950 model; a longer, 133-inch wheelbase, extended rear deck and fender line, and eight chrome chevrons mounted behind the rear-fender louver.

The Series Sixty interior was upholstered in a choice of four fabric colors—green, tan, blue, or gray. The seats and seat backs were pleated in either broadcloth or whip cord. The door panels, in contrasting tone, had a smooth center portion bracketed by pleated sections. Like the headliner, the wool-pile carpeting was of a lighter tone that matched the general color scheme. The instrument and trim panels were similarly painted. As in previous years, the Sixty Special's front-seat back was fitted with a robe cord, a combined ashtray and lighter, and assist grips. Model-year output of the $4,142 Series Sixty Special was 18,631, up 4,876 units from the 1950 level.

Production of the Series Seventy-Five moved up smartly in 1951, with a total of 1,085 Limousines priced at $5,405 assembled. The front compartment of the Limousine was again trimmed in black leather. Pleated seat cushions contrasted with plain black-leather door panels and black trim moldings. Once again the front headliner was of black imitation leather. A new feature was the use of black wool-pile carpeting rather than the black rubber of 1950. Also revised was the molding for the front-seat back, which was now finished in Carpathian-burl, walnut grain.

The seven-passenger Sedan featured an interior of Bedford cord or broadcloth in either gray or tan. Both the rear seat and seat backs were tufted, while the wide bolsters were of a plain design. Slightly less expensive than the limousine at $5,200, the Sedan's production level of 1,090 virtually matched the limousines.

For use in the rental or livery business, Cadillac again offered a Series Seventy-Five Business Sedan. This model had been available in 1950, but only one was constructed. Output in 1951 was again very limited, reached only 30 units. Not surprising, this was the final year for the business Sedan. Its interior, for 1951, was trimmed in tan broadcloth. Extra-wide auxiliary seats enabled six passengers to be carried in the rear compartment.

1951 Series Sixty-Two Sedan.

1951 Series Sixty-Two Convertible.

CADILLAC VITAL STATISTICS: 1951

Series	Model	Body Type	Factory Price ($)	Weight (lbs.)	Production (#)
61	6169	4 dr Sedan	2940	3839	2300
	6137	2 dr Coupe	2831	3807	2400
62	6219	4 dr Sedan	3528	4062	54,596
	6237	2 dr Coupe	3436	4081	10,132
	6237D	Coupe de Ville	3843	4156	10,241
	6267	2 dr Convertible Coupe	3987	4377	6117
60	6019	4 dr Sedan	4142	4234	18,631
75	7523	4 dr Sedan 8p	5200	4621	1090
	7523L	4 dr Bus Sedan 8p			30
	7533	4 dr Imp Sedan 8p	5405	4652	1085

1951 Series Sixty-One Coupe.

1951 Series Sixty-Two Coupe.

CADILLAC'S DOMESTIC COMPETITION

Although greater challenges lay ahead, 1951 was a year when both Packard and Chrysler made it very clear that they had by no means resigned themselves to Cadillac's hegemony in the fine-car field. Yet, measured by the crucial sales results, these thrusts were easily parried by Cadillac.

Packard had started work on a new look for its outdated models in mid-1949, and the new models were ready for public perusal beginning on August 24, 1950. Although they lacked any startling styling features, the Twenty-Fourth Series models were excellent examples of contemporary American design. Major Packard trademarks, such as its arched grille outline, spear-shaped side trim, cormorant hood ornament, and cloisonne wheel-cover medallions, were successfully blended into a body whose wide expanses of glass gave it a fresh, airy appearance.

Packard was still four years away from having its new, overhead-valve V-8 ready for use, which meant 1951 would once again be a straight-eight year for Packard. In a move that surely disturbed long-time Packard loyalists, the 356 cubic-inch engine was not available. It was replaced in the Custom models by a nine-main-bearing version of the 327-cubic-inch eight rated at 155 horsepower. This made sense from a manufacturing point of view, but did little to heighten Packard's status vis-à-vis Cadillac.

Even more serious was Packard's further withdrawal from direct competition with Cadillac. Packard divided its 1951 models into four lines: 200, 250, 300, and 400. The 200 line represented over 71 percent of Packard's model-year output of 100,713 cars, and were most definitely not comparable with the Series Sixty-One Cadillacs. More appropriately regarded as Packards intended to lure away Cadillac customers were the 250 Series Convertible and Mayfair models priced at $3,391 and $3,239. The latter was Packard's first two-door hardtop. These Packards, except for the very early models, were trimmed and detailed to put them in close proximity to Packard's top models, making them very appealing vehicles. Unfortunately, their late introduction date of March 16, 1951, limited output to just 4,640 cars.

Packard's line became sparse above the 250 Series, with only a four-door body style offered in the 300 and Patrician 400 lines. Their output was predictably low: 15,309 and 9,001, respectively. Against either car, the Fleetwood Sixty Special was a formidable opponent, and its output of 18,631 cars made it the obvious choice of the marketplace while the Series Sixty-Two Coupe De Ville and Convertible had no competitors from Packard at all. The hardtop body style had come from nowhere to capture 9 percent of the new car market in 1951. Packard's decision not to offer such a model in the 400 Series was a costly and a shortsighted decision, roughly analogous in its folly with Chrysler President Keller's belief that millions of Americans wanted to sit in cars with their hats on.

The major news from Chrysler was mixed. Its Imperial was still saddled with a basically unimaginatively styled body shell with a dated two-piece windshield. But improvements made the Imperial a more distinctive and attractive automobile. Chrysler also added Convertible and two-door, hardtop-body styles to the Imperial line and officially proclaimed the Imperial a separate model. Of far greater significance was the Imperial's new ohv V-8 engine, which with 180 horsepower had a definite power advantage over Cadillac's V-8.

Based largely on the strength of this engine, Chrysler received *Motor Trend* magazine's Engineering Achievement Award in 1951. *Motor Trend* admitted that its criteria for determining the winner of its competition did not include such factors as suspension, upholstery, appearance, comfort, ease of driving, and visibility. These were areas that were also important to consumers. In addition, the Chrysler engine with its hemi-heads couldn't make up for other Chrysler shortfalls. The best Chrysler had to offer customers who weren't keen about shifting gears in an expensive car were two versions of fluid drive: Fluid-Matic, which was standard on the Imperial, and the Crown Imperial's standard Fluid-Torque. Neither of these eliminated the clutch pedal from Chrysler's most expensive products. This deficiency became even more glaring when the prices of the Crown Imperial Sedan and limousine were $6,623 and $6,740.

Imperial production increased substantially for 1951, reaching 27,698. This was far below Cadillac's level of 103,200, but represented a significant increase from the 11,064 Imperials assembled in 1950.

Also enjoying a major production increase was the Lincoln Cosmopolitan of which 15,813 were manufactured. The Cosmopolitan, unlike Chrysler, did not have a modern, new engine to offer buyers nor did it follow Packard's lead and present a product with fresh styling. On the other hand, efforts to improve performance in the L-head V-8 were starting to pay off. With a higher rear-fender line, bolder taillights, a larger rear window, and a simple, but attractive grille format, the 1951 Cosmopolitan's appearance represented a definite improvement over older models.

Clearly shaping up was round two in the "Great American Luxury Car Contest." Cadillac, by most measurements, had been the winner of the first round by a large margin. It had been first in adopting new styling, a styling innovator via the rear fender fin, first with the popular two-door hardtop, and, until 1951, had enjoyed a monopoly in its class with the ohv V-8.

Cadillac's efforts had not been unrewarded. In 1951 *Popular Mechanics* magazine's "Owner's Reports" on Cadillac, Packard and Chrysler provided evidence of just how successful Cadillac's postwar strategy had been. Among Cadillac owners, 82 percent rated their cars "excellent." Packard's score in the same category was 64 percent. Chrysler's was 67 percent. This strong position came on the heels of evidence that Cadillac enjoyed a clear-cut edge over Packard and Chrysler in terms of customer loyalty. Of those Cadillac owners responding to the *Popular Mechanics* poll, 79 percent had previously owned a Cadillac, and 90 percent indicated they would buy another one in the future. Packard's previous ownership was far lower at 33 percent. In addition, Packard's weak model representation in the top price class was reflected by the small proportion (only 6 percent) of Patrician owners among the Packard owners surveyed. In contrast, 88 percent of the Cadillac owners participating had purchased either Series Sixty-Two or Sixty Specials. As far as their next purchase was concerned, only 66 percent of the Packard owners indicated it would definitely be a Packard.

Chrysler outpointed Packard in all three categories, but it failed to match Cadillac's popularity. Sixty-seven percent of the Chrysler owners rated their cars excellent, 63 percent were previous Chrysler owners, and 77 percent said they would buy another Chrysler.

SPECIFICATIONS

Cadillac specifications and options were unchanged from 1950.

1952

The Motor Car That Marks a Half-Century of Automotive Supremacy

NINETEEN FIFTY-TWO wasn't a record-breaking year for Cadillac, at least in terms of production. Model-year output dropped to 90,259 cars, with calendar-year assemblies totaling 96,880. This fallback to pre-1950 levels was due to a variety of factors, not the least of which can be credited to shortages and material restrictions caused by the Korean war and a long steel-industry strike. As a consequence, industry-wide production for the year fell to 4,337,400 or over a million cars less than in 1950.

Cadillac was opposed by Lincoln, which, for the first time since the prewar years, was an automobile that on all counts was a formidable challenger. The latest Cadillac was an automobile whose appearance was little changed from 1951, but it was an appearance that enjoyed a high level of public acceptance and was far from dated. Furthermore, 1952 was Cadillac's Golden Anniversary, and Cadillac not only offered a few styling features to commemorate the occasion, but also bolstered them with several significant engineering developments.

Then there was the matter of the horsepower race. Cadillac's rating of its V-8 had remained unchanged since 1949. Now, with the arrival of Chrysler's 180-horsepower Hemi V-8, that type of conservatism was cast aside. The great American horsepower race, for better or worse, was about to begin, and Cadillac was going to be in its midst.

CHANGES AND IMPROVEMENTS

Identifying the 1952 models as Golden Anniversary Cadillacs were gold-cast V and crest emblems on the hood and rear deck. As in 1951, the Series Sixty and Seventy-Five models had Fleetwood script on their trunk lids. A subtle change, not immediately detected, was the deeper angle of the V and the reshaped crest, which was lower and wider than before. Appearing only on the 1952 models were the gold-colored, winged

Cadillac crests on the side grille extension, which closely resembled the form of the standard prewar Cadillac radiator badge. No longer used was the "waffle" insert for this grille element. The optional fog lights now carried "Cadet Visor" bezels similar to those embracing the headlights.

Linking Cadillac's styling and technical changes for 1952 were the standard dual-exhaust exits that were integrated into the rear bumper. These were part of an exhaust system consisting of two independent exhaust pipes (not headers) for each cylinder bank that entered identical sets of resonators and mufflers. Also increasing the efficiency of this system were larger exhaust ports.

Along with Buick and Oldsmobile, Cadillac offered a four-barrel carburetor (either a Carter WFCB or a Rochester 4GC unit) in 1952. Both Lincoln and Chrysler had to once again see Cadillac be first in the field with a significant and widely publicized innovation since Lincoln's first use of a four-barrel carburetor came a year later with Chrysler's waiting until 1954. The Cadillac setup used a progressive linkage to provide use of the primary barrels for normal, part-throttle operation. When the accelerator was fully depressed, the secondary barrels were opened to supply additional intake capability. This feature, along with a new intake manifold and larger exhaust valves, enabled Cadillac to claim power ratings of 190 horsepower at 3,800 rpm and 322 lb-ft of torque at 2,400 rpm.

With the exception of the Series Seventy-Five Fleetwoods, all Cadillacs had a new Dual-Range Hydra-Matic as their standard transmission. For the Series Seventy-Five, it was a $186 option. The most attractive feature of the four-speed Hydra-Matic was its new performance range, which allowed the driver to keep it in third gear for as long as desired.

Performance of the 190-horsepower Cadillac with Hydra-Matic was impressive. During 1952, *Motor Trend* tested 20 American cars, and none of them exceeded its Cadillac Series Sixty-Two test car's top speed of 109.6 mph. In second place was the 106.0 mph Chrysler

Saratoga. In its test of a Series Sixty-Two with an identical 3.36:1 rear axle (a 3.07:1 ratio was a no-cost option), *Science and Mechanics* reported a top speed of 105.2 mph. Whereas *Motor Trend's* best time from zero to 60 mph was 13.2 seconds, *Science and Mechanics* attained an extremely rapid 0- to 60-mph time of 10.89 seconds. In the standing-start quarter-mile test, the Series Sixty-Two was *Motor Trend's* fastest car with a time of 18.4 seconds. The Chrysler was well back at 19.5 seconds; the Packard 300, slow still at 20.7 seconds; and the Lincoln well off the pace at 21.6 seconds.

Chrysler had scored a point against Cadillac by introducing power steering in 1951. But for 1952, General Motor's Saginaw power steering was a $198.43 option for all Cadillacs. It was generally praised for its retention of road feel while at the same time providing effortless operation. Also debuting was the $53.36 Automatic Eye (also offered as an option by Oldsmobile), which was developed by the Guide Lamp Division of General Motors. This device, which was mounted on the left side of the dash, contained a prismatic condensing lens, which, upon catching the light of an oncoming car, depressed the Cadillac's high beam until the car had passed.

The only major chassis change for 1952 concerned the use of larger 2.5 × 12-inch, ribbed, front-brake drums for all models. In 1950 and 1951, only the Series Seventy-Five had brakes with these dimensions. All other Cadillacs had 2.5 × 11-inch brakes front and rear. The Series Seventy-Five, however, continued to use rear brakes of a 12-inch diameter while 11-inch units were fitted to the remaining 1952 Cadillac models. Thanks to its larger brakes, the Series Sixty-Two Cadillacs had the best pound per square inch of brake-lining ratio of any American car. These brakes, as expected, gave the Cadillac good braking performance. Under normal use conditions, fade was very unlikely; and even after 32 panic braking stops from speeds ranging from 20 mph to 60 mph, *Science and Mechanics* reported its Cadillac's brakes were still performing well.

Motor Trend revised its "Car-of-the-Year" evaluation procedure to, it claimed, place less emphasis on power. In 1951, Chrysler had received this award, to Cadillac's chagrin no doubt; but for 1952, all was smiles at Cadillac as *Motor Trend* reported that on the basis of performance, handling, safety, economy, and maintenance, it had awarded its Engineering Achievement Award to Cadillac. In *Motor Trend's* view, Cadillac had built the best car among the vehicles it had tested in 1952.

DIFFERENCES AMONG MODELS

With the elimination of the Series Sixty-One line, Cadillac offered three series of automobiles for 1952. The Series Sixty-Two Sedan along with Series Seventy-Five models had higher rear deck lines with what Cadillac described as "slipstream styling." Its interior, as well as that of the Coupe, was upholstered in two-tone combinations of dark broadcloth and either cord or patterned cloth of a lighter color. The seat-back insert

and cushions were deeply tufted, and the upper door panels were trimmed in dark broadcloth, divided into 6-inch squares. The door bottoms were in a lighter tone, while the wool carpet was of a harmonizing shade. A simulated-leather finish protected the extreme lower-seat facing. The two-tone colors offered were dark and light gray, brown broadcloth with tan cord or patterned cord, dark and light green, and a pale blue combined with the darker blue.

The Series Sixty-Two Convertible interior was tailored in leather. Three two-tone and two single colors were offered. Solid-color selections were red and black. If a two-color scheme was desired, Cadillac provided a choice of three light-metallic, dark-leather combinations: brown/tan, dark/light green, and dark/light blue. In these arrangements, both the seat-back and cushion inserts were trimmed in the light metallic color with the front and rear bolsters of the darker shade. The front-seat back was similarly divided into an upper section of the darker-tone leather and a recessed lower region finished in the light leather. The robe cords were covered in the dark leather. Like the seats, the door panels had a diagonally tufted leather pattern of two colors. If the single-color interior was selected, both the seats and the door panels were in a single color. A chromed Cadillac crest was mounted in the center of each interior door panel. The kick panels were of a ribbed chrome.

Coupe de Ville interiors featured leather bolsters and door panels in light matching tones with dark, cord-cloth seats and backs. The four color combinations exclusive to the Coupe de Ville were shadow blue fabric/light blue metallic leather, dark gray cord cloth/light gray leather, green cloth/light green leather, and brown nylon fabric/tan leather. The robe cords were covered in a light colored leather. The dark-toned carpeting was color-coordinated with the upholstery. The door and kickpads were in patterned chrome. Chrome roof bows and garnish moldings continued to be key features of the De Ville interior. As on the Convertible, a chrome Cadillac crest was centrally mounted in each door panel.

The output of 70,255 Series Sixty-Two models represented the bulk of Cadillac's 1952 model production. Leading the way was the $3,636 Sedan of which 42,625 were built. Next was the $3,962 Coupe de Ville whose 11,165 production level put it just ahead of the less costly $3,542 hardtop Coupe whose production reached 10,065.

Contributing 16,110 cars to Cadillac's model-year total was the $4,720 Series Sixty Special. In addition, 1,400 Series Seventy-Five Sedans, priced at $5,361 and 800 of the $5,572 Imperial Sedans were manufactured.

The Series Sixty Special, again recognized by its unique exterior trim and long, 133-inch wheelbase, was available in any of eight interior, two-tone color combinations. The choices offered included dark green/pastel green, tawny brown/golden tan, dark gray/light gray and dark blue/light blue. The seats and seat-back inserts were trimmed either in light cord or in light-toned plain broadcloth. Light-toned metallic leather was tailored into heavily padded door piping that

1952 Series Sixty-Two Coupe.

1952 Series Sixty-Two Convertible.

1952 Series Sixty-Two Coupe de Ville.

CADILLAC VITAL STATISTICS: 1952

Series	Model	Body Type	Factory Price ($)	Weight (lbs.)	Production (#)
62	6219	4 dr Sedan	3684	4140	42,625
	6237	2 dr Coupe (HT)	3587	4173	10,065
	6237D	2 dr Coupe de Ville	4013	4203	11,165
	6267	2 dr Convertible	4163	4418	6400
60	6019	4 dr Sedan	4323	4255	16,110
75	7523	4 dr Sedan 8p	5428	4698	1400
	7533	4 dr Imp Sedan 8p	5643	4733	800

1952 Series Seventy-Five Limousine.

contrasted with the door sidewall broadcloth finished in a harmonizing shade. This light- and dark-toned motif was repeated in the cushion and seat-back piping. The lower rear-seat bottoms and seat sides were faced in dark leather. The same regions of the front seat were covered in a dark-toned cloth. Additional Series Sixty Special interior features included chrome window moldings, integral armrests in the door panels, a dark leather robe cord, and assist handles.

The front compartment of the Series Seventy-Five Limousine was virtually identical to that of the 1951 model. The rear compartment of the Series Seventy-Five Imperial limousine and the eight-passenger Sedan were identical. The rear-seat cushions and seat backs were in a tufted style with wide plain bolsters and harmonizing leather welts. Customers could select either Bedford cord or broadcloth in shades of light tan or light grey. The garnish moldings, door panels, and floor carpeting were in a harmonizing pattern.

The instrument panel used by all models was distinguished from the 1951 version by its new gold and brushed-silver crest. Both the Series Sixty-Two and Sixty Special Sedan were available in twelve new solid and five two-tone exterior colors. Respective choices for the Coupe de Ville totaled thirteen and six. The Convertible, whose top was available in black, tan, blue and green, could also be ordered in any of the solid colors offered for the Coupe de Ville.

CADILLAC'S DOMESTIC COMPETITION

The challenge posed by Cadillac's opposition to what was obviously a line of cars worthy of being its Golden-Anniversary offering ranged from an almost stand-pat Chrysler and Chrysler Imperial lineup to dramatically redesigned and repowered Lincolns, with moderately restyled Packards boasting power brakes (two years before Cadillac made them available) somewhere in the middle of this spectrum. Unlike the Imperial, which if not in name then certainly in basic appearance was associated with lower-priced automobiles, the 1952 Lincoln was a car that was unsoiled by any such state of affairs. For the first time since the age of the Lincoln-Zephyr, the Lincoln name was reserved exclusively for automobiles clearly intended to be compared with the Cadillac. Emphasizing this point was the introduction of the new Capri series, which were more expensive than the former top-ranked Cosmopolitans. After struggling with a less-than-successful body style from 1949 through 1951, Lincoln, with its 1952 cars, produced an automobile that some observers regarded as worthy of comparison with the original Continental.

Furthermore, the Ford Motor Company, painfully aware of the requirements for any successful opposition to the Cadillac juggernaut, had made the development of an ohv V-8 for the 1952 Lincoln a top priority. The only mistake Ford made in this strategy was to introduce this 317.5-cid V-8 with a modest 160 horsepower, which was exceeded by both Cadillac and Chrysler. In the next few years, this would change; and with its thoroughly modern suspension (the 1952

Lincoln was the first American car to use a balljoint, rather than kingpin front suspension) and more power, the Lincoln would emerge as a high-performance luxury automobile.

Meantime, it made a startling recovery in 1952. Comparing 1951 Cosmopolitan sales with those of the 1952 Cosmopolitan and Capri models shows the new version's sales improved by over 72 percent to 27,271. A great advance to be sure, but barely 30 percent of Cadillac's output. Furthermore, Cadillac would enter the 1953 model year with a backlog of 90,000 car orders at a time when James M. Roche, its general sales manager, could report that the demand for its cars was at the highest level ever experienced by the division.

Packard's output of its Twenty-Fifth Series for 1952 of 62,921 was as in earlier years composed mainly of lower-priced models. Thus in the price ranges where it competed with Cadillac, Lincoln, and Chrysler, Packard had produced only 15,881 cars. Packard's output, like that of its peers, had been held down by the five-week strike in the steel industry. The resumption of production wasn't the biggest news to come from Packard's East Grand Boulevard plant by a long shot, for taking over its presidency was James J. Nance, formerly of General Electric and determined to restore Packard to a place of prominence among American automobiles. Nineteen fifty-three was shaping up as quite a year.

SPECIFICATIONS

Engine

Type: V-type, ohv, 8 cylinders
Bore × stroke: 3.8125 × 3.625 inches
Displacement: 331 cubic inches
Horsepower: 190 @ 4,000 rpm
Torque: 322 lb-ft @ 2,400 rpm
Compression ratio: 7.5:1
Fuel system: Carter WFCB or Rochester 4GC, four-barrel carburetor
Electrical system: 6-volt

Chassis/Drivetrain

Transmission: Dual-range Hydra-Matic (standard on all models except Series 75)
Frame: X-type, reinforced side bars with deep X-member junction
Rear axle: Hypoid, semifloating, offset differential housing
  Ratio for Series 60 Special and Series 62: 3.36:1, optional, 3.07:1
  Series 75: 3.77:1
Front suspension: Independent, helical coil
Rear suspension:
  Semielliptic leaf springs, 54.5 × 2 inches
  Series 75: 56.5 inches × 2 inches
Steering: Recirculating ball-type, overall ratio: 25.47:1
Tires: Low-pressure 4-ply
  Series 75: 6-ply, 8.20 × 15

Brakes: Four-wheel hydraulic, 12-inch drums, 241.5 square inches of braking area, 258.5 square inches on Series 75

Dimensions

Wheelbase:
    Series 62:   126 inches
    Series 60 Special: 133 inches
    Series 75:   147 inches
Width: 80.1 inches
Front/rear tread: 59/63 inches
Overall length:
    Series 62 Sedan: 215.5 inches
    Series 62 Coupe and Coupe de Ville: 220.5 inches
    Series 60 Special: 224.5 inches
    Series 75:   236.25 inches

Popular Options

Full-size wheel discs: $28.40

Hydra-Matic (Series 75): $186
Windshield washer: $11.36
Oil filter: $11.34
Fog lamps: $36.91
Outside mirror: $6.24
E-Z eye glass: $45.52
Heating-ventilating system: $113.66
Signal-seeking radio: $129.22
Automatic push-button radio: $112.47
Power steering: $198.43
Autronic light control: $53.36
White sidewall tires (Series 62 and Series 60 Special): $33.76
Power windows (standard in Coupe de Ville and Convertible: $138.64
Full wheelcovers
Wheel-trim rings
External sun visor
Vent shades
Spotlights

1953

The Motor Car That Begins a Second Half-century of Automotive Leadership

"THE YEAR 1953," proclaimed Cadillac, "is certain to go down in history as a milestone in Cadillac progress and development. For the motor cars that Cadillac presents . . . brings to fruition all the good and wonderful things Cadillac has pioneered in the past fifty years—and at the same time, herald a wholly new era in automotive advancement. The 1953 Cadillac is in everyway, the finest motoring creation ever to bear the Cadillac name . . ."

CHANGES AND IMPROVEMENTS

With this grand vision in mind, General Manager Don E. Ahrens closed out the 1952 Cadillac model year by announcing that Cadillac would start production of its 1953 cars with a backlog of 90,000 orders. To meet the demand, he reported that Cadillac would be expanding its manufacturing facilities. James M. Roche, Cadillac's general sales manager, added that the demand for cars was at the highest level ever experienced by the division.

This situation seemed to suggest that Cadillac was headed for another record output and with model-year production reaching 109,651 (calendar-year output was 103,538), Cadillac came close to equaling its 1951 record. The reason why it didn't exceed that year's mark was due to a fire in August that destroyed General Motors Hydra-Matic plant at Livonia, Michigan. The result was a shutdown of Cadillac operations for nearly a month. When production resumed on September 8, the Cadillacs leaving the assembly line were equipped with Buick-supplied Dynaflow transmissions. These Cadillacs, totaling approximately 28,000 units, were fitted with 3.36:1 instead of the normal 3.07:1 rear axle in order to partially compensate for Dynaflow's slower than Hydra-Matic acceleration. Cadillac specified either a Carter WCFB, model 20885 or a Rochester 4GC, model 700621 in place of the Carter WCFB, model 2005S and Rochester 4GC, model 7005100 carburetors for its Dynaflow models.

Cadillac did not use the Dynaflow term in its advertising, selecting instead "Twin Turbine" to identify Dynaflow-equipped Cadillacs. These cars also had a redesigned converter pump cover, flywheel housing, and rear-bearing extension. Although the bumper-positioned exhaust outlets were retained, the exhaust system was reshaped. Even so, the difference between Cadillacs with these two transmissions was apparent. Using Drive range only, a Hydra-Matic Cadillac would accelerate from 0 to 60 mph in approximately 15 seconds. The Dynaflow version was about 2 seconds slower. On the other hand, Dynaflow provided somewhat more rapid midrange acceleration. The Dynaflow-equipped Cadillac also delivered slightly fewer miles to the gallon, as well as less engine braking.

Cadillac did not change the displacement of its V-8 engine for 1953, but incorporated a number of changes, enabling it to claim 210 horsepower at 4,150 rpm and 330 lb-ft of torque at 2,700 rpm. Cadillac said that this engine, "the result of over 37 years of experience in the design of V-8 engines, brings unprecedented power, smoothness, responsiveness, and economy to automotive performance . . . one that will set a new world's standard for performance and efficiency."

Nonetheless, Cadillac was being conservative in its power ratings, since the following year the horsepower would climb to 230 without any change whatsoever in the engine's specifications. The reason for this approach was simple; at 210 horsepower, Cadillac remained America's most powerful automobile with a 115-mph top speed and a 0 to 60-mph time of under 13 seconds.

The use of a new high-lift, cam-and-valve mechanism enabled the valves to open wider. In 1952, intake and exhaust valves opened respectively at 14 and 24 degrees; for 1953, these increased to 22 and 27 degrees. In addition, slightly larger exhaust valves with a stem diameter of 0.3417 instead of 0.3410 inches were used. Contributing to an increased compression ratio of 8.25:1, up from 7.5:1, were longer aluminum-alloy pistons and a reshaped combustion chamber that decreased flame travel while increasing gas turbulence. Nineteen fifty-three was also the first year Cadillac used a 12-volt electrical system.

Whereas 1952 models had used a standard 3.36:1 axle ratio, those for 1953 were equipped with a 3.07:1 unit. In comparison tests, Cadillac reported that the newer model would deliver an average mileage of 18.2 mpg as compared with the 16.2 mpg achieved by the 1952 Cadillac. At the same time, the 210-horsepower engine more than compensated for use of a numerically lower rear axle. Tests at the General Motors Proving Grounds showed the new model 100 feet ahead of its predecessor after just 1,000 feet of an acceleration test.

Since new body shells were on tap for 1954, the 1953 models were restyled not only to conform to Cadillac's conservative, yet relentless evolutionary policy of change, but to serve as a platform to prepare the public for what was planned for 1954. By this time, the form of Cadillac's front bumper guard had acquired unmistakable sexual overtones, as evidenced by its "Dagmar" nickname, acquired because of its similarity to the physical assets of a well-endowed television sensation of the time.

In 1953, the Cadillac bumper guards really were no longer a key part of the bumper design. Sensually shaped, they nestled within the cozy confines of Cadillac's egg-grate grille work, displacing the parking/directional/fog lamps, which were moved to the outer grille extensions. The circular parking/directional light was set in a small panel with five thin, horizontal ribs that matched similar grille elements on either side. If installed, the optional fog lights maintained this integrated form because of the raised elements on their surface. Continued from 1952 were the gold-colored V (which was wider for 1953) and hood emblem.

The 1953 hood was both wider and lower. Also altered was the goddess ornament, which was more streamlined than in 1952. All Sedan and hardtop models had a lighter and more airy appearance thanks to the elimination of the rear-window division bars. Cadillac made its first major change in hubcap design since 1947 with a new optional wheelcover that had the Cadillac disc deeply recessed within a concaved center section.

Once again, "Cadet-Visor" headlight bezels were a key feature of Cadillac's front-end appearance. This time around they protruded further than in earlier years. It's fair to say that it was love at first sight between these eyelids and American car owners, as this styling feature quickly became an industry cliche.

Cadillac also was the industry trend setter, as evidenced by the proliferation of rear-fender fins and scoops as well as V-type emblems among American automobiles.

Assuming the same "bulletlike" shape as the front bumper guards (Cadillac also identified them as "grille guards") were the rear bumper guards. Cadillac also modernized the form of the rear-fender stone guard. As always, Cadillac made certain this change wasn't too radical, noting "this new guard retains the familiar characteristics that have made it a sparkling hallmark of Cadillac recognition and appearance . . . and yet, it adds a new distinctive note to Cadillac styling for 1953

by giving the rear fender bulge the modern tailored, trim look."

Concluding the list of Cadillac styling changes for 1953 were new optional wheel discs, which did not have the series of concentric rings set within the concave surface as did the 1952 units. Also changed was the surface on which the Cadillac crest was positioned. Instead of being only moderately curved, it was now prominently domed. Cadillac claimed that "in addition to styling advantages, these new Cadillac wheel discs reduce wind, noise, and wind drag to a new low point in streamlined automotive design."

Experienced Cadillac watchers had no difficulty in detecting the changes made in the Cadillac's interior for 1953. The Cadillac crest mounted, as in 1952, in the center instrument panel was now gold and brushed silver instead of all silver on Series Sixty-Two models. The other Cadillacs continued to carry Fleetwood script in the same position. Also altered was the clock face, which had a light-toned insert and four rather than 12 hour numerals. Debuting in 1952 was a two-tone steering wheel with light-toned, simulated-leather hand grips, a less cluttered center pad, and a dash mounting for the Hydra-Matic quadrant. The fuel and temperature gauges continued to have white needles against a chrome background. A feature not found on other American luxury cars was the Cadillac interior mirror, which had an up-and-down adjustment. Continued from 1952 was the symmetric arrangement of the twin map lights mounted above the radio and the dual vent knobs positioned below the speaker.

Even though Packard had offered cars with air conditioning back in 1939, it wasn't until 1953 that this comfort option became widely available, as both General Motors and Chrysler, as well as Packard, announced that their cars would be offered with this feature. On this point, Lincoln was far behind its competition, not offering air conditioning until the 1955 model year.

Cadillacs with this $619.00 option were easily identified by their fresh air scoops located on the rear fenders and the transparent plastic outlets on the parcel shelf. Key elements of this system, produced by General Motors' Frigidaire Division, included a rotary compressor mounted on the engine's right side and a condenser located ahead of the radiator. The refrigeration unit was positioned in the trunk, which had a negative impact on available luggage space.

DIFFERENCES AMONG MODELS

The most popular (a total of 47,316 were produced) of the 1953 Cadillacs once again was the Series Sixty-Two Sedan, which Cadillac described as "a perfect motor car for both family and business." Its interior featured light-toned tufted upholstery in either nylon cord or broadcloth with contrasting dark tufted bolsters and trim in broadcloth. The doors were trimmed in light-toned sidewall cloth with light and dark metallic-finish moldings. Simulated, light-toned leather covered the tops of the armrests. Polished, tinted, stainless-steel, door kickpads were used along with door hardware fin-

1953 Eldorado Convertible.

1953 Series Sixty Special.

CADILLAC VITAL STATISTICS: 1953

Series	Model	Body Type	Factory Price ($)	Weight (lbs.)	Production (#)
62	6219	4 dr Sedan	3666	4201	47,316
	6237	2 dr Coupe	3571	4189	14,353
	6237D	Coupe de Ville	3995	4252	14,550
	6267	2 dr Convertible	4144	4476	8367
	6267S	Eldorado Convertible	7750	4799	532
60	6019	4 dr Sedan	4305	4337	20,000
75	7523	4 dr Sedan 8p	5604	4801	1435
	7533	4 dr Imp Sedan 8p	5818	4853	765

ished in brushed and bright chrome. The rear compartment was equipped with a wide center armrest as well as built-in side armrests. The rear shelf was finished in simulated leather. Eight interior trim combinations were offered for the Series Sixty-Two Sedan.

The Series Sixty-Two Coupe interior was detailed in the same fashion and, like the Sedan, was available in eight choices. As was the Series Sixty-Two Sedan, the Coupe was fitted with a textured-weave carpet colored to harmonize with the interior trim. Both the steering column and instrument were painted to match the interior.

Although considerably more expensive ($3,995 to $3,571) than the Coupe, the Series Sixty-Two Coupe de Ville was marginally more popular. Its production totaled 14,550 to the Coupe's 14,353. Cadillac depicted the Coupe de Ville as "one of the most dramatically styled on the American road." It became ever "more beautiful," continued Cadillac, "with the optional wire wheels, available on all 1953 Cadillacs, adding an extra note of excitement." Continued from 1952 was the gold-colored "Coupe de Ville" script located on the rear roof pillar.

The Coupe de Ville's eight interior combinations featured nylon fabrics and leather. Four were offered with a new V-and-crest pattern for the seats and seat-back inserts along with dark leathers in contrasting tones. Color combinations included green, tan, gray, and blue. Continuing to give the Coupe de Ville interior added distinction were its chrome roof bows and moldings.

Depicted as "low, beautiful and graceful of tone . . . perhaps the most exciting of all 1953 Cadillacs," The Series Sixty-Two Convertible was available in any of seven new interiors, consisting of solid-tone leather in red or black and two-tone combinations of metallic synthetic leather and natural leather in green, tan, and blue. In the latter versions, pleated seat-back inserts and cushions were upholstered in the metallic leather edged by darker leather. White leather cushions and seat-back inserts in either light blue or green were also offered. A new interior-door design also found in the Coupe de Ville featured a Cadillac crown mounted in the dip of the V'ed center panel. The Convertible's door was paneled in two shades of leather and a wide, stainless-steel kick panel. The Convertible top was offered in black, tan, blue and green. Once again hydro-electric windows were standard on both the Coupe de Ville and Convertible.

Output of the Fleetwood Series Sixty Special increased sharply in 1953, moving from 16,110 in 1952 to 20,000 units. Externally, the Sixty Special retained its eight rear-fender-mounted vertical louvers and rear-deck V and gold Fleetwood script. Joining these features was a dramatically broader, chrome, lower-body trim running from the front-fender cutout to the rear bumper. Twelve solid and five two-tone color combinations were offered.

The Series Sixty interior color choices were dark green, brown, gray, and blue, with contrasting lighter-tone trim. The seat and seat-back inserts were trimmed in light-toned Bedford cord fabric, plain broadcloth, or the new V-and-crest pattern cloth. Each version had tailored, narrow 1-inch piping. The deeply cushioned bolsters were styled in dark-toned broadcloth, while the seat sides were faced in dark cloth and leather. Other features that added to the distinctively luxurious mode of the Sixty Special interiors included an extra-wide center armrest, and a V and crown mounted on the back of the front seat.

The front-seat back area below the leather robe cord was finished in 1-inch, light-toned broadcloth piping. Both the seat top and lower-seat side, as well as the seat

1953 Orleans Show Car.

sides, were faced in dark leather. The Series Sixty interior door design was much more conservative than that of the lesser models. At the top, two narrow, dark-metal-finish panels were divided by an "ostrich-skin" insert. This material was also used for the center portion of the dash panel. The main-door section carried a raised, rectangular inner panel. Twelve interior trim styles were available.

Neither the eight-passenger Series Seventy-Five Sedan nor the Limousine was a big seller for Cadillac, as shown by their respective 1953 totals of 1,435 and 765. Yet they remained of great value to Cadillac as prestige showpieces. A total of 12 different interior selections was offered, including six two-tone combinations in gray, blue, tan, and brown, plus six solid shades of tan, gray and blue. The seat fabrics were broadcloth and Bedford cord.

Limousine models, as was Cadillac's policy, were fitted with a hydraulically controlled partition between the front and rear compartments. The chauffeur's seat was covered in either blue or black leather; and on both the Limousine and eight-passenger Sedan, the front-seat upholstery had a tufted motif with wide plain bolsters and harmonizing leather edging. In the rear, a new center armrest joined the side armrests with built-in lighters, ashtray, and electric clock.

IMPACT OF LE MANS ON CADILLAC

By 1952, American interest in motor sport and sports cars had grown to proportions that attracted the attention of virtually every American manufacturer. Actually the independent manufacturers, more mindful of the need to carve out small and hopefully profitable niches in the market than their "Big Three" competition, had been pioneers in the development of American sports cars. For example, in the 1950 Le Mans race, in addition to the Cunningham Cadillacs, a Nash-Healey had represented the United States. Indeed, with a fourth-place finish, it had done extremely well. This car was the start of an agreement between Nash-Kelvinator and an ambitious Englishman, Donald Healey, who, when beginning his own automobile company after World War II, had sensed that a latent market for sports cars in America was beginning to surface. As a result, he had come to terms with Nash-Kelvinator President George Mason; and by 1951, Nash-Healey two-seaters were available.

While the Nash-Healey relied on Donald Healey for much of its design, the Crosley Hotshot Super-Sports two-seater was a pure American design. Moreover, these Crosleys, first available in 1949, were real pioneers of the postwar, American sports-car movement. These developments, along with the efforts of Americans such as Brooks Stevens, Sterling Edwards and Frank Kurtis, all of whom produced sports or sports-type cars in small numbers in the early fifties, paved the way for the major American companies to follow their lead.

Actually, as suggested by the prewar Buick Y-Job and Chrysler Thunderbolt, the large producers had long been aware of the value of "Dream Cars" as devices to measure public attitudes about advanced styling ideas. Not surprisingly, therefore, when General Motors showed its LeSabre and Buick XP-300 in 1951, they were, in spite of their two-seater capacity, far removed from the spartan nature then regarded as crucial to the contemporary sports cars.

General Motors followed up these two cars with a very ambitious 1953 Motorama show that featured "high-performance" two-seaters from every automotive division except Pontiac. Only one of these, the Corvette, could realistically be termed a sports car. Yet Cadillac's version, the "Le Mans" (critics who objected to Cadillac's use of this hallowed name apparently chose to ignore Cunningham's achievements in the 1950 race), both pointed the way toward future Cadillac styling themes and preceded the arrival of the limited-production Eldorado model in the 1953 model year.

The Le Mans, along with the Chevrolet Corvette, Buick Wildcat, and Oldsmobile Starfire, featured both a fiberglass body and General Motor's "panoramic" windshield, which would soon gain as much social acceptability as Cadillac's rear-fender fin. The Le Mans predictably aroused the ire of the conservative, neo-traditional, sports-car enthusiasts who had developed a litany of excuses for the anemic performance of the 54.4-horsepower MG-TD. What they failed to see was the appeal of the Le Mans as a sporty two-seater that, if not suitable for competition, was ideal for personal, luxurious motoring.

Compared with a production Series Sixty-Two Convertible, the Le Mans was 5.5 inches lower, with a height of 51 inches to the top of its windshield. Overall length, at 196 inches, was nearly 20 inches less than that of the Convertible. The Le Mans' weight was approximately 400 pounds less than the Convertible's 4,200 + pounds.

Introduced earlier on the LeSabre was the Le Mans' rain switch, which automatically raised its orlon top if a shower occurred while the car was unattended. Another interesting convenience feature was the Le Mans' "memory" seat. When the car door was opened, the electrically controlled seat slid back to allow for ease of entry and exit. When the door closed, the seat returned to its former position.

Powering the Le Mans was a 331-cid Cadillac V-8 with a 9.0:1 compression ratio, dual carburetors, and a rating of 250 horsepower at 4,500 rpm. A modified Hydra-Matic was also fitted, which allowed for higher rpm shift levels and provided the Le Mans with quick acceleration. Zero to 60-mph times were under 9 seconds with the transmission not shifting into fourth gear until approximately 87 mph. The stock Hydra-Matic shifted from third to fourth gear between 73 and 79 mph.

Cadillac, which eventually built three (each slightly different from the other) Le Mans models, allowed the press to sample the Le Mans at the General Motors Proving Ground. The general consensus—that they really weren't sports cars—was no surprise, but their overall performance and acceleration put them well out of classification as mere show cars.

In appearance, the Le Mans was what was expected from Cadillac: a blend of old and new features with a hint here and there of what was in store for production Cadillacs a few years into the future. The grille was very similar to that of the upcoming 1954 Cadillacs, as was the shape of its taillights. Another feature destined for extensive use on production Cadillacs, was the form of the Le Mans' turbine-wheel hubcaps. At the rear, Cadillac endowed the Le Mans with prominent dual exhausts that had large circular openings protruding from the outer-bumper units. Contrary to Cadillac's partiality toward massive front and rear bumpers, the rear of the Le Mans was left relatively exposed, with a series of seven vertical bars placed along the lower body region.

With the Le Mans wowing Motorama show-goers from coast to coast, Cadillac produced an equally important contributor to its ever-growing image as America's finest automobile. The prime mover in what was to become the Cadillac Eldorado was General Motors' vice-president of styling, Harley Earl. Almost always unerring in his reading of public taste, Earl had, after the end of World War II, recognized in the embryonic American sports-car movement an opportunity for General Motors. As a result, work began at GM in 1951 on the styling of the car destined to become the production model Corvette.

THE ELDORADO

In a similar fashion, Earl wanted to add a limited production, ultra-luxurious Convertible to the top of the Cadillac line as the crowning example of its status among American automobiles. The result, the Eldorado, or model 62675X of the Series Sixty-Two line, was first available during the 1953 model year with a price of $7,750. The Eldorado possessed a dazzling array of standard equipment features, including Hydra-Matic, white sidewall tires, leather upholstery, fog lamps, genuine chrome wire wheels, interior vanity, exterior mirrors, signal-seeking preselector radio, power steering, power windows and seat, dual front and rear heating system, and windshield washer.

Exterior finish choices included any of Cadillac's 12 standard 1953 colors and four colors exclusive to the Eldorado: Aztec red, azure blue, alpine white, and artisan ochre. Depending on the body color selected, the interior was finished in red, blue, or black with white accents. The Eldorado dash was topped by a plastic royalite, antiglare cover that wrapped around into the door panels. It was color-matched to the interior. A gold Eldorado crest was mounted on the chrome face of the panel. Eldorado script was also installed on the door sills.

In appearance, the Eldorado mixed standard production Cadillac features with enough special touches to convince observers that this was not a typical 1953 Cadillac. Most apparent was the Eldorado's wraparound windshield, a feature it shared in the 1953 model year with Oldsmobile Fiesta. Also obvious was the Eldorado's 58.5-inch height due to its altered body and lower (by 1-inch) chassis. By comparison, the Series Sixty-Two Convertible's height was 61.125 inches.

Automobile designers have long argued over the issue of who should receive credit for developing the dipped-door beltline feature; but regardless of its origin, this feature complemented the Eldorado's front and rear fender line in a grand fashion. At the back of its door, the Eldorado was only 37 inches high. Also accentuating this sporting profile, by providing a slight uplift for the Eldorado's rear deck, was the metal panel that covered the Convertible's top well. The Eldorado top, constructed of a special orlon fabric and fitted with an inner rubber liner, was available in either black or white.

CADILLAC'S DOMESTIC COMPETITION

The intensity of Packard's effort to climb back into the ring in direct competition with Cadillac was exemplified by the reintroduction of the Clipper name for use by Packard's medium-priced cars and the introduction, in January 1953, of the Packard Caribbean. This six-passenger convertible, as Packard historians have noted, with a price of $5,210 was intended to compete more with the Buick Skylark than the Cadillac Eldorado. Nonetheless, it was an important plus for Packard's prestige-building campaign. The top-of-the-line Packard Cavalier and Patricians were nicely restyled; and with four-barrel carburetors and 8.0:1 compression ratios, their straight-eight engines were rated at 180 horsepower, which still placed them last in the luxury-car power standings.

On the other hand, Packard President James Nance put forth a strong effort to correct some of the mistakes made by his successors by not filling out Packard's top-ranked series with models corresponding to those available from Cadillac. For example, he upgraded the Packard convertible and hardtop models to Patrician status and offered three new models for 1953—the $6,531 Derham Formal Sedan, the $6,900 Henney Executive Sedan, and the $7,100 Corporation Limousine. All three were mounted on a 148-inch wheelbase. Production of these cars totaled only 175 units. This low output was indicative of Packard's essential weakness. Total model-run production was a respectable 89,730 cars; but of these, Cavalier and Patrician output numbered just 18,217, including 750 Caribbeans.

A look at Lincoln's fortunes, on the other hand, indicated that the strategy it introduced in 1952 was paying handsome dividends. Total model-year output rose by nearly 50 percent from the 1952 level to reach 40,762 cars. Of these, 14,122 were Cosmopolitans and 26,630 were the more costly Capri models.

That this increase was achieved with automobiles virtually unchanged in appearance from 1952 speaks well for Lincoln styling. Yet the 1953s also enjoyed the benefits of a far more powerful 205-horsepower engine. Along with its outstanding suspension system, this V-8 enabled Lincoln to sweep the first four places in the production car division in the Pan-American Road Race in Mexico. Although more than one automotive publication crowned the 1953 Lincoln "America's fastest automobile," the Cadillac turned in a higher speed, 110.85 mph to the Lincoln's 107.88 mph, at the Daytona Speed Week competition in early 1953.

In sharp contrast to Lincoln's sales and racing success and Packard's energetic efforts to make it a more meaningful competitor, Chrysler's 1953 performance was typical of a car maker in trouble. Nineteen fifty-three was the year the seller's market finally dried up; and as buyers became more selective, those with the means to purchase expensive automobiles stayed away from the Chrysler and Chrysler Imperial in droves.

While Imperials did have a distinctive eagle hood ornament and a higher-mounted, rear-fender chrome spear, they were hardly sufficient to stir up much excitement. Long overdue, and therefore having limited impact on Imperial's fortune, was the introduction of the fully automatic Powerflite transmission in June 1953 as standard equipment on all Imperials.

The combination of little that was new and a rapidly aging image pushed Imperial output to just 9,019 cars from the 1953 level of 27,700. New Yorker production of 76,518 was deceptive since the Saratoga line was dropped for 1953 and replaced by the New Yorker on a 121.5-inch, rather than 131.5-inch, wheelbase. In effect, the New Yorker label was now being applied to a broader price range of automobiles than previously.

SPECIFICATIONS

Engine

Type: V-type, ohv, eight cylinders
Bore × stroke: 3.9375 × 3.625 inches
Displacement: 331 cubic inches
Horsepower: 210 @ 4,150 rpm
Torque: 330 lb-ft @ 2,700 rpm
Compression ratio: 8.25:1
Fuel system: Four-barrel, down-draft carburetor (various Carter WCFB and Rochester VGC models) with equalized manifold
Gas tank capacity: 20 gallons

Chassis/Drivetrain

Front suspension: Independent knee action, helical-coil springs
Rear suspension: Hypoid, semifloating, differential offset to provide for straight-line drive, semi-elliptic springs, 54.5 inches × 2 inches
    Series 75: 56.5 × 2 inches
    Series 60 Special and Series 62 ratio: 3.07:1
    Series 75: 3.77:1
Steering: Recirculating ball-type, overall ratio: 25.47:1
Electrical system: 12-volt
Transmission: Hydra-Matic, fluid coupling, two normal driving ranges, low-gear range and reverse (standard on Series 60 and 62, optional at $186 for Series 75). Because of Hydra-Matic plant fire, Dynaflow also used. Standard Series 75 transmission: three-speed synchromesh, 11-inch semicentrifugal clutch

Frame: X-type, reinforced side bars with deep X-member junction
Tires: Low-pressure 4-ply, 8.00 × 15
    Series 75: 6-ply, 8.20 × 15, Supplied by U.S. Royal, Firestone, and Goodrich
Brakes: Four-wheel hydraulic, front and rear dimensions: 2.5 × 12 inches, 258.5 square-inch braking area

Dimensions

Wheelbase:
    60 Special: 130 inches
    Series 62: 126 inches
    Series 75: 147 inches
Width:
    Series 62, Series 75: 80.125 inches
    Series 60 Special: 80.625 inches

Height:
    Series 62 Sedan
    Series 60 Special: 62.68 inches
    Series 62 Convertible: 60.125 inches
    Series 62 Coupe, Coupe de Ville: 60.937 inches
    Series 75: 64.06 inches
Front/rear tread: 59/63 inches

Overall length:
    Series 62 Coupe and Convertible: 220.68 inches
    Series 62 Sedan: 215.68 inches
    Series 60 Special: 224.68 inches
    Series 75: 236.56 inches

Popular Options

Hydra-Matic (optional for Series 75): $186
Hydraulic window lifts (standard for Series 62 Convertible, Coupe de Ville, optional on all other models)
Heating and ventilation system: $199
Power steering: $177
Signal-seeking radio with preselector and antenna: $132
Rear compartment remote-control signal-seeking radio with preselector and antenna: $214 (Series 75 only)
White sidewall tires: $48
E-Z tinted glass: $46
Autronic eye: $53
Chrome wire wheels: $325
Air conditioning: $619
Outside sun visor
Vent shades
License-plate frames
Windshield washers
Fog lamps
Interior visor vanity mirror
Exterior mirrors (two)
Instrument panel anti-glare cover
Wheel discs
Wheel-trim rings
Spoke-wheel discs
Seat covers (nylon, paratwill, tartan plaid, plastic)

1954

As Always—The Standard of the World!

FOR THE THIRD TIME in the postwar era, Cadillac, in 1954, introduced an all-new body shell. Identified as the General Motors' "C" body, it was also used by the Buick Super and Roadmaster. Following past practice, its appearance contained no surprises, reinforced Cadillac's image as the most admired car in America, and maintained Cadillac's reputation for distinctiveness. General Manager Don Ahrens, who admitted to striving to produce "the finest car in the world," described the latest Cadillac as a "blending of a multitude of totally new features and traditional Cadillac features . . . " Critics were less than overwhelmed by the new model's appearance. A writer covering the 41st Detroit Automobile Show for a European publication considered Cadillac's new front end as extremely ugly. Also singled out for negative comment was the 1954 model's rear overhang and increased weight. From 1948 to 1954, the weight of a Series Sixty-Two Sedan had ballooned from 4,200 to 5,100 pounds.

Much of this bad mouthing was swept away by Cadillac's extraordinary appeal. It was the only American car to enter the second year of the buyer's market with an order backlog; and measured either in terms of styling or technical innovations, Cadillac remained a formidable competitor to any other American automobile.

CHANGES AND IMPROVEMENTS

As anticipated by many, the 1954 Cadillac contained many styling elements of the 1953 Le Mans show car and Eldorado limited production model. Both the form and spirit of the 1941-1947 models was rekindled by the very clean cellular texture of the grille. After years of reducing the intersecting grille members to just a single horizontal unit and five vertical bars, Cadillac started the process all over again! In line with this finer grille form was a slimmer Cadillac crest and V for the front hood.

A high degree of modernity was provided by the bumper's gull-wing form and the continued sensational shape of the twin guards. The outer grille extensions carried four horizontal bars that ran into those of the main-grille portion. This had not been the case in the Le Mans, whose 1953-type grille outriggers looked a bit ill at ease with the rest of its grille structure. After being exiled to the outer-grille regions in 1953, the directional/parking lights were moved inward on the main grille surface. They were larger than those of 1953.

Representing Cadillac evolution at its best were the elongated front-fender extensions over the headlights, which sheltered chrome headlight surrounds. Instead of being circular, they were pulled slightly outward at their equator lines.

In profile, the 1954 Cadillac appeared both lower and longer than its immediate predecessors. This was not an illusion since the Series Sixty-Two models had a 129-inch wheelbase, up three inches from 1953. The Series Sixty Special wheelbase was extended to 133 inches from 130 inches, while the Series Seventy-Five Cadillac's wheelbase now measured 149.8 inches, an increase of just over 3 inches in one year.

Similarly, the overall length of the new Cadillacs was substantially greater. The smallest Cadillac, the Series Sixty-Two Sedan, measured 215.6 inches bumper to bumper, with all other Series Sixty-Two models extending from front to rear 223.4 inches. In turn, the Series Sixty Special stretched out 227.4 inches, which was eclipsed by the 237.1-inch measurement of the Series Seventy-Five Fleetwood. This did not, however, make the Series Seventy-Five the nation's longest passenger car, since Packard's Henney-built Executive Sedan and Corporate Limousine edged it out with a measurement of 238.5 inches. This loss to Packard obviously counted for little, since only 100 of the Henney Packards were built compared with Cadillac's production of 3,135 Series Seventy-Five models.

Accentuating Cadillac's extended length was a lower height, which averaged 1.5 inches less than in

1953. Enabling the driver to view the right front fender was a 1.68-inch lower hoodline. All models now had full body-length chrome underscores (this feature had previously been absent from Series Sixty-Two models), which, in contrast with that used for the 1953 Series Sixty Special, was a bit thinner and more graceful.

The latter change was, in the view of most Cadillac watchers, less significant than the 1954's new rear-fin form. Lifted virtually intact from the Le Mans, its upsweep was more abrupt than previously. Another Le Mans feature finding its way to production was the 1954 Cadillac's circular, dual-exhaust outlet.

Continuing previous practice, Series Sixty Special and Seventy-Five Series Cadillacs carried Fleetwood script above the trunk-lid-mounted V, while other models had a similarly located Cadillac crest.

Even if its impact had been somewhat diluted by its installation on the Eldorado and Oldsmobile Fiesta in 1953, the use of General Motors' panoramic windshield on all its 1954 models except for Chevrolet and Pontiac, enabled Cadillac to score another styling coup over its competitors. Like the tail fins of 1948, the wraparound windshield of 1954 had its share of detractors and controversy. Rumors that they would crack when the car was jacked up, claims of visual distortions, and charges that the net result was of questionable merit were common. Within a few years, the wraparound windshield would wrap over as well as around before gradually receding back to a more conventional form. But in the mid-fifties, it was the rage and a popular feature among owners of 1954 Cadillacs. In *Popular Mechanics'* poll of Cadillac drivers, 72 percent rated it excellent.

Adoption of the wraparound windshield necessitated use of what Cadillac described as "continental-type venti-panes." These were "one of the leading new style changes in the 1954 Cadillac . . . one that is almost certain to be copied in the years ahead." Since all General Motors cars would have wraparound windshields in 1955, Cadillac was clearly making the most of proprietary information!

In any case, Cadillac claimed that use of these rectangular vent windows, in conjunction with vertical pillar posts, provided "exceptionally strong roof support . . . exactly the amount of draft-free ventilation desired" and contributed to "the eye-catching beauty of the car as well."

Automotive safety was not yet a strong public issue in 1954, but Cadillac also noted that the latest models provided greater safety due to a new "side-welded body construction and by the welding of rear quarter panels and rear fenders into a single, extra-strong and rigid unit."

When installed in Sedan bodies, the Cadillac windshield had a narrow, 2-inch chrome visor across its top. This feature was not found in either hardtop or convertible models, but all 1954 Cadillacs had their heater air intakes mounted directly below the windshield base. This was part of a revised interior heating system that included heating ducts installed in the front doors with exits in the rear passenger area.

Hardtop Cadillacs had a reshaped rear-window pe-

rimeter in what Cadillac called the "Florentine" style. Its most identifiable feature was the shape of its extremities, which curved backward to blend into the downward sweep of the side window frames. Another styling feature (inspired by the 1953 Eldorado) shared by the Cadillac hardtop and convertible models were the belt-line dip, which corresponded with the front-rear fender line. All models had new upper-door reveal mountings that extended outward above the windows. Cadillac claimed this "style first" enabled the door windows to be opened slightly during rainy weather to provide ventilation and prevent window fogging.

Both the front and rear seat were spacious, measuring 64.75 inches and 65.2 inches, respectively. The Cadillac dashboard, which by 1953 was beginning to appear rather dated, was modernized for 1954. The form of the speedometer insert was basically unchanged, but the large center of vertical chrome slats was eliminated. An insert of chrome horizontal stripes, separated by satin black grooves, extended from the dash panel into the door panel. Locations of the radio and clock were unchanged from 1953. The Cadillac nameplate, consisting of gold Cadillac script on a background of brushed chrome, was located just above the ashtray. For Series Sixty Special and Series Seventy-Five models, Fleetwood script was used. Covering the upper dash surface was a leather-like vinyl material identified as Elascofab.

The Cadillac chassis, while completely redesigned and 35 percent stiffer than previously, continued to consist of channel-section side rails and an I-beam, V-shaped cross-member. Given added strength were the mounts for the engine, suspension, and steering components. The added length of the new frame provided not only a 3-inch longer wheelbase, but an additional 2 inches of rear leg room and a wider, 60-inch (up from 59.12 inches) front tread. Rear tread was unchanged at 63.10 inches.

Cadillac's basic ride and handling package wasn't substantially changed, but there were measurable and detectable changes. Providing more consistent ride control were new double-end shocks that reacted more quickly to spring flexing on small bumps and controlled spring response to harsh road conditions. This improved performance was maintained year round thanks to a new high-viscosity, aircraft-type fluid that was less susceptible to temperature changes than the previous fluid used. Additional chassis-suspension changes included a 2-inch lower position of the engine in the frame, a higher roll center, and increased wheel travel, resulting in significantly improved handling and cornering. Cadillac wasn't producing sports cars, but its lower center of gravity and reasonable 51 to 49 percent front-rear weight distribution made it ideal for long-distance, open-road runs. Enhancing this asset was the extensive use of soundproofing installed on the fire wall, trunk roof, and hood.

Customers were assured that "with the introduction of the great 1954 Cadillac engine, Cadillac once again reaffirms its position as the master builder of the V-8 power plant." While not of the same magnitude as the changes made in Cadillac's chassis and styling, those found in the latest Cadillac V-8 provided more responsive performance, improved economy, and quieter operation. Among these refinements were smoother intake manifolding, use of a wide-lobe cam, a slight increase in valve lift, a minor change in valve timing, and the adoption of aluminum-alloy pistons. A new starter motor plus a 12-volt distributor and voltage regulator were also introduced. Cadillac continued to use both Carter and Rochester, four-barrel carburetors; but those used in 1954 carried different model designations. The Carter WCFBs used were models 21435, 21095, and 21105. Rochester model 7006963 carburetors were used on cars with air conditioning. Those Cadillacs not so equipped used a model 7006963. Horsepower and torque ratings were now 230 horsepower at 4,400 rpm and 330 lb-ft of torque at 2,700 rpm.

Added to the Cadillac option list was a two-section, signal-seeking, preselector radio. A touch of the selector bar above the dial caused the radio to select the strongest signal in the area. Another new-for-1954 option was a Bendix Hydravac power-brake system, which allowed for normal brake operation if the power unit failed. Cadillac also increased brake lining area to just over 211 square inches. These longer-wearing linings also had a 0.5-inch-wide center groove to dissipate heat more rapidly.

The list of standard Cadillac equipment was extended to include windshield washers, an outside rear-view mirror, oil filter, vanity mirror, and power steering, which, as a 1953 option, had been ordered by 93 percent of new Cadillac buyers. Its design was refined to provide a lowering of the steering ratio to 21.5:1 from 25.47:1. For the first time since they had been available, Cadillac provided full-size wheel discs on all models as standard equipment. These were identified by their concave center section and raised, flat-surfaced hub bearing a Cadillac crest. A series of concentric inner rings lead up to the outer section.

DIFFERENCES AMONG MODELS

Winding up its 1954 road testing program, *Motor Trend* (November 1954) named the Cadillac Series Sixty-Two Sedan as the hottest performing car of the year. The other semifinalists in this competition were the Buick Century, Chrysler New Yorker Deluxe, Lincoln Capri, and Oldsmobile Super 88. *Motor Trend* used seven performance measurements to determine the winner: elapsed times from zero to 30 and 60 mph; standing-start quarter-mile time; elapsed times to accelerate from 10 to 30 mph, 30 to 50 mph, and 50 to 80 mph; and the car's maximum speed. In three of these categories (zero to 30 mph, zero to 60 mph, and 50 to 80 mph), the Cadillac had the best times of 3.7, 11.3, and 12.7 seconds, respectively. In the quarter-mile run, it tied the New Yorker Deluxe for second place with a mark of 18.4 seconds behind the Buick Century's 17.9-second time. In the 10 to 30 mph contest, it finished second to the Century's 3.0-second time by 0.4 seconds. The Chrysler was the fastest *Motor Trend* test car, but the Cadillac, at 113.0 mph, was a mere 0.1 mph slower. From 30 to 50 mph, the winner was the Chrysler with a run of 4.9

seconds. Cadillac's 5.7 seconds placed it third behind the 5.2-second time of the Buick Century.

Aiding and abetting Cadillac's V-8 in giving the 1954 model its excellent performance was a vastly improved Hydra-Matic transmission. Carried over from 1953 were its two Drive ranges, which were combined with numerous refinements of design and construction.

The Series Sixty-Two Sedan and Coupe shared an interior design featuring two-tone combinations of wool gabardine or wool gabardine with patterned nylon. Six color shades of gray, blue and green were offered. This all-new interior motif was highlighted by seat cushions and seat-back inserts of light-toned wool gabardine or patterned nylon with dark-toned bolsters and seat-cushion sides. The upper- and lower-door panels were of the light-toned upholstery color, with the latter finished in the same tufted pattern as the seat cushions and inserts. A leather-grained vinyl cover was used for the door armrests and seat scuff pads. Stretching across the front door was a narrow stainless-steel molding with a grille opening at the door edge, serving as the heater outlet for the rear compartment. The door and ventpane handles were mounted in a panel insert of alternating chrome and satin-black horizontal ribs.

Convertible interiors were again leather finished. Solid colors available were red, black or natural. The two-color choices consisted of seat cushions and seat backs in light blue or green metallic with white leather bolsters and trim or dark blue and green metallic with light blue and green metallic bolsters and trim. Along with the Coupe de Ville, the Convertible's door panels and seat pattern continued to be highlighted by a V-line styling theme. For 1954 a broad-angled V extended across the door's full length. The lower-door panel was covered by 2-inch wide bands. On Convertibles, these were leather; on the Coupe de Ville, they were either nylon or a floral patterned tapestry, depending on the upholstery selected. The door panel housing the window controls was identical to that of the Series Sixty-Two. Both the Coupe de Ville and Convertible used seat backs with deeply V'ed bolsters. The Convertible top was available in blue, black, tan, or green. A matching snap-on cover was also standard.

External identification of Series Sixty-Two models, in addition to their overall dimensions, was aided by the continued use of front and rear V-and-crest emblems and narrower (in comparison with the Series Sixty Specials), lower rear-fender trim.

In light of the sweeping changes accomplished in 1954, it was no great surprise that the Eldorado was now based on the Series Sixty-Two Convertible body. This change was accompanied by a substantial price reduction to $5,738. In turn, this was a key contributor to a healthy increase in output to 2,150 units. Cadillac didn't hold anything back in promoting the Eldorado, noting "the Eldorado blends the beauty and excitement of contemporary sports design with the basic soundness and excellence of the industry's finest engineering. Its remarkable 'dropped door' styling gives the Eldorado an unusually low silhouette—while its panoramic windshield three-piece fiberglass top cover, chrome panels and gold-plated crest on the rear fenders,

1954 Series Sixty Special.

1954 Series Sixty-Two Sedan.

1954 Series Sixty-Two Convertible Coupe.

1954 Series Sixty-Two Coupe de Ville.

CADILLAC VITAL STATISTICS: 1954

Series	Model	Body Type	Factory Price ($)	Weight (lbs.)	Production (#)
62	6219	4 dr Sedan	3933	4330	33,845
	6237	2 dr Hardtop Coupe	3838	4347	17,460
	6237D	Coupe de Ville	4261	4409	17,170
	6267	2 dr Convertible	4404	4598	6310
	6267S	Eldorado Convertible	5738	4809	2150
60	6019	4 dr Sedan	4683	4490	16,200
75	7523	4 dr Sedan 8p	5875	5031	889
	7533	4 dr Imp Sedan	6090	5093	611

wire wheels and many other unusual styling features give the Eldorado a character all of its own."

Priced at just $1,334 above the cost of the Series Sixty-Two Convertible, the Eldorado was a bargain both in terms of prestige and equipment. Externally, it was immediately identified as an ultra-fancy Cadillac with a broad expanse of ribbed aluminum sweeping across the lower portion of the rear fenders, in addition to the above-mentioned features. Exterior color choices consisted of Aztec red, azure blue, alpine white, and Apollo gold.

The Eldorado's interior was entirely new, with all-leather seats with French seams, saddle-stitched piping, and raised leather welts. Four solid colors—red, yellow, black, or blue—were offered. Any of these colors could be joined with white to form a two-tone color scheme. An embossed V and Cadillac crest highlighted both the front- and rear-seat back bolsters.

Equally exotic was the Eldorado's door-panel styling. Beginning at the bottom, stainless-steel moldings lead to a panel of 0.75-inch wide horizontal risers of light-tone leather. This unit contained a tapered insert of smooth-finished, dark-tone leather on which was mounted a Cadillac crest. The upper-door region was covered by yet another material, diamond-patterned Dinco, in blue and silver. The window- and door-insert panel was of alternating satin-black grooves and raised chrome lines. Rear side panels followed a similar pattern.

The upper-dash surface was covered with fine-grain Elascofab. The dash emblem carried Eldorado script in 18-carat gold on a brushed chrome background. All interior hardware was of either bright or brushed chrome. A feature unique to the Eldorado was its dual sun visors of translucent, smoke-gray plastic. A Rox Point, dark-tone carpeting was used for the floor, heel pad, and lower portion of the front-seat back.

The 1954 Series Sixty Special Sedan carried noticeably thinner, bright trim along its lower body sill. This made it possible to reposition the traditional rear-fender louvers lower on the rear fender. Both the rear deck and dash carried gold Fleetwood script.

Twelve interior choices were offered in a light-pattern nylon, an all-wool broadcloth, or a V-crest pattern nylon matched with a dark-toned, plain, all-wool broadcloth. The seat-cushion inserts were upholstered in lighter fabrics divided into 1.25-inch piping. The bolsters and cushion sides were finished in darker harmonizing tones. Four basic colors were available: gray, blue, brown, and green. All seam welts were either dark-toned genuine leather or fine-grain Elascofab.

As expected, door panels were very conservative. A smooth-surfaced, stainless-steel kickpad was used with a light-toned panel set within a rectangle of dark-toned sidewall cloth, outlined in fine stainless-steel molding. The armrests were covered in genuine dark-toned leather. Each rear door was fitted with power window controls and an ashtray.

Once again the Series Seventy-Five models were available in either Limousine or eight-passenger Sedan form. This body style successfully combined Cadillac's new styling with the traditionally restrained format typical of these large vehicles. "New dignity and bearing are apparent," said Cadillac, "throughout its exterior styling."

Six solid color interiors were offered, combining Bedford cord or plain broadcloth with light gray, light blue, or light tan bolsters. The front compartment of the limousine was upholstered in black leather when either gray or tan was selected for the rear. If blue was specified, the front compartment was finished in blue leather. The front seats were upholstered in 3-inch wide welts. A new feature for 1954 was an electric front-seat adjustment. A wool-pile carpet was used for the front floor with a Kinkimo covering at the rear.

Both the front and rear seats of the Sedan, and those in the rear of the Limousine, had tufted seat cushions and seat backs with deeply recessed buttons. The front-seat back of both versions continued to house the two auxiliary seats when their use was not required. Its appearance was similar to that of the 1953 models. Among the changes made was a reshaped insert for the cloth, the addition of a Cadillac crest and revised trim moldings.

DREAM BOAT FLEET

Cadillac's "Dream Boat" fleet for 1954 consisted of three cars: the Park Avenue, the La Espada, and El Camino. Since the Park Avenue is best examined in the context of the Cadillac Eldorado Brougham's development, its salient features will be found in Chapter 13.

The La Espada and El Camino were, respectively, convertible and hardtop versions of the same basic two-place automobile. Each had a 115-inch wheelbase, an overall length of 200.6 inches, and an overall width of 79.9 inches. Front and rear tread measured 59 inches. At 51.7 inches, the La Espada was just 0.2 inches lower than the El Camino.

Both cars were equipped with Hydra-Matic and Cadillac's 230-horsepower, production V-8. Their fiberglass bodies were attractive, highlighted by high, razor-edged fins, described by Cadillac as "supersonic," separate headrests for the bucket seats flowing back onto the rear deck, and tapered body creases extending from the twin-pod taillights forward into the door. A brushed-aluminum panel with horizontal fluting served both as an engine-heat outlet and an intake for passenger-compartment ventilation. At the front, Cadillac introduced a dual headlight system. The La Espada/El Camino hood line was extremely low, and its forward protruding form was later used for the 1959 production models.

Cadillac strongly hinted that the styling of these cars would be seen again by describing the El Camino as possessing "the link of today with the future." The gull-wing bumper format of the 1954 production models was used in modified form. Body color for the La Espada was "Apollo Gold," with the El Camino finished in a "Pearlescent Silver" paint.

The instrument panel and door hang-ons, along with the convex shoulders and sides of the center console, were covered with gray leather. A contrasting gun-metal gray was used for the leather finish on the seat inserts, bolsters, and upper side-wall sections. The steering-wheel rim was wrapped in gray nylon cord. Hand-brushed aluminum was used for the instrument dial insert, while the lower-door panels had a fluted aluminum finish.

The El Camino's fixed, hand-brushed aluminum top had front and rear fiberglass saddles and, said Cadillac, provided "aero-dynamic qualities." Its headlining was perforated gray Naugahyde, which Cadillac said, "provides an acoustical effect further reducing any possible operational sound." A rear luggage shelf constructed of Pearlescent silver fiberglass was also installed. The floors of both cars were covered by a gray nylon-loop carpet.

CADILLAC'S DOMESTIC COMPETITION

Because of the Livonia fire and the slow start-up of Hydra-Matic production at Willow Run, Cadillac's 1954 model year didn't begin until January 1954, which held output to 96,680 cars. The calendar output of 123,746 was obviously far more representative of Cadillac's popularity, especially since it exceeded Ahren's goal of 117,000 cars.

When the 1954 models debuted, General Sales Manager James M. Roche said Cadillac was hoping to win 50 percent of the high-priced car market. At year's end, he had achieved his objective, as the following chart indicates:

Car	Model-Year Sales	% of Luxury Car Market
Cadillac	96,680	53.24
Chrysler (New Yorker)	40,084	22.07
Packard (excluding)	7,892	4.34
Lincoln	36,993	20.37
Total	181,589	100.00

Chrysler's performance, in absolute terms, was actually improved from 1953, although total Chrysler marque output, which included Windsor and New Yorker, was down from 170,006 to 104,985. The explanation for this inconsistency takes into consideration several factors. The Chrysler V-8 now developed 235 horsepower, which put it ahead of Cadillac, which certainly was not an insignificant development.

This was "driven home" at the 1954 Daytona Speed Week where a factory-prepared Chrysler averaged 117.065 mph for a two-way run through the measured mile. Another Chrysler was second at 116.90 mph. A 1954 Cadillac was third at 113.635 mph. With both fully automatic transmission and air conditioning, Chrysler was no longer perceived as a laggard in the area of convenience features. Lastly, although their styling was clearly dated, the New Yorker Deluxe and Imperials were attractively restyled.

On the other hand, Packard, even after squeezing 212 horsepower out of its straight-eight, offering another version of its Caribbean convertible, and sending its Balboa one-off model on the show circuit, was simply outclassed with the obsolete look of its basic body shell, which dated back to 1951.

Lincoln's model-year output dropped somewhat from its 1954 level, but the increased popularity of the Capri, whose production increased from 26,630 to 29,582 suggested that Lincoln's success in the Mexican Road Race (it won its third successive victory in the 1954 race, with a 1954 Cadillac finishing in third position, just 3 minutes behind the leading Lincoln) had not been for naught.

Another perspective of the relative strength of these marques comes from a review of production during the calendar year. From January through December 18, 1954, Cadillac turned out 117,903 cars, up 13.7 percent from 1953. Chrysler's output of all models was 94,651, down 38.8 percent; Packard's total was 26,365, down 65.7 percent; and Lincoln assembled 34,718 cars or 11.9 percent less than in 1953. The industry as a whole produced 5,258,115 cars, a drop of 10.9 percent from 1953.

When the 1955 models appeared, it seemed as if the entire American automotive industry had discovered the 1948-1949 Cadillacs. Plymouth, Pontiac, Packard, Chevrolet, and Pontiac unwrapped their ohv V-8s; and virtually without exception, every model in the market seemed to have rear-fender forms that were inspired by Cadillac's efforts.

SPECIFICATIONS

Engine

Type: V-type, ohv, eight cylinders
Bore × stroke: 3.8125 × 3.625 inches
Displacement: 331 cubic inches
Horsepower: 230 @ 4,400 rpm
Torque: 330 lb.-ft. @ 2,700 rpm
Compression ratio: 8.25:1
Carburetor: Four-barrel down-draft with equalized manifolding
Electrical system: 12-volt
Transmission: Hydra-Matic three-speed automatic, consisting of a fluid coupling and automatically actuated gear sets, providing two driving ranges, a low-speed range, and reverse

Chassis/Drivetrain

Frame: X-type, reinforced side bars with deep X-member junctions
Rear axle: Hypoid, semifloating, differential housing offset to provide for straight-line drive
Series 60 Special, Series 62 ratio: 3.07:1,
Optional ratio (standard on air-conditioned equipped cars): 3.36:1
Series 75 axle ratio: 3.77:1
Front suspension: Independent, helical-coil springs
Rear suspension: Five-leaf semielliptic, 56.5 × 2.5 inches
Series 75: six-leaf units
Steering: Hydraulic power steering, overall ratio 21.5:1
Tires: Low-pressure, 4-ply, 8.00 × 15
Series 75: 6-ply, 8.20 × 15
White sidewalls optional

Dimensions

Wheelbase:
    Series 60 Special: 133 inches
    Series 62:   129 inches
    Series 75:   149.75 inches
Width: 80 inches
Front/rear tread: 60/63.1 inches
Overall length:
    Series 60 Special: 227.437 inches
    Series 62 Sedan: 216.437 inches
    Series 62 Coupe and Convertible: 223.437 inches
    Series 75:   237.187 inches

Popular Options

Power brakes: $48
Radio: $120
Heater: $129
Air conditioning: $620
Power windows and seat: $124
Chrome wire wheels: $325
White Sidewall tires: $49
E-Z Eye tinted glass
Autronic eye

1955

The Car of Cars

SPEAKING AT A PRESS PREVIEW of Cadillac's 1955 models in Detroit on November 1, 1954, Cadillac General Sales Manager James Roche was the picture of confidence. Cadillac was winding up the 1954 calendar year with another record output, and it was carrying over a backlog of 90,000 orders. Even if the changes for 1955 were not radical, Cadillac had invested over $18 million in their development. Furthermore, Cadillac had just completed a $24 million expansion program, giving it over 5 million square feet of manufacturing space. In sharp contrast, Packard had suffered a major setback in 1953 when Briggs, the source of its bodies, was purchased by Chrysler. Shortly thereafter, Chrysler advised Packard that it would have to look elsewhere for its body shells. As a result, all Packard operations had to take place in its 760,000 square-foot Conner Avenue, Detroit plant. This spelled disaster for Packard.

With just a single assembly line, Packard missed its golden and last real opportunity to gain acceptance as a luxury-car producer. Instead, cars of notoriously bad quality plagued Packard, compounding a late introduction date (January 17, 1955, compared with Cadillac's November 18, 1954, debut), problems with its Twin Ultramatic automatic transmission, and a lackadaisical advertising program. This wasn't the way to surround the Packard name with the same aura of prestige that was associated with Cadillac.

This intangible virtue enjoyed in abundance by Cadillac took all sorts of forms. One of the more graphic examples was that of 71-year-old George W. Morris, board chairman of the National Office Supply Company, who purchased six 1955 Cadillacs. Taking the view that "you can't take it with you," Mr. Morris used one of his Cadillacs for personal use and handed over the remaining cars to his sons and daughters.

Cadillac, quite correctly, took efforts to remind its past, present, and future customers "that the responsibility of leadership is more than an inheritance at Cadillac. It is the day-to-day, practical measure by which every Cadillac advancement and innovation is judged." One look at Cadillac's 1955 sales and production performance provides another measure of how Cadillac was regarded by the public. James Roche had predicted Cadillac would sell 150,000 of its 1955 models. Actual model-year output was 140,777, with model-year production reaching 153,334. Registrations no doubt brought a smile to Mr. Roche's face; they totaled 141,038.

CHANGES AND IMPROVEMENTS

Cadillac's appearance was, as expected of a car only in the second year of a three-year styling cycle, moderately changed for 1955. On all models except for the Series Seventy-Five, which retained the 1954-style side trim, the side-body spear was linked to the now abbreviated rear-fender grille to form a 90-degree angle. The form of the simulated air scoop was now much narrower and simpler in design. Extended to all models except for the Series Seventy-Five was the Florentine rear-roof backlight form introduced on the 1954 hardtop models. Eliminated from the Series Sixty-Two and Sixty Special Sedans was the chromed belt molding used on those models since 1950. But what Cadillac could take away, it could also add; and in this case, it was the Sixty Special that received chrome trim for its center and rear ventpane posts.

Up front, the gull-wing bumper form was continued with the larger bullets placed higher and further apart. The circular parking lights were moved into the outer grille extensions. Cadillac continued to use a cellular concept for its grille, which now had larger openings and narrower dividing bars. Both the hood ornament and V-and-crest were moderately reshaped.

Viewed from the rear, the 1955 Cadillac could be distinguished from the 1954 model by the six vertical chrome strips installed on the lower deck panel.

When the Cadillac V-8 had entered production in 1948 with 331 cubic inches and 160 horsepower, its horsepower-per-cubic-inch output had stood at 0.48 hp/cid. Now, eight years later, its displacement remained at 331 cubic inches; but with a rated output of 250 horsepower at 4,600 rpm, its output per cubic inch had risen to 0.75. Peak torque was increased to 350 lb-ft at 2,800 rpm. The major factors behind these higher ratings were a redesigned combustion chamber, providing a 9.0:1 compression ratio, larger four-barrel carburetor, and wider valve openings, which necessitated a change in rocker-arm design. Also introduced in the 1955 engine was a more rigid crankshaft and a new water pump.

Cadillac also flip-flopped its standard and optional rear-axle ratio, with 3.36:1 being standard (except for the Series Seventy-Five, which was equipped with a 3.77:1 unit) and 3.07:1 optional. Cadillac said this was strictly a merchandising move since "in 1954, 3.07 was [the] standard 'economy' axle and 3.36 was offered as optional 'performance' axle. Field reports indicated that customers confused the two and ordered 'economy' when they wanted 'performance.' As a result, the change, which is more consistent with industry-wide designations, was made this year."

The result, in conjunction with its more powerful engine, made Cadillac one of America's best performing automobiles. At the Daytona Beach Speed Week, Cadillac won first place in the 1-mile (from a standing start) acceleration runs, with a speed of 80.428 mph, easily defeating the far-lighter 1955 Chevrolet, which finished second at 78.158 mph. Other "hot" cars vanquished by Cadillac included a Buick Century, timed at 77.436 mph, and a Chrysler 300, which finished fifth at 76.840 mph.

The 300-horsepower, limited production (only 1,725 were built in 1955) Chrysler 300s took first and second in the flying-mile competition with speeds of 127.80 mph and 126.543 mph. Nonetheless, Cadillac's third place finish at 120.478 mph was respectable, putting it ahead of both a Buick Century and a Chrysler New Yorker.

Enhancing the improved straightaway performance of Cadillac's more powerful engine were numerous running gear changes. Stiffer rear springs and revalved shock absorbers plus altered steering geometry reduced lean-in turns. Providing more positive road feel was a revamped power steering unit, which now required approximately seven instead of three pounds of pressure before it provided assistance.

As did most manufacturers, Cadillac introduced tubeless tires on its 1955 models. A small, but welcomed improvement was made in the windshield wiper mechanism to allow a greater area of the windshield to be cleaned in each sweep. The optional E-Z Eye glass was now tinted gray instead of green.

CHANGES IN THE ELDORADO

Making the transition from dreamland to reality were the rear fender fins of the Eldorado, which were virtually identical to those seen earlier on the La Espada and El Camino. Contrary to Cadillac's post-1947 practice, this new form placed the tail and backup lights at the base of the fin in jetlike nacelles. Extending from these enclosures was a long side spear, becoming progressively narrower as it streaked across the rear fender.

Anticipating the widespread attention the new Eldorado would attract, Cadillac noted, "its styling alone represents a daring departure. Indeed, in the modeling of its sweeping rear fenders, it foretells the styling others must surely follow in the future." Correctly predicting the future when the Eldorado would be a valued possession of car collectors, Cadillac depicted it as "destined to be one of the most prized cars of the decade . . . beautiful to see . . . thrilling to drive . . . and uniquely satisfying to own."

As in 1955, the Eldorado was characterized by a wide-body belt molding and fiberglass top boot. Not used, and for good reason, were rear fender skirts. This change showed off the Eldorado's new cast-aluminum, heavy-gauge steel "Sabre-Spoke" wheels, which had been developed by Cadillac in cooperation with Kelsey-Hayes and Alcoa. These wheels, in slightly different form, had appeared on a number of GM Dream Cars, including the 1955 Le Mans as well as the La Espada and El Camino.

Color choices for the Eldorado's all-leather interior were expanded to include five solid colors—black, blue, beige, gray or red. All but beige could also be combined with white leather trim. Seat cushions and seat backs were formed in padded biscuits with recessed, chromed concave buttons. The smooth bolsters dipped to form two V-shaped regions. Covering the floor was a dark-toned, loop-pile insert with aluminum-ribbed rubber floor mats front and rear. The door panels were styled in a smooth, light-toned upper section and a darker, square-patterned lower portion. Added were door pockets with openings concealed by leather flaps with snap fasteners. Exterior colors for the Eldorado included all standard Cadillac tones plus four special Eldorado paints.

Powering the Eldorado was Cadillac's 331 cubic-inch V-8, modified to produce 270 horsepower at 4,800 rpm and 345 lb-ft of torque at 3,200 rpm. This latter output was identical to that of the standard engine, but was produced at a higher (by 400 rpm) engine speed. Cadillac, noting that engine made "the Eldorado one of the most responsive cars on the road," offered it on a "strictly limited" basis as a $161 option for the Series Sixty-Two and Series Sixty Special models.

This raised the prospect of Cadillacs capable of exceptionally quick acceleration. The Series Sixty-Two Sedan could accelerate from 0 to 60 mph in 10 seconds. It also weighed 400 pounds less than the Eldorado, which needed just over 11 seconds for the same run. Thus an Eldorado-engined Sixty-Two would have no difficulty in attained 0 to 60-mph times well under the 10-second level.

To achieve its higher output, the Eldorado engine was equipped with a revamped intake manifold carrying two Carter 4GC, four-barrel carburetors. A large, triangular air cleaner with a chrome V emblem was installed. Helping the Eldorado make the most of its 270 horsepower was a reworked Hydra-Matic (standard on all models) with higher shift points and a 3.36:1 rear axle.

DIFFERENCES AMONG MODELS

Once again interior designs for all Cadillac models were drastically altered. For the Series Sixty-Two Sedan and Coupe, seat backs and cushion inserts were divided into four biscuits with a single, center-mounted button. Segmenting the front and rear seats into distinct left- and right-side units was a pleated panel in a darker tone. The standard upholstery choices consisted of dark and light gabardine or dark gabardine with a diamond-patterned nylon.

Door panels featured stainless-steel moldings, a simple geometric pattern with a Cadillac crest at its center, and the usual panel insert for the door and ventpane handles.

The Series Sixty-Two Convertible's leather interior used horizontally pleated seat inserts with smooth-surfaced dividers. As before, the seats were available in solid colors of red or black. Two-tone choices were expanded to six: light blue metallic with either white or dark blue trim, Tangier tan metallic with light gray trim, light green metallic with dark green trim, and red with white trim.

Eleven standard interiors were available for the Coupe de Ville, combining button-and-biscuit seats and seat backs in one of two patterns of metallic nylon fabrics with leather trim. Included in this selection were three new "glamour-trim" styles consisting of V-pattern metallic nylon and leather trim. Color selections were black/Tangier tan, Wedgewood green/green and gold/white.

"In all the world," said Cadillac, "there is no other motor car quite like the Cadillac Series Sixty Special. In this single model, traditionally a four-door sedan, every artistry of Cadillac craftmanship and every forward-looking feature of performance, styling and graciousness are superbly integrated."

1955 Series Seventy-Five Limousine.

1955 Series Sixty Special.

External identification of the Sixty Special was enhanced by the 12 (up from eight in 1954) rear-fender vertical louvers, rear-deck Fleetwood script, and slender centerpost, which Cadillac noted was "so vastly reduced in thickness that it brings to this sedan the airy feeling of a hard-top design."

As with other Cadillacs, the Sixty Special was offered in over 200 exterior color selections. Interior choices included broadcloth, patterned nylon, and metallic nylon in contrasting tones of gray, blue, tan, and green. The 12 standard interiors were offered in a trim pattern of light-toned seat cushions and seat-back inserts with V-shaped dark-toned seat backs. The door panels featured a smooth, stainless-steel kickpad, a lower panel of dark-toned horizontal risers, a midsection of light-toned body cloth, and an upper, light-toned metal panel. A Glamour-Line trim option combined beige, square-pattern, nylon seat and seat-back inserts with Tangier-tan leather bolsters and trim. Regardless of the color or trim selected, all Sixty Specials were fitted with deep nylon-loop-pile carpeting in harmonizing dark-toned shades.

The Fleetwood Seventy-Five Cadillacs, which were again offered as eight-passenger Sedans or Limousines equipped with a power-operated dividing glass partition, retained the 1954 model midbody side trim with a 1955-style, full-length, rear-fender vertical molding. As with the Sixty Special, the Seventy-Five carried Fleetwood lettering on its trunk lids.

Interiors of the Series Seventy-Five featured contrasting shades of tan, gray, or blue in light-toned Bedford cord or broadcloth. Seat cushions and seat-back inserts had three wide, horizontal sections separated by a center panel of six narrower, vertical stripes. The bolsters and seat faces were light colored, the cushions and inserts of a darker shade. Door coverings had a four-part lower panel bearing a center-mounted Cadillac crest. The door scuff pad, floor, and rear seat bottom were covered in a deep, textured Kinkomo carpeting.

The Series Seventy-Five Imperial Limousine, which Cadillac asserted was "the most luxurious chauffeur-driven car in America," had a leather-upholstered front seat as well as looped nylon-pile carpeting. If gray or tan rear upholstery was selected, a black-leather front seat

CADILLAC VITAL STATISTICS: 1955

Series	Model	Body Type	Factory Price ($)	Weight (lbs.)	Production (#)
62	6219	4 dr Sedan	3977	4375	44,904
	6237	2 dr Hardtop Coupe	3882	4364	27,879
	6237D	Coupe de Ville	4305	4428	33,300
	6267	Convertible	4448	4631	8150
	6267S	Eldorado Convertible	6286	4829	3950
60	6019	4 dr Sedan	4728	4545	18,300
75	7523	4 dr Sedan 7p	6187	5020	1075
	7533	4 dr Imp Sedan 8p	6402	5113	841

1955 Series Sixty-Two Coupe de Ville.

was installed. The specified color for cars with a blue rear compartment was also blue.

CADILLAC'S DOMESTIC COMPETITION

Packard, as we've observed, was severely handicapped in its efforts to regain the glory of bygone days. In retrospect, 1955 was its do-or-die year. It was a year when the industry established a new production output; and riding this crest, Packard attracted considerable public interest because of its revamped styling, torsion-bar suspension system, and powerful V-8 engine. If Packard's production and quality problems could have been avoided, it's likely that far more than 16,833 Senior Packards would have been assembled. But sales momentum, once lost, was never regained. Packard's image was dulled by sloppy assembly, and this seriously weakened its ability to remain a viable competitor in the fine-car field.

Once again Packard challenged the Eldorado with its Caribbean model, which was by any measure a worthy competitor, boasting a 352-cubic-inch, 275-horsepower V-8, four-wheel torsion-bar suspension, and distinctive (if a bit gaudy) styling. The Caribbean's base price of $5,892 placed it slightly below that of the Eldorado; but when comparably equipped, the two cars finished the price war in a virtual dead heat. This was not the case when their production figures were compared, since only 500 Caribbeans were built, compared with 3,950 Eldorados.

Also experiencing a significant (27 percent) decline in production was Lincoln, whose output of 1955 models totaled 27,222. Lincoln had two all-new and very significant cars ready for introduction in 1956. In the meantime, Lincoln enthusiasts had to be content with a 1955 model that, while still attractive, was stylistically dated.

Beneath the Lincoln's familiar form was its first in-house designed and built automatic transmission, Turbo-Drive, and a larger, 341-cubic-inch V-8, rated at 225 horsepower and 332 ft-lb of torque. Lincoln also introduced dual exhausts and air conditioning in 1955.

1955 Series Sixty-Two Sedan.

1955 Series Sixty-Two Convertible.

Both of these were overdue since Cadillac had been using dual exhausts on its cars since 1952 and had introduced air conditioning on the 1953 models.

Chrysler called it the "Hundred Million Dollar Look," and from any perspective, it was sensational. The entire line of Chrysler Corporation cars shared in what was for Chrysler a revolutionary change in design philosophy. Gone was the boxy, pragmatic look, replaced by (in light of what was yet to come) modestly finned rear fenders, flowing lines, flashy side-trim and body-color schemes, and distinctive front ends.

The Imperial was now a separate marque, and its emancipation from Chrysler-Imperial status was celebrated in fine fashion. Both its front- and rear-end designs were strongly influenced by Chrysler's K310 show car of 1952 and reflected an ability to combine classic themes with contemporary lines without submitting to a slavish imitation of Cadillac's styling elements.

The Imperial line still lacked a model-for-model compatibility with Cadillac, and total output of 11,432 cars was a reminder of just how strongly entrenched Cadillac's position had become. It was clear that if any of Cadillac's three American counterparts were to gain ground in the luxury-car field, they would need more than new styling, advanced engineering, and powerful V-8s. These were merely the building blocks of Cadillac's success. Cadillac had become the symbol of achievement, the goal of up and coming Americans, the ultimate expression of the American Dream come true. Cultivated over the years by careful attention to styling continuity, that upon occasion was set off in a new direction by radical styling breaks with the past, and a reputation for engineering leadership, this image would be hard to surpass.

To break Cadillac's dominance would require a series of sensational products, creative marketing, and time. This concept was not alien to Packard, Lincoln, and Chrysler; and if Studebaker-Packard President James Nance had had his way, Packard would have offered a spectacular car in 1957. But instead, Studebaker-Packard's near-collapse in 1956 led only to a 1957 Packard based on Studebaker components that in no way could be regarded as an alternative to a Cadillac. In contrast, Chrysler would, in 1957, offer another new Imperial whose appearance was even more soul stirring than the 1955. Lincoln, as noted, had two new cars ready for 1956 introduction; and one of them, bearing the Continental name, would expand the traditional upper limits of the American luxury-car market to include ultraexpensive, limited-production vehicles. Cadillac would trail Lincoln into this territory, but its Eldorado Brougham would, with the reborn Continental, make automotive history.

SPECIFICATIONS

Engine

Type: V-type, ohv, eight cylinders
Bore × stroke: 2.8125 × 3.625 inches
Displacement: 331 cubic inches

Horsepower: 250 @ 4,600 rpm (Eldorado 270 @ 4,600 rpm)
Torque: 350 lb.-ft. @ 2,800 rpm
Compression ratio: 9.0:1
Carburetor:
    Carter WCFB or Rochester 4GC, four-barrel, down-draft carburetor with equalized manifolding
    Eldorado: two Rochester 4GC, four-barrel carburetors
Electrical system: 12-volt
Transmission: Hydra-Matic three-speed as in 1954

Chassis/Drivetrain

Frame: X-type, reinforced side bars with deep X-member junction
Rear axle:
    Hypoid, semifloating, offset differential, 3.36:1 ratio
    Series 60 Special and Series 62 ratio: 3.07:1 optional (except on Eldorado and air condition equipped cars)
    Series 75 ratio: 3.77:1
Front suspension: Independent, helical-coil springs
Rear suspension: Five-leaf semielliptic, 56.5 inches long, 2.5 inches wide
    Series 75:   six-leaf units
Steering: Hydraulic power steering, overall ratio 21.3:1
Tires: Low-pressure, 4-ply, tubeless, 8.00 × 15
    Series 75:   6 ply, 8.20 × 15
    Whitewalls optional at extra cost

Dimensions

Wheelbase:
    Series 60 Special: 133 inches,
    Series 62:   29 inches,
    Series 75:   149.75 inches
Width: 80 inches
Front/rear tread: 60/63.1 inches
Overall length:
    Series 60 Special: 227$\frac{7}{16}$ inches,
    Series 62 sedan: 216$\frac{7}{16}$ inches,
    Series 62 Coupe and Convertible: 223$\frac{7}{16}$ inches,
    Series 75:   237$\frac{3}{16}$ inches

Popular Options

Power brakes (standard on Eldorado): $48
Signal-seeking preselector radio: $132
Heater: $129
Air conditioning: $620
Power windows: $108
Four-way power seat: $70
Vertically adjustable power seat (available only with four-way power seat): $54
White sidewall tires
E-Z Eye tinted glass
Fog lamps

1956

The Gauge Against Which the World's Motor Cars Will Be Measured

IN 1956, Cadillac produced its millionth automobile: an Eldorado convertible. It was a milestone far out of the reach of other American luxury cars and one that underscored Cadillac's position among American cars. To no one's real surprise, the annual Crowell-Collier automotive survey reported that 92.9 percent of all Cadillac owners would buy another one if they were in the market for a new car. Well back in second place was Buick with a score of 80 percent.

This huge reservoir of new Cadillac buyers provided Cadillac dealers with a steady supply of previously owned cars for those car buyers wanting a Cadillac but unable to afford (yet) a new model. The result on used Cadillac prices was impressive. For example, during 1956, the only 1950 and 1951 American cars listed in the *Used Car Red Book* for more than $1,000 were Cadillacs. Furthermore, Cadillacs of that vintage had an average retail price double that of any other used American car regardless of original price. Consistently producing cars of quality, possessing good performance and up-to-date styling, that were expertly promoted had paid Cadillac handsome dividends.

The production/sales results of 1956 clearly showed that Americans still regarded the Cadillac with considerable respect, affection, and desire. In spite of an overall industry downturn in production from 1955's record output of 7,942,200 to 5,801,900, Cadillac, even in the face of a revitalized Lincoln, had, at midyear, set a new retail delivery record of 81,143 cars. Granted, this was a mere dozen over the old mark; but when the final tally had been completed, a grand total of 154,577 Cadillacs for the model year had been produced, making 1956 the latest "Best Ever" year for Cadillac.

CHANGES AND IMPROVEMENTS

Key changes in the Cadillac engine and Hydra-Matic transmission plus continued close attention to styling updates made 1956 an important year for Cadillac. For the first time since its introduction in 1949, the Cadillac engine was increased in size, from 331 to 365 cubic inches, by use of a larger, 4.0-inch, rather than 3.8-inch bore in conjunction with an unchanged 3.625-inch stroke. Nonetheless, it still ranked behind Lincoln and Packard, which boosted their engines to 368 and 374 cubic inches, respectively.

With a 9.75:1 compression ratio, the Cadillac developed 285 horsepower at 4,600 rpm and 400 lb-ft of torque at 2,800 rpm. Either a Carter WCFB or Rochester 4GC four-barrel carburetor with 1.093-inch primary and 1.1875-inch secondary venturis was used. A more dependable fuel flow to the carburetors was provided by relocating the fuel pickup closer to the rear of the fuel tank.

The Eldorado engine continued to use twin, four-barrel carburetors. These carburetors had greater venturi area than those used on the single carburetor engine and were the sole source of the Eldorado's increased output of 305 horsepower at 4,700 rpm and 400 lb-ft of torque at 3,200 rpm. This engine gave Cadillac the highest horsepower/cubic inch ratio in the luxury-car field with 0.83 horsepower per cubic inch. Packard, which claimed 310 horsepower for its Caribbean V-8, was a very close second at 0.82. Lincoln's 285 horsepower V-8 reported in at 0.77; while the Imperial, with 280 horsepower, developed 0.79 horsepower for each of its 354 cubic inches.

In light of what were increasingly regarded as overly optimistic, wishful-thinking horsepower claims, Cadillac's ratings were considered accurate. The procedure under which they were attained was known as General Motors Corporation Engine Test Code 20, which mandated a number of stringent conditions. For example, the generator was required to be turning but did not have to be charging. Both the fuel and water pumps had to be operating, and the stock exhaust manifold was installed. The major deviations from normal operation status consisted of the removal of the air cleaner, no intake manifold heat, no fan operation, and manual advancement of the spark to maximize torque output.

The 365-cubic-inch Cadillac V-8 had the same external block dimensions, cylinder-bore centers, and cylinder-head dimensions as its predecessors. Yet, such components as its cylinder block, pistons, piston rings, crankshaft, main bearing caps, exhaust manifolds, cam, valve springs, guides, and exhaust valves were new. This major revision made possible Cadillac's claim that it embodied "the greatest number of important advancements since the introduction of the famous short-stroke, large-bore Cadillac engine in 1949." The cylinder block had reinforced bulkheads and recored water jackets, while the deep-forged, 71-pound crankshaft had larger, by ½ inch, main bearing journals measuring 2⅝ inches in diameter. The Cadillac cam with a 324 degree duration and 102 degrees of overlap belied the smooth operation of its hydraulic valve lifters, which didn't begin to pump up until rpms exceeded the 5,000 mark.

The Cadillac V-8's higher compression ratio was achieved by the combination of the added displacement and a reduction in the volume of the combustion chambers. No fundamental changes were made in Cadillac's piston design except for a stronger crown, pin-boss support, and skirt. Cadillac had, back in 1949, decided to use a wedge- rather than a hemispheric-shaped combustion chamber because of its ability to combine smooth performance with a high compression ratio. The latest version kept the gases in a highly agitated stage, which provided a smooth burning of the fuel/air mixture.

Changes to the Cadillac's intake system included reshaping of the intake ports to provide a slightly faster fuel flow. No change was made in the intake valve's diameter, which remained at 1¾ inches. The exhaust valve head diameter was increased to 1⁹⁄₁₆ inches from 1½ inches. Exhaust-port area was increased by approximately 9 percent as was the capacity of the cast-iron exhaust manifolds. The net weight increase due to these changes was only 30 pounds. The 285-horsepower V-8 now weighed 680 pounds, with the Eldorado version coming in at 700 pounds.

Along with this redesigned engine, the 1956 Cadillacs featured a revamped, "controlled coupling" Hydra-Matic that virtually eliminated the power surges on up and down shifts common to older Hydra-Matics. On those models, the gear-ratio changes were accomplished by the engaging or disengaging of two multiple-disc clutches and the corresponding tightening or releasing of two bands on revolving drums. This system worked satisfactorily, but peak performance was difficult to maintain since proper timing of these procedures depended on extremely precise adjustment.

The new Hydra-Matic used a one-way clutch, in place of the band and multiple-disc clutch, that needed no adjustment. This was an expensive ($32 million in tooling costs) undertaking that, in essence, revised Hydra-Matic's basic design philosophy. A small fluid coupling added to the front clutch, described as a "dump-and-fill" unit, when empty of fluid provided torque multiplication. On the other hand, if conditions called for direct drive through a lockup of the front planetary gears, it filled with fluid. The entire cycle of filling and emptying of fluid was completed in approximately 1 second. As a result, abrupt shifting was virtually eliminated. The gear ratios of this Hydra-Matic were 3.96:1 (first), 2.55:1 (second), 1.55:1 (third), and 1:1 (fourth).

A criticism by 1955 Cadillac owners that their cars were too slow in reverse was answered by provision of a 4.3:1 ratio for reverse. Another important change was the inclusion of a mechanical parking pawl that protected against emergency-brake failure. As a result of this feature, the Hydra-Matic quadrant now read P, N, D_1, D_2, L, R.

As installed with a single-plate, transmission-fluid cooler (the Eldorado engine had a standard two-plate cooler), the Hydra-Matic weighed 208 pounds. General Motors' Detroit Transmission Division, which built the Hydra-Matic, used aluminum for its bell housing and rear-bearing retainer in order to reduce the transmission weight.

Acceleration of the typical 1956 Cadillac was marginally improved. For example, a Cadillac Series Sixty-Two Sedan could complete the 0 to 60-mph run in just under 11 seconds with the standard 3.07:1 rear axle. This time could be improved by the optional 3.36:1 unit offered for all Series Sixty-Two models, as well as the Sixty Special. All Series Seventy-Five Eldorados and Eldorado-engined cars had the 3.36:1 gear set as their standard axle.

Saginaw continued to produce Cadillac's standard power steering, but the 1956 version was a smaller, lighter and more efficient concentric gear unit rather than the bevel-gear-in-rack system of 1955. Among its advantages was quicker steering due to a 19.5:1 instead of 21.3:1 overall ratio. This reduced steering-wheel turns lock-to-lock by 10 percent. The point at which the steering became power assisted when the car was in motion was also lowered from 3.5 to 3 pounds of pull on the steering wheel. A new parking valve reduced the maximum pull on the steering wheel when the car was at rest from 12 to 6 pounds, making parking a much easier task.

Cadillac's power-brake system now combined the master and vacuum-power cylinders into a single, smaller unit that offered the advantage of easier servicing. Drivers were quick to notice the reduced pedal pressure demanded of this unit. Cadillac regarded the new arrangement as an important safety feature, citing the pedal's lower level as reducing the time needed for an operator to apply the brakes. In addition, it called attention to the reduced pedal travel needed for rapid braking.

There were no changes made in the rear spring rates for the 1956 Cadillacs that were fitted with five rear-leaf springs. Series Seventy-Five cars had six-leaf springs. But the combination of an increased 0.5 degree in the front wheel caster and the new power steering system made a noticeable improvement in Cadillac's highway handling. Contemporary road tests praised the Cadillac for its quick steering response, stability, and overall agility.

Nineteen fifty-six wasn't a year of major styling change. Instead it exemplified Cadillac's unequaled proficiency in maintaining a strong styling continuity with recent models, while giving owners of older Cadillacs plenty of visual encouragement to move up to a new model.

The grille grid, now constructed of aluminum, was of a finer texture. The oval parking/directional signal lights were positioned in the bumper below the wing guards. A gold Cadillac script unit was boldly inscribed on the left side of the grille. Cadillac also chose 1956 to reshape its crest and V. The result was a wider-angle V and a lower as well as wider crest.

One of the year's movie releases, "The Solid Gold Cadillac," starring Judy Holiday and Paul Douglas, also featured a gold-painted and detailed Eldorado Convertible. What better time, then, for Cadillac to offer a gold-colored alternative to the standard satin-finished grille? This was optional at no extra cost on Eldorados and at a slightly added cost for other models. The Sabre-Spoke wheels were also available in this gold finish at no additional cost.

This transformation was accomplished by an electrochemical process in which a layer of aluminum oxide was built up over the cast or stamped aluminum base. The component was then dipped into a color dye and chemically sealed.

Whether satin or gold colored, the Cadillac's grille was part of a front end intended to emphasize Cadillac's lower and wider look. Both the hood and fenders were flatter, the hood ornament was broader and horizontally ribbed "reflector shields" were situated on each side of the headlamps.

At the rear, Cadillac's bumper/exhaust exit scheme was rearranged to position the oval exhaust higher in the bumper. This was just one change contributing to a smoother rear-deck appearance. The bumper height was increased, the six vertical trim moldings were eliminated, and the license-plate bracket was now mounted in the lower bumper region. Depending on the model, the rear-deck V embraced gold block letters reading Cadillac, Eldorado, or Fleetwood.

When viewed in profile, the 1956 Cadillacs appeared to be considerably longer than previously. Actually this was an illusion created by the use of a longer front-fender crest line, which now extended nearly to the front door's leading edge and the adoption of the 1955 Eldorado's rear-fender spear. On the 1956 regular-production Cadillacs, this appendage was emphasized by chrome trim and nine vertical uprights. Cadillac described this arrangement as "slip-stream rear fender styling." A new addition to Cadillac's rear-fender fin format was a thin chromed molding outlining the top of the rear fender and taillight. Cadillac also reshaped the rear fender "louver" by extending the six horizontal dividers further forward.

All Cadillacs with the exception of the Eldorado were slightly reduced in overall length. The Series Sixty-Two Sedan, still 7 inches shorter than other Series Sixty-Two models, now extended 214.9 inches instead of 216.3 inches. The remaining Series Sixty-Two Cadillacs measured 221.9 inches, down from 223.2 inches. The Series Seventy-Five model's overall length of 235.7 inches was 14 inches less than in 1955.

Similarly, the Eldorado now took slightly less time to sweep past awed pedestrians as its length was 222.2 inches, down from 223.3 inches in 1955.

Cadillac made only passing reference to the new crest-V arrangement for 1956, describing it as a "new, wider V." But even a casual review of its appearance revealed many changes. The reangled V was joined by a reshaped crest far wider than in 1955. In addition, the crest's components were reshaped and rearranged to create an impression of modernity.

Unlike 1949, when Cadillac, with its Coupe de Ville, along with counterparts from Oldsmobile and Buick, had marked an industry milestone with the introduction of the two-door hardtop, it lagged behind both marques in including four-door pillarless hardtops in its model lineup. This slow response to what was a popular trend was made even more unexplainable by Cadillac's early promotion of four-door hardtop styling with its 1953 Orleans showcar.

In any case, Oldsmobile and Buick offered hardtop sedans in 1955, leaving Cadillac in the slightly embarrassing situation of trailing along a year later, with such lesser lights as Chevrolet, Pontiac, Ford, and Rambler. On the other hand, there were no Imperial, Lincoln, or Packard four-door hardtops; and in its first year of availability, the Cadillac Sedan de Ville, with a production total of 41,732, became Cadillac's most popular model. More Sedan de Villes were built than Packard's total output of 13,432 cars and the Imperial's production of 10,684 cars combined. It also nearly matched Lincoln's record 50,322 output. For its part, Cadillac introduced the Sedan de Ville "as a magnificent companion to the world-famous Coupe de Ville . . . [it] brings to its owner all the comfort, spaciousness and convenience of a four-door model, yet retains all the brilliance and spirit of the coupe design."

Cadillac, responding to a poll of its dealers and salesmen that indicated 41 percent of its customers preferred a center–dash-positioned glove box, redesigned the dash of its 1956 models around this feature, which was also found in the 1956 Packard. Another customer desire that Cadillac responded to was the indication by 37 percent of those interviewed that they would like dual ashtrays up front bracketing the glove box. Their wish was Cadillac's command; and this feature, as well as dual lighters, was found on the 1956 models.

Other changes included a single-color steering wheel with a slimmer, yet still protruding center post and an instrument cluster with a sun shade. The speedometer, with white figures on a black background, was easy to read, but the broad chrome band along the lower-dash edge remained a bothersome source of reflections. Cadillac continued to use warning lights for the generator discharge and oil pressure indicators. The rectangularly shaped clock and radio were located to the driver's right in a band of mesh trim that extended across the rest of the dash. Placed directly in front of the passenger was a gold Cadillac crest and script reading "Nineteen-fifty-six."

Since power brakes were now standard on all models (in 1955 they had been standard on the Eldorado and a $48 option for other Cadillacs), a new, double-hung brake pedal, large enough for left or right foot use was used. A Cadillac exclusive was the optional, interior manual control for the driver's side exterior mirror. This was particularly useful if the optional, six-way power seat was installed. Also unique to Cadillac was an electrically operated radio antenna that superseded the older vacuum-activated model. Cadillac also increased the comfort quotient of its cars by offering a remote-control, trunk-lid lock and a six-way power seat with variable settings.

Cadillac provided 86 possible interior trim variations, ranging from natural and metallic leathers to silver-patterned nylons, Bedford cords, and rich-looking broadcloths. There were 23 basic exterior colors, including 4 different shades of gray that enabled nearly 500 two-tone color combinations to be offered.

NEW MODELS

Cadillac introduced both the Sedan de Ville and a new hardtop Eldorado model, the Eldorado Seville, on October 24, 1955, nearly a month earlier than the debut date of November 18, 1955, for the rest of its 1956 offerings. Like Packard, which also offered a hardtop version of its Caribbean for 1956, Cadillac recognized the value of broadening its base in this small, but lucrative band of the luxury-car field.

"In the two years since the Eldorado was first introduced," said Cadillac, "it has won itself a unique place in the hearts of motorists everywhere. Though the Eldorado name originally designated only the Convertible model, it will include for 1956 both an open and a closed car. The first of these—the spectacular Biarritz—is a true achievement in advanced design and engineering . . . In every way it is a true masterpiece of Cadillac craftsmanship." The Seville was described as "an inspiration to behold . . . a revelation to ride in . . . an education to drive . . . a 'dream car' in actual production . . . Deliberately designed and manufactured as the most exclusive motor car of our time, the Eldorado Seville represents Cadillac's highest achievement in automotive quality and craftsmanship."

The Seville, along with the Eldorado Biarritz, was priced at $6,501, which included virtually every option except air conditioning, E-Z-Eye glass, automatic headlight dimmer, remote-control trunk lid, spotlights, and the no-cost optional gold finish for the grille and Sabre-Spoke wheels. Incidentally, Cadillac, along with Packard, was the first American manufacturer to offer air conditioning on its Convertible models.

Identifying the Eldorados as the latest models were, in addition to the grille format seen on all 1956 Cadillacs, their twin, vertical-blade hood ornaments and altered rear-bumper form, which now carried vertical grooves in the outer panels and enclosed larger, oblong exhaust outlets. The bumper's center panel was widened considerably, enabling the license-plate bracket to be included in its surface.

The Seville's padded top was covered in a new Vicodec material (which was also available on the Convertible) in a choice of blue, green, tan, ivory or black.

Both cars used the same interior styling, with narrow, 1-inch pleating and V-shaped, smooth-surfaced bolsters with miniature chromed Cadillac crests. Door panels consisted of a chrome kick panel with three grid inserts, a section of 1-inch vertical pleats with concealed pockets, topped by a bullet-shaped, smooth-surfaced leather section framed by bright molding. Above this segment, which included the arm rest, was light-toned leather and the insert for the vent wing and door handle.

The Biarritz used an all-leather interior in solid red, black, blue or green or in combinations with white bolsters.

For the Seville, several nylon fabric choices were added to the above leather upholsteries. These joined white or green leather bolsters with Florentine-pattern, metallic nylon in black, blue, green, or red. Colors for the Seville's Vicodec top were the same as those offered for the Biarritz and Series Sixty-Two Convertible.

Productions of these automobiles totaled 6,050 units, of which 3,900 were Sevilles. Cadillac was justifiably proud, depicting them as having been "deliberately created to establish a new level of motor car excellence . . . In their unique acceptance, they are, without question, the leading representation of the great Cadillac name."

DIFFERENCES AMONG MODELS

Cadillac described the Series Sixty-Two Sedan as "far more exciting in appearance" than previous examples . . . with its new slip-stream rear fender styling . . . its brilliant new grille assembly . . . and its wonderful new color combinations."

External identification of all Series Sixty-Two Cadillacs, in addition to those features already mentioned, included the elimination of the bright trim from the rear fender's lower edge and the use of a thin chrome strip on the rear-fender fairing, which led to eight vertical bars.

Series Sixty-Two Sedan and Coupe upholstery choices consisted of blue, beige, green, or gray Heatherstone-patterned nylon matched with bolsters of all-wool gabardine. Another alternative scheme provided light gray, green, or blue, Lurex-threaded, frost-pattern nylon with white Elascofab bolsters.

When the latter scheme was selected, the seat cushions and seat backs were finished in tufted biscuits with deeply recessed buttons. If all-cloth upholstery was installed, the upper half of the seat back was a smooth-surfaced gabardine.

Door and side panels combined a darker-toned biscuit pattern with smooth upper surfaces, carrying a thin chrome strip that dipped into a V below a Cadillac crest. Floor carpeting was a thick, dark-toned nylon frieze.

Interior choices for the Series Sixty-Two Convertible were based on new seat and side door-wall formats. The seat cushion and lower portion of the seat backs were covered by a 2.5-inch-wide piping running from front to rear. The remaining portion of the seat back was smooth finished with a rectangular insert highlighted by exposed stitching. Running along the top and sides of the front seat backs was a bright chrome molding.

1956 Series Sixty-Two Sedan de Ville.

1956 Series Sixty-Two Coupe.

Upper door panels were covered with light Elascofab, a second panel of light-toned, painted metal and a satin-black and chromed grid insert for the door and ventpane handles. Dark-toned leather extended across the center section with a wide V separating the smooth-faced leather from a lower region of vertically pleated Elascofab. A bright chrome kickpad was installed. A nylon-frieze carpeting was standard.

Color choices consisted of solid black, beige, or red plus combinations of black/white, light blue/white, black/aquamarine, light green/white, and red/white.

The Convertible's Vicodec top was available in white, black, light blue, beige, and light green.

Interiors for the Coupe and Sedan de Ville models were identical. The seat cushions and lower half of the seat backs were covered by one of two fabrics in 2.5-inch

CADILLAC VITAL STATISTICS: 1956

Series	Model	Body Type	Factory Price ($)	Weight (lbs.)	Production (#)
62	6219	4 dr Sedan	4296	4430	26,222
	6237	2 dr Hardtop Coupe	4201	4420	26,649
	6267	Convertible	4766	4645	8300
	6239D	4 dr Sedan de Ville	4753	4550	41,732
	6237D	2 dr Coupe de Ville	4624	4445	25,086
	6237S	Eldorado Seville	6556	4665	3900
	6267S	Eldorado Biarritz	6556	4880	2150
60	6019	4 dr Sedan	5047	4610	17,000
75	7523	4 dr Sedan 8p	6613	5050	1095
	7533	4 dr Limousine 8p	6828	5130	955

1956 Series Sixty-Two Convertible Coupe.

piping. The choices included black nylon, in what Cadillac identified as a stardust pattern consisting of white, blue and yellow stars against a black background; or white, green, and pink stars against a black background. The factor determining which of these was used was the color of the leather bolsters, which carried a rectangular panel with raised stitching. Side panels and doors used a similar arrangement with a panel of leather-grained Elascofab added to the upper door panel.

For the Series Sixty Special, 1956 was historically significant since it closed out the era of pillared, four-door Series Sixty Specials that had begun in 1938. Cadillac gave a touch of perspective to its description of the Sixty Special, depicting it as "long regarded as the perfect representative of Cadillac's incomparable beauty and quality. Appropriately enough, there is but one model in this world-renowned series . . . a four-door sedan."

Missing from the Sixty Special's exterior were the expected rear-fender trim marks. Instead, Cadillac covered the entire rear-fender fairing with a ribbed chrome molding. In the years just ahead, an elaborate rear-fender chrome embellishment would be the keystone of Series Sixty styling.

Twelve interior choices were offered for the Sixty Special. Three nylon fabrics for the 1.5-inch pleated seat cushions and seat backs were offered with either all-wool broadcloth or leather bolsters and trim. The five basic colors available in various patterns were light gray, light blue, light green, and gold. A chrome-lined molding ran across the sides and forward edges of the seats. A gold-plated V and crest were positioned on the rear of the front-seat back.

Providing added distinction to the pleated lower portion of the door panel was a bright and brushed chrome insert with a gold-plated Cadillac medallion. The remaining panel subdivisions were finished, respectively, in leather-grained Elascofab and leather. Cadillac characterized the 1956 Seventy-Five as the car that came to mind first "if the average motorist were asked to name the one most luxurious and distinguished motor car in the world."

The interiors of the eight-passenger Sedan and Imperial limousine were available in Bedford cord with broadcloth bolsters in light blue, light gray, dark gray, or brown. As an alternative, light gray, light blue, or beige broadcloth was also offered. The limousine once again featured an electrically operated partition between the front and rear compartments. The limousine's front seat was available in either black or blue leather. Dark-toned KinKomo carpeting was used, except for the front compartment of the limousine where looped-nylon pile was installed.

As in 1955, both Series Seventy-Five models had full-length rear-fender verticals and a separate body-side chrome spear.

CADILLAC'S DOMESTIC COMPETITION

This was a year when Packard, sad to say, slipped away from view as one of America's great automobiles. Val-iant, desperate, but ultimately futile efforts were made to maintain Packard's credibility as a luxury car beyond 1956. During the year, Packard provided plenty of examples that it had finally learned what was needed to effectively compete with Cadillac. Its production and quality problems were largely resolved, Packard featured a first-rate innovation in the form of the Twin Traction, limited slip differential, optional seat belts, and, on four-door models, an electric door lock, and a clever merchandizing feature, "Touch-Button Ultramatic," push-button automatic controls that put it on a par with Chrysler's introduction of this feature. A long overdue move was to remove the Packard name from the Clipper models. It was an action that should have been taken years earlier.

Packard also countered, as we've noted, Cadillac's expansion of the Eldorado series with a hardtop Caribbean, but it proved to be neither a parry nor a thrust since only 539 Caribbeans (263 hardtops and 276 convertibles) were built. More successful was Packard's effort to be first in the luxury-car, horsepower-engine displacement race with the Caribbean's 310-horsepower, 374-cubic-inch V-8.

With the Clipper established as an upper–medium-priced automobile, Packard also belatedly recognized the tremendous sales success of Cadillac's Series Sixty-Two models, which in 1956 represented, with a total production of 128,452, over 83 percent of total Cadillac output. Its reaction was the Packard Executive, which, if priced too close to the Clipper at $3,465 (sedan) and $3,560 (hardtop), at least expanded Packard's market span without seriously diluting its name. The production of 2,815 Executives, or over 20 percent of total Packard output is indicative of what could have been if Packard had taken a similar step years earlier.

Chrysler's Imperial, with a 3-inch longer (to 133 inches) wheelbase, revised side trim, bolder rear-fender lines, and new four-door hardtop, had a total production run of 10,682 cars, down slightly from the 1955 level of 11,430.

Far more impressive and indicative of Lincoln's aggressive approach to luxury-car marketing were the new sales records set by the 1956 Lincolns. We've already mentioned Lincoln's 1956 production in regard to the successful debut of Cadillac's Sedan de Ville, but it's certainly worth emphasizing two additional points: Lincoln sales were up over 83 percent from 1955 and its production of 50,322 1956 Lincolns would not be exceeded until 10 years had passed.

Lincoln did not contest Cadillac Series Seventy-Five Fleetwoods with equivalent offerings, and it lacked a model that compared directly with the Sedan de Ville. In most other areas, however, its cars, divided in Capri and more expensive Premiere series, were positioned to compete head on with the Series Sixty-Two Cadillac.

In a switch of thinking, Lincoln abandoned the road-racing heritage of the 1952-1955 models in favor of 126-inch wheelbase cars with an overall length of 223 inches. Their styling was futuristic, with a wraparound windshield, deeply hooded headlights, simple side trim, and a beautifully tapered rear fender line.

Lincoln substantially updated its V-8 engine, boosting its displacement in the process to 368 cubic inches. Horsepower was raised to 285, from 225 in 1955.

These cars were correctly perceived as the first serious threat to Cadillac since the end of the war and were accompanied by an even more impressive vehicle, the Continental Mark II whose introduction on October 6, 1955, at the Paris Auto Show opened a new era in American luxury-car history. Cadillac wouldn't formally introduce its champion in this new arena of competition until December 1956; but prior to that date, it had made it abundantly clear that the Continental would not have the rarified environment of the $10,000+ American automobile all to itself.

SPECIFICATIONS

Engine

Type: V-type, ohv, eight cylinders
Bore × stroke: 4 × 3.63 inches
Displacement: 365 cubic inches
Horsepower: 285 @ 4,600 rpm
    Eldorado: 305 @ 4,700 rpm
Torque: 400 lb.-ft. @ 2,800 rpm (Eldorado 3,200 rpm)
Compression ratio: 9.75:1
Carburetor: Carter WCFB, four-barrel model 2371S
    Eldorado: Two Carter WCFB or Rochester four-barrel carburetors
Electrical system: 12-volt
Transmission: Hydra-Matic, three-speed automatic, controlled coupling

Chassis/Drivetrain

Unchanged from 1955

Dimensions

Wheelbase:
    Series 62 and Eldorado: 129 inches
    Series 60 Special: 133 inches
    Series 75: 149.8 inches
Width: 80 inches
Front/rear tread: 60/63.16 inches
Overall length:
    Series 62 Sedan: 214.9 inches
    Other Series 62: 221.9 inches
    Eldorado Biarritz and Seville: 222.2 inches
    Series 60 Special: 225.9 inches
    Series 75: 235.7 inches

Popular Options

Air conditioning: $540
E-Z Eye tinted glass
Autronic eye
Signal-seeking radio
Electrically operated antenna
Heater
Power windows
Gold-finish grille
Two-way power seat: $81
Six-way power seat: $97 (standard on Eldorado, available for 62 Coupe and Sedan)
Remote-control trunk lid lock
License-plate frame
Fog lamps
Spotlights
Door guards
White sidewall tires

1957

Finest Expression of Motordom's Highest Ideal

IN THE 1956 CALENDAR YEAR, Cadillac sold 140,843 cars or 2.43 percent of the industry's total. Although fewer than the 153,334 Cadillacs sold in 1955, this total enabled Cadillac to increase its market penetration from the 1.93 percent of 1955 and move up from tenth to ninth position in the industry standing.

Although this placed Cadillac in an extremely advantageous position for the 1957 model year, it was soon apparent that it was to be a year of intense competition. For the second consecutive year, Cadillac faced a revitalized opponent, this time in the form of the Imperial, which, on the basis of its new styling and engineering features, enjoyed over a 300 percent production increase. The output of 37,557 Imperials (in 1956 just 10,684 had been built) placed it behind Lincoln, which turned out 41,123 (35,223 Premieres and 5,900 Capris) cars. Cadillac remained far ahead with a model-year total of 146,841 cars, which was 7,736 cars less than in 1956.

This drop of approximately 5 percent compared favorably with the overall performance of General Motors' 1957 model cars in comparison with Chrysler's line of new products whose rear-fender fins and torsion-bar front suspensions were clearly the big news stories from Detroit. While GM's output slumped almost 9 percent to 2,816,400 from 3,062,400, Chrysler's increased over 40 percent to 1,222,300 from 870,300.

The loss of upward sales momentum by the 1957 Cadillac, coming on the heels of a similar decline in 1956 and preceding four years when model-year output would fall short of the 1956 level, has made it tempting to regard the 1957 Cadillacs as automobiles falling a bit short of expectations. This perception has been enhanced by the 1957 (and of course, the 1958's) close proximity to the radically styled 1959 models, which makes them conservative-appearing automobiles by comparison.

Most of this has been altered by the passage of time. From a contemporary perspective, the 1957 Cadillacs are seen as significant automobiles whose styling represented a bridge between design eras at Cadillac and whose level of workmanship maintained Cadillac's tradition of excellence. On this point, Chrysler paid dearly for its record 1957 output. Too often Chrysler Corporation cars, poorly assembled, quickly rusted and fell victim to various mechanical maladies. It's certainly worth noting that at least one road test of a 1957 Imperial mentioned water leaks and rattles, while contemporary Cadillac evaluations found little to fault in Cadillac's construction.

CHANGES AND IMPROVEMENTS

With the exception of the Series Seventy-Five eight-passenger Sedan and Limousine models, and, of course, the Convertible, all 1957 Cadillacs used a pillarless hardtop roof design. Cadillac was the only American manufacturer to adopt this policy in 1957.

The Series Sixty-Two line consisted of two- and four-door hardtops, the Convertible Coupe, plus Coupe de Ville and Sedan de Ville versions of the two- and four-door models. The Eldorado segment of the Series Sixty-Two Cadillacs consisted of the Biarritz Convertible and Seville Hardtop.

Following previous practice, the Series Sixty Special Fleetwood was available only as a single model—a four-door hardtop. Carried over from 1956 were the earlier-mentioned Series Seventy-Five models.

Cadillac shared a new General Motors C-body with the Buick Super and Roadmaster models, but exterior panel interchangeability was very limited. The four-door hardtop Buicks and Cadillacs shared only their roof panels and deck lids, while two-door hardtops only used the same roof panels. Both marques used identical windshields and back lights. The Series Seventy-Five line had many exclusive body parts including the rear quarter, roof, and rear-door panels. A change made on the 1957 C-body, which GM said reduced manufacturing costs, was the elimination of the deck-opening upper panel and the subsequent lengthening of the deck lid.

Wheelbase for the Series Sixty-Two models was increased a half inch to 129.5 inches, while those for the Series Sixty Special and Series Seventy-Five remained unchanged at 133 and 149.75 inches, respectively. Changes in overall length were minor. That of the Series Sixty-Two increased by one inch to 215.9 inches on four-door hardtops, while remaining models recessed by the same amount to 220.9 inches. Series Seventy-Five Cadillacs grew from 235.7 to 236.2 inches.

To give some perspective to these dimensions, a comparison of the 133-inch wheelbase, 224.4-inch overall length Series Sixty Special to the largest Lincolns and Imperials is helpful. The Lincoln, with a 126-inch wheelbase, had an overall length of 224.6 inches; the 129-inch wheelbase Imperial's overall length was 224.0 inches. The Crown Imperial, on a 149.5-inch wheelbase, stretched across 244.7 inches of pavement.

From any angle, the new Cadillacs had a clean, uncluttered, and well-coordinated appearance that, on initial overview, disguised the extent of its new form. But after a few minutes of closer study, the Cadillac's appearance not only remained pleasing, but tended to blossom into full bloom as one of GM's best efforts.

All models were lower for 1957. The height of the Series Sixty-Two and the Sixty Special dropped from 62 inches to 59.1 inches. That of the Series Seventy-Five went from 63.9 inches to 61.6 inches. These reductions, plus a 3.5-inch lower hood line and a deeper windshield with forward-slanting A-posts, contributed to a sleeker profile.

Not continued from 1956 was the roof-visor feature. The form of the windshield was repeated in the rear backlight with rearward sloping C-posts. Although the windshield was larger, with an area of 1,412.1 square inches, compared with the 1956 version's 1,206 square inches, total glass area was reduced on the 1957 Cadillacs. It varied from model to model; but as an illustration, that of the Series Sixty Special dropped from 4,264 to 3,949.2 square inches.

A sense of fleetness was enhanced by the removal of rear fender skirts (the 1957s were the first postwar models without this feature) and rearranged side trim. Absent was the long, side chrome piece that, in 1956, ran from the grille to the rear fender louver. The use of a higher and wider front-wheel cutout and an extended fender crease line that faded into the front door panel was far more attractive.

With the same degree of success, Cadillac restyled its rear-fender format for 1957. The big news was the abandonment of the high-mounted tail and backup lights, which, following the Eldorado's lead, now were positioned just above the exhaust exits in separate circular nacelles. Of course Cadillac wasn't abandoning the rear-fender fin. For 1957, it was actually more evident than ever before, but its thinner shape and angular shape was neither too extreme nor overly modest. These shapely fins with their narrow chrome stripes flowed down to meet the low-mounted dual rear lights and join the vertically arranged exhaust exits to contribute to a very clean rear appearance.

The uplift these fins gave to the Cadillac's rear fenders was emphasized by the use of a fender spear that was now one of Cadillac's major styling features. It was mounted much higher on the fender than previously and extended forward to join the rear fender louver. In turn, this feature took on a fresh appearance, positioned where the old gravel fender shield had once been and having its horizontal bars trail after, rather than lead into the windstream.

Series Sixty-Two models carried a gold Cadillac crest and V in 1957. This had been the practice from 1948 until 1956 when the Sixty-Two models combined the V with Cadillac lettering. Series Sixty Special and Series Seventy-Five models continued to have Fleetwood nameplates on their rear decks.

The Cadillac's front grille again consisted of an anodized aluminum insert. Its gridwork divisions were slightly larger. The familiar gull-wing bumper shape was once again reformed and relocated. Black rubber inserts made them a bit more innocent appearing; and along with the center crossbar, they now served as the grille's upper perimeter. Cadillac's goddess hood emblem, which dated back to 1930, was relegated to option status in 1957.

Cadillac still used single headlamps, but their fender lids were fully chromed instead of having grille inserts as in 1956. This secondary grille theme wasn't dropped since gridwork bars extended into the front fenders from a location directly below the headlights. Matching the shape of the rear lights were the dual parking/directional lights mounted in the lower extremities of the bumper.

Series Sixty-Two Sedans and Coupes, as well as the Sixty Special and Seventy-Five had a gold-colored, anodized-aluminum, Cadillac script mounted on their front fenders. The remaining Cadillacs carried model name identification at this spot. The Cadillac crest was moved to the upper area of the rear-fender fin on the Series Sixty-Two. The other Cadillacs did not carry this ornamentation. Bolder-appearing wheelcovers with more prominent turbine vanes and concentric inner rings helped accentuate the new thinner white walls that were available for $54.95.

The new Cadillac body shell marginally reduced most interior dimensions. For example, on the Series Sixty Special, rear shoulder room was reduced from 59.4 to 57 inches while that available to front-seat passengers was reduced a half inch to 59 inches. Front headroom dropped from 35.8 to 34.6 inches, and rear headroom was reduced to 34.7 from 35.1 inches. Front and rear hip room also was slightly less, but front leg room increased from 43.3 to 44.8 inches.

More apparent were the Cadillac's rearranged instrument panel, standard front-seat center armrests, safety padding of the front-seat back, and two-spoke, recessed-center steering wheel. For the most part, the instruments were well grouped, large, and legible. The 0 to 120-mph speedometer read horizontally and included a trip as well as a total mileage odometer. The red warning lights for the generator and oil pressure, along with gauges for the temperature, fuel level, as well as the directional signal indicator, were placed in close proximity to the speedometer. The center-mounted dash box had its push button mounted off center to faciliate use by the driver.

A similar arrangement grouped the controls for the radio. This unit priced at $164.25, including a power antenna and rear speaker, was a combined search-tuner, push-button manual model that could also be fitted with a foot-operated remote control unit. Cadillac was one of the few American manufacturers to mount the front radio speaker on the transmission tunnel directly below the dash.

Grouped to the driver's left were controls for the lights and windshield wipers and washers. The latter feature was standard on all models, but the wipers were dated, two-speed vacuum-activated units. No electric wipers were available. The electric clock was positioned close to the passenger in a chrome strip that stretched across most of the instrument panel. When the optional power windows were fitted, their master controls were located on the left hand extension of the instrument panel. If the optional ($128.85 on all models except Series Seventy-Five whose system was priced at $179.00) heater/defroster was installed, its four-unit controls were installed to the right of the steering column. As in 1956, the right-side sun visor had a vanity mirror as standard equipment. Unlike 1956, when rear robe cords had been standard on all models, they were found only on the Series Seventy-Five Sedans in 1957.

Cadillac discarded the traditional ladder-type frame with X-members in 1957 for what it described as a "tubular-center X-frame" with approximately 18 percent greater beam stiffness and torsional rigidity as compared with the older version. This setup eliminated the side rails and used outrigger hangers to attach the body to the frame. All stress was taken through the tubular-center X-frame. The cross-member arms were of box-section steel, with the front and rear cross-members constructed of channel-section steel.

Cadillac offered many reasons for adopting this frame. The elimination of frame side-members flanking the passenger compartment allowed the goal of a lower-body profile to be attained without any significant loss of interior space. At the same time, tooling costs were kept low by using one basic frame for all three Cadillac series. This was possible since the wheelbase could be altered by changing the center section. The use of the same frame-forming tools for the front and rear extending beams made it easy to accommodate the needs of the various body styles, particularly the Convertible. The weight of the Cadillac chassis thus varied with its application. For example, that of the Series Sixty-Two Sedan weighed 412 pounds, that of the Series Sixty-Two Convertible weighed 549 pounds. Overall, the 1957 frame was nearly 4 percent lighter than in 1956. In addition, Cadillac reported that there was no metal-to metal contact between body and frame to transmit road noise and vibration to the interior.

Suspension changes were not significant. Cadillac continued to use semielliptical rear springs, which now were mounted outside of the frame. The front suspension remained a coil-spring type but now featured ball joints rather than kingpins. This design

was used in all General Motors' 1957 cars, but Cadillac's adoption trailed Lincoln by five years. Among the positive effects of this change was greater resistance to front-end dive during braking, less free-wheel play, and steadier steering.

Other changes reported by Cadillac for 1957 included modified shock absorbers for a softer ride; a two-piece propeller shaft (used in 1956 on Series Seventy-Five models) with three universal joints and a new, rubber-cushioned center bearing; quieter differential gears due to a 50- rather than a 45-degree angle of the teeth; and a stronger, hardened carbon-steel, rear-axle shaft, thicker rear-axle housing, and larger rear-axle bearings.

Front-spring rates were unchanged for all models except the Series Sixty-Two Convertible, Series Sixty Special, Eldorados, and Series Seventy-Five models. All of these had slightly stiffer springs. These changes resulted in Cadillacs with riding qualities matching or exceeding those of any contemporary automobile. A road weight approaching three tons was apparent if the Cadillac was rushed through sharp turns, but the combination of a responsive engine and smooth-shifting transmission made the Cadillac the ideal car for long-distance driving.

Along with Buick, Cadillac was unique among GM's 1957 models to continue using 15-inch wheels. Standard tire size on Series Sixty and Sixty-Two was 8.00 × 15, four-ply, with 8.20 × 15, six-ply for the Series Seventy-Five. All models were available with white sidewalls as optional equipment. Those for the Series Sixty-Two and Sixty Special were larger, 8.20 × 15 tires.

The 1957 Cadillacs had slightly less brake-lining area than in 1956 as the effective swept area dropped to 210.32 from 221.96 square inches. The Series Seventy-Fives went from 233.64 to 233.32 square inches.

Changes in the General Motors Hydra-Matic transmission were limited to internal modifications intended to make shifts smoother and the repositioning of the transmission cooler nearer the bottom of the radiator.

Leaving its engine displacement unchanged at 365 cubic inches put Cadillac behind the leaders in engine-size standings. Buick boosted its biggest engine to 364 cubic inches, but Oldsmobile produced the biggest engine of any GM auto division with a 371 cubic-inch V-8. Lincoln shared a 368-cubic-inch V-8 with the Mercury Turnpike Cruiser and Chrysler's Imperial outranked them all at 392 cubic inches.

Cadillac's horsepower rating increased to 300 at 4,800 rpm.Peak torque remained unchanged at 400 lb-ft, but it was now reached at 3,200 rpm rather than 2,800 rpm. The Cadillac's four-barrel carburetor, either a Carter model 27795 or a Rochester model 7010100, had larger secondary bores than those units used in 1956. Internal changes included the use of larger combustion chambers that retained their wedge-shapes, a compression ratio boost to 10.0:1, and a new "high intensity" cam providing the same 0.451 inches of valve lift while slightly altering the valve-train timing.

Cadillac engineers improved the V-8's breathing ability by rerouting the intake ports and using 1.875- rather than 1.750-inch diameter intake valves. This latter change necessitated the use of exhaust valves that were proportionally smaller. They now measured 1.437 instead of 1.562 inches. Other minor changes included pistons with cam ground regions for reduced oil consumption, improved piston cooling, and, on cars with air conditioning, a vent tube added to the fuel filter that returned fumes to the fuel tank. Its purpose was to reduce the possibility of vapor lock. Also adopted were new rocker arms, motor mounts, starting motor, higher output generator, battery and battery box, and higher-capacity fuel pump.

The use of a 3.07:1 axle in 1957 instead of the 3.37:1 unit of 1956 basically cancelled out the impact of Cadillac's added horsepower on its performance while improving its fuel economy. A typical 0- to 60-mph time was now 11 seconds.

DIFFERENCES AMONG MODELS

Seven interior two-tone color combinations were listed for the Series Sixty-Two Sedan and Coupe. Four Neptune-pattern metallic nylons in blue, gray, green, and beige were offered in conjunction with matching Glacial Mist metallic nylon bolsters and trim. A Grecian-pattern metallic nylon in light gray, light blue, and light green was paired with Elascofab bolsters and trim in corresponding colors. A dark-toned, deep-pile, nylon-blend carpeting was standard. Door panels featured a dark-toned painted upper surface, a middle region, and armrest in light-toned Elascofab, and a bottom panel of metallic nylon. The window, door, and mirror controls were mounted lower on the door than in 1956.

For the Series Sixty-Two Convertible, three solid, all-leather interiors of black, tan, and Dakota red were offered. The seat cushions and seat-back inserts had a biscuit design highlighted with concave, chromed buttons. The upper-seat portions had vertical, 1-inch wide piping. When the new front center armrest was not in use, its shorter height helped create the impression that the Convertible was equipped with front bucket seats. A similar recess on the back served as the location for the rear radio speaker.

If two-tone leather was desired, the Convertible could be finished in any of five seat/bolster-trim combinations. The Convertible's door panel carried a pleated-leather insert surrounded by fine-grained Elascofab. Extended across the insert (which also was the location of the leather-covered armrest) was a horizontal chrome molding with a stylized V and Cadillac crest. A ribbed kick panel was also used.

While Cadillac regarded the Convertible's interior as "styled in keeping with the zest and the spirit of youth," it considered the Coupe de Ville as "truly an aristocrat." "Thus," said Cadillac, "its interior conveys all the charm, taste, and graciousness that the name implies."

Coupe de Ville buyers selected from eight upholstery alternatives. Four combined a Sahara-pattern, metallic nylon cloth with matching leather bolsters and trim in gray, blue, beige, and green. Three brocade-pattern metallic nylons in gray, blue, and green were offered with matching leather bolsters and trim. Yet another combination, mountain laurel and black Corinthian-pattern metallic nylon with mountain laurel leather bolsters and trim was available.

The seat cushions and seat backs used the tufted-biscuit, recessed concave, chromed-button format. The remaining upper portion was finished in 1-inch piping. Chromed roof bows extended across the light-toned, perforated Elascofab headliner.

Door panels were the same as the Convertible's except that the main panel was finished in upholstery fabric. Carpeting was in a deep-pile nylon blend.

The interior of the Sedan de Ville was available in the same patterns and colors as the Coupe de Ville. Its seats did not have the centrally located indents.

Described as the "symbol of Cadillac leadership in the luxury car field," the Series Sixty Special was making its first appearance as a pillarless four-door sedan. Its longer rear deck, in comparison with the Series Sixty-Two models, was accentuated by a broad, brush-finished, stainless-steel rear-fender panel.

Any of its interiors, said Cadillac, "were designed to please the most disarming eye." Seat cushions and seat-back inserts featured 2-inch-wide piping contrasting with bolsters of either fine-textured metallic nylon or leather. Ten upholstery and color choices were offered. All four doors had full-width armrests containing an ashtray and cigarette lighter. Above the armrest were two Elascofab panels separated by a light-toned strip of lacquered metal matching the pleated headliner's moldings. Set within the armrest molding was a chromed Cadillac crest. Above the ribbed kick panel were vertical pleats of the seat upholstery. A heavily tufted, deep-pile, nylon-blend carpeting was installed.

The debacle that Studebaker Packard suffered in 1956 effectively eliminated Packard from the fine-car market. In turn this left Cadillac's Eldorado Seville and Biarritz unchallenged in their field.

Viewed head-on, the Eldorado's appearance almost paralleled that of other 1957 Cadillacs. The only real tip-off that this was not a typical model were the lack of a hood ornament and the twin-fin "bunny ears" ornaments mounted on the front fenders. Also apparent were the front-fender gold script that read either Biarritz or Seville and the simulated rectangular-shaped air vents.

But Cadillac was merely teasing the on-lookers, setting them up for a look at rear-fender fins it described as "the most rakish ever included in an American production automobile." Most Americans were accustomed to Cadillacs with fins, but the Eldorado combined a curvaceous rear-deck and fender form with slender metal fins whose chrome-coated upper edges made them look like super-sized X-acto knife blades. Protruding from the area directly below the fins were the taillights, slightly recessed within chrome nacelles. Emphasizing the Eldorado's exclusive rear deck design was a three-piece pod encasing the circular backup and directional lights. As the bumper curved into the rear-

1957 Sixty-Two Eldorado Biarritz Convertible.

1957 Series Sixty-Two Sedan.

CADILLAC VITAL STATISTICS: 1957

Series	Model	Body Type	Factory Price ($)	Weight (lbs.)	Production (#)
62	6239	4 dr Hardtop Sedan	4781	4595	32,342
	6237	2 dr Hardtop Coupe	4677	4565	25,120
	6267	Convertible	5293	4730	9000
	6239D	4 dr Sedan de Ville	5256	4655	23,808
	6237D	2 dr Coupe de Ville	5116	4620	23,813
	6237S	Eldorado Seville	7286	4810	2100
	6267S	Eldorado Biarritz	7286	4930	1800
60	6039	4 dr Sedan	5614	4755	24,000
70	7059	Eldorado Brougham	13,074	5315	400
75	7523	4 dr Sedan 9p	7440	5340	1010
	7533	4 dr Imp Sedan 9p	7678	5390	890

1957 Series Sixty-Two Sedan de Ville.

1957 Series Sixty-Two Eldorado Seville.

1957 Series Sixty-Two Coupe.

fender, it linked up with the bright chrome work surrounding the wheel cutout.

The net result was a sleek, impressive machine that was one of the best examples of the short (relatively) hood-long, rear-deck idiom. One casualty of the Eldorado's sleek new look was the hidden under-the-tailfins gas filler. The 1957 Eldorados sported a discreet door opening to the filler tube at the joint between the rear-fender trim and the bumper wraparound.

Included in the Eldorado's base price of $7,196 was a long list of spectacular standard equipment. The Sabre spoke wheels (a $350.000 option for other Cadillacs) were provided in either gold or silver finish and were joined by the six-way power seat, radio-rear speaker-power antenna combination, whitewall tires, remote trunk control, heater and defroster, license-plate frames, and fog lights, as well as the features found on all 1957 Cadillacs. In addition, the anodized gold grille was a no-cost option. Still listed as optional equipment was air conditioning, E-Z Eye glass, and the Autronic-Eye headlight control.

Seville interiors were offers in two metallic leather choices: Sabre blue and Elysian green. Other leather choices consisted of either black or Kiowa red seats and seat backs with white bolsters and trim. Four additional cloth and leather interiors were also available.

Centered in each bolster was a chromed Cadillac medallion. The Seville and Biarritz shared a similar door-panel format of pleated and smooth leather, a wide chrome kickpanel, and a top door surface of Elascofab.

If any of the Seville's metallic nylon upholsteries were selected, that material replaced the leather-pleated door section. The Seville's headliner was of perforated Elascofab with chrome roof bows.

The Biarritz interior choice list included four all-leather alternatives: black, Sabre blue metallic, copper metallic, Elysian green metallic, and Kiowa red. In addition, black or Kiowa red leather seats and seat backs could be combined with white bolsters.

Color choices for the Biarritz's Viodec Convertible top consisted of white, black, Sabre blue, copper, and Elysian green.

The standard Eldorado engine was the 300-horsepower, 365-cubic-inch V-8. It was possible to order as an option a 2, four-barrel version rated at 325 horsepower at 4,800 rpm and 400 ft-lb of torque at 3,300 rpm. Unlike 1956, this engine was not available for other Cadillac models.

Cadillac abandoned the "Imperial" description for its Series Seventy-Five Limousine models in 1957. This made good sense. After all, why give any rival free advertising? Both the Limousine and the Sedan version had nine-passenger ratings, although there was no actual change in interior accommodations from those of the eight-passenger, 1956 models.

The latest Seventy-Fives carried Cadillac's new styling with considerable grace. "Impressively big and beautiful" was Cadillac's summation of their visual impact. Aside from an imposing size, 149.75-inch wheelbase, 236.2-inch overall length, the Series Seventy-Fives featured doors extending into the roof for added ease of entry and exit.

As in 1956, the floor, along with the door scuff-pad, lower seat, and sidewalls, was carpeted in the same material, which for 1957 was a heavily tufted, deep-pile, nylon blend. The rear of the front-seat back and the upper regions of the doors and sidewalls were covered by a teakwood grain Dinoc panel. The front-seat back carried an electric clock, leather-covered robe cord, and two assist handles also leather covered.

The Seventy-Five's interior styling was changed only slightly from 1956, with rectangular biscuits and deeply recessed buttons on the seat and seat backs. A contrasting, smooth-surfaced panel extended across the upper seat-back portion. A Bedford cord could be ordered with harmonizing all-wool bolsters and trim in light gray, beige, dark gray, or brown.

Also available were two all-broadcloth interiors in either light gray or beige. All upholstery selections included leather or leather-grained Elascofab at points likely to receive extra-hard wear.

The Limousine was available in the same colors and fabrics as the Sedan except for the front compartment, which was again trimmed in Black leather stitched in

1957 Series Sixty Special.

2-inch piping. An added feature was a folddown armrest.

CADILLAC'S DOMESTIC COMPETITION

Although it was long overdue, Chrysler Corporation's decision to market the Imperial as a separate marque rather than as a Chrysler Imperial gave its image a much needed boost. This move was not simply an empty gesture because it accompanied the introduction of an Imperial that shared only its 392-cubic-inch, 325-horsepower engine and three-speed TorqueFlite transmission with the Chrysler line.

This Imperial was an automobile to be reckoned with. Its styling, marking, one of the postwar era's peaks, represented the high-water mark of Chrysler designer Virgil Exner's "Flight-Sweep" styling. Never again would there be an Imperial that was as distinctive, as handsome, and original as the 1957 model. Moreover, this was an automobile whose front torsion-bar suspension gave it a degree of roadability unequaled by either Cadillac or Lincoln. Also suggesting that Chrysler had seized the initiative from Cadillac and had become the nation's leader in terms of styling and technical innovation was the Imperial's continued use of push-button transmission controls and optional dual headlights. Chrysler wasn't infallible, of course; and while it deserved credit for equipping the Imperial with variable-speed electric wipers, the use of a push-button, direction-signal system that could not be switched off except by the motion of the steering wheel seemed to defy logic.

The Imperial's wheelbase and overall length were reduced, respectively, to 129 and 224 inches from the 1956 dimensions of 133 and 229 inches. These changes were hardly noticed since the Imperial's height of 56.7 inches (lower than both Cadillac's and Lincoln's) and greater width of 2.5 inches give it the appearance of being longer than before.

Public reaction to the new Imperials was extremely positive. In the first month of 1957 model production, Imperial sales increased 91 percent over the equivalent 1956 level. For the full model year, Imperial output totaled 37,557 cars as compared with the 1956 mark of 10,684.

If there were weak points in the Imperial challenge, they escaped immediate notice. Nonetheless, they were there and would be more apparent in the years to follow. Among them were the Imperial's level of workmanship. It's fair to say that the Imperial escaped the worst of Chrysler's notoriously poor, quality-control illnesses. Yet there were complaints of water leaks, rattles, and poor assembly standards.

Furthermore, the Imperial, while effectively matching Cadillac's spread of Series Sixty-Two and Sixty Special models with its Imperial and Imperial Crown models, fell short of offering a strong challenge to the Series Seventy-Five Cadillacs. Chrysler could not construct a limousine version of the Crown Imperial in the United States without incurring a substantial loss on each model. As a result, it contracted with Ghia of Italy to hand-build limousine models on a limited basis.

These cars had a 149.5-inch wheelbase, overall length of 244.7 inches, and a 58.5-inch height. Coordinating the assembly of these cars and ironing out their electrical system difficulties kept Chrysler busy. The output of Ghia-Crown Imperials was very low, amounting to only 37 cars in 1957. In the meantime, Cadillac turned out 890 Series Seventy-Five Limousines and 1,010 eight-passenger Sedans. Imperial did not offer an eight-passenger Crown-Imperial model.

None of these marketing policies were incapable of remedy. More serious and increasingly apparent would be Chrysler's inability to keep the Imperial's appearance up-to-date. While Cadillac benefited from the economic advantages of sharing its main body structure with Buick, the Imperial stood alone in the Chrysler manufacturing system. Initially this gave it the advantage of distinctiveness, but it also meant Chrysler wouldn't be giving the Imperial a new unit-body every few years. Furthermore, Chrysler wasn't noted for its success in revamping body styles between model changeovers. The result would spell trouble for Imperial in the years to come.

Lincoln, after having been completely redesigned in 1956, offered a 1957 line that was, if not "all new," substantially revised. Lincoln's popularity, therefore, held up quite well with production totaling 41,123 cars. The view that the 1957 model was visually more pleasing than the 1957 version was far from unanimous, however.

The most striking elements of Lincoln's 1957 look were its canted rear-fender fins, which made Cadillac's appear extremely modest by comparison, and the use of "Quadra-lites" consisting of two conventional headlamps and smaller road lights mounted vertically. This setup allowed Lincoln to appear a bit more modern than Cadillac.

Overall, however, the Lincoln's styling was not as coordinated as in 1956. It seemed strained and overdone, changed merely for the sake of change and not to achieve a new styling theme. Lincoln did attempt to break away from Cadillac's lead by abandoning the rear-bumper, exhaust-exit setup in favor of exhausts that were rerouted to a location beneath the rear bumper. Nonetheless, Lincoln still trailed Cadillac in a number of areas. For example, 1957 was the first year Lincoln offered a four-door hardtop Sedan, an automatic headlight dimmer, a radio with two speakers, a remote control and power antenna, and a six-way power seat.

These overdue additions aside, Lincoln had, in less than 10 years, reestablished its presence in the fine-car field. Furthermore, it had made automotive history a year earlier with the Mark II Continental, a car that ushered in an all-too-brief age when Lincoln and Cadillac took their rivalry to a level reminiscent of the classic era of custom bodied V-12 KA and KB Lincolns and V-16 Cadillacs.

SPECIFICATIONS

Engine

Type: V-type, ohv, eight cylinders

Bore × Stroke: 4.0 inches × 3.625 inches
Displacement: 365 cubic inches
Horsepower: 300 @ 4,800 rpm
    Eldorado optional engine: 325 @ 4,800 rpm
Torque: 400 lb-ft @ 2,800 rpm
    Eldorado optional engine: 400 lb-ft @ 3,300 rpm
Compression ratio: 10.0:1
Carburetor: Four-barrel Rochester (2 four-barrels on
    325-horsepower engine)
Electrical system: 12-volt, 170 amp-hr Delco battery
Transmission: Hydra-Matic, four-speed automatic
    with controlled fluid coupling

Chassis/Drivetrain

Frame: X-type, tubular
Rear axle: Hypoid, semifloating
    Standard: 3.07:1 ratio
    Optional: 3.36:1
    Eldorado with 325-horsepower engine:
        3.36:1 standard
    Series 75:   3.77:1 standard
Front suspension: Independent, helical-coil springs
Rear suspension: Five-leaf, semielliptic, 56.5 inches
    × 2.5 inches
    Series 75:   six-leaf units
Steering: Hydraulic power, Saginaw unit, overall
    steering ratio: 19.5:1
Tires:
    Tubeless, 4-ply 8.00 × 15
    Whitewall option and all Eldorados: 8.20 × 15
    Series 75:   8.20 × 15, 6-ply

Dimensions

Wheelbase:
    Series 62, Eldorado Biarritz, and Seville: 129.5
        inches
    Series 60 Special: 133 inches
    Series 75:   149.8 inches
Width: 80 inches

Front/rear tread: 61/61 inches
Overall length:
    Series 62 Sedan and Sedan de Ville: 215.9 inches
    Series 62 Coupe, Coupe de Ville, Convertible:
        220.9 inches
    Eldorado, Biarritz, and Seville: 222.1 inches
    Series 60 Special: 224.4 inches
    Series 75:   236.2 inches

Popular Options

Air conditioning: $474.30
    Series 75: $587.45
Automatic heating system: $128.85
    Series 75: $179.00
    Standard on Eldorado
Radio power antenna, and rear-seat speaker: $164.25
    Standard on Eldorado
Autronic eye: $48.20
Fog lamps: $41.00
    Standard on Eldorado
Sabre-Spoke wheels: $350.00
    Standard on Eldorado
Six-way power seat:
    Series 62: $97.35
    Convertible, De Ville, and Series 75: $80.60
Remote-control trunk-lid lock: $43.00
    Standard on Eldorado
Gold-Finish grille: $26.85
    Standard on Eldorado
E-Z Eye glass: $45.55
License-plate frames: $15.00
    Standard on Eldorado
Two-tone paint: No extra cost
Power windows: $108.15
    Standard on all models except Series 62 hardtops
White sidewall tires: $54.95
    Standard on Eldorado

Brougham

America's Most Advanced, Limited-production Motor Car

MOST CONTEMPORARY REPORTS of the 1953 Motorama show contain flattering descriptions of the Corvette prototype on display. This is as it should be. After all, the Corvette went into production in June 1953 as the "first of the Dream Cars come true" and gradually evolved into one of the world's finest sports cars.

ORLEANS/PARK AVENUE

All but ignored by the automotive journalists of the day was one of the Cadillacs on display: the Cadillac Orleans. The reason for this somewhat neglected status was simple. The bulk of its body design was identical to the 1953 production models; its wraparound windshield was available on the Eldorado Convertible; and in terms of exotic, dream-car dash and class, the Orleans was left at the starting gate by the Le Mans two-seater.

The Orleans' impact on Cadillac history was soon to be apparent and profound. Automotive historians had long debated the issue of who should receive credit for developing the first two-door, hardtop body style; but when it comes to assigning authorship for the first four-door, pillarless Sedan, there's no dispute—it was Cadillac and the car was the Orleans.

The following year, its body style appeared in grand style as the Park Avenue Motorama show car. While easily identifiable as a Cadillac, the Park Avenue's uniquely formed fins, front-grille arrangement, and side trim gave it a look of its own. Whereas the Orleans' roof seemed ungainly high, that of the Park Avenue was an integrated part of its overall form, flowing in a smooth curve from the windshield to the back light. In addition, the Park Avenue's top, like that of the El Camino, was of hand-brushed aluminum.

The Park Avenue was an automobile whose transformation into a production model would be relatively easy, and this is essentially what Harley Earl proposed to Cadillac General Manager Don Ahrens in early 1954. Ahrens, who was striving to make Cadillac the finest car in the world, was aware at this point that

the Ford Motor Company was planning to introduce the Continental Mark II in the fall of 1955.

Ever since the demise of the original Lincoln Continental at the end of the 1948 model year, Ford had been haunted by the spectre of that classic automobile. Enthusiastic owners let it be known that they would forgive Ford for dropping the Continental only after a successor was produced. At the same time, Lincoln dealers maintained that they needed such a car to draw would-be Cadillac owners into their showrooms to become Lincoln owners.

The Ford Motor Company wasn't in a position to deal with these demands until the early fifties when the residue from years of mismanagement had been scraped away and a new generation of corporate talent was firmly in place. In mid-1952, after the potential market for a new Continental had been evaluated, Ford decided to proceed with preliminary cost and price studies. Since Rolls-Royce was then selling fewer than 150 cars a year in the United States, the view at Ford that a revived Continental would probably lose money for the company was correct.

The value of the Continental was not to be measured in terms of the profit-or-loss margin per car, however. If it was perceived as a car clearly superior to Cadillac, Ford would have achieved the nearly impossible. To do this required a car far out of the ordinary. Cadillac had for years been the best-balanced of America's luxury cars. Not always the leader in every category, it had been very good in all of them; and this, plus the benefits of its styling and engine coups, had contributed significantly to its tremendously favorable public image. Any car that was going to eclipse Cadillac had to be demonstrably superior in virtually every area, including styling and engine performance.

On the critical issue of image, Ford was willing to bet that demographics would work in favor of the Mark II Continental, quickly being perceived as the ultimate American automobile. In spite of the low sales level of the Rolls-Royce, it could be argued that there were enough Americans with incomes above $50,000 willing to pay an exclusive price for an exclusive automobile. For years Cadillac had appealed to the man on the way up. Now, the Ford executives hoped there were too many Cadillacs on the road. The Continental would appeal, they reasoned, to the man (or woman) who has already arrived, who would regard its high price as an advantage.

ELDORADO BROUGHAM

Whether it was the uneasiness this news created at Cadillac or the intensity of Earl's call for a premium model Cadillac that gave life to the Eldorado Brougham project remains an undecided issue. Clearly, Cadillac could not allow the high development costs involved to serve as blinders to the challenge posed by the Mark II. It was a threat coming from a company with the wherewithal to make it stick. Regardless of the prime catalyst's origin, the Brougham program moved into hand-built prototype stage during 1954 with the 1955 Motorama show as its target. The Continental Mark II would, it was apparent, easily beat the Brougham to production, and Cadillac would have to make the best out of trailing Lincoln to the marketplace with a new prestige automobile.

The appearance of the first-generation Eldorado Brougham predicted, in many ways, key design features of the 1957 mass-produced Cadillacs. Examples included its elongated front-fender accent line, low rear-fender spear and ribbed rear-fender trim, which was adopted by the 1957 Series Sixty Special. The Brougham's divided rear-bumper arrangement was destined for the 1957 Eldorado Biarritz and Seville. Up front were dual headlights obviously pointing to the future. The Cadillac goddess hood ornament linked the Eldorado Brougham to Cadillacs past and yet to be. Retained from the Park Avenue was the brushed-aluminum roof panel and rear window collar. The Brougham's interior had special lounge seats, a unique instrument panel, and a vanity case. Overall length and height were 216 inches and 54 inches, respectively.

Cadillac described the Chameleon Green Brougham displayed at the 1955 Motorama in glowing terms, noting, "it features low, sweeping lines . . . graceful contours of roof and hood, a unique pillarless door design . . . and great areas of vision." Somewhat awkwardly, at least in view of the impending arrival of the production model Continental Mark II, Cadillac added that "the fabulous Eldorado Brougham offers still further evidence of Cadillac's leadership in automotive styling . . . and promises continued progress in Cadillac's crusade to build greater quality into the American motorcar."

When the Motorama show reached San Francisco, Don Ahrens announced that the Eldorado Brougham would go into production during 1955 and output would be held to 1,000 units per year. The price would be, he added, around $8,500. Obviously not eager to give the Continental Mark II any free publicity, he described the Eldorado Brougham as a car that "will make people forget about the Rolls-Royce."

By September 1955, with the Continental ready for an October 21, 1955, introduction, Cadillac could only report that production planning for the Eldorado Brougham was progressing. Two weeks before its official debut, the Continental made its world premier at the 42nd Paris Show. The best Cadillac could do was display the Eldorado Brougham in production prototype form.

While Ford reaped a publicity bonanza during the rest of 1955, Cadillac was still nearly 18 months away from the start of Eldorado Brougham production. For the 1956 Motorama, the Brougham appeared in production form along with a Dream Car version, the Eldorado Town Car. Finally, on December 4, 1956, Cadillac formally announced the Eldorado Brougham. Beginning on December 8, 1956, it displayed a production model with body number three at the New York Automobile Show.

One of the first tasks awaiting James M. Roche, who moved up from Cadillac's general sales manager to replace Don Ahrens as its general manager effective December 31, 1956, was to promote the Eldorado Brougham. He placed it in the context of Cadillac history as representing "the climax of long years of research and experimentation by our engineers and designers in their continuous search for a better way to build the best automobile . . . and the experiment has been a success . . . We feel that it represents achievement of the goal we set out to attain—and more."

The first Eldorado Broughams were shipped to Cadillac dealers on March 11, 1957, and their price of $13,074 was considerably more than that of the Continental Mark II, which listed for $9,517. Actually the Brougham's price was a bargain, since years later its actual cost of production to Cadillac was estimated to be approximately $23,000. By way of comparison, the contemporary Rolls-Royce Silver Cloud sold for $13,550, f.o.b. principal ports of entry, and it's doubtful Rolls-Royce was selling its cars at a loss.

BROUGHAM'S STYLE

Unlike the Continental Mark II, which was patterned closely along the lines of the original version, and thus bore no resemblance to contemporary Lincolns, the Eldorado Brougham was instantly identified as a modern Cadillac. This close proximity to less expensive and far more common models probably worked to the Brougham's disadvantage since the owner of a $13,000 automobile expected part of the price to provide a degree of visual exclusiveness. The Eldorado Brougham did have its own special look, but it came only from altering existing Cadillac styling themes.

For example, its front end contained the usual combination of gull-winged split bumpers with rubber tips and an egg-crate grille. Mounted directly below the main lights was a circular "sound wave" opening for the Brougham's four-horn system, which consisted of three "sea shell" plus one "trumpet" horn operating simultaneously. Running across the windshield base line was a very pronounced air intake that Cadillac claimed had a greater intake capacity than existing systems. Recessed in the top of each front fender was a two-piece, finely meshed, rectangular grille that served as a vent for the engine compartment. Unlike those on other Cadillacs and most other American cars, the Eldorado Brougham's hood was forward-hinged on a cross-over panel. Even with standard dual lamps, the Brougham's hooded headlights looked familiar, as did the secondary lighting arrangement, which included rectangular fog lamps.

Cadillac was quite proud of this headlight system, which incorporated an Autronic Eye dimming system, calling it "a true four headlamp system pioneered by Cadillac." It was claimed to provide "vastly improved night illumination in both city and country driving as compared with the present two headlamp system." The outer lamps had both high and low beams and were intended for city driving. The low beam had greater wattage than existing systems. The high beam provided a spotlight effect. They were intended for country driving in conjunction with the high beams of the outer lamps. Cadillac claimed the combined wattage of this setup exceeded that of the high beams of two lamp systems and provided the driver with maximum visibility without creating a glare in the eyes of approaching drivers.

The Brougham's fins were virtually identical to those used on the 1956 Motorama Eldorado Town Car and contained delicately curved taillights. The rear bumper was divided into three sections with the innermost position recessed to house the license plate. The two outer pieces served as housing for the dual oval exhaust ports and the circular backup and combination directional/stop lights.

Exterior identification of the Eldorado Brougham was limited to Eldorado lettering above the front hood and rear deck-mounted V and a small front-fender crest reading "Eldorado Brougham by Cadillac." A total of 15 acrylic exterior colors were offered. The standard Brougham wheel consisted of a cast aluminum center with a steel rim with an integral ribbed design. A relatively small hubcap with a Cadillac crest was used.

Cadillac and U.S. Rubber developed a special low-profile, 8.40 × 15 tire, the U.S. Royal 140, for the Brougham. With 4 plies of a high-grade rayon cord, its cross-section was more oval than round. Its 1-inch-wide, white-sidewall size was soon adopted by other manufacturers.

As expected, the Eldorado Brougham had a stainless-steel roof and a four-door hardtop body design. This featured rear-hinged back doors that, along with the front doors, were fitted with rotary locks whose latching plates were mounted on a stand just 14 inches above the floor. This arrangement eliminated the center side pillar found on conventional four-door hardtops.

If the Eldorado Brougham disappointed those who expected a startling new appearance, it pleased individuals who delighted in an automobile reflecting meticulous workmanship, close attention to details, and having virtually every imaginable feature as standard equipment. Cadillac's commitment to the latter point reflected its desire to make the Eldorado Brougham an example of its technical expertise rather than an automobile cast in the shadow of an earlier age.

Thus air conditioning was standard, not optional as was the case with the Continental Mark II, and it was joined by grey-tinted glass in the rear window plus a heating system providing a front compartment unit with two rear, under-seat heaters that could be operated individually by rear-seat passengers. The six-way, power-seat idea was not unique, yet the Continental's was a four-way system. The Brougham's incorporated a "Favorite Position" control in the left front armrest. When a front door was opened the seat moved down and back to provide maximum ease of entrance or exit. When all doors were closed and the driver seated, the seat returned to the position indicated on the three controls. It was also possible to select two separate seat positions by using the red arrows on each dial for one driver and the green arrows for the second. Additional power-operated equipment included the brakes, steering and windows, including the ventpanes.

An alphabetical listing of the Eldorado Brougham's standard equipment fully substantiates Cadillac's claim that it was the "most completely equipped motor car in production today."

Eldorado Brougham Standard Equipment

Air cleaner, dry-pack type
Arm rest, center front
Arm rest, center, rear, custom fitted
Cadillac air conditioner
Cadillac power brakes
Cigarette lighters (two in front and rear)
Clock, electric
E-Z Eye glass
Fog lamps
Front seat adjustment, six-way, electric
Glove compartment, custom fitted
Headlight dimmer, automatic
Heater, front and rear
License frames
Lights, courtesy or map, glove bar, luggage compartment, back-up, directionals, front ashtrays
Oil filter
Outside mirror, left-side, remote-control
Parking brake warning signal
Radio, transistor
Rear-view mirror, three-way, E-Z Eye
Remote-control trunk-lid lock
Special wheels, set of 5, forged aluminum and steel
Visors, dual sun, translucent, tinted plastic
White sidewall tires, high-speed, low-profile, 8:40-8:20 × 15
Window Lifts, electric, including ventpanes
Windshield Washers

The preselector, all-transistor radio had, in addition to the front speaker, a rear unit mounted on the top center of the rear-seat back. When both the radio and ignition switches were turned on, it automatically rose to roof height. For "country reception," an override switch was provided, allowing the antenna to rise to its full height.

Getting underway in an Eldorado Brougham was

accomplished in a subdued but nevertheless spectacular fashion. The driver initiated the process by turning the ignition to the ON position. Then, when the Hydra-Matic gear selector was moved to either Neutral or Park, the engine was started automatically. When the car was placed in any Drive gear, all doors automatically locked to the center pillar. In addition, a switch was incorporated into each rear door that prevented shifting of the transmission into a driving position if either of the rear doors were open. If the unthinkable (a power failure) occurred, the door locks could be operated manually. Also, the inside rear-door handles would be operative.

BROUGHAM'S INTERIOR

The interior appointments of the Eldorado Brougham were, as expected, luxurious. Trim styles and colors included a choice of mouton or high-pile-nylon Karakul carpeting among the 44 standard interiors offered. In addition, two special-order trim styles were offered at extra cost. Cadillac, noting that "the rear seat of the Brougham is designed for maximum comfort for two passengers," promoted the Brougham as a five-passenger automobile. Although it differed in details, the general layout of the Brougham's instrument panel was patterned after that of the standard 1957 Cadillac. The Brougham's was fitted with gauges having 270-degree swept hands for the fuel level, coolant temperature, oil pressure, and ammeter. Providing backup for these were red telltale lights for low oil and air pressure (in the car's suspension system), battery discharge, low fuel level, and high coolant temperature.

In place of the conventional clock, a unit with a rather curious drum face was used. Along with the radio, it was placed in the thin cove extending across the panel from the instrument cluster to the passenger's door. As on other 1957 Cadillacs, this cove had a chrome finish to which was added a delicately curved Eldorado Brougham script. The Brougham's sun visors were polarized plastic, which became darker as they were tilted closer to the windshield.

The control for the power-operated trunk lid was found in the left corner of the glove box. This system was also activated by the insertion of the key in the trunk lock. The inner-door surface served as the receptacle for six metal, magnetized gold-finish drinking cups as well as a cigarette case, tissue dispenser, vanity compact, lipstick, and stick cologne. Two recessed lights provided illumination. A similar arrangement was found in the rear, where a center armrest, mounted over the drive-shaft tunnel, divided the seat into space for two occupants. When opened, it revealed a small storage compartment containing a note pad and pencil, portable vanity mirror, and a perfume atomizer filled with Arpege, Extrait de Lanvin.

BROUGHAM'S ENGINE

The Brougham's engine was the 325-horsepower, twin-four-barrel carburetor, 365-cid V-8 offered as an option for the Eldorado Biarritz and Seville models. Hydra-Matic transmission was standard as was a 3.36:1 rear axle. The Saginaw power-steering system had an overall ratio of 19.5:1 with 4.5 turns lock-to-lock. The turn circle measured 53 feet.

Like that used on other 1957 Cadillacs, the Brougham's frame was produced by the A.O. Smith Company and was of "Tubular Center-X" design. For use on the Eldorado, it provided a 126-inch wheelbase and a 61-inch front and rear tread. The front suspension consisted of the unequal length A-arms, tubular shocks, and spherical joints with built-in anti-drive control, as introduced on other 1957 Cadillacs. At the rear, the Brougham used a high-roll center, four-link suspension with an upper control yoke and two lower trailing, control links.

None of these elements represented a major shift from established design patterns; but by introducing the Eldorado Brougham with a true air-suspension system, Cadillac made automotive history. Unfortunately, this arrangement soon gained a reputation for less than stellar performance; and although air suspension systems were widespread among 1958 cars (General Motors made them available on all 5 of its car lines), they proved to be a short-lived phenomenon among American automobiles.

Components of the Brougham system included an air compressor with an electric motor, an accumulator tank with normal pressure range of 100 to 120 psi, four rubber air domes replacing the springs at each wheel, and a leveling system with one unit up front and two at the rear. In operation, the compressor supplied air to the accumulator tank, with a 500-cubic-inch capacity, which, in turn, was connected to the air domes fitted with a rubber diaphram and a piston.

In operation, the air domes maintained a pressure of approximately 75 psi. As the load grew greater, this pressure was appropriately increased by air from the accumulator trunk, usually without calling the compressor into operation. In addition, the leveling system, which was solenoid controlled, responded quickly to restore the Brougham to an even keel whenever sudden load changes occurred. The load levelers also made any needed correction whenever the ignition was turned on. Yet another attraction was the car's "quick jack-up" feature, which was controlled by a handle under the dash. This enabled the driver to bring the leveling system into operation in a fully pressurized mode, raising the car to its maximum height; useful for travel across steeply pitched roads or rutted surfaces.

From Cadillac's perspective, there were five basic reasons for the use of air suspension on the Eldorado Brougham. The first was its ride characteristics. Compared to steel springs, the air bag's ride rate was 10 percent less, resulting in a more pleasing body motion to passengers. Next was the appeal of a car whose ride characteristics were independent of the passenger load. Regardless of the weight being carried, the ride remained the same. Cadillac also maintained that the air suspension's damping quality was superior to that of an equivalent setup using steel springs and

1957 Eldorado Brougham.

Eldorado Brougham Town Car.

shock absorbers. As far as handling was concerned, Cadillac claimed that the Brougham's was exceptionally good. Finally the air suspension was cited as a contributor to the Brougham's low 55.5-inch height.

On the debit side of this ledger were several major shortcomings. The most serious involved air leaking from fittings and valves. The result would be a Brougham in a "down-at-its-knees" position until the compressor was activated to restore it to normal level. Eventually Cadillac offered a kit to convert the Brougham to standard front-coil springs.

CADILLAC'S DOMESTIC COMPETITION

In contrast to the Brougham's sophisticated suspension and extensive list of standard features, its arch rival, the Continental Mark II, was designed along more conservative lines and, with fewer accessories included in its base price, was, at $9,517, considerably less expensive. The Continental's suspension was obviously less involved than the Brougham's, consisting of front-coil and semielliptic rear springs.

Lincoln subjected to six hours of dynometer testing prior to installation. Thus it developed 285 horsepower at 4,000 rpm and 402 lb-ft at 3,000 rpm. The 1957 models were slightly more powerful: 300 horsepower at 4,800 rpm and 415 lb-ft at 3,000 rpm. In 1958, the Eldorado Brougham adopted a triple Rochester, two-barrel carburetor system that provided 335 horsepower at 4,800 rpm and 405 lb-ft at 3,400 rpm. At the same time, its compression ratio was boosted to 10.25:1.

With a 56.25-inch height, width of 77.50 inches, and overall length of 218.40 inches, the Mark II was dimensionally the Brougham's twin; but its styling philosophy, patterned after the original Lincoln Continental, gave it a totally different appearance.

Although a second version was offered in 1958 and continued in production through 1960, the production of the original Eldorado Brougham ceased in July 1958. By that time, only 704 had been built. Just a year earlier, in August 1957, production of the Continental, which totaled 4,660, had ended.

The Brougham never really had a chance of outselling the Continental. By May 1956, for example, when 3 Broughams were being tested at the GM proving ground in Mesa, Arizona, 928 Continentals had been built, and they were being produced at the rate of 26 per week.

In retrospect, both cars were magnificent examples of two different goals: the production of an ultra-sophisticated engineering tour de force (the Eldorado Brougham) and the resurrection of a classic automobile in modern garb (the Continental). Both cars were built to exacting tolerances and standards that were the equal of any other automobiles then available. Their failure to survive in the marketplace was due more to the trend away from such examples of conspicuous consumption that took hold in 1957-1958 rather than in their concept. They were cars out of step with the times.

SPECIFICATIONS

Engine

Type: Eight cylinders, ohv
Bore x stroke: 4.0 x 3.625 inches
Displacement: 365 cubic inches
Horsepower: 335 @ 4,800 rpm

Torque: 405 lb-ft @ 3,400 rpm
Compression ratio: 10.25:1
Carburetor: 2 four-barrel carburetors
Electrical system: 12-volt, 11-plate, 72-watt battery
Transmission: Hydra-Matic four-speed automatic with controlled fluid coupling

Chassis/Drivetrain

Frame: Tubular-center X-frame
Rear axle: Semifloating 3.36:1 ratio
Front suspension: Unequal A-arm, tubular shock absorbers, self-leveling air bags
Rear suspension: Four-link, upper-control yoke; 2 lower links, tubular shock absorbers, self-leveling air bags
Steering: Hydraulic, Saginaw unit, overall steering ratio 19.5:1
Tires: 8.40 x 15, four-ply

Dimensions

Wheelbase: 126 inches
Width: 78.5 inches
Front/rear tread: 61/61 inches
Overall length: 216.3 inches

1958

Motordom's Masterpiece

SOCIAL CRITICS of the American automobile had a field day in 1958. Not until publication of Ralph Nader's *Unsafe At Any Speed* was there a book critical about Detroit that received the attention of John Keats' *The Insolent Chariots* that was released in 1958.

Apparently Keats wasn't alone in believing that American cars had become too large, too gaudy, and too fuel thirsty since foreign car sales took off at a rapid pace during 1958. The leader was the Volkswagen, which sold nearly 80,000 cars during the year.

Among American manufacturers, the big surprise was American Motors, which, after having been pressed to the brink of disaster, started to show signs of life with its Rambler. For the rest of the industry though, 1958 was a disaster. Total model-year production of the five major American producers; General Motors, Ford, Chrysler, American Motors and Studebaker-Packard, totaled just 4,244,000 cars—a far cry from the 6,115,400 units turned out just a year earlier.

Cadillac wasn't immune from the automotive sales virus as its output fell to 121,778 cars, which represented a drop of 25,063 cars from the 1957 level. However, its competitors fared far worse at the hands of the car-buying public. Lincoln attempted to match Cadillac on a model-for-model basis with an enormous creation whose length of 227 inches stretched beyond the outer limits of all Cadillacs except the Series Seventy-Five by a foot.

Sheer size couldn't carry the day for Lincoln as its production sagged to 29,684. The revitalized Imperial also had a disappointing model run, with its output reaching only 16,102 cars. This represented an abysmal drop for an automobile only in the second year of its styling cycle.

Against this backdrop of an industry reduced to the infamous "You Auto Buy Now" sales campaign in response to a sales famine, the 1958 Cadillacs stand out as examples of Cadillac's ability to withstand turbulence in the marketplace with a minimum amount of storm damage. This tremendous asset would ironically not be perceived by writers in the future. Nearly 30 years later, automotive journalists would be eagerly writing about Cadillac's demise, while ignoring both the strong sales of its current models and passing by on one of the most important stories of the 1980s—Cadillac's realignment of its market posture to embrace a new group of buyers while not alienating its traditional customers.

Similarly, the 1958 models, when new, did not receive the degree of attention that their styling and engineering features warranted. Apparently it was difficult to work hard at Detroit bashing and maintain an unjaundiced view of your victims at the same time.

Regardless of how anyone felt about the American automobile of the late fifties, the concession had to be made that it was an era when styling distinctions between marques was at, or near, an all-time peak. Thirty years later, it took the impact of a major reorganization of General Motors for its top executives to relearn just how important that was to sales success. Just as in 1948 and 1958, owners of expensive automobiles weren't keen about their cars being nondescript variations of a styling theme, virtually identical to that of a far lower-priced car.

There was just a bit of uneasiness created when the appearance of a 1958 Chevrolet was compared with that of a 1958 Cadillac; but overall, there was little danger that an Impala would be confused for a Sixty Special.

CHANGES AND IMPROVEMENTS

Ever since 1941, Cadillac had used one variation after another of an egg-crate form for its front grille. For 1958, something new was added to the expected. At each intersection of the six horizontal and 27 vertical fins were found what Cadillac, rather unfortunately, called "bright, concave, bullet-like projectiles." Within Cadillac, these were less eloquently, but certainly less ominously, referred to as "clothes pins." In any case, they made a major contribution to a front-end bearing little resemblance to that of the 1957 model.

Unknown to most automobile enthusiasts was the technological story behind these "clothes pins." Cadillac had for years maintained a keen interest in applying new engineering or manufacturing concepts to the design of its cars. In turn, this open-mindedness encouraged its suppliers to offer Cadillac a steady flow of fresh ideas. One of these, the Doehler-Jarvis Division of the National Lead Company, acting on the foundation of work done in Germany, developed an expertise enabling them to be pioneers at producing extruded, tapered cylindrical parts in the United States.

This achievement came to the attention of Clarence Morphew, who, in 1956, was assigned to Cadillac's body engineering group. Taking advantage of an opportunity to combine a new manufacturing technique with the need for a fresh approach to grille design, Morphew began the process which led to the 1958 Cadillac grille midway through the 1956 model year.

In its manufacturing process, Doehler-Jarvis used two 120-ton, impact extrusion presses to turn out 3,000 grille pieces per hour. After buffing, they were shipped to Cadillac, which used between 50,000 and 60,000 each day. Cadillac assumed responsibility for anodizing them either gold or silver to suit customer preference.

While this procedure was being sorted out, Cadillac committed itself to a far more ambitious expansion plan. Ever since postwar production had begun, it had been apparent that it was only a matter of time before additional space would be needed. Cadillac production engineers were the equal of any in the world but the task of producing nearly 150,000 cars in the same area where once 50,000 had been built was stretching things just a bit!

Cadillac resisted the temptation to commit a very large sum of money to the construction of an entirely new complex in favor of searching out existing facilities that, when refurbished, would provide the same amount of manufacturing space at a considerably lower cost.

While Cadillac was in the market for a good used building, it just so happened that American Motors was eager to sell some old property where Hudson cars had once been built. Eventually, the site of Hudson's main plant on Detroit's east side was sold to a group of businessmen who converted it into a parking lot. As an artifact of the automotive industry, Hudson's body plant located near Gratiot Street and Conner Avenue, had a happier fate, since it was purchased and renovated by Cadillac.

When Cadillac acquired this property, it was both obsolete and rundown, but its 1 million square feet of manufacturing space was what Cadillac needed. Turning it into a modern facility was well within Cadillac's capability.

The total cost of this operation was only one third the expense of building a new facility. The "new" addition to Cadillac's operation, known as Plant Four, served as the location for its press shop, screw machine shop, and rear-axle fabrication operation, and was ready for the 1958 model year.

This was accomplished without any shutdown or loss of production time which was no mean feat. In terms of sheer size, this was an undertaking of major

proportions, which, at the time, was regarded as the most complex industrial switchover in history. Approximately 350 machines with an aggregate weight of 70,000 tons were relocated.

Cadillac took this opportunity to update its press operations; and as a result, 64 new presses plus 16 new pieces of equipment capable of multiple functions joined the 145 presses that were moved to the new site. Among the components produced in Plant Four were front fenders, hoods and hood inner panels, bumper sections, various stainless-steel and aluminum trim items and a number of small stamped parts.

The new presses represented a significant advance in automation. For example, presses for the hood now included automatic feeding of the press and the movement of parts to the next production station. Also increased was the number of machines capable of doing a variety of tasks simply by changing the dies.

The space vacated by these operations in Cadillac's main plant did not remain vacant for long as it was quickly filled by an advanced transfer machine line for the manufacture of cylinder heads and blocks. Here too, the emphasis was on a heightened level of quality, enhanced productivity, and increased multifunction capability of machinery.

Yet another unheralded, but prime example of Cadillac's continuous policy of product improvement was the adoption of a new process of chrome plating for the 1958 models. Actually, this had been applied on a limited basis during the 1957 model run. Credit for this development went to the Metal & Thermit Corporation, which in 1953 developed the means by which the chrome plating applied to a component made from nickel possessed a much greater resistance to corrosion than did those plated by current means.

The source of this problem had long been known. Tiny cracks, apparently inherent in plating, enabled corrosion to attack the base metal. Some of the sources of corrosion were road salt and acid rain. Unfortunately the use of thicker chrome plating failed to remedy the situation since the minute cracks would remain.

Initially, the new plating process was limited to either a matte or satin finish; but within a short time, success was achieved in developing a bright chrome finish with the same crack-free properties. Cadillac's Polishing and Plating Division then devised an accelerated acetic-acid, salt-spray test in which the vastly superior resistance to corrosion of the new material was apparent.

Aside from this obvious advantage, adoption of the new plating process, although slightly more expensive than the system it replaced, provided Cadillac with several additional advantages. These included a higher acceptance rate of finished items and the discovery that the plating could be applied to other surfaces besides nickel. Among these were stainless steel. Superior plating of recessed areas was also achieved.

Highlighting the list of technical developments keyed to the public's perception of engineering prowess was the extension of the Eldorado Brougham's air suspension system as an extra cost option for all other Cadillacs. All cars regardless of their suspension system moved down the same assembly line. Cadillac maintained close control of the quality of the air suspension throughout its manufacturing process. Before the air cushions were accepted for assembly, they were carefully checked in an accelerated test at a pressure of 150 psi even though ordinary operating pressure was only 125 psi. The acceptable pressure loss rate was one psi in a 24-hour period.

Accompanying the availability of the air suspension was a new rear suspension that used coil springs and four links arranged in essentially the same format as on the Eldorado Brougham. The result was a roll center approximately 5.88 inches higher than in 1957. This resulted in both improved cornering and stability.

Displacement of the Cadillac engine was unchanged at 365 cubic inches. There were a number of changes that contributed to improved fuel economy and higher power outputs, which now stood at 310 horsepower at 4,800 rpm and 405 ft-lb of torque at 3,100 rpm. Heading this list were revised valves. The intake valve's head size was unchanged at 1.875 inches, though its length was increased to 4.794 from 4.675 inches. The exhaust valves now had a head diameter of 1.50 inches, up from 1.437 inches. Its length was increased from 4.692 to 4.815 inches. A higher (10.25:1) compression ratio was achieved by use of a new combustion chamber that utilized a recessed contour in the piston head to increase gas turbulence. Also used was a recontoured camshaft.

The standard Eldorado engine, which was available optionally on all other models, used a triple, two-barrel carburetor setup to push horsepower up to 335 at 4,800 rpm. Its torque rating was the same as the standard engine, but it was produced at 3,400 rpm.

The appearance of the Cadillac that carried these technical refinements was substantially changed from that of the 1957 models. Cadillac told its sales staff that "seldom is the introduction of any motor car greeted with such enthusiastic welcome as that habitually accorded the introduction of a new Cadillac." Perhaps that welcome was a bit muted in 1958, but the car that Cadillac was offering was distinctively a Cadillac, with a look that made the sales personnel's task a relatively easy one in a difficult sales year.

Aside from the new grille form, the Cadillac's front end was dominated by its standard dual headlights from whose heavily chromed shells emanated the front-fender chrome spear. Mounted just above the wraparound front bumper was a chrome-simulated air intake. Not content to provide the 1958 model with just a new grille insert, Cadillac also altered the grille's shape as well. The twin bumper guards lost their gull-wing shape and no longer extended to the upper level of the grille. Instead they were set lower and further apart. The twin parking/directional lamps were replaced with single units nestled directly below the bumper guards.

On all but the Eldorados, the rear-fender fin shape was essentially that of the 1957. Outlining the fin profile was a chrome molding. Both the Series Sixty-Two and Seventy-Five carried gold block "CADILLAC" letters near the uppermost portion of the fin. For the Series Sixty Special gold script reading "Sixty Special" was installed in the same location.

DIFFERENCES AMONG MODELS

These permutations were just the first of many exterior trim differences among the Cadillac series for 1958. All Series Sixty-Two models had twin-blade hood ornaments and very thin, bright trim strips extending back along the front-fender crown line. This trim scheme was also used for the Series Seventy-Five. The Series Sixty Special did not have any hood ornamentation, but its fender molding began with a high fin and terminated with chromed engine-ventilator grilles similar to those used on the 1957 Eldorado Brougham. A stylized Cadillac crest with block letters reading "Cadillac" was positioned at the rear of the front fender just below the side chrome spear on the Series Sixty-Two Sedans, Coupe and Convertible. Except for reading either "Sedan de Ville" or "Coupe de Ville," the same badge was used for those Series Sixty-Two models. While the Sixty Special did not have this feature, the Series Seventy-Five models carried one reading "Fleetwood."

But this product differentiation still didn't satisfy the Cadillac designers who gave the Series Sixty Special one of the most distinctive and controversial rear-fender trim panels ever to appear on an American car. To fully appreciate the audacity of their efforts, consider first that used on the Series Sixty-Two and Seventy-Five models. It combined a thin chrome line, accentuating the side crease extending forward from the taillight unit and terminating just before the rear edge of the front door. Mounted just ahead of the rear-fender cutout were five chrome, "simulated stone guards," which to long-time Cadillac watchers seemed to be remnants of the bold "airscoop stone guard" of earlier days.

There was none of this sort of sentimentality for the Sixty Special. A broad rocker-panel trim piece, extending into the lower door region, lead the eye of the beholder to a magnificent expanse of grooved anodized aluminum with a border of stainless steel, ranging from the final quarter of the rear door to the rear bumper. Added drama was achieved by incorporating the rear fender skirt into this pattern.

Viewed from the rear, Series Sixty-Two Cadillacs were identified by their trunk-lid-mounted crest and concave bumper with simulated exhaust outlets at its extremities. This latter feature was found on all 1958 Cadillacs. The Cadillac V-8 still had dual exhausts, but they exited demurely below the bumper.

The same view of the Sixty Special was, to say the least, distinctive. The bumper carried four vertical ribs on either side of the license-plate insert. Extending across the trunk lid was a textured molding containing rectangular backup lights above which were positioned bold block letters reading "Fleetwood." Unlike the Series Sixty-Two and Seventy-Five models, the Sixty Special had two, rather than one circular taillights.

Cadillac added an extended deck model to the Series Sixty-Two line for 1958. Compared with the standard Sedan, its length was 225.3 inches instead of 216.8 inches. Alert Cadillac shoppers recognized this car for what it was, the Sedan de Ville with the less elaborate interior appointments of the Sedan and Coupe.

1958 Series Sixty-Two Eldorado Seville.

1958 Series Sixty-Two Sedan de Ville.

1958 Series Sixty-Two Coupe de Ville.

1958 Series Sixty-Two Convertible.

1958 Series Sixty-Two Extended Deck Sedan.

1958 Eldorado Brougham.

All three models were available in seven two-tone interiors, of which three were nylon Morrocan cloth with turquoise, bronze, or white thread against a black background.

The interior of the Series Sixty-Two Convertible, which was offered in four solid and four two-tone leather combinations was now highlighted by a broad bolster whose bottom edge formed a wide-angled V. The seat backs and cushions were covered with large rectangular biscuits with recessed buttons. If the optional radio was fitted, its speaker was installed inside a recessed area at the top of the rear seat. The Convertible top was available in white, black, blue, tan, or green.

De Ville interior selections consisted of nine combinations of patterned nylon with leather. The seats had a slim V-crest in their center, which was accentuated by the bolster's V-line. The fabric seating areas were separated by a leather divider.

Interiors of the Series Sixty were available in either all cloth or cloth-and-leather combinations. If one of the latter were chosen, the seat cushions and seat backs were crafted in 2-inch-wide piping, while the bolsters were finished in smooth leather. The all-cloth alternatives had rectangular biscuits with deeply recessed buttons.

The interiors of the Series Seventy-Five models were, said Cadillac, "immaculately tailored in classic simplicity." With the Limousine's front compartment finished in black leather, the interior of the Sedan and the rear compartment of the Limousine were offered in wool cord and broadcloth combinations of gray, beige, and brown tones.

"Eldorado Biarritz interiors," said Cadillac, were "truly in a class by themselves." Finished in imported, deep-grained leather, their color choices included copper, silver, green metallic, white and black, vermilion and white, vermilion, or black.

The interiors for the Eldorado Seville were equally exciting, combining a crest cloth with leather in eight color variations.

CADILLAC'S DOMESTIC COMPETITION

The most startling aspect of the new Lincolns was their appearance. At the front were canted, dual headlights and a simple mesh-grille design. The Lincoln's profile was relatively free of chrome trim. The Premiere and Capri models had a simple chrome spear, while the Continental carried only a rocker-panel strip and model identification. All versions relied on their extensive amount of body creases and contours for visual impact.

The rear view was somewhat cluttered with a form of the car's fender fins conflicting with the circular shape of the deck insert.

With the Continental Mark II not available, Lincoln moved to compete with Cadillac on a much broader base. Thus there were 10 models available, including four Lincoln Continental Mark III models. These were set off from the less expensive Capri and Premiere versions by their reverse-slant rear windows and six taillights.

Powering the 1958 Lincolns was a new 430-cubic-inch V-8 with 375 horsepower.

The Imperial, in contrast with both Lincoln and Cadillac, was left almost unchanged for 1958. Principal changes included a finer grille meshwork; round, instead of square, parking lights; introduction of an automatic speed control, and an electromechanical door-locking system. Both of these were firsts among American cars.

There was a Packard for 1958, but like the 1957 Clipper, it was based on a Studebaker body. It was in no way a car comparable to previous Packards nor to the contemporary Cadillac, Lincoln, and Imperial.

The 1959 model year promised to be an interesting one. Lincoln, frustrated by the failure of its massive 1958 models to make even modest inroads into Cadillac's lead, would attempt to make them more attractive to the public.

Imperial, although little changed, would be

CADILLAC VITAL STATISTICS: 1958

Series	Model	Body Type	Factory Price ($)	Weight (lbs.)	Production (#)
62	6239	4 dr Hardtop Sedan	4891	4675	13,335
	6239E	4 dr Extended Deck	5079	4770	20,952
	6237	2 dr Hardtop Coupe	4784	4630	18,736
	6267	Convertible	5454	4845	7825
	6239D	4 dr Sedan de Ville	5497	4855	23,989
	6237D	2 dr Coupe de Ville	5251	4705	18,414
	6237S	Eldorado Seville	7500	4910	855
	6267S	Eldorado Biarritz	7500	5070	815
60	6039	4 dr Hardtop Sedan	6232	4930	12,900
70	7059	Eldorado Brougham	13,074	5315	304
75	7523	4 dr Sedan 9p	8460	5360	802
	7533	4 dr Limousine 9p	8675	5425	730

somewhat more popular than in 1958. But neither of these developments could compare in sheer sensationalism to the 1959 Cadillacs. Whatever would be later said about their appearance, in 1959, while Lincoln sales declined, those of Cadillac rose by over 17%.

SPECIFICATIONS

Engine

Type: V-type, ohv, 8 cylinders
Bore × stroke: 4.0 × 3.625 inches
Displacement: 365 cubic inches
Horsepower: 310 @ 4,880 rpm
    Eldorado: 335 @ 4,800 rpm
Torque: 405 lb-ft @ 3,100 rpm
    Eldorado: 405 lb-ft @ 3,400 rpm
Compression ratio: 10.25:1
Fuel system: Carter four-barrel carburetor
    Eldorado: triple, two-barrel carburetors
Electrical system: 12-volt
Transmission: Hydra-Matic with two drive ranges, low range, and reverse. Controlled fluid coupling on forward gear set

Chassis/Drivetrain

Frame: Tubular-center X-type with U-shaped rear section
Rear axle: Hypoid, semifloating, offset differential
Standard ratio: 3.07:1
    Eldorado, Eldorado-engined models, Series 75: 3.36:1 (3.77:1 optional for Series 75)
Front suspension: Spherical joint, independent with helical-coil springs
Rear suspension: Four-link drive, helical-coil springs
Steering: Power-assisted, overall ratio: 19.5:1
Brakes: Power-assisted, effective brake-lining area: 210.32 square inches
    Series 75: 233.72 square inches

Tires:
    Low-pressure, four-ply, 8.00 × 15
    Series 75: six-ply, 8.20 × 15

Dimensions

Wheelbase:
    Series 62: 129.5 inches
    Series 60: 133 inches
    Series 75: 149.75 inches
Front/rear tread: 61/61 inches
Overall length:
    Series 60: 225.3 inches
    Coupe de Ville, Series 62 Coupe, Convertible: 221.8 inches
    Series 62 Sedan: 216.8 inches
    Sedan de Ville, Series 62 Extended Deck: 225.3 inches
    Eldorado Seville, Biarritz: 223.4 inches
    Series 75: 237.1 inches
Eldorado Brougham specifications unchanged from 1957 except for use of the triple, two-barrel carburetor system

Popular Options

Eldorado engine
Air suspension: Standard on Eldorado Brougham
Heating and ventilating system
E-Z Eye glass
Preselector radio
Power windows and seats: power windows and fore-and-aft power front seat standard on Series 62 Convertible, Coupe de Ville, Sedan de Ville, 60 Special, Series 75
Six-Way power front seat: Standard on Eldorado Brougham, Biarritz, Seville
    optional for 62 Sedans and Coupe
Power front vent windows: standard on Eldorados and 60 Special
Air conditioning
Autronic eye
Fog lamps

1959

The World's Most Eloquent Possession

CADILLAC EMERGED from the rocky 1958 model year relatively unscathed. Its sales were down by 6% from 1957, but its market penetration was greater than at any other point in its history—not a bad place to be with a sensationally styled new car to be measured against warmed-over offerings from Imperial and Lincoln.

General Motors had been caught off guard in 1957 when Chrysler, taking a corporate-wide deep breath, gambled on its multihundred-million-dollar "Forward Look." But, as we've seen, neither the 1957 Imperial nor, for that matter, the enormous 1958 Lincoln were able to do much more than ripple the surface of the luxury-car market. Nonetheless, General Motors wasn't inclined to encounter any repetitions of Chrysler's audacious behavior with cars cast in a conservative mold.

The 1959 GM cars, if not exactly the product of a knee-reflect action were certainly a reaction to Chrysler's boldness. If the customer wanted a car with fins, then General Motors would provide them in abundance. Moreover, they would take forms and shapes unequaled by Chrysler.

This is confirmed by a brief look at the GM lineup. Chevrolet had its "gull-wing" rear deck, Pontiac split its rear-fender line into twin "V's," with Oldsmobile adopting a front-to-rear fender line, climaxing in high-flying oval light pods crowned by chrome spears. Buick, which had been battered badly in both 1957 and 1958, launched its new cars with canted fins arrogantly stretching the full length of the car.

For Cadillac was reserved the honor of taking GM's styling counterattack to literally its highest level. To some, the rear-fender fins of the 1959 Cadillac remain today, as they did back then, a ludicrous expression of excess, ostentation, and plain bad taste. To others, time has mellowed their criticism somewhat, and they regard them as manifesting contemporary American tastes; graphic expressions of a society still reacting to the deprivations of World War II by a headlong plunge into material excess. A third point of view is less introspective: the fins looked good back then and they remain attractive today.

Since over 142,000 new Cadillacs were sold in 1959, it's apparent that Cadillac's flamboyant appearance captured the imagination of a good many Americans who regarded those soaring fins as badges of honor signifying their arrival (or continued presence) in the world of the rich and well-heeled.

Of course, it wasn't just the size and stature of Cadillac's tailfins that made automotive news in 1959. The entire GM line was given body shells linking them together via a familial similarity that had never before been so apparent. This could only be taken so far; after all, each division had its own clientele to consider, and the folks at Cadillac (or for that matter, Pontiac, Oldsmobile, or Buick) weren't particularly eager to have their cars mistaken for a Chevrolet Bel Air.

As a result, while all the GM cars looked, and were, huge, they were able to both maintain distinctive exterior appearances and save GM a bundle of money by sharing many internal body components.

CHANGES AND IMPROVEMENTS

In the midst of the mass of styling cliches that resulted, Cadillac rear-fender fins were the most memorable. If nothing else, their sheer size overwhelmed all others offered by Detroit that year. Their uppermost height of 38 inches was up 3.75 inches from the level of the 1958 Cadillac's, which made them barely 16 inches below the roofline of the lowest 1959 Cadillac. Exceeding the height of the 1959 Chrysler New Yorker's by 2.5 inches, they were magnificent symbols of Cadillac's position relative to its competition. Cadillac described them as "gracefully tapered; chrome-edged . . . with twin, nacelle-like contours containing the projectile-shaped red lenses of the tail stop and turn signal lamps."

They were also, although the public wasn't then aware, Cadillac's ultimate expression of what was then an 11-year styling idea. Never again would Cadillac tailfins soar so high. There were, after all, limits that even Cadillac had to accept. Beginning in 1960, they would begin to recede; and just four years later, they would make their last appearance on a Cadillac.

Already, with the 1959 models, Cadillac swept past convention out of its path by eliminating its bullet-type front bumpers. In their place, Cadillac used massive, twin-nacelle pods for the parking and directional lights that, in conjunction with the standard dual headlights, gave the Cadillac an eight-lamp lighting system up front.

The grille insert was similar to that used in 1958 with rows of square metal studs interrupted by a single horizontal bar. No hood ornament was fitted, which emphasized the broad expanse of the Cadillac hood. This was no mere illusion since the Cadillac's overall body width was 81.1 inches. Still in use was Cadillac hood-mounted "V" and crest identification, which was restyled and slimmed down for 1959.

Cadillac had long since abandoned headlight eyebrows, but the extension forward of the front fender crowns and leading hood surface served to make the Cadillac's appearance on the highway even more imposing. Equally dramatic was the view of a 1959 Cadillac as it cruised out of sight down the interstate. The chromed, shielded, and taillight-bedecked fins were joined by a massive extravaganza of chrome that only the most modest of observers could describe as a bumper. In reality, it might have served that purpose; but as a manifestation of Cadillac's role as an American status symbol, it was surely more successful. Extending backward from the outer surfaces were two high, chrome-coated pods from which it seemed a blast of flaming jet exhaust was imminent. But they served no such awesome purpose; instead, only a pair of benevolent, backup lights resided therein.

This arrangement made no provision for the twin exhaust outlets that had been integrated into Cadillac's rear bumper layout since 1952. Dual exhausts were still standard, but they now exited discreetly beneath the rear bumper.

Impacting only slightly less upon America's ocular senses than Cadillac's rear-fender profile was the expanse of glass found on its 1959 hardtop models. Up front a new compound, curved windshield took the panoramic design to its next logical stage of progression: a wrap up and over into the roof line. This "Vista-Panoramic" windshield measured 1,740.1 square inches on the six-window sedans and 1,711.8 square inches on the Coupe and four-window Sedans. Two-door hardtops used a back light whose width of 25.75 inches totally overwhelmed the 18-inch-wide window of 1958.

Two completely different roof lines were used for the four-door hardtop Cadillacs. The six-window model, with a small, stationary, triangular-shaped rear window, was offered in the Series Sixty-Two, De Ville, and Series Sixty Special Fleetwood lines. It used a conventional rear-window form that followed the roof-line curve and, with very-thin rear pillars, made wrap-

around vision a reality rather than a figment of an ad copy writer's imagination.

The four-window version used a nearly flat roof line in union with a back light that was both more vertical and more expansive in its wraparound form than that of the six-window version. This body style, offered in both Series Sixty-Two and Sedan de Ville form, proved less popular with customers than the six-window version, as the following indicates:

Production - 1959

Series 62 six-window	23,461
Series 62 four-window	14,138
Sedan de Ville six-window	19,158
Sedan de Ville four-window	12,308

Far less controversial than any aspect of the 1959 Cadillac's exterior form was its newly styled instrument cluster. *Motor Life* magazine regarded it as the most legible to be found on any 1959 GM car.

All Cadillacs with the exception of the Series Seventy-Five models used the same 130-inch wheelbase and had an identical overall length of 225 inches. This slight increase in wheelbase (up 0.5 inches) for the Series Sixty-Two and modest shrinkage (down by 3 inches) in the Series Sixty Fleetwoods had mixed effects on interior dimensions. Although seat-cushion heights were dropped as much as three inches on some models (the front seat on the Sixty Special was just 9.5 inches above the floor), front headroom was marginally reduced. For example, that of the Series Sixty-Two Sedan went from 35 to 34.8 inches. A more significant loss was experienced by rear-seat occupants of a Series Sixty-Two whose headroom dropped to 33.2 from 34.9 inches. Front and rear leg room was essentially unchanged.

Cadillac's suspension, like that of the 1958 model, was designed to allow installation of the optional air system in place of the conventional coil-spring system on the assembly line with a minimum amount of difficulty. Changes in the air system consisted of a redesigned accumulator tank identified by its short, squat shape and vertically mounted position. The previous model had been long and narrow with a horizontal mount. Minor valving changes also took place.

Cadillac was striving hard to remove any remaining traces of roughness in its ride, and this effort lead to the use of the inert gas Freon 12 in its shock absorbers. In conventional shocks the mixing of air and oil eventually adversely affected the shock's performance. This was eliminated on the 1959 Cadillac by surrounding the oil chamber with Freon 12 in a plastic envelope. The result was a more road-worthy, more stable, and better handling automobile.

Accompanying these changes was an improved Saginaw power-steering unit with a larger rotary valve whose faster steering ratio (18.9:1 instead of 19.5:1) was negated by a larger turning radius on most models of 27 feet, 7 inches, up nearly 3.5 feet from 1958. Overall,

Cadillac's power steering received good grades. One magazine, *Car Life*, ranked it number one of all systems available on American cars.

Additional detail changes to Cadillac's running gear included the elimination of a rear pump from Hydra-Matic (it had previously been included only for use in push-starts) and the use of a standard 2.94:1 rear axle in place of the 3.09:1 ratio of 1959. The exceptions were cars with air conditioning and/or the Eldorado Q-engine. These Cadillacs were fitted with a 2.21:1 rear axle and an automatic-choke control moved to the exhaust area of the intake manifold for quicker action. For the first time, an automatic temperature compensator was built into the choke system for smoother idling.

The use of a new crankshaft lengthened the Cadillac V-8's stroke an additional quarter-inch to 3.875 inches, which, with an unchanged 4-inch bore, boosted displacement to 390 cubic inches. Along with a higher (10.5:1) compression ratio, redesigned intake manifold with larger passages, and reshaped exhaust valves that improved gas flow, these changes pushed horsepower up to 325 at 4,800 rpm. Torque was now 410 lb-ft at 3,100 rpm.

DIFFERENCES AMONG MODELS

Both Eldorado models lost their distinctive appearances in 1959, since, for the first time since 1954, they shared the same body form as the standard Cadillac models. It was still fairly easy, however, to pick out a Biarritz or Seville from the rest of the Cadillac line. Both models carried chrome block lettering along the lower portion of the front fender, a three-level rear-deck grille insert and their own brand of side trim. Their form was voluptuous, to say the least, sweeping downward from the windshield corner post to embrace the rear-bumper nacelles before swinging back to the front fender cut out along the rocker panel.

Eldorados were also identified by their special triple-decker, rear-cove grille and "V" inserts for the backup lights. Unique wheel covers had always been part of the Eldorado package and 1959 was no exception. Though not everyone believed abandoning the Sabre-Spoke design of previous years was a good idea, the new form, which included 12 vanes surrounding a dished center portion with Cadillac crest, was not unattractive.

Both models were identically priced at $7,401, which represented a $99 price reduction from 1958. This assumed more significance in light of Eldorado's greatly expanded list of standard equipment features. The Eldorado's price included power brakes, steering, and Hydra-Matic, dual backup lights, windshield washers, two-speed electric wipers, outside rear-view mirror, E-Z Eye rear-view mirror, interior vanity mirror, two-way power seat, and heater. To these items were added fog lamps, remote control for the rear deck, radio with antenna and rear speaker, front power vent windows, six-way power seat, electric door lock, license frames, electric clock, four cigarette lighters (two-front, two-rear), white sidewall tires, and air suspension. The only items not standard on the Eldorados were air conditioning, cruise control, automatic headlight dimmer, and shaded and/or tinted glass. Reserved exclusively for the Eldorado Biarritz as a no-cost option were individual bucket seats. Only 99 Eldorados left the factory with this feature.

Both models used an upholstery design with horizontal pleating in an alternating long-short pattern with buttons at each intersection. Surrounding these inserts on all sides were wide bolsters. Common to the Seville and Biarritz were all-leather interiors in white or blue. Sevilles were also available in cloth/leather combinations in any of six colors: gray, blue, slate, green, bronze, and red. Reserved for the Biarritz were six additional all-leather interiors of black, gray, slate, green, bronze, or red.

The Series Sixty-Two line consisted of four- and six-window Sedans, Coupe, Convertible, Coupe de Ville, as well as four- and six-window Sedan de Ville sedans. Interiors of the four- and six-window Sedans were identical, with patterned 1.25-inch piping for the seat cushions and seat backs bracketed by smooth-surfaced Elascofab bolsters. Seven 2-tone combinations were offered. A deep, loop-pile carpeting was used.

The Series Sixty-Two Coupe was available in the same interior color combinations and seat design with the exception of the rear-seat back, which had a recessed section embossed with a Cadillac crest and crown.

Eight all-leather interiors were offered for the Series Sixty-Two Convertible. Its seats and seat back featured 2.5-inch wide piping with a single row of recessed buttons in each seat section. The upholstery selections offered were black, blue, saddle tan, turquoise, green, and red. White bolsters and trim were available with red and black seats and seat backs. The Convertible top was available in ivory, black, green, buckskin, or blue.

De Ville interiors were highlighted by two new upholsteries, a metallic nylon Coronado cloth with Lurex threads set in a ribbed pattern and a block-patterned Camdem cloth that had a softer finish. Front and rear seats were fitted with a 10-inch-wide recessable center armrest. All interior selections combined leather bolsters and trim with seat cushions and seat backs furnished in 2.5-inch-wide piping. A single row of recessed buttons extended across the cushions and backs. Seven 2-tone choices similar but not identical, to these for the standard Series Sixty-Two were offered. A Trieste, loop-pile, nylon-blend carpet was used for the floor, lower-cowl side walls, door panels, and seat cushions.

Aside from their interiors, De Ville models varied in external trim from the standard Series Sixty-Two models. They lacked the styled Cadillac crest found on the low front fender of these cars and carried model identification script on their rear fenders.

1959 Eldorado Biarritz Convertible.

1959 Sedan de Ville.

CADILLAC VITAL STATISTICS: 1959

Series	Model	Body Type	Factory Price ($)	Weight (lbs.)	Production (#)
62	6239	4 dr Hardtop Sedan 4W	5080	4770	14,138
	6229	4 dr Hardtop Sedan 6W	5080	4835	23,461
	6237	2 dr Hardtop Coupe	4892	4690	21,947
	6267	Convertible	5455	4855	11,130
63	6339	4 dr Sedan de Ville 4W	5498	4825	12,308
	6329	4 dr Sedan de Ville 6W	5498	4850	19,158
	6337	2 dr Coupe de Ville	5252	4720	21,924
60	6029	4 dr Sedan	6233	4890	12,250
64	6437	Eldorado Seville	7401	4855	975
	6467	Eldorado Biarritz	7401	5060	1320
69	6929	Eldorado Brougham	13,075	4890	99
75	6723	4 dr Sedan 9p	9533	5490	710
	6733	4 dr Limousine 9p	9748	5570	690

1959 Coupe de Ville.

1959 Series Sixty Special.

1959 Series Seventy-Five Limousine.

1959 Eldorado Brougham.

BROUGHAM

Cadillac introduced the 1959 Eldorado Brougham at the January 1959 Chicago Automobile show. By this time, its existence was, in a sense, no longer required since its arch rival, the Continental Mark II, was no longer in production. But if the Brougham's demise followed too closely after the Continental's, it might appear as if Cadillac lacked a mind of its own.

The manufacturer's suggested retail price for the Eldorado Brougham remained unchanged at $13,075. At the same time, Cadillac moved to reduce the Brougham's manufacturing costs by adopting numerous mechanical and body components from the mass-production models. As a result, the following items were interchangeable between the Eldorado Broughams and the standard Cadillac models: floor pan, inner lower-body panels, door pillars and hinges, front bumpers, front wheel-lip moldings, rear-fender skirts, headlight bezels, seat frames, instrument panel, dashboard, and grille insert. Adopted with slight modifications were the inner door panels and rear bumper. Nonetheless, none of the Brougham's outer sheet metal interchanged with that of the standard Cadillacs. Its wheel covers were identical to those used on the 1959 Fleetwood models.

As in 1957 and 1958, the Brougham body was custom built by Pinin Farina. The chassis, engine, and other mechanical components were shipped to Genoa and then transported to Farina's plant in Turin. There the bodies were hand-built on bucks and forms Farina constructed from a full-sized plaster model provided by Cadillac.

The result carried plenty of examples of careful handcraft, such as seams hammer-welded without the use of solder, extensive use of sealer to prevent rust, and fabricated chrome trim. Yet, like the bodies Pinin Farina supplied to Ferrari, not every line or curve on the Brougham's body matched those on the other side!

This minor bother aside, the Eldorado Brougham was, if less distinctive than its predecessor, an extremely handsome automobile with surprisingly restrained styling. The two designers most involved with its appearance were Dave Holls and Chuck Jordan. At one point, in January 1958, a full-sized clay mockup of the Brougham was developed without fins in response to a request by General Motors President Harlow Curtice. This bold approach didn't, of course, materialize; but the Brougham's relatively conservative fin forms pointed toward the 1960 Cadillacs. Furthermore, its thin roof line, with slender C-posts and non-wraparound backline, was a corporate mainstay during the early sixties, a time when General Motors produced extremely attractive models in all its price divisions. The Brougham also lead General Motors away from the compound curved, panoramic windshield with a nonwraparound version that later appeared (in smaller form of course) on the 1960 Corvair. The following year, all five GM cars followed suit. What a magnificent trend breaker that Brougham windshield was. The rake-back angle was 61 degrees, and its 3-foot width was several inches greater than the standard Cadillac's.

The use of body trim on the Brougham was restrained, limited to a narrow side-rub rail; a small Cadillac coat of arms above the dual headlights; a modest, almost nondescript hood ornament, and a third Cadillac crest positioned low on the rear deck. Naturally, the Brougham wouldn't have been a Cadillac without a bold rear bumper; but here again, restraint rather than unbridled extremism was the theme. The outer bumper pods contained the stoplights. A simple bright piece, significantly thinner than the grid bar found on standard models, ran the full width of the trunk. Viewed head-on the Brougham presented a tidy, well-coordinated face. The bumper/auxiliary light format was identical to that of other 1959 Cadillacs. The lack of a center bar and a more prominent grid work linked the Brougham's front grille to those used in the Cadillacs of the late forties and early fifties.

The Brougham was available in 15 acrylic lacquers, none of which were offered for other Cadillac models. Fewer (15 rather than 44 as in 1958) upholstery combinations were available for the 1959 Brougham. When leather was specified, the seats were tufted, plain door trim was fitted, and Mouton carpeting was installed on the floor. Broadcloth seats were either plain or striped and had plain bolsters with only a limited amount of stitching. The door trim carried three rows of horizontal stitching and either nylon or wool Karakul carpeting was specified. All interiors used a broadcloth headliner.

Absent from the Brougham's interior were the silver drinking cup, perfume container, vanity case, cigarette holder, and digital clock that were installed on the 1957-1958 models. This didn't mean the new Brougham's occupants were denied appointments befitting a $13,000 automobile. Up front, a brushed, stainless-steel panel with an Eldorado Brougham emblem was installed on the dash cove. The front-seat back had a wood veneer insert that carried a rectangular clock. Behind the rear seat, on the window shelf, were two locking storage bins on each side of the radio speaker. Other nice touches included a magazine rack along the front-seat back and wood-veneer appliques on the front-seat side panels. The trunk-mounted battery was isolated from other trunk contents by a carpeted cover. The entire luggage area was padded and sound-sealing insulating material was installed on the deck lid's inner surface.

The Brougham's air suspension and 345-horse-power engine were identical to those systems available on other Cadillacs.

Total production of 1959 Broughams was just 99 units, placing them in the ranks of the rarest postwar luxury vehicles extant.

CADILLAC'S DOMESTIC COMPETITION

While Cadillac production climbed upward by 17 percent, Lincoln's declined by 9 percent to 26,906. With the evidence clearly indicating that the public was less than enthralled with the shape, form, and format of the super-sized Lincoln, the best the company could do was to lose as little of its market share as possible until the near-revolutionary models of 1961.

For 1959, this meant a Lincoln with minor appearance changes, such as a revised grille, reshaped front bumper, and altered taillights. The most important technical change consisted of a reduction of the engine's compression ratio to 10.0:1 from 10.5:1, which pushed horsepower down to 350 from 375.

Along with greater attention to quality control, Lincoln also dropped the Capri model name, adopted a Continental Mark IV designation, and offered both Town Car and Limousine models. These cars, built by the Hess and Eisenhardt Company of Cincinnati, Ohio, were not big sellers. Output of the Town Cars was just 78, while that of the Limousine totaled 49 units.

Chrysler Corporation lost $33.8 million in 1958, a reflection of the weak car market as well as the first backlash from its notoriously bad quality control of 1957. As far as the Imperial was concerned, the most important development was the transfer of its production from Chrysler's Jefferson Avenue plant to a 1-million square-foot facility at Warren Avenue in Dearborn, which was reserved only for Imperial assembly.

Changes to the Imperial's appearance included a new grille with protruding teeth, reminiscent of that found on old DeSotos, revised side trim that was dominated by a longer spear, and replacement of Imperial body script with block letters. Mechanical refinements included an automatic, self-leveling rear suspension and a swivel seat option.

Like Lincoln, Imperial offered limited production, high-prestige models. The Imperials were constructed by Ghia of Italy and were identified as the Ghia Crown Imperial. These cars on a 149.5-inch wheelbase with an overall length of 244.7 inches were very rare. Only seven were built in 1959. This compared with 31 in 1958 and 36 in 1957. Total Imperial production moved up to 17,262 from 16,102 in 1958.

SPECIFICATIONS

Engine

Type: V-type, ohv, eight cylinders
Bore × stroke: 4 × 3.875 inches
Displacement: 390 cubic inches
Horsepower: 325 @ 4,800 rpm
    Eldorado: 345 @ 4,800 rpm
Torque: 430 lb-ft @ 3,400 rpm
    Eldorado: 435 lb-ft @ 3,400 rpm.
Compression ratio: 10.5:1
Carburetor: Carter AFB, 4-barrel
    Eldorado: triple Rochester model 7015901, two-barrel carburetors
Electrical system: 12-volt
Transmission: Hydra-Matic planetary gearset

Chassis/Drivetrain

Frame: Tubular-center X-type
Rear axle:
    Hypoid semifloating, 2.94:1 ratio
    3.21:1 optional, standard on air-conditioned cars
    Series 75: 3.36:1, 3.77:1 optional
Front suspension: Independent, direct-action, coil springs, torsion-rod stabilizer
Rear suspension: Helical-coil springs
Steering: Power steering with overall ratio of 18.9:1
Tires: 8.0 × 15
    Series 75, Eldorado: 8.20:1

Dimensions

Wheelbase: 130 inches
    Series 75:   149.5 inches
Width: 81.1 inches
Front/rear tread: 61/61 inches
Overall length: 225 inches
    Series 75:   244.8 inches

Popular Options

AM radio with rear speaker
AM radio with remote control
Six-way power seat
Power windows
Power front vent windows
Air Conditioning
Air suspension
Autronic eye
Cruise control
E-Z Eye glass
Fog lights
White sidewall 8.20 × 15 tires

1960

A New Era of Motoring Elegance

WHAT A DIFFERENCE a year can make. In 1959, opinions about Cadillac's appearance were sharply divided. Just a year later, critics were almost unanimous in praising the 1960 model for its excellent styling. Some journalists went so far as to say it was the most attractive Cadillac the marque had yet produced. Devotees of the prewar V-16, not to mention those fans of the 1938-1941 Series Sixty Special, probably felt their hackles rise when they read such glowing commentary, but even the most avid of classic Cadillac enthusiasts were likely to regard the new models as well-designed automobiles.

Not only did the 1960 Cadillac represent a major styling step forward from the 1959 model; but in comparison, the contemporary Lincolns and Imperials appeared awkward and dated. Yet, its designers had managed to maintain the styling continuity linking all postwar Cadillacs in a string of gradually unfolding design evolution.

CHANGES AND IMPROVEMENTS

With the exception of overall width, which was reduced slightly to 79.9 from 81.1 inches, the Cadillac's external dimensions were unchanged. But the sheet metal that filled up the space between those extremes was elegant in a restrained, almost conservative fashion, reflecting the influence of the 1959 Eldorado Brougham.

Cadillac's description of its 1960 models underscored the view that its styling represented a graceful retreat from the extreme levels of 1959. "The motor car that will represent Cadillac on the highways of the world during the year of 1960," it explained, "advances the Cadillac tradition of excellence to an extraordinary degree. The car is now more inspiring to behold . . . more rewarding to ride in . . . more exciting to drive . . . and more wonderful to own than at any previous moment in Cadillac history. A classic new profile . . . a restrained use of adornment . . . and a grille of such elegance that it might have been crafted by a

master jeweler—these mark the 1960 Standard of the World as a dramatic step forward in contemporary motor car design."

If the fins of 1959 were remembered for their extremism, then those found on the 1960 Cadillac were memorable as examples of good taste. Arching gradually to a narrow peak, they remained one of Cadillac's prime styling elements. They now were incorporated into a single, sweeping line that extended the entire length of the car. Unlike Lincoln and Imperial, whose flanks were conglomerates of creases, chrome spears, and awkward bits and pieces of trim going every which way, Cadillac limited its body embellishments to a simple, thin chrome strip running back from the front fender well and, on Series Sixty-Two models, a narrow front-fender bar carrying Cadillac lettering and crest. The De Ville models compensated for the lack of this latter item by featuring script nameplates on their rear fenders. Another variation of these details was used to emphasize the status of the Eldorado Biarritz and Seville models. They carried bright trim the full length of the body sill before arching upward along the upper fender line. Also fitted was Eldorado lettering on the front fenders behind the headlights.

Eliminated from the front grille of all models was the large bar divider that had given the 1959 model a two-tier appearance. The grille now consisted of bright metal "dots" set in a field of vertical and horizontal bars. The front bumper/secondary lighting arrangement retained the individual parking/directional light system, but their squared-off form made them less conspicuous and more carefully coordinated into Cadillac's overall styling theme than in 1959.

The rear deck-taillight-bumper arrangement followed a similar philosophy. The narrow taillights gradually reversed their curve to meet large oval pods at each end of the bumper, containing vertically stacked, oval backup, and stop lights.

Ornamentation was restrained on all models. On Series Sixty-Two models, the trunk lid was embellished by a Cadillac "V" and crest and a narrow chrome strip along its lower edge. Filling the area between the lid and bumper was a fine-mesh insert. Series Sixty and Seventy-Five models used a similar arrangement in which Fleetwood script replaced the crest and V. The same area on Eldorado models was filled by a two-tier version of the front-grille design. Along with a narrow chrome bar across the trunk lid containing Eldorado lettering, this gave them an especially smart appearance. Both the Eldorado Seville and Series Sixty Special were available with a grained, fabric-top covering dyed to match the body color. This feature, soon to set off a vinyl-top craze among American cars, was outlined by narrow chrome molding.

Also destined to be found on future products from other American manufacturers were the Cadillac's amber-colored directional light indicators, which were removed from the dash to a location in the chrome strip running along the front fender.

Since only 101 were assembled, few Americans had the opportunity to view first hand the 1960 version of Cadillac's $13,074 Eldorado Brougham. This was unfortunate since they were handsome, aristocratic automobiles with design features that would be incorporated into Cadillac's mass-produced models in 1961. An example of this was the Brougham's lower body "skeg" line, which creased the body to form a horizontal fin. In both 1961 and 1962, this would be a key element of Cadillac styling. This feature had been seen on the Cadillac XP-74 Cyclone show car and could be traced back as far as 1954 to the La Espada Dream Car.

Other detail changes included moving of the small Farina cloisonné emblem from the front to rear fender, placement of Brougham nameplates on the hood and rear splash panel, and removal of the hood ornament. Unlike those on other Cadillacs, the Brougham's fins did not have light inserts. This feature required using twin, circular rear lights mounted in concave, brushed-aluminum panels within the outer bumper uprights. In turn, the backup lights consisted of rectangular units mounted low on the bumper. Yet another identifying feature of the 1960 Eldorado Brougham was the absence of any bright work on its lower rear-deck panel.

Cadillac presented the Eldorado Brougham to the public in a manner intended to leave no doubt in anyone's mind about its status among the world's leading luxury cars. "Here, beyond conjecture," said Cadillac, "is the finest expression of the new era of automotive elegance . . . Its individual styling and its dramatic and exclusive range of colors mark the Eldorado Brougham as a motor car that stands out—even among Cadillacs. Let it appear on any motoring scene and it will be immediately recognized as an achievement unparalleled in motoring history."

None of Cadillac's technical highlights for 1960 were, by themselves, of sufficient magnitude to create much of a stir, but collectively they represented a worthwhile effort to make the latest Cadillac a superior car to its predecessor. A first for Cadillac, as well as for the industry, was a vacuum-controlled parking brake that automatically released the brake whenever the car was

put in gear with the engine running. As a result, it was virtually impossible to drive the car with the parking brake on. Furthermore, since the brake would not lock when the car was in gear, it had value as a true emergency brake. Two other significant braking developments were self-adjusting brakes and finned, rear brake drums. The former system operated whenever the brakes were applied with the car moving in reverse. The finned drums were part of a system that included larger wheel cylinders.

No changes were made either in the Cadillac's standard spring or optional air suspension, which continued to be standard on both Eldorado models and the Eldorado Brougham. The springs were now 10 percent softer, which further enhanced Cadillac's reputation for possessing an ultra-smooth ride. The price paid was a tendency to float and sway over road dips and curves.

Whether Cadillac drivers ever subjected their cars to the sort of treatment that brought out these undesirable characteristics is problematic. What is certain is that most of them noticed, and welcomed, the use of a narrower and thinner transmission case, which resulted in a 1-inch lower and 3-inch narrower tunnel hump.

DIFFERENCES AMONG MODELS

All three Series Sixty-Two models (Coupe, four- and six-window Sedans) were offered in interiors of fawn, blue, or gray Cortina cord, as well as turquoise, green, Persian sand, or black Caspian cloth. The seat bolsters were Florentine-grain vinyl in complementary colors. The Series Sixty-Two Convertible's interior was available in Florentine leather, in solid tones of silver, blue, green, saddle, red, or black. Combinations of black with silver or red and white were also offered. Newly designed wheelcovers incorporating alternating concentric rings of bright chrome and black or white enamel or brushed chrome were standard on all models.

De Ville models (Coupe, four- and six-window Sedans) were available with numerous interiors. Among the choices were Chadwick cloths with matching Florentine-leather bolsters in fawn, green, gray, and Persian sand. Additionally, De Villes were offered in Cambray cloth/Florentine-leather combinations in three color schemes.

External identification of the Sixty Special was not difficult. A dark red cloisonné crest was mounted on the front fenders, the rear fenders were adorned with nine chrome-accented louvers, and a broad chrome bar extended along the entire lower body from the rear edge of the front fender cutout to the rear bumper structure. The fabric top was finished in tones to match the body color.

Ten interiors were available: Clarion cloth in turquoise, gray, or Persian sand with matching Florentine-leather bolsters, Cardinal cloth in Lorarno blue, green, or fawn with matching bolsters, black Cardinal cloth with white Florentine-leather bolsters, and wool broadcloth in gray, Lorarno blue, or Sage tan.

Both the Seville and Biarritz were equipped with

1960 Series Seventy-Five Limousine.

1960 Eldorado Biarritz Convertible.

CADILLAC VITAL STATISTICS: 1960

Series	Model	Body Type	Factory Price ($)	Weight (lbs.)	Production (#)
62	6239	4 dr Sedan 4W	5080	4775	9984
	6229	4 dr Sedan 6W	5080	4805	26,824
	6237	2 dr Hardtop Coupe	4892	4670	19,978
	6267	Convertible	5455	4850	14,000
De Ville	6339	4 dr Sedan de Ville 4W	5498	4815	9225
	6329	4 dr Sedan de Ville 6W	5498	4835	22,579
	6337	2 dr Coupe de Ville	5252	4705	21,585
60	6029	4 dr Sedan	6233	4880	11,800
64	6437	Eldorado Seville	7401	4855	1075
	6467	Eldorado Biarritz	7401	5060	1285
69	6929	Eldorado Brougham	13,075		101
75	6723	4 dr Sedan 9p	9533	5475	718
	6733	4 dr Limousine 9p	9748	5560	832

1960 Coupe de Ville.

1960 Sedan de Ville, 6-window Model.

1960 Series Sixty Special.

Sabre-spoke wheels. A textured-vinyl fabric top was installed on the Seville. Both could be ordered in any of the 15 standard Cadillac colors, as well as five exclusive colors.

Seville interiors were available in combinations of Cardinal cloth and Florentine leather in Sierra rose, Lorarno blue, Dundee green and heather, beige-metallic Cardiff leather with beige Florentine-leather bolsters, or in red or white Cardiff leather with white Florentine-leather bolsters.

Biarritz interiors were finished in Cardiff leather in white, silver metallic, Lorarno blue, beige, black, Dundee green, or red with matching Florentine-leather bolsters and trim.

Seating areas in both the Series Seventy-Five Sedan and Limousine models were finished in gray tones of Bedford cord and wool broadcloth. The chauffeur's compartment was trimmed in gray, fawn, or black Florentine leather.

CADILLAC'S DOMESTIC COMPETITION

Cadillac's opposition was, in 1960, conforming to one of its classic patterns that, as in the past, provided essentially ineffective competition. The Imperial, after its twin challenges of 1955 and 1957, was, in effect, spinning its wheels. Caught up in the third facelift of the 1957 body, it was progressively becoming less attractive and losing contact with the basic purity of line marking the 1957 models. Particularly unfortunate (for Chrysler) was the Imperial's huge and ungainly rear fender fins that were out of touch with public attitudes toward automotive styling.

Chrysler's lack of success in revising the four-year-old Imperial body while maintaining a basic styling theme had a counterpart in the arrangement of its interior. The use of a flattened steering wheel was a novel idea intended to improve visibility of the Imperial instruments. But why not arrange them in a more logical fashion to begin with? While neither Cadillac nor, for that matter, Lincoln were beyond criticism for their dash arrangements, Cadillac's was relatively free of ornamentation, well positioned, and recessed to eliminate reflection.

In contrast, the Imperial's dash seemed intended more to impress rather than please. For example, the turn-indicator switch was placed to the left of the

1960 Series Sixty-Two Convertible

1960 Eldorado Brougham.

instrument cluster for the sake of symmetry and at the expense of easy operation.

To Imperial's credit was full instrumentation with nonglare electroluminescent lighting, four-way directional light flashers, and its Auto Pilot speed-control system. Imperial had pioneered this feature in 1958 and, for 1960, updated it to become the best of its kind. Unlike Cadillac's Cruise Control and Lincoln's Speed Control, the revamped Auto Pilot did not have to be reset manually each time the brakes were applied. Instead, it reengaged automatically as soon as the desired cruising speed was reached.

Imperial's real forte was its handling; and once again, the latest models were clearly superior to both Cadillac and Lincoln.

If Imperial's output of 17,707 cars, down nearly 20 percent from 1959, was sending a message to Chrysler that the Imperial wasn't exactly the top choice among American luxury-car buyers, then Lincoln's production of 24,820 cars, down 8 percent from the previous year, has to be regarded as a duplicate expression. Basically, the big Lincolns and Continentals never recovered from their bad start in 1958. From 1958 through 1960, Lincoln lost ground to Cadillac at an alarming rate, which, at year's end, left it with just half of its 1958 market penetration. Nineteen-sixty would be the last year for this body shell; and in more ways than one, it had been a gigantic fiasco, based on the false premise that the way to surpass Cadillac was with a car of overwhelmingly huge proportions.

The net result for 1960 was a car with styling that pleased few customers and engineering developments that were headlined by a less powerful engine and a new rear-suspension system. Not mourned was elimination of air suspension as a Lincoln option. The Lincoln 430-cubic-inch V-8 remained the industry's largest; but now with a two; rather than a four-barrel carburetor, its 315-horsepower rating was the lowest in its class.

Not surprisingly, with a standard 2.93:1 axle ratio, it was also the slowest from zero to 60 mph with a time of over 14 seconds. In contrast, the Imperial required slightly more than 12 seconds. Even with the smallest V-8 developing 325 horsepower (25 less than Imperial), Cadillac was the champ, recording a zero to 60-mph time of under 11 seconds.

Curiously, Lincoln was the only American car not entered in the 1960 Mobilgas Economy Run. This might have been just as well for Cadillac since the combination of its 2.89:1 axle ratio and big, lazy V-8 with a small carburetor might have made for a Lincoln victory. As it turned out, the Imperial easily beat Cadillac with a 20.5036 mpg average to Cadillac's 18.8170 mpg.

With gas selling for under 30 cents a gallon, a victory in the Economy Run had limited impact in the luxury-car market. Nineteen sixty was another Cadillac year.

SPECIFICATIONS

Engine

Type: V-type, ohv, eight cylinders

Bore × stroke: 4.0 × 3.875 inches
Displacement: 390 cubic inches
Horsepower: 325 @ 4,800 rpm
   Eldorado: 345 @ 4,800 rpm
Torque: 430 lb.-ft. @ 3,400 rpm (Eldorado: 435 lb.-ft. @ 3,400 rpm)
Carburetor: Carter four-barrel, model 2814S
   Eldorado: 3 two-barrel
Electrical system: 12-volt
Transmission: Hydra-Matic, three-speed automatic; controlled fluid coupling provides two drive ranges, Low range, and reverse

Chassis/Drivetrain

Frame: Tubular-center X-frame
Rear axle:
   Hypoid, offset differential, 2.94:1 ratio, with 3.21:1 optional
   3.21:1 provided with air-conditioned cars and when 345-horsepower engine is installed
   Series 75 models: 3.36:1 axle, with 3.77:1 optional
Front suspension: Spherical ball joints with independent helical-coil springs
Rear suspension: Four-link drive with helical-coil springs
Air suspension: Standard on Eldorado Brougham, optional at extra cost for other models
Steering: Power steering standard with over-all steering ratio of 18.9:1
Tires: Low pressure, 4-ply, tubeless, 8.00 × 15,
   Series 75:   6-ply, 8.20 × 15,
   Whitewall 8.20-15 tires optional at $57

Dimensions

Wheelbase: 130 inches
   Series 75:   149.75 inches
Width: 79.9 inches
Front/rear tread: 61/61 inches
Overall length: 225 inches
   Series 75:   244.8 inches

Popular Options

Air Suspension: $215
Cruise control
Power windows: $118
Power vent windows: $73
Six-way power seats: $85-$113
Guide-matic headlight control: $97
Power door locks:
   Two-door: $46
   Four-door: $77
Air conditioning:
   Series 60, 62: $474
   Series 75: $624
E-Z Eye glass: $52
Heater: $129
Fog lamps: $43
Radio with rear speaker: $165, with remote control: $247
Remote-control trunk lid: $59

1961

A New Inspiration for all Motordom

IF, BY 1961, anyone had any doubts as to who was calling the shots in the luxury-car field he or she merely had to ponder the following situation. Nineteen sixty-one was a year of dramatic new policy at Lincoln. Abandoning the huge size and bulk of the 1958-1960 era, Lincoln introduced a trim, elegantly styled car with an 8-inch shorter wheelbase and with nearly 15 inches removed from its overall length. No less dramatic was the combining of the best of Lincoln's past with the promise of a brighter future by naming this outstanding motor car the Lincoln Continental. Moreover, it was offered as either a four-door hardtop or a convertible. The latter was the first such example in the luxury-car field since the prewar years.

The Lincoln Continental's styling borrowed from no other manufacturer; and even today, it is regarded as one of Ford Motor Company's most outstanding achievements. But there was even more to the Lincoln Continental, since a major effort was made to raise its level of quality to a point perceptibly above previous Lincoln standards. To drive this point home, Ford sold the Lincoln Continental with a two-year/24,000-mile warranty. At a time when the norm was a ninety-day/3,000 mile commitment, this was a dramatic statement of confidence in the Lincoln Continental.

It came as no real surprise to anyone that *Car Life* awarded the Lincoln Continental its first Engineering Excellence Award, praising it as a car with numerous attributes such as beauty, comfort, longevity, and reliability.

Regardless of the media's response to the Lincoln Continental, it remained unclear whether Lincoln's change of course would be sufficient to challenge Cadillac's bellwether position in the luxury-car field, since Cadillac was also making some major moves in its design direction. Yet, even the most partisan of Cadillac's supporters found it hard to accept Cadillac's 3-inch cut in overall length, elimination of the Eldorado Brougham, and reduction of the Eldorado line to a single convertible version in the Series 62 line as equal in magnitude to Lincoln's truly revolutionary move for 1961.

Yet if sales meant much (and in Detroit they meant everything), all of Lincoln's efforts hardly mattered. Production totaled a miserable 25,164 units, barely 300 cars more than in 1960. Lincoln obviously did harm to itself by not offering more than two body styles; but even then, would they have enabled it to come that much closer to Cadillac's output of 138,379 cars?

Once again Cadillac's unequaled public image, buoyed by effective advertising and further buttressed by a look that was new without being extreme, had carried the day. Not everyone, of course, was satisfied with the latest Cadillacs. Some felt it had moved too rapidly away from the extremely fluid form of the 1960 model. Others considered the latest Cadillac as having too much of a rocketship look. Another group of critics liked many of the individual aspects of its appearance, but felt the overall effect was overladen with styling clichés.

Then there were those who didn't care for the Cadillac's shorter length. In any case, the era of this compact Cadillac was short-lived. Just a year later, the Cadillacs were longer; and not until the early seventies would any automotive journalist write seriously about a "compact Cadillac."

CHANGES AND IMPROVEMENTS

Although the demise of the Eldorado Brougham left Cadillac without representation in the ultra-expensive car field, many of its individual styling features were found on the 1961 models. Cadillac executives had not been pleased with initial styling proposals for 1961 and had decided to rely on the Brougham as the primary inspiration for 1961. Specific influences were easy to identify. Among these were the Brougham's lower-body skeg line and nonpanoramic windshield. These changes, in the context of an all-new body, achieved the annual Cadillac objective of maintaining styling continuity while providing the appearance of newness that attracted a healthy harvest of customers.

Therefore, the front-grille design still was highlighted by a gridwork of rectangular divisions with chrome dots on alternating horizontal bars. As part of the chiseled look, itself vaguely suggestive of the razor-edged styling found on some early postwar Rolls-Royce and Bentley models, the grille now protruded forward at an obtuse angle. Along with the cutback of the front fenders, exposing the large, chromed-headlight shell, this form created an impression of greater front length than actually existed.

Cadillac, in offering a shorter car in 1961, was tampering with an element that made plenty of Cadillac dealers nervous. Indeed, one criticism they had of the 1961 model was that it was too short. This didn't fall on deaf ears, for the 1962 Cadillacs had their front hoods extended by 4.575 inches. Could it be that this change in itself accounted for the sales increase of 21,461 cars that Cadillac enjoyed in 1962?

Having abandoned, in evolutionary fashion, use of massive bumpers with huge torpedo-shaped guards, Cadillac now offered a less-menacing front bumper, consisting of a lower unit carrying circular parking/directional lights in recessed shells and a slightly protruding center bar, which, at best, could evoke only the slightest memory of what had once sprung forward from a Cadillac front end.

At the rear, things were just a bit cluttered, due not to an excessive amount of trim, but because, in a mixture of horizontal and vertical shapes, the fender fins and twin light pods eagerly competed for the viewer's attention.

Perhaps there was just too much of a good thing back there. The age of extreme-sized rear bumpers to ward off real or imagined enemies was, however, part of the past. Now the byword was simplicity; and following the form of the front bumper, the rear unit was highlighted by a thin center element extending outward, thus conforming to the skeg line's shape.

Having taken the movement to provide ever-increasing amounts of glass area and corresponding thinner cornerposts as far as glass manufacturing technology allowed, Cadillac began to pull away from that extreme position in 1961. Of course there wouldn't be anything resembling a sudden retreat; that would be unbecoming. Thus Cadillac's Series Sixty-Two models continued to offer two types of roof lines providing vast expanses of glass area. The two-door versions adopted a tall back light with an impressive sweep of glass area.

With nowhere else to take this theme and a more conservative styling philosophy rapidly gaining the upper hand, Cadillac used a formal roof line for the Series Sixty Special. Imperial, to give Chrysler its due, had used a relatively small rear window on its 1960 Le Baron model to distinguish it from lesser Imperials. The same concept applied to the Sixty Special, along with its familiar chevrons on the leading edge of the rear fenders plus small, model name plates on the front fenders, gave this Fleetwood a limousine look in a smaller size.

All Cadillacs except the Limousine had identical lengths of 222 inches until the introduction of the Town Sedan de Ville model in early 1961. This model, whose production totaled only 3,756 units, was identical to the Sedan de Ville in all respects save one: its rear overhang was reduced by 7 inches, which resulted in a length of 215 inches.

The development of this model was a response to reports from dealers in urban areas that some customers of the 1959-1960 Cadillacs weren't happy about their length. A survey conducted in 17 large cities indicated that 30 percent of Cadillac sedan buyers were interested in a smaller car.

Cadillac depicted the Town Sedan as "created especially for urban driving." It was "the perfect answer for those who—because of more limited garaging and parking facilities—require a lesser overall length, yet are reluctant to accept anything less than Cadillac elegance, spaciousness, comfort and performance."

As the Town Sedan's low production level indicates, customer interest was at best lukewarm. This model was also offered in 1962, but slow sales limited output to only 2,600 cars, and it was dropped from the 1963 Cadillac lineup. General Motors' Chairman Frederic Donner took this disappointment in stride. He considered the Town Sedan a valuable addition to Cadillac's image since by offering customers a choice that they apparently didn't really want, Cadillac was effectively refuting the charge that they were out of touch with current market trends.

No one really noticed (at least that's what Cadillac hoped) that air suspension wasn't available for 1961. This much maligned system whose virtues were overwhelmed by its admitted shortcomings, the most notorious and perhaps most exaggerated being a tendency to leak, simply wasn't worth continuing in the face of the controversy it generated.

Far less divisive was the response to Cadillac's revision of its front suspension for 1961. On the surface, it seemed hardly worthy of more than a passing glance. The replacement of one lower control arm and three connecting points by a unit with two mounts really didn't seem to count for much. But the results were significant. Not only did this change improve stability, but it allowed the front brakes (which were now finned like those at the rear) to be moved further into the air stream for better cooling. At the same time, Cadillac also installed larger wheel cylinders. The net result was better brakes with less fade.

Attention to the steering geometry and power steering also made for some worthwhile changes in Cadillac's driving characteristics. The turning circle was reducing 3 feet to 43 and a lower (18.2:1) steering ratio reduced the turns lock-to-lock to 3.66. Finally, increasing the steering wheel's diameter 1 inch to 16 inches contributed to Cadillac's quicker and easier response to changes in direction.

Cadillac received good grades for its handling, maneuverability, and smooth operation from the road testers for the nation's automotive magazines. *Car Life*, April 1961, concluded that when its size was taken into consideration, the Coupe de Ville handled very well.

Motor Trend, April 1961, noted that, in both its 1960 and 1961 test cars, no mechanical sounds were detected and that passengers in a 1961 Cadillac were likely to hear outside sounds only when the windows were lowered.

Contributing to this aspect of Cadillac's performance was the extensive use of rubber sound-insulation mountings. New for 1961 were rubber bushings for all suspension joints and a rubber support for the driveshaft carrier bearing. Cadillac even went so far as to install a copper strap from the suspension to the frame to eliminate tire static from the radio.

In the industry, the trend in 1961 was to reduce the number of engine options available. Cadillac did its part by dropping the Q-engine both as the standard engine for the Eldorado Biarritz and as an option for other Cadillacs. All models were now powered by the 390-cubic-inch V-8 with a single Rochester, four-barrel carburetor, 10.5:1 compression ratio, and 325 horsepower at 4,800 rpm. Maximum torque was 430 lb-ft at 3,100 rpm.

On a model-for-model comparison, Cadillacs were somewhat lighter than their Imperial and Lincoln Continental counterparts, although no Cadillac body style really matched up with the Lincoln Continental four-door hardtop and convertible. This resulted in a virtual dead heat in competitive acceleration times between an Imperial and a Cadillac, with both cars reaching 60 mph in approximately 10.5 seconds with their standard rear-axle ratios of 2.94:1 (Cadillac) and 2.93:1 (Imperial). The Lincoln Continental engine, with a single, two-barrel carburetor, was rated at 300 horsepower at 4,100 rpm and 465 lb-ft at 2,000 rpm. Its 0- to 60-mph time was in the vicinity of 13 seconds.

Cadillac was the only member of this trio to offer optional axle ratios of 3.21:1, 3.36:1, and 3.77:1. The first of these was mandatory for cars with air conditioning. *Car Life*, June 1961, tested an air-conditioned Coupe de Ville and reported that the results were so good that they had to check the gear ratio to make certain Cadillac hadn't slipped in a nonstandard axle. The results from *Car Life* showed a 0- to 60-mph time of 9.5 seconds; a standing-start quarter-mile run of 17.1 seconds and 78.7 mph; and an estimated top

speed of 115 mph. Ready for testing, this Cadillac weighed 5,080 pounds.

Of interest in any discussion of Cadillac performance was the dropping of the dual-exhaust system in 1961 and the installation on cars for the California market of a crankcase ventilator system.

DIFFERENCES AMONG MODELS

Cadillac's interior, like its exterior, conveyed the notion that Cadillac was America's number one motorcar in a conservative fashion. Entrance into the rear passenger compartment of four-door models was made easier thanks to doors that were 6 inches wider and opened outward 7.5 inches further. A new dash layout with a bin-type glove box continued Cadillac's policy of exercising restraint in the use of chrome trim, while making certain that all controls were within easy reach of the driver. Few cars in the world were so operator-friendly. Without a stretch or even the slightest exertion, the driver could lock all doors, open or close all windows, adjust the outside mirrors, set the cruise control, and, if the car was so equipped, determine the optimum seating position with the six-way power seat.

The five Series Sixty-Two models—Coupe, four- and six-window Sedans, and the Convertible—did not carry the Cadillac name, nor for that matter any series identification on their bodies. Their front and rear decks were fitted with a wide-angle V below the Cadillac crest, which was also positioned on the front fender just below the trim line.

Interior appointments for the closed models consisted of Canberra cloth in gray, green, blue, fawn, or rose. A Chilton cloth was also available in sandalwood, turquoise, or black. Both formats used Florentine-grain vinyl bolsters in complementary colors.

For the Sixty-Two Convertible's Florentine-leather interior, eight color selections—black, blue, sandalwood, saddle, green, red metallic red, and white—were listed. Seat bolsters were either black or metallic red.

All De Ville models (Coupe de Ville, four- and six-window Sedan de Villes, and the Town Sedan) carried de Ville script on their front fenders just behind the

1961 Series Sixty-Two Coupe.

1961 Coupe de Ville.

1961 Series Sixty-Two Convertible.

CADILLAC VITAL STATISTICS: 1961

Series	Model	Body Type	Factory Price ($)	Weight (lbs.)	Production (#)
62	6239	4 dr Sedan 4W	5080	4660	4700
	6229	4 dr Sedan 6W	5080	4680	26,216
	6237	2 dr Hardtop Coupe	4892	4560	16,005
	6267	Convertible	5455	4720	15,500
De Ville	6339	4 dr Sedan 4W	5498	4715	4847
	6329	4 dr Sedan 6W	5498	4710	26,415
	6399	4 dr Town Sedan	5498	4670	3756
	6337	Coupe de Ville	5252	4595	20,156
Eldorado	6367	Eldorado Biarritz	6477	4805	1450
60	6039	4 dr Sedan	6233	4770	15,500
75	6723	4 dr Sedan 9p	9533	5390	699
	6733	4 dr Limousine 9p	9748	5420	926

headlights. Unlike their Series Sixty-Two counterparts, the De Villes did not have fender-mounted Cadillac crests.

Eight interior choices were offered: gray, fawn, or green Covington cloth; black or turquoise Coronel cloth; and Cromwell cloth in blue, sandalwood, or rose. All three cloth patterns were accompanied by Florentine-leather bolsters in appropriate shades.

The Eldorado Biarritz, which Cadillac proclaimed as, "beyond doubt the most beautiful convertible ever created," carried Biarritz front-fender script and was available in eight ostrich-grain leather tones with Florentine-leather trim: sandalwood, nautilus blue, white, topaz, mauve, black, or metallic red. Bucket-type front seats were available as a no-cost alternative to the conventional bench seats.

Cadillac's Fleetwood models—the Sixty Special, and Series Seventy-Five Sedan and Limousine—demonstrated Cadillac's ability to blend the conservative appearance that attracted buyers to these cars into a new style with a minimal amount of compromise.

In the case of the Sixty Special, Cadillac said its designers had "achieved new luxury, spaciousness and good taste." Primary styling features included a small Fleetwood, front-fender badge, Fleetwood lettering on the rear deck, and six chrome chevrons on the rear fenders just ahead of the taillights.

Sixty Special interior fabrics included a fine-textured Cambridge cloth in blue, sandalwood, or green with matching Florentine-leather bolsters. Also offered were three other themes: black Cambridge cloth with white Florentine-leather bolsters; gray, fawn, turquoise, or rose Crestwood cloth with matching bolsters; and gray or fawn broadcloth.

Interiors for the Seventy-Five Sedan and Limousine, which did not carry the front-fender Fleetwood emblem found on the Sixty-Special, consisted of either a wool broadcloth in gray or fawn or a Calais cord available in those colors, as well as dark gray with matching broadcloth bolsters and trim. The chauffeur's compartment of the Limousine was available in black, gray, or fawn Florentine leather.

CADILLAC'S DOMESTIC COMPETITION

Seldom had affluent Americans enjoyed the choice in domestic fine cars as they did in 1961. The Lincoln Continental, at 212.4 inches, was significantly smaller than either Cadillac or Imperial, and its styling was undeniably superb. Imperial was at the other extreme, America's largest automobile, unable, it seemed, to break away from the series of facelifts that rendered each successive model less attractive and more ungainly than its predecessor.

An effort was made in 1961 to blend some styling elements from the thirties in the form of free-standing head- and taillights with a body conceived during the halcyon days of soaring tail fins and long, sweeping body forms. The results, if spectacular, were not entirely successful. Once again, the Imperial appeared to be designed without a clear sense of purpose or direction.

The Imperial's interior layout did little to alter this impression. The odd-shaped steering wheel made few converts, and the twin towers of push-button controls ran a distant third in esthetic appeal to the corresponding arrangements found in the Lincoln Continental and Cadillac.

Imperial still used a front-torsion bar, rear leaf-spring suspension setup, but opinions were divided as to whether it remained the top-handling car in its class. *Motor Trend* rated it as number one, but was critical of its maneuverability at low speeds and in traffic. In fact, it regarded the Imperial as the poorest car in this respect. Similarly, *Car Life* placed the Imperial's overall driving characteristics third in a class of three.

Equally open to question was the efficacy of Imperial's slogan for 1961: "America's Most Carefully Built Car." Its literal accuracy was difficult to ascertain objectively and in comparison with Cadillac's long-lived "Standard of the World" (admittedly also difficult to substantiate) rallying cry, seemed lacking in self confidence.

Lincoln Continental's forte for 1961 was its styling, followed closely by its name; an amalgamation of two of the most respected titles among American automobiles. As it had done in 1952, Lincoln was once again attempting to convince the public that less was more. The age of unbridled application of chrome trim was already in its twilight years, but the Lincoln Continental's extremely sparse use of body bright-work still came as a shock.

These two features—a much smaller physical size and a design that forsook body creases and chrome spears for a form linking the Lincoln Continental to the earlier Continental—made it one of the most distinctive cars built in America.

Technically, the new Lincoln Continental broke no new ground. Although its overall ride and handling characteristics were improved, they will still inferior to Cadillac's. Surely prompting negative reaction from prospective customers was the Lincoln Continental's limited trunk space (which, in the convertible, dropped to almost zero when the top was lowered) and its restricted rear leg room. This latter weakness was particularly evident when the front seat was moved to its most extreme rear position.

While certainly an elegant feature evocative of the classic era, the rear-hinged rear door also resurrected the old "suicide door" expression. It's unlikely that this arrangement posed any serious safety hazard. But to make certain that no mishaps would occur, the Lincoln Continental had a dash-mounted warning light that alerted the driver that a rear door was unlocked. The Lincoln Continental was the only Ford automobile to use the 430-cubic-inch V-8 in 1960. It remained the largest American V-8 in production.

Like the Imperial, the design of the Lincoln Continental was marked by individual features that were outstanding. But on balance, it fell short of the mark as a car capable of generating sales enthusiasm approaching that of the 1961 Cadillac. It was a bold gamble that, in the ensuing years, provided only a modest growth in Lincoln sales. For example, it wasn't until 1965 that output rose above the 40,000 mark; and even then, that was some 622 cars under Lincoln's level for 1953. By contrast, Cadillac was producing 184,435 cars in 1965, nearly 72,000 more than in 1953.

SPECIFICATIONS

Engine

Type: V-type, ohv, eight cylinders
Bore × stroke: 4.0 × 3.875 inches
Horsepower: 325 @ 4,800 rpm
Torque: 430 lb-ft @ 3,400 rpm
Compression ratio: 10.5:1
Carburetor: Carter four-barrel
Electrical system: 12-volt
Transmission: Hydra-Matic, three-speed automatic; controlled fluid coupling on forward gear set, two drive ranges, low range, and reverse

Chassis/Drivetrain

Frame: Tubular-center X-frame with new, front-frame members
Rear axle:
  Hypoid, offset differential: 2.94:1 ratio, 3.21:1 optional
  Air-conditioned cars: 3.21:1 axle
  Series 75 ratio: 3.36:1 standard, 3.77:1 optional
Front suspension: Independent, spherical joints, helical-coil springs. New rubber-mounted strut rods and rubber bushings
Rear suspension: Four-link drive, helical-coil springs, rubber bushings
Steering: Power-assisted with 18.2:1 ratio, turning angle increased from 36° to 38.5°

Tires: Low-pressure, 4-ply, tubeless
  Series 75:   8.00 × 15
  Optional: 6-ply, 8.20 × 15, white sidewall (standard for Biarritz)

Dimensions

Wheelbase: 129.5 inches
  Series 75:   149.75 inches
Width: 79.8 inches
Front/rear tread: 61/61 inches
Overall length: 222 inches
  Town Sedan: 215 inches
  Series 75:   242.3 inches

Popular Options

Power windows: Standard on all models except Series 62
Power ventpanes: Standard on Eldorado Biarritz and 60 Special
Six-way power seat: Standard on Eldorado Biarritz with bench front seat
Power door locks
Cruise control
Air conditioning
Power deck-lid lock
Power headlight control
Fog lamps
Heater
Rear-window defogger
Signal-seeking preselector radio
E-Z Eye tinted glass
Floor mats
Cushion topper
Seat belts

1962

For 60 Years, the Standard of the World

CADILLAC'S 60TH ANNIVERSARY was in 1962. In contrast, Lincoln and Imperial seemed mere upstarts. After all, when the first Lincoln was constructed in August 1920, Cadillac had been building cars for 18 years. When Walter P. Chrysler's Chrysler Imperial debuted in 1925, total Cadillac output exceeded 22,500 cars.

Having endured the hard times that destroyed many of its competitors, Cadillac was, in 1962, offering its customers the largest choice of fine cars available from a single producer in the world. Underscoring Cadillac's preeminence in its field was the assertion that "in all its distinguished history, Cadillac has never created a motorcar so finely crafted, so meticulously refined, so progressively engineered" as the 1962 model.

Nineteen sixty-two was a good year for the industry because every major manufacturer enjoyed a substantial boost in output. Overall, 6,935,200 American cars were produced in 1962 compared with 5,516,400 the previous year. Cadillac's share was impressive: 158,528 cars built in the calendar year and an all-time record output of 160,840 for the model year. Percentage-wise, Cadillac's increase from 1961 of 16.2 percent trailed both Imperial's 16.9 percent and Lincoln's 23.4 percent. But this interpretation offered sparse encouragement to Chrysler and Ford since Cadillac's increased output of 22,461 cars exceeded total production of 1962 Imperials by over 8,000 cars and came within hailing distance of the Lincoln Continental's 25,164 model-year assemblies. So much for the talk at Chrysler and Ford about closing the gap with Cadillac.

Certainly there was nothing mysterious about Cadillac's strategy for 1962. In essence it was a repeat of what had held it in good stead for years. Cadillac gently massaged its external appearance, refined and sharpened its attention to the myriad of small details that collectively pampered the Cadillac owner in virtually every conceivable way and then topped off the package with some solid and worthwhile technical improvements and innovations.

CHANGES AND IMPROVEMENTS

No changes were made in Cadillac's overall length and width, but a squarer roof line was joined by a flatter back light and a lower overall height of approximately 2.2 inches on all sedans except for the Series Seventy-Five models, which remained unchanged. This still left the Lincoln Continental the lowest car in its class even though its sedan-model height rose slightly to 53.7 from 53.5 inches. The real object of attention for tape-measure-packing car nuts was the height of Cadillac's tail fins. They were losing attitude and dropping fast. For 1962, they shed their chrome caps and a total of 2 inches. This was accomplished with the greatest of ease since it was accompanied by a much cleaner and more coordinated rear-end design with vertical-mounted, obtuse-angled, and rectangularly shaped taillights. The most interesting feature of what first appeared as not much more than a typical year-to-year styling revamp was the use of clear white lenses, allowing the tail, brake, and backup lights to be incorporated in a single unit. In this setup, the bulb burned white or red as required. This made for a very neat rear-deck arrangement, the only element of which could be criticized was the full-length beauty panel placed just below the deck lid. The problem wasn't its appearance, which blended nicely into the Cadillac's overall format. Rather, the issue was the shadow of suspicion it cast that suggested Cadillac had followed Lincoln's lead on that point.

Up front though, there wasn't any implication of Cadillac's looking over its neighbor's fences. Rather, it was a return to the format of 1954-1957 when the simple egg-crate form reigned supreme. Gone was the peaked leading edge, replaced by an upright grid network, subdivided by a wider center bar, and carrying Cadillac script in its lower right corner. Directly below the dual headlights were bumper-mounted, rectangular-shaped parking/directional lights. For years, Cadillac designers had tacked on a small appendage to the outer grille; and in 1962, it came into its own becoming functional element of Cadillac's lighting system as a cornering light activated by the turn-signal lever whenever the headlights or fog or parking lights were on. This worthwhile safety feature spread its 50-candle power beam across a 30-degree arc.

Also making Cadillac a safer automobile was its new dual braking system. Strange as it seems, the only other American car to offer this feature was Rambler, a point that American Motors gleefully pointed out in its ads. The Cadillac system used dual master cylinders with separate pistons and reservoirs for the front and rear wheels. Therefore, the car still had adequate emergency braking in the event that one of the lines was damaged. It also was still possible to use the parking brake as an auxiliary brake if necessary. This system was further refined for 1962 with a new diaphragm providing a smoother release and more positive locking.

Cadillac's quest for an ever smoother and quieter ride was responsible for the use of more sound-deadening, dense rubber material under the floor pan and the cowl section separating the front door and fenders. Also directed toward the same objective was the use of new exhaust-pipe mounts, drive-line "improvements," and "specially cut" gears for the transmission. Similarly, Cadillac upgraded the operating standards of its V-8 by selectively fitting bearings for a closer fit. Owners of air-conditioned Cadillacs were assured of the system's quieter operation due to use of a redesigned fan clutch and a smaller, lighter, but more powerful six-cylinder Freon compressor.

No changes were made in the basic arrangement of Cadillac's suspension, but revised front spring rates, revalved shock absorbers, and new front and rear suspension bushings contributed to a smoother ride.

All Cadillacs, except the Town Sedan and Park Avenue models (which continued to use a 21-gallon fuel tank) now had a 26-gallon fuel capacity. Apparently, Cadillac was now convinced that the luxury quotient of its cars now made it possible for drivers to extend their time on the road between fill-ups.

Minor, but still noticeable changes for 1962 included incorporation of a heater into Cadillac's standard equipment list and a number of changes in the optional, automatic trunk control, which now had a vacuum-operated release and a mechanical locking system.

DIFFERENCES AMONG MODELS

The three Sixty-Two hardtop models, the Coupe, Sedan, and Town Sedan (the new name for the short-deck Sedan), were available in three cloth interior patterns in eight color combinations. Cotillion cloth, with either matching or harmonizing, coated fabric bolsters, was offered in black, sandalwood, maize, and laurel. Cromwell and Copley cloth (also combined with coated fabrics) were offered in green and gray, respectively.

The Convertible's natural-grain leather interior was offered in white, black, blue, maize, saddle, green, sandalwood, or red. The carpeting, instrument panel, and steering wheel were colored to either harmonize or match the interior. Completing the Convertible's color theme was the coated, fabric-top boot. In place of the standard front bench seat, bucket seats were available on the Convertible at extra cost.

With the exception of the Town Sedan, the Sixty-Two models did not carry exterior body-trim identification. Series Sixty-Two Coupe and Sedan models were the only Cadillacs not fitted with power front-seat adjustment and windows.

Apparently not discouraged by the weak sales of the Town Sedan during 1961, Cadillac added a version to the De Ville line identified as the Park Avenue Sedan de Ville. It was described as "specially designed with a shorter rear deck for easier parking and garaging." Carried over from 1961 were the Sedan de Ville six- and four-window models plus the Coupe de Ville. The addition of the Park Avenue to the De Ville series made for some interesting model nomenclature. Officially, the short-deck De Ville was identified as the Park Avenue Sedan de Ville; and as such, it carried Park Avenue script on its rear fender. Both the four- and six-window Sedan de Villes carried Sedan de Ville script in the same location.

Three cloth upholstery patterns, in combination with natural-grain leather, were offered for the De Ville model's Fleetwood interiors. The eight colors available were black, gray, blue, sandalwood, maize, turquoise, green, and laurel.

Exclusive to the Park Avenue were leather bench seats in white, black, sandalwood, and red. These same choices were available for the Coupe de Ville and four-window Sedan de Ville when equipped with their front bucket-seat option. Standard on all De Villes were power front-seat and window controls, as well as front and rear center armrests (except for the Convertible, which had a front armrest only).

"It is unlikely," said Cadillac, "that any material possession speaks so eloquently of a man's good taste and achievement as does the distinctive Fleetwood Sixty Special Sedan." The Sixty Special was a car that, said Cadillac, "almost writes its owner's biography."

Cadillac also depicted the Sixty Special as a car possessing "correctness of styling," an opinion supported by its appearance. A formal roof line with a reduced-area rear window; five, rather demure chevrons on the C-pillar; a small Fleetwood emblem on the front fender, and a cross-hatched rear-deck grille made the Sixty Special an easy car to identify. The Sixty Special's Fleetwood interior was offered in fabric-leather combinations or all-wool broadcloth.

Depicted as the "industry's most magnificent limited production Convertible," the Eldorado Biarritz was once again based on the Series Sixty-Two Convertible. But with its exclusive exterior trim and interior upholstery choices, the Biarritz was set apart from its less expensive kin. Unlike 1961, when Biarritz script was mounted on the front fender, the latest model carried a Cadillac crest just before the windshield pillar.

1962 Series Sixty-Two Town Sedan.

1962 Series Sixty-Two 6-Window Sedan.

CADILLAC VITAL STATISTICS: 1962

Series	Model	Body Type	Factory Price ($)	Weight (lbs.)	Production (#)
62	6229	4 dr Sedan 6wd	5213	4640	16,730
	6239	4 dr Sedan 4wd	5213	4645	17,314
	6289	4 dr Town Sedan	5213	4590	2600
	6247	2 dr Coupe	5025	4530	16,833
	6267	2 dr Convertible	5588	4630	16,800
DeVille	6329	4 dr Sedan 6wd	5631	4660	16,230
	6339	4 dr Sedan 4wd	5631	4675	27,378
	6389	4 dr Park Avenue Sedan	5631	4655	2600
	6347	2 dr Coupe	5385	4595	25,675
Eldorado	6367	2 dr Convertible	6610	4620	1450
60	6039	4 dr Sedan	6366	4710	13,350
75	6723	4 dr Sedan 9p	9722	5325	696
	6733	4 dr Limousine 9p	9937	5390	904

Extending rearward to the bumper was a thin, chrome trim strip. The Biarritz interior, available with bucket front seats in place of the bench seat at no extra cost, was offered in seven shades of leather as well as a Cannes cloth-and-leather combination.

Completing the Cadillac lineup for 1962 were the two Fleetwood Seventy-Five models—the Sedan and the nine-passenger Limousine. Along with the design changes found on other 1962 Cadillacs, the Series Seventy-Five models also differed from the 1961 versions by the absence of chrome trim along their center door pillars. Interior formats for 1962 were also changed. The driver's compartment on the Limousine was again finished in black or optional fawn and gray to harmonize with that in the rear compartment, which was finished in either cord or broadcloth upholstery.

CADILLAC'S DOMESTIC COMPETITION

As I've noted, both the Lincoln Continental and Imperial were more popular with the public in 1962. Lincoln made only moderate appearance changes, concentrating instead on refinements to enhance its position in the marketplace. Thus, the new models were identified by their front- and rear-grille inserts, which were of a small rectangular design rather than the mesh-type of 1962. The wide center-grille bar was replaced by a simpler and thinner version. Other detail changes included higher, by 1 inch, headlights, narrow-band, white sidewall tires (the older, wide-type was still available), and hubcaps with Lincoln Continental lettering in place of the Continental emblems used in 1961. Convertible models featured top profiles that approximated the squared-off form of the hardtops.

Added to the Lincoln Continental's option list were a number of new items, including remote-control exterior mirrors, automatic headlight dimmer, automatic rear-deck release, electric antenna, and power vent windows, all of which had been earlier offered by Cadillac.

The general manager of the Lincoln-Mercury Division, Ben D. Mills, outlined a strategy that he hoped would bring the Lincoln Continental closer to Cadillac in the public's view. Not surprisingly, he enunciated a policy that Cadillac had been employing for many years: "Change for the sake of change will not be characteristic of this luxury automobile," he said. "Instead of a different looking car each year, our goal is to make changes which will help us build as perfect a luxury automobile as possible."

Surely, this should have been adopted by Imperial years earlier. Rather than expending resources on annual front-end designs that collectively seemed to be a series of grimaces rather than a look of success, while concurrently attempting to blend neo-Ionic shapes and forms with fins that were passé, Chrysler should have strived for the creation of a distinctive "Imperial look."

Belatedly, it came close to this goal in 1962. The fins were finally gone and in their place were simple, rear-fender forms with narrow character lines that flowed into a loop below the rear-deck lid. At their top were taillight elements whose shapes evoked memories of the 1955-1956 model. Side trim was less involved than in 1961, and a divided front grille with thin horizontal bars blended nicely with the free-standing headlights.

Unfortunately, Chrysler, in the early sixties, was in the midst of one of its traumatic passages through management shakeups. In late April 1960, Chrysler President Lester Colbert was replaced by his hand-picked successor, William C. Newberg. He barely had time to settle in when he was forced out 64 days later because of his financial connection with a number of Chrysler component suppliers. What followed was painful to behold. Colbert returned as president, under attack not only by Newberg but by Chrysler stockholders who weren't pleased with Chrysler's big drop in sales and profits in 1961. Eventually Lynn Townsend emerged as Chrysler's president to give the corporation a new sense of direction and purpose that, not incidentally, reaped it some record profits.

Yet this tidal wave of change swept away the chief architect of the Imperial look, Virgil Exner, who was replaced by Elwood P. Engel as Chrysler's styling chief. Engle came to Chrysler from Ford where he had been responsible for the overall design of the 1961 Lincoln Continental. An Imperial cast in the mold of a Lincoln Continental was in Chrysler's future.

SPECIFICATIONS

Engine

Type: V-type, ohv, eight cylinders
Bore × stroke: 4.0 × 3.875 inches
Displacement: 390 cubic inches
Horsepower: 325 @ 4,800 rpm
Torque: 430 lb-ft @ 3,400 rpm
Compression ratio: 10.5:1
Carburetor: Carter four-barrel
Electrical system: 12-volt
Transmission: Hydra-Matic, three-speed automatic; controlled fluid coupling on forward gear set, two drive ranges, low range, and reverse.

Chassis/Drivetrain

Frame: Tubular-center X-frame
Rear axle:
    Hypoid offset differential: 2.94:1 ratio, 3.21:1 optional
    Air-conditioned models: 3.21:1 axle
    Standard Series 75 ratio: 3.36:1, 3.77 optional
Front suspension: Spherical joints with independent helical-coil springs, rubber-mounted strut rods and rubber bushings
Rear suspension: Four-link drive, helical-coil springs and rubber bushings
Steering: Power steering with overall ratio of 18.2:1, turning angle of 38.5°
Tires: Low-pressure, 4-ply tubeless, 8.00 × 15
    Series 75: 6-ply, 8.20 × 15, white sidewall tires
    Optional: 8.22 × 15 (standard for Biarritz)

Dimensions

Wheelbase: 129.5 inches
    Series 75:   149.75 inches
Width: 79.8 inches
Front/rear tread: 61/61 inches
Overall length: 222 inches
    Town Sedan and Park Avenue Sedan: 215 inches
    Series 75:   242.3 inches

Popular Options

Cruise control
Six-way power seats
Power Ventpanes: Standard on Eldorado Biarritz,
front and rear on Sixty Special
Fog lamps
Signal-seeking radio
Seat belts (all Cadillacs had built-in anchoring)
Air conditioning
Power door locks
Controlled differential
Rear-window defogger
Soft-ray glass
Power headlight control
Power deck-lid lock
Cushion toppers
Door-guards (stainless steel door-edge guards)
License-plate frames

1963

Can a Cadillac Surpass Its Own Great Reputation?

"CAN A CADILLAC surpass its own great reputation?" Those were the opening words of Cadillac's 1963 showroom brochure. Before the reader had time to ponder the question, Cadillac quickly supplied the answer: "The 1963 Cadillac does just that. In beauty . . . in luxury . . . in performance." That this was more than just another example of the hype found in most sales literature is indicted by *Car Life* magazine's conclusion after testing a Series Sixty-Two Park Avenue that the Cadillac was as fine a car as any currently available.

These views were bolstered by Cadillac's model-year production. For the second successive year, the division established a new output record. For 1963, Cadillac production reached 163,174. This was clearly the start of a great Golden Age for Cadillac since in each successive model year until 1971 production would exceed the mark of the previous year.

CHANGES AND IMPROVEMENTS

Literally powering Cadillac into this streak of production records and unequaled popularity was a new V-8 engine. The old engine had reached the point where, if its performance was still laudatory, the outer limits of its development had been breached. No doubt, it was an engine that many at Cadillac parted with reluctantly. Its place in automotive history was both secure and dramatic. As the engine that opened the American market to a new level of quiet, smooth operation in conjunction with performance that cast previous standards aside with ease, the original Cadillac V-8 knew no equals. When first introduced, it produced 160 horsepower from 331 cubic inches. Fourteen years later, it was displacing 390 cubic inches and developing 325 horsepower; put another way, a 103 percent in horsepower with an increase in displacement of 21 percent.

A production life of nearly a decade and a half was a long one for any engine, however, and just about everyone at Cadillac involved in engine engineering and production knew the time was at hand to take advantage of technological developments to move Cadillac's high standard of operation to even loftier levels.

This outlook provided the basis for the design objectives established for the new Cadillac engine; improved product quality via the use of the latest machine and tool design, and a design responsive to the significant boosts in compression ratio and power that were anticipated in the future.

Whether it was because America had become so inured to the arrival of new V-8s or because of the superficial similarity of the new Cadillac V-8 to the old model, the debut of the latest engine from Cadillac attracted only a relatively modest amount of attention. Cadillac described it as a "greatly refined" engine; but beyond references to its lighter weight and quieter and smoother operation, it seemed content to leave matters at that. Perhaps it felt its customers were content to trust its good judgment and didn't need any detailed engineering analysis to convince them of the new V-8's statue.

Although the new V-8 used the same 4.0-inch bore and 3.875-inch stroke, as well as identical 4.625-inch bore centers as its predecessor, the only components interchangeable between them were their valves, rocker arms, cylinder heads, and connecting rods. An entirely new cylinder block was used that contributed to the assembled engine's more compact dimensions. Compared with the 1962 V-8, the new model was 1 inch lower, 4 inches narrower, and 1.188 inches shorter.

The major factor in reducing the engine's length was the mounting of the water, fuel, and oil pumps along with the oil filter and distributor at the engine's front on aluminum die-castings. In addition, this arrangement improved accessibility and yielded a 30-pound weight saving. Not as obvious, but also contributing to the engine's reduced length was the use of the third rather than the fifth main bearing to accept the crankshaft bearing thrust. This shortened the

117

crankshaft and allowed use of a simpler and more effective rear oil seal. Instrumental in lowering engine height were the use of shorter, by 0.5 inch, pistons, which reduced the necessary deck height and 0.445-inch lower head gasket faces. A new over-under intake manifold helped matters by dropping the level of the carburetor. The new pistons, which were, at 20.48 ounces, slightly lighter than before, followed the old design but had the heat-dam groove removed. In turn, they required shorter pushrods, which meant a narrower engine.

A much higher level of strength and rigidity was achieved for the engine block by changing the walls, bulk heads, and reinforcing ribs. Cadillac had its own foundry for pouring engine blocks and, for many years, had been turning out what were fashionably called in the sixties "thin-wall" castings. When the block for the 1963 engine was fully machined, it weighed 142.86 pounds which compared favorably with the 173.75-pound weight of the old block.

Riding in the lighter block was an entirely new crankshaft whose five bearings now measured 3 inches rather than the previous 2.625 inches. Normally the resulting increase in rigidity and resistance to flexing came at the cost of substantially increased internal friction, but Cadillac reported this was not the case with the new V-8. Weighing 59 pounds, or 11 pounds less than that of the 1962 engine, this crank was constructed of GM Arma steel with cored holes through the main-bearing journals. The crank pins were solid, but the two end pins were drilled out, and counterweights smaller than those used on most V-8s were used.

Cadillac promised its customers that the new V-8 was "quieter and smoother in operation then ever before." This was achieved by careful attention to the details of engine assembly and production. For example, bearing clearances were, at 0.004-inch per inch of diameter, among the closest in the world. The overall accuracy of mating parts, cylinder bore alignment, and surface finishing was to similarly high standards. In practice, the new engine made good on Cadillac's promise but the general consensus was that its exhaust note was just a bit more audible than those of recent models.

This noise really was of little consequence or concern. What was more important was its inherent responsiveness to future expansions and power increases. In its initial stage, this engine's displacement, torque, and horsepower were identical to those of the final version of the original Cadillac ohv V-8. Down the road it would be expanded to 500 cubic inches to become the world's largest displacement engine with a great future ahead of it!

New for Cadillac (but old hat for Chrysler Corporation, which had started using an alternator in 1960) was a Delcotron alternator. The normal unit had a 45-ampere output, but cars with air conditioning had 52-ampere versions. In either case, this change provided improved electric output and reduced weight.

Cadillac's efforts to reduce road noise were concentrated on what it described as its "true-center drive line." Cadillac claimed that "the advanced design and precision assembly of this unit isolate and cancel vibrations and driving impulses." The basis of Cadillac's boast was a new two-piece drive shaft divided by a double, constant-velocity universal joint. The rear section of the drive shaft was far shorter than the front and was not adversely affected by change in the car's passenger or luggage load.

The most apparent change in the appearance of the new Cadillacs was the forward extension of the front fenders by 4⅝ inches. Nineteen sixty-three was a year when Cadillac's front-end design was in transition from one styling motif to another. Thus, the center divider bar (which was on the way out) was joined by a multiplane grille (which was on the way in). Playing backup to these two themes were the familiar egg-crate grille bars. Once again, the area directly below the headlights became part of the grille and carried small circular parking lights. This change made 1963 the first year since 1955 that Cadillac's front bumper did not contain auxiliary lights of some sort.

Speculation that Cadillac might soon abandon its tail fins was widespread as it once again lowered their height. Their presence was further deemphasized by the abandonment of the clever white/red-lense arrangement after just one year of use. In its place, Cadillac stacked the stop/taillights above the backup lights in vertical nacelles. Their much larger size made the slender tail fin lights clearly the junior partners in Cadillac's rear lighting arrangement.

Added to Cadillac's list of optional equipment were a number of new items, including a six-position adjustable steering wheel. Adjustments were made by lifting a lever on the left side of the steering column, moving the wheel up or down to the desired angle, then releasing the lever to lock the wheel in the desired position. Also debuting in 1963 was an AM-FM transistor radio option in addition to the older AM model. On this point, Cadillac was both trailing and leading Lincoln, which had offered a transistorized radio in 1961, but not an AM-FM model until 1963. Cadillac also simplified the controls of its air-conditioning system (which had been installed on well over half of all 1962 Cadillacs). A single control panel provided a range of temperature choices from very cool to very warm.

Cadillac offered enough options (143 interior options alone were available—an all-time record) and accessories that it reported the 1963 model could be built in so many variations during a ten-year period that there wouldn't be a single duplication.

The longer front fenders, along with the toned-down rear-fender fins, gave the 1963 Cadillacs an appearance very close to that of the 1959-1960 Eldorado Brougham. Also contributing to this impression was the virtual elimination of all side-body contours. The grille retained its gridwork and center dividing bar, but the higher placement of the headlights, side-grille extensions, and positioning of small, circular parking lights directly below the headlights, rather than in the bumper, added up to a new and very clean front-end appearance.

DIFFERENCES AMONG MODELS

All Series Sixty-Two models, except for the Convertible, were available in interiors of Carelton, Claridge, and Caravelle fabrics, in narrow piping with smooth bolsters and trim. Color choices included gray, dark blue, light blue, sandalwood, rose, turquoise, green, and a black and white combination.

For the Convertible, which, like other 1963 Cadillacs, was offered in 16 exterior colors, eight leather interiors with either matching or contrasting trim and carpet were available. The Convertible's seat combined a biscuit design and deeply recessed buttons with smooth bolsters.

This was the final year for the Park Avenue Sedan de Ville model. Cadillac promoted this model as "a handsome choice for town and country motoring . . . . For no more gracious and luxurious town car exists in the world than this elegant Cadillac creation." But apparently the combination of the same interior room as other De Ville models with a shorter rear deck wasn't what most Cadillac buyers were interested in. For the model year, only 1,575 of these short-deck models were produced.

Like the four- and six-window Sedan de Villes and Coupe de Ville models, the Park Avenue carried model script identification at the extreme end of the rear fenders. Also distinguishing the De Villes from the standard Series Sixty-Two models were the ribbed panels for their rear-deck-bumper inserts. Those on the Sixty-Two versions were smooth. All De Ville interiors were available in a choice of Cambria, Clarendon, or Cameo cloth patterns, joined with leather trim in eight color selections. Also offered were all-leather seats and trim in white, black, sandalwood, or red. Both the front and rear seats had Cadillac crests embossed just above the center armrest. A tufted-biscuit-recessed-button design, in conjunction with smooth bolsters was used for all De Villes.

"Among all the manufactured products of man," said Cadillac, "few can claim the excellence of design, dedication of assembly, and universal acceptance that is accorded the Eldorado Biarritz." As a limited production (only 1,825 were produced in 1963) and expensive ($6,609) automobile, the Biarritz was, in its styling, closely related to that other Cadillac prestigious heavyweight, the Series Sixty Special Sedan. Neither car carried any side-body trim save for broad, full-length, rocker-panel brightwork and a Fleetwood emblem on their rear fenders. Also shared by both cars was a cross-hatched, rear-deck insert. No trunk-lid ornamentation was used for either car. Eldorado block lettering was mounted on the Biarritz's right side lid, while the Sixty Special carried Fleetwood lettering in the same location. A nice touch was the use of wheel covers with inner surfaces color-keyed to the body.

The Biarritz's grained-leather interior was offered in eight colors, and customers could select two "individual sports-type" front seats in place of the regular three-passenger, full-width seat. If the former were selected, a center-mounted console could be installed. In either case, the Biarritz seats had narrow pipings embraced by raised side bolsters. Door and side panels carried wood-grain inserts.

In addition to the points of interest already mentioned, the Sixty Special was distinguished

1963 Series Sixty-Two Convertible

1963 Coupe de Ville. Its framed-in rear window was 38% smaller in area than the 1962 version.

1963 Series Sixty-Two 4-Window Sedan.

CADILLAC VITAL STATISTICS: 1963

Series	Model	Body Type	Factory Price ($)	Weight (lbs.)	Production (#)
62	6229	4 dr Sedan 6wd	5214	4610	12,929
	6239	4 dr Sedan 4wd	5214	4595	16,980
	6257	2 dr Coupe	5026	4505	16,786
	6267	2 dr Convertible	5590	4545	17,600
De Ville	6329	4 dr Sedan 6wd	5633	4650	15,146
	6339	4 dr Sedan 4wd	5633	4605	30,579
	6389	4 dr Park Avenue Sedan	5633	4590	1575
	6357	2 dr Coupe	5386	4520	31,749
Eldorado	6367	2 dr Convertible	6608	4640	1825
60	6039	4 dr Sedan	6366	4690	14,000
75	7523	4 dr Sedan 9p	9724	5240	680
	7533	4 dr Limousine	9939	5300	795

externally by the five chevrons positioned in its C-roof pillar. Interiors were offered in leather, fabric, and leather or soft wool broadcloth. All were color coordinated.

The Series Seventy-Five Limousine and nine-passenger Sedan continued to use the old-style panoramic windshield, which other Cadillac models had abandoned after the 1960 model year. Also unique to the Series Seventy-Five models, among the 1963 Cadillacs, was their pillared sedan style. None of these factors detracted from the extremely clean styling of the Series Seventy-Five, which was characterized by the sweep of its narrow, full-body-length side trim.

The Sedan's interior in either cord or broadcloth was available in black, beige, or gray. The Limousine's driver compartment was finished in leather.

CADILLAC'S DOMESTIC COMPETITION

While Cadillac production was up by 2,334 cars for the 1963 model year, the levels for Lincoln Continental and Imperial remained almost unchanged. Imperial's took a slight dip to 14,108 from 14,337, with Lincoln Continental production edging up just 172 units to 31,233.

In style, the Imperial showed off the first influence of Chrysler's new styling boss, Elwood P. Engel. The full force of his impact would be felt in 1964, but already the Imperial's rounded, flowing lines were giving way to sharper edges and squared-off corners. Still in use were the free-standing headlights and rear-deck pseudospare-tire cover. This latter feature was to have a life of its own under Engel, who made it a prime styling feature of this 1964 "Continentalized" Imperial. Swept away, however, were the Imperial's gun-sight rear lights and the divided grille scheme of 1962. The latter feature was replaced by an equally attractive arrangement of horizontal bars with thin, vertical spaces surrounding a prominent Imperial emblem. In total, this was quite impressive and original.

The demise of the Imperial's distinctive rear lights was more difficult to accept. True, their demise was in line with Chrysler's move to disassociate itself from fins, but their elimination cost Imperial one of its most unique styling features. In their place were thin, vertical taillights that were uncomfortably close in form to those found on 1963 Valiants. That must have made owners of two-door V-100 Valiants happy. It's not likely that owners of an $8,000 LeBaron Imperial shared the same degree of exuberance.

Still arousing murmurs of discontent was the Imperial's squared-off steering wheel, which forced drivers to adjust to a wheel which measured 14.7 inches at its narrowest before growing to 17.7 inches. This type of gimmickry was in contrast to the Imperial's use of flared brake drums that increased effective brake lining from 251 to 287 square inches and revised suspension strut-wheel stops that permitted a 3-degree increase in the front wheels' arch of motion. In turn, this reduced the Imperial's turning circle to 47.5 feet.

Other technical changes for 1963 included a rear-wheel, parking-brake system in place of the older transmission unit and a lever, mounted to the left of the transmission push buttons that locked the transmission in Park. Imperial also introduced an automatic parking-brake release. This system, which followed by two years a similar Cadillac setup, set engine vacuum to disengage the step-on emergency brake when the transmission was placed in Drive. No significant changes were made to Imperial's 413-cubic-inch V-8, which continued to produce 340 horsepower at 4,600 rpm.

Imperial, along with the other Chrysler-built automobiles, had a five-year, 50,000-mile warranty that, along with use of aluminized steel in the exhaust system and greater anticorrosion techniques, helped the corporation earn nearly $162 million in 1963, an all-time record.

At long last the Lincoln Continental had broken the curse that had affected all but one previous postwar efforts to establish a bastion deep in Cadillac territory that could serve as a springboard for future assaults on Number One's position, namely a decline in sales in the years following introduction of a new body style. The reason was deceptively simple. Lincoln had established a visual identity of its own that did not quickly become dated, and backed it by an equally obvious commitment to quality. After achieving these goals, Lincoln then had the good sense not to tamper with the basic elements of success.

As a result, the latest Lincoln Continental differed visually only in details from its immediate predecessor. The grille used a mesh insert with bold vertical bars; directional lights were amber colored, and the rear deck was raised to provide a much-needed increase in luggage space. For the first time since the introduction of the Lincoln Continental, the rear grille insert differed in form from that at the front of the car.

Like the Imperial, which gained an additional 4.5 inches of rear leg room thanks to a new roof line, the Lincoln Continental's rear-seat occupants found accommodations slightly more commodious than before. A modest increase in front knee room was also provided.

Lincoln's V-8 remained the industry's largest. Changes in piston and combustion-chamber design and the return of a four-barrel carburetor after an absence of four years (it had been dropped for the 1960 models) resulted in a horsepower increase to 320 at 4,800 rpm. This made the Lincoln Continental a fairly strong performer, accelerating from zero to sixty mph in approximately 11 seconds. Accompanying this improvement was the installation of the flared, aluminum brake drums on all models instead of just convertibles as had been previous policy.

The emergence of the Lincoln Continental as a stable challenger to Cadillac wasn't the only change occurring in the luxury-car field in the early sixties. Historically, the Ford Mustang, introduced in April 1964, is given credit for being the first car fully exploiting the emerging youth market of the sixties. But a year earlier, both Pontiac with its Grand Prix model and, to a lesser degree, Oldsmobile with its Starfire, had shown that the market previously targeted for the original four-seater Ford Thunderbird was also very broad, very substantial, and very lucrative.

Now at the lower part of its traditional price spectrum, Cadillac was in competition with a number of cars whose style and performance were clearly intended to appeal to relatively young and affluent car buyers. It took only a limited awareness of market trends to conclude that at the upper end of Cadillac's price range there might also be buyers lurking, eager to pay premium prices for personal-luxury automobiles with room for four passengers and their luggage.

As had been the case in the past, both Cadillac and Lincoln, but sad to say, not Chrysler, began to prepare for entry into this new field. Their efforts wouldn't be visible for a few years. The time would pass quickly, though, as each attempted to refine their existing models to place them in the strongest possible position to enter a new phase of the luxury-car wars.

SPECIFICATIONS

Engine

Type: V-type, ohv, eight cylinders
Bore x stroke: 4.0 x 3.875 inches
Displacement: 390 cubic inches
Horsepower: 325 @ 4,800 rpm
Torque: 430 lb-ft @ 3,400 rpm
Compression ratio: 10.5:1
Carburetor: Rochester 4-barrel, model 710930
Electrical system: 12-volt

Transmission: Hydra-Matic, three-speed automatic; controlled fluid coupling on forward gear set, two drive ranges, low range, and reverse

Chassis/Drivetrain

Frame: Tubular-center X-frame
Rear axle: Hypoid, offset differential, Standard ratio: 2.94:1, 3.21:1 optional;
Air-conditioned cars: 3.21:1 standard
Series 75 standard ratio: 3.30:1, 3.77:1 optional
Front suspension: Independent with spherical joints, helical coil springs, rubber-mounted strut rods, rubber bushings
Rear suspension: Four-link drive with helical-coil springs and rubber joints
Steering: Power steering with overall ratio of 18.2:1, turning angle of 38.5°
Tires: Low-pressure, 4-ply, tubeless, 8.00 x 15
Series 75: 6-ply, 8.20 x 15
Whitewall tires, 8.20 x 15 optional

Dimensions

Wheelbase: 129.5 inches
Series 75: 149.75 inches
Front/rear tread: 61/61 inches
Overall length: 223 inches
Park Avenue Sedan: 215 inches
Series 75: 243.3 inches

1964

More Tempting Than Ever

THE SHIFTING ABOUT of the luxury-car market, if not strong enough to send little more than minor seismic shocks throughout its foundation, necessitated a reevaluation of what exactly was a luxury car. One of the industry's prime source of data, R.L. Polk & Co., suggested that the traditional "Big-Three" concept (Cadillac, Lincoln, and Chrysler) was now obsolete, by arbitrarily stating that any car with a suggested list price of $4,101 or higher was a luxury car. Quite a few cars then crossed into that field, including the Oldsmobile Starfire, Ford Thunderbird, Studebaker Avanti, Chevrolet Corvette, Chrysler New Yorker, and Buick Riviera.

Cadillac general manager Harold G. Warner, in early 1963, had redefined Cadillac's perception of the fine-car field by including any car with a price above $5,000. During 1963, Cadillac made a study of the high-income class that was its home base and, in Warner's words, concluded, "The heart of the Cadillac market, people who earn more than $20,000 per year, is growing rapidly." This trend was so strong that Cadillac estimated its size would increase from 866,000 in 1959 to 960,000 in 1964, and by 1965 would exceed the one million mark.

By reshaping Cadillac's market, Warner also was changing Cadillac's status from the market's dominant force to that of a major player, since its share of the market fell from 64 percent to 32 percent. This was expected to sharpen the skills of Cadillac salesmen, while focusing Cadillac's attention, from Warner down through the ranks, on the buyers of what were now regarded as Cadillac's competitors as a new source of sales. These were people, in Warner's view, who were paying a Cadillac price but not getting a Cadillac.

Warner's basic strategy to push Cadillac sales higher than ever had three key components. The first was, of course, to develop the capacity to produce enough cars to supply that market. This resulted in a $55 million expansion program. Cadillac also was determined to move out of the old, established pattern of marketing its cars through a series of distributors.

Overall, the industry had moved away from this system to one involving factory zone offices. The first stage of this transition took place in 1958 when the first Cadillac zone office, in Oklahoma City, was opened. By 1960, Cadillac entered into its final five year contract with its distributors; and in July 1962, a new sales manager, Lee N. Mays, came over from Chevrolet, where he had been assistant sales manager.

Mays, although coming to Cadillac with firsthand knowledge of virtually every aspect of sales operation at Chevrolet, was not expected to pattern Cadillac's zone system after Chevrolet's. Instead, his basic task was to bring Cadillac's staid sales system unto a higher plane of aggressive operation leading to increased sales satisfaction and improved merchandising.

Next came a move that required a steady, calm hand at the helm. One result of the nation's technologic explosion was both a challenge and an opportunity for Cadillac: the existence of a potential market of highly paid scientists and engineers. They could obviously afford a Cadillac; but since they were younger, they were attracted to cars with a youthful image. Warner's task was to hold onto Cadillac's conservative design, which had evolved into an extremely attractive automobile for its traditional customers, while reaching out to the new class of young affluents.

This new outlook was apparent in Cadillac's advertising campaign for its new models which went on sale October 3, 1963. Both in ad copy and layout, the appeal was to youth and performance. This wasn't, of course, nearly as blatant as promotions for Detroit's super cars such as the GTO, but the ads showed younger men and women and far fewer individuals with gray hair. Even the settings of the ads began to change toward an accent on youth.

CHANGES AND IMPROVEMENTS

Cadillac wasn't about to become the rage of the nation's drag strip; but it was, thanks to a new automatic transmission and a large, more powerful engine, ready to assume a clear margin of performance superiority over its peers. The path to increased torque and horsepower was an easy one. Having successfully launched its new engine the year before, Cadillac now increased its displacement 10 percent to 429 cubic inches by use of a 4.13-inch bore, up 0.125 inches from 1963, and a larger 4-inch instead of a 3.875-inch stroke. No change was made in valve size (1.875 inch diameter for intake, 1.50-inch diameter for exhaust), although the cam was slightly altered. The single exhaust system was carried over, but now used slightly larger-diameter tubing. With a 10.5:1 compression ratio and a Carter AFB, four-barrel carburetor (a Rochester unit was used in 1963), the Cadillac engine produced 340 horsepower at 4,000 rpm. Maximum torque was 480 lb-ft at 3,000 rpm.

Retained for use by the Series Sixty-Two and Fleetwood Seventy-Five models was the three-speed Hydra-Matic, improved via increased cooling and a stronger reverse gear. The remaining Cadillacs were equipped with a new Turbo Hydra-Matic, which from virtually every viewpoint was a vastly superior transmission. For starters, it weighed less, just 168 pounds, some 30 pounds less than Hydra-Matic. A key contributor to this weight reduction was the use of a die-cast aluminum casing.

The new transmission essentially was a Hydra-Matic gear box linked to a torque converter. This remedied two basic shortcomings of the older model: its relative complexity and high manufacturing costs. By virtue of the torque converter, the Turbo Hydra-Matic shifted smoother and experienced no "blind spots," where the car's speed was too high for one gear and too low for another.

Among the numerous desirable features of this transmission was an altitude compensator involving an aneroid-bellows arrangement, which expanded or contracted with changes in altitude. In turn, this activated a valve adjusting transmission-line pressure. Also introduced on this transmission was a kickdown system using electrical switches and a solenoid to shift gears rather than the older setup of mechanical rods and levers.

Combined with Cadillac's 340-horsepower engine, Turbo Hydra-Matic gave the 1964 models performance unmatched by either Lincoln or Imperial. Both *Motor Trend* (March 1964) and *Car Life* (July 1964) reported 0- to 60-mph times of 8.5 seconds with what was apparently the same Sedan de Ville with a 3.21:1 axle ratio (cars without air conditioning had 2.94:1 axles). *Car Life* extended its acceleration data up to 100 mph and reported the Cadillac could attain that speed from rest in just 23.5 seconds. Identical standing-start quarter-mile speeds of 86 mph were reported, but *Car Life*'s time of 16.4 seconds was slightly better. Similarly, the Cadillac in the hands of the *Car Life* staff reached a higher top speed of 121 mph compared to *Motor Trend's*, mark of 115 mph. Although *Car Life*'s enthusiasm was a bit more muted than *Motor Trend's*, both publications praised Cadillac's performance as far beyond that normally associated with a large, luxury automobile.

These words of praise were joined by favorable comments from England's *The Autocar*, which carried a road test of a Coupe de Ville in its August 7, 1964, issue. Its test crew loved the smooth, seemingly limitless flow of power from its engine and excellent handling and stability.

The Autocar also praised the Cadillac's high-speed stability, resistance to cross winds, and ability to corner rapidly without an excessive amount of body roll. Back in the United States, *Motor Trend* and *Car Life* reached similar conclusions. Both publications regarded Cadillac as the class act among American luxury cars in this respect.

All three magazines were far less happy with the performance of Cadillac's brakes. They continued to be finned, cast-iron drums measuring 12 × 2.5 inches front and rear, with a total swept area of 378 square inches. *Motor Trend* reported they could sustain only two maximum stop tests from 115 mph before fading completely. In the hands of *Car Life* testers, the Cadillac survived only one 80 mph to 0 stop. *The Autocar* also found them fully extended after just one stop from maximum speed.

Better brakes were part of Cadillac's future; but in 1964, the future had arrived as far as state-of-the-art air conditioning was concerned. Cadillac modestly called it Comfort Control and just stood back as the words of praise for this very advanced air-conditioning unit poured in.

The goal of this system, the maintenance of a constant interior temperature regardless of outside conditions, was achieved with such efficiency that a Cadillac owner could, by operating just two controls, enjoy an unvarying driving environment for the full term of ownership.

Essentially, Comfort Control combined the heating and air-conditioning units into one inter-responsive system. One control enabled the operator to select any temperature on a dial reading from 65° to 85°. A second sliding lever had four settings: High-Low Blower and High-Low Defroster. The system would then function automatically (if just a bit noisily) as needed. Air entering the interior was either warmed or cooled and passed through a dehumidifer as demanded by a sensing valve. Behind the scenes, three "thermistors," positioned at the outlet of the heater/air-conditioning unit as well as other locations both in and out of the car, monitored temperature changes. When a change took place, a voltage charge was fed to a two-transistor amplifier, which boosted the voltage and sent it to a transducer. This unit was a 10-inch steel tube containing a single strand of heat-sensitive wire, which either expanded or contracted to cause a needle valve at the end of the tube to open or close. A power servo was then activated to open or close the door of the comfort system. In addition, the power servo also controlled the blower speed and the location inside the car where the incoming air would be discharged. If maximum cooling was called for, the servo also shut off water flow to the heater core.

More visible, if less sensational than Comfort Control, was Cadillac's new Twilight Sentinel option, which incorporated three photo cells to automatically turn on the headlights at dusk and turn them off at dawn when, of course, the engine was running. Its control was adjustable for sensitivity and included a delay action that kept the headlights on for up to 90 seconds after the ignition was switched off.

Also offered for the first time was a factory-installed, rear-window defogger. Improving the responsiveness of the power-window system was a deactivator switch, enabling the driver to override individual window switches in case of an emergency. Improving the neat appearance of the Cadillac dash was the moving of the automatic, headlight-dimming photo cell to the left headlight hood, where it was incorporated in the trim strip.

If Cadillac was determined to enhance its reputation for technical prowess with these engineering developments, it also seemed equally willing to slow down its styling evolution to a crawl. This was hardly a disadvantage as Cadillac was maintaining an appearance that was difficult to criticize and extremely appealing to its clientele. By this time, it was clear that its tailfins were steadily shrinking toward oblivion. But the process was slow, deliberate, and measured, with their height for 1964 reduced by 1 inch. Also evident was a flatter rear deck and a reformed grille that had been brought forward more on a single plane then previously and divided into two sections by a horizontal strip painted in the body color. Cadillac's front end was now very clean, free from excessive trim, and extremely well coordinated. The traditional Cadillac crest and V was the only adornment on the hood. The twin fender spears, while ornamental, also served as receptacles for the directional signal indicators. The grille design was of timeless simplicity, the simple egg-crate form that had become almost the hallmark of a Cadillac. For 1964, even Cadillac's front parking/directional lights, for so long, objects whose shape and position had been changed as part of the annual model change, became part of the grille work. Now the parking/directionals were hidden behind extensions of the grille, to be seen only when in use.

Having gone nearly full circle from the extreme (1959) to the sublime (1964), Cadillac would not abandon the look inherited from the 1960 Eldorado Brougham until 1969; and then it would again borrow, not from an outside source, but rather from a sensational new model bearing its name, the 1967 Fleetwood Eldorado.

Measured either in terms of production or by the remarks of critics, Cadillac had clearly moved onto a new plateau of excellence in 1964. Model-year production was up moderately to 165,959—a small gain of 2,825 cars, but a new record nonetheless.

The expression of praise for the 1964 Cadillac had a genuine ring of admiration for what seemed to be a newly discovered (or perhaps previously underrated) example of automotive excellence. *Motor Trend*, which had tested virtually all the world's luxury cars, considered, on a dollar-value basis, the Cadillac as the hands-down winner in terms of quality, comfort, and overall performance. *Car Life*, which brought a strong European orientation to its evaluation of American automobiles, admitted that its initial perception of the Cadillac was of a vastly overrated status symbol. But at road-test end, it had adopted a different view. Then it considered the latest Cadillac as the physical manifestation of the famous 1911 Cadillac "Penalty of Leadership" advertisement. Being the leader decreed that the Cadillac was subjected to a hypercritical evaluation by *Car Life*, which admitted to having been very impressed by the competence and quality of its test car.

The Autocar also positioned its evaluation of the 1964 Cadillac in an historical perspective. In its view, the latest Cadillac was, like the earliest single-cylinder models, a car whose construction put a premium on quality.

DIFFERENCES AMONG MODELS

The three Series Sixty-Two models (Coupe, four- and six-window Sedans), as in 1963, did not carry an exterior series identification. All three were equipped with a rear center, folding armrest; rear corner reading lights, front courtesy and map lights; electric clock; and visor vanity mirror. Except for the Coupe, two front and two rear cigarette lighters were installed.

Two interior cloth patterns, either Dusmuir or Doncaster, in combination with a coated fabric, were offered in seven color combinations.

As was its practice, Cadillac touted the competitiveness of the Sixty-Two Series in its price class. It was priced, Cadillac noted, "favorably with many models of smaller, less respected cars . . . and actually surpasses them in economy, dependability, and long-lasting value."

The De Ville Series was reduced to four body styles—Convertible, Coupe, and four- and six-window Sedans—with the dropping of the Park Avenue Sedan de Ville for 1964. Once again, all versions carried specific model script on the extreme end of their rear fenders except for the Convertible, which was fitted with De Ville identification.

Convertible interiors with perforated leather in the seat and seat-back inserts were available in nine color combinations. Both the Convertible and Coupe de Ville were available with leather trim and bucket seats. Also offered for the Coupe de Ville were two fabric patterns in eight colors. The Sedan models could be upholstered in either Dover or Dorchester cloth with harmonizing leather trim. Eight color selections were offered.

Cadillac revamped its Fleetwood Series for 1964 to include four models: the Eldorado Convertible, Sixty Special Sedan, and the Limousine and Sedan Series Seventy-Five versions. The inclusion of the Eldorado Convertible in the Fleetwood series and the corresponding elimination of the Eldorado Biarritz was, if more an exercise in semantics than a change of substance, an overdue development. For too long, the Eldorado had been, in spite of its limited production and top-flight appointments, classified as a Series Sixty-Two model. Placing it among the Fleetwoods made much more sense.

1964 De Ville Convertible.

CADILLAC VITAL STATISTICS: 1964

Series	Model	Body Type	Factory Price ($)	Weight (lbs.)	Production (#)
62	6229	4 dr Sedan 6w	5236	4575	9243
	6239	4 dr Sedan 4W	5236	4550	13,670
	6257	2 dr Coupe	5048	4475	12,166
De Ville	6329	4 dr Sedan 6w	5655	4600	14,627
	6339	4 dr Sedan 4w	5655	4575	39,674
	6357	2 dr Coupe	5408	4495	38,195
	6267	2 dr Convertible	5612	4545	17,900
Eldorado	6367	2 dr Convertible	6630	4605	1870
60	6039	4 dr Sedan	6388	4680	14,550
75	7523	4 dr Sedan 9p	9746	5215	617
	7533	4 dr Limousine 9p	9960	5300	808

1964 Series Sixty-Two 4-Window Sedan.

1964 Sedan de Ville 4-Window Sedan.

1964 Series Seventy-Five Limousine.

The most startling feature of the latest Eldorado was the absence of rear fender skirts. Other changes included the removal of the Eldorado lettering from the rear deck in favor of a center-mounted Fleetwood wreath and crest. On all Fleetwoods, the crest swung to one side to provide access to the trunk lock. The interior of perforated leather was offered in any of eight colors. Console and front bucket seats were optional.

The only Fleetwood model to carry body-mounted Fleetwood lettering was the Sixty Special, which had this identification above the burnished chrome molding, running the full body length to integrate with the rear bumper. Another interesting styling twist was the relocation of the Sixty Special's side-body wreath and crest from its 1963 rear location to the rear C-pillar, where chrome chevrons had previously been located.

Highlighting the interior of the Sixty Special as well as the De Ville Convertible was door inserts and a new, flexible, assist handle (also found on the Series Seventy-Five models) of hand-rubbed, imported, African Baku wood paneling. Two cloth patterns, wool broadcloth, and all-leather upholsteries in a wide variety of colors were offered for the Sixty Special.

The Fleetwood Series Seventy-Five models continued to use the old compound-curved windshield and side trim from the 1963 model. Their interiors featured wool broadcloth, cord cloth, or leather. The Limousine's chauffeur compartment was in a harmonizing leather finish.

CADILLAC'S DOMESTIC COMPETITION

The 1964 Imperials were, to no one's surprise, restyled, more popular versions of the previous model. Chrysler, overall, had an excellent year, reaching its highest sales level since 1955. Moreover, this momentum would extend into 1965 when output reached 224,000 for a new Chrysler division mark. Imperial, with its new look, was the darling of the statistician. After all, who couldn't love a car whose production soared by 65 percent, whose early-season sales rate was nearly twice that of a year earlier and that finished the year with its share of the market increased by 50 percent?

Measured in terms of actual cars produced, this imposing paper performance was a bit less impressive. Model-year production of 23,285 was an increase of 9,177 cars over 1963's level, but that still left Imperial trailing Cadillac by 142,674 cars. Since the Chrysler New Yorker series edged into Cadillac's price range, it might seem appropriate to include their output in any Cadillac-Imperial comparison. The only New Yorkers priced competitively with the least expensive Series Sixty-Two Cadillacs were the six- and nine-passenger Town & Country Sedan Wagons, base priced, respectively, at $4,903 and $5,010, and the $5,344 four-door hardtop. Their total output was almost insignificant for comparison purposes.

Cadillac's sales, as well as its calendar-year output, slipped from their 1963 levels. Sales fell 7,595 cars to 151,638, and 6,207 fewer cars were produced in 1964 than in 1963 when 158,528 cars were assembled. One consequence was lower sales per Cadillac dealership.

Sales per outlet fell from 91 in 1963 to 88 in 1964. At the same time, Imperial sales per dealer moved up from 11 to 15, while those of Lincoln Continental increased to 36 from 31 per dealer.

Cadillac's modest downturn was attributed to a month-long strike at General Motors that pushed down total corporate-car output to 3,956,610 units from the 4,077,254 level of 1963. Overall, the industry set a new all-time production mark of 7,745,888, with both Chrysler and Ford enjoying their best production years since 1955.

No doubt, the Imperial's rise in popularity was of concern at Lincoln where output rose only to 32,969. The spector of an Imperial, styled by the same man who was responsible for the 1961 Lincoln Continental, must have been painful to ponder!

The similarity between the Elwood P. Engel-designed Imperial and the Elwood P. Engel-designed Lincoln Continental was apparent in their roof lines, rear window shape, chrome fender strips, and inboard grille-mounted headlights. Furthermore, the Imperial's front bumper form, with its prominent upward thrust into the forward edge of the fenders, revealed a Lincoln parentage. Even in details, the Imperial mimicked the Lincoln Continental look. For example, since 1961, a Continental logo had been placed on the rear C-pillar of Lincoln Continental Sedans. Guess what Engel put on the 1964 Imperials?

To be sure, there were enough differences between the two cars to save the Imperial from appearing as a Lincoln Continental clone. At the front, the two-piece grille of 1962 was resurrected; and at the rear, Engel blended his conception of a spare-tire mount into the Imperial's squared-off deck. Left at that, this would have been a neat, if not exactly original shape suggestive of the Continental Mark II. But Engel didn't stop there. Instead he added what was viewed as a propeller-shaped appendage enclosing the Imperial's rear lights and serving as an integral part of the bumper. This left a great deal to be desired. The pseudo-tire cover was little more than a design cliché that went out in 1956 (it was a big deal on Nash and Hudson models that year); and as far as the pusher-propeller was concerned, the sooner it was removed, the better. That didn't happen until 1967.

In essence, Imperial was buying short-run gains at the expense of a solid foundation for future expansion. Ten years later, Imperial production would total 14,426, or barely more than half of what it had been in 1964. Lincoln's would be 93,985, some two and a half times that of 1964. Cadillac's output, after reaching a record 304,839 in 1973, dropped back to 242,220 in 1974.

Lincoln Continental's strong suit in 1964 was its appearance—it was almost identical to that of the 1961 model. Of course, progress at Lincoln had not stood still. The 1964 version of the Lincoln Continental was far more refined than its 1961 counterpart and substantially improved over 1963. The most significant development was a longer, by 3 inches, 126-inch wheelbase, in conjunction with wider rear doors and revamped upper body or greenhouse section. The curved side glass of previous years was superseded by straight glass. The tumble-home angle (the angle between the body beltline and roof) was decreased from 23.5 degrees to 14 degrees, and the roofline was raised by half an inch. The net result was more front and rear hip and head room, plus expanded rear knee and leg room. Also enlarged was the Lincoln Continental's luggage capacity.

Modest exterior changes included wheel covers with Continental emblems, a more apparent front grille mesh and a modification of the rear grille work to include dual bumper inserts. Technical improvements included an automatic parking-brake release, a longer, 20-inch wiper blade, heavier axle gear and 15-inch tires.

Interiors were almost completely revised, with a more elegant dash layout, with trip odometer, fuel warning light, and integral air-conditioning outlets. For the first time, an automatic parking-brake release was used on the Lincoln Continental.

The bulk of Lincoln Continental sales continued to be of the four-door hardtop Sedans. Of 36,297 cars sold, just 3,328 were Convertibles.

With Cadillac's larger engine and new transmission making it the easy winner in any three-way performance contest, the only issue left to decide was who would be second. *Car Life's* test of all three luxury cars credited them with identical top speeds of 121 mph. In acceleration, the Lincoln Continental finished second to Cadillac in the standing-start quarter mile with a speed of 78 mph. The Imperial, though trailing behind at 75 mph in this contest, easily out-paced the Lincoln Continental's 0- to 60-mph time of 11.8 seconds with a mark of 10.4 seconds.

Nineteen sixty-four had been a year when all three luxury-car manufacturers could find good news in their sales summaries. But only one was just three model years away from establishing what once was considered impossible, the output of 200,000 automobiles. In the interim, Cadillac would set two more model-year records and, in 1965, do what had once been unthinkable—abandon its tail fins.

SPECIFICATIONS

Engine

Type: V-type, ohv, 8 cylinders
Bore × Stroke: 4.13 × 4.0 inches
Horsepower: 340 @ 4,600 rpm
Torque: 480 lb-ft @ 3,000 rpm
Compression ratio: 10.5:1
Fuel system: Carter AFB, four-barrel with equalized manifolding
Electrical system: 12-volt, 13-plate battery, high-capacity, 42-amp generator
     55-amp on air-conditioned cars and Series 75

Chassis/Drivetrain

Transmission:
     De Ville, Series 60 Special, Eldorado: Turbo Hydra-Matic, three-speed automatic
     Series 62, 75:   Hydra-Matic, three-speed
Frame: Tubular-center X-frame
Rear axle: Hypoid, offset differential housing, 2.94:1 ratio standard 3.21:1 optional
     Series 75 ratio: 3.36:1 standard, 3.77:1 optional
Front suspension: Independent with spherical joint, helical coil-type springs, rubber-mounted strut rods, and rubber bushings
Rear suspension: Four-link drive, helical-coil springs, rubber bushings
Steering: Power-assisted, 18.2:1 overall ratio, 38.5° turning angle
Brakes: Power-assisted, self-adjusting, finned front and rear drums, split hydraulic master cylinder; effective brake lining area: 221.8 square inch
     Series 75:   233.72 square inch
Tires: Low-pressure, 4-ply, tubeless, 8.00 × 15
     Series 75:   6-ply, 8.20 × 15

Dimensions

Wheelbase: 129.5 inches
     Series 75:   149.75 inches
Width: 79.7 inches
Front/rear tread: 61/61 inches
Overall length: 223.5 inches
     Series 75:   243.8 inches

Popular Options

Comfort control
Twilight sentinel
AM radio
AM/FM radio
Cruise control
Power windows
Power front seat
Power door lock
Power deck lock
Guide-matic headlight control
Seven-position steering wheel
Controlled differential
Rear-window defogger
Soft-ray glass
License-plate frames
Seat belts
Eldorado C-note horn
Rubber floor mats
Spare-tire cover
Right-side exterior mirror

1965

It Leaves No Other Logical Choice in Fine Cars

THE 1965 MODEL YEAR got off to a slow start for Cadillac. The Cadillac factory closed on July 8, 1964, to begin conversion to the 1965 model year and reopened August 24 with an additional 471,000 square feet of manufacturing space added to the Clark Avenue plant in Detroit. This shutdown, which was the longest in its history, "gave" Cadillac the capacity to produce 800 cars daily. But a month later, on September 25, Cadillac's drive toward a 207,000-car model year was brought to an abrupt end by a United Auto Worker's strike that lasted into December.

However, this was a year of greatness that couldn't be denied. Cadillac called 1965 "the most extensive model change in the history of Cadillac—in both styling and engineering" and that enthusiasm was transformed into two milestones: the highest production and sales levels in Cadillac's history. The breakdown of Cadillac's performance in its factory and dealerships was as follows:

Calendar-year production: 196,595
Calendar-year sales: 189,661
Model-year production: 181,435

CHANGES AND IMPROVEMENTS

Leading off the array of changes for Cadillac that were as always carefully packaged in a style that preserved both a link with the past while edging delicately into the future was a new perimeter frame for all models except the Series Seventy-Five, which continued use of the older cross-braced frame. The new unit consisted of box-section beams with an upward sweep at the rear, built-up torque boxes between the beams, and a front subframe for the engine and suspension. This latter unit extended from the front suspension cross-member to the channel-section, rear motor-mount cross-member, which enabled the torque boxes to absorb and dampen engine vibration (which was also reduced thanks to a new engine mounting system) and road noise before

they could reach the main-body-carrying frame. Use of a single-piece propeller shaft with constant velocity joints plus the moving of the engine 6 inches further back in the chassis made a smaller propeller tunnel possible. In addition, the new chassis design increased Cadillac's front and rear tread by 1.5 to 62.5 inches.

The new D-series body, which Cadillac shared with senior-model Buicks and Oldsmobiles, featured curved side glass, thinner door sections, and a lower passenger floor height. Appearance-wise, Cadillac's version of this body bid adieu to what had been, beyond any doubt, the most copied styling feature of the postwar years.

Actually, Cadillac was hedging just a bit on its removal of rear-fender fins on the 1965 models since a small "bevel" edge atop the combined bumper-taillight unit captured the spirit, if not the absolute form, of rear fenders of Cadillacs past. It was a master stroke, the final retreat with grace and dignity having been made easier by first emphasizing the vertical taillight arrangement with the 1962 models. It couldn't have been done better by anyone else in the world. Cadillac barely acknowledged the passing of this era, instead noting that "distinguishing every 1965 Cadillac is the smart rear-fender and taillamp assembly, which forms an integral part of the clean, smooth rear deck styling."

In profile, the appearance of the 1965 models was characterized by a softer roof line, along with a distinctive three-plane design that created a definite shadow stripe along the body's lower surface. On all models, side trim, in the pattern of previous years, was very restrained. Complementing the new body styling were curved, frameless side windows.

At the front, added emphasis was placed on the angled form of the bright and satin-finished grille (which reverted to a massive one-piece mesh unit with a small Cadillac script in its lower right corner) by thrusting the front fenders further forward. At the same time, the vertical stacking of the headlights was destined for a short life at Cadillac. After the 1968 model run, they would revert to a horizontal arrangement. Back in evidence were the Cadillac's front parking lights, which now were housed in rectangular receptacles in the bumper. Less apparent was the optional Guide-Matic headlamp control which was mounted behind the grille.

The cornering lights were now an integral part of the front bumper design. For 1965, they were larger and redesigned to provide increased illumination.

Mounted at the top of the front fenders were small crown ornaments housing the directional signal indicator. Cadillac explained that this enabled the driver to "be fully aware of the signal operation at all times without taking his eyes from the road—a distinct advantage in traffic."

Cadillac's 340-horsepower, 429-cubic-inch engine was virtually unchanged for 1965, but its Turbo Hydra-Matic transmission now was fitted with variable stator blades, providing improved performance in the 15 to 50 mph speed range. The stator blade's normal 32-degree pitch was, when the accelerator was partly depressed, changed to 51 degrees, which allowed the engine to pick up some 700 to 800 rpms. When the car was at idle, the vanes maintained their high position, which reduced the Hydra-Matic's tendency to creep at stoplights. This transmission also had smoother upshifts due to the torque load now being taken off the gearset by an over-running sprag clutch, which transferred its load to a spring-cushioned, multiple-disc clutch running in oil.

The latest Hydra-Matic transmission was standard in all Cadillacs except for the Series Seventy-Five, which retained the fixed stator model and a two-piece drive shaft. Its axle ratio was 3.36:1, with all other models having a 2.94:1 unit.

One of Cadillac's most publicized new options for 1965 was its $80.65 automatic level control, which consisted of a small, under-hood-mounted compressor that either pumped up or deflated the Delco "Superlift"

rear shocks whenever there was a change in the car's passenger or trunk load. Another exclusive Cadillac option was the tilt and telescoping steering wheel produced by General Motors' Saginaw Steering Gear Division. This provided the six angle/height choices as before in conjunction with 3 inches of in-and-out travel.

Supporting these highly visible features were numerous technical refinements. A quieter and longer-lasting "co-axial" exhaust system was introduced, consisting of a heavy, open-ended tube running through the middle of the resonator. It made a substantial reduction in engine noise and, since it enabled the system to operate at a higher temperature, provided a much longer muffler life.

Cadillac, along with Oldsmobile and Buick, introduced a cross-flow radiator on its 1965 models that provided better deaeration of the coolant, as well as a lower hood line. Another change seen on cars without air conditioning was the elimination of the thermostatic fan clutch and fan shroud by a change in the shape and position of the fan blades. Contributing both additional front leg room and easier servicing was the positioning of most components for the Comfort Control system under the hood.

Replacing the Series Sixty-Two models was the Calais series, which was described by Cadillac as "a brilliant combination of Cadillac quality and practicality." The Calais series consisted of three models: two- and four-door hardtops and a pillard four-door Sedan. Standard interior appointments consisted of seven combinations of Delhi or pin-striped Delmar cloth and coated fabrics.

DIFFERENCES AMONG MODELS

Aside from their more elaborate interiors, the De Ville models were distinguished from their Calais

1965 Series Seventy-Five Limousine.

1965 Series Sixty Special.

1965 Calais Sedan.

1965 Coupe de Ville.

counterparts by the De Ville script found on their rear fenders plus a bright, brushed chrome rear-cove molding.

The De Ville Convertible was offered in 11 interior color combinations with perforated leather in the seat and seat-back inserts. Convertible-top colors consisted of white, black, blue, green, and sandalwood. The Sedan and Coupe models were available in eight standard fabric and leather combinations. As options, seven choices of perforated leather were offered.

After sharing a 129.5-inch wheelbase chassis with lesser Cadillacs from 1959 to 1964, the Series Sixty Special experienced two major design changes for 1965: the return to an exclusive, 133-inch wheelbase chassis and the adoption of a four-door, pillared, Sedan body style. This return of the Sixty Special to its traditional stature in the Cadillac line was accompanied by the

availability of a Fleetwood Brougham option priced at $199. The most apparent feature of the Brougham was its padded and textured vinyl top, available in white, black, blue, and sandalwood. The rear quarter panel carried both the Fleetwood crest and wreath plus Brougham script. These touches were applied to an automobile that was cleanly styled with a broad, full-length, lower body trim and unique, egg-crate, rear-deck-cove insert.

Sixty Specials, with or without the Brougham feature, were available in a wide choice of interiors including five combinations of leather and Devon cloth and five choices of embroidered Danforth cloth. At added cost, seven colors of perforated leather were offered.

The repositioning of the Sixty Special was just one aspect of a general model realignment that eliminated

1965 Fleetwood Brougham.

CADILLAC VITAL STATISTICS: 1965

Series	Model	Body Type	Factory Price ($)	Weight (lbs.)	Production (#)
62	68269	4 dr Sedan	5144	4490	7721
	68239	4 dr Sedan (HT)	5144	4500	13,975
	68257	2 dr Coupe (HT)	4959	4435	12,515
De Ville	68369	4 dr Sedan	5554	4555	15,000
	68339	4 dr Sedan (HT)	5554	4560	45,535
	68357	2 dr Coupe (HT)	5312	4480	43,345
	68367	2 dr Convertible	5528	4690	19,200
Eldorado	68467	2 dr Convertible	6604	4660	2125
60	68069	4 dr Sedan	6351	4670	18,100
75	69723	4 dr Sedan 9p	9553	5190	455
	69733	4 dr Limousine 9p	9762	5260	795

the Eldorado Biarritz as a Series Sixty-Two model and placed it, as the Eldorado Convertible, into the Fleetwood series.

CADILLAC'S DOMESTIC COMPETITION

The old Imperial body shell was, by 1965, nearing the end of its production life. Appearance changes were minimal, limited to a new grille with both horizontal and vertical dividing bars and glass covers for the headlamps. The former feature was found, in a modified form, on the Chrysler 300 series, while all 1965 Chryslers featured the tempered-glass headlamp windows. Along with upgraded interiors and ride characteristics, the Imperials were equipped with what Chrysler called the "Sentry Signal." If engine-coolant temperature increased to a dangerous level or if the fuel level or oil pressure dropped below specific levels, a red "check-gauge" signal was illuminated.

No changes were made in the Imperial's engine specifications, but use of a different cam improved overall performance.

Like Imperial, the Lincoln Continental was also in line for a major restyling, and its changes for 1965 were not extensive. Yet a new front bumper and grille arrangement made the new model readily identifiable. Ribbed parking lights were positioned above the front bumper edges; and the grille, with a protruding center section, was highlighted by a series of horizontal bars. For the first time since 1961, the Lincoln Continental was not fitted with rear-deck grille-work. A new option for Sedans was a vinyl top. Lincoln scored a major technical coup over both Cadillac and Imperial by supplying power front disc brakes as standard equipment on the Lincoln Continental.

Once again, Lincoln Continental sales and production levels rose substantially. For the 1965 calendar year, output totaled 45,470 cars, with 40,180 models produced.

Imperial's performance was less spectacular. Its calendar-year total was 16,422, with model-year assemblies reaching 18,399. Respective Lincoln Continental and Imperial sales were 42,636 and 17,214.

The Lincoln Continental's production for 1965 was impressive, but the fact that it still was below the 1956 level of 47,670 weakened its use as an example of Lincoln's success in making inroads into Cadillac's position. Cadillac's strength was underscored by the production of its three millionth car, a 1965 Fleetwood Brougham on November 4, 1964. Since 1945, Cadillac had produced 2,467,909 of those cars. In comparison, total 1945-1965 Lincoln output was 676,666 cars. Imperial from the time it was established as a separate marque in 1955 had produced 197,618 cars. In contrast, Cadillac would sell over 200,000 cars in 1966.

SPECIFICATIONS

Engine

Type: V-type, ohv, eight cylinders
Bore × stroke: 4.13 × 4.0 inches
Displacement: 429 cubic inches
Horsepower: 340 @ 4,600 rpm
Torque: 480 lb-ft @ 3,000 rpm
Compression ratio: 10.5:1
Fuel system: Single, Carter AFB, four-barrel carburetor

Chassis/Drivetrain

Front suspension: Independent, coils springs, upper A-arms, tubular shocks, anti-roll bar
Rear suspension: Coil springs, four-link, tubular shock absorbers
Steering: Power-assisted, turns lock-to-lock: 3.7
Electrical system: 12-volt
Transmission: Turbo Hydra-Matic, three-speed with variable-vane torque converter.
Frame: Perimeter design
    Series 75: X-braced
Tires: 8.00 × 15
    Series 75: 8.20 × 15
    Eldorado: 9.00 × 15
Brakes: Hydraulic, dual-master cylinder

Dimensions

Wheelbase:
    Calais, De Ville: 129.5 inches
    Series 60 Special: 133 inches
    Series 75: 149.8 inches
Width: 79.9 inches
Overall length:
    Calais, De Ville: 224 inches
    Series 60 Special: 227.5 inches
    Series 75: 243.8 inches
Front/rear tread: 62.5/62.5 inches

Popular Options

Twilight sentinel
Guide-matic
Cruise control
Seat belts
Rear-window defogger
Radio-foot control
Eldorado horn
Air conditioning
Soft-ray tinted glass
Power-door locks
Radio with rear speaker
AM/FM radio
Adjustable steering wheel
Remote-control trunk lock
White sidewall tires

1966

The Car of Cars

IF BY CHANCE there was anyone in 1966 who still didn't understand just how Cadillac had become the world's best-selling luxury car, its advertising agency, McManus, John & Adams, Inc., was delighted to enlighten them. "The reasons for Cadillac's overwhelming popularity," it explained, "are numerous. Among the most important are its advanced engineering and meticulous craftsmanship. Cadillac's styling and luxury are renowned for dignity and good taste. Its alert performance and handling rival many sports cars. No other motor car in the luxury field retains its value as long or as well as Cadillac."

The momentum built by years of close attention to these building blocks of success was given added acceleration in 1966 by the deployment of numerous new items for testing and evaluation of Cadillac models before they were released for production. Standing out from the dynamometers, hot and cold rooms, and machines testing the viability and durability of individual components was a $250,000 Road Simulator, which firmly held a test car in the grip of its four hydraulic pistons. This device could be programmed to simulate any known road condition, making it possible to determine in seconds what had previously consumed hours of over-the-road testing.

In a curious turn of events, while at least one automotive journal, *Car & Driver*, November 1965, noticed that Cadillac's very cautious approach to annual model changes was European in nature, Mercedes-Benz was marking the first anniversary of the formation of Mercedes-Benz of North America, Inc., which provided the basis for a much greater presence in the American luxury car field.

Mercedes, for a time in the late fifties, had been closely tied to Studebaker-Packard, which served as its American distributor. The formation of Mercedes-Benz of North America on March 1965 as a subsidiary of Daimler-Benz A.G. reflected a more long-term approach to planning and market development. Although this move reduced initially the number of Mercedes dealers, it also uplifted their quality. Whereas sales in 1965

increased only moderately to 11,994 from 11,234 in 1964, sales per dealer increased from 33 to 55, which put Mercedes-Benz retailers second only to Volkswagen among foreign-car dealers.

As was Cadillac, Mercedes-Benz was a name long associated with quality and prestige. Its symbol, the three-pointed star, like Cadillac's "Standard of the World" slogan, was known the world over. Also linking the two companies was their marketing strategy of blanketing several price ranges with automobiles closely linked together by style, design, and reputation. Mercedes' market space was broader than Cadillac's, ranging from a $3,955 Model 200 four-door Sedan to the 600 Grand Mercedes, seven-passenger Sedan retailing for $25,582.

In 1966, Mercedes-Benz stood twenty-second in sales in the United States, behind such marques as Studebaker and Simca and barely ahead of Renault. Within a few years, however, Mercedes-Benz would emerge not only as a viable participant in the American luxury-car market, but as an automobile that would foster a major change of strategy at Cadillac.

In 1966, it was still business as usual at Cadillac, with a combination of conservative styling changes and several new options proving sufficient to move the marque into a new sales/production level.

CHANGES AND IMPROVEMENTS

Actual styling changes were minor, including a coarser grille-mesh network with a wider center bar, the moving of the rectangular-shaped parking lights from the bumper into the grille, and the addition of a horizontal divider to the tulip-shaped taillight/bumper structure. What created the most stir was the absence of chrome trim on the 1966 models. It was still there, of course, but its application suggested that its supply at GM Design was harshly rationed.

Rather than being chromed as in 1965, the areas around the headlights, the lower front-fender panels and tops, plus the cornering light region were now painted to match the body color. This treatment was even applied to the lower half of the rear bumpers. Gone forever were soaring dorsal fins and wave upon wave of bright chrome.

Instead, what was increasingly becoming second nature to Cadillac, an intrinsic sense of good taste, proportion, and restraint, was also manifested by its interior with a functional layout enhanced by a number of new features and options. The most apparent of these was an AM-FM stereo radio system. It incorporated four speakers, two placed within the left and right upper cover of the instrument panel, with the others located at the outer portions of the rear-shelf package. To make certain nearly equal volumes of sound reached passengers, regardless of their location in the car, a cross-fire speaker system was used in which the left-front and right-rear speakers operate in tandem as did those on the right front and left rear. This option was offered on all Cadillacs except the Seventy-Five models, which were available with an AM radio with rear-compartment controls located on the right-hand armrest.

With changes in interior temperature controlled by the Climate-Control air-conditioning unit, Cadillac solved the cold-seat-on a-frosty-morning syndrome with a built-in front-seat warming system priced at $78.95. This utilized a carbon yarn developed by Union Carbide, which was woven into pads installed in the front seat backs and cushions. Operating whenever the key was turned or when the heater fan operated, it used 150 watts to heat the cushions to a temperature ranging between 85 and 105 degrees Fahrenheit.

Other new interior features and options debuting in 1966 included headrests, an ignition switch reducing the possibility of the key being moved past OFF to Accessory and thus draining the battery, a smoother operating tilt and telescoping steering wheel, four-way hazard warning flashers, and the positions of master power door locks in each front-door panel. The controls for the six-way power seats were now located on the driver's side of the front seat.

All 1966 Cadillacs (except Series Seventy-Five) had a new, variable-ratio, power-steering unit that substantially improved low-speed maneuverability, while reducing steering-wheel turns lock-to-lock from 3.6 to 2.4. The geometry of the worm and sector unit inside the steering gear box was altered so that, as the steering wheel was turned away from a center position, the ratio became much faster, changing from 16.7:1 in the straight-ahead position to 11.5:1 in the full-turn position. In 1965, the constant ratio had been 18.2:1. As a consequence, much less movement of the steering wheel was required to handle major turns. Because of higher-power steering-pump output and pressure, there was no increase in steering effort. This meant that with even less movement of the steering wheel now required for minor changes in direction, the Cadillac's response on the straightaway was faster and more finely controlled.

The introduction of the variable-ratio steering allowed the steering arm and upper tie-rod pivots to be raised for improved stability and handling. At the same time, the rear upper control arm was altered to reduce pitching and bottoming on severe bumps. Rounding out changes in the Cadillac suspension were more durable shock absorbers, that as before eliminated any mixing of air with shock-absorber fluid by using a gas-filled nylon envelope in place of the air space found in conventional shocks plus the use of two-ply, four-ply rated tires on all except the Seventy-Five Series, which had standard four-ply, eight-ply tires. A slight change in the rear, upper control arm reduced suspension pitch and bottoming on severe bumps.

Cadillac wouldn't offer power front discs until the introduction of the Fleetwood Eldorado in 1967. They would not be available on remaining Cadillacs until the 1970 model year. In the interim, Cadillac improved its drum-brake system by replacing the composite iron and steel rear drums of earlier years with all-cast-iron units. At the same time, effective lining area was increased to 377 square inches.

Changes to Cadillac's perimeter frame were so extensive as to warrant an ''all new'' description. It was now fully boxed along its length for greater torsional rigidity, and a heavier-gauge steel was used for key frame members. Finally, two additional, forward-frame braces were added for extra strength, rigidity, and quietness.

In size, Cadillac's 429-cubic-inch V-8 fell behind both the Lincoln Continental's and Imperial's, both of which were substantially increased in displacement for 1966. The Imperial unit now measured 440 cubic inches, with the Lincoln Continental V-8 becoming the industry's largest at 462 cubic inches.

During the 1965 model run, some Cadillacs had exhibited an unbecoming tendency to consume inordinate amounts of oil. This was traced to the loss of ''spring'' conformity of the aluminum pistons. To resolve this problem and to increase engine durability, new ''autothermic,'' steel pistons and redesigned oil rings were used. Also introduced were new oil-pan seals that Cadillac claimed provided both higher compression and better sealing, plus a more durable, stamped, metal water-pump impeller with a ceramic seal. The rear main bearing now had a relief groove that deflected excessive oil into the pan, reducing the load on the rear seal by nearly 90 percent.

Replacing the Carter AFB, four-barrel carburetor was a Rochester unit developed for the California-mandated Air-Injection Reactor. This reduced the variation in off-idle operation from the previous 6 percent norm to virtually zero after final factory adjustment. The system used a vane-type air pump to supply pressurized air to tubes positioned close to the exhaust valves, where it oxidized unburned hydrocarbons to meet California air-quality standards.

Cadillac, justifiably regarding the quietness of its car's interior as ''a matter of pride and pleasure for Cadillac owners,'' added a new molded, one-piece sound barrier between the engine and interior to all its 1966 models. Insulation was also installed in the rear quarter panels to reduce tire noise. With the exception of the Seventy-Fives, all Cadillacs used new rubber door moldings to cut down on wind noise. Also found on all

Sedans but the Seventy-Five models was a layer of felt sound deadener and Tuflex insulation between the steel top and headliner. Other contributors to Cadillac's quieter operation were a 1.5-inch-thick under-hood fiberglass insulation pad and thicker front floor insulation consisting of two layers of jute sandwiching a rubber compound beneath the carpeting. At the rear, carpeting had an additional jute layer.

The Calais series was accurately described as "the easiest step to the 'car of cars'." Model for model, the Calais, priced at $5,171 (Sedan and Hardtop Sedan) and $4,986 for the Coupe, represented stiff competition for what Cadillac regarded as "comparably equipped cars of lesser reputation."

Exterior identification consisted of Cadillac script on the trunk lid and Calais script on the rear quarter panels. Sixteen body colors were offered along with eight interior trim selections. Among the latter was Danbury cloth in blue, gray, green, and beige with harmonizing vinyl bolsters, as well as a Delrio cloth in black, turquoise, gold, and copper with color-blended vinyl trim.

Production of the pillared Sedan fell 7,940 units to just 4,575 cars. The other two Calais models fared a bit better in the marketplace. Output of the Hardtop Sedan was virtually unchanged at 13,025 as compared with 13,975 in 1965. Coupe production moved moderately down from 12,515 to 11,080.

Accounting for nearly half of all 1966 Cadillacs produced for the 1966 model year were the four De Villes, whose output reached 142,190, a handsome increase from 1965's mark of 123,080. Leading the De Ville field was the Hardtop Sedan priced at $5,581 of which 60,550 were built. Reflecting the limited appeal of pillared models during the era of hardtop mania was the lackluster 11,860 output of the identically priced Sedan de Ville. Indicating strong consumer interest was the production of 50,580 Coupe de Villes with a base price of $5,339. Adding 19,200 units to the De Ville's production total was the $5,555 De Ville Convertible.

DIFFERENCES AMONG MODELS

Externally, De Ville models were distinguished from Calais counterparts by the De Ville script on the rear fenders. Contributing to the 171 upholstery options offered by Cadillac was a wide variety of De Ville interiors. Standard for the Convertible was leather with perforated seat and seat-back inserts in red, black, blue, turquoise, green, gold, and antique saddle. Leather interiors were also offered for the closed models in black, white, medium blue, saddle antique, light gold, and red.

Numerous cloth and leather upholstery combinations for the De Ville line were available. Among the more popular were Desmond cloth in various textures and a diamond-weave Desmond cloth, both accompanied by leather bolsters. Among the Desmond colors were turquoise, black, gold, and copper. The Danube cloth tones included beige, gray, blue, and green.

All Cadillacs were, of course, depicted as "The Standard of the World," but efforts were made to differentiate them. For example, the Calais was the "Standard of the World in luxury and practicality." The De Ville was the "Standard of the World in glamour and excitement." Reserved for the Fleetwood was "Standard of the World in magnificence and dignity."

In contrast to its status as a $199 option for the Sixty Special in 1965, the Fleetwood Brougham became a separate model for 1966. All Fleetwoods again carried the familiar Cadillac wreath and crest on the hood and rear deck. Fleetwood lettering was positioned just behind the front wheel cutout. Fleetwoods also had full-length chrome rocker panels and a ribbed insert for the rear-deck trim panel.

Fleetwood interiors were available in nonperforated leather in white, black, blue, antique saddle, gold, and red. Also offered was a Damask cloth in conjunction with leather bolsters. Colors offered in this combination consisted of gold, midnight blue, turquoise, and crimson. A Dartmoor cloth pattern could be selected in black, blue, and beige. Also available was Delmont cloth with embroidered inserts in blue, gray, and beige. The Eldorado Convertible's leather interior with perforated seat and back inserts was finished in green, black, white, midnight blue, gold, vermillion, and antique saddle. Bucket seats were available at extra cost.

The most popular Fleetwood model was the $6,995 Brougham, of which 13,630 were produced. Well back in second place was the $6,378 Sixty Special, whose

1966 Calais Hardtop Sedan.

production totaled 5,445. Eldorado Convertible output remained almost static, at 2,250 it was up only 125 units from 1965. Its price was reduced slightly to $6,631 from $6,754.

The Fleetwood Seventy-Fives, which in 1966 received both a styling and engineering redesign making them virtually identical in those areas to other Cadillacs, were produced in significantly greater numbers than in 1965. Output of the nine-passenger Sedan, priced at $10,312, was 980 units; that of the $10,521 Limousine was 1,037.

CADILLAC'S DOMESTIC COMPETITION

After five years of cautious, calculated change, Ford was still reluctant to make any major changes in the Lincoln Continental's appearance. As a result, the 1966 models retained the essential character of earlier models even though they had all-new body sheet metal. This disappointed critics who were expecting more than a rehash of established ideas, but the new model, with another five inches added to its overall length, attained the goal of its designers—a greater share of the luxury-car market. Also helping the cause was the Lincoln Continental's 340-horsepower V-8. At 462 cubic inches, it was the industry's largest.

More important that these developments was the introduction of a two-door hardtop, whose $5,485 price put it directly in competition with Cadillac's $5,339 Coupe de Ville. The goal for Lincoln Continental's 1966 model-year production was 50,000; and with output of this new model reaching 15,766, actual output amounted to 54,755, easily shattering the old Lincoln record established back in 1956 of 50,322.

Imperial, like Lincoln Continental, pushed past Cadillac's 429-cubic-inch engine with a larger, 440

1966 De Ville Convertible.

CADILLAC VITAL STATISTICS: 1966

Series	Model	Body Type	Factory Price ($)	Weight (lbs.)	Production (#)
Calais	68269	4 dr Sedan	5,171	4460	4575
	68239	4 dr Sedan (HT)	5,171	4465	13,025
	68257	2 dr Coupe (HT)	4,986	4390	11,080
De Ville	68369	4 dr Sedan	5,581	4535	11,860
	68339	4 dr Sedan (HT)	5,581	4515	60,550
	68357	2 dr Coupe (HT)	5,339	4460	50,580
	68367	2 dr Convertible	5,555	4445	19,200
Eldorado	68467	2 dr Convertible	6,631	4500	2250
Brougham	68169	4 dr Sedan	6,695	4665	13,630
60	68069	4 dr Sedan	6,378	4615	5445
75	69723	4 dr Sedan 9p	10,312	5320	980
	69733	4 dr Limousine 9p	10,521	5435	1037

cubic-inch engine whose 350 horsepower at 4,400 rpm made it the most powerful in its field. New features included a tilt and telescope steering wheel and an improved automatic headlight system that switched from high to low beam when a car approached within 1,200 feet.

Styling changes were minor. The front grille still housed the headlights, but they were no longer fitted with glass covers. A new grille mesh was suggestive of the 1964 Lincoln Continental. At the rear, Chrysler, finally deciding that enough was enough, abandoned the old pseudo-spare wheel hump in favor of a raised center section. In contrast to Cadillac's limited use of chrome, the Imperial's propeller-shaped bumper structure and prominent center-mounted circular emblem were more suggestive of past chrome fantasies then of a more progressive styling philosophy.

Chrysler could refer to 1966 as Imperial's third best year; but with both Cadillac and Lincoln Continental output soaring to new levels, the output of 13,742 Imperials, down over 4.600 from 1965 and well off its all-time mark of 1957, was hardly much to cheer about.

While Imperial would begin to slip toward oblivion as a gussied-up Chrysler model, both Cadillac and Lincoln Continental would blaze forward with exciting new products for the rapidly emerging personal luxury-car market.

SPECIFICATIONS

Engine

Type: V-type, ohv, eight cylinders
Bore x stroke: 4.13 x 4.0 inches
Displacement: 429 cubic inches
Horsepower: 340 @ 4,600 rpm
Torque: 480 lb-ft @ 3,000 rpm
Compression ratio: 10.5:1
Fuel system: Rochester or Carter, four-barrel carburetor
Electrical system: 12-volt, 13-plate, 73-amp battery, high-capacity 42-amp generator (55 amp on air-conditioned cars)

Chassis/Drivetrain

Transmission: Turbo Hydra-Matic torque converter
Frame: Fully boxed with hidden bulk head
Rear axle: Hypoid, offset housing, Semifloating, 2.94:1 ratio, with 3.21:1 optional
  Series 75 and air-conditioned cars: 3.21:1 standard
Front suspension: Independent, spherical joints with helical-coil springs, rubber bushings, hydralic, direct-acting shock absorbers
Rear suspension: Four-link drive, helical-coil springs, rubber bushings, hydraulic direct-acting shock absorbers
Steering: Variable-ratio power steering, except for Series 75. Ratio varies from 16.7:1 to 11.5:1
  Series 75:   18.2:1
Tires: 2-ply, 4-ply rating, 9.00 x 15 on all models except 4-ply, 8-ply rating
  Series 75:   8.20 x 15

Dimensions

Wheelbase:
  Calais, De Ville and Fleetwood Eldorado Convertible: 129.5 inches
  Series 60 Special and Brougham: 133 inches
  Series 75:   149.8 inches
Width: 79.9 inches
Front/rear tread: 62.5/62.5 inches
Overall length:
  Calais, De Ville, Fleetwood Eldorado Convertible: 224 inches
  Fleetwood 60 Special and Brougham: 227.5 inches
  Series 75:   244.5 inches

Popular Options

Automatic climate control: $484.15
  Standard on Series 75
Automatic level control: $78.95
  Standard on Series 60 Special and Brougham, Series 75
Controlled differential: $52.65
Cruise control: $94.75
Rear-window defogger: $26.35
  (not available for De Ville Convertible, Series 75)
Door-edge guards
Power-door locks: $68.45 (not available for Series 75)
Power six-way front seat: $83.15 (available for all models except Series 75) Limousine and De Ville Convertible unit provides vertical and angle adjustment, available only with bucket seats. Eldorado Convertible with bucket seats has fore and aft only (plus angle on driver's side)
Hazard Warning Flashers
Guide-matic headlight control
Front seat headrests: $40.15
License frames
Padded vinyl roof: $136.85, available only for De Ville Sedan, Coupe de Ville and Series 75
  Standard on Fleetwood Brougham
AM radio: Front and rear compartment controls, separate option on Series 75
AM-FM radio
AM-FM stereo radio: $287.90
Front-seat warmer: $78.95
Reclining front-passenger bucket seat: De Ville and Eldorado Convertible only
Soft ray glass
Tilt and telescope steering wheel: $89.50 (not available for Series 75)
Remote-control trunk lock: $52.10
Twilight sentinel: $28.45
Power vent windows: $71.60
  Standard on 60 Special Sedan, and Brougham, Eldorado
  Optional for Calais, De Ville, and Series 75
Power windows, Calais only, standard all other models
White sidewall tires:
  Standard for Eldorado Convertible
  Size 9.00 x 15 optional for Calais, De Ville, Series 60 Sedan, and Brougham
  Series 75: size 8.20 x 15

1967

A Whole New Luxury-Car Concept

IN MANY RESPECTS, the introduction of the Eldorado was the beginning of a new era for Cadillac. True, its name, having been applied successively to a Motorama show car, limited production Convertibles and hardtops, super-luxurious Sedans, and specially trimmed Convertibles, had been around for a long time. But usage hadn't diluted its prestige—Eldorado still connotated "extra-special Cadillac."

Moreover, this was a car targeted specifically at customers who had previously never seriously considered purchase of a Cadillac. It didn't, for example, possess the commodious accommodations for all occupants that for so long had been a Cadillac virtue. Then there was the matter of appearance. The Eldorado could be identified as nothing else but a Cadillac, yet what a Cadillac! Rather than maintaining the careful grooming and refinement that enabled Cadillac's styling continuity to be unequaled among American cars, this vehicle stood out in the crowd.

Its close-coupled styling, long hood, and short deck were mature manifestations, but manifestation nonetheless of the pony cars that were then the rage of young Americans. Cadillac was really up to something!

ELDORADO'S BEGINNINGS

In terms of its drivetrain, one of the Eldorado's early ancestors was the La Salle II sports car shown at the 1955 Motorama. This was a nonoperative display; but shortly thereafter, a running version appeared under the somewhat boxy lines of a GMC show truck, the Universelle. Front-wheel drive at that time was a novelty among American cars, but most certainly not unknown elsewhere in the world. Indeed, Walter Christie had demonstrated an awesome front-wheel drive creation for American racing in the early years of the twentieth century. In the classic era of the twenties and thirties, the L29 and 810 Cord models had front-drive designs, but their demise seemed to close the book on its use in conjunction with large displacement engines.

This perspective gained credibility by events in Europe. In 1932 Citroen first offered its "Traction Avant" front-wheel drive cars, but their engines were on the small side, displacing less than two liters. In 1955, this long-lived series was replaced by the DS19, which startled the automotive world with its iconoclastic design. Again, it was front-wheel drive powered by a small four-cylinder engine.

While the revolutionary front-wheel-drive Austin/Morris Mini with its transverse-mounted engine was being launched in 1959, General Motors was evaluating an experimental front-wheel-drive automobile powered by a Cadillac 429-cubic-inch V-8. Shortly thereafter, Cadillac began exploratory work, with the approval of general manager Harold Warner, on a car to fill the vacuum created by the demise of the Eldorado Brougham.

The third conduit of the process leading to the Eldorado began with the rejection by Cadillac in 1960 of a proposal by the Special Projects Studio (under the close control of GM Design Chief William Mitchell) for a new automobile, the La Salle II. After being turned down by Cadillac, it was eagerly accepted by Buick and became the 1963 Riviera.

Roughly paralleling the introduction of the first-generation Riviera was the involvement of Cadillac along with Oldsmobile and Buick in a new E-body project leading to a new Riviera, as well as the 1966 Toronado and 1967 Eldorado. The primary reason for this three-way marriage was economic. Oldsmobile had, since 1961, been seeking corporate approval to develop a full-sized, front-wheel-drive car. But it was hard pressed to justify the large costs involved for a car whose market was relatively small. The solution was to bring Cadillac and Buick into the project. Eventually Buick elected to stay with a conventional drivetrain. This decision had a counterpart at Ford Motor Company where plans for a front-wheel-drive Thunderbird were also set aside.

Until 1964 the E-body project was coordinated by

the General Motors Engineering Staff, at which point each division was assigned responsibility for product development. Prior to Cadillac's decision to go front-wheel drive, styling had to follow two design patterns, one for front, the other for rear drive. Also to be resolved was the basic styling philosophy characterizing the new car and whether it would have two or four doors. During the La Salle II project, a four-door version was also developed. Ironically, the Thunderbird debuted a new model that had four doors at the time of the Eldorado's introduction. Its 1967 production was 24,967 compared with an output of nearly 53,000 two-door models.

Before the Eldorado's form was finalized, GM Design endured a series of trials and tribulations. Initial proposals didn't excite management, which regarded them as too close to the looks of the Riviera and uncomfortably similar to the Thunderbird.

When the 1967 Eldorado appeared, however, it was acclaimed as a major styling triumph. Praise was almost unanimous for its crisp, tailored lines with their razor edges and its blending of neoclassic forms with contemporary performance.

Car Life even went so far as to compare the Eldorado with the original Lincoln Continental. That must have thrilled everybody at Cadillac (and for opposite reasons, the folks at Ford). The comparison was worth making. Both cars possessed the long hood (the Eldorado's extended over 6 feet to become the longest on any 1967 Cadillac) and short deck so often found on cars of the classic era. Each of them provided rear-seat accommodations that were better suited for other purposes than for passenger use, mechanical specifications promising good performance, and, perhaps most important of all, styling that was both distinctive and suggestive of a high price tag.

The Eldorado was a car that added a new dimension to the luxury-car field—one characterized by a heightened sensation of individuality and accentuated by tasteful luxury. It was a design destined to successfully stand the test of time to remain an automobile as visually appealing today as in 1967.

ELDORADO'S STYLE

The Eldorado front end took the typically Cadillac cross-hatch grille arrangement to its ultimate expression. Broad and low, it was unencumbered by any extraneous ornamentation save for the elegant Cadillac script on the driver's side. Cadillac was now positioned diametrically opposite to its outlook of the late fifties as far as chrome trim was concerned, and an examination of the Eldorado body seemed to suggest that whatever trim it did have had been applied in a miserly, begrudging manner. A narrow bar ran the length of the 6-foot hood, leading to a wreathed Cadillac crest. Side trim consisted of a narrow rub-bar and a body-bottom shield extending from stem to stern.

Another touch of refined elegance to the Eldorado's appearance was provided by the pronounced V-shape of its rear window. Initially this form had appeared on the windshield of an early styling concept.

When the La Salle II proposal was under

development in 1960, a key styling element was the use of dual, vertical fender nacelles behind whose grilles were vertically stacked headlights. It wasn't until 1965 that this feature was put into production on the Riviera. The Eldorado picked up on this theme, although its headlights hid behind the grille when not in use. The pointed front fenders, in concert with the angular grille work with its forward thrusting center plus angular-shaped rear fenders, gave the Eldorado a chiseled, razor-edged appearance that contrasted dramatically not only with the E-bodied Riviera and Toronado but every other car on the road.

Cadillac stylists worked hard to give the Eldorado's rear deck an appearance that matched the front's combination of simplicity and elegance. Again, the key word was restraint. The rectangular backup lights were, like the front parking lights, mounted high on the bumpers, the simple Cadillac crest and wreath were placed just above the centrally positioned gas-filler door cover, and an Eldorado identification bar was located to its extreme right. The vertical taillights were separated into two sections by a slender chrome bar that capped the upswept bumper. Seen on no other Cadillac were the Eldorado's slotted disc wheels.

Vying with the Eldorado's styling for the lion's share of the public's attention was the front-wheel-drive arrangement, although the arrival of the Toronado a year earlier took away some of its novelty. As on rear-drive Cadillacs, the variable, stator-torque converter was attached to the rear of the engine. But then matters changed drastically. What remained of the Turbo Hydra-Matic, the planetary gear box, and controlling elements were rotated 180° and mounted, facing forward, along the left side of the engine. A new, 2-inch-wide, Hy-Vo chain, a product of the Hydra-Matic Division and Borg-Warner's Morse Chain Division, transferred power from the converter, across and through the transmission gear sets, to a differential bolted to the transmission's front where it was split between the two front wheels. The differential used a planetary-gear set rather than the usual ring-gear pinion. The driving chain was not fitted with any tensioner since all chains were run in on devices that prestretched them. The sprockets had bonded-in, rubber-cushioning devices for driveline smoothness, and the entire chain consisted of 2,294 individual pieces.

The front suspension consisted of upper and lower A-arms, torsion bars, and a 1.062-inch, link-type antiroll bar. The ride rate, at 140 lb/in was significantly stiffer than that of other 1967 Cadillacs. For example, that of the Calais was 86 lb/in. A drop-center live axle with parallel, single-leaf springs and four telescopic shocks were mounted vertically and horizontally in pairs. As standard equipment, the Eldorado was fitted with the automatic level-control system.

Cornering and handling characteristics of the Eldorado were, if not of sports-car caliber, precise and brisk. After all, the Eldorado was a large automobile with a 120-inch wheelbase, 79.9-inch width, and 221-inch overall length. In contrast, the dimensions of the front-wheel-drive Toronado were wheelbase, 119 inches; width, 78.5 inches; and overall length, 211 inches.

In most driving conditions, it was almost impossible to determine if the Eldorado was front or rear drive, although it cornered flatter than other Cadillacs. Only when hard pressed did the Eldorado reveal that approximately 60 percent of its weight was carried by the front wheels. A major plus for the Eldorado was the standard, variable-rate power steering that with just 2.7 turns lock-to-lock made it surprisingly agile.

With just 15 pounds for each of its 340 horsepower to put in motion, the Eldorado's 429-cubic-inch V-8 gave it brisk acceleration, although not as good as that of a 360-horsepower Riviera Gran Sport or the 385-horsepower Oldsmobile Toronado. Typical acceleration times were 0 to 60 mph in 9 seconds and the standing-start quarter mile in 17 seconds at 84 mph with the standard 3.21:1 rear axle. Top speed was 130 mph.

Eliciting strong negative reactions were the Eldorado's standard drum brakes, which measured 11 × 2.75 inches (front) and 11 × 2.00 inches (rear). *Car Life* found the Eldorado's deceleration rate of 19 to 20 ft/sec^2 inferior to that of a 1966 Calais. *Motor Trend* reported a 60-mph to 0 stopping distance of 224 feet, which was identical to a 1966 Chrysler Town & Country station wagon with an 840-pound payload. This weak point didn't escape the scrutiny of *Car & Driver*, whose test car needed 386 feet to come to a halt from 60 mph. Front disc brakes measuring 11 × 1.25 inches were offered at $105.25 and lowered that figure to 312 feet with far better directional stability. *Car & Driver*, rejecting Cadillac's view that this option was for the "performance-minded customer," argued they should be included in the basic Eldorado package.

ELDORADO'S INTERIOR

As expected of a Fleetwood model, the Eldorado appointments were of a very high quality. Its standard Strato-bench seat was available in any of 18 upholstery selections, including a Dalmatian cloth and a combination of Carien cloth and vinyl.

The instrumentation included a large, easily read speedometer with white letters on a matte black background, round warning lights for oil pressure and battery, an electric clock plus gauges for fuel supply and coolant temperatures. Because of contoured outer sections and a raised center portion, the standard seats could be regarded as semibuckets, True bucket seats with leather upholstery were also available.

Although dual, interior door handles had been offered on the first Buick Riviera in 1963, they were equally welcomed by rear-seat passengers on the Eldorado. One sign of the times was the size of the Eldorado's steering wheel—its diameter was equivalent to the horn rings on the 1958 Cadillac. A new forced-air ventilation system exiting through slotted vents on the inner sides of the rear fenders was introduced on the Eldorado, which became the first postwar Cadillac without front-vent windows.

The Eldorado has been credited with a major role in pushing Cadillac sales for the third successive year to a new record high. For the model year 17,930 were produced; and at times, Cadillac dealers had a three-month backlog of Eldorado orders. Even matched against far less costly personal cars, the $6,277 Eldorado did well. Toronado output, after reaching nearly 41,000 in 1966, fell to 21,790. Assemblies of the Buick Riviera totaled 42,799, while the Thunderbird continued to reign supreme among the personal cars, producing 52,989 two-door and 24,907 four-door models. All of these cars had significantly lower base prices than the Eldorado. The most expensive Thunderbird Landau four-door began at $4,825, the Deluxe Toronado at $4,869, and the Riviera at $4,469.

Promotion of the Eldorado, even for Cadillac, was characterized by a surprising degree of understatement and restraint. There were two reasons for this. First, there was no desire to arouse sentiment that it was a radically new design. Secondly, Cadillac wanted to incorporate the Eldorado into its lineup with a minimum amount of confusion as to its status. What better way was there than to depict it as the "world's finest personal car," an automobile that along with other 1967 Cadillacs offered "the only real choice in luxury motor cars."

Equally evident was Cadillac's pride in bringing this significant new car to market. In Cadillac's view, the Eldorado was a "dramatic blend of the best of two motoring worlds . . . [combining] the spirit and action of a true performance car with the comfort and five-passenger spaciousness of a true luxury car . . . the one car that must be seen to be believed, driven to be appreciated, and owned to be fully enjoyed."

DIFFERENCES AMONG MODELS

Obviously, Cadillac wasn't about to ignore the multitudes of would-be and repeat customers for its conventional models in 1967. The format for 1967 was unchanged from earlier years, a mix of styling changes carefully chosen to promote customer interest but not at the expense of instantly rendering the preceding models obsolete, buoyed by some solid engineering refinements and advances.

Heading up the latter were laminated, mylar-printed circuits for the instrument panel and, for quieter operation, a new fan clutch and modified body mounts. No changes were made in engine displacement, horsepower, torque, or compression ratio levels. Cadillac was still concerned about oil consumption and introduced new production-line cylinder-bore techniques as well as new oil rings for better immediate oil economy. Also altered were the specifications for the four-barrel Quadrajet carburetor.

In profile, a downward-sloping, side-panel character crease, in conjunction with a sharply peaked fender line, gave the rear fenders, if not a finned look, then surely a high-style appearance.

Like the Eldorado's, the grille work on the rest of the 1967 Cadillacs continued the traditional cross-hatched format, while extending it downward into a section just below the bumper crossbar. As in 1966, the rectangular parking lights were mounted high in the

1967 De Ville Convertible.

1967 Fleetwood Brougham.

1967 Calais Sedan.

1967 Coupe de Ville.

1967 Fleetwood Eldorado.

CADILLAC VITAL STATISTICS: 1967

Series	Model	Body Type	Factory Price ($)	Weight (lbs.)	Production (#)
Calais	68269	4 dr Sedan	5215	4520	2865
	68249	4 dr Sedan (HT)	5215	4550	9880
	68247	2 dr Coupe (HT)	5040	4445	9085
De Ville	68369	4 dr Sedan	5625	4575	8800
	68349	4 dr Sedan (HT)	5625	4550	59,902
	68347	2 dr Coupe (HT)	5392	4505	52,905
	68367	2 dr Convertible	5608	4500	18,200
Eldorado	69347	2 dr Coupe (HT)	6277	4590	17,930
60	68069	4 dr Sedan	6423	4685	3550
Brougham	68169	4 dr Sedan	6739	4735	12,750
75	69723	4 dr Sedan 9p	10360	5335	835
	69733	4 dr Limousine 9p	10571	5450	965

grille. At the rear, the tail, stop, and backup lights were integrated into the vertical bumper elements.

Throughout the year, Cadillac production ran at record or near-record levels. When the model year ended, output stood at an even 200,000, with calendar-year production totaling 213,161. Both were new records.

Except for the replacement of the Eldorado Convertible by the front-wheel-drive Eldorado, no changes were made in Cadillac's model lineup. The three Calais models (Sedan, Hardtop Coupe, and Sedan) were depicted as representing "an unusual standard of value for the Standard of the World." Eight interior selections in an exclusive Calais Duet-pattern cloth with vinyl trim or all vinyl were offered. Like all Cadillacs, the Calais models were available in 16 standard and 5 optional Firemist exterior colors.

In spite of attractive prices (Pillared Sedan: $5,215, Coupe: $5,040), production of the Calais series slumped in a year of overall record Cadillac output. Only 21,830 were assembled (2,865 Sedans, 9,880 Hardtop Sedans, and 9,085 Coupes), a sharp drop from the 28,680 level of 1966.

Cadillac's most popular series, the De Ville, was again available in four models: Coupe, Sedan, Hardtop Sedan, and Convertible. The $5,025 Sedan, the least popular of the De Villes, with an output of 8,800 cars, was offered in 17 leather or cloth and leather interiors. Its hardtop counterpart, priced at $5,025, was, by far, not only the choice of De Ville buyers, but also Cadillac's number one seller as evidenced by its production level of 59,902 cars. Its interior could be upholstered in 19 leather or cloth and leather choices, including two bucket-seat options.

Output of 52,905 Coupe de Villes placed this $5,392 two-door hardtop in the number two sales slot at Cadillac. Listed among its 19 interiors in leather or cloth and leather were two cloth and perforated-leather patterns. Also offered were leather bench or bucket seats.

The $5,608 De Ville Convertible, whose output was 18,200 cars, could be ordered in 13 leather interiors. The bucket-seat option was offered in four choices of perforated leather.

The Fleetwood Sixty Special, as in 1966, was offered in either Sedan or Brougham form. The latter, priced at $6,739 to the Sedan's $6,423, was identified by its padded roof (available in five colors) with wreath crest and Brougham script on the C-pillar. This up-market model's production easily exceeded the Sedan's by a margin of 12,750 to 3,550.

Standard Sixty Special equipment included power-operated front and rear vent windows and automatic-level control. Broughams were given added distinction thanks to their rear-compartment, folddown vanity trays, which lowered from the front-seat backs, individual swivel-type reading lamps, and carpeted folddown footrests.

Both versions could be upholstered in one of 21 variations of cloth, leather and cloth, or all leather.

Both versions of the Fleetwood Seventy-Five, the $10,360 Sedan and the $10,571 Limousine, were offered in five exclusive interiors, including light gray Devonshire with embroidered inserts for the seat backs. Limousines continued to be fitted with a glass partition and leather-upholstered chauffeur's compartment. Respective output of these nine-passenger Cadillacs were 835 (Sedan) and 965 (Limousine).

CADILLAC'S DOMESTIC COMPETITION

Cadillac's introduction of the Eldorado plus its strong sales performance contrasted with a little-changed package from Lincoln Continental and a nearly 17 percent downturn (from 54,755 to 45,667) in Lincoln Continental output. The decision to offer a four-door Convertible in 1961 had been a novel one, but the idea never caught on with the public; and after seven years of poor sales, Lincoln decided enough was enough and made 1967 the last year for this model. Of 45,607 Lincoln Continentals built for the model run, only 2,278 were soft tops.

External changes from 1966 were very minor, taxing the talents of the most knowledgeable Lincoln Continental watcher. Vertical bars were added to the grille, the taillight inserts were altered; and on Sedans and hardtops, a Continental logo was placed on the rear side roof panel. Rendering the hood ornament harmless to the touch was its new spring mounting.

Technical changes, aside from the mandatory safety features, consisted of a dual hydraulic-braking system (Cadillac had been using its version since 1962); a new interior ventilation system, known as Fresh-Flow; and a revised automatic transmission, Select-Shift Turbo Drive. As its name implied, it offered both manual and automatic gear shifting.

Imperial at long last received a new unit-body shell for 1968. At face value, this long overdue development suggested Chrysler was, as in 1955 and 1957, about to market an Imperial capable of providing serious competition to both Cadillac and Lincoln Continental. The promise was less than what was delivered since the Imperial's new full, unitized body was that shared by other lesser Chryslers. Defenders of this move were quick to note that Cadillac shared its basic structure with several Oldsmobile and Buick models. Thus, they maintained, what was wrong with Imperials' doing likewise with Chrysler? The fault was not in the concept but its application.

Chrysler management, after being rocked by the sales disasters of the early sixties (at one point in 1961 Chrysler Corporation's entire share of the market had dwindled down to under 11 percent), had become increasingly obsessed by the idea of joint responsibility, the creation of consensus by committee, and a resultant moving away from the daring-to-risk-all mentality that characterized its triumphs of 1955 and 1957.

The result was an Imperial that looked as if it had been designed by a committee. Moreover, the Chrysler C-body of 1967 was already in its third model year; and in overall form, a 1967 Imperial bore an embarrassing similarity to a 1965 New Yorker. Making matters worse was the amalgamation of the Lincoln Continental's influence with styling cliches lifted from contemporary Cadillacs.

Not surprisingly, Imperial output while making an impressive percentage increase, still languished well below the 20,000 mark, reaching only 17,614 cars. Once again, it had been a Cadillac year with record production and sales records underscored by the successful introduction of the Eldorado. On the horizontal, however, was Lincoln's response, the Lincoln Continental Mark III, which would prove a worthy sales competitor to the Eldorado.

SPECIFICATIONS

Engine

Type: V-8, ohv
Bore × stroke: 4.13 × 4.0 inches
Displacement: 429 cubic inches
Horsepower: 340 @ 4,600 rpm
Torque: 480 lb-ft @ 3,000 rpm
Compression ratio: 10.5:1
Fuel system: Rochester Quadrajet, four-barrel, down draft carburetor
Electrical system: 12-volt, 13-plate battery, high-capacity 42-amp generator (55 amp on air-conditioned cars)

Chassis/Drivetrain

Transmission: Turbo Hydra-Matic torque converter with variable stator (except Series 75)
Frame: Fully boxed perimeter frame with hidden bulk heads
    Eldorado: Boxed perimeter designed for front-wheel drive
Rear axle:
    Rear-drive models: Hypoid, offset housing, semifloating 2.94:1 ratio, with 3.21:1 available
    Air-conditioned cars and Series 75: 3.21:1 standard
Front suspension: Independent spherical joints with helical-coil springs. Rubber-mounted strut rods and rubber bushings, telescopic shock absorbers, and stabilizer bars
    Eldorado: torsion bars
Rear suspension: Rear-drive models: four-link drive, helical-coil springs, rubber bushings, telescopic shock absorbers
    Eldorado: single-leaf springs, beam axle, two horizontal and two vertical telescopic shock absorbers

Steering: Variable-ratio power steering standard, except for Series 75. Ratio varies from 16.7 to 11.5:1.
    Series 75: 18.2:1
    Eldorado: 16.3:1
Tires: Low-pressure, two-ply tubeless 9.00 × 15
    Series 75: four-ply, 8.20 × 15

Dimensions

Wheelbase:
    Calais: 129.5 inches
    Series 60 Special and Brougham: 133 inches
    Eldorado: 120 inches
    Series 75: 149.8 inches
Width: 79.9 inches
    Eldorado: 80.0 inches
Front/rear tread: 62.5/62.5 inches
Overall length:
    Calais: 224 inches
    Series 60 Special and Brougham: 227.5 inches
    Eldorado: 221 inches
    Series 75: 244.5 inches

Popular Options

Automatic level control: $79
    Standard on Fleetwood models
Reclining right front seat with adjustable headrest (except for Eldorado, available only with bucket seats)
Automatic climate control: $516
Cruise control: $95
Power door locks
Twilight sentinel
Tilt and telescope steering wheel: $90
Padded vinyl roof: $132, available on De Ville, Series 75 and Eldorado
    Standard on Brougham
AM radio: $162
AM-FM radio: $188
AM-FM stereo radio: $288
Adjustable front-seat headrests: $53
Six-way power seat
Front-seat warmer
Guide-matic power headlamp: $50
Power trunk lock: $52
Controlled differential
Rear-window defogger: $27
Door-edge guards
White sidewall tires
Firemist paint: $132
Soft-ray glass: $51

1948 Series 75 Limousine. (Owner: Mitchell Near; Photographer: Jackie O'Rourke)

1949 Series 62 Convertible. (Owner: Dominic Lombardo)

1954 Series 62 Sedan. (Owner: Mark Maslanka; Photographer: Jackie O'Rourke)

1956 Coupe de Ville. (Owner: Nancy Renzi; Photographer: Jackie O'Rourke)

1956 Series 60 Special. (Owner: Phil Gilter)

1957 Series 62 Convertible. (Owner: Carmen Ferri)

1958 Fleetwood 60 Special. (Courtesy: Jackie O'Rourke)

1959 Coupe de Ville. (Owner: Low Borini; Photographer: Jackie O'Rourke)

1962 Park Avenue Sedan. (Owner: Leonard Sherwood; Photographer: Jackie O'Rourke)

1966 Sedan de Ville. (Owner: Gary Livingston; Photographer: Jackie O'Rourke)

1969 Sedan de Ville. (Courtesy: Special Interest Auto Sales, Otego, N.Y.)

1970 Sedan de Ville. (Courtesy: Special Interest Auto Sales, Otego, N.Y.)

1977 Coupe de Ville. (Courtesy: George Lundin)

1979 Seville. (Courtesy: Gary Enck's Car Store, Otego, N.Y.)

The symbol of Cadillac as used in 1979.

1980 Seville: July 6, 1977. (Courtesy: General Motors Design)

1980 Seville: March 22, 1978. (Courtesy: General Motors Design)

1985 De Ville: September 21, 1978. (Courtesy: General Motors Design)

Styling of the 1986 Eldorado as of May 20, 1981. (Courtesy General Motors Design)

Styling of the 1986 Seville as of January 28, 1982. (Courtesy General Motors Design)

Styling of the 1986 Seville as of March 30, 1983. (Courtesy General Motors Design)

1948 Series 75 Limousine (above).   40 years later: The 1987 Allanté (below). <small>(Courtesy General Motors, Cadillac Motor Car Division)</small>

1968

The Exceptional Motoring World of Cadillac

JUST AS IT HAD IN 1949, Cadillac for 1968 followed the debut of a sensationally styled automobile with the introduction of an all-new V-8 engine. With the sense of perspective appropriate to an automobile manufacturer of its stature, Cadillac portrayed this new engine with the proper mixture of conservative and dramatic comments. In announcing the 1968 models, which went on sale on September 21, 1967, Cadillac general manager Calvin J. Werner said the "heart of the performance-durability story for the 1968 models is Cadillac's completely new V-8." This was, said Cadillac, "the biggest, smoothest engine ever put in a production motor car . . . This new engine represents the fourth major Cadillac development in V-8 engine design since Cadillac introduced America's first production V-8 fifty-three years ago . . . It is almost like having two engines, one to give you remarkable road performance, the other to power all the luxuries that make driving a Cadillac so uniquely pleasurable. Yet the new Cadillac 472 V-8 is smoother, significantly quieter, more efficient and more reliable than any of Cadillac's previous great engines."

SPECIFICATIONS FOR THE NEW V-8

Indeed, the new engine's credentials were world-class. No other passenger-car engine in production exceeded its 472-cubic-inch displacement or output of 525 lb-ft of torque. Moreover, Cadillac was at ease touting both its newness and road worthiness. Its chief engineer, Carlton A. Rasmussen, reported; "all but four small parts of this engine are new and it is the product of many thousands of design hours over a three-year period and more than two million miles of testing. The result is an engine that sets new industry standards of smoothness and effortless performance." "We have capitalized," added Calvin Werner, "on our 53 years of V-8 engine design and manufacturing experience to produce an engine to satisfy the needs of our Cadillac owners."

No longer did Cadillac's engine trail behind Chrysler and Imperial in sheer size. Its displacement boost for 1967 was a big one, up 43 cubic inches with new bore and stroke measurements of 4.30 and 4.06 inches, respectively. While it didn't come to pass, the ultimate displacement potential of this engine was in the area of 600 cubic inches. Yet its external dimensions were virtually identical to the superseded 429 cid engine. Weight increased, but it was a moderate 80 pounds and was due mostly to increased cylinder-wall thickness.

This contributed to one of Cadillac's three goals for this engine—a measurable reduction of noise and vibration. Two other objectives were improved durability and a reduction in the total number of engine parts. At the same time, Cadillac, recognizing that more, not less, emission controls would be forthcoming from Washington, became the first American automobile manufacturer to produce an engine with an integrated air-injection emission control. Since the overwhelming majority of Cadillacs were equipped with air conditioning, the cylinder-block casting also included the system's compressor mounting brackets.

Another feature worthy of note was a metal temperature monitoring device located in the cylinder head. This was connected to a warning system, including a buzzer and red warning light, to alert the driver to engine overheating. Cadillac reported that "unlike former systems based on water temperature alone, this system alerts the driver in time to prevent engine damage if cooling system conditions become abnormal."

Contributing to the 472 engine's anticipated long life and minimal noise output were numerous applications of modern technology. The crankshaft was now a stiffer cast unit of ductile iron providing increased bearing surface area. The piston skirt was lengthened and cast Armasteel was now used for the connecting rods. Providing increased protection from fluid leads were "hydrodynamic" oil seals developed by GM Research, which, along with Cadillac, also devised a new cylinder-bore finish. Also contributing to reduced oil consumption were redesigned piston rings. Improved serviceability was provided by a self-contained, single-unit oil pump and the mounting of the oil filter directly on the cylinder block.

In addition, explained Mr. Rasmussen, "extensive noise reduction considerations were made in the basic design of the crankshaft, bearings, belt drive system and valve train area. Electronic computers were used in the camshaft design, and the intake manifold was designed to serve double duty as a tappet valley cover for isolating noise."

Aside from these major revisions, the introduction of the new Cadillac V-8 was accompanied by numerous small refinements such as a quick-set choke, carburetor shafts coated with a low friction surface, heavier battery cables, a 15-plate battery, and a more powerful starter motor.

As it had done in previous years when a new or redesigned engine had been adopted, Cadillac took this opportunity to implement significant quality improvements and operation efficiencies into its engine assembly procedure.

Of the 167 machine tools used in the engine machining department, all but 44 were new. Characteristic of these advanced units was an ability to produce components with extremely fine tolerances with a minimum of variation. Typical of the means by which important savings were realized was the precise foundry operation, which enabled the combustion chambers to be used in an as-cast condition.

Beginning with this engine, Cadillac switched from use of a cast Armasteel crankshaft to one of modular steel supplied by General Motors' Central Foundry Division. Its counterweights were also suitable for use in their as-cast condition, which further reduced matching expenses. To make certain no untoward problems arose during final balancing operations a prebalancing machine was used. In the final balancing operation, the tolerance was 0.25 ounce.

Cadillac's 10.5:1 compression ratio (unchanged from 1967), 375 hp at 4,400 rpm, and 525 lb-ft of torque at 3,000 rpm, was superior to the corresponding specifications of the 460-cubic-inch Lincoln and 440-cubic-inch Imperial engines. At the same time, they enabled Cadillac to make drivetrain changes leading to smoother and quieter operation with no sacrifice in performance. The most important of these was the abandonment of the variable-pitch torque converter in favor of one with fixed-pitch status. With so much torque available, there was no loss in either performance or flexibility. At the same time, the redesigned Turbo-Hydramatic, along with a higher 2.94:1 rear axle ratio and higher-capacity differential gear, provided smoother and more economical operation. Front-wheel disc brakes were optional in all 1968 Cadillacs. The regular line used units with a new single-piston, floating caliper design. The Eldorado continued with the four-piston caliper design, offered in 1967, but with a tandem booster for improved performance.

CHANGES AND IMPROVEMENTS

Cadillac depicted its 1968 models as "Elegance in Action," which in less lofty terms meant that no one should look for any startling styling changes. But as was so often the case, a side-by-side, wheel-to-wheel examination of a 1968 Cadillac with a 1967 revealed some surprising changes. The first to be apparent was the 6.5-inch longer hood line, which accompanied the use of concealed windshield wipers. This latter feature, viewed by some critics as little more than a styling ploy, was defended by Cadillac as "reducing glare and providing an exceptional view ahead."

The traditional Cadillac cross-hatched grille was superseded by one with a new header bar plus thinner and narrower bars, which gave it a predominately horizontal appearance. The larger parking/directional lights were mounted slightly higher in the grille. They operated whenever the headlights were on. All 1968 model cars were required to carry side running lights. Cadillac's close attention to detail was evident in how it responded to this government mandate. Rather than simply tacking the rear units on as an afterthought, its designers incorporated them into the design of the rear-bumper uprights. Even more impressive was the Eldorado's arrangement. Its rear marker lights were located within the wreath and crest emblem just ahead of the rear bumper. Eliminated from the rear lighting arrangement, which now utilized larger lenses, were the vertical dividers used in 1967. A key styling feature was the new sculptured deck lid with a raised surface that blended into a beveled edge similar to the Eldorado's.

Installed on all models was a larger, rectangular, remotely controlled driver's-side mirror. It was shrouded to eliminate buffeting by the air stream. A right-hand, rear-view side mirror was available as a dealer-installed option on all models except the Series Seventy-Five Cadillac on which it was standard. The last vestiges of the turbine influence on Cadillac wheel-cover design, which after reaching its zenith in 1957 before going into a radical remission, was eliminated from the 1968 models. The main appearance features of the new covers were their peripheral black and chrome rings surrounding a brushed-finish recessed center, which served as the background for the Cadillac crest. The overall effect was very similar to the 1965 version. The wheels on which these covers were mounted now had what Cadillac described as an "additional safety hump" on the inside bead for better tire retention in case of a tire failure. Additional safety-related changes included stamped door hinges, edge-crush provisions for the padded sun visors, padded windshield pillars, and reduced reflectivity for interior bright finishes. In order to improve collision protection for the middle passenger, the center automatic-climate-control outlet was more deeply recessed than in 1967. It was constructed of impact-absorbing plastic with breakaway retainers. The inside rear-view mirror now bent away from either a forward or side impact. Similarly, the ventilation-window crank handles, which now were flatter and had rounder edges, would bend away upon side impact. All front-seat backs were fitted with more padding than on previous models. Offered as optional equipment on all 1968 Cadillacs were lower and softer head restraints.

Completing the list of standard safety features were door buttons made of a flexible material; a brake failure warning system; and an improved, higher-capacity windshield-washer system that cleaned a larger portion of the windshield. The washer delivered fluid to the windshield before the first cycle of the wipers. A new antitheft feature was a buzzer that operated when the key was in the ignition and the driver's side door opened.

That Cadillac established new record sales and production figures in 1968 wasn't really much of a surprise to anyone. This was a very good year for the industry overall, with output reaching the 8,848,507 level. What attracted attention was the sheer strength of the Cadillac surge. Model-year output was 230,003 cars, up from 200,000 the year earlier. In 15 years, Cadillac had more than doubled its production, while Lincoln's had grown only some 8 percent and Imperial's had remained almost static.

DIFFERENCES AMONG MODELS

The 1968 Calais Cadillacs, the least expensive line, were, with the elimination of the four-door pillared Sedan, available either as a two-door hardtop or a four-door hardtop Sedan. The rear-deck insert had a satin finish, Calais script was installed on the rear fenders, and the Cadillac V and crest were mounted on the front hood and rear deck. No lower-body edge trim was installed.

Added to the list of Calais standard features were power windows with a power-control panel on the driver's side controlling all windows, in addition to the single switches at each window for individual operation. Included in the Calais's base price were Turbo-Hydramatic, power steering and brakes, electric clock, ash receiver light, courtesy lights, automatic glove box and trunk lights, remote-control outside mirror, door-panel warning reflectors, three-speed electric wipers and washers, full wheelcovers, passenger visor-mounted vanity mirror, trip odometer and seat belts.

Six interiors of patterned DaKarta cloth with vinyl trim, as well as two, extra-cost, leather-textured vinyl upholsteries, were offered. Like all Cadillacs, the Calais was available in 16 standard colors, sable black, regal silver, arctic blue, Caribe aqua, Kashmir ivory, chestnut brown, Normandy blue, silverpine green, Sudan beige, San Mates red, Grecian white, summit gray, emperor blue, Ivanhoe green, Baroque gold, and regent maroon. Five Firemist colors—spectre blue, rosewood, topaz gold, monterey green, and Madeira plum—were available on all Cadillacs at additional cost.

The most popular Cadillac model of 1967, the Hardtop Sedan de Ville, was, as in 1968, one of four models offered in the De Ville Series, the others being the Convertible, Coupe de Ville, and Sedan de Ville. All carried ribbed, rear-deck inserts and individual model script on their rear fenders, with the exception of the Convertible which had De Ville script.

The De Ville models, said Cadillac, represented "by far the widest and certainly the most desirable cars" in their price range. Once again the public agreed, as the De Ville's production run of 164,472 cars indicates. De Villes shared their 129.5-inch wheelbase and 224.7-inch overall length with the Calais models. In addition to the items included as standard Calais features, all De Ville Cadillacs were equipped with a power front seat and illuminated door-panel reflectors.

The De Ville Convertible was offered with any one of 11 standard leather interiors. A choice of five harmonizing, fabric-top colors was available. All other models were available with optional leather interiors in eight color selections. Included in the leather package was rosewood-veneer wood paneling. All models, except

1968 Coupe de Ville. Exterior changes for 1968 included redesigned cornering lights and new side marker lights.

for the Convertible, could be appointed in any of eight different, patterned-cloth, leather-bolster color combinations.

The Fleetwood series, which encompassed the Brougham, Sixty Special, Seventy-Five Sedan and Limousine, as well as the Eldorado, was described by Cadillac as representing "the supreme achievement in grand and gracious motoring."

Both the Brougham and Sixty Special were, as they had been since 1966 when the Brougham's status was changed from that of a trim package to a full-fledged model, pillared four-door Sedans.

Joining the list of standard features the Brougham and Sixty Special did not share with lesser Cadillacs was automatic-level control plus front and rear power ventpanes. With a 133-inch wheelbase and overall length of 228.2 inches, these Cadillacs would be easy to identify even if they did not have Fleetwood exterior appointments. These consisted of a Fleetwood wreath and crest at the front and rear of the car, Fleetwood block letters on the lower front fender just behind the fender wheel, full-length, lower-body molding, and outlined rear-deck panels with Fleetwood lettering inscribed on the passenger-side unit. Setting the Brougham apart was its padded roof, available in five colors and highlighted by a small wreath, crest, and Brougham script.

Eighteen interiors in cloth, leather, or cloth and leather combinations were available. The eight leather interiors were extra-cost options, while three Damsel and four DuBarry cloth and leather combinations plus three all-cloth colors in a Dunstan pattern with embroidered backrests were standard choices for both the Sixty Special and Brougham. Exclusive to the

1968 Fleetwood Brougham. Highlighting Cadillac styling in 1968 was a sculptured rear deck providing additional trunk space.

CADILLAC VITAL STATISTICS: 1968

Series	Model	Body Type	Factory Price ($)	Weight (lbs.)	Production (#)
Calais	68249	4 dr Sedan (HT)	5491	4640	10,025
	68247	2 dr Coupe (HT)	5315	4570	8165
De Ville	68369	4 dr Sedan	5785	4680	9850
	68349	4 dr Sedan (HT)	5785	4675	72,662
	68347	2 dr Coupe (HT)	5552	4595	63,935
	68367	2 dr Convertible	5736	4600	18,025
Fleetwood Eldorado	69347	2 dr Coupe (HT)	6605	4580	24,528
60 Special	68069	4 dr Sedan	6583	4795	3300
Brougham	68169	4 dr Sedan	6899	4805	15,300
75	69723	4 dr Sedan 9p	10629	5300	805
	69733	4 dr Limousine 9p	10768	5385	995

1968 Fleetwood Eldorado. Styling changes for 1968 included relocated parking lamps and a longer hood to accommodate concealed wipers.

1968 De Ville Convertible.

1968 Sedan de Ville.

On June 10, 1968, the three-millionth postwar Cadillac, a gold De Ville Convertible, was built. From left to right: James Roche, GM chairman (and former Cadillac general manager), Harold G. Warner (Cadillac's general manager in 1963 when the two-millionth postwar Cadillac was built), and Don E. Ahrens (in charge of Cadillac in 1956 when the first millionth postwar Cadillac was built).

Brougham were two carpeted, folding footrests and two large, storage pockets in its rear passenger compartment.

The Fleetwood Eldorado's two standard interiors of Diamond pattern or Deaville cloth and vinyl were each offered in four color choices. Leather interiors in 12 color combinations were available at extra cost. Of all the 1968 Cadillacs, only the Eldorado at 221 inches was unchanged in overall length. But the added length of the rear-drive models was, at 0.7 inches, insignificant. On the other hand, the Eldorado's appearance was far more extensively changed than normally expected of an automobile entering its second model year.

The most significant alterations took place at the front where the parking lights were now positioned in the leading edge of the front fenders. To accommodate the new concealed, windshield-wiper system the Eldorado's hood length was extended 4.5 inches. At the rear, reshaped larger taillights, more visible from the side and rear, blended into the trailing edge of the rear fenders. Added to the taillight housing was narrow chrome trim.

"No cars in all the world," said Cadillac, "are more in evidence at important social occasions or more appreciated in the business community than the magnificent Fleetwood Limousines." As it did with the Series Sixty Special and Brougham models, Cadillac, in this pre-fuel crisis era, regarded the sheer size of the Series Seventy-Five Sedan and Limousine as sales assets rather than debits. Thus, it noted: "More than twenty feet long with a wheelbase of 149.8 inches, the Seventy-Five Sedan and Limousine provided motoring luxury and spaciousness without compare." Cadillac pulled out all the stops in equipping these flagships of its automobile fleet. Joining the list of standard features found on other Fleetwoods was a right-side, manually operated, exterior rear-view mirror, automatic climate control air conditioning, and a rear-window defogger. While power steering was standard, it was not the variable ratio unit.

The formal roof line (a padded roof was optional), 149.8-inch wheelbase, and 245.2-inch overall length of the Seventy-Five models impacted mightily on one's visual senses. Both cars had the same rear-deck and hood trim as the Fleetwood Brougham and Sixty Special. To these items were added small wreath and crest plates on the rear fenders and a demure Fleetwood plaque to the Limousine's C-pillar. The Sedan had power vent windows with the Limousine equipped with a glass-partitioned, leather-upholstered chauffeur's compartment. The standard color was black with gray available as an option.

Five interiors were offered as standard selections for the Seventy-Five models. These included dark-blue DuBarry cloth and leather and light-gray Dunstan cloth with embroidered inserts. Both versions were equipped with a full-width folding seat for three additional passengers. Rear controls in the Limousine allowed occupants to raise or lower windows, turn on reading lamps, tune the radio, activate the automatic climate control, and raise or lower the glass partition. Overall,

Cadillac offered 141 interior combinations: 70 in cloth, 67 in leather, and 4 in vinyl.

The latest Cadillac, being after all a conglomeration of mechanical components assembled and designed by fallible humans, was not flawless nor faultless. But it was by any reasonable standard, an outstanding automobile. Tom McCahill, who drove a Fleetwood Brougham from coast to coast, reported in *Mechanix Illustrated*, June 1968, that it came close to being, in his view, one of the world's best automobiles. He considered it far and away the top American prestige car. Among the attributes he singled out for praise were its comfort, roadability, and general performance.

AUTOCAR'S TEST DRIVE

As it had done in both 1961 and 1964, the British magazine *Autocar* tested a contemporary model (a Coupe de Ville) owned by Cadillac enthusiast, J. C. Bamford. Cadillac sales in Great Britain were negligible; and due to its sheer size, any modern Cadillac was really out of its realm on most British roads.

To many *Autocar* readers, the Cadillac was not merely a foreign car, but one whose philosophy of design was truly alien. Thus *Autocar* went to some efforts to provide readers with a new perspective of the Cadillac. It explained that although it was one of America's most expensive cars, it did not compare in price to Rolls Royce nor did it have the same level of craftsmanship. On the other hand, the *Autocar* noted that while 2,000 Rolls Royces were being built in 1967, Cadillac was busy turning out over 213,000 cars!

Autocar wasn't terribly enthused by the Coupe de Ville's design and construction, which it characterized as obsolete. But it also found much to praise in its operation, particularly the Cadillac's ability to effortlessly provide outstanding performance. Indeed, *Autocar* elevated Cadillac to a pedestal, considering it superior to all cars it had ever tested in terms of its ability to deliver effortless and silent performance. All that and more from an engine capable of moving a 5,354-pound automobile from 0 to 60 mph in 9.9 seconds, completing the standing-start, one-quarter mile in 16.9 seconds at 81 mph, and reaching 100 mph from rest in 27.6 seconds. McCahill's test car, a Fleetwood Brougham, was a bit quicker, reaching 60 mph from rest in 8.7 seconds; 100 mph in 25.6 seconds. Moreover, the *Autocar* test car delivered excellent fuel economy. At a constant 60 mph, it averaged 16.2 mpg; and even while maintaining a speed of 100 mph, traveled 10.3 miles on a single gallon.

This particular Cadillac was not equipped with the optional power, front disc brakes and, predictably, *Autocar* wasn't thrilled with the standard drum system, which it concluded was incapable of making a stop from 100 mph to 0 in a manner considered acceptable. As a result, *Autocar* noted the folly of having mandated safety padding, while a superior disc-brake system remained an option. Cadillac was trailing both Imperial and Lincoln Continental by not adopting front disc brakes as standard equipment on all its models.

Imperial had done so since 1967, Lincoln Continental since 1966. Cadillac would not provide them across the board until 1970.

CADILLAC'S DOMESTIC COMPETITION

Neither Lincoln Continental nor Imperial came anywhere near remotely approximating Cadillac's production/sales performance in 1968. Lincoln Continental output for the model year, at 46,904, was up only 1,237 units from the mediocre level of 1967. Imperial, running true to its tradition, experienced a decline of 2,253 cars, closing out its model run with 15,361 assemblies.

Both Lincoln and Imperial failed to offer automobiles with significant styling or technical changes; although the introduction of the Lincoln Continental Mark III on April 5, 1968, as a 1969 model, ushered in an age when Cadillac's supremacy in every aspect of the luxury-car field would no longer be considered a foregone conclusion.

The standard Lincoln Continentals, like other American cars, had front and rear side running lights which, in its case, were incorporated in the front parking lights and rear taillights. Other changes included a revised grille grid, the removal of the hood emblem, and a revamped roof line for the coupe model. Except for necessary pollution controls, the Lincoln Continental's 460 cid V-8 was unchanged from 1968. Technical refinements included detail changes to the Select-Shift Turbo-Drive transmission and a "controlled crush" front structure to improve the car's "crashability." Changes to the interior were, like those of other cars, mainly keyed to new government regulations, involving additional padding, an energy-absorbing steering column, and redesigned instrument panel dash knobs. Added to Lincoln Continental's option list was a rear-window defogger and a reclining passenger seat equipped with a power-operated headrest.

As the last version of a body style scheduled for replacement in 1969, the Imperial's appearance contained few surprises, being limited mainly to a new grille arrangement embracing the leading edges of the front fenders.

Technically, the most interesting feature offered by Imperial was a semihigh-performance-engine option, the "440 Dual," which was fitted with a dual-snorkle air cleaner and dual exhausts. No change in the Imperial's rated horsepower of 350 at 4,400 rpm was made for the addition of these items. Indeed, the power output of the 1968 Imperial engine remained unchanged from 1967 even though larger-diameter exhaust valves were used.

For the third straight year, Imperial Crown coupes could be ordered with the $597.40 Mobile Director option, which included a front passenger seat that revolved 180° to face the rear seat across a folding, miniconference table complete with a gooseneck light.

Imperial's market penetration remained low. Production, at 15,361 cars, was down by just over 2,200 units from 1967. A new body would boost sales in 1969; but even then, output would remain far below the two-decade-old mark of 37,557 set back in 1957.

As the sixties drew to a close, three fundamental factors dominated the luxury-car field. Foremost was Cadillac's dominant position in its field. But this supremacy was to come under increasing challenge from Lincoln, which had successfully embraced Cadillac's marketing philosophy without compromising its uniqueness. Of equal concern to Cadillac was the steady upward climb of Mercedes-Benz sales in the United States. This was a development Cadillac could ignore only at its own peril. It chose not to. Just a few years later, it was surveying Mercede-Benz owners to determine what the appeal of this German automobile was to its American buyers. Who would have thought, in 1968, with Cadillac sales at an all-time peak that just seven years later it would market a much smaller model whose intended target carried a three-pointed star?

SPECIFICATIONS

Engine

Type: V-8, ohv
Bore × stroke: 4.30 × 4.06 inches
Displacement: 472 cubic inches
Horsepower: 375 @ 4,400 rpm
Torque: 525 lb-ft @ 3,000 rpm
Compression ratio: 10.5:1
Fuel system: Rochester Quadrajet, four-barrel downdraft
Electrical system: 12-volt, 15-amp battery, high-capacity 42-amp generator (55-amp on air-conditioned cars)

Chassis/Drivetrain

Transmission: Turbo Hydra-Matic torque converter with fixed stator
Frame: Fully boxed perimeter frame with hidden bulkheads (Eldorado: Boxed perimeter for front-wheel drive)
Rear axle:
　Rear-drive models: Hypoid, offset differential, redesigned for increased torque of 472 cid V-8, 2.94:1 ratio
　Eldorado: 3.07:1
　Series 75: 3.21:1
Front suspension: Spherical joints with helical-coil type springs, torsion bars on Eldorado
Rear suspension: Four-link drive, helical-coil springs, single-leaf springs with four shock absorbers on Eldorado
Steering: Variable-ratio power steering standard on all models except Series 75
　Overall ratio: 16.6:1
　Series 75: 18.2:1
　Eldorado: 16.3:1
Tires: Low-pressure, 2-ply tubeless, 9.00 × 15
　Series 75: 8.20 × 15, 4-ply

Dimensions

Wheelbase: 129.5 inches
    Fleetwood 60 Special, Brougham: 133.5 inches
    Series 75:   149.8 inches
    Eldorado: 120 inches
Width: 80.0 inches
Front/rear tread: 62.5/62.5 inches
    Eldorado: 63.5/63 inches
Overall length: 224.7 inches
    Brougham and Series 60:   228.2 inches
    Series 75:   245.2 inches
    Eldorado: 221 inches

Popular Options

Disc brakes

Automatic cruise control
Tilt and telescope steering wheel
Automatic climate control
Six-way power seat
Twilight sentinel
Power vent window
Power door locks
Padded vinyl roof
AM-FM radio
Remote-control trunk lock
Front-seat head restraint
Guide-Matic headlamp dimmer
Controlled differential
Soft-ray tinted glass
White sidewall tires
Auxiliary horn
Rear shoulder belts

1969

A Masterpiece from the Master Craftsmen

IF NOT FOR labor stoppages resulting from strikes, Cadillac, in 1969, would have established another model-year production record. As it was, 1969 model output totaled 223,267 units, down just 6,736 from 1968. For the calendar year, the results were more sensational, as output easily shattered the quarter-million level by peaking at 266,798.

When the Cadillac line was introduced on September 26, 1968, it was obvious that 1969 would feature a rarity in the postwar luxury-car market: a hammer and tongs, no holds barred, no mercy asked or given battle between a Cadillac model and a challenger from one of its adversaries. In this sales drama, the two protagonists were the Cadillac Eldorado and the Lincoln Continental Mark III.

LINCOLN MARK III

Lincoln introduced the Mark III, as a 1969 model, on April 5, 1968. Ford Motor Company was partial to that time of year for unveiling important new products. Four years earlier, for example, the first Mustang had been announced in April 1964. Sales of the far more costly Mark III didn't even approach those of the Mustang. But they clearly indicated that Ford had another success on its hands that would make a significant contribution to Lincoln's market strength.

The Ford Motor Company, like General Motors, chose to spread out the development costs for its entry into the personal luxury-car field by utilizing many components and design features from another automobile. In this case, the Mark III's associate car was the Ford Thunderbird, which, having added a four-door model in 1967, was already considered a competitor to Cadillac.

One look, however, at a Mark III quickly dispelled any preconceptions of the "Baby Lincoln" as merely a spruced-up Thunderbird. Lincoln did have familial connections with other Ford Motor Company products in mind when it designed the Mark III, but the T-Bird wasn't part of the strategy. Instead, the Mark III, as its name implied was intended to be evaluated in the context of the original prewar Lincoln Continental and its short-lived (1955-57) successor, the Mark II.

Lincoln admitted that with the Eldorado into its second model year, the Mark III was a response to a move Cadillac had made first. But the Lincoln-Mercury management wasn't willing to concede that Ford had been slow to react to a market that seemed far from reaching a saturation point. Rather, they pointed to the Mustang and Cougar as cars that Ford had chosen to give a higher priority.

Unlike the Eldorado, the engineering of the Mark III followed along conventional lines with coil springs at all four wheels and a rear-wheel drivetrain. Compared with the Eldorado, its 117.2-inch wheelbase was 2.5 inches shorter, while overall length at 216.5 inches was 4.5 inches less. At 79.5 inches, the Mark III was just a half inch narrower than the Eldorado. Its engine, a 460-cubic-inch V-8 with 365 horsepower and 500 lb-ft of torque, provided competitive performance.

As noted, the Mark III's appearance bore a strong resemblance to the earlier models, particularly the Mark II. This was especially evident in the Mark III's rear-deck tire bulge, side-body character line, and roof profile. A minor shock was the shape of the Mark III's grille, which bore a close similarity to that associated with Rolls-Royce.

This bit of design plagiarism apparently had anything but a negative impact on Mark III output, which totaled 7,770 in 1968. The next year, things really began to heat up between the Mark III and the Eldorado, as their respective model-year totals were 23,088 and 23,333. The Eldorado emerged the winner but by a razor-thin margin of 245 cars! Two years later, as the Mark IV, the Lincoln surged ahead of the Eldorado's output by over 8,000 units. This was undeniably a great achievement for Lincoln, made more impressive by an even larger margin over the Eldorado the following year. As embarrassing as this was to

Cadillac, it was not to be a permanent situation. Nor would it be a sales bonanza for Lincoln without a price, since the evidence was strong that a good portion of the Mark's sales success was gained at the expense of other Lincoln products.

CHANGES AND IMPROVEMENTS

While this free-for-all in tails and top hats was unfolding, the remaining 1969 Cadillacs displayed styling clearly influenced by the Eldorado. This new outer skin for the Cadillac cost approximately $16 million. It was highlighted by prowlike front fenders with sharper upper edges and narrower profiles made possible by the positioning of the headlights horizontally on each side of a grille that was noticeably higher and narrower than previously. To some, the net result, rather than closely associating all Cadillacs with the Eldorado, bore too much similarity to the Lincoln Continental's front end.

At the rear, there was just a hint of the good old days as Cadillac abandoned, at least for a time, the combination taillight-bumper format in favor of bolder vertical taillights that, combined with a high and narrow rear-fender line, came tantilizingly close to being fins.

Additional exterior changes included a longer (by 2.5 inches) hood and elimination of the cowl vents and front ventpanes on all body styles. Coupe models adopted Eldorado's "vertical break," rear-window design.

Changes in the Eldorado's appearance were of the minor variety except for the abandoning of hidden headlights in favor of exposed models positioned to conform with those on other Cadillacs.

Technical changes included a redesigned frame, a larger-capacity automatic Climate Control system, and a sealed-engine coolant system. A welcome addition as standard equipment in all models were power, front disc brakes.

DIFFERENCES AMONG MODELS

The two Calais models, the Hardtop Sedan and Coupe, were, like all Cadillacs, available in 16 standard and five optional Firemist colors. A total of eight interiors in either Decameron cloth with leather-textured vinyl trim or all-vinyl were available.

Interior selections for the Coupe de Ville totaled 17; for the Hardtop Sedan de Ville, 16; for the Sedan de Ville, 14; and for the Convertible, 10. Cadillac exploited both this wide choice of colors and interiors as well as the particular virtues of each De Ville model. For example, it claimed that "the Coupe de Ville can be expected to return a higher percentage of its original cost at trade than any other car built on the land." The Hardtop Sedan de Ville was depicted as the automobile "that attracts more buyers than any other single luxury car in the world," while the Sedan de Ville was lauded for combining "spirited performance . . . with spacious six-passenger roominess." Finally, in regard to the De Ville Convertible, it was claimed that "for the youthful zest of top-down motoring, Cadillac has no peer among luxury cars."

Both the Fleetwood Sixty Special and Fleetwood Brougham were available in 19 interiors, including cloth and Sierra-grain-leather combinations. The Brougham's padded vinyl roof was offered in any of six colors.

The Fleetwood Eldorado, described as "the third edition of a motor car already a classic in its time," was, like other Fleetwood models, equipped with Automatic Level Control. Its list of available interiors totaled eighteen.

For the Fleetwood Seventy-Five Limousine and nine-passenger Sedan, five interior choices were offered. Regardless of color selected, the Limousine's front compartment was finished in Black leather.

1969 Coupe de Ville. Front-end changes included horizontal headlamps and combined parking and cornering lamps that wrapped around the front fender.

CADILLAC'S DOMESTIC COMPETITION

If both Cadillac and Lincoln were to be applauded for vigorously responding to the challenges of a shifting luxury-car market, what was to be said for Imperial? More than ever, it appeared as a car struggling for identity, lacking a solid base on which to plan future products, slowly drifting back to its former status as a glorified Chrysler while, at the same time, attempting unsuccessfully to emulate Cadillac's recipe for success.

It's true, Imperial production did advance in 1969 to 22,077, but that total, even if it was an increase of 6,716, was less than that of either the Eldorado or the Continental Mark III. Chrysler said its 1969 cars were "fuselage-styled" but they didn't mention which aircraft had donated its main body section for inspiration. The

swollen jowls of the Imperial suggested that the B-52 wouldn't be a bad guess.

While the Imperial's new appearance attracted few plaudits, Lincoln Continental was bidding farewell to one that had served well. The next year Lincoln would introduce a new body, the first since 1961. Changes for 1969, therefore, weren't extensive; a new front end, that made some people wonder who (Cadillac or Lincoln) was copying from whom, along with taillights now located within the rear-bumper confines.

Cadillac wouldn't have an all-new body in 1970 to match Lincoln's move, but it would offer something not found on any other automobile in the world—an engine displacing 500 cubic inches.

1969 Hardtop Sedan de Ville. All rear-drive Cadillacs had restyled Eldorado-like front fenders. For 1969, the hood was extended 2.5 inches, and the cowl vent louvers at the rear of the hood were eliminated.

CADILLAC VITAL STATISTICS: 1969

Series	Model	Body Type	Factory Price ($)	Weight (lbs.)	Production (#)
Calais	68249	4 dr Sedan (HT)	5660	4630	6825
	68247	2 dr Coupe (HT)	5484	4555	5600
De Ville	68369	4 dr Sedan	5954	4640	7890
	68349	4 dr Sedan (HT)	5954	4660	72,958
	68347	2 dr Coupe (HT)	5721	4595	65,755
	68367	2 dr Convertible	5905	4590	16,445
Fleetwood Eldorado	69347	2 dr Coupe (HT)	6711	4550	23,333
60 Special	68069	4 dr Sedan	6779	4765	2545
Brougham	68169	4 dr Sedan	7110	4770	17,300
75	69723	4 dr Sedan 9p	10841	5430	880
	69733	4 dr Limousine 9p	10979	5555	1156

1969 Fleetwood Brougham. The Brougham and Sixty Special had exclusive roofs with a design line accenting the roof perimeter, creating a formal effect.

1969 Fleetwood Eldorado. Changes to the Eldorado included a finely textured grille, new wheel discs, and exposed headlamps.

SPECIFICATIONS

Engine

Type: V-type, ohv, 8 cylinders
Bore × stroke: 4.30 × 4.06 inches
Displacement: 472 cubic inches
Compression ratio: 10.5:1
Horsepower: 375 @ 4,400 rpm
Torque: 525 lb-ft @ 3,000 rpm
Fuel system: Rochester Quadrajet four-barrel carburetor
Electrical system: 12-volt, 15-plate battery, 42-amp generator, 55-amp on air-conditioned cars

Chassis/Drivetrain

Frame: Perimeter-type, fully boxed with hidden bulkheads
Front suspension: Independent, spherical joint, helical-coil springs, rubber-mounted strut rods and rubber bushings, Eldorado: torsion bars
Rear suspension: Four-link drive, helical-coil springs, rubber bushings

Eldorado: Single-leaf springs with two horizontal and two vertical shock absorbers
Rear axle: Hypoid, offset differential, 2.94:1 ratio
Series 75:   3.21:1
Driving axle ratio for Eldorado: 3.07:1
All models except Eldorado available with controlled differential
Brakes: Power-assisted, composite-finned rear drums, disc front, split hydraulic master cylinders
Steering: Variable-ratio power steering on all models except Series 75, 16.6:1 overall ratio

Popular Options

Power-door locks
Automatic climate control
Tilt and telescope steering wheel
AM radio
AM/FM radio
AM/FM stereo radio
Dual comfort seats (driver's and driver/passenger), standard on Brougham
Remote-control trunk release
Cruise control
Twilight sentinel

1970

Is It Any Wonder Cadillac Owners Continue to Return to Cadillac?

IN 1970, for the sixth consecutive year, Cadillac established a new divisional, model-year production record. This achievement, resulting in 238,745 Cadillacs being built, was made under less than favorable economic conditions—a major GM strike plus a general economic downturn and in the face of the first all-new Lincoln Continental since 1961. This latter development pegged a moderately restyled Cadillac against an automobile with the significant advantage of freshness on its side.

The ability of Cadillac to sustain its upward sales momentum ran counter to the efforts of its competition. Imperial's output fell by nearly 50 percent, with Lincoln Continental's, in spite of offering a new product, dropping slightly to 59,127. Cadillac's general manager, George R. Elges, admitted that Cadillac's changes for 1970 were subtle; but at the same time, he regarded them as important innovations that maintained Cadillac's standing as America's number one prestige product.

CHANGES AND IMPROVEMENTS

If not exactly fitting into the category of an innovation, the 1970 Eldorado's standard engine aroused as much attention as any other technical development of recent years. This wasn't due to any great technologic breakthrough but rather because of its size. For the first time in automotive history, a production model was offered with a standard engine displacing 500 cubic inches. Given contemporary trends, it's unlikely that the likes of this engine will ever be seen again. Cadillac attained this peak with ease and without complication. All that was required was an increase in the engine's stroke to 4.304 from 4.06 inches, and there were 500 cubic inches, turning out 400 horsepower at 4,400 rpm and 550 lb-ft of torque at 3,000 rpm.

Less startling and certainly less exciting was Cadillac's adoption of a new ductile-iron steering knuckle. Since George Elges readily admitted that

"Cadillac owners rarely seek out a new model line's engineering achievements," it's likely that this seemingly esoteric development passed them by totally unacknowledged. But in practice, it proved to be more reliable and durable than the previous system. Furthermore, it combined the knuckle, steering arm, and disc-brake support plate, which were previously hand-assembled, into a single unit, thus lowering production costs. "The durability of this imaginative design," said Carl Rasmussen, "has been dramatically demonstrated in over a half-million miles of road testing under all conditions. In all those miles, we have had outstanding success. In addition, the design has been extensively tested on laboratory endurance equipment with equal success."

Fitting into the same category of unnoticed, unappreciated, but worthwhile improvements for 1970 was a new cooling fan with flexible, stainless steel blades. This both improved engine cooling and air-conditioner performance, which was also enhanced by virtue of a larger-capacity condenser. Concurrently, since the fan ran at a slightly reduced speed, there was less wear on the water pump and belt. For improved exhaust emission, Cadillac replaced the air injection used previously with a controlled combustion system, which included a carburetor preheat system and an altered spark advance. Cadillacs sold in California were also fitted with an evaporative emission control system. All models were equipped with a new steering pump with fewer parts and potential leak points. All Cadillacs were available with a vacuum-type, speed-control system activated by pressing a button on the end of the turn signal level. This feature was available only on the Eldorado in 1969.

Rear-drive models were equipped with a completely new rear-axle assembly that not only was quieter, more durable, and easier to service than the unit it replaced, but also was reported to possess the highest torque capacity of any passenger-car unit in production. This axle, which had been under development for six years, combined an integral carrier housing and a straddle-mounted pinion. "The new axle has improved access to the differential, a replaceable ring gear and pinion and improved adjustment procedures for greater ease of servicing by mechanics in the field," reported Carl Rasmussen. He also noted that "the straddle-mounted pinion provides greater rigidity with the added advantages of increased torque capacity, quietness and durability."

In this new design, the pinion was supported by a total of three bearings, unlike the two-bearing setup used by most passenger cars. The pinion was also offset 2.25 inches below the axle center line, which was the largest in the industry. This allowed a lower drive line to be adopted. To ensure reliability, hundreds of car tests and a half-million miles of laboratory tests were performed on this axle design before it was released for production. Accompanying this change was a 1-inch tread increase and the installation of standard equipment, belted, bias-ply fiberglass tires on all models.

While following after Pontiac, which introduced a radio antenna embedded in the windshield on its 1969 Grand Prix, Cadillac both adopted this item in 1970 and offered an industry-first AM/FM signal-seeking stereo radio as an option on all models but the Seventy-Five Series. Described by Cadillac as "the ultimate in listening pleasure with four-speaker stereo sound," its tuning bar was fitted with a "Stereo Only," setting which limited FM radio selections to those stations broadcasting in stereo. This radio plus the AM/FM model with front and rear speakers (No AM-only radio was available in 1970) could be linked to the foot-control switch, which allowed the driver to change stations by simply tapping the floor-mounted button. Also available was an eight-track stereo tape player.

With a new styling cycle scheduled to begin in 1971, the latest Cadillacs were carefully tailored to maintain styling continuity between two design eras. There were plenty of changes to be sure—a new grille, revised taillights, and rear bumper to cite three examples. But the 1970 model was closely linked to the 1969 models, which, in turn, was like the 1968 and so on back in Cadillac's history.

Furthermore, no one needed to possess clairvoyance to declare that the 1970 model would be like the 1971. Past, present, and future were, in any postwar Cadillac, combined in a fashion that was the envy of the auto industry. The latest models appeared longer because of new cornering lights with horizontal chrome trim, the extension of the rear quarter into the taillight, and a horizontal design line that extended the full body side.

Additional detail changes for 1970 consisted of a grille format using 13, rather than seven, as in 1969, vertical bars to create a finer texture. Elegantly formed winged Cadillac emblems were placed on the forward section of the front fender to replace the V on the hood of Calais and De Ville models. For the veteran Cadillac owner, this brought back fond memories of Cadillacs from an earlier day, in particular those of 1941 and 1942. All Fleetwoods retained a hood-mounted wreath and crest. Moderately changing the front end's lines was the use of body color painted, rather than chromed, headlight surrounds. Also contributing to the Cadillac's fresh appearance were new wheel discs with radial fins.

Cadillac turned away from the "wraparound" taillight format of 1969 in favor of a concave, V-shaped vertical lens that housed the taillight, stoplight, and directional signal. The rear bumper was incorporated into the rear lighting arrangement. This vertical motif was extended by the reflective marker, which was now located directly below the taillight in the outer ends of the bumper. Small, rectangular backup lights with a wider and brighter beam were placed close to the license-plate receptacle.

Summarizing Cadillac's styling changes for 1970, George Elges noted, "Cadillac customers can personalize their 1970 car from a variety of 21 exterior colors, 15 of which are new. Also, there are seven vinyl-roof color options." Beside the availability of new fabrics in 167 combinations of cloth, vinyl, and leather, interior changes were highlighted by much greater use of wood-grain appliques on the dash and side-panel insert, a steering wheel with slimmer spokes, and new center pad. The horn could be activated from an insert in each spoke and one in the center padded section. The driver controls were easier to reach, and the instrumentation was both more legible and convenient. A tamper-proof odometer was also introduced.

DIFFERENCES AMONG MODELS

Once again production of the Calais series trailed far behind equivalent De Ville models. But Cadillac stubbornly continued trying to convince would-be Calais buyers of their virtues. "The most practical way," said Cadillac, "to discover Cadillac luxury and distinction is with the Calais Coupe. It possesses all of Cadillac's uncompromising excellence, yet competes in price with cars of lesser stature that do not come equipped with many of the Calais' standard features." True enough, but interest in the $5,637 Coupe was so moribund that only 4,724 were produced. The Hardtop Sedan, priced at $5,813, didn't fare much better with an output of 5,187.

Externally, Calais were set apart from the identically sized De Ville by their Calais signature script placed on the rear fenders just ahead of the headlight-bumper structure and the use of square, rather than rectangular (as on other models) backup lights.

Interiors for both the Coupe and Hardtop Sedan were offered in six color choices of Dorian cloth and Sierra-grain vinyl trim. All-vinyl interiors in either black or antique medium beige were optional.

The sheer scope of interior choices offered for the De Ville models partially explained the tremendous popularity of these Cadillacs. The output of just one model, the Hardtop Sedan De Ville (83,274) was greater than that of Lincoln (53,127) and Imperial (11,816) combined. Cadillac wasn't fooling when it said that "in all the world, the Hardtop Sedan De Ville stands pre-eminent in popularity among luxury-car motorists." Perhaps modesty prevented it from adding that the sec-

1970 Hardtop Sedan de Ville. New taillights with concave, V-shaped vertical lens were introduced in 1970.

1970 Fleetwood Eldorado. Its 500-cubic-inch V-8 was the largest production-car engine in the world.

ond most popular choice was the Coupe de Ville. Its output which totaled 76,043, also exceeded that of Lincoln and Imperial.

Coupe de Ville interiors numbered 16 in 1970, nine were all leather, the rest combined leather trim with either Dubonnet or Dynasty cloth seats. For the Hardtop Sedan de Ville, the choice was narrowed to 15: 3 Dynasty cloth-and-leather, 4 Dubonnet cloth-and-leather, and 8 all-leather selections.

The Sedan de Ville, which along with the De Ville Convertible was in its last year of production, was available with the same cloth-and-leather interiors offered for the Hardtop Sedan. Only six all-leather choices were listed. Of all the De Ville models, it was the least popular, as its production total of 7,230 indicates.

It wasn't the most startling of developments by any means, but the De Ville Convertible bid farewell to the new car world by becoming the first Cadillac soft-top available with a rear-window defogger. All in all, Cadillac said the Convertible was "without a doubt, . . . the most exciting way to enter the spirited seventies." Ten all-leather interiors, each with a contrasting carpeting could be selected for the Convertible. As in all De Ville models upholstered in leather, the Convertible was fitted with oriental tamo wood in its door and instrument panel.

Changes in the Eldorado's successful format were not extensive. The rear taillights were resculptured, providing a more slender appearance. Replacing the fine-mesh grille of the 1969 Eldorado, which in effect was now found on the rear-drive models, was a unit with five prominent horizontal bars forward of narrower vertical fins. Beneath the Eldorado script was a not exactly immodest badge that read "8.2 LITRE," which Cadillac informed prospective customers was "the internationally recognized metric equivalent of 500 cubic inches.

As in 1969, the Eldorado's turn signals were placed in the leading edge of the front fenders. For 1970, their lenses were embossed with the winged crest found on the other Cadillac models.

After having been moved to a point just above the midbody crease line in 1969, the Eldorado name, in block letters, returned to its original location directly

behind the front fender cutout. Running between the wheel cutouts, along the body shadow line, was a chrome-trim spear. Also changed was the form of the taillights, which were thinner than previous models.

Eight all-leather and seven duplex cloth interiors were offered for the Eldorado. These interiors, its exclusive engine, front-wheel drive, and distinctive styling combined to add substance to Cadillac's claim that the Eldorado was "purposefully built to be the world's finest personal car . . . One designed for the motorist who deserves unusually spirited performance, individual styling and all the elegance and comfort for which Cadillac is renowned."

Similarly the Fleetwood Sixty Special Sedan and its alter ego, the Fleetwood Brougham, were once again the leaders of their price class. Both models now were fitted with a full-length body-rub item, in addition to their broad lower-body-trim rails. Unlike those found on the Calais and De Ville models, which were all-chrome, all Fleetwoods used moldings with raised vinyl inserts. The insert's color was color-keyed to the body color. If the Fleetwood was equipped with a vinyl top, the insert's color matched the roof's. Common to all Fleetwoods were the traditional crest and wreath embellishments for the hood and rear deck. Standard on the Fleetwood Brougham was its padded cross grain roof and the Brougham crest and name plate mounted on the C-pillar. Both the Brougham and Sixty Special were offered with 7 leather interiors, 4 selections of all Divan cloth, and 4 Dumbarton cloth and leather combinations. The Brougham also was fitted with carpeted, rear footrests and oriental tamo wood on the doors and instrument panel.

The Brougham's modest price (at $7,285, it was only $331 more costly) relative to the Sixty Special made it far and away the winner in the production race between these two Cadillacs: 16,913 to 1,738. Ever since the Brougham's debut in 1966 as a separate model, it had outsold the Sixty Special. There was little logic, therefore, to continue the latter model in Cadillac's lineup. Thus, 1970 was the "standard" Sixty Special's final year.

Predictably, Cadillac saved plenty of superlatives to describe the Fleetwood Seventy-Five nine-passenger Sedan and Limousine. They offered, said Cadillac,

The Eldorado's 500-cubic-inch, 400-horsepower engine.

All 1970 rear-drive models used a new rear axle with the highest torque capacity of any American-built passenger car.

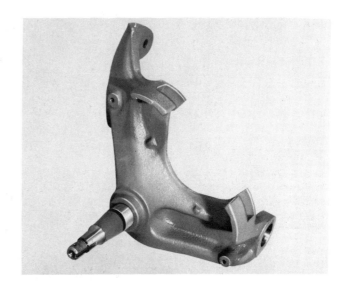

A new integral steering knuckle under development for seven years was introduced in 1970.

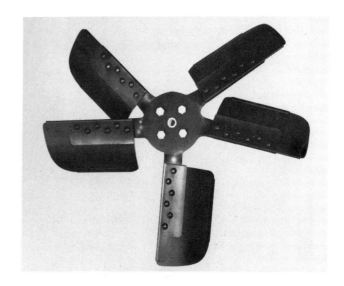

The 1970 Cadillacs were fitted with a fan having flexible stainless steel blades. By running at slightly slower speeds than previously, it reduced wear on the water pump and belt.

1970 Coupe de Ville. Headlight bevels on 1970 models were trimmed in body color.

1970 Fleetwood Brougham.

CADILLAC VITAL STATISTICS: 1970

Series	Model	Body Type	Factory Price ($)	Weight (lbs.)	Production (#)
Calais	68249	4 dr Sedan (HT)	5813	4680	5187
	68247	2 dr Coupe (HT)	5637	4620	724
De Ville	68369	4 dr Sedan	6118	4690	7230
	68349	4 dr Sedan (HT)	6118	4725	83,274
	68347	2 dr Coupe (HT)	5884	4650	76,043
	68367	2 dr Convertible	6068	4660	15,172
Fleetwood					
Eldorado	69347	2 dr Coupe (HT)	6903	4630	23,842
60 Special	68069	4 dr Sedan	6953	4830	1738
Brougham	68169	4 dr Sedan	7284	4835	16,913
75	69723	4 dr Sedan 9p	11,039	5530	876
	69733	4 dr Limousine	11,1178	5630	1240

"splendor that is unmatched in all of motordom. No other motor cars are so luxuriously appointed for comfort, convenience and privacy." As in earlier years, the Limousine was fitted with a glass partition separating the chauffeur's compartment from the rear passenger area. Once again, the front seat was upholstered in leather. The interior of the Sedan, and the Limousine's passenger region, was offered in five upholstery choices, a Decordo cloth, a Dumbarten cloth-leather combination, plus a Divan cloth available in medium blue, light gray, or medium beige.

Cadillac had long since relinquished corporate performance leadership to other GM automotive divisions by 1970, but the arrival of the 400-hp/500-cid Eldorado engine rekindled interest in its acceleration and top-speed capability. With a road weight just a hundred or so pounds shy of the 2½-ton mark, the Eldorado was not to be counted among America's muscle cars. Yet it was certainly capable of spirited motion when called upon with a 0 to 60-mph mark of approximately 9.5 seconds, a top speed approaching 125 mph, and standing-start marks of 16.3 seconds and 80 mph.

Undoubtedly, Cadillac could have, in 1970, produced a Grand Touring version of the Eldorado. But its primary interest was in offering an Eldorado that appealed to somewhat younger drivers than did other Cadillacs, while maintaining the road decorum of the larger models.

CADILLAC'S DOMESTIC COMPETITION

While the Eldorado had, when introduced in 1967, been compared with that other great front-wheel-drive car of an early day, the 1937 Cord, because of their design relationship, the 1970 Lincoln Continental aroused memories of that car because of its front-end appearance. With concealed headlights and a hood-grille arrangement that carried unmistakable overtones of the old "coffin-nosed" Cord, the new Lincoln was a formidable-appearing automobile. This kinship was shortlived. As the Mark III gained in popularity, it made far more sense for the Lincoln Continental to copy that car's "classic" grille form and beginning the next year this process began.

Major engineering and design changes included use of a body-frame chassis rather than the unit-body construction of 1961-1969 and the abandonment of the center-opening format for four-door models. Influencing this change was both its lower construction cost and the results of a survey that found the older setup unattractive to Cadillac owners.

Certainly an important feature of the new Lincoln Continental body was its expanded interior space. Although it was a mere 0.8 inches longer, 2.3 inches higher and a 0.1 inch narrower, the new car offered significantly increased interior accommodations.

While the Lincoln Continental was just catching up with Cadillac by featuring hidden windshield wipers and "Stardust" metal-flake paint options, it was out front with its optional Kelsey-Hayes, "Sure-Track" anti-skid braking option and rear backlight embedded with heat wire to melt accumulated snow and ice.

Changes to the Mark III were not extensive, the most important being new wheelcovers, revised parking and taillights, concealed wipers, a standard vinyl roof, revamped interior, and several new features including a time-delay, interior light system. A point of major interest was the standard equipment status of the Sure-Track system on the Mark III, which was intended to counter the Eldorado's image of superior technology.

Once again these two cars finished a very close, model-year production run. The Mark III closed its 1970 books at 21,432 cars with Eldorado ahead at 23,842.

If Lincoln was enjoying the fruit of early efforts to establish its cars as worthy competitors to Cadillac, the Imperial was in the final throes of a failed policy, indecisive planning and poor marketing strategy. Increasingly regarded as an up-market version of the New Yorker, the Imperial was only moderately altered (both in terms of styling and engineering). The inevitable result, in face of the new Lincoln-Continental, the existence of the Mark III and Eldorado models, and of course, the Cadillac, more appealing than ever, was a precipitous drop in Imperial's popularity as only 11,816 were produced for the model year.

The handwriting on the wall was clear, the Imperial's days were numbered. On the other hand, for Cadillac it was moving towards a 70th anniversary celebration in 1972 by offering new styling for the 1971 models, that would, to no one's real surprise, establish another sales record.

At the same time, what once would have been dismissed as sheer poppycock, rumors that a small, down-sized Cadillac was in the works were beginning to be taken seriously. If Imperial was on the way out as a Cadillac competitor, its place was being filled by the Teutonic heavyweight, Mercedes-Benz.

SPECIFICATIONS

Engine

Type: V-type, ohv, eight cylinders
Bore × stroke: 4.3 × 4.06 inches
    Eldorado: 4.3 × 4.304 inches
Displacement: 472 cubic inches
    Eldorado: 500 cubic inches
Horsepower: 375 @ 4,400 rpm
    Eldorado: 400 @ 4,400 rpm
Torque: 525 lb-ft @ 3,000 rpm, Eldorado: 550 lb-ft @ 3,000 rpm
Compression ratio: 10.0:1
Fuel system: Rochester, four-barrel Quadrajet, Model 4MV
Electrical system: 12-volt, 15-plate battery, 42-amp generator, 55 amp on air-conditioned cars

Chassis/Drivetrain

Transmission: Turbo Hydra-Matic
Frame: Boxed perimeter type
Rear axle: (rear-drive models):   2.93:1 ratio
    Series 75:   3.15:1
    Eldorado driving axle ratio: 3.07:1

Front suspension: Independent, helical-coil springs,
     rubber-mounted strut rods
  Eldorado: torsion bars
Rear suspension: four-link drive, helical-coil springs,
     rubber bushings
  Eldorado: single-leaf springs with two horizontal
     and two vertical shock absorbers
Steering: Variable-ratio power steering standard
  Series 75: fixed-ratio system standard
  Overall steering ratio: 16.6:1
  Series 75: 18.2:1
  Eldorado: 16.3:1
Tires: Low-pressure, L78 × 15, bias-belted, fiberglass,
     tubeless, black sidewalls.

Dimensions

Wheelbase: 129.5 inches
  Fleetwood 60 Special and Brougham: 133 inches
  Fleetwood 75: 149.8 inches
  Eldorado: 120 inches
Width: 79.8 inches
Front/rear tread: 63/63 inches
  Eldorado: 63.5/63

Overall length: 225.0 inches
  Series 60 Special and Brougham: 228.5 inches
  Series 75: 245.5 inches
  Eldorado: 221.0 inches

Popular Options

Automatic climate control: $516
Automatic level control: $79 (standard on all
     Fleetwoods)
Firemist paint: $205
Cruise control: $95
Rear-window defogger: $28-37
Soft-ray glass: $53
Guide-matic headlight control: $51
Power door locks: $68, $116 (Series 75)
Signal-seeking AM/FM radio with rear control: $289,
     $222 (without rear control)
AM/FM stereo: $322
AM/FM radio: $188
Tilt and telescoping steering wheel: $95
Trumpet horn: $15
Remote-control trunk lock: $53
Twilight sentinel: $153, $158 (Eldorado)
White sidewall tires: $40, $46 (Series 75)

1971

The New Look of Leadership

THE WINDS OF CHANGE were still sweeping gently across the American automotive landscape in 1971. But their strength would grow in intensity until most vestiges of the way the industry once did business would be swept away. As the nation's most visible automotive manifestation of the good life, Cadillac, perhaps more than any other American automobile, would undergo a product change easily equalizing in scope those that took place in the Great Depression. The words of Cadillac's vintage "Penalty of Leadership" advertisement would serve as a clarion call for the division to marshall all its creative talents and resources. The focal point of this effort was not just another record sales year, but the means by which Cadillac's survival would be assured in an automotive market far different from that of the years since 1945.

With the exception of persistent rumors about the development of a small Cadillac and the growing presence of Mercedes-Benz on the American road, the 1971 models, released for sale on September 29, 1970, were entering a market that, if in its twilight years, was little changed from those of the past few years. Imperial showed disturbingly clear evidence of a terminal illness, while Lincoln continued to keep the pressure on with its Lincoln Continental and Mark III models.

In this context, the first all-new Cadillacs since 1961 did what most of their predecessors had done, establish another sales record. Granted, this was for the calendar year not the model year (respective figures were 267,868 and 188,537), with labor disputes responsible for the poor model-year output.

CADILLAC QUALITY

The reaching by Cadillac of a new production mark was accompanied by the extension, for the first time, of Cadillac production to facilities in Linden, New Jersey. This not only ended an era when all Cadillac operations were situated at one location, but also called for close ties between Detroit and Linden to ensure that the new plant maintained Cadillac's standard of quality.

This was a matter, obviously, of no small importance to Cadillac, which had over the years developed an unyielding attitude toward any variations in the quality of its product. By 1971 this approach had several key facets that required the full-time attention of 850 employees, as well as the involvement of many thousands of other workers.

The director of quality assurance was a 30-year Cadillac veteran, Charles Ford, who believed the keys to high quality were communication, education, motivation, and the means to act rapidly when changes were called for.

The monitoring of Cadillac quality was facilitated by its relatively small size as compared with other General Motors automotive divisions. Turnover among Cadillac's 10,500 employees was among the lowest in the industry, and this stability enhanced both job competence and pride in a job well done. Cadillac didn't take for granted, however, that slip-ups wouldn't take place. At the end of each work day, approximately 50 people from such diverse departments as purchasing, engineering, manufacturing, service, reliability, and Fisher Body took a new Cadillac home for an overnight checkout. These workers were selected at random, and the next day they reported what they thought of the cars. This program, which began when Harold Warner was Cadillac's general manager, not only yielded information on what was found wrong, but what features could be improved.

Another source of valuable information came in the form of the daily–car-audit data, which contained detailed reports on approximately two dozen cars randomly selected from the assembly line that were thoroughly inspected and subjected to an 18-mile test over a variety of road conditions.

Similarly, an Early Drive Program evaluated the operating performance of the cars first built in a model run. Each week a number of cars were subjected to a multihundred-mile evaluation by reliability engineers. On a daily basis, each car shipped was checked against

169

a list of 40 appearance and functional items. These results were reviewed daily by executives from the manufacturing, purchasing, and reliability departments. Other aspects of Cadillac quality included a Failure Mode Prevention Analysis that sought out operations susceptible to quality problems and film presentations to workers after completion of the changeover for 1971 model production, explaining why it was important to turn out a top-quality product. To ascertain that the Linden plant adhered to the same quality principles, five reliability engineers on assignment there had a daily telephone conference with their counterparts in Detroit.

CHANGES AND IMPROVEMENTS

"Although the 1971 Cadillacs are completely new in appearance," said Cadillac general manager George R. Elges, "we have maintained those unique traditions that have set this car apart from all others." While still maintaining the required styling link with earlier models, the 1971 Cadillacs were extremely modern-appearing automobiles. In key areas such as windshield shape, the contour of the side windows, and the flow of fender lines and body contours, the impression was of flowing, curvaceous forms that Cadillac characterized as "tubular" in contrast with the sharp edges of the 1970 models. One result, a sensation of spaciousness, was due to the new body's increased shoulder width and larger glass areas.

Having resisted the temptation to adopt the original front-wheel-drive Eldorado's concealed headlights for its remaining models, Cadillac achieved an equally dramatic effect by using separate chrome nacelles for the headlights, moving them several inches apart and placing a winged Cadillac emblem in the resulting space. At the same time, a front-fender crease extended across the hood to create a more unified appearance than in 1970. A deeper, bumper center section and a prominent, hood character line emphasized the grille's vertical theme. For the first time since 1958, bumper uprights figured prominently in Cadillac's front-end design. This wasn't a signal that Cadillac would immerse itself in nostalgia. The primary purpose of these items, fitted with integrated vinyl guards, was to provide greater impact and parking protection. Also marking the 1971 model's appearance were bumper-mounted directional/parking lights, slimmer windshield pillars, and radially finned wheelcovers.

In profile, the latest Cadillacs were characterized by a strong design line that dropped well below the rear fender line and a secondary crease line that proved, if any one still had any doubts, that Cadillac designers didn't have to rely on chrome trim or fins to create an imposing appearance. The side spear was raised slightly with the side marker located horizontally at the rear of the side trim.

The rear lights and bumper was reminiscent of those used in 1965 and 1966. Adding emphasis to the V-shape of the body contour was the arrowhead form for the bumper uprights, which contained one of the largest taillight lenses ever to appear on a nontailfinned Cadillac. Three-element backup lights bracketed the receptacle for the license plate.

To be sure that Cadillac's interior designers received their fair share of recognition for their efforts on the 1971 model, George Elges told the press corps that "the 1971 Cadillac interior story is as dramatic as the exterior styling." For the new models, the instrument panel was completely redesigned. One result was the angling of all controls toward the driver. Even though the clock was moved to the right-hand side of the instrument panel directly in front of the passenger, it, too, was canted toward the driver.

As an antitheft measure, the hood release on all models was relocated inside the car. Other revisions consisted of lower seat backs for improved side and rear vision, a horn pad, and a rear-view mirror mounted directly to the windshield.

To improve serviceability, all warning lights were located on the right side of the instrument panel where the bulbs were easily accessible. Also, the upper-door panel could be removed independently from the lower sections to expose the door/window mechanism for adjustment or replacement. Similarly, the top cover of the instrument panel could be taken off without removing the windshield moldings for quicker access to the speedometer and other elements.

These were just some of the changes representative of Cadillac's efforts to enhance customer satisfaction with their cars. Cadillac's national service manager, Robert M. Phillips, noted, "The advancements introduced this year are aimed at reducing customer maintenance and repair costs and expediting proper service diagnosis."

Under the hood, a goal of rearranging components in a practical and systematic manner to improve serviceability and appearance resulted in the relocation of the cruise control and automatic level control to more accessible positions. Also arranged in a more serviceable fashion were the engine hoses and electrical wiring. A new cover panel for the radiator not only improved the overall appearance and helped keep the underhood area cleaner but provided a more visible position for owner and service instruction decals. Some other results of these changes were a more accessible oil dip stick and easier removal of the rocker-arm covers and other components.

"Coupled with the totally new distinctive look of the 1971 Cadillac," Robert Phillips noted, "we feel these refinements in the area of serviceability will help meet the changing and rising levels of expectations of our customers."

These expectations were also met by a host of small detail changes that collectively made a measurable improvement in Cadillac's driving comfort and operating efficiency. For example, polyurethane foam was now used in the seat construction and a new buzzer on the twilight sentinel indicated that the manual headlight switch had been pulled out. Thus the headlights would not be turned out by the twilight sentinel. Found on all cars were new, variable steering ratios for more precise steering and a larger, 27-gallon fuel tank. The air-conditioning system provided a 20 percent greater air flow through repositioned outlets.

All 1971 Cadillacs were also equipped with honed tire treads to provide perfect roundness. Unlike tires for other Cadillacs, which were honed by the supplier, on Eldorados this operation was performed on the assembly line. Another feature found only on the Eldorado was a side-terminal sealed battery. Eldorados, along with commercial models, were equipped with a new Delco Remy alternator with an integral solid-state regulator.

Having a long-lasting impact on future engine trends was the corporate decision by General Motors to equip all its 1971 automobiles with engines capable of operating on 91-octane unleaded gasoline. Concurrently, the five GM automotive divisions began to move away from using gross horsepower ratings to SAE net figures, which were based on SAE standard J245. This continued to use a dynamometer to measure output, but now required the engine to be in an "as installed" condition with a complete exhaust system, manifold heat-riser, air cleaner, and, if used, a preheat system. These units, along with all emission controls, had to be operating.

Such an arrangement differed sharply from the old system where, under the pressure of the horsepower race, it was tempting, in order to claim a high-power output, to conduct tests under very unrealistic conditions. For example, engines would have their air cleaners and exhaust systems removed, carburetor mixtures and spark timing would be set for peak performance, and the intake-manifold heat would be sealed off. For 1971, Cadillac supplied both gross and net power ratings.

The results of General Motors' action were engines with sharply lowered compression ratios and reduced power output. The 472-cubic-inch engine had its gross horsepower drop from 375 at 4,400 rpm to 345 at 4,400 rpm. Respective figures for the Eldorado's 500-cid V-8 were 400 hp at 4,400 rpm and 365 hp at 4,400 rpm. SAE net horsepower rating were 220 at 3,800 rpm (472-cid engine) and 235 at 3,800 rpm (500 cid engine).

The reduction of the Cadillac engine's compression from 10.0:1 to 8.5:1 was accomplished by the use of newly designed aluminum-alloy, slipper-type pistons, changes in the cylinder-head design, and a cam with greater overlap between the intake and exhaust-valve timing to aid in reducing nitrous-oxide emissions. The Quadrajet, four-barrel carburetor featured a new purging system to utilize stored fuel vapors and to minimize emissions to the atmosphere.

All 1971 Cadillacs were equipped with the evaporative emission-control system used only on cars destined for California in 1970. In this setup, vapors generated in the fuel tank were separated from the fuel in a new stand-pipe and then stored in a charcoal canister when the car was parked. They were burned in the engine when the vehicle was operating.

Cadillac was the only American manufacturer to equip its 1971 engines with the General Motors AIR (Air Injection Reactor) exhaust emission system, which incorporated the Saginaw steering air pump. In addition, a Controlled Combustion System (CCS) was used to meet federal and state emission standards. All engines were equipped with a single exhaust system with the muffler positioned ahead of the resonator. The purpose of this change was to extend exhaust system life.

Aside from these changes, there was enough technical news from Cadillac to allow George Elges to note that "engineering improvements are also significant in the 1971 Cadillac story." Leading the way, in the sense that most new Cadillac drivers could detect the result, was a significant improvement in what Cadillac identified as "rolling smoothness" and an equally dramatic reduction in road noise. These were credited to the use of new body mounts with 15 percent greater rubber volume, shock-absorber revision, modified front and rear suspension, and new engine mounts.

An unheralded, but praiseworthy safety development was a new, stronger, front-end structure, consisting of frame bumper mountings and stiffer sheet metal that was developed through new computer techniques. This provided a 45 percent increase in energy absorption in the event of a front-end impact.

Improving brake performance on all models were new front and rear brake assemblies of larger capacity.

A new optional fiber-optic-lamp monitoring system, which indicated proper bulb function, was available on all models. The front-lamp monitor, positioned on the top of the front fenders, checked the headlights, parking lights, and directionals. The rear unit, placed on the package shelf, maintained vigil over the taillights, stop lights, and rear directionals. Included in this system was a light on the instrument cluster that operated when the windshield-washer fluid level was low.

DIFFERENCES AMONG MODELS

Once again, the Eldorado and Lincoln Continental Mark IV ran a production race that literally wasn't decided until the last working day of the model year. The final tally put the Eldorado out front, 27,368 to 27,091 Mark IVs. This margin of less than 300 units was of small comfort to Cadillac, since it had required the introduction not only of a totally restyled Eldorado but the addition of a Convertible model. It was evident that the once unthinkable was about to happen; a Lincoln would outsell a comparable Cadillac.

Unlike those on other Convertibles, the Eldorado's top did not infringe upon rear-seat accommodations. When lowered, it folded inward behind the seat, providing full-width seating and recessing into a near-flush boot.

The Eldorado's restyling was characterized by two distinct themes. First, the bridge between its appearance and that of other Cadillacs was narrowed considerably. The Eldorado still possessed a distinctive appearance but now it was more a matter of details rather than basic form.

Concurrently, the Eldorado retained a degree of individuality within the Cadillac family via the resurrection of some memorable Cadillac styling

1971 Fleetwood Eldorado Coupe. Its fixed rear quarter-panel window was depicted as "a style leader of the future."

1971 Fleetwood Eldorado Convertible. Both Eldorado models were restyled for 1971.

CADILLAC VITAL STATISTICS: 1971

Series	Model	Body Type	Factory Price ($)	Weight (lbs.)	Production (#)
Calais	68249	4 dr Hardtop Sedan	6075	4710	3569
	68247	2 dr Hardtop Coupe	5899	4635	3360
De Ville	68349	4 dr Hardtop Sedan	6498	4730	69,345
	68347	2 dr Hardtop Coupe	6264	4685	66,081
Fleetwood Eldorado	69347	2 dr Hardtop Coupe	7383	4675	20,568
	69367	Convertible	7751	4730	6800
60 Special Brougham	68169	4 dr Sedan	7763	4815	15,200
75	69723	4 dr Sedan	11,869	5510	752
	69733	4 dr Limousine	12,008	5570	848

The Eldorado's new "stand-up" Cadillac crest was spring-mounted both to resist vandalism and meet safety requirements.

The 1971 Cadillac front end was highlighted by a new front end structure with a 45 percent increase in energy absorption.

The 1971 Cadillac instrument panel was completely redesigned, with the cluster controls angled toward the driver and located for maximum visibility.

1971 Fleetwood Sixty Special Brougham. The rear-quarter mounted opera light was optional.

1971 Coupe de Ville.

Cadillac's most popular model, the Sedan de Ville, and the newest Cadillac, the Eldorado convertible, make a very attractive pair.

elements from earlier days. To cite several examples, the midbody-chrome strip harked back to the 1946-1947 models, as did the front and rear fender contours, which contrasted sharply with the format used for the 1967-1970 Eldorado. Equally reminiscent of the past, especially the 1950-1954 models, was the Eldorado's vertical, rear-fender "windsplit." Then there was the matter of the Eldorado's standard, rear-fender skirts and upright hood ornament. The latter was perhaps the most elegant example of its type ever to adorn a Cadillac and the first to be found on a production Cadillac since 1958.

Both the Eldorado's front parking/directionals and taillights were attractive renditions of the original model's divided rear-lighting arrangement. Yet the use of a neoclassic front-hood line and a beveled rear deck easily overshadowed this linkage with the 1967 Eldorado. To add a touch of individuality to the Eldorado, accent body stripes in eight colors were offered.

The Eldorado Coupe had exclusive coach windows, which Cadillac eagerly noted "add to its classical, personal car appearance." Eventually, like the original tail fins of 1948, they would appear on virtually every American car from the Continental Mark III to Chrysler's K-car. Summing up the Eldorado's styling, George Elges observed, "The tailored and chiseled lines of the '71 model draw parallels between the great era of the fine classics and the new Eldorado."

Standard on the Eldorado Convertible was a pliable leather interior offered in 10 colors. These were also available for the Coupe. In addition, the Coupe was offered with a textured Dorado cloth in medium blue, black, dark jade, or maize, as well as a smooth Dalton cloth in dark blue, medium aqua, beige, or heather. On both models, an oriental tamo-wood insert was installed in the doors and instrument panel. Dante cloth, a detailed matelasse cloth was pique stitching, was available in five colors in combination with leather. Also offered was Daphne cloth in four colors, as well as Sierra-grain leather in 10 colors. Door inserts were accentuated with oriental tamo wood. This material was also used for the instrument panel.

The aristocratic lines of the Brougham were shared by the Seventy-Five Sedan and Limousine. Aside from its longer length and side opera windows, the Seventy-Five differed from the Brougham only in the absence of a lower–body-trim molding.

The Seventy-Five's Daphne cloth interior was offered in medium beige and medium gray. Also available was Dante cloth and leather combinations in black or dark blue. The chauffeur's seat in the Limousine was covered by a fine-piped black leather.

The lowest-priced Calais series continued to offer two models, a Coupe and Sedan, both in hardtop-body configuration. With the introduction of the Eldorado Convertible, the De Ville version was dropped, leaving the De Ville series with the same body styles as the Calais. De Villes were distinguished by their full-length, lower-body molding (which was not found on the Calais) and model script identification on the front fender. In contrast, Calais carried Cadillac script in that location.

De Ville interiors were also far more elaborate than the Calais. A Debonaire cloth with leather and vinyl trim was offered in jade, dark blue, or medium beige. Also available was a Dumbar cloth in five colors and 10 color selections of Sierra-grain leather. Exclusive to the De Ville were upper-door and instrument-panel inserts of a Florentine-textured metal. All told, 156 interior-trim combinations were available for the 1971 Cadillac.

The most impressive expression of Cadillac's new-body form was found on the Fleetwood Sixty Special Brougham and Series Seventy-Five models. In the case of the Sixty Special, it assumed a distinction in the Cadillac model line approaching that enjoyed by the 1948-1949 and 1958 versions. The main source of this exclusiveness was its roof, which Cadillac said was "reminiscent of the classic V-16's of the '30's." The padded, cross-grain, vinyl-roof covering extended between the doors whose windows were framed in narrow chrome trim. As in 1970, the side trim of the Brougham carried a vinyl insert color keyed to the vinyl top. Fleetwood lettering on the rear-deck lid and front fenders, full-length lower-body trim, and an optional opera light, mounted adjacent to the Brougham script in the rear C-pillar, underscored the visual impact of this very impressive product.

Accompanying the Eldorado's styling changes was use of a new frame with a longer, 126.3-instead of 120.0-inch wheelbase. At the rear, helical-coil springs replaced the single-leaf springs used up through 1970. In addition, larger rubber bushings were adopted for a quieter, softer ride. These developments made a significant change in the Eldorado's ride character. While the precise steering and strong directional characteristics of earlier Eldorados were retained, they were now joined by the soft ride and isolation from road noise associated with rear-drive Cadillacs.

Receiving surprisingly little attention relative to its importance as a safety feature was the Eldorado's $210 Track Master option, a computerized rear-wheel, skid-control braking system. The Eldorado, as well as all 1971 Cadillacs, was fitted with the industry's largest (9.5 in. × 8 in.) brake power booster.

CADILLAC'S DOMESTIC COMPETITION

Imperial's presence in the luxury-car market was further eroded by the elimination of the Crown series in 1971. This left only two LeBaron models, a two-door and a four-door hardtop, to face nine Cadillacs and three Lincoln Continentals. Styling changes were minimal, consisting of rectangular doors for the hidden headlights, Imperial lettering across the hood front and rear-quarter panels, and reshaped side-marker lights. The rear-quarter roof panel now carried LeBaron identification.

Without anything startling or new, the Imperial's popularity remained static as production dropped slightly to 11,558 from 11,816 in the 1970 model year. The most newsworthy development from Imperial was the availability of the $351.50 Sure Brake antiskid option. While Cadillac's Track Master and Lincoln's

Sure-Track systems operated only on the rear wheels, the Chrysler unit affected all four wheels. This technical edge wasn't able to overcome buyer resistance to a car too close in appearance to less expensive Chrysler products that suffered from careless assembly procedures and a lack of design direction.

Lincoln, in sharp contrast, enjoyed its best production year ever by turning out a record 62,642 cars. With Mark III sales running at a very strong pace, Lincoln moved to capitalize on its popularity by altering the Lincoln-Continental's grille slightly to bring it closer in form to the Mark III's. At the rear, the taillights were divided vertically rather than horizontally as in 1970.

The commemoration by Lincoln of its completion of half a century of production was marked by a 1971 ½ model, the "Golden Anniversary Continental," which had exterior Town Car identification, the owner's initials in black and gold on the front doors, a dash-panel-mounted plaque and 22-karat gold keys.

Both Cadillac and Lincoln were poised to reach new model-year records in 1972 that would serve only as targets to be shattered the following year. There seemed to be little reason to doubt that for the rest of the decade the upward spiraling sales of luxury cars would continue. Yet the first of two severe shock waves that would strike deep into the bedrock of the American automobile industry was just over the horizon. Gas crunch, gas hogs, and gas lines were ready to enter the average American's vocabulary.

SPECIFICATIONS

Engine

Type: V-type, ohv, eight cylinders
Bore × stroke: 4.30 × 4.06 inches
   Eldorado: 4.30 × 4.304 inches
Displacement: 472 cubic inches
   Eldorado: 500 cubic inches
Horsepower: 345 @ 4,400 rpm (net hp 220 @ 2,800 rpm)
   Eldorado: 365 @ 4,400 rpm (net hp 235 @ 3,800 rpm)
Torque: 500 ft-lb @ 2,800 rpm (net torque 410 ft-lb @ 2,400 rpm)
Compression ratio: 8.5:1
Fuel system: Quadrajet, four-barrel downdraft with equalized manifold
Electrical system: 12-volt, 15-plate battery, side terminals on Eldorado, 42-amp generator
   80-amp on all 75 models
   63-amp on all other air-conditioned cars
   Generator with integral regulator on Eldorado and Series 75

Chassis/Drivetrain

Transmission: Turbo Hydra-Matic, torque-converter with fixed stator, three speeds: low, intermediate, and high
Frame: perimeter with boxed side rails, new front members added
Rear axle: 2.93:1 ratio
   3.07:1 front driving axle on Eldorado
   3.15:1 ratio standard on Series 75, optional on all others except Eldorado
Front suspension: Integral steering knuckle, independent, helical-coil springs, rubber-mounted strut rods, rubber bushings
   Eldorado: torsion bars
Rear suspension: Four-link drive, helical-coil springs, rubber bushings
Steering: Variable-ratio power steering standard
   Series 75:   fixed-ratio system
   Overall steering ratio of 16.6:1
   Series 75: 19.5:1
   Eldorado: 16.3:1
Tires: low-pressure, 178-15, bias-belted, fiberglass, tubeless, blackwall

Dimensions

Wheelbase:
   Calais, De Ville: 130 inches
   Fleetwood 60 Special Brougham: 133 inches
   Fleetwood 75:   151.5
Front/rear tread: 63.6/63.3 inches
   Eldorado: 63.66/63.59 inches
Overall length:
   Calais, De Ville: 225.8 inches
   Fleetwood 60 Special Brougham: 228.8 inches
   Fleetwood 75:   247.3 inches
   Eldorado: 221.6 inches

Popular Options

Automatic climate control
Automatic level control (Calais, De Ville)
Cruise control
Dual comfort seats
Soft-ray tinted glass
Firemist paint
AM/FM radio
AM/FM signal-seeking stereo radio
Tilt and telescope steering wheel
Twilight sentinel

1972

Out of a Tradition of Excellence

THIS WAS CADILLAC'S 70th anniversary year, and, if not a year of startling styling or technical developments, certainly memorable as Cadillac's best sales year to date. Registration of Cadillacs totaled 257,795, up nearly 5,000 cars from 1971. Model-year production of 265,365 cars, plus 2,500 commercial chassis, was also a new record.

No changes were made in Cadillac's model lineup, which consisted of Coupe and Sedan models in the Calais and De Ville series, plus five Fleetwood models: Brougham, Eldorado Coupe and Convertible, and the Seventy-Five Sedan and Limousine.

CHANGES AND IMPROVEMENTS

Styling revisions were minor. The traditional cross-hatch grille continued but with a strong horizontal accent, giving it a "floating effect." The parking lights were moved from the lower bumper area to locations between the headlights, which continued to be set in individual bezels. The winged Cadillac crest separating the headlights in 1971 was incorporated in the cross-hatched parking-light lens. All standard Cadillacs now had a narrow, center-hood molding and the V emblem returned to the hood and rear-deck lid of the De Ville and Calais models.

No longer found in the rear deck of all models were the louvers previously required for the "flow through" ventilation system, which was redesigned to use vents positioned in the body-lock pillars. A close look at Cadillac's rear taillights revealed that the thin, vertical chrome trim of 1972 had been replaced by a winged crest embossed on the lens.

Both front- and rear-bumper impact capability on all Cadillacs was increased, the front bumper to 5 mph (car-to-car), the rear to 3.25 mph. To achieve these ratings, the front bumper was moved 0.75 inches forward to provide for more deflection distance to the sheet metal and by redesigning the bumper reinforcements and hanger brackets. Impact strips were

again used on the front-bumper guards. All standard models were available with white, full-width impact strips for the front and rear bumpers. Because of the new bumper arrangement, overall length on all models was extended by 1.6 inches.

Aside from the installation of grille bars across the defroster openings at the base of the front windshield on all models (intended to prevent items from falling into the air duct), interior changes were cosmetic. Rosewood inserts were added to the dash of De Ville models. The Brougham used a fruitwood inlay, while wood-like carvings were installed on the Eldorado. All Cadillacs were fitted with a detachable litter box mounted to the right-hand shroud foundation, ashtray lids bearing the Cadillac crest, bright trim moldings for the seat side and back panels, and softer molded head restraints.

On all Cadillacs built after January 1, 1972, a combined lap-and shoulder-belt system with a light and buzzer "buckle-up" alert system was installed. This also included a new roof-rail, shoulder-belt stowage feature.

In tune with Cadillac's long-standing emphasis on a soft and smooth ride for its customers, refinements were made in the frame, body reinforcements, shock absorbers, and body mounts. The front suspension on standard Cadillacs was modified to accept a new wheel spindle plus an integral wheel hub and disc-brake rotor. Unlike 1971, when the Trackmaster rear skid control was available only for the Eldorado, it was offered for all Cadillac models in 1972. At the same time, Cadillac, along with the rest of the industry, had to cope with the constraints new emission regulations placed on engine operation. Cadillac noted that, since 1960, it had, on the average, reduced hydrocarbon emission by 80 percent and those of carbon monoxide by about 66 percent. To improve engine starting for 1972, Cadillac used a recalibrated choke and carburetor. Driveability (not exactly one of the best features of 1971 American-made automobiles) was improved by replacing the older transmission-controlled spark advance with a speed-controlled unit, thus allowing lower-speed transmission shift points.

Increasing the reliability of the air-conditioning system was a new Freon-level monitoring sensor that immobilized the system when the Freon charge was low. This made it less likely that, unbeknown to the driver, serious (and costly) damage would be done to the compressor. Relocation of the in-car sensor to the instrument panel's top surface rendered the air-conditioning system more sensitive to the sun load. Also relocated was the trunk light, which improved trunk illumination.

DIFFERENCES AMONG MODELS

Cadillac commemorated its 70th year by adopting a historical theme for its full-line prestige catalog, in which a famous Cadillac model of the past provided the backdrop for the current models. In the case of the Calais Sedan, its companion was the 1938 Sixty-Special. Unfortunately, that car's timeless appeal failed to affect the popularity of the Calais, which remained abysmally low. Total Sedan output was 3,875 units, that of the Coupe only 3,900. Both models were again identified externally by their front-fender-mounted Cadillac script and Calais script on the lower right portion of the rear-deck lid.

A new fabric, Mayfair Cloth, with vinyl bolsters was the Calais' standard interior. Color choices consisted of black, dark blue, medium aqua, dark jade, medium mauve, and medium beige. At extra cost, full vinyl upholstery in either antique saddle or black was offered.

Model identification for the Sedan and Coupe de Ville models was moved from the lower front fender to the C-roof pillar in 1972. Once again, a full-length, lower-body molding was used. The De Ville interior was offered in three forms: Majestic cloth with leather and vinyl trim in medium mauve, dark blue, and black, and dark covert; Medley cloth with leather bolsters in medium aqua, dark jade, and medium blue; or all leather in any of 12 trim combinations. Standard features not found in the Calais models included a rear, center armrest and two, rear-compartment cigarette lighters.

The Fleetwood Sixty-Special Brougham retained its distinctive appearance features for 1972: Fleetwood lettering on the front fenders and rear deck; hood and rear deck-mounted Cadillac crest and wreath emblem; and a four-door, pillared Sedan style. Giving an even smoother look to the Brougham's standard padded roof was the elimination of the center pillar seam.

Seating comfort on the Brougham was improved by the use of rubber, rather than poly, cushion pads, a cored-poly seat back, and a change in the seat cushion's wire gauge. A new interior, a crushed velour cloth trim called Medici, that Cadillac noted was "a forerunner of a completely new line of interior trim materials" was introduced in beige. Also offered was Sierra-grain leather in any of nine colors, Matador cloth in a choice of four colors, or Minuet cloth in one of three colors. Both of these cloth choices were new for 1972.

Included in the Brougham's standard equipment were rear-seat reading lights, light monitors, and dual-comfort front seat with separate controls for the driver and passenger sections.

The two Eldorado models, the Coupe and Convertible, retained their unique status among Cadillac's lineup because of having front-wheel drive and exclusive use of the 500-cubic-inch V-8. Cadillac general manager George R. Elges, in introducing the latest Eldorado, remarked that "it will be exciting as ever and feature the tailored and chiseled lines that set this luxury personal car apart from all others."

Exclusive to the Eldorado was a new grille that was

1972 Fleetwood Sixty Special Brougham.

1972 Sedan de Ville. For 1972, the parking lamp was moved out of the bumper area to a location between the headlamps.

1972 Fleetwood Eldorado Convertible. A new option for 1972 was the hard plastic boot cover.

1972 Coupe de Ville. The V emblem returned to the rear deck of both De Ville and Calais models in 1972. The rear deck louvers from 1971 were eliminated since the "flow through" ventilation system now used vents in the body lock pillar.

remarkably similar to that used on the standard Cadillacs in 1971. Compared with the 1971 Eldorados, the new models had a wider grille-gridwork and a wider chrome molding over the grille. The headlights also received new moldings.

Joining these detail changes was the placement of Eldorado script on the upper-grille molding. Viewed from the side, the latest Eldorado was identified by the placement of the Eldorado script just below the front cornering lamps. The same script replaced the Eldorado block lettering of 1971 on the lower right corner of the trunk lid.

Debuting in 1972 were new Eldorado wheelcovers with concentric satellite rings surrounding the center hub. These were vented to improve brake cooling. As optional equipment, a two-piece, hard-plastic boot cover, "the hide-a-way top," was offered that gave the Convertible an extremely clean appearance.

The Convertible's standard Sierra-grain leather interior was offered in nine colors. If white leather was selected, a choice of four carpet colors was available. Color choices for the Convertible top consisted of white, black, dark blue, covert, and beige. Both the Eldorado Coupe and Convertible now had standard, Dual Comfort front seats. Coupe interior selections consisted of four colors of Morocco cloth or Mandate cloth in medium aqua, medium beige, or dark jade. Optional leather upholstery was available in 12 different colors.

Added to the Eldorado line at midyear was the limited-edition Custom Cabriolet model, which retailed

1972 Fleetwood Eldorado Coupe. Highlighting the Eldorado's appearance were new chrome moldings over the grille and headlamps plus wheel discs with concentric rings that were open for brake cooling.

CADILLAC VITAL STATISTICS: 1972

Series	Model	Body Type	Factory Price ($)	Weight (lbs.)	Production (#)
Calais	C49-N	4 dr Hardtop Sedan	5938	4698	3875
	C47-G	2 dr Hardtop Coupe	5771	4642	3900
De Ville	D49-B	4 dr Hardtop Sedan	6390	4762	99,531
	D47-J	2 dr Hardtop Coupe	6168	4682	95,280
Fleetwood Eldorado		2 dr Hardtop Coupe	7681	4966	7975
		Convertible	7360	4880	32,099
60 Special Brougham		4 dr Sedan	7636	4858	22,750
75		4 dr Sedan	11,948	5620	995
		4 dr Limousine	12,080	5742	960

for $360 above the Coupe's $7,360 base price. It featured a padded (all 1972 Cadillac vinyl roofs were padded), elk-grain vinyl covering for the rear roof portion. Its installation was marked by a custom rolled edge around the back window, a French seam shaping the vinyl around the glass, and a chrome strip running around the perimeter. The vinyl was offered in seven colors: white, black, medium blue, medium gold, light beige, dark green, and dark brown.

"With such elegance," asked Cadillac, "what more would you want in the Eldorado Custom Cabriolet?" The answer to this question was the electronically operated sunroof, which pushed the Cabriolet's price up another $645.

"An understated opulence pervades Seventy-Five interiors" was how Cadillac depicted the accommodations for occupants of the Fleetwood Seventy-Five, nine-passenger Sedan and Limousine. For the latter model, the chauffeur's seat was furnished in black leather. Otherwise, two new fabrics, Minuet cloth in pewter or beige and Matador cloth, in combination with leather could be selected. The colors offered for the interior were black or dark blue.

No longer found on the Seventy-Fives were the outside air scoops previously needed for the air-conditioning system.

CADILLAC'S DOMESTIC COMPETITION

Like Cadillac's, production of its arch rival, Lincoln, reached a record level in 1972 of 94,560. Pacing this

(Top left) Details of the Fleetwood Brougham's front-end design. The bumper guards were standard on all models. The rubber impact strips were standard on the vertical bars and optional on the bumper bar face. (Bottom left) A rubber impact strip for the rear bumper was optional for the rear-drive Cadillacs. Impact capability in the rear was increased to 3.25 mph car-to-car situations. (Right) Details of the Eldorado's optional rear bumper rubber impact strips.

achievement was the popularity of the Mark IV, which, in the classic idiom, was "longer, lower, and wider." At the same time, the Mark IV didn't abandon the basic form that had proved so successful for the Mark III. Thus, the new model had a longer hood, a shorter deck, and a neoclassic front end with hidden headlights. Standard engine for the Mark IV as well as the Lincoln Continental continued to be a 460-cubic-inch V-8.

The result was a 79 percent increase in Mark IV production to 48,591, far ahead of the Eldorado's own record output of 40,774 cars (32,099 Coupes, 7,995 Convertibles). What had once been considered a postwar impossibility—a Lincoln that was more popular than a Cadillac—had become a reality.

Perhaps the greater irony of this very significant achievement by Lincoln was the means by which it was accomplished. Rather than developing an automobile with innovative engineering, Lincoln had paid close attention to details and image. The Mark IV was carefully assembled and used top-quality interior appointments. At the same time, its styling offered little that was new or daring. Instead, the emphasis was on established clichés that obviously linked the Mark IV with the original Continental. This paid handsome dividends—one Mark IV came off the assembly line late in 1971 as the 100,000th Mark built since 1939.

SPECIFICATIONS

Engine

Type: V-type, ohv, eight cylinders
Bore × stroke: 4.32 × 4.06 inches
    Eldorado: 4.30 × 4.304 inches
Displacement: 472 cubic inches
    Eldorado: 500 cubic inches
Horsepower: 220 @ 4,000 rpm
    Eldorado: 235 @ 3,800 rpm
Torque: 365 lb-ft @ 2,400 rpm
    Eldorado: 385 lb-ft @ 2,400 rpm
Compression ratio: 8.5:1
Carburetor: Quadrajet, four-barrel downdraft, new purging system included to utilize stored fuel vapors and minimize emissions
Electrical system: 12-volt, 15-plate battery, side terminals on Eldorado, 42-amp generator
    80-amp generator on Series 75
    63-amp generator used on all other air-conditioned cars
    Generator on Eldorado and Series 75 had an integral regulator
Transmission: Turbo Hydra-Matic, three-speed torque-converter with fixed stator

Chassis/Drivetrain

Frame: Perimeter frame with boxed side rails. New front members provided added protection with increased energy absorption.
Rear axle: 2.93:1 ratio

3.15:1 standard Series 75 and optional for trailer hauling and mountains used on all models
Eldorado driving axle ratio: 2.93:1
Front suspension: Integral steering knuckle, independent, helical-coil springs, rubber-mounted strut rods, spindle with integral hub and rotor
    Eldorado: torsion-bar independent suspension
Rear suspension: Four-link drive, helical coil springs
Steering: Variable-ratio power steering standard
    Series 75:   fixed-ratio
Overall Ratio:
    Calais, De Ville, and Brougham: 17.8
    Eldorado: 16.3:1
    Series 75:   19.5:1
Brake: Power-=assisted, self-adjusting. Front discs; rear: composite-finned drums, split hydraulic master cylinder for independent operation of front and rear units.
    Lining areas: 158.5 square inches
    Eldorado: 125.64 square inches
Tires: L75 × 15

Dimensions

Wheelbase:
    Calais, De Ville: 130.0 inches
    Brougham: 133.0 inches
    Eldorado: 126.3 inches
    Series 75:   151.5 inches
Width: 79.8 inches
Front/rear tread: 63.3/63.3 inches
    Eldorado: 63.66/63.59 inches
Overall length:
    Calais, De Ville: 227.4 inches
    Brougham: 230.4 inches
    Eldorado: 223.2 inches
    Series 75:   248.9 inches

Popular Options

AM/FM radio: front and rear speakers
AM/FM signal-seeking radio: four speakers
AM/FM stereo radio with eight-track speaker: four speakers
Radio foot control: for signal-seeking radio only
Remote-control right-side mirror: Standard on Series 75
Automatic climate control: Standard on Series 75
Trailering package (not available for Series 75)
Trackmaster
Twilight sentinel
Cruise control
Tilt and telescope steering wheel
Six-way power seat adjuster
Electrically operated sunroof: Available for Brougham, Eldorado, and De Ville models with vinyl roofs
Power-door locks
Remote-control truck lock
Automatic level control: Standard on Fleetwood models
Rear-window defogger: Standard on Series 75

1973

The Legend and the Life–Style

CADILLAC INTRODUCED its 1973 models on September 21, 1972. Just a few months later on January 1, 1973, Robert D. Lund became its general manager, succeeding George R. Elges. Although the Arab oil embargo began later in the year, it had no effect on the popularity of the new Cadillac models. For the model year, production reached another record of 304,639 cars. And when the five millionth Cadillac, a blue Sedan de Ville, was completed on June 27, 1973, the vision of a 400,000-car model run did not seem unrealistic.

Although work on a small-sized Cadillac was well along, Lund wasn't content to wait for its arrival to mount a counterattack against Mercedes-Benz, which sold 41,000 cars in the U.S. during 1972. Virtually all were in Cadillac's price range and three-quarters were priced above $9,300. Lund, who was eager to enlarge Cadillac's owner base, acknowledged the obvious; that anyone who sold cars in Cadillac's field was considered a threat. In 1973 though, his response was modest, involving a new ad campaign emphasizing young professionals owning Cadillacs and the selection of a Cotillion-white Eldorado Convertible to pace the 57th Annual Indianapolis 500. This was only the second time (the first was in 1931) that a Cadillac had served as the Indy Pace Car, though La Salles had performed in this capacity in 1927, 1934, and 1937. Also of historical interest was the Eldorado's celebrity status as only the second front-wheel-drive car (preceded by the Cord in 1930) to pace the field at Indianapolis.

CHANGES AND IMPROVEMENTS

Given its starring role in the prerace events at Indy, it was appropriate that the Eldorado was the most changed member of the 1973 Cadillac line. While Continental Mark IV sales had surged ahead of the Eldorado in 1972, Cadillac's had reached a new record level, which the division claimed had been limited not by sales losses to the Mark IV but because of limited production facilities. Nonetheless, Cadillac was determined not to allow Lincoln to establish an insurmountable lead in a prestigious and highly profitable market. The result was a substantially restyled Eldorado whose appearance indicated a return to a theme of elegant simplicity rather than a reliance on ornamentation, which characterized the appearance of the 1971-1972 models. It's likely that George R. Elges had this in mind when he remarked that the 1973 Eldorado retained "the classic look of its predecessors, but with exterior styling changes in the grille, lighting, side moldings and ornamentation."

Absent from the 1973 models was the rear-fender, vertical divider and the large chrome collar for the rear taillight. The taillights were slightly reduced in size while retaining the basic form of the older units. Along with the backup lights and license-plate holder, they were relocated out of the impact area. The side chrome now extended nearly the full length of the body from just behind the front-wheel cutout to a point before a circular Fleetwood crest, which also served as the side-marker lamp. The 8.2-litre badge was eliminated, while the Eldorado script was repositioned from above the running light to a spot below the side spear and just behind the front-wheel cutout.

All 1973-model American automobiles were required to carry front bumpers capable of absorbing the impact of a 5-mph collision and rear bumpers with a similar 2½-mph capability. This mandate substantially altered the appearance of most domestic automobiles. All Cadillacs used a Delco, energy-absorbing mounting system for their front bumpers, while a new urethane, energy-absorbing unit was used at the rear.

In order to provide the necessary front-bumper deflection capability without adding an inordinate amount of front-end length, the hoods on all Cadillac models were shortened (the Eldorado's was also a bit

183

flatter) and the grille was mounted directly to the bumper. George Elges explained that "this allows both the grille and bumper to telescope beneath the hood during impact."

Accompanying the new Cadillac rear-bumper system was revised rear styling highlighted by a new lighting arrangement in which the taillights were located in the upper half of the bumper. The stoplights were placed on the lower portion, protected from damage by impact strips. Both the backup lights and license-plate insert were moved upward away from the impact area.

Accentuating the standard Cadillac's very smooth side view were wheelcovers without the turbine ring of 1972, having a simple, yet elegant appearance. Adornment of the center portion was limited to the Cadillac crest and several concentric rings.

DIFFERENCES AMONG MODELS

The Eldorado's front bumper retained its multiplane outline, with the center upright moved further apart and linked with a center bar. Greater use was also made of rubber inserts. The new bumper system added 0.7 inches to the Eldorado's overall length. Cadillac also installed a bolder cross-hatched grille insert on the 1973 Eldorado. This change was accompanied by a reshaping of the parking/directional lights into smaller, divided square units at the base of the front fenders where they joined the cornering lights (also now segmented) to create a wraparound effect. The space previously reserved for the parking/directional lights now carried a winged Cadillac emblem. At the rear, the bumper consisted of a straight horizontal section with small, vertical side elements. The rear deck was flatter along its rear face. A larger opera window was used on the Coupe.

The Eldorados, along with other 1973 Cadillacs, were offered in 15 standard and six Firemist colors. Of this total, 19 were new. Eight vinyl-roof options were listed for the Eldorados, including two new colors—Gold and Metallic Taupe. Common to all vinyl roofs was a new center seam.

Like all 1973 Cadillacs, the Eldorado's interior featured "soft-pillow" door panels, a redesigned and fully illuminated windshield-wiper control, and a new clock face with Roman numerals. Door-panel appliques with a carved-wood effect were installed. The Coupe's interior was again available in cloth or optional leather. The Manchester fabric had a houndstooth pattern and was available in seven colors. The leather option was offered in 12 colors. Once again, the Custom Cabriolet was included in the Eldorado line. Available with or without a sunroof, it featured a back roof with padded, elk-grain vinyl and a chrome "halo."

As in 1972, the Eldorado Convertible's interior could be fitted with nine choices of Sierra-grain leather. These were included among the 153 interior combinations Cadillac offered in 1973.

The Eldorado's 500-cubic-inch engine retained its 8.5:1 compression ratio and 235 net horsepower at 3,800-rpm rating for 1973, but peak torque was down from 410 lb-ft at 2,400 rpm to 385 lb-ft at 2,400 rpm. The primary reason for this reduction was the use of a cam with greater overlap between the intake and exhaust-valve timing to reduce nitrous-oxide emission. An exhaust-gas recirculation system (EGR) was added to all engines to further reduce NOx (oxides of nitrogen) emission. A reduction in exhaust noise was achieved by use of mufflers, resonators, and exhaust pipes acoustically superior to their 1972 counterparts. A lower, engine operating noise level was achieved by revising the engine pulleys and the air injection reactor (AIR) pump. Installed on all engines was the integral regulator generator used only by the Eldorado and Series Seventy-Five models in 1972. Similarly, the side-terminal battery used only by the Eldorado in 1972 was installed on all 1973 Cadillacs. Except for the Eldorado, all Cadillacs used a new serviceable, centering-ball feature in their constant-velocity joints. All transmissions were filled with a new transmission fluid with a

1973 Fleetwood Eldorado Convertible. Among its new features were a hood with a flatter profile, parking lights that wrapped around the fender into the cornering lamps, and a much bolder cross-hatched grille.

100,000 mile (50,000 miles for heavy-duty conditions) service life. Additional technical/design changes included shock absorbers fitted with Teflon piston rings for more consistent ride and handling characteristics and heavier-gauge boxed-chassis side rails.

The rest of the Cadillac model line received, in addition to their new bumper system, only cosmetic changes. The grille now had a strong, vertical-bar emphasis, and a new "console" assembly placed the head and parking lights in a single unit. A strong family relationship to the Eldorado was achieved by use of slender bumper guards moved farther apart to line up with the outer reaches of the grille and a center portion dividing the grille into upper and lower sections.

Change came slower and in more subtle ways to the Series Seventy-Five nine-passenger Sedan and Limousine. Aside from the changes incorporated in the general Cadillac appearance for 1973, the latest versions were also identified by their Fleetwood script rather than block-letter body identification and three new interiors:

Potomac gray cord, Medici beige velour, and Magi in either black or dark blue with matching leather bolsters. For added rear-compartment privacy, a Landau top was offered, which eliminated the two small side windows.

Specific series identification for the two Calais models, as well as those for other standard Cadillacs, was the same as in 1972. Also continued for the Calais was the standard Mayfair cloth upholstery and full vinyl option. All models except Calais were fitted with new wood-grain instrument and door-panel inserts and interiors.

For the De Villes, this meant rosewood vinyl inserts and a multitextured Medallion cloth-weave upholstery in dark blue, dark taupe, dark jade, and black. Also offered was a Mirabelle fabric in dark teal or medium beige. Once again, leather upholstery in 12 colors was available.

"As always," said Cadillac, "the Series Sixty Special Brougham was special even in the special world of Cadillac." For 1973, the Brougham's Medici crushed-

1973 Fleetwood Eldorado Coupe. Both the tail and backup lamps were new. Overall length was reduced as a result of new deck lid design. Incorporated into the wreath and crest on the rear quarter panels were a reflex and side marker light.

CADILLAC VITAL STATISTICS: 1973

Series	Model	Body Type	Factory Price ($)	Weight (lbs.)	Production (#)
Calais	C49	4 dr Sedan (HT)	6038	4953	3798
	C47	2 dr Coupe (HT)	5866	4900	4202
De Ville	D49	4 dr Sedan (HT)	6500	4985	103,394
	D47	2 dr Coupe (HT)	6268	4925	112,849
Fleetwood Eldorado	L47	2 dr Coupe (HT)	7360	4880	42,136
	L67	2 dr Convertible	7681	4966	9315
60 Special Brougham	B69	4 dr Sedan	7765	5102	24,800
75	F23	4 dr Sedan	11,948	5620	1017
	F33	4 dr Limousine	12,080	5742	1043

1973 Coupe de Ville. Rear-drive Cadillacs had new tail lamps located in the upper half of the bumper away from the normal impact area.

(Top left) A new option for 1973 was this illuminated vanity mirror. The lamps were located on each end of the mirror, and their intensity was controlled by a switch. (Top right) An electrically heated rear window defogger was optional on all models except the Fleetwood Seventy-Five, which had a hot air defogger as part of its comfort control system. (Bottom left) Cadillac's outside temperature gauge was integrated with the left outside mirror. (Bottom right) Cadillac radios were available with either the windshield-mounted antenna or this power unit, which receded automatically into the fender when the radio or ignition was turned off and rose when turned on.

velour interior was extended to include four colors: dark blue, maize, and taupe, as well as beige. Also available in four colors was a patterned Magi cloth and Sierra-grain leather, again offered in nine colors. Added to the Brougham's interior appointments was a swivel lamp providing adjustable lighting for the front passengers.

Options for the Brougham were sparse, exemplified by a lap robe and pillow, exterior opera lights, and a deluxe trim package consisting of deep-pile, two-toned shag carpeting, rubber-backed floor mats, and shirred elastic pockets on back of the front seats.

In relation to the purchase of accessories for their cars, Cadillac's general manager George R. Elges observed that "Cadillac owners are known to be discriminating in the selection of optional equipment." In a sense, this interest in personalizing a new Cadillac explains both the poor sales of the Calais and the steady popularity of the Series Sixty Special. The former, perceived as too common, actually became a rare sight because of its presupposed status. On the other hand, the strong sales of the Sixty Special encouraged Cadillac to introduce the Brougham option in 1965. Almost predictably, it became far more popular than the "standard" Sixty Special, which lead to that model's demise after the 1970 model year. Now the cycle began anew with the introduction of the $750 Brougham d'Elegance option.

Broughams with this feature carried "Brougham d'Elegance" script on their rear-roof panel; a stand-up wreath and crest hood ornament; special wheel discs; and a thickly padded, elk-grain vinyl roof. The interior extended the use of Medici cloth beyond the seats to such regions as the front-seat backs, robe cords, door-trim pads, door-pull straps, retractable assist straps (not found on the standard Brougham, and front-seat-back pockets. Other Brougham d'Elegance appointments included deep-pile carpeting with matching floor mats and additional bright and brushed moldings.

The popularity of options among new Cadillac owners was apparent by the percentage of cars purchased in 1972 with a long list of extra-cost features. To cite some examples, 99.6 percent had automatic climate control and Soft-ray glass, 96.7 percent were equipped with electric-seat adjusters, 94.7 percent with power-door locks, 89.3 percent with vinyl roofs, and 72.3 percent with the tilt and telescope steering wheel. Light monitors, which were only in their second year as a Cadillac option, were ordered by 92.8 percent of Cadillac buyers.

It was with good reason that Cadillac added new items to its list of factory-installed options in 1973. These included a power antenna for the three radio options, which receded automatically into the fender when the radio or ignition was turned off and rose when turned on. Another new option was an electrically heated rear-window defogger for all models except the Fleetwood Seventy-Five (whose rear-compartment comfort control system included a hot-air defogger). Except for the Series Seventy-Five models, all Cadillacs could be ordered with steel-belted radial (ply) tires with a 40,000-mile warranty.

Rounding out the list of new options for 1973 was an outside temperature gauge integrated with the remote-controlled, left outside, rear-view mirror and a theft-deterrent system designed to provide greater security for the vehicle, its contents, trunk and engine compartment. This system was automatically armed when the door was closed. Upon entering the car, the driver had to turn on the ignition system within approximately 20 seconds or the alarm system would activate, causing the headlights and taillights to blink and the horn to blow intermittently. This device also sensed disturbances in the car's electrical system.

CADILLAC'S DOMESTIC COMPETITION

Calendar-year output for Cadillac was a new, all-time record of 302,554. Lincoln's was also a new mark at 128,073.

The appearance of both the Continental and Mark IV were little changed from 1972. More noteworthy was the introduction of a Town Coupe option for the Lincoln Continental and the first of the special-decor options for the Continental Mark IV, the Silver Luxury Group option. Its main features included silver paint and vinyl top and a red velour interior. Lincoln, like Cadillac, offered an optional antitheft alarm system.

While Eldorado output moved up to 51,451, this wasn't enough to keep pace with that of the Mark IV, which totaled 69,437. But there was a dark side to the Mark IV's success in that it was now outselling the standard Lincolns, whose output of 58,636 cars fell far short of the De Ville's 216,243. Cadillac's position in the center of the luxury-car market remained strong, while, as the future would show, it was only a matter of time before the Eldorado would overtake the Mark IV in sales.

This contest, however, was only a small element of a major sales battle being waged between Ford and General Motors. While GM enjoyed a tremendous advantage because of the large numbers of Chevrolet, Pontiac, Oldsmobile, Buick, and Cadillac owners who were accustomed to buying another GM car every two or three years, Ford could also point to some significant developments of its own. In 1972, for example, Ford's profit of $870 million represented an increase of 59 percent from the 1969 mark. At the same time, GM's $2.1 billion profit had grown just 26 percent from 1969. Ford had also increased its profit margin by 0.6 percent compared with GM's 0.1 percent.

Lee Iacocca, Ford's president, noted that the overhauling of the Lincoln-Mercury Division and the introduction of the Mark Continentals had given Ford 29 percent of the luxury-car market compared with Cadillac's 68 percent. Ford was also quick to note that since 1969, sales of the Lincolns, Marks, and Thunderbirds increased 47 percent while their profits had increased nearly 700 percent.

There was hardly a lack of factual data encouraging to Cadillac, however. When the 1973 models were introduced, Cadillac general manager George R. Elges reported production was scheduled for 286,000 units or 6.8 percent more than the 267,787 units built in the

1972 model year. Actual output was nearly 14 percent higher.

Even so, Cadillac could not afford any degree of complacency. The appreciation of the Mark IV Continental as a worthy competitor was a strong catalyst for product development at Cadillac but equally pressing was the growing presence of Mercedes-Benz, which set another sales record in the American market for 1972.

At the 1973 model press preview, George Elges reported that Cadillac hadn't yet made a decision to produce a smaller luxury car to compete in that market where Mercedes and other cars such as Jaguar were in control. He did admit that Cadillac had built two prototypes, but these were depicted as concept automobiles rather than as the basis for a production model. But, unbeknown to the public, before the final 1973 Cadillac had been assembled, the decision had been made—a new-sized Cadillac would be built.

SPECIFICATIONS

Engine

Type: V-type, ohv, eight cylinders
Bore × stroke: 4.30 × 4.06 inches
    Eldorado: 4.30 × 4.304 inches
Displacement: 472 cubic inches
    Eldorado: 500 cubic inches
Horsepower: 220 @ 4,000 rpm
    Eldorado: 235 @ 3,800 rpm
Torque: 365 lb-ft @ 2,400 rpm
    Eldorado: 385 lb-ft @ 2,400 rpm
Compression ratio: 8.5:1
Fuel system: Quadrajet, four-barrel, down-draft carburetor
Electrical system: 12-volt, 15-plate battery, side terminals, 42-amp generator
    Series 75: 80-amp
    All other air-conditioned cars: 63 amp
Transmission: Turbo Hydra-Matic, three-speed torque converter with fixed stator

Chassis/Drivetrain

Frame: Perimeter frame, boxed side nails
Rear axle: Hypoid 2.93:1 ratio
    3.15:1 standard on Series Seventy-Five, optional for trailer hauling and mountainous area use on all models except Eldorado
    Driving axle for Eldorado: 3.07:1
Front suspension: Integral steering knuckle, independent, helical-coil springs, rubber-mounted strut rods, rubber bushings, tubular shock absorbers
    Eldorado: torsion bars
Rear suspension: Four-link drive, helical-coil springs, rubber bushings
Steering: Variable-ratio power steering
    Series 75: fixed ratio

Overall steering ratio: 17.8-9.0
    Eldorado: 16.1-14.3
    Series 75: 19.5:1
Brakes: Power brakes, self-adjusting, disc front, composite finned rear with split, hydraulic master cylinder for independent operation of front and rear brakes
Tires: L78 × 15 (tubeless, blackwall standard)

Dimensions

Wheelbase:
    Calais, De Ville: 130 inches
    Fleetwood 60 Special Brougham: 133.0 inches
    Eldorado: 126.3 inches
    Fleetwood 75: 151.5 inches
Width: 79.8 inches
Height:
    Calais Coupe and Coupe de Ville: 54.6 inches
    Calais Sedan and Sedan de Ville: 54.6 inches
    Fleetwood 60 Special Brougham: 55.5 inches
    Eldorado Coupe: 53.9 inches
    Eldorado Convertible: 54.3 inches
    Fleetwood 75: 58.1 inches
Front/rear tread: 63.3/63.3 inches
    Eldorado: 63.66/63.59 inches
Overall length:
    Calais, De Ville: 228.5 inches
    Fleetwood 60 Special Brougham: 231.5 inches
    Eldorado: 222.0 inches
    Fleetwood 75: 250.0 inches

Popular Options

AM/FM stereo with eight-track tape player, four speakers
AM/FM signal-seeking stereo with four speakers
AM/FM with front and rear speakers
Automatic power-operated antenna
AM/FM signal-seeking stereo with passenger compartment controls (only radio available for the Fleetwood 75)
Outside thermometer
Automatic climate control
Electrically operated sunroof: Available for Brougham, Eldorado Coupe, and De Ville with vinyl roofs
Cruise control
Tilt and telescope steering wheel
Lighted vanity mirror
Lamp monitors
Power door locks
Twilight sentinel
Steel-belted radial tires
Remote-control trunk lock
Remote control right-side mirror: Standard on Fleetwood 75
Six-way, power-seat adjuster
Deluxe robe and pillow
Trailering package
Track master
Rear-window defogger: Standard on Fleetwood 75
Automatic level control
Theft-deterrent system

1974

More Than Ever, America's Number One Luxury Car

CADILLAC PRODUCTION, like that of most American cars, tumbled from the lofty height of 1973. Cadillac's decline, of 62,509 to 242,330 cars was substantial, yet Cadillac actually increased its percentage share of the market.

A relatively good year didn't detract from the facts, however. Cadillac suffered a 20.6 percent decline in output at a time when the most popular article to be found in the nation's automotive journals was a variation on the "what's the best car to own in a gas crisis" theme.

One reaction by Cadillac was a large showroom brochure titled "Cadillac is the quality car that makes sense for today." Found inside, sandwiched between color covers, was a black and white insert labeled "What long-time Cadillac owners are saying about the mileage and performance of their 1974 Cadillacs." Their remarks combined plaudits about traditional Cadillac virtues with uncustomary comments about fuel efficiency.

CHANGES AND IMPROVEMENTS

The improved mpg performance of the 1974 Cadillacs was achieved at the same time California mandated a one-third reduction in nitrogen oxides on all 1974 cars sold within its borders. Cadillac's response was a further reduction in engine compression ratio from 8.5:1 to 8.25:1, achieved by raising the combustion-chamber roof approximately 0.10 inch and closing in one side of the combustion chamber to concentrate the mixture more closely around the spark plug. This "fast-burn" combustion chamber allowed an ignition timing closer to the ideal for 91-octane fuel. The cam timing was also changed to give less overlap than before.

Also installed on the Quadrajet carburetor was a snorkle-type air cleaner that supplied the engine with cooler air from outside the engine compartment. This feature also served as a muffler for engine noise. Other contributors to a reduction in engine noise were a fan clutch, high-damping engine mounts, and an acoustical network of sound-deadening materials, including double-door seals. To improve starting at moderate temperatures, a vacuum reindexing feature was added to the choke.

As an option, Cadillac, like Buick and Oldsmobile, offered the Delco-Remy High Energy Ignition (HEI) with an electronic solid-state ignition and a coil that could deliver up to 37,500 volts, or between 50 and 75 percent more than the standard ignition system. This unit eliminated the points, condenser, cam, and rubbing block, thus improving reliability as well as performance. Nonetheless, power ratings again were reduced. Peak net horsepower now stood at 205 at 4,000 rpm.

While Cadillac was scrambling to meet more stringent emission controls and escalating fuel-economy demands, it also had to contend with a governmental mentality that was taking increasing delight in discovering new, so-called safety requirements for the industry to meet. The overall impact of these regulations has long been hotly disputed; but in the midseventies, they required the delivery of money and talents from other projects to satisfy them. Jim McDonald, then general manager at Chevrolet, summed up the sentiment at General Motors by remarking: "There's only so much money left over after safety and emissions."

Perhaps the prime example of these questionable regulations was the 1974 bumper law that called for the infamous pendulum test in which each bumper was assaulted six times by a pendulum that could be arranged by the testers in any sequence of angles and positions they desired. Most GM cars, including Cadillac, used Delco self-restoring "Enersorber" units in their front- and rear-bumper systems.

Fortunately, there were areas where government chose not to intervene that still allowed for substantial innovations and improvements to take place. For example, Cadillac introduced, along with Buick and Oldsmobile, a "Controlled Windshield Wiper" option that provided an adjustable delayed wiper action with up to 10 seconds between wipes. Hardly noticed and barely mentioned, except by the most informed of Cadillac salesmen and owners, were new radiator hoses made of a stronger material with a "Fiber 13" polymer.

Changes in the more traditional Cadillac mode, namely those intended to increase passenger comfort, were paced by a new air-conditioning system with improved air distribution and control. Even here, however, the need to improve Cadillac fuel economy influenced the air conditioner's design, as the latest version included provisions for more efficient performance under moderate temperature conditions.

Option innovations and additions included steel-belted radial tires for all models; a space-saver spare tire; power-operated, mast-type antenna for all radios; and, for the trunk-lock option, an electric rather than spring-powered, pulldown feature.

One byproduct of the government's bumper rules was the government becoming a silent partner in the design of new American cars. Fortunately, in the case of the 1974 Cadillac, this new state of affairs did not impact negatively on its appearance. In the time-honored tradition of previous years, styling changes for 1974 were cautious and decidedly conservative. Yet they were well conceived and effectively coordinated to give the latest Cadillac dignified and sophisticated lines. "A legend becomes a life style" aptly suited the 1974 Cadillac.

By using new white on gray bumper impact strips and color-keyed, flexible urethane-filler material, the Cadillac's stylists turned what could have been a liability into an asset. The new model's front and rear bumpers were among the most attractive and restrained to appear on a postwar Cadillac. Due to the new rear-bumper system, which telescoped into the rear-fender extensions and utilized Delco energy absorbers, overall length for all models was increased 2.2 inches. The top of the rear bumper was, in comparison with its 1973 location, lower; and the horizontal stop, backup, and taillights were relocated in a urethane body-colored bezel for improved protection. This element was easily removed to facilitate servicing of the lamps and bulbs.

On rear-drive models, the headlights were moved back together and further inboard to provide room at the fender's outer surface for the auxiliary lights. These were now placed in a two-tier format that carried over to the body side where the front marker and cornering lights were neatly arranged to complete a single, multifunction system. When not used, the parking light lenses appeared white; when operating, they had an amber glow.

Because of the all-new, rear-quarter panels, which had a lower profile at the top of the fender, plus longer body moldings and redesigned wheel discs, the Cadillac's side view differed markedly from that of the 1973 model.

For the first time since 1949, there was not a true two-door hardtop in the Cadillac model lineup. The Coupe de Ville remained available, but its pillared side window was described as a "private quarter window." An era in Cadillac history ended with nary a whisper

with Cadillac calling the new model "a quite sensation." Cadillac general manager Robert D. Lund, commenting on this change, observed, "A striking change to the Coupe de Ville and Calais Coupe . . . had been accomplished by the new design of a fixed rear-quarter window."

Significant changes were made in Cadillac's interior design for 1974. All models used a new wood-grained instrument panel placing all warning lights in a narrow "information ban" extending from just to the driver's left to the dash center point. Bracketing the warning lights were the fuel gauge and a new crystal-controlled digital clock, which, because of its middash location, was easily read by the driver as well as all passengers. Just in case anyone was uncertain about the make of car they were riding in, a Cadillac script and crest were mounted near the extreme right of the information ban. The speedometer, transmission indicator, and turn-signal lights were placed in a chrome housing over the steering column. The speedometer now read to 100 mph, making it both easier to read and, in the view of some, a contributor to highway safety. The center-pad area contained four air-conditioning outlets, each with individual shut-off controls and, at the extreme left, the windshield-wiper/washer control. All other controls were placed in a lower, wood-grained vinyl panel. Standard on all models except the Eldorado Convertible (which had a lap belt interlock) was a three point shoulder-lap belt interlock system.

Also debuting was a very attractive three-spoke steering wheel with a flat surface and a distressed-pecan, wood-grained vinyl inlay around the circumference. The center rim, also covered in this material, carried three chrome dividers pointing to a Cadillac crest. On Fleetwood models the familiar wreath was added.

DIFFERENCES AMONG MODELS

Highlighting the Eldorado's visual appeal was a new "superfine" grille mesh topped by a broad chrome ledge with diminutive Cadillac script at its far right, a new striping pattern extending around the hoodline to points just short of the rear-door openings and revamped wheel discs with a sunray outer region rather than the concentric-ringed motif of 1973.

At the rear, the trunk deck was beveled as in 1973. The taillights, while following the general pattern found on other Cadillacs, had a center lighted section as well as two side units. The stop lights were set inboard as on the rest of the Cadillac models. Eldorado Coupe and Custom Cabriolet models carried small Fleetwood identification (the wreathed Cadillac crest) in their side quarter windows. In addition, bolder side-body striping accentuated the Eldorado's body lines. New wheelcovers with a "pancake" center section surrounded by a narrow band of fins were also installed.

The most significant technical change found on the Eldorado for 1974 was the use of a rear stabilizer bar.

Eldorados were available in Coupe, Custom Cabriolet, and Convertible form. As before, the Custom Cabriolet version was offered with or without a sunroof. Interior color and material choices for the Eldorado were

1974 Fleetwood Sixty-Special Brougham.

1974 Sedan de Ville. Cadillac's new rear bumper outer units telescoped into the fender extensions upon impact. The horizontal stop, backup, and tail lamps were relocated in a body-colored bezel above the bumper.

1974 Coupe de Ville. Highlighting its appearance was a fixed rear-quarter window and the extension of the body side molding forward of the front wheel, where it blended into the new cornering lamps.

1974 Fleetwood Eldorado Coupe. Eldorados also had a new rear bumper that telescoped into the rear fender extensions.

1974 Fleetwood Eldorado Convertible. A fine mesh grille plus wider and lower bumper guards were key elements of its new front-end design.

1974 Coupe de Ville. The front end of the rear drive models was significantly changed for 1974. The bumper impact strips were standard and were silver gray in color to blend into the chrome bumper.

numerous. A new fabric was three-toned Mohawk, which was joined by Meridan bolsters. The Mohawk/Meridian combination was available in saddle, black, dark blue, medium jasper, medium gold, and terra cotta. Leather upholstery could be ordered in 14 different trim combinations. The Medici crushed-velour trim was offered in dark blue, amber, or terra cotta.

Standard on the Eldorado Convertible was soft Sierra-grain leather in dark blue, medium jasper, antique light sandalwood, saddle, gold, terra cotta, scarlet, black, or white. The white leather was available in 6 carpet colors, including lime and cranberry.

Calais series Cadillacs were again offered in either Coupe or Sedan styles. The former was in pillared form. Calais script was found on the rear fender just ahead of the taillight assembly. The Cadillac V and crest were mounted on the front hood and rear deck. No lower-body trim was used, but the lower edge of the rear-fender skirt was edged in chrome as was the front-fender cutout surround.

The Calais' new standard interior, Minosa, was described by Cadillac as a "multitoned and delicately ornate fabric . . . [a] lively departure for the series." It was offered in black, dark blue, medium jasper, and medium gold. The vinyl bolsters were of matching colors as were the "soft-pillow" door panels. Optional was an expanded vinyl upholstery in either antique medium saddle or black.

In addition to the standard equipment found on the Calais models, the De Ville Cadillacs carried rear, center armrests, rear cigar lighters, and a power front seat. The Sedan de Ville, described as "a perennial favorite," and the Coupe de Ville, as well as the other 1974 Cadillacs, were available in 15 new colors, including three new nonmetallic shades: jasper, Apollo yellow, and conestoga tan. The Firemist paints, whose acrylic base gave them added elements of color, luster, and gloss, were offered in six new colors: pharaoh gold, terra cotta, regal blue, Victorian amber, cranberry, and Persian lime.

The Sedan de Ville's soft-pillow door panels carried distressed-pecan, wood-grained vinyl inserts. The seats, redesigned to feature hidden tie-downs, were available in numerous colors and materials including a new multicolored fabric, Maharajah, with leather borders offered in medium jasper, dark blue, saddle, gold, and terra cotta. Also offered was Mardi Gras, a two-toned striped velour—the first velour offered in the De Ville series. Customers could also specify leather seats in 14 trim combinations.

Exterior features of the De Ville models consisted of either Sedan de Ville or Coupe de Ville script on the rear fender plus rocker-panel trim.

Broadening the appeal of the De Ville line were a "Special Edition" option, the D'Elegance package. Priced at $355 for the Sedan de Ville and $300 for the Coupe de Ville, the D'Elegance package consisted of a "see-through" standup crest on the hood, a D'Elegance script on the sail panel behind the quarter window, and vinyl-tape accept striping on the hood, sides, and rear deck.

Interior distinctions consisted of a two-toned Mardi Gras upholstery available with matching leather in four colors: white-on-black, medium amber, terra cotta, and dark blue. In addition deluxe door pads trimmed in Mardi Gras, storage pockets on the back of front seats and deep-pile carpeting with color-matched, carpet-covered mats were also included.

A $220 Cabriolet feature for the Coupe de Ville was an exterior-roof design utilizing a sheer chrome strap, surrounded with vinyl welds that also bordered the back roof section. When combined with an electrically operated sunroof, its price rose to $842. In either case, the interior was the same as that of the standard Coupe de Ville. If desired, the d'Elegance and Cabriolet options could be jointly installed on a Coupe de Ville. For the first time in the Calais series, a padded, cross-grained vinyl roof was offered as an option.

The Fleetwood Sixty Special Brougham, which was depicted as a "Cadillac in the grand manner," continued to use the 133-inch wheelbase chassis of previous years. Its standard equipment list extended outward from that

CADILLAC VITAL STATISTICS: 1974

Series	Model	Body Type	Factory Price ($)	Weight (lbs.)	Production (#)
Calais	C49	4 dr Sedan (HT)	7545	4979	2324
	C47	2 dr Coupe	7371	4900	4449
De Ville	D49	4 dr Sedan (HT)	8100	5032	60,419
	D47	2 dr Coupe	7867	4924	112,201
Fleetwood 60 Special Brougham	B69	4 dr Sedan	9537	5143	18,250
Eldorado	L47	2 dr Coupe	9110	4960	32,812
75	F23	4 dr Sedan	13,120	5719	895
75	F33	4 dr Limousine	13,254	5883	1005

The new instrument extended in one continuous sweep from one side of the car to the other.

Details of the new rear bumper design utilizing Delco energy absorbers. The top surface of the bumper was lower, and the horizontal lights were relocated in a urethane body-colored bezel.

The 1974 front-end format featured a new lamp arrangement.

of the De Ville models to include a padded vinyl roof, Automatic Level Control, a Dual Comfort front seat, carpeted footrests, plus front and rear reading lights.

Interior choices included, new for 1974, Morroco, a substantial and ornate matelasse, and the crushed velour Medici. Broughams with cloth trim had seat fabric incorporated in their assist straps and door pulls. Sierra-grain leather was available in nine colors, including terra cotta.

As in 1973, the Fleetwood Brougham was offered with the $750 Brougham d'Elegance option, consisting of the Medici crushed-velour interior with a new pique-stitch design in black, dark blue, terra cotta, or amber. The Medici format was also incorporated in the trim on the door, seat back, storage pockets, and pull straps. Also installed was deluxe deep-pile floor and floor-mat carpeting. External features consisted of a hood-mounted, standup wreath and crest; Brougham d'Elegance script on the roof sail panel; and turbine-style wheel discs with center-located wreath and crest.

Cadillac described the Talisman option for the Fleetwood as "our ultimate in individual luxury and comfort." This expensive, $2,450, option provided four ("and only four," said Cadillac) seats separated by large center rests. The front unit contained provision for an illuminated writing pad with a pen and pencil along with a lockable storage compartment. The rear unit contained a holder for a vanity mirror and a storage bin. The seats and console were covered with Medici cloth in one of four available colors. Other interior areas finished in Medici included the sail panels, pillars, and door panels. In addition, sculptured laurel-wreath moldings were used to accent the door pads and instrument panels. Also included were seat-back pockets, assist straps, and deep-pile carpet and carpeted mats.

Exterior features of a Fleetwood Talisman included a padded, elk-grained vinyl roof; turbine Fleetwood wheel discs; standup wreath and crest hood ornament; plus Fleetwood Talisman script on the sail panel. Prospective customers were told, "Webster defines 'Talisman' as 'something producing apparently magical or miraculous effects.' So does Cadillac."

Once again depicted as "the flagships" of the Cadillac lineup were the nine-passenger Fleetwood Seventy-Five Sedans and Limousines. Their standard equipment list, in addition to the items found on a De Ville, included Automatic Level Control, carpeted footrests, full-width folding seats, a rear-compartment control panel, rear-window defogger and Automatic Climate Control. Both versions were available in Medici or, on "special request," the d'Elegance interior in blue only. Also offered was Morocco, depicted as an ornate matelasse in either black or medium saddle with matching leather bolsters. For what Cadillac regarded as "more conservative tastes," a gray cord fabric, Potomac, was offered.

As always, the visual impact of the Series Seventy-Five models was stunning. Their impressive length in excess of 21 feet, privacy-type rear window, and six-light side window was sufficient to impress most onlookers.

Specific exterior identifications included Fleetwood script on the front fenders, behind the wheel housing, and on the rear deck, plus the familiar Fleetwood wreath-and-crest design on the hood and trunk. For added privacy, a Landau top, which eliminated the rear coach window, was available. On a special order basis, the Limousine was available with the d'Elegance option.

CADILLAC'S DOMESTIC COMPETITION

Like Cadillac's, Lincoln's model-year output was adversely affected by the Arab oil embargo. As Cadillac's production fell from record heights, so did Lincoln's, declining 26 percent to 93,985 cars. As had been the case since 1970, Mark production ran ahead of Continental output. Respective totals for 1974 were 57,316 and 36,669. This placed the Mark IV comfortably ahead of the Eldorado's total of 40,412, but left the Lincoln Continental far outstripped by the popularity of the remaining Cadillac models.

Primary styling changes for the Lincoln Continental consisted of wraparound signal lights mounted in the leading edge of the front fenders. A similar format was used at the rear on the taillights. These changes increased the visual link between the Continental and the Mark IV. Simplifying the front-end appearance was apparently a major goal of Lincoln stylists since they eliminated the trim on the headlight covers and used thinner vertical bars for the Continental's grille. All Lincolns had, as required, new federal collision bumpers.

The Continental Mark IV was little changed in appearance, save for new wraparound taillights and front-end bumpers. Joining the Silver Luxury Group Option was a Gold Luxury Group Option with a gold Diamond Firepaint and contrasting gold-flare, levant-grained vinyl roof. A mid-1974 offering was the saddle and white trim option, which combined a white body finish with a saddle vinyl roof. The seats were covered in white leather with saddle accent striping.

Chrysler gave the Imperial a new front end that was embarrassingly similar to that of the original 1969 Mark III Continental. Chrysler even had the audacity to place Imperial script over the right headlight panel, the same place as "Continental" was found on the Mark III.

Whether the 1974 Imperial's appearance was an improvement over the "Fuselage" model of 1973 was questionable. Production dropped to 14,426 units; and with Chrysler, already the weakest of the Big Three, on the verge of a severe retrenchment in the face of a serious economic recession, the Imperial was first in line to be dumped overboard.

While Chrysler was undergoing a retreat that would leave it without a serious competitor in the fine-car field until 1981, Cadillac was putting the final touches on an automobile that would expand the perimeter of that market as dramatically and successfully as had the Eldorado in 1967. The Seville had arrived!

SPECIFICATIONS

Engine

Type: V-type, ohv
Bore × stroke: 4.30 × 4.06 inches
  Eldorado: 4.30 × 4.304 inches
Displacement: 472 cubic inches
  Eldorado: 500 cubic inches
Horsepower: 205 @ 4,000 rpm
  Eldorado: 210 @ 3,800 rpm
Torque: 365 ft-lb @ 2,000 rpm
  Eldorado: 380 lb-ft @ 2,000 rpm
Compression ratio: 8.25:1
Fuel system: four-barrel carburetor
Electrical system: 12-volt, 15-plate battery, side terminals, 42-amp generator
  75: 80-amp
  All other cars: 63-amp

Chassis/Drivetrain

Transmission: Turbo Hydra-Matic, three-speed automatic, torque-converter with fixed stator
Frame: Perimeter-type with heavy-gauge, boxed side rails
Rear axle: Rear-drive models: 2.93:1
  Eldorado driving axle: 3.07:1
    3.15:1 standard on 75 models, optional on all others except Eldorado
Front suspension: Independent, helical-coil springs, integral steering knuckle, rubber-mounted strut rods, rubber bushings, telescopic shock absorbers with Teflon piston rings
  Eldorado: torsion-bar suspension
Rear suspension: Four-link drive, helical-coil springs, rear stablizer bar in Eldorado
Steering: Variable-ratio power steering with 17.8:1 overall ratio standard
  Series 75: fixed ratio, 19.5:1
  Eldorado ratio: 16.1:1
Tires: Low-pressure, L78-15 bias-belted, fiberglass tubeless

Dimensions

Wheelbase: 130 inches
  Fleetwood 60 Special Brougham: 133 inches
  Fleetwood 75: 151.5 inches
  Eldorado: 126.3 inches
Width: 79.8 inches
Front/rear tread: Front: 63.5 inches, rear: 63.3 inches
  Eldorado: front: 63.7 inches, rear: 63.6 inches
Overall length: 230.7 inches
  Fleetwood 60 Special Brougham: 233.7 inches
  Fleetwood 75: 252.2 inches
  Eldorado: 224.1 inches

Popular Options

Automatic climate control: $523 (standard on 75 models)

Airbag restraint system: $225 (Calais, De Ville, Eldorado Coupe only)
Automatic level control: $77 (Calais, De Ville)
Cruise control: $95
Electric rear-window defogger: $64 (blower-type standard on 75, not available on Convertibles)
Deluxe robe and pillow: $85
Door-edge guards: $6 (two-door)
  $10 (four-door)
Power door locks: $69 (two-door with automatic seat-back release activated on the side the door is opened)
  $79 (four-door)
  $115 (75 models)
Dual-comfort front seat: $108 (standard on Fleetwood Brougham, available on Eldorado and De Villes)
Floor mats (front and back): $17 (all except 75 models and Eldorado)
  Eldorado, one-piece front and rear: $20
  Twin rubber front mats for Series 75: $11
Soft-ray tinted glass: $57
Guidematic headlamp control: $49
Trumpet horn: $15
Bumper impact strips: $24 (except 75)
Lamp monitors: $48
Illuminated vanity mirror: $43
License-plate frame: $6
Right body-side, remote-control exterior mirror: $27 (except 75)
Opera lamps: $52 (Brougham and 75 only)
Firemist paint: $132
Special Firemist paint: $200
AM/FM radio: $203
AM/FM radio with tape player: $426
AM/FM signal-seeking stereo radio: $340
  With passenger-compartment control for Series 75: $430
Padded vinyl roof:
  De Ville, Calais: $152
  Eldorado Coupe: $157
  75 models: $741
Six-way power seat:
  Calais: $120
  De Ville, all Fleetwoods except Limousine: $89
  Passenger seat with Dual-Comfort option: $120
  Driver's seat only with Dual-Comfort option: $89
Eldorado Convertible shoulder harness: $33
Tilt and telescope steering wheel: $94
Electrically operated sunroof (De Ville, Calais, Brougham, Eldorado Coupe
  Vinyl-roof option required on De Ville, Calais and Eldorado Coupe: $610
Theft deterrent system (activates horn and flashes exterior light if security of interior, trunk or hood is violated): $80
Outside thermometer (mounted on base of left side mirror): $15
L78 × 15D white sidewall tires: $41
  Series 75: $47
LR78 × 15B white sidewall radial tires: $156
  Calais and De Ville: $162
Eldorado convertible hard boot: $40

Trailering package (heavy-duty equipment for towing trailer with loaded weight between 2,000 and 6,000 pounds): $65 (all models except Series 75)

Automatic trunk-lock release (operated by control button inside glove box. When lid is brought to a nearly closed position, the power lid lock secures it. A warning light on instrument panel indicates when lid is unlocked): $60

Trunk mat: $80

Twilight sentinel: $42 (standard on Series 75)

Leather upholstery: $195 (leather seat cushion and back inserts, (De Ville and Eldorado Coupe models only)

Extended vinyl upholstery: $184 (Calais only)

Turbine wheel discs: With wreath around Cadillac crest for Fleetwood Brougham and 75, without wreath for De Villes and Calais

Track master

Controlled cycle windshield wiper: $25

High-energy ignition system

Lamp monitor (front-fender monitor shows if low- and high-beam headlight, parking light, and front turn signal are functioning. Monitor visible through rear-view mirror shows if taillight, stop light, and turn signals are functioning. A third monitoring system shows, by means of a warning light on the instrument panel, when windshield washer fluid is low.)

Fleetwood Brougham d'Elegance: $750
    Custom Cabriolet: $220 (Coupe de Ville)
        $842 with sunroof
    Custom Cabriolet: $220 (Coupe de Ville)
        $840 with sunroof
    Custom Cabriolet: $385 (Eldorado Coupe)
        $1005 with sunroof
    De Ville d'Elegance:
        $355 (Sedan)
        $300 (Coupe)
    Fleetwood Brougham Talisman: $1,800
        With leather trim: $2,450

1975

A Standard for the World in American-built Cars

CADILLAC FOUND ITSELF, on the eve of the Seville's introduction, the focal point of unaccustomed media attention. Cadillac was still far and away the dominant force in the luxury-car field, but the advances of Mercedes-Benz and Lincoln had pushed its share of the market back from 72 percent in 1968 to 62 percent in 1974.

SAFETY PROBLEMS

At the same time, Cadillac had not been immune from the stigma of safety recalls and criticism from Ralph Nader's Council for Automotive Safety. In late August 1972, Cadillac had recalled 3,872 of the 1972 model Series Seventy-Five Sedans and Limousines, as well as commercial-chassis vehicles for replacement of rear-axle shafts. It was reported that these had been improperly tempered and could break, causing a rear wheel to fall off. Less than a month later, on September 11, Cadillac had to announce another recall involving 37,000 1972 Cadillacs to search out approximately 5,000 cars with rear-axle shafts that were too long and could ultimately cause the rear brakes to fail.

These disquieting developments preceded published revelations about a presentation by John DeLorean to the triennial meeting of General Motors' 700 top executives at the Greenbriar Hotel in White Sulphur Springs, West Virginia. Reportedly, he admonished his audience that the defects and recalls of GM's cars effectively cancelled out the best efforts of the company's advertising. Turning to the future, DeLorean was depicted as declaring that poor product quality could undermine owner loyalty and reduce public confidence in General Motors' credibility.

In early May 1973, the Center for Auto Safety issued a report that claimed 1969 and 1970 model Cadillacs carried an electrical relay that constituted a serious fire hazard. This set off a verbal brawl between GM and the Center. General Motors' first response was a strong denial that any safety hazard existed. At worst, it said, a failure in the relay would result in a loss of the high-speed function on the air-conditioner and heater blower. It did concede that a high number of relay failures had been noted among the 275,000 Cadillacs involved.

The Center's counterattack asserted that three painful burns, one of which required hospital treatment, had resulted from the relay malfunction. Claiming that, in some cases, Cadillacs had also been burned, the Center quoted General Motors' internal documents showing (it claimed) the relay failures burned up much of the car's wiring and even the car itself.

General Motors replied that "there is no evidence in our file or any files that we know of that would support any such assertion." It added it did have data on four fires, all of which were confined to either the instrument panel or under the hood. None, it said, showed any burns to individuals. In response to the Center's charge that General Motors had engaged in a coverup to avoid a recall to protect Cadillac's "Standard of the World" image, General Motors denied there had been any coverup and that it had eventually redesigned the relay.

The next safety-related issue concerned the Pitman arm (which connects the steering shaft to the steering linkage) on 1959-1960-model Cadillacs. The Center for Auto Safety, which was no longer affiliated with Ralph Nader, cited reports of numerous crashes and injuries plus several deaths. The National Highway Traffic Safety Administration (NHTSA) said its investigation didn't show any deaths or injuries but rather a number of accidents caused by Pitman arm failure due to metal fatigue from repeated stresses during low-speed turns and parking maneuvers. NHTSA added that the failure occurred "frequently and without warning." Thus there was "an unreasonable risk of accidents, injuries and deaths to drivers and passengers."

General Motors, insisted there wasn't a safety-related defect in the Pitman arm, noted there had been only two accidents that could be attributed to the arm. It added that "if a safety-related defect existed, we'll recall them."

After this episode, Cadillac had to make its most

embarrassing public statement of 1973. On November 25, 1973, the division announced it was recalling 380,000 of its 1971-1972 models (all types except the Eldorado) to have dealers install a lubrication fitting on part of the steering linkage. This was to remedy a lubrication problem in the steering linkage that could lead to other problems, possibly resulting in impaired steering control. A Cadillac spokesman said the problem had caused three accidents but no injuries or deaths.

The only real public image plus, and it was a small one, Cadillac gained from this was that the recall was at Cadillac's initiative and not due to the National Highway Traffic Safety Administration or the Nader group.

Unfavorable publicity for Cadillac also found its way into the news in 1974. In an initial finding, the Department of Transportation reported that 411,000 General Motors cars, including 1970 Cadillacs (no Eldorados), with Cruise Control could experience motor-mount failures that could cause the accelerator to jam in a high-speed position. General Motors said it had received 12 reports of injuries and accidents allegedly caused by motor-mount failures on Buicks but none involving Cadillacs.

Five months later, on October 31, 1974, Cadillac had to accept the unfavorable reaction to its announcement of a recall of 270,000 1973 and 1974 models to check for a possible steering-linkage problem. This recall applied to all 1973 Cadillac models and a small number of early 1974 models. No Eldorados were involved.

Cadillac made clear that it hadn't received any accident reports, but said a lack of lubricant could exist in some parts, which, in conjunction with an accumulation of road salt and moisture, could cause corrosion and binding. This ultimately could lead to a loss of steering control. Under this recall, Cadillac dealers installed a lubrication fitting in the steering assembly and would replace any parts if necessary.

An age of criticism about the automobile's impact upon society, its claim on resources, and a counter-culture mentality prompted a slew of books and countless articles in general proclaiming the love affair of Americans with the automobile had come to an end that would eventually be reputed by the severest critic of them all, the American consumer. But for a time, these self-appointed doomsday prophets held center stage.

Cadillac, long considered the epitome of American automotive desires, was clearly in a vulnerable position. Once again the "Penalty of Leadership" came back to haunt Cadillac in a perverse fashion. But Cadillac's response was a far stronger endorsement of the basic premises inherent in the original meaning of "The Penalty of Leadership." Cadillac was willing to take major risks to maintain not only the continued loyalty among its current clientele, but to make its products attractive to younger buyers. One obvious example was the introduction of the Seville; the second, an aggressive marketing strategy for its existing full-sized models;

and, perhaps most dramatic of all, the planning of dramatically resized models for 1977.

Viewed in retrospect, the 1975 and 1976 full-sized Cadillacs are correctly seen as the products of an automotive age entering their twilight time. Like the classic cars of the 1930s, they were of magnificent proportions, perhaps a bit wastefully extravagant, yet at the same time worthy of admiration for an uncompromising commitment to quality that would never go out of style.

CHANGES AND IMPROVEMENTS

Cadillac was eager to have its 1975 product recognized for virtues other than quality and status, however. Thus, the 1975 Cadillac was described by its manufacturer as "efficient as it is elegant . . . rugged as it is rewarding."

Cadillac wasn't going to abandon appearance and convenience features as key selling points, but it came out swinging in reaction to a growing public perception of Cadillac as a "gas guzzler" and the spate of recalls that had tarnished its reputation for producing cars of unquestioned quality. Thus Cadillac's improvements in fuel economy and its rigid durability tests received primary emphasis in its 1975 sales brochure.

Standard in all models was the 500-cubic-inch Eldorado engine, which was now equipped with a catalytic converter as well as a new electric choke that Cadillac said improved both fuel economy and driveability. Included as standard equipment on the Cadillac engine was the High Energy Ignition System, which, in conjunction with the catalytic converter and use of unleaded gasoline, allowed for up to 22,500 miles between tuneups.

Three important changes in the Cadillac's drivetrain—a "tighter" torque converter; a lower 2.73:1 rear-axle ratio on all models except the Series Seventy-Five Limousine and nine-passenger Sedan; plus standard steel-belted radial tires, which, compared with bias-belted tires, reduced drag as much as one third—made major contributions to an improved fuel efficiency of the 1975 models.

Available on all models, except the Limousine and nine-passenger Sedan, was electronic fuel injection, which, said Cadillac, "can result in a host of advantages for the car owner—including increased fuel economy." Also reflecting Cadillac's economy theme was a new "Economy" setting for the Automatic Climate Control system, which allowed the system to operate with the compressor disengaged, and an optional "Fuel Monitor." This provided two lights on the dash that were intended to encourage economical driving habits. A green light glowed when the car was being operated efficiently. An amber light operated if the verdict was inefficiency. Also included was a red light on the fuel gauge to indicate a low-fuel level.

Cadillac was rightfully proud of the attractive appearance of its latest models. There was nothing extreme or startling in their styling, but adoption of rectangular headlights completed the wraparound format of Cadillac's front lighting system that had been introduced in 1974. Eliminated was the two-tier arrangement of the parking and turning lamps. Replacing the wide-spaced grid of the 1974 grille was a finer, deeper mesh encased in a more prominent grille shell carrying Cadillac script on the driver's side. The greater grille height was emphasized by a squared-off hood line. Also redesigned were the front—fender-mounted light monitors, which now were color coded to indicate if the high or low beam as well as the parking and directional lights were functioning. As before, the rear-monitor system, which reported on the status of the taillights, stop lights and turn signals, was visible through the rear-view mirror.

Cadillac's "space-age" instrument panel was moderately changed for 1975 with improved graphics for the digital clock. Also introduced were new hinged, door-pull handles (except on Calais, which retained door-pull straps) with specific designs identifying each series.

It was a bit self-conscious, especially in light of all those unhappy recalls and acrimonious remarks by its critics, but Cadillac said with pride that "beneath those great Cadillac looks is a great car." Specific points that Cadillac wanted to make certain its customers were aware of included new engine mounts; stainless-steel, corrosion-resistant, rear brake lines; and lighter batteries. "Yet," added Cadillac, "perhaps the most meaningful test is reflected in this fact: Of all the Cadillacs ever built since 1902 more than forty-four percent are still on the road."

DIFFERENCES AMONG MODELS

The Calais Sedan, as well as all Cadillac four-door, six-passenger Sedans, now was fitted with a side coach window. Automatic Climate Control, previously an option, was now included as standard equipment. The Calais' standard Morgan plaid interior was offered in dark blue, crimson, or black, all with matching vinyl bolsters. Also available was black or dark-brown vinyl upholstery or Morocco matelasse fabric in saddle. A new option was the $843 glassdome Astroroof.

The De Ville series, again consisting of the Coupe de Ville and Sedan de Ville, carried exterior model script on the rear fenders, as well as a new seat and door-panel design. Numerous interior trim choices were offered, including Maharajah, as before a multicolored pattern, two velours, Manhattan, offered in gold, crimson, and rosewood, or a black Mardi Gras. In addition, a muted plaid known as Metamora, available in orange, jasper, or saddle, was offered along with leather upholstery in 10 colors.

Both De Villes were available with the $350 d'Elegance package consisting of a see-through stand-up hood crest plus accent striping on the hood, sides, and rear deck. Interior consisted of the Manhattan two-toned, crushed-velour upholstery in dark blue, rosewood, crimson, or saddle with leather cushion bolsters and back inserts in matching colors. The hinged door handles had simulated wood plaques. The deep-pile carpeting had color-coordinated, carpeted floor mats.

The Coupe de Ville continued to be available with the Cabriolet option now priced at $236. As in 1974, it consisted of a vinyl roof and a sheer chrome accent strip. It could be combined with either the Astroroof or the $668 electrically operated sunroof.

Cadillac abandoned the Sixty-Special designation in 1975, thus ending a tradition begun in 1938. The Fleetwood Brougham now had an AM/FM, signal-seeking stereo radio, as well as dual interior reading lamps as standard equipment. Brougham customers could select from numerous interior choices. A soft leather was available in nine colors; a new, ornate Monticello velour in six colors; or a Moselle fabric in black, jasper, or saddle.

For the third consecutive year, Cadillac offered two Special Edition options for the Fleetwood Brougham, the $784 Brougham d'Elegance package and the $1,788 Fleetwood Talisman. The former, which Cadillac said was "so majestic it attracts admirers wherever it goes,"

CADILLAC VITAL STATISTICS: 1975

Series	Model	Body Type	Factory Price ($)	Weight (lbs.)	Production (#)
Calais	C49/H	4 dr Hardtop Sedan	8,377	5087	2500
	C47/G	2 dr Hardtop Coupe	8,184	5003	5800
De Ville	D49/B	4 dr Hardtop Sedan	8,801	5146	63,352
	D47/J	2 dr Hardtop Coupe	8,600	5049	110,218
Fleetwood Eldorado	L47/H	2 dr Hardtop Coupe	9,935	5108	35,802
	L67/E	Convertible	10,354	5167	8950
Brougham 75	B69/P	4 dr Sedan	10,414	5242	18,755
	F23/R	4 dr Sedan	14,218	5720	876
	F23/S	4 dr Limousine	14,557	862	795
Seville	6S69	4 dr Sedan	12,479	4232	16,355

1975 Coupe de Ville. All rear-drive Cadillacs had a new grille and front fenders. Rectangular head lamps were used on all 1975 models.

1975 Sedan de Ville. Both the Sedan de Ville and the Calais Sedan has a new fixed rear-quarter window.

was identified by its stand-up wreath and crest hood ornament, "Brougham d'Elegance" script on the rail panel of the padded elk-grained vinyl roof, and turbine-type wheel discs with wreath and crest ornamentation. As in 1975, the Brougham d'Elegance was available in four interior trim combinations, which for 1975 included upper-door-trim pads and seat-back storage pockets. The choices this year included a softer Sierra leather in nine colors and a shirred-stitch, Medici crushed velour in dark blue, rosewood, black, and gold. Standard on all Brougham d'Elegance Cadillacs was a 60-40 Dual Comfort front seat with a six-way power adjuster on the driver's side.

Apparently not every customer impressed with the

1975 Fleetwood Sixty Special Brougham. The appearance of the Brougham was enhanced by its wider white wall steel-belted radial tires.

The 1975 Eldorado grille was highlighted by larger rectangular openings and bolder vertical fins. New urethane fender extensions deflected and moved rearward when the bumper was impacted.

1975 Fleetwood Eldorado Coupe and Convertible. The Coupe now used a larger fixed rear-quarter window. Its running mate was the only domestic luxury convertible available. Both versions had a new grille and vertical front bumper outer bar. Also evident was the absence of rear fender skirts.

Cadillac began production of its Electronic Fuel Injection System in early February 1974. Its "brains," a small analog computer, were held by Jo Ann Fry of Cadillac's engineering department.

Prior to being routed to a new, fully computerized shipping center, Cadillacs fresh from the assembly line were assigned computerized traffic control instructions.

1975 Cadillacs awaiting shipment from their computer-assigned locations. Depending on their final destination, Cadillacs were shipped via truck or tri-level or stac-pac railcar.

The 1975 Cadillac's Climate Control unit now had a new economy setting for 1975. This feature was also found on some late 1974 models.

Close-up of the 1975 Cadillac's rectangular head lamps.

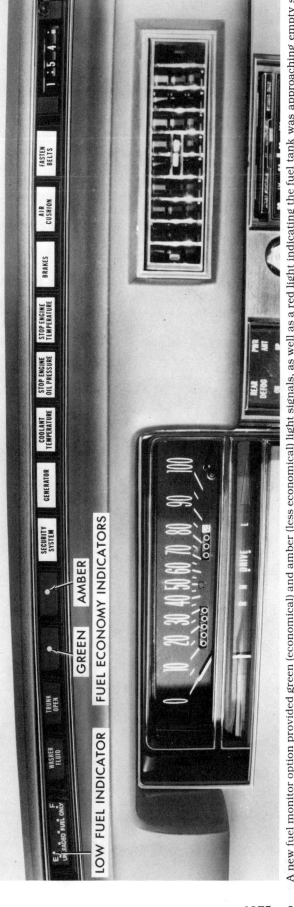

A new fuel monitor option provided green (economical) and amber (less economical) light signals, as well as a red light indicating the fuel tank was approaching empty status.

luxury of the 1974 Fleetwood Talisman had accepted Cadillac's logic of making it a four-passenger automobile. Thus, for 1975, Cadillac offered a compromise. Individual front seats were still installed but the rear seat was now full-sized.

After quoting Webster's definition of Talisman as "something producing apparently magical or miraculous effects" for the second year in a row in its sales material, Cadillac explained that "very simply, it is our ultimate in personalized luxury and comfort." The front seats were divided by a fabric-trimmed console with an illuminated and lockable storage compartment. The door inserts had sculptured moldings, and the Medici crushed-velour interior was available in gold, rosewood, black, and dark blue. Exterior appointments consisted of the elements found on the Brougham d'Elegance with "Fleetwood Talisman" script on the rail panel.

Both Series Seventy-Five models, the Limousine and nine-passenger Sedan were offered in a Moselle black knit upholstery with matching leather bolsters, Medici dark blue crushed velour, or a Potomac Graystone cloth upholstery.

The Eldorado coupe and Convertible models, which Cadillac described respectively as "one of the world's most exciting cars" and "one of a kind," were the most changed, appearance-wise, of Cadillac's carryover models. Their front end now carried rectangular headlights and a cross-hatched grille with larger divisions and bolder bars. Gone was the wraparound light style of 1974, replaced by a narrow, rectangular, horizontally mounted cornering light and vertically-positioned directional/parking lights. The Eldorado also lost its soft, flowing front-rear fender line to far sharper forms. Adding emphasis to this more forceful appearance was the abandonment of the rear-fender skirt, a larger rear-wheel opening, and a shorter side-body chrome spear, which now ran between the front and rear-fender wheels. On Coupe models, the rear side window was enlarged and reshaped to correspond to the upward kick of the rear fender.

Matching the impact of these changes were the Eldorado's revamped interiors. A Sierra-grain leather interior was offered in a wide range of colors, including light blue, dark crimson, rosewood, dark brown, medium orange, dark blue, medium jasper, light sandlewood, black, and white. In addition, the Metamora plaid-cloth pattern could be selected in orange, jasper, or saddle. Monticello velour was offered in six colors. The most sensational interior was the new Mosaic check, a black and white checkerboard cloth pattern. The Eldorado dashboard carried a simulated wood insert with a raised Eldorado script. Also new for 1975 were molded door-panel inserts with a hand-carved gunstock design.

A plaid "Morgan" cloth highlighted the 1975 Calais interiors.

CADILLAC'S DOMESTIC COMPETITION

In comparison with Cadillac's sales performance, Lincoln had its second best year in its history. Output of 101,843 cars was exceeded only by the 128,073 level of 1973. Once again, Mark IV output exceeded the Eldorado's, but the comfortable margin of earlier years had slipped away to a paper-thin edge of superiority. The final tally for 1975 showed 47,115 Mark IVs built to 44,752 Eldorados.

Unlike the Eldorado, the Mark IV was almost unchanged visually from 1974. Its standard vinyl roof, for example, now had chrome molding that, like the Eldorado's, gave it a "halo" effect. More importantly, the Mark IV now had, as standard equipment, four-wheel disc brakes, a feature the Eldorado would not have until 1976.

The Continentals were restyled with a more sharply squared-off roof line and reshaped front grille and taillights. In order to provide dealers with a more direct competitor to Cadillac's Calais models, Lincoln introduced, in late April 1975, a Continental Coupe from whose standard equipment list a sufficient number of items had been deleted to reduce its price to $8,799. It's doubtful that the close proximity of its introduction date of April 28 to the April 22, 1975, debut of the Seville was merely coincidental.

This was the final year for the Imperial until it was born again in 1981 as part of the "New Chrysler Corporation." Not surprising, changes were very minor for this end of the line model. Production totaled 8,830 cars.

SPECIFICATIONS

Engine

Type: V-type, ohv, eight cylinders
Bore × stroke: 4.30 × 4.304 inches
Displacement: 500 cubic inches
Horsepower: 190 @ 4,000 rpm
Compression ratio: 8.50:1
Carburetor: four-barrel
Lubrication: Full-pressure, full-flow oil filter
Electrical system: 12-volt, 15-plate battery, side terminals, 63-amp generator
    Limousine: 80-amp
Transmission: Turbo Hydra-Matic, three-speed automatic, torque-converter with fixed stator

Chassis/Drivetrain

Frame: Perimeter-type with heavy-gauge boxed side rails

A new 50/50 dual comfort seat was an exclusive Fleetwood Eldorado option for 1975.

Rear axle (rear-drive models):   2.73:1 ratio
    Limousine: 3.15:1
    3.15:1 available on all models except Eldorado
Front suspension: Integral steering knuckle; independent, helical-coil spring; rubber-mounted strut rods, and rubber bushings. Telescopic shock absorbers have Teflon piston rings.
    Eldorado: torsion-bar suspension
Rear suspension: Four-link with helical-coil springs, Eldorado had rear stabilizer bar
Steering: Variable-ratio with 17.8:1 ratio
    Eldorado: 20.0:1 variable ratio
    Limousine: 19.5:1 fixed-ratio system
Tires: GM specification, steel-belted radials, LR78-15 white sidewalls on all models; LR78-15B with wide-stripe whitewalls optional on all models except Limousine.

Dimensions

Wheelbase: 130 inches
    Fleetwood Brougham: 133 inches
    Limousine/9-passenger Sedan: 151.5 inches
    Eldorado: 126.3 inches
    Seville: 114.3 inches
Width: 79.8 inches
    Seville: 71.8 inches
    Eldorado: 79.8 inches
Front/rear tread: 63.3/63.3 inches
    Eldorado: 63.7/63.6 inches
    Seville: 61.3/59 inches
Overall length: 230.7 inches
    Fleetwood Brougham: 233.7 inches
    Limousine/nine-passenger Sedan: 252.2 inches
    Eldorado: 224.1 inches
    Seville: 204 inches

Popular Options

Electronic fuel injection
Illuminated entry system

Glass dome astroroof
AM/FM stereo with eight-track player
Passenger recliner seat: Available on Eldorado with passenger-side, six-way power adjuster
Sunroof*
Theft-deterrent system
Lighted vanity mirror
Remote-control trunk-lock release
Cruise control
Air-cushion restraint system*
Fuel monitor system
Tilt and telescope steering wheel
Track-master skid control
Twilight sentinel
Controlled-cycle wiper
Wide-stripe whitewalls: (1.6-inch width) compared with standard 0.75-inch width. Not available for Limousine/9-passenger Sedan
Special wheel discs: Standard on Brougham d'Elegance and Fleetwood Talisman, offered without wreath for De Ville and Calais
Automatic level control: Standard on Fleetwood models
Leather interior: Standard on Convertible, expanded vinyl on Calais
Passenger-side, power Seat Adjuster: Available on Fleetwood, Brougham, Eldorado, De Ville
Remote-control right side mirror: Standard on Limousine/9-passenger Sedan
Outside thermometer
Trailering package (not available for Limousine/9-passenger Sedan)

Firemist paint
Carpeted floor mats

----

*Not available for Convertible and Limousine/9-passenger Sedan.

Seville

International-size Luxury

IN OCTOBER 1974, Bernd Harling of Mercedes-Benz described M-B as "the moving target." It had become, he said, "the ideal of an industry," in spite of selling only some 40,000 cars in a market of close to 10-million annual sales. As Harling saw the American automobile scene, it was in a time of "dramatic reversals in buyer demand" back and forth from small to big cars that had sent all the major players searching for "swing-proof cars that are immune to the vagaries of buyer preference." In a thinly disguised reference to General Motors, he noted that "corporations with huge market research staffs and single car lines that have sold as many as three million cars a year are suddenly looking towards Mercedes-Benz for the answer."

Much of what Harling said was right on target. Almost overnight, all manner of vehicles had been appearing with pseudo-Mercedes grilles and body shapes. However, General Motors' interest in Mercedes-Benz was far more deeply rooted than Harling implied.

Over four years earlier, some Mercedes-Benz owners had received a questionnaire from Cadillac that, in essence, was intended to ascertain how they would react to a Cadillac that, at least in dimensions, would be similar to the Mercedes. At that time, over 29,000 Mercedes-Benz automobiles were sold in the United States. In contrast to Cadillac's output of over 158,000 (its second best year to that point), this minor achievement seemed to be of little importance.

Yet a closer look revealed that, in growing numbers, individuals with substantial incomes who normally were prime targets for Cadillac salesmen had abandoned the Standard of the World for the three-pointed star. Furthermore, Mercedes wasn't the only foreign manufacturer who was making inroads into Cadillac's domain. Other intruders bore Jaguar and BMW nameplates. Aside from their foreign origin, these automobiles shared several common denominators. All were, size-wise, similar to such U.S. compacts as the Chevrolet Nova, had relatively conservative styling that wasn't quickly outdated, and had no-nonsense, business-like interiors. But it was the Mercedes that, in terms of size, quality, styling, and interior design, represented the single most formidable challenge to Cadillac.

SEVILLE'S DEVELOPMENT

The first steps taken by General Motors in response to this situation came shortly after the survey of Mercedes drivers had been completed. It's important to point out that this project, which would lead to the 1975 Seville, was not a reflex action by Cadillac to the 1973 oil embargo. That situation persuaded GM to accelerate its development, but that's a long way from being a crash project as some auto journalists had depicted the Seville's development.

When the Seville debuted in April 1975, Cadillac Marketing Director Gordon Horsburgh reported that the demand for a Cadillac of its type had existed for five to seven years. Certainly the advocating of a small Cadillac by several of General Motors' outside directors didn't hurt the Seville's case! But at the same time, not everyone in the corporate power structure embraced the concept of a Cadillac with less than six-passenger capacity without some severe misgivings. Reportedly found among this group was GM President Ed Cole. Even after this issue was resolved, plenty of heated verbal exchanges that often lasted half a work day added plenty of zest to the Seville's evolution. But more often than not, these were over detail not format.

In the early stages of the Seville's evolution, there was at least an outside chance that it would come to market with either a Wankel engine or front-wheel drive or even both. There were plenty of proponents of these ideas, such as styling boss, Bill Mitchell, GM President Ed Cole, and Wankel project manager, Robert Templin, who were also close to the Seville's development to push it in those directions. But the high costs involved, the problems GM encountered with the Wankel, and the relatively limited production output envisioned for the Seville brought those ideas to a dead end.

For a time, the Opel Diplomat was considered a possible base for the Seville. There was plenty of logic behind such a move if it actually had been made. The Diplomat was a strong challenger to the 280 SE Mercedes-Benz; and with its 230 horsepower, Chevrolet-derived, 327-cubic-inch V-8, it was a strong, 125-mph, top-speed performer. It also was widely regarded in Europe as an outstanding automobile that could easily stand comparison with Mercedes, Jaguar, and BMW.

It was, therefore, with good reason that Cadillac concluded a number of clinics where the Opel Diplomat, along with 11 other high-priced automobiles, were displayed. Although there obviously was no engine or suspension evaluation included, of the several thousand individuals who completed a detailed questionnaire, approximately 90 percent rated the Diplomat superior to the Mercedes-Benz. The Seville was to be a made-in-America automobile, but the shipping costs and operational problems inherent in transplanting German assembly procedures in the United States were sufficient to abandon this plan.

Already in domestic production as the Chevrolet Nova, Pontiac Ventura, Oldsmobile Omega, and Buick Apollo, was GM's X-body platform, which in most critical dimensions was similar to most of the Seville's intended competition. The decision to base the Seville on the X-body had been derided by at least one critic of the industry as an example of the American auto industry's inability to do little better than a decent improvision when facing a challenge from abroad. But this charge holds little water. So many changes were made in adopting the X-car to Cadillac's standards that it was given a K-body designation; and in its final form, only a few components (front subframe, rear subframe cross members, and rear floor pan) were interchangeable between the two designs. The Seville's body was built by the Fisher Fleetwood Plant in Detroit where other Cadillac bodies were constructed.

A second disparaging rumor about the Seville concerned its tooling costs. To hear the critics, it was a money eater, rampantly running over its budget. This was more myth than fact. The Seville's tooling costs were high, reaching the $100 million mark. But Bob Templin unequivocally stated that there were no significant cost overruns.

When work first began on the Seville in late 1970, Cadillac's chief engineer was Carl Rasmussen, but by January 1973, when full-size design proposals had been completed, he had been succeeded by 44-year-old Bob Templin, a long time (since 1950) Cadillac man who was returning from work on the Wankel project. Templin's Cadillac background provided a solid anchor for the Seville's development. As Templin later remarked, "The Seville is a car engineered for the excellent performance characteristics long associated with Cadillac." In other words, Cadillac, while sending out the Seville as a conquest car, was "doing it my way" rather than slavishly copying Mercedes.

Obviously, this philosophy had to be carried over into the Seville's appearance. The initial proposal from the Advanced Cadillac Studio, headed by Stan Parker under the direction of Irv Rybicki and his assistant Jack

Humbert, completed during the winter of 1972-1973, was a classy-looking, semifastback code named La Salle. With plenty of side-glass, rear-fender skirts, and sloping rear deck, it possessed a distinct, original appearance.

An alternative proposal, the Le Scala, retained the La Salle's rear-deck profile while combining a round-wheel opening with a low and wide version of Cadillac's "classic" egg-crate grille. These were to become major elements of the Seville's appearance. Still unresolved was the form its roof line would take.

Key developments taking place during the summer of 1973 tilting the scale toward the Seville's final form included a private showing of a full-size fiberglass model of the new small Cadillac for GM's Board of Directors and a product clinic at Anaheim, California, in July. There the various fiberglass proposals for the new Cadillac were displayed, along with its intended competitors, to a very select audience. The result, according to Gordon Horsburgh, reinforced the styling trend toward the notchback body. Thus by November 1973, the basic form of the Seville was completed, and final GM approval came in 1974. These developments were not taking place within a tranquil social and economic environment. The 1973 OPEC oil embargo with its resulting doubling of gasoline prices, limited gallonage sales, and long lines at the gas pumps seemingly signaled the end of the road for the large American automobile.

The response at Cadillac was dramatic. Stylists put in a four-month tour of two-shift work days; and within nine months (from January to September 1974), the Seville's engineering design was completed.

Development of the Seville was an expensive undertaking. Nearly $1 million was spent on its tooling and designing. This price tag would have been much higher if not for the use of innovative computer applications. For some design and die preparation, a specialized Fast Fourier Transforms (FFT) computer program enabled engineers to both bypass some of the customary steps involved in design and tooling and identify early on areas in need of revision. When the Seville's design was completed, the computer tapes were used by tape-controlled die shops to cut the dies.

On the surface, the Seville's suspension appeared very conventional. At the front was a straight-forward, independent unit with A-arms and coil springs. Also familiar was the Seville's live rear axle with leaf springs. Although the lack of an all-independent rear suspension was a disappointment to some, a closer look at the Seville's underpinning revealed numerous examples of Cadillac's close attention to detail. Bob Templin, when the Seville debuted, explained the goal of its designers in regard to ride and handling characteristics: "In the development of the Seville, we directed a maximum effort toward engineering a machine with a quiet ride and extremely precise, responsive handling."

Thus, while the Seville's front suspension was conventional, it had 2 degrees of positive caster which provided excellent straight line stability and accurate steering. Also contributing to the latter was the Seville's variable ratio (from 14.0 to 16.2:1), Saginaw power steering, which provided 3.25 turns lock-to-lock. Helping to minimize the transferral of high-frequency road disturbances from the spring path to the frame were small rubber spacers placed between the front coil springs and the upper spring tower. Helping to limit the transfer of road disturbances to the steering wheel was a specially tuned steering-linkage damper. At the rear, Teflon separators were placed between each of the five leaf springs to reduce interleaf friction and help the springs maintain their original characteristics throughout the vehicle's life.

Also influencing the Seville's road manners was a 0.62-inch rear-stabilizer bar to help control roll during cornering. The Seville's shock absorbers were expensive Delco units with pliacell gas chambers with a tent-like rubber seal separating the moving sections of the shock. With gas on one side and oil on the other, aeration of the oil was virtually nonexistent. These units, with their large-diameter bushings, were similar to those used on the larger Cadillacs.

Included in the Seville's rear suspension was a Delco leveling system. In 1975, the Seville was the only American car to have this feature as standard equipment. The automatic leveler, which was operated by a small compressor mounted on the engine, either inflated or deflated rubber springs mounted coaxially around the upper portion of the rear shock absorbers on command from a load sensor. Up to an 800-pound load limit, this system could maintain a nearly constant rear-suspension level and spring travel.

Since the 450SE Mercedes was equipped with four-wheel disc brakes, the lack of a similar arrangement on the Seville disappointed some critics. The Seville engineers looked high and low through the GM parts inventory, but there was nothing on hand, including the Corvette's disc-brake system that would fit into the Seville's design. Thus the Seville came to market with 11.0-inch, ventilated disc brakes up front and rear 11-x-2-inch finned drums whose diameter was 1.5 inches greater than those used on the GM X-cars. Helping to fill out the Seville's full-fender openings were 15-inch wheels with a 6-inch rim width on which were mounted Firestone steel-belted, 6R78-15B radial tires.

When General Motors introduced the Seville to the press early in 1975 at its Arizona test facility, it had a 450SE on hand for comparison purposes. This might have appeared to be an act of extreme arrogance on Cadillac's part to those who regarded the Mercedes as one of the world's finest automobiles. Of that there can be no doubt, but also beyond doubt was the Seville's ability to come away from a tire-to-tire contest with the 450SE with honor. The Mercedes, with its independent rear suspension, enjoyed an advantage over the Seville on rough road surfaces; but on smooth roads, the Cadillac's combination of ride and control put it among the ranks of the world's most competent Sedans. Although the Seville's absolute cornering power (in the region of 0.65 G) was inferior to the Mercedes, it was able, on *Road & Track's* 100-ft-radius handling circle, to maintain a slightly faster (32.7 mph to 32.5 mph) speed than the 450SE.

Cadillac had for years maintained not only a demanding standard of silence and smooth operation but also one of the world's highest levels of quality control. It was thus a virtual mandate that the Seville would measure up to these criteria.

Perhaps the single most important contribution to the Seville's silky smooth performance was the means by which its front subframe, which carried the front wheels, suspension, engine, and transmission, was attached to the main body structure. Six "Isoflex" rubber mounts, bonded with upper and lower steel plates, served as the mounting system. These cushions had a stiffer lateral-movement characteristic than in the other two movement modes and, along with twin Delco shock absorbers, effectively dissipated most of the impact energy generated by the various front-end components.

Although the Seville's 350-cubic-inch (5.7 liter) V-8 was manufactured by Oldsmobile, the installation of Bendix electronic fuel injection and a Cadillac-designed intake manifold provided more power and torque than a pure stock Oldsmobile version plus excellent driveability.

The earlier announcement that electronic fuel injection (EFI) would be an option for all Cadillacs except for the Limousine and commercial-chassis models made the availability of EFI on the Seville less sensational than it might have been otherwise. The fact remained, however, that the Seville was the first American car to be available with fuel injection as standard equipment.

ELECTRONIC FUEL INJECTION

This system of delivering the air-fuel mixture to the cylinders dated back to the 1920s, when the Robert Bosch firm in Germany provided a unit for installation on diesel engines. After its recovery from the destruction of World War II, the Daimler-Benz was, by 1952, capable of producing one of the world's most advanced sports cars, the 300SL. Two years later, as a production model, it again was a sensation as the first automobile offered to the public with fuel injection as standard equipment.

Meanwhile, in the United States, a number of firms were cognitive of fuel injection's potential both in terms of performance and its significance as an example of technical expertise. In a crash program, Chevrolet won the race to become the first American manufacturer to offer fuel injection. In 1957, it was available at $538 for both the Corvette and its regular production-model Sedans.

For a time, it seemed as if every automobile producer was intent on jumping aboard the fuel-injection bandwagon. Among the automobiles available with fuel injection were Pontiac, Chrysler, and Rambler. But this proved optimistic as the availability of large-displacement V-8s with triple two-barrel or dual four-barrel carburetors offered levels of performance previously unattainable in domestic automobiles at lower prices. The Corvette continued to offer a fuel-injection engine. But that, too, was dropped after the 1965 model year.

Despite this sequence of events, engineers recognized some solid pluses for fuel injection. Surely not the least of its advantages was the elimination of some old-fashioned components, such as the manifold heat riser and carburetor choke that had justifiably bad reputations for orneriness and misbehavior.

Another attraction of fuel injection was its impact on intake-manifold design. Unlike the manifold used for engines with carburetors, a unit intended for a fuel-injection system did not have to be compromise between volumetric efficiency (cool manifolding) and fuel vaporization (hot manifolding). Whereas a carburetor could deviate as much as 15 percent in its air-fuel mixture to separate cylinders, a fuel-injection system delivered an identical air-fuel charge to each cylinder. Thus, while the former imbalance forced engineers to set a carburetor to deliver a mixture richer than needed for good fuel economy, the fuel injection could be set to operate very near its theoretical limit.

The bane of high-performance engines with carburetors—fuel starvation and surge in hard cornering and severe braking conditions—was also almost unknown in a fuel-injected engine. Lurking just out of the engineering limelight was the attractiveness of a fuel-injected engine to designers who were eager to take full styling advantage of its low profile.

Arrayed against these factors were three simple, but solid realities. Fuel injection was expensive, complex, and required a well-trained service staff to keep it functioning properly. But between the age of high performance and the era of fuel shortages and stringent emissions regulation, a dramatic cost reduction of electronic components took place, and the long dormant electronic fuel-injection system awoke to a bright future.

Bendix had begun research with EFI in the early fifties with a 1953 Buick V-8 fitted with what was described as a "vacuum-tube controlled system." Following on the heels of this program was interest by Robert Bosch, which lead to a licensing agreement and joint development work. From this point, the next crucial juncture was a Cadillac-Bendix engineering program that commenced in 1973.

The attractiveness of EFI, magnified tremendously by the availability of relatively inexpensive components, was its ability to take the inherent advantages of fuel injection to a new plateau of finesse. Relegated to a stage of technical obsolescence was the old mechanical system with its complex arrangement of linkage, cams, pluggers, and injection pumps.

In its place was a system that isolated each operation of the engine and treated them independently. The result was a fuel-air mixture supplied to each cylinder tailored to meet very specific conditions and demands at any given moment. This had obvious implications for meeting and not deviating from emissions control specifications in "real-world" driving conditions.

Unlike its role as a high-performance enhancer two decades earlier, the fuel-injection system of the midseventies soon gained a reputation for providing improved driveability and emissions performance. Nonetheless, the use of EFI on the big, 500-cubic-inch Cadillac V-8 increased horsepower to 215 from 190 and torque output from 360 to 400 ft-lb. Since the injectors used on the Seville had a lower flow rate, the horsepower increased only moderately (to 180 from 170) over its carburetored counterpart. This did, however, provide a payoff in terms of fuel economy.

The Seville's EFI consisted of four basic units: fuel delivery system, air induction system, primary sensors, and the electronic control unit (ECU). The latter element was a preprogrammed analog computer with four customer-developed circuits, as well as others calibrated to particular cars. In addition, the ECU controlled other operations, including exhaust gas recirculation (EGR).

The Seville's design theme was distinctive yet unmistakably that of a Cadillac. The Seville's tail lamps wrapped around the rear fenders and incorporated both the side marker lamps and the side and rear reflexes.

Front armrests of the Seville contained the power door lock switches and power seat adjuster controls.

The Seville carried traditional Cadillac script just above the rectangular head lamps.

The Seville's instrument panel positioned the telltale and warning lights in the information band which stretched across the upper portion of the panel.

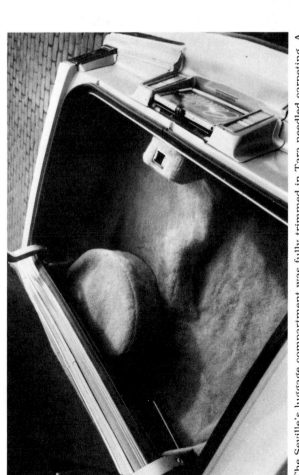

The Seville's luggage compartment was fully trimmed in Tara needled carpeting. A General Motors specification stowaway spare tire was standard equipment.

Five sensors continuously monitored engine operating conditions and transmitted data to the ECU for analysis of fuel requirements. The engine conditions under scrutiny were manifold absolute pressure, throttle position, engine speed, engine coolant temperature, and intake air temperature. The sensors for the last two items were identical and thus interchangeable.

Cadillac built the intake manifolds, which were shipped to the Bendix plant at Troy, Michigan, where they were joined to the injector's fuel rail and throttle body. Bendix calibrated the system prior to returning it to Cadillac for engine installation.

Additional primary units of the EFI system included an electric booster pump, supplied by AC, which was mounted on the fuel tank. It delivered fuel to the main fuel pump, a Robert Bosch unit, which was positioned directly ahead of the left rear wheel. This pump maintained a nominal pressure of 39 psi and delivered fuel at a rate of 33 gph. Any excess fuel was rerouted back to the tank. Since these two electric pumps increased the demand on the Seville's electrical system, an 80-amp generator was fitted. The Seville also was the first passenger car to be fitted with the new Delco Freedom battery.

The eight fuel injectors supplied by both German and Japanese companies were separated into two groups. On one engine revolution, cylinders 1, 2, 7, and 8 received fuel. On the next revolution, fuel was delivered to cylinders 3, 4, 5, and 6.

PRODUCTION OF THE SEVILLE

Seville production began on March 26, 1975, on a 14.5-cars per hour, two-shift schedule in Cadillac's West assembly complex at the Clark Avenue plant. Conversion of this facility, which had previously been used for Eldorado production, began in February 1975. The next vehicle to appear on the assembly line as the last Eldorado, number 275,260, to be built at West was completed was a bulldozer that, along with others of its kind, crashed through the rear wall to begin dismantling the old equipment.

Retooling of the plant, which for a time was known as "Omaha Beach," took place round the clock, seven days a week, and was completed in six weeks. Among the innovative manufacturing techniques installed were conveyor-carried pedestals for assembly of the engine and rear-axle components and a Delco computer, which tested the Seville's optional equipment in one operation.

Long before it became fashionable, Cadillac made a strong effort to acquaint its work force with the Seville and their role in its success. They were invited to view the first prototype mounted on a turntable in the engineering building as well as a slide presentation on the new plant's features. Both production foremen and key hourly personnel were involved in a five-week training plan.

When operational, the production line moved at low speed to ensure maximization of high-quality control standards. In many ways, the enthusiasm of the Seville workers took on the nature of a group assembly operation.

Cadillac was, even after these steps, taking no chances with the Seville's quality. To ensure everything was in its place and operating properly, the first 2,000 Sevilles were exactly alike: metallic silver with gray upholstery and fully optioned. This gave the line workers plenty of experience in a short time span as well

CADILLAC VITAL STATISTICS: 1976

Series	Model	Body Type	Factory Price ($)	Weight (lbs.)	Production (#)
Seville	S69	4 dr Sedan	12,479	4232	43,772
Calais	C49	4 dr Sedan (HT)	8825	5083	1700
	C47	2 dr Coupe	8629	4989	4500
De Ville	D49	4 dr Sedan HT	9265	5127	67,677
	D47	2 dr Coupe	9067	5025	114,482
Fleetwood Eldorado	L47	2 dr Coupe	10,586	5085	35,184
	L67	2 dr Convertible	11,049	5153	14,000
60 Special Brougham	B69	4 dr Sedan	10,935	5213	24,500
75 Sedan	F23	4 dr Sedan 9p	14,889	5746	981
75 Limousine	F33	4 dr Limo 9p	15,239	5889	834

as in ironing out repair procedures since all the cars were identical.

With a list price of $12,479, the Seville was one of America's most expensive automobiles, and a perusal of its list of 64 standard equipment items (which began with ''Accent Paint Stripe'' and concluded with ''Wheel Discs'' helped ease the anguish of long-time Cadillac owners who might have been having a difficult time understanding why a small Cadillac was so expensive.

Among the Seville's more prominent standard features were power windows; six-way power driver's seat (two-way operation was provided for the passenger); AM-FM signal-seeking stereo radio; automatic, temperature-control air conditioning; digital clock; electric trunk-lid release; automatic parking-brake release; and an intermittent setting for the three-speed wipers. Although the Seville was the most fully equipped Cadillac built, there were still another 28 items available as either factory- or dealer-installed optional equipment. These included Firemist paint, Astroroof, cruise control, a heavy-duty cooling system, an illuminated entry system, Guide-Matic headlight control, and leather upholstery.

The only real shortcomings in the Seville's interior relative to its foreign competition were the use of false rosewood in its door panels and dash and the lack of gauges found in its ''information band.'' This battery of tell-tale and warning lights was, however, nicely arrayed across the upper portion of the panel facing the driver. The lack of any annoying reflections from its dull black surfaces (when all was well) was commendable, but a comprehensive display of accurate gauges would have been welcome.

Bob Templin perceived the Seville as a car virtually devoid of compromise. Beyond any doubt, the Seville was that type of an automobile. It was a landmark Cadillac that proved a worthy alternative to its foreign competition while still maintaining identity as a Cadillac.

SPECIFICATIONS

Engine

Type: V-type, ohv, eight cylinders
Bore x stroke: 4.057 x 3.385 inches
Displacement: 350 cubic inches
Horsepower: 180 @ 4,400 rpm
Torque: 275 lb-ft @ 2,000 rpm
Compression ratio: 8.0:1
Fuel system: Electronic fuel injection
Electrical system: 12-volt Freedom battery, 80-amp generator
Transmission: Turbo Hydra-Matic, three-speed, 400 series

Chassis/Drivetrain

Rear axle: Salisbury type with 8.5-inch ring gear, 2.56:1 standard ratio
    Optional: 3.08:1
Front suspension: Unequal-length, upper-lower suspension arms, coil springs, 1-inch-diameter stabilizer bar, hydraulic shock absorbers
Rear suspension: multiple-leaf springs, 0.57-inch stabilizer bar, hydraulic shock absorbers, Automatic Level Control
Steering: Variable-ratio power steering, overall ratio: 16.4-13.8
Brakes: Front ventilated discs; rear, 11-inch, finned cast-iron drums
    Total swept area: 350.8 square inch
Tires: GM specification, steel-belted radial, wide white sidewall, GR78-15B

Dimensions

Wheelbase: 114.3 inches
Width: 71.8 inches
Front/rear tread: 61.3/59 inches
Overall length: 204 inches

Popular Options

Accessory engine block heater
AM/FM stereo signal-seeking radio with weather band
AM/FM stereo radio with integral tape player
Astroroof
Automatic door-locking system
Controlled differential
Cruise control
Deluxe robe and pillow
Door guards
Firemist paint
Carpeted floor mats
Guide-matic headlamp control
Heavy-Duty cooling system
Illuminated entry system
Illuminated vanity mirror (passenger side)
Leather upholstery
License frames
Performance axle ratio
Power seat-back recliner
Rear shoulder belts
Rear-window electric defogger
Sunroof
Theft deterrent system
Trailer towing package
Trunk mat
Twilight sentinel
Wheel discs, deluxe and turbine

1976

Whatever You Want in a Luxury Car

CADILLAC MADE ONLY MINIMAL CHANGES in its products for 1976. This hardly came as a surprise since it was well known that Cadillac, along with the other GM automotive divisions, was going to make a near-revolutionary move in 1977 by resizing its cars to a new standard. This would put GM out front of its competitors and thus in harm's way if the public, rejecting the notion that smaller is better, embraced the older-style, large-sized models still offered by Ford and Chrysler. Cadillac had scored a point over Lincoln by being the first domestic manufacturer to have an entry in the internationally sized market with the Seville, but whether customers long accustomed to Cadillacs with wheelbases of 130 and more inches would accept models with wheelbases nearly a foot shorter was unknown.

As the 1976 model-year began there was plenty of good news for Cadillac to dispel any lingering doubts as the design for 1977 was finalized. General manager Edward C. Kennard reported that while industry-wide sales had declined almost 15 percent during the 1975 model year, Cadillac's had increased nearly 10 percent over 1974 levels to 256,362. This lead him to predict 1976 sales of approximately 281,000, which would be only 7,500 short of Cadillac's best-ever model sales year of 288,504 cars, set in 1973.

This provided the basis for more positive words from Mr. Kennard, and he made the most of it. "Cadillac," he noted, "accounted for 34.5 percent of total high price group purchases, an increase of four percentage points from 1974, and almost 40 percent of domestic high price group buys, up five percentage points from the year before."

Kennard also had encouraging words about the Seville's success based on surveys of Seville buyers conducted by Cadillac. The results showed that approximately 45 percent of principal Seville drivers were women. The median driver age was 55.7 years, with 30 percent of the owners surveyed having taken at least some post-college graduate work. That median age was a bit on the high side, but the trade in and shopping patterns for Seville indicated its success against foreign competition. Twenty-five percent of Seville buyers said they considered buying another model Cadillac, while 41 percent said they considered a luxury import.

Following this pattern, a total of 16 percent said another Cadillac model would be their second choice if the Seville were not offered, and 23 percent named a luxury import as their second choice. Of those questioned, 19 percent owned another Cadillac, while 22 percent were owners of a foreign car. "Thus," reported Cadillac, "this means the Seville is doing an excellent conquest job for Cadillac and General Motors, especially in diverting luxury import sales."

In Kennard's view, the Seville had "greatly contributed to increased showroom traffic and outstanding sales, providing dealers with product flexibility and owners with luxury of choice when combined with full-size Cadillacs."

Those models, as noted earlier, were marked by subtle interior and exterior changes. Although in their final production year, they were leaving the automotive scene styled, said Cadillac, "to further personalize the existing customer appeal of an already successful automobile."

CHANGES AND IMPROVEMENTS

The changes that were made were predictable. The traditional cross-hatched grille theme remained but now with recessed, finely meshed accent lines. The cornering lights were changed by virtue of two horizontal, chrome-strip inserts.

DIFFERENCES AMONG MODELS

The Calais Coupe, along with the Coupe de Ville was now available with an exterior opera lamp similar to

1976 Calais Coupe. A new grille design with recessed accent lines was used in 1976. The wire wheel discs on this Calais were a new option for 1976.

1976 Sedan de Ville. Turbine wheel discs as installed on this De Ville were optional for all 1976 Cadillacs except Eldorado models.

CADILLAC VITAL STATISTICS: 1976

Series	Model	Body Type	Factory Price ($)	Weight (lbs.)	Production (#)
Seville	S69	4 dr Sedan	12479	4232	43,772
Calais	C49	4 dr Sedan (HT)	8825	5083	1700
	C47	2 dr Coupe	8629	4989	4500
De Ville	D49	4 dr Sedan HT	9265	5127	67,677
	D47	2 dr Coupe	9067	5025	114,482
Fleetwood Eldorado	L47	2 dr Coupe	10,586	5085	35,184
	L67	2 dr Convertible	11,049	5153	14,000
60 Special Brougham	B69	4 dr Sedan	10,935	5213	24,500
75 Sedan	F23	4 dr Sedan 9p	14,889	5746	981
75 Limousine	F33	4 dr Limo 9p	15,239	5889	834

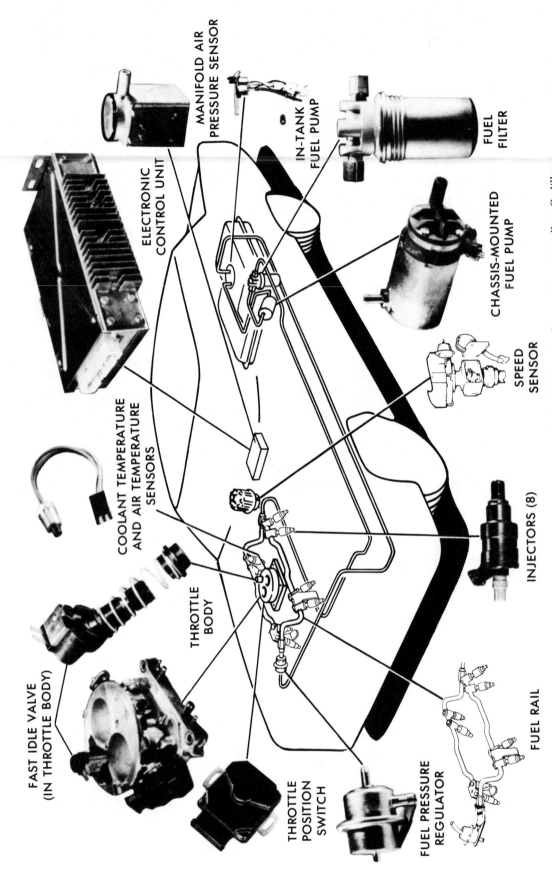

MANIFOLD AIR PRESSURE SENSOR

IN-TANK FUEL PUMP

FUEL FILTER

ELECTRONIC CONTROL UNIT

CHASSIS-MOUNTED FUEL PUMP

SPEED SENSOR

COOLANT TEMPERATURE AND AIR TEMPERATURE SENSORS

INJECTORS (8)

FAST IDLE VALVE (IN THROTTLE BODY)

THROTTLE BODY

FUEL RAIL

THROTTLE POSITION SWITCH

FUEL PRESSURE REGULATOR

Detail of Cadillac's Electronic Fuel Injection System. Components were provided by Delco and Bendix Corporation, as well as Cadillac.

1976 Seville. Its Federal fuel economy ratings were 21 mpg highway and 15 mpg city.

The 1976 Fleetwood Eldorado Convertible and the first Cadillac, 1916 Type 53. Since 1946, Cadillac had produced nearly 354,000 convertibles.

that used in the Coupe de Ville d'Elegance package and on the Fleetwood Brougham and Seventy-Five models. Also found in Calais and de Ville Coupes was a new vinyl-roof treatment with a top molding that was a continuation of the door-belt molding.

The standard interior for the Calais Coupe and Sedan remained Morgan plaid in several new color combinations, including blue-green/gray-black, black/gray/red, blue/gray/black, and red/gray/black. An all-vinyl interior was offered in either antique light buckskin or black. All full-sized Cadillacs used new Rosewood-grain trim for the instrument panel. As in 1975, appropriate series identifications were placed in the panel facing the front-seat passenger.

De Ville exterior identification remained unchanged from 1975. Interiors were revised to feature a new ribbed knit material, Magnan, which was offered in black, dark blue, light ivory-gold, light buckskin, dark blue-green, and dark firethorn. Also debuting was a Merlin plaid in dark blue-green or dark firethorn. Continued from 1975 was the Manhattan velour in blue and light buckskin, and leather which was now offered in 11, rather than 10 colors.

The De Ville d'Elegance option featured what Cadillac described as "a new expression of comfort—Cadillac contoured Pillow Seating." Joining the see-through, stand-up hood emblem and accent striping from 1975 were 50/50 Dual Comfort front seats and, on the coupe, opera lights. Both the Coupe de Ville and Coupe de Ville d'Elegance were available with the Cabriolet roof option.

The signature trim for the Fleetwood Sixty Special Brougham now comprised styled block letters in matching car color. Standard on the latest model were Dual Comfort 60/40 front seats with a center, folddown armrest. Like all Cadillacs, the Brougham was offered in 15 standard and six optional Firemist paint colors, of which 13 were new for 1976.

Once again, Cadillac offered two "Special Editions" of the Fleetwood Brougham, the Brougham d'Elegance and the Fleetwood Talisman. The latter option had individual front seats (and a full-width rear seat) trimmed in crushed-velour Medici in either dark blue or black. The front seats were divided by a console equipped with an illuminated and lockable storage compartment. Exterior features included Talisman identification on the roof panel, a padded, Elk-Grain vinyl roof and turbine-vaned wheel discs.

The contoured pillow seats for the Brougham d'Elegance were trimmed in Mansion knit available in light gray, black, dark blue, dark blue-green, and light buckskin. The seat backs were fitted with storage pockets. Also included in this package was deep-pile carpeting, turbine-vaned wheel covers (which, along with wire-wheel discs, were available for all 1976 Cadillacs except Eldorados), opera lamps, 50/50 Dual Comfort front seats, a padded, Elk-Grain vinyl roof and brushed-chrome door moldings.

Both the Fleetwood Seventy-Five Sedan and Limousine, with their "Executive-Size Luxury" were offered with either a Medici crushed-velour interior in black or dark blue or a light gray Magnan knit interior.

Entering its tenth year as a front-wheel-drive automobile, the Eldorado was fitted with new wheel discs with a black center hub area. At the front, the Cadillac script was moved upward onto the hood from its previous position on the top-grille frame. The Eldorado taillight now carried a single, continuous red lens set in a large bezel frame.

Far more noteworthy was the adoption of four-wheel disc brakes as standard Eldorado equipment. The Eldorado, as did all Cadillacs, used the Delco "Freedom" battery, first introduced on the Seville. In addition to never needing water, its advantages over the batteries previously used included smaller size, lighter weight, and a visible charge indicator.

The Coupe was also available with the same leather interiors as the Convertible, as well as two fabric upholsteries. A Mansion knit was offered in dark blue, light ivory-gold, light buckskin, and black. The Merlin plaid could be ordered in either dark blue-green or dark firethorn.

Midway through the model year, Cadillac introduced a Custom Biarritz option for the Eldorado Coupe listing for $1,831. It consisted of a Cabriolet roof with reduced-size back and rear quarter windows, both of which had "razor-edge" outlines, and a rear vinyl insert accentuating the aluminum cross-over roof molding. Running from the car's rear to the hood, where it widened into a "spear-like" design, was a stainless-steel accent molding with black grooves and a brushed center area.

Additional body identification for the Custom Biarritz consisted of Biarritz script; a passenger-side, remote-control mirror; additional accent stripes on the front fenders, doors, and rear-quarter panels; a padded, Elk-grain roof with opera lamps; and special, color-coordinated wheel discs. In conjunction with an all-leather interior, five exterior colors were offered: Innsbruck blue, Cotillion white, Academy gray, Sable black, and firethorn.

The Seville was now offered with the full range of Cadillac exterior colors. Added to its option list were the Astroroof and sunroof features, which were now available on all models except for the Series Seventy-Five Cadillacs. Among 43,772 Sevilles produced in 1976 was the five millionth postwar Cadillac, built during April 1976.

Providing what Cadillac regarded as "additional customer value benefits" were a number of revisions in existing options as well as several new features. Examples of the former was the refinement of the illuminated entry system to provide interior/exterior illumination until the ignition was turned on and the redesigning of the theft-deterrent system with a specific arming sequence to prevent false triggering of the system.

New options for all series consisted of an automatic door-locking system, which locked all doors when the shift lever was moved to Drive position. Also debuting was a power-operated, passenger-seat-back recliner (for models with 50/50 Dual Comfort front seats), and a weather-band feature for AM/FM stereo radios. This offered weather information, in those areas which it was transmitted, by depressing a button.

THE CONVERTIBLE

Cadillac promoted the Eldorado Convertible as the "End of an Era," which in 1976 seemed all too true as prevailing governmental attitudes toward automotive design seemed to doom the American Convertible. This didn't happen, and in eight years, the Cadillac Convertible would be reborn in Eldorado Biarritz form. In 1976, however, it appeared that government edicts aside, the Convertible's fate was sealed.

Throughout Cadillac history, there had always been an open car since the first Model A Cadillacs of 1902 were offered with a detachable top. In 1916, Cadillac first used the term "convertible" in reference to one of its Type 53 models.

The golden years of the Cadillac Convertible were after World War II with the mid-1960s being the peak production years. From 1963 through 1966, for example, Cadillac produced, on the average, approximately 20,000 soft tops annually. All told, from 1946 through 1970, Cadillac produced 353,786 Convertibles. But as the following shows, popularity of the Cadillac Convertible gradually slipped.

Cadillac attributed the decline in Convertible model popularity to the "corresponding increase in the use of automobile air conditioning, hardtop coupes with vinyl-roof styling, and more frequent, high-speed expressway travel."

Whatever the reason for its demise, Cadillac ushered out the Eldorado Convertible in style. "It's not often," it reported, "that a collector's item can be classified as such even before its production has been completed. This, however, is the unusual and unique aspect of the 1976 Cadillac Fleetwood Eldorado Convertible." To make even more of a lasting impression, Cadillac turned out the last 200 Convertibles with identical finishes; white body with red and blue trim. Savoring the Eldorado's 1975 sales victory over the Mark IV Continental, George Kennard added, "The interest in the last Convertible . . . should further enhance our popularity over the nearest competitor." The full range of the Convertible's Sierra-grain leather interior included eight colors: white, antique light gray, black, antique light blue, antique dark blue-green, light ivory-gold, antique light buckskin, and antique dark firethorn. Convertible tops were offered in black, ivory, white, buckskin, dark blue, firethorn and dark blue-green.

CADILLAC'S DOMESTIC COMPETITION

Cadillac's 1976 model production total of 304,485 cars was just short of surpassing the all-time mark of 304,839, set back in 1973. But sales, as measured by 1976 calendar-year registrations, were the best ever for Cadillac totaling 293,176 cars.

Lincoln production, like Cadillac's, came tantalizingly close (124,756) to its record level of 128,073, also set in 1973. In the Eldorado-Mark IV production contest, the Lincoln, in spite of the

Cadillac Convertible Production: 1946-1976

Year	Model/Series	Subtotals	Production
1946	Series 62	-	1,342
1947	Series 62	-	6,755
1948	Series 62	-	5,450
1949	Series 62	-	8,000
1950	Series 62	-	6,986
1951	Series 62	-	6,117
1952	Series 62	-	6,400
1953	Series 62	8,367	
	Eldorado	532	8,899
1954	Series 62	6,310	
	Eldorado	2,150	8,460
1955	Series 62	8,150	
	Eldorado Biarritz	3,950	12,100
1956	Series 62	8,300	
	Eldorado Biarritz	2,150	10,450
1957	Series 62	9,000	
	Eldorado Biarritz	1,800	10,800
1958	Series 62	7,825	
	Eldorado Biarritz	815	8,640
1959	Series 62	11,130	
	Eldorado Biarritz	1,320	12,450
1960	Series 62	14,000	
	Eldorado Biarritz	1,285	15,285
1961	Series 62	15,500	
	Eldorado Biarritz	1,450	16,950
1962	Series 62	16,800	
	Eldorado Biarritz	1,450	18,250
1963	De Ville	17,600	
	Eldorado Biarritz	1,825	19,425
1964	De Ville	17,900	
	Eldorado Biarritz	1,870	19,770
1965	De Ville	19,200	
	Eldorado	2,125	21,325
1966	De Ville	19,200	
	Eldorado	2,250	21,450
1967	De Ville		18,200
1968	De Ville		18,025
1969	De Ville		16,445
1970	De Ville		15,172
1971	Eldorado		6,800
1972	Eldorado		7,975
1973	Eldorado		9,315
1974	Eldorado		7,600
1975	Eldorado		8,950
1976	Eldorado		14,000

Eldorado's healthy output increase to 49,184, was the winner with 56,110 cars produced.

The ability of the Mark IV to widen its production lead over the Eldorado after it had narrowed to just 2,393 cars in 1975 was due more to the introduction of four new Designer Series models rather than to any major revisions. Both the Mark IV and Continental were, except for the Designer Series option and emission-fuel economy technical changes, essentially unchanged from 1975.

Nineteen seventy-seven, against this backdrop, was going to match a facelifted Continental against all-new, smaller Cadillacs; a new Mark V against a stand-pat Eldorado, and, midway through the model year, Lincoln's response to the Seville, the Versailles.

SPECIFICATIONS

Engine

Type: V-type, ohv, eight cylinders
Bore × stroke: 4.30 × 4.304 inches
Displacement: 500 cubic inches
Horsepower: 190 @ 3,600 rpm
Torque: 360 lb-ft @ 2,000 rpm
Compression ratio: 8.5:1
Fuel system: Four-barrel Quadrajet carburetor
Electrical system: 12-volt Freedom battery, 3,500-watt, 66 plates, side terminals, no filler/vent cap, 63-amp generator
   Series 75:   80-amp

Chassis/Drivetrain

Transmission: Turbo Hydra-Matic 400 Series, three-speed automatic (425 series on Eldorado)
Frame: Perimeter type with heavy-gauge, boxed side rails
Rear axle: Rear-drive models: Hypoid type with ring gear, 2.73:1 ratio
   Series 75:   3.15:1 (available on other models)
   Eldorado driving axle: Spiral-bevel, 2.73:1 ratio, 3.07:1 available
Front suspension: Upper and lower arms, coil springs, (torsion bars in Eldorado), integral knuckle arm and caliper support, integral hubs and rotors on spindles (except for Eldorado), rod and link stabilizer, hydraulic double-action shock absorbers
Rear suspension: Four-link drive, coil springs, hydraulic double-action shock absorbers, Automatic Level Control (except for Calais, De Ville)
Steering: Variable ratio
   Series 75:   constant ratio
Overall ratios:
   Calais, De Ville, Brougham: 17.8 to 9.0:1
   Eldorado: 20.0 to 17.7:1
   Series 75:   19.5:1
Tires: GM specification, steel-belted radials, white stripe, LR78-15-B
   Series 75:   LR78-15-D
Brakes (all models except Eldorado:
   Front: ventilated discs
   Rear: 12-inch finned cast-iron, molded asbestos linings, total swept area: 428.5 square inches
   Eldorado front and rear: single-piston sliding calipers, ventilated discs, total swept area: 448 square inches

Dimensions

Wheelbase:
   Calais, De Ville: 130 inches
   Fleetwood Brougham: 133 inches
   Series 75:   151.5 inches
   Eldorado: 126.3 inches
Width: 79.8 inches

Height:
   Calais, De Ville Sedans: 54.3 inches
   Calais, De Ville Coupes: 53.8 inches
   Fleetwood Brougham: 55.3 inches
   9-passenger Sedan: 57.4 inches
   Limousine: 57.2 inches
   Eldorado Coupe: 54.1 inches
   Eldorado Convertible: 54.5 inches
Front/rear tread: 63.3/63.3 inches
   Eldorado: 63.7/63.6 inches
Overall length:
   Calais, De Ville: 230.7 inches
   Fleetwood Brougham: 233.7 inches
   Series 75:   252.2 inches
   Eldorado: 224.1 inches

Popular Options

Electronic fuel injection (not available for Limousine/9-passenger Sedan)
Weather-band radio
Door-lock system
Astroroof (not available for Convertible and Limousine/9-passenger Sedan)
Sunroof
Theft-deterrent system
Illuminated entry system
Illuminated vanity mirror
Fuel monitor system
Stereo with 8 track player
Power recliner seats: With 50/50 Dual Comfort front seats
Opera lamps
Wire wheel discs
Disc wheel with black hub (not available for Limousine/9-passenger Sedan)
Air-Cushion restraint system (not available for Convertible and Limousine/9-passenger Sedan)
Manual Recliner: Driver's seat on models with 50/50 Dual Comfort seats
Trackmaster Skid-Control (not available for Eldorado)
Twilight sentinel
Guide-Matic headlamp control
Controlled-cycle wipers
Trailering package (not available for Limousine/9-passenger Sedan)
Controlled differential (not available for Eldorado)
Automatic Level Control: Standard on Fleetwood series
Remote-control trunk-lock and electric pulldown
Tile and telescope steering wheel
Leather interior: standard on Eldorado Convertible and Custom Biarritz option
Remote-control, right-side mirror: Standard on Limousine/9-passenger Sedan and Custom Biarritz option
Outside Thermometer: Mounts on based of left-side mirror
Firemist metallic paint
Carpeted floor mats
Performance axle: Seville only

1977

The Next Generation of the Luxury Car

CADILLAC GENERAL MANAGER Edward C. Kennard introduced the 1977 Cadillacs on September 3, 1976. By any measurement, he was in charge of Cadillac at a time of considerable consequences. Looking back at the success of the 1976 models, Kennard noted that "Cadillac's domestic deliveries for the 1976 model year will reach 300,000 cars for the first time in our history." This milestone came on the threshold of Cadillac's 75th anniversary, a year that Kennard predicted would see Cadillac continue to produce "the highest quality automobiles" at a record level.

However, 1977 was not to be a year when Cadillac, as it had done so well for so many years, would avoid any extremes and instead, follow an established pattern of success. Rather, Cadillac was breaking with a tradition nearly a half century old that equated automotive luxury and prestige with an automobile's physical size. For years, Cadillac had reaped benefits from this perception, but now it was part of a corporate program that saw every GM automotive line introduce vehicles dramatically reduced in size from their 1976 counterparts. Cadillac was, as it had been so many times in its history, out front of its domestic competition in a crucial and trend-setting area.

CHANGES AND IMPROVEMENTS

The newest Cadillacs hardly qualified as compacts; but in comparison with the 1976 models, their new dimensions were startling. The De Ville, on a 121.5-inch wheelbase, was now 9.5 inches shorter. The Fleetwood Brougham, also with a 121.5-inch wheelbase, was 12.5 inches shorter. The Limousine, on a 144.5-inch wheelbase, extended 244.2 inches, down 8 inches from 1976. The width of all models, except for the Seville and Eldorado, was reduced by nearly 3.5 inches to 76.4 inches. Dimensions for the latter two cars were virtually identical to those of 1976. Average weight reductions exceeded 950 pounds per car.

Elaborating on this last development, Edward Kennard noted that "our engineers accomplished dramatic weight savings in many areas of the new models through the use of advanced computerized technology and durable, light-weight materials." Separated into its components, the Cadillac's weight reduction became even more impressive. The single most important change took place in the Cadillac's body, which now was 109 pounds or 28 percent lighter. Other representative reductions were the engine at 93 pounds (down 12 percent), bumpers at 69 pounds (down 27 percent), and the front sheet metal down 21 percent.

Recognizing Cadillac's special position among GM products, general manager Kennard noted, "With the corporate objective of developing lighter, smaller, more efficient cars, Cadillac was especially challenged to retain the interior roominess and comfort associated with our luxury tradition." No doubt, long-time Cadillac owners, apprehensive about the prospect of smaller, mainline Cadillacs, were relieved to hear Mr. Kennard report that "we have met that challenge." Indeed, the Fleetwood Brougham's front and rear leg room was unchanged, while the rear leg room of the Sedan de Ville increased by 1 inch.

One casualty of the resizing project was Cadillac's broad model range. Gone from the lineup were the Calais models, the nine-passenger Sedan, and, as noted earlier, the Eldorado Convertible. What remained were the Coupe and Sedan de Villes, the Fleetwood Brougham, Eldorado Coupe, Seville, an eight-passenger Limousine, and a seven-passenger formal Limousine.

This apparently was of no concern to Edward Kennard who observed, "We are in the most exciting period of change and innovation that Cadillac has ever known. Smaller and lighter cars, fewer models but more product flexibility, and improved performance and economy."

In appearance, the latest models were instantly identified as Cadillacs, albeit very new Cadillacs. Overall, the impression was of automobiles styled to conform to a taut overall design theme. Hood, fender, and front-rear deck lines were sharply defined. Aided by full rear-wheel openings along with a familiar Cadillac front grille/lighting arrangement, they blended together to achieve this objective.

At the rear, the taillight and side-marker lights were integrated into a single vertical unit positioned directly above the bumper's outer upright. The trunk lid was more squared off than in 1976, conforming to the overall design philosophy and enhancing luggage capacity. Both the front and rear bumpers used dual, rubber, horizontal-strip inserts that added to bumper protection and to creating an impression of width. All models were offered in 15 standard and six optional Firemist paint colors, 18 of which were new for 1977.

Interiors were completely redesigned. The instrument panel retained the information band with telltale and warning lights behind an opaque surface when not illuminated. A new type of odometer was used with a simplified reset feature with fingertip control. Clustered together in a "center-control area," accessible to both the driver and passenger, were the radio, climate controls, air-conditioner outlets, and accessory switches. On a separate control panel to the left of the steering column were the "driver-only" controls for the headlights, cruise control, and windshield wipers. An exclusive Cadillac feature, found on all models but the Seville, was a new seat-belt system with increased belt movement, flexibility, and retractors concealed in the side pillar.

All models used a new two-spoke steering wheel with a high-gloss, simulated rosewood trim, which was also used for the dash and interior trim in all Cadillacs except for the Eldorado, which used a low-sheen rosewood.

Engineering developments, which Kennard described as "representative of the most advanced automotive techniques in the industry, including many which were developed in conjunction with our Seville project," were headed by the use of a 15 percent smaller and lighter-weight engine with a 4.08-inch bore and 4.06-inch stroke, displacing 425 cubic inches. Its maximum net horsepower was 180 at 4,000 rpm. With an 8.2:1 compression-ratio, peak torque was 320 lb-ft at 2,000 rpm. Use of this engine was also an historical turning point since it was the first time in postwar history that Cadillac had reduced the size of its overhead-valve V-8. The Electronic Fuel Injection option continued to be available for the De Ville, Brougham, and Eldorado models. A Turbo Hydra-Matic 400 transmission was standard on all models. A 2.28:1 axle ratio (2.73:1 on California cars) was used for all models except for the Limousines, which were fitted with 3.08:1 units. The high altitude ratio was 3.08:1 except for the Eldorado's which was 3.07:1.

Basic chassis design was little changed from 1976. At the front were coil springs, hydraulic direct-action shocks, and a link-type stabilizer. At the rear, the four-link, coil-spring arrangement was continued. All models except the De Villes were fitted with standard equipment Electronic Level Control.

The results of Cadillac's efforts to improve its automobile's resistance to corrosion promoted Kennard to claim that "Cadillac's use of contemporary techniques and materials make our 1977 cars the most corrosion free automobiles we've ever manufactured." Specific anticorrosion features included the use of zinc-rich primers, deadeners, plastisol, hot-melt sealers, and wax coatings in strategic locations. In addition, Cadillac made use of galvanized steel, a zinc-iron alloy, zincrometal, which was steel coated with zinc paint on one side before forming and bi-metal (stainless steel laminated to aluminum) moldings.

Always a strong point, Cadillac's optional equipment list was buttressed by a new AM/FM stereo radio with 23-channel citizen's band controls and an integral AM/FM-CB power antenna that retracted into the front fender when the radio wasn't in operation. The conventional AM/FM stereo radio now featured digital display for time, date, elapsed trip time, and station. Exclusive to Cadillac was a "scan" feature built into the signal-seeking bar directly above the station selector button. When the scan button was used, the signal-seeking device scanned the radio dial, providing the car's occupants with a 10-second sample of each radio signal. When a desired station was heard, a second push of the scan button locked in the station. A technical improvement found in all Cadillac stereo radios was new circuitry that minimized unwanted FM signals.

All Cadillacs were available with a new and more sophisticated Electronic Cruise Control using micro-circuitry and incorporating new "resume" and "advance" controls. The automatic trunk-lock release option was now wired through the ignition system, which prevented its operation unless the ignition was in the "on" position.

DIFFERENCES AMONG MODELS

The demise of the Calais line placed the De Villes in the unaccustomed position of being the most affordable Cadillacs. Since De Ville prices were up, on average, nearly $750, there clearly was no effort to have the De Villes become Calais Cadillacs with an up-market name!

No hardtop models were offered in any Cadillac line. Both the De Ville Sedan and Coupe carried model identification on the side roof panel. Larger wheel covers were standard with a Cadillac crest mounted on a black background.

De Ville interiors were available in two cloth fabrics: Aberdeen (a color-coordinated, horizontal line design) or a more conservative, ribbed Dynasty cloth. These two choices were offered in 10 colors. A leather option could also be selected from white, black, antique, light blue, antique medium sage green, antique light yellow gold, antique light buckskin, antique medium saffron, red, and claret.

Both De Villes could be ordered with the $650 d'Elegance option, which for 1977 began with pillow-style seats in a Medici crushed-velour cloth available in claret, medium saffron, dark blue, and light buckskin. In addition to the seats, the Medici cloth covered the upper-door pads, door-pull-strap inserts, and front-seat-back assist straps. Other d'Elegance components

1977 Coupe de Ville. The opera lights, accent stripes, and wire wheel discs on this De Ville were optional.

1977 Sedan de Ville. Styling of the latest Cadillacs was highlighted by well-defined edges originating at the front end and running the full length of the car.

1977 Coupe de Ville. Rear styling details included vertical tail and side marker lamps positioned above the outer rear bumper. The rear deck was more sharply sculptured than in 1976.

1977 Fleetwood Brougham with optional d'Elegance package.

1977 Fleetwood Eldorado Coupe. For 1977, the Eldorado featured a unified grille-headlight format. Individual Eldorado lettering was located on the hood directly above the grille.

1977 Seville. A new vertical grille and amber park and turn signal lights were introduced in 1977.

included high-pile carpeting, 50/50 Dual Comfort front seats, and exterior accent striping and body-side moldings with vinyl inserts matching body color.

The Coupe de Ville was again offered with the Cabriolet roof package priced at $348. It consisted of vinyl covering in 13 coordinated colors for the rear roof section with bright roof molding and a Cadillac crest mounted on the sail panel.

Almost unnoted, except perhaps by veteran Cadillac watchers who lamented any break with its glorious heritage, was the elimination of the Sixty Special designation from the Fleetwood Brougham identification.

The Brougham was, of all Cadillac models, the most drastically affected by the new design philosophy, being nearly 900 pounds lighter and more than 12 inches shorter than the 1976 model. On the same wheelbase as the De Villes, its physical prominence among stand-

ard Cadillacs was drastically diminished. It was not, however, all that difficult to visually distinguish a Fleetwood Brougham from a De Ville. Unique to the Brougham was a tapered center-door pillar, a smaller "custom-trimmed" rear window, opera lights, wheel covers with body-color center hubs, and Fleetwood body-side and rear-deck identification Brougham script was placed on the sail panel. Standard was a padded, Tuxedo-grain vinyl roof.

The Brougham's interior was finished in a new Florentine velour fabric available in light gray, dark blue, medium sage green, light yellow-gold, light buckskin, and claret. Also debuting was a smooth-finish Dover fabric offered in black, dark blue, light buckskin, or claret. In addition, 11 combinations with leather in the seating areas were offered.

The Brougham d'Elegance package, unchanged in price at $885 from 1976, was similar to the earlier

CADILLAC VITAL STATISTICS: 1977

Series	Model	Body Type	Sug. Retail Price ($)	Weight (lbs.)	Production (#)
Seville	S69	4 dr Sedan	13,359	4192	45,060
De Ville	D69	4 dr Sedan	10,020	4222	95,421
	D47	2 dr Coupe	9810	4186	138,750
Eldorado	L47	2 dr Coupe	11,187	4955	47,344
Fleetwood Brougham	B69	4 dr Sedan	11,546	4340	28,000
Fleetwood	F23	4 dr Sedan	18,349	4738	1581
	F33	4 dr Formal Sedan	19,014	4806	1032

version consisting of pillow-style seats in Florentine velour cloth offered in light gray, dark blue, light buckskin, and claret with 50/50 Dual Comfort front seats, high-pile carpeting, and vinyl-backed floor mats. Both the upper-door pads and the inserts for the door-pull straps and front-seat-back assist straps were in Florentine cloth. Once again, three roof-mounted assist straps were installed. Added to normal Brougham body trim was d'Elegance script on the sail panel and accent striping. Turbine-vaned wheel discs were installed.

Cadillac depicted the 1977 Fleetwood Limousine and Formal Limousine as "the next generation of the Limousine"; and although their wheelbase and overall-length dimensions were still imposing, their reductions were indeed the turning of the tide. But it's certain that few Limousine buyers could have then imagined that less than 10 years into the future, Cadillac would be offering a front-wheel-drive limousine with a 134.4-inch wheelbase and a 218.6-inch overall length!

For 1977, the Formal Limousine retained the movable glass partition between the front and rear compartments and black leather front seat used on earlier Limousines. Interior trim also was cast in the conservative mood of previous years, consisting of dark blue Florentine velour plus a light gray or black Dover cloth.

Although all Broughams were equipped with four-wheel disc brakes, De Villes and Limousines continued use of a front-disc-rear-drum brake system.

While understandably not attracting attention to the extent of the main-line models, the 1977 Eldorado Coupe was noteworthy for its new front end, which unified the grille and headlights into a horizontal format. Extending across the width of the headlights and grille was a bright, brushed-chrome molding, which, in turn, was capped by Eldorado lettering. The vertical chrome crests on the bumper end caps now had black backgrounds.

At the rear, an altered vertical tail lamp, similar in shape to those on the down-sized models, was used. Cadillac continued to offer the Custom Biarritz option for the Eldorado.

For the first time since its introduction, the Seville, which Cadillac continued to call "international size," was moderately restyled. Cadillac had a strong sales performer in the Seville, and its popularity continued to spiral upward in 1977. Shrugging off the challenge offered by Lincoln's Versailles (which the Seville outsold by a 3 to 1 ratio), its model-year production totaled 45,060.

The Seville shared with other Cadillacs such technical advancements as the new scan-radio features and improved cruise control. Along with the Eldorado and Brougham, it was fitted with rear disc brakes for 1977. A subtle, but discernable change in the Seville's suspension could be traced to the elimination of the hydraulic shocks previously used between the front subframe and body plus the use of stiffer isoflex mountings.

Visually, the 1977 Seville was identifiable due to a new grille with vertical accents and amber parking/directional signals. The lower lip of the hood now carried a chrome strip on which the Cadillac script was applied. On previous models, it had been located just above the inner-most, driver-side headlight. For the first time, the Seville was offered with a painted metal roof in addition to its customary padded vinyl roof. As was the case with all Cadillacs except for the Eldorado, the Seville's vinyl roof used the new Tuxedo-grain material. All told, Cadillac offered 16 vinyl-roof choices for 1977, three of which were exclusive to the Seville.

The Seville's standard interior was a new Dover knit cloth. Leather/vinyl trim remained available as an option.

CADILLAC'S DOMESTIC COMPETITION

Lincoln countered Cadillac's resized 1977 offerings with a formidable line consisting of a restyled Mark V, a slightly altered Continental, and its response to the Seville, the Versailles. The latter model was introduced on March 28, 1977, and had a first model-year output of 15,434 cars. The Versailles was based on a model already in production, in this case, the Ford Granada/Mercury Monarch. From the beginning, the Versailles failed to match the sales momentum enjoyed by the Seville; and after the 1980 model year, it was withdrawn from production. Unlike Cadillac, which gave the first-generation Seville an appearance quite unlike that of other Cadillacs, the Versailles was closely patterned after that of the current Mark V and Continental. As a result, it did little to broaden Lincoln's market range. At the same time, the Versailles too easily betrayed its heritage. It wasn't far off the mark to depict it as a customized Monarch.

Overall, however, 1977 was a sensational production year for Lincoln with a new, all-time mark of 191,355 cars. Also reaching an all-time high was the registration of 191,351 new Lincolns during 1977. Of these, 80,321 were Mark Vs, whose new look kept all of the sales appeal of earlier models. At the same time, Continental output moved up substantially to 95,600 units.

The Mark V's tremendous success at a time when Eldorado output dropped back to 47,344 balanced the lackluster public response to the Versailles. Moreover, Cadillac could point to some impressive accomplishments such as a new production total of 350,813 cars and a new registration mark of 325,724.

As for Mercedes-Benz (obviously not a domestic product), its sales moved up 5,517 units to 48,722. Regardless of the Seville's success, it was apparent that Mercedes-Benz had become a permanent and formidable presence in the American luxury-car market.

SPECIFICATIONS
Fleetwood Brougham, De Ville, and Limousines

Engine

Type: V-8, ohv, eight cylinders
Bore × stroke: 4.082 × 4.060 inches
Displacement: 425 cubic inches
Horsepower: 180 @ 4,000 rpm
Torque: 320 lb-ft @ 2,000 rpm

Compression ratio: 8.2:1
Fuel system: four-barrel Quadrajet
Electrical system: 12-volt Delco-Remy 87-5, 3,500 watt, 66 plates, side terminals, no filler/vent caps, 63-amp generator

Limousines and models with EFI (electronic fuel injection) and trailering package: 80-amp

Chassis/Drivetrain

Transmission: Turbo Hydra-Matic 400 Series, three-speed automatic
Frame: Ladder-type, welded X-members
Rear axle: Hypoid type, 2.28:1 ratio
2.73:1 standard for California EFI
California carburetor, federal high altitude and Limousine: 3.08:1 standard
Front suspension: Independent, coil springs, link-type stabilizer bars, hydraulic direct-action shock absorbers
Rear suspension: Four-link drive, coil springs, hydraulic direct action shock absorbers, Automatic Level Control (except De Villes)
Steering: Variable-ratio power steering except for constant ratio on Limousines
Overall ratios:
De Ville, Brougham: 17:1-15:1
Limousines: 20.0-20.6:1
Brakes: De Villes and Limousines: front-ventilated drums, rear-finned cast-iron drums with molded asbestos lining,
De Ville: 11-inch diameter
Limousine: swept area: 12-inch diameter
De Ville: 375 square inches
Limousine: 425.3 square inches
Brougham: Ventilated discs front and rear, molded asbestos lining, swept area: 474 square inches
Tires: steel-belted, radial (ply) whitewalls
De Ville: GR78-15B
Fleetwood Brougham, Limousine models: NHR78-15B

Eldorado

Engine

Same as De Ville, Brougham, Limousine

Chassis/Drivetrain

Transmission: Turbo Hydra-Matic 400 Series, three-speed automatic
Frame: Perimeter type with heavy-gauge, boxed side rails
Driving axle ratio: 2.73:1
2.03:1 available for high-altitude use
Front suspension: Torsion bars with separate hub and rotor, link-type stabilizer, hydraulic direct-action shock absorbers
Rear suspension: Four-link drive, coil springs, direct-action shock absorbers, Automatic Level Control

Steering: Variable-ratio power steering, overall ratio 20.05-18.0:1
Brakes: Ventilated discs with single-piston sliding calipers, swept area: 448 square inches, molded asbestos lining
Tires: Steel-belted radial (ply) whitewalls, LR78-15B

Seville
Unchanged from 1976, with the exception of rear disc brakes replacing drum units and steering ratios changed from 16.4-13.8 to 16.4-13.6:1

Dimensions

Fleetwood Brougham, De Ville and Limousine (all others unchanged from 1976)
Wheelbase:
De Ville, Brougham: 121.5 inches
Limousine: 144.5 inches
Width: 76.4 inches
Front/rear tread: 61.7/60.7 inches
Overall length:
De Ville, Brougham: 221.2 inches
Limousine: 244.2 inches

Popular Options

AM/FM stereo radio with eight-track tape player, four speakers: $254
Eldorado, Brougham: $100
AM/FM stereo radio with signal-seeker and scanner, four speakers: Standard on Seville
AM/FM stereo push-button radio with digital display
AM/FM stereo push-button radio with citizens band: $386
Eldorado, Brougham: $230
Automatic Level Control: $100 (standard on Brougham, Eldorado, Limousines, Seville)
Remote-control trunk-lock release: Standard on Seville
Tilt and telescope steering wheel: Standard on Seville
Remote-control right-side mirror: Standard on Limousines, Seville, Eldorado Custom Biarritz
Illuminated outside thermometer
Firemist paint
Accent striping: Standard on Limousines, Seville, Eldorado Custom Biarritz
Door-edge guards
Front and rear license frames
Trumpet horn
80-amp Generator: Standard on Limousines and with EFI engine
Performance axle: No-charge feature (not available for Limousines)
Trunk mat
Power seat adjuster: Available for Limousines, standard on others
Electronic fuel-injected engine: $702 (not available for Limousine, standard on Seville)
Astroroof (not available for Limousines)
Sunroof (not available for Limousines)
Vinyl roof: Standard on Brougham and Limousines

Automatic door-lock system: $101 (standard on Seville)

Theft-deterrent system

Illuminated entry system

Illuminated vanity mirror

Fuel monitor system

Dual Comfort 50/50 front seats: Standard on Brougham and Seville, available for De Villes only

Power-recliner passenger seat: Available for Dual Comfort 50/50 front seats

Power-recliner driver seat: Available for Dual Comfort 50/50 front seats

Power-recliner passenger seat back: Available for De Ville with leather seating areas

Opera lamps: Standard on Brougham and Limousines, available for De Villes

Wire wheel or turbine-vaned wheel discs

Cruise control

Rear-window defogger

Twilight sentinel

Guide-matic headlight control

Controlled-cycle wipers: Standard on Seville

1978

Behind the Great Name . . . Great Cars

ANNOUNCING THE 1978 CADILLACS on September 12, 1977, Cadillac General Manager Edward C. Kennard noted that "Cadillac has been the pinnacle of success in every area of the luxury-car market since we began seventy-six years ago. When change is necessary, we've led the way, and continue to do so today."

CHANGES AND IMPROVEMENTS

The big year for necessary change had been 1977, and for 1978 no major interior or exterior alterations were made. "Nonetheless," Kennard added, "we're making important refinements to further accent the individuality of our automobiles. Our designers concentrated on those items that make Cadillacs the most imitated cars in the world."

DIFFERENCES AMONG MODELS

Appearance-wise, these refinements were subtle. The De Ville, Brougham, Limousine, and Eldorado models shared a bolder horizontal grille design and, with the exception of the Eldorado, new rear bumpers with vertical taillamps incorporated in the bumper outers.

For the first time, De Ville, Brougham, and Seville models were available with optional, full-chrome wire wheels featuring a hexagonal center hub and Cadillac-crest insert plus a theft deterrent mounting. The standard De Ville wheel covers were also restyled to feature narrow turbine vanes surrounding a series of concentric rings at whose center was a Cadillac crest.

The optional, padded vinyl top for the Coupe and Sedan de Ville models was now custom-trimmed to create a "tucked" effect around the back window. The De Villes, as well as the Broughams, were also offered with an optional package featuring chrome moldings, rear-deck accent stripes, and body side moldings color-keyed to the car's exterior color.

Although Cadillac's interior design was essentially unchanged, a close look revealed some minor revisions. For example, the six-way, power-seat controls were now

consolidated with other switches on the left-hand armrest of all 1978 De Ville, Brougham, and Limousine models, and the mirror control was moved forward on the armrest. Seat-back pockets were added to the front seats of both the De Villes and Fleetwood Broughams.

Two new interior upholsteries, a Hampton woven cloth and a Random velour, were offered for the De Villes. The velour was available in six shades: light gray, yellow, beige, dark green, mulberry, light blue, or black. Choices for the Hampton cloth were either light blue or mulberry. Twelve selections of Sierra-grain leather for the seating areas (the rest of the seat area was trimmed in vinyl) were also available.

Shortly after production began, all Cadillacs, except the Seville, which continued to use a Tuxedo-grain padded top, were available with padded elk-grain tops. Sixteen color choices were offered.

Sedan de Villes with the available Electronic Fuel Injection system, as well as all Sedan de Villes for California delivery and most Fleetwood Broughams, were equipped with an aluminum hood, which weighed 45 pounds less than the conventional version. "Its use," explained George Kennard, " will enable us to keep these Sedan de Ville models, with their heavier equipment load, within the 4,500 pound E.P.A. weight class, and also allow us to accumulate the real world experience with these units to plan their expanded useage in the future."

The most significant technical change for the Fleetwood Brougham was a new Electronic Load Leveling System, which was also standard equipment for the Eldorado, Limousine, and Seville models and optional for the De Ville series. In operation, an electronic sensor determined when load leveling was necessary, and a green instrument panel indicator light informed the driver when the "Level Ride" compressor was activated.

Visually, the latest Brougham was identified by its new wreath and crest ornamentation on a brushed-chrome molding. Also standard were body-color-coordinated wheel discs.

1978 Seville Elegante. The Elegante was offered in two color combinations: two-tone brown, or black and platinum. The steering wheel was covered in either gray or saddle leather to match the interior color combination.

1978 Eldorado Biarritz. Features of the Biarritz included its padded vinyl roof, chrome moldings, accent striping, color coordinated wheel discs, opera lights, Biarritz script, and interior appointments.

1978 Coupe de Ville. New rear bumpers for 1978 carried the tail lamps and side marker lights in the outer section. The locking wire wheel discs remained optional.

The Brougham interior, with new door-pull handles, was offered in seven shades of Florentine velour (mulberry, light gray, black, light blue, dark green, yellow, and light beige) as well as 11 vinyl/leather choices.

Foreseeing the time when the first-generation Sevilles would become a contemporary classic, Cadillac depicted the 1978 model as "a car of timeless design." Given its outstanding lines and proportions, most critics applauded Cadillac's restraint in providing the Seville with 1978 model-year styling cues. The most apparent change was the extension of the paint accent stripe

CADILLAC VITAL STATISTICS: 1978

Series	Model	Body Type	Sug. Retail Price ($)	Weight (lbs.)	Production (#)
Seville	S69	4 dr Sedan	14,710	4179	56,985
De Ville	D69	4 dr Sedan	10,924	4236	88,951
	D47	2 dr Coupe	10,584	4163	117,750
Eldorado	L47	2 dr Coupe	12,401	4906	46,816
Fleetwood					
Brougham	B69	4 dr Sedan	12,842	4314	36,800
Limousine	F23	4 dr Sedan	20,007	4772	848
	F33	4 dr Formal Sedan	20,742	4858	682

1978 Sedan de Ville. All full-size Cadillacs had a new horizontal grille and raised script on the hoodface. De Ville models had a special sail panel crest and scripted nameplate.

across the rear-deck lid where it combined with new bumper guards.

Introduced as one of Cadillac's two "specialty cars" (the other was the Eldorado Biarritz) was the Seville Elegante, which, Cadillac said, "bespeaks the inherent luxury and versatility of Cadillac's international size automobile. It's elegant and sport at the same time."

The Elegante was offered in two duotone finishes, platinum and sable black, or western saddle Firemist and Ruidoso brown. Chrome-plated wire wheels with long-laced spokes were standard as was a full-body-length chrome molding with etched black grooving. In addition, the Elegante featured a one-piece, rear-window molding and Elegante script on the rear roof pillar. Optional for the Seville, but not available for the Elegante, were exterior opera lamps.

Cadillac noted that the Elegante interior was "luxurious, even by Seville's demanding standards."

1978 Fleetwood Brougham. Key identification features of the Brougham included color-coordinated wheel discs, opera lamps, vinyl roof, and tapered center pillar.

1978 Seville. A new grille was introduced for 1978.

Leather/vinyl seat and door trim with segments of perforated leather and suede-like accent stripes was offered in antique gray or antique medium saddle. The steering-wheel rim was wrapped in matching leather.

The Elegante's exclusive 40/40 Dual Comfort front seats were fitted with storage pockets for rear passenger use. The driver and front-seat passenger shared a center console featuring a folddown armrest, interior light, rear-floor courtesy lamps, a writing table, pen, and provision for a tape storage cabinet or telephone installation.

At Cadillac's new model introduction, George Kennard explained that "the Elegante package was researched at auto show displays for two years, and received with great enthusiasm by our most demanding, discriminating, prospects and owners. We plan to build 5,000 Seville Elegante models during 1978."

The Seville continued to be powered by the 350-cubic-inch, electronically fuel injected V-8 engine. For 1978, it was fitted with a new Electronic Spark Selection control that, when added to the High Energy Ignition System, automatically advanced or retarded engine spark as conditions warranted. Cadillac reported this improved the Seville's estimated fuel economy by about 1 mile per gallon. Beginning in March 1978, the Seville was available with a 350-cubic-inch, diesel V-8 option.

The latest Eldorado sported a grille very similar to that used by the De Ville, Fleetwood Brougham, and Limousine models. Its gridwork, however, was of a finer texture. Interior choices began with four shades of a Halifax knit or a Random velour offered in three colors. Also available was a vinyl/Sierra-grain leather combination in 12 single tone and three, 2-tone color selections.

George Kennard, at the start of the model year, reported that "for 1978 we're again planning to personalize between thirty-five and forty percent of our Eldorados with the well received Biarritz optional package."

The Custom Biarritz was once again easily recognized by its fully padded, elk-grain roof; back and rear quarter-window size; black-accented, stainless-steel body molding; special striping; and body-color-coordinated wheel discs. The Biarritz leather/vinyl interior with 50/50 pillow-type seats was offered in antique medium saddle, white, dark carmine, antique yellow, or antique light blue.

For the Fleetwood Limousine and Fleetwood Formal Limousine, a Florentine velour interior was offered in light gray, black, or dark blue. The Formal Limousine was equipped with a divided 45/45 front seat, a black-leather seating area, and a sliding glass partition between the driver and passenger compartments. Included in the traditional Limousine appointments were two folddown rear seats. Available for both Cadillacs was a Landau-bar roof trim in either full or Cabriolet style.

Also continued in Cadillac's "Special Edition" category were the De Ville d'Elegance, Coupe de Ville Cabriolet, and Brougham d'Elegance.

Cadillac made only minor changes in its optional equipment offering for 1978. For the first time, an AM/FM stereo radio with 40-channel citizens band controls and an integral eight-track tape player was offered.

Available in limited quantities for the Fleetwood Brougham and Seville was a radio with these features as well as an electronic programmer and crystal-controlled frequency synthesizer.

New rear deck styling features of the Seville consisted of lamp insignias and fully-extended deck lid striping. Use of Electronic Spark Selection Control improved highway fuel economy by approximately 1 mpg.

CADILLAC'S DOMESTIC COMPETITION

Changes to the three lines of Lincolns—Continental, Mark V, and Versailles—were not extensive. The Versailles was virtually a carryover model, while a 400-cubic-inch V-8 became the standard powerplant for the Continental and Mark V.

The most interesting development was the offering of the elaborate and, with a price tag of some $8,000, very expensive, Diamond Jubilee Edition of the Mark V. This was a dramatic way of commemorating the 75th anniversary of the Ford Motor Company.

Total production of 1978 Lincolns consisted of 88,087 Continentals, 72,602 Mark Vs, and 8,931 Versailles.

SPECIFICATIONS

Engine

Unchanged from 1977

Chassis/Drivetrain

Unchanged from 1977

Popular Options

In addition to those offered in 1977, Cadillac now made available:
AM/FM stereo radio with signal-seeker, 8-track tape player and digital display: Available only for the Fleetwood Brougham and Seville
AM/FM stereo radio with tape player and citizens band

1979

More Than Ever, An American Standard for the World

NINETEEN SEVENTY-NINE was a year when eras crashed together in explosive fashion. For Cadillac, it marked a record production year with output totaling 381,113 automobiles. It was a sensational way to end the decade. At the same time, Cadillac introduced a dramatically resized Eldorado whose new format was given a ringing endorsement in the marketplace. Model-year production reached 67,437, a new record. At the same time, the popularity of the Seville took a slight dip, falling to 53,487 units, down from its peak year of 1975. A dramatically restyled front-wheel drive Seville would be introduced in 1980, but its popularity would never approach that of the first-generation Sevilles, which are now recognized as modern classics.

These transitions of design, while exciting to the new luxury-car buyers and the subject of future research efforts by automotive historians, paled alongside the explosive chain reaction set off by the 1979 Iranian revolution. Once again, gas shortages and long lines at the gas pumps became the norm. Worse yet, a dazzling period of oil-price increases set the stage for America's most severe economic recession since World War II.

Few Americans knew or cared about Iran when the 1979 Cadillacs were introduced. From any perspective, they possessed tremendous market appeal. Cadillac had, with the introduction of the Seville in 1975 and the downsizing of its main line models in 1977, adapted to the new automotive era with the same degree of elegance as it had exited from the age of fins.

Cadillac was riding on a crest of self confidence and public acceptance that was evident in its sales literature. Under the general theme of "What makes a Cadillac a Cadillac?" the 1979 model was aptly depicted as an automobile that, like its predecessors, was "a Cadillac right for its day," a car that stood as a "symbol for excellence." While readily admitting that its image as both an "American standard for the world" and a "superb luxury car" were key assets, Cadillac was eager to move beyond this point to emphasize other virtues such as its road manners, reliability, stamina,

advanced engineering, and quality. Thus sales brochures were aptly sprinkled with phrases such as "a totally capable road machine . . . one tough automobile . . . extensive use of space-age technology" and "attention to detail."

DIFFERENCES AMONG MODELS

The bastion of Cadillac strength remained its Fleetwood Brougham and De Ville models. Exterior styling changes were minor. Tradition reigned supreme at the front as the timeless Cadillac cross-hatched grille was retained, changed only by the placement of the Cadillac script directly on the broad upper-grille ridge instead of on the lower-hood surface as in 1978. At the rear, a new taillight lens design was used.

Technical changes were similarly low-key. A new exhaust-gas recirculating system with rise tubes was used that improved mixing and reduced emissions and fuel consumption. To accommodate the use of high-pressure (32 psi) tires, the Cadillac's suspension was restructured and retuned.

Fleetwood Brougham interiors were available in 11 shades of leather (for the seating areas only) or a new Dante knit cloth in six colors. De Ville customers were also offered the same leather selection or any of six colors of the standard Durand knit cloth.

The Fleetwood Limousine and Formal Limousine models continued to be equipped with two folddown auxiliary seats. Both interiors were offered in dark blue, slate gray, or black Dante cloth. The Formal Limousine's front compartment was black with black-leather seating areas.

As expected of a model scheduled for a major change in 1980, the last of the rear-drive Sevilles was only slightly changed from 1979. Burled walnut replaced the rosewood appointments on the dash and door control areas. Also used was a new, two-spoke steering-wheel design. The standard Seville interior combined new Dante and Roma fabrics in six color choices. Sierra-grain leather for the seating areas was also available in 11 colors. A Tuxedo-grain, padded vinyl roof was standard with an uncovered metal top available at no extra cost. The Seville Elegante, which, said Cadillac, "combines the superb qualities of Seville with elegant refinements you might expect only in custom-crafted automobiles," was offered in a two-tone, slate Firemist exterior and a sable black interior. Additional features included accent striping, full-length side molding with etched black grooving and Elegante script. The seating areas and door panels were finished in breathable, perforated-leather inserts with suede-like vinyl trim. The floor covering was Tangier carpeting. All Sevilles

were equipped with larger batteries with increased reserve capacity. To improve fuel economy, all Seville axle ratios were lowered. No doubt the most obscure change for 1979 was the use of a convex, rather than a flat-surfaced, right-side exterior mirror.

Eldorado enthusiasts would have little to do with these piddling changes for 1979. Their favorite Cadillac was reshaped, reformed, resized, and repowered so dramatically that Cadillac described it as a "new breed of Eldorado."

As in the mid-sixties when Cadillac shared development of the new E-body with Oldsmobile and Buick, work on its successor was a joint project of these

1979 Sedan de Ville.

This 1979 Fleetwood Brougham d'Elegance features optional two-tone paint and wire wheel covers.

three divisions. Unlike 1967, however, when Buick opted to remain with a rear-drive system, all three versions (Cadillac Eldorado, Buick Riviera, and Oldsmobile Toronado) now used front-wheel-drive.

Over the years, the Eldorado had consistently outsold the Toronado and Riviera, a fact that gave Cadillac a stronger role in the E-body project than in any other General Motors car project involving more than one automotive division. Under direct Cadillac responsibility were its frame, rear suspension, and electronic-leveling system designs. Oldsmobile was

assigned its front suspension and steering, and Buick took charge of brake design. While the Fisher Body Division handled body design, the typical distinctions among Eldorado, Riviera, and Seville were assured by each division's autonomy over outer-body sheet metal and engineering.

As had happened on so many occasions, Cadillac, with the 1979 Eldorado, broke stride with an established pattern, while producing a car that was unmistakably a Cadillac. The only body style available, a two-door hardtop coupe, clearly was inspired by the

1979 Coupe de Ville with the optional Phaeton package.

CADILLAC VITAL STATISTICS: 1979

Series	Model	Body Type	Sug. Retail Price ($)	Weight (lbs.)	Production (#)
Seville	S69	4 dr Sedan	16,224	4180	5887*
De Ville	D69	4 dr Sedan	12,093	4212	93,211
	D47	2 dr Coupe	11,728	4143	121,890
Eldorado	L57	2 dr Coupe	14,668	3792	67,436
Fleetwood Brougham	B69	4 dr Sedan	14,102	4250	42,200
Limousine	F23	4 dr Sedan	21,869	4782	957
	F33	4 dr Formal Sedan	22,640	4866	1068

*Includes 3,400 Seville Elegantes

rectilinear forms introduced by the 1975 Seville. But this was no copy-cat automobile. Its squared-off roof line, upright backlight, and sharply defined rear-fender and trunk line were masterfully coordinated with a dramatically swept back windshield. This was also noteworthy due to its flush body mounting made possible by installation from inside the car. The classic Cadillac front end and bold wheel-well openings helped make the Eldorado one of the handsomest of Cadillacs.

Moreover, this was a Cadillac true to a tradition of engineering excellence. A four-wheel independent suspension system was used with long, longitudinal, front torsion bars and rear trailing arms. A link-type stabilizer was part of the standard front suspension, and hydraulic direct-action shock absorbers were used at all four wheels. Contributing to lower maintenance costs

were new permanently seated wheel bearings that never needed lubrication. Incorporated into the rear suspension was an electronic, automatic load-leveling system that responded more rapidly to weight changes than earlier Cadillac systems. The key to this quicker action was a small sensor mounted on a rear cross-member, which activated an air compressor that increased pressure within the rear shock to compensate for heavy loads.

This system, the Eldorado's front-wheel drive, and fully independent suspension were three elements of what Cadillac called "the big five" features of the Eldorado. The two remaining components, which, added Cadillac, made the Eldorado "one of the world's best engineered cars," were its four-wheel disk brakes and 5.7 liter, electronic fuel-injected V-8 engine. The

1979 Seville.

The 1979 Eldorado Biarritz was the first Eldorado since the 1957 Eldorado Brougham to have a stainless steel roof cap.

former used single-piston sliding calipers and ventilated discs to provide a total swept area of 396 square inches. The lining material was molded asbestos into which were incorporated audible wear indicators.

At first glance, the use of the same 350-cubic-inch, 170-horsepower V-8 installed in the Seville seemed inappropriate for an automobile that over the years had been powered by some of Cadillac's most potent V-8s. But the Eldorado weighed 1,150 pounds less than its predecessor; and in contemporary road tests, it proved capable of respectable zero to 60-mph times of just under 10 seconds.

Among the key contributors to the Eldorado's lower weight (its shipping weight was 3,792 pounds) was its all new chassis and perimeter frame, which represented a 224-pound weight reduction. The 12.2-inch, torque converter, Turbo Hydra-Matic 325, whose design was strongly influenced by Cadillac, weighed 50 pounds less than the 1978 version. With a 114-inch wheelbase and 204-inch overall length, the 1979 Eldorado was 20 inches shorter than the older model. This smaller size reduced the Eldorado's turning circle by 5 feet to 38.4 feet, undoubtedly welcome, but of questionable virtue to long-time Eldorado owners who liked their car's expansive interior. Any fretting about this was needless. The Eldorado did lose some hip room and was now given a four-passenger rating capacity. But those four occupants enjoyed an interior with added leg and head room. Moreover, thanks to the new rear suspension plus a lower rear cross-member, more trunk space was available.

As expected of a Cadillac with a base price of $14,668, the Eldorado's interior was elegant. Critics who, when pressed, often conceded that they approached any Cadillac with a built-in negative bias, regarded it as yet another Sybaritan excess. A more objective view, and more certainly the overwhelming consensus of the Eldorado admirers, was that Cadillac was right on target by depicting it as "a new breed of luxury." The wide, flat-face dash was finished in simulated burl-walnut, which was also applied to the door panels. All instruments and controls were clustered in close proximity of the driver for ease of viewing and operation. The top of the dash was covered in a leather-like synthetic material extending over both ends of the dash to conceal the new side-window defogger vents. The split bench-front seat was equipped with a standard, six-way (two-way manual adjustment for passenger) electric adjustment. Additional standard equipment included an AM/FM stereo radio with digital display, automatic climate control, variable-speed windshield wipers (with a washer-fluid, low-level indicator light), electric windows, power steering and brakes, an electric trunk release, plus an illuminated entry system that featured a "halo" lens around the door-key lock cylinder. The standard Eldorado interior was finished in the Dante knit cloth in a choice of six colors or, as an option, 11 shades of leather seating areas.

Once again, the "ultimate" Eldorado was the Biarritz version. Its external distinctions consisted of a cabriolet roof treatment with a brushed, stainless-steel front portion and a wider chrome molding crossing the roof area and extending forward to the front fenders. Other Biarritz features included cast-aluminum wheels, accent striping, opera lamps, and Biarritz script. A total of six body/vinyl roof combinations were available.

The interior appointments were highlighted by tufted-pillow seating available in either Dante cloth or leather seating areas in a choice of five colors. A one-piece Tangier carpet was fitted as were individual, rear-seat reading lamps and a leather-trimmed steering wheel. Five Special Edition versions of the 1979 Cadillac were offered, said Cadillac, as a "further expression of luxury of choice in action, . . . a delightful way to express your individuality."

Although Cadillac had not offered a true Convertible since 1976, a link was maintained with the past via the Custom Phaeton Coupe, which Cadillac explained "reflects the excitement reminiscent of the classic Cadillac Convertibles." Its primary features consisted of brushed-chrome moldings with flush-mounted opera lights and Cadillac crest, reduced-size quarter windows and backlight, a Convertible-like roof treatment, and Phaeton script on each rear quarter panel. Also part of the Phaeton package (which was also available in four-door form as the Custom Phaeton Sedan), were wire-wheel disks and accent striping. Interior fittings included 45/55 Dual Comfort front seats, leather seating areas, and a matching leather-trimmed steering wheel.

Continued from 1978 were the Brougham d'Elegance, De Ville d'Elegance and Cabriolet options. The Brougham d'Elegance now used new Dante and Roma knit upholstery, while the De Ville version featured a Venetian velour. The Cabriolet, again offered only for the Coupe de Ville, was available in 17 elk-grain, vinyl-roof colors, one more than in 1978.

When the model year began, Cadillac offered the Oldsmobile-built, 5.7-liter diesel V-8 as an option for the Seville and Eldorado. Later it became available for the Fleetwood Brougham and De Villes. When the international situation prompted government allotments of gasoline and, in some areas, odd-even license-plate-number days for fillups, the availability of diesel engines gave Cadillac a major selling point. At the same time, the standard 25-gallon fuel tanks of the De Ville and Fleetwood Brougham enabled Cadillac to proclaim they were "miles ahead of the imports in estimated driving range . . . from Mercedes-Benz 450 SEL to Honda Civic!" At the same time, Cadillac was quick to point out the substantial improvements in fuel economy attained by its car since 1974. For example, the latest Fleetwood Brougham and De Ville had a 55 percent better EPA estimated mpg than their 1974 counterparts. The Eldorado's 13-mpg EPA estimate was 62 percent greater than the 1974 model.

These credentials made the 1979 Cadillac, in its manufacturer's view, a "Long Distance Runner . . . designed with our nation's priorities in mind."

CADILLAC'S DOMESTIC COMPETITION

With the arrival of the 1979 Eldorado, the first stage of Cadillac's resizing was complete. In contrast, Lincoln was still offering traditionally sized Continental and Mark V models in 1979. But the end was in sight; and in 1980, both Lincolns were significantly reduced in size.

The 1979 versions were changed only in detail, although the availability of Collector Series models gave them a measure of distinction. No doubt their popularity gave Cadillac product planners the chills. Total production for the model year was 189,546, not far from the all-time record set in 1977 of 191,355 cars. But when the gasoline crisis hit its stride in the summer months, Lincoln sales dropped dramatically. The Versailles, sporting a new, more formal, squared off roof line finally began to show some signs of life in the marketplace. Its production for the model year increased to 21,007 cars. But this still represented a poor showing against the Seville, then in its fifth year of production in a form basically unchanged from 1975. Thus when the new Seville debuted in 1980, the Versailles was nowhere to be seen.

SPECIFICATIONS

Except for the following, specifications and options were unchanged from 1978.

Engine

Electrical system: Delco Remy, F4 Freedom 12-volt battery

Chassis/Drivetrain

Rear-axle ratio: 2.28:1
   Limousines: 3.08:1

Eldorado

Engine

Type: V-type, ohv, eight cylinders
Bore × stroke: 4.057 × 3.385 inches
Displacement: 350 cubic inches
Horsepower: 170 @ 4,200 rpm
Torque: 275 lb-ft @ 2,000 rpm
Compression ratio: 8.0:1

Fuel system: Cadillac open-loop electronic fuel system
Electrical system: Delco Remy, F4 Freedom 12-volt battery, 80-amp generator
Transmission: Turbo Hydra-Matic-325, three-speed

Chassis/Drivetrain

Frame: Ladder-type with welded-in X-members
Driving axle: Spiral, bevel-ring gear and pinion, 2.19:1 ratio
Front suspension: Independent torsion bar, link-type stabilizer bar, hydraulic direct-action shock absorbers
Rear suspension: Independent trailing arms, coil springs, hydraulic direct-action shock absorbers, Electronic Level Control
Steering: Power-assisted with hydraulic shock absorber damper, overall ratio: 14.0:1
Brakes: Single, sliding-piston ventilated discs front and rear, molded asbestos linings, total swept area: 396 square inches
Tires: GM specifications steel-belted radials, wide white stripes, P205/75R15

Dimensions

Wheelbase: 114 inches
Width: 71.5 inches
Front/rear tread: 59.3/60 inches
Overall length: 204 inches

Popular Options

Electrically Controlled Mirror
Two-tone exterior (not available for Limousine)
Stereo cassette player
Convex, remote-control right-side mirror: Standard for Fleetwood Brougham and Limousine
Cast-aluminum wheels: Standard on Biarritz, available for Eldorado
Wire-wheel discs (not available for Limousine)

1980

An American Standard for the World

AS WITH ALL General Motors full-sized models, the Cadillac de Ville and Fleetwood Brougham models carried new sheet metal over virtually unchanged chassis/running gear. Unlike earlier years when such an extensive change would be manifested in a new styling theme, the 1980 Cadillac looked remarkably similar to the 1979 models. The explanation for this was simple: The changes for 1980 were intended primarily to meet tight federal fuel economy and exhaust-emissions standards.

If that had been the only factor affecting the 1980 Cadillac's fortunes in the marketplace, it's likely GM would have established another sales record. But instead, the economy, plunging into recession, sent automobile sales downward. Before the sales charts began to plot a painfully slow recovery, over 25 percent of the auto industry's workers were unemployed.

CHANGES AND IMPROVEMENTS

All rear-drive Cadillacs had the same width and wheelbase as in 1979; but with lower hood and fender lines plus a higher trunk lid, their air drag was reduced by some 10 percent. Also aiding fuel economy was a drop in weight of approximately 200 pounds. The standard engine for all models was a 368-cubic-inch V-8 derived from the discontinued 425-cubic-inch engine. For those who relished the days when every Cadillac was equipped with a 500-cubic-inch V-8, this engine's peak 145-horsepower output was a bit of a shock. Optional for all models except the Limousine was the 350-cubic-inch diesel V-8.

Cadillac regarded its major technical development for 1980 as the Digital Electronic Fuel Injection System standard on all Eldorados and Sevilles with the 6-liter V-8 engine, except those intended for sale in California. This system used two injectors electronically controlled by a digital microprocessor monitoring numerous operating variables, including barometric and manifold pressure, engine temperature, and the aging of components.

The microprocessor also was the basis of an on-board computer diagnostic system that activated a "check engine" dash light when service was required. At a Cadillac dealer, a diagnostic system, which shared controls and a digital display system with the Electronic Climate Control system, was used by service technicians to identify the specific area needing service. When the work was completed, a push of a button displayed an "all-clear" signal.

DIFFERENCES AMONG MODELS

All rear-drive models had two additional inches of rear leg room due to their new bodies. De Ville models had several new, standard-equipment features, including left- and right-hand side mirrors and "Dual-Spot" map/courtesy lamps. A new wheelcover with the Cadillac crest mounted on a dark red background was also used for the 1980 De Villes. Both versions carried model identification script on the roof sail pillar.

Interior selection for the De Villes included a Durand knit with Renaissance-velour inserts in six colors or 10 shades of upholstery with leather seating areas.

The interior for the De Ville's d'Elegance option was a Venetian velour in four shades: slate gray, light beige, dark claret, and dark blue. The Tampico carpeting extended to the lower door region. Door-pull handles replaced the standard straps and a "De Ville d'Elegance" script was mounted on the glove box. The Sedan was equipped with three, roof-mounted assist straps.

Both models had d'Elegance script designation on their sail pillars, but only the Coupe version had standard opera lamps. The Cabriolet option for the Coupe de Ville combined a chrome, crossover roof molding and an elk-grain vinyl roof cover available in 15 colors. A French seam surrounded the rear window.

Initially the Fleetwood Brougham was available only in four-door form; but at midyear, a two-door version was added. For 1980, the Fleetwood Brougham, which was depicted as "the Cadillac of Cadillacs," was

The 1980 Eldorado Biarritz was identified by its custom cabriolet roof with a stainless steel cap and by wide chrome moldings. All Eldorados had new multislot design wheel covers.

1980 Sedan de Ville. Both De Ville and Brougham models had a stiffer roof profile with a sharpened crease line running the full length of the body side.

1980 Coupe de Ville. The aerodynamics of the De Ville and Brougham Cadillacs included a higher profile rear deck.

1980 Fleetwood Brougham. Exclusive to the Brougham was a standard electroluminescent opera lamp mounted in the body center pillar.

1980 Eldorado. A more graphic grille design was used in 1980.

1980 Seville Elegante. Aside from its new body lines, the Seville also had new cast-aluminum wheels with brushed chrome hub cap and wreath and crest ornamentation.

Details of the Seville's MPG, ECC, and CB radio displays.

A new heated outside rearview mirror was offered in combination with the rear-window defogger option.

The 1980 Seville's luggage compartment, with a flat floor, had 1.7 cubic feet more usable space than the older model's.

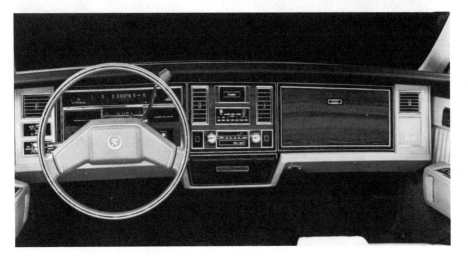

The Seville's full-width dash panel had simulated teak woodgrain inlaid with simulated butterfly walnut.

ELECTRONIC CONTROL MODULE

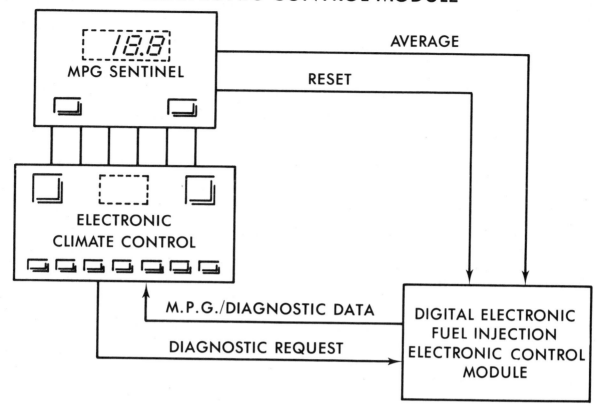

Interaction sequence of Cadillac's electronic system.

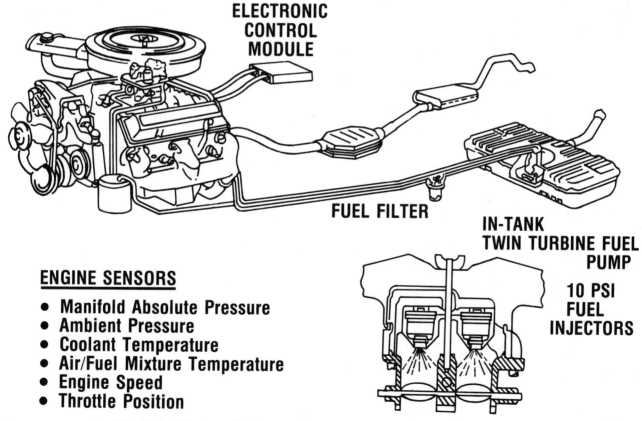

ENGINE SENSORS

- Manifold Absolute Pressure
- Ambient Pressure
- Coolant Temperature
- Air/Fuel Mixture Temperature
- Engine Speed
- Throttle Position

Primary components of the Digital Electronic Fuel Injection System.

easily identified by its limousine-style rear window, electroluminescent opera lamps mounted in the center pillar, and wider rocker-panel molding. Wheelcovers now had a red background for the familiar wreath and crest identification, which was also found on the hood (in stand-up ornament form) and rear deck.

The Fleetwood interior of Heather knit cloth with Raphael inserts and a center-mounted wreath was offered in slate gray, dark blue, dark green, saddle, light beige, and dark claret. Also installed was extra-thick carpeting, door-pull handles, and a wreath and crest plaque mounted ahead of the door release. De Ville models had similar identification highlighted with a Cadillac crest. The Brougham's optional interior with leather seating area was available in 10 shades.

Broughams with the d'Elegance package carried d'Elegance sail-panel script. Interior appointments included roof-mounted assist straps and Brougham d'Elegance script on the glove box. The standard d'Elegance interior of Heather and Raphael knits set in a pillow-style format was available in slate gray, dark blue, saddle, dark claret, and light beige. Colors for the optional leather (seating areas only) trim consisted of light beige, slate gray, saddle, dark blue, and dark claret. Both versions carried embossed wreaths (two-front, two-rear) on the upper-seat bolsters. Completing the d'Elegance package was Tampico carpeting and deluxe carpeted floor mats.

The twin flagships of the Cadillac fleet, the Fleetwood Limousines, had improved acoustics, which further improved their reputation for quiet operation. The Limousines' interiors were finished in dark blue, slate gray, or black Heather cloth and high-pile carpeting. The front compartment of the Formal

Limousine was black with black leather on the seating areas. These were the only Cadillacs to carry Fleetwood script on their front fenders.

The Eldorado was visually unchanged except for a new pillar-style Heather knit interior in six colors. The Cabriolet roof treatment of textured elk-grain vinyl was offered in 15 colors, including matching Firemist tones. Carried over from 1979 was the Biarritz option highlighted by a wide chrome molding that, after crossing the roof, continued forward to the front fenders, sail-pillar-mounted opera lamps, Biarritz script, and accent stripes.

The Biarritz interior, set in a tufted pillow-style format, was available in seven selections of leather for seating areas. As an alternative, a slate gray, Heather knit cloth was offered. A one-piece, plush-pile Tampico carpeting was installed along with individual, rear-seat reading lamps and a leather-trimmed steering wheel.

Initially the Biarritz was offered with cast-aluminum wheels; but early in November 1979, wire wheelcovers became standard with the aluminum wheels a no-cost option. At the same time, diesel-powered Seville and Seville Elegante models received the wire covers as standard with the aluminum wheels optional at no cost. On the other hand, Sevilles with Digital Fuel Injection (electronic in California) now had cast-aluminum wheels standard with the wire wheelcovers a no-cost option.

As an alternative to the fuel-injected, 6-liter V-8, the Eldorado was available with the 105-horsepower diesel V-8. In this form, the Eldorado was tested by *Motor Trend* (August 1979) and received less than a ringing endorsement. High on the list of *Motor Trend* disappointments was the Eldorado diesel's inability to

CADILLAC VITAL STATISTICS: 1980

Series	Model	Body Type	Sug. Retail Price ($)	Weight (lbs.)	Production (#)
Seville	S69	4 dr Sedan	20,477	3911	45,544*
De Ville	D69	4 dr Sedan	13,282	4084	49,188
	D47	2 dr Coupe	12,899	4048	55,490
Eldorado	L57	2 dr Coupe	16,141	3806	68,150†
Fleetwood Brougham	B69	4 dr Sedan	15,564	4092	29,659
	B47	2 dr Coupe	15,307	NA	2300
Limousine	F23	4 dr Sedan	23,509	4629	790
	F33	4 dr Formal Sedan	24,343	4718	822

*Includes 6,200 Seville Elegantes
†Includes 16,465 Eldorado Biarritzes

match the traditional levels of smoothness and power common to a modern Cadillac. Although Mercedes-Benz had been offering diesel-powered luxury cars for decades, the spector of black exhaust smoke emitting from a Cadillac tailpipe added to the cacaphony of a diesel engine's clatter seemed out of tune with the image many Cadillac owners had of the Eldorado.

Viewed from that perspective, Cadillac's decision to make the 350-cubic-inch diesel the standard engine for the 1980 Seville was a daring move. But far more controversial was the Seville's new styling for 1980. To place the Seville in historical perspective, it impacted the visual senses as profoundly as had the 1948 and 1959 Cadillacs.

While those memorable Cadillacs were sensational because of their futuristic motifs, the Seville achieved notoriety by reaching back to the late thirties for its styling theme and then pulling it rudely into the declining years of the twentieth century. The 1980 Seville was one of the final designs supervised by William Mitchell, who was attracted to the 1954 Rolls-Royce Silver Wraith, with a body designed by Hooper and Company. The similarity between these two cars was remarkable. The Cadillac's rear deck, side-window shape, and side-trim sweep were patterned very closely after those found on the Rolls-Royce.

In 1968, Daimler of England had introduced its DS420 Limousine, which transformed the grace of the Hooper Rolls into a singularly unattractive form. On the basis of William Mitchell's comments, Cadillac Seville historian Thomas Falconer concluded that it was this Daimler that initially was Bill Mitchell's inspiration for the Seville.

Until it was superceded in 1986 by a severely downsized model, this version of the Seville was a favorite subject of journalists never quite able to decide if they were at ease with the Cadillac's appearance. Regardless of their judgments, its primary designer, Wayne Cady, had delivered on his promise of a unique Cadillac.

In its first model year, the new Seville's sales totaled 39,480. They then proceeded to decline in 1981 and 1982 to 26,622 and 22,334, respectively. But in those dark years for the automotive industry, these were respectable figures. Cadillac described the Seville as "quite possibly the most distinctive car in the world today . . . A masterpiece of classical and contemporary elements united in an undeniably beautiful automobile."

The dramatic outline of its rear deck was further accentuated by the roof line's downward sweep and the razor-edged, rear-window surround. The front end's appearance was nearly as sensational, dominated by the combination of a sharply sloped windshield and a neoclassic grille with vertical bars. Regardless of automotive history's final verdict on the 1980 Seville, the subsequent adoption of many of its features by both Lincoln and Chrysler speaks for itself.

Whereas the first-generation Seville had been of unit-body construction, its replacement reverted back to a separate body-chassis arrangement joined at 14 points. This change was mandated by the need to further rationalize the Seville's production into overall corporate planning. This made it possible to build Sevilles at the General Motors Assembly Division plant at Lincoln, New Jersey, along with Eldorado, Toronado, and Riviera models. The Seville may have been visually unique; but beneath its controversial form, it was a virtual mechanical twin to the Eldorado.

Thus its front suspension consisted of unequal-length, upper and lower A-arms with torsion bars and an antisway bar. The rear wheels rode on short stub axles and were controlled by coil springs and splayed trailing arms. The telescopic shock absorbers with their pneumatic height adjustments were mounted to the rear of the trailing arms. The standard power-assist, recirculating ball steering required three turns lock-to-lock and guided the Seville through a 38.4-foot turning circle. Four-wheel, 10.4-inch vented disc brakes were used as were 6.0-x-15-inch cast-aluminum wheels on which were mounted Goodyear Polysteel P205/75R-15 radial tires. As an option, Uniroyal Seal antipuncture tires were available.

When the Seville was announced on September 26, 1979, Cadillac anticipated that between 50 and 60 percent would be diesel powered. This proved to be wildly optimistic; since of the 39,344 Sevilles produced during the 1980 model run, 63.2 percent were equipped with a gasoline engine.

With only 105 horsepower at 3,200 rpm and 205 lb-ft of torque at 3,200 rpm, the diesel, equipped with a Roosa-Master mechanical fuel injection system, provided the Seville with performance that at best could be described leisurely; at worst, it was depicted as lethargic. A typical time from 0 to 60 mph was 20 seconds, and well over 21 seconds was required to move the Seville from a standing start through the quarter-mile to a speed of approximately 63 mph.

As an alternative in all markets except California, where the older 5.7-liter (350-cid) V-8 (now with a 160-horsepower rating) was required, Cadillac offered its new 368-cubic-inch gasoline V-8. This engine was equipped with a state-of-the-art digital, electronic fuel-injection system. Among its salient features was a pulse-time system that injected fuel from a new throttle body. The digital microprocessor (on the basis of information provided by sensors monitoring manifold absolute pressure, ambient barometric pressure, engine coolant temperature, incoming fuel-air mix temperature, engine speed and throttle position) provided consistent starting, idling, and overall performance regardless of operating conditions.

A readout on the dash (incorporated in the air-conditioning control functions) progressively scanned 25 engine functions. This information was fed into the computer, which recorded any temporary fault. The fuel-injection system also automatically diagnosed the problem and, if possible, bypassed the problem until it was remedied.

The Seville also used electronic control for its suspension leveling system and radio tuning. The latter unit was an AM/FM/CB/eight-track unit with a scanning function and integral digital clock. It also gave the driver the capability to monitor the CB while listening to the regular radio. But even more emphatically placing the Seville's owner/operator directly in the midst of its comprehensive electronics system was the interior climate adjustment system. By a mere push on either the red or blue button, the Seville's interior temperature was raised or lowered by a 1-degree increment.

Use of a new body and front-wheel drivetrain had a favorable impact on the Seville's interior and luggage capacity. The latter was 1.7 cubic feet larger (up to 14.5 cubic feet) due to the new exterior shape, use of a fully inflated compact spare tire and the new independent rear suspension. Interior space was enhanced by the nearly flat floor area. Replacing the information-band dash of 1975-1979 was a new dash with a two-tier arrangement of instruments that were easily seen by the driver. Mounted in the center were the air-conditioning controls above which was found, on gasoline-engined cars, the MPG Sentinel system. On diesel Sevilles, this area was filled by a plate carrying Cadillac script. Bordering the information/control elements of the Seville dash was a network of simulated teakwood grain with butterfly walnut inlays plus simulated chrome-plated plastic striping. The roof-mounted, twin map-light unit contained space to install an optional garage–door-opener transmitter. The Seville's standard interior of Heather cloth was available in a wide range of colors as was the optional saddle leather interior.

Cadillac continued to offer an expensive ($2,934) Elegante option package for the Seville. For 1980, it provided customers with a choice of three exterior, two-tone color schemes: sable black/Sheffield gray Firemist, Sheffield gray Firemist/Norfolk gray, and Canyon rock/desert sand Firemist, all separated by a thin red, hand-applied pinstripe. Initially unique to the Elegante was its sweeping side trim, but this was found on virtually all Sevilles in addition to the standard midbody trim bar. Elegante models also carried Elegante script on the C-pillar.

All Elegante interiors had leather upholstery in either light beige or slate gray with large Cadillac crests embossed into the backrest centers. As in 1979, the Elegante Seville had 40/40 Dual Control rear seats.

When the Seville was introduced, Cadillac general manager Edward C. Kennard described it as the "first Sedan to combine front-wheel drive with fully independent four-wheel suspension, four-wheel disc brakes, electronic leveling control, electronic climate control and cruise control." This package of sophisticated elements combined with the Seville's appearance was intended to bolster its credentials in the sales fray with BMW and Mercedes for customers in their early thirties with sufficient disposable income to purchase a $20,000 automobile.

Pushing in the opposite direction, however, was the lack of a sporting-type suspension option. Cadillac chief engineer Robert Templin reported in late 1979 that the Seville's demographics indicated little interest in such an option. This decision, which was later rescinded, and the failure of the strategy to fit the Seville with a standard diesel engine illustrated just how fluid the luxury-car market had become. By all measurements, offering a diesel-engine option in 1978 appeared to be perfectly timed. At that point, Mercedes was offering four diesel models: 240D, 300D, 300CD and 300SD. Fully 52.2 percent of Mercedes sold that year were diesel powered. In 1979, Cadillac seemed to be following a similar track as approximately 20 percent of its Sevilles were produced with diesel engines. But as earlier noted, diesel-Seville sales in 1980 were well off Cadillac's projections. It's highly unlikely that the availability of the gasoline engine as a "cost-saving" option for $316 less was a factor in this preference. In 1981, the last year the diesel was the standard Seville engine, it was installed in only 25.4 percent of the Sevilles produced. After that, the diesel's popularity as an option dwindled rapidly. Apparently Cadillac was unable to follow the diesel trail blazed by Mercedes.

Offering the Seville with an optional sports touring suspension probably had limited impact on its sales as the Eldorado, which was available with the same setup, gradually emerged as the Cadillac perceived to have a more sporting image. At the same time, Eldorado sales increased substantially from 1980 to 1984, while those of the 1984 Seville were only slightly above those of the 1980 model.

This reasonably priced ($95) option, which after first being identified as the Sport Handling Package was soon renamed the Touring Suspension, made both Cadillacs competent road machines far closer to the Mercedes-Benz/BMW scheme of things than their standard versions. The stiffness of the front torsion bars was increased 39 percent, while the front antisway bar measured 32 mm in diameter or 19 percent larger than the standard version. Other changes at the front involved the use of firmer shock-absorber valving and stiffer suspension bushings. At the rear, the spring rates were increased 19 percent, and a 20 percent larger, 24-mm, antisway bar was used. The power-steering unit required 25 percent greater effort, and 70 series radial tires were used in place of the base 75 series.

The impact these changes had upon Cadillac handling was startling. Driving an Eldorado or Seville with Touring Suspension was not totally alien to drivers more familiar with a BMW or Mercedes. Its steering was firm; and when cornered at a brisk pace, the Cadillac had minimal body lean.

CADILLAC'S DOMESTIC COMPETITION

Although 1980 wasn't a record year, Cadillac's sales totaled 213,002 units. In its class, the Eldorado's sales of 52,142 (model-year production was 52,685) were greater than those of Lincoln's Mark VI by a 12,552 margin. Moreover, neither the Oldsmobile Toronado nor Buick Riviera, with respective sales of 37,051 and 42,917, were its equals.

The Seville's supposed challenger from Lincoln, the Versailles, unchanged for 1980 and scheduled to be discontinued at model-year end, had an output of only 4,784 cars.

When introduced, the 1979 Lincoln Continental had been called "the last traditionally full-sized American car." In other words, it was an anachronism.

It was common knowledge that its replacement and that for the Mark V would be all-new models with significantly reduced dimensions. These cars were introduced on October 12, 1979, just in time to face the economic unpleasantness of that time.

For the first time, the Mark, now in VI form, was available in a four-door version as well as the Coupe model. This move plus the decision to bring the Continental and Mark into closer manufacturing compatibility while maintaining a very close styling contact with previous models resulted in some serious problems for Lincoln. Years later, Lincoln would extol the appearance of its products as unique among American cars, but in 1980 their styling seemed unimaginative and dated.

The transformation of a form previously used on cars with wheelbases and overall length of 120 inches and 230 inches onto vehicles with 114- and 117-inch wheelbases and overall lengths of 210 and 219 inches met with a lukewarm reception in the marketplace that was soon chilled down to solid ice as the economy worsened.

SPECIFICATIONS

Engine

De Ville, Fleetwood Brougham, Limousine, Eldorado

Type: V-8, ohv, eight cylinders
Bore × stroke: 3.8 × 4.06 inches
    California Eldorados: 4.057 × 3.385 inches
Displacement: 368 cubic inches
    California Eldorados: 350 cubic inches
Horsepower: 140 @ 3,800 rpm
Torque: 265 lb-ft @ 1,400 rpm
Compression ratio: 8.2:1
    California Eldorados: 8.0:1
Fuel system: Quadrajet, four-barrel carburetor
    Eldorado: Digital electronic fuel injection (closed-loop electronic fuel injection for California Eldorados)
Electrical system: Freedom II, Delco Remy F18, 12-volt batteries

Seville (optional for Fleetwood Brougham, De Ville, Eldorado)

Type: V-8, ohv, eight cylinders, diesel
Bore × stroke: 4.05 × 3.385 inches
Displacement: 350 cubic inches
Horsepower: 105 @ 3,200 rpm
Torque: 205 lb-ft @ 1,600 rpm
Compression ratio: 22.5:1
Fuel system: Diesel injectors
Electrical system: Two Freedom II, Delco Remy F18 12-volt batteries

Chassis/Drivetrain

Transmission:
    De Ville, Fleetwood Brougham, Limousine (with gasoline engine): Turbo Hydra-Matic 400, three-speed automatic
    With diesel engine: Turbo Hydra-Matic 200, three-speed automatic
    Eldorado, Seville (all engines): Turbo Hydra-Matic 325, three-speed automatic
Frame: All models: separate full frame, ladder construction with welded-in X-members
Rear axle: Rear-drive models: hypoid type
    De Ville and Brougham: 2.28:1 ratio
    California De Villes, Brougham: 2.56:1
    Limousines: 3.08:1
Final drive:
    Eldorado: Ring gear and pinion, hypoid, 2.19:1 ratio
    Seville: 2.41:1 ratio
Front suspension Rear-drive models: Independent coil springs, link-type stabilizer bar; hydraulic, direct-action shock absorbers
    Eldorado, Seville: independent torsion bars, link-type stabilizer bar; hydraulic, direct-action shock absorbers
Rear suspension: Rear-drive models: coil springs, four-link drive; hydraulic, direct-action shock absorbers, Electronic Level Control standard on Limousine
    Eldorado, Seville: independent trailing arm, coil springs; hydraulic, direct-action shock absorbers, Electronic Level Control.
Steering: Power assisted with hydraulic shock-absorber damper (except De Ville, Brougham), overall ratios: 17.1-15.1:1
    De Ville, Brougham: 20.0-20.6:1
    Limousine: 14.0:1
    Eldorado, Seville: 15.0-13.0:1
Brakes:
    De Ville, Brougham, Limousine: Front: ventilated discs
Rear: composite cast-iron steel drums, 11-inch diameter, 375.1-square-inch swept area
    Limousine: 12-inch diameter, 425.3 square inches
    Seville, Eldorado: single-piston sliding caliper, ventilated rotors, disc brakes front and rear, 396-square-inch swept area.
Tires:
    De Ville, Brougham: GM specification steel-belted radial, wide white stripe, P215/75R15
    Limousine: HR78-15-D
    Seville, Eldorado: P205/75R

Dimensions

Wheelbase:
    De Ville, Brougham: 121.4 inches
    Limousine: 144.5 inches
    Seville, Eldorado: 114 inches
Front/rear tread:
    De Ville, Brougham, Limousine: 61.7/60.7 inches
    Seville, Eldorado: 59.3/60.6 inches

Overall length:
 De Ville, Brougham: 221.0 inches
 Limousine: 244.1 inches
 Seville: 204.8 inches
 Eldorado: 204.5 inches

Popular Options

Long-distance cruise package (25-gallon fuel tank and electronic cruise control):   available for De Ville, Fleetwood Brougham, 5.7-liter diesel V-8 (not available for Limousine)

Theft-deterrent system

Astroroof: Special order required for Limousine

Vinyl roof: Standard on Fleetwood Brougham, Limousine

Electrically controlled mirrors

Rear-window defogger and heated outside mirrors

Two-tone exteriors

1981

Answering Today's Needs with Tomorrow's Technology

AFTER FOLLOWING UP the introduction of a reengineered and styled Eldorado in 1979 with an equally sensational, but far more controversial, Seville, it would not have been surprising if Cadillac, in 1981, had decided to consolidate the benefits of these developments and offer a product line with only cosmetic changes. In normal times that might have been possible. However, the early Eighties were years when no one who wished to still be building cars at decade's end dared conduct business as usual.

CHANGES AND IMPROVEMENTS

Added to Cadillac's optional equipment list was a new radio (for a total of five) with an integral "Symphonic Sound System" premium cassette-tape player. Also now available on all Cadillacs except Limousines was a memory seat system, making it possible to preset and store two separate driver-seat positions.

Beyond this point, Cadillac marked 1981 with two bold thrusts, one of which, the introduction of the modular displacement V-8-6-4 engine, brought unfortunate consequences. This engine's design was based on a simple premise: the typical automobile needed the full power developed by all its cylinders only on occasion. Most of the time, only a fraction of the engine's output was required to overcome friction, wind resistance, etc. It seemed feasible, therefore, to develop a V-8 engine that would, according to driver demands and road conditions, operate on four, six, or eight cylinders. By pursuing this engineering project, Cadillac was accepting certain risks and dangers that, in practice, approached worst-case condition proportions.

For years, Cadillac had, by both word and deed, promoted its image as a leader of automotive engineering and technology. On the same elevated plane of public awareness was its close association with the V-8. For nearly 70 years, Cadillac had been producing V-type engines. It had set the pace for V-8 design in both 1936 and 1949. No automotive company

had so tightly intertwined such an engine design into its public image as had Cadillac.

The Eighties dealt harshly with the established order of things, however, and it appeared to many that the V-8, already swept off the lofty pedestal where cubic-inch displacement of 400 cubic inches was common, was headed for extinction, doomed to serve as clumsy stepping stones to an era of high mpg, mini-displacement, four-cylinder engines.

Cadillac had already stepped back from its 500-cubic-inch V-8 by adopting a 425-cubic-inch V-8 in 1977 and a 368-cubic-inch version in 1979. Now it seemed the time was right for the variable displacement V-8-6-4. In form, this was a marvelous piece of machinery, allowing the valves either to function normally or, in certain cylinders, remain closed. This was achieved by moving the fulcrum of the rocker arm from the pivot point to the end of the valve stem. An internal selector mechanism supplied by Eaton allowed this transition to take place without disruption of the normal function of the cam, lifter, and pushrod. In six-cylinder operation, cylinders one and four were deactivated. When the engine was in its four-cylinder mode, cylinders one, four, six, and seven didn't operate. Cadillac owners, in effect, had three engines at their disposal: a 368-cid V-8, a 270-cid V-6, and a 184-cid V-4. In its V-8 mode, the Cadillac engine developed 140 horsepower at 3,800 rpm. Peak torque was 265 lb-ft at 1,400 rpm.

The heart of this system, which operated only in the transmission's Drive range, was a microprocessor called the Electronic Control Module (ECM) by Cadillac. It received information from sensors monitoring such conditions as intake-manifold pressure, ambient pressure, engine coolant temperature, manifold charge temperature, engine revolutions, vehicle speed, transmission ratio, throttle position, and exhaust-gas composition. The computer then selected the appropriate number of cylinders to operate on the basis of three factors: optimum fuel economy, emissions, and driveability. It controlled the fuel flow from a new digital fuel-injection system with a twin-injection throttle body. This system was standard on the 1981 De Ville, Fleetwood, Brougham, Limousine, and Eldorado gasoline models and optional for the gasoline Seville.

Since a Cadillac needed only 40 horsepower to cruise at 55 mph, the rationale for this unit seemed impeccable. When cruise control was used, the driver could select a speed where only four cylinders were required. If more power was needed, the microprocessor brought cylinders back into operation two at a time. Cadillac reported that at highway speeds between 55 and 60 mph, a Cadillac with this system had a 3- to 4-mpg economy advantage over a model with a conventional V-8. Standing-start performance, which was conducted with the engine operating on all cylinders, was, if far off the pace of earlier models unfettered by various mandates and controls, respectable. Zero to 60 mph required approximately 11.5 seconds, the standing-start quarter-mile was completed in 18.4 seconds at a speed of 75 mph. Top speed was an honest 100 mph.

The Environment Protection Agency reported, after testing a V-8-6-4 Cadillac, that in city driving the engine would operate on eight cylinders 60 percent of the time; on six cylinders 3 percent, and on four cylinders the remaining 37 percent. Highway operation was dramatically different. There the engine's use of all eight cylinders fell to just 4 percent. Six-cylinder usage was just 8 percent, leaving the engine functioning as a V-4 for 88 percent of the time. Drivers could sense the movement of the engine in and out of its various modes, but this impression was minimized, at least when cruise control was used, by tighter control over the amount of tension in its activator chain linkage.

Coexisting with the V-8-6-4 engine was a revamped MPG Sentinel that informed the driver of both instantaneous and average mpg plus the number of cylinders currently operating. The information from the Sentinel also was used for an electronic digital readout (in metric and English) of the number of miles able to be traveled based on current mpg and the amount of fuel remaining.

Fuel economy results from road tests of the V-8-6-4 Cadillac sent conflicting signals to would-be buyers. *Car and Driver* (April 1981) tested a De Ville Sedan and found its fuel consumption very disappointing. Over 1,500 miles, it returned only 11 mpg. In contrast, a test by *Motor Trend* (January, 1981) of a V-8-6-4 Eldorado found it capable of 6 to 10 percent better fuel economy than its EPA ratings of 15 mpg city, 22 mpg highway. Unfortunately, the modulated displacement engine's notoriety extended well beyond its fuel consumption as it quickly gained a reputation for unreliability. As a result, its use after 1981 was limited to Limousine models.

DIFFERENCES AMONG MODELS

In appearance, however, Cadillac's carryover models offered little that was new. A more finely textured grille in traditional Cadillac cross-hatch design was used for the De Ville, Fleetwood, Brougham, and Limousines. Interior changes were also minor. De Villes now had

pillow-style seats available in four colors of Heather knit cloth. The leather-upholstery option in 10 colors used new ribbed seating areas. Sedan de Villes with V-6 gasoline engines were offered with the first automatic seat-belt system available in a General Motors full-sized car. As the door was opened, shoulder and lap belts extended outward across the seat, allowing easy entry or exit. When the door was closed, a retractor assembly, housed in the center console, spooled in the belt slack. By depressing a "comfort release" button and pulling out the belt, front-seat occupants could obtain an additional half inch of belt slack.

Fleetwood Brougham interiors had biscuit-sculptured seats with Cadillac wreaths embroidered on the armrests. Door-trim panels carried Fleetwood script. Bright chrome moldings were added to the door armrests, along with new door courtesy-lamp ornamentation. The standard Brougham interior, a Heather knit cloth with patterned Raphael-velour inserts, was offered in six colors. The optional leather trim had tucked seating areas. Nine shades of leather were offered.

The eight-passenger Fleetwood Limousine and seven-passenger Formal Limousine models retained their conservative interior appointments with a choice of either dark blue or black heather cloth available for the rear seating area.

A number of changes, including a grille insert finely-textured like the standard Cadillac's, were seen in the 1981 Eldorado. Also redesigned were the optional (standard on Biarritz) wire wheelcovers now with a larger center medallion with a red background. Optional for the first time on all Eldorados except the Biarritz, where they remained standard, were opera lamps.

The Eldorado instrument panel again was trimmed in simulated teak woodgrain. The door panels received new wood-grain appliques and the pull strap used in 1980 was replaced by a swing handle.

The Seville continued to have a V-8 diesel as its standard engine. But it was hardly the engine of choice for Seville buyers as 75 percent selected either the V-8-6-4 engine, which was portrayed as the Seville's standard gasoline engine, or the optional, at-no-cost 252-cubic-inch V-6 produced by Buick. This was the first V-6 engine ever offered by Cadillac and was also available in all other Cadillacs except Limousines. On front-wheel-drive models, it was linked to a three-speed transmission. All other applications used a four-speed transmission with a converter clutch. This V-6 also had the distinction of being the only engine Cadillac offered in 1981 that did not have a fuel injection system.

All 1981 Cadillacs with the 5.7-liter, 350-cubic-inch V-8 diesel were fitted with a fuel tank-sending unit that had been phased in during the 1980 model year. It included a water separation system as well as a "water-in-fuel" detection system using a capacitive probe. The driver was alerted to the latter situation by a telltale light on the dash illuminated by an electronic module. The fuel-tank system could hold substantial amounts of water that was passed in very small quantities through the fuel system without harm to engine components.

1981 Sedan de Ville. A fine-textured grille was introduced for 1981.

1981 Fleetwood Brougham Coupe. Exclusive to the Broughams were chrome belt moldings, larger rocker moldings, special wheelcovers, and electroluminescent opera lamps.

CADILLAC VITAL STATISTICS: 1981

Series	Model	Body Type	Sug. Retail Price ($)	Weight (lbs.)	Production (#)
Seville	S69	4 dr Sedan	23,000	3898	34,436*
De Ville	D69	4 dr Sedan	14,769	4067	55,100
	D47	2 dr Coupe	14,345	4016	54,145
Eldorado	L57	2 dr Coupe	17,550	3822	79,158†
Fleetwood Brougham	B69	4 dr Sedan	17,420	4115	31,500
	B47	2 dr Coupe	16,978	4069	8300
Limousine	F23	4 dr Sedan	26,242	4629	610
	F33	4 dr Formal Sedan	27,163	4717	590

*Includes 5,715 Seville Elegantes
†Includes 18,515 Eldorado Biarritzes

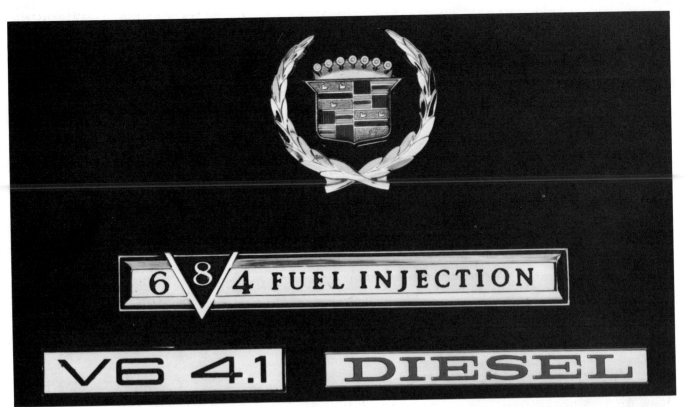

Significant Cadillac plaques for 1981.

The 1981 Seville Eleganté was available in four exclusive two-tone color combinations. An "Elegante" script was located on the sail panel.

1981 Eldorado. A fine textured grille and a front air dam were distinguishing features for 1981.

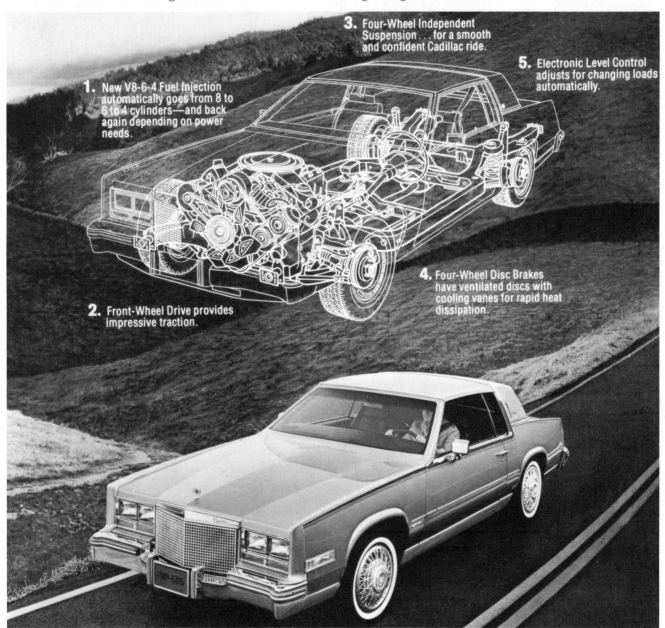

3. Four-Wheel Independent Suspension . . . for a smooth and confident Cadillac ride.

5. Electronic Level Control adjusts for changing loads automatically.

1. New V8-6-4 Fuel Injection automatically goes from 8 to 6 to 4 cylinders—and back again depending on power needs.

4. Four-Wheel Disc Brakes have ventilated discs with cooling vanes for rapid heat dissipation.

2. Front-Wheel Drive provides impressive traction.

1981 Eldorado Biarritz. Redesigned wire covers with a large center medallion were introduced for 1981. The opera lights standard on the Biarritz were now optional for all Eldorados.

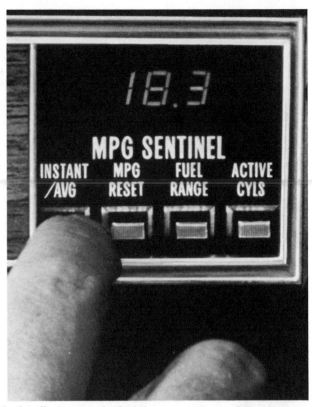

The MPG feature was standard on all Cadillacs with the V-8-6-4 engine. In this illustration, the Cadillac is operating on four cylinders and averaging 18.3 mpg.

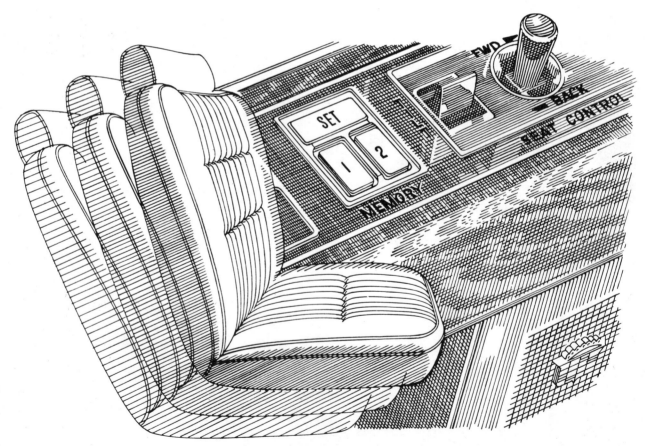

All Cadillacs except the Limousines were available with the Memory Seat option. This feature stored two seat positions in its memory.

If the fuel was contaminated with more water than the fuel system could tolerate, the engine would not run and prompt removal of the water was a necessity. To facilitate this, a new siphoning system was used that allowed drainage of the water without the need to remove the tank from the vehicle. For 1981, the diesel engine was also equipped with roller tappet camshafts to reduce wear. Use of new noise control components contributed to quieter operation. Under most operating conditions, the oil-change interval was now 5,000 instead of 3,000 miles as in 1980.

Changes to the Seville's exterior consisted of a front air dam (also installed on Eldorados) that Cadillac claimed provided better aerodynamics and contributed to fuel economy plus winged Cadillac crests for the horizontally positioned taillights. These replaced the unadorned crests used in 1980 and were very similar to those found on the 1941 Cadillac. Both the standard aluminum wheel cover and the optional wire-wheel cover had gold-colored wreath and crest ornamentation on a red background. Standard on all models was the brushed and bright side-accent molding from the 1980 Elegante.

The 1981 Seville Elegante, depicted as "the ultimate Cadillac," continued to have an "Elegante" script designation on the sail panel. It was offered in four exclusive, two-tone color combinations: Sheffield firemist/sable black, superior blue metallic/twilight blue, desert sand firemist/briarwood brown, and mulberry gray firemist/bordeaux red. Each of these also had a matching interior. Except for the addition of a center console with a removable three-compartment tray on standard models, Seville interiors were unchanged from 1980.

All 1981 Sevilles and Eldorados were equipped with a new fluid, windshield-washer system. This unit sent an oscillating stream of solvent at such a high frequency to the windshield that it appeared as a fan of fluid. The washer nozzles were mounted directly on the top of the cowl and, by being located positively against each windshield wiper stop, provided accurate aim for the spray stream in the wipe pattern.

Another feature introduced on the latest Sevilles and Eldorados was higher pressure (32 psi) tires designed to improve fuel economy because of their lower rolling resistance. Cadillac announced it was "making life tougher for car thieves" by marking for life major body parts of 1981 Sevilles and Eldorados. The 17-character vehicle identification number (VIN) of each car, printed in a security film label that could not be altered or used again, was found on the front fender, hood, right front door, rear-deck lid, and rear body structures. The labels could be authenticated by viewing in retro-reflective light. Some 1980-model Sevilles and Eldorados produced during this project's pilot stage also carried these labels.

Available for the first time on Eldorados and Sevilles equipped with the V-8-6-4 or 5.7-liter, diesel V-8 engine was a digital instrument-panel cluster with digital displays of vehicle speed, fuel level, and fuel range on those cars with the gasoline engine. The electronic climate control, first offered on 1980 Eldorados and Sevilles, was now standard as was a new "low-fuel" warning light. The 1981 models also had adhesively attached body-side moldings that aided in corrosion resistance as well as providing for more accurate alignment.

CADILLAC'S DOMESTIC COMPETITION

Aside from minor trim changes and optional color availability, the major development at Lincoln was the use of new model designations and the dropping of the Versailles. The Lincoln Continental now was labeled the Lincoln Town Car, available either in standard form or in the Signature Series. The two- and four-door Town Cars were priced respectively at $14,574 and $14,985. In Signature Series form, their prices were increased by $1,214.

The Continental Mark VI was continued virtually unchanged except for additions to its standard equipment that included wire-wheel covers and a number of passenger-comfort features. Puncture-resistant tires, offered by Cadillac in 1980, were now available as an option. The 351-cubic-inch V-8 was no longer available. Instead, the 302-cubic-inch V-8 with electronic fuel injection was used.

Registrations of new Lincolns dropped to 61,775 in 1981 from the 1980 level of 72,740. Calendar-year retail sales, totaling 63,830 included 29,178 Town Cars. This was, however, to mark the end of Lincoln's retreat from its 1978 peak level, as it would in subsequent years begin to recover from the doldrums of the early Eighties.

Chrysler, in 1980, was still a year away from introducing its compact K-cars, which after a rocky launch catapulted the company and Lee Iacocca into international fame as the comeback kids of the century. On the surface, the rebirth of the Imperial on what essentially was the Chrysler Cordoba chassis, suspension, brakes, and engine platform (which in turn had been derived from the 1976 Aspen/Volare) seemed out of step with the "New Chrysler Corporation's" pragmatic approach to survival. But there was money to be made in the luxury-car market; and with a price tag of $18,311, Chrysler expected a fair return on a projected 1981 production run of 25,000 Imperials. This proved grossly inflated as total sales from late 1980 through 1983 amounted to 9,927 Imperials.

All Imperials were built at Chrysler's Windsor, Ontario, plant on a special assembly line by workers with a minimum of 25 years of assembly experience at Chrysler. Quality was the byword for the Imperial. Compared with other Chryslers, many of its body panels were of heavier steel and all components were blueprinted. After review by a road simulator and a 5.5-mile road test, every chassis/suspension component was retorqued to factory specifications. Assembly procedures were stringent. Many, such as the fitting of major body components and soldering, were done by hand, and the body was wet-sanded prior to the application of the second paint coat. To make certain the Imperial's interior was super-quiet, a great deal of sound-deadening material, along with 63 suspension isolators, was installed.

Powering the Imperial was a 318-cubic-inch V-8 with a unique, continuous-flow, electronic fuel-metering system that Chrysler said involved 24 new Chrysler patents and was backed by three years of testing on over 100 cars that had amassed over 1-million miles.

Styling of the 1981 Imperial combined a front end reminiscent of the older models and a rear deck strongly suggestive of the 1980-1981 Seville's. The result was not unattractive but not particularly original either.

SPECIFICATIONS: 1981

De Ville, Fleetwood, Brougham, Limousine, Eldorado

Engine

Type: V-type, ohv, eight cylinders, V-8-6-4 modulated displacement format
Bore × stroke: 3.8 × 4.1 inches
Displacement (V-8 formal):   368 cubic inches
Horsepower: 140 @ 3,800 rpm
Torque: 265 lb-ft @ 1,400 rpm
Compression ratio: 8.2:1
Fuel system: Digital fuel injection
Gas-tank capacity: Approximately 24.6 gallons

Standard: Seville
(Available: De Ville, Fleetwood Brougham, Eldorado)

Type: V-type, ohv, eight cylinders, diesel
Bore × stroke: 4.05 × 3.385 inches
Displacement: 350 cubic inches
Horsepower: 105 @ 3,200 rpm
Torque: 205 lb-ft @ 1,600 rpm
Compression ratio: 22.5:1
Fuel system: Fuel injection
Gas tank capacity: Approximately 27 gallons

Available: De Ville, Fleetwood Brougham, Eldorado, Seville

Type: V-type, ohv, six cylinders
Bore × stroke: 3.965 × 3.40 inches
Displacement: 252 cubic inches
Horsepower: 125 @ 3,800 rpm
Torque: 210 lb-ft @ 2,000 rpm
Compression ratio: 8.0:1
Fuel system: Two-barrel carburetor
Gas-tank capacity: Approximately 25 gallons

Chassis/Drivetrain

All physical dimensions unchanged. Except for the following, all other specifications were unchanged for 1981.

Electrical system: Diesel engine: Two Delco Remy, Freedom 20 II batteries, 80-amp generator, all models
Rear-axle ratios:
   De Ville, Fleetwood Brougham with V-8-6-4 and diesel engines: 2.41:1, with V-6:   3.23:1
   Eldorado and Seville with V-8-6-4 and diesel engine: 2.41, with V-6:   2.93:1

Popular Options

Memory seat: Available only with Dual Comfort seats
Theft-deterrent system
Automatic lap/shoulder belts: Available for V-6 Sedan de Ville only
Astroroof (not available for Limousine)
Leather-trimmed steering wheel: De Ville and Brougham
Vinyl roof: Standard on Brougham
Electrically controlled mirrors
Rear-window defogger with heated outside mirrors
Two-tone colors (not available for Brougham and Limousine)
Illuminated entry system: Standard on Brougham, available for De Ville
Puncture-sealing tires
Illuminated vanity mirrors
Dual Comfort 45/55 front seats: Standard on Brougham, Eldorado, Seville, available for De Ville
Power-recliner driver seat
Power-recliner passenger seat
Opera lamps: Available for De Ville, standard on Brougham
Wire wheels
Wire-wheelcovers
Turbine-vaned wheelcovers: Available for De Ville and Brougham
Electronic cruise control
Twilight sentinel: Standard on Brougham, Eldorado and Seville
Guide-matic headlamp control
Controlled-cycle wiper system: Standard on Brougham, Eldorado, Seville
Heavy-duty ride package: Available for De Ville, Brougham
Power trunk lock and pulldown: Standard on Eldorado, Seville
Tilt and telescope steering wheel: Standard on Brougham
Firemist paints
Carpeted floor mats
Accent striping: Standard on Brougham, Eldorado, Seville

Electronic level control: Standard on Eldorado, Seville
Automatic door locks: Standard on Eldorado, Seville
Door-edge guards
Front and rear license frames
Trumpet horn
100-amp generator: Available with V-8-6-4 and diesel
   engines only

Heavy-duty cooling system
Three-channel, garage-door opener
Symphonic sound system
Engine block heater: Standard with diesel engine
Illuminated thermometer
Trunk mat
Trailering package

Cimarron

A New Kind of Cadillac for a New Kind of Cadillac Owner

WHEN CADILLAC was introducing the first examples of its down-sized automobiles in 1977, work was beginning within General Motors on a new line of products intended to compete with Japanese-built cars. Cadillac didn't become involved in the J-car project until March 1980, barely one year before production began in 1981. This late entry into a project for which General Motors had high hopes as an import fighter limited Cadillac's influence over its basic design. This was not an insurmountable obstacle to the creation of a new Cadillac. After all, the De Villes, Brougham, Sevilles, and Eldorados shared components with other GM automobiles. The contracted time frame for the Cimarron's development brought some interesting results. The Cimarron grille was rushed to completion in 24 hours, and its suspension system, which proved to be one of its strongest points, went from concept to final form in seven days.

While Pontiac and Chevrolet had as their J-car adversaries Toyota and Nissan, the targets for Cadillac's J-car were such up-scale imports as the Audi 5000, BMW 320i, Volvo GLE, and Saab 900S. Early marketing seminars held in Ohio with the Cimarron's identity masked indicated that confirmed foreign-car enthusiasts were impressed with the Cimarron's overall quality and the level of its interior appointments. Buoyed by these results, Cadillac wasn't bashful about comparing the Cimarron with these cars.

As had been the case with the 1975 Seville, the purpose of the Cimarron was not to extend Cadillac into an existing market to carry off conquest sales. Rather, it was a defensive move, with both short- and long-term objectives. Immediately facing Cadillac was the challenge to bounce back from the poor 1980 automobile market. But as important as a stronger 1981 performance was, the need to ensure a steady source of new Cadillac customers in the years to come was of greater significance. For years, Cadillac had successfully promoted its products as those best exemplifying success American-style. But far less likely than their

parents to accept this scenario had been the much written about and analyzed "Baby Boomers." By 1980, they, along with many slightly younger Americans, were employed in positions providing incomes of $35,000 or more per year. When it came to spending their money on a new automobile, these buyers were displaying a tendency to think foreign. Selected statistics from 1980 graphically illustrate the result.

Marque	1980 Retail Sales
Cadillac Fleetwood/De Ville	126,151
Cadillac Eldorado	52,142
Cadillac Seville	34,709
BMW	37,017
Audi 5000	27,796
Saab	13,327
Volvo	56,429
Peugeot	13,093

In total, sales of BMW, Audi, Saab, Volvo, and Peugeot were certainly enough for any American manufacturer to wish they were in its column. Moreover, individuals who, for example, purchased an "entry-level" BMW model 320i were likely to accumulate a high dosage of marque loyalty. The next time around, they would probably upgrade their purchase and remain within the BMW fold. It didn't take a great deal of perception to recognize what this implied for Cadillac over the long haul. In this perspective, George Kennard's comment that the Cimarron offers "more quality and functional features than many imports" was far more than a passing comment. It was a statement that he hoped many car buyers would agree.

Cadillac also had to deal with another assault on its position from Japan. Quickly moving out from the beachheads secured by their economy models, the Japanese manufacturers were successfully penetrating the highly profitable upper strata of the American market with such models as the Toyota Cressida, Datsun 810, Maxima, and Honda's Accord and Prelude. An even more ominous note was struck by their sales records than those of the Europeans.

Marque	1980 Sales
Datsun Maxima	9,440
Toyota Cressida	11,628
Honda Accord	185,977
Honda Prelude	50,676

CIMARRON'S DEVELOPMENT

Against this sombering statistical backdrop, George Kennard introduced the Cimarron on May 8, 1981. His remarks reflected Cadillac's hopes for its latest model. The Cimarron was, he said, "a new kind of Cadillac for a new kind of Cadillac owner . . . Cimarron will appeal to all fine car buyers, but especially to affluent young Americans interested in smaller cars with characteristics different from the traditional American luxury car." These potential customers, in Kennard's view, differed dramatically from traditional Cadillac buyers in their automotive priorities. "They are not," he explained, "as concerned with a vast passenger seating area or even interior quiet. What they want is a car that offers a good road feel and excellent fuel mileage, a car with quality and value in their terms."

Overall, Kennard expected Cimarron customers would come from four major groups: the just-mentioned youth market, those interested in a quality second car, retired persons, and "the fuel and energy conscious."

Initially it appeared that the Cimarron was not registering with younger car buyers. *Popular Mechanics* (February 1982) reported that 60 percent of 1982 Cimarron owners were over age 50 and that nearly one-third were previous Cadillac owners.

Whereas the Chevrolet and Pontiac J-cars were available in four forms: two- and four-door notchback Sedans, a two-door hatchback, and a station wagon, the Cimarron was offered only in the four-door body style. Dimensionally, it was virtually identical to its Chevrolet and Pontiac siblings. Its wheelbase was 101.2 inches, width measured 65 inches, and its height stood at 53.3 inches. The Cimarron's drag coefficient was a so-so 0.43.

Powering the J-cars was an all-new, 1.8-liter (112 cubic inch) pushrod, overhead valve, four-cylinder engine with a 9.0:1 compression ratio and General Motors' Computer Command Control. Both the block and the crossflow design head were cast iron. Carburetion was by a two-barrel Rochester Varajet mounted on an aluminum intake manifold. Maximum net horsepower was 85 at 5,100 rpm. The engine's peak torque of 100 lb-ft was developed at 2,800 rpm.

Chevrolet was given the responsibility for the J-car engine and from the very beginning had to fend off criticism that it had bungled the job by developing an all-new engine around old-fashioned technology. There seemed to be a good deal of logic in that criticism. After all, in an age of overhead cams and aluminum cylinder heads, the J-engine did look a bit archaic with pushrods and cast-iron heads.

Chevrolet was quick to challenge this view. It maintained that all existing four-cylinder engine configurations were examined at the onset of the J-car engine project. At the top of the criteria against which various engine formats were evaluated was fuel economy, particularly in city driving.

Also limiting the options open to the engine designers were physical dimensions imposed by the J-car's overall design. The engine had to fit into what was, in effect, a box beyond whose length, width, and height it could not extend. Because of these factors, a V-4 design was eliminated (too wide) as was an overhead arrangement (too fast an idle speed was needed to compensate for limited low rpm power).

Chevrolet also maintained that the use of pushrods rather than an overcam and cast iron instead of aluminum made it possible to produce the J-engine at a lower cost than competitors' engines. At the same time, Chevrolet portrayed the J-engine as having numerous contemporary design features. Examples cited included short length; chain-driven pushrods; five-bearing crankshaft; compact, fast-burn combustion chamber, and thin-wall castings.

Compared with existing American-made, four-cylinder engines, the 1.8-liter J-four seemed to fulfill many of Chevrolet's claims. For example, its 47.8-hp/liter output was superior to the Ford Escort (43.1 hp/liter) and the Chrysler K-car (38.2 hp/liter).

Although this engine's horsepower/liter output was the best of any non-turbo-charged American engine, it was subjected to tremendous criticism in the press for the poor performance it delivered. While the term also referred to its initially weak sales level, the labeling of the Cavalier as the "Cadaver" was not atypical.

In the specific case of the Cimarron, *Car and Driver* (June 1981) was critical of its noise at high revolution levels (the four cylinders' red line was 6,000 rpm). Both *Car and Driver* and *Motor Trend* attained a 0 to 60-mph time of 13.7 seconds, virtually identical to those of the Honda Accord and Audi. *Road and Track* (November 1981) managed a best run of only 15.9 seconds from 0 to 60 mph. This put the Cimarron in the uncomfortable position of being, along with the J-2000 Pontiac, slower than any gasoline-engine car recently tested by *Road and Track*.

A brighter, though not unblemished, picture of the Cimarron emerged from test sessions on the skid pad and over twisting roads. Its lateral acceleration on a 100-foot radius circle was 0.742 g, virtually on a par with the Audi 4000 and BMW 320i, which recorded respective figures of 0.743 g and 0.731 g.

The Cimarron, like all J-cars, was a front-wheel-drive vehicle with its engine mounted transversely in the chassis. The basic suspension system consisted of trailing arms connected by a transverse member, coil conical springs, vertical tubular shocks, and an antisway bar. As formulated for the Cimarron, the suspension consisted of the same rear springs as used on the base-level Cavalier, antisway bars (28 mm front, 19 mm rear) from the Chevrolet F41 handling package, and special shock-absorber valving, and dual-rate

1982 Cimarron.

Instrumentation of the Cimarron include a tachometer, voltmeter, and oil pressure gauges.

The Cimarron was equipped with forged aluminum wheels and P195/70 R13 blackwall steel-belted radial tires.

The Cimarron's remote control outside mirror was electrically operated.

A deck lid luggage rack was a Cimarron option.

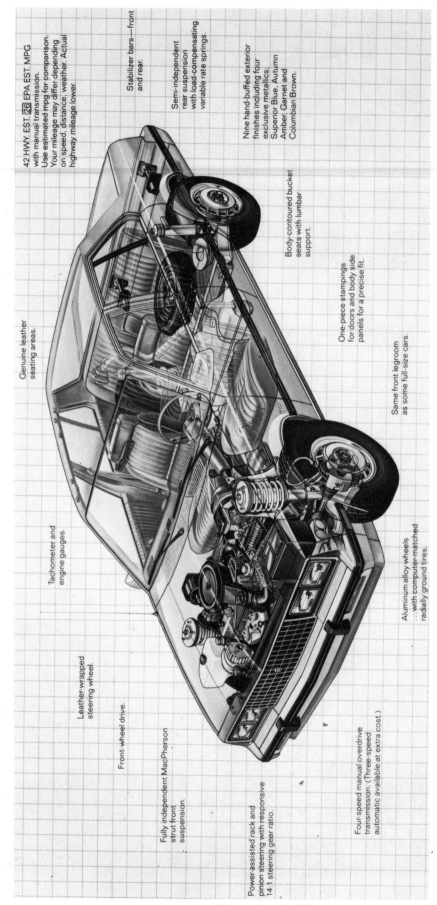

42 HWY. EST. 26 EPA EST. MPG with manual transmission. Use estimated mpg for comparison. Your mileage may differ depending on speed, distance, weather. Actual highway mileage lower.

Stabilizer bars—front and rear.

Semi-independent rear suspension with load-compensating variable rate springs.

Nine hand-buffed exterior finishes including four exclusive metallics; Superior Blue, Autumn Amber, Garnet and Columbian Brown.

Body-contoured bucket seats with lumbar support.

Genuine leather seating areas.

One-piece stampings for doors and body side panels for a precise fit.

Same front legroom as some full-size cars.

Tachometer and engine gauges.

Leather-wrapped steering wheel.

Aluminum alloy wheels ...with computer-matched radially ground tires.

Front-wheel drive.

Fully independent MacPherson strut front suspension.

Power-assisted rack and pinion steering with responsive 14:1 steering gear ratio.

Four-speed manual overdrive transmission. (Three-speed automatic available at extra cost.)

A phantom view of the Cimarron illustrating many of its attributes.

suspension bushings developed by Cadillac. To limit transmission of mechanical noise to the interior, large upper-axle insulators were installed. Also used was the 14:1 ratio rack and pinion steering from the F41. With power steering, the Cimarron's wheel moved from lock-to-lock in just 2.9 turns. The steering unit was located behind the engine and attached with insulators to the firewall. The bushings used for the Cimarron's front lower A-arms and upper shock-absorber mounts were stiffer than those found on other J-cars. Yet their composition was such that the harshness, noise, and vibration often associated with high-caliber cornering was absent from the Cimarron.

The Cimarron's standard tires were Goodyear blackwall, P195/7OR13, steel-belted radial tires. These were available as options for other J-cars, but those intended for the Cimarron were tested electronically to detect any out-of-round spots. If any were detected, they were ground to conform with the tread belt. Similarly, the forged-alloy, 5.5- x -13.5 wheels supplied exclusively by Alcoa were spun to determine their heavy spot where the air-valve stem hole was drilled. When the tire and

With room for four passengers and an interior volume index of 101 cubic feet, including the trunk, the Cimarron was classified as a compact car.

The Cimarron's profile was attractive.

wheel were joined, their high and low points were matched to ensure the best possible dynamic balance and vibration-free "ride."

Common to all GM J-cars was a front-disc, rear drum-brake setup. Unique to the Cimarron were its vented front rotors. The 9.7- x -0.5-inch discs were fitted with sintered metallic pads. At the rear, the 7.8- x -1.8-inch, cast-iron drums had semimetallic, riveted brake shoes. These provided the Cimarron with good braking performance. A stop from 60 mph was completed in approximately 175 feet, and wheel hop under deceleration was minimal. Included in the Cimarron's standard power-brake system was a tandem diaphragm vacuum booster and an electrically operated auxiliary pump that supplemented the engine for adequate brake assist under extreme operating conditions.

CIMARRON ROAD TESTS

As a total handling package, the Cimarron fell short of matching the speeds of the BMW 320i or Audi 4000 through the *Road & Track* 700-foot-long slalom. The best the Cadillac could score was 56.3 mph, while the BMW passed through at 58.6 mph. The Audi was even quicker at 60.2 mph. Singled out for criticism by *Road & Track* was the Cimarron's steering response, which it considered numb. Yet it had to concede that down a twisting two-lane road, the Cimarron felt well balanced and was at least the equal of the BMW.

Car and Driver, whose Cimarron road test appeared in its August 1981 issue, reached similar conclusions about the Cimarron's handling and cornering. Both publications praised it for having excellent road insulation and ride. On its favorite test loop, *Car and Driver* found the Cimarron nearly the equal of the best European sports Sedan. Again, rough road performance was less-exemplary, nor did its power steering provide sufficient feel.

While *Road & Track* returned its Cimarron with little enthusiasm for its performance, however, *Car and Driver* took a more positive tact. It saw the Cimarron as a good beginning, a major step forward for Cadillac, and a car that had in its basic design the wherewithal to be a world-class car. *Motor Trend*, in comparing the Cimarron with the Audi 4000, found the Cadillac's steering input at least equal to the Audi's, and, on wide sweeping turns, its handling superior. Overall, when various bias and prejudices toward Cadillacs were factored in, the road-test results lent a fair degree of credibility to Cadillac's assertion that the Cimarron's suspension "provided impressive performance relative to such overall handling characteristics as cornering capability, roll stiffness, and lateral acceleration capability."

While by no means unanimous nor overly generous in praise for the Cimarron, initial press reaction also tended to support Edward Kennard's claim that "the Cimarron combines the size, ride and functional design of fine European road cars with the traditional quality and value of Cadillac."

CIMARRON'S INTERIOR

The Cimarron's base price of $12,131 provided sufficient room within its five digits for a long list of standard equipment items. Perhaps the most historic was a four-speed manual transmission, the first hand-shifter offered by Cadillac since 1953. Its short, stubby shifter was, except for its knob, encased in a leather-like rubber cover and moved precisely through a tight gate. Its ratios of 3.53, 1.95, 1.24, and 0.81 (fourth gear was overdrive) were a bit too widely spaced for the 2.0-liter engine; but nonetheless, the fact that a three-speed automatic transmission was an option for a modern Cadillac was a newsworthy occurrence.

Another sure sign of changing times at Cadillac was the absence of any interior plastic-wood appliques.

The Cimarron was the first four-cylinder Cadillac built since this 1905 Model D.

Instead, the Cimarron driver was treated to complete instrumentation, including gauges for the oil pressure, water temperature, voltmeter, and fuel. Matching the circular size and shape of the speedometer was a tachometer. The instrument-panel retainer was of one-piece construction to minimize rattles. Exclusive to the Cimarron was its brushed, gray metallic instrument-panel surface. Integrated in the side air-conditioning outlets were side-window defogger vents. Five interior color selections, including two exclusive to the Cimarron, were available. The seating, which proved very comfortable for four adults, featured leather seating areas. The remaining upholstery areas were finished in pleated vinyl. A swing-down center armrest was provided for the rear seat. Thick, cut-pile carpeting was installed and the hand-brake lever was mounted between the front seats. The front bucket seats were designed to provide a lumbar and lateral support. They were equipped with adjustable headrests and mechanical seat-back recliners. Map pockets were installed on the front-seat backs and the front-door panels. The three-spoke steering wheel was leather-wrapped.

Additional equipment found on the Cimarron included air conditioning, intermittent windshield wipers, power steering and brakes, electric exterior mirrors, reclining front bucket seats, digital clock, halogen quad headlights, tinted glass, AM/FM stereo radio with four speakers, and buffed paint. For those customers who wanted even more features, Cadillac listed 18 additional pieces of optional equipment, including power windows ($216), power seats ($183), power door locks ($42), tilt steering wheel ($88), and deck-lid release ($29). Unique among the J-cars was the Cimarron's sporty-appearing deck-lid rack.

CIMARRON'S EXTERIOR

The Cimarron's exterior appearance was, as expected, cast in the same mold as the Chevrolet Cavalier and Pontiac J-2000. With only 11 months available, its stylists didn't exactly have much time on their hands. Even so, as a total package, the Cimarron was equipped with features not offered on either the Chevrolet Cavalier and Pontiac J-2000. To prove this point, Cadillac offered the following chart as evidence.

Cimarron Exclusives
(as compared to Cavalier and J-2000)

Exterior

Four metallic paint selections
Dual-color, painted accent stripes
Copper, nickel, and chrome-plated bumpers

Interior

Perforated-leather seating area
Adjustable, contoured, front-seat headrests
Front-seat back pockets
Leather-wrapped, steel-spoked steering wheel
Dual-note horn
High-density carpet

Center-supported sun visors
Fabric-covered interior-garnish moldings
Fully trimmed trunk with edge-bound carpet and acoustical insulation
Warning chimes for seat belt, ignition, and headlamp-on alert
Padded glove-box door with color-keyed inner panel
Custom-fitted, color-keyed air-conditioning outlets
Upgraded front console
Upgraded instrument-panel pad with stitching
Rear-seat armrest
Deluxe dome and reading lamps
Low-fuel warning indicator

Chassis/Drivetrain

Tuned touring suspension
Radially ground, single-sourced tires
Custom-forged, aircraft-type, aluminum-alloy wheels

While not fitted with a Fleetwood body, the Cimarron's construction was of high quality and the beneficiary of modern manufacturing techniques. Key contributors to body quality included: one-piece door stampings (eliminated joints and weld marks); one-piece stamping for four-door frame (eliminated joints and welds, made possible higher precision-fitting of doors); new door-latching mechanisms (maintained uniform door alignment and operation); new "super-soft" weatherstripping (reduced door closing effort); and mitered joints instead of butt joints for finish moldings.

In producing the Cimarron, the Fisher Body Division made extensive use of robotics, lasers, and gamma-ray machines. Components such as the hood and trunk lids were assembled with robotics to a $\frac{1}{10}$-inch tolerance, which was only one-third of previous tolerances. Most of the welds during the early stages of body assembly (for a total of 450 spot welds per body) were performed by robots. Gamma-ray detection systems determined if parts automatically welded inside components such as doors were actually there and in the proper location. The dimensional accuracy of metal openings around doors, deck lids, tail lamps, and windows were checked by robotic optical scanners using two beams of laser light.

With "fit and finish" emerging as one of the customer's prime considerations in evaluating a new automobile, Cadillac placed a high priority on the Cimarron paint quality. A good starting point was the basic form of the J-car body, which was designed to eliminate corners that were inherently difficult to paint. To ensure a smoother finish, the water used in cleaning car bodies before painting was repeatedly filtered to remove dirt. Body areas likely to suffer dings and scratches prior to painting were coated with a special solution that made them shine like a painted surface, thus making it possible to refinish any blemishes prior to painting. No lead solder was used on the Cimarron body, thus eliminating its filings as a source of paint imperfections. Additional changes in the painting process included oil sanding to improve finish smoothness and luster, multiapplication of sealers after electroposition of the paint and the relocation of various operations away from the paint department to reduce risk of paint contamination.

To provide the Cimarron with a high degree of corrosion protection, Fisher Body used a specially coated steel, an improved primer paint process, aluminum, plastics, and various types of sealers and wax-based sprays in its assembly. Components such as the hood, fenders, doors, trunk lids, rocker and quarter panels were fabricated from special metals, including galvanized steel, zincrometal, zinc-iron alloy, and aluminum.

If not the most distinctive Cadillac ever built, the Cimarron was certainly among the most pleasing to the eye. Given the boldness and change in direction the Cimarron symbolized for Cadillac, its styling was very acceptable. The quad headlights bracketed a simple rectangular, cross-hatched grille carrying a Cadillac crest in its center. At the rear, winged Cadillac emblems were found on the taillight lenses. Flanking the taillights were amber-colored turn indicators. On either side of the rear license-plate openings were rectangular backup lamps. Cimarrons were offered in nine exterior, buffed paint selections, including four exclusive color choices. Dual-color, painted accent stripes were standard. With the tendency of GM designers to apply extraneous trim to their creations in full remission, the Cimarron was clear-hooded, flanked, and decked. Simple side-body molding with a functional purpose was used; and aside from the trunk lock/opener, the only element on the rear deck was a ''Cimarron by Cadillac'' plaque. The only other place on the Cimarron where its name was found was the door panel.

Cimarron production began on March 14, 1981, at General Motors' South Gate, California, plant; and at year's-end, production totaled 14,604 cars.

The Cimarron was regarded as a 1982 model and publicly introduced on May 21, 1981. Initial sales were limited to 242 single-line Cadillac dealers. By September 1981, when Cimarron output was greater, they were available through all 1,600 Cadillac dealers.

SPECIFICATIONS

Engine

Type: L-4, ohv
Bore x stroke: 3.5 x 2.9 inches
Displacement: 112.11 cubic inches
Horsepower: 85 @ 5,100 rpm

Torque: 100 ft-lbs @ 2,800 rpm
Compression ratio: 9.0:1
Fuel system: two-barrel, Rochester carburetor

Chassis/Drivetrain

Front suspension: Independent, trailing arms, coil springs, tubular shocks, 28-mm stabilizer bar
Rear suspension: semiindependent, trailing arms, coil springs, vertical shock absorbers, 19-mm stabilizer bar
Steering: Rack and pinion, 14:1 overall ratio
Electrical system: 12-volt
Transmission: four-speed manual, all synchromesh
Frame: Unit construction
Tires: Steel-belted radial P195/70 R13, blackwall
Brakes:
   Front: 9.7- x -0.5-inch vented discs
   Rear: 7.9- x -1.8-inch cast-iron drums

Dimensions

Wheelbase: 101.2 inches
Width: 65.0 inches
Height: 52.0 inches
Overall length: 173.0 inches
Front/rear tread: 55.4/55.2 inches

Popular Options

Three-speed automatic transmission
California emissions system
Carpeted floor mat
Cruise control
Deck-Lid luggage rack
Door-edge guards
Engine block heater
Heavy-duty battery
Heavy-duty radiator
High-Altitude emissions package
Lighted-visor vanity mirror
Power door locks
Power windows
Power seats, 6-way driver and passenger
AM/FM stereo radio with cassette tape player and extended range-rear speakers
Electric remote deck-lid release
Tilt steering column
Trunk mat
Vista-vent removable sunroof
White stripe tires

1982

Best of All, It's a Cadillac

FOR EIGHTY YEARS, Americans have trusted Cadillac to lead the way. And their confidence has been rewarded. The first American production car with a V-8 engine. The first V-16. The first Diesel V-8 as standard equipment. And now another first: the remarkable new HT-4100 power system.'' That's the way Cadillac introduced an era of small V-8 engines to its clientele.

NEW V-8 ENGINE

This new V-8 engine, standard in all models except for the four-cylinder Cimarron and Fleetwood Limousines, which continued to use the V-8-6-4 engine, had a 3.46-inch bore and 3.31-inch stroke, resulting in a displacement of 249 cubic inches. Just six years earlier, Cadillacs had been equipped with 500-cubic-inch V-8s! Anyone who suggested GM in general or Cadillac in particular didn't change with the times were themselves out of touch with reality.

Not only was this engine the smallest American-made V-8, but it was also the first domestic powerplant since the Vega to use an aluminum cylinder block. Cadillac put plenty of design distance between its V-8 and that four-cylinder Chevrolet engine. Aside from the obvious differences, only the outer case of the Cadillac engine was aluminum. All the working surfaces were manufactured of iron. Unlike the Vega's high-silicon 390 alloy block, the Cadillac's iron liners were relatively easy to manufacture and provided excellent heat transfer. The cylinder block, which weighed a mere 42 pounds, was die cast (rather than the usual sand cast) of aluminum alloy 380 at General Motors' Central Foundry facility in Bedford, Indiana, which had the capacity to produce 1,400 engines daily. Contributing significantly to the cylinder head's low weight was the design of the aluminum intake manifold, which was carried deep into the cylinder head, and the use of a separate aluminum, rocker-arm support structure.

This was by no means a revolutionary design, but a number of interesting features were apparent. Certainly a good starting point was the combination of lightweight construction and good fuel economy with the inherent smoothness of a V-8. Among the features enhancing these attributes were fast-burn (physically midway between a wedge and hemi-shape) combustion chambers, integrated emissions systems designed around digital, electronic, throttle-body fuel injection (DFI) and closed-loop controls.

The DFI system was equipped with an electronic control module (ECM), a digital microprocessor that controlled the electronic spark timing, fuel metering, and idle speed. The DFI had a built-in compensation capability for variations in attitude, temperature, and accessory load.

A significant feature of the DFI was its ability to perform a number of diagnostic functions since the ECM constantly monitored the engine control system, engine sensors, and activators. Included in the information delivered to the ECM was manifold pressure, ambient barometric pressure, engine coolant temperature, air/fuel mixture temperature, engine speed, throttle position, exhaust gas oxygen, and vehicle speed. Malfunctions, even if temporary, were memorized, and the driver was alerted by way of a ''check-engine'' light on the instrument panel. This system also substituted backup system valves for malfunctioning sensors to keep the car running until needed repairs could be made.

It was possible for a Cadillac service technician to ''interrogate'' the ECM and receive diagnostic information on an instrument-panel digital display. The system could also verify the accuracy of the repair.

In production, the Cadillac V-8 had a low scrap rate and minimal losses in machinery since the initial casting weight was only 60 pounds. By using iron cylinder liners, any defect (each liner was monitored during its machining) involved the scrapping of only that liner rather than the entire cylinder block.

The cylinder heads were also of cast iron and were of a very compact design, while still having deep skirts for crankcase rigidity. The aluminum intake manifold extended well into the head and included most of the intake port area. The use of separate, aluminum rocker-arm supports made the use of separate valve-seat inserts and guides unnecessary. Other key components constructed of aluminum included the pistons and the water and oil pumps.

Compared with the 5.7-liter diesel V-8, the 4.1-liter Cadillac weighed 353 pounds less. Matched against Cadillac's 368-cubic-inch V-8, its weight advantage was 209 pounds. But this was a small displacement engine and that translated into a dramatically reduced power output. The HT-4100 developed 125 horsepower at 4,200 rpm and 190 ft-lb of torque at 2,000 rpm. These were respectively 15 horsepower and 70 lb-ft less than the ratings of the 368-cubic-inch V-8.

Cadillac maintained that drivers were more concerned about low speed (0 to 15 mph) acceleration than the traditional 0 to 60-mph mark. Toward this end, the transmission and final drive ratios were altered to maximize the use of the engine's limited output. Nonetheless, the sensation of modern-day Cadillacs accelerating from 0 to 60 mph in 15 seconds did take some getting used to unless a driver was switching over from a diesel-powered car.

Production of these V-8s began in July 1981 at Cadillac's new engine plant in Livonia, Michigan. Located on a 38.6-acre site with 857,000 square feet of space, the plant, working at full capacity, could produce 1,400 engines daily.

Cadillac claimed that one of the "most thorough engine testing systems in North America" ensured the high quality and reliability of these new engines. Examples of advanced technology found on Livonia's 17 machine- and component-assembly and test lines were numerous.

The result was significantly increased productivity, improved quality, and less damage to precision parts during manufacture and assembly. On machinery lines, a technique identified as "in-process" gauging involved the use of automatic gauging stations that determined if critical dimensions were being met in machinery parts. This equipment had the ability to automatically accept or reject the parts.

In addition, many machines, through "automatic tool compensation," produced parts to specific dimensions, holding tolerances within set limits. If the machine began to exceed these limits, it automatically readjusted the tools to the established specifications. Throughout the plant, tool changes were scheduled according to the wear rates.

Common to all major machining and assembly lines were numerous applications of automatic processes. On the engine assembly line, the crankshaft, for example, was automatically inserted by a machine into the engine block. Later, at another station, the crankshaft and piston/rod assembly were automatically tested to proper rotating torque. Crankshaft insertion was also automatic.

Controlling bolt tightening of such components as the main-bearing caps, oil pan, cylinder heads, intake manifold, and valve train were torque-sensing units. If any bolt wasn't tightened according to specifications, the pallet carrying the engine was automatically flagged

and routed to a repair area. The particular torque control unit discovering the discrepancy placed a reader card on the block that told the repair person exactly which bolt or bolts were not properly torqued.

To set timing, each engine was "cold motored" without fuel. This process eliminated variations in engine timing. When completed, all engines were routed to one of 14 stations where they underwent computer-controlled testing of various engine functions. These tests included running torque, breakaway torque, thermostat opening, water temperature, intake vacuum, fuel inlet pressure, timing, and oil pressure. This process began when the completed engines were lowered (automatically, of course) onto work pallets. Each pallet was labeled with a code number on a magnetic strip. This information was transmitted by an automatic reader to one of the hot-test computers, which automatically established the test limits for each engine. A second scanner read bar codes that identified the engine model type and serial number. This information also went to the computer.

Prior to the start of the engine check, the integrity of the test-stand electronics were checked to ensure valid results. The engines were first pressurized to check for oil and water leaks. If any were found, the engine was automatically routed to the repair area.

Before fuel was added, the engine was externally motored and checked for oil pressure, turnover torques, and timing. The engine was then started and subjected to drive and load conditions in simulated in-car operation. Next followed a series of rpm tests ranging from 1,000 to 3,000 rpm. Among the items tested were exhaust pressure, crankcase pressure per cylinder, intake vacuum, and individual cylinder performance. After final computer testing of timing and oil pressure plus another leak check, an employee examined the engine for oil leaks and excessive noise. If any problems were detected, that information could be entered into the computer from a control panel.

When the engine passed all tests, it was automatically routed to final shipment. If the computer found the engine failed one or more of its tests, it was sent to one of five light-repair stands. Any engine requiring major repairs was taken out of the hot-test area. Following corrections, the engine was once again sent through the complete hot-test cycle.

The computers used in this operation could store up to 20,000 engine records at any time. Beyond that level, all records were stored permanently on either magnetic tape or disc. This made it possible for the assembly plant, dealer, or service department to have access to an engine's history whenever needed.

Potentially equal in importance to Cadillac's ability to meet its foreign and domestic competition of the 1980s was what Cadillac called "The Livonia Opportunity." This team approach to plant operation was developed by a joint, 12-member, Cadillac-United Automobile Workers Local 22 planning committee. Under this system, production teams of approximately 15 employees were formed from assembly, machining, on-line inspection, material handling, cleaning, and resident skilled trades. Each team, formed according to product line or major function, met at least one hour weekly to work on problem solving or to improve product quality.

Leading the group was the team coordinator (a Cadillac supervisor) and an assistant team coordinator who was an hourly employee. To facilitate the team's operation, all employees were given training in a problem solving/decision-making process. Each team was expected to meet plant production goals, maintain quality control systems, perform preventive maintenance, maintain good housekeeping and safety practices, and counsel other teams when necessary.

At the Livonia plant, all traditional nonskilled job classifications were incorporated in a single, "Quality Operator" unit. At the same time a "pay-by-knowledge" policy was adopted. Under this system, as an employee learned more jobs on the team, his or her pay level increased over the base rate.

Facilitating these plans was a selection process for team coordinators involving both union representatives and quality operators. Team coordinators received two weeks' training in team problem solving and decision making, as well as a course in teaching these methods to team members. In addition, all quality operators received a week of analytical trouble-shooting training that included the complete tear-down and rebuilding of an engine.

A key element in the success of this approach to industrial management and plant operation was the maintaining of an atmosphere of openness and trust. Efforts toward this end included expanded meetings between and among various groups, articles in union and divisional publications, and feedback to the teams on relevant performance variables. Certainly not the least important change at Livonia was the elimination of traditional salaried/hourly distinctions in areas such as cafeterias, locker rooms, parking lots, and dress codes.

OTHER CHANGES AND IMPROVEMENTS

Linked to the HT-4100 V-8 was a new four-speed overdrive, Turbo Hydra-Matic 325-4L transmission. With a lockup torque converter for the top two gears, this smooth-operating transmission contributed to the Cadillac's improved 18-mpg city and 26-mpg highway EPA fuel ratings by reducing engine rpms by 33 percent at cruising speeds.

Also contributing to this improved fuel economy, as well as reducing shifting between gears as road conditions changed, were new shift points and clutched, torque-converter engagement modes. For example, on all cars except for California Eldorados and Sevilles, the third to fourth gear shift was made at 24 mph, while the converter engaged the fourth gear only at speeds of 48 mph or greater. Making the latter operation less apparent to the Cadillac's driver and occupants was inclusion of a "poppet valve" release in the converter.

Also introduced with the HT-4100 V-8 were new engine/transmission mounts designed to isolate engine noise and improve idle quality plus rigid engine accessory mounts. All HT-4100 engined Cadillacs also used a new, more compact power steering pump and fluid reservoir.

Standard on all Cadillacs with the HT-4100 engine was a Fuel Data Panel providing drivers with the capability to "call up" pertinent fuel economy information at the touch of a button. For example, instantaneous miles-per-gallon readouts, to the nearest mile per gallon, were displayed by pushing the "Instant/Average" button on the panel keyboard. Average miles per gallon, accurate to $1/10$ mpg, were called up by pushing this button a second time.

In a similar fashion, one push of the "Range/Fuel Used" button reported the fuel range, while a second push displayed the amount of fuel consumed. The anticipated fuel range reflected the number of miles or kilometers (Cadillacs for export displayed a liters-per-100 kilometers figure) that could be expected with the fuel remaining in the tank based on average miles per gallon over the last 25 miles or 40 kilometers.

If the Fuel Data Panel "Reset" button was pushed while either average mpg or fuel used was being displayed, computation of those two items was retained in the computer memory until the "Reset" was pushed again.

Most likely, the participants in this fuel economy test would notice the Cadillac's softer ride for 1982, which was accomplished by revising the front springs and body mounts on the De Ville and Fleetwood Brougham models.

DIFFERENCES AMONG MODELS

Available as a "Credit Option" for the Fleetwood Brougham, De Villes, Eldorado, and Seville was the 4.1-liter V-6 engine. "If you're looking for a car with the comfort, ride, roominess and quality of a Cadillac, combined with the advantages of V-6 power," said Cadillac, "this is an excellent choice." All V-6 Cadillacs had standard four-speed, automatic overdrive transmissions. Diesel Cadillac customers could select either a four-speed overdrive or a three-speed automatic transmission.

On all 1982 Cadillacs except the Cimarron and Fleetwood Limousine, the electronic climate control panel displayed, on demand, the outside temperature. All Cadillacs used new premium, extended-range rear speakers with heavy ceramic magnets for increased power-handling capacity and dual-cone construction for extended frequency response.

After first being offered on the 1981 Eldorado and Seville, Cadillac's "iso-mount" electronically powered antenna was now standard on the 1982 De Ville, Fleetwood, Brougham, and Fleetwood Limousine. This antenna used a rubber-isolated motor and mechanical drive mechanism to isolate what Cadillac depicted as "undesirable antenna extension and retraction noise" from the interior.

Yet another feature, a fluidic windshield washer system provided full-coverage spray on the windshield viewing area. First introduced on the 1981 Eldorado and Seville, it was installed on all new De Villes, Fleetwood Broughams, and Limousines.

1982 Seville Elegante. New bumper stripes were found on the latest Sevilles. Added to its option list was a remote lockable fuel filler door.

The 1982 Eldorado Touring Coupe had many distinguishing external features, including body-colored headlight and taillight bezels and black-finished windshield reveal moldings.

The 1982 Eldorado Biarritz continued to feature a cabriolet roof, stainless steel roof cap, wide bright moldings, and opera lights as standard equipment. Common to all Eldorados was a new multicolored Cadillac crest ornamentation on the tail lamp lenses.

1982 Sedan de Ville. All De Villes had new black bumper rub strips with white center sections. Also evident was a center hood molding.

1982 Sedan de Ville. The latest De Ville and Brougham models had new rear ornamentation for the tail lamps.

1982 Coupe de Ville. All 1982 rear-drive models had revised front grille work with a vertical accent for 1982.

The 1982 Fleetwood Brougham Sedan retained its closed-in rear window design.

1982 Fleetwood Brougham Coupe d' Elegance.

On the other hand, the latest Eldorados and Fleetwood Broughams were equipped with the low-drag, front disc brakes introduced a year earlier on the De Ville and Fleetwood Brougham. For 1982, the front-brake calipers were modified to allow the linings to retract further, thus decreasing rubbing action against the rotors and providing for improved fuel economy.

Among the numerous detail changes for 1982 was an optional, remote-locking, fuel filler door for all models except the Cimarron. For the De Ville models, a "tone" generator replaced the warning buzzer for key-in-ignition alert. Added to the Eldorado and Seville option list were all-season puncture-seating tires. These could not be ordered for the Touring Coupe or any car with the Touring Suspension package.

Understandably, in light of these major technical

A 1982 Sedan de Ville equipped with the new standard wheelcovers for 1982.

The new 4.1 liter V-8 introduced for 1982.

developments, styling changes for 1982 were extremely limited. All models, except for the Seville and Cimarron, had a new grille with twin horizontal dividers. The grille was flanked by flush-mounted lights and modules with the parking/directional lights located directly under the headlights. De Villes were also fitted with a new hood-center molding, black bumper rub strips with white center stripes, and taillight lenses featuring horizontal dividers and traditional winged Cadillac crests.

Standard interior for the Coupe and Sedan de Ville consisted of Heather knit cloth with matching Dundee ribbed-cloth inserts. Five colors were available: slate gray, dark redwood, dark gray blue, saddle tan, and dark brownstone. Seats with leather seating areas were optional in eight colors.

Both De Villes could be ordered with the d'Elegance option consisting of pillow-style seats in Venetian velour. They were available in all standard De Ville interior colors except for dark redwood. Also included in this package were 50/50 Dual Comfort front seats, deluxe carpeting and floor mats, altered trim design (three roof-mounted assist straps were added to the Sedan's interior), and exterior accent striping and opera lamps. All De Villes, Fleetwood Broughams, and Limousines used the basic 1981 instrument-panel design.

Fleetwood Brougham Coupe and Sedan models carried the usual Fleetwood details, such as a stand-up hood wreath and crest ornament, body identification, accent striping, bright belt molding, and larger rocker-panel trim. The Coupe had a standard Cabriolet roof with electroluminescent opera lamps, which was a $398 option for the Coupe de Ville, while the Sedan had a full-length vinyl roof that was also available for the Sedan de Ville.

Fleetwood interiors featured seats with an exclusive Heather knit with patterned Raphael-cloth inserts in five colors or eight optional leather-upholstery choices. A Cadillac wreath was embroidered on the center armrest along with embroidered "Fleetwood" script on each door-trim panel.

Cadillac extended the scope of the Brougham d'Elegance option for 1982, which was available in either cloth or leather in any interior color offered on the Fleetwood Brougham. The 50/50 Dual Comfort front seats were standard, along with special interior-trim design and deluxe carpeting and floormats. Exterior identification consisted of wheel covers incorporating a matching body color and script identification.

With prices of $18,567 (Sedan) and $18,096 (Coupe), the Fleetwoods were priced approximately $2,800 above the $15,699 De Ville Sedan and $15,249 Coupe. In addition to the already mentioned items, the Fleetwood Brougham's prices included an Illuminated Entry System, which, when the front door handle was pushed, illuminated the keyhole and turned on the interior courtesy lights. The Fleetwoods also featured Twilight Sentinel, Dual Comfort 55/45 front seats (including a six-way, driver and passenger, power seat adjuster and a manual, passenger seat-back recliner), tilt and telescope steering wheel, controlled-cycle wipers, adjustable rear-seat reading lamps, and a remote trunk-lid release and power pulldown system.

Identification of a 1982 Seville was via the HT-4100 engine emblems found on the front fenders of all Cadillacs with this V-8 and gray, rather than black as

CADILLAC VITAL STATISTICS: 1982

Series	Model	Body Type	Sug. Retail Price ($)	Weight (lbs.)	Production (#)
Cimarron	G69	4 dr Sedan	12,131	2524	25,968*
Seville	S69	4 dr Sedan	23,433(A)	3731	23,098†
De Ville	D69	4 dr Sedan	15,699	3839	53,870
	D47	2 dr Coupe	15,249	3783	44,950
Eldorado	L57	2 dr Coupe	18,716(B,C)	3615	66,933‡
Fleetwood Brougham	B69	4 dr Sedan	18,567	3866	32,150
	B47	2 dr Coupe	18,096	3825	5180
Limousine	F23	4 dr Sedan	28,003	4628	514
	F33	4 dr Formal Sedan	28,983	4718	486

A - Seville Elegante $27,312
B - Eldorado Biarritz $22,111
C - Eldorado Touring Coupe $20,691

*Includes 3,877 Cimarrons with four-speed manual transmission
†Includes 3,100 Seville Elegantes
‡Includes 14,915 Eldorado Biarritzes

4.1 LITER 90° V-8
MAJOR COMPONENTS

ROCKER ARM COVER
CHROME PLATED STEEL

EXHAUST MANIFOLD
CAST IRON

CYLINDER HEAD
CAST IRON

CYLINDER
DOUBLE-HONED
CAST IRON

PISTON
CAST ALUMINUM
WITH LOW TENSION
RING ASSEMBLY

CRANKSHAFT
AUTOMATICALLY BALANCED
NODULAR IRON

OIL PAN
ZINC-PLATED STEEL

THROTTLE BODY
FUEL INJECTION UNIT
WITH IDLE SPEED CONTROL

INTAKE MANIFOLD
CAST ALUMINUM

CRANKCASE
DIE-CAST
ALUMINUM

BEARING
STEEL-BACKED
ALUMINUM

MAIN BEARING CAP
CAST IRON

FRONT COVER
ALUMINIZED STEEL

COOLANT PUMP
DIE-CAST ALUMINUM
WITH HIGH-EFFICIENCY
IMPELLER

Major components of the HT 4100 engine.

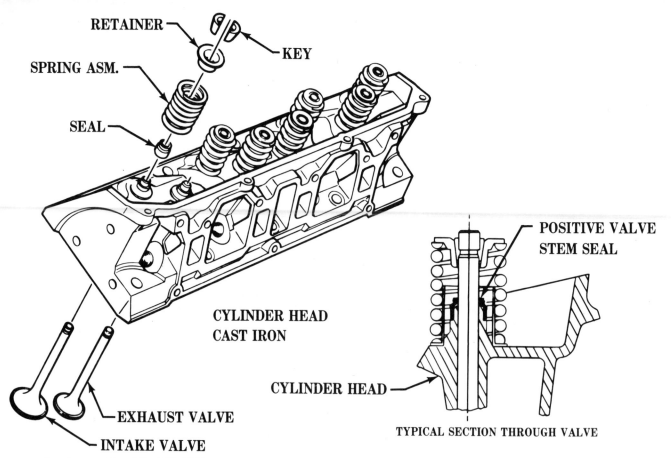

RETAINER

KEY

SPRING ASM.

SEAL

POSITIVE VALVE
STEM SEAL

CYLINDER HEAD
CAST IRON

CYLINDER HEAD

EXHAUST VALVE

INTAKE VALVE

TYPICAL SECTION THROUGH VALVE

Cylinder head assembly of the HT 4100 engine.

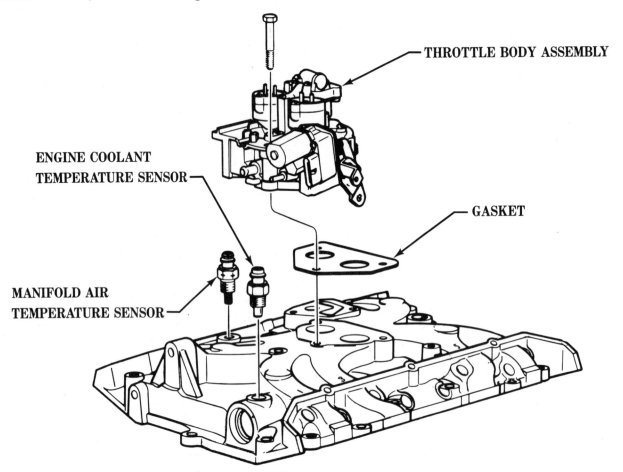

THROTTLE BODY ASSEMBLY

ENGINE COOLANT
TEMPERATURE SENSOR

GASKET

MANIFOLD AIR
TEMPERATURE SENSOR

Fuel injection and intake manifold details of the HT 4100 V-8.

in 1981, bumper moldings. Like all Cadillac models except for the Cimarron and Fleetwood Limousines, the Seville was also available with the 5.7-liter diesel V-8 or 4.0-liter V-6.

All diesel-powered Cadillacs continued to use a water-separation unit and a water-in-fuel detection system. Also carried over was a diesel–fuel-line heater introduced during the 1981 model year. It was operational when the ignition was on and the under-hood temperature was 20 degrees Fahrenheit or less. A new feature for the V-6 engine was a warm-engine, idle speed control that compensated for accessory-load variations.

Interiors of the $23,433 Seville were offered in Heather cloth in the same five colors as in the other series. Eight colors of leather were available for the stitched seating areas.

Priced $3,095 above the Seville was the Seville Elegante whose two-tone body finish (available in Sheffield gray firemist/sable black, desert dusk firemist/brownstone, or red cedar firemist/Colorado copper) was divided by a sweeping two-tone French curve. Additional exterior identification was provided by burnished and bright side moldings, accent striping, and Elegante script on the sail panels.

The Elegante interior featured tucked-leather seating areas in three Sierra-grain colors, a complementary leather-trimmed steering wheel (optional for the base Seville), deluxe Tampico carpeting and floor mats, and a leather-topped front console. The Elegante's individual front seats were separated by a center console with an integrated folddown armrest, two removable storage compartments, coin holder, and courtesy lights. For 1982, the Seville was equipped with new 45/50 split front seats. The Elegante continued to use a 40/40 split front-seat arrangement.

Midway through the model year, Cadillac offered a $398 Cabriolet option for the Seville, which simulated the appearance of a Convertible top. Thus it featured padded roof bows and a top rear-seam cover in four colors.

Standard equipment for all Sevilles included electronic level control, Twilight Sentinel, Dual Comfort front seats, controlled-cycle wipers, rear-window defoggers, adjustable rear-seat reading lamps, exterior accent striping and molding, wire-wheelcovers or aluminum-alloy wheels, remote-control lid release, and power pulldown and spare-tire cover.

In the twilight of their model cycle, Cadillac's Fleetwood eight-passenger Limousine and seven-passenger Formal Limousines were imposing vehicles priced at $28,003 and $28,983, respectively. These were the only 1982 Cadillacs to use the 6.0-liter, V-8-6-4 modulated displacement engine.

Robots were used for difficult or repetitive material handling activities at the Cadillac Livonia plant.

As in previous years, both versions had two folddown, rear-compartment auxiliary seats with a sliding glass partition installed on the Formal model. The front seats of the Limousine were finished in Heather cloth in either black or dark gray. On the formal Limousine, the front seat was black with leather in the seating areas.

Exterior revisions to the front-wheel-drive Eldorado consisted of a vertically accented grille, multicolored Cadillac crest ornamentation on the taillight lenses, and black bumper rub stripes with a white center stripe.

Standard Eldorado interiors were in the five-color, Heather ribbed-cloth/Dundee cloth bolster format with Cadillac wreaths embroidered into the seat back. Optional leather was available in eight colors.

The Eldorado Biarritz, tagged at an additional $3,335, was, with considerable justification, described by Cadillac as "the ultimate 'dream machine'." Its standard interior featured leather seats in five colors, a leather-trimmed steering wheel, Tampico carpeting, and rear-quarter reading lamps. Both the base Eldorado and the Biarritz featured new 45/50 split front seating. All Eldorado instrument panels were trimmed in simulated teak woodgrain with a center display of the Fuel Data Panel, Electronic Climate Control, and Electronically Tuned Radio readouts.

Unchanged from 1981, was the Biarritz's custom Cabriolet vinyl roof with a brushed, stainless forward section, wire-wheel discs, opera lights, Biarritz sail-panel script and wide bright moldings.

Appeal of a completely different form was found in a new Cadillac model for 1982, the Eldorado Touring Coupe. Cadillac, depicting the Special Edition as "created for the person who loves to drive," gave it a grand send-off: "The leather-wrapped steering wheel tightens under your grip as you turn toward the sky. Wide blackwall tires grip the pavement. And for a fleeting moment, you, the road and your Eldorado become one." This sort of prose, cast more in the mold of Ned Jordan's "Somewhere West of Laramie" style rather than Cadillac's "Penalty of Leadership" format was apropos for a Cadillac that, in many respects, was one of the most important of its postwar models.

Two years earlier, in February 1980, Cadillac had introduced a sports handling package for both the Eldorado and Seville, consisting of higher-rate front and rear springs, front and rear antiroll bars with diameters of 0.32 mm and 0.24 mm, respectively, and stiffer front shock absorbers. Although this didn't arouse a great deal of public attention, it marked the beginning of an energetic effort by Cadillac engineering for the expansion of the Eldorado line to include a special sports

Computers were used to monitor many operations at the Cadillac Livonia plant. Shown is William T. Lesner, assistant superintendent of production, reviewing the status of the engine block line.

model. An after-market facsimile of what these engineers had in mind appeared as the Penske/RS, which Roger Penske's Downer, California, Cadillac dealership offered for $950 above the price of a fully equipped (including Sport Suspension) model. This handsome machine had a distinctive grille with vertical bars, genuine wire wheels, and Goodyear Sixty-Series NCT tires. Cadillac had long ago abandoned its "King of Chrome" mentality, but most of which was installed on the 1980 Eldorado was either removed or blacked out by Penske.

The appearance of the 1982 Eldorado Touring Coupe, which retailed for $1,950 above the normal Coupe's price, was equally startling. Virtually all brightwork was body-colored or finished in black. Specifically, the windshield reveal, quarter-window channel moldings, and windshield wipers were black-finished. The headlight and taillight bezels were body-colored and solid-black bumper rub strips were installed. The lower body trim remained, but it now had a purposeful ribbed gray surface. Initially, only a sterling silver finish with red over black accent striping was offered. Later in the season, a black body color was added.

Mounted on the aluminum alloy wheels available on all Eldorados and Sevilles were, in place of the standard Seventy-Five Series tires, Goodyear blackwall P225/70R15, steel-belted radial tires. The wheels and tires were match-mounted for rolling smoothness. In lieu of the stand-up crest and wreath found on other Eldorados was a circular cloisonne hood ornament suggestive of those found years earlier on the rear deck of the Jaguar XK 150. It carried a Cadillac crest embraced by lettering reading "Eldorado Touring Coupe."

Additional components of the Touring Suspension, which was also offered for any Eldorado and Seville, included a 32-mm-diameter front stabilizer bar, in place of the standard 30-mm model. The rear unit was enlarged 18 percent to 24 mm. The front suspension bushings were 16 percent stiffer. Joining shock absorbers with increased shock absorber valving were 18 percent stiffer front torsion bars and rear springs with a 14 percent higher rate. The power steering provided the same quick, 2.9 turns lock-to-lock response as on the standard Eldorado, but with 20 percent greater steering effort for increased feedback to the driver.

A Touring Suspension plaque on the instrument

Use of automatic torque monitoring controls, such as this unit tightening cylinder heads to the engine block, reduced variations between assemblies of the HT-4100 engine.

panel was a nice touch, but more important as far as getting Cadillac's point across was the replacement of the normal Eldorado split bench seat with a set of reclining bucket seats usually found in the Cimarron. The net result, with one exception, was a competent sports tourer that intruded into the traditional genre of BMW, Mercedes-Benz, and Jaguar. The shortcoming was its engine's limited power output. The TC Eldorado weighed in at over 3,800 pounds, which translated into a weight-per-horsepower ratio of 30.4:1. What was needed was a dose of classic Cadillac V-8 power or a turbocharger such as Pontiac had earlier adopted for its Firebird.

While not intended for the same type of roadwork as the Touring Suspension, Cadillac did offer a heavy-duty package for the Fleetwood Brougham and De Villes. It provided, said Cadillac, ''added ride firmness when driving on rough roads—whether they be in the city or country.'' Primary components consisted of electronic level control, larger-diameter rear stabilizer bar, heavy-duty shock absorbers, increased spring rates, and steering damper.

Having been originally introduced as a 1982 model earlier in the year, the Cimarron was left all but unchanged. The sole new feature was a full-width rear seat with a folddown center armrest and front–seat-back pockets. Three new options offered for the Cimarron were the power Astroroof, Twilight Sentinel system, and electronically tuned radio.

The Cimarron's nine exterior color selections included sable black, cotillion white, sterling silver (light-silver metallic), superior blue (medium-blue metallic), arroyo tan (medium tan), autumn amber (medium amber metallic), garnet (medium-red metallic), Columbian brown (dark-brown metallic), and charcoal (dark-gray metallic).

All other Cadillacs were available in 11 standard paints of which only sable white, cotillion white, and sterling silver were shared with the Cimarron. The additional colors were almond (light tan), brownstone (medium-brown metallic), Colorado copper (medium-copper metallic), redwood (dark-red metallic), slate gray (light gray), colonial yellow (light yellow), steel blue (light-blue metallic), and twilight blue (dark-blue metallic).

Cadillac's optional Firemist paint was available in seven colors, one of which, autumn maple (dark-red metallic) was available only for the Seville and Eldorado. The remaining Firemist colors were desert dusk (light-brown metallic), jade gray (medium-green metallic), Nugget (light-gold metallic), red cedar (light-copper metallic), azure blue (light-blue metallic) and Sheffield gray (medium-gray metallic).

In addition, De Villes were available in four optional, two-tone paint combinations; Eldorados in five; and Sevilles in seven, two-tone combinations. The Seville Elegante was offered in the previously identified choice of three exclusive, two-tone paint combinations.

One of the 14 hot-test stands at Cadillac Livonia.

Although Cadillac abandoned the 5.7-liter diesel engine as the Seville's standard engine for 1982, it still, as has been noted, offered diesels for all models except Fleetwood Limousines and the Eldorado Touring Coupe. Cadillac answered its own question: "Why a Diesel Cadillac?" by responding: "Very simply, it's the only way to get Cadillac roominess, Cadillac comfort, that Cadillac ride and impressive fuel economy all in the same automobile."

In terms of their miserly fuel consumption, the diesel Cadillacs were excellent performers. All were credited with at least a 20 EPA estimated mpg and 33 highway mpg ratings. Cadillac reported that an owner of a diesel Eldorado who drove 15,000 miles annually would save $420 in fuel costs compared with a 1981 Eldorado with the standard gasoline engine.

Although Cadillac cited resale value as "the last reason for buying a diesel Cadillac," it noted that a 1980 diesel Eldorado or diesel Seville was, according to the September 1982 *NADA Used Car Guide*, worth an average of $200 more than a comparable gas-powered model. When diesel Fleetwood Broughams and De Villes were compared with their gasoline-engined counterparts, their resale advantage was seen to be $750.

This was an impressive economic argument in favor of an engine option priced at $351. This did not, however, make it a persuasive one. For example, in 1980 when the Seville's standard engine was the 5.7-liter diesel, 36.8 percent were so equipped, an impressive jump from the 20.1-percent level of 1979. The next year, the diesel's share of Seville output dropped to 25.4 percent. In 1982, with the diesel relegated to option status, only 11.9 percent were diesel equipped.

CADILLAC'S DOMESTIC COMPETITION

The focal point of the Cadillac-Lincoln confrontation was in the Seville-Continental arena in 1982. The Continental was downsized in wheelbase from 114 to 108.7 inches, which reduced its overall length to 201.1 inches. Compared with the Seville, the Continental's wheelbase was 5.5 inches shorter; while in overall length, the Cadillac was just 3.6 inches longer. The Continental was offered only as a four-door Sedan and was based on the Ford Fairmont/Mercury Zephyr platform. Suspension consisted of a modified MacPherson strut, coil-spring front system with a four-

Automated parts storage was a key feature of the Cadillac Livonia plant. This unit holds bore liners ready for additional processing.

link, coil-spring arrangement at the rear.

Carried over from 1981 was the Continental's 302-cubic-inch V-8, which was also found in other Ford products. Despite its humble origins, this V-8, with 131 horsepower at 3,400 rpm and 220 lb-ft of torque, in union with the standard, four-speed automatic overdrive, enabled the 3,700-pound Continental to easily outperform the slightly heavier Seville. The Cadillac's small V-8 was just giving away too many cubic inches to the Lincoln. From 0 to 60 mph, the Continental needed just a bit over 12 seconds, whereas the Seville required approximately 15 seconds.

Like the Seville, the Continental was available with a V-6 engine, a 231-cubic-inch unit also used for the Thunderbird, Cougar, XR-7, and Granada. Its ratings were 120 horsepower at 3,800 rpm and 190 lb-ft of torque at 2,400 rpm. Continentals with this engine virtually matched the Seville's 0 to 60-mph time; but in both highway speed passing ability and quarter-mile acceleration, the Seville was the quicker car.

A far more startling similarity was found in the appearance of the two cars. There was no reason to doubt Lincoln's claim that the Continental's design had been finalized long before the 1982 Seville debuted. Nonetheless, Cadillac, by virtue of being first with its rear-deck format, enjoyed the advantage of having the Continental being regarded as more a follower than an innovator.

Sales of the 1982 Lincolns rebounded strongly from the low point of 1981, totaling 93,068. Of these, 22,430 were Continentals and 27,844 were Mark II models.

Chrysler's reborn Imperial, carried over virtually intact from 1981, except for a price boost to $20,988 from $19,491, had sales of just 2,601 units.

Cadillac remained far and away the nation's best-selling luxury car with a volume of 249,295, up 18,030 from 1981. Of this total, 154,229 were De Ville and Fleetwood models. Rounding out the Cadillac sales picture were 57,263 Eldorados, 24,229 Sevilles, and 13,774 Cimarrons.

SPECIFICATIONS

Engine

Standard: De Villes, Fleetwood Broughams, Sevilles, Eldorado

Type: V-8, ohv, aluminum block
Bore × stroke: 3.47 × 3.31 inches
Displacement: 249 cubic inches
Horsepower: 125 @ 4,200 rpm
Torque: 200 ft-lb @ 2,200 rpm
Compression ratio: 8.5:1
Fuel system: Digital Fuel Injection

Credit Option: De Villes, Fleetwood Broughams

Type: V-6, ohv, diesel

Employee training in process at Cadillac Livonia. These workers are involved in a complete tearing down and rebuilding of an engine.

Bore × stroke: 3.965 × 3.4 inches
Displacement: 252 cubic inches
Horsepower: 125 @ 3,800 rpm

Standard: Fleetwood Limousines

Type: V-8-6-4
Bore × stroke: 3.8 × 4.06 inches
Displacement: 368 cubic inches
Horsepower: 140 @ 3,800 rpm
Torque: 265 lb-ft @ 1,400 rpm
Compression ratio: 8.2:1
Fuel system: Digital Fuel Injection

Optional: All Models
(except Fleetwood Limousines, Cimarron, Eldorado Touring Coupe

Type: V-8, ohv, diesel
Bore × stroke: 4.057 × 3.385 inches
Displacement: 350 cubic inches
Horsepower: 105 @ 3,200 rpm
Torque: 205 ft-lb @ 1,600 rpm
Compression ratio: 22.5:1
Fuel system: Fuel injection

Standard: Cimarron

Type: L-4, ohv
Bore × stroke: 3.5 × 2.9 inches
Displacement: 112.4 cubic inches
Horsepower: 88 @ 5,100 rpm
Torque: 100 ft-lb @ 2,800 rpm
Compression ratio: 9.0:1
Fuel system: Rochester Varajet, two-barrel carburetor

Chassis/Drivetrain

Front suspension (rear-drive models): Independent coil, link-type stabilizer bar, hydraulic, direct-action shock absorbers
Rear suspension (rear-drive models): Four-link coil springs, direct-action shock absorbers
Eldorado and Seville: Independent trailing arms, coil springs, hydraulic, direct-action shock absorbers, electronic level control
Cimarron: Front suspension: Independent, Mac-Pherson struts, coil springs, tubular shocks, stabilizer bar; Rear suspension: semiindependent, trailing arms, coil springs, vertical shock absorbers, stabilizer bar
Steering: Variable-ratio power steering
Rear suspension (rear-drive models): Four-link coil springs, direct-action shock absorbers
Overall steering ratios:
  De Villes, Fleetwood Broughams: 17-15:1
  Fleetwood Limousines: 20.0-20.6:1
  Eldorado: 14:1
  Seville: 15-13:1
  Cimarron: rack and pinion, 14:1
Electrical system: 12-volt, Delco Remy F-18, Freedom II battery
  Diesels: two Delco Remy F-20, Freedom II batteries, 80-amp generator, (70 amp: V-6 engine)
Transmission:

De Ville, Fleetwood Brougham models with HT-4100 V-8 or V-6: four-speed automatic with overdrive and clutched torque converter
De Ville, Fleetwood Brougham with diesel: four-speed automatic with overdrive (or available three-speed) and clutched torque converter
Fleetwood Limousine: three-speed automatic
Cimarron: four-speed manual
Tires: GM specification steel-belted radials
  De Ville, Fleetwood Brougham: wide white stripe, P215/75R15
  Limousine: HR78-15 x6JJ heavy-duty wheels
  Eldorado and Seville (except for Eldorado Touring Coupe): wide white stripe, P205/75R15
  Cimarron: Blackwall, P195/17R13

Dimensions

Wheelbase:
  De Ville, Fleetwood Brougham: 121.4 inches
  Limousine: 144.5 inches
  Eldorado, Seville: 114 inches
  Cimarron: 101.2 inches
Width:
  Coupe de Ville, Fleetwood Brougham Coupe: 75.3 inches
  All other rear-drive models: 70.6 inches
  Eldorado, Seville: 70.6 inches
  Cimarron: 65.0 inches
Front/rear tread: all rear-drive models: 61.7/60.7 inches
  Eldorado, Seville: 59.3/60.0 inches
  Cimarron: 55.4/55.2 inches
Overall length:
  De Ville, Fleetwood Brougham: 221 inches
  Limousine: 244 inches
  Eldorado: 204.5 inches
  Seville: 204.8 inches
  Cimarron: 173 inches

Popular Options

Memory seat
Remote-locking fuel filler door
Theft-deterrent system
Digital instrument cluster: Eldorado and Seville only, not available with V-6 engine
Astroroof
Leather-trimmed steering wheel
Full vinyl roof: Sedan de Ville
Electrically controlled mirrors
Rear-window defogger with heated outside mirrors
Two-tone exteriors (not available for Fleetwood Broughams, Eldorados, Biarritz)
Illuminated entry system: Standard on Fleetwood Brougham
General Motors Continuous Protection Plan
Puncture-sealing tires (not available with touring suspension)
Illuminated vanity mirrors
Dual Comfort front seats: Available for De Ville models, standard on Fleetwood Broughams, Eldorado, Seville
Power-recliner driver seat: With Dual Comfort seats only

Power-recliner passenger seat: Available with Dual Comfort seats and for De Ville notchback seats only

Opera lamps: Standard on Fleetwood Broughams, Eldorado Biarritz (not available for Seville)

Wire wheels: Available for De Villes and Fleetwood Broughams

Wire Wheelcovers: Standard on Seville

Aluminum alloy wheels: Available for Eldorados, no-cost option for Seville

Turbine-vaned wheelcovers: Available for De Villes only

Electronic cruise control

Twilight sentinel: Standard on Fleetwood Broughams, Eldorado and Seville

Limited slip differential: Available for De Villes and Fleetwood Broughams

Remote trunk-lid release and power pulldown: Standard on Fleetwood Broughams, Eldorado, Seville

Tilt and telescope steering wheel: Standard on Fleetwood Broughams

Accent body striping: Standard for Fleetwood Broughams, Eldorados and Sevilles

Electronic level control: Standard on Eldorado and Seville

Symphonic sound system: Cassette player with automatic tape reverse

Combination cassette player and built-in citizens band radio

Eight-track tape player

40-channel citizens band radio and eight-track tape player

Tri-band AM/FM/CB power antenna: Standard with CB Transceiver

Automatic door locks

Door-edge guards

Three-channel garage-door opener

Trumpet horn (not available for Seville)

Front and rear license frames: Standard on Seville

100 Amp generator: Available with HT-4100 and diesel engine

1983

What Makes a Cadillac a Cadillac?

A QUICK REVIEW of Cadillac's 1983 model lineup suggested it was a year of only minor changes. Measured by traditional standards, this assessment seemed to be correct. Yet, this was also a year when Cadillac strengthened its existing models' competitiveness by introducing numerous refinements and innovations. Moreover, in the case of the Cimarron, the changes made in its design resulted in an automobile that was shaking off the aftermath of a slow start and evolving into an extremely competent and appealing performance sedan.

CHANGES AND IMPROVEMENTS

All of Cadillac's C-body cars (the De Ville, Fleetwood Brougham, and Limousine models) featured a moderately altered front grille distinguished by the use of new, clear-lens parking/directional lights, and the relocation of Cadillac script from the top bolster to the lower left corner of the grille.

Changes to the side appearance were limited to wheelcovers with new center emblems and the use of two-color accent stripes. Still available were single-color accents.

At the rear, the 1983 models were identified by the stylized, crowned-V emblem located beneath the Cadillac script (or Fleetwood on the Broughams and Limousines).

DIFFERENCES AMONG MODELS

As in 1982, it was easy to differentiate a Brougham from a De Ville because of its reduced-size rear window (Sedans only), bright belt moldings, larger rocker-panel trim, wheelcover design (shared with the Fleetwood Limousine), and electroluminescent opera lamps.

Interiors of both the De Villes and Fleetwood Broughams were appointed in a knit fabric in a choice of five new colors. Of the 10 optional leather-trim colors offered for the De Villes, six were new. Similarly, six of the eight leather choices for the Fleetwood Broughams

were being offered for the first time. The Brougham interiors were set off by sculptured seats with the Cadillac wreath embroidered on the center armrests. An embroidered Fleetwood script was located on each door panel.

All De Villes, Fleetwood Broughams, and Limousines carried over the 1982 instrument-panel design. Its primary feature was a center control section providing both the driver and front-seat passenger easy access to the radio, electronic climate control, and Fuel Data Panel.

Also continued were the d'Elegance special edition options for both series. The De Ville d'Elegance models were highlighted by pillow-style seating, six-way power seat adjusters for the front-seat occupants, and deluxe carpeting and floor mats. Found on the Sedan were three roof-mounted, passenger-assist handles.

Broughams with d'Elegance appointments featured a tufted-seat design in either cloth or optional leather trim, special wheelcovers, interior and exterior d'Elegance script identification, and the carpeting, floor mats, and passenger-assist handles included in the De Ville package.

The standard engine for all 1983 Cadillacs, except Fleetwood Limousines and Cimarron, was the 4.1-liter, HT-4100 V-8. Its horsepower was boosted to 135 at 4,400 rpm from 125 at 4,200 rpm, while torque was increased to 200 lb-ft at 2,200 rpm from 190 lb-ft at 2,000 rpm.

The primary sources for this extra (and welcomed) power were revisions made in the engine's exhaust system. The addition of an exhaust crossover restrictor to the intake manifold gasket limited the amount of exhaust gas passing through the manifold, thus reducing manifold temperature, improving engine efficiency, and therefore increasing power output.

On De Villes and Fleetwood Broughams, the exhaust system was modified by the use of a larger-diameter kickup pipe, retuned muffler, and the addition of a resonator to reduce exhaust back pressure. This system was very similar to those used on the Eldorado and Seville.

Also contributing to both the performance and overall driveability of the 4.1-liter V-8 were transmission shift-point recalibrations, modifications to the torque converter, and revised cruise-control, third-gear acceleration rates.

No longer offered was the Buick-built, 4.1-liter V-6 engine. Still available as an option on all Cadillacs except Fleetwood Limousines and the Cimarron was

Oldsmobile's 5.7-liter diesel V-8. Its popularity (only 2.2 percent of 1983 Sevilles were diesel-powered) continued to slide, although its availability enabled Cadillac to claim it was the world's only automobile producer to offer customers a choice between a fuel-injected gasoline V-8 and a diesel V-8. The only transmission supplied for these models was the four-speed automatic. The standard engine for the Fleetwood Limousine models remained the 6.0-liter, modulated displacement V-8-6-4 with digital fuel injection.

The 1983 Cimarron was given a new front-end look thanks to a grille with strong vertical accents and standard fog lights and a lower valance panel. Also added was a circular "Cadillac Cimarron" hood emblem.

The deck lid luggage rack remained a Cimarron option. The rear deck lid identification now simply read *Cimarron*.

Exterior changes to the Eldorado were restricted to the placement of the Cadillac script in the grille's lower left corner, use of clear lens for the front parking/directional lights and a new center emblem for the standard wheelcover. A new option for the base Eldorado was the aluminum wheel with a small hubcap and exposed chrome lug nuts that was part of the Touring Coupe's equipment. Both that model and the Eldorado Biarritz were continued for 1983.

The Eldorado's fabric interior was trimmed in a ribbed-knit cloth with new minichecked cloth inserts. A choice of four colors was available. Ten optional leather/vinyl trim colors (six of which were new) were also offered for the base model. The Biarritz interior of Sierra-grain leather/vinyl design was available in six color combinations, four of which were new.

For 1983 the leather/vinyl interior of the Touring Coupe was available only in saddle tan. Exterior color choices were sable black or Sonora saddle, a medium-amber metallic Firemist color.

Production of the Seville increased substantially in 1983 to 30,430 (calendar-year sales totaled 33,522) from 19,998 in 1982. At least in part, this was due to a new marketing policy that moved much of the equipment

1983 Eldorado Biarritz. All Eldorados had a *Cadillac* script added to their grille in the upper left corner. Clear lens park and turn signals were new for 1983.

1983 Seville Elegante. For 1983, the Seville was given a grille with finer vertical accents. Cadillac script was now located in the lower left grille corner. Other changes included a tapered hood center molding and clear secondary lamp lenses.

previously standard on the Seville onto its option list. This reduced the Seville's base price from $23,433 to $21,440. Among the items no longer standard on the Seville were the heated exterior mirror, interior lighted vanity mirror, Twilight Sentinel, tilt/telescopic steering wheel, and wire-wheelcovers.

Numerous detail changes were made to the Seville's design. The grille now had finer vertical bars and a grid-mounted Cadillac script. Also apparent was a slimmer upper molding for the grille, which gave the Seville's front end a sleeker appearance. These changes, along with the clear-lensed parking/directionals contributed to the Seville's strong Cadillac family identity. Also altered was the hood center molding, which was now tapered and smaller than in 1982. For the first time, the Seville was available with the aluminum wheels previously restricted to Eldorados.

The base-Seville interior joined knit cloth to minichecked-fabric inserts in a choice of four new colors. Nine (six of which were new) leather/vinyl interiors were optional.

Seville Elegante interiors continued to be highlighted by their individual front seats, front center console with integrated folddown center armrest, front map pocket, twin individual storage compartments, spring-loaded coin holder, and courtesy lights. The Elegante's leather seating area was color-coordinated with the exterior, which was available in four two-tone paint combinations.

All Sevilles and Eldorados featured new multi-

1983 Eldorado Touring Coupe.

1983 Coupe de Ville.

1983 Sedan de Ville. Common to all De Ville, Brougham, and Fleetwood Limousines was the *Cadillac* grille script and clear-lens park and turn signal lamps.

Added to the De Ville models was a new emblem located beneath the *Cadillac* script.

function warning chimes. Warnings for the driver's seat belt, key-in ignition, and headlights-on had their own distinctive chime tones.

Both Cadillac models were offered with the full Cabriolet roof option that was, said Cadillac, "designed to capture the distinctive and sporty styling associated with classic Cadillac Convertibles." It was constructed of a "Diamond-Grain" vinyl that closely resembled the appearance of a true Convertible top.

All Cadillacs, except for the Cimarron, were available in 12 standard and six optional Firemist colors. This selection consisted of the following: sable black, Balboa blue (light-blue metallic), gray fern (medium-silver metallic), loden green (dark green-gray metallic), royal maroon (dark-red metallic), midnight blue firemist (dark-blue metallic), flaxen firemist (gold metallic), briar firemist (light-brown metallic), Sonora saddle firemist (medium-amber metallic), beech firemist (dark-amber metallic), and autumn maple firemist (medium-red metallic). All De Villes, Fleetwood

1983 Fleetwood Brougham Sedan.

The optional digital instrument panel for the Seville and Eldorado provided readings of fuel level, speed, and fuel range from English to metric.

Broughams, and Limousines were also available in a choice of 18 vinyl-roof colors, 12 dual-color accent stripe combinations, and 14 single-accent stripe colors.

For the Eldorado, there were 18 vinyl-roof colors and 12 dual-color accent stripe selections. Both the Eldorado and Seville featured 15 single accent-stripe colors. De Villes and Eldorados were also available in six optional two-tone paint combinations. The Seville offered seven optional two-tones.

The Cimarron was offered in 10 exterior colors of which the following were available for all Cadillacs: cotillion white, silver sand (silver metallic), Hatteras blue (medium-blue metallic), cameo ivory (light yellow), woodland haze (light-tan metallic), and sand gray. Additional Cimarron colors were antique saddle (dark-amber metallic), briar brown (medium-brown metallic), midnight-sand gray (dark-gray metallic), and garnet medium-red metallic). Thirteen dual-color accent stripes were also available for the Cimarron.

Cadillac took a major step forward in the area of automotive-installed radio and tape units with the availability of the Delco-GM/Base Premium Sound System as an option for the Eldorado and Seville (other Cadillac models received electronically tuned radios and cassette tape players plus improved performance front speakers). Cadillac's claim that it was "the first automotive sound system to be specifically tuned to the acoustics of the individual car series in which it is offered" underscored the significance of this new feature.

Delco Electronics, which had introduced the first automobile instrument panel radio in 1936, was General Motors' automotive and computer division, and was regarded as one of its most advanced operations, particularly in the area of technologic innovations for automobiles.

The Bose Corporation, founded by Dr. Amar Bose in 1964, had been in the high-fidelity field since 1968,

Standard on all 1983 Cadillacs except the Cimarron and Limousine models was an outside temperature feature located on the Electronic Climate Control display panel.

CADILLAC VITAL STATISTICS: 1983

Series	Model	Body Type	Factory Price ($)	Weight (lbs.)	Production (#)
Cimarron	G69	4 dr Sedan	12,215	2639	19,294
Seville	S69	4 dr Sedan	21,440	3844	34,115*
De Ville	D69	4 dr Sedan	16,441	3993	70,423
	D47	2 dr Coupe	15,970	3935	60,300
Eldorado	L57	2 dr Coupe	19,334	3748	84,660†
Fleetwood Brougham	B69	4 dr Coupe	19,182	4029	38,300
	B47	2 dr Coupe	18,688	3986	5200
Limousine	F23	4 dr Limousine 8p	29,323	4765	492
	F33	4 dr Formal Limousine	30,349	4852	508

*Includes 3,685 Seville Elegantes
†Includes 17,250 Eldorado Biarritzs and 2,463 Commemorative Edition Eldorados

developing an international reputation for its research in sound perception. As installed in the Seville and Eldorado, the speakers and amplifiers of the Delco-GM/Bose system were designed to provide "acoustically customized sound" by taking into account such individual acoustic characteristics as the shape and location of windows, upholstery, carpeting, and even the position of the driver and passenger.

The system's components included an electronically tuned receiver, integral cassette tape player mounted in the front instrument panel, plus four speaker/amplifier enclosures. Two of these were mounted in the rear package shelf. The others were mounted in each of the lower front-door panels.

These units were rigidly constructed with high-density foam gaskets to eliminate unwanted vibration and resonance. Fiberglass was used for acoustical damping to minimize distortion caused by standing waves. Each enclosure also included a tuned port to enhance bass response. The speakers used heavy ceramic magnets and a low-impedance design to provide both high-power handling capacity and sound pressure levels. Within each speaker enclosure was a small, lightweight amplifier delivering 25 watts of power.

Cadillac claimed that this sound system encompassed more new technology than any other home or auto unit currently available, and a review of its individual features provided impressive evidence to support this assertion. For example, its automatic circuits adjusted both band width and stereo separation reception to match the signal being received. Automatic compensation for signal strength provided sensitivity to weak signals without the danger of overloading from a nearby transmitter.

At low-volume levels, a "Full-Time" loudness control automatically provided bass boost, resulting in fuller, richer sound reproduction. A "Dynamic Noise Reduction" control contributed to a reduction of high-frequency hiss on cassette tapes as well as AM and FM reception. Also included was a built-in Dolby-tape noise reduction, which automatically reduced high frequency hiss on Dolby-encoded cassette tapes. Yet another feature, a "Tape Equalization" switch, provided the correct frequency response for the playback of both chromium dioxide and metal tapes, as well as ferric-oxide types.

CIMARRON CHANGES

Cadillac's latest model, the Cimarron, was treated to a major overhaul of its design, a move resulting in substantially improved sales, which for 1983 totaled 19,188, up over 5,400 cars from calendar-year 1982. Of this total, approximately 20 percent was to customers switching from a foreign make.

The most criticized feature of the original Cimarron, its relative lack of power, was at least partly remedied by the use of a larger, 2.0-liter (121-cubic-inch) engine in place of the 1.8-liter unit. The increased displacement of this pushrod four came from a longer, 3.51-inch stroke. Also altered was the compression ratio, which was raised from 9.0 to 9.3:1.

Other significant design changes included high-swirl intake ports and a new piston design that increased gas turbulence and provided more complete combustion; revised camshaft and valve train; a new mechanical vacuum pump and timing chain; and a new pulse-air delivery system on all Cimarrons with automatic transmission or for sale in California. This helped control hydrocarbon and carbon-monoxide emissions.

Replacing the electronically controlled carburetor of 1982 was a Rochester, single-bore, throttle-body fuel injection system with a more accurate ECM "black box." This new unit, which enabled Cadillac to announce that "carburetors on Cadillacs have gone the way of steering tillers, running boards and rumble seats," provided measurable advancements in four important areas: overall operation (smoother), standing starts (virtually no "bog-down"), improved cold-start characteristics, and better throttle response throughout the entire rpm range. The Cimarron engine now also featured built-in fuel, spark, and idle-speed compensation for consistent performance under varied operating conditions.

The Cimarron's 88-horsepower rating was unchanged, but it was now delivered at 4,800, rather than 5,100 rpm. Torque output improved measurably to 110 lb-ft at 2,400 rpm as compared with the older level of 100 lb-ft at 2,800 rpm.

Joining these technical improvements was a new Isuzu-built, five-speed manual transmission that eliminated most of the complaints critics had about the wide-ratio four-speed used in 1982. With ratios of 3.92, 2.15, 1.33, 0.92, and 0.74, the new gear box contributed to better standing-start acceleration, provided less rpm drop between shifts, and gave the driver a choice of two overdrive ratios.

Less spectacular but still noteworthy was the use of a higher (2.70:1), torque converter ratio for the three-speed automatic transmission. The final drive ratios of the manual and automatic transmissions were, respectively, 3.83 and 3.18 to 1.

Cadillac claimed a 0 to 60-mph time for the 1983 Cimarron of 14.5 seconds. Yet tests of two Cimarrons by *Motor Trend* indicated the Cimarron was capable of 0 to 60 mph in the 12.59- to 12.85-second range.

The Cimarron continued to use the basic chassis system of 1982, but here, as with its engine, Cadillac made changes both noteworthy and easily detected. A development that reduced engine shake-at-idle and lessened the transfer of engine noise into the passenger compartment was the use of new bushing-type transmission mounts in place of the older opposed-pad arrangement. Also contributing to a quieter Cimarron were new, rear-shock absorbers with lower-mount bushings.

Found in the Cimarron's front suspension were new-design MacPherson struts with gas-filled pliacells that were exclusive to the Cimarron among the GM J-cars, plus shock absorbers filled with a special low-friction fluid. The valving in both the struts and rear shock absorbers was altered to provide a softer and flatter ride. At the top of the MacPherson struts were urethane jounce bumpers that were more compressible and thus possessed superior damping characteristics than the rubber rings they replaced.

The Cimarron remained an expensive ($12,215, up a moderate $84 from 1982) and a well-equipped automobile in its base form. A new option, the Astroroof, included a rear tilt-up feature as well as a built-in wind deflector and integral sun shade. The standard AM/FM stereo Delco radio had new front speakers and separate bass and treble slide controls. The optional sound system added an automatic-reverse cassette system with DNR, a built-in five-band equalizer and tape equalization.

Interior appointments were left essentially unchanged, although a front-seat, folddown center armrest was now standard. Exterior styling changes, while limited, were effective in separating the Cimarron from the other, far less expensive J-cars. In 1982, the Cimarron's front end appearance made comparison with a Chevrolet Cavalier both inevitable and embarrassing. For 1983, the Cimarron grille format with prominent vertical bars gave it a much needed Cadillac look.

On this point, it's worth noting that the Cimarron was gradually shedding its stepchild status. Admittedly, the rear deck still carried the notorious "Cimarron by Cadillac" plaque. But, like other 1983 Cadillacs, the Cimarron sported Cadillac script in the lower left corner of its grille and a new lay-down circular emblem on the hood read "Cadillac Cimarron."

Standard for the Cimarron was a lower valance panel and two, 25-watt tungsten halogen fog lamps, delivering 6,500 candela each. They were operated by an on-off switch mounted on a concentric ring surrounding the headlight switch.

Also distinguishing the new Cimarron was the addition of Cimarron script just above the body side molding on each front door. At the rear, a "2.0 Liter Fuel Injection" plaque was positioned on the left side of the trunk lid. More aggressively styled aluminum wheels rounded out the Cimarron's 1983-model appearance changes. These now were highlighted by a gray metallic-painted vaned pattern surrounding a small center hubcap and exposed lug nuts.

The Cimarron's interior was revised by the addition of a Sierra-grain, door-panel insert bordered by vertical welts. A wider door-handle trim plate was installed, which included the power door-lock switch if that option was ordered. As standard equipment, a folddown center armrest was installed for the front seat. Six interior selections, five of which were new, were offered for the Cimarron.

To provide for more clarity and accuracy, the 1983 speedometer increments were marked every 1-mile/hour. Those for the tachometer had 100-rpm divisions, while the voltmeter's were marked in 2-volt segments.

Listed among the Cimarron's options was a revised power Astroroof featuring power-assisted opening and closing, a rear tilt-open capability, a pop-up front air deflector, and a sliding headliner sunshade. Also changed was the deck-lid luggage rack, which now had

black accents; fixed black "tie-downs," and black protective-slat rub stripes. A new option was a garage-door opener and retainer.

Beginning on June 1, 1982, all Cadillac Cimarron production took place at the GM Assembly Division Plant in Janesville, Wisconsin. This was an old plant, in operation for nearly 60 years, that was subjected to an extensive expansion and renovation project, resulting in its transformation into what Cadillac general manager Edward C. Kennard described as "the most modern body assembly plant within General Motors." Among Janesville's most advanced features was the use of over 50 robots in the body fabrication and assembly departments, plus "Robo-gate" welding and "Car-Trac" conveyor systems.

The specific purpose of the Robo-gate system was to improve precision body building. Each Cimarron body shell was securely and accurately positioned within a Robo-gate fixture for welding. Initially, light robots completed approximately 50 welds to establish the body's dimensional accuracy. Beyond this point, the body was delivered to another series of robots performing a sequence of respot and final-weld operations. Throughout these operations, the Car-Trac conveyor kept the body at the proper height and position. Commenting on the total Janesville operation, Edward C. Kennard noted that it was "tuned to building a highly dimensionally accurate body on a consistent basis. The use of robots and other high technology applications is designed to provide a degree of consistently high quality and accuracy unheard of in the past."

Beyond these procedures, the Cimarrons were subjected to numerous extra-care assembly operations. These included a metal finisher and inspector in the body shop whose task was to, said Cadillac, "give all Cimarrons special attention." Two workers were appointed to the trim shop to make certain all Cimarron seats were in excellent condition. Receiving special attention was the proper line-up of welts and the removal of any wrinkles in the leather. In the paint shop, extra oil sanding was undertaken to ensure a quality finish.

Before being released, finished cars were sent to the "Cimarron Quality Center" where four employees checked each car for proper fluid levels and fluid systems integrity, electrical equipment operation, paint finish, molding alignments, interior cleanliness, and interior protective coverings. In addition, the workers cleaned the windows; waxed and buffed the hood, roof, and deck lid; and checked the car against its order sticker to determine that all specified options had been installed.

Cimarron's market position was strengthened by the availability, as a 1983½ model, of the special edition Cimarron D'Oro, featuring a sable black exterior with gold-tone accents. This theme was further accentuated by black-finished bumpers, headlight bezel, drip rail and window reveal moldings, wheel-opening and rocker-panel moldings, door handles, door trunk lid and fuel-filler door-lock cylinders, and a fixed-mast radio antenna.

Gold-tone appointments consisted of the grille, lay-down hood ornament, hood accent stripes, bumper rub strips and body side molding, Cimarron trunk-lid script, "2.0 Liter Fuel Injection" trunk-lid plaque, and the winged Cadillac crest taillight ornamentation. Completing the exterior features was D'Oro gold-toned, front-fender identification and aluminum-alloy wheels with gold-toned accents.

The Cimarron D'Oro interior provided saddle-leather-trimmed seating; gold tinted, brushed-finish, steering-wheel spokes; gold-toned steering-wheel, horn-pad emblem; and "Cimarron D'Oro" instrument plaque.

CADILLAC'S DOMESTIC COMPETITION

Three basic forms of Lincolns were offered for 1983: Lincoln Continental, Lincoln, and Mark VI. The Continental, in the second year of its downsizing, no longer was available with a V-6 engine. Instead, a 5.0 liter with fuel injection was standard, as was an automatic overdrive transmission. All Continentals were four-door Sedans with the base level, identified as the Signature Series, beginning at $20,985. Special Designer Editions, the Valentino and Givenchy, were also offered. The Valentino was identified by its walnut metallic-over-tan finish, while the Givenchy had a black-over-silver color scheme.

Among the items added to the Continental's standard equipment list was a locking fuel-filler door. New options for all Lincolns included an automatic dimming day-night mirror and an antitheft alarm system.

Continental sales fell to 13,691 in the 1983 calendar year, a drop of 8,739 cars from the 1982 level.

The Mark VI for 1983 offered an optional "simulated-carriage-Convertible" roof for four-door models, along with revised Designer Series' Bill Blass two-door and Emilio Pucci four-door models. Respective base prices for the two- and four-door models were $20,229 and $20,717. The Givenchy Mark VI model was dropped.

Mark VI sales moved slightly upward to 28,257 from 27,844. Lincoln sales continued to rebound from the low level of 1980-1981, reaching 59,626 for 1983.

All Lincolns were four-door models on a 117.3-inch wheelbase with an overall length of 219 inches. In addition to the base model, Signature and Cartier Designer Series versions were offered. Now listed as standard Lincoln equipment were AM/FM stereo radio, speed control, tilt steering column, intermittent wipers, and twin remote-control exterior mirrors.

Chrysler's $18,685 Imperial was still available; but as sales of 1,122 units indicated, its impact on the luxury-car market was almost imperceptible.

SPECIFICATIONS

Engine

Standard for Models except Fleetwood Limousines and Cimarron

Type: V-8, ohv
Bore × stroke: 3.46 × 3.31 inches

Displacement: 249 cubic inches
Horsepower: 135 @ 3,200 rpm
Torque: 200 lb-ft @ 2,200 rpm
Compression ratio: 8.5:1
Fuel system: Digital fuel injection
Electrical system: 12-volt, Freedom II battery

Standard for Fleetwood Limousines

Type: V-8-6-4, ohv
Bore × stroke: 3.8 × 4.1 inches
Displacement: 368 cubic inches
Horsepower: 140 @ 3,800 rpm
Torque: 265 lb-ft @ 1,400 rpm
Compression ratio: 8.2:1
Fuel system: Digital fuel injection
Electrical system: 12-volt, Freedom II battery

Optional for All Models (Except Fleetwood Limousines and Cimarron)

Type: V-8 diesel, ohv
Bore × stroke: 3.3 × 3.5 inches
Displacement: 350 cubic inches
Horsepower: 105 @ 3,200 rpm
Torque: 200 lb-ft @ 1,600 rpm
Compression ratio: 22.7:1
Fuel system: Digital fuel injection
Electrical system: 12-volt, Freedom II battery, 80-amp generator

Standard for Cimarron

Type: L-4, ohv
Bore × stroke: 3.50 × 3.51 inches
Displacement: 121 cubic inches
Horsepower: 88 @ 4,800 rpm
Torque: 110 lb-ft @ 2,400 rpm
Compression ratio: 9.3:1
Fuel system: Digital fuel injection
Electrical system: 12-volt, Freedom II battery

Chassis/Drivetrain

Transmission: Four-speed automatic overdrive, five-speed manual standard for Cimarron
Frame:
  De Ville, Fleetwood Brougham, Limousine, Eldorado, Seville: Ladder-type with welded X-members
  Cimarron: unit body frame
Rear axle:
  De Ville, Fleetwood Brougham, Limousine, Eldorado, Seville: Hypoid type, 3.42:1 ratio, 3.73:1 available for high-altitude use
  Limousines: 3.08:1
Driving axle ratio for front-wheel drive models:
  Eldorado, Seville: 3.15:1, 3.36:1 for high-altitude use
  Cimarron: 3.83:1, 3.18:1 with optional three-speed automatic transmission, 3.43:1 for high-altitude use
Optional ratio for diesel-powered cars: 2.93:1

Front suspension:
- De Ville, Fleetwood Brougham, Limousines: Independent, coil springs, link-type stabilizer bar, hydraulic, direct-action shock absorbers
- Eldorado, Seville: Independent, torsion bars, link-type stabilizer bar, direct-action shock absorbers
- Cimarron: Independent, MacPherson struts, coil springs, stabilize bar, direct-action shock absorbers

Rear suspension:
- De Ville, Fleetwood Brougham, Limousines: Four-link drive, coil springs, direct-action shock absorbers
- Eldorado, Seville: Independent, trailing arms, coil springs, direct-action shock absorbers, electronic level control
- Cimarron: Coil springs, stabilizer bar, direct-action shock absorbers

Steering: Power-assisted, overall ratio
- De Ville, Fleetwood Brougham: 17:1-15:1
- Eldorado, Cimarron: 14:1
- Seville: 15:1-13:1
- Formal Limousine, Limousine: 20:1-20.6:1

Tires: Steel-belted radial (ply) white sidewalls standard equipment except for Cimarron and Eldorado Touring Coupe, De Ville and Fleetwood Brougham: P215/75 R15
- Eldorado, Seville: P205/75 R15
- Eldorado Touring Coupe: P225/70 R15
- Formal Limousine, Limousine: HR78-15/D
- Cimarron: P195/70 R15

Dimensions

Wheelbase:
- De Ville, Fleetwood Brougham: 121.5 inches
- Eldorado, Seville: 114 inches
- Formal Limousine, Limousine: 144.5 inches
- Cimarron: 101.2 inches

Width:
- Coupe De Ville, Fleetwood Brougham: 75.4 inches
- Sedan De Ville, Formal Limousine, Limousine: 75.3 inches
- Eldorado: 70.6 inches
- Seville: 70.9 inches
- Cimarron: 65.0 inches

Front/rear tread:
- De Ville, Fleetwood Brougham, Limousine models: 61.7/60.7 inches
- Eldorado, Seville: 59.3/60.6 inches
- Cimarron: 55.4/55.2 inches

Overall length:
- De Ville, Fleetwood Brougham: 221.0 inches
- Eldorado: 204.5 inches
- Seville: 204.8 inches
- Limousine models: 244.3 inches
- Cimarron: 173.1 inches

Popular Options

Electronically tuned radio and cassette player
Extended-range rear speakers
Delco-GM/Bose premium sound system
Astroroof
Wire-Wheel
Custom wheels
Power door locks
Power seats
Tilt steering wheel
Cruise control
Power windows
Rear-window defogger

1984

The Cadillac of Convertibles Is Here!

CHANGES FOR 1984 were very modest. Cadillac had expected to have its new generation of front-wheel-drive models ready for a late 1983 debut, but their introduction was delayed by quality problems with the new Hydra-Matic planned for them. This setback meant that the 1984 model line would essentially consist of carryovers from 1983.

BIARRITZ

The exception to this pattern was the offering of the first production Cadillac Convertible since 1976. As in those days, the Eldorado was chosen for this singular honor. What was different was the mode of production used for the 1984 reincarnation. The new Eldorado Biarritz Convertibles began life as normal Coupes prior to their shipment to the ASC Corporation. Its owner, Heinz Prechter, had begun conversion of Buick Riviera Coupes into Convertibles in 1983.

In the case of the Cadillac, the result was an elegant, distinctive product. The rear quarter windows lowered automatically whenever the top was folded or raised. In order for the top to operate, the transmission lever had to be positioned in Park. The only color available for the roof was white. In contrast to the standard Eldorados, which were offered in a choice of 12 standard and six optional Firemist colors (as well as 15 single accent-stripe colors), the Biarritz Convertible's color selection was limited to cotillion white, Hatteras blue, and autumn maple.

As a Biarritz, the Convertible used numerous styling cues from the Coupe version, including wide bright accent moldings for the door and fenders, deck-lid accent striping, Biarritz script nameplates and wire-wheelcovers.

Interior appointments featured a leather-wrapped steering-wheel rim, deluxe carpeting and floormats, as well as a multibutton, tufted-seat design in leather/vinyl trim. Interior color selections were limited to three choices: white with dark blue accents, white with dark carmine (red) accents, and dark carmine.

The power-operated top was made of a diamond-grain vinyl and included a glass rear window and a color-coordinated cloth headliner. This latter feature, aside from giving the interior a neat, tailored appearance, also provided noise insulation. A power top switch was located on the instrument panel to the left of the radio controls. If necessary, the top could also be raised or lowered manually.

Providing a protective covering for the top when it was lowered was a removable, soft-vinyl boot that snapped onto the rear-belt moldings. A storage bag was provided for the boot when it was not in use.

Aside from the obvious removal of the car's top, there were numerous frame, body structure, and suspension modifications completed before the final product was ready for shipping. Frame alterations included heavier-gauge front, center, and rear side rails and reinforced cross-member braces. These were intended to provide a balance of soft ride with a solid road feel.

Body structural changes included inner rocker reinforcements, radiator support cross-rods, numerous braces, and door-wedge reinforcements. A rear-wheelhouse sound absorber-barrier was installed to reduce transmission of outside noise into the passenger compartment. Cadillac also retuned the suspension and body structure on those Eldorados equipped with the diesel engine.

The Biarritz Convertible used numerous components from the Eldorado Touring Suspension System, including higher-rate front and rear stabilizer bars; front torsion bars; rear coil springs; and P225/70R15, steel-belted, radial whitewall tires.

None of this came together inexpensively. The base price of the Biarritz Convertible was $31,286 or $10,944 above that of the Coupe; $7,547 higher than a Biarritz Coupe and $8,965 above the cost of an Eldorado Touring Coupe.

CHANGES AND IMPROVEMENTS

The 4.1-liter V-8 continued as the standard engine for all Cadillacs except the Fleetwood Limousines and Cimarron. All, except those for California delivery, were fitted with a new, dual-bed, monolithic catalytic converter that was 50 percent lighter than the older unit it replaced. In addition, because of a faster warmup rate, it provided improved catalytic efficiency and emissions control. Another plus was the improved driveability permitted because of additional fuel enrichment. All but those V-8s intended for high-altitude use had recalibrated electronic emissions controls.

In order to accommodate this new converter, modifications to the exhaust system were necessary, including a revised Y-pipe, converter hanger, and intermediate pipe on all cars. Found on the Eldorado and Seville were revised exhaust pipes and a retuned muffler.

The 4.1-liter engine was given a new external appearance because of its new, black-painted, rocker-arm covers and oil-filter cap. New graphics consisted of a recessed silver-tone stripe with black "HT-4100" identification on the rocker covers plus a similar silver-tone band, reading "Digital Fuel Injection V-8" on the air cleaner cover.

The diesel V-8 was again offered in all Cadillac models except the Fleetwood Limousines, Eldorado Biarritz Convertible, and Cimarron and on cars intended for use in California. The only change of consequence was the installation of a new fast-glow plug system using dual-coil, positive temperature coefficient plugs. Cadillac reported that these plugs self-regulated their power to match heating requirements and to prevent their burnout should the ignition key be left on unintentionally.

The Limousines had, as their standard engine, the 6.0-liter, modulated displacement V-8-6-4 with digital fuel injection.

Cadillac's legendary long list of options was strengthened by the improvement of existing features. All radios except the Delco-GM/Bose system now used extended frequency range rear speakers and a new standard AM/FM stereo radio, the Delco Series 2000, was introduced. The theft-deterrent system, which was standard on the Biarritz Convertible and optional for all other Cadillacs except the Cimarron, was revised to include a new driver-seat presence switch that detected the presence of any object weighing 40 pounds or more in the driver's seat. A heavy-duty Freedom III battery was optional for all gasoline-engined Cadillacs except Cimarron.

DIFFERENCES AMONG MODELS

As the newest addition to the Eldorado line, the Biarritz Convertible shared numerous detail changes for 1984 with its running mates. The major side-body appearance change was the use of car-colored side moldings and low-gloss, black door-trim bezels. Low-gloss, black instrument-panel bezels and air-conditioning outlets were among the changes made in the Eldorado's interior. Other dash revisions included a new headlight switch knob, reshaped center air-conditioning outlets, a resized Fuel Data Panel, and, on diesel-engined cars, a resized "Cadillac" trimplate. Also restyled was the steering-wheel horn pad, which now had a stitched appearance around the center Cadillac emblem, and sculptured, raised areas on the steering-wheel spokes.

The fabric interior of the base Eldorado was again trimmed in a knit cloth with minichecked inserts. The optional leather trim had a new, vertically ribbed seat design. The Biarritz continued its tufted, multibutton leather/vinyl design.

Left unchanged from 1983 was the Eldorado Touring Coupe and its components. Its interior was available only in saddle leather/vinyl trim. Exterior color choices were limited to either sable black with accent stripes of dark black over light saddle or Sonora saddle firemist (medium-amber metallic) with dark beech-over-orange accents.

The Seville shared with the Eldorado a number of changes, such as car-colored body side moldings and low-gloss black finishes for the door trim, instrument-panel bezels, and air-conditioning outlets.

For 1984, the Seville's horizontal taillight design was revised to include a clear outer and a red inner lens, incorporating the "floating," horizontally winged Cadillac crest as found on the 1983 models. As was the case with all 1984 model Cadillacs, the engine identification plaque was removed from the front fender. Also altering the Seville's appearance were optional aluminum wheels with a center hubcap and exposed-chrome lugnuts. For the first time, the Seville Elegante was available in 12 single colors, as well as four, two-tone combinations. Seville color choices were identical to those of the Eldorado. Base models of both the Seville and Eldorado were offered with the full Cabriolet roof option in diamond-grain vinyl.

The base Seville interior for 1984 used new seat and door trim with a multibutton, tufted-pillow design in knit cloth or optional leather/vinyl. The door panels had a horizontally sewn pattern and an embroidered Seville script. As with the Eldorado, a restyled horn pad plus a revised and reshaped instrument panel were adopted for 1984.

In spite of numerous refinements, Cimarron production plateaued in 1984, reaching 18,014 units, down 1,174 cars from 1983. Heading up the list of Cimarron changes was a new cross-hatch grille that, said Cadillac, was "designed to provide a bold distinctive look." Four new color inserts for the body side molding, bumper rubstrips and endcaps were offered in white, red, orange, and, for the D'Oro option only, gold. Ten exterior and 13 dual-color accent stripes were offered for the Cimarron. The D'Oro was available only in sable black.

At the rear, styling refinements included a rearranged lighting system with horizontal taillights carrying flush-mounted, winged Cadillac crests as in 1983. New amber turn signals and white backup lights were located below the taillights.

Significant interior changes included new heating/ventilating/air conditioning push-button con-

The 1984 Eldorado Biarritz was the first convertible from Cadillac since 1976. It featured a removable soft vinyl boot.

1984 Eldorado Biarritz Convertible. The convertible top was available in white only.

1984 Eldorado Biarritz Coupe. A new feature was a car-colored body side molding.

1984 Eldorado with full cabriolet roof option.

1984 Eldorado Touring Coupe.

1984 Seville with full cabriolet top. For 1984, the Seville's tail lamps were revised to include a clear outer lens and a red inner lens with a winged Cadillac crest.

1984 Sedan de Ville. All De Villes, Fleetwood Broughams, and Limousines had a gold-tone Cadillac crest ornamentation added to their park and turn signals.

1984 Fleetwood Brougham Sedan d'Elegance.

The 1984 Cimarron used a cross-hatch grille and new stripe-insert colors for the bumper rub strips.

trols, making operation of these systems more convenient. Amber annunciator lights now indicated the mode selected. A push-button, four-speed, blower-motor control allowed selection of the desired blower speed. Again, annunciator lights indicated the blower speed selected. A detented temperature control provided smooth operation and, with 24 click stops, precise control.

Also added to the Cimarron interior was a push-button, trip-odometer control and new trim plates for the dash and console with a fine, beige-tone grid pattern. Joining the standard, perforated–leather-trimmed seats was an optional cloth/leather combination featuring a woven velour cloth with a diamond-shaped pattern for the seating surfaces and the center and upper portion of the front headrests. Seat bolsters were trimmed in leather. This interior was available in dark blue, sand gray, and dark briar brown.

More important, as far as bringing the Cimarron closer to the mainstream of its market, where road performance was one of the dominant sales factors, were the numerous changes found in its technical makeup for 1984. These consisted of increased-diameter, front stabilizer-bar bushings; larger-diameter, rear stabilizer bar; redesigned front-jounce bumpers; and a new rear, shear-type, upper shock-absorber mount.

Rear-end styling changes for the Cimarron included a new lighting arrangement with horizontal stop and taillights with winged Cadillac identification plus amber turn signals.

CADILLAC VITAL STATISTICS: 1984

Series	Model	Body Type	Sug. Retail Price ($)	Weight (lbs.)	Production (#)
Cimarron	G69	4 dr Sedan	12,614	2563	23,396*
Seville	S69	4 dr Sedan	22,468	3804	44,397†
De Ville	M69	4 dr Sedan	17,625	3981	68,270
	M47	2 dr Coupe	17,140	3940	46,340
Eldorado	L67	2 dr Convertible	31,286	3926	3300
	L57	2 dr Coupe	20,342	3734	99,001‡
Fleetwood Brougham	W69	4 dr Sedan	20,451	3962	39,650
	W47	2 dr Coupe	19,942	4005	4500
Limousine	F23	4 dr Limo 8p	30,454	4765	462
	F33	4 dr Formal Limo 7p	31,512	4855	631

*Includes 1,498 Cimarron D'Oros
†Includes 4,400 Seville Elegante
‡Includes 21,195 Eldorado Biarritzes

Enhancing both serviceability and general overall performance was a single engine-emission wiring harness, a rubber-isolated throttle cable, new Electronic Control Module, and a modified automatic-shift lever handle incorporating a new Park-lock feature. Also revised was the electronic cruise control option, which now had a new vacuum reservoir providing more precise speed control as well as a new "accel" mode for controlled acceleration.

The full-sized De Ville, Brougham, and Limousine models shared several minor appearance changes such as the car-colored body side moldings found in all 1984 Cadillacs, except the Cimarron, gold-tone horizontally winged Cadillac crests on the front parking/turn signal and taillight lenses. The rear lights also had gold-tone accents. If any of these Cadillacs was equipped with the optional 5.7-liter diesel V-8 engine, a "DIESEL" engine identification plaque was installed on the left rear side of the deck lid.

All De Villes, Broughams, and Fleetwood Limousines were available in 12 standard and five optional Firemist paint colors, 17 vinyl-roof colors, 12 dual-color, accent-stripe combinations, and 15 single accent-stripe colors. Five optional two-tone paint combinations were also offered for the De Villes.

The only interior change of consequence was the use of the same restyled steering-wheel pad used on the Seville and Eldorado.

Even if 1984 wasn't a great leap forward for Cadillac, it was a solid sales success year. Total sales rose from the 1983 level of 309,337 to 320,017 cars. The small sales decline of the Eldorado and Cimarron were more than offset by significantly higher sales of the Seville, De Ville, and Fleetwood models.

CADILLAC'S DOMESTIC COMPETITION

Even with little new to offer either technically or stylewise, both the Lincoln and Continental models had strong sales increases in 1984. The Continental's sales moved up to 31,110 cars while the Lincoln's increased 41,243 cars to 90,869. Sales of the Mark, now in VII form, moved up only slightly to 29,496 from 28,257.

But this very dramatically restyled and engineered car in the form of its LSC model was a far cry from the Signature and Designer Series Continentals. Its combination of electronic air suspension, four-wheel disc brakes, front-rear sway bars, and 302-cubic-inch V-8 linked to a four-speed automatic transmission placed the LSC in direct competition with the Eldorado Touring Coupe.

Ford described the Mark VII as "the first car in the United States to offer integrated, front-mounted aerodynamic headlamps, and the first to use an exclusive electronic three-way leveling air-spring suspension system that adjusts for passengers and luggage."

The air-spring system for the LSC with larger front and rear stabilizer bars and higher air springs was 40 percent stiffer than that used for the Mark VII. It was also equipped with quick-ratio power steering, wide 15-inch, cast-alloy wheels and a performance axle.

SPECIFICATIONS

Unchanged from 1983.

Dimensions

Unchanged from 1983.

Popular Options

Unchanged from 1983 except for addition of Series 2000 radios for Eldorado and Seville, Citizens Band transceivers, and Freedom III battery.
Astroroof: $1,225
Vista vent: $300 (Cimarron)
Eldorado Biarritz package: $3,395
Seville Elegante package: $3,879
GM-Delco/Bose music system: $895
D'Oro package: $350

1985

The Cadillac of Tomorrow Is Here

THE INTRODUCTION of front-wheel-drive De Ville and Fleetwood Cadillacs on April 5, 1984, marked yet another watershed in Cadillac's postwar history. As with the introduction of rear-fender fins in 1948, the adoption of the ohv V-8 in 1949, the debut of the front-wheel-drive Eldorado in 1967, and the presentation of the Seville in 1975, Cadillac was making fundamental changes that would have long-term ramifications.

CHANGES AND IMPROVEMENTS

The C-body used by the new Cadillac, shared with the Oldsmobile 98 and Buick Electra, was, when compared with its rear-wheel-drive counterparts, far smaller. Wheelbase, at 110.8 inches was 10.7 inches shorter; overall length was just 195 inches, a reduction of 26 inches, and width, at 71.7 inches, was 3.7 inches less.

This downsizing was even more dramatic than that of 1977, since it was accompanied by a strong effort to retain Cadillac's traditional customers while also appealing to younger clients with equally impressive incomes. This was no easy task to accomplish. Cadillac's repeat customers were conservative and not known for a high receptivity to change. On the other hand, the hoped-for conquest sales were oriented toward technical sophistication and a perception of value based on tangible road performance rather than images and status.

To expedite this "Bi-Model" approach, Cadillac advertising and sales material emphasized the technical advances and advantages the new models possessed. Since the new models were more expensive than those they were intended to replace (the timetable for the ending of rear-drive model production had to be revised repeatedly due to the dramatic drop in oil prices and customer loyalty to the older models), Cadillac worked hard to convince customers that the new model had more value than the larger version. This program was known as "Compensatory Consumer Value" (CCV) and was closely related to market research indicating that customer impressions of the front-wheel-drive Cadillacs

improved dramatically after a demonstration drive. In essence, Cadillac was offering a car that it hoped would be perceived as offering all that the older models did in a more graceful, contemporary form. At the same time, it was putting distance between itself and the apparently outdated living room-on-wheels approach to luxury-car design.

Overall, the final form of the C-body Cadillac had to conform to five mandated requirements: no significant loss of interior space; seating for five adults; continuation of traditional Cadillac comfort; ease of entry/exit; good luggage accommodation, and maintenance of Cadillac's luxury-car image.

The styling theme that resulted was described as "contemporary elegance" and was characterized by three elements seen on previous GM front-wheel-drive models: a sharply sloped windshield; a near-vertical, rear-window profile; and a high, nearly horizontal rear deck. The result, in Cadillac's view, was a "distinctive exterior styling theme designed to be both aesthetically pleasing and functional." Primary design elements included a door-into-roof design incorporating a hidden drip molding; a cross-hatch pattern grille with Cadillac script identification in its lower left corner, plus a stand-up wreath and crest hood ornament. Additional Cadillac marque identification was found on the rear deck and on the vertical tail lamps, which had winged Cadillac crest ornamentation. The Cadillac's exterior carried two, color base coats with clear acrylic finishing coats.

C-BODY CADILLACS

The C-body Cadillacs had four-wheel independent suspension, consisting of coil-spring and MacPherson struts at all four wheels. At the rear, the coil springs were mounted inboard from the struts. The front struts were connected to wide-based lower arms. The springs were mounted atop the struts and were designed to collapse within themselves during compression.

Cadillac noted that this design contributed to the C-body's low hood line. Cadillac used a "warm set" manufacturing process that reduced the tendency of the springs to sag with age and provided a more consistent trim height and front-wheel alignment. Electronic Level Control was included as standard equipment.

All 1985 Cadillacs, except for the Cimarron, had the 4.1-liter V-8 as their standard engine. For 1985, the external appearance of the 4.1-liter V-8 was altered by use of new air-cleaner graphics and rocker-arm covers. With a 9.0:1 compression ratio, its power ratings for 1985 remained unchanged at 125 hp at 4,200 rpm and 190 lb-ft of torque at 2,200 rpm. When used on the C-body Cadillacs, the V-8 gained the distinction of being the only transverse-mounted V-8 currently offered in a front-wheel-drive production automobile by any manufacturer in the world.

Cadillac offered the 4.3-liter V-6 diesel engine as a no-cost option for the front-wheel-drive De Villes and Fleetwoods. Among its features were fast-glow plugs providing a wait-to-start time of 6 seconds at 0° Fahrenheit, fuel-line and engine-block heaters, a water-in-fuel indicator, and a new design accessory drive belt. Improving both cold starting performance and idle speed quality was an electronic controller. Incorporated in this unit were new diagnostic functions that continuously monitored the engine control system for proper operation. An important addition to all Cadillac diesel engines was an improved fuel system. An in-tank, metered, water-pickup valve continuously removed water from the fuel tank and transported it through the fuel line to a water-separating filter located in the fuel-conditioner unit. Also found on the 1985 diesels was a remote, filter drain valve that included a water drain hose running from the conditioner unit to the left side of the engine compartment. This allowed the draining of contaminated fuel into a removal container located in the engine compartment. With a displacement of 262 cubic inches and a 22.8:1 compression ratio, the V-6 diesel was credited with 85 hp at 3,600 rpm and 165 lb-ft of torque at 1,600 rpm.

Included in the Engine Control Module of the front-wheel-drive De Ville, Fleetwood, and Seventy-Five Limousine was an Electrical System Check that monitored for the proper charging system. If the system was operating under certain high-load conditions, the ECM would increase engine idle speed and generator output. If there was a problem in the system, the instrument panel alerted the driver.

Yet another electronic unit, the Body Computer Module (BCM), was standard equipment for the C-body Cadillacs with either gasoline or diesel engines. The BCM was a digital control system controlling 13 major convenience functions. Under its control, for example, were the heating, ventilating, and air-conditioning system. If needed, it could, for example, provide continuous air-conditioner compressor operation at idle. On the other hand, it would disengage the compressor during wide-open throttle acceleration for maximum engine output.

Interior temperature control was improved thanks to the ability of the BCM to anticipate the loss of a set temperature before it was felt by vehicle occupants by monitoring engine coolant and air-conditioning refrigerant temperatures.

Also monitored by the BCM were the air-conditioner's refrigerant level and pressure. The driver was alerted if it either became low enough to reduce cooling capacity or if the system should be serviced before it was operated. Like the Engine Control Module, the Body Computer Module stored any malfunctions of body-related systems and displayed them during servicing. It also included controls to actuate certain components to aid in diagnosis, as well as displays to confirm that a problem has been properly corrected.

Owners were saved from potentially expensive compressor repair bills by the BCM's response to possibly damaging, low refrigerant levels by shutting down the compressor and preventing damage until service was completed. The driver was alerted of this situation by an instrument panel tell-tale light.

The BCM also possessed a "Returned Accessory Power" function, enabling operation of the power windows and remote trunk-lid release for 10 minutes after the ignition had been turned off or until the car door was opened.

All Cadillacs with the Digital Fuel Injection, 4.1-liter V-8 had a standard equipment Fuel Data Center. One push of the "Instant/Average" button on the panel keyboard provided an instantaneous mpg readout to the nearest mile per gallon. A second push of the same button brought forth an average mpg reading accurate to one-tenth of a mile per gallon. The first push of the "Range/Fuel Used" provided the estimated driving range. This was based on the average mpg recorded over the previous 25 miles or 40 kilometers. The amount of fuel consumed was indicated by pushing this button a second time. To begin computations again, the "Reset" button was depressed while the average mpg or fuel used data was displayed.

The only transmission offered for the De Ville, Fleetwood, and Fleetwood Seventy-Five Limousine models with the 4.1-liter V-8 was the Turbo Hydra-Matic 440, four-speed automatic. This transmission was also used by Buick Electra and the Oldsmobile 98, but exclusive to Cadillac was a Microprocessor-controlled viscous converter clutch (VCC) made by Eaton. This arrangement used a heavy silicone fluid moving through a series of concentric grooves within the viscous clutch rather than spring dampers to couple the turbine shaft to the engine. Due to its extremely high viscosity, the fluid allowed only minimal slippage while eliminating the lockup sensation felt with the spring engagement. Furthermore, since this system allowed the converter clutch to lock up at speeds between 20 and 30 mph, which was some 20 mph less than with the conventional system, the transmission could be geared for improved efficiency and smooth driveability.

General Motors committed 2.5 billion dollars to the C-body program, which included the construction of two new assembly plants at Orion, Michigan, and Wentzville, Missouri. De Ville and Fleetwood Cadillacs were constructed along with the Oldsmobile 98 at Orion, while the Wentzville plant was used to produce the

Buick Electra and Park Avenues as well as the Olds 98.

Both facilities were virtually physically identical and, at $600 million each, equally expensive. Their role in General Motors' future was made clear by GM President F. James McDonald, who noted when they opened: "The most advanced and expensive technology in these plants is there for one reason—to give our employees the best possible tools for producing consistently high-quality vehicles."

A tour of the Orion plant was a visit to a Valhalla for the high-tech worshiper. Over 1,000 computers were in operation, and from start to finish, automobile production was closely monitored by electronic systems. Of the 4,869 welds in each C-body, 93 percent were done by automatic Robogator Cartrac welders. In contrast, 82 percent of the welds required in the older C-body were done with manual welding guns.

Joining the automated welding system as a key factor in meeting the stringent body-assembly tolerances established for the C-car was the use of single set weld fixtures. Assembly of the older cars invited wide discrepancies in tolerances because numerous fixtures were employed, each of which required adjustment to remedy a problem. The new philosophy used fewer, but more accurate (and expensive) tools.

Throughout the assembly process, GM used state-of-the-art inspection techniques. For example, a laser-beam, "Gapsight," unit operated on the welding lines, and each underbody unit moved through an inspection station where the location of the weld points was examined. In both cases, operators were alerted to discrepancies. If the Gapsight system detected a movement away from the target tolerances, an orange light on the machine began to flash. If the part had deviated out of bounds, a red light flashed. At all times, a manual printout, as well as statistical process control data, was provided for each inspection.

Every underbody unit was checked at over 30 weld points, and "Go" or "Not Go" lights on a control point flashed depending on the results.

Not the least of the Orion plant's advanced manufacturing techniques was adoption of the "just-on-time" deliver-inventory system. Unlike older GM plants where up to 90 percent of all components were delivered by railroad, the Orion plant received up to 75 percent of its material by truck. This, along with the relatively close proximity of nearly three-fourths of the plant's suppliers to Orion, allowed inventories of engines and transmissions, for example, to drop from the typical seven-day supply to under a six-hour inventory.

Delivering material to assembly stations were several dozens of unmanned transporters, part of the Automated Guided Vehicle System (AGUS). These devices, traveling on over 19,000 feet of buried cable, were computer controlled to deliver parts to where they were needed. Each unit was equipped with sensors stopping its operation if anything was obstructing its path. When the way was clear, the Automated Guided Vehicle went on its way.

DIFFERENCES AMONG MODELS

Both the Coupe de Ville and Fleetwood Sedan were available with an optional Formal Cabriolet roof with a tuxedo-grain vinyl cover and narrow "textured-lace" moldings around the roof periphery and windows. A new model, the Fleetwood Coupe, had, as standard equipment, the Formal Cabriolet feature with electroluminescent opera lamps, closed-in rear window, wide lower rocker panel/moldings, and "silk-screen" identification. As with all Fleetwoods, the Coupe had standard "floating-center" wire wheel discs. These were optional on the De Villes whose standard wheelcover had a center hub with the Cadillac wreath and crest.

Cadillac depicted the front-wheel-drive model interiors as "designed to provide optimal elegance, spaciousness, luxurious appointments, functional efficiency and operating convenience, as well as isolation from noise." Common to all models were low-effort power-window switches providing both a light, tactile feel with an audible feedback. In addition, these switches were shape-identified: convex for "up" and concave for "down." Cadillac claimed that new front-seat designs offered improved lumbar support for added passenger comfort.

Both De Ville and Fleetwood Cadillacs had standard front and rear folddown center armrests and a six-way power driver-seat adjuster. The standard De Ville seat design of horseshoe-shaped bolsters in Heather velour and main-seat sections of horizontally striped Augusta cloth was offered in six colors. The same style was also available in a Sierra-grain leather trim.

The standard Fleetwood interior also used the Heather cloth for the seat bolster, but with a squared-off horseshoe-shaped design in combination with vertically piped Wheaton cloth in a small herringbone pattern. An embroidered Cadillac wreath was located on the upper seat back. A selection of six colors was offered. A Sierra-grain leather trim in the same style and in 10 colors was optional. If desired, the Fleetwood's standard manual driver and passenger seat-back recliners could be replaced by optional power units.

A new digital instrument cluster was set in a padded dash panel with simulated butterfly walnut trim and integral side-window defogger outlets. The instruments were backlit by a blue-green vacuum fluorescence, which Cadillac said provided "a high-contrast, glare-free appearance." The gauges could be set to read in either metric or English units by the touch of a button. The speedometer was fitted with a quartz, electrical swing-needle movement utilizing a speed sensor signal, thus eliminating the traditional speedometer cable. The trimmed steering wheel carried a center wreath and crest emblem and simulated walnut-grain trim. A leather-wrapped wheel was optional.

Following previous practice, a Sedan D'Elegance package for the Fleetwood was available. For 1985, it consisted of "Fleetwood D'Elegance" script on the lower portion of the rear quarter window (all Fleetwoods had etched glass identification in this area), deluxe Tampico carpeting and floor mats, and seats trimmed in a tufted multibutton design.

When the 1985 models were introduced on September 19, 1984, a significant new eight-passenger Fleetwood Seventy-Five Limousine was announced. This car, along with the seven-passenger Formal

1985 Coupe de Ville.

1985 Fleetwood Coupe.

1985 Sedan de Ville.

Limousine, which was offered later in the model year, were based on the front-wheel-drive Fleetwood.

Compared with its rear-wheel-drive predecessor, the new Limousine was shorter by 25.7 inches, had a wheelbase reduced by 10.1 inches and weighed nearly 1,200 pounds less. Yet it retained previous passenger capacity. Contributing to this significant weight reduction was the use of sheet molding compound (SMC) for its rear doors, hood, and roof insert. SMC consisted of chopped fiberglass, resin, and a filler folded into sheets and then molded into those components.

Cadillac's front-wheel-drive body configuration made the Limousine one of the most distinctive cars of its class. Highlighting its exterior appearance was the Formal Cabriolet roof design fitted with opera lamps on the sail panel and, as on other Fleetwoods, series identification on the rear quarter windows. In addition, aluminum-alloy wheels with a silver wreath and crest mounted on a dark maroon background were standard.

The Limousine's interior was available in either a standard Heather knit cloth or optional Sierra-grain leather. Both were offered in black, dark blue, or gray. The front seat was of 45/55 Dual Comfort design. Rear-seat occupants enjoyed several new standard conveniences. These included a power-operated, rear-door unlatch system plus a revamped electronic control panel that featured a digital outside-temperature display and controls for the optional, electronically tuned AM/FM stereo/cassette player.

As with the other front-wheel-drive models, the Limousine was fitted with a rear center, high-mount stop light measuring approximately 4.5 square inches.

1985 Fleetwood Coupe.

1985 Fleetwood Sedan.

Government regulations required its use on all 1986 model cars, but Cadillac reported that "GM decided to use the lamp early on some Cadillac models to gain experience with it and indicate its support for the regulation."

As with the rear-drive Fleetwood Brougham, the Seville and Eldorado models were continued with only modest detail changes. Available for the Seville was a new, optional aluminum-alloy wheel with radial fins and medium-gray accents. The center hubcap with brushed and bright metal surfaces had a gold wreath and crest on a silver background.

All Seville and Eldorado models, except for the Eldorado Touring Coupe, could also be equipped with optional spoked, aluminum-alloy wheels with bright

machined outer surfaces, interlacing aluminum spokes, and black-painted brake-vent opening areas. The snap-on center hubcap had a Cadillac crest mounted on a dark maroon background.

The limited-production Eldorado Biarritz Convertible had, as a new option, an electric rear-window defogger.

Of much greater consequence were the changes found in the Cimarron. Each year, sales had crept upward as Cadillac made the Cimarron more and more "the Cadillac of Smaller Cars." For 1985, this transformation began with the use of the same Sierra-grain leather interior as used in larger Cadillacs. If desired, a new combination of Ripple cloth and the Sierra-grain leather sealing areas was available at no

1985 Fleetwood Seventy-Five Limousine.

1985 Fleetwood Seventy-Five Limousine.

extra charge. Also found in the Cimarron's interior was a new two-spoke, leather-trimmed steering wheel. Seven items previously available as options were standard on the 1985 Cimarron. These included power antenna, cruise control, electric power locks, six-way power driver's seat, tilt steering wheel, power trunk-lid release, and electric power windows. Exterior revisions included a redesigned hood and front end.

The special edition, Cimarron D'Oro, continued into 1985 with larger, aluminum-alloy, 14- x -6-inch wheels with Goodyear Eagle GT/P205R14 tires, plus a grooved, lower-body, side accent molding (available on other Cimarrons as an extra-cost option) painted to match the body color. For 1985, the D'Oro was available in either cotillion white or bordeaux red.

The Cimarron's 2.0-liter engine was unchanged in its basic specifications, but performance was improved due to the use of a new V-5 air-conditioning compressor, which could vary its displacement from 9.2 to approximately 1 cubic inch depending on evaporator requirements.

Of far greater consequence for the Cimarron's ability to compete with the performance of such cars as the Audi 4000S Quattro and BMW 318i was the availability of General Motors' 2.8-liter V-6 engine. Compared with the base engine's 85 horsepower and 110 lb-ft of torque, this multiport, fuel-injected engine had 125 horsepower at 4,800 rpm and 159 lb-ft of torque at 3,600 rpm. With 46 percent more power, the V-6 Cimarron accelerated from 0 to 60 mph in just over 10 seconds. Its quarter-mile performance with the standard four-speed manual transmission with overdrive was equally impressive: 17.5 seconds and 78 mph.

Cadillac correctly noted that, for 1985, "the V-6 is only half the story," since a required option for V-6 Cimarrons was a suspension system with softer front springs and larger-diameter stabilizer bar; Delco gas-charged, twin-tube front struts (in place of the standard pliacell units); and rear Bilstein-Delco, single-tube, gas-charged shock absorbers instead of the pliacells used on four-cylinder Cimarrons.

Cadillac modestly summed up these changes with an off-hand "so there is quite a bit of technology packed into what appears to be conventional MacPherson front

A 1985 Seville Elegante fitted with a new optional spoked aluminum-alloy wheels.

1985 Fleetwood Brougham Sedan d'Elegance.

struts and rear shock absorbers." Not so self-effacing was the V-6 Cimarron's skid-pad performance, which yielded a 0.83-g number.

The Eldorado, which, along with Seville, was destined for major resizing and reshaping in 1986, was, as mentioned earlier, little changed for 1985. A new option for the Convertible was an electric rear-window defogger. The Touring Coupe was available in either a brodeaux-red or sable-black finish.

Both the Seville, unchanged from 1984, and all Eldorados, except for the Touring Coupe, were offered with Cadillac's new optional, spoked aluminum-alloy wheel. The Seville Elegante was fitted with a new "Inner Shield" windshield which had a two-part plastic layer applied to its inner surface. This feature was intended to reduce facial lacerations when an occupant contacted the windshield in an accident and prevent glass splinters from entering the vehicle's passenger compartment due to outside impact.

Cadillac cautioned that since the plastic layer didn't have the same abrasive resistance as glass, abrasive cleaning agents, or any type of metal scraper should not be used. The "Inner Shield" windshield was offered initially only on the Seville Elegante due to a very limited manufacturing capacity.

Cadillac expanded its list of available options to include a new digital-instrument cluster that could be set to read in English or metric units at the touch of a button. The Cimarron's unit also provided bar graphs for battery volts, engine-coolant temperature, fuel level, oil pressure, and tachometer. Offered for all models except the Cimarron was an electronically controlled, day/night inside rear-view mirror that automatically was dimmed in response to glare from the headlights of vehicles following behind. When this condition no longer existed, the mirror was switched back to the normal position.

A small control panel beneath the mirror included the photosensor, adjustable distance sensitivity dial, a green dim telltale, and the on-off switch. By setting the illuminated thumb-wheel distance dial from 1 ("near") to 9 ("far"), the driver could match the mirror's performance to his or her sensitivity to glare. Also introduced on the De Ville and Fleetwood Cadillacs was an electrically powered Astroroof with a glass panel that could be either retracted or tilted up. When retracted, an air deflector automatically popped up in the front.

The 1985 De Ville and Fleetwood models were available in 11 standard exterior clearcoat, three optional Firemist, and two optional Pearlmist paint colors. Firemist paint was characterized by the use of numerous metal-flake particles held in suspension within the paint. Pearlmist, in madeira, plum, or black cherry, contained extremely fine mica platelets encapsulated within a molecular deposition of iron oxide. As the sunlight penetrated these minute translucent particles, it was reflected by the color pigment and refracted through the mica fragment.

In addition, both vinyl roofs and accent striping were offered in 16 colors. The Fleetwood Seventy-Five Limousine was offered in four clearcoat colors: cotillion white, sable black, commodore blue, platinum, and

CADILLAC VITAL STATISTICS: 1985

Series	Model	Body Type	Sug. Retail Price ($)	Weight (lbs.)	Production (#)
Cimarron	JG69 (4 cyl)	4 dr Sedan	12,962	2538	
x	JG69 (V-6)	4 dr Sedan	13,447	2665	21,140*
Seville	KS69	4 dr Sedan	23,359	3803	39,755†
De Ville	CD69	4 dr Sedan	18,571	3396	101,366
	CD47	2 dr Coupe	17,990	3324	39,500
Eldorado	EL57	2 dr Coupe	20,931	3724	76,401
	EL57	2 dr Biarritz	24,326		19,435
	EL67	2 dr Convertible	32,105	3915	2300
Fleetwood	CB69	4 dr Sedan	21,040	3422	52450
	CB47	2 dr Coupe	21,069	3346	3000
Brougham	DW69	4 dr Sedan	21,402	4020	NA
	DW47	2 dr Coupe	20,798	3977	NA
75	CH23	Limousine	32,640	3583	405‡

*Includes 1,250 Cimarron D'Oros
†Includes 3,235 Seville Elegantes
‡Includes 16 Formal Limousines

black cherry pearlmist. Five vinyl roof colors and 10 accent colors were available.

The Fleetwood Brougham, Seville, and Eldorado models (except for the Touring Coupe) were offered in 12 clearcoat colors: cotillion white, sable black, silver frost, academy gray, gossamer blue, commodore blue, aspen green, sage green, chamois, sandalwood, burlwood brown, and bordeaux red. All were available in Firemist colors of desert frost, autumn maple, corinthian blue, cranberry, and charcoal. Restricted to the Eldorado and Seville was Flaxan firemist.

Eldorados were available in 18 vinyl-roof colors (as were Sevilles); 25 dual-color, accent-strip combinations; and 15 single accent-stripe colors. Both models could be fitted with any of four full Cabriolet roof-treatment colors. For the Fleetwood Brougham, there were 17 vinyl-roof colors; 25 dual-color, accent-stripe combinations; and 15 single accent-stripe colors.

CADILLAC'S DOMESTIC COMPETITION

Lincoln's 1985 models were visually near-twins to their 1984 counterparts; but on several fronts, they continued to gain recognition as serious challengers to Cadillac. All models with the 5-liter V-8 engines sold in Oregon, Washington, Alaska, California, and Hawaii, plus 5-liter Givenchy and Valentino models were fitted with a four-wheel anti-lock braking system. This unit used an electronic digital computer connected to deceleration sensors at all four wheels. When one wheel began to slow down at a faster rate than the other, the computer adjusted brake line pressure to prevent wheel lockup.

The Continental Mark VII LSC received an engine with 185 hp (55 more than in 1985) that made it the fastest accelerating, American luxury car. Its 0 to 60-mph time was less then 9.5 seconds. Continued from 1984 were the LSC's special suspension components.

SPECIFICATIONS

Engine

Standard on all Models Except Cimarron

Type: V-8, aluminum block, ohv
Bore × stroke: 3.46 × 3.31 inches
Displacement: 249 cubic inches
Horsepower: 125 @ 4,200 rpm
Torque: 190 lb-ft @ 2,200 rpm
Compression ratio: 9.0:1

No-cost Option for Front-wheel-Drive De Ville and Fleetwood

Type: V-6, diesel
Bore × stroke: 3.965 × 3.4 inches
Displacement: 262 cubic inches
Horsepower: 85 @ 3,600 rpm
Torque: 165 ft-lb @ 1,600 rpm
Compression Ratio: 22.5:1

No-cost Option for Fleetwood Brougham, Eldorado, Seville

Not available for California delivery and for Eldorado Biarritz, Convertible, and Touring Coupe
Type: V-8, diesel
Bore × stroke: 4.051 × 3.358 inches
Displacement: 350 cubic inches
Horsepower: 105 @ 3,200 rpm
Torque: 205 ft-lb @ 1,600 rpm
Compression ratio: 22.5:1

Standard: Cimarron

Type: V-4, ohv
Bore × stroke: 3.50 × 3.51 inches
Displacement: 121 cubic inches
Horsepower: 88 @ 4,800 rpm
Torque: 110 lb-ft @ 2,400
Compression ratio: 9.3:1
Fuel system: Digital fuel injection
Electrical system: 12-volt, Freedom II battery

Optional: Cimarron

Type: V-6, ohv
Bore × stroke: 3.50 × 2.99 inches
Displacement: 173 cubic inches
Horsepower: 125 @ 4,800 rpm
Torque: 159 lb-ft @ 3,600 rpm
Compression ratio: 8.9:1
Fuel system: Digital fuel injection
Electrical system: 12-volt, Freedom II battery

Front-wheel Drive De Ville and Fleetwood

All Others unchanged for 1985
Front suspension: Independent, MacPherson struts with integral, pliacell shock absorbers, coil springs, stabilizer bar
Rear suspension: Independent, coil springs, super-lift shock absorbers, stabilizer bar, Electronic Level Control
Steering: Power, rack and pinion, 18.4:1 ratio
Electrical system: 12-volt, Freedom II battery (Freedom III with V-6 diesel), 120-amp generator (94 amp with diesel)
Transmission: Four-speed automatic with overdrive and viscous converter clutch (four-speed automatic with overdrive and torque converter clutch with V-6 diesel)

Chassis/Drivetrain

Chassis/body: Unit construction, isolated power-train cradle
Final drive ratio: 2.97:1 for 4.1 liter V-8
2.14:1 for V-6 diesel
Tires: GM specification, steel-belted, all-season, white stripe, P205175R14 on 14- × -6-inch wheels

Dimensions

Wheelbase: 110.8 inches
  Fleetwood 75 Limousine: 134.4 inches
Width: 71.7 inches
Front/rear tread: 60.3/59.8 inches
Overall length: 195 inches
  Fleetwood 75 Limousine: 218.6 inches

Popular Options

Automatic day/night inside rear-view mirror
Astroroof
Trunk release and power Pulldown
Controlled-cycle wiper system
Cruise control
Rear-window defogger with heated exterior mirrors
Dimming sentinel
Automatic door locks
Garage-door opener
Illuminated entry system
Memory seat
Electrically powered exterior mirrors
Power reclining front seats
Front-passenger, six-way Power Seat
Dual comfort 45/55 front seats
Trumpet horn
Power trunk release
Twilight sentinel
Illuminated visor vanity mirrors
Tri-band antenna
Delco-GM/Bose symphony sound system
Delco-GM 2000 series receiver with cassette tape player
Universal citizens band transceiver cabriolet roof:
  Coupe De Ville only
Digital instrument cluster

Firemist paint
Pearlmist paint
Leather-trimmed steering wheel
Theft-deterrent system
Wire wheel discs
Aluminum-alloy wheels
Heavy-duty Delco-GM Freedom III battery (4.8-liter V-8)
  Puncture-sealing tires

Additional Eldorado and Seville Options

Opera lamps: Standard on Biarritz, not available on
  Convertibles or Touring Coupe
Spoked Aluminum-Alloy Wheels (not available on
  Touring Coupe)
Touring suspension (not available on Convertible)
White-lettered P225170R15 tires: Available on
  Touring Coupe only
Full Cabriolet roof (not available on Biarritz,
  Convertible, Touring Coupe, Seville Elegante)

Additional Cimarron Options

AM/FM stereo, signal-seeking scanner radio with digital
  display
Cassette Player and five-band graphic equalizer
Lower-body side molding: Standard on D'Oro
Heavy-duty battery
2.8-liter V-6
Gas-charged suspension: Required with V-6 engines
13-inch narrow stripe, whitewall tires (not available on
  D'Oro)
Three-speed automatic transmission
14- x -6-inch aluminum-alloy wheels with Goodyear GT
  P205/60R14, steel-belted radial blackwall tires:
  Standard on D'Oro

1986

The Cadillac Promise

TWENTY YEARS AFTER Cadillac had first used the term "Seville" in reference to the 1956 Eldorado Coupe, a new Seville model was announced. Since the third form of the Seville was again a distinct Cadillac line, the latest model naturally invited comparison with earlier versions. The first Seville, bowing in May 1975, had startled those who naively assumed Cadillac was slow to respond to market changes by its "international size." For its time, the first Seville was a radically smaller Cadillac. Compared to a 1975 Sedan de Ville, it was 26.8 inches shorter and 951 pounds lighter.

SEVILLE CHANGES

In the years that followed, the Seville gained recognition for its complement of standard equipment, technical competence, and, with the introduction of the Seville Elegante in 1978, adherence to Cadillac's tradition of offering special-edition versions of its products.

The 1980 model with its controversial styling never equaled the highest sales levels of its predecessor. But by the end of the 1985 model run, over 413,000 Sevilles had been built. During those years, the Seville's basic character was both supplanted and refined by a number of developments lead by the touring suspension offered in mid-1980. Then came the digital instrument cluster (1981), the fuel data panel (1982), and a Delco-GM/Bose premium sound system (1983).

Providing the capstone to this era of Seville design development was the Commemorative Edition offered during the 1985 model run. It featured gold-accented exterior trim; a "Commemorative Edition" sail-panel plaque; steering-wheel, horn-pad emblem; and dual-tone seating areas.

The 1986 model, while startlingly different in appearance from its predecessor, disappointed some critics who found it too similar to other GM products such as the Oldsmobile Calais and Pontiac Grand Am. Be that as it may, Cadillac's assertion that "since its introduction more than a decade ago, the Cadillac Seville has gained a reputation for classic styling, innovative engineering, advanced electronics, and sophisticated chassis and suspension systems" was upheld by the latest version.

The fundamental design philosophy on which the 1986 Seville was based placed a high priority on precise fit of exterior panels and aerodynamics. The Seville wasn't a leader in the former category, but its drag coefficient of 0.37 was a marked improvement over the 1985's 0.50 number. Contributing to the Seville's aerodynamic efficiency was its basic low front-end, high rear-deck design, supported by door-into-roof styling with hidden drip moldings, flush-mounted windshield and bumpers, and integrated outside mirror.

Although tradition survived in the form of a standard wreath-and-crest hood ornament, much of the Seville's front-end appearance was the result of new manufacturing concepts and the drive for a smooth, air-cheating form. The classic Cadillac grille form survived along with "Cadillac" script on the lower right corner, but its small size was clearly a sign of the times as were the composite tungsten-halogen headlights. Their aerodynamic form combined parabolic reflectors and low and high beams into a single assembly. This system still used separate and interchangeable bulbs for each beam function.

Also evident throughout the Seville were many examples of a body designed purposely without complex forms to ensure superior assembly fit. The Seville's front bumper, of a new design, used a fiberglass-reinforced plastic beam. With hydraulic energy absorbers, this bumper met a 5-mph guideline established by General Motors, whereby only cosmetic bumper damage would be sustained at that speed or lower. Externally, this system was highlighted by dropped centers and full body-color fascias of reinforced urethane plastic. Also manufactured of this material was a lower valance panel that also served as an air dam.

In profile, the Seville showed off 14-inch, aluminum-alloy wheels; full wheel openings; a grooved lower-body trim panel; and Seville script on the front cornering lights. The fuel filler door, previously positioned behind the license plate, was now located on the left quarter panel. At the rear, a flush-filling rear window was accentuated by bright and black reveal moldings. A wreath and crest ornamentation as well as Seville script was installed on the rear deck. Most of the underbody hardware was enclosed by a lower-body fascia. These appointments, plus horizontally oriented taillights with winged Cadillac crests, were among the few details that were carryovers from the old Seville.

Cadillac reported that "the roof outline of the 1986 Seville is reminiscent of the original 1975 models." The squared-off roof line shared by these two Sevilles substantiated this claim, but this was really just a superficial similarity. The latest model's door-into-roof construction and hidden drip moldings were just two features that put a decade's distance between the cars.

A new instrument panel for the Seville was described by Cadillac as "sophisticated but driver-friendly." The basic format consisted of two fully padded tiers with a two-tone color scheme. The upper level contained most of the Seville's controls and displays, including the instrument cluster and control panels for the lights, windshield wipers, cruise control, exterior mirrors, and radio. The lower panel contained the climate-control information center, air-conditioning duct and three air-conditioning outlets (another outlet was positioned on the left side of the upper panel), defroster grille, and fixed front side-window defogger outlets. The lower panel also was home for the glove box.

Highlights of the driver information center included a 20-character, alphanumeric matrix display with an English/metric conversion switch for the displays.

Standard on the Seville was a two-spoke steering wheel with a hand-stitched, leather-wrapped rim. Two horn switches were provided, one located in the center hub, the second on the right portion of the steering-wheel spoke area. Interior appointments were representative of what Cadillac depicted as the "Seville's first-class luxury." The seats (front-bucket, rear-bench) had a cloth-leather trim combination and manual driver- and passenger-seat recliners. The trim design consisted of narrow vertical piping on the knit-cloth seat back and cushion inserts and leather bolster. A new one-piece door panel with a formed cloth pillow rolled at the top edge of the door.

Like the front-wheel-drive De Ville and Fleetwood, the Seville used Cadillac's HT-4100 engine mounted in a transverse position. In its latest version, this engine was equipped with a new high-output, 120-amp generator that was lighter than yet provided improved performance over the unit used in 1985. Also more efficient than its predecessor was a cross-flow aluminum radiator that replaced the older copper-brass unit.

Improving fuel economy was a new "cross-under," low back-pressure, exhaust system that was a one-piece welded unit from the catalytic converter back. Also redesigned was the electronic control module that provided 15 percent greater computational capability and increased memory than in 1985. The result was a higher degree of engine system control over a wide range of operating conditions.

Cadillac claimed a 0 to 60-mph time for the base Seville of approximately 12.5 seconds, which was some 2 seconds quicker than a 1985 model. Aside from the 1986's lighter weight, a prime contributor to this improved acceleration was the Seville's new four-speed automatic transmission with a viscous-damped converter clutch similar to that used on the front-wheel-drive De Ville and Fleetwood. Its first-gear ratio of 2.92:1 was significantly higher than the 2.74:1 used in 1985. A 2.97:1 final drive ratio, along with a 1.63:1 torque-converter ratio as well as the Seville's improved aerodynamics, zero-drag disc brakes, and low rolling resistance tires, contributed to fuel economy figures of 17-mpg city and 26-mpg highway, which were 6 and 18 percent improvements, respectively.

The Sevilles were depicted by their manufacturer as "outstanding handling Cadillacs with a refined degree of well-controlled, smooth, quiet-ride quality. These attributes are designed to appeal to the technically sophisticated younger affluents." Obviously, Cadillac had not forgotten the original reason for the Seville's existence!

In other words, beneath the Seville's conservative appearance was a chassis design/suspension system that indicated Cadillac had learned much from the earlier Seville Eldorado Touring Suspension options. Indeed, Cadillac, with justification, noted "the Seville's base suspension combines the best handling elements of previous touring suspension offerings with the excellent isolation qualities inherent in the new vehicle design."

Replacing the older body, separate frame design was an internally-constructed body frame with six frame insulators isolating the body from the drivetrain and front suspension frame. Also intended to provide the same results, namely traditional Cadillac operating characteristics with a more sophisticated road performance, was the use of engine mounts that improved both idle-speed smoothness and transmission shift feel.

Particularly interesting was the use of powerplant-mount brackets of high aluminum content. For example, the left transmission mount-bracket assembly, made from two aluminum-alloy forgings, had nearly half the mass of a structurally comparable steel bracket. It provided excellent durability and dimensional accuracy.

Abandoning the old torsion-bar suspension in favor of a MacPherson strut system, the new Seville had a softer ride than in 1985. Yet the combination of a large-diameter front stabilizer bar, new lower control arms, and Cadillac-specified strut valving and spring rates provided a higher level of cornering roll control.

At the rear, the Seville once again had independent suspension, but unless you were closely associated with Corvettes, the view was absolutely shocking—in place of the expected coil springs was a transverse leaf spring! Furthermore, it was made of fiberglass. This spring provided a longer fatigue life than the older steel coils as well as being compact, lightweight, and corrosion free. In the standard suspension, it functioned both as a ride spring and a roll stabilizer. Thus, no stabilizer bar was installed on the standard Seville.

Another new feature—teflon-lined, control-arm outer bushings—also enhanced the Seville's roadability by enabling a high radial rate to be tuned in for precise handling while still maintaining a low torsional rate for excellent isolation. Continued as standard equipment was an electronic level-control system similar to that used in 1985. The most important change was the relocation of the air compressor from the engine compartment to the rear suspension support assembly. Now installed on the compressor was a new body-mounted, air-intake filter intended to minimize both intake noise and water intrusion into the system.

As mentioned earlier, the Seville was fitted with four-wheel disc brakes of a new zero-drag design. A change in the angle of the caliper-seal groove made it possible to have full piston retraction to eliminate the drag formerly caused by friction between the linings and rotor. Further refinements included a new power-assist electric vacuum pump, a multistroke parking-brake pedal designed to hold on a grade with less pedal effort, and a two-piece caliper-brake design for easier brake servicing.

Superseding the old recirculating ball steering was a new power-assisted rack and pinion system with a 11.5:1 ratio. The 1985 Seville's ratio was 15:1-13:1. Contributing to this system's crisp operation was a stiff, front-frame cross-member; modified, low-flow, steering gear valve; and a front-end sheet-metal crossbrace that reduced compliance in the body structure.

The Seville's standard, low-rolling resistance tires were P20517OR14, steel-belted radial whitewalls with a mud and snow rating.

The optional Touring Suspension used 15-inch wheels with Goodyear Eagle GT P215/6OR15 tires. Cadillac reported that these tires' "low-profile, high-performance design (available either in black or white-wall format) with bold, aggressive tread contributes to increased cornering capability and quick steering response." Other components of the Touring Suspension were a larger-diameter front stabilizer bar, the addition of a stabilizer bar to the rear suspension, specifically tuned components, and higher effort steering. Available only with the Touring Suspension were 15-inch aluminum-alloy wheels. They were similar in appearance to the standard wheels except for their broad brake-vent openings.

SEVILLE ELEGANTE

Continuing the policy first enacted in 1978, Cadillac offered the Seville in Elegante form. Standard on this model, and optional for the base Seville, was a thin, brushed, and bright accent molding on the fender, door, and quarter panels, which served as the dividing line for a unique midtone paint treatment. On the base Seville, a two-tone paint scheme was standard; whereas on the Elegante, the lower rocker color matched that of the upper body. This treatment was optional for the base Seville. Also found on the Elegante were wire wheel discs (also listed on the Seville's optional equipment list)

with a bright outer periphery and center hub mounting, and a Cadillac wreath and crest plus Elegante script screened on the lower rear quarter-panel window.

The Elegante interior had a new, Cadillac-exclusive bucket-seat design. The seat trim consisted of a narrow horseshoe bolster of genuine leather enclosing a leather upper with an embroidered wreath. The lower section included a soft-cloth insert and both the seat back and cushion inserts had a narrow V-groove down the center. All-leather upholstery was also available for the Elegante. Located in the upper portion of the driver and front-passenger seatbacks of Elegante Sevilles were "briefcase-type" map pockets with foldover tops.

Both a power recliner for the front seats and a new power lumbar adjustment were standard on the Elegante. This latter feature consisted of an inflatable pillow located within the lower front seatbacks. A control switch along the outer side of the seat cushion controlled a small air compressor to inflate or deflate the pillow as desired.

A new option for the Seville that was standard on the Elegante consisted of reversible, two-sided carpeted floor mats, one side matching the floor carpet and the reverse side having a short-nap carpeting. Since these were symmetrical, they could be switched from side to side.

All Sevilles were equipped with an antilacerative Inner Shield windshield. Applied to its inner surface was a 0.015-inch-thick layer of polyvinylbutyl and a 0.005-inch-thick top mylar cover. Another worthwhile feature was the inclusion of standard transluscent sunshade extensions that slide out from the inboard side of the sun visors. They were a valuable safety asset when the visor was pivoted to block sunlight from the side windows.

PRODUCTION OF SEVILLE

The Seville was built in General Motors Buick-Oldsmobile-Cadillac (B-O-C) Detroit-Hamtramck Assembly Center, which Cadillac described as "the most modern, most efficient and most quality-oriented automotive production complex in the United States."

At the heart of this operation were the people who built the cars, and the operating philosophy of the employees who were organized along a team concept was as enlightening as a review of the plant's sophisticated equipment. "We at the Detroit-Hamtramack Assembly Center," it read, "are a team dedicated to assembling world-class products for our customers in a clean and safe plant by recognizing the skills and abilities of each individual. We encourage the participation and development of everyone, in an atmosphere of trust, respect, pride and open communications to ensure job security, profitability and progressiveness in a changing environment."

To facilitate the transfer of this outlook into reality, the average assembly-line worker received approximately 200 hours of training. For the typical skilled trades person, the hours of classroom and laboratory training exceeded 2,100 hours—the equivalent of a full work year. All told, over 2 million hours of employee training took place to ensure the plant's effective operation.

The sheer size of the Detroit-Hamtramck plant was imposing: 77 acres under one roof, fully air-conditioned, 21 miles of conveyor lines, approximately 2,000 programmable devices and numerous applications of laser cameras.

In the body shop, which was among the world's most highly automated, electric robots or flexible automation performed 97 percent of all spot welding. Throughout the sequential assembly processes, numerous checks, including on-line laser cameras, were used to ensure the maintaining of proper dimensional specifications.

The plant's paint system, which was a model for future GM plants, began with a high-pressure cleaning system followed by an eight-step phosphate washing process involving both sprays and immersion in an electrically charged primer that was attracted to the sheet metal. Another primer coat was applied by a system that flowed the paint on with centrifugal force.

The final paint operations were computer controlled for each color and were performed in a new modular paint-booth system with a stop-and-go capability. This allowed for better consistency of paint applications, minimal dust problems, and the separation of two-tone vehicles from single-color treatments. Each Seville received two coats of its base color followed by two coats of clear enamel. Throughout the production process, each car carried a small transponder that identified itself to the in-plant computer system. In this way an electronic history of the car was established.

The Seville was also the subject of what was depicted as "the most comprehensive corrosion protection plan in Cadillac history." The goal was ten years usage with no perforations or loss of functions. To achieve this, all of the Seville's body panels (except the roof) and exposed body structural components were of two-sided galvanized metal. Cadillac also provided special anticorrison treatment to over 100 chassis areas. To support this program, over 250,000 miles of corrosion durability testing was scheduled for the Seville.

DIFFERENCES AMONG MODELS

The Eldorado, as it had been since the 1980 model year, was virtually identical, technically, to the Seville. Moreover, its appearance, though as a two-door model, was very similar to the Seville's.

Also linking the Eldorado to the Seville was its history, which had taken it from an origin as a limited production model in 1953 to a key role in the Cadillac lineup. Both cars in their new form were intended to bolster Cadillac's status both among affluent customers who would normally not consider a Cadillac, as well as Cadillac's traditional buyers.

Historically, the Eldorado name had been attached to some of Cadillac's most memorable postwar models. Among the greatest was the Eldorado Brougham of 1957, which Cadillac calculated would have sold for $48,774 in 1986 dollars.

Not until 1967, with the advent of the front-wheel-drive model did Eldorado production begin in earnest.

Of the 926,000 + Eldorados built by the end of the 1986 model run, over 96 percent, or over 891,000, were front-wheel-drive models.

As it had with the Seville, Cadillac observed the Eldorado's upcoming change with a Commemorative Edition during the 1985 model year with exterior and interior gold accents as well as two-tone leather trim. For 1986, Cadillac promised its successor would be a "formidable driver's coupe which promises to be another in a long line of Cadillac successes."

Physically, the Eldorado was identical in size to the Seville, with a 108-inch wheelbase, overall length of 186.2 inches, and a 53.7-inch height.

Aside from the obvious two-door, four-door distinction the Eldorado's styling was set apart from the Seville's by its body-colored, side-body molding, cornering lamps placed within the stainless-steel molding of the front bumper, and vertically positioned taillights. Eldorado script was found on the fenders ahead of the front wheel openings.

Interior appointments and features of the Eldorado and the Biarritz version followed the format established by the standard Seville and Seville Elegante. Standard on all Eldorados was a new front floor console that included an illuminated ashtray and cigarette lighter, transmission shifter (which had been column mounted in 1985), rotating cup holder, spring-loaded coin retainer, and two storage compartments.

The console was color-coordinated with the interior, and the self-adjusting shifter trim plate had a textured-aluminum precision grid. Similar trim distinctions were found on the dash of these models. For the Biarritz, it was of American walnut. On both models, the transmission shifter had a black hand-stitched, leather-wrapped handle.

In all aspects of its technical specifications and equipment availability, the Eldorado was identical to the Seville. Like the Seville, it was produced in the new Detroit-Hamtramck Assembly Center.

The introduction of these two new models came little more than a year after the arrival of the front-wheel-drive De Ville and Fleetwood, which Cadillac had depicted as the most advanced cars in its history. Changes for 1986 were depicted as "product refinements" intended to "further enhance quality, appearance, function and performance."

The De Villes were given a wide, bright rocker molding plus the closed-in rear window formerly restricted to the Fleetwood. The Fleetwood Sedan now was fitted with the previously optional Format Cabriolet vinyl roof. The optional 14-inch, aluminum-alloy wheels had new center flush-mounted hubcaps with a silver wreath and crest on a dark red background.

De Ville seats had improved lateral support thanks to a new seat design with a formal sew pattern which was offered in either knit cloth or leather. The optional leather upholstery for both the De Ville and Fleetwood now included leather front-seat headrests.

On the Coupe de Ville, the vertically mounted assist handles were relocated from the front-seat back to the lock pillar. Replacing the light butterfly, walnut instrument panel and door-trim plates used on 1985 De

1986 Eldorado with optional wide body side accent molding.

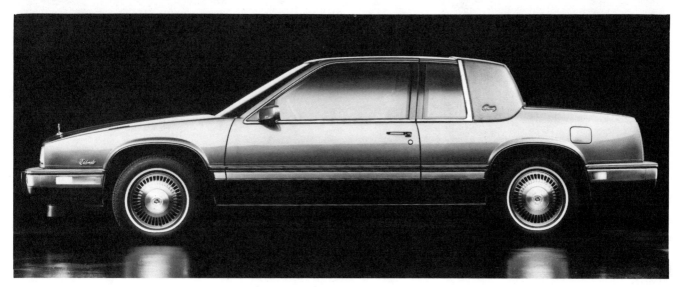

1986 Eldorado Biarritz.

CADILLAC VITAL STATISTICS: 1986

Series	Model	Body Type	Sug. Retail Price ($)	Weight (lbs.)	Production (#)
Cimarron	JG69 (4 cyl)	4 dr Sedan	13,128	2575	
	JG69 (V-6)	4 dr Sedan	13,738	NA	24,534
Seville	KS69	4 dr Sedan	26,756	3428	19,098
De Ville	CD69	4 dr Sedan	19,669	3378	129,857
	CD47	2 dr Coupe	19,990	3319	36,350
Eldorado	EL57	2 dr Coupe	24,251	3365	21,342
Brougham	DW69	4 dr Sedan	21,265	4020	49,137
75	CH23	Limousine	33,895	3637	650
	CH33	Formal Limousine	36,934	3736	350

1986 Eldorado Biarritz interior.

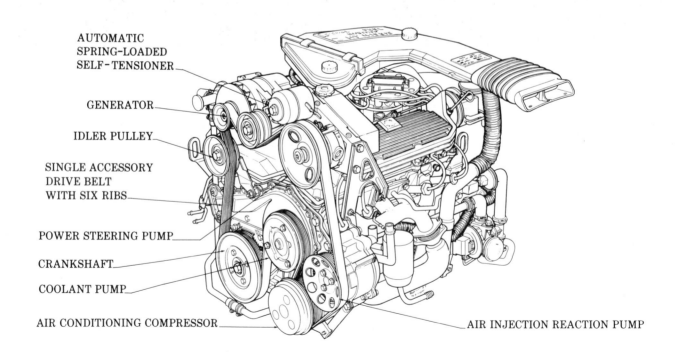

AUTOMATIC
SPRING-LOADED
SELF-TENSIONER

GENERATOR

IDLER PULLEY

SINGLE ACCESSORY
DRIVE BELT
WITH SIX RIBS

POWER STEERING PUMP

CRANKSHAFT

COOLANT PUMP

AIR CONDITIONING COMPRESSOR

AIR INJECTION REACTION PUMP

1986 Seville Elegante.

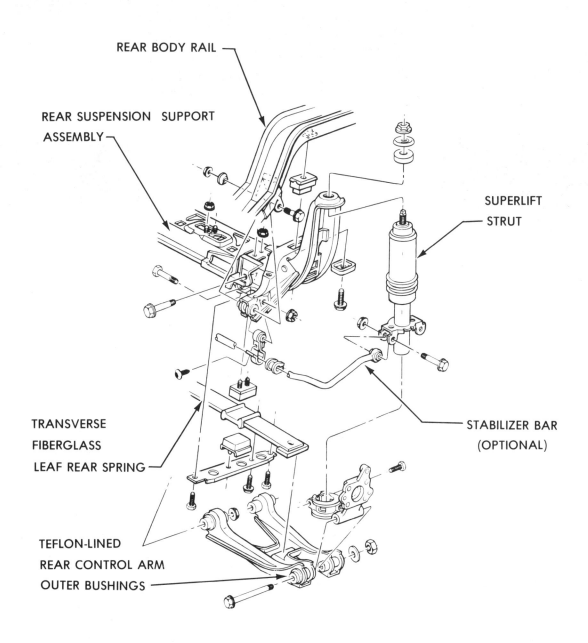

REAR BODY RAIL

REAR SUSPENSION SUPPORT
ASSEMBLY

SUPERLIFT
STRUT

TRANSVERSE
FIBERGLASS
LEAF REAR SPRING

STABILIZER BAR
(OPTIONAL)

TEFLON-LINED
REAR CONTROL ARM
OUTER BUSHINGS

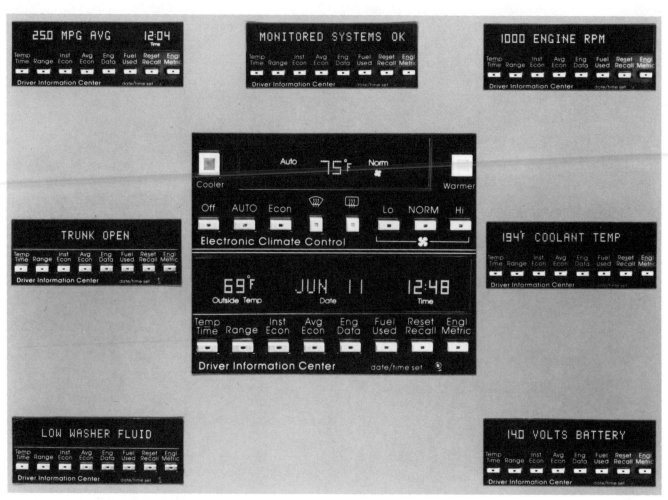

Details of the Climate Control Driver Information Center as installed in the 1986 Eldorado and Seville.

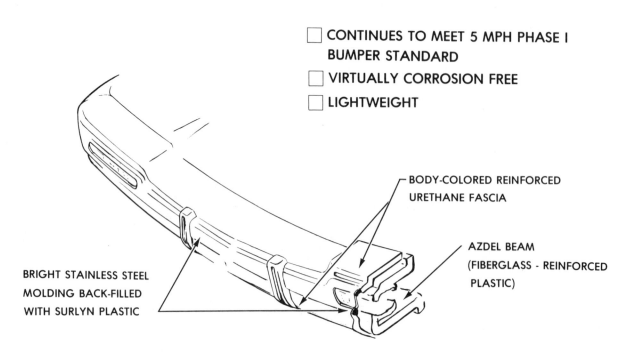

☐ CONTINUES TO MEET 5 MPH PHASE I BUMPER STANDARD

☐ VIRTUALLY CORROSION FREE

☐ LIGHTWEIGHT

BODY-COLORED REINFORCED URETHANE FASCIA

AZDEL BEAM (FIBERGLASS - REINFORCED PLASTIC)

BRIGHT STAINLESS STEEL MOLDING BACK-FILLED WITH SURLYN PLASTIC

Features of the Eldorado and Seville front and rear bumper system.

The optional cellular telephone for the Eldorado and Seville was positioned in the front center armrest.

1986 Cadillac Touring Coupe.

Ville and Fleetwood models was a cherry woodgrain. The Fleetwood d'Elegance used American walnut-trim plates. Added to the instrument panel was a low brake-fluid warning indicator. All De Villes and Fleetwoods also had, as standard equipment, the sunshade extensions installed on the Eldorado and Seville. The digital instrumentation cluster remained an option for the De Ville but was now standard for the Fleetwood. Both series had new electric mirror controls relocated from the instrument panel to the driver's door armrest. These mirrors (color keyed to the car's exterior) were optional for the De Ville and standard on the Fleetwood.

In place of the vertically mounted spare-tire arrangement of 1985, the latest De Villes and Fleetwoods used a lay-down tire storage. This change was associated with a new exhaust system routing and the use of a modified, rear stabilizer bar. Additional 1986 improvements included reduced deck-lid closing effort and quieter operation of the electric window lifts and door locks.

All of these Cadillacs were also available with an optional cellular telephone, located on De Villes and Fleetwoods within the front, center folddown armrest. On the Seville and Eldorado, it was positioned in the

1986 Cimarron D'Oro with its new Tungsten-halogen headlights and grille design.

1986 Fleetwood Brougham d'Elegance.

locking storage compartment of the front console armrest. An overhead microphone was mounted on the outboard side of the driver's sun visor (De Ville and Fleetwood) or in the overhead console between the sun visors (Seville and Eldorado).

A "radio mute module" integrated the telephone within the cars' sound system. This allowed the front speakers or the telephone handset to be used for conversation. It also automatically decreased the volume of the radio through the rear speakers when the system was in operation.

Changes to the standard HT-4100 V-8 increased its horsepower rating to 130 at 4,200 rpm with peak torque moving up to 200 lb-ft at 2,200 rpm. These higher outputs were attributed to use of a revised intake manifold; a less restrictive, electric, early fuel-evaporation heating grid; and throttle-body bores providing increased air flow into the engine. Providing 15 percent greater computational capability and more memory was a new electronic control module. Cadillac reported that benefits from its use included "improved performance

feel, better idle speed control, improved acceleration feel, and smoother driveability."

All HT-4100 engines were also equipped with stainless-steel exhaust manifolds in place of the older cast-iron units of 1985. These both reduced overall weight and helped raise the operating temperature of the catalytic converter, thus reducing hydrocarbon emission more effectively. Making engine sounds less apparent to occupants were new "hydro-elastic" engine mounts.

Changes to the De Ville/Fleetwood power-assisted, rack and pinion steering consisted of a revamped steering control valve, resulting in enhanced, straight-ahead steering feel and a 19.4:1, rather than 18.4:1, base steering ratio.

Cadillac had signaled its intention to provide sporting versions of its new front-wheel-drive models by offering the optional ride-and-handling touring package during 1985. A similar move had preceded the introduction of the Eldorado Touring Coupe in 1982.

That model was no longer available. Instead,

1986 Sedan de Ville.

A 1986 Coupe de Ville with optional Formal Cabriolet Roof.

Cadillac offered De Ville-based Touring Coupe and Sedan versions. The key ingredients of the ride-and-handling Touring package consisted of 15-inch, aluminum-alloy wheels with Goodyear Eagle GT P215/65R15 blackwalls, replacing the standard P205/75R14 whitewalls, a larger, 18-mm to 12-mm, rear stabilizer bar, 18.4:1 ratio steering, tighter front and rear strut valving, and high front and rear spring and suspension bushing rates.

Numerous styling-appointment features identified the Touring models. Their interiors were fitted with gray leather seating areas, rear leather headrests, a leather-wrapped steering-wheel rim, and leather insert for the horn pad, leather gear-shift lever and steering-wheel tilt lever knobs, glove-box identification plaque reading either "Touring Coupe" or "Touring Sedan," and Cadillac script door-sill plates.

Cadillac had no intention of keeping these cars' existence a secret—thus their external appearance was intended to draw attention to their status as performance models. At the front, an air dam, carrying fog lights (provided with covers), was installed that wrapped rearward to the front wheel openings. The gray bumper strips had silver inner accents that blended nicely with a wide gray rocker molding. Car-colored outside mirrors (electrically operated) and tail-lamp bezels were fitted as was a rear deck-lid spoiler positioned between the fender endcaps. The rear

window carried either "Touring Coupe" or "Touring Sedan" identification. The Touring Coupe was also fitted with removable vertical louvers for its side quarter windows. Body-color choices for the Touring models were restricted to platinum, academy gray, cotillion white, and sable black.

Overall, Cadillac's 1986 color selections for the De Villes, Fleetwoods, and Fleetwood Seventy-Five Limousines numbered 16. Two of these Pearlmist paints, black cherry and black emerald, were identified as Richelyn R colors. They achieved their unique status due to their metallic appearance achieved without the use of metal in the pigment. In place of the customary use of small aluminum flakes, these paints used color pigments mixed with extremely fine mica platelets encapsulated within a molecular deposition of iron oxide. When sunlight penetrated these particles, it was both reflected and refracted by the mica fragments. Cadillac reported that the overall effect was "one of luminous, enriched color that actually diversifies, depending upon the angle of sunlight striking the automobile's surface."

For example, the black cherry could appear as solid black, solid violet, solid reddish violet, metallic reddish violet, or metallic magneta. Similarly, black emerald might appear as solid black, dark rich green, or metallic emerald.

Another benefit of Pearlmist paint was its long-term

Details of the 1986 Seville's standard digital instrumentation.

1986 Eldorado America II Special Limited Edition.

durability and protection from the elements provided by the iron-oxide mica coating, which both absorbed and dissipated ultraviolet radiation.

Available for all front-wheel-drive De Villes and Fleetwoods, as well as the Seville and Eldorado, was a new electronic, antilock braking system. Its primary components consisted of a small, modular-design hydraulic unit, a digital electronic control unit, and four wheel sensors. The front wheels were controlled separately, the rear wheels as a single unit.

In practice, the speed sensors at each wheel alerted the electronic control unit of an imminent lockup based on the rotational speed of the wheels. This computer then modulated the braking effect of each wheel via solenoid valves up to 12 times a second to optimize whatever traction was available from the road surface.

The latest Fleetwood Seventy-Five Limousines shared the revisions and additions found in the 1986 Fleetwoods. Both versions had Dual Comfort front seats trimmed in standard knit cloth or optional leather trim. The Formal Limousine had black seating areas for the front seats.

Also included in its appointments was the customary center partition with sliding glass, a front compartment with two removable storage compartments, controlled-cycle wiper systems, separate rear-heater and air-conditioning unit, and tilt and telescope steering wheel.

Changes to the Cimarron for 1986 consisted of wraparound rear taillights requiring the use of modified rear quarter panels. Also apparent were shorter, rear-bumper endcaps. As did all 1986 American automobiles, the Cimarron had a standard center, high-mounted stop light.

The D'Oro model had its own front-grille treatment involving composite tungsten-halogen headlights, wraparound and side markers, and lowered front-bumper center section. As in 1985, the D'Oro package featured gold styling accents; grooved car-colored, lower-body accent molding, 14-inch, aluminum-alloy wheels with gold accents; Goodyear Eagle P205/6OR14 low-profile tires; foglight cover; and identification plaque.

Cimarron interior appointments were refined to include added leather trim for the manual shift-lever boot and knob, as well as a leather-wrapped, parking-brake handle. As a credit option, a new Morgan cloth-and-leather upholstery was offered as an alternative to the standard Sierra-grain leather interior. Joining the Cimarron's radio lineup was the Delco-GM/Bose sound system.

No changes of consequence were made in the Cimarron's power train and chassis. Cimarrons with the V-6 engine continued to use a fully gas-charged suspension with front Delco struts and Bilstein-Delco shocks at the rear. The front stabilizer bar was increased from 28 to 30 mm, and stiffer spring rates were specified.

The grande dame of the Cadillac line, the Fleeetwood Brougham, and its special-edition version, the Fleetwood Brougham d'Elegance, were originally scheduled to be manufactured only through December 1985. No changes, except for the use of the center high-

mounted stop lamp beginning in September 1985, were anticipated. But the appeal of this "traditional" Cadillac to "traditional" Cadillac buyers forced a rethinking of this strategy. Not only was the December 1985 production deadline abandoned; but in mid-February 1986, a 1986 version was introduced. This was a car, said Cadillac, "for luxury-car enthusiasts who 'Think Big'."

Replacing the HT-4100 V-8 was a 5.0-liter V-8 engine with a 140 horsepower rating and four-barrel carburetion. A "5.0 liter" plaque on the trunk lid identified these revised models. Aside from this change, the Brougham was put on a weight-reduction program that resulted in the use of tubular front stabilizer bars and lightweight coil springs. Base models also used aluminum, internal seat frames and reduced mass-carpeted floor mats in order to save weight. In the same spirit, Broughams were available with aluminum wheels for additional weight savings. The d'Elegance models could be purchased with lightweight, center-retention, wire-wheel discs.

Whereas once it had been the benchmark for the era of resized luxury cars, the Brougham was now seen in a totally different perspective. John O. Grettenberger explained: "While it remains the longest, tallest and heaviest production luxury car in America, the Fleetwood Brougham also offers a bigger emphasis on performance in 1986. The combination of a larger, more powerful engine and extensive component weight reduction makes the Fleetwood Brougham the only automobile in the world that combines Cadillac engineering excellence with the spaciousness and comfort of a rear-wheel-drive luxury car. Many American luxury-car buyers still demand the ammenities of a rear-wheel-drive, full size car. The revisions to the 1986 Cadillac Fleetwood Brougham, along with a more competitive price, make it an unsurpassed value in the market today."

CADILLAC'S DOMESTIC COMPETITION

The 1986 Lincoln Town Car rode into 1986 on the crest of all-time high sales. Depicted as offering "traditional full-size comfort," the Town Car was powered by the same 5.0-liter V-8 as in 1985. For 1986, this engine was equipped with sequential, multiport electronic fuel injection. The Signature and Cartier Designer series offered equipment beyond that included on the standard Town Car such as a power deck-lid pulldown, rear floor mats, and articulated front-seat headrests. During the model year, a Ford JBL Audio-System with 12 speakers was offered as an option for all three series.

The Lincoln Continental was also available with this sound system. In addition, the Continental's standard equipment list included Lincoln's Anti-Lock Brake System. Refinements included "twin-comfort lounge" front seats with a new cloth-trim fabric and four-way, articulated, front-seat headrests.

The Givenchy designer series had a new two-tone paint treatment of midnight black over red velvet, glamour clearcoat metallic.

Powering the Lincoln Mark VII was the same

5.0-liter V-8 with multiport electronic fuel injection as used on other Lincolns. Numerous features previously available only as options became standard Mark VII equipment for 1986. These included a six-way power passenger seat, power seat recliners, keyless entry system, power deck-lid pulldown, and dual external heated mirrors. The Bill Blass designer series had a new color scheme of sandalwood clearcoat metallic over a lower-body treatment of dark sandalwood clear-coat metallic.

The LSC version of the Mark VII had a high output, 5-liter V-8 even stronger than in 1985 thanks to a new tuned intake manifold and tubular headers. It produced approximately 8 percent more horsepower and torque as compared with the 1985 engine. Official power ratings were 200 horsepower at 4,000 rpm and 285 lb-ft of torque at 3,000 rpm. This translated into 0 to 60-mph times of 8.3 seconds, considerably beyond the capability of a Cadillac Eldorado. The Mark VII was also equipped with Lincoln's Anti-Lock Brake System and "European-style" mechanical analog gauges.

SPECIFICATIONS
Seville, Eldorado

Engine

Type: V-8, aluminum block, ohv
Bore × stroke: 3.46 × 3.31 inches
Displacement: 249 cubic inches
Horsepower: 130 @ 4,200 rpm
Torque: 200 lb-ft @ 2,200 rpm
Fuel system: Digital fuel injection
Electrical system: 12-volt battery, 120-amp generator
Transmission: Turbo-Hydramatic, four-speed automatic with overdrive and viscous converter clutch

Chassis/Drivetrain

Frame: Body frame integral construction
Front suspension: Independent, MacPherson struts, stabilizer bar, coil springs, Pliacell shock absorbers integral with struts. Final drive ratio 2.97:1
Rear suspension: Independent, single transerve fiberglass spring, electronic level control, superlift shock absorbers; stabilizer bar on Touring suspension optional
Steering: Power-assisted rack and pinion, 16.5:1 overall ratio

Brakes: Power, four-wheel vented disc, zero drag, 10.25 × 1 inch (front), 10.0 × 0.5 inch (rear)
Tires: Steel-belted, all-season radial white sidewall, P205/7OR14
Touring suspension uses Goodyear Eagle GT P215/6OR15

Dimensions

Wheelbase: 108 inches
Width:
    Eldorado: 71.3 inches
    Seville: 70.9 inches
Front/rear trend, 59.9/59.9 inches
Overall length: 188.2 inches

De Ville and Fleetwood (Front-wheel-drive)

Engine

Same as Seville/Eldorado

Chassis/Drivetrain

Unchanged from 1985 except steering ratio: 19.4:1; and engine ratings: 130 hp @ 4,200 rpm and 200 lb-ft of torque @ 2,200 rpm

Cimarron

Unchanged from 1985

Fleetwood Brougham

Unchanged from 1985 except a 5.0-liter V-8 with four-barrel carburetor and 140 hp @ 3,200 rpm is fitted.

FL Popular Options

Cellular telephone: Eldorado, Seville
Astroroof
Automatic day/night mirror
Dimming sentinel
Rear-window defogger
Automatic door locks
Passenger-Seat power recliner
Six-way front passenger seat
Trunk-Lid pulldown
Delco GM/Bose symphony sound system
Delco-GM electronically tuned received with cassette player
Wire wheels: Fleetwood Brougham

1987

There Is a New Spirit That Drives Cadillac

THE INTRODUCTION OF the Allante coincided with the arrival of the "new spirit of Cadillac." This didn't mean that Cadillac's latest models were drastically redesigned and restyled, but rather that, thanks to numerous refinements, they were even more capable and appealing than in 1986.

Cadillac divided its "new spirit" into five sections, in each of which a particular Cadillac was highlighted. The "Sporting Spirit" Cadillac was the Cimarron, the "Contemporary Spirit" Cadillacs were the De Ville and Fleetwood models; the "Classic Spirit" of Cadillac was represented by the Brougham, the "Driving Spirit" was the Eldorado, and the "Elegant Spirit" was the Seville.

Not included in this delineation were the Series Seventy-Five and the revived Fleetwood Sixty Special models. But Cadillac made up for these omissions by noting that "its heritage of advanced technology, quality craftsmanship and limousine luxury are embodied" in the latest Seventy-Fives. The Sixty Special was described as a "new top-of-the-line vehicle for 1987."

THE SPORTING SPIRIT

Beginning its sixth year of production, the Cimarron adopted the composite, tungsten headlight system introduced on the 1986 D'Oro model, which was not carried into 1987. Its use was accompanied by a new molded front-end fascia and wraparound side markers that also functioned as side lights. More important to the Cimarron's image was the adoption of a "second-generation" V-6 engine; an all-new, five-speed transmission; and revised suspension components as standard equipment.

The new engine, with 125 instead of 120 horsepower, featured an aluminum head with a centralized sparkplug location and canted valve design for a faster burning combustion chamber. In addition, the engine's compression ratio was boosted to 8.9:1 from 8.5:1. Other engine refinements included stone-microfinished, crankshaft working areas and improved

engine fluid sealing. The multiport fuel injection system was retained, but its timing was now direct-fire via a computer-controlled coil ignition system instead of the older conventional mechanical distributor.

Changes to the front suspension, which included the use of revised element bushings and stabilizer bar, were intended to improve ride quality without any sacrifices in the Cimarron's handling characteristics. Coinciding with the installation of the five-speed manual transmission was the use of equal-length driveshafts and a lower engine mounting.

THE CONTEMPORARY SPIRIT

Both the De Ville and Fleetwood d'Elegance Cadillacs were 1.5 inches longer because of a new rear-quarter/bumper extension and taillamps. The most apparent appearance changes were the dual-stacked, red reflex appliques centered between the taillights and the license-plate opening. At the front a restyled grille, composite headlights, a new hood header molding, restyled side markers and cornering and reflex lamps were used.

Nine new exterior colors in addition to five two-tone paint treatments for the Sedan de Ville were offered. The Coupe de Ville was available with the Formal roof and a new-for-1987 cloth-textured Cambria top.

Interior appointments for the De Ville included a Contessa Royal Prima fabric with Sierra-grain leather seating areas optional. Whereas the De Villes used the Contessa fabric for the vertical piping in combination with Royal Prima bolsters, all portions of the Fleetwood d'Elegance upholstery were finished in Royal Prima. Also setting the two interiors apart were the cherry wood-grain trimplates for the De Ville and the American walnut versions installed in the Fleetwood d'Elegance.

Detail changes to these models' accoutrements included new power rear-door locks with a lock-only function, refined power window motors that dampened operational sound, the relocation of the optional cellular telephone microphone to the center armrest for improved voice reception, and the operation of the radio/cassette player and washers added to the retained accessory power feature.

Engineering refinements included use of deflected, disc front-strut valving; a new two-piece front-strut mount; new shear-type rear-strut mounts; and "hydro-elastic" engine mounts that collectively resulted in smoother and quieter ride characteristics. Reducing noise level at idle was the elimination of the front-fender-mounted vacuum pumps on cars without cruise control and limitation of its use on cars with cruise control only when the system was engaged. Both series were also fitted with revised rear-drum brakes and master cylinders that provided less pedal travel and improved modulation. The optional ride-and-handling package was continued as were the De Ville Touring Coupe and Sedan models.

THE SIXTY SPECIAL

Although initial 1987 model production was set at a modest 2,000 units, the return of the Fleetwood Sixty Special to the Cadillac lineup was a clear signal that Cadillac's more aggressive marketing plan for the rest of the decade and beyond included a return to product concepts of the past as well as radical new proposals.

As had so often been the case in earlier years, the Sixty Special had its own exclusive wheelbase, which for 1987 was 115.8 inches, 5 inches longer in the rear-door area than that of the Fleetwood d'Elegance. The Sixty Special had the same front and rear styling of that model plus rear-door sail panels and stainless-steel/aluminum-composite rocker moldings that were 5 inches longer. Cadillac noted that "the wider sail panels lend a more formal look both inside and out, and afford limousine-like privacy for rear-seat passengers."

In addition to the amenities of the Fleetwood d'Elegance interior, the Sixty Special's had several exclusive features, such as rear passenger-compartment footrails and a rear overhead console. Also standard was the Cadillac/Teves electronic anti-lock braking system and a full vinyl top.

THE DRIVING AND ELEGANT SPIRITS

Visually the Eldorado and Seville, after being completely redesigned and re-engineered in 1986, were virtually unchanged for 1987. There were some noteworthy technical refinements. Both cars used new "hydro-elastic" engine mounts with a three-way hydraulic action, vehicle sensitive rear seat belts, and carried vehicle identification tags on major body components. If these tags were removed, a telltale tracing was left behind.

A single-point AIR emission system replaced the older port AIR injection to improve overall emission-system operation. Also utilized was a new transmission aneroid modulator that compensated for changes in ambient temperature. This translated into more consistent engine performance in varied altitude driving conditions.

Along with recalibrated chassis and suspension components that Cadillac said resulted in "an improved combination of ride and road management," the Seville and Eldorado were fitted with larger Goodyear P205/75R14 tires. The optional touring suspension available for both cars included 15-inch wheels, Goodyear Eagle GT tires, a rear stabilizer bar, specifically tuned suspension components, and higher effort steering.

Cadillac explained that the use of front and rear deflected disc struts "improved road feel by momentarily allowing shock absorbers to become more compliant than their typically harsher handling counterparts, then quickly stiffen to provide firm road feel and control."

Neither the Eldorado nor the Seville were equipped with a conventional speedometer. Instead, the speedometer and odometer used electric signals generated at the transmission by a speed sensor. Incorporated into the body computer module was a nonvolatile memory circuit that retained odometer information even when the battery was disconnected.

Standard on the base Eldorado were finely striped, steel-gray trimplates for the instrument panel, steering wheel, and console. Genuine American Walnut trimplates were optional on the base Eldorado and standard on the Biarritz.

Cashmere and leather seating areas were standard on the base Eldorado and the Biarritz with Sierra-grain leather seating areas optional. The Biarritz featured a power lumbar support as well as full-power, front-seat controls and power recline. The same power lumbar support, which consisted of an inflatable pillow located within the lower front-seat back of the driver and front passenger seats, was standard in the Seville Elegante.

All Sevilles had a two-spoke steering wheel with a foam-padded, hand-stitched, leather-wrapped rim. The transmission gear-selector lever was also leather-padded and color-coded to match the steering wheel.

A dual-tone exterior was standard for the Seville. The Elegante was finished in a two-color midtone finish. A monotone finish was available on both models and the base Seville was available in the midtone finish as well.

Cadillac warrantied the Seville and Eldorado (as well as all other models for 1987) against rust-through for five years or 100,000 miles. The entire braking system of the Seville and Eldorado, including brake pads, was warrantied for five years or 50,000 miles.

THE SERIES SEVENTY-FIVE

The Fleetwood Seventy-Five Limousine featured the same front and rear styling revisions as the Sedan de Ville plus a grooved, 6-inch-wide rocker molding made of a stainless-steel/aluminum composite with a single-rib accent groove. Overall length was now 220 inches or 1.5 inches greater than in 1986.

THE CLASSIC SPIRIT

The popularity of the only rear-drive Cadillac, the Brougham (whose sales increased by over 30 percent during 1986), required Cadillac to extend its 1986

1987 Cimarron.

1987 Sedan de Ville.

1987 Fleetwood d'Elegance.

1987 Fleetwood Sixty Special.

1987 Seville.

1987 Fleetwood Seventy-Five Limousine.

production run through July, a month longer than originally anticipated. The latest version received a new cross-hatched grille, revised header molding, and new parking/directional signal lamps. Other changes included the addition of red reflexes to the rear panel; a Cadillac, rather than Fleetwood, rear-deck script; and Brougham, instead of Fleetwood Brougham, script on the quarter panels. The Brougham's gold parking lamp and rear taillight crests were replaced by silver versions.

Standard interior trim consisted of a Royal Prima cloth with Sierra-grain leather seating areas optional. The Brougham d'Elegance continued to use a tufted-pillow design. All Broughams were also available with a new tricolor interior.

Technical changes were minor, represented by altered engine-accessory mounts and the use of a roller valve lifter.

CADILLAC'S DOMESTIC COMPETITION

Changes to the three Lincoln series were limited for 1987. The Continental was highlighted by a new variation of the Givenchy Designer Series. The veteran Town Car was virtually identical to the previous model, although a compact disc player was available as an option to supplement the standard quality sound system.

The most impressive of all Lincolns, the Mark VII LSC, was once again offered with two versions of its fuel-injected, 5.0-liter V-8 with 150 horsepower or a high-output version with 200 horsepower. Pivoting front vent windows were now optional, and the corrosion protection was upgraded.

SPECIFICATIONS

All specifications were unchanged for 1987 except for the following:

Dimensions

Overall length:
    De Ville, Fleetwood d'Elegance: 196.5 inches
    Series 75:   220 inches

Series 60 Special

Wheelbase: 115.8 inches
Width: 71.7 inches
Front/rear tread: 60.3/59.8 inches
Overall length: 201.5 inches

Popular Options

Two-tone paint
Cellular telephone
Automatic day/night interior mirror
Full Cabriolet roof
Astroroof (not available with full Cabriolet roof)
Delco-GM/Bose symphony sound system
Delco AM Stereo/FM Stereo Electronically Tuned Receiver with Cassette tape player
Antilock braking system

1987 Eldorado Biarritz.

1987 Brougham.

Allanté

The Realization of a Dream

THE ALLANTÉ is General Motors' new passenger car flagship. With that pronouncement, Cadillac General Manager John O. Grettenberger introduced what, in terms of its impact on the division, could be the most significant Cadillac model of the postwar era.

DEVELOPMENT OF THE ALLANTÉ

Its origin was, in one respect, similar to that of the 1948 model. In both cases, there was a need for Cadillac to break out of the styling mode that gave many General Motors' cars styling parity. But the automotive market of 1987 bore little resemblance to that of 1948. Among the more important changes were its internationalization and fragmentation. Both of these changed the fundamental structure of the luxury-car market and the number of firms competing in each of its subdivisions.

Cadillac was not lacking in exposure to the market's ultra-luxury segment. Half a century ago, its V-16 automobiles were regarded by many objective critics as at least the equal of the contemporary Rolls-Royce; and although production was extremely limited, the Eldorado Brougham of 1957-1960 was a modern manifestation of Cadillac's ability to substantiate its "Standard of the World" slogan.

In 1982 when the controversy over the Seville's styling was still stirring, work began on what became the LST or Luxury Two-Seater project. This identification was important to the Allanté's development as a unique automobile that, while destined to be compared with other ultra-luxury automobiles, really was not a direct competitor to any one of them.

Cadillac had often been maligned for depicting the Cimarron the "Cadillac of small cars"; but the point of this statement, often missed by over-zealous critics eager to fault Cadillac for every real or imagined misdeed, was that Cadillac was making a strong effort to set the Cimarron apart from other competitive marques.

Admittedly this wasn't an easy task, given the Cimarron's J-car base, but a similar philosophy carried over to the Allanté produced startling results.

The Allanté was in the same market slot as the Mercedes-Benz 560SL, Porsche 928S, BMW 635SCi, and Jaguar XJ-S. Like each of those cars, it was designed according to a special agenda, reflecting both its maker's heritage and perspective of quality, luxury, and performance. Overall, this implied that the Allante design would be an intelligent expression of sophistication rather than a manifestation of brute performance or neotraditional sports-car handling and driving characteristics.

Aside from providing the product needed to move Cadillac into the ultra-luxury class, the luster of the Allanté was expected to shine benevolently on Cadillac's image. At a time when Cadillac was resurrecting the Series Sixty Special and enhancing the Cimarron's performance, the arrival of the Allanté and the tremendous fallout of publicity it generated boded well for Cadillac's efforts to more aggressively market its products.

With projected first-year output pegged at just 7,800 units, the Allanté, as a low-volume, high-priced car, did not easily fit into Cadillac's domestic production operations. A link-up with a relatively low-volume producer was both a necessity and one that offered a real plus—a close relationship with a prestigious "Old World" name.

Cadillac entered this phase of Allanté development with an open mind. Its chief engineer, Warren Hirshfield, visiting the 1982 Turin, Italy, auto show, made several on-site inspections of a number of Italian design/production facilities. It didn't take long for the resources of Pininfarina and its impressive design-development-production operation to emerge as Cadillac's choice for the project.

Later, citing a 1932 V-16 dual-cowl phaeton that was the first Cadillac to be bodied by Pininfarina, Cadillac noted: "The Allanté is the most significant re-

1987 Allanté.

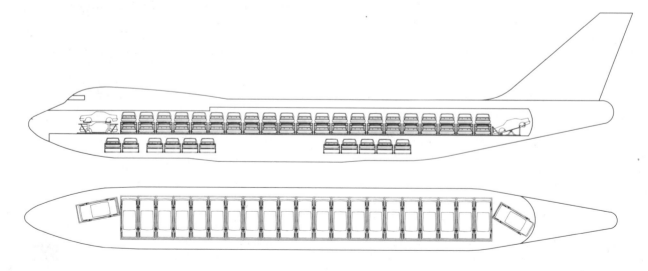

1987 Allanté Convertible.

Details of a Boeing 747 model fully loaded with Allanté bodies.

338   *Cadillac—America's Luxury Car*

Cadillac General Manager John O. Grettenberger demonstrating how 56 Allanté bodies fit into a Boeing 747 with tolerances of just 1 inch.

John O. Grettenberger surveys the interior of a Boeing 747 used in the Allanté Airbridge.

sult of a quarter-century of continuing cooperative efforts between Pininfarina and Cadillac.''

Both this background and the two firms' close proximity in terms of styling philosophy and commitment to quality made what could have been a difficult task relatively easy. What Cadillac wanted, a car with the Cadillac look and a style that was both distinctive and not easily dated, was what Pininfarina was capable of delivering.

Powering the Allanté was a specially tuned version of Cadillac's 4.1-liter V-8, developing 170 horsepower at 5,300 rpm and 230 lb-ft of torque at 3,200 rpm. Among its unique features were low-friction pistons, low-restriction intake ports, magnesium rocker-arm covers, and an aluminum oil pan specific to the Allanté.

Providing what Cadillac called ''state-of-the-art fuel delivery'' was an electronic, sequential-port, fuel-injection system. Unlike other electronic systems, this unit sprayed a precisely metered fuel charge into each port at the exact instant of introduction. Found only on the Allanté was a staged, two-barrel throttle body intended to produce a smooth transition from normal operating speeds to wide-open throttle.

In the early stages of Allanté development, consideration was given to use of a rear-drive system based on the technology existing in the form of the Opel Senator and Corvette. But this approach never moved far from ground zero. Both Pininfarina and Cadillac were advocates of front-wheel-drive systems; and as a result, the Allanté was based on the GM-30 platform, which had been in production since 1986 as the Cadillac Eldorado, Buick Riviera, and Oldsmobile Toronado.

ENGINEERING FEATURES

Cadillac was quick to emphasize that the Allanté was unique among General Motors cars, noting that it was ''engineered from the beginning as a Convertible'' and that it ''has a structural integrity exceeding previous international standards to serve as a sound foundation for suspension components designed to deliver world-class ride and handling.''

MacPherson struts were used at the front and rear in conjunction with front coil springs and a single, composite, polyester-fiberglass, transverse-leaf spring at the rear. All components, as compared with the Eldorado's, were recalibrated for use on the Allanté. Thus, very few parts, including, for example, the Allanté's deflected disc valving, were interchangeable with the Eldorado.

Exclusive to the Allanté in 1987 were its low-profile, high-performance, P225/60VR15 Goodyear Eagle VL tires mounted on 15-×-7-inch forged aluminum wheels. These tires were engineered by Goodyear specifically for the Allanté and combined the cornering power of a high-performance tire with the quiet, smooth ride of a luxury-car tire.

The 0.82-lateral-g cornering capability of the Allanté was impressive; but perhaps even more important for the Allanté's stature, which Cadillac observed was ''in the tradition of the great grand touring cars,'' was its road performance. Cadillac's chief engineer reported, ''When cornering briskly in the Allanté, you only have to set the steering angle once.

Secondary corrections are unnecessary. We have developed a car that is free from front-wheel-drive symptoms. It is possible to go from a normal road load to wide-open throttle in a turn without steering corrections.''

With 50 more horsepower than other Cadillacs with the 4.1-liter engine, the Allanté's zero to 60-mph acceleration time of 10 seconds, if not the equal of the Mercedes-Benz 560Sl, which was capable of the same run in 8 seconds, was delivered with traditional Cadillac smoothness. Likely to become an option early in the Allanté's performance life, a five-speed Getrag manual transmission will enhance its acceleration ability.

Initially the only transmission offered was a dramatically reworked version of the Turbo Hydra-Matic with a Turbo Hydra-Matic F7 designation. The major thrust of its redesign was to enhance its ability to cope with the Allanté's 230 lb-ft of torque.

For well over a decade, Cadillac had been a leader in the area of automotive electronics. In keeping with its status as General Motors' flagship automobile, the Allanté had an on-board electronic capability unequaled by any other car in General Motors' history. Indeed, with a combined systems memory capacity of 90.7 K bytes, the Allanté's total on-board memory was more than twice that of the Cadillac de Ville.

Symbolizing the leading-edge status of Allanté automotive electronics technology was its use of electronic signal-multiplexing, which, explained Cadillac, was ''the employment of a single wire to do the task of many wires by using digitally encoded pulses to transmit information between vehicle lighting control modules.'' One of many results of this system's adoption was the use of a single wiring harness and a resultant reduction in the number of wiring interconnects in the Allante electrical system.

TESTING AND QUALITY CONTROL

The testing of the Allanté, which had the distinction of being the only automobile in the world to be evaluated on a test track designed, built, and tested exclusively for its use, was extensive. The track, measuring 2.5 miles in length, was located just a few hundred feet from the Detroit-Hamtramck Assembly Center. ''In our testing procedures, just as in all aspects of the building of the Allanté,'' said John Grettenberger, ''we decided to go the extra mile—actually the extra two and a half miles.''

After completion, each Allanté was driven for 25 miles before being shipped to Cadillac dealers. This evaluation involved two occupants, a trained test driver and a passenger, a technician whose job it was to scrutinize every aspect of Allanté performance, including acceleration, braking, handling, ride quality, and quietness. At the conclusion of this ''final examination,'' the technician's responsibility was to make any adjustments before releasing the car for delivery.

Prior to shipment to the United States, each Allanté was also subjected to a rigid quality control by Pininfarina. In total, the electrical and electronic systems of each Allanté were tested at eight different stages of assembly in the United States and Italy. Each engine was also operated for 48 hours on a dynamometer.

Commenting on the Allanté's predelivery scrutiny, John Grettenberger noted, "We think Allanté is destined to be the finest automobile in its class, and our testing procedures are an important step in making our beliefs a reality."

PRODUCTION OF THE ALLANTÉ

For the Allanté, reality began with the shipment of two-piece GM-30 platforms plus 107 American-made components such as instrumentation, air conditioning, and electronics to a new Pininfarina facility built especially for the Allanté program at San Giorgio, a Turin, Italy, suburb. Shipment was by Lufthansa or Alitalia Boeing 747s.

Pininfarina began the construction process by reducing the size of the front and rear pan members and then welding them together. The body was then assembled and painted. Pininfarina was also responsible for construction of the Allanté interior. For shipment to the Detroit-Hamtramck Assembly Center, the bodies were placed in specially designed, high-strength, aluminum-alloy cargo modules and taken by trucks, also fitted with specially designed bodies, to Turin's Caselle Airport, where the 747s, each carrying 33 cargo modules capable of containing 56 Allanté bodies, were loaded. The initial schedule called for three round trips weekly.

This "Airbridge," depicted by Cadillac as the "world's longest assembly line," extended 3,300 air miles from Turin to Detroit. "The Airbridge," explained Grettenberger, "gives us the world's longest assembly line, is another automotive first for Cadillac, and is entirely consistent with every other aspect of this distinctive automobile's unique development." Further emphasizing the point that this was far more than a mere attention-grabber, Grettenberger went on to note, "The Allanté's manufacturing techniques and unique organizations and people programs represent innovations that could signal a revolution in automotive assembly."

When the Allanté modules arrived at the Detroit Metropolitan Airport after a 12-hour flight from Italy, they were moved by motorized carriers to the Detroit-Hamtramck Assembly Center where the bodies were removed from the modules and placed on the assembly line.

The engine and suspension system of the Allanté were built using a "stop-station assembly" procedure in which automated guided vehicles (AGVS) moved each engine and chassis unit from station to station with each employee performing 10 or 11 operations. Each Allanté received 23 in-process checks and inspections that included the use of specifically designed testers.

The domestic production of the Allanté took place in just a 1-acre section of the Hamtramck installation (which covered 77 acres under one roof) and involved 110 Cadillac technicians. Over 1,500, or about half of the Hamtramck work force, initially applied for these jobs. The screening process for the Allanté positions was conducted by a joint task force of Cadillac management and the United Auto Workers. Each Allanté technician received a minimum of 200 hours in specific Allanté hands-on training, in addition to the hundreds of hours of training each employee first received at Hamtramck. Those workers performing more complex production processes received up to 500 hours of intensive training.

Forty Allanté assembly technicians received further information and training at the Pininfarina facility in Italy. Upon their return to the United States, these individuals assisted in the training of their 70 coworkers.

ALLANTÉ'S EXTERIOR

Cadillac reported that the Allanté's exterior "was designed to be understated but unmistakably a Cadillac." It possessed, therefore, some typical Cadillac styling themes such as a cross-hatched grille and, like most Cadillacs built after the early sixties, had very clean lines devoid of extraneous trim. The result was elegance cast in a conservative mode, a format that was not extreme nor quickly dated. All-in-all, it was a car with the look of success both as a new car and, 20 years down the road, a desirable collectible.

Positioned on each side of the grille, which carried a prominent Cadillac wreath and crest, were flush-mounted Carello headlights with built-in fog lamps. In profile, the low nose and high deck of the Allanté suggested good aerodynamics, which was confirmed by its 0.34 drag coefficient.

Side-body contours emphasized the Allanté's wedge shape. The only model identification found on the Allanté's flanks was the Pininfarina name and crest placed on the lower front fender. The rear taillights carried the words "Cadillac" on the left and "Allanté" on the right. The required center, high-mounted light was positioned in the rear-deck lid and carried Cadillac identification in outline form.

Four exterior colors were available: pearl white, silver metallic, maroon metallic, and gold metallic. Each Allanté received four coats of paint; two of color and two clear. Except for the hood, rear-deck lid, and the removable hardtop, the Allanté body was constructed of two-sided galvanized steel. The aluminum roof, which weighed 60 pounds, had four latch contact points and an electric pulldown to ensure proper release and securing. The Convertible top with glass rear-quarter windows was, when lowered, stored beneath a molded boot.

The results of testing prompted John Grettenberger to comment, "Allanté owners will find that even with the top down, they will be able to carry on a conversation in normal tones and they won't have to worry about their hair being tousled."

ALLANTÉ'S INTERIOR

The Allanté was fitted with Recaro seats with a two-way electronic adjustment and a built-in memory enabling them to assume one of two programmable positions. They also had a separately programmable exit position. All-leather upholstery was offered in Burgundy or natural leather.

Instrumentation combined both digital and analog displays, with the latter, including a 150-mph speedometer, created electronically. All main readouts were liquid crystal displays. The tachometer was equal in size to the speedometer, and the Driver Information Center (DIC) presented such information as current time, outside temperature, and, when appropriate, "Headlights Secured."

The DIC also displayed fuel economy, driving range, average speed, and elapsed time to a preset destination. These readings, as well as the secondary instrument displays, could be shut off at the touch of a button, leaving the driver with only the speedometer and tachometer readings. The displays, however, had a reactive feature that enabled them to reappear should new information enter the system.

Supplementing the trunk's 13-cubic-feet capacity was a storage area behind the seats, which was also accessible through the trunk, that had a capacity of 3 cubic feet.

A Delco-Bose stereo system was standard, and the only option, aside from the choice of interior colors, was a cellular telephone. Along with this item came an AM/FM cellular-telephone retractable antenna.

Working at full capacity, Cadillac's production capacity for the Allanté was just 7,800 units a year. Thus there would be just a few hundred more Allantés available than were Series Sixty Cadillacs back in 1948. Like that venerable model, the Allanté signaled a new beginning a break with the past, and a promise for the future.

Nearly 50 years of postwar Cadillac history notwithstanding, the arrival of the Allanté was a statement that the best of Cadillac was yet to come.

SPECIFICATIONS

Engine

Type: V-type, 8 cylinders, aluminum block, iron cylinder heads
Displacement: 249 cubic inches
Horsepower: 170 @ 4,400 rpm
Torque: 230 lb-ft @ 3,200 rpm
Fuel system: Electronic port fuel injection
Electrical system: 12-volt
Transmission: Hydra-Matic F-7, four-speed automatic

Chassis/Drivetrain

Driving axle: 2.95:1 ratio
Front suspension: Independent, MacPherson struts, lateral and trailing arms, coil springs, stabilizer bar
Rear suspension: Independent, MacPherson struts, transverse leaf spring
Steering: Power-assisted, rack and pinion
Tires: Goodyear Eagle VL, P225/6OR-15

Dimensions

Wheelbase: 99.4 inches
Width: 73.4 inches
Overall length: 178.6 inches

Options

Cellular telephone

1988

The Only Way to Travel Is Cadillac Style

Key elements of the Eldorado's new look included front and rear bladed fenders, extension of the rear fender forward into the C-pillar, and new rear fender extensions.

The 1988 Allanté included a power decklid pulldown as standard equipment. Two new exterior colors—red and black—were added for 1988.

The 1988 Seville had a more sharply defined front end: a new hood with a raised power dome and new header molding, grille, and bumper guards.

Although the 1988 Cadillac Fleetwood d'Elegance had minimal exterior changes from 1987, it featured many technical changes, including revised suspension and engine mount rates. In addition, ten previously optional features were now standard.

The most visible exterior change on the 1988 Cimarron was the body-colored lower-body grooving, which was now standard.

A significant reduction in wind noise and improvement in fit and finish were achieved on the 1988 Brougham through revision of the vertical drip moldings.

With the new 4.5-liter V-8, the 1988 Fleetwood Sixty Special is the quickest Cadillac in over a decade, with a 0 to 60 mph time of 9.9 seconds. The 1987 model's time was 12.8 seconds.

The latest Cadillac V-8 has a displacement of 273 cubic inches—up nearly 10 percent from 1987. With 155 horsepower at 4,000 rpm and 240 lb.-ft. of torque, it makes the 1988 models the best performing Cadillacs since the 8.2-liter models of more than a decade ago.

1989

New Models

The 1989 Cadillac Sedan de Ville has a longer, 113.8-inch, wheelbase. Its overall length is almost nine inches greater than the 1988 version's.

Powering all front-wheel drive Cadillacs, including the 1989 Eldorado, is Cadillac's 4.5-liter aluminum block V-8. It is rated as the most reliable General Motors powerplant, exceeding "world class" quality, reliability, and durability (QRD) standards in Cadillac testing as defined by the average of the four highest rated powertrains sold in the United States.

1989 Cadillac Seville. Revisions in the suspension of the Cadillac Seville for 1989 include new variable rate front coil springs and revalved front MacPherson struts. Michelin all-season tires are standard. The interior features six-way power seats for the driver and passenger.

The length of the Coupe De Ville has been increased by nearly six inches for 1989. Both De Ville bodies are redesigned with extended front and rear overhang, larger trunks, and improved aerodynamics. Their drag coefficient has been lowered to 0.39.

Standard on the limited-edition 1989 Seville Touring Sedan (STS) is a "European-feel" road package that is optional for the Seville. It includes a stiffer, 33 mm, front stabilizer bar and the addition of a solid, 16 mm, rear stabilizer bar. While the touring package for the Seville includes 15-×-6-inch styled aluminum wheels equipped with P215/65R15 Goodyear tires, the STS has wider 15-×-7-inch alloy wheels.

After an absence of two years, the Fleetwood Coupe returns to the Cadillac line for 1989. Along with the Sedan version, the Coupe features full rear wheel skirts and American walnut interior trim.

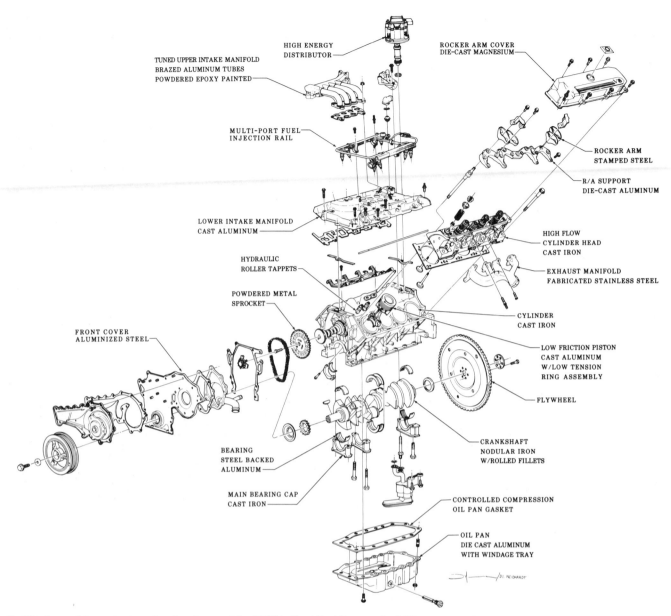

HIGH ENERGY
DISTRIBUTOR

ROCKER ARM COVER
DIE-CAST MAGNESIUM

TUNED UPPER INTAKE MANIFOLD
BRAZED ALUMINUM TUBES
POWDERED EPOXY PAINTED

MULTI-PORT FUEL
INJECTION RAIL

ROCKER ARM
STAMPED STEEL

R/A SUPPORT
DIE-CAST ALUMINUM

LOWER INTAKE MANIFOLD
CAST ALUMINUM

HIGH FLOW
CYLINDER HEAD
CAST IRON

HYDRAULIC
ROLLER TAPPETS

EXHAUST MANIFOLD
FABRICATED STAINLESS STEEL

POWDERED METAL
SPROCKET

CYLINDER
CAST IRON

FRONT COVER
ALUMINIZED STEEL

LOW FRICTION PISTON
CAST ALUMINUM
W/LOW TENSION
RING ASSEMBLY

FLYWHEEL

BEARING
STEEL BACKED
ALUMINUM

CRANKSHAFT
NODULAR IRON
W/ROLLED FILLETS

MAIN BEARING CAP
CAST IRON

CONTROLLED COMPRESSION
OIL PAN GASKET

OIL PAN
DIE CAST ALUMINUM
WITH WINDAGE TRAY

Cadillac's most important engine development for 1989 is the Allanté's use of a 4.5-liter tuned, fuel-injected V-8. With 200 horsepower @ 4300 rpm and 270 lt-ft of torque @ 3200 rpm, the Allanté is capable of 0 to 60 mph times of 8.5 seconds and quarter-mile runs of 16.6 sec @ 83 mph. Its top speed now exceeds 130 mph.

The last remaining example of traditional Cadillac rear drive and V-8 power, which Cadillac first introduced in 1915, is the 1989 Brougham. In its latest version, this Cadillac boasts of a new grille and interior appointments. Although base curb weight exceeds 4,000 pounds, the Brougham's EPA rated fuel economy of 24 mpg highway and 17 mpg city excludes it form the federal "Gas Guzzler" excise tax.

Index

THE
MANAGED
Health Care Handbook

Third Edition

Peter R. Kongstvedt, MD, FACP
Partner
Ernst & Young LLP
Washington, DC

AN ASPEN PUBLICATION®
Aspen Publishers, Inc.
Gaithersburg, Maryland
1996

Library of Congress Cataloging-in-Publication Data

The managed health care handbook / [edited by] Peter R. Kongstvedt. --
3rd ed.
p.   cm.
Includes bibliographical references and index.
ISBN: 0-8342-0733-8
1. Managed care plans (Medical care)--United States--Management.
I. Kongstvedt, Peter R. (Peter Reid)
[DNLM: 1. Managed Care Programs--organization & administration--
United States. W 130 AA1 M26 1996]
RA413.M28 1996
362.1'0425--dc20
DNLM/DLC
for Library of Congress
96-13500
CIP

Orders: (800) 638-8437
Customer Service: (800) 234-1660

About Aspen Publishers • For more than 35 years, Aspen has been a leading professional publisher in a variety of disciplines. Aspen's vast information resources are available in both print and electronic formats. We are committed to providing the highest quality information available in the most appropriate format for our customers. Visit Aspen's Internet site for more information resources, directories, articles, and a searchable version of Aspen's full catalog, including the most recent publications: **http://www.aspenpub.com**
Aspen Publishers, Inc. • The hallmark of quality in publishing
Members of the worldwide Wolters Kluwer group.

Editorial Resources: Ruth Bloom

Library of Congress Catalog Card Number: 96-13500
ISBN: 0-8342-0733-8

Printed in the United States of America

This book is dedicated to my family:
my late father, Gerald Nicholas Kongstvedt;
my mother, Elizabeth Pearson Kongstvedt;
my sister, Chris Lieberman;
and especially my wife, Sheryl, and my son, David

Table of Contents

CHAPTER 21—MANAGING UTILIZATION OF ANCILLARY AND EMERGENCY SERVICES 330

Peter R. Kongstvedt

CHAPTER 22—MANAGED BEHAVIORAL HEALTH CARE SERVICES 341

Donald F. Anderson, Jeffrey L. Berlant, Danna Mauch, and William R. Maloney

CHAPTER 23—PHARMACEUTICAL SERVICES IN MANAGED CARE 367

Henry F. Blissenbach and Peter M. Penna

CHAPTER 59—ERISA AND MANAGED CARE 944

Jacqueline M. Saue and Gregg H. Dooge

CHAPTER 60—EFFECTIVE UTILIZATION OF LEGAL SERVICES 967

James L. Touse

AFTERWORD—WHAT MIGHT THE FUTURE HOLD? 976

*Frederick B. Abbey, Garry Carneal, Peter D. Fox, Robert E. Hurley, Peter R. Kongstvedt,
Jerry R. Peters, Jacqueline M. Saue, Craig Schub, Roger Taylor, and Carlos Zarabozo*

Contributors

Frederick B. Abbey, MPA
National Director, Legislative and Regulatory
 Services
National Health Care Practice
Ernst & Young LLP
Washington, DC

Donald F. Anderson, PhD
Leader, National Behavioral Health Consulting
 Team
William M. Mercer, Incorporated
San Francisco, California

John P. Anton
Vice President, National Marketing
CIGNA Employee Benefits Companies
Atlanta, Georgia

Jeffrey L. Berlant, MD, PhD
Senior Consultant, National Behavioral Health
 Unit
William M. Mercer, Incorporated
San Francisco, California

Henry F. Blissenbach, PharmD
President, Diviersified Pharmaceutical
 Services
SmithKline Beecham Corporation
Minneapolis, Minnesota

Christine C. Boesz
Vice President, Government Programs
NYLCare
New York, New York

Thomas W. Bone, MCHA
Director of Business Development
State Health Care Division
Electronic Data Systems, Inc.
Phoenix, Arizona

Alexandre B. Bouton
Epstein Becker & Green, PC
Washington, DC

John F. Boyer, PhD
Vice President, Strategic Planning and Contract
 Administration
MAXIMUS, Inc.
McLean, Virginia

Garry Carneal, Esq.
Vice President, Legal & State Departments
Americal Association of Health Plans
Washington, DC

Stephen M. Cigich, FSA
Consulting Actuary
Milliman & Robertson, Inc.
Milwaukee, Wisconsin

Richard J. Coffey, PhD
Director, Program and Operations Analysis
University of Michigan Hospitals
Ann Arbor, Michigan

Ronald M. Davis
Senior Vice President, Operations and Customer
 Service
PacifiCare Health Systems, Inc.
Cypress, California

Gregg H. Dooge
Foley & Lardner
Milwaukee, Wisconsin

Robert S. Eichler
Vice President
Scheur Management Group, Inc.
Newton, Massachusetts

Allan Fine, MBA
Senior Manager, Health Care Strategy
  Consulting Practice
Ernst & Young LLP
Chicago, Illinois

Peter D. Fox, PhD
President
PDF Incorporated
Chevy Chase, Maryland

Dana E. Frank
Continuous Quality Improvement Coach,
  Western Region
PacifiCare Health Systems, Inc.
Cypress, California

Kathleen M. Griffin, PhD
President and Chief Executive Officer
Griffin Management, Inc.
Scottsdale, Arizona

Dale F. Harding
Senior Manager, East/Great Lakes Healthcare
  Practice
Ernst & Young LLP
Islin, New Jersey

Fred L. Horowitz, DMD
Executive Vice President of Business
  and Market Development
Dental Benefit Providers
Bethesda, Maryland

Robert E. Hurley, PhD
Associate Professor, Department of Health
  Administration
Medical College of Virginia
Richmond, Virginia

Terry A. Jacobs, JD
National Director of Insurance Tax Services
Ernst & Young LLP
Washington, DC

Mark S. Joffe, Esq
Law Offices of Mark S. Joffe
Washington, DC

Gregory L. Johnson, PhD
Director of Time Loss Management
Ernst & Young LLP
San Francisco, California

Leonard J. Kirschner, MD, MPH
Vice President, Health Care Initiatives
State Health Care
Electronic Data Systems, Inc.
Phoenix, Arizona

William G. Kopit
Associate, Health Law Section
Epstein Becker & Green, PC
Washington, DC

Anthony M. Kotin, MD
National Practice Leader for Clinical
  Effectiveness
Integrated Healthsystems Consulting Practice
Towers Perrin
Chicago, Illinois

Thomas J. Kuhlman, FSA
Principal, Health and Welfare and Retirement
  Practices
Towers Perrin
Chicago, Illinois

Glenn L. Laffel, MD, PhD
Senior Vice President for Medical Affairs
Preferred Health Systems LLC
Bethesda, Maryland

Jean D. LeMasurier
Director, Division of Policy and Program
  Improvement
Office of Managed Care
Health Care Financing Administration
Balitmore, Maryland

Sarah S. LeRoy, RN, MSN, CPNP
Clinical Nurse Specialist, Pediatric Cardiology
University of Michigan Medical Center
Ann Arbor, Michigan

Gregory J. Lippe
Senior Manager
Ernst & Young LLP
Milwaukee, Wisconsin

Edward H. Lipson, MD
National Director of Time Loss Management
Human Resource Consulting Group
Ernst & Young LLP
New York, New York

William R. Maloney
Principal, Behavioral Healthcare Practice
William M. Mercer, Incorporated
San Francisco, California

Danna Mauch, PhD
Partner, Integrated Health Strategies, Inc.
Cambridge, Massachusetts

Robin L. McElfatrick
Senior Consultant
Scheur Management Group, Inc.
Newton, Massachusetts

Joel L. Michaels
Michaels, Wishner & Bonner PC
Washington, DC

Catherine M. Mullahy, RN, CCRN, CCM
President
Options Unlimited
Huntington, New York

David B. Nash, MD
Director of Health Policy
Thomas Jefferson University
Philadelphia, Pennsylvania

Margaret E. O'Kane, MHS
President
National Committee for Quality Assurance
Washington, DC

Norman C. Payson, MD
President and Chief Executive Officer
Healthsource, Inc.
Hooksett, New Hampshire

Peter M. Penna, PharmD
Vice President of Managed Pharmacy
CIGNA HealthCare
Hartford, Connecticut

Jerry R. Peters, Esq.
Partner, Health Care Practice Group
Latham & Watkins
San Francisco, California

David W. Plocher, MD
Principal, Health Care Consulting Practice
Ernst & Young LLP
Minneapolis, Minnesota

Robert Reese
Partner
Ernst & Young LLP
Detroit, Michigan

Janet S. Richards, BSN, MS, CNAA
Assistant Director of Nursing
University of Michigan Hospitals
Ann Arbor, Michigan

Christine C. Rinn, Esq
Principal
Michaels, Wishner & Bonner PC
Washington, DC

James A. Rodeghero, PhD
Partner, Health Care Management Consulting
  Practice
National Director, Physicians Compensation
  Consulting
Ernst & Young LLP
Los Angeles, California

Phillip G. Royalty, JD, CPA
National Director of Health Care Tax Services
Ernst & Young LLP
Washington, DC

Richard B. Salmon, PhD, MD
Corporate Medical Director
Healthsource, Inc.
Hooksett, New Hampshire

Jacqueline M. Saue, JD
Partner
Foley & Lardner
Washington, DC

Barry S. Scheur, JD
President
Scheur Management Group, Inc.
Newton, Massachusetts

Craig Schub
Senior Vice President, Government Programs
PacifiCare Health Systems, Inc.
Cypress, California

Pamela B. Siren, RN
Director of Clinical Development
Lazo, Gertman & Associates
Waltham, Massachusetts

Larry Sobel
Deputy Director of Managed Care Operations
Senior Health Care Program Analyst for the
  Deputy Assistant Secretary for Defense for
  Health Services Financing
Washington, DC

Richard L. Solit, MD
Fellow, Office of Health Policy and Clinical
  Outcomes
Resident, Department of Surgery
Thomas Jefferson University Hospital
Philadelphia, Pennsylvania

C. David Spencer, PhD, MD
Medical Director
Blue Cross Blue Shield of the National Capitol
  Area
Washington, DC

Roger S. Taylor, MPA, MD
President and CEO
Connecticut Health Enterprises
Monroe, Connecticut

James L. Touse, JD
Vice President and General Counsel
Group Health Plan, Inc.
St. Louis, Missouri

Tracey Thompson Turner, MA
Director of Investor Relations
Healthsource, Inc.
Hooksett, New Hampshire

Eric R. Wagner, MBA
Vice President for Managed Care
Medlantic Healthcare Group
Washington Hospital Center
Executive Director
WHC Physician-Hospital Organization
Washington, DC

James A. Williams
Senior Vice President of Information Services
Chief Information Officer
PacifiCare Health Systems, Inc.
Cypress, California

Susan Wintermeyer-Pingel, RN, MSN, OCN
Clinical Nurse Specialist,
  Hematology/Oncology
University of Michigan Medical Center
Ann Arbor, Michigan

Barbara J. Youngberg, BSN, MSW, JD
Vice President of Insurance, Risk & Quality
  Management
University HealthSystem Consortium
Oak Brook, Illinois

Carlos Zarabozo
Social Science Research Analyst
Special Analysis Staff
Office of the Associate Administrator for Policy
Health Care Financing Administration
Baltimore, Maryland

Preface

When the first edition of this book was written and published, managed health care was still occasionally referred to as an alternative delivery system. The alternative has now become mainstream. As the American health care system has evolved to embrace managed care, however, managed health care itself has continued to evolve at an equally rapid pace. This evolution (or in some cases, mutation) means that new approaches to managing cost, quality, and access will be created; some will fail, others will succeed and lead to still more changes in the near future.

The second edition of this book referred to a state of "permanent white water" to describe the health care environment. For some, this means class III rapids; for others, it means Niagara Falls. Now more than ever, individuals involved with the management of health care need to be quick and adaptive. As the best white water river guides know, you don't fight the current, you use it to your advantage.

The rate of the rise of health care costs has been variable. The shocking increases experienced in the early 1990s have slowed in the mid-1990s, but there is no guarantee that they will continue to do so. Managed health care has been effective in holding down the rate of rise, but many of the fundamental reasons that lead to rises in health care costs are still with us today, including:

- rapidly developing (and usually expensive) technology
- cost shifting by providers to pay for care rendered to patients who either cannot pay or are covered by systems that do not pay the full cost of care

- shifting demographics as our population ages
- high (and not unreasonable) expectations for a long and healthy life
- the current legal environment, which has led to defensive medicine
- administrative costs related to the care that is delivered
- wide variations in efficiencies and quality of care that is rendered by all types of providers (professional and institutional)
- serious inequities and variations in incomes among all types of providers (regardless of efficiency or quality)
- fewer available public dollars to pay for health care in entitlement programs
- a myriad other reasons

In the 3-year interval between the publication of the second edition of this book and the third, there have been enough changes in the health care system to warrant a considerable revision and expansion of this text. Many chapters have been entirely rewritten, some have been modified and expanded, and many new topics are addressed for the first time.

The primary mission of this book remains unchanged: to provide a strategic and operational resource for managers in the field. It is based as much as possible on actual operations of managed care plans rather than on purely theoretical models. In a field this complex, many topics can be discussed, but not always to the degree one would like or with the emphasis with which all would agree. The information in this book is not intended to be the total, final, or best solution to any issue in managed health care. Rather, we present possible solutions and multiple approaches to problems as well as information that managers should be aware of when running managed care operations.

Beyond its primary mission, this book is intended to be a useful resource to managers who are considering entering the field, to middle managers in the field who are trying to advance their careers, to senior executives in the industry with a little less experience than they would like, to medical directors new to managed care, to physicians in group practice or integrated delivery systems who are charged with managing their peers and colleagues in a risk arrangement with a managed care plan, to hospital administrators trying to cope with the plethora of health care plans banging on their doors, to corporate benefits managers charged with controlling health care costs for employees, to academicians or students working to gain an understanding of how these things work, and to regulators who must administer the rules of play.

The chapters do not really need to be read in order, although they are presented in a logical order; neither do all chapters need to be read to gain understanding. Chapters cross-reference each other when necessary. There is a glossary at the back of the book for those times when the acronyms run heavy or the terms become obtuse.

The book is intended to provide practical advice based on the experiences, both firsthand and observed, of managers and experienced consultants in the industry as it exists today. The book is also highly biased: my biases as well as those of the contributing authors. There is no shortage of impassioned opinions in this industry, and many of those opinions are held with nearly religious zeal. That means that there will be those who disagree with what they read here, and some of what will be presented in the following pages will become outdated, perhaps even as the book is published. Still, the information in this book has been created with a single focus: to enable the reader to succeed better in the world of managed health care.

Peter Reid Kongstvedt
McLean, Virginia

Acknowledgments

I wish to acknowledge and thank the following individuals for their help during the creation of this new edition of *The Managed Health Care Handbook*. First, I want to thank Jack Bruggeman for getting things rolling, painful as that was. I also wish to thank Amy Martin and Bob Howard for their help in collecting research information and tracking and assisting the progress of the book in its protracted first stages. Ruth Bloom and Barbara Priest carried out the difficult task of copy editing the text and finding the errors and vagaries that I missed in compiling the manuscript; their efforts are much appreciated.

Lisa Shreve of AAHP (formerly GHAA/ AMCRA) provided some good referrals and advice while I was planning the content. I wish to express sincere thanks to Nina Lane and especially to Erin Carlson for their invaluable help in collecting research information from the AAHP library. My appreciation is also expressed to Ron Klar for stimulating discussions about provider practice profiling in past years. Although I cannot name them all, since to do so would double the size of this book, I thank my many colleagues and friends in the managed care industry with whom I have had the pleasure both to work beside and to compete with over the years.

I can only express my appreciation and gratitude to my long-suffering and neglected wife and son for putting up with me during the many months I was an utter boor and bore during the creation of this book. Last, I want to give heartfelt thanks to the many readers of previous editions for the support and kind words that have fueled my ability to do it again.

Part I

Introduction to Managed Health Care

"Grasp the subject, the words will follow."

Marcus Porcius Cato [Cato the Elder]
(234–149 B.C.)
CAIUS JULIUS VICTOR,
Ars Rhetorica, I [4th century A.D.]

"You know more than you think you do."

Benjamin Spock, M.D. (b. 1903)
Baby and Child Care (1945)

Chapter 1

An Overview of Managed Care

Peter D. Fox

Managed care is rapidly dominating the health care financing and delivery system in the United States. To illustrate, health maintenance organization (HMO) enrollment reached 51 million in 1994. Although the estimates are less reliable, by all accounts the number of persons enrolled in preferred provider organizations (PPOs) and their variants rivals the number enrolled in HMOs.[1] Even traditional plans are adopting principles of managed care; for example, hospital precertification and large case management, daring innovations as recently as a decade ago, have become the norm in indemnity insurance. Public sector, notably Medicare and Medicaid, reliance on managed care is growing rapidly.

Managed care has also become a big business. Some 36.7 million HMO enrollees are in multistate firms, including nonprofits such as Kaiser and the HMOs owned by the various Blue Cross and Blue Shield plans (which operate largely autonomously).[2] Many of the large managed care companies are traded on the New York Stock Exchange and other stock exchanges, and the general business press regularly reports their profits along with the compensation of the chief executive officers, which can amount to millions of dollars annually.

When one thinks of managed care, one should distinguish between the techniques of managed care and the organization that performs the various functions. Managed care can embody a wide variety of techniques, which are discussed throughout this book. These include various forms of financial incentives for providers, promotion of wellness, early identification of disease, patient education, self-care, and all aspects of utilization management.

A wide variety of organizations can implement managed care techniques, of which the HMO has the potential to align financing and delivery most closely by virtue of enrollees' being (with some exceptions) required to use network providers. Managed care techniques can also be employed directly by employers, insurers, union–management (Taft-Hartley) trust funds, and the Medicare and Medicaid programs. They can also be implemented by PPOs, organizations that allow enrollees to be reimbursed for care delivered by nonnetwork providers, although the enrollees face higher out-of-pocket payments (i.e., cost sharing) if they do. Finally, a variety of hybrid arrangements have evolved, one example is the point-of-service (POS) program, which operates as a PPO except that, to receive the highest level of benefits, the enrollee must obtain a referral from a primary

Peter D. Fox, Ph.D., is an independent consultant, located in Chevy Chase, MD, specializing in managed care. His clients have included HMOs, PPOs, provider groups, employers, Taft-Hartley trust funds, government agencies, and foundations. He is the author of numerous articles and books.

The author is most grateful for the helpful comments of John Gabel (Group Health Association of America), Peter Kongstvedt (Ernst & Young), Kenneth Linde (Principal Health Care), Robert Lurie (HealthCare Connections), Margaret O'Kane (National Committee for Quality Assurance), and George Strumpf (Health Insurance Plan of Greater New York).

care physician who is part of the contracted network. Increasingly, the arrangements are difficult to characterize, let alone profile statistically, in a meaningful manner.

MANAGED CARE: THE EARLY YEARS (BEFORE 1970)

Whatever its role today, managed care had humble origins and struggled to survive in its early years. To some extent it still struggles today, as evidenced by the controversies, mostly at the state level, surrounding "any willing provider" legislation and other legislative proposals that constrain the development of managed care (see Chapter 2). This section addresses the development of HMOs and other managed care organizations rather than focusing on techniques.

Sometimes cited as the first example of an HMO, or prepaid group practice as it was known until the early 1970s, is the Western Clinic in Tacoma, Washington.[3] Starting in 1910, the Western Clinic offered, exclusively through its own providers, a broad range of medical services in return for a premium payment of $0.50 per member per month. The program was available to lumber mill owners and their employees and served to assure the clinic a flow of patients and revenues. A similar program was developed by a Dr. Bridge, who started a clinic in Tacoma that later expanded to 20 sites in Oregon and Washington.

In 1929, Michael Shadid, M.D., established a rural farmers' cooperative health plan in Elk City, Oklahoma by forming a lay organization of leading farmers in the community. Participating farmers purchased shares for $50 each to raise capital for a new hospital in return for receiving medical care at a discount.[4] For his trouble, Dr. Shadid lost his membership in the county medical society and was threatened with having his license to practice suspended. Some 20 years later, however, he was vindicated through the out-of-court settlement in his favor of an antitrust suit against the county and state medical societies.[5] In 1934 the Farmers Union assumed control of both the hospital and the health plan.

Health insurance itself is of relatively recent origin. In 1929, Baylor Hospital in Texas agreed to provide some 1,500 teachers prepaid care at its hospital, an arrangement that represented the origins of Blue Cross. The program was subsequently expanded to include the participation of other employers and hospitals, initially as single hospital plans. Starting in 1939, state medical societies in California and elsewhere created, generally statewide, Blue Shield plans, which reimbursed for physician services. At the time, commercial health insurance was not a factor.[6]

The formation of the various Blue Cross and Blue Shield plans in the midst of the Great Depression, as well as that of many HMOs, reflected not consumers demanding coverage or nonphysician entrepreneurs seeking to establish a business but rather providers wanting to protect and enhance patient revenues. Many of these developments were threatening to organized medicine. In 1932, the American Medical Association (AMA) adopted a strong stance against prepaid group practices, favoring, instead, indemnity type insurance. The AMA's position was in response to both the small number of prepaid group practices in existence at the time and the findings in 1932 of the Committee on the Cost of Medical Care—a highly visible private group of leaders from medicine, dentistry, public health, consumers, and so forth—that recommended the expansion of group practice as an efficient delivery system. The AMA's stance at the national level set the tone for continued state and local medical society opposition to prepaid group practice.

The period immediately surrounding World War II saw the formation of several HMOs that are among the leaders today. They encountered varying degrees of opposition from local medical societies. They represent a diversity of origins with the initial impetus coming, variously, from employers, providers seeking patient revenues, consumers seeking access to improved and affordable health care, and even a housing lending agency seeking to reduce the number of foreclosures. The following are examples of other early HMOs:

- The Kaiser Foundation Health Plans were started in 1937 by Dr. Sidney Garfield at the behest of the Kaiser construction company, which sought to finance medical care, initially, for workers and families who were building an aqueduct in the southern California desert to transport water from the Colorado River to Los Angeles and, subsequently, for workers who were constructing the Grand Coulee Dam in Washington state. A similar program was established in 1942 at Kaiser shipbuilding plants in the San Francisco Bay area. Kaiser Foundation Health Plans now serve 16 states and the District of Columbia and, as of July 1, 1994, had 7.3 million members.

- In 1937, the Group Health Association (GHA) was started in Washington, D.C. at the behest of the Home Owner's Loan Corporation to reduce the number of mortgage defaults that resulted from large medical expenses. It was created as a nonprofit consumer cooperative, with the board being elected periodically by the enrollees. The District of Columbia Medical Society opposed the formation of GHA. It sought to restrict hospital admitting privileges for GHA physicians and threatened expulsion from the medical society. A bitter antitrust battle ensued that culminated in the U.S. Supreme Court's ruling in favor of GHA. In 1994, faced with insolvency despite an enrollment of some 128,000, GHA was acquired by Humana Health Plans, a for-profit, publicly traded corporation.[7]

- In 1944, at the behest of New York City, which was seeking coverage for its employees, the Health Insurance Plan (HIP) of Greater New York was formed. HIP is currently licensed in New York, New Jersey, and Florida and, as of July 1, 1994, had 1.1 million members.

- In 1947, consumers in Seattle organized 400 families, who contributed $100 each, to form the Group Health Cooperative of Puget Sound. Predictably, opposition was encountered from the Kings County Medical Society. Group Health Cooperative remains a consumer cooperative and had 588,000 members as of July 1, 1994.[8]

Only in later years did nonprovider entrepreneurs form for-profit HMOs in significant numbers.

The early independent practice association (IPA) type of HMOs, which contract with physicians in independent fee-for-service practice, was a competitive reaction to group practice-based HMOs. The basic structure was created in 1954, when the San Joaquin County Medical Society in California formed the San Joaquin Medical Foundation in response to competition from Kaiser. The foundation established a relative value fee schedule for paying physicians, heard grievances against physicians, and monitored quality of care. It became licensed by the state to accept capitation payment, making it the first IPA model HMO.

THE ADOLESCENT YEARS: 1970–1985

Through the 1960s and into the early 1970s, HMOs played only a modest role in the financing and delivery of health care, although they were a significant presence in a few communities, such as the Seattle area and parts of California. In 1970 the total number of HMOs was in the 30s, the exact number depending on one's definition.[9] The years since the early 1970s represent a period of vastly accelerated developments that are still unfolding.

The major boost to the HMO movement during this period was the enactment in 1973 of the federal HMO Act. That act, as described below, both authorized start-up funding and, more important, ensured access to the employer-based insurance market. It evolved from discussions that Paul Ellwood, M.D., had in 1970 with the political leadership of the U.S. Department of Health, Education, and Welfare (which later became the Department of Health and Human Services).[10] Ellwood had been personally close to Philip Lee, M.D., Assistant Secretary for

Health during the presidency of Lyndon Johnson (and again in the Clinton administration), and participated in designing the Health Planning Act of 1966.

Ellwood, sometimes referred to as the father of the modern HMO movement, was asked in the early Nixon years to devise ways of constraining the rise in the Medicare budget. Out of those discussions evolved both a proposal to capitate HMOs for Medicare beneficiaries (which was not enacted until 1982) and the laying of the groundwork for what became the HMO Act of 1973. The desire to foster HMOs reflected the perspective that the fee-for-service system, by rewarding paying physicians based on their volume of services, incorporated the wrong incentives. Also, the term *health maintenance organization* was coined as a substitute for *prepaid group practice*, principally because it had greater public appeal.

The main features of the HMO Act were the following:

- Grants and loans were available for the planning and start-up phases of new HMOs as well as for service area expansions for existing HMOs.
- State laws that restricted the development of HMOs were overridden for HMOs that were federally qualified, as described below.
- Most important of all were the "dual choice" provisions, which required that employers with 25 or more employees that offered indemnity coverage also offer two federally qualified HMOs, one of each type—that is the closed panel or group or staff model, or the open panel or IPA/network model—if the plans made a formal request* (the different model types are discussed in Chapter 3). Most HMOs were reluctant to exercise the mandate, fearing that

---

* For workers under collective bargaining agreements, the union had to agree to the offering.

doing so would antagonize employers, who would in turn discourage employees from enrolling.

The statute also established a process under which HMOs could elect to be federally qualified. To do so, the plans had to satisfy a series of requirements, such as meeting minimum benefit package standards set forth in the act, demonstrating that their provider networks were adequate, having a quality assurance system, meeting standards of financial stability, and having an enrollee grievance system. Some states emulated these requirements and adopted them for all HMOs that were licensed in the state regardless of federal qualification status.

Obtaining federal qualification has always been at the discretion of the individual HMO, unlike state licensure, which is mandatory. Plans that requested federal qualification did so for four principal reasons. First, it represented a "Good Housekeeping Seal of Approval" that was helpful in marketing. Second, the dual choice requirements ensured access to the employer market. Third, the override of state laws—important in some states but not others—applied only to federally qualified HMOs. Fourth, federal qualification was required for the receipt of federal grants and loans that were available during the early years of the act. In 1994, 50.8 percent of HMOs nationally, accounting for 70.6 percent of all enrollment, were federally qualified.[11] Federal qualification is less important today than it was when managed care was in its infancy and HMOs were struggling for inclusion in employment-based health benefit programs, which account for most private insurance in the United States. (Federal Qualification is discussed further in Chapter 54.)

Ironically, in its early years the 1973 legislation may have retarded HMO development, earning it the nickname of the "Anti-HMO Act." This occurred for two reasons. The first stems from a compromise in Congress between members having differing objectives. One camp was principally interested in fostering competition in the health care marketplace by promoting plans that incorporated incentives for providers to constrain costs. The second camp, while perhaps sharing the first objective, principally saw the HMO Act as a precursor to health reform and sought a vehicle to expand access to coverage for individuals who were without insurance or who had limited benefits. Imposing requirements on HMOs but not on indemnity carriers, however, reduced the ability of HMOs to compete.

Of particular note were requirements with regard to the comprehensiveness of the benefit package as well as open enrollment and community rating. The open enrollment provision required that plans accept individuals and groups without regard to their health status. The community rating requirement limited the ability of plans to relate premium levels to the health status of the individual enrollee or employer group. Both provisions represented laudable public policy goals; the problem was that they had the potential for making federally qualified HMOs noncompetitive because the same requirements did not apply to the traditional insurance plans against which they competed. This situation was

largely corrected in the late 1970s with the enactment of amendments to the HMO Act that reduced some of the more onerous requirements. The federal dual choice provisions were "sunsetted" in 1995 and are no longer in effect.

The second reason that HMO development was retarded was the slowness of the federal government in issuing the regulations implementing the act. Employers knew that they would have to contract with federally qualified plans. Even those who were supportive of the mandate, however, delayed until the government determined which plans would be qualified and established the processes for the implementation of the dual choice provisions.

The Carter administration, which assumed office in 1977, was supportive of HMOs. In particular, Hale Champion, as undersecretary of the U.S. Department of Health and Human Services, made issuance of the regulations a priority. As can be seen from Figure 1–1, rapid growth ensued, with enrollment rising from 6.3 million in 1977 to 29.3 million in 1987.

Politically, several aspects of this history are interesting. First, although differences arose on

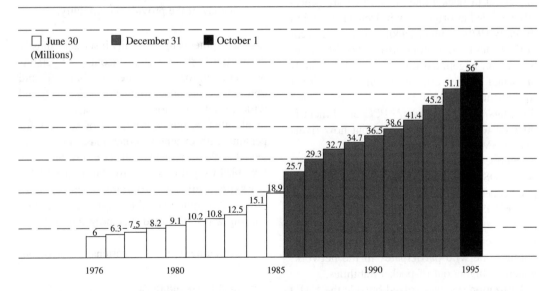

Figure 1–1 Number of people receiving their care in HMOs, 1976–1995. *1995 estimate based on Group Health Association of America's 1994 HMO performance report. *Source:* American Association of Health Plans (formerly GHAA/AMCRA). *Patterns in HMO Enrollment*, p. 3 (Washington, D.C., 1995).

specifics, the congressional support for legislation promoting HMO development came from both political parties. Also, there was not widespread state opposition to the override of restrictive state laws. In addition, most employers did not actively oppose the dual choice requirements, although many disliked the federal government in effect telling them to contract with HMOs. Perhaps most interesting of all has been the generally positive interaction between the public sector and the private sector, with government fostering HMO development both through its regulatory processes and also as a purchaser under its employee benefits programs.

Other managed care developments also occurred during the 1970s and early 1980s. Of note was the evolution of PPOs. Although there is no widely accepted legal definition, PPOs are generally regarded as differing from HMOs in two respects. First, they do not accept capitation risk; rather, risk remains with the insurance company or self-insured employment-based entity (employer or Taft-Hartley employer–union trust fund). Second, enrollees may access providers that are not in the contracted network, but they face disincentives for doing so in the form of higher out-of-pocket liabilities. PPOs are generally regarded as originating in Denver, where in the early 1970s Samuel Jenkins, a vice president of the benefits consulting firm of The Martin E. Segal Co., negotiated discounts with hospitals on behalf of the company's Taft-Hartley trust fund clients. Starting in 1978, Jenkins negotiated discounts with physicians.[12] PPO enrollment is difficult to estimate accurately but now rivals that of HMOs.

Intermediate between the HMO and the PPO is the POS plan. It is sometimes referred to as a gatekeeper PPO. To avoid financial penalties under POS, the enrollee must designate a primary care physician, who in turn authorizes any referral services. Self-referral to a specialist, including one who participates in the network, generates higher out-of-pocket liabilities.

Utilization review evolved outside the HMO setting between 1970 and 1985, although it has earlier origins:

- In 1959, Blue Cross of Western Pennsylvania, the Allegheny County Medical Society Foundation, and the Hospital Council of Western Pennsylvania performed retrospective analyses of hospital claims to identify utilization that was significantly above the average.[13]
- Around 1970, California's Medicaid program initiated hospital precertification and concurrent review in conjunction with medical care foundations in that state, starting with the Sacramento Foundation for Medical Care.[14]
- The 1972 Social Security Amendments authorized the federal Professional Standards Review Organization (PSRO) program to review the appropriateness of care provided to Medicare and Medicaid beneficiaries. Although its effectiveness has been debated, the PSRO program established an organizational infrastructure and data capacity upon which both the public and private sectors could rely.
- In the 1970s, a handful of large corporations initiated precertification and concurrent review for inpatient care, much to the dismay of the provider community.

Developments in indemnity insurance, mostly during the 1980s, included encouraging persons with conventional insurance to obtain second opinions before undergoing elective surgery and widespread adoption of large case management—that is, the coordination of services for persons with expensive conditions, such as selected accident patients, cancer cases, and very low–birthweight infants. Also during the 1980s, worksite wellness programs became more prevalent as employers, in varying degrees and varying ways, instituted such programs as:

- screening (e.g., for hypertension and diabetes)
- health risk appraisal
- promotion of exercise (whether through having gyms, conveniently located show-

ers, or running paths, or simply by providing information)

- stress reduction
- classes (e.g., smoking cessation, lifting of heavy weights, and the benefits of exercise)
- nutritional efforts, including serving healthy food in the cafeteria
- weight loss programs
- mental health counseling

For both employers and managed care organizations, wellness and prevention have become integral components of managed care (see Chapter 17).

MANAGED CARE COMES OF AGE: 1985 TO THE PRESENT

The last decade has seen a combination of innovation, maturation, and restructuring. These are briefly discussed below.

Innovation

Three areas of innovation are discussed. First, in many communities hospitals and physicians have collaborated to form physician-hospital organizations (PHOs), principally as vehicles for contracting with managed care organizations. PHOs are typically separately incorporated, with the hospital and the physicians each having the right to designate half the members of the board. Most PHOs seek to enter into fee-for-service arrangements with HMOs and PPOs, although an increasing number accept full capitation risk. Other variants on integrated delivery systems are described in Chapter 4.

Whether PHOs are an important development or little more than a transitional vehicle is hotly debated. Some have been successful as provider units of health care plans, particularly those that have accepted capitation risk from HMOs. The skeptics argue, however, that most PHOs are hospital and specialty dominated, whereas one of the success factors in managed care is a strong primary care orientation. Other reasons for skep-

ticism are that most PHOs allow all physicians with admitting privileges at the hospital in question to participate rather than selecting the more efficient ones and that the physicians are commonly required to use the hospital for outpatient services (e.g., laboratory tests) that might be obtained at lower cost elsewhere, hence hurting the ability of the PHO to be price competitive. Finally, some PHOs suffer from organizational fragmentation, inadequate information systems, management that is inexperienced, and lack of capital.

A second innovation has been the development of carve-outs, which are organizations that have specialized provider networks and are paid on a capitation or other basis for a specific service, such as mental health, chiropractic, and dental. The carve-out companies market their services principally to HMOs and large self-insured employers. Similar in concept are groups of specialists, such as ophthalmologists and radiologists, that accept capitation risk for their services (sometimes referred to as subcapitation) through contracts with health plans and employer groups. One controversy surrounding carve-out arrangements is whether they result in fragmented care for the patient. Such specialty-based networks are also discussed in Chapter 13.

A third set of innovations is those that have been made possible by advances in computer technology. Vastly improved computer programs, marketed by private firms or developed by managed care plans for internal use, have become available that generate statistical profiles of the use of services rendered by physicians. These profiles serve to assess efficiency and quality and may also serve to adjust payment levels to providers who are paid under capitation or risk-sharing arrangements to reflect patient severity. These topics are discussed in greater detail in Chapter 27.

Another example of the impact of computer technology is a virtual revolution in the processing of medical and drug claims, which is increasingly being performed electronically rather than by paper submission and manual entry. The result has been dramatically lower administrative costs—claims costs now are typically less than twice the price of a first-class postage stamp—and far superior information; an example of the latter is allowing the pharmacist at the time a prescription is dispensed to receive information about potential adverse effects. Management information systems can be expected to improve in the next few years as providers, almost universally, submit claims electronically. In addition, providers are likely to be assigned unique identification numbers, enabling profiling systems to combine data across multiple payers. Electronic data interchange and management information systems are discussed further in Chapter 28.

Maturation

Maturation can be seen from several vantage points. The first is the extent of HMO and PPO growth. Between 1992 and 1994, only a 2-year period, HMO enrollment rose 23 percent, reaching 51.1 million.[15] As mentioned earlier, PPO enrollment is difficult to estimate but approaches that of HMOs. Employers have come to rely on managed care at the expense of traditional indemnity insurance, as seen in Figure 1–2, with many no longer offering traditional insurance at all.

Medicare and Medicaid have also increasingly relied on managed care. Many HMOs regard Medicare risk contracting (i.e., capitation arrangements that HMOs enter into with the Medicare program) as an essential part of their business strategy, although the penetration is considerably below that of the working-age population. In April 1995, some 2,540,000 Medicare beneficiaries were enrolled in HMOs having Medicare risk contracts, an increase of 31 percent in a single year.[16] (See Figure 1–3). Even more impressive, after several flat years the number of plans with Medicare risk contracting increased 75 percent in 2 years (Figure 1–4). The reasons include the realization that Medicare can be profitable; employer demands for HMO options for retirees; reluctance to ignore a major market at a time when HMOs are consolidating and, in some cases, fighting for survival; and the perspective that the plans that account for a high proportion of a provider's revenue will acquire competitive advantage because they have leverage in negotiating reimbursement arrangements. (Medicare and managed care are discussed further in Chapters 46 and 47.)

State Medicaid programs, too, have turned to managed care, and, like employers, many are re-

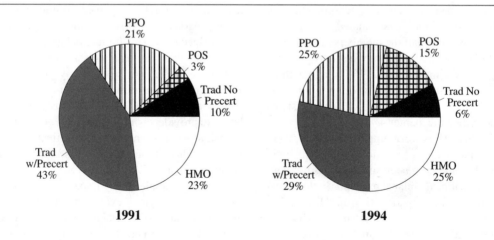

1991   **1994**

Figure 1–2 Market share by health plan type, 1991 and 1994. Trad, traditional; precert, precertification. *Source:* Courtesy of KPMG Peat Marwick, LLP, 1994, Washington, D.C.

moving the fee-for-service option. As of June 1994, 7.8 million beneficiaries were in managed care, representing 23.2 percent of the total Medicaid population, an increase from 11.8 percent just 2 years before.[17] Some 4.0 million of the 7.8 million beneficiaries were in HMOs, with the balance being under less restrictive arrangements, mostly so-called primary care case management (PCCM) programs, which entail beneficiaries electing a primary care physician, who must approve any referrals to specialists and other services. Under the PCCM programs, providers are generally paid a fee for service, except that the primary physician may receive a small (e.g., $2.00) monthly case management fee. (Medicaid and managed care are discussed further in Chapter 48.)

Another phenomenon is the maturation of external quality oversight activities. Starting in 1991, the National Committee for Quality Assurance (NCQA; see Chapter 37) began to ac-credit HMOs. The NCQA was launched by the HMO industry in 1979. It became independent in 1991, however, with the majority of board seats being held by employer, union, and consumer representatives. Many employers are demanding or strongly encouraging NCQA accreditation of the HMOs with which they contract, and accreditation is coming to replace federal qualification as the "Good Housekeeping Seal of Approval."

In addition, performance measurement systems (report cards) are evolving, although they are at an early stage. The most prominent is the Health Plan Employer Data and Information Set (HEDIS; see Chapter 28), which was developed by the NCQA at the behest of several large employers and health plans. The indices of quality that are part of the performance measurement system are incomplete but will be improved over time. Shortcomings include a focus on what is easily measurable and the lack of health out-

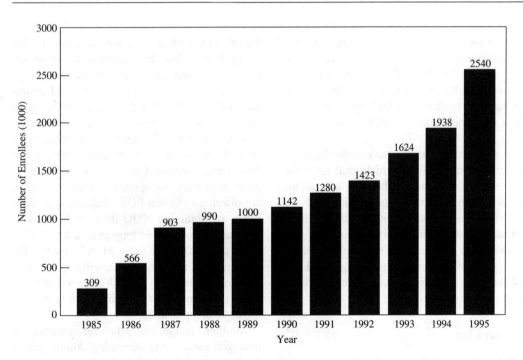

Figure 1–3 Medicare risk enrollees (month of April). *Source:* Data from *Managed Care Contract Reports*, Health Care Financing Administration, Baltimore, Maryland.

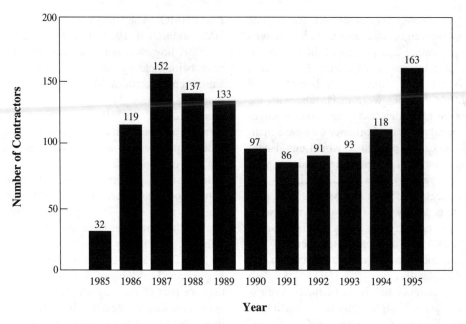

Figure 1–4 Medicare risk contractors (month of April). *Source:* Data from *Managed Care Contract Reports*, Health Care Financing Administration, Baltimore, Maryland.

come measures. In a related development, several consumer-oriented magazines regularly carry articles assessing HMOs in their respective communities. As more and more of the insured lose access to traditional indemnity plans, the issue of HMO performance will become more salient.

Another form of maturation is the focus of cost management efforts, which used to be almost exclusively inpatient hospital utilization. Practice patterns have changed dramatically in the last 20 years, however, and inpatient utilization has declined significantly. Although hospital utilization still receives considerable scrutiny, greater attention is being paid to ambulatory procedures such as the use of diagnostics and specialists.

Restructuring

Perhaps the most dramatic development is the restructuring that is occurring and that reflects

the interplay between managed care and the delivery system. The definitional distinctions are blurring as managed care organizations undergo a process of hybridization. Staff and group model HMOs, faced with limited capital and a need to expand into new territories, are forming IPA components. Meanwhile, some IPAs have created staff model primary care centers while continuing to contract with physicians in independent practice for specialty services. HMOs are offering PPO and POS products, and some PPOs are obtaining HMO licenses. HMOs are also contracting with employers on a self-funded rather than a capitated basis, whereby the risk for medical costs remains with the employer, not to mention a variety of hybrid arrangements. In short, the managed care environment is becoming more complicated.

Another change, and a natural evolution of managed care, is the increasing dominance of the primary care physician, who assumes responsibility for overseeing the allocation of resources. Most managed care organizations regard gaining the loyalty of primary care physicians as critical to their success. The "food chain" analogy has become a popular one, with primary care physicians rising above specialists and hospitals in the "food chain" hierarchy. Contributing to this role reversal is the excess supply in many specialties, with primary care physicians being in tight supply, a phenomenon that varies geographically. The role reversal has been a mixed blessing for primary care physicians, who may feel caught between pressure to reduce costs on the one hand and, on the other hand, the need to satisfy the desires of consumers, who may question whether the physician has their best interests at heart in light of the financial incentives to limit resource consumption.

Finally, consolidation is notable among both health care plans and providers. The multistate managed care firms, including the Kaiser plans but excluding the Blue Cross and Blue Shield plans, which operate largely autonomously, accounted for 60 percent of all enrollment nationally in 1994.[18] Mergers are continuing to occur, as exemplified in 1995 by United Health Care, a publicly traded managed care company headquartered in Minnesota, purchasing Metra-Health, which in turn combined all the health insurance lives, managed care and indemnity, of the Travellers and Metropolitan insurance companies.

FUTURE ISSUES FACING MANAGED CARE

This chapter concludes with observations regarding managed care and how it has, and will, evolve with regard to the interplay between the public and private sectors; the role of quality in the new competitive, and managed care–dominated, environment; the locus of decision making on coverage of expensive and marginally effective technologies; and how the nation will address problems that managed care and competitive delivery mechanisms cannot solve and may exacerbate, notably access to coverage for

the uninsured and the financing of graduate medical education.

Interplay between the Public and Private Sectors

One of the themes of this chapter is the generally positive interplay between the public and private sectors. HMOs, which are private entities, have proven themselves to be viable mechanisms for delivering care to Medicare and Medicaid beneficiaries. At the same time, government at all levels has contributed much to managed care growth. One of the earlier examples of a large employer contracting with HMOs on a dual choice basis was the agreement between the U.S. Office of Personnel Management and Kaiser Foundation Health Plans setting forth the terms under which Kaiser would be offered to federal employees. Today, federal, state, and local (including school district) government employees constitute the largest accounts of many HMOs. In addition, the HMO Act of 1973 provided a major impetus for HMO development. Even before then, the California Medicaid program represented one of the first examples of inpatient precertification and concurrent review. Also, many private plans have adopted diagnosis-related groups for hospital reimbursement and the resource-based relative value scale for physician reimbursement, both developed by Medicare for its fee-for-service program.

Ironically, many in the provider community, which is hardly unified, now look to the government for protection, such as by lobbying for laws that limit the ability of managed care plans to select the providers that are in their networks. A significant segment of the provider community appears to prefer government regulation to marketplace competition.

Role of Quality

The role of quality in employer contracting decisions as well as in consumer choice among plans is unclear. HMOs pay considerable attention to enrollee satisfaction and regularly conduct surveys of both enrollees and disenrollees. Satisfaction may not equate to technical quality, however. Managed care should have as its objective maximizing value, not minimizing cost. The degree and manner in which quality will enter into employer contracting decisions and consumer choice, thereby affecting financial performance and market share, are unclear.

Of particular concern to some is how the chronically ill, especially those with rare conditions requiring specialized care, will fare under capitated arrangements. By one estimate, chronic illness accounts for 80 percent of all medical costs.[19] HMOs focus considerable attention on the more prevalent conditions, such as diabetes and asthma (which are also the focus of HEDIS measures). How good is their performance in caring for persons with complex or rare chronic conditions? Unfortunately, the research literature has little to say on this question, which should be a matter of empirical study, not anecdotes or preconceived views. Also debated is the role of the specialist versus the primary care physician in caring for persons with certain chronic conditions, such as congestive heart failure and chronic obstructive pulmonary disease, both prevalent among the elderly in particular. Should the cardiologist or pulmonologist be allowed to serve as primary care physician for patients with these respective conditions?

Technology Assessment and the Coverage Determination Process

Another issue is the technology assessment or coverage determination process, that is, the process for making decisions about when new procedures or services are no longer experimental as well as when procedures in general, some in use for many years, are not effective. For example, when is a particular form of transplantation no longer experimental? Subscriber and employer contracts, indemnity or HMO, routinely exclude coverage of procedures that are investigational or experimental. There is not a uniform set of guidelines or a review process for

determining when a procedure is no longer investigational or experimental, however. As a result, coverage denials are often litigated. Whether the courts are the best locus of decision making about what should be accepted medical practice is doubtful.

The extent to which such decisions should be within the province of the individual health care plan is debated among the HMOs themselves. Competition among health care plans based on the restrictiveness of their benefit interpretations is of questionable social merit. Segments of the HMO industry hold that such coverage decisions should be made by an external body, perhaps a public–private partnership, that establishes guidelines for all health care plans even while recognizing that such guidelines will always allow room for interpretation. Others oppose constraining individual plan latitude in coverage determinations.

This issue is not new with the advent of managed care. Under capitated systems, however, the plans have both more medical information about enrollees and greater incentive to scrutinize what is covered than is the case under conventional insurance.

Financing of Access for the Uninsured and for Graduate Medical Education

Finally, the growth of competitive delivery systems affects the nature of public policy debate for a broad gamut of issues. Even matters such as priorities for biomedical research are not immune. Managed care, however, places into particularly sharp relief the question of financing of access for the uninsured and graduate medical education. With regard to access, on the one hand managed care provides a vehicle for covering all populations efficiently; on the other hand it reduces the financial capacity of providers, operating in a more price competitive environment, to care for the uninsured.

Much of the cost of graduate medical education has traditionally been financed through higher fee-for-service billings. These costs are principally stipends to residents and interns along with the costs of supervision and those associated with services and procedures that are principally didactic in nature. Medicare reimburses hospitals for its share of these costs, which are incorporated into the county-specific rates at which Medicare pays HMOs. HMOs are not required to contract with teaching hospitals, however, which are often more expensive than their nonteaching peers. These hospitals need to be price competitive to survive, reducing their ability to support the teaching function.[20] The topic of academic health centers and managed care is also discussed in detail in Chapter 15.

CONCLUSION

Unmanaged care is no longer affordable, but several forces continue to fuel its growth. Purchasers of care, public and private, are unwilling to tolerate the growth in medical costs of the last several years. Purchasers also question the wide and unexplained variations in practice patterns among geographic areas and delivery systems, raising suspicions of widespread waste. Further fueling the growth of unmanaged care are the excesses in provider supply, such as in the numbers of specialists and hospital beds, leading to intense competition for limited health care dollars. Because medical care is such a personal matter, managed care will continue to generate anxiety among some consumers and to raise issues of societal values and public policy.

REFERENCES AND NOTES

1. Group Health Association of America (GHAA), *Patterns in HMO Enrollment*. (Washington, D.C.: GHAA, 1995). These figures include PPO and point-of-service products as well as pure HMO products. The principal sources of data on HMO enrollment are GHAA and InterStudy. They differ slightly in the data collected and the numbers reported. Both are regarded as generally reliable.

2. InterStudy, *Competitive Edge (Part II: Industry Report)*. February 1995; 5, No. 1. Minnetonka, Minn.

3. T.R. Mayer and G.G. Mayer, HMOs: Origins and Development, *New England Journal of Medicine* 312 (1985): 590–94.

4. G.K. MacLeod, "An Overview of Managed Care in *The Managed Care Handbook*, 2d ed., ed. P.R. Kongstvedt (Gaithersburg, Md.: Aspen, 1993), 3–11.

5. Mayer and Mayer, HMOs: Origins and Development.

6. P. Starr, *The Social Transformation of American Medicine* (New York, NY: Basic Books, 1982), 295–310.

7. InterStudy, *Competitive Edge*.

8. InterStudy, *Competitive Edge*.

9. Mayer and Mayer, HMOs: Origins and Development.

10. G.B. Strumpf, "Historical Evolution and Political Process," in *Group and IPA HMOs*, ed. D.L. Mackie, D.K. Decker (Gaithersburg, Md.: Aspen, 1981), 17–36.

11. InterStudy. *Competitive Edge*.

12. J.J. Spies, et al., "Alternative Health Care Delivery Systems: HMOs and PPOs," in *Health Care Cost Management: Private Sector Initiatives*, ed. P.D. Fox, et al. (Ann Arbor, Mich. Health Administration Press, 1984), 43–68.

13. J.E. Fielding, *Corporate Cost Management*. (Reading, Mass.: Addison-Wesley, 1984).

14. Fielding, *Corporate Cost Management*.

15. GHAA, *Patterns in HMO Enrollment*. These figures include PPO and POS products as well as pure HMO products.

16. U.S. Department of Health and Human Services (DHHS), *Medicare Care Contract Report* (Rockville, Md.: DHHS, 1995).

17. Health Care Financing Administration (HCFA), *National Summary of Medicaid Managed Care Programs and Enrollment* (HCFA, 1994).

18. InterStudy, *Competitive Edge*.

19. K.N. Lohr, et al, Chronic Disease in an General Adult Population: Findings from the Rand Health Insurance Experiment, *Western Journal of Medicine* 145 (1986): 537–545.

20. For a discussion of the managed care issues facing academic health centers, see P.D. Fox and J. Wasserman, Academic Medical Centers and Managed Care: Uneasy Partners. *Health Affairs* 12 (1993): 85–93.

SUGGESTED READING

Davis, K., Collins, K.S., and Morris, C. 1991. Managed Care: Promise and Concerns. *Health Affairs* 13 (4): 3–46.

Iglehart, J.K. 1993. The American Health Care System. *New England Journal of Medicine* 328 (12): 896–900.

Chapter 2

Managed Care and Health Care Reform: Evolution or Revolution?

Frederick B. Abbey

In this era of national debate on reforming our national health care system, the health care industry awaits legislative decisions that may affect its future. Cost containment and incremental reforms are the prevailing themes of the 104th Congress as this chapter is written. Failure of the previous Congress to build support for comprehensive reforms and universal access has reshaped the political agenda in Washington. Political debate has shifted from universal access to cost containment because of the issues that the new Republican leadership is juggling, including:

- reducing the federal deficit
- balancing the federal budget
- addressing the insolvency of the Medicare Trust Fund
- decreasing the size of government

Rather than look at health care reform as a single sweeping overhaul of the current system, we now can examine its impact in the context of continuous change. As we contemplate the future of health care delivery, the contentious debate of 1994 provides a menu of proposals that will be considered during the continuing process of changing our financing and delivery systems.

How should managed care organizations view these reforms? This chapter presents the drivers of federal health care policy and four major areas of policy development. Each of these areas illustrates incremental policy steps that Congress has taken, and may take in the future, to move more Americans toward a managed care system.

FEDERAL HEALTH POLICY DRIVERS

The outlook for incremental change in the health care delivery system is also supported by the nature of our political process and the fragmentation of the health care industry. Because the health care industry represents one seventh of the U.S. gross domestic product, it understandably generates a multitude of perspectives in this debate. Each perspective will attempt to advocate for a particular position and as a result will contribute to the compromises that form legislation.

In the 1980s, Congress increased the scope and frequency of legislative activity, which reduced federal payments to most providers of care. Consequently, the health care industry increased its self-advocacy in the legislative process. In the midst of the health care reform debate, there are at least 837 Washington care–related associations and coalitions representing different points of view—more than triple the number a decade ago.[1] These various

Frederick B. Abbey is a partner in the Washington, D.C. office of Ernst & Young LLP. He is the National Director of Legislative and Regulatory Support. For 8 years, he served as a federal official in policy development at the U.S. Department of Health and Human Services and the Health Care Financing Administration.

Ernst & Young staff members Peter Gunter, Mike Treash, Kirby McIlyar, and Sue Carrington also contributed to this chapter.

viewpoints, coupled with the American public's perception that our health care system has major problems, resulted in nearly 300 members of the 103rd Congress sponsoring health care reform legislation.[2] In the legislative process, the multitude of perspectives will need to be addressed so that any resulting proposal can be supported publicly and ultimately enacted. The health care industry is enormously complex, and each group views itself as a potential winner or loser under reform proposals.

In analyzing these proposals, we see that no one approach will be adopted; rather, the political process represents the public and special interest forces that will continue to be evident after the enactment of any initial bill. Despite wide support in the 103rd Congress for changes in our health care delivery and financing system, no legislation was enacted. The primary reason for inaction was that most approaches were global, involving enhanced government roles and representing significant change. Reform legislation, however, will probably be introduced and enacted in every Congress into the next century.

The health care system has multidimensional effects on federal, state, and private sector spending as well as on business innovation and competitiveness. The drivers of federal health policy include:

- the U.S. budget deficit, $203 billion annually
- the public debt, $5 trillion and growing
- the Medicare Trust Fund, approaching insolvency by 2002
- state budget shortfalls, strapped by an average 12 percent Medicaid growth rate
- public perception of change and reluctance to accept larger roles for the government
- an aging population and changing demographics, represented by a 23 percent increase in the over-85 population

These issues will continue to limit the government's ability to expand rapidly its role in health care.

The federal budget is composed of seven pieces, with more than half of spending being devoted to entitlement and mandatory programs (Figure 2–1).[3] The federal deficit has long been a problem and will continue to be; recent estimates project that the deficit will exceed $300 billion by the year 2003.[4] Medicare and Medicaid will continue to fuel federal spending at a steady rate of 10 percent each year for at least the next 10 years.[5] Consequently, the government's ability to address other domestic issues is hindered. Health care entitlement programs continue to be the source of funding cuts to reduce the deficit and allow other concerns to be addressed. Public debt is growing at a rate exceeding 50 percent of the gross domestic product.[6] Congress is continuing efforts to reduce the deficit and has set 2002 as a goal. Thus, regardless of the political interests of those who would expand government's role in health care, the economic budget realities will preclude the government from taking on long-range health care commitments.

Republican congressional promises to balance the budget by 2002 have forced politicians to take immediate action to reduce Medicare expenditures while shoring up the Hospital Insurance (HI) Trust Fund. In fact, in 1996, for the first time ever, the HI Trust Fund will be paying out more in benefits than it takes in from payroll taxes. The situation will only worsen when the Baby Boomers age into retirement beginning in 2010. Medicare enrollment is expected to jump from its current 33 million enrollees to 70 million by the year 2030.[7] The $270 billion reduction proposed by the House and Senate for the fiscal year (FY) 1996 budget, however, will only extend Medicare solvency several years, to 2005. This solvency issue will continue to plague lawmakers until systematic change is implemented to control utilization and define the federal government's contribution up front.

If federal commitment to the elderly is to continue, a more efficient health care delivery system will be required. States are also being forced to reduce spending and raise taxes to fund Medicaid programs with out-of-control expenditure

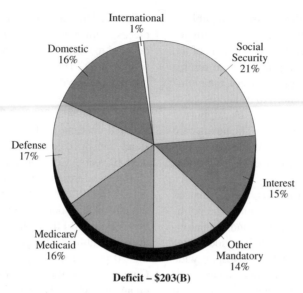

Figure 2–1 The federal budget. *Source:* Reprinted from "The Economic and Budget Outlook for Fiscal Years 1995–1999," with permission of Congressional Budget Office, © 1995.

growth that is expected to more than double in the next 5 years. State funding provides the single largest source of Medicaid financing and has grown at an average annual rate of 12 percent.[8] The increase in Medicaid financing has prohibited states from meeting other community needs, such as education, road improvements, and crime prevention. With federal regulations limiting fundraising measures for Medicaid, such as donations and provider taxes, states now strongly support improved access to care and cost containment.

Rising health care costs reduce profits and divert money from investments in business expansion. Many employers have taken steps to contain these costs, but the growing number of uninsured forces health care organizations to shift the burden to the insured population. A more efficient delivery system would slow the growth of health care expenditures, enabling more Americans to afford insurance and abating the cost-shifting trend.

Members of the more conservative 104th Congress have focused more on the insurance

coverage problems of the middle and upper classes. These proposals increase purchasing power for small employers, simplify administrative reporting, ensure portability, and extend guarantee issue and renewal in group markets. Unlike the broad health reform efforts of the 103rd Congress, these provisions are popular with employers, employees, providers, and lawmakers alike. Specific suggestions include applying credit earned under an individual plan toward a group policy, offering different levels of coverage under the Consolidated Omnibus Reconciliation Act (COBRA), and allowing former employees to join individual plans after exhausting their COBRA coverage.

MAJOR AREAS OF POLICY DEVELOPMENT

The incremental health care reform efforts and proposals for entitlement restructuring have many interrelated elements. There are four areas, however, that provide insight into how federal policy is slowly moving toward a managed care system: Medicare payment policies (see Chapter 46), Medicaid payment policies (see Chapter 48), federal fraud and abuse regulation (see Chapter 56), and regulation of managed care at the state level (see Chapter 53).

Medicare Payment Policies

Budget pressures and the impending insolvency of the HI Trust Fund have forced lawmakers to consider immediate solutions to curb the escalating costs of the Medicare program. Whether Congress simply adopts price control mechanisms or restructures Medicare, the changes will not stop with this Congress. These cost containment forces that promote change will surface again, and participants in the health care system will have to be flexible to adjust accordingly (Figure 2–2).

Medicare future state growth rates of about 5 percent, needed to keep the HI Trust Fund in actuarial balance, have required that the system reduce the utilization of services. The 104th

Congress proposals to reduce Medicare's expenditure growth rate include payment reductions and delivery system restructuring. Choice is key in the future delivery model. Individuals will be asked to select a type of health plan based on information about cost, access, quality, and benefits. Legislative proposals establish the following:

- market area information to distribute information to the elderly about health plan options
- medical savings accounts (MSAs) to allow direct government funds to be deposited into a self-directed financing account
- catastrophic plan to "piggyback" the MSA with flexible deductibles that are less than $10,000
- multi–managed care plans to allow new organizational models into the Medicare market [i.e., point-of-service (POS) products, preferred provider organizations (PPOs), and provider-sponsored plans]

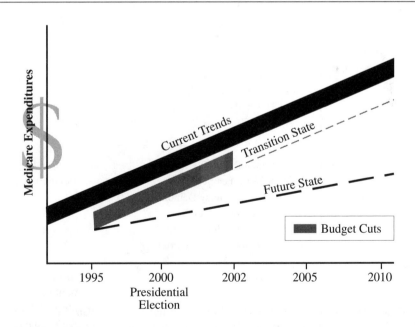

Figure 2–2 2001, the next wave. *Source:* Courtesy of Ernst & Young LLP, 1995, Washington, D.C.

- fee-for-service (FFS) plans to maintain the current traditional coverage
- budgetary safeguards to allow a Medicare budget target to set MSA, health plan, and FFS payments

These proposals contain a mix of prescriptions to control utilization by establishing more managed care organizations and by allowing beneficiaries to control the flow of health care expenses from their own MSA. Alternatively, the proposals also require an initial and probably subsequent reductions in FFS payments.

The Medicare program has been a major source of the federal government's experience with managed care. As Congress considers the evolving federal role in managed care, it is likely to take into account Medicare's direct and indirect experience in formulating new policies. Medicare history with managed care stems from a belief that health care delivery can be more ef-

ficiently deployed under a prepaid coordinated system and that the Medicare program can contain its costs. The concept of developing and expanding fixed price payments for certain defined services is a well-established trend (Figure 2–3). Two sets of policies affect managed care organizations: the Medicare managed care contracting policies, and the fragmented at-risk payment methods.

Medicare Risk-Based Contracting Program

Lawmakers are targeting managed care efficiencies to reduce Medicare spending from the current annual growth rate of 9.1 percent to 6.5 percent. Thus a great deal of regulatory and demonstration project activity is taking place in the Medicare risk-based contracting program (for a full discussion, see Chapters 47 and 48). Since 1982, Medicare has encouraged health maintenance organizations (HMOs) to provide coverage to enrolled Medicare beneficiaries in

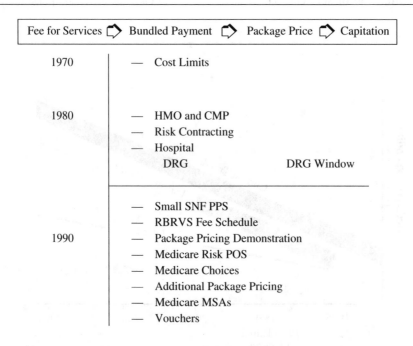

Figure 2–3 Medicare payment policy development. CMP, competitive medical plan; DRG, diagnosis-related group; SNF, skilled nursing facility; PPS, prospective payment system; RBRVS, resource-based relative value scale. *Source:* Courtesy of Ernst & Young LLP, 1994, Washington, D.C.

return for a fixed prepaid premium. In 1985, the Medicare risk program began paying HMOs a fixed monthly amount set at 95 percent of the actuarial estimate of what it would have typically reimbursed health care providers and practitioners for covered services.

The program has had limited success in attracting the participation of beneficiaries and health plans. As of July 1995, there were 250 health plans (165 of which are risk contracts) enrolling 3.5 million beneficiaries.[9] Although only 9.5 percent of Medicare beneficiaries are enrolled in a Medicare HMO, 74.0 percent of seniors currently live in an area where a managed care plan is available. Managed care is most popular with Medicare beneficiaries in those states with overall high levels of HMO penetration: Minnesota, Florida, Arizona, and California. Penetration levels in these states have exceeded 30 percent of the Medicare market.

Policy development in the future will probably focus on refining the basis of payment to prepaid plans. A General Accounting Office report, which is disputed by many managed care executives, states that beneficiaries with chronic health conditions were less likely to enroll in HMOs and that the payment rates failed to reflect a healthier-than-average enrolled population.[10] The Medicare method of adjusting the prepaid payment rates by studying age, gender, and a few other patient characteristics failed to account for a patient's health status. As a result of the enrollment of healthier beneficiaries in HMOs and the lack of a health status adjuster in the payment rate calculation method, Medicare spent nearly 6 percent more than it would have if enrollees had not joined HMOs. As Congress considers health care reform legislation, it will be concerned about developing payment methods with rates that will attract health plan participation and cost containment goals.

Hoping to ease seniors into managed care, Congress enacted Medicare Select, a preferred provider arrangement of hospitals for first-dollar coverage. Hospitals waive the $716 Part A deductible to increase their market share by joining a hospital network, and health plans pass on the savings in the form of lower premiums. Medicare Select was enacted in 15 states in 1990 as a demonstration project. After renewing Medicare Select in 1993, Congress decided in June 1995 to extend the program to all 50 states permanently.

The Health Care Financing Administration (HCFA) recently launched a pilot project called Medicare Choices in nine cities to test different types of managed care arrangements for seniors. The demonstration project, running 3 to 5 years, is the first step to opening up the Medicare managed care market to PPOs, POS plans, HMOs serving rural markets, and integrated delivery systems (IDSs) other than HMOs. Alternatively, Congress could forgo the demonstration phase of this policy development and create new plan criteria for IDSs.

Future policy areas under the Medicare program will continue on both the managed care and the FFS front. The fragmented policy changes will shift financial risk to the provider/practitioner community. This risk shift will contribute to the integration of services into new types of risk-bearing organizations. On the HMO front, Medicare will probably develop a risk adjuster to its premium setting calculations.

Fragmented at-Risk Payment Methods

The Medicare program has initiated efforts to reduce hospital inpatient costs, physician expenditures, outpatient costs, and virtually every other area of service. At-risk payments have been developed for hospital inpatient stays using the diagnosis-related group (DRG) system of patient classification with a prospective pricing method. Over time, the government will extend the definition of a hospital stay to incorporate more pre- and poststay services. In 1990, Congress enacted legislation that extended the definition of a hospital stay to include certain diagnostic services that are performed before an admission. This resulted in maintaining the integrity of the at-risk (i.e., DRG) payment and providing a payment intended to cover all the services around the treatment of a particular diagnosis in a hospital stay. As technology and practice patterns change, Congress is expected to consider extending this DRG window to postdischarge services.

The HCFA began a Medicare demonstration project in an effort to reduce costs and improve quality of care for two open heart surgery procedures commonly performed on Medicare-eligible patients (DRGs 106 and 107).[11] Under the demonstration, hospitals and physicians are paid a single negotiated price to provide coronary artery bypass graft (CABG) surgeries to Medicare patients. About 145,000 CABG procedures are performed annually on Medicare beneficiaries.[12] In the first 2 years, four of the seven participating hospitals developed cost-saving quality care protocols for the 2,552 surgeries, resulting in a savings of more than $14 million.[13] Improved case management on each patient reduced length of stay, increased hospital/physician communication, permitted greater savings, and improved quality of care. The participating hospitals reported no compromise in patient care. In fact, patient reaction was extremely positive.

Each of the hospitals is committing resources to change clinical practice patterns and administrative procedures, demonstrating the success of the effort. Hospital officials and physicians believe there is developing proof that their discrete and manageable approaches to specific surgical categories are making a difference in cost reduction without compromising quality. This bundled payment approach will probably be considered for other types of high-volume procedures (e.g., hip replacement) involving hospital- or facility-based services coupled with physician services.

In addition to DRGs and bundled pricing, the federal government is considering changing its reimbursement methods for other types of providers from a cost-based to a risk-based approach. There will probably be many legislated activities in the remainder of the 1990s to convert FFS or cost-based reimbursement systems into risk-based sites. In this way, Medicare can limit its financial responsibility for paying for covered services by shifting the risk to the provider/practitioner community. Two likely providers that will be transitioned to risk-based sites are home health agencies (HHAs) and skilled nursing facilities (SNFs).

In response to home health care expenditures rising at a rate of 40 percent per year, Congress is considering a proposal to move toward a prospective payment system (PPS). This system would be based on prospectively determined per visit rates subject to episode limits. If enacted, it would take effect in 1997 and would establish limits by discipline: skilled nursing care, physical therapy, speech pathology, occupational therapy, social services, and additional services. The objective would be to control the number of visits that a beneficiary receives under an episode of care. This proposal is based on an earlier demonstration project.

The project is being implemented in two phases. Phase 1 tested a per visit PPS on 26 HHAs in five states: California, Florida, Illinois, Massachusetts, and Texas.[14] Initial findings indicated no significant change in either agency costs or program expenditures with the implementation of this payment method. In early July 1995, phase 2 of the project began instituting a per episode payment method. This involves a single payment for all Medicare-covered home health services furnished during the first 120 days of an episode of home health care. The rate will be subject to an annual adjustment in the HHA's case mix.[15]

Rapid growth in Medicare SNF program expenditures has prompted Congress to address payment policy reform options. Program expenditures have grown at an alarming rate, from $0.4 billion in 1980 to $8.0 billion in 1994.[16] Greater utilization due to changes in the benefit accounts for much of the increase since 1987.[17] Several payment policy options have been proposed in an effort to control rising costs. Two such proposals are facility peer groups based on the type of facility or geographic location and adjustments based on the SNF case mix. Another option would be payments combining acute hospital and postacute care. Such bundling services would include not only SNF payments but also payments for postacute services, such as home health care and rehabilitation services. Details on the various choices have not yet been outlined for Congress to decide on a specific payment reform method.

Ambulatory services constitute the remaining large part of the delivery system under Medicare that will be transitioned to a risk-based reimbursement system. Congress has given the Department of Health and Human Services a mandate to search for a way to pay for hospital outpatient care under a PPS similar to that used for inpatient services. A new patient classification system, similar to DRGs, was developed to serve as the basis of payment for a visit-based outpatient PPS. The system is referred to as ambulatory patient groups (APGs) and was designed to be the basis of payment in an outpatient PPS. APGs serve as a patient classification scheme that reflects the amount and type of resources used in an ambulatory patient visit. Patients in each APG exhibit similar clinical characteristics for resource utilization and costs. Currently, there are roughly 300 APGs that describe the complete range of services provided in the outpatient setting.[18] Congress has not particularly focused on APGs' potential for holding down outpatient costs, however (APGs are discussed in Chapter 14).

Since January 1992, physician services have undergone a change in the reimbursement system, from one that standardized the payments to a resource-based fee schedule that bases payments on the amount of time, effort, and overhead associated with specific patient visits. The standardization of the Medicare reimbursement system will enable the Medicare program to consider ways to bundle payments with other providers and to continue shifting the financial risk away from the federal government.

Medicare is moving toward managed care on multiple fronts. It has capitated enrollees into health plans as well as bundled or packaged prices into new service areas. Both shift financial risk, but to different degrees. The fragmented FFS system of DRGs and package pricing serves two roles: first, to define or limit federal Medicare payments, and second, to prepare health care providers incrementally for greater risk of capitated payments.

Medicaid Payment Policies

In its 30 years of existence, Medicaid has improved access to medical services for many of the poor in America. Despite its successes, the program today has numerous limitations resulting from its basic design and financing. The discussions about national health care system reform have moved policymakers to review where Medicaid is, how it got there, and how it might be made more efficient. Medicaid transition toward integration with a private health insurance–based model has begun as states have moved aggressively into a managed care arena (this topic is discussed more fully in Chapter 48).

Budget pressures have drawn lawmakers' attention to Medicaid. The FY 1996 budget blueprint calls for $185 billion in savings over 7 years. Medicaid would be block granted to states, and the federal contribution would be capped at a 4 percent annual growth rate. States would have greater flexibility in how they distribute money and structure the health care delivery system. States would be held responsible for running the program with the predetermined federal contribution, however.

As with Medicare, the Medicaid program has its roots in a fragmented benefit and reimbursement structure. Historically, health care providers and practitioners were compensated through a variety of methods that differed from state to state. Before 1980, Medicaid generally reimbursed hospitals using the same cost-based principles adhered to by the Medicare program since its 1966 inception. Changes in statute in 1980 and 1981 permitted states to develop their own methodologies for reimbursing hospital inpatient services provided that their rates were appropriate for an efficiently run hospital. Most states have now moved to a PPS in which a predetermined amount would compensate a hospital for a defined service. Many states follow the DRG classification system used by Medicare to reimburse for hospital inpatient services. Other states use a contracting process in which they contract directly with hospitals to provide for inpatient services. These payment systems place an organization at financial risk to provide all services incidental to a hospital stay and thereby require more active management of the patient compared with earlier reimbursement methods. Throughout the last 30 years, Medicaid payment rates have not kept up with hospital costs, and today they cover, on the average, only about 78 percent of these costs.[19]

Physicians and outpatient services have also experienced incremental payment policy changes. States have historically established maximum allowable charges that provided the ceiling for physician and other individual practitioner payments. Over time, states have moved to adopt fixed FFS schedules. Like hospital inpatient services, Medicaid payment rates for physician services now average about 73 percent of what would have been reimbursed using Medicare principles of reimbursement.[20]

Despite Medicaid's poor payment rates and cumbersome eligibility and administrative processes, it is generally the single largest program in each state's budget. Federal and state Medicaid dollars combined account for 12 percent of the nation's health care spending. In recent years, annual Medicaid spending growth has exceeded 25 percent.[21] The absolute dollars involved, the growth rates, and the competing public policy demands have encouraged states to look for alternatives to contain costs and increase health care service and accessibility for the nation's poor.

Federal and state lawmakers are looking to managed care to improve access and control spiraling costs in the Medicaid program. As of June 1994, approximately 7.3 million Medicaid recipients were enrolled in managed care plans.[22] The Medicaid statute provides a number of options that allow states to pursue innovative methods of delivery and financing of Medicaid services. Figure 2–4 outlines Medicaid payment policy milestones. Since 1981, several freedom of choice waivers were enacted that allowed

states to lock Medicaid recipients into cost-effective alternative systems. A second type of waiver permitted states to offer an enhanced home and community services benefit to a defined population. Both types of waivers shared several characteristics: targeted enrollment of individual patients, defined formal contracts between the state Medicaid agency and the provider/payer network, and a case manager or gatekeeping function. Beyond these general attributes, Medicaid managed care organizational structure varies by program and by state.

As of 1995, states have moved to enroll about 25 percent of the entire Medicaid population in some 340 Medicaid managed care plans in 42 states.[23] However, only 10 states have chosen full-risk capitation plans for their Medicaid population.[24] Four states—California, New York, Maryland, and Michigan—account for 32 percent of the total Medicaid managed care enrollment.[25] Eight states have more than 25 percent of their Medicaid population enrolled in managed care plans (Figure 2–5).

Concerned over state flexibility in dealing with federal rules, the Clinton administration expedited the processing of Medicaid waiver requests. States that have greatly expanded their Medicaid program to include those who previously did not qualify (i.e., the previously uninsured), however, will be forced either to do more with less money or to cut their beneficiary roles. For example, Hawaii has expanded eligibility to those individuals who are up to 300 percent of the federal poverty level, and Oregon has expanded eligibility to those up to 100 percent of the federal poverty level.[26] Questions remain as to whether states will change their managed care strategy if previously eligible individuals lose coverage under the 4 percent growth cap.

The next wave of Medicaid managed care, however, will occur in long-term care, which accounts for nearly 70 percent of all Medicaid outlays. In fact, 93 percent of all Medicaid expenditures are still made on an FFS basis. Although 70 percent of Medicaid beneficiaries are women and children on aid to families with dependent

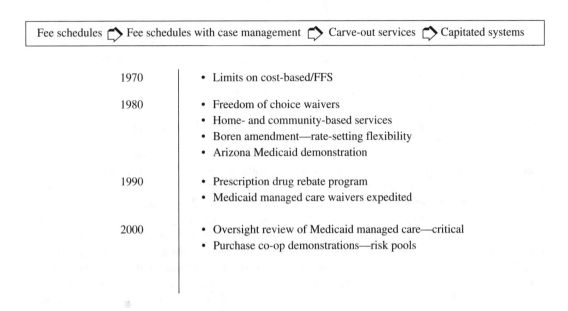

Figure 2–4 Medicaid managed care payment policies. *Source:* Courtesy of Ernst & Young LLP, 1994, Washington, D.C.

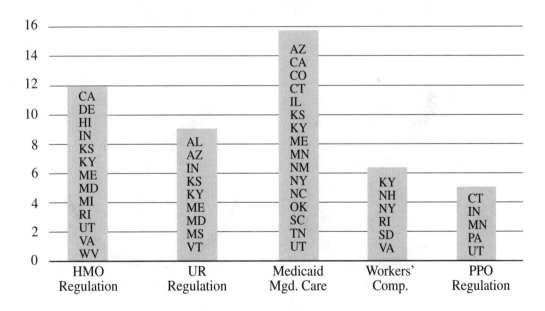

Figure 2–5 1994 managed care regulations. UR, utilization review. *Source:* Reprinted with permission from Major Health Legislation in the States: 1994, *Intergovernmental Health Policy Project*, pp. 138–141, The George Washington University, © 1995.

children (AFDC), they account for only 30 percent of Medicaid expenses[27] (Figure 2–6).

The success of managed care in containing costs and providing quality health care services is under considerable scrutiny. As policymakers examine the number of states pursuing managed care and the associated enrollment increases, we would expect to see an agreement among policymakers as to the degree of success of managed care in meeting these objectives. The Kaiser Commission on the Future of Medicaid, in its review of the more than 100 published studies in the literature, indicated that "it is difficult to draw definitive conclusions or to generalize about the successes or failures of managed care."[28] Despite mixed reports on Medicaid managed care, federal policy will continue to allow managed care to grow in hopes that money will be saved.

Since 1981, there have been numerous legislative proposals to change the federal financial relationship with the states over the Medicaid program. Vouchers, federal budget caps, and block grants are being considered. The return for this changed relationship between the federal and state governments limits the federal budget

responsibility and increases the states' flexibility to operate the program. Therefore, financing changes are likely to expedite the use of managed care because this is already the accepted method.

Fraud and Abuse Regulation

Managed care and the federal fraud and abuse regulatory process have evolved simultaneously (Table 2–1). Although many initial efforts to limit fraud and abuse were designed to protect the fiscal integrity of the public reimbursement programs (Medicare and Medicaid), more recent efforts have focused on defining appropriate provider relationships with ancillary services. The latter strategy could pose the most significant challenges to managed care providers. Within physician-directed or -owned vertically integrated systems (see Chapter 4), a significant portion of revenue can come from ancillary providers in the form of referrals for certain services. Such services include diagnostic imaging, clinical laboratory, radiation therapy, physical therapy and occupational therapy, ambulatory surgery, home infusion therapy and other home

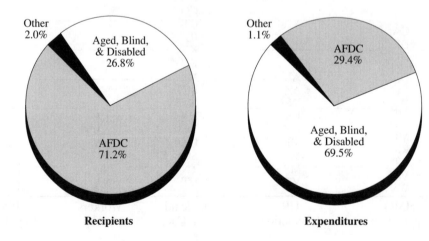

Figure 2–6 Medicaid recipients and payments, 1992. *Source:* U.S. House of Representatives, Overview of Entitlement Programs: 1994 Green Book.

Table 2–1 A Fraud and Abuse Continuum

Federal Legislation	Regulatory Guidance	Purpose
1970s		
Medicare/Medicaid Antifraud and Abuse Amendments	Correspondence	Protecting fiscal integrity
Office of Inspector General created		Protecting beneficiaries
1980s		
Medicare/Medicaid Patient, Program Protection Act	Safe harbors	Limiting financial gain
Medicare physician ownership restrictions	Fraud alerts	
1990s		
Physician ownership restrictions expanded, extended to Medicaid	Internal Revenue Service memoranda	Controlling utilization
Future		
Managed care oversight	New statute	Assessing reasonableness

Source: Courtesy of Ernst & Young LLP, 1994, Washington, D.C.

health services, durable medical equipment, parenteral and enteral nutrients and supplies, and outpatient prescription drugs.

The Medicare/Medicaid amendments of 1993 would prohibit physician referral to such entities if an ownership relationship exists unless such services are provided in office.[29] Members of the 104th Congress, however, seem more sympathetic to providers' complaints about the ambiguity and complexity of the self-referral regulations. Republicans and Democrats alike support legislation to require the Department of Health and Human Services to offer timely advisory opinions to inquiring providers.

As part of efforts to control utilization of services among private and public payment plans, however, health care reform might seek to limit further managed care referrals. HMOs have previously been exempt from such limitations because the HMO maintains ownership of such services. Physicians typically have no ownership interest; they are employed either as staff of the HMO or under contract as part of a medical group or as an independent practice association member. In physician-owned vertically inte-

grated systems, however, such ownership interests must be structured to prevent violation. As further models develop (e.g., physician–hospital organizations, group practices without walls, and integrated provider organizations) to position providers for managed care contracting, federal scrutiny will address the extent to which such relationships are designed to generate referrals.

Also, as managed care becomes more integral to Medicare, regulators will focus on plans' fiscal integrity. The Office of the Inspector General (OIG), Health and Human Services is now examining premium payments to risk-based HMOs. The current system, based on the average adjusted per capita cost, will be evaluated to understand better the variables (demographics, eligibility, and geography) used in calculation and whether they adequately reflect the risk of a given population. The financial solvency of all managed care plans will be closely scrutinized. Plans lacking a solid financial base are considered a threat to both beneficiaries and providers.

The federal legislative trends in antifraud and abuse demonstrate an increasing need for federal oversight. Beginning with a focus on program fiscal integrity and beneficiary protection, oversight turned in the late 1980s to controlling utilization of services. Now, as the federal government gains experience with capitation, it will evaluate more closely the reasonableness of payment to plans. Medicare and Medicaid are already being evaluated in this context as federal payments under such managed care programs increase rapidly and certain plans post profits.[30] Plans and providers should be prepared for close federal scrutiny of certain components of their managed care relationships (e.g., quality of care, patient access to providers, and other utilization controls as well as calculations for premium and payment amounts) as part of the OIG's ongoing investigations.

In this era of politically risky Medicare and Medicaid reductions, politicians frequently cite the inefficiencies and fraud present in the system. Attempting to deflect political criticism for Medicare cuts, lawmakers often point to an OIG study that says that 10 percent ($17 billion) of the Medicare budget in 1996 ($177 billion) will be consumed by fraud and abuse in the system. It is difficult to pin down the amount of fraud and abuse that is happening. As the perceived threat of supervision and prosecution ebbs and tides, so does the number of questionable practices.

Regulating Managed Care at the State Level

The federal government has often enacted national reforms in response to legislative trends on the state level. While politicians in Washington were debating comprehensive reform, several states enacted legislation in 1993 and 1994 that expanded access and attempted to control rising health care costs. The public's uneasiness over government control of the health care system, however, has led several of these states to reconsider and roll back their comprehensive initiatives. State regulation of managed care organizations is also discussed in detail in Chapter 53.

With the demise of federal health care reforms, the Employee Retirement Income Security Act (ERISA; see Chapter 59) is the primary federal law affecting state activities. It excludes self-insured plans from meeting state-imposed mandated benefit structures, administrative requirements, or enforcement mechanisms. Many state laws have been challenged based on assertions that they are preempted by ERISA. ERISA's original intent was to allow large, multistate employers to administer benefits uniformly across state lines. The law's impact on the health care market has increased significantly, however, as insurance companies have created products that allow smaller groups to self-insure.

Some states believe that ERISA was substantially weakened by a recent Supreme Court ruling (April 1995) upholding New York's practice of imposing surcharges on hospital bills. States are interpreting the ruling as an opening that allows them to impose provider taxes that they can use to fund increased access to care. ERISA plans had argued that the surcharges "relate to" self-insured plans by having an indirect effect on the choices made by insurance buyers, including ERISA plans. The New York law required hospitals to collect surcharges from patients covered by HMOs with low Medicaid enrollments and commercial insurers but not from a Blue Cross/Blue Shield plan. The law had the effect of adding as much as 24 percent to the bill of patients covered by commercial insurers and 9 percent for HMO patients.

Because states have traditionally regulated insurance products, their approach to policy contains far greater detail and clarity than that of the federal government. Historically, some states concentrated on regulating Blue Cross/Blue Shield and commercial health plans, leaving managed care plans to operate in an environment relatively free of regulation. Other states have for many years heavily regulated the managed care industry. In recent years, the increasing penetration of a variety of managed care plans has prompted a greater need for more market oversight in most parts of the country.

Legislators are becoming increasingly concerned that competitive pressures and risk-sharing contractual agreements are skewing health plans' incentives toward withholding care. As a result, they have developed regulations that are collectively referred to as health plan accountability laws. These laws cover a variety of issues, including the following:

- *Grievance procedures*—Provide standards to ensure that covered persons will have the opportunity for equitable resolution of their grievances.
- *Health information confidentiality*—Establish standards for the collecting, using, and disclosing of information gathered in connection with health plans.
- *Credentialing*—Ensure that participating health professionals meet specific minimum standards of professional qualification.
- *Utilization review*—Establish criteria for a health plan's quality assessment and quality improvement activities to evaluate, maintain, and improve the quality of health care services.
- *Quality assurance*—Ensure criteria for a health plan's quality assessment and quality improvement activities to evaluate, maintain, and improve the quality of health care provided to covered persons.
- *Provider contracting*—Ensure availability, accessibility, and quality of health care by establishing requirements for standards, terms, and provisions under which the provider will deliver services or supplies.

In some states, utilization management laws have evolved from guidelines detailing the activities that health plans must perform to rules determining how much plans can restrict access to care through utilization management techniques. More than half the states have enacted laws addressing concerns such as how much insurers can interfere with clinical decision making and the rights of providers and health plan members to appeal adverse utilization review decisions. Laws establishing minimum stay re-

quirements for obstetric cases, the most recent trend in managed care legislation, may spill over to other types of medical care.

Both the federal government and the states have advocated managed care as a way to control health care costs. Recent legislation has shown, however, that the state and federal governments are moving in opposite directions on at least one front. Prompted by provider lobbies fearful of being locked out of managed care plans, states began to limit the ability of managed care plans to create exclusive provider networks (so-called any willing provider statutes). A survey by the Medical Group Management Association found that at least 12 states have enacted one or more any willing provider laws (Figure 2–7). Twenty-one states have passed some type of freedom of choice legislation, either pure or contingent, whereby enrollees may be covered for services provided by a nonnetwork provider or practitioner who agrees to HMO requirements for the encounter(s).[31]

The pace at which any willing provider laws are being enacted has slowed as states have been presented with data showing the possible adverse impact of the laws on health care costs. Also, as managed care demonstrates cost savings over FFS coverage, federal policymakers are reconsidering the appropriateness of open panel requirements. A recent survey stated that any willing provider laws would increase private sector health spending by $74.7 billion between 1996 and 2002.[32,33] Several federal reform proposals introduced in both the 103rd and 104th Congress would preempt such measures and permit managed care plans to build closed panels of providers. This gives managed care advocates further reason to seek congressional legislation to bypass state laws and create uniformity across markets for building provider networks (see state regulation of managed care organizations, Chapter 53).

CONCLUSION

As the health care reform debate continues throughout the remainder of this century and

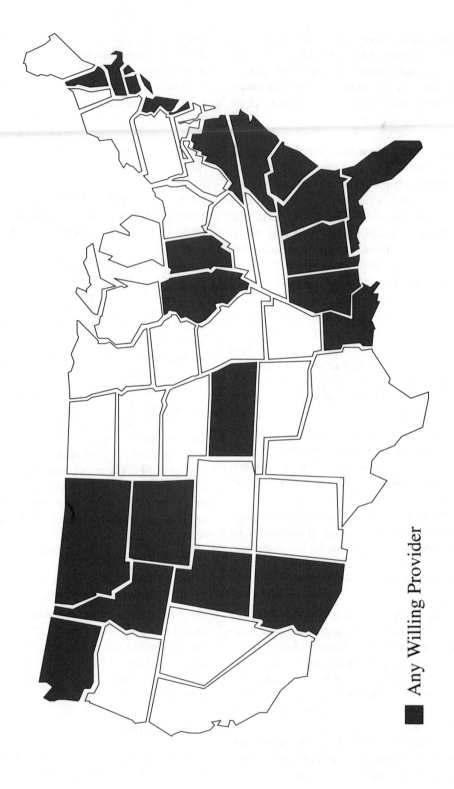

Figure 2-7 Open panel laws. *Source:* Data from Medical Group Management Association, 1995.

■ Any Willing Provider

possibly into the next, managed care will be a central component. At the heart of the debate is the struggle to accept that an IDS has greater benefit than one that relies on sole practitioners and FFS. At the federal level, the debate ranges from the government's running a fee-driven health program to standardizing a private health plan market that is held accountable for cost and quality of service. In the meantime, health care is likely to continue on the path of incremental changes that will moderately support the continued development of managed care plans in each marketplace.

To allow continuation of these incremental changes, Congress will need to address several other areas; each area will have an independent and a collective impact on the development of managed care organizations:

- defining a health benefits package that would be standardized in all markets
- deciding the level of responsibility and risk to be assumed by health care consumers
- legitimizing IDSs on provider-sponsored health plans as a model of managed care
- establishing administrative reporting requirements to support fiscal integrity and development of practice guidelines
- determining the role of supplemental insurance
- initiating changes in tax laws to limit the amount of employer-deductible health coverage expenses
- implementing changes in tax laws so that money accumulated in employees' MSAs is tax exempt
- refining the definition of an insurance company to clarify the requirements of tax exempt organizations
- affirming the role of academic health centers

Examination of the incremental health care and entitlement reform legislation enacted in the remainder of this century will illuminate the future direction of the private market and the public sector. The complex task of defining new roles and responsibilities among the federal and state governments, patients, businesses, insurers, and health care providers/practitioners cannot be completed with the enactment of any one piece of legislation. As we saw in 1994, that was too revolutionary for America. After all, the country has not had a revolution in hundreds of years and is not about to start one with Medicare, Medicaid, and health care reform!

REFERENCES AND NOTES

1. National Health Council (NHC), *Health Groups in Washington—A Directory*, 12th ed. (Washington, D.C.: NHC, 1993).

2. Roper Center, *Time, Cable News Network Poll* (Stamford, Conn.: Roper Center, 1995).

3. Congressional Budget Office (CBO), *The Economic & Budget Outlook* (Washington, D.C.: CBO, 1994), 39.

4. Congressional Budget Office (CBO), *Reducing the Deficit: Spending and Revenue Options* (Washington, D.C.: CBO, 1995), 5.

5. Congressional Budget Office, *Reducing the Deficit.*

6. Concord Coalition, *The Zero Deficit Plan* (Concord, Mass.: Concord Coalition, 1995), 8.

7. Medicare Trustees, *Medicare Trustees' Report* (Washington, D.C.: Medicare Trustees, 1995).

8. Health Care Financing Administration (HCFA), Office of Legislative and Inter-Governmental Affairs, *Medicaid Fact Sheet* (Washington, D.C.: HCFA, 1995).

9. Health Care Financing Administration (HCFA), *Monthly Report* (HCFA, 1995).

10. General Accounting Office (GAO), *Changes to HMO Rate Setting Method Are Needed To Reduce Program Costs* (Washington, D.C.: GAO, 1994).

11. Participant Hospitals, *The Medicare Participating Heart Bypass Demonstration Project, Interim Report to the Nation* (Washington, D.C.: National Press Club, 1993), I-1.

12. Boston University Medical Center Hospital, Medicare Participating Heart Bypass Demonstration Project.

13. Participant Hospitals, *The Medicare Participating Heart Bypass Demonstration Project*, I-4.

14. Prospective Payment Assessment Commission, *Interim Analysis of Payment Reform for Home Health Services* (Congressional Report C-94-02, 1 March 1994), 5.

15. P. Hoffman, CFO, Outreach Health Services, testimony before the House Ways and Means Committee (20 July 1995).

16. J. Ratner, Government Accounting Office, testimony before the House Commerce Committee (20 July 1995).

17. Prospective Payment Assessment Commission, *Prospective Payment System for Medicare's Skilled Nursing Facility Payment Reform* (Congressional Report C-92-01, March 1992), 5.

18. Health Care Financing Administration (HCFA), *Final Report: Design and Evaluation of a Prospective Payment System for Ambulatory Care* (Washington, D.C., HCFA, 1994).

19. Congressional Research Service, U.S. House of Representatives, *Medicaid Source Book: Background Data and Analysis* (Washington, D.C.: Congressional Research Service, 1993), 19.

20. Congressional Research Service, *Medicaid Source Book*, 20.

21. Kaiser Family Foundation's Commission on the Future of Medicaid, testimony before the House Subcommittee on Health Ways and Means (2 February 1994).

22. Health Care Financing Administration *Review*, Spring 1995.

23. Ernst & Young LLP, *Health Care Data Reference Card* (Cleveland, Ohio: Ernst & Young LLP, 1995).

24. Ernst & Young LLP, *Medicaid Managed Care* (Cleveland, Ohio: Ernst & Young LLP, 1995).

25. Kaiser Family Foundation's Commission, *Medicaid and Managed Care Discussion Brief* (Kaiser Family Foundation's Commission, 1994).

26. Health Care Financing Administration *Review*, Spring 1995.

27. U.S. House of Representatives, *1994 Green Book* (Washington, D.C.: House of Representatives, 1994).

28. Kaiser Family Foundation's Commission, *Medicaid and Managed Care: Lessons from Literature* (Kaiser Family Foundation's Commission, 1995).

29. Committee on the Budget, U.S. House of Representatives, *Conference Report* (Report 103–213 to accompany H.R. 2264, 4 August 1993), 807.

30. Office of the Inspector General (OIG), *Workplan for Fiscal Years 1994 and 1995* (Washington, D.C.: OIG, 1995).

31. Medical Group Management Association, August 1995.

32. V.H.I. Lewin, *The Cost of Legislative Restrictions on Contracting Practices* (1995).

33. Health Leadership Council, press release (21 June 1995).

SUGGESTED READING

Blumenthal, D. 1995. Health Care Reform: Past and Future. *New England Journal of Medicine* 332 (7): 465–468.

Helms, R.B. (ed.). 1993. *American Health Policy: Competition and Controls*. Washington, D.C.: AEI Press/American Enterprise Institute.

Iglehart, J.K. 1993. Health Care Reform: The Labyrinth of Congress. *New England Journal of Medicine* 329 (21): 1593–1596.

Chapter 3

Types of Managed Care Organizations

Eric R. Wagner

The various types of managed health care organizations were reasonably distinct as recently as 1988. Since then the differences between traditional forms of health insurance and managed care organizations have narrowed substantially. More recently, the distinctions between health care providers and health care insurers have blurred substantially. In contrast to the situation ten years ago, when managed care organizations were often referred to as alternative delivery systems, managed care is now the dominant form of health insurance coverage in the United States.

Originally, health maintenance organizations (HMOs), preferred provider organizations (PPOs), and traditional forms of indemnity health insurance were distinct, mutually exclusive products and mechanisms for providing health care coverage. Today, an observer may be hard pressed to uncover the differences among products that bill themselves as HMOs, PPOs, or managed care overlays to health insurance. For example, many HMOs, which traditionally limited their members to a designated set of participating providers, now allow their members to use nonparticipating providers at a reduced coverage level. Such point-of-service (POS) plans combine HMO-like systems with indemnity systems, allowing individual members to choose which systems they wish to access at the time they need the medical service. Similarly, some PPOs, which historically provided unrestricted access to physicians and other health care providers (albeit at different coverage levels), have implemented primary care case management or gatekeeper systems and have added elements of financial risk to their reimbursement systems. Finally, most indemnity insurance (or self-insurance) plans now include utilization management features in their plans that were once found only in HMOs or PPOs.

As a result of these recent changes, the descriptions of the different types of managed care systems that follow provide only a guideline for determining the form of managed care organization that is observed. In many cases (or in most cases in some markets), the managed health care organization will be a hybrid of several specific types.

Some controversy exists about whether the term *managed care* accurately describes the new generation of health care delivery and financing mechanisms. Those commentators who object to the term raise questions about what it is that is managed by a managed care organization. These commentators ask: Is the individual patient's

Eric R. Wagner is Vice President for Managed Care at Medlantic Healthcare Group and Washington Hospital Center where he is responsible for the development of managed care strategy, negotiation of participation agreements, and maintenance of relationships with managed care plans. In addition, he serves as Executive Director of and has operational responsibility for the WHC Physician-Hospital Organization. Previously, Mr. Wagner was with the health care strategy and managed care practice of an international professional services firm. He has more than 14 years of experience in the health care industry specializing in managed care strategy, development, operation, and finance and has published several books, chapters, and articles on managed care evaluation, development, negotiations, and provider compensation.

medical care being managed, or is the organization simply managing the composition and reimbursement of the provider delivery system?

Observers who favor the term *managed care* believe that managing the provider delivery system can be equivalent in its outcomes to managing the medical care delivered to the patient. In contrast to historical methods of financing health care delivery in the United States, the current generation of financing mechanisms includes far more active management of both the delivery system through which care is provided and the medical care that is actually delivered to individual patients. Although the term *managed care* may not perfectly describe this current generation of financing vehicles, it provides a convenient shorthand description for the range of alternatives to traditional indemnity health insurance.

A simplistic but useful concept regarding managed care is the continuum. At one end of the continuum is managed indemnity, with simple precertification of elective admissions and large case management of catastrophic cases superimposed on a traditional indemnity insurance plan. Similar to indemnity is the service plan, which has contractual relationships with providers addressing maximum fee allowances, prohibiting balance billing, and using the same utilization management techniques as managed indemnity (the nearly universal, although not exclusive, examples of service plans are Blue Cross/Blue Shield plans). Farther along the continuum are PPOs, POS products, open panel [individual practice association (IPA) type] HMOs, and closed panel (group and staff model) HMOs. As you progress from one end of the continuum to the other, you add new and greater elements of control and accountability, you tend to increase both the complexity and the overhead required to operate the plan, and you achieve greater potential control of cost and quality. This continuum is illustrated in Figure 3–1.

This chapter provides a description of the different types of managed health care organizations and the common acronyms used to represent them. A brief explanation is provided for each type of organization. In addition, this chapter includes descriptions of the five most common forms of HMOs, the original managed care organizations, and their relationships with physicians.

TYPES OF MANAGED CARE ORGANIZATIONS AND COMMON ACRONYMS

The managed care and health care industries have spawned a large number of acronyms to describe their distinctive organizations; many people have described these acronyms as a confusing alphabet soup of initials. Nevertheless, knowledge of a few key acronyms makes an understanding of the managed care environment easier.

HMO

HMOs are organized health care systems that are responsible for both the financing and the delivery of a broad range of comprehensive health services to an enrolled population. The original definition of an HMO also included the aspect of financing health care for a prepaid fixed fee (hence the term *prepaid health plan*), but that portion of the definition is no longer absolute, although it is still common.

In many ways, an HMO can be viewed as a combination of a health insurer and a health care delivery system. Whereas traditional health care insurance companies are responsible for reimbursing covered individuals for the cost of their health care, HMOs are responsible for providing health care services to their covered members through affiliated providers, who are reimbursed under various methods (see Chapters 7, 9, 10, 11, and 12).

As a result of their responsibility for providing covered health services to their members, HMOs must ensure that their members have access to covered health care services. In addition, HMOs generally are responsible for ensuring the quality and appropriateness of the health services they provide to their members.

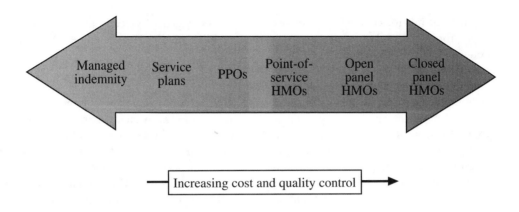

Figure 3–1 Continuum of managed care.

The five common models of HMOs are staff, group practice, network, IPA, and direct contract. The primary differences among these models are based on how the HMO relates to its participating physicians. These relationships are described in more detail in a subsequent section of this chapter.

PPO

PPOs are entities through which employer health benefit plans and health insurance carriers contract to purchase health care services for covered beneficiaries from a selected group of participating providers. Typically, participating providers in PPOs agree to abide by utilization management and other procedures implemented by the PPO and agree to accept the PPO's reimbursement structure and payment levels. In return, PPOs often limit the size of their participating provider panels and provide incentives for their covered individuals to use participating providers instead of other providers. In contrast to individuals with traditional HMO coverage, individuals with PPO coverage are permitted to use non-PPO providers, although higher levels of coinsurance or deductibles routinely apply to services provided by these nonparticipating providers.

PPOs sometimes are described as preferred provider arrangements (PPAs). The definition of a PPA is usually the same as the definition of a PPO. Some observers, however, use the term *PPA* to describe a less formal relationship than would be described by a PPO. The term *PPO* implies that an organization exists, whereas a PPA may achieve the same goals as a PPO through an informal arrangement among providers and payers.

The key common characteristics of PPOs include the following:

- *Select provider panel*—PPOs typically contract with selected providers in a community to provide health services for covered individuals. Most PPOs contract directly with hospitals, physicians, and other diagnostic facilities. Providers are selected to participate on the basis of their cost efficiency, community reputation, and scope of services. Some PPOs assemble massive databases of information about potential providers, including costs by diagnostic category, before they make their contracting decisions.
- *Negotiated payment rates*— Most PPO participation agreements require participating providers to accept the PPO's payments as

payment in full for covered services (except for applicable coinsurance or deductibles). PPOs attempt to negotiate payment rates that provide them with a competitive cost advantage relative to charge-based payment systems. These negotiated payment rates usually take the form of discounts from charges, all-inclusive per diem rates, or payments based on diagnosis-related groups. Some PPOs have established bundled pricing arrangements for certain services, including normal delivery, open heart surgery, and some types of oncology.

- *Rapid payment terms*— Some PPOs are willing to include prompt payment features in their contracts with participating providers in return for favorable payment rates. For example, a PPO may commit to pay all clean claims submitted by its providers within 15 days of submittal in return for a larger discount from charges.

- *Utilization management*—Many PPOs implement utilization management programs to control the utilization and cost of health services provided to their covered beneficiaries. In the more sophisticated PPOs, these utilization management programs resemble the programs operated by HMOs. Unlike indemnity plans where failure to comply with utilization management precertification programs increases the financial liability to the member (or covered insured), many PPOs impose the financial penalty for noncompliance on the participating provider, who may not balance bill the penalty to the member (of course, if the member uses a nonparticipating, or out-of-network provider, the financial penalty for noncompliance falls back on the member).

- *Consumer choice*—Unlike traditional HMOs, PPOs generally allow covered beneficiaries to use non-PPO providers instead of PPO providers when they need health services. Higher levels of beneficiary cost sharing, often in the form of higher copayments, typically are imposed when PPO beneficiaries use non-PPO providers.

Exclusive Provider Organization

Exclusive provider organizations (EPOs) are similar to PPOs in their organization and purpose. Unlike PPOs, however, EPOs limit their beneficiaries to participating providers for any health care services. In other words, beneficiaries covered by an EPO are required to receive all their covered health care services from providers that participate with the EPO. The EPO generally does not cover services received from other providers, although there may be exceptions.

Some EPOs parallel HMOs in that they not only require exclusive use of the EPO provider network but also use a gatekeeper approach to authorizing nonprimary care services. In these cases, the primary difference between an HMO and an EPO is that the former is regulated under HMO laws and regulations, whereas the latter is regulated under insurance laws and regulations or the Employee Retirement Income Security Act of 1974 (see Chapter 59), which governs self-insured health plans.

EPOs usually are implemented by employers whose primary motivation is cost saving. These employers are less concerned about the reaction of their employees to severe restrictions on the choice of health care provider and offer the EPO as a replacement for traditional indemnity health insurance coverage. Because of the severe restrictions on provider choice, only a few large employers have been willing to convert their entire health benefits programs to an EPO format.

POS Plan

Capitated and Primary Care PPOs

These are hybrids of more traditional HMO and PPO models. The following are characteristics of these types of plans:

- Primary care physicians are reimbursed through capitation payments (i.e., a fixed payment per member per month) or other performance-based reimbursement methods (see Chapter 9).

- There is often an amount withheld from physician compensation that is paid contingent upon achievement of utilization or cost targets.
- The primary care physician acts as a gatekeeper for referral and institutional medical services.
- The member retains some coverage for services rendered that either are not authorized by the primary care physician or are delivered by nonparticipating providers. Such coverage is typically significantly lower than coverage for authorized services delivered by participating providers (e.g., 100 percent compared with 60 percent).

Traditional HMOs may offer similar benefit options through an out-of-plan benefits rider or POS option.

Open Access or POS HMOs

Many HMOs have recognized that the major impediment to enrolling additional members and expanding market share has been the reluctance of individuals to forfeit completely their ability to receive reimbursement for using nonparticipating providers. These individuals consider the possibility that they would need the services of a renowned specialist for a rare (and expensive to treat) disorder and believe that the HMO would not refer them for care or reimburse their expenses. This possibility, no matter how unlikely, overshadows all the other benefits of HMO coverage in the minds of many individuals.

An expanding number of HMOs (and insurance carriers with both HMOs and indemnity operations) have adopted a solution to this problem: They provide some level of indemnity type coverage for their members. HMO members covered under these types of benefit plans may decide whether to use HMO benefits or indemnity style benefits for each instance of care. In other words, the member is allowed to make a coverage choice at the POS when medical care is needed.

The indemnity coverage available under POS options from HMOs typically incorporates high deductibles and coinsurance to encourage members to use HMO services instead of out-of-plan services. Members who use the non-HMO benefit portion of the benefit plan may also be subject to utilization management (e.g., preadmission certification and continued stay review). Despite the availability of out-of-network benefits, studies have found that most POS plans experience between 65 percent and 85 percent in-network usage, so that POS plans retain considerable cost control compared with indemnity type plans.

There are two primary ways for an HMO to offer a POS option: via a single HMO license approach, or via a dual license approach. The single license approach means that the HMO provides the out-of-network benefit using its HMO license. In many states, this restricts the total dollar amount of out-of-network care to 10 percent or less. The dual license approach is more flexible in that the health plan uses an HMO license to provide the in-network care and an indemnity license to provide the out-of-network coverage. Dual license obviously requires either that a single company possess both licenses (e.g., a commercial insurance carrier with a subsidiary HMO) or that the HMO partner with a licensed insurance carrier. In a few cases, an HMO has contracted with an indemnity carrier to front the indemnity portion but has retained the bulk of the risk for medical expenses through the funding arrangement with the carrier.

As discussed in Chapter 36, this hybrid form of health benefit coverage represents an attractive managed care option for many employers and their covered employees, particularly when the employer is looking toward point of service as a consolidation of existing indemnity coverage and multiple HMOs in the group (i.e., total replacement coverage). Coverage under HMO

POS plans recently has been the fastest growing segment of health insurance.

Self-Insured and Experience-Rated HMOs

Historically, HMOs offered community-rated premiums to all employers and individuals who enrolled for HMO coverage. The federal HMO Act originally mandated community rating for all HMOs that decided to pursue federal qualification. Community rating was eventually expanded to include rating by class, where premium rates for an individual employer group could be adjusted prospectively on the basis of demographic characteristics that were associated with utilization differences. Such characteristics often included the age and sex distributions of the employer's workforce and the standard industrial classification of the employer.

Although community rating by class provided HMOs with some flexibility to offer more attractive rates to selected employer groups, many employers continued to believe that their group-specific experience would be better than the rates offered by HMOs. Some HMOs developed self-insured or experience-rated options in response to the needs expressed by these employers.

Under a typical self-insured benefit option, an HMO receives a fixed monthly payment to cover administrative services (and profit) and variable payments that are based on the actual payments made by the HMO for health services. There is usually a settlement process at the end of a specified period, during which a final payment is calculated (either to the HMO by the group or to the group by the HMO). Variations in the payment arrangement exist and are similar in structure to the different forms of self-funded insurance programs.

Under experience-rated benefit options, an HMO receives monthly premium payments much as it would under traditional premium-based plans. There typically is a settlement process, where the employer is credited with some portion (or all) of the actual utilization and cost

of its group, to arrive at a final premium rate. Refunds or additional payments are then calculated and made to the appropriate party.

The HMO regulations of some states and federal HMO qualification regulations preclude HMOs from offering self-insured or experience-rated benefit plans. HMOs avoid these prohibitions by incorporating related corporate entities that use the HMO's negotiated provider agreements, management systems, utilization protocols, and personnel to service the self-insured line of business.

Rating and underwriting methodologies are discussed in detail in Chapters 43 and 44.

Specialty HMOs

Specialty HMOs have developed in some states to provide the benefits of the HMO model to limited components of health care coverage. Dental HMOs have become common as an option to indemnity dental insurance coverage (see Chapter 51). Specialty HMOs serving other health care needs (e.g., mental health) have also developed in certain states where they are permitted under the insurance or HMO laws and regulations. One challenge to the formation of such HMOs is that state laws often define a broad range of health services that are required to be offered by licensed HMOs; other states, however, have regulations to allow so-called single specialty HMOs.

Managed Care Overlays to Indemnity Insurance

The perceived success of HMOs and other types of managed care organizations in controlling the utilization and cost of health services has prompted entrepreneurs to develop managed care overlays that can be combined with traditional indemnity insurance, service plan insurance, or self-insurance (the term *indemnity insurance* is used to refer to all three forms of coverage in this context). These managed care overlays are intended to provide cost control for insured plans while retaining the individual's freedom of choice of provider and coverage for out-of-plan services. The following types of managed care overlays currently exist:

- *General utilization management*—These companies offer a complete menu of utilization management activities that can be selected by individual employers or insurers. Some offer, or can develop, panels of participating providers within individual markets and bear a strong resemblance to PPOs.

- *Specialty utilization management*—Firms that focus on utilization review for specialty services have become common. Mental health and dental care are two common types of specialty utilization management overlays.

- *Catastrophic or large case management*—Some firms have developed to assist employers and insurers with managing catastrophic cases regardless of the specialty involved. This service includes screening to identify cases that will become catastrophic, negotiation of services and reimbursement with providers who can treat the patient's condition, development of a treatment protocol for the patient, and ongoing monitoring of the treatment. See Chapter 18 for further discussion of this topic.

- *Workers' compensation utilization management*—In response to the rapid increases in the cost of workers' compensation insurance, firms have developed managed care overlays to address what they claim are the unique needs of patients covered under workers' compensation benefits. Managed care and workers' compensation programs are discussed in detail in Chapter 52.

Physician–Hospital Organizations

As their name implies, physician–hospital organizations (PHOs) are organizations that generally are jointly owned and operated by hospitals and their affiliated physicians. These organizations typically are developed to provide a vehicle for hospitals and physicians to contract together with other managed care organizations to provide both physician and hospital services. They represent one approach taken by providers who are implementing integrated delivery systems.

In their simplest form, PHOs are separately incorporated entities in which physicians and one or more hospitals are shareholders or members. These members execute provider agreements with the PHO under which they delegate responsibility for negotiating agreements with managed care organizations (or, in some cases, employers) to the PHO and agree to accept as reimbursement the PHO's payment schedules.

PHOs can offer several advantages for providers who develop them. They may increase the negotiating clout of their individual members with managed care organizations. They provide a vehicle for physicians and hospitals to establish reimbursement and risk-sharing approaches that align incentives among all providers. They can serve as a clearinghouse for certain administrative activities, including credentialing and utilization management, thereby reducing the administrative burden on their individual physician and hospital members. Finally, they provide an organized approach for physicians and hospitals to work together on managed care issues, including utilization management and quality improvement.

PHOs may also offer advantages to some managed care organizations. For organizations that are new to a market, they can provide a means of rapidly establishing a panel of participating physicians and hospitals. Also, if the managed care organization delegates claim processing responsibility to the PHO, they can provide a means of reducing operating costs.

Despite their potential for benefits to health care providers and managed care organizations, many observers believe that PHOs have fallen far short of their promise. Recent surveys suggest that PHOs have achieved only limited success in contracting with managed care plans and generally have not implemented medical management programs.[1] Among the reasons for the lack of success for PHOs are the following:

- Managed care organizations in many markets have achieved great success in enrolling large panels of participating physicians and hospitals. For these organizations, PHOs may offer little or no benefit.

- Although many PHOs have professed strong interest in assuming financial risk for delivering health services by accepting capitation-based payments, many managed care organizations have been reluctant to cede global capitation payments because they continue to earn margins by managing the utilization and cost of health services. These margins would be reduced or eliminated if they passed capitated risk along to PHOs.

PHOs and other forms of integrated delivery systems are discussed in detail in Chapter 4.

HMO MODELS

The five commonly recognized models of HMOs are staff, group, network, IPA, and direct contract. The major differences among these models pertain to the relationship between the HMO and its participating physicians. Until recently, individual HMOs usually could be neatly categorized into a single model type for descriptive purposes. Currently, many (if not most) HMOs have different relationships with different groups of physicians. As a result, many HMOs cannot easily be classified as a single model type, although such plans are occasionally referred to as mixed models. The HMO model type descriptions now may be more appropriately used to describe an HMO's relationship with certain segments of its physicians. The following sections provide brief descriptions of the five common HMO model types. Further discussion can be found in Chapters 1, 7, and 8.

Staff Model

In a staff model HMO, the physicians who serve the HMO's covered beneficiaries are employed by the HMO. These physicians typically are paid on a salary basis and may also receive bonus or incentive payments that are based on their performance and productivity. Staff model HMOs must employ physicians in all the common specialties to provide for the health care needs of their members. These HMOs often contract with selected subspecialists in the community for infrequently needed health services.

Staff model HMOs are also known as closed panel HMOs because most participating physicians are employees of the HMO and community physicians are unable to participate. A well-known example of staff model HMOs is Group Health Cooperative of Puget Sound in Seattle, Washington. Many staff model HMOs are incorporating other types of physician relationships into their delivery system.

Physicians in staff model HMOs usually practice in one or more centralized ambulatory care facilities. These facilities, which often resemble outpatient clinics, contain physician offices and ancillary support facilities (e.g., laboratory and radiology) to support the health care needs of the HMO's beneficiaries. Staff model HMOs usually contract with hospitals and other inpatient facilities in the community to provide nonphysician services for their members.

Staff model HMOs can have an advantage relative to other HMO models in managing health care delivery because they have a greater degree of control over the practice patterns of their physicians. As a result, it can be easier for staff model HMOs to manage and control the utilization of health services. They also offer the convenience of one-stop shopping for their members because the HMO's facilities tend to be full service (i.e., they have laboratory, radiology, and other departments).

Offsetting this advantage are several disadvantages for staff model HMOs. First, staff model HMOs are usually more costly to develop and implement because of the small membership and the large fixed salary expenses that the HMO must incur for staff physicians and support staff. Second, staff model HMOs provide a limited choice of participating physicians for potential HMO members. Many potential members are reluctant to change from their current physician and find the idea of a clinic setting uncomfortable. Third, some staff model HMOs have experienced productivity problems with their staff physicians, which have raised their costs for providing care. Finally, it is expensive for staff model HMOs to expand their services into new areas because of the need to construct new ambulatory care facilities.

Group Model

In pure group model HMOs, the HMO contracts with a multispecialty physician group practice to provide all physician services to the HMO's members. The physicians in the group practice are employed by the group practice and not by the HMO. In some cases, these physicians may be allowed to see both HMO patients and other patients, although their primary function may be to treat HMO members.

Physicians in a group practice share facilities, equipment, medical records, and support staff. The group may contract with the HMO on an all-inclusive capitation basis to provide physician services to HMO members. Alternatively, the group may contract on a cost basis to provide its services. There are two broad categories of group model HMOs, as described below.

Captive Group

In the captive group model, the physician group practice exists solely to provide services to the HMO's beneficiaries. In most cases, the HMO formed the group practice to serve its members, recruited physicians, and now provides administrative services to the group. The most prominent example of this type of HMO is the Kaiser Foundation Health Plan, where the Permanente Medical Groups provide all physician services for Kaiser's members. The Kaiser Foundation Health Plan, as the licensed HMO, is responsible for marketing the benefit plans, enrolling members, collecting premium payments, and performing other HMO functions. The Permanente Medical Groups are responsible for rendering physician services to Kaiser's members under an exclusive contractual relationship with Kaiser. Kaiser is sometimes mistakenly thought to be a staff model HMO because of the close relationship between itself and the Permanente Medical Groups.

Independent Group

In the independent group model HMO, the HMO contracts with an existing, independent, multispecialty physician group to provide physician services to its members. In some cases, the independent physician group is the sponsor or owner of the HMO. An example of the independent group model HMO is Geisinger Health Plan of Danville, Pennsylvania. The Geisinger Clinic, which is a large, multispecialty physician group practice, is the independent group associated with the Geisinger Health Plan.

Typically, the physician group in an independent group model HMO continues to provide services to non-HMO patients while it participates in the HMO. Although the group may have an exclusive relationship with the HMO, this relationship usually does not prevent the group from engaging in non-HMO business.

Common Features of Group Models

Both types of group model HMOs are also referred to as closed panel HMOs because physicians must be members of the group practice to participate in the HMO; as a result, the HMO is considered closed to physicians who are not part of the group. Both types of group model HMOs share the advantages of staff model HMOs of making it somewhat easier to conduct utilization management because of the integration of physician practices and of providing broad services at its facilities. In addition, group practice HMOs may have lower capital needs than staff model HMOs because the HMO does not have to support the large fixed salary costs associated with staff physicians.

Group model HMOs have several disadvantages in common with staff model HMOs. Like staff model HMOs, group model HMOs provide a limited choice of participating physicians for potential HMO members. The limited physician panel can be a disadvantage in marketing the HMO. The limited number of office locations for the participating medical groups may also restrict the geographic accessibility of physicians for the HMO's members. The lack of accessibility can make it difficult for the HMO to market its coverage to a wide geographic area. Finally, certain group practices may be perceived by some potential HMO members as offering an undesirable clinic setting. Offsetting this disadvantage may be the perception of high quality associated with many of the physician group practices that are affiliated with HMOs.

Network Model

In network model HMOs, the HMO contracts with more than one group practice to provide physician services to the HMO's members. These group practices may be broad-based, multispecialty groups, in which case the HMO resembles the group practice model described above. An example of this type of HMO is Health Insurance Plan of Greater New York, which contracts with many multispecialty physician group practices in the New York area.

Alternatively, the HMO may contract with several small groups of primary care physicians (i.e., family practice, internal medicine, pediatrics, and obstetrics/gynecology), in which case the HMO can be classified as a primary care network model. In the primary care network model, the HMO contracts with several groups consisting of 7 to 15 primary care physicians representing the specialties of family practice and/or internal medicine, pediatrics, and obstetrics/gynecology to provide physician services to its members. Typically, the HMO compensates these groups on an all-inclusive physician capitation basis. The group is responsible for providing all physician services to the HMO's members assigned to the group and may refer to other

physicians as necessary. The group is financially responsible for reimbursing other physicians for any referrals it makes. In some cases, the HMO may negotiate participation arrangements with specialist physicians to make it easier for its primary care groups to manage their referrals.

In contrast to the staff and group model HMOs described previously, network models may be either closed or open panel plans. If the network model HMO is a closed panel plan, it will only contract with a limited number of existing group practices. If it is an open panel plan, participation in the group practices will be open to any physician who meets the HMO's and group's credentials criteria. In some cases, network model HMOs will assist independent primary care physicians with the formation of primary care groups for the sole purpose of participating in the HMO's network.

Network model HMOs address many of the disadvantages associated with staff and group model HMOs. In particular, the broader physician participation that is usually identified with network model HMOs helps overcome the marketing disadvantage associated with the closed panel staff and group model plans. Nevertheless, network model HMOs usually have more limited physician participation than either IPA model or direct contract model plans.

IPA Model

IPA model HMOs contract with an association of physicians—the IPA—to provide physician services to their members. The physicians are members of the IPA, which is a separate legal entity, but they remain individual practitioners and retain their separate offices and identities. IPA physicians continue to see their non-HMO patients and maintain their own offices, medical records, and support staff. IPA model HMOs are open panel plans because participation is open to all community physicians who meet the HMO's and IPA's selection criteria.

Generally, IPAs attempt to recruit physicians from all specialties to participate in their plans.

Broad participation of physicians allows the IPA to provide all necessary physician services through participating physicians and minimizes the need for IPA physicians to refer HMO members to nonparticipating physicians to obtain services. In addition, broad physician participation can help make the IPA model HMO more attractive to potential HMO members.

IPA model HMOs usually follow one of two different methods of establishing relationships with their IPAs. In the first method, the HMO contracts with an IPA that has been independently established by community physicians. These types of IPAs often have contracts with more than one HMO on a nonexclusive basis. In the second method, the HMO works with community physicians to create an IPA and to recruit physicians to participate in it. The HMO's contract with these types of IPAs is usually on an exclusive basis because of the HMO's leading role in forming the IPA.

IPAs may be formed as large, community-wide entities where physicians can participate without regard to the hospital with which they are affiliated. Alternatively, IPAs may be hospital based and formed so that only physicians from one or two hospitals are eligible to participate in the IPA.

Hospital-based IPAs are sometimes preferred by HMOs over larger, community-based IPAs for at least two reasons. First, hospital-based IPAs can restrict the panel of the IPA to physicians who are familiar with each other's practice patterns. This familiarity can make the utilization management process easier. Second, by using several hospital-based IPAs, an HMO can limit the impact of a termination of one of its IPA agreements to a smaller group of physicians.

Most HMOs compensate their IPAs on an all-inclusive physician capitation basis to provide services to the HMO's members. The IPA then compensates its participating physicians on either a fee-for-service basis or a combination of fee for service and primary care capitation. In the fee-for-service variation, IPAs pay all their participating physicians on the basis of a fee

schedule or a usual, customary, or reasonable (UCR) charge approach and withhold a portion of each payment for incentive and risk-sharing purposes. Under the primary care capitation approach, IPAs pay their participating primary care physicians on a capitation basis and pay their specialist physicians on the basis of a fee schedule or UCR approach. The primary care capitation payments are based on fixed amounts per member per month and usually vary depending on the HMO member's age and sex. The IPA typically withholds a portion of both the capitation and fee-for-service payments for risk sharing and incentive purposes. Compensation for primary care is discussed in Chapter 9.

IPA model HMOs overcome all the disadvantages associated with staff, group, and network model HMOs. They require less capital to establish and operate. In addition, they can provide a broad choice of participating physicians who practice in their private offices. As a result, IPA model HMOs offer marketing advantages in comparison with the staff and group model plans.

There are two major disadvantages of IPA model HMOs from the HMO's perspective. First, the development of an IPA creates an organized forum for physicians to negotiate as a group with the HMO. The organized forum of an IPA can help its physician members achieve some of the negotiating benefits of belonging to a group practice. Unlike the situation with a group practice, however, individual members of an IPA retain their ability to negotiate and contract directly with managed care plans. Because of their acceptance of combined risk through capitation payments, IPAs are generally immune from antitrust restrictions on group activities by physicians as long as they do not prevent or prohibit their member physicians from participating directly with an HMO.

Second, the process of utilization management generally is more difficult in an IPA model HMO than it is in staff and group model plans because physicians remain individual practitioners with little sense of being a part of the HMO. As a result, IPA model HMOs may devote more administrative resources to managing inpatient and outpatient utilization than their staff and group model counterparts. Notwithstanding this historical disadvantage, recent analyses suggest that some IPA model HMOs have overcome the challenge and have succeeded in managing utilization at least as well as their closed panel counterparts.

Direct Contract Model

As the name implies, direct contract model HMOs contract directly with individual physicians to provide physician services to their members. With the exception of their direct contractual relationship with participating physicians, direct contract model HMOs are similar to IPA model plans. A well-known example of a direct contract model HMO is US Healthcare and its subsidiary HMOs.

Direct contract model HMOs attempt to recruit broad panels of community physicians to provide physician services as participating providers. These HMOs usually recruit both primary care and specialist physicians and typically use a primary care case management approach (also known as a gatekeeper system).

Like IPA model plans, direct contract model HMOs compensate their physicians on either a fee-for-service basis or a primary care capitation basis. Primary care capitation is somewhat more commonly used by direct contract model HMOs because it helps limit the financial risk assumed by the HMO. Unlike IPA model HMOs, direct contract model HMOs retain most of the financial risk for providing physician services; IPA model plans transfer this risk to their IPAs.

Direct contract model HMOs have most of the same advantages as IPA model HMOs. In addition, direct model HMOs eliminate the potential of a physician bargaining unit by contracting directly with individual physicians. This contracting model reduces the possibility of mass termination of physician participation agreements.

Direct contract model HMOs have several disadvantages. First, the HMO may assume additional financial risk for physician services

relative to an IPA model HMO, as noted above. This additional risk exposure can be expensive if primary care physicians generate excessive referrals to specialist physicians. Second, it can be more difficult and time consuming for a direct contract model HMO to recruit physicians because it lacks the physician leadership inherent in an IPA model plan. It is more difficult for nonphysicians to recruit physicians, as several direct contract model HMOs discovered in their attempts to expand into new markets. Finally, utilization management may be more difficult in direct contract model HMOs because all contact with physicians is on an individual basis, and there may be little incentive for physicians to participate in the utilization management programs.

CONCLUSION

Managed care is on a continuum, with a number of plan types offering an array of features that vary in their abilities to balance access to care, cost, quality control, benefit design, and flexibility. Managed care plans continue to evolve, with features from one type of plan appearing in others and new features continually being developed. There is no one single definition of the term *managed care* that has endured in the past or will survive into the future.

REFERENCE AND NOTE

1. Ernst & Young LLP, *Physician–Hospital Organizations: Profile 1995* (Washington, D.C.: Ernst & Young LLP, 1995).

SUGGESTED READING

Boland, P. 1993. *Making Managed Healthcare Work: A Practical Guide to Strategies and Solutions.* Gaithersburg, Md.: Aspen.

Dasco, S.T. and Dasco, C.C. 1996. *Managed Care Answer Book.* New York: Panel Publishers.

Ernst & Young LLP. 1995. *Physician–Hospital Organizations: Profile 1995.* Washington, D.C.: Ernst & Young LLP.

Hale, J.A. 1988. *From HMO Movement to Managed Care Industry: The Future of HMOs in a Volatile Healthcare Market*. Minneapolis, Minn.: InterStudy.

Rahn, G.J. 1987. *Hospital-Sponsored Health Maintenance Organizations.* Chicago, Ill.: American Hospital Publishing.

Shouldice, R.G. 1991. *Introduction to Managed Care.* Arlington, Va.: Information Resources Press.

Traska, M.R. 1996. *Managed Care Strategies 1996.* New York: Faulkner & Gray.

Wagner, E.R. 1987. *A Practical Guide to Evaluating Physician Capitation Payments.* Washington, D.C.: American Society of Internal Medicine.

Wagner, E.R, and Hackenberg, V.J. 1986. *A Practical Guide to Physician-Sponsored HMO Development.* Washington, D.C.: American Society of Internal Medicine.

Chapter 4

Integrated Health Care Delivery Systems

Peter R. Kongstvedt and David W. Plocher

The concept of integrated health care delivery systems (IDSs) is neither new nor novel. Kaiser Permanente Health Plans, Group Health of Puget Sound, the Henry Ford Health System and others have operated as IDSs [albeit as health maintenance organizations (HMOs) rather than as providers] for many years, in some cases for more than half a century. Even before managed care came to play as dominant a role as it does today, an increase in vertical integration was predicted by Paul Starr in 1982 in his book *The Social Transformation of American Medicine*, albeit in a form somewhat different from what is currently occurring.[1]

Managed care has placed increasing pressures on providers of health care both to reduce costs and to maintain or improve quality as well as find ways to protect their market share. The prospect of impending reform of the American health care system, whether through regulatory reform or marketplace-driven reform, provides even greater impetus for change. This has led to the still-evolving desire on the part of health care providers to become aligned. Such alignment provides, at least theoretically, greater economies of scale, the ability to deploy clinical resources most cost effectively, a greater ability to influence provider behavior, and greater negotiating strength. Whether these and other goals can be met through integration is not always

clear at the outset, and certain types of integration models appear to have greater potential than others. It must also be borne in mind that effective control of medical utilization by any model of managed care organization (MCO) will achieve greater and longer-lasting savings than will any economies of scale.

This chapter provides an overview of the more common forms of IDSs. The taxonomy is that in general use at the time of this writing. It is expected that, because this is an area in continual evolution (as is managed care in general), these terms and definitions will not remain constant. Even if the nomenclature changes, however, many of the concepts discussed here will remain valid. The closely related topic of joint ventures, mergers, and acquisition between payers and providers is discussed in Chapter 5.

IDSs may be described as falling into three broad categories: systems in which only the physicians are integrated, systems in which the physicians are integrated with facilities (hospitals and ancillary sites), and systems that include the insurance functions. Within the context of the first two categories, IDSs fall along a rough continuum. Figure 4–1 illustrates the common names used for such organizations. As one proceeds from one end of the continuum to the other, the degree of integration increases, as does the potential ability of the organization to operate effectively in a managed care environment. Also, the complexity of formation and operation, required capital investment, and political difficulties increase from one end of the continuum to the other. The primary political

David W. Plocher, M.D., is a principal in the Minneapolis office of Ernst & Young LLP, an international accounting and consulting firm.

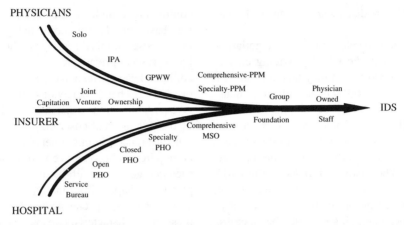

Figure 4–1 Types of integrated health care organizations. IPA, independent practice association; GPWW, group practice without walls; PPM, physician practice management; PHO, physician–hospital organization; MSO, management services organization.

difficulty encountered in the development of these systems, or at least the systems that are tightly managed, is that not all providers can participate. This can present a significant challenge for both hospital and physician leadership that, if not addressed deftly, can result in a career limiting move by the responsible executive.

As this chapter is written, comprehensive health reform has not been enacted at the federal level and has been carried out only erratically in a few states. It is safe to assume, however, that the regulatory framework will continue to evolve (see Chapters 2, 53, and 56), which will alter the form and methods used in alignment but not the need for IDSs.

INDEPENDENT PRACTICE ASSOCIATIONS

The first type of IDS to be described is the independent practice association (IPA), a form that has been in existence for several decades and was even codified to some degree by the original HMO Act of 1973. The IPA is a legal entity, the members of which are independent physicians who contract with the IPA for the sole purpose of having the IPA contract with one or more HMOs. IPAs are usually not for profit,

although that is not an absolute requirement. The term *IPA* is often used synonymously (and inaccurately) with terms for any type of open panel HMO (see Chapter 3); although the use of the term in this fashion is now widespread, it is not technically accurate. The true IPA is discussed here.

In its common incarnation, the IPA negotiates with the HMO for a capitation rate inclusive of all physician services (for a detailed discussion of such forms of reimbursement systems, see Chapter 9). The IPA in turn reimburses the member physicians, although not necessarily using capitation. The IPA and its member physicians are at risk for at least some portion of medical costs in that, if the capitation payment is lower than the required reimbursement to the physicians, the member physicians must accept lower income. It is the presence of this risk sharing that stands the IPA apart from a negotiating vehicle that does not bear risk. It is also the reason that true IPAs generally are not subject to antitrust problems (unless the IPA was formed solely or primarily to keep out competition). The usual form of an IPA is as an umbrella organization for physicians in all specialties to participate in managed care. Recently, however, IPAs that only represent a single specialty have emerged;

specialty IPAs are discussed in Chapters 12 and 13.

The IPA may operate simply as a negotiating organization, with the HMO providing all administrative support, or it may take on some of the duties of the HMO, such as utilization management (UM), network development, and so forth. The IPA generally has stop-loss reinsurance, or the HMO provides such stop-loss coverage, to prevent the IPA from going bankrupt (see Chapter 9). The history of IPAs in the early years of HMOs was variable, and a number of IPAs did indeed go out of business. Recently, IPAs have been enjoying considerable success, especially in the western part of the country. The hospital usually has no role in a traditional IPA, although some hospitals have begun sponsoring IPA development as an alternative to a physician–hospital organization (PHO) structure, which is discussed later.

Advantages of an IPA

There is a current, although undocumented, resurgence of interest in IPAs as a vehicle for private physicians to contract with managed care plans. It stops well short of full integration but has more ability to share risk and obtain HMO contracts than many PHOs. It is also a model that is more easily understood and accepted by many managed care executives, who may cast a wary eye on less traditional models. The newly dominating IPAs are those that allow more convenient geographic access, have succeeded in bearing risk, and have limited specialist membership. They may be the only model available in nonurban areas, where one to two physician offices are the norm. Finally, in contrast to staff models, IPAs require much less capital to start up and operate, and some managers feel that IPAs motivate their physicians more successfully than models that depend on salary.

Disadvantages of an IPA

The IPA is inherently unwieldy because it is usually made up of a large number of independent physicians whose only commonality is the contracting vehicle of the IPA (well, perhaps they have other loci of commonality, but not for the purposes of this discussion). The IPA's ability to preserve private practice also means its inability to leverage resources, achieve economies of scale, or change behavior to the greatest degree possible. An IPA that accepts a high degree of risk for medical costs may be found by the state insurance commissioner to be an HMO and be required to become licensed, with all the issues that go along with being a licensed health plan (see Chapter 53). Finally, many IPAs contain a surplus of specialists, resulting in upward pressure on characteristic resource consumption (although see Chapters 12 and 13 for a discussion of specialty IPAs).

PHYSICIAN PRACTICE MANAGEMENT ORGANIZATIONS

Physician practice management (PPM) organizations are recent arrivals in the integration scene. PPMs may in some ways be viewed as variants in management services organizations (MSOs), but unlike the MSO described below (in the discussion of physician–hospital vertical integration), PPMs are physician only. In other words, there is no involvement by the hospital. Some managed care taxonomists refer to these organizations as physician-only MSOs, but that convention is not the predominant one as this chapter is being written.[*] The operations of a full MSO are described in a later section of this chapter.

Recently, some large PPMs have been branching into more activities than physician-only management. These activities include joint ventures in PHO development and even the purchase of insurance licenses. Thus PPMs, like everything else in managed care, continue to make classification a high challenge indeed.

---

[*] Not that there is much stability in the naming of new types of organizations in managed care. As the field evolves, or perhaps mutates is more accurate, terms and labels will mutate as well.

For-Profit, Comprehensive PPMs

In a melding of Wall Street and the physician's office, entrepreneurs have capitalized for-profit PPMs operating independent of hospitals. These have most often purchased physician practices, beginning with primary care groups but including certain large specialty groups as well, and have signed multiyear contracts with those physicians. The physicians may be given varying degrees of equity participation in the PPM (the equity model PPM) and a voice in governance. In some cases, the PPM may not necessarily offer equity to all physicians. The PPM may offer equity only to those physicians who are early participants, or it may offer equity in exchange for the value of the acquired practice but not offer equity if it pays cash for the practice.

These entities may be attractive to some practitioners who, exasperated by the business pressures of practice, would prefer selling to an entity specializing in managing physician practices as opposed to a possibly distrusted hospital or may simply feel that a PPM has more capability to manage a practice than a hospital. As these entities become publicly traded, a further attraction to physicians is based on seeing their equity grow. Recent successes in such PPMs have been complicated by changes in identity as noted earlier, for example through the purchase of an HMO or small insurance company (thus producing taxonomist cognitive dissonance).

In general, the PPM provides management for all support functions (e.g., billing and collections, purchasing, negotiating contracts, and so forth) but remains relatively uninvolved with the clinical aspects of the practice. In many cases, the physician remains an independent practitioner, although the PPM owns all the tangible assets of the practice. The PPM usually takes a percentage of the practice revenue, often at a rate equal to or slightly below what the physician was already experiencing for overhead. The physician agrees to a long-term commitment as well as noncompetition covenants.

Although the early track record appears promising, it is far too soon to articulate clear advantages and disadvantages. Compared with hospitals and insurers acquiring practices, as discussed in Chapter 5, the PPM is theoretically able to be more nimble and is better able to give physicians an investment return. All practice acquisitions make the physician an employee (or employeelike) for many years, however, with all the attendant motivational concerns. The guiding principle behind the early success of PPMs may be the virtue of an IDS that is physician driven as opposed to hospital or insurer driven. This advantage derives in part from the fact that physicians control or direct between 75 percent and 90 percent of health resources consumed.

Specialty PPMs

A variation on the comprehensive PPM theme, the specialty PPM has taken most of the comprehensive PPM features into consideration for a single specialty's market share preservation or expansion. The most common specialties involved are oncology and cardiology, and multistate networks are now in place. Other specialties involved include ophthalmology, radiology, anesthesiology, and occupational medicine. The specialty PPM is a variant of a specialty network, which is also discussed in Chapter 13.

The early experience with this PPM variant is at least as promising as the experience with the comprehensive PPM. Promises will probably be fulfilled only if two conditions are met, however: the ability to bear financial risk, and willingness on the part of the PPM's customers to deal with another carve-out vendor. Although the first point is an obvious managed care fundamental, the second requirement may need clarification. We can consider the emergence of disease management vendors a valuable model (see Chapter 20). The vendors that are concentrating narrowly on rare, expensive diseases, such as hemophilia, have made some inroads. The typical HMO medical director may be willing to carve that out and devote internal case manager skill to more common conditions. The field of oncology may be viewed as too common, however, and therefore intrinsically embedded in the HMO's operations (note that disease management vendors, for example those specializing in hemophilia, usually do not employ their own hemophilia experts but rather contract with them *and* provide more customized care management).

The potential ability of an oncologist PPM to survive this caveat is enhanced by the presence of a less aggressive buyer, such as a preferred provider organization. Alternatively, if the oncologist PPM happens to have its oncologist network in place in a given city before the HMO provider relations manager begins recruiting specialists, this oncologist PPM could become the dedicated oncologist network for the HMO. Finally, an HMO may choose to use such a specialty PPM because it allows the HMO to improve quality and lower cost compared with using a less organized network of private specialists.

Advantages of PPMs

The primary advantage of a PPM is that its sole purpose in business is to manage physicians' practices. This means that it will either have or obtain expertise that is not usually resident in either a hospital or a payer (other than a group or staff model HMO). Also, the PPM has the ability to bring substantial purchasing power to bear though combining the purchasing needs of several hundred (or potentially more) physicians. The PPM can also provide a greater sense of ownership to the participating physicians in an equity model, thus helping align incentives and goals.

Disadvantages of the PPMs

The primary disadvantage is that the PPM may not achieve sufficient mass in the market to influence events substantially, or negotiate favorable terms. Also, the physicians may chafe under the long terms usually required and may

not change their practice habits sufficiently to be truly effective in managed care; this last issue becomes especially critical if the PPM is seen more as a vehicle to negotiate fees than as a system to lower costs and improve quality. These PPMs often lack strong physician leadership; business leadership comes from nonphysicians. Finally, investor-owned PPMs are businesses that are expected to return a substantial profit; they are not philanthropic institutions. If that profit is not forthcoming, it may be anticipated that the investors will begin to demand action, some of which may not be palatable to the participating physicians.

GROUP PRACTICE WITHOUT WALLS

The group practice without walls (GPWW), also known as the clinic without walls, is a significant step toward greater integration of physician services. The GPWW does not require the participation of a hospital and, indeed, is often formed as a vehicle for physicians to organize without being dependent on a hospital for services or support. In some cases, GPWW formation has occurred to leverage negotiating strength not only with MCOs but with hospitals as well.

The GPWW is composed of private practice physicians who agree to aggregate their practices into a single legal entity, but the physicians continue to practice medicine in their independent locations. In other words, the physicians appear to be independent from the view of their patients, but from the view of a contracting entity (usually an MCO) they are a single group. This is differentiated from the for-profit, physician-only MSOs described earlier by two salient features: First, the GPWW is owned solely by the member physicians and not by any outside investors, and second, the GPWW is a legal merging of all assets of the physicians' practices rather than the acquisition of only the tangible assets (as is often the case in an MSO).

To be considered a medical group, the physicians must have their personal income affected by the performance of the group as a whole. Although an IPA will place a defined portion of a physician's income at risk (that portion related to the managed care contract held by the IPA), the group's income from any source has an effect on the physician's income and on profit sharing in the group; that being said, it is common in this model for an individual physician's income to be affected most by individual productivity.

The GPWW is owned by the member physicians, and governance is by the physicians. The GPWW may contract with an outside organization to provide business support services. Office support services are generally provided through the group, although as a practical matter the practicing physicians may notice little difference in what they are used to receiving.

Advantages of the GPWW

The GPWW enjoys an advantage over some other models in that it has the legal ability to negotiate and commit on behalf of all the members of the group. Unlike a PHO, where the physicians remain independent private practitioners, the GPWW *is* a legal group and can legitimately bargain with MCOs or other organizations. The GPWW also has the ability to achieve some modest economies of scale, similar to those found in MSOs. The most common subset of these services includes centralized billing, centralized scheduling, group purchasing, and data sharing. Less often, the GPWW centralizes recruiting and can help with employee leasing. The GPWW is free of hospital influence (at least theoretically) and therefore is able to have greater flexibility.

Perhaps the key advantage of the GPWW is that income is affected by the performance of the group as a whole. Therefore, the GPWW has some ability to influence practice behavior. If a member physician is practicing in such a manner as to affect adversely the group as a whole, considerable peer pressure can be brought to bear. The group can even proceed to expel a physician member if the problems are serious and are not rectified.

Disadvantages of the GPWW

The primary disadvantage of the GPWW is that the physicians essentially remain in independent practice. Except for obvious practice behavior, the physicians continue to practice in the manner to which they have become accustomed. The ability of the group actually to manage practice behavior is thus seriously limited to only those elements that are gross outliers (e.g., exceptionally long lengths of stay). Thus optimal efficiencies are not achieved. Although there is some alignment of incentives, disparate goals still exist.

The ability of a GPWW to accept risk-based reimbursement (e.g., capitation) is enhanced but is not optimal. The GPWW is potentially capable of negotiating with MCOs for such contracts, but distribution of income and risk usually defaults to those methods used by IPAs (see Chapter 9).

The very feature that attracts many physicians, independence from a distrusted hospital, is also a source of GPWW weakness. That is, new sources of capital, information systems, and management expertise must be explored (such as an insurance partner; see Chapter 5).

Finally, the GPWW structure generally does not have as strong a leadership as is seen in a true medical group. This, along with the other disadvantages noted, may lead to a relative instability in the structure. Some managers in the industry believe that the GPWW concept is transitional to a more traditional medical group. Furthermore, although sharing of certain administrative services represents an improvement in overhead, there are many more economies of scale to be found in a true, or consolidated, medical group practice.

CONSOLIDATED MEDICAL GROUP

The term *consolidated medical group*, or *medical group practice*, refers to a traditional structure in which physicians have combined their resources to be a true medical group practice. Unlike the GPWW, in which the physicians combine certain assets and risks but remain in their own offices, practicing medicine as they always have, the true medical group is located in a few sites and functions in a group setting; in other words, the physicians occupy the same facility or facilities. This means a great deal of interaction among members of the group and common goals and objectives for group success.

Traditional medical groups are totally independent of the hospital. Even so, it is common for the group to identify strongly with one or more hospitals. Although this is good for the hospital as long as relations are good, it can be devastating to a hospital if relations sour or if the group is motivated to change hospitals for any reason. Some hospitals sponsor medical groups, but those operate more like other models discussed later in this chapter.

The group is usually a partnership or professional corporation, although other forms are possible. Usually the more senior members of the group enjoy more fruits of the group's success (e.g., higher income, better on-call schedules, and so forth), although one hopes not to an abusive degree. New members of an existing group who pass a probationary period often are required to pay in a substantial contribution to the group's capital to join, which can create an entry barrier to growth. Other groups employ new physicians for a lengthy period to control the finances of the group as well as to give all parties the opportunity to see whether it is a good fit. In any event, it is common for the group to require physicians to agree to a noncompetition clause in their contract to protect the group from a physician defecting and taking patients away from the group. A discussion of the general management of medical groups is beyond the scope of this chapter. Physician compensation in such groups is discussed in Chapter 10.

Advantages of Medical Groups

Medical groups have the ability to achieve substantial economies of scale, have strong negotiating leverage, and have the ability to influence physician behavior. Groups are usually attractive to MCOs because they not only deliver a large block of physicians with one contract but also have the ability to manage their own resources. The group can also decide to make a change in resource use (e.g., change hospitals) that can have a rapid and substantial positive effect on managed care.

Although the capital investment required of partners or group shareholders can be an entry barrier, it is also an exit barrier, promoting greater stability. An additional exit barrier is seen in the form of a noncompetition clause required of member physicians, again promoting stability, which is desirable in the eyes of a managed care plan. Medical groups are often able to recruit new physicians more easily because they offer an improved life style compared with that of solo practice, which allows them to grow along with a managed care plan. On the whole, medical groups are in a superior position to benefit from managed care compared with many other models, and certainly compared with independent private physicians.

Disadvantages of Medical Groups

Medical groups can certainly have serious problems, such as uncontrolled overhead or poor utilization patterns. If these problems are not rectified, the impact of failure is felt to a far higher degree than is the case if a single physician or small group fails. If the group has markedly disproportionate compensation or life style differences between the senior members and the new physicians, the turnover of new members can be unacceptably high. Medical groups can also inflate their own opinions of their worth, impeding effective contracting.

Medical groups can become calcified in their ways and be less able to change than individual physicians. This is a serious problem if compounded by the group being top heavy with subspecialists and, in turn, treating primary care physicians (PCPs) as second-class members. If the group is unwilling to consider redistributing the rewards to the PCPs, it may suffer defections of those physicians, which will make the group less desirable from a managed care standpoint.

PHOs

The PHO is an entity that, at a minimum, allows a hospital and its physicians to negotiate with third party payers. PHOs may do little more than provide for such a negotiating vehicle, although this could raise the risk of antitrust. PHOs may actively manage the relationship between the providers and MCOs, or they may provide more services, to the point where they may more aptly be considered MSOs (see below).

In its weakest form, the PHO is considered a messenger model. This means that the PHO analyzes the terms and conditions offered by an MCO and transmits its analysis and the contract to each physician, who then decides on an individual basis whether to participate.

In its simplest and more common version, the participating physicians and the hospital develop model contract terms and reimbursement levels and use those terms to negotiate with MCOs. The PHO usually has a limited amount of time to negotiate the contract successfully (e.g., 90 days). If that time limit passes, then the participating physicians are free to contract directly with the MCO; if the PHO successfully reaches an agreement with the MCO, then the physicians agree to be bound by those terms. The contract is still between the physician and the MCO and between the hospital and the MCO. In some cases, the contract between the physicians and the MCO is relatively brief and may reference a contract between the PHO and the MCO.

PHOs are generally considered the first step on the evolutionary ladder in vertical integration with respect to practitioners and facilities. They often form as a reaction to market forces from managed care. PHOs are considered the easiest type of vertically integrated system to develop (although they are not actually that easy, at least if done well). They also are a vehicle to provide some integration while preserving the independence and autonomy of the physicians.

By definition, a PHO requires the participation of a hospital and at least some portion of the admitting physicians. Often, the formation of the PHO is initiated by the hospital, but unless the leadership of the medical staff is also on board it is unlikely to get far. It is not uncommon for a PHO to be formed primarily as a defensive mechanism to deal with an increase in managed care contracting activity. It is also not uncommon for the same physicians who join the PHO already to be under contract with one or more managed care plans.

The PHO is usually a separate business entity, such as a for-profit corporation. This requires thorough legal analysis for the participating not-for-profit, tax exempt [Internal Revenue Code 501c (3)] hospital because the hospital could lose its tax exempt status if access to tax exempt financing confers an advantage to the PHO's balance sheet (see Chapter 56).

Initial capitalization and ownership occur with varying formulas, but most strive toward equal ownership between the physicians and the hospital. The hospital may put up the majority of the cash, however. For the sake of practitioner motivation, physician equity is considered a desired feature.

Ongoing revenue to the simplest form of PHO may be a nonitem because the entity could serve only as a cost center for the hospital. As the PHO takes on various MSO functions, however, participating providers pay a fee for those services. Third party payers also may pay an access fee.

Governance can evolve similarly. That is, in its simplest form hospital administrators may run the entity. Most PHOs are establishing formal governing boards, however. Board composition is usually equally divided between hospital administrators and physicians, with attention being given to primary care representation within the physician component.

PHOs fall into two broad categories: open and closed. These are described separately because MCOs often view them that way.

Open PHOs

The open PHO is one that is open to virtually any member of the medical staff of the hospital. There will often be minimum credentialing requirements (see Chapter 8), but not necessarily even that. Open PHOs are almost universally specialty dominated; in other words, there are disproportionately more specialists in the PHO than there are PCPs. The creators of the open PHO are often the specialists themselves, who become concerned that MCOs are selectively contracting, thereby reducing the amount of business that the specialists (as a group) are doing. The medical staff then approach the hospital administration to form the PHO primarily to allow all the members of the medical staff to participate with MCOs. In this situation, PCPs are usually courted but may still be relegated to secondary citizenship, even if unconsciously.

Some open PHOs claim that, although their genesis is an open format, the ultimate goal will be to manage the membership and remove those physicians who are unable to practice cost effectively. MCOs view such claims with skepticism, although it is certainly possible. The political reality of an open PHO is that it is quite difficult to bring sufficient discipline to bear on medical staff members who wield a high level of influence. This is currently complicated by the continued dichotomy of payment mechanisms, in which a certain portion of reimbursement to the hospital rewards cost effectiveness (e.g., prospective payment, capitation, and package or bundled pricing), whereas other forms of reimbursement reward the opposite (e.g., fee for service and simple discounts on charges). Finally, one must never underestimate the influence of the medical staff, particularly when they are united; failure to attend to the needs of the medical staff may be a serious career limiting move on the part of the hospital chief executive officer (CEO). In light of this, some PHOs have featured hospital CEOs permitting more than half the board seats to be occupied by physicians, although some are hospital-based physicians; in the case of not-for-profit PHOs, however, physicians may not represent more than 20 percent of the governance, regardless of the hospital's desire (see Chapter 56 for a discussion of this issue).

One last note regarding PHOs: The "PO" portion of a PHO may be a different model entirely. As an example, a GPWW or an IPA could represent the physician portion of the PHO. Although the most common model at the time of this writing is one in which the physicians remain independent and contract individually with the PHO, it is by no means the only method of organization.

Closed PHOs

The primary difference between a closed PHO and an open one is the proactive decision to limit physician membership in the PHO. This is clearly more difficult politically than an open model, but it carries greater potential for success. The two general approaches to limiting membership are by specialty type and by practice profiling.

Limitations by specialty type are most common and most easily done. The most common limitation is the number of specialists, to address the imbalance of PCPs and specialists found in an open PHO. In fact, it is not uncommon to find closed PHOs having a disproportionate number of PCPs on the governance board as well as in the membership of the PHO. Although an extreme demonstration of this concept is the primary care–only PHO that simply subcontracts with certain specialists, the PHO usually places limits on the number of specialists of any given specialty type beyond primary care for equity sharing and/or membership status. This limitation on the number of specialists is most often accomplished by projecting the enrollment (or covered lives) that the PHO is expected to cover over the next several years and then recruiting specialists according to predetermined ratios of specialists needed for that enrollment.

The second type of limitation involves practice profiling and is more difficult to carry out for technical reasons. This type of limitation requires the PHO to examine some objective form of practice analysis (it could be a subjective analysis, but that would probably raise a restraint of trade issue). Based on that analysis, physicians are invited to join the PHO or not. This is difficult to accomplish unless the PHO has access to adequate data, which is most uncommon. The closed PHO may be impeded in its quest to demonstrate selectivity by those states enacting any willing provider legislation and needs to be aware of any possible antitrust issues (see Chapter 57 for a discussion of both issues).

As part of ongoing recredentialing, the PHO also regularly reevaluates the number of physicians required in each specialty. If the PHO has the ability to capture and analyze data regarding practice behavior and clinical quality (see Chapters 25 and 27), those data may be used in managing the physician membership and, ultimately, in ending the participation agreement with any physicians who repeatedly depart from the PHO's practice guidelines. Such analyses are difficult to perform properly. It is important for the PHO (or for any type of IDS, for that matter) that accepts full risk to negotiate the right to receive claims data on all members for whom the PHO has the full capitated risk because otherwise the PHO will not have sufficient data to analyze all medical costs.

Advantages of a PHO

The primary advantage of a PHO is its ability to negotiate on behalf of a large group of physicians allied with a hospital. This advantage can be ephemeral if no MCO wishes to negotiate (see below), but it may be very real if the hospital and key members of the medical staff are attractive to MCOs and are not already under contract. Closed PHOs are more attractive to MCOs than open ones. Of course, if the providers have already contracted with the MCO and threaten to pull out (i.e., boycott the MCO) unless the MCO uses the PHO, a serious antitrust problem may arise. If the MCO has not already contracted with the providers, the PHO may be an expeditious route to developing a delivery system capability. Even in those situations where a contract already exists, contracting through the PHO may

represent a sufficient improvement in terms such that an MCO will be willing to switch from direct contracting to using the PHO; for example, the PHO may be willing to provide performance guarantees. Finally, physicians may view the PHO as a facilitator in landing direct contracts with self-insured employers, with the Health Care Financing Administration for Medicare risk contracts, and with the state for managed Medicaid contracts.

A second advantage of a PHO is its theoretical ability to track and use data and to manage the delivery system, at least from the standpoints of UM and quality management. Once again, this advantage is more likely to be found in a closed PHO than in an open one, primarily because a closed PHO has a greater concentration of events over fewer physicians.

The third advantage of a PHO is that it is the first step to greater integration between a hospital and its medical staff. Although a PHO by itself may result in improved relations, those relations can quickly sour if the PHO consumes time, energy, and money but fails to yield results. If the PHO does result in a better ability to contract or yields economic rewards, then its mission is successful, at least for the near term. If the PHO does not succeed, or if success appears to be short lived, then the PHO may be the base from which a more integrated model may be built.

Disadvantages of a PHO

The chief disadvantage of a typical PHO is that it often fails to result in any meaningful improvement in contracting ability. In many cases, MCOs already have provider contracts in place and see little value in going through the PHO. Even worse, an MCO may see the PHO as little more than a vehicle for providers to keep their reimbursement high.

Open PHOs are at a significant disadvantage if the MCO (or employer, in the event that the PHO chooses to contract directly with employers) does not want all the physicians in the PHO to be participating with the health plan. MCOs often want the right to select the providers and are unlikely to give up that ability. Even closed PHOs may suffer from this problem if the MCOs specifically wish to avoid contracting with certain physicians who are members of the PHO.

MCOs may view the PHO as a barrier to effective communication with the physicians and a hindrance to fully effective UM. Unless the PHO has a compelling story to tell regarding its ability to manage utilization, the MCO may believe that it can do a better job without the PHO's interference. Alternatively, if the health plan has relatively unsophisticated UM capabilities, or if the plan is too small to be able to devote adequate resources to UM, the PHO may represent an attractive alternative.

Because PHOs are relatively loose in their structure, and because the physicians may still be completely independent, the PHO's ability to affect provider behavior is rather limited. This can have an impact not only on UM but also on getting the entire organization to make necessary changes.

In a 1995 study performed by Ernst & Young LLP, the majority of PHOs were young, had little enrolled membership, had little systems support, and did not have full time management, especially medical management.[2] It is possible, and even likely, that by the time this book is published that PHOs in the aggregate may have improved their performance and infrastructure. If not, then it is probable that PHOs will not be long-term entities.

Regrettably, there have been a few cases where a hospital and medical staff with existing managed care contracts formed a PHO with the intent of using the PHO to improve their negotiating strength, only to lose the existing managed care contract and be unable to replace it with anything better. In other words, the PHO actually harmed them because it was considered undesirable by the MCO. Because PHOs do allow the participating physicians to contract directly with the MCO in the event that the MCO does not offer terms agreeable to the PHO, this risk is usually minimal.

Specialist PHOs

A recent variant of the PHO has emerged over the past few years. The specialist PHO has taken the general closed PHO concepts down to the level of a single specialty. Common specialties involved are cardiology and pediatrics; psychiatric PHOs also have existed for many years. Their track record is too brief in most cases for definitive observations, but the value placed on them by the market should follow the logic described above under specialist PPMs, except that this entity brings with it an expensive facility.

MSOs

An MSO represents the evolution of the PHO into an entity that provides more services to the physicians. Not only does the MSO provide a vehicle for negotiating with MCOs, but it also provides additional services to support the physicians' practice. The physician, however, usually remains an independent private practitioner. The MSO is based around one or more hospitals. The reasons for the MSO's formation are generally the same as for the PHO, and ownership and governance issues are similar to those discussed earlier.

In its simplest form, the MSO operates as a service bureau, providing basic practice support services to member physicians. These services include such activities as billing and collection, administrative support in certain areas, electronic data interchange (such as electronic billing), and other services.

The physician can remain an independent practitioner, under no legal obligation to use the services of the hospital on an exclusive basis. The MSO must receive compensation from the physician at fair market value, or the hospital and physician could incur legal problems (discussed in Chapter 56 as well as below). The MSO should, through economies of scale as well as good management, be able to provide those services at a reasonable rate.

The MSO may be considerably broader in scope. In addition to providing all the services described above, the MSO may actually purchase many of the assets of the physician's practice; for example, the MSO may purchase the physician's office space or office equipment (at fair market value). The MSO can employ the office support staff of the physician as well. MSOs can further incorporate functions such as quality management, UM, provider relations, member services, and even claims processing. This form of MSO is usually constructed as a unique business entity, separate from the PHO. Because they are their own corporations, legal advisors are finding advantages in characterizing these as limited liability corporations, but alternatives exist.

The MSO does not always have direct contracts with MCOs for two reasons: Many MCOs insist on having the provider be the contracting agent, and many states will not allow MCOs (especially HMOs) to have contracts with any entity that does not have the power to bind the provider. The physician may remain an independent private practitioner under no contractual obligation to use the hospital on an exclusive basis. It should be noted here that there are IDSs that operate under the label of MSO that actually do purchase the physician's entire practice (possibly including intangible values such as good will) and function much like a more fully integrated system, as discussed later in this chapter.

Advantages of an MSO

The primary advantage of an MSO over a PHO is the ability of the MSO to bind the physician closer to the hospital, although not as a contractual obligation to use the hospital on an exclusive basis. The MSO certainly has the ability to bring economies of scale and professional management to the physician's office services, thus potentially reducing overhead costs. The MSO may have the potential ability to capture data regarding practice behavior, which may be used to help the physicians practice more cost effectively. This develops when the MSO contains more advanced functions, such as UM and claims processing.

Disadvantages of an MSO

The disadvantages of an MSO are similar to those of a PHO in that the physician may remain an independent practitioner with the ability to change allegiances with relative ease. Also, when the MSO does not employ the physician, it has somewhat limited ability to effect change or to redeploy resources in response to changing market needs.

Special problems arise with MSOs, problems that can be compounded by MSOs that purchase assets from a physician's practice. These are the problems of the transaction being perceived as inuring to the benefit of the physician in an illegal manner and of fraud and abuse for federally funded patients. These issues are briefly discussed later in this chapter and in detail in Chapter 56.

FOUNDATION MODEL

A foundation model IDS is one in which a hospital creates a not-for-profit foundation and actually purchases physicians' practices (both tangible and intangible assets) and puts those practices into the foundation. This model usually occurs when, for some legal reason (e.g., the hospital is a not-for-profit entity that cannot own a for-profit subsidiary, or there is a state law against the corporate practice of medicine), the hospital cannot employ the physicians directly or use hospital funds to purchase the practices directly. It must be noted that, to qualify for and maintain its not-for-profit status, the foundation must prove that it provides substantial community benefit.

A second form of foundation model does not involve a hospital. In that model, the foundation is an entity that exists on its own and contracts for services with a medical group and a hospital. On a historical note, in the early days of HMOs many open panel types of plans that were not formed as IPAs were formed as foundations; the foundation held the HMO license and contracted with one or more IPAs and hospitals for services.

The foundation itself is governed by a board that is not dominated by either the hospital or the physicians (in fact, physicians may represent no more than 20 percent of the board) and includes lay members. The foundation owns and manages the practices, but the physicians become members of a medical group that, in turn, has an exclusive contract for services with the foundation; in other words, the foundation is the only source of revenue to the medical group. The physicians have contracts with the medical group that are long term and contain noncompetition clauses.

Although the physicians are in an independent group, and the foundation is also independent from the hospital, the relationship in fact is close among all members of the triad. The medical group, however, retains a significant measure of autonomy regarding its own business affairs, and the foundation has no control over certain aspects, such as individual physician compensation (see Chapter 10).

Advantages of the Foundation Model

The primary advantages of this model pertain to legal constraints that require the foundation's creation in the first place. Because the construction of this entity is rather unwieldy, it is best suited to those states in which it is required (e.g., California, at the time this chapter is being written) so that a not-for-profit hospital can proceed with a fully integrated model. That said, the foundation model provides for a greater level of structural integration than any other model discussed to this point. A not-for-profit foundation may also be better able to access the bond market for capital in an advantageous manner.

Because the foundation clearly controls the revenue that the medical group will get, it has considerable influence over that group. The foundation also has the ability to rationalize the clinical and administrative resources required to meet obligations under managed care contracts (and fee for service, of course) and can achieve greater economies of scale. If the foundation consolidates medical office locations, these economies are improved, as is the foundation's

ability to provide more comprehensive services to enrolled members. A foundation also has the ability to invest required capital to expand services, recruit PCPs, and so forth. For these reasons, a foundation model may be viewed quite favorably by a contracting MCO.

Disadvantages of the Foundation Model

The primary disadvantage of a foundation model is that the physicians in the medical group are linked only indirectly to the foundation and the business goals of that foundation. Although that indirect link is quite strong, the medical group remains an intermediate organization (vaguely analogous to an IPA) that can operate in ways that are potentially inconsistent with the overall goals of managed care. One example of this becoming a problem would be a medical group that is seriously top heavy with specialists and in which PCPs are treated as second-class members. Another example would be a group that compensated member physicians based on fee for service or other measures that are easily gamed, leading to less than optimal control of utilization and quality.

Related to this issue is a built-in potential for conflicts between the governance boards of the hospital and the medical group. If the goals and priorities of those two organizations are not completely aligned (and they rarely are), then it is possible for serious disputes to arise, which impede success.

The last main disadvantage is the not-for-profit status of the hospital and foundation. Because of that status, the foundation must continually prove that it provides a community benefit to maintain its status. The risk of private inurement (discussed below) is also heightened. As this book is being written, several not-for-profit hospitals, to compete against foundation models, have formed PHOs and MSOs (both for-profit and not-for-profit entities) allowing well over 20 percent board representation by physicians. These developments have been permitted by a favorable interpretation of regulatory requirements, although their ultimate corporate stability is still undetermined (see Chapter 56).

STAFF MODEL

Not to be confused with the staff model HMO (see Chapter 3), a staff model in the context of this chapter refers to an IDS owned by a health system rather than by an HMO. The distinction is whether the primary business organization is a licensed entity (e.g., an HMO) or primarily a provider. This distinction is not always easy to observe, and in some cases the only way to make any distinction is to look at the genesis of the parent organization: Was it founded to be a health plan or founded to be a provider? If the distinction rests on history only, then it is meaningless.

The staff model is a health system that employs the physicians directly. Physicians are integrated into the system either through the purchase of their practices or by being hired directly. The system is often more than a hospital, being rather a larger, more comprehensive organization for the delivery of health care. Because the physicians are employees, the legal issues that attach to IDSs using private physicians are attenuated.

Advantages of Staff Models

Staff model IDSs are theoretically in a good position to be able to rationalize resources and to align goals of all the components of the delivery system. Physicians are almost always paid based on a salary, and incentive programs can be designed to reward the physicians in parallel with the goals and objectives of the system (see Chapters 7, 10, and 11). Far greater economies of scale are achievable, and capital resources can be applied in a businesslike manner. Staff models also have a greater ability to recruit new physicians because there is no cost to the new physician and the income stream to the new physician begins immediately. The ability to manage the physicians in the system is also at least theoretically enhanced. The problems of taxable status, private inurement, and fraud and abuse are greatly diminished. MCOs generally consider staff model IDSs as desirable business partners, assuming that cost, quality, and access are acceptable; the exception would be if the staff model chooses to pursue obtaining its own HMO license, thus becoming a direct competitor and threat to a contracting MCO.

Disadvantages of Staff Models

One key problem with staff models is when management assumes that, simply because the physicians are employees, they can be managed in a manner similar to that of other employees of the system; that is a false and unproductive assumption. Physicians are highly intelligent and highly trained professionals who must operate clinically with considerable autonomy. Any health system that does not recognize these qualities is bound to have difficulties with its medical staff.

Despite the previous statement, staff models often run into problems with physician productivity. Salaried physicians are obviously no longer motivated to see high volumes of patients, as they are under fee for service. Staff models may be most attractive to physicians who do not wish to practice full time or who wish to limit their hours. Some staff model HMOs have had such problems with low productivity that they have at least partially eroded the economies of scale that are available in tightly integrated systems. Staff models, although having a somewhat easier time recruiting than a medical group, suffer from the doppelgänger of easy entry, easy exit. Physicians in staff models often feel little loyalty and are more easily recruited away than physicians who have an investment in a group.

The last disadvantage is the high capital requirement to build and operate the system. Once adequate patient volume is coming through, staff models can have excellent financial performance. Until then, however, they are heavily leveraged. Expansion of an existing system likewise requires a great deal of capital investment.

PHYSICIAN OWNERSHIP MODEL

The physician ownership model refers to a vertically integrated system in which the physicians hold a significant portion of ownership (i.e., equity) interest. In some cases, the physicians own the entire system; in other cases, the physicians own less than 100 percent, but more than 51 percent. The physicians' equity interest is through their medical group(s). Physicians holding equity as simple shareholders could raise problems with Medicare fraud and abuse (see below and Chapter 56). It is theoretically possible for physicians to own equity through a limited partnership, although that format would require serious legal review. It is also possible to craft a model in which physicians own less than 50 percent as a group, but it is not clear whether that model would survive legal scrutiny (see below) or whether it would confer the same advantages as the model described here.

The physician ownership model operates with features combining those of the staff model and MSO. Unlike the situation with the staff model, the medical groups have a strong role in the overall management of the system, and the physicians (at least those physicians who are partners in the group) have a clear vested interest in the system's success.

Advantages of the Physician Ownership Model

The advantages of the physician ownership model are similar to those enumerated for the staff model above. In contrast to the staff model, this model enjoys a powerful advantage by virtue of the physician ownership: total alignment of goals of the medical group and the health system. Because the physician owners' success is tied directly to the overall success of the entire organization, there is far less of a problem with conflicting goals and objectives (within the boundaries of human nature). Because of this alignment, strong physician leadership is present, which is more effective in managing the medical groups. Finally, this model can choose

either to contract with or to own the hospital rather than be dominated by the hospital.

Disadvantages of the Physician Ownership Model

The primary disadvantage of the physician ownership model is the high level of resources required to build and operate it. Large capital resources are required to acquire the personnel, facilities, and practices necessary to provide comprehensive medical services, an adequate level of managerial support, and the required infrastructure. The source of this capital is primarily the physicians' practices, although outside access to capital is certainly possible. Related to that issue is the generally high buy-in cost to new physician partners, which may be a barrier to some physicians joining the group as other than employees.

As this chapter is being written, it is unknown whether models in which physicians are significant equity holders will face problems with the fraud and abuse provisions discussed below and in Chapter 56, but it is possible. This is because the physicians receive an economic reward for patient services that is unrelated to their own services.

VIRTUAL INTEGRATION

Goldsmith argues that it is possible, and even likely, that many of the structurally rigid vertical integration models are not going to succeed.[3] He argues that success will be more probable with models of virtual integration, in which more or less independent parties come together for the purpose of behaving like an IDS under managed care but retain their own identities and mission. This virtual integration requires an alignment of the financial incentives among the parties as well as an alignment of business purpose.

In a virtual integration, each of the major segments of the health care system—the physicians, the institutional providers, the payers/MCOs, and the ancillary providers (e.g., pharmacy)—act in concert for a common cause, but none is an employee or subdivision of another. This allows each party to manage its own affairs and meet its own financial goals without being managed by another segment of the industry. In this model, there is greater horizontal integration (e.g., between hospitals, between physicians, and so forth), with each of those horizontally integrated systems then forming relationships with other parts of the health care system.

GLOBAL CAPITATION

Global capitation applies to IDSs that are capable of accepting full or nearly full risk for medical expenses, including all professional, institutional, and many ancillary services as well. This differs from the full capitation described in Chapter 9, which applies to primary care groups accepting full risk for all professional services but not for institutional or ancillary services. Global capitation includes institutional as well as professional services, and the party accepting the capitation payment is a large, vertically integrated organization with presumably greater resources. Even though the IDS has accepted global capitation, it often purchases reinsurance to protect it against catastrophic cases; that reinsurance is either provided by the HMO or purchased by the IDS from a reinsurer.

Many IDSs accept a percentage of premium revenue from an HMO rather than a fixed capitation. Although these forms of revenue are similar, they are not the same. A percentage of premium may be affected by underwriting and marketing issues (primarily in commercial enrollment; in Medicare and Medicaid, percentage of revenue and capitation are nearly the same). As discussed in Chapters 43 and 44, if underwriting is poor and there is a revenue shortfall from the standpoint of covered lives, the percentage of that shortfall passed on to the IDS will mirror the percentage of revenue it is receiving from the MCO.

Although the HMO may have capitated the IDS, the IDS still faces the issue of how to divide up the revenue and risk among the parties. In a sense, global capitation simply transfers the burden of payment and management from the HMO to the IDS, but the fundamental issues remain. If the IDS employs the physicians, then it is relatively easier to distribute income.

Many IDSs, however, are combinations of private and employed physicians. Even hospitals that employ physicians usually still rely on private physicians for at least some services, and often the genesis of the IDS was to allow the hospital and private physicians to remain competitive in a managed care environment. Therefore, the IDS that accepts global capitation must still figure out how to allocate risk and reward. The managers of the IDS must be realistic and recognize that individual physicians will be unable and unwilling to bear a high level of financial risk (e.g., how many individual physicians could afford to pay $200,000 as their share of overutilization?) but will usually demand a disproportionate share of financial reward. Although risk and reward are always related, the IDS management must be careful to incent the physicians properly as well as to avoid the legal problems of private inurement and fraud and abuse regulations. Reimbursement of physicians is discussed in Chapters 7, 8, and 10.

The last major issue in global capitation is who is actually the licensed health plan. If an IDS accepts global capitation, then a state's insurance department may require the IDS to become licensed as an HMO. This issue is discussed below and in detail in Chapter 53. Regulation of IDSs accepting full-risk capitation is an area undergoing considerable change, and the reader will need to keep aware of applicable regulations and laws.

PROVIDING THE INSURANCE FUNCTION

Until this point, this chapter has concentrated on vertical integration of practitioners and facilities. The MSO and PHO models are examples of delivery systems that can expand horizontally (by finding other PHO partners and forming a regional network—the super PHO—with convenient geographic access) and then become independently capable of direct contracting with self-insured purchasers. This capability requires incorporating most of the typical insurance functions. These usually begin with claims processing but may extend to ownership of the insurance license itself.

Options for an IDS to converge with insurance functions include the following: The insurer buys the hospital and physician groups, an integrated provider network buys or builds the insurance function, or the insurer and the integrated provider network form a joint venture with shared ownership (or perhaps a looser relationship). All these options, and more, are discussed in greater detail in Chapter 5. An integrated provider network may also rent an insurance function; for example, it may pay several dollars per subscriber per month for third party administrator (TPA) functions and possible insurance licensure fronting services.

Clearly, when dealing with purchasers that are not self-insured, the IDS or MSO needs to incorporate all the classic insurance functions, including underwriting and actuarial rate development, as it takes on risk. The IDS also needs to have an insurance license. Many small insurance companies and TPAs are willing to price their role in this scheme competitively and are capable of avoiding the double digit overhead associated with the largest insurance companies. One must be cognizant, however, that many of these TPAs are not capable of carrying out sophisticated managed care functions. It is also possible for an IDS to contract with an insurer to front the license, that is, to use the insurer's license to back up the IDS's activities.

Advantages

A joint venture between an IDS and an insurer or MCO has several advantages. Both parties bring assets to the venture (at least theoretically): The IDS brings a network, some medical management, the ability to accept some level of risk for medical expenses, and a framework for contracting, and the insurer or MCO brings a license (and its ability to meet the attendant capi-

tal and regulatory needs), possibly an enrolled subscriber base, and expertise in functions such as claims processing, member services, and the like. See Chapter 5 for more discussion of these issues.

Disadvantages

The main disadvantage of an IDS assuming the insurance functions is that it may fail to carry them out competently, and failure would have far-reaching effects. The activities of an insurance company or MCO go well beyond medical management, and it would be naive for the management of an IDS to believe that those functions do not require expertise or that they are not fraught with complexities.

The pursuit of the insurance partner requires great caution. Too many insurance entities are configured as indemnity claims processors, incapable of understanding the subtleties associated with managing care. Significant capital may be required to structure the new entity. A large organization perceived to have deep pockets that has gotten closer to the provision of care will also need to evidence due diligence in credentialing providers to minimize the risk associated with negligent credentialing.

Governance and control of a joint venture may be a sensitive area. Although joint representation on the board is likely to be required, controlling representation may become a contentious issue. Control is generally subject to the Golden Rule (whoever has the gold makes the rules), but supermajority rights may help address control concerns by the minority partner.

Finally, these relationships often begin as nonexclusive. When the stakeholders have multiple alliances, true allegiance and true alignment of motivation are difficult to achieve. Gradually, consolidation will require a deliberate "choosing up sides" evolution. As noted earlier, for more detailed discussion see Chapter 5.

LEGAL PITFALLS

There are many legal pitfalls in the development and operation of IDSs, and this chapter cannot possibly address them all. A few particular legal problems are especially worthy of note. Two related issues are the problems of private inurement and fraud and abuse; the other two especially noteworthy issues are problems of antitrust and licensure requirements. Readers are urged to review these and other legal issues in Chapters 53, 56, 57, and 58, and in the numerous other sources of material available in the literature. More important, competent legal counsel should be obtained before and during any operational activities involving these types of IDSs or any other integration activity not discussed here.

Private Inurement

This issue is one raised primarily by the Internal Revenue Service (IRS), which has set rules against the inurement of private benefits from activities of a tax exempt organization. The tax exempt organization pertinent to these discussions is usually a hospital but could be any tax exempt vehicle. The issue at hand is that a tax exempt organization cannot do any business that provides more than incidental monetary benefit to private individuals. Specifically, if a hospital provides services to a physician at less than fair market value, provides a below-market (or forgiven) loan to a physician, or purchases a practice at greater than fair market value, then the physician has benefited in a manner not allowed by the IRS. As this chapter is being written, there is also the possibility that a PHO that has majority or even parity board representation by physicians would be considered an organization created for the private inurement of the physicians; it is not known whether that position will be held.

Fraud and Abuse

The federal government, through Medicare and Medicaid, has developed regulations regarding what it considers fraud and abuse in the provision of services to federally funded patients. These regulations are extensive, and this chapter will not be able to review them. One pertinent

portion of these regulations is similar to the issue discussed above, that of hospitals providing a financial benefit to physicians over what would be considered fair market value. In this case, the federal government views such an offense as fraudulent payments in return for referrals of federally funded patients to the hospital, in other words, kickbacks. This problem would apply to any hospital or provider that serves Medicare or Medicaid patients, regardless of the taxable status of the provider.

A key to avoiding this problem (including the problem of private inurement), in addition to competent legal counsel, is to pay or charge only fair market value. If a hospital purchases a physician's practice, it must have that practice valued by an independent firm that is competent to conduct valuation studies. If a hospital provides services to a physician (e.g., facilities, billing and collection, and so forth), it must charge fair market value and manage those services in a businesslike fashion. The exact same caveat applies to a hospital system infusing capital into physicians' practices or into an IDS: The capital infusion must be based on reasonable business terms and must be recovered over time, just as any investment. It must be stressed that even strict adherence to these guidelines may not guarantee that there will be no problem with charges of fraud and abuse; the federal government is likely to examine each individual situation on its merits.

A special problem under the fraud and abuse regulations of the federal government relates to prohibitions against self-referral by physicians, the so-called Stark amendments.* Although this is easily avoided for some situations (e.g., a private physician cannot refer a Medicare or Medicaid patient to a radiology facility that the physician owns), the application of these regulations is not necessarily as clear as it might be to a physician-owned IDS. There are Safe Harbor provi-

---

* Named after California Representative Fortney "Pete" Stark; the actual provisions are included as amendments to the Omnibus Reconciliation Act of 1993.

sions for some licensed HMOs and for certain clinical activities that are an integral part of a physician's practice, but whether these provisions would apply to certain forms of IDSs that are owned or controlled (even partially controlled) by physicians is unclear. As an example, GPWWs and fee-for-service MSOs may have an exposure. This is a new area of law that has not been fully clarified; competent legal counsel is critical here because the penalties for noncompliance with these federal regulations can be severe. At the time of writing, there appears to be a bit of loosening of these restrictions, but it is unclear as to how this issue will be resolved (if it ever is), and there is debate in Congress that could affect how this problem manifests.

Antitrust

It is well beyond the scope of this chapter to discuss antitrust in any depth, but a general point may be made. If an IDS is perceived to have been formed primarily to stifle competition, then it may be found in violation of antitrust provisions. Examples of so-called per se violations of antitrust law would include competitors agreeing to fix prices (either minimums or maximums!), sharing pricing information, agreeing to divide the market among themselves, and so forth. Although per se violations refer to actions that are clearly wrong, other activities may be subject to the rule of reason, in which there are good procompetitive reasons for the activity even though there may be some elements that could be perceived as antitrust. For example, an IDS may encompass greater than 20 percent to 30 percent of the total number of providers in a community but can clearly demonstrate that resources are rationalized and competition has increased. Again, competent counsel is required to review this issue. Antitrust issues are also discussed in Chapter 57.

Licensure Provisions

Except in situations where the IDS is part of a joint venture with a licensed insurer or MCO (see Chapter 5), if an IDS takes on too much risk for medical expenses, the state insurance department may conclude that the delivery system should be the licensed entity, not the HMO or insurance company that contracted with the delivery system. This problem has occurred in some states in which well-organized IPAs or PHOs took full capitated risk, and the insurance department forced the IPA or PHO to cede back a portion of that risk to the HMO or else obtain an HMO license of its own. As of the time of this writing, the National Association of Insurance Commissioners had issued a policy statement that IDSs that accept risk will require licensure as HMOs. Although this policy statement does not have the force of law, it carries considerable stature. See Chapter 53 for more discussion of this topic.

The costs associated with becoming a licensed entity are not trivial and can easily exceed several million dollars, including capital necessary to meet statutory reserve requirements. Furthermore, compliance with licensure regulations is a resource- and capital-consuming task that many provider organizations will not be willing to take on. An interesting variation sometimes occurs: An IDS becomes a licensed HMO but only sells services to other HMOs (in other words, it does not market directly to enrollees). How much risk is too much in the eyes of a state insurance department? That issue is not at all clear as this chapter is being written.

CONCLUSION

IDSs have existed for quite some time, but under current pressures they are evolving rapidly. The more a system is truly integrated, and the more the goals and objectives of all stakeholders can be aligned, the greater the likelihood of success. IDSs may provide a viable vehicle for managed care plans to deliver services to their members, but no one should assume that the presence of an IDS does not also bring a large set of challenges, both managerial and legal. If those challenges cannot be overcome or managed, the downside of failure in an IDS is potentially more severe than if smaller, unintegrated medical groups fail. When designed and implemented well, however, the IDS can show advantages over many conventional managed care models.

REFERENCES AND NOTES

1. P. Starr, *The Social Transformation of American Medicine* (New York, N.Y.: Basic Books, 1982).
2. Ernst & Young LLP, *Physician–Hospital Organizations: Profile 1995* (Washington, D.C.: Ernst & Young LLP, 1995).
3. J.C. Goldsmith, The Illusive Logic of Integration, *Healthcare Forum Journal* (September/October 1994): 26–31.

SUGGESTED READING

Beckham, J.D. 1995. Redefining Work in the Integrated Delivery System. *Healthcare Forum Journal* May/June: 76–82.

Boland, P. 1994. *Organized Delivery Systems. Managed Care Quarterly*, 2.

Burns, L.R., and Thorpe D.P. 1993. Trends and Models in Physician–Hospital Organizations. *Health Care Management Review* 18:7–20.

Coddington, D.C., Moore, K.D., and Fisher, E.A. 1994. *Integrated Health Care: Reorganizing the Physician, Hospital, and Health Plan Relationship*. Englewood, Colo.: Center for Research in Abulatory Health Care Administration/MGMA.

Coile, R.C. 1994. Year 2000 Scenario for Physician-Hospital Organizations. *Topics in Health Care Financing* 20 (4): 75–83.

Conrad, D. and Hoare, G. (eds.). 1994. *Strategic Alignment: Managing Integrated Health Systems*. Ann Arbor, Mich.: Health Administration Press/AUPHA.

Dasco, S.T. and Dasco, C.C. 1996. *Managed Care Answer Book*. New York, N.Y.: Panel Publishers.

DeMuro, P.R. 1994. Integrated Delivery Systems. *Topics in Health Care Financing* 20.

Ernst & Young LLP. 1995. *Physician–Hospital Organizations: Profile 1995*. Washington, D.C.: Ernst & Young LLP.

Fine, A. 1993. *The Integrated Health Care Delivery Systems Manual*. New York, N.Y.: Thompson Publishing Group.

Fine, A. (ed.). 1995. *Integrated Health Care Delivery Systems: A Guide to Successful Strategies for Hospital and Physician Collaboration*. New York, N.Y.: Thompson Publishing Group.

Korenchuk, K.M. 1994. *Transforming the Delivery of Health Care: The Integration Process* (2nd ed.). Englewood, Colo.: Center for Research in Abulatory Health Care Administration/MGMA.

Traska, M.R. 1996. *Managed Care Strategies 1996*. New York, N.Y.: Faulkner & Gray.

Chapter 5

Acquisitions, Joint Ventures, and Partnerships between Providers and Managed Care Organizations

Peter R. Kongstvedt and David W. Plocher

As the health care environment continues to evolve, many new types of health care delivery systems are forming [see Chapter 4 for a discussion of different forms of integrated health care delivery systems (IDSs) as well as common operational characteristics of these systems]. The new IDSs are continuing to evolve and explore new ways to interact on both the health care delivery side and the payer and management side. At the same time, managed care organizations (MCOs), including health maintenance organizations (HMOs), are exploring new ways to approach the delivery of health care services and are continuing to evolve in their own right.

As the health care marketplace evolves, new opportunities are created for providers and health plans to relate to each other. These opportunities include MCOs acquiring physician practices and even hospitals, hospitals acquiring physician practices, insurers acquiring hospitals or physician practices, proprietary physician practice management (PPM) companies acquiring physician practices, provider systems becoming licensed health plans, and joint ventures between provider systems and MCOs.

There is no clear trend in these activities save one: In highly competitive markets with moderate or high levels of managed care penetration, it is becoming increasingly difficult to be in solo (or small group) private practice. Whether through negative pressures, such as decreasing

economics and increasing hassle, or through positive pressures, such as the ability to cash in by selling a practice and turning the administrative burden over to professional management, physicians are coming together either on their own or under the umbrella of a larger organization. Beyond that, this is an area that remains in a state of rapid evolution.

THE GRASS *MUST* BE GREENER!

There is a truly astonishing lack of knowledge transfer between the provider industry and the payer industry, especially the managed care industry. This high level of naiveté is coupled with a natural tendency to consider the other party in a less than flattering light because the other party is considered the one causing most of the problems.

There is a widespread belief by providers that payers are corrupt incompetents who do little for their money. After all, what could be easier? A claim comes in, a check goes out! How dare they create all the hassle they do! Worse yet, they extract unfairly huge sums of money, enriching themselves at the expense of funds that should be spent on direct patient care. Get rid of them! Cut out the middle man, and life will be simple once again!

Alternatively, there is a belief by many MCO managers that most providers are really greedy entrepreneurs whose main goal in life is to suck money out of the system. It would all be easier if the MCO simply had direct control of providers. After all, what could be simpler? Patients come

David W. Plocher, M.D., is a principal in the Minneapolis office of Ernst & Young LLP, an international accounting and consulting firm.

in, you treat them! The only thing that's required is to order the physicians to behave (after all, they're employees now), and they'll straighten up. Get that private practice, fee-for-service (FFS), rip-off mentality under control, and life will be a lot better for all concerned (except for those recalcitrant, avaricious physicians whom you brutally throw out and whose bedraggled countenance then gives proof to the adage that Cheaters Never Prosper).

Such characatures, such mean parodies, are not representative of the real world. Although it is undeniable that a small percentage of individuals on both the provider side and the payer side may behave in such a reprehensible way, in fact the huge majority do not. Each discipline is in reality far more complex than the other appreciates. If the insurance and managed care industries were really so simple and inexpensive to operate, someone would have taken over the market by now, performing at a high level at little cost. Conversely, if it were simple to care for patients, medical texts would be slim, it would take 6 weeks to learn medicine, and all physicians would work 6-hour days for princely incomes. Mature and thoughtful individuals recognize that the core skills and experiences of each party are necessary.

GENERAL TRENDS

Heavily Penetrated Markets

A heavily penetrated market [e.g., one in which HMO or point-of-service (POS) enrollment is 25 percent or more of the total population] is often one in which it is common (although not absolutely necessary) to find a few plans dominating the market in terms of size and financial performance. Entry by new plans is difficult, although possible.

If an MCO in such a market is large and currently successful, it has little impetus to change. An exception may occur if the MCO wishes to introduce an entirely new product, however. For example, an HMO may be highly successful in the commercial market but decide to enter into a market in which it has little experience, such as Medicare or Medicaid. Another possible exception may occur if the MCO wishes to tie up a strong IDS to prevent the IDS from contracting with a strong competitor. An IDS may offer an established MCO such preferable pricing or provide access to such highly desirable providers that are otherwise unavailable that the MCO may be willing to give up its direct relationship with the providers and agree to work through the IDS. To entice the MCO to change, the advantages must be significant.

If the MCO is large and troubled, that may be an impetus to change its contracting to take advantage of what an IDS can offer. For example, if the MCO is losing money, it may find that entering into global capitation contracts allows it to cap its costs, thus controlling premium rate increases. If an MCO is a new entrant into a heavily penetrated market, then there is great impetus to partner with the provider system. This approach allows the newly entering MCO to have a delivery system quickly and to construct a risk-sharing arrangement that will protect it from excessive medical costs (at least theoretically).

Underpenetrated Markets

Underpenetrated markets (e.g., markets with less than 20 percent HMO and POS enrollment) have relatively limited experience with advanced managed care activities. In such markets there is a much greater impetus to consider creative options by both MCOs and IDSs. Partnering with providers may fast-track an MCO's market entry ahead of its competitors.

Conversely, some hospital systems are pushing aggressively to become licensed HMOs as a preemptive move, sometimes even in advance of working out their integration strategy. This is seen as a way to keep MCOs out of their service area. In such a situation, the IDS is used as the vehicle for health care delivery. This is discussed further below.

In any event, underpenetrated markets offer greater opportunities for joint ventures and partnerships between payers and providers as well as opportunities for IDSs to approach the market in creative ways. Table 5–1 describes the continuum of strategic debate culminating in the environment in which acquiring an HMO license would only subtract majority market share from other payers.

ACQUISITION OF PROVIDERS BY MCOs

One increasingly common approach to integrating providers and payers is the outright acquisition of provider practices or provider facilities by MCOs such as HMOs and Blue Cross/ Blue Shield (BCBS) plans. Primary care practices are being purchased at an astonishingly fast pace, to the extent that it has become a seller's market. This pace cannot continue, and it is likely that such activities will decline as desirable practices become rare, at which point it will change into a recruiting strategy. Acquisition of specialty practices is not occurring at the same rate but is clearly occurring. Numerous forms of physician practice acquisitions are possible and are described in Chapter 4. A brief discussion of these activities follows.

This enthusiasm for primary care physician (PCP) practice acquisition is based on the central role of these physicians as the gateway at the POS. This has been enforced by the requirement for PCP selection during open enrollment. There may be new POSs developing, however. Exhibit 5–1 summarizes cautionary notes regarding the rampage toward PCP acquisition.

Table 5–1 Likelihood of Success of a Provider-Based System Acquiring an HMO License

Managed Care Market Penetration (%)	Strategy
< 5	Possible success
5–20	Proceed with caution
20–30	Worry and spend more money
> 30	Don't bother

Acquisition of Physician Practices

Perhaps the leading type of organization that is purchasing physician practices is the hospital, as illustrated in Table 5–2. The chief reasons for

Exhibit 5–1 Reasons Why Pursuit and Acquisition of PCP Practices Require Restraint

- PCPs are not distributed evenly across cities and regions. Some regions, such as the upper midwestern and western United States, have a surplus of PCPs in larger cities.
- Specialty referral guidelines, according to some criteria vendors, permit nearly direct access to specialists for certain conditions.
- Mature delivery systems often perform better with direct access to specialists for certain conditions (e.g., chronic congestive heart failure, type I diabetes, refractory adolescent asthma, acquired immunodeficiency syndrome, rheumatoid arthritis, depression, and others) based on peer reviewed evidence supporting superior outcome as measured by parameters varying from episode cost of care to functional status.
- Mature delivery systems further deploy demand management methodologies that, through nurse triage lines and self-help literature, avoid an unnecessary office visit for a minor, self-limiting symptom or arrange a direct referral to a specialist (see Chapter 17).
- Advanced MCOs may staff outpatient clinics with up to four nonphysician practitioners to every family practitioner.
- There is early activity in retraining specialists to become PCPs.
- Advanced hospitals do not need PCPs for conducting rounds; care has been assumed by an intensivist or hospital-based physician.
- Over the past 10 years, MCOs have prospered without buying practices; they simply have designed motivational contracts. In fact, putting a PCP on salary does *not* align incentives and may cause productivity problems.
- Some staff model HMOs have found that they cannot support the high cost associated with employing physicians and cannot necessarily provide all the revenue necessary to meet income needs; they have therefore privatized the physicians into a closely aligned true medical group.

acquiring practices are the desire to control the primary care referral base, enhancing the hospital's ability to negotiate with MCOs, and the need to prevent a competing hospital from acquiring the practices. Hospitals also hope that, by controlling primary care practices, they will be in a better position to obtain and successfully manage capitation.

Private or proprietary PPMs are also acquiring practices. Usually organized on a for-profit basis, PPMs are frequently able to achieve more efficient management and economies of scale, thereby producing a profit while maintaining physician income. These PPMs, like hospitals, see practice acquisitions as giving them a stronger negotiating position, at least when the company represents a substantial part of the physician marketplace. Many of these companies are also seeking capitation contracts, but in general they desire to cut out the hospital from any profit and control. PPMs are also discussed in Chapter 4.

Physician practices are also in the market to purchase or merge with other practices, with the goal of becoming sizeable, independent medical groups. Large groups provide for increased coverage of clinical conditions and back-up (such as on-call responsibilities). More important from a managed care standpoint, large groups, especially primary care groups or multispecialty groups with strong primary care, have an increased negotiating strength and a greater ability

to accept risk (as discussed in Chapter 9). Large groups also tend not to want to share profits with hospitals, although joint ventures or other sharing between large groups and hospitals certainly does occur.

As described in Chapter 3, HMOs have historically relied on contracting with private physicians (in open panels), contracting with large medical groups (in group and network models), or employing physicians directly through recruiting efforts (in staff models). HMOs are now acquiring practices as well, as in open panel plans becoming mixed models through practice acquisition or group and staff model plans absorbing practices into existing structures. HMOs are acquiring practices for several reasons. The HMO may need to expand its delivery system to meet access needs, the acquired group may bring rapid increases in membership, or (not insignificant) the HMO may wish to prevent other parties from increasing their negotiating leverage at the HMO's expense. The ability of the HMO to manage the culture clash is often a challenge.

Although high demand for primary care services tends to create a seller's market, hospitals must pay only fair market value or run the risk of violating private inurement guidelines (if not for profit) and fraud and abuse regulations (for any type of hospital); see Chapter 56 for a discussion of this problem. Nonhospitals do not have such restrictions but still need to valuate practices and determine whether it is worth it to overpay. Practice acquisition has a bell-shaped curve. After a relatively short period, most desirable practices are aligned or purchased, at which point a physician-based strategy changes from an acquisition to a recruiting strategy.

Table 5–2 Health Care Systems Owning /Managing Group Practices

Type of System	Number of Owned Practices	
	1993	1994
For Profit	48	99
Religious	364	604
Secular (Not for profit)*	295	416
Overall change 1993–1994	57.4%	

* Includes other system types not shown.

Source: Reprinted with permission from *Modern Healthcare.* Copyright Crain Communications, Inc. 740 N. Rush St., Chicago, IL 60611.

Pitfalls of Physician Practice Acquisition

Beyond the problems of private inurement and fraud and abuse violations discussed in Chapter 56, there are some common problems encountered when organizations acquire physician practices. The first is the recognition that the ability to manage those practices is often not present in an insurer or even a hospital because that is not its core business competence. Also, it is distressingly common that, once a practice is acquired, productivity is sharply reduced, particularly if the physicians are guaranteed an income regardless of how well the practice is performing. The issue of physician compensation when one moves from a private practice setting to an organizational setting, especially when managed care makes up a large component, is a complex one and is addressed in Chapter 10.

Acquiring a large number of physician practices provides a remarkable ability to lose money if the endeavor is not properly managed. Maintaining physician income, investing in improvements in administrative infrastructure, and managing risk are serious activities. If practice acquisition has been carried out to obtain capitation, then the risk associated with that capitation must be managed or even more money can be lost.

An acquisition strategy requires a real commitment by the organization. If the organization does not achieve a critical mass of practices, then a great deal of capital is tied up for questionable value. Even in the event that critical mass is not achieved, however, the organization may be able to parlay a partially adequate network into a reasonable deal with an IDS that has the other parts. If that is not possible, then the organization may need to consider selling practices later in the context of a broader transaction.

An additional pitfall in physician practice acquisition is the inappropriate acquisition of varying types of physicians in surplus for the delivery system. Table 5–3 serves as a reference for physician need by specialty in *advanced* managed care markets.

Acquisition of Hospitals and Institutions by MCOs

Acquisition of hospitals by MCOs is still relatively uncommon but not unheard of, and certainly many established HMOs, such as Kaiser Permanente in California, have owned hospitals for a long period of time. Hospital acquisition is obviously a much larger event than physician

Table 5–3 Enrollment Required per Specialists

Specialty	Enrollment
Medical	
Allergy	76,923
Cardiology	35,088
Dermatology	40,000
Endocrinology	125,000
Gastroenterology	66,667
Hematology/oncology	52,632
Infectious disease	117,647
Nephrology	125,000
Pulmonary disease	74,074
Rheumatology	181,818
Surgical	
Obstetrics/gynecology	9,615
General surgery	16,219
Neurosurgery	117,647
Ophthalmology	27,397
Orthopedics	16,393
Otolaryngology	32,258
Plastic surgery	285,714
Thoracic surgery	1,000,000
Urology	33,333
Hospital Based	
Radiology	12,821
Anesthesiology	13,793
Pathology	32,258
Other	
Psychiatry	20,833
Emergency medicine	15,873
Neurology	83,333

Source: Reprinted with permission from J.P. Weiner, "Forecasting the Effects of Health Reform on U.S. Physician Workforce Requirements: Evidence From HMO Staffing Patterns, *JAMA,* Vol. 272, No. 3, pp. 222–230, © 1994, American Medical Association.

practice acquisition. The capital requirements are obviously higher because, if the hospital is profitable, then the price is high and if the hospital is unprofitable, then capital requirements in the future will be high. Rarely does enough management expertise exist in an insurer or HMO to deal with the problems of hospital management, so that the MCO runs a higher than normal risk of failing to manage the hospital properly. Also, it must be noted that several group and staff model HMOs have elected to sell hospitals that they once owned and have likewise elected not to buy or build hospitals in expansion markets despite a history of owning their own hospitals.

Before even considering hospital acquisition, the MCO needs to decide that the hospital or hospital system adds critically needed capabilities that are unavailable in a more cost-effective way. If the MCO does acquire a hospital, what effect will this have on other hospitals with which the MCO currently contracts? Will it be seen as a competitive threat? Will it have a negative effect on contracts already in place? Will it influence a hospital-based IDS's decision to enter the insurance business?

Acquisition of Other Types of Providers

In unusual circumstances, an MCO may consider acquiring specialized providers, such as pharmacy, laboratory, radiology, rehabilitation, home care, and so forth. It is uncommon for MCOs to pursue such acquisitions because the MCO is usually able to achieve far greater savings through capitation and deep discounts in contractual arrangements. It may be worthwhile, however, if the MCO is unable to negotiate a favorable contract.

DE NOVO START-UP OF PRACTICES

Beyond provider acquisition, there is an increasingly common strategy to start up practices de novo or to supplement existing practice structures through recruiting and expansion.* A number of insurance companies are starting primary care practices in key urban areas, building out facilities, and recruiting PCPs. Although the focus is managed care, the practices are often also expected to generate FFS income from other sources, at least initially. It is unknown if insurer-managed practices will prove to be a durable model. In addition, most hospitals are ac-

---

* No discussion of building new hospitals in a managed care environment is provided because there is already an oversupply of hospital beds, and it makes little sense to build a new one except to replace an existing one.

tively recruiting PCPs for the same reasons they wish to acquire practices.

The cost of starting a practice is only slightly less than that of acquiring one because an existing practice has a revenue stream. The revenue stream from an existing, acquired practice may not be stable, however. For example, when an insurer purchases a practice, that practice's contracts with competing health plans are unlikely to be renewed. Furthermore, dramatic reductions in the productivity of acquired practices often occur and may make "building" less expensive if the physicians can be fully utilized in 12 to 18 months.

PROVIDERS BECOMING LICENSED HMOs

On the opposite end of the spectrum of practice acquisition is the desire by many provider systems to become licensed health plans. Provider-based preferred provider organizations (PPOs) are quite common, provider-based HMOs less so.

When a provider-sponsored HMO is created, emotions are often the driver. Physicians and hospital executives are often angry about corporate salaries and shareholder profits in proprietary HMOs, believing that the money should be put into medical care instead. There is also a highly naive belief that HMO "interference" adds little value, and there exists a clear lack of understanding of the complexities of the business, including a lack of recognition of how HMOs have driven down the cost of medical care. Coupled with this, provider-sponsored plans often perform little or no market research, assuming that they will simply be able to access the market based on the quality reputation of their system.

There are positive reasons for provider-sponsored plans to come into existence as well. There is a growing belief that perhaps capitation is acceptable, and in fact capitation may be seen as a way to get the profit in the risk. There is less recognition that there *is* a lot of risk (after all, it is referred to as the assumption of risk, not the assumption of profit).

Provider-sponsored HMOs have had a poor track record. There are several common reasons for past (and some future) failures. Adverse selection has been a problem for provider-sponsored plans because a patient is always a member, but not vice versa. In other words, provider-sponsored plans often attract existing patients, particularly patients who are high utilizers of medical services, but may not have as much success attracting new members who have no particular medical needs and who are therefore more likely to choose a health plan based on cost.

Many provider-sponsored plans have had mixed success at changing a predominantly FFS mentality in their network. In other words, many of the physicians in such plans have tended to continue to practice in a way more conducive to revenue maximization under FFS than to controlling cost, often because provider-sponsored plans have continued to use FFS as the predominant method of reimbursement.

Finally, provider-sponsored HMOs have had a decreased ability to manage physicians effectively or lower costs. The reasons for this are many, but they include the political nature of the governance structure, a dominance of the delivery system by specialists, and the large and often nonselective nature of the physician panels. Also, often the same physician who is causing serious utilization problems for the HMO is also providing a great deal of FFS revenue to the hospital through high utilization in non-HMO patients.

Even if provider-sponsored HMOs are able to overcome the problems of the past, they face new risks. As discussed in Chapter 56, if a hospital is the sponsor (or provides funds to the plan), it runs the risk of violating private inurement (if it is not for profit) and federal fraud and abuse regulations. For example, if an HMO that is jointly owned by a hospital and physicians goes into a deficit position and the hospital simply covers the losses while keeping the physicians whole, it is possible that the Internal Revenue Service would consider that a violation.

A provider-sponsored plan, especially one sponsored by a hospital, must carefully gauge the reaction of contracting MCOs to the IDS's becoming a direct competitor. There are now numerous examples of HMOs canceling or not renewing contracts with hospitals because the HMO did not want to subsidize a new competitor. This is most characteristic of heavily penetrated managed care markets.

Although the track record of provider-sponsored plans has been poor, some provider-sponsored HMOs are now succeeding. These HMOs frequently develop an arm's length relationship with the provider system, operating as a business in their own right. Successful provider-sponsored HMOs find that, to manage health care costs, they must adopt effective, HMO-like management of utilization, quality, and access. In other words, there is less the elimination of the middle man than the recreation of it.

JOINT VENTURES BETWEEN PROVIDERS AND HEALTH PLANS

Joint ventures between providers and licensed health plans are a potentially effective way to approach the marketplace. Well thought out joint ventures recognize that each party has domain expertise in a defined activity, and by combining strengths the new entity created by the joint venture can bring synergy to the marketplace. There are numerous issues that must be resolved and continually managed, however, if such joint ventures are to succeed.

The first issue to resolve is who is actually going to be in the joint venture. There are multiple possible combinations of organizations. On the health plan side, there are insurance companies, BCBS plans, PPOs, and HMOs. On the provider side, there are hospital-based IDSs, physician-only organizations, and hospitals as standalone organizations.

Health Plans

A provider system needs to look at the type of health plan with which it wishes to partner and understand the pros and cons. HMOs offer resident expertise in utilization management techniques and unique aspects of marketing in a managed care environment. An existing HMO license provides far faster access to the market than if a health plan or insurer must file for licensure and spend the time going through the licensure process. As discussed earlier, however, an HMO that is large and successful may feel no compelling need to partner with a provider system except under special circumstances.

Insurance companies generally fall into three broad categories: those companies that specialize in the large market (i.e., sell insurance to large companies), companies that specialize in the small group and individual market, and regional companies that service a specific region of the country. Provider systems need to look at those characteristics as they assess a potential partner. For example, an insurer specializing in the large group market may be able to deliver a large block of business through several large employers; conversely, a large group insurer may have relatively little market share and may not realistically be able to penetrate a market. An insurer that specializes in small group business may have excellent relationships with brokers that will increase market exposure; conversely, such an insurer may rely so heavily on medical underwriting to exclude bad risk that the product languishes in the market. A regional carrier is in many ways well suited to partnering with a provider system because it already has good market penetration and does not get distracted by concerns in distant locations; conversely, a regional carrier may have little expertise in managed care or may choose to exit the health insurance business altogether (while remaining in the life and property–casualty business).

BCBS plans have been relatively aggressive in forming joint ventures with provider systems, perhaps stemming from their roots as service plans (see Chapter 3). BCBS plans often have the capability of delivering reasonably good market share, although they may not want to share the most profitable segments of their portfolio. BCBS plans also tend to be more careful about offending the other providers in their service area, so that true partnering can sometimes be a more difficult process.

IDSs

Joint ventures between MCOs and IDSs are the most obvious pairing. The most fundamental question that the MCO needs to answer is whether the IDS has the capability of succeeding in a managed care environment. An MCO needs to feel comfortable that the IDS is capable of managing the risk. If an IDS is fully capitated and fails, the MCO suffers along with the IDS. Therefore, the IDS needs to be able to demonstrate its capabilities to manage utilization, quality, and access (especially in primary care) as well as provide and use data and properly align the financial incentives of all the parties (especially the physicians).

When approaching a joint venture, the parties need to address how the premium will be divided. One approach is to divide a percentage of premium revenue. This is a viable approach, but the parties must recognize that it is possible to transfer more risk than potential profit in such a setting. Furthermore, percentage of premium places some of the IDS's revenue under the influence of nonmedical capabilities of the health plan, the most important of these being underwriting and rating (see Chapters 43 and 44). If the rates are incorrect, a disproportionate amount of the error will be passed on to the IDS. Nevertheless, this approach has merit in that it is straightforward and places both parties subject to market pressures. Underwriting errors are most important in commercial accounts because Medicare and Medicaid revenue tends to be driven by regulation, not market forces.

Capitation is the other method of dividing revenue. Under capitation, the IDS receives fixed per member per month dollars, adjusted for age, sex, and product type, that are not influenced by rating or underwriting. A discussion of capitation is found in Chapters 9, 12, and 14.

The other critical issue is a clear understanding of the division of responsibilities. Although it would seem obvious that the IDS should provide medical services and the MCO should market and provide administration, the actual division of responsibilities is not always that clear. For example, how will the administrative costs associated with medical management be treated? State regulatory bodies and outside accreditation agencies may allow a certain level of delegation of some functions from an HMO to a provider system, but they will not allow the HMO to abdicate its ultimate responsibility.

It is in the best interest of each party to be assured that the other party is carrying out its responsibilities competently and efficiently. A joint venture in which one party insists that the other party not be allowed any influence in certain activities is counterproductive from a standpoint of continuous improvement and is potentially disastrous if one of the parties is grossly incompetent, but the incompetence does not become apparent until far too late.

Physician-Only Organizations

There are many organizations that are physician only. These organizations include independent practice associations (IPAs), large group practices, and proprietary MSOs (all these types of organizations are discussed in Chapter 4). Many physician-only organizations expressly wish to exclude the hospital from any joint venture or partnership, believing that there will be superior financial performance if hospital services are simply purchased on the medical spot market through per diems (see Chapter 14).

If the physician organization is able to bring critical mass to a delivery system and has sufficient capital and resident management expertise, then it may well be able to deliver on its promise. Some physician organizations, particularly in the western United States, have grown quite large and are able to provide good access to members as well as strong internal management. In advanced situations, these groups manage the entire medical expense portion of the premium (i.e., 80 to 85 percent of the total premium revenue).

Hospital(s)-Only Organizations

A joint venture between an MCO and a hospital on a standalone basis is an unusual configuration because physicians are absolutely critical to success, and independent physicians may be suspicious of a hospital–payer axis. In a rural area, however, the hospital may be ready for a joint venture, but the physicians are still disorganized and not inclined to take an aggressive role. In such instances, the hospital and the MCO may allow for future participation by physicians.

For a joint venture between an MCO and a hospital sans physician partners to be successful in an urban area, the hospital needs to employ the physicians directly, and to have a critical mass of physicians, especially PCPs. If there are insufficient numbers of physicians or an inadequate geographic coverage, then the hospital will have a difficult time living up to its obligations in a joint venture. Alternatively, the hospital (or MCO) must have a concrete ability to deliver a physician network on a contractual basis (mimicking an open panel HMO; see Chapters 3 and 8), which may be somewhat more difficult when the physicians do not feel part of the ownership or governance of the joint venture.

Ownership in a For-Profit Joint Venture

Ownership issues in a joint venture need to be considered carefully. It is not always easy to change once it is set. Corporate structures that may be used include:

- a not-for-profit corporation
- a not-for-profit taxable corporation
- a for-profit corporation
- a limited liability corporation
- a limited liability partnership
- a general partnership
- a limited partnership

In an equity type of organization, the joint venture must address whether each party will hold equal or unequal percentages of equity. It is not unusual for there to be an unequal distribution of equity, with one party contributing more resources or having greater negotiating leverage. In those situations, and even in situations with equal ownership or control, the partners must address the role of supermajority rights to all parties. Examples include changing the bylaws and allowing new partners to join.

Method of Distribution of Profits and Losses

The joint venture must pay extra attention to how it will distribute profits *and* losses, and equal attention must be paid to each possibility. As a general rule, there is a requirement for risk and equity position to be related. Some joint ventures, particularly from the provider's perspective, seek to have no profits at all because it is their goal to distribute all the income to the providers directly rather than face double taxation (i.e., the income is taxed as profit to the organization, and then each provider is in turn taxed on his or her income).

What about funding losses? Although insurers and HMOs have a straightforward way of funding losses, provider systems may not. There is frequently a strong desire by the physicians to enjoy profits, but the organization must have a realistic view of the ability of physicians to accept a high level of loss. In other words, the physicians' desire to receive profit does not match their ability to absorb significant losses. There are significant problems with hospitals protecting physicians from loss while allowing them to share in profit, including the dangers of private inurement (in the case of not-for-profit hospitals) and potential fraud and abuse violations. Examples of approaches to funding losses may include a hospital choosing to retain earnings versus distributing the wealth to provide a cushion for loss, carrying losses forward, or funding losses through interest-bearing notes payable. The mechanism for funding losses needs to be clearly understood before those losses are incurred. See Chapter 56 for further discussion of the legal risks inherent in this issue.

When profits or surpluses are shared, how are funds distributed to providers? Possible channels for distribution include the following:

- through the IDS
- through the hospital(s)
- via a corporate shell
- directly with individual hospitals
- through the physicians
- via an IPA or other shell
- directly with individual physicians

Responsibility versus Authority To Carry Out Designated Functions

Although on its surface a joint venture would seem naturally to assign roles to each party, the parties have a vested interest in ensuring that the other party carries out its responsibilities effectively and competently. There is a clear role for mutual oversight and reporting. Furthermore, some states will not allow an HMO to delegate final responsibility for key functions. For example, a provider system may assume responsibility for managing utilization and quality, but the HMO may retain final authority on authorizations and require regular reports on quality and utilization statistics. Conversely, the provider system may want assurances that the HMO is performing its underwriting duties competently and is receiving the budgeted per member per month premium revenue.

Exclusivity Issues

Whether a joint venture is an exclusive relationship is often a difficult area to negotiate. Usually each party, in a form of corporate polyandry or polygamy, demands that the other party be exclusive with it but requires the right to enter into deals with other parties. This has some reason behind it. It is not common for a single payer to be able to provide enough business to a provider system to make up for loss of business from other payers, and it is equally uncommon for a provider system to be able to provide adequate geographic coverage to an MCO's total medical service area.

The parties may negotiate exclusivity based on a single product (e.g., an HMO product) or to a confined geographic area (e.g., a defined set of ZIP codes). The parties may also agree that they cannot be totally exclusive but will limit other similar arrangements to no more than two to four other parties. Attention must be paid to possible antitrust problems in this area as well (see Chapters 56 and 57). An example in schematic form of one such dual identity is illustrated in Figure 5–1.

Prenuptial Agreements, or Planning for Divorce

None of the parties should enter into a joint venture or partnership with the belief that it will fail. After the parties have resolved how to divide up the profits, negotiations often halt. It is wise and necessary, however, to plan for the possibility that either the new organization will fail or the parties will choose to part company.

If failure is defined as insolvency, then it is likely that the plan either has been seized by the state insurance department or has been sold to a larger (and more competent) organization. A plan can fail without becoming insolvent, however, by simply languishing in the market or facing continual losses that the parties no longer wish to fund. In that event, the parties may agree to dissolve or sell the organization, and some attention should be paid to how that decision gets made and the rights and responsibilities of each party once that direction is set.

It is also possible for the parties to come to a point where they no longer wish to continue with each other. The plan may be performing poorly, but one party wants to continue while the other wants to quit; or the parties may have had a bellyful of each other and no longer want to be in business together. The parties should negotiate under what circumstances a party can leave the business, under what terms (e.g., under what circumstances could they simply walk away, pay money, receive money, and so forth), and how disputes will be resolved other than by using the courts.

Finally, it is possible that one or more parties to the joint venture has cashing out as its main goal. It must be decided ahead of time how that can occur. For example, does the other party

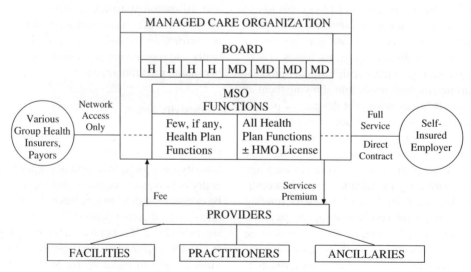

Figure 5–1 Schematic of a dual-identity model.

have the right of first refusal? Does it have the right to veto or approve a potential acquirer? How will the fair market value be set? These and many other issues should be agreed to before it is too late.

CONCLUSION

Evolution of the American health care system is occurring rapidly, and there are numerous opportunities to enter into relationships with providers that were not possible until now. Some of these new organizations will succeed, some will fail, but an understanding of the issues will help improve the odds of success. As provider systems and MCOs enter into these new relationships, it is worthwhile remembering the advice of fictional detective Nero Wolfe to his faithful dogsbody Archie Goodwin: Use your intelligence guided by your experience. And keep your sense of humor; it helps.

Suggested Reading

Coddington, D.C., Moore, K.D., and Fisher, E.A. 1994. *Integrated Health Care: Reorganizing the Physician, Hospital, and Health Plan Relationship*. Englewood, Colo.: Center for Research in ambulatory Health Care Administration/MGMA.

Herzlinger, R.E. 1992. *Creating New Health Care Ventures*. Gaithersburg, Md.: Aspen Publishers.

Korenchuk, K.M. 1994. *Transforming the Delivery of Health Care: The Integration Process* (2nd ed.). Englewood, Colo.: Center for Research in Ambulatory Health Care Administration/MGMA.

Taylor, R. 1995. Health Plans and Providers: How New Partnerships are Evolving in a Volatile Environment. *Medical Interface* 8 (1): 95–100.

Traska, M.R. 1996. *Managed Care Strategies 1996*. New York, N.Y.: Faulkner & Gray.

Chapter 6

Elements of the Management Control and Governance Structure

Peter R. Kongstvedt

It is not really possible to deal comprehensively with the topic of the elements of management control structure in one chapter of a book. There are myriad courses, texts, and other learning resources available to the reader that deal with the basic elements of management. For the purposes of this chapter, it is assumed that the reader has a working knowledge of business and management, so that certain fundamental aspects of management are not discussed here (e.g., how to read a balance sheet, write a job description, or construct an organizational chart). What follows in this chapter is a brief overview of certain management control elements as they pertain specifically to managed care. Detailed discussions of these activities are the topics of much of this book.

Ironically, there is no standardization of management governance or control structure in managed care; for example, the function, or even the very presence, of a board of directors will vary from plan to plan. The function of key officers or managers, as well as of committees, will likewise vary depending on the type of organization, the ownership, and the motivations and skills of the individuals involved. Because each plan will construct its own management control structure to suit its needs, only a few of the most common elements are described in this chapter.

BOARD OF DIRECTORS

Many, although not all, types of managed care plans will have a board of directors. The make-up and function of the board will be influenced by many factors (discussed below), but the board has the final responsibility for governance of the operation. Examples of plans or managed care operations that would not necessarily have their own boards include the following:

- preadmission certification and medical case management operations of insurance companies
- preferred provider organizations (PPOs) developed by large insurance companies
- PPOs developed for single employers by an insurance company
- employer-sponsored/developed plans (PPOs and precertification operations)
- health maintenance organizations (HMOs) or exclusive provider organizations set up as a line of business of an insurance company

These operations or plans are subsidiaries of larger companies; those companies do have boards of directors, but their boards are involved with oversight of the entire company, not the subsidiary operation. PPOs or HMOs that are divisions of insurance companies may be required to list a board on their licensure forms, but that board may have little real operational role.

Board Make-Up

All HMOs have boards, although not all those boards are particularly functional. This is especially true for HMOs that are part of large national companies. Each local HMO is incorporated and required to have a board, but it is not uncommon for the chains to use the same two corporate officers (perhaps with one local representative; see below) as the board for every HMO. Again, the board fulfills its legal function and obligation, but the actual operation of the HMO is controlled through the management structure of the company rather than through a direct relationship between the plan director and the board.

There are legal requirements for boards, particularly for HMOs. Those requirements are spelled out in each state's laws and regulations; for federally qualified HMOs, there are federal regulations as well. A common (although recently less so) requirement for HMOs is the necessity for member representation; new start-up operations may be exempt from that requirement for a period of time. Many state regulations require that at least one third of the board be members of the plan. In the case of the national HMO companies, that often translates into one individual who meets periodically with two corporate officers for brief board meetings. In the case of community-based HMOs, that may mean that multiple board seats (up to one third) are held by members.

Board make-up will also vary depending on whether the plan is for profit, in which case the owners' or shareholders' representatives may hold the majority of seats, or not for profit, in which case there will be broader community representation. Some not-for-profit health plans are organized as cooperatives, in which case the board members are all members of the plan. Not-for-profit plans that are not cooperatives are generally best served by board members who are truly independent and have no potential conflicts of interest; provider-sponsored not-for-profit plans may be restricted to no more than 20 percent of board seats being held by providers. The use of outside directors rather than plan officers as directors in any case will be dictated by local events, company bylaws, and laws and regulations (including the tax code for not-for-profit health plans). Provider-sponsored for-profit plans may have majority representation by providers and so must take special precautions to avoid antitrust problems.

Function of the Board

As stated earlier, the function of the board is governance: overseeing and maintaining final responsibility for the plan. In a real sense, the buck stops with the board. Final approval authority of corporate bylaws rests with the board. It is the bylaws that govern the basic structure of power and control not only of the plan officers but of the board itself.

The fiduciary responsibility of the board in an operating plan is of paramount importance. General oversight of the profitability or reserve status rests with the board, as do oversight and approval of significant fiscal events, such as a major acquisition or a significant expenditure. In a for-profit plan, the board has fiduciary responsibility to protect the interests of the stockholders.

Legal responsibilities of the board also may include review of reports and document signing. For example, a board officer may be required to sign the quarterly financial report to the state regulatory agency, the board chairperson may be required to sign any acquisition documents, and the board is responsible for the veracity of financial statements to stockholders.

Setting and approving policy represent another common function of an active board. This function may be as broad as determining the overall policy of using a gatekeeper system, or it may be as detailed as approving organizational charts and reporting structures. Although most policies and procedures will be the responsibility of the plan officers, an active board may set a policy regarding what operational policies must be brought to the board for approval or change.

In HMOs and many other types of managed care plans, the board has a special responsibility for oversight of the quality management (QM) program and for the quality of care delivered to members. Usually this responsibility is discharged through board (or board subcommittee) review of the QM documentation (including the overall QM plan and regular reports on findings and activities) and through feedback to the medical director and plan QM committee.

In freestanding plans, the board also has responsibility for hiring the chief executive officer (CEO) of the plan and for reviewing that officer's performance. The board in such plans often sets the CEO's compensation package, and the CEO reports to the board.

Active boards generally have committees to take up certain functions. Common board committees may include an executive committee (for rapid access to decision making and confidential discussions), a compensation committee (to set general compensation guidelines for the plan, set the CEO's compensation, and approve and issue stock options), a finance committee (to review financial results, approve budgets, set and approve spending authorities, review the annual audit, review and approve outside funding sources, and so forth), and a QM committee (as noted above).

Board Liability Issues

Any board faces the problem of liability for its actions. This is especially so in a board made up of outside directors and in the board of a not-for-profit organization. This is not to say that a board must always make correct decisions (it may make an incorrect decision, but it must do so in good faith), although being right is usually better than being wrong. Rather, a board should act in ways to reduce its own liability, and such actions will also be consistent with good governance. It is beyond the scope of this chapter to discuss fully board liability and prevention, but a few general comments may be made. Examples given in this section do not constitute legal opinions but are simply provided to help illustrate possible issues. The reader is urged to consult competent legal counsel as needed to understand board liability fully.

It is of paramount importance that board members exercise their duties to the benefit of the plan and not in their own self-interest. Con-

flict of interest is a difficult problem and can surface more readily than one might suppose. Examples of such conflicts would include actions that preferentially profit the board members, actions that are more in the interest of the board members than the plan (e.g., influencing how services are purchased by the plan), taking advantage of proprietary information to profit, and so forth. It is certainly possible for an action to benefit both the plan and the board members, but extra care must be taken to ensure that the action is first in the interest of the plan. In many cases, a board member with an obvious conflict of interest will abstain from voting on an issue or may even absent himself or herself from discussing the issue at all.

The board must also take care that it operates within the confines of the plan bylaws. In other words, the board cannot take any action that is not allowed in the bylaws of the organization. Examples of such actions might include paying an individual beyond the normal reimbursement policies, entering into an unrelated line of business, and so forth.

Board members must also perform their duties with some measure of diligence. For example, if plan management provides board members with information they need to decide properly on a course of action or a policy, it is incumbent on the board members to understand what is being provided and to ask however many questions are necessary to gain an adequate understanding to make an informed decision. Related to this is a duty actually to attend board meetings; although this would seem obvious, some board members may be so lax in their attendance as to provide virtually no governance or oversight. In any event, thorough documentation of the decision-making process is valuable, and those records should be maintained for an appropriate length of time.

As mentioned earlier, the board's primary responsibility is to the plan or organization and to the shareholders in the event that the plan is for profit. The board may also have some measure of responsibility to other individuals or organizations if the plan acts in such a way as to harm another party illegally. For example, if a health plan knowingly sets a policy not to perform credentialing of physicians and a panel physician commits malpractice, it is possible that the board (which either agreed to the policy or failed to change it) may have some liability.

Regardless of how the board is made up, it is important for there to be adequate director and officer liability insurance as well as insurance for errors and omissions. The need for such insurance may be attenuated by certain provisions in the company's or plan's bylaws holding the board members and officers harmless from liability. This issue requires review by legal counsel. The reader is referred to Chapter 38 for an in-depth discussion of risk management.

KEY MANAGEMENT POSITIONS

The roles and titles of the key managers in any plan will vary depending on the type of plan, its legal organization, its line of business, its complexity, whether it is freestanding or a satellite of another operation, and the local needs and talent. There is little consistency in this area from plan to plan. How each key role is defined (or even whether it will be present at all) is strictly up to the management of each plan. What follows, then, is a general overview of certain key roles.

Executive Director/CEO

Most plans have at least one key manager. Whether that individual is called a CEO, an executive director, a general manager, or a plan manager is a function of the items mentioned earlier in this chapter (e.g., scope of authority, reporting structure of the company, and the like). For purposes of discussion, this key manager will be referred to as an executive director.

The executive director is usually responsible for all the operational aspects of the plan, although that is not always the case. For example, some large companies (e.g., insurance companies or national HMO chains) have marketing reporting vertically to a regional marketing di-

rector rather than through the plan manager. A few companies take that to the extreme of having each functional area reporting vertically to regional managers rather than having all operations coordinated at the local level by a single manager; thus reporting is a function of the overall environment, and there is little standardization in the industry.

In freestanding plans and traditional HMOs, the executive director is responsible for all areas. The other officers and key managers report to the executive director, who in turn reports to the board (or to a regional manager in the case of national companies). The executive director also has responsibility for general administrative operations and public affairs.

Medical Director

Almost by definition, managed care plans will have a medical director. Whether that position is a full-time manager or a community physician who comes in a few hours per week is determined by the needs of the plan. The medical director usually has responsibility for provider relations, provider recruiting, QM, utilization management, and medical policy.

Some plans (e.g., simple PPOs) may only use the medical director, or a medical consultant, to review claims, perhaps to approve physician applications, and to review patterns of utilization. The spectrum of medical director involvement parallels the intensity of medical management activities. Usually the medical director reports to the executive director.

As a plan grows in size, particularly if it is a complex plan such as an HMO, the need for the medical director to leverage time becomes crucial. If the medical director gets bogged down in day-to-day minutiae, his or her ability to provide leadership in the critical areas of utilization, quality, network management, and medical policy becomes dramatically reduced.

There are two approaches commonly employed to deal with this problem. The most common is bringing in an associate medical director. An associate medical director usually starts as a part-time position, but as the plan grows in size and complexity the position may evolve into a full-time function, and in fact there may be many associate medical directors in large plans. The role of the associate medical director is often defined as a subset of the overall duties of the medical director; for example, this person may focus primarily on utilization management or QM. This concept of adding qualified staff is not different from basic management practices for any specialized activity, but health plan managers are occasionally slow to realize the value of adding physician managers when they may be quick to realize the value of adding multiple layers of management in other operational areas.

The second approach to the issue of dealing with medical management in a large plan is to decentralize certain functions. For example, in a closed panel plan (e.g., a staff model HMO or a multisite group practice) it is common practice to assign management responsibilities to a physician at each geographic site. This on-site physician manager may have responsibility for utilization and staffing at the site or other duties as necessary. In an open panel setting (e.g., an open panel HMO), the network may be divided up into regions, and associate medical directors may be assigned responsibilities for designated regions. In either case, management must be realistic about the time and resources required for these associate medical directors to do their jobs. The skills, motivations, and compensation for decentralized or delegated medical management must be carefully thought through, and of course the medical director retains ultimate accountability.

Finance Director

In freestanding plans or large operations, it is common to have a finance director or chief financial officer. That individual is generally responsible for oversight of all financial and accounting operations. In some plans, that may include functions such as billing, management information services, enrollment, and underwriting as well as accounting, fiscal reporting, and

budget preparation. This position usually reports to the executive director, although once again some national companies use vertical reporting.

Marketing Director

This person is responsible for marketing the plan. Responsibility generally includes oversight of marketing representatives, advertising, client relations, and enrollment forecasting. A few plans have marketing generating initial premium rates, which are then sent to finance or underwriting for review, but that is uncommon. This position reports to the executive director or vertically, depending on the company.

Operations Director

In larger plans, it is not uncommon to have an operations director. This position usually oversees claims, management information services, enrollment, underwriting (unless finance is doing so), member services, office management, and any other traditional backroom functions. This position usually reports to the executive director.

COMMITTEES

Again, there is little consistency from plan to plan regarding committees. Nonmedical committees may be limited to the member grievance committee (see Chapter 30). Other nonmedical committees are often ad hoc, convened to meet a specific need and then dissolved. Most plans tend to have standing committees to address management issues in defined areas, but that is idiosyncratic from plan to plan.

In the medical management area, committees serve to diffuse some elements of responsibility (which can be beneficial for medical–legal reasons) and allow important input from the field into procedure and policy or even into case-specific interpretation of existing policy. These aspects are discussed in greater detail in Chapter 58.

Some examples of common medical management committees are given below. The actual formation, role, responsibility, and activity of any committee are local calls. More information about each of these areas can be found in the pertinent chapters of this book.

QM Committee

This topic is discussed in Chapter 25. This is one area where a committee is essential for oversight of the QM activity, setting of standards, review of data, feedback to providers, follow-up, and approval of sanctions. A peer review committee may be a subset of the QM committee, or it may be separate.

Credentialing Committee

This important topic is discussed in Chapters 8, 57, and 58. This committee may also be a subset of the QM committee, or it may be separate. In new plans with heavy credentialing needs, it is probably best for the committee to be separate.

Medical Advisory Committee

Many plans have a medical advisory committee, whose purpose is to review general medical management issues brought to it by the medical director. Such issues may include changes in the contract with providers, compensation, changes in authorization procedures, and so on. This committee serves as a sounding board for the medical director. Occasionally it has voting authority, but that is rare because such authority is really vested with the board.

Utilization Review Committee

This committee reviews utilization issues brought to it by the medical director. Often this committee approves or reviews policy regarding coverage. This committee is also the one that reviews utilization patterns of providers and approves or reviews the sanctioning process (for utilization reasons) against providers.

Sometimes this committee gets involved in resolving disputes between the plan and a provider regarding utilization approval and may be involved in reviewing cases for medical necessity. In large plans, this function may be further subdivided into various specialty panels for review of consultant utilization. This committee may be a subset of the medical advisory committee, or it may be freestanding.

Pharmacy and Therapeutics Committee

Plans with significant pharmacy benefits often have a pharmacy and therapeutics committee. Pharmacy is discussed in Chapter 23. This committee is usually charged with developing a formulary, reviewing changes to that formulary, and reviewing abnormal prescription utilization patterns by providers. This committee is usually freestanding.

MANAGEMENT CONTROL STRUCTURE

Control structure refers to issues such as reporting responsibility, spending (and other commitment) authority, hiring and firing, the conduct of performance evaluations of employees, and so forth. Each plan will set these up to fit its situation and needs. Although these issues are too diverse to be addressed in this chapter, a wealth of material on all these functions can be found in the general management literature.

One item that is of special significance is the monthly operating report (MOR). Most tightly run managed care plans develop an MOR to use as the basic management tool. The typical MOR reports the month- and year-to-date financial status of the plan. Those data are backed up with details regarding membership, premium revenue, other revenue, medical costs (usually total and broken out into categories such as hospital, primary care, referral care, ancillary services, and so forth), marketing costs, administrative costs, other expenses, taxes (if appropriate), and the bottom line. Results are generally reported in terms of whole dollars and per member per month. This issue is discussed in detail in Chapter 40.

How much detail is reported routinely or on an ad hoc basis is a local call. The point here is that managed care, especially in tightly run plans, is so dynamic that managers cannot wait for quarterly results. Managers must have current and reliable data from which to manage. Sutton's law dictates that you must "go where the money is," and that can only be done if the MOR tells you where to look. In the case of hospital utilization, one cannot even wait for the MOR but must have daily reporting (see Chapter 17).

Various other types of reports are described throughout this book. What reports and routine reviews a manager needs to run the business is a decision each plan must make. If the plan is not producing an MOR, however, it is probably not managing optimally.

CONCLUSION

The basic functions of governance and control in HMOs are similar to those in any business, although the specifics regarding the board of directors, plan officers, and responsibilities of key managers vary tremendously from plan to plan.

Suggested Reading

Bader, B.S. 1994. Governance of Community-Based Integrated Healthcare Delivery Systems. *Health System Leader* 1 (9): 4–12.

Coile, R.C. 1994. *The New Governance: Strategies for an Era of Health Reform.* Ann Arbor, Mich.: Health Administration Press/American College of Healthcare Executives.

Part II

The Health Care Delivery System

"When one's all right, he's prone to spite
The doctor's peaceful mission.
But when he's sick, it's loud and quick
He bawls for a physician."

Eugene Field (1850–1895)
Doctors, st. 2 [1890]

Chapter 7

Primary Care in Closed Panel Plans

Peter R. Kongstvedt

This chapter deals with issues involving primary care physicians (PCPs) in closed panel health plans, that is, group and staff model health maintenance organizations (HMOs) or large group practices in which managed care provides the majority of practice income. Although primary medical care can and is delivered by consultants, this chapter restricts its scope to PCPs.

Conventional definitions of primary care encompass internal medicine, family practice, and pediatrics. Obstetrics/gynecology (OB/GYN) is generally considered specialty care, although it is not uncommon for HMOs to allow self-referral by members to OB/GYN physicians for certain services (e.g., Pap smears). In that context, many of the comments regarding PCPs will hold equally well for OB/GYN physicians in closed panels because issues of recruiting, compensation, and so forth will be similar.

Many of the issues discussed in this chapter will also apply to large integrated delivery systems (IDSs), at least those IDSs that either employ physicians or have a tight relationship with a large medical group (see Chapter 4 for a discussion of different IDS models). Last, issues germane to primary care in closed panels may also hold relevance in open panels, particularly for private medical groups of ten or more physicians that have a significant level of managed care participation.

NEEDS ASSESSMENT

To assess a closed panel's needs for PCPs, you must look at realistic staffing ratios, availability, scope of practice, and acceptance.

Staffing Ratios

In closed panel HMOs, staffing ratios look at the number of PCPs relative to the number of members. There are significant differences in staffing ratios depending on the size of the health plan and whether there is a considerable Medicare and/or Medicaid population being served. Staffing ratios are also occasionally addressed in state regulations; for example, in Pennsylvania a minimum staffing ratio of 1 physician per 1,600 members is required. Staffing ratios will be discussed in terms of full-time equivalents (FTEs), although most closed panel plans in fact use part-time providers on their staff. There are two common units of measurement for staffing: physicians per members (e.g., 1:1,300), and physicians per 1,000 members (e.g., 0.8:1,000). This chapter will use the latter convention.

Based on research published in 1995, there appear to be some differences in staffing ratios between large and small closed panel HMOs, with the difference occurring at approximately 80,000 members. In plans with less than 80,000 members, the weighted mean PCP staffing ratio (rounded) was 0.89:1,000, with a standard deviation of 0.68; for plans with more than 80,000 members, the weighted mean PCP staffing ratio (rounded) was 0.66:1,000, with a standard deviation of 0.51. The weighted mean staffing ratio for all physicians (not just PCPs) was 2.8:1,000 for small plans and 1.2:1,000 for large plans.[1]

These data compare with data published in 1992 obtained at an earlier point in time from essentially the same sources, in which large, closed panel plans that served a primarily commercial population had an average PCP staffing ratio of 0.8:1,000 and an average physician staffing ratio of 1.3:1,000. Plans that were smaller had more than twice those ratios. In the 1992 data, the ratios per 1,000 members, by specialty type, were 0.3 for full-time general/family practice, 0.3 for internal medicine, 0.2 for pediatrics, and 0.1 for OB/GYN.[2] When one is looking solely at general pediatricians for *pediatric* enrollees (as opposed to all enrollees, which is what the other ratios look at), recent data report 0.54:1,000 for large plans and 0.79:1,000 for small plans.[3]

These figures may vary considerably from plan to plan. Some private, for-profit, closed panel plans have used primary care staffing ratios of 0.6:1,000, and some large, well-known, closed panel plans use ratios closer to 1.2:1,000.

As noted in the data, the size of a health plan has a clear impact on staffing ratios. Economies of scale are achievable in large plans. Plans that have a large medical staff also have the ability to cover clinic sites more easily, so that there is less need for overstaffing simply to ensure the presence of a provider at a site. Smaller plans not only need to ensure site coverage (assuming that they have more than one site to cover) but must staff for growth as well.

The scope of clinical practice by the PCPs has an effect on staffing. If PCPs are performing many procedures that might otherwise go out to referral specialists, there will be a need for more generous staffing. For example, if family practitioners are performing obstetrical services, some of their time will be taken up with prenatal care

and deliveries, so that greater staffing will be required to meet the primary care needs of the members.

Medicare members utilize more services, including office visits, than commercial members. Commercial enrollees younger than 65 have an average of 3.6 to 3.8 physician encounters per year, of which 2.5 are primary care visits. Medicare members average 7.0 encounters per year for Medicare risk enrollees and 6.4 encounters per year for Medicare cost enrollees[4]; these data refer to total physician encounters, not necessarily those for primary care only, and do not include encounters with nonphysicians. Nevertheless, the implications for staffing are clear: Staffing needs are greatly increased when a substantial Medicare population is served. In the previously cited study, the majority of closed panel HMOs increased their staffing ratios for Medicare members to a mean of 1.6 per 1,000 Medicare enrollees.[5]

The effect of Medicaid members is less clear. In one set of data, Medicaid HMO members received approximately 13 percent more ambulatory care and were hospitalized 52 percent more frequently than commercial members.[6] This has led at least one researcher to conclude that a Medicaid member requires 21 percent more physician time than a commercial member.[7] In one study examining actual staffing patterns in HMOs, however, plans with Medicaid members did indeed show a higher median physician-to-member ratio than plans without Medicaid members, but there was no statistical correlation with the number of physicians per 100,000 members.[8] Therefore, the need for increased staffing for HMOs with Medicaid members is likely to be higher than in a commercial population, but the degree of increase is not obvious.

Staffing ratios are useful guides for management to use when addressing recruiting needs, but they are also useful when addressing issues of efficiency and productivity. Ratios that are lean may, over time, erode the level of service and cost effectiveness of a plan. For example, if you run at 0.5:1,000 or tighter for an extended period, the stress level of the PCPs may rise as they try to meet the demand for services by members. When that happens, the harried PCPs will have less time and patience for evaluating problems and will be inclined to refer the member to a consultant to deal with any but the most routine care. Furthermore, the attitude of the PCPs will degenerate and be reflected back to members during office visits.

Ratios that are significantly richer may over time become an insupportable overhead cost. If overstaffing continues for too long, productivity could take a nose dive, and efforts to improve it will be met with resistance. Once low productivity levels become institutionalized, it is often quite difficult to improve them because you are demanding more work for no increase in compensation, and the usual result is the retort that plan management's demands for greater productivity will have a serious negative impact on patient care quality. A more detailed discussion of productivity is presented later in this chapter.

Availability

The availability of high-quality physicians may have an impact on staffing ratios. Although there are many things that may affect physician availability, two important elements are the cycle of physician training and the desirability of your practice situation.

Virtually all residency programs begin and end in midsummer. Usually a resident fresh out of training will want to decompress for a few weeks or more, so that physicians from training programs often are not available to start until August or September. Even for physicians a few years out of training, it is not uncommon for them to have signed 1-year contracts, so that they also may not be available until the late summer. If a physician has been out of training for a number of years and is in private practice or is coming out of the military, there is much more variability in availability.

If you are in a situation where there is sufficient variation in physician availability to make recruiting difficult, you may have to overstaff in the summer and fall to be able to serve projected

increases in membership in January and February because many open enrollments occur in the fall.

Scope of Practice

The scope of clinical skills that the physicians in your group have will also affect your staffing needs. If the PCPs perform a large variety of procedures or if supervision of midlevel practitioners is required (e.g., family practitioners performing routine obstetric procedures, internists performing stress tests and reading electrocardiograms, or PCPs supervising physician assistants), there will be an incremental decrease in the amount of time available for regular office care.

You may wish to recruit a PCP with special skills rather than recruit a consultant, and this too may have an effect on your staffing ratios. For example, your PCPs may be sending all the routine flexible proctosigmoidoscopies out to a gastroenterologist. If your plan is large enough, you may consider recruiting specifically for an internist skilled in that procedure, even though it would alter your staffing ratios slightly downward. The same argument may exist for stress testing or a number of other high-volume procedures that a well-trained PCP can perform as well as a consultant.

One concern with this idea, which applies equally to adding consultants (see Chapter 12), is that once such a resource becomes easily available, utilization tends to rise. The service is often seen as free, and other PCPs will tend to request it more readily. Furthermore, if a physician truly enjoys doing the procedure, he or she may tend to recommend it more often as an unconscious means of displacing other less enjoyable clinical activities (e.g., routine health assessments).

Acceptance

Your needs may be affected by the acceptability of your current PCPs by your target markets, the medical community as a whole, and your membership. For example, you may require the addition of only one PCP according to the staffing ratios, but your plan is located in a community where family physicians are not generally accepted. To provide adequate coverage, you may have to consider adding an internist and a pediatrician, even though it ostensibly makes your staffing ratios too high for half the year.

NONPHYSICIAN PROVIDERS

Closed panel plans are more likely to use nonphysician providers (i.e., physician assistants, advanced practice nurses, nurse practitioners, clinical nurse specialists, or certified nurse-midwives) to deliver some medical care to their members. In a previously cited study, 65 percent of closed panel plans reported the use of nonphysician providers, with a mean ratio of 0.08:1,000.[9] In a 1992 report, fully 86 percent of closed panel plans reported using nonphysician providers (compared with 48 percent of open panel plans), 52 percent of plans used physician assistants, 52 percent of plans used nurse practitioners, and 28 percent of plans used certified nurse-midwives.[10]

Well-qualified nonphysician practitioners are generally found to be a great asset to a plan in that they are able to deliver excellent primary care, provide more health maintenance and health promotion services, tend to spend more time with patients, and receive generally good acceptance from most members. In many states, nurse practitioners (and, in a smaller number of states, physician assistants) have the authority to write prescriptions.

Nonphysician providers may also play an important role in the management of chronically ill patients. They may provide the primary locus of coordination of care or case management for patients with diseases such as chronic asthma, diabetes, and the like. In a similar vein, nonphysician providers may take a key role in managing high-risk patients, using practice protocols for prevention and health maintenance in this population. Certified nurse-midwives not only may provide services for routine deliveries but may in fact provide primary gynecological care using practice guidelines and protocols.

Most plan managers use slightly different staffing ratios for nonphysician providers than for PCPs. For example, a nonphysician provider may be considered between 0.5 and 0.8 FTE for PCP staffing purposes. The primary reasons for this are the tendency for nonphysician providers to spend more time with their patients (which often accounts for their popularity with their patients), the fact that nonphysician providers generally do not make hospital rounds and are less likely to perform procedures, and the need for the nonphysician provider to staff cases with a physician. The physician who staffs such cases may also have a slightly diminished productivity strictly from the point of view of personally seeing patients.

The availability of nonphysician providers varies widely from state to state and correlates strongly with a favorable state practice environment.[11] The practice environment includes such variables as the ability to write prescriptions, the ability to practice in a (relatively) autonomous manner for certain situations, and the ability to receive direct reimbursement. Many elements of the practice environment will also have an impact on a nonphysician provider's efficiency.

RECRUITING

Practice Attributes

The desirability of your practice opportunity clearly affects the availability of physicians. Geographic location, climate, plan size and history, reputation, and life style potential will all have an impact. The presence of other well-qualified and congenial physicians on your staff will also improve your recruiting potential because a collegial atmosphere with support from fellow physicians is an important element in making your plan desirable from the PCP's standpoint.

Table 7–1 lists attributes deemed desirable in a study of physicians at the Lovelace Clinic in New Mexico. It is likely that any HMO or medi-

Table 7–1 Practice Attribute Rating by Physicians Employed at Lovelace Clinic, New Mexico (*N* = 76)

Practice Attribute	Mean*	Standard Deviation	Rating as Very or Extremely Important (%)
Quality of care provided	4.66	0.58	95
Amount of clinical time spent on patients	4.19	0.68	84
Number of hours worked per week	4.18	0.78	80
Interaction with colleagues	4.14	0.69	80
Professional autonomy	4.00	0.79	77
Salary	4.01	0.77	76
Geographic location	4.04	0.84	75
Call schedule	4.08	0.87	74
Nonsalary fringe benefits	3.87	0.75	71
Input into managerial decisions	3.7	0.87	55
Amount of administrative time	3.07	1.04	32

* Scoring: 1 = least important, 5 = most important. *Source:* Reprinted from N.B. Fisher, H.L. Smith, and D.P. Pasternok, "Critical Factors in Recruiting Health Maintenance Organization Physicians," *Health Care Management Review*, Vol. 18, No. 1, pp. 51–61, © 1993, Aspen Publishers, Inc.

cal group would find a slightly different constellation of attributes considered desirable by physicians, but in general these attributes would still be considered.

Timing

New managers who are recruiting physicians for the first time often underestimate how long it takes to recruit well-qualified PCPs. Although physicians coming out of training programs are usually not available until middle to late summer, they frequently have decided where they are going by the preceding fall or winter. There are always exceptions, and there are certainly excellent physicians who have not decided by the time they are done with their residency programs, but that is not the norm. According to one large study, the average time it takes to recruit a physician for a closed panel HMO is 9 months.[12]

Even for PCPs who have been in practice and desire to make a change, the process is a long one. Physicians, like other people, do not wish to contemplate another change, so they will take their time in choosing their next location. If they are well qualified, they can afford to be choosy and explore many opportunities.

In general, the window for recruiting is most open between November and April, although opportunities do exist all year long. As a rule of thumb, it is best to plan on beginning the recruiting process at least 5 to 9 months before new physicians are required to be on board. This gestation period may be cut short if you are lucky, in which case you may have to decide whether you are willing to add the new PCP(s) to your staff early.

Sources

Two of the most effective methods of finding candidates for recruiting are word of mouth and professional relationships. Clinical chairpersons as well as the medical staff often have frequent contact with other physicians. Such contact may be collegial (e.g., at the hospital, in a specialty society, and so forth), through a teaching program, through personal friendships, and through friends of friends. Some HMOs and medical groups pay staff physicians a recruiting bonus for initiating contacts with physicians who are later successfully recruited.

Spontaneous inquiries occur randomly. If your plan is in a desirable location, you can count on frequent inquiries. If a physician is already in your community or once lived there and wishes to return, he or she may contact you directly.

Advertisements in professional journals are another common method of making contact with PCPs interested in making a change. The lead time for getting the ad in the periodical can be quite long, so plan ahead. Some managers hold that it is enough to run the ads every other issue rather than every issue. State medical societies also have journals, which are good places to run ads, especially in your home state and the states surrounding your plan. Examples of national medical journals that routinely run advertisements include the following:

- *American Journal of Obstetrics and Gynecology*
- *Annals of Internal Medicine*
- *Journal of the American Medical Association*
- *Journal of Family Practice*
- *Pediatrics*
- *New England Journal of Medicine*

Newspaper advertisements are less useful, although some widely circulated newspapers, such as the *New York Times*, do run ads for physicians in their areas. Military publications, such as *Military Press* and *Stars and Stripes*, may reach physicians who will be completing their service and are looking for civilian practice opportunities.

Letters to cooperative residency programs may be useful, especially if the program director is willing to post your letter on a common bulletin board where residents can see it. Recruiting physicians on site at a training program is not often allowed, so some large plans host informal off-site gatherings for residents of area programs. If your plan participates as a training site for a residency program, you will have a reasonably good chance of recruiting some of the residents who rotated through.

Direct mail can be quite effective. Mailing labels may be obtained from a number of sources, such as the American Medical Association and Business Mailers, Inc. Preparing a professional-looking brochure is important, although a well-written letter will still have an impact. Because preparing a direct mailing can be labor intensive, you may wish to contract with an outside agency to collate the material, stuff the envelopes, and so on. Your brochure or letter should contain, at a minimum, the following elements:

- a description of the health plan in terms of its size, the number of medical facilities (or clinics, if you use that term), medical services available, current physicians on staff, and any unique points about the plan
- a description of the hospitals, their location, their size, their services, and so forth
- a description of the community and its positive points, such as colleges or universities, special cultural and recreational offerings, religious and social organizations, shopping and dining, and the weather

Professional Recruiting Agencies

A carefully selected professional agency can be a resource in locating and recruiting physicians. When you do your own recruiting, you will be dismayed at the number of responses you get from poorly qualified candidates. Separating out the well-qualified candidates from the unqualified, as well as weeding out the tire kickers, can be an exhausting chore for someone not trained in it. Even worse, you may inadvertently pass over an important piece of information about a candidate, or not look for it at all, and have a disastrous outcome. For those plans or medical groups that do not have a professional physician recruiting department, the use of an external recruiting agency may be worthwhile.

Professional recruiters will not be able to guarantee a placement, nor can they guarantee that a candidate who does get placed with you will ultimately work out. They can, however, remove a great deal of the burden from you in the recruiting process. They may also have access to candidates who are looking to change but who do not wish to contact anyone directly for fear of compromising their current position.

Such help does not come cheap, although fees for placements are quite variable. The most you might see is 30 percent of the physician's first-year salary, but lesser fees are more common. For example, a recruiter may charge a straight fee of $15,000 or $20,000 for a placement. Some recruiters require a retainer to be paid at the beginning with the balance contingent on placement, whereas others work strictly on contingency. It is common for a recruiter to give you a discount for multiple placements in a year. Fees are sometimes negotiable, although if you negotiate the fee down too low the recruiter may be less motivated to help you.

In selecting a recruiting agency, be sure to check the agency's references. Try to get an idea of how many physicians it has placed, whether it has successfully placed PCPs in groups similar to your own, how long it took on average, and whether the physicians are still there. If you are unfamiliar with contracts, be sure to have the agency's contract reviewed by an attorney before signing.

Initial Selection of Candidates To Consider

After you have responses from candidates, you need to select whom you will consider asking in for an interview. Although this process will be easier if you have been using a professional recruiter, it cannot be eliminated entirely. It is important to evaluate inquiries and respond promptly to initiate contact while the candidate is still available and interested.

The curriculum vitae is the first source of data for you to use and should describe the physicians' credentials and current situation, their training, where they went to medical school,

where their postgraduate training took place, and specialty board certification or eligibility (some specialties, such as OB/GYN, require a certain amount of practice experience before certification is given). Most board certifications are now time limited; although physicians who received their board certification before that board's setting a time limitation may have their certification status unaffected, physicians who receive their certification after that may have to renew their certification every 10 years.

From either the cover letter or a phone call, try to ascertain the professional goals and needs of the PCP. For example, a physician may simply be looking for someplace to park for a year while a spouse finishes training. In that case, you need to decide whether that is acceptable.

The process of checking the credentials of a candidate should be thorough; shortcuts must not be taken, even if your group is suffering from understaffing. Failure to perform credentials checking properly not only opens the group up to a serious legal liability but may compromise care to the members, cause a serious embarrassment to the group, and result in the need to recruit again under even more stress, especially because it was found in one well-known study that up to 5 percent of physicians applying for positions in ambulatory care clinics misrepresented their credentials in their applications.[13] A more thorough discussion of physician credentials checking is found in Chapter 8; the process in closed panels should contain all the elements found in open panels plus those items discussed specifically in this chapter.

Finding out the malpractice history is an important exercise. Usually it is enough simply to ask the candidates to list any malpractice claims that were judged against them or settled with an award. It is not uncommon for a physician to have been sued or even to have settled a case to avoid costly and lengthy litigation, even though the physician may have been perfectly innocent. Do not allow the presence of a malpractice history alone to deter you from considering a candidate, but look closely at that history for evidence of a pattern or of a truly malfeasant act.

You should find out what type of malpractice insurance the potential candidate currently has. You want to know who the carrier is, whether the insurance is on a claims-made or occurrence basis, and whether the candidate has or will purchase tail coverage if necessary. In other words, if candidates have the occurrence type of malpractice insurance (which is becoming uncommon), they are covered for any claim arising against them in the future for events that occurred during the time they had the policy. If they have the claims-made type of coverage (the most common type), their coverage ends as soon as the premiums stop. To continue coverage for future claims arising from events that occurred during the policy period, they must buy tail coverage. Tail coverage can be quite expensive (for example, an OB/GYN in practice for 10 years may have to pay well over $75,000 for tail coverage), and you need to determine whether your plan would have to provide it to attract the candidate. If you do provide it, you may want to consider a 3-year forgiveness of the cost. In other words, you will pay for the coverage, but its cost is considered a loan to the new physician. For each year the physician practices with your group, you forgive a third of the original loan. If the physician leaves before 3 years are up, he or she has to repay whatever portion of the loan remains.

Under no circumstances may you refuse to consider a candidate for reasons of age, sex, religious beliefs, race, or any other elements considered under the Equal Employment Opportunity Act.

Before inviting a physician to your plan for an interview, conduct a telephone interview. This may reveal, for example, that the candidate has little or no communication skills, is unable to speak the same language as your members, or has unreasonable demands. This will also give you an opportunity to explore further reasons why the candidate wants to be considered for your group.

Reference checks are usually done at this point but are occasionally done after the candidate has come in for an interview. There are two types of reference checks: formal letters of reference, and telephone reference checks. Ask your candidates to submit three letters of reference from physicians who have known them professionally in their current position. If that is not possible for reasons of confidentiality, reserve the right to check those references after a job offer has been made, and ask for references from the next most recent position. It is unusual in this litigious era for reference letters to do anything except either state what percentage of time the candidate spends walking on water or simply confirm employment, revealing no information whatsoever except that the candidate was employed.

Telephone reference checks are more useful because they are confidential, and you may sometimes be able to read between the lines. The most useful telephone conversations occur between physicians. When nonphysicians question physicians about the competence of another physician, negative responses are likely to be muted. Again, it is unusual for a reference to say negative things for fear of a lawsuit, even after you have assured him or her of complete confidentiality.

You may wish to telephone references who have not been provided by the candidate (only after the candidate has given permission for you to do reference checks; it could be devastating if the current employer or medical group does not know that the candidate is looking to leave). Such references could include the president of the candidate's local medical society, the chief of staff where the candidate currently has active privileges, or, in the case of physicians just completing training, the director of the residency program.

The National Practitioner Data Bank

A special type of reference check was created by the Health Care Quality Improvement Act of 1986: the National Practitioner Data Bank (NPDB). In addition to providing immunity from antitrust lawsuits, the act requires hospitals, health plans, malpractice carriers, and state

licensure boards to report settled or lost malpractice suits and adverse acts, sanctions, or restrictions against the practice privileges of a physician. In the first full year of operation, the NPDB
reported that the annual rate of licensure actions
was 2.7 per 1,000 physicians (0.0 to 9.7 per
1,000), that the annual rate of clinical privileges
actions was 1.4 per 1,000 physicians (0.0 to 3.6
per 1,000), and that there were an average of
21.1 medical malpractice payments per 1,000
physicians.[14] By the end of 1994, the NPDB reported the following statistics: The data bank
contained more than 97,500 reports, of which 82
percent were related to malpractice payments,
with licensure reports making up most of the
rest; it had processed more than 4.5 million requests for information; and 8 percent of queries
were matched with a report.[15] The act is further
discussed in Chapter 26.

The act also states that any hospital or HMO
may contact the NPDB to obtain information
about a physician and that, if the hospital or
health plan fails to do so, it will be assumed that
it did so anyway. In other words, there is a potential for liability on the part of the plan if it fails to
check with the NPDB and hires a physician who
has a poor record as reported in the data bank,
and there is a malpractice problem later on. Information about the NPDB may be obtained by
writing to:

> National Practitioner Data Bank
> P.O. Box 10832
> Chantilly, VA 22021
> 1-800-767-6732

Interview Process

After candidates to interview are selected, the
plan needs to send the candidates adequate information about the plan, the practice environment,
and so forth. The next step is to invite them to the
plan. The trip should be arranged so that as little
work as possible is required of the candidates.
You should prepay the air fare, arrange to have
someone meet them at the airport, have the hotel
arranged, and so forth. It is good form to invite

spouses as well, but that may be delayed until a
second interview.

The interview should be scheduled carefully.
Plan for the candidate to meet with other PCPs in
the plan, the chief of staff of the appropriate
medical department, and other plan executives
as necessary (e.g., the marketing director, the
nursing or operations director, the executive director, and so forth).

A visit to the main hospital that the PCP
would be using is also important. Hospitals are
usually quite accommodating about giving tours
to prospective new physicians. If there is time,
an informal tour of the community is helpful,
with an emphasis on the types of neighborhoods
that are available to live in. If the candidate and
spouse have both come, you may wish to arrange
for a real estate agent to give the spouse a tour
while the candidate is interviewing.

Try not to leave large blocks of time where the
candidate has nothing to do and feels adrift. The
same goes for the spouse (unless the spouse
wants to be left alone; inquire first). This carries
over to the evening if the candidate is staying
overnight. A dinner invitation is appropriate, although the candidate may feel too tired and may
wish to decline, in which case you should gra-
ciously accept the refusal.

It is important to schedule an exit interview
with the candidate. This meeting allows the
medical director to find out how the candidate
views the situation and to ascertain a level of interest (although it is unusual to hear an outright
rejection at this point, even if the candidate is no
longer interested). Likewise, this final meeting
allows the candidate to ask any last minute questions or clarify any information that may have
been obtained during the visit.

After the initial interview is complete, be sure
to follow up promptly within 7 to 14 days. If you
are no longer interested, it is still good form to
send a letter thanking the candidates and indicating that the final selection did not include them
but that you appreciate their interest and wish
them luck. If you are still interested, arrange for
a second visit, this time for the candidate and
spouse to see the community. Assuming that you

have satisfactorily completed the reference check, you will want to make an offer of employment at that time. The candidate may wish to think it over and review the contract. If that is the case, ask for an answer within a fixed time frame, such as 3 weeks.

When offering a contract, you will wish to include a provision that, if the candidate has falsified any information or has failed to provide complete information, you have the right to terminate the contract. If you have not been able to complete the reference check because of confidentiality issues, you will wish to be able to contact references at the candidate's current location upon the candidate's acceptance of your offer, and final acceptance by you is contingent upon that last reference check.

COMPENSATION

The issue of compensation of physicians in medical groups and IDSs is a complicated topic and is discussed in full in Chapter 10. An overview of some of the issues is provided here. The basic tenet of compensation for PCPs in closed panels is that they should be on approximate parity with their fee-for-service colleagues. This does not refer to gross income but includes benefits (e.g., malpractice insurance, health and life insurance, retirement, and so forth), duty requirements (e.g., frequency of being on call, hours worked, and so forth), bonus pay, and net take-home pay. Because physicians do not look at gross dollars alone when assessing a practice opportunity, neither should you. Further discussion about factors leading to physician retention is found later in this chapter.

Straight Salary

A straight salary is the most common payment mechanism in staff model HMOs and is often found in group models as well, where the group's salary costs are passed back directly to the plan. Some private group practice groups use straight salary, although usually as a base, after which productivity, medical costs, or other

modifiers are applied. Although it is rare for a staff model to use some form of risk, group models may use withholds on salary. Bonus arrangements are commonly attached to salary plans as well.

Capitation

Some group model closed panel plans capitate a medical group (or groups) that makes up the physician panel. In that case, the plan negotiates the overall capitation rate with the group, and the group then decides how to compensate the physicians. Again, salary with a bonus plan is the most common arrangement within the group (with or without a withhold), although some groups use fee for service, and a few capitate individual providers. A more thorough discussion of both capitation and fee for service in managed care is found in Chapter 9.

Benefits

Benefits are a vital part of the total compensation package. Whether the plan pays straight salary and provides the benefits directly to the physicians or the group is capitated and provides the benefits itself, benefits are an integral part of compensation.

The following are benefits that are almost universally provided to physicians as part of their compensation:

- malpractice insurance
- life insurance
- health insurance
- continuing medical education time and funds
- professional licensure fees
- vacation and sick leave

Benefits that are quite commonly provided as well, but perhaps not in every case, include:

- dental insurance
- disability insurance

- auto allowance and parking fees at hospitals
- professional society dues
- retirement plan
  1. 401(k)
  2. simplified employee pension plan individual retirement account
  3. tax deferred annuity

Finally, the following are benefits that are not routinely provided but that you may wish to consider for special circumstances:

- book and journal allowance (separate from continuing medical education funds)
- paid time off for nonplan activities
  1. research
  2. jury duty
  3. military leave
  4. volunteer work
- compensation time
- extended leave without pay
- in-plan moonlighting
  1. extended hours
  2. urgent care
- sabbatical program
- paternity leave (maternity leave is assumed to be provided)
- deferred compensation
- profit sharing
- low-interest unsecured loans

Risk and Bonus Arrangements

Bonus plans are common in closed panels, whereas risk arrangements are less so. In capitated groups, there is the inherent risk that the capitation payment represents all the money there is; in a sense, that is a clear risk. Again, the reader is referred to Chapter 10 for an in-depth discussion of compensation of physicians in medical groups and IDSs.

The most common mechanism to deal with risk in a closed panel is a withhold. In a withhold, part of the capitation payment (e.g., 20 percent) or salary (e.g., 10 percent) is withheld until the end of the year. That withhold is used to cover excess medical expenses. If there is still money in the withhold, the physicians receive it. For a more complete discussion of risk arrangements, refer to Chapter 8.

Bonus plans are most often based either on total plan performance or on medical cost alone. When bonus is based on total plan performance, it may be affected by things outside the physician's control, such as membership growth, underwriting criteria, premium yield, and so forth. This will be perceived as unfair in the event that no bonus is paid. On the other hand, it clearly points out that everyone is in it together.

Bonus based on medical expense only is more closely related to actions under the control of the physicians. For example, if the plan outperforms budget on per member cost for medical services, 10 percent of the total base salary is paid as a bonus. When medical expense is measured on a per member per month or per member per year basis rather than on whole dollars, there can be no charge that the bonus is based on anything outside the physician's control.

Bonus plans may pay straight bonus to every physician, or they may be tied to performance evaluations. It is unwise to pay bonus on the basis of a few single criteria for individual PCPs because any single criterion can be manipulated to the benefit of the PCP but to the detriment of the plan. If bonus is to be paid to PCPs on a differential basis, you are better off using a broader performance evaluation system. Such performance evaluation systems are discussed in Chapter 11.

The amount of bonus available may be calculated as a percentage of the total base salary paid during the year or as a percentage of savings over budget. If a percentage of savings is used, you need to determine whether there will be an upper limit on the bonus. For example, you may wish to share savings of per member per month medical expenses on a 50:50 basis with the physician group, but only to a maximum of 20 percent of the total base salary paid.

If you intend to pay a bonus on the basis of making the budget targets (e.g., paying 10 percent of base salary if the per member per month medical expense targets are met), be sure to include the amount of the bonus payment in your overall accruals for physician salary and benefits. If you are going to pay on the basis of exceeding budget only, then you will not have to face an unexpected expense.

CREDENTIALING

The process of credentialing new physicians in closed panels is basically one of making sure that they have the necessary documents to allow them to practice with your group. This use of the term *credentialing* differs from its use in open panels. In the open panel setting, credentialing refers primarily to checking references and documentation (e.g., licensure verification, malpractice insurance, and so forth); this activity is discussed in an earlier section of this chapter.

In open panels, it is the physician's responsibility to have the necessary documentation to practice; in closed panels, it is the plan's responsibility to obtain it for the physician so that the physician can practice in the group. Because some of the documents require a lengthy lead time, you should plan to begin as soon as the physician has signed an employment contract.

Obtaining a state license to practice medicine takes the longest amount of time. If the physician has licenses in many other states, it lengthens the process because the state must check with each other state to determine whether the PCP's license is valid.

The Drug Enforcement Agency (DEA) number allows a physician to prescribe scheduled narcotics. Although it is a federally issued permit, the number is good only for one state location. Therefore, even if the physician has a DEA number from another state, he or she must reapply for a new number. Some states also issue narcotics numbers.

After state licensure has been obtained, the physician must obtain malpractice insurance. If your plan has a group policy, it is a simple matter to add the newcomer. If candidates had claims made through malpractice insurance, they will need a tail coverage policy to cover against suits that may haunt them from the past. Your carrier may insist on seeing evidence of such coverage before issuing a new policy, and you should as well.

Once state licensure and malpractice coverage have been obtained, the physician must apply for hospital privileges at your participating hospitals. An application for membership in the county and state medical societies may also be made at that time.

ORIENTATION

Time invested in proper orientation will be time well spent. If your plan has been understaffed for some time, there will be pressure to get the new PCP seeing patients as soon as possible, or perhaps after half a day of brief overview. The new PCP will learn the ropes eventually, but if you want to foster a good attitude and help the new PCP learn his or her way around more efficiently, spend the time with a good orientation program.

Plan the orientation to expose new PCPs to all the personnel with whom they will be interacting in the future. Have those individuals review the important elements of their areas. When new PCPs understand what is expected of them and what to expect from others in the plan as well as the technical components of practicing in your group, they will be more comfortable. Consider orientation administrative preventive medicine. Exhibit 7–1 lists some topics that may be appropriate for an orientation program.

Although you may spend 3 or 4 days going over orientation material, there is no way a new PCP will be able to absorb all the information about your plan in that short time. Therefore, for the first few weeks it is best to schedule a reduced patient load. For example, you may want

Exhibit 7–1 Suggested Topics for Orientation of Closed
Panel Physicians

- Plan mission, values, and strategic plan
- Physician leadership roles
- Expectations
  — Of the plan for the physician
  — Of the physician for the plan
- Productivity
- Plan practice manual or principles of practice
- Scheduling and appointments
  — Appointment system, including control of the schedule
  — Scheduling of procedures
  — Schedule of regular hours and on-call hours
- Patient responsibilities and clinical duties
- Utilization management policies and procedures
  — Authorization policies and procedures
  — Forms and paperwork
  — Consultants
  — Institutions
  — Case management and clinical pathways
  — Ancillary services
  — Affiliated providers
- Nonclinical duties
- Meetings and committees
- Continuing medical education
- Quality management program and peer review
- Administrative forms and paperwork
- Plan subscription agreement and plan schedule of benefits
- Plan member grievance procedures

to schedule only half the normal number of appointments for the new PCP to see. It is also helpful to assign an experienced nurse to the new PCP to help explain the forms, assist in getting laboratory and radiology studies, help with preadmission requirements, and so forth. After 2 or 3 weeks, the new PCP may be assigned a permanent nurse or aide if such a change is necessary.

Many groups use a buddy system for the first few weeks as well. This means that an experienced plan physician in the same specialty as the new PCP is designated to help the new PCP acclimate to the system. This extends to the new PCP taking phone calls with the experienced PCP (the first call, actually; the new PCP takes the call, and then, if more than advice is needed, the new PCP in turn calls the experienced PCP to review procedure). By designating another physician to help out the new PCP, there is less chance of the new PCP feeling reluctant to ask for help.

In a few large group and staff model HMOs and medical groups, the orientation program is highly formal. These HMOs or groups may dedicate numerous days to training, either in a large block or, more often, spread out over a longer period, such as a year. For example, the program may have formal, didactic classes to teach the fundamentals of managed care, how capitation and financing work, how utilization and quality are managed, and so forth. The group may also develop formal training in standards of care and treatment protocols, methods of improving communications with members, risk management, the treatment of common conditions, and other medical topics. The reader is referred to the literature for further discussion of these interesting approaches to formal training of physicians in managed care.[16]

PRODUCTIVITY

Measuring outpatient productivity in closed panel managed care plans is far more complicated than measuring it in a standard fee-for-service setting. Because the economic incentives in fee for service are so straightforward, productivity is a simple product of how much a physician bills and collects. In managed care, one is trying to practice cost effectively and yet provide high-quality care. Therefore, the measures must be modified.

One common unit of measurement involves looking at the number of patient visits per unit time (e.g., visits per day). Other common measures are visits per hour, per session (usually half a day, but that can be subtly altered), per week, per month, and per year. The larger the time scale, the less the influence of minor factors. For example, if you measure visits per session but fail to define a session rigidly, you will not know whether all the visits are occurring in the space of 2 hours, 3 hours, and so on. The problem with larger time scales is that they are slow to respond to changes and will be less sensitive indicators of current productivity. A reasonable combination is to look at visits per day or per week on average for a month and then have a rolling 12-month average for the year to date.

In the fee-for-service setting in 1993, the mean outpatient productivity by PCPs was 76.1 office visits per week, with the breakdown by specialty going from 62.0 visits per week for internal medicine (including Medicare visits), 99.6 visits per week for pediatrics, 109.5 visits per week for family practice, and 86.9 visits per week for OB/GYN. Hospital rounds add to these numbers as follows: The mean number of hospital visits per week in 1993 was 20.7, with the breakdown by specialty going from 31.5 rounds per week for internal medicine (including Medicare visits), 19.0 rounds per week for pediatrics, 14.4 rounds per week for family practice, and 17.4 visits per week for OB/GYN.[17]

Comparing productivity in closed panel HMOs with that found in private practice is not always easily done. Although it is perfectly reasonable to expect somewhere around the private practice level of productivity from PCPs on your staff, productivity in staff and group model HMOs is estimated to be approximately 83 percent of that found in fee-for-service practice.[18] In addition, recently there has been an increase in the number of female physicians: In 1992, women accounted for 16 percent of practicing physicians; in 1994, more than 40 percent of medical students were women.[19] Although two studies have reported that, in private practice, on average female physicians work approximately 85 percent as many hours as male physicians (primarily because of increased family responsibilities), most experienced medical directors find that life style issues are present with a large number of physicians who are recruited into group or staff model HMOs regardless of gender.[20] In one large study, reasonable and regular work hours and salary were the most important reasons for staff model HMO physicians to join.[21] These issues must be clearly understood and accounted for not only during the recruiting process but also during the management of productivity.

Using productivity as an absolute measure can cause problems. Just as in an uncontrolled fee-for-service setting, if you pressure the PCPs too heavily to get productivity up, the easiest thing for them to do is start churning the patients (e.g., refer sick patients out and schedule 35 blood pressure checks per day). This is obviously counterproductive in a managed health care plan. The point is to have a reasonable expectation of PCP productivity and stick to it but not rely inappropriately on productivity in measuring how well the plan is doing. If studies of appointment availability show reasonable accessibility to care, and if the medical expenses are well controlled (including salary and benefits for the medical staff), you may feel little need to apply pressure to improve productivity.

RETENTION OF QUALITY PHYSICIANS

Physician turnover in group and staff model HMOs, once a chronic problem, is now relatively modest. A review of young HMO physicians reported more than 82 percent are satisfied with their practice.[22] One recent study of 27 group and staff model HMOs reported that the mean turnover rate of physicians who left or were dropped from the staff was 5 percent; and the two most common reasons were departure from practice due to retirement, death, or change in career (61 percent) and departure from the service area (66 percent).[23] These data are supported by data from the Lovelace Clinic study cited earlier, which also reported a turnover rate of 5 percent.[24] Interestingly, in the earlier cited study the percentage of physicians who reported that they would be likely to leave was more than 16 percent, with a higher level of self-reported intention of leaving being found among non-

Hispanic minority physicians.[25] No plan or group wants to lose quality physicians. Therefore, the medical leadership and plan management (if they are not one and the same) need to be attentive to some issues that may lead a physician to choose to leave for other than the two reasons cited above.

Issues of physician autonomy tend to rise quickly to the surface in tightly managed closed panels, and perceived lack of autonomy is the leading reason for dissatisfaction in physicians in closed panels.[26–28] Because tight medical management equates with frequent physician management, some physicians grow uncomfortable with practicing in a fishbowl environment. Closely related to this is the heavy use of practice protocols; although such protocols may be necessary for the efficient and effective practice of medicine, they extract a price in perception of autonomy.[29] Physicians generally would prefer a practice where there is no retrospective secondary evaluation of their decisions and where they are the unquestioned authority. Situations such as this are becoming more rare with increasing intervention by third party payers, but the image of the autonomous, hard-working, well-compensated physician is one that is placed in front of physicians as the ideal throughout training and

---

Exhibit 7–2 Items To Consider for Physician Retention in Closed Panels

Longevity-related benefits, within limits (must use great care so as not to make physicians with less longevity into second-class citizens, or attrition will occur from below)
- Cafeteria style
- Flex time of some sort
- On-call responsibilities
  1. Amount
  2. When
- Participation in profit sharing
- Vesting schedule for tail malpractice insurance and relocation expenses
- Sabbatical time
- Tuition aid for dependents
- Increasing vacation time
- Stock options
- Preferential opportunity for investment in plan
- Personal financial counseling
- Retirement plan with vesting schedule on plan-matching contributions

On-call responsibilities for all physicians
- Outside back-up
- After-hours telephone triage system

Physician input into support staff

Staff development for physicians beyond continuing medical education
- Telephone skills

- Stress management
- Coping skills
- Handling difficult patients
  1. Entitled demanders
  2. Other hateful patients
- Communications skills
- Time management skills

Formal recognition programs

Career path development

Encouragement of academic affiliation

Social events with professionals

Utilization of group or staff physicians for larger task force objectives

Participation in and encouragement of research

Professional newsletter

Development of survey instruments
- Structured exit interviews
- Profile of high-quality physicians who are likely to remain with the group

Training programs for ancillary and support staff
- Telephone skills
- Stress management
- Coping skills
- Handling difficult patients (as above)
- Communications skills
- Time management skills

beyond. This issue becomes especially critical in the recruiting and retention of physicians right out of residency training, who have little knowledge of how difficult the real world of private practice can be.

Other reasons that a physician may feel stress or choose to leave include a narrow range of problems seen in practice, the stress of dealing with demanding patients, high demands for productivity with little or no financial incentive, and lack of control over workload.[30] One large study reported that workload and scheduling were actually the leading causes of burnout in staff model HMO physicians, with lack of influence and autonomy issues being second.[31] It is not possible to create practice Nirvana for a physician, but recognition of these issues may help address them, presumably at an affordable cost. In the earlier cited report, it is important to note that the onset of burnout and dissatisfaction occurred in the first 2 to 5 years of employment, arguing for the fact that attention to this issue must take place early in a physician's career with the plan.[32]

Another problem in closed panels is that there is no real entry or exit barrier. Few closed panels require new physicians to ante up $50,000 for a partnership or place physicians in the position of trying to sell their equity stake if they leave. Because of that, group and staff model HMOs are convenient places for physicians to practice for a few years while trying to figure out what they ultimately want to do.

Although one can argue that new physicians cost less than experienced ones (thus reducing overhead), the cost to the plan of high physician turnover is large. When one factors in recruiting costs, such as recruiters' fees, advertising, time spent interviewing candidates, travel costs, and so forth, the costs are considerable. New physicians also do not know the system as well, which reduces efficiency in medical management. Last, problems of member satisfaction and plan reputation are markedly exacerbated by high physician turnover.

Exhibit 7–2 presents some ideas that could be incorporated into a closed panel to promote re-

tention of high-quality physicians; a plan may choose to incorporate some of these ideas but could not possibly use them all. One key caution is not to develop a system that entrenches a few senior physicians with all the longevity benefits and allows new physicians little hope of attaining those benefits, thereby continuing the turnover problem.

CONCLUSION

The development and maintenance of a high-quality medical staff in a closed panel health plan take a great deal of thoughtful attention and work, but the reward is high. Ensuring that compensation (both monetary and nonmonetary) is comparable with the community norms, properly orienting new physicians, paying considerable attention to proper incentive programs and performance requirements, and keeping in touch with the short- and long-term needs of the medical staff are necessary management tasks.

REFERENCES AND NOTES

1. T.H. Dial, T.H., et al., Clinical Staffing in Staff- and Group-Model HMOs, *Health Affairs* (Summer 1995): 168–180.
2. Group Health Association of America (GHAA), *HMO Industry Profile, Vol. 2: Physician Staffing and Utilization Patterns* (Washington, D.C.: GHAA, 1992).
3. Dial, et al., Clinical Staffing.
4. Group Health Association of America (GHAA), *HMO Industry Profile* (Washington, D.C.: GHAA, 1994).
5. Dial, et al., Clinical Staffing.
6. Group Health Association of America (GHAA), *HMO Industry Profile* (Washington, D.C.: GHAA, 1992).
7. J.P. Weiner, Forecasting the Effects of Health Reform on U.S. Physician Workforce Requirement, Evidence from HMO Staffing Patterns, *Journal of the American Medical Association* 272 (1994): 222–230.
8. Dial, et al., Clinical Staffing.
9. Dial, et al., Clinical Staffing.
10. J. Packer-Thursman, The Role of Midlevel Practitioners, *HMO Magazine* (March/April 1992): 28–34.
11. E.S. Sekscenski, et al., State Practice Environments and the Supply of Physician Assistants, Nurse Practitioners,

and Certified Nurse-Midwives, *New England Journal of Medicine* 331 (1994): 1266–1271.

12. S.E. Palsbo and K.B. Sullivan, *The Recruitment Experience of Health Maintenance Organization for Primary Care: Final Summary Report* (Washington, D.C.: Group Health Association of America, 1993).

13. W.A. Schaffer, et al., Falsification of Clinical Credentials by Physicians Applying for Ambulatory Staff Privileges, *New England Journal of Medicine* 318 (1988): 356–357.

14. F. Mullan, et al., The National Practitioner Data Bank—Report from the First Year, *Journal of the American Medical Association* 268 (1) (1992): 73–79.

15. R.E. Oshel, et al., The National Practitioner Data Bank: The First Four Years, *Public Health Reports* 110 (4) (July/August 1995): 383–394.

16. T. Defino, Educating Physicians in Managed Care, *Health System Leader* (May 1995): 4–12.

17. American Medical Association (AMA), *Socioeconomic Characteristics of Medical Practice 1994* (Chicago, Ill.: AMA, 1994).

18. Weiner, Forecasting the Effects of Health Reform.

19. R.A. Cooper, Seeking a Balanced Physician Workforce for the 21st Century, *Journal of the American Medical Association* 272 (1994): 680–687.

20. Cooper, Seeking a Balanced Physician Workforce.

21. D. Murray, Doctors Rate the Big HMOs, *Medical Economics* (January 1995): 114–120.

22. L.C. Baker, et al., What Makes Young HMO Physicians Satisfied?, *HMO Practice* 8 (1994): 53–57.

23. M. Gold, *Arrangements between Managed Care Plans and Physicians, Results from a 1994 Survey of Managed Care Plans, Mathematica Policy Research and the Medical College of Virginia* (report submitted to the Physician Payment Review Committee, 7 February 1995).

24. N.B. Fisher, et al., Critical Factors in Recruiting Health Maintenance Organization Physicians, *Health Care Management Review* 18 (1993): 51–61.

25. Baker et al., What Makes Young HMO Physicians Satisfied.

26. Fisher et al., Critical Factors.

27. R.A. Schmoldt, et al., Physician Burnout: Recommendations for HMO Managers, *HMO Practice* 8 (1994): 58–63.

28. Baker et al., What Makes Young HMO Physicians Satisfied.

29. Baker et al., What Makes Young HMO Physicians Satisfied.

30. E. Freidson, Prepaid Group Practice and the New "Demanding Patient," *Milbank Memorial Fund Quarterly* 51 (1973): 473–488.

31. G. Deckard, et al., Physician Burnout: An Examination of Personal, Professional, and Organizational Relationships, *Medical Care* 37 (1994): 745–754.

32. Deckard, et al., Physician Burnout.

SUGGESTED READING

American Medical Association (AMA). 1995. *Socioeconomic Characteristics of Medical Practice 1994/1995*. Chicago, Ill.: AMA.

Felt, S., Frazer, H., and Gold, M. 1994. *HMO Primary Care Staffing Patterns and Processes: A Cross-Site Analysis of 23 HMOs*. Washington, D.C.: Mathematica Policy Research, Inc.

Fisher, N.B., Smith, H.L., and Pasternok, D.P. 1993. Critical Success Factors in Recruiting Health Maintenance Organization Physicians. *Health Care Management Review* 18 (1): 51–61.

Hammon, J.L. 1993. *Fundamentals of Medical Management*. Tampa, Fla.: American College of Physician Executives.

Konrad, T.R., et al. 1989. *The Salaried Physician: Medical Practice in Transition*. Chapel Hill, N.C.: University of North Carolina at Chapel Hill.

Nash, D.B. (ed.). 1994. *The Physician's Guide to Managed Care*. Gaithersburg, Md: Aspen Publishers.

Palsbo, S.E., and Sullivan, C.B. 1993. *The Recruitment Experience of Health Maintenance Organizations for Primary Care Physicians: Final Report*. Washington, D.C.: Health Resources and Services Administration.

Shouldice, R.G. 1991. *Introduction to Managed Care*. Arlington, Va.: Information Resources Press.

Chapter 8

Primary Care in Open Panel Plans

Peter R. Kongstvedt

DEFINITIONS

One must begin with definitions of what will be considered primary care. In virtually all systems, care rendered by physicians in the specialties of family practice, internal medicine, and pediatrics is considered primary care. Many obstetrics/gynecology (OB/GYN) specialists feel that they, too, deliver primary care to their patients. They argue that they are often the only physician a young woman sees for many years. This is true in the case of generally healthy young women, but it is not always so when medical problems not involving the female reproductive tract occur. In at least one program designed to retrain OB/GYN physicians to provide a broader range of primary care, the results were quite disappointing, with a high dropout rate and a high level of dissatisfaction with broad primary care being seen among the OB/GYNs.[1]

Still, a number of plans that capitate primary care or otherwise use primary care physicians (PCPs) as case managers (i.e., use a gatekeeper system) also include OB/GYN as primary care for OB/GYN services and split the care (and often the capitation) between the OB/GYN and an internist or family practitioner. Plans that use this method must define what services are to be delivered by each. For example, the OB/GYN may be seen without referral for Pap smears and pelvic examinations, for pregnancy, and for ster-

ilization procedures; in fact, more than 71 percent of surveyed health maintenance organizations (HMOs) in one study allowed self-referral to OB/GYN.[2] For any other problems, the member must see the PCP for either treatment by or referral to another specialist and perhaps even for referral back to the OB/GYN whom she has chosen for services beyond those defined as being allowed under the self-referral option.

In general, it is probably easier to define OB/GYN as a specialty service and treat it as any other specialty. For marketing reasons as well as medical acceptability in the community, however, most plans make special arrangements for routine Pap smears and obstetric services while still requiring coordination with the PCP for all other care.

NETWORK DEVELOPMENT

Young or newly forming plans will concentrate primarily on network development. Mature plans will concentrate more on network maintenance (discussed later in this chapter), although recruiting to fill in areas with suboptimal access will always be an ongoing process, particularly during periods of high growth or expansion into a new service area. The initial section of this chapter discusses recruiting in an environment in which physicians contract directly with the plan; similar issues would apply in the case of an integrated delivery system (IDS) or management services organization (MSO) that needs to recruit physicians (see Chapter 4 for a discussion of IDSs).

The ease of developing a network is influenced by many factors. Markets that are heavily saturated with managed care plans may have difficulty recruiting PCPs (or consultants) if those providers see no need to sign up with yet another plan. Conversely, competition may be so fierce, or there may be so many (underutilized) providers, that recruiting will be easier. In any event, recruiting PCPs for open panels is best done by means of an orderly approach. Without proper planning, the time line will be substantially drawn out, and the physician panel may not complement hospital choices or market needs.

Setting Priorities

If you are beginning from scratch, you are likely to start with a few easy recruits (often friends of the medical director or physicians with whom contact has already been made). That will rarely be sufficient by itself, so that there is a need to recruit systematically to achieve an acceptable panel size and configuration.

Consider geographic needs first. This generally breaks down into two main considerations: the need to target potential new members, and the need to use certain hospitals (discussed in Chapter 14). In the first case, you should already have identified your primary target markets (e.g., a large and growing suburban–industrial community). In the second case, you may have selected a high-quality hospital and need to recruit physicians from that medical staff in preference to physicians who practice only at a noncontracting hospital, even if it is in the targeted area.

Priorities will also be affected by the availability, acceptability (to you, to your potential members, and to the rest of the medical panel), scope of practice, and practice capacities of physicians in target areas. If you have more than one geographic high priority for recruiting but there is a major difference in the ease with which you

will be able to recruit qualified and acceptable physicians, you will want to give early attention to the area from which it will be the easiest to recruit. This is for two reasons. First, the success of your physician recruiters will be enhanced with the amount of successful experience they have, and second, there is often a chain reaction when your panel reaches critical mass. In other words, when there are enough physicians already on your panel, it becomes more acceptable or even competitively necessary for physicians to join.

Access Needs

In addition to the broad geographic needs and hospital-related needs, it is important to assess accessibility in general. There are a number of ways to do this. One method is to look at the number of physicians per 1,000 members. One large survey, now dated, reported the mean total physicians per 1,000 members in mature open panel plans to be 36.92, and the mean total PCPs per 1,000 members was reported as 14.43.[3] This last ratio equates to 71 members per physician, which may represent an average enrollment but does not necessarily predict capacity.

It is more useful to look at the number of members whom each physician must accept (on the basis of contractual terms, see Chapter 55), such as 200 members per PCP. The ratios of physicians to members in open panels can vary tremendously depending on the age of the plan, geographic access needs, the product lines being sold (e.g., a Medicare risk product may require a higher number of physicians than a commercial product), maturity of the marketplace in general, the number of open practices, and marketing needs.

Another useful measure is geographic accessibility. This is generally calculated through one of two methods: drive time, and number of PCPs by geographic availability. Drive time refers to how long members in the plan's service area have to drive to reach a PCP (or a PCP with an open practice, that is, one still accepting new patients). In general, drive time should be no more than 15 minutes, although 30 minutes may be appropriate for certain rural areas. A drive time of 20 minutes may be acceptable for access from a purely medical viewpoint, but it may not be as acceptable in a heavily urbanized market.

Analyzing the number of PCPs by geographic availability is also useful. Generally, you want to be able to provide at least two PCPs within 2 or 3 miles of each ZIP code from which your plan will be drawing members (the density is usually greater in urban areas and less in rural areas). Another measure of geographic availability is the radius from where the members live (e.g., two PCPs within an 8-mile radius for urban areas and two PCPs within a 20-mile radius for rural areas). Again, these ratios may represent a minimum configuration and will not necessarily be acceptable in your marketplace.

Identification of Candidates

Selection of candidates to recruit is based on a number of sources. First is the personal acquaintances of the medical director. These are often the easiest physicians to recruit, but they are relatively few in number.

Second, the list of physicians with privileges at the hospitals with which you are contracting should be used. The hospital administrator will frequently be able to guide you toward those physicians you should approach early and those you should avoid. The hospital executive staff is often helpful in enhancing the environment for recruiting because in many situations the physicians will value highly the judgment of the hospital administration. An important caveat is in order here: Sometimes the reason a physician is considered desirable from the hospital's point of view is the fact that the physician admits a lot of patients, and a heavy user of hospital services is not always the most desirable from the point of view of a managed care plan. It is therefore crucial that the plan retain independent judgment about whom to recruit and why.

A third source for identification of candidates is the physician list of your competitors. In general, unless your competition has signed the phy-sicians to an exclusive agreement, you will have an easier time signing up these physicians because they have already made the commitment to join a managed health care plan panel.

Fourth, the local county or state medical society may be a good source for obtaining mailing labels. You can rent the list for a single label run, or the society may actually provide the labels for a reasonable fee. If possible, you want this broken down by primary care and by ZIP code.

Last, if all else fails (or simply as a back-up), there are the Yellow Pages. Although the phone book provides the most complete list, it is absolutely unselective and must be used only with extreme caution.

One special method of identifying candidates is available only to large insurance carriers, and that is claims data. A large carrier may already have sufficient data on hand from indemnity business to be able to make an initial evaluation of which physicians practice cost effectively and which physicians have been pillaging the system for years. Claims data may also provide a crude method of assessing quality, for example by identifying physicians with abnormally high rates of certain procedures (e.g., hysterectomies) or those who frequently use outmoded treatments (e.g., routine tonsillectomies). Although interpretation of indemnity claims history is not as easy as it first appears, clear outliers are not difficult to identify if there are sufficient data to draw statistically valid conclusions. In other words, a large database is of no value if there are insufficient transactions at the level of individual providers in an area. The subject of provider profiling is addressed in greater detail in Chapter 27.

Timing

You need to develop a realistic time frame within which to work. You also need to give the physician recruiters a reference to use in recruiting so as not to let one step of the recruiting process overshadow the others. Each aspect of physician recruiting should have set goals for both number and duration. Begin the time frame with first contact and continue through successful completion, which occurs when both the physician and your plan sign the contract. In a new start-up, you may want to begin the time frame with the start of the enterprise and include physician identification as the first step.

Each plan and community will have its own special characteristics, but in general the time between the first letter to the physician and the first telephone contact should be no more than 7 to 10 days. If it is longer than that, the physician will have forgotten you.

The time between the first telephone contact and the first visit should likewise be no more than 7 to 10 days, although a busy physician's schedule may necessitate a slightly longer lead time. Try to avoid scheduling the first visit during normal office hours because the physician, who is under pressure to see patients, will be unable to give enough time and thought to the discussion. A lunch meeting (you bring the deli tray) or a meeting on an afternoon off or just after office hours is best. This first visit should last about 1 hour and involve explaining the concept and the contract, determining the level of interest, and obtaining initial information about the physician and the practice. This is also the time for the recruiter to obtain an initial impression of the ambiance of the physician's office for marketing purposes.

If possible, you wish to obtain closure (actually, contingent closure) on the second visit. Generally, allow 1 or 2 weeks between the first and second visits, and make the appointment for the second visit during the first one. In some cases, physicians will want to have their attorney look at the contract, and you will need to allow sufficient time for that. In any event, have a definite time for follow-up and potential closure.

In general, it is best to keep the pressure on. If you allow too much time to elapse between contacts or steps, your ease in getting a signed contract will be diminished. It is preferable to keep the entire time from first letter to signed contract or signed letter of intent to 2 months or less.

As discussed below under credentialing, the contract or letter of intent is contingent on the credentialing process. If a physician does not meet the standards of your plan, you reserve the right not to add that physician to your panel.

Role of the Recruiter

The key personnel in this process are the physician recruiters. In some plans, recruiters are drawn from the marketing department; in others, they are part of the provider relations department. The use of marketing representatives for physician recruiting may be necessary during the first few months of a new start-up plan, but the function is really best carried out by people who have more understanding and empathy with physicians and who will be responsible for maintaining the relationship after a physician has joined the panel. The recruiters are supervised by a director or manager of provider relations.

The recruiters make the telephone calls and do the leg work. They must be able to explain to the physician and the physician's support staff any necessary details to facilitate an informed decision. This includes all the aspects of physician compensation, best and worst case scenarios, the scope of covered services, covered benefits to members, benefits to the physician for joining, operational policies such as authorization systems and preadmission requirements, and any other pertinent information. A detailed understanding of the reimbursement system is, of course, critical (compensation models are discussed in Chapter 9).

The number of recruiters will depend on the number of physicians you hope to add to the panel and the geographic area you want to cover. In the early phases of a start-up, when there is an intense need for physician recruiting, you may need three to five individuals. Later, during a controlled growth phase, recruiting is handled by the regular provider relations staff.

Role of the Medical Director

In addition to making the personal contacts in the recruiting process, the medical director has at least two other primary responsibilities in recruiting (besides credentialing, as discussed below).

First, the medical director adds prestige and legitimacy to the endeavor. The medical director endorses the plan, both explicitly and implicitly, by being the medical director. If the medical director has been in the area for some time, this local endorsement may be the deciding factor in new plans looking to recruit physicians.

It is important for the medical director to understand the plan and its policies. This seems obvious, but there have been cases where medical directors have been recruited solely to add prestige and have been unaware of how the plan actually operated. This poses two serious problems. The medical director may promise things that are not possible, and he or she may quit in an embarrassing huff after finding out how things really work. Fortunately, over the past few years, the level of management expertise found in medical directors of open panels has increased significantly, and the medical director is much more likely to be able to manage the process than have to be managed.

The second primary recruiting responsibility of the medical director is closing certain difficult cases. There will be times when the physician recruiter has done all the preparatory work but a sought-after physician will be hesitant about signing. In these cases, the medical director's personal contact may be the deciding factor.

TYPES OF CONTRACTING SITUATIONS

There are a number of possible types of contracting situations with which an open panel may have to deal in developing a network. The subject of the contract itself is addressed in Chapter 55, and reimbursement is discussed in Chapter 9. This discussion focuses on the types of situations that may present themselves regardless of specific contracting and reimbursement issues.

Individual Physicians

This is the most common category of contracting in open panels, which is not surprising

given the large number of solo practitioners in many parts of the country. In this model, the physician contracts directly with the health plan and not through any third party or intermediary. The advantage to the plan is that there is a direct relationship with the physician, which makes it cleaner and simpler to interact. The disadvantage is that it is only one physician, and therefore the effort to obtain and maintain that relationship is disproportionately great.

Small Groups

Not substantially different from individual physicians, small groups usually operate relatively cohesively. The advantage to the plan is that the same amount of effort to obtain and maintain a small group yields a higher number of physicians. Plans generally prefer to contract with small groups for that reason. The disadvantage is that, if the relationship with the group needs to be terminated (for whatever reason, theirs or yours), there is greater disruption in patient care.

Multispecialty Groups

Multispecialty groups represent a special category. Relatively uncommon in certain parts of the country, they are occasionally the dominant practices in certain areas. The advantage of contracting with multispecialty groups is that you obtain not only PCPs but specialty consultants as well. This provides for broader access (including specialists to whom other PCPs may refer) and allows for existing referral patterns to continue.

One disadvantage is that multispecialty groups sometimes are dominated by the specialty or referral physicians in the group, which may lead to inappropriate utilization of referral services. Another potential disadvantage is the case where, by accepting the group, you are forced to accept a specialist whose cost or quality is not what you desire (although not so bad as to prevent contracting with the group). Again, as a general rule, if relations with large groups founder, there is a greater likelihood that there will be disruptions in patient care.

Independent Practice Associations

The independent practice association (IPA) is the original form of open panel plan. In the early 1970s, it was envisioned that open panel plans would all be IPA model plans. In this situation, there is actually a legal entity of an IPA, which contracts with physicians and in turn with the health plan. The advantage to the plan is that a large number of providers come along with the contract. Furthermore, if relations between the IPA and the health plan are close, there may be a confluence of goals, which benefits all parties.

There are two primary disadvantages to contracting with IPAs. The first is that an IPA can function somewhat as a union. If relations between the IPA and the health plan are arm's length or problematic, the IPA can hold a considerable portion (or perhaps all) of the delivery system hostage to negotiations. This fact has not been lost on the Justice Department of the federal government. IPAs that function as anticompetitive forces may encounter difficulties with the law.

The second disadvantage is that the plan's ability to select and deselect individual physicians is much more limited when contracting through an IPA than when contracting directly with the providers. If the IPA is at risk for medical expenses, there may be a confluence of objectives between the plan and the IPA to bring in cost-effective and high-quality providers and to remove those providers whose cost or quality is not acceptable. Unfortunately, the IPA has its own internal political structure, so that defining who is cost effective or high quality, as well as dealing with outliers, may not match exactly between the plan and the IPA. If the plan has the contractual right to refuse to accept or to departicipate individual providers in the IPA, that obstacle may be avoided, although the purely political obstacles remain.

IDSs

Many hospitals have been exploring methods of developing organizations that will legally and structurally bind the physicians to the hospital. Sometimes these are referred to as physician–hospital organizations (PHOs) or MSOs. In addition to hospital-based IDSs, there are physician practice management companies (PPMs) and physician-only MSOs. These and other forms of IDSs are discussed in further detail in Chapter 4. The positive and negative ramifications that apply to IPAs are similar to those for IDSs (including their antitrust risk) and have been discussed above. In addition to those issues, there are two other broad issues that relate specifically to hospital-based organizations.

First is the link between a hospital's own willingness to do business with a plan and the plan's willingness to do business with the PHO or MSO. In other words, the hospital may refuse to contract with the plan or may not provide favorable terms unless the plan brings in the PHO, perhaps even on an exclusive basis. That obviously removes control of that entire portion of the delivery system (physicians and hospital), leaving the plan at the mercy (or abilities) of the PHO or MSO to achieve the goals of the plan. If the PHO or MSO is at significant risk for medical expenses, there may be confluence of goals.

The second issue relates to the reasons that the PHO formed in the first place. If the hospital has the goals of keeping beds filled and keeping the medical staff happy (and busy), the selection process for choosing which providers are in the PHO may be weighted toward those physicians who admit a lot of patients to the hospital, a criterion that may not be ideal from the plan's perspective. Another reason that the PHO may have formed was to circle the wagons, that is, to resist aggressive managed care. In that event, there may be a real mismatch between how the plan wants to perform medical management and how the PHO will allow it to occur. Issues of control of utilization management, quality management, and provider selection become difficult to resolve.

Nonetheless, IDSs can function effectively. If the organization is formed with a genuine understanding of the goals of managed care, a genuine willingness to deal with difficult issues of utilization, quality, and provider selection, and a willingness to share control with the health plan, it is possible to work together.

PPMs are similar to IPAs in some regards, except that the bond between the physician and the PPM is generally quite tighter than that found in a typical IPA. PPMs often desire to contract with a plan with the specific intent of not including the hospital in any risk sharing. This is done to allow the PPM to buy hospital services on the medical spot market through per diem reimbursement (see Chapter 14) and keep the savings (and profit) from lower utilization.

The primary advantage to a health plan in contracting with an IDS is the ability to have a network in rapid order. This may be a primary driver in the case of a plan entering into a new market or one that is already competitive, and it may in fact be the only way an HMO can get a network. This last issue will be especially true if a large number of physicians have sold their practices to hospitals or PPMs. A plan that needs to expand its medical service area quickly or is expanding into entirely new geographic areas may find that contracting through IDSs allows it to achieve its expansion goals and be first to market.

An additional advantage may occur if the IDS is willing to provide a substantial savings to the plan, better than what would be available on a direct contract basis. If the plan is entering into a new product line (e.g., Medicare risk or Medicaid), the plan may desire to share the risk for medical costs through aggressive capitation with the IDS.

The last broad condition that may make contracting with an IDS the most desirable option is when an insurer with little or no managed care experience desires to enter into the managed care arena (such a strategy may be the only alternative to death by attrition for some insurers in markets with heavy or growing managed care

penetration). In this case, the non–managed care health insurer plans to capitalize on the IDS's (hoped for) ability to manage utilization and quality.

It should be noted that, in certain states, HMOs are not allowed to contract solely with the IDS but must have contracts directly with the physicians. The contract may be brief and encompass no more than standard hold harmless language (see Chapter 55) and then reference the contract between the IDS and the physician and the contract between the IDS and the plan. This requirement is meant to ensure that each and every individual physician understands and agrees to certain provisions required under state law, such as the prohibition on balance billing. See Chapter 56 for more discussion of legal issues in IDSs.

Faculty Practice Plans

Faculty practice plans (FPPs) are medical groups that are organized around teaching programs, primarily at university hospitals. An FPP may be a single entity or may encompass multiple entities defined along specialty lines (e.g., cardiology or anesthesiology). Plans generally contract with the legal group representing the FPP rather than with individual physicians within the FPP, although that varies from plan to plan.

FPPs represent special challenges for various reasons. First, many teaching institutions and FPPs tend to be less cost effective in their practice styles than private physicians. This probably relates to the primary missions of the teaching program: to teach and to perform research. Cost effectiveness is a secondary goal only (if a goal at all).

A second challenge is that an FPP, like a medical group, comes all together or not at all. This again means that the plan has little ability to select or deselect the individual physicians within the FPP. Related to that is the lack of detail regarding claims and encounter data. Many FPPs simply bill the plan, accept capitation, or collect encounter data in the name of the FPP rather than in the name of the individual provider who performed the service. This means that the plan has little ability to analyze data to the same level of detail that is afforded in the rest of the network.

A third major challenge is the use of house officers (interns and residents in training) and medical students to deliver care. In teaching hospitals, the day-to-day care is actually delivered by house officers rather than by the attending faculty physician, who functions as a teacher and supervisor. House officers and medical students, because they are learning how to practice medicine, tend to be profligate in their use of medical resources; they are there to learn medicine, not simply to perform direct service to patients. Furthermore, experience does allow physicians to learn what is cost effective, and house officers and medical students have yet to gain such experience. Nevertheless, there is some evidence that intensive attention to utilization management by faculty can have a highly beneficial effect on house staff.[4]

The last major issue with teaching programs and FPPs is the nature of how they deliver services. Most teaching programs are not really set up for case management. It is far more common to have multiple specialty clinics (e.g., pulmonology, cardiology, or vascular surgery) to which patients are referred for each specific problem. Such a system takes on characteristics of a medical pinball machine, where the members ricochet from clinic to clinic, having each organ system attended to with little regard for the totality of care. This leads to enormous run-ups in cost as well as continuity problems and a clear lack of control or accountability.

Despite these difficulties, there are good reasons for health plans to contract with teaching programs and FPPs other than the societal good derived from the training of medical practitioners. Teaching programs and FPPs provide not only routine care but tertiary and highly specialized care as well, care that the plan will have to find means to provide in any event. Teaching programs also add prestige to the plan by virtue of their reputation for providing high-quality

care, although that can be a two-edged sword in that the participation of a teaching program may draw adverse selection in membership.[*]

Most teaching programs and FPPs recognize the problems cited above and are willing to work with plans to ameliorate them. For example, they may be willing to extend a deep discount to a managed care plan in the recognition that the plan's ability to control utilization is limited and therefore must be made up on price. Teaching programs may occasionally be willing to accept a high level of risk for medical expenses, but that can be a problem for them because of the risk of adverse selection mentioned above. Risk for defined services (e.g., laboratory or radiology) may be more acceptable.

See Chapter 15 for a detailed discussion of academic medical centers and managed care.

CREDENTIALING

It is not enough to get physicians to sign contracts. Without performing proper credentialing, you will have no knowledge of the quality or acceptability of physicians, nor will you have any idea whether they will actually be an asset to your plan. Furthermore, in the event of a legal action against a physician, the plan may expose itself to some liability by having failed to carry out proper credentialing. In one well-known study, up to 5 percent of physicians applying for positions in ambulatory care clinics misrepresented their credentials in their applications; how that might translate for an HMO or other managed care organization (MCO) where physicians are likely to be more stable in their com-

---

[*] In other words, if there is more than one health plan competing in a single group account (e.g., an employer group) for membership, members with serious illnesses may choose the health plan affiliated with a teaching program to ensure access to high-quality tertiary care. That means that sicker members join that health plan and less sick members join the health plan that does not have such an affiliation. This issue does not come up if the plan is the sole carrier in an account or if all the competing plans use the teaching program, but it is a clear problem if there are multiple plans competing freely for members in a single account.

munity is unknown.[5] In most plans, the medical director bears ultimate responsibility for credentialing along with a credentialing committee, although the activities of credentialing are usually carried out by the provider relations department.

The credentialing process is a critical one and should be carried out during the recruiting process and, if necessary, after the contract or letter of intent is signed. Periodic recredentialing (usually every 2 years) should also take place. Recredentialing may be less extensive than primary credentialing, but more sophisticated plans are adding new elements to the recredentialing process, including looking at measures of quality of care, member satisfaction, compliance with plan policies and procedures, and utilization management.

As this book is being written, a new organization has come into existence: the third-party credentialing verification organization (CVO). The CVO performs primary credentialing on a physician, and then the HMO or PPO relies on the CVO for that credentialing verification. The purpose of this is to reduce the need for an individual physician to be required to provide identical credentialing data to numerous MCOs; in addition, the MCO can obtain the data in a more timely fashion, and the data will be complete on the first pass. The chief problem with this approach is the requirement by many regulators and outside accreditation agencies that the HMO conduct primary source verification (i.e., obtain the information directly rather than relying on another party to obtain it). The National Committee for Quality Assurance (NCQA; see Chapter 37) has created a CVO certification program to allow third party CVOs to meet NCQA standards in credentialing to perform credentialing for MCOs.[6]

If the credentialing process is incomplete at the time the physician is ready to sign, then a provision must be included in the signed document (either the contract or the letter of intent) indicating that the final contract is contingent upon the plan's completing the credentialing process. If the predetermined standards are not met, then the plan will be unable to accept that physician in its panel. A word of warning: It is more difficult than one might imagine to tell physicians that the plan is not going to accept them after they have signed a contract.

The elements illustrated in Exhibit 8–1 are some examples of data that should be captured in the credentialing process.

Verification of Credentialing Data

Primary verification of the elements in Exhibit 8–1 should also be performed as appropriate. Verification of data may be obtained from a number of sources, including the National Practitioner Data Bank (NPDB; see below) and those noted in Exhibit 8–2.

NPDB

A special type of credentialing requirement and reference check was created by the Health Care Quality Improvement Act of 1986. This act, an important law for managed care plans, is discussed in Chapters 7 and 57. The reader is urged to refer to those chapters and to become familiar with the credentialing aspects of this act. An early report from the NPDB stated that the annual rate of licensure actions was 2.7 per 1,000 physicians (0.0 to 9.7 per 1,000), that the annual rate of clinical privileges actions was 1.4 per 1,000 physicians (0.0 to 3.6 per 1,000), and that there were an average of 21.1 medical malpractice payments per 1,000 physicians.[7] By the end of 1994, the NPDB reported the following statistics: The data bank contained more than 97,500 reports, of which 82 percent were related to malpractice payments, with licensure reports making up most of the rest; it had processed more than 4.5 million requests for information; and 8 percent of queries were matched with a report.[8]

Office Evaluation

If the plan is contracting directly with physicians, it will probably desire to perform a direct evaluation of the physician's office. If the plan

Exhibit 8–1 Elements of Credentialing

Basic elements

- Training (copy of certificates)
  1. Location
  2. Type
- Specialty board eligibility or certification (copy of certificate)
- Current state medical license (copy of certificate)
  1. Restrictions
  2. History of loss of license in any state
- Drug Enforcement Agency (DEA) number (copy of certificate)
- Hospital privileges
  1. Name of hospitals
  2. Scope of practice privileges
- Malpractice insurance
  1. Carrier name
  2. Currency of coverage (copy of face sheet)
  3. Scope of coverage (financial limits and procedures covered)
- Malpractice history
  1. Pending claims
  2. Successful claims against the physician, either judged or settled
- National Practitioner Data Bank status
- Medicare, Medicaid, and federal tax identification numbers
- Social Security number
- Location and telephone numbers of all offices
- Yes/no questions regarding:
  1. Limitations or suspensions of privileges
  2. Suspension from government programs
  3. Suspension or restriction of DEA license
  4. Malpractice cancellation
  5. Felony conviction
  6. Drug or alcohol abuse
  7. Chronic or debilitating illnesses

Additional elements

- Hours of operation
- Provisions for emergency care and back-up
- Use of nonphysician (i.e., midlevel) practitioners
- In-office surgery capabilities
- In-office testing capabilities
- Languages spoken
- Work history, past 5 years
- Areas of special medical interest
- Record of continuing medical education

Exhibit 8–2 Credentialing Data Verification Sources

Graduation from medical school (any one of the following):

- Confirmation from the medical school
- American Medical Association Master File of Physicians in the United States
- Confirmation from the Association of American Medical Colleges
- Confirmation from the Educational Commission for Foreign Medical Graduates for international medical graduates licensed after 1986
- Confirmation from state licensure agency, if the agency performs primary verification of medical school graduation

Valid license to practice medicine (any one of the following):

- State licensure agency
- Federation of State Medical Boards
- Primary admitting facility if the facility performs primary verification of licensure

Completion of residency training (any one of the following):

- Confirmation from the residency training program
- American Medical Association Master File of Physicians in the United States
- Confirmation from the Association of American Medical Colleges
- Confirmation from state licensure agency, if the agency performs primary verification of residency training

Board certification (any one of the following):

- American Board of Medical Specialties Compendium of Certified Medical Specialists
- American Osteopathic Association Directory of Osteopathic Physicians
- Confirmation from the appropriate specialty board
- American Medical Association Master File of Physicians in the United States
- Confirmation from state licensure agency, if the agency performs primary verification of board status

Source: National Committee for Quality Assurance, 1995 NCQA Reviewer Guidelines for the Standards for Accreditation.

has contracted through an IDS, it is more likely to forgo such a review if the IDS has already performed the review to the satisfaction of the plan. In some cases, the plan may choose not to perform an office review because of the associated cost or the need to get the network up quickly or for fear of offending physicians; these are inadequate reasons.

There are two main items to evaluate in a physician's office: capacity to accept new members, and office ambiance. In addition, the plan or IDS may review the office from the standpoint of a quality management process, compliance with Occupational Safety and Health Administration guidelines, presence of certain types of equipment (e.g., a defibrillator), and so forth. If capacity and ambiance are the only review areas, the evaluation is best accomplished by having the recruiter visit the office and may be performed in one fairly short visit. A more detailed review will require a trained health professional, usually a nurse, and may take an hour or two.

In addition to asking physicians directly how many new members they will accept (and usually including that in the contract), the recruiter should ask to examine the appointment book. In this way, the recruiter can get a reasonably good idea of how much appointment availability the physician has. For example, if there are no available appointment slots for a physical examination for 6 weeks or more, the physician may be overestimating his or her ability to accept more work.

The recruiter can also get an idea of how easy it is for a patient with an acute problem to be put on the schedule. This may be examined by looking at the number of acute slots left open each day and by looking at the number of double-booked appointments that were put in at the end of each day.

In addition, the recruiter can assess less tangible items, such as cleanliness of the office, friendliness of the staff toward patients, and general atmosphere. Hours of operation can be verified, as can provisions for emergency care and in-office equipment capabilities.

MEDICAL RECORD REVIEW

Many plans require a review of sample medical records by the medical director. The purpose of this is to assure the medical director that physicians do indeed practice high-quality medicine and that their practice is already cost effective. Some physicians object to submitting to this review, but if it is required for participation, and if the physician is assured that it is strictly confidential and not a witch hunt, there should be fewer problems. Because the physician presumably has no plan members whose charts can be reviewed, care will need to be taken to protect the identity of the patients because the plan has no legal right to access confidential medical records.

If the plan already has a quality assurance program that involves chart review, a physician should agree to the initial review as a matter of course. Sometimes it is not objections by the physicians that form the impediment to this review but rather the embarrassment of the medical director in having to perform it.

COMPENSATION

Compensation of PCPs in open panels is discussed in detail in Chapter 9.

ORIENTATION

In all enterprises, time invested in the beginning to ensure real understanding is time well spent. Therefore, a planned approach to orientation of a newly added PCP will pay off in improved compliance with your plan's procedures and policies, in increased professional satisfaction on the part of the PCP, and in increased member satisfaction. Orientation is aimed at two audiences: the PCP and the PCP's office staff. Exhibit 8–3 lists some topics to consider in orienting physicians, and Exhibit 8–4 lists some topics for orienting their office staff.

NETWORK MANAGEMENT

Maintenance of the professional relationship with physicians in the network recently has as-

Exhibit 8–3 Suggested Topics for Orientation of Open Panel Physicians

- Plan subscription agreement and schedule of benefits
- Authorization policies and procedures
- Forms and paperwork
- Utilization and financial data supplied by plan
- Committees and meetings
- Quality management program and peer review
- Recredentialing requirements
- Member transfer in or out of practice
  —Member initiated
  —Physician initiated
- Plan member grievance procedure
- Schedule of compensation from plan
- Contact persons in plan
- Affiliated providers
  —Primary care
  —Consultants
  —Institutions
  —Ancillary services

Exhibit 8–4 Suggested Topics for Orientation of Office Staff

- Plan subscription agreement and schedule of benefits
- Authorization policies and procedures
- Forms and paperwork
- Member transfer in or out of practice
  —Member initiated
  —Physician initiated
- Plan member grievance procedure
- Member eligibility verification
- Member identification card
- Current member list and eligibility verification
- Affiliated providers
  —Primary care
  —Consultants
  —Institutions
  —Ancillary services
- Contact persons in plan
  —Names
  —Telephone numbers
- Hours of operation

sumed a far greater role in managed care than at any previous time in the industry's history. The saturation of managed care plans in some communities, coupled with increasing interventions by third party payers (commercial, Medicare, and Medicaid) limiting providers' ability to cost shift to other fee-for-service payers, has placed increasing strain on physicians and has clearly colored how they view participation with managed care plans. Failure to service the network properly can lead to defections or closure of practices to your plan, difficulty with new recruiting, and a slow downward spiral. Even for those plans that have not properly maintained their networks, however, it is never too late to put in the effort because it is certainly possible to recover from a poor history.

If the plan contracts with an IDS for its network, that does not mean that obligations to maintain the network cease. Many of the issues discussed here remain under the control of the plan and will continue to exert a strong influence over the physicians in the contracted network. The IDS will have the burden of responsibility for network maintenance and must therefore also pay attention to these issues. It is imperative that *both* the plan and the IDS pay close attention to network maintenance and not rely solely on one party for this vital function. If both parties are not actively involved, there is the strong possibility of network problems degenerating into finger-pointing, in which case both parties lose.

The Physician's View of Managed Care

To maintain the network, it is first important to understand how physicians view managed care. These issues are discussed at length in Chapter 26 but are mentioned briefly here. An understanding of these elements allows provider relations staff to key in on those items that are important to physicians.

In general, physicians see managed care as a general threat and pain in the neck. The issue of loss of or impingement on autonomy is perhaps the most emotionally charged issue there is. There are organizational demands on physicians as well: compliance with a restricted referral and hospital panel, increased bureaucratic overhead, multiple plans that use different forms and procedures, and an inability to rid themselves easily of difficult patients (so-called entitled demanders[9,10]).

Managed care often places the physician in an adversarial relationship with a patient (actually less often than one would think, but it only takes a few). This is uncomfortable because physicians are not trained for it.[11] This most often comes up in the guise of clearly unnecessary or medically marginal care that is demanded by the patient, but it may also occur when something is medically necessary but not a covered benefit; this issue most often appears under the term *patient advocacy*.

Some physicians have a real fear that managed care can lead to decreased quality of care. This has never really been proven, and there are now some data specific to open panel plans that show good quality of care along with lower utilization.[12–15] Nevertheless, the fear remains, and coupled with this is a fear of increased malpractice liability. The Wickline case, combined with threats of legal action by members demanding certain services, has increased the anxiety level of practicing physicians.

Managed care often results in a demand to discount fees or, more important, restricts the ability of a physician to cost shift into the plan as other payers (especially government programs) squeeze down. In plans with capitation or withhold mechanisms, some income is placed at risk, a situation generally not greeted with enthusiasm.

Last, most managed care plans are quite poor at providing appropriate feedback to physicians. Feedback is often sporadic, usually coinciding with annual payouts (or lack thereof) of risk pools. Routine useful information, such as the status of risk pools and utilization data, is often inadequate. In fact, in some plans the physicians hear from the plan only when there is a problem,

such as overutilization, and never at all when performance is good.

In the face of all these issues, many physicians in fact are quite satisfied with their participation in managed care. Their incomes are maintained or enhanced, their patients are able to receive medical care without economic barriers to access, and they enjoy participating in a more structured delivery system that has the ability to deal with issues of cost and quality.[16] In general, physicians who are satisfied with their participation have been able to make an attitudinal adjustment more successfully than their colleagues who are not satisfied.[17]

Maintaining the Network

This topic is so important that most of the key elements are discussed in a separate chapter. The reader is referred to Chapter 26, which examines changing provider behavior, because changing behavior involves many issues that are important to network maintenance. The issues of data and feedback, the use of positive feedback, translation of goals and objectives, autonomy needs, quality of care, role conflict, understanding the insurance functions of the plan, plan differentiation in the marketplace, and discipline and sanctioning will not be repeated here.

In most plans, there are individuals who are solely responsible for maintaining communications with the physician panel, both PCPs and consultants, and with the physicians and their office staff. The roles of these provider relations representatives are to elicit feedback from the physicians and office staff, to update them on changes, to troubleshoot, and generally to keep things running smoothly.

The importance of this function cannot be overstated. Some care must be taken in selecting the individuals who will fill this role. Unless provider relations staff are mature and experienced, they may fall into the trap of forgetting for whom they are actually working. It is appropriate and necessary for them to represent the PCPs' point of view to plan management, but it is inappropriate if they find themselves siding against the health plan in the event of a dispute unless the plan is egregiously at fault. The provider relations staff must seek to prevent rifts, not foster them.

Provider relations are similar to customer relations, but an even better metaphor is that of a business partner. In a customer relation, the customer is always right; in a health plan, neither the plan nor the physician is always right. It is perhaps more useful to strive to be seen as a reliable and desirable business partner to the providers with whom you do business under contracts and agreements. Provider relations must therefore be proactive rather than simply reactive.

In addition to the items discussed in Chapter 26, the plan should have a well-developed early warning system for troubleshooting. Such a system could include regular on-site visits by provider relations staff (and occasionally by the medical director) and regular two-way communications vehicles. Changes in patterns, particularly patterns in utilization and compliance with plan policy and procedure, will often be a sign that the relationship is going awry. Last, close monitoring of the member services complaints report can yield crucial information; physicians will often tell their patients what they think and what they intend to do long before they tell the plan.

Removing Physicians from the Network

Beyond the elements referred to above, another function of network maintenance is the determination of whom not to keep in the plan. In any managed care plan, there will be physicians who simply cannot or will not work within the system and whose practice style is clearly cost ineffective or of poor quality. Quality is discussed in Chapter 25, and sanctions for reasons of poor quality are discussed in Chapter 57; quality-related actions will not be repeated here. The point of this section is not whether those physicians practice poor medicine (that judgment need not be made) but whether their practice style is one that the plan can afford.

A plan may also choose to terminate physicians because the physician panel is too large. This is rarely an issue for PCPs because most plans can always use wider access to primary care for both medical delivery and marketing reasons. Specialty networks (see Chapter 13) are a different matter, and plans may reduce the size of the specialty network to concentrate business or achieve better discounts and more control. The exception in primary care is likely to occur when a plan makes a wholesale commitment to an IDS and, as part of that commitment, agrees to terminate any PCPs who are not part of the IDS. In this situation, plans will usually resist terminating existing PCP relationships but may agree no longer to recruit new PCPs who are not part of the IDS (unless the IDS cannot provide sufficient PCPs in a geographic region).

Regarding the issue of unacceptably costly practice style, the plan must develop a mechanism for identification of such practitioners that uses a combination of claims and utilization data (see Chapter 27) and some type of formal performance evaluation system. If identified providers are reluctant to change, even after the medical director has worked closely with them, then serious consideration should be given to terminating them from the panel. In fact, if a plan is in serious financial difficulties stemming from the behavior of the network providers, management may decide to act unilaterally (assuming that the contract between the plan and the providers allows either party to terminate without cause upon adequate notice) and to departicipate those (presumably few) providers whose practice behavior is so far out of line that there will be an immediate positive impact on plan performance.

There are any number of objections to removing a physician from the panel. Asking the members to change physicians is not easy or pleasant, benefits managers get upset, and invariably the physician in question is in a strategic location. The decision often comes down to whether you want to continue to subsidize that physician's poor practice behavior from the earnings of the other physicians (in capitated or risk/bonus types of reimbursement systems) and from the plan's earnings or drive the rates up to uncompetitive levels. If those are unacceptable alternatives, then the separation must occur.

In some states, organized medicine has succeeded in persuading the state legislatures to pass due process laws, putting the plan in a position of having to follow potentially cumbersome and bureaucratic procedures to terminate a physician for any reason (without requiring the physician to follow those same procedures in the event that he or she wants want to quit the plan). In these situations, the plan has no choice but to conform; the cost of such conformance is generally minimal compared with the economic consequences of failing to take action. The primary problem with these types of laws (other than the long period of time it requires to go through the process) is the possibility that a physician whose practice style is truly not a match for managed care may prevail, through utterly procedural measures, and continue to practice in the plan, with negative consequences for the rest of the network.

Once the decision has been made to departicipate a provider from the network, it is best to act promptly. Some HMOs, however, contractually require a physician to participate until the entire membership has had a chance to change plans (which may take a year unless the physician's member panel is small), but that option can be quite costly because the physician will have no incentive to control cost once he or she has been notified of termination. In those cases, the contract usually also allows the plan to increase the amount of withhold (e.g., from 20 percent up to 50 percent) to cover excess costs. In preferred provider organizations there is usually no need for such arrangements because the member may still see that physician, albeit at a higher level of coinsurance.

CONCLUSION

Network development requires an orderly project management approach, whether such development is undertaken by a health plan or by an IDS. It is equally important to invest in proper orientation of new physicians and their office staff. Maintenance of the relationship between the physicians and the plan is a key element of success that is gaining increasing importance as plans become ever more competitive in the marketplace. The plan or IDS must be willing to departicipate a provider in certain circumstances to deliver the proper combination of quality and cost effectiveness that is a requirement of managed care.

REFERENCES AND NOTES

1. T. Defina, Educating Physicians in Managed Care, *Health System Leader* (May 1995): 4–12.

2. Group Health Association of America (GHAA), *HMO Performance Survey* (Washington, D.C.: GHAA, 1994).

3. Group Health Association of America (GHAA), *HMO Industry Profile, Vol. 2: Physician Staffing and Utilization Patterns* (Washington, D.C.: GHAA, 1991).

4. J.R. Woodside, et al., Intensive, Focused Utilization Management in a Teaching Hospital: An Exploratory Study, *Quality Assurance and Utilization Review* 6 (1991): 47–50.

5. W.A. Schaffer, et al., Falsification of Clinical Credentials by Physicians Applying for Ambulatory Staff Privileges, *New England Journal of Medicine* 318 (1988): 356–357.

6. National Committee for Quality Assurance (NCQA), *CVO Certification Program 1995–1996* (Washington, D.C.: NCQA, 1995).

7. F. Mullan, et al., The National Practitioner Data Bank— Report from the First Year, *Journal of the American Medical Association* 28 (1992): 73–79.

8. R.E. Oshel, et al., The National Practitioner Data Bank: The First Four Years, *Public Health Reports* (July/August 1995): 383–394.

9. E. Friedson, Prepaid Group Practice and the New "Demanding Patient," *Milbank Memorial Fund Quarterly* 51 (1973): 407–411.

10. J.E. Groves, Taking Care of the Hateful Patient, *New England Journal of Medicine* 298 (1978): 883–887.

11. N. Daniels, Why Saying No to Patients in the United States Is So Hard, *New England Journal of Medicine* 314 (1986): 1380–1383.

12. J.E. Ware, et al., Comparison of Health Outcomes at a Health Maintenance Organization with Those of Fee-for-Service Care, *Lancet* 1 (1986): 1017–1022.

13. I.S. Udvarhelyi, et al., Comparison of the Quality of Ambulatory Care for Fee-for-Service and Prepaid Patients, *Annals of Internal Medicine* 115 (1991): 394–400.

14. E.M. Sloss, et al., Effect of a Health Maintenance Organization on Physiologic Health, *Annals of Internal Medicine* 106 (1987): 130–138.

15. C.M. Clancy and B.E. Hillner, Physicians as Gatekeepers—The Impact of Financial Incentives, *Archives of Internal Medicine* 149 (1989): 917–920.

16. R. Schultz, et al., Physician Adaptation to Health Maintenance Organizations and Implications for Management, *Health Services Research* 25 (1990): 43–64.

17. H.R. Reames and D.C. Dunstone, Professional Satisfaction of Physicians, *Archives of Internal Medicine* 149 (1989): 1951–1956.

SUGGESTED READING

Felt, S., Frazer, H., and Gold, M. 1994. *HMO Primary Care Staffing Patterns and Processes: A Cross-Site Analysis of 23 HMOs*. Washington, D.C.: Mathematica Policy Research, Inc.

Fisher, N.B., Smith, H.L., and Pasternok, D.P. 1993. Critical Success Factors in Recruiting Health Maintenance Organization Physicians. *Health Care Management Review* 18 (1): 51–61.

Greeley, H.P. and Woods, K.A. 1994. *Credentialing in the Managed Care Environment: A Guide for Managed Care Organizations and Health Care Networks*. Marblehead, Mass.: Opus Communications.

Nash, D.B. (ed.). 1994. *The Physician's Guide to Managed Care*. Gaithersburg, MD: Aspen.

Palsbo, S.E. and Sullivan, C.B. 1993. *The Recruitment Experience of Health Maintenance Organizations for Primary Care Physicians: Final Report*. Washington, D.C.: Health Resources and Services Administration.

Chapter 9

Compensation of Primary Care Physicians in Open Panel Plans

Peter R. Kongstvedt

Managed care organizations (MCOs), primarily health maintenance organizations (HMOs), frequently use some form of risk-based reimbursement to pay physicians, especially primary care physicians (PCPs).* Specialty care physicians may also be paid under some form of risk-based reimbursement, although with less frequency than occurs with PCPs; reimbursement of specialty care physicians is discussed in Chapter 12. This chapter provides an overview of the most common risk-based methods to reimburse PCPs.

All risk-based reimbursement systems require a change in attitude from unmanaged fee for service (FFS). Economic reward comes from lowering *total* health care costs. Depending on the design of the reimbursement system, the financial reward may be directly or indirectly related to total health care costs. Financial reward may be only partially related to utilization and may also be affected by member satisfaction and quality (see Chapter 11). Reimbursement systems may be perceived as primarily punitive, as primarily reward based, or as a system that shares with providers the savings achieved from

good management of medical utilization. Those perceptions are driven partially by the design of the reimbursement system and partially by the HMO's attitude to the management of that system.

A reimbursement system is simply one of the many tools available in managed care and has limited ability to achieve desired goals in the absence of other tools, such as competent management of utilization and quality. Neither the divisions by provider type nor the reimbursement mechanisms described here are found often in a pure state. Managed care is marked by a high degree of continual change and variation.

BASIC MODELS OF REIMBURSEMENT

This chapter addresses reimbursement of PCPs in open panels. This is distinct from the compensation of individual physicians in organized groups or integrated delivery systems (IDSs); that topic is discussed in detail in Chapter 10. It is possible (and even likely in the case of IDSs) that these methods of reimbursement will be used on an individual physician basis in such groups, but not necessarily. In the case of organized groups, this chapter discusses only the reimbursement of the group, rather than any one physician in that group by the MCO. In the case of IDSs, if the IDS accepts risk for primary care services, it will still need to apply these methods to compensate the physicians within the IDS, even if that method is different from how the IDS is compensated by the MCO.

---

* PCPs are assumed to be in the specialties of family practice, internal medicine, and pediatrics; general practice (i.e., non–board certified general practitioners) is also considered primary care in those plans that contract with general practitioners. Obstetrics and gynecology, while sharing some attributes of primary care, are generally treated as specialties by HMOs. Physician extenders, such as physician assistants and clinical nurse practitioners, are generally treated as being associated with PCPs and so are not discussed separately.

There are two basic ways to compensate open panel PCPs for services: capitation and FFS. Large surveys have reported that approximately 60 percent of open panel plans use capitation and that the remainder use FFS (with a rare and puzzling small percentage of salary), as illustrated in Figure 9–1.[1] Another study reports that 69 percent of HMOs use capitation to reimburse PCPs; the difference between these two reports is probably due to sampling techniques but is not terribly important.[2] This distribution of reimbursement methods has been relatively stable for the past several years, although there is no guarantee that it will remain so.[3,4]

CAPITATION

Capitation is prepayment for services on a per member per month (PMPM) basis. In other words, a PCP is paid the same amount of money every month for a member regardless of whether that member receives services and regardless of how expensive those services are.

Scope of Covered Services

To determine an appropriate capitation, you must first define what will be covered in the scope of primary care services. Include all services that the PCP will be expected to deliver, including preventive services, outpatient care, and hospital visits. Certain areas are difficult to define, for example diagnostic testing, prescriptions, surgical procedures (what if the same procedure is performed by the PCP and by a referral physician?), and so forth. Other services, such as immunizations, office care, and so forth, are easier to define. If a plan is unable to define primary care services easily, a good reference is published by Milliman & Robertson, a national actuarial firm.[5] Defining the scope of covered services forms the basis for estimating the total costs of primary care.

Many performance-based compensation systems also hold the PCP accountable for non–primary care services through either risk programs or positive incentive programs, both of which

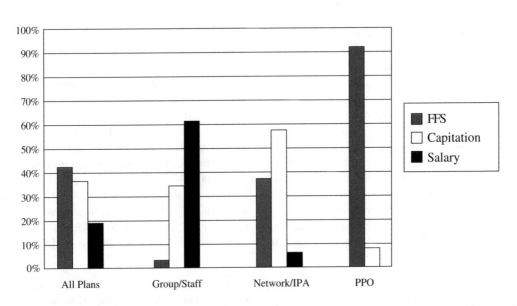

Figure 9–1 Primary care reimbursement. IPA, independent practice association; PPO, preferred provider organization. *Source:* Reprinted from *Arrangements Between Managed Care Plans and Physicians: Results from a 1994 Survey of Managed Care Plans*, 1995, Physician Payment Review Commission.

are discussed later in this chapter. For such programs, the same exercise of categorizing what and how services are defined should be carried out for specialty or referral services, institutional care, and ancillary services. Essentially, you need to be able to estimate costs for each of the categories you will capitate or track for capitated or at-risk PCPs.

Calculation of Capitation Payments

The issue of expected costs in defined categories is beyond the scope of this chapter; greater discussion can be found in Chapters 42 and 43. Most plans use an actuary to set these cost categories initially, but if you have been in operation for some time and have a data system capable of tracking the detail, estimating costs in categories is simply a matter of collating the existing data. If you do not have that experience or cannot draw upon it, you will have a more difficult time. In those cases, it is frequently necessary to have an actuary develop the data on the basis of your geographic area, the benefits you will offer, and the controls you will put in place. In fact, it may be best to consult an actuary in any case, even though it is not inexpensive.

A plan wishing to convert from an FFS system to capitation will have to calculate the capitation equivalent of average FFS revenues for the physicians. In other words, calculate what physicians would receive from FFS for that membership base, assuming appropriate utilization.[*] This figure may then be discounted or not, depending on your situation. In plans where you fully expect the PCPs to receive a substantial bonus from control of utilization, a discount may be appropriate. In most cases, however, you will not wish to discount PCP services heavily.

As a rough example, if a physician receives approximately $45.00 per visit (collected, not just billed), and you can reasonably estimate a visitation rate of three primary care visits per member per year (PMPY),[*] then multiplying 3 × $45.00 and dividing the result by 12 (to get the revenue per month) yields $11.25 PMPM. That could approximate the capitation rate. This example is crude and does not take into account any particular definition of scope of covered services, actual visitation rates for an area, visit rate differences by age and sex, average collections by a physician, effect of copays, or differences in mean fees among different specialties, so that it should not be used in capitating primary care services.

If your plan uses a risk/bonus arrangement, it is useful to be able to demonstrate to physicians that if utilization is controlled they will receive more than they would have under FFS. For example, if your plan uses a blended capitation rate of $11.25 PMPM and there are in fact three visits PMPY, and if good utilization control yields a bonus of $2.25 PMPM from the risk pools, then the physician receives a year-end reconciliation that blends out to $13.50 PMPM, or $54.00 per visit.

Variations by Age and Gender

Most capitation systems vary payments by the age and gender of the enrolled member to take into account the differences in average utilization of medical services in those categories. For example, the capitation rate for a member younger than 18 months of age might be $34.00 PMPM to reflect the high utilization of services by newborns.[†] The capitation rate may then fall to $12.00 PMPM for members 1 to 2 years of age, $7.00 PMPM for members 2 to 18 years of age, $10.00 PMPM for male members 18 to 45 years of age, and $14.00 PMPM for female members 18 to 45 years of age (reflecting the

---

[*] In other words, if high utilization is one of the primary reasons to convert from FFS, it would not be appropriate simply to memorialize the high utilization rates when one is calculating a capitation equivalent; it is more appropriate to calculate the capitation on the basis of what utilization should be.

---

[*] The actual rate is closer to 3.3 to 3.6 (see Chapter 7), but it is easier to use 3.0 for the purposes of illustration.

[†] This includes immunizations unless the plan carves out immunization costs from the capitation rate; this is discussed later in the chapter.

higher costs for women in their childbearing years), and so forth.

Those plans without the capability of capitating by age and gender must take special care in developing capitation rates. This is a particular problem when one is recruiting pediatricians because utilization of services by members in the first 18 months of life is quite high. In plans that capitate an independent practice association (IPA) or an IDS with a single payment, the issue will remain. Unless the IPA or IDS has worked out an equitable method of distributing funds, the plan may need to provide support in this area.

Variations by Other Factors

It is possible, although not common, to vary capitation by factors other than age and sex. One example would be to vary capitation on the basis of experience, either expected or real. In this case, the capitation calculations would need to factor in the experience of each account group. In other words, if an account had an unusually healthy population of enrollees (e.g., all healthy, young nonsmokers who use seat belts and advocate nonviolence), the capitation would be factored downward; the reverse would be true for a group with high expected utilization (e.g., all hypertensive, overweight asbestos workers who smoke and drink heavily before racing on their motorcycles, without helmets, to buy illegal drugs). On a prospective basis, this could be done with standard industry codes in a manner similar to that used in developing premium rates under some forms of community rating (see Chapters 43 and 44). In the case of actual experience, a commercial account's retrospective experience could be used to adjust capitation payments up or down on a prospective basis. It is also possible to adjust capitation based on current health status, through the use of health status questionnaires and physical examinations, but that is cumbersome to administer and is not likely to reflect the actual premium collected from the account from which the members came. The reader is referred to the literature for

further discussion of methods of risk adjustment.[6] In all cases, the calculation of capitation would be highly complex compared with simple age and sex adjustments.

Another, more easily analyzed factor is geography. Even in the same statistical metropolitan area, there may be considerable differences in utilization. For example, in the Washington, D.C. metropolitan area there are highly significant differences in utilization among some counties in Maryland, northern Virginia, and the District of Columbia (Blue Cross/Blue Shield of the National Capitol Area, unpublished data, 1989–1992). In such situations, it may be appropriate to factor in geographic location when capitation payments are calculated.

Practice type may occasionally be a legitimate capitation factor. As an example, internists argue that the case mix they get is different from the case mix family practitioners get. This has not been borne out in any research, but there is some evidence that even in the same stratum of age and sex specialty internists (e.g., cardiologists) have sicker patients than general internists[7] (it must also be pointed out that the same investigators noted that, after adjustment for patient mix, there was a whopping 41 percent higher level of utilization in unmanaged FFS systems compared with HMOs[8]). The actual mix of services delivered in the office may also differ by specialty type (Blue Cross/Blue Shield of the National Capitol Area, unpublished data, 1989–1992). University teaching programs tend to attract adverse selection from the membership base and may have a legitimate claim in that regard (see Chapter 15).

There may be straightforward business adjustments to capitation as well. One example that occurs in certain plans is an adjustment for exclusivity. In this case, the plan pays a higher capitation rate to those providers who do not sign up with any other managed care plans (there are usually no restrictions against participating with government programs or indemnity carriers). Such arrangements may raise the potential for antitrust actions, but that is dependent on the particular situation.

In any event, if factors other than age and sex are to be used to adjust capitation, the calculations become highly complex, and communicating these factors to the participating providers becomes far more difficult. The plan must also guard against an imbalance in factors that lead to a higher than expected (or rated for) capitation payout over the entire network. In other words, adjustments lead not only to increases in capitation but to decreases as well.

Carve-Outs

Occasionally, capitation systems allow for certain services normally considered covered to be carved out of the capitation payment. For example, immunizations may not be paid under capitation but may be reimbursed on a fee schedule. As a general rule, carve-outs should only be used for those services that are not subject to discretionary utilization. In the case of immunizations, the medical guidelines for administering them are clear cut but subject to change (e.g., there may be an increase in the number of immunizations that are to be given in the first years of life), and there is little question about their use. That would not be the case, for example, for office-based laboratory testing. If your plan reimburses capitation for all services but pays fees for office-based laboratory work, you may see a rise in routine testing.

Risk

There are two broad categories of risk for capitated PCPs: service risk and financial risk. Service risk refers to the PCP receiving a fixed payment but not being at risk in the sense of having potentially to pay money out or not receive money as a result of risk. Service risk is essentially the fact that, if service volume is high, then the PCP receives relatively lower income per encounter, and vice versa. Although the PCP may not be at obvious financial risk, the PCP does lose the ability to sell services to someone else for additional income in the event that his or her schedule fills up with capitated patients at a rate that is higher than that used to calculate the

capitation. This issue is irrelevant if the PCP has slack time in his or her appointment book but can be an issue if the PCP is extremely busy. It is common for PCPs to feel that their capitation patients are abusing the service by coming in too frequently, but the perception often is more grievous than the reality.

Financial risk refers to actual income placed at risk regardless of whether the PCP has a service risk as well. There are two common forms of financial risk: withholds and capitated pools for non–primary care services. Figure 9–2 illustrates relative percentages of MCOs that use withholds and incentives as part of their capitation of PCPs.

THE FEDERAL GOVERNMENT'S PHYSICIAN INCENTIVE RULE*

Proposed limitations on physician incentive payments were first published in the *Federal Register* as a proposed rule on December 14, 1992. On March 27, 1996, HCFA and Health and Human Service's Office of Inspector General (OIG) published a final rule governing physician incentive arrangements entered into by Medicare risk and cost contractors and HMOs with risk-comprehensive contracts with Medicaid State Agencies. The effective date of the regulation varies depending on the requirements, but health plans with Medicare and/or Medicaid contracts must comply with the requirements by the dates noted later in this section.

This final rule is significant for several reasons. The media and courts have increased their scrutiny of physician incentive arrangements. The definition of "substantial financial risk" is likely to be used in lawsuits alleging that an HMO's incentive arrangements were unreasonable and encouraged underutilization of serv-

---

* The section entitled "The Federal Government's Physician Incentive Rule" was written by Mark S. Joffe, a contributor to this book, and a leading expert in this area of law and regulation. The author is indebted to him for allowing this section to be included in this chapter.

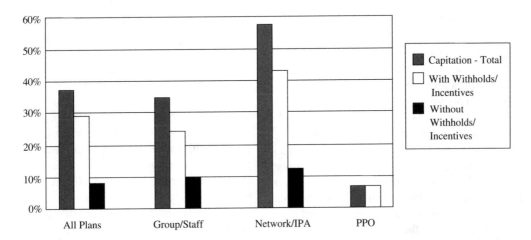

Figure 9–2 Primary care capitation and risk. PPO, preferred provider organization. *Source:* Reprinted from *Arrangements Between Managed Care Plans and Physicians: Results from a 1994 Survey of Managed Care Plans,* 1995, Physician Payment Review Commission.

ices. Further, it is likely that states will either use this rule as a framework for adopting laws to regulate physician incentive arrangements in the commercial sector or as a rationale against adopting such laws.

Background

Due to increasing attention to financial compensation arrangements and concern regarding their impact on physician behavior[9], in 1986, Congress passed legislation which prohibited hospitals and prepaid plans from "knowingly making a payment, directly or indirectly, to a physician as an inducement to reduce or limit services provided with respect to Medicare and Medicaid beneficiaries." Through amendment, the effective date of the law, as it applied to HMOs, was delayed twice. In 1990, the law was amended to repeal the application of the prohibition to HMOs. A new provision was added to Section 1876 of the Social Security Act which allows HMOs and CMPs to offer physician incentive arrangements that meet certain regulatory and statutory requirements. This final rule, published on March 27, 1996, implements that

amendment to Section 1876 to provide that the affective organizations must:

1. not operate a physician incentive plan that directly or indirectly makes specific payments to a physician or physician group as an inducement to limit or refuse medically necessary services to a specific individual enrolled with the organization;

2. disclose to HCFA their physician incentive plan arrangements in such detail as to allow HCFA to determine compliance of the arrangements with HHS regulations; and

3. in instances in which a physician incentive plan places a physician or physician group at "substantial financial risk" for services not directly provided, provide the physicians or physician groups with adequate and appropriate stop-loss protection and conduct surveys of currently and previously enrolled members to assess the degree of access to services and the satisfaction with the quality of services.

The Final Rule

Scope of Regulation

This rule applies to HMOs and CMPs with Medicare contracts under Section 1876 of the Social Security Act and to most plans with Medicaid risk comprehensive contracts (including Health Insuring Organizations or HIOs) operating under Section 1903(m) of the Social Security Act. For these entities, the rule only applies to payment arrangements applicable to services provided to Medicare beneficiaries and Medicaid recipients under the contracts.

In addition, the rule applies to entities other than federally qualified HMOs that seek an exception from the compensation arrangement prohibition under the physician self referral law. These entities may include HMOs without Medicare or Medicaid contracts, preferred provider organizations and prepaid health plans with Medicaid contracts.[10] For these entities, the rule applies to any payment for the provision of Medicare or Medicaid covered services.

The statute provides authority to HCFA to regulate only those arrangements that put a physician or physician group at risk for services which they order but do not directly furnish. It does not apply to incentive arrangements for services which a physician or physician group directly provides.

Criteria for the Determination of Substantial Financial Risk

Under the rule, a physician or physician group is considered to be at substantial financial risk if the incentive arrangements place the physician or physician group at risk for amounts beyond the risk threshold if the risk is based on the use or cost of referral services. The risk threshold is 25 percent of total potential payments from the HMO. If the patient panel size over which risk is spread is greater than 25,000 patients and is not the result of pooling patients enrolled in different lines of business or that are patients of more

than one physician group, the arrangement is deemed not to put physicians at substantial financial risk.

Withholds. Withhold arrangements will be considered to put physicians or physician groups at substantial financial risk if the amount withheld is greater than 25 percent of total potential payments from the HMO or if the amount withheld is less than 25 percent but the physician or physician group is liable for amounts exceeding 25 percent of total potential payments.

Bonuses. Bonuses will be considered to put physicians or physician groups at substantial financial risk if the bonus is greater than 33 percent of total potential payments minus the bonus. In such a case the risk threshold continues to be 25 percent because the bonus not received constitutes 25 percent of the maximum amount that may be paid to the physician or physician group.

Withholds plus bonuses. Arrangements that combine withholds and bonuses will be considered to put physicians or physician groups at substantial financial risk if the withhold plus bonuses equal 25 percent of total potential payments.

Capitation. Capitation payments will be considered to put physicians or physician groups at substantial financial risk if the difference between the maximum possible payment and the minimum possible payment is more than 25 percent or if the maximum and minimum amounts are not clearly defined in the contract. As a result, all HMOs that capitate physicians or physician groups for services that the physicians or physician groups do not directly provide must delineate the amounts at risk for such services or have the arrangement considered to place the physicians at substantial financial risk. Further, the HMO must provide a stop loss mechanism so that the risk for referrals is limited to less than 25 percent of the physicians' or physician groups' total potential payments. Arrangements without such stop loss protection will also be considered to place physicians at substantial financial risk.

Other incentive arrangements. Any other incentive arrangement will be considered to place physicians or physician groups at substantial financial risk if the physician or physician group is at risk for more than 25 percent of total potential payments.

Requirements for Physician Incentive Plans That Place Physicians at Substantial Financial Risk

Under the statute, HMOs that place their physicians or physician groups at substantial financial risk must provide adequate stop loss coverage and conduct enrollee surveys. These requirements extend to financial arrangements between physician groups and physicians who are at risk for referrals as well as intermediary organizations, such as PHOs, and physician groups or physicians. (It is unclear, however, whether the HMO can assign to the intermediary group the responsibility to pay for stop loss coverage.)

To comply with the enrollee survey requirement, the rule requires that the enrollee surveys must:

1. include all current Medicare/Medicaid enrollees in the organization and those who have disenrolled (other than because of loss of eligibility or relocation) in the past 12 months, or a statistically valid sample;

2. be designed, implemented, and analyzed in accordance with commonly accepted principles of survey design and statistical analysis;

3. address enrollees/disenrollees satisfaction with the quality of the services provided and their degree of access to the services; and

4. be conducted no later than one year after the effective date of the incentive plan and at least every two years thereafter.

To comply with the requirement to provide adequate stop loss protection to physicians or

physician groups placed at substantial financial risk, the rule allows HMOs to provide either aggregate or individual stop loss protection. If the HMO provides aggregate stop loss protection it must cover 90 percent of the cost of referrals that exceed 25 percent of total potential payments.

If the HMO provides individual stop loss protection, the limit per individual must be decided based on the size of the physician panel, and the stop loss protection must cover 90 percent of the costs of referral services that exceed the per patient limit. If the panel includes less than 1,000 patients, the stop loss limit must be $10,000; for panels of up to 10,000 patients, the limit must be $30,000; for panels not greater than 25,000 patients, the limit must be $200,000; and for panels greater than 25,000 that are the result of pooling patients, the limit must be $200,000. The rule allows for two methods of pooling patients: (a) including commercial, Medicare, and/or Medicaid patients in the calculation of the panel size and (b) pooling together, by the HMO, several physician groups into a single panel.

Finally, in the preamble to the rule, HCFA clarifies that the requirement to *provide* adequate stop loss protection means that the HMO either pays the premium or if the physician or physician group wishes to purchase the coverage, the HMO reduces the level at which the stop loss protection applies by the cost of the stop loss.

Disclosure Requirements

An HMO is required to disclose to HCFA information concerning its physician incentive plan as required or requested. The disclosure must include the following information in sufficient detail to enable the agency to determine whether the incentive plan complies with the rule:

1. whether referral services are covered by the incentive plan

2. the type of incentive arrangement, e.g. capitation, withhold or bonus

3. the percentage of any withhold or bonus

4. the amount and type (e.g. aggregate or individual) of any stop-loss insurance

5. the panel size and whether patients are pooled (including the method of pooling)

6. any capitation payments made to primary care physicians for the most recent year broken down by the percent paid for primary care services, referrals to specialists, and hospital or other types of provider services

7. for HMOs required to conduct beneficiary surveys, survey results

The HMOs must submit this information to HCFA when the HMO applies for a contract, when the HMO applies for a Medicare service area expansion, and within 30 days of a request by HCFA. In addition, an HMO must notify HCFA at least 45 days before changing the type of incentive plan it uses, changing the amounts of risk or stop loss protection or expanding the risk formula to cover new referral services. While this requirement is a refinement of the language from the proposed rule which required notification "each time there is a change in the incentive plan," it remains broad. Clarification may be required after this requirement is implemented to avoid imposing an undue burden on HMOs.

An HMO is also required to disclose information about whether it uses incentive arrangements for referrals, the types of incentive arrangements it uses, whether it provides stop loss insurance and the results of its enrollee survey (if required) to any Medicare beneficiary who requests this information.

Subcontracting Arrangements

The final rule contains requirements related to subcontracting arrangements. The requirements applicable to HMOs with subcontracts are broken into two categories.

First, HMOs that contract with physician groups that place individual physician members at risk for services they do not directly furnish

are required to disclose only arrangements that put physicians at substantial financial risk. In addition, the HMO must provide adequate stop loss insurance and conduct enrollee surveys.

Second, HMOs that contract with intermediate entities (including IPAs that contract with one or more physician groups and PHOs) are required to disclose all physician incentive arrangements that put physicians or physician groups at risk for services they do not directly furnish, regardless of whether they are at substantial financial risk. Because an IPA that contracts only with individual physicians is considered a physician group, it would appear that HMOs that contract with IPAs that contract with any physician group will be required to disclose any and all of the incentive arrangements between the IPA and individual physicians. It is not clear at this point whether HMOs will be required to disclose the arrangements with individual physicians under this requirement. Further, while HMOs contracting with intermediary entities are subject to stop loss and survey requirements if substantial financial risk is imposed, it is not clear whether the HMO or the intermediary entity must pay for the stop loss insurance. In contrast to other provisions of the rule that require the HMO to *provide* stop loss insurance, under the intermediary entity provision, HMOs are required to *meet* the stop loss provision.

Penalties

Determination of noncompliance may result in civil money penalties, intermediate sanctions, and/or contract termination for Medicare or withholding of Federal financial participation for Medicaid. The civil money penalties may be as high as $25,000 for each determination of noncompliance. In addition, HCFA can suspend the enrollment of individuals into noncomplying plans or suspend payments for new enrollees in Medicaid. State Medicaid agencies have the authority to enforce compliance of HMOs with Medicaid contracts.

Issues

The physician incentive rule raises several issues for HMOs:

- Does an HMO want to be viewed as transferring substantial financial risk? If so, what form of stop loss will it adopt? If not, how will the HMO restructure its incentive arrangements to limit the amount of risk transferred for referrals?

- How will HCFA choose to perform its oversight functions in relation to this rule given its limited resources?

- What changes to a physician incentive plan will trigger the HCFA disclosure requirements? Will there be a threshold regarding the significance of the changes?

- What happens if an HMO cannot restructure its incentive arrangements or meet the stop loss requirements by May 28, 1996? It may be possible that although HMOs technically have to meet this requirement by that date, the agency would understand that this may be difficult and may be considering allowing an additional reasonable time for compliance which has yet to be determined; there is no guarantee, however, that this will happen.

Effective Dates

HMOs with contracts or agreements as of March 27, 1996 must comply with the disclosure requirements of the rule, except for the requirements on capitation payments and survey results, by May 28, 1996 or by the renewal date of the contract, whichever is later. Requirements for disclosure on capitation payments and survey results and the requirement to conduct enrollee surveys must be complied with by May 27, 1997. HMOs must comply with all other requirements (including the stop loss requirement)

by May 28, 1996. At the time of this writing, the final rule is still open for commentary, so it is possible, although not likely, that there could still be some further modification.

WITHHOLDS AND RISK/BONUS ARRANGEMENTS

One common risk arrangement is the withhold. A withhold is simply a percentage, for example, 20 percent, of the primary care capitation that is withheld every month and used to pay for cost overruns in referral or institutional services. In the earlier example of $11.25 PMPM, a 20 percent withhold would be $2.25. The PCP would actually receive a check each month for the difference between the capitation rate and the withhold, in this case $9.00; the remainder, in this case $2.25, is held by the plan and used at year end (or whenever) for reconciliation of cost overruns. The amount of payment withheld varied from 5 percent to 20 percent in one survey, with few plans reporting routine withholds greater than 20 percent (in fact, concern was registered that withholds greater than 20 percent could have a risk of incenting inappropriate underutilization).[11]

Many plans also have a clause in their physicians' contract that states that the plan may increase the amount of withhold in the event of cost excesses beyond what is already being withheld. For example, the withhold can be increased from 20 percent to 30 percent if referral costs are out of control. The general guideline is to cover the actual and accrued expenses through the capitated pools and the withhold.

Although there are a few plans that have attempted to put the entire PCP capitation payment at risk for cost overruns, this is unwise. If a PCP's entire capitation payment is withheld, that is tantamount to indentured servitude and may lead to serious service problems. It is better to limit the maximum risk at which the primary care capitation may be placed (e.g., 50 percent, although even that level of withhold cannot be sustained for long).

CAPITATION POOLS FOR REFERRAL AND INSTITUTIONAL SERVICES

When capitation exists for primary care services, payment for referral services and institutional services is often made from capitation funds or pools as well. The services themselves may be paid for under a number of mechanisms (FFS, per diem, capitation, and the like), but the expense is drawn against a capitated fund or pool. There are a variety of ways that HMOs handle these types of risk pools, and some common methods will be described. It must be stressed that the illustration that follows probably does not exist in the real world exactly as it appears here. In those HMOs that use this approach, there is usually considerable variation; the illustration also reflects models that were more prevalent roughly a decade ago; mature HMOs have undergone considerable changes since then.[12] Nevertheless, the illustration provides a common basis for understanding this type of model. Figure 9–3 illustrates schematically how some of these risk pools operate.

There are three broad classes of non–primary care risk pools: referral (or specialty care), hospital (or institutional care, regardless of whether it is inpatient, outpatient, or emergency department), and ancillary services (e.g., laboratory,

radiology, pharmacy, and so forth). Many HMOs also have a fourth pool, usually called "other," in which they accrue liabilities for such things as stop-loss or malpractice and in which the physicians have no stake (see below). Some HMOs combine the ancillary services into the "other" pool, which is the model illustrated in Figure 9–3. It is not uncommon for these risk pools to be handled in different ways regarding the flow of funds and levels of risk and reward for the physicians and the plan.

As an example, the PCP receives an $11.25 PMPM blended capitation rate for primary care services (in other words, the blend of all the age and sex capitation rates for that physician's membership base comes out to $11.25 PMPM). For each member, $22.00 PMPM is added to a capitated pool for referral services, and $40.00 PMPM is added to a capitated pool for hospital or institutional inpatient and outpatient services. The PCP does not actually receive the money in those pools; the plan holds onto it. Any medical expenses incurred by members in that PCP's panel will be counted against the appropriate pool of funds. At the end of the year, a reconciliation of the various pools is made (see below).

As with primary care, the scope of covered services must first be defined. For example, will home health be covered under institutional or

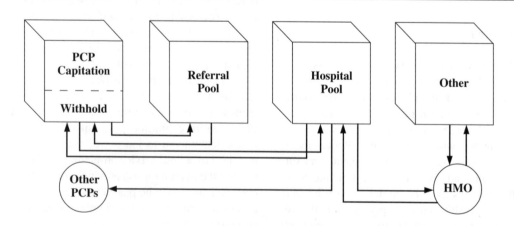

Figure 9–3 Capitation risk pools.

referral (probably institutional because it reduces institutional costs), and will hospital-based professionals (radiology, pathology, and anesthesia) be covered under institutional or referral? The same exercise is carried out with any category for which capitated funds will be accrued.

What if not all the withhold is used (if the plan employs a withhold system) or there is a surplus in either the referral pool or the institutional services pool? First, any surplus in one pool is generally first used to pay for any excess expenses in the other pool. For example, if there is money left in the referral pool but the institutional pool has cost overruns, the extra funds in the referral pool are first applied against the excessive expenses in the hospital pool, and vice versa.

After both funds are covered, any excess money is shared with or paid to the physicians. In general, only those physicians with positive balances in their own risk pools receive any money. For example, a PCP has referral services funds tracked for his or her own patients. If the cost of services for those members leaves a positive balance in the referral pool, and if there is money left in the institutional services pool on a planwide basis, the PCP receives a pro rata share of the money. In other words, risk is shared with all physicians in the plan, but reward may be tracked individually. In another example, some plans have decided to disburse positive balances in referral and institutional funds on the basis of both utilization and measures of quality and member satisfaction; a discussion of such incentive programs is found in Chapter 11.

The degree to which an individual PCP's pools will have an impact on year-end bonus disbursements may vary. If the decision is to minimize risk to individual PCPs, then you will want to set low threshold protection or stop-loss (see below) and minimize or even stop tracking expenses against an individual PCP's pools while those expenses are still low. For example, if a PCP has a member with acquired immunodeficiency syndrome (AIDS), the referral expenses will be paid either out of the planwide referral

capitation pool or out of a separate stop-loss fund and will not count against the individual PCP's referral risk fund after referral expenses have reached $2,500. In this way, high-cost cases, which could wipe out an individual PCP's risk pool, will have less effect than that PCP's ability to control overall referral expenses in the rest of the member panel.

It is common, although not absolute, for a plan to pay out all extra funds in the referral pool but only half the funds in the hospital pool. In some cases, there is an upper limit on the amount of bonus a PCP can receive from the hospital pool. The justification for this is that the plan stands a considerably greater degree of risk for hospital services and therefore deserves a greater degree of reward. Furthermore, it is often a combination of utilization controls and effective negotiating that yields a positive result, and the plan does most of the negotiating.

Medical Expenses for Which the PCP Is Not at Risk

Even in plans that use withholds and risk/bonus arrangements, there are sometimes certain medical expenses for which PCPs will not be at risk. For example, a plan may negotiate a capitated laboratory contract; laboratory capitation is then backed out of the referral and primary care capitation amounts and accounted for separately. If the PCP orders laboratory services from another vendor, that cost is deducted from his or her referral pool; otherwise, laboratory cost and use have no effect on the PCP's compensation.

Other examples of such nonrisk services might include any type of rider benefit (e.g., vision or dental) or services over which PCPs have little control, such as obstetrics. Another example would be defined catastrophic conditions (e.g., persistent vegetative state), where the PCP is taken out of the case management function by the plan and the plan's case management system takes over the coordination of care (see Chapters 18 and 20). The danger here is that there will be pressure to include too much in this category, thereby gutting the entire concept of capitation. Once a service has been taken out of the at-risk category, it is exceedingly difficult to put it back in.

Reinsurance and Stop-Loss or Threshold Protection

The degree of risk to which any physician is exposed needs to be defined. As mentioned earlier, it is common for a plan to stop deducting expenses against an individual PCP's pool after a certain threshold is reached for purposes of the year-end reconciliation. There are two forms of stop-loss or threshold protection: costs for individual members, and aggregate protection.

As an example of individual case cost protection, if a PCP has a member with leukemia, after the referral expenses reach $2,500 they will no longer be counted against the PCP's referral pool, or, more commonly, only 20 percent of expenses in excess of $2,500 will be counted against the referral pool. The uncounted expenses will be paid either from an aggregate pool or from a specially allocated stop-loss fund.

It is possible to vary the amount of threshold protection by the size of a PCP's member base to reduce the element of chance. For example, if a PCP has fewer than 300 members, the threshold is $2,000; if the PCP has more than 800 members, the threshold is $4,000. It is equally common for a threshold to exist for hospital services, although the level is much higher, for example $30,000. As alluded to earlier, the lower the threshold, the less the effect of high-cost cases on individual capitation funds and the greater the effect of overall medical management. On the other hand, if the threshold is too low there may be a perverse incentive to run up expenses to get them past the threshold. Multitiered thresholds also create an artificial barrier to the PCPs' acceptance of new members. For example, if the threshold for 300 members or fewer is less than that for 301 members or more, PCPs may resist adding members above the 300 limit so as to protect the lower threshold level. Tiered thresholds can be time limited to prevent this problem.

Aggregate protection is not as common. As an example of aggregate protection, the plan may reduce deductions to 20 percent or even stop deducting referral expenses after total expenses for an individual PCP reach 150 percent of the capitation amount. Providing aggregate stop-loss protection on the basis of a percentage of total capitation allows such protection to be tied to the membership base of the PCP. This is another way of ensuring that a PCP's capitation will not be totally at risk.

The combination of threshold protection and risk sharing across the physician panel serves to reduce any individual PCP's exposure to events outside his or her control. It is frustrating to manage all your cases properly but receive no reward because one seriously ill patient had high expenses.

In any case, providing threshold protection to an individual physician is important, and you need to remember to budget for its cost. Although such stop-loss protection can be paid from the aggregate of all the physician's referral funds, that ensures that there will be a draw on the withhold (if there is one). Because positive referral balances will be paid back to PCPs, negative balances will need to be funded through the withhold, so that there can never be a full return of the withhold. Therefore, it is preferable to budget a line item for stop-loss expense and to reduce the referral allocations by that amount.

It is likewise important for there to exist a mechanism for peer review of excess expenses to determine whether they were due to bad luck or poor case management. In the latter situation, the plan must have recourse to recovering all or part (up to the contractually agreed-upon maximum individual physician risk) of the excess costs from a physician who failed to provide proper case management.

Individual versus Pooled Risk

All forms of financial risk are affected by how the HMO handles the issue of individual risk versus pooled risk. In other words, to what degree is an individual physician at risk for his or her performance compared with the degree to which that risk is shared with some or all other PCPs? It is human nature to wish to share the downside risk (and pain) with others but to keep the upside (profit) for oneself.

In one large survey, 25 percent of plans reported using individual risk pools, 12 percent reported using risk pools of 2 to 50 physicians, and 63 percent used risk pools of more than 50 physicians.[13] In those plans that do track risk pools individually, it is more common for only one pool (usually referral), if any, to be tracked on an individual basis while the withhold, if any, and hospital pool are aggregate.

Although many HMOs contract directly with PCPs, there are many that contract through the vehicle of the IPA,* physician–hospital organization (PHO), management services organization (MSO), or other form of IDS (see Chapter 4 for discussions of these organizations). The HMO capitates the IPA or IDS, but that organization may or may not capitate the PCPs. In fact, many of these organizations pay the PCPs on a FFS basis using one or more of the performance-based FFS reimbursement methods described below.

Even when there is no intervening organization, the issue of who actually is being capitated, and for what, still remains. Is it the individual PCP, a subset of the total network of PCPs (i.e., pools of doctors or PODs), or the entire network of PCPs? The answer may not be the same for each category or risk. For example, a plan may wish to capitate PCPs individually for their own services, combine them into PODs for purposes of referral services, and use the performance of the entire network for purposes of hospital services.

A plan can also choose to use different categories for risk and for reward. For example, a

plan may spread risk across the entire network but only reward a subset of PCPs. An example was given earlier in which positive balances in withholds or referral pools were used to offset deficits in the hospital pool; any remaining surplus balance would only be paid to those PCPs with a positive balance.

There are common and predictable problems with individual risk. The majority of those problems relate to the issue of small numbers. As noted earlier, luck can have as much or more of an impact on utilization as good management, at least in small member panels. As a PCP's panel grows to more than 500 members, this problem starts to lessen, but it persists. This is one of the most important reasons that an HMO will contractually require a PCP not to close his or her practice to the HMO until that PCP has 250 or more members (see Chapter 55); it is the identical reason that a PCP should desire to have a large panel enrolled. When PCPs have good utilization results, they generally desire to keep the reward for their hard labor; when results are poor, they frequently feel that they have been dealt an abnormally sick population of members and should not be held accountable for the high medical costs.

The larger the number of dollars at stake, the more dangerous the problem of small numbers becomes to an individual PCP. Although stop-loss and reinsurance somewhat ameliorate the problem, the problem remains. This is the very reason that plans may be willing to use individual pools for referral services but will not do so for hospital services, where the dollars are substantially higher.

The other major problem with individual risk is the ability of some PCPs to game the system. In other words, to enhance income the PCP manages to get his or her sickest patients to transfer out of the practice, with a resulting improvement in that individual PCP's medical costs. Although all plans prohibit PCPs from kicking a member out of their practice because of medical condition, a wily and unethical PCP can find a way to do so and remain undetected. Related to this issue is the concern that individual risk incents a

---

* The term *IPA* is often used to describe any HMO that uses private physicians practicing in their own offices (as opposed to a group or staff model HMO), but in fact the term technically refers to an actual legal entity. See Chapter 3.

PCP to withhold necessary medical care (discussed below). Although this charge has been leveled at the HMO industry for many years, it has never been proven.

Last, there have been cases of HMOs requiring an individual PCP (or small group) actually to write a check to the plan to cover cost overruns in medical expenses (as opposed to simple reconciliation of accidental overpayments). This has usually occurred when the plan agreed not to keep the withhold (in response the PCP's plea to improve cash flow) but to track it nonetheless. Whenever a PCP is required to pay money back to the plan, a severe problem in provider relations is likely to occur.

If the plan chooses to pool risk across the entire network, then the flip side of individual risk occurs: The impact of any individual PCP's actions are diluted so much as to be undetectable. If a PCP is having good results, then he or she may resent having to cover for the problems of colleagues with poor results (of course, no one objects to being helped out when one's own results are poor). If the plan does not track individual results, then it will have little capability of providing meaningful data to individual physicians to help them better manage medical resources.

Because of these two extremes, many plans have chosen to use PODs for at least some financial risk management. PODs are a subset of the entire network, although there is no standard size. A pool may be a large medical group, an aggregation of 10 to 15 physicians, or made up of all participating PCPs in an entire geographic area. A POD could also be made up of the physicians in a PHO or MSO that accepts risk. The common denominator is that the number of members enrolled in practices in the POD will be sufficient to allow for statistical integrity but small enough to allow the pool to make changes that will be seen in utilization results. The chief risk is that PODs require support from the plan in the form of data and utilization management.

It should not be assumed that PODs are a panacea; they are not. If a POD fails, the repercussions are greater than if an individual physi-

cian fails because far more members are affected and the dollars are higher. There are times when using individual risk and reward is best, times when the entire network should be treated as a single entity, and times when PODs will make sense. Medical managers should be aware that there is evidence that individual risk/bonus arrangements elicit strong changes in behavior whereas aggregated risk/bonus arrangements do not.[14]

FULL-RISK CAPITATION

Full-risk capitation refers to the PCP receiving money for all professional services, primary and specialty, but not hospital services (although the group may still be on an incentive program regarding hospital utilization management). The PCP not only authorizes the referral but actually has to write a check to the referral specialist. This was once marginally popular but is currently uncommon because there were a number of problems in the past with such systems when the PCPs did not have sufficient funds to cover specialty costs and members were exposed to balance billing. There has been a recent resurgence of interest in this form of capitation as PCPs band together into large groups or other forms of collective activity such as IPAs, PHOs, and MSOs.

Full-risk capitation is generally not supportable by other than a large group or organized system of PCPs. The more the primary care group can capitate specialists for services, the less the danger of having insufficient funds. Many state insurance departments, however, will not allow a provider to subcapitate; that is, the insurance department believes that only a licensed HMO, not another provider, may capitate a provider (see Chapter 53).

Any group accepting full-risk capitation needs strong financial management skills and good computer systems support. Of considerable interest is one substantial study that looked at how physicians at such a form of financial risk managed their own utilization. The physicians employed techniques identical to traditional HMO utilization management, including the use of a PCP gatekeeper, an authorization system, practice profiling, clinical guidelines, and managed care education (see Chapters 17, 18, and 19 for discussions of these techniques).[15] It should be noted that many HMOs are reluctant to enter into such arrangements, unless they are convinced that the physicians will be able to manage utilization because they do not wish to be exposed to the risk of failure.

REASONS TO CAPITATE

The first and most powerful reason for an HMO to capitate providers is that capitation puts the provider at some level of risk for medical expenses and utilization. Capitation eliminates the FFS incentive to overutilize and brings the financial incentives of the capitated provider in line with the financial incentives of the HMO. Under capitation, costs are more easily predicted by the health plan (although not absolutely predictably because of problems of out-of-network care). Capitation is also easier and less costly to administer than FFS, thus resulting in lower administrative costs in the HMO and potentially lower premium rates to the member.

The most powerful reasons for a provider to accept capitation from an HMO are financial. Capitation ensures good cash flow: The capitation money comes in at a predictable rate, regardless of services rendered, and comes in as prepayment, thus providing positive cash flow. Also, for physicians who are effective medical case managers as well as cost-effective providers of direct patient care, the profit margins under capitation can exceed those found in FFS, especially as FFS fees come under continued pressure. The main nonfinancial reason for a provider to accept capitation is that it eliminates any disagreements over the level of fees that the provider may charge a patient, thus providing some level of insulation regarding finances and the provision of health care.

PROBLEMS WITH CAPITATION SYSTEMS

The most common problem with capitation is chance. As mentioned earlier, a significant element of chance is involved when there are too few members in an enrolled base to make up for bad luck (or good luck, but nobody ever complains about that). Physicians with fewer than 100 members may find that the dice simply roll against them, and they will have members who need bypass surgery or have cancer, AIDS, or a host of other expensive medical problems. The only way to ameliorate that is to spread the risk for expensive cases through common risk-sharing pools for referral and institutional expenses and to provide stop-loss or threshold protection for expensive cases.

The problem of small numbers is especially acute in the early period of a PCP's participation with the MCO unless the MCO is failing to grow. To deal with this, and to entice PCPs to participate, some HMOs have offered to pay the PCP on a FFS basis for the first 6 months or until the PCP has more than 50 enrollees, whichever comes first. A few HMOs have offered to pay capitation but have guaranteed that the PCP would receive the higher of capitation or FFS in that first 6 months. A few HMOs have even agreed to pay FFS until the PCP has more than 50 members without any time limit, but that is unwise because it may disincent the PCP to enroll an adequate number of members.

Another frequent problem is the perception of the physicians and their office staff of capitation. Although many practices have now acclimated to capitation, there is a feeling that capitation is really "funny money." When PCPs are receiving a capitation payment of $11.25, this is sometimes unconsciously (or consciously) confused with the office charge. In their minds, it appears as though everyone is coming in for service and demanding the most expensive care possible, all for an office charge of $11.25. It is easy to forget that many of the members who have signed up with that physician are not even coming in at all. It only takes 10 percent of the members to come in once per month to make it seem as if there is a never-ending stream of entitled demanders in the waiting room. The best approach to this is to make sure that the plan collects data on encounters so that the actual reimbursement per visit can be calculated.

The last major perceived problem is inappropriate underutilization. An argument made against capitation in general, and against risk/bonus arrangements in particular, is that you are paying physicians not to do something, and that is dangerous.[16-20] Although there was one spectacular case of fraud in south Florida in the mid-1980s where providers were placed on individual risk arrangements and serious quality problems were noted, that was a failure of management and regulation. In fact, not only is there no real evidence that capitation or risk/bonus systems have led to poor quality (a fact that the sources noted earlier in this paragraph have themselves all conceded), but there is some evidence that managed care systems have provided equal or better care to members than uncontrolled FFS systems even while lowering costs.[21-29]

Under a well-crafted capitation program, you are not paying physicians to underutilize services; you are sharing the savings of cost-effective care. In an unmanaged FFS system, there is a direct relationship between doing something and getting paid for it; under capitation, the reward is removed from the action. In other words, the capitation check does not change each month depending on services. Furthermore, by carefully constructing a stop-loss or threshold protection program, you can attenuate the effect of high-cost cases on capitation funds. Spreading the risk over more than one physician can lower the effect of single cases on a physician's reimbursement, but at the cost of not recognizing individual performance. In addition, it must be kept in mind that HMOs, with their lack of deductibles and high levels of coinsurance, lower economic barriers to care, thus improving access to care.

In the final analysis, it is the obligation of plan management to monitor the quality of services and to ensure that there is no inappropriate underutilization of services. One can argue that in a well-managed plan identification of poor quality is easier because there is more access to data and a tighter quality assurance system, and that is exactly how the plan must approach this issue.

One last issue should be raised, although it is not a problem per se but something to be aware of. In a capitated system, savings from decreased utilization may not always result in direct savings to the plan. In other words, if primary care services undergo a reduction in utilization, the capitation payments will not go down, just as they will not go up when there is increased utilization. If a system uses capitation extensively for primary care, specialty care, and hospitalization, there may be no reduction in expenses even if controls result in a dramatic lowering of utilization rates. On the other hand, such reductions will result in less pressure to increase capitation and premium rates the next year.

EFFECT OF BENEFITS DESIGN ON REIMBURSEMENT

Benefits design may have a great effect on reimbursement to PCPs in capitated programs, although the effect may be felt in any reimbursement system that relies on performance. The three major categories of benefits design that have such an impact are reductions in benefits, copayment levels, and point-of-service (POS) plans.

Benefits Reductions

Because many managed care plans have adopted greater flexibility in benefits design in response to marketplace demands, the underpinnings of actuarial assumptions that were used to build capitation rates have become less reliable. If a plan has adopted exclusions for preexisting conditions, has imposed waiting periods, or does not offer benefits that have usually been covered, the related expenses for those conditions are no longer applicable to the reimbursement rate. In other words, the capitation rate may now be higher than actually required. The impact of benefits reductions on primary care services is usually not so great as to warrant changing previously acceptable capitation rates, but that is not an absolute.

Benefits changes have a greater impact on risk pools. For example, if mental health and chemical dependency coverage is carved out of the PCP managing system and turned over to a dedicated management function (a common occurrence in managed care; see Chapter 22), then concomitant reductions in the referral and hospital risk pools are warranted. The same is true if an account wanted to carve out pharmacy services to another vendor (e.g., a national company that administers a card and mail-order program).

Copayment Levels

Copayment levels can have an immediate impact on capitation rates, both for PCP capitation and for risk pool allocations. The amount of capitation due a PCP will be different with a $3.00 copay compared with a $10.00 copay. For example, if a capitation rate were calculated to be $11.25 on the basis of three visits PMPY at $45.00 per visit, then application of a $10.00 copay would reduce the capitation amount to $8.75 ($45.00 − $10.00 = $35.00; three visits × $35.00 = $105.00; $105.00 ÷ 12 months = $8.75 PMPM). The same issue applies for calculating contributions to referral risk pools and hospital risk pools. For example, if consultant care has a $10.00 copay, then estimated consultant visit costs would have to take the copay into account. The same is true for hospital care if copays of $100.00 or $200.00 are applied.

The effect of copays and cost sharing on utilization is real, although it differs with respect to the amount of out-of-pocket expense to which the member is exposed.[30–32] It should be noted, however, that cost sharing does not necessarily selectively reduce inappropriate hospitalization (in other words, although total utilization may be reduced with cost sharing, the change in utilization may not reflect a change in whether the uti-

lization was appropriate in the first place).[31] Deciding whether to adjust capitation rates on the basis of expected utilization differences from copays is difficult. Explaining such adjustments to PCPs is no easy task either because changes in utilization are population based, and any individual member may or may not change his or her behavior.

Adjusting capitation rates for copays is not easily done if there are widespread differences in copay amounts among different accounts. For example, if 50 percent of the members have a $3.00 copay, 35 percent have a $5.00 copay, and 15 percent have a $10.00 copay for primary care services (not to mention different copays for referral services), calculating the appropriate capitation can be difficult. Even so, it is worth doing unless the variations are minor or infrequent.

POS Plans

For the purposes of this discussion, POS plans are those that allow members to obtain a high level of benefits by using the HMO or gatekeeper system while still having insurance type benefits available if they choose to use providers without going through the managed care system. For a discussion of POS, see Chapter 3.

Because members with POS benefits are not totally locked into the managed care plan, utilization occurs both in network and out of network. Although the plan can actuarially determine the level of in-network and out-of-network use for the entire enrolled group, that cannot be said for an individual physician's member panel. This has an obvious impact on capitation rates.

Some plans attempt to adjust capitation rates on the basis of prospective in-network utilization. That usually means a reduction in the capitation rate. Other plans attempt to make adjustments on a retrospective basis, although this is a terribly difficult exercise in provider relations when a PCP is asked to refund a percentage of the capitation payment he or she had received all year. In either event, it is no easy task to explain to a PCP who feels underpaid anyway that you are going to pay even less. An alternative is not to reduce the capitation rate, but that can result in a windfall for the PCP whose POS members never come in for services (or, on a more pernicious note, for the PCP who does not provide adequate access for POS members, thereby driving them out of network for services). This has become so difficult that many plans capitate PCPs for pure HMO (i.e., not POS) members and pay FFS for POS members. This creates problems due to the schizophrenic reimbursement systems and results in what psychologists refer to as cognitive dissonance. Many HMOs with high levels of POS membership simply do not capitate all and use FFS exclusively. Figure 9–4 illustrates relative percentages of MCOs that use different reimbursement systems for different product types.

POS makes it difficult to measure the performance of PCPs as well. For example, if performance is based only on in-network utilization, one good way to look like a stellar performer is subtly to encourage POS members to seek services out of network. If PCPs are held accountable for all services, both in network and out of network, then they may argue that it is not fair that they are held accountable for utilization that is completely out of their control. Although this issue is not easily resolved, many plans with extensive experience in POS have chosen to fold out-of-network utilization into the performance-based reimbursement system, whether capitation or FFS. To attenuate the problem of lack of control by an individual PCP, the risk or reward system is spread out among groups of PCPs or the entire network, thereby maintaining actuarial integrity.

Although capitating individual PCPs is a challenge with POS, it is certainly possible to capitate a large group or an IDS. In most cases, a prospective adjustment is made to the capitation rate based on the actuary's best estimate of in-network versus out-of-network utilization. Out-of-network claims are paid by the plan from the funds that had been backed out of the capitation rate. Surpluses (or a percentage of surpluses) in that pool of funds may be returned to the group or IDS to encourage it to find ways of getting its enrolled members to seek care in network, thus reducing out-of-network utilization.

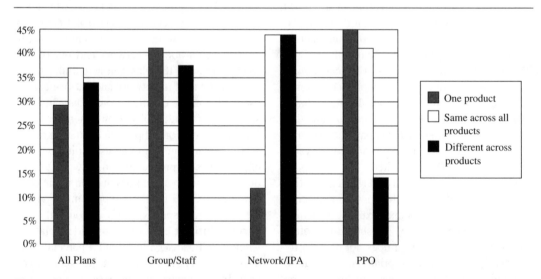

Figure 9–4 Variation in reimbursement models by product. *Source:* Reprinted from *Arrangements Between Managed Care Plans and Physicians: Results from a 1994 Survey of Managed Care Plans*, 1995, Physician Payment Review Commission.

FFS

There are some veterans of managed health care who hold that the FFS system of American medicine is the root of all the problems we face with high costs. Although that is simplistic, there is some truth to it, particularly when there are no controls in place. In a system where economic reward is predicated on how much one does, particularly if procedural services pay more than cognitive ones, it is only human nature to do more, especially when it pays more. The reward is immediate and tangible: A large bill is made out, and it usually gets paid. Doing less results in getting paid less. On the other side of the argument, FFS results in distribution of payment on the basis of expenditure of resources. In other words, a physician who is caring for sicker patients will be paid more, reflecting that physician's greater investment of time, energy, and skills.

In a managed health care plan, FFS may be used to compensate physicians and may be the method of choice in certain situations. For example, in a simple preferred provider organization (PPO), FFS will be virtually the only option available (except in the rare and oxymoronic capitated PPO). The reasons for an HMO to use FFS reimbursement are varied and have not been systematically studied. One dynamic is that FFS is frequently more acceptable to physicians, so that many HMOs use FFS to get more physicians to sign up, at least in an HMO's initial period of development. This is especially true in markets where managed care penetration is low; where managed care penetration is high, PCPs often prefer capitation. As noted earlier, HMOs may also capitate IPAs or PHOs, but those organizations actually pay FFS to the physicians. Also as noted earlier, certain products, such as POS, also are difficult to capitate, leading many HMOs with a large POS enrollment to use FFS. Last, some HMOs simply believe that FFS is a good way to reimburse PCPs and have operated that way for more than 20 years.

There are two broad categories of FFS: straight FFS and performance-based FFS. The first category is less common in HMOs but nearly universal in PPOs and Blue Cross/Blue Shield service plans. In some cases, an HMO may not even be allowed to use straight FFS because the PCPs are required to be at some level of financial risk for the HMO to qualify for licensure.

Performance-based FFS simply refers to the fact that the fees that the PCPs ultimately receive will be influenced to some degree by performance. Whether performance refers to overall plan performance, performance of only one segment of medical costs (professional costs, for example), or performance of the individual PCP is quite variable. How performance affects the fees is likewise variable. Figure 9–5 illustrates the relative percentages of MCOs using straight FFS versus performance based FFS. Both these forms of FFS are described in the following.

Standing Risk

In an FFS plan, determining who will stand risk for services is a major issue. This may run from a situation where the plan stands virtually all the risk, such as in a simple PPO or indemnity plan, to a system where the risk is shared fully with the providers, such as in an HMO. The no balance billing clause (see Chapter 55) is highly important to a tightly managed FFS plan. This clause states that the physician will only look to the plan for payment of services and will accept payment by the plan as payment in full. In other words, if the plan has to reduce or otherwise alter the amount of payment, the physician will not look to the member for any additional fees.

Determination of Fees

Usual, Customary, or Reasonable

The historical method of fee determination is the usual, customary, or reasonable (UCR) fee. In some cases, this is really a euphemism for the physician sending a bill and the plan paying it. There is little uniformity to UCR because it represents what the physician usually bills for that

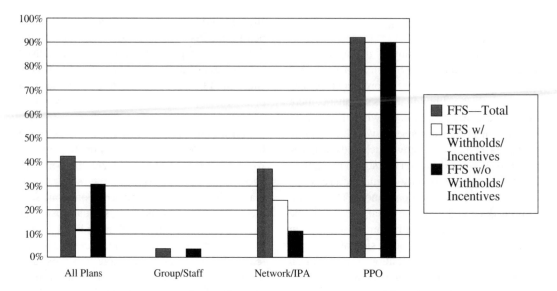

Figure 9–5 FFS and risk/incentives for PCPs. PPO, preferred provider organization. *Source:* Reprinted from *Arrangements Between Managed Care Plans and Physicians: Results from a 1994 Survey of Managed Care Plans*, 1995, Physician Payment Review Commission.

service, and there can be tremendous discrepancies among physicians' fees for the same service. One common methodology for determining UCR is to collect data for charges by current procedural terminology (CPT) code, calculate the charge that represents the 90th percentile, and call that the UCR maximum. When a claim is submitted, it is paid in full if it is lower than the 90th percentile; if it is higher than the 90th percentile, it is paid at the UCR maximum. Some plans use different technologies to determine what is reasonable and arrive at allowances different from the 90th percentile. Still other plans negotiate a further percentage discount of the UCR (e.g., 20 percent) and use that to pay claims.

The advantage to using a percentage of UCR is that it is extremely easy to obtain. Most physicians will gladly accept a discount on fees if it ensures rapid and guaranteed payment. The problem is that there is nothing to prevent the physician from increasing the fees by the same percentage as the discount, although excessive fee hikes will bump into the fee maximum.

Some plans require the physician to notify the plan of a fee hike, but in truth there is little that the plan can or will do if it has no real clout.

Relative Value Scales

The use of a relative value scale (RVS) has gained popularity in FFS plans. In this system, each procedure, as defined in CPT, has a relative value associated with it. The plan pays the physician on the basis of a monetary multiplier for the RVS value. For example, if a procedure has a value of 4 and the multiplier is $12, the payment is $48.

A classic problem in using an RVS and negotiating the value of the multiplier has been the imbalance between procedural and cognitive services. Until recently, in most available RVS systems, as in FFS in general, procedures have more monetary value than cognitive services. In other words, there is less payment to a physician for performing a careful history and physical examination and thinking about the patient's problem than for doing a procedure involving needles, scalpels, or machines. This has changed with the adoption of the resource-based relative value scale (RBRVS) by the Health Care Financing Administration (HCFA) for Medicare.

RBRVS has addressed to some extent the imbalance between cognitive and procedural services, lowering the value of invasive procedures (e.g., cardiac surgery) and raising the value of cognitive ones (e.g., office visits). The HCFA has imposed this on all physicians for Medicare recipients. Many large insurers are following suit in setting their determination of reasonable fees, although they lack the statutory ability to require acceptance of that fee as payment in full unless there is a contractual agreement to do so by the provider.

Negotiated Fee Schedule, Fee Maximum, or Fee Allowance

Fee allowance schedules are quite useful and common. In this case, the plan determines what it considers the correct FFS, usually on the basis of CPT codes, and the physician agrees to accept those fees as payment in full. This has the advantage of allowing the plan to control determination of payment for services on a uniform basis. In essence, this is an RVS that has already been multiplied. It is common practice to pay a percentage discount off charges subject to the fee schedule maximum. As mentioned above, the use of RBRVS is becoming a common method of building the fee allowance schedule.

Of special concern in the use of a fee schedule or RVS is the possibility of an antitrust violation. This is of particular concern in physician-sponsored plans. You do not really want a group of competing physicians to get together and set fees. It is preferable to use nonphysicians or an outside agency to perform this task.

Global Fees

A variation on FFS is the global fee. A global fee is a single fee that encompasses all services delivered in an episode. Common examples of global fees include obstetrics, in which a single fee is supposed to cover all prenatal visits, the delivery itself, and at least one postnatal visit, and certain surgical procedures, in which a single surgical fee pays for preoperative care, the surgery itself, and postoperative care.

Some plans are using global fees to cover primary care as well. In this case, the plan must statistically analyze what goes into primary care to calculate the global fee. That analysis must include the range of visit codes as well as all covered services that occur during primary care visits (e.g., electrocardiography, simple laboratory tests, spirometry, and so forth). The analysis will vary by specialty type (i.e., internal medicine, family practice, and pediatrics).

The analysis then builds by specialty a composite type of visit. The average type of visit for internal medicine, for example, may be an intermediate visit, and 20 percent of the time an electrocardiogram is performed, 30 percent of the time a urinalysis is performed, and so forth (these figures are fictitious and should not be used for actual fee calculations). The plan then builds up the global fee by putting together the pieces, for example $42 for the office visit, $7 for the electrocardiogram ($35 × 0.2), and so forth.

The chief value of a global fee is that it protects against problems of unbundling and upcoding. With unbundling, the physician now bills separate charges for services once included in a single fee; for example, the office visit is $45, the bandage is $10, starch in the nurse's uniform is $3, and so forth. Upcoding refers to billing for a procedure that yields greater revenue than the procedure actually performed; an example is coding for an office visit that is longer than the time actually spent with the patient. Global fees offer no protection against churning, which is the practice of seeing patients more often than is medically necessary to generate more bills; in fact, global fees, if not managed correctly, may exacerbate a problem with churning.

Plans that use global fees often tie them to performance. For example, utilization targets may be set for some or all medical services. How a PCP or group of PCPs performs against these targets may be used to set the global fees. For example, PMPM targets are set for primary care, referral care, institutional care, and ancillary services. Performance of a group of PCPs is measured against those targets on a rolling 12-month basis, and performance against those targets is used to adjust prospectively the next quarter's global fee up or down. Targets are modified by age, sex, product type (e.g., pure HMO versus POS), or any other variables that are appropriate. Targets are also modified for the effect of stop-loss against catastrophic cases. In other words, measurement of performance is similar to that used in capitated systems.

A performance-based global fee system is a hybrid of capitation and FFS. Unlike capitation, there are generally no payouts from capitated risk pools (e.g., referral pools), so that there is no dollar-for-dollar relationship between utilization and reimbursement. Like capitation, PMPM targets in all categories of medical expense are monitored, and reimbursement is still associated with good performance. Also like capitation, there is a statistical build-up to determine reimbursement. Like FFS, payment is only made if services are rendered, and no payments are made if there are no services.

This last feature makes such systems attractive to employer groups that have much lower than normal utilization (i.e., those that have healthy employees and dependents who require fewer services than a typical capitation calculation assumes) and to POS plans where the plan desires to reward performance but needs to address both in-network and out-of-network utilization. As discussed earlier, under capitation you run the risk of paying twice for services under POS, once through capitation, and again through out-of-network claims.

Withholds

As with capitation, many plans that use FFS withhold a certain percentage of the fee to cover medical cost overruns. For example, the plan may be using a negotiated fee schedule that amounts to a 20 percent discount for most physi-

cian fees. The plan then withholds an additional 20 percent in a risk pool until the end of the year. In effect, physicians receive what amounts to 60 percent of their usual fee but may receive an additional 20 percent at the end of the year if there were no excess medical costs that year.

It is possible to try to create profiles of physicians' utilization patterns to distribute more equitably the withhold funds in the event that some, but not all, of the withhold is used to cover extra medical costs. Unfortunately, this is difficult in an FFS system if there is no gatekeeper model in place. Most plans simply return remaining withhold funds on a straight pro rata basis, although some plans return withhold on a preferential basis to PCPs as opposed to specialty care physicians.

Mandatory Reductions in All Fees

In a plan where risk for medical cost is shared with all the physicians and where straight CPT codes are used to reimburse on an FFS basis, there must exist a mechanism whereby fees may be reduced unilaterally by the plan in the event of cost overruns. This is the usual method in an HMO and may be employed in a strongly controlled PPO as well.

For example, the plan may be using a fee schedule that is equivalent to a 20 percent discount on the most common fees in the area. In the event that medical expenses are over budget and there is not enough money in the risk withhold fund to cover them, all physicians' fees are reduced by a further percentage, say an additional 10 percent, to cover the expenses. At this point, the effective discount is 30 percent, although this would really be 50 percent in the event that a withhold system was in place, all the withhold funds had been used, and there were still excess medical liabilities.

Budgeted FFS

Related to mandatory fee reductions, budgeted FFS is used in a few plans. In this variation, the plan budgets a maximum amount of money that may be spent in each specialty category. This maximum may be expressed either as a PMPM amount (e.g., $7.50 PMPM) or as a percentage of revenue (e.g., 5.6 percent of premium revenue). As costs in that specialty category approach or exceed the budgeted amount, the withhold in that specialty, not across all specialties, is increased.

This approach has the advantage of focusing the reimbursement changes on those specialties in which excess costs occur rather than on all specialties in the network. The disadvantage is that this may not be provider specific; in other words, all specialists are treated the same, and there is no specific focus on individual outliers. Plans that do not use gatekeepers to manage care may find this type of approach useful, and one model uses this form of reimbursement in lieu of any type of precertification requirements on the physicians.[33] This type of system usually only works when there are regular reports and practice profiles provided to the physicians (see Chapters 26 and 27), and when the enrolled membership is very large in order to ensure statistical integrity.

Sliding Scale Individual Fee Allowances

Related to budgeted FFS is the sliding scale individual fee allowance. In this model, PCP performance is again measured against benchmark targets in all categories of medical expense with appropriate protection for expensive outlier cases. On the basis of performance, the PCP's reimbursement may vary from 70 percent of allowable charges up to 110 percent if performance exceeds targets.[34] Although this system still allows for upcoding and unbundling, it does vary by individual on the basis of performance and could be applied to groups of physicians as well as to individuals.

POS and Performance-Based FFS

As discussed earlier, a central issue facing plan management in applying performance-based FFS under POS is determining whether to include out-of-network costs in the performance evaluation of PCPs. At first blush, it does not seem fair to do so because such expenses are not under the control of the PCP. The best way to make one's performance profile look good, however, is to force members to seek care out of network (through poor service), thereby subverting the ultimate goal of cost control. Therefore, most plans are now including out-of-network expenses into performance evaluations and are working with PCPs to encourage in-network use by members. Related to that, it is important for plans to set performance parameters accurately that vary by product type; in other words, if you expect 30 percent out-of-network use by members under POS, that assumption must find its way into the PMPM standards against which you measure a PCP's performance.

PROBLEMS WITH FFS IN MANAGED HEALTH CARE PLANS

There are two significant problems with using FFS in managed health care plans. These problems can become markedly exacerbated if the plan starts to get into financial trouble.

The first problem is churning. This simply means that physicians perform more procedures than are really necessary and schedule patient revisits at frequent intervals. Because most patients depend on the physician to recommend when they should come back and what tests should be done, it is easy to have a patient come back for a blood pressure check in 2 weeks instead of a month and to have serum electrolytes measured (unless laboratory services are capitated) in the physician's office at the same time. Few patients will argue, and the physician collects for the work.

Few physicians consciously churn, but it does happen, even if unconsciously. The more serious problem comes when the plan reduces the fees because of medical expense overruns. When this happens, a "feeding frenzy" can occur. In effect, physicians start to feel that they have to get theirs first. If the fees are lowered 10 percent this month, what might happen next month? Better to get in as many visits as possible this month because next month may bring a 20 percent fee reduction. This creates a self-fulfilling prophecy, and the inevitable downward spiral begins.

The only effective approach to churning is tight management (or switching to capitation). Some plans develop physician peer review committees to review utilization. These committees have the authority to sanction physicians who abuse the system. This has some slowing effect if there are enough reviewers and not too many physicians to review. The actions of such committees should follow a process that includes warnings and a probationary period in which expectations for improvement are clearly outlined. Other plans apply differential withholds selectively on those providers whose utilization is clearly out of line, although defining that takes some care.

Better still, manage the plan so that few sanctions are necessary. This means controlling referrals, controlling hospital and institutional utilization, and negotiating effective discounts with providers and hospitals. It also means closely monitoring utilization and billing patterns by PCPs and acting when necessary. Performance-based programs such as those described earlier can also be applied to lessen the impact of churning, but this problem still remains in any FFS plan.

On the other hand, if cost overruns bring fees down to grossly unacceptably low levels, utilization may decrease simply because the plan does not pay enough to get providers to do the work. That is a potentially problematic situation that can lead to inappropriate underutilization.

The second major problem is upcoding (sometimes referred to as CPT creep) and unbundling. As mentioned earlier, upcoding refers to a slow upward creeping of CPT codes that pay more; for example, a routine office visit becomes an extended one, a Pap smear and pelvic examination become a full physical examination, or a cholecystectomy becomes a laparotomy. Unbundling refers to charging for services that were previously included in a single fee

without lowering (or lowering sufficiently) the original fee.

These problems are best monitored by the claims department in coordination with whichever department is responsible for data analysis. There are two useful approaches. The first is to look for trends by providers. Individuals who are trying to game the system will usually stand out. If there is one physician who has 40 percent extended visits compared with 20 percent for all the other physicians in the panel, it may be worth further review (this topic is addressed in Chapter 27). The second approach is to automate the claims system to rebundle unbundled claims and to separate for review any claims that appear to have a gross mismatch between services rendered and the clinical reason for the visit (this topic is addressed in Chapter 31). The problems of upcoding and unbundling may also addressed through the use of global fees, as discussed earlier in this chapter.

CONCLUSION

To be effective, an MCO, whether it is an HMO or an IDS, must align the financial incentives and goals of all the parties: the health plan and the providers who deliver the care. Capitation, and to a somewhat lesser extent performance-based FFS, do that in ways that traditional FFS does not.

In a tightly managed plan, such as an HMO, capitation will be more consistent with the overall goal of controlling costs. Although capitation is initially harder to calculate, and although it is sometimes harder to gain acceptance for it from physicians, this system has less likelihood of leading to overutilization than FFS. Problems of inappropriate underutilization must be guarded against with effective monitoring and an effective quality assurance system.

FFS can be used as well but requires a different set of management skills. It is easier to install and is often more acceptable to physicians, but it can quickly get out of control unless it is watched carefully. New products such as POS require new approaches to reimbursement because classic approaches are not ideally suited. As managed care evolves, reimbursement may be expected to evolve further.

The reimbursement system is a tool, and like any tool it has limitations. A hammer is the correct tool for pounding and removing nails, but it is poor for cutting wood and drilling holes. In the same way, a reimbursement system is a powerful and effective tool, but it can only be effective in conjunction with other managed care functions: utilization management, quality management, provider relations, and the many other activities of a well-run MCO.

REFERENCES AND NOTES

1. M. Gold, et al., *Arrangements between Managed Care Plans and Physicians: Results from a 1994 Survey of Managed Care Plans* (Washington, D.C.: Physician Payment Review Commission, 1995).

2. InterStudy, *The InterStudy Competitive Edge* (St. Paul, Minn.: InterStudy, 1994).

3. Group Health Association of America (GHAA), *HMO Industry Profile, Vol. 2: Physician Staffing and Utilization Patterns* (Washington, D.C.: GHAA, 1991).

4. Gold, et al., *Arrangements between Managed Care Plans and Physicians.*

5. R.L. Doyle and A.P. Feren, *Healthcare Management Guidelines, Vol. 3: Ambulatory Care Guidelines* (Milliman & Robertson, 1991).

6. N. Goldfeld, Risk Adjustment, Reinsurance, and Health Reform, *Managed Care Quarterly* 2 (1994): 82–94.

7. R.L. Kravitz, et al., Differences in the Mix of Patients among Medical Specialties and Systems of Care: Results from the Medical Outcomes Study, *Journal of the American Medical Association* 267 (1992): 1617–1623.

8. S. Greenfield, et al., Variations in Resource Utilization among Medical Specialties and Systems of Care: Results from the Medical Outcomes Study, *Journal of the American Medical Association* 267 (1992): 1624–1630.

9. The 1996 law grew out of abuses by Paracelsus Hospital under the Medicare fee-for-service program. The hospital created incentives that rewarded physicians for each patient that the physician released from the hospital under a certain number of days.

10. For simplicity, this Supplement refers collectively to all the organizations to which the physician incentive law and implementing rule applies as "HMOs."

11. A.L. Hillman, et al., HMO Managers' Views on Financial Incentives and Quality, *Health Affairs* (Winter 1991): 207–219.

12. N. Schlackman, Evolution of a Quality-Based Compensation Model: The Third Generation, *American Journal of Medical Quality* 8 (1993): 103–110.

13. Hillman, et al., HMO Managers' Views on Financial Incentives and Quality.

14. L. Debrock and R.J. Arnould, Utilization Control in HMOs, *Quarterly Review of Economics and Finance* 32 (1992): 31–53.

15. E.A. Kerr, et al., Managed Care and Capitation in California: How Do Physicians at Financial Risk Control Their Own Utilization?, *Annals of Internal Medicine* 123 (1995): 500–504.

16. A.L. Hillman, Health Maintenance Organizations, Financial Incentives, and Physicians' Judgments, *Annals of Internal Medicine* 112 (1990): 891–893.

17. A.L. Hillman, Financial Incentives for Physicians in HMOs—Is There a Conflict of Interest?, *New England Journal of Medicine* 317 (1987): 1743–1748.

18. A.L. Hillman, et al., How Do Financial Incentives Affect Physicians' Clinical Decisions and the Financial Performance of Health Maintenance Organizations?, *New England Journal of Medicine* 321 (1989): 86–92.

19. M.D. Reagan, Toward Full Disclosure of Referral Restrictions and Financial Incentives by Prepaid Health Plans, *New England Journal of Medicine* 317 (1987): 1729–1734.

20. General Accounting Office (GAO), *Medicare: Physician Incentive Payments by Prepaid Health Plans Could Lower Quality of Care* (Washington, D.C.: GAO, 1988), GAO Publication GAO/HRD-89-29.

21. J.E. Ware, et al., Comparison of Health Outcomes at a Health Maintenance Organization with Those of Fee-for-Service Care, *Lancet* 1 (1986): 1017–1022.

22. I.S. Udvarhelyi, et al., Comparison of the Quality of Ambulatory Care for Fee-for-Service and Prepaid Patients, *Annals of Internal Medicine* 115 (1991): 394–400.

23. E.M. Sloss, et al., Effect of a Health Maintenance Organization of Physiologic Health, *Annals of Internal Medicine* 106 (1987): 130–138.

24. C.M. Clancy and B.E. Hillner, Physicians as Gatekeepers—The Impact of Financial Incentives, *Archives of Internal Medicine* 149 (1989): 917–920.

25. N. Lurie, et al., The Effects of Capitation on Health and Functional Status of the Medicaid Elderly: A Randomized Trial, *Annals of Internal Medicine* 120 (1994): 506–511.

26. P. Braveman, et al., Insurance-Related Differences in the Risk of Ruptured Appendix, *New England Journal of Medicine* 331 (1994): 444–449.

27. A. Relman, Medical Insurance and Health: What about Managed Care? *New England Journal of Medicine* 331 (1994): 471–472.

28. J.P. Murray, et al., Ambulatory Testing for Capitation and Fee-For Service Patients in the Same Practice Setting: Relationship to Outcomes, *Medical Care* 30 (1992): 252–261.

29. M.F. Shapiro, et. al., Out-of-Pocket Payments and Use of Care for Serious and Minor Symptoms, *Archives of Internal Medicine* 149 (1989): 1645–1648.

30. J.P. Newhouse, et al., Some Interim Results from a Controlled Trial of Cost Sharing in Health Insurance, *New England Journal of Medicine* 305 (1981): 1501–1507.

31. K.F. O'Grady, et al., The Impact of Cost Sharing on Emergency Department Use, *New England Journal of Medicine* 313 (1985): 484–490.

32. A.L. Siu, et al., Inappropriate Use of Hospitals in a Randomized Trial of Health Insurance Plans, *New England Journal of Medicine* 315 (1986): 1259–1266.

33. Cleveland MCO QualChoice Is Using Risks and Incentives To Determine Provider Fees, *Managed Healthcare* (June 1994).

34. D.E. Church, et al., An Alternative to Primary Care Capitation in an IPA-Model HMO, *Medical Interface* (November 1989): 37–42.

SUGGESTED READING

Pauly, M.V., et al. 1992. *Paying Physicians: Options for Controlling Cost, Volume, and Intensity of Services.* Ann Arbor, Mich.: Health Administration Press.

Wozniak, G.D. 1995. *Evaluating Capitation Payments: A Guide to Calculating Benchmark Capitation Rates.* Chicago, Ill.: American Medical Association.

Chapter 10

Physician Compensation in Groups and Integrated Delivery Systems

James A. Rodeghero

BACKGROUND

Any discussion of physician compensation must address issues ranging from macroeconomics to individual emotion. This chapter recognizes three fundamentals that anchor any discussion of physician compensation. First, there is an unstoppable trend for physicians to practice medicine as employees or in structured contexts where reimbursement and compensation are externally managed rather than based on their own efforts. Second, as society addresses increasing health care costs, physicians' incomes will come under more scrutiny and pressure from employers, payers, and patients challenging the value of medical services. Third, the very nature of compensation theory and practice presumes that compensation itself (i.e., monetary rewards) is a determinant of and/or a reward for the practice of medicine and should be a central factor in the management and reward of physicians.

The day-to-day challenges in managing physician compensation are grounded in the changing health care system context and the realities

of each individual organization's situation. Only in recent years have large numbers of physicians become employees or contracted with payers, hospitals, and other provider organizations. The rise of integrated delivery and financing systems (see Chapter 4)* brings physicians into central roles, where their impact may rapidly expand. With these changing contexts come increasing pressures to control health care costs, and physicians, as high earners, find themselves the focal point of cost cutters, regulators, and payers.

The broad movement of physicians into the employed/contracted context is part of a more important shift in the overall roles of physicians in health care delivery. No longer the owner-operators of cottage enterprises, physicians cannot exercise total independence in either the medical or the business aspect of their practices. Furthermore, although physicians are surrendering much of their prior independence, they are assuming new risks under capitated reimbursement. As physicians assume economic risk in capitation contracts, they essentially underwrite the medical risks of increasingly large populations of managed care plan members.

In this context, the determinants of rewards from medical practice are shifting from individual effort/volume to the selective delivery of

James A. Rodeghero, Ph.D., is a Partner at Ernst & Young LLP's Los Angeles Health Care Management Consulting practice and is the National Director for Physicians Compensation Consulting. His area of expertise emphasizes physician compensation and management programs, and he has worked in all areas of the industry including acute care hospitals, HMOs and managed care organizations, and freestanding group practices. He is experienced in the design and implementation of management and reward systems for all levels of health care industry providers, executives, and employees.

* The term integrated delivery and financing systems represents the current nomenclature, adding the financing function to the delivery functions typically attributed to integrated delivery systems based on the clear trend toward inclusion of an underwriting, risk assumption, or other financial interest in integrated organizations.

care, from effective management of a small business (medical practice) to satisfaction of employment standards in large organizations; and from independent judgment to compliance with protocols. Factors such as patient (i.e., customer) satisfaction, resource management, and organizational compliance are new to physicians and the source of confusion and frustration as they seek success in their practices. The challenges felt by physicians are second only to those felt by employers searching for the holy grail of the "best" physician pay plan.

This chapter explores the background, mechanics, and outcomes of various approaches to rewarding medical practice. The impact on physician earnings of the changing health care industry and the reciprocal impact that employed physicians are creating are discussed. Although the "best" plan may remain elusive in the near term, this chapter seeks to define the directions where successful approaches to physician rewards may be found and to present alternative approaches and pay plan designs structured to address the issues facing the industry. It is important to note that the discussion differentiates between compensation and reimbursement, the latter referring to organizational level payments or direct premium payments. Although reimbursement may often constitute the physicians' compensation plan [as with direct distribution of per member per month (PMPM) payments] or define the pay plan's key characteristics [as in staff model health maintenance organizations (HMOs)], the discussion focuses on compensation, defined as the individual physician level pay plan. The reader is also encouraged to review physician compensation issues discussed in detail in Chapters 7, 9, 11, and 12.

TRADITIONAL CONCEPTS IN PAY PLAN DESIGN

Before proceeding with a discussion of specific issues in rewarding physicians, let us review the basic concepts and assumptions in compensation plan design and the implications for physicians. Without going too deep into the

concepts and precedents in reward management, we should consider those traditional issues from which we may better craft a strategy for physicians' rewards. Admittedly, many traditional industrial compensation models will not apply with physicians, but we can learn some useful techniques, and avoid making some mistakes, from the traditional rationales.

At the risk of oversimplification, we can identify three basic factors in compensating anyone for anything: need, desire, and ability. These factors apply to both the employer/contractor* and the physician and should always be considered when one is designing compensation programs.

First and foremost, there is a definable need for any employer or contractor to provide a market wage for any labor services. Calibration of physician incomes to market norms to establish the need-to-pay level will require a common denominator for the services being priced, and although it may be straightforward to define a common standard for many labor classifications, the practice of medicine has historically represented an exceptionally robust range of behaviors, resource requirements, and outcomes. As a simple example, primary care physicians' value in the market is reported across a range of more than 200 percent.[1] This range is a reflection of the wide variation among physicians' activities, procedures, and practice contexts.

Second, we can discuss the rationale and design of reward systems in terms of the employer's desire to provide a certain level of rewards. These goals are often described in terms of market norms, such as the median or third quartile, reinforcing the market linkages discussed above. Organizations espousing a relatively high competitive pay level are often challenged to ensure sufficient funding. For example, those organizations targeting physician salaries at above-average market levels may find it impossible to fund incomes under discounted or capitated reimbursement.

---

* We refer to the contracting entity (e.g., HMO, independent practice association, and so forth) as the contractor.

Analysis of market data should underlie any effort to ensure that physicians' salary and total compensation levels reflect actual market practices. Figure 10–1 highlights the variability in market pay comparisons based on different subgroup breakdowns. It also highlights how a hybrid market norm may be drawn from the comparative data to support the broadest level of competitiveness. Note that comparisons between the two charts (salary and total compensation) can be used to benchmark incentive or variable pay levels.

The organization's ability to fund physician labor costs may be the most critical factor in pay plan design. Under fee for service and discounted procedure-based reimbursement, the ability to fund physician labor is directly measurable. Capitated reimbursement blurs the direct linkage between volume and individual physicians' contributions. This leads some managed care organizations to define pay plan goals not in terms of competitive rates but rather in relation to internal economics. For example, staff model HMOs may set boundaries on physician labor expenses as a percentage of total health care delivery costs.

Funding issues in physician compensation hold an importance not seen in traditional employment situations. Under traditional (indemnity) reimbursement and in independent practices, physicians' incomes are funded directly from collected professional (and technical) fees. The resulting range of individual earnings has been due to factors largely within physicians' control, so that the range of their earnings is considered an accurate reflection of productivity.

Now we find that the economics of many physicians' practices are largely driven by external forces, and employers and contractors have redefined physician roles. Under many forms of managed care reimbursement, increased physician activity only increases costs, thus eroding profitability. Whereas budgeting for physician labor costs may be straightforward under fee for service, accounting for the value of physicians' labor under capitated reimbursement raises the paradox of establishing the remunerative value of a commodity that, by its very exercise, raises costs.

PAY PLAN DESIGN ISSUES

In actual practice, there will be relatively few basic pay plan designs from which to choose. Any physicians' pay plan development effort seeking the best model for a specific context will depend on a few primary considerations:

- *Practice context*—The physicians' practice setting and relationship to the payers or contracting organization may define the amount and type of compensation. Free-standing contracted groups [with or without management services organizations (MSOs; see Chapter 4)], staff model HMOs, independent practice associations (IPAs) or preferred provider organizations (PPOs), and hospital-based practices all require different reward schemes.

- *Available remunerative elements or pay vehicles*—Options for delivering rewards to physicians may be chosen from fixed or variable cash compensation (salaries and bonuses/incentives), equity-based, profit sharing, or dividend income (in some settings), benefits and perquisites; and nonmonetary rewards (recognition, research opportunities, and the like).

- *Regulatory and payer considerations*—Special restrictions in tax exempt settings may limit the ability to use some income deferral vehicles or share profits and may create special reporting issues.

- *Risk and economics*—With the trend toward capitation and risk sharing, traditional practice economics have been turned upside down. As discussed above, defining and ensuring the funding for physicians' earnings are now more complex than in fee-for-service reimbursement, and the willingness and ability of all parties to share or assume risk further affect the design of the pay plan.

Annual Base Pay

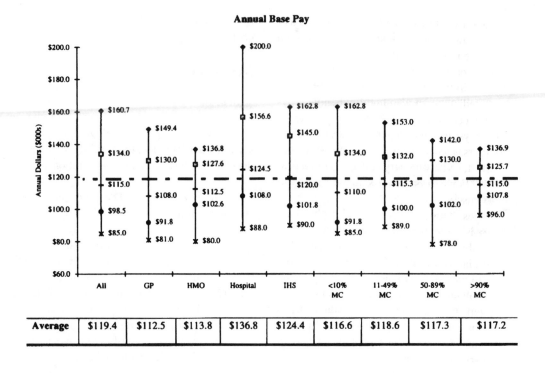

| Average | $119.4 | $112.5 | $113.8 | $136.8 | $124.4 | $116.6 | $118.6 | $117.3 | $117.2 |

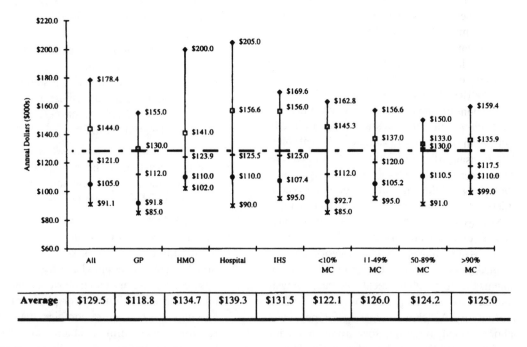

| Average | $129.5 | $118.8 | $134.7 | $139.3 | $131.5 | $122.1 | $126.0 | $124.2 | $125.0 |

Figure 10–1 Internal medicine market norms. Hypothetical "hybrid" midmarket (median) pay ranges are indicated by dashed lines. GP, group practice; HMO, health maintenance organization; IHS, integrated health care system; MC, managed care. *Source:* Courtesy of Ernst & Young LLP, Washington, D.C.

In a perfect world we could address these issues in an integrated fashion and seek an optimal solution, but most often the design of physician pay plans occurs under a transitional state with imperfect information, limited strategic clarity, and immediate operational or financial needs.

First, let us explore the impact of practice context on physician pay plan design. Many contextual factors, such as the type and size of the business unit, will directly affect physicians' rewards. For example, large clinical settings lend themselves to operational and scheduling economies that make it easier to structure workloads around common standards. An increased ability to manage the level and amount of physician work allows a more structured approach to pay, such as the use of salaries rather than variable pay.

Conversely, in dispersed clinics, under multiple plans, and/or under mixed reimbursement, the organization may use higher levels of variable (at-risk) pay. This approach reflects the variability among physician practices and allows the employer/contractor to build variability into compensation commensurate with reimbursement mix.

Other factors will affect the level and type of variable or risk-based pay in a physician plan, and the risk and economics that define the reimbursement profile should be tightly integrated with the physicians' reward plan. Risks associated with the effect of resource management on compensation are the most typical in managed care practices, and most plans have one or more mechanisms to pass risk through to the physicians.

For example, many salary-based managed care pay plans put some of the physicians' base rate at risk through withhold amounts. This compensation plan mirrors many group level PMPM reimbursement plans. A physician's annual pay rate may be set at $140,000, but a flat amount or percentage (e.g., 20 percent, reducing the effective salary to $121,000) is held back until year end to cushion cash flow and hedge against utilization overruns. The amount of at-risk pay is generally calibrated to the total group/plan risk

pool withhold for economic and equity reasons, and other measures of physician contribution may affect payouts.

The structure of this at-risk compensation should be balanced to reflect both the physicians' risk profile and the employer's/contractor's expectation that variable pay will affect behavior. Also the reality of differential specialty overall pay rates will affect the design of any variable pay component: Cash flow and life style factors may preclude large relative amounts (e.g., 40 percent or more) of at-risk pay for primary care providers, but many high earners can bear, and perhaps will be better motivated by, relatively large incentives.

The level of risk in the pay plan should also reflect the extent to which physicians' efforts and outcomes reflect true manageable variability. Common or low-variability activities are best managed and rewarded through base (salary) or fixed compensation. For example, if physicians' schedules can be managed to result in similar visit volumes, then that component of pay is best compensated within the salary component.

Efforts to standardize the practice of medicine will probably never fully succeed, however. The extent to which physicians' practices can be standardized will be determined both by organizational systems and controls and by physicians themselves. Most organizations would, if given the opportunity, opt to institutionalize practice behaviors as a cost containment and quality assurance strategy, and many physicians would prefer the income security of a steady practice volume and salary. Physicians, however, may also balk at what they see as the practice of "cookbook medicine" under such managed situations. Most important, the nature of the practice of medicine will always include activities and responsibilities that cannot be standardized across clinical settings, practitioners, patients, and illnesses.

The primary regulatory and payer considerations in structuring physician pay plans are limited to tax exempt organizations and the treatment of federal and state reimbursement.

Restrictions in tax exempts include the need to justify the reasonableness of compensation levels and plan design, the need for caps (maximums) on physician earnings, and sanctions against inurement or private benefit. Restrictions on pension and deferred rewards in tax exempts may limit the organization's ability to deliver long-term rewards, security, and tax advantages.

The primary restrictions created by federal (Medicare) and state (Medicaid) payers are self-referrals within physicians' practices and the ability of physicians to derive direct income from ancillary or technical services. The Stark regulations define Medicare's limits on referrals and ancillary income and prescribe substantial fines for violations. These fraud and abuse guidelines also define the safe harbors within which physicians and groups may operate and derive benefit from ancillary operations.

Implementation of the Stark I regulations provided a precursor for the reclassification of ancillary activities from revenues to liabilities under managed care. Practices with large ancillary components either have been forced to accept reduced incomes from divesting ancillary operations or have redistributed these earnings in compliance with the regulations.

The immediate effect of the Stark regulations (only the first generation, Stark I, has been implemented at this time) has been to reduce physicians' earnings in a practice with significant ancillary income if the practice is forced to divest any ancillary business interests. Alternatively, if the practice can retain its other revenue sources, the effect is felt through the group as a redistribution of compensation.* Even in primarily fee-for-service practices, these factors are creating a more "managed care–friendly" reward context as the relative importance (i.e., amount) of ancillary income is diluted.

Fraud and abuse regulations have another indirect impact on managed care physician compensation. As might be expected, as practices have lost, or been forced to redistribute, ancillary revenues, their willingness to enter into integrated service agreements via contracts, acquisitions, or mergers increases. Integrated delivery systems may be able to retain the ancillary revenue sources in other business units and may have the financial ability to compensate physicians at historical levels based on compensable outcomes other than volume of technical or referral fees. As long as indemnity reimbursement motivates increased technical charges, however, retaining ancillary services in mixed reimbursement practices may be dysfunctional.

GENERAL DESIGN ALTERNATIVES

Although the above litany of issues may seem to present an impossible challenge as we seek to design the best pay plan in a given context, most approaches to physician compensation reflect relatively few different designs. Each of these is reviewed separately.

Productivity Plans

Traditional productivity-based pay plans, including income distribution schemes in group practices, have direct implications for structuring physicians' rewards under managed care. These fully variable plans' greatest, and most problematic, impact comes from the historical psychological impact of decades of piece-rate pay.* Few occupations or professions have enjoyed such high relative earnings coupled with immediate linkages between productivity and rewards. Coupled with physicians' innate achievement orientation, this reinforcement scheme gets much of the credit (or blame) for the

---

* Under Stark I, allowable ancillary revenue cannot be distributed to the physician who orders the test or controls the services rendered; hence, the proscription against self-referral.

---

* Pure productivity pay plans, even many with draws, are essentially fully variable or full-risk variable pay plans. This also applies to most such plans that use a draw or other fixed component when that component is adjusted frequently based on changing volume.

high levels of productivity, technology advancement, and tertiary outcomes reflected in the U.S. health care industry. The emphasis on production and volumes under traditional pay plans becomes dysfunctional under managed care, however, and may confuse physicians' motives in integrated delivery systems. Certainly, increased resource utilization and patient visits are problematic under capitation and are increasingly being negatively rewarded under discounted reimbursement.

Many physician practices have used productivity surrogates to provide the feel of a production-based system under mixed reimbursement, and some find such plans effective under full capitation. The most typical of this genre use relative value units (RVUs) to calibrate each physician's productivity.* The total RVUs, or the physician's relative contribution to total group RVUs, are then used to distribute available labor funds or to establish incentive payouts.

Although RVU productivity plans are presently enjoying great popularity as a transitional approach, they risk significant problems when not coupled with strong resource management programs under managed care reimbursement. More than one group has experienced the negative impact of diluted or nonexistent risk pools due to overutilization. When physicians feel motivated to increase their earnings by increasing their RVUs under managed care, they may take two steps forward and one step back (or, worse yet, one step forward and two steps back) by increasing their individual percentage of a diluted income pool.

The use of productivity-based pay plans may even affect a group's ability to contract for capitated members when a payer organization feels that production pay plans may lead to overutilization or quality problems. It is always in a payer's best interest for physicians to be satisfied with their pay plan and pay levels simply

because motivated physicians can provide better and more personable patient care. Enlightened payers therefore seek those medical groups where the physicians are not demotivated by the inverse impact of productivity-based pay under fixed reimbursement.

Direct Distribution Plans

The managed care era equivalent of the productivity-based pay plan model is demonstrated in full capitation models where net premium income is distributed directly to physicians. As in productivity plans, the total net income attributable to individual physicians is computed and allocated. Income sources typically include all PMPM revenue plus net risk pool distributions. In this plan, reimbursement is paid directly to the physicians, thus providing the perfect linkage between the plan's goals and the physicians' reinforcement.

Computing each physician's PMPM income is typically based on paneled members or a visit/encounter measure. Risk pool distributions may be similarly based, or they may be computed based on tabulation of each physician's resource, inpatient, and specialty utilization. These latter computations may become complex under multiple plans. In this context, risk pools are often distributed on the physician's volume (members and visits), which is adjusted based on a moderator variable, such as a rating of resource management outcomes.

The direct distribution approach provides a direct link between net pay and each individual physician's total volume and managed care effectiveness. It assumes an individual (rather than group) level of service delivery, however, and in its purest form puts the individual physician fully at risk for underwriting health care costs for the covered members.

Salary-Only Plans

In some contexts, physicians are best rewarded with fixed compensation only. For example, physicians entering practice from resi-

---

* Most RVU pay plans have their roots in the Medicare resource-based relative value scale, which is the basis for Medicare reimbursement levels.

dency are best paid a straight salary if they cannot yet produce sufficient volumes to participate in incentive-based pay. Some managed care organizations have used salary-only plans under structured practice contexts, such as staff model HMOs, and government facilities have historically paid physicians via salary alone. Hospital-based practitioners are one other group that is often paid only in fixed pay.

Salary-only plans are most attractive for their administrative simplicity and for those practitioners who are not able or willing to accept compensation risk. Although it may seem unlikely that physicians would prefer fixed compensation, many find that, as patient populations shift among payers and volumes become unpredictable, their best option is the security of a salary-only pay package.

The primary drawbacks to salary-only plans are the high fixed cost basis created by physician salaries and the absence of linkages between physicians' behaviors and overall practice outcomes. In salary-only models, productivity, resource utilization, and quality assurance must be managed through other (nonmonetary reward) mechanisms.

Salary plus Variable Pay Plans

The salary-only model seems attractive from an administrative perspective and is preferred by some practitioners, but most organizations and individuals see the merit of using variable compensation for creating linkages between physicians' rewards and the variable costs and outcomes of their services.

The design of the salary/fixed component in these pay plans must reflect a concern not only for salary levels, which may be defined in relation to market norms or funding ability, but also for the relative level of incentive or variable pay. We can think of the process of setting salary and incentive as either a forward or reverse engineering exercise.

Salary and incentive levels (i.e., target amounts) should be set within an a priori structure based on market norms, the organization's

funding ability, and historical physician earnings (or a combination thereof). For example, the employer may, based on historical earning trends, specify a targeted salary level at the market median for most practitioners. Market-sensitive hiring rates will be set, with caps or maximums being set high enough to reward those who exceed basic expectations.

These three pay targets are generally structured as a range, often with steps that provide rapid early career growth slowing in later years.* Figure 10–2 illustrates a typical approach to salary range structure. This approach presupposes adequate funding for the aggregate labor cost of all employed physicians. Also, when setting salaries based on market norms, one must isolate salaries and total cash compensation (salaries plus bonuses/incentives) in survey data to ensure accurate analysis. Assuming that the targeted salary level is economically prudent, incentive opportunities are then designed as incremental earnings.

The level (amount) of potential incentive earnings must have administrative caps (maximums) in tax exempt delivery systems and is limited in all organizations to the available funding. Therefore, organizations with high relative salary levels often find that their ability to structure and fund incentives is limited. As noted earlier, this relative impact is quite different at the primary care level compared with the subspecialist pay level. It is often necessary to provide high fixed compensation in competitive markets, but these high salaries may limit the organization's ability to fund incremental (incentive) earnings. In practices where some physicians may be able to generate high volumes under fee for service or discounted procedure-based reimbursement, however, this approach can provide significant upside motivation.

Conversely, salaries and incentives can be reverse engineered by starting with available labor funds and backing into the relative amount of

---

* This "maturity curve" earnings relationship is typical of professional services, including physicians in solo and group practice.

Salary Range	Entry	I	II	III	IV - Target	V	Max
Maximum $150,000						$150,000	$150,000
					$137,500	$131,300	$135,000
Target $125,000				$149,100	$125,000	$118,200	
			$135,500	$135,500	$112,500		
		$126,500	$123,200	$122,000			
	$115,500	$115,000	$110,900				
Entry $105,000	$105,000	$103,500					

Figure 10–2 Illustrative salary ranges (based on Figure 10–1 market data for internal medicine).

pay in fixed and variable components. Alternatively, the design can be anchored in market norms for total cash compensation, with the respective elements being computed as percentages of the total. For example, available income (from all sources) for a clinic, department, or single specialty may provide an average of $160,000 cash compensation for each of ten physicians.[*] If 20 percent of the available cash is allocated to incentives, then physicians' salaries will average $128,000. Similarly, salaries and incentives could be anchored using absolute dollar amounts. For example, all physicians may have a $20,000 incentive opportunity regardless of specialty. Base rates would be adjusted to reflect this withhold amount.

One final design option for setting salaries and incentive opportunities is afforded in practices where high volumes, favorable reimbursement, and low relative costs allow competitive salaries plus significant incentive opportunities. One might expect this set of conditions to occur only under fee-for-service reimbursement, but many predominantly managed care practices find that they can fund such programs where

their physicians generate high patient volumes with effective specialty and ancillary utilization.

MEASUREMENT ISSUES

The adage "We measure what we can, and we get what we measure" applies as much to designing pay plans as to other aspects of business. Under fee-for-service reimbursement, measuring a physician's productivity or value is easy and direct. In transitioning from fee for service to managed care reimbursement, the measurement of physicians' contributions and productivity must change. The shift in measures simply reflects the changing (appropriate) practice behaviors, but the direct link between pay and the measures creates special pressures.

The most typical first-generation productivity measures (as managed care reimbursement becomes significant to the practice) use a form of fee-for-service equivalent, RVUs, visits/encounters, or paneled members. Any or all of these measures may be effective in calibrating total volume/productivity for the purposes of allocating performance-based rewards. Although most evolving performance measures continue to focus on productivity or utilization, new measures are being designed to capture better the full value that physicians provide to man-

---

[*] Similar examples can be structured by setting the total compensation limit/target based on market norms rather than internal funding economics.

aged care plans and delivery systems (see Chapter 11). Furthermore, as reimbursement shifts, any pay plan must evolve its measurement focus and technology. Table 10–1 illustrates one model for changing the measurement of physician contribution as the organization's reimbursement profile shifts further toward managed care and capitation (or discounts).

Under predominantly managed care reimbursement, measuring physicians' performance must move beyond traditional volume-based measurement. In practices where fixed (capitated) reimbursement is reallocated based on RVUs or fee-for-service equivalent charges, there is the risk of overdistribution. That is, available funding may be depleted as a result of poor resource management, thereby limiting upside incentive opportunities. This impact may justly be felt by the highest producers if they achieved that status by churning or other dys-

Table 10–1 Adapting Measurement to Changing Reimbursement

Factors	Current State	Transitional "Next-Generation" Model	End State I	End State II
Practice profile	Primarily fee for service (FFS)* Managed care < 25%; 21% of annual visits capitated High Medicare	Add-risk contracting	Primarily capitated primary care delivery model	Primarily managed, but not capitated, primary care model
Primary productivity indicators	FFS production, measured as adjusted net revenue (ANR)	Blended ANR and capitation FFS–equivalent revenue	Risk pool retention	Volume, measured in terms of panel size, available slots, encounters
Secondary indicators	Access, protocol compliance, quality, patient satisfaction	Cost efficiency, encounters, quality, access, satisfaction	Volume, quality, access, patient satisfaction	Cost efficiency, quality, access, satisfaction
Primary core role	Full-time practitioner	Full-time practitioner	Gatekeeper/care manager	Gatekeeper/care manager
Implications for pay plan design	Maintain productivity focus for experienced physicians in mature practices Ensure linkage to mission, strategy, and managed care initiatives through 20% professional	Productivity must be redefined to accommodate economic benefits of efficient capitated (i.e., risk) management Salaries will take precedence over incentives as measurement changes	Salary will be primary pay component, with bonuses for risk pool distribution of group performance	Salary will be primary plan component, but incentives will include blended productivity component

* Includes discounted procedure-based payment.

functional activity. Even appropriate practice behaviors can be negatively reinforced, however, when managed care reimbursement is distributed based on individual productivity. Again, only when effective resource management and quality assurance programs are in place can productivity-based pay plans ensure the appropriate rewards for the right practice behaviors under managed reimbursement.

Measurement issues affect the design and administration of both fixed compensation and incentives. Most fixed pay plans assume a nominal or threshold level of activity as justification for receiving the base salary of the fixed pay component. This assumption may be operationalized as predefined production/volume levels as preconditions for receipt of the full-time equivalent (FTE) salary.*

The transition away from traditional productivity-based measurement under managed care presents the greatest current challenge in ensuring prudent and motivating physician pay plans. As noted above, historical approaches to productivity assessment (professional collections) and transitional approaches (RVUs) carry the risk that physicians will maximize their incomes via inappropriate activity and resource utilization.

Specific examples of physician performance/contribution measures are presented below, as is a discussion of the design and administrative issues in ensuring pay–performance linkages.

THE ROLE OF BENEFITS IN TOTAL COMPENSATION

As physicians find themselves increasingly in employed status, the value and structure of benefits packages become more important. As noted earlier in Chapter 7, most employed physicians enjoy competitive benefits, traditionally structured to include the following:*

- health and welfare benefits, including medical, dental, and prescription benefits

- disability and survivor benefits, including short- and long-term disability and life insurance

- retirement and savings plans, including qualified or nonqualified retirement plans, 401(k) or 403(b) (in tax exempts) savings plans, annuities, and other programs (see below)

- employment benefits, including paid time off (vacations, holidays, etc.), business expense reimbursement, and so forth

- medical malpractice coverage, often including tail coverage for physicians entering employment from existing practices (see Chapter 7)

- professional expense account, including reimbursement for continuing medical education, professional development, memberships, certifications, licensure, subscriptions, and other qualified expenses

Basic benefits programs vary widely in actual costs as a result of coverage, structure, and population differences. In many contexts, physicians are necessarily covered by existing employee benefits packages.[†] For example, hospitals acquiring medical practices typically extend their current benefits plans to cover the physi-

---

*One may argue that such plans, in which some objective measure of production or volume is directly linked to salary levels, are not salary plans at all because the fixed income component essentially varies based on the same (typically) productivity measure used to assign incentive pay.

---

*Physicians aligned with managed care delivery systems via reimbursement contracts are generally not eligible for participation in the system's benefits packages. These physicians' benefits are typically provided, funded, and administered within the medical group, with or without direct allocation of costs to the individual physician.

[†] Regulatory restrictions on multiple benefits plans within employers, designed to preclude two-tier plans where executives receive disproportionate value (especially in retirement plans), limit most organizations' ability to structure special programs for physicians or other employee categories.

cians and their staffs. Benefits programs may add 20 percent to 30 percent to direct (cash compensation) labor costs, and the plans in large organizations, especially those with union employees, may be significantly more costly than those in freestanding medical practices. These employers are often challenged to demonstrate the value of any increase in costs to physicians who would not incur such expenses in their own businesses.

Retirement and deferred income benefits warrant special discussion. This class of benefits has become a critical component in structuring competitive pay plans for employed physicians. Physicians in private and group practice have generally enjoyed the benefits of other business owners in the ability to defer income and structure their retirement plans to meet their individual tax, security, and income context.

The use of individual retirement accounts, Keogh accounts, trusts, and annuities in medical groups generally allows a higher level of retirement plan funding than in typical employer plans. Considerations in tax exempt organizations further restrict the ability to structure such plans for highly paid individuals (i.e., executives and physicians). Finally, qualified retirement plans are limited to contributions based on a maximum of $150,000 in cash income (salaries and incentives/bonuses).* Whereas employers can provide supplemental benefits to offset this regulatory cap, the potential costs for large numbers of employed physicians may limit employers' ability to fund such plans broadly.

The net effect of the regulatory and economic context in employment settings is to limit the level of income deferral and retirement funding options. Legal, administrative, risk management, and financial issues keep many organizations from providing special supplemental ben-

efits for physicians, although such programs are gaining wider appeal.

Employers may directly supplement retirement or deferred benefits for physicians in for-profit entities or through the use of intermediary financial devices, such as insurance or trusts, in tax exempts. Supplemental benefits in tax exempt organizations must be subject to a risk of forfeiture and other constraints, making these plans generally unattractive to physicians.

COMPENSATING MEDICAL DIRECTORS AND ADMINISTRATIVE PHYSICIANS

The expanding numbers and roles of practicing physicians in managed care delivery systems are creating parallel growth in the numbers and types of administrative roles for physicians. Typically, physicians fill one or more of three administrative roles under managed care: direct clinical line management, functional or staff support, or professional affairs/development. These roles may be in any type of organization, including hospitals, IPAs, PPOs, MSOs, HMOs, and medical groups.

Administrative physician roles are compensated with a variety of approaches, generally reflecting the organization's relative level of sophistication and maturity in the utilization of physicians in such roles. Many organizations with less than full-time administrative roles simply provide hourly reimbursement for meetings and functional activity. This approach is simple but may not provide rewards for the actual value of the services rendered. More than one hospital has found that time spent in meetings increases when it is compensated but that outcomes may not improve.

Many organizations are moving to the use of formal compensation arrangements for administrative physicians, in which the amount, type, and value of the physician's services are calibrated to pay levels. Such plans may also use multiple pay elements, such as salaries plus incentives, to link activities to rewards. This approach can be adapted to a wide variety of physi-

---

* These plans have formal structures based on either defined contributions (by the employer, set as a percentage of salary or a fixed amount or based on company profits) or defined benefits (at retirement); qualified plans must also comply with federal regulations ensuring adequate funding and securitization of benefits.

cian roles and for full- or part-time responsibilities.

The structure of medical director compensation packages is often anchored in the physician's historical practitioner earnings. Although most organizations would agree that administrative roles should be rewarded based on actual responsibilities and not the incumbent physician's prior practice income, attracting qualified practitioners into administrative roles often demands compensation levels above those available for clinical practice.

When administrative physicians maintain an active clinical practice, administrative compensation should be structured to represent accurately the relative amount of effort and time committed to the nonpractitioner role. Many organizations put caps on the medical director's practitioner earnings, especially if this income is based on productivity, to ensure that energies are not diverted from critical administrative duties.

Structuring medical director pay packages around the relative value of the job should begin with a definition of all core ongoing responsibilities, including documentation of activities, time commitments, authorities and controls, and expected outcomes. This core job can then be priced in relation to external and internal benchmarks to set a fixed salary that covers all ongoing duties. Incentives may be appropriate for motivating extra effort, rewarding special projects or initiatives, or producing incremental operational/financial results.

Under this approach, compensation packages for medical directors may take on the nature of typical executive pay plans (except for any clinical compensation component). This approach will afford the opportunity to align medical directors' incentives with organizational priorities. As in any executive pay plan, however, defining performance standards and expectations and measuring of results may present new challenges.

Performance indicators for administrative physicians may be based on process goals, such as chairing meetings or developing and administering policies. As physician roles become more

directly linked to the organization's management and clinical activities, pay can be linked to measurable outcomes. For example, incentives for medical directors with quality assurance or utilization management responsibilities can be linked to the total practice's performance on the same quality assurance and utilization management measures used in individual physicians' incentives. The reader should note, however, that based on recent court actions (as discussed in Chapter 58), a medical director should not be financially incented to deny payment for specific cases.

COMPENSATING HOSPITAL-BASED PRACTITIONERS

Hospitals have traditionally provided some level of reimbursement/compensation for some specialties operating within hospital units. Such arrangements may be structured as direct compensation agreements when the physicians are employed or as contracts between the institution and a hospital-based medical group. Pathology, radiology, anesthesiology, and emergency medicine are the units most often providing compensation to hospital-based practitioners.

Compensation to hospital-based specialists is most often linked to administrative, quality assurance, and other nonpractitioner duties. Under typical relationships, the physicians bill and collect separately for the professional fee revenue from their practice. The level and structure of compensation from the hospital may range from token payments to recognize the physicians' administrative presence to significant amounts tied to broad management responsibilities. Unfortunately, the general level of documentation of these roles and the sophistication of the economic linkages suggest that many such relationships are not truly structured as reward plans.

Many hospitals are shifting these payments from fixed payments to more complex group level pay plans similar to those described above for medical directors. By structuring some or all of the hospital-based specialist group's income as incentives linked to predefined goals, the hospital can begin to shift physicians' focus as both administrators and as practitioners.

This shift is largely in reaction to the recognition that hospital-based specialists can have a significant impact on resource management efforts but that incentives to these physicians to comply with cost containment initiatives may negatively affect their own professional incomes. Physicians whose professional reimbursement is calibrated in fee-for-service or other volume measures present special problems for hospitals and MSOs being paid under capitation or other fixed reimbursement arrangements.

Examples of incentive programs for hospital-based medical groups may include specified bonus opportunities linked to achievement of predefined utilization or quality goals. Arrangements where physicians share directly in cost reductions are generally proscribed in most hospitals, but plans that rely on fixed (and capped) payments for predefined goals may be appropriate. These plans may also include "circuit breakers" or other mechanisms to ensure that payments to physicians are made only when the total institution hits its mission/strategy, operational, and financial targets.

COMPENSATION IN FACULTY PRACTICE PLANS UNDER MANAGED CARE

Special considerations apply when one is compensating practitioners in faculty practices under managed reimbursement. Because faculty practices often represent the higher levels of care (tertiary or quaternary) and costs in a community, they may not always be perceived as the best choice as a source of practitioners for managed care plans, but faculty plans find themselves increasingly seeking participation in managed care plans to ensure their patient base.

Physicians in many faculty practices are paid with salaries plus bonuses tied to patient care volumes and/or professional contribution. Funding may be from mixed sources, including academic stipends (i.e., tuition), research grants, and professional fees. The relative mix of fund-

ing sources may not be well defined for individual practitioners, and total physician labor costs may not be fully self-funded from internally generated revenues. These pay plans are not well suited for the distribution of managed care reimbursement. The lack of incentives for effective resource utilization or high-volume patient loads limits the typical faculty practice pay plan under managed reimbursement.

Operational changes and a shift in practice behaviors are often required to align faculty practices with the new protocols in managed care. Considerations such as scheduling and staffing models may have more impact on the ability to design appropriate physician pay plans than other issues. As operating practices change in response to shifting reimbursement, faculty practices will increasingly adopt pay plans similar to those in managed care medical groups and HMOs.

In fact, many faculty practice plans are under significant pressure to generate higher patient care revenues to support their compensation expense. Many are seeking managed care relationships as a result. Incentives to increase volumes while managing resources are inherent in these new reimbursement contracts, and the physicians are quickly learning the new practice styles required to maintain their earnings. The role of academic health centers in managed care is discussed further in Chapter 15.

CASES AND EXAMPLES

Implementing an RVU Plan

The simplest path to an RVU-based pay plan leverages existing RVUs as reflected in the Medicare resource-based relative value scale tables. All patient encounters and procedures are coded for RVU credit, and the resulting totals supplant fee-for-service collections as the measure of physician productivity. Compensation is typically delivered via both salaries and incentives/bonuses.

As an example, in a mostly primary care organization (with only a few selected specialists), an RVU plan is used to set thresholds for both assigning full-time salaries and allocating incentives when excess income is available. RVUs are tracked for all patient care activity, and special RVUs have been designed to capture the relative value of inpatient and administrative duties. No distinctions are made for different types or levels of reimbursement.

Salaries are set against market norms by specialty, with steps being taken to bring new graduates from a competitive entry point to the market median in 3 years. An FTE salary is contingent on providers' meeting a minimum annual total RVU goal. New hires' RVU goals are tailored to their relative experience, their specialty, and an analysis of market dynamics. Seniority is rewarded with a 3 percent above market median salary adjustment for each 5 years in practice within the group. All physicians are shareholders after 3 years. Schedules, call responsibilities, and committee assignments are standardized and rotated to equalize these activities over time.

When the group produces excess net income after all expenses, including physician salaries and benefits costs, the pool is distributed to all physicians as follows: Twenty percent of the available pool is distributed equally, with each individual physician's actual payment being adjusted up or down based on profile ratings; and 80 percent of the available pool is distributed proportionately based on each physicians' relative contribution to RVU production above the group aggregate target.

The group has made significant investments in information systems and provides departmental and individual feedback (and comparisons) on managed care measures monthly. Data include inpatient days and length of stay, number of encounters, average RVUs, total RVUs, out-of-plan referrals, direct laboratory and imaging expense, and patient satisfaction survey scores. A confidential summary of any complaints and the findings from any chart reviews are included.

The group has been able to fund the annual incentive pool each year, but total incentive pools were disappointing at first. Peer review committees now conduct chart audits of all practitioners whose monthly statistics are rated as outliers (20 percent above or below the comparison group median or beyond externally defined ranges). Physicians participate in their own chart review, receiving confidential feedback and coaching from the committees and support staff (quality management and utilization management) as appropriate. These controls have reduced resource utilization and churning, significantly increasing the incentive pool last year.

Multispecialty Group Rewards under Managed Care

Many large multispecialty groups have embraced (or been forced to participate in) managed care plans. Some have developed, acquired, or merged with health plans. Managing the reward plan across specialties ranging from pediatrics to neurosurgery under mixed reimbursement presents special problems.

Although the short-term reimbursement context may include substantial fee-for-service opportunities for some subspecialties, most physicians are experiencing pricing and volume decreases. Staffing models may require substantial revision under managed care as fewer specialists and more primary care practitioners are required to service the patient population.

For example, a large multispecialty group (more than 150 physicians) has integrated with a community hospital, has created a proprietary health plan with 35,000 lives, and contracts for 55,000 more (most are for full risk). More than 69 percent of the medical group's professional fees come from capitation. The parent system is tax exempt, creating new limits on pay levels and plan designs as well as new reporting requirements.

Many specialists continue to receive substantial fee-for-service referrals, whereas most primary care physicians' practices are now mostly capitated. All physicians' productivity is tracked as fee-for-service equivalent collections by imputing the average reimbursement amount per procedure/visit for capitated patients.

Salaries are set based on an annual analysis of group trends (productivity and costs), group and system budgets, and market norms (collected in a proprietary survey of similar practices). Salary targets for each specialty are linked to the norms, within internal budgetary funding limits, commensurate with relative productivity. That is, if fee-for-service obstetrics/gynecology equivalent productivity is at the third quartile of the benchmark, the target salary for these physicians is set at the competitive cash compensation third quartile.

Total budgeted salaries are always set below projected net income both to ensure a cash flow cushion and to increase the group's ability to fund the incentive pool. Adjustments are made (±10 percent) to the target rate to reflect individual physician performance, citizenship, and a number of managed care measures generated by the health plans. When net income exceeds budgeted levels, an incentive pool is funded and distributed based 75 percent on relative productivity and 25 percent on professional criteria.

The pay plan has had some issues with high utilization among specialists, but most problems have been resolved by staffing adjustments or salary reductions. Internal committees reviewing quality and resource utilization are linked with those in the owned health plan and the hospital, creating multiple review points to recognize problems early. The group expects capitation to increase to more than 80 percent in the coming years and has plans for further specialty staffing reductions with an expansion in primary care.

DESIGNING PERFORMANCE MEASURES

Any non–productivity-based pay-for-performance plan will require formal measurement of physician performance and, ideally, outcomes. Although job performance measurement is a relatively mature exercise in traditional employment contexts, the technology for reliably measuring a physician's performance is still evolving.

Some general trends have appeared, and a wide variety of appraisal models have been developed and shared. Some groups and delivery systems rely on the health plan's existing measures of outcomes, patient satisfaction, resource utilization, and volumes to calibrate their pay plans; others use industry standards, such as those in the Healthplan Employer Data and Information Set (HEDIS; see Chapter 28) database or used in accreditation by the National Committee for Quality Assurance (NCQA; see Chapter 37).

Although the use of industry standard models saves time and effort and allows comparisons with norms, many organizations recognize the need for customized measures matched to their own practice and reimbursement profile. The general industry standard approach to performance appraisals provides only nominal direction for this context, but the evolving "profiling" model used with physicians shows promise.

A physician profile is a tool that measures how an individual physician's performance compares with a predefined set of standards. Many organizations link profile ratings to incentive earnings. Because profiling standards generally include professional qualifications and behaviors as well as comparisons with similar practitioners within the group, physicians may be more receptive to this approach than to purely subjective evaluations or financial measurement only. Profiling is also discussed in Chapters 26 and 27, and non–utilization-based incentives are also discussed in Chapter 11.

Steps for building a profiling tool may include the following:

1. *Develop performance categories.* Performance categories should be developed based on the most important input and output factors directly affected by physician behavior. Examples might include productivity or volume, resource utilization, quality of care and service, financial performance, and professionalism.

2. *Define measures.* Specific measures must be defined for each performance category, ideally emphasizing objective measurement or behaviorally anchored ratings. Using the above examples, typical measures could include those listed in Table 10–2.

3. *Define data collection method.* Ratings scales, data reporting and recording formats, and administrative protocols should be carefully defined to maximize the accuracy and reliability of the profiling information. When possible, data should be taken directly from available sources, such as system reports on patient volumes, costs, and referral tracking. Any data elements collected via subjective ratings should be anchored with behavioral indicators. For example, peer ratings of work habits should be grounded in specific indicators, such as attendance and communication, not wholly subjective ratings.

4. *Develop standards for comparison.* Profiles should be compared among physicians and with normative data when possible. Most organizations track internal historical trends as one key benchmark.

5. *Build a reporting protocol.* The success of any profile plan will depend largely on the timeliness, accuracy, and user-friendliness of the reports used to track and manage results. Implementing a good profiling plan may require a significant investment in computer and accounting systems as well as implementation and ongoing communication with physicians. Because these measurements will affect the physicians' incomes and be instrumental in guiding their behaviors, the organization should recognize the need for both competent technical design and effective communications.

6. *Link to rewards.* The final step includes building linkages to physicians' earnings. Minimal standards for profile scores are typically used to determine continued employment and eligibility for salary increases. Profile scores are also typically used to define incentive payouts.

The link between profile scores and incentive earnings will depend on the structure of the incentive plan itself. If incentives are either targeted at a percentage of salary or based upon the retrospective distribution of withheld earnings, profile scores above a predefined threshold may trigger a full incentive distribution. Similarly, scores above or below the expected standard may increase or decrease payouts.

For example, many profiling schemes rely on structured ratings using a scale such as that

---

Table 10–2 Measures for Performance Categories

Productivity/ Volume	Resource Utilization	Quality of Care	Financial Performance	Professionalism
Appointment access	Ancillary and	Clinical outcomes	Cost control/	Citizenship
Number of encounters	specialty referrals	Patient satisfaction	overhead	Professional
Available patient	Inpatient days	tion	Profitability or net	development
contact hours	Length of stay		income	Community service
Panel size	Home health or		Risk pool retention	
RVUs, fee-for-	subacute referrals			
service equivalent				
collections, net				
fees				

shown in Exhibit 10–1. The ratings and linkages to the incentive payouts can be varied to reflect different ratings schemes, and different measures on the profile can be weighted to reflect relative importance.

CONCLUSION

An effective physician compensation model will reflect a thoughtful application of general compensation plan concepts to each organization's and practice context's operational and reimbursement profile. The variety of situations during the rapid transition from indemnity reimbursement and productivity-based compensation toward managed care precludes any "one size fits all" answers, but as the scope of medical practices grows through mergers, acquisitions, and network integration, more commonalties will appear among pay plans.

The most prevalent current trend in managed care practices is the reliance on fixed or salary income for most physicians. As the funding economics for physicians' compensation become more integrated with system financial results, these salary plans must rely on market surveys to calibrate relative pay levels and develop internal measures of key performance indicators to administer cash compensation based on relative performance.

Most employers include bonus or incentive opportunities in the physician pay plan, typically funding the pool based on total group available net income. Incentive plans in integrated systems may be paid based on achieving system or business unit budget and strategy goals. Most incentives are still allocated primarily based on the physician's relative patient volume, but the use of resource management protocols has helped ensure that specialty productivity is focused at the right level for the right patients.

Although many predict the inevitability of a future in which physicians are paid via salaries and bonuses based on group results with contin-

---

Exhibit 10–1 Structured Rating for Physician Profiles

Rating	Level	Definition
5	Outstanding	Results consistently and significantly exceed standards and are recognized as exceptional by peers, superiors, and patients.
4	Exceeds Standards	Results often exceed expectations and reflect above-average effort and impact.
3	Normal/Acceptable	Competent performance of the type and level expected.
2	Needs Improvement	Results generally meet expectations but require improvement in some areas.
1	Unacceptable	Consistently fails to meet minimum standards.

Each individual's overall rating across all performance measures determines allocation of the targeted incentives using the following scale:

Overall Rating ⇨	<2.0	2.1–3.0	3.1–4.0	4.1+
Incentive Payout ⇨	0%	80%	100%	110%

ued reductions in specialty earnings, this outcome is by no means assured. Increasing sophistication in resource utilization, contracting, and risk management among physicians is increasing profitability and earning under managed care. Although staffing levels for specialists remain relatively high, their effective utilization in managed care contexts can still produce relatively high earnings.

Physicians' professional roles and total system impact will probably lead them to a new leadership role in integrated systems. The current transition state is reallocating revenues and compensation costs while trying to reduce overall health care expense. Physicians will continue to be motivated to increase their patient volumes to maintain and increase earnings potential. The primary change in successful physicians' practices will not be a reduction in earnings. These physicians will continue to generate high volumes and incomes, but they will substantially change their practice styles to reflect managed care reimbursement and integrated system dynamics.

REFERENCE AND NOTE

1. Ernst & Young LLP, *Physician Compensation Survey* (Washington, D.C.: Ernst & Young LLP, 1995). This value represents the range for primary care providers (family practitioners, internists, pediatricians, and some obstetrian /gynecologists).

SUGGESTED READING

Konrad, T.R., et al. 1989. *The Salaried Physician: Medical Practice in Transition*. Chapel Hill, N.C.: University of North Carolina.

Pauly, M.V., Eisenberg, J.M., and Radany, M.H. 1992. *Paying Physicians: Options for Controlling Cost, Volume, and Intensity of Services*. Ann Arbor, Mich.: Health Administration Press.

Chapter 11

Non–Utilization-Based Incentive Compensation for Physicians

Peter R. Kongstvedt

Physician compensation is an area with a great deal of variation. In managed care it is difficult to use any single criterion or small set of criteria for judging performance. As discussed below, it is relatively easy to game a system that has only a few elements, and that can lead to problems. Basic methods of compensation of primary care physicians (PCPs) is addressed in Chapter 7 (for closed panels) and Chapter 9 (for open panels), compensation of specialty care physicians (SCPs) is addressed in Chapter 12, and compensation of physicians in medical groups and integrated delivery systems is addressed in Chapter 10. Although those chapters do give the reader a sense of the complexity of reimbursement issues, it is often believed by many that physician compensation in managed care focuses solely on issues of utilization and cost. It is accurate to state that the alignment of financial incentives between the managed care organization and the physicians is highly important in managed care, but it is inaccurate to state that there is no interest in aligning physician incentives with goals that are not based on utilization. Therefore, although many managed care organizations combine utilization and non-utilization financial incentives, this chapter focuses on incentive compensation programs that rely on standards of performance outside utilization management.

CLOSED PANELS COMPARED WITH OPEN PANELS

Obviously, there are significant differences between closed and open panels that affect formal physician performance evaluations. In closed panels it is easier to observe behavior, and a greater reliance on subjective evaluations is possible. Closed panels also frequently include both PCPs and SCPs, both of whom may authorize services and may care for a regular panel of patients. Formal performance evaluations in closed panel managed care plans similar to what is discussed in this chapter have been in use for many years.[1]

In open panels, the issues may be confused by existing risk/bonus systems in the private practice setting that often reward physicians strictly on the basis of utilization or productivity. Such systems generally place a greater reliance on objective measures. Furthermore, open panels tend to focus more on PCPs than on both PCPs and SCPs. It is certainly possible to construct an open panel performance evaluation program for SCPs as well as PCPs, and the principles will be the same. This chapter focuses on PCPs, looks at both types of systems, and makes suggestions for methods that may work in one or the other. Although most performance evaluation systems have been applied to PCP managing plans (i.e., gatekeeper plans), it is also possible to apply them to preferred provider organizations.[2]

THE VALUE OF FORMAL PERFORMANCE EVALUATIONS

Beyond the intellectual challenge, there are some practical uses for formal performance evaluations. What follows are examples for closed panels, open panels, or both.

Annual Compensation Adjustments in Closed Panels

Formal performance evaluations are quite useful in groups that use merit raises to adjust annual compensation. If a group uses strict percentage raises, or perhaps tails off the percentage after time but still handles raises in an across-the-board manner, adding an element of merit to the process of getting a raise can help reward the types of behavior one wishes to encourage.

Few physicians will argue that there are various levels of contributions from the closed panel medical staff. In a private fee-for-service practice, the less you collect, the less money you get. In a managed care setting, the criteria are not all that clear, and there may be no built-in reward structure for superior performance. Formal evaluations provide that structure.

In prepaid groups, where the idea of performance-based compensation may be too volatile to implement fully, it is possible to combine an element of across-the-board raise with a performance-based raise. For example, if a plan has budgeted a 6 percent increase in physicians' base salary, one could allocate 3 percent for an across-the-board (or cost of living) raise, and the remaining 3 percent would be based on performance. Compensation in medical groups is discussed in Chapter 10.

Bonus Distribution in Open or Closed Panels

In open panels, year-end payouts from withhold or risk-sharing pools are frequently based strictly on utilization, either individual or aggregate. It is possible for a plan to budget for a bonus or to use some profit or withhold for incentive compensation payments based on performance evaluations.[3–6] This allows the plan to reward individual performance by some physicians beyond low utilization.

Behavior Modification

Certainly the purpose of any system that has an impact on compensation is geared toward modifying behavior. Even if you have chosen not to use a formal evaluation process for adjusting compensation or bonus distribution, or in those years when there is no bonus to distribute, there remains merit in its use. Most professionals are motivated to do a good job simply for its own sake but often lack sufficient feedback. A formal system for performance evaluations is designed to provide such feedback. In addition, systems that collect and disseminate data will produce what is referred to as the sentinel effect: The very fact that the organization is observing behavior will cause that behavior to change, usually in the direction the organization wants it to.

Feedback of information to physicians will allow them to examine and perhaps modify their performance based on available data. Because frequent feedback about performance has a more significant impact than an annual review, it is generally desirable to provide such feedback on a quarterly or semiannual basis unless constraints in data processing, personnel, or money require that feedback be given only annually.

Documentation of Substandard Performance

Documenting and tracking substandard performance also represents one of the elements of formal performance evaluation. Beyond the issues of discipline and sanctions (see Chapter 26), there will certainly be instances where performance is not so poor as to warrant immediate termination or probation but where improvement is clearly required. A system that provides information about utilization and nonutilization performance is an excellent vehicle for documenting needed improvements. This allows the plan to indicate clearly the need for improvement and provides the necessary documentation in the event that the plan or group feels compelled to terminate the relationship with the individual physician.

PROBLEMS WITH EVALUATION SYSTEMS

Evaluating physician performance is unique in managed health care. As mentioned earlier, traditional fee-for-service has a straightforward reward system: The more you collect, the more you are rewarded. Because that often works in opposition to the goals of managed care, different criteria are necessary.

At first, it would appear that simply reversing the economic reward would work. In other words, the less physicians utilize services, the more money they get. Unfortunately, not only does that method fail to take into account certain behaviors that have no direct impact on utilization [such as member satisfaction, participation with the quality management (QM) program, or compliance with administrative procedures], but it may also be subject to inappropriate manipulation or, worse yet, inappropriate underutilization.

Objective Criteria

The use of strictly objective criteria has recognized drawbacks. Examples of strictly objective criteria include utilization rates (e.g., hospital rates, referral rates, and ancillary testing), overall medical cost [e.g., per member per month (PMPM) cost], productivity (e.g., visits per day), and so forth. The major problem with strictly objective criteria is that they can be gamed. The two major games played with objective criteria are churning and "buffing and turfing."

Churning is the major complaint against fee-for-service medicine but can be equally prevalent in some managed care environments that rely heavily on productivity measures. Churning is simply increasing the revisit rate of existing patients more than is medically necessary. For example, it is just as easy to schedule a hypertension recheck in 4 weeks as in 8 weeks. Furthermore, a revisit is a lot easier than a new patient, so that the temptation can arise to see many revisits rather than allow the time for lengthy visits from new patients. Of course, if productivity is *not* tracked and rewarded in a closed panel system or medical group, overhead and costs will rise while access declines.

Buffing and turfing can occur in any plan with an undue emphasis on low utilization and when the compensation and reward structure for physicians is heavily weighted toward individual physicians having low utilization profiles. Buffing and turfing refers to a physician's culling sick patients out of the practice to make the utilization profiles look better. Buffing refers to a physician's making this practice appear (to the plan) to be justifiable, and turfing refers to transferring the sickest patients to other physicians for care to look like a low-utilizing provider.

This problem is not to be confused with the common excuse for failing to control utilization: "But I've got all the sick patients!" It is up to the medical director to determine whether there is validity to that. Buffing and turfing refer specifically to physicians trying to dump their high-cost patients on other physicians.

Subjective Criteria

Strictly subjective criteria are just as problematic as strictly objective criteria. Examples of strictly subjective criteria can include judgments about attitude, professionalism, demeanor, and the like. The principal problems with subjective criteria are the variability of interpretation and charges of favoritism and bias.

The very nature of subjective criteria demands variability in interpretation. Although a subjective category may be defined, performance in that category will be judged on the basis of the evaluator's opinion rather than on a set of numbers. This is certainly legitimate because presumably the manager making the judgment has a reasonably good idea of what he or she wants to see. It is still true, however, that different managers may judge the same behavior in different ways.

Charges of favoritism and bias are much more serious. If strictly subjective criteria are used, and if a negative evaluation is given to a physician, the manager may find that the physician does not accept the results, and charges of favoritism or bias may ensue. This can be of great concern if disciplinary actions are necessary and could theoretically lead to legal action against a plan.

CATEGORIES FOR EVALUATION OF PHYSICIAN PERFORMANCE

As we have seen, the use of strictly objective or subjective criteria can cause problems. It is therefore often useful to use both types of evaluation criteria in assessing physician performance. There are clearly objective items that can be measured and evaluated, items that a medical manager will consider important, such as utilization or productivity. The same is true for subjective measures, such as participation, attitude, and so forth. The real issue is to combine objective with subjective in such a way as to avoid as much as possible the disincentive aspects of concentrating too heavily on any one category. It is unlikely that any plan will use all categories discussed; rather, plan management will choose what is important to the plan's particular situation.

Categories for Evaluation in Closed Panels

This section discusses suggested categories for evaluation of physician performance in closed panels. These categories are listed in Exhibit 11–1 and are discussed below. In any individual plan, certain categories will have more or less importance, and there are surely categories that are not even mentioned here. Unlike the situation in open panels, where utilization results may have a direct economic impact on a

Exhibit 11–1 Possible Categories for Evaluation in Closed Panels

- Productivity
- Medical charting
- Dependability and efficiency
- After-hours call duty
- Medical knowledge
- Management of patient care
- Management of outside resources
- Patient relations
- Staff relations
- Attitude and leadership
- Participation

physician, in many closed panels a physician's utilization-based performance will require increased attention during this process.

It is important that the physicians in the group buy in to the process and not feel that it is being forced upon them. It is up to medical management to decide what behavior it wishes to motivate and then to present the concept to the practicing physicians. Allowing the physicians to have input into developing the criteria against which their performance will be judged is crucial to gaining acceptance and cooperation with the program.

What follows are areas that one may wish to consider for evaluation of closed panel physician performance. A general idea of how the category is defined is also given, although before using these categories one would want to define more specifically just what aspects of behavior would be evaluated.

Productivity

This category looks at volume of work and efficiency. Whatever standard a plan sets, such as number of visits per week, hours worked, and so forth, would be used as the judgment criterion. One could add an element of time management as well. Productivity is discussed in Chapter 7.

Medical Charting

This would evaluate a physician's outpatient charts for legibility, timeliness, thoroughness, and compliance with whatever system is being used (e.g., chart format, face sheets, medication sheets, and so forth).

Dependability and Efficiency

This category would include arriving on time for work, sticking to the schedule, and complying with administrative aspects of the plan, such as properly using the forms.

After-Hours Call Duty

This category looks at responsiveness, appropriate use of emergency medical resources, proper documentation, ensuring continuity of care through follow-ups or transfer of care to the appropriate primary physician, and any other aspects of care delivered through the after-hours on-call mechanism.

Medical Knowledge

This evaluates the level of medical knowledge, amount of technical skill, evidence of proper medical judgment, awareness of limitations in skills and knowledge, and appropriate use of continuing medical education opportunities.

Management of Patient Care

Closely related to the category of medical knowledge, this category looks at how the basic medical skills are translated into action and how that relates to cost effectiveness. This category would include both outpatient and inpatient care. Examples include logical and efficient plans for diagnosis and treatment, proper discharge planning, appropriate follow-up intervals, and so forth. The common thread is how patient care is handled by the physician being evaluated rather than by a consultant.

Management of Outside Resources

This category looks at a physician's use of outside resources, including consultants and an-

cillary services, both diagnostic and therapeutic. Evaluations of appropriateness, cost-effective use, and maintenance of continuity would be made.

Patient Relations

This category looks at a physician's ability to communicate effectively with patients, the quality of patient relations, and any concerns regarding member satisfaction. Member surveys may be conducted to obtain the opinions of members after their encounter; telephone surveys generally yield more data than mail-based surveys.

Staff Relations

This looks at a physician's ability to communicate and cooperate with other members of the medical staff, including a physician's working relationship with support staff.

Attitude and Leadership

Attitude looks at a physician's enthusiasm, interest, commitment, flexibility, responsiveness, and so forth. Although essentially this is a measure of positive attitude, one may wish to add specifics about what is considered most important in judging attitude. Leadership refers to a physician's ability to train others and to motivate and lead as well as to his or her decision and communication skills in nonmedical matters.

Participation

Closely related to attitude, participation refers specifically to participation in plan committees and meetings. This looks at attendance, contribution, and initiative in taking responsibility.

Categories for Evaluation in Open Panels

This section discusses possible categories for formal performance evaluation in open panels; again, this list is not exhaustive, and a plan would not necessarily use all the categories. These categories are much more objective than subjective, in keeping with the management structure of open panels. They are listed in Exhibit 11–2 and are discussed below.

Exhibit 11–2 Possible Categories for Evaluation in Open Panels

- Utilization
  - Hospital utilization
  - Referral utilization
  - Ancillary utilization
- Productivity and access
  - Productivity
  - Access
  - Panel size and status
- Compliance with administrative procedures
  - Cooperation with precertification and authorization requirements
  - Compliance with use of the plan network
  - Use of electronic data interchange
  - Cooperation with other plan policies and procedures
- QM
  - Participation with and results of the QM program
  - Continuing medical education
- Patient relations and member satisfaction

Utilization

Utilization is included in this section, but not in any detail. It is included only because many open panel plans that have incentive programs include utilization data as part of the total program and do not necessarily separate these data from the final incentive result. Issues such as adjustments for case mix and severity are important, and data used in medical management and practice profiling are discussed in greater detail in Chapters 26 and 27.

Hospital utilization. This could measure days per 1,000 (annualized) or could be subdivided to look at the admission rate and the average length of stay. Cost on a PMPM basis may also be tracked. The plan may include ambulatory surgery as well. Values that are either too high or too low could require additional review.

Referral utilization. One could look at referrals per member per year (PMPY), total referral costs PMPM, both, or other common measures of referral utilization, such as referrals per 100 primary encounters. Values that are either too low (e.g., fewer than 0.5 referral PMPY or less

than $30 PMPY) or too high (e.g., more than 3 referrals PMPY or more than $100 PMPY) could require additional review.

Ancillary utilization. This category would measure the physician's use of laboratory, radiology, pharmacy, or whatever ancillary service the plan wished to observe. Members' use of the emergency department is often measured as well, although that may be part of hospital utilization.

Productivity and Access

Productivity. Productivity is generally measured as office visits PMPY. Too low a number (e.g., fewer than 1.5 visits PMPY) could indicate either good luck or denied access. Too high a number (e.g., more than 5) could indicate either bad luck or inefficient case management.

Access. Accessibility can be measured in several ways. One easy measure is the total number of office hours available, and the plan may wish to reward the availability of increased office hours, especially nights and weekend hours. The plan may also perform on-site office reviews and examine the appointment book of the physician to determine how long it takes to get an appointment.

Panel size and status. Some plans want to incent large panels and will therefore provide incrementally higher incentives to larger panels (up to a limit; the plan does not want to incent such large panels that access is hampered). The plan may also want to encourage physicians to keep their panels open to new members of the plan and will provide incentives for the PCPs to keep their panels in an open status. Because most plans require PCPs to keep their panels open to a set number of members (e.g., 250 members), this incentive may be used only for panels with more than the minimum required number of members.

Compliance with Administrative Policies and Procedures

In addition to clinical behavior, the plan benefits from high compliance with administrative policies and procedures.

Cooperation with precertification and authorization requirements. This measures the physician's compliance with the plan's requirements for precertification and authorization of services and is measured as a percentage. For example, 88 percent of admissions for a physician are precertified, and 95 percent of referrals are prospectively authorized. There is no value that can be too low; the scale is linear rather than bell shaped.

Compliance with use of the plan network. This measures a physician's use of the plan network, both consultant and hospital. The more a physician uses nonparticipating providers, the worse the compliance. A certain amount of background noise (e.g., from out-of-area emergencies) is to be expected, especially with point-of-service plans.

Use of electronic data interchanges. Electronic communications between the plan and the physicians improve efficiencies and timeliness. Therefore, the plan may wish to provide an incentive to practices that are linked electronically to the plan's computers for defined activities such as encounters, authorizations, claims, and reimbursement.

Cooperation with other plan policies and procedures. Beyond the policies and procedures for precertification and authorization, this measures compliance with encounter tracking, participation in meetings and committees, fee structures, and so forth. This measure may be somewhat subjective.

QM

Participation with and results of QM program. This would look at a physician's cooperation with the QM program and the results of actual audits and focused chart reviews. Failure to cooperate would result in either no points or a negative score or evaluation. Standards of care for such things as health maintenance or common problems (e.g., hypertension) would be evaluated, and a cumulative score would be developed. For example, 85 percent compliance with standards for a particular audit would yield a result equal to 85 percent of the maximum possible score.

Continuing medical education. The plan may wish to provide incentives for physicians to comply with enhanced continuing medical education programs. Although such compliance is often required for state licensure or for recredentialing (see Chapter 8), the plan may wish to incent particular forms of continuing education or may even wish to provide the programs directly to the physicians. For example, additional training in preventive care may be desired, or the plan may want to focus on defined clinical conditions.

Patient Relations and Member Satisfaction

These data are obtained from member services reports (see Chapter 30). Evaluations could include the rate at which members transfer out of the practice, the rate at which the physician asks to remove members from the practice, and complaints or grievances about the physician.

Another source for member satisfaction data is member surveys. Periodic mail or telephone surveys with a well-designed survey instrument can yield valuable information about patient satisfaction and perceived quality of service.

MEASURING THE CATEGORIES AND PRODUCING A RESULT

Although you may wish to use the above categories simply for discussion, there is utility in quantifying the results of the evaluation. For example, if you are using a formal evaluation system for allocating bonus or incentive payments, it is extremely useful to have the results of the evaluation tie directly to the amount of money that is paid out.

To facilitate measurement, it is sometimes helpful, although not required, to assign relative weights to each category. These weights would reflect the importance of that category in the overall scheme of things. For example, you may decide that medical charting is less important than cost-effective use of resources. Regardless of whether you use a weighting factor, it is quite helpful to translate the evaluation of performance in each category into a numeric value or score. For example, you may use a scale of 1 to 5 or 1 to 10. The better the performance in that category, the higher the number.

For categories in which the result depends on achieving a norm, a bell-shaped curve could be used. For example, if PCP encounters are expected to be 3.5 visits PMPY, then 5 points could be awarded for visits of 3.0 to 4.0 visits PMPY, 3 points for 1.5 to 2.9 or 4.1 to 5.0 visits PMPY, 2 points for 0.5 to 1.4 or 5.1 to 6.0 visits PMPY, and so forth. If you are using weighting factors, you would then multiply the score by the weight to achieve a numeric result. For example, if a score of 5 is given and the weight is also 5, the score would be 25. The last step is to tabulate the results. For example, if you were using an evaluation system with 11 categories, a scale of 1 to 5, and no weighting factor, the highest possible result or score would be 55.

If you are using an evaluation system for allocating bonus or adjusting annual base compensation, the numeric result would be used to calculate the amount of payout as described in the examples provided below.

Closed Panel Example

The following example illustrates the use of a formal evaluation system for allocation of bonuses in a group or closed panel plan. Assume that there are 50 physicians eligible to participate in a year-end incentive equal to $500,000. Assume also that the medical leadership has chosen to focus on the following areas of concern and with the following weights: productivity (weight, 5), utilization management and resource use (weight, 3), member satisfaction (weight, 3), and attitude and participation (weight, 2). Each category is evaluated on a scale of 1 to 5, so that the highest possible score would be 65 for any single physician [(5 × 5) + (5 × 3) + (5 × 3) + (5 × 2) = 65]. After all the physicians are evaluated, the total points for each physician are added together to yield a

maximum number of points. In this case, assume that the grand total equals 1,250 (an average score of 25 for the 50 eligible physicians). Therefore, each point is worth $400 ($500,000 ÷ 1,250). Multiplying each physician's score by $400 results in the incentive payment; for example, a score of 50 would result in an incentive payment of $20,000. The medical leadership may also choose to pay no incentive to any physician with a score less than a certain number (e.g., lower than 15), thus slightly increasing the amount available to those who remain eligible.

Open Panel Example

How complex one makes an incentive program will be dependent on the plan's goals for the program, the level of sophistication in the physician panel, the size of the panel to be covered under the program, and the amount of money available for incentive compensation. Some plans pay incentive compensation from utilization-based risk pools (such as referral or institutional; see Chapter 9); other plans budget incentive compensation as a separate line item independent of utilization. In open panels, it is also quite useful to look at both behavior and the size of the membership base for which a physician is responsible, with greater potential rewards going not only to those physicians who demonstrate desired behavior but also to those whose panel size is large.

In a small, stable, and sophisticated individual practice association, one may use all the above-mentioned categories for evaluation. In a large and heterogeneous direct contract model open panel, the focus may be more narrow. The following examples illustrate some different ways to approach an open panel.

Many physicians in private fee-for-service practice complain about the administrative burden placed on them by managed care. That complaint is partially legitimate, although if utilization is controlled the economic reward should offset the hassle factor. Nevertheless, one may agree to compensate through incentive compensation for those items that are important to the plan but do not necessarily result in a direct utilization-based economic reward (e.g., QM, compliance with administrative procedures, and member satisfaction). In this example, payment of performance-based incentive compensation is not influenced by utilization results or the status of any utilization-based risk/bonus pool. The incentive compensation is funded on a PMPM basis and as a distinct line item. Points are assigned for each category, and a minimum score (say, 50 percent of the total possible points) must be achieved for the physician to participate in the incentive compensation program.

In this example, assume that there are 180 PCPs in a direct contract open panel health maintenance organization (HMO). Because of problems with member satisfaction, it is decided to pay out incentive compensation based 40 percent on member satisfaction and 30 percent each on compliance with administrative procedures and QM. For simplicity's sake, assume that translates to 40 possible points for member satisfaction and 30 possible points each for compliance and QM. Funding is at $0.30 PMPM, and there are 60,000 members in the HMO, so there is $216,000 potentially available (60,000 × 12 × $0.30) at year end.

Member satisfaction is measured by telephone surveys of members who have seen the PCP in the past 6 months, transfer rates out of the practice, and member complaints and concerns. Compliance with administrative procedures is measured by looking at compliance with precertification requirements (measured as a percentage of hospital admissions and outpatient surgeries that are precertified), encounter form submission (measured against a statistical average, 3.2 visits PMPY for example), and compliance with the referral authorization system (measured by timeliness and completion of the referral authorization form and use of participating providers). QM is measured by compliance with standards of care set by the QM committee for both routine health maintenance and disease-specific process audits. For example, a set number of charts are audited for a fixed set of criteria; if the PCP meets the criteria 90 percent of the

time, then the score would be 90 percent of the maximum number of possible points. If a PCP refuses to participate in the QM program, or if the PCP has been sanctioned by the QM committee, no participation in the incentive program is allowed.

The plan may choose to pay out only on the basis of the PMPM allocation to any individual PCP, or it may choose to pay out the entire incentive pool but only to those PCPs who are eligible to participate. In other words, if half the network qualifies, the plan must choose whether to pay out only half the incentive pool (based on the assumption that PCPs who fail to qualify increase the overhead cost to the plan because of their poor habits) or to pay out the entire incentive pool but only to half the network.

In the case of only paying out an individual PCP's allocation, the plan simply pays out the individual PCP's PMPM allocation times the total member months for a qualifying physician times the percentage of the maximum score received. For example, assume that a single PCP has 700 members and has achieved a rating of 85 percent on member satisfaction, 75 percent on compliance, and 80 percent on QM. The calculation would then be ($0.30 × 700 × 12) × [(0.4 × 0.85) + (0.3 × 0.75) + (0.3 × 0.8)] = $2,028.60.

In the situation where the entire fund is to be paid out to qualifying PCPs, the following calculations illustrate disbursement of incentive compensation. First, membership must be factored into the score. One simple method is to multiply the score by the membership base that the PCP covers; for example, if a PCP has achieved results as noted above, the total score would be (700 × 12) × [(0.4 × 0.85) + (0.3 × 0.75) + (0.3 × 0.8)] = 6,762. Next, the entire incentive fund must be divided by the total number of available points to assign a value to each point; for example, if 70 PCPs qualify to participate and the aggregate point value of those 70 PCPs is 444,500, then each point is worth ($216,000 ÷ 444,500) = $0.486. Last, each PCP has his or her individual total points multiplied by the point value; in our example that would be (6,762 × $0.486) = $3,286.33.

Some managers feel that, if a PCP has already received a substantial bonus from the utilization risk/bonus pools (in a capitated system), then incentive compensation should be reduced, and they therefore include a negative factor for bonus already received. In that way, the incentive program preferentially rewards PCPs who were good case managers but who experienced more than their share of bad luck in terms of adverse selection. This method of adjustment is not common.

CONCLUSION

Most managed care products have similar benefit designs. As the industry matures, the plans that survive will no doubt be those that motivate health care providers to provide cost-efficient service. As efficiencies standardize across plans, price competition intensifies and creates a marketplace where plans can only distinguish themselves on service. Performance evaluation in health care therefore should reward cost efficiency and high-quality service.

Formal evaluations of physician performance can and should be made in a managed care plan, and appropriate incentives can be provided. Professional behavior may be evaluated with a combination of objective and subjective criteria. Ex-

cessive emphasis on any one area must be avoided to prevent inappropriate manipulation of the system. Even in the absence of monetary rewards associated with an evaluation system, feedback regarding behavior is still a useful tool for a medical director.

REFERENCES AND NOTES

1. C.M. Cooper, Formal Physician Performance Evaluations, *Journal of Ambulatory Care Management* 13 (1980): 19–33.

2. M. McGuirk-Porell, et al., A Performance-Based Quality Evaluation System for Preferred Provider Organizations, *Quality Review Bulletin* (November 1991): 365–373.

3. N. Schlackman, Integrating Quality Assessment and Physician Incentive Payment, *Quality Review Bulletin* (August 1989): 234–237.

4. N. Schlackman, Evolution of a Quality-Based Compensation Model: The Third Generation, *American Journal of Medical Quality* (1993): 103–110.

5. J. Beloff, "AV-Med Health Plan of Florida: The Physician Incentive Bonus Plan Based on Quality of Care," in *Making Managed Healthcare Work: A Practical Guide to Strategies and Solutions*, ed. P. Boland (Gaithersburg, Md.: Aspen, 1993): 322–330.

6. C. Morain, HMOs Try To Measure (and Reward) "Doctor Quality," *Medical Economics* (6 April 1992): 206–215.

Chapter 12

Contracting and Reimbursement of Specialty Physicians

Peter R. Kongstvedt

In previous years, some health maintenance organizations (HMOs) had difficulties contracting with specialty care physicians (SCPs).* In more recent years, the oversupply of SCPs in some markets, along with the increasing penetration of managed care organizations (MCOs), has led SCPs in those markets actively to pursue contracts with MCOs. Concomitant with that shift in attitude, many HMOs and other forms of MCOs, such as preferred provider organizations (PPOs) and even some integrated delivery systems (IDSs; see Chapter 4), have closed their panels to new SCPs and have even departicipated some SCPs with existing contracts. In that environment, MCOs find contracting for specialty services to be relatively easier than in the past. In a number of such markets, some plans have also required that any participating SCPs agree to follow established practice guidelines in addition to accepting the other terms and conditions of participation.[1]

In other markets, SCPs remain in strong financial positions or may not be overrepresented (at least not by desirable candidates), or managed care may not yet be in a strong market position. In those cases, an MCO, especially an HMO, will need to be aware of the reasons that contracting for specialty services is of high priority and of the reasons that an SCP may wish to contract with the MCO.

This chapter discusses common issues involved in SCP network development and contracting and in the reimbursement of SCPs. The reader is also referred to Chapter 13 for a discussion of specialty networks as organizations in their own right.

Perhaps the most obvious reason for a plan to contract with SCPs is to save money by having a financially advantageous agreement, such as a discounted fee schedule, or to lower risk for medical costs through capitation. There are other reasons in addition to obtaining financial terms. For an HMO, the issue of subordinated funds for uncovered liabilities is very real. Regulatory reserve requirements include calculations that are based on the number of real or expected visits to outside providers who have not signed a contract containing the National Association of Insurance Commissioners' (NAIC) no balance billing clause (see Chapter 55 for a discussion of this issue). Just as important, contractual arrangements will aid in getting and holding an SCP's attention, will help in the administration of an authorization system, will allow the plan to forecast and budget medical expenses more accurately, and will help ensure access to care for the members of the health plan.

An SCP will be acutely interested in the total volume of referrals. If the plan intends to restrict the size of the referral panel significantly (or has already done so), and if the plan has a reasonable membership base, then one can easily calculate the expected number of referrals. In addition, time really is money. Most SCPs will value a plan's ability to turn around a claim quickly. If

---

*For purposes of this discussion, SCPs refer not only to physician SCPs but to nonphysicians as well, such as psychologists, physical therapists, and the like. The chapter is most germane, however, to physician specialists.

SCPs do not understand the value of rapid claim turnaround, their office manager will. Of course, if the plan cannot turn the claim around in a reasonable amount of time (e.g., 30 days or sooner), it will have considerable difficulty in negotiating and maintaining contracts.

In tightly managed plans with well-functioning prospective authorization systems, being able to guarantee payment for authorized services for covered benefits is valuable. Elimination of uncertainty will be worth a measure of peace of mind to most SCPs. If a plan depends heavily on retrospective review and claims adjudication, however, it may not be able to guarantee payment.

Some contracts will provide a regular revenue stream for the SCP. This is most valuable in capitated arrangements but holds for other arrangements as well. Depending on the payment mechanism agreed on and the volume of work that the SCP will do, this can be a powerful incentive, especially in an overcrowded medical market or to an SCP just getting started.

An SCP may also hope to see an increase in fee-for-service (FFS) referrals. This is important only in open panel arrangements or in those closed panels that do a significant amount of FFS work. Because most physicians prefer to work with those SCPs whom they know and trust, a contractual arrangement that leads to that type of relationship will be valuable. The reverse is also true: An SCP may contract with your plan to prevent the disruption of FFS referrals or as a favor to a valued primary care physician (PCP) who has been a good source of referrals. Last, an SCP may contract simply to prevent a competitor from getting there first. There is often fierce competition among SCPs, although most physicians are reluctant to admit it.

HOW MANY SCPs?

The number of SCPs of each type with which a plan needs to contract is not an easy calculation. Many plans have between two and three times as many SCPs as PCPs, whereas some aggressive systems in the western United States have equal numbers of SCPs and PCPs. Certain specialties, such as general surgery, orthopedics, and obstetrics and gynecology, and some of the medical subspecialties (e.g., cardiology and gastroenterology) need to be adequately represented at each major hospital with which a plan contracts. Other specialties, such as neurosurgery or cardiothoracic surgery, need only be represented at those hospitals to which the plan refers members for appropriate treatment.

In one widely read article, the number of SCPs required was estimated to be between 80 and 110 per 100,000 population depending on the type of MCO, as illustrated in Table 12–1 (adjustments for Medicare and Medicaid were noted in the article).[2] There was, however, considerable variation in staffing ratios for all types of plans and all specialties. In another study, group model HMOs were used to project the number of covered lives needed for each of a variety of specialists in nonrural areas, as illustrated in Table 12–2.[3] In both these cases, the projections were based on maximum efficient use of SCPs and not on other considerations, as discussed below; therefore, they probably repre-

Table 12–1 Physician Requirements per 100,000 Population

Sector	Overall	Primary Care	Specialty Care
Staff/group HMO	146.4	65.9	80.5
IDS and IPA	124.4	55.9	68.5
Managed FFS	171.0	61.6	109.4
Open FFS	180.1	64.8	115.3

Source: Weiner JP. Forecasting the Effects of Health Reform on US Physician Workforce Requirements: Evidence from HMO Staffing Patterns. *JAMA.* 1994;272(3):222–230.

Table 12–2 Group Model HMO Covered Lives per Physician

Type of Practice	Number of Enrollees
Family practice and general internal medicine	2,250
Pediatrics	6,000
Obstetrics/Gynecology	7,000
General surgery	15,000
Anesthesiology	17,000
Radiology	20,000
Orthopedics	20,000
Mental health	20,000
Ophthalmology	25,000
Otolaryngology	35,000
Cardiology	35,000
Dermatology	35,000
Cardiovascular surgery	35,000
Gastroenterology	50,000
Neurosurgery	150,000

Source: Reprinted with permission of *The New England Journal of Medicine* , The Marketplace in Health Care Reform–The Demographic Limitations of Managed Competition, *The New England Journal of Medicine SPECIAL REPORT,* Vol. 328, p. 150, © 1993, Massachusetts Medical Society.

sent a far more draconian reduction in the need for SCPs than actually exists or is likely to exist in the United States, even in nonurban markets. The alert reader will note that Table 12–2 is actually slightly more generous than ratios noted in Table 5–3, which is quite severe.

An MCO or IDS must balance between the lowest possible number of SCPs required for the purposes of medical management and a somewhat higher number of SCPs required for the purposes of access and marketing. In other words, an MCO or IDS may have a higher number of SCPs than would be required to provide specialty services in the most efficient manner to provide good access to services by members and PCPs, thus improving satisfaction and retention of both members and PCPs.

PRIMARY VERSUS SPECIALTY CARE DESIGNATION

It is not uncommon, especially in open panel HMOs and in IDSs, for the same physician to desire to be designated as both a PCP and an SCP. The usual argument is that the SCP, almost always a medical subspecialist, performs a significant amount of primary care, perhaps as much as half their practice time. In some cases, the same physician also wishes to be able to see a member for primary care and then to refer that member back to himself or herself at a later time for specialty services (i.e., get paid first to see the member as a PCP and then get paid a second time to see the same member as an SCP). It is uncommon and foolish to allow physicians to be able to authorize referrals back to themselves and get paid twice to provide care for the same member.

In some cases, a plan will make the decision based on criteria such as an objective review of a physician's practice and thereby designate the physician as a PCP or an SCP. In other cases, the plan may allow a medical subspecialist to self-designate but will prohibit that physician from being both a PCP and an SCP. It is also possible for a physician to be a PCP for his or her own panel of members but to take referrals as an SCP from other PCPs who are not associated with that physician in some way, such as in the same multispecialty group.

There is conflicting evidence on how costly SCPs are versus PCPs in overall use of medical resources to deliver similar episodes of care. Several studies support the notion that SCPs are far more costly than PCPs in managing care.[4,5] It is likely that some of this variation is caused by a different mix of cases and severity because SCPs do get sicker patients on average than PCPs.[6] There is also some evidence that, for certain chronic conditions, medical specialists are more efficient in their use of resources than PCPs.[7]

As a plan takes on a sizeable Medicare or elderly population, there may be many instances where a specialty-trained physician will function more efficiently than a PCP who does not have the same depth of training in a particular clinical area. This is especially true for certain complex conditions, such as acquired immuno-deficiency syndrome (AIDS), and it may be true for other chronic and complex medical conditions.

It is not at all unreasonable for a specialty-trained internist to function as a PCP, especially in an open panel type of MCO or in an IDS. As managed care increases its penetration in the health care market, and as the supply of physicians who are trained specifically as PCPs is strained, this issue will take on even greater importance.

CLOSED PANELS: IN-HOUSE AND OUTSIDE CONTRACTS

Closed panel plans, such as staff or group model HMOs (or large primary care group practices with a significant managed care practice), must carefully weigh the advantages and disadvantages of bringing an SCP in house to join the medical staff rather than contracting out for services. The need to bring an SCP in house may arise if the volume of referrals is high, if the plan is unable to obtain satisfactory contracts outside, if there are questions about the quality of care being delivered by outside SCPs and there are no good alternatives, if there is patient dissatisfaction, or if there are problems with proper utilization control.

Balanced against this are issues that may militate against the decision to bring an SCP in house. Providing adequate on-call coverage could be a problem. If there is only one of that type of SCP and cross-coverage with another in-house SCP is not possible, the SCP could burn out; if coverage previously had been provided by outside SCPs who now no longer receive referrals, they may be less than cooperative about sharing calls.

Another potential problem can arise if there is a large geographic area to cover. If the plan uses multiple hospitals covering a wide territory or if there are multiple medical centers, the SCP may not be able to provide sufficient coverage, and

the volume of referrals coming back inside may decrease. Even if referrals can be tightened up on an outpatient basis, attention must be paid to emergency care, especially for surgery, obstetrics, orthopedics, and cardiology.

CREDENTIALING

Credentialing of SCPs is performed the same way as it is for PCPs; credentialing is discussed in Chapter 8 and is not repeated here. It should be noted that many MCOs require SCPs to be fully board certified or board eligible and make no exceptions.

TYPES OF REIMBURSEMENT ARRANGEMENTS

This section discusses reimbursement of SCPs on the basis of the financial relationship between the plan and the SCPs as a whole. It is possible that a contracting entity, such as a group or a management services organization, may accept reimbursement from the plan but compensate individual physicians in a separate manner. The compensation of physicians in groups and IDSs is discussed in Chapter 10.

As illustrated in Figure 12–1, approximately 20 percent to 30 percent of HMO specialists are paid through capitation as the predominant form of reimbursement.[8,9] The majority of SCPs are paid through FFS, the rest through other mechanisms, such as salary, retainer, hourly, and so forth. Exhibit 12–1 lists some of the common (and less common) methods. The most appropriate method for use in any given situation will be predicated on the goals of the plan, the SCP, and each party's ability actually to manage within the terms of the agreement.

Charges and Discounts

The simplest arrangement to understand, although a highly unsatisfactory one, is straight FFS. The SCP sends a claim, and the plan pays it. Then why bother to contract at all? The an-

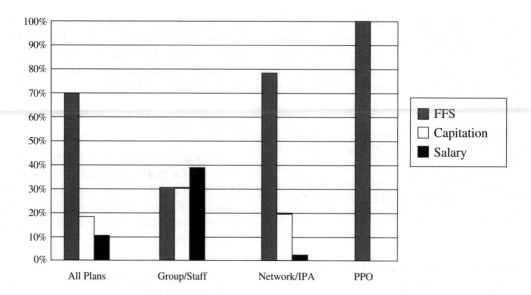

Figure 12–1 Predominant form of reimbursement for SCPs. IPA, independent practice association. *Source:* Reprinted from *Arrangements Between Managed Care Plans and Physicians: Results from a 1994 Survey of Managed Care Plans*, 1995, Physician Payment Review Commission.

swer is to get the SCP to agree to the NAIC sole source of payment clause (see Chapter 55). Although certainly not a preferred arrangement, occasionally it is all an MCO can get, particularly in high-cost specialties (e.g., neurosurgery) when there are no good alternatives or in small start-up plans without a significant enrollment. Paying straight charges is uncommon.

Another simple arrangement is discounted FFS. There are two variations here: a straight discount on charges, such as 20 percent; and a discount based on volume or a sliding scale. In the latter type, the degree of discount is based on an agreed-upon set of figures. For example, for an obstetrician who performs 0 to 5 deliveries per month there is a 10 percent discount, for 6 to 10 per month there is a 15 percent discount, and so forth. Many plans combine a discount arrangement with a fee maximum. The fee maximum is a fee allowance schedule (see below); the plan pays the lesser of the SCP's discounted charges or the maximum allowance.

Relative Value Scale or Fee Allowance Schedule

The most common form of FFS is the relative value scale, such as the resource-based relative value scale (RBRVS), or a fee allowance schedule. The RBRVS is discussed in Chapter 9. The difference between a relative value scale and a fee allowance schedule is that in the former each procedure is assigned a relative value, usually on the basis of current procedural terminology revision 4 (CPT-4). That value is then multiplied by another figure (the conversion factor) to arrive at a payment. Rather than negotiate separate fees, one negotiates the conversion factor. In a fee allowance schedule, the fees for procedures (again, usually on the basis of CPT-4) are explicitly laid out, and the SCP agrees to accept those fees as full payment unless the discounted charges are less than the fee schedule, in which case the plan pays the lesser of the two. The majority of MCOs that use FFS use the RBRVS,

Exhibit 12–1 Models for Reimbursing SCPs

- Charges
- Discounts
- Fee allowances
- Global fees
- Changing schedules based on performance
- Capitation (with or without carve-outs)
- Retainer
- Hourly and salary
- Outpatient and professional diagnosis-related group or ambulatory patient groups
- Withholds
- Penalties
- Periodic interim payments or cash advances

and the majority of those set the conversion factor somewhat higher than that used by Medicare.[10]

The real utility of RBRVS or a fee allowance schedule is the avoidance of unanticipated fee hikes. If you have simply negotiated a discount on charges, the discount can easily be made up by raising fees. This may be partially offset by contractually requiring notice for any fee increases, assuming that you can and will actually spot the stray fee hike, but that still leaves you with the problem of administering a jumble of different agreements. It is far preferable to have one uniform method of handling claims.

Performance-Based FFS

Performance-based FFS for SCPs is similar to that discussed for PCPs in Chapter 9. The most common examples are through withholds and fee adjustments in an independent practice association (IPA), in which all physicians are treated the same regardless of whether they are PCPs or SCPs. A few IPAs have attempted to adjust fees based on each specialty, so-called budgeted FFS. In this approach, each specialty has a per member per month (PMPM) budget

(e.g., $2.50 PMPM for cardiology), and actual costs are measured against that budget. If costs exceed budget, then fees are lowered, but only for that specialty, and vice versa if costs are better than budget. Although this is an interesting variation, it takes a highly sophisticated tracking system, sound actuarial analysis, and a large membership base to ensure with statistical integrity that utilization patterns are based on provider behavior rather than on random chance. A variation on FFS is the global fee, flat rate, or case rate. These are discussed later in this chapter.

Capitation

Although only 20 percent to 30 percent of HMOs use capitation as the predominant form of reimbursement to SCPs, a much higher percentage of plans do use capitation to reimburse individual specialties (in other words, FFS is the predominant method, but capitation is still used for some SCPs), and there may be some level of risk sharing as well. This is illustrated in Figure 12–2. It is important to note that, in the same study that produced these numbers, fully 79 percent of all HMOs planned to increase the use of SCP capitation.[11]

SCP capitation is in general simpler than PCP capitation, as discussed in Chapter 9. Again, capitation refers to a fixed payment PMPM for services. The capitation payment may be adjusted for age, sex, and product type, but not as universally as is found in PCP capitation. You first must calculate the expected volume of referrals, the average cost, your ability to control utilization, and your relative negotiating strength. Your plan may have past data to guide you, or you may need to depend on an actuary or your best assumptions to derive the correct capitation amount. Please refer to Chapter 42 for more discussion of capitation and utilization rates.

Although theoretically the same utilization issues apply to specialty care as to primary care, the numbers involved in SCP capitation are often significantly smaller for any given specialty

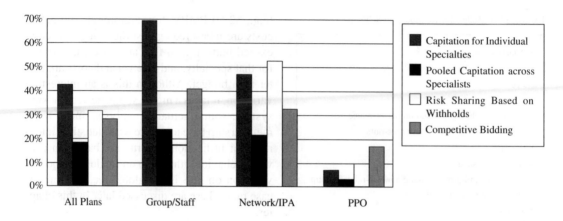

Figure 12–2 Capitation to individual specialists. *Source:* Reprinted from *Arrangements Between Managed Care Plans and Physicians: Results from a 1994 Survey of Managed Care Plans*, 1995, Physician Payment Review Commission.

(even though specialty PMPM costs as a whole are usually 1.5 to 2 times higher than those for primary care). For example, PCP capitation may average $14.00 PMPM, and the capitation for neurology may be $0.55. Thus adjustments based on demographic variables become very small indeed and may not be worth the effort. Because the numbers can be smaller, an SCP requires a much larger number of members for capitation to have meaning. Where a PCP may achieve relative stability in capitation at a membership level of 400 to 600, an SCP may require triple that number or more to avoid the problem of random chance having more effect than medical management on utilization. Capitation of SCPs can be challenging, particularly if you have a lot of point-of-service (POS) benefits in your plan (see Chapter 3 for a discussion of POS).

Capitation clearly has the advantages of allowing you to budget for expected medical costs and to place a degree of risk and reward on the SCP, and the financial incentives encourage the SCP to be a more active participant in controlling utilization. If done properly, capitation can be valuable both to the SCP and to your plan, a genuine win–win situation. If done poorly, it can be a chronic headache. Figure 12–3 illustrates the relative percentages of the various specialties that are capitated as of the time of this text writing.

In FFS plans, it is probably not a good idea to capitate SCPs before capitating PCPs. If you do so to any great degree, you may find that you have obligated more money than you intended to SCP capitations, to the detriment of primary care and hospital funds. There may be exceptions to this, such as physical therapy or mental health and chemical dependency, but those are infrequent.

Organizational Models for Capitating Specialty Services

Capitating for specialty services has some complexities compared with PCP capitation. When PCPs are capitated, a member must choose a PCP and it becomes a straightforward issue of tracking that membership. Specialty capitation is different in that any given SCP will provide care to patients of multiple PCPs, and there is no requirement on the part of a member

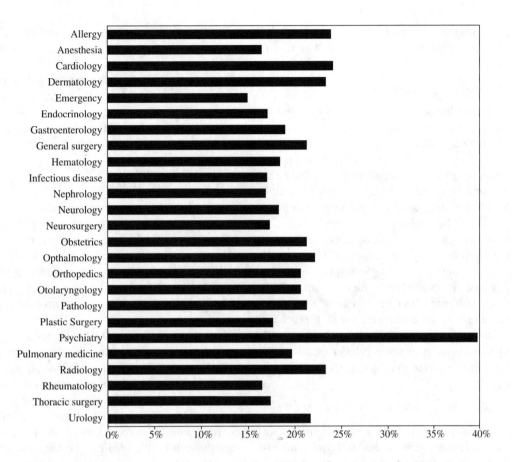

Figure 12–3 Percentage of SCPs capitated as of 1994, part 1 and 2. *Source:* Reprinted with permission from Industry Report Data as of January 1, 1994, *The InterStudy Competitive Edge*, Vol. 4, No. 1, p. 49, © 1994, InterStudy Publications.

to choose a SCP.* Because of these issues, HMOs must use alternative methods to determine how to capitate SCPs. Some of these methods are described as follows.

---

* The common exception to this last point is obstetrics and gynecology (OB/GYN). More than 71 percent of HMOs allow members to self-refer to OB/GYNs, although those OB/GYNs generally do not have the authority to refer the member to another specialist.[12] Many of those plans require all female members over the age of 12 to choose an OB/GYN, and the plan in turn capitates that OB/GYN in a fashion similar to that used for PCPs (although the capitation rate is less frequently varied by age and, of course, sex).

Organized Groups

The easiest form of SCP capitation is through organized medical groups. In some cases, the group is a multispecialty group, inclusive of primary and specialty care. In that case, it is assumed that any member assigned to a PCP in that group will likewise be assigned to the SCPs in the group.

Organized single-specialty groups are also good candidates for capitation. If the group is large enough, then the group may be capitated for the entire network. If it is not large enough to cover the entire medical service area, then the group may be capitated for that portion of the geographic medical service area that it can cover.

Geographic Distribution

Geographic distribution is closely related to the way an organized medical group is capitated. The reason to discuss it separately is that it involves the same principle applied to a smaller group. In essence, a small (e.g., two or three physicians) specialty group accepts capitation for all relevant specialty services in a defined portion of the medical service area but not the entire service area. For example, a group of general surgeons might be capitated to cover all services rendered at a single hospital. In an urban area, a capitated SCP might cover all PCP practices located in a particular set of ZIP codes. Because it is not uncommon for PCP practices (or SCP practices, for that matter) to have multiple locations, assignment is based on whatever office is considered the physician's principal office.

Specialty IPAs

Specialty-specific IPAs are not common, but the recent increase in vertical integration activities (such as physician–hospital organizations) has led to an increase in interest in this form of specialty capitation. The specialty IPA operates like a standard IPA, as described in Chapter 9. The specialty IPA accepts capitation from the HMO but usually pays FFS to the participating specialists. Capitation of individual SCPs within the specialty IPA is certainly possible but is rarely seen because specialty IPAs are often created to preserve the opportunity for multiple, unrelated SCPs to participate with aggressive HMOs. Whether specialty IPAs will remain viable is unknown.

Disease Management Companies

A new variation on single group capitation is capitation for single specialty services to a specialty corporation (e.g., a vendor that specializes in cancer services or cardiac care). The corporation employs physicians and support staff and provides facilities and ancillary services. The corporation is then responsible for providing all specialty services within the HMO's medical service area. This approach is best suited to specialty care that is not usually associated with emergencies, unless the vendor's employed physicians are on staff at all the HMO's participating hospitals.

Single Specialty Management or Specialty Network Manager

This method is uncommon but may increase as managed care experiments with different methods of capitating specialty services. It involves the HMO contracting with one single entity to provide all services within a single specialty, but that entity does not actually provide all the services. There are two basic approaches.

In one approach, an HMO capitates a single specialist (i.e., an individual physician) to manage all services in that specialty for all HMO members, even though the SCP cannot personally provide the services. This contracted SCP, the specialty network manager, must then subcontract with other specialists to provide services throughout the medical service area. The specialty network manager either makes or loses money, depending on how efficiently specialty services are managed. The specialty network manager may subcapitate with other SCPs if that is allowed by the state insurance department (many states will not allow a provider to capitate another provider; see Chapter 53), or may pay FFS. In any event, the primary SCP acts like a second gatekeeper in that PCPs need to work through the primary SCP to access specialty care for members. Sometimes the primary SCP receives the full capitation payment and must pay the other SCPs directly, or the HMO may administer the claims payments and provide the accounting and reporting for the primary contract holder. In fact, the HMO may wish to do so to track performance on a real-time basis as well as to protect members from possible nonpayment of claims by the primary contract holder.

In the other approach, an HMO contracts with a single institution for single specialty services (e.g., the HMO contracts with a local university faculty practice plan for all cardiology services). The contracted institution is then responsible to arrange for specialty services that it cannot provide itself. The primary specialty contract holder receives the capitation payment and must then administer payment to subcontractors. In some cases, the administrative cost to the primary contractor may be greater than the total capitation payment because it is often a manual process.

By PCP Choice

A theoretically interesting (although seldom used) method of capitating SCPs is through the mechanism of PCP choice. This model requires each PCP to choose which SCP from the applicable specialties will be used on an exclusive basis. The presence of choice means that multiple SCPs have agreed to a capitation rate but that no single SCP has exclusive rights. The plan is then required to track the members assigned to those SCPs by virtue of being on the PCP's panels and to pay the SCP capitation based on that. Although this is interesting and has great logic and appeal, most HMO management information systems are not capable of handling it, and the administrative headache would be great.

COMMON PROBLEMS WITH SPECIALTY CAPITATION

There are some common problems that need to be addressed before you capitate SCPs. If you fail to explore these issues, you may find yourself in the position of having to live with a year-long arrangement that is to your disadvantage.

The pressure to capitate frequently comes as a result of uncontrolled utilization. Referrals are high, expenses are out of control, and there is high negative variance to budget. The pressure to capitate is to prevent costs from going even higher and to bring some predictability to medical expenses. This is usually the wrong time to

capitate. Be assured that the SCP knows exactly how much you have been paying and will not eagerly agree to a capitation rate that amounts to a substantial discount, unless the plan (and the PCPs) is willing to change SCPs. It is far preferable to control utilization before negotiating a capitation rate. If you do not, you may be locked into the higher rate for at least a year. Of course, if the SCP, not the PCP, is the cause of inappropriately high utilization, then you really should look for a new SCP.

Another common problem is being able to control the flow of referrals. It is easy to assume that, once you cut a deal with an SCP, all you need to do is notify the PCPs and/or members and your problems are solved. This is not so. Disrupting old referral patterns is tough, and you may find that you do not have the system capabilities to respond proactively to referrals outside the capitated system. Furthermore, your capitated SCP may not be able to provide adequate geographic or emergency coverage. When referrals go outside your capitated system, you are essentially paying for them twice. This problem virtually defines a POS plan, which is why capitating SCPs in a POS plan is problematic.

One possible approach to the geographic coverage problem is to capitate only for an appropriate geographic primary care base. This balkanization of the specialty base frequently is more acceptable, unless the capitating specialty group has wide coverage.

Capitation may actually serve to increase utilization. If the PCPs who are controlling the referrals, and perhaps even the medical director of the plan, see capitation as putting a lid on expenses, there is far less pressure to control utilization because it appears that the service costs the same regardless of use; you could almost say that it is free! If you fail to control utilization of capitated services, you will have a most unpleasant surprise when the contract comes up for renegotiation. Most SCPs will keep track of what they would have made in FFS equivalents. If you have failed to control utilization, the capitation rate may be equivalent to an unacceptable discount on charges. You will either have to give in, find a new SCP, or hang tough. In each of those cases, someone loses.

The other problem with high levels of SCP utilization is the increase in other forms of utilization as well. As noted earlier, there is evidence that at least for many routine types of conditions SCPs use more resources than PCPs. Increases in institutional and ancillary services may follow increases in SCP referrals.

The last major problem encountered in capitation is the issue of carve-outs. A carve-out is a particular service that the SCP does not include in the capitation rate. For example, ophthalmologists may capitate for all services except cataract extractions, for which they will give you a 25 percent discount on charges. The problem here is that you may find yourself with an unexplainably high rate of cataract extractions. If the service is one for which only the SCP can reasonably judge the need, and that service is a carve-out, you have a potential problem. In all fairness, it is unlikely that you will be the victim of outright fraud, but it still makes for some uneasiness.

A variation of the carve-out problem arises when the SCP cannot or will not handle all the services. If you capitate for all services but the SCP refers out for the delivery of some of those services, you may wish to consider deducting those costs from the capitation payment. There are no consistent guidelines here. If the service is one that the SCP truly cannot perform (e.g., an ophthalmologist who does not do retinal surgery), then you can probably budget properly and not roll that expense into the capitation rate, thereby avoiding having to adjust the rate frequently and pressuring the SCP (perhaps inappropriately) not to refer cases. On the other hand, if the SCP can perform the service but simply does not (e.g., an ophthalmologist who is never available on Wednesday afternoons), then it is appropriate to deduct those expenses from the capitation payment. If you intend to do so, you must be clear about your intentions from the start and place appropriate language in the contract.

OTHER FORMS OF SPECIALTY PHYSICIAN REIMBURSEMENT

Retainer

A retainer is identical to what is commonly used with law firms. You simply pay a set amount to an SCP every month and reconcile at periodic intervals on the basis of actual utilization, either as a prenegotiated fee schedule or on some other objective measure. This ensures availability of the SCP to members and provides for the steady income desired by the SCP while still allowing payment on the basis of actual utilization. One issue to address early is whether the reconciliation goes both ways or whether it only goes up. That issue surfaces more often than one would expect.

Hourly and Salary

Just as it sounds, with hourly and salary arrangements the plan pays an SCP an hourly rate or salary for performing services. In essence, you are buying block time. This works to your advantage if you contract with an already busy SCP because there will be little incentive for him or her to stretch out sessions. This type of arrangement is common in emergency departments or other settings when a physician needs to be available for a defined time period. This also works if you need to buy on-call coverage to back up an in-house SCP. Hourly and salary arrangements lend themselves more to closed panel than open panel plans.

Case Rate, Global Fee, or Flat Rate for Procedures

Case rates, global fees, or flat rates are single fees that are paid for a procedure, and the fee is the same regardless of how much or how little time and effort are spent. For example, many plans use the same flat rate for either a vaginal delivery or a cesarean section, thereby eliminating any financial incentive to perform one or the other; this has been associated with a decrease in the cesarean section rate, although there may be other factors affecting this rate as well.[13]

Related to the flat rate is the global fee. A global fee is a flat rate that encompasses more than a single type of service. For example, a global fee for surgery may include all preoperative and postoperative care as well as one or two follow-up office visits. A global fee for obstetrics may include all prenatal and postnatal care.

Global fees must be carefully defined as to what they include and what may be billed outside them. For example, if ultrasound is billed outside the global fee for a delivery, you will need to monitor its use to determine whether any providers are using (and billing for) an abnormally high number of ultrasounds per case.

Bundled Case Rates or Package Pricing

Bundled case rates refer to a reimbursement that combines both the institutional and the professional charges into a single payment. For example, a plan may negotiate a bundled case rate of $20,000 for cardiac bypass surgery. That fee covers the charges from the hospital, the surgeon, the pump technician, and the anesthesiologist as well as all preoperative and postoperative care. Bundled case rates sometimes have outlier provisions for cases that become catastrophic and grossly exceed expected utilization.

Diagnosis-Related Groups and Ambulatory Patient Groups

These are important topics for hospital reimbursement but currently have limited utility in SCP reimbursement other than through bundled case rates, as discussed above. Further discussion of these two methods is found in Chapters 13 and 14.

Periodic Interim Payments and Cash Advances

Occasionally, a plan may use periodic interim payments (PIPs) or cash advances with SCPs. In the case of PIPs, the plan advances the provider a set amount of cash equivalent to a defined time period's expected reimbursable charges. As claims come in from that SCP, the claims are taken against the PIP, but the PIP is routinely replenished. In this way, the SCP gets a positive cash flow as well as the use of the plan's money interest free. Cash advances are simply that: The plan advances the provider a set amount of cash and then carries it as a receivable on the books. In the event that the relationship between the SCP and the plan terminates, the final claims are taken against the cash advance.

Neither of these techniques can be recommended for routine use. In either case, the advanced cash may not be treated as a liability by the SCP but rather simply as a payment, which makes it difficult to recover the funds. Capitation will accomplish much of what a PIP is intended to accomplish and is a preferred method. It is possible that in a plan with a heavy POS enrollment this method may be employed, but even then it is probably not necessary.

RISK/BONUS ARRANGEMENTS

In addition to whatever reimbursement arrangement you make with an SCP, there are times when it is mutually advantageous to add an element of risk and reward. This is almost always done in the context of utilization but could conceivably be tied to other objectives as well. These types of arrangements are best suited to those specialties in which the SCPs themselves control a major aspect of utilization and in which there is a sufficient volume of referrals to rule out random chance playing too large a role in the results. Risk and reward arrangements are far easier to do in a pure HMO environment than in a PPO (where they may not be allowed by state regulations) or a POS plan.

In setting risk and reward levels, keep in mind that you do not want to make the risk or reward so great that it has the potential of having a serious negative impact on clinical decision making. It is better policy to devise a reimbursement mechanism that fairly compensates an SCP up front for appropriate and judicious use of clinical resources and then sets a risk or bonus level that, while still being attention getting, is not potentially seriously injurious to the fiscal health of the SCP. You do not want to put the SCP, the plan member, or yourself in the position of having economics override proper medical care. What you do want is a risk or bonus arrangement that will help focus the attention of the SCP on controlling unnecessary utilization. Also, as noted in Chapter 9 regarding PCP risk/bonus arrangements, a plan with a Medicare risk contract must be aware of the possible limitations on the total amount of risk to which a physician may be subject without requiring the plan to undertake detailed member surveys.[14]

Set Targets

There are a number of objective criteria that one can use in setting targets for risk/bonus arrangements. A frequent one is average length of stay (e.g., setting a target of 1 or 2 days average length of stay for normal vaginal deliveries). A variation would be total bed days per 1,000 members (e.g., all surgical bed days per 1,000 members for the total plan membership, or whatever geographic base you choose).

Another possibility is PMPM cost. You need to define carefully the cost area, such as professional, hospital, all inclusive, and so on. If you have the systems capabilities to track accurately, this method has the advantage of being tied more directly to the bottom line of your plan.

Another method is to look at a particular medical expense as a percentage of premium revenue. This is less useful because, although it ties directly to your plan's margin, it can lead to disputes that are based on your premium rates and yield.

Avoid setting targets for productivity. If you set a risk or bonus on the basis of seeing a certain number of patients per hour or any of the other usual FFS incentives, you could have the problem of churning.

Define the Risk or Bonus

You must define the amount of payment that will be at risk or the amount that will potentially be available for bonus. For example, in a capitation situation it may be 10 percent or 20 percent of the total capitation payments for the year (in whole dollars). Next you must choose between a straight bonus arrangement for exceeding goals or a risk/bonus band in which the SCP is at risk for failing to meet goals and may achieve a bonus for exceeding them (in other words, a withhold on payment, possibly combined with a bonus plan).

After you have set the goals and amount of risk and reward, determine the spread of bonus payments. For example, achieving a 2 percent reduction in length of stay yields a 1 percent bonus up to a maximum of 10 percent of the total payments for the year. Be as specific as possible to avoid disputes later, and be absolutely sure that you can accurately track whatever objectives you set.

A simple warning here: Be sure that you have done a financial model of the possible outcomes of a bonus arrangement. You do not want to set up an arrangement where the bonus negates any savings achieved from meeting the goals. If the bonus will be paid simply for meeting goals and you have included those goals in your budget, be sure to include the bonus in your budget and reported medical benefit expenses as well. This should be obvious, but occasionally it is overlooked.

A frequently encountered criticism of bonus arrangements is that you are paying a provider to deliver reduced (i.e., inferior) care. This should simply not be the case. You are sharing the savings that high-quality, cost-effective medical care produces; furthermore, any providers caught trying to line their pockets by delivering inferior care will be terminated from participation in your plan. It is the SCP's responsibility to provide high-quality care. It is your responsibility to make sure that the SCP is properly reimbursed and to monitor the quality of care delivered.

NON–UTILIZATION-BASED INCENTIVE COMPENSATION

Some MCOs may wish to consider non–utilization-based incentive compensation. Described in detail in Chapter 11, this is an incentive program that rewards SCPs based on factors other than utilization, although it is certainly possible to combine a utilization-based and non–utilization-based program. Typical factors would include adherence to practice protocols or clinical pathways (see Chapters 19 and 25), member satisfaction (see Chapters 11 and 30), PCP satisfaction, and other forms of outcomes measures.

PROHIBITION OF SUBAUTHORIZATIONS

Of all the contractual terms (see Chapter 55), in a tightly controlled managed care plan with a primary care authorization system there must be a clear understanding that the SCP is not allowed to authorize services for a member but must obtain authorization from the PCP or the health plan. This includes hospitalizations, ancillary testing, and referrals to other SCPs.

There are some common occurrences of this problem. One example is the SCP who owns an expensive piece of diagnostic equipment; although there may be no genuine plan to do unnecessary testing, there is still a subtle pressure to use the machine and generate some revenue from it. If such self-authorizations are prohibited contractually, either the SCP will be forced to contact the PCP and discuss the need for the test, or the SCP will not be allowed to bill for the test (remember the sole source of payment clause).

Another common occurrence is the SCP choosing to hospitalize the member. Although hospitalization may be appropriate, your ability to manage the case is severely hampered if you do not know about it until it is all over. In most managed health care plans, hospitalization requires either preadmission review by the plan's utilization management department or authorization from the PCP and health plan. It is crucial to ensure that you will be able to manage hospi-

tal cases concurrently, and that means preadmission notification and authorization. See Chapter 17 for further discussion about utilization management.

The last common occurrence is the problem of referrals to other SCPs. If the plan allows an SCP to refer to another SCP without obtaining authorization, the member can start getting shunted from one SCP to another like a game of medical air hockey. Not only is that an inefficient and expensive way to deliver medical care, but the lack of continuity has implications for the quality of care as well.

How tightly you enforce this will vary in certain circumstances. For example, an obstetrician may only need to notify the plan when a member is admitted for a delivery and would not require PCP preauthorization at all. If an SCP is capitated for all office services, that capitation may include office procedures and tests as well (e.g., office radiology for an orthopedist). Even without capitation, you may decide to allow selected SCPs to perform certain studies because it is simply necessary for the delivery of care (e.g., allowing neurologists to order magnetic resonance imaging). These exceptions must be carefully thought through, and reimbursement for them should not encourage overutilization.

The point of this is not to make a system so rigid that it becomes impossible to deliver proper care but to have a system that allows you to manage the health care that is delivered by timely intervention when it is appropriate and to direct the care in the most cost-effective way possible. It is certainly possible that a tightly run plan could allow SCPs to function as managing physicians in certain circumstances (e.g., for active AIDS cases), but that is an analysis that each plan must make for itself.

CONCLUSION

Medical care delivered by SCPs is a crucial element in the cost and quality of health care. The roles of the SCP are continuing to evolve in managed care, as are the organizational structures that SCPs are using to contract for services.

Reimbursement arrangements and contracts are tools that codify and clarify the responsibilities of each party to the other. They will not solve your problems and will not take the place of good management. Remember: A 20 percent discount will not make up for poor utilization control, and nothing will make up for poor quality of care.

REFERENCES AND NOTES

1. Atlantic Information Services, Inc., *Provider Contracting and Capitation* (Washington, D.C.: Atlantic Information Services, 1993).

2. J.P. Weiner, Forecasting the Effects of Health Reform on U.S. Physician Workforce Requirements: Evidence from HMO Staffing Patterns, *Journal of the American Medical Association* 272 (1994): 222–230.

3. R. Kronick, et al., The Marketplace in Health Care Reform: The Demographic Limitations of Managed Competition, *New England Journal of Medicine* 328 (1993): 148–152.

4. S. Schroeder and L. Sandy, Specialty Distribution of U.S. Physicians—The Invisible Driver of Health Care Costs, *New England Journal of Medicine* 328 (1993): 928–933.

5. S. Greenfield, et al., Variations in Resource Utilization among Medical Specialties and Systems of Care: Results from the Medical Outcomes Study, *Journal of the American Medical Association* 267 (1992): 1624–1632.

6. R. Kravitz, Differences in the Mix of Patients among Medical Specialties and Systems of Care: Results from the Medical Outcomes Study, *Journal of the American Medical Association* 267 (1992): 1617–1623.

7. M. May, Resource Utilization in Treatment of Diabetic Ketoacidosis in Adults *American Journal of Medical Sciences* 306 (1993): 287–294.

8. M. Gold, et al., *Arrangements between Managed Care Plans and Physicians: Results from a 1994 Survey of Managed Care Plans* (Washington, D.C.: Physician Payment Review Commission, 1995).

9. InterStudy, *The Interstudy Competitive Edge* (St. Paul, Minn.: InterStudy, 1994).

10. Gold et al., *Arrangements between Managed Care Plans and Physicians.*

11. Gold et al., *Arrangements between Managed Care Plans and Physicians.*

12. Group Health Association of America (GHAA), *HMO Performance Survey* (Washington, D.C.: GHAA, 1994).

13. E.B. Keeler and M. Brodie, Economic Incentives in the Choice between Vaginal Delivery and Cesarean Section, *Milbank Memorial Fund Quarterly* 71 (1993): 365–404.

14. *Federal Register* 57 (14 December 1992): 59024–59040.

SUGGESTED READING

Palsbo, S.E. and Sullivan, C.B. 1993. *The Recruitment Experience of Health Maintenance Organizations for Primary Care Physicians: Final Report.* Washington, D.C.: Health Resources and Services Administration.

Pauly, M.V., Eisenberg, J.M., and Radany, M.H. 1992. *Paying Physicians: Options for Controlling Cost, Volume, and Intensity of Services.* Ann Arbor, Mich.: Health Administration Press.

Chapter 13

Specialty Networks from the Specialist's View

Allan Fine

As managed care grows more dominant in today's markets, purchasers of health care services are increasingly concerned about the value they are receiving for their health care dollars. Astute purchasers have begun to examine and question variations in cost, treatment, and outcomes among providers. They want to know, for example, which institutions are able to show that patients undergoing total hip replacements have long-term improvements in mobility and long-term reduction of discomfort and pain. As a result, they have begun to react unfavorably to health care services delivered on a fragmented basis. Many of their concerns are well grounded because most providers also are self-critical of episodic treatment intervention and the lack of coordination of medical care.

The frustration common to both purchasers and providers is the difficulty of demonstrating

Allan Fine, M.B.A., is a Senior Manager in Ernst & Young LLP's Health Care Strategy Consulting Practice. He serves in a leadership role in the firm's managed care and integrated delivery systems practice. He has assisted clients in developing managed care strategic plans, conducting market and medical staff assessments, developing and implementing integrated systems, regional and national networks, and affiliations. In addition, he has helped clients design and implement direct contracting arrangements, develop marketing and sales strategies for various managed care initiatives, and conduct new product development; assisting with managed care contract negotiations, and conducting managed care operational assessments. Mr. Fine is a frequent speaker and writer on topics related to managed care, integrated delivery systems, relationships between providers and employers, and marketing and sales strategies.

the relationship of quality and value with the provision of health care services. Pressures for accountability are mounting on providers. As a result, providers, particularly specialists, are struggling with the challenge of providing services for less money in a system that once rewarded them based primarily on production (i.e., volume and number of procedures).

The current and anticipated excess capacity of both hospitals and physicians also has made the situation distressing for specialists. Some have argued that the problem of excess capacity stems from a maldistribution of physicians. Regardless, it is apparent that there is a surplus of specialists. Many specialists are beginning to see their incomes decline, as Figure 13–1 and Table 13–1 illustrate.

Second, the demands of managed care organizations, insurers, and other purchasers on providers to improve health care services without raising prices are changing the roles of specialists and primary care physicians (PCPs). When patients access the health care network by presenting themselves to the PCP for treatment, the PCP assumes the role of risk manager for the medical group.

Like PCPs, specialists are being asked to assume at least a portion of the economic responsibility of caring for a certain population by furnishing services to patients on a discounted fee-for-service basis or in a capitated (per member per month) arrangement with the group. Increasingly, this has led to a deselection of specialists, especially if panels are large. Likely candidates include specialists with consistent

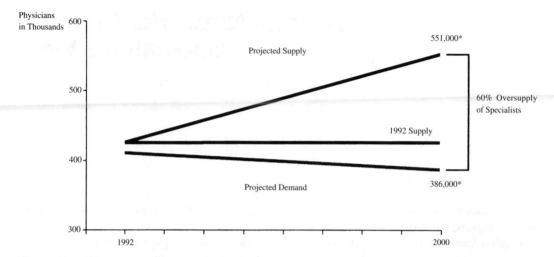

Figure 13–1 Projected physician surplus. *Data represent 83 percent of all known active, nonfederal physicians in the United States and exclude residents and fellows. *Source:* Reprinted with permission from J.P. Weiner, Forecasting the Effects of Health Reform on U.S. Physician Workforce Requirements: Evidence From HMO Staffing Patterns, *JAMA*, Vol. 272, No. 3, pp. 222–230, © 1994, American Medical Association.

patterns of overutilization, low volume, or little commitment to the panel's managed care objectives.

For example, a large physician group in northern California terminated contracts with specialists who saw the fewest independent practice association (IPA) patients. It was estimated that those eliminated drew less than 5 percent of their incomes from the IPA. "We didn't terminate them because they were bad doctors," said the group's administrator. "It's just that they didn't have much of a stake in the organization."[1(p.27)] He said that a smaller group of physicians can better develop and follow practice protocols. By seeing more IPA patients, the remaining physicians will be more committed to the IPA's success. In addition to reducing the number of specialists, some medical groups also are eliminating internal clinical departments, such as anesthesiology or radiology, in favor of outside contractors.

Others would argue that the better approach is not to downsize or eliminate physicians from the physician panel but instead to increase the number of patients and then support them by adding additional PCPs. In highly competitive markets, however, this strategy may not be effective because the pool of potential new members may be limited.

The focus of this chapter is specifically to address the topic of specialty networks from the viewpoint of the specialists themselves. The reader is referred to Chapters 4, 10, and 12 for related information.

ASSESSING MARKET CONDITIONS

Every geographic area is different in terms of demographics, psychographics, health care demand and supply, and degrees of managed care competition and penetration. Even so, there is a growing number of markets where managed care penetration either has precipitously increased or is expected to increase and where the following conditions apply:

- PCPs tend to be unaligned or, if aligned, only with one or two large groups.
- Specialists predominantly practice in solo or small group practices.

Table 13–1 Projected Surplus by Specialty

Specialty	Projected Supply in Year 2000*	Projected Demand in Year 2000*	Percentage Range of Surplus
Neurosurgery	4,285	1,449–2,736	57–196
Plastic surgery	5,204	1,882–2,311	125–177
Cardiology	14,999	7,002–9,792	53–114
Anesthesiology	28,161	14,426–16,143	74–95
Ophthalmology	17,141	9,014–10,946	57–90
Neurology	8,265	4,542–5,400	53–82
Radiology	26,324	15,706–18,496	42–68
General surgery	33,058	20,313–21,815	52–63
Gastroenterology	7,346	4,752–4,967	48–55
Orthopedics	19,896	13,103–16,537	20–52

*Data represent 83 percent of all known active, nonfederal physicians in the United States and exclude residents and fellows.

Source: Reprinted with permission from J.P. Weiner, Forecasting the Effects of Health Reform on U.S. Physician Workforce Requirements: Evidence From HMO Staffing Patterns, *JAMA*, Vol. 272, No. 3, pp. 222–230, © 1994, American Medical Association.

- Hospital-driven physician–hospital organizations (PHOs) and physician IPAs are not accomplishing integration objectives, prompting both the hospitals and the physicians to reevaluate these approaches and simultaneously consider other options.
- Activities of management services organizations are underdeveloped.
- Low to moderate levels of managed care enrollment exist currently, but increases in network development, marketing, and penetration are expected.
- Growing numbers of specialists are interested in exploring how best to create stronger groups or IPAs and align with PCPs to create viable multispecialty physician organizations.

In assessing the market, additional information that is generally quite useful (as discussed below) includes:

- the number and location of specialists (for each type of specialty under consideration)
- comparison of those numbers with anticipated need

- the existence of specialty-specific capitation contracts (see Chapter 12)
- a profile of the existing payers, and the dynamics of those organizations in the marketplace
- willingness of those payer organizations to contract with specialty organizations

Emerging specialty networks should conduct a situation assessment that will enable them to identify the competition and evaluate their strengths and weaknesses; understand the concerns of insurers, managed care organizations, and employers; determine the level of commitment and interest of network physicians; understand the needs of PCPs; and identify other specialty institutions, tertiary/academic centers, community hospitals, ambulatory surgical centers, or other providers offering similar services. A market assessment should follow, enabling the specialty network to probe further when meeting with insurers, managed care organizations, and employers. Issues that should be considered in meetings with these organizations include attitudes toward specialty facilities/networks; volume of specialty services utilized;

interest in contracting for specialty services; types of contractual/payment arrangements sought; current plan design, steering mechanisms, utilization review, provider selection criteria, and referral patterns; and the role of PCPs.

The specialty network also must consider the extent of current competition and the likelihood of increased competition as neighboring physicians aggregate by forming group practices. The network should evaluate the competition in terms of reputation of other providers, market penetration, existing contractual relationships, referral patterns, and cost of services.

There is no single approach, structure, or plan of organization that guarantees the successful formation of a multispecialty medical group that will be able to generate a sufficient volume of business to remain profitable for any given market condition. Understanding the market dynamics, however, will enable specialists or sponsoring organizations to set their strategies better.

Some medical groups, hospitals, and health maintenance organizations (HMOs) have established programs to retrain specialists in primary care. "Specialists make excellent primary care physicians for patients with chronic diseases such as cancer and diabetes, but that doesn't mean a specialist can deliver primary care to a general population—or wants to," said one group's chief executive officer.[2(p.101)] As managed care takes hold, some specialists may also find it more satisfying and lucrative to retrain in primary care or become physician managers and assume positions in integrated networks. One unknown is whether managed care plans will recognize retrained specialists as PCPs. Where state law permits, specialists increasingly may play such a role. In California, which allows obstetricians to act as PCPs, one medical group instituted a primary care training program for that specialty, although it is as yet unclear whether that program will succeed.

Other specialists will relocate to geographic areas where their particular services are still in demand in a fee-for-service environment. Those specialists, however, who refuse to adapt quickly to market changes—capitation, clinical and referral protocols designed to lower costs, utilization review, and so forth—should begin accelerating their retirement plans.

DEVELOPING SPECIALTY NETWORKS

Developing a specialty managed care network requires the organization to consider the following checklist of concerns for network development:

- *Marketability.* What is the market's current managed care penetration? Most experts agree that, once the market hits the 20 percent level, the time is ripe to form a managed care organization because it shows that employers are being drawn to managed care.

- *Governance and structure.* Is the proposed organization willing to act collectively to initiate an employer- and consumer-friendly approach to decision making? Will the product give employers more value for the money now being spent on care and services? The group must be able cooperatively to develop utilization and cost reviews that will yield efficient operations. Purchasers want networks to be accountable for the care they provide. There is a growing trend toward purchasers seeking long-term relationships with provider networks. Emphasis will be placed on cooperative relationships.

- *Linkages to PCPs and other providers.* Establishing linkages with PCPs is essential to the long-term viability of a specialty network. Consistent with the views of purchasers, the role of PCPs is becoming more pronounced in terms of diagnosis and treatment. Evolving specialty networks should identify PCPs currently involved in capitated programs and determine their appropriate entry point into the network. In some instances, the specialty network may seek to identify existing or emerging primary care networks with which to develop linkages. In addition, the specialty network may wish to explore relationships with existing PHOs or other provider organizations. The exception to a tight linkage with PCPs is in those situations where a specialty network contracts directly with an HMO for all services in that specialty (e.g., cardiac care or oncology); in that case, linkages will be built after the contract is signed, as opposed to being built to produce the referrals in the first place.

- *Clear delineation of responsibilities*. Referral guidelines should be established that shift responsibility for patient care to the specialty network for the appropriate intervention and then return the patient to the PCP. The specialty network should develop intake systems that support this collaborative and nonadversarial approach. Such an approach is particularly important when the specialty network is in a capitated referral arrangement with a managed care organization. In such instances, the health plan is ultimately responsible for the care of its members. The health plan will supervise the health treatment plan to be sure that the specialty network is proceeding according to the capitation referral agreement.

- *Purchaser expectations and service differentiation*. What kinds of services do employers and health plans want? Failure to follow standards can reduce efficiency and lead to perceptions by consumers of low-quality care. As purchasers evaluate various options for purchasing health care services, they will begin to apply criteria enabling them to access value from their purchasing decisions. Purchasers will attempt to differentiate among providers offering similar services. Increased competition will exist for specialty care as specialty networks are formed. When evaluating the purchase of specialty services, purchasers will probably attempt to identify network providers who are defined by the provision

of a particular service(s) or procedure(s) typically representing high profile or high cost.

- *Quality and cost*. Can the group distinguish itself from competitors? Networks must be able to collect increasingly detailed data to improve quality measurement and comply with growing government data reporting requirements. Obtaining data from a large number of physicians is difficult, so the network must bear that in mind as it determines its size and configuration. Consumers will also want access to such reports. Purchasers increasingly will select specialty providers on the basis of the expertise that they possess related to a particular procedure or service. Purchasers are attracted to specialty networks where the negotiated prices are tied to the procedure, with physicians, hospital, and ancillaries being bundled into one price. Selected networks will often assume risk in the form of a capped price. Is the group prepared to accept lower income? Such a measure may be necessary if a group wishes to increase its market share. Groups also must know their bottom lines so that they will not offer services at too low a price at the outset.

To satisfy payers, specialty networks must be focused on becoming effective in terms of quality and outcomes. Interfacing with PCPs in a supportive role is essential. For some groups, this may mean contracting with local, state, regional, or national managed care networks, especially in situations where a payer wishes to form a partnership with a health care organization for one type of service. In such instances, there are several advantages for physician members, including more opportunities to educate PCPs about appropriate utilization of specialty services, internal maintenance of claims and outcomes data for more effective utilization management, and higher quality of care through internal peer review and strict credentialing policies.

When market conditions warrant, health care purchasers have indicated a willingness to consider long-term relationships with specialty groups. In one case, for example, a large, multistate HMO successfully recruited physician groups in one competitive region for a minimum of 5 years and up to 10 years in some cases.[3] The HMO sought the long-term relationship because it believes that such agreements create stability for health plan enrollees in terms of physician choice. Such relationships also alleviate the acceleration of nonmedical costs by reducing the volume of paperwork involved in annual contracting negotiations and other administrative transactions. It is hoped that the long-term agreements also will help improve customer service and more effectively identify best clinical practices.

MEDICAL STAFF ASSESSMENT

The value of conducting a medical staff assessment is that it will allow the parties seeking to form a specialty network to ascertain the potential participating physicians' level of interest in and knowledge of managed care. One measure that can be used to evaluate their level of interest is their receptivity to working on gaining efficiencies (e.g., sharing information about performance and practice management, common information systems, etc.) through collaborating in forming the specialty network.

It is important for the parties organizing the specialty network to understand and evaluate the needs and concerns of PCPs who may become part of, or affiliated with, the specialty group. Issues that should be considered include their experience with managed care and capitation; use of specialty services, perceptions of the specialty network and its physicians, the optimal referral process, and methods to eliminate duplication of services.

ORGANIZATIONAL FORM

Objectives in selecting the organizational form should consider such operational issues as contracting, utilization management, management/support functions, and provision of professional services. The specialty network may be formed primarily as a contracting vehicle, but it could perform services itself as well as provide management services in support of the professional activities of its participants.

The network has a choice among various organizational forms depending on its intended functions and objectives. Examples include the professional corporation, the taxable nonprofit corporation, the tax exempt corporation, the limited liability corporation, and the limited partnership, among others. Each has a different role and can provide different results, depending on the network's role and functions, its investment needs and objectives, and its anticipated tax situation.

A major consideration for the development of a specialty network relates to its needs for capital and the potential sources of this capital. The extent of capital needs will be a function of the scope of the network's activities (e.g., contracting, service provision, management service organization functions, and geographic scope). Increased demand for integrated specialty care has recently prompted initial public offerings by single-specialty practice management companies. For example, one firm raised $115 million to fund an acquisition strategy, and another firm, which will integrate eye care, raised $40.3 million.[4] Several firms have formed to organize PCPs or multispecialty groups. There is also an emerging market for companies/networks that can manage expensive cases (e.g., diabetes, cardiovascular disease, orthopedics, and the like).

Attention must be given to investment objectives both in terms of the structuring of the network as well as in terms of the structuring of the financing. In some instances, fraud and abuse concerns will play a role in defining investment opportunities and the structure of investment.

PACKAGE PRICING

Package pricing, which is also discussed in Chapters 12 and 14, enables the purchaser to predict health care expenses better by establishing a separate, predetermined rate or rate structure for a specific diagnosis or procedure that covers a broad range of services, usually over a given time period. Covered services typically include those of physicians and other professionals who might otherwise bill separately for their services during the period covered by the packaged price; the institutional or facility costs are likewise usually addressed in the package price. The expectation is that administrative and clinical costs can be reduced and patient satisfaction improved because a single claim will be generated.

Provider Motivations in Package Pricing Arrangements

Specialty providers are increasingly becoming interested in package pricing arrangements because they believe that, through these contracts, they will gain access to new markets and have a greater potential to retain existing patients. Additionally, they feel that they will gain experience in care management within a budget.

In general, benefits of package pricing to the provider include:

- potential gain of market share

- guarantee of reimbursement amount

- potential to secure an exclusive or semi-exclusive contract with a purchaser

- gain of prestige and potential free advertising

- ability to learn how to render care under capitation

Also, one packaged contract can lead to acquiring others. Some providers have found that they can gain an advantage on their competitors because they may be the first organization to package a new service or procedure and they therefore become the "expert." Such an approach will enable them to emphasize that a particular episode of illness is their specialty.

Considerations in Package Pricing

It is important for specialty networks to consider multiple variables that can influence the success of a package pricing arrangement. At a minimum, they need to do the following:

- specify what is included and excluded

- define the specific length of time for which care will be offered

- offer something desirable to the purchaser other than the episode of care with a specific competitive price (e.g., extensive locations, ease of administration, quality of providers, or completeness of package, describing all possible contingencies)

- be able to identify their own costs

- know their risks, exposure, and capabilities

- understand the purchaser's needs

Specialty networks must recognize that unambiguous definitions are essential to developing a strong package pricing arrangement. The following are examples:

- *clinical exclusions*—specify exclusively what procedures are covered in the package arrangement

- *nonclinical exclusions*—specify what pre- and postoperative services are covered

- *carve-outs*—specify any separate pricing for service components that may or may not occur in the performance of the packaged price service

- *effective dates*—specify effective dates of the proposal and by what date the proposal needs to be accepted for it to apply

- *payment requirements*—specify discount levels against charges (when appropriate), outlier provisions (i.e., when an alternative reimbursement mechanism comes into play for expensive cases), and the payment cycle

Specialty Service Contracting/Package Pricing

Specialty networks can position themselves to be considered by purchasers for specialty services contracting, but it will require the network to identify appropriate customers and services that are priced competitively and can be rendered efficiently, resulting in positive outcomes. Characteristics of the appropriate customer for a provider contemplating specialty service contracting could include the following:

- The purchaser has enough beneficiaries needing the service.
- The purchaser has the ability to channel these prospective patients to the provider network.
- The purchaser is at financial risk for the service.

Clearly, the service to be package priced must have physician support; that is, physicians must be willing to incorporate their fees with the institutional or facility component into the global price and to practice as efficiently as possible.

Determining the appropriate price for the packaged service requires conducting a competitive pricing analysis. An internal pricing assessment is essential because it will enable the specialty network to identify its own costs for providing such services and the margin that it must realize to achieve certain targets.

Some specialty networks have the capacity to offer high quality care at generally below national average rates because they have experience in performing an above-average number of procedures in a given specialty, resulting in economies of scale. Therefore, they can successfully negotiate fixed competitive rates for high-cost procedures. Purchasers are selecting certain centers of excellence and specialty networks according to criteria that improve the likelihood of a positive outcome, both clinically and financially.

ANTITRUST CONSIDERATIONS

Both the Department of Justice and the Federal Trade Commission have issued guidelines concerning the antitrust scrutiny of physician organizations, primarily concentrating on the number of specialists in a given market that may "safely" be included within a specialty physician preferred provider arrangement. These guidelines, in addition to general antitrust principles, must be considered in the design of a specialty network, thus ensuring that physician participation is not at a level that would prompt concerns from the antitrust agencies. Typically, the more integrated the group, the more effectively it can engage in contracting with lower antitrust exposure. Geographic considerations also play a key role. If, for example, the network consists of one significant group per market in a number of markets, such that the participants would not otherwise be considered competitors, the network would have more flexibility in its contracting approaches than would be the case if its structure involved the effort to develop a joint venture among physicians who would otherwise be competitors. Competent legal counsel is required to address this issue.

MOVING FROM RHETORIC TO ACTION

Unfortunately, there are many situations where the specialists are disenchanted and are critical of both the hospitals' and their colleagues' initiatives (or lack thereof) in terms of dealing with managed care, but despite these frustrations they are complacent about taking any actions. Often this self-imposed paralysis is attributed to:

- lack of clarity about which path to pursue
- unwillingness to confront reality
- perceived lack of capital
- distrust of their colleagues
- fears of alienating their colleagues and therefore jeopardizing their referral streams

- unwillingness to share information about the clinical performance and financial management of their offices

The ability of specialists to transition from the stage of simply complaining and engaging in self-pity to taking tangible action in exploring opportunities for organizing will vary depending on market conditions and the degree of personal impact that managed care has had on their practices. If specialists are serious about developing specialty networks, then they should consider taking the following steps:

1. A core group of specialists meets with its own partners or group members to discuss integration and options and to reconfirm interest in moving ahead with the development of a selective multispecialty group practice or specialty network.

2. The core group meets with hospital(s) management to describe directions and to ascertain the hospitals' interest in working with and/or providing capital for multispecialty group or specialty network planning and development.

3. The core group meets with primary group representatives to increase understanding of group integration and goals and to ascertain their interest in working collaboratively.

4. The core group begins to define criteria (i.e., structural, process, and outcome) for physician participation in the group and to identify a "short list" of likely group members.

5. The core group gathers information from likely participants regarding:
   - current patient load characteristics
   - physician referral relationships
   - information and management systems
   - productivity and compensation arrangements

6. The core group defines charges for subcommittees dealing with issues related to:

- credentialing and criteria for participation
  - —Who will be the participating physicians?
  - —How will they be selected?
- medical care management and protocols
- contracting criteria and objectives
- management processes and infrastructure
- revenue will be divided
- means for reducing operating costs
- what incentives and/or controls will be required

Regarding operating cost reduction, there are various approaches for reducing operating costs, such as sharing the costs of space and equipment, office staffing, billing and collection services, information systems, and all other overhead. If all participating physicians are required to adopt the same operational protocols and business systems, economies of scale can be achieved, administrative burdens reduced, clinical performance improved, and operating margins increased. Given disparate systems, however, the current investments of each individual practice may be devalued as a result. Therefore, developing common management services may be achieved in the following approaches:

- Evaluate current practices, select the best, and extend/convert all others.

- Redefine requirements and acquire or develop new capabilities.

- Purchase services and "turnkey" systems from an experienced vendor.

Capitation is the mechanism that does the most to align the incentives and behaviors of PCPs and specialists. The most advanced multispecialty groups in the most aggressive managed care markets have demonstrated that alignment can be achieved when:

- the majority of revenue received is capitated
- physician base compensation is fixed or salaried, removing incentives to order more care to increase income (see Chapters 7 and 10)
- productivity, quality of care, and professional development incentives are in place and balanced (see Chapters 7, 10, and 11)
- surpluses are shared among all participants

IMPLEMENTATION REQUIREMENTS

Participating physicians contemplating the formation of a specialty network should be poised to address several objectives:

- Define the requirements for local/regional acceptance of:
  1. a specialty physician group practice or IPA
  2. a multispecialty group practice including PCPs
  3. an integrated PHO or network
- Based on the requirements of the marketplace, define appropriate organizational structures, governance, and marketing processes.
- Develop a plan for implementation.

The implementation plan should contain milestones and time frames and identify the parties responsible for completion of the various implementation tasks. This plan becomes a vehicle for communication with various audiences as well as a work plan for those responsible for implementing operations. Typical components of the implementation plan are listed in Exhibit 13–1.

PARTING ADVICE FOR SPECIALISTS

As specialists contemplate their future under managed care and capitation, they may wish to consider the following parting advice:

Exhibit 13–1 Components of an Implementation Plan

Description of the business
- Goals and objectives
- Products/services
- Customer identification
- Regions of operations
- Roles of the principles
Design and development
- Information management
- Care management
Operations
- Geographic location
- Facilities
- Care delivery
- Business processes, policies, and procedures
- Human resources
Management team
- Organization
- Key management personnel
- Management compensation and ownership
- Board of directors
- Management assistance and training needs
- Supporting professional services
Financial plan
- Pro forma operating and capital budgets
- Cash flow and balance sheet forecasts
Schedule
Critical risks and problems to be resolved

- Prepare for partnerships.
- Affiliate with the best subspecialists in a given specialty.
- Decide which referral relationships make sense financially, and terminate others.
- Be prepared for the relentless cost control necessary under flat payments.
- Be able to demonstrate effective management of the financial aspects associated with rendering care if there is the realistic expectation of obtaining managed care contracts.
- Collect your own data on utilization and quality as opposed to relying on purchasers' information.
- Apprise purchasers of your patient satisfaction rating should you possess such data.

CONCLUSION

It will become increasingly difficult for specialists to practice as solo practitioners. Their ability to gain access to covered lives, coupled with the challenge of developing the systems and practice protocols vital to practicing successfully under a managed care structure, will be limited significantly as solo practitioners. In addition, specialists will increasingly be held accountable by purchasers and payers in the same manner as hospitals and PCPs. Specialists organizing in a precipitous manner, however, will not adequately respond to the challenges raised by managed care.

Organizing specialty groups and/or networks requires a thoughtful and deliberative strategy that initially establishes goals and objectives that will serve as the basis for future decision making regarding credentialing, medical management protocols, systems, and operational and financial issues. A due diligence of all potential and existing partners in the group or network must be secured to ensure that the members of the combined entity are capable of both working together and offering demonstrable value to the marketplace. The pressures and challenges confronting specialists may appear daunting, but the process of organizing according to a well-conceived strategic plan will actually preserve the viability of the group throughout this tumultuous period.

REFERENCES AND NOTES

1. *Health Alliance Alert*, 5/12/95, Faulkner & Gray.
2. *Modern Healthcare*, 4/17/95, Crain Communications.
3. *Modern Healthcare*, 6/19/95, Crain Communications.
4. *Modern Healthcare*, 7/10/95, Crain Communications.

SUGGESTED READING

Rowe, C.S. 1994. The Impact of Managed Care on Specialty Practices. *Medical Group Management Journal* 41(5): 36–41.

Chapter 14

Negotiating and Contracting with Hospitals and Institutions

Peter R. Kongstvedt

Hospital contracting is one of the most important tasks that an executive director and other appropriate plan managers face. Hospital executives likewise need a thorough understanding of the issues involved in contracting with managed care organizations (MCOs). Although there are a few states (e.g., Maryland) that are so heavily regulated that there is little or no latitude allowed in reimbursing hospitals, in general this represents an area of tremendous potential for creativity.

REASONS TO CONTRACT

The reasons for a plan to contract with hospitals are obvious and much the same as those for contracting with consultants; this is discussed in Chapter 12 and will not be repeated here. It should be noted that, because of the amount of money involved with hospital care, the issues take on greater importance for any given contract. This is particularly true for both required reserves for uncovered liabilities (see Chapter 40) and the impact of favorable pricing. In some cases, failure to have adequate contracts with hospitals will lead to a rejection of state licensure for an MCO or federal qualification for health maintenance organizations (HMOs) and competitive medical plans (see Chapter 54 for a discussion of federal qualification).

The reasons for a hospital to agree to a contractual arrangement are likewise similar to those of a consultant. The hospital will be acutely interested in improving, or in some cases holding onto, a volume of inpatient days and outpatient procedures. This becomes crucial if the hospital is suffering from a low occupancy rate. A hospital will also be interested in a plan's ability to turn around a claim; the time value of money is even more important to a hospital than to a consultant because the amount of money is so much greater and because the public sector (i.e., fee-for-service Medicare and Medicaid) is a notoriously slow payer.

Guaranteed payments for authorized services for covered benefits will also be valuable, especially if the hospital has been absorbing losses as a result of denial of payments from a retrospective review process. As with consultants in an open panel, a hospital may hope to see an increase in regular fee-for-service patients; because physicians prefer not to perform rounds in multiple hospitals, this is a genuine possibility.

Last, a hospital will contract to shut out a competitor. Competition among hospitals is usually much more open than competition among physicians and is usually a regional issue; a hospital will have a reasonably defined service area from which most of its admissions come. If an MCO is willing to limit the number of participating hospitals in each service area, this becomes a strong negotiating point.

HOSPITAL NETWORK DEVELOPMENT

Selecting Hospitals

Selecting which hospitals for an MCO to approach is done by balancing a number of variables. In a small or rural market there may be a limited choice (see Chapter 50). In most cases, though, there will be some latitude. Before beginning the selection process, plan managers must first decide how much they are willing to limit the choices in the plan.

Generally, the more the MCO is willing to limit the number of participating hospitals, the greater its leverage in negotiating. Limiting the number has potential disadvantages as well. If the MCO strictly limits itself to just a few hospitals, it may have a competitive disadvantage in the marketplace because prospective members and accounts often use hospitals as a means of judging whether to join an MCO; therefore, if the plan fails to include a sufficient selection of hospitals, it may see disappointing marketing results. On the other hand, if the MCO refuses to limit the number of hospitals, it will have considerable difficulty in extracting favorable agreements and in managing utilization.

A certain number of hospitals will be required to cover a medical service area effectively. In some small communities, a single hospital may be able to serve the entire population, but that is rare. It is important to map out the hospital locations relative to the defined service area and to look for overlap among competing hospitals.

Selecting which hospitals to approach first in a service area is a combination of hard data—such as occupancy, cost, and services offered—and judgment about the hospital's willingness to negotiate and the perception of the public and physician community about the hospital's quality. It does little good for an MCO to make an agreement with a hospital that is perceived as inferior. Likewise, it is less than optimal to contract with a hospital that does not do high-volume obstetrics if there is a regional competitor that does because the plan will be less attractive to young families.

In some instances, the presence of a well-run integrated delivery system (IDS; see Chapter 4) will make a particular hospital attractive. This is most likely to be the case if a plan is a new entrant to the market, is introducing a new service line, or has been unable to create an attractive network from a marketing standpoint. The IDS

may be in a position to accept considerable financial risk, such as total capitation, which may be desirable to an HMO that wishes to limit financial risk.

If the hospital is a sponsor or joint venture partner in an MCO, the choice factors become rather clear. If a hospital is an enthusiastic supporter of the MCO, or if there is a long history of a good working relationship, that should also be taken into consideration.

Finally, consolidation in the hospital industry has been occurring at a rapid pace. In many cases, this leads to the creation of a system with multiple hospitals. The MCO is then in a position of negotiating a broader contract with the system for services at multiple sites. The system may also demand a higher level of preference or even exclusivity in exchange for favorable terms. Although consolidation does not always bring value, the potential of cost reduction and rationalization of clinical services may allow the new system to provide care far more efficiently than individual hospitals, thus allowing for a considerable price advantage.

General Negotiating Strategy

An MCO's ability to negotiate successfully with the hospitals in its area will depend on a number of things. Chief among them are the personal abilities of the negotiator, the size of the plan, the MCO's ability actually to shift patient care, and the track record of the MCO in being able to deliver what was promised. A new start-up operation has considerably less clout than an existing large plan. If the new start-up can demonstrate genuine potential for significant growth, that may help offset the weakness of having little to offer but promises.

Setting an overall strategy is important to the ultimate success of an MCO's hospital network. It is certainly possible to approach the project of hospital negotiations by using the managerial equivalent of Brownian motion, but the end results could be disappointing.

The strategic plan should address both regional and planwide issues. There may be one set of criteria for primary care services in a service area and a different set for tertiary services. After plan managers have selected the hospital they wish to approach first, they must then select the hospitals to approach next if the initial hospital either is unwilling to come to agreement or offers too little to make the agreement worth the risk. The plan managers may find that they will want to approach some hospitals for tertiary services on a much wider regional basis than for primary care. If the MCO does not intend significantly to restrict its hospital panel, then it should first select those hospitals with the most marketing value.

Data Development

After selecting individual hospitals to approach, make a worksheet for each and one for the entire service area as well. Estimate the hospital's occupancy rate (these data may be available from the local or state health department or the American Hospital Association[1]) and operating margin (this, too, may be available at the health department or may be published in the hospital's annual report).

Estimate the total number of bed days the plan currently has in the hospital. If the plan is a new start-up, estimate the total number of bed days the medical director believes can be controlled and over what time span (be honest here). Estimate as well the number of bed days the plan can realistically shift into the hospital or, if necessary, away from the hospital. This estimate will be affected by geographic accessibility and acceptability of such case shifting by members and physicians. It is helpful to both parties if the bed days are categorized at least into broad categories such as medical–surgical, obstetrics, intensive care, mental health, and so forth.

Last, calculate the whole dollars associated with all the above estimations or facts. Plan management will want to know what whole dollar amount the plan represents to the hospital now and in the future. Calculate what happens if utilization shifts into and out of the hospital and

what percentage of the hospital's gross income that would represent.

Goal Setting

Markets with Low Managed Care Penetration

In markets that do not have high levels of managed care penetration (e.g., where managed care, primarily HMOs, accounts for less than 30 percent of *total* health care), it is axiomatic that medical services are bought at the margin. As with purchasing an automobile or furniture, it is unusual to pay the sticker price. This goes for primary care, consultant care, and, most important, hospital services. If a hospital ward is fully staffed but running at less than full occupancy, the marginal cost of filling another bed on that ward is minor compared with the revenue. It is unlikely that the hospital will call in extra nurses, hire extra support staff, buy new equipment, or take out more insurance to care for a 10 percent increase in bed days; those costs are relatively fixed. The marginal costs (such as laundry, food, drugs and supplies, and the like) are less than the fixed overhead.

Because of this, a hospital has room to maneuver in negotiating. This does not mean that you can expect a hospital to reduce its charges by half (unless its charges are grossly inflated to begin with), but you can reasonably expect effective discounts of 20 percent to 30 percent if you are able to deliver sufficient volume. Certain for-profit hospitals are actually managed to show a profit at less than 50 percent occupancy. In those cases, even greater discounts may sometimes be obtained because much of the added revenue to the hospital goes right to the bottom line. Conversely, such high-margin hospitals may feel little pressure to increase their occupancy if they have a decent market share and may be difficult to deal with because they hope to freeze you out.

After you have developed the worksheet referred to above, take your assumptions regarding how much you can shift into the hospital and apply the desired discount. If a hospital has a low occupancy rate, or if it has less than a full occupancy rate but is enjoying healthy profit margins (or reserves if it is not for profit), and you can deliver or remove a significant volume of patients, you may be able to achieve a good discount. If the hospital is running above 90 percent occupancy, your prospects of substantial savings are not as good.

Include outpatient procedures in the calculations. It is increasingly common to find that outpatient procedures, if paid on a discounted charges basis, are actually more expensive than identical procedures done in an inpatient setting. Hospital managers have not been idly watching utilization shift to the outpatient department; they have adjusted charges to enhance revenues.

Markets with High Managed Care Penetration

In markets with high levels of managed care penetration, the dynamics may look considerably different. In those markets the margin has been reduced, and few payers are paying full charges. Public sector fee-for-service reimbursement (i.e., Medicare and Medicaid) certainly does not pay full charges, and if managed care accounts for most of the rest, as well as a considerable portion of the public sector, then charges become relatively meaningless, and a hospital's ability to absorb payment differentials is diminished. In such markets, MCOs, especially HMOs, are most likely to use a reimbursement system that is unrelated to charges (see below). The MCO and the hospital must then balance the actual cost to provide the service (if the hospital has a cost accounting system, which is not always the case), the ability to provide volume to offset fixed costs, the market power and desirability of the parties, and the cost of not doing business together.

Markets with high managed care penetration also tend to have high levels of hospital consolidation. This changes the dynamic as noted earlier. In addition, the levels of sophistication increase on all sides. More creativity comes into play, and the MCOs and hospitals find themselves operating more as business partners (or at least close acquaintances) and less as arm's length contracting entities. Although price and clinical services are still the most important factors, the ability of the parties to operate together becomes of greater importance. The ability to interface administratively, the ability to resolve operating problems, and similar factors play heavily in the negotiating strategy.

Last, in such markets there is often a desire on the part of the hospitals, through their IDS, to accept greater amounts of risk for medical expenses because there is the perception that there is greater margin in that form of reimbursement. Paradoxically, large and successful HMOs may have little incentive to do so because it could erode their margin as well as increase the possibility of failure if the IDS is unable to manage the risk. These issues often become key negotiating points in crafting a long-term relationship between MCOs and hospitals.

Responsibilities and Timing

Plan Management

The key players in hospital negotiations from the health plan side are the executive director, the medical director, and the finance director. It is the responsibility of the executive director to initiate the contact, set the stage or tone, and be sure that the executive director of the hospital feels comfortable with the plan's commitment to proceed fairly, openly, and honestly. It is not always necessarily the role of the executive director actually to negotiate the details of the agreement, because it is unlikely that the executive director of the hospital will be doing so. Nevertheless, a relationship between the chief executive of the MCO and the chief executive of the hospital is important to establish. Large HMOs may have an officer who is responsible for managing relations with hospitals, and that individual may also be the most senior person in the plan who will manage the process. In small plans or in early start-ups, or sometimes for political reasons, the executive director may end up carrying the ball all the way through.

The role of the finance director is to work closely with the plan's executive director (or the officer responsible for hospital contracting) and the hospital's finance director or controller. In many cases, the actual negotiation takes place at this level. The finance director should not have the authority actually to sign off on the agreement because the controller of the hospital will surely not have this authority, and it further serves a useful purpose to be able to break the negotiations to confer with the executive director back at the plan. Because the hospital may not believe the numbers produced by the plan, it falls to the finance director of the plan to present those numbers in a credible and understandable way (not only the numbers now but the numbers the plan expects).

In addition to evaluating the quality of the institution and helping elucidate the political climate, the medical director needs to be able to convince the hospital administrator that the plan will genuinely shift the patient caseload as necessary. If the medical director cannot persuade the hospital that the plan is able to move patients in or out, the plan will have lost a key advantage in the negotiations. This need not be done in a heavy-handed way or as a naked threat. It suffices for this issue to be brought out in a businesslike and unemotional way.

It is important to set a realistic time schedule. The degree to which plan management achieves success in its hospital negotiations will be reflected in the amount of effort put into the negotiating process. It is not realistic to think that one can obtain favorable pricing and contracts with a number of hospitals in less than 2 or 3 months (and perhaps considerably longer). It will take time to do the preplanning work, for the hospital to digest what is being proposed, for the hospital to make a counter offer and for the plan to counter that, and so on. After that, each side's lawyers will want to review the contract language.

Conversely, try not to let too much dust collect on the proposal before either following up or approaching another hospital as an alternative. There is no reason for the hospital to hurry the process unless it believes that delaying will mean losing the contract. If the plan has proposed a reduction in what it is currently paying, the hospital will obviously prefer to keep collecting revenue under the existing terms as long as possible unless the plan is promising a sizeable increase in volume that it is not now getting.

Hospital Management

The chief executive officer (CEO) or executive director of the hospital must set the overall strategy for managed care contracting. Managed care is now far too important to delegate to a lower level individual in the organization. Many hospital CEOs may not be comfortable with this role because their training and experience are in the operations of the clinical facility, and they may choose to delegate the development of managed care strategy to another officer or director. This is perfectly acceptable and may even be necessary, but the CEO should be fully knowledgeable about the terms and strategies and accept ultimate responsibility for them. In many cases, it is important for the hospital CEO to establish a good working relationship with the CEO of the MCO to indicate the level of importance that the hospital holds for the MCO and to work through any obstacles in the negotiating process. It also allows the CEO to understand better the goals and strategies of the MCO.

As noted above, it is common for a hospital to appoint a high level individual to be the primary source of managed care relations. It is a serious mistake to use an individual who is not sufficiently senior in the system or one who cannot make any decisions. The MCO will become frustrated in dealing with a lower level functionary, and this will impede success. This individual may have primary responsibility for all aspects of the negotiation, including financial analysis, operational issues, and reimbursement terms.

The hospital's finance director must be closely involved in the process as well. Unless the MCO is of trivial size, managed care revenues need to be carefully analyzed as described above (and if the MCO is of trivial size, there better be a pretty compelling reason if the hospital is to provide it with favorable terms). Of special concern is the ability of the hospital to meet its direct costs for providing care; if the MCO's reimbursement terms do not even cover direct cost, then the hospital is in trouble. How much the MCO's terms contribute to the hospital's indirect costs and margin is at the core of the negotiation, along with the usual issues of market strength, services offered, and ability to shift volume.

The hospital should have a medical director involved as well. In the past, hospital medical directors were primarily involved with issues of credentialing and privileges, clinical services, recruiting, and so forth. In a market with high levels of managed care penetration, the medical director needs to be heavily involved in clinical aspects of the relationship with the MCO, including clinical efficiency, utilization management, quality management, and member satisfaction. The hospital must be able to provide quality services efficiently and to manage its costs to prosper under managed care reimbursement terms.

Last, it is now common for hospitals to have some form of IDS, and the MCO may or may not be willing to contract with it. In the event that the IDS does indeed accept a significant level of risk for medical expenses, then the IDS and hospital will need to apply managed care utilization management techniques or face a negative financial result.

TYPES OF REIMBURSEMENT ARRANGEMENTS

There are a number of reimbursement methodologies available in contracting with hospitals, except in those states where regulations prohibit creativity. Exhibit 14–1 lists a number of methods that have been used by plans. Lack of imagination is the only real impediment to negotiating, although many plans have found that their inability to handle administratively what is otherwise a bright idea has led to problems such as high administrative cost, frequent

Exhibit 14–1 Models for Reimbursing Hospitals

Charges
Discounts
Per diems
Sliding scales for discounts and per diems
Differential by day in hospital
Diagnosis-related groups
Differential by service type
Case rates
 • Institutional only
 • Package pricing or bundled rates
Capitation
Percentage of premium revenue
Bed leasing
Periodic interim payments or cash advances
Performance-based incentives
 • Penalties and withholds
 • Quality and service incentives
Outpatient procedures
 • Discounts
 • Package pricing or bundled rates
 • Ambulatory patient groups

errors, and disputes over reconciliations. Figure 14–1 provides a snapshot of the four most common forms of hospital reimbursement as of the time this book was written. It is possible, and even likely, that the percentage distribution of these methods will change, and perhaps change rapidly. A brief discussion of these reimbursement methodologies follows.

Straight Charges

The simplest (albeit least desirable) payment mechanism in health care is straight charges. It is also obviously the most expensive, after the option of no contract at all. This is a fallback position to be agreed to only in the event that you are unable to obtain any form of discount at all, but it is still desirable to have a contract with a no balance billing clause in it (see Chapter 55) for purposes of reserve requirements and licensure.

Straight Discount on Charges

Another possible arrangement with hospitals is a straight percentage discount on charges. In

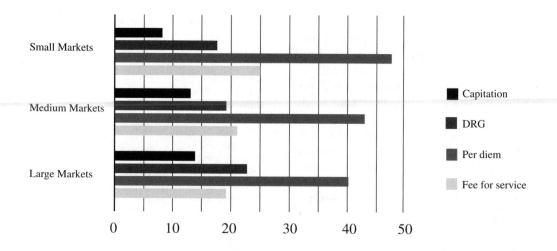

Figure 14–1 HMO reimbursements to hospitals. DRG, diagnosis-related group. *Source:* Reprinted with permission from Regional Market Analysis Reporting Data as of July 1, 1994, *The InterStudy Competitive Edge*, Vol. 5, No. 1, p. 46, © 1995, InterStudy Publications.

this case, the hospital submits its claim in full, and the plan discounts it by the agreed-to percentage and then pays it. The hospital accepts this payment as payment in full. The amount of discount that can be obtained will depend on the factors discussed above. This type of arrangement is not infrequent in markets with low levels of managed care penetration but is uncommon in markets with high levels of managed care.

Sliding Scale Discount on Charges

Sliding scale discounts are an option, particularly in markets with low managed care penetration but some level of competitiveness among hospitals. With a sliding scale, the percentage discount is reflective of the total volume of admissions and outpatient procedures. Deciding whether to lump the two categories together or deal with them separately is not as important as making sure that the parties deal with them both. With the rapidly climbing cost of outpatient procedures, savings from reduction of inpatient uti-

lization could be negated by an unanticipated overrun in outpatient charges.

An example of a sliding scale is a 20 percent reduction in charges for 0 to 200 total bed days per year with incremental increases in the discount up to a maximum percentage. An interim percentage discount is usually negotiated, and the parties reconcile at the end of the year based on the final total volume.

How the plan tracks the discount is also negotiable. You may wish to vary the discount on a month-to-month basis rather than yearly. You may wish to track total bed days, number of admissions, or whole dollars spent. Whatever you finally agree to, be sure that it is a clearly defined and measurable objective.

The last issue to look at in a sliding scale is timeliness of payment. It is likely that the hospital will demand a clause in the contract spelling out the plan's requirement to process claims in a timely manner, usually 30 days or sooner. In some cases you may wish to negotiate a sliding scale, or a modifier to your main sliding scale, that applies a further reduction based on the plan's ability to turn a clean claim around quickly. For example, you may negotiate an additional 4 percent discount for paying a clean claim within 14 days of receipt. Conversely, the hospital may demand a penalty for clean claims that are not processed within 30 days.

Straight Per Diem Charges

Unlike straight charges, a negotiated per diem is a single charge for a day in the hospital regardless of any actual charges or costs incurred. In this most common type of arrangement, the plan negotiates a per diem rate with the hospital and pays that rate without adjustments. For example, the plan will pay $800 for each day regardless of the actual cost of the service.

Hospital administrators are sometimes reluctant to add days in the intensive care unit or obstetrics to the base per diem unless there is a sufficient volume of regular medical–surgical cases to make the ultimate cost predictable. In a small plan, or in one that is not limiting the number of participating hospitals, the hospital administrator is concerned that the hospital will be used for expensive cases at a low per diem while competitors are used for less costly cases. In such cases, a good option is to negotiate multiple sets of per diem charges based on service type (e.g., medical–surgical, obstetrics, intensive care, neonatal intensive care, rehabilitation, and so forth) or a combination of per diems and a flat case rate (see below) for obstetrics.

The key to making a per diem work is predictability. If the plan and hospital can accurately predict the number and mix of cases, then they can accurately calculate a per diem. The per diem is simply an estimate of the charges or costs for an average day in that hospital minus the level of discount.

A theoretical disadvantage of the per diem approach, however, is that the per diem must be paid even if the billed charges are less than the per diem rate. For example, if the plan has a per diem arrangement that pays $800 per day for medical admissions, and the total allowable charges (billed charges less charges for noncovered items provided during the admission) for a 5-day admission are $3,300, the hospital is reimbursed $4,000 for the admission ($800 per day × 5 days). This is acceptable as long as the average per diem represents an acceptable discount, but it has been anecdotally reported that some large, self-insured accounts have demanded the lesser of the charges or the per diems for each case (i.e., laying off the upper end of the risk but harvesting the reward). Such demands are to be avoided because they corrupt the integrity of the per diem calculation.

A plan may also negotiate to reimburse the hospital for expensive surgical implants provided at the hospital's actual cost of the implant. Such reimbursement would be limited to a defined list of implants (e.g., cochlear implants) where the cost to the hospital for the implant is far greater than is recoverable under the per diem or outpatient arrangement.

Sliding Scale Per Diem

Like the sliding scale discount on charges discussed above, the sliding scale per diem is also based on total volume. In this case, the plan negotiates an interim per diem that it will pay for each day in the hospital. Depending on the total number of bed days in the year, the plan will either pay a lump sum settlement at the end of the year or withhold an amount from the final payment for the year to adjust for an additional reduction in the per diem from an increase in total bed days. It may be preferable to make an arrangement whereby on a quarterly or semiannual basis the plan will adjust the interim per diem so as to reduce any disparities caused by unexpected changes in utilization patterns.

Differential by Day in Hospital

This simply refers to the fact that most hospitalizations are more expensive on the first day. For example, the first day for surgical cases includes operating suite costs, the operating surgical team costs (nurses and recovery), and so forth. This type of reimbursement method is generally combined with a per diem approach, but the first day is paid at a higher rate. For example, the first day may be $1,000 and each subsequent day is $600.

Diagnosis-Related Groups

As with Medicare, a common reimbursement methodology is by diagnosis-related groups (DRGs). There are publications of DRG categories, criteria, outliers, and trim points (i.e., the cost or length of stay that causes the DRG payment to be supplemented or supplanted by another payment mechanism) to enable the plan to negotiate a payment mechanism for DRGs based on Medicare rates or, in some cases, state regulated rates. First, though, the plan needs to assess whether it will be to its benefit.

If it is the plan's intention to reduce unnecessary utilization, there will not necessarily be concomitant savings if it uses straight DRGs. If the payment is fixed on the basis of diagnosis, any reduction in days will go to the hospital and not to the plan. Furthermore, unless the plan is prepared to perform careful audits of the hospital's DRG coding, it may experience code creep. On the other hand, DRGs do serve to share risk with the hospital, thus making the hospital an active partner in controlling utilization and making plan expenses more manageable. DRGs are perhaps better suited to plans with loose controls than plans that tightly manage utilization.

Service-Related Case Rates

Similar to DRGs, service-related case rates are a cruder cut. In this reimbursement mechanism, various service types are defined (e.g., medicine, surgery, intensive care, neonatal intensive care, psychiatry, obstetrics, and the like), and the hospital receives a flat per admission reimbursement for whatever type of service to which the patient is admitted (e.g., all surgical admissions cost $6,100). If services are mixed, a prorated payment may be made (e.g., 50 percent of surgical and 50 percent of intensive care).

Case Rates and Package Pricing

Whatever mechanism a plan uses for hospital reimbursement, it may still need to address certain categories of procedures and negotiate special rates. The most common of these is obstetrics. It is common to negotiate a flat rate for a normal vaginal delivery and a flat rate for a cesarean section or a blended rate for both. In the case of blended case rates, the expected reimbursement for each type of delivery is multiplied by the expected (or desired) percentage of utilization. For example, a case rate for vaginal delivery is $2,000, and for cesarean section it is $2,600. Utilization is expected to be 80 percent vaginal and 20 percent cesarean section, and therefore the case rate is $2,120 ($2,000 × 0.8 = $1,600; $2,600 × 0.2 = $520; $1,600 + $520 = $2,120).

Although common, case rates are certainly not necessary if the per diem is all inclusive, but a plan will want to use them if it has negotiated a discount on charges. This is because the delivery suite or operating room is substantially more costly to operate than a regular hospital room. For example, you may negotiate a flat rate of $2,100 per delivery. The downside of this arrangement is that you achieve no added savings from decreased length of stay. The upside is that it makes the hospital a much more active partner in controlling utilization.

Another area for which a plan would typically want to negotiate flat rates is specialty procedures at tertiary hospitals, for example coronary artery bypass surgery or heart transplants. These procedures, although relatively infrequent, are tremendously costly.

A broader variation is package pricing or bundled case rates. As discussed in Chapters 12 and 13, the package price or bundled case rate refers to an all-inclusive rate paid for both institutional and professional services. The plan negotiates a flat rate for a procedure (e.g., coronary artery bypass surgery), and that rate is used to pay all parties who provide services connected with that procedure, including preadmission and postdischarge care. Bundled case rates are not uncommon in teaching facilities where there is a faculty practice plan that works closely with the hospital.

Capitation or Percentage of Revenue

Capitation refers to reimbursing the hospital on a per member per month (PMPM) basis to cover all institutional costs for a defined population of members. The payment may be varied by age and sex but does not fluctuate with premium revenue. Percentage of revenue refers to a fixed percentage of premium revenue (i.e., a percentage of the collected premium rate) being paid to the hospital, again to cover all institutional services. The difference between percentage of revenue and capitation is that percentage of revenue may vary with the premium rate charged and the actual revenue yielded. Although capitation and percentage of premium revenue are essentially the same for public sector programs (i.e., risk contracts for Medicare and Medicaid), that is not the case for the commercial sector. In the event that the plan fails to develop rates properly or perform underwriting (or gets caught up in a price war), a proportionate percentage of that shortfall will be passed directly to the hospital. In both cases, the hospital stands the entire risk for institutional services for the defined membership base; if the hospital cannot provide the services itself, the cost for such care is deducted from the capitation payment.

For this type of arrangement to work, a hospital must know that it will serve a clearly defined segment of a plan's enrollment and that it can provide most of the necessary services to those members. In these cases, the primary care physician is clearly associated with just one hospital. Alternatively, if the plan is dealing with a multihospital system with multiple facilities in the plan's service area, it may be reasonable to expect that the hospitals in the system can care for the plan's members on an exclusive basis. It

is possible for capitation to be tied to the percentage of admissions to a hospital. For example, the capitation rate is $35 PMPM. The plan has 10,000 members, and 50 percent of admissions go to that hospital that month. The payment therefore is $35 × (10,000 × 0.5) = $175,000. This is quite uncommon, however.

The hospital must also perform aggressive utilization management to see any margin from capitation; if utilization management is carried out so as to ruffle the least number of feathers of attending staff, the hospital will pay a stiff price. There needs to be a clear definition of what is covered under the capitation and what is not. For example, the capitation may include outpatient procedures, but the plan and hospital need to account for outpatient procedures that are being performed outside the hospital's domain. Will home health be part of the capitation, and, if so, what agency? It is preferable not to place the hospital at risk for services it cannot control. The hospital also needs to be provided with stop-loss insurance to protect it against catastrophic cases; for example, the plan may reimburse the hospital at a low per diem for all days of a case after it has been in the hospital for a number of days (e.g., beyond 30 days in a year). Alternatively, the plan may pay a percentage of charges after a certain charge level has been reached, and the plan's own reinsurance comes into play.

The advantage of capitation is that it is not only budgetable but succeeds in laying off all or most of the risk for institutional expenses. The hospital becomes a full partner in controlling utilization, and the plan has less need to control. The problem is that the plan will see none of the savings for improved utilization control. Another problem can arise if the hospital refuses to share any of the savings (calculated as though there were a per diem or discounted charges model) with the physicians who are controlling the cases; if you pursue such an arrangement, the HMO may want to include provisions for a bonus plan between the hospital and the physicians.

Point-of-service (POS) plans with an out-of-network benefit make capitation methods difficult to use. As discussed in Chapter 9, capitation in POS may mean having to pay twice for a service: once under capitation and again if the member seeks service outside the network. In areas where there are no real alternatives to a certain hospital (e.g., a rural area or an area where a hospital enjoys a monopoly), this problem may not be material, but that is the exception. Capitation tied to the percentage of admissions to that hospital, as mentioned earlier in this chapter, may also attenuate this problem. The alternative is to deduct out-of-area costs from the capitation payment. Closely related to this is the idea of global capitation, in which an IDS accepts capitation or percentage of premium revenue in exchange for total risk for medical services. This is discussed in Chapter 4.

The last issue of which you need to be aware in this arrangement is that some state insurance departments may consider this degree of risk transfer too much. It may be reasoned that, if the health plan is not actually assuming the risk for services, then it is not really a health plan at all but only a marketing organization. In such a case, there may be a question as to who should really hold the certificate of authority or license to operate the health plan. This issue is discussed in Chapter 53.

Bed Leasing

A relatively uncommon reimbursement mechanism is bed leasing. This refers to a plan actually leasing beds from an institution, for example paying the hospital $350 per bed for 10 beds regardless of whether those beds are used. This ensures revenue flow to the hospital, ensures access to beds (at least some beds) for the plan, and is budgetable. It is perhaps best used in those situations where a plan is assured of a steady number of bed days with little or no seasonality. The problem with bed leasing is that there is no real savings from reducing utilization unless contract terms allow the plan to lease back the beds to the hospital if they are not being used.

Periodic Interim Payments and Cash Advances

Once common but now rare, periodic interim payments (PIPs) and cash advances are methods whereby the plan advances a hospital cash to cover expected claims. This cash advance is periodically replenished if it gets below a certain amount. Claims may be applied directly against the cash advance or may be paid outside it, in which case the cash advance serves as an advance deposit. The value of this to a hospital is obvious: positive cash flow. PIPs and cash advances are quite valuable to a hospital and will generate a discount in and of themselves.

Performance-Based Reimbursement

The largest portion of reimbursement to hospitals is likely to be done under one or more of the methods described above. Capitation is clearly an example of performance-based reimbursement, in that the hospital only profits if it can provide services at a low cost and a high level of quality. Beyond that, there are other forms of performance-based reimbursement, although they are not common at this time.

Penalties and Withholds

As with physician services (see Chapters 7 and 9), occasionally penalties or withholds are used in hospital reimbursement methods. As an example, a plan may negotiate with a hospital to allow the hospital's own utilization management department to perform all the utilization management functions (see Chapter 17). As part of that negotiation, goals are set for average length of stay and average admission rate. Part of the payment to the hospital may be withheld, or, conversely, the plan may set aside a bonus pool. In any event, if the goals are met or exceeded, the hospital receives its withhold or bonus, and vice versa. One complication with this is the possibility that a hospital can make its statistics look good by simply sending patients to other hospitals; this is similar to problems encountered with physician capitation. If a service area is clearly defined, or if the hospital is capitated, then it may be easier to apply a risk or reward program. The reader should be aware, however, that there is evidence that financial penalty models applied to hospitals have little or no effect on utilization or physician performance.[2]

Service and Quality Incentives

An alternative approach to financial penalties associated with utilization levels is to provide the hospital incentives for improving its quality and service as well as its business operations. In one model, hospitals receive an incentive payment that is affected by three broad variables: satisfaction with services (measured by surveys of patients and physicians), clinical care (measured by looking at complication rates, average length of stay, and other measures), and business structural support for managed care (e.g., electronic data interchange, case management support, and other aspects).[3] In another model, hospitals receive modest incentives based on outcomes for certain clinical procedures (Blue Cross/Blue Shield of Minnesota, unpublished data, 1993).

Outpatient Procedures

As mentioned earlier, the shift from inpatient to outpatient care has not gone unnoticed by hospital administrators. As care has shifted, so have charges. It is not uncommon to see outpatient charges exceeding the cost of an inpatient day unless steps are taken to address that imbalance.

Discounts on Charges

Either straight discounts or sliding scale discounts may be applied to outpatient charges. Some hospitals argue that the cost to deliver highly technical outpatient procedures actually is greater than an average per diem, primarily because the per diem assumes more than a single day in the hospital, thereby spreading the costs over a greater number of reimbursable days. Some plans have responded by simply admitting patients for their outpatient surgery, paying the per diem, and sending the patient home. Many plans negotiate the costs of outpatient surgery so that they never exceed the cost of an inpatient day, whereas other plans concede the problem of front-loading surgical services and agree to cap outpatient charges at a fixed percentage of the per diem (e.g., 125 percent of the average per diem).

Package Pricing or Bundled Charges

Plans may negotiate package pricing or bundled charges for outpatient procedures. In this method of reimbursement, all the various charges are bundled into one single charge, thereby reducing the problem of unbundling and exploding (i.e., charging for multiple codes or brand new codes where previously only one code was used). Plans may use their own data to develop the bundled charges, or they may use outside data (one such source is published by Milliman & Roberston, a national actuarial firm[4]). Bundled charges are generally tied to the principal procedure code used by the facility. Bundled charges may also be added together in the event that more than one procedure is performed, although the second procedure is discounted because the patient was already in the facility and using services.

Related to this approach are tiered rates. In this case, the outpatient department categorizes all procedures into several different categories. The plan then pays a different rate for each category, but that rate covers all services performed in the outpatient department, and only one category is used at a time (i.e., the hospital cannot add several categories together for a single patient encounter).

Ambulatory Patient Groups

Ambulatory patient groups (APGs) were developed by 3M Health Systems under a contract with the Health Care Financing Administration (HCFA), primarily for use with Medicare.[5] As this book is being written, APGs have not been put into use, although the HCFA has recommended that they be phased in over several years. The commercial market, however, has begun actively to use APGs.[6]

APGs are to outpatient services what DRGs are to inpatient ones, although APGs are based on procedures rather than simply on diagnoses and are considerably more complex. As with bundled charges (discussed above), under APGs all the services associated with a given procedure or visit are bundled into the APG reimbursement. More than one APG may be billed if more than one procedure is performed, but there is significant discounting for additional APGs.

CONCLUSION

Reimbursement mechanisms and contracts with hospitals, as with consultants, are tools. The importance of these tools cannot be overestimated, and an MCO must craft these tools with all the skills it has available. It is possible and desirable to develop win–win situations with hospitals, and that can be a pivotal issue in the ultimate success of a plan.

REFERENCES AND NOTES

1. American Hospital Association (AHA), *American Hospital Association Guide to the Health Care Field* (Chicago, Ill.: AHA, 1995).

2. L. Debrock and R.J. Arnould, Utilization Control in HMOs, *Quarterly Review of Economics and Finance* 32 (1992): 31–53.

3. C. Sennett, et al., Performance-Based Hospital Contracting for Quality Improvement, *Journal of Quality Improvement* 19 (1993): 374–383.

4. R.L. Doyle and A.P. Feren, *Healthcare Management Guidelines, Vol. 3: Ambulatory Care Guidelines* (Milliman & Robertson, 1991).

5. R.F. Averill, et al., *Design and Evaluation of a Prospective Payment System for Ambulatory Care, Final Report* (Health Care Financing Administration Cooperative Agreement 17-C-99369/1-02, Health Care Financing Administration, 1995).

6. S. Larose, Preparing for Ambulatory Patient Groups, *Capitation and Medical Practice* 1 (1995): 1, 4–6.

SUGGESTED READING

Profiles of U.S. Hospitals. 1995 Baltimore, Md.: HCIA, Inc.

Pyenson, B.S. (ed.). 1995. *Calculated Risk: A Provider's Guide to Controlling the Financial Risk of Manged Care.* Chicago, Ill.: American Hospital Publishers.

Chapter 15

Academic Health Centers and Managed Care

Richard L. Solit and David B. Nash

Academic health centers (AHCs) have symbolized the great technological advancements and specialization in patient care that have occurred in this century. They have been successful in their classic mission to train health professionals, foster basic and clinical research, and provide the highest quality of patient care. As a result, applications to medical schools, clinical revenues, and research discoveries are at record highs.

These traditional ways face an uncertain future in today's rapidly changing health care environment, however. Public generosity toward research and education is tempered by a strong deficit-lowering sentiment in the nation. Furthermore, with the failure of comprehensive health reform, medical educators have lost confidence in the certainty of future public support for education, research, and patient care in the academic setting. This would not present an insurmountable problem if the historical subsidization of education and research by profitable clinical activities continued indefinitely. It is clear, however, that this cannot continue as the purchasers of health care seek continued cost containment through managed care. As a result,

the AHC is forced to compete in the marketplace on cost and quality. This may leave little support for less profitable activities and requires a transformation of the current structure.

An understanding of the complex interaction among patients, physicians, hospitals, insurers, employers, and government agencies is necessary before one develops a strategy for the managed care market. The traditional role played by each party is in a state of flux. Definitions of a few of the terms used in this discussion therefore may be helpful. Providers deliver care to patients and include hospitals and physicians. Insurers provide various financing arrangements as defined by a specified benefits plan for purchasers and beneficiaries (or patients). The purchasers of health care include patients, employers, and government agencies, such as Medicare and Medicaid, who pay premiums to insurers or pay providers directly for services. Managed care is defined as the integration of financing with the delivery of health care services. Therefore, managed care organizations (MCOs) provide plans or products that integrate the health care financing activities of insurers with the delivery of care by providers for purchasers. Insurers are increasingly becoming MCOs as they go beyond simply paying for services rendered in a fee-for-service (FFS) system to managing provider activity and in turn arranging the delivery of care. Providers are also becoming MCOs by providing financing and delivery of health care services when they contract directly with purchasers. Some MCOs, such as staff model health maintenance organizations (HMOs), provide fi-

Richard L. Solit, M.D., is a fellow in the Office of Health Policy and Clinical Outcomes and a resident in the Department of Surgery at Thomas Jefferson University, Philadelphia, Pennsylvania.

David B. Nash, M.B.A., M.D., is the director of the Office of Health Policy and Clinical Outcomes and Associate Professor of Medicine at Thomas Jefferson University, Philadelphia, Pennsylvania.

nancing and delivery within one system and assume both the provider and insurer role. Stemming from the rapid changes in the industry, this terminology is somewhat artificial. Further discussions of the evolving taxonomy of MCOs and integrated provider systems are found in Chapters 3 and 4.

This chapter defines the challenges to academic medicine in terms of changing market mechanisms and financial support for AHCs and demonstrates how the unique organizational and cultural environment within the AHC contributes to the problem and obstructs potential solutions. Potential strategies must integrate primary and specialty care with network formation to secure a solid patient base. Furthermore, the AHC must create and cultivate stakeholders in its mission to support necessary but nonprofitable activities. Internal changes to meet these new demands require innovation and leadership in realigning incentives, managing information and outcomes, and reinventing education and research. Finally, anticipating change to improve market position and profitability will prove valuable as rapid change continues.

DIMENSIONS OF THE PROBLEM

With the rapid growth of managed care, AHCs face multiple financial challenges that threaten their ability to perform their traditional academic mission. The potential loss of public funds that directly and indirectly support medical education, research, charity, and complex care take on new implications in the context of the challenges presented by managed care. It is important to recognize that managed care is a reflection of the change in societal values and attitudes. It is the response of the free market to two decades of runaway medical inflation caused by a cost-plus system that encouraged unlimited use of medical services. Although the AHCs benefited immensely in this environment, continued reliance on the structure and culture of the past is the real threat to their viability. Salvation lies in recognizing that "they can no longer operate as specialty-driven institutions largely divorced from the trends that favor lower costs, less hospitalization, and more primary care."[1(p.407)] The dimensions of the problem will be examined here in terms of the interaction between the barriers to organizational change and the changes in market mechanisms and financial support for academic medicine. The reader is also referred to Chapters 1 and 2 for an overview of the broad forces at play in managed care.

Change in Market Mechanisms

Many feel that the multiple roles of AHCs make them noncompetitive in this changing environment. Excluding the direct cost of teaching, a 1991 study places the average cost of care per admission at $6,000 in AHCs compared with $4,400 in nonteaching hospitals.[2] Because clinical activities under capitation become cost centers, like the programs they support, managed care plans avoid contracting with teaching hospitals. According to predictions by the University HealthSystem Consortium (an organization of 70 AHCs that helps its members with the business of medicine), the movement toward managed care has created a clear trend toward markedly lower utilization of secondary and tertiary services with fewer admissions and shorter lengths of stay. These data suggest that hospital admissions and revenues would decline by 25 percent and 50 percent respectively, in aggressively managed markets. Similarly, contributions to revenues by specialists would decline by approximately 30 percent. Given that an average of 40 percent of medical school revenues are derived from professional and hospital services, academic funding will suffer considerably under these conditions.[3]

To respond to the threat of declining revenues, academic leaders must focus on the market mechanisms that create the environment in which they will operate. The paradigm shift in health care toward cost containment occurred in 1982, when prospective payment was introduced for Medicare. Although this did not control the growth of medical expenditures, a clear message was sent that the 20-year era of cost-plus medicine was over. Real changes, however, occurred only with an increasing role of the purchasers of health care and the subsequent shift in financial risk allocation from these purchasers to insurers, providers, and patients.

Increasing Role of Purchasers

The importance of the purchasers, who bear the burden of health insurance premiums, cannot be overstated. The separation of the consumer (patient) from the provider by third party payers (insurers) has removed the normal economic mechanism that controls utilization, namely cost to the consumer. The vast majority of Americans are sheltered from the direct cost of rising premiums because health care is a benefit funded either by their employer through pretax payroll deductions (37 percent of insured Americans) or by the taxpayer through Medicare and Medicaid (42 percent of insured Americans).[4] Rampant medical inflation increased this responsibility immensely and forced these purchasers to be the most significant catalyst for the movement toward managed care.

Because the consumer is sheltered from the rising cost of health care premiums in addition to the direct cost of care, there is no market mechanism to control demand for health services and, in turn, total costs. Simply stated, total medical expenditures depend on the product of the volume of services and the price for these services. Although discounted FFS and price controls in the form of diagnosis-related groups (DRGs) for hospitals slowed the rate of medical inflation for Medicare, true cost reduction in the absence of demand control requires a reduction in the volume of services provided. For years after DRGs were introduced, AHC revenues were not drastically threatened because physicians still controlled the flow of patients into the system and could therefore continue to generate volume in an atmosphere of price control. Intense use of services continued along with a shift toward FFS outpatient services.

Private industry, and now Medicare and Medicaid, are increasingly attracted to managed care.[5–7] Approximately 65 percent of employees

of large firms were enrolled in managed care plans by 1994. This had grown from 47 percent in 1991. Only 6 percent remain in traditional indemnity plans that use no utilization control.[8] Even though this is an employer decision rather than a beneficiary preference, reports indicate a high level of patient satisfaction.[9] Many states have followed the example set by employers and now encourage managed care for Medicaid beneficiaries. Since 1987, the Medicaid population in managed care has doubled to 12 percent. See Chapter 48 for a discussion of Medicaid and managed care. The Health Care Financing Administration has also encouraged HMOs for Medicare beneficiaries since the early 1980s. Although enrollment is growing at an annual rate of 12 percent, projected growth by 1994 was only 6 percent of the estimated 36 million beneficiaries.[10] See Chapters 46 and 47 for a discussion of Medicare and managed care.

Utilization control is the undeniable result of increasing purchaser involvement in cost containment. Purchasers have long noted regional variation in practice patterns as well as lower levels of spending per capita in other industrialized countries. As the level of medical inflation has continued, they have turned to managed care as a mechanism for removing "fat" from the current system. The government considered regulatory mechanisms and forms of universal health care used in other nations to control total expenditures. Instead, the private market concentrated on changing incentives from FFS that produced independent profit centers to managed care with annually capitated cost centers.[11] The result was minimal premium increases and some reductions by 1995.[12]

This distinct about face from the previous culture of overutilization is the fundamental threat to the AHC. The decline in the utilization of high technology and other AHC services directly reduces revenues that have traditionally subsidized "unprofitable" activities such as education, research, and unreimbursed patient care. Academic leaders must also recognize that economics is not the only factor promoting managed care. Although health spending decreased by 1 percent for American industry in 1994, employers are not yet satisfied.[13] They want further information about quality and experience to improve their purchasing decisions. Purchasers and their beneficiaries are concerned with determining quality and appropriateness of care based on definable outcomes and physician accountability. MCOs are responsive to these needs, and the managed care culture supports deliberate evaluation of outcomes, accountability, utilization control, primary care, disease management, and integration of care for defined populations.[14] If viewed broadly as the integration of financing with the delivery of services, whether through capitation or a combination of financial mechanisms, managed care is seen by purchasers as essential for transforming medicine into an efficient, high-quality industry for the 21st century. See Chapter 36 for additional discussion of the topic of what employers want from managed care.

Shift in Financial Risk Allocation

The most important factor in the proper allocation of resources is the proper allocation of financial risk among patients, purchasers, insurers, and providers. When patients assume risk, they gain in the form of savings through demand control. When risk is assumed by insurers and providers, profit is achieved by more efficient delivery of fewer services. Insurers are in the best position to assume risk for catastrophic conditions, whereas providers are in the best position to control utilization on a case-by-case basis.

Purchaser involvement led to utilization control by shifting financial risk to insurers and providers. The ideal strategy is to allocate financial risk to the party that is most able to manage utilization and outcomes effectively. Even though purchasers are the least able party to manage processes and outcomes, they assumed the greatest risk under a cost-plus FFS system in the form of ever increasing insurance premiums or direct costs for self-insured businesses (see Chapter 59). The patient has had no motivation to constrain utilization. Additionally, AHCs, like all

providers, could profit from overutilization while passing along all costs resulting from inefficiencies. Under managed care, capitation allows for a fixed budget and transfers financial risk to insurers and providers. Future attempts to distribute more risk to employees through increased deductibles and copayments are likely.[15,16]

Change in Financial Support

Three interrelated factors directly decrease support for the academic mission. First, employers are selecting health plans largely on the basis of cost because there is little information available about differences in quality.[17,18] The perceived superiority of care in AHCs no longer guarantees continued utilization or funding of their services. In effect, the focus on price by purchasers has transformed medicine into a commodity market. Second, the failure of legislative health care reform in late 1993 (see Chapter 2) means that academic centers must face the threat of diminishing revenues under managed care with no likelihood of greater government support. Third, the loss of federal support, in the context of the purchaser shift toward a commodity view of health care, may lead to elimination of the financial support derived from the clinical revenues of academic providers.

Medicine as a Commodity

Most types of insurance have traditionally acted as commodities in the market. Because commodities are usually indistinguishable, commodity businesses compete solely on price and cannot keep market share at prices above others in the marketplace. Conversely, health insurers, and especially Blue Cross/Blue Shield and indemnity plans (see Chapter 3) as well as providers such as AHCs, have enjoyed a noncommodity identity. In the past, they could increase prices without losing market share. Profitable organizations were high-cost producers. The shift toward competition based solely on price suggests that medical care has transformed into a commodity in which the products offered are virtually indistinguishable. Reports indicate that patients are willing to change plans for a price differential as low as $5.00.[19] Unless services can be distinguished through measures of quality or overcapacity decreases dramatically, AHCs must become low-cost producers.

Studies comparing the quality and satisfaction of managed care patients demonstrate equal quality.[20] Reports also indicate that HMOs consistently perform better in preventive care with a greater proportion of mammography, general physical, pelvic, and rectal examinations.[21,22] Even more important, these results are disseminated in the financial papers and general media, exposing purchasers to data suggesting that care provided to managed care enrollees is indistinguishable from that provided through traditional indemnity insurance.[23] Therefore, academic pursuits are not immune to economic forces, and the feeling of superior quality of care at AHCs cannot be taken for granted. Private insurers, and now Medicare and Medicaid, will not pay higher prices to support increased costs incurred by AHCs for teaching, research, and indigent care because they no longer perceive greater quality of services in AHCs.[24]

Graduate Medical Education

The academic mission has been subsidized by a process with no logic and no basis in proper allocation of society's resources. Public support for education, indigent care, and research has traditionally been hidden in Medicare payments as adjustments for graduate medical education (GME). The indirect cost of GME as well as uncompensated care was factored into DRG payments to hospitals with resident training. There were two unanticipated results from these hidden payments. First, there was a dramatic rise in accredited programs for GME, which increased by 21 percent from 1983 to 1991.[25] Second, these hidden payments supported managed care profits. When the Heath Care Financing Administration targeted payments to managed care organizations at 95 percent of projected FFS levels as defined by geographic area, it included direct and indirect support for GME in these capitated

payments. There was no obligation for MCOs to pass along these funds for educational activities. In addition, enrollment of healthier patients may have increased expenses for the remaining FFS population, raising the measured FFS levels the following year and in turn further increasing payments to MCOs.[26,27] Many would argue that the federal subsidy for GME does not properly allocate the nation's limited capital resources.

The federal government has never supported undergraduate medical education, and the failure of health care reform eliminated assurances of continued support for GME. As Medicare increasingly turns toward managed care, GME funding no longer reaches academic institutions. In conjunction with diminishing federal support, an avoidance of AHC services by purchasers and insurers resulting from the shift toward a commodity view of health care leads to a divergence of medical center and medical school goals.

Historically, medical schools and their associated teaching hospitals have prospered by supporting each other. The linkage of GME support to Medicare payments resulted in a mutual financial dependence between the medical school and academic providers. The academic hospital and its physicians gained surplus revenues for the teaching they provided in two ways. First, they benefited directly from inflated Medicare payments. Second, higher prices and volume were achieved from the perception that the professor is the expert and delivers the highest-quality care. In return, physicians and hospitals provided the medical school with financial support and a large, comprehensive patient base for students and residents.

With the introduction of managed care, divergent needs exist between academic providers and medical schools. Association with the medical school may no longer provide the hospital and faculty the benefit of increased payments through Medicare and increased referrals through reputation. As described earlier, lack of outcome measures showing better quality converts medicine to a commodity market based on price. Therefore, academic providers can no longer maintain higher prices. Conversely, the medical school benefits less from association with the hospital. The health care system of the future will not revolve around the hospital, and the inpatient environment does not provide fully the education needed for managed care. Instead of handling all aspects of care, hospitals will only care for those patients who cannot be cared for in other settings. Furthermore, separation of GME payments from Medicare along with declining revenues means that medical schools cannot count on hospitals for continued financial support. Association with the hospital and faculty plans may also present a conflict of interest in attempts to align with other providers or MCOs that are able to add to the teaching patient base or act as new sources of support.

As hospitals and medical schools realign their goals for survival, common areas will present for continued collaboration, but the paradigm shift suggests that the two need not remain inextricably linked.[28] Acting independently, they will be free to pursue alliances with other competing organizations. Unless the teaching hospital and academic faculty pursue a strategy that addresses proper training for managed care, the medical school will need to look elsewhere for an appropriate teaching environment. Even with successful adaptation to managed care, hospitals alone cannot support the academic mission. The cost of education and research will require funding by the federal government or comprehensive support from the managed care industry. Funding for medical schools must be separated from the revenues of the medical centers.

Barriers to Organizational Change

The unique organizational and cultural structure of the traditional AHC is an impediment to adaptation to a competitive environment. Although the AHC has been tremendously successful under the FFS system, its present structure appears ill suited to enable it to adapt to the rapid changes affecting the industry. The changes in market mechanisms and financial support provide an incredible challenge for the AHC. How can the AHC create a cultural and organizational structure that improves competitiveness, fosters education and research, contributes to efficient use of resources, and maintains a high level of technical quality? The traditional culture, based in physician autonomy, presents the strongest barrier to collaboration. A market in transition further prevents changes by providing conflicting incentives to providers. Finally, the current information structure, based in a billing function, does not allow for accurate determination of cost bases, processes, and outcomes for services and education.

Traditional Culture

The structure of the AHC is the product of a culture that fostered great clinical and technical advances over the last half century. This structure is based in a culture or system in which the physician is the main focus. The hospital is the physician's workshop; the medical school is the physician's classroom. Autonomy of the individual physician results from revenue generation. In an FFS, the individual physician controls access and therefore generates revenues for the AHC. Within the hospital, specialists who can generate a large volume of services through procedures and hospital admissions have developed a great deal of power. This system defines the physician as the knowledgeable decision maker. The autonomy of the individual is so important, however, that bias and habits often replace true outcomes-based decision making (see Chapter 26 for a discussion of this issue).

Because the culture of the AHC is centered on the individual physician, it revolves around the needs of the departments of various specialties. Stemming from the frustration that many feel in dealing with the divergent needs of different departments, these departments have often been described in a derogatory manner as fiefdoms. This political entrenchment prevents beneficial change, and individual power struggles destroy the ability of the AHC to act in a rational, cohesive manner. Given that purchasers increasingly insist on cost effectiveness, a culture that obstructs fundamental change will increasingly weigh on the AHC. The present structure forms a bias against primary care, population focus, outcomes-based decision making, and sound business principles.

The Transition Market

The profits of today are a barrier to the profits of tomorrow. Continued revenues for individuals and autonomous departments, as a result of incomplete capitation and utilization control, obstruct attempts at changing the traditional culture of the AHC. With this dichotomy in place, the AHC remains a revenue center, while increasing capitation and its resulting shift in financial risk transform it to a cost center. The AHC still needs the individual physicians, in particular the specialists, to generate revenues in the current hybrid environment. Therefore, the needs for future viability of the AHC do not coincide with the needs for today's profitability. A transition market dictates that the timing of strategic actions takes on great importance. Additionally, change that precedes the arrival of fierce competition requires leadership that will alter the traditional culture by creating a common vision for those with a stake in the AHC.

Information Structure

The absence of information regarding clinical processes and cost structures is a significant barrier to effective competition. For the majority of physicians, current information systems perform a billing function and do not provide information about clinical processes and their underlying cost structures. A few hospitals have internal cost accounting systems that can be used to evaluate physician practice patterns and overall institutional averages by diagnosis. These hospitals, however, do not usually have this information available in a timely manner for immediate clinical use and feedback.

As AHCs assume increased financial risk and the economics begins to resemble a commodity market, internal cost and process accounting becomes necessary for success. Profit under capitation can only occur at the margin between revenues and costs of services provided, and only the low-cost provider in a commodity market

can profit because there is little price flexibility. This involves creating higher margins that result from cost controls and aggressive cost analysis. Information systems of the future must combine clinical resources such as guidelines and protocols with accurate cost data to manage process and outcome effectively.[29]

With improved information management, medical centers can withstand poor economic environments and strengthen their market positions by driving weaker competitors from the market. Problems in operations can be identified more easily as well. Furthermore, improved profit margin allows growth without debt and accumulation of funds for the academic mission. Management information systems and the use of data for medical management are discussed in Chapters 28 and 29.

STRATEGIES FOR SUCCESS

Attempts at uniformity and standardization aimed at reducing variability in treatment are a first step toward lowering costs within academic health centers. As purchasers shift their focus from cost to value, however, an information-based industry such as health care requires a new system or culture that promotes decentralized decision making and accountability to purchasers. Impediments to cooperation are especially strong from the physician perspective. Hospital administration has always depended on physicians to provide care for patients. Physicians, however, have not relied on outside parties for strategy, marketing, capital allocation, and cost structure, to name a few. Success with cultural change in the AHC will depend more on effective leadership than traditional corporate management to create a clear mission and vision, foster cooperation and collaboration, and promote appropriate physician education.

Because managed care will ultimately limit the number and types of specialists and reduce hospital overcapacity, AHCs must alter their training and culture. Success will depend largely on leadership and its ability to find innovative ways of maintaining a patient base, transforming the traditional culture, and creating new stakeholders in the academic mission. In addition, the AHC must reinvent education and research in the context of these strategies. Because the literature on this subject is largely anecdotal, a framework for potential solutions must be based on common trends in the industry. As a result of rapid changes in the industry, current information often comes from non–peer reviewed journals and news sources.

Innovation and Leadership

Given the speed with which the market is evolving, successful strategies will not be known until they are tried and tested. Projects attempting to delineate strategies for dealing with educational funding have begun. The Council on Graduate Medical Education is expected to release its sixth report specifically dealing with the effect of managed care on the physician workforce and medical education. The University HealthSystem Consortium commissioned two task forces that conducted research in an attempt to identify effective organizational structures and models for the delivery of care in the evolving managed care environment. They determined that a quick and radical response to the eventual dominance of managed care and integrated delivery systems (IDSs; see Chapter 4) is needed to maintain the clinical income required to support the academic mission.[30] Although a complete review and analysis of this work are beyond the scope of this chapter, it is apparent that survival for the AHC will ultimately depend on innovation and a responsiveness to change.

Managed care is rooted in the notion that health care can be managed. Who will be management in an AHC, however, and how do you manage highly skilled people in an information-oriented industry? Traditional management evolved from the industrialization of manufacturing. Before industrialization, craftsmen produced goods while educating apprentices, a process similar to medical education today. By simplifying production processes into small, definable tasks, less skilled workers could produce similar goods more efficiently. Labor became more interchangeable, but the new system needed managers to supervise and control the process. Simplification of the processes meant skilled labor was no longer required, and apprentices disappeared. Unfortunately, innovation and creativity were effectively removed from the labor force. In the end, thinking resided with management, and anything but obedience by workers led to chaos in production.

The industrialization of medicine parallels that of manufacturing in certain ways. There is a drive toward standardization through the use of guidelines, protocols, and benchmarking. Standardization implies simplification and the need for less skilled labor. In addition, the lure of standardization is that the generalist will be able to replace the specialist without needing the same knowledge or experience. Medicine, however, is a complex, knowledge-dependent process. Although improved information capabilities foster the industrialization of medicine, they also require a different form of management.

Systems play an important role in defining management and producing outcomes. Although traditional corporate culture has defined the manager as the knowledgeable decision maker, traditional medical culture has given the physician this role. Knowledgeable people, however, tend to lack an understanding of the complexity of skills they do not possess. Without experience or training in financial and managerial skills, physicians could "manage" medicine successfully, albeit inefficiently, because price and ultimately cost were unimportant. In a commodity business, where aggressive cost control and differentiation are essential, management takes on greater importance. Similarly, managed care executives who have successfully capitalized on overcapacity, negotiating substantial price discounts, believe that they can "deskill," simplify, and in effect control processes they cannot fully understand.

As with any imperative, the outcome is inevitable regardless of individual or group opposition. The market imperative for change created by the purchasers of health care leads to the inevitability of the industrialization of medicine. Network formation is clearly necessary in the evolution of medical organizations. Network formation does not automatically lead to system improvement, however, and a primary care strategy for negotiating capitated contracts does not intrinsically lead to greater physician productivity and competitiveness (see Chapters 4 and 5). The ultimate challenge for the AHC will be what to do with networks once they are formed. Furthermore, what role will the primary care physician hold within a newly created system?

Innovative ways of maintaining the AHC patient base, and in turn clinical revenues, are a top priority. Strategies for integrating hospital, generalist, and specialist services into functional networks are essential for successful positioning in the marketplace. Concurrently, the creation and cultivation of stakeholders in the academic mission are of paramount importance to supplement revenues that cannot be maintained as a result of the changes in support for GME. Collaboration with new stakeholders can reinvent education and research in the academic environment. Although innovation is necessary for survival in the short run, anticipating change is essential for prosperity in the long run.

Maintaining a Patient Base

Maintaining a patient base is fundamental for the financial survival of academic physicians and hospitals. For the university, it is mandatory for maintaining quality educational and training programs. As a result of the market forces discussed earlier, total inpatient and specialty service volume will decline as care shifts away from AHCs and toward less expensive settings. To remain viable, AHCs must focus on gaining covered lives through risk sharing and capitated contracts as well as on maintaining their share of the remaining FFS market. In addition, as discussed elsewhere in this book, in an environment of capitation providers want and need more members than patients because most of the money in a capitated system comes from mem-

bers of health plans who use few or inexpensive medical services. This issue is especially important for AHCs, which stand a greater than normal risk of adverse selection in an enrolled population (see Chapters 42 through 44 for detailed discussions of risk selection).

Consolidation between academic and nonacademic hospitals is expected and will leave the remaining institutions in a stronger financial position. Furthermore, declining support for AHCs may lead to a contraction in the number of medical schools and residency programs, which, one hopes, will leave the remaining institutions with more adequate funding. Current strategies for maintaining a patient base by an AHC rest upon network formation in combination with primary and specialty care strategies.

Network Formation

Maintaining clinical revenues requires satisfying the demands of purchasers of health care for access, low cost, appropriate care, ease of contracting, and patient satisfaction. The marketplace response has been the formation of networks that can eventually serve as the backbone for IDSs. Positioning by insurers, hospitals, and AHCs to create service networks of primary care physicians and specialists has reached a rapid pace.[31,32] Networks provide access to geographic areas, reduce the cost of capital, and foster information systems development. As a result, network formation is expected to increase market share and reduce operating costs. Networks are useful to AHCs in preserving the academic mission by educating primary care physicians and retraining specialists in a managed care environment.[33] Additionally, an IDS allows the creation of insurance products that can be marketed directly to purchasers such as employers, Medicare, and Medicaid. By integrating the financing and delivery of care with networks, AHCs can become MCOs in their own right and can profit from greater risk sharing.

Large networks do not always equate with purchaser satisfaction, however. After encouraging market consolidation into three large HMOs, employers in Minnesota decided to negotiate contracts directly with smaller groups of physicians and hospitals. This move occurred for two simple reasons. First, the health plans were engaging in price wars instead of focusing on medical care. Second, they wanted to get employers and health plans "out of the middle" between patients and their physicians.[34] This will give providers such as AHCs an opportunity to develop networks that eliminate the "middleman." Yet, within any delivery system, care will continue to be influenced, if not managed, by parties other than individual physicians. Therefore, elimination of MCOs that have provided value through innovative management of care in combination with the creation of delivery systems may be shortsighted. Ultimately, though, this example reinforces for everyone involved that networks must satisfy purchasers by providing measurable quality care to patients.

AHCs can form primary care networks, hospital networks, or a combination. Primary care networks often require significant capital compared with hospital networks. Positioning in the marketplace can range from forming networks providing a full range of services for a capitated population to providing services to other networks, employers, and insurers in the form of niche, secondary, and tertiary focused services. These strategies are not mutually exclusive and will probably coexist in the future. A network can be created by acquisition of hospitals or physician practices, partnering with established MCOs, and joint ventures with local physician groups and community hospitals.[35] See Chapter 5 for more discussion of these options.

Primary Care Strategy

Current thinking stresses the importance of a primary care strategy for success in a market dominated by managed care. Whether loosely associated or acquired, physicians who will accept capitated payments for defined populations are the prerequisite for negotiating broader arrangements. The adoption of a primary care strategy by the AHC has other important benefits. Besides revenue generation through capitated payments, an environment is created

within the academic setting for education and research in managed care.

Some options for gaining covered lives through primary care include purchasing existing practices, affiliating with existing practices or MCOs, or forming a teaching staff model HMO. Each has different risks and rewards. Purchasing practices and building staff model systems require large capital expenditures. The University of Pennsylvania is pursuing a strategy of purchasing physician practices in Philadelphia and the surrounding metropolitan area. It anticipates needing 150 primary care physicians who will form the backbone of an integrated network capable of caring for defined populations. This capital-intensive strategy will probably cost $100 million.[36] The university does not expect to compete directly with insurers but instead will provide a full range of services to MCOs in the area. Across the river in Philadelphia, Thomas Jefferson University has formed the Jefferson Health System through an agreement with several suburban hospitals.[37] This is a less expensive strategy for affiliating with generalists who can eventually assume risk for defined populations. Another approach might consist of partnering with a strong MCO and taking a role as its sole provider. By reducing the fixed cost per covered life and avoiding the complexity of managing primary care, the risk created by building the infrastructure needed for primary care is avoided.

There are a few caveats that must be noted in forming a primary care strategy, however. First, it cannot be used as mechanism to provide patients for continued specialty and tertiary care. This will continue to encourage overutilization, raising premiums for insurers and purchasers and resulting in poor competitiveness. Second, the AHC must attract healthy members to profit on capitated contracts. Converting the present patient population to a risk contract will be financially dangerous if the patients are an older or sicker group. Excellence in well baby care, sports injuries, and general obstetrics and gynecology may attract younger and healthier enrollees.[38] A focus on the ability to treat complex cases may be a disadvantage, leading to adverse risk selection by patients requiring access to costly tertiary care.

Third, the AHC must recognize that the immediate importance of primary care physicians in network formation is gaining covered lives. Competitiveness based on expected reductions in specialist use or improved population health through preventive care will depend on primary care physicians of the future.[39] Although health care expenditures for American industry decreased in 1994, it is unclear whether managed care as it exists today lowers overall costs or just allows a selection bias, reducing the proportion of sick and elderly in these plans.[40] There is no doubt that fierce competition leads to lower prices. Continued price reductions based on real changes in the delivery of health services, however, will depend on increased physician productivity created with a combination of system improvements and innovative physician training.

Specialty Strategy

The role of the specialist in managed care and network formation is a more challenging issue. FFS, global packaging, and capitation arrangements will probably remain in varying combinations. Further growth of managed care is expected to lead to continued decreases in the use of specialty and tertiary services. To maintain current levels of specialist revenue, AHCs would need to serve larger populations. The number of managed care enrollees needed to support current levels within any particular AHC would differ depending on whether the AHC provides all the specialty services needed by a defined HMO population or only a portion of referral services for the members of various managed care plans. Furthermore, the number of enrollees needed to support revenues varies widely among specialties.[41] Examples of such numbers can be found in Chapters 12 and 13.

Options include broader than normal geographical linkages with community providers and insurers as well as increased referrals within their primary service areas. A reliance on refer-rals from community physicians to teaching hospitals is not viable, however, as the market moves increasingly toward managed care.[42] As stated earlier, primary care cannot be viewed as a means to support specialist and tertiary services. The corollary is that a specialty strategy should be structured to support market needs for such services. AHCs must recognize that, although the current goal of MCOs is to reduce specialty use, elimination is impossible. In the ideal, the goal is the elimination of inappropriate utilization. Although fewer high-priced specialists will be needed, this area can continue to provide a large portion of revenue for the AHC. It is possible that AHCs will have a long-run competitive advantage in situations requiring complex care or the use of new technology for chronic, difficult to manage conditions. Real differences would allow lower per member per month premiums for covered lives within AHC integrated networks. Also, consolidation among AHCs may parallel consolidation of specialty services. The remaining providers will be a combination of low-cost providers and providers of excellence who can demonstrate superior results at a reasonable premium. This may allow the expansion of local and broader referral bases. Arbitrary designations as "centers of excellence" in the absence of superior results, however, will require aggressive marketing in an attempt to differentiate services from the competition.

The battle between producing services within the organization or network versus subcontracting to more efficient providers is a fundamental challenge to all organizations within managed care. Therefore, centers of excellence and integrated networks are not mutually exclusive. Outsourcing often allows more efficiency and less risk for organizations. If the AHC can package specialty and tertiary care for a price below the marginal cost for other networks and managed care organizations, it can create revenues outside of its own capitated contracts. This requires aggressive tertiary marketing that segments and satisfies different customer needs. Unfortunately, adverse risk selection to plans offering these services may eliminate AHC competitive advantage and make these services unappealing to other organizations. Therefore centers of excellence may exist only for a minority of complex cases or procedures such as transplantation.[43]

Transforming the Traditional Culture

AHCs must compete with service-oriented community providers to survive. Clearly, the clinical faculty must offer price-competitive and user-friendly services. Clinical training needs to focus on more relevant and emerging practice situations. Finally, the AHC must delineate funding streams and identify cross-subsidies taking place among teaching, research, and patient care enterprises. This can strengthen clinical training and the financial positions of the AHC and faculty.[44]

Leadership is essential for overcoming the barriers to such organizational changes. By stressing the inevitability of managed care, academic leaders can use market imperatives to begin the process toward transforming the traditional culture. The system must encourage centralized capital allocation and information management in the context of flexible, decentralized delivery of care. Focusing attention on accountability to purchasers for the cost and quality of care is an important first mechanism for fostering cooperation within the AHC. Next, managing outcomes through information and aligning incentives can promote a common vision within the AHC. New organizational structures will depend on functional production rather than departmental orientation, and the traditional risk-averse culture must evolve to take financial risk. Ultimately, though, the challenge for academic leaders may be to prepare for the inevitable external jolt of fierce competition that can unite powerful internal interest groups and successfully guide their institutions to a competitive position.[45]

Accountability

Although the traditional academic culture based in physician autonomy presents a barrier to collaboration, the threat of extinction will be the ultimate catalyst forcing cooperation. The need for provider accountability to purchasers is one market imperative for change within the AHC. Normal market mechanisms always make the seller accountable to the buyer, but the presence of third party payers and purchasers has altered these normal market forces and eliminated provider accountability. By altering the physician's ability to control the stream of revenues, managed care has taken the once autonomous physician and made him or her accountable to the market. Interference in autonomy through imposed practice guidelines and utilization review is a function of providers' past unwillingness to be accountable for the resources they use. Physician accountability assumes that individual physicians determine outcomes, and the question of whether provider accountability and autonomy are mutually exclusive is left to be determined.

Providers assume that, by engaging in risk contracts, they may retain their autonomy while becoming accountable to the consumer. Problems defined in terms of individual physicians, however, often lead to inappropriate solutions. As a result, defining the challenges faced by AHCs as a function of systems as opposed to individuals implicitly alters the culture. Essentially, good people can have bad results depending on the system in which they operate. This was clearly demonstrated in the 1994 cardiac surgery report cards released in New York state.[46] As a result of a poor report card, a system flaw was found and corrected at one hospital in the study. Yet ranking this particular surgeon last implied that the problem was with the individual physician.

As the New York report card indicates, defining the problem in terms of individuals is too simplistic. The assumption of financial risk under capitation by individuals creates accountability for outcomes that may depend on institutional structures or societal issues, such as violence, pollution, life style, diet, alcohol, tobacco, and illicit drug use. By emphasizing the need for group accountability, a common goal is created, and a cultural shift that embraces managed care can begin.

Information Sharing and Outcomes

Response to external pressure for proof of value by purchasers is another market imperative for cooperation within the AHC. Employers want information about value based on measures of cost and quality. AHCs have always claimed superior results. Now they must be able to document these results to justify higher fees for their services. Current information systems perform a billing function and do not provide information about clinical processes and their underlying cost structures. As AHCs assume increased financial risk and the economics of the health care system more resemble those of a commodity market, information about internal cost and process becomes necessary for success. Information systems of the future must combine clinical and financial data to manage process and outcome effectively.[47]

The 1994 report cards released for cardiac surgery in New York once again provide insight into the motivation for cooperation. Because the results suggested problems with individual physicians, purchasers may view report cards as a mechanism to improve care by eliminating poorly performing physicians. The usual argument against the use of such information is that it is not statistically significant for the individual physician and low-volume providers. This fact will not end requests for better outcomes measurements. Although providers will continue to block the release of outcomes data because they fear that the results may be misleading to the public, the marketplace will prevail. Successful integration provides statistically significant samples from which outcomes can be measured. Good results will promote increased market share for providers who are willing to cooperate.

Besides creating valid report cards, linking process to outcomes improves quality and controls costs. There is tremendous variation in the clinical and economic performance of individual providers.[48] Continuous internal evaluation involves separating practice bias and habits from truly effective clinical principles. Ideally, there is a method to promote the best health possible for each individual patient. Medicine, once impervious to standardization because of its complexity, can benefit from application of newer information techniques. The process of identifying best practices is a result of normal industrialization. Although clinical intuition cannot be ignored, a database that knows how 100,000 patients responded to a particular treatment compares favorably with a physician who has seen 100 patients. The initial step toward coordinating efforts at creating clinical pathways and practice protocols depends on elucidation of unexplained clinical variability that increases costs without improving outcomes (see Chapter 19). Information management using clinical pathways can determine the best of a multitude of alternatives. Using these breakthroughs in information technology and statistics, "complex calculations incorporating the clinical variability that physicians have struggled with for centuries" may provide the ability to determine best practices.[49(p.A8)] In the ideal, one clinical approach will be better, more cost effective, and less risky than another. When raw data are transformed into comparative clinical information, the decision process, management structure, and processes of the institution transform as well.

Many MCOs are using information with traditional management techniques that control, instead of improve, processes. Although the technology to examine complex variables in care exists, the information gained is only as good as the data used and the people who interpret them. Real gains in productivity will result from greater provider use of information in managing processes and outcomes rather than standardization and managerial control.[50] Protocols should be viewed as a way of gaining feedback to improve quality. By evaluating the current processes and adjusting practice patterns to align with cost containment and quality goals, overall value can be optimized. Information transforms opinion and clinical bias into the rational weighing of alternatives. Information also shifts control of process to the point of service.

AHCs cannot rely on MCOs for information. Controlling data is strategically important and operationally essential. Fundamentally, it is an important core competence regardless of strategy. There is evidence to show that, as MCOs become more sophisticated with information management, they are less likely to share financial risks and rewards with providers. Since they profit from retaining financial risk and controlling utilization, decapitation occurs because MCOs often choose discounted FFS options over global packaging and capitation.[51,52] Aggressive utilization management with a per diem fee schedule in lieu of capitation allows an MCO to retain the financial benefits of lowered utilization. MCOs may also fear that shifting financial risk to providers eliminates their major function as insurers. Once at risk, providers can obtain their own licenses, bypass MCOs, and contract directly with purchasers. With or without capitation, information management using efficient systems and meticulous records is vital for continuous internal evaluation within the AHC. Academic leaders must stress that technological and information demands have become too complex and require a collaborative framework between the medical staff and hospital administration.

Reinventing Education and Research with New Stakeholders

Because hospitals and medical schools cannot determine the true cost structure for the activities in which they engage, there are vast disagreement as to whether residents are a burden that promotes inefficiency and noncompetitive care or an inexpensive source of highly trained labor that creates a competitive advantage. Clearly, residents enhance productivity after an initial learning period. Residents are less effective as substitutes for primary care, and there is pressure to keep them in the hospital, where low cost and high skill allow a competitive advantage.[53] But is it ethical to train people for jobs that will not exist?

Education must parallel, and prepare students for, the workforce as it is, not as it has been. Because the current trend is toward ambulatory and primary care, physicians must be trained in this way and in these settings. Effective management should lead to improved education. Controlling the desire to use all available technology requires more oversight and teaching on the part of faculty. Although current educational efforts are based on advancement of medical knowledge, future education will include a focus on efficient and effective delivery of quality care.

The introduction of managed care has created divergent needs between academic providers and medical schools. Although alterations in the culture of the AHC may lead to improved financial strength and an improved patient base, the real cost of education and research may place an insurmountable burden on clinical support for these activities. For example, Tulane University sold 80 percent of its hospital to Columbia/HCA Hospital Corporation while continuing to channel its 20 percent share of the profits to support the academic mission.[54] Meeting the challenges created by managed care involves reconciling the academic mission with the demands of the marketplace. In addition, communication of the importance of the academic mission by academic leaders can foster the creation and cultivation of new stakeholders with an interest in the educational and research value provided by the AHC.

The traditional sources for support, namely the clinical activities of the medical center and the federal government, will remain important. Support for medical education has always been provided by the federal government, and in all likelihood this will continue in some form. Although there may be heavy political negotiation regarding the necessary funding of education and research, the focus must shift toward proper allocation of resources. AHCs can gain public support for endeavors that promote the public good, but not as a proxy to continue inefficiencies. Separation of federal subsidies from Medicare payments is in the best interest of the university. As discussed earlier, the current system of indirect and disguised support is inefficient and unreliable. Restructuring funding for education would markedly diminish reliance on indirect GME funding provided through clinical revenues and eliminate unintended subsidies to local MCOs. Ultimately, educational funding should flow directly to the medical school. Continued federal subsidies in any form will require lobbying to promote the true value of the AHC.

Federal action will also be extremely important to help with adverse patient selection, ensuring that hospitals and physicians in the academic setting are properly reimbursed for more complex cases. AHCs, however, must be able to prove that their patient population has greater needs that require additional support. Pressure by AHCs can promote discussions of public policy issues, such as undergraduate and graduate education, research funding, and care for the indigent.[55] Support will come with increased political involvement concerning the use of these funds, however.

Support from clinical operations will also continue, possibly for different reasons than today. Systems that remain fully integrated with the university can only profit from and support the academic mission if education is also fully integrated and adds value to the system. This may be the crux of reinventing education. Academic providers may find that association with the medical school helps recruit and retain top physicians.[56] As a result, the institution will have an opportunity to select and recruit the best and brightest before its competition.

Consolidated tertiary care hospitals will still need and support training of qualified specialists, but the classic tertiary hospital of today will not control the majority of physician training. In response, Harvard Medical School is attempting to bring the academic and managed care cultures together by forming a partnership with the Harvard Community Health Plan. This is the first medical school department to be based in a freestanding HMO, turning the teaching hospital structure into a "teaching HMO" that creates a practice setting for education and research in a managed care environment.[57,58]

Aside from government and clinical subsidies, the most likely stakeholders in the academic mission are MCOs, pharmaceutical manufacturers, and medical device companies. By providing new avenues for income and investment, new stakeholders reduce university reliance on clinical and federal funds. By way of complex joint ventures, universities are already forming relationships with other stakeholders in the academic mission, such as pharmaceutical companies and medical device manufacturers. Collaboration with these new organizations gives industry access to academic experience and resources. For example, Duke University has formed a business unit called the Duke Clinical Research Center. It will compete directly with private companies that perform clinical trials for drug and medical device companies. Other ventures will promote the development of information tools that improve the quality and cost effectiveness of care.[59]

A NEW ROLE FOR MCOs

Few MCOs have formal relationships with AHCs other than through contracts for tertiary services. First, MCOs find that it is difficult to provide the cost-effective care needed to survive under the influence of the needs and culture of teaching hospitals.[60] This is especially true because MCOs seek to limit specialist use while the traditional academic culture encourages its use. Second, university medical centers in urban areas offer few services that are not available in community hospitals and from specialists in private practice.[61] A change in the AHC culture is important to overcome barriers to collaboration with outside MCOs. It is also clear, however, that MCOs will need to embrace the advantages of supporting academic endeavors. As the chief executive officer of a major insurer commented, "We recognize that AHCs have educational costs. We just aren't going to pay for them."[62]

Nevertheless, there are powerful reasons for MCOs to collaborate with AHCs. Simply put, education and research will become more critical in transforming managed care and medicine in the future. The major benefits from managed care have come through macro-management, which has reinvented the financing of health services. The resulting change in financial incentives has promoted a population-based, cost-effective perspective that rests with defining appropriate care. In response, provider organizations are adopting management techniques that were previously only used by insurers.[63] Innovation in the future, however, will increasingly depend on micro-management of the delivery of care. Reports of increasing physician management of care at the clinical level represent a fundamental transformation in the practice of medicine.

Undoubtedly, MCOs and providers will struggle in defining their respective roles in decision making. This is a fundamental conflict between management and labor in highly technical, specialized service industries. Given the importance of knowledge in today's information society, however, the power of implementation ultimately lies with the service provider.[64] The role of capital assets in the delivery of services will continue to diminish. At the same time, labor's inexorable transformation from an expense to an asset requires a dedicated investment.[65]

Consequently, provider education and training are important in creating value for managed care. The quality of primary care graduates is already a concern to MCOs that employ them, and shortages of primary care physicians have been reported as a limiting factor in the growth rates of staff and group models HMOs in particular.[66] An unwillingness to support education could have deleterious long-term effects for MCOs. Without new financial supporters, current educators could dramatically decrease the training of their competition, ultimately raising expenses for MCOs. Partnerships with medical centers will allow greater input into the training needs of a MCO and ensure an adequate supply of well-trained physicians. This is not an abstract concept; as private practices affiliate or merge, the ability of an MCO to purchase practices or to contract with existing groups becomes more dif-

ficult. If an MCO has an established and good relationship with an AHC that is training the types of physicians most attractive to the MCO, then recruiting becomes at least a bit easier.

Next, the growth of managed care has highlighted the need for outcomes research while simultaneously diminishing the funds available. The philosophy of managed care emphasizes appropriate care based on outcomes analysis. Yet (with some exceptions) MCOs do not support research in this area.[67] The fight for survival may provide the impetus for innovative management techniques within successful AHCs. Through association with medical centers, MCOs can benefit from continued improvements that result from systematic research on best practices and outcomes measurements. Furthermore, as MCOs have increasing responsibility for older and sicker populations, they will require further advances in basic and clinical resources.[68,69] Many AHCs have extensive experience with complex cases, Medicare populations, and indigent populations, which are becoming a greater source of revenue for MCOs. The AHC provides a legitimate source for research into health service delivery, with dissemination of literature that influences the definition of medically acceptable and appropriate care.

Examples of support for the academic mission by MCOs appear regularly in many of the rapidly changing local markets. In the area of direct support for education and research, US Healthcare (an open panel or independent practice association model HMO operating primarily in the northeast) has a managed care fellowship at Thomas Jefferson University in Philadelphia. This unique collaboration, one of the few in the country, is designed to train physicians for influential roles in MCOs. In addition, US Healthcare has joined the Jefferson Cancer Center to promote clinical research in health services.

Despite long-term benefits for the support of AHCs by MCOs, fierce price competition may leave little excess revenue for such direct support. The collaboration between Sanus Health Systems, a subsidiary of New York Life Insurance, and Duke University Medical Center goes beyond direct support for the academic mission and transforms the relationship between MCOs and AHCs from contractor and contracted to equal partners. The new health management and benefits company, WellPath Community Health Plans Holdings, splits ownership and decision making between the two organizations. Sanus sees this partnership as an opportunity to take advantage of the excellent relationships already established between the academic medical center and hospitals and physicians in the community. The success of the venture, however, focuses on effective community-based care and is not a mechanism for steering patients to Duke for specialized care. Contracts will be created with other hospitals, including other tertiary care centers.[70] MCOs interested in creative approaches to contracting with AHCs must recognize the importance of shared ownership and decision making with academic centers and providers.

In addition to the above, many MCOs have developed attractive primary care networks and affiliations with community hospitals. An MCO that is newly entering the market or is entering into a new line of business, such as Medicare or Medicaid, may find contracting with the AHC and its network to be an efficient way to get into the market and that negotiating a global capitation (with stop-loss protection) is an equally efficient way to attenuate the risk for health care costs. As AHCs learn more about the management of health care resources, they are ever more willing to accept that level of risk, especially in partnership with an MCO that can provide the kind of data and support necessary for the AHC to succeed.

CONCLUSION

The threat to the traditional financing of the academic mission by the spread of managed care presents many challenges for academic health centers. Still, opportunities exist for improved patient care amid physician doom and gloom. Surely, bright individuals with a stake in this mission can respond to the challenges outlined in this chapter. Physicians appreciate and foster the scientific model. AHCs are positioned to create the "new" science of medical practice, promoting the industrial revolution in medicine. Although altered, the AHC will remain the centerpiece of American medicine.

REFERENCES AND NOTES

1. J.K. Iglehart, Rapid Changes for Academic Medical Centers: Second of Two Parts. *New England Journal of Medicine* 332 (1995): 407–411.

2. J.K. Iglehart, Rapid Changes for Academic Medical Centers: First of Two Parts. *New England Journal of Medicine* 331 (1994): 1391–1395.

3. University Hospital Consortium, Responding to a Dynamic Health Care Marketplace: Implementation Strategies for Academic Health Centers (presented at the University Hospital Consortium 1995 Research Conference, St. Petersburg, Fla., 2–3 February 1995).

4. Office of National Cost Estimates, Health Care Financing Administration, *1991–1992 Hospital Fact Book* (Sacramento, Calif.: California Association of Hospitals and Health Systems, 1992).

5. R.S. Brown, et. al., *Does Managed Care Work for Medicare? An Evaluation of the Medicare Risk Program for HMOs* (Princeton, N.J.: Mathematica Policy Research, Inc., 1993).

6. D.G. Clement, et al., Access and Outcomes of Elderly Patients Enrolled in Managed Care, *Journal of the American Medical Association* 271 (1994): 1487–1492.

7. Managing Medicaid, *American Medical News* (19 December 1994): 11.

8. University Hospital Consortium, Responding to a Dynamic Health Care Marketplace.

9. J.P. Kassirer, Academic Medical Centers under Siege, *New England Journal of Medicine* 331 (1995): 1370–1371.

10. HMOs Are Changing the Face of Medicine, *New York Times* (11 January 1995): A1.

11. U.E. Reinhardt, The Bounty Hunters, *Imaging Economics* (July/August 1995): 9–10.

12. A.J. Slomski, Employers to Doctors: It's Time for REAL Savings, *Medical Economics* (August 1995): 34–48.

13. Reinhardt, The Bounty Hunters.

14. University Hospital Consortium, Responding to a Dynamic Health Care Marketplace.

15. Slomski, Employers to Doctors.

16. Demand Management: A "New" Strategy To Solve Our Health Care Ills, *Managed Care Update* (July 1995): 3–10.

17. Reinhardt, The Bounty Hunters.

18. Managed Care Maelstrom, *American Medical News* (25 July 1994): 1.

19. University Hospital Consortium, Responding to a Dynamic Health Care Marketplace.

20. S. Greenfield, et al., Outcomes of Patients with Hypertension and non–Insulin-Dependent Diabetes Mellitus Treated by Different Systems and Specialties: Results from the Medical Outcomes Study, *Journal of the American Medical Association* 274 (1995): 1436–1474.

21. D.J. Shulkin and A.H. Rosenstein, "Towards Cost-Effective Care," in *The Physicians Guide to Managed Care*, ed. D.B. Nash (Gaithersburg, Md.: Aspen, 1994), 119–159.

22. Clement et al., Access and Outcomes of Elderly Patients Enrolled in Managed Care.

23. Large Study Finds Certain Patients Fare as Well in HMOs as in Insurance Plans, *Wall Street Journal* (8 November 1995): B13.

24. University Hospital Consortium, Responding to a Dynamic Health Care Marketplace.

25. University Hospital Consortium, Responding to a Dynamic Health Care Marketplace.

26. J.K. Iglehart, Academic Medical Centers Enter the Market: The Case of Philadelphia, *New England Journal of Medicine* 333 (1995): 1019–1023.

27. P. Fox and J. Wasserman, Academic Medical Centers and Managed Care: Uneasy Partners, *Health Affairs* 272 (1993): 85–93.

28. K. Pallarito, New York's Academic Medicine Goes Ape, *Modern Healthcare* (28 August 1995): 34–41.

29. S.R. Craig, Practicing Medicine under Capitation: One Group's Experience, *Internist* (May 1995): 8–9.

30. University Hospital Consortium, Responding to a Dynamic Health Care Marketplace.

31. Iglehart, Rapid Changes for Academic Medical Centers: Second of Two Parts.

32. Iglehart, Academic Medical Centers Enter the Market.

33. University Hospital Consortium, Responding to a Dynamic Health Care Marketplace.

34. Employer Groups Rethink Commitment to Big HMOs, *Wall Street Journal* (21 July 1995): B1.

35. University Hospital Consortium, Responding to a Dynamic Health Care Marketplace.

36. Iglehart, Rapid Changes for Academic Medical Centers: Second of Two Parts.

37. Iglehart, Academic Medical Centers Enter the Market.

38. Craig, Practicing Medicine under Capitation.

39. B. Starfield, Is Primary Care Essential?, *Lancet* 344 (1994): 1129–1133.

40. Brown, et al., *Does Managed Care Work for Medicare?*

41. J.E. Billi, et al., Potential Effects of Managed Care on Specialty Practice at a University Medical Center, *New England Journal of Medicine* 333 (1995): 979–983.

42. Iglehart, Academic Medical Centers Enter the Market.

43. University Hospital Consortium, Responding to a Dynamic Health Care Marketplace.

44. J.E. Kralewski, et al., Can Academic Medical Centers Compete in a Managed Care System?, *Academic Medicine* 70 (1995): 867–872.

45. Kralewski, et al., Can Academic Medical Centers Compete in a Managed Care System?

46. Death-Rate Rankings Shake New York Cardiac Surgeons, *The New York Times* (6 September 1995): A1.

47. M. Clare, et. al., Reducing Health Care Delivery Costs Using Clinical Paths: A Case Study on Improving Hospital Profitability, *Journal of Health Care Financing* 21 (1995): 48–58.

48. HMOs Are Changing the Face of Medicine.

49. Medicine's Industrial Revolution, *Wall Street Journal* (21 August 1995): A8.

50. E.J. Proenca, Why Outcomes Management Doesn't (Always) Work: An Organizational Perspective, *Quality Management in Health Care* 3 (1995): 1–9.

51. M. Gold, et al., Behind the Curve: A Critical Assessment of How Little Is Known about Arrangements Between Managed Care Plans and Physicians, *Managed Care Research and Review* 52 (1995): 307–341.

52. University Hospital Consortium, Responding to a Dynamic Health Care Marketplace.

53. Fox and Wasserman, Academic Medical Centers and Managed Care.

54. Academic Centers—and GME—Face Growing Market Pressure, *American Medical News* (18 September 1995): 1.

55. Reinhardt, The Bounty Hunters.

56. Market Changes Hasten Oversupply of Physicians, *American Medical News* (8 August 1994): 1.

57. G.T. Moore, et al., The "Teaching HMO": A New Academic Partner, *Academic Medicine* 69 (1994): 595–600.

58. Managed Care and Academia Join To Build "Teaching HMO's," *ACP Observer*, (April 1995): 1.

59. Getting Down to Business at Duke's Medical School, *Wall Street Journal* (29 August 1995): B1.

60. Fox and Wasserman, Academic Medical Centers and Managed Care.

61. Kralewski, et al., Can Academic Medical Centers Compete in a Managed Care System?

62. University Hospital Consortium, Responding to a Dynamic Health Care Marketplace.

63. E.A. Kerr, et al., Managed Care and Capitation in California: How Do Physicians at Financial Risk Control Their Own Utilization?, *Annals of Internal Medicine* 123 (1995): 500–504.

64. P.F. Drucker, The Coming of the New Organization, *Harvard Business Review* (January/February 1988): 45–53.

65. B.J. Reilly, et al., Traditional Decision-Making Questioned: It's Time for New Thinking for a New Age, *Business Forum* (Winter/Spring 1993): 25–30.

66. Moore, et al., The "Teaching HMO."

67. HMOs Value Research—If Others Pay for It, *American Medical News* (20 November 1995): 1.

68. Academic Centers—and GME—Face Growing Market Pressure.

69. Managed Care and Academia Join To Build "Teaching HMOs."

70. Sanus Offers Multiple-Option Plan with N.C. Academic Medical Center, *Managed Care Outlook* (17 November 1995): 1–3.

SUGGESTED READING

Nash, D.B. 1994. *The Physician's Guide to Managed Care.* Gaitherburg, Md: Aspen Publishers, Inc.

Weitekamp, M.R. and Ziegenfuss, J.T. 1995. Academic Health Centers and HMOs: A Systems Perspective on Collaboration in Training Generalist Physicians and Advancing Mutual Interests. *Academic Medicine* 70(1): S47–S53.

Chapter 16

Managed Care and Community Health Centers

C. David Spencer

Community health centers (CHCs) have been major providers of primary care for medically underserved populations for more than 30 years. Initiated during the 1960s, these community-based centers have often been the sole providers of care for Medicaid recipients as well as for those with neither private insurance nor public subsidy. Most have received grant support from the Bureau of Primary Health Care of the Department of Health and Human Services. There are more than 700 such CHCs, serving an estimated 7.5 million individuals in both rural and urban sites. To receive federal grant funding, they must be located in medically underserved areas, such as inner cities and rural sites. Approximately 30 percent of those served are covered by Medicaid, about 10 percent are covered by Medicare, a small percentage have private insurance, and 40 percent have no coverage at all.

As states' Medicaid funds face financial crisis, they are turning to managed care concepts and contracts to try to stem the tide of rising costs. Through a variety of approaches, including those linked to the so-called waiver stipulations by the Health Care Financing Administra-

tion (HCFA; see Chapter 48), they have launched a substantial initiative in this direction. These two trends—CHCs' long-standing provision of care to the Medicaid population and the uninsured, and managed care's increased involvement in the Medicaid market—have converged on the doorstep of the state house. This chapter presents a brief historical and current description of these trends and their operational implications to facilitate the closer merging of these two health care delivery systems.

BRIEF HISTORY

CHCs

In the 1960s, the federal government provided grants to establish community-based health centers. Initially called neighborhood health centers, these programs were soon expanded to serve both urban and rural populations, including migrant farm workers, and eventually programs were created for health care for the homeless. For simplicity, we will refer to all these as CHCs. A given CHC not infrequently receives a combination of federal, state, and some private grants and therefore has a commitment to serve a combination of designated recipients. Most CHCs are federally qualified health centers (FQHCs). To have this designation, a CHC must fulfill a set of regulatory requirements in regard to both structure and operational performance, including quality standards. By meeting these, CHCs qualify for cost-based reimbursement from Medicaid and Medicare rather than the

C. David Spencer, Ph.D., M.D., has served as a medical director for 8 years in community health centers and 17 years in managed care. He has been a consultant for the Bureau of Primary Health Care of the U.S. Public Health Service and for community health centers, assisting in their preparation for managed care. He is currently Medical Director of Blue Cross/Blue Shield of the National Capitol Area. He is a board-certified internist and is also a surveyor for the National Committee for Quality Assurance.

usual fee-for-service method. These cost-based global fees for provider visits are derived from the HCFA's cost-based methodology. Through this method, a CHC is paid a set global fee for any Medicaid or Medicare visit, regardless of complexity. CHCs are concerned that transition to capitation or health maintenance organizations' (HMOs') discounted fee for service will seriously cut into the revenues needed to support that part of their operations, particularly given the special needs of their populations. Such fears have, in fact, become a reality in some states.

Because CHCs provide care for a substantial number of uninsured, the need for grant funding will continue. Federal funding for these programs has fluctuated over time but over the past 5 years has remained essentially level, despite the increase in demand driven by the continued increase in the number of uninsured. This financial squeeze has led to a significant change in the policy direction toward expanding the population served to include more insured, including members of HMOs (Figure 16–1) and active

participation of CHCs in contracting with state Medicaid managed care arrangements.

Thus CHCs face a major change in their strategy while continuing their mission to ensure care for the traditionally underserved in their geographic areas and communities. The Bureau of Primary Health Care has provided managed care technical support to CHCs.[1-5]

Managed Care and Medicaid

Medicaid contracts are not new to the managed care industry. In the 1980s, some HMOs ventured into the Medicaid arena. A few were successful financially, primarily through effective hospital utilization management. Most HMOs, however, steered away from Medicaid, fearing financial loss from adverse selection. In the early Medicaid–HMO contracting, relatively small populations of Medicaid recipients voluntarily signed up for the HMO option with a capitation contract between the state and the HMO. Some of these early Medicaid-contracted HMOs

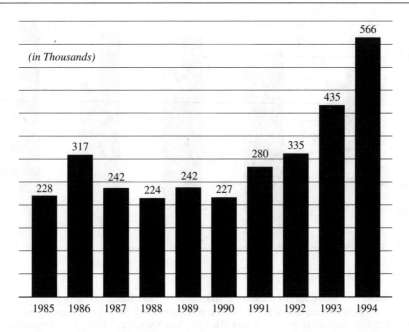

Figure 16–1 Prepaid enrollment in FQHCs, 1985–1994. Data from Bureau of Primary Health Care, U.S. Department of Health and Human Services, Health Resources and Services Administration.

were derived from large urban CHCs. With the current increase in states' turning to managed care, HMOs have been sizing up the Medicaid market, and an increasing number have seen it as an important source of revenue. Figure 16–2 shows this trend.

The more recent experience with managed care in this arena has been varied. Experiences in Tennessee with the statewide TennCare program have pointed out the potential for problems.[6] That program suffered from too rapid an implementation and consequent inadequate planning of both fiscal and operational details. In general, however, it is clear that state legislatures are turning more and more to managed care, and managed care must decide whether and how to meet the challenge of providing care for the Medicaid populations. For more details on the overall Medicaid–managed care history and current status, see Chapter 48. For a detailed dis-

cussion of the waiver programs, see Holahan, et al.[7] and Vladeck.[8]

TYPES OF CONTRACTS INVOLVING MANAGED CARE AND CHCs

A variety of contractual arrangements involving CHCs and managed care have emerged. Each represents the outcome of the many factors unique to a particular state: geography, politics, history regarding managed care, strength and numbers of CHCs, and the direction the state has taken in its effort to control costs. As this chapter is being written, many states had programs that were HCFA approved via 1115 waivers; other states have been able to proceed with substantial initiatives, however, even in the absence of waiver-associated programs. As of the fall of 1995, more than 135 HMOs or other managed care plans have contracts with CHCs. Although

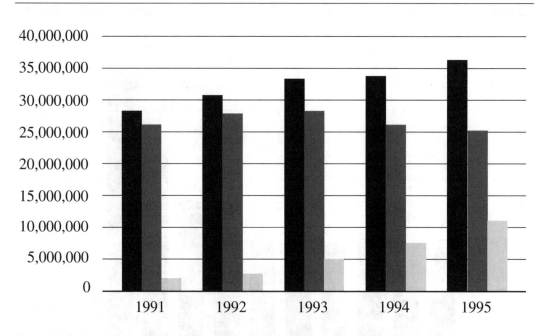

Figure 16–2 Comparison of Medicaid fee for service and managed care. Black bars represent the total Medicaid population, heavily stippled bars represent the fee-for-service population, and lightly stippled bars represent the managed care population. *Source:* Reprinted from Office of Managed Care, HCFA, U.S. Department of Health and Human Services, *Medicaid Managed Care Enrollment Report*, U.S. Government Printing Office, 1995, Baltimore, Maryland.

the number of combinations and permutations of networks and linkages found are too numerous to detail, it is possible to describe four basic types of models as follows.

CHC Contracts with State Medicaid To Provide Case Management as well as Primary Care

These contracts are referred to as primary care case management programs, in which Medicaid recipients are given a choice of a primary care provider. This physician is to serve as the personal physician and gatekeeper. For a per person per month fee, this physician is to provide primary care and to authorize all other services, including specialty, emergency, hospital, or other. These physicians receive, in addition to the case management fee, payment for their direct provision of primary care. For CHCs that are FQHCs, that is in the form of a global visit fee. For CHCs or physicians that do not have the FQHC designation, it is a fee-for-service payment.

In this model, the primary care provider bears no financial risk for referred services, nor is there any financial penalty to the primary care provider for unauthorized services. The state may choose not to pay for the unauthorized care, in which case the specialist or hospital does not get paid. In a few states, primary care providers are given a bonus at the end of the year if the expenses for the state as a whole are under budget. There are no published data indicating whether this case management approach has resulted in either savings to the states or better coordination of care for the recipients. Theoretically, it is unlikely that, without risk sharing on the part of the primary care provider, there is sufficient incentive to result in substantial cost savings. On the other hand, for a CHC in a small rural town, it could be feasible to enhance coordination of care and therefore foster more appropriate use of resources. In a large urban setting, this would be much more difficult.

The case management payment can nevertheless be a useful mechanism to reimburse CHCs for their actual case management practices (e.g.,

coordination of care with institutional providers and local agencies, mental health care, and so forth) and could be added as a "wraparound" to any capitation contract that the CHC is under, be it directly with the state or via an HMO. Such wraparound funding has been enacted in some states. In these instances, where combined with at-risk arrangements, the expenditure to coordinate care for these difficult populations would benefit all parties, including CHCs and HMOs. To be effective, this program requires good referral and hospitalization information and tracking systems. The role of managed care is relevant only if the case management is part of, or an adjunct to, a larger managed care contract.

CHC Subcontracts with a Managed Care Organization To Provide Primary Care and, in Some Instances, a Portion of Other Services as well

This type of contract represents the next step on the continuum of at-risk arrangements for CHCs. Such a contract places the CHC in a contractual agreement with a managed care organization to provide primary care. In general, CHCs seek contracts under which they assume risk for services that they directly manage or control. A variant of this is the provision of some additional services that the CHC arranges with local providers and for which the CHC bears some or all financial responsibility. These may include such services as laboratory, radiology, and some specialty services. If the CHC does include these additional components, they must be defined and include some stop-loss protection or shared risk, particularly if they are major portions with potential high-cost overruns.

It is not infrequent for this contract to be based upon a combination of capitation and negotiated fee for service or discounted charges. That is, the CHC might receive a per member per month payment and in addition be reimbursed on a negotiated fee scale for services rendered. To provide incentive, there may be a percentage withhold, usually in the range of 5 percent to 10 percent of the capitation amount, to be calculated at the end of the year. This withhold usually is partially dependent upon the performance of the CHC in regard to referrals and hospitalization, even if the CHC has not taken on those areas as a full at-risk portion. The HMO may use profiling (see Chapter 27) as a basis for calculating the amount of the withhold to be paid at the end of the year. Because there are many possible variations, it is essential that both the CHC and the HMO be clear about these reimbursements and withholds before signing the contract.

Contracts such as these between CHCs and HMOs may include both Medicaid and commercial HMO enrollees. It will be important to both the CHC and the HMO to have systems adequate to track these populations.

CHC Contracts with State Medicaid for All Services

In this model, the CHC expands to become an HMO. This has been the least common route for CHCs. As of 1995, there were only ten such HMOs. Most were CHCs that expanded and formed satellites, built up contracts with local institutional providers over the years, and eventually became full-service HMOs. They also expanded their population base to serve substantial numbers of commercially insured individuals. Whether all these will continue to exist as separate entities or will merge or be acquired remains to be seen. Most of these HMOs are in a strong position to contract with the state, either alone or as part of a larger network.

CHC Becomes Part of an Integrated Services Network Linked to Other CHCs and Other Providers, Including Hospitals

This model is the one toward which most CHCs are moving, with the encouragement of the Bureau of Primary Health Care. In most instances, the beginnings of a statewide organization of CHC have been initiated by the state primary care organization. The latter organizations exist in most states, providing a forum for CHC administrators and clinicians to solve problems and work on legislative matters. In the past couple of years in a number of states, the primary care organizations have formed separate organizations to contract with the state or with a managed care organization. In some states, these organizations are forming full-service HMOs.

In most states, this process of linkage among CHCs, managed care organizations, and the Medicaid program is still in the planning stages. It is not clear what the future of the waiver programs will be, particularly with the uncertain future of state block grants.

Within the integrated services network model, there are many different types of arrangements. For example, in one urban setting several CHCs have contracted with a local hospital, which in turn has linked with another hospital and with local physicians to form an integrated delivery system. It is this system that will contract with a large HMO contracted with the state. Such a model is able to maintain local coordination of the delivery sites. It avoids the geographic dislocation that occurs when a managed care organization has failed to sign up local specialty providers, resulting in decreased access for Medicaid recipients. In other states, for example those in which there are large rural areas in which the only providers are small CHCs, a statewide CHC network may contract directly with the state for primary care services. As of the fall of 1995, 120 CHCs were participating in a total of 20 operating integrated networks, and more than 300 more were in planning and negotiating stages.

GOALS AND ATTRIBUTES OF CHCs AS CONTRACTORS

CHCs are undergoing a major paradigm shift. Historically, their image was as a service agency driven by a philosophical concern for the medically underserved. Their major financial focus was their grant funding with a minimum of billing activity. Over the past 10 years that has changed as grant funds have decreased and CHCs have moved to expand their patient and revenue base to include a higher proportion of insured. Over the past 4 or 5 years, CHCs have gained increasing experience with patients who are members of commercial HMOs.

CHCs have a number of attributes that make them well suited to continue providing care for Medicaid populations. These are described as follows.

Experience

Their long-standing experience in treating and arranging care for people of low income and differing cultural and ethnic backgrounds has taught them much about how to provide care to these populations. They have established close linkages with local health departments, Medicaid and public assistance offices, local mental health centers, and other agencies to deal with special problems. They are knowledgeable about how to accomplish continuity of care through outreach, education, and systems for follow-up of high risk-individuals. They have provided language translation and transportation and have shown the critical role that these services provide.

Rural Presence

In many rural areas, CHCs are the only providers of primary care. This means that, for Medicaid programs, they are the only link with those recipients. They also are generally organized with multiple delivery sites, often with satellites in the remote areas. See Chapter 50 for additional discussion of rural HMOs.

HMO-Like Attributes

CHCs have always been structured with multidisciplinary teams of providers, with physicians working with nurse practitioners, physician assistants, midwives, social workers, nutritionists, and others in a coordinated team. This can provide a cost-effective and comprehensive approach to care. Studies have shown that CHCs perform as well in regard to utilization and financial performance as other HMO network providers.[9] Many CHCs have been effective sites for training of these providers and have formal linkages with schools of medicine, nursing, and social work and physician assistant training programs.

CHCs are accustomed to working with limited resources. In the past, they were limited strictly by the size of the grant. Salaries have been modest to low. Many have utilized community volunteers to assist in the delivery of services. In many cases, a strong commitment to service has helped in retention of talent.

CHCs are accustomed to working with computer systems. This expertise has been driven by the requirements for reporting, both internally and to funding sources, their activities and finances. More recently, CHCs are expanding their computer capabilities to encompass clinical quality assurance, utilization management, and more sophisticated financial systems, thus preparing for managed care.

Quality assurance programs have always been a required feature of CHCs. In the early years of the 1970s, problem-oriented medical records were instituted in all grant-funded CHCs, and studies have shown high quality of care.[10] Over the succeeding years, clinical quality measures expanded and became a part of the annual grant review by the Bureau of Primary Health Care. The bureau developed, with the input of physicians and other providers, standard sets of measures. These measures are similar to those required by the National Committee for Quality Assurance (NCQA) as standards for HMOs. Over the past 2 years, in some regions CHCs have begun to pool their quality improvement clinical data by means of a shared computer database to measure CHC performance in the aggregate.

Some CHCs have sought and received external accreditation, either from the Joint Commission on Accreditation of Health Care Organizations or from the Association for the Accreditation of Ambulatory Health Care (AAAHC). The Bureau of Primary Health Care provides technical assistance to CHCs as they bring their standards and performance in line with expectations of accrediting organizations (see Chapter 37 for a discussion of accreditation in managed care).

CHCs have always emphasized preventive services and health education based upon the need for special measures, particularly for populations of linguistic, socioeconomic, and cultural diversity. They have carried out these functions as individual health centers, in collaboration with local health departments, and through involvement in school health programs.

Case management and outreach are integral parts of CHC's structure and function. In recent years, CHCs have developed approaches to case management that have included close linkages with case managers in agencies such as welfare departments and community mental health centers. The need for these linkages will continue. In some CHCs the local Medicaid offices have established an on-site eligibility worker. The outreach functions have historically been more common in those programs that are serving migrant farm workers, a population that is not and will not be covered by Medicaid. Nevertheless, outreach is important to HMOs for certain high-risk individuals, such as high-risk pregnant women. Early intervention programs are found increasingly in HMOs that are trying to decrease the incidence and costs of premature births. In fact, two of the Health Plan Employer Data and Information Set (HEDIS) measures focus on improving prenatal care (see Chapter 28 for a discussion of HEDIS).

Perhaps most important is that CHCs have over the years established rapport and continuity of care with their patients, including the Medicaid recipients. This has been true even for times when these individuals lose their eligibility because the CHC has continued to provide their care under its sliding fee schedule program. In some communities, other providers have refused to see Medicaid patients, and in fact they may continue to say no to contracts with Medicaid-contracted entities, including HMOs. This places even more responsibility upon the local CHC to be the provider of care. As long as the state-contracted programs for Medicaid under-

stand the value of a community base, CHCs will be ideally suited for being primary care providers.

GOALS AND ATTRIBUTES OF HMOs AS CONTRACTORS

Managed care organizations are engaged in a highly competitive battle for survival. To compete successfully, HMOs must capture market share, offer competitive premium rates, and provide attributes that are satisfactory to payers (both private and public), providers, and consumers. They must be well capitalized and have financial reserves that meet state regulatory requirements. Over the past several years, demand for quality has increased. The NCQA has become the predominant accrediting organization for HMOs, and the achievement of accreditation has assumed a new level of importance in the industry. In fact, an increasing number of payers are placing importance on NCQA accreditation in their choice of health plans for their employees. Some states have legislated that HMO licensure be contingent upon attaining NCQA accreditation.

Managed care organizations that want to survive know that they must become active participants in state efforts to provide more universal coverage. In the shorter range, the Medicaid-eligible population is a large potential market. All these factors add to the incentive for managed care to enter the Medicaid scene.

From the point of view of state Medicaid agencies, HMOs offer many strengths:

- They have a substantial track record of cost savings. Obviously, the reality is that some HMOs have been effective and responsible in this regard whereas others have not. The rate of increase in premiums has slowed, however, and in some instances the premiums actually have decreased.

- For state Medicaid agencies, the opportunity to shift the financial risk to other entities offers an opportunity to budget for a given year and decrease or eliminate worries about cost overruns. At the same time, such a shift cannot be carried out without adequate reserve requirements.

- HMOs have over the years developed computer information systems capable of dealing with large populations. Currently, most state Medicaid systems have not been adequate to handle the increased requirements of tracking referrals, profiling providers, and dealing with the financial complexities of a managed care approach.

- HMOs provide expertise in managing provider networks with multiple reimbursement systems. Network management requires communication and tracking patterns of care, including quality of records and patient care, referral practices, hospitalization trends, and patient satisfaction.

- Management of large contracts with hospitals and with payers is also part of HMOs' expertise. As integrated systems have increased, they have become more complex, and effective contract management is critical.

- Finally, HMOs have developed methodologies for dealing with the complexities of other processes involved in marketing and enrolling large numbers of groups and individuals and maintaining compliance with the multiple regulatory requirements that exist within health care.

On the other hand, HMOs have some new challenges that they must acknowledge:

- In general, they have had minimal experience dealing with low-income populations. They may not recognize the importance to their business needs of addressing cultural and language differences and the importance of health education. They have had few links with local agencies that serve the poor and can continue to offer support.

- Some states have begun to require that HMOs enroll Medicaid populations. In such situations, HMOs may comply with reluctance and inadequate planning. This can seriously compromise the quality and efficiency of the process of care.

- By virtue of the size of some HMOs, sudden and major dislocations of both patients and providers may occur when contracts change. Furthermore, large HMOs that are not based locally may fail to include local specialists in their network (often because such individuals refuse to sign up) and thereby cause members (both commercial and Medicaid) to travel long distances to receive specialty care. This disruption of community-based care is a concern and must be dealt with prospectively.

- Strong competitive pressures may force HMOs to pay CHCs capitation amounts that are not adequate to cover the range of primary care services currently being provided by those CHCs. In a few states, additional funding is being allotted for the "enabling" services of transportation, language translation, outreach, and case management. In some cases the funding goes directly to the CHCs and in others it may be passed through the HMO.

STEPS THAT CHCs MUST TAKE

CHCs must embark upon a number of steps to develop new paradigms and practices that will sustain their mission in a managed care environment. There must be an understanding that the changes that are occurring are rapid and will force change or extinction. CHCs should consider the following:

- Gain a thorough understanding of the basic concepts of managed care. Although many features of managed care are common to CHCs, an essential change is the fiscal responsibility for care of a defined group of people, some of whom are users (i.e., actually come to the center for care) and some of whom are nonusers (i.e., are enrolled but have not yet received care). This concept of a closed system is the key to managed care and is distinct from the user-driven orientation that CHCs (and traditional fee-for-service providers) have had.

- Achieve an understanding of the local environment in regard to both populations to be served and the role, orientation, and business goals of other individual and institutional providers. Prior linkages have evolved over the years among CHCs, hospitals, specialists, academic centers, and other CHCs. These long-standing collaborations have provided a solid base for formal contracting and the formation of integrated service networks. This process of linking can be confusing because, in most communities, there are multiple contracts and networks among the providers. Such complexities, however, do not preclude the possibility of new linkages that include the CHCs. CHCs should explore the current and possible future roles of managed care organizations in the area and in the state.

- Work with the state primary care association or state association of CHCs to explore statewide or areawide possibilities. This has been successful in several states. Clinicians must be included in these deliberations because clinical issues, such as selection of specialists in the network, are critical features. CHCs must learn in detail what has transpired in other states.

- Look critically at productivity within the CHC. Providers may react negatively to the term *productivity*, but it is an essential ingredient of both fee-for-service and capitation systems. Clinicians must recognize that these are pressured times with limited resources, and both access to care and financial viability depend upon establishing clear productivity goals and adhering to them. In primary care, the unplanned nature of problems presented by patients requires flexibility in scheduling, so that each patient receives adequate time and atten-

tion while overall numbers of visits and/or staffing ratios are maintained. In a capitation system, there must be a combination of optimal visits in a given provider's schedule and the use of a team approach that emphasizes efficient management of a patient's episode of illness and of his or her long-term health care. Productivity issues are also addressed in Chapter 7.

- Develop or obtain computer systems adequate to accomplish the information needs of both grant-funding requirements and managed care operations. In most cases, the new components or modules that will be required will include the following:

  1. enrollment data that ideally interface with eligibility and enrollment data systems at the level of the state or the state-contracted managed care organization, thus allowing regular electronic or tape transfer

  2. a utilization module for tracking referrals, hospitalization, and other out-of-center services

  3. a clinical module for linking diagnoses and procedures with other components to carry out quality improvement programs

  4. modifications of present financial systems to accommodate accounting that are capable of handling a variety of revenue sources (e.g., capitation contracts, fee schedules, and other contractual arrangements). Such systems must include authorization/denial features for proper processing of claims.

- Bring current quality management and improvement programs in line with NCQA standards. Fortunately, current Bureau of Primary Health Care requirements for CHCs take them a long way toward achieving this goal, but there will be additional requirements. Consider working toward and achieving accreditation as a CHC through accreditation by either the Joint Commission or the AAAHC. Some CHCs have accomplished this and feel that it has both improved their quality and given them a stronger position in the market-driven environment. For small centers, this may be an unnecessary step.[11]

• Further develop cost accounting systems in preparation for building a capitation rate (see Chapter 42). Initial per member per month cost estimates are likely to be inaccurate. Until you have tracked a panel of patients over time, you will lack the information that includes costs of members who are enrolled but have not previously appeared for care (i.e., the nonusers). To the extent that the existing Medicaid system in your state can provide utilization data, incorporate them into the estimates. Some CHCs have negotiated a phase-in period of 2 years to allow time for tracking of expenses. Some states have provided additional funding such that the CHC revenues will match calculated FQHC (global fee) reimbursement.

• Look carefully at opportunities for taking on at-risk services beyond primary care. Some CHCs have been successful in developing shared risk subcontracts for other services, such as specialty care, some radiology, laboratory, and in some cases inpatient care, with risk sharing being provided either through commercial insurance or as a provision in their contract with the state or managed care organization. For such shared risk arrangements to succeed, the CHC must have adequate systems for tracking and controlling these outside services.

• Recognize that the managed care model requires close integration of clinical issues in management decisions, and include clinicians in planning and management. The CHC's medical director must provide this clinical input and leadership. Examples of issues requiring medical input are defining which services can be provided directly by the CHC and which require outside contracts and selecting software that can handle clinically related data.

• Develop new approaches for delivering care that emphasize longitudinal rather than episode-focused care. Although CHCs have a long tradition of a team approach, the use of some services has been limited because of nonreimbursement by fee for service. Examples include case management, nutrition, and health education. Under capitation, reimbursement systems change, and inclusion of these services can result in cost savings without decreased revenues for the CHC. This is particularly true for patients with chronic illnesses.

• Learn how to evaluate and negotiate contracts with managed care, including at-risk arrangements, financial payments, liability issues, and credentialing and termination of providers.

STEPS THAT HMOs SHOULD TAKE

Managed care organizations first face a decision as to whether they are going to move into the Medicaid arena and, if so, how. The issues entering into this decision are dealt with elsewhere in this book. Nevertheless, managed care organizations must consider the following factors while determining whether to contract with CHCs:

• Become informed about the existing models and experiences of other HMOs. In this chapter it is not possible to outline fully the many variants of the four basic models. The structures that have emerged have placed the managed care organization in a variety of positions. The best contracts are those in which the strengths of the CHCs in providing needed primary care to the Medicaid population are matched with the capabilities of the HMO in dealing with large systems and providing financial stability.

• Explore the current role and geographic distribution of CHCs in your market area or potential area. The HMO can act as a catalyst for the CHCs to link with each other and with local institutional providers. Are there rural areas in which the CHC is the sole provider?

• Engage in dialogue with the state primary care association as well as the state Medicaid agency to understand potential linkages. Have they formed an integrated services network? What are its strengths and shortcomings?

• Pay attention to local factors in each of the market areas. The best control of utilization and expenses will occur where there is no disruption of local provider networks (e.g., between CHCs and local specialists and hospitals). People of low income will not readily travel to providers outside their area.

• Recognize that current providers of care for Medicaid recipients will need some phase-in time to adjust their systems to capitation. Also, their continued provision of case management and enabling services can save costs in the long run.

• Work with the CHCs to help establish relationships with the community. CHCs represent a valuable resource linked with programs within the community that are low cost or no cost and are important in meeting health care needs with potential decreased cost for the HMO.

• Be sure that the enrollment mechanisms with the state and with other providers are carefully planned and have adequate lead time. When this process is carried out too hastily, major problems can result. For example, in some states Medicaid recipients were given a choice of providers before the providers and HMOs had completed their contracting.

• Bring representation from the CHCs to your advisory committees or boards of directors. As is true in the non-Medicaid arena, the closer the links between the HMO and providers, the greater the chance of success with activities such as clinical guidelines and adherence to utilization and quality programs.

• Establish mechanisms for regular sharing of important data with the CHCs, with opportunities to discuss performance and to highlight strengths and weaknesses.

CONCLUSION

The movement of Medicaid programs to managed care is a difficult task, filled with unexpected potential pitfalls. In this chapter, we have focused on two types of organizations that are currently playing a role in this transition. Each brings strengths and weaknesses to the table. The successful ventures will be the ones that acknowledge these factors and work toward mutually beneficial goals.

REFERENCES AND NOTES

1. R. Abrams, et al., Performance of Community Health Centers under Managed Care, *Journal of Ambulatory Care Management* 18 (1995): 77–88.

2. U.S. General Accounting Office (GAO), *Report to the Chairman, Committee on Labor and Human Resources, U.S. Senate; Community Health Centers: Challenges in Transitioning to Prepaid Managed Care* (Report GAO/HEHS-95-138, May 1995).

3. Bureau of Primary Health Care (BPHC), *The Integrated Service Network Development Initiative; The First Cohort* (Washington, D.C.: BPHC, 1995).

4. National Association of Community Health Centers (NACHC), *America's Health Centers* (Washington, D.C.: NACHC, 1995).

5. Bureau of Primary Health Care (BPHC), *Integrated Service Networks and Federally Qualified Health Centers* (Washington, D.C.: BPHC, 1995).

6. D.M. Mirvis, et al., TennCare—Health System Reform for Tennessee, *Journal of the American Medical Association* 274 (1995): 1235–1241.

7. J. Holahan, et al., Insuring the Poor through Medicaid 1115 Waivers, *Health Affairs* 14 (1995): 200–216.

8. B.C. Vladeck, Medicaid 1115 Demonstrations: Progress through Partnership, *Health Affairs* 14 (1995): 217–220.

9. Abrams, et al., Performance of Community Health Centers.

10. B. Starfield, et al., Costs vs. Quality in Different Types of Primary Care Settings, *Journal of the American Medical Association* 272 (1994): 1903–1908.

11. C.D. Spencer, *Accreditation and Community Health Centers* (National Association of Community Health Center, January, 1996).

SUGGESTED READING

Lewin-VHI/MDS Associates for U.S. Department of Health and Human Services, HRSA, Bureau of Primary Health Care. 1994. *Community Health Centers' Performance Under Managed Care: Executive Summary*. McLean, Va.: U.S. Department of Health and Human Services, Bureau of Primary Health Care/National Clearinghouse of Primary Care Information.

Samuels, M.E. and Shi, L. 1993. *Physician Recruitment and Retention: A Guide for Rural Medical Group Practice*. Englewood, Colo.: Center for Research in Ambulatory Health Care Administration/MGMA.

U.S. Department of Health and Human Services, HRSA, Bureau of Primary Health Care. 1994. *Managed Care Internal Operations Self-Assessment Tool for Federally Qualified Health Centers*. McLean, Va.: U.S. Department of Health and Human Services, Bureau of Primary Health Care/National Clearinghouse of Primary Care Information.

U.S. Department of Health and Human Services, HRSA, Bureau of Primary Health Care. 1994. *Managed Care Market Area Self-Assessment Tool for Federally Qualified Health Centers*. McLean, Va.: U.S. Department of Health and Human Services, Bureau of Primary Health Care/National Clearinghouse of Primary Care Information.

Part III

Medical Management

"You can't always get what you want.
But if you try sometimes
You just might find
You get what you need."

Mick Jagger (1969)

Chapter 17

Managing Basic Medical–Surgical Utilization

Peter R. Kongstvedt

The management of utilization is a critical function of any managed care organization, especially a health maintenance organization (HMO). When one analyzes where the premium dollars go, between 70 percent and 90 percent go into the provision of medical services. While ensuring access and high quality, the fundamental purpose of a managed care plan is to manage utilization, thereby reducing health care costs.

There are many facets to the management of utilization, and these facets are addressed in numerous chapters in this book. As managed care has become more prevalent, the divisions among the management of specialty physician care, inpatient care, outpatient care, and indeed all aspects of health care delivery have become progressively blurred. This chapter will concentrate on basic medical–surgical care. Utilization of primary care services (as well as other professional services) are addressed in the section on demand management. Utilization of specialty services and institutional services is also discussed in later sections of this chapter. The reader is referred to other chapters of the book for discussions of the following:

- large case management (LCM)
- disease management
- long-term and subacute care
- managing utilization of ancillary and emergency services
- changing provider behavior in managed care plans
- clinical pathways

- managed mental health and substance abuse services
- pharmaceutical services in managed care
- quality management
- use of data and reports in medical management

ADMINISTRATIVE COST VERSUS MEDICAL LOSS RATIO

Experienced HMO managers know well that investment in utilization management (UM) is well leveraged in the classic sense of the word leverage. In other words, there is a high rate of return for money spent in this activity in the form of lower health care costs. The degree of leverage will vary from plan to plan, but a recent review of 13 quarters of data on 14 large open panel HMOs performed by an investment analyst confirms this finding.[1]

DEMAND MANAGEMENT*

Demand management refers to activities of a health plan designed to reduce the overall requirement for health care services by members.

---

* The author is indebted to David W. Plocher, M.D., a contributor to three other chapters in this book, for his invaluable work in summarizing the information paraphrased in the demand management section of the chapter.

In addition to helping lower health care costs, these services may provide a competitive advantage to a plan by enhancing the plan's reputation for service and by giving members additional value for their premium dollar. Demand management services fall into five broad categories, which are briefly discussed below.

Nurse Advice Lines

Nurse advice lines provide members with access to advice regarding medical conditions, the need for medical care, health promotion and preventive care, and numerous other advice-related activities. Such advice lines have been in use in closed panel HMOs for many years (where they are occasionally referred to as triage nurse lines). Plans may staff these lines with their own nurses or may purchase the service from any one of a number of commercial services. Hours of operation are almost always extended and may be 24 hours (especially if a plan uses a commercial service). A geographically large plan or a commercial service is likely to use a toll-free line to make it easier for members to access the service.

Special market segments, such as Medicare and Medicaid, may benefit from dedicated programs. Attention to the special problems and concerns of seniors will go a long way to improving their health status and can be a major contributor to the overall management of care in this population. Easy access to medical advice in the Medicaid population may allow these members to avoid a trip to the emergency department.

Self-care programs have been evaluated since the early 1980s with typical results around $2.50 to $3.50 saved for every dollar invested.[2] A fever health education program at Kaiser decreased pediatric clinic utilization by 35 percent for fever visits and 25 percent for all acute visits.[3] In another study, the combination of a 24-hour nurse advice service with a self-care program (see below) resulted in a savings of $4.75 per dollar invested, and the self-care program alone resulted in a savings of $2.40 per dollar invested.[4]

Self-Care and Medical Consumerism Programs

This activity refers to the provision of information to members to allow them to provide care for themselves or to evaluate better when they need to seek care from a professional. Member newsletters with medical advice are used extensively by HMOs. The most common example of a more proactive approach is a self-care guide provided by the plan. These books are generally written in an easy-to-understand manner and provide step-by-step advice for common medical conditions as well as preventive care. Information about the wise use of medical services or how to be an informed consumer would also fall into this category. In one structured study in a staff model HMO, the targeted use of such self-care manuals resulted in decreased outpatient visits and a 2-to-1 return on the cost of the program.[5] Other studies have reported savings of $2.40 to $2.77 per dollar invested.[6]

Shared Decision-Making Programs

This activity refers to making the member an active participant in choosing a course of care. Although this general philosophy may be prevalent in routine interactions between patients and physicians, this activity is more focused. Shared decision-making programs provide great depth of information to patients regarding specific procedures. By receiving this information, patients are able to gain a deeper understanding not only of the disease process but also of the treatment alternatives. Some HMOs that use these programs will not finalize authorization for certain elective procedures (e.g., transurethral resection of the prostate) until the member has completed the shared decision-making program.

A number of commercial services have appeared in the past few years to produce these programs. Many use interactive CD-ROM, videotape, and computer programs to provide the information. Supplemental access to a nurse advice line as well as the ability to discuss the alternatives with the physician after the patient has reviewed the material are also routine.

Medical Informatics

Medical informatics is a broad term that applies to the use of information technology in the management of health care delivery. The broader topics of the use of data in medical management are discussed in Chapter 27. For the purposes of this section, medical informatics refers to the use of information technology in helping manage demand for services. There are two broad categories to be mentioned: the use of informatics by the member, and the use of informatics by the plan.

Use of informatics by the member might include access to an on-line service, such as one that provides health-related information to members. Business-related information as well as electronic mail and communications with the plan may also be available. The plan may do this through a dedicated direct dial-in service, or it may do so through a more public arena; several plans have developed sites on the World Wide Web.

Related to this, many plans have placed kiosks in easily accessible locations. These locations might include on the site of a large employer, in the lobby of the health plan, in a large medical facility, or in a public area such as a shopping mall. The kiosk provides information regarding prevention and certain common medical conditions and may also provide access to business information, such as the types of benefits available.

The plan may use information systems to anticipate demand for services or to analyze how demand for services can be better managed. For example, an analysis of the use of urgent care or emergency services may be related to hours of operation, location of primary care, work patterns at a large employer, and so forth. By looking for patterns, the plan may be able to develop strategies for lowering demand for one type of service by substituting another type of service.

Preventive Services and Health Risk Appraisals

Preventive services are a hallmark of the HMO industry. Common preventive services include immunizations, mammograms, routine physical examinations and health assessments, and counseling regarding behavior that the member can undertake to lower the risk of ill health (e.g., smoking cessation, dietary counseling, stress reduction, and so forth). Counseling and education may also be applied to specific clinical conditions; for example, in one study of a managed indemnity plan, an employer held worksite prenatal education programs and found that participants in the educational programs had an average cost per delivery that was $3,200 less than that for nonparticipants.[7]

The health risk appraisal is a tool designed to elicit information from a member regarding certain activities and behaviors that can influence health status. Self-reported information about obvious behaviors, such as smoking and alcohol use, as well as less obvious behaviors, such as the use (or really lack of use) of seat belts, gun ownership, and so forth, is obtained. That information is then used in a computer program to produce a profile of an individual's health risks and what modifications of behavior may improve that individual's life expectancy. This information is usually also provided to the member's primary care physician (PCP), who will then be in a better position to counsel the member.

In plans that have a large Medicare enrollment, the plan may take extra steps in performing an initial assessment. The most common of these extra activities is an in-home assessment of the new Medicare member. A trained nurse or medical social worker may determine, for example, that if the plan gives the new Medicare enrollee a bath mat or shower chair it will significantly reduce the risk of a hip fracture from falling in the bathtub. An inventory of the member's diet may also yield valuable information that will enable the new member's provider to improve health status by lowering sodium intake or lowering saturated fats in the diet. A review of medications may reveal a compliance problem that, if corrected, could prevent complications from a chronic condition.

SPECIALTY PHYSICIAN UTILIZATION MANAGEMENT

The management of utilization of referral physicians and consultants (both physicians and nonphysicians) is an area of great importance. In most managed health care plans, the costs associated with non–primary care professional services will be substantially greater than the cost of primary care services, often between 1.5 and 2.0 times as high. This is due to the increased fees associated with consultant services and to the hospital-intensive and procedure-oriented nature of those services; in other words, more than half the costs of consultant services may be associated with hospital or procedural cases.

Often overlooked are the associated utilization costs generated by consultants. It is not only the fees of the consultants themselves that add to the cost of care but also the cost of services ordered by consultants, such as diagnostic studies, facility charges for procedures, and so forth. One 1987 study in a non–managed care environment found that each referral from a PCP generated nearly $3,000 in combined hospital charges and professional fees within a 6-month period after the referral.[8] It may be safely assumed that the value of a referral has increased considerably since 1987. These costs are not routinely added to the cost of consultant services when data are compiled, but control of consultant services will often lead to control of these outside services as well.

Definitions

The definition of referral or consultant services includes physician fees that are not considered primary care, in other words all physician fees that are not from general internists, family physicians, and general pediatricians. If you have chosen to include obstetrics and gynecology (OB/GYN) as primary care, then you will need to decide which of the services provided by OB/GYNs (e.g., surgery, routine Pap smears and pelvic examinations, colposcopy, and so forth) are included as primary care and which are consultant care.

In general, most managed care plans count consultant physicians and nonphysician professionals (e.g., psychologists) in the consultant cost category, and ancillary services (e.g., laboratory, radiology, pharmacy, and the like) are dealt with separately. In keeping with that, control of ancillary services utilization is addressed separately in Chapter 21.

Data

To manage consultant services, you must first be able to capture utilization and cost data in an accurate and timely manner. If you do not have that ability, your efforts to control utilization in this category will be severely hampered. The issue of data capture and reporting is discussed further in Chapter 27.

There is no set standard for reporting data on referral utilization as there is for hospital utilization. Nevertheless, certain measures are used frequently and found useful by managers. In HMOs that do not have any benefits for services provided without an authorization from a PCP, a useful measure is referrals per 100 encounters per PCP. In this measure, one counts the total number of referrals made by a PCP for every 100 primary care encounters. This correlates to a referral percentage. For example, 11 referrals per 100 encounters per PCP equals a referral rate of 11 percent.

More commonly used is the referral rate per 1,000 members per year. Like the measurement of hospitalization rate, this looks at an annualized referral rate for every 1,000 members. Although this is less directly related to a PCP encounter than referrals per 100 primary care encounters, the nomenclature is standard across many types of plans.

It is important to know whether you are counting initial referrals or total visits to a referral consultant. In other words, if you are only counting the initial referral or authorization, you may be missing a large portion of the actual utilization. It is not uncommon, especially in loosely controlled systems, for a single referral to generate multiple visits to a consultant. For example, if a PCP refers a member with the request to evaluate and treat, this is carte blanche for the consultant to take over the care of the patient, and succeeding visits will be to the consultant and not to the PCP.

It is therefore far more useful to track actual visits. Better yet is to track both initial referrals and actual visits because that will give you a clearer idea of how the consultants are really handling the cases. In a tightly controlled system, such as an HMO with a strict policy granting authorization for one visit only for any referral, the numbers may be close to being the same. In a system with loose controls, the number of actual visits may exceed the initial referral rate

by two to three times. Specialty visit rates in commercial HMOs average 1.2 encounters per member per year (PMPY), with a range of 0.8 to 1.3 encounters PMPY; visits to medical specialists were slightly higher than for surgical specialists.[9] Figure 17–1 illustrates specialty visit rates in HMOs.

Selection of Referral and Consulting Providers

As mentioned in Chapter 8 and discussed in Chapter 27, the ability to select providers on the basis of a demonstrated pattern of practice can have a considerable impact on referral expenses. There are large differences in the efficiency of practice among providers within each specialty, and if patients are preferentially sent to those consultants and referral specialists who demonstrate cost-effective practice, the plan can achieve considerable savings.

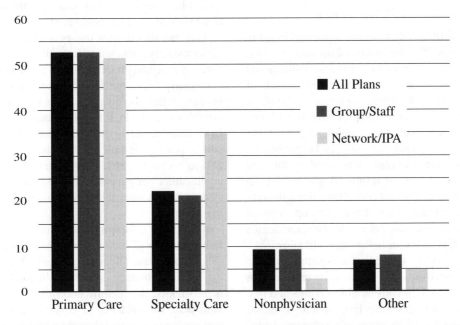

Figure 17–1 Specialty physician visit rates in HMOs as a percentage of total ambulatory encounters. IPA, independent practice association. *Source:* American Association of Health Plans (formerly GHAA/AMCRA) 1992 Utilization Data Supplement to the Eighth Annual HMO Industry Survey, (Washington, D.C.).

This is especially important in plans that allow self-referral to consultants by members, such as preferred provider organizations (PPOs) or point-of-service (POS) plans; see Chapter 3 for a description of these types of plans. If you have a loose system that allows open access to any consultant at any time other than through selection of providers, you can exert little control except perhaps by making fee adjustments after enough documentation of overutilization. The problem with using fee adjustments to control utilization (i.e., adjusting a consultant's, or the entire provider panel's, fees downward as utilization goes up) is that it can lead to an "I'd better get mine first" mentality. In that situation, providers may begin churning visits and increasing utilization to increase revenues, worried that next month the fees may be adjusted even lower. This issue is discussed in Chapter 9.

Evaluating referral practice behavior is no easy task and must be done over a long period of time on a significant number of events. See Chapter 27 for further discussion of this topic.

Authorization System

Authorization systems are discussed in detail in Chapter 29. The utility of an authorization system is mentioned here because without one you have a markedly diminished chance of effectively controlling referral utilization. Through educative techniques, you may be able to decrease consultant utilization somewhat, but unless there is a primary care gatekeeper or case manager system in place, it is not likely that you will achieve optimal results. If you have been able carefully to select consultants through practice pattern analysis, you may get improvement in referral expenses, but not to the same degree that a PCP authorization system will allow.

The corollary to this is the possibility that a PCP can deliver many of the same services as a consultant, but at considerable savings and in a more appropriate setting. Even in non–managed care systems, PCPs manage a substantial proportion of their patients' care.[10] Therefore, the reason for a PCP authorization system to manage consultant costs is twofold: to reduce consultant utilization through services delivered by the PCP, and to manage those referrals that are made.

The remainder of this chapter will assume that there is some type of authorization system in place. That system can be rigid or loose.

Methods To Achieve Tight Control of Specialty Physician Services

Single Visit Authorizations Only

As discussed in Chapter 29, a system that allows only one visit per authorization is necessary for optimal control. There are common exceptions to that, which are listed below. In essence, every time a member is referred to a consultant, the PCP gatekeepers (or care coordinators, or whatever you choose to call them) must issue a unique authorization. That authorization is good for one visit and will only be used to pay one claim. Claims submitted by the consultant with multiple charges will be compared with what was authorized, and only the authorized services will be reimbursed.

This sounds strong in theory, and it is strong. Unfortunately, it is sometimes difficult to enforce. A mechanism for review of claims that do not exactly match the authorization must be put in place so that you do not penalize members and consultants if the PCP fails to document the authorization correctly. It is also sometimes difficult in practice to pull out overcharges or add-ons to a claim, particularly when the claims adjudicators get overworked. Nonetheless, this system is both workable and necessary for optimal control.

It is vital to inform members through full and fair disclosure of such a system before they enroll in your plan. The usual methods of informing members include enrollment literature, new member kits, the identification card issued by your plan, the evidence of coverage certificate that you issue to a member, the referral form itself, the plan newsletter, and even signs in your consultants' offices. Consultants will usually agree to allow signs in their offices when they understand that improving compliance with authorization procedures will enhance their revenue both by speeding up claims processing and by a decreased bad debt load.

After you have informed members, you must periodically reinform them. Most people will not remember everything they hear, even after hearing it multiple times. There will always be some who deny ever knowing about the need for authorization, but you can only do the best you can.

As noted above, there are common exceptions to the rule of one authorization per visit. These include chemotherapy and radiation therapy for cancer, obstetrics, mental health and chemical dependency therapy, physical therapy, and rehabilitation therapy. You may choose other exceptions in your plan. For example, you may automatically allow one or two home health visits after short-stay obstetrics.

Even for these exceptions, however, you should not have open-ended authorizations. There should be an absolute limit on the number of visits that can be authorized at once. For example, you may wish to limit initial mental health referrals to two or three visits and then require the therapist to discuss the case with the PCP or mental health case manager before any further authorizations are allowed (see Chapter 22). Physical therapy should likewise be limited to an initial number of visits, and then the therapist must discuss the case with the physician before any further authorizations are issued. For chemotherapy cases, the oncologist should discuss the case with the PCP and outline the exact course of treatment, which could then be authorized all at once. The overriding principle is that open-ended authorizations are simply blank checks. If you allow them, you will pay the price.

Prohibition of Secondary Referrals and Authorizations

Another facet of controlling referral utilization is the prohibition of secondary referrals by consultants. This means that a consultant cannot authorize additional referrals for a member. In other words, if a consultant feels that a patient needs to see another consultant, that must be communicated back to the PCP, who is the only one able to issue an authorization for services.

This extends to revisits back to the consultant and to testing and procedures as well. For example, if a consultant has an expensive piece of diagnostic equipment in the office, there may be a subtle pressure to use it to make it pay for itself. One widely noted study looking at physician ownership of radiology equipment documented a fourfold increase in imaging examinations as well as significant increases in charges among physicians who used their own equipment compared with physicians who referred such studies to radiologists.[11] Similar results have been reported for laboratory services and a wide variety of ancillary services.[12,13]

The issue of physician-owned diagnostic and therapeutic equipment or services is a difficult one to address and one that is coming under increasing pressure from government regulation, at least for Medicare.[14] Perhaps the best method for dealing with this issue is simply to prohibit or markedly restrict the use of such services. Most managed care plans contract with a limited number of vendors for such ancillary services and may limit referral to only those vendors. The topic of ancillary services is discussed in Chapter 21.

Even in the absence of those types of pressures, secondary referrals may simply be unnecessary. For example, an endocrinologist may be concerned about a referred patient's chest pain and may refer the patient to a cardiologist when in fact the patient's PCP had worked up the problem and was tracking it carefully. This happens more often than one might think because a patient may not always communicate or even understand the previous care he or she has received, and the PCP may not have considered it necessary to put that information into the referral letter or form.

Last, the prohibition on secondary authorizations extends to procedures, including hospitalizations. A consultant must obtain the authorization from the PCP or the plan (depending on the plan's policy about precertification) before any procedures (e.g., colonoscopy) or admission to the hospital. This is not to be punitive but to ensure that such things are done in the most cost-effective manner possible. For example, a referral surgeon may not be aware of the preadmission testing program, may use a noncontracting hospital, or may be used to admitting the patient the day before surgery simply as a convenience. By requiring authorization, such problems can be detected and dealt with easily.

Review of Reasons for Referral

It is the responsibility of the medical director to review the reasons for referral by the PCPs. In the tightest of all systems, this review takes place before the actual referral is made. In other words, the medical director or associate medical director must approve any authorization prospectively. This system is obviously cumbersome and may be seen as demeaning to the PCPs, but it is definitely tight, even if prohibitively expensive. It is perhaps most suitable for a tightly controlled closed panel plan or a training program where interns and residents are involved.

More acceptable is retrospective review of referrals. In this case, the medical director or associate medical director reviews referral forms after the fact, although preferably not long after. Reviews may be of all referrals, which potentially achieves tight control but is unrealistic, or of randomly selected referrals, which will be less tight but still quite useful. More useful is to evaluate PCP referral rates and patterns as well as utilization patterns of referral physicians to determine where retrospective review will have the greatest potential impact.

The preferred vehicle for review is the referral form (or authorization form), which contains the reasons for referral. If the referral form does not contain clinical information, or if referral authorizations are captured electronically, then periodic chart review, similar to a quality assurance audit, needs to be used.

In this review, the medical director is looking at reasons for referral that are inappropriate or poorly thought out. It is surprising how often one encounters reasons for referral such as "Please evaluate and treat." This is a blank check. Another commonly encountered referral is one in which the patient's complaints are simply echoed (e.g., "Patient complains of pain in foot"). In these cases, one is not sure what the referring physician even bothered to do.

A referral should be made after adequate thought and course of action have been taken. The referring PCP should indicate why the patient is being referred, what the PCP thinks the diagnosis is or what he or she is concerned about, what has already been done, and what exactly the PCP wants the consultant to do. By failing to indicate the results of their own work-up or significant findings on the patient's history and physical examination, PCPs make themselves look lazy and make the job of the consultant that much more inefficient.

When the medical director encounters sloppy reasons for referral, it is not necessary to reprimand or embarrass the PCP. It is more appropriate to discuss the case clinically, suggesting options that the PCP may have tried before referring or ways in which the referral could have been more effective. The ultimate goal of these discussions is to foster that type of internal questioning behavior in the PCP so that the medical director will not have to do it. You want each PCP to consider all the options before making a referral and to make referrals count. This often means breaking old habits, but then that is what medical management is about.

Self-Referrals by Members

It is a chronic problem in managed care plans with authorization systems to have members referring themselves to consultants for care. In POS plans that have benefits for self-referral, plan design allows this. In either an HMO or a POS plan, new members who are not used to the system and signed up because of the benefits offered may not recall or note the requirements for authorization and are more apt to self-refer and later be surprised that there is reduced or no coverage for the service.

In these situations, you need to consider your policy on first offenders. Many HMOs will pay for the first self-referral if it is a new member, if the plan recently changed to an authorization system, or if plan managers want to be nice. In such cases the plan documents a warning so that benefits for self-referral may be denied on subsequent occurrences. Most POS plans do not cover any self-referrals at the higher level of benefits, but some will remind the member via their explanation of benefits statement that the benefits would have been higher if the member had obtained authorization.

LCM By Specialty Physicians

Even in HMO or POS plans, there may be times when the plan may wish to have a referral specialist function as a PCP. This would occur when a member has a chronic and high-cost problem that is clearly outside the scope of a PCP's training and practice. In those events, the plan's LCM function becomes proactive in managing the case (see Chapters 18 and 20). As part of the case management, the patient may no longer be the responsibility of a PCP, but care may be coordinated with a specialist who functions as the PCP for that case only. For example, a member with active and aggressive acquired immunodeficiency syndrome may be better cared for by an infectious disease specialist rather than a PCP, although that assumption may not hold in every case. The point is that the plan's LCM function may choose this route on occasion rather than force the PCP to manage catastrophic cases.

Compensation and Financial Incentives for Specialty Physicians

Financial arrangements are discussed in detail in Chapter 12, so only two pertinent issues are reiterated. Capitation is a powerful and effective

tool for controlling consultant utilization but can be a trap if not used wisely. You are urged to review the section on capitation in Chapters 9 and 12 before using it. Simple capitation arrangements alone without proper controls on utilization, such as an authorization system and review of reasons for referral, can lead to serious overutilization unless the referral physician is able to exert strong controls on utilization without managerial controls.

Financial incentives or risk/bonus arrangements for PCPs and contracting consultants can be quite useful, especially incentives for PCPs. As discussed elsewhere, this is not an attempt to bribe a physician but to share the savings of cost-effective practice. Incentives should not be so great as to raise the danger of inappropriate underutilization but should be enough to have a genuine effect.

INSTITUTIONAL UM

Utilization of hospital (or, more accurately, institutional) services usually accounts for 40 percent or more of the total expenses in a managed health care plan. That amount can be even greater when utilization is excessive. Control of these expenses is therefore prominent among most managers' priorities.

The expense of any medical service is a product of the price of that service times the volume of services delivered. Pricing for institutional services is discussed in Chapter 14; this chapter focuses on managing the volume of institutional services. Simple reduction of bed days may be of value but can lull the inexperienced manager into a sense of complacency. Control of institutional utilization is therefore to be understood in context with control of other areas of utilization as well.

Measurements

Definition of the Numbers

First, you must choose exactly what you will measure and how you will define that measurement. It is common for most plans to measure bed days per 1,000 plan members per year (a formula to calculate this is given below). Deciding what to count as a bed day is not always straightforward, however.

In some plans, outpatient surgery will be counted as a single day in the hospital. This is done on the assumption that an outpatient procedure will cost the plan nearly the same as or sometimes more than a single inpatient day. Some plans count skilled nursing home days in the total, and some add commercial, Medicare, Medicaid, and fee for service into the total calculation. In some plans the day of discharge is counted; in most it is not (unless it is charged for by the hospital). Whether to count nursery days in the total when the mother is still in the hospital or only if the newborn is boarding over or in intensive care also needs to be decided.

As a general rule of thumb, most plans count commercial days separately from any other days, especially Medicare days. If you have a significant Medicaid population, you may wish to track it both separately and together with commercial. Most plans do not count outpatient surgery as an inpatient day but report out that number separately; likewise, most plans report skilled nursing days separately.

How to count nursery days is a difficult decision. If you use the assumption that skilled nursing days are not counted as hospital days because the cost is so much less, the same assumption may be made for nursery days while the mother is in the hospital. In most hospitals, the nursery charges for a normal newborn are relatively low. If the newborn requires a stay beyond the mother's discharge, the charges usually are higher. If the neonate is in the intensive care unit, charges will obviously be quite high. If you have negotiated an all-inclusive per diem rate or a case rate that takes normal nursery days into account while the mother is in the hospital, you may have no need to count them separately. If you must pay a high rate for nursery, you will probably want nursery days counted in the total. Many plans separate obstetric days from medical–surgical days and report on each. The same issue may apply to mental health days.

Further discussion about utilization reports can be found in Chapter 27.

Formulas To Calculate Institutional Utilization

The standard formula to calculate bed days per 1,000 members per year is relatively straightforward. You may use it to calculate the annualized bed days per 1,000 members for any time period you choose (e.g., for the day, the month to date, the year to date, and so forth).

When calculating bed days per 1,000, use the assumption of a 365-day year as opposed to a 12-month year to prevent variations that are due solely to the length of the month. The formula is as follows:

$$[A \div (B \div 365)] \div (C \div 1,000)$$

where A is gross bed days per time unit, B is days per time unit, and C is plan membership.

This may be broken into steps. Exhibit 17–1 illustrates the calculation for bed days per 1,000 on a single day; Exhibit 17–2 illustrates the calculation for bed days per 1,000 for the month to date.

Expected Utilization and Variations

Inpatient utilization is almost always lower in HMOs than in any other type of health plans. Table 17–1 provides examples of utilization data under a variety of different options. Note that the data in Table 17–1 are for 1993, the most recent year available for analysis at the time of this writing. Utilization figures in some parts of the country are at least 20 percent lower than those illustrated in Table 17–1, even in 1995.

There are two common reasons for variations in hospital utilization rates across the country. One reason is easily understood; the other is not. Easily understood is the relationship between how tight the UM program you have is and its results. The tighter you make the program, and the more actual medical management is going on, the lower your utilization numbers will be. Conversely, if you choose for various reasons not to enforce a UM program stringently (e.g.,

Exhibit 17–1 Example of Bed Days for a Single Day

Assume:	Current hospital census = 10 Plan membership = 12,000
Step 1:	Gross days $= 10 \div (1 \div 365)$ $= 10 \div 0.00274$ $= 3,649.635$
Step 2:	Days per 1,000 = 3,649.635 ÷ (12,000 ÷ 1,000) $= 3,649.635 \div 12$ $= 304$ (rounded)

Therefore, the days per 1,000 for that single day equals 304.

Exhibit 17–2 Example of Bed Days for the Month to Date (MTD)

Assume:	Total gross hospital bed days in MTD = 300 Plan membership = 12,000 Days in MTD = 21
Step 1:	Gross days MTD $= 300 \div (21 \div 365)$ $= 300 \div 0.0575$ $= 5,217.4$
Step 2:	Days per 1,000 in MTD $= 5,217.4 \div$ (12,000 ÷ 1,000) $= 5,217.4 \div 12$ $= 435$

Therefore, the days per 1,000 for the MTD equals 435.

you may not be marketing a tight system), you will have proportionate increases in the hospitalization rate.

Less easily understood are the profound geographic variations in inpatient utilization. Rates of utilization on the east coast are consistently and significantly higher than those on the west coast.[15] In fact, there are geographic variations in utilization in cities of similar size that are not terribly far apart and even significant geographic variations in a single metropolitan service area[16–20] (Blue Cross/Blue Shield of the National Capitol Area, unpublished data). There is no rational explanation for this from the standpoint of the patients. The answer must lie with the practice habits of physicians in different areas. At the very least, this perplexing disparity based on geography points out that significant improvement in utilization may be achieved, especially in the eastern United States.

Despite low utilization in HMOs and other forms of managed care plans, there are researchers who strongly believe that there remains a significant amount of unnecessary utilization even now. The most aggressive of these opinions is found in a report by Milliman & Robertson, in which the authors state that almost 60 percent of inpatient utilization is unnecessary.[21] Table 17–2, adapted from that report, lists "optimally managed" admits per 1,000 and days per 1,000 for commercial and Medicare enrollees.

Reimbursement of Hospitals and Financial Incentives

Financial incentives are important tools for helping manage hospital utilization. This topic is addressed in Chapters 7, 9, and 12, and the reader is referred to those chapters.

Common Methods for Decreasing Utilization

Control of institutional utilization may be best presented by discussing the key categories for managing the process: prospective, concurrent, and retrospective review and LCM (i.e., catastrophic case management). Prospective review means that the case is reviewed before it happens, concurrent review means that review occurs while the case is active, and retrospective review occurs after the case is finished. LCM refers to managing cases that are expected to result in large costs to provide coordination of care that results in both proper care and cost savings.

Prospective Review

Precertification. Precertification refers to a requirement on the part of the admitting physi-

Table 17–1 Hospital Utilization Rates, 1993

	Commercial			Medicare			Medicaid		
Type of Plan	BD/K	Discharges/K	ALOS	BD/K	Discharges/K	ALOS	BD/K	Discharges/K	ALOS
Indemnity									
and HMO	273.1	61.2	4.46	2474	309	8.0	930.1	165.4	5.62
HMO (all plan									
types)	242.2	66.3	3.8	1526	224.5	7.0	568	132.1	3.8
Staff	251.5	71.1	3.7	1501	209.6	7.0	439	124.9	3.5
Group	242.0	67.0	3.6				N/A	N/A	N/A
Network	197.5	58.9	3.6	1565	228.3	N/A	480	122.0	3.6
Independent									
practice									
association	262.9	68.6	4.0				603	142.7	3.7

Note: Indemnity and HMO data cannot be accurately separated. Indemnity and HMO data combined exclude Medicare, Medicaid, workers' compensation, government pay, uninsured, nonpay, and no charge. Indemnity-only utilization is estimated to be approximately 20 percent higher than noted for commercial. For Medicare, staff and group figures are combined, and network and independent practice association numbers are combined.

Abbreviations: BD/K, bed days per 1,000; discharges/K, discharges per 1,000; ALOS, average length of stay.

Source: Courtesy of Ernst & Young LLP, Washington, D.C.

Table 17–2 Optimal Utilization Levels, July 1, 1993

	Commercial Optimally Managed		Medicare Optimally Managed	
Category of Service	Admits per 1,000	Days per 1,000	Admits per 1,000	Days per 1,000
Inpatient Hospital				
Nonmaternity				
Medical	21.24	72.99	132.66	598.27
Surgical	15.23	57.50	66.22	404.48
Psychiatric	2.00	13.78	1.51	14.65
Alcohol/drug	0.70	4.05	0.61	3.97
SNF/ECF	0.50	4.00	32.50	544.10
Maternity				
Mother	15.50	26.14	0.00	0.00
Well newborn		26.14	0.00	0.00
Nondelivery	2.75	5.64	0.00	0.00
Grand Total (excluding SNF/ECF)	57.42	180.10	201.00	1,021.37
Grand Total (including SNF/ECF)	57.92	184.10	233.50	1,565.47

Abbreviations: SNF, skilled nursing facility; ECF, extended care facility.

Source: Courtesy of Milliman & Robertson, Inc., Brookfield, Wisconsin.

cian (and often the hospital) to notify the plan before a member is admitted for inpatient care or an outpatient procedure. There is a widespread and rather erroneous belief that the primary role of precertification is to prevent unnecessary cases from occurring. Although that may occasionally happen (particularly in workers' compensation cases, see Chapter 53), it is not the chief reason for precertification.

There are three primary reasons for precertification. The first is to notify the concurrent review system that a case will be occurring. In that way, the UM system will be able to prepare discharge planning (discussed below) ahead of time as well as look for the case during concurrent review rounds. In some instances, the LCM function (see below) may be notified if the admission diagnosis raises the possibility that it will be a highly expensive case (e.g., a bone marrow transplant).

The second major reason for precertification is to ensure that care takes place in the most appropriate setting. Perhaps an inpatient case is diverted to the outpatient department, or a case is diverted from a nonparticipating hospital to a participating one or to a facility that has been designated as a center of excellence for a selected procedure.

The third reason is to capture data for financial accruals. Although it is unlikely that a plan can capture every case before or while it is taking place, a mature plan that is running well can capture the vast majority of cases, perhaps 90 percent to 95 percent. By knowing the number and nature of hospital cases as well as potential catastrophic cases, the plan can more accurately accrue for expenses rather than have to wait for claims to come in. This allows management to take action early and to avoid nasty financial surprises. Accrual methodology is discussed in Chapter 40.

In any case, for inpatient cases the plan usually assigns a length of stay guideline at the time the admission is certified. This topic of length of stay is discussed below. The plan may also use the precertification process to verify eligibility of coverage for the member, although most

plans have a disclaimer stating that ultimate eligibility for coverage will be determined at the time the claim is processed.

In the case of an emergency or urgent admission, it is obviously not possible to obtain precertification. In that event, there is usually a contractual requirement to notify the plan by the next business day or within 24 hours if the plan has 24-hour UM staffing. Most plans have contractual language with both the physicians and the hospitals imposing financial penalties (e.g., a percentage of their fee or a flat penalty) for failure to obtain certification. For plans that allow members to seek care from noncontracted providers (e.g., in POS plans), the responsibility to contact the plan rests with the members if they choose not to see a network physician; in such cases, most plans impose benefits penalties (e.g., a higher coinsurance or a flat penalty rate) on a member who fails to obtain proper precertification.

Preadmission testing and same day surgery. One of the easiest, and also one of the most common, methods for cost control is preadmission testing and same day surgery. A member who is going to be hospitalized on an elective basis has routine preoperative tests done as an outpatient and is admitted the same day the surgery is to be performed. Both these policies are confirmed at the time of precertification.

For example, a member has elective gallbladder surgery scheduled for 10:00 A.M. on Thursday. On Tuesday the member goes to the hospital for the preoperative tests. The results are made available to the admitting physician, who performs the admission history and physical as an outpatient and either delivers the results to the hospital or calls them in on an outside line to the hospital's transcription department. The member arrives at the hospital at 6:00 A.M. on Thursday, is admitted, and has surgery as scheduled.

In many health plans, the plan has made arrangements for laboratory work to be done with a contracted laboratory at reduced rates or will have in-house capabilities to perform the laboratory work. Occasionally, a hospital will refuse to accept the results of these laboratories. If the laboratory is accredited and licensed, the hospital has little grounds to require you to use its laboratory, electrocardiography, and radiology services for preoperative admission testing. In these cases it falls to the plan's management team to discuss this with the hospital administrator and negotiate an agreement for the hospital to accept your laboratory work or to agree to perform the work at equivalent costs to you. If the hospital refuses to cooperate, you need to decide whether you want to direct the elective cases to another, more cooperative hospital.

Mandatory outpatient surgery. It has become popular for health plans to produce mandatory outpatient surgery lists. These are essentially lists of procedures that may only be performed on an outpatient basis unless prior approval is obtained from the plan medical director. This is used by so many third party payers that you do not need to make one from scratch if you do not wish to; simply look at what other similar plans (or even Medicare) are using. One byproduct of this popularity is that no two lists are identical, which causes some confusion with physicians and hospitals. Although there is consensus on many common procedures (e.g., a carpal tunnel release), there are always procedures that are migrating from inpatient to outpatient (e.g., at the time of this writing, outpatient cardiac catheterization had become popular only in the last few years).

As mentioned earlier in this chapter and elsewhere, be sure that you will actually achieve the desired savings before instituting mandatory outpatient surgery requirements. In some cases, hospitals or freestanding outpatient surgery facilities have charges that are equal to or greater than those for an inpatient day. In other cases, the facility charge may be lower, but the unbundled charges for anesthesia, recovery, supplies, and so on can drive the cost higher than anticipated. These issues are discussed in Chapter 14.

Concurrent Review

Concurrent review means managing utilization during the course of a hospitalization (as opposed to an outpatient procedure). Common techniques for concurrent review involve assignment and tracking of length of stay, review and rounding by UM nurses, and discharge planning. The roles of the medical director, the PCP, and the attending or consulting physicians are discussed later in this chapter, as is the relationship between concurrent review and LCM.

Assignment of length of stay. A common approach to hospital utilization control is the assignment of a maximum allowable length of stay (MaxLOS), which sometimes appears in the guise of an estimated length of stay, but with teeth. With the MaxLOS, the plan assigns a length of stay on the basis of the admission diagnosis, and that is all the plan will authorize for payment. For example, an admission for a routine surgical admission may be assigned 3 days. It is assumed that the patient will be admitted on the day of surgery and will go home 3 days later. Any stay beyond that day is not covered. In those plans that cannot or will not restrict payment, the MaxLOS is used only to trigger greater involvement by the medical director.

The MaxLOS is determined by International Classification of Diseases, Ninth Revision, Clinical Modification code, or diagnostic code, although diagnosis-related groups (DRGs) are similar in concept. Selecting a norm for the MaxLOS is not always easy given regional variations. Looking at the local fee-for-service experience may or may not be helpful, depending on your area's history in achieving good control of utilization. If you have no other source, a number of organizations and companies sell such data, and American Association of Health Plans publishes data on a few selected procedures.

The advantage of using MaxLOS designations is threefold. First, it allows you to cover a relatively large geographic area with few personnel, which may be necessary in a new start-up open panel plan. Second, such a list has the power of legitimacy and does not require that you negotiate every time. Third, it is relatively mechanical and requires less training of plan personnel. This last may be true for the person issuing the MaxLOS designation, but it is still important to verify, usually through the UM nurse, that the diagnosis is accurate.

The problem with using MaxLOS designations is also threefold. First, it is easy to get complacent. If you choose certain values for MaxLOS designations, you may fail to evaluate continually whether those are in fact the correct values. Second, designated time becomes free time. In other words, there is less incentive to evaluate critically every day in the hospital for appropriateness and alternatives if plan personnel and the physician feel that there is still time on the meter. Third, using such a mechanical system often achieves less than optimal results. Intensive medical management by qualified personnel should produce better control of utilization, but such personnel are not always available. The topic of concurrent review against criteria is discussed below.

You must also know what the consequences of exceeding the MaxLOS will be. In many plans, exceeding the MaxLOS results in either a denial of payment for services rendered after the MaxLOS has been reached or a reduction in payment, usually by a percentage amount. If you have failed to inform your membership of a MaxLOS program and you do not have sole source of payment clauses with your providers and hospitals (see Chapter 55), you may not be able to enforce a MaxLOS designation easily.

Role of the UM nurse. The one individual who is crucial to the success of a managed care program is the UM nurse. It is the UM nurse who will be the eyes and ears of the medical management department, who will generally coordinate the discharge planning, and who will facilitate all the activities of utilization control.

Staffing levels for UM nurses will vary depending on the size of the geographic area, the number of hospitals, the size of the plan, and the intensity with which UM will be performed (e.g., by on-site hospital rounding). It is common for plans to staff one UM nurse for every 6,000 to 8,000 members, assuming that the UM nurses will be making rounds on all hospitalized pa-

tients and that utilization is reasonably tightly controlled, but not on a 24-hour basis. Staffing ratios have considerable variation, however, with one study reporting the average number of full-time nurse reviewers at 0.16 per 1,000 enrollees, with a range of 0.01 to 0.8 per 1,000.[22] Plans that perform telephone review only may staff at ratios that are half the average. It is also necessary to provide clerical support to do intake, to follow up on discharge planning needs, to take care of filing, and so forth.

The scope of responsibilities of the UM nurse will vary depending on the plan and the personalities and skills of the other members of the medical management team. In some plans, the role simply involves telephone information gathering. In other plans, there will be a more proactive role, including frequent communication with attending physicians, the medical director, the hospitals, and the hospitalized members and their families; discharge planning and facilitation; and a host of other activities, including active hospital rounding.

The one fundamental function of the UM nurse is information gathering. Information about hospital cases must be obtained in an accurate and timely fashion. It falls to the UM nurse to be the focal point of this information and to ensure that it is obtained and communicated to the necessary individuals in medical management and the claims department.

Necessary information includes admission date and diagnosis, the type of hospital service to which the patient was admitted (e.g., medical, surgical, maternity, and so forth), the admitting physician, consultants, planned procedures (type and timing), expected discharge date, needed discharge planning, and any other pertinent information the plan managers may need.

In some plans, information gathering is done strictly by telephone; in other plans, hospital rounding is done in person by the UM nurse. When the telephone is used, it is used first to check with the admitting office to determine whether any plan members were admitted and then to check with the hospital's own UM department to obtain any further information.

Telephone rounding is usually done in cases where there is too much geographic area to cover and the plan cannot yet justify adding more UM nurses (e.g., in a start-up individual provider association or PPO covering five counties). It may also be done in those instances where a hospital refuses to give the UM nurse rounding privileges on hospitalized plan members. There are certain instances where a plan may in fact delegate rounding and review to the hospital's UM department, but those are rare; examples include arrangements where the hospital is at significant financial risk (e.g., through capitation or DRGs, or when an IDS has accepted global capitation [see Chapter 4]). The other time telephone rounding is used is when there are not tight controls on utilization, and the function is one of looking for clear outliers rather than trying to achieve optimal utilization control.

Rounding in person is far superior to telephone rounding. When rounds are conducted daily by a UM nurse on every hospitalized member, you will obtain the most accurate and timely information, and you will obtain information that you might not get otherwise.

For example, in a good quality management program (see Chapter 25), the rounding UM nurse will be able to watch for quality problems or significant events that would trigger a quality assurance audit. A rounding nurse will also be able to pick up information about a patient's condition that may affect discharge planning, information that the attending physician may have failed to communicate (e.g., the need for home durable equipment that must be ordered).

The UM nurse may also be able to detect practice behavior that increases utilization simply for the convenience of the physician or hospital. For example, a patient may be ready for discharge but the physician missed making rounds that morning and will not be back until the next day, or the hospital rescheduled surgery for its own reasons and the patient will have to spend an extra and unnecessary day. In situations such as these, the UM nurse must not be put into an adversarial position but should refer such cases to the medical director.

Personal rounding by the plan's UM nurse has the added advantage of increasing member satisfaction. Many people feel uncomfortable talking to physicians and welcome the chance to express their fears or feelings to the UM nurse. In other cases, inquiring about how members are feeling can let them know that you care about them as people and that you are not simply trying to get them out as fast as you can.

In the situation where a hospital refuses to grant rounding privileges to the UM nurse (an increasingly uncommon occurrence), a frequent excuse is that there is already a UM department in the hospital. That is usually not adequate for your needs and does not address the specific member satisfaction and quality assurance needs of your plan. Another frequent excuse is protecting the confidentiality of the patients. That does not hold if the plan's UM nurse is only rounding on plan members (who have agreed in their application to allow access to records). If a hospital refuses to cooperate with you on allowing the plan's UM nurse to round, you must seriously question your willingness to do business with that hospital. In most cases, a hospital will cooperate fully and willingly.

The heart of concurrent review is the evaluation of each hospital case against established criteria. Many plans, especially open panel plans and PPOs, use published or commercially available criteria for such reviews to facilitate evaluation by the UM nurses.[23-26] Experienced nurses use such criteria as an aid in managing utilization, but they do not blindly depend on them. It is possible to keep a patient in the hospital for less than adequate reasons but still meet criteria; the seasoned UM nurse is able to evaluate each case on its merits.

Most plans have now automated this function to improve the efficiency of the UM nurses. Software allows the MaxLOS to be generated automatically from the admission diagnosis or procedure. Member and benefit eligibility is checked, diagnostic and procedure codes are generated from entered text, review criteria are automatically displayed for both admission and concurrent review, unlimited text may be entered to allow tracking, census reports are produced, statistics are generated, and so forth. UM software also links to the claims system so that claims are properly processed, including special instructions from the nurses.

Good discharge planning starts as soon as a patient is admitted into the hospital, or even before. The physician and the UM nurse should be considering discharge planning as part of the overall treatment plan from the outset. This planning includes an estimate of how long the patient will be in the hospital, what the expected outcome will be, whether there will be any special requirements on discharge, and what needs to be facilitated early on.

For example, if a patient is admitted with a fractured hip and it is known from the outset that many weeks of rehabilitation will be necessary, it is helpful to contact the facility where the rehabilitation will take place to ensure that a bed will be available at the time of transfer. If it is known that a patient will need durable medical equipment, the equipment should be ordered early so that the patient does not spend extra days in the hospital waiting for it to arrive.

An often overlooked aspect of discharge planning is informing the patient and family. If the patient and family do not know what to expect, they may be surprised when the physician tells them that the patient is being discharged. This is especially true if the patient has received hospital care in the past and has certain expectations. Informing the patient and family from the start about when they can expect discharge, how the patient will be feeling, what they might need to prepare for at home, and how follow-up will occur will all help smooth things considerably.

In the case of short-stay obstetrics, if the patient and family are not prepared for the homecoming, there may be tremendous pressure on the physician to keep the mother and child in the hospital so that everyone can get a little more rest. Unfortunately, the hospital is far too expensive for that. Active discharge planning for short-stay obstetrics is crucial. If your plan offers a home health visit to mothers who have had a short-stay delivery, that should be confirmed on admission.

Discharge planning is an ongoing effort beginning with admission or preadmission screening. The UM nurse is in the ideal position to coordinate discharge planning. In addition to making sure that all goes smoothly to effect a smooth and proper discharge from the hospital, the UM nurse can follow up with the member by telephone after discharge to ensure that all is well.

PCP model. There are two basic models for managing hospital cases: the PCP model and the attending physician model. In the PCP model, the PCPs are expected to manage the care of their patients in the hospital even when patients are hospitalized for care delivered primarily by consultants or specialists; most commonly this occurs either when the patient is hospitalized for surgery or when the patient has a drawn-out course of treatment (e.g., recovery from a stroke). In the PCP model, the most important functions of the member's PCP are also the most obvious: to make rounds every day and to coordinate the patient's care.

In the first cited instance, care from a consultant, it is all the more important for the PCP to round daily. This serves a number of purposes. First, it helps ensure continuity of care while the patient is in the hospital (e.g., the PCP may be able to add pertinent clinical information as needed). Second, it provides a comforting presence for the patient, a presence that results not only in better bonding between physician and patient but in providing emotional support. Third, it allows for continuity after discharge because the PCP is aware of the clinical course and discharge planning. Fourth, it helps control unnecessary utilization.

Utilization control by the PCP is highly effective in the setting of a member receiving hospital care from a consultant. The PCP is able to discuss the case with the consultant and suggest ways to decrease the length of stay (e.g., home nursing care) that the consultant is not used to considering. The PCP will presumably know the patient well enough to determine the patient's ability to do well in alternative situations.

The PCP will also be able to communicate effectively with a consultant in the event that the consultant failed to see the patient on rounds. For example, if a busy surgeon misses a patient on rounds because the patient was in the bathroom, the surgeon, because of a heavy operating room schedule, may not make it back to see that patient until late at night. If the patient is actually ready for discharge, the PCP can communicate with the surgeon that morning and arrange for discharge.

There will be situations where the PCP is unable to make rounds in person. This happens most frequently when a member is admitted to a tertiary hospital where the PCP does not have privileges. For example, cardiac bypass surgery may be done at a teaching hospital with a closed medical staff. In these situations, it is important for the PCP to be in frequent telephone contact with the attending physician on the case to keep up with developments and to aid in the discharge planning process. For example, the PCP may be comfortable in accepting the patient back in transfer during the recovery period or may be able to suggest home nursing care. In addition to controlling utilization, this helps ensure continuity of care, and the attending physician will almost always remark to the patient about how attentive the PCP has been about the case.

Equally important to good medical management is for the PCP to avoid the trap of "That's the way it's always been done and it's good enough for me!" The PCP has responsibility not only over the physical health of the member but over the financial health of the plan as well. The PCP must be open to evaluating new methods of treatment and to considering high-quality but cost-effective ways of caring for people.

As a corollary, PCPs must be confident and assertive about their own abilities. It is an unfortunate byproduct of the highly specialized nature of medicine that there are times when a PCP is looked down upon by a consultant. Certainly a consultant who depends on the PCP for referrals will not knowingly exhibit behavior that the PCP

will find offensive, but there often remains an unspoken agreement that the consultant will call the shots once the patient is admitted.

There are a number of objections that a PCP may raise concerning getting involved with patients admitted to a consultant's service. First, the PCP may feel intimidated by the consultant's knowledge about the medical problem. When this happens, there is no reason why the PCP cannot read up on the subject, at least in a major medical text, and ask questions. Also, it is the PCP's patient, and the consultant is a consultant. It is the role and responsibility of the PCP to follow the care of the patient and to be aware of the medical issues involved. The simple act of asking the consultant questions about that care is appropriate and necessary and will frequently result in improved understanding by all parties as well as improved utilization control.

There is the possibility that the PCP will view such questioning as confrontational and will be unwilling to question the competence of the consultant. It is important to point out that the PCP is not questioning the consultant's competence (assuming that the consultant is indeed competent) but rather is discussing the case and asking the consultant his or her opinion about alternatives. The fear of such confrontations is far greater than the reality. The PCP has nothing to be shy about; PCPs are trained physicians specializing in primary care, and the consultant is helping care for the PCP's patient, not vice versa.

Specialist physician responsibilities. Even in a PCP model the consultant has responsibilities as well as the PCP. The interaction between consultant and PCP is highly important to good medical management and utilization control. Beyond that, it is reasonable for the plan, through the medical director, to communicate certain expectations of all consultants. It has been clearly shown that even in intensive care units, where little discretion would be expected in treatment decisions, HMOs have 30 percent to 40 percent lower utilization (measured by length of stay, charges, and use of ventilators) compared with fee-for-service plans even when adjusted for case mix, thus pointing out that consultants and specialists in a managed care environment have considerable effect on resource use.[27]

First, you expect all consultants to be aware of and to cooperate with your plan's policy on testing, procedures, and primary care case management. Second, plans that use PCPs as gatekeepers or managing physicians should expect consultants to be in communication with PCPs about their patients and to provide written reports on consultations (some plans go so far as to refuse payment to a consultant until the PCP receives a written report). Third, care should be directed back to the PCP as soon as it is possible to do so, so that the consultant reinforces the plan's philosophy of primary care. Last, the consultant cannot subauthorize further care for the member without first discussing the case with the PCP involved. The PCP may already have worked up a problem that the consultant is seeing for the first time, or the PCP may be able to perform the medical duties that the consultant is requesting; for example, a surgeon may call a cardiologist to evaluate chest pain even though the PCP is an internist who is aware of the patient's condition.

In a loosely controlled plan there will be fewer expectations of the consultant than in a tightly controlled plan. As has been mentioned numerous times, the better the control of utilization you hope to achieve, the more you have to deal with practice patterns and physician behavior. Consultants are able to add significantly to the cost of care not only from their own fees but through additional fees generated by extra days in the hospital and through testing, procedures, and secondary referrals to other consultants.

Rounding physician model. In the rounding physician model, sometimes called the designated admitting physician model, one physician is designated to care for all admissions of a group or health plan to a given hospital or hospital service (e.g., to a medical service). This model is not infrequently found in group and staff model HMOs and is beginning to appear in some open panel HMOs as well. The PCP in-

deed relinquishes responsibility for the admission, and the rounding physician assumes responsibility.

The rounding or designated physician may be on site on a full-time basis or may simply carry a lighter outpatient load, devoting greater time to rounding on hospitalized patients. In the large closed panels as well as the open panel plans that are adopting this system, it is more common for the designated physician to be on site full time at the hospital.

The reasoning behind this approach is that a dedicated on-site physician will be closer to the care that the patient is receiving and in a better position to coordinate needed services as well as closely monitor care for quality and appropriateness. On a secondary note, large groups find that this increases their overall efficiency because this model avoids many physicians going into the hospital for just one or two visits.

In some plans, it is not practical for the PCP to follow all cases in the hospital even though the plan may not have a formal rounding physician program in place. Reasons may include high use of teaching hospitals with closed medical staffs, communities where PCPs simply do not hospitalize cases (which can occur in both urban and rural areas), and plans that do not use a PCP gatekeeper system. In any case, the attending physician in this situation is usually a specialist or consultant and has responsibility to manage the case and to interact with the plan. The responsibilities of the attending physician in this model are little different from those of the PCP. Interaction with the plan is necessary, and the consultant needs to cooperate with plan policies and procedures. The main difference in this model is the person with whom the UM nurse and medical director interact.

Medical director's responsibilities. In addition to monitoring all the elements discussed in this chapter, there are a few specific functions that the medical director should be performing. The medical director will have to become involved in the most difficult cases from a management standpoint. This does not necessarily refer to those cases where the difficulty is medical but rather to those cases where there is difficulty with the PCP, a consultant, a hospital, or the member or member's family. There are times when the medical director must deal with uncooperative individuals, and this is certainly a difficult responsibility. The medical director must take a compassionate, caring, but firm and fair stance when dealing with difficult people. It is often easiest simply to give in, but that can only be done so many times before it becomes a habit that damages the plan's effectiveness. The ability to empathize and sympathize with someone's point of view and to recognize what the real issues are in a dispute is not the same as acquiescing. Although there are indeed times when the medical director will want to loosen the reins, it is important for the medical director to remain firm when the situation is clear and to back up his or her subordinates and the PCPs when they are right.

If the medical director is only heard from when there is a problem, his or her effectiveness will be diminished. It is important for there to be reasonably frequent contact with PCPs and important consultants even when all is well. This can be especially useful when discussing cases. If the medical director discusses cases, suggesting alternatives if appropriate even when there is no pressing need to make a change, the participating plan physicians will be much more accepting of the medical director's opinions when change is needed (assuming that the medical director has useful opinions in the first place, of course).

The usefulness of frequent contact cannot be overestimated. By asking thoughtful questions in a nonthreatening manner and by constantly stimulating thought regarding cost-effective clinical management, the medical director may slowly reinforce appropriate patterns of care. The most successful outcome of such contacts occurs when physicians begin asking themselves the questions the medical director would ask and begin improving their practice patterns on that basis.

A task that the medical director should perform for optimal utilization control is reviewing the hospital log daily. This may seem an onerous task, and it can be, but it is the only way the medical director will consistently spot problems in time to do something about them. For example, finding that surgery was not done on the same day as admission may prompt a call to the PCP or surgeon to prevent that same thing happening again. If possible, it is even better for the medical director to review the hospital log with the UM nurse early enough in the day for meaningful action to be taken, which is usually before noon, when many hospitals automatically charge for another day. Large plans with highly competent UM nurses and UM departments may get to a point where the medical director need not review every case every day but simply will review any problem cases or outliers. Even in these situations, the medical director should periodically review every case to be certain that the UM department is performing as well as expected.

Retrospective Review

Retrospective review occurs after the case is finished and the patient is discharged. Retrospective review takes on two primary forms: claims review and pattern review.

Claims review. Claims review refers to examining claims for improprieties or mistakes. For example, it is common for plans to review large claims to verify whether services were actually delivered or whether mistakes were made in collating the claims data. In such large cases, the plan may actually send a representative on site to the hospital to review the medical record against the claims record.

Pattern review. This refers to examining patterns of utilization to determine where action must be taken. For example, if three hospitals in the area perform coronary artery bypass surgery, the plan may look to see which one has the best clinical outcomes, the shortest length of stay, and the lowest charges. The plan may then preferentially send all such cases to that hospital. Pattern review also allows the plan to focus UM efforts primarily on those areas needing greater attention (i.e., Sutton's law: Go where the money is!).

One other use of pattern review is to provide feedback to providers. Although not as powerful as active UM by the plan's own department, feedback can have an effect in and of itself.[28] When combined with other management functions and financial incentives, feedback can be a useful management tool.

Alternatives to Acute Care Hospitalization

There are many instances where patients are ill or disabled but not to the extent that they need to be in an acute care hospital. Despite that, that is where they often stay. The reasons for this are many. In some cases, the patient started out needing the services of an acute care hospital (e.g., a patient had surgery but the recovery phase requires far fewer resources than are available in the hospital). In other cases, there is simply no place for the patient to go (e.g., a patient is recovering from a broken femur but lives alone). In a few cases, a patient is kept in the hospital for the convenience of a physician who does not want to make house calls or rounds at another institution. Last, there are times when a patient is kept in the hospital simply because "That's the way it's always been done!"

Skilled or intermediate nursing facilities and subacute facilities. A useful alternative to consider is the skilled or intermediate nursing facility or subacute facility (subacute care facilities are discussed in detail in Chapter 24). This is best suited for prolonged convalescence or recovery cases. For example, if a patient with a broken femur requires more traction than can be provided safely at home and requires many months to recover, the cost for a bed day in a nursing facility will be greatly reduced compared with that in the acute care hospital. The same goes for rehabilitation cases, such as stroke or trauma to the brain, when the damage is too extensive for the patient to go home immediately. Although there are few (if any) reasons anymore to admit someone for uncomplicated back pain, if one of your physicians does so, a nursing facility is the most appropriate place for the bed rest to take place.

Recently, the subacute care industry has begun to focus on making its facilities a practical alternative to an acute care hospital for a larger variety of medical cases. For example, some subacute care facilities provide a cost-effective location for the administration of chemotherapy that requires close supervision. The treatment of many medical conditions, such as acute pneumonia or osteomyelitis, when the patient is too sick to be cared for at home may be done in a subacute facility. In some cases, the patient may be able to be cared for at home, but it is still more cost effective to deliver the therapy in the subacute facility as a result of the more favorable pricing achievable through economies of scale. For a subacute facility to vie effectively for this type of business, it must transform itself into something other than a nursing home.

The main problem with the use of subacute facilities or nursing homes is objections from the patient or the family, particularly in the case of young patients. There is a stigma attached to nursing homes that makes some people associate them with warehouses for the elderly. To overcome this, you need to take a proactive approach.

First, contract only with those nursing and subacute facilities that meet your (and implicitly your members') demands for pleasant surroundings. You may find a better price elsewhere, but try to imagine yourself or your loved ones staying at the facility for a month and see if it would be acceptable. A good nursing facility will be interested in working with you on making the option acceptable by ensuring that your patients will be given a private room (a private room in a nursing facility is still less costly than a semiprivate bed in an acute care hospital) or at least will be placed in a room with another patient with a similar functional status.

Second, discuss the alternative with the patient and the family well in advance of the actual move. Nothing is as distressing as suddenly finding out that you will be shipped out in the morning to a nursing home. If possible, have the family visit the nursing facility to meet the staff and see the environment before the patient is transferred.

Last, do not abandon the patient. In other words, have someone, preferably the physician and the UM nurse, visit the patient on a regular basis. It is easy to rationalize that, because the patient is in the nursing facility for long-term care, you do not need to visit often; after all, the nurse would call if there were a problem. That may be true from a medical standpoint, but it is not true from a human relations standpoint.

How you handle using a nursing facility will have an impact on your marketing. If you coldly shunt people into a nursing facility simply to save money, you will rapidly get a reputation for placing your needs over those of your members. Members will complain to their benefits managers or to other potential members, and you will develop problems in enrollment. If, however, you handle the option with caring and compassion, taking the time to alleviate the emotional distress that may be caused, you will find that most people will be quite understanding and accepting of this alternative.

The other issue to consider in the use of nursing facilities is monitoring the case in regard to your benefit structure. It is easy for a case to go from prolonged recovery to permanent placement or custodial care. It can be emotionally wrenching both for the member's family and for you to face up to the end of benefits. The problem of who will pay for long-term custodial care is a national dilemma, and it becomes personal when a family is faced with high costs because the benefits your plan offers do not continue indefinitely.

If it is possible or likely that benefits will end, it is wise early on to make the benefits structure clear to the family. This does not have to be done in a cold and calculating manner but rather by laying out all the possibilities so that the family members can begin early planning themselves.

Step-down units. As an alternative to freestanding nursing facilities, many hospitals with excess capacity have developed step-down units. Even if they have not, many hospital administrators are willing to consider it in your negotiations.

In essence, a step-down unit is a ward or section of a ward that is used in much the same way as a skilled nursing facility. A patient who requires less care and monitoring, such as someone recovering from a hip replacement (after all the drains have been removed), may need only bed rest, traction, and minimal nursing care. In recognition of the lesser resource needs, the charge per day is less.

The step-down unit has the advantage of being convenient for the physician and UM nurse and is more acceptable to the patient and family. It also does not require transfer outside the facility. Although the cost per day is sometimes slightly higher than that of a nursing facility, the difference may be worth it in terms of member acceptability.

Outpatient procedure units. In many instances, performing a procedure in an outpatient unit is less expensive than admitting a patient for a 1-day stay. This is not always true because, with the increased popularity of outpatient surgery, some hospitals have raised their outpatient unit charges to make up the lost revenue. As discussed in Chapter 14, you must pay attention to outpatient charges when negotiating with hospitals.

Freestanding outpatient facilities are also an alternative. These may be affiliated with a hospital or may be independent. As with hospitals, you can and should negotiate the charge structure so that you indeed save the costs that outpatient surgery should allow.

Hospice care. Hospice care is that care given to terminally ill patients. It tends to be supportive care and is used most often when such care cannot be given in the home. It is not always covered by health plans, but it does sometimes take the place of acute care hospitalization and should be considered when appropriate.

Home health care. Home health agencies are proliferating, and home care is becoming increasingly accepted. Services that are particularly amenable to home health care include nursing care for routine reasons (e.g., checking weights, changing dressings, and the like), home intravenous treatment (e.g., for osteomyelitis, certain forms of chemotherapy, and home intravenous nutrition), home physical therapy, respiratory therapy, and rehabilitation care.

You should have little trouble negotiating and contracting with home health agencies for services. It is becoming popular for hospitals to have home health care services to aid with caring for patients discharged from their facility, and you may be able to negotiate those services with your overall contract. Furthermore, as Medicare continues to tighten down payments for home care, many agencies are looking for alternative sources of revenue. As with hospitals or any other providers of care, home health and high-technology home care agencies need to be evaluated in terms beyond simple pricing breaks. An active quality management program, the presence of a medical director, and evidence of attention to the changes that are constantly occurring in the field are all requisites for contracting.

A warning about home health services is in order. Because the physician and UM nurse seldom visit the patient receiving home health care, it often defaults to the home health nurse to determine how often and how long the patient should receive services, and this can lead to some surprising bills. It is highly advisable to have a firm policy regarding how many home health visits will be covered under a single authorization and stating that continued authorization requires physician review.

LCM and Disease Management

LCM, also referred to as catastrophic case management, refers to specialized techniques for identifying and managing cases that are disproportionately high in cost; disease management refers to the same activity, but focused on a defined set of diseases. For example, active acquired immunodeficiency syndrome can be an expensive disease process, as can a high cervical spinal cord injury, a bone marrow transplant, and many other events. This highly important

subject is discussed in detail in Chapter 18 as well as Chapter 20, so that only brief discussion will occur here in the context of overall management of medical–surgical utilization.

Identification of large cases may be straightforward because the patients are in the hospital the first time you identify them. This is the case for trauma. Other cases may be identified before they are ever hospitalized. For example, examining the claims system for use of dialysis services may identify an end-stage renal disease patient. Proactively contacting patients with potentially catastrophic illnesses not only can save the plan considerable expense by managing the care cost effectively but can also result in better medical care because the services are coordinated.

Prenatal care is a specialized form of LCM because active coordination occurs before the newborn is delivered. Prenatal LCM involves identification of high-risk pregnancies early enough to intervene to improve the chances of a good outcome. With the staggering costs of neonatal intensive care, it only takes a few improved outcomes to yield dramatic savings. Methods for identifying cases include sending out information about pregnancy to all members, reviewing the claims system for pregnancy-related claims, asking (or requiring) the PCPs and obstetricians to notify the plan when a delivery is expected, and so forth. After the UM department is informed of the case, the member may be proactively contacted, and a questionnaire may be given to assess for risk factors (e.g., young maternal age, diabetes, medical problems, smoking or alcohol abuse, and so forth). If risk factors are noted, then the plan coordinates prenatal care in a proactive manner. Although it is impossible to force a member to seek care and to follow up on problems, it is possible to increase the amount and quality of prenatal care that is delivered. A special problem exists when the pregnant patient is also abusing drugs; close coordination with the substance abuse program must then occur.

The degree to which the plan can become involved in LCM is in part a function of the benefits structure. In a tightly run managed health care plan, it is common for the UM department to be proactive in LCM; in simple PPOs, LCM is often voluntary on the part of the member (in other words, if the member chooses not to cooperate, there is little impact on benefits). Even in situations requiring strictly voluntary cooperation by the members and physicians, it is surprising how often LCM can be highly effective.

In addition to the standard methods of managing utilization, LCM often involves two other techniques. First is the use of community resources. Some catastrophic cases require support structures to help the member function or even return home. Examples of such support include family members, social service agencies, churches, special foundations, and so forth. The other common technique is to go beyond the contractual benefits to manage the case. For example, if the benefits structure of the group has only limited coverage for durable medical equipment, it may still be in the plan's interest to cover such expenses to get the patient home and out of the hospital. In self-funded groups, the group administrator may actually be willing to fund extracontractual benefits simply as a benefit for an employee or dependent who is experiencing a terrible medical problem.

In any event, the hallmark of LCM is longitudinal management of the case by a single UM nurse or department. Management spans hospital care, rehabilitation, outpatient care, professional services, home care, ancillary services, and so forth. It is in the active coordination of care that both quality and cost effectiveness are maintained.

CONCLUSION

The provision of basic medical–surgical services involves a broad continuum of care. Managing utilization of these services must focus on managing basic demand, managing referral and specialty services, and managing institutional services.

The control of referral and specialty services affects not only professional expenses but also costs associated with testing and procedures, including hospitalization, that may be generated by the consultant. The ability to select only those consultants and referral specialists who practice cost effectively can yield cost savings, but optimal control depends on an authorization system, and lack of such a system will hamper your abilities to decrease consultant utilization meaningfully over the long term.

The control of hospital or institutional utilization is one of the most important aspects of controlling overall health care costs. The methods used to control hospital utilization vary from relatively weak and mechanical to tightly controlled, longitudinally integrated, and highly labor intensive. The control of hospital utilization is a function that must be attended to every day to achieve optimal results, and special attention must be paid to LCM to produce the greatest savings.

REFERENCES AND NOTES

1. Sherlock Company, *P.U.L.S.E.* Analysis (Gwynedd, Pa.: Sherlock Company, 1995).

2. D.M. Vickery, et al., Effect of a Self-Case Education Program on Medical Visits, *Journal of the American Medical Association* 250 (1983): 2952–2956.

3. J.S. Robinson, et al., The Impact of Fever Education on Clinic Utilization, *American Journal of Diseases of Children* 143 (1989): 698–704.

4. M.A. Goldstein, Emerging Data Show Programs are Effective, *Modern Healthcare* (21 August 1995): 126–130.

5. V.D. Elsenhans, Use of Self-Care Manual Shifts Utilization Pattern, *HMO Practice* (June 1995).

6. M.A. Goldstein, Emerging Data Show Programs are Effective, *Modern Healthcare* (21 August 1995): 126–130.

7. W.N. Burton and D.A. Hoy, First Chicago's Integrated Health Data Management Computer System, *Managed Care Quarterly* 1 (1993): 18–23.

8. J.K. Glenn, et al., Physician Referrals in a Competitive Environment: An Estimate of the Economic Impact of a Referral, *Journal of the American Medical Association* 258 (1987): 1920–1923.

9. Group Health Association of America (GHAA), *1995 Sourcebook on HMO Utilization Data* (Washington, D.C.: GHAA, 1995).

10. A.J. Dietrich, et al., Do Primary Physicians Actually Manage Their Patients' Fee-for-Service Care?, *Journal of the American Medical Association* 259 (1988): 3145–3149.

11. B.J. Hillman, et al., Frequency and Costs of Diagnostic Imaging in Office Practice—A Comparison of Self-Referring and Radiologist Referring Physicians, *New England Journal of Medicine* 323 (1990): 1604–1608.

12. Office of the Inspector General, *Financial Arrangements between Physicians and Health Care Businesses: Report to Congress* (Washington, D.C.: Department of Health and Human Services, 1989; Department of Health and Human Services Publication OAI-12-88-01410).

13. State of Florida Health Care Cost Containment Board, *Joint Ventures among Health Care Providers in Florida* (Tallahassee, Fla.: State of Florida, 1991), 2.

14. Omnibus Budget Reconciliation Act of 1989.

15. Health Care Knowledge Resources, *Length of Stay by Diagnosis and Operation* (Ann Arbor, Mich.: Health Knowledge Resources, 1991).

16. M.R. Chassin, et al., Variations in the Use of Medical and Surgical Services by the Medicare Population, *New England Journal of Medicine* 314 (1986): 285–290.

17. H.L. Smits, Medical Practice Variations Revisited, *Health Affairs* (Fall 1986): 91–96.

18. J. Wennberg and A. Gittelsohn, Variations in Medical Care among Small Areas, *Scientific American* (April 1982): 120–135.

19. J. Wennberg, et al., Are Hospital Services Rationed in New Haven or Overutilized in Boston?, *Lancet* 1 (1987): 1185–1189.

20. M.R. Chassin, et al., Does Inappropriate Use Explain Geographic Variations in the Use of Health Care Services? A Study of Three Procedures, *Journal of the American Medical Association* 258 (1987): 2533–2537.

21. D.V. Axene and R.L. Doyle, *Research Report: Analysis of Medically Unnecessary Inpatient Services* (Milliman & Robertson, 1994).

22. S.K. Kelley and J.J. Trutlein, A Survey of Human Resources in Managed Care Organizations, *Physician Executive* 18 (1992): 49–51.

23. R.L. Doyle, *Healthcare Management Guidelines, Vol 1: Inpatient and Surgical Care* (Milliman & Robertson, 1990).

24. InterQual, *The ISD—A Review System with Adult Criteria* (Chicago, Ill.: InterQual, 1991).

25. InterQual, *Surgical Indications Monitoring SIM III* (Chicago, Ill.: InterQual, 1991).

26. Utilization Management Associates, *Managed Care Appropriateness Protocol (MCAP)* (Wellesley, Mass.: Utilization Management Associates, 1991).

27. J. Rapoport, et al., Resource Utilization among Intensive Care Patients: Managed Care vs. Traditional Insurance, *Archives of Internal Medicine* 152 (1992): 2207–2212.

28. J.E. Billi, et al., The Effects of a Cost-Education Program on Hospital Charges, *Journal of General Internal Medicine* 2 (1987): 306–311.

SUGGESTED READING

Doyle, R.L. *Healthcare Management Guidelines: Inpatient and Surgical Care.* Milliman & Robertson. Updated periodically.

Doyle, R.L. and Feren, H.P. *Healthcare Management Guidelines: Ambulatory Care.* Milliman & Robertson. Updated periodically.

Gray, B.H. and Field, M.J. (eds.). 1989. *Controlling Costs and Changing Patient Care? The Role of Utilization Management.* Washington, D.C.: National Academy Press.

Hammon, J.L. (ed.). 1993. *Fundamentals of Medical Management: A Guide for New Physician Executives.* Tampa, Fla.: American College of Physician Executives.

Chapter 18

Case Management and Managed Care

Catherine M. Mullahy

THE CASE MANAGER'S ROLE

Managed care and case management are not interchangeable concepts. Managed care is a system of cost containment programs; case management is a process. It is one component in the managed care strategy. The following definition of case management has been adopted by the Commission for Case Manager Certification (CCMC), the developers of the credentialing process for case managers: "Case management is a collaborative process which assesses, plans, implements, coordinates, monitors, and evaluates the options and services required to meet an individual's health needs, using communication and available resources to promote quality, cost-effective outcomes."[1(p.1)] CCMC goes on to clarify the role by stating that case management is not episodic or restricted to a single practice

Catherine M. Mullahy, B.S., R.N., C.R.R.N., C.C.M., is a nationally recognized case management consultant and spokesperson for the case management industry. She is a founder and president of Options Unlimited, a medical case management and benefits consulting firm in Huntington, New York, serving individuals, corporations, insurers, and third party administrators nationwide since 1983. She is a member of the Certified Case Manager Commission (CCMC) and chair for CCM Compliance Review. She also serves on the Individual Case Management Association (ICMA) Advisory Board and chairs the Standards of Practice and Ethics Committee for the Case Management Society of America. Ms. Mullahy is a frequent lecturer and has contributed to numerous publications. Her book, *The Case Manager's Handbook*, was published in 1994 and is in its second printing.

setting, but occurs across a continuum of care and addresses ongoing individual needs.

Case managers work in the provider sector in hospitals, rehabilitation facilities, home health agencies, infusion care companies, and other practice settings as well as in the payer sector, representing employers through third party administrators (TPAs) or self-administered programs or being employed within health maintenance programs or by major insurance carriers. Independent case managers, professionals working outside the medical care provider and claims payer systems, can be found in any of the practice settings mentioned and may also be working directly for a patient or other family member.

Case managers are not the claims police. Ensuring cost-effective treatment does not mean that case managers are overrated number crunchers who review treatment simply to find the cheapest scenario. Case managers are coordinators of care, catalysts, problem solvers, facilitators, impartial advocates, and educators. They are professional collaborators with physicians and negotiators with durable medical equipment providers, home health care agencies, therapists, and many other providers. They make certain that the patient is following the treatment plan prescribed by the physician and that the equipment delivered to the home is the equipment that was ordered, not the super deluxe version of the same bed that just happens to cost $400 more per week. As a liaison with insurance claims staff, they clarify claims information. With benefits personnel, they sometimes pursue alternatives to the plan package in the best interests of the patient and the payer.[2]

Patient Profile: Not Every Case Needs a Case Manager

For years, it has been known that the greatest portion of health care costs is generated by the 3 percent to 5 percent of the patient population that is at high risk, critically injured, or suffering from a chronic disease. As an example, in one 10-month period one firm (a client of the author) spent more than $1.8 million in health care benefits for its employees and their dependents (2,520 covered lives). Fully half that dollar total was distributed to 30 individuals (4 percent of the employees). This means that half the benefit dollars spent, more than $900,000, was focused on 1.1 percent of the total covered population. Twenty-two employees spent $588,702; expressed differently, 3 percent of the employees accounted for 32 percent of the group's total in paid claims, or less than 1 percent of those covered spent 32 percent of the dollars. This is the singular message for the reader to understand: You don't have to manage all the patients all the time. You do have to track complex cases, those patients who are most likely to fall through the cracks in our health care delivery system because of the layers of care they require.[3]

By developing systems to identify and manage the high-risk, high-cost cases from day 1 [cancer, acquired immunodeficiency syndrome (AIDS), stroke, transplant, head injury, severe burns, high-risk pregnancy, high-risk neonates, spinal cord injuries, neuromuscular diseases, etc.], case management promotes quality care and contains costs. By wrapping the case management approach around all lines of medical coverage, case managers can be appropriately attentive to potentially problematic cases, more creative in problem solving, and better able to address spiraling expenses before they take off. As a bonus, case management also tackles three other problem areas that push up employer costs and concerns: employee morale, decreased production, and absenteeism. A case manager's

professional intervention and guidance improve employee morale by providing direct communication and personal attention, help return employees to the job more quickly, and help eliminate repeated occurrences of the same afflictions.[4]

Throughout the course of care, the case manager will work in four major areas of activity: medical, financial, behavioral/motivational, and vocational[5]:

1. Medical activities—Encompasses all those activities a case manager performs to ensure that the patient receives the most effective medical and nursing care, including:
   - Contacting the patient in the hospital, in the rehabilitation unit, or at home
   - Contacting the members of the medical treatment team (the physician, nursing staff, rehabilitation therapists, etc.) to discover the patient's course of progress and needs; utilizing the information in discharge planning and the initial needs assessment
   - Arranging for all services required for discharge or relocation (equipment, home nursing care, therapy, transportation, transfer to another facility, home utilities, etc.); coordinating efforts with the primary nurse, discharge planner, or social services administrator to eliminate duplication of services and to conserve benefit dollars
   - Visiting with the family
   - Checking the home for safety factors and architectural barriers and arranging for any needed safety aids and modifications
   - On follow-up, reevaluating equipment, ensuring that supplies are replenished, monitoring home nursing services, and arranging for equipment repair; evaluating activities of daily living, home programs, and modifications to treatment

- Identifying problems, providing health instruction, and referring the patient back to the physician or other health team member when appropriate
- Identifying plateaus, improvements, regressions, and depressions; counseling accordingly or recommending help
- Making personal visits or contacting the physician to clarify the diagnosis, prognosis, therapy, activities of daily living, expected permanent disability, and so on
- Assisting in obtaining payer authorizations for any modalities of treatment recommended
- Acting as a liaison between the physician and the insurance company when necessary
- Sharing pertinent information about the patient with the physician and working together with the physician to achieve the best outcome

2. Financial activities
   - Counseling the patient or family on budgeting and notifying creditors
   - Identifying financial distress and referring the patient or family to appropriate community resources
   - Helping the patient or family sort and prioritize unpaid bills
   - Acting as a liaison among the insurance company, referral source, and patient to alleviate financial and other problems or misunderstandings

3. Behavioral/motivational activities
   - Exploring the patient's feelings about himself or herself and his or her injury or illness and helping the patient with the associated trauma and frustration
   - Monitoring the family's feelings regarding the patient's illness and observing the family's ability or inability to manage under new emotional stress

- Offering reassurance and information about the patient's condition
- If qualified, counseling in the areas of marital discord, role reversal, dependency, and sexual problems arising from the injury or illness

4. Vocational activities
   - Obtaining a history of education, employment, hobbies, and job skills and uncovering vocational interests and future goals
   - If appropriate, overseeing psychovocational testing, work evaluations, schooling, on-the-job situations, transportation, and anything else needed to assist the patient in becoming or remaining gainfully employed
   - Assisting the patient in using the recuperative period in a constructive fashion (studying, upgrading skills, preparing for job interviews, etc.)
   - Visiting the patient's place of employment and talking with the personnel director or immediate supervisor about the employer's expectations and the patient's needs
   - Completing a job analysis and discussing the possibility of the patient's return to work in the same job, perhaps after job modification or lightening of duties
   - Sharing the above information with the physician at appropriate time

On-Site versus Telephonic Case Management

Case management is not a hands-on role. Case managers are not actively practicing nurses, clinicians, or caregivers. They do not diagnose an ailment, prescribe a medication, or set the course of treatment. They do offer their expertise and observations to suggest alternative care options. Using on-site visits and information-gathering conversations, a case manager can make sure that a noncompliant patient is following the treatment plan outlined by the physician or note the possible complications from the medications recommended by the patient's otolaryngologist but never mentioned to his or her cardiologist.

Although case managers do not offer hands-on care, they cannot always be effective if they never make an on-site visit. Telephone work, which is part of case management, is necessary for maintaining lines of communication without driving up costs. Telephonic case management is particularly effective for preventive and case-screening measures and for tracking low-intensity patients or patients who have improved to the point where in-person case management is no longer needed. Using only telephonic case management, however, so that all communication among the case manager, patient, family, physician, and payer occurs over the phone, can lead to oversights in care, especially in cases where the patient is noncompliant, undereducated, or poor. The vulnerability of the patient coupled with the legal and monetary exposure of the provider and payer may call for at least a minimum of on-site interaction.[6]

Telephonic case management is almost always less expensive than on-site case management. If it can be established that care decisions were made based only on dollars to be saved, employers, providers, payer groups, and case managers could be held liable in a wrongful action suit. To protect their interests and liabilities, it behooves each party to be fully aware of how care decisions are made. It is the case manager's responsibility to say "No, I must be on site to review this case rather than manage it solely by phone" or "No, I'm unable to put that plan into action" if she or he feels that the level of care being provided is substandard or places the patient at too great a risk. Providers need to maintain accurate outcomes data, and payers should use case managers as their eyes and ears. When payers and employers become involved in determining who will provide how much care and when, they must make sure they know exactly what they are paying for and how care decisions

are made. Periodic on-site visits by a case manager will make this possible.

CASE MANAGERS IN MANAGED CARE

An integral part of the managed care process, case managers are introduced to patients and cases in a variety of ways. The case manager may be a member of the discharge planning team employed on site at a hospital; part of a major insurer's in-house case management team, an independent case manager working on contract for an employer or TPA, a community-based social worker/case manager; or a staff member at a rehabilitation facility, infusion therapy company, home health agency, or other provider location. The referral source might be an insurance company with clients covered under workers' compensation, auto, or group medical plans; a TPA that is paying claims for a client company; or a corporate human resources manager. It might be a state Medicaid office with case management services within a line of insurance or a population segment, such as high-risk newborns or children who are dependent on technological medical assistance. Case managers are also contacted directly by families seeking to monitor the care of an out-of-state relative or friend, for example. There are individuals and firms providing a broad range of case management services and those specializing in specific diseases or patient groups, such as premature infants, diabetics, or patients with Alzheimer's disease, AIDS, or breast cancer, for example.

For optimum outcomes, a case manager will be called in on the case as early as possible. If case management services are strategically coordinated with preadmission review and concurrent review services, early intervention and its benefits often occur. There are times, however, when a case manager is not notified until a case has reached a threshold of $30,000—a little late in the game but not entirely past the point of no return.

Although many managed care organizations employ case managers as part of their utilization management departments, in other situations case management services are obtained from an independent case management service. In those instances, case management services are usually billed on an hourly basis; preadmission and concurrent review services, on the other hand, are customarily purchased at a capitated rate or on a per case basis. These per case fees may be calculated on an hourly basis for the time each reviewed case takes or on a flat fee basis, whereby a set fee is established for each review conducted. Services may be covered by language in the benefit plan or requested as an alternative to policy benefits. Sometimes part of a comprehensive managed care program, case management services are offered in conjunction with preadmission review and concurrent review. In these cases, all three services might be offered at a capitated rate or on a standalone (per service per case) basis.

THE CASE MANAGEMENT WORK FORMAT AND PROCESS

Money is pouring into our health care system, but improved treatment and services are not flowing out at the same rate. Case management is a catalyst that pushes performance to more cost-effective levels, promoting better outcomes and the maintenance of quality care (Figure 18–1).

Gathering and Assessing Information

A case manager's approach to a new case is influenced by the referral source (generally the payer) and the line of insurance; his or her latitude in creatively and effectively managing a case will vary with the amount the payer has at risk. Generally, the self-insured employer, paying dollar-for-dollar for benefits, is more interested and involved in the case management process and more readily approves out-of-plan benefits to make the most of benefit dollars. On the other hand, a large employer paying a capitated, one-rate-fits-all fee to a major insurer for its employees' health benefit coverage is of-

ten less inclined to work with a case manager on an individual case.

Appropriate and effective case management is only possible when the information gathered is accurate and thoughtfully analyzed. This gathering process will include conversations with the major players: the referral source or payer, patient, family, physicians, and other key members of the medical treatment team. The case manager will introduce himself or herself and the role of case management, making certain that each person understands what the case manager will bring to the table. Medical records must be consulted and employers and attorneys contacted as needed. The right questions must be asked. For example, when the case manager speaks with the patient, the query "Are you taking your medication?" cannot stand on its own. It should be followed by "Are you taking it as prescribed? What other medications are you currently taking? What other pills, vitamins, or supplements are you taking?"

Furthermore, all data must be carefully considered. Too often, case managers fall into the habit of transferring information from their notes to a report without asking themselves the same direct questions they should be asking their patients, payers, and providers, such as "What is hindering better progress here? What can I do to encourage more response from the patient's family? Should I aggressively pursue this seemingly needed service on an out-of-plan basis?"

The words *initial needs assessment* carry a variety of meanings depending on the listener. An initial needs assessment is the case manager's first activity, undertaken to prepare a report to the referral source (payer), and will include a description of the patient and his or her condition, diagnosis, and prognosis together with the case manager's recommendations and other information. Some clients think of an initial needs assessment as a four-page document prepared by the case manager after on-site visits with the claimant, family, physician, and employer. Others feel that an extensive phone call will cover their needs (and their liability), or they will request that the case manager visit with

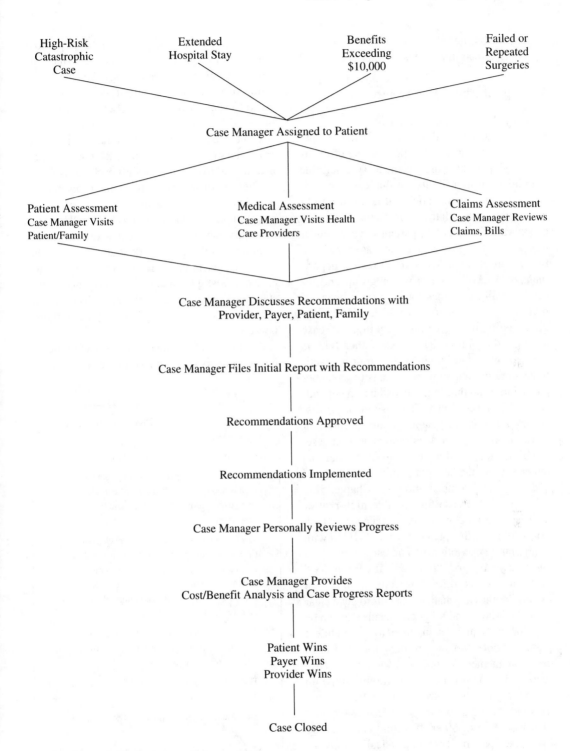

Figure 18–1 Case management work format flowchart. *Source:* Reprinted from C.M. Mullahy, *The Case Manager's Handbook*, p. 109, © 1995, Aspen Publishers, Inc.

the patient but no other participants in the care plan during the initial needs assessment.

Talking with the Referral Source

Before beginning an initial needs assessment, the case manager needs to know whether the patient is covered under the specific line of insurance paying for case management. To determine the client's responsibility on this case, for this individual, under this policy, it is not too rudimentary to start with the basics: What is the line of insurance, and is this patient covered under this policy? Suppose the case manager works in the preadmission and concurrent review department of a health care provider group and receives a call that James Jones has just been admitted to the hospital with which the provider group is affiliated. Upon checking, the case manager determines that James' father John is covered by a plan in which the group's practitioners are participating physicians (or member physicians) and that James is listed as a dependent on his father's plan. The case manager discovers, however, that James' injury occurred at work, making it a workers' compensation case. James is not eligible for benefits under his father's group medical plan but may be covered under workers' compensation (see Chapter 52).

To assess the case for possible high-risk or long-term cost factors, the case manager will ask "How long has this patient been ill?" Even with a minimum description—"The car accident occurred 2 years ago," "It's a spinal cord injury," or "This is his third hospitalization in 18 months"—the case manager begins to get a clear picture of short- and long-term needs and can be alert for any required adjustment to the treatment plan, the potential requirement for long-term case management, or the need for a closer case review. The person in a coma rarely jumps up during week 2 to return to his or her normal lifestyle; hence a long-term case management plan would be in order. If an individual citing lower back pain has been in physical therapy for 3 years, a wake-up call to the treating physician might be in order.

Other questions for a case manager to put to a referral source include the following: What dollars are available for how long? Are there any limits or restrictions on the type of care provided? Type of care facility? Length of stay? Is there coverage for a skilled nursing facility versus an acute care center? Does the provision for home nursing services include 24-hour care, or is it limited to one 4-hour shift each day?

The line of insurance itself indicates certain questions to a case manager. In workers' compensation cases, one such question is "How did the injury happen?" This might be one in a series of injuries at the same work station, causing the case manager to urge the employer's risk manager to investigate that job procedure and/or job station before another employee is disabled and before the employer is facing a wrongful injury lawsuit.

A wrap-up of questions to cover with the referral source is given in Exhibit 18–1.

Exhibit 18–1 Referral Source Communication Tips

1. A referral call is made to the case manager.

2. The case manager gets the appropriate business details and confirms the needs of the referral source (e.g., expectations, fees, format and time frame for reports, etc.).

3. The case manager requests case background (e.g., the status of the patient, the diagnosis and the prognosis, the type of insurance coverage, the patient's eligibility under the policy, the policy benefit limits, the plan's flexibility, the restrictions on care, etc.).

4. The case manager confirms the initial needs assessment and report parameters in writing to the referral source and/or payer.

5. The case manager makes a follow-up call to review the confirmation letter.

6. The case manager documents all conversations.

Source: Reprinted from C.M. Mullahy, *The Case Manager's Handbook*, p. 120, © 1995, Aspen Publishers, Inc.

Talking with the Patient

The case manager's objective when interviewing the patient is to gain an overview of the patient's current medical history, the particular individual, and the situation as well as to encourage the patient to be participatory in his or her own care program. Initial questions will center on the patient's understanding of the medical diagnosis and prognosis. How does the patient view his or her situation? The individual might answer "My doctor told me I have lupus." The case manager must follow this up by asking "What do you think that means? Will it affect your life style?" By listening carefully to patient responses, a case manager will be able to determine the individual's level of understanding and acceptance (or denial) of the problem.

The case manager should never assume that a patient has the ability to understand the diagnosis, the ability to accept the diagnosis, or enough information and an adequate understanding of that information to be a cooperative, compliant participant in the health care plan. Perhaps the family is withholding information from the patient in a misguided effort to protect him or her. Perhaps the referral source, the physicians, and the case manager all have a clear understanding of the patient's condition—a malignant tumor that has already metastasized to other organs—but the patient and family have no concept of what this means in terms of the future. They might have heard the information but have chosen to edit it to a version that is easier or more convenient to accept. "I had a growth, but it was removed and I'm fine now." "Dad can go back to his job in 2 weeks, and my college tuition will be no problem."

A case manager also needs to be able to spot those who want to be lifelong members of the health care delivery process. Turning a chronic headache pattern into an undetectable brain tumor allows one some respite from life's greater responsibilities.

A crucial line of questioning, often overlooked by all members of the medical system (including case managers) centers on medica-

tions. There is a gap, the distance between life and death, between what a patient perceives as a problem and what the medical profession knows is a problem. Regardless of whether the patient thinks they are of interest, the case manager should ask to see all pills and medications being taken, including over-the-counter capsules and herbal vitamins. The case manager should also ask which of these the patient is taking, how often the patient is taking them, and what the patient thinks they are for. Patients sometimes halve their doses, stop taking medications midway through the prescription, or take them only on the days when the presenting problem presents itself. In some cases, this medical manipulation has no significant consequences. In other cases, the ill effects are harrowing.

Also important are questions regarding the patient's vocation and avocations. Is this person actively involved in a church? Members might provide the family with care respite. Is he or she an avid golfer, fisher, skeet shooter? Does he or she enjoy work? An optimistic person, fully experiencing life, is more likely to be a cooperative patient than the individual who is not participatory by nature. Someone seeking to get back to all life's business will follow the treatment plan; someone who was recently laid off may choose a "disability mentality," where the illness becomes his or her job and social life.

At the end of her interview, the case manager should obtain a signed consent form (Exhibit 18–2) from the patient or the patient's guardian. This will enable the case manager to review the patient's medical records and to share information regarding the patient with his or her physician(s) and attorney, if the case is in litigation.

Talking with the Family

Families affected by an injury or illness often will experience role changes, dependency shifts, anxiety, anger, and an inability to make decisions, particularly in long-term cases. Because of this, it is helpful for a case manager to interview the family early on to determine family dy-

Exhibit 18–2 Patient Consent Form

Authorization

I, _____, hereby request and authorize any hospital, physician, or other person who has attended or examined me, or who may hereafter attend or examine me for _____
_____
to disclose any and all information obtained thereby, relative to this injury or illness, to Options Unlimited. I further authorize that this information may be shared with other professionals, agencies, or insurance companies who may be involved in the provision or payment of services that may be necessary.

_____   _____
            (Date)   (Signature of Party)

_____   _____
                                                  (Signature of Guardian)

Witness: _____

Source: Reprinted from C.M. Mullahy, *The Case Manager's Handbook*, p. 130, © 1995, Aspen Publishers, Inc.

---

namics. Is the family taking an overprotective stance with the patient? Is the family spokesperson presuming to speak for the patient (e.g., "He needs to eat more," "She isn't sleeping well.")? Is there so much fear associated with this illness that other members of the family are developing symptoms, having emotional outbursts, or consulting the bottle in an effort to regain a feeling of balance or control in their lives?

In many ways, the patient's health will be supported by the emotional and physical health of the family. The case manager not only will want to gauge the strength of the family structure but also will want to compile a "medical family tree." Do certain illnesses run in the family? Does the 42-year-old man recuperating after a heart attack have a family with a history of cardiac disease and middle-age deaths?

The case manager needs answers to the following questions. What was the prime caregiver's role in the family before this illness? Did he or she run the household? Hold down a job? Does the caregiver still have those responsibilities in addition to caring for the patient? How

is he or she reacting to the illness? Is the caregiver physically and emotionally capable of supporting and caring for the patient?[7]

All these elements will influence the case management plan and in some cases dictate what the case manager will hope to accomplish. For example, the family with three active, inquisitive, dial-turning children under age 7, plus an infant who requires oxygen is going to need part-time home nursing assistance after discharge; also helpful will be an oxygen system with outdoor tanks, removing the siblings' temptation to tamper.

Talking with the Treating Physician

When a case manager works as a collaborative partner with a physician as well as all other members of the treating medical team, there is greater opportunity to track the patient's progress, ensure that the patient is and remains participatory and compliant, and that each element of the treatment plan is carried out appropriately. To build such partnerships, a case manager should schedule a personal meeting with the physician at his or her convenience when the case is complex. In less medically complex or physically distant cases, a telephone conversation with the treating physician is effective.

The case manager will ask questions such as: What is the diagnosis? What is the treatment plan and prognosis? What do you think will be the outcome for this person, both short term and long term? Do you anticipate any complications? What have you told the patient? What do you think the patient understands?[8] This last is important because the patient, the physician, and the case manager all need to be speaking the same language. Patients often choose to "forget" the components of a condition that they have difficulty accepting. This affects the treatment plan. It is the case manager's job to make certain that the patient has all the information the physician needs him or her to have to be able to cooperate and follow the treatment plan.

If the case manager knows up front that there is a limit on care dollars, he or she has the responsibility to make the physician aware of the limit and share in the goal of using the money in the best way possible. Although some care options may be ideal, the expenses connected with them make them poor first choices. An alternative plan may not be the ideal, but it will not pose any risk to the patient and may buy care and services over a longer period of time.[9]

Independent Medical and Second Opinion Examinations

In some cases, an independent medical or second opinion examination will be requested. A case manager's involvement is linked to the type of examination performed. An independent medical examination is generally utilized by insurance carriers to determine the diagnosis, the need for continued treatment, the degree of disability (partial or total), the duration of a disability (temporary, long term, or permanent), and the patient's ability to return to work. Independent medical examinations are requested when

treatment appears excessive, when the recovery time appears overly extended, or when there is a delay in the patient's return to work schedule. They are also employed upon request to authorize surgery, expensive equipment, or unusual diagnostic testing or when there is an increase in the number of treating professionals. The physician conducting the examination most often remains in a nontreating role. A case manager may assist in setting up the examination and may accompany the patient but in most instances will not be present at the examination.

Also used to determine a diagnosis, a second opinion examination is often performed to help clarify a complex medical picture or to prepare alternatives to the current or proposed treatment. In group medical plans, a second opinion examination is sometimes required before certain surgical procedures that the carrier or the latest utilization review statistics show to have a high usage rate (e.g., hysterectomies, hip replacements, cardiac bypass, disc surgery, etc.). Such examinations are also called for when there is a conflict between potential treatment plans, when a questionable treatment is underway, or when the existing treatment plan is not achieving the expected outcome. The case manager who arranged for the second opinion examination is usually in attendance, and the physician conducting the examination often will become a treating physician.

To get the most benefits from independent medical and second opinion examinations, a case manager should thoroughly understand the purpose of any examination ordered and be specific as to what should be addressed in the physician's report. The examining physician should be given as much information as possible (operative reports, diagnostic test reports, radiographs, computed tomography scans, etc.) and be given enough time to review all the data before the actual examination. After reviewing the physician's report to confirm that it is responsive to the initial request for information, the case manager should speak to the physician to discuss findings and clarify any unanswered issues.[10]

Talking with Service and Equipment Providers

Many case managers find it helpful to work with one representative at a durable medical equipment, home medical equipment, or home health care agency. In this way, equipment, services, contracts, and billing can all be reviewed in one phone call. In addition, it helps case managers get answers when they need them, and often answers are needed immediately (especially on Friday afternoons, when it seems that every patient in the country is simultaneously declared ready for discharge).

Before selecting providers or arranging for services, a case manager should review the benefit plan contract to make certain that its language supports the use of home nursing visits, durable medical equipment, and the like. It is the case manager's responsibility to verify that the contract he or she arranges agrees with plan language and will be approved when the bill for the services/equipment finally arrives in a claims department.

Questions case managers should ask include the following: What are the options included with this piece of equipment? What specifically is it designed to do? What are the terms—lease, rent, rent with option to buy, outright purchase? This patient will be using this equipment for at least 6 months; what discount will you offer for a long-term rental? Is repair service available 24 hours a day? What are the costs for various levels of service? What services do your homemakers provide, and how do they differ in price and services from those of the home health aides?

Talking with Community Resources

The case manager need not spend benefit plan money just because it exists. There are numerous local, county, and state agencies as well as disease-specific organizations, foundations, and philanthropic groups that provide services, guidance, and/or equipment free of charge. The United Way, Meals on Wheels, I Can Cope programs, and loaner wheelchairs from the Ameri-can Cancer Society are all examples of available assistance. Easter Seals offers support on a sliding scale for children and adults with disabling diseases. Some local volunteer fire departments provide free ambulance services.[11]

Planning

Case management is a process of identifying and solving problems. The first and key issue is whether the treatment is appropriate and being provided in the best possible setting. If the patient is not being well served, the case manager can help create a better system of care. The case manager's evaluation of the patient's current status will be the foundation for the case management plan. The case manager must look at what the patient's needs are and how they can best be met in terms of quality and cost. One factor should never drive the others; there must be equilibrium among the three. Given the patient's diagnosis, current medical status, and medical history, is the treatment plan attaining the most desirable results? Does it appear that it will lead to an eventual recovery, or have there already been too many complications? Is the treatment plan sound? Is it appropriate, reasonable, and really necessary for this patient? Is it forcing the patient into any undue hardship or discomfort?

Is the patient in the most appropriate and most cost-effective setting for his or her problem? For example, John is in the hospital, his surgery has been completed, and now he is being observed and given medication, pain, or infusion care services, or physical therapy. Does he have to remain in the hospital? Once patients can be effectively managed without all the expensive support services of an acute care facility, they should be moved to a more appropriate and less costly arena for care: the home or another setting (see Chapters 17 and 24 for a brief discussion of alternative treatment settings).

During assessment and planning, the case manager will also be evaluating the money available and the exposure faced. Whose pocket is it, and how deep is it? If unlimited dollars are available, should they be spent whatever way the providers want regardless of necessity? Sometimes this attitude does prevail. Case managers need to look for the "value-locked dollar" for a demonstration that the treatment is necessary and reasonable, will achieve good results, and is the most cost-effective way to provide the requisite care.[12]

Reporting

A case manager's report back to the referral source, payer, or internal personnel (in the case of a comprehensive health plan) should reflect those things about which the payer is most concerned. If the case manager is on staff at a health maintenance organization (HMO) and the lines of insurance are predominantly group medical, reports will address medical issues for the most part. In a disability case where the client is the employer, the case manager needs to focus on return to work issues. In a workers' compensation case, carriers are responsible for both medical costs and lost earnings. This payer will want to know the extent of medical involvement, the severity of injury, and the likelihood of some permanent incapacitation. When reporting to a claims supervisor, the case manager will want to include specific medical information and parenthetical explanations to help the reader interpret the medical terms (and to help educate them regarding information they are likely to see about the diagnosis or prognosis in other reports). The frequency and length of case management reports should be confirmed with the referral source.

Reports should be written at least once a month. All pertinent case activity should be recorded in a specific, regular format. Clients should not be punished with months' worth of casework attached to a large invoice. By reporting in manageable increments of 3 to 4 weeks, case managers gain better control of client files and invoicing and keep the payer up-to-date on the case. Significant activity or events requiring clarification should be reported in a timely fashion, first by phone and subsequently through written documentation (within a few days).

How extensive should reports be? Some payer organizations have specific guidelines, limiting initial report writing time to 2 hours or even half an hour. Others request a verbal report, asking that the case manager not even take the time to send a document or even a fax. In this type of situation, the case manager needs to educate the referral source. Case management reports have practical and legal value as documents chronicling case management activity.

Suppose the case manager, during a phone conversation, reports to the payer a previously undocumented call to the patient or the physician. Will either of them remember this exchange of information? What if the case moves into litigation? What if the patient takes a turn for the worse? Especially when planning services, negotiating services, or putting alternative plans in place, case managers need to document decisions and their implementation. This is just good case management administration.

Regardless of the client's (payer's) needs, case management reports should follow a certain format and contain the same basic information: the name of the referral source, the mailing address and phone number for reporting, the line of insurance, the date of occurrence of the accident or injury, the name of the insured, and the name of the claimant or patient. In addition, they will include pertinent information obtained from the payer, patient, family, physician(s), employer, medical records, and other medical professionals; a review of the policy coverage and limits; any suggested alternative treatment program, and a discussion of relevant community resources.[13]

Obtaining Approval from the Payer

Once the case management plan has been devised and the report has been sent to the client, the case manager must then obtain approval to proceed with the recommendations in the report. There are always going to be times when case managers have to use their own judgment and consider whom they are representing. An employer or referral source might say directly "I want John out of that facility; it's too expensive." If the case manager feels that the patient is in the most appropriate center and there is no less costly setting, he or she cannot allow the client to override his or her professional judgment. The case manager cannot service the client first and the patient last; the interests of the patient must always predominate. Case managers are not in the business of protecting the federal or corporate health budget at the expense of patients' well-being and safety.[14]

Coordinating and Monitoring: Putting the Plan into Action

Plans are sometimes put in motion as early as the initial evaluation stage. The case manager may not have gathered all the information or submitted a report when he or she gets the go-ahead to put services in place. When an involved case has been referred from a company with which the case manager has worked before, the company might request a verbal report from on site. During that phone conversation, the case manager might obtain approval to begin the recommended intervention.

The case manager not only has the responsibility to put appropriate services in place but also should make certain that the services and treatments put in place remain high quality in nature, cost effective, and necessary; he or she needs to monitor the case. Sometimes a client company will want a case manager to make a one-time visit, arrange for services, and be done with the case. Then who is watching for changes in the patient's needs or tracking and assisting with increases or decreases in services: the home infusion company or home care agency, which obviously has a stake in the case's progression? Who is tracking the continued adherence to the physician's treatment plan?

The monitoring process varies from case to case. It may include semimonthly home visits by the case manager or periodic phone calls made by the patient to the case manager. In active cases where multiple services are in place, the case manager must make monthly on-site visits.

If there are no services in place but the patient has been discharged and asked to take specific medications or dress a wound in a certain way, the case manager will make check-in calls to see how the patient is coping. When a patient sounds ill or acknowledges problems, the case manager should call the treating physicians and assess the situation. Perhaps the treatment plan needs to be reevaluated.[15]

Evaluating the Plan

Along with monitoring the medical treatment plan and its effectiveness, the case manager will evaluate and reevaluate the case management plan over the course of intervention. Is the treatment working? Have any complications developed? How is the family coping? Does the caregiver need a respite? Each case will go through modification and redevelopment. Changes in patient status will require new measures of care.

The case manager should review the treatment plan and the patient's progress at least once every 30 days. Short-term referrals, which generally run less than 3 months and are characterized by intense activity at the outset that tapers off as the patient improves, are always reassessed before the patient's discharge from a facility or program. Long-term programs, such as geriatric care, are evaluated at intervals of 3, 6, or 9 months. In a brain or spinal cord injury, care may be evaluated at 1-year intervals. Long-term care evaluations can become challenging because the goal of case management is stability; in some cases, things can go smoothly for long periods of time, and there will seemingly be nothing to report.

Furthermore, quality of life is less easily measured than the quantity of money spent on care. Is a continuation of the program warranted? Are the dollars spent on John's care every day worth it? Treatment might be necessary for a 6- to 9-month period, but the patient may not require facility services for that entire time. Although making great strides in the first 2 months, the patient may show no further improvement after 3 months. Perhaps the patient has hit a plateau and needs a break from the rigorous therapies. The next step might be to place the patient in a less expensive day program and then perhaps return him or her to the inpatient facility for another round of intensive therapy if improvement again becomes noticeable.

Over the course of care, as a treatment facilitator the case manager maintains communication with the treating physicians to share concerns and observations regarding developing conditions and with physical therapists, social workers, community center personnel, employers, and anyone else who may contribute to the patient's care and welfare. The case manager may need to reestablish ties to a specialist to request assistance.[16]

UTILIZATION REVIEW: PREADMISSION REVIEW, CONCURRENT REVIEW, AND CASE MANAGEMENT

Generally speaking, utilization reviews fall into three categories: prospective (before the event, called preadmission or precertification), concurrent (during the event), and retrospective (after the event). Each type of review uses certain criteria to determine whether there is a need for further action, decision, or intervention and to evaluate the necessity and efficiency of the use of medical services. In addition to tracking the appropriateness of medical care and expenses, the review process itself can also be used to identify cases for case management if the organization or reviewer is aware of the red flags that indicate a need for case management intervention, such as multiple hospital admissions; certain International Classification of Diseases, Ninth Revision, Clinical Modification (ICD-9-CM) diagnostic codes; and claims for apnea alarms, electric hospital beds, or infusion care services. These red flags are discussed further in the next section. Suffice it to say that, from a case management perspective, the opportunity to explore alternatives, assist the patient, and preserve benefit dollars is already missed when the case manager is confronted with a claim for $42,000 resulting from a hospital stay of 28 days. Could the patient have gone to a skilled facility for 14 of those days? Were nursing and other services in the home a possibility? With alternatives, would there have been opportunities for fee negotiations? These are questions without answers and a $42,000 price tag.

It is amazing that carriers, TPAs, and employer groups often set up a preadmission review program without linking it to some kind of case management program. Reviews are performed in a management vacuum; it is assumed that there are no savings to be gained. Furthermore, except for those possibly realized through the denial of a few days in the hospital or avoidance of an inpatient stay, there will not be any savings to record. Without a connection to case management, preadmission review accomplishes nothing more than maintaining a census of inpatient admissions. Also, preadmission review alone, without concurrent review, is incapable of reducing lengths of stay or allowing alternative care plans to be considered.

The maximum opportunity for success exists when one organization provides preadmission and concurrent review along with case management services. Too often, particularly in organizations other than large HMOs, one company does the reviewing and another provides the case management. The delays that inevitably occur in identifying a high-cost case, referring it to a case management vendor, assigning the case, and actually managing the case make the system ineffective; an ongoing process of evaluation, identification, assessment, planning, and implementation could be the ideal. The key in case management is how the case manager gets involved and how soon. For example, one has missed an opportunity if a case manager starts working with a spinal cord–injured patient 20 or 30 days after the initial hospitalization. Earlier involvement could have resulted in a transfer of this patient to a spinal cord injury treatment center and the prevention of some complications that have now occurred, which will be more costly to treat and will prolong the period of rehabilitation.

Case managers are facilitators who have expertise in understanding complex cases and the ability to effect change. They assist patients by getting information and expediting the delivery of services. To perform effectively, case managers need to work within a system that allows involvement to occur at an optimum time. Because a seemingly simple procedure can unexpectedly become complex and expensive, each admission needs to be reviewed as it occurs. This does not mean that each case will require case management intervention. Most will not. The strategy of reviewing each case, however, will promote better outcomes for patients and payers.

The sample case presented in Exhibit 18–3 was created for an organization to illustrate what would probably occur with and without an integrated system in place. Exhibit 18–4 is a letter designed to be sent to plan participants to explain the advocacy role of the case manager and the nature of the case management process.[17]

As an example, this author once received a referral from a claims department after it was notified by a provider who had conducted the preadmission review 7 weeks earlier and noted a diagnosis of cancer of the stomach. A claims examiner now had the end-of-month printout and had also just received a claim for 1 week of total parenteral nutrition (TPN) and "other" services totaling $10,000. The examiner thought a case management referral was in order. It was, but it came a little too late. The services continued for a second week as arranged; the provider refused to negotiate retrospectively to lower costs because he knew his services were payable at 100 percent (he knew that the patient's benefit plan would pay the full price for his services because he called the claims department and learned this from a customer service representative). The patient died after a second admission to the hospital. Perhaps the TPN services could have been negotiated more cost effectively; perhaps a hospice program could have been arranged, allowing the patient to die at home with his family around him; perhaps money could have been

saved, too. In this instance, there was preadmission and concurrent review and case management as well as a benefit plan that would have permitted alternatives, yet because each system functioned independent of the others, in a vacuum, realizing an alternative was impossible.

When preadmission and concurrent review and case management functions are integrated, the coordination can avoid duplication of involvement, help a claims department manage its workload, assist in the development of prevention and wellness programs, support the evaluation of use of benefits, and expose the need to redesign plans.[18]

PREADMISSION AND CONCURRENT REVIEW CASE MANAGEMENT REPORTS

Preadmission and concurrent review summary reports (Exhibit 18–5) and other documentation of case events constitute an ongoing profile of a case. Case-specific reports (Exhibit 18–6) help establish a case history and can be used to track the details of a case, which can be extremely helpful if the patient moves from low- to high-risk status. Produced for all hospital admissions, all scheduled pregnancies, and all emergency cases, case-specific reports incorporate notes made by nurse reviewers. They are valuable for internal use in a preadmission and concurrent review department, provide the rationale for case management referral, contain important background information for the case manager assigned to the case, and are also forwarded to the claims examiner.

The review summary report in Exhibit 18–5 shows that only one patient out of ten was referred for case management. One review summary prepared by this author showed a surprisingly high incidence of admission for pregnancy complications for one employer group, and it led to the formation of a maternity screening and management program and the prevention of two premature births. The savings to the group far outweighed the costs of the managed care program.[19]

Exhibit 18–3 Case Sample without (Example A) and with (Example B) Preadmission Review, Concurrent Review, and Case Management

---

Example A

Mr. Jones enters the hospital as recommended by his physician for a diagnosis of pneumonia. As prescribed by his medical plan, he contacts ABC Insurance Co. to advise of his scheduled admission. ABC's representative obtains basic information concerning hospital, treating physician, and possibly the proposed length of stay for this admission (5 days).

The notification procedure is completed, there is no follow-up of this patient, and eventually this individual will be discharged.

The hospital claim is eventually received by ABC, and it is then noted that the actual stay was for 21 days at a cost of $22,500.

Example B

Mr. Jones, as prescribed by his medical plan, contacts ABC Insurance Co. to advise of his scheduled admission, and the representative obtains information concerning diagnosis, length of stay, name of treating physician, hospital, etc. This information is then faxed to Options Unlimited, where it is screened for follow-up.

The Options Unlimited nurse contacts the patient and treating physician and obtains additional information, including medical history, other hospital admissions, etc. She is in agreement with the treating physician for length of stay (which for this man would be 5 days).

Now on day 5, the Options Unlimited nurse contacts the hospital utilization review nurse to determine whether, in fact, the patient will be discharged. The utilization review nurse advises that there has not been a good result thus far with the current antibiotic and that further hospitalization was indicated. The Options Unlimited nurse confers with the treating physician, who discusses the case further and hopes that an additional 3 days will result in success.

On day 7, the Options Unlimited nurse contacts the treating physician, who reports continued lack of response. He will try a different antibiotic. The patient will need perhaps another 7–10 days of hospitalization.

Because of the extended stay, requests for additional days, and the uncertain treatment plan, the decision is made to refer for an on-site case management assessment.

A visit by the case manager to the patient and treating physician uncovers additional problems, but the result is that the physician agrees to discharge the patient home on intravenous antibiotics (rather than continue the inpatient stay).

The patient is discharged to his home on day 7 of this hospital admission. Antibiotic therapy and nursing services are provided in his home. The Options Unlimited case manager has arranged the services with the input from the physician, negotiated fees for these services, and monitored the patient for the desired outcome and eventual discontinuation of these services. After a 5-day course at home, the patient is switched to antibiotics by mouth and is permitted to return to work.

Results

Example A:

Action:	Pay claim (obtain discount if possible, audit the claim) of $22,500.00
Savings:	None
Questions:	1) Were all the costs necessary?
	2) Was a 21-day stay necessary?
	3) Were there other alternatives?

Results

Example B:

Pay:	Hospital claim of $7,499.94
Pay:	Claim for home antibiotic therapy and nursing services of $1,250.00 ($250/day × 5 days)
Pay:	Case management fees of $800.00
Total:	$9,549.94
Savings:	$12,950.06
Questions:	1) Were the costs appropriate? Yes
	2) Were the patient and the plan well served? Yes

Source: Reprinted from C.M. Mullahy, *The Case Manager's Handbook*, pp. 182–183, © 1995, Aspen Publishers, Inc.

Exhibit 18–4 Letter Explaining Case Management to Plan Participants

---

Employees:
ID (SSN) #:
Claimant/Patient:
Physician:
Hospital:
Date of Admission:
Employer Group:

TO: XXXXXXXXXXXX
       XXXXXXX
       XXXXXXXXXXXX, XX XXXXX

We received notification of the above hospital admission on _____. Please be advised that this is an advisory notice only and does not imply payment of the claim/bill that will be received for this hospital confinement. It further does not imply payment for any of the services that may be related to the confinement, i.e., surgeon, anesthesia, etc.

A Nurse Case Manager will be following the patient's progress during the hospital stay. It is also possible that a nurse case manager may be in contact with you either via telephone or in person, should this seem appropriate.

All claims received by the plan administrator for _____ will be reviewed and considered and will be subject to the terms of your medical plan. This includes but is not limited to preexisting conditions, plan limitations and exclusions, cosmetic vs. medical need, uncovered services, etc., and co-payments and deductibles.

If there are any changes in the case-related information above, please notify the Nurse Case Manager at 1-800-555-1212. If you have any additional questions or concerns about this or other medical matters, please feel free to call us.

Thank you in advance for your anticipated cooperation.
Very truly yours,

_____

Nurse Case Manager, OPTIONS UNLIMITED
cc: File@J.J.#01481

Source: Reprinted from C.M. Mullahy, *The Case Manager's Handbook* p. 184, © 1995 Aspen Publishers, Inc.

RED FLAGS: INDICATORS FOR CASE MANAGEMENT

Cases that benefit most from case management commonly involve the most expensive services. Use of these services is thus a red flag. Other indicators include a high frequency of admissions in a short period and an unusually lengthy hospital stay. A stay of 10 days or longer for a surgical hospitalization indicates multiple problems or complications now and points to problems down the road as well. This is where a case manager's clinical knowledge, his or her feel for what constitutes a big case, comes into play. Exhibit 18–7 shows a tip sheet developed for the claims department of one TPA. It includes red flags for case management intervention as well as indicators for claims review.

Different red flags should be used for different lines of insurance. When looking for case management indicators, a case manager will not apply the same dollar limit per claim in a workers' compensation case as in a group medical case. In workers' compensation, for each

Exhibit 18–5 Sample Preadmission and Concurrent Review Summary Report

Group # - 001   Third Party Administrator   1/1/93-1/31/93

Date Reported	Emp SS#	Patient Name	Diagnosis	Type	Date of Admission	Date of Discharge	Status
1/2/93	000000000	J. Smith	Fracture	Emerg	1/1/93	1/2/93	Closed
1/3/93	000000000	C. Jones	Norm Delivery	Emerg	1/25/93		Open
1/5/93	000000000	K. Williams	Lump in Breast	Sched	1/8/93		Open
1/7/93	000000000	S. Allen	Myocardial Infar	Emerg	1/11/93	1/18/93	Refer CM
1/12/93	000000000	T. Hans	Herniated Disc	Sched	1/21/93	1/25/93	Closed
1/14/93	000000000	L. Mooney	Miscarriage	Emerg	1/13/93	1/14/93	Closed
1/16/93	000000000	J. Bono	Appendicitis	Emerg	1/15/93	1/18/93	Closed
1/18/93	000000000	N. Strong	Derangement Knee	Sched	1/25/93		Open
1/25/93	000000000	P. Duffy	Depression	Sched	1/28/93		Psych
1/28/93	000000000	I. Grello	Pregnancy	Sched	3/25/95		Open

Total Admissions for Period = 9   Total Discharged = 5   Total Referred for Case Management = 1

TOTAL CASES FOR PERIOD = 10

Source: Reprinted from C.M. Mullahy, *The Case Manager's Handbook*, p. 189, © 1995, Aspen Publishers, Inc.

lost-time injury there is an established guideline, and if the injured person is still out of work a month beyond the date calculated using the guidelines, then that fact becomes a red flag (see Chapter 52).[20,21]

Other indicators of a problem include the following: extension of treatment, treatment recommended by a physician at his or her physician-owned facility, a patient receiving physical therapy and chiropractic manipulation at the same time, a variety of practitioners consulting on a seemingly straightforward case, a case that continually passes its return to work date, and a patient taking large numbers of pain medications or antidepressant medications.

In group medical coverage, the concerns will be different. Group plans cover employees and their dependents, and a case manager might target catastrophic illnesses, premature deliveries, cancer cases, and other chronic and devastating long-term diseases such as AIDS or multiple sclerosis. Other things to watch for include multiple hospitalizations, multiple physicians, expenses beyond a certain threshold (e.g., $10,000), and particular kinds of services, such as chemotherapy, radiation therapy, and infusion care.[22]

TIMING CASE MANAGEMENT INTERVENTION

At what point in the review process should a referral be made for case management intervention? As discussed earlier, there are some basic indicators or red flags to look for, and there are other, less specific, more individualized considerations. Some indicators may actually be evident during the first call from a hospital admis-

Exhibit 18–6 Sample Preadmission and Concurrent Review Case-Specific Report

---

CareWatch ID#: 00676
Date Reported: 08/31/93
Reported by: RENY
Group/Carrier:
Employee Info:

Name:	G. Jones	SSN: 123-45-6789
Address:	12 Amhurst St., Mid-Island, N.Y.	
Hire Date:	03/01/91	Effective Date of Coverage: 06/01/91
Telephone:		

Patient Information:

Name:	G. Jones	DOB: 01/25/67	Age: 26
Relation:	Employee	Sex: Male	
Confinement Type:	Emergency		
Admission Date:	08/28/93	Length of Stay: 2 Days	
Discharge Date:	08/30/93		

Procedure: initial hosp. care/eval. and management
Hospital: COMM. HOSPITAL
Address: ROUTE 111
    SMITHTOWN, NY 11787
Telephone: (516) 979-9800   Faxphone:
Admitting Physician Information:
Doctor: Dr. J. Kahn
Telephone: (516) 555-1212   Faxphone:
Diagnosis: hemorrhage—cerebral

CASE REMARKS

9/3/93: t/c to hospital, claimant was discharged on 8/30/93 but could not give me any other info. CTR t/c to MD, spoke w/ Evelyn Spencer, who said that the claimant has an app't. with the MD today and she will call me back after he has been seen by the MD. CTR t/c to claimant, who said he felt dizzy and went to the ER, he was admitted to ICU and had a CAT scan, was told he had an elevated BP and is on medication. He continues to feel dizzy sometimes and gets tingling in his tongue. Has an appt. today at 12:30 PM. Will f/u on 9/8/. CTR

9/8/93: t/c to claimant - per family member he is having some type of outpt. test today. f/u with claimant 9/9. IK

9/9/93: t/c to MD - told me that claimant was readmitted to hosp. for one day 9/8 to have arteriogram done. Diagnosis is seizure disorder and AV malformation and he was started on Dilantin. Will be referring him to neurologist. Will f/u with claimant. MF

9/10/93: t/c to claimant - still feels dizzy, has appt. with his MD today. Will f/u with claimant 9/14 for outcome and neuro. appt. IK

9/14/93: t/c to claimant - per his father, he has an appt. with neurologist Dr. Kahn (didn't have no.) tomorrow at 1 PM; he still has dizziness and numbness of tongue. f/u with claimant/MD 9/16. IK

9/16/93: t/c to claimant - told me that he had appt. with neurologist yesterday and that he referred him to another MD (neurosurgeon?) and that appt. is for next week 9/22. (claimant did not know the name of MD offhand). Continues to take Dilantin and continues to feel dizzy, even though he stopped smoking. Claimant mentioned that MD might have to operate on his brain because "there is something wrong with blood vessel in his brain." Obtained Dr. Kahn's phone number 516-555-1212. Will f/u with MD. MF

9/16/93: t/c to MD - not in because of holidays. Will be back in office on 9/21 after 1 PM. MF

9/21/93: t/c to Dr. Kahn - per Sue pt. has AVM, will not be seen again in MD's office until sometime around 10/12, not aware of ref. to another MD, not aware of potential for surg. at this time. f/u with claimant to obtain name and no. of referral MD. IK

9/21/93: t/c to claimant - no answer x 2. IK

9/24/93: t/c to claimant - left message on answering machine. MF

9/30/93: t/c to claimant - no answer. Will try one more time tomorrow if no answer or return call, then will close case. MF

10/01/93: t/c to claimant - no answer x 2. IK. MULTIPLE attempts made to contact claimant; per MD office no further therapy scheduled at this time. Case closed. IK

MONITOR FILES FOR FUTURE CLAIMS*************

(continues)

Exhibit 18–6 continued

CareWatch ID#: 00954
Date Reported: 11/08/93
Reported by: BARBARA
Group/Carrier:
Employee Info:

Name:	G. Jones	SSN: 123-45-6789
Address:	12 Amhurst St., Mid-Island, N.Y.	
Hire Date:	03/01/91	Effective Date of Coverage: 06/01/91
Telephone:		

Patient Information:

Name:	G. Jones	DOB: 01/25/67	Age: 26
Relation:	Employee	Sex: Male	
Confinement Type:	Emergency		
Admission Date:	10/30/93	Length of Stay: 4 Days	
Discharge Date:	11/03/93		

Procedure: initial hosp. care/eval. and management
Hospital: COLUMBIA PRESBYTERIAN MED CTR.
Address: 207 ST & BROADWAY
          NEW YORK, NY 10032

Telephone:	(212) 305-2500	Faxphone:

Admitting Physician Information:

Doctor:	Dr. Z. Binder	
Telephone:	(212) 555-1212	Faxphone:
Diagnosis:	hemorrhage—cerebral	

CASE REMARKS
CASE KNOWN TO OPTIONS FROM PREVIOUS ADMISSION - VERY DIFFICULT TO FOLLOW - CLAIMANT DID NOT RETURN PHONE CALLS.

11/8/93: t/c Dr. Binder Office. MD not available. will have secretary (Aline) call me back. vc

11/8/93: t/c to hospital pt info. patient discharged 11/3/93. vc

11/8/93: t/c claimant. No answer. vc

11/8/93: t/c hospital medical records. Dept closed (hrs. 9-12, 2-3:45) direct #212-555-1212

11/9/93: t/c to MD - MD is away, per Aline, residents are following claimant. She will get info. from them and return call. MF

11/9/93: t/c from Aline at Dr. Binder's office - told me that claimant is being followed by Dr. Sachs and that I should speak to Pat his secretary for further info. Number is 212-555-1212. Transferred me to that number - according to Pat, MD is away and she could not tell me about hosp. stay. Claimant does not have a follow up appt. yet, she has to call him this week and set something up. Told me that claimant did not have surgery and during hosp. stay claimant was under the care of Dr. Frank 212-555-1212. MF

11/9/93: t/c to Dr. Frank - not in yet, left message with secretary, Lisa. MF

11/10/93: t/c to Dr. Frank - not in yet; left message with secretary, Lisa, for MD to call-back. BR

11/11/93: t/c to claimant - spoke to man who rents a room from claimant's father. Told me that claimant does not live here anymore. Claimant's father is out right now, he will give him my phone number for him to call me back with number where claimant can be reached. MF

11/11/93: t/c to claims. Renee will pull most recent claims and check on address and call me back. MF

11/11/93: t/c to MD office - spoke to Lisa who told me that she gave the MD the messages. She will speak to him again and try to get info and call me back. Asked if she had claimant's address and phone number and she transferred me to billing to speak to Terry. Per Terry, claimant does not appear to be in computer system at office or with hosp. Check system several times. Told me to call back after 1 PM and speak to Carmen and perhaps she could help. MF

11/12/93: t/c to Dr. Frank claimant had a minor cerebral hemorrhage. Dx. is arterial malformation of the brain; Dr. Sachs is performing surgery at a later date; (212) 555-1212; individual not in any danger; need to contact Dr. Sachs for more detailed info. JG/br

11/15/93: t/c to Dr. Sach's office/Pat: they have been unable to contact claimant; he needs to see Dr. Sachs & then surgery can be scheduled. BR

(continues)

Exhibit 18–6 continued

11/15/93: t/c to claims Renee says claimant admitted to Community Hosp. of W. Suffolk on 11/3

11/14/93: t/c to C.H.O.W.S./UR Dept./Mrs. King - claimant adm. 11/13 via ER with seizures; was in ICU - now on telemetry; under the care of Dr. Zeller, (516) 555-1212 has no additional info @ this time. BR

11/15/93: t/c to Dr. Sachs/Pat - given above info; she will inform MD to f/u with Dr. Z; BR

11/15/93: t/c to Dr. Zeller's office - informed of pending consult with Dr. S # given; Dr. Zeller in with patient; will call with claimant when finished. BR

11/15/93: t/c from Dr. Zeller, claimant c/o numbness of tongue which MD feels is seizure activity; Dilantin increased - c/o dizziness; CAT scan WNL; EEG pending; will be disch. tonight or tomorrow; f/u with Dr. S. BR

11/15/93: t/c to claimant; spoke with father; corrected birthdate obtained (12-06-34): will f/u with claimant tomorrow to schedule CM assessment; in rm 254 -, father & son work for the same company. BR

CASE REFERRED FOR CASE MANAGEMENT.

Source: Reprinted from C.M. Mullahy, *The Case Manager's Handbook*, pp. 190–193, © 1995, Aspen Publishers, Inc.

sions department, treating physician, or patient's family to a preadmission review department or company. A preterm delivery, a high-risk pregnancy, a cerebrovascular accident in a teenager, a spinal cord injury, and a traumatic brain injury with coma are all conditions for which there is a high probability of a lengthy hospital stay, a need for additional care and services upon discharge, high costs, and benefits to be gained through case management.

Other conditions also merit an early referral, not necessarily because of a particular diagnosis but because of surrounding circumstances. For instance, diabetes is not by itself a condition that would necessarily promote a case management referral, but the fourth hospital admission in 2 months of a patient with diabetes might. Why are these readmissions occurring? Is the patient noncompliant or noneducated? Is the treating physician a retiring family practitioner? Might an endocrinologist be needed?

Let's look at a patient with an admitting diagnosis of cellulitis. At first glance, this is not a case for case management referral. As the patient's stay in the hospital continues, though, we learn more about this 46-year-old woman: She is also hypertensive, had a coronary bypass 2 years earlier, is diabetic, and weighs 250 pounds, clearly morbidly obese for her height of 5 feet 4 inches. This woman might eventually require a below-knee amputation secondary to her multiple conditions. The potential for this

occurrence warrants an assessment by a case management professional. Patients such as this woman would probably be overlooked by a system for case management referral that is driven solely by one ICD-9-CM code or one set dollar limit. Each similar case presents such substantial opportunities for improved outcomes, prevention of complications, and reduction of expenses that not referring becomes a costly risk.[23]

BEYOND THE CASE MANAGEMENT BASICS

Case Management's Contribution to Claims Management

By helping identify the small percentage of claimants responsible for generating the majority of claims and the bulk of benefit payouts (those in need of case management intervention) and educating claims administrators regarding medical issues, case managers serve a vital function in claims departments. They help insurers and TPAs look good to employers/payers by better managing benefit dollars, help patients get care approval in a timely fashion, and help speed the claims administration process *without* losing patients through the cracks in the system.

Nothing speaks louder to a client than a report taken from its own group experience. With a claims run, the case manager can show that, out of a group of 500 with total claims paid of

Exhibit 18–7 CareSolutions™ Red Flags and AccuClaim™ Red Flags

CareSolutions Red Flags

- **Diagnosis:**

Cancer	Neuromuscular Diseases	Head Injury	Psychiatric
AIDS	Spinal Cord Injuries	Severe Burns	Multiple Trauma
Stroke	Alcohol & Substance Abuse	Hi-Risk Pregnancy	Hi-Risk Infant
Transplant	Cardiovascular	Chronic Respiratory	

- **Potential Treatment:**

Ventilator Dependent	TPN/Enteral	Home Care
IV Antibiotics	Extended ICU	Chemo

- **Frequent Hospitalizations:** 3 Admits Same Year/Same or Related Problem

- **Cost of Claim:** Same illness over $10,000 Year-to-Date

- **Location of Claim:** Complex Care Delivered in Rural Setting, Small Hospital, or Facility w/Poor Outcome History/Diagnosis

- **Patterns of Care:** Failed or Repeated Surgeries, Hospital Acquired Infections, Malpractice Concerns

----

- **Diagnostic Codes:** ICD9CM - Case Management Referral Indicators

042-044	HIV Infection	644	Early or threatened labor
140-239	Neoplasms (Cancer)	655-656	Fetal abnormality
250	Diabetes w/complications	710	All collagen (SLE+)
252	(possible mult. hosps., coma, renal, eye, neuro)	714	Rheumatoid arthritis w/inflammatory polyarthropathies
277	Cystic Fibrosis, porphyria, metabolic disorders (multi hosps.)	740-759	Congenital Anomolies, Spina Bifida, Cardiac Septal defect
279	Immunity deficiency disorders (repeat hosps.)	760-763	Maternal causes of Perinatal morbidity & mortality
286-287	Coagulation defects (repeat hosps.)	765.1	Premature birth
290-299	Psychoses	800	Fx vault of skull
300-316	Neurotic, personality & other non-psychotic mental disorders	806	Fx of vertebral column w/SCI
330-337	Hereditary & degenerative diseases of CNS (Alzheimer's, Huntington Chorea)	850-854	Intracranial injury excluding those w/skull Fx
340-349	CNS disorders, MS, CP, Quadriplegic, Paraplegic, Anoxic brain damage	860-869	Internal injury of chest, abdomen & pelvis
358	Myasthenia Gravis (repeat hosps.)	870-879	Open wound of head, neck & trunk
359	Muscular Dystrophy (repeat hosps.)	925-929	Crushing injury (may involve extensive trauma)
430-438	Cerebral vascular disease, car. hemorrhage	948	Burns over 25% of body
496	COPD	952	SCI without spinal bone injury
501-503	Asbestosis & Silicosis	994	Effects of external causes - lightning, drowning, strangulation
584-586	Renal failure	996-999	Complications of surgical & medical care

(continues)

Exhibit 18–7 continued

AccuClaim Red Flags

- **Surgical & Anesthesia Claims:** All claims over $1,000.00 & all cases with more than 2 line items should be referred for a medical review. Alert for GYN, Orthopedic, Plastic Surgery. If the surgical claim is referred, corresponding anesthesia claims should be referred also to verify complexity of claimed procedure.
  Information to Obtain: 1) Operative Report 2) Anesthesia Time 3) R&C Charges for EACH CPT code.
- **Podiatrists:** All claims that exceed $800.00 should be referred.
  Information to Obtain: 1) Operative Report if a surgical procedure is being billed 2) R&C charges for EACH CPT code.
- **Physical Therapy & Occupational Therapy:** Claims that exceed 6 weeks of treatment should be referred.
  Information to Obtain: 1) PT evaluation 2) Therapy progress notes that include long- and short-term goals and the Range of Motion results 3) Letter of Medical Need from treating MD w/diagnosis, frequency of treatment & estimated duration.
- **Chiropractic Care:** Claims that exceed $300.00 should be referred.
  Information to Obtain: 1) Complete copy of the medical records; NO summaries. Include diagnosis, treatment plan, frequency of treatment, estimated duration.
- **Durable Medical Equipment:** This is an area of extreme abuse and overutilization of services and fees. The following claims should be referred: oxygen concentrators & related equipment, hospital beds, wheelchairs, ANY monitors, respirators/ventilators, requests for home modifications (ramps, etc.).
- **Home Health Services:** All claims for nursing, aides or related services should be referred.
  Information to Obtain: 1) Itemized bills 2) Nursing notes
- **Infusion Care Services:** All claims for the following infusion services should be referred: IV antibiotics & other medications, TPN (Total Parenteral Nutrition), chemotherapy, analgesia (pain medications)
  Information to Obtain: 1) MD's prescription 2) Itemized billing for medications, nursing & related services & supplies.
- **Any of the following should be referred:** 1) Appeals 2) Difficult Providers 3) Ambulatory Surgical Center 4) Large Hospital Bills: over 7 days LOS; to review for LOS, medical needs vs. custodial
- **Procedure Codes:** CPPT Accu-Claim Referral Indicators

Integumentary System
11000-11044	For Cosmetic vs. Medical
15780-15791	For Cosmetic vs. Medical
15810-15840	For Cosmetic vs. Medical
17304-17310	For Cosmetic vs. Medical
19318-19500	For Cosmetic vs. Medical

Musculoskeletal
27290-	Amputation
27590-27598	Amputation

Pulmonary System
30400-30630	For Cosmetic
31300-31660	Laryngectomy - Tracheotomy, etc.
32310-32545	Lung Surgery

Cardiovascular
33200-33220	Pacemaker Surgery
35450-35458	Vascular vs. Cosmetic
37799	Unlisted Procedure
38999	Unlisted Procedure
39599	Unlisted Procedure

Digestive
41100-41155	Mouth, Tongue (for cancer)
43600-43640	Stomach (Biopsy, etc.)
44100-44340	Intestinal
47100-47135	Liver

Urinary System
50200-50380	Kidney, incl. Transplant
51550-51597	Bladder (especially for cancer)

Maternity
59000-59100	High-Risk Procedures
59120-59140	High-Risk Procedures

Nervous System
61304-61576	Craniectomy
62180-62258	Spine
64999	Unlisted Procedure

Eye and Ear
65771	Radial Keretotomy
69300	Cosmetic
69399	Unlisted Procedure
68899	Unlisted Procedure

Source: Reprinted from C.M. Mullahy, *The Case Manager's Handbook,* pp. 210–212, © 1995, Aspen Publishers, Inc.

$200,000, fewer than 20 individuals (4 percent) filed claims totaling 80 percent ($160,000) of that sum. With this information in hand, a case manager can work with the claims administrator and the employer/payer to improve that claims experience. When the few cases are properly managed, the whole group benefits from lower claims costs.[24] (It must be emphasized that a case manager's work is accomplished without compromising the patient's/employee's right to privacy. A case manager can save a company big bucks; the chief executive officer has no need to know, and will never know, the name of the individual in each case.)

Using a computer program, a case manager can conduct a group run; it may be defined to include all workers' compensation cases, all short-term disability cases, all cases lasting longer than 1 year, all hospital admissions, and so forth. The purpose is to begin examining the claims experience of the group to answer the question: Where have all the dollars gone? Gone to lower back pain every one? Gone to four riveters all injured at the same worksite over a period of 3 years?

As an example, for one of this author's clients, a group claims run was prepared as a way to find those patients in need of case management intervention. For the first check, we cast a wide net: all hospital admissions (this field could be narrowed later by setting specific length-of-stay parameters). The first month's claims run showed that 1 percent of the group generated 34 percent of the claims; the next month, 2 percent generated 67 percent of the total. In the third month, 2 percent of the group was responsible for 73 percent of the benefit dollars paid, and 0.3 percent (three employees) accounted for 44 percent of the total. This 3-month run also showed us those cases requiring costly care from month to month, a clear indicator for case management intervention.[25]

Case managers also work with individual reports. Let's assume that the specific limit for this report is $15,000. The first patient that the computer identifies has claims for one hospitalization and one major surgical procedure, a colostomy. The surgery was successful and the postoperative problems minor; there was no real opportunity here for case management to have a major impact. The next individual who has reached the $15,000 limit has a series of claims for an unresolved ulcer of the foot, diabetes, hypertension, and vascular disease. This patient is a health care time bomb. What's the real problem here? Why isn't the ulcer healing? Is this person receiving appropriate care? When reports break out claims history by ICD-9-CM or current procedural terminology codes, the case manager can ascertain the presenting problems and procedures taken to alleviate those problems; actual claims files will indicate potential difficulties, such as complications from the interaction of various medications. Case managers can use the tools of the claims department to help resolve health issues, and claims departments can use the skills of case managers to better their service.[26]

Cost/Benefit Analysis Reports

Cost/benefit analysis reports are one form of case management documentation; they illustrate in financial terms that the money spent on case management services (and the services that are put in place as part of an alternative care plan) translates into dollar savings, or dollars spent versus dollars saved. The report format can be customized or modified to meet client company needs, and report citations may change as a case management program develops. Generally, a cost/benefit analysis report should include an overview of the case management intervention (a brief narrative), a summary of the intervention, case management fees, savings (avoided charges, potential charges, discounted and/or negotiated reductions, and reductions in services, products, and equipment), actual charges, gross savings (potential charges minus actual charges), net savings (gross savings minus case management fees), and the status of the case (open or closed).

There are many opportunities for case managers to improve treatment quality, outcome, and life style for patients. Arranging for home care can increase patient morale and save money; additional savings are realized when a case manager asks providers for prompt-pay discounts or reduces the level of care or hours of care through continual assessment of the patient's progress. Reductions, discounts, negotiated rates, all-inclusive per diem rates, and "freebies" (the free ambulance service provided by some community fire departments, for instance) are examples of hard savings reported in a cost/benefit analysis report.

Soft savings are more difficult to quantify but should be reported as well. A case manager is referred a patient who, in previous months, had an admission every 1 to 2 months for diabetic complications and an emergency hospital stay of 5 to 7 days. The case manager discovers that this patient does not understand his diagnosis, is minimally compliant, and frequently ignores dietary restrictions and blood and urine testing. During the case management intervention of 3 months, the case manager spoke to the patient's physician regarding these problems, referred the patient for formal education and a diet counseling program, and involved him in daily monitoring of his own progress. The pattern of admissions and complications was halted. Over 6 months of case management intervention, there were no further hospital admissions. The dollars in acute care that could have been spent, but were not, are soft savings.[27]

Combined with outcomes data (and including outcomes data as part of the summary of case management intervention), cost/benefit analysis reports chart the success of alternative treatment plans and serve as strong arguments for the effectiveness of case management and managed care.

Wellness Programs

A good case management program should come full circle, with outcomes data providing the rationale for wellness programs designed to address the problems before they arise so that employers and payers spend even less money

treating them and patients are relieved of having to live through the treatments. If a preadmission and concurrent review program or a claims report sequence is pointing up patients whose illnesses are protracted and all of them are smokers, perhaps a "smoke out" wellness program is needed. If every third worker in the warehouse has been out on disability for lower back pain, a case manager might design a wellness program incorporating exercise, review of and instruction on improved lifting patterns, and a facility review to make site modifications as needed to reduce the lifting injuries. As mentioned earlier in the chapter, effective pregnancy counseling and case management intervention can prevent premature labor and the problems arising from low-birthweight infants.

Once a company puts a case management program in place, the next best step is to use the case management outcomes data wisely to reduce its exposure and liabilities by addressing those areas where it is most vulnerable.

24-Hour Coverage Programs

As in wellness programs, 24-hour coverage programs take the best offered by case management and managed care programs and puts it to broader use. Combining total health care and disability management, 24-hour coverage is a program that coordinates all aspects of health care management. This eliminates the oversight, duplication of services, and paper chase encouraged when care and management of care are split into categories based on whether the slip on the ice occurred on the job (workers' compensation) or at home (group medical coverage), includes a jaw injury (dental coverage), or removes the patient from the workforce for 3 months (short-term disability). Rather than pass this individual from management system to management system, 24-hour programs coordinate the entire care program as it moves from site to site and coverage plan to coverage plan. This puts the focus back on the patient and his or her care, better managing his or her needs and therefore better managing the costs. See Chapter 52 for additional discussion of this topic.

Disease Management

At the time of this writing, there is a great deal of discussion about disease management, which has striking similarity to case management. An article in the April 1995 issue of the *Journal of Subacute Care* defined disease management as a coordinated care strategy, citing Blue Cross/ Blue Shield of Michigan's National Coordinated Care Management program as an example of

> ... a new strategic direction for managing customer healthcare experience. The program presents an opportunity to enhance patient care and decrease benefit costs by identifying and selecting chronically ill individuals who represent high-cost users of medical care and linking those individuals with appropriate providers and outpatient interventions. The program involves three separate but integrative components: 1) Identification; 2) Intervention; and 3) Monitoring and Evaluation, that are designed to provide a comprehensive approach to the management of an individual patient's care.[28(p.17)]

Sound familiar? Look again at the description of case management at the beginning of this chapter and the section on the case management work format and process to see just how familiar. See also Chapter 20 for additional discussion of disease management.

In *Medical Marketing & Media* (January 1995), there was less consensus expressed as to exactly what disease management covers. It was summarized, however, as "a system of viewing healthcare disease by disease and examining the interrelated elements in the treatment process with outcomes research to improve quality and lower costs."[29(p.48)] The article positioned disease management as a new "income zone" for pharmaceutical companies to jump into. Some phar-

maceutical executives quoted described disease management as "a work in process" and "embryonic," but others have moved far beyond the infant stage. One major pharmaceutical house is aiming at 50 programs "as quickly as we can do them," according to the individual in charge of the firm's disease management ventures. In the piece, he defined disease management as "An integrated system of customized interventions, measurements, and refinements to current processes of care designed to optimize clinical and economic outcomes within a specific disease state by facilitating proper diagnoses, maximizing clinical effectiveness, eliminating ineffective or unnecessary care, using only cost-effective diagnoses and therapeutics, maximizing the efficiency of care delivery and improving continuously."[30(p.53)] It has yet to be seen whether the pharmaceutical industry will succeed in this activity because many medical managers may be reluctant to allow the drug companies to carry this out on their behalf.

BEYOND REFORM

Case management was improving outcomes and preserving benefit dollars long before *health reform* became a catch phrase bandied about in political circles, and case management will continue to help maintain quality care while making the most of the dollars available. As an integral part of effective managed care programs, case management is a long-term solution to a long-term problem: the attempt to find a balance in our health care delivery system for patients, families, physicians, employers, and payers confronted by diverse health care challenges, new medical technologies, broad ethical questions, and the real lack of monies to fund every treatment humans can think of. As a managed care technique, it works. As a health care profession, it is here to stay.

REFERENCES AND NOTES

1. P. McCollom, Position Statement by the Interim Commission for Certification of Case Manager (Paper pre-

sented at the meeting of the Certified Case Manager Interim Commission Committee, Orlando, January 1995), 1.

2. C. Mullahy, *The Case Manager's Handbook* (Gaithersburg, Md.: Aspen. 1995), 4.

3. Mullahy, *The Case Manager's Handbook*, xv.

4. Mullahy, *The Case Manager's Handbook*, xvi.

5. Mullahy, *The Case Manager's Handbook*, 173–175.

6. Mullahy, *The Case Manager's Handbook*, 11.

7. Mullahy, *The Case Manager's Handbook*, 131.

8. Mullahy, *The Case Manager's Handbook*, 134.

9. Mullahy, *The Case Manager's Handbook*, 135.

10. Mullahy, *The Case Manager's Handbook*, 138, 142–145, 148.

11. Mullahy, *The Case Manager's Handbook*, 340.

12. Mullahy, *The Case Manager's Handbook*, 156–160.

13. Mullahy, *The Case Manager's Handbook*, 161–165.

14. Mullahy, *The Case Manager's Handbook*, 169–170.

15. Mullahy, *The Case Manager's Handbook*, 170–172.

16. Mullahy, *The Case Manager's Handbook*, 172–173.

17. Mullahy, *The Case Manager's Handbook*, 177–181.

18. Mullahy, *The Case Manager's Handbook*, 188.

19. Mullahy, *The Case Manager's Handbook*, 188, 194.

20. See, for example, P. Reed, *The Medical Disability Advisor: Workplace Guidelines for Disability Duration* (Horsham, Pa.: LRP Publications, 1991). Many physicians use this as a reference.

21. See, for example, Milliman & Robertson guidelines. This set of guidelines is followed by the health plans of more than 50 million Americans, among them Prudential, Cigna, US Healthcare, Kaiser Permanente, and many Blue Cross/Blue Shield plans.

22. Mullahy, *The Case Manager's Handbook*, 207, 209–213.

23. Mullahy, *The Case Manager's Handbook*, 186–187.

24. Mullahy, *The Case Manager's Handbook*, 216.

25. Mullahy, *The Case Manager's Handbook*, 217.

26. Mullahy, *The Case Manager's Handbook*, 222, 225.

27. Mullahy, *The Case Manager's Handbook*, 245–248.

28. S.P. Falcon, et al., National Coordinated Care Management: Focused Disease Management Strategies for the 21st Century, *Journal of Subacute Care* 3 (1995): 16–19.

29. W.G. Castagnoli, Is Disease Management Good Therapy for an Ailing Industry?, *Medical Marketing & Media* 30 (1995): 46–53.

30. Castagnoli, Is Disease Management Good Therapy, 53.

SUGGESTED READING

Books

Benefits Source Book. Updated annually. Marietta, Ga.: Employee Benefit News, Enterprise Communications.

Driving Down Health Care Costs: Strategies and Solutions 1996. Updated annually. New York: Panel Publishers.

Garner, J.C. 1996. *Health Insurance Answer Book*, 4th ed. New York: Panel Publishers.

Health Care Financing Administration. 1995. *Best Practices of Managed Care Organizations.* Baltimore, Md.: Health Care Financing Administration.

Mullahy, C.M. 1995. *The Case Manager's Handbook* Gaithersburg, Md.: Aspen Publishers.

Schwartz, G.E., et al. 1989. *The Disability Management Sourcebook.* Washington, D.C.: Washington Business Group on Health and Institute for Rehabilitation and Disability Management.

Thorn, K. 1990. *Applying Medical Case Management: AIDS.* Canoga Park, Calif.: Thorn.

Youngs, M.T. and Wingerson, L. 1995. *The Medical Outcomes & Guidelines Sourcebook.* New York, N.Y.: Faulkner & Gray.

Periodicals

Business & Health, Five Paragon Drive, Montvale, NJ 07645, (201) 358-7200.

Business Insurance, 740 North Rush Street, Chicago, IL 60611-2590, (800) 678-9595.

Case Management Advisor, 3525 Piedmont Road, NE, Building Six, Suite 400, Atlanta, GA 30305, (800) 688-2421.

The Case Manager, 10801 Executive Center Drive, Suite 509, Little Rock, AR 72211, (501) 223-5165.

The Journal of Care Management, 35 East Main Street, Westport, CT 06880, (203) 454-2300.

Managed Healthcare News, 201 Littleton Road, Suite 100, Morris Plains, NJ 07950-2932, (201) 285-0855.

Risk & Insurance, 747 Dresher Road, Suite 500, Horsham, PA 19044-0980, (215) 784-0860.

Risk Management, 205 East 42nd Street, New York, NY 10017, (212) 286-9364.

Chapter 19

Critical Paths: Linking Outcomes for Patients, Clinicians, and Payers

Richard J. Coffey, Janet S. Richards,
Susan A. Wintermeyer-Pingel, and Sarah S. LeRoy

Critical paths are important tools to link patients, clinicians, and managed care organizations (MCOs) and other payers to achieve both high-quality and cost-effective care. Critical paths have proved to be effective tools to improve the planning, coordination, communication, and evaluation of care. This chapter provides an overview of the concepts, approach, and uses of critical paths and provides guidance for developing and implementing critical paths based upon knowledge gained at the University

Richard J. Coffey, Ph.D., is Director of Program and Operations Analysis at the University of Michigan Hospitals and an Adjunct Associate Professor of Industrial and Operations Engineering at the University of Michigan, Ann Arbor, Michigan. Dr. Coffey has authored more than 40 articles and chapters, co-authored two award-winning books, and given more than 100 presentations at regional, national, and international conferences.

Janet S. Richards, M.S., R.N., C.N.A.A., is Assistant Director of Nursing at the University of Michigan Hospitals, Ann Arbor, Michigan. She has programmatic lead for the Coordinated Care Program at the hospitals.

Susan A. Wintermeyer-Pingel, M.S.N., R.N., O.C.N., is a clinical nurse specialist at the University of Michigan Medical Center and participates in the center's Coordinated Care Program, working with the adult hematology/oncology population. She co-authored the chapter entitled "Clinical Paths and Patient Care Documentation" in *Clinical Paths: Tools for Outcomes Management*, published in 1994, and has presented topics related to management of critical pathways both nationally and locally.

Sarah S. LeRoy, M.S.N., R.N., is a clinical nurse specialist in pediatric cardiology at C.S. Mott Children's Hospital in the University of Michigan Medical Center in Ann Arbor, Michigan.

of Michigan Medical Center (UMMC) and other organizations. In a managed care environment, there is greater emphasis on coordination of services and efficient use of resources across multiple settings, such as inpatient, outpatient, and home.

Critical paths foster collaborative goal setting among multiple care providers for specific case types. Outcomes that have been discussed and agreed upon by a whole team are more likely to be achieved because they have a team focus. Changes or variations in outcome trends are more likely to be explored and acted upon. There is less chance of confusion for the patient, the family, the care provider, or the payer concerning the intent of care and expected outcomes.

Development of outcomes related to processes for their achievement (the path) are more likely to assist payers and health care providers to agree upon resources for care provision. Data support the process, particularly when benchmarking has been incorporated into the pathway development. Critical paths help health care providers have input into the payer's guidelines for reasonable care.

BACKGROUND AND TERMINOLOGY

Critical path method (CPM), program evaluation and review technique (PERT), project management, and related approaches have their roots in construction, industrial, and military applications, where there is a need to coordinate multiple contractors and activities to complete a project on time and within limited resources. Within the health care industry, several different terms are used, including *critical paths*, *CareMaps®* (Center for Case Management, South Natick, MA), *clinical pathways*, *clinical guidelines*, *clinical protocols*, *CPM*, and *algorithms*. There are no universally accepted definitions of these terms, although the underlying concepts and tools are similar. It is most important that you understand the concepts; then you can choose terminology that you consider best for your organization. Some operational definitions are given for this chapter.

Coffey and colleagues described the basics of critical paths as they have been applied in health care: "A critical path is an optimal sequencing and timing of interventions by physicians, nurses, and other disciplines for a particular diagnosis or procedure, designed to minimize delays and resource utilization and to maximize the quality of care."[1(p.45)] "A critical path is the sequence of activities that takes the most time to complete."[2(p.15)]

When first introduced, the term *critical path* may cause some confusion in health care organizations because of multiple interpretations of the term *critical*. Clinically, the term *critical* refers to the urgency of a patient's clinical condition, as for patients admitted to the critical care unit or those with critical injuries. From the perspective of CPM, however, *critical* refers to the sequence of activities that takes the most time. Most clinicians are comfortable using this meaning of critical path. If, however, clinicians object to the term *critical path*, you may alternatively choose to use terms such as the following:

- *clinical path*, which emphasizes coordination of all clinical activities
- *time-limiting path*, which clarifies that the goal is to coordinate resources and care to minimize the duration of care[3,4]
- *CareMaps®*, which clarifies that the map describes the care provided.[5,6]

CareMaps® also include outcome information.

Schriefer offers a useful distinction between the general terms associated with pathways and those associated with algorithms or guidelines:

> The pathway provides an overview of the entire production process from start to finish, not only pieces in the process, and can be used to reduce variation in the production process.... Conversely, algorithms often guide clinicians through the 'if, then' decision-making process, such as a variation from a pathway. Algorithms, which were initially developed for handling complex mathematical equations, usually address patient responses to a particular treatment or condition.[7(pp.485–486)]

SCOPE AND USES OF CRITICAL PATHS

Depending upon requirements, there are several different scopes of critical paths.[8] The different scopes can be thought of as how something is viewed through a microscope at different levels of magnification. The contrast of these scopes is particularly important for MCOs. Sample scopes include the following:

- *Inpatient care*—These critical paths are initiated either at the time of admission or at the time of a surgical procedure and typically end at the time the patient is discharged. As length of stay is shortened, some critical paths now include selected pre- and posthospitalization care as well.
- *Complete episode of care*—These critical paths begin at the time the patient presents at the physician's office requiring diagnosis and end when the patient has completed all therapeutic care related to that episode of illness. This scope of critical path application addresses care across multiple geographic settings, including inpatient care in a hospital, outpatient care at a clinic or physician's office, and home care.

- *Specialized applications*—CPM can also be used for specialized applications, such as for ambulatory surgery patients, renal dialysis patients, or managing patients in an intensive care unit. As an example, UMMC is currently developing a model for managing the care of outpatients in a new cough and dyspnea clinic.

- *Life and health management*—These critical paths are developed for management of chronic conditions. These might be used to coordinate the care of patients with hypertension, asthma, cancer, or other illnesses to achieve the highest-quality and most cost-effective care practices.

The scope chosen affects the geographic setting of care and the resources involved. The scope for critical paths will be addressed again later in relation to creating an environment for critical paths.

Critical paths have many important uses. Some of the key are as follows:

- *Clarification of the "big picture" of planned care*—Traditionally, physicians write orders each day, but often other members of the care team are unaware of the overall plan for care. Lacking knowledge of an overall plan, nurses, pharmacists, therapists, ancillary departments, and others carry out each day's orders but cannot plan ahead. Hence breakdowns in communication and delays are common. Critical paths direct care toward agreed-upon end points that are expected outcomes.

- *Planning and coordination of care*—During development of critical paths, the teams of physicians, nurses, pharmacists, therapists, and others discuss the coordination of appropriate care based upon data, expert opinion, and consensus. Thus the different specialties and disciplines are acting in a coordinated, rather than independent, manner.

- *Establishment of expectations*—Critical paths developed by a multispecialty, multidisciplinary team establish specific expectations of actions, timing, and outcomes for everyone.

- *Reduction in the variation of care*—An almost uniform outcome of using critical paths is reduction in the variation of care.

- *Education and orientation*—Critical paths provide an excellent tool to educate staff, students, and others regarding treatment plans and expected outcomes. This represents a substantial deviation from the normal way of educating house officers or residents, medical students, nurses, and others.

- *Benchmarking*—Critical paths provide an excellent mechanism to study alternative care plans in terms of their patient outcomes. Many hospitals compare critical paths and learn from those with the best outcomes.

- *Communication among clinicians, patients, families, payers, and others*—Probably one of the best uses of critical pathways is to communicate the planned care and expected outcomes among clinicians, patients, families, payers and others. MCOs, for example, might approve services based upon the critical path.

- *Improved working environment*—The process of developing and using critical paths encourages cooperation and mutual understanding of everyone's role in providing high-quality, cost-effective care. This leads to an improved working environment.

ENVIRONMENT FOR CRITICAL PATHS

Successful development and use of critical paths is not just a matter of learning the analytical technique. Administrative support of this process is crucial to the success of implementing such a program. Commitment to dedicating time to critical path development, training, monitoring, and data analysis must be in place to meet pathway outcomes successfully.

Success is vitally tied to creating the right environment for critical paths with all the people involved. Establishing an environment where development of, education in, and use of critical paths prosper is fostered by the following.

Urgency To Change

Change only occurs if people perceive a reason to change. Lacking a satisfactory answer to the question "Why change?", physicians, nurses, other clinicians, payers, and others will continue to practice as they have in the past. Business, government, and payers are creating an urgency to control costs without sacrificing quality of care by working "smarter and better."

Champions

The cooperation of respected clinicians from all disciplines is necessary for broad acceptance. Look for teams of physicians, nurses, pharmacists, therapists, and others who believe that critical paths will help them. Working with these champions to demonstrate success with pilot studies in those areas will encourage broader participation.

Willingness To Challenge Current Practices and Boundaries

It is important that the environment encourage clinicians and support staff to challenge current practices critically, such as current clinical protocols, settings where care is provided (e.g., inpatient, outpatient, and home), roles of individuals providing services to achieve the desired outcomes (e.g., physicians, registered nurses, physician assistants, and family members), and timing of activities. One of the keys to challenging the boundaries is to think about the whole episode of care, not just the inpatient portion. If other settings are considered, the time in a hospital may be short or even zero, but the total time for which the patient's care is managed may be substantial.

Standardization versus Independence

One of the most significant changes facing physicians is the introduction of more standardization of clinical practice rather than the independent, autonomous practices of the past. Many physicians object to critical paths, algorithms, and other guidelines as "cookbook medicine." For critical paths to succeed, the environment must encourage physicians and other clinicians to standardize care to the extent that it is helpful and then address appropriate exceptions. The idea is to reduce unnecessary variation in care rather than replace critical thinking.

Managed Care Scope

For broad-scope critical paths to be used, it is important that MCOs cover the same scope of services as addressed by the critical path. For example, a broad-scope critical path addressing the complete episode of care related to a knee replacement might address prehospitalization care in the physician's office, preadmission testing, inpatient care, outpatient physical therapy, durable medical equipment, and home care. If the MCO only covers inpatient care and selected outpatient therapy, however, clinicians will tend to utilize these more expensive services and minimize services that result in direct costs to the patient. Thus MCOs should consider extending coverage of services when broad-scope critical paths demonstrate cost effectiveness and quality.

APPROACH TO DEVELOPING CRITICAL PATHS

The approach may vary with the organization and the team, but the following steps provide a useful approach to developing a critical path.[9,10]

Select the Diagnosis, Procedure, or Condition for the Path

Although this may sound obvious, there are some cautions. There should be an urgency for change and a champion. In addition, it may be helpful to do an initial sensitivity analysis of where costs and problems exist. If, for example, 80 percent of the costs for a surgical patient are associated with the surgical procedure, spending large amounts of time on a postsurgical critical path may address postsurgical length of stay but may miss the major opportunity to reduce costs.

Define the Scope of the Critical Path

Will the critical path address inpatient stay only, inpatient plus outpatient follow-up care, the whole episode of care, or another scope?

Select a Multidisciplinary Team

As with quality improvement projects, the team should include all the key clinical and nonclinical staff involved with the scope of care encompassed by the critical path.

Flowchart the Process and Collect Baseline Information

Most critical path efforts begin with flowcharting the current process and documenting current practices and outcomes through chart review. This approach helps team members understand the complexities, precedent relationships, and current variations in practices within the process before instituting change. Time estimates for different activities are helpful to clarify understanding. Collecting benchmark information and critical paths for the same diagnosis, procedure, or condition also provides useful baseline information. If another organization is found to achieve similar outcomes with a substantially shorter length of stay or at substantially lower cost, further information should be gathered about how that organization achieves those results.

Identify Outcomes

When you are developing a critical path, it is important to begin by defining the specific de-

sired patient outcomes. Ideally, these outcomes should be defined as final goals related to the patient's functional status. When outcomes are defined, it is helpful to think in terms of what specific outcomes the patient must achieve by doing the following:

- Define the outcome criteria for discharge from the hospital, to return home, and to return to daily activity. The focus here should be the most important criteria. All clinical activities should be addressed as part of the critical path, but some are not as important to the overall progress toward these outcomes. It is useful to contrast patient outcomes related to physiological progression or functionality versus system outcomes, such as the patient being transferred or discharged. Focusing on the system-generated boundaries may distract attention from more creative alternatives to achieving the desired patient outcomes. These same outcomes are used to develop the tool for monitoring variance from the pathway and planned outcomes.

- Be specific. Use objective, quantitative terms and measures to the extent that this is practical.

- Be alert to changes in criteria due to new clinical practices, new technology, changing resources available in different settings, and/or other changes. For example, UMMC has been able to change the discharge criteria related to stable heart rhythm by using a home care agency with experienced cardiac care nurses to monitor patients at home.[11] In this case, the discharge criteria are achieved earlier in the treatment course and have resulted in the emergence of a new critical path.

Define Intermediate Patient Care Objectives

Although not currently done by most teams at UMMC, the next logical step in defining the critical path is to define intermediate patient care objectives necessary to achieve the desired outcomes. Care planning should be based upon the clinical and support activities required to achieve the intermediate patient care objectives leading to the major outcome criteria. To the extent possible, the intermediate objectives should be related to the patient's condition rather than system outcomes or constraints.

Determine Activities To Achieve Outcomes

Next, identify all the activities required to accomplish the outcomes and intermediate objectives. There may be some confusion between activities and events when you are describing the care plan. Activities are actions that require time and resources to complete, whereas events are milestones that have zero time. Activities are often grouped into categories such as consults, tests, patient activities, treatments, medications, diet, and patient and family education. Including events may be helpful for clarity purposes.

Determine Precedent Relationships

An activity that must be completed before a subsequent activity can begin is called a precedent. Certainly, care providers understand precedent relationships within the scope of their own practice. Formalizing the sequence of activities and the precedent relationships is difficult but important, however, particularly for coordination among professions. In part, this is difficult because care providers have different conceptual frameworks of how care should be organized, different information, and different involvements and priorities for activities. More formalized definitions of precedent relationships and activity times stimulate important discussions that often result in more efficient care. To identify the precedents for each outcome, intermediate objective, and activity, you ask "What must be completed before this can begin?" The flowchart/network format, which provides a visualization of the process, is helpful in reaching

consensus and discovering opportunities for improvement.

Question Current Practices

During development and use of a pathway, it is important that all current practices be questioned. Simply replicating current practice in pathways is an acceptable place to start, but improving practice requires serious questioning of what, when, who, where, how, and why. What criteria are *really* necessary for the patient to be ready to be discharged? What care can be provided at home or on an outpatient basis? What intermediate patient care objectives or outcomes are really necessary to accomplish the desired outcomes? What activities contribute? What activities are unnecessary or not directly related to the key discharge criteria? Why do we do this? Do different practices really result in different outcomes? The purpose of asking these questions is to challenge current practices objectively, to identify those activities that are pertinent to attaining and improving outcomes, and to eliminate or give less attention to those that are less important to outcomes.

As a mechanism to create more innovative ideas, it may also be helpful to pose the questions as "Why *can't* we do such and such," which asks whether hard evidence exists to prove that an approach might not work. Asking the "why not" questions stimulates more creative approaches. If no counterevidence exists, then a new approach can be tested to determine its effectiveness.

Determine Activity Times

Some health care organizations discuss the time requirements of activities in general but do not determine times for every activity. This provides a useful understanding of the process. To calculate the critical path, however, the times of all activities must be determined. Different approaches can be used to estimate activity times. Initially, most teams develop consensus estimates involving small interdisciplinary efforts.

Analyses of charts can provide frequency data and times of certain events from which activity times can be estimated. After a pathway is in use, analyses of variations can provide additional data. Formalized time studies are the most accurate but are done infrequently. CPM calculations use average time estimates, whereas PERT calculations use three time estimates: optimistic, most likely, and pessimistic. It should be noted that activity durations can be changed by changing processes, productivity, or the amount of resources allocated to an activity. For example, after a coronary artery bypass graft (CABG) procedure, an aggressive monitoring of intake, output, and patient weight can shorten the amount of time needed for the patient to "dry out" or reduce to his or her preoperative weight.

Determine the Critical Path

You can find the critical path by summing the times of the respective activities and intermediate outcomes to calculate the total duration of each path through the network or flowchart. The path with the longest time requirement is the critical path. Because the critical path is intuitive to the clinical team, formal calculation of the critical path and float/slack times for paths of shorter duration may not be done. These calculations are done most easily by computerized project management software, and many such programs for personal computers are available.

Implement and Monitor Pathways

Once consensus is reached on a pathway, the pathway is implemented and monitored. Pathways should be viewed as guidelines for coordinated care that regularly change based upon changes in practice, new technologies, and resources available in different settings. Consequently, it is acceptable to initiate pathways without 100 percent clinician agreement. Clearly, at times the patient condition requires alterations in pathway activities. Outliers are allowed and documented along with the out-

comes. Those data are then used subsequently to review and revise the pathway. By analyzing data comparing variations in practice, costs, and outcomes, the clinicians are able to reduce future variations.

USE OF CRITICAL PATHS

In practice, the large majority of clinician effort involves the use of critical paths in daily care of patients after the pathways are developed. Most health care organizations assign a case manager, a pathway coordinator, or another member of the health care team to monitor all patients on critical paths. Richards and colleagues describe a sample process to initiate and use critical paths for an inpatient care episode as follows[12]:

1. The pathway coordinator is notified of the admission.
2. The head nurse or designee assigns an appropriate bed on the unit.
3. The pathway coordinator starts the patient on the pathway by:
   - documenting in the unit log (handwritten or computer database)
   - entering dates on preprinted orders
   - entering dates on the pathway
   - placing completed pathways in a plastic folder on the bedside chart and in the main chart
4. The pathway coordinator talks with the admitting physician to clarify any questions related to caring for this patient while looking at the clinical pathway and preprinted orders.
5. The pathway coordinator talks with the nurse providing care for this patient to clarify any questions.
6. Variance documentation takes place throughout the admission and upon discharge; the pathway coordinator completes the variance record and the unit log.

7. Ongoing communication between outpatient and inpatient care providers facilitates smooth transition of patient care throughout the continuum.

The critical path serves as an important tool for daily communication about and coordination of clinical activities, support activities, expected outcomes, and the patient's progress. The critical path, however, is only one tool in the process of care for the patient. Any program that uses a pathway must have a method to evaluate the patient's progress while on the pathway and to evaluate the effectiveness of the pathway.

Variances from expected activity along the critical path or inability to meet intermediate objectives must be monitored. Because these are constantly monitored, action can be taken proactively when a variance is identified. In some cases, this allows for corrective action before variances occur. For example, if a physician orders a complete blood count and chemistries to be drawn every day and the pathway specifies that these are to be drawn on days 1, 3, and 5, timely monitoring can prevent these tests from being repeated unnecessarily by having the orders changed. Although retrospective monitoring takes place, this is less than optimal because variances may already have occurred.

It is also necessary to identify critical events or activities that have a direct impact on pathway outcomes and are schedule dependent. Examples of these are the ordering of needed consults and initiation of discharge planning. Although the pathway may describe when you should begin these activities, the variance tool describes the last point at which they can be achieved before the delay will affect an outcome or resource use. Another example might be that the pathway describes that the patient should begin an ambulation protocol within 6 hours of return from surgery. The outcome is that the patient walks the length of the hallway independently by the time of discharge. The team may decide that an intermediate outcome is that the patient walks at least so many feet by 24

hours after surgery. If the patient cannot meet the intermediate outcome time frame, a consult may be needed, and the consult time must be built in so that the patient can still meet the intended 3-day discharge time.

Another example of critical events or activities that affect pathway outcomes is a 5-day course of continuous 24-hour chemotherapy where completion of 5 days (120 hours) of chemotherapy is one of the pathway outcomes. A critical event or activity that must occur every day is the initiation of each bag of chemotherapy, on time and infused over the appropriate hours, to meet the final outcome of the required amount of drug given over 5 days or 120 hours. A variance in this process would be the development of patient toxicities resulting in delay of chemotherapy; this is a patient variance. On the other hand, if the day 1 bag is hung late because of a delay in nursing time to initiate, this is a clinician variance.

Documentation of variances from the critical path is important both to the care of the patient and to the continued improvement of the care processes and critical paths. As Richards and colleagues state:

> When a variance occurs between expected and actual treatment plan of care, documentation should identify the variance, its type (patient, clinician, or system), and its effect on outcomes achievement. This should be followed by a review of aggregate data about multiple patients and the long-term outcomes achieved. Only patient variances should be addressed in the patient record. For legal reasons, clinician and system variances are tracked and recorded separately as part of a more confidential quality assurance document. Variance data collection routinely has been labor-intensive, especially when the information is collected in narrative form. When variances are collected outside the patient record they should

be recorded in a quantitative format that is user-friendly and clear, allowing clinicians to use the data to identify trends requiring timely action plans.[13(pp.35–36)]

ALTERNATIVE FORMATS AND SAMPLE USES

Critical path methods include a number of formats for information displays and associated calculations that can further enhance understanding and provision of health care services. Although some of these formats are not normally used, they offer an opportunity for enhancement of critical paths, particularly as the pathways become computerized. This section briefly summarizes four key formats: the activity/precedent table format, the Gantt chart format, the flowchart/network format, and the resource format; it also provides an interpretation of float/slack time. A more complete description is provided by Coffey et al.[14] Some computer programs include additional formats or views. All the formats or views are interrelated. Thus if you change the number of hours or days required for an activity in one view, the other views change to reflect the longer time period. Also, the same information, such as precedent relationships, can be discussed using different formats. In choosing formats, it is best to use those that are easiest to understand and readily allow involvement by members of the team.

Activity/Precedent Table Format

After the desired outcomes are defined, the next step in the methodology discussed above is to define all the necessary activities and their relationships. The activity/precedent table is helpful for listing all the activities and reviewing their required precedents, durations, and resource requirements. Calculated start times, finish times, and float/slack times may be displayed in this table also. Use of the activity/precedent table forces a formal consideration of the prece-dent relationships and duration of all activities, which in turn raises questions about availability of ancillary services and other resources to expedite patient recovery. The relationships among activities are more difficult to understand in this format than in the flowchart/network format because there is no indication of which activities are on the critical path. Also, it is difficult to visualize which activities are done on the same day. An activity/precedent table is illustrated in Figure 19–1.

Gantt Chart Format

A Gantt chart shows the beginning and ending times for each activity on a bar chart along a time line in the units being used. Most health care organizations that are currently implementing critical paths use a form of the Gantt chart listing the activities to be done each day. This is the most common form of representing a pathway or CareMap®. It presents a concise, easy to understand picture of the activities, and in some cases expected outcomes, for each day. The activities are typically organized into groups of consults, tests, patient activities, treatments, medications, diet, and patient and family education. The Gantt chart format is particularly helpful in communicating which activities are being done during each time period. It provides an excellent tool for communication among staff, patients, and family members and is useful for teaching, orientation, and education of clinicians related to care requirements. Although it is useful to display activities by day for communication purposes, it may be more useful to use smaller time units, such as hours, for planning, coordination, and evaluation.

This format does not work well to illustrate the precedent relationships among activities, nor does it identify which among all the activities listed are on the critical path. Some computer software programs have partially solved this deficiency by including lines linking the information on the Gantt chart to show precedence-related activities. This is illustrated in Figure 19–2.

ID No.	Activity Name	Duration (hours)	Precedent Activities
1	Thoracic Surgery Clinic Visit	3	None
2	Anesthesia Clinic Visit	3	1
3	Physical Therapy Visit	1	1
4	Preop Assessment	1	2,3
5	Preop Identification of Postdischarge Caregiver	1	4
6	Pre- and Postop Patient and Family Teaching	1	5
7	Operative Procedure CABG	6	6
8	Pharmaceutical Support	16	7
9	Hemodynamic Monitoring	16	7
10	Cardiac Monitor	16	7
11	Maintain Ventilator Support	16	7
12	Stabilize Hemodynamics	1	8,9,10
13	Discontinue Hardwire Monitor	1	12
14	Discontinue Hemodynamic Monitoring	1	12
15	Adequate Blood Gases, with Reduced Oxygenation	1	11
16	Extubate	2	15
17	Transfer to Step-Down Unit	1	13,14,16
18	Cardiac Monitoring via Telemetry	48	17
19	Discontinue Telemetry	24	18
20	Normal or Preop Cardiac Rhythm	0	19
21	Monitor Intake and Output, Vitals, etc. (ongoing)	0	17
22	Diuretic Protocol	36	21
23	Monitor Weight	1	22
24	Weight Approaching Preop Weight	0	23
25	Increasing Activity (plus other related activities)	85	17,27,28
26	Bowel Movement	1	25
27	Wean to Nasal Cannula	3	16
28	Discontinue Nasal Cannula	34	27
29	Room Air × 24 Hours	24	28
30	Tolerates Activity on Room Air	0	29
31	Discharge	4	20,24,26,30
32	Positive Life Style Activities		31
33	Postop Appointments Kept		31
34	Weight at Preop Level		31
35	Cardiac Rhythm Stable		31
36	Activity at Least at Preop Level		31

Figure 19–1 Excerpt from a sample activity/precedent table for uncomplicated CABG Patients. *Source:* Reprinted from R.J. Coffey, J.E. Othman, and J.I. Walters, Extending the Application of Critical Path Methods, *Quality Management in Health Care*, Vol. 3, No. 2, p. 24, © 1995, Aspen Publishers, Inc.

Flowchart/Network Format

The flowchart/network format graphically illustrates the precedent relationships among activities and shows the critical path. This format displays the activities in the care process as a flowchart. The initial flowchart of the current process may be used as a first step but may be refined as precedent relationships and activity durations are revised. It is helpful to involve direct care providers in creating the flowchart. Using the flowchart may allow creation of the pathway in less time because it is easier to visualize the relationships of activities than in other formats. It is particularly helpful for discussions about existing or changing precedent relationships, clinical practices, and sequences of activities. People can actually see the critical path. There may be one or more critical paths of equal duration. Flowcharts require more space than the tables of activities and can be quite large. This format does not work well to communicate what will be done each day. Manually generated networks seldom have supplemental information, such as durations of activities or float times, but some computerized project management programs display this additional information on the flowchart/network format. This is illustrated in Figure 19–3.

Resource Format

There are entry and output forms of the resource table. The data entry table, which is sometimes an extension of the activity table, is used to enter the amounts of different resources required for each activity. If the activity duration is significantly altered, it may alter the resource requirements. As with the required activities and precedent relationships, the resource requirements must be challenged carefully. For example, things that previously were done by a physician in an intensive care unit might possibly be done by a nurse in an acute care unit or even by a visiting nurse in a patient's home. The resource requirements by activity differ from the activity times. The activity time is the amount of

	Postop Period of Operative Day	Postop Day 1	Postop Day 2
Treatment	Maintain ventilator support until extubation Wean to nasal cannula Hardwire monitoring Vital signs monitored Hemodynamic monitoring Cardiac output every 4 hours Pharmaceutical support Initiate diuretic protocol	Oxygen by nasal cannula Telemetry Vitals every 4 hours Pharmaceutical support Continue diuretic protocol	Room air Monitor intake and output tid Vitals every 4 hours Telemetry Pharmaceutical support Continue diuretic protocol
Patient Activity	Bed rest until extubated Up in chair at bedside	Ambulate to tolerance qid	Increase ambulation to tolerance qid
Diet	NPO Advance to clear liquids	No added salt, low-cholesterol solid diet	No added salt, low-cholesterol solid diet
Discharge Planning		Assess additional home care needs Transfer to step-down unit	
Teaching	Explain ICU procedures Explain transfer to step-down unit	Reinforce incentive spirometer use Reinforce increasing activity	Reinforce increasing activity
Medications	Potassium as needed Magnesium as needed Diltiazem 30 mg tid Nitroglycerine 1 ug/kg	Diltiazem CD once a day	Potassium as needed Diltiazem CD once a day
Tests	Electrolytes (potassium × 3) CBC Arterial blood gases Chest X-ray Pulse oximetry	Electrolytes Pulse oximetry	

Figure 19–2 Excerpt of activities by day for uncomplicated CABG patients. *Note:* This Gantt chart is for illustration only and should not be used as a standard of care. *Source:* Courtesy of University of Michigan Hospitals, Ann Arbor, Michigan.

chronological time required to complete the activity. The resource requirement is the amount of time or resources required during the activity. For example, it may take 16 hours of pharmaceutical support for a CABG patient, yet the resource requirement during that period may be 1 hour of registered pharmacist time and 1 hour of registered nurse time.

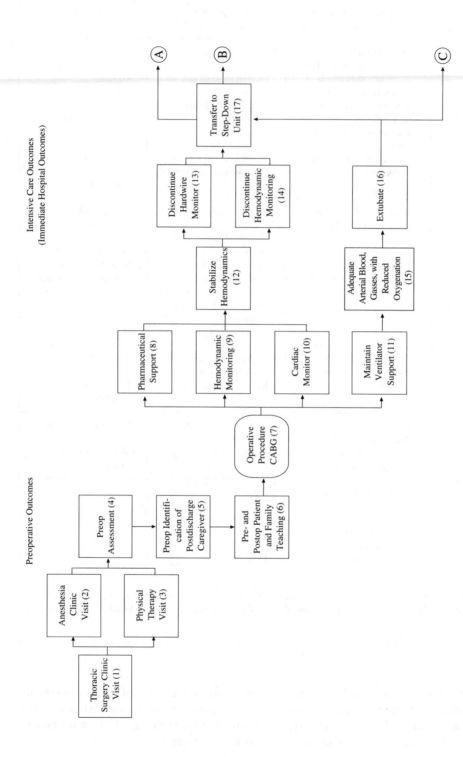

Figure 19–3 Excerpt from a sample flowchart of activities and outcomes for uncomplicated CABG patients. *Note:* This figure is for illustration only and should not be used as a standard of care. *Source:* Reprinted from R.J. Coffey, J.E. Othman, and J.I. Walters, Extending the Application of Critical Path Methods, *Quality Management in Health Care*, Vol. 3, No. 2, p.20, © 1995, Aspen Publishers, Inc.

(continues)

Home Care Outcomes

Hospital Discharge Outcomes

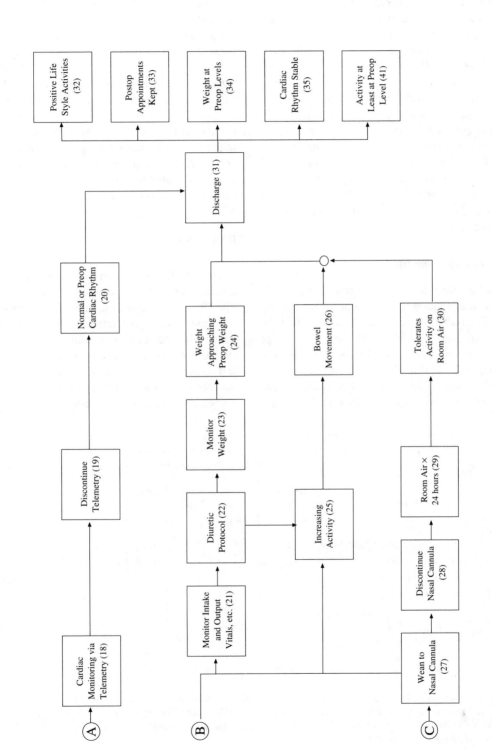

Figure 19–3 continued

As with estimating activity times, resource requirements may be derived from consensus estimates of the respective professionals, estimates derived from times in patient charts, analyses of variances, or time studies. Resource requirements by activity are not part of the critical path work to date in health care. The resource format can be helpful to plan and schedule resource requirements and to evaluate changes in resource use as more patients are placed on computerized critical paths. Like the Gantt chart, this format does not communicate precedent relationships, nor does it have information about the duration of the activity. A resource table is illustrated in Figure 19–4.

Float/Slack Time Information

All tasks not on the critical path have slack or float time. Float time is the amount of time by which an activity or task can be delayed without delaying something else. Although this concept is not currently used in health care, knowing the amount of float time is helpful in prioritizing activities, particularly in clinical situations where the path is constrained. Free float is the amount of time by which an activity can be delayed without delaying any other activity. Total float is the amount of time by which an activity can be delayed without delaying the finish date but may cut into the float times of its successor activity(ies). A path with a relatively large float time allows for more tolerance of uncontrollable variation. Clinicians must be extremely vigilant if the float time is zero or small because delays of these activities will delay the outcomes or discharge. Although conceptually simple, the calculations related to float time are detailed and best done by a computer program.

RESULTS

The results associated with implementing critical paths fall into two general categories. The first is improved planning, coordination, and communication related to the care of patients. The second is quantitative measures of changes in length of stay, resource use, costs, and so forth. Based upon the perceptions of the patients, clinicians, and payers involved, critical paths and variance tools are useful to focus and

		Staff Time Requirements				Equipment	
ID No.	Activity Name	Physician Time	Nurse Time	Tech/PA Time	Other	Room	Other
1	Thoracic Surgery Clinic Visit	1		0.5	0.75	Exam Rm.	
2	Anesthesia Clinic Visit	0.5			0.75	Exam Rm.	
3	Physical Therapy Visit			1		Exam Rm.	Spirometer
4	Preop Assessment		0.5				
5	Preop Identification of Post-discharge Caregiver		0.5				
6	Pre- and Postop Patient and Family Teaching		0.5				Booklet
7	Operative Procedure CABG	24	12	24	16	OR	

Figure 19–4 Sample resource table for uncomplicated CABG patients. *Note:* This resource table is for illustration only and should not be used as a standard of care. *Source:* Reprinted from R.J. Coffey, J.E. Othman, and J.I. Walters, Extending the Application of Critical Path Methods, *Quality Management in Health Care*, Vol. 3, No. 2, p. 26, © 1995, Aspen Publishers, Inc.

improve planning, coordination, teamwork, and communication. They help communicate expectations among clinicians, patients, family members, and payers.

Of particular interest to health care administrators and payers are the quantitative results related to length of stay, resource use, costs, and the like. Based upon work at UMMC and other health care organizations, critical paths do have a positive impact on these quantitative measures. We will provide some selected examples.

At the C.S. Mott Children's Hospital in the UMMC, data were analyzed for a sample of 300 inpatients admitted to the pediatric cardiology service included on one of the critical pathways for 19 diagnoses/procedures.[15] Charts were analyzed for 130 patients before the critical paths were initiated, and these were compared with results for 170 patients after the critical paths were initiated. Cost and readmission data were obtained from patient accounting and admitting, respectively. After implementation of case management with critical paths, 76 percent (130 of 170) of the patients were discharged within the expected length of stay, an increase from 66 percent (86 of 130) of patients in the pre–case management group ($\chi^2 = 3.89$, $p = .05$). The average length of stay decreased by 0.2 day for 11 of 14 diagnoses/procedures in the case managed group. The incidence of readmissions was not significantly changed after initiation of case management, at only 1.2 percent (2 of 170 patients) compared with 1.5 percent (2 of 130 patients) before case management. Discharge readiness was not assessed in patients hospitalized less than 72 hours. At the time of assessment before discharge, 67 of 69 assessed parents (97 percent) reported readiness for their child's discharge within 24 hours. Follow-up assessment approximately 2 weeks later revealed that parental perception of discharge readiness was highly reliable, with 95 percent agreement (i.e, same or better rating of readiness). With respect to charges for the surgical procedures, however, the data regarding average billed charges for eight cardiac surgical procedures suggested a mean increase of 13.4 percent, without adjustment for changes in hospital costs, over a multiyear period.

Multiple clinical services have implemented critical paths within the adult hospital of UMMC. The following are selected examples of quantitative results. For thoracic surgery, average lengths of stay decreased significantly for the four key procedures with pathways, as illustrated in Table 19–1. Some of the procedures had multiple critical paths. The changes in other resource use, as measured by relative value units

Table 19–1 Average Length of Stay for Thoracic Surgery Patients

	Length of Stay (Days)	
Unit and Procedure	Before Critical Path (4/1/90–1/1991)	2 Years after Critical Path (4/1/92–12/31/92)
Intensive care unit		
Heart transplant	12.10	8.47
CABG (first time)	4.60	2.53
Esophagectomy	3.60	0.80
CABG (revision)	6.29	2.73
Routine unit		
Heart transplant	14.60	10.44
CABG (first time)	8.50	6.90
Esophagectomy	12.70	11.99
CABG (revision)	6.83	6.58

Table 19–2 Average Length of Stay for Orthopedic Surgery Patients

| | Length of Stay (Days) | |
Procedure	Before Critical Path (1/1/92–12/31/92)	After Critical Path (1/1/93–12/31/93)
Posterior spinal fusion	10.40	8.39
Total knee arthroplasty	6.39	5.65
Total knee arthroplasty (revision)	8.20	6.33
Total hip arthroplasty	7.24	6.52
Total hip arthroplasty (revision)	10.52	9.26

(RVUs) to eliminate pricing changes, varied. For four of seven procedures, resource RVUs decreased, and for three of seven, resource RVUs increased. For orthopedic surgery, average lengths of stay decreased significantly for the five key procedures with pathways, as illustrated in Table 19–2. Four of the five procedures also experienced decreases in resource use as measured by RVUs. For urology, Figure 19–5 illustrates length of stay calculated for many of the diagnoses and procedures with critical paths. Although the length of stay was decreasing before the critical paths were implemented, the length of stay after implementation decreased faster.

CONCLUSION AND RECOMMENDATIONS

Critical paths are important tools to link patients, clinicians, and MCOs, and other payers to achieve both high-quality and cost-effective care. Critical paths have different scopes of use, including inpatient care, an entire episode of care, and management of chronic conditions. They are developed collaboratively by multidisciplinary teams of physicians, nurses, pharmacists, therapists, dietitians, and other clinicians to coordinate the care of a patient with a specific diagnosis or procedure. To be most effective, critical paths are focused upon achieving

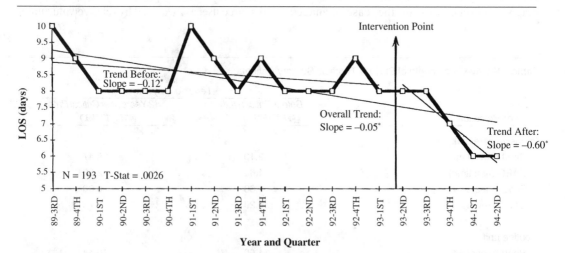

Figure 19–5 Radical prostatectomy without complications: Mean length of stay and trend lines, all patients, before and after 6/21/93 intervention. Total RVU consumption, 881,318. * The slope of the trend line reflects the average increase (or decrease, if negative) in days per quarter (per patient). *Source:* Integrated Inpatient Management Model (IIMM), University of Michigan Medical Center, Ann Arbor, MI.

patient care outcomes and intermediate objectives as quickly as possible, while avoiding wasted resources.

Critical paths have demonstrated effectiveness in planning and coordinating care; establishing expectations; reducing variation of care; educating and orienting staff; communicating among patients, clinicians, payers, and others; benchmarking best practices; and reducing length of stay and costs. Successful development and use of critical paths are not just a matter of learning the analytical technique. Success vitally depends upon creating the right environment for critical paths, including having urgency for change, champions for critical paths, willingness to challenge current practices and boundaries, payers and MCOs covering the same scope of care as the critical paths, and administrative support.

REFERENCES AND NOTES

1. R.J. Coffey, et al., An Introduction to Critical Paths, *Quality Management in Health Care* 1 (1992): 45–54.
2. R.J. Coffey, et al., Extending the Application of Critical Path Methods, *Quality Management in Health Care* 3 (1995): 14–29.
3. Coffey, et al., Extending the Application of Critical Path Methods.
4. S. Wintermeyer-Pingel, et al., Coordinated Care Variance Data Collection: A "Time Limiting Pathway" Approach (Paper presented at the National Leadership Conference on Management of Quality, Ann Arbor, Mich., 4 November 1993).
5. K. Zander, Estimating and Tracking the Financial Impact of Critical Paths, *Definition* 5 (1990): 1–3.
6. K. Zander, Care Maps: The Core of Cost/Quality Care. *The New Definition* 6 (1991): 1–3.
7. J. Schriefer, The Synergy of Pathways and Algorithms: Two Tools Work Better Than One, *Joint Commission Journal on Quality Improvement* 20 (1994): 485–499.
8. Coffey, et al., An Introduction to Critical Paths.
9. Coffey, et al., An Introduction to Critical Paths.
10. Coffey, et al., Extending the Application of Critical Path Methods.
11. A. Frantz, Cardiac Recovery in Home: Improving Quality while Reducing Cost, *Remington Report* 7 (1993): 14–15.
12. J.S. Richards, et al., "Clinical Paths and Patient Care Documentation," in *Clinical Paths: Tools for Outcomes Management*, ed P.L. Spath (Chicago, Ill.: American Hospital Association, 1994): 33–44.
13. Richards, et al., "Clinical Paths and Patient Care Documentation."
14. Coffey, et al., Extending the Application of Critical Path Methods.
15. K. Uzark, et al., The Pediatric Nurse Practitioner as Case Manager in the Delivery of Services to Children with Heart Disease, *Journal of Pediatric Health Care* 8 (1994): 74–78.

SUGGESTED READING

Griffin, M. and Griffin, R.B. 1994. Critical Pathways Produce Tangible Results. *Health Care Strategic Management* 12(7): 1, 17–22.

Handley, M.R., Stuart, M.E., and Kirz, H.L. 1994. An Evidence-Based Approach to Evaluating and Improving Clinical Practice: Implementing Practice Guidelines. *HMO Practice* 8(2): 75–83.

Health Care Financing Administration. 1995. *Best Practices of Managed Care Organizations*. Baltimore, Md.: Health Care Financing Administration.

Standards of Medical Care: The Comparative Guide to Medical Practice Guidelines and Outcomes Research. 1994. Washington, D.C.: R & R Publishing, Inc.

Thomasson, G.O. 1994. Participatory Risk Management: Promoting Physician Compliance with Practice Guidelines. *The Joint Commission Journal on Quality Improvement* 20(6): 317–329.

Youngs, M.T. and Wingerson, L. 1995. *The 1996 Medical Outcomes & Guidelines Sourcebook*. New York, N.Y.: Faulkner & Gray.

Chapter 20

Disease Management

David W. Plocher

DEFINITION

Disease management is a prospective disease-specific approach to delivering health care spanning all encounter sites and augmenting the physician's component visits with interim management through nonphysician practitioners specializing in the target disease. Disease management redirects the intervention efforts toward the outpatient setting for several chronic disorders and captures information from all sites of care for each patient with that disorder into a single longitudinal episode. It is on this comprehensive knowledge base that patients are tracked continuously, thereby adding new opportunities for patient education at encounter sites other than the hospital or physician's office. This allows a more prospective approach to managing a disease, improving the likelihood of altering its natural history. That is, exacerbations of the disease can be prevented or reduced in frequency and severity. The resulting performance report is unique for this approach to a disease because it represents resource consumption from all sites of care, values global episode changes over time, and adds to routine economic measures the impact on morbidity, satisfaction, functional status, and, when advanced, population health status. This can be cast in a realistic light for the busy primary care physician as follows: The internist or family practitioner will typically see a patient with diabetes or chronic congestive heart failure every three months in the office. Other than a rare visit to the emergency department or hospitalization, each office encounter is a brief, isolated time for the physician to become aware of a patient's circumstances and to offer educational information. Disease management programs employ nonphysician practitioners to telephone and visit these patients during each intervening three month period, for a variety of purposes, including morbidity assessment, education, and assistance with medication compliance.

RATIONALE AND REQUIREMENTS FOR SUCCESSFUL DEMONSTRATIONS

This lengthy definition is necessary to explain the newness of the concept. Figure 20–1 displays schematically where disease management fits on the background of other established interventions in care management.

The connectivity depicted favors a disease manager who is operating within a vertically integrated delivery system with alignment of incentives among all constituents. This permits capture of information from and dissemination of educational material to encounter locations that are physically and geographically discontinuous.

David W. Plocher, M.D., is a principal in the Minneapolis office of Ernst & Young LLP with the Health Care Consulting practice. His managed care activities include design and implementation of integrated delivery systems and the national direction of development and deployment of care management techniques, including demand management and disease management.

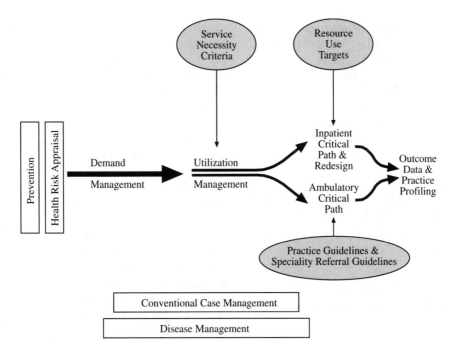

Figure 20–1 Interventions in care management.

Disease managers are also most motivated if they are at financial risk. Conversely, the fee-for-service physician is not financially rewarded for struggling through the innovations discussed in this chapter. There is one exceptional circumstance: the purchaser mandates. Recently, The Foundation for Accountability, a large purchasing group, has announced intentions to direct market share toward those delivery systems showing measurement and performance capabilities in five conditions: asthma, type I diabetes, cardiovascular disease, acquired immunodeficiency syndrome (AIDS), and cancer.

Primary prevention programs have usually been discussed on a continuum that precedes the scope of classic disease management. That is, many primary preventive efforts do not select a single disease to prevent but rather emphasize generic nutrition, exercise, stress reduction, and so on. Conversely, we do not yet have a method for prevention of type I diabetes. Therefore, the

prevention theme within disease management is oriented to exacerbation prevention. This includes a more sensitive outpatient detection mechanism, such as the newly designed health risk appraisal instruments, to help discover that emergency-department-visit-to-be.

When this prospective reconnaissance is supplemented by telephone nurse triage services that include directions for self-care, we begin to see an amelioration of the expected course for common disorders. This ranges from a dramatic reduction for office and emergency department visits for pediatric fevers (as in the Harvard Community Health Plan Pediatric Fever Pilot) to extensive counseling for type I diabetics that reduces annual care costs. These approaches to demand management are discussed further in Chapter 17.

In summary, the disease manager will deploy techniques in secondary prevention, patient empowerment through education, demand management, and enhanced data management. Information systems will be key in determining success, beginning with analysis of practice pattern variants and progressing toward new outcome measures.

The performance requirements of such a data warehouse can be summarized as follows:

- Data are captured from all sites of care.
- Data are edited and cleansed.
- Severity adjustment is conducted with methodology validated independently.
- Reports are generated and benchmarks are provided:
  1. charges and cost
  2. mortality and morbidity
  3. functional status, health status, and satisfaction

There will be a real value in such information for the delivery system medical director who needs to find comparisons, norms, and benchmarks for each disease's annual cost of care and other outcome parameters.

CARVE-OUTS

Although industry analysts often represent carve-outs as a synonym or variation of disease management, this chapter will not incorporate a lengthy discussion of this entity. Chapters 12 and 13 address specialty-selective contracting in detail. Carve-outs usually produce a separate provider network as a capitated subcontractor. This chapter will instead concentrate on the new approach for managing patients with certain diseases, looking at improving the processes of care inside a delivery system.

For the sake of complete taxonomy, the main disease management carve-outs are divided between common and rare conditions. Common disease carve-outs have been in place for many years for patients with mental illness and substance abuse (see Chapter 22). More recently, oncology carve-outs have replicated this

mode.[1–4] Rare diseases are amenable to a carve-out when there is a large enrollment in the delivery system. It then becomes problematic for the medical director to divert care management resources from asthma, congestive heart failure (CHF), and type I diabetes to create new guidelines for conditions such as hemophilia. Recently, vendors have come to the rescue for this purpose, and preliminary performance data are encouraging. For example, the annual cost of care for hemophilia could be reduced by 30 percent.

It must be emphasized that various other forms of specialty contracting (e.g., package pricing for coronary artery bypass) have not risen to the level of disease management. They are concerned about the hospitalization component only. Taxonomists might classify them as single-procedure preferred provider organizations.

CONVENTIONAL CASE MANAGEMENT AND DISEASE MANAGEMENT

The decade of the 1980s featured flourishing case management programs. Table 20–1, a comparison of these two care management techniques, helps answer the case manager's question "What else do we need?" In short, disease managers are better equipped to accomplish what the profession has wanted to do:

- achieve better control of episode cost of care
- reduce morbidity
- improve functional status
- improve patient and physician satisfaction
- acquire more meaningful outcome data (e.g., medication compliance)
- develop an improved ability to bear financial risk for the service

SELECTION OF DISEASES

Advanced delivery systems have experimented with this model of care management for

Table 20–1 Comparison of Conventional Case Management and Disease Management

Case Management	Disease Management
Goal Streamlining components Critical path component cost control	*Goal* Integrating components Improving long-term outcome
Emphasis Treatment of sickness, especially in a complex inpatient	*Emphasis* Prevention and education • for patients, families, and physicians • for common outpatient conditions • low technology nonsurgical • prescription drug-managed
Scope Patient often has multiple diseases	*Scope* Patient is initially evaluated for a single disease
Timing Periodic inspection	*Timing* Prospective and concurrent
Guidelines Generic Externally imposed	*Guidelines* Customized to diagnosis Internally designed
Caregivers Generalists Nurses (primarily)	*Caregivers* Specialists Multidisciplinary team
Data sources • Primarily inpatient (tracks length of stay, profit margin per confinement, mortality) • Not integrated Lacks ability to bear financial risk	*Data sources* • All points of service (tracks annual episode of care cost, medication compliance, functional status) • Integrated Increased ability to bear financial risk

a large number of conditions. Pharmaceutical manufacturers have promoted this model for dozens of diseases for which their product represents one of the treatment options. After struggles with cost versus benefit, the feasibility tests have produced the following short list of diagnoses that appear currently to deliver the largest early impact. They are ranked here in approximate order of success.

1. asthma; adolescent, refractory
2. CHF
3. diabetes, type I
4. AIDS
5. cancer, as managed by carve-outs mentioned above

It is important to understand the criteria that these conditions must meet. The following series of observations seem to be most valuable in prioritizing the selection:

• high dollar and high volume
• high rate of preventable complications, so that emergency department visits and hospital readmissions can be influenced
• short time frame during which alterations in natural history can show a measurable impact (i.e., 1 to 3 years), coinciding with the most common time interval after which subscribers change health plans
• chronic outpatient-focused conditions that are common, low technology, and nonsurgical

- disease episodes lend themselves to discrete coding boundaries
- high rate of variability in patterns of therapeutics from patient to patient and from physician to physician (most variation is easily measured in resource use, but other outcome measures should pertain, such as prescription drug selection)
- high rates of patient noncompliance with the therapeutic regimen (this noncompliance must be amenable to change by education; education is directed at patients, family members, *and* physicians)
- current care patterns show multiple referrals from primary care physician to several specialists
- practice guidelines on optimal treatment exist or can be developed
- consensus is achievable on what constitutes good quality, which outcomes to measure, and how to improve them
- there are no constraints on intervention (e.g., lack of access to home care services)

EXPERIENCE FROM EARLY DEMONSTRATIONS

Adolescent Refractory Asthma

The performance observed in the first pilots of disease management is best described with adolescent refractory asthma. Most pilots begin with refractory adolescents, because of the above tests, and extend to adults later. Less than 5 percent of asthmatics are classified as severe, and nearly half the claims costs for all asthmatics occur in the emergency department and hospital.[5] More important is the observation that only 10 percent to 20 percent of asthmatics receive inhaled steroids, considered the cornerstone of therapy. The reason appears to be that inhaled bronchodilators are overused because of their ability to provide instant relief. Finally, physicians are not the most frequently encountered caregiver. Asthmatics see their pharmacist five times more often. This has raised the posi-

tion of the pharmacist in disease management programs to that of a true provider and educator, sometimes with financial incentives. Ironically, this opportunity is lost when subscribers are financially motivated to use mail order programs for inhaler refills. Compensatory efforts include visits by home nurses specializing in asthma and various phone and mail prompts.

The entire continuum of asthma care is displayed in Figure 20–2. The contrast between a hospital-based case manager's role and that of the disease manager is dramatic.

Results from individual delivery system implementation of disease management for asthma are consistent over all regions in the United States. The most important observations include the following:

- reduction in hospitalizations by half or more
- reduction in emergency department visits by half or more
- abrupt increase in the use of inhaled steroids
- decrease in reliance on bronchodilators
- improved functional status, as measured by:
  1. ability to work
  2. quality of sleep

Other Conditions

The role of specialized nurse managers and intensive home care is applicable to a variety of conditions, ranging from hemophilia to AIDS. For reasons of space, an abbreviated series for type I diabetes and CHF is described below.

Type I Diabetes

Context. Five percent of Americans are diabetic, and employers pay as much as 20 percent of their medical claims for this disease. The nonmedical claim costs add up a further tally for employers in the form of reduced productivity at work, absenteeism, and short- and long-term disability.

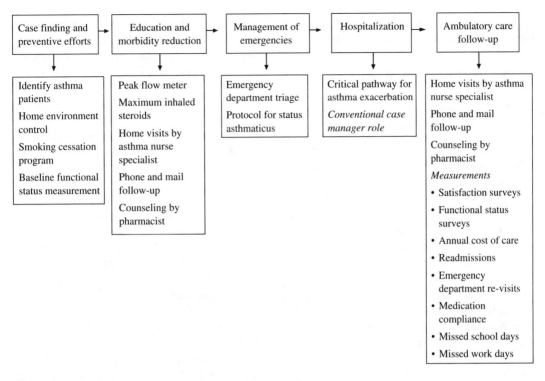

Figure 20–2 Continuum of care for adolescent refractory asthma.

Caregivers. As with asthma, the diabetic will see a pharmacist twice a month but the physician as infrequently as three times a year.

Short-term impact. Emergency department visits and hospitalizations for ketoacidosis are reduced. A southwestern health plan has demonstrated half the usual admission rate, attributed largely to intensified educational efforts.

Long-term impact. The literature has recently documented the success of tighter control (beyond intensive education) in reducing retinopathy, neuropathy, and nephropathy;[6] the risk of weight gain; a threefold increase in severe hypoglycemia[7] and at least triple care costs.[8]

CHF

Context. Many primary care physicians have been insufficiently aggressive in using angiotensin-converting enzyme (ACE) inhibitors and other preload and afterload reducers for this population, especially for the CHF subset with systolic dysfunction. There has been further difficulty separating the CHF patient subset with diastolic dysfunction, for which digoxin is not primary therapy and agents that control the heart rate, such as ß blockers or calcium channel blockers, are indicated. Both types of patients have also been subject to excessive diuresis, which makes them refractory to the indicated agents or compromises renal function.

Caregivers. The combination of more direct access to cardiologists as well as clinic nurses and home care nurses specially trained in CHF is changing these episodes.

Short-term impact. CHF readmissions and annual cost of care have been reduced. This success and recent data are displayed at the end of this chapter, serving as examples for measurement when pilots are being constructed.

Long-term impact. Expanded use of ACE inhibitors has reduced mortality from CHF.[9]

CAVEATS FROM THE MARKET

The Skeptical Health Maintenance Organization Medical Director

Several medical directors have adopted a hold-out posture until better data are available. The additional labor embedded in these new processes must be weighed against the suggested annual cost of care reductions. More important for a delivery system trying to be comprehensive in all services is the threat of a carve-out. That is, the conditions best suited for disease management are so common that their services are already completely intertwined with the health maintenance organization's operations. Carving them out to a subcontractor would interrupt the continuity of care and produce disintegration, according to several medical directors. These medical directors also observe that patients do not present with a single disease, but often at least two. They are not in favor of disconnected treatment locations and protocols.

The Suspect Pharmaceutical Manufacturer

Most delivery systems will not consider allowing a drug supplier to "front" a disease management pilot. This risks using a therapeutic agent that is not the drug of choice. It is also anti-innovation because newer products from competitors, blockbuster drugs or otherwise, must have a chance to prove their worth. The middle ground with some medical directors has been partnering as long as the supplier shares risk and offers some of its competitors' agents.

Poor Prioritization

In an effort to manage high-volume conditions better, several medical directors have selected hypertension and hyperlipoproteinemia as target diagnoses for disease management pilots.

Of the criteria that must be met, frequency and variability appear applicable. These are diseases subject to some of the heaviest marketing by pharmaceutical manufacturers, and pilots are underway. These two conditions are not necessarily the best selection for an early success, however.

First, the conditions have no symptoms. Therefore, patients are not going to experience instant gratification through compliance and will be refractory to education efforts, which has been summarized as the primary care physician's quandary: "It's hard to make an asymptomatic patient feel better." Second, there is an early increase in cost of care when randomly screened subscribers acquire these diagnoses and begin drug therapy. Finally, the return on investment for the delivery system cannot be achieved in a 1- to 3-year time frame because the sequelae of those conditions are at least 10 years away. All this is not to suggest that these patients should be abandoned but only to remind the delivery system chief financial officer where the first disease management pilot might be more effectively directed. A hypertension pilot is more reasonable when the subscriber base is projected to have low turnover and treatment costs are variable and excessive, allowing for management cost reductions within a year.

GETTING YOUR PILOT PROGRAM STARTED

There are several key steps in the pilot start-up process:

1. Prioritize disease selection:

   • Make it pertinent to the demographics of your covered lives.

   • Begin with two "Top-10" diagnosis lists, one by frequency or volume and one by total charges.

2. For the first condition selected, flowchart care processes across all sites in your delivery system, including self-care.

3. Conduct focus groups with a homogeneous group of patients carrying that diagnosis to validate patient needs and preferences as well as to articulate bottlenecks in the delivery system.

4. Using the flowchart, discover each cost driver.

5. Identify opportunities for patient and family education.

6. Using the flowchart, discover determinants of important clinical outcome measures.

7. Assign working groups to each cost/outcome driver to engage in formal process value optimization, including literature search for evidence-based support.

8. Prepare for major information systems investment.

9. Define episode duration and establish performance measures specific to the diagnosis beyond cost and resource use (e.g., morbidity, functional status, and satisfaction).

10. Use data to motivate physicians.

11. Consider restructuring financial incentives for caregivers.

12. Restructure caregivers to become a cross-functional team, changing roles and responsibilities for each caregiver.

Learning is accelerated by searches and surveys that reveal process and outcome from early efforts around the country. In light of the critical role of information capture and reporting, three examples are offered here. The first example is illustrated in Figure 20–3 and Table 20–2. These episode reports are remarkable in their ability to capture drug and nondrug costs, including drug side effect management. In view of the wide 95 percent confidence intervals, however, the differences among therapeutic agents do not appear significant.

The next example is illustrated in Figures 20–4 through 20–6. These episodes are more completely constructed with narrower confidence intervals, possibly related to large sample sizes. Of

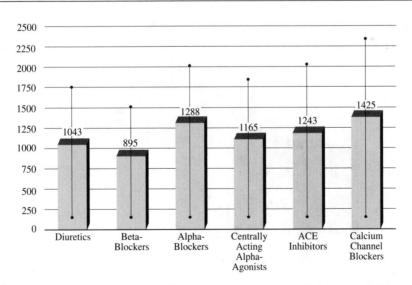

Figure 20–3 Mean annual cost per drug (dollars) for drugs with comparable blood pressure control. ACE, angiotensin-converting enzyme. *Source:* Reprinted with permission from S.H. McBride, Taking a long-term view of hypertension, *Managed Healthcare*, pp. 519–520, © 1995, Advanstar Communication, Inc.

Table 20–2 Mean Annual Cost per Drug per Cost Category for Drugs with Comparable Blood Pressure Control (Values Expressed as Mean ± Standard Deviation)

Drug Category	Acquisition Cost ($)	Supplemental Drug Cost ($)	Laboratory Cost ($)	Clinic Visit Cost ($)	Side Effect Cost ($)	Total Cost ($)
Diuretics	133 ± 107	232 ± 203	117 ± 32	298 ± 102	263 ± 480	1043 ± 667
β Blockers	334 ± 170	115 ± 192	56 ± 32	187 ± 87	203 ± 418	895 ± 545
α Blockers	410 ± 151	290 ± 290	114 ± 30	227 ± 69	256 ± 485	1288 ± 697
Centrally acting α agonists	285 ± 224	295 ± 338	125 ± 52	267 ± 114	193 ± 390	1165 ± 658
Angiotensin-converting enzyme inhibitors	444 ± 301	291 ± 315	95 ± 33	218 ± 87	195 ± 400	1243 ± 800
Calcium channel blockers	540 ± 219	278 ± 398	87 ± 29	214 ± 84	306 ± 642	1425 ± 962

Source: Reprinted with permission from S.H. McBride, Taking a long-term view of hypertension, *Managed Healthcare* , pp. 519–520, © 1995, Advanstar Communications, Inc.

further interest, measurement parameters go beyond dollars to variations on patient satisfaction.

Finally, Exhibit 20–1 and Table 20–3 depict advantages for elderly patients, with substantial risk factors beyond age alone, whose CHF is managed using principles of disease management. The main outcomes are a reduction in the rate of readmission due to recurrent heart failure by 56.2 percent, and improved life quality scores.

THE FUTURE

Speculations about the future of disease management include the following:

- Information technology advances hold the greatest promise for improvement, starting with the electronic longitudinal patient medical record and including on-line educational services for patients.

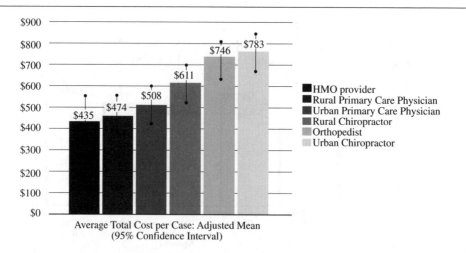

Average Total Cost per Case: Adjusted Mean
(95% Confidence Interval)

■ HMO provider
■ Rural Primary Care Physician
■ Urban Primary Care Physician
■ Rural Chiropractor
■ Orthopedist
■ Urban Chiropractor

Figure 20–4 Total direct outpatient costs per episode of low back pain, adjusted for baseline functional status, sciatica, income, duration of pain, and workers' compensation. HMO, health maintenance organization. *Source:* Adapted from T.S. Carey et al., *New England Journal of Medicine*, 1995, Vol. 333, p. 916. Copyright 1995. Massachusetts Medical Society. All rights reserved.

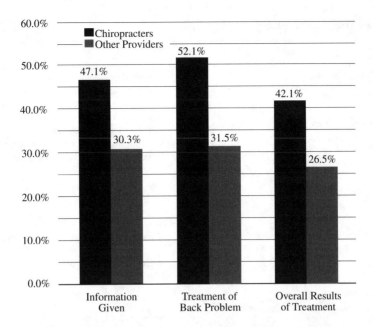

Figure 20–5 Satisfaction with treatment of acute low back pain: Percentage of patients answering"excellent" in response to satisfaction survey. Chiropractors, $n = 606$; other providers, $n = 1,027$; $p < .001$. A one-way analysis of variance, or the Kruskal-Wallis test was used for continuous data; the Pearsons chi-square test was used for categorical data; nonparametric Kaplan-Meier methods were used for data on time to functional recovery. *Source:* Adapted from T.S. Carey et al., *New England Journal of Medicine*, 1995, Vol. 333, p. 917. Copyright 1995. Massachusetts Medical Society. All rights reserved.

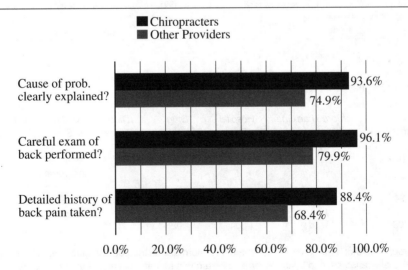

Figure 20–6 Perception of care in treatment of acute low back pain: Percentage of patients answering "yes" to satisfaction survey. Chiropractors, $n = 606$; other providers, $n = 1,027$; $p < .001$. A one-way analysis of variance, or the Kruskal-Wallis test was used for continuous data; the Pearsons chi-square test was used for categorical data; nonparametric Kaplan-Meier methods were used for data on time to functional recovery. *Source:* Adapted from T.S. Carey et al., *New England Journal of Medicine*, 1995, Vol. 333, p. 915. Copyright 1995. Massachusetts Medical Society. All rights reserved.

Exhibit 20–1 Disease Management in CHF

Study design
   Randomized controlled trial

Population
   Seniors older than 70 years ($N = 282$)
   Risk factors in addition to age

Duration
   90 days

Care patterns
   Disease management (treatment group, $n = 142$)
   Conventional management (control group, $n = 140$)

Functional status measure
   Chronic Heart Failure Questionnaire
   • Has shown responsiveness to improvement in
     health status
   • Has demonstrated validity (e.g., in measuring
     shortness of breath)

Treatment group interventions
   Cardiovascular nurse education
   Booklet specific for geriatric patients with CHF
   Diet instruction
   Social services consultation
   Medication analysis by geriatric cardiologist
   Intensive postdischarge home care
   • Visits
   • Phone contacts

*Survival (for 90 days without readmission from subset
of survivors of the initial hospitalization)*
   Treatment group: 66.9%
   Control group: 54.3%
   $p = .04.$

90-Day episode cost
   Treatment group: $4,815 $2,178
   Control group: $5,275 $3,236
   Difference: $460 $1,058*

* $p = 0.03$.

Table 20–3 Disease Management in CHF

Group	Readmissions	More Than One Readmission	Hospital Days	Drug Compliance	Daily Drug Doses	Quality of Life Scores	Understanding CHF
Treatment	53	9	556	82.5%	2.7	Greater improvement	Greater
Control	94	23	865	64.9%	3.0	—	—
p	.02	.01	.04	.02	.01	.001	.001

The two study groups were compared by students' t-test for normally distributed continuous variables, by the chi-square test for discrete variables, and by the Wilcox rank-sum test for categorical and abnormally distributed continuous variables.

- Continuous updates in optimal treatment guidelines will drive improvements in care.
- Customized programs for Medicare and Medicaid populations will be necessary, relying heavily on outreach programs.
- Interventions must include attention to the patient's psychosocial needs rather than focus only on clinical morbidity because care-seeking behavior is often not directly related to burden of illness. This will raise the value of demand management programs.
- Treatment decision support systems will need to rediscover the role of patient choice in the equation for controversial circumstances.
- Progression is necessary from concentrated efforts on the single disease toward better coordination of care for patients with two or more diseases.
- Health risk appraisals need to become better cost risk predictors.
- Population health management will require using both disease-specific functional status measures and health status measures.

REFERENCES AND NOTES

1. B. Kurowski, Cancer Carve-Outs: Can They Fulfill the Promise of Managed Care?, *Oncology Issues* (November/December 1994): 10–13.
2. R. Rundle, Salick Agrees to Provide Cancer Care at Fixed Price to Florida HMO Patients, *Wall Street Journal* (14 July 1994): B7.
3. Salick Signs First Capitated Oncology Contract, *Modern Healthcare* 24 (1994): 14.
4. C. Sardinha, Seeking Cancer Know-How, PCA Signs Carve-Out Deal with Salick, *Managed Care Outlook* (1994).
5. National Jewish Center for Immunology and Respiratory Medicine, *Your Guide to National Jewish* (Denver, Colo.: National Jewish Center for Immunology and Respiratory Medicine, 1987).
6. DCCT Research Group, The Effect of Intensive Treatment of Diabetes on the Development and Progression of Long-Term Complications in Insulin-Dependent Diabetes Mellitus, *New England Journal of Medicine* 329 (1993): 977–986.
7. DCCT Research Group, Adverse Events and Their Association with Treatment Regimens in the Diabetes Control and Complications Trial, *Diabetes Care* 18 (1995): 1415–1427.
8. DCCT Research Group, Resource Utilization and Costs of Care in the Diabetes Control and Complications Trial, *Diabetes Care* 18 (1995): 1468–1478.
9. L. Kober, et al., A Clinical Trial of the Angiotensin-Converting Enzyme Inhibitor Trandolapril in Patients with Left Ventricular Dysfunction after Myocardial Infarction, *New England Journal of Medicine* 333 (1995): 1670–1676.

SUGGESTED READING

Disease State Management: Identifying an Rx for Savings. *1995. Business & Health,* 13, pp. 11–15.

Griffin, M. and Griffin, R.B. 1994. Critical Pathways Produce Tangible Results. *Health Care Strategic Management* 12(7): 1, 17–22.

Lumsdon, K. 5 April 1995. Disease Management: The Heat and Headaches over Retooling Patient Care Create Hard Labor. *Hospitals and Health Networks,* pp. 34–42.

Peterson, C. May/June 1995. Disease Management. *HMO Magazine,* pp. 39–47.

Peterson, C. September/October 1994. Pharmaceutical Integration: Going Vertical. *HMO Magazine,* pp. 50–54.

Regardie, J. 30 January–5 February 1995. Providers Turn to "Disease Management" To Cut Costs: Practice Targets Conditions Requiring Pricey Treatment. *Los Angeles Business Journal.*

Rohl, B.J., Meyer, L.C., and Lung, C.L. 1994. Asthma Care Map for Decision Making. *Medical Interface* 7(2): 107–110.

Rohl, B.J., Meyer, L.C., and Lung, C.L. 1994. An Individualized, Comprehensive Asthma Care Treatment Program. *Medical Interface* 7(3): 121–123, 134.

Terry, K. April 1995. Disease Management: Continuous Health-Care Improvement. *Business & Health,* pp. 64–72.

Chapter 21

Managing Utilization of Ancillary and Emergency Services

Peter R. Kongstvedt

This chapter addresses those medical services that are generally considered ancillary services by most managed care plans. These services are a collection of services that are provided as an adjunct to basic primary or specialty services and include almost everything other than institutional services as described in Chapter 14 (although institutions can provide ancillary services). Ancillary services and emergency services are sufficiently different that each must be discussed in its own section. The two categories often cost the health plan roughly the same amount of money, but for different reasons.

ANCILLARY SERVICES

Ancillary services are divided into diagnostic and therapeutic services. Examples of ancillary diagnostic services include laboratory, radiology, nuclear testing, computed tomography, magnetic resonance imaging, electroencephalography, electrocardiography (ECG), and cardiac testing (including plain and nuclear stress testing, other cardiac nuclear imaging, invasive imaging, echocardiography, and Holter monitoring). Examples of ancillary therapeutic services include cardiac rehabilitation, noncardiac rehabilitation, physical therapy (PT), occupational therapy, and speech therapy.

Pharmacy services are a special form of ancillary services that account for a significant measure of cost and have been subject to tremendous inflation. This important topic is discussed separately in Chapter 23. Mental health and substance abuse services may also be considered ancillary from a health plan's standpoint but are really core services, albeit discretely defined. Those services are discussed in Chapter 22.

Ancillary services are unique in that they are rarely sought out by the patient without a referral by a physician. For example, it is certainly possible that an individual could self-refer to a rehabilitation center, but it is likely that the center would require a referral from a physician before accepting the individual into the program. Diagnostic studies almost universally require physician referral. One exception is the freestanding diagnostic center that has medical staff whose sole purpose is to guide a patient through the diagnostic work-up that the patient seeks (e.g., a freestanding cardiac testing center whose advertisements appeal to people who want those tests done). Because those types of centers are out of a plan's control, as are freestanding urgent/convenience care centers, the only real way to control them is economically. If those centers do not have a contract with the plan, or if the plan requires authorization from a contracted physician to pay in full, then the plan does not have to pay such freestanding centers. In the case of a health maintenance organization (HMO), the plan does not have to pay at all. For a preferred provider organization (PPO), a point-of-service (POS) plan, or a managed indemnity plan, the plan may or may not have a partial payment liability, depending on the service agreement and schedule of benefits.

Because most ancillary services require an order from a physician, it is logical that control of such services is dependent on changing the utilization patterns of physicians. As discussed below, the other primary method of controlling costs of ancillary services is to contract for such services in such a way as to make costs predictable. Even with favorable contracts, however, controlling utilization of ancillary services by physicians remains an essential ingredient to long-term cost control.

Physician-Owned Ancillary Services

There is compelling evidence that physician ownership of diagnostic or therapeutic equipment or services, whether owned individually or through joint ventures or partnerships, can lead to significant increases in utilization of those services. As mentioned in Chapter 12, there are three studies that documented this phenomenon in diagnostic imaging, laboratory, and a remarkably wide range of other services.[1-3] Physician self-referral is now restricted by the Health Care Financing Administration for Medicare services (see Chapter 46), and many private plans have followed suit, especially if they are enrolling public sector (i.e., Medicare or Medicaid) members.[4]

Actually tracing ownership or fiduciary relationships is not always easy. The ancillary services may have a completely separate provider name and tax identification number, may have a separate billing address (perhaps not even in the same geographic area), and may otherwise appear to be an independent vendor. Tracking unusually high rates of referral to a given provider of ancillary services (see Chapter 27) may be the only clue to such potential utilization abuse. Many plans are also clearly prohibiting physician self-referral in their provider contracts (unless expressly allowed by the plan) and are requiring the physicians to disclose any fiduciary relationship with such providers.

It is neither practical nor desirable to place too heavy a restriction on physicians' ability to use services or equipment that they own to deliver routine care. For example, orthopedists cannot properly care for their patients if they cannot obtain radiographs. In some cases, a physician may be the only available provider of a given service (e.g., in a rural area). In other cases, it may actually be more cost effective to allow physicians to use their own facility. The point here is that physician-owned services must not be allowed to become a lucrative profit center, one that is subject to abuse.

Managed care plans deal with this issue in a number of ways. One method is to have an outright ban on self-referral other than for carefully designated services. For example, a cardiologist may be allowed to perform in-office exercise tolerance testing but be prohibited from referring to a freestanding cardiac diagnostic center with which he or she has a fiduciary relationship. Another method is to reimburse for such physician self-referred services at a low margin (not so low as to cause the physician to lose money but low enough to prevent any profit) or to include it in the capitation payment (see Chapters 9 and 12). The last common method is to contract for all ancillary services through a limited network of providers and require the physicians and members to use only those contracted providers for ancillary services; this is discussed later in this chapter.

The advent of integrated delivery systems (IDSs; see Chapter 4) has complicated this issue somewhat. It is not always clear whether the ancillary services are owned by the physician or the IDS, and those services may be included in an all-encompassing global capitation rate in any event. The regulatory environment is changing in this arena, however, which is particularly important for those managed care organizations (MCOs) that are contracting for public sector business (Medicare and Medicaid; see Chapters 46, 47, and 48). The reader is referred to Chapter 56 for additional discussion of the topic of fraud and abuse in physician-owned ancillary services in the setting of IDSs.

Data Capture

The ability to control utilization of ancillary services will be directly related to your ability to capture accurate and timely data (see Chapters

26 and 27). If you have a tight authorization system (see Chapter 29), you may get prospective data. If your claims management system is capable, you should be able to get retrospective data. If you have no way to capture data regarding ancillary services, you will have great difficulty controlling utilization. Lack of data will also make contracting problematic because no vendor will be willing to contract aggressively without having some idea of projected utilization.

Data elements that you need to capture include who ordered the service [this is sometimes different from the physician of record; for example, a member may have signed up with a primary care physician (PCP), but the referral physician ordered the tests], what was ordered, what is being paid for (in other words, are you paying for more than was ordered?), and how much it is costing.

The ability to look at patterns of usage in ancillary services is quite valuable. For example, it would be useful to know that of ten family practitioners there is one who routinely orders double the number of radiographs compared with the other nine. There may be a perfectly good reason for this, but you will never know unless you can identify that pattern and look for the reasons.

Financial Incentives

Ancillary services utilization is commonly incorporated into primary care reimbursement systems that are performance based (e.g., capitation or performance-based fee for service). In one study, capitation with risk sharing combined with education and feedback (see below) led to a clear reduction in the use of ambulatory testing while having no adverse impact on outcomes.[5] The topic of financial incentives is discussed in Chapters 7, 9, 11, and 12.

Feedback

The issue of monetary gain leading to excessive use of ancillary services has been discussed

earlier in this chapter, but there are a number of nonmonetary causes of excessive testing; such causes include the quest for diagnostic certainty, peer pressure, convenience, patient demands, and fear of malpractice claims.[6]

There is evidence that physicians will modify their use of ancillary services when given feedback on their performance. Simple feedback regarding test ordering behavior has led to modest reductions in use.[7] This response has been confirmed for simple feedback, and somewhat greater decreases have been seen when feedback was combined with other written guidelines or peer review.[8,9]

Feedback to physicians regarding their use of ancillary services is therefore a worthwhile endeavor. Feedback should include comparisons with their peers and should be properly adjusted for factors that affect utilization (e.g., age and sex of patients, specialty type, and the like). Feedback should also contain adequate data to allow a physician to know where performance may be improved. See Chapter 27 for further discussion about using reports and practice profiling.

Control Points

Irrespective of physician self-regulation of the use of ancillary services, many plans apply additional controls over ancillary utilization. The most common of these are briefly discussed as follows.

Indications for Use

The first control point to discuss is indications for use of services. This is not an easy means of controlling ancillary services, but it has the potential of producing the best control and fostering high quality. In essence, this means using standards of care. Like protocols and clinical pathways (see Chapter 19), standards of care outline the events and thought processes that should occur before physicians refer for ancillary or consultant services.

Standards of care are especially useful in certain types of services. Theoretically, one could develop standards of care for virtually any service, but because review of such standards is time consuming, it is not worth it in all cases. For example, unless a plan is experiencing a tremendous cost overrun connected with urinalyses, there will be no marginal benefits to developing a protocol for when a urinalysis is required and when a urine dip test will do.

Cardiac testing is another matter. Cardiac testing, particularly stress testing and imaging, is quite expensive and increasingly common. Indications for cardiac testing have been published in medical journals, and texts and algorithms are available, but the ordering of cardiac testing sometimes defies rationality. As mentioned earlier in this chapter, a scattershot approach may be used by some physicians that results in test ordering simply as an effort to turn something up. Concentration on this service via chart reviews for appropriateness may yield interesting results and give you direction in developing standards for ordering.

There are now multiple sources for clinical protocols. In the example of cardiac testing, a reasonable approach is to enlist several highly respected cardiologists to use published protocols as a beginning and then tailor the algorithms, protocols, or standards rather than simply impose the protocol without input from plan physicians. A well-reasoned, referenced, and well-presented approach to cardiac disease will benefit the patient and result in lower costs.

The problem with using standards of care is that it exposes you to charges of practicing cookbook medicine. If you are imposing arbitrary requirements on physicians, that charge has the ring of truth. If, however, you are using the best and latest in medical intelligence as well as respected journals and experts to develop the standards, then you are simply expecting high-quality medical practice and thoughtful care of the patient. That having been said, some plans have found that adherence to good protocols has such a beneficial effect that those plans require specialists to agree to follow such protocols and guidelines as a condition of their participation with the health plan.[10]

Test of Reasonableness

If you do not have standards developed, or if you choose not to do so, there are still other approaches. The first is a continual test of reasonableness: Will the test or therapy help? In other words, will the test provide a piece of information that will have an effect on the care of the patient, or at least on the diagnosis or prognosis? In too many cases, tests are ordered only because they have always been ordered. A good example of that is the routine admission chest radiograph. Despite multiple articles in the medical literature, admission chest radiographs get ordered for many people who do not need them.[11-13] The same issue may apply to many other routine studies (e.g., preoperative ECGs or laboratory screening for otherwise healthy patients[14,15]).

Another example is long-term PT for patients who no longer show improvement but who continually complain to their physician. For example, a patient complains of lower back pain, but a diagnostic work-up has yielded a negative result. The patient may not be losing weight or exercising as instructed but is still demanding that something be done. The physician orders PT because it is easy to do and because the patient likes the attention. This is clearly not cost effective, but it happens.

Limits on Authority To Authorize

Limiting the authority to authorize ancillary services will also help control their use. An HMO can limit the authority to authorize services to the PCP only. In that case, a consultant must discuss the case with the PCP, and the PCP must actually order the test or therapy. This is not always practical, and there are legitimate reasons in some plans to allow certain consultants to order ancillary services; for example, orthopedists need to be able to order radiographs, cardiologists need to be able to do ECGs, and so forth.

On the other hand, as discussed earlier in this chapter, you need to watch out for the physician who has purchased an expensive piece of equipment and is hoping to increase revenue from its use. In those cases, allowing the physician to bill the plan for tests or procedures done with that equipment may cause problems. Again, one must be reasonable in this. Certain specialists use certain pieces of equipment routinely (e.g., gastroenterologists use colonoscopes), and you may not want to hamper that unduly. What you do want to avoid is paying for someone else's amortization needs.

Limits on Services Authorized

Another standard feature of managed care is limiting the number of visits for therapy without prior approval. This refers not only to having a limited number of visits that are covered in your schedule of benefits but also to having a limitation on the number of visits that a member may receive without reauthorization.

For example, you may allow up to three or four visits to PT, but for any more the PCP must receive a case report, or the therapist must discuss the case with the physician or the plan's case manager. At that point a treatment plan is developed, and the correct number of visits is authorized.

There will be exceptions to this last technique. In cases where the absolute treatment need is known, proper authorizations for the entire course of treatment may be made. An example is radiation therapy or home intravenous treatments. In such cases, the treatment plan is worked out in detail before therapy is initiated. The number of treatments required and their duration are known and may be authorized at the beginning.

Failure to control prospectively the use of ancillary therapy may result in the number of treatments or visits required in a particular type of therapy exactly equaling the level of benefits your plan offers. Much preferred is a rational approach to treatment with review of the case by the member's physician or the plan's case management function (as appropriate) and a definite treatment plan with periodic reassessments required.

Contracting and Reimbursement for Ancillary Services

Closed panels have the option of bringing certain ancillary services in house. It is up to management to do the cost/benefit analysis to determine whether that is the best course of action. One thing to keep in mind, though, is that controlling utilization is no less difficult when the service is in house because referral for that service is often seen as free and certainly as convenient.

For open panel plans or closed panels that do not have the services in house, the services must be contracted for. A plan usually has its choice of hospital-based (sometimes that is the only choice), freestanding or independent, or office-based service. The choice will be made on the basis of a combination of quality, cost, access, service (e.g., turnaround time for testing), and convenience for members. Unlike physician services, ancillary services usually may be limited to a small subset of providers. This allows for greater leverage in negotiating as well as greater control of quality and service.

In HMOs or plans that have absolute limitations on benefits for ancillary services, ancillary services often lend themselves to capitation. When capitating for ancillary services, you need to calculate the expected frequency of need for the service and the expected or desired cost and then spread this over the membership base on a monthly basis. Plans that allow significant benefits for out-of-network use (e.g., a POS plan) may still capitate, but only for the in-network portion; out-of-network costs will have to be paid through the regular fee allowances. If the capitated provider strictly limits access or cannot meet demand, the plan could end up paying twice: once through capitation and a second time through fee for service. It is possible, although uncommon, for a POS plan to have no out-of-network benefits for some ancillary services, thus more easily allowing for capitation; this may be difficult from a regulatory standpoint if the ancillary services are clearly part of the basic medical benefit. Simple PPOs generally are unable to capitate and must therefore depend on fee allowances.

Capitating for ancillary services clearly makes the provider of the service a partner in controlling costs and helps you budget and forecast more accurately. The benefit to the provider of the service is a guaranteed source of referrals and a steady income. In diagnostic services, great economies of scale will often be present (this is especially true for diagnostic laboratory services). In those services where the provider delivering the service may be determining the need for continued services (e.g., PT), capitation will remove the fee-for-service incentives that may lead to inappropriately increased utilization. As with all capitation contracts, you must take care that the service is not seen by the providers as free, which may lead to uncontrolled utilization. Again, as with all capitation arrangements, be sure that you can direct all (or at least a defined portion) of the care to the capitated provider, and do not allow referrals to noncontracted providers.

Certain types of ancillary services require greater skill in capitating than others. If an ancillary service is highly self-contained, then it is easier to capitate; for example, PT usually is limited to therapy given by the physical therapists, and does not involve other types of ancillary providers. Home health, on the other hand, is often a combination of home health nurses and aids, durable medical equipment, home infusion and medication delivery (which includes the cost of the drug or intravenous substance as well as the cost to deliver it), home PT, and so forth. Some plans have successfully capitated for home health services, although those have tended to be larger plans with sufficient volume to be able to predict costs accurately in all these different areas. Other plans have been able to capitate only parts of home health (e.g., home respiratory therapy) but have had less success in other forms. In those cases, a combination of capitation and fixed case rates (e.g., for a course of chemotherapy) may yield positive results.

A recent variant on capitation is similar to the single-specialty management organization or specialty network manager discussed in Chapter 12. In this case, a single entity accepts capitation from the plan for all of a particular ancillary service (e.g., PT). That organization then serves as a network manager or even an independent practice association. The participating ancillary providers may be subcontractors to the network manager and be paid either through subcapitation or through a form of fee for service, but in any event, the network manager is at risk for the total costs of the capitated service (the participating ancillary providers are usually at risk as well through capitation, fee adjustments, withholds, and so forth).

Some plans that capitate for ancillary services are employing risk and reward systems to ensure high levels of quality and satisfaction. For example, a plan may withhold 10 percent of the capitation or set up an incentive pool to ensure compliance with service standards, such as accessibility, member satisfaction, responsiveness to referring physicians, documentation, and so forth.

Plans that do not have the option of capitating may still achieve considerable savings from discounts. Because ancillary services are often high-margin businesses, it is usually not difficult to obtain reasonable discounts or to have a negotiated fee schedule accepted for ancillary services. Related to that for therapeutic ancillary providers are case rates or tiered case rates. In this form of reimbursement, the ancillary provider is paid a fixed case rate regardless of the number of visits or resources used in providing services. For home health that is inclusive of high-intensity services such as chemotherapy or other high-technology services, the plan may pay different levels of case rates depending on which category of complexity the case falls into. These types of reimbursement systems are appealing but often quite hard to administer, requiring manual administration by both the plan and the provider.

The exception to being able to obtain substantial discounts and savings is when there are a limited number of providers offering the service. Beyond exotic testing and therapy, this is usually not the case unless the plan is located in a rural area. In general, high savings can be achieved through good contracting.

EMERGENCY DEPARTMENT

Exactly opposite the situation with ancillary services, use of the emergency department (ED) is usually at the discretion of the members themselves rather than due to referral from a physician. Physicians do refer patients to the ED, but that is only a source of inappropriate expense if the physician is using the ED as a way of avoiding seeing the patient. For the most part, when a patient is sent to the ED by a physician, it is because there is a legitimate concern that there may be a significant medical problem. There are, however, concerns about cost-effective use of the ED even in that circumstance, and these are discussed later in this chapter. In those plans where the physicians are at risk for medical services, the cost of ED care must be built into that risk arrangement.

Nurse Advice Lines

As discussed in Chapter 17 in the section on demand management, many plans now use 24-hour nurse advice lines. These advice services may be provided by the plan's own advice nurses, or a plan may contract with a company that expressly provides the service for customers in a wide geographic area. In this form of ED utilization management, members are strongly encouraged to call a toll-free 800 number before going to the ED (unless the member has a truly life-threatening emergency such as a bleeding wound or a heart attack). The member then discusses his or her symptoms and medical history with the advice nurse over the telephone. In virtually all advice services of this kind, the nurse uses a clinical protocol to evaluate the member's complaint and then renders advice about what the member should do, possibly including going to the ED. In the event that a referral to the ED is authorized by the advice nurse, the nurse may

then follow up with the ED to determine the member's disposition. This latter feature has the added value to the plan of tracking possible admissions to notify the utilization review system.

This approach is rapidly gaining popularity and appears to be highly beneficial. In one remarkable situation, four competing health plans joined together to form a not-for-profit association to provide the same service to all their combined members not only to manage the cost but also to provide uniform services to all their managed care members.[16]

Prior Approval by the PCP

Managed care plans that use PCPs to coordinate care have the opportunity to bring some measure of control to ED use. There have been some studies documenting decreased usage of ED services in PCP case manager plans, but these studies have been most positive when looking at Medicaid populations.[17,18] There is evidence that good access to primary care in and of itself lowers use of ED services, so that the positive effect in the Medicaid population may be more related to accessibility to care in a population with chronic access problems than to a structural method to lower utilization.[19] In fact, there is one study involving children that was able to document only a modest reduction in ED use despite the presence of a gatekeeper system.[20] Requiring members to seek authorization from PCPs (in an HMO or POS system) may thus yield some savings in utilization, but results may not be what you would hope to see.

Alternatives to the ED

There are alternatives to ED care that you may wish to explore. Late office hours will provide a lot of the care that members go to EDs to receive. If not all physicians or offices offer evening and weekend hours, those that do may wish to cover for those that do not (with appropriate compensation, of course). Some MCOs have included extended hours in their PCP incentive compensation programs (see Chapter 11). Freestanding urgent care centers are found in most communities. These are sometimes less expensive than EDs, but not always. Ancillary services or professional fees can erode any savings from the room charge, and again you have no control of the case. Nonetheless, you may consider contracting with an urgent care center if you can negotiate a good fee structure or a flat fee and ensure that the service will not be abused. Urgent care facilities or late office hours have a way of becoming predominantly for convenience care, and that can be expensive.

Know Each ED

Although the ED may be a lesser aggregate cost than some specialties, it is important to bear in mind that a single ED is usually more costly than any single specialist. It is therefore worthwhile for plan management to apply at least as much attention to the relationship between the plan and the ED as it does to the relationship between the plan and individual specialists. It is also important to bear in mind that each ED tends to have its own culture, just as each hospital does. Regular visits by provider relations and utilization management staff may aid in communications between the ED and the plan and help identify problems that can be resolved. It also allows the ED to understand how the plan works beyond simply receiving payment denial notices. This level of communication becomes even more important as a plan takes on a significant Medicaid population because many Medicaid recipients are used to using the ED as a source of primary care.

Contracting

Many plans contract for special rates with both freestanding urgent care centers and EDs of hospitals. A plan may negotiate a flat rate for all cases to remove the incentive to unbundle and upcode charges. That rate may be deeply discounted if the plan agrees preferentially to send urgent care visits to that facility through the plan's after-hours advice line, through the PCPs, or through the provider directory sent to each member. This has the added value of service to the members because, if the discount is deep enough, the plan may be more willing to allow urgent care visits than if it is paying full charges at an ED. In the case of flat rates, occasionally a plan will negotiate several tiers of flat rates to differentiate routine ED visits from severe trauma cases or other forms of high-cost emergencies.

Self-Referral

Except for serious or life-threatening conditions, when a person goes to an ED without seeking advice from the physician or advice nurse first, the cost can be quite high for a problem that did not need to be cared for in that setting unless the plan has negotiated a deeply discounted flat rate, as discussed above. In cases where the plan denies payment for inappropriate self-referral to the ED, the plan must allow the member to appeal that decision (see Chapter 30), especially to avoid charges of arbitrariness. In cases of payment denial, the plan needs a clear policy on whether to allow the ED then to bill the member for the uncovered charges. Although many plans refer to balance billing prohibitions in their contracts and thus require the ED to absorb the cost, it is more fair to allow the ED to bill the member, although collecting that money may sometimes be difficult. This last issue is especially problematic in public sector programs (i.e., Medicare and Medicaid), and the ED may in fact never collect the denied charge.

One effective approach to the problem of members inappropriately self-referring themselves to the ED is a limitation on coverage. It has been shown that adding a deductible or copay for ED visits can reduce ED utilization without having an adverse effect on health.[21] Some plans have a higher copayment or coinsurance for ED visits than for visits to contracting urgent care centers (some of which may actually be hospital EDs) to direct where members seek care. Most plans waive the ED copay if admission is required.

Most plans also review ED claims that come in cold (i.e., when there is no prior authorization). If the ED visit is not found to be medically necessary, then coverage is denied. Some plans may elect to pay the claim for the first offense, especially for a new member of the plan. If that happens, the member should always get a letter explaining that payment was made but that hereafter he or she will have to get authorization first (unless it is a life-threatening condition) or future claims will be denied.

Education may have some effect on members' use of ED services. Educating members is done through the usual means of newsletters, pamphlets, the member identification card, and so forth. Some plans also promote self-help through education, self-help medical reference manuals, and the like, as discussed in Chapter 17.

Hidden Costs

There are hidden costs associated with ED visits. The ED charges themselves are made up of the room charge, testing, therapy, a professional component, and take-home items or medication. That in itself routinely runs several hundred dollars. The hidden expenses come from losing control of the patient's care.

When a member is seen in the ED, the care is often rendered by the ED medical staff. If the member needs admission, he or she may be admitted to a physician who is not participating in your plan. When that happens, you have lost control of the care of the patient and will have less impact on future events.

In those cases, the plan may have the option of refusing to pay the charges or paying only part of them. That will help achieve some savings, but at the cost of goodwill from the member, and you have still not controlled the actual use of services. It is far better to work hard to develop and maintain a notification system that functions reliably.

The goal of a notification system is to educate both the plan members and the staff of the local EDs that a plan physician must be notified for all cases involving plan members. When hospital administrators know that the level of reimbursement (or even reimbursement at all) will be dependent on plan notification, that will provide a strong incentive for the staff of the ED to work with you. Notification will allow participating plan physicians to gain immediate control of the case and to direct care in the most appropriate fashion.

You must take care not to make the system so difficult that proper medical care is hampered. The ED staff must understand that in serious cases, or when there is sufficient concern, they must take action as necessary. In those cases, the patient should be evaluated and treatment initiated if necessary, but the plan physician or the plan's utilization management department should be notified as soon as possible without jeopardizing the care of the patient. Certainly the ED receptionist can notify the plan physician in those cases where the ED physician is unable to leave the patient's side.

In cases where the physician has referred the member to the ED, you still want to have a system where the physician is kept aware of the course of events. At an absolute minimum, a plan physician should be required to handle an admission from the ED to avoid losing control of the care of the patient. That requirement also allows for continuity of care, and patients have a positive reaction when their own physician handles the case. Latitude must be given for the realities of covering on call. It will not always be possible for any single physician to handle all admissions, but that physician should have a coverage mechanism worked out that provides for this.

Nonparticipating EDs

Because virtually all HMOs, and even PPOs, do not contract with the entire universe of available hospitals in the community (rural communities being the obvious exception), there will be

Chapter 22

Managed Behavioral Health Care Services

Donald F. Anderson, Jeffrey L. Berlant, Danna Mauch, and William R. Maloney

Management of behavioral health (BH) treatment and costs presents special challenges. For the purposes of this chapter, BH services include mental health and substance abuse or chemical dependency services. Unique factors contributing to these special challenges include the following:

- destigmatization of mental illness and chemical dependency, which has led to a greater willingness on the part of the general public to seek help for these problems

- erosion of social support systems, including fragmentation of traditional extended and nuclear family structures

Donald F. Anderson is national practice leader for behavioral health benefits at William M. Mercer, Incorporated, a human resources consulting organization. He has extensive experience in the evaluation of managed mental health and substance abuse programs.

Jeffrey L. Berlant is William M. Mercer, Incorporated's senior consultant for mental health and substance abuse services. He has broad experience in evaluation of both public and private sector managed mental health and substance abuse programs.

Danna Mauch is a partner in the behavioral health consulting firm of Integrated Health Strategies, Inc. She has extensive experience in strategic planning, operations management, systems evaluation, and the development and implementation of innovative and managed care programs.

William R. Maloney is a principal in William M. Mercer, Incorporated's Behavioral Healthcare Practice in San Francisco. His consulting specialty is the evaluation of information management systems for managed behavioral health applications.

- increased complexity and stress in society, which have resulted in increased incidence and manifestation of BH symptoms

- advances in medication and psychological therapeutic techniques, which have promoted more effective treatment of more disorders

- proliferation of private hospitals during the 1970s and early 1980s as a result of high profit margins, cheap capital investment, elimination of certificate-of-need laws in several large states, and exemption from reimbursement by diagnosis-related groups

- tightening during the 1990s of public sector BH funding at the federal level, which resulted in increasing pressure on local government agencies to contain costs

Added to these pressures is the fact that many BH problems tend to be chronic and recurrent, requiring periodic treatment, sometimes intensive in nature, throughout the lifetime of the affected individual. Finally, BH diagnostic categories do not lend themselves to by-the-book utilization management with standardized length of stay and treatment protocols for specified diagnoses. The range of accepted treatment approaches for a given BH diagnosis can be broad, and severity of illness and service requirements cannot be inferred without detailed information about social context and specific symptoms.

Substantial efforts at managing BH treatment and costs first emanated from health maintenance organizations (HMOs). Early HMOs, for the most part, were wary of BH coverage. Some plans offered only diagnosis and consultation; others arranged for discounted fee-for-service care for members. The HMO Act of 1973 required only minimal BH benefits, such as crisis intervention and a maximum of 20 visits for outpatient services. No benefits for inpatient care, chronic or recurrent conditions, and chemical dependency were required. Later in the 1970s and 1980s, increasing numbers of HMOs expanded BH benefits as a result of consumer demand and legislation enacted in a number of states that required richer benefits.[1]

During the late 1970s and 1980s, when insurers and self-insured employers began instituting general utilization management techniques to help control their indemnity plan health benefit costs, it became clear that these approaches were far less effective in controlling BH costs than other medical benefit costs. Thus the scene was set for development of a niche industry of specialized managed BH organizations to contract directly with HMOs, indemnity insurers, and self-insured employers and to apply specialized techniques in managing these costs. Employers traditionally have been the ultimate payers for most BH treatment managed by specialty BH entities (whether in-house HMO, insurance carrier based, or freestanding). Increasingly in recent years, government BH agencies have become purveyors and/or purchasers of managed BH services as budgets have constricted, federal regulations have been administered more flexibly, and accountability has migrated to local government levels. The following describes managed BH care as it undergoes transformation and reinvention during an era of ferment and change.

KEY TREATMENT PRINCIPLES

Special Issues and Common Problems

Any managed care organization (MCO) venturing into management of BH care faces the dilemma of how to address potentially large unmet treatment needs that place demands on scarce resources and may compete for resources from other medical care specialties. Several factors limit BH resources: a historical pattern of poor insurance benefits for BH care, particularly stemming from benefit reductions put into place during the late 1980s; a historical legacy of underinvestment and avoidance of treatment of BH disorders left by pioneering general medical–surgical HMOs; biases underestimating the prevalence, morbidity, and mortality of BH disorders; and apprehension over assuming the moral hazard of coverage for a large and poorly delineated pool of service needs.

On an operational level, it has been difficult to establish the boundaries of BH service obligations. The concept of medical necessity begins to blur when the causes of the disorder encompass social, personality, and biological factors and when necessary services often must address stabilization of social supports; these are factors that are not universally recognized as medical needs. From the perspective of designing a delivery system, this need for social stability as a critical prerequisite for clinical stability requires a broader, more diverse continuum of programs and services than is seen in the general medical–surgical realm.

As a result recent advances in diagnostics, psychopharmacology, and psychotherapeutic techniques, there is a growing demand for powerful new treatment options during a time of shrinking resources. All these factors enhance the need for incisive management of BH care.

Goals of Treatment

Ideally, the goal of treatment for the health plan should be to improve the BH status of a defined population. A well-managed system should aim to reduce suicide and homicide rates, substance abuse–related impairments, and mortality and morbidity from accidents related to substance abuse or mental disorders. A well-managed system should improve the clinical status of a population in terms of symptomatic distress levels and improve life functioning in several areas.

Another central goal of managed BH care should be conservation and rational allocation of resources to optimize return on expenditures. Finding the correct balance between conservation of resources and provision of the appropriate mix of effective services is the fundamental task for managed care.

Objectives of Treatment

There are a number of important clinical objectives for a managed care system to pursue: rapid symptomatic relief, protection of the physical safety of the patient and others, satisfaction of the patient/client and family, and improved life functioning. To conserve resources, managed care systems need to invest in cost-effective treatments and high-return therapeutic activities and to maximize medical cost offsets (decreased costs for general medical and surgical care).

Strategic Approaches

Historically, MCOs have regarded BH care services cautiously. Coming down strongly on the side of conservation of resources, at least in terms of short-term, direct costs of care, they have pursued two general strategies: controlling demand and controlling supply.

Typical strategies for controlling demand make use of the established fact that demand for mental health services is price sensitive. Techniques employed that are based on this price sensitivity include setting higher copayments and deductibles, delaying access to treatment, and limiting benefits, including imposing lifetime ceilings on BH benefits. Typical strategies for controlling supply have included benefit restrictions, program limitations, gatekeepers, triage systems, and waiting lists.

Benefit and program restrictions have at times been profound, severely limiting or excluding mental health services entirely from the benefit package, excluding certain diagnostic-specific disorders or chronic illnesses, and providing few or no psychiatric inpatient services and little or no long-term outpatient treatment. Some contracts have excluded certain member groups from coverage, such as the mentally retarded and people with organic psychoses, alcoholism, and/or intractable personality disorders. Others have limited or refused to provide court-ordered services, thereby reducing liability for uncooperative clients. Some contracts have excluded geriatric patients, violent or assaultive patients, primary substance abusers, heroin-dependent persons, and people with sexual dysfunction, severe learning disabilities, or attention deficit hyperactivity disorder. Virtually all managed care plans use some form of utilization review (UR). Although many use primary care practitioner (PCP) gatekeeping, large HMOs (those with more than 200,000 enrollees) usually allow self-referral. Large case or catastrophic case management is also used.

Beyond a certain point, however, limitations on services can result in underservice of legitimate needs. To meet the BH care needs of a population better, MCOs are exploring strategies for improving the clinical value received for each BH dollar.

From a clinical perspective, managed care should favor:

- use of multiple clinical pathways, providing simpler treatment plans for uncomplicated cases and more intensive treatment plans for exceptional cases

- development of a network of effective, efficient providers selected and retained on the basis of demonstrated superior clinical performance

- matching of the treatment problem with the optimal provider

- selection of treatment innovations and clinical best practices to optimize effective and efficient patient response

- minimal disruption of everyday social role obligations

- treatment at the least restrictive but most effective level of care, favoring community-based over facility-based services

- measurement and tracking of clinical performance, focusing on clinical outcomes, management of resources, and efficiency of response

- systematic methods for helping treatment-refractory patients gain access to highly skilled, specialized services, including the use of centers of excellence for specific problems

- reducing relapse through identifying and planning for ongoing support for therapeutic and social needs

Finally, there is a need for the collective management of aggregate clinical expenditures in comparison with budgeted resources, concurrently identifying reasons for unexpected excessive expenditures and incisively constructing corrective action plans. It is a powerful strategic concept in managed care to tie useful clinical information to financial information in such a manner that changes in clinical practices can target high-risk areas.

Methods of Treatment

Specialized managed BH care is rooted in four key principles of clinical treatment: alternatives to psychiatric hospitalization, alternatives to restrictive treatment for substance abuse, goal-directed psychotherapy, and crisis intervention.

Alternatives to Psychiatric Hospitalization

Partial hospitalization programs (PHP; i.e., day, evening, and/or weekend nonresidential programs) have been proved to be effective alternatives to hospital inpatient treatment in many outcome studies.[2] In a plan with adequate coverage for alternatives to inpatient services, and with informed decision making as to which patients can benefit from these alternatives, eco-

nomical and effective treatment can be provided to acutely ill patients in a PHP setting.[3,4]

Alternatives to Restrictive Treatment for Substance Abuse

Research does not provide evidence that inpatient or residential substance abuse treatment is superior to outpatient or PHP approaches.[5,6] The central question of which patients truly need inpatient treatment and which can benefit equally well from outpatient or partial hospitalization has yet to be answered definitively. In the absence of support for the superiority of inpatient programs for the general treatment population, specialized managed BH systems tend to emphasize the more economical alternatives.

Goal-Directed Psychotherapy

The research literature supports the effectiveness of brief, goal-directed psychotherapeutic approaches for a number of problems.[7,8] Specialized managed BH care systems generally emphasize an interpersonal rather than an intrapsychic focus of therapy. These systems also place emphasis on therapy that is designed to be brief and time limited and not just a truncated version of long-term therapy.

Crisis Intervention

Successful managed BH systems are designed to make use of crisis intervention as a key service in the overall constellation of services. Research has demonstrated that short-term, intensive support of individuals during life crises or periodic acute episodes of psychiatric illness is an effective way to diminish the incidence of future crises and can substantially reduce the inappropriate use of psychiatric care.[9]

Additional clinical methods, utilized especially when managed care principles are applied to the care of severely ill persons, include the following:

- accurate behavioral diagnosis and attention to potential medical and neurological diagnostic issues

- detection and management of substance abuse

- prompt access to services for high-risk clients

- effective management of safety issues

- coordination of services from other agencies and multiple providers

- prevention of relapse through specialized clinical and case management services and adoption of a longitudinal treatment perspective for chronic disorders

- integrated use of multidisciplinary providers for exceptional cases, driven by a coherent, comprehensive treatment plan

- intensive community treatment of high-risk patients

- use of social stabilization measures to reduce relapse

Bridging

Integral to effective BH care services is the capacity to bridge from mental health and substance abuse treatment services to closely allied and interactive general health and medical care, social services, and long-term care.

The Ideal Continuum of Care

Despite historical separation of substance abuse and mental health treatment programs, effective systems integrate treatment programs that tailor the appropriate mix of services to each individual's treatment needs.

Basic Core Services

Entry into the system requires an intake function, not necessarily geographically centralized, to triage cases, gather initial data, establish the presence of a BH disorder requiring treatment, determine the clinically appropriate level of care and mix of service types, and refer the patient to appropriate services. Immediate access to emergency evaluation services is also essential.

Mobile emergency services should also be available on a 24-hour basis for on-site evaluations of the need for acute inpatient services and to provide stabilization services as an alternative to hospitalization. Other important emergency services include the capacity to schedule next-day outpatient appointments and to provide psychiatric nursing back-up for problems that might arise after hours.

Patients who are not stabilized despite on-site interventions may require 24-hour observation and assessment by a multidisciplinary team in a short-term behavioral crisis unit providing 1 to 5 days of 24-hour voluntary or involuntary observation, containment of assaultive or self-destructive behavior, and treatment of acute psychiatric emergencies. Because of the high prevalence of dual diagnoses, chemical dependency detection and treatment protocols as well as staff with specialized training in both chemical dependency and mental disorders should be standard components for all basic services as well as for inpatient and residential programs.

Specialized Treatment Services

Substance abuse. Few patients with substance abuse problems require inpatient treatment. Patients with mild to moderate withdrawal symptoms or significant drug craving symptoms who need more than social support to maintain abstinence can be referred for ambulatory detoxification with daily medical management and monitoring by a physician–nurse practitioner team, including administration of medications as needed.

Patients with more severe problems need at least three types of alternative treatment levels:

1. social detoxification centers for those who require removal from their usual living environment as a result of an inadequate support system

2. residential rehabilitation for medically supervised detoxification when moderate withdrawal symptoms are present or when there is a problem with compliance with instructions

3. inpatient medical detoxification, usually in a general hospital setting, for patients with severe withdrawal syndromes of an imminently life-threatening nature, such as delirium tremens or withdrawal seizures

A full spectrum of nonintensive outpatient chemical dependency treatment services should be available, including brief alcohol and drug counseling, maintenance counseling for individuals who need long-term support, and medication services for those requiring long-term chemical stabilization.

Most patients who are unable to control substance use despite outpatient efforts can benefit from a PHP or intensive outpatient program, including standardized, systematic group education and therapy, core information about chemical dependency, and development of peer supports. Standard treatment packages may include an initial intensive phase with at least 20 evenings of treatment followed by progressively less intensive treatment for the remainder of at least 1 year. Drug counselors in the intensive outpatient program discourage drop-out by contacting patients who fail to attend meetings to determine whether relapse is occurring and to encourage return to treatment.

For those patients who relapse despite best therapeutic efforts and completion of treatment in the intensive phase of an intensive outpatient program, the continuum of care needs to provide several levels of care and therapeutic programs:

- residential chemical dependency rehabilitation with 24-hour supervision during initial rehabilitation treatment to identify and correct factors interfering with the ability to receive successful treatment at an outpatient level, once these factors have been removed, discharge to an intensive outpatient program can proceed

- relapse prevention programs providing specialized, more individualized techniques to address unmet treatment needs

and specialized aftercare for those for whom standard methods are ineffective

- therapeutic halfway houses, linked to participation in a relapse prevention program, for those who repeatedly fail outpatient efforts

Mental health. The vast majority of patients with mental health problems need only outpatient therapy services, including brief (fewer than 12 sessions) individual, group, and family psychotherapy; medication management services; and, for those at risk of relapse and deterioration, long-term maintenance therapy. Complicated cases need a designated primary therapist, who is responsible for formulating and implementing a master treatment plan and for coordinating referrals to other outpatient services. Complicated cases may require individualized services, such as on-site clinical case management assistance, social service interventions, and wraparound services.

Patients who are unable to succeed by using only outpatient therapy services need access to intensive outpatient services. These may consist of crisis services, such as daily intensive individual, group, or family therapy sessions or outpatient medication visits; home-based or school-based therapeutic services, including in-home family therapy; or modular outpatient programs with an array of psychoeducational modules combined with specialized individual outpatient services and interdisciplinary treatment team involvement.

For more severely ill patients who cannot be served adequately by outpatient or intensive outpatient services, multidisciplinary PHPs provide several hours of structured, integrated, modular treatment and psychoeducational services per day throughout the week and weekend. PHP replaces the range and intensity of services, except for 24-hour supervision and security, previously found in inpatient psychiatric programs.

Some patients require brief removal from troubled environments for stabilization of potentially life-threatening situations or situations that may cause family disintegration. As an alternative to acute hospital services or a behavioral crisis unit, the availability of crisis/respite house services may avert the need for a more restrictive and intensive facility placement. Such settings provide brief removal from a destructive or dangerous social situation or from an excessively strained family system for periods up to 2 weeks to allow stabilization of the living environment, placement in a more suitable living placement, or investigation by protective service agencies. Ideal applications of this level of care would be runaway adolescents with oppositional behavior and limited substance abuse problems, battered spouses with highly disruptive adjustment disorders, self-mutilating nonpsychotic patients, and chronically mentally ill patients with families needing respite from excessive care needs or unremitting levels of conflict.

Despite intensive efforts, return home is infeasible in some situations because of excessive long-term danger related to family violence or conflict, risk of violence by the patient, or predatory sexual behavior on the part of the patient. For such patients, community-based residential treatment services, such as a range of residential alternatives for out-of-home placement, need to be available, including therapeutic homes under the care of a family with parenting training and therapeutic group homes for small groups of adolescents and chronically ill adults with frequent disruptive behavior or without the skills to live independently or semiindependently.

Some children or adults may require placement in conventional large residential treatment centers for modification of subacute dangerous behaviors that exceed the skills capacity and security of community-based therapeutic services. Such centers provide 24-hour, tightly coordinated behavioral modification and medication treatment services, preferably with programs designed to prepare patients as rapidly as possible for placement in less restrictive therapeutic settings.

Psychiatric acute care facilities remain essential for patients requiring high-security and highly intensive treatment for imminently life-threatening conditions.

Dual diagnosis. To address the treatment needs of the large population of patients with both mental disorders and substance abuse disorders, the continuum of care should include two general types of program elements: routine surveillance and cross-training in both disciplines at all levels of care, and specialized dual-diagnosis programs to facilitate simultaneous treatment of both types of disorders when simpler treatment methods fail.

For more severely ill dual-diagnosis patients, outpatient programs need to address abuse of a wide range of substances because polysubstance abuse is highly prevalent among dual-diagnosis patients. Intensive day and evening programs are needed for motivated patients with dual diagnoses, including psychotic mental disorders without severe residual symptoms, personality disorders without severe behavioral disturbance, and moderately severe coexisting anxiety, mood, and posttraumatic stress disorders. In these specialized dual-diagnosis treatment programs, abstinence may be a goal rather than a prerequisite for entry. An ideal system will make provision for programs integrating interventions from both psychiatric and substance abuse treatment camps: continuous treatment teams, monitored medication compliance, behavioral skills training to prevent both psychiatric relapse and lapses into substance abuse, close monitoring of drug abuse, modified 12-step groups, behavioral reinforcement programs (such as a token economy) to reward abstinence and healthier behaviors, and assertive case management to reengage poorly compliant participants. Specialized dual-diagnosis treatment programs may exist at the level of the crisis house, social detoxification house, behavioral crisis unit, PHP, community therapeutic residential program, large-scale residential treatment center, or acute inpatient service.

BENEFIT PLAN DESIGN

The starting point for managing benefits in any managed BH program is the underlying benefit plan. BH benefit design, like all health benefit design, needs to address two key issues: coverage limits and incentives.

Coverage Limits

Coverage limits are essentially a fail-safe to limit benefit cost at levels beyond which the plan will not pay, even for medically necessary, cost-effective treatment. Coverage limits can include maximum days, visits, or dollar amounts and can be based on level of care (e.g., inpatient, PHP, or structured outpatient), type of disorder (e.g., acute psychiatric, chronic, custodial, or specific diagnosis), type of treatment (e.g., psychosurgery, psychoanalysis, or nutritionally based therapies), and/or type of provider [e.g., physician, psychologist, social worker, or marriage, family, and child counselor (MFCC)]. The optimal benefit design for a managed BH program will provide adequate coverage for inpatient treatment and its alternatives as well as for treatment providers from various professional disciplines.

Levels of Care

Traditional indemnity plans and many HMO plans limit coverage to inpatient hospital care and minimal outpatient care for mental health problems and inpatient detoxification and may cover inpatient rehabilitation for substance abuse. To support a comprehensive managed BH program, the benefit should cover a number of levels of care (Table 22–1).

Day/Dollar Limits

A recent survey of specialized managed BH organizations (D. Anderson and K. Anderson, unpublished data, 1991) revealed current practice regarding coverage limits in plans where some degree of specialized BH management is in effect (Exhibit 22–1). When asked to characterize optimal coverage limits, respondents advocated raising deductibles (to $500 for individuals and $1,200 for families), raising mental health outpatient annual dollar limits (to $6,000 to $8,000), raising substance abuse structured outpatient annual dollar limits (to $6,000 to $12,000), and raising the lifetime BH combined maximum (to $125,000 to $130,000).

Types of Disorders

Another way that some managed BH plans limit plan liability is through limiting covered disorders. Survey respondents indicated considerable variation in the types of disorders covered by plans featuring BH management (Table 22–2). Some plans also exclude coverage for specific *Diagnostic and Statistical Manual IV* (DSM-IV) diagnostic categories, such as learning disorders and autism, as well as medical diagnoses with potential psychiatric treatment regimens, such as obesity.

Types of Treatment

Many plans built around specialized BH management limit the specific treatments covered. Table 22–3 indicates variation among respondents as to coverage of selected types of treatment. Many plans also exclude from coverage such treatments as biofeedback and electroconvulsive therapy.

Types of Providers

Many traditional indemnity plans have covered only the services of practitioners holding

---

Table 22–1 Managed Mental Health Benefits: Covered Levels of Care

Mental Health	Substance Abuse
Hospital inpatient services	Detoxification (inpatient, noninpatient residential, and outpatient)
Nonhospital residential treatment	Hospital rehabilitation
PHP/day treatment	Nonhospital residential rehabilitation
Individual/group outpatient treatment	Structured outpatient rehabilitation
Crisis intervention	Individual/group outpatient rehabilitation
Outreach services	

Exhibit 22–1 Typical Day/Dollar Limits in Plans with Specialized Mental Health/Substance Abuse Management

Annual deductibles:	$250 individual/$750 family

Annual dollar maximum:
Mental health
  Inpatient
  Residential $25,000–$30,000
  PHP
  Individual/group
    outpatient $1,200–$3,500
Substance abuse
  Inpatient
  Residential $15,000–$20,000
  Structured outpatient $4,000–$9,000
  Individual/group
    outpatient $1,300–$1,500

Annual day/session maximum:
Mental health
  Inpatient   35–40
  Residential   45–60
  PHP   40–45
  Individual/group
    outpatient   35–40
Substance abuse
  Inpatient   30–40
  Residential   35–40
  Individual/group
    outpatient   35–40

Annual family out-of-pocket limit (stop loss): $4,000
Lifetime course of treatment limit (substance abuse): 2
Lifetime maximum (mental health/substance abuse): $45,000–$50,000

Courtesy of William M. Mercer, Inc., San Francisco, California.

Table 22–2 Typical Coverage of Disorders in Plans with Specialized Mental Health/Substance Abuse Management

Category of Disorder	Percentage of Plans Offering Coverage
DSM diagnoses	100
Chronic mental disorders	71
Sexual addiction	21
DSM V codes	7
Codependency	7
Nicotine addiction	7
Custodial care	0

Courtesy of William M. Mercer, Inc., San Francisco, California.

Table 22–3 Typical Coverage of Treatment Types in Plans with Specialized Mental Health/Substance Abuse Management

Category of Treatment	Percentage of Plans Offering Coverage
Brief problem-focused therapy	93
Long-term psychodynamically oriented therapy	64
Psychosurgery	15
Nutritionally based therapies	7

Courtesy of William M. Mercer, Inc., San Francisco, California.

Table 22–4 Typical Coverage of Provider Types in Plans with Specialized Mental Health/Substance Abuse Management

Category of Provider	Percentage of Plans Offering Coverage
MD	100
PhD psychologist	93
MA social worker	87
MA psychiatric nurse	87
MFCC	83
MA psychologist	73
Certified alcoholism counselor	57

Courtesy of William M. Mercer, Inc., San Francisco, California.

medical and doctoral degrees for outpatient BH psychotherapy. HMOs and managed indemnity BH plans have expanded coverage to a broader range of mental health professionals. Table 22–4 indicates patterns of provider coverage for plans with specialized BH management. Some plans also cover pastoral counselors and family practitioners for BH services.

Incentives

The greater the incentives to access and comply with the managed BH system, the greater the impact of the system. Exclusive of HMO BH coverage, most employers are not comfortable with a plan that offers no BH coverage outside the managed system. For this reason, most managed BH plans tend to offer point-of-service choice with differential coverage. The typical managed indemnity plan offers a zero deductible in-network benefit with a coinsurance of 20 percent. Out-of-network coverage typically will feature a deductible of $250 with 50 percent coinsurance.

In one survey, respondents indicated that an optimal coinsurance differential would be 40 percent (e.g., 10 percent in network and 50 percent out of network). Managed BH plans typically do not publish a preferred provider list. For practical purposes, then, coverage differentials actually apply to the plan member accessing a gatekeeper and accepting channeling to a network provider rather than accessing a provider directly without going through the gatekeeper.

RISK ASSESSMENT AND CAPITATION

General issues relative to risk contracting and capitation are covered thoroughly in Chapters 9, 10, and 12; our purpose here is to touch on some issues of particular relevance to BH.

Definitions

For our purposes here, we define capitation as the provision of a defined scope of BH services for a defined population for a fixed period of time for a fixed fee per population member. Risk, in this context, is defined as the possibility that BH care expenditures will exceed a specified amount of revenue (i.e., the capitation amount).

Sources of Risk

Whether the payer or provider is at risk, or if there is a sharing of risk, there are a few key factors that determine the magnitude of overall risk:

- *Insufficient information*—Although in some circumstances historical utilization and cost data can form the best basis for predicting future expenditures, these data frequently are neither complete nor easily accessible. To the extent that the data are flawed, risk increases.
- *Excess demand*—Even if historical data are accurate, utilization of services may exceed that which would be predicted based on historical trends. Particularly in instances where real or perceived access to the services covered by the benefit is enhanced, pent-up demand may unexpectedly boost costs, especially in the early stages of implementation of a capitated system.
- *Large claim risk*—The smaller the size of the capitated population, the larger the impact of isolated catastrophic expenses incurred by individual population members. Actuarial principles determining capitation levels are based on having a large enough population over which to spread the risk (see Chapters 42 and 43).

Although such factors as population demographics, historical experience, and diagnosis can help predict risk, there are no perfect predictors of risk. It is vitally important that entities accepting risk be equipped with an actuarial analysis of the magnitude of risk and that they establish an adequate dedicated safety net of reserve to deal with likely fluctuations in claims experience.

Special BH Capitation Issues

Given the current state of the BH service delivery system nationally, the following issues must be addressed carefully and seriously as capitation is implemented.

Underservice

In any capitated system, an overarching concern is the possibility of restriction of access and resulting underservice. Although this concern is not restricted to BH systems, it is particularly important that reliable monitoring of access, quality of care, and satisfaction take place. It is also vital that the capitated entity be at risk not only for cost but also for meeting measurable performance standards pertaining to access, quality, and outcomes.

Cost Shifting

As discussed above, it has been difficult to establish the boundaries of BH service obligations. To the extent that treatment of BH problems can involve interventions addressing social, personality, and biological problems, entities capitated for BH services can easily become victims or perpetrators of attempts to shift costs. This issue is particularly sensitive in the emerging public/private partnerships involving public BH agencies, BH integrated delivery systems, and MCOs/HMOs (discussed below). It is of key importance to develop and obtain agreement on clear protocols and processes to determine responsibility among agencies with overlapping constituencies and separate capitation arrangements.

Preparedness

Perhaps the single most important issue for BH is the preparedness of the key players to participate knowledgeably and effectively in capitated service delivery models. The current enthusiasm for implementing capitated arrangements, and thereby for "pushing down" accountability and control to the lowest possible level, must be tempered by taking a hard look at the capacity of the front-line players to accept and sustain risk while managing the care. Whether one focuses on BH provider organizations competing for capitated contracts or on county BH agencies faced with capitation from state and federal funding sources, the issues are the same.

Information

Information is a key determinant of magnitude of risk. Do these entities have access to sufficient and accurate information in the required format? Have they built a sufficient specialized infrastructure, particularly information systems, to analyze and manage the information (see below)? If large claims are a significant driver of risk, do they have a large enough "locked-in" population to make such risk sustainable? Do they have the resources to conduct an actuarial analysis of their level of risk? Do they have sufficient dedicated safety net reserves to cope with possible fluctuations in costs?

UTILIZATION MANAGEMENT

Utilization management in specialized BH programs falls into two general categories: UR and case management. In practice, distinctions between the two disciplines often become blurred, but it will be instructive to discuss them separately.

UR

In the mid-1980s, when an increasing number of employers had installed UR systems to help contain the costs of indemnity plans, it became clear that UR conducted by nonspecialized staff with general medical backgrounds was ineffective when applied to BH cases. As a response, specialized BH UR developed that employed specialized staff applying BH-specific utilization criteria. Specialized UR typically includes preadmission certification of inpatient BH cases and concurrent review of inpatient and residential cases (and sometimes of outpatient cases) to determine the presence or absence of medical necessity of treatment. Operational characteristics of effective specialized UR programs are as follows:

- Telephone-based treatment review is conducted by credentialed BH professional reviewers, usually master's level psychiatric nurses, master's level social workers, and doctoral and master's level psychologists.

- Reviewers as a group are trained and experienced in inpatient and outpatient BH treatment for adults, adolescents, and children.

- Initial and concurrent review episodes involve direct contact with the primary clinician instead of, or in addition to, the facility UR nurse.

- High level back-up clinical supervisory staff are readily available for front-line reviewers. Such back-up staff include, at a minimum, board-certified adult and child/adolescent psychiatrists and a certified addictionologist.

- Medical necessity/level of care criteria employed by reviewers are age and diagnosis specific and behaviorally descriptive and encompass all levels of care, including, for example, nonhospital residential programs and PHPs. Criteria are tested and retested continually and modified as needed on an ongoing basis.

UR construed narrowly as determination of medical necessity is typically installed as a means of protecting against abuses in a traditional fee-for-service plan. Although specialized BH UR has proved to be somewhat more effective in containing costs than nonspecialized UR, utilization management has been far more effective in conjunction with a specialized BH network with point-of-service choice.[10] This comprehensive approach to managing BH care generally invokes case management as the utilization management tool of choice.

Case Management

As comprehensive managed BH programs evolved during the late 1980s and early 1990s, the case management function crystallized as a focal point for promoting cost-effective, quality BH care. BH case management encompasses traditional UR but extends beyond it into a broader form of patient advocacy, addressing the longitudinal course of care as well as discrete episodes of intensive treatment. Comprehensive case management includes four overlapping components:

1. promoting correct diagnosis and effective treatment: assisting plan members to access the best level, type, and mix of treatment; keeping alert to opportunities for enhancing the quality and efficacy of care; acting to make the provider and patient aware of these opportunities (UR strives to exclude payment for unnecessarily intensive treatment, whereas case management strives to direct patients into effective forms of treatment at appropriate levels of intensity)

2. promoting efficient use of resources: helping the patient/family access the most effective resources with the minimum depletion of family finances and finite available insurance dollars (directing patients into effective care may be the most potent cost-saving method of all)

3. preventing recidivism: monitoring progress subsequent to intensive treatment episodes; encouraging and, if necessary, helping arrange for interepisode care to prevent recidivism

4. monitoring for and containing substandard care: identifying potential quality of care defects during treatment; investigating and, when needed, intervening to ensure remediation

Comprehensive case management goes beyond determination of medical necessity and seeks to promote enhancement of the quality, efficacy, and continuity of care. As such, it is a more demanding discipline than simple UR. It is practiced optimally by qualified front-line case management staff with a minimum of 5 to 10 years of relevant clinical experience who are thoroughly trained in case management techniques, backed up by readily available doctoral level advisors with relevant clinical experience (including managed care experience), and supported by well-articulated systems to assist with the case management task. Examples of such systems include the following:

- *Triage systems*—Every managed BH system must devise a mechanism for directing cases to the proper case manager. This includes, for example, ensuring that cases with medical issues are directed to a psychiatric nurse rather than to a social worker and that substance abuse cases are directed to case managers specifically qualified and experienced in this area.

- *Quality screens*—Diagnosis-based criteria for the use of case managers, delineating typical best practice patterns of high-quality care for specific problems as well as screens for common quality of care defects, should be employed routinely as cases are reviewed. Such screens assist in early identification of mismatches between treatment plans and diagnosis as well as pinpoint more subtle opportunities to enhance quality and efficacy of care (e.g., when providers may be unaware of or unwilling to use superior treatment methods).

CHANNELING MECHANISMS

A key aspect of any managed BH system is a channeling mechanism to assess initially and then direct an individual to the appropriate type and intensity of treatment. This gatekeeper function is crucial to the effectiveness of the managed BH program and is fraught with potential implementation problems. Who should conduct the initial assessment to determine whether there is a BH problem for which an evaluation and treatment plan are in order? Who should conduct a thorough clinical evaluation and formulate a treatment plan? Who should carry out the treatment plan? The candidates for some role in the gatekeeper function may include an employee assistance program (EAP), a PCP in a general managed medical system, and/or a specialized BH case manager and designated assessor clinician belonging to a contracted BH provider network.

In practice, the gatekeeper role in a managed BH system is often divided among a number of

system participants. EAP counselors may be credentialed to make direct treatment referrals for certain types of cases but may be required to review decisions with a case manager before making other types of referrals. PCPs may have full authority to treat mental health problems, may have authority to refer cases directly for BH treatment with notification to the BH managed care system, or may yield all authority over BH treatment to the BH manager. It is of the utmost importance that protocols detailing roles and responsibilities of all concerned be carefully worked out, understood, and agreed to.

The EAP as Gatekeeper

EAPs play a unique role in corporate America, serving as a wide open point of access for employees and dependents with various problems and concerns. Before the advent of specialized BH systems, EAPs were often the only reliable source of information and guidance for individuals needing BH services. In this role, it has long been one of the functions of the EAP to assess an individual's BH status and, if necessary, to make a referral for treatment.

The positive aspect of involving EAP counselors as gatekeepers for the managed BH benefit is that they are numerous and generally knowledgeable and cast a wide net. They are likely to come in contact with people early, when problems of living have not necessarily grown to become major BH problems. Drawbacks of assigning gatekeeper responsibilities to EAP counselors include the fact that not all are clinically credentialed and qualified, that virtually none has the medical background to enable identification of medical and medication problems that may mimic or underlie BH problems, and that some may not be philosophically in tune with the goals of the managed BH program.

The PCP as Gatekeeper

Many managed medical care programs (including many HMOs) restrict direct access to mental health practitioners and require the approval of the PCP before mental health specialists may be consulted. In some managed care programs, the PCP is expected to diagnose and treat common, uncomplicated mental disorders.

The advantage of investing gatekeeping responsibility in the PCP is that it encourages continuity of care and concentrates authority over preventing unnecessary use of all specialty services in the hands of one person. A major disadvantage of using PCPs as gatekeepers for BH services is that medical clinicians have been shown to be dramatically less likely to detect or treat mental disorders than mental health specialists.[11] Historically, HMOs have gradually acknowledged the value of allowing direct access to mental health services. A recent longitudinal study of a large number of HMOs demonstrated that only 22 percent allowed self-referral for mental health services in their first 2 years of existence, 51 percent allowed self-referral after 2 to 5 years, and 80 percent allowed self-referral after 16 years.[12]

The Mental Health/Substance Abuse Case Manager and Assessor as Gatekeepers

Most specialized managed BH systems are organized to utilize some combination of case managers and designated assessor-clinicians within the contracted provider network as gatekeepers/channelers to appropriate treatment. Some systems rely on case managers to conduct a fairly detailed initial assessment over the telephone and to make referrals for treatment on that basis for all but the most complex cases, which are referred to a field clinician for further evaluation. Other systems routinely channel virtually every case to one of a group of specially designated assessors for detailed face-to-face evaluation and treatment planning.

In either instance, important triaging occurs at the outset. Many systems are able to case-match referrals to assessors or treatment clinicians on the basis of the therapist's specialty interests, gender, language, ethnicity, and so forth. Among systems that encompass a broad spectrum of mental health providers (e.g., those holding degrees in medicine, psychiatry, psychology, social work, or nursing), few have developed a practical theory or usable criteria for matching cases to specific provider disciplines.

PROVIDER NETWORKS

Assembling and administering a specialized BH provider network involves a more labor-intensive selection and monitoring process than is usually required for a general medical provider network. Some of the criteria could apply to any network; examples are geographic accessibility, inclusion of a full continuum of care, willingness to negotiate favorable rates in exchange for channeling of patients, willingness to cooperate with utilization management procedures and standards, and structural evidence of quality, such as appropriate credentials, current licensure, certification, and the like. Some other issues related to continuum of services, practice patterns, and practice philosophy are uniquely relevant to specialized BH networks.

Network Development Staff

All managed BH organizations offering a specialized network-based product employ network development staff dedicated to assembling and administering networks of contracted BH providers. These staff may be located at a central administrative location or at several local offices throughout the region or country, but typically they reside in the local area of a network during its start-up phase. Network development staff typically include experienced BH clinicians, who are responsible for evaluating the clinical skills of prospective network members, and individuals experienced in managed care administration and provider contracting, who are responsible for negotiating contract terms and administering the network after it is established.

Network Development Process

Generally, managed BH organizations adhere to a network development process that includes the following seven steps.

Step 1: Establish the Size and Scope of the Network

To pinpoint the size and scope of the network, the organization must take into account the benefit design to be administered (i.e., the range of provider types covered), the demographic characteristics of the population to be served, area geographic characteristics (e.g., physical or psychological barriers to provider access), and any specific payer requirements related to the size and composition of the network.

The above factors influence the characteristics of a network in any particular area, but certain general rules of thumb apply across most specialized BH networks:

- No plan member has driving time of more than:
  - —1 hour to a full-service hospital
  - —30 minutes to an emergency department
  - —30 minutes to an outpatient substance abuse program
  - —30 minutes to an individual provider
  - —30 minutes to an assessor

- Network coverage ratios should be at least:
  - —1 individual provider per 1,000 covered members
  - —1 assessor per 3,000 covered members

- The distribution of network providers by discipline generally falls within these ranges:
  - —20 percent to 30 percent psychiatrists
  - —20 percent to 30 percent doctoral-prepared psychologists
  - —40 percent to 60 percent master's level providers (psychologists, social workers, nurses, and MFCCs)

Step 2: Assess and Determine Fees/Rates

Providers in the area to be developed are surveyed to determine current prevailing fees by discipline and sometimes by procedure within discipline. From analysis of these data, maximum fees are usually fixed at a standard by discipline across the entire network in the given geographic area. Individual provider fees are usually pegged at a level reflecting approximately a 10 percent discount from the median. Some organizations actually establish the maximum fee at the 75th or 80th percentile, arguing that it is more cost effective to pay close to top dollar to attract the best practitioners but to be vigilant when it comes to evaluating practice philosophy and practice patterns. Hospital and substance abuse treatment program rates typically are not fixed but are negotiated on a program-by-program basis. Typical discounts for these programs are in the range of 25 percent to 40 percent of regular charges and are usually contracted on an all-inclusive per diem basis (see Chapter 14).

Step 3: Identify Targeted Providers

Once the size of the network and the fees are established, the task is to identify providers who will actually be enrolled in the network. Important factors in identifying the targeted group include minimizing disruption of ongoing therapeutic relationships for the plan population to be served, identifying providers who have a good reputation in the community for quality and competence, and identifying providers who are likely to work compatibly in a managed care environment.

Good sources of information about providers include payer (employer or insurer) staff, who can identify providers historically utilized by plan members and who probably have some knowledge of specific BH providers; EAP counselors, who have ongoing relationships with BH providers to whom they have referred patients; and community providers with whom the BH organization itself has had favorable past experience. If these sources are not available or are not sufficient to identify a large enough target group, less selective sources such as professional association listings, state licensing registers, or the phone book are used.

Step 4: Contact Providers

Once a targeted group of providers is identified, contact is made by mail or telephone. Information about network requirements and potential channeling of patients is provided, and providers are invited to indicate interest. Depending on how much advance work has been done to identify likely candidates, response rates range from 10 percent to 50 percent.

Step 5: Obtain In-Depth Information via Application

Providers expressing interest in network membership are asked to complete a detailed application. Although the content and length of application forms vary, forms generally cover such areas as credentials, certification, licensure, specialization/specialized training, years of experience, treatment philosophy, hours available, percentage of practice available to network subscribers, fees, and so forth.

Step 6: Conduct a Site Visit/Interview

Anywhere from 10 percent to 30 percent of providers completing the application typically are eliminated as a result of failure to pass the screening process (most BH organizations have a formalized set of screens that are applied to applications to narrow the field of eligible network participants). Virtually all organizations conduct an in-person site visit to facility-based programs before approving them for network membership. With individual providers, there is considerably more variation. Many organizations rely completely on written applications, some include a telephone interview, some conduct face-to-face site visits/interviews for selected providers, and a few require site visits/interviews for all individual providers admitted to the network. Some common selection criteria are listed in Exhibit 22–2.

Step 7: Select Providers for Network

Results of analysis of applications, interviews, and site visits typically are reviewed formally by a credentialing committee that includes

Exhibit 22–2 Common Selection Criteria for Providers

Facilities
- Must provide a continuum of levels of care (not only acute inpatient)
- Average length of stay for acute inpatient cases < 10 days

Psychiatrists
- Accustomed to filling medication management role in conjunction with other therapists handling individual therapy
- Usual practice pattern involves referring patients to psychologists and social workers for individual therapy
- Work primarily with serious, complicated conditions

Psychologists
- Usual practice pattern involves referring to physician for medication evaluation when appropriate
- Do not routinely test all patients unless specifically indicated

Social workers
- Demonstrated experience in treating sociofamilial issues
- Experienced with assessment, especially in community mental health center settings

Nurses
- Some general medical nursing experience
- Demonstrated current knowledge of psychopharmacology

All practitioners
- Knowledge, experience, and training in goal-focused, brief therapy techniques
- Experienced in multidisciplinary treatment approaches
- Routinely use peer support system to discuss difficult cases
- Demonstrated familiarity with community resources

Courtesy of William M. Mercer, Inc., San Francisco, California.

top level clinical and administrative staff. Approved providers receive a contract, the final terms of which are negotiated by network development staff with oversight from top level operations and legal staff. Managed BH contracting issues do not differ significantly from those involved in general managed care contracting, which are dealt with in Chapters 8 and 55.

QUALITY ASSURANCE

Quality management (QM) refers to activities designed to prevent and/or correct quality problems. In managed BH systems, core QM activities are focused on the qualifications and behavior of case managers and providers and (to some extent) on the treatment results achieved by providers. The following is a delineation of common elements of internal QM programs for managed BH organizations.

UR/Case Management

Internal QM programs should include the following elements designed to ensure quality in the UR/case management process:

- *Credentialing/recredentialing*—Typical requirements are that case managers have at least master's level BH clinical credentials, have a minimum of 3 to 5 years of clinical experience, and maintain current licensure and certification to practice. Many organizations consistently exceed these standards in practice; for example, it is not uncommon for incumbent case managers in a given setting to average 10 to 15 years of clinical experience at various levels of care.
- *Clinical rounds*—Staff must participate in educationally oriented interdisciplinary conferences that include senior clinical staff.
- *Formal supervision*—Provision must be made for regular direct supervision and coaching of case managers by clinically qualified supervisors.
- *Clinical audits*—Routine internal audits of case management notes must be performed with attention to administrative and clinical performance, routine feedback to case managers, and individualized remedial activities when standards are not met.
- *Data tracking*—Staff-specific, diagnosis-specific outcome data must be tracked

(e.g., average length of stay) with comparison to norms, analysis of implications for case management technique, and feedback to case managers.
- *Inservice training*—Inservice training programs for case managers must be shaped and driven by the findings of the internal QM monitoring system.

Network Providers

Internal QM systems in BH programs should include the following elements to ensure quality in the provider network:

- *Credentialing/recredentialing*—Minimum requirements usually include academic credentialing, licensure, certification, confirmation of criterion level malpractice insurance, and clearing of malpractice history. Some organizations independently check licensure directly with state licensing boards and perform direct checks on legal actions concerning malpractice. Recredentialing should be done on a continual basis (e.g., every 2 years), including systematic reminders to providers when current licensure or insurance is about to expire.
- *Case manager ratings*—Routine global ratings of providers by case managers per contact episode must be based on cost effectiveness, quality of care, and degree of cooperation with the managed care system.
- *Provider profiling*—Diagnosis-based provider profiling must be based on measures of cost and utilization with feedback to providers on network norms. This topic is also addressed in Chapter 27.
- *Treatment chart audits*—There must be routine audits of provider treatment charts, often focused on profile outliers, with feedback to providers.
- *Provider communications*—These include bulletins, newsletters, memoranda, and so forth to network providers addressing ad-

ministrative and clinical issues; these are driven by findings of the internal QM system.

- *Provider education*—Provision must be made for formal education programs for providers driven by findings of the internal QM system.
- *Provider satisfaction surveys*—The plan must conduct routine monitoring of network provider satisfaction with clinical and administrative requirements of the managed care system and provide the opportunity for constructive suggestions for system changes.
- *Outcome monitoring*—There must be diagnosis-specific, provider-specific tracking of outcome measures, including patient satisfaction, recidivism/relapse, mental and/or physical health status change, mental and/or physical claims costs, and functional change (through employer-based data such as absenteeism rates and productivity measures).

External Quality Assurance Monitoring

It has been suggested that the incentives and conflicts of interest inherent in a managed BH program are too great to be overcome entirely by internal self-regulation. In recognition of this problem, some state and federal regulatory agencies and employer/payers have instituted routine external quality monitoring of managed BH systems. The results of such external auditing activities reveal considerable variation in performance among managed BH organizations and within organizations over time and at different service delivery locations.

Routine monitoring of the quality of patient care services may be a useful check and balance mechanism. Audits of treatment records and case management records can reveal significant areas for improvement in the service delivery system not otherwise detected by internal quality assurance methods. Determining these areas may help improve the MCO's quality of care and its competitive position. Following are some

examples of variation and common weaknesses in systems.

Utilization Criteria

Most organizations have criteria that specify clear, behavioral criteria for various levels of care. Some organizations, however, have adopted criteria that do not provide clear guidance to the case manager. In these cases, general, nonbehavioral criteria are difficult to apply with any precision. In some other instances, criteria are clear but inefficient. For example, some organizations use published 50th percentile norms to assign initial lengths of stay, thus missing the opportunity to influence cases for which earlier discharge would be reasonable and achievable.

As specialized BH MCOs have matured, there has been a growing consensus among organizations concerning the essential criteria for inpatient care. There has also been serious attention paid to indications for outpatient care and elaboration of UR criteria for intermediate levels of care in the continuum of care.

Staff Qualifications

Some organizations lack case managers or even supervisory personnel with relevant BH background and experience. Some lack doctoral level advisors who can engage in matched peer review with doctoral level providers. Some programs have physicians without psychiatric or substance abuse background functioning as psychiatric medical directors.

Inservice Training

Some organizations select inservice training programs on the basis of apparently random or arbitrary topic selection rather than needs identified through an internal QM system. Many have no inservice training, orientation, or QM oversight applied to doctoral level advisors. Some have no discernible inservice training program at all.

Quality of Care Problem Identification

Analysis of random samples of case management notes in more than 100 audits of managed

BH systems has consistently identified clinically significant quality of care problems in 25 percent to 50 percent of cases (National Medical Audit, unpublished data, 1994). Identified problems include misdiagnosis, subtherapeutic or toxic medication dosages, unexplored medical complications, mismatch of diagnosis and treatment plan, and mismanagement of dangerous behavior. Over time, the prevalence of such problems has not diminished, and specialized MCOs have yet to devise effective methods for improving care at the point of UR. In general, review programs document detection of and action on these problems in only a small minority of cases, although informal activity is believed to occur in some programs. When problems are identified by case managers in these programs, action by doctoral level advisors can also be too rare an occurrence. The potential for conserving resources through methodical improvement of the quality of care remains unexplored territory.

Provider Credentialing

At the most minimal level of QM for a provider network, the BH system warrants to payers and direct consumers that all network providers meet certain baseline credentialing standards. Some programs fail to document and confirm credentialing thoroughly and independently when providers are admitted to the network, and many programs fail consistently to recredential on a continuing basis to ensure that network members continue to meet basic requirements.

Progress in Outcomes Measurement, Tracking, and Assessment

The ultimate gateway to true continuous quality improvement is keyed to the reliable measurement of treatment outcomes and analysis of the relationship among treatment approach, provider type, case management technique, and treatment outcome. Some BH programs have begun to track treatment outcomes in a number of ways, and joint meetings between MCOs and large provider entities have been held to stimulate consensus on proposed tentative conceptual

schemes and data measurement tools. There remains, however, great variation among programs and providers in the degree of conceptual development of these approaches, in the sophistication of information systems available to put data to use, and in the extent of agreement about appropriate measures and methods.

Special Issues and Common Problems in Establishing Effective Utilization Management/QM in an MCO for BH

There has been a progressive homogenization of specialized carve-out BH MCOs. Competitive pressures to provide managed care services at lower prices have made it increasingly difficult to engage in more than narrow UR activity. Yet the larger strategic need is to promote more effective care and to generate more clinical value for every BH care dollar. Increasingly limited MCO dollars also limit investment in clinical information systems (infrastructure) and in processes for data aggregation and analysis necessary for the development of outcomes tracking systems.

PROVIDER STRUCTURES FOR INTEGRATED DELIVERY SYSTEMS TO MEET MANAGED CARE OBJECTIVES

An earlier discussion in this chapter focused on aspects of network formation from the perspective of MCOs. Market changes are rapidly moving the BH delivery system toward mergers of providers themselves into vertically or horizontally integrated systems and toward the integration of providers and MCOs. Therefore, in this section the focus will be aspects of network formation from the point of view of such emerging systems. A detailed discussion of integrated health care delivery systems is also found in Chapter 4.

Importance of Planned Integrated Delivery Systems

The nature of psychiatric and addiction disorders and the secondary disabilities that manifest as a result of the severity and persistence of these disorders underscore the importance of integrated delivery systems. A range of treatment interventions must be simultaneously available to address numerous and discrete demands for crisis intervention, stabilization and relief of acute symptoms, and continuing treatment and psychoeducational support for recovery and relapse prevention.

Historical Structures: Public and Private

Integrated service delivery systems can offer better access and accountability while safeguarding against clinical risk and cost drifting. Historical BH delivery structures in the private sector were one dimensional (a hospital) or two dimensional (a hospital and outpatient clinic). These limited structures were inadequate to address the heterogeneity of the client population and its needs. Interventions more intensive than an outpatient visit were either carried out in expensive hospital settings or not available. Public care systems began to develop a broader range of services in the 1960s under the umbrella of comprehensive community mental health centers (CMHCs).

Until the advent of managed care, CMHCs represented the majority of comprehensive and integrated care systems. Managed BH care organizations adopted community mental health approaches and became leaders in creating integrated service delivery networks, initially for the private sector and for Medicaid and Medicare recipients more recently.

Move to Provider Networks

Integrated service delivery systems have a comprehensive array of services organized to meet the needs of a defined population and geographic base. Fully integrated systems in BH care comprise acute and intensive care services, continuing care and relapse prevention, and community support and long-term care. Integrated care systems provide a single point of

clinical and fiscal accountability to patients and payers, promoting access, managing utilization, and ensuring quality.

Integration has been achieved through consolidation and/or affiliation of providers into defined delivery networks. As discussed in Chapter 4, the model of a physician–hospital organization, which is familiar to health practitioners, is less common in BH care. More common are preferred provider organizations, which are designed to link individual and small group practitioners and are established by hospitals, insurers, and MCOs. Horizontal networks, comprising provider organizations in similar lines of business (i.e., a hospital *or* CMHC *or* residential provider) are most often formed to consolidate a broader geographic and client base, to achieve management efficiencies, and to position the combined organizations to compete for managed care business. Vertical networks incorporate hospitals with ambulatory service providers. In the BH arena, this may include acute care services or a combination of acute, continuing, and long-term care services (i.e., hospitals *and* CMHCs *and* residential providers).

Issues in Establishment of Networks

A number of issues must be addressed in the formation of a successful BH services delivery network. Among the steps to be taken are the following:

- Confirm patient and payer demand to ensure an adequate client and financing base for efficient operation of the network.
- Define the terms of membership and governance structure for both core and affiliated members.
- Identify and implement the legal structure(s) that best fit the mission of the network and the culture of the core members.
- Acquire network development staff with capabilities in marketing, system development, and information management.

- Initiate the marketing and development functions in conjunction with core members of the network to attract business that is key to the maintenance and growth of the network.

- Determine the size and scope of the network consistent with the mission and the market.

- Profile, recruit, and select providers based on planning and marketing results.

- Set network provider fees, costs model, and rate structure for capitated reimbursement and risk management.

Key Operational Challenges

Providers contemplating the formation of a network face numerous operational challenges. Although the initial will to coalesce may be driven by external forces in the regulatory, financing, and competitor environment, an internal will must be formulated if the network is to succeed in bringing together previously independent organizations to:

- adopt common practice standards required by multiple payers

- share reporting and information about clients, utilization, and cost of care

- form a firm commitment to quality assurance and improvement

- develop the capacity to demonstrate and evaluate outcomes of treatment and service interventions provided

- set aside individual agency interests and competition to survive in the BH reimbursement environment

Factors in and Constraints on Carve-In and Carve-Out Strategies Varying by Eligibility Population

To succeed in the current reimbursement environment, BH networks require the capacity to integrate internally across programs and facilities and externally with primary health care providers. Carve-out approaches, where both reimbursement and management of BH benefits are administered separately from broader health benefits, persist where payers believe that separate administration strengthens accountability, lowers cost, and/or improves access to care (see Chapter 36). Carve-outs are most common in the private sector in areas where benefits were historically generous, utilization was high, and the provider community was well developed. In the public sector, the strategy has been focused most often on the disabled population that represents the greatest risk, clinically and financially.

Carve-in approaches are most frequently found in HMOs that provide all health and BH services for a single capitated rate and limit even specialty service utilization to providers within the organization or network. Carve-in strategies are viewed as useful in controlling inappropriate health utilization driven by behavioral disorders and in promoting more integrated care. BH delivery systems must organize to accept payment on a carve-out basis as well as on a carve-in basis if volume is to be maintained and growth achieved. This capacity is particularly important in the short term to preserve continuity with clients whose insurance coverage may shift and to mitigate the financial impact of low HMO expenditures and subcapitated payments for BH. The capacity to play on both terms is considered essential to positioning for the long term, for which the forecast is greater integration between physical health and BH.

Recent Trends in Network and MCO Integration

As the profit margins become thinner and providers gain sophistication in care management, the utility and affordability of carve-out BH care management diminishes. In recognition, MCOs and provider networks have begun to merge. Combined, these new organizations offer service, utilization management, and insurance functions directly to primary purchasers of health care.

INFORMATION SYSTEMS

BH care information systems are a subset of general health care informatics. Consequently, many of the issues facing the automation of BH care processes mirror those facing health care generally. This section focuses on the balance that BH systems must reach between the necessarily unique BH features and those features that both types of systems hold in common. Information systems in managed care are also discussed in Chapter 28.

Unique Features of BH Systems

An information system designed specifically for BH diverges functionally in several ways from similar medical–surgical systems. Good BH systems include, for example, DSM-IV diagnosis codes (including all axes). They allow for residential and partial care settings, nontraditional treatment alternatives, and BH testing. Many of the most important methods for delivering BH services under managed care involve the use of intensive, noninpatient, alternative care settings. These alternatives are incompatible with the basic inpatient/outpatient structure and coding schemes of typical medical–surgical systems.

Developers of the best BH management information systems recognize the more long-term nature of BH problems and have structured system functions to accommodate this reality. These systems smoothly handle issues of multiple and extended authorizations for all levels of care, review and approval of treatment plans, and episodes of care that are routinely longer than those in medical–surgical systems. Contracting and provider modules have well-developed BH credentialing and profiling systems and allow for provider searches on the full range of provider experience, treatment preferences, and education. A wide range of contracting options should be accommodated and utilization against these contracts tracked.

Level of Integration

Although good BH information systems have many features that distinguish them from typical medical–surgical systems, there are many functions that can be shared between the BH and corresponding medical–surgical systems. More important, there are many functions that by definition must be the same. One example is eligibility information. In most cases, the BH benefit is part of a larger medical benefit, and therefore the eligibility information for the two benefits must be the same.

Typically, the BH system relies on the corresponding medical–surgical or employer system for eligibility information. The level of integration between these corresponding systems determines the eligibility file access alternatives. The level of integration can be represented as a continuum with highest level being a single system for both medical–surgical and BH and the lowest level being two independent systems with incompatible eligibility file structures.

At the high integration end of the continuum, BH processing is accomplished on the medical–surgical information system. Historically, this has led to significant functional compromises in the quality and specificity of the BH data, but it does have the positive effect of making access to the eligibility file simple. Because the BH staff are using the same system as the medical–surgical staff, they have access to the same eligibility functions and access the same eligibility file. No transfer of eligibility information between systems is required.

At the other end of the integration continuum, there are many independent BH systems that have varying degrees of compatibility with the employer systems or medical–surgical systems from which they must obtain their eligibility data. In the worst case, the BH staff must either access the medical–surgical system themselves for the eligibility data or rely on paper printouts or phone calls to the medical–surgical staff.

The center point of the integration continuum includes maintaining duplicate eligibility files on each system. This requires transferring the data from one system to the other over a leased line or by tape. Duplicating the files leads to new issues, including scheduling the replication process, reconciling the files, and accessing the original file between replications when eligibility questions arise.

The best integration options utilize client/server approaches. In these cases, there is only one eligibility file which is maintained on its own eligibility server. When either a user of the medical–surgical system or a user of the BH system checks the eligibility of a client, the respective system sends a message or remote procedure call to the eligibility server, which returns with the appropriate eligibility and demographic data. The user is unaware that the system has accessed an external resource to answer the query.

This last approach allows the BH system the independence required to preserve its unique BH functions without requiring the duplication of files that need to be accessible to all systems. It also makes it easy to develop BH-specific data files that contain information not required by medical systems. These files can be accessed by the BH client application at the same time as the shared eligibility file. The result for the user of the BH system is an answer that contains information from both the unique BH file and the systemwide eligibility file.

Key Issues

The key to a successful BH information system is found in the balance between unique system functions and data and those functions and data that must be integrated with the remainder of the benefit plan. Eligibility is an example of a function that must be well integrated. Other examples include accumulators against benefit plan maximums, integrated claims files, member service systems, and contracting.

Many other system functions and data, as indicated above, must be developed independently. The quality of the service provided is compromised when these functions are combined because the medical–surgical information systems do not support the unique needs of BH

care. Treatment planning provides a good example. Medical–surgical applications have not been designed to accommodate treatment plans before the delivery of the service. There is much less variability in the possible treatments, and they are typically not delivered over the longer time spans that BH care requires. Consequently, medical–surgical systems do not analyze treatment plans and progress against treatment plans in determining the appropriateness of services delivered. In BH, however, this is the main method of precertification and concurrent review. It is much more efficient and effective to develop this function and the others mentioned above as separate mental health modules or as an entirely independent system.

PUBLIC–PRIVATE SYSTEMS INTEGRATION

BH is unique in the health care world for the dominant role that the public sector has played in the financing and delivery of care. Approximately two public dollars are spent for every private dollar in the financing of psychiatric and addiction treatment services. Moreover, publicly financed and operated systems historically have cared for individuals with the most serious forms of illness, contrary to tertiary care practices in the medical–surgical arena, where the sickest people more often access care in the best staffed teaching hospitals.

The BH field moved from a medical to a psychosocial model of care in the last 30 years to support the decongregation of public psychiatric hospitals and the development of community-based care. Considerable technology was developed in community mental health and addiction services for the management of care in alternative and less costly settings. Adoption of these practices was key to the success of the early managed BH care organizations.

Managed BH care was formally established in response to private sector demand for an alternative to unregulated and growing use of inpatient and outpatient care. Emergence of managed care in the public sector has, in the main, been driven by a desire to manage cost or the benefit combined with aspirations to improve access, quality, and outcomes of the care provided. Despite the fact that first-generation BH managed care developed from public sector approaches, the advent of managed care in the public sector has been accompanied by the notion that the private sector is more consistent and considered in its approach, which can therefore benefit the public sector. This implied notion has created some misunderstanding and disappointment.

Managed care has also been accompanied by a government privatization effort that has (more than managed care techniques) promoted public–private systems integration. Opportunities for a positive fusion of public and private sector technologies and competence are a great benefit accrued to patients at a time when the amount and cost of service benefits are being reduced. Through privatization and managed care initiatives, those with the most serious disorders now have access to the best hospitals at more affordable rates. At the same time, privately insured persons now have access to less restrictive and broader types of care. The interactive effects of public sector community treatment technology and private sector quality improvement and information management hold great promise for consumers of care.

The promise of public–private systems integration can be realized through a deliberate and planned approach to implementation of a reformed system. Steps to be taken include the following:

- Understand the shifting roles of government players in the local environment as public health and medical assistance programs reframe their policy, regulatory, financing, and provider roles

- Analyze the case mix characteristics and utilization patterns among publicly insured persons to identify client risk groups and project utilization and cost associated with their care.

- Assess political and regulatory challenges to implementing new provider arrangements, service models, and reimbursement rates.

- Evaluate the potential for integration of publicly and privately insured persons at the provider level to reduce segregation, maximize resources, and improve access.

- Establish a process and standards for quality assurance and improvement of all care programs.

- Incorporate the voice and interests of consumers in the planning, delivery, and evaluation of accountable services.

- Develop benchmarks to guide monitoring of client utilization and professional practice patterns as a safeguard against underservice.

- Frame agreements and a plan for allocation of savings as a return on public investments.

EMERGING ISSUES

As with managed health care in general, the field remains highly dynamic, with new issues emerging. Among the more salient emerging issues in BH care are the following.

As noted above, BH providers are challenged to integrate horizontally to achieve comprehensiveness of service continuum, geographic base, and covered lives. They are also challenged to integrate vertically to complete continuums with primary health and tertiary care providers. BH providers/networks require the capacity to operate as, and to accept varying payments on, both carve-in and carve-out bases.

The potential for medical cost offset as a result of timely and targeted psychiatric and addiction treatment is recognized but infrequently measured. As data emerge and full-risk capitation arrangements grow, the demand for behavioral treatment in primary and tertiary care settings grows. A substantial proportion of the highest-cost tertiary care patients have psychiatric and substance abuse disorders that increase morbidity and mortality if left untreated. The implications for redistribution of resources to BH are dependent upon the ability of the BH field to produce data and to educate payers and practitioners.

Legal, ethical, cultural, and values challenges that have been commonplace in public care systems are emerging in managed BH care systems. Legally mandated civil commitment has produced uncontrolled expenses in length of stay and legal representation, driving financial risk to a capitated system. Providers face challenges in rationing care under managed and capitated arrangements, where fiscal incentives promote underservice. As managed care penetration increases, particularly among publicly insured clients, demands increase for providers to be culturally competent, for treatments to be culturally fit, and for programs to be culturally accessible.

CONCLUSION

This chapter has outlined some of the key aspects, issues, and recent developments in specialized managed care programs addressing BH treatment. In overview, BH presents unique management problems that are increasingly being addressed through specialized managed care systems with specific and separate operational guidelines, managed care personnel, provider networks, and QM approaches.

REFERENCES AND NOTES

1. M.J. Bennett, The Greening of the HMO: Implications for Prepaid Psychiatry, *American Journal of Psychiatry* 145 (1988): 1544–1549.

2. A.H. Schene and V.P. Gersons, Effectiveness and Application of Partial Hospitalization. *Acta Psychiatrica Scandinavica* 74 (1986): 335–340.

3. J.S. Rosie, Partial Hospitalization: A Review of Recent Literature, *Hospital and Community Psychiatry* 38 (1987): 1291–1299.

4. L.R. Mosher, Alternatives to Psychiatric Hospitalization, *New England Journal of Medicine* 309 (1983): 1579–1580.

5. H.M. Annis, Is Inpatient Rehabilitation of the Alcoholic Cost Effective? A Composition, *Advances in Alcohol and Substance Abuse* 5 (1986): 175–190.

6. L. Saxe and L. Goodman, *The Effectiveness of Outpatient vs. Inpatient Treatment: Updating the OTA Report* (Hartford, Conn.: Prudential Insurance Company, 1988).

7. R. Husby, et al., Short-Term Dynamic Psychotherapy: Prognostic Value of Characteristics of Patient Studies by a Two-Year Follow-Up of 39 Neurotic Patients, *Psychotherapy and Psychosomatics* 43 (1985): 8–16.

8. M.J. Horowitz, et al., Comprehensive Analysis of Change after Brief Dynamic Psychotherapy, *American Journal of Psychiatry* 143 (1986): 582–589.

9. H.G. Whittington, "Managed Mental Health: Clinical Myths and Imperatives," in *Managed Mental Health Services*, ed. S. Feldman (Springfield, Ill.: Thomas, 1992), 223–243.

10. D. Anderson, How Effective Is Managed Mental Health Care?, *Business and Health* (November 1989): 34–35.

11. K.B. Wells, et al., Detection of Depressive Disorder for Patients Receiving Prepaid or Fee-For-Service Care, *Journal of the American Medical Association* 262 (1989): 3298–3302.

12. M. Shadle and J.B. Christianson, The Organization of Mental Health Care Delivery in HMOs, *Administration in Mental Health* 15 (1988): 201–225.

SUGGESTED READING

Austin, M.J. and Blum, S.R. 1995. Public Sector Planning for Managed Mental Health Care. *Administration and Policy in Mental Health*, 22, pp. 201–356.

Burton, W.N. and Conti, D.J. 1991. Value-Managed Mental Health Benefits. *Journal of Occupational Medicine*, 33, pp. 311, 313.

D'Alesandro, A. (ed.). 1994. *Managed Behavioral Health Care: Provider Training and Development Manual*. Clearwater, Fla.: American Board of Certified Managed Care Providers/Of Course Publications.

Feldman, J.L. and Fitzpatrick, R.J. 1992. *Managed Mental Health Care: Administrative and Clinical Issues*. Washington, D.C.: American Psychiatric Press.

Gartner, L. and Mee-Lee, D. 1995. *The Role and Current Status of Patient Placement Criteria in the Treatment of Substance Use Disorders*. Rockville, Md: U.S. Department of Health and Human Services.

Goodman, M., Brown, J., and Dietz, P. 1992. *Managing Managed Care: A Mental Health Practitioner's Survival Guide*. Washington, D.C.: American Psychiatric Press.

Migdail, K.J. and Youngs, M.T. (eds.). 1995. *1995 Behavioral Outcomes & Guidelines Sourcebook*. New York, N.Y.: Faulkner & Gray.

Milstein, A. 1994. Evaluating Psychiatric and Substance Abuse Case Management Organizations. In S.A. Shueman, W.G. Troy, and S.L. Mayhugh, eds: *Managed Behavioral Health Care: An Industry Perspective,* pp. 222–240. Springfield, Ill.: Charles C. Thomas.

Mrazeki, P.J. and Haggerty, R.J. 1994. *Reducing Risks for Mental Disorders*. Washington, D.C.: National Academy Press.

National Advisory Mental Health Council. 1993. Health Care Reform for Americans with Severe Mental Illnesses: Report of the National Advisory Mental Health Council. *American Journal of Psychiatry*, 150, pp. 1447–1465.

Shueman, S.A., Troy, W.G., and Mayhugh, S.L. (eds.). 1994. *Managed Behavioral Health Care: An Industry Perspective*. Springfield, Ill.: Charles C Thomas, Publisher.

Chapter 23

Pharmaceutical Services in Managed Care

Henry F. Blissenbach and Peter M. Penna

Before 1973, pharmacy, as a covered benefit, was not a significant part of the benefit dollar. Often it was not even a standard component of the benefit. The trend toward inclusion of a prescription drug benefit as part of a managed care benefit package has evolved, however, and at present is a standard component of health benefits.

In tandem with this desire to include drug coverage as a benefit has been the growing number and complexity of medications available to affect the quality and length of life. As with all components of health care, the costs have been increasing annually. Throughout the entire health care industry, prescription costs are placing financial stress on payers and budget managers of health care plans. To the individual who has health care coverage and a prescription drug benefit as part of that coverage, medications are considered an entitlement. The economics of a prescription drug benefit, however, require continued assessment of the appropriateness and necessity of drug use and subsequent aggressive, and sometimes controversial, interventions to manage cost.

The challenge to an appropriate pharmaceutical management program is to control costs without adversely affecting the quality of care and, equally important, providers' and recipients' perceptions of the quality of care. To decrease, cut back, not cover, or omit something previously perceived as a benefit is not well accepted by plan members. Additionally, providers often perceive these same changes as a threat to their independence to practice medicine or pharmacy.

Managing a pharmaceutical benefit requires an understanding of the components of that benefit. When we contract with members of our managed care organizations (MCOs) to provide a quality drug benefit, we mean that we will allow physicians to prescribe medicines that will either cure an acute illness or increase the length and/or improve the quality of life. Our responsibility is to contain the cost of these medicines without depriving individuals of necessary medicines while at the same time improving quality (or at least not degrading it).

Henry F. Blissenbach, Pharm.D., is President of Diversified Pharmaceutical Services, a subsidiary company of SmithKline Beecham Corporation in Minneapolis, Minnesota. He also holds an academic appointment in the College of Pharmacy at the University of Minnesota. Dr. Blissenbach is a member of the American Society of Hospital Pharmacists, the American Pharmacy Association, and the American College of Clinical Pharmacy, and has been actively involved in an advisory capacity with many pharmaceutical manufacturers and managed care entities. His research interests include cost containment of pharmaceuticals and disease management with therapeutics, and he has published numerous articles in these areas, most recently dealing with cost containment issues in managed care.

Peter M. Penna, Pharm.D., is Vice President of Managed Pharmacy for Cigna HealthCare, based in Hartford, Connecticut. His area of expertise is pharmacy benefit design and management as a part of comprehensive health care systems in staff, IPA, and PPO models. His areas of focus include formulary systems, changing prescriber behaviors, contracting for pharmaceuticals, and using pharmacists to promote the best overall therapy for the patients enrolled in a health care system.

COST OF DRUGS

The percentage of the total health care expenditure that pharmaceuticals represent is a highly scrutinized area of economic concern to the public, payers, and policymakers. The pharmaceutical industry as a whole, including the manufacturers, wholesalers, and dispensers of the product, has been widely criticized because drug products are perceived to be expensive without adequate evidence of cost effectiveness. Yet as Dr. P. Roy Vagelos, past chair and chief executive officer at Merck and Company, states, "even if each of the medicines that may eventually be found to prevent or treat diseases become tremendous commercial successes, patient cost for the medicines would be far less than the cost of the diseases."[1(p.252)]

The producer price index (PPI) and the consumer price index (CPI) are the two barometers typically used to measure price changes over time. Both have been used recently in comparison with drug costs to demonstrate excessively escalating pharmaceutical costs. The PPI measures change over time of the prices received by manufacturers, suppliers, or producers of products. Although the PPI for all prescription products grew 78.3 percent between 1981 and 1986, in recent years the percentage increase has fallen below the 10.1 percent per year average between 1981 and 1986 to approximately 9.0 percent. In the mid-1990s, it has dropped even lower as drug companies have responded to the challenge of health care reform.

The CPI measures the average change in retail prices paid by consumers for the product. The CPI further differentiates drug products according to their product type. Prescription drugs are reflected in the CPI-Rx. Between 1981 and 1986, this component increased by almost 80.0 percent, an average rate of 10.2 percent. As with the PPI, the CPI-Rx average dropped during subsequent years. After a slight increase in 1989 to 9.5 percent, the CPI-Rx maintained at about 9.0 percent for several more years until further erosion in 1994.

What does this mean in terms of overall cost to the MCO when providing a drug benefit program? As Table 23–1 shows, since 1988, when drug expenditures accounted for approximately 6 percent of the premium, drug costs have accounted for approximately 10 percent of operating expenses. Since that time, drug costs as a percentage of operating expenses have continued to run higher than drug expenditures as a percentage of premium. In other words, MCOs seemingly have been reluctant to charge the premium payer an amount equivalent to the percentage of operating expense that the drug benefit consumes. Hence for most MCOs offering a pharmacy benefit, the drug benefit program has often served as somewhat of a loss leader.

As we will see throughout this chapter, it is becoming more important to manage the cost of the pharmaceutical benefit than to save money. If MCOs choose to continue to operate at a loss for the drug benefit program, managing the amounts of these losses becomes paramount.

THE PHARMACY BENEFIT

Before we discuss policies, procedures, and services necessary to ensure successful management of the pharmacy benefit, we need to review what a managed care pharmacy benefit includes. Typically each member of an MCO that offers a prescription drug benefit can receive prescriptions as a covered benefit as long as the following criteria are met:

- The individual must be eligible for coverage by the MCO. An eligible member is the primary card holder or dependent of the card holder. The eligible member or employee usually must present identification designating that he or she is a member of that MCO.

- In some cases, the prescription must be written by a contracted prescriber (i.e., an eligible prescriber on record with the MCO). When the MCO closes its physician prescriber list and requires prescriptions to be written only by contracted physicians, the pharmacist must determine eligibility.

Table 23–1 Drug Expenditures as Percentage of Premium and Operating Expenses

Expenditure	Year	Total	Type of MCO			
			Staff	Network	IPA*	Group
Percentage of Premium	1988	6.0	3.4	5.4		6.9
	1989	5.5	4.0	5.5		5.7
	1990	6.2	5.1	6.2		6.3
	1991	7.1	5.9	7.9		7.1
	1992	8.8	7.2	9.0	9.1	8.4
	1993	8.3	N/A	6.8	8.9	8.1
	1994	8.6	6.7	8.8	9.1	8.4
Percentage of Operating Expenses						
	1988	10.0	5.0	12.0		11.0
	1989	10.0	5.0	10.0		11.0
	1990	9.0	6.0	10.0		9.0
	1991	11.0	9.0	10.0		11.0
	1992	9.0	8.0	10.0	10.0	8.0
	1993	12.0	8.0	9.0	13.0	11.0
	1994	10.0	8.0	9.0	11.0	12.0

* IPA, independent practice association.

Source: Courtesy of Hearst Marion Roussel Legal Department, Cincinnati, Ohio.

- Prescriptions for over-the-counter medications are ordinarily not covered; only prescriptions that are legend will be covered. A legend drug is one labeled "Caution: Federal law prohibits dispensing without a prescription." Even if the medication is a legend drug, however, that does not necessarily mean that it is covered.

- Most MCO's now have formularies. If a formulary is open, it is merely a list of preferred drugs; drugs prescribed but not on the list will still be covered. If the formulary is closed, then only drugs on the formulary will be covered.

- Many MCOs require that specific guidelines be met before certain drugs will be covered.

- Prescriptions must be filled at designated pharmacies; these are drug stores that have a contractual agreement with the MCO. The covered member cannot take the prescription into any drug store to have it filled but must remain within the network.

- If the medication is available generically, it will be reimbursed at a generic rate and probably will be dispensed as a generic equivalent. Often, the member has the option of paying the difference between the generic and the branded products.

- For the member to receive the prescription, a deductible or copay is usually required. Members are expected to pay a portion of the cost of their prescriptions.

CERTIFICATE OF COVERAGE

The pharmacy benefit is typically defined in a document called the certificate of coverage or certificate of benefits that the MCO provides to the member to describe his or her covered health care benefits. Before any cost management or cost containment procedures can be implemented, the benefit certificate must have language to allow these procedures. Once benefit language changes are in place, these need to be communicated and explained to members and to providers. This entire process often takes considerable time for approval and implementation. Many cost management efforts can be accomplished without changes being required in the certificate of coverage, however.

The certificate typically addresses the fact that medications are eligible for coverage if they meet certain criteria and are medically necessary and appropriate for treatment of the illness. Generally, the treatment must also be consistent with medical standards of the community and prevent the patient's condition from worsening. The fact that a provider recommends a certain medication or service does not necessarily mean that it is eligible for coverage under the contract.

Typically excluded from pharmacy benefit programs are services or prescription drugs that the MCO determines to be experimental or unproven, services or prescription drugs that are not generally accepted by the medical community as a standard of care, and others. Typical exclusions include anorexant drugs, cosmetic medications, and vitamins. All MCOs allow the member an appeal process should there be a disagreement with a coverage decision.

Do therapeutic qualifications alone automatically qualify a drug for coverage? Covered drug decisions can also be based on a determination that an individual's life will be better in terms of quantity or quality. In other words, quality and outcome qualifications can be included when coverage of a medication is determined.

MANAGED HEALTH CARE AND THE PHARMACY BENEFIT

When one refers to a prescription drug benefit, ordinarily the implication is that someone other than the recipient is paying for the benefit. In other words, the receiver of the service is not the payer for the prescription. There are still a significant number of individuals who pay for their prescriptions out of their own pocket, but the percentage of the population that has partial or total prescription drug coverage is increasing yearly. The largest group without a benefit comprises retirees.

How the Benefit Is Received

There are several ways that prescription services are obtained, and each of these has its own characteristic method of payment.

Recipient of Service Pays Entire Cost of Prescription

Until recently, this was the most common way that prescriptions were obtained. The recipient would call or visit the physician, the physician would write a prescription, and the recipient would take the prescription to a pharmacy, have it filled, and pay the cost of the product plus the service. Competition then entered the pharmacy marketplace, driving some of the product and service fees downward and somewhat decreasing prescription costs.

Partial Pay for Both Recipient and Third Party

Partial payment plans for drug benefit programs usually require an identification card designating eligibility. These programs are further classified as managed or unmanaged programs. The managed card program traditionally has been associated with MCOs. More recently, for quality and cost reasons, self-insured employers and even indemnity insurance plans with prescription drug riders are moving from unmanaged to managed card programs.

Prescription drug benefit programs with a partial payment requirement on the part of the recipient are increasing in popularity, and variations in the partial pay amount are significant factors in enabling the payer to manage the drug benefit cost. The common variations are as follows:

- *Copayments*—Typically these are handled at the point of service. This mechanism requires a designated dollar amount in exchange for the product or service. In other words, a prescription is presented at the pharmacy, and upon delivery of the prescription to the recipient, the recipient pays a copayment amount. Sometimes the copayment is the same for a branded or generic, formulary or nonformulary prescription; other times there is a higher copay for branded than generic drugs. The copayment may vary from $3.00 to $20.00 per prescription, with lower copays being more common.

- *Deductibles*—Typically these are associated with indemnity insurance plans and sometimes with self-insured employer groups. They are gaining popularity in health maintenance organizations (HMOs) and preferred provider organizations (PPOs), particularly now that calculation and notification of up-to-date deductibles via on-line point-of-service claims processing systems are common. The prescription deductible, like any other medical service deductible, requires a designated out-of-pocket expenditure before the pharmacy benefit coverage comes into effect. Although the deductible should be approximately 25 percent to 35 percent of the annual drug cost, because these are prospectively determined amounts they most often are underestimated and rarely reach an appropriate percentage of partial payment. In the past, insurers and other payers have gambled that recipients would "shoe box" the receipt for services and would not file a claim for the eligible amount. With the increasing cost of prescription drugs, the decreasing comparative percentage of salary increases compared with prescription cost increases, and the ease of recordkeeping via on-line point-of-service claims processing systems, however, the shoe box effect is becoming less and less apparent.

- *Coinsurance*—This is most common with indemnity insurance plans. Each time the benefit is used, a designated percentage is applied to the total cost of the prescription. In other words, a drug benefit plan with 20 percent coinsurance would require the recipient to pay 20 percent of the cost of the prescription each time it is obtained.

Again, because they once relied on the shoe box effect, indemnity insurance plans are finding that unmanaged drug benefit riders with coinsurance applications are experiencing high costs.

Recipient Has No Partial Payment: Third Party Pays All

This method of payment typically is associated with state and federally financed programs. In these Medicaid type programs, the recipient is not required to pay out of pocket any part of the drug benefit. There are a few exceptions to this. Some states have initiated minimal copayments ($0.25 to $1.00) on the part of the Medicaid recipient. Government funded programs are typically managed by legislative regulations, and special interest groups have made managing a drug benefit system for state Medicaid programs difficult at best. Provider reimbursement fees are usually legislated, and discounts off the average wholesale price (AWP) of the product are determined by Congress. Because federally and state funded programs have been experiencing higher drug expenditures than the private sector, however, both levels of government are requiring more management applications to these programs.

Components of a Pharmacy Benefit

A prescription drug benefit has several components. These components depend on whether the benefit is unmanaged or managed. An unmanaged program is simple to facilitate and, with minor exceptions, allows the eligible recipient to have prescriptions filled, with the pharmacy collecting the designated copay, deductible, or coinsurance.

A well-managed prescription drug benefit, on the other hand, can be complex and includes the following characteristics:

- appropriate benefit design
- point-of-service claims adjudication and processing

- a contracted and discounted pharmacy network
- an aggressive generic substitution program
- a cost-effective drug formulary program
- discounts from manufacturers via volume purchase or market share programs
- financial and utilization management reporting
- budgeting appropriateness based on accurate information

The Providers

Staff model or closed panel HMO. This type of MCO often employs its own pharmacists and owns its in-house pharmacies. The MCO assumes all the risk for the prescription drug service and is the oldest form of prepaid pharmaceutical services in the country. The MCO-employed pharmacists dispense medications to plan members at MCO-owned pharmacies. The primary advantages of a staff model MCO prescription benefit are as follows:

- The MCO saves administration cost because there are no claims processed for reimbursement.
- Program changes (e.g., drug formularies, copayment, etc.) are made easily because all affected providers are employed by the MCO.
- The MCO can take advantage of volume purchasing because of a large in-house prescription volume.
- Because physicians and pharmacists work for the same organization, it's easier to develop consensus on benefit management strategies.

There are also some disadvantages:

- This system requires a considerable capital investment by the MCO to provide pharmacy space, drug inventory, and staff.

- Lack of evening and after-hours emergency service and convenient accessibility often creates problems for plan subscribers.
- Difficulty in establishing pharmacist–patient relationships is sometimes experienced.

Some staff model MCOs also agree to cover over-the-counter (nonprescription) medications.

Independent practice association or open panel HMO. The base of pharmacy benefit programs in independent practice associations (IPAs) and open panel MCOs is contracted provider networks. Pharmacies are not owned; neither is the pharmacist's salary paid by the MCO. Instead, these are established freestanding community pharmacies. Pharmacy participation in the limited pharmacy network is, for the most part, determined by the MCO.

Advantages include the following:

- Pharmacies are conveniently located for patient/member accessibility.
- The MCO can provide pharmaceutical benefits without a considerable investment in facility space, drug inventory, and pharmacy staff.
- The pharmacy network can expand easily as growth requirements emerge.
- The MCO can take advantage of competition in the marketplace to generate discounts.

There are also disadvantages:

- Administrative expenses increase as a result of claims processing and reimbursement.
- This decentralization of pharmaceutical services makes it more difficult to implement program, policy, and procedural changes.
- Criteria are necessary for selection of participating pharmacies to ensure nonviolation of existing laws.

- Managing the benefit is more difficult because physicians, pharmacists, and administrators have few common interests.
- Policies regarding reimbursement for pharmacy services must be determined and established.

PPO. This benefit may look like a traditional MCO benefit with an IPA flair because there is a pharmacy network that is typically contracted and limited. A PPO benefit may also resemble an indemnity insurance benefit if it is not tightly managed, although this is losing favor. Most PPOs have not been able to manage their pharmaceutical costs as well as the MCOs, primarily because PPOs tend to be more provider sensitive and have been reluctant to implement aggressive cost management applications, as have the MCOs.

Indemnity insurance plan. Typically unmanaged, these may utilize a prescription card program within a relatively large pharmacy network. Under this mode, all pharmacies located in the geographic service area are generally afforded the opportunity to provide pharmacy services to the indemnity insurance subscriber. Ordinarily, these operate under a pay-and-submit approach with few or no benefit restrictions. Mail order pharmacy may be a component. Some indemnity plans function in a major medical approach, in which the subscribers pay out of pocket and then submit claims to the insurance plan for reimbursement (after deductible and coinsurance).

Advantages of this program include the following:

- Card programs deliver some level of control over ingredient cost and dispensing fee.
- Such programs maintain a strong freedom of choice concept, preserving long-standing pharmacist–patient relationships.
- Subscribers are not forced to drive considerable distances to have their pharmaceutical needs fulfilled.

- Mail order programs achieve good control of ingredient cost and dispensing fee and are convenient for members on long-term medications.

The following are some disadvantages:

- As one might expect, the costs associated with operating an open pharmacy network are much greater than those of the other two alternatives.
- Plans that use card programs must print and distribute administration manuals, participating pharmacy agreements, claims reimbursement forms, and the like, all of which contribute to total administrative cost.
- Such plans are unable to take advantage of competition in the marketplace to drive significantly discounted fees.
- Mail order programs may result in waste when a prescription is changed in midcourse or when a member loses eligibility shortly after receiving a 90-day supply.

Self-insured benefits. The advantages and disadvantages are similar to those for indemnity insurance.

Government/medicaid programs. Traditional non–managed care public sector programs utilize contracted pharmacy networks and have the same advantages and disadvantages discussed above. They are usually card and point-of-service programs and are often unmanaged. Many public sector programs, however, are moving to managed care (see Chapters 46, 47, and 48) and operate much the same as HMOs.

Determining Pharmaceutical Benefit Costs

How does one determine the true cost of a pharmaceutical benefit? How should that benefit be priced? What is its overall value? How does your cost compare with that of other MCOs and competitors? Trying to provide a pharmacy benefit program without knowing the answers to these questions puts managers at a distinct disadvantage.

Before management approaches can be initiated to control pharmaceutical expenditures, it is necessary that managed care understand the cost of the program and the degree of responsibility that each of the components of that cost has to the overall bottom line.

The cost of pharmacy benefit can be determined by applying the following formula:

$$\text{Total drug cost} = (\text{ingredient cost} + \text{dispensing fee} - \text{copay}) \times \text{number of prescriptions}$$

Total drug costs can be calculated either as a per member per month (PMPM) or per member per year (PMPY) expenditure. The actual prescription cost is represented by the values in parentheses (ingredient cost + dispensing fee – copay). If the intent is to decrease overall pharmacy benefit expenditures, we need to determine the percentages that each component represents. Although the prescription cost is often the cost indicator, PMPM costs are a more accurate indicator. An example is illustrated in Exhibit 23–1.

The next step is to determine high or low status and to react accordingly. As you can see by the above formula, there are several ways to reduce or control the PMPM cost:

- *Reduce ingredient cost*—This is accomplished by maximizing generic substitution, reimbursing for generics only according to a maximum allowable cost (MAC) list, implementing a drug formulary to manage utilization, and using volume purchase (rebate) or discount contracting.

- *Decrease dispensing fees*—Take advantage of the competition in the marketplace to ensure the lowest acceptable dispensing fee.

- *Increase copays*—Increase the member's (or subscriber's) out-of-pocket responsibility for a portion of the drug benefit. This

Exhibit 23–1 Illustration of PMPM Drug Cost

Assume:
  Ingredient cost = $18.00
  Dispensing fee = $2.50
  Copay = $7.00
  Number of prescriptions = 0.6 PMPM

Then:
  PMPM drug cost = ($18.00 + $2.50 – $7.00) × 0.6
  = $8.10

can act as a disincentive for utilizing the drug benefit and could increase total costs if members do not get necessary prescriptions to manage their disease.

- *Decrease the number of prescriptions*— The total number of prescriptions written by physicians multiplies the prescription cost. Outlier prescribers, once identified, can be evaluated for cost effectiveness and notified if appropriate to try to bring them toward the norm.

Managing the Pharmacy Benefit

Adequately and appropriately managing a pharmacy benefit consists of two integral pieces: management of the cost and management of the quality of that benefit. Successful pharmacy benefit management applications have proved that drug costs can be managed without adversely affecting quality of care.

Benefit design. The manner in which the pharmacy benefit is designed determines how the pharmacy benefit works. Simply stated, the benefit identifies for both the member and the provider the terms and extent of the coverage. All determinants of coverage hinge on the benefit design. The actual benefit design depends on several factors: competition, government regulations and requirements, union or employer specifications, dollars available, and the like. The real art of prescription benefit design is choosing where to save money and where compromises are possible. The benefit design should define prescription medications, describe refill restrictions (if any), list products or services excluded from the benefit, state payment responsibilities of the member, specify limits on the number of medications allowed with each transaction, and identify approved prescribers and providers. Also, generic and formulary requirements as well as allowances for investigational or experimental medications should be listed.

Claims adjudication. Once the benefit design has been finalized, a process must be implemented to reimburse for benefit coverage, unless of course the prescription is filled in a pharmacy owned by the managed care plan. Whether the pharmacist adjudicates the claim electronically or a claims processor at the plan performs this task, this procedure includes the following:

- verification of eligibility on the basis of enrollment information provided by the payer
- verification of coverage on the basis of the benefit design of the group
- verification of copay
- verification of reimbursement amount to the pharmacy in accordance with prearranged or contracted specifics

Enrollment information/eligibility verification. Of utmost importance is the verification of eligibility before a claim is paid. Todays' point-of-service verification capabilities allow for assurance to the provider as to the authenticity of the eligibility.

Eligibility verification is accomplished simply: The member presents an eligibility card, and the provider verifies the member as eligible. Although some plans still use printed eligibility lists, the majority of pharmacies have moved to on-line point-of-service eligibility verification and claims processing.

Electronic claims adjudication. Not so long ago, all pharmacy claims were submitted on paper. The primary disadvantage was that, although the recipient of the prescription could present an identification card indicating eligibility for coverage, often eligibility had terminated

without adequate notification to the provider; or the pharmacist would have a claim returned without payment because of a change in eligibility; or incorrect payment was received by the pharmacist; or the wrong amount of copayment was collected. All these increase the frustration level of the pharmacist and often put members at odds with the pharmacist in terms of who owes money to whom.

Electronic claims processing reduces all these and allows for the point-of-service coordination of benefit services such as deductible, copayment, and coverage limits. When the pharmacist enters the prescription on line, that pharmacist receives up-to-date eligibility status and knows that acceptance by the on-line system ensures payment. Additionally, the delay in receiving payment for the prescription is decreased significantly, and rejected claims are eliminated.

Interestingly, the driving force behind point-of-service eligibility systems has been not the pharmacist but the payer.[2] Cost containment pressures are forcing health care plans to take a hard look at the cost of paying for bad claims. Most payers have included a point-of-service requirement as part of pharmacy network contracting.

Pharmacy Provider Networks

Limitations on the number of pharmacies to provide services for enrolled members are typical of managed care plans. Like hospital and physician networks, pharmacist networks have been limited to provide a network exchanging volume for price. Limiting the pharmacy network allows the MCO to accomplish two objectives: lower dispensing fees and improve compliance with policies and procedures. In most large cities, the available pharmacy network is generally larger than necessary to fill the prescriptions of the plan's membership. MCOs will take advantage of that competitive marketplace to obtain discounts. Reimbursement is a function of supply and demand.

Part of the pharmacy benefit cost management process is an analytical evaluation of the current pharmacy network. According to the Marion Merrell Dow *Managed Care Digest*, all model types of MCOs increase their reliance on contracted pharmacies annually.[3] Only 11 percent of MCOs utilize in-house pharmacies to fill prescriptions, 74 percent use contracted pharmacies, and 14 percent use a combination of in-house and contracted pharmacies. More MCOs use a combination of chain and independent drug stores, and there has been a yearly increase in the use of drug store chains.

For the contractual arrangement to be successful, the payer must be willing to restrict covered members' access to pharmacies. When this happens, there may be an initial negative reaction. If the plan is large enough, one can also expect the local pharmacist associations to organize against the plan's decision. When a plan is deciding to decrease the pharmacy network, the negative reaction should be weighed carefully against the benefit. The standard within the managed care industry, however, is to provide the pharmacy benefit through a restricted pharmacy network.

Mail order pharmacy is increasing in popularity nationally, such that 55 percent of managed care plans offer a mail order component.[4] Employers offering a self-insured pharmacy benefit have offered mail order usually as an option. This has also been an especially popular method for retirees to receive prescriptions at a discounted rate. Those MCOs offering mail order as a component of the pharmacy benefit should require the mail order dispenser to follow the same policies and procedures as the rest of the pharmacy provider network. Formularies, MAC reimbursement, eligibility verification, copay collections, and all other procedures must be followed. Usually, the mail order companies are willing to compete even more aggressively than the members of the pharmacy network. Mail order pharmacies may be especially good at ensuring generic and therapeutic substitution.

The final type of prescription vendor is the physician dispenser. Several companies offer repackaging services to physicians' offices as part of a system to dispense prescriptions. Some MCOs allow physician dispensers as part of the pharmacy benefit system, but the physician must accept the same discounted reimbursement as the rest of the pharmacy network. This includes a percentage discount from the AWP of the product and the discounted dispensing fee. Physician dispensers primarily dispense short-term medications and usually have few or no refill capabilities. The popularity of this system in MCOs is low, and usually there is little interest on the part of the physician to fill prescriptions for third party payers; as pressure increases on physicians to accept lower capitation and fee rates, however, some may look for ways to provide more services and hence get more reimbursement.

Ingredient Cost

There are several approaches to managing this significant cost portion of the equation, each method is dependent on the design of the drug benefit.

Generic Drug Policy

When the patent expires on a previously brand-only medication, usually other manufacturers competitively distribute the same drug. The quality indicators of a generic program are covered later in this chapter; the advantage to this is that the generic medication is significantly less costly than the branded medication. Almost 90 percent of MCOs require the use of generics, and approximately 40 percent of MCO prescriptions are filled with generic drugs.[5] The average generic cost is anywhere from 40 percent to 70 percent less than the equivalent branded product cost.

The components of an aggressive generic program include generic reimbursement according to a MAC reimbursement rate. Because there are multiple manufacturers of generic medications, each pricing at different AWPs, and because most pharmacies participate in some form of purchasing group arrangement, the difficulty in identifying the true average price of a generic medication has created the MAC reimbursement process. This process allows the payer to set a price for a specific generic medication and indicates to the pharmacist the maximum amount that will be reimbursed as the ingredient cost. The determination of the MAC is highly technical and work intensive.

Remember that generic utilization numbers can be misleading. An MCO could have an extremely high generic utilization rate and yet not maximize generic cost savings. This is exactly what happens when a MAC list is not part of the reimbursement policy.

If exceptions are included in the benefit design that allow the pharmacist to be reimbursed for prescriptions at other than the MAC, benefit costs will increase. These exceptions are a benefit design allowing the physician and/or member to request the branded product at the expense of the plan. Commonly called a dispense-as-written (DAW) policy, this request may be generated by the physician by writing "dispense as written" on the prescription. It may also be generated by a verbal request on the part of the member to receive the branded product rather than the generic. This will decrease the number of prescriptions dispensed generically and will cause a significant increase in the average ingredient cost. A well-managed pharmacy benefit program allows for member payment of the difference between the generic and the branded product should either the physician or the member request this option. Anything short of this will unnecessarily cost the plan money.

AWP Discounts

The AWP of a medication implies that it is the purchase price of the medication or ingredient from a drug wholesaler. Fews things are more confusing or more difficult to determine than the purchase price of a medication. Hence the claims processor or the third party payer utilizes an independent source, or pricing vendor, to determine the AWP of the medication. This AWP reference has become the standard of payment for the ingredient, and this reference source is usually part of the pharmacy contract.

To complicate the issue further, there are usually discrepancies between the actual purchase price of the ingredient by the pharmacy and the designated AWP per the pricing source. Like sticker prices on automobiles, the reference source purchase price and the actual purchase price are typically different. Hence a negotiated discount off the referenced AWP is a standard part of the pharmacy contract. This discount is often more important to the pharmacist than the dispensing fee because the AWP of the ingredient will continue to inflate over time, whereas the dispensing fee is generally the same over time. The current marketplace allows the AWP discount for branded products to be in the 10 percent to 18 percent range. The differential factor is the competition within the marketplace. The AWP discount for generic drugs is significantly higher (estimated to be in the 40 percent to 60 percent range). Managers should not concentrate on AWP discounts for generics but rather should utilize a MAC rate.

Drug Formularies

The decision to require a drug formulary in a managed care environment is one that mandates careful planning. More and more MCOs are realizing the value of the drug formulary in managing costs and are moving toward aggressive formulary management. Most MCOs are using formularies (96 percent), and almost 50 percent of plans have closed formularies.[6]

A drug formulary is best defined as a dynamic, comprehensive list of drugs designed to direct physicians to prescribe the most cost-effective medications. The list is organized by therapeutic class; the selection criteria for the drugs on the formulary are primarily patient care (therapeutics) and secondarily cost.

A drug formulary must meet three criteria to be successful:

1. It must reflect the practice of medicine in the community. Attempting to restrict physicians from using medications that have become a standard of practice in the

community will be a difficult endeavor indeed.

2. It must be responsive to the therapeutic needs of the physicians. If physicians are not able to find medications that are necessary to treat patients and are continually requesting exceptions to the formulary, the effort to enforce a formulary will serve neither the physicians nor the patients. In other words, it must be therapeutically appropriate.

3. It must be representative of cost-effective therapy. This is where most formularies that are nothing more than drug lists fall short. All drug formularies provide community standards and therapeutic necessities. The true differentiating criterion among formularies, however, is the ability to ensure community standards in a cost-effective manner.

When a drug formulary is used in an appropriate manner, quality of care is improved. Furthermore, by moving toward a closed or mandatory status and maximizing volume purchase contracts, a drug formulary can save upward of 10 percent or more on the pharmaceutical benefit cost.

The formulary development process is extremely important to the success of a formulary system. Educating physicians that the drug formulary is coming ensures implementation without undue delay. A simple statement in the physician newsletter that the MCO has decided, via its medical staff advisory committee, to implement the drug formulary is useful.

A formulary committee or pharmacy and therapeutics committee comprising physicians, clinical pharmacists, and sometimes representatives from the administrative offices of the health plan is necessary to give adequate documentation to the drug formulary process. Certain physician specialties are a must for this committee, including family practice, internal medicine, pediatrics, and gynecology. These physicians prescribe the majority of the medications for the members of health plans and thus deserve the largest representation on the committee. Often, for various reasons, other specialty areas are represented (e.g., psychiatry, dermatology, and surgery). Usually the internal medicine representatives on the committee have subspecialty areas for which input can be provided. In situations where there is no expertise on the committee (e.g., infectious disease, rheumatology, cardiology, and so forth), those specialists can be asked to attend on an ad hoc basis. Maximum success can be ensured if the formulary is developed at the local level, but with oversight, coordination, and some direction from the central office. A written protocol addressing the process to be used for additions to the drug formulary is beneficial.

After the formulary document has been approved, it is ready to be sent to the providers and promoted as the cost-effective, quality document that it is intended to be. Directions explaining how to use the document need to be included. The document should be formatted to be as simple and easy to follow as possible. There needs to be an index to which providers can turn to find immediate formulary information and a therapeutic categorization that facilitates identification of drugs available for certain disease entities. There is some work being done currently with electronic formularies on the physician's personal computer.

The promotion of the formulary also needs to include information about what happens if providers do not follow the formulary. This can be part of the endorsement on the front end, simply stating that there will be a monitoring process in place that will identify physicians who are continually not complying with the drug formulary, that these physicians will be contacted if they do not follow the formulary, and that consistent outliers (without justification) will be dealt with.

Drug formularies in the staff model MCOs are generally followed without question. In the IPA model MCO, however, providers are typically private practice physicians and pharmacists who see the formulary as a hindrance to or constraint on their ability to practice their profession. Furthermore, the providers may participate with multiple plans, each with a slightly different formulary. Therefore, the plan should expect provider pharmacies to call physicians about nonformulary medications, and the physicians should follow the advice of the pharmacist when they are called in terms of changing to a formulary drug.

Last comes the question of assessing the success of the formulary. This is easier if you determine the percentage of prescriptions that are written in compliance with the formulary than if you apply financials to that formulary in a retrospective process. If cost-effective guidelines were followed in developing the drug formulary, however, then the logical assumption is that the higher the formulary compliance, the more cost effective the drug formulary.

With respect to compliance in those environments where there is a voluntary formulary, a compliance rate of greater than 95 percent should be expected. In an open formulary environment, however, a high compliance rate does not necessarily mean cost effectiveness. Obviously, the easiest way to obtain 100 percent compliance is to put all medications on the formulary. A mandatory closed formulary with high compliance will achieve the greatest savings.

The institution of a drug formulary system also requires notification of the members of the plan that their medications will now be required to be prescribed per a drug formulary. Often, if this is a new policy, a period of grandparenting can be put in place so that individuals who are stabilized on a particular medication that will no longer be a part of the drug formulary can continue to use that medication. It is important to understand that the intent of the drug formulary is not to restrict medications from individuals who need them but rather to change physician prescribing behavior to the most cost-effective therapeutics.

Volume Purchasing and Rebates

The fourth mechanism in managing ingredient cost is volume purchase contracting, com-

monly called rebates. This is the mechanism by which the pharmaceutical manufacturer agrees to a volume-driven discount contract in exchange for formulary considerations. Most pharmaceutical companies have formed a managed care department to understand and interface with MCOs. Most companies have contractual relations with MCOs already and share utilization of their products. Although a couple of the manufacturers have fought the MCOs' attempts to manage cost, the gamble that their freedom of product choice philosophy will outlast cost containment has almost disappeared. The necessity for MCOs and the pharmaceutical industry to work as allies is becoming more obvious. Both industries have the pharmaceutical product as their focal point, and both have much to gain by cooperative efforts in proving the value of their product.

Why should pharmaceutical companies agree to contract with MCOs? Why should they discount their products? There are a number of important reasons:

- It often is the only way the MCO will accept the company's product on the drug formulary. Most medications newly marketed today are therapeutically equivalent to a product currently in existence and probably already on the formulary.

- The plan in essence becomes an extension of the industry sales force. Because the product has been given formulary status, it serves as an endorsement for the product.

- Once an established relationship exists, the plan preferentially reviews newly marketed products in a way that ensures the partner company the greatest opportunity for inclusion on the formulary.

- Most closed panel plans will cooperate with the partner company to facilitate local representatives' accessibility to providers, at least for those products that are already on the formulary. The ability to see physicians and pharmacists is essential for pharmaceutical sales representatives.

- Formulary decisions provide a spillover effect; that is, physicians will tend to prescribe formulary products for all their patients, not just those belonging to the MCO.

Quantitative Drug Utilization Review

An integral part of managing pharmaceutical costs is the development of drug utilization review (DUR) programs. DUR and drug utilization evaluation programs offer the prospect of saving money both by restraining the use of unnecessary or inappropriate drugs and by preventing the adverse effects of misused medications.[7] DUR programs assess the appropriateness, safety, and efficacy of drug use. Under the heading of utilization review, we have tended to blend together cost and quality considerations in managing pharmacy benefits. Realistically, the emphasis has been on the cost side; there are various reasons for this, including convenient access to cost data and the completeness of those data. Because plans are effectively managing the cost aspects of cost utilization, the demand for proof that the therapeutics/quality of care considerations are not being affected by these cost considerations continues to arise. Hence it is best to separate the DUR process into quantitative and qualitative elements. Quality is discussed later in this chapter. Realistically, quantitative DUR answers the questions "How costly? How often? For whom? By whom?" The properties of quantitative DUR are as follows:

- It describes patterns of drug utilization and cost.
- It quantitates drug utilization and cost.
- It identifies areas and categories to be used for qualitative DUR.
- It identifies areas for education.
- It is not based on any predetermined criteria for standards.
- It can be used to describe the quality of drug use.

In essence, quantitative DUR selects the therapies to be reviewed. Data are collected, and those data are analyzed and reported. Based on findings, certain management and educational applications are then put into effect. To determine the significance of the quantitative information, we can use a comparative analysis when looking at results. In other words, for each of the therapeutic categories indicated, we compare our data with national or national utilization data in that therapeutic category to determine whether we are significant outliers.

Success with any program of DUR demands a management information system capable of providing information. The ability to tie in all components of the information, not just pharmacy, to analyze the entire picture will ensure therapeutically cost-beneficial decisions. Differences in therapeutic utilization are driven by various factors, and it should not be inferred that inappropriate utilization is always the cause. Both local and national dynamics as well as patient demographics need to be considered before assumptions and action plans are made.

Audits

Often receiving less attention within the managed care pharmacy benefit than other more common cost management applications, the auditing process is extremely important. The auditing function is performed essentially for fraud and abuse detection. Fraud can be perpetrated by the member as well as by the provider. Reports focusing on the following should ensure that reasonable attempts to identify fraud are in place:

- generic utilization by pharmacy
- number of prescriptions dispensed costing more than $100 per prescription
- number of prescriptions dispensed indicating dispense as written

Although abuse generally is unintentional, sometimes it is not. From a quality of care standpoint, and certainly from a cost management perspective, providers and members abusing the system need to be identified and dealt with. Thanks to today's on-line electronic claims processing systems, abuse is becoming increasingly difficult to commit. The requirement on the part of most MCOs for pharmacies to have the on-line capability of checking for duplicate prescriptions, prescriptions filled too soon, and multiple providers is becoming the norm.

An additional audit process that needs to be implemented is one to ensure the integrity of the volume purchase or rebate contracting program. The pharmaceutical industry is aware of the possibility of fraud on the part of the provider and the potential for paying rebates for medications that are not dispensed. The successful total audit program that the plan must have in place should include determination of fraud or abuse by providers and members and protection when pharmaceutical industry rebate contracts exist.

MANAGEMENT OF QUALITY

Quantitative DUR deals with generics, formularies, dispensing fees, and other efforts to ensure cost-effective prescription drug benefits. One necessity is the ability to reduce pharmacy costs without compromising quality. Accomplishing this requires an efficient and reliable data system, quality assurance and utilization review processes, and assessment according to criteria standards.

Defining quality has always been difficult. Most often it is a subjective rather than objective measure. The necessity to ensure the provision of safe and effective drug therapy to health plan members is a focal point of managed care. A structured program with continuous collection and analysis of information, in conjunction with authority to compare this information against a previously established standard, ensures the quality of the pharmaceutical benefit program. With the majority of the emphasis today seemingly being on cost, those MCOs that are successfully managing cost do so by a process focusing on the quality of care rather than solely on cost management.

Therapeutics

Drug Formulary

A well-managed drug formulary process can ensure the quality of the drug formulary document and is a critical component of the overall quality process. Over and above any cost considerations in the drug formulary decision is the comparable therapeutic advantage of one product over another. This review process includes the following:

- *Product therapeutic review*—The comparative review of the therapeutic advantages of one product over another (i.e., the indications, the uniqueness, and the value of this product compared with the therapeutic alternatives available to physicians). Those drugs offering little or no therapeutic advantage may be rejected unless there is a significant cost advantage.

- *Pharmaceutics*—The characteristics of the drug in terms of its absorption and metabolism. The therapeutic advantage of a long-acting drug preparation compared with a short-acting drug needs to be determined. Once-a-day therapy, which is typically more expensive compared with multiple daily dosing, is a part of the therapeutic evaluation. If dosing several times throughout the day in fact will not affect the quality of the care, this determination can then be part of the cost containment strategy.

- *Side effects/adverse effects*—Determining a product's profile in comparison with another with regard to the likelihood of adverse effects. Patient tolerance or intolerance to the medication means that compliance will be questionable. The drug formulary should assure the prescriber that the adverse effect profile of this medication has been considered and that a determination of appropriateness for drug formulary status has been attained. These types of formulary assessments are relatively easy to make, and the literature comparing products is readily available.

- *Effectiveness*—For some products in new therapeutic categories, there are serious concerns about overall effectiveness. Typically, these are biotechnology products or those for previously untreatable conditions. Many of these are released with poor or limited documentation of efficacy (and sometimes safety) because of public pressure to make available something that "might help." Formulary committees have significant challenges in dealing with these products. They need to balance patient and provider demand with the very real possibility that for some patients these drugs may do more harm than good.

Step Therapy

A mechanism that is often employed with success within staff model MCOs but is more difficult to institute in IPA models is step therapy. Step therapy refers to the steps that a physician is encouraged to follow when prescribing medications to treat a specific illness. Step therapy for any disease for which step criteria have been initiated implies that, unless the treatment modality is part of step 1, it should not be instituted without justification. As an example, step 1 for hypertension could be salt restriction, weight reduction, and exercise. If this fails to lower blood pressure, step 2 could be choosing any medication within the therapeutic categories of thiazide diuretics or ß blockers. Step 3 might include angiotensin-converting enzyme inhibitors or calcium channel blockers. If these fail, step 4 would be the addition of another drug from the step 2 category, and step 5 could be the introduction of medication choices from other therapeutic categories.

Step therapy typically is designed according to nationally or community accepted criteria, often developed by the National Standards Committee on Therapeutic Modalities. These step therapies can also be adapted institutionally and often become a standard of practice for the community. The difficult political aspect of step therapies is that physicians often interpret them as dictatorial in terms of their freedom to practice medicine. Claiming that individualization of patient care often runs counter to step therapy, some physicians will refuse to follow or even acknowledge step therapy but rather will insist on practicing medicine according to the standards and guidelines with which they are more familiar. Step therapy is being incorporated into prescribing according to outcome criteria.

The concept of disease management is related to step therapy in that experts determine the best approach to a disease, outlining successive strategies that can be used to control increasingly resistant candidates. There is intense interest by the pharmaceutical industry in disease management. Industry executives hope that this can be an entry for them into more sophisticated relationships with managed care systems. There will probably be some short-term gains, but managed care plans at the leading edge are moving beyond disease management to care management, which incorporates the total patient. This topic is discussed in further detail in Chapter 20.

Community Standards

Like step therapies, community standards imply an identifiable standard by which prescribers are to prescribe. Unlike step therapy, however, community standards are often more subjective than objective. It is difficult to determine how one establishes community standards. They may well be determined according to accumulated data, which essentially means that community standards are similar to the community norm, or they could be determined by a representative group of specialists in a particular area who blatantly state that treating a medical problem in a manner different from their recommended way does not meet an acceptable standard of care.

Ensuring the quality of a managed pharmacy benefit program requires attention to community standards. Possibly more from a feasibility and dependability perspective, utilizing expertise in the community to determine standards allows the MCO to defend its decisions. Many physicians and attorneys discourage the use of prescribing according to community standards. They point out the lack of organization in determining these standards and the potential inappropriateness of this method. Nonetheless, the practice of medicine according to community standards utilizes patterns within the community that are known to be credible.

Outcomes Management

According to Paul Ellwood, founder of the Excelsior, Minnesota–based managed care research firm InterStudy, outcomes management is defined as "a tool to use in the everyday management of MCOs. It would measure and compare the impact of ordinary medical care on the patient's quality of life."[8(p.3)] Undoubtedly, outcome information will be part of both cost management and quality of care programs within the MCO. Decisions will be easier and much more defensible and will have with enhanced credibility if they are based on outcomes. The public will be better assured that the quality of the pharmacy benefit not only is safe and effective but will result in a more positive outcome. To date, little is still known about how expenditures for pharmaceutical therapeutic agents can positively affect health care outcomes compared with other treatments. As we accumulate the necessary information, the data are analyzed and the results disseminated, but progress has been disappointing.

We can anticipate that the results will show the pharmaceutical logic of interventions that improve both cost and the outcomes of health care. As new medications emerge, the value of the outcome will be weighed against the cost of the therapy. Reimbursement for new and expensive agents may be denied unless the quality of therapeutics based on outcome has been demonstrated. Justification for coverage of high-cost drugs will be an increasingly difficult and data-intensive task but will ensure quality of care. Integration of database should simplify the task so that MCOs can readily determine the benefits of one drug versus another.

Patient/Member Expectations of the Pharmacy Provider

The primary expectation of the members of the MCO is that, when they present a prescription to the pharmacist, the prescription will be filled accurately and will be indicated as a treatment modality for the problem with which they presented to their physician. Although they are not directly involved with the quality assurance associated with ensuring that expectations are met, they believe that there is a process in place by which the quality of that service is protected. Unlike the situation with physicians, however, where credentialing is a standard dictating whether one is an eligible participant in the health plan (see Chapter 8), the pharmacies rather than the pharmacists are credentialed. The credentialing of the pharmacist is left to the regulatory agencies appointed by the state to ensure the competency of the practitioner pharmacist.

Along those same lines, the assurance of the quality of the pharmacy is also often overseen by a state regulatory agency. Within the pharmacy practice acts of each state, specific qualifications are described for a pharmacy to meet the licensing requirements. Some plans have elected to go beyond this, requiring certain quality of care enhancements such as 24-hour service and on-line utilization review programs. Each of these enhancements forces the plan to walk a tighter line between deeply discounting a pharmacy network and increasing the services required by the pharmacist and at the pharmacy. The best indicators of lack of quality in pharmacy services are obtained by audits, as addressed earlier in this chapter, and by encouraging member feedback concerning service at the participating pharmacy.

HMO Expectations of the Pharmacy Provider

Like the member, the plan expects the pharmacist to dispense the prescription accurately and in a cost-effective manner. Additionally, the plan requires the pharmacist to follow all aspects of the contract between the plan and the pharmacy. In other words, all policies and procedures addressed in the pharmacy contract must be adhered to.

The plan also often expects the pharmacy to participate in a utilization review program, audit processes, and other services of value to the plan. If this is the case, the plan will have expectations of the pharmacy beyond the normal dispensing of prescriptions in a quality manner in exchange for an agreed-upon reimbursement rate.

Point-of-Service Review

The universally increasing popularity of point-of-service claims adjudication has facilitated the likelihood of on-line utilization review. One does not have to think too far down the line to imagine a situation where a prescription will be entered into an on-line claims adjudication system, the reason for the medical intervention will be checked via compatible information systems, and the appropriateness of the medication prescribed for that medical intervention will be analyzed. Currently, on-line point-of-service systems at the least ensure checking for drug interactions; checking for age, sex, and pregnancy interactions; checking for therapeutic duplication; and checking for allergies.

QUALITATIVE DUR

Earlier in this chapter we addressed the quantitative aspects of DUR. This is the aspect of utilization review associated with cost containment. The other aspect is qualitative DUR. The properties of qualitative DUR are the following:

- criteria-based or standard-based processing
- determination of the appropriateness of drug therapy prescribing and dispensing
- direct relationship of information generated to the quality of patient care

In starting the process of qualitative DUR, objectives need to be identified and stated. Criteria for drug use need to be created that define quality and standards for measurement. Data are then collected and analyzed. When there is failure to meet criteria, causes are identified. Subsequently an intervention takes place, and there should be a reassessment of the results of that intervention. If necessary, the original objectives are modified. There is then documentation and dissemination of the DUR process and results.

As an example, consider a drug interaction. The objective is to perform concurrent DUR of a drug interaction and to inform pharmacies and prescribers of the presence of such an interaction. By using criteria defining quality standards, one collects the information to identify patients who are receiving the drugs in combination and then notifies physicians who have prescribed this drug, informing them of the problem. Last, one monitors the results and then documents and disseminates this information.

Qualitative utilization review can be directed at the member, physician, or pharmacy. Each can be performed prospectively, concurrently, or retrospectively. Today, the approach usually is essentially retrospective, primarily because of the lack of sophistication of on-line electronic point-of-service systems in providing the necessary information to do concurrent utilization and because the majority of the data currently are in a retrospective format. The exception would be for drug interactions, allergies, and duplicate therapy.

The following are the elements necessary to provide a qualitative DUR program:

- electronic point-of-sale review of drug therapy to alert the dispensing pharmacists of a potential problem
- retrospective data analysis (patient, prescriber, or pharmacy specific) to identify and evaluate concerns
- clinically based screening criteria that use decision tree analysis

- evaluation of drug therapy for specific targeted populations
- definition of mechanisms for intervention and follow-up to identify problems
- definition of mechanisms to assess the impact of intervention
- integration of DUR with other databases providing medical diagnosis and financial cost

There are definitely some challenges to a quality-driven DUR program. If we are going to utilize successfully the combination of quantitative and qualitative review to provide a safe and cost-effective pharmacy benefit program to members, the following must be addressed:

- Technology needs to be available for plan-performed qualitative DUR, both concurrently and prospectively.

- We need to move from case review analysis to drug therapy process intervention.

- We spend too much time analyzing cases; our movement to an action plan is often too slow.

- Currently the patient and pharmacist are at the center of concurrent DUR intervention and managed care environments. The prescriber must be brought into the loop.

- We need to develop patient outcome–driven DURs. Outcome is the next logical step from quality assurance. Realistically, it is difficult to make cost-effective determinations without knowing outcomes.

MEASUREMENT OF SUCCESS

The successful management of a pharmacy benefit program can be determined from two aspects: the overall ability to manage the cost of that program, and the dependability of the quality.

First, with regard to cost management, as a manager of a pharmacy benefit program your re-

quirements to manage costs are based on your ability to maintain pharmaceutical expenditures within a predetermined budget. Without any doubt, the emphasis is not only on managing costs but on reducing costs. Cost containment programs drive the budget each year. A portion of the pharmaceutical expenditure, the manufacturer's cost, is becoming more predictable. The utilization factor, that is, the shifting in utilization trends from less expensive to more expensive therapeutics to treat the same illnesses, is becoming more difficult to predict and typically has a bigger impact. You can consider that you are practicing successful cost management, or cost containment, if in fact you continue under budget in a pharmacy benefit as well as maintain pharmaceutical indicator costs (PMPM, ingredient costs, and prescription costs) at or under the national average for an MCO similar to yours. Anything less than this should be considered an inability to manage appropriately and should give the plan manager an incentive to find management support for the pharmacy benefit program.

Some leading edge plans now look at pharmacy expenses in light of total health care expenses. The emphasis is not on reducing each line-item cost (e.g., drugs, laboratory, radiology, emergency visits, etc.) but on the bottom line. These plans have recognized that the goal should be to maximize the return on investment made in each cost center. As such, drug costs may go up, but if managed appropriately total costs will go down because effective drug use will decrease hospital stays, emergency visits, and so forth.

Quality is a much more difficult parameter by which to measure success. Certainly, the DUR programs addressed earlier in this chapter will help and, if followed, will provide the documentation for any internal or external agency requiring it. Because quality is often such a subjective entity, however, the development of subjective criteria to determine quality is helpful. A successful quality-run program can be based on the results of these subjective criteria. Again, utilizing the averages or norms found in similar plans for member utilization beyond the cost of the service will help ensure and document a successful quality of care–driven pharmacy benefit program. Simply taking the information available via a retrospective information system, applying this information against comparable information, and then documenting action taken to investigate, and change if necessary, inappropriateness in the pharmacy benefit will ensure quality.

PHARMACY BENEFIT MANAGEMENT: THE NEXT PHASE

This chapter has attempted to point out the future of pharmacy benefit programs. Essentially, pharmacy programs can be divided into three specific areas, each of which is going to have significant application to success and even to the continuance of coverage of prescription drugs in the future.

We Will Be Paying More Attention to Truly Managing Costs, Not Cost Shifting

In the past few years, we have made many successful applications to managing the pharmacy benefit cost profile. We have moved to an on-line claims and adjudication system, we have increased significantly the utilization of generics, we pay pharmacists according to a MAC schedule for generic medication, we have instituted drug formularies, we have successfully negotiated discounts from the pharmaceutical manufacturers, and we have discounted our pharmacy networks. Even so, drug costs continue to increase at percentages that are considered inappropriate. The reason is, quite simply, cost shifting. As an example, the increase in the therapeutic categories in the number of drugs within a category is staggering. One only needs to look at the angiotensin-converting enzyme inhibitor category, the calcium channel blocker drugs, or the cephalosporin category to realize that the number of medications available to treat the same medical problems reads like a menu in a restaurant.

Statistics indicate that, with each new therapeutic entity within the category, the utilization does not just divide among the group but actually increases. In other words, with each new drug that is marketed within the therapeutic category, utilization of medications within that therapeutic category increases manyfold. We can no longer continue to add therapeutic entities of all kinds to our drug formularies. Medications that offer no therapeutic benefit will not be allowed formulary status, and as the utilization creep begins to emerge criteria will be developed by which the offending medication will be eliminated.

Prior Authorization Will Increase; Usual and Customary Prescribing Will Become a Thing of the Past

As medication types, medication capabilities, and medication expenses all increase, the only response to managing the utilization of the most expensive medications is by the prior authorization process. Many drugs today, all of which are presumably better than previously available medications to treat similar medical problems, do not need the formulary or nonformulary status. In other words, many of these drugs now fit into a "formulary-if" category. Too many medications are valuable for a certain population, and our current system of a product being either covered or not covered no longer applies. Hence there is a need for a prior authorization process for many of these medications.

To make the prior authorization process feasible from both an administrative and a compliance standpoint, we must be able to develop an acceptable and easy system. On a local level, this means accessibility to MCO case managers to ensure the appropriate application of the prior authorization process. On a national scope, this means telephone access by toll-free numbers to centrally located case managers. In both cases, the cooperation of the provider, including the pharmacist and physician, is a must. We will not be able to continue the same "covered, yes–covered, no" approach that we currently have.

Outcomes Information Will Be Used To Make Decisions

Adequate resources will be available to develop sound outcome methodologies. Large-scale measurement of health outcomes, with feedback to all decision makers, will help ensure that quality is maintained and costs are managed. Drug costs are increasing at a faster rate than other health care costs, and these inflationary trends are not compatible with the continuance of coverage for a pharmacy benefit service. Therapeutic decisions in our managed care environment will be based on results as identified in outcomes.

CONCLUSION

The purchasers of the managed care benefit seek both quality and price. Expectations run high, and pressure is tremendous to keep costs at a minimum while meeting these high expectations. Reimbursement for services continues to be a focal point of disagreement between the MCO and the provider. The pharmaceutical industry has recently experienced for the first time hands-on intervention by the federal government into its pricing policies. Past years have noted significant efforts to manage the costs of the pharmacy benefit. DUR, subsequent outcome results, action plans, and implementation of these action plans will dictate the future.

REFERENCES AND NOTES

1. P.R. Vagelos, Are Prescription Drug Prices High?, *Science* (1991).
2. Part 1: The New Claims Systems, *Drug Topics* (February 1988).
3. Marion Merrell Dow, *Managed Care Digest, MCO Edition* (Marion Merrell Dow, 1991).
4. Ciba-Geneva, *Pharmacy Benefit Report, 1995, Facts and Figures* (Geneva, Switzerland: Ciba-Geneva, 1995).
5. Ciba-Geneva, *Pharmacy Benefit Report*.
6. Ciba-Geneva, *Pharmacy Benefit Report*.
7. R. Atlas, Editorial, *Drug Benefit Trends* 4 (1992): 3.
8. T. Marcinko, Outcomes Management: Medicine under the Microscope, *Managed Care Insights* (1990): 3.

SUGGESTED READING

Barnett, A.A. (ed.). 1995. *1995 Drug Outcomes Sourcebook.* New York, N.Y.: Faulkner & Gray.

Navarro, R.P. 1994. Capitation for Pharmacy Services. *Medical Interface* 7(7): 88–90.

Navarro, R.P. 1994. The Evolving Pharmacy Benefit Market. *Medical Interface* 7(5): 65–67, 70.

Navarro, R.P. 1994. The Future of Managed Care Drug Formularies. *Medical Interface* 7(4): 62–64.

Chapter 24

Subacute Care and Managed Care

Kathleen M. Griffin

Subacute care has emerged in response to pressures from third party payers to provide a less costly alternative treatment setting to acute hospital care. Subacute care is provided both in specialty hospitals and in subacute skilled nursing facilities and units. It has been estimated that as of 1995 there were approximately 720 subacute providers with 27,050 beds. In 1994, these providers reportedly admitted 270,000 patients, accounting for 8.1 million patient days and $3.4 billion in revenues. Approximately 73 percent of admissions were Medicare beneficiaries. Most of the remainder were covered by managed care plans.[1]

SUBACUTE CARE DEFINED

Definitions of subacute care have been prepared by a number of organizations. The definitions developed by two organizations, the National Subacute Care Association (NSCA) and the Joint Commission on Accreditation of Healthcare Organizations, appear to contain the key components reflected in most other definitions (see Appendix 24–A).

SUBACUTE CARE CATEGORIES

In spite of the promulgation of definitions of subacute care by the NSCA and the Joint Com-

mission, there remains a great deal of confusion about exactly what subacute care is. This confusion is due, in part, to the lack of a federal definition of subacute care and, in part, to the fact that subacute care is commonly provided in three different settings: specialty hospitals, hospital-based skilled nursing facilities, and freestanding skilled nursing facilities. Each setting tends to focus on one or two of the following four categories of subacute care:

1. transitional subacute care
2. general subacute care
3. chronic subacute care
4. long-term transitional subacute care

Hospital-based subacute skilled nursing units typically focus on the first category, transitional subacute care. Subacute nursing facilities usually can be classified as general subacute or chronic subacute care units. Specialty hospitals (most often long-term care; prospective payment–exempt hospitals) focus on long-term transitional subacute care. Appendix 24–B depicts the categories of subacute care, reflecting the key differences in service intensity and length of stay parameters.

SUBACUTE PATIENTS

Subacute patients vary in acuity levels and exhibit a variety of problems. Subacute patients generally include the following:

Kathleen M. Griffin, Ph.D., is President and Chief Executive Officer of Griffin Management, Inc., in Scottsdale, Arizona.

- medically complex patients who are chronically ill or have multiple medical problems or disorders; these patients need medical monitoring and specialized care but can be managed in a subacute setting

- respiratory care patients who require ventilator weaning or ventilator care programs as a result of a respiratory disease, injury, or impairment or who require medical and nursing care as well as therapies to recover from an acute respiratory episode

- recuperating surgery patients who need rehabilitative therapy but no longer need intensive care services

- patients who require rehabilitation for a variety of reasons, most frequently after orthopedic surgery or a stroke

- patients with brain injuries as a result of ischemic or hemorrhagic stroke, blunt trauma, or penetrating trauma

- cardiovascular patients who require a cardiac recovery or rehabilitation program, often related to congestive heart failure or cardiovascular surgery

- patients with such medical conditions as septicemia or osteomyelitis who require short-term intravenous therapy

- oncology patients who require radiation oncology services, chemotherapy, pain management, and rehabilitation

- wound management patients with chronic wounds (e.g., pressure ulcers, necrotic wounds, or peripheral vascular disease ulcerations) related to diseases that need management before the wounds will heal

Although patients of all ages may suffer one or more of these disorders, the vast majority of subacute patients are geriatric patients.

SUBACUTE PROVIDERS

Although managed care organizations are increasingly becoming payers for subacute care, especially with the growth of Medicare risk health maintenance organizations as discussed in Chapters 46 and 47, Medicare continues to be the major payer for subacute services. As a result, provider settings for subacute care, to a great extent, reflect the idiosyncrasies of the health care reimbursement system.[2] The three most common types of settings for subacute care are hospital-based subacute skilled nursing facility units, subacute units in freestanding skilled nursing facilities, and long-term care hospitals.

Hospital-Based Subacute Skilled Nursing Facility Units

Hospital-based subacute skilled nursing facility units allow the hospital to create a continuum of care. Patients who no longer require the intensity of services typically found on the medical–surgical floor of an acute care hospital can be transferred to a subacute unit, where the sophisticated diagnostic, monitoring, and emergency response capabilities are available but the intensity of services is less. Moreover, the programs in the subacute unit are oriented toward a patient's optimal functional independence at the time of discharge.

To be eligible for favorable reimbursement by Medicare, the hospital-based subacute unit must be licensed as a skilled nursing facility unit. The result is that the hospital's performance under the Medicare prospective payment system (PPS) is improved. Hospitals reduce their inpatient lengths of stay for Medicare patients by utilizing the subacute skilled nursing facility unit as a stepdown or transitional facility.

In addition to reduced hospital stays for Medicare patients and the concomitantly improved margins on such patients, the hospital is able to reallocate certain Medicare expenses from the hospital to the subacute skilled nursing facility unit as a new cost center. As a result, a portion of Medicare costs previously allocated to an inpatient area subject to Medicare's PPS can be distributed to a cost-based, extended care reimbursement area.

For managed care organizations, hospital-based subacute units provide a low-cost alternative setting for patients who are not medically stable enough to be transferred to a subacute unit in a freestanding nursing facility or for patients who simply require a few additional days of inpatient care before being discharged home. The location of the subacute unit in the hospital facilitates patient–physician interaction and enhances the integration of services between the subacute unit and the hospital. For example, although the subacute unit's nursing staff usually will be different from the nurses who cared for the patient on the medical–surgical floor, rehabilitation and respiratory staff members who provided services to the patient while he or she was in a hospital bed may continue to provide services to the same patient in the hospital-based subacute unit. The subacute unit also can benefit from the hospital's quality improvement programs, infection control procedures, and management information system.

Although it is clear that there are many system and patient management benefits to hospital-based subacute units, the costs of patient care in these units typically are greater than the costs for care in subacute units in freestanding nursing facilities. In 1994, the average cost per day for Medicare patients in hospital-based skilled nursing facilities was $435; for Medicare patients in freestanding nursing facilities the cost was $275.[3]

Subacute Units in Freestanding Skilled Nursing Facilities

The creation of a subacute unit in a freestanding skilled nursing facility usually involves the establishment of a distinct area within the facility that is separated from the areas of the building dedicated to long-term care services. Subacute units in freestanding skilled nursing facilities have separate nursing stations, patient rooms, and common areas, so that subacute patients and long-term care residents and their families do not mix.

Subacute units in freestanding nursing facilities typically are positioned as a low-cost alternative to the hospital setting. Average managed care reimbursement as of 1994 for patients in subacute units in freestanding skilled nursing facilities ranged from $250 and $550 per day.[4]

From the provider's perspective, the greatest challenge to the freestanding skilled nursing facility that has created a subacute unit is to ensure that there is a cultural paradigm shift from a long-term care, custodial focus to a short-term recovery and rehabilitation focus, wherein the patient will be discharged home or to a less costly level of care in 2 to 4 weeks. To achieve this conceptual shift, the most successful subacute units in freestanding skilled nursing facilities have staff who are dedicated to the subacute unit and are separate from the nursing, rehabilitative, and social services staff for the long-term care residents. In addition, the successful subacute unit employs a medical director who is different from the administrative medical director for the long-term care facility. Other components of successful subacute units are specific programs of care, outcome measures, subacute unit–specific admission and discharge criteria, and care protocols that help ensure that patients in the subacute unit receive the services they need in a cost-effective manner.

Long-Term Care Hospitals

Long-term care hospitals are one of five types of hospitals that may be excluded from Medicare PPS reimbursement. Instead of being paid prospectively on the basis of diagnosis-related groups (DRGs), the PPS-exempt long-term care hospitals are paid a specific amount per Medicare discharge. The amount is established based on the individual hospital's costs during its initial year of PPS-exempt operations.

Long-term care hospitals provide services to patients who continue to require intensive or other acute inpatient care. The patients in long-term care hospitals usually have complex medical conditions and multisystem failures that require more intensive care, monitoring, and emergency back-up resources than are available in freestanding subacute nursing facility units. Patients may be admitted to long-term care hospitals directly from the intensive care unit of an acute care general hospital.

Subacute programs in long-term care hospitals provide more hours of nursing care per patient day (6.5 to 9.0 hours) than are typically provided in subacute programs in hospital-based or freestanding skilled nursing facilities. Also, average lengths of stay are longer than in skilled nursing facility subacute care units. Patients in subacute programs in long-term care hospitals have an average length of stay of 40 to 80 days.

Although the costs of care in subacute and long-term care hospitals usually are higher than the costs of subacute care in skilled nursing facility subacute units, the costs in long-term care hospitals can be considerably less than the costs in an intensive care unit in an acute care general hospital.

Specialty Hospital–Based Subacute Skilled Nursing Facility Units

Both long-term care hospitals and PPS-exempt rehabilitation hospitals may create subacute skilled nursing facility units within the hospital. The subacute unit within a long-term care hospital would focus on medically complex patients who have met certain goals in the long-term care hospital and who no longer need the same intensity of services. Such patients would require continued inpatient care for their medical conditions, however, to be discharged home or to a long-term care facility.

Freestanding acute rehabilitation hospitals may create subacute skilled nursing facility units for patients who either are not medically stable enough to benefit from an intensive acute physical rehabilitation program or are unable to tolerate an intensive rehabilitation program (e.g., 3 hours or more of rehabilitation daily) but can benefit from a less rigorous program (e.g., 1 to 2 hours daily). Although the average length of stay for patients in the acute rehabilitation hospital may be 18 to 20 days, the average length of

stay for patients in the slower paced, less intensive rehabilitation program in the subacute skilled nursing facility unit in the rehabilitation hospital may be 20 to 30 days. Typically, the costs of care in the subacute skilled nursing facility unit of the specialty hospital would be less than the costs for acute care in the specialty hospital.

SUBACUTE CARE WITHIN A CONTINUUM OF CARE

Subacute care cannot be viewed as independent from other levels of care within the care continuum. Appropriate utilization of subacute care requires an effective case management system that ensures that the patient receives the right care, at the right time, in the right setting, and for the right cost. The case management system must focus on the patient's condition and medical needs, level of family and/or other social support systems available, the services that are available within the continuum, the location of those services, and the health benefits available to the patient. Table 24–1 shows how transitional subacute care and general subacute care fit into a care continuum, and contrasts the subacute care levels with other components of the care continuum, such as intermediate/custodial care, skilled nursing care, acute rehabilitation, and acute care.

As health care providers in the United States convert from nonaffiliated, independent provider entities into integrated delivery systems (see Chapters 4 and 5), the four categories of subacute care are expected to be components of every system. During the current transition period from multiple independent providers to integrated provider networks, however, utilization of subacute care, as with other postacute health care levels, has tended to be stratified and fragmented. The regulatory requirements for subacute providers within skilled nursing facilities, whether hospital based or freestanding, have served as barriers to easy transition of patients between the acute and subacute settings. For example, to transfer a patient from an acute hospi-

Table 24–1 Subacute Care within the Care Continuum

| Characteristics | Acute Rehabilitation (from Lowest Acuity to Highest Acuity) | | | | | |
| | Nursing Facilities | | | Hospital | | |
	Intermediate	Skilled	General Subacute	Acute Rehabilitation	Transitional Subacute	Acute
Patients (residents)	Restorative care	Medically stable/ rehabili-tation	Medically stable/ rehabilita-tion	Medically stable, need acute rehabilitation	Medically sick/highly complex care	Medically unstable, invasive proce-dures, most complex care
Physician visits	Monthly	Monthly	Weekly to biweekly	Daily	3 to 7 times/ week	Daily
Nursing hours	< 2.5, LPN/ CNA	2.5 to 3.5, 1 RN, LPN/ CNA	4.0 to 4.5, 1 RN, LPN/ CNA	5.5 to 7, RNs and assistants	5.5 to 6.5, RNs and CNAs	6.5 to 9, RNs
Respiratory therapy	No	Rarely/as needed (if any)	Rarely/as needed (if any)	5 to 7 times/ week, 3 hours/day	24 hours on site	24 hours on site
Rehabilitation	Rare	3 to 5 times/ week	5 times/ week	5 to 7 times/ week, 3 hours/day	Daily therapy	Daily therapy
Pharmacy, laboratory	Contract	Contract	Contract	Pharmacy: on site 24 hours Laboratory: may be contracted	24 hours on site	24 hours on site
Average length of stay	2 years or longer	30 to 60 days	10 to 40 days	15 to 25 days	5 to 30 days	4 to 8 days
Discharge	Death	Long-term care or home	Long-term care, home, or acute rehabilita-tion	Home or general subacute care	Home (long-term care rare)	Home or skilled nursing facility

Abbreviations: RN, registered nurse; LPN, licensed practical nurse; CNA, certified nurse aide.

tal bed to a subacute skilled nursing facility bed in an adjacent unit within the hospital, the patient must be formally discharged from the hospital and formally admitted to the subacute care unit. The admission procedures to the subacute care unit must comply with federal and state nursing facility regulations. Compliance with these regulations often means the completion of a substantial amount of paperwork related to the admission process.

Nevertheless, active case management within an integrated delivery system, wherein an individual patient's care is managed by the same case manager throughout the continuum, can help ensure that the transfer of a patient to the most appropriate level of care within the continuum occurs as seamlessly as possible. The reader is also referred to Chapters 17 through 20 for additional discussion of utilization management and the continuum of care.

PAYMENT FOR SUBACUTE CARE

Although the majority of subacute patients have Medicare as a primary payer, increasingly managed care organizations are including subacute care in their hospital or health care system agreements. Managed care organizations and subacute providers negotiate payment under a variety of arrangements:

- *Discounted fee for service:* The provider typically agrees to furnish subacute care services at a discount from its standard charges. The discount may be a percentage of the standard charge for all services or may be specific to the service or category of service.

- *Per diem:* The managed care organization pays the provider a fixed rate for each day that an enrollee is treated within the provider's subacute care facility or unit. The per diem rate may be specified in a contractual arrangement or may be negotiated for each patient admission.

- *Per case:* The managed care organization pays the provider a fixed rate for each case of inpatient treatment. The rate will vary depending on service category or patient category. This payment methodology is similar to the hospital DRG payment under Medicare.

- *Capitation:* In this arrangement, the provider receives from the managed care organization a fixed payment per enrollee per month. For that monthly fee, the provider agrees to furnish specified subacute care to the payer's enrollees. The number of enrollees, as opposed to the utilization of services, controls the providers' revenues.

Today, the most common payment arrangement between managed care organizations and subacute providers is the per diem payment. In the contract between the subacute provider and the managed care organization, certain items and services typically will be included in the per diem rate, and items or services over which the provider has less control often will be excluded. Table 24–2 lists usual inclusions and exclusions from a per diem rate negotiated between the managed care organization and the subacute care provider. Per diem rates also may vary based on patient acuity as well as resources required by the patient. Often, subacute care providers utilize a patient acuity measurement system to define subacute care levels, and each level has a different per diem payment amount. An example of subacute care per diem payment levels is shown in Table 24–3.

Subacute care providers may include a stop-loss provision for patients whose acuity levels increase significantly during their inpatient stay in the subacute care unit or facility. Conversely, the managed care organization may include stipulations in the agreement that the patient will be reviewed weekly to determine whether a less expensive level of subacute care or discharge home or to a long-term care facility is appropriate for the patient.

Table 24–2 Items and Services Typically Included or Excluded in a per Diem Rate for Subacute Care

Inclusions	Exclusions
Room and board (semiprivate)	Special beds
Nursing and personal care	Ventilators
	Respiratory therapy
	Intravenous antibiotics
Medical social services	Third-generation pharmaceuticals
Recreation/activities program	Traction equipment
House toiletries	Prosthetic devices
Patient/family education	Laboratory tests
Surgical dressings	Radiology services
Dietary consultation	Parenteral formulas, supplies, equipment
Case management	

SELECTING A QUALITY SUBACUTE PROVIDER

In most areas of the United States, managed care organizations have an array of subacute providers from which to select. Certain indicators of quality may be used as benchmarks in the selection process.

Accreditation

The size of the subacute provider marketplace and the number of alternative settings for managed care organizations have spurred the need for an agreed-upon set of national standards against which to judge performance, monitor service delivery, and determine the outcomes of care. Although some states are exploring or have special licensing categories for subacute care, Medicare does not differentiate subacute care from the skilled nursing benefit for Medicare beneficiaries. During the past several years, however, two accrediting organizations have created standards for subacute providers: the Joint Commission and the Commission on Accreditation of Rehabilitation Facilities (CARF).

The Joint Commission has created a protocol for accrediting subacute programs.[5] The foundation for the subacute protocol is the existing standards for long-term care, with the intent of those standards being tailored to the needs of subacute patients, particularly in areas related to time frames, staff qualifications, organizational structure, leadership, and safety and equipment management. In addition, standards for comprehensive rehabilitation, medical credentialing and privileging, and respiratory care have been added to form the Joint Commission's subacute accreditation protocol. The subacute protocol incorporates the following major sections:

- patient rights and responsibilities
- admission
- patient assessment and evaluation
- patient care
- continuity of care
- leadership
- human resources management
- information management
- quality assessment and improvement
- plant, technology, and safety management
- infection control

CARF is the national accrediting agency that establishes standards for organizations serving persons with disabilities. Subacute providers may be accredited if they demonstrate compliance with the standards for one of the categories of comprehensive inpatient medical rehabilitation.[6] Comprehensive inpatient medical rehabilitation programs may seek accreditation in one or more of the three existing categories depending on the licenses they hold. Category 1 is reserved for acute rehabilitation programs within facilities licensed as hospitals. Categories 2 and 3 are reserved for subacute rehabilitation.

In selecting subacute providers, managed care organizations may wish to ascertain whether the provider is accredited according to the Joint Commission subacute protocol. If the subacute unit includes a rehabilitation program, it would be desirable to determine whether the unit has obtained CARF accreditation as a medical rehabilitation program.

Table 24–3 Subacute Care/per Diem Payment Levels

Level of Care	Level of Payment
Subacute care: special	Special arrangements Patients with specialized care needs 6.0+ nursing hours per patient day 0.0 to 2.0+ hours of therapies per patient day
Subacute care tier III	Patients requiring intense medical, nursing, and/or rehabilitative interventions/ procedures *Definition of intense:* 4.5 to 6.0 nursing hours per patient day (with up to 50% professional nursing time) and 0.0 to 2.0 hours of rehabilitation therapies per patient day
Subacute care tier II	Patients requiring moderate to minimal medical and nursing procedures and moderate rehabilitative interventions *Definition of moderate:* 4.0 to 4.5 nursing hours per patient day (with up to 45% professional nursing time) and 0.0 to 1.5 hours of rehabilitation therapies per patient day
Subacute care tier I	Patients requiring minimal medical, nursing, and/or rehabilitative interventions *Definition of minimal:* 3.5 to 4.0 nursing hours per patient day and up to 1.0 hour of rehabilitation therapies per patient day
Skilled nursing care	Patients requiring skilled care with minimal medical and rehabilitation intervention 2.5 to 3.5 nursing hours per patient day (with less than 30% professional nursing time) 0.0 to 2.0+ hours of rehabilitation therapies per patient day

Programs of Care

The subacute provider should have clearly defined protocols, care paths, or programs for the key categories of patients whom they serve. Admission criteria, continuing stay criteria, and discharge criteria should be clearly delineated for each program. Programs may include one or more of the following:

- *Medically complex/postsurgical:* Patients in this program may require the following types of care:

    1. Active treatment of disease under the direction of a physician (e.g., administering intravenous medications, epidural medications, agents by continuous infusion pump, hypodermatoclysis monitoring/evaluating signs and symptoms of condition change; teaching care to the patient and/or significant others; providing respiratory therapy and care; performing hemodialysis and peritoneal dialysis; evaluating effective intervention through laboratory values, signs, and symptoms)

    2. Postsurgical care (managing and evaluating drains and tubes, performing complex dressing changes, evaluating and assessing changes in wounds)

    3. Pulmonary care (managing tracheotomized patients)

    4. Nutrition management (enteral and parenteral feedings; monitoring the effect

of intervention and therapeutic diets through weight, tissue turgor, wound healing, and laboratory values)

- *Wound management:* Patients in this program may need complex treatment and dressing procedures, whirlpool treatment and debridement, electrical stimulation, specialty beds and pressure-reducing devices, frequent laboratory evaluation, teaching, and ongoing assessment of the effectiveness of treatment by changes in wound status.
- *Rehabilitation:* These patients typically have medical complications or frailties that preclude their ability to tolerate or benefit from acute rehabilitation services. Patients with orthopedic conditions, strokes, degenerative neurological disorders, and other medical complexities may require the combination of intensive nursing care and a low-intensity rehabilitation program.
- *Cardiopulmonary recovery/rehabilitation:* Patients in this program may have been hospitalized because of congestive heart failure or suspected myocardial infarction or for cardiovascular surgical procedures. These patients typically are deconditioned as both a cause and an effect of acute treatment, possibly exacerbated by their stay in the intensive care unit or by their course of treatment, resulting in malnourishment, weakness, frailty, and poor physical stamina. Patients also may have complicating comorbidities that require that the subacute services be provided in an environment that allows immediate access to the high-technology equipment and services of the acute hospital.
- *Respiratory:* Patients for subacute care typically have respiratory infections, pneumonias, or chronic obstructive pulmonary disease with medical complications. Many of the respiratory patients will be on ventilators and are admitted to the subacute unit for ventilator weaning, intensive care, and intravenous infusions with antibiotics.

Clinical Staff

Clinical direction of a subacute program should be provided by a physician who is qualified by virtue of training and experience in the area(s) related to the program being offered. In addition to the medical program director, a medical staff of credentialed and privileged physicians should be created so that physicians can serve as either attending or consulting staff in the subacute unit or facility. A dedicated clinical staff for the subacute care unit or facility should report to a program director, who is responsible for the overall management of the subacute program. An interdisciplinary clinical team should include nursing and medical staff, social services staff, rehabilitation therapists, respiratory therapists, dietitians, pharmacists, and, as appropriate, psychologists and pastoral counselors.

Case Management

A case management system should involve appropriate coordination of care, allocation of resources, and an effective communication system with payers, families, physicians, and referral sources. The case management function usually is provided by a registered nurse. The goal of case management is to help the patient attain appropriate goals by the most cost-effective means. Case management is discussed further in Chapter 18.

Outcome Measurement System

An outcome measurement system should include an ongoing, organized, systematic method of evaluating the results of interventions and services relative to patient and family goals and expectations. The outcomes to be achieved in a subacute program include the resolution of medical problems and functional improvement. A key outcome for subacute care includes a reduction of rehospitalizations as well as a reduced risk of utilization of health care services after discharge from subacute care. The reader is referred to Chapter 25 for further discussion of outcomes measurement.

Cost-Effective, Quality Care

The subacute program should incorporate admissions procedures that are as simplified as possible, given the need to comply with regulatory requirements. Throughout the subacute care program, the focus should be achieving optimal results in a reasonable time period so that the patient can be discharged home or to a less costly level of care. Operations should support patient and family dignity, realistic goal setting, and early preparation and planning for discharge.

CONCLUSION

The subacute care industry has rapidly evolved into a recognized niche within health care. Its continued growth will be dependent on a clear demonstration of the cost-saving potential of moving patients out of high-cost acute care hospitals and into low-cost subacute care units and facilities and on patient outcomes that demonstrate that subacute program treatment interventions have positive long-term effects. With the growth of managed care, cost-effective, quality subacute levels of care will continue to be important components of the continuum of health care.

REFERENCES AND NOTES

1. H.M. Ting, *Subacute Care: Analysis of the Market Opportunities and Competition* (Newport Beach, Calif.: Center for Consumer Health Care Information, 1995).

2. T.N. McDowell, Jr., "An Overview of Provider Reimbursement: Medicare, Medicaid, and Managed Care," in *Handbook of Subacute Health Care*, edited by K.M. Griffin (Gaithersburg, Md.: Aspen, 1995), 39–58.

3. B. Vladeck, Testimony before the House Ways and Means Subcommittee on Health, July 1995.

4. McDowell, "An Overview of Provider Reimbursement."

5. Joint Commission on Accreditation of Healthcare Organizations, *Subacute Care Protocol* (Oakbrook Terrace, Ill.: Joint Commission, 1994).

6. Commission on Accreditation of Rehabilitation Facilities (CARF), "Standards for Comprehensive Inpatient Rehabilitation Programs," in *1995 Standards Manual and Interpretive Guidelines for Medical Rehabilitation* (Tucson, Ariz.: CARF, 1995).

SUGGESTED READING

Fisher, C. 1995 (July). Facilities, Hospitals, Working Together. *Provider,* 43–45.

Fogel, L.A. and Grossman-Klim, K. 1995 (October). Getting Started with Subacute Care. *Healthcare Financial Management,* 64–65, 68, 70 ff.

Griffin, K.M., ed. 1995. *Handbook of Subacute Health Care.* Gaithersburg, Md.: Aspen Publishers, Inc.

Griffin, K.M. 1995. A New Option for Postoperative Patients: Hospital-Based Subacute Care. *Surgical Services Management* 1, no. 3, 37–40.

Kothmann, W.L. 1995 (October). Is Subacute Care Feasible? *Healthcare Financial Management,* 60–63.

Maher, L.A. 1995 (July). Is Subacute Care Worth Your Money? *Business and Health,* 18–24.

Market Focus: Subacute Care. 1995. *BNA's Managed Care Reporter* 1, no. 10, 228–230.

Shriver, K. 1995 (January 22). What's New is Subacute Care. *Modern Healthcare,* 34–37.

NSCA and Joint Commission Definitions of Subacute Care

The NSCA defines subacute care as follows[1]: Subacute care is a comprehensive and cost-effective inpatient program for patients who have had an acute event as a result of an illness, injury, or exacerbation of a disease process; have a determined course of treatment; and do not require intensive diagnostic and/or invasive procedures. The severity of the patient's condition requires physician direction, intensive nursing care and significant utilization of ancillaries, and an outcomes-focused interdisciplinary approach utilizing a professional team to deliver complex clinical interventions (medical and/or rehabilitation). Typically short term, the subacute level of care is utilized as an inpatient alternative to an acute care hospital admission or as an alternative to continued hospitalization.

- *Comprehensive:* Subacute care programs are designed to provide the full range of medical, rehabilitation, and professional services required to provide efficient and effective care for the specific medical conditions treated within a program.
- *Cost effective:* Subacute programs are designed to maximize value to patients and payer sources through the delivery of necessary, appropriate care with optimal outcomes in the lowest-cost setting.
- *Outcome orientation:* Subacute programs are designed to achieve quantifiable, measurable outcomes, such as (but not necessarily limited to) functional restoration, clinical stabilization, avoidance of medical complications or exacerbation of a disease process, and discharge to the patient's least restrictive living environment.
- *Professional staffing:* Subacute interventions, because of their duration, complexity, and intensity, are provided under the direction of a physician. An interdisciplinary team provides a coordinated program of care. The team may include a physician, nurses, therapists, social workers, psychologists, pharmacists, dietitians, case managers, discharge planners, and other professionals.
- *Program description:* Programs are organized around patient populations with related treatment or service needs that result in common goals, measures of outcomes, treatment plans, and resources delivered at similar levels of intensity. Subacute programs may include medical rehabilitation and respiratory, nutritional, cardiac, oncologic, and wound care programs. Levels of intensity for specific disciplines will vary from program to program but will generally range from 3.5 to 8.0 nursing hours per patient day with up to 5 hours per patient day for therapy as well as appropriate use of nutrition, laboratory, pharmacy, radiology, and other ancillary services.
- *Site of care:* The site of care is not a distinguishing characteristic of subacute care. Subacute programs can be delivered in a variety of settings, including acute hospitals, specialty hospitals, freestanding skilled nursing facilities, hospital-based skilled nursing units, outpatient ambulatory centers, residential living facilities, and home health settings. Most existing subacute programs are inpatient programs serving as an alternative to prolonged acute hospitalization. Given the existence of a broad range of treatment and cost alternatives to acute hospitalization, however, the site of care should not be a limiting factor

in the delivery of subacute services. Distinctions among subacute services should be focused on program differences, not settings.

- *Continuum of care:* Subacute care is essential to the development of a complete continuum of care. Subacute programs are necessary components of vertically integrated health care systems.

The definition developed by the Joint Commission is as follows[2]: Subacute care is comprehensive inpatient care designed for someone who has an acute illness, injury, or exacerbation of a disease process. It is goal-oriented treatment rendered immediately after, or instead of, acute hospitalization to treat one or more specific active complex medical conditions or to administer one or more technically complex treatments in the context of a person's underlying long-term conditions and overall situation. Generally, the individual's condition is such that the care does not depend heavily on high-technology monitoring or complex diagnostic procedures. Subacute care requires the coordinated services of an interdisciplinary team including physicians, nurses, and members of other relevant professional disciplines who are trained and knowledgeable in assessing and managing these specific conditions and in performing the necessary procedures. Subacute care is given as part of a specifically defined program, regardless of the site. Subacute care is generally more intensive than traditional nursing facility care and less intensive than acute care. It requires frequent (daily to weekly), recurrent patient assessment and review of the clinical course and treatment plan for a limited (several days to several months) time period, until the condition is stabilized or a predetermined treatment course is completed.

REFERENCES AND NOTES

1. National Subacute Care Association, *Definition of Subacute Care* (Bethesda, Md.: National Subacute Care Association, 1995).
2. Joint Commission on Accreditation of Healthcare Organizations, *1995 Survey Protocol for Subacute Programs* (Oakbrook Terrace, Ill.: Joint Commission, 1995).

Categories of Subacute Care

TRANSITIONAL SUBACUTE CARE

Transitional subacute care can be described as short-stay (5 to 30 days) hospital stepdown care. Nursing care averages 5.5 to 6.5 hours of direct care per patient day. Fifty percent to seventy percent of the direct nursing care is provided by licensed nurses. Transitional subacute units are utilized for patients who require daily medical care and monitoring; highly skilled and intensive nursing care; an integrated program of therapies, both rehabilitative and respiratory; and heavy utilization of pharmaceutical and laboratory services. Days in this type of subacute care unit serve as replacement hospital days to effect a significant reduction in acute hospital days. In other words, a transitional subacute unit actually serves as a substitute for continued hospital stays, not as an alternative hospital discharge placement. For example, stroke patients may be transferred to a transitional subacute unit on day 4 or 5 of hospitalization in the acute hospital, and coronary bypass patients who are not off the ventilator within 4 or 5 days may be transferred for a weaning program. Transitional subacute units will have a variety of physician program directors or consultants, a dedicated staff of acute or critical care nurses, 24-hour respiratory therapy, and 7-day-per-week rehabilitation therapies.

GENERAL SUBACUTE CARE

General subacute units are most often utilized for patients who require medical care and monitoring at least weekly, short-term nursing care at a level of approximately 3.5 to 5.0 hours per patient day, and rehabilitative therapies that may extend from 1 to 3 hours per patient day. Short stay in nature (10 to 40 days), general subacute care units focus on patients who require rehabilitation, wound care, or intravenous therapies with few other significant medical complications. Although there is some overlap in the clinical programs between transitional subacute units and general subacute care facilities, the key difference is the acuity level of the patients. A sizable number of patients in the general subacute units are geriatric because younger patients at these acuity levels tend to be cared for by home health services.

The goal of both transitional subacute units and general subacute units is to manage the patient's recovery or rehabilitation in a cost-effective manner and to discharge the patient home or, in some cases, to a less expensive level of care, such as long-term care or an assisted living facility.

CHRONIC SUBACUTE CARE

Chronic subacute units manage patients with little hope of ultimate recovery and functional independence, such as ventilator-dependent patients, long-term comatose patients, and patients with progressive neurological disease. Typically, these patients require nursing care at the level of the general subacute unit (3 to 5 hours per patient day), medical monitoring biweekly to monthly, and restorative therapies, usually provided by nursing staff with guidance from rehabilitation therapists. These patients either will eventually be stabilized so that they can be discharged home or to a long-term care facility or will expire. Their average length of stay is 60 to 90 days.

LONG-TERM TRANSITIONAL SUBACUTE CARE

Long-term transitional subacute facilities most often are licensed as hospitals rather than as nursing facilities. They usually are reimbursed through the Medicare PPS as long-term care hospitals and have average lengths of stay of at least 25 days. The overall average length of stay for long-term transitional subacute care is 40 to 80 days. Typically, these facilities provide care for acute ventilator-dependent or medically complex patients. Because they are hospitals, attending physicians visit the patients daily. Nursing staff tend to be primarily registered nurses, and nursing hours per patient day may range between 6.5 and 9.0 depending on the types and acuity levels of the patients.

Chapter 25

Quality Management in Managed Care

Pamela B. Siren and Glenn L. Laffel

There are a variety of approaches to quality management in the managed care setting. These approaches are complementary and employ the principles of measurement, customer focus, and statistically based decision making. This chapter provides an overview of quality management in managed care, from traditional quality assurance to modern performance assessment and continuous improvement. It is hoped that readers will be able to utilize both methods once they have completed this chapter.

TRADITIONAL QUALITY ASSURANCE

Advocacy for performance assessment in health care can be traced to E.A. Codman, a surgeon who practiced at Massachusetts General Hospital in the early 1900s. He was among the first advocates of systematic performance assessment in health care. His efforts included evaluation of the care provided to his own patients.

Pamela B. Siren, R.N., is the Director of Clinical Development with Lazo, Gertman & Associates in Waltham, Massachusetts. Her area of expertise is quality management in health care. She has designed strategies to identify and address opportunities for improvement in clinical performance in a variety of health care settings. She is the former Director of Clinical Improvement of Blue Cross and Blue Shield of Massachusetts.

Glenn L. Laffel, M.D., Ph.D., is the Senior Vice President for Medical Affairs at Preferred Health Systems. He is recognized internationally for his work on the health care application of total quality management and is the founding editor of *Quality Management in Health Care*.

In the 1960s and 1970s, the introduction of computers and large administrative datasets (used initially to support Medicare claims processing) permitted investigators to use powerful epidemiological methods in their analyses of practice variations and related phenomena. In this period, Avedias Donabedian developed three criteria for the assessment of quality that are still used today: structure, process, and outcome.[1] His approach to quality assessment of care has stood the test of time and remains useful in managed care settings.

Structure Criteria

Structural measures of health care performance focus on the context in which care and services are provided. These measures provide inferences about the managed care organization's (MCO's) capability to provide the services it proposes to offer. Structural measures include board certification of physicians, licensure of facilities, compliance with safety codes, recordkeeping, and physician network appointments. Many such requirements are delineated in federal, state, and local regulations that govern licensing or accreditation and mandate periodic review and reporting mechanisms.

Accreditation and regulatory bodies have traditionally emphasized structural criteria because of their ease of documentation. Purchasers support this tradition by requesting such information in their contract negotiations with MCOs. The role of the MCO's leadership in improving performance is increasing and is evaluated by accrediting agencies through assessment of committee function. The MCO needs a complete understanding of its leadership's role in performance improvement.

As MCOs form into integrated delivery systems, the structural criterion of performance assessment becomes more complex. The regulations and standards that may govern MCOs, such as those of the National Committee for Quality Assurance (NCQA; see Chapter 37), may be different from the standards to which member hospitals are held accountable, such as those of the Joint Commission on Accreditation of Healthcare Organizations. Reconciliation of at least the minimal and widely accepted standards within the MCO and across an integrated delivery system is the first step to developing structural measures and evaluating structural performance and its impact on the quality and cost of health care delivery.

Structural measures generally do not offer adequate specificity to differentiate the capabilities of providers or organizations beyond meeting minimum standards. In addition, the relationship between structure and other measures of performance, such as outcomes, must be clarified to ensure that enforcing structural standards leads to better results.[2]

Process Criteria

The second traditional criterion for health care quality assessment is process. Process of care measures evaluate the way in which care is provided. Examples of care process measures for MCOs include the number of referrals made out of network, health screening rates (e.g., cholesterol), follow-up rates for abnormal diagnostic results, and clinical algorithms for different conditions. Such measures are frequently evaluated against national criteria or benchmarks. Process of service measures are also frequently used. These include appointment waiting times and membership application processing times.

As with structural measures, it is important to link process measures to outcomes. Although the field of outcomes research is growing, the link between many health care processes and key outcomes has not always been clearly defined.

Outcome Criteria

The third traditional category of quality assessment is the outcome of care or service. Traditional outcomes measurements include infection rates, morbidity, and mortality. Relatively poor outcomes performance generally mandates careful review. Exhibits 25–1 and 25–2 illustrate common outcome criteria used to assess quality of inpatient and outpatient care. Unfortunately, although outcomes measures are purported to reflect the performance of the entire system of care and service processes, they often offer little insight into the causes of poor performance.

Despite the limitations of current outcomes assessment, most MCOs have systems in place to assess for adverse events. These screening criteria are often evaluated during the utilization review process to detect sentinel events. Some of these same measures are being applied to the peer review process within the MCO.

Peer Review and Appropriateness Evaluation

In addition to Donabedian's three quality criteria, peer review and appropriateness review have been key components of the traditional quality assurance model. Because of their applicability to managed care, they are discussed here.

Peer Review

Peer review involves a comparison of an individual provider's practice either by the provider's peers or against an acceptable standard of care. These standards may be developed within the MCO (e.g., practice guidelines), be described by national professional associations, or be required by a regulatory or legislative agency. Cases for peer review are identified either as outliers to specific indicators or through audits of medical records. Peer review has tradi-

Exhibit 25–1 Examples of Events among Hospitalized Patients That May Indicate Inadequate Quality of Care

Adequacy of discharge planning
- No documented plan for appropriate follow-up care or discharge planning as necessary, with consideration of physical, emotional, and mental status/needs at the time of discharge

Medical stability of the patient at discharge
- Blood pressure on day before or day of discharge: systolic, < 85 mm Hg or > 180 mm Hg; diastolic, < 50 mm Hg or > 110 mm Hg
- Oral temperature on day before or day of discharge > 101°F (rectal, > 102°F)
- Pulse < 50 beat/min (or < 45 beat/min if patient is on a ß blocker) or > 120 beat/min within 24 hours of discharge
- Abnormal results of diagnostic services not addressed or explained in the medical record
- Intravenous fluids or drugs on the day of discharge (excludes the ones that keep veins open, antibiotics, chemotherapy, or total parenteral nutrition)
- Purulent or bloody drainage of postoperative wound within 24 hours before discharge

Deaths
- During or after elective surgery
- After return to intensive care unit, coronary care, or special care unit within 24 hours of being transferred out
- Other unexpected death

Nosocomial infections
- Temperature increase of more than 2°F more than 72 hours from admission
- Indication of infection after an invasive procedure (e.g., suctioning, catheter insertion, tube feedings, surgery)

Unscheduled return to surgery within same admission for same condition as previous surgery or to correct operative problem (excludes staged procedures)

Trauma suffered in the hospital
- Unplanned removal or repair of a normal organ (i.e., removal or repair not addressed in operative consent)
- Fall with injury or untoward effect (including but not limited to fracture, dislocation, concussion, laceration)
- Life-threatening complications of anesthesia
- Life-threatening transfusion error or reaction
- Hospital-acquired decubitus ulcer
- Care resulting in serious or life-threatening complications not related to admitting signs and symptoms, including but not limited to neurological, endocrine, cardiovascular, renal, or respiratory body systems (e.g., resulting in dialysis, unplanned transfer to special care unit, lengthened hospital stay)
- Major adverse drug reaction or medication error with serious potential for harm or resulting in special measures to correct (e.g., intubation, cardiopulmonary resuscitation, gastric lavage), including but not limited to the following:
  1. Incorrect antibiotic ordered by physician (e.g., inconsistent with diagnostic studies or patient's history of drug allergy)
  2. No diagnostic study to confirm which drug is correct to administer (e.g., culture and sensitivity)
  3. Serum drug levels not measured as needed
  4. Diagnostic studies or other measures for side effects not performed as needed (e.g., blood urea nitrogen, creatinine, intake and output)

Source: Health Care Financing Administration, 1986.

Exhibit 25–2 Examples of Inpatient Diagnoses That May Indicate Inadequate or Improper Outpatient Care

- Cellulitis (extremities)
- Dehydration of child with severe diarrhea (younger than 2 years)
- Diabetic coma–ketoacidosis
- Essential hypertension
- Gangrene (angiosclerotic, extremities)
- Hemorrhage secondary to anticoagulant therapy
- Hypokalemia secondary to potassium-depleting diuretic
- Low-birthweight infant (premature, < 2,500 g)

- Malunion or nonunion of fracture (extremities)
- Perforated or hemorrhaging ulcer (duodenal, gastric)
- Pregnancy-induced hypertension (preeclampsia, eclampsia, toxemia)
- Pulmonary embolism (admitting diagnosis)
- Readmission of same condition within 14 days
- Ruptured appendix
- Septicemia (admitting diagnosis)
- Status asthmaticus
- Urinary tract infection (bacturia, pyuria)

Courtesy of Blue Cross and Blue Shield Association, Chicago, Illinois.

tionally been used as an informal educational tool. It is typified by morbidity and mortality conferences currently in existence.

Peer review has its limitations. First, opportunities for improvement may be missed by a paradigm that rests on conformance with standards. Deming emphasized that meeting specifications does not result in constant improvement but rather ensures the status quo.[3] Second, studies have shown that there is poor interreviewer reliability among panels of physician reviewers and that the level of physician agreement regarding the quality of care is only slightly higher than the level expected by chance alone.[4] Third, peer review is limited by the scope of the indicators or processes under review. Despite these limitations, peer review continues to serve an important role in MCOs' quality management programs.

Appropriateness Evaluation

Appropriateness evaluation reviews the extent to which the MCO provides necessary care and does not provide unnecessary care. Appropriateness review frequently occurs before an elective clinical event (admission or procedure). Procedures or admissions most frequently selected for appropriateness review include those for which there is a wide variation of opinion as to their usefulness or effectiveness and those that have been notably expensive. Examples of procedures frequently selected for appropriateness review include hysterectomy, coronary artery bypass surgery, and laminectomy. The proposed indication for the event is compared with a list of approved indications obtained from a professional society or a specialty vendor or designed by the MCO itself. Appropriateness review is intended to identify and minimize areas of overutilization.

Appropriateness review provides a snapshot of a care decision and does not lend itself to an understanding of the events that may have preceded the admission or procedure in question. In addition, this review does not evaluate the effectiveness of the procedure once it has been authorized.

COMPONENTS OF A QUALITY MANAGEMENT PROGRAM: BUILDING ON TRADITION

The traditional quality assurance model provides a sound foundation for a modern quality management program. The quality assurance model can be improved, however, with an infusion of systems thinking, customer focus, and knowledge for improvement.

First, systems thinking offers a method for assessment and management of performance with a clear aim or purpose. The traditional quality assurance model does not incorporate this important concept. Lacking a shared aim, payers and providers risk forming a disconnected, inefficient network. This disconnected network will eventually engage in contradictory and inefficient behaviors. Organizational goals can be achieved first by identifying customer needs of an organization, unifying the purpose within the organization, and expanding the shared purpose across the integrated delivery system. For further information about systems thinking and organizational goal setting, the reader is referred to the work of Peter Senge.

Second, the cornerstone of a modern quality management program is customer focus. The traditional quality assurance model was driven, in part, by regulations and accreditors without explicit knowledge of what the customer (member, purchaser, provider) needed. The modern quality management program identifies key customers, measures customer needs, and improves processes to meet those needs.

Finally, an enhancement of the traditional quality assurance model is knowledge for improvement. According to Moen and Nolan, three fundamental questions can be used as guides for improvement efforts[5]:

1. What are you trying to accomplish? Information gained from understanding customer needs, the current process and outcome performance, and expected performance will assist the MCO in answering this question.

2. How will you know that a change is an improvement? Establishing performance expectations before implementing an improvement activity assists the MCO in understanding whether a change is an improvement and minimizes any potential confusion between measures of utilization and indicators of quality.

3. What changes can be made that will result in an improvement?

To develop tests and implement changes, the plan-do-study-act cycle is used as a framework for an efficient trial and learning model. The term *study* is used in the third cycle to emphasize this phase's primary purpose: to gain knowledge. Increased knowledge leads to a better prediction of whether a change in a current process will result in an improvement.[6]

A PROCESS MODEL FOR A MODERN QUALITY MANAGEMENT PROGRAM

Figure 25–1 depicts a model for a modern quality management program that enhances the traditional quality assurance model such that it includes the above dimensions. The remainder of this chapter discusses the eight key steps in developing a modern quality management program.

Understand Customer Need

Understanding customer need (Figure 25–2) is the basis of all quality management programs. Juran and Gyrna described a customer as anyone who is affected by a product or process.[7] Three categories of customers are external customers, internal customers, and suppliers. External customers of an MCO include members or benefactors and purchasers. Internal customers include the departments and services within the MCO, such as claims processing and member education, as well as the health care professionals themselves. Customer needs may be clear or dis-

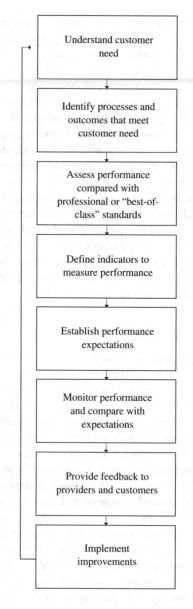

Figure 25–1 Continuous improvement process.

guised, rational or less than rational. These needs must be discovered and served.[8] Negotiating and balancing the needs of these diverse and sometimes conflicting customer groups represent a challenge for MCOs, as they do for any organization.

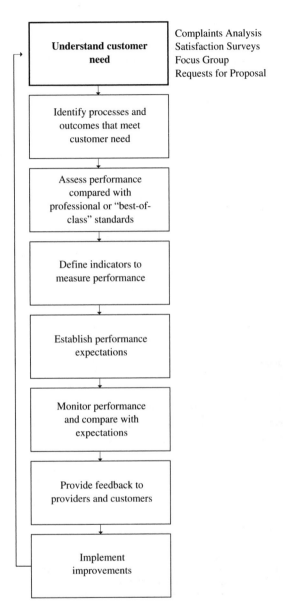

Complaints Analysis
Satisfaction Surveys
Focus Group
Requests for Proposal

Figure 25–2 Continuous improvement process—understand customer need.

Methods to understand customer need are as diverse as the customer groups. Customer complaints are a usual signal of a quality problem. Low levels of complaints, however, do not necessarily mean high satisfaction. Frequently, dissatisfied customers will purchase services elsewhere without ever registering a complaint. Most MCOs have a formal process to survey their membership for satisfaction with care or services (Exhibit 25–3). Yet despite the burgeoning number of satisfaction surveys, a study has shown that only two of ten health care organizations conducting patient satisfaction surveys were using them as a regular feedback device to administrative and clinical departments.[9] Through marketing initiatives, MCOs are proactively determining customer needs through focus groups and interviews. These processes are designed to identify customer expectations and real (versus stated) need. The Hospital Corporation of America (now Columbia/HCA) finds it useful to identify several levels of customer expectation. At level I, a customer assumes that a basic need will be met; at level II, the customer will be satisfied; at level III, the customer will be delighted.[10] Results from member satisfaction surveys and market analyses are an integral part of strategic quality planning.

A fundamental principle of quality improvement theory is the necessity for economically meaningful partnerships between purchasers and suppliers. Purchasers, MCOs, and hospitals are negotiating contracts based on performance measurement. To illustrate this concept, US Quality Algorithms, Inc., a subsidiary of US Healthcare, has implemented the CapTainer[SM] compensation system, which combines base payments with an annual performance-based distribution. The CapTainer[SM] system is based on a contracting process that includes the setting of performance targets, the development of a schedule for progress toward them, and the construction of a purchase/compensation schedule that translates improvement into a performance-based distribution.[11] The size of the performance-based distribution is related to progress toward goals and to the financial implications of changes in hospital or MCO operating procedures. Partnerships between MCOs and hospitals, and the positive economic relationships they imply, are only realistic and possible if the

Exhibit 25–3 Examples of Satisfaction Surveys*

How would you rate:	Excellent	Very Good	Good	Fair	Poor
The thoroughness and technical skills of the:					
Attending doctor					
Nursing staff					
Consulting doctors					
Other personnel (lab, x-ray, etc.)					
The friendliness and compassion of the:					
Attending doctor					
Nursing staff					
Consulting doctors					
Other personnel (lab, x-ray, etc.)					
The explanations, instructions, and responses to questions by the:					
Attending doctor					
Nursing staff					
Consulting doctors					
Other personnel (lab, x-ray, etc.)					
Admission process (timeliness, friendliness, convenience)					
Explanation of your rights as a patient					
Discharge instructions and arrangements					
Food quality and service					
Appearance and cleanliness of the hospital					
Overall quality of care provided by the attending doctor					
Overall rating of this hospital					
Satisfaction with the outcome of your procedure (if applicable)					

Would you recommend this hospital to a friend or loved one?   ❏ Yes   ❏ No

Would you recommend your attending doctor to a friend or loved one?

© U.S. Quality Algorithms (USQA), 1991

How would you rate each of the following:	Excellent ◄——————► Poor 10 9 8 7 6 5 4 3 2 1	No Opinion 0
Nursing Care		
Emergency Room Services		
Laboratory Department		
Quality Assurance/Improvement Program		
Utilization Review Department		
Social Services/Discharge Planning		
Medical Records		
Bed availibility		
Patient satisfaction with the hospital		

Please rate the following clinical departments:	Excellent ◄——————► Poor 10 9 8 7 6 5 4 3 2 1	No Opinion 0
OB/GYN		
General Surgery		
Orthopedics		
Urology		
Cardiology		
ENT		
Other _____		
Other _____		

Would you refer a family member to this hospital? ❏ Yes ❏ No   © U.S. Quality Algorithms (USDA), 1991

* This example includes selected questions from USQA's survey of members and USQA's survey of physicians.

Source: © *Journal on Quality Improvement.* Oakbrook Terrace, IL: Joint Commission on Accreditation of Healthcare Organizations, 1993, p. 377. Reprinted with permission.

values of delivering care in a managed environment are shared.[12]

Negotiating and balancing the diverse groups of customer needs represent a challenge. Juran and Gyrna stated that it is important to recognize that some customers are more important than others. It is typical that 80 percent of the total sales volume comes from about 20 percent of the customers; these are the "vital few" customers who command priority.[13] Within these key customer groups, there is a distribution of individual customers that also may have a hierarchy of importance, such as a government agency, a gold card purchaser account, or an academic teaching center. Explicit understanding of the needs of all the MCO customer groups will minimize situations in which one customer's needs are met to the exclusion of another's.

Identify Processes and Outcomes That Meet Customer Need

Identification of processes and outcomes that meet customer need is the next step of the continuous improvement process model (Figure 25–3). How do customers view the MCO's quality? To begin with, they want to know whether the MCO meets their expectations. MCOs are expected to treat members who are ill and to maintain the health and functional capabilities of those who are not. To treat sick patients, MCOs first have to make it easy for them to access services and second must provide them with appropriate care. Purchasers and members value access and appropriateness.[14] Purchasers also value assessments of disease screening activities, service quality, and encounter outcomes to the extent that they support or embellish information about access and appropriateness.[15] Similarly, purchasers know that to maintain health and functional capacity, MCOs must support prevention of illness and management of health status. Therefore, the two key processes in this step are treating disease and managing health.

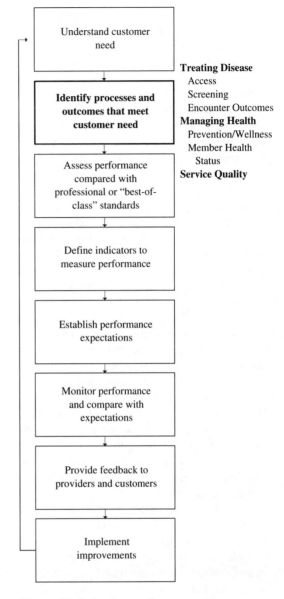

Figure 25–3 Continuous improvement process—meet customer need.

Treating Disease

Access. The Institute of Medicine defines access as "the timely use of personal health services to achieve the best possible outcomes."[16(p.4)]

In an MCO, access encompasses geographical convenience and availability of providers.

For purchasers and members alike, access is an absolutely critical area. For example, a 1993 study found that 93 percent of Americans considered access to services very important in their choice of a health system, and 76 percent of the same group felt that accessibility might decline given the incentive structure created by capitation.[17] Of related interest, Americans in all demographic categories consistently indicate that they will not accept the waits characteristic of other countries' health systems (up to 6 months for heart surgery in Canada, up to 4 months for a specialist appointment in Britain).[18] Finally, surveys of MCO disenrollees repeatedly show that a majority of those who left the MCO of their own volition chose to leave because they were dissatisfied with access to service.

In addition, studies have concluded that communities where people perceive poor access to medical care have higher rates of hospitalization for chronic diseases (asthma, hypertension, chronic obstructive pulmonary disease, congestive heart failure, and diabetes).[19] It has been suggested that improving access to care is more likely to reduce hospitalization rates for chronic disease than changing patients' propensity to seek health care or eliminating variation in physician practice style.[20]

Screening. Disease screening measures assess the MCO's performance in detecting the medical conditions of its membership at an asymptomatic, treatable stage. Familiar examples of disease screening include mammography, Pap smear testing, cholesterol screening, and sigmoidoscopy. Disease screening measures defined as screening rates per eligible population are easy for consumers to understand. The measures, however, are not immune to the controversies of timing of disease screening. In addition, purchasers tend to view screening activities as useful and cost effective even though the evidence to support this is weak. Nevertheless, screening processes are likely to remain important to purchasers.

In the future, outcomes of screening may supersede the quantification of screening in terms of its importance to consumers and purchasers alike. After all, screening does not assess the patient's benefit from early detection. For example, an effectiveness measure in screening breast cancer may someday be two outcome measures—the stage of breast cancer at diagnosis and the 5-year mortality rate for breast cancer—rather than only mammography rates over time.

Encounter outcomes. Encounter outcome measures evaluate the results of specific clinical encounters, such as a hospitalization or an office visit. Included in this category are the traditional assessments of mortality, readmission rates, adverse events, provider empathy, and satisfaction. Traditionally, encounter outcome measures have been confounded by small sample sizes, case mix adjustment issues, and unreliable data collection methods. These problems have made it difficult to compare data across systems or even within an MCO over time. Purchasers are likely to continue asking for encounter outcomes for high-volume clinical conditions. Because of the methodological issues mentioned, however, purchasers are likely to set relatively low performance standards in these areas.

Managing Health

Prevention/wellness. The next set of key processes comprises those associated with prevention of illness. Prevention activities are designed to keep the membership free of disease. Examples of prevention programs include smoking cessation, nutritional counseling, and stress reduction. Measures of prevention include the percentage of eligible patients enrolled in one of the above programs, immunization rates, and first trimester prenatal care visit rates. Such prevention programs assess process performance. As discussed earlier, the effectiveness of such programs is questionable without a link to outcomes. High disenrollment rates make it hard for MCOs to realize long-term benefits from prevention programs. At least in the short term, it appears that consistently poor performance in this area would dampen a purchaser's enthusiasm for a particular MCO.

Member health status. The evaluation of a member's health status may include assessment of functioning in physiological terms (e.g., blood pressure or laboratory tests), physical terms (e.g., activities of daily living), mental or psychological terms (e.g., cognitive skill and affective interaction), social terms (e.g., ability to engage in family work or school), and other health-related quality of life areas (e.g., pain, energy, sleep, and sex).[21] Two purposes are served by health status evaluations. First, members at risk for need of services can be identified before a catastrophic event. Second, a member's health status assessment can serve as an outcome measure for care or treatment received. The recent popularity of health status assessment stems from two ideas. The first is that members' perceptions of their health are both important and easy to obtain.[22] The second is that health systems should be accountable not only for treating disease and managing health, but for enhancing members' well-being as well.

Although it is believed that purchasers will rely heavily on member health status measures in their assessments of MCO quality, the Health Care Advisory Board recently articulated a persuasive countervailing opinion.[23] According to the Advisory Board, health status data are not likely to play a prominent role in MCO selection. The Advisory Board called attention to two facts in presenting its argument. First, member health status is influenced by factors beyond the control of the MCO, including genetic predisposition to illness, sociodemographic factors, dietary and exercise habits, and so forth. Second, most systems exhibit member turnover rates of 10 percent or higher, and this makes it difficult to link health status to activities in any one system. According to the Advisory Board, purchasers are unlikely to hold MCOs accountable for (much less make a decisive negotiating decision in light of) the health status of its members. Only time will tell how much member health status measures will play as a role in MCOs.

Service Quality

Service quality measures evaluate the timeliness, responsiveness, and courtesy with which the MCO serves its members. These attributes are of obvious importance to MCO members. The impact of managed care and the balance of cost and quality will continue to be evaluated. Although there are numerous studies showing high levels of member satisfaction with MCOs, it is worthy to note that the results were less than favorable for the MCOs in one recent survey. A total of 2,374 adults were randomly selected and interviewed over an 11-month period. Nonelderly sick persons in managed care plans reported lower out-of-pocket expenses but more problems getting the health service or treatment they or their physicians thought was necessary. The study also found that sick people in managed care plans were more likely to be unhappy with both general and specialist physician care. In addition, managed care enrollees were more likely to report difficulty getting access to specialist care and diagnostic tests and waited longer for medical care. Compared with patients in fee-for-service plans, sick or disabled patients in managed care plans were more likely to complain that their general physician:

- provided medical care that was not correct or appropriate (5 percent fee-for-service patients, 12 percent managed care patients)

- failed to explain what he or she was doing (6 percent fee-for-service patients, 12 percent managed care patients)

- neglected to explain how and when to take prescriptions at home (4 percent fee-for-service patients, 10 percent managed care patients)

- made them wait a long time for an appointment (7 percent fee-for-service patients, 17 percent managed care patients) or a long time in the waiting room (18 percent fee-for-service patients, 26 percent managed care patients)[24]

In addition to these service quality assessments, some MCOs are following their industry counterparts by offering service guarantees for members who are not satisfied with services received during an office visit; for example, qualified member dissatisfiers may result in the repayment of a monthly premium.

Assess Performance Compared with Professional or "Best-of-Class" Standards

The third step of the continuous improvement process model (Figure 25–4) is assessing the MCO's performance compared with a professional or "best-of-class" standard. This concept of comparison was discussed earlier. The modern quality management program includes the components of performance assessment as described for appropriateness evaluation and peer review but also includes the processes of benchmarking and outcomes assessment.

Appropriateness Review

As discussed for the traditional quality assurance model, appropriateness indicators evaluate the extent to which the MCO provides necessary care and does not provide unnecessary care in the service location best suited for quality and cost efficiencies. Purchasers understand that they cannot obtain good value from an MCO unless it provides appropriate services, so that these indicators are as important as those for accessibility.

Unfortunately, improving the assessment of appropriateness has been dogged by methodological problems, such as adjusting the data for case mix (discussed later), and the surprising lack of data from controlled trials that would define appropriate care in the first place. This issue affects the evaluation of both overutilization and underutilization of services.

In response to these challenges, the MCO can do two things. First, the MCO can identify minimum performance standards for high-cost diagnoses and use them to select processes having excess utilization. Second, the MCO can demonstrate evidence of consistent success and/or an

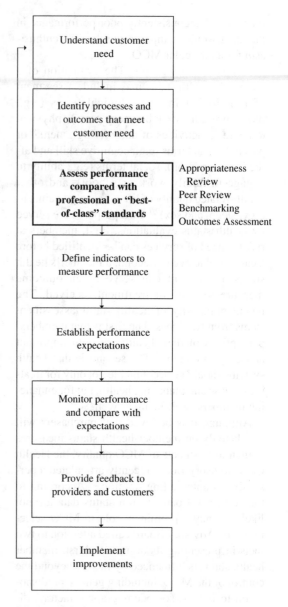

Figure 25–4 Continuous improvement process—compare performance.

improvement trend in clinical appropriateness indicators. If these two approaches are employed, purchasers seem inclined to offer MCOs some flexibility in the short run even if some isolated indicators suggest that there may be quality problems.

Peer Review

As discussed previously, peer review involves a comparison of an individual provider's practice against an accepted standard of care. A key difference between peer review in a traditional quality assurance model and that in a modern quality management model is the topic of comparison.

Benchmarking

A third method of assessing and comparing an MCO's performance is benchmarking. Benchmarking was popularized by Robert Camp of Xerox (Rochester, New York) over the last 20 years. Camp and Tweet define benchmarking as "the continuous process of measuring products, services and practices against the company's toughest competitors or those companies renowned as industry leaders."[25(p.229)] Two types of benchmarking may be used by MCOs. First, internal benchmarking identifies internal functions to serve as pilot sites for comparison. This type of benchmarking is particularly useful in newly integrated delivery systems with multiple, diverse component entities.[26] The second type of benchmarking is external or competitive benchmarking. Competitive benchmarking is the comparison of work processes with those of the best competitor and reveals which performance measure levels can be surpassed.[27] The benchmarking process can be applied to service and clinical processes for knowledge of current performance.

Outcomes Assessment

A fourth method for an MCO to assess performance is through outcomes assessment. An outcomes assessment may be performed on the MCO's ten high-volume or high-cost diagnoses or procedure groups. An outcomes assessment permits the MCO to assess its own performance over time and to identify variation within the MCO. Davies and others have outlined three core activities for an outcomes assessment[28]:

1. Outcomes measurements are "point-in-time" observations.
2. Outcomes monitoring includes the process of repeated measurements over time, which permits causal inferences to be drawn about the observed outcomes.
3. Outcomes management is the application of the information and knowledge gained from outcome assessment to achieve optimal outcomes through improved decision making and delivery.

The purpose of an outcomes assessment is to provide a quantitative comparison among treatment programs, to map the typical course of a chronic disease across a continuum, or to identify variations in the outcome of care as potential markers of process variation.[29]

Define Indicators To Measure Performance

Defining indicators to measure performance is the fourth step of the continuous improvement process model (Figure 25–5). The MCO may apply the quality criteria (structure, process, and outcome) as discussed for the traditional quality assurance model. In addition, it is useful for MCOs to evaluate their process and outcomes by populations of customers served. The MCO quality management matrix (Figure 25–6) is a diagram of how this may occur. A key issue faced by MCOs in indicator definition and analysis is case mix adjustment.

Case mix adjustment is the process to correct data for variations in illness or wellness in patient populations. It is a statistical model that takes into account specific attributes of a patient population (e.g., age, sex, severity of illness, chronic health status, etc.) that are beyond the control of the MCO or health provider.[30] This adjustment is particularly important in comparative analyses between providers or among MCOs.

Case mix adjustment permits fair comparisons among same-population groups because it accounts for preexisting phenomena that may

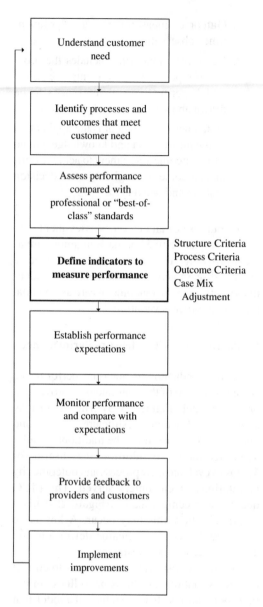

Figure 25–5 Continuous improvement process—measures of performance.

affect the outcome of care. Potentially required variables in a broadly useful risk adjustment system include the following[31]:

- demographic factors
- diagnostic information

- patient-derived health status
- claims-derived health status
- prior use of all services
- prior use of nonelective hospitalization
- prior use of medical procedures

Issues of case mix affect the analysis of both inpatient and outpatient care. The problem, however, is more serious for some performance measures than for others. Case mix is important for clinically oriented indicators such as appropriateness and encounter outcomes. It also has a significant impact on assessments of health status, resource use, and member satisfaction. Case mix is not nearly as important for measures of access and prevention and thus these measures should be considered for physician profiles and report cards. The topic of case mix adjustment exceeds the scope of this chapter; Chapter 27 provides a discussion of this issue.

Establish Performance Expectations

Establishing performance expectations is the fifth step of the continuous improvement process model for an MCO (Figure 25–7). Performance expectations are defined by understanding customer needs (step 1), evaluating the performance of the processes and outcomes designed to meet those needs (step 2), and comparing performance against "best-of-class" standards either internal or external to the MCO (step 3). Purchasers have had an influence on establishing performance expectations. In 1990, Digital Corporation identified priority areas where quality improvement efforts might promote better outcomes. Digital began this effort with the development of health maintenance organization (HMO) standards and by setting expectations in the areas of utilization management, access, quality assurance, mental health services, data capabilities, and financial performance.[32] Digital examined its health care costs and used weightings that drew on multiple data sources to identify priority areas to be considered by the

Population		Treatment of Disease				Managing Health		
Key Function	Access	Appropriateness	Screening	Encounter Outcomes	Prevention	Health Status	Service Quality
Primary Care	# of PCPs with open panels # days for routine physical		Mammog-raphy Cholesterol		Childhood immuniza-tion Adult immuniza-tion		Member satisfac-tion
Senior Care		% seniors with > 7 prescrip-tions					
Specialty Care							
High Risk OB Care							
Other High-Volume or Special Need Population							

Figure 25–6 Quality management matrix. PCP, primary care physician; OB, obstetrics. *Source:* Adapted from N. Goldfield. Case Mix, Risk Adjustment, Reinsurance, and Health Reform. *Managed Care Quarterly*, Vol. 2, No. 3, p. iv. © 1994, Aspen Publishers, Inc.

participating plans. Clinical indicators selected for performance measurement and improvement included mental health inpatient readmissions and inpatient days per patient, cesarean section rates, prenatal care in the first trimester, screening mammography rates, asthma inpatient admissions, and blood pressure screenings. The results from these measurements were not meant to be used punitively but rather enabled Digital to gauge the participating managed care plans in terms of their success in managing specific aspects of health care.

Monitor Performance and Compare with Expectations

Following established expectations, the sixth step is the actual monitoring of performance and comparison with expectations. The frequency of monitoring is determined by the indicators the MCO has selected to measure performance. An MCO can compare its performance against its own over time and against other MCOs if the same indicator definitions are used.

Provide Feedback to Providers and Customers

The seventh step of the continuous improvement process model (Figure 25–8) is providing feedback. Two methods of feedback are discussed here: profiling assesses the performance of individual providers, and report cards assess overall MCO performance.

Profiling

Profiling focuses on the patterns of an individual provider's care rather than that provider's specific clinical decisions (see Chapter 27). The practice pattern of an individual provider—hos-

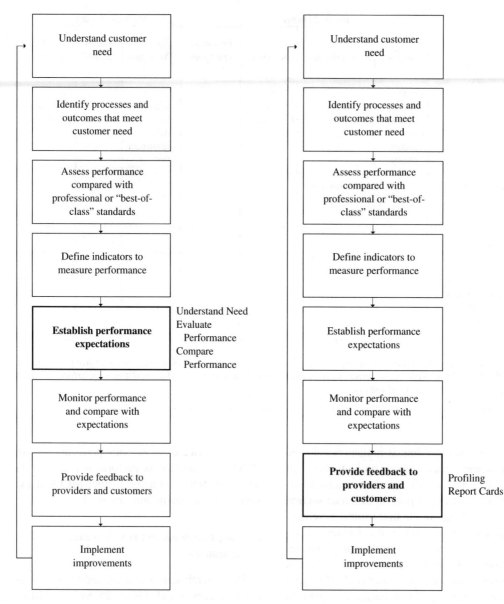

Figure 25–7 Continuous improvement process—establish expectations.

Figure 25–8 Continuous improvement process—feedback.

pital or physician—is expressed as a rate or a measure of resource use during a defined period and for a defined population.[33] The resulting profile can then be compared against a peer group or a standard. MCOs are using profiling to measure providers' performance, to guide quality improvement efforts, and to select providers for managed care networks.[34]

The Physician Payment Review Commission (PPRC) has suggested several guidelines for effective physician profiling.[35] According to the PPRC, profiles first must be analyzed for a well-defined population. Second, they must include a sufficient number of observations to ensure that differences are not due to chance. Third, they should include adjustments for case mix. Finally, profiles must be analyzed for a small enough organizational unit that the parties involved can be responsible for the results and take the necessary courses of action for improvement. A successful profiling system defines an episode of care, accounts for severity of illness and comorbidities, and identifies all the resources used per episode of care.[36] Most profiling systems rely heavily on standard billing information, such as diagnosis-related groups, categories in the tenth revision of the *International Classification of Disease*, and current procedural terminology codes.

Examples of measures used in provider profiling include average wait time to schedule a routine physical, number of hospital admissions, number of referrals out of network, number of emergency department visits, member satisfaction, percentage compliance with the MCO's clinical practice guidelines, and, if applicable, the percentage of children receiving appropriate immunizations and the cesarean section rate. Profiling is discussed further in Chapter 27.

Report Cards

Report cards have become a popular method of conveying performance within an individual MCO with multiple geographic sites or across many diverse MCOs. The purpose of a report card is to provide customers (purchasers and consumers) with comparable quality and cost information in a common language for the purpose of selecting a health plan. Purchasers have formed groups across the country to facilitate the development of a standardized approach to health plan performance measurement. For example, in 1993, 27 corporate and government purchasers of health care formed the Massachusetts Health Care Purchaser Group. The group challenged the health plans in Massachusetts to submit data on six clinical indicators: mammog-

raphy screening, prenatal care, cesarean section rate, hypertension screening, asthma admission rate, and mental health admissions after an inpatient stay[37] (Exhibit 25–4). Each health plan was compared with the clinically significant average range, and a consumer-friendly pie chart graphic was used to summarize performance (Figure 25–9).

The NCQA, a nonprofit group that accredits HMOs, organized a national test pilot report card demonstration for 21 health plans representing 9.6 million enrollees. The NCQA judged the plans on a subset of the Health Plan Employer Data and Information Set (HEDIS; see Chapter 28) measures: standard measures of quality, member satisfaction, membership enrollment, and resource utilization measures.

The report card concept is equally valuable when applied to internal customers of the MCO. Key quality measures can be tracked, trended, and utilized for strategic quality planning and to assess the effectiveness of improvement efforts. For example, in 1993, the northern California region of Kaiser Permanente released a self-assessment that it referred to as its report card.[38] This report card is organized into seven categories: childhood health, maternal care, cardiovascular disease, cancer, common surgical procedures, other adult health, and mental health/substance abuse. In designing categories, developers selected areas that affected many enrollees and tried to depict care from the patient's perspective (i.e., what would the patient need during the course of his or her illness?) The report card assessed enrollee satisfaction as a separate entity.

The benefits of the report card movement include the stimulus for MCOs to build the capacity to produce performance information and strengthen data quality. Public disclosure of performance information also lends itself to plan, provider, and hospital accountability. The main limitation of the report card movement continues to be measurement. Although the NCQA and HEDIS have made moves to standardize measurement, there continues to be variation in measurement, coding, and clinical classifica-

Exhibit 25–4 Massachusetts Health Care Purchaser Group Clinical Indicators

Mammography Screening Rate:	Percentage of members aged 52–64 who were continuously enrolled in the plan during 1991 and 1992 who received mammograms.
Hypertension Screening Rate:	Percentage of members aged 52–64 who were continuously enrolled in the plan in 1991 and 1992 who were screened for high blood pressure.
Asthma Admission Rate:	The number of hospital admissions for asthmatics of both sexes between the ages of 1 and 19 and ages 20 and 64 divided by the number of enrollees in the plan of the same age cohorts over a 1-year period.
Prenatal Care Rate:	The percentage of pregnancies among women who delivered babies and who were continuously enrolled for 7 months in 1992 for which prenatal care was received during the first trimester of pregnancy.
Cesarean Section Rate:	The percentage of all deliveries in 1992 that were performed by cesarean section.
Mental Health Readmission Rate:	Males and females aged 18–64 years continuously enrolled in a given health plan for the previous 2 years, and hospitalized with a discharge date in the second year for psychiatric care. There were two measures: the average number of individual hospital admissions per patient, and the average number of mental health hospital days per patient for all hospital admissions.

Source: © *Journal on Quality Improvement.* Oakbrook Terrace, IL: Joint Commission on Accreditation of Healthcare Organizations, 1995, p. 169. Reprinted with permission.

tion. Additionally, there is variation in the administrative source datasets that plans use to obtain their measurements. Risk adjustment and a broader clinical focus are opportunities for improvement. Finally, no conclusion can be drawn about processes or outcomes that are not assessed by the report card measurements.

Implement Improvements

The eighth step of the continuous improvement process model (Figure 25–10) is implementation of improvements. Current strategies employed by MCOs as tools to improve health care delivery processes and outcomes are practice guidelines, case management, improvement teams, and consumer education.

Practice Guidelines

Clinical practice guidelines are systematically developed statements to assist practitioners and patients in making decisions about appropriate health care for specific clinical circumstances. Guidelines offer an opportunity to improve health care delivery processes by reducing unwanted variation. An appointed committee of the Institute of Medicine recommended the following attributes of guideline design[39]:

- *Validity:* Practice guidelines are deemed valid if they lead to the health and cost outcomes projected for them.

- *Reliability/reproducibility:* If given the same evidence and development methods, another set of experts would come up with the same recommendations and the guidelines are interpreted and applied consistently across providers.

- *Clinical applicability:* Guidelines should apply to a clearly defined patient population.

	Provider															
	5	8	14	13	2	11	9	6	16	1	10	15	3	4	7	12
Mammography	◑	○	●	◔	○	◕	◑		●	◑		◑	◑	◔	◕	◑
Prenatal Care: NonMedicaid	◑	◑	◑	○	◑	◔	○	◑	●	◑		◑	◑	◔	◑	◑
Medicaid	◑			○	●	◑				◕	◕	◑		◑		
C-Section: NonMedicaid	◑	◑	◑	○	◑	◑	◑	◑	◕	◔		◑	◑	◕	◑	◑
Medicaid	◑			◑	◑					◑	◑	◔	◑	◑		
Hypertension	◕	◑	◔	◑	◑	◑				◑			◑	◑	◑	
Asthma-Adult: NonMedicaid	●	◑	◑		◑	○	◕	◔	○	○		◑	●	●	◑	
Medicaid					◔	◔					●	●	●			
Asthma-Child: NonMedicaid	●	○	◑	◑	●	○	○	○	○	○		●	●	●	◑	
Medicaid	◑		◑	◑	◕	◑					●	●		◑		
Mental Health: Admissions (0 in 1991)	◑	◑	◑	◑	◑	○	◑		◑	◑		◑	◑	◕		◔
(> 0 in 1991)	○		◑		◔	◕			◑				◔	◑		
Mental Health: Days (0 in 1991)	◔	◑	◕	◔	◕	◔	○		●			○	◑	◑		
(> 0 in 1991)	◑		◑	◑	◕	◕	○		●			○	◑	◑		

Legend
○ Better than the average range
◔ Better than the mean, but within the average range
◑ Within the average range
◕ Worse than the mean, but within the average range
● Worse than the average range

Figure 25–9 Massachusetts Health Care Purchaser Group 1992 Summary Table. *Source: Journal on Quality Improvement*. Oakbrook Terrace, IL: Joint Commission on Accreditation of Healthcare Organizations, 1995, p. 171. Reprinted with permission.

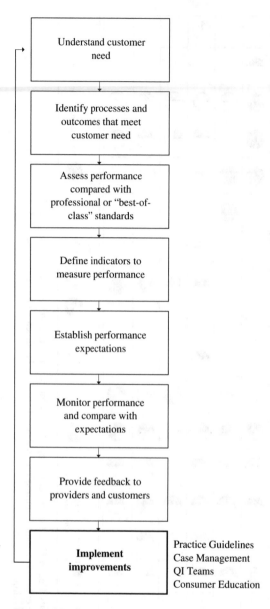

Figure 25–10 Continuous improvement process—implement improvements. QI, quality improvement.

- *Clinical flexibility:* Guidelines should recognize the generally anticipated exceptions to the recommendations proposed.
- *Multidisciplinary process:* Representatives of key disciplines involved in the process

of care should participate in the guideline development process.

- *Scheduled review:* Guideline evaluation should be planned in advance and occur at a frequency that reflects the evolution of clinical evidence for the guideline topic.
- *Documentation:* Detailed summaries of the guideline development process should be maintained that reflect the procedures followed, the participants involved, the evidence and analytical methods employed, and the assumptions and rationales accepted.

In addition to a development process, guideline programs also have an implementation process. The first step in designing an implementation strategy for clinical guidelines is to identify the forces driving and restraining clinical practice change.[40] Thus, an MCO may want to convene a group of local content experts along with its own medical leadership to initiate guideline planning and adoption. An effective implementation team strengthens the driving forces for the guideline and weakens the restraining forces for a given clinical practice change. Performance assessment is measured on two levels. First, the gap between prior and optimal practice is measured to assess the degree of implementation. Second, feedback may given to providers to reinforce the change in clinical practice. As an example, the following is a summary of United HealthCare's guideline implementation process[41]:

1. Prioritize your objectives.
   - Select guidelines that:
   —are likely to be accepted by physicians
   —have a cost impact for the health plan
   —affect a quality issue for patients
   —affect a large population
   —fulfill a regulatory issue
2. Document the need to change.
3. Look for guideline credibility.

4. Get the word out.

5. Use timely feedback to physicians.

6. Remember, you are dealing with a system.

Practice guidelines are not without limitations. Studies have shown that traditional methods of guideline dissemination have not resulted in significant changes in practice.[42,43] Frequently, guidelines are not designed to be implemented directly into practice. This has a particular impact in preferred provider organizations (PPOs) and independent practice associations (IPAs), where there are multiple and varied processes. An MCO can facilitate the implementation of guidelines through the corresponding development of algorithms, summaries, laminated cards, medical record tools, and reminder systems. Second, as mentioned earlier in this chapter, meeting specifications does not necessarily result in constant improvement but rather may maintain ensuring the status quo.[44] Guidelines should be designed with flexibility to encourage improvement and innovation.

Clinical pathways and protocols are discussed in detail in Chapter 19.

Case Management

Case management is a model of patient care delivery that restructures and streamlines the clinical production process so that it is outcome based.[45] Case management, like practice guidelines, can reduce unwanted variation. As a model, case management mobilizes, monitors, and rationalizes the resources a patient uses over the course of an illness. In doing so, case management aims at a controlled balance between quality and cost.[46]

Case management plays an integral part in an MCO's quality management program. First, a case manager is an integral part of the health care team and participates in establishing an individualized treatment plan with the member, physician, and MCO. Second, case management can be applied to the identification of members at risk for high-dollar, catastrophic illness. After identification of these members, case managers monitor their care on an ongoing basis to assess whether quality care is being provided in an appropriate setting. The case manager plays an important role as a resource manager for the MCO. Third, case managers can evaluate the implementation and effectiveness of practice guidelines.

To date, little evidence exists regarding the long-term effectiveness of case management in MCOs or integrated delivery systems. The effectiveness of case management, however, has been studied in preventive services and community mental health. A number of studies have shown that maternity care coordination and preventive services improve child health and are cost effective but are underused.[47–54] Replicated findings suggest that case management during pregnancy increases infant birthweight.[55,56] Other studies have found that community mental health clients who received case management used more community services than those not receiving case management.[57–61] This finding has led researchers to speculate that case management of clients' vocational, educational, housing, social, recreational, and financial needs may improve their quality of life, which consequently reduces their need for rehospitalization.[62,63] These effectiveness evaluations are important to MCOs because the performance of these key functions (prenatal care and mental health care management) is a measure used for evaluation by purchasers in HEDIS.

Large case management is discussed in detail in Chapter 18.

Quality Improvement Teams

A third tool employed by MCOs to facilitate improvement of health care delivery is the quality improvement team. MCOs are complex organizations that span job functions and geography. The tasks required to produce the outputs of a quality management program require diverse talents and skill sets. The variety of network configurations (e.g., staff model HMO, PPO, and IPA) requires a method to incorporate provider input from a variety of perspectives.

Quality improvement teams offer an alternative in an environment where administrative expense must be controlled and minimized. Teams outperform individuals acting alone or in larger organizational groupings, especially when performance requires multiple skills, judgments, and experiences.[64]

There are several well-known phenomena that explain why teams perform well. First, the broader skill mix and know-how facilitate the team's response to multifaceted challenges, such as innovations, quality, and customer service. Second, in developing clear goals and approaches to problem solving, teams can support real-time resolution and initiative. Finally, teams provide a unique social dimension that enhances the economic and administrative aspects of work. By surmounting barriers to collective performance, team members build trust and confidence in each other's capabilities. This supports the pursuit of team purpose above and beyond individual or functional agendas.[65]

How can teams be applied to quality management in an MCO? Examples include a team consisting of MCO leaders, purchasers, members, and providers setting the evaluation and improvement agendas for the MCO by prioritizing goals. Alternately, a cross functional team may evaluate the disease- or population-specific needs of a member group and test interventions, such as practice guidelines, for care improvement. Finally a team could form to design an MCO's strategy to meet accreditation requirements. Teams can be chartered to address most issues faced by an MCO as long as an explicit purpose and a defined time frame for completion have been identified.

Consumer Education

Many MCOs' quality management programs include evaluation of the effectiveness of consumer education. Consumer education is targeted at beneficiaries so that they can become effective health care consumers and participate in meeting the aforementioned needs of treating disease and managing health. Examples of consumer education utilized by MCOs include telephone resource lines, health risk appraisals, worksite-based consumer education programs, and consumer health education materials. Many MCOs have developed and provide members with self-care guidelines for preventing illness and treating common complaints at the time of enrollment. These topics are also discussed in Chapter 17.

SETTING THE IMPROVEMENT AGENDA

After the implementation of step 8, the MCO must evaluate whether the improvements actually made a change and met customer need. If not, the cycle begins again with step 1. If improvements did occur and customer needs were met, the cycle can begin again for new or unaddressed customer needs.

How can an MCO design such a cycle? MCOs have limited resources with which to assess and improve performance, and strategic decisions must be made to target resources effectively. An MCO's leadership group may begin the cycle of improvement by applying the following criteria:

1. Identify which customer need is being addressed by the proposed project.

2. Evaluate the strength of the evidence for the need to improve.

3. Assess the probability that there will be a measurable impact.

4. Determine the likelihood of success.

5. Identify the immediacy of impact in meeting the customer's need.

CONCLUSION

Consumers and purchasers of health care are demanding quality at a reasonable price. To address this need, a quality management program in a managed care setting must be designed to reflect complex delivery systems and diverse customer groups. Success in managing cost and optimizing health outcomes begins with an understanding of customer needs, assessment of performance to meet those needs, and continuous improvement. Attention focused on the provision of appropriate care in an appropriate setting will continue to shape the quality resource programs in MCOs. The need to assess the impact of these shifts of care from one segment of the delivery system to another will continue to grow as the shifts progress.

As a part of a health delivery system, MCOs have an opportunity to affect the health status of populations through their actions and thus have a responsibility to assess and measure these effects. To achieve these goals, an MCO must have a focused aim and a process for achievement, such as that summarized in Figure 25–11. This eight-step process can be implemented on a diverse scale, such as in an IPA or network model, or at a staff model site. Improvement opportunities have many degrees of success in diverse organizations, as identified in Figure 25–12. A variety of methods—practice guidelines, case management, outcomes management, and others—have been introduced and, no doubt, will continue to evolve.

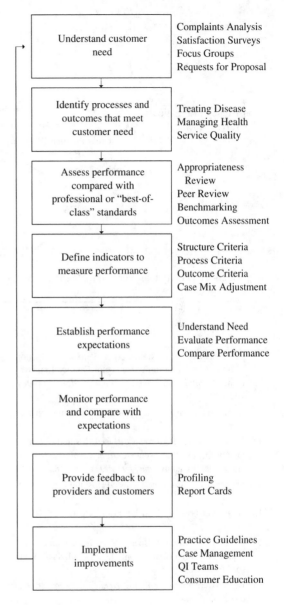

Figure 25–11 Continuous improvement process—summary. QI, quality improvement.

REFERENCES AND NOTES

1. A. Donabedian, *Exploration in Quality Assessment and Monitoring: The Definition of Quality and Approaches to Its Assessment*, Vol. 1 (Ann Arbor, Mich.: Health Administration Press, 1980).

2. S.M. Shortell and J.P. LoGerfo, Hospital Medical Staff Organization and Quality of Care: Results from Myocardial Infarction and Appendectomy, *Medical Care* 19 (1981): 1041–1056.

3. M. Walton, "Improve Constantly and Forever the System of Production and Service," in *The Deming Management Method* (New York, N.Y.: Putnam, 1986), 66–67.

4. R.L. Goldman, The Reliability of Peer Assessments of Quality of Care, *Journal of the American Medical Association* 267 (1992): 958–960.

5. R.D. Moen and T.W. Nolan, Process Improvement, *Quality Progress* 9 (1987): 62–68.

6. G.J. Langley, et al., The Foundation of Improvement, *Quality Progress* 6 (1994): 81–86.

7. J. Juran and F. Gyrna, "Understanding Customer Need," in *Quality Planning and Analysis*, 3d ed. (New York, N.Y.: McGraw-Hill, 1993), 240–252.

8. Juran and Gyrna, "Understanding Customer Need," 241.

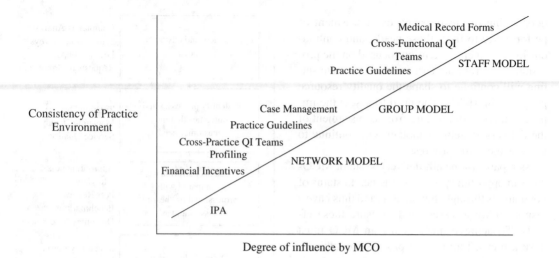

Figure 25–12 Quality management tools for a variety of MCOs. QI, quality improvement.

9. C.W. Nelson and J. Niederberger, Patient Satisfaction Surveys: An Opportunity for Total Quality Improvement, *Hospital Health Service Adminstration* 35 (1990): 409–427.

10. Juran and Gyrna, "Understanding Customer Need," 243.

11. C. Sennet, et al., Performance-Based Hospital Contracting for Quality Improvement, *Joint Commission Journal on Quality Improvement* 9 (1993): 374–383.

12. Sennet, et al., Performance-Based Hospital Contracting, 380.

13. Juran and Gyrna, "Understanding Customer Need," 241.

14. Health Care Advisory Board, *Next Generation of Outcomes Tracking* (Washington, D.C.: Health Care Advisory Board, 1994), 1–57.

15. Health Care Advisory Board, *Next Generation of Outcomes Tracking.*

16. M. Millman, ed., *Access to Health Care in America: Institute of Medicine (U.S.) Committee on Monitoring Access to Personal Health Services* (Washington, D.C.: National Academy Press, 1993), 4.

17. What about Quality of Care?, *PR Newswire* (14 September 1993): 3–6.

18. R.B. Alta, Canadian Way: Universal, But Not Immediate Access, *Modern Healthcare* 6 (1989): 36.

19. A. B. Bindman, et al., Preventable Hospitalization Rates and Access to Health Care, *Journal of the American Medical Association* 274 (1995): 305–311.

20. Bindman, et al., Preventable Hospitalization Rates, 305.

21. P.B. Batalden, et al. Linking Outcomes Measurement to Continual Improvement: The Serial "V" Way of Thinking about Improving Clinical Care, *Joint Commission Journal on Quality Improvement* 20 (1994): 167–180.

22. E.C. Nelson, et al., Patient-Based Quality Measurement Systems, *Quality Management in Health Care* 2 (1993): 18–30.

23. Health Care Advisory Board, *Next Generation of Outcomes Tracking.*

24. Robert Wood Johnson Foundation, *Sick People in Managed Care Have Difficulty Getting Services and Treatment* (Princeton, N.J.: Robert Wood Johnson Foundation, 1995).

25. R.L. Camp and A.G. Tweet, Benchmarking Applied to Health Care, *Joint Commission Journal on Quality Improvement* 20 (1994): 229–238.

26. Camp and Tweet, Benchmarking Applied to Health Care, 230.

27. Camp and Tweet, Benchmarking Applied to Health Care, 230.

28. A.R. Davies, et al., Outcomes Assessment in Clinical Settings: A Consensus Statement on Principles and Best Practices in Project Management, *Joint Commission Journal on Quality Improvement* 20 (1994): 6–16.

29. Davies, et al., Outcomes Assessment in Clinical Settings, 11.

30. M. Pine and D.L. Harper, Designing and Using Case Mix Indices, *Managed Care Quarterly* 2 (1994): 1–11.

31. N. Goldfield, Case Mix, Risk Adjustment, Reinsurance, and Health Reform, *Managed Care Quarterly*, 2 (1994): iv.

32. M.A. Bloomberg, et al., Development of Indicators for Performance Measurement and Improvement: An HMO/Purchaser Collaborative Effort, *Joint Commission Journal on Quality Improvement* 19 (1993): 586–595.

33. P.R. Lee, et al., Managed Care: Provider Profiling, *Journal of Insurance Medicine* 24 (1992): 179–181.

34. L.M. Walker, Can a Computer Tell How Good a Doctor You Are?, *Medical Economics* 71 (1994): 136–147.

35. Physician Payment Review Commission (PPRC), *Conference on Profiling* (Washington, D.C.: PPRC, 1992).

36. Walker, Can a Computer Tell?, 138.

37. H. Jordan, et al., Reporting and Using Health Plan Performance Information in Massachusetts, *Joint Commission Journal on Quality Improvement* 21 (1995): 167–177.

38. Executive Director's Office, Kaiser Permanente Medical Group, *Reporting on Quality KPMG Forum* (Oakland, Calif.: Kaiser Permanente Medical Group, 1993), 1–16.

39. Institute of Medicine, Committee to Advise the Public Health Service on Clinical Practice Guidelines, *Clinical Practice Guidelines: Directions for a New Program* (Washington, D.C.: National Academy Press, 1990).

40. M.R. Handley, et al., An Evidence-Based Approach to Evaluating and Improving Clinical Practice: Implementing Practice Guidelines, *HMO Practice* 8 (1994): 75–83.

41. L.N. Newcomber, Six Pointers for Implementing Guidelines, *Healthcare Forum Journal* (July/August 1994): 31–33.

42. J. Kosecoff, et al., Effects of a National Institutes of Health Consensus Development Program on Physician Practice, *Journal of the American Medical Association* 258 (1987): 2708–2713.

43. J. Lomas, et al., Do Practice Guidelines Guide Practice: The Effect of a Consensus Statement on the Practice of Physicians, *New England Journal of Medicine* 321 (1989): 1306–1311.

44. Walton, "Improve Constantly and Forever," 67.

45. K. Zander, Nursing Case Management: Strategic Management of Cost and Quality Outcomes, *Journal of Nursing Adminstration* 18 (1988): 23–30.

46. K.K. Giullano and C.E. Poirier, Nursing Case Management: Critical Pathways to Desirable Outcomes, *Nursing Management* 22 (1991): 52–55.

47. S.L. Gortmaker, The Effects of Prenatal Care upon the Health of the Newborn, *American Journal of Public Health* 69 (1979): 653–660.

48. J.A. Showstack, et al., Factors Associated with Birth Weight: An Exploration of the Roles of Prenatal Care and Length of Gestation, *American Journal of Public Health* 74 (1984): 1003–1008.

49. D.R. Cohen and J.B. Henderson, *Health, Prevention, and Economics* (New York: Oxford University Press, 1988).

50. R. Currier, Is Early and Periodic Screening, Diagnosis and Treatment (EPSDT) worthwhile?, *International Journal of Rehabilitation Research* 2 (1979): 508–509.

51. P.H. Irwin and R. Conroy-Hughes, EPSDT Impact on Health Status: Estimates Based on Secondary Analysis of Administratively Generated Data, *Medical Care* 20 (1982): 216–234.

52. W.J. Kelle, Study of Selected Outcomes of the Early and Periodic Screening, Diagnosis, and Treatment Program in Michigan, *Public Health Reports* 98 (1983): 110–119.

53. W.L. Manning, The EPSDT Program: A Progress Report, *Indiana Medicine* 78 (1985): 320–322.

54. J.S. Reis, et al., A Synopsis of Federally Sponsored Preventive Child Health, *Journal of Community Health* 9 (1984): 222–239.

55. C.C. Korenbrot, et al., Birth Weight Outcomes in a Teenage Pregnancy Case Management Project, *Journal of Adolescent Health Care* 10 (1989): 97–104.

56. P.A. Buescher, et al., An Evaluation of the Impact of Maternity Care Coordination on Medicaid Birth Outcomes in North Carolina, *American Journal of Public Health* 81 (1991): 1625–1629.

57. D.A. Bigelow and D.J. Young, Effectiveness of a Case Management Program, *Community Mental Health Journal* 27 (1991): 115–123.

58. A. Borland, et al., Outcomes of Five Years of Continuous Intensive Case Management, *Hospital Community Psychiatry* 40 (1989): 369–376.

59. J.L. Franklin, et al., An Evaluation of Case Management, *American Journal of Public Health* 77 (1987): 674–678.

60. P.N. Goering, et al., What Difference Does Case Management Make?, *Hospital Community Psychiatry* 39 (1988): 272–276.

61. J. McRae, et al., What Happens to Patients after Five Years of Intensive Case Management Stops?, *Hospital Community Psychiatry* 41 (1990): 175–180.

62. Bigelow and Young, Effectiveness of a Case Management Program.

63. Goering, et al., What Difference Does Case Management Make?

64. J.R. Katzenbach and D.K. Smith, *The Wisdom of Teams. Creating the High Performance Organization* (Boston, Mass.: Harvard University Press, 1993), 9.

65. Katzenbach and Smith, *The Wisdom of Teams*, 18.

SUGGESTED READING

Books

Couch, J.B. (ed.). 1991. *Health Care Quality Management for the 21st Century*. Tampa, Fla.: American College of Medical Quality and the American College of Physician Executives.

The Deming Management Method. 1986. New York, NY: Putnam.

Juran, J.M., and Gyrna, F.M. 1993. *Quality Planning and Analysis*. New York, NY: McGraw-Hill.

Goldfield, N., Pine, M., and Pine, J. 1992. *Measuring and Managing Health Care Quality: Procedures, Techniques, and Protocols*. Gaithersburg, Md.: Aspen Publishers.

Katzenbach, J.R., and Smith, D.K. 1993. *The Wisdom of Teams: Creating the High Performance Organization*. Boston, Mass.: Harvard University Press.

Senge, Peter, 1993. *The Fifth Discipline: The Art and Practice of the Learning Organization*.

Senge, Peter, and Kleiner, Art. 1994. *The Fifth Discipline Fieldbook*.

Youngs, M.T. and Wingerson, L. 1995. *The 1996 Medical Outcomes and Guidelines Sourcebook*. New York, N.Y.: Faulkner & Gray.

Journals

Joint Commission Journal on Quality Improvement. Joint Commission on Accreditation of Healthcare Organizations, One Renaissance Blvd., Oakbrook Terrace, IL 60181.

Quality Management in Health Care. Aspen Publishers, Inc., 200 Orchard Ridge Dr., Gaithersburg, MD 20878.

Newsletter

Eye on Improvement. Institute for Healthcare Improvement, P.O. Box 38100, Cleveland, OH 44138-0100.

Chapter 26

Changing Provider Behavior in Managed Care Plans

Peter R. Kongstvedt

The practice behavior of physicians in a managed care organization (MCO) is the most important element in controlling cost and quality. As mentioned in Chapters 7, 8, and 57, this process begins at the front door. Selecting physicians who already practice high-quality, cost-effective medicine is the best way to achieve success, although profiling physicians, as discussed in Chapter 27, is no easy task. Even in the best of worlds, however, one cannot be assured that every physician participating in the plan will be solid gold, and realities of marketing and delivery system needs dictate that adequate geographic coverage be present, even when that means accepting some B players rather than all A players.

The best contractual arrangements in the world will be of little value if there are poor utilization patterns or a lack of cooperation with plan policies and procedures. There will be some physicians in the medical community who will not modify their practice behavior. There will also be some physicians who are frankly hostile and some whom, for various reasons, you will not want participating in your plan regardless of how friendly or cooperative they are. The majority of physicians, however, will want to cooperate and be valued participants.

Given these realities, the purpose of this chapter is to present some of the issues involved in modifying the practice behavior of those participating physicians who can and will work with the plan. Financial incentives are clearly a useful method of aligning financial and behavioral goals and are discussed separately in Chapters 7, 9, 10, and 11; nonfinancial approaches are the topic of this chapter.[1,2]

INHERENT DIFFICULTIES IN MODIFYING PHYSICIAN BEHAVIOR

Physicians are professionals with an inordinately large set of built-in biases. This is due to their training, the current environment of medical practice, and the types of pressures now being brought to bear upon them. There is also great heterogeneity in attitudes and prior training in cost containment.[3] None of these issues is unique to the medical profession, but their combination and depth make for a number of inherent difficulties in changing behavior.

What follows is a brief discussion of some of the more important issues. It is wise for managers to be sensitive to these issues. It is wise for mangers to be sensitive to these issues, although that does not mean that they should fail to apply proper management techniques.

Strong Autonomy and Control Needs

There is perhaps no more emotionally charged issue than autonomy and control. Physicians are trained to function in an autonomous way, to stand up for themselves, and to be the authority. It is difficult for them to accept a role in which another entity has control over their professional activities, whether it is managed care, peer review, or practice guidelines.[4,5] Because of that, physicians participating in MCOs often feel antagonistic when they perceive that their control has been lost or lessened. By definition, managed care introduces elements of management control into the arena of health care delivery, control that clearly reduces the physician's autonomy. In one large study, physicians who entered into contracts with health maintenance organizations (HMOs) expected lower earnings, lower quality of care, and lessened autonomy; neither earnings nor quality declined, but there remained a general perception that physician autonomy did decline.[6] In a different study, physicians maintained a mildly negative attitude toward practicing medicine in an open panel HMO setting, yet their perceived negative attitudes regarding autonomy and income were not supported by actual facts abut their practice when they were asked specific questions about these issues.[7] At least one other study, however, has shown that practicing under managed care does not produce a uniformly lower level of satisfaction.[8]

There has been an increase in the amount of external control over the years. HMOs, preferred provider organizations (PPOs), indemnity plans with managed care elements (e.g., preadmission authorization requirements), Medicare, and Medicaid are all programs that have been increasing their control over medical practice as health care costs have risen. The degree of control will vary considerably depending on the type of program involved, but managed health care, particularly tightly managed HMOs, currently exerts the greatest degree of external control outside medical residency training. The greater the degree of external control, the greater the danger of overt or covert resistance to achieving the goals of the plan.

Many of the issues discussed in the course of this chapter are pertinent to ameliorating some of the anxieties that arise in dealing with control issues. It is probably not unreasonable to point out that failure of the private sector and the physician community to control medical costs in the nation will lead to even greater interventions by nonphysicians charged with bringing medical costs under control. Enlisting the physician's help in achieving the plan's goals is possible by empowering the physicians within the system. Suggestions for some specific approaches to the issues of control needs follow.

Control of Where Care Is Received

Virtually all managed care plans will have some controls over where members receive their care. In a simple PPO, that control will be confirmed to a differential in benefits that is based on whether a member uses participating hospitals and physicians. In a tightly managed HMO, the plan will allow only the use of participating providers, and even then only for certain services. For example, the HMO may have an exclusive contract for mammography; even though all the participating hospitals have the ability to perform mammography, only one provider will be allowed to do it and get paid.

If a plan intends to have a highly restricted panel of participating providers, it is sometimes helpful to elicit the opinions of those physicians already in the panel, even though the final decision will still rest with the plan. For example, if the decision has been made to use only two or three orthopedic groups to provide services, the primary care physicians could be canvassed for nominations of groups to approach. The plan should clearly state that it is not having a majority rule vote but is looking for people to approach; the final selection will be based on a combination of the plan's regular credentialing and quality assessment process, the group's willingness to cooperate with plan policies and procedures, and cost.

Control of Patient Care

Much more volatile than the above, control of patient care is a real hot button with most physicians. This control can range from the retrospective review of claims that is found in most plans to the mandatory preauthorization of all nonprimary care services that is found in most HMOs. The greater the degree of plan involvement in clinical decision making, the greater the chances of antagonism between physicians and plan managers, but also the greater the degree of medical cost control.

Because management of medical services is the hallmark of managed care, it is neither possible nor desirable to eliminate it. How that control is exercised will have a great effect on its acceptance and success, however. If the plan intervenes in an arbitrary and heavy-handed manner, there will be problems. If interventions are done with an element of understanding and respect, there should be greater cooperation.

The techniques described in a later section of this chapter are particularly important here. Frequent and regular contact, both positive and negative, will help a great deal. Discussing cases and suggesting and soliciting alternatives for case management will yield better results than arbitrary demands for improvement.

Control of Quality

The most common objection that physicians will actually voice about managed care is that it reduces the quality of care. Regardless of whether that argument is a smoke screen for purely economic concerns, the issue is still a valid one. Any system that requires the use of a restricted network of providers and has an authorization system has the potential of reducing the quality of care delivered. Despite the fact that numerous studies of quality in managed care have shown care to be equal or superior to unmanaged care (see Chapter 9 for references), this feeling persists.

The best approach here is to place responsibility for participating with the plan's quality management (QM) program squarely with the physicians themselves. It is vital to have a properly constructed QM program so that participation is meaningful. A solid QM program will allow the physicians to feel that the plan genuinely does have an interest in quality and should allow for some pride in participation. A more detailed discussion of QM programs is found in Chapter 25.

Role Conflict

It is often stated the physicians are trained to be the patient's advocate. This is partially true, but that notion presupposes a system whereby a patient, like a plaintiff or defendant in a lawsuit, needs an advocate. In fact, physicians are trained to be the patient's caregiver, that is, the coordinator and deliverer of medical care.

The issue of advocacy arises when a physician feels that the needs of the plan and the needs of the patient are in conflict.[9] When that happens, the physician feels genuinely torn between being the patient's advocate and the plan's advocate. This most frequently comes up when the patients request or demand a service that is not really necessary or is medically marginal. Physicians feel on the spot if they must deny the service, putting themselves in a role conflict with their patients: "Just whose side are you on, anyway?" This is a difficult situation that is handled better by some physicians than others.[10]

Plan managers need to acknowledge this conflict, even though there may be less conflict in reality than in perception. Because of poor provider understanding of the insurance function (discussed below), the conflict may come up when the physician feels a service is medically necessary that in fact is not a covered benefit. In some cases, there is poor understanding of the difference between what is actually medically necessary and what is essentially a convenience. The health plan is not in the business of denying truly needed services, assuming that they are covered under the schedule of benefits; denial of such services would be ethically and financially foolish.

What the health plan is in the business of doing is cutting the fat out of the system. The physician is charged with conserving the resources, primarily economic, of the plan to ensure availability of those resources to those who truly need them. It is the physician who will best be able to determine what is really needed and what is really not, and that will help provide more appropriate allocation of those resources. The plan's utilization management efforts are (or should be) aimed at aiding the physician in carrying out the function.

Poor Understanding of the Insurance Function of the Plan

As mentioned above, some of the problems of role conflict stem from a poor understanding of the insurance aspect of the plan. HMOs in particular are marketed as offering comprehensive benefits, even though there are clearly certain exclusions and limitations, just as there are for any form of health coverage. Physicians often do not differentiate between what is medically necessary and what is a covered benefit.

Every plan has certain exclusions and limitations of coverage. For example, a member may require 3 months of inpatient psychiatric care, but the plan only covers 30 days. Another example is an experimental transplant procedure. In each case, an argument can be made that the treatment is necessary, but it is not a covered benefit under the plan's schedule of benefits.

Plan management may make exceptions to the exclusions and limitations policy, but that should only be done rarely and after much thought. In some cases, it will be clearly cost effective to do so (e.g., providing 30 days of home durable medical equipment to avoid a hospitalization). In other cases, it will not be. If frequent exceptions are made, it can lead to an open-ended commitment to provide lifetime noncovered services, a commitment that the plan cannot afford if it is to remain in business.

Helping a physician understand the insurance nature of the plan and that there are limitations to coverage will be a wise investment on the part of the plan managers. It is often of great help for the plan to play the role of the black hat here; in other words, plan management contacts the member in such cases to reinforce that it is a contract (i.e., schedule of benefits) issue and not a matter of the physician being callous and hard hearted.

Bad Habits

All of us have habits and patterns in our lives. Most physicians have habits and patterns in their practices that are not cost effective but are difficult to change. One example is the practice of not seeing patients or making rounds on Wednesdays; the physician's partner may not feel comfortable discharging a partner's patient, so the stay is lengthened by an extra day. Another example is a physician who keeps a routine, uncomplicated surgical patient in the hospital for 4 days, stating "That's the way I've always done it, and it's worked just fine for me!"

This problem is a touchy one. It is usually poor form bluntly to accuse a physician of bad practice habits. The frontal assault is generally met with the indignant question, "Are you questioning my judgment?" You are not, of course; you are questioning a bad habit.

It is preferable to lead physicians to the appropriate conclusion themselves. If you discuss the issue objectively, present supporting information, and ask physicians to examine critically the difference in practice behavior, a number of physicians will arrive at the conclusion that their old habits must change. By allowing physicians gracefully and quietly to make the change, you run less risk of creating the need for a rigid defensive posture on their part.

In some cases, that will not work. If calm and rational discussions fail to effect a change, firmer action is needed; physicians may cooperate but may tell the patient that the health plan is making them do it. In most cases, that type of grumbling will go away after a short while. If it does not, the medical director must counsel these physicians about appropriate behavior, especially in this litigious era. If there is an adverse outcome, even though it had nothing to do with the changed practice pattern, the chances of a lawsuit are probably heightened if those types of comments have been made.

Poor Understanding of Economics

Even though physicians and their business managers are becoming more sophisticated about managed care, there is still a surprising lack of understanding of its economics, especially in capitated or other performance-based reimbursement systems. There may be little understanding of the withholds and incentive pools, or physicians may feel so distant from those pools that there is little or no effect on behavior.

It is worthwhile to have continual reeducation about the economics of the plan as it relates to the physician's income. Related to this is the need for accurate and timely feedback to the physicians about their economic status on the basis of payments and utilization. Inaccurate feedback is far worse that no feedback at all.

The hoary old cliche that money talks is absolutely true. Because of that, plan management should always be aware of the whole dollars involved in compensating physicians. A small number, such as an $11.25 per member per month capitation payment, may seem like "funny money" to a physician, but if that $11.25 per member per month really means $40,000 per year, that has a considerable impact on the financial health of a practice. Helping physicians realize the contribution that the plan is making to their bottom line can be eye opening.

Poor Differentiation Among Competing Plans

Considerable difficulty arises when there is little or no differentiation among competing plans; this is essentially a problem in open panels. In many HMOs, particularly when the state or federal government sets standards, the benefits may be the same, and the provider network may be similar or the same; the only difference is the rates (at which point the situation takes on the ominous characteristics of a commodity market).

This becomes a problem when each plan has different internal policies and procedures with which the physicians and their office staff must comply. If a physician is contracting with three or more plans, the frustration involved with trying to remember which one wants what can be quite high. This problem is exacerbated when

the same patient changes to a different managed care plan. For example, on Friday Mr. Jones was with the ABC Health Plan, but when he came in for his return appointment on Monday he had switched to the XYZ Health Plan; the office staff did not take notice, which resulted in claims or authorization denials. This can be a real morale problem with the physician's office staff. When frustration rises, compliance fails.

This is best addressed by increased attention and service to the physicians and their office staff. Frequent and timely communications will help, and the more that is done in person the better because newsletters have a way of getting to the bottom of the parakeet cage without being read.

In this area, nonmonetary issues can have as much impact as monetary ones. Examples include difficult-to-use forms that require a lot of unnecessary writing, frequent busy signals on service lines, and inconsistencies in responses to questions. It cannot be overstressed that prompt and courteous responsiveness to questions and concerns is required. You do not have to give the answer that you think physicians will want to hear; you do have to give an answer or response that is consistent, clear, and reasonably fair.

GENERAL APPROACHES TO CHANGING BEHAVIOR

Translating Goals and Objectives

A useful way of looking at communications between plan management and physicians is to consider the concept of translation. It is easy to overlook the fact that managers and physicians may have radically different ways of viewing matters relating to the delivery of health care services to plan members.

For example, the area of cost containment is rife with possibilities for opposing views. Physicians frequently look upon cost containment measures as unnecessary intrusions into their domain, whereas nonphysician managers view the same measures as the only way to control headstrong physicians. Translating the goal of cost containment into terms that are both understandable and acceptable to both parties will take you far toward obtaining cooperation and acceptance. To ensure that the economic resources will be available to compensate providers and to make services available at all to patients, cost containment must take place.

Rewards Are More Effective Than Sanctions

A tenet of behavior modification theory is that positive interactions or rewards are more effective at achieving long-term changes in behavior than negative interactions or sanctions. Furthermore, it is rarely good policy for managers to impose their will on others in an arbitrary manner. In some cases it is necessary, but if it is done as a matter of course, cooperation will not be enthusiastic. In the worst case, it can lead to widespread dissatisfaction and defection from the plan. Even without such attrition, overt cooperation can occur, but covert sabotage undoes any progress made. This can be especially true with physicians. Unlike regular employees, physicians (even in closed panel operations) behave with a great deal of autonomy and power.

In the context of this discussion, rewards refer primarily to forms of positive feedback and communication about good performance. Clearly, good case management should yield economic rewards as well, but positive feedback from plan management will be a reward system all in its own. Other rewards could include continuing education seminars about managed care, small gifts or acknowledgments for good work, and so forth.

Although it is unrealistic to expect that every physician will embrace every policy and procedure that plan has, the odds in favor of cooperation will increase when the interaction between the physician and the plan are more positive than negative. This is not to be confused with capitulation on necessary policies and procedures: There were once plenty of physician-friendly health plans that are now little more than smoking rubble. Rather, this is to emphasize that too heavy a hand will eventually cause problems.

Be Involved

It is shocking how often managers of health plans fail to maintain an active involvement with the participating physicians. Frequently the only communications with the physicians are occasional newsletters or memos, claims denials, and calls from the utilization management department harassing the physicians about hospital cases. Those types of interactions will not add to the luster of plan management in the physicians' eyes.

Frequent and regular contact, through scheduled meetings, personal visits, or telephone calls, will help create an environment for positive change. If the only time physicians hear from the plan is when there is a problem, they will try to avoid contact in the future and will tend to have decreased responsiveness to the plan's needs.

Offer advice, suggestions, and alternatives, not just demands to change something. Ask intelligent questions about the clinical issues at hand, and solicit advice about alternative ways to provide the care. Work to get to the point where physicians will be asking themselves the same questions you would ask without your having to ask them.

Involvement is a two-way proposition. It is fair and reasonable to expect the practicing physicians to participate in plan committees to help set medical policy, monitor quality, and so forth. Soliciting active participation in such functions helps promote a sense of ownership on the part of the involved physicians and will clearly give the plan some valuable input. Whether the plan compensates the physicians for the time spent on such activities is a local decision, but an honorarium is common.

PROGRAMMATIC APPROACHES TO CHANGING PHYSICIAN BEHAVIOR

Formal Continuing Medical Education

Formal continuing medical education (CME) is the provision of additional clinical training through seminars, conferences, home study, and so forth. The hallmark of CME is that it provides CME credits by virtue of the accreditation of the sponsoring body. This method of information dissemination, while traditionally the most prevalent, has mixed effectiveness when it comes to changing behavior. One large review found little evidence that traditional CME changed patient outcomes or changed behavior.[11] Another study, however, found that changes in behavior did occur when the curriculum was *designed* to change specific types of behavior.[12] A more recent and extensive review of CME (which specifically excluded programs that were tied to financial incentives) supports the conclusion that traditional CME can have a small effect on behavior, with a somewhat greater effect on behavior when the techniques of academic detailing (e.g., one-on-one education focused on specific issues), reminders (e.g., specific reminders at the time of a patient visit), and possibly the additional influence of opinion leaders are brought into play.[13]

Based on this evidence, formal CME will remain a useful tool for disseminating clinical information and will be a useful adjunct in changing physician behavior in general. Formal CME is not currently a useful tool for a managed care plan to use to change specific physician behavior compared with other available methodologies.

Data and Feedback

As mentioned in other chapters, particularly Chapter 27, data regarding utilization and cost are an integral part of a managed care plan. The value of data is not restricted to plan managers; data are equally important to individual physicians. If the only data physicians get are letters at the end of the year informing them that all their withhold is used up, they can credibly argue that they have been blindsided.

Providing regular and accurate data about an individual physician's performance, from both a utilization and (for risk/bonus models) an economic standpoint, is vital to changing behavior.

Most physicians will want to perform well, but they can only do so when they can judge their own performance against that of their peers or against plan norms.

The research literature is actually a bit mixed in its support for feedback as a means of changing behavior, although the preponderance of the research data is positive. There are numerous studies showing significant reductions in utilization and costs in response to feedback about individual physician behavior.[14–22] There are, however, some studies that are more ambiguous regarding the role of feedback or report that feedback has little lasting effect unless continuously reinforced.[23–29]

When one is reviewing the possible reasons for feedback being shown to be ineffective (at least in the long run), it is possible to conjecture on some conditions that improve the effectiveness of feedback. First, the physicians must believe that their behavior needs to change, whether for clinical reasons, for economic reasons, or simply to remain part of the participating panel in the plan; if physicians do not believe that they need to change, then feedback provides nothing of value. Feedback must also be consistent and usable; in other words, a physician must clearly understand the data in the report, be able to use that information in a concrete way, and be able to keep using it to measure their own performance. Feedback needs to be closely related to what a physician is doing right at that time; in other words, feedback about behavior that is remote in time or infrequent is less likely to be acted upon. Feedback must be regular to sustain the changed behavior; feedback that is sporadic or unsustained is likely to result in behavior returning to the condition before the feedback caused any change to begin with. Last, feedback that is linked to economic performance is more likely to produce substantial change than feedback that is not so linked.

Practice Guidelines and Clinical Protocols

Practice guidelines and clinical protocols refer to codified approaches to medical care.

Guidelines may be for both diagnostic and therapeutic modalities, and they may be used to guide physicians in the care of patients with defined diseases or symptoms or as surveillance tools to monitor practice on a retrospective basis. Clinical pathways or protocols are discussed in great detail in Chapter 19, and the reader is urged to review this chapter.

Many physicians have an initial negative reaction to practice guidelines. They feel that guidelines make for "cookbook medicine" and do not allow for judgment or that guidelines represent a high risk in the case of a malpractice suit (because guidelines provide a template against which all actions will be judged). Nevertheless, practice guidelines have been gaining in popularity, at least among medical managers.

Implementing practice guidelines is not always easy, particularly in an open panel setting. There is frequently a lack of enthusiasm on the part of the physicians, and the plan's ability actually to monitor the guidelines is limited. Generally, the plan's QM process is best able to monitor the use of guidelines (see Chapter 25), although there may be some ability to use the claims system to do so as well.

Attempting to put comprehensive practice guidelines into place in a managed care plan is a daunting task. In an open panel, it will be exponentially more difficult. There is some evidence that simple publication of practice guidelines alone may predispose physicians to consider changing their behavior but that such guidelines by themselves are unlikely to effect rapid change.[30,31] When such protocols are accompanied by direct presentations by opinion leaders (so-called academic detailing), then changes are more sustained.[32] Last, as discussed in Chapter 19, clinical pathways that are developed by the physicians who will then use those pathways, especially in the inpatient setting, are most likely to have significant effects, at least for the type of care that the pathway addresses, and there are multiple interventions that can improve compliance with the guidelines.[33]

CHANGING THE BEHAVIOR OF INDIVIDUAL PHYSICIANS

Stepwise Approach to Changing Behavior Patterns

Changing the behavior of an individual provider involves a stepwise approach. The first and most common step is collegial discussion. Discussing cases and utilization patterns in a nonthreatening way, colleague to colleague, is generally an effective method of bringing about change.

Far less common is positive feedback.* This is an even more effective tool for change but one that most managers fail to use to any great degree. Positive feedback does not refer to mindless or misleading praise but to letting a physician know when things are done well. Most managers get so involved in firefighting that they tend to neglect sending positive messages to those providers who are managing well. In the absence of such messages, providers have to figure out for themselves what they are doing right (the plan will usually tell them what they are doing wrong), and that may not be optimal.

Persuasion is also commonly used. Somewhat stronger than collegial discussion, persuasion refers to plan managers persuading providers to act in ways that the providers may not initially choose themselves. For example, if a patient requires intravenous antibiotics for osteomyelitis but is otherwise doing well, that patient is a candidate for home intravenous therapy. Some physicians will resist discharging the patient to home therapy because it is convenient to follow the case; keeping the patient in the hospital is a lot easier in terms of rounding. The physician must then be persuaded to discharge the patient because of the cost effectiveness of home therapy.

_____

* The use of the term *positive feedback* here is different from the use of the term *feedback* regarding data. Although both forms of feedback provide information to the provider regarding performance, data feedback is objective; positive feedback in the context of this section refers to subjective information from plan managers.

Firm direction of plan policies, procedures, and requirements is the next step after persuasion. If a physician refuses to cooperate with the plan to deliver care cost effectively, and if discussion and persuasion have failed, a medical director may be required to give the physician firm direction, reminding him or her of the contractual agreement to cooperate with plan policies and procedures. Behind firm direction is the implied threat of refusal to pay for services or even more severe sanctions. It is clearly a display of power and should not be done with a heavy hand. When giving firm direction, it is best to not allow oneself to be drawn into long and unresolvable arguments. Presumably the discussions and even the arguments have already occurred, so that it is pointless to keep rehashing them. This is sometimes called a broken record type of response because, rather than respond to old arguments, the medical director always gives the same response: firm direction.

The last steps are sanctions and termination. Sanctioning should rarely be required, and termination is so serious that these topics are discussed separately below.

One last thought in this section: Avoid global responses to individual problems. When managers are uncomfortable confronting individual physicians about problems in behavior, a dysfunctional response is to make a global change in policy or procedure because of the actions of one or two physicians. That type of response frequently has the effect of alienating all the other physicians who have been cooperating while failing to change the behavior of the problem providers. If a policy change is required, make it. If the problem is really just with a few individuals, however, deal with them, and do not harass the rest of the panel.

Discipline and Sanctions

This section discusses the most serious form of behavior modification. Sanctions or threats are only applied when the problem is so serious that action must be taken and when the provider fails to cooperate. In some cases the provider may be willing to cooperate, but the offense is so serious that sanctions must be taken anyway. An example of this is a serious problem of quality care, such as malpractice resulting in death or serious morbidity. In any event, the sanctioning process has legal overtones that must be kept in mind.

Plan management may initiate disciplinary actions short of a formal sanctioning process. In most cases, such discipline is helpful in creating documentation of chronic problems or failure to cooperate. Discipline may involve verbal warnings or letters; in either case, the thrust of the action is to document the offensive behavior and to describe the consequences of failure to cooperate.

One example of discipline is sometimes called ticketing. It is called that because it is similar to getting a ticket from a traffic cop. This is a verbal reprimand about a specific behavior; the behavior and corrective action are described, as are the consequences of failure to carry out the corrective action. The manager refuses to get into an argument at that time and requires the offending provider to make an appointment at a future date to discuss the issue (similar to a court date). This allows tempers to cool off a bit and ensures that the disciplinary message does not get muddied up with other issues. When a manager issues a ticket, there should be a document to file that describes what transpired. Ticketing works best in a closed panel or medical group; it is less effective in an open panel setting.

A more formal approach is an actual disciplinary letter. Like a ticket, the letter describes the offending behavior and the required corrective action and invites the provider to make an appointment to discuss the issue. In the case of a verbal ticket or a disciplinary letter, the consequences of failure to change errant ways is initiation of the formal sanctioning process.

Formal sanctioning has potentially serious legal overtones. Due process, or a policy regarding rights and responsibilities of both parties, is a requirement for an effective sanctioning procedure, at least when one is sanctioning for reasons of quality. The Health Care Quality Improvement Act of 1986 has formalized due process in the sanctioning procedure as it relates to quality and must be adhered to in order to maintain protection from antitrust action (see Exhibit 26–1).[34] Although this act was primarily aimed at hospital peer review activities, HMOs are specifically mentioned, and other forms of managed care may be implied in the future.

Following the requirements of the act regarding due process is cumbersome and is obviously the final step before removing a physician from the panel for reasons of poor quality care. Because it is such a drastic step, compliance with the act, including the reporting requirements, is the best protection the plan has against legal action.

It should be emphasized that the act applies to peer review activities that result in actions against physicians for quality problems. If a physician fails to cooperate with contractually agreed-to plan policies and procedures, the plan may have reason to terminate the contract with the physician for cause. Even in that case, it may be wise to have a due process policy that allows for formal steps to be taken in the event that the plan contemplates termination. Presentation of facts to a medical advisory committee made up of physicians who are not in direct economic competition with the involved physician provides a back-up to plan management. Such a committee may be able to effect changes by the physician where the medical director may not. Finally, the backing of a committee underscores that severe sanctions are not arbitrary but the result of failure on the part of the physician, not plan management.

There may arise situations where a physician's utilization performance is such that there is a clear mismatch with managed care practice philosophy; in other words, the plan simply cannot afford to keep the physician in the panel. The quality of the physician's medical care may be adequate, and there may have been no gross lack of cooperation with plan policies and procedures, but the physician simply practices medicine in such a style that medical resources are heavily and inappropriately overuti-

lized. In such cases, the medical director must assess whether the physician can change his or her behavior. Assuming that the medical director concludes that the provider in question cannot change (or change sufficiently) or has failed to change despite warnings and feedback, the plan may choose to terminate the relationship solely on the basis of contractual terms that allow either party to terminate without cause when adequate notice is given (see Chapter 55).

When the plan departicipates a physician in this way, it is often not subject to a due process type of review. The reason is that the separation is based on practice style and fit, not accusations of rule breaking or poor quality. Although this may not seem fair at first blush, in point of fact most contracts certainly allow physicians to terminate if they feel the fit is poor; plans have the same right, even if they do not exercise it frequently. Terminating physicians in this manner has the potential for creating adverse relations in the network if there is the perception that the plan is acting arbitrarily and without reason. On the other hand, assuming that the terminated physician does indeed practice profligately, the other physicians in the network are probably aware of it, so that there may not be as much shock and surprise as one might think. Even so, such steps are drastic and should not be taken frequently or lightly. Recently, some state legislatures have passed laws or regulations restricting a plan's ability to terminate a physician.

CONCLUSION

Changing physician behavior is crucial to the success of any managed care pan. Physicians are unique in their strong need for autonomy and control, potential for role conflicts, uneven understanding of the economics or insurance functions of managed care, and ingrained practice habits. Plan managers can exacerbate the difficulties in changing physician behavior by failing to be responsive and consistent, failing to differentiate their plan from other plans, failing to provide positive feedback, failing to address specific problems with providers early, and fail-

Exhibit 26–1 Health Care Quality Improvement Act of 1986: Requirements of Due Process

(a)...a professional review action must be taken

    (1) in the reasonable belief that the action was in the furtherance of quality health care,

    (2) after a reasonable effort to obtain the facts of the matter,

    (3) after adequate notice and hearing procedures are afforded to the physician involved and after such other procedures as are fair to the physician under the circumstance, and

    (4) in the reasonable belief that the action was warranted by the facts known after such reasonable effort to obtain facts and after meeting requirements of paragraph (3)...

(b)...A health care entity is deemed to have met the adequate notice and hearing requirement of subsection (a)(3) with respect to a physician if the following conditions are met (or are waived voluntarily by the physician):

    (1) Notice of Proposed Action—The physician has been given notice stating—

        (A)(i) that a professional review action has been proposed to be taken against the physician,

           (ii) reasons for the proposed action,

        (B)(i) that the physician has the right to request a hearing on the proposed action,

           (ii) any time limit (of not less than 30 days) within which to request such a hearing, and

        (C) a summary of the rights in the hearing under paragraph (3).

    (2) Notice of Hearing—If a hearing is requested on a timely basis under paragraph (1)(B), the physician involved must be given notice stating—

        (A) the place, time, and date of the hearing, which date shall not be less than 30 days after the date of the notice, and

        (B) a list of the witness (if any) expected to testify at the hearing on behalf of the profession review body.

    (3) Conduct of Hearing and Notice—

        (A)...the hearing shall be held (as determined by the health care entity)—

        (i) before an arbitrator mutually acceptable to the physician and the health care entity,

        (ii) before a hearing officer who is appointed by the entity and who is not in direct economic competition with the physician involved, or

        (iii) before a panel of individuals who are appointed by the entity and are not in direct economic competition with the physician involved;

    (B) the right to the hearing may be forfeited if the physician fails, without good cause, to appear;

    (C) in the hearing the physician has the right—

        (i) to representation by an attorney or other person of the physician's choice,

        (ii) to have a record made of the proceedings, copies of which may be obtained by the physician upon payment of any reasonable charges associated with the preparation thereof,

        (iii) to call, examine, and cross-examine witnesses,

        (iv) to present evidence determined to be relevant by the hearing officer, regardless of its admissibility in a court of law, and

        (v) to submit a written statement at the close of the hearing; and

    (D) upon completion of the hearing, the physician has the right—

        (i) to receive the written recommendation of the arbitrator, officer, or panel, including a statement of the basis for the recommendations, and

        (ii) to receive a written decision of the health care entity, including a statement of the basis for the decision.

Source: Healthcare Quality Improvement Act of 1986, 45 U.S.C. §11101–11152, section 412.

ing to take a stepwise approach to managing change.

Systematic approaches to changing physician behavior can be used successfully for many aspects of practice. Continuing education, creation and dissemination of practice protocols, and data feedback are all useful techniques, especially when combined with financial incentives.

When reasonable efforts to get a physician to change are unsuccessful and the problems are serious, discipline and sanctions must be applied. Due process must be followed before termination for poor quality, and it may be useful in other settings as well. In the final analysis, it is the plan's responsibility to effect changes in provider behavior that will benefit all the parties concerned and to take action when necessary.

REFERENCES AND NOTES

1. A.L. Hillman, et al., HMO Managers' Views on Financial Incentives and Quality, *Health Affairs* (Winter 1991): 207–219.

2. A.L. Hillman, et al., How Do Financial Incentives Affect Physicians' Clinical Decisions and the Financial Performance of Health Maintenance Organizations?, *New England Journal of Medicine* 321 (1989): 86–92.

3. H.L. Greene, et al., Physicians Attitudes Toward Cost Containment: The Missing Piece of the Puzzle, *Archives of Internal Medicine* 149 (1989): 1966–1968.

4. S.J. O'Connor and J.A. Lanning, The End of Autonomy? Reflections on the Postprofessional Physician, *Health Care Management Review* 17 (1992): 63–72.

5. J.W. Salmon, et al., The Futures of Physicians: Agency and Autonomy Reconsidered, *Theoretical Medicine* 11 (1990): 261–274.

6. R. Schultz, et al., Physician Adaptation to Health Maintenance Organizations and Implications for Management, *Health Services Research* 25 (1990): 43–64.

7. G.J. Deckard, Physicians Responses to a Managed Environment: A Perceptual Paradox, *Health Care Management Review* 20 (1995): 40–46.

8. L.C. Baker and J.C. Cantor, Physician Satisfaction under Managed Care, *Health Affairs Supplement* (1993): 258–270.

9. E.J. Emanuel and N.N. Dubler, Preserving the Physician–Patient Relationship in the Era of Managed Care, *Journal of the American Medical Association* 273 (1995): 323–329.

10. R.O Anderson, How Do You Manage the Demanding (Difficult) Patient?, *HMO Practice* 4 (1990): 15–16.

11. D.A. Davis, et al., Evidence for the Effectiveness of CME: A Review of 50 Randomized Controlled Trials, *Journal of the American Medical Association* 268 (1992): 1111–1117.

12. C.W. White, et al., The Effectiveness of Continuing Medical Education in Changing the Behavior of Physicians Caring for Patients with Acute Myocardial Infarction: A Controlled Randomized Trial, *Annals of Internal Medicine* 102 (1985): 686–692.

13. D.A. Davis, et al., Changing Physician Performance: A Systematic Review of the Effect of Continuing Medical Education Strategies, *Journal of the American Medical Association* 274 (1995): 700–706.

14. S.A Myers and N. Gleicher, A Successful Program To Lower Cesarean Section Rates, *New England Journal of Medicine* 319 (1989): 1511–1516.

15. J.E. Wennberg, et al., Changes in Tonsillectomy Rates Associated with Feedback and Review, *Pediatrics* 59 (1977): 821–826.

16. L.M. Frazier, et al., Academia and Clinic: Can Physician Education Lower the Cost of Prescription Drugs? A Prospective, Controlled Trial, *Annals of Internal Medicine* 15 (1991): 116–121.

17. K.I. Marton, et al., Modifying Test-Ordering Behavior in the Outpatient Medical Clinic, *Archives of Internal Medicine* 145 (1985): 816–821.

18. D.M. Berwick and K.L. Coltin, Feedback Reduces Test Use in a Health Maintenance Organization, *Journal of the American Medical Association* 255 (1986): 1450–1454.

19. J.E. Billi, et al., The Effects of a Cost-Education Program on Hospital Charges, *Journal of General Internal Medicine* 2 (1987): 306–311.

20. J.E. Billi, et al., The Effects of a Low-Cost Intervention Program on Hospital Costs, *Journal of General Internal Medicine* 7 (1992): 411–416.

21. L.M. Manheim, et al., Training House Officers To Be Cost Conscious: Effects of an Educational Intervention on Charges and Length of Stay, *Medical Care* 28 (1990): 29–42.

22. E. Zablocki, ed. "Sharing Data with Physicians," in *Changing Physician Practice Patterns: Strategies for Success in a Capitated Health Care System*, (Gaithersburg, Md.: Aspen, 1995), 1–22.

23. F.J. Dyck, et al., Effect of Surveillance on the Number of Hysterectomies in the Province of Saskatchewan, *New England Journal of Medicine* 296 (1977): 1326–1328.

24. J. Lomas, et al., Opinion Leaders vs. Audits and Feedback to Implement Practice Guidelines: Delivery after Previous Cesarean Section, *Journal of the American Medical Association* 265 (1991): 2202–2207.

25. Failure of Information as an Intervention To Modify Clinical Management: A Time-Series Trial in Patients with Acute Chest Pain, *Annals of Internal Medicine* 122 (1995): 434–437.

26. P. Axt-Adam, et al., Influencing Behavior of Physicians Ordering Laboratory Tests: A Literature Study, *Medical Care* 31 (1993): 784–794.

27. T.A. Parrino, The Nonvalue of Retrospective Peer Comparison Feedback in Containing Hospital Antibiotic Costs, *American Journal of Medicine* 86 (1989): 442–448.

28. S.B. Soumerai, et al., Improving Drug Prescribing in Primary Care: A Critical Analysis of the Experimental Literature, *Milbank Memorial Fund Quarterly* 67 (1989): 268–317.

29. A.R. Martin, et al., A Trial of Two Strategies To Modify the Test-Ordering Behavior of Medical Residents, *New England Journal of Medicine* 303 (1980): 1330–1336.

30. J. Kosecoff, et al., Effects of the National Institutes of Health Consensus Development Program of Physician Practice, *Journal of the American Medical Association* 258 (1987): 2708–2713.

31. J. Lomas, et al., Do Practice Guidelines Guide Practice? The Effect of a Consensus Statement on the Practice of Physicians, *New England Journal of Medicine* 321 (1989): 1306–1311.

32. S.B. Soumerai and J. Avorn, Principles of Education Outreach ("Academic Detailing") To Improve Clinical Decision Making, *Journal of the American Medical Association* 263 (1990): 549–556.

33. A.G. Ellrodt, et al., Measuring and Improving Physician Compliance with Clinical Practice Guidelines: A Controlled Intervention Trial, *Annals of Internal Medicine* 122 (1995): 277–282.

34. Healthcare Quality Improvement Act of 1986. 45 U.S.C. §11101–11152, section 412.

SUGGESTED READING

Berenson, R.A. 1991. Commentary: A Physician's View of Managed Care. *Health Affairs* 10:106–119.

Chernov, A.J. 1993 (February). Managed Care and the Doctor–Patient Relationship. *Medical Interface*, 30–32.

Delio, S.A. and Hein, G. 1995. *The Making of an Efficient Physician*. Englewood, Colo.: MGMA.

Eisenberg, J.M. 1986. *Doctors' Decisions and the Cost of Medical Care*. Ann Arbor, Mich.: Health Administration Press.

Greco, P.J. and Eisenberg, J.M. 1993. Changing Physicians' Practices. *New England Journal of Medicine* 329:1271–1274.

Mittman, B.S. and Siu, A.L. 1992. "Changing Provider Behavior: Applying Research on Outcomes and Effectiveness in Health Care. In *Improving Health Policy Management: Nine Critical Research Issues for the 1990s*, eds. S.M. Shortell and U.E. Reinhardt. Ann Arbor, Mich.: Health Administration Press, pp.195–227.

Moynihan, J.J. 1994. Using EDI for Utilization Management. *Healthcare Financial Management* 48(7): 73.

Nash, D.B., ed. 1994. *The Physician's Guide to Managed Care*. Gaithersburg, Md.: Aspen.

Zablocki, E. 1995. *Changing Physician Practice Patterns: Strategies for Success in a Capitated Health Care System*. Gaithersburg, Md.: Aspen.

Chapter 27

Using Data in Medical Management

Peter R. Kongstvedt

Of all the activities involved in managing health care, the use of data in medical management continues to take on ever increasing importance. It is the ability of medical managers to use data intelligently to manage the health care delivery system that will ultimately separate out those plans that truly excel from those plans that are, at best, adequate performers. This is not to say that the other management activities described in this book have less merit; rather, the opposite is the case: the use of data allows those activities to be carried out more effectively (of course, no data in the world can change someone's personality). It is important to bear in mind, however, that information is not magic; one cannot press ALT-F4 and have utilization suddenly drop. Data and information are merely powerful tools for the medical manager to carry out necessary functions.

This chapter should be read in the context of a managed care plan's specific needs and in conjunction with the information presented in other chapters. It is the intention of this chapter not to be highly redundant and review all the possible reports that can be produced by a plan's management information system (MIS) but rather to concentrate on those reports specific to utilization and medical management that will help medical directors carry out their job. Clearly, the need for these types of reports will be influenced by the configuration of your plan and the types of controls and incentives in place. Not all the reports discussed in this chapter will be helpful, and there will certainly be situations where there are necessary utilization reports that are not discussed here. It is up to the medical director to decide what reports are necessary, and it is up to the director of MIS to provide them. The reader is also referred to Chapter 28 for an in-depth discussion of systems issues in managed care.

GENERAL REQUIREMENTS FOR USING DATA TO MANAGE THE HEALTH CARE DELIVERY SYSTEM

Data Characteristics

For data to be used at all for managing health care costs, certain basic requirements must be met. First, the data must have integrity. Errors are common, especially in data that require manual entry (i.e., data entered via keystrokes); such errors must be prevented when possible and identified and corrected when present. In some plans, especially large insurance companies, the database may not even use all the available information; for example, to hold down personnel costs, the plan may only key in the first three digits of the diagnostic code (each keystroke costs money!) and thus may not be able to refine diagnostic data.

It is not unusual for data to come from multiple sources. For example, a health plan may use more than one system to administer different activities (e.g., enrollment and billing on one system, general ledger on another, utilization management on another, and claims on still another). It is also possible that multiple plans, or a combination of a plan and a provider system, such as an integrated delivery system (IDS; see Chapter 4), will desire to combine data to improve the robustness of the database. In such cases, the data must be integrated into a common database, again bringing up the problems of conformance in meaning. This leads to a requirement to standardize a format for use in data analyses.

Data must be consistent and mean the same thing from provider to provider. For example, one provider may code differently from other providers for the same procedure, and a hospital may code an event differently from the attending physician. Diagnostic coding is particularly problematic when one is analyzing data from physician outpatient reports. Because diagnostic coding is not important in determining what a physician is paid (except for those claims systems that match diagnostic code to procedure code), there is a great deal of laxity in diagnostic coding for office visits. Procedure coding tends to be more accurate because there is a direct relationship between what a provider codes as having been performed and what the provider gets paid (except in capitated systems). Accuracy, however, does not rule out creative coding, upcoding, or even fraud in the form of deliberate coding inconsistencies. For example, one surgeon may bill for a hysterectomy, and another surgeon may bill for an exploratory laparotomy, removal of the uterus, removal of the ovaries, and lysis of adhesions, all of which generate a fee. The need for consistency may mean having to change or otherwise modify data to force conformance of meaning.

Data must also be valid: They must actually mean what you think they mean. Even when there is great attention to diagnostic coding, the reason for the visit may not be related to everything that gets done (e.g., a patient is seen with the diagnosis of hypertension but also gets a hearing test), or the diagnostic code may not be the same as the underlying disease (e.g., a patient is seen for an upper respiratory infection, but the relevant diagnosis is emphysema). In addition to coding validity, it is important to validate data against other potential sources of the same data; for example, physician identification data may be kept in two separate databases, which may not match.

The measures must be meaningful. It is of no value (other than academic) to measure things that have no real impact on the plan's ability to manage the system or a physician's ability to practice effectively. Even worse, there is potential harm in producing reports that purport to mean one thing but really mean another.

The sample size must be adequate. Measuring encounters or referral statistics by physician is of little value if a physician has only 20 members in the panel. Even large databases may fall prey to this problem if the claims and clinical data are spread over too large a provider base, so that there are insufficient data for any given provider. Even when there are sufficient outpatient data for participating primary care physicians (PCPs), there frequently are insufficient data regarding inpatient admissions to be meaningful, even in large insurance claims databases.[1,2]

The data must encompass an adequate time period. Simple snapshots in time do not reveal the true picture. This is particularly important when one is looking at total health care resource consumption of patients. It is even more important when one is trying to determine whether a provider's behavior is consistent. Analyses that encompass long periods of time need to be viewed with the knowledge that practice patterns and behavior do indeed change over time, and that must be taken into account when long time periods are compared with short ones for the same types of episodes.

General User Needs

There are certain general needs that must be considered to make data more useful to end users. Raw data have no immediate value to the typical manager. Users must be able to access usable data as directly as possible. If a manager must stand in line to supplicate the priests of MIS to get critical information, opportunities will be lost. Access must also be as timely and easy as possible.

The ability of managers to have considerable flexibility with data is also desirable. If a manager must accept a hard-coded report and cannot cut the data in another fashion without a lot of wasted time and coding expense, then that manager will be trapped into managing only with whatever information the programmers have allowed for.

Ability To Use System Data with Other Tools

It is important that managers be able to obtain data from the system and use those data with other analytic tools. Advanced statistical analysis programs can be useful to the medical department in performing practice profiling (discussed below) or other trend analyses. The ability to export or download data into other plan programs, such as spreadsheets or database programs in personal computers, is also desirable. The ability to transmit analyzed data to physicians' offices is a feature that will become more important over time.

Format

How reports are formatted is a matter of taste and the MIS department's ability to produce the requested format. The easiest type of report for MIS to produce is one that tabulates columns of numbers. That is also usually the type most deadly to a busy manager. An already overburdened medical director has better things to do than sift through 20 pages of printout looking at raw numbers of referrals for each physician to get an idea of the referral rate.

The best types of report formats for senior plan managers usually are ones that can fit onto one or two 8" × 11" sheets of paper. Those reports should summarize the important data, indicate the outliers and deviations from the norm (or from preset standards), and indicate whether the manager will need to seek more detail. If managers need the raw data, they can always ask for them. For example, a 2-page report giving the overall referral rate for the plan and the annualized referral rate per 1,000 members per year for each PCP for the month and the year to date may be sufficient by itself. If there are PCPs who are grossly over the norm, the medical director can then ask for the detail behind the report.

Graphic reports (especially color graphics) are highly useful for conveying large amounts of information quickly to busy managers. This is particularly true when one is presenting data to managers and providers who are not used to looking at reports. Unfortunately, most mainframe computer systems are not set up to produce graphic reports, so that data must be entered (or downloaded and then imported) into a personal computer before the graphs can be produced. This is a cumbersome process and not amenable to mass production. As computers and software become more sophisticated and interlinked through client-server systems, production of graphic reports will become more common.

Routine and Ad Hoc Reports

To manage information wisely, you need to decide which reports you will want on a routine basis and which reports you will want to call on an ad hoc or as needed basis. For example, in a stable open panel plan, it is unnecessary for the medical director to receive a monthly report listing the recruiting activity or membership for each participating physician. That information, if it is needed, could be provided once per quarter. On the other hand, the medical director or associate medical director will usually want a hospital report on a daily basis.

The basic rule of thumb is to ask for routine reports for those functions that require constant management and will provide sufficient data to show trends and aberrations. Routine reports should allow you to decide when to focus on specific areas for further investigation. For example, watching the trend in referral costs could reveal an upswing that would result in your requesting detail about utilization by specialty. That in turn could lead to a need to look at utilization by individual providers in a single specialty. Save the highly detailed reports for infrequent intervals or ad hoc requests. Time spent deciphering cryptic reports is time spent not managing.

Further discussion of what types of summary reports may be useful follows. The message here is that reports for busy managers should be concise, readable, and easily interpreted and allow the manager to request further detail as needed. One common problem is overkill with detail. Judging by the stacks of computer printouts that are seen holding up the ceiling, reports in some plans must be valued by weight. It is easy to believe that the more data and detail the better. When that happens, you get the classic problem of not seeing the forest for the trees, with the manager spending more time grinding through reports than managing. Computers are wonderful tools, but they can smother you with data. Know what to ask for and when to ask for it.

FOCUS

Reports may be focused in a variety of ways to reveal useful information. For example, the overall admission rate for the plan may be normal, but a report focusing on where the patients are admitted may reveal that most of the admissions are to high-cost or even nonparticipating hospitals. What follows is a general guide to the different ways in which data can be focused.

Plan Average

Plan average simply looks at the average performance for the entire plan. It is useful in that it will relate closely to the plan's financial performance. For example, if the plan is over budget in medical expense, a plan average report that reveals hospital admissions to be greatly over budget will allow management to focus on that

first. It also allows for comparative data between plans that may have somewhat different types of arrangements for the delivery of care.

Plan average is limited because it is relatively insensitive to specific causes of problems. That can be an advantage in some circumstances, however. In plans that manage by trying to keep performance clustered around a norm, that norm can sometimes be one of mediocrity. If the plan average reports and the provider-specific reports tie closely (i.e., there are no real outliers in performance), and if the plan is not doing as well as it should, then it is clear that there is a general problem of attitude or skills in the managers themselves and not a problem with a few recalcitrant providers or hospitals.

Plan average reports are frequently required by regulatory agencies and are also useful for reporting the overall performance of the plan to participating physicians and corporate parents. Plan average reports also function as the backdrop against which other reports are viewed. A plan with multiple lines of business, such as commercial, Medicare, and Medicaid, will probably create additional plan average reports that focus on each line of business.

Health Center, Individual Practice Association, Provider Organization, or Geographically Related Center

The purpose of this focus is to provide midlevel managers with data for their own areas of responsibility. In many plans, especially large or geographically diverse ones, it is common to divide up responsibility into manageable units. The problem of span of control in large or diverse plans can be a very real one. In closed panels this often refers to a health center or a small number of geographically related health centers. In open panels, this usually refers to discrete multiple individual practice associations (IPAs), subunits within the overall health plan (e.g., pools of doctors [PODs]), or geographically divided territories. In plans that contract with vertical IDSs, such as physician–hospital organizations or management services organizations (see

Chapter 4 for a discussion of such systems), it will be important to develop reports focused on each individual IDS.

Individual Physician

Most managed care plans produce reports that focus on individual physicians. This may refer to PCPs who are functioning as gatekeepers or care coordinators but may apply equally to open access health maintenance organizations (HMOs) or preferred provider organizations (PPOs). Virtually all the types of utilization reports discussed later in this chapter are amenable to focusing on individual physicians.

Physicians become understandably paranoid about the plethora of reports that are produced about them. They feel that they are being judged by machines or by standards that fail to take into account any extenuating circumstances and that their fate will be decided on the basis of sterile reports. In truth, it is the ability to report the behavior of individual physicians that provides managed care plans with their most powerful tool and physicians with their greatest source of both concern and potential help.

Care must be taken when one is using physician-specific reports. The medical director must look behind the data of the report for the reasons for the reported performance. This is not to say that any behavior should be rationalized, and physicians are as adept as anybody in arguing that they are different and should not be held to the same standards as anyone else. Rather, this is to say that individual physician performance reports need to be used intelligently and properly.

Service or Vendor Type

This type of report refers to the entity delivering the service (e.g., a hospital or a type of referral specialist). Focusing reports on those delivering the service (sometimes referred to as vendors) will be of great value when one is negotiating contracts and will allow for improved utilization control. These types of reports also help focus on areas where attention should be

directed. Remember Sutton's law: Go where the money is!

Employer Group

This type of report tracks utilization and other data by enrolled group. For those plans that are allowed to experience rate, this will be necessary to develop the actual cost experience; even for those plans that must community rate, these data will tell you whether you have a problem with a particular group that may need to be addressed (see Chapters 43 and 44 for discussions of underwriting). Also, some large employers are demanding such data as a requisite for offering your plan to their employees.

HOSPITAL UTILIZATION REPORTS

Routine hospital utilization management reports may be divided into two categories: the daily log and monthly summaries. Many plans now automate their utilization management systems (see Chapter 17). In addition to producing reports as discussed below, these systems allow for on-line access to far more information than would be practical on a printed report. Nevertheless, printed reports regarding hospital utilization remain useful to medical managers, who may review them in a manner and time not possible if they were required to stare at a computer terminal.

Daily Log

It is almost a requirement for a managed care plan to produce a daily hospital log. This document serves as a working tool for the utilization management nurse and the medical director in controlling institutional utilization. Its design should be directed toward providing the necessary information to manage cases actively that are current or prospective. Data should be sorted and printed by whatever management criteria make sense. For example, you may wish to print each hospital's census separately so that the utilization review nurse can take it when making hospital rounds. In plans where associate medical directors will have primary responsibility, you may want to print the log so that it sorts by geographic region, IPA, IDS, or health center.

Useful information for any daily log includes elements illustrated in Exhibit 27–1. Information on a daily log that is also useful in most types of health plans is illustrated in Exhibit 27–2.

Monthly Summary

A monthly summary report of hospital utilization should also be produced. This differs somewhat from the daily log because it is used to identify patterns for overall management rather than to serve as a mechanism for performing concurrent utilization review. A monthly report might include the data illustrated in Exhibit 27–3 for both the month ended and the year to date.

OUTPATIENT UTILIZATION

Although daily reports are necessary for controlling hospital utilization, in only the most tightly managed health plans will that be necessary for controlling outpatient utilization. In general, outpatient utilization control is usually best done by using monthly reports, both routine and ad hoc. Reports should include data both for the month ended and for the year to date. Data may also be reported by month on a 12-month rolling basis. Data for such reports might include the elements illustrated in Exhibit 27–4, depending on the needs of medical management.

Categories of outpatient or ambulatory care may be divided into several components, each of which has its own unique characteristics. Office visits for primary care, including any testing or procedures, is one such category, as is the related category of office visits for specialty care. Ambulatory procedures are a different matter, however, as is the setting for the procedure. The identical procedure may be performed in a physician's office, an ambulatory care center, or the outpatient department of a hospital.

Exhibit 27–1 Minimum Data Elements for a Daily Hospital Log

Current census
- Name of patient
- Hospital
- Diagnosis and procedures
- PCP
- Admitting physician
- Consultants or specialists
- Admission date
- Length of stay to date
- Free text narrative with clinical information
- In-network compared with out-of-network status

Hospital statistics
- Days per 1,000 today
- Days per 1,000 month to date

Prospective admits and outpatient surgeries

Exhibit 27–2 Additional Useful Data Elements for a Daily Hospital Log

Service type (as part of current census)
- Medicine
- Surgery
- Pediatrics
- Gynecologic surgery
- Obstetrics
- Mental health
- Chemical dependency
- Intensive care unit/cardiac care unit
- Neonatal intensive care unit
- Rehabilitation
- Outpatient surgery

Estimated length of stay or maximum length of stay
Admissions and discharges today and month to date
Authorization or denial status
Catastrophic case report
Line of business code
- Commercial
- Medicare
- Medicaid
- Self-insured versus fully insured
- Special accounts

Some plans have addressed the issue of ambulatory care, especially outpatient procedures, by using statistical groupings. One method is ambulatory patient groups (APGs), a method developed under contract by 3M Systems for the

Exhibit 27–3 Sample Data Elements for a Monthly Summary of Hospital Utilization*

Plan statistics
- Days per 1,000
- Admissions per 1,000
- Average length of stay
- Average per diem cost
- Average per case (per admission) cost
- Emergency department visits and average cost

Hospital- and provider-specific statistics
- Days per 1,000
- Admissions per 1,000
- Average length of stay
- Average per diem cost
- Average per case (per admission) cost
- Emergency department visits and average cost

Statistics by service type (see Exhibit 27–2)
- Days per 1,000
- Admissions per 1,000
- Average length of stay
- Average per diem cost
- Average per case (per admission) cost

Retrospective authorizations

Pended cases for review

In-network compared with out-of-network statistics

Number and percentage of denied days

* The plan will want to produce these statistics not only for the entire plan but for major lines of business as well (i.e., commercial, Medicare, Medicaid, self-insured versus fully insured, and so forth). The plan may also want to report year-to-date.

Exhibit 27–4 Sample Data for a Monthly Summary of Outpatient Utilization*

Primary care encounter rates
- Visits per day (closed panels only)
- Visits per member per year (annualized)
- Percentage of new visits
- Revisit interval rates (to look for churning)

Preventive care
- Immunization rates
- Mammography
- Pap smears
- Other

Laboratory/pathology utilization per visit

Radiology utilization per visit
- Total
- Focused (e.g., magnetic resonance imaging)

Prescriptions
- Prescriptions per visit or prescriptions per member per year
- Average cost per prescription
- Percentage generic

Referral utilization
- Referral rate per 100 primary care visits or per 1,000 members per year
- Comparison of PCP referral rate with peer group referral rate
- Initial referrals only compared with total referral visits
- Cost per referral by PCP, plan average, and specialty
- Number of visits and cost by specialty
  1. Top specialty referrals for each PCP
  2. Average cost per visit
  3. Per member per month cost by specialty

Out-of-network specialty care in point-of-service plans
- Percentage of total specialty care
- Cost
- Specialty and utilization categories

Ambulatory procedures
- By ambulatory patient groups
- By ambulatory care groups and ambulatory diagnosis groups
- By diagnostic or procedure code

Ancillary care
- Physical therapy and other rehabilitation therapies
- Podiatry
- Eye care
- Oral surgery
- Other

* The plan will want to produce these statistics not only for the entire plan but for major lines of business as well (i.e., commercial, Medicare, Medicaid, self-insured versus fully insured, and so forth). The plan may also want to report year-to-date.

Health Care Financing Administration for use in Medicare (Medicare has yet to use them as this chapter is being written, but a number of private health plans have adopted them for reimbursement purposes; see Chapter 14). APGs are to outpatient services what diagnosis-related groups (DRGs) are to inpatient ones, although APGs are based on procedures rather than simply on diagnoses and are considerably more complex. Under APGs, all the services associated with a given outpatient procedure or visit are bundled into the APG reimbursement. More than one APG may be billed if more than one procedure is performed, but there is significant discounting for additional APGs. There are 297 APGs, and if the number of events is quite high, a plan may analyze them all; most plans, however, will probably need to cluster the APGs into sets to achieve statistical validity.

Another statistical approach is to use ambulatory care groups (ACGs), a methodology that focuses on a resource-based measure of burden of illness.[3] Ambulatory patients are monitored for all encounters, and each encounter is classified as one of 34 ambulatory diagnosis groups (ADGs) based on medical resource used over a 1-year period and on the expectation of recurrence of that diagnosis over time. The set of ADGs for each patient is then combined with measures of age and sex to assign the patient to 1 of 51 mutually exclusive ACGs. ADGs and ACGs may also be looked at independently.[4] ACG and ADG methodology requires a high level of statistical sophistication, and the programming is not always found in the plan's MIS.

As has been mentioned earlier, once you decide on the routine reports, you can use those to decide what reports to request on an ad hoc basis. For example, if total expenses for cardiology appear to be high, you could investigate further by requesting reports that show who is ordering the referrals, what ancillary testing is being done, which specialists are seeing the patients and how much are they charging, and so forth.

Open access systems, or systems that do not use a PCP gatekeeper model, present special problems in monitoring utilization. In a PPO or managed indemnity plan, there will be no physician-specific membership base to use as a denominator. In HMOs that allow open access to specialists or allow specialists to self-authorize revisits or secondarily to authorize referrals to other specialists, there will be no way to measure specialist utilization against a fixed membership base (the base is only for the PCPs, not the specialists).

In these situations, you must be willing to accept less precise methods of measuring utilization of referral services and specialist utilization. Reports should focus on those areas under the control of the specialist as well as the PCP. Examples of such data elements are illustrated in Exhibit 27–5.

PROVIDER PROFILING

Closely related to all the issues discussed in this chapter is provider profiling. Profiling means the collection, collation, and analysis of data to develop provider-specific profiles. Such profiles have a variety of uses, but the most important ones are producing provider feedback reports to help the providers modify their own behavior, recruiting providers into the network, and choosing which providers may not be (or are not) the right fit with the plan's managed care philosophy and goals. Other uses include determining specialists to whom the plan will send certain types of cases, detecting fraud and abuse, determining how to focus the utilization management program, supporting performance-based reimbursement systems, and performing economic modeling.

The initial focus of many physician profiling activities has been inpatient care. A hospital case is usually easily definable (except for cases that are transferred or readmitted), and the physicians delivering care are usually identifiable. The cost of inpatient care has also led to this focus. Basic hospital care profiling (adjusted for case mix and severity; see below) combined with feedback to physicians and active intervention has been shown to reduce length of stay effectively.[5] Recent activity has shifted to considering outpatient care as well because it has been recognized that care occurs across a continuum rather than in isolated episodes.

Some provider profiling systems simply look at the behavior of the provider against certain norms. Comparison against norms is certainly necessary, but it is fraught with difficulties. The chief difficulty is defining the norm, but an attendant difficulty is choosing what to look at. Most profiling activities focus solely on the actions of the provider. It is better to attempt to examine provider behavior from the standpoint of total health care resource consumption and outcome, including resources not directly delivered or billed by the provider, and to look at true episodes of care and outcomes as opposed to constellations of single visits.

Exhibit 27–5 Sample Data for an Open Access Model Plan

Outpatient Services
- Average number of visits per member per year
- Average number of visits per member per year to each specialty
- Diagnostic utilization per visit
  1. Laboratory
  2. Radiology and imaging
  3. Other
- Average cost per visit
- Procedures per 1,000 visits per year (annualized)
  1. Aggregate
  2. By procedure for top 10 by specialty type
  3. By individual specialist
- Average cost per episode (as defined for each sentinel diagnosis) over a defined time period, including charges not directly billed by provider

Inpatient Services
- Average total cost per case, including charges not billed by provider, for hospitalized cases
- Average length of stay for defined procedures
- Average rate of performance of a procedure, such as:
  1. Cesarean section rate
  2. Hysterectomy rate
  3. Transurethral prostatectomy rate
  4. Cardiac procedures
- Readmission rate or complication rate
- Use of resources before and after the hospitalization

Episodes of Care

Episodes of care are defined as time-related intervals that have meaning to the behavior you are trying to measure. Episodes may vary considerably both by clinical condition and by the provider type that is being measured. In the case of obstetrics, obvious measures such as cesarean section rate and average length of stay are important but will not reveal the full picture. Looking at the entire prenatal and postnatal episode may reveal significant differences in the use of ultrasound and other diagnostics or perhaps a great deal of unbundled claims during the prenatal period. In the case of some medical conditions, the episode may extend over the course of years. Furthermore, it is possible in patients with multiple medical conditions to have overlapping episodes of care, making it more difficult to sort out what resources are being used for what episode.

Related to the issue of episode is the problem of identifying which provider is actually responsible for care. As an example, an internist may be responsible for the care of a diabetic but may have little responsibility for managing that patient's broken leg other than to refer the patient to a cost-effective orthopedist. This issue is also difficult regarding hospitalized patients. It is not uncommon for the admitting physician not to be the attending physician, especially when surgery is involved.

The hallmark of episode definition is the ability to link up all the health care resources into a defined event. This may mean diagnostic services (e.g., laboratory or imaging), therapeutic services (e.g., physical therapy), consultations, outpatient visits, and inpatient visits. In other words, it must be a patient-based analysis rather than a provider-based one; the analysis of the behavior of providers is a product of examining what happens to their patients.

Adjusting for Severity and Case Mix

Case mix and severity are always issues of contention when one is profiling providers: Providers with costly profiles will always complain that they have the sickest patients. When you are performing profiling, the issue of severity must be accounted for. One technique for doing so is to use severity of illness indicators. Severity of illness is most often used in hospital cases (using, for example, 3M's all-patient DRGs, which assign patients to DRGs and adjust that based on four levels of severity), but it may be applied to outpatient care as well (with some difficulty by using, for example, APGs, ACGs, and ADGs). Statistical manipulation, such as trimming in outlier cases, is also commonly employed (i.e., if only a few cases are outliers, one brings those cases back to the mean).

Adjusting for severity and case mix is important and cannot be bypassed. It is interesting to note, however, that it probably accounts for only a small amount of the variation noted in practice behavior. At least one study has reported that adjusting for severity and case mix significantly reduced the number of physicians who appeared to be outliers, although there was some discussion as to whether the methodology actually made genuine outliers look normal.[6,7] Other studies have reported that these adjustments accounted for little of the variation in practice that was found.[8–10]

Practices will also have differences in the age and sex make-up of their patient panel that must be accounted for. Geographic differences may also account for utilization variations. These must be factored into any profiling report. Even within a single specialty there will be differences in how "specialized" a specialist is. For example, a specialist may have a larger percentage of primary care or may not care for patients in the intensive care unit. The plan therefore will want to look at the degree to which a physician is truly a specialist in his or her mix of routine and complex cases.

Comparing the Results of Profiling

Practice profiles are of no use unless the results are compared with some type of standard. There are certain problems inherent in comparisons of provider profiles. All these problems are resolvable, but medical managers need to be aware of them before embarking on profiling.

The usual way of comparing profiling results is to provide data for each individual practice in comparison with one or more of the following:

- *Plan average results*—This standard is simply the average for the entire plan. It is the crudest method of comparison.

- *IPA, POD, or IDS*—A variation on plan average, this compares the practice only with other practices within a smaller set of providers than the entire network. This approach may be combined with multiple

other approaches when a plan contracts through organized provider systems. Another variation on this is geography even in the absence of organized provider groups.

- *Specialty or peer group*—This compares each practice only with its own specialty. For example, internists are only compared with other internists.

- *Peer group adjusted for age, sex, and case mix/severity of illness*—This is the most complicated approach, as noted earlier, but provides the most meaningful comparative data.

- *Budget*—This compares the profile with budgeted utilization and cost, a necessary activity when providers are accepting full or substantial risk for medical expenses.

It is not always clear what specialty a physician really is practicing. Most plans have provider files that indicate what specialty type a physician has self-indicated, but it is surprising how often that information does not match up with specialty indicators in the claims file. Of course, plans that perform comprehensive verification of board specialty status will have more accurate data than plans that depend on self-reporting by physicians. Even when the specialty designation is accurate, there is no guarantee that the provider actually makes a living at that specialty.

The problem of provider specialty definition is particularly acute when one is looking at primary care. Many board-certified medical specialists actually spend a considerable amount of time performing primary care, whereas others spend the majority of their time practicing true specialty medicine. This has great implications for how a plan will evaluate performance of specialists as well as PCPs when comparisons with peers are used (as they almost always are). A related issue is determining which physicians will be considered specialists at all because the plan may not want to send referrals to a specialist who is not particularly active in his or her designated specialty.

Even when the issue of specialty definition is resolved, there remains the problem that no two practices are exactly alike. As an example, either general internists perform flexible sigmoidoscopies, or they do not. If one looks only at charge patterns, the internist who performs the procedure will look more expensive compared with the internist who does not, but that analysis will fail to pick up the fact that the internist who does not perform flexible sigmoidoscopies instead refers them all to a gastroenterologist who charges more than the first internist (of course, the first internist could be overutilizing the procedure, but that is a separate part of the analysis).

The next issue is the problem of providers who behave as though they are in a group but are not legally connected and do not appear as a group in the plan's provider file. An example would be two physicians who share an office, share on-call duty, and see each other's patients but who have different tax numbers and billing services. The reason that this is important in managed care is that, if the plan contracts with one but not the other, the member may wind up seeing the nonparticipating physician and be subject to balance billing. Even if the physicians agree not to balance bill, the plan still may not actually want the other physician in the network, even on an occasional basis.

Related to the above is the ability to detect linkages between practices and ancillary services. Examples include orthopedists who own physical therapy practices and neurologists who have a proprietary interest in a magnetic resonance imaging center.

Incorporation of Other Data

Many plans incorporate other data into a provider profile analysis. Claims and encounter data are enormously useful, as are data from hospital episodes, but there are additional sources of data as well. Credentialing data (see Chapters 8 and 57) may be automated and referenced. Data from member services, such as complaints, transfer rates, or administrative problems, may be incorporated (see Chapter 30). Data from the quality management program (see Chapter 25) and member satisfaction are now included in the profiling reports and even compensation programs of advanced managed care organizations (see Chapter 11).

Feedback

Medical management reports should not be confined to plan managers. As mentioned in several chapters in this book (especially Chapter 26), feedback to providers is a useful adjunct to other medical management activities. Feedback to providers must be clear, easy to understand, and accurate.

Feedback should be meaningful and useful to both parties, not just the plan or the provider. When feedback reports are clearly linked with performance expectations, and when such reports can help a provider alter a behavior in a positive way (which will in turn benefit that provider), then feedback may be successful. This is especially true when feedback is linked to the financial incentive system.

Providers will alter their behavior in response to feedback for a variety of reasons. Natural competitiveness and peer pressure may exert influence. More important, the opportunity to increase market share and to improve their revenue will be a powerful reason to respond to feedback. Fear of possible adverse actions by the plan may also play a role if a provider is a clear outlier and if feedback provides a concrete measure of expectation by the plan.

Hospitals may benefit from feedback reports as well. Hospitals are providers in their own right, even though the physicians on staff give the orders. Nevertheless, hospitals have their own policies and procedures that influence how care is rendered, and hospitals certainly have their own billing practices. Hospitals can also have a strong role in influencing the practice behavior of the physicians on staff and can work effectively with managed care plans to effect changes.

Feedback is not always effective in changing behavior, however. The topic of changing physician behavior, including the use of data and feedback, is discussed in Chapter 26.

Focused Utilization Management

As noted earlier, profiling provides medical managers with the ability to focus utilization management more efficiently. Some providers may perform at such a high level of cost effectiveness that the plan can essentially rely on feedback and case management support rather than on more traditional methods of managing utilization; in other words, those providers would need little oversight or intervention by the plan. In other cases, the plan may determine that heightened levels of utilization review and precertification are required for some providers who are clear outliers.

Profiling and data management may also reveal systemwide issues of utilization that require a broad approach. For example, it may be found that emergency department usage is uniformly high and not due to a small number of outlier physicians. In that case, a focused approach to demand management (see Chapter 17) would have greater utility than focusing on individual physician behavior.

Last, profiling will enable the medical director to determine which specialists should receive more referrals and preferential business in contrast to those specialists who are less cost effective, of lesser quality, or simply too low volume in a competitive market.

CONCLUSION

Medical management reports are powerful and absolutely necessary tools for managers of health plans. Routine reports need to be simple to read and compact and must provide only those data required generally to manage the plan. They need to provide managers with sufficient information to order ad hoc, detailed reports required to solve specific problems that are flagged by the routine reports. Provider profiling is taking on an ever greater role in managed care but remains a complex area. Data overload is a frequent and

deadly problem in managed care, but intelligent use of reports should prevent that from occurring. As systems evolve, the ability of managers to access useful information directly and manipulate it as needed will provide a clear competitive edge.

REFERENCES AND NOTES

1. R.D. Lasker, et al., Realizing the Potential of Practice Pattern Profiling, *Inquiry* 29 (1992): 287–297.
2. R. Nathanson, et al., Using Claims Data To Select Primary Care Physicians for a Managed Care Network, *Managed Care Quarterly* 2 (1994): 50–59.
3. B. Starfield, et al., Ambulatory Care Groups: A Categorization of Diagnoses for Research and Management, *Health Services Research* 26 (1991): 53–74.
4. J. Weiner, et al., Development and Application of a Population Oriented Measure of Ambulatory Care Case-Mix, *Medical Care* 29 (1991): 452–472.
5. G. Bennett, et al., Case Study in Physician Profiling, *Managed Care Quarterly* 2 (1994): 60–70.
6. S. Salem-Schatz, et al., The Case for Case-Mix Adjustment in Practice Profiling: When Good Apples Look Bad, *Journal of the American Medical Association* 272 (1994): 871–874.
7. H.G. Welch, et al., Case-Mix Adjustment: Making Bad Apples Look Good, *Journal of the American Medical Association* 273 (1995): 772–773.
8. Bennett, et al., Case Study in Physician Profiling.
9. Nathanson, et al., Using Claims Data To Select Primary Care Physicians.
10. H.G. Welch, et al., Physician Profiling: An Analysis of Inpatient Practice Patterns in Florida and Oregon, *New England Journal of Medicine* 330 (1994): 607–612.

SUGGESTED READING

Betty, W.R., et al. 1990. Physician Practice Profiles: A Valuable Information System for HMOs. *Medical Group Management* 37: 68–75.

Blackwood, M.J. 1994. Utilization Management and Data Acquisition: A Case Study. *Benefits Quarterly* 10(3): 38–42.

Boll, A. and McCafferty, C. 1994. Why Managed Care Needs Encounter-based Systems. *Healthcare Infomatics* 11(2): 78, 80.

Braham, R.L., and Ruchlin, H.S. 1987. Physician Practice Profiles: A Case Study of the Use of Audit and Feedback in an Ambulatory Care Group Practice. *Health Care Management Review* 12: 11–16.

Doubilet, P., et al. 1986. Use and Misuse of the Term "Cost Effective" in Medicine. *New England Journal Medicine* 314: 253–256.

Eisenberg, J.M. 1989. Clinical Economics: A Guide to the Economic Analysis of Clinical Practices. *Journal of the American Medical Association* 262: 2879–2886.

Goldfield, N., and Boland, P. 1996. *Physician Profiling and Risk Adjustment*. Gaithersburg, Md.: Aspen Publishers, Inc.

Gotowka, T.D., et al. 1993. Health Data Analysis and Reporting: Organization and System Strategies. *Managed Care Quarterly* 1: 26–34.

Harris, J.S. 1991. Watching the Numbers: Basic Data for Health Care Management. *Journal of Occupational Medicine* 33: 275–278.

Hughes, R.G., and Lee, D.E. 1991. Using Data Describing Physician Inpatient Practice Patterns: Issues and Opportunities. *Health Care Management Review* 16: 33–40.

Kenkel, P.J. 1995. *Report Cards: What Every Health Provider Needs to Know About HEDIS and Other Performance Measures*. Gaithersburg, Md.: Aspen Publishers.

Nathanson, P., Noether, M., et al. 1994. Using Claims Data to Select Primary Care Physicians for a Managed Care Network. *Managed Care Quarterly* 2(4): 50–59.

Physician Payment Review Commission. 1992. *Physician Payment Review Commission Conference on Profiling*. Washington, D.C.: Physician Payment Review Commission.

Wang, H., Sharp, V., and Coulter, C. 1994. Creating an Information System for Evaluating HMO Performance. *Managed Care Medicine* 1(5): 43–44, 46–49.

Operational Management and Marketing

"We could manage this matter to a T."

Sterne
Tristram Shandy, bk. II, ch. 5, 1760

Operational Management and Marketing

Chapter 28

Information Systems Operations and Organization Structures

Robert Reese

Numerous contributing items have caused many health care organizations to view their information systems (IS) operations differently from other operations. The lack of enterprise-wide technology-enabled systems and the focus of available applications on internal operating procedures led many health care organizations in the past to view their IS operations as an operating expense. As efforts have been made to control or reduce costs, many organizations have focused on reducing their operating costs by targeting IS operations in the budget wars.

Today, health care organizations, specifically managed care organizations (MCOs), better understand the ability of technology-enabled systems to lower their operating costs and manage the entire enterprise. Technology-enabled systems are now viewed as an investment in the future of the enterprise rather than an expense. As a result, many health care organizations are exploring the most efficient means of building and supporting technology-enabled systems throughout their enterprises.

The health care industry, however, lags behind other industries, such as manufacturing and banking, in its investment in information technology. In fact, health care organizations spend, on average, about 2 percent of their operating expenses on information technology, whereas heavy manufacturing companies spend 6 to 8 percent and banking firms spend from 8 to 12

percent.[1] As a result of minimal investment, information technologies in many hospitals can be characterized as disjointed service-specific applications with little internal or external connectivity.

The managed care industry is no exception to this low level of investment. In a review of Ernst & Young managed care clients conducted in the fall of 1994, IS expenditures were expected to be in the range of 1.4 percent to 2.2 percent of revenues. The bulk of the expenditures in this study was expected to be in the areas of application software. The focus was to be enhancing clinical competency, particularly outcomes analysis and demand management. Additionally, money was to be used to expand the use of technology to enhance the primary and specialty physicians' knowledge and use of established regional and national practice guidelines to improve overall patient care.

This low level of investment is quickly changing, as evidenced by the 1995 Health Information Management Systems Society survey.[2] In that survey, 80 percent of the chief information officers (CIOs) who responded indicated that their IS budgets were growing. In addition, the vendor marketplace for health care information technology is growing. In October 1995, the *New York Times* noted that "health care could be the biggest growth market [for vendors of information technology] in the 1990s, exceeding $20 billion in sales annually by the turn of the century."[3(p.41)]

As managed care contracting and capitation expand to dominate the U.S. market, low-cost

Robert Reese is a partner with Ernst & Young LLP in Detroit, Michigan. He specializes in information technology issues relative to managed care.

health care providers who can quickly and efficiently share information will have a distinct advantage. MCOs and integrated delivery systems (see Chapter 4) have already begun to transition themselves toward reduced cost by leveraging new technologies and providing value through information management among physicians and patients and between payers and providers.

GENERAL ORGANIZATION STRUCTURE AND REPORTING RELATIONSHIPS

Organizational structure and reporting relationships are vital to the successful management of the IS operations within the MCO. A CIO is necessary to oversee the entire MCO as well as to represent IS operations on the enterprise's strategic planning committee. The CIO's main responsibility is to align the IS operations with the strategic direction of the MCO as well as to ensure that targeted efficiencies are achieved.

An IS strategic planning committee should be established to oversee the continuum of IS operations. This committee should identify a vision statement that is consistent with the MCO's operations to direct all business decisions and initiatives within the IS department. The MCO's chief operating officer and a representative from finance should participate on this committee to help ensure alignment with the MCO's strategic and financial direction.

Directors of IS operations, depending on the size of the organization, should have responsibility for each of the separate operating entities (e.g., claims and benefits administration, ambulatory care services, etc.) within the MCO. Their primary responsibility is to ensure alignment with the strategic direction within their entity and to oversee the day-to-day IS operations. The directors should be members of the IS strategic planning committee. Within each entity, IS teams should be established to support and meet the needs of a specific customer base.

Purchasing, hardware support and maintenance, employee training, and application support should function independent of the MCO's operating entities and should operate under the leadership of individual directors. As members of the IS strategic planning committee, these directors should be under the direction of the committee. A sample organizational structure is illustrated in Figure 28–1.

ANNUAL OPERATING GOALS WITH QUARTERLY UPDATES FOR REFINEMENTS

Because of the strong alignment between effective technology-enabled systems and the success of the MCO, it is important that IS operations, the means of building and supporting the technology-enabled systems, be included in the MCO's strategic plan and be given specific operating goals that help move the MCO in the direction of its strategic plan. The IS operating goals should be developed annually in conjunction with the MCO's strategic plan. Goals should include at least the following: the MCO's strategic goals, the IS divisions' supporting strategic goals, a list of approved IS projects that have been included in the annual capital budget, IS staffing and educational requirements, the annual IS budget, and long-term (3- to 5-year) IS plans. Built-in quarterly reviews and updates prevent getting off track or falling behind.

COST MANAGEMENT

When structuring contractual agreements with their customers (or internal departments) in the past, many organizations closely examined the operating procedures of the primary business and included IS operations as free or set-fee support for the primary business process. This type of IS cost structuring increases the difficulty of IS providing quality service and provides no means to link the size of the customer base supported to the level of information technology provided.

As an effective component of cost accounting, a mechanism to help manage IS costs is to charge each customer or department for the rela-

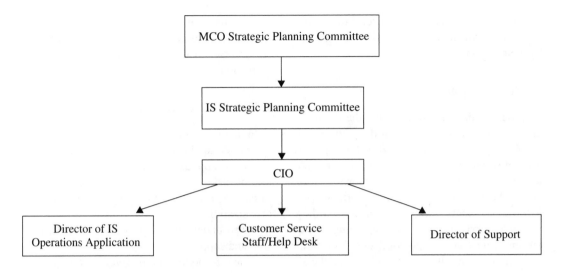

Figure 28–1 Sample IS organizational structure.

tive amount of IS services utilized on a per member per month (PMPM) basis. The PMPM effectively increases or decreases IS revenues as the customer base, and the resulting amount of IS support, grows or shrinks.

CLIENT RELATIONSHIPS

The IS department generally has more customers than any other department within the MCO. Its customers or clients include every staff member who uses the IS and every staff member who utilizes the data (reports and so forth) produced by the IS. All the constituencies may make requests to the IS department about the format and content of reports, the format and content of user workstation screens, and application errors. This flexibility places a significant responsibility on the department to manage its staff and prioritize user requests.

One of the goals of a progressive IS organization is to help users become more proactive, responsible, and accountable for identifying systems needs and assisting with implementations. To meet the daily and long-term needs of the users and the members of the MCO, an effective

IS department must develop an enterprisewide user support philosophy.

Client Support Philosophy

In the past, most IS departments have operated in a reactive mode to client end-user requests for application enhancements and/or support. Often, the end-user would have to track down an individual within the IS division to issue a request. The schedule of the IS department would often determine the priority level of the request. IS would then react to the request by developing and implementing a solution. Most commonly, the solution would address only the immediate request and not the long-term impact as time became a limiting factor and more requests were being made. In this scenario, the end-user had little input into how the IS department prioritized or completed user requests, and users often became disillusioned and frustrated.

In an effort to provide quality community service today, MCOs are implementing quality initiatives throughout their organizations. Effective IS services, whether owned or outsourced, are beginning to develop service level agreements, customer teams, and user satisfaction surveys to provide the level of service expected by their customers.

Service Level Agreements

Under the direction of the CIO, the IS strategic planning committee should develop service level agreements that clearly define the expected level of service that IS operations are to provide to their customers and a recourse for scenarios where the level of service falls short. Service level agreements, also known as guiding principles, serve as boundaries regarding expectations, roles, and responsibilities for senior management, the user community, and the IS department. The agreement should address such areas as expectations of support provided by each party, the working relationships among the three parties, how IS-related projects are coordinated from project initiation through postimplementation, and benefits realization. The agreement should also drive the philosophy of the customer teams and satisfaction surveys.

Customer Teams

Today, MCOs are assigning teams to work with each constituency. These teams develop an understanding of the business issues facing the customer and work with the customer to develop systems (people, processes, and technology) to improve the business process. In this manner, MCOs are taking a proactive approach to improving operations and reducing costs.

User Satisfaction Surveys

User satisfaction surveys are tools that review the effectiveness of the IS operations and provide insight into possible operational improvements within the MCO. User satisfaction surveys should be used annually or semiannually and should include questions relating to the following: IS operations improvement opportunities, upcoming legislative or client issues that

could affect the business, and training requirements. When used effectively, user satisfaction surveys can provide a tremendous amount of information.

INTELLECTUAL PROPERTY

In many organizations, it is common practice to develop applications in house and then interface those applications with a packaged application or make modifications to the packaged application directly. For legal reasons, the organization adding to the package application needs to understand fully the issues of ownership and support.

When an organization develops an application and then integrates it with a packaged solution, the vendor that developed the original package may gain ownership rights to the application. The same holds true for modifications made to the source code of the package solution in that the organization that developed the original package gains the ownership rights of the modifications. Before signing the software licensing agreement, the organization should negotiate with the vendor to retain the right to any software developed by the organization.

Support agreements can also be affected by in-house source code and/or package modifications. In almost all cases, when modifications are made to any source code or package by anyone other than the company that originally produced the package, the vendor will no longer support the product. Support issues are important to understand because in-house modifications to an application may adversely affect the IS operations and thus the MCO.

OUTSOURCING VERSUS OWNERSHIP

Although many readers may assume that information technology is an internally managed function, this is not always strictly the case. As a result of the expertise required to purchase, install, and manage IS operations within an organization, many health care companies choose to contract with outside vendors to provide the information technology to meet their needs. For some MCOs, outsourcing all or part of their IS operations has significant potential to provide quality customer service while reducing operating costs. The central issue is to examine closely each function that the IS division performs, compare those functions with vendors' products and services, and identify areas that may benefit from outsourcing.

The level of outsourcing, as in other industries, can vary significantly from providing limited application support to providing complete IS staff and technology. Similarly, the types of organizations that provide outsourcing services range from consulting firms, to health care IS hardware and software vendors, to neighboring (noncompeting) or organizationally related health care organizations with excess resources.

Outsourcing has (or can have) many benefits. The most notable benefit is when another company, whose service is its core competency, can provide the service in a more cost-effective and cost-efficient manner than can be achieved by providing the service in house. Outsourcing can allow an organization to focus on its core business while providing access to state-of-the-art technology and scarce resources. From a cost standpoint, it can preserve capital resources while reducing and providing for predictable operating costs. Some additional benefits include guaranteed levels of service, shared risk, and improved user satisfaction.

Areas that commonly reap benefits from outsourcing are management, purchasing, hardware support and maintenance, employee training, specific application support, and application development. Outsourcing the purchasing function often leads to volume discounts, consistencies among purchased equipment, and better inventory tracking and control. Outsourcing other areas often improves quality while reducing necessary staffing levels. Again, each area being considered for outsourcing should be examined closely and weighed against the value of ownership of that area.

Many of the outsourcing contracts over the past 5 years have involved some form of upfront payment by the vendor. Some of the payments provided cash for capital equipment acquired as part of the contract. In return, the vendor received a long-term annuity agreement. The term, usually 10 to 15 years, enabled the vendor to begin to expect a certain level of cash flow. It was this guaranteed cash flow that enabled many of the vendors to experience substantial increases in the value of their companies. Because the cost of technology (most notably hardware) has dropped dramatically, however, clients now realize that they are paying far more than the vendor's true cost plus margin. It is for this reason, along with other lesser issues, that many of the outsourcing agreements of the past are being renegotiated. MCOs should regard outsourcing as an option when deciding to focus on core services.

HARDWARE CONSIDERATIONS

Mainframes, Minis, and Personal Computers

A variety of hardware environments, including mainframes, midrange systems, minis, and personal computers (PCs), exist for today's MCO. As would be expected, support issues vary among these environments. In general, mainframe and midrange systems require greater support resources than minis and PCs. Mainframe and midrange systems are often proprietary systems, making little or no use of industry standards and requiring a great deal of time and effort to interface with other systems. Most mainframe and midrange applications are written in a first- or second-generation programming language and do not maximize the potential of the powerful development tools and commercial applications that are available for the mini and PC environment.

Conversion/Migration

Although most organizations simply cannot afford to replace all their legacy systems at one time, migration of these legacy systems to more open, distributed network models is common. It should be noted that, during the migration period, both environments must be supported.

A support consideration when the organization is moving from a mainframe or midrange system to a more distributed system is the migration (conversion) itself. This process is complex and requires numerous resources, both user and IS operations involvement, and a strong organizational commitment to be successful. Conversion strategies and work plans should be developed in advance for all the following: infrastructure migration, application migration, process improvement (developing new procedures to capitalize on the efficiencies of the new applications), training schedules, and job definitions.

"Throw-Away" Solutions

Once the decision has been made to migrate from one environment to another, IS resources should focus on performing the migration. As is often the case, organizations will attempt to migrate to a new platform while continuing normal operation on the existing platform. Attention should be paid to reducing the number of throw-away solutions, that is, those solutions made specifically for a system that will soon be obsolete. Efforts should also be made continuously to eliminate the development of short-lived (single-use) system solutions. This is more likely to occur in the mini and PC environments because thousands of commercial applications can be purchased and installed quickly to fulfill immediate needs.

INTERCONNECTIVITY

The term *interconnectivity* refers to an enterprise's ability to allow multiple, disparate systems to share information from department to department, from the hospital to other entities in the enterprise, and from the enterprise to the insurance company or employer. The opportunities are significant. The following sections discuss some of the current and emerging trends in interconnectivity.

Types of Interconnectivity

Some in the health care IS industry have noted that the lack of spending in health care information technology has resulted in the technical and financial impossibility of acquiring a single system solution to meet all an MCO's needs. One study noted "Given the multitude of competing interests, a single, monolithic IS is a virtual impossibility in the near future."[4(p.189)] Therefore, methods for integrating disparate systems are essential to develop effective enterprisewide solutions.

System interconnectivity is occurring within institutions through system integration and between provider institutions and MCOs through electronic eligibility verification, authorizations, claim submission, and remittance advice receipts. In addition, interconnectivity exists between MCOs and banks through electronic reimbursement [electronic funds transmission (EFT)] and between hospitals and suppliers through electronic inventory management. In health care today, interconnectivities that occur among health care applications are primarily financial in nature (e.g., submitting a claim for payment, transferring funds electronically, and sending automated remittance advices to providers).

Managed care has already seen significant advances in interconnectivity with the development of patient eligibility and provider referrals. As the health care industry emerges into the information age, interconnectivity will include the exchange of financial and clinical information within and external to the enterprise and the full support of a computer-based patient record.

System Integration

The goal of integrating the various system platforms is seamless access to any network application and/or data through a single workstation. Although it is possible to maintain disjointed hardware and software systems, successful integration of all systems in the managed care network is vital to cost-effective support of interconnectivity. With disjointed hardware and software systems, building and managing the network interfaces necessary for seamless access are labor intensive.

Successful systems integration includes all the following components: universal cabling plans, integrated network electronics and components, telecommunication systems, an application integration gateway (interface system), application services (E-mail and file transfer), and enterprise network management tools.

Integration requires connectivity or the ability to plug any device into the system (network). Connectivity is not possible without common, enterprisewide (universal) cabling because various systems must be able to communicate at the lowest possible level. Integrated network electronics and components are necessary to achieve seamless access (i.e., the ability for users to traverse the network without needing to know where the information resides).

Managed care systems, at a minimum, must support the integration of multivendor applications and key strategic applications. The application integration gateway, necessary for traversal across the network, refers to the point where independent application services are reduced to their lowest common denominator. Enterprise network management tools give system administrators the ability to manage network security and transactions at each access point across the network.

Electronic Data Interchange Initiatives

Electronic data interchange (EDI) is a means for IS operations to exchange information in a common, standard methodology. Although many organizations, such as the American National Standards Institute (ANSI) and the Workgroup on Electronic Data Interchange, are working toward EDI standards, EDI is not yet fully developed for the health care industry. Numerous providers and MCOs are aiding in the definition and development process. Reportedly, 13 percent of all hospital IS budget increases in 1995 were attributable to advances in EDI.[5]

When EDI permeates the health care industry, the need for individual interface applications will be eliminated, thus allowing virtually all systems to share information more easily. More important, with the successful implementation of EDI, critical work flow procedures within health care facilities and the industry could be reengineered to eliminate and streamline many of the existing paper- and labor-intensive functions. As a result of EDI, the entire manner in which health care providers deliver services could change, leaving only the basic mission statement—to improve the health of our communities—unchanged.[6]

Implementing EDI across the enterprise continuum can be a difficult task. Once implemented, however, further EDI requirements can be expanded with little effort. One common example of an EDI initiative outside the health care industry is bar coding. Walk into a grocery store and look at the bottom or side of any product on the shelves, and you will see a one-inch square bar code with a number of lines varying in width and a series of numbers. The bar code is a standard in the industry, and a product can be taken to any grocery store and recognized by the bar code scanner. In the food services industry, the bar code allows both suppliers and grocers to inventory their products easily, and the grocer's need to maintain a large inventory is virtually eliminated. The status of the grocer's supply is electronically routed to the distributor. In addition, both the grocer and the supplier can easily track the purchasing patterns of their customers.[7] The distributor can deliver goods "just in time" to the grocer, eliminating labor- and paper-intensive inventorying.

The same EDI scenario can apply in a health care provider organization (e.g., in a hospital system or a closed panel health maintenance organization) in the daily provision of medical treatment. For example, while treatment is being administered to the patient, the caregivers can record the information into wireless, hand-held computers as opposed to making notes on paper. This information is critical to the ongoing treatment of the patient, and its usefulness can be maximized through the interconnected computerized medical record. The medical information can be sent instantaneously to appropriate caregivers throughout the facility, significantly reducing charting time, missing charts, and unnecessary or duplicated tests and facilitating the next steps in the treatment process. In addition, supplies could be ordered, treatment charts and work orders outlined and distributed, progress reports updated, surgeries and radiologic tests scheduled, and billing information accumulated and submitted. If necessary, providers from other facilities could also be notified. All this is happening at the same time as treatment is being administered.[8]

Electronic transfer of information is already occurring between and within institutions through nonstandard, proprietary formats. Individual interface programs are being written to exchange information between applications and organizations. Although EDI is not fully developed within the health care industry, standards are emerging for appointment scheduling, electronic eligibility verification, automated authorization and referrals, electronic claims submission, EFT, electronic remittance advice (ERA), and computerized medical records.

Eligibility Verification

In a managed care setting, various means of electronic verification are important to give health care service providers immediate and accurate service parameters for the patient, such as enrollment, eligibility, and benefits information. The utilization of electronic eligibility verification at the service entry point significantly reduces efforts to verify these service parameters, thus reducing manual intervention to obtain the information and reducing the number of noncovered treatments performed.

Although some argue that the patient can present an identification card indicating cover-

age, it is often the case that coverage has terminated without adequate notification to the provider. The provider must contact the MCO at each patient registration or risk providing services to ineligible patients, thus raising administrative costs and hassles for both organizations. Frequently, providers must write off services performed because the patient did not have coverage at the time of service or needed prior authorization or because the wrong amount of copayment was collected. With electronic eligibility verification, when the clerk enters the patient's name, up-to-date eligibility status is received, and the provider can be assured of payment. This reduces unnecessary ineligible claims for both the provider and the payer, along with the attendant costs and frustrations.

Within the industry, the electronic eligibility and benefits inquiry standard being developed is the ANSI ASC X12 (270 and 271).

Authorizations and Referrals

A key component in managed care is the presence of a system to monitor care for medical necessity. Interconnected information systems can greatly increase the effectiveness and efficiency of managed care authorization systems. As with electronic eligibility verification for members (patients), the MCO can provide an immediate automated authorization, or permission, to the provider of care.

The MCO determines which types of services and providers require preauthorization. To receive reimbursement, the provider [primary care physician (PCP) or specialist] must obtain authorization from the MCO to perform a service or refer a patient to another physician. The request to the managed care company can be made electronically at the provider site. The electronic request may be as simple as an electronic form that the provider completes on line and transmits to the plan. Most electronic authorization systems are more complex, however, containing editing fields to ensure that the referral or admission is to a participating provider and requiring that key data elements be provided. An electronic authorization system may also provide automatic information transfer (e.g., member status and demographics). More sophisticated systems could ensure that the referral provider is participating and can gather clinical information (from the patient's electronic medical record) and compare it with standard protocols before processing the authorization.[9]

The MCO may review the request and electronically provide authorization or denial for the service, or in some cases it may automatically issue an authorization number (e.g., in many MCOs, the PCP has the ability to refer to any participating specialist without prior review by the MCO). The authorization number can become part of the patient's master file and can be attached to the electronic claim when it is submitted. As a result, the need for hospital and physician office personnel to enter data, mail information, and speak directly with the MCO is significantly reduced. In addition, automated authorization systems can easily provide reports to the MCO for provider profiling (usage patterns) and to estimate incurred but not reported (IBNR) costs. The standard for electronic referrals is in development.

Electronic Claims Submission

Electronic claims submission is a mechanism that the Health Care Financing Administration (HCFA) and payers are utilizing to reduce paper flow and increase the accuracy and timeliness of claim submission. As patients receive treatment throughout the integrated delivery network, health care service providers electronically produce and submit the appropriate claim forms to the appropriate payer. As noted above, much of the patient and treatment information necessary for proper submission of the claim is generated from the provider's information system, thus reducing the labor necessary to complete paper forms as well as inadvertent data inaccuracies. Delays from using a mail service are also eliminated. The electronic claim forms flow directly into the payer's system while other MCOs' databases are queried and checked for duplicate ben-

efit requests. Specific claim and cost information of MCOs can also be made available to enable a health care facility to manage its claims appropriately.[10] For the MCO, this reduces the need for claim processors, as discussed in Chapter 31.

Over the past 5 years, the HCFA has been phasing in mandatory electronic claims submission for both Medicare A and Medicare B. As MCOs began to see the benefits and became more technology enabled, many also began accepting electronic claim submissions. The HCFA and payers are using many different standards for claims submission, however. This variability requires providers (hospitals and physicians) to spend many hours of programming time and funds to meet the data format requirements of the payers to which they send claims. Fortunately, an EDI standard, ANSI ASC X12 (837), is being developed for electronic claims and is a major step in the attempt to reduce health care administrative costs nationwide.

EFT/ERA

After proper claim submission and adjudication, reimbursement to providers can be sent electronically. Funds can be transferred from the payer's financial institution to the provider's financial institution, and an electronic notice of reimbursement or electronic remittance advice (ERA) can be sent directly to the provider. In addition, concurrent updates of payer and provider database information can reduce operating costs.

HCFA implemented EFT and ERA in 1993 for Medicare A and Medicare B. Again, as a result many payers also began to reimburse and notify providers in this manner. The electronic processing saves printing and mailing costs for the payer, and providers can save data entry costs when they automatically post the remittance voucher within their own systems. An EDI standard, ANSI ASC X12 (835), has been developed and is in use for EFT and ERA.

Computerized Medical Records

A common, enterprisewide medical record supports the concept of data integration. Immediate, accurate information is vital to controlling operating costs. By developing one common computerized medical record, the ability to reduce unnecessary, duplicative procedures is significantly enhanced, paper flow is reduced, the number of lost documents is reduced, and more accurate and reliable treatment is administered. Because a patient's history and medical information can be accessed at any time in an organized, legible format, the computerized medical record can also help clinical staff provide better care to the patient. Unnecessary tests resulting from unavailable patient records are eliminated.

According to an Institute of Medicine report, a computerized medical record should do the following[11]:

- record and organize clinically all transactions, encounters, and events

- streamline and guide the business of the caregiver or caregiving team

- add substantively to the body of medical knowledge

- support population and epidemiological studies

The report defined the computer-based patient record as an "electronic record that resides in a system specifically designed to support users through availability of complete and accurate data, practitioner reminders and alerts, clinical decision support systems, links to bodies of medical knowledge, and other aids."[12(p.110)] The report also noted that a patient's medical record is unavailable 30 percent of the time during clinical evaluation and that 11 percent of laboratory tests are reordered because the first test results are lost.

According to Kenneth McCarty, director of the Pittsburgh Cancer Institute's (PCI's) Endocrine Laboratories, "Participating physicians could access necessary patient records instantly, regardless of where and when the clinical and laboratory information was generated."[13(p.131)] By connecting with the networking infrastructure at PCI, community physicians can analyze the various diagnostic and treatment alternatives available to their patients and can readily access experts. An alarms-and-alerts subsystem of the network will notify health care professionals when they have not entered all the information necessary for each patient or when they need to order additional procedures.

The EDI standard for electronic medical records is HL7.

Claim Liability of IBNR Services

IBNR refers to the amount of money that the plan needs to accrue for services that have been performed by providers but not yet reported to the MCO (see Chapter 40). This lapse results from a lag in the provider's process between providing a service and submitting a claim to the MCO. IBNR is determined actuarially from past experience and the MCO's IS operations, including authorization information, and represents a liability to the MCO.

The MCO's management IS should provide regular reporting of actual claims paid statistics. The most common method of reporting claims paid statistics is through system-generated lag reports. A lag report summarizes claims paid by the month of service and the month of payment. The lag report is so named because of the lag, or lapse of time, between when services are rendered (date of service) and when the MCO actually receives the billing for such services.[14]

In an MCO with EDI links to all its providers, IBNR will be significantly reduced. Each time a service is provided, the information will be directly submitted to the MCO, and the lag will be minutes instead of days or months. This is particularly true for participating providers, but it holds the potential to be true even for emergency or urgent services provided by nonparticipating providers as well.

DATA REPOSITORIES

Enterprisewide data repositories are relational databases that bring together snapshots of transactional data from multiple systems to provide a single source of data for executive decision making, customer management, patient care, and end-user applications. According to Inmon, a data repository or warehouse is a collection of data in support of management's decisions. The data are subject oriented rather than application oriented; integrated or transformed into a consistent format; nonvolatile, meaning that the snapshot never changes; and time variant, with snapshots over a period of 5 years or more.[15]

MCOs have historically led the way in developing large repositories of encounter data. In the early 1980s, MCOs, specifically those linked with health care–focused teaching institutions, began to analyze the data contained in these repositories to improve their negotiating position with payer organizations and employers. At that time, computer hardware was not capable of sufficiently managing the huge volumes of data contained in a repository. As technology advanced, MCOs began to review more broadly the large-scale data repositories of clinically related services.

Although still in its infancy stages, data warehousing is becoming more popular. The Gartner Group has predicted that more than 90 percent of all information processing organizations will implement this technology within 5 years, and some industry analysts feel that its implementation is a key success factor for competing in the managed care environment.[16] The implementation of central data repositories is considered a key success factor primarily because data warehousing supports business process redesign and has been, in many cases, the first step in the reengineering process.

Data within a repository are stored according to the structure of the database model, either central or relational. Central databases are characterized by centralized control through a single hardware platform with a database management system serving both operations and enterprise decision support. With central databases, end-user functional needs are more difficult to meet. This is especially apparent when the community physician user group and other user groups are not utilizing the same central hardware platform. Relational databases, although efficient in enabling storage and extraction functions, do not meet enterprise decision support needs for analysis and comparisons because decision support functions frequently involve complex queries and comparisons of cross-tabulated data.

Development of the data warehouse often occurs in opposite sequence to the standard systems development life cycle: implementation followed by data integration, testing, programming, design of the decision support system, analysis, and requirements definition. For this reason, cost justification is difficult because benefits are not understood at the outset. Historically, benefits of established data warehouse implementations have been measured in terms of differentiation of product/services with increases in market share, improved production efficiency as evidenced by increased revenue per unit cost, and improved management through a better understanding of the profitability of products and services.

Data warehousing supports on-line transaction processing, on-line analytical processing, enterprise decision support, executive IS, business process redesign, legacy refurbishment, clinical workstation development, clinical decision support, distributed processing, and client-server implementation. Although distributed client-server standards-based environments are supported fully by many data warehouse vendors, specific characteristics such as management preferences, technology infrastructures, products and services, and market volatility make each data warehouse organizationally specific. Individual organizational characteristics and long-term strategic plans will drive the structure of the storage of information within the database because each type of database is suited to meet different needs.

THE NATIONAL COMMITTEE FOR QUALITY ASSURANCE AND THE HEALTH PLAN EMPLOYER DATA AND INFORMATION SET REPORTING

The National Committee for Quality Assurance (NCQA; see Chapter 37) in 1993 revised the data reporting standard for MCOs. The second release of the standard known as the Healthplan Employer Data and Information Set (HEDIS 2.0) established performance criteria in more than 60 categories. These performance measures establish a baseline for commercial purchasers in their effort to evaluate MCOs in terms of provision of health care services to their employees and family members. The HEDIS reporting standards as of 1995 (version 2.5) are expected to be revised again (to HEDIS 3.0) in the fall of 1996. In addition, there is a Medicaid-specific version of HEDIS 2.5 at the time of this writing that modifies the dataset (by deleting some types of reports and requiring others) to be more useful in the Medicaid environment.

As one can see from this schedule of updates, any discussion here of the individual data elements in HEDIS is bound to become outdated within a relatively brief period of time. Nonetheless, it is important for the reader to understand HEDIS and to be aware of the increasing importance of HEDIS in the purchaser and regulatory communities. As one reviews the data elements in HEDIS, it becomes clear that most MCOs should be, and usually are, collecting these data and producing similar reports for internal uses. By way of example, Exhibit 28–1 lists the basic data elements in HEDIS 2.5; the reader is urged to obtain the most recent release of HEDIS from the NCQA (2000 L Street, N.W., Suite 500, Washington, D.C. 20036) and to become familiar with the required data reports and their interpretation.

HEDIS requires a significant level of IS technology and staff support to represent effectively the performance of the MCO. The clinically focused user of IS requires an enhanced ability not only to display data in the aggregate but also to perform a "drill-down" through the information.

Related to this issue is the difficulty in interpretation of what the data are actually supposed to report. The primary function of HEDIS 2.5 was to address this very issue. It is obviously of great value to any external body in reviewing data to have consistency of meaning and report integrity on a plan-to-plan comparative basis. As HEDIS continues to mature, the ability of plans to capture and report data in a consistent manner will continue to improve.

The data analysis necessary to support HEDIS reporting requires a thorough understanding of the business requirements of the MCO. This is critical given that the interpretation of the data is influenced by the behavior of the MCO in relating to the purchasers of health care in the community. From this understanding of the business, a high-level data model can be constructed. The data model should depict each data value and the interrelationships that exist. An iterative process of reviewing the data, interpreting their use, and refining the model is critical to the development of the HEDIS report set.

Development of a robust data model will permit the use of relational database tools to support the creation of the clinical and financial analysis reports necessary to support HEDIS reporting. These relational database tools will enable the managed care leadership to perform detailed longitudinal studies of its experience with a defined population and to identify possible interventions. An example is determining the impact of implementing an early intervention program for children younger than 5 years living in a certain geographical region. The reporting tools can perform the detailed analysis necessary to determine the value of the program in assessing the overall level of health care in the area.

CONCLUSION

"Health care delivery systems need flexibility with empowered users to meet and surpass the competition in managed care entrainments. Ideally,

Exhibit 28–1 Categories of Data Reports in HEDIS 2.5

Quality
- Preventive medicine
  1. Childhood immunization
  2. Cholesterol screening
  3. Mammography screening
  4. Cervical cancer screening
- Prenatal care
  1. Low birthweight
  2. Prenatal care in first trimester
- Acute and chronic disease
  1. Asthma inpatient admission rate (optional)
  2. Diabetic retinal examination
- Mental health
  1. Ambulatory follow-up after hospitalization for major affective disorders

Access and patient satisfaction
- Access
  1. Percentage of members ages 23–39 and 40–64 with plan visit in previous 3 years
  2. Number and percentage of PCPs accepting new patients
  3. Provision of plan access standards for various types of visits and telephone response
- Member Satisfaction
  1. Percentage of members who are satisfied with the plan
  2. Provision of plan satisfaction surveys

Membership and utilization
- Membership: enrollment/disenrollment
- High occurrence/high cost: frequency and average cost of nine diagnosis-related group categories and frequency of seven selected procedures
- Inpatient utilization (general hospital/acute care): medicine/surgery, maternity and newborns
- Ambulatory care utilization: outpatient visits, emergency department visits, and ambulatory surgery/procedures
- Inpatient utilization (nonacute care): stays in nursing homes, rehabilitation facilities, and hospice, transitional and respite facilities
- Maternity: total deliveries subdivided by vaginal births and cesarean sections; optional reporting of vaginal births after cesarean section
- Newborns: well and complex newborns differentiated by length of stay
- Mental health: treatment on the basis of inpatient, day/night, and outpatient location; readmission rate for major affective disorder
- Chemical dependency: treatment on the basis of inpatient, day/night, and outpatient location; readmission rate for chemical dependency
- Outpatient drug utilization: average costs and number of prescriptions per member

Finance
- Rate trends for 5 years
  1. Actual expense PMPM
  2. Expected rate trend assumption
- Indicators of financial stability
  1. Years in business
  2. Total membership
  3. Total revenue
  4. Net income
  5. Net worth
  6. Debt-to-service ratio
  7. Overall loss ratio
  8. Administrative loss ratio
  9. Medical loss ratio
  10. Operating profit margin
  11. Days cash on hand
  12. Ratio of cash to claims payable
  13. Days in receivables
  14. Days in unpaid claims
  15. Admitted reserves under statutory regulations (tangible net worth)
  16. State minimum reserve requirements
- Narrative information of rate trends, financial stability, and insolvency protection

Health Plan Management and Activities
- Percent of PCPs board certified
- Percentage of specialty care physicians board certified
- Turnover in physician network for primary care
- Recredentialing
- Physician compensation
- Clinical management
  1. Quality assessment and improvement
  2. Preventive care and health promotion
  3. Case management
  4. Utilization management
  5. Risk management

Source: Courtesy of the National Committee for Quality Assurance, Washington, D.C.; 1996.

enterprise data could be transformed into strategic information and implemented via package parameters. Clerical workers would be converted to knowledge workers, empowered with preconceived information that would be used during the operations of health care delivery."[17(p.98)]

Health care in the 1990s has been characterized by tremendous change, the need to reduce costs overall within the industry, and the development of new processes and methods to provide better patient care. In 1994, Wendy Herr, vice president of the Healthcare Financial Management Association, testified before the House Ways and Means Health Care Subcommittee. In urging Congress to adopt standard electronic patient and processing practices for health care, Herr advocated "the development of legislation to simplify health care administrative processes rather than waiting for a complete reform package."[18] Even without such legislation, MCOs and providers throughout the United States have been diligently working to streamline their processes and invent new ways to reduce operating costs while providing high-quality care to the patient. IS and information technology are key to an MCO's ability to thrive and compete successfully in the health care marketplace.

REFERENCES AND NOTES

1. T. Reynolds, Informatting the IDS, *HIMSS News* 6 (1995).
2. Health Information Management Information Systems Society (HIMSS), *Conference Survey* (HIMSS, 1995).
3. L.M. Fisher, Health Care Is Being Pulled into the Computer Age, *New York Times* (21 October 1995).
4. J.D. Ladd and R.D. Reese, Traveling the Information Superhighway, *Michigan Hospitals* (1994).
5. HIMSS, *Conference Survey*.
6. Ladd and Reese, Traveling the Information Superhighway.
7. Ladd and Reese, Traveling the Information Superhighway.
8. Ladd and Reese, Traveling the Information Superhighway.
9. P. Kongstvedt, ed., *The Managed Care Handbook*, 2d ed. (Gaithersburg, Md.: Aspen, 1993).
10. Ladd and Reese, Traveling the Information Superhighway.
11. Institute of Medicine, *The Computer-Based Patient Record: An Essential Technology for Health Care* (Institute of Medicine, 1991).
12. Institute of Medicine, *The Computer-Based Patient Record*.
13. Ladd and Reese, Traveling the Information Superhighway.
14. Kongstvedt, *The Managed Health Care Handbook*.
15. W.H. Inmon, *Building the Data Warehouse* (New York, N.Y.: Wiley, 1993).
16. R.E. Gilbreath, Health Care Data Repositories: Components and a Model, *Healthcare Information Management* 9 (1995).
17. Reynolds, Informatting the IDS.
18. Ladd and Reese, Traveling the Information Superhighway.

SUGGESTED READING

Austin, C.J. and Sobczak, P.M. 1993. Information Technology and Managed Care. *Hospital Topics*, 71(3): 33–37.

Coady, S.F. 1993. Where are the Data? *Managed Care Quarterly*, 1(3): 40–44.

Gotowka, T.D., Jackson, M., and Aquilina D. 1993. Health Data Analysis and Reporting: Organization and System Strategies. *Managed Care Quarterly*, 1(3): 26–34.

Kenkel, P.J. 1995. *Report Cards: What Every Health Provider Needs to Know About HEDIS and Other Performance Measures*. Gaithersburg, Md.: Aspen Publishers.

Rontal, R. 1993. Information and Secision Support in Managed Care. *Managed Care Quarterly*, 1(3): 3–14.

Strategies for Transitioning from Legacy Systems to New Systems. *The Singer Report*. Boston, Mass.: Charles Singer, Inc.

Wang, H. Sharp, V., and Coulter, C. 1994. Creating an Information System for Evaluating HMO Performance. *Managed Care Medicine* 1(5): 43–44, 46–49.

Chapter 29

Authorization Systems

Peter R. Kongstvedt

One of the definitive elements in managed health care is the presence of an authorization system. This may be as simple as precertification of elective hospitalizations in an indemnity plan or preferred provider organization (PPO) or as complex as mandatory authorization for all non–primary care services in a health maintenance organization (HMO). It is the authorization system that provides a key element of management in the delivery of medical services.

There are multiple reasons for an authorization system. One is to allow the medical management function of the plan to review a case for medical necessity. A second reason is to channel care to the most appropriate location (e.g., the outpatient setting or to a participating specialist rather than a nonparticipating one). Third, the authorization system may be used to provide timely information to the concurrent utilization review system and to large case management. Fourth, the system may help finance estimate the accruals for medical expenditures each month (see Chapter 40).

DEFINITION OF SERVICES REQUIRING AUTHORIZATION

The first requirement in an authorization system is to define what will require authorization and what will not. This is obviously tied to the benefits design and is part of full and fair disclosure marketing requirements in that, if services require authorization, the plan must make that clear in its marketing literature.

There are no managed care systems that require authorization for primary care services. PPOs and HMOs require members to use providers on their panels, and most HMOs require members to choose a single primary care physician (PCP) to coordinate care, but this does not require an authorization. Defining what constitutes primary care services is another issue and is addressed in Chapters 7 and 8.

The real issue is determining what non–primary care services will require authorization. In a tightly controlled system, such as most HMOs (with a few rare exceptions), all services not rendered by the PCP require authorization. In other words, any service from a referral specialist, any hospitalization, any procedure, and so forth require specific authorization, although there may be certain exceptions, such as an optometry visit or a routine Pap smear from a gynecologist. In less tightly controlled systems, such as many PPOs and most indemnity plans, the requirements are less stringent. In those cases, it is common for authorization only to be required for elective hospitalizations and procedures, both inpatient and outpatient.

The tighter the authorization system, the greater the plan's ability to manage utilization. An authorization system per se will not automatically control utilization, although one could expect some sentinel effect. It is the management behind the system that will determine its ultimate effectiveness. If the medical director is unable or unwilling to deal with poor utilization behavior, an authorization system will have only a marginal effect. If the claims department is unable to back up the authorization system, it will quickly be subverted as members and providers learn that it is little more than a burdensome sham.

In any plan, there will be times when a member is unable to obtain prior authorization. This is usually due to an emergency or an urgent problem that occurs out of area. In those cases, the plan must make provision for retrospective review of the case to determine whether authorization may be granted after the fact. Certain rules may also be defined regarding the member's obligation in those circumstances (e.g., notification within 24 hours of the emergency). Be careful that such requirements do not allow for automatic authorization if the plan is notified within 24 hours but only for automatic review of the case to determine medical necessity.

DEFINITION OF WHO CAN AUTHORIZE SERVICES

The next requirement of an authorization system is to define who has the ability to authorize services and to what extent. This will vary considerably depending on the type of plan and the degree to which it will be medically managed.

In PPOs that are tightly controlled, there may be a requirement for PCP authorization (the so-called "gatekeeper" PPO). In loosely controlled PPOs and in managed indemnity plans, there is usually only a requirement for authorization for elective hospitalizations and procedures, but that authorization comes from plan personnel and not from the PCP or any other physician.

For example, if a participating surgeon wishes to admit a patient for surgery, the surgeon first calls a central telephone number and speaks with a plan representative, usually a nurse. That representative then asks a number of questions about the patient's condition, and if predetermined criteria are met, and after the member's eligibility is confirmed (if the plan has that capability), an authorization is issued. In most cases, the surgery must take place on the day of admis-

sion, and certain procedures may only be done on an outpatient basis.

It is common practice in HMOs to require that most or all medical services be authorized by the member's PCP. Even then, however, there can be some dispute. For example, if a PCP authorizes a member to see a referral specialist, does that specialist have the ability to authorize tests, surgery, or another referral to himself or herself or to another specialist? Does a PCP require authorization to hospitalize one of his or her own patients?

A relatively common exception to this practice is in the area of mental health and substance abuse (MH/SA). As discussed in detail in Chapter 22, MH/SA services are unique and often lend themselves better to other methods of authorization. Plans or even the accounts themselves may carve out MH/SA from the basic health plan and treat it as a standalone function.

Another exception to the PCP-only concept occurs in HMOs that allow specialists to contact the plan directly about hospitalizations. In these cases, the referral to the specialist must have been made by the PCP in the first place, but the specialist may determine that hospitalization is required and obtain authorization directly from the plan's medical management department. Plans that operate this way generally do so because the PCPs have no real involvement in hospital cases anyway and because there is no utility in involving them in that decision.

There are a few non-HMO managed care organizations (MCOs) that are experimenting with the use of nurse advice lines for authorizations. In these plans (usually "gatekeeper" PPOs or point-of-service plans), the member calls a nurse to request an authorization to see a specialist rather than going through a PCP. While theoretically eliminating an unnecessary PCP visit, it is in fact likely to lead to significantly higher utilization than occurs in a PCP model. Plans attempting to use this model must employ good risk management techniques (see Chapter 38) and good physician profiling (see Chapter 27).

In any type of managed care plan, there may be services that will require specific authorization from the plan's medical director. This is usually the case for expensive procedures such as transplants and for controversial procedures that may be considered experimental or of limited value except in particular circumstances. This is even more necessary when the plan has negotiated a special arrangement for high-cost services. The authorization system not only serves to review the medical necessity of the service but ensures that the care will be delivered at an institution that has contracted with the plan.

As mentioned above, the tighter the authorization system, the better the plan's ability to manage the care. For optimal control, only the PCP should be able to authorize services, and that pertains to all services except those that specifically require the approval of the plan's medical director or to MH/SA services in those plans that have carved out that piece. In other words, even if a member is referred to a specialist, only the PCP can actually authorize any further services, such as diagnostic tests, rereferral, or a procedure. This is the tightest form of a gatekeeper or case management model. As discussed below, it requires the use of unique authorization numbers that tie to specific bills, and the claims department must be able to back that up. As one backs away from that degree of tight control, utilization will tend to increase.

CLAIMS PAYMENT

A managed care health plan does not exist as an absolute dictator; you cannot issue blindfolds and cigarettes to members who fail to obtain authorization for services. The only recourse a plan has is to deny full payment for services that have not been authorized. This pertains equally to services obtained from nonparticipating providers (professionals or institutions) and to services obtained without required prior authorization.

In an HMO, payment can be completely denied for services that were not authorized. Point of service (POS) is unique and is discussed below. In most PPOs and in indemnity plans, if an inpatient admission is not authorized but is considered a covered benefit, payment may not be denied, but the amount paid may be significantly reduced. For example, a plan pays 80 percent of charges for an authorized admission but only 50 percent of charges for a nonauthorized admission or perhaps imposes a flat dollar amount penalty for failure to obtain authorization.

In certain cases, a plan may deny any payment for a portion of the bill but will pay the rest. For example, if a patient is admitted the day before surgery even though same-day admission was required, the plan may not pay the charges (both hospital and physician) related to that first day but will pay charges for the remaining days.

In a PPO where a contractual relationship exists between the provider and the plan, the penalty may fall solely on the provider, who cannot balance bill the member for the amount of the penalty. In the case of an indemnity plan (or a PPO in which the member received services from a nonparticipating provider), the penalty falls on the member, who must then pay more out of pocket.

POS is a special challenge for authorization systems and claims management (a discussion of claims management may be found in Chapter 31). It is necessary to define what is covered as an authorized service and what is not because services that are not authorized will still be paid, albeit at the lower out-of-network level of benefits. Because POS is sold with the expressed intent that members will use out-of-network services, it is not always clear how a service was or was not authorized.

Common examples of this issue are illustrated as follows. If a PCP makes a referral to a specialist for one visit and the member returns to that specialist for a follow-up, was that authorized? If a PCP authorizes three visits but the member goes four times, does the fourth visit cascade out to an out-of-network level of benefits? If a PCP refers to a specialist and the specialist determines that admission is necessary but the member is admitted to a nonparticipating hospital, is that authorized? What if the member is admitted to a participating hospital but is cared for by a mix of participating and nonparticipating physicians? What if a member is referred to a partici-pating specialist who performs laboratory and radiology testing (even though the plan has capitated for such services); is the visit author-ized but not the testing? What if the member claims that he or she had no choice in the matter?

The list of "what ifs" is a long one. Most plans strive to identify an episode of care (e.g., a hos-pitalization or a referral) and to remain consis-tent within that episode. For example, the testing by the specialist referenced above would be de-nied and the specialist prohibited from balance billing, or an entire hospitalization would be considered either in network or out of network. In any case, the plan must develop policies and procedures for defining when a service is to be considered authorized (and when it is considered in network in the case of hospital services that require precertification in any event) and when it is not.

A quirky but vexing problem in POS can occur when a claim is received before the authorization arrives. It is increasingly common for providers to submit claims electronically (in fact, some MCOs now require it), but far less common for authorizations to be submitted; as noted below, paper-based authorization systems remain prevalent at the time this book is being written. Thus, the claim arrives well before the authorization. In an HMO, the plan can pend (see below) the claim for a week to see if an au-thorization is forthcoming. In a POS plan, how-ever, a claim without an authorization will im-mediately cascade out and be paid at the out-of-network level of benefits. The angry member and provider then resubmit, and the plan readjudicates, all at a high cost. The solu-tion, of course, is to aggressively move to elec-tronic authorizations (see below).

CATEGORIES OF AUTHORIZATION

Authorizations may be classified into six types:

1. prospective
2. concurrent

3. retrospective
4. pended (for review)
5. denial (no authorization)
6. subauthorization

There is value in categorizing authorization types. By examining how authorizations are ac-tually generated in your plan, you will be able to identify areas of weakness in your system. For example, if you feel that all elective admissions are receiving prospective authorization and dis-cover that in fact most are being authorized ei-ther concurrently or, worse yet, retrospectively, you will know that you are not able to intervene effectively in managing hospital cases because you do not know about them in a timely manner. A brief description of the authorization catego-ries follows.

Prospective

Sometimes referred to as precertification, this type of authorization is issued before any service is rendered. This is commonly used in plans that require prior authorization for elective services. The more prospective the authorization, the more time the medical director has to intervene if necessary, the greater the ability to direct care to the most appropriate setting or provider, and the more current your knowledge regarding uti-lization trends.

Inexperienced plan managers tend to believe that all authorizations are prospective. That na-ive belief can lead to a real shock when the man-ager of a troubled plan learns that most claims are actually being paid on the basis of other types of authorizations that were not correctly categorized. This is discussed further below.

Concurrent

A concurrent authorization is generated at the time the service is rendered. For example, the utilization review nurse discovers that a patient is being admitted to the hospital that day. An au-thorization is generated, but by the nurse and not by the PCP. Another example is an urgent service that cannot wait for review, such as setting a broken leg. In that case, the PCP may contact the plan, but the referral is made at the same time.

Concurrent authorizations allow for timely data gathering and the potential for affecting the outcome, but they do not allow the plan medical managers to intervene in the initial decision to render services. This may result in care being inappropriately delivered or delivered in a setting that is not cost effective, but it also may result in the plan's being able to alter the course of care in a more cost-effective direction even though care has already commenced.

Retrospective

As the term indicates, retrospective authorizations take place after the fact. For example, a patient is admitted, has surgery, and is discharged, and then the plan finds out. On the surface, it appears that any service rendered without authorization would have payment denied or reduced, but there will be circumstances when the plan will genuinely agree to authorize services after the fact. For example, if a member is involved in a serious automobile accident or has a heart attack while traveling in another state, there is a clear need for care, and the plan could not deny that need.

Inexperienced managers often believe not only that most authorizations are prospective but that, except for emergency cases, there are few retrospective authorizations. Unfortunately, there are circumstances when there may be a high volume of retrospective authorizations. This commonly occurs when the PCPs or participating providers fail to cooperate with the authorization system. A claim comes in cold (i.e., without an authorization), and the plan must create one after the fact if it finds out that the service was really meant to be authorized. The plan cannot punish the member because it was really the fault of the PCP, so that claim gets paid.

Most plans have a no balance billing clause in their provider contracts (see Chapter 55) and

may elect not to pay claims that have not been prospectively authorized, forcing the noncompliant providers to write off the expense. That will certainly get their attention, but it comes at some cost in provider relations. Even so, sometimes it becomes necessary if discussions and education attempts fail.

If the plan's systems allow an authorization to be classified as prospective or concurrent regardless of when it is created relative to the delivery of the service, it is a sure thing that retrospective authorizations will occur but not be labeled retrospective; for example, the PCP or specialist will say "I really meant to authorize that" or "It's in the mail" and will call the authorization concurrent. Another possibility is that claims clerks may be creating retrospective authorizations on the basis of the belief that the claim was linked to another authorized claim (see below).

In a tightly managed plan, the ability to create a retrospective authorization is strictly limited to the medical director or utilization management department, the ability to create prospective authorizations does not exist once the service has actually been rendered, and concurrent authorizations cannot be created after 24 hours have passed since the service was rendered.

Pended (for Review)

Pended is a claims term that refers to a state of authorization purgatory. In this situation, it is not known whether an authorization has been or will be issued, and the case has been pended for review. This refers to medical review (for medical necessity, such as an emergency department claim, or for medical policy review to determine whether the service is covered under the schedule of benefits) or to administrative review. As noted above, if a plan is having problems getting the PCPs or participating providers to cooperate with the authorization system, there will be a significant number of pended claims that ultimately lead to retrospective authorizations.

Denial

Denial refers to the certainty that there will be no authorization forthcoming. As has been discussed, you cannot assume that every claim coming into the plan without an associated authorization will be denied because there are reasons that an unauthorized claim may be paid.

Subauthorization

This is a special category that allows one authorization to hitchhike on another. This is most common for hospital-based professional services. For example, a single authorization may be issued for a hospitalization, and that authorization is used to cover anesthesia, pathology, radiology, or even a surgeon's or consultant's fees.

In some plans, an authorization to a referral specialist may be used to authorize diagnostic and therapeutic services ordered by that specialist. Great care must be taken to control this. If not, the phenomenon of linking will occur. Linking refers to claims clerks linking unauthorized services to authorized ones and creating subauthorizations to do so. For example, a referral to a specialist is authorized, and a claim is received not only for the specialist's fees but for some expensive procedure or test as well, or a bill is received for ten visits even though the PCP intended to authorize only one. The claims clerk (who is probably being judged on how many claims he or she can process per hour) may then inappropriately link all the bills to the originally authorized service through the creation of subauthorizations, thereby increasing the costs to the plan.

STAFFING

Plan personnel required to implement an authorization system properly are the medical director, an authorization system coordinator (whatever that person's actual title), and the utilization review nurses. Various clerks and telephone operators will also be required; the number of these depends on the size of the plan and the scope of the system.

The medical director has three primary roles. The first is to interact with the plan's PCPs and specialty physicians to ensure cooperation with the authorization system. Second, the medical director is responsible for medical review of pended claims. That does not mean that the medical director will have to review every claim personally but rather that it is ultimately the medical director's responsibility. In some instances the case will be reviewed by the member's PCP; in others it will be more appropriate for a nurse reviewer or even the medical director (or designee) to perform the primary review. Third, the medical director will sometimes have interactions with members when payment of a claim is denied. Although the claims department usually sends the denial letters and responds to inquiries, it is common for members to demand a review of the denied claim on the basis of medical necessity or a belief that the PCP really authorized the service. In those cases, the medical director will often be involved.

The authorization system needs a coordinator to make sure that all the pieces fit together. Whether that responsibility falls to the claims department, the utilization department, the medical director's office, or general management is a local choice. In a small plan, the role of coordinator usually falls to a manager with other duties as well, but as the plan grows it is best to dedicate that function.

The coordinator's primary purpose is to track the authorization system at all its points. All systems can break down, and the coordinator must keep track of where the system is performing suboptimally and take steps to correct it. In some cases that will require the intervention of others because an authorization system has ramifications in the PCP's office, the hospitals, the utilization review department, the claims department, member services, and finance. If no one is in charge of maintaining the authorization system, people will tend to deny their responsibilities in making it work.

Some thought must be given to the relationship of the authorization system to the utilization review coordinators. Specifically, how much can the utilization review coordinator authorize? It makes sense to allow some ability to create authorizations, especially subauthorizations for hospital services, but you must decide whether you will allow the utilization review coordinators to create primary authorizations, particularly for hospital cases. It is common in large HMOs for nurse case managers involved in large case management to have the ability to authorize services without the need to go through a PCP (see Chapter 18 for a discussion of this activity).

COMMON DATA ELEMENTS

The needs of your plan will dictate what data elements you actually capture. In some plans, the management information system will be able automatically to provide some of this information, so you would not have to capture it at the time the authorization is created. The data elements that are commonly captured in authorization systems are illustrated in Exhibit 29–1.

In systems where there are clinical requirements for authorization, the system then must determine what the requirements are on the basis of the diagnosis. For example, if a plan has preset criteria for authorization for cataract surgery, those requirements may be reviewed with the physician when he or she calls in for authorization. The same issue applies to mandatory outpatient surgery: If admission is being requested, the procedure may be compared with an outpatient surgery list to determine whether the physician needs to justify an exception. Such reviews should only be done by medically trained personnel, usually nurses. In the case of disagreements with the requesting physician, the medical director must be able to contact the physician at that time or as soon as possible. It becomes less common for a plan to deny authorization based on medical necessity as the plan matures and the participating physicians become more conversant in definitions of medical necessity; the other

Exhibit 29–1 Data Elements Commonly Captured in an Authorization System

Member's name

Member's birth date

Member's plan identification number

Eligibility status

- Commercial group number or public sector (i.e., Medicare and Medicaid) group identifier
- Line of business (e.g., HMO, POS, Medicare, Medicaid, conversion, private, or self-pay)
- Benefits code for particular service (e.g., noncovered, partial coverage, limited benefit, full coverage)

PCP

Referral provider

- Name
- Specialty

Outpatient data elements

- Referral or service date
- Diagnosis (ICD-9-CM, free text)
- Number of visits authorized
- Specific procedures authorized (CPT-4, free text)

Inpatient data elements

- Name of institution
- Admitting physician
- Admission or service date
- Diagnosis (ICD-9-CM, diagnosis-related group, free text)
- Discharge date

Subauthorizations (if allowed or required)

- Hospital-based professionals
- Other specialists
- Other procedures or studies

Free text to be transmitted to the claims processing department

values of the authorization system remain important, however.

When an authorization is made, the system also must be able to generate and link an authorization number or identifier to the data, so that every authorization will be unique. In tightly controlled plans, any claim must be accompanied by that unique authorization number to be processed.

METHODS OF DATA CAPTURE AND AUTHORIZATION ISSUANCE

There are three main methods of interacting with an authorization system: paper based, telephone based, and electronic.

Paper-Based Authorization Systems

Paper-based systems generally work in plans that allow the PCP to authorize the service without prospective review by the plan. If plan preapproval is necessary before an authorization is issued (except for infrequent services, such as transplants), a paper-based system will not be responsive enough. If, however, the PCP has the authority to authorize services, a paper-based system will be adequate, although not state of the art.

This type of system depends on the PCP (or other authorizing provider) filling out an authorization form, which may be used as a referral or admission form as well. A copy of the form is sent to the plan, which enters the authorization data into its system. Claims submitted to the plan may or may not require a copy of the authorization form, depending on plan policy.

The advantages of paper-based systems are as follows. They are less labor intensive than telephone-based systems and therefore require less overhead for the plan. Although electronic systems are even more labor efficient, they require a higher level of sophistication and support than paper-based systems. Data entry can be done in batch mode because there is little need for real-time interaction. They also tend to be more acceptable to physicians because they are less intrusive regarding clinical decision making, run less risk of violating patient confidentiality, and do not have the problem of busy signals or a physician being placed on hold during a busy day in the office.

The main disadvantage of paper-based systems is that there is less opportunity to intervene at the time the authorization is made. Once an authorization is issued, it is nearly impossible to reverse it. You may be able to alter future behavior, but neither the physician nor the member will easily accept an after-the-fact reversal of an authorization. Another disadvantage is that it increases the administrative burden on the physician, particularly if he or she is participating in multiple plans, each with its own complicated set of forms. Paper authorizations can also get lost in the mail (or mail room) and lend themselves to data entry errors (e.g., digit transpositions). Lastly, as noted earlier, paper authorizations may arrive at the plan after an electronic claim has been received and adjudicated.

Telephone-Based Authorization Systems

Telephone-based systems rely on the PCP or office staff to call a central number and give the information over the phone. If clinical review is required, it is done at that time. Telephone-based systems have the built in potential of clogging up and leading to poor service. If the system is unresponsive, or if PCPs get frequent busy signals or are put on hold, they will stop calling. The investment in a responsive telephone-based system will be paid back in a reduction of pended claims and retrospective authorizations.

Collecting the data and issuing an authorization number may be done either manually or by an automated system. It is extremely rare for a health plan not to use computers for claims payment, although a new start-up plan could certainly perform this function manually for a brief period. Because authorization is linked to claims payment, there must be an interface between the two systems.

One approach is to collect all the data on manual logs and then enter them into the claims system through batch processing. Another approach is to automate the entire process. If you have systems capabilities to do so, you may wish to have your authorization clerks or nurses enter the data directly into the computer. Be aware, though, that computer systems can delay you with slow screens, complicated menus and entry screens, downtime, training problems, and a host of other problems. Some computer systems are made for batch entry, making real-time entry too inefficient. In those situations, you may wish to use a manual log for data capture and authorization issuance until your automated system is well tested. You should also be able to use a manual system as a back-up on a moment's notice.

The advantages of telephone-based systems are that they can be more responsive and timely, have greater potential for directing care to the appropriate location and provider, and have the potential of reducing the administrative burden on the PCP's office staff. The disadvantages are that they increase the administrative burden on the plan and, if not run efficiently, can generate great ill will with the PCPs.

Electronic Authorization Systems

Electronic authorization systems are still not as common as paper- or telephone-based systems, but their popularity is growing. Electronic systems require participating physicians and hospitals to interface electronically with the plan, usually through a personal computer or a dumb terminal in the office. Generally, electronic communications with providers focus on claims submission and payment, but authorizations are equally possible.

Electronic authorizations may be nothing more than an electronic form that the provider completes on line and transmits to the plan. The authorization system may be more complex, using editing fields to ensure that the referral or admission is to a participating provider and requiring key data elements to be provided. An electronic authorization system may also provide automatic information transfer (e.g., member status and demographics). It is also possible for an electronic system to gather clinical information and to compare it with protocols before processing the authorization, but currently that is more conjecture than fact.

Electronic systems generally enter the authorization data directly (or via electronic batch entry) into the management information system, so that the need for personnel to enter data is re-duced. Such systems require a high level of expertise by the plan and a certain level of sophistication by the providers themselves. Electronic systems and data interchange are discussed in Chapter 28.

AUTHORIZATION SYSTEM REPORTS

The reports needed from an authorization system will depend on the complexity of the system and your management needs. Obviously, the one absolutely necessary report function is linking incoming claims to authorized services.

Hospital logs and reports are discussed in greater detail in Chapter 17. The authorization system should be able to print out a report indicating prospective admissions and procedures, current admissions and procedures, and retrospectively authorized cases. Cases pended for review should also be reported, with data indicating when the claim was received, when it was reviewed, and its current status.

Outpatient reports are also discussed in greater detail in Chapter 27. Reports from the authorization system could include summaries of authorizations by type for each PCP expressed as ratios, for example total authorizations per 100 encounters per PCP or per 1,000 members per year (annualized), with a breakdown of prospective compared with concurrent compared with retrospective, and so forth. Authorization types may also be expressed as a percentage of the total number of authorizations for that PCP. For example, the total authorization rate may be 8 per 100 encounters per PCP with 50 percent prospective, 40 percent concurrent, 6 percent retrospective, and 4 percent pended (if it is denied, it is not an authorization, although it is still quite useful to report denial statistics by provider as well).

A valuable report is a comparison of authorization types with paid claims. This is basically looking at the percentage of claims that have been authorized prospectively, concurrently, and so forth. This is valuable in determining your ability to capture the data in a timely fashion. It will be inversely proportional to your plan's rate of incurred but not reported claims.

These reports will allow you to identify noncompliant providers or providers who comply but not in a timely fashion. The medical director will be able to focus on those providers who either do not obtain authorizations or do so in a way that does not allow for active medical management by the medical director (if that is needed). These reports, along with a report on the number and nature of open authorizations (i.e., authorizations for services for which a claim has not yet been received), will also allow the finance department to calculate more accurately the accruals and incurred but not reported

factor for the plan, reducing the chances of nasty surprises later.

CONCLUSION

An effective authorization system is a requirement of any managed care plan. Whether that system is all encompassing or pertains only to certain types of services is dependent on the type of plan. Key elements to address are what services require authorization, who has the ability to authorize, whether secondary plan approval is required, what data will be captured, how they will be captured, and how they will be used.

Chapter 30

Member Services and Consumer Affairs

Peter R. Kongstvedt

All managed health care plans need a member services, customer services, or consumer affairs function. For purposes of discussion, in this chapter the term *member services* is used synonymously with the terms *customer services* and *consumer affairs*. Member services are not to be confused with membership services; the latter term is sometimes used to describe the operational area responsible for processing enrollment applications and sending out membership cards and evidence of coverage documents. Member services, in the context of this chapter, refers to the department responsible for helping members with any problems, handling member grievances and complaints, tracking and reporting patterns of problems encountered, and enhancing the relationship between the members of the plan and the plan itself.

Managed care plans are far more complicated than simple indemnity insurance plans (as if those were simple!). Members are required to choose a primary care physician (PCP), to follow rules for accessing health care (e.g., obtaining an authorization from their PCP for referral services), to understand complex benefits structures, and so forth. Health maintenance organizations (HMOs) are complicated enough; point-of-service (POS) plans are even more complicated and have different levels of coverage depending on how the member accesses services (intentionally or not). See Chapter 3 for a description of these types of plans.

The central point is that plans that manage access to care through the use of a restricted pro-vider panel and an authorization system need to have a system to help members use the plan, a system to monitor and track the nature of member contacts, and a mechanism for members to express dissatisfaction with their care because members have less ability simply to change providers. Likewise, plans that have the ability to deny or reduce coverage for nonauthorized services need a mechanism for members to seek review of claims that have been denied or covered at a lower than expected level of benefits. Managed care or not, any plan that provides for the financing of health care must have a system to manage member problems with those payments (see Chapter 58). Last, the plan must have a mechanism for members to get help addressing routine business issues, such as change of address, issuance of identification cards, and so forth.

When a plan has delegated a large measure of responsibility to an integrated delivery system (IDS; see Chapter 4), then some care needs to be taken as to how member services will function. The IDS will have a higher than normal level of control over all aspects of the medical encounter, including access to care, the authorization system, availability of providers, and so forth. In some cases, the IDS will actually perform many traditional member services functions. It is important that there be consistency between the plan and the IDS and that there be clear distinctions between the responsibilities of the plan and those of the IDS. It is preferable for the plan to perform all member services functions, but if the

IDS is to perform some of them, then it is necessary that the plan receive accurate and timely data from the IDS member services department. It is equally important for the plan to share its member services data with the IDS.

TRAINING AND STAFFING

The amount of training required for member services representatives before they are allowed to interact with members varies from plan to plan. It is common for large and complicated plans to require new representatives to spend 2 to 3 months in training before they begin actually interfacing with members, and even then the first few weeks are monitored by the supervisor. Smaller or less complicated plans generally require less training. It is a clear mistake to skimp on training because how the member services representative performs will have a direct impact on member satisfaction and perhaps on the legal risk profile of the plan. Remember: Each and every interaction that members have with the plan will either reaffirm their decision to join or cause them to wonder whether they made a mistake; that goes for member services encounters as well as for medical encounters.

Staffing of this department is a function of both the scope of responsibilities of the representatives and the complexity of the plan. For highly complex plans with significant growth, complicated products such as POS, and active outreach (discussed below), staffing ratios may be as generous as 1 representative for every 3,500 members. Plans with benefits designs that are simpler and more consistent, those that have stable membership levels, and those that generally have good service levels may staff at a ratio of 1 representative for every 7,500 members.

The degree to which a plan can automate certain routine customer calls may have a substantial effect on staffing ratios as well and can clearly improve responsiveness in the eyes of the member. If the member services representative is required to look up information manually, such as benefits (base plan and riders), claims history, the provider directory, and so forth, that will reduce efficiency and the member's satisfaction with the interaction. In addition, if the member services representative is required to access multiple, awkward screens, many of which may actually add no value to the transaction, then work required will be disproportionately high. Automation will also help the member services representative resolve the problem or issue on that first call, thereby lowering the amount of follow-up work required and thus administrative cost.

It is common in large plans to organize the department into dedicated service units. Such units are responsible for a limited number of accounts, particularly if those accounts are large. In that way, the representatives working in the unit are better able to be familiar with a limited set of benefits issues, to gain knowledge about particular problems unique to an account, and to be more responsive to the accounts. Dedicated service units are sometimes required by large employers before you can obtain their business.

ACCESSING MEMBER SERVICES

How a member accesses the plan is also important to understand and manage. Traditional telephone lines must be adequate in number and must be properly automated in function (e.g., automatic call distribution, sequencing, etc.), depending on plan size. Large plans usually also have a toll-free line for use by members outside the local area code of the plan's service center. The use of direct inward dialing can relieve a member from having to grind through several automated menus. This means that the member's identification card or member handbook lists different numbers for different needs. For example, a plan may have a dedicated, direct inward dial-in line for members to select a new PCP, to obtain a new identification card, or to resolve a problem.

Some plans allow members access by personal computer through bulletin boards or dedicated on-line services. A few large plans and insurers have also developed Web sites on the

World Wide Web of the Internet, allowing E-mail through that vehicle as well as access to nonconfidential information. Plans that provide for such electronic communications from members must be careful about security, and members are usually limited to sending E-mail and other routine transactions.

Related to communication by personal computer is the electronic kiosk, which the plan may place in its lobby, on site at a large employer, or in a public area such as a shopping mall. This kiosk allows access to generally available plan information and, in the case of a kiosk at an employer site, may allow the member to perform certain functions such as choosing a PCP or sending an electronic message.

Mail and paper communication remains highly important and must be managed properly. All correspondence must be logged and tracked, policies and procedures must be in place regarding the routing of correspondence, and master files need to be kept of both incoming and outgoing correspondence. In a small plan, this is usually done with the actual paper documents; large plans frequently use imaging technology to store the massive amounts of paper documents, the originals of which may then be stored off site for a number of years. It is important to ensure that paper correspondence receives the same attention that telephone calls do and have time standards for response.

PERFORMANCE STANDARDS

Member services departments generally have responsiveness requirements as part of their performance standards. Such standards generally revolve around a few simple measures. Performance standards must be tailored to meet the standards that the members would expect, not simply what the plan chooses to measure. For example, a plan may measure telephone responsiveness by measuring how long it takes an operator to answer once that operator receives the call; such a measurement might fail to capture the fact that the member had to wade through

seven menus of a voice-response unit to get there, resulting in 3 minutes of frustration by the member.

Telephone responsiveness is usually measured by how many times the telephone rings on average, the elapsed time (in seconds) before it is answered by a representative, and what percentage of calls are abandoned before they are ever answered. For example, a plan may have a goal of less than 2 percent of callers hanging up because their call did not get through and 80 percent of all calls being answered in 20 seconds or less.

Timeliness of response is also measured against standards. This is done by tracking the percentage of calls that are resolved on the spot (i.e., no follow-up is required); for example, the standard may be that 90 percent of calls require no follow-up. For problems or questions that require follow-up, there are usually standards for how long that takes (e.g., 90 percent of outstanding inquiries or problems are resolved within 14 days and 98 percent within 28 days). Similar standards apply to written correspondence.

Individual service representatives are usually monitored for both productivity and quality. Productivity may be measured by tracking the number of contacts per day or per hour, the length of time each contact takes to complete, and the percentage of contacts that are resolved on the first call. Quality is usually monitored through silent monitoring of the calls themselves. This refers to the supervisor or manager listening to random calls for each service representative and then making a qualitative judgment about how well the service representative handled the call. It is not enough to take and give information when a member has a problem or complaint; the representative must apply communication techniques developed for customer service to be optimally effective.[1] Some plans routinely send follow-up questionnaires to members after the member services inquiry or complaint is resolved to solicit feedback about the process as well as to reinforce the notion that the member is important.[2]

SERVICE AND HELP

Member services is responsible for helping members use the plan. New members commonly have less than complete (or even no) understanding of how the plan operates, how to access care, how to obtain authorization for specialty services (in a PCP case manager type of plan), and so forth. These are services to members as opposed to complaint and concern resolution, which is discussed later. Although the broad issues are generally the same across product lines, plans often find differing levels of need for each of these types of services in the commercial, Medicare, and Medicaid markets.

PCP Selection

In plans that use PCPs to access care, member services will frequently be called on to help members select a PCP. This may occur because the member failed to select a PCP in the first place, particularly in a POS plan in which the member has no intention of using the HMO part of the plan. Even in POS, it is best to require the member to select a PCP because it is not known whether the member will change his or her mind later and because the plan really does want to encourage the member to use the managed care system.

Another reason that a member may need to select a new PCP is if a participating PCP leaves the network for any reason or if the PCP's practice closes because it is full but that information did not get into the most recent provider directory (or the member did not realize that a tiny, asterisk superscript meant that the practice was closed). One other common reason for change is that the member and the PCP simply were not the right match for each other, and the member is requesting a change to another PCP. This often occurs when a member is new to the system, and it occurs particularly often when managed care is installed as a replacement for all other insurance (as with most POS plans), thus requiring new members who never wanted to go into a managed care plan to select a PCP.

In any event, member services is generally responsible for helping the members with this problem. Many plans have more information about PCPs available on line to the member services representative than is available in the directory, and representatives may be able to help the member select a PCP on the basis of special information, such as languages spoken, training, hours available, and so forth. Some plans, especially closed panel plans, have highly informative physician directories available for this purpose that they mail to the member.

Identification Cards

Although this chapter does not address the basic issues of entering enrollment information and issuing identification cards, it is inevitable that some members will have problems with their cards, and then member services will need to resolve those problems. Common problems include lost cards, cards that were sent to the wrong address, incorrect information on the card, and changes required because of change of status (e.g., the subscriber got married).

Outreach

An outreach program can be of great benefit in preventing member complaints and problems. An outreach program is one that proactively contacts new members and discusses the way the plan works. By reaching out and letting members know how the authorization system works, how to obtain services, what the benefits are, and so forth, the plan can reduce confusion.

Virtually all HMOs, as well as other types of plans, mail an information pack to new members. This pack typically includes not only the new identification card but also descriptive language about how to use the plan, how to access care, and how the authorization system works; information about coordination of benefits (see Chapter 32); an updated provider directory (possibly with maps in the case of a closed panel); and a description of how the pharmacy benefit works (see Chapter 23) if the member has such a benefit. Some plans may also include a copy of the benefits description and even possibly the group master contract or legal schedule of benefits. Some plans also include a "Member Bill of Rights" outlining the member's rights and responsibilities. Closed panels also include hours of operation and telephone numbers for the health centers as well as how to access urgent care. Medical groups in network model plans, medical groups in open panel plans, and IDSs may also provide such information on a direct basis and not as part of materials sent by the HMO.

Many plans accomplish a more aggressive and effective outreach program by conducting a telephone-based outreach program. Telephone outreach requires a carefully scripted approach during the contact. Development of scripts allows the plan to use less thoroughly trained personnel to carry out the program; when questions arise that are not easily answered from the script or when problems are identified, the member may be transferred to an experienced member services representative. This also gives the member a chance to ask questions about the plan, especially when those questions do not come up until the member has heard about the plan from the outreach personnel. It is worthwhile to bear in mind that, for many members who are low utilizers, this contact may be the most important one; clearly, it is in the plan's interest to retain such members. Outreach is most effective when carried out during both daytime and early evening hours to ensure that contact is made.

Telephone outreach is especially useful when the plan undergoes a large enrollment surge. The level of problems that members experience with a managed care plan is generally highest during the initial period of enrollment (because new members are still unfamiliar with the way the plan operates), and outreach can help ameliorate that issue. The sooner the members understand how to access the system, the sooner the burden on the plan to deal with complaints and grievances will diminish.

MEMBER COMPLAINTS AND GRIEVANCES

Complaints Compared with Grievances

Complaints by members may be generally defined as problems that members bring to the attention of the plan; they differ from grievances in that grievances are formal complaints demanding formal resolution by the plan. Complaints that are not resolved to the satisfaction of the member may evolve into formal grievances. It is clearly in the best interest of the plan to try and resolve complaints before they become formal grievances because there are greater legal implications and member satisfaction issues involved with grievances.

Resolution of complaints is usually informal, although the plan should have a clear policy for investigating complaints and responding to members. Despite the informal nature of complaint resolution, it is extremely important for the member services department, or in fact any staff member, to document carefully every contact with a member when the member expresses any dissatisfaction. For complaints, the member services representative should keep a log of even casual telephone calls from members as well as notes of any conversations with members while he or she is trying to resolve complaints. Concise and thorough records may prove quite valuable if the complaint turns into a formal grievance. Such documentation also helps in data analysis, as discussed later in this chapter.

Grievance resolution is distinctly formal. State and federal regulations require HMOs to have clearly delineated member grievance procedures, to inform members of those procedures, and to abide by them. Clearly defined grievance and appeals procedures are usually required in insurance and self-funded plans as well (see Chapter 59). As a general rule, members may be contractually prohibited from filing a lawsuit over benefits denial until they have gone through the plan's grievance procedure. Conversely, if a plan fails to inform a member of grievance rights or fails to abide by the grievance procedure, the plan has a real potential for liability. Suggested steps in formal grievance resolution follow later in this chapter.

Claims Problems Compared with Service Problems

Member complaints and grievances fall into two basic categories: claims problems and service problems. Service problems fall into two basic categories as well: medical service and administrative service.

Claims Problems

Claims problems generally occur when the member seeks coverage for a service that is not covered under the schedule of benefits or is not considered medically necessary or when the member had services rendered without authorization and the plan denied or reduced coverage. In the first two situations, the plan must rely on both the schedule of benefits and determinations of medical necessity by the medical department. In the case of denial or reduction in payment of claims already incurred, the issue of plan policy and procedure is also present because this situation arises from cold claims received without prior PCP authorization.

For prospective denial or reduction of coverage, the plan should respond to the member with the exact contractual language upon which it bases its denial of coverage. There also needs to be a mechanism in place for second opinions by the medical director or designee in those cases where there is a dispute over medical necessity. The medical director must be careful not to confuse these two issues: There may be times when a service can be considered medically necessary but the plan does not cover it under the schedule of benefits.

Cases involving denial or reduction in coverage for services already incurred are a bit more complex. The claims department of the plan will receive a claim without an authorization for services. As discussed in detail in Chapter 31, the plan must have clear policies and procedures for processing such claims. In the case of an HMO without any benefits for out-of-network services, the plan may pend or hold the claims to investigate whether an authorization actually does exist (or should have been given). If an authorization for services ultimately is given, the claim is paid; if no authorization is forthcoming, the claim is denied. The plan may occasionally wish to pay the claim even without an authorization in certain circumstances, such as a genuine emergency, an urgent problem out of the area, or a first offense of a new member.

In POS plans an unauthorized claim is not denied (assuming that it is covered under the schedule of benefits), but the coverage is substantially reduced. As discussed in Chapter 29, it is not always clear when a service was actually authorized and when the member chose to self-refer. The plan must have clear policies to deal with these claims because it is impractical to pend every unauthorized claim, POS being predicated on a certain level of out-of-network use.

In those instances where the claim is ultimately denied or coverage is reduced, members need an appeal mechanism. It is conceivable that the plan's claims payment policies will not envision every contingency, that the claims investigation mechanism will not always be accurate, or that there may be mitigating circumstances involved. There may be a genuine conflict of opinion over whether the member followed plan policies or over issues such as medical necessity. In the case of denial of a claim, the member needs to be informed of appeal rights; whether such information is required when one is processing POS claims is not clear, but most plans do not do so under the assumption that nonauthorized claims are a result of voluntary self-referral by the member and that coverage has not been denied but only paid at the out-of-network level.

Service Problems

Service problems include medical service and administrative service problems. Medical service problems could include a member's inability to get an appointment, rude treatment, lack of physicians located near where the member lives, difficulty getting a needed referral (difficult at least in the opinion of the member), and, most serious, problems with quality of care. Administrative problems could include incorrect identification cards, not issuing an identification card at all, poor responsiveness to previous inquiries, not answering the telephone, lack of documentation or education materials, and so forth.

Member services personnel need to investigate service complaints and get a response to the member. When the complaint alleges quality of care problems, the medical director needs to be notified. If investigation reveals a genuine quality of care problem, the matter requires referral to the quality assurance committee or peer review committee (see Chapters 6 and 25). In most cases, the real problem may be one of communication or of a member demanding a service that the physician feels is unnecessary. In those cases, the member services personnel need to communicate back to the member the results of the investigation or to clarify plan policy regarding coverage.

In all cases of service problems, the key to success is communication. If member services communicates clearly and promptly to all parties, many problems can be cleared up. Such communication must not be confrontational or accusatory. It is important for member services always to keep in mind that there are at least two ways of looking at any one situation and that there is rarely a clear-cut right or wrong.

FORMAL GRIEVANCE PROCEDURE

As indicated earlier, plans (HMOs at least) are required to have a formal grievance procedure, and the responsibility for implementing it falls to the member services department. State regulations (and federal regulations for federally qualified HMOs and competitive medical plans) often spell out the minimum requirements for the procedure. Such requirements may include timeliness of response, who will review the grievance, what recourse the member has, and so forth. Plans are also usually allowed to have a

limitation on how long a member has to file a grievance; for example, if a member fails to file a grievance within 90 days after the problem arises, he or she may lose the right under the plan's grievance procedure to file. Such restrictions may not ultimately prevent lawsuits, but they probably serve to strengthen the plan's position.

Each plan must review applicable state and federal regulations to develop its grievance procedure; the procedure should also be reviewed by the plan's legal counsel to evaluate its utility as a risk management function (see Chapter 38). A general outline of a suggested grievance procedure follows.

Filing of Formal Grievance

Assuming that the plan has been unable satisfactorily to resolve a member complaint, the member must be informed of and afforded the opportunity to file a formal grievance. This is usually done with a form specific to that purpose. The form usually asks for essential information (e.g., name, membership number, parties involved, and so forth) and a narrative of the problem. The form may also contain space for tracking the grievance and responses by other parties.

Investigation of Grievance

During the time period that begins when the form is received and ends when the plan responds, the grievance needs to be investigated. This may include further interviews with the member, interviews with or written responses from other parties, and any other pertinent information. The time period may be set by law or may be set by the plan, but it should not exceed some reasonable period (e.g., 60 days). At the end of that time period, the plan responds to the member with its findings and resolution. The response includes the requirements for the member to respond back to the plan if the resolution is not satisfactory.

Appeal

If the member's grievance is not resolved to his or her satisfaction, the member has the right to appeal. This appeal may involve having the case reviewed by a senior officer of the company or by an outside reviewer. This first appeal is usually done without any formal hearings or testimony but rather is based on the material submitted for review by both the plan and the member. Again, the plan usually sets a reasonable time period for requesting the appeal (e.g., 30 days) and a reasonable time period for the review to occur (e.g., 30 days).

Formal Hearing

If the plan's response is still not satisfactory to the member, some plans afford the member a right to request a formal hearing. There is usually a time limitation (e.g., 15 working days), during which the member must request the hearing or forfeit the right to a hearing. If the plan has a formal hearing right, then once the plan receives a request for a formal hearing the plan has an obligation to respond in a timely manner (e.g., 15 working days). The response is notification of when and where the hearing will take place. The hearing should be scheduled within a reasonable time period (e.g., 15 working days).

The purpose of a formal hearing is to afford the member a chance to present his or her case in person to an unbiased individual or a panel of unbiased individuals. To that end, the hearing officer or the voting members of the hearing panel should not have participated in the earlier decisions, if possible; plan managers who have been involved before will surely participate, but not necessarily as the hearing officer or as voting members.

It is common to use a panel for formal hearings. Panels may be made up of board members, providers (who are not involved with the member on a professional basis), lay members of the plan, or managers from the plan who do not participate in member services issues except for grievances. It is best to use a panel size of odd numbers, preferably five or seven, to prevent ties. There should be a panel chairperson to function as the hearing officer. If a single hearing officer is used, that individual should be the board chairperson, the president of the corporation, or an independent person capable of understanding the issues (e.g., an attorney specializing in health care).

The hearing provides the member the opportunity to present the grievance and any pertinent information. The plan does likewise, usually by having the member services representative present the plan's case. The executive director and medical director may likewise present testimony.

It is a bad idea to ask the member's provider to appear at the hearing in those cases where the provider has been involved in the grievance. This carries the potential of disrupting the physician–patient relationship and of placing the provider in a no-win situation, and it can have implications for future legal action against the provider or plan. Any information from the provider should be presented by the medical director.

A resolution of the grievance is rarely given to the member at the close of the hearing. When the hearing is over, the member is told that he or she will be informed of the results within a set time period (e.g., 15 working days). After the member and staff have left, the voting members of the panel discuss the case and reach a resolution. That resolution is communicated in writing to the member and any other pertinent parties, along with the statement that the member has the right of further appeal to arbitration or the government agency, as appropriate.

Arbitration

In some states, arbitration is allowed. This may occur before or after appeal to the state agency (see below). In those states where arbitration is allowed, and if the plan wishes to pursue it (or if it is required), the plan would comply with the regulations regarding arbitration in terms of selection of the arbitrator(s) and the form of the hearing.

Appeal to Government Agencies

In all cases, if the member is not satisfied with the results of the formal hearing, he or she has the right to appeal to the appropriate government agency. Usually, most members are commercial members; that is, they are members who are neither federal employees nor beneficiaries of entitlement programs but who enroll through a private company or are employees of the state or municipal government. For commercial members, the state insurance department has jurisdiction. In cases where the grievance involves quality of care, the health department may have jurisdiction.

Federal employees, or those who are covered under the Office of Personnel Management (OPM), have the right of appeal to the OPM. The OPM specifically reserves the right in its contract with health plans to resolve and rule on grievances by members who are federal employees. Members who are covered under entitlement programs (Medicare and Medicaid) have the right to appeal to the respective government agency; for Medicare that means the Health Care Financing Administration, and for Medicaid it refers to the state's human services (or welfare) department.

Lawsuits

Although not a part of a plan's grievance procedure, the last legal remedy for a disgruntled member is legal action. If the plan carefully follows its grievance procedure, the chances of a successful lawsuit against it are small. If the plan fails to follow proper policy and procedure, the chances become pretty high. See Chapter 38 for a full discussion of risk management.

DATA COLLECTION AND ANALYSIS

The member services department should be responsible for collecting, collating, and analyzing data. Data may be considered in two broad categories: data regarding general levels of satisfaction and dissatisfaction, and data regarding medical and administrative problems (trends analysis).

Satisfaction Data

Satisfaction data may include surveys of current members, disenrollment surveys, telephone response time and waiting time studies (these may be done in conjunction with the quality management department, but they are essentially patient satisfaction studies), and surveys of clients and accounts (although marketing rather than member services may perform many of these studies).

Member surveys are particularly useful when done properly. Even when a managed care plan is the sole carrier in an account (e.g., a replacement POS plan), surveys help the plan evaluate service levels and ascertain what issues are important to the members. Surveys may be focused on a few issues that the plan wants to study, or they may be broad and comprehensive.[3]

In an environment where members have multiple choices for their health care coverage, member surveys will be geared toward issues that influence enrollment choices. It is easier and less expensive to retain a member than it is to sell a new one. Of special importance are those members who do not heavily utilize medical services because their premiums pay for the expenses of high utilizers and because such members tend to disenroll more often than members who utilize services heavily.[4] Surveys designed to analyze what makes those low-utilizing members leave or stay (or join in the first place) can lead to the development of targeted member retention programs. Some plans develop direct mail campaigns that include giveaways or promote services available to low utilizers (e.g., health promotion) to have those members place a sense of value on their membership in the plan.

Trends Analysis

Problems that are brought to the plan's attention not only require resolution but need to be analyzed to look for trends. If a problem is sporadic or random, there may be little required other than helping the individual member as needed. If problems are widespread or stem from something that is likely to cause continual problems, then the plan must act to resolve the problems at the source. Such resolution may mean changing a policy or procedure, improving education materials to the members, dealing with a difficult provider, or any number of events. The point is that plan management will not know of chronic problems if the data are not analyzed.

Many plans now automate their member services tracking systems. Such automation not only serves to help member services track and manage individual problems but also serves as a method to collect and collate data. Each member contact with the plan is entered into the computerized tracking system and assigned a category (or multiple categories if necessary); issues involving providers are generally tracked not only by category but by provider as well. Repeat or follow-up calls are also tracked but usually still count as only one problem or inquiry.

Producing regular reports summarizing the frequency of each category as well as the frequency of problems or complaints by provider (along with monitoring of the rate at which members transfer out of a provider's practice) allows management to focus attention appropriately. An example of the types of categories that a plan may track is given in Exhibit 30–1. This example applies primarily to HMOs or POS plans and is by no means exhaustive; conversely, it is unlikely that a plan would use all these categories.

PROACTIVE APPROACHES TO MEMBER SERVICES

Most member services departments become complaint departments. When that happens, the plan not only loses a valuable source of member satisfaction but runs the risk of burning out the personnel in the department. It is emotionally draining to listen to complaints all day. Even the

satisfaction of successfully resolving the majority of complaints can be inadequate if there is nothing else the plan is doing to address satisfaction. In addition to analyzing the sources of dissatisfaction and complaints to resolve the problems at the source, the plan might consider the following suggestions.

Member Suggestions and Recommendations

Soliciting member suggestions and recommendations can be valuable. This may be done along with member surveys, or the plan may solicit suggestions through response cards in physicians' offices or in the member newsletter. There are times when the members will have ways of viewing the plan that provide valuable insight to managers. Although not all the suggestions may be practical, they may at least illuminate trouble spots that need attention of some sort.

Affiliations with Health Clubs and Health Promotion Activities

Managed care plans frequently develop affiliations with health clubs and other types of health-related organizations. This serves to underscore the emphasis on prevention and health maintenance, allows for differentiation with competitors, and provides value-added service to the member. Access to or sponsorship of various health promotion activities falls into the same category.

A special type of health promotion is the provision of health advice from nurses available on the telephone. This is meant not as a replacement for physician advice but rather as a supplement. Advice may range from helping a member deal with a minor illness to explaining and educating about surgical procedures. This may be done in tandem with distribution of self-help medical books and other health promotion literature. Some closed panel plans are providing this type of service to a remarkable degree. These plans have well-designed education materials, such as interactive videos, literature, and personal edu-

Exhibit 30–1 Examples of Categories for a Member Contact Tracking System

Enrollment issues
- Selecting a PCP
  - Practice closed
  - Never selected
  - Special needs
- Changing PCP
  - Dissatisfied with PCP
  - PCP no longer participating with plan
  - Geographic reasons
- Identification card(s)
  - Never received
  - Errors on card
  - Change in information
  - Lost card
- Change in enrollment status
  - New dependent
  - Delete dependent
  - Student or disabled dependent verification
- Change in address
  - Subscriber
  - Dependent(s)
- Need evidence of coverage or other documentation
- Need new directory of providers

Benefits issues
- Questions
  - Physician services (primary care, specialty care)
  - Hospital or institutional services
  - Emergency services
  - Ancillary services (pharmacy, other)
  - POS benefits questions
- Complaints
  - Copayment or coinsurance levels
  - Limitations on coverage
  - Did not know benefits levels

Claims issues
- In-network
  - Claims denied (HMO)
  - Claim cascaded to lower level of benefits (POS)
  - Unpaid claim (provider submitted, member submitted)
  - Received bill from provider
  - Coordination of benefits
  - Subrogation/other party liability
- Out of network
  - Claim denied (HMO)
  - Claim cascaded to lower level of benefits (POS)

  - Unpaid claim (provider submitted, member submitted)
  - Received bill from provider
  - Coordination of benefits
  - Subrogation/other party liability

Plan policies and procedures
- Authorization system for specialty care
- Precertification system for institutional care
- Second opinion procedures
- Copayments and coinsurance
- Unable to understand printed materials or instructions
- Complaint and grievance procedures

Plan administration
- Personnel rude or unhelpful
- Incorrect or inappropriate information given
- Telephone responsiveness problems
  - On hold
  - Unanswered calls
  - Call not returned
- Complaints or grievances not addressed satisfactorily

Access to care
- Unable to get an appointment
- Too long before appointment scheduled
- Office hours not convenient
- Waiting time too long in office
- Problems accessing care after hours
- Too far to travel to get care
- No public transportation
- Calls not returned

Physician issues
- Unpleasant or rude behavior
- Unprofessional or inappropriate behavior
- Does not spend adequate time with member
- Does not provide adequate information
  - Medical
  - Financial
  - Administrative (e.g., referral process)
- Lack of compliance with use of plan network
- Lack of compliance with authorization policies
- Does not speak member's language
- Speaks negatively about the plan

Perceived appropriateness and quality of care
- Delayed treatment
- Inappropriate denial of treatment

(continues)

Exhibit 30–1 continued

- Inappropriate denial of referral
- Unnecessary treatment
- Incorrect diagnosis or treatment
- Lack of follow-up
  —Physician visit
  —Diagnostic tests

Medical office facility issues
- Lack of privacy
- Unclean or unpleasant
- Unsafe or ill equipped
- Lack of adequate parking

Institutional care issues
- Perceived poor care in hospital
- Discharged too soon
- Hospital or facility staff behavior
  —Rude or unpleasant behavior
  —Unprofessional or inappropriate behavior
  —Speak negatively about the plan
- Facility unclean or unpleasant
- Facility unsafe or ill equipped
- Problems with admission or discharge process
- Other administrative errors

cation. For certain types of procedures, such as transurethral prostatectomy, the member must participate in an interactive video before making a choice regarding an elective procedure. Some open panel plans are also providing such services either through their own personnel or through contracts with outside firms. Many advanced managed care plans are using this type of service to help reduce the demand for physician-related services; see Chapter 17 for more discussion of this topic.

CONCLUSION

Member services are a requirement of any managed care plan. The primary responsibility of member services is to help members resolve any problems or questions they may have. Member services must also track and analyze member problems and complaints so that management can act to correct problems at the source. Mechanisms to resolve complaints and grievances not only are required by law but make good business sense. Plan management should not be satisfied with a reactive member services function but should take a proactive approach as well.

REFERENCES AND NOTES

1. C.R. Bell and R. Zemke, Service Breakdown: The Road to Recovery, *Management Review* 76 (1987): 32–35.

2. S.W. Hall, Targeting Member Needs with Technology, *HMO Magazine* (July/August 1993): 55–56.

3. Group Health Association of America (GHAA), *GHAA's Consumer Satisfaction Survey*, 2d ed. Washington, D.C.: GHAA, 1991.

4. W. Wrightson, et al., Demographic and Utilization Characteristics of HMO Disenrollees. *GHAA Journal* (Summer 1987): 23–42.

SUGGESTED READING

Furse, D.H., Bucham, M.R., et al. 1994. Leveraging the Value of Customer Satisfaction Information. *Journal of Health Care Marketing* 14(3): 16–20.

Gold, M. and Woolridge, J. 1995. Surveying Consumer Satisfaction To Assess Managed-Care Quality: Current Practices. *Health Care Financing Review* 16: 155–173.

Hall, S.W. 1993. Targeting Member Needs with Technology. *HMO Magazine* 34(4): 55–56.

Kenkel, P., ed. 1995. Centered Information. *Managed Care Quarterly* 3(4).

Noe, T.J. 1994. Bypassing the Busy Signal. *HMO Magazine* 35(3): 81–82, 83.

Polonski, G.J. 1995. Customer Complaints: A Managed Care Firm's Best Weapon in CQI. *Medical Interface* 8(1): 111–117.

Youngs, M.T. and Wingerson, L. 1995. *The 1996 Medical Outcomes & Guidelines Sourcebook*. New York, N.Y.: Faulkner & Gray.

Chapter 31

Claims and Benefits Administration

Robert S. Eichler and Robin L. McElfatrick

The claims and benefits administration department is literally where the buck stops, or goes, within a managed care organization (MCO). When all else is said and done in terms of other corporate functions (sales, enrollment, utilization management, etc.), the bottom line is that somewhere between 75 percent and 93 percent of all premium dollars are paid out for medical care in capitation and claims payments combined. The effectiveness of the claims department can literally either make or break the company. It is precisely this point that provides MCOs with the impetus to pay close attention to their claims and benefits administration responsibilities.

Claims and benefits administration is not an independent function that gathers, records, and manages all the information necessary to do its job effectively. Instead, claims is part of an integrated organization and process that is actually downstream of and dependent upon many other functions and departments within the MCO.

Historically, within indemnity insurance and even in most MCOs, claims and benefits administration functions were viewed (and positioned) as back room operations. Little attention was given to their positioning within the organization, their internal structures, and even their physical settings. In today's MCOs the realization of the importance of the claims and benefits administration function has meant an elevation of its status. Claims and benefits administration is now viewed as being equally important as other core organizational functions, such as medical management and finance.

Throughout this chapter, we attempt to place equal focus on management and operations tasks to assist readers in establishing new claims and benefits administration functions or in evaluating existing ones. The subject of other party liability (OPL) is discussed separately in Chapter 32.

Robert S. Eichler is Vice President of The Scheur Management Group, Inc. His area of expertise is managed care systems and claims and other party liability operations. He has assisted clients in system strategy, evaluation, selection and customization, operational evaluation and reengineering, claims and other party liability audits, and functional analyses. He has also designed and developed software to support other party liability and provider credentialing operations.

Robin L. McElfatrick has experience encompassing 23 years in HMOs, indemnity plans, and managed care consulting and serves The Scheur Management Group, Inc. clients in organizational analysis, operations, medical management, MIS assessments, claims, and coordination of benefits. Her work with clients ranging from small IPAs to a major national health care firm has included a wide variety of operations and systems-related assignments.

CLAIMS: POSITIONING, PURPOSE, AND OPPORTUNITIES

To understand the purpose of and opportunities presented by claims and benefits administration functions, one must understand this area's positioning within the organization.

Positioning

Claims and benefits administration is really a "middleman" between various internal and external groups. Claims comes between sales and enrollment and group accounts when providing benefits coverage. It also comes between the providers and customer service when processing claims and providing reimbursement for those services. You will, no doubt, know of many other examples where claims assumes a "middleman" position.

In examining the strategic positioning of claims and benefits administration, it is fair to say that the function lies at the last point in the flow of organizational activities where the company has an opportunity to "make it right" (the first time around) with the provider and/or member customer. Other than sales and enrollment functions, where the MCO faces employer and member customers and has a chance to make positive first impressions, conduct of the claims and benefits administration process frequently presents the first real occasion for the MCO to demonstrate its ability to deliver on its service promise. Groups, members, and providers expect prompt and accurate payment of claims. It is often these first demonstrations of service abilities that form the basis of the purchasers', members', and participating providers' lasting opinions about an MCO's performance.

Many MCOs get caught up in internal conflict and argument over what went wrong, why, and who is to blame when claims and benefits administration functions are performed less than optimally. When asked to explain or account for high backlog or claims error rates in claims production, frustrated claims examiners, supervisors, and managers typically respond with statements like these: "If only the enrollment records were timely and accurate, I'd be able to get these claims out faster." "How can I process a claim when the authorization is never in the system when I need it?" "If given more automation through systems support, the claims shop would make fewer errors." Although all these conditions may be true at times, they are internal is-sues that customers could care less about. When claims decisions are delayed or payments are inaccurate, the customer forms one opinion and one opinion only: This MCO cannot deliver on the promises it makes.

Rather than get caught up in the quagmire of backpedaling to correct customers' dissatisfaction with claims service, the MCO must employ preemptive strategies and tactics to ensure a successful claims and benefits administration operation.

Purpose

The first step in ensuring the success of the claims and benefits administration process is to define clearly and agree on its purpose both within the department and between the department and other corporate areas or functions. Claims and benefits administration fulfills the following five basic purposes for the MCO and its customers.

Plan Contract Administration

MCOs have several different contracts with many types of individuals or entities. Claims and benefits administration is concerned with meeting relevant contractual obligations that the MCO has made to groups, members, and providers. Claims-related contractual obligations include benefits (see below), processing time frames, reimbursement methodologies and amounts, appeal mechanisms, and grievance procedures. To meet these obligations, claims and benefits administration must establish and maintain adequate work flow and control procedures to ensure timely and appropriate processing of claims, appeals, and grievances and must coordinate with and rely on assistance from other areas within the MCO. Reimbursement methodologies and amounts are translated into pricing fee schedules and guidelines that should be automated to ensure consistency in and timeliness of application.

Benefits Administration

For each group and individual contract, claims and benefits administration is responsible for ensuring coverage for the benefits program defined. Contracts typically describe benefits for eligible members in general terms and by category of care and include benefit limitations, member cost-sharing obligations, and exclusions. To administer contractually provided benefits, claims and benefits administration must translate the more generally described benefits into specific coverage issues, to the point of defining what is covered (or excluded) by CPT-4 procedure codes. The task of translating coverage issues into specific procedure codes is often tedious but is absolutely necessary if claims are to be processed accurately and on time. As an example, if the benefit description includes coverage for durable medical equipment (DME), including repairs, when medically necessary and appropriate, are all types of wheelchairs covered? Do repairs include routine service? Member cost sharing via coinsurance, copayments, and deductibles must also be interpreted specifically to be applied correctly at the claim line item level.

Medical Management Policy Administration

A common overriding premise in an MCO benefits program is that covered services must also be medically necessary and appropriate. Medical necessity and appropriateness is a concept that is administered on a claim- or case-specific basis given individual clinical circumstances. The most frequently occurring examples of medically necessary and appropriateness decisions are those that are made before the provision of care. In these circumstances the MCO establishes, contractually and with its providers, the types of services and procedures that require prior approval by MCO medical management staff. Prior approval is translated into referral authorizations and precertifications, which serve as instructions to the claims and benefits administration staff in handling subsequent claims. The second most frequently occurring case of medical policy administration is when the claims and benefits administration department coordinates with medical management to define those types of cases that must receive

clinical review for coverage determination and those that can be processed by claims staff given specific guidelines and procedures.

Member and Provider Service

Although most MCOs maintain separate member and provider service functions, the core of what the claims and benefits administration department does is provide service to these customers. Claims and benefits administration fulfills a large percentage of the total service promise that the MCO has sold. When claims are processed incorrectly or late, providers' cash flow is affected, which can (although typically prohibited in MCO–provider contracts) result in balance billing to members. At a minimum, providers and members are pitted against each other when MCO claims functions do not run smoothly. The member and provider services departments rely on claims and benefits administration staff to solve claims riddles. No matter how well trained the staff of these other departments are, they will never understand, and cannot reasonably be expected to understand, all the nuances of claims adjudication.

Liability Protection

By virtue of its contractual obligations, the MCO holds itself out as responsible for coverage of defined benefits in the types, quantities, time frames, and reimbursement amounts specified. Anything less or more creates an unnecessary liability for the organization. All claims errors, whether they result in overpayment or underpayment, present additional and unnecessary financial liability to the MCO. Overpayments, which are often, but not always, detected or reported, inflate medical expense at worst (if undetected or unreported) and increase administrative expense at best (if adjusted). Underpayments, which are almost always reported, require adjustment and additional payment, thereby increasing administrative expense. Some state regulatory agencies or legislative bodies impose fines on MCOs that do not meet defined claims processing time frames. The third area of liability risk that a claims and benefits administration shop may impose on an MCO is related to the timeliness of claims decisions and payments. In the last decade there has been precedent in several areas of the country for compensatory, and even punitive, damage awarded to members of MCOs who have held that delayed coverage and/or payment decisions resulted in roadblocks to needed medical care.

Opportunities

Even with all the obligations and risks inherent in the act of processing a claim and with all the difficulties implicit in the positioning of the claims operation, claims and benefits administration presents a situation rich in opportunities. The first opportunity is the prospect of providing excellent service to provider and member customers. The challenge to MCOs is to operate by design versus chance when organizing, staffing, managing, and coordinating the necessary resources and activities to effect optimum claims and benefits administration operations. No less attention and fewer resources should be committed to this function than to any other function within the MCO.

For claims and benefits administration management and staff, there is the opportunity to establish and maintain effective relationships with corporate colleagues. To do its job well, the claims and benefits administration department must coordinate with and develop constructive working relationships with virtually every other function within the organization. It is the responsibility of management in all organizational areas to ensure, directly or through delegation, that the necessary integrated policies, procedures, information, and work flows exist to enable the claims operation to run effectively.

Because of the relative positioning of claims and benefits administration within the MCO (i.e., downstream of most other corporate functions and "middleman" for others), the opportunity exists within claims to identify weak spots in both precedent and subsequent processes. Although one may consider this a tenuous position to be in, if handled judiciously and in politically appropriate ways, reporting issues and working with colleagues to resolve problems in other areas can be significant assets to the corporation.

The various tasks associated with claims and benefits administration often require review of contracts and other corporate documents for clarification and guidance. In doing so, claims and benefits administration staff have an opportunity to observe any extant inconsistencies between documents and/or loopholes in particular documents. Left unresolved, these issues can create confusion and ambiguity on the part of customers and unnecessary liability on the part of the MCO.

The outcome of the claims and benefits administration process is the creation and maintenance of a total rendered care database. This database is the source of information for innumerable, important corporate functions and activities. For example, claims and encounter data are used for quality assurance (QA) and quality improvement studies, the development and reporting of utilization management statistics, and the development of capitation and premium rates. All these activities rely on the completeness, accuracy, and timeliness of the database, again an opportunity for claims and benefits administration.

ORGANIZATIONAL STRUCTURE AND STAFFING

Organizational Positioning within the Company

The claims function within an MCO holds a unique position in that it can be viewed alternatively as a primarily financial or operational function. Add to this equation claims processing's heavy reliance upon, and contribution to, the definition of management information services (MIS) requirements, and strong arguments may be made for placing claims processing under the control of finance, operations, or MIS. In spite of the financial focus (i.e., that claims processing is, in effect, a highly complex accounts payable function), it is precisely the degree of operational complexity that places it more effectively under the auspices of operations. The financial components of claims work—the generation of checks, the recovery of overpayments due to OPL, retroactive terminations, claims processing adjustments, and so forth—can be controlled effectively through direct coordination with appropriate contacts in the finance area. Similarly, despite the high degree of MIS involvement, both claims and MIS functions have substantial areas of responsibility that require specialized expertise that is not interdependent. Claims, for example, combines significant operational flow and areas of intelligent intervention (clinical expertise, reinsurance, and OPL recovery operations) that, although requiring system support, extend beyond the ability to codify decision-making processes. MIS, too, has responsibilities (technical and plant operations and other functional areas requiring significant MIS support) that extend beyond the focus of claims functions. Therefore, these two functions, although codependent, if combined do not contribute to efficient or effective plan management.

More effectively, claims is under the direction of a director or vice president on equal footing with the directors of MIS, finance, medical management, and so forth. This organizational structure appears to be more effective than one in which a claims manager reports to finance or operations because it gives the claims function the importance it needs within the organization.

Organization within Claims

The director or vice president of claims is the planner, coordinator (with other areas), and strategist; he or she is knowledgeable about all aspects of the organization and knows contracts and local legislative and regulatory requirements. A sample job description is included in Table 31–1, and a sample organizational chart is shown in Figure 31–1. Reporting to the director, the manager is the direct controller over line operations. The manager is responsible for designing, monitoring, and managing work flow;

maintaining procedural documentation; conducting staff training and development; and resolving claim-specific and work flow problems. Other positions within claims include a number of supervisors (depending on the size of the shop and the span of management) reporting to the manager and a hierarchy of examiners (junior and senior).

Supervisors may be organized to encompass responsibility for equivalent, comprehensive processing steps for all claims within a line of business or for particular customers, or they may be designated as responsible for specific functional areas (e.g., clerical support staff, data entry, pended claims resolution, OPL, QA, and so forth). Typically, designation as an examiner reflects experience and authority. Additionally, the examiner level may indicate expertise in a particular specialized claim type by line of business (e.g., Medicare claims), by function (e.g., training, OPL, or QA) or complexity of provider contract (particularly if contract terms cannot be supported by MIS). Finally, claims operations include a number of clerical support personnel: secretary(ies) to the director, manager, and supervisors as well as mail room support for the activities of incoming document control, microfilming (if performed), and sorting and support for file room document storage and retrieval.

The various choices for structuring the claims department carry implications for smooth work flow through the department. In small plans, the ability to define specialized units within claims is contraindicated by the necessity for cross-training to provide coverage for absenteeism. In larger plans, management will have the luxury of designing the organizational structure according to functional requirements and corporate strategy (e.g., customer-driven units in combination with similar alignment through marketing, enrollment, benefits and medical management, and customer service). More often, the organizational structure of the department may be driven by MIS deficiencies. For example, if the system cannot support differentiated benefits and product rules, claims units may be divided by line of business or employer group so that examiner

Table 31–1 Sample Job Descriptions

Title/Goal	Tasks Required	Experience
Claims Director: Plans and strategizes claims operational support of business lines, groups, products, and contracts. Knowledgeable about all aspects of the organization.	Coordinates (with other areas within the company and with peer companies) and develops interdepartmental operational strategies. Develops and monitors annual budget. Through auditing and internal reporting, proactively identifies negative or positive trends and develops recommendations for change. Establishes and maintains cost-effective and high-quality relationships with contracted vendors for OPL, equipment maintenance, third party claims coding, or procedure review vendors. Maintains current industry knowledge through association memberships, annual meetings, etc. Payment authority up to $XXX.	Thorough knowledge of contracts, laws, and regulations relating to managed care claims processing and related functions. Demonstrated management ability to budget and administer a claims program. Master's degree in health care administration preferred. Equivalent experience acceptable.
Claims Manager: Plans and manages the activities of the claims administration department to ensure the achievement of stated department and plan goals and objectives.	Oversees all activities related to claims processing. Establishes standards of performance for each unit, including training, policies and procedures, auditing, and other performance measurement techniques. Evaluates and monitors staff performance with respect to complaint handling and resolution. Develops and implements cost control measures. Identifies areas for improvement in communication, benefit structure, and plan administration. Resolves high level problems related to claims, eligibility, or benefits. Payment authority up to $XXX.	Knowledge of laws and regulations relating to managed care claims processing and related functions. Knowledge of managed care computer systems, features, and reporting. Knowledgeable about employment practices, budgeting, and general management functions. Demonstrated management ability to coach, train, and administer a claims program. Bachelor's degree preferred. Equivalent experience acceptable.
Claims Supervisor: Plans and supervises the activities of subunits within the claims department to ensure that department, plan, and regulatory requirements are met for output, quality, timeliness, and service.	Supervises employees' daily activities, delegates work, and trains and coaches employees regularly regarding performance. Resolves problems related to claims, eligibility, or benefits. Provides necessary information to related plan units and their systems. Prepares materials for the grievance committee. Reviews and releases claims up to $XXX. Prepares routine reports for the manager on productivity, error rates, complaint rates, financial recordkeeping, and other activities.	Thorough knowledge of claims processing regulations, systems, and procedures, preferably in a managed care setting. Demonstrated supervisory background and experience. Ability to work with computer programs to perform analysis and word processing. Education and experience equivalent to 2 years of college education, 3–5 years of claims processing adjudication experience, preferably in a managed care setting.
Claims Examiner: Reviews and pays health claims up to a certain complexity level.	Pays claims within authorization limits according to established quality and service standards. Determines eligibility of members, acceptability of evidence submitted, and necessity for additional information or review. Resolves issues before claims payment to avoid readjudication. Refers complex claims or claims falling out of standard procedure guidelines to senior examiner or supervisor. Provides routine reporting of work volume and productivity as required by the supervisor. Analyzes all relevant materials for the processing of claims up to $XXX.	High school education. Minimum of 1–3 years of claims processing experience in an environment of multiple plan benefits and provider contracts.

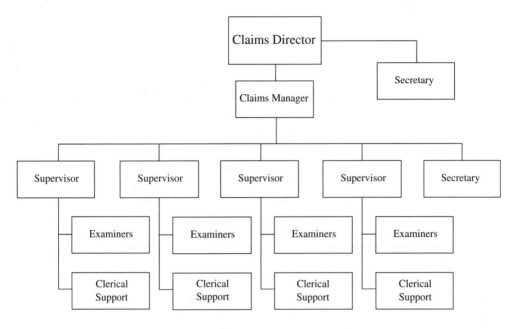

Figure 31–1 Claims department organizational structure.

knowledge and proficiency may compensate during claims processing. Likewise, if the complexity of provider pricing arrangements is not supported by automation, claims may default to designated units by provider type.

The critical element in structuring an effective work flow through the organizational structure is determining communication requirements among and between the units and designing efficient methods for claims to cross organizational structural boundaries without the respective units succumbing to finger-pointing for lost or substandard work. Figures 31–2 and 31–3 show the impact of organizational structure on work flow.

Staffing

Although Table 31–2 gives some indication of administrative, examiner, and clerical full-time equivalent (FTE) employees required for various ranges of members enrolled in the plan, it is important to include in any staffing equation

the number and complexity of products serviced, the number and complexity of reimbursement methodologies used, and the degree and quality of automated support that may be brought to bear upon the claims adjudication process. A high degree of complexity in any of these areas or a lack of system support for these or any adjudication and pricing functions will require a greater number of FTEs. Table 31–1 provides general guidelines for claims staff tasks and required expertise.

CLAIMS OPERATIONS MANAGEMENT

For claims and benefits administration, operations management means the base resources, methods, processes, procedures, and systems employed to form the foundation of a successful department. Although unfortunately there is no magic formula for arriving at the exact best configuration of these elements for each MCO, each of these components is a direct contributor to overall success or failure. Careful planning,

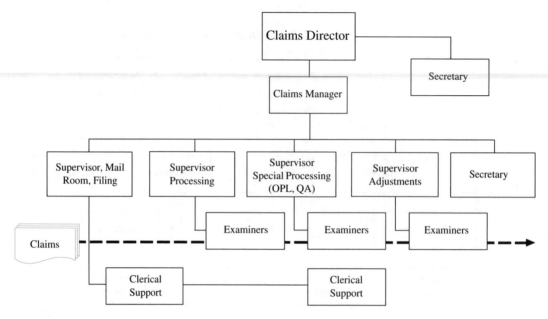

Figure 31–2 Impact of organizational structure on work flow: Supervisory units organized by function.

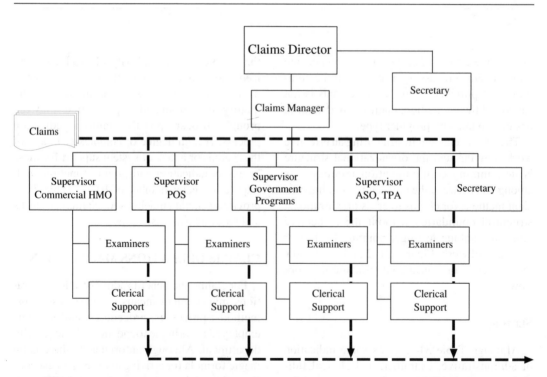

Figure 31–3 Impact of organizational structure on work flow: Supervisory units organized by line of business or customer-driven unit. HMO, health maintenance organization; POS, point of service; ASO, administrative services only; TPA, third party administrator.

Table 31–2 Claims Staffing Ratios by Health Maintenance Organization Model and Membership: Average Ratio of Staff to Members

Model/Membership	Total Staff	Analysts	Clerks
Model			
Staff	1:4,711	1:18,958	1:22,164
Group	1:3,697	1:20,176	1:17,305
Independent practice association	1:4,899	1:12,465	1:21,808
Membership			
< 25,000	1:3,135	1:6,483	1:8,000
25–50,000	1:4,653	1:13,518	1:17,166
51–100,000	1:4,630	1:13,549	1:21,498
101–200,000	1:4,237	1:24,731	1:25,561
> 200,000	1:7,938	1:19,085	1:38,867

Source: Courtesy of Warren Surveys, Rockford, Illinois. For further information call 815/877-8794.

implementation, and maintenance of each of these operational factors are essential to claims and benefits administration.

Inventory Control

To control inventory, there must first be agreement as to just what inventory is. Webster's dictionary defines *inventory* as "A detailed, often descriptive, list of articles, giving the code number, quantity and value of each." The key words here are *detailed*, *articles* (claims and encounters), *code number* (type of claim), and *quantity and value of each*.

Most other businesses that you can think of rely on inventory control as a means of managing and accounting for assets. In an MCO, cash obtained through premium revenue is the primary source of assets; capitation and claims expense are the primary sources of liabilities. Claims and benefits administration must effectively control its inventory in support of corporate management of assets and liabilities. The inventory control responsibility includes a definition of inventory, what an acceptable level is, how to evaluate current inventory, how to control it (including retrieval as necessary), and how to report on it.

Mechanisms for inventory control include clearly written procedures (including definitions, categories, methods, etc.), a sound inventory process that occurs at reasonable intervals, ways to record receipts on a timely basis and to monitor the movement of those receipts throughout the process, automation support, work flow simplicity, and assigned responsibility and authority for controlling inventory. Basic principles, or rules, of inventory management include the following:

- All receipts need to be logged in to the mainframe claims processing system within a day or two of their receipt.

- When claims are transferred (permanently or temporarily) to another department, they need to be noted as a transferral. If a claim (or copy of a claim) goes to another department, there should be an agreed-upon time frame for the return of that transaction, and that time frame should be monitored actively.

- Work to be done should be stored centrally to the extent possible. File integrity must be maintained to ensure that work to be done is not misplaced.

- Control and recording mechanisms should be checked periodically to make sure they are still effective and accurate.

The essence of inventory control is accounting for all units of work on hand by category of work/transaction, defining where these transactions are in terms of their processing, and verifying the validity of ongoing counting. Basically all units of work on hand get counted. All claims and transactions, no matter what their form, get counted: paper, electronic, or tape submissions; encounters (sometimes called statistical claims); suspended or pended claims; requests for adjustments; and authorizations and referrals (if done in your claims shop). There may be other transactions as well (e.g., member-submitted claims, laboratory billings that come in on computer printouts, and telephone and written inquiries).

You may ask: Why count everything if claims and encounters are our main responsibility? The answer is that a complete and detailed inventory will tell you much more than what you have on hand. It is a measure of productivity. You can see how well your current work flow facilitates movement of claims and other transactions through your department. You can test staffing levels, task allocation, and grouping of tasks. You can identify problems, such as bottlenecks in the flow, aged claims in suspense, illogical groupings of tasks, and counting problems.

For each work unit, you want to know type and processing stage:

- *electronic receipts:* in preparation, received but untouched, or received and processed (again, by type of claim)
- *paper claims/encounters:* in preparation (in the mail room), to be processed (on the shelf/desk to be done), to be entered (if done by operations rather than claims examiners), or processed
- *suspended/pended transactions* (electronic or paper; claims or encounters): by suspense/pend status (why suspended), suspense age (how long in that status), and if resolved
- *authorizations and referrals* (if entered within claims): by processing stage and type

A key principle in the management of inventory is front-end control. Under this principle, everything, be it new receipts that come into the department or documents returned from internal or external sources, is date stamped, counted, categorized, batched, and recorded at the point of its receipt. Batches are rational units, groupings of work that can be done in reasonable periods of time (e.g., claims to be processed in batches of 25). The practice of front-end control enables management to ensure that all units of work are accounted for from the minute they are received within the department.

In addition to required definitions and principles, inventory control can be aided significantly through automation support. Electronic data interchange enables MCOs to receive claims electronically, thereby negating the need to count in batch and store receipts manually until they are processed. Although there needs to be a reconciliation procedure between what the biller submitted electronically and what the MCO received, electronically received transactions should, for the most part, be capable of being controlled and processed automatically.

The ability to log transactions into the claims processing system as they are received but before they are processed is critical. Computerized logs, on the mainframe or in personal computer applications, are important to track movement of claims into and out of the department before they are finalized. The claims processing system should be able to support predetermined age and status assignment categories for claims as they move along in the various processing stages. This is particularly true for suspended claims.

Reporting can also be significantly supported through automation. These reports need to be thorough yet usable. Certain automation aids, such as optical character recognition, can cut certain inventory control steps considerably and ensure a greater level of accuracy.

The last significant area of automation support for inventory control is document filming, archiving, and retrieval. Microfilming and optical character recognition are the most commonly used forms of document imaging at present. Although a surprisingly large number of claims and benefits administration operations still maintain hard copy claims files for retrieval, unless there is a relatively small membership in the MCO and/or the MCO is very new, automated forms of imaging and retrieval are much more efficient for claims operations.

An outcome of inventory control is productivity measurement. By virtue of the fact that inventory management includes a running count of what came into and went out of the department, it necessarily captures and records individual and departmental productivity counts. Accounting for and managing pended/suspended claims is also an integral part of inventory control. Because pended transactions usually represent the largest single category of aged claims, it is necessary to track their location, status, and age within each location and status at all times. Aggregate pend counts are routinely tracked and reported in inventory processes.

To keep ongoing inventory counts and control, it is necessary to create a starting point with a physical inventory of all work on hand and to proceed from that point with daily counts of receipts, productivity, and remaining inventory. Daily counts are produced in two forms—individual and departmental—and rely on ongoing counting measures among physical inventories. For each job function with the claims and benefits administration department, a daily count sheet is filled out and collected for tabulation into a departmental total. Daily count sheets should be simple for ease in completing and should capture units of work received by type; transactions completed by type; transactions pended, suspended, or remaining on the desk by type; and date of receipt of the oldest claim and the oldest encounter on the desk. Weekly reporting consists of a summary of daily counts. See

Exhibit 31-1 for a sample claims and benefits administration productivity/inventory report.

There are two basic levels of claims reporting: departmental reporting and plan reporting. Departmental reporting is detailed and specific; it encompasses all the information you need to manage your shop. It should cover, at a minimum, all claims/encounter productivity and inventory (beginning, received, processed, and ending) by work unit and type of claim/encounter, nonclaim inventory and production (adjustments, internal inquiries, authorizations, and referrals; if applicable, written and telephone inquiries from providers and members; and walk-ins if they are handled by claims), number of weeks' work on hand (volume divided by average weekly production), oldest claim to be worked and date being worked (for new receipts), and a comments or notes section for things such as resource expenditure (total hours worked, regular and overtime), systems availability (any significant downtime), unavailability of staff (due to holidays, absenteeism, training/seminar time, etc.), or any other reasons for variances in normal productivity and inventory.

Claims reports for others in the MCO are generally less detailed and focus on the main work responsibilities of the department and their status. Plan reporting of claims and benefits administration inventory and productivity is usually limited to total production and inventory by work unit and type of claim/encounter, number of weeks' work on hand, oldest claim to be worked, and special inventory issues, such as certain types of claims that are being given priority or explanations of major variances.

To maintain an accurate count of all work on hand, it is necessary to perform a physical inventory on a periodic basis. With a physical inventory, all units of work are counted by work unit, type of transaction, and stage in processing. As the work is counted, the batches are labeled to avoid recounting. All work is then tallied. The results of the physical inventory are then compared with the count balances that are run from week to week (again, by type of claim/work unit and processing stage). The physical inventory

Exhibit 31–1 Sample Claims Productivity/Inventory Report

Unit	Inventory	IP	OP	1500	ENCS	OTHER	TOTAL
MAIL/PREP	BEGINNING						
DATE OF OLDEST WORK	RECEIVED						
	PROCESSED						
_____	ENDING						
TAPE & ELECTRONIC RECEIPTS							
EXAMINERS	BEGINNING						
DATE OF OLDEST WORK	RECEIVED						
	PROCESSED						
_____	ENDING						
DATA ENTRY	BEGINNING						
DATE OF OLDEST WORK	RECEIVED						
	PROCESSED						
_____	ENDING						
SUSPENSE	BEGINNING						
DATE OF OLDEST WORK	RECEIVED						
	PROCESSED						
_____	ENDING						

OTHER WORK: PRODUCTIVITY AND INVENTORY

	AUTH/CERTS	REFERRALS	INTERNAL QS	EXTERNAL QS
BEGINNING				
RECEIVED				
PROCESSED				
ENDING				

TOTALS	BEGINNING	RECEIVED	PROCESSED	ENDING
CLAIMS	_____	_____	_____	_____
ENCOUNTERS	_____	_____	_____	_____
AUTH/REF	_____	_____	_____	_____
INQUIRIES	_____	_____	_____	_____

counts, by category, are then reconciled to the weekly running counts. Reasons for possible discrepancies are then identified. Some common culprits are live claims sent to other departments, claims done at home (cottage industry), claims buried on someone's desk, and erroneous batch labeling. Sometimes a partial inventory is called for. A good example is suspended claims that show up in the system but cannot be accounted for in live claims.

Pended Claims Management

Pended/suspended claims typically account for the largest portion of a claims and benefits administration department's problem cases. Although the terms *pend* and *suspend* are often used synonymously, some MCOs differentiate between claims that examiners place on hold (pends) and those that are placed on hold automatically by one or more systems edits (suspends). In this discussion, both types of transactions are addressed.

The volume of pended/suspended claims is directly linked to the accuracy and completeness of predecessor functions (e.g., enrollment, provider relations, utilization management, etc.) and the number, type, and logic of edits that are defined in the claims module (and any related "side-car" modules, such as rebundlers, software programs that roll up and reprice fragmented bills as well as apply industry-standard claims adjudication conventions) of the computer system. Computerized edits may be set to force on-line examiner resolution, suspend claims that fail criteria for examiner intervention, or adjudicate automatically based on predetermined and preprogrammed guidelines. Electronically submitted claims that do not pass system edits will necessarily result in suspension or system resolution. Claims may be pended/suspended for a variety of reasons, including some of the most common reasons, as described in Table 31–3.

The management of pended/suspended claims requires constant vigilance on the part of claims staff. The first consideration is careful planning

for and understanding of the rules that will be applied to the claims adjudication process manually, by the computer system, and in combination. Not only must claims and benefits administration staff understand the circumstances that will cause claims to be pended/suspended, but staff in other areas whose functions manage data that are accessed in claims adjudication must also understand their impact on the process. Claims rules should be developed and administered based on a combination of program requirements (contract issues, regulations, etc.) and standard industry practices.

The second key to pended/suspended claims management is the predetermination of guidelines and procedures for addressing pend/suspend situations when they occur. For every category of pended/suspended claims, there should be documented policy and procedure to address which department (and individual) will provide the necessary information/decision needed to resolve the issue, what information/documentation will be needed by that individual, the procedure and time frame for conveying information/documentation to the decision maker, the time frame for response, how decisions are conveyed back to the claims department or individual staff member (for cases resolved within claims), the time frame and responsibility for completing the pended/suspended claim within the computer system, and a process (with contact person) to follow when predetermined guidelines and procedures do not work. One of the best ways of developing such policy and procedure is to sit down with staff in the supporting areas to review the reasons for pended/suspended claims and agree on what exactly will occur for each type of transaction.

The last, but certainly not the least important, factor in pended/suspended claims management is a satisfactory tracking and monitoring mechanism. The ideal process begins with an adequate pended/suspended claims and encounter report. A computer-generated report should be produced at routine intervals (and be available on an ad hoc basis) and should include, at minimum, member name, member identification number,

Table 31–3 Reasons for Claims Being Pended/Suspended

Issue	Description
Eligibility	Member eligibility not found, date(s) of service before or after eligibility effective dates, claim date(s) of service within preexisting condition period, member primary with alternate insurance carrier (the MCO would be secondarily liable for this dependent member in the presence of alternate insurance), student eligibility in question, group premium in arrears, and/or individual premium in arrears.
Provider	Provider not in system, member not assigned to this primary care provider, provider's claims flagged for suspense, provider suspended/terminated, provider not approved for this procedure, provider not eligible for date(s) of service, and provider not a member of billing group.
Utilization management (UM)	Precertification required but not in system (no match), referral authorization required but not in system (no match), claim exceeds limits of precertification or referral authorization, claim does not match with provider in referral authorization or precertification, specified field(s) of information missing from referral authorization or precertification (number of visits/days, admission date), and procedure flagged for UM review.
Claims line item	Validity edits: Date(s) of service after claim receipt or current date and invalid information (dates of service, type of service, place of service, procedure/modifier code, diagnosis code, units of service, and/or charge). Consistency edits: Procedure–place inconsistency, procedure–type inconsistency, place–type inconsistency, procedure–gender inconsistency, diagnosis–gender inconsistency, and procedure–member age inconsistency. Claims rules edits: Claim dates of service past filing limit, submitted/allowed charges require supervisory review, procedure allowed charge exceeds predetermined maximum (supervisory/UM review required), possible subrogation or workers' compensation, related surgical procedures, no price in fee schedule, billed care in surgical follow-up (same provider), duplicate suspect, second lifetime procedure reported, bilateral procedure for unilateral diagnosis, unbundling (fragmented charges), concurrent care, cosmetic procedure (requires medical record), new patient procedure with established patient, assistant surgery by same provider, obsolete procedure, and selected procedures reported on same date of service.

claim number, date of receipt, date pended/suspended, provider name/number, dates of service (to and from), total charge, pend/suspend reason (code and explanation), number of days in status, and examiner. The report should be sorted in pend/suspend reason order so that all the same and grouped pend/suspend reasons are printed together in a subsection. Next, it is crucial to designate an individual to be responsible for reviewing the report on a routine basis (usually weekly), distributing its various sections, and following up with the appropriate MCO staff on individual claims that are nearing or have

exceeded their predetermined pend/suspend reason aging factor. The individual who reviews and manages this report must be empowered to work with others (inside and outside claims and benefits administration) to resolve claims/encounters on a timely basis and to recommend modifications to related policy and procedure.

Task Allocation and Work Distribution

It is helpful while claims work flow is being designed to consider the variety of tasks in which the claims department engages. In addition to processing bills, the department is responsible for answering correspondence, correcting prior claims processing errors (adjustments), assembling information to support appeals and grievance processes, reducing liability through administrative procedures such as OPL, and reinsurance claims submission. The department also engages in activities to monitor and continually improve the quality of its work, to provide training to its staff, to identify fraud, and to contribute to special studies regarding utilization or payment patterns. The claims department may be responsible for the configuration of the system to maintain benefits logic and provider contract pricing arrangements. Some of these tasks combine with the overall flow of claims through the department, some are specialized subroutines within the claims process, and others are separate from the main flow of claims payment. By defining the tasks, mapping their flow(s) in the context of the claims process, and determining the volume of work attributable to each task, department management will recognize those tasks requiring dedicated, specialized staff.

Claims themselves can be categorized to determine the most appropriate staff assignment. Generally, claims categorized by type identify an implied level of processing difficulty. Typical definitional categories, in order of increasing complexity, are office visit, laboratory, radiology, surgical, ancillary, and hospital (outpatient and inpatient). Finally, there are a variety of specialized facility claims, such as those for nursing homes, drug and alcohol detoxification centers, and mental health clinics. Categorization by complexity allows management to assign staff to tasks according to skill level. Secondarily, such claim delineations tend to mirror dollar value ranges, which is another control mechanism for authorizing more highly skilled examiners with authority to pay claims up to higher dollar thresholds. Mail room procedures can include sorting claims by type to accomplish appropriate work allocation among examiners of various skill levels.

Because one of claims' responsibilities is to record all utilization rendered to eligible members, it becomes the claims department's task to enter encounters as well as pay claims. Encounters, also called statistical claims, are bills for services where reimbursement is made by virtue of salary (staff model health maintenance organizations) or capitation payment. Statistical claims, because they have no inherent financial impact upon the plan, may be assigned to less highly skilled examiners. This presupposes that mail room sorting procedures can identify and separate encounters from payable claims. Increasingly complex provider reimbursement arrangements, which reimburse a provider alternatively by capitation or fee basis depending upon the place of service and the service provided, are making it more difficult to identify encounters from claims at this preliminary stage.

Correspondence that is easily identifiable as not an acceptable bill format should be separated from claims in the mail room and given over to staff assigned to researching and responding to correspondence issues. Correspondence will include requests for information, response forms to OPL questionnaires, letters initiating the formal appeal process, and so forth. Some types and volumes of mail received merit identification and forwarding to additional, specialized examiners (OPL is a prime example). Inventory and turnaround time (TAT) control mechanisms should be in place to ensure resolution of correspondence issues, just as they are for claims.

The requirement for a claim adjustment may enter the claims area from a number of sources and in a variety of formats. Management should consider a formal policy for identifying valid adjustment requests. Some requests will arrive in the mail and therefore deserve consideration for their impact upon mail room flow and tasks. These could be in the form of correspondence or returned checks. Claim adjustments are usually made by more highly skilled examiners. Even so, claim adjustments should not be made by sequestered specialists. Claims requiring adjustment constitute an important feedback mechanism for claim process quality, and they create their own information flow back to the department. Claim adjustments, categorized by type of adjustment, provider requiring adjustment, and processor responsible for the initial process, may indicate the need for system configuration review, revision of operational policy, or staff training.

Once the task categories are identified and their proportional volumes determined, tasks may be grouped logically according to a number of parameters to determine the appropriate assignment allocation according to plan staffing resources. Table 31–4 shows how various tasks can be allocated according to logical position with respect to claims processing as well as required skills.

Claims processes are controlled straightforwardly enough by monitoring input and output measures. Control of ancillary tasks may be accomplished through similar means focused on the input and output of the subtask. Claims and pended claims control standards and measures are discussed in separate sections of this chapter. The control of logically separate tasks can be accomplished by establishing, for each task, initiating events, interim milestones achievable through the application of measurable tasks, and recognizable goals. For example, the initiating event for reinsurance claim submission is the acquisition of a single claim, or an aggregate number of claims, whose total value reaches a threshold over which the reinsurer is liable for the cost of the claim. Identification of reinsurance situations will require a combination of examiner or system notification of single claims over the reinsurance amount threshold and continual monitoring of claims and authorization history to identify claim combinations that meet the threshold. Interim tasks involve preparing the claim with its supporting documentation, submitting the claim, tracking the receivable amount, and working with the reinsurance claim examiner to resolve any issues. The goal is reached when the reinsurance check has been received, deposited, and appropriately recorded.

Monitoring of task allocations is an ongoing process. Any of a number of events can affect the volume of work that makes up a task, including enrollment of large groups, deployment of new products or business lines, improved systems support, more expert staff, and so forth. It is therefore important not only to obtain and re-

Table 31–4 Task Allocation

Required Skill Set	Examiner (by Skill Level)	Research/ Analyst	Investigative/ Personal Contact
Part of claims flow			
Encounters, claims	X		
Specialized subset of claims flow			
Correspondence review		X	X
Information development for various pend types		X	X
OPL		X	X
Separate from claims flow			
Adjustments, training	X	X	
Reinsurance claim submission		X	
System configuration		X	
Processing returned checks		X	
Special studies		X	
Appeals, grievance support development		X	X

view snapshots of work productivity but also to evaluate trends identified by a series of such measures.

Work Flow

Work flow design of claims processing considers the processing points for claims from receipt by the organization through adjudication to final disposition and storage. Note that the initiating event is receipt by the organization, not simply receipt by the claims department within the organization. Statutory requirements and the plan's own processing standards stipulate claims processing within a certain time period of their having been received irrespective of their entry date into a controlling automated information system. The plan is compelled to implement and document inventory control mechanisms, manually if necessary, to identify and track claims from the moment the organization receives them.

Work flow design should combine claim inventory control functions with claim processing functions so that claims processing is as efficient as possible. As an example, if hard copy claims are sorted in the mail room, they may as well be counted there simultaneously for the purpose of inventory control. As they are counted, they should be batched and placed for data entry or claims examiner retrieval. Design the work flow so that claims picked up for one purpose are not replaced in the identical stage of processing but move toward the next processing step. Handle transactions as few times as possible while maintaining and documenting inventory control points.

Claims processing is akin to assembly line production: Each logical step of adjudication requires certain readily available information in the same way that production assembly requires component parts. As claims are entered into an information system for processing, the system provides much of the necessary information pertaining to claim adjudication. Depending upon the system, certain information may only be available to claims examiners via reference

works, claim guidelines, or communications with other plan areas. Clearly, the facility with which claims examiners access and retrieve additional information pertaining to claim adjudication directly affects productivity and accuracy. A corollary to the production model view of claims is that other plan departments involved in resolving pended claims are part of the claims production line. It may be necessary to reinforce the requirement for timely resolution of claims-related questions from plan departments that are not usually attuned to production-oriented work management.

Claims work flow should be reevaluated periodically. In addition to major events that affect work flow design, such as system development or conversion, new product deployment, or different pricing arrangements, management should be aware of innovative desk procedures that either embellish upon or stray from published operational documentation. Where desk procedures improve upon existing work flow, they should be incorporated into claims documentation. In some cases, individual desk flows may run contrary to established guidelines or negatively affect the process farther down the assembly line. In these cases, corrective action should be taken.

In addition to the effects of organizational structure upon work flow mentioned in the preceding section, claims work flow follows one of two principle designs: on-line adjudication or batch adjudication. Although electronic claims submission presupposes batch adjudication, the processing method and claims submission format are distinct events and are considered separately here. In on-line adjudication, examiners entering claim information into the system follow all adjudication steps, attempting to bring the claim to final disposition (either payment or denial). In some instances, the examiner may have to pend a claim while additional information is requested of the provider or member or for review in another area, such as medical management or OPL. In batch processing, the system performs minimal verification steps upon the data as they are entered to ensure that the claim meets minimal data requirements defining a valid claim. Such system verification of data format, syntax, and validity is generally referred to as edits. Later, system operations staff initiate a computer program that performs all adjudication steps on a batch of claims. Many claims, with valid data elements, involving adjudication and pricing criteria that can be codified within the system are brought to final disposition without human intervention. Claims requiring decisions that cannot have been programmed or configured into the system are suspended, or pended, for claims examiner intervention, research, and resolution.

Both methods, on-line and batch adjudication, have inherent merits and problems. The batch method is appealing because data entry tasks are allocated to employees of an appropriate, lesser, skill level rather than to more expensive claims examiners. Once entered, many claims are adjudicated (pass through) without more costly claim examiner intervention. A typical target is an 80 percent or better pass-through rate. To the detriment of batch processing, data entry clerks who are less skilled in identifying unreasonable-looking data may not make simple adjustments to the data as they are entered that would permit a better pass-through rate. Claims, once pended, may require extra time-consuming steps of retrieval of the hard copy for additional information not contained in the system that contributes to an examiner's ability to process a claim. Claims managers must be comfortable managing the virtual flow of reported pends as opposed to the more tangible flow of claims through a department in on-line processing. The decision to use on-line or batch processing is generally dictated by the combined effects of system capability and management predisposition.

Electronic claims submission promises to reduce claims data entry tasks. Electronically loading provider claims into a system will also force the plan to engage in batch claim processing. For those plans that are accustomed to resolving claims in real time with on-line edits, this will result in maintaining and managing two operational flows: one for manual data entry claims processed to completion on line, and a batch review and resolution of the previous day's pend report based on electronic claims that failed to process.

PRODUCTIVITY

Although some believe that performance standards are archaic, unnecessary, and stifling when it comes to creativity, the largest part of the responsibility of claims and benefits administration is production oriented: processing claims accurately and on time. For this reason, productivity must be closely monitored and managed. Productivity management starts with the establishment of goals. Before goals can be established, several things must be considered:

1. What is the nature of the work to be accomplished?
   - volumes of claims, encounters, and other work units
   - types of work units and their relative degree of complexity (e.g., encounters versus hospital claims)
   - fluctuations in volumes and mix by season and over time
   - completeness of receipts
2. Who will accomplish the work?
   - FTEs
   - areas of expertise and task allocation
   - experience, training, and cross-training
   - current productivity by type of work unit
3. What tools and other resources are available to support the work effort?
   - management and supervision
   - policy and procedure
   - work flow
   - degree of automation
   - assistance from other departments (e.g., utilization management, provider relations, and enrollment)

Once these areas of information are identified and analyzed, it is time to observe the current processes and time frames for producing (completing) the various units of work within the claims and benefits administration department. What this requires is actual observation, over time, of the completion of each work unit type, collection of information about the observation processes and results (units of work completed, interruptions and delays, etc.), projection of productivity over the period of a work day, and consideration and allowance for normal downtime (time away from desk, interruptions, etc.).

For example, if you are trying to determine a reasonable productivity goal for processing hospital claims, you will want to observe a trained and established claims examiner processing hospital claims in the typical way under typical circumstances. Because one period of observation of one claims examiner cannot reasonably be used to establish productivity goals for the processing of hospital claims overall, it will be necessary to conduct several observations, preferably of two or three claims examiners.

To illustrate the degree of variability that the above-described factors can have on productivity, consider a temporary claims agency employee who was asked to quantify claims productivity in the various temporary assignment environments where he had worked most recently (Exhibit 31–2). The individual was asked to describe the claims processing environment of six recent MCO assignments, to indicate whether productivity standards had been established, and to quantify his productivity (mixed claim types). Keep in mind that claims examiners from a good temporary agency can typically achieve higher productivity than full-time permanent employees because temporary staff are not subject to the same level of interruption as employees.

It is clear from Exhibit 31–2 that productivity varies greatly depending on whether claims are prescreened, the degree of adjudication automation, the number of claims entry screens, and even the number of work hours in a day. What we cannot determine from this illustration is the degree to which productivity was affected by other factors, such as volume and type of work units, completeness of receipts, policy and procedure, and support by other departments.

Productivity, and therefore the productivity standard, also vary depending on whether the individual is a new or established claims examiner. Productivity standards are typically set at a lower level for new examiners for a set period of time after a training process has been completed. The idea behind this temporarily lowered productivity standard is to allow a relatively new employee time to concentrate on quality while gradually building productivity to desired levels. It is often the case that a new employee will be given the easier types of transactions (e.g., encounters and specialty referrals) to process initially and be allowed to progress at a reasonable pace toward processing the more complicated transactions (ancillary and hospital claims).

Monitoring performance in relation to productivity goals is essential. The reasons to monitor performance to goals are obvious in some respects and not so obvious in others. Obvious reasons include gaining an objective measure of individual performance (for employee evaluations and merit increases) and a tool to use in managing departmental inventory levels and staffing. The more inconspicuous reasons for monitoring performance in relation to productivity goals, on an aggregate level and at an individual level, are as follows:

- Overall low productivity can signal one problem or a combination of problems: standards are unreasonably high, systems and/or other support resources are inadequate, departmental morale is low, outside interruptions are detracting from processing time, and the like.

- Overall high productivity, assuming that it is significantly higher than standards on a consistent basis, usually indicates that the standards are artificially low and need to be reevaluated.

Exhibit 31–2 Variability of Claims Productivity Based on Processing Environment

Temporary Assignment 1
System: large commercial
Number of claims screens: 3
Estimated automation: 90%
Productivity standard: 13.3/hour, 100/7.5-hour day
  Comments: Claims had not been prescreened, standard deemed too low, examiner indicated that a reasonable standard would have been 16/hour, 120/7.5-hour day.

Temporary Assignment 2
System: large commercial
Number of claims screens: 4
Estimated automation: 60%
Productivity standard: none set
  Comments: Claims had not been prescreened, two-computer system in use (claims prescreened in one and processed in the second), examiner indicated that a reasonable standard would have been 11.25/hour, 90/8-hour day.

Temporary Assignment 3
System: large commercial
Number of claims screens: 2
Estimated automation: 40%
Productivity standard: 20/hour, 150/7.5-hour day
  Comments: Claims had been prescreened, standard was not met by permanent or temporary employees because of "systems problems," examiner indicated that a reasonable standard would have been 13.3/hour, 100/7.5-hour day.

Temporary Assignment 4
System: "home grown"
Number of claims screens: 2
Estimated automation: none (manual)
Productivity standard: 15/hour, 120/8-hour day
  Comments: Claims had not been prescreened, manually adjudicated claims were entered via two claims screens, examiner indicated that standard was reasonable.

Temporary Assignment 5
System: "home grown"
Number of claims screens: 2
Estimated automation: none (manual)
Productivity standard: 12.5/hour, 100/8-hour day
  Comments: Claims had not been prescreened, manually adjudicated claims were entered via two claims screens, examiner indicated that standard was reasonable.

Temporary Assignment 6
System: "home grown"
Number of claims screens: 6
Estimated automation: 80%
Productivity standard: 12.5/hour, 100/8-hour day
  Comments: Claims had not been prescreened, standard deemed too high, examiner indicated that a reasonable standard would have been 10/hour, 80/8-hour day.

- Individual low productivity can often be attributed to inadequate training, lack of understanding (of standards, policies, procedures, etc.), poor work habits, personal problems, or just plain poor performance.
- Individual high performance, assuming that it is significantly higher than standards on a consistent basis, usually signals a "star" performer but can also mark an individual who is capable of, and should be, handling more complicated work. Although quite unusual, an occasional "star" performer has been known to have manipulated work so as to get the easiest transactions by type or within type.

Standards are obviously needed to plan and manage the work of the claims and benefits ad-ministration function, but they are also necessary to monitor performance in relation to standards as a mechanism by which to identify and resolve problems. Any significant variation in productivity that is not attributable to a known cause (e.g., system downtime or absenteeism) should be evaluated immediately. Part of the evaluation process includes asking departmental staff why they think productivity is off the standard(s). As problems arise, signaled by variations in productivity, their root causes need to be identified and addressed.

TAT

TAT, in its most general sense, is the measure of the claims and benefits administration department's responsiveness to its provider and member clients. It is expressed in calendar days and measures the time from receipt of a claim to final disposition (payment or denial and notification). TAT also measures the time frames for all the points between claim date of receipt and date of final disposition (e.g., date of receipt to date of system entry). The act of establishing goals for and recording and tracking TAT yields a tool with which to monitor and manage the timeliness of claims processing.

Receipt to final disposition TAT goals are established based on certain relevant considerations:

- *contractual and regulatory requirements:* those commitments defined in MCO provider agreements and/or established by state legislation or regulatory mandate (e.g., Medicare and Medicaid)
- *provider billing cycles:* local billing practices, especially of large provider groups and/or high-volume billers, the idea being to manage TAT to minimize duplicate claims submission
- *competitor practice:* maintaining a par with local competitors in the timeliness of claims payments to remain attractive to contracting providers
- *MCO cash flow:* the balancing of TAT with cash flow to meet all other TAT requirements without releasing payments too early

In establishing TAT goals, consideration is also given to the types of claims (or units of work) that are handled. For example, encounters (or statistical claims) record patient care but do not result in provider payment. The TAT goal for encounters can be longer than for non-statistical claims, but encounters should be processed on a regular basis to provide necessary rendered care data to MCO management. The TAT goal for clean claims (those submitted with all information required for adjudication) is typically lower than for nonclean claims. Even the Health Care Financing Administration (HCFA) recognizes the difference between these two cat-

egories of claims and requires that Medicare managed care contractors process 95 percent of clean claims in 24 days and 95 percent of all other claims within 60 days.

To ensure the timely processing of claims overall, incremental TAT goals are assigned to the various points at which a claim may be stopped temporarily during processing. Date of receipt to date of systems entry is an important incremental TAT because it establishes front-end control of each transaction. The ideal goal for TAT from date of receipt to date of entry is 1 to 2 days. Pended/suspended claims are assigned TATs per pend/suspend reason to ensure that the issues causing the pend/suspend are addressed promptly. When pended/suspended claims require the intervention of areas other than claims and benefits administration, pend type–specific TATs are agreed upon between claims and the various other support areas (e.g., enrollment, medical management, provider relations). Reasonable TATs are also assigned to claims requiring development for additional information and those requiring OPL (coordination of benefits, subrogation, and workers' compensation) investigation.

Ongoing tracking and monitoring of TATs are imperative to manage the claims and benefits administration function effectively. There are several tools that the claims manager should have at his or her disposal for tracking and monitoring claims TATs:

- *pended/suspended claims report:* a listing, by category of pend/suspend in oldest (from date of receipt) first descending order within category, of all pended/suspended claims (document control number, member name and number, provider name and number, dollars charged, pend/suspend reason, age in house, and age in pend/suspend status)
- *claim status by date of receipt:* a listing by date of receipt (expressed in ranges; e.g., received within 1 to 10 days, received within 11 to 20 days, etc.) of total claims (number, charged dollars, and paid dollars)

and claims by processing status (to be paid, in process, in review, and denied)

- *paid claims report:* a listing of the detail (member, provider, diagnosis, date of service, received date, processed date, charge, cost sharing, paid amount, etc.) of all claims by type of claim (e.g., facility or professional, and potentially more detailed categories within these two general types) that have completed processing (to final disposition) as of the current date and for a specified preceding time period, including summary totals
- *check register:* a listing, sorted by MCO-specified provider number and provider name, of all claims to be paid in the next check run, including the number of claims and the aggregate amount to be paid
- *lag claims report:* a listing within date category (e.g., in 15- or 30-day increments, 1 to 15 days from date of service, 16 to 30 days from date of service, 31 to 45 days from date of service, etc.) of claims that shows the time between date of service and receipt and the length of time between date of service and payment

Monitoring of encounter and claim TATs is an ongoing and continual process that involves routine review of reports to determine whether overall and incremental TATs are being met and, if not, to determine where the bottlenecks are. Once bottlenecks are identified, they must be addressed immediately. Problems may include insufficient staffing and task allocation for front-end control, systems adjudication and edit logic, delays in resolving pended/suspended claims, delays in check runs, and the like. It is the claims and benefits administration manager's job to qualify and quantify each issue and bring about its resolution.

STAFF TRAINING AND DEVELOPMENT

Staff training and development are as necessary to claims and benefits administration as they are to any other department/function within the MCO. In staffing a managed care claims and benefits administration department, it is essential to hire experienced claims examiners, preferably those with experience in managed care claims adjudication. Some MCOs make the mistake of believing that an indemnity claims examiner can make an automatic transition to managed care claims processing with little or no training. The differences between indemnity and managed care programs, especially in the areas of provider network service delivery and medical management, make the two types of claims processing decidedly different.

As new staff come into the department, the ideal training situation involves MCO orientation and 3 to 8 weeks of classroom training (depending on skills and experience upon hire) with a subsequent on-the-job training probationary period, during which time the new employee has close supervision and a 100 percent quality check of his or her work. Regardless of the format and length of training, there is a plethora of information and skills that claims and benefits administration staff must have. Table 31–5 lists those information and skill needs.

If you are taking over an existing claims and benefits administration department and are not quite sure of the adequacy of staff training and development to date, a self assessment can assist in determining training and development needs. An easy way to conduct a self-assessment of training and development needs is to design a survey instrument to be completed by each employee. The instrument should be designed to provide an easy method for respondents to define their total training and development needs related to general skills, knowledge of the MCO, and functional/technical and interface knowledge about other key departments. Such a survey is typically presented to employees during a departmental meeting, where an explanation of the purpose of the project as well as a review of the instrument itself can be provided.

Once surveys are completed, tabulation is performed by grouping responses of employees

Table 31–5 Claims Information and Skill Needs

Information/Skills Area	Description
Overall knowledge of MCO	Organizational structure, corporate mission and goals, group account information, membership information, products offered, service area, corporate groups/committees, history of MCO, major competitors, medical management philosophy, center locations and hours (staff model), physician staff (staff model), contracting provider network, reimbursement mechanisms and methods, major functions of all departments, regulatory parameters, MCO marketing practices
Claims functional knowledge/skills	Enrollment regulations and guidelines, medical underwriting (if applicable), coding schema (ICD-9-CM diagnosis and procedure, CPT-4, and HCPCS), medical terminology, benefit programs (covered, denied, and limited benefits; cost sharing applications), claims department work flow and task allocation, claims mail handling, document filing and retrieval, claims filing limitations and TATs, inventory control mechanisms, referral and precertification processes, medical necessity and appropriateness guidelines, pended claims resolution and management procedures, OPL processing, suspect duplicate claims processing, out-of-area claims processing, member claims processing, claims quality standards and review process, productivity standards and performance measurement, adjustment processing, responding to claims status/disposition questions, claims development (for additional information) process, benefit interpretation process, check and explanation of benefits/remittance production and schedule, claims appeals process, overpayment and refund processing, computer system knowledge (claims processing screens, provider inquiry, claims history, enrollment inquiry, pricing file inquiry, computer edits, all code files, referral and precertification screens, pend/suspense resolution screens, adjustment screens, etc.), all other claims policies and procedures
Knowledge of and coordination with other areas/functions	Enrollment and billing, provider relations and contracting, utilization management, quality improvement, finance, legal, member services, internal auditing, etc.
General skills	Letter writing, telephone techniques, handling irate callers, problem solving, computer skills, personal computer skills, stress management, research skills, time management, dealing with conflict

with similar job functions. This method is employed to reduce skewing that would occur if all responses, regardless of job-specific knowledge required, were grouped together. For example, all responses may be grouped for tabulating and analyzing training needs on general skills and overall MCO knowledge. Responses of clerical workers, however, should not be grouped with those of more technical respondents when training needs associated with claims adjudication processes are tabulated.

An analysis of tabulated survey results should be conducted in concert with a review of claims QA results (i.e., the nature and volume of errors detected during routine claims quality audits). Using these two sources of information, a training and development program can be formulated with reasonable assurance that it will meet individual and departmental needs while addressing issues on a priority basis.

Although the exact nature of and resources for training will vary depending on the age, level of experience, and size of the claims department, the following are some tips for developing and conducting effective training and development sessions:

- Begin training on those issues that will effect the greatest improvement in claims payment errors and development of the rendered care database.

- Focus initial training on those individuals with the greatest rate of self-reported need and those with the highest related error rates.

- To ensure consistency of training among the smaller groups, standard materials should be prepared and used. Materials should include documented policies and procedures, live claims samples, relevant forms, anonymous quality audit results, prints of claims system screens, and the like.

- Active participation as well as question and answer sessions should be employed, with results being documented and disseminated. Depending on availability of equipment, videotaping of sessions may also be helpful.

- Feedback mechanisms to evaluate the effectiveness of training should be developed and used for all sessions.

- After training, claims QA examiners should focus on newly presented materials and how well they are applied in the production environment. Feedback and remedial training should be conducted as necessary.

- The outcome of training sessions should result in a package of materials suitable for use in training new employees and for use as a procedure/reference manual for existing employees.

- Coding schemes and medical terminology are most effectively taught using commercially available training tools and packages. Training needs in the area of general

skills are probably best met though personal development plans by employees.

Staff training and development should also include consideration of cross-training and job enrichment. On an individual employee basis, a manager or supervisor should determine, along with input from the employee, a plan for increasing job skills and experience. Those employees who are able, willing, and ready (as determined by quality and productivity performance levels) for cross-training and additional or increasingly complex responsibilities should be given those opportunities. Outside courses and special seminars (through universities, professional and trade organizations, software manufacturers and distributors, etc.) should also be used as resources to meet training and development needs.

QUALITY

Quality is the measure of the accuracy and completeness of the product of the claims and benefits administration process. Quality cannot be neglected in favor of productivity; the two go hand in hand. The overall goal of claims QA is to assist in effecting continuous quality improvement of departmental work. There is also an individual performance component of claims QA, and by measuring and evaluating individual quality, retraining, coaching, and counseling needs can be identified. The key is to use claims QA as a tool to ensure quality performance rather than as a stick to apply to individuals who make errors.

The first step in ensuring a quality process is to develop standards. There are three measures of claims quality. Overall accuracy is the percentage of claims paid correctly in every respect, with no errors. Payment accuracy is the proportion of claims for which the payment amount is correct but other processing errors are identified (incorrect payee, match to wrong authorization, etc.). Financial accuracy is determined by dividing the sum of all overpayment and underpayment amounts by the total amount paid. Table 31–6 shows typical industry standards for the three types of claims quality (accuracy) measures.

As you can see by the industry standards, financial errors are weighted more heavily than procedural errors. In the case of an acceptable level of financial errors, where only 1 percent of claims dollars are paid erroneously, that 1 percentage point can translate into hundreds of thousands of dollars in error over the course of a year for a relatively large claims shop. The percentage of financial errors is calculated as the sum of overpayments and underpayments divided by the net of overpayments and underpayments.

The next step in developing a QA process for claims is to identify auditing criteria, that is, what specific fields in the claim and associated records (e.g., eligibility, referral authorization, etc.) will be audited, what will be acceptable as accurate, and what will be considered an error. There are basically three major issues to be considered in performing an audit:

1. Was the claimant eligible at the date of service? There is little room for dispute on this particular question.

2. What was the provider's status and payment arrangement? This refers to whether the provider was a contract or noncontract provider as well as whether contractual reimbursement obligations were followed accurately. This is also relatively straightforward.

3. Were written MCO policies, procedures, and guidelines followed when the claim was adjudicated? This does not mean that the policies, procedures, and guidelines

represent acceptable levels of control. It merely is meant to indicate whether the organization complies with its own rules, however appropriate or inappropriate they are. Examples of this criterion as it would be applied include the following:

• Were the services authorized or referred by a plan primary care physician (PCP) or participating physician?

• Were contractual obligations with respect to benefits, exclusions, limitations, and conditions appropriately applied?

• Was the paid amount accurate, including any copayments, deductibles, and so forth?

• Was the coding accurate? Put another way, were all the data elements translated and entered into the computer system in such a way as to create an accurate and appropriate record of rendered care?

• Was the right person paid?

All these items should be noted on a claims QA audit worksheet. With this information in hand, a representative sample of each claims examiner's work is reviewed on a routine basis, and accuracy and error types and numbers are recorded.

The flow of the actual quality review process may go accordingly:

1. Every morning, or at some predetermined interval, the reviewer gets the report of the previous day's productivity by analyst. Conversely, it may be easier to do the quality review at the point of the examiner completing a batch of work.

2. The reviewer then manually and randomly selects X claims for every examiner [claims/encounters can be paid (processed) or pended/suspended].

Table 31–6 Industry Standards for Claims Quality

Accuracy Category	Industry Standards		
	Acceptable	Good	Excellent
Overall	90.0	95.0	98.0
Payment	95.0	97.0	99.0
Financial	99.0	99.3	99.6

3. The reviewer audits each claim (against the checklist) and checks it in the system (he or she will need to access enrollment records, preauthorization and precertification records, and claims/encounter screens).

4. The reviewer completes the claims QA audit worksheet. The claim form and prints of enrollment records, preauthorization and precertification records, and claims/encounter screens are kept for those claims where the reviewer identifies a potential error.

5. The reviewer meets with every claims examiner to review:

   • the audit worksheet only where there is no potential error

   • the audit worksheet plus copy(ies) of claim documentation if there is one or more suspected errors

6. The reviewer and the examiner reach consensus on whether a suspected error is, in fact, an error. Here it is important also to reach agreement on the cause of the error.

7. Confirmed errors should be corrected in the system by the examiner that day, with confirmation of the fix (by the reviewer) being documented on the audit worksheet. The reviewer will typically instruct the examiner (on the audit worksheet) as to the adjustment to be made. Certain errors may not get adjusted; it is up to the judgment of the reviewer.

8. If the reviewer and the examiner cannot reach consensus on whether a particular issue is an error, the claims manager or supervisor should be the tie breaker.

9. Actual errors are recorded in a log for the individual and in aggregate for the department.

Before the actual audit is instituted on a routine basis, it is important to discuss the process with departmental staff. Review and discuss standards and calculations to evaluate performance against standards. Determine your short-term and long-term goals regarding standards. You may want to shoot for good performance for the first few months and for excellent performance thereafter. Discuss how quality standards and measurement will be applied to new staff versus seasoned staff. New employees may require 100 percent claims review, whereas 10 percent to 20 percent review for established examiners may be sufficient. Also, the standards themselves may be somewhat relaxed for an initial training period.

Discuss and determine how significant problems (errors) will be resolved. If everyone is making the same types of errors, is more training indicated? Do policies need clarification? Coordination with other areas for changes in interdepartmental procedures may be indicated. Raise the subject of claims quality as a performance measure whereby repeated/voluminous errors (given clear policy and adequate training) can and should be used as a measure of individual performance. Although this is not the overall purpose for claims QA, there must be some objective way to measure the quality of individual performance. Also discuss with staff how the process will help the department and the organization (e.g., as a continuous process for improvement; to identify areas for policy and procedure clarification, retraining, and so forth; to let the rest of the organization know the quality of the claims department's product; and to identify problems upstream and downstream of claims).

Start the claims QA process, and report results intradepartmentally for the first few reporting periods. This will give everyone a chance to experience the process, work out the kinks, and make any refinements that are indicated. Set a target date for reporting departmental quality to the organization as a whole. Anyone in the program (reviewers and the reviewed) should feel comfortable with raising issues (problems, enhancements, etc.) at any time. Review program results periodically, perhaps every quarter, to determine whether quality has improved and is at the desired level, what improvements in policy and procedure (intra- and interdepartmentally) have occurred as the result of the program, and what program changes, if any, are indicated.

As the results of quality reviews are known and the financial impact is calculated, claims management is in a position to determine what steps should be taken operationally, procedurally, and in terms of resources. In many cases, claims audits result in the promulgation or tightening up of policies, procedures, and guidelines. The results may also spur management to consider dedicating additional staffing or technology resources or to focus more closely on a particular identified problem area, such as claims backlog, poor coordination of benefits performance, or unclear precertification or referral authorization instructions.

POLICY AND PROCEDURE

Policy and procedure are the mainstay of the claims and benefits administration department. Policy statements are different from procedures in that they provide direction as to what is to occur and why. Procedures define, specifically, the steps involved in carrying out policy, the responsible person/department, and the required time frames. As an example, a policy statement may say that clean claims are to be processed within 30 calendar days of their receipt, but the related procedures would specify the steps to be taken in processing a claim, who is responsible for each step, and the time frame for processing. Procedures will also provide specific instructions for defined exceptions. The combination of policy statements and procedures provides a complete set of instructions for the given topic.

Without appropriate policy and procedure as supports, the claims department can anticipate delayed, erroneous, and inconsistent claim decisions. All too often, claims guidelines exist, but in the form of a variety of memoranda, charts, cheat sheets, and notes based on verbal instructions. Those documents that do exist often speak

mostly to the mechanics of getting the claims processed rather than the application of managed care principles. A comprehensive policy and procedure manual, including administrative, coordinative, and medical–operational policies and procedures, is required to provide staff with the direction needed to ensure an accurate, timely, and consistent work product.

There are basically three types of claims policies and procedures: administrative, coordinative, and medical–operational. Administrative policies and procedures instruct staff on processes internal to the claims department, including such things as work flow, TAT, inventory and productivity reporting, claims adjustments, and work distribution. Coordinative policies and procedures address the ways in which claims staff interact with other departments/functions to acquire information or decisions necessary to complete processing of claims. An example of a coordinative policy and procedure is a description of the kinds of cases and methods used between claims and enrollment when eligibility issues delay the processing of a claim. Medical–operational policy consists primarily of internal guidelines and instructions used in MCO authorization of care and in adjudication of resultant claims. The purpose of developing such policy is to ensure that coverage of services is provided within the context of what is medically necessary and appropriate, what is reasonable in terms of billing practice, and what is provided for in terms of the purchased benefit plan(s). Guidelines for adjudicating claims for related surgical procedures and "incident to" billings are examples of medical–operational policy and procedure. Table 31–7 provides a list of the most frequently seen claims policies and procedures by type.

As you can see, there is a large number of policies and procedures required for claims and benefits administration, which may seem daunting to a new claims shop. The numerous required medical–operational policies and procedures may only be developed through collaboration between claims and medical management because they require clinical knowl-

Table 31–7 Claims Policies and Procedures by Type

Type	Description
Administrative	Adjustments; appeals and grievances; application of copayments, coinsurances, and out-of-pocket maximums; authority limits; claims codes; claim forms and documentation; claim definition and TAT requirements; claims QA; coding schemes used; computer screens; confidentiality; duplicate suspect processing; flowcharts and procedures; level of care coding; manual pricing; OPL; overpayment recovery; pended claims procedures and management; plan information; and terms and definitions
Coordinative	Alternate insurance information updates, authorization matching, benefit interpretation, claim check reconciliation, eligibility updates, grievances, group eligibility, incurred but not reported tracking, medical review, member eligibility, member services interfaces (questions, adjustments, OPL information), OPL information from utilization management, pended claims interfaces, providers' claims inquiries, provider flagged, provider not on file, refund processing, reinsurance processing, and unfunded claims liability
Medical–operational	Allergy testing, injections, and serum; ambulance transportation services; ambulatory surgery; anesthesia services; authorizations (referral, precertification, case management, concurrent review, treatment plan); benefits, exclusions, and limitations; bilateral procedures; cardiac procedures; concurrent inpatient care; cosmetic and discretionary services/procedures; cosurgeons; diagnostic studies; dialysis; DME; emergency care; endoscopic procedures; experimental/investigative services and procedures; global fee surgery; home infusion; home health care; hospice care; immunizations and other injections; incidental services and supplies; individual consideration procedures and services; inpatient preoperative and postoperative care; medical–surgical supplies; mental health and substance abuse services; minor surgery and medical care by same physician; multiple intensive care unit visits; mutually exclusive procedures; observation beds; obsolete procedures; obstetrical services–global fees; occupational therapy; out-of-area care; orthotics and prosthetics; physical therapy; physician assistants, certified nurse anesthetists, and nurse practitioners; podiatry services; preadmission testing; preexisting conditions; procedures with diagnosis restrictions; providers under supervision; rehabilitation services; related and unrelated multiple surgeries; repeat initial inpatient examinations; repeat new patient code procedures; risk management; speech therapy; skilled nursing facility care; specialist-to-specialist referrals; sterilization/reversal and fertility services; surgical assistants; temporomandibular joint dysfunction; transplants; unbundled services/procedures; and urgent care

edge for medical necessity and appropriateness. A claims rebundling software package will apply many standard medical necessity and appropriateness guidelines to claims, thereby lessening the degree of required manual adjudication. Additionally, many other types of claims guidelines can be applied through user-defined computer system edits (e.g., procedure–gender, age–procedure, diagnosis–procedure, and procedure–frequency edits). Policies and procedures that require coordination between claims and the various different functional areas (e.g.,

enrollment, member services, provider relations, MIS, etc.) should also be developed jointly. Information/guidelines for many of the policy and procedure items noted should come primarily from other areas of the organization, with claims adding relevant policy and procedure language (e.g., enrollment guidelines).

A standard format is recommended, as is consistency in who approves and signs off on policy and procedure. Within the standard format, there should be a note of which lines of business or products are affected by each policy and procedure. One recommended format includes the following:

- *policy header information:* policy name and number, effective date of policy, new or revised (if revised, the name, number, and date of the superseded policy), products/groups affected, and approved by (chief operating officer, chief executive officer, finance, medical director and perhaps others, depending on the nature of the policy)
- *body of policy:* statement(s) of MCO policy; rationale for the policy (definitions, reasons for the MCO's decision, explanations of the intent of the policy, description of new technologies, etc.), and operational instructions and implications (specific guidelines on how to deal with cases covered by this policy; includes specific circumstances under which services will be authorized/covered and detail at the level of diagnosis and procedure codes)

COORDINATION WITH OTHER DEPARTMENTS/FUNCTIONS

To do its job effectively, the claims and benefits administration department must establish and maintain positive working relationships with many other departments/functions within the MCO. Most of these departments/functions are upstream of claims and provide critical information to enable adjudication of claims; some are downstream of and rely on information from claims. When any of these relationships weakens or breaks down, the claims adjudication process is obfuscated and, most often, delayed. It is the claims manager's responsibility to effect and preserve affiliations with all corporate colleagues and to facilitate the necessary coordination with claims and benefits administration.

For each area or department with which claims must coordinate, the terms of a mutually beneficial relationship must be negotiated, and specific procedures must be developed, agreed upon, implemented, and monitored. One way to

start is to identify information and process needs for each area of coordination and from there to develop procedures and standards. Exhibit 31–3 describes, for five of the major areas/functions with which claims coordinates, procedures/guidelines, standards, information exchange, and desired outcomes.

When procedures/guidelines and standards are developed between claims and its various corporate colleagues, there must also be monitoring and feedback mechanisms to evaluate the effectiveness of the coordination and to fix problems once they arise. Good working relationships are based on mutual understanding and trust, accountability for specific procedures and standards, frequent feedback, and open communication.

SYSTEMS SUPPORT

Claims processing relies heavily upon, and contributes to the definition of, MIS requirements. System application design rests on two pillars. The first is the design of the data structures, or files, that record your information. The second is the application's ability to manipulate the information in ways that serve the user in performing operational tasks.

Minimum requirements of an automated system begin with the definition and presence of data elements necessary to process claims. This function of the system is essentially that of an electronic filing cabinet. Within the model of claims as an assembly line production environment, the system should, at a minimum, provide required data elements for examiner review and decision during claim adjudication. The technological aspects of the data structures are not of concern here. Instead, consider the level of system support available to claims processing by identifying data elements included in the database that contribute to efficient claims adjudication and those critical elements that are absent. In addition to demographic, medical, and payment information about each claim, the system should provide eligibility information about the member, benefits information, participatory sta-

Exhibit 31–3 Claims Coordination with Other Departments: Accountability and Goals

---

Enrollment and Billing

- *Procedures/guidelines:* Eligibility, medical underwriting or waiting period stipulations, unpaid premium (withholding claims payment), identification and maintenance of alternate insurance information, identifying and billing for paid services after termination (retroactive)
- *Standards:* Timeliness of eligibility verification, TAT for responses on problem cases, time frame for retroactive terminations (how far back)
- *Information exchange:* Updated name and address, alternate carrier information (new or updated) and incurred care (retroactive eligibility requests)
- *Desired outcomes:* Routine communication and problem-solving methods, compliance with enrollment and underwriting regulations, limited adjustments (especially if they are based on lack of information), and no overpayments

Provider Relations

- *Procedures/guidelines:* Provider not on file, provider flagged, resolving claims questions, required claims adjustments
- *Standards:* Information required for questions, TAT for responses from claims, TAT for responses from provider relations
- *Information exchange:* Open communication about claims inventory/backlogs, information about billing anomalies
- *Desired outcomes:* Accurate and timely provider claim processing, accurate submission of claims by providers, feedback on the quality of the claims operation

Utilization Management

- *Procedures/guidelines:* Matching claims to referral authorization records, matching claims to precertification records, claims requiring medical review, procedures without prices, medical necessity and appropriateness, claims without authorizations/precertifications, experimental procedures

- *Standards:* TAT for establishing authorization and precertification records, TAT for medical review/special pricing, TAT for updating authorizations and precertifications, identifying and recording potential OPL
- *Information exchange:* Utilization anomalies, information to update authorization and precertification records, claims information related to managed cases
- *Desired outcomes:* Appropriate payments (based on medical necessity and appropriateness), enable medical review (when indicated), collaboration on development of medical/operational policy and procedure, assist finance in estimating incurred but not reported costs

Member Services

- *Procedures/guidelines:* Resolving claims questions, required claims adjustments, updating member information
- *Standards:* Information required for questions, TAT for responses from claims, TAT for claims adjustments
- *Information exchange:* Additional claim information, alternate carrier information, OPL information
- *Desired outcomes:* Timely and satisfactory resolution of members' claims questions/issues, knowledgeable representatives who can answer most questions, minimal disruption to productivity (due to unnecessary inquiries and adjustments), feedback on the quality of the claims operation.

Finance

- *Procedures/guidelines:* Claims adjustments due to refunds/adjustments and check register audit and reconciliation
- *Standards:* TAT for refunds/adjustments, TAT for check register audit and reconciliation
- *Information exchange:* Changed payees and check register anomalies
- *Desired outcomes:* Correct and timely payments, minimal claims adjustments, accurate claims records

---

tus and contracting information about the provider, and a record of any events of medical management activities that affect final claim disposition or payment amount. A comprehensive list of the data elements that should be available within the system are included in Table 31–8.

The second parameter defining the minimum level of system support for claims processing is

Table 31–8 Claims System Information

Type	Elements
Group record	Account and subaccount identifiers, benefit plans purchased by accounts and subaccounts, eligibility period, premium payment status, eligibility rules (e.g., pre-existing conditions, waiting periods, student age limitations)
Member record	Member identifiers, alternate carrier information, relationship to subscriber, group affiliation, PCP selection, member benefit accounting, eligibility period
Benefit record	Description of covered services and procedures, benefit limitations and maximums, benefit exclusions and benefit cost sharing at the CPT-4, HCPCS, and ICD-9-CM procedure code levels
Provider record	Contracted and credentialed network providers, reimbursement methodologies, eligible services, tax identifier, payment location, practice relationships and network affiliations, contract period, payment status, covering physicians, risk-sharing mechanisms
Price	A series of reimbursement tables: capitation (procedure specific), planwide fee schedules (procedure specific), provider-specific fee schedules (case rates, procedure-specific rates, per diems, percentage of charge, percentage of fee schedule), other plan- and/or provider-specific tables (resource-based relative value scale, relative value units, ambulatory patient groups, diagnosis-related groups), location-specific tables at the procedure level
Authorization record	Medical management parameters to define preapproved procedures, provider, number of services and time frame, case management identifier and to identify third party liability (TPL) potential
Code files	Place of service, type of service, procedure codes with modifiers, diagnosis codes (identify TPL potential), remittance and explanation of benefits codes (denials, limitations, reductions, cost sharing, etc.), pend reasons, adjustment reasons, processor codes
Claim rules	A series of tables that define benefit coverage issues, including medical necessity and appropriateness, validity and consistency edits (gender–procedure, age–procedure, place–procedure, provider/specialty–procedure, type–procedure, diagnosis–procedure, lifetime–procedure, etc.), rebundling rules, reinsurance amounts, duplicate parameters, processor limitations, claim to authorization record matching parameters, table of procedures that allow assistants
Accounts payable information	A table mapping procedure codes or ranges and/or type of service codes to financial revenue codes
Vendor record	A record that identifies the payee, including tax and discount information

the extent to which it supports operational tasks. This aspect of system support can be divided into two major functions: the application of logic to assist with adjudication, and general ease of use. Application logic in support of adjudication can itself be divided into two categories: validity edits during data entry that ensure proper data type and format, and the more involved logic that performs adjudication and pricing steps. The processing steps described in detail in the next section provide a map of claims processing decisions that must be followed, whether claims are processed with system support (on line or in batch mode) or entirely manually. Steps of particular importance are eligibility verification, adjudication of the claim within the limitations of benefits, the ability to select and apply contract reimbursement methodology, the ability to apply medical management rules by matching claims to appropriate authorization records, and the ability to perform final pricing calculations.

System ease of use relates to the system's ability to present information in a manner that supports desk procedure tasks. Claim records ought to be able to be presented in a number of sort orders: by claim number (to work through a batch of claims or to retrieve claims listed in a pend report), alphabetically by provider (provider relations), alphabetically by member (case history), by date (member/customer service), and so forth. It should be possible to scroll through the information easily, to search by various fields (e.g., to find a particular claim or claims for a particular member, group, or provider), and to locate claims occurring on a particular date. Are appropriate reference file lookups available to assist with data entry (procedure and diagnosis codes)? Can the user move from one record to another easily? If the user scrolls in one direction past the desired record, does the system scroll back? Is it possible to jump easily from reviewing a claim to reviewing an entirely different set of data (e.g., eligibility information such as group premium payments or medical management data such as an authorization record)? Does the system provide menus for navigation (for novice users) as well as support commands (for expert users who know exactly what they need to look for)?

System ability to support claims processing contributes significantly to efficient and accurate claims processing. To the extent that the managed care system fails to support eligibility, product, line of business, medical management requirements, and payment arrangements, a plan will have to make up for system inadequacies through increased manual processing. Increased manual processing is a detriment to the claims process in two ways. First, work flows will be compounded to ensure that claims of a specific type are routed to examiners who are trained to handle them. Second, individual interpretation of adjudication rules are prone to misjudgment, and pricing is prone to calculation errors. Manual claims adjudication is slower, less accurate, and less consistent.

Systems involve increasingly complex configuration in direct proportion to the amount of flexibility they offer, such as varied eligibility rules, products, or benefits packages; different rules regarding necessity for referral or precertification authorization; and complex reimbursement methodology. Irrespective of the company area that controls the information in related subsystems, it becomes claims' responsibility to ensure the correct implementation of configuration parameters, the controlling logic rules that support claims processing. Successful system support of claims adjudication relies upon correct and timely system configuration. More than translating business rules into system parameters and logic, maintenance of system configuration requires timely acquisition of clear and specific business rules from other areas in the company in mutually acceptable formats.

Eligibility rules (e.g., preexisting conditions, waiting periods, and student age limitations) vary per group. Plan enrollment processes, which generally focus on entry of member data, need to include transmittal of eligibility rules to claims. Likewise, the benefits that make up a product must be loaded into the system. Any new product development or revision of benefits to suit a particular employer group must be transmitted to claims for codification into the supporting system. The effort required to interpret benefits into a system in particular is often underestimated. Covered and excluded benefits must be listed not generically by type, as they are in marketing materials and member contracts, but as specific procedures or ranges that will cause claim payment or denial. Claims should solicit medical management direction while codifying benefits as well for those procedures, such as reconstructive surgery, where coverage depends upon medical necessity. Additionally, medical management and claims must work together to determine the parameters for claim and authorization record matches. The reimbursement methodologies stipulated in provider contracts must also be codified in the system. Again, as with benefits, definitions of reimbursements according to procedure type and location must be translated into specific procedure codes and place of service types to support automated claim adjudication. As a corollary to requiring timely and precisely stated information from other company areas, system codification requires management sign-off from those areas that parameters have been loaded properly.

Administration of system configuration is a distinct function within claims, one that requires prompt turnaround, accurate coding, and its own QA controls. Correct configuration substantially increases claims accuracy, timeliness, and consistency, all of which contribute to provider and member satisfaction with plan service.

CLAIMS BUSINESS FUNCTIONS

Whether your claims process is fully or partially automated or entirely manual, the following business functions contribute to the adjudication of any particular claim. To accommodate many of these steps and processes, information from other areas within the organization must be gleaned and codified into the computer system to serve as guidelines in the adjudication of claims. It is important to note that these steps and processes must be continually evaluated and updated because they rely on information and guidelines that are subject to change over time. The accompanying flowchart (Figure 31–4) depicts the entire flow of claims processing starting with preparation.

Determination of Liability

The first step in claim adjudication determines the plan's liability based on the contrac-tual relationship between the plan and the patient. Membership eligibility steps determine the relationship of the member to the contract holder (direct contract or dependent membership), compare the service date(s) for the claim with the effective dates of the policy, and evaluate whether the member has coverage through another group health plan that could be responsible for the primary payment of the claim under the terms of coordination of benefits. Based on the member's eligibility status through a particular employer group account, further conditions of eligibility are determined. If group premiums are in arrears for the period in which the service date of the claim occurs, there may be cause to withhold payment. Group-specific rules regarding age cut-offs for dependent members may apply. Proof of full-time student status in an accredited continuing education program may be required. Through the establishment of eligibility as a member of an employer group, the particular product and its specific list of benefits may be retrieved. Benefits, in addition to listing covered and excluded services, list member contribution amounts applicable toward claim payment (copayments, coinsurance, and deductibles). Member annual and lifetime benefits limits may limit the plan's liability with respect to the particular claim. Out-of-pocket limitations may curtail the member's responsibility for copayments if they have already been met. Depending upon the health care product, the amount of the plan's liability for the rendered services may differ based on the member's adherence to medical management policies. The member's relationship to the provider of services is reviewed to determine whether the provider is the member's PCP, a specialist within the network to whom the member was referred by his or her PCP, or an out-of-network provider. The combination of information obtained from the member and group records begins to shape a picture of the proportionate shares of plan and member liability. Additional information regarding adherence to medical management guidelines will be found in a matching authorization record (if any). Final pricing will

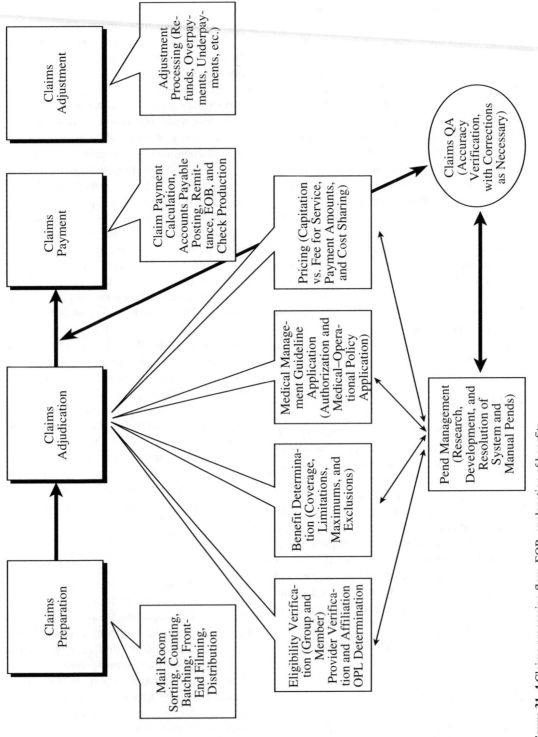

Figure 31–4 Claims processing flow. EOB, explanation of benefits.

necessarily take into account the plan's contractual arrangement with the provider.

Benefit Administration

Although benefits are defined in evidence of coverage documents and are summarized in benefits brochures provided by the MCO, many instances will arise where an interpretation must be issued to state more specifically what the MCO's position is regarding coverage for specific services. With the introduction of new benefits packages where more than just copayments are modified, interpretation activities will intensify. It must be remembered that every benefit is covered only within the context of medical necessity and medical appropriateness as determined by the MCO and within the rules regarding eligibility, use of the participating delivery system, and so forth.

Benefits interpretations involve decisions of what the MCO will and will not cover from an insurance perspective. This function is not to be confused with medical policy determinations, which involve decisions regarding the conditions under which the MCO will consider services medically necessary and/or nonexperimental in nature.

The process of interpreting benefits within an MCO must be a managed, monitored, and documented activity for several reasons:

- Once a benefit has been interpreted, the interpretation must be consistently applied and consistently communicated whenever the same issue is raised (by marketing, member services, provider relations, or elsewhere).

- Benefit determinations can have an impact on all operating areas, from finance (because of the costs associated with the benefit) to claims (which must pay in accordance with the interpretation) and all other operating areas.

- The degree to which an interpretation meets needs may vary from operating area to operating area. For example, marketing needs for coverage of a benefit may not be consistent with good medical practice or with product pricing. As a consequence, decisions may have to balance competing demands.

The interpretation of benefits within the MCO should be a centralized function and must also be responsive to the need to resolve interpretation issues in a timely and well-considered fashion. An executive level committee is the typical vehicle for interpreting benefits within an MCO. The committee may consist of the chief executive officer/chief operating officer, the director of health services or medical director, one representative from claims, and one representative from the marketing department. The committee convenes on an ad hoc basis as issues arise for interpretation. Participation from the Finance Department may be included for purposes of determining financial impact of benefit interpretations. The committee should hold itself to a TAT standard for rendering benefit interpretation decisions.

Determinations will frequently require research regarding the exact nature of a procedure or service as well as clinical circumstances and considerations. Such determinations may require a joint effort involving both a benefits interpretation and a medical policy decision.

When benefits interpretation decisions are reached by the committee, they should be documented in a standard format and provided to all staff who need to have such information (e.g., claims, member services, health services, provider relations, etc.). Many MCOs maintain benefit interpretation manuals for this purpose.

Information to members, providers, and groups regarding covered benefits must be both accurate and consistent. Failure to provide accurate information may wrongfully deny a member needed services or may obligate the MCO to provide services that were not contemplated in the development of premiums/rates. When an MCO employee is asked a question regarding coverage of services, procedures, supplies, and the like, responses must be based word-for-word on one of two sources:

1. The first response provided should be an exact presentation of the applicable evidence of coverage language and must include a search for covered benefits and a search for any exclusions or limitations. It must further include a common warning regarding the medical necessity of all MCO covered services.

2. If the exact evidence of coverage language does not answer the question, the benefits interpretation manual should be searched to determine whether an interpretation has been reached that satisfies the question, again with the medical necessity requirements being kept in mind.

If neither of these two sources answers the question, the question should be referred to the benefits interpretation committee. If a question needs to be referred either because the answer is not clear or because there appears not to have been an interpretation that addresses the question, a standard form may be used to convey the needed benefit interpretation and any supporting documentation to the committee. Although the committee should be responsive to requests for interpretation, the person posing the question should be clearly told that getting an answer may take several days.

The benefit interpretations themselves should be sufficiently detailed and specific as to provide exact claims adjudication guidelines. For example, stating in a benefit interpretation that ambulance transportation is covered in full does not give a claims examiner enough detail to adjudicate a claim properly. The level of detail needed includes answers to the following questions: Is mileage, in addition to the transport charge, reimbursable? Is transportation between two hospital facilities covered? Is air ambulance coverable? Is transportation from the hospital to home covered? If an ambulance is summoned but the patient refuses transportation, is the MCO financially responsible? Is medical necessity to be questioned (only certain diagnoses are coverable)? Is transportation from the hospital to a nursing home, or vice versa, covered? A benefit interpretation should address all these coverage issues thereby allowing the claims examiner to make an informed benefit coverage decision.

Pricing

Pricing claims involves the determination of three things: the contractual reimbursement amount, member cost sharing, and OPL. The majority of claims are priced by the MCO's computer system once planwide and individual fee schedules, capitation tables, diagnosis-related group/ambulatory patient group tables, global fees, deductible and copayment tables, secondary payment calculation formulas, provider records, and vendor records are established. The key in a new MCO is to identify the individuals and departments responsible for these initial setups and to establish the means for ongoing maintenance of the various files and tables as existing provider agreements are updated and new arrangements are entered into. Benefit design changes and implementation of new products will also effect changes/additions to pricing information.

Although claims and benefits administration does not typically own or control the various fee schedules, tables, formulas, and provider/vendor records required to establish pricing rules and automate the process, the pricing component of claims adjudication relies on the timeliness and accuracy of these data to produce precise claims payments. For this reason, the astute claims manager understands all the inputs to claims pricing and maintains effective working relationships with those individuals responsible for provider contracting and associated computer systems set-up and maintenance. Although pricing files are not usually under the purview of claims and benefits administration, information about new contracts and changes to existing ones must be conveyed to claims on a routine and timely basis. The need for this information stems from claims QA requirements and the need, on occasion, to be able to price claims manually until the computer system parameters are established and implemented. Many audits have resulted in findings of erroneous claims payments due to inaccurate interpretation/set-up of computer pricing files.

Many MCOs use a transmittal sheet to convey (from contract administration) provider identification and payment and payee information to claims and benefits administration. The transmittal sheet is modeled after the various data requirements in the MCO's computer system provider, pricing, and vendor files and, when sent to claims, either includes a copy of the signed contract or references the exact contract (and addenda) by name and number (which claims can then reference to sample contracts on file).

Member cost sharing through deductibles, copayments, and coinsurances (and circumscribed by out-of-pocket maximums) is also typically driven by computer system tables that are established initially and updated for new or modified benefit designs. As with pricing file information, the need for cost sharing information stems from claims QA requirements and the need, on occasion, to be able to price claims manually.

Following are some examples of cost sharing provisions and how they are applied:

- *Physician office visits:* Only one copayment is assessed for each office visit regardless of the number and type of service performed and reported for that visit. The copayment need not be assessed only against evaluation and management CPT-4 codes. For example, if the only service reported is suture removal, any applicable copayment is assessed against the suture removal code.

- *Chiropractic services:* Coinsurance applies to all covered services rendered, including, but not limited to, manual manipulation of subluxation and radiology. Coinsurance applies to all services regardless of place of service.

- *Inpatient admission:* Copayment is waived for a second admission resulting from a transfer from one acute care facility to another (look for a transfer code in the discharge disposition field of the UB-92). Emergency department copayment is waived when the visit results in an inpatient admission. When there is a readmission for the same condition any applicable inpatient admission copayment is also assessed against the second admission.

- *Female and male sterilization:* The copayment applies to each of these surgical procedures and is always assessed against the professional fee.

- *DME and prosthetics:* The DME and prosthetic out-of-pocket maximum is calculated per benefit year; coinsurance applies to all DME and prosthetics charges.

- *Out-of-pocket maximums:* The individual and family out-of-pocket maximums apply per benefit year and include the member cost sharing (deductible, copayment, and coinsurance) portion of covered services.

OPL also affects claims pricing. For coordination of benefits when your MCO is secondary, the payment on a claim is generally reduced to the difference between the primary MCO's payment and the usual and customary charge for the services in question. Depending on the specific state's regulations concerning workers' compensation and any arrangement that the MCO may have made with the workers' compensation carrier, your MCO will either price and pay claims as if it were fully liable (and recoverable through the workers' compensation carrier) or deny services that are confirmed as being coverable by workers' compensation (see Chapter 52). Subrogation cases, because they are typically carried out over an extended period, usually result in initial full claims payment by the MCO with liens applied to whatever monies may be gleaned through settlement or court award. It should be noted that each state has its own regulations for OPL, and their effects on claims pricing will differ depending on their content. Refer to Chapter 32 for more details.

Customer Service

Because one of the five basic functions of claims and benefits administration is to provide, by way of claims processing, service to both member and provider customers, it is important for the department to interact with and get feedback from those departments whose sole purpose is customer contact (see Chapter 30). As a measure of overall performance, the claims department should track claims-related inquiries, complaints, and grievances from both members and providers. The primary way to do this is through review of reports provided by member services and provider relations. When specific categories of claims-related questions/complaints occur in any significant volume and/or over a period of time, it is incumbent on claims and benefits administration to determine the cause(s) of the problem(s) and to work within the department and with member service/provider relations personnel to resolve the issues.

The relationships between claims and these departments should be such that:

- claims management sits in periodically on member services and provider relations staff meetings, and vice versa
- claims management is designated as a review point for grievances
- provider relations, on behalf of claims, returns to a particular provider for correction a complete batch of claims submitted incorrectly
- claims gives priority to resolving predefined, specific claims issues related to member/provider complaints
- claims staff occasionally accompany provider relations staff on site visits to providers' locations to provide orientation on claims submission or to resolve voluminous claims-related issues

- member services staff collect and report to claims updated alternate carrier information about individual members

Claims should also provide management of these two departments, among others, with routine inventory, productivity, and quality statistics. Maintaining effective relationships with member services and provider relations is essential.

Adjustments

There are two types of adjustments: clinical/clerical, which may involve spelling errors, coding errors, and omissions, and financial adjustments. Clinical/clerical adjustments make changes that do not affect payment but rectify inaccurately recorded utilization information. These are important for providing accurate information to support the analysis of the plan's utilization patterns to estimate future liability (see Chapter 40), to support physician profiling (see Chapter 27), and to support appeals and grievance processes (see Chapter 30). Financial errors involve claim corrections for payment errors (wrong payee or wrong amount). Financial adjustments may or may not involve clinical adjustments as well. Usually the two are intertwined, as when the wrong number of units, visits, or days affects both clinical information and payment calculation.

Adjustments are triggered by returned checks, customer/provider service calls, and a variety of other transactions. Methods for achieving adjustments differ from system to system. Effectively, the original claim information is nullified by the creation of a reversal claim record. Subsequently, the correct claim is entered. This methodology provides for the ability to recreate a snapshot of prior months' activities, as well as to provide for year-to-date information. Difficulties arise when corrective claims are entered after the prior period's finances are closed out.

Management will want to maintain information about the types of claims that are susceptible to readjustment, categories of adjustment, and processors responsible for erroneous claims. The adjustment process itself is subject to QA, along with all other claims transactions, to ensure that they are made correctly. Claims adjustments, rather than being a reactive step to correct processing errors, can then be used proactively to identify system configuration errors, benefits design ambiguities, and processor training issues.

Management Reporting

Claims operations management reporting is required internally to claims and benefits administration, within the operations division and companywide. The term *claims operations management reporting* refers to standard information about inventory, productivity, and quality. Intradepartmentally, it will be necessary to have, on a daily basis, individual claims examiner and aggregated departmental reports of inventory and productivity.

Departmental reporting starts with the mail room function, wherein, on a daily basis, total receipts are sorted (by type and category), recorded, and totaled. The exact format of a claims mail room daily count sheet will depend on the degree of sorting that is done. For example, and depending on task allocation within the claims shop, some claims mail room functions may sort paper claim submissions into inpatient UB-92s, outpatient UB-92s, encounter HCFA-1500s, specialist HCFA-1500, ancillary HCFA-1500s, and member-submitted claims; other shops might simply sort by UB-92s and HCFA-1500s. Additional types of receipts may include correspondence, explanations of benefits, explanations of Medicare benefits, medical records, duplicate coverage inquiry responses (for coordination of benefits), refund checks, and other miscellaneous documents. In any event, a daily count of all receipts into the department is completed by mail room staff and forwarded to the claims manager or supervisor.

The second departmental report is an individual count sheet for each person contributing to daily productivity. On this daily report, there is a count of beginning desk inventory (claims/encounters), receipts, pended/suspended transactions, processed work (including transactions released from pending/suspension and completed), and ending desk inventory. For those individuals who are responsible for the majority of the daily production (i.e., claims examiners or resolution analysts, depending on task allocation and job title), the daily inventory and productivity report also includes a section for comments about extraordinary circumstances. These are circumstances that detract from an examiner's ability to produce fully, such as system downtime/slowness, training time, and the like.

The statistics on these individual reports are combined with other information to produce a daily departmental inventory and productivity report. Other information that will be shown on a daily departmental inventory and productivity report includes oldest date of receipt in house by type of claim and information about electronic receipts, productivity, and inventory.

These daily reports are consolidated into a weekly inventory and productivity report for internal departmental purposes and then into a monthly report that is shared with operations management and claims' other corporate colleagues. The weekly and monthly reports are similar to daily reports except that they provide a snapshot of a week's or month's activity (versus a day's). These manually produced reports provide a running count of receipts, production, and inventory by category of work, are compared on a routine basis with physical inventory counts and system-produced reports, and are reconciled. An accurate count of inventory must include all work to be done, not just those transactions that have been entered into the computer system. Also, it is customary for inventory descriptions to differentiate not only among categories of work on hand but also, within categories among the various stages of incomplete work (on the shelf, logged, and pended).

Weekly consolidation of all claims' inventory and production reporting is critical to ongoing inventory control because it enables management to identify quickly and manage variation in workload among units. This type of evaluation, coupled with redeployment of resources (based on workload, by unit), allows the department to maintain some parity in the age of work on hand, ensuring that oldest claims are worked first.

Claims business function reporting refers to the ability to determine and report on, at any given point in time, key statistics such as percentage of paid and denied claims, lag time and outstanding claims liability, and OPL savings for input to other MCO management functions. The following statistics must be routinely tracked and monitored by claims management:

- monthly and annual receipts (numbers and dollars)
- average number of claims on hand (numbers and dollars)
- average productivity (by examiner and in aggregate, daily and weekly)
- weeks' work on hand (volume divided by average weekly productivity)
- claims pended by type of pend and in total (number, percentage, and dollars)
- denied claims (number, percentage, and dollars)
- average claims per member
- OPL savings (coordination of benefits, subrogation, and workers' compensation) by avoidance, diversion, and recovery

Not only does this information provide valuable input to other management functions, but it also assists in the effective management of the claims and benefits administration function (e.g., anticipating and planning for reduction of backlogs, staffing projection, performance management, etc.).

Claims Business Functions Reporting

In addition to reporting on the status of claims work flow and inventory, a second set of claims reports focuses on the analysis of the way the business is conducted. Utilization reports are used to manage, on an individual case basis and in aggregate, the cost of health care, which is the overwhelming expense category for any health care concern. Analysis of these kinds of reports provides a forecast for liability trends and informs the plan of corrective policy and operational steps that may be taken. Examples of this type of report include paid claims versus denied claims and claims lag to anticipate incurred but not reported costs. Claims and encounter reports may be evaluated to monitor the adequacy of capitation, to serve as the basis for reevaluation and renegotiation of capitation rates, and to determine those types of care that can be better managed through capitation (versus fee-for-service) arrangements.

On an individual provider basis, these reports will be used to profile practice patterns to be used as a tool to ensure, over time, the appropriate and medically necessary use of health care resources. Utilization data serve as an indicator of product and pricing needs to remain viable in the long term while providing necessary benefits and coverage to the membership base.

Reports extracted from the paid (or processed) claims file may also be used to modify existing benefits packages to the extent that reported services serve as indicators of actual utilization versus covered services. Medical management, specifically the QA function, uses the claims database as a source for claims-based studies regarding quality of care and adherence to practice protocols, preventive health service guidelines, and other clinical standards. The QA function also uses the claims database as a repository from which to select sample cases for special studies (e.g., all members with a reported diagnosis of diabetes mellitus) and to identify aberrant clinical practices. As previously mentioned, finance routinely makes use of many reports that use as their basis the claims history file.

CONCLUSION

Claims and medical management together form the core of plan operations and control. Those plans that dedicate resources to marketing, product development, customer service, and other activities to the exclusion of claims operations run the risk of failing to deliver to plan customers what they have purchased or contracted to receive. Claims is where the plan has a direct relationship with all its customers (providers, members, and groups) and where all preceding relationships and information therefrom come together. Additionally, the plan relies on information created in the process of adjudicating claims to understand and manage many other aspects of its business. The quality of claims and benefits administration significantly determines the plan's overall success.

Chapter 32

Other Party Liability and Coordination of Benefits

Barry S. Scheur, Robin L. McElfatrick, and Robert S. Eichler

With one exception, the claims processing function reports cost but does not control cost. Control of cost is exercised through medical management, provider contracting, and other means. Only a properly structured claims process, however, can provide the data that will permit the plan to control cost. The exception is other party liability (OPL). In the case of OPL, the claims process does control cost by obtaining reductions in the net cost of medical services provided through the avoidance, diversion, or

Barry S. Scheur, J.D., is President of The Scheur Management Group, Inc., a management and consulting firm specializing in the conceptualization and implementation of effective managed care solutions. In addition to having written and lectured extensively on both operational and futuristic trends in managed care, his advice and counsel have been sought by hundreds of HMOs, physician groups, insurance companies, and major employers.

Robin L. McElfatrick has experience encompassing 23 years in HMOs, indemnity plans, and managed care consulting and serves The Scheur Management Group, Inc. clients in organizational analysis, operations, medical management, MIS assessments, claims, and coordination of benefits. Her work with clients ranging from small IPAs to a major national health care firm has included a wide variety of operations and systems-related assignments.

Robert S. Eichler is Vice President of The Scheur Management Group, Inc. His area of expertise is managed care systems and claims and other party liability operations. He has assisted clients in system strategy, evaluation, selection and customization, operational evaluation and reengineering, claims and other party liability audits, and functional analyses. He has also designed and developed software to support other party liability and provider credentialing operations.

recovery of costs that should be borne by other parties. OPL is an integral part of the claims management process and depends upon the effective conduct of claims processing.

Although traditionally indemnity plans have reported OPL savings as a percentage of premium, health maintenance organizations (HMOs) typically report such savings in the same manner as other financial factors: as a per member per month (PMPM) value. Alternatively, HMOs may report OPL savings as a percentage of net paid claims amount. An aggressive OPL program, for an organization in a metropolitan area where double-income families are the norm and in a jurisdiction that permits subrogation, can expect to save from $3.50 to $4.50 PMPM (in 1995 dollars), or roughly 3.5 percent to 4.5 percent of net paid claims.

DEFINITIONS

OPL may be divided into distinct categories by the manner in which costs that may be avoided are identified and in the processes, operational and legal, by which to effect the cost avoidance. Plans often lump all the categories under one definitional term (usually, inaccurately, *coordination of benefits*, COB) and suffer the financial consequences of reduced savings from these activities because the differentiating operational nuances are also lumped together. The following definitions clarify the distinctions between the two categories of OPL. Whether or not the exact terminology presented here is adopted in a particular plan, clear terminology consistently understood within the claims department and throughout the organization provides a foundation for effective OPL activities.

OPL activities usually encompass three kinds of mechanisms by which the costs of health care delivery that should be paid by someone other than the plan are avoided by the plan or are diverted to or recovered from an alternative payer: COB, third party recovery (TPR), and nonplan liability. COB and TPR are usually grouped under the heading of insurance and liability recovery or OPL. The three mechanisms are operationally handled in quite different ways.

COB

COB is an administrative process whereby plans coordinate the reimbursement of health care services for members covered by two or more plans. If a patient has costs that are payable by the plan under the certificate of benefits that applies to the patient as a member of the plan, and some or all of the costs may also be payable by another health insurance coverage held by the patient, then the respective primary and secondary payment obligations of the two coverages are determined by the Order of Benefits Determination Rules contained in the National Association of Insurance Commissioners (NAIC) Model COB Regulation, as interpreted and adopted by the various states. Primary means that the carrier is responsible for costs of the claim up to the benefit limit of the coverage. Secondary means that the carrier is responsible for any unpaid balance of the total allowable expenses, up to what it would have paid if it had been primary within the claim determination period. The definition applies to group health benefits and, in some jurisdictions, to nongroup (or direct pay) health benefits. The definition also applies to the health care portion of automobile insurance. Auto insurance is usually secondary to the plan. Personal injury protection is secondary to the plan.

The definition also applies to Medicare. The rules that apply to Medicare (at the time of this writing) are as follows: If the member is still employed, Medicare is always secondary to the plan (with the single exception of end-stage renal disease after an 18-month period). If the member is totally disabled, Medicare is primary. If the member is retired, the plan is primary from age 65 to 70, and Medicare becomes primary at age 70.

COB is the process of applying the NAIC rules to determine the costs for which the plan is primarily responsible and the costs for which the plan would be in a secondary position if applicable alternative coverage exists. If the plan is secondary for any costs, COB is the process of discovering whether any applicable alternative coverage is (or may be) in effect. If applicable alternative coverage is (or may be) in effect and the plan is secondary, COB is the process of avoiding those costs for which another carrier is known to be liable by denying the claim, diverting those costs for which the plan is secondary to the alternative carrier (if the costs have not already been paid by the plan), or recovering those costs for which the plan is secondary to the alternative carrier. Medicare and Medicaid coordination is a special case of COB.

The term *avoidance* applies when the plan is made aware before paying the claim that another party is responsible and simply denies part or all of the claim, forwarding it to the correctly liable party for payment. The term *diversion* applies when the plan pends a claim for COB determination and does not pay it until the COB process is performed. This process is commonly referred to as "pursue and pay" or "chase and pay." The term *recovery* applies when the plan pays the entire claim and then performs the COB process in an effort to recover that portion of the costs of the claim for which the plan is in a secondary position under the NAIC rules. This process is commonly referred to as "pay and pursue" or "pay and chase."

TPR (Subrogation)

Subrogation is a legal process whereby the plan may seek reimbursement from a third party that is legally responsible (at fault) for claims arising from a negligent act or omission. TPR encompasses accident, malpractice, and other negligence and omission events. Workers' compensation is a special case of TPR. Case identification methods include medical record notations, examination of specific diagnoses that are often accident related, and others. As a legal process, subrogation is not permitted in all jurisdictions, such as Virginia. In others, such as California, although subrogation is not permitted, the organization is permitted to recover TPR savings to the extent that the member recovered monies in a tort case where a portion of the damages was afforded for the costs of medical care provided by the plan and with the member's prior consent. Such stipulations will both complicate the operational steps required to secure TPR recovery and inhibit a plan's overall TPR program effectiveness. TPR operations must identify which situations merit investigation for possible third party liability, conduct the investigation, make the determination, and pursue reimbursement when appropriate.

TPR issues typically take a considerable time to resolve. In almost every case the claim is paid before the process is initiated; the process is therefore usually "pay and chase." Funds reimbursed for medical costs on TPR claims are recoveries.

Nonplan Liability Claims

Nonplan liability claims are claims that the plan is not responsible for paying because the services are not covered under the applicable statement of benefits or under plan policy as defined in the applicable member handbook. Common occurrences include services provided to members before plan coverage applies or after plan coverage has terminated, claims improperly billed to the plan on which the plan takes an adjustment from the provider (which may rebill elsewhere), claims with incorrect billing amounts that were paid and the error was discovered later, and costs not covered under the

member's contract or for which required approval has not been obtained.

These situations are commonly confused with COB. The distinction to be made is that if the cost is not a covered cost, then there is no plan liability to pay the cost; hence there is no subsequent determination to be made of the plan's primary or secondary liability for any portion of the cost. Nonplan liability claims are not, strictly speaking, OPL and are not addressed further in this section.

CONTRACTUAL SUPPORT/ REQUIREMENTS

COB and TPR, like nonplan liability claims, rely upon legally binding contractual language in a number of plan documents: the group certificate of coverage, the subscriber agreement or certificate of coverage, and provider agreements. Subscriber application forms should also contain a statement regarding the plan's right to receive and release information pertaining to these functions over the subscriber's signature. The impetus behind contractually binding language supportive of COB and TPR is that, without it, the plan has no legal footing for reducing liabilities through either of these activities. Provider agreement language delineates the administrative responsibilities of providers and the plan with respect to OPL operations and the right of recovery.

Group and Member Agreements

The language in the subscriber and group agreements should conform to state regulations (if any) regarding COB and subrogation. Most states have adopted some form of the NAIC Model COB Regulation and promulgate sample language. Although in many instances COB and TPR are handled within the same section in plan contracts, the distinctive legal basis for their respective operations merits separate contract sections. At a minimum, the COB section should include the following subsections: definitions, order of benefits determination rules, effect on benefits, right to receive and release information, responsibility and cooperation of members, and right of recovery.

Definitions include the following:

- identification and description of a plan for purposes of coordinating benefits among plans
- a total allowable expense as any health benefit for which the member is covered, at least in part, by at least one of the coordinating plans
- a claim determination period as the time frame encompassing incurred claims within which the total allowable expense is applied for coordination purposes (generally 1 calendar year)
- order of benefits determination rules, which identify which plan is to be primary and which secondary for a particular member in a given set of circumstances
- effect on benefits, which describes the reduction of benefits when the plan is secondary with respect to another plan and the notion that benefits may be rendered as either services provided or reimbursement for services
- right to receive and release information, which secures the plan's right to communicate whatever information, medical or administrative, it deems necessary to other parties to carry out the COB function
- responsibility and cooperation of members, which bind the member to comply with plan requests for information, signatures on forms or statements, and so forth for the plan to exercise its COB right (the plan may include some teeth in its COB provision here, stating noncompliance as grounds for claim denial and/or member termination)
- right of recovery, which secures the plan's right to recover money from any involved party for reimbursement of benefits provided by the plan as primary where it sub-

sequently discovered it should have been secondary

It is particularly important to define a total allowable expense in such a way as to encompass the provision of services, the typical benefit within a managed care setting, as a benefit paid. Furthermore, the NAIC Model COB Regulation allows the allowable expense to be defined as the reasonable and customary cost of services provided irrespective of any particular provider reimbursement arrangement. A commonly misunderstood notion is the member credit bank, or credit reserve amount, as it applies to COB. Although these terms are generally known, they are rarely seen within state COB regulations or model language or in plan agreements and are not present at all in the NAIC Model COB Regulation. Hence plans often assume that they are not required to implement member-specific tracking of COB savings. The concept and obligation of a member bank are built into COB by virtue of defining the total allowable expense within the context of a claim determination period. Where savings have been obtained on behalf of a particular member for a specific claim at one time in the period, such savings are traceable and available to pay out on behalf of that member for other claims in the period where the combination of benefits from coordinating plans comes up short against providers' usual and customary charges. The challenges in drafting effective, legally binding COB language include attaining appropriate readability scores as well as reducing the member perception that COB is a loathsome burden that serves to reduce the quality of services or benefits expected of the plan. Effective language in plan marketing materials may assuage this effect.

TPR subsections should include definitions, right of subrogation or recovery (in accordance with state regulations regarding subrogation), effect on benefits, right to receive and release information, responsibility and cooperation of members, and right of recovery. These subsections are comparable with those describing

COB, differentiating the administrative basis for COB from the liability foundation of TPR.

Provider Agreements

COB and subrogation language should be included in provider agreements for two purposes: to establish the operational responsibilities of each of the parties with respect to identifying and transmitting COB information, and to establish and secure the right of retainership of COB and subrogation savings and recovery dollars. Particularly in a managed care setting where providers have accepted some level of risk by virtue of reimbursement arrangements based on other than episode of care, providers will contend that, with reduced reimbursement arrangements, they should be able to recapture reimbursement through OPL activities. The intent of the typical hold-harmless clause is at stake here: May the provider balance bill where it is known that a secondary insurer, not the member, will pay? The plan, on the other hand, has actuarial calculations as the foundation of its reimbursement arrangements, calculations that presumably take into account the fact that the plan's net payable liability is reduced by virtue of OPL. The plan also has, on its side, the NAIC Model COB Regulation definition of a plan as excluding providers of health care. COB is a function specifically performable by and among health plans. The NAIC model does not address COB in a capitated reimbursement environment at all.

A healthy approach acknowledges that, without providers' assistance in identifying and transmitting OPL information to the plan, the plan's net reduction due to OPL activities suffers. The far-thinking plan will structure provider agreements to include and reward provider responsibilities with respect to OPL information gathering and transmittal with specific monetary guarantees. Compensation could include allocation of a savings pool or outright payment, to a maximum, of either a percentage of the claim value or a fixed amount for a newly identified OPL of which the plan had no prior knowledge. Contract language that addresses these issues

fairly and comprehensively lays the groundwork for effective operations and obviates misunderstandings regarding reimbursement.

See Chapter 55 for further discussion of provider agreements.

ORGANIZATIONAL PLACEMENT (WITH DEDICATED STAFF)

COB and subrogation activities are closely integrated yet distinct from the mainstream of claims processing. To some degree, decisions relating to organizational structure depend upon the level and sophistication of claims transaction information system support. With appropriate automation, claims examiners may perform routine processing of OPL claims where alternative coverage has already been identified. Even in these most sophisticated shops, however, the labor-intensive and manual tasks of identifying new potential cases and investigating alternative coverage via phone and mail require and deserve dedicated staff. If the claims processing automation does not include appropriate adjudication of COB secondary payments, calculation of savings, and retention and management of member credit reserve amounts, then these functions also fall within the purview of dedicated OPL staff. In larger plans (generally, those with more than 50,000 members), a second division of labor occurs between COB and TPR tasks. Although both activities share comparable investigative tasks to disclose either the existence of alternative group coverage or the potential for subrogation, resultant COB activities involve administrative duties relating to data management of alternative coverage information and specialized claim adjudication. TPR activities focus instead on paralegal type activities: establishing and updating lien amounts and negotiating settlement amounts with often adverse attorneys.

The specialized and dedicated team of OPL analysts may work under a supervisor or manager reporting to the claims director. In some instances, the OPL unit is set on par with the claims department, reporting directly to a director of operations or finance. Either design recognizes the highly specialized skills required to perform a set of tasks distinct from the routine claims adjudication process. Furthermore, it recognizes and encourages implementation of incentives based on effective work whose goal is reduced liability (value of claims processed) as opposed to routine claims processing with its incentives for productivity (volume of claims processed).

COB: BASIC PROCEDURE DEFINED

In its most simplistic form, effective COB comprises two operational flows: Information regarding members with other coverage is discovered and retained, and such information is brought to bear upon claims during adjudication. The first flow involves staff from across almost all plan departments. Marketing and sales staff encourage prospects to include alternative coverage information on plan applications. Enrollment should reinforce the requirement for this information by rejecting as incomplete any applications without COB information. Provider relations staff may be privy to COB information contained in medical charts. Medical management staff can routinely ask regarding alternative coverage or the occurrence of an accident as the initiating factor behind the requirement for care. Customer services uses customer contact as an opportunity to discover subrogation potential and forwards such information to OPL staff routinely. Also, customer services staff will respond to general subrogation questions and will forward questions regarding complicated cases or aspects of cases to OPL staff for response. Claims examiners may recognize COB- or TPR-related information on claims forms (e.g., check boxes regarding accidents or other payment sources), or explanations of benefits paid may be included with the bills. In any event, the plan must structure the conduits for such information so that it can be applied at the time of claim payment. Generally, the information should accumulate to a central repository to ensure its consistency and obviate any redundancy. The OPL unit is responsible for maintaining this database,

including investigating incomplete information. The OPL unit is also responsible for the second flow: applying alternative coverage knowledge to claims.

In point of fact, the two operations are intertwined. Rarely does a plan acquire COB information on more than 5 percent of its membership from up-front gathering mechanisms such as enrollment applications. Conversely, even if it did acquire COB information before a claim submission, there is little likelihood that each of the members researched would submit claims before the information was out of date and therefore inaccurate. A more productive method of working is to apply the order of benefit determination rules to claims as they are submitted to determine if, in the presence of other coverage, the plan would be secondary. A statistical analysis of claims data usually shows this to be the case for most of a plan's dependent member claims. The potential for COB could be anywhere from 25 percent of claims to 60 percent or more. Restated, between 25 percent and 60 percent of claims are likely to be for dependent members for whom a plan will be secondary if other coverage exists for these members. Potential COB claims include claims for spouses and children where the spouse's birthday falls earlier in the year than that of the plan's subscriber. The volume of claims to be investigated for other COB coverage is usually reduced by ignoring claims under a certain dollar amount. The NAIC Model COB Regulation stipulates that COB should be performed for all claims except those under $50. The plan should analyze its paid claim data to determine a reasonable dollar threshold under which to ignore investigations for new COB.

Investigative efforts are then applied to these claims' members to determine the existence of other coverage. Not all potential COB claims (claims for dependent members) result in COB savings. Factors that contribute to reduced COB include situations in which one spouse does not work and, when both spouses work, one does not receive health benefits through his or her employer. Upon verification of the existence of other coverage, if the claim has been pended during this investigative process ("chase and pay"), then the claim may be diverted to the appropriate carrier. A duplicate coverage inquiry (DCI) is the process and document used to contact another plan thought to be primary for the claim and member in question. The process and document seek to determine the exact liability status of the alternative plan and the already made or intended payment for the services in question. The plan would initiate recovery efforts for such paid claims.

Although these tasks can be performed on a manual basis, they are executed much more efficiently and require much less human resource given computer systems support. Information system support can usually identify claims where alternative coverage information is known but is incapable of identifying and pending claims in the absence of known COB information where, as a result of the dependent relationship of the member to the subscriber, the plan would be secondary if there were other coverage.

SUBROGATION: BASIC PROCEDURE DEFINED

Subrogation operations begin with identification of cases for investigation using a combination of automated screening of the claim, referral/authorization records for selected diagnoses, and input from various other sources of provider/member/attorney contact (claims, provider relations, medical services, etc.). Suspected cases, once identified, will be pended (temporarily) for investigation. Subsequent tasks include written correspondence and telephone investigation (with members, employers, attorneys, providers, and third parties) as a means to follow up on any additional information needed. Upon the confirmation of a case, OPL staff release the associated claims from pending status to pay them. Staff determine which cases will be handled in house and which ones will be referred to outside entities. The de-

cisions on the type of cases to be handled in house versus outside entities will be reevaluated periodically based on case volume, number of cases going to litigation, and any changes in the laws governing TPR. For those suspected subrogation cases to be handled in house, staff will contact the member to determine whether a claim has been made and whether an attorney has been hired. Initial letters to the member and to the member's attorney (if one has been retained) explain the plan's recovery rights and the need for information; provide a questionnaire that solicits all necessary data about the accident/injury; request, on a standard form, the member's signature acknowledging the plan's recovery rights, confirming the member's duty to provide information, and assigning payment to the plan of any claim the member may have on account of the accident; and give notice of lien and provide copies of bills (claims).

Subsequent to establishing a case, examiners notify all parties on a timely basis of the plan's subrogation interest in the settlement. As a standard, the following parties will be notified: the member, the third party (if applicable), all insurance carriers involved, and all attorneys involved (plaintiff and defendant). After these initial contacts, and on a periodic basis (every 30 to 60 days), examiners request a status report from attorneys and insurers as well as update lien amounts and check court files to determine whether a lawsuit has been filed and to monitor the lawsuit once it has been filed. The defined tasks presume the development of internal tracking reports to provide information about the amount and age of outstanding liens and to flag cases for the next follow-up steps.

In settlement of cases, OPL staff (or corporate counsel for selected cases) follow all relevant laws/principles/regulations, including reasonableness, in the pursuit of plan expense recoveries. Settlement applies to the member's acceptance of a recovery amount from the third party (or his or her liability insurer) or the plan's acceptance of all or a portion of the monies due it for the cost of claims expense incurred for a specific subrogatable event.

The procedures for identifying, managing, and settling workers' compensation claims are similar to those of general subrogation cases, of which workers' compensation is a subset. These cases have the additional research resource of state employment agencies or boards that consolidate and coordinate workers' compensation claims. See Chapter 52 for further discussion of workers' compensation.

ACCOUNTING FOR OPL

The OPL staff are responsible for realizing savings as the result of discovery and investigation activities. Savings are retained and tracked in concert and cooperation with claims/encounter processing staff, corporate legal counsel, providers, and other insurers. Mechanisms and communications links between claims and insurance and liability recovery staff are necessary to pend potentially duplicative payments and to unpend and adjudicate claims for secondary liability. Complete claims and encounter detail must be available to the OPL staff to produce a "bill" to the alternative carrier or provider if a duplicative payment has already been made and must be recovered. Providers must understand their roles and be contractually liable to return plan payments that are duplicative of alternative carrier remittances. Offsetting, an alternative to COB recovery, requires communication and cooperation between COB and accounting staff.

"Chase and pay" presupposes the acceptance, philosophically, that costs avoided, diverted, or recovered through COB and TPR programs are not revenue but rather reduced claims liability. Furthermore, reduced claims liability via accrual must be considered at least as valuable as a recovery. If one contemplates a comparison of the administrative expenses associated with "pay and chase" and "chase and pay" programs, an additional impact can be seen. Savings gleaned through recoveries (cash receipts) require claims adjustments as well as accounting adjustments. When savings result from diversion, claims are readjudicated before final payment rather than being paid and later adjusted. The plan not only reduces administrative costs but realizes the immediate cash flow advantage of reduced claims payment. When diversions and avoidances are accounted for, the claims expense reduction is booked based on the actual amount of savings as they occur. Recoveries require an accrual of the estimated amount of recovery and the reversed or adjustment of that accrual when the cash is received.

Accounting for Diversions

Unlike "pay and chase," which reaps its cost reduction benefits by way of cash receipts (recoveries), "chase and pay" accrues savings via avoidance and diversion. Within the "chase and pay" context, there are still, albeit minimal, cash receipts resulting from recoupment of erroneously paid Medicare claims, retroactive enrollment (the plan or alternative carrier) causing duplicate carrier payment, or cases where the plan simply exercises its judgment to pay a claim before concluding the investigation. This may be particularly true with long-term subrogation cases. For the most part, "chase and pay" is considered an alternative COB process.

Upon conversion to a "chase and pay" accrual system, a plan will experience almost immediate reduction in cash receipts. In the short term, administrative expense will increase as a result of additional case volumes and new operational procedures. This should be more than offset by reduced claims liability and, over time, an additional reduction in administrative expense because far fewer claims will require adjustment.

There are several financial accounting guidelines and procedures that must be established to ensure accurate accrual processing. They include the development of an automated accounting system to record accruals as a suspect or positively identified claim is released from its pend status. The information system should be investigated to determine whether it has the capability to perform the requisite accounting functions. If not, manual procedures will need to be implemented to perform this function. The information system will need to be able to record and report savings by individual member; category or source of savings, that is, avoidance (accrual), diversion (accrual), and, for the exception, recovery (cash receipt); type of accrual or cash receipt, that is, COB, workers' compensation, subrogation, and Medicare; individual account and established account groupings; and line of business (e.g., benefits product).

The automated accounting system should be capable of relating accruals and recoveries to incurred but not reported (IBNR) cost and lessening the IBNR by the sum of the values of avoidances, diversions, and recoveries. This may need to be accomplished manually through the use of specified reports produced by the automated accounting system. There should be a mechanism for the automated system to transfer accrued savings and recoveries from one employer account to another when a member is covered under two separate risk group accounts. Finally, financial accounting for OPL includes the ability to establish and maintain a benefits reserve bank account on each member for whom avoidances, diversions, or recoveries are booked. Amounts on credit in the reserve bank will be applied to a plan's secondary payments when benefits for a specified claim have been exhausted. The automated accrual system must provide accurate data on such transactions to the claims payment system. On a calendar year-end basis, these accounts will require zero balancing of unused savings (including avoidances, diversions, and recoveries).

A critical issue in establishing a financial accounting system for OPL is the development and implementation of a standard definition and calculation methodology for accruals. Claims, legal, and finance personnel must all operate with the same knowledge and understanding. By definition, the savings for an avoidance or diversion (accrual) is the amount that the plan would have paid had it been primary minus any amount that it will pay or has paid as secondary payer or from the credit reserve bank. Hospital discounts/differentials should be applied before accruals are calculated for claims. When the alternative, primary carrier is billed via DCI, however, it is the total allowable expense or, in this case, the provider's charge(s), that is requested as payable.

When savings are realized vis-à-vis recoveries (cash receipts), it is the exact amount of money recovered that is booked as savings. This amount does not affect the claims payment amount to the provider. An illustrative example is given in Exhibit 32–1. Here, the plan's secondary payment is made within the terms of total allowable expense as any claim at least a portion of which is covered under at least one of the plans covering the patient for whom the claim is made. The secondary payment, when added to the primary payment, is attempting to total to the usual and customary charges for the service(s) rendered. The amount charged in these examples is presumed to be a usual and customary charge. The plan is liable in a secondary payer position up to the amount it would have paid as primary. The savings are calculated as the remainder of what the plan would have paid as primary less the secondary payment.

The alternative payer primary payment in the second example in Exhibit 32–1 is set at such an extreme minimal amount for illustrative purposes. There are times (e.g., mental health benefits) when the primary payer's deductible amount and/or benefit amount result in a payment allotment similar in principle to this example, where the total benefits available from the two plans covering a particular member are still less than the charged amount. Again, the total of the two plan payments are attempting to reach the usual and customary charge. The assumption here is that we have experienced a savings of $3,000 within the year for this particular member. The savings are then available to pay for subsequent claims where the sum of an alternative's primary payment plus the plan's primary payment would not come up to the usual and customary changes. The previous bank amount of $3,000 is reduced by $39 to permit the plan secondary payment of $99. $99 is paid so that it, together with the primary payment, reimburses the usual and customary $100 charge for the services. The plan's payment limit is al-

Exhibit 32–1 Savings Accounting Examples

Example 1: Total Allowable Benefits

Charge:	$100.00	
Plan benefit:	$96.00	
Alternative primary payment:	$64.00	(Assumption: indemnity applies small deductible, pays 80% of remainder)
Plan secondary payment:	$36.00	
Plan COB savings:	$60.00	

Example 2: With a Credit Reserve

Previous bank amount:		$3,000.00
Charge:	$100.00	
Plan benefit:	$60.00	
Alternative primary payment:	$1.00	
Plan secondary payment:	$99.00	
Plan COB savings:	–39.00	
New bank amount:		$2,961.00

---

ways what it would have paid as primary plus any available credit reserve amount accrued for this particular patient. If there were no positive bank amount for this member from which to draw, the maximum of the plan's secondary payment is the allowed amount, in this example $60. The credit reserve or bank amount is zero balanced at the beginning of each claim determination period.

Accounting for Recoveries

Conversion to an accrual system, although requiring new or modified accounting procedures, will also require maintenance of the existing cash recovery accounting process. Allowed charges, savings, and payment amounts will need to be calculated and recorded differently depending on whether the accrual or cash receipt method of savings has been applied. In general, the accrual method will most often apply to COB savings, and the cash receipt method will

most often be used in subrogation and other OPL cases. Guidelines for accounting for recoveries should be developed along the following lines: as reductions to claims expense if realized within X months and during the same calendar year as the date on which the claim(s) was paid and as revenue if realized beyond these limits.

To account for OPL, the finance department will need to develop a process for communicating avoidances and agreement on posting practices, to achieve common understanding of bank credit reserve and reasonable cash value and their applications, to develop and implement procedures between finance and OPL to reconcile booked and reported savings, and to arrive at a common understanding of the effects of accruals and recoveries on IBNR.

OPL POLICY ISSUES

Effective OPL requires proactive, assertive behavior in the pursuit of all OPL. This philosophical approach to claims liability requires innovative cooperation and responsible behavior on the part of subscribers, providers, employers, and other carriers. Success can only be accomplished when policy issues are identified and resolved, effects on constituents are anticipated, and rules and expectations are developed and communicated to everyone.

The key policy decision, upon which others are contingent, is whether to convert from "pay and chase" to "chase and pay." Given a positive response to this issue, the following policy considerations must be addressed:

- To what degree and in what ways will subscribers be held to their contractual obligations to provide alternative carrier information? Will claims be denied for failure to respond to questionnaires/inquiries, and, if so, at what point in OPL processing?
- Will providers be expected to bill and receive payment from known or newly identified alternative carriers before billing the plan? Will the plan deny claims when this procedure is not followed?

- How will employers be expected to participate in the OPL program? Will the plan expect employers periodically to canvass employees for alternative carrier information? Will employers be required to provide case-specific information for COB, subrogation, and workers' compensation claims? What actions, if any, will be taken by the plan for lack of cooperation?
- Does the plan intend to develop and implement a benefit credit reserve?

Operational policies to be decided upon include the following:

- What is an acceptable claims payment delay time for OPL processing?
- Considering the need to maintain data integrity, who will adjust/readjudicate claims?
- What controls are necessary?
- At what point in OPL processing are cases closed?
- Are they paid or denied if not successfully concluded?
- What incentive options are most likely to produce the desired results?
- Who, internally and externally, should be included in an incentive program? If adopted, what overriding principles are to be used in the administration of an incentive program?

OPL IN A CAPITATED ENVIRONMENT

The capitation issue has not been adequately addressed by the NAIC in its most recent version of the Model COB Regulation. Nevertheless, it appears that an approach to COB and TPR can be constructed that will be perceived as favorable in terms of compensation from the sponsoring participants, will retain a legal basis under the diversion of claims to alternative primary carriers according to the NAIC Model COB Regulation, and has the potential for yielding

significant savings and recoveries from this often overlooked source of revenue.

The NAIC Model defines two terms that are specifically applicable in approaching the capitation question. The term *plan* means, in its major context, an organization providing benefits or services to enrollees on a group basis. Many insurers and state regulators have considered HMO plans to fall within this definition, but the revisions to the NAIC Model COB Regulation in 1985 clearly indicated that an HMO is, for the purposes of COB, to be considered a plan. It is the plan that is permitted under the NAIC Model to coordinate benefits. It should be noted that no reference is made to the ability of the provider or institution to coordinate benefits with those of a carrier or other form of plan. Because the COB process envisioned by the NAIC Model guarantees payment to the providers and/or facilities regardless of whether benefits or services are provided by one or more plans, neither a provider nor a facility is strictly entitled to engage in direct COB.

The second definition of relevance concerns what is meant by the term *benefits*. In an HMO setting, benefits are usually provided in the form of direct services rather than merely, as to carriers, facilitating the payment for such services. In such a situation, the NAIC Model also clearly indicates that, where benefits are provided in the form of services, the plan that is coordinating is entitled, if applicable, to be credited with or reimbursed the reasonable cash value of the services provided or arranged. This means that the coordinating plan would be entitled to any reduction in costs occasioned by its voluntary determination to coordinate benefits.

The underlying assumption about capitation rates is that it is understood that the providers are capitated with a prebudgeted amount for COB and TPR being built into those rates. In other words, the capitation formulas have been derived on the basis that a plan is entitled to all proceeds (consistent with the language of the NAIC Model) reimbursed or diverted as a result of COB or TPR. In one sense, a provider (physician or hospital) receiving capitation that then, on the basis of a denied claim by one of the plans, bills and collects from another carrier for services provided or arranged through that plan is actually collecting twice for the provision of the identical service. This clearly was not intended as part of the capitation process, nor does it fall within the spirit or letter of NAIC Model COB Regulation. It cannot be forgotten, however, that much of the COB and TPR information upon which a plan relies is furnished through providers and participating hospitals. Therefore, the following process is being proposed that will both satisfy the underlying purpose of COB and TPR and reward providers/facilities and their respective staffs for their cooperation in making this program as effective as possible.

The Capitation Process: Physicians

The plan's negotiated agreement with physician providers should explicitly acknowledge that physician capitation contains an amount that has been budgeted to include COB and TPR savings/diversions (amount paid by another) arising out of professional services provided by physicians. The participating physicians will agree, either contractually or implicitly, to cooperate with the plan to maximize revenues derived from the COB and TPR process. This will include the gathering of information about other coverage by office staff and the refraining from billing by individual physicians for services for which the COB and TPR component has been built into the provider's capitation. At the end of each mutually agreed-upon period, the amount of actual COB and TPR recoveries and diversions achieved by the plan will be compared with the amount budgeted for that period of time. A formula should be derived splitting any excess amounts in an equitable manner between the plan and the capitated physician(s). Any deficit from amounts budgeted will be borne by the plan.

The Capitation Process: Hospitals

The concept of paying a hospital an incentive for assisting a carrier in diverting COB claims away from itself is one utilized by a number of commercial carriers. Carriers in a number of states have an arrangement with hospitals by which the carrier pays the hospital up to the lesser of a fixed amount or a percentage of the value of the COB claim diverted away from it when the hospital has provided information about other coverage not previously existing in the carrier's database. A bonus payment mechanism could be worked out for hospitals that assist in providing managed care plans with undetected COB or TPR information. As an alternative, a similar risk-sharing arrangement as utilized for the physician providers could be applied in the case of hospitals. Both approaches—award sharing vis-à-vis budget and direct bonus payments—should be presented to each facility with which a managed care plan interacts.

Although the rules governing TPR are different (the plan is attempting to shift all costs arising out of an accident or injury to another party), the same budgeting, reward mechanism, and bonus program could be applied. Generally, TPR claims amount to a smaller percentage of revenue or PMPM income than those for COB. The plan budget for COB/TPR amounts could be subdivided into their two respective categories with various incentive mechanisms determined separately.

CONCLUSION

All the functions, processes, and relationships described in this chapter depend on senior management support. The function of senior management as it relates to an OPL operation is to engender corporate understanding and support of the OPL effort and to provide the necessary policy and resources with which to succeed. Resource support includes competent and adequate OPL staff; direct access to corporate legal counsel when necessary; systems availability and support; commitment to assistance in discovery, including data capture documents and procedures to convey such data on a timely and regular basis; contractual support for plan rights to coordinate benefits and subrogate; and availability of all utilization data (claims, encounters, and referrals) and the ability to replicate claims/referrals efficiently and to produce fee-for-service–equivalent bills for any capitated care. Policy support includes identification and corporatewide adoption of common terms and definitions; for designated states, adoption and practice of the NAIC Model, including, but not limited to, total allowable expense and its implications, benefit credit reserve, and order of benefits determination; adoption and practice of state legislation and regulation regarding the plan's right to subrogate and collect from third parties; "pay and chase" versus "chase and pay" for COB; and whether to deny claims payment absent response to investigation activities.

OPL activities are a complex process. In addition to establishing and maintaining an effective operational engine that identifies, researches, and adjudicates OPL claims, coordinated and consistent policy throughout the plan and extending to providers, members, and group customers is required so that the proper incentives are built into the program to encourage the disclosure of other coverage or subrogation information. The most common flaws are member disincentives for disclosure (i.e., perception that benefits will be reduced or denied), provider disincentives for contributing to the process (i.e., additional administrative tasks resulting in lowered reimbursement), and staff disincentives (i.e., promotion of the number of cases processed rather than valuing effective procedures that contribute to the plan's OPL financial goals).

SUGGESTED READING

Jordan, M. 1986. *COB and the New NAIC Model COB Regulations*.

Scheur, B. 1988. *Making COB Work for Your Plan: Why COB Plans Often Fail*. Newton, Mass.: Scheur Management Group.

Chapter 33

Optimizing Health Plan Operations

Ron M. Davis, James A. Williams, and Dana E. Frank

Managed care organizations (MCOs) have enjoyed vast popularity and success over the last decade. Enrollees in health maintenance organizations increased from 9 million to more than 36 million between 1980 and 1990.[1] Market forces driving the health care industry, however, are undergoing dramatic changes. Shifting demographics, new technologies, increasing consumer pressure to lower costs, regulatory changes at the state and national levels, and a rapidly consolidating marketplace have irrevocably altered the context in which MCOs do business. This new context has forced MCOs to formulate new goals, new strategies, and new ways of operating to remain an essential part of health care in the decades to come. To this end,

there has been an industrywide trend toward radically reevaluating and reconceptualizing key operating systems and technologies to ensure that they are as simple, flexible, and consumer focused as they need to be in this competitive and volatile climate.

One process that MCOs are using to bring about breakthrough improvements in performance is reengineering, a tool that requires not only a serious commitment of time, resources, and talent but also a significant leap of faith. This chapter discusses the concept of reengineering in general, why its principles are important to MCO operations in today's marketplace, and how to use information technology to make it work. For the purposes of this chapter, operations are defined as administrative activities that support member services and production areas such as contract administration, capitation, enrollment, billing, and claims.

WHAT IS REENGINEERING?

Its most well-known proponents, Michael Hammer and James Champy, describe reengineering as "the fundamental rethinking and radical redesign of business processes to achieve dramatic improvements in critical, contemporary measures of performance such as cost, quality, service, and speed."[2(p.81)] Reengineering is an act of imagination, looking into the future to see what could be instead of working with what exists now. Reengineering, also known as process innovation or reinventing the corporation, is not incremental improvement or

Ron M. Davis is Senior Vice President of Operations and Customer Service for PacifiCare Health Systems, Inc. PacifiCare is one of the leading managed health care companies in the United States, serving more than 1.7 million members and owning the nation's largest Medicare risk program. Mr. Davis has over 15 years of experience in all facets of the managed care industry and recently led PacifiCare's reengineering efforts.

James A. Williams is Senior Vice President of Information Services and Chief Information Officer of PacifiCare Health Systems, Inc. Mr. Williams has more than 25 years of experience in the information services field and is responsible for overseeing PacifiCare's enterprisewide electronic data and information systems.

Dana E. Frank is Continuous Quality Improvement (CQI) Coach for PacifiCare's Western Region, responsible for directing the region's CQI efforts. Ms. Frank has over 10 years of experience in the health care management consulting field and recently served as PacifiCare's internal consultant for reengineering.

downsizing; instead, it forces companies to start with the future and work backward as if existing methods, people, and departments did not exist. In addition to asking "How can we do what we do at a lower cost, faster, and better?," reengineering asks "Why do we do what we do at all?"

Corporations have traditionally built their systems and departments based on models created during the Industrial Revolution. Proponents of reengineering assert that these models no longer work in today's world and that they inhibit a corporation's ability to take advantage of new technology and to adapt to change in general. Reengineering requires companies to look past existing models, assumptions, and infrastructures to see the underlying key processes that bring value to the customer. Cross-functional teams are assembled to ask the following question of each process: "Would we do it this way if we could start from scratch tomorrow?" If the answer is no, the process is a candidate for reengineering.

Reengineering a process demands intuition, creativity, and a completely different type of analysis. Instead of focusing exclusively inward, reengineering examines each process in terms of how it serves the customer, extending the boundaries of what is considered a process well beyond the walls of the MCO. Because new processes usually transcend old structures, the work must be performed in different ways. Less emphasis is put on checks and controls that require layers of management. More emphasis is put on giving information and authority to those closest to the work. Teams, case managers, and process owners see a process through from beginning to end instead of having discrete departments perform tasks assembly line style.

Reengineered processes are ultimately organized around outcomes, not tasks. For example, instead of looking at how to process purchase orders faster, a reengineering team may look at how to get goods delivered and paid for faster and may design a new process that makes purchase orders unnecessary.

Although reengineering's primary focus is the process, reengineering also demands a significant change in corporate culture. Compensation, recruitment, job descriptions, and career paths must be changed to reflect new business priorities. By starting over with an open mind and rejecting the frameworks and assumptions of the past, reengineering enables organizations to pursue their business strategies in new and unexpected ways, producing the kind of breakthroughs that can catapult a corporation ahead of its competition.

WHY SHOULD MCOs REENGINEER?

As the health care industry undergoes fundamental changes, MCOs need to prepare for the future by doing several things simultaneously: They must expand their client/provider bases, lower operating costs, improve the quality of medical care, and attempt to stand out in a crowded commodity marketplace by offering diverse products, demonstrated value, and convenience to customers. This is not a modest endeavor; it is a major undertaking that only the most determined organizations will accomplish. The reengineering process spurs MCOs to examine their underlying structures and assumptions, discard what is no longer useful, embrace new technology, and meet the future with confidence.

Growing Pains and Cost Control

The most immediate change that MCOs have to address is the consolidation of the health care marketplace. MCOs, hospitals, private physicians, and providers of every kind are rushing to merge, acquire, and form new partnerships to survive (also see Chapter 5). Growth at this pace invariably comes with growing pains. Newly consolidated MCOs often find themselves weighed down by multiple layers of bureaucracy, by redundancy when several departments perform the same task in different ways, and by incompatible information systems. The more an MCO grows, the more staff it requires to support this complex accumulation of old structures, rules, and departments, eventually producing an organization that is slow to respond to customer needs and unable to control operations costs. This is a weak position to be in for several reasons, the most compelling of which is that employer groups and other consumers are applying ever-increasing pressure to lower premiums. General and administrative cost ratios that were considered acceptable 10 years ago will push an MCO toward bankruptcy today.

Reengineering can help MCOs through such growing pains. The most successful MCOs have used the concepts of reengineering to establish large-scale, highly flexible, integrated organizations that operate with a uniform set of work practices and information systems, significantly lowering transaction costs. These centralized systems could not have been created from existing systems that were built according to outmoded market assumptions.

Bringing New Value to Consumers and Medical Professionals

Lowering costs is only a temporary competitive advantage for MCOs; it must be combined with high-quality and convenient services, a local focus, and the ability to develop new products quickly to attract and retain new customers. For example, reengineering has helped MCOs reconceptualize their customer service and claims processing divisions, changing them from internally focused, quota-driven departments into divisions that are evaluated in terms of customer satisfaction.

Cultivating a superior network of medical professionals is another key to MCO success. Instead of using technology solely to extract information from medical providers, reengineered MCOs use technology to furnish health-related information and technical support to providers, thus improving the quality of care and provider satisfaction. This new focus improves an MCO's ability to attract the best medical professionals.

Reengineering also makes it possible for MCOs to expand upon the concept that made them popular in the first place: preventive medi-

cine. MCOs that reengineer are able to shift resources away from routine operations and toward the development of services that keep members healthy.

Starting Fresh with New Information Technology

There is an information technology revolution underway, and MCOs cannot afford to be left behind. With membership predicted to double within the next decade, MCOs must overcome their fear of the new and use this explosion of technological options to innovate.

Currently, most MCOs use information systems based on unconnected production units and old technology designed to meet the needs of one type of delivery system, such as fee for service, staff model, or capitation. Today's MCOs, however, may offer several delivery options and need information systems that are flexible enough to move among delivery models and to support the long-term goals and vision of the company. If given unlimited resources (a rare occurrence), a reengineering team can design entirely new systems with new technology. A more conservative (and common) approach is to use new technology to develop ancillary systems to connect to the existing central information system, making the most of the original investment.

Several technological advances are making it easier than ever before to concentrate medical management on total patient care, allowing for more continuity of care, enhancing member satisfaction, and reducing duplication of work and factual errors. Examples of such innovations include electronic data interchange (EDI), client-server applications, imaging, and voice response systems, all of which play a critical role in reengineering health plan operations. The reader is also referred to Chapter 28 for additional discussion of information systems. The availability of these information technologies has dramatically increased the potential benefits of reengineering operations. Already automated processes such as claims adjudication can become radically more efficient when hooked up to EDI and imaging technology. The money saved on each claim processed can translate into millions of dollars in additional margin for a medium to large MCO.

EDI

EDI allows electronic information to travel across geographical, business, and industry boundaries, improving accuracy and speed by minimizing duplication and unnecessary paperwork. Information that once existed only on paper or in multiple forms on multiple computer systems can now be created on one personal computer (PC) and then electronically routed wherever it needs to go.

Several large health care companies are developing standards that will enable the seamless transfer of medical records, patient radiographs, laboratory results, and E-mail among hospitals, primary care physicians, specialists, pharmacies, and ancillary providers. This is no easy task, however, because the various entities that make up our health care industry resemble warring tribes, each defending its familiar turf and computer language. This atmosphere will not prevail, however. Soon enough, all players will have to agree on a common language that will allow them to exchange electronic information across all segments of the industry, thus speeding the arrival of integrated health delivery systems.

EDI promises to save billions from the annual national health care bill. Some experts predict savings of up to $42 billion by the turn of the century from costs cut on claims and electronic fund transmissions alone.[3]

Intelligent Workstations

The evolution of intelligent workstation technology is an important factor in the shift away from the transactional mindset typical of the fee-for-service environment and toward the analysis and management of information at the decision-making nexus. Intelligent workstation technology takes data out of the exclusive domain of the central office and brings information to every-

one who needs it—physicians, provider office staff, employer groups, and reengineering teams—thus bringing the answers closer to the questions.

Client-server architecture, which leverages the use of intelligent workstations, is a boon for reengineering teams. Previously, developing new systems required a significant investment of time and resources, putting a damper on creativity and risk taking. Intelligent workstations allow reengineering teams to design and test new systems via prototyping, a speedy and virtually risk-free endeavor. Prototyping allows MCOs the luxury of experimenting with several different approaches to problems, thus encouraging innovation.

Imaging

Imaging technology makes it possible to transfer the written word directly to the computer screen. Imaging, combined with document work flow software, has the power to shorten process time by hours, days, and even weeks by reducing data processing time. Almost any paper record can now be scanned directly into a PC to serve as a static electronic record or, using optical character recognition software, to be funneled into a database or word processing application. Document work flow software also makes it possible to move a scanned image between applications.

Data Warehouses

Data warehouses organize data to meet both internal and external information needs. These centralized stores consolidate data across multiple administrative systems into a unified format, ready to be accessed via EDI. This allows the user to access and analyze only as much information as needed in the decision-making process, saving time and resources.

Employer groups are asking MCOs to provide increasingly sophisticated information about the quality of the medical care they are buying. The Healthplan Employer Data and Information Set (HEDIS; see Chapter 28) was created to rate MCO performance and to provide that information to consumers. Data warehouses allow MCOs to produce relevant consumer-directed information, not just data for internal use, this is now a necessity for getting high HEDIS scores and attaining full accreditation from the National Committee for Quality Assurance, a nonprofit organization that performs quality-oriented accreditation reviews on MCOs (also see Chapter 37).

Voice Response Technology

Voice response technology, which allows members and providers to call an automated attendant for answers to frequently asked questions, provides a quick and easy way to access information. Members and providers appreciate the fast response and 24-hour, 7-day-a-week availability of information, and MCOs save money, time, and resources.

WHAT DOES A REENGINEERED MCO PROCESS LOOK LIKE?

The following are examples of how the concepts of reengineering can be applied to MCO operations. This list is by no means exhaustive, nor will these examples be appropriate for all MCOs.

Several Functions Are Combined into One Expanded Job

Before Reengineering

Sales and underwriting are separate departments. Sales staff are given financial incentives to make sales. Underwriting staff are motivated to assess accurately the MCO's risk when considering a contract with a new employer group. A salesperson, equipped with promotional material and charm, goes out into the field to bring in new business. Once a potential sale is discussed, the salesperson collects member demographic data from the employer group and brings them back to the home office to hand off to the underwriting division. Underwriting may take up to 2 weeks to come up with a quote for the salesper-

son to bring back to the employer group. Sales must go back to the employer group several times before a contract is made.

After Reengineering

A newly trained underwriting salesperson goes out into the field equipped with promotional material, charm, and a laptop computer. This computer is loaded with decision-support software and data that allow the salesperson to enter demographic information, analyze it, develop a quote, and negotiate on the spot, a significant competitive edge. Only the most complex cases require the expertise of the underwriting staff. New incentives are devised for sales staff based on long-term outcomes instead of the number of sales.

Workers Are Empowered To Make Decisions

Figure 33–1 shows an overview of a customer services reengineering project cycle. Note that measuring and reacting to member satisfaction results represent an iterative process.

Before Reengineering

The MCO provides a different customer service 800 number for every division, such as claims, dental, prescriptions, and so forth. These numbers are staffed by customer service representatives with limited information and authority. They may use computers, but they do not have access to on-line data. If the member has a nonroutine question, the customer service representative has to take it to a supervisor and then call the member back or refer the member to a different telephone number. The customer service representatives have been trained to get through calls quickly. They are evaluated with respect to how many calls they process in a day, not how many queries are answered or problems solved.

After Reengineering

The MCO eliminates all but one 800 number for customer service by product line (e.g., com-

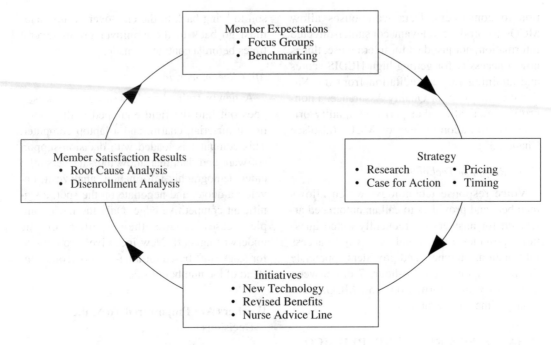

Figure 33–1 Customer service reengineering cycle.

mercial or Medicare and Medicaid). Customer service representatives work with a computer system that is connected to a database linked to all MCO divisions, such as claims, dental, and so forth. They are also extensively trained in the protocols of each division and are given the authority to make judgment calls. When they get a call from a member wanting to know whether a particular service is covered, they have the information and authority to say yes or no. If they need to refer to a member's enrollment form, they can call up the imaged form on the screen. A low percentage of calls are referred to other sources or require a call-back. Customer service representatives are evaluated based on how many calls they are able to resolve themselves within the first member contact. The system is evaluated in terms of overall member satisfaction: how many complaints are received, how fast complaints are resolved, and how long it takes to relay relevant information.

Work Is Performed According to Process Flow

Before Reengineering

The enrollment staff are in charge of keying data manually from member enrollment forms into the computer system. The data must be carefully checked for accuracy, and the forms must be filed. The forms are physically routed to other locations when needed by another department.

After Reengineering

Instead of focusing on how to enroll new members more quickly and accurately, a brave soul on the reengineering team asks "Why do *we* have to enter the information on the computer?" The MCO takes advantage of imaging and interactive technology to create systems by which members enroll themselves, entering in their own information on a networked PC at the employer group using dial-in technology, using a voice response unit, or filling in paper forms that can be scanned easily by the MCO. New member information is available immediately, and processing time and inaccuracy are reduced.

Bureaucracy Takes a Back Seat to Customer Convenience

Before Reengineering

A member with a minor rash calls his primary care provider and is told that he must come in for an examination before getting a referral to a dermatologist. The member comes in, and the primary physician makes a determination based on the presenting symptoms. The member is handed a referral and then must make an additional appointment with the dermatologist.

After Reengineering

A member with a minor rash calls an 800 number and is connected to a nurse. The member describes the rash and other symptoms to the nurse, who in turn uses her own training and a networked computer equipped with diagnostic algorithms to make the decision to send the member to a dermatologist. The nurse also enters the member's symptoms and the referral into the computer, which generates a record that is sent to the primary physician. Alternatively, the diagnostic algorithms may suggest methods for self-care.

There are several advantages to this system: Members are saved an extra trip to the physician's office, thus enhancing their satisfaction with the health plan; members are more likely to report symptoms early if all they have to do is make a phone call, reducing the need for more expensive interventions later; and many unnecessary physician visits are eliminated, giving primary physicians more time to spend with seriously ill members.

HALLMARKS OF REENGINEERING

Reengineering takes on a different form in every corporation where it is applied, but there are several universal goals that are achieved when reengineering is successful. Exhibit 33–1 lists the hallmarks of reengineering.

REENGINEERING STEP BY STEP

Reengineering proceeds in four phases. Exhibit 33–2 gives an overview of the major steps within each phase. The start-up or mobilization phase of reengineering is critical to set the foundation for successful reengineering projects. Figure 33–2 shows the flow of activities for phase I in more detail.

CRITICAL SUCCESS FACTORS

Reengineering is not a casual commitment; it has the potential to disrupt every aspect of business for a significant period of time. There is no guaranteed recipe for success, but there are several key factors that must stay constant for reengineering to work.

Key Elements

Sponsorship

The board of directors and all top executives need to be whole-heartedly invested in the reengineering process, presenting a united front to staff. They must authorize enough staff time and money to give the project a chance. Ambivalence from the top will quickly sabotage all efforts to change; the leading cause of reengineering failure is lack of active participation by senior managers. Because reengineering is cross-functional, it must be led by those with the seniority to combine, create, and dissolve entire departments. Senior management must also be willing to assign reengineering duties to the most talented and indispensable staff members; reengineering will not work if carried out only by those with extra time on their hands.

Link to Strategy

Reengineering is not a substitute for a coherent business strategy. Instead, it is an effective

Exhibit 33–1 Hallmarks of Reengineering

Dramatically improved performance: Companies that have successfully reengineered experience unprecedented reductions in costs and upswings in profit, customer satisfaction, and market share.

Focus on process: Instead of focusing on individual tasks, entire cross-functional business processes are redesigned from beginning to end.

Shattered assumptions: Conventional wisdom is replaced with unconventional wisdom. All assumptions are analyzed, and most are discarded.

New context for doing business: A new context is created that gives everyone a sense of starting fresh, which in turn inspires creativity and high performance.

Simplicity: Reengineering strives to eliminate complexity and multiple layers of administrators. Instead of preserving discrete functions for individuals, the reengineering team combines functions and increases individual authority so that one person can handle a process from start to finish.

Intelligent use of information technology: New technology is not used merely to upgrade existing systems; it is used to encourage innovation. New services are created that bring value to the customer.

Focus on the customer: Reengineering is based on the premise that businesses exist to create value for their customers and that businesses should make it easy for customers to do business with them. Reengineering demands that companies look beyond financial reports to see themselves honestly through their customers' eyes. Customer complaints are seen as valuable sources of information and are used to reveal root problems.

means by which to execute that strategy. If an organization is headed in the wrong direction, reengineering will only serve to take it there faster.

Case for Action

An MCO must be willing to evaluate and confront its true competitive situation honestly and then to identify all barriers to significant change. The case for action must be so compelling that no one in the organization will think that there is any feasible alternative to reengineering. The case for reengineering must be presented in a written vision statement that is persuasive but not exaggerated.

Vision and Goals

Clear vision, a compelling case for action, and dramatic goals are essential. It is not enough to make saving money on operating costs a goal; it must be combined with creating new value for the customer to keep staff interested and motivated. Keeping the focus on the customer and the competition will also help preempt some of the inevitable turf battles. Goals must be translated into terms that are meaningful to all participants. A strong vision will inspire management and staff to reassess assumptions constantly and to counteract the inertia of habit and routine.

Best Practices and Benchmarking

Researching MCO best practices and benchmarking with other organizations outside the health care industry can be a valuable source of breakthrough ideas and are important components of the case for action. For example, automatic teller machine technology has been used in hospitals to dispense medication automatically. Consequently, prescription and dosage accuracy and patient billing have improved dramatically.

Communication

Clear and frequent communication is vital. Senior management must constantly articulate support for reengineering efforts to keep everyone motivated, confident, and interested in the reengineering process. All the relevant facts, positive and negative, should be shared with staff to justify the changes taking place and to counteract the rumor mill.

Harness Contention

Traditionally, conflict and contention have been perceived as counterproductive. In reengineering, the opposite is true. Conflict can provide a catalyst for innovation and eventually stimulate trust. Those charged with assessing the company's competitive situation must be fearless. They must break through the usual silences

Exhibit 33–2 Reengineering Step by Step

Phase I: Mobilization

1. Develop reengineering vision and case for action linked to overall strategic plan
2. Create high-level process map
3. Establish guidance and leadership structure
4. Formulate reengineering strategy
5. Determine process prioritization
6. Once processes are identified and mapped, companies typically use four criteria to determine which processes require reengineering and to establish the order in which they should be addressed:
   - *Dysfunction*—Which processes are causing the most distress?
   - *Importance*—Which processes have the greatest impact on the corporation's customers?
   - *Best practices*—How do we compare with the competition in terms of process cost, speed, quality, and service?
   - *Feasibility*—What is the probability that reengineering this process will succeed?
7. Select process to start
8. Assign team members and project manager
9. Allocate resources and create a schedule

Phase II: Process diagnosis

1. Develop process understanding and define scope of process

- Create detailed process maps
- Conduct time/value analysis

2. Develop understanding of customer needs
3. Identify weaknesses in existing design
4. Set targets and create vision for new design
5. Create action plan for "quick hits"

Phase III: Process redesign

1. Create breakthrough process design concept
2. Develop detailed process design
3. Redesign entire business infrastructure, and align incentives
4. Build laboratory prototype
5. Test, learn, and modify

Phase IV: Transition/implementation

1. Formulate transition strategy
2. Implement initial field release
3. Implement succeeding releases
4. Develop supporting infrastructure
5. Roll out and institutionalize
6. Establish ongoing continuous quality improvement effort
7. Devise system to measure results continuously

---

about certain pet projects, challenge the preferences of senior management, and face their own role in the company's failures. It is natural for staff members to worry about reengineering themselves out of a job. The challenge is to come up with new jobs that will support the organization's new goals.

Empowerment

Reengineering should be structured in such a way that all staff have a personal stake in the outcome. Reengineering must be led from the top, but reengineering teams should also include staff members who have informal authority over key resources and over opinion networks. In a truly empowered environment, workers have the trust, the training, the judgment, and the self confidence necessary to accept authority and responsibility.

Process Mapping

Process mapping is defined as the graphical depiction of business processes. Process maps provide an analytical framework to identify and quantify the benefits from reengineering and to provide information for the process diagnosis phase. By mapping current business processes, hand-offs of work among functions or departments (which introduce delays in process completion) can be identified and eliminated.

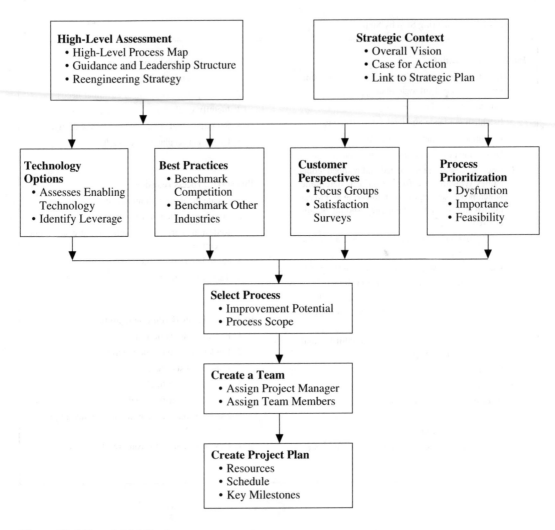

Figure 33–2 Phase I: Mobilization.

Process maps are used to provide a baseline of common understanding among team members and to provide the platform for redesign efforts.

There are many types and styles of process maps that are used to analyze and redesign work flow for reengineering initiatives. Practitioners usually start with a high level process map that depicts the core business processes of the entire enterprise. More detailed process maps are then developed during the process diagnosis and redesign phases.

Quick Hits/Momentum

The process diagnosis and redesign phases should be accomplished in less than 6 months, but the transition/implementation phase may take longer, depending upon monetary, technological, and human resource requirements. Therefore, a certain amount of instant gratification is necessary to keep everyone interested and invested in the reengineering project. To ensure the success of the more central, long-term goals, build in some tasks that are sure to have immediate positive results.

Change Management

Reengineering teams need to consider carefully how radical change will affect employees. Staff being asked to expand their responsibilities dramatically should feel as if they are benefiting from this stretch. If an employee's job is reengineered, the incentives/rewards associated with that job must also be changed to reflect the new goals. It is also important to budget enough time and money to retrain staff to use new technologies and complete new processes. Fundamental cultural change takes time and commitment. Reengineering will not succeed in the long run if the human component is ignored.

Key Personnel

The right people can make or break a reengineering campaign. The following are common roles and responsibilities that emerge in companies that are committed to reengineering.

Reengineering Leader

The leader is a senior executive who has enough clout to instigate a rigorous process that could change the company's very reason for existing. This person must have the leadership and persuasive powers to keep people interested in and supportive of the process, even as their work lives are radically disrupted.

Process Owner

The process owner is a senior manager with line responsibility for the process that is being reengineered. The process owner's primary role is to make reengineering happen at the process level. Because most traditional companies lack end-to-end process owners, responsibility for processes is fragmented across organizational boundaries. In practice, process owners are usually managers who manage one of the functions involved in the process that will undergo reengineering. The process owner may participate in reengineering team meetings and is responsible for executive sponsorship of the project.

Project Manager

A new breed of manager must emerge to oversee reengineering efforts: the project manager. As the title suggests, this manager will oversee a particular project or process, not a department, and will have no investment in preserving existing systems or departments. The project manager reports to either the reengineering leader or the process owner.

Reengineering Team

The team is a group of five to ten people dedicated to the reengineering of one specific process. The team produces the ideas and plans for reengineering and then implements the reinvented process. Reengineering teams are self-directed, and their client is the process owner. It is helpful to have a dedicated project manager to serve as team leader, coach, and facilitator.

Teams should be composed of process insiders as well as outsiders, and members should be selected from the organization's best and brightest staff. Insiders understand how things work now; outsiders bring in new ideas and attitudes. Human resources and information technology staff are important team participants. Team members need to be allowed to give 75 percent to 100 percent of their time to reengineering to sustain focus.

Steering Committee

The reengineering steering committee comprises senior managers, including the process owners, who plan and oversee the organization's overall reengineering strategy. The reengineering leader chairs this group, and the reengineering czar (see below) serves as a facilitator. It may be necessary to create a steering committee at the beginning of the reengineering effort, but it is considered optional. As the reengineering effort matures, executive leadership should take over this role.

Reengineering Czar

The reengineering czar acts as the leader's chief internal consultant for reengineering. The czar is responsible for coordinating all ongoing reengineering efforts and develops and maintains the organization's arsenal of reengineering approaches. The czar is also responsible for providing reengineering consulting to each individual process owner, project manager, and process team, drawing from his or her own knowledge or engaging appropriate outside expertise.

MEASURING SUCCESS

Because reengineering is expensive, it is important that benefits from the reengineered processes outweigh the investment to get there. Hidden costs, such as diverted staff time, must be added to obvious costs, such as consultant fees and information system development. The initial planning process should include a detailed model of expected results. Once reengineering is underway, results must be measured carefully and constantly to justify the initial outlay of resources. At the most basic level, reengineering should significantly reduce operations costs, increase transaction speed, and improve information accuracy. The long-term benefits can be measured in terms of customer satisfaction and increased revenue. Customer satisfaction should be continually measured by analyzing complaints and holding focus groups.

The ultimate goal of reengineering is to bring about a fundamental change in the context for doing business, but this context should not remain static. Reengineering should be a continual process, working alongside other long-term management initiatives such as total quality management, to keep an MCO in touch with its customers and ready to evolve with the marketplace.

THE FUTURE OF MCO OPERATIONS

MCOs are in the unique position of being able to collect data from a variety of settings over long periods of time, and they will soon be able to analyze data in such a way that they can spot trends, make forecasts, and set standards and protocols for their provider networks. Information systems that now have only the capability to record events and analyze data after the fact will soon be able to help providers make decisions not only about referrals and diagnostics but also about actual courses of treatment. On-line utilization review systems that track approvals/denials, efficacy of care, staff productivity, and accuracy are on the cutting edge now but will be standard soon, along with electronic medical records linked to automated medical libraries, telephone information and advice lines, and other member-directed preventive services.

As discussed in Chapters 4 and 5, what are now considered alternative provider groups, such as physician–hospital organizations, integrated service networks, large group practices, and management service organizations, will be common, enlarging the pool of entities in the business of risk bearing or underwriting. MCOs will have to find ways to collaborate with these entities or risk becoming redundant.

Today's health care delivery systems are designed to manage illness. Tomorrow's will be designed to keep people healthy. The biggest challenge facing MCOs is to use new ideas and technologies to transform their corporate culture, management, and information systems from those that support disease management into those that support wellness, a fundamental shift in context that will require the tools of reengineering.

REFERENCES AND NOTES

1. HCIA, Inc., *The Guide to the Managed Care Industry* (Baltimore, Md.: HCIA, 1994).

2. M. Hammer and J. Champy, *Reengineering the Corporation* (New York, N.Y.: HarperCollins, 1993).

3. Medical Interface, *The EDI Movement Marches On* (Bronxville, N.Y.: Medical Interface, 1994).

SUGGESTED READING

Barr, S. 1995. Grinding It Out: Why Reengineering Takes So Long. *CFO*, January.

Davenport, T.H. 1993. *Process Innovation: Reengineering Work Through Information Technology*. Boston, Mass.: Harvard Business School Press.

Hall, G., Rosenthal, J., and Wade, J. 1993. How to Make Reengineering Really Work. *Harvard Business Review*, November/December.

Hammer, M. 1990. Reengineering Work: Don't Automate, Obliterate. *Harvard Business Review*, July/August.

Hammer, M., and Champy, J. 1993. *Reengineering the Corporation: A Manifesto for Business Revolution*. New York, N.Y.: Harper Business.

Harrington, H.J. 1991. *Business Process Improvement: The Breakthrough Strategy for Total Quality Productivity and Competitiveness*. New York, N.Y.: McGraw-Hill, Inc.

The Horizontal Corporation. 1993. *Business Week*, 20 December.

Goss, T., Pascale, R., and Athos, A. 1993. The Reinvention Roller Coaster: Risking the Present for a Powerful Future. *Harvard Business Review*, November/December.

Leebov, W., and Scott, G. 1994. *Service Quality Improvement: The Customer Satisfaction Strategy for Health Care*. Chicago, Ill.: American Hospital Publishing.

McKinney, R., and Childress, R. 1992. Moving Toward Self-Directed Work Teams in a Service Environment: Creating a Customer Service Advantage Through Teams at Aetna Health Plans. *HMOs and Managed Care: Proving Their Advantages in an Era of Reform*. Washington, D.C.: American Association of Health Plans (formerly GHAA).

Stewart, T.A. 1993. Reengineering: The Hot New Management Tool. *Fortune*, 23 August.

Stewart, T.A. 1995. The Corporate Jungle Spawns a New Species: The Project Manager. *Fortune*, 10 July.

Treacy, M., and Wiersma, F. 1995. *The Discipline of Market Leaders*. Boston, Mass.: Addison-Wesley.

Wheatley, M.J. 1992. *Leadership and the New Science*. San Francisco, Calif.: Berrett-Koehler.

Chapter 34

Assessing the Market for Managed Care

Eric R. Wagner

The managed care industry has been characterized during the last two decades by alternating periods of rapid growth and expansion followed by slower growth and consolidation. The early to mid-1980s saw rapid enrollment growth in health maintenance organizations (HMOs), initial development of preferred provider organizations (PPOs), and an explosion in the total number of managed care plans in the United States. The success of the industry during this period led many to attempt to emulate the achievements of those who had entered during the early phase of the cycle.

Unfortunately, many who entered the managed care industry during the mid-1980s failed to assess adequately local market conditions or their potential to thrive. Compounding this failure to investigate their market environment, the health insurance industry in which managed care plans compete for business entered the downturn

---

Eric R. Wagner is Vice President for Managed Care at Medlantic Healthcare Group and Washington Hospital Center where he is responsible for the development of managed care strategy, negotiation of participation agreements, and maintenance of relationships with managed care plans. In addition, he serves as Executive Director of and has operational responsibility for the WHC Physician-Hospital Organization. Previously, Mr. Wagner was with the health care strategy and managed care practice of an international professional services firm. He has more than 14 years of experience in the health care industry specializing in managed care strategy, development, operation, and finance and has published several books, chapters, and articles on managed care evaluation, development, negotiations, and provider compensation.

phase of its own underwriting cycle. The results were devastating to the industry.

Enrollment growth in managed care plans flattened. The number of HMOs actually dropped as some plans ceased operations and others were merged with or acquired by stronger plans. The largest HMO company in the country at that time declared bankruptcy and ultimately shrank to a fraction of its former size. In the process, many physicians, hospitals, and other providers discovered the true impact of the hold-harmless clause (see Chapter 55) when their claims went unpaid, shareholders and bondholders of public HMO companies lost several hundred million dollars, and health care coverage for many enrollees was disrupted.

Although the managed care market contraction of the late 1980s had many causes (see Chapter 39), it is clear that the failure of many managed care plans to assess market conditions before expanding or forming new plans featured prominently in at least some of the industry's disasters. Unlike events in the movie *Field of Dreams,* where "if you build it, they will come," when the plans were built, customers did not come.

Market assessments cannot guarantee success for managed care plans; nevertheless, properly performed assessments can help reduce the risks that confront the development of complex new managed care ventures. Market assessments also provide valuable information to assist sponsors of managed care plans in deciding whether (and how) to enter particular markets. Finally, market assessments can help identify features to include in plan design to respond to consumer preference. The elements of a properly performed market assessment include the following:

- identification of the product or service to be marketed
- definition of what or who is the market
- review of market demographics and conditions
- understanding of the regulatory environment
- profile of competition
- analysis of employers and their needs

WHAT ARE WE PLANNING TO SELL?

The range of types of managed care organizations and the products they offer has broadened considerably during the last decade (see Chapters 3, 35, and 36). As a result of these changes, we must identify clearly what managed care products or services we intend to evaluate in the market assessment.

The types of managed care organizations that could be evaluated during a market assessment range from full-fledged HMOs to individual practice associations or physician–hospital organizations (PHOs; see Chapter 4). Although these types of organizations are not necessarily mutually exclusive, offering one product could seriously reduce the success of another. For example, a health care provider that offers a PHO could find its prospects dramatically diminished by developing an HMO that is perceived to compete with other HMOs in the market (see Chapter 5).

Similarly, different products may appeal to different segments of the market and should be evaluated differently. For example, an existing managed care organization may wish to offer a Medicaid product line. The process for performing a market assessment for this product would be different from the process for a point-of-service product oriented toward the commercial market.

WHAT OR WHO IS THE MARKET?

The definition of what or who is the market for the purposes of the market assessment is dependent on the managed care products to be offered. Table 34–1 illustrates the target markets for some selected types of managed care products.

REVIEW OF MARKET DEMOGRAPHICS AND CONDITIONS

Market demographics and local market conditions have a large influence on the potential success of managed care organizations and their individual product lines. Among the elements of market demographics that should be evaluated as part of the market assessment are population characteristics, health services utilization rates, employment and commuting patterns, and Medicare characteristics. Medicaid is likewise important to assess, but the Medicaid market operates in a very different manner and is therefore discussed separately in Chapter 48.

Population Characteristics

Population characteristics in a local market area can be a large determinant of whether a managed care organization will achieve success. Issues of population growth, age distribution, mobility, and income distribution should all be considered part of the market assessment.

Population Growth

Areas with more rapid population growth generally are more favorable for the development of managed care organizations. As a result of the influx of individuals from outside the area, there often is a larger population base of people who lack established physician–patient relationships. These individuals generally are more likely to enroll with HMOs because they will not face disruption in their provider relationships. In addition, areas with rapid population growth have a built-in potential for premium and in-

Table 34–1 Examples of Target Markets

Type of Managed Care Product	Target Markets
Traditional HMO products	The market for traditional HMOs generally is restricted to larger employers (e.g., 100 or more employees) that are willing to offer more than one benefit option to their employees.
Point-of-service HMO products	The market for point-of-service products is broader than the market for traditional HMOs. It includes larger employers that may offer a point-of-service plan either as a benefit option to their employees or as a single health benefit option. It also includes smaller employers, perhaps those with as few as 5 employees.
PPO products	The market for PPO products generally is limited to larger, self-insured employers, although many indemnity insurance companies have included PPO options in their small group products. These products typically are offered as a replacement for traditional indemnity insurance coverage.
PHOs	The market for most PHOs generally is limited to other managed care organizations. Although some PHOs have attempted to market themselves directly to self-insured employers as alternatives to other forms of managed care organizations, effectively as replacements for HMOs, PPOs, or indemnity insurance, market research indicates that such PHOs have achieved only limited success in securing direct contracts.

Source: Health Care Financing Administration.

come growth for managed care organizations. Managed care organizations with stable or expanding market shares are virtually guaranteed revenue growth at least equal to the population growth rate.

Age Distribution

Areas with populations that are relatively younger generally offer better opportunities for managed care organizations. Managed care organizations often are more attractive to these individuals for at least three reasons. First, younger families may be more price sensitive than their middle-aged counterparts and may find the premium rate advantages of managed care plans attractive. Second, younger families find the coverage of preventive services, including immunizations, well-child visits, and periodic physical examinations, to be an appealing characteristic of managed care plans. Finally,

younger families may not be as committed to more traditional forms of health insurance and delivery and may be more willing to choose managed care plans.

Mobility

Relatively transient population areas often are more favorable for managed care plan development and enrollment. As in the case of areas with rapid population growth, individuals in more transient areas are more likely to enroll with HMOs because they will not face disruption in their provider relationships.

Income Distribution

Market areas with larger segments of the population in the middle income brackets generally are more favorable to enrollment in managed care plans. Conversely, individuals in relatively affluent areas with large disposable incomes may not be as favorably disposed toward managed care plans because they are not as price sensitive to out-of-pocket health care costs and because of the limits that are placed on provider choice.

Health Services Utilization Rates

Health services utilization rates within a market area may be an important indicator of the success that can be attained by a managed care organization within a market area. Several elements are important to consider.

First, the utilization rates experienced by existing HMOs and managed care plans in the market area provide a benchmark against which potential new managed care organizations can evaluate themselves to test whether they will be competitive in the market. Information about utilization rates can be calculated from information contained in quarterly and annual statements, which HMOs generally are required to file with state insurance departments. These annual statements contain information concerning the HMO's enrollment, financial performance, and health services utilization. For example, it is possible to calculate the following for individual HMOs from information contained in the statements: inpatient utilization for commercial, Medicare, and Medicaid enrollees, average premium revenue per member per month for commercial, Medicare, and Medicaid enrollees, and average inpatient hospital expenses per patient day.

Second, existing utilization rates in the market area can be compared with the utilization rates for HMOs to gain an understanding of the extent to which utilization patterns must be changed to be competitive. Two examples of how utilization rates can be used in market assessments are as follows:

1. Some suburban markets or rural markets have substantially lower utilization rates than their adjacent metropolitan areas. These areas may provide opportunities for new managed care plans to develop with built-in utilization advantages. Such utilization advantages may be translated into pricing and premium rate advantages.

2. Conversely, analysis of current utilization rates in a market area may reveal that inpatient hospital utilization is substantially higher than it will need to be to compete effectively with existing managed care plans. The assessment may conclude that it would be too difficult to alter medical practice patterns and reduce utilization rates sufficiently to offer a competitively priced benefit plan. Alternatively, if the HMO believes that it can aggressively manage utilization, it may see high rates as an opportunity to differentiate itself quickly in the market, although such aggressive utilization management is often easier said than done in markets with high levels of utilization.

The review of utilization rates should be stratified into each of the key market segments (e.g., commercial, Medicare, and Medicaid) that may be served by a managed care organization because each of these segments exhibits different utilization characteristics. Separate information about utilization rates for competing HMOs typically is available in quarterly and annual statements for commercial, Medicare, and Medicaid enrollees. In addition, organizations such as the American Association of Health Plans in Washington, D.C. prepare aggregate analyses of the utilization experience for HMOs based on national surveys. This information can be used to establish comparative targets for expected utilization rates on a regional basis.[1]

As with other elements of the market assessment, analysis of utilization rates contributes only one dimension to reaching conclusions about market feasibility. Other elements of the assessment may lead to different conclusions, and the analyst will need to take all these elements into account in making decisions.

Employment and Commuting Patterns

Managed care organizations need to analyze the employment and commuting patterns within their prospective market areas to understand two key aspects of their implementation and operation. First, the location of employment centers helps managed care plans understand where their marketing activities need to be concentrated. In addition, to the extent that metropolitan areas span multiple states, employment patterns may lead HMOs to seek licensure in multiple states to market to employers in an urban area and their employees who reside in suburban areas in adjoining states.

Second, commuting patterns help managed care organizations identify the geographic areas in which they need to develop participating provider panels. For example, a managed care plan may intend to focus its marketing efforts on employers located in the central portion of a metropolitan area. Research on commuting patterns for this area could indicate that a majority of employees reside in particular suburbs. The managed care plan might then choose to devote most of its physician and provider recruitment efforts in those suburbs.

Figure 34–1 provides an example of how information concerning employment and commuting patterns can be illustrated and examined. In this example, a managed care organization intended to pursue development of a new HMO in Wales County (the names of geographic areas have been altered to protect the organization). It intended to develop a provider network only within the county and to seek licensure only within a single state. Based on review of the employment and commuting patterns, the managed care organization concluded that it would need to be licensed in at least two states. In addition, it concluded that employers in the metropolitan area located in Northumberland County, where many Wales County residents were employed, were unlikely to offer the HMO if it did not have a provider that covered at least four counties. Based on these commuting patterns, the managed care organization would have needed to be

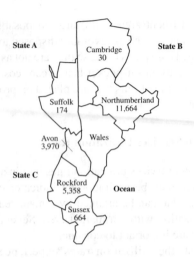

Figure 34–1 Example of commuting patterns. *Source:* Courtesy of Ernst & Young, LLP, Washington, D.C.

licensed in two states and to have an extensive provider network to provide the geographic coverage demanded by the market.

Medicare Characteristics

Many HMOs have entered, or are considering entering, into contracts with the Health Care Financing Administration (HCFA) to serve Medicare beneficiaries under the Medicare risk contracting program. One of the key variables that must be considered as part of the market assessment is the rate of payment that will be made by the HCFA for beneficiaries who enroll with HMOs in the market area.

The method used by the HCFA for calculating HMO payment rates has been controversial almost from the outset of the risk contracting program. Although the rate calculation considers other factors, one of the most important elements is the adjusted average per capita cost (AAPCC; see Chapter 46) in which the beneficiary resides. There are separate AAPCCs calculated for Part A and Part B benefits for each county in the United States. The combined AAPCC (adjusted for the demographic characteristics) provides a proxy for the payment that will be made by the HCFA for each enrolled Medicare beneficiary (actual payments are based on the AAPCC times adjustment factors for the beneficiary's age, sex, and institutional status).

There are wide variations in the amounts of the AAPCC from region to region. For example, the highest AAPCC for 1995 ($678.90 for Bronx, New York) was almost 3.5 times the lowest AAPCC ($196.51 for Harding County, New Mexico). There also has been little consistency among rates within metropolitan areas. For example, there is a 50 percent difference between the highest and lowest AAPCCs for selected jurisdictions in Washington, D.C., and its suburbs, as illustrated in Table 34–2.

Although the HCFA's methodology for calculating the AAPCC is supposed to be based at least in part on costs in each county, many observers believe that the differences between the AAPCC for adjacent jurisdictions cannot be explained based on true cost or utilization differences. As a result, the rate differences can create opportunities for HMOs to enter markets with relatively high AAPCC rates and avoid markets with relatively low rates.

The market assessment should consider both the actual level of the AAPCC for the market area and how the AAPCC compares with national averages and adjacent market areas. In the absence of an ability to explain wide differences among AAPCC rates for adjacent markets, a managed care organization may conclude that it would not enter the market for Medicare beneficiaries in counties with relatively low AAPCC rates. Conversely, it may find that portions of its local market area would be attractive because the AAPCC is relatively high.

Another characteristic that should be considered in evaluating the Medicare market for managed care organizations is the current market share of HMOs among Medicare beneficiaries in the market area. Information is available from the HCFA concerning the total number of Medicare beneficiaries and the number enrolled with HMOs for each county in the United States.

The percentage of beneficiaries enrolled with

Table 34–2 Selected 1995 AAPCC Rates

Jurisdiction	Overall AAPCC
District of Columbia	$539.97
Montgomery County, Maryland	$426.48
Prince Georges County, Maryland	$543.30
Alexandria, Virginia	$407.22
Arlington County, Virginia	$396.31
Fairfax County, Virginia	$360.50

Source: Health Care Financing Administration.

HMOs varies widely from one area to another, even among areas with relatively high levels of enrollment in HMOs within the commercially insured population. Many counties on the west coast have more than 40 percent of their Medicare beneficiaries enrolled in HMOs. In contrast, many areas on the east coast with high overall HMO penetration have less than 10 percent of their Medicare population enrolled in HMOs. This market share information provides an indicator of how easy or difficult it may be to enroll Medicare members in a managed care organization.

PROFILE OF COMPETITION

One of the key components of a market assessment is the development of a profile of organizations that are potential competitors to the planned managed care organization. This profile should be designed to answer at least two questions: Can the market area support a new managed care organization or product line, and how should the managed care organization's products, benefit, plans, pricing, and promotion be structured to compete most effectively against existing or potential competitors?

The profile of competitors should be prepared by reviewing publicly available information from regulatory filings, including annual statements, rate filings and actuarial analyses (if available), certificates of coverage, marketing materials, and provider directories. Key information that should be considered in the competitor profile includes the following:

- overall level of managed care enrollment in the market area (if managed care organizations already have achieved significant market share, such as more than half of commercial enrollment, it may be difficult for new organizations to enter the market successfully)
- key operating statistics for each of the competing plans, including the following information:
  1. enrollment by market segment (e.g., commercial, Medicare, and Medicaid)
  2. enrollment growth by market segment for the previous 3 years
  3. inpatient and outpatient utilization experience by market segment
  4. average per capita premium rates by market segment
  5. average equivalent inpatient per diem rates
  6. average per capita expenses by category
  7. reserves
  8. profitability
- types of benefit products offered (e.g., traditional HMO, point of service, Medicare risk contract, Medicaid, PPO)
- relationships with physicians and other providers, including style of the relationships (i.e., confrontational or partnership), types of reimbursement and risk-sharing mechanisms, and level of participation (e.g., broad or narrow panel)

Information gained from the competitor profile can be used to help assess the feasibility of entering the market. For example, average per capita premium rates can be used as a benchmark for establishing the maximum premium rates that can be charged for a new managed care product. In addition, the competitor profile can help managed care organizations decide how to position their products, to both consumers and their participating providers.

UNDERSTANDING OF THE REGULATORY ENVIRONMENT

The regulatory scheme in the United States for health insurance, HMOs, and other managed care organizations is based on a combination of state authority and federal oversight (see Chapters 46, 53, and 54). As a result, the regulatory environment in each state and market area is different. In some market areas, there may be an interplay between state regulations for adjacent states that make up the market area.

Although it is beyond the scope of this chapter to describe each regulatory approach, it is important to consider the impact of state requirements during the market assessment to help make decisions about products and structure. Two key issues should be considered:

1. Most states regulate HMOs under different laws and regulations than other forms of health insurance. Under the theory that "if it looks like a duck, talks like a duck, and walks like a duck, it is a duck," state regulators are likely to require health benefit plans with HMO-like characteristics to be controlled under the state's HMO legislation. This may have implications for the ability to offer point-of-service benefit options or other types of indemnity-like coverage.

2. A few states have enacted regulatory schemes for PPOs. These regulations impose requirements concerning structure, marketing, and other issues. Entities interested in developing PPO products should inquire about their ability to offer the products under the state's regulatory scheme.

Providers that are interested in developing and offering PHOs or other types of integrated delivery systems should consider whether such organizations are required to obtain licensure from state regulators. Although most states, as of 1995, allow PHOs to contract with licensed health plans on a full-risk capitation basis, they would not allow them to contract directly with employers or government agencies on the same basis (see Chapter 53). Because this is an evolving area of regulation, organizations should investigate the current status with their state insurance commissioner or other agency.

The results of the regulatory assessment should be considered as part of the overall market assessment in evaluating whether development of the proposed managed care organization is feasible or desirable.

ANALYSIS OF EMPLOYERS AND THEIR NEEDS

Thus far, the components of the market assessment have focused on aggregate level information that is publicly available. If these components are supportive of development of a managed care organization or product line, the next step in the process is to consider the needs of individual employers and their employees who are located within the market area.

The process of analyzing employer needs begins with identifying the major employers that are located within the market area. The definition of what constitutes a major employer depends on the size of the market area under consideration. Within major metropolitan areas, major employers generally are limited to those with 500 or more employees. In midsize areas, major employers may include all employers with 100 or more employees. In small market areas, major employers may include all employers with more than 50 employees.

In any event, the first step in the process is to collect information from the local chamber of commerce or other organization about major employers, numbers of employees, and key contacts. The competitor profile is prepared by conducting a survey using a combination of written questionnaire, telephone interview, or personal interview with the human resource manager for each major employer. The survey should be designed to elicit information from each employer about the following:

- health benefit options offered to employees and dependents
- health insurance funding mechanisms (e.g., fully insured, self-funded, or combination)
- current health insurer(s), third party administrators, and managed care plans
- premium rates or costs for each benefit plan option
- required employee contributions
- level of satisfaction with each current benefit option and provider of service
- level of interest in offering a new benefit option
- process for determining which available benefit plans to offer (e.g., proposals, negotiations, request for proposals)
- timeline for benefit decisions, including dates for required rate quotations and open enrollment
- role of local management and corporate or regional management (if applicable)

The employer survey is most effective when it is conducted by experienced professionals through personal, face-to-face interviews or telephone interviews. Although written questionnaires can produce valuable information, personal interviews provide an opportunity for the surveyor to probe for additional details and to evaluate the nuances of the conversations with employer representatives.

The results of the analysis of employers and their needs should be an assessment of the likelihood that employers will offer the proposed managed care product to their employees and, if so, whether it will be offered exclusively or as a benefit option. If employers are willing to offer the product, the analysis will provide useful information for projecting enrollment in the managed care organization.

CONCLUSION

All the information and analyses compiled as part of the market assessment should be reviewed and considered in reaching decisions about whether a particular market can support a proposed managed care organization or product. Often, different items of information lead to contrary conclusions. As a result, the evaluator must consider all available information and assess whether it suggests a likelihood of success or failure. This assessment frequently results in changes in strategy or approach for implementing the managed care product. A managed care plan must also recognize that the information and analyses may be quite different for different segments of the market (e.g., commercial, Medicare, and Medicaid), leading to different conclusions and approaches to each segment.

A thorough understanding of market dynamics, coupled with adequate data and informed analyses, will enable a managed care organization to position itself better to enter a new market, increase its penetration in an existing market, and expand its services.

REFERENCE AND NOTE

1. See, for example, Group Health Association of America, *HMO Industry Profile 1995*. (Washington, D.C.: American Association of Health Plans).

SUGGESTED READING

Ellis, B. and Brockman, B. 1993. Changing Competition in Health Care Marketing: A Method for Analysis and Strategic Planning. *Health Marketing Quarterly* 10 (3-4): 5–21.

Heckley, P.H. 1993. Market Research and Product Positioning: Developing, Implementing, and Using Market Research. In: P. Boland (ed.). *Making Managed Healthcare Work: A Practical Guide to Strategies and Solutions*. Gaithersburg, Md.: Aspen Publishers.

Chapter 35

Marketing Managed Health Care Plans

John P. Anton

Marketing is key to a managed care organization's (MCO's) expansion and member/customer retention. It seeks to determine existing and changing market demand, to help the MCO meet that demand, and to persuade current and prospective members and customers that the organization best meets their needs.

In doing so, members of the marketing staff must be ambassadors who can convince people in other parts of the MCO to support the marketing effort. They must have diplomatic and negotiating skills that enable them to improve or maintain their position in tense situations, turning possible adversarial situations into agreements. Finally, the marketing staff must possess and exercise investigative skills so that they can uncover hidden information, analyze it, and use it to develop marketing strategies.

This chapter discusses how to develop information to help sell your plan and compete successfully. It then discusses product and marketing diversification, prospecting, marketing communications, sales promotions, the marketing staff, and client retention.

John P. Anton is Vice President of National Marketing for CIGNA Employee Benefits Companies. Before joining CIGNA, he was Vice President and Executive Director of Georgia Medical Plan, an Atlanta health maintenance organization. Earlier, he was responsible for Medicare and Medicaid contracts for the Health Care Financing Administration's Southeast Region, coming to that position from The Traveller's Companies, where he was a claims manager for more than 9 years.

MARKET RESEARCH

The goal of market research is to enable an MCO to survive and grow. Market research identifies markets and submarkets by such variables as geographic area, industry type, case size, and competitor. It enables the MCO to determine what that particular market wants, the factors that influence its choices, and how the market or its demands and needs may change in the future. The MCO that does not know its market or does not respond to market interests or demands is living on borrowed time.

Benefits

Market research can help you determine whether a market is viable for your organization and can keep you from wasting your marketing efforts. For example, market research may reveal that a particular city, industry, or number of prospective companies has a consistent history of rejecting your model of health plan. It may tell you that a market is shrinking because of industry turndowns, company relocations, or closings. It may show that a market is saturated or alert you to client and prospect moves to reduce the number of MCOs offered to employees. On the other hand, market research may reveal opportunities such as an increasing receptiveness to managed care, unserved areas, a company's pending decision to move to or start a new operation in your area, or increasing interest in a particular market niche (e.g., mental health and substance abuse or vision care services).

Market research may indicate the approaches you can take to market the plan. For example, it can help you determine whether the health care business in the community allows direct selling or whether you will have to sell through established brokers or respond to consultants' requests for proposals (RFPs) on behalf of an employer. You can also use market research to tell you which brokers control which accounts.

You may find that market research can even help you with specific client approaches. Having a sense of a prospect's specific needs can help your organization present its potentially unique value to a prospect [e.g., "We operate health maintenance organizations (HMOs) in the three Texas cities where you have operations, and we have preferred provider organizations (PPOs) that can serve your Oklahoma City and St. Louis employees"].

Competitive intelligence, a specialty area of market research, helps you identify your competition and its strengths. It may reveal a tough-to-break lock on the market by a formidable competitor, or it may reveal a competitor's weaknesses, such as member dissatisfaction with the time it takes to get an appointment with a physician or a lack of providers close to where members live. Competitive intelligence may provide early warning of a competitor's activities, such as an acquisition, that may result in a temporary disruption for its clients. While the competition fumbles the ball, you can move in.

Market research can give you important data for plan design and pricing. You can learn about an area's demographics, income, and average health care costs. Research may alert you to health care outliers, which represent an uncommonly high rate of certain treatments that may indicate overutilization or costly overtreatment. Research can tell you about a market's potential or special needs. For example, you may find that an area has a greater than average need for pediatricians or for clinics with a bilingual staff.

Market research is not only a tool for new business prospecting, however. Your consumer research and member surveys can help you retain clients by keeping tabs on what they most appreciate and what they dislike. In turn, you may be able to enjoy a double benefit of market research by recycling your research and survey results as a marketing tool. For example, if the results are impressive, tell clients and prospects the results of your member satisfaction surveys.

Market Research Resources

Your market research needs and resources will determine your choice of research methodology. For example, you would not use a focus group to identify a community's demographics. Your budget, staff, and skills also will affect whether you can or cannot employ an outside organization to conduct market research for you.

You can gather a considerable amount of market information for relatively little cost and moderate time investment. The U.S. Department of Labor's Bureau of Labor Statistics (BLS) conducts extensive surveys. The results it publishes sometimes break down findings by region or even standard metropolitan statistical areas, as does the Department of Commerce's Bureau of the Census. Your local, state, or university library may have some BLS or Census Bureau documents and be able to provide you with guidance, as may your local or state Chamber of Commerce. They can probably also point you to other useful surveys conducted by nonfederal agencies.

Several of the large benefits consulting organizations conduct their own national surveys on managed care topics and provide the published results for anywhere from $25 to a few hundred dollars. Dunn & Bradstreet, which has sales offices around the country, may be able to conduct specialized research on your organization's behalf, obtaining information about local employers by sales, industry, and size of employer; information about their insurance programs; and names of such key contacts as company chief executive officers, chief financial officers, benefits managers, and human resource directors.

The major polling organizations, such as Louis Harris and Associates, the Roper Organization, Gallup & Robinson, and Yankelovich

Clancy Shulman, as well as smaller polling and research organizations often conduct market research for health care organizations, as do the major benefits consulting organizations. Be a careful shopper, though, because prices can vary tremendously.

A growing number of university libraries now offer fee-based information services, where library staff conduct research for client projects. A clipping service may also be helpful in alerting you to trends and developments among local or national employers.

Informal Market Research

Some of the most productive research you can undertake will be less scientific and methodical in approach. You probably already conduct informal market research. Whenever you build a relationship with brokers or employers, you develop resources that can provide you with information you cannot obtain otherwise.

One highly effective method that MCOs use to build their informal information bases is organizing luncheon or breakfast programs with groups of brokers, consultants, and employers to discuss benefits or health care issues. It is a far less expensive research approach than organizing a focus group, and it also builds goodwill.

You may get a pleasant surprise when you find how willing the different segments of the benefits community are to participate in these discussions. For example, brokers often will talk freely about what sells and what does not. These programs also serve them well: They learn about your organization, which helps put them in a better position to serve their clients; they know their feedback will help make you serve their clients better; their discussions help them reinforce their control over their accounts; and they learn from other brokers.

Community organizations can also serve as launchpads for you to establish employer relationships, as will any opportunities for involvement in health care coalitions. They give you the chance to listen to what the organized business community is saying and what people in the community are complaining and talking about. In looking for ways to meet local employers, look also to your board members for referrals to people they know.

Your informal market research may be particularly helpful in evaluating subtle differences in market wants. Every product has the potential to meet more than one market need. Just as automobiles are alternately marketed as cars, as transportation aids, as status symbols, and as life style enhancers, a managed care market's hot buttons will vary. Is the market looking for health care or insurance? Better service? Cost control? Better employee relations and retention? A way to meet the health needs of employees? Ease of benefits administration? Also what does a particular market or prospect have in mind when it repeats that word on everyone's lips: *quality*? The answers to these questions tell you how to project your organization.

PRODUCT AND MARKETING DIVERSIFICATION

The Diversification Explosion

A decade ago, the managed care industry's membership was generally composed of PPOs, three or four models of HMOs, and indemnity plans with managed care features. They tended to specialize in the same thing: basic medical coverage. Since then, we've seen a bewildering explosion of managed care products, services, and market diversification, including:

- point-of-service (POS) plans, which provide different coverage levels, depending on whether the participant obtains health care services from a PPO, a nonnetwork provider, or an HMO

- open-ended HMOs, which allow members to self-refer to other providers and still receive coverage, although at a reduced rate

- greater MCO interest in serving particular market segments, such as the Medicare (see Chapters 46 and 47), retiree, Medicaid (see Chapter 48), armed services and Department of Defense (see Chapter 49), and workers' compensation (see Chapter 52) markets

- alternative financing arrangements, such as administrative services only for self-funded clients, minimum premium pricing, experience rating, and so forth
- a growing number of optional benefits marketed as plan enhancements or as standalone products that can be sold separately (e.g., an HMO may offer vision care either as an optional plan enhancement to health coverage or as a standalone benefit, where the employer contracts with another organization for basic health benefits and with the HMO only for vision coverage)
- MCOs providing separate services or lines of business, such as utilization review services, claims administration, or workers' compensation medical services

Several related factors are driving the trend toward wider variety and specialization, including cost control concerns, the search for better ways to price and deliver care, and competitive pressures. To stay within the focus of this chapter, we will primarily restrict our attention to competitive concerns.

Diversification Advantages

The MCO that can offer several different financial arrangements as well as add-on and standalone products enjoys a competitive advantage because it has a better chance of being able to fulfill employers' differing needs. That versatility also enables it to promote an image of expertise and competence.

Standalone products may appeal to an employer that at that time only needs that one extra benefit. A standalone product also provides a toe-in-the-water low-risk chance to test the MCO. From the MCO's perspective, it is an opportunity for cross-selling additional products. For example, if an employer becomes a client for an HMO's network on a PPO basis, the HMO

gains more of an opportunity to acquaint the employer with its other products and services.

Diversification Disadvantages

Diversification can also be dangerous. Developing new products, financial arrangements, or the administrative and financial systems to sell existing products such as add-ons or standalones can be costly. New products can be difficult to price without historical data to guide underwriting. Standalone products are vulnerable to adverse selection. Certain market segments, particularly the public sector (Medicare and Medicaid), entail administrative complexities and the uncertainty of changing requirements and reimbursement formulas.

New products or attempts to serve special market segments also carry the risk of taking away the MCO's attention and resources from what it knows best. Worse yet, they may take its attention and resources away from areas that need improvement.

Making the Choice

The decision to offer specialty products or to pursue a certain market segment should be based upon the findings of several areas in the MCO, including administrative, financial, and medical. The marketing area's contribution to the decision initially lies in its market research function to determine whether the market wants and will pay for the new products or marketing ventures.

What if market research indicates considerable market demand for a product that would dangerously stretch the MCO's resources? Fortunately, there are ways to add new products and financial arrangements without risking large investments in time and money. For adding standalone or add-on products, a private label approach may hold the solution. In this kind of arrangement, you contract with a specialty vendor to allow you to market its product under your name in such a way that the arrangement is not visible to the employer/employee. This approach holds little risk to the MCO, has low start-up costs, takes little time to set up, and takes advantage of the vendor's economy of scale and expertise.

Other kinds of arrangements are also possible. For example, a joint venture arrangement with an insurance company may allow a freestanding HMO to develop POS products. Reciprocating agreements with other MCOs outside your coverage area may allow you to expand the number of locations you offer. Joint marketing arrangements or alignments, where your organization and another help sell each other's products and services, present another possibility. This approach may be appropriate for MCOs and third party administrators, who may see the same prospects for related but noncompeting reasons.

MOVING AHEAD

The trend of increasing specialization and variety is apt to continue in the years ahead. Several driving forces are likely to propel interest in certain areas.

Cost Drivers

Costs are continuing to increase unevenly in the health care sector. As new technologies are introduced and as new treatment modalities occur, some conditions become ever more expensive to treat. In a more confined example, workers' compensation costs have been escalating at incredible rates in recent years. In most states, restrictive laws prevent employers from directing workers' compensation claimants only to managed care providers, where costs would be less and claimants would get back to work sooner. As cost pressures build, some states are beginning to relax restrictions on employers' abilities to direct claimants to managed care. This issue is discussed in detail in Chapter 52.

Health Drivers

The nation's interest in fitness is extending beyond the life span of a craze and may become a permanent life style component. If so, wellness and health promotion programs could become a more frequently expected part of standard benefit packages.

Age Drivers

The cohort of aging Baby Boomers will swell the ranks of retirees in the years ahead. Employers that provide retiree benefits are already under pressure from accounting rules to reduce their current and future estimated retiree costs. These forces may drive employers to look to managed care plans to reduce those costs. Meanwhile, more MCOs may begin pursuing the retiree and Medicare markets (see Chapters 46 and 47) to replace the retiring active employees they would otherwise lose as members.

Reform Drivers

Public pressure to reform the health care system will continue to grow. The pressure to increase access will focus on and intensify in every area of the health care delivery system, including MCOs. MCOs will inevitably begin serving more Medicaid recipients (see Chapter 48) and small employers, either because they see them as profitable new markets or because they are forced to serve them by legislative and regulatory directives.

PROSPECTING

Establishing Relationships

As discussed earlier, your involvement in health coalitions, business organizations, and the broker community as part of your informal market research can help you develop a network of information resources and contacts. Utilizing this network, your current customer base, and your board, can help you spend more of your time in referral prospecting instead of cold calling.

Listening is crucial to establishing a relationship. Your initial objective is not to make a sale but to get a meeting with a prospect, a potential client, where you can conduct some market research and develop the opportunity to ask for another referral. Managed care marketing requires a high level of buyer trust. As a result, sales are rarely quick, and relationships play a crucial role.

Identifying Primary Prospects

Primary prospects are the people who make the initial decision about whether an employer should affiliate or contract with a MCO. The decision maker will vary. It could be the benefits manager, human resources director, chief executive officer, or chief financial officer.

Sometimes the initial decision maker is not even the employer. For example, your market research or conversation with an employer or broker may reveal that a case is broker controlled, or you may find that the employer is using a consultant to evaluate MCOs, requiring you to direct your attention there. Perhaps the employer will not make a move until its union gives an O.K.

Brokers and Consultants

In many markets, brokers and consultants play critical and somewhat overlapping roles. Both advise employers about their selection of a benefits provider, but brokers receive a commission as compensation based on a percentage of the premium as stated in the MCO's commission schedule. Consultants are more often employed on a project basis and are paid directly by the employer. It is possible for an employer to use a broker for most of its benefits needs and to hire a consultant for work on a specific project.

How do you find out whether an employer uses a broker? It is part of market research to determine who controls business in the community. Also, an employer will tell you whether it has a broker of record, or a broker can produce a letter from the employer stating that it is the broker of record.

A case may be broker controlled, in which case the employer essentially delegates decision making about its benefits plan to a broker. In these cases, it will be to your benefit to work with the broker. Some MCOs choose not to approach employers through brokers as a matter of policy, but that means they are effectively cut out from a portion of the market.

Health Care Purchasing Cooperatives

Health care purchasing cooperatives, also known as purchasing alliances, coalitions, and a variety of other names, are collections of small employers and/or individuals who use a collective approach to purchase health care coverage. In some states, such purchasing cooperatives were created by state law under market reform. In other cases, the small market purchasers banded together under their own initiative.

In the case of state-mandated purchasing cooperatives, it may be possible for a small employer or individual to purchase health coverage either independently or through the cooperative. In such conditions, it is inevitable that the purchasing cooperative will draw adverse selection because healthy people will have access to cheaper coverage on their own. Even so, a health plan may be required to offer coverage through the cooperative. If the cooperative is the only vehicle for a small employer to purchase insurance, then there remains the possibility of adverse selection, but it is much diminished.

In the case of independently formed purchasing alliances, the members of the alliance may have applied strict underwriting criteria (see Chapters 43 and 44), so that no adverse risk is present. Prospecting in this type of environment will be a combination of meeting the purchasing alliance's requirements and retail selling to the individual members.

Responding to RFPs

An employer seeking a managed care provider will often issue an RFP to solicit bids directly or through a consultant or broker. Although the MCO's response to an RFP is an essential step in the marketing process, this cannot replace the relationship-building process. An RFP is only a formal step. The informal marketing steps before and during the RFP response period can have a great bearing on the MCO's success in responding to the RFP.

First, consultants and employers do not simply conduct a mass mailing of RFPs to every known MCO. Formally or informally, they assess prospective organizations and send RFPs only to a selected list. If the RFP issuer does not consider your organization a known, active player in the community with the qualities the employer seeks, it may not even send you an RFP.

Second, consultants and employers do not develop RFPs in a vacuum. If you have a relationship with the employer and/or consultant, you may have an opportunity to influence the content of an RFP with your suggestions and comments about the capabilities it should examine before it is issued.

Third, having a relationship with the consultant and employer allows you to push for an opportunity to meet with the employer during the RFP process to identify its key buying issues. By meeting with the employer, you can determine the relative weights of importance the buyer attaches to different parts of the RFP. That meeting also provides you the opportunity to present your company in the best possible light. A good consultant will only present a factual, unbiased picture of your organization and all the others that respond. You do not want the consultant to be the only person representing your company to the employer.

The RFP will vary substantially by the size of the account and the employer's or consultant's level of experience. Smaller cases may use a less formal process than an RFP; for example, they may use a request for information (RFI) simply to request financial information, general information, and the MCO's schedule of benefits and prices. The RFI may be as simple as a request for the MCO to quote community rates for a prospective customer and to provide some demographic information about the plan's customer base, such as age, sex, and ZIP codes of residences in the community rate quote.

At the other extreme, more sophisticated consultants and employers may use an RFI to gather preproposal information. The RFI may ask significant questions about your company, organizational structure, membership, profitability, how it manages care, how it manages quality, its member services, how it pays claims, where it is located, its service area, and how it interfaces with the home office. The RFI issuer will then analyze responses to develop an RFP and also to determine the MCOs to which it will send the actual RFP. The RFP itself is more concerned with financial data and will ask you to give information about your claims, experience, and proposed benefits design.

Typically, the last question in an RFP will ask why your plan is best suited for the employer. This is another area where your market research investment can pay dividends. It can tell you about specific needs of the employer not addressed elsewhere in the RFP that you can emphasize here. Similarly, on the basis of your competitive intelligence research findings, you can use this question to highlight the advantages you have over other MCOs.

Sometimes the answer to this last question can be decisive in winning a managed care contract. Isn't it nice that you have all that solid market research to guide you?

Employee and Dependent Prospecting

Managed care marketing does not stop with the employer's agreement. The marketing process must also identify its competitors and prospective members and develop targeted messages to guarantee increased plan enrollment.

The competition will certainly include the other MCOs that the employer offers, if any. If the employer will still provide an indemnity plan option, that too is a competitor. Finally, your competition will include the plan you replace. Even if it is gone, it will still be in the minds of employees, and they will compare it with your plan.

What does, or did, the competition offer? Your enrollment people need to understand how your program differs from its competition so that they can identify the high points of your program. There are several possible points of comparison:

- *Benefits*—When the MCO is competing with or replacing an indemnity plan, there are apt to be significant coverage differences. What are the points to push on your side?
- *Process*—The employee's procedure for obtaining health care from your organization will differ substantially from that for the indemnity process and possibly from that for other MCOs (e.g., procedures may differ between PPOs and HMOs and possibly even between HMO model types, such as closed panel and open panel models).
- *Premiums*—Although your MCO's benefits and process may be similar to those of other organizations, the premium levels may differ.
- *Accessibility*—The locations your MCO offers in relation to where employees work and live may differ from those of other managed care providers.

Your analysis of the competition should go hand in hand with your analysis of the buyer's employees and dependents. Your enrollment team will need to know, for example, their average age, their education levels, whether they are blue or white collar, where they live, and their probable buying decisions.

Some rough generalizations may be helpful. Younger employee populations are likely to place more importance on well-child care, child care accessibility, and obstetrical care. Cost is an issue with all groups, but it is more so with blue collar groups. Physician quality, too, is important to all groups, but high-income groups are more likely to be interested in details about the program, provider backgrounds, and provider accessibility than in a $5 difference in premium.

Although these generalizations can be useful in a broad sense, the information you can gather through the relationships you established can be more helpful. If possible, meet with the company's human resources and benefits people to learn their perceptions of what matters to employees. Find out whether the broker or consultant on the case has any knowledge of employee interests or applicable survey information. If the plan serves union members, ask union representatives for their perceptions of employee concerns.

Your relationship with the employer can be a critical factor in the enrollment process. Ideally, the employer will:

- provide names and addresses of employees so that you can mail materials to them
- distribute your materials to employees at the workplace
- make employee attendance at enrollment meetings mandatory
- allow spouses, who may be the actual decision makers in the family when it comes to health care, to attend enrollment meetings

Managed care serves both employer and employee in different but complementary ways. That requires the preparation of different messages for each. For example, the employer may appreciate the gatekeeper role of the primary care physician in controlling overutilization and its attendant expenses. The gatekeeper function, however, does not serve as a buy signal to employees and dependents. To the employee and dependent, presenting the primary care physician as their personal physician who will walk them through the system, make sure their needs are met, and serve as an advocate for their health needs speaks more to that audience's interests and still accurately portrays the primary care physician's role.

Whatever employer-oriented messages you develop for the prospecting process and whatever employee- and dependent-oriented messages you develop for the enrollment process should be consistent with the messages you present in your marketing materials. This consistency can reinforce your messages at every step of the marketing process.

MARKETING COMMUNICATIONS AND SALES PROMOTION

Advertising, public relations, and sales promotion are related but distinctly different activities that MCOs can use to convey positive messages about their plans to employers and employees/prospects. To capitalize on the strengths of these tools and to deploy these resources effectively, it pays to develop marketing communication strategies through an integrated approach rather than as separate promotional activities.

Start the marketing communications planning process with a review of your market research findings to identify your target business and consumer audiences. Only after you have a firm view of your intended audiences can you begin building an integrated marketing communication strategy. Next, identify the key messages you want to deliver to your target audiences. For example, if your market research tells you that consumers are most concerned about the quality of care they receive, their ability to choose where their care comes from, and cost, you will want to develop overall messages relating your plan or products to these concerns.

As you develop overall messages, develop specific, supportive statements. For example, one overall message may be that the plan provides quality care. Your supportive statements for this might inform audiences about your physician credentialing process and the primary care physician's role to ensure that care is appropriate.

Identifying overall messages and position statements allows you to develop an effective integrated marketing approach that protects you from presenting a fragmented image. Advertising, public relations, collateral materials, direct mail, and sales promotional items all have different and overlapping capabilities and limitations. If you give your range of promotional materials a consistent message and look, however, you can present a capable and unified message that is stronger than the sum of its parts.

Advertising

Advertising is one of the most effective means available to build name recognition and is good for communicating a broad, overall message. At best, however, it can only grab attention and give a few brief reasons for strengthening preference for your plan. Radio and television advertising, for example, give too little time to communicate more than a single idea. Print advertising, too, has only a few moments to capture and hold readers' attention before readers turn the page. Billboards can raise name awareness, but they barely provide enough space to deliver even a brief, simple message. Advertising is also expensive.

High costs and lack of space or time are not the only reasons why advertising is best for communicating only a broad message and establishing name recognition. Advertising tends to go to a broad audience. A large portion of any advertising message will be wasted on listeners, viewers, and readers who are not in your target audience. Also, if you offer a variety of products and present a message about a specific product, you may reach an audience whose employer offers one of your other products. Your plan could then end up competing against itself.

Public Relations

Public relations activities encompass a far greater range than the damage control role popularized in the media. They include, for example, working with the media to develop articles for trade, newspaper, and business and consumer publications. Public relations includes planning promotional events, such as organizing or participating in a health promotion worksite wellness fair. It may also include arranging local speaking opportunities for the plan's management or sponsoring a business and health meeting for an audience of employers.

With business and public interest in health care delivery at an all-time high, opportunities abound for a plan's management to speak at business and industry meetings. Seminars for employers, where the theme is clearly informational rather than marketing oriented, have great potential for establishing a plan's management as a knowledgeable, professional group. In an industry where trust and relationships are paramount, that is a goal worth pursuing.

Community events, such as road races, health screenings, and lectures on health issues that are open to the public, present a way to reach out to potential members. On the local level, the mere act of reminding people that you are in the community can enhance the name of your company. Community events may require large amounts of money, however. You will want to identify which events and locations best reach your target audience. For example, schools are a good place to start.

Public relations activities, like advertising, can build name recognition and communicate single messages. They can also help establish goodwill and a sense that the plan is a member of and serves the community. Also like advertising, however, public relations is limited in the number of messages it can deliver.

Collateral Materials and Direct Mail

Collateral materials generally include any printed materials about the MCO and its products and services. Brochures, provider directories, member handbooks, newsletters, stuffers, posters, and data sheets all fall into the collateral materials category. Direct mail, however, refers to transmitting the message in a targeted fashion. For example, you can distribute collateral materials such as product brochures at an enrollment meeting, at a health fair, or as part of a direct mail promotion.

In contrast to advertising and public relations, with collateral materials and direct mail you can exercise much greater control in limiting the audience you reach. Although you can use direct mail to communicate general messages, that audience selectivity also gives you the opportunity to deliver specific information for a particular audience in greater detail than you can with advertising. For an employee audience, however,

you will want your collateral materials written simply so that everyone can understand the options you offer.

Although collateral materials and direct mail offer great flexibility, advertising and promotion are still necessary activities because they help create the conditions for direct mail and collateral materials to work. Name recognition, credibility, and a favorable impression of the plan are preconditions that must be met before recipients of direct mail and collateral materials are likely to read them.

Also, unlike the situation with advertising, the distribution channels for collaterals and direct mail are tightly controlled and are not always easily accessible. Will the employer distribute your materials? Will the employer provide employees' names and home addresses? If you do not have an employer's support, you may not be able to reach much of your intended audience.

Promotional Items and Services

Sales promotions can include both objects and services. The objects are usually giveaways, such as health education materials for members, or incentives, such as a T-shirt for achieving an exercise goal or an infant car safety seat as an incentive to enroll in a prenatal care program. Services include access to free information, free blood pressure screening, discounts on health- or sports-related purchases, free sports physicals, and discounted memberships in health clubs or day care centers.

Sales promotional items are generally the weakest part of the promotional effort. They cannot deliver a competitive message, and they may draw more attention to themselves than to the plan. They can be costly and are often given either to people who are already in the plan or to people who have no intention of joining.

In a market where there may be few or no differentiating factors between your plan and another, however, sales promotional items and services can make a difference. They serve as attention getters and reminders. Also, when your price is the same as or higher than that of a competitor, they communicate a value-added message: "Yes, you pay a little more here, but you get more." When they are clearly linked to your product, sales promotional items can also provide a tangible reminder of another message: "We believe in keeping you healthy."

YOUR MARKETING TEAM

Should Staff Specialize?

The larger carriers and HMOs have separate sales and marketing teams. Their marketing staffs gather research and data on what to sell and how to sell, and they play a role in product development and market research. Their sales teams sell. In other organizations, the same staff have both sales and marketing functions, which is the model discussed here. Although some specialization is necessary for maximum effectiveness, there are probably as many schools of thought about marketing staff specialization as there are ways to develop that specialization.

The possibilities are many. Some MCOs have marketing staff dedicated to or specializing by prospect size, geography, product line, or new business versus current customers. The degree and type of specialization will depend in part on the marketing staff's size and experience and the market. The marketing director may also want to consider individual personalities and experience in assigning staff responsibilities.

The marketing staff members will have various levels of expertise. Some will be new without any established client relationships and without the expertise to establish relationships. Others may be competent at selling smaller cases but lack the expertise to establish and deal with more technically astute and experienced clients. Some may be great for selling small case HMO-only business but cannot handle the financial considerations of a larger case looking for a POS plan and experience rating.

Just as they will differ in experience, marketing staff members will have different personality traits and related skills. Some will work well as hunters, who are best at drumming up new busi-

ness, and others will serve better as closers, who negotiate and finalize the sale. Still others may work well with consultants and are able to wend their way through the maze that often entails.

It is worthwhile to note that many MCOs that specialize in public sector markets (Medicare and Medicaid) do in fact have specialty sales and marketing forces for those specific product lines. Between the regulatory requirements in these lines and their unique marketing and sales challenges, it is usually not optimal for sales and marketing personnel trained in the commercial market to cover the public sector markets as well.

Sales versus Service Representatives

Should your salespeople be responsible for servicing accounts? In part, that depends on the size of the marketing organization. There is value in requiring the person who sells to be the one who services the account. After all, the individual sellers and buyers already have established relationships. Not every seller is a good service person, however, and not every service person is a good seller. Also, managed care is a service-intensive business. If sales people retain responsibility for service, you take their time away from generating new business.

Some MCOs, especially the larger ones, balance these concerns by having an account management team to service accounts. Regardless of who has account servicing responsibilities, however, the marketing staff members should maintain communications and a relationship with customers. This may provide them with an early warning of client dissatisfaction and the opportunity to remedy problems. It also provides opportunities for cross-selling of additional products and for getting referrals to new prospects.

Product Specialists

Should your marketing team specialize by product in the commercial market? It is more realistic for smaller organizations to expect everyone to be a generalist with an overall knowledge of all the products the organization sells. More experienced generalists can become specialists in certain products, so that anyone can go to them for assistance and advice.

Large, diverse health care organizations that market a range of HMOs, PPOs, POS plans, and other combinations are more likely to have product specialists, at least in the product development area. The sales operation should consider the potential pitfalls of specialization carefully, however. Jealousy and resentment can flare if certain staff members are rewarded with exclusive privileges to sell in-demand, highly profitable products. Also, having product specialists may give the appearance of a fragmented organization and a confusing impression to the broker community.

Sales Compensation

Organizations with separate sales and marketing staffs should compensate them through different arrangements. Marketing staff who do not have a sales function can be compensated through typical salary arrangements. In addition, bonuses tied to performance and/or profitability may be appropriate. Staff members who have a sales function should be compensated in large part through an incentive compensation (IC) program. IC uses a carefully structured set of rewards to provide selling incentives. Generally, it compensates individual salespeople on the basis of a percentage of the income that their sales generate.

The MCO can base its specific IC structure on a number of different factors, depending upon the sales staff's responsibilities and what the organization wishes to emphasize. For example, some MCOs base their IC program upon a sold case's membership size.

Where sales people also service an account, some MCOs use a formula based on the net member gain compared with gross membership. By tying IC to net retention, the IC structure rewards the salespeople for servicing the account and preventing disenrollment on the back side. For example, if a case has a membership of 500,

but 400 members of the employer's group do not stay with the plan, the sales staff on the case would only get credit for 100 members.

Still other MCOs base IC on premium dollars and revenue brought into health plans instead of on membership numbers. This gives the sales team an incentive to sell premium increases instead of offering lower premiums to encourage a quick sale.

A common goal underlying these different arrangements is tying IC into the profitability of membership. After all, the ultimate goal of the MCO is not simply to sell coverage but to make money. An IC program that rewards salespeople simply on the basis of case size may tempt salespeople to sign up every risk they can and withhold information from the underwriting and/or financial departments.

In addition to an IC program, MCOs can use a bonus program tied into business profitability, either that of the entire plan or that of the book of business that the sales representative is responsible for selling and servicing. This gives the sales staff a stronger commitment to the overall financial soundness of the organization and to helping you manage its risk.

Last, as noted in Chapter 48, some MCOs tie the IC program of the sales and marketing staff to the IC program for the underwriting staff. This aligns the incentives of both sales and underwriting to obtain credible information, create profitable rates and benefits structures, and encourage sales.

The Health Plan Staff's Importance to the Sales Process

The sales team is only part of the MCO's team. The organization's medical director, provider relations staff, member services department, quality assurance staff, and providers all have marketing roles. Every encounter or interaction that a member or employer has with the plan either confirms or undermines the sale.

Business concerns about quality have moved into the health care arena. Health plan site visits are now critical to the sales process. Employers are asking MCOs to show them how their system works and who will handle their account. Presenting the health care delivery system and demonstrating how quality is monitored are becoming increasingly significant in the sales process. The medical director can lend critical credibility to the plan's reputation for quality and control.

IT IS NEVER OVER

Despite your best efforts, your plan is bound to lose customers and members. Some disenrollments will be involuntary. A customer's headquarters in a faraway city may consolidate the plan for all locations with another MCO. A member may lose eligibility because of a change in employment status or marital status.

Although there is little you can do to prevent involuntary disenrollment, you will want to try to keep voluntary disenrollment to a minimum. Even when the marketing department does not have a direct role in servicing an account, it should still keep in touch with the three primary customers of an account to determine whether their needs are being satisfied.

First, the technical person with day-to-day responsibilities, usually the benefits manager, has administrative needs. Second, the person with financial responsibilities requires financial information and cost savings data. Third, individual members need to stay satisfied.

The member services department plays a critical role in both member and customer retention. If a member has problems, often the customer's human resources person who deals with employee-raised issues will hear about it. It is important that the human resources person and the member services department people get to know each other and begin a bonding process. The account manager should maintain open communications with customers so that the organization has a chance to identify problems and work to resolve them. Member services are discussed in greater detail in Chapter 30.

Open communications with accounts also means that, when you become aware of a problem, you notify the broker, union, and/or employer immediately. You will not be able to prevent all disenrollments. Small cases especially are apt to swap providers at renewal time for penny-saving differences. If an account does not renew and that comes as a surprise, however, then shame on you. You probably were not maintaining relationships and communicating effectively with the employer.

CONCLUSION

Sales and marketing provide that which allows a managed care plan to exist at all: members. Without members, there is nothing for an MCO to do, and without growth an MCO will stagnate in the market. Although sales and marketing bear primary responsibility for this activity, all plan personnel are involved in the process. Every single encounter a member has with the plan, whether clinical or administrative, either confirms or refutes his or her decision to enroll. A well-run sales and marketing organization and a well-run plan are both required for success.

SUGGESTED READING

Chakraborty, G., Ettenson, R., and Geath, G. 1994. How Consumers Choose Health Insurance. *Journal of Health Care Marketing* 14 (1): 21–33.

Clark, C.S., and Schuster, T.B. 1994. Managed Care Innovation and New Product Development. *Journal of Ambulatory Care Management* 17 (1): 18–28.

Cooper, P.D. 1994. *Health Care Marketing: A Foundation for Managed Quality* (3rd ed.). Gaithersburg, Md.: Aspen Publishers.

Health Care Financing Administration. 1995. *Best Practices of Managed Care Organizations.* Baltimore, Md.: HCFA.

Shea, W.F. 1994. The People Side of the Healthcare Marketing. *Group Practice Managed Healthcare News* 10 (3): 12, 20–25.

Vitberg, A.K. Making the Grade: Critical Lessons for Improving Your HMO's Marketing Performance. *HMO Magazine* 34 (3): 15–16, 18.

Chapter 36

The Employer's View of Managed Health Care: From a Passive to an Aggressive Role

Anthony M. Kotin and Thomas J. Kuhlman

Over the years, the term *managed care* has meant different things to different people. Some see managed care as an intrusion into freedom of choice through limited access, whereas others see it as a bona fide opportunity for employers truly to manage their health benefit expenditures and for employees to become better educated health care consumers and have access to quality-driven, accountable health care providers.

Despite differing views and experience, managed care is the direction of the future. Fanned by the flames of increasing need to control cost and the congressional push toward managed Medicare and Medicaid, managed care will continue to grow, change, and mature, expanding into small markets all across America. This chapter focuses on how the employer's interest in managed care has evolved, moving from a passive purchaser to more aggressive, vocal, and hands-on management of company-sponsored health care plans.

HEALTH MAINTENANCE ORGANIZATIONS: THE EARLY YEARS

In the early 1970s, managed care was essentially limited to, and defined by, health maintenance organizations (HMOs). A dramatic boost was provided by Congress and the Nixon administration, both of which were largely responsible for their early success. HMOs first appeared in the 1940s but failed to spread beyond California and parts of the Midwest until lawmakers passed the HMO Act of 1973 (P.L. 93-222). The act promised financial support to HMOs that offered a minimum level of benefits to enrollees, charged premiums based on communitywide health care costs, and met certain other criteria for federal qualification.

The new law gave federally qualified HMOs the right to mandate employers (i.e., forcing employers to offer the HMO option to employees), a critical factor in ensuring enrollment growth. Mandating meant that employers that had heretofore failed to recognize the potential of HMOs in providing comprehensive medical care at a reasonable cost (including preventive, acute, and chronic care) could now be forced to offer them alongside traditional fee-for-service medical plans. A full discussion of federal qualification is found in Chapter 54.

Federal financial support, coupled with employer mandates, clearly enabled some HMOs to

Anthony M. Kotin, M.D., is the National Practice Leader for Clinical Effectiveness for the Integrated Healthsystems Consulting Practice of Towers Perrin. His expertise is in managed care, with experience as a practitioner, as medical director for an IPA and an HMO, and as an executive in a large commercial carrier. He works with large employers to help evaluate the clinical quality and medical management effectiveness of their health plans.

Thomas J. Kuhlman, F.S.A., is a Principal and head of the Health and Welfare and Retirement practices in the Chicago office of Towers Perrin. As an actuary and consultant, he has worked with many major corporations to help define their employee benefit strategies, particularly those relating to managed care. He played an integral role in the initial development of the Minneapolis large employer health care coalition.

develop faster than they might have otherwise. Expanded enrollments were not accompanied by philosophical change among employers. The growth of HMOs did not necessarily equate with employers embracing the concept of managed care. Indeed, the employer mandate was a mixed blessing to HMOs. It opened the door while at the same time generating employer hostility to the concept of HMOs. It has taken many years to overcome the negative impact of the mandates. In fact, at the same time that employers were adding HMOs to their health care programs, many began to pursue other means of cost control.

MANAGED INDEMNITY PLANS

The HMO Act was widely acknowledged as a government effort to help bring the health care costs primarily of Medicare and Medicaid under control. Its passage preceded the intensified cost control effort in the private sector. Health benefit costs rose steadily throughout the 1960s but began to skyrocket in the early 1970s. Employers remained largely unaware of the advancing cost of care until the early to mid-1980s and entered the era of cost containment at a time when it would seem that HMOs could have played a valuable role. Nonetheless, early private sector strategies were aimed at controlling costs while attempting to maintain the traditional fee-for-service environment.

Surgical Second Opinions

Surgical second opinions were among the first tactics to emerge. They were introduced in the early 1970s by Dr. Eugene McCarthy of Cornell University Medical Center in conjunction with the United Store Workers. He suggested that benefit plans require a second opinion before reimbursing certain surgical procedures. This would serve as a means of stemming the increasing frequency of surgeries and thereby would reduce or eliminate inappropriate physician and hospital expenses. This requirement remained fairly common in fee-for-service plans until the

early 1980s, when program evaluations began to indicate that the cost of second opinions equaled or exceeded the savings they generated. Focused reviews targeting high-cost procedures replaced the early second opinion programs and probably played a role in furthering the emergence of a new player, the utilization review vendor.

Utilization Review

As medical science developed throughout the 1970s and 1980s, experts began to examine and question treatment patterns that had long been part of mainstream medicine. As a result, management protocols used to guide medical, surgical, and pharmacological decisions began to emerge through consensus building in the industry.

Plan Design

Even while incorporating elements such as these in their health plans, employers continued to use the time-honored strategies of plan design and employee cost sharing to control company costs. Deductibles and out-of-pocket limits rose steadily, and employees became responsible for more and more of their health care premiums, particularly for dependent coverage (Figures 36–1 and 36–2).

EMPLOYERS CONFRONT THE DELIVERY SYSTEM

Despite early employer efforts to control health care utilization and their own share of the costs, overall health care cost inflation has continued to exceed the consumer price index, with total expenditures nationwide exceeding 7 percent of the gross national product (GNP) in 1975 being 16 percent of the GNP in 1995 (Figure 36–3). The realization that cost sharing with employees had its limits as a result of decreasing inflation together with smaller salary increases led employers to look for other ways to manage health care costs. Perhaps as a result of the frustration that grew with their increasing awareness

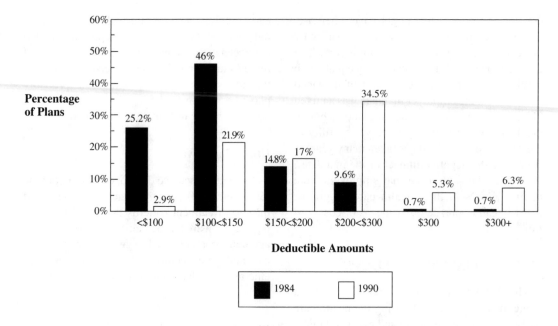

Figure 36–1 Comprehensive indemnity plans, 1984 and 1990: Individual deductibles. *Source:* Courtesy of Towers Perrin, New York, New York.

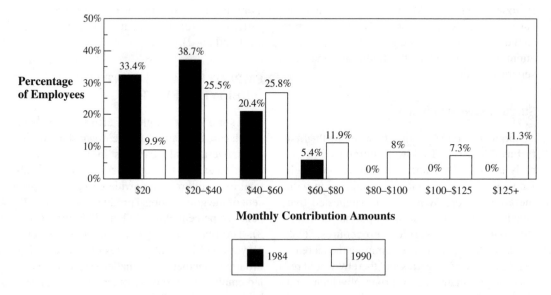

Figure 36–2 Comparison of contribution amounts, 1984 to 1990: Family coverage. *Source:* Courtesy of Towers Perrin, New York, New York.

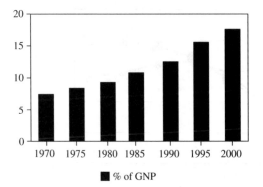

Figure 36–3 National health expenditures as a percentage of GNP. *Source:* Health Care Financing Administration.

of the perverse incentives at work in the U.S. health care delivery system, employer strategies in the middle to late 1980s began more directly to target the system itself.

Preferred Provider Organizations

HMOs enjoyed significant enrollment growth throughout the 1980s, but their market share did not stand unchallenged. Many employers refused to accept HMOs as managed care alternatives and were committed to creating programs that did not carry their stigma. Still reluctant to forgo the flexibility and provider choice features inherent in fee-for-service medicine, employers experimented with yet another alternative to HMOs: the preferred provider organization (PPO). PPOs grew tremendously beginning in 1983, as shown in Figure 36–4.

Early PPOs did not include utilization controls in their discounted fee-for-service physician contracts, leaving participating physicians simply to render additional services to compensate for lower fees. To enhance network utilization, employees were given financial incentives (e.g., 100 percent reimbursement or waiver of the deductible) to use participating providers, with the cost of these incentives often offsetting any potential savings. Large networks, typical of PPOs, made it likely that physicians would not

see enough additional patient volume to make discounted fees worth their while. Without control over a substantial amount of the provider's patient volume, PPOs had difficulty persuading physicians to comply with cost controls such as utilization review.

HMO Consolidation

By the late 1980s, it was becoming clear that unmanaged PPOs did not have the firepower necessary to provide long-term, comprehensive cost control. Employers' HMO offerings had grown in numbers as a result of their passive approach to the selection of their HMO participants. Compounding the problem, indemnity plan costs began their death spiral, their rates increasing disproportionately as younger, healthier employees chose HMO coverage, leaving the high utilizers in the indemnity plan. Finally, the practice of shadow pricing, calculating HMO premiums to shadow indemnity plan premiums, reduced the savings potential offered by the HMOs and provided little incentive for competition among them.

In response to these problems, employers embarked on the path toward HMO consolidation. In general, they sought to reduce the number of HMOs they offered and to use the enrollment leverage they gained among the winners to accomplish more effective cost control overall. A number of management techniques surfaced as part of this new, aggressive strategy.

Coincident with the consolidation movement, employers intensified their demands for utilization data from the HMOs and argued that premiums should reflect actual results for their own employee populations rather than the frequently higher community rates that the HMOs charged. HMOs that were not federally qualified had the flexibility to experience rate their plans. Now, even federally qualified HMOs are able to achieve some degree of rating flexibility through amendments to the HMO Act passed in 1988.

These amendments also phased out the employer mandate provision in 1995, so that HMOs are now competing head to head with indemnity

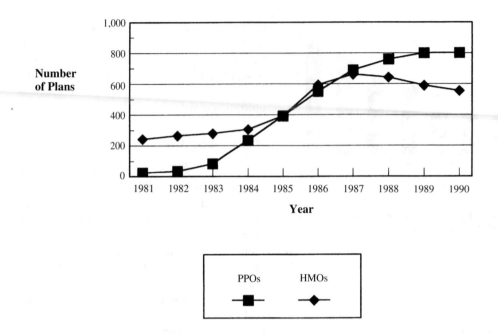

Figure 36–4 Prevalence of HMOs and PPOs, 1981 to 1990. *Source:* Health Care Financing Administration.

plans and other managed care programs for employer business. Although most HMOs abandoned federal qualification well before 1988, the amendments, along with the phase-out of federal funding, clearly marked the end of a significant chapter in HMO development and encouraged them to become more aggressive in the marketplace.

Carve-Outs

Employers who were interested in offering elements of managed care to all employees without having to worry about the negative feedback resulting from a complete alteration of traditional health insurance benefits often felt much more comfortable in selectively carving out discrete benefits for stricter management. Mental health and substance abuse (MH/SA), a poorly understood, costly, and emotional area, became safe ground to tread upon as a bona fide first step into fully managed benefits. The vendor organi-

zations offered their own employee assistance program or would work intimately with an existing one as a means of providing easy access to the network and management process. Even though the coverage limitations were as strict as in any HMO plan design, the management of these clinical issues was typically more proactive and thus palatable to the employee. Employee acceptance of this specific, fully managed health care product was not problematic. This topic is discussed in detail in Chapter 22.

Similar to the MH/SA carve-outs are the managed pharmacy plans. This area was commonly overlooked by the benefits staff because it represented 6 percent to 8 percent of medical spending and for a long time was felt to be uncontrollable anyway because the employee could not affect which drugs were being prescribed. Several companies began to offer card plans and mail order benefits, which greatly accelerated the cost of drug coverage. It became apparent in the late 1980s that drug costs, although still representing a small percentage of the whole, were escalating at a much greater rate than other elements of medical cost. This, then, became a second area where tighter managed care controls could be put in place without suffering a serious pushback from employees. This topic is discussed in detail in Chapter 23.

The inevitable result of the success of these carve-outs has been the new movement toward vendors of "demand" and "disease" management. Employers, however, are becoming more wary of this increasingly fragmented approach to employee health benefits. Even with the positive cost reduction impact of mental health and drug managers, there is growing concern over the interface issues that are not being addressed. It is well known that much of the cost of medical care emanates from mental health problems. The problem is ensuring that care is rendered in the most appropriate venue; often, the clinical interface required to accomplish this between mental health vendors and medical network providers never occurs. Similarly, the inability to marry drug utilization data from the pharmacy benefit manager with diagnosis and medical utilization information greatly diminishes the management of the total patient.

POINT-OF-SERVICE MANAGED CARE EMERGES

From the employer perspective, the most difficult aspect of HMO coverage to accept was its all-or-nothing coverage arrangements. Employees resisted the inflexibility of annual enrollments and did not want to sacrifice their benefits completely when using nonparticipating physicians or hospitals. In 1987, one employer took an aggressive, novel approach to tackling these issues.

Aiming to develop a long-term cost control strategy in the face of substantial retiree health care liabilities (which now must be reported on company financial statements as required by the Financial Accounting Standards Board), Allied-Signal negotiated with Cigna to use the insurer's HMO network to deliver health care to all Allied

employees wherever the HMOs were available. The new wrinkle was that employees could decide, at the point of service (POS), whether they wanted to be treated by an HMO physician or a provider of their choice. In either case, Cigna would cover the expense, albeit at differing levels of benefits. This was one of the early, and certainly among the most visible, new-generation managed care programs that are now well known as POS plans.

To encourage the use of Cigna's provider networks, Allied required employees to select a network primary care physician at the time of enrollment and imposed significant reimbursement differentials between in- and out-of-network services (i.e., no deductible or coinsurance for in-network care and deductibles of 1 percent of pay for individuals and 4 percent of pay for families, along with 80 percent coinsurance, for out-of-network care).

Another significant component of this program was Cigna's guarantee that Allied would experience a low rate of annual cost increase over the 3-year period of the contract. Despite the fact that the financial results of this pioneering program would eventually prove to be less favorable for Cigna than for Allied, it did not take long for other major carriers to develop and market similar products.

POS and Employer Expectations

As they began dealing more directly with managed care organizations (MCOs), employers began to develop higher expectations for results. Generally, employers are now interested in choice (provider access), cost effectiveness (provider discounts and risk sharing), and quality and outcomes in the delivery of health care.

POS plans employ several key components geared to meet these expectations. Most important, appropriately aligned financial risk sharing among all parties—network manager, employer, providers, and employees—drives the system. A primary care physician serves as medical manager, controlling and monitoring all care delivered to the employee or dependent. Finally, the network manager (a role that was initially filled by insurance carriers but now includes other entities, such as HMOs and in some instances integrated delivery systems such as physician–hospital organizations) generally takes responsibility for quality of care, network development and maintenance, claims processing, client reporting, and other relevant services.

What Makes POS Work?

The critical characteristic of POS plans is their ability to combine broad access to care with effective cost control by offering PPO-like elements of choice overlaid with HMO-like utilization and cost management. These features satisfy both employers and employees, and the combination does, in fact, seem to work. Ninety-one percent of employers with network-based managed care who participated in a Towers Perrin telephone survey in early 1992 believed that managed care was meeting company objectives, and 73 percent said their employees were as satisfied or more satisfied with their benefits than before.[1]

HOW DO EMPLOYERS CHOOSE MCOs?

The MCO and plan design purchasing decision by employers is heavily dependent upon the size of the employer. There are several reasons for this, but fundamentally it has to do with the amount of resource, financial and human, that is available to make purchase decisions and then manage health benefits, as illustrated in Table 36–1.

The Small Group Employer: 0 to 50 Lives

This cohort is nearly always purchasing on price. First, they are sold their benefits through brokers and agents that understand price issues more clearly than they understand managed care. These employers are subject to purchasing indemnity type plans that have minimal coverage as a cost hedge or will look to HMOs as the primary source of cost mitigation. If they are di-

rectly contacted by HMO sales personnel, they will select on network and price. Their size prohibits any ability to risk share, and they do not have staff or interest in outcomes. They also do not have the ability to self-fund. They simply want affordable, adequate coverage. In the Twin Cities, several hundred small employers have joined together to form a purchasing cooperative, which gives them leverage and a promise of price stability over a several-year period.

The Medium Group Employer: 50 to 500 Lives

The purchasing habits of groups of this size are variable. Price sensitivity is still significant. The nature of the employer is still local, and thus network composition is important. Brokers and agents remain the primary distribution channel. This group does have the capability in many markets to self-fund. This makes the purchasing decision more complex, so that, if the company does not have an in-house benefits coordinator, it becomes heavily dependent upon brokers and agents for decision support. Only on the high end do these companies employ benefits consultants. This group sees customer service as an important determinant, and in the larger companies quality of care issues can begin to play a role in decisions.

The Moderate Group Employer: 500 to 2,000 Lives

These companies have in-house benefits departments and at the larger end can be multisite. They will commonly rely upon benefit consultants to aid in decisions. Although they value price, the quality of service, network, and responsiveness to member needs are now important. Flexibility of plan design may become an important driver. These companies, if geographically centralized, can be influential with a given health plan and may be able to engage in risk-sharing arrangements. If they are multisite and have a common administrator, they still may be able to engage in risk sharing, but the admin-

Table 36–1 Employer Selection Process by Size of Employer

Employer Size	Plan Flexibility	Price	Sales Approach	Human Resources Staff	Self-Funding	Network Quality	Access	Reporting
Small (< 50 employees)	1+	4+	Direct/agent/brokers	No	No	3+	2+	0
Medium (50–100 employees)	2+	3+	Direct/agent/brokers	No	Some	3+	2–3+	1+
Moderate (500–2,000 employees)	3+	3+	Broker/consultant	Yes	Many	3–4+	3+	2–3+
Large (> 2,000 employees)	4+	2+	Consultant	Yes	Most	3–4+	4+	4+

Ratings are made on a scale of 1+ to 4+. 1+ reflects issues of little importance, 4+ reflects issues of significant importance.

Source: Courtesy of Towers Perrin, New York, New York.

istrative complexity will mitigate the willingness of the MCO to be aggressive. Customer reporting becomes a larger issue at this size. These employers may have multiple plan offerings and may in fact offer multiple HMOs in a given location, creating contribution strategies that place plan cost variations on the employees.

The Large Group Employer: More Than 2,000 Lives

These plans are commonly multisite. Self-funding is prevalent, and many are even self-administered. Nearly all have benefits staffs and utilize consultants to facilitate strategy and purchasing decisions. These employers have traditionally been the market drivers for creativity in plan design, medical management policies, measurement tools, and network composition. Their initial strategy in the market was to look for single plan administrators for PPO/POS programs and to supplement each locale with an HMO offering. This is now moving toward a local market strategy: Large groups are looking for the best vendor in each market and coordinating

management through a central administrative organization. Quality of care, reporting, customer/member service, and elaborate risk-sharing arrangements are important. As a result of the cost, financial and organizational, of moving business, contractual arrangements are frequently multiyear.

EMPLOYER ACTIVISM IN MANAGED CARE

By far the most interesting development associated with POS is the degree to which employer participation has increased. Employers initially did little actively to encourage the use of HMOs and PPOs, essentially insulating themselves from day-to-day health care delivery. By contrast, new risk-sharing arrangements and the fact that employers are forcing employees to choose to use a network have encouraged employers to play an active role in network or network manager selection. For example, in-depth, on-site evaluations have become a principal part of the network selection process, as illustrated in Table 36–2. These hands-on techniques help educate employers about the inner workings of the MCO, establish a rapport between the parties, and clarify the employer's objectives for network management.

Employer Coalitions

One of the most interesting phenomena that has arisen with this new employer activism is the emergence of employer-led health care coalitions. No coalition is more demonstrative than the Business Health Care Action Group in the Twin Cities. In 1992, 14 employers decided collectively to purchase health care for their combined employee population in the Twin Cities (potentially 35,000 members). After developing a common POS design, the group decided to select providers and an administration that could deliver their goals of:

- reducing (or eliminating) unnecessary care
- developing a quality-based focus that would yield cost savings
- involving the employers directly in working with the providers
- educating/involving employees and dependents more directly in achievement of the goals

The group selected HealthPartners, a merger of two HMOs (MedCenters and Group Health Plans), to develop and administer the network. This initiative also led to the development of the Institute for Clinical Systems Integration (ICSI), which is charged with developing and monitoring the continuous quality improvement initiative related to the development of practice standards, outcomes studies, measurement systems,

---

Table 36–2 Network Evaluation Concerns

Characteristic	Fundamental Questions
Provider network	Is the network constructed and managed in such a way as to offer a full range of medical services and to provide enough access to care efficiently for the needs of the employees? Are the providers credentialed according to National Committee on Quality Assurance (NCQA) standards?
Quality of care	Is there a documented quality management process in place? If the network is not NCQA accredited, is it striving to achieve it or some other external quality validation?
Customer service	Is there a member-oriented program staffed by well-trained and properly incented individuals? Are service levels monitored, and is historic performance documented?
Medical management	Is the medical management staff properly trained, and do staff follow a well-documented, consistent process in the course of medical reviews? Is there an external peer review process in place for appeals?
Network management	Is there a professional staff responsible for provider interface? Is there a documented program for routine field visitations?
Information systems	Can the network produce standard utilization, cost, and quality management reports? Can the network provide all Health Plan Employer Data Information Set measurements?
Financial performance	Is the network financially viable? Is the overall medical loss ratio adequate to sustain the program successfully?

Source: Courtesy of Towers Perrin, New York, New York.

and other key quality-focused efforts. The employers are represented directly on the ICSI board.

After 3 years, the coalition has grown substantially and has been successful in achieving its quality-focused goals. Cost savings have followed the quality-based efforts. Planned future efforts will focus on achieving competition with the various health care systems (i.e., hospitals, clinics, physician–hospital organizations, etc.) within the health plan.

Exclusive Provider Organizations

The exclusive provider organization (EPO) in the context of this chapter refers to the creation by many employers of a select network of institutions and physicians to provide a narrowly defined set of services through an EPO. This plan element may occur even when an employer offers a traditional PPO or POS plan, but because of real or perceived needs in a particular clinical area, the employer will create an HMO-like benefit. Common examples would be EPOs of transplantation networks, cardiovascular networks, and high-risk pregnancy networks. With an EPO benefit, the employee essentially loses the POS option of provider selection to have access to a highly specialized group of providers. Often, these benefits include nontraditional coverage, such as travel for dependents or significant others as well as per diem living expenses.

Direct Contracting

In this era of intense consolidation and the desire of various components of the system to attempt to integrate vertically, more provider organizations exist in a form that allows them to contract directly with employers. Most examples of this involve locally defined networks or medical groups where an employer has a geographically concentrated population and elects to have a local provider organization provide some or all medical services to its employees. Some direct contracting relationships take the form of on-site company health departments.

Companies that have successfully employed this type of model include MGM-Grand in Las Vegas and Delta Airlines in Atlanta. It will be interesting to watch as the provider market continues to reinvent itself to see whether this mode of benefit plan delivery will continue to evolve. Direct contracting issues and concerns are illustrated in Table 36–3.

Coordinated Multisite Network Administration

Large national employers are faced with the reality that there are no MCOs that have the best health network in every market they serve. Although contracting with the large national multiline insurers was thought to be the most efficient model, this is falling increasingly into disfavor. These employers are frequently faced with managing and analyzing the performance of dozens, if not hundreds, of individual health plans, all with their own enrollment protocols, accounting procedures, and reporting processes. Employer activism is driving a movement that seeks to place more oversight and control over all MCOs into one common location. This network administration area (either internal or contracted out) is charged with maintaining consistency of process and outcome across the disparate members of the MCO partnership. In the spirit of total quality management, this centralized oversight will serve to export best practices across the various MCOs. In the spirit of cost and quality management, it will make contracting decisions more consistent and well founded. Fundamental to the overall management effort is the need to have performance standards for consistent evaluation of the MCOs. The standards can include the following:

- access to providers
- timeliness (appointments, wait times, etc.)
- cost
- accreditation (e.g., the National Committee on Quality Assurance, the Utilization Review Accreditation Commission, etc.; see Chapter 37)

Table 36–3 Direct Contracting Concerns

Characteristic	Fundamental Questions
Providers	How will prospective network providers be identified in a community? Who will be responsible for provider credentialing? Who has the final say in provider selection or elimination?
Contracting	What will be the basis of provider fee negotiations? Will performance guarantees be negotiated? Who will be responsible for conducting the negotiations?
Reporting	How and by whom will management reports be generated?
Quality	Who will be responsible for quality management, and how can necessary corrections or improvements be ensured?
Members	Where will customer services be provided? Who is in control of the members appeals process?
Risk	What are the relevant liability issues? How is the responsibility determined?

Source: Courtesy of Towers Perrin, New York, New York.

- utilization or clinical goals (preventive care, cesarean section rates, etc.)
- customer (or member) service goals
- administrative goals (reports, response time, billing, etc.)
- member satisfaction
- specific goals in certain areas (e.g., mental health)

These standards are typically monitored on a networkwide basis using a variety of data from national managed care databases, Health Plan Employer Data Information Set (HEDIS) reports (see Chapter 28), and specific HMO survey instruments. MCOs that do not meet the standards may be eliminated or replaced or may have their membership frozen until they develop and execute action plans focused on improving their results.

The coordination efforts also include developing contribution strategies to support the employers' health care goals, consistent management of the enrollment process (e.g., collecting and maintaining primary care physician elections), developing appropriate communication materials, and handling/monitoring member service issues. Many employers have decided to outsource this MCO management activity to consulting firms and other organizations that provide this service.

Demand and Disease Management

Discussed in Chapters 18 and 20 in greater detail, these more refined quality and cost management products are of increasing interest to the employer market. Although felt to be largely the province of the health plans, many large paternalistic employers are using these programs as a supplement to their standard benefit plans. In the instance of demand management, these programs typically take the form of wellness promotion efforts. They include monthly publications, self-help books, and telephone decision support lines. Disease management programs are in their infancy. From the employer perspective, they are mostly being sold as worksite surveillance programs. As noted in Chapter 20, their early focus has been hypertension management, asthma management, and diabetes and cholesterol monitoring.

Proactive Involvement in Managed Medicare for Retirees

The Financial Accounting Standards Board's 106 rules require that the liability for the potential health care costs of a corporation's retired population be reported on its balance sheet. This has had a profoundly negative impact on older companies with large numbers of retirees. The enrollment of Medicare recipients into Medicare HMOs relieves the company of this liability. A consortium of more than 50 large corporations has taken an aggressive approach to the market regarding proactively moving its Medicare retirees into HMO plans across the country. The effort has involved an in-depth on-site capabilities assessment to find health plans that are felt to have those components necessary to deliver quality care to this population. Once the approved health plans have been determined, the employers will be embarking upon a focused communications program aimed at maximizing enrollments into these selected plans.

Proactive Evaluation of Managed Care Results and Success

Employers are developing specific criteria and standards that serve as benchmarks for measuring network capabilities: network management, provider network development and maintenance, medical management, quality and clinical outcomes, member services, and financial performance. Employer coalitions in many cities have begun to develop report cards that are based upon individual health plan performance across all members of the coalition. Some of these efforts have even been able to get data that include the entire health plan experience, thus allowing the community to understand what the health care issues are and where potential for improvement exists.

Employer familiarity with and monitoring of network operations play a critical role in keeping local networks ever vigilant. In addition to performance guarantees, these collaborative efforts have emerged as effective tools for ensuring that the networks meet mutually agreed-upon objectives.

HEDIS

This data tool, discussed in Chapter 28, was largely the result of an employer-driven effort to equilibrate the analysis of health plan performance. With its clear definitions of how data are to be collected and reported, it represents the best effort to date toward being able to measure plans against one another.

24-Hour Products

Although employers have been wishing for a more proactive approach to the total health care of their employees, their inherent corporate structure has served as a roadblock for 24-hour products to become reality. Traditional divisions between corporate benefits and risk management departments serve only to perpetuate the disruption of an individual's total health care.

THE FUTURE OF POS

POS is a good way to introduce employees to the concept of managed care and is proving to be a strong, effective strategy in the current health care environment. It is not, however, likely to be the last frontier of managed care. Instead, POS may provide a long and fruitful transition to true managed care, the HMOs or HMO-like programs that were so unpopular only a few decades ago. Managers are already looking at tightening their provider networks, which will make even non–HMO-based networks more like HMOs than ever before.

Notably, some HMOs are moving in the opposite direction. About half of all HMOs are already offering their own POS (or open-ended) products to attract employees. Although they are doing so to retain and expand their market share, they do run the risk of eroding the comparatively effective cost control that was their strength for years.

Meanwhile, employees have willingly embraced managed care, as evidenced by Towers Perrin's telephone survey of employers and corroborated by its earlier survey of plan participants.[2] If in-network utilization continues to increase and networks are held to the quality standards that keep employees happy with the care they receive, employers will be less reluctant to offer network-only benefits. Furthermore, as more and more claims are covered in the networks, it may become possible for employers to provide only catastrophic benefits out of network.

CONCLUSION

Employer concern with rising health care costs has led to a variety of strategies over the years. Initially reluctant to forgo the advantages of fee-for-service indemnity plans, employers encouraged providers and third party administrators to develop cost controls that would work within that environment. Now in the era of health care reform and increased political activism, the provider landscape is changing at an ever accelerating rate. Managed care networks, once a large city phenomenon, are now emerging in small town and rural states throughout the country. This will markedly enhance the opportunities for multisite employers to develop true comprehensive managed care strategies. It will also allow small businesses to assess the cost effectiveness of managed care. Last, the small group market may cease to be a direct purchase market.

The progression from relative disinterest in managed care to increasing activism may, in the long run, lead to aggressive promotions of lock-in HMOs, direct contracts, or owned or operated medical facilities. In the interim, employers will have learned enough about health care delivery that they can be confident in their ability to shape policy and practice in this area. The learning process has also brought refinements and enhancements that put the private sector today in a better position to control the cost, quality, and delivery of health care.

REFERENCES AND NOTES

1. Towers Perrin, *Managed Care: Employers Perspectives* (New York, N.Y.: Towers Perrin, 1992).
2. Towers Perrin, *Managed Care: The Employee Perspective* (New York, N.Y.: Towers Perrin, 1991).

SUGGESTED READING

Carroll, M.S. 1993. Managed Care Programs: An Employer Perspective. *Topics in Health Care Financing* 20(2): 10–16.

Driving Down Health Care Costs: Strategies and Solutions. 1994. New York, N.Y.: Panel Publishers.

Lipson, E.H. 1993. What are Purchasers Looking for in Managed Care Quality? *Topics in Health Care Financing* 20(2): 1–9.

Vogel, D.E. 1994. The Health Maintenance Organization Must Focus on Maximizing Value. *Managed Care Quarterly* 2(1): 80–82.

Chapter 37

External Accreditation of Managed Care Plans

Margaret E. O'Kane

Concurrent with the growth of managed care has been the development of a consensus among purchasers, regulators, consumers, and providers that an appropriate oversight infrastructure be established to ensure that quality of care is not affected negatively. Three accreditation organizations, each of which specializes in a different organizational type of managed care organization (MCO), have developed in response to these concerns. The various organizational types and the quality issues associated with each type are described in this chapter.

All the accrediting bodies were developed with the purpose of responding to external demands for accountability. For health maintenance organizations (HMOs), the oldest organizational form, the intent of the accreditation program is to standardize what has become a maze of different customer and regulatory requirements around a national evaluation process with independent governance and a broad base of support. Preferred provider organizations (PPOs) and utilization review (UR) firms have attempted, by establishing their accreditation

Margaret E. O'Kane is President of the National Committee for Quality Assurance (NCQA), an independent nonprofit organization located in Washington, D.C. In addition to developing the Healthplan Employer Data and Information Set (HEDIS 2.0/2.5), the NCQA accredited nearly half the nation's health maintenance organizations (HMOs) by the end of 1995. Previously, Ms. O'Kane served as Director of Quality Management for the Group Health Association, a staff model HMO with approximately 150,000 members. Before that, she was Director of the Medical Directors Division for the Group Health Association of America.

programs, to head off incipient regulatory initiatives in many states and also to respond to the demands of their customers for assurances about the integrity of their functions. As discussed below, there are important differences among the accreditation programs that reflect to some degree the differences among the organizations that are the focus of their respective review processes.

Because the Utilization Review Accreditation Commission (URAC) was established largely to respond to provider concerns, a major emphasis is placed on reducing the "hassle factor" and creating a degree of uniformity among UR processes. In late 1995, the American Accreditation Program, Inc. (AAPI) announced its intention to merge with URAC. Before this announcement, AAPI had emphasized reducing risk and liability for the purchaser of services and assessing the value of a particular PPO. Organizations accredited by AAPI will be transferred to URAC and recognized as AAPI accredited for a period of 18 months. For the National Committee for Quality Assurance (NCQA), the major emphasis is on the quality of care and service that the organization delivers to its enrollees and those mechanisms that the organization has established for continuous improvement in quality.

There are two other organizations that accredit some MCOs. In 1994, the Joint Commission on Accreditation of Healthcare Organizations announced the creation of a network accreditation program applicable to a variety of organizational types. The Accreditation Association for Ambulatory Health Care also accredits HMOs under its ambulatory care accreditation program. Because neither of these programs has accredited more than a handful of MCOs, however, they are not within the scope of this chapter.

TYPES OF MANAGED CARE

The simplest type of MCO is the UR firm, which does not typically include a defined delivery system. Most often, the UR function is performed by these firms on behalf of purchasers of health care to manage health care costs for individuals who have traditional indemnity health insurance. PPOs, prepaid MCOs, and HMOs will sometimes contract with UR firms to perform this function, although these organizations typically perform UR functions themselves.

A PPO is an insurance arrangement wherein patients are encouraged through financial incentives (e.g., lower copayments and deductibles) to use a defined network of providers. Preferred providers are usually selected based on their willingness to discount fees or the insurer's assessment that the preferred providers provide more cost-effective care. PPOs often have a UR function that applies both to the preferred providers and to care received outside the defined network.

The most comprehensive form of managed care is the HMO. An HMO or prepaid MCO is an organized prepaid health care system that is responsible for the provision of comprehensive health services to an enrolled population in return for a predetermined payment. The prepaid MCO includes a defined delivery system that serves a defined population with a defined set of benefits. Prepaid MCO primary care physicians are usually either capitated (i.e., they receive a fixed monthly payment for providing services to specific enrollees), salaried, paid on a fee-for-service basis with a withhold, or paid on some other type of performance-based reimbursement schedule (see Chapters 7, 9, and 10 for detailed discussions of physician reimbursement). These payment arrangements, which were developed with the expressed intention of giving financial incentives to manage resources effectively, have led to criticisms that they produce an incentive for providers to underserve patients.

The prepaid MCO usually also has a defined network of specialists, who may be paid on a capitated, salaried, discounted fee-for-service, or other basis (see Chapter 12 for a detailed discussion of specialist reimbursement). Prepaid MCO members are usually allowed to receive services only from contracted providers. Together with the financial incentives, it is this lock-in feature of prepaid MCOs that has led policymakers to require active quality assurance programs for prepaid MCOs as a condition of licensure (see Chapter 53) or federal qualification (see Chapter 54).

Although the above definitions are technically correct, the reality in the managed care marketplace is far more complex. Not only have the boundaries among the various MCO types become blurred, but there is a blurring of the definitions within each model type. The results of this hybridization have produced staff model HMOs offering point-of-service products and PPOs experimenting with capitated payment methods for providers. The point-of-service HMO product is essentially a blend of the HMO and the PPO, giving the patient the option of leaving the HMO network while retaining some coverage through an indemnity wraparound (with higher copayments and deductibles).

The primary MCO types may be viewed as points along a continuum of medical management. At one end of the continuum, the UR firm does not seek to define a delivery system or to ensure most aspects of quality. For the most part, its approach to quality management addresses only one of the many complex components that determine clinical quality: elimination of unnecessary services.

When effective, UR helps prevent services from being delivered that are inappropriate in the sense that they are not medically necessary. Sometimes this results in positive gains in improvements in the quality of care, as when patients avoid the risk of unnecessary or ineffective procedures such as unwarranted hysterectomies or carotid endarterectomies. There are real limitations to effective quality management with only a UR system, however, such as no control over who provides medical services, an inability to credential providers, and an inability to monitor for underutilization, misdiagnosis, or incompetent use of the right treatment.

Moving along the continuum, PPOs can achieve more medical management than UR firms. Because there is a defined system of preferred providers, the plan has the opportunity to select providers who meet certain defined criteria of quality as well as of price or economical practice style. Because it is not possible to link patients to a given physician within the PPO, however (patients do not select a single gatekeeper type physician), it is not easy or common for PPOs to perform systematic evaluations of the quality of care across providers.

Prepaid MCOs or HMOs offer the most opportunity for medical management by ensuring that many of the complex issues that affect the quality of care in the system are addressed. Like the PPO, the prepaid MCO can establish quality standards for entry into its provider network through its credentialing process. Because there is a defined system of providers within which patients must seek care, it is also possible to evaluate the quality of care by applying defined criteria. When problems occur within the delivery system, it is possible to seek out their origin and implement actions for improvement. With the defined system of providers comes greater potential for exposure to legal liability for the performance of providers and thus an additional incentive to develop management processes and oversight systems.

QUALITY ASSURANCE AND IMPROVEMENT SYSTEMS IN MCOs

As noted in the preceding discussion, there is a range of possible strategies for quality assurance and improvement in the various types of MCOs. In general, the managed care industry is shifting away from the traditional quality assurance approach in favor of the quality improvement model. The following discussion covers some possible quality assurance and improvement techniques given the attributes of the various delivery systems. Quality management is also addressed in Chapter 25.

The reader should be aware that there is wide variation in quality assurance and improvement activities even within similar types of organizations. Thus, although it is theoretically possible for a PPO to have more control over the quality of care received by its enrollees than a UR firm can achieve for the population it serves, if the PPO has few or inadequate mechanisms to ensure the quality of its provider network, the quality will be no better than that of unmanaged care. Worse, if the PPO's preferred providers were selected on the basis of price alone, it is possible that they may be lower in quality than the average provider in an area. Although there is somewhat more homogeneity among HMOs because of accreditation and regulatory requirements, the emphasis on quality assurance and improvement still varies among organizations.

Quality assurance activities of the UR firm can be geared toward ensuring that the system is effective in terms of avoiding unnecessary services, that it does not prevent or delay unacceptably the provision of services that are necessary, and that providers and patients are satisfied. To these ends, firms may monitor the performance of UR nurses, review denied cases, monitor readmissions as a possible outcome of premature discharge, and survey member and provider satisfaction. Although a number of states have enacted regulations for UR firms, few address the need for quality assurance mechanisms.

As noted in the discussion above, because PPOs have a defined set of hospital and/or physician providers, it is possible for them to use quality as a criterion for participation. With regard to physicians, this can range from minimal credentialing, including proof of licensure and hospital privileges, to more selective criteria, such as board certification or demonstrated compliance with defined clinical quality standards. Again, there are few regulatory mechanisms for PPOs and little information available either about what proportion of PPOs have quality assurance programs or about the efficacy of those quality assurance programs that do exist.

This section describes some of the prevalent types of quality assurance that currently exist in the managed care sector. Because there are many new and exciting technological developments taking place, and because purchasers of health care are demanding that managed care systems assume more accountability for the quality of their systems, quality assurance is a rapidly evolving and increasingly important aspect of managed care systems. Although it is not possible to detail here all the types of quality assurance mechanisms that are currently being used in managed care systems, what follows is a description of quality assurance activities that are frequently in use today.

Establishment of Practice Guidelines and Evaluation of Performance against Guidelines

A technique that has great appeal in that it sets out expectations in advance is the measurement of performance against criteria that are linked to generally accepted practice guidelines. Thus a plan may study immunizations in children to determine, for example, the proportion of children who are up to date for measles, mumps, and rubella immunizations. Likewise, the plan may study the proportion of women older than 50 years who received a mammogram in the past year. An important limitation of this technique is the shortage of generally accepted practice guidelines. Currently, there are widely accepted guidelines for preventive services, for many pediatric services, and for many services in obstetrics/gynecology. With the continued development of practice guidelines by the American Medical Association, specialty societies, and the federal government, it is expected that their use will increase in the next 5 to 10 years.

This type of monitoring has the advantage of allowing assessment of system performance with the goal of overall improvement. Interestingly, the widespread use of practice guidelines first originated with UR under the rubric of UR criteria, as UR criteria were used for preauthorization of certain surgical procedures. This process introduced to the general American health care system the notion that there are generally accepted decision rules that can be applied to the practice of medicine.

Monitoring of Outcomes of Selected Services

As discussed above, monitoring of the outcomes of care and effects on the health status and well-being of patients is an important way of assessing system performance. Outcome measurement has some important shortcomings and usually needs to be supplemented by detailed review of the process of care to work systematically for quality improvement. An additional complicating factor for MCOs is that they may not have a large enough population base of enrollment to perform meaningful analyses of specific conditions. Nevertheless, some large systems have been able to conduct extremely valuable analyses of the outcomes of their care in such areas of medicine as prenatal care and cancer screening, and they have been able to demonstrate improvement in performance after new interventions have been put in place.

Credentialing and Recertification Systems

As previously noted, one of the advantages of a defined delivery system is the ability to ensure that only high-quality providers participate in the system. Prepaid managed care systems and PPOs are able to evaluate the qualifications, if not the actual performance (with a few notable exceptions), of the physicians they hire, contract with, or designate as preferred when there is a systematic and thorough application, credentialing, and recredentialing process. Other providers (e.g., hospital and home health agencies) that contract with or are part of a preferred system should undergo some kind of credentialing or quality systems review as well.

The initial physician credentialing process generally includes verification of licensure, Drug Enforcement Agency certification, graduation from medical school and a residency program, and board certification. Work history is reviewed, which may include an evaluation of references. There is generally both an extensive interview process and an initial probationary period before the physician achieves permanent status with a group or staff model MCO.

Independent practice association (IPA) models and PPOs may not review work history in detail because they generally contract with independent practitioners. Many plans also review professional liability claims history. Hospital privileges in good standing are generally a prerequisite for physicians who wish to contract with IPAs. Prepaid MCOs increasingly request information about potential hires or contractor physicians from the National Practitioner Data Bank.

Many IPA model MCOs also conduct a review of the private practitioner's office before signing a contract. Besides allowing the plan to ensure that the office meets basic standards of safety, cleanliness, comfort, and patient privacy, this review also offers the opportunity for the plan to ensure that there are adequate medical record systems and sufficient appointments available for those new enrollees who may select the provider.

Perhaps even more important than the initial credentialing process is the process of performance review and recertification (recredentialing) that managed systems conduct periodically, usually every 2 years. Besides the review of the structural credentials that is repeated from the initial credentialing process, this recertification allows for the review of the actual performance of the practitioner, including information from member satisfaction surveys, results of quality reviews, and review of utilization patterns and member complaints.

Although credentialing was not traditionally a high priority in every MCO, it has become increasingly important both because of the interest of purchasers and consumers in strong credentialing systems and because the courts have increasingly held that managed care plans with defined delivery systems have a responsibility to try to ensure the quality of those systems (see Chapter 57). Further discussion of credentialing is found in Chapter 7 (for closed panel plans) and Chapter 8 (for open panel plans).

Medical Records Standards

One common quality improvement technique among MCOs is the review of documentation in medical records against a set of standards. The challenge of conducting such studies is often greater in the IPA model because of the various charting styles among independent practitioners.

Sentinel/Adverse Event Monitoring

One methodology used frequently by prepaid plans is the investigation of adverse events. Originally introduced in hospital risk management programs as generic occurrence screening, the method has intuitive appeal because it deals with defined events and because it avoids many technical issues of case finding.

The review methodology identifies a list of sentinel or adverse events that indicate potential problems with the care provided before the event. The original examples from hospitals include events such as unplanned transfer to the intensive care unit, unplanned return to surgery on the same admission, and surgery and myocardial infarction on the same admission. Typically the case that is identified by the generic screen is subjected to peer review, and the reviewing physician renders an opinion as to whether the adverse event resulted from a problem with the quality of care.

The system has been adapted for use in managed care quality assurance programs. Although some MCOs use the generic hospital screens to monitor the quality of their hospital care, many use a different set of screens that were intended to identify potential deficits in the quality of ambulatory care that may have caused the hospital admission. Some examples include ruptured appendix, complications of diabetes, and late-stage breast cancer. Examples of both types of screens are found in Chapter 25.

Member Satisfaction Surveys

Another widely used quality improvement technique is the member satisfaction survey. Although most prepaid MCOs conduct a survey of general member satisfaction, a number of organizations also have developed specialized satisfaction surveys to focus on more specific aspects of care in their systems. Some MCOs now conduct surveys with a large enough sample size to allow analysis at the individual primary care physician level. In some cases, the member satisfaction score is used to adjust the physician's reimbursement (see Chapter 11). One large staff model prepaid MCO conducts "How was your visit?" surveys, wherein all the patients seeing a given physician within a given week are surveyed at the end of their visit. The results are used to provide detailed feedback to the physicians. Other organizations have used patient satisfaction surveys to assess hospital and specialty care.

Evaluation of Adequacy of Follow-Up Care

Risk management case files are replete with cases of patients who were harmed because of the failure to follow up on abnormal tests, radiographs, or symptoms. Most often, these failures result not from the error of any particular individual but from a failure of the system, such as a laboratory slip that never got filed or was filed before the abnormal result was noted and the next step was taken, or a patient who was not at home to receive a phone call to schedule follow-up care and then was lost to the system. Although these events are no more likely to occur in managed care systems than elsewhere in the delivery system, managed care systems are in a better position to improve their processes because they have some degree of control over an entire delivery system.

Control over the Delivery System

The degree of control that an MCO exerts over its delivery system will vary depending upon factors such as ownership, degree of integration, and local market conditions. Likewise, the ability of the MCO to influence its enrollees' behavior varies with the nature of the insurance arrangement. Depending on the specific situation, quality improvement can be achieved through one or a combination of strategies, such as internal quality improvement, cooperation, education, market influence, and provider deselection. Nevertheless, the prepaid MCO has a degree of control over all the components of the provider system and its enrollees that is unmatched in the other types of MCOs. The prepaid MCO has the greatest potential impact on quality both in terms of ability to deliver high-quality care and in terms of ability to compromise on quality. For this reason, expectations for quality assurance activity have been greater for prepaid MCOs than they have been for the other forms of managed care.

DEVELOPMENT OF ACCREDITATION PROGRAMS FOR MANAGED CARE

As previously discussed, there were similarities in the origins of the accreditation programs for the three dominant forms of managed care. These included the desire to be accountable to external customers; the desire to avoid or provide an alternative to burdensome, state-specific regulatory processes; and the desire to respond to allegations of poor quality from various provider groups. For the three different sectors of managed care, the evolution and the dominant impetus were different, and these differences are reflected in the focus of their review process, governance of the organizations, and the actual operation of the process.

ADMINISTRATIVE ISSUES RELATED TO MCOs

One impetus came from concerns about the administrative burden these systems may impose on individual physicians and hospitals. *Administrative burden* is a term that has traditionally been used to refer to the preparation of claims and related information needed for a provider to obtain reimbursement for services. With the advent of precertification (i.e., requirements imposed by payers that certain services be approved in advance), UR activities now constitute an increasing proportion of the administrative burden. Quality assurance and improvement programs also impose administrative burden, such as special data collection efforts, the retrieval of medical charts for retrospective review, and requirements to participate in quality assurance committees and projects. To date, however, the burden associated with UR has been far more extensive than that associated with quality review. In general, the type and extent of administrative burden imposed on individual physicians and hospitals depend on the types and numbers of MCOs involved.

Different approaches to UR impose different degrees of administrative burden on physicians and hospitals. Prospective UR generally refers to the prior approval of certain surgical procedures and may involve both ambulatory and inpatient surgery. Concurrent review generally takes place during an approved hospitalization; authorization has been given for a specified period of time, and any additional days of stay require a second approval. Retrospective review, used extensively in both quality review and UR, involves the analysis of the appropriateness of care after it has been provided.

Prospective and concurrent reviews are far more intrusive than retrospective review and have the potential, under certain circumstances, to disrupt the physician–patient relationship. Under prospective and concurrent review, the attending physician's judgment may be brought into question in full view of the patient. In addition, both physician and patient may become involved in lengthy appeals processes in the event that a procedure or continued hospital stay is denied. Prospective and concurrent review processes do afford some financial protection to patients in that the patient and provider are put on notice before the provision of services that the costs of those services will not be covered by insurance. Under retrospective UR, a patient with indemnity coverage might be held financially accountable for services provided but judged to be medically unnecessary after the fact.

ACCREDITATION OF UR ORGANIZATIONS

The leading accreditation organization for UR is URAC.

History and Governance

URAC was established in December 1990 from an initiative led by the American Managed Care and Review Association (AMCRA), a trade association for UR firms, PPOs, and HMOs.[*] AMCRA's goal was to address providers' concerns and frustration with the diversity of UR procedures and with the growing impact of UR on physicians and hospitals. As a result of this provider frustration, legislative initiatives were underway in a number of states to pass legislation that, according to managed care advocates, would severely limit the impact of UR in some instances and make it impossible to conduct UR in others. The URAC accreditation process was developed in large part as a response and alternative to these legislative initiatives. In late 1994, URAC announced its intention to develop standards and an accreditation program for health care networks ineligible for NCQA accreditation.

URAC's board of directors includes representatives from the American Medical Association, the American Hospital Association, the American Nurses Association, the American Psychiatric Association, the Washington Business Group on Health, the National Association of Insurance Commissioners, the National Association of Manufacturers, the United Auto Workers Union,

---

[*] In 1995, AMCRA merged with Group Health Association of America to form a single trade association for MCOs, the American Association of Health Plans (AAHP).

AAHP, the American Medical Peer Review Association, Blue Cross/Blue Shield Association, and the Health Insurance Association of America.

Goals of URAC

URAC's goal is to improve continually the quality and efficiency of the interaction between the UR industry and the providers, payers, and purchasers of health care. The URAC accreditation process is specifically designed to reduce the hassle factor for providers, and the standards are not designed to evaluate the adequacy of UR criteria and protocols. URAC standards are designed to foster this goal and to:

- encourage consistency in the procedures for interaction between UR organizations and providers, payers, and consumers of health care
- establish UR standards that cause minimum disruption to the health care delivery system
- to establish standards for the procedures used to certify medical services and to process appeals of certification determination
- provide the basis for an efficient process of credentialing and accrediting UR organizations
- provide consistent standards and an accreditation mechanism that can be applied efficiently nationwide for those states that choose to regulate UR organizations

URAC Standards

The following is a synopsis of the URAC standards.[1] Copies of the URAC standards and application materials can be obtained by writing to URAC, 1130 Connecticut Avenue N.W., Suite 450, Washington, D.C. 20036.

Applicability

The URAC standards apply to prospective and concurrent UR for inpatient admissions to

hospitals and other inpatient facilities as well as to outpatient admissions to surgical facilities.

Responsibility for Obtaining Certification

The standards specify that a UR organization shall allow any licensed hospital, physician, or responsible patient representative, including a family member, to assist in fulfilling that responsibility.

Information upon Which Utilization Review Is Conducted

This standard specifies that UR organizations shall collect only the information necessary to certify the admission, procedure or treatment, and length of stay. The standard stipulates that the UR organization shall not routinely request copies of medical records on all patients reviewed but only when a difficulty develops in certifying the medical necessity or appropriateness of the admission or extension of stay. In such cases, only the pertinent sections of the records are to be requested. The standard specifies that UR organizations may request copies of medical records retrospectively for purposes such as auditing the services provided, quality assurance, and evaluation of compliance with the terms of the health benefit plan or UR provisions. In most cases, the standard states that health care providers should be reimbursed for copying costs.

This standard also specifies the maximum data elements that can be required by the UR organization, including categories of information such as patient, enrollee, attending physician/provider, diagnosis/treatment, clinical status, and facility, and information necessary for concurrent review, such as additional days/services proposed with reasons for extension. For admissions to facilities other than acute medical–surgical hospitals, added information may be required about history of present illness, patient treatment plan and goals, prognosis, staff qualifications, and 24-hour availability of staff. The standard does allow for additional information to be requested for such specific review functions as discharge planning or catastrophic case management. Second opinion information may also be required. The standard also allows for additional information to be requested where there is significant lack of agreement between the UR organization and the health care provider regarding the appropriateness of certification during the review or appeal process.

Procedures for Review Determinations

The standards require that reviews be conducted in a timely manner. For most cases, certification determinations are to be made within 2 working days of receipt of the necessary information about a proposed admission or service. The UR organization may require a discussion with the attending physician or a completed second opinion review. The standards stipulate that the UR organization may review ongoing inpatient stays but may not conduct daily review of all such stays.

The standards also specify that the organization must have in place procedures for providing notification of its determinations. There is considerable detail concerning the required contents of these procedures. The UR organization is also required to have procedures to address the failure of a health care provider, patient, or their representative to provide the necessary information for review.

Appeals of Determinations Not To Certify

The standard specifies that the right to appeal shall be available to the patient or enrollee and to the attending physician. The standard also defines minimum elements of the appeals process, including provision for an expedited appeals process. Other requirements include notification by the UR organization to the patient or enrollee, provider, and claims administrator no later than 60 days after receiving the required documentation on the appeal; provision for review of the original decision not to certify by a physician who did not make the original decision not to certify; and the opportunity for the attending physician who has been unsuccessful in an attempt to reverse a determination not to certify to

be provided the clinical basis for that determination upon request.

Confidentiality

UR organizations are required to have written procedures that include certain minimum elements. The standard stipulates that summary data shall not be considered confidential if they do not provide sufficient information to allow identification of individual patients. The standards also cover the accuracy and proper disclosure of provider-specific information.

Staff and Program Requirements

The standard requires that UR staff be properly trained, credentialed, monitored, supervised, and supported by written clinical criteria and review procedures. Review criteria and procedures are to be established with appropriate involvement from physicians and periodically evaluated and updated. The standard requires that a physician review all decisions not to certify for clinical reasons and utilize clinical peers in second and third level review activities.

The standards require written documentation of an active quality assessment program, including the scope and mechanisms for monitoring, evaluation, and organizational improvement of all clinical review activities and UR processes and services. The program must also include an evaluation of specific action plans to improve or correct deficiencies and must communicate the results of quality improvement studies.

Accessibility and On-Site Review Procedures

The standards specify requirements for accessibility, including a toll-free telephone line that must be available during regular business hours in the provider's local time zone with written procedures for handling after-hours calls. There are detailed requirements for the conduct of on-site hospital reviews.

Review Process

The URAC accreditation process begins with a desktop review of a detailed application.[2] The reviewer then verifies the answers on the application telephonically. If the applicant did not pass the telephone review, a letter is sent to the applicant notifying him or her of this. At this time, the applicant is given 90 days to correct the deficiency. An extension of the 90-day period can be granted for an additional 90 days if a request is made in writing to the accreditation committee.

If URAC staff are unable to verify information telephonically, or if they cannot interpret the information that is given telephonically, they will ask for a recommendation from the accreditation committee. The accreditation committee will recommend either an on-site inspection by URAC staff, for which the applicant organization will pay expenses, or a nonaccreditation decision (which will be made by the executive committee of the URAC board of directors).

If the organization meets the minimum criteria for accreditation, the reviewer's recommendation is forwarded to the accreditation committee, which reviews the information with all organizational identifiers deleted. If the accreditation committee decides to recommend accreditation, the application is sent to the executive committee of the board of directors for final approval. Accreditation is granted for a 2-year period.

PREFERRED PROVIDER
ACCREDITATION

Like the industry itself, PPO accreditation is currently in a state of transition. Traditionally, AAPI stood as the only PPO accreditation body. In December 1994, however, the board of directors of URAC voted to expand the scope of URAC's accreditation process to include the accreditation of non–risk-assuming networks. It is anticipated that this accreditation process will be designed for the accreditation of noncapitated PPOs, physician–hospital organizations, hospital–physician organizations, IPAs, and integrated delivery networks ineligible for NCQA accreditation. In the last quarter of 1995, AAPI announced its intention to merge with URAC. In addition, a number of the more highly organized PPOs expressed interest in undergoing NCQA accreditation.

Although AAPI merged with URAC in 1996, a brief history and description of the AAPI standards and process is still in order. Established in May 1989 by the American Association of Preferred Provider Organizations and MedStrategies, Inc., a PPO development consulting firm, AAPI was founded "to develop, field test, and demonstrate the value of a PPO accreditation program."[3(p.22)] MedStrategies currently handles the marketing and administration of the process.

According to AAPI promotional materials, the AAPI accreditation process focused on the following areas:

- *Managed care network*: This part of the accreditation process reviews the scope and stability of the provider network, how out-of-panel referrals are controlled, and how patient access is handled.

- *Provider selection*: The review process examines the objective criteria used in the selection of providers of each type, the consistency of application of the criteria, and verification of data submitted by potential providers and establishes that there is a periodic credentialing and recredentialing process.

- *Payment methods and levels*: The review team reviews payment levels (and decides whether they are competitive and equitable), the flexibility of the PPO in responding to purchasers' needs, how the reimbursement level fosters incentives for efficient provider behavior, and how fee increases are monitored and controlled.

- *Utilization management*: This part of the review assesses the comprehensiveness and effectiveness of utilization management activity, the training and experience of program staff, the standards or criteria used by the program, and the degree of integration of utilization management data and analysis with the PPO's management information system.

- *Quality assessment*: The process reviews the comprehensiveness of the quality assessment program, training and experience of staff, what quality data are generated, the effectiveness of the program in identifying and correcting quality problems, and whether quality assessment data are used in provider credentialing.
- *Management/administrative capabilities*: The team assesses such factors as the PPO's organizational structure, the experience of management and supporting staff, management information systems, how the PPO is marketed, and the content and scope of the patient and provider relations programs.
- *Legal structure*: The team assesses the legal structure of the PPO, evaluates its provider and purchaser contracts, reviews the organization's litigation history, and examines the adequacy of arrangements for due process. The team also examines how antitrust issues are handled.
- *Financial stability*: The accreditation process evaluates the PPO's past and current financial stability through review of its financial statements, the budget process, and accounting controls. A determination of the adequacy of the organization's reserves and insurance coverage is also made.

Because AAPI did not publish its standards, it is not possible to ascertain exactly how compliance with these standards is assessed.

The Review Process

AAPI's accreditation process has three steps:

1. The PPO completes a 100-page questionnaire that covers the eight accreditation components.
2. The questionnaire is reviewed by AAPI's primary accreditation team, which con-

sists of a PPO administrator, a physician, and an attorney.

3. A team of PPO professionals with specific expertise in medicine, law, finance, UR, management information systems, and administration conducts a site visit.

The purpose of the site visit is to verify questionnaire answers, gather additional information, examine records, and interview PPO staff. The site visit typically lasts 2 days. In each of the eight accreditation areas, AAPI gives the PPO a numeric grade based on a 100-point total. Each component is also rated by level (levels I, II, and III). The higher the level, the greater the PPO's degree of complexity and sophistication. Accreditation decisions are made by the site visit teams. AAPI does not currently have a board of directors.

Types of Accreditation

AAPI grants full accreditation to PPOs that meet established standards in each of the eight component areas. Full accreditation is effective for 2 years. Provisional accreditation is granted for 6 months if a PPO meets five of the standards. If the deficiencies are met within the 6-month period, the PPO is fully accredited. If they are not met, the PPO is denied accreditation. After the expected merger with URAC, PPOs with AAPI accreditation will be grandparented into the URAC process for a period of 18 months.

ACCREDITATION OF HMOs OR PREPAID MANAGED CARE SYSTEMS

The NCQA accredits prepaid MCOs and HMOs, including traditional staff and group model HMOs, network and IPA model HMOs, mixed models, open-ended HMOs or point-of-service products, and PPOs that meet the eligibility criteria. Eligible organizations must provide comprehensive health care services to enrolled members through a defined benefit package in both ambulatory and inpatient settings, have been in operation and actively caring for members for at least 18 months, have an active quality management system, and have access to essential clinical information about their patients. Copies of the NCQA accreditation standards and application materials can be obtained by contacting NCQA, Publications Department, 2000 L Street N.W., Suite 500, Washington, D.C. 20036; voice: (202) 955-3500; fax: (202) 955-3599; or on the Internet: www.ncqa.org/

History

The NCQA was established in 1979 by Group Health Association of America and the American Association of Foundations for Medical Care (now AMCRA), the trade associations at that time for HMOs. Original NCQA governance was by the HMO industry.

In 1987, HMO industry leaders, believing that the NCQA provided a good base for external quality review, studied a broader role for the NCQA and began a process to separate it from the trade associations and make it independent, a recognized prerequisite for its credibility. As part of that process, the board was restructured to empower purchasers and other users.

In 1988, the Robert Wood Johnson Foundation funded a series of meetings to explore interest in the purchaser community in NCQA's potential as an independent external review organization. The group of purchaser representatives, benefits managers from Fortune 500 companies who were at the leading edge of external quality assessment, gave a resounding mandate for the NCQA to go forward. In late 1989, the foundation awarded the NCQA a grant to support its development as an independent entity. As evidence of industry support, the grant required that matching monies be raised from the managed care industry. Industry contributions demonstrated support, and the NCQA was officially launched in March 1990. By the end of 1996, NCQA will have reviewed over half the nation's HMOs. In 1996, NCQA began pilot testing two new certification programs for credentialing verification organizations (CVOs) and managed behavioral health care organizations (MBHCOs).

Reviewers

NCQA review teams typically consist of an administrative reviewer and three or more physician reviewers. Administrative reviewers are nonphysician clinicians or quality assurance experts with extensive experience in quality assurance in managed care. Physician reviewers are medical directors, associate medical directors, or directors of quality management from MCOs.

Areas of Review

Quality Assurance

The first and most intensive area of NCQA review is an organization's own internal quality control systems. To meet NCQA standards, an organization must have a well-organized, comprehensive quality assurance program accountable to its highest organizational levels. The program's scope and content must be broad, covering the full spectrum of services included in its delivery system; the program should focus on important aspects of care and service and address clinical issues with major impact on the health status of the enrolled population.

Quality assurance must be coordinated with other management activity. Contracts with physicians and other health care providers must be explicit about the need to cooperate with the plan's own quality activities or about the contractor's delegation of quality assurance responsibilities. An organization must actively monitor any delegated quality assurance activity. Finally, and most important, an organization must be able to demonstrate program effectiveness in improving its quality of care and service.

The NCQA establishes compliance with its standards by thorough on-site review of an organization's quality assurance program description and related policies and procedures, quality assurance studies, projects and monitoring activities, quality assurance and governing body minutes, interviews with key staff, tracking of issues uncovered by the quality assurance system to ensure resolution, and documented evidence of quality improvement.

Credentialing

The review process includes a thorough review of an organization's credentialing system. The NCQA requires that the MCO conduct primary verification of such credentialing information as licensure, malpractice history, good standing of hospital privileges, Drug Enforcement Agency certification, and so forth. Additionally, for IPA model organizations, the NCQA requires the MCO to conduct a structured review of primary care physician offices before contracting.

An important part of ensuring delivery system integrity is periodic recertification or reappointment of providers. Aside from reverifying the paper credentials, the NCQA requires a periodic performance appraisal to include information from quality assurance activity, risk and utilization management, member complaints, and member satisfaction surveys. Organizations delegating credentialing responsibility retain responsibility for ensuring that it meets NCQA standards. Compliance with credentialing standards is ascertained by reviewing an organization's credentialing policies and procedures, sampling individual provider files, conducting interviews with relevant staff, and tracking issues identified through the complaint system or quality assurance findings.

In 1995, the NCQA released standards and began pilot testing a program to certify CVOs. A CVO is any organization that verifies the credentials of physicians (e.g., medical school diploma, board certification, and malpractice history) and/or other practitioners for MCOs. Increasing numbers of MCOs are delegating responsibility for certain aspects of the physician credentialing process to these independent organizations, and the NCQA believes that this certification program will eliminate the need for duplicative reviews.

Current NCQA standards require the credentialing policies of a CVO to be reviewed and approved by each of the health plans with which it contracts. Certification by the NCQA will now stand as sufficient evidence for survey teams, however. In addition to reducing the burden at the time of a survey, the CVO certification program has the potential to reduce administrative costs for physicians contracting with multiple MCOs.

Utilization

Utilization management, a keystone of effective managed care, is an important determinant of both the cost and the quality of an MCO. NCQA standards for utilization management seek to establish that an organization has an organized system for utilization management, that review decisions are made by qualified medical professionals, that the organization has written utilization management protocols based on reasonable scientific evidence, that there are adequate appeals mechanisms for physicians and for patients, that decisions and appeals are processed in a timely manner, and that the utilization management system monitors for underutilization as well as overutilization. An organization must actively monitor any delegation of utilization management. The process includes review of utilization reports, committee minutes, and individual case files, as well as interviews with relevant staff.

Member Rights and Responsibilities

To meet NCQA standards, an organization must have written policies that recognize such member rights as voicing grievances and receiving information regarding the organization, its services, and its practitioners. These written policies must also address such member responsibilities as providing information needed by the professional staff and following practitioners' instructions and guidelines. The NCQA requires an organization to have a system for resolving members' complaints and grievances, to aggregate and analyze complaint and grievance data, and to use the information for quality improvement.

NCQA standards require communication to members of certain types of information about how the health plan works, including the organization's policies on referrals for specialty care; provisions for after-hours and emergency coverage; covered benefits; charges to patients; procedures for notifying patients about terminations or changes in benefits, services, or delivery sites; procedures for appealing decisions regarding coverage, benefits, or relationship to the organization; disenrollment procedures; and complaint and grievance procedures. The standards require that member information be written in readable prose and be available in the languages of the major population groups served. Organizations must also have mechanisms ensuring confidentiality of specified patient information and records.

Finally, an organization must have mechanisms to protect and enhance member satisfaction with its services, including member satisfaction surveys, studies of reasons for disenrollments, and evidence that the organization uses this information to improve its quality of service.

Preventive Health Services

HMOs have traditionally prided themselves on their commitment to preventive health services. Moreover, because they serve defined populations, HMOs are in a better position than the fee-for-service system to ensure that preventive services are used appropriately. NCQA preventive services standards require adoption of specifications (clinical policies or practice guidelines) for the use of preventive services, communication of this information to providers and patients, and yearly measurement of performance in the delivery of two such services chosen from a list developed by the NCQA. These results are audited by the NCQA.

Medical Records

The NCQA supplements management systems review with a sample of ambulatory records to assess both the quality of documentation and the quality of care. NCQA physician reviewers, guided by a 21-item medical record review form, assess the adequacy of diagnosis, the appropriateness and continuity of care, and the use of preventive services.

Review Process

At the time of application, the applicant organization fills out a preliminary information form, which contains detailed descriptions of the plan's delivery system, including information about delegated quality assurance, utilization management, and credentialing activity. The NCQA uses this information to determine the size and composition of the review team and the duration of the on-site review, both of which are used to determine the price of the review. Before the review, the applicant organization fills out a detailed preassessment information form, which contains information regarding the plan's compliance with each of the accreditation standards.

The on-site review typically lasts 3 days and includes extensive review of documentation such as minutes of quality assurance committee and board meetings; policies and procedures relating to various areas of the standards; provider contracts; quality assurance studies, reports, and case files; utilization management review criteria, reports, and files; credentialing files; complaint and grievance files; and member satisfaction and disenrollment surveys. Interviews are conducted with the chief executive officer; the medical director; the directors of quality assurance, utilization management, provider relations, and member services; members of the quality assurance committee; a member of the board of directors; and participating physicians. The review team reviews for evidence of compliance with each of the NCQA standards and presents a summary of its findings of fact at the end of the site visit. A member of the review team prepares a report that is submitted to the NCQA.

The report is reviewed by NCQA staff and the NCQA Review Oversight Committee. This committee makes compliance determinations for each of the NCQA standards as well as for the overall accreditation decision.

Accreditation Decisions

The NCQA publicly releases the name and accreditation status of all health plans, and in June 1996 it will begin releasing two-page accreditation summary reports for all health plans reviewed after July 1995. Full accreditation status is awarded when the NCQA determines that the organization is in full or substantial compliance with the group of NCQA standards in each category and that, with respect to any standard with which the organization is not in full compliance, there is no issue of sufficient significance that, in the NCQA's judgment, requires additional action before the organization can qualify for full accreditation.

One-year accreditation is awarded when the NCQA determines that the organization is in significant compliance with the group of standards within each category but, with respect to any standard or standards for which the organization is not in full compliance, that further action by the organization is required to achieve full accreditation status and that achievement of compliance with such standards can best be evaluated by the NCQA over a period of time not to exceed 1 year. A resurvey of the organization is conducted within the 12-month period after the accreditation determination to assess the extent to which deficiencies have been corrected.

Provisional accreditation is awarded when the NCQA determines that the organization is in partial compliance with the group of standards for each category and, with respect to any standard for which the organization is not in full com-

pliance, there is no deficiency that, in the NCQA's judgment, poses a potentially significant risk to quality of care. A resurvey of the organization is conducted within the 12-month period after the accreditation to assess the extent to which deficiencies have been corrected.

Denial/revocation occurs when the organization fails to comply with the group of standards within a category in such a significant way that the NCQA determines that a denial or revocation is warranted or, if a particular deficiency is identified, in the NCQA's judgment it poses a potentially significant risk to quality of care.

CONCLUSION

This chapter has presented a summary of the three primary organizations that currently accredit MCOs. Like the organizations they review, the three organizations vary in their goals and in their approach to external review. Although they vary considerably in their approach, all hold the potential for rationalizing and consolidating current external review processes for state, federal, and individual purchasers that are sometimes duplicative and/or contradictory in their requirements and that, in some cases, have a detrimental impact on managed care programs. Ultimately, however, their effectiveness must be judged in terms of their ability to improve the quality of care and service that MCOs provide to their customers.

REFERENCES AND NOTES

1. Utilization Review Accreditation Commission (URAC), *Standards* (Washington, D.C.: URAC, 1994).

2. Utilization Review Accreditation Commission (URAC), *Accreditation Process* (Washington, D.C.: URAC, 1994).

3. N.N. Bell, The AAPI Accreditation Program, *Medical Interface* (April 1991): 22–27.

Chapter 38

Risk Management in Managed Care

Barbara J. Youngberg

Risk management has been in a period of evolution almost since it first became an important function in the health care setting. In the mid-1970s, the health care risk management profession emerged in response to the malpractice crisis surrounding the availability of liability insurance.[1] Although the basic concepts for health care risk management were adopted from the insurance industry, over the past two decades the discipline of health care risk management has taken on many important characteristics and unique functions. Risk management in many functions of a managed care organization (MCO) are discussed in various chapters throughout this book, especially those in the section on legal and regulatory issues and those that discuss managing quality and utilization. Although there are clear risks associated with benefits administration, contracting, and other activities, the bulk of risks in managed care is associated with the provision of health care services and coverage decisions surrounding that care. In addition, providers face risks associated

with managed care beyond those faced by health plans. Therefore, this chapter focuses particularly on those issues.

Risk management has changed from an activity that sought solely to transfer risk through the purchase of commercial insurance or the financing of risk through the establishment of a self-insured trust or investment fund to a profession where education, proactive risk control and risk modification, and risk financing and risk transfer are merged into a partnership. The overall goals of the partnership enable the organization to be responsive to the needs and demands of the health care industry and to provide safe and effective care to patients. The organizational goals of ensuring financial stability in the event of an adverse outcome are still consistent with the goals of the health care risk manager, but risk managers also find that their work takes them out of the finance department and into those clinical and operational areas where the risks are created.

Specific objectives in risk management programs relate to the organization's desire to ensure survival, maximize efficiency, and sustain growth and effectiveness. This is accomplished through the identification, control, management, elimination, transfer, or financing of risk. Achievement of these objectives is accomplished by interacting with internal and external customers of the organization that demand low-risk, high-quality, cost-effective service. Management may have different priorities in seeking efficiency and growth, particularly as managed care continues to dominate the marketplace.

Barbara J. Youngberg, B.S.N., M.S.W., J.D., is Vice President of Insurance, Risk & Quality Management for the University HealthSystem Consortium (UHC). In this capacity she has responsibility for the design and management of group professional liability and provider excess insurance programs and for supporting risk and quality management for 70 academic medical centers in the U.S. and Switzerland. Ms. Youngberg is also on the faculty of the Loyola University College of Law—Health Law Institute and the Chicago Medical School—Finch University College of Health Sciences.

The primary targets or strategies of management could relate to gaining market share, increasing the overall number of relationships and contracts with payers, increasing sales or service volume, ensuring continuity of performance, maintaining the quantity of controlled resources, or other items expected to produce desired long-term financial results. These targets may be sought without appropriate consideration of the inherent risks that may also be assumed by adopting those strategies.

The goals identified to achieve market success may not be the most efficient or effective strategies from a risk management perspective. To achieve favorable results from both a risk management and an organizational perspective, the risk manager must recognize how the internal and external changes in health care created by managed care influence or enhance risk. The risk manager should begin to plan a strategy by first identifying how the organization is influenced from a risk perspective due to managed care (Exhibits 38–1 and 38–2). After this assessment, the risk manager should work with administration to determine critical success factors that will define risk management success for the organization (Exhibit 38–3).

Once the key measures of success have been agreed upon, the risk manager can develop a plan to protect the organization and help it progress. The risk manager's role and the challenges posed by that role will not differ significantly if the risk manager is employed by an MCO, a hospital that seeks to be the hub of an integrated delivery system, or a network that forms to be able to compete under managed care. Thus this chapter has been written to focus on the key risk management issues created by managed care as opposed to a specific job that a risk manager might assume given potentially differing structures. Many of the legal and risk management challenges created by managed care will exist regardless of the employer. The customers of the risk manager will include not only those in administration and finance but also physicians, nurses, and external customers. As managed care becomes more prevalent, risk manag-

Exhibit 38–1 Internal Environment Assessment

From	To
Focus on acute care hospital	→ Part of an integrated delivery system or network
Focus on clinical risk	→ Increasingly complicated with diverse risks
Focus on patients as customers	→ Many customers identified
Risks contained within single like entities	→ Risks extremely varied and increasingly complex
Reactive approach	→ Proactive approach
Multiple managers with autonomy	→ Streamlined individual management with shared responsibility
Focus on individual incidents	→ Focus on "big picture," requiring ability to track, trend, and benchmark
Data generated for internal use	→ Risk management data provided to payers and consumers
Risk management activities centralized and well defined	→ Risk management activities shared or delegated
Monopolistic	→ Focus on free market
Volume-driven staffing	→ Organization streamlined by function
Internal stability	→ Chaotic environment with multiple changes
Physician driven	→ Market driven
Professional roles clearly defined	→ Roles of health care professionals blurred by multidisciplinary and crossfunctional training

Source: Reprinted from B. Youngberg, Risk Management Strategic Planning for a Changed Health Care Delivery System, *Managing the Risks of Managed Care*, p. 25, © 1996, Aspen Publishers, Inc.

ers must develop new knowledge and utilize existing and new skills and techniques to identifying the new risks created, design creative strategies for managing those new risks, and provide education and information to an ever increasing and divergent customer base.

Exhibit 38–2 External Environment Assessment

From	To
Managing episodes of care	→ Managing covered lives
Managing illness	→ Managing health
Primary risk of clinical exposure	→ Organizations at significant financial risk due to changes in payment
Appropriate care determined and quality defined by providers	→ Reimbursable care and definition of quality determined by payers and legislators
Ethical decisions regarding health care made by hospitals and providers	→ Ethical standards set by consumer and various legislators
"Hospital-contained" risks	→ Risks prevalent in many settings, varied, and unique
Risk management reliant on conceptual and philosophical skills	→ Risk management requiring enhanced technical and theoretical skills while retaining interpersonal and communication skills
Privileged data not shared	→ Data widely shared

Source: Reprinted from B. Youngberg, Risk Management Strategic Planning for a Changed Health Care Delivery System, *Managing the Risks of Managed Care*, p. 26, © 1996, Aspen Publishers, Inc.

Exhibit 38–3 Organizational/Risk Management Critical Success Factors

Develop a systematic process for proactively identifying the nature and severity of risks created or acquired through the expansion into diverse health care services that might include for-profit activities.

Collaborate on a methodology for quantifying the financial risk inherent in managing the care of populations through capitated arrangements or other payer-driven financing strategies.

Determine the risk tolerance of the organization, and design the most advantageous risk transfer and risk sharing program.

Develop a strategy for managing and controlling the clinical, administrative, and contractual liabilities arising out of delivering care in the changing health care environment.

Develop and provide innovative strategies and tools that will contribute to improvement of patient care and service.

CHANGES IN THE HEALTH CARE ORGANIZATION RELATED TO MANAGED CARE

Managed care initially started out as "discount medicine," but it has now evolved to actual management of medical care by providing the patient with the appropriate level of care in the appropriate setting. In his book *Making Managed Health Care Work: A Practical Guide to Strategies and Solutions,* Peter Boland states the following: "Managed care alters the decision making of providers of health care services by interjecting a complex system of financial incentives, penalties, and administrative procedures into the doctor–patient relationship. Managed care often attempts to redefine what is best for the patient and how to achieve it most economically."[2(p.3)]

This statement implies altering and directing care to gain a cost advantage, which is risky if it is at the real or even perceived sacrifice of quality. Managed care administrators, insurance providers, and risk managers are becoming increasingly aware of the development of new case law associated with managed care, particularly how quality or access is limited by strict utilization or financial restrictions and how that limitation can pose a significant financial risk to the organization. Learning how to identify proactively these and other potential new exposures associated with managed care and how to control or eliminate them will be a challenge and will be at the core of the risk manager's responsibility.

Historically, MCOs have faced minimal professional liability exposure, especially compared with other health care organizations. In large part, this is the result of the broad and well-publicized protection provided by the Employer

Retirement Income Security Act of 1974 (ERISA; see Chapter 59).[3] That protection includes barring jury trials and punitive damage awards, limiting compensation to medical expenses, and preempting actions against an MCO for the "administration" of a ERISA-qualified employee benefit plan.[4] The Federal Employee Health Benefits Act (see Chapter 45) can also afford some protection for federal employee benefit plans.[5] These statutory protections have their limits, however, and the risk manager must develop a clear understanding of the new risks that may be created under managed care and are not afforded statutory protection and must develop strategies to manage them.

The changes in the organization relative to managed care create new operational and clinical risks and opportunities for risk management. No longer are the risks contained within the walls of a provider organization; rather, the risks now follow the patients to whom the MCO has agreed to provide services. This may result in making the environment more difficult to control for the risk manager. In addition, with the movement away from high-technology specialties, many organizations may find the need to identify and engage providers with a focus on primary care and prevention. This group of professionals may include physicians but may also include nurse practitioners, physician assistants or extenders, social workers, and other health care professionals. Credentialing, reappointment, privilege delineation, and definition of the scope of service for an enhanced range of caregivers will be essential components of the risk manager's job.

OPERATIONAL RISKS UNDER MANAGED CARE

Operational risks are enhanced under managed care. For example, a provider organization becomes more complex as it attempts to compete by becoming part of an integrated delivery system (see Chapter 4). New business risks can create corporate liability, both direct and indirect (vicarious). A risk manager whose responsibility is to manage the risks of the MCO must be mindful of the business and clinical risks created. Managed care plans can pose the following risk concerns that will be new challenges for the organization's risk manager:

- coordinating the appropriate amount and level of care, by appropriate providers, through utilization management activities

- negotiating arrangements with selective providers with proven skills and competence to provide comprehensive services identified in the contracts

- ensuring that the financial incentives provided by the contract are sufficient to sustain the organization and that the potential for catastrophic financial risk is understood and appropriately funded for or transferred (Relative to financial risk management, the risk manager should also be cognizant of the potential double-edged sword created by the use of financial incentives to providers. In a positive sense, these types of incentive structures can help support the provision of efficient, effective, and appropriate service. They can also, however, be seen as a reward system that inappropriately incents physicians to deny needed care to patients in exchange for increased compensation.)

- understanding the nature of the new clinical risks created and proactively designing systems or structures to eliminate or control them

Figure 38–1 illustrates the relative risk for managed care structures based upon the degree of influence and relationships that the MCO maintains with its providers.[6] It is only through an analysis of the MCO's business and an understanding of the relative risk associated with that business that one can develop a comprehensive risk management plan to ensure that all risks created are eliminated, managed, controlled, or transferred.

Figure 38–1 Relative risk for managed care structures. PPO, preferred provider organization; IPA, independent practice association; HMO, health maintenance organization.

MANAGING CORPORATE NEGLIGENCE

Direct Liability

Corporate negligence claims arising from managed care pose new risks for the risk manager. Corporate liability claims are based on the premise that the health care entity or MCO has a legal duty to protect the patient from harm. This responsibility can be deemed to be abrogated when negligent providers are employed by the MCO and render care to patients that is determined to be negligent. The need to develop rigorous screening procedures for potential staff members and to follow those procedures is an important risk management function in this new environment and should be carefully monitored to verify adherence.

Under the doctrine of corporate negligence, an MCO and its physician administrators may be held directly liable to patients or providers for failing to investigate adequately the competence of health care providers whom it employs or with whom it contracts, particularly where the MCO actually provides health care services or restricts the patient's/enrollee's choice of physician. MCOs and their physicians administrators may be held liable for bodily injury to patients/enrollees resulting from improper credentialing of physicians or for economic or compensatory damages to providers as a result of credentialing activities (e.g., unlawful exclusion from provider networks or staff decertification). The doctrine of corporate negligence may also apply to other managed care activities besides credentialing, such as performance of utilization review.

Under the theory of negligent or improper design or administration of cost control systems, an MCO and its physician administrators may be held liable when they design or administer cost control systems in a manner that interferes with the rendering of quality medical care or corrupts medical judgment. To date, most litigation involving allegations of negligent administration of a cost control system have involved utilization review activities of MCOs.

MCOs and their physician administrators are also susceptible to antitrust liability for violations of federal and state antitrust laws, which generally prohibit the unlawful restraint of trade, monopolies, price fixing and discrimination, group boycotts, illegal tying arrangements, exclusive dealing, and other arrangements that are anticompetitive. Antitrust problems may arise when entities engage in collective actions that reduce competition in a given market. Antitrust problems can arise early in a market where managed care encourages the combining of the services of former competitors to facilitate service delivery. A balancing test must be performed to ensure that the benefits gained by combining outweigh the danger posed by limiting competition of those entities outside the agreement. Managed care networks are also likely to face an increased number of antitrust lawsuits from providers and competitors as they gain increased market share. The larger an MCO becomes in a particular area, the fewer opportunities available to the provider who is not part of the network. This issue is discussed extensively in Chapter 57.

In addition, MCOs and their physician administrators face corporate exposure to direct liability for various forms of discrimination, for example discrimination in benefit design, underwriting, claims adjudication, credentialing, treatment, employment, and contracting. The following pieces of legislation may give rise to allegations of discrimination in specific managed care plans:

- the Family and Medical Leave Act of 1993
- the Americans with Disabilities Act of 1992
- the Civil Rights Act of 1991
- the Age Discrimination in Employment Act of 1967, including the Older Workers Benefit Protection Act of 1990
- Title VI of the Civil Rights Laws of 1964, as amended (1983), including the Pregnancy Discrimination Act of 1978
- the Civil Rights Act of 1966, Section 1981
- the Fifth and Fourteenth Amendments of the U.S. Constitution

In addition, MCOs and their physician administrators face corporate liability for invasion of privacy of providers for improper dissemination of information regarding credentials or competence to the National Practitioner Data Bank or other third parties or of patients/enrollees for improper dissemination of their records or information pertaining to their health. They may also be sued by providers, patients, or employees for defamation, particularly in connection with their peer review activities. In such an event, however, they may be entitled to qualified immunity under the Health Care Quality Improvement Act of 1986 (HCQIA).

Vicarious Liability

Under the theory of vicarious liability or ostensible agency, hospitals have been held vicariously liable for the acts, errors, and omissions of their independent contractors. By definition, a provider is an independent contractor in independent practice associations and direct contract models. Therefore, the MCO should not be re-

sponsible for negligent acts unless the MCO has given the impression that these providers are acting as agents of the MCO. The decisions of the courts to uphold claims based on ostensible agency depend on many factors, applicable state statutes, the ability of the plaintiff's attorney to demonstrate the apparent agency relationship, and other aspects of the provider–MCO relationship as viewed by the courts.

Because "appearance" or perception seems to be the major issue driving the ostensible agency argument, it might be wise for the risk manager to consider some of the circumstances that might lead the public to assume that an agency relationship exists and to make the necessary arrangements to control these potential exposures. Factors that may give rise to the presumption of the existence of an agency relationship include:

- supplying the provider with office space
- keeping the provider's medical records
- employing other health care professionals, such as nurses, laboratory technicians, and therapists, to support the physician provider
- developing promotional or marketing materials that allow a relationship to be inferred

The risk manager may wish to review documents provided to patients to ensure that the physician is described as an independent practitioner and that there is a clear distinction between those services provided by the MCO and those provided by the physician.

CLINICAL RISKS

Managing clinical risks has been an activity of pivotal importance for the health care risk manager. This activity continues to be important, but there have been changes in its complexity under managed care. Specific risks that require control and relate to the provision of clinical care include risks associated with credentialing, risks associated with clinical decision making (e.g., rationing of care), risks associated with utilization review, and risks associated with adhering to externally imposed standards of care.

Credentialing

Credentialing is a risk management function that considers who the health care provider is in the MCO and what the provider can do.[7] In an effort to facilitate the credentialing process and reduce administrative burdens and costs, some entities may choose to participate in a joint credentialing process. This process might include a consolidation of credentialing procedures and a sharing of the information requested as part of the process. It will be important to have appropriate releases signed by the professional being credentialed so that there can be no subsequent claims for breach of confidentiality.

In general, a credentialing process must be developed that allows for the successful selection and retention of high-quality providers who understand and support the mission and vision of the organization or network with which they work. See Chapters 7, 8, and 57 for further discussion of credentialing.

Measures that might be instituted to prevent or limit liability associated with credentialing include establishing realistic criteria, ensuring that the data being measured and evaluated are accurate, conveying and evaluating the criteria on a consistent basis, and creating a paper trail clearly tying quality to the economic credentialing process.[8] The following is a checklist for risk managers to keep in mind when setting up a credentialing process[9]:

- Review credentialing criteria for compliance with state statutes, standards for MCOs, Joint Commission on Accreditation of Healthcare Organizations standards, Medicare conditions of participation, National Committee for Quality Assurance, and court decisions.
- Review policies, procedures, bylaws, and contracts to ensure that all credentialing criteria are clearly stated.

- Review application forms for compliance with standards and local, state, and federal regulations.
- Review credentialing policies and procedures of other hospitals, facilities, and credentialing services whose credentialing decisions are used instead of an internal process.
- Review protocols for investigating and verifying an applicant's credentials. Do these protocols minimize the risk of inadequately screening and verifying the credentials of practitioners?
- Observe the methods by which these protocols are applied in reviewing individual applicants. Are protocols applied equally to all applicants whether they are well known or not?
- Evaluate the organizational structure of the credentialing process. Are checks in place to minimize the involvement of direct economic competitors in the credentialing process? Does the structure minimize the risk of creating antitrust liability?
- Review due process provisions to ensure that practitioners who are denied medical staff membership or have had privileges restricted are afforded a fair hearing in accordance with federal and state laws and standards.
- Require all practitioners to report claims, disciplinary proceedings, or adverse actions taken against them at other facilities or hospitals. Ensure risk management access to these records.
- Ensure that HCQIA regulations are complied with and that information from the National Practitioner Data Bank is used appropriately in credentialing and privileging determinations.
- Establish rapport with practitioners to facilitate open communication, education, and resourcefulness regarding risk management issues.

Clinical Decision Making

One of the most frequently verbalized fears relative to managed care is that it will create a system whereby care is predicated on a person's ability to pay or upon an externally imposed system of values that dictates which medical conditions are appropriate for specific types of intervention. In general, when these issues and concerns are voiced they relate to the denial of interventions deemed to be extraordinary or experimental to patients with terminal conditions or conditions where the treatment may not result in a cure but may only serve to delay inevitable furtherance of the disease. Although much of the discussion thus far seems to be fueled more by fear than fact, making care decisions based on reasons other than best medical judgment is risky and thus should be avoided. Risk managers can assist in limiting these types of risks by determining that policies are in place that clearly indicate that care decisions are not predicated on the ability of the patient to pay or the willingness of the payer to reimburse but rather are based on sound medical judgment that is rendered consistent with appropriate professional standards of care. Many of these decisions also are linked to an area of well-developed case law in managed care, that law related to utilization review activities.

Utilization Management Issues

Controlling the parameters of care through a well-detailed utilization review process is an important component of cost controls associated with managed care. Court cases have demonstrated that a plan's utilization review process is an operational exposure with the potential for considerable financial risk. A well-structured utilization review program is designed to limit the potential risks associated with attempts to structure care around predetermined criteria. The program should allow for retrospective, concurrent, and prospective review of care provided under the managed care plan. It should be remembered that underutilization presents real threats to quality and risk just as overutilization presents threats to cost control.

Emerging Case Law

The seminal case describing the liability that can attach to an organization with inappropriate utilization criteria is *Wickline v. State of California*.[10] This case addressed the legal implications of preadmission certification of treatment and length of stay authorization. In this case, suit was brought against the state of California alleging that its agency for administering the medical assistance program was negligent when it only approved a 4-day extension of the plaintiff's hospitalization when an 8-day extension was requested by the physician. Plaintiff's attorney alleged that the discharge was premature, resulting in the ultimate amputation of the plaintiff's leg. The physician requesting the 8-day extension did not appeal the decision of the state agency. Neither the hospital nor the physician was the defendant in this action.

A jury returned a verdict in the plaintiff's favor on the grounds that the plaintiff had suffered harm as a result of the negligent administration of the state's cost control system. The trial court's decision was reversed by the appellate court, which found that the state had not been negligent and therefore was not liable. The court held that the state was not responsible for the physician's discharge decision and that a physician who complies without protest with limitations imposed by third party payers when the physician's medical judgment dictates otherwise cannot avoid ultimate responsibility for the patient's care. The court did acknowledge, however, that an entity could be found liable for injuries resulting from arbitrary or unreasonable decisions that disapprove requests for medical care. The court emphasized that a patient who requires treatment and is harmed when care that should have been provided is not provided should recover for the injuries suffered from all those responsible for the deprivation of such care, including, when appropriate, health care payers. The court went on to say that third party payers can be held legally accountable when medically inappropriate decisions result from defects in the design or implementation of cost containment mechanisms. The court concluded from the facts at issue in this case that the California cost containment program did not corrupt medical judgment and therefore could not be found liable for the resulting harm to the plaintiff.

In another case, *Wilson v. Blue Cross of California*, plaintiffs alleged that their son's suicide was directly caused by the utilization review firm's refusal to authorize additional days of inpatient treatment.[11] The patient had been admitted for inpatient psychiatric care for depression, drug dependency, and anorexia. His physician recommended 3 to 4 weeks of inpatient care, but the utilization review firm only approved 10 days. The patient was discharged and committed suicide less than 3 weeks later by taking a drug overdose. The trial court granted summary judgment in favor of the defendants. The appellate court reversed this decision, concluding that the insurer could be held liable for the patient's wrongful death if any negligent conduct was a substantial factor in bringing about harm. Testimony of the treating physician indicated that, had the decedent completed his planned hospitalization, there was a reasonable medical probability that he would not have committed suicide. The court concluded that whether the conduct of the utilization review contractor's employee was a substantial factor in the patient's suicide was a question of fact precluding summary judgment and remanded the case for further review. On retrial, the jury entered a verdict in favor of the defendants.

Litigation for utilization review decisions may also be brought under theories of bad faith and breach of contract based on the contractual nature of the relationship between the MCO and its patient members.

Reducing Utilization Management Exposure

The risk manager attempting to work with providers in the organization can provide the following advice to assist physicians in the reduction or elimination of exposures related to utilization review:

- Devise a comprehensive utilization management program that integrates with quality and risk management. Individuals performing utilization management functions should utilize patient outcome indicators as a means of identifying quality of care or risk problems.

- Physicians must exercise independent medical judgment that meets with the standard of care. Utilization management decisions should not influence the physician's clinical decisions in any way that the physician would consider truly harmful to the patient.

- Providers must advise the MCO of their medical judgment. The physician needs to be aware of each plan's utilization review process and to advise the plan of his or her medical judgment in clear terms. If a disagreement arises, the physician may need to support the validity of the clinical recommendations with documentation as to the medical necessity. Including diagnostic test results and providing an opinion as to the possible adverse outcomes should the request be denied will also be helpful.

- Develop a "fast-track" second opinion program. Providers need to support the development of a system that can quickly render a second opinion in case of disagreement surrounding clinical judgment. Ideally, the second opinion should be rendered by a health care professional whose skill and training are commensurate with those of the provider whose judgment is being questioned.

- The patient should be informed of any issues that are being disputed relative to the physician's recommended treatment plan and the MCO's coverage decision. Alternative approaches and the potential cost and outcome of those approaches should be discussed with the patient. Also, the patient should be informed that, if the plan continues to deny coverage, the patient may be responsible for payment. The patient should continue to be informed throughout the appeal process.

- Exhaust the appeals process. In the event that the treating physician firmly believes that the MCO has made an incorrect decision, then the best defense in cases of treatment denials is staunch patient advocacy. The physician should request to speak to the medical director in charge of the utilization decision and explain the rationale behind the intended treatment. If a plan continues to deny coverage for a service that the physician feels is necessary, the process that allows for a second opinion fails to support treatment, and the physician continues to believe that the denial of coverage is in error, then the decision should be appealed aggressively. All avenues of appeal should be exhausted. If unsuccessful, the physician should inform the patient of treatment opinions without regard to coverage. The patient must ultimately decide whether to continue treatment at his or her cost. If the patient should wish to proceed at his or her own expense, the physician should have the patient sign an informed consent signifying awareness that such expenses may not be covered by the health plan.
- Ascertain that insuring agreements include coverage for utilization review activities.

Externally Imposed Practice Guidelines or Standards of Care

Many clinicians are particularly concerned about the development of practice guidelines that seek to define appropriate services that should be provided to a patient given a specific condition. In some instances, these guidelines are used to support utilization management

decisions; in others, they may be developed in attempts to define best practice. Although developers often argue that best practice determinations are predicated on an evaluation of effectiveness, some providers believe that under managed care best practice really means lowest cost. To avoid the risks that are likely to be associated with the use of guidelines, clinicians should be assured that the existence of a guideline does not in and of itself create a standard of care and that guidelines, although they may be instructive, do not set standards of care (although well-developed guidelines should articulate agreed-upon standards of care; see Chapter 19). Risk managers should advise clinicians that, despite the existence of a guideline, their skill and judgment based on a careful assessment of the patient's condition can and should preempt the recommendations of a guideline. Case law, at least to date, supports this position.

MULTISITE CHALLENGES

The sheer number of sites where clinical care may be provided or that have affiliation or network agreements makes it essential that the risk manager create tools that can empower staff at these sites to understand and manage their own risks. Risk management will increasingly become a responsibility of all staff who will rely on the risk manager for support and advice but will ultimately be responsible for on-site control of risks inherent in the operation of their business. Tools that are developed should focus on those proactive strategies that enable all health care professionals working in a particular area to identify issues unique to their area that may give rise to risk and to modifying those risks in a manner that will allow for a safer environment with staff increasingly aware of the risks inherent in providing care in a specific area or setting. Tools that contain specific questions about an area can be developed and are useful for assisting managers and clinicians in recognizing and managing their own risks.

THE CONVERGENCE OF FINANCIAL AND RISK MANAGEMENT

Capitation

Managed care contracts create both opportunity and risk for health care organizations. Under many contracts the reimbursement from payers is capitated, with the health care organization receiving a fixed sum per member per month regardless of the intensity of services that the member receives. Understanding the financial risks assumed under these contracts and either funding for those risks or transferring them to a third party require many of the same skills that the risk manager uses to mange the clinical risks that are part of all health care organizations. Once the total risk being assumed is quantified, the risk manager, working with the chief financial officer or managed care plan administrator, can evaluate the best ways either to fund for or to transfer this risk.

Financial Incentives and Cost Control Programs

Incentive payment systems link provider compensation to the provision of cost-effective health care. An incentive system is meant to encourage providers to render only care that is necessary and appropriate (see Chapters 7, 9, 10, and 11). Financial incentives can take a variety of forms, and depending on the outcome of care patients may view the incentive programs as having influenced their providers' medical decision making.

Cases are beginning to emerge that allege that physicians whose salaries are based in part on an incentive structure that predicates payment for services based on utilization of services make treatment decisions based more on their financial reward than on the well-being of the patient. It is imperative that financial incentives be structured in such a way that they do not have the appearance of encouraging this type of behavior.

Whether the cost control program of the MCO creates a financial incentive for physicians to provide inadequate treatment was raised in a recent legal opinion.[12] The case involved a delay in the diagnosis of cervical cancer due to the failure of the primary care physician to order a Pap smear. In this case, an MCO participant brought suit against the MCO alleging that the contractual agreements between the MCO and its providers encouraged physicians not to refer patients to specialists. The court found that the plaintiff had offered evidence establishing that the cost control system contributed to the delay in diagnosis and treatment. A formal opinion on this issue was never rendered, however, because the case was settled during trial for an undisclosed amount.

In another well-publicized case, *Fox v. HealthNet*, a California jury awarded nearly $90 million to the estate of a breast cancer patient arising from the refusal of the MCO to pay for a bone marrow transplant; $77 million was awarded as punitive damages.[13] The MCO considered this procedure experimental and would not pay for any experimental treatment until it was proven effective. According to reports in the press, testimony at trial included that of two women for whom the MCO had approved identical treatments as proof that the treatment might have worked.[14] Furthermore, it was shown that the physician executive who denied payment for the bone marrow transplant received bonuses based on the denial of costly medical procedures. The jury concluded that the MCO acted in bad faith, breached its contract of care with its subscriber, and intentionally inflicted emotional distress.

This case represents a good example of how denial of access to treatment can expose an MCO to liability. It also demonstrates how the emotional impact and negative publicity associated with the denial of treatment, even if the treatment has not been proven effective, can influence the ultimate decision and the damage award. In a managed care environment, the primary care physician, in conjunction with the MCO, acts as a gatekeeper in determining what hospital or specialty physician services should be provided. The failure to meet the applicable standard of care in making these decisions can expose the primary care physician and the MCO to liability. In the Fox case, the treating physician recommended the treatment with the support of the two other MCO physicians who had used it for the two witnesses in the case, and the MCO, as gatekeeper, refused to pay for it.

These cases reveal that courts are willing to impose liability on MCOs when inappropriate medical decisions result from defects in the design or implementation of the cost containment programs, breach of contract, or bad faith in the denial of payment. The impact of an MCO's financial incentives to contain costs has also been tested. If financial incentives result in inadequate treatment being rendered, the MCO could be held liable. These cases indicate that members will seek redress if harmed as a result of the administration of cost control programs which deny them access to care, which delay care, or which deny payment for necessary care.

Avoiding Liability Associated with Cost Control Programs

The design and administration of cost control programs should promote efficient care but must not corrupt the medical judgment of the physician. If an MCO overrides the medical judgment of the physician, it could be held liable for the consequences of the treatment or discharge decision. To avoid liability in this regard, an MCO needs to ensure that its financial incentive and cost control programs include procedures that accomplish the following:

- utilize medical necessity criteria that meet acceptable standards of medical practice
- review all pertinent records in determining the necessity of treatment
- contact the treating physician before certification is denied
- allow sufficient time to review the claim before denial
- ensure that medical personnel approving payment denials are appropriately trained,

have met established minimum qualifications, and have the requisite knowledge to assess the appropriateness of care
- maintain policies and procedures that ensure that operations do not interfere with the physician–patient relationship regarding the duration and level of medical care
- carefully document procedures used to deny certification of care (coverage restrictions need to be adequately described in materials given to MCO members, especially with respect to experimental or investigational treatments)
- devise a mechanism for communication of programs to members, especially financial incentive programs

RISK FINANCING

The professional liability and business risks that are associated with managed care have fairly consistently been insurable under standard insurance contracts. Many creative products and concepts are being developed for the control or minimization of the financial risks that are inherent in capitated contracts or for the balance sheets fluctuations that are possible during a period of time when there is considerable volatility in the financing of health care services. The concepts underlying the financing of all these risks are the same and are consistent with the risk financing skills that were practiced by many risk managers before the emergence of managed care.

UTILIZING THE RISK MANAGEMENT PROCESS TO CONTROL THE RISKS OF MANAGED CARE

The risk management process is generally structured around loss reduction techniques (which include the identification of risk, the elimination of risk whenever possible, and the control or management of risk when it cannot be entirely eliminated) and loss transfer (techniques which include determining the economic risk associated with various types of loss and selection of the best methods either to finance risk internally or to transfer those risks to a third party, generally through the purchase of insurance). These processes can be successful in managing the emerging risks that are created by a managed health care system. Obviously, the techniques will need to be tailored to the specific needs of each organization, particularly as managed care becomes increasingly dominant.

Because it is essential that the risk manager understand the scope of potential risk in the hospital, health network, or integrated delivery system, the first step will be to develop effective communication links with those parts of the organization that are responsible for the strategic growth of the hospital into a managed care partner or into the hub of a managed care network. Anticipating risk and being able to plan for it will greatly enhance the likelihood that risks created by the new delivery model will be capable of being controlled. Educating all staff, including administration and health care providers, about the emerging risks that are associated either with the delivery system created by managed care or with the clinical delivery system that is more decentralized because of managed care will be an important function for the risk manager. The risk manager may achieve the greatest success by developing tools that can be used by others to assess and manage their own risk. Making each member of the health care team responsible for managing the risks created by this complicated new health care delivery model will be the only way to ensure success.

CONCLUSION

Risk managers must continually monitor emerging risks and design comprehensive strategies for managing them. Unlike the traditional role of the risk manager in a hospital, where a single person or a designated risk management staff is central to the risk management effort, in an MCO or integrated delivery system everyone will have to become engaged in the process of proactively identifying and managing risks. A brief checklist follows that will assist the risk manager in managing the process of providing health care in a managed care environment:

- Design department-, unit-, or function-specific assessment tools that can be used easily by managers and clinicians to assess risks associated with specific environments or activities. Make risk management everyone's responsibility!
- Continually monitor case law and developing trends in managed care and design a system to provide information about new developments to all staff working in the MCO or network.
- Never underestimate the importance of a rigorous credentialing process that allows for the careful screening of all health care providers—physicians and advanced practitioners. Make certain that this process is in compliance with state and federal law and that it measures both credentials and competence.
- Verify that a comprehensive process exists for utilization management activities. Ascertain that decisions about patient care are based on the best interest of the patient, not primarily the financial interest of the provider or the MCO.
- Develop a system that allows risk managers to be involved in the assessment of potential new business opportunities or entities before their becoming part of the organization or network. This will allow for a clear understanding of the risks to be assumed and for the development of a plan to control, eliminate, or transfer those risks.
- Develop the risk management role as one of a consultant whose advice and expertise are sought whenever issues of potential liability arise.

REFERENCES AND NOTES

1. B. Youngberg, *Essentials of Hospital Risk Management* (Gaithersburg, Md.: Aspen, 1990).

2. P. Boland, *Making Managed Health Care Work: A Practical Guide to Strategies and Solutions* (Gaithersburg, Md.: Aspen, 1993).

3. Employee Retirement Income Security Act of 1994, 29 U.S.C. Section 1001 et. seq.

4. *Corcoran v. United Healthcare, Inc.*, 965 F.2d 1321 (5th Cir. 1992), cert. denied, 113 S.Ct. 812 (1992).

5. Federal Employees Health Benefits Act, 56 U.S.C.A., Section 8901 et. seq.

6. R.J. Hester, "Managed Care Liability Concerns," in *1992 Health Care Law Update* (Florida Bar Lecture Program, 1992).

7. B. Youngberg, *Managing the Risks of Managed Care* (Gaithersburg, Md.: Aspen, 1996).

8. C.S. Doyle, Managing the Risks of Managed Care, *Journal of Healthcare Risk Management* 14 (1995): 3–7.

9. S. Hagg-Rickert, Medical Staff Credentialing and Privileging Determinations: The Emerging Role of the Risk Manager. *Perspectives in Healthcare Risk Management* 11 (1991): 2–4.

10. *Wickline v. State of California*, 192 Cal.App.3d 1630, 239 Cal. Rptr. 810 (Ct. App.); cert. granted, 727 P.2d 753, 231 Cal. Rptr. 560 (1986); review dismissed, case remanded, 741 P.2d 613, 239 Cal. Rptr. 805 (1987).

11. *Wilson v. Blue Cross of California*, 271 Cal. Rptr. 876 (Cal. Ct. App. 1990), review denied, No. S017315, 1990 Cal. LEXIS 4574 (Cal. 1990).

12. *Bush v. Dake*, File No. 86-25767 No-2 (Mich. Cir. Ct. 1987).

13. *Fox v. HealthNet*, No. 219692 (Cal Super. Ct. 1992).

14. *Los Angeles Times* (7 April 1994): D-1.

SUGGESTED READING

American Society of Healthcare Risk Management. *Journal of Healthcare Risk Management*. Chicago, Ill.: American Hospital Association. A quarterly journal devoted to relevant risk management issues.

Benda, C.G. and Rozovsky, F.A. 1996. *Managed Care and the Law*. Boston, Mass.: Little, Brown & Co.

Berkowitz, S. 1991. *Managing Risks and Quality in Hosptial Related Managed Care: A Guide to Hospitals*. Chicago, Ill.: The Institute on Quality Care and Patterns of Practice, The Hospital Research and Education Trust, American Hospital Association.

Creed, B.B., Corcoran, M.E., and Leitner, M. 1993. "Managing the Legal Risks of Managed Care Programs." pp. 390–395. *Driving Down Health Care Costs: Strategies and Solutions*. New York: Panel Publishers.

Harding, J. 1994. Risk Management in an IPA Setting. Part I. *Physician Executive* 20 (5): 32–37.

Harding, J. 1994. Risk Management in an IPA Setting. Part II. *Physician Executive* 20 (6): 21–24.

Thomasson, G.O. 1994. Participatory Risk Management: Promoting Physician Compliance with Practice Guidelines. *The Joint Commission Journal on Quality Improvement* 20 (6): 317–329.

Youngberg, B.J. 1996. *Managing the Risks of Managed Care*. Gaithersburg, Md.: Aspen.

Youngberg, B.J. 1994. *The Risk Manager's Desk Reference*. Gaithersburg, Md.: Aspen.

Chapter 39

Common Operational Problems in Managed Health Care Plans

Peter R. Kongstvedt

As in most enterprises, managed health care plans are prone to problems that are common to their own industry. The most common problem for start-up plans is inability to gain market share. That problem, languishing in the market, is not addressed in this chapter. The reader is referred to Chapter 35 for an in-depth discussion of marketing issues, including common pitfalls and problems. The focus of this chapter is operational problems rather than the problems of gaining membership.

Whether a problem occurs and how serious that problem is will depend on a variety of factors. None of the problems and common mistakes that are discussed in this chapter occurs in a vacuum. Certain problems will be exacerbated by the presence of other, concurrent problems. In some types of plans the relative dangers will be far less than in others. The purpose of this chapter is to discuss these common problems and mistakes to help make a manager aware of them. Early detection could prevent severe damage to the plan.

Not all these problems would be found in the same plan at the same time, and rarely will only one problem exist at a time. In general, troubled health plans will have problems in logical combinations. For example, if significant problems are occurring with expenses that are incurred but not reported (IBNRs), it is likely that the plan will be having problems with claims processing and inaccurate utilization reports as well.

In some cases, the problems discussed in this chapter will be serious only in plans that assume

full financial risk [i.e., health maintenance organizations (HMOs), full risk-bearing preferred provider organizations (PPOs), and individual practice organizations (IPAs) that take full responsibility for enrolling members, collecting premiums, paying providers, and so forth]. Other problems, especially those that relate to medical management, may be found in organizations that accept limited risk as well as organizations accepting full risk (e.g., medical groups, contracting IPAs within an HMO, or any other organization responsible for delivering medical services).

Regardless of how a particular organization is configured, it is worthwhile understanding the potential common problems that any health plan can encounter. This may allow you to see whether a plan is running into trouble, even if you yourself do not have responsibility for that particular area of management. It will also allow you to analyze the competition better and develop strategies for success.

UNDERCAPITALIZATION OF NEW PLANS

A classic problem in business, undercapitalization is just as troublesome for health plans as for any other business. Losses can mount more quickly than anticipated, and if the pricing strategy was too low, losses can continue for quite some time. It is not uncommon for new plans to spend between $2 million and $7 million before getting to breakeven status. The best way to handle this is to prevent it by using an experienced actuary and financial consultant to estimate losses before breakeven and to do so under a number of different scenarios.

Once a plan is operational, if it is undercapitalized and not amenable to fast repairs (e.g., sharp reductions in administrative cost or medical cost or rapid increases in premium revenue), there are a limited number of responses available to management. One response is to try to get the providers to assume the expenses, perhaps through mandatory fee reductions or promissory notes, or to use a reimbursement methodology that places provider systems at full risk for medical expenses (which is a complicated strategy; see Chapter 5). The other routes involve obtaining money from outside sources, either as debt or by selling equity. In any of these cases, you are obviously dealing from a position of weakness and will usually pay the price of failing to obtain adequate capital before commencement of operations. Failing even that, the plan may wind up in a forced merger with a healthy plan, in receivership to creditors, seized by the state insurance department, or having to declare bankruptcy or even fold. All these last options may be considered a career limiting move on the part of management.

PREDATORY PRICING OR LOW-BALLING

This refers to premium rates that are intentionally well below the actual cost of delivering care. This is usually found in start-up plans, although a mature plan may low-ball to preserve or rapidly gain market share in response to a competitor's rates. Price undercutting is a venerable tradition in a capitalistic system and has great utility in enhancing one's competitive stance. Buying market share is not necessarily a mistake under all circumstances, but it is a risky strategy that must be undertaken with great care.

There is a crusty old cliché in business that goes "You can't buy widgets for a dollar, sell them for eighty cents, and make it up on vol-

ume." This is even more true in managed health care than in manufacturing. The manufacturer may hope to sell a service contract with the widget and recoup the loss or raise the price of widgets after a few months. In a health plan, all you sell is service; there are no benefits riders that will make up for a grossly underbid base premium. Furthermore, once you sign up a group for a set premium rate, you usually have to live with that rate for at least a year. Even in accounts in which the plan is not bearing financial risk for medical expenses (such as an administrative services only account), the plan may suffer a financial penalty if it has guaranteed medical expense trends, and it will doubtless suffer a tarnished reputation for effective management, veracity, or both.

The purpose of low-balling is to drive enrollment up and buy market share. If you low-ball a rate so that you lose $5 per member per month (PMPM), and if you succeed in increasing enrollment by 5,000 members, you have succeeded in increasing your losses to $5,000 \times \$5$ PMPM, or $25,000 per month, or $300,000 per year. You cannot make it up on volume.

Occasionally, managers may low-ball primarily to cover high overhead costs (in other words, to get some cash flowing in) rather than as an attempt to get market dominance. In those cases, the losses from the fixed overhead are in fact attenuated by the premium revenue brought in, at least initially, even though the medical loss ratio is unacceptably high. Low-balling may provide a short-term fix for highly leveraged plans such as closed panels, but the long-term result is the same: As enrollment increases, the overhead required to provide service increases as well, leading to a continuing loss situation that may become more severe than anticipated.

In addition to sustained losses, low-balling is a market strategy that appeals to the most price-sensitive consumers. That can be a set-up for a raid by a competitor who low-balls the rates even further. Unless another strategy is available, the plan could then end up in a price war and never recoup its losses.

None of this is to say that a plan may not have to hold rates down or even lower them for competitive reasons. It is to say that low-balling should never be the only competitive strategy. It should really be used only as an adjunct to a long-range strategy, and even then only with caution. Far too many plans have found that their pockets were not as deep as they thought or that they underestimated how deep those pockets would need to be.

A common and critical mistake by plan managers facing price competition is to lower the rates to unrealistic levels and simply budget expenses lower, usually medical expenses. Unless there is a clear and believable strategy for lowering those expenses, the savings will not materialize. It is not enough to order the medical director to harass the physicians and get costs down; there needs to be a more cogent plan for reducing expenses. Sadly, a manager under pressure frequently indulges in a combination of magical thinking and rule by decree. In other words, by decreeing that expenses must be reduced, the other managers will magically figure out how to do that despite not having succeeded the previous year. The lesson here is that, if the rates are intentionally lowered, managers had better figure out specifically how they are going to reduce expenses in each category. If they cannot come up with a clear plan for each category, they should budget the loss.

Assuming that the decision has been made to try to recover some of the losses, the main question is whether to raise the rates in one breathtaking rate hike or to phase in the rate increase over a number of years. That decision must be made by analyzing the plan's financial resources, the market conditions, the customers' willingness to put up with a rate hike, the danger of losing significant enrollment in that group (which may or may not be a bad thing, depending on the degree of losses you are sustaining in the group; in turn, this may lead to adverse selection, which is discussed below), and the plan's ability to control expenses. Of course, if the situation is bad enough, the state insurance commissioner may wind up making the decision unilaterally.

OVERPRICING

The antipode of low-balling, overpricing simply refers to rates that are unacceptably high in the marketplace. This is usually found in mature plans, but occasionally it occurs in new plans that anticipate high costs or that have incurred unusually high preoperational expenses. Overpricing is becoming more rare in the current, highly competitive marketplace because purchasers simply will not overpay when good, less expensive alternatives exist. Nevertheless, overpricing is not extinct, and it remains an identifiable and even predictable problem for health plans.

There are five primary reasons for overpricing:

1. a panic response to previous low-balling
2. excessive overhead
3. failure to control utilization properly
4. adverse selection
5. avarice

The fifth reason, avarice, is obvious and will not be addressed in this chapter except to note that the competitive marketplace may help hold down excessive prices that are based on greed.

A panic response to previous low-balling is not unusual. As losses mount, plan management feels unable to weather the losses and tries to make up the revenue quickly. This is particularly true when a plan is being pressured by investors or regulators or when the plan's financial reserves are projected to be dangerously low. If the low-balling strategy has driven out competition (not a likely event), exorbitant rate hikes may occur simply as a natural course.

Excessive overhead may also lead to overpricing. If plan management is unable to improve efficiency, the price must be paid. Excessive overhead may occur in any plan. It occurs in new starts when required administrative support has been estimated on the basis of enrollment projections that fail to materialize. In mature plans, excessive overhead usually is traced to a combination of internal politics, or turf battles, and management's unwillingness or inability to explore new methods of managing the plan. An additional cause of excessive overhead in a mature plan is the plan developing multiple and creative products and/or reimbursement systems that require significant manual intervention.

Excessive medical expense is the most common reason for overpricing. It is far easier to raise prices than to deal with the causes of overutilization. The usual rationalization goes something like this: "The reason we have the highest rates is that we have the best physicians, and so we have the sickest patients. It's all adverse selection!" In these cases, the plan has often marketed benefits comparable to or better than those of competing HMOs and has assumed utilization rates similar to those of tightly run HMOs (after all, if you call yourself an HMO, you should perform like one, right?) but has imposed fewer controls on physicians and hospitals. Rather than impose restrictions and tighten management, administrators indulge in the common fantasy that they are doing the best they can and it is all the fault of external events.

Bear in mind, however, that excessively high rates do indeed lead to adverse selection. This is especially true in two situations. The first situation is when an account allows more than one health plan to market to employees, in contrast to a total replacement account, where no competing health plans are allowed to market. In a multiple-choice environment, if the plan becomes too expensive for most people, only those facing high medical costs will choose to enroll because the plan's premiums are still less than the coinsurance and deductibles they would face with the competition. A related phenomenon has been a classic problem with indemnity insurance when multiple HMOs are offered: Despite high premium rates in the indemnity plan, individuals with high medical costs and an affinity with a provider not in the managed care plan will enroll at almost any premium cost.

The second common situation is in a free-choice environment, such as is found in a purchasing cooperative or in the public sector market (i.e., Medicare). In this situation, analogous to what was just described above, each individual can choose among several alternatives. A high-priced plan with a large provider panel will remain attractive to sick individuals, and healthy individuals may choose a less expensive plan despite a smaller network because they feel healthy and have bills to pay (and can thus use the savings for other needs). This situation is especially dangerous for provider-sponsored health plans that may easily enroll existing patients but not attract members with few health problems.

UNREALISTIC PROJECTIONS

Any and all categories of revenue and expense are subject to unrealistic projections and expectations, but two stand out: overprojecting enrollment and underprojecting medical expenses.

In new plans, it is common to overestimate enrollment. The reasons are probably a combination of high optimism, inexperience of the marketing director, failure to forecast and reforecast enrollment correctly on an account-specific basis, and an unrealistic start date. Unless the marketing director is a seasoned veteran, the forecast may include accounts considered sold that were only being polite, a factor may be added for new business even when the source and probability of that business are in doubt, or a standard penetration factor may be used that fails to address competitiveness in the account. If the plan does not go operational when anticipated, or if the delivery system is weaker than the anticipated delivery system used to forecast enrollment, significant negative variations in projected growth can occur.

Certainly unanticipated events can blindside even the most experienced marketing director. Competing or invading plans may spark a price war, or a regulator may delay certification for unexpected reasons. For all these reasons, the best marketing projections are conservative ones. Some executive directors feel that enrollment projections should always be high to motivate the director of marketing through his or her bonus. Unfortunately, enrollment projections drive financial projections, so that care must be taken, especially in new plans.

Underprojecting medical expenses, or overestimating the ability to manage utilization, is equally common in new plans. As has been mentioned earlier, naive managers sometimes assume that if they call themselves an HMO or a PPO and put some rudimentary controls in place, they will have the same results as an experienced and successful plan. If the medical director is inexperienced, or if the physicians in the panel are not used to tight medical management, it is unlikely that good utilization results will occur, unless by good luck.

Luck can also be bad. During the early stages of a plan's life, enrollment will be small enough that a few bad cases can have an excessive impact on expenses. A common and critical mistake for new plan managers to make is to project utilization as though there will be few serious cases. When the cases occur, management keeps factoring out the cost of caring for those sick patients and measures utilization on the basis of the remaining members. Clearly, if one factors out sick patients, utilization will always look reasonable. This mistake can be partially offset by purchasing adequate reinsurance, but that comes at a cost.

UNCONTROLLED GROWTH

Rapid growth is usually greeted with applause. In fact, many readers of this book may be saying to themselves "I wish we had such problems," but rapid growth is not always a good thing (dandelions come to mind). Certainly growth is a necessary ingredient to long-term success, but if growth is too rapid it can lead to problems that are long in resolving.

Closely related to the problem of overextended management (see below), the problem of uncontrolled growth is a bit more generalized: Rapid growth not only may quickly outstrip the ability of the plan's managers to keep up but

may outstrip the system's capabilities as well. Dysfunctional patterns can set in, such as referral patterns or utilization behaviors that are more difficult to change after the fact than if they were addressed early on. Because the systems and management capabilities in the plan may now be inadequate, the developing problems will not be picked up until they are serious.

Rapid growth also means rapid expansions in the delivery system. The same attention paid to recruiting and credentialing in the development stages may not be present, and there may be little or no time spent properly orienting new providers to the plan's policies and procedures. That ultimately leads not only to inefficient practice patterns but to frustration on the part of those new providers.

Conversely, rapid growth can lead to saturation of the delivery system before there is adequate recruiting to take up the volume. This becomes especially problematic when practices begin to close more quickly than directory printing can accommodate, and new groups are enrolled with inaccurate directories of providers (or directories are distributed with addendums falling out onto the floor). In many cases, the physician practices will decide to close before they even notify the plan, and new members are signed up for those practices only to be turned away when calling for an appointment.

Service erosion is common when growth has been too rapid. Identification cards are not produced on time (or are produced inaccurately), claims are not paid properly, telephone calls to the plan are not answered in a timely or quality manner, evidence of coverage statements are not sent out on time, inadequate information is given to new members, and so forth. Poor service leads to a vicious cycle of ever-escalating problems resulting in a poor reputation from which it takes a long time to recover.

Rapid growth may also result in insufficient claims reserves. In periods of rapid growth, the usual methods of calculating claims reserves and IBNR become less reliable. This issue is discussed below. Last, rapid growth may lead to inadequate reserves. If reserves were adequate for a small plan, utilization in a plan suddenly grown large may take those reserves down to a dangerously low level. A plan's ability to withstand the cyclic nature of the insurance business, or just a run of bad luck, is tied directly to the amount of reserves available.

One approach to the problem of rapid growth is to limit increases in enrollment through decreased offerings and marketing. This has been done by a few plans in the past and is a viable approach. The risk in this is that your competition may pick up the members, and you will never catch up. For that reason, most plan managers are reluctant to turn off the tap unless it is a critical situation.

It is preferable to have plans for dealing with rapid growth before your back is against the wall. Plan for expansion of the plan's information and computer systems. Groom potential candidates for managerial promotion; you may even consider delegating certain responsibilities before such delegation is required. Some amount of physician recruiting activity should always be occurring, especially in areas without a great deal of capacity, although the rate of actual contracting needs to be coordinated with projected enrollment increases. Careful attention to staffing levels and training lead times in service areas such as claims and member services will help a great deal, although if projected enrollment does not occur, the overhead to the plan can become crushing.

IMPROPER IBNR CALCULATIONS AND ACCRUAL METHODS

As discussed in Chapter 40, the calculation and booking of liabilities in managed care plans are different from those found in most other industries. There have been quite a few health plans where accruals were based on the bills that came in the mail that month or on historical data only. A health plan that is standing risk for medical services must estimate accurately the cost of those services and accrue for them. If the costs are simply booked as they come in, disaster is certain.

The usual culprit here is failure to accrue properly for expenses that are IBNR. With data from lag studies and the plan's information system (i.e., the authorization and encounter data systems) as well as prior experience, sufficient accruals must be made each month for all expenses regardless of whether the bills came in. Calculation of proper accruals and IBNRs becomes especially difficult in plans that are experiencing rapid growth. A new member contributes to revenue on day 1 but generally does not incur medical services until some later date. Also, new members are not familiar with the plan and may not comply with policies and procedures, incurring medical costs that the plan will ultimately have to pay but are not well controlled. If the plan fails to perform good lag studies, the problem can be compounded. For all the reasons discussed earlier, a rapidly growing plan will have a diminished capacity to capture data accurately and will have lessened efficacy of utilization controls. Rapid growth should always lead management to consider boosting IBNRs.

In plans that have failed to accrue properly for expenses, actual expenses may exceed accruals as early as the first 6 months. The malignant feature of this problem is that it can go inexorably on for another 6 months or even more, especially if the plan is experiencing a claims processing problem, as most plans undergoing rapid growth do. Each month's accruals have to be adjusted for expenses related to past months, and financial performance suffers not only for performance to date but for past periods as well. The plan cannot stop the financial hemorrhage quickly because the expenses were already incurred and will keep rolling in. Monthly performance gets muddied up with adjustments for prior performance, and managers find themselves chasing their tails. This problem becomes intensified if the plan is generating inadequate premium revenue either through intentional low-balling or through faulty rate calculations.

This problem has accounted for a disproportionate number of health plan failures. It does not occur as an isolated problem and is usually accompanied by serious claims processing problems and inadequate controls on utilization. Failure to accrue properly is preventable with vigilance and early detection.

FAILURE TO RECONCILE ACCOUNTS RECEIVABLE AND MEMBERSHIP

Typical managed care plans have considerable changes occurring in membership each month. When the plan is standing risk for medical expenses, capitates providers, capitates administration fees, books some accruals based on PMPM historical cost, and so forth, it is vital to have as accurate a reconciliation of membership as possible. Most important, accounts receivable are tied directly to membership and billing.

It is common for plans to have difficulty with this activity. In some accounts (e.g., the federal employee health benefit program), the account is chronically late in providing accurate enrollment information. In other cases, the plan receives information from an account but never properly reconciles it every month because it is such a labor-intensive process. In any case, if the plan pays medical expenses for members who are no longer eligible or fails to collect premiums for members who are newly enrolled, losses are sure to follow. Even more devastating is the need to make a huge downward adjustment on the balance sheet to write off an uncollectible receivable.

OVEREXTENDED MANAGEMENT

What may have been appropriate or even generous staffing at the start-up stage can become understaffing after significant growth, especially if that growth has been rapid. The problem is more complex than the number of management bodies available; it is really one of span of control and experience of managers.

It is not uncommon in any industry for management requirements to change over time. Frequently, the methods used by the pioneers become dysfunctional as plans reach significant size. Tight control concentrated in a few managers, overreliance on central decision making, heavy hands-on involvement by senior managers, and so forth all can lead to paralysis and calcification as a plan becomes large and complex. The few managers with the control are unable to keep up with all the necessary details and demands of running operations, and failure to delegate properly prevents the plan from recruiting and retaining talented second level managers.

As a plan grows, its ability to change and adapt to the competitive environment becomes diminished. All the details necessary for proper operations become overwhelming. If senior managers are personally responsible for all these details, they may be unable to keep up, and things will get missed. Change becomes even less likely when overloaded managers cannot handle the prospect of having to learn yet another set of management skills while still having to use the old ones. This becomes demoralizing to subordinates and providers when plan management is seen as unresponsive, inattentive, or both.

A full discussion of appropriate delegation of authority and responsibility is beyond the scope of this chapter. Here it is sufficient to point out the dangers inherent in failing to create proper tiers of management as a plan grows. This is not to imply that senior managers should insulate themselves from the operations of the plan, overdelegate, or drive up administrative costs for no good reason. Rather, it is to emphasize that health plans are complex organizations, and nobody can do it all.

FAILURE TO USE UNDERWRITING

As this book is being written, the topic of small group market reform is being actively debated both at the federal level and in many states. Such reforms would sharply limit the degree to which a plan may medically underwrite accounts (i.e., choose whether to offer coverage and under what terms). That is, plans would not be able to turn down any valid group for coverage because of medical conditions, although the plan may be able to use such information in premium rate development. Such market reform is currently sporadic but is likely to become more widespread.

Even in the face of market reform, underwriting has a place, and in the desire to grow proper underwriting guidelines may be neglected. This is most likely to occur in a new plan that is trying to grow, but it can occur in any plan where marketing representatives and managers are inadequately supervised at the same time that they are being pressured to produce growth. Proper information must be obtained and acted upon both to determine what product to offer (or even whether the group qualifies for coverage under any circumstances) and to determine proper premium rates.

The plan's approach to rate setting must also occur in the context of the market, or problems in adverse selection are bound to occur. If a plan uses standard book rates or basic community rating (see Chapters 43 and 44) but the competition uses more advanced rating methodologies, then it is likely that the risk selection will be skewed. Conversely, if advanced approaches to rating are used simply to lower the price, then the plan will not obtain the required premium revenue in the budget.

FAILURE TO UNDERSTAND SALES AND MARKETING

When the plan is offered in an account with multiple other carriers or plans competing to enroll employees, then marketing managed care is essentially retail selling. It is much harder to assess the actuarial risk accurately in a multiple choice environment because it is possible to enroll only those members who have high medical needs, or vice versa. In other words, the possibility of adverse selection occurring within a group is very real. This is a particular problem in a highly competitive market, where the pressure on the marketing department is high. If the sales representative is on a pure commission basis, the pressure may be overwhelming. If emphasis is placed on the ease of access to high-cost specialists and hospitals, and if any restrictions to that

access are downplayed, it can lead to adverse selection within an otherwise normal risk group.

This issue is especially important to provider-sponsored health plans. Provider-sponsored plans often look at members as patients and fail to understand that a health plan needs more members than patients. There will always be a pool of relatively young and healthy people who will choose price over provider selection because they have pressures on their lives greater than health-related issues (e.g., they feel healthy and need to pay their mortgage). A provider-sponsored health plan that markets primarily to the patients of the providers will never enroll enough new members who are not patients of anybody and thus will have adverse selection.

FAILURE OF MANAGEMENT TO UNDERSTAND REPORTS

Difficult as it may be to believe, managers may not always understand how reports are developed and written. A report may be labeled as one thing, but the data that are put into the report are really something else. For example, there may be a report that gives the rate of disenrollment from the plan. Depending on how the management information services (MIS) department inputs the data or how the computer was programmed, the disenrollment rate may include any member who changes status (e.g., goes from single to family) or coverage (e.g., changes jobs but continues with the plan under the new group). If that is the case, the disenrollment rate will be spuriously high. Failure to understand the meaning behind the disenrollment rate can lead to inaccurate forecasting and budgeting. Failure to understand the data elements in medical management and utilization reports is obviously far more serious.

To prevent this, senior management should be involved in developing the formats of reports and deciding what data will be used. The decisions about how to collect data and how to input them should not be made solely by the MIS department. In the event that the plan has experienced changeover in managers, it is important for the new manager not to assume anything and to ask explicitly what data go into each report. This last may seem embarrassing to a manager, but that type of compulsive behavior could prevent a serious mistake in the future.

FAILURE TO TRACK MEDICAL COSTS AND UTILIZATION CORRECTLY

This is a special subset of the problem just discussed, that of failure of management to understand reports. The problem of tracking medical expenses and utilization is so important that it merits discussion by itself.

As growing plans develop problems with operations (the authorization system, claims, or data gathering in general), medical expense and utilization reports frequently suffer. If the plan is accruing for IBNRs based on historical data because current data are inaccurate, expenses may be allocated to categories primarily because that is where the expenses have been found before. For example, if a plan historically has had high costs in orthopedics, and if the data system is unable reliably to provide current utilization data, finance may accrue expenses to orthopedics even if the medical director has been able to reduce costs in that area. It may take 6 months for the data to come through the system that show a reduction in orthopedics expenses, but by that time the medical director has resigned in frustration.

Another example would be a plan that has an authorization system for referrals but that system allows for subauthorizations, automatic authorization of return visits, and self-referral. Because of the loose nature of the system, the finance department cannot rely on it when calculating accruals. If there is a concomitant problem with claims processing, then there will be no timely and accurate data about utilization. In that case, finance will calculate accruals by using lag studies and best guess numbers and will assign the expenses where they fell as the claims were processed. In this way, high expenses may really be reflective of a combination of two things: what was happening in utilization some time

back, and what types of claims were processed that month.

If the calculation of these numbers is sufficiently removed from senior management, and if the medical director does not know how the numbers are derived, tremendous efforts may be expended in dealing with problems that are neither timely nor high priority. As mentioned in Chapter 25, a plan's ability to implement continuous quality improvement in its business operations will be hampered if efforts are wasted trying to solve problems that are not indicative of the true problems facing management.

Closely related is the problem of not properly tracking utilization. For example, if a plan has an authorization system for referrals that tracks initial referrals from the primary care physician but fails to track subauthorizations, self-referrals, and repeat visits adequately, the referral rate may be grossly inaccurate. Another example would be a plan that is able to report high rates of utilization but is unable to provide the details about who is responsible.

In a perverse twist, in those cases where data are presented in an inaccurate or inadequate form but the medical director understands why that is so, a false sense of complacency can develop. For example, if a hospital utilization report consistently and inaccurately reports high utilization for a certain physician (perhaps because that physician represents a three-physician group), the medical director may continually make adjustments when reviewing the report and fail to recognize a genuine increase in utilization.

SYSTEMS INABILITY TO MANAGE THE BUSINESS

As a health plan grows in the marketplace, it must continue to evolve to meet ever-changing needs. When the plan does so, it is not uncommon that the MIS is unable to change at the same pace without a prohibitively high cost in programming and time. Manual workarounds are put into place, custom programming is undertaken, and soon MIS is a cat's cradle of code and administrative costs have escalated. Multiple systems are used to manage different parts of the business, and they do not tie or even match up. This problem is quickly compounded when innovative managers invent new ways of doing business (e.g., invent a new reimbursement system) that appears to make sense but cannot be supported by MIS. Eventually the plan ends up migrating to an entirely new system, with the attendant headaches that accompany any conversion.

Unfortunately, the most obvious way to prevent this problem is also the least useful: Never change anything. A health plan that fails to change and innovate soon becomes stale in the market and begins losing to the competition. Therefore, what is most important is for information systems managers to be involved in management policies and procedures so that alternative approaches are explored and the entire team understands the systems implications of policy changes. Even more important, the information systems managers need to be able to engage in strategic planning to stay in front of the demands of the industry. As discussed in Chapter 28, MIS must be flexible and designed such that change is accommodated at an acceptable cost.

FAILURE TO EDUCATE AND REEDUCATE PROVIDERS

An all too common sin of omission is the failure to educate providers properly. As discussed in Chapters 7 and 8, proper orientation of new providers and office staff is an important success factor. All too often, the providers are simply given a procedure manual and a metaphorical kiss on the cheek. Even in those situations where proper orientation has taken place, it is unlikely that the information will stick unless there are already a large number of patients coming in through the plan. This is even more of a problem when there are a number of competing health plans, each with its own unique way of doing things.

Just as important as the initial orientation is a program of continuing education in the proce-

dures and policies of the plan. Regular maintenance of the knowledge base of the providers and their office staff will help prevent problems caused solely by lack of communication.

Examples of this problem abound in most open panels. Physicians may fail to use the authorization system properly, may provide or promise benefits that the plan does not cover, may allow open-ended authorizations to specialists, and so forth. Although none of these occurrences is dangerous in itself, all can be additive. In a large plan, failure to communicate properly with providers can lead rapidly to a loss of control. Far more energy is spent trying to repair damage than would have been spent in maintenance.

FAILURE TO DEAL WITH DIFFICULT OR NONCOMPLIANT PROVIDERS

Perhaps the most difficult of all the tasks of a medical director is dealing with difficult and noncompliant physicians. The same task applies to nonphysician providers, but that is generally easier for most medical directors. Because dealing with difficult physicians is so onerous to physician managers, they tend to avoid it or at least procrastinate. Assuming that the plan is reasonably well run and not subject to a justified physician mutiny, difficult physicians, like difficult patients, make up only a tiny minority of the total panel but consume an inordinate amount of managerial energy. Failure to deal with such physicians has both direct and indirect ramifications.

The direct result of failing to deal with an uncooperative physician is the expense associated with that physician's utilization of resources. This problem is obvious, although easy to rationalize away ("Well, maybe they have sicker patients"). If the physician's utilization behavior really is a problem, it may be worthwhile to calculate in whole dollars the cost of that overutilization.

The indirect results are less obvious. The most important is the effect on members. If the physician has a truly bad attitude, that will be transmitted to members. For example, the physician may tell members that they need services but the plan will not allow it. A little bit of this "blame the bogeyman" behavior can be tolerated and understood, but if it becomes chronic, the plan can find itself fighting off unwarranted attacks by members and employee benefits managers. Other indirect effects include promoting a poor attitude among the other physicians and lowering the morale of the plan staff who have to deal with that particular physician.

The most frequent objection to dealing with difficult physicians is that the plan needs them because they are so prestigious or popular. In many cases, that physician also has a large number of members, and there are fears that if the physician leaves or is kicked out, the plan will lose membership. It is up to plan management to determine whether the plan is worse off with or without the physician. Do not let numbers of members alone make that determination (remember, if you are losing on each member, you cannot make it up on volume). Regarding the issue of prestige, it is far worse to have that physician bad mouthing your plan directly to the members than it is to have him or her deriding you in the hospital lounge (where he or she is probably doing it anyway). You may also find that the members stick with the plan and agree to change physicians.

If education and personal appeals fail to effect the needed change, you must take action. Failure to take action is the mark of weak and ineffectual management.

CONCLUSION

This chapter presents some of the common problems that can occur in managed care plans. There are few plans in existence today that have not experienced at least a few of these difficulties at some point. The list is not exhaustive, and there are certainly many other difficulties that a plan can experience. The important point is to recognize that managed care plans do indeed develop predictable problems and must be ever vigilant for their emergence.

SUGGESTED READING

Christianson, J.B., et al. 1991. State Responses to HMO Failures. *Health Affairs* 10: 78–92.

Coyne, J.S. 1993. Assessing the Financial Performance of Health Maintenance Organizations: Tools and Techniques. *Managed Care Quarterly* 1: 63–74.

Health Care Financing Administration. 1995. *Best Practices of Managed Care Organizations*. Baltimore, Md.: HCFA.

Meigham, S.S. 1994. Managing Conflict in an Integrated System. *Topics in Health Care Financing* 20 (4): 39–47.

Part V

Finance and Underwriting

"Being good in business is the most fascinating kind of art. . . . Making money
is art and working is art and good business is the best art."

Andy Warhol
(1928–1987)
From A to B and Back Again, ch. 6, 1975

Chapter 40

Operational Finance and Budgeting

Dale F. Harding

The challenge to manage successfully a managed care organization (MCO) lies in the financial manager's ability to produce timely, accurate financial reports. The interaction between operational managers and financial managers is key to achieving this goal. Overall financial management of an MCO begins with the MCO's product pricing strategies. Strategic pricing is based on an assessment of the competition, targeted profitability, the MCO's estimate of costs incurred for the provision of health care, and its ability to control costs, in particular, medical costs. Detailed operating budgets are then developed under the same assumptions used in the pricing strategy. Financial managers rely significantly upon information captured and monitored by operational departments to develop the detailed budgets.

Information provided by operational departments is also used as the basis for certain accounting estimates recorded in financial statements. The financial manager's ability to report on actual results, analyze budget variances, and assess the reasonableness of pricing strategies in a timely manner is dependent upon the support of operating functions.

In this chapter, through a review of the components of the financial statements of a health

Dale F. Harding is a senior manager in the East/Great Lakes Healthcare Practice of Ernst & Young LLP. Dale has been with the firm for over eleven years, focusing on the insurance and health care fields. She spends most of her time working on financial audits and financial management projects for managed care organizations.

maintenance organization (HMO), key information and operational procedures that the financial manager will need and rely upon are discussed. The discussion addresses typical problems that occur in gathering information and provides insight into challenging the integrity of information.

BACKGROUND

Accounting policy for MCOs is set by many regulatory entities. MCOs are primarily regulated at the state level, although certain federal regulations may be imposed if an MCO offers federally regulated products such as Medicare risk contracts. State regulation may be imposed by both the Department of Insurance and the Department of Health. Additionally, there are many publicly held MCOs that are subject to the rules and regulations of the Securities and Exchange Commission (SEC).

The state's Department of Insurance is generally concerned with the fiscal solvency of the MCO to ensure that the health benefits of enrollees will be provided. The state's Department of Health is generally concerned with quality of care issues as well as access to care issues, including the location of providers within specific geographic boundaries and the mix of primary care physicians and specialists to serve the population within these boundaries.

Financial management of MCOs must consider the interests of each of the users of financial information, whether they be senior management, insurance regulators, the SEC, tax authorities, or investors. Balancing the concerns of each interested party represents a challenge for the financial manager. Senior management is concerned with the profitability of products and market segment performance. Management will require internal reporting that focuses on line of business management and also meets regulatory reporting requirements. Regulators are concerned with protecting the insured members and focus on liquidity of the MCO. The SEC is concerned with the protection of investor interests. Balancing conservatism and positive performance with the best return on investment is a difficult task.

The requirements imposed by the state's Department of Insurance and Department of Health can be found in the state laws and regulations. The National Association of Insurance Commissioners (NAIC) is an organization comprising the state commissioners of insurance, who set guidelines at a national level. The NAIC has no governing authority over the individual states, however. Generally, states will introduce legislation modeling NAIC guidelines. The NAIC has adopted an annual statement report format that has been adopted by most states. The financial information is prepared in accordance with statutory accounting practices (SAP). Other financial statement users (lenders, the SEC, and investors) require that financial statements be prepared in accordance with generally accepted accounting principles (GAAP). The American Institute of Certified Public Accountants (AICPA) issued an audit and accounting guide for health care providers that provides additional guidance on audit, accounting, and reporting matters for prepaid health plans.

The financial manager should also be aware of the continuous changes taking place in the regulatory arena. For many states, managed care market penetration has historically been minimal, and legislation has not kept pace with recent growth in managed care. Many varieties of MCOs or managed care strategies are emerging, such as physician–hospital organizations (PHOs), integrated delivery systems, management services organizations, direct contracting

arrangements among employers and providers, and so forth (see Chapters 3 and 4), and regulators acknowledge that there is little or no legislation governing these emerging areas (see Chapters 53 and 56). For example, many regulators have imposed policy (absent legislative authority) to exercise financial restrictions on PHOs or other provider organizations that contract directly with self-insured plans. Other developments include the NAIC's committee to develop risk-based capital requirements for health insurers, including HMOs, which will impose stricter minimum capital requirements. An exposure draft was issued by the AICPA updating the audit and accounting guide for health care providers and is slated for an effective date in late 1996. In 1994, expanded financial disclosure requirements regarding changes in claims reserves were imposed on health insurers. Although these new requirements are not yet required for MCOs, they may be required in the future.

FINANCIAL STATEMENT COMPONENTS

Operating Statement

A typical profit and loss statement for an HMO is depicted in Exhibit 40–1. For internal management reporting purposes, the ability to develop profit and loss reports by product line/market segment is critical to the financial management process. Assumptions and financial benchmarks may vary widely by product or market segment. For example, medical cost estimates are based on utilization patterns and provider reimbursement strategies that will differ by product and market segment. Likewise, administration of lines of business may be different. For example, the costs associated with supporting a Medicare or Medicaid product will differ from those associated with the commercial population because the customers have unique service needs and because dedicated staff with specific skill sets will be needed to service Medicare and Medicaid enrollees. Pricing is based on the medical cost and administrative

Exhibit 40–1 Sample Profit and Loss Statement for an MCO—Percentage of Total Revenue

Revenue
Premiums earned: 90
Other income: 5
  Total revenue: 100

Expenses
Health care expenses: 84
General and administrative expenses: 11
  Total expenses: 95

Income or loss before income taxes: 5

Exhibit 40–2 Allocation of Operating Revenue Dollar (Median Results as of December 1993)

Health care expenditures:	79% (HMOs with fewer than 50,000 enrollees);
	84% (HMOs with 50,000 enrollees or more)
Administrative expenses:	11%
Profit margin:	3–5%

Source: Courtesy of Hoescht Marion Roussel, 1994, Cincinnati, Ohio.

cost components; therefore, premium pricing by product will vary consistent with the variations in these cost components. In the following discussion of the components of the financial statement, keep in mind the importance of segregating the reporting by product line or market segment. Analyzing financial results by line of business not only will enhance management's ability to understand the fluctuations from budgeted results but will provide information needed to redirect strategies to preserve the overall success of the operation.

Premium Revenue

Premium revenue is the primary revenue source for HMOs. Premiums are generally received in advance of the coverage period, which is usually monthly. Premium rates are generally effective for a 12-month period. Rates or rating methodologies are usually filed with and must be approved by the state's Department of Insurance. MCOs may file revisions to the rates or methodology, which will also be subject to approval by the Department of Insurance. New rates will not be effective for existing groups until the renewal of the annual contract.

Premiums are actuarially determined, as discussed in Chapter 43. Premiums are intended to cover all medical and administrative expenses as well as to provide a profit margin (Exhibit 40–2). Premium rates are therefore directly related to medical expense and administrative ex-

pense projections. If the premium rates are not adequate to cover the actual medical expenses and administrative costs, expected profit margins will diminish. If losses for a line of business are anticipated, a premium deficiency exists. Under GAAP accounting, because premium rates are fixed until the end of the coverage period, the aggregate anticipated net loss for the line of business may need to be recorded immediately, not ratably over the remaining coverage period.

Certain premium rates may not be controlled by the MCO, such as those for Medicare risk contracts or Medicaid. These rates are set by the government. For example, Medicare premium rates are based upon the adjusted average per capita cost (AAPCC) rates set by the federal government. The sufficiency of these rates therefore is dependent, in part, on the federal government's ability to capture and analyze data when determining the AAPCC rates and also on the ultimate product benefit design and the ability of the MCO to manage benefits and expenses to the rates. It is then the responsibility of the MCO to be able to perform medical management and administrative expense management so that the premium is sufficient to cover costs and yield a profit (see Chapter 46).

Rating methodologies derive rates based on an evaluation of demographic data (e.g., the age and sex mix or geographic location) of the population to insure. Rates may be determined using a community rating methodology or an experience rating methodology. Community rating is often used for small groups (less than 50 subscribers) or individuals, and experience rating is used for large groups. In many states community rating is mandatory for small groups and individuals. States may also mandate community rating for all groups regardless of size.

Basic community rating entails the application of a standard rate to all groups within the community being underwritten. The standard rate is applied to groups on the basis of the number of rate tiers quoted, the average family size, and the contract mix assumed for the group. Rate tiers are developed based on the age and sex of members as well as the classification of single versus family. Community rating by class considers an adjustment to the basic rate for specific demographics and/or industry classification of the group. Adjusted community rating allows for adjustments to the base rate for group-specific information other than demographics and industry classification.

The experience rating methodology develops a group rate based on a group's actual experience. After determining actual past experience, expenses are trended forward. Experience-rated contracts can be retrospectively rated or prospectively rated. Retrospective rate adjustments allow for an adjustment to the current period premium based on actual experience. The premium adjustment should be accrued in the current financial statement period and may need to be estimated if the settlement date is subsequent to the end of the accounting period. Prospectively rated premiums provide for increases in rates in the next contract period based on the actual experience of the previous period. When premium adjustments are prospectively rated, there are no accounting entries required in the current reporting period. Rating and underwriting are discussed in greater detail in Chapters 43 and 44.

Revenues are recorded in the financial statements as a function of the underlying billing process. The effectiveness of the billing process is further dependent upon the membership or enrollment process. Membership data must be gathered in sufficient detail from the enrollment forms to allow for the proper classification of the enrollee to ensure that the appropriate rates are charged. Timely updating of enrollment records for changes in membership status not only ensures the accuracy of rates charged but also ensures that medical services are only provided to active enrollees. Furthermore, compliance with billing and enrollment procedures may affect whether the MCO will incur costs for health care services provided to inactive enrollees. Subscribers, providers, and the MCO each have contractual obligations related to updating and verification of the enrollee's status. Failure to meet contractual obligations to maintain enrollment records properly and accurately could result in additional costs to the MCO. Therefore, the financial manager should have the information needed to ensure that revenue is being billed for all active enrollees and that business processes are functioning in a manner to prevent loss due to noncompliance with contract terms.

Premium billing may occur under two methods: self-billing or retroactive billing. The self-billing method permits the subscriber (or the group) to adjust the invoice for changes in enrollment. In this situation, the amount billed and recorded as premium revenue receivable will differ from the actual amounts paid by the group. Differences in the amount billed and received require adjustment to revenue and accounts receivable records. A secondary process should include communication of changes to ensure timely updating of enrollment records and notification of enrollment changes to providers. If processes are not in place to ensure that such differences are reconciled and resolved on a timely basis, revenue and accounts receivable may not be recorded properly in the financial statements, and health care benefits may be provided to individuals who are no longer insured.

The retroactive billing method results in adjustments to be recorded in the next month's billing cycle. Under this method, payments made by the group should equal amounts billed. Any changes in enrollment will be adjusted on the next billing. Any changes in enrollment noted should also be forwarded to the appropriate department to ensure updating of enrollment records.

For either billing method, the financial manager must develop a methodology of estimating adjustments affecting the current accounting period. Because the actual adjustments are not known until payment is received or reported in the next billing cycle, an estimate of expected adjustments should be accrued in the current reporting cycle.

Certain large commercial or government clients remit payment without detailed hard copy explanation of the adjustment. These customers often request electronic data transfer for billing purposes. Financial managers should be aware that significant resources may be needed to service these customers. Information systems personnel will be needed to deal with technical aspects of the electronic data transfer process. Support personnel with specific training will be needed to handle the unique challenges associated with large accounts. The process of reconciling the MCO's records with the customer's records can be time consuming but is absolutely necessary. The financial manager should monitor the status (timeliness and completeness) of the reconciliations of these accounts to ensure that any potential problems with the reconciliations do not also affect other financial statement components, such as medical expense accruals.

Other Revenue Sources

Because many HMOs offer preferred provider organization (PPO) products, a growing revenue source is fee revenue derived from PPO members. Subscribers selecting a PPO product generally pay an access fee for use of the provider network established by the MCO. For example, PPO product fees are generally based on a specified per member per month charge. Fees for PPO products vary depending upon the level of service. There is a base fee for accessing the provider network, but enhanced services such as utilization management or providing a gatekeeper mechanism to manage utilization would

increase the PPO access fee charged. Pricing of access fees should consider costs of performing administrative functions related to maintaining the provider network, such as credentialing, contract negotiations, and monitoring physician practice patterns.

Coordination of benefits (COB) recoverable is another source of revenue for the HMO. MCOs must have sufficient procedures in place to identify recoveries of costs under COB. COB usually exists when there is a two-wage earner family and individuals will have insurance coverage under two policies with a different insurer or health plan. Policies and procedures are established by insurance organizations to determine which insurer or health plan will serve as the primary or secondary payer. Procedures need to be in place to ensure that costs that are the responsibility of the other carrier are recovered. The data necessary to perform this procedure are usually gathered during the enrollment and billing process. Again, accuracy and completeness during the enrollment process are key to securing the data necessary to determine the amounts recoverable.

There are two primary methods of recovering COB: pay and pursue, and pursue and pay. Under the pay and pursue method, claims are paid, and COB recovery is sought later from the other carrier. Under pursue and pay, the claim net of any COB is paid. To ensure that medical expenses are not recorded net, it is important that gross claim costs and COB recoverable are identifiable by the financial manager. See Chapter 32 for a detailed discussion of this issue.

Reinsurance recoverable is another source of income to the MCO. Reinsurance against catastrophic claims or claims in excess of specified dollar limits is often obtained to reduce the risk of individual large losses for the MCO. MCOs may forego obtaining reinsurance based on the cost versus benefit of the coverage. The financial manager needs to perform a risk assessment to determine whether stop-loss insurance is appropriate. Procedures need to exist to ensure that costs recoverable under reinsurance are identifiable, so that the MCO receives the full benefit to which it is entitled under the reinsurance arrangement. Reinsurance premiums should be recorded as health care costs, and reinsurance recoverable should be shown net of health care costs.

Another source of income for HMOs is interest income. Excess cash is generally invested in short-term instruments to ensure cash availability for the payment of claims.

Medical Expenses

Table 40–1 summarizes the breakdown of medical costs among hospital, physician, and ancillary services. Medical expenses may be incurred on a capitated basis, fee schedule, or per diem arrangement. Another form of reimbursement that is similar to capitation is percentage of premium. Capitation and percentage of premium represent risk transfer arrangements. Risk transfer arrangements place the providers at risk if utilization exceeds expected results. Reimbursement strategies are discussed in more detail in Chapters 9, 12, and 14.

Medical expenses reported in the financial statements should represent paid claims plus accruals for claims reported but unpaid and claims incurred but not reported (IBNR). The development of the accruals for both reported and unreported claims is an accounting estimate whereby the accuracy of the estimate is dependent upon the data captured by operations personnel and communicated to the financial managers. For reported claims, the incidence of claims is known (e.g., estimated length of stay for inpatient service, number of referred visits for outpatient services, etc.), and the type of claim is known (e.g., inpatient procedure codes, type of outpatient service, etc.). The costs related to the claim incident must be estimated. For reported claims there is less unknown, and there can be more accuracy when ultimate costs are projected, although the ultimate disposition of the claims must still be estimated.

For IBNR claims, both the incidence of claims and the type of claims are unknown and must be estimated. IBNR estimates are often developed with the assistance of actuaries. A preferred methodology for estimating IBNR is the development of loss triangles (Table 40–2). These triangles graphically depict the lag between either the date of service and the payment date or the date of service and the date the claim is reported. From the lag analysis, completion factors are developed to estimate the remaining claims to be reported or paid at each duration. Claim severity, or the estimated average claim costs, is then used to calculate the total projected costs yet to be incurred. The total projected costs are the basis for accruals to be recorded in the financial statements for the IBNR claims.

Loss triangles are often developed separately for hospital and physician claims. Physician claims can also be further analyzed by type of specialty claim where appropriate. Also the IBNR claims analysis should be segregated by line of business. Although greater level of details can assist in a more refined estimate, caution should be used when one is developing estimates from small population sizes. The smaller the base population, the less precise the estimates. It is prudent to limit the level of detail used in the analysis.

As discussed above, the adequacy of the estimates for reported claims developed by financial

---

Table 40–1 Typical Health Plan Medical Costs

Category	Percentage of Expenses
Hospital	
Inpatient:	28
Outpatient:	11
Total hospital:	39
Physician services	
Primary care:	12
Specialty care:	20
Total physician services:	32
Other medical services:	5
Ancillary services:	15
Prescription drugs:	9
Total health care expenditures:	100

Source: Data from Milliman & Robertson *Health Cost Guidelines* 1993.

Table 40–2 Loss Triangles

Inpatient Services
Claims Paid by Month of Receipt

Service Month	Jan	Feb	Mar	Apr	May	Jun	Jul	Aug	Sep	Oct	Nov	Dec
Jan	10	100	150	50	35	2	1		1		4	1
Feb		7	126	164	44	22	1	1		6		
Mar			24	89	201	33	46	53			5	1
Apr				12	109	177	3	25	2	2	1	
May					1	188	156	45	59	3	4	2
Jun						3	255	189	67	55	4	1
July							9	163	198	84	54	8
Aug								33	127	199	87	62
Sep									27	244	149	88
Oct										17	155	205
Nov											5	104
Dec												12
Total	10	107	300	315	390	425	471	509	481	610	468	484

Inpatient Services
Completion Factors by Month of Receipt

Service Month	Cur	+1	+2	+3	+4	+5	+6	+7	+8	+9	+10	+11	Total
Jan	0.03	0.31	0.73	0.88	0.97	0.98	0.98	0.98	0.99	0.99	1.00	1.00	
Feb	0.02	0.36	0.80	0.92	0.98	0.98	0.98	0.98	1.00	1.00	1.00		
Mar	0.05	0.25	0.69	0.77	0.87	0.99	0.99	0.99	1.00	1.00			
Apr	0.04	0.37	0.90	0.91	0.98	0.99	1.00	1.00	1.00				
May	0.00	0.41	0.75	0.85	0.98	0.99	1.00	1.00					
Jun	0.01	0.45	0.78	0.90	0.99	1.00	1.00						
Jul	0.02	0.33	0.72	0.88	0.98	1.00							
Aug	0.06	0.31	0.71	0.88	1.00								
Sep	0.05	0.53	0.83	1.00									
Oct	0.05	0.46	1.00										
Nov	0.05	1.00											
Dec	1.00												
Jan–Jun	0.02	0.36	0.78	0.87	0.96	0.99	0.99	0.99	1.00	1.00	1.00	1.00	

managers is dependent upon the availability of data from the operating areas within the MCO. These data are usually developed from the utilization management program. Inpatient care, excluding nonemergency care, typically requires preauthorization; therefore, if the utilization managers are keeping accurate records of admissions and length of stay statistics, the data needed by the financial managers to estimate admissions and cost of services should be readily available. For outpatient services and specialist services, referrals are usually required for more services. Again, if the utilization management program is properly monitoring outpatient and specialist utilization and is maintaining accurate records of referrals, the data needed to estimate outpatient and specialist visits should be readily available to the financial manager. To be usable, the authorization information must be carefully controlled so that authorizations unlikely to be used are eliminated before ultimate utilization is estimated. It is extremely important that the utilization managers understand the significance of their responsibilities in that utilization managers not only are vital to controlling overall utilization but also provide necessary information to predict medical costs accurately, prepare reports on financial results, and develop budgets and financial forecasts. See Chapter 29 for a detailed discussion of authorization systems and types of authorizations.

Because the tools used by the financial managers to estimate medical costs also rely heavily on the accuracy of paid claims data, the claims processing department also plays an important role in financial management. The accuracy of claims data and the timely processing of claims will affect the reliability of the data used to develop the loss triangles. The extent of any backlogs in claim processing must be communicated in timely fashion to the financial manager. See Chapter 31 for a detailed discussion of claims.

Loss triangles represent the most frequently used method to estimate claim costs. Other analyses can also be performed to substantiate further the reasonableness of the estimates for IBNR claims. Analyzing the monthly trends in claims costs or loss ratios by service type (inpatient, outpatient, physician services by specialty, etc.) within product lines and on a per member per month basis provides a basis for determining whether the overall trends in claim costs are consistent with expected results and, where appropriate, industry benchmarks. Factors that may affect the trends include:

- significant changes in enrollment
- unusual or large claims (isolated occurrences versus changes in utilization/cost patterns)
- changes in pricing or product design

- seasonal utilization or reporting patterns
- claim processing backlogs
- major changes to the provider network or reimbursement methods

Each of these factors provides a basis for explaining fluctuations when one is preparing trend analyses. It is important to note, however, that significant changes in enrollment also affect the financial manager's ability to determine reasonable estimates used in financial statements. For example, during periods of enrollment growth, it is difficult to estimate medical cost trends because there is little history associated with the current enrollment base and revenue begins on the first day of enrollment but medical costs generally do not; this may lull an inexperienced financial manager into believing that the medical costs ratio is low. In times of significant disenrollment, there is a risk of adverse selection. Adverse selection exists when the characteristics of the remaining population of insureds are weighted toward a high-risk group. Significant disenrollment often occurs when it is generally not an optimal condition for the enrollee to maintain the current coverage. Usually, those insureds with less choice (e.g., those who are unable to opt for other coverage because of current health status) remain enrolled. Medical cost estimates must be adjusted under these circumstances.

Administrative Expenses

Administrative expenses include salaries as well as sales, marketing, and other operating expenses. Administrative expenses also vary by product and market segment. Administrative expenses can be measured using percentage of premium and per member per month benchmarks. Administrative expenses may also be tracked by functional area (e.g., finance, sales, underwriting, member services, etc.). Administrative expenses will vary with volume as a result of economies of scale. In growth periods, administrative expenses tend to be high as a percentage of premium.

Tracking of administrative expenses by product and market segment allows management to identify whether the appropriate resources are being allocated to product lines. Additionally, if the HMO experience rates certain groups, management needs to track adequately costs associated with a particular group's business to ensure that costs are appropriately allocated to the group and are recovered. The financial manager should also be aware that certain products or market segments, such as government groups and Medicare or Medicaid, place limits on administrative expense allocations to these product lines.

Balance Sheet

Cash and Investments

Cash and investments represent a significant balance sheet account for an HMO. The major source of cash is premium revenue. An HMO's investment portfolio usually consists of short-term investments because cash outlays for claims are frequent. As a result, the financial manager is not significantly affected by investment strategies, and typically there is limited investment risk associated with an HMO's investment portfolio. Because cash does churn quickly through the HMO, management may benefit from implementing strong cash management practices, such as using lock-box arrangements for premiums.

Premium Receivable

Another significant balance sheet account is premium receivable. Premiums are generally collected monthly; therefore, problems with the aging of accounts will probably arise from many old items that are not reconciled often. Unreconciled differences may occur when billing problems exist or as a result of discrepancies in the enrollment records of the MCO in comparison with customer records.

Timely update of membership records ensures the accuracy of premium billings and further ensures that claims are paid appropriately. Policies and procedures to ensure timely updating of membership records protect the MCO from paying claims for terminated members or ensures the recoverability of amounts paid incorrectly. In general, if membership records are not up to date and the MCO bills incorrectly for terminated or inactive members, upon remittance a group will adjust the payment accordingly. If the MCO does not have procedures in place to reconcile remittances to billed amounts, premium receivable records will show amounts outstanding and past due. Because of the large number of individual members within a group and the potentially large number of billings, management must monitor closely the status of premium reconciliation procedures.

The reconciliation process related to premium receivable for government accounts is usually a more complex problem. For example, federal and state employers often remit premium on a cycle that differs from the normal billing cycle of the MCO. The remittances by these institutions are consistent with the institution's payroll cycles. Premium is remitted only for those employees noted as active on the payroll. There are many events that affect the active status of federal and state employees (e.g., leave of absence, summer recess for educators, etc.), but these employees may still be eligible for health benefits. For this reason, the MCO will bill and accrue for premium that will not be paid until the employee's status on the institution's records is reinstated to active status. Often, MCOs that provide coverage to federal and state groups will have dedicated resources to support the reconciliation process.

The reconciliation process for certain large groups may also be complex. The high enrollment volume or the need to accept enrollment data in compatible electronic format may present a challenge for the MCO.

Other Assets

The significance of other assets of an MCO will vary. Another typical large asset may be fixed assets, particularly if the HMO is organized as a staff model HMO and owns and operates physician offices.

Unearned Premiums

Unearned premiums are premiums received by the MCO that at the close of the financial reporting period have not been earned, principally because the premiums are for the ensuing month and are in actuality premiums received in advance. Because most MCOs bill on a monthly basis, unearned premium is generally not a major accounting issue. If premiums are billed and collected other than monthly (e.g., quarterly), an unearned premium reserve would be required.

Claims Payable and IBNR

As discussed earlier, the basis for the recording of claim reserves, including IBNR, is dependent upon information provided by other operating areas of the MCO. Claim liabilities are separated between hospital claims and physician claims. In addition to the matters discussed for medical expenses, the financial manager should prepare further analyses of claim reserves and IBNR estimates.

The financial manager should compare the actual claim payments since the close of the accounting period with the original estimates. Significant differences in the actual results compared with estimated results should be investigated. Information obtained from the investigation should be considered when the sufficiency of current estimates is evaluated.

Risk Pool Liabilities

As discussed in Chapter 9, reimbursement strategies may provide for risk pools, which will require the MCO to maintain accurate records of payment withholds from hospitals and physicians. Amounts payable to the providers from the withhold should be maintained in separate accounts. In addition, shortfalls in the risk pool that must be recovered from the providers need to be evaluated to ensure that the amounts are recoverable, and where necessary the financial manager should consider the need for a provision for unrecoverable amounts. Additionally, any contributions to be made by the MCO for its participation in a risk pool should be appropriately accrued in the financial statements.

Equity

The MCO will need to track its SAP and GAAP basis equity. The statutory balance sheet may permit certain surplus notes to be classified as equity for purposes of determining statutory net worth (issues regarding statutory net worth are discussed below). Surplus notes are obligations to investors that meet certain requirements of the state insurance laws, which are generally subordinated to all obligations of the MCOs. Repayment of surplus notes is subject to the approval of the state's commissioners of insurance. Other transactions affecting equity that are subject to the approval of the state's commissioners of insurance include restrictions on the payout of dividends.

REGULATORY REPORTING CONSIDERATIONS

Generally, HMOs are required to file quarterly financial statements with the state Department of Insurance, which are due 45 days after the close of the quarter. An annual statement filing is also required. The annual filing is due March 1. Many states also require the filing of a certification on claims reserves prepared by a licensed actuary. Audited financial statements are also required; the filing deadline may vary by state but is generally June 1. Any differences in the amounts reported in the audited financial statements and the annual filing due on March 1 must be disclosed in the footnotes to the audited financial statements. Depending on the applicable state's requirements, the audited financial statements may be prepared on either an SAP basis or a GAAP basis.

GAAP focuses more on the matching of revenue and expenses in a given reporting period to measure the earnings of an entity. The state insurance departments that have jurisdiction over the MCO are concerned with the MCO's ability to pay claims in the future. For example, certain expenditures (e.g., capital assets) may benefit future earnings ability and therefore are likely to be capitalized and expensed ratably over future periods for GAAP. However, such costs are expensed immediately in accordance with SAP because monies expended are no longer available to pay future liabilities.

There are many differences between SAP and GAAP accounting that are generally based on the premise of the state insurance department's ability to determine liquidity of the MCO. Some of the major differences include the following:

- treatment of certain assets and investments as nonadmitted under SAP (e.g., fixed assets other than electronic data processing equipment, past due premium receivables, certain loans and other receivables, and investments not authorized by statute or in excess of statutory limitations)
- deferred tax accounts
- carrying value of investments in subsidiaries (which is primarily affected by limitations in the carrying amount and the amortization period of goodwill)

The state Department of Insurance imposes minimum statutory capital requirements for HMOs. The NAIC adopted a model act for HMOs that specified that minimum capital for HMOs should be determined as follows:

- the greater of $1,000,000, or
- 2 percent of annual premium as reported on the most recent annual financial statement filed with the commissioners of insurance on the first $150 million of premium and 1 percent of annual premium on premium greater than $150 million, or
- an amount equal to the sum of 3 months' uncovered health care expenditures as reported on the most recent financial statement filed with the commissioners, or
- an amount equal to the sum of:
  1. 8 percent of annual health care expenditures except those paid on a capitated basis or a managed hospital payment

basis as reported on the most recent financial statement filed with the commissioner, and
  2. 4 percent of annual health care expenditures paid on a managed hospital payment basis as reported on the most recent financial statement filed with the commissioner

Managed hospital basis means agreements wherein the financial risk is primarily related to the degree of utilization rather than to the cost of services. *Uncovered expenditures* means the costs to the HMO for health care services that are the obligation of the HMO, for which an enrollee may also be liable in the event of HMO insolvency and for which no alternative arrangements have been made that are acceptable to the commissioner.

Many states are in the process of adopting the NAIC model act. Other states maintain separate minimum surplus requirements. The requirements of each of the states generally call for plans of action when an entity's capital falls within a close range of the minimum requirement.

Although the states' minimum requirements have provided a means to measure the financial viability of an insurance entity, the states' requirements were often a flat minimum and disregarded the size of an entity or the differing degrees of risk to which different entities are exposed. Insurance entities' exposure to risk has become more diverse, and although some are conservative in investment and underwriting practices, others have been more aggressive. The NAIC began examining existing capital requirements and concluded that consumers should be further protected by having companies that assume a more aggressive, risk-taking approach be subject to higher capital requirements. Risk-based capital requirements have been developed for life and health insurers and property/casualty insurers. A working group was formed in 1993 to develop a separate risk-based capital formula for health organizations, including traditional health insurers, HMOs, Blue Cross/Blue Shield plans, and health service plans.

Integrated delivery systems have some risk characteristics that may differ from those of other insurers. Traditional indemnity insurance companies in general invest extensively in marketable securities, and the risk-based capital formulas currently in place address the risks associated with this investment strategy. Although MCOs may invest excess cash in low-risk, short-term securities, they also will often invest directly in the provider operation (e.g., they will own and operate hospitals, medical groups, or outpatient facilities), which contributes directly to the MCO's ability to control quantity and cost of services. MCOs may also control costs through risk transfer arrangements with providers, such as negotiated fee schedules, budgets, and capitation rate agreements. These reimbursement arrangements are not generally available to the traditional indemnity carrier.

The goals of the working group are to develop a seamless system of risk-based capital requirements that will be appropriate for the existing environment and will accommodate future evolution as well. The goals are aimed at facilitating an even playing field for health insurers, Blue Cross/Blue Shield plans, HMOs, and others while not compromising the development of innovations in the health care finance field. A health organization risk-based capital formula proposed by the American Academy of Actuaries is under review by the working group. The working group has been asked to work with the academy to develop a simplified formula to be presented to the NAIC at its March 1996 meeting. Any changes to the formula will probably not be approved before mid-1996. If this timetable is met, changes that would affect HMOs will probably be effective for calendar year end 1997, but HMOs would be able to measure where they stand using the formula that is expected to be proposed in mid-1996.

The regulatory environment under which MCOs operate is continuously changing to meet market changes, and entities need to prepare

themselves in particular to meet the challenges imposed by new or expected legislation.

BUDGETING AND FINANCIAL FORECASTING

The importance of maintaining detailed budgets has been discussed throughout this chapter. Financial forecasts, which project activity and results beyond the current period, are also important management tools. Financial forecasts often are prepared when new product lines are introduced, particularly for the purposes of determining capital needs to invest in new lines of business.

When one is preparing current year budgets or projecting results for future periods, it is important to build the projections at a detailed level. This would include developing projections by product line. A baseline projection representing the best estimate of results should be developed first and variations from the baseline projection that are more conservative or optimistic can be developed later and evaluated. Building the projections begins with detailed enrollment projections developed from an analysis of the market and total targeted population for each market segment. Management should then estimate the market share anticipated to be captured. The enrollment projections should be reviewed with the sales and marketing departments and compared with the detailed sales plan. Where possible, membership projections for targeted accounts should be reconciled to the overall enrollment projections.

Based on historical experience or, for new products, industry benchmarks, medical costs should be extended from the enrollment projections. Medical cost estimates should be developed at a detailed level with separate calculations for inpatient costs, outpatient costs, and ancillary benefits costs, such as mental health and substance abuse, vision, dental, and pharmacy. Inpatient cost projections should be benchmarked against an overall per member per month cost and should identify the assumed days per thousand, overall length of stay targets, or, where appropriate, per case or per diem costs. Outpatient and ancillary benefit costs will probably be compared with per member per month cost benchmarks and, where applicable, per case costs. These projected costs should be evaluated for consistency with historical experience and negotiated or proposed (but realistic) changes in reimbursement arrangements. For future years, medical costs should be trended for inflation and also should consider the impact of utilization management and reimbursement strategies that may change over time.

Administrative costs should be developed from detailed staffing plans and detailed budgets for supplies and system development costs. The operating departments should prepare staffing requirements that consider the need for additional staff as enrollment grows. Once the detailed budgets are developed, the overall costs on a per member per month basis and as a percentage of premium should be determined and compared with historical experience and industry benchmarks.

The MCO also needs to consider pricing of products. As previously discussed, certain pricing, such as the pricing of Medicare risk products, is not controlled by the MCO. Pricing will therefore be a function of enrollment projections and mandated rates. For products under the control of the MCO, the financial manager should consider the desired profit margin and determine the premium to charge to achieve a profit margin based on the medical costs and administrative costs developed as discussed above. The premium rates then must be evaluated against competition, and the process of reevaluating the initial set of enrollment assumptions begins. For example, based on desired rates and competitor rates, will the market retention used in enrollment projections be achievable?

The process of financial forecasting is an iterative process. Management will begin to reevaluate all initial assumptions. Targeted profit margins may need to be adjusted to revise the premium rates for competitive purposes. Management will probably challenge the aggressiveness or conservativeness of administrative budgets.

The financial forecasting process must also include the development of a projected balance sheet. This is particularly important to evaluate the impact of the projected growth in operations on minimum capital requirements. Additionally, the forecasting process should require variations from the baseline projections to determine the risks and exposures if the actual results fall short of the baseline and also to project the impact if actual results are better than expected. Cash flow analyses are also important to ensure that cash will be generated from operations or to determine the extent to which cash reserves will be needed, particularly as new lines of business are pursued.

CONCLUSION

Whether the financial manager is developing budgets or financial forecasts or preparing financial statements, he or she must depend on the information prepared and maintained by the operating departments. This information is an integral part of the financial manager's decision-making process. Communication among the various functional areas in the MCO will be key to the successful operation of the entity. Timely financial reporting enhances management's ability to determine performance against anticipated results and redirect its strategies to minimize exposure to loss and preserve a favorable financial performance.

SUGGESTED READING

Coyne, J.S. 1993. Assessing the Financial Performance of Health Maintenance Organizations: Tools and Techniques. *Managed Care Quarterly* 1(3): 63–74.

Mensah, Y. M., Considine, J.M., and Oakes, L. 1994. Statutory Insolvency Regulations and Earning Management in the Prepaid Healthcare Industry. *Accounting Review* 69 (1): 70–95.

Peterson, C.E. 1994. Standards for Capitilization and Solvency. *HMO Magazine* 35 (4): 13–14, 16.

Chapter 41

Taxation of Managed Health Care Plans

Terry A. Jacobs and Phillip G. Royalty

Managed health care plans take a variety of forms. The requirements to qualify for tax exempt status vary depending on the type of plan involved. Also, classification as an insurance company has important tax consequences. The following is a general discussion of the tax treatment of managed care plans.

HEALTH MAINTENANCE ORGANIZATIONS

A health maintenance organization (HMO) represents one segment of today's rapidly

---

Terry A. Jacobs is the National Director of Insurance Tax Services for Ernst & Young LLP, based in Washington, D.C. He oversees the firm's technical tax services and helps clients identify and strategically respond to issues and opportunities arising from a changing business environment and legislative, regulatory, and tax policy changes. Mr. Jacobs previously served as Attorney Advisor to the Assistant Secretary of the Treasury for Tax Policy and has worked with the Internal Revenue Service on tax matters relating to insurance companies and products. He received a Masters degree in Accounting and a Juris Doctor degree from the University of Iowa in 1981, and a Masters degree in Law in Taxation from Georgetown University in 1988.

Phillip G. Royalty, JD, CPA, is a partner in the National Tax Department of Ernst & Young LLP based in Washington, D.C. He is the firm's National Director of Health Care Tax Services. Before joining Ernst & Young, Mr. Royalty was a tax law specialist with the Internal Revenue Service National Office in Washington, D.C. He graduated Phi Beta Kappa from the University of Kentucky in 1973, and received his law degree from the University of Kentucky College of Law in 1976.

changing health care industry. The principal activity of an HMO is to arrange for medical treatment to members in exchange for fixed payments from each member. Benefits generally include primary physician care, specialist physician care, medical care for emergencies out of the HMO's service area, and hospital care.

An HMO assumes an obligation to satisfy a member's loss from obtaining primary physician benefits and contracts with its affiliated physicians to provide those benefits. An HMO does not typically indemnify its members for physician care. HMOs may provide benefits on what is referred to as a point-of-service or open-ended basis. Under this type of arrangement, the HMO member receives partial reimbursement for primary physician care rendered by a physician who generally is unaffiliated with the HMO. The HMO's arrangements with providers to offer the other types of benefits (e.g., hospital care) vary widely.

Types

HMOs differ based on the structure of the physician organization that delivers care to its members. Some common types of HMO models include the staff model, group model, open panel and independent practice association (IPA) model, network model, and mixed model. Caution should be exercised when one is using these terms because their definitions are not consistent throughout the health care and insurance industries.

Under the staff model, salaried physicians are employed by the HMO. The salary may include profit sharing or productivity bonuses. If care cannot be provided by the staff physicians, the HMO contracts with medical specialists for the care. Under the staff model, all premiums and other revenue accrue to the HMO.

Group model HMOs contract with one group of physicians in private practice. The HMO usually compensates the group by paying a fixed monthly amount for each member of the HMO. This payment is referred to as capitation. The space and medical equipment used in providing care can be owned by the group practice or by the HMO. Physicians can be organized as a partnership, professional corporation, or other association that contracts to provide health care services to members of the HMO. If the group practice cannot provide all the services required by the members, the practice group typically subcontracts with other medical providers for the service. A network model is a variation of the group model. A network model HMO contracts with two or more physician groups.

Open panel model HMOs contract directly with physicians practicing independently; alternatively, the HMO contracts with an IPA, a group representing physicians, which in turn contracts with the individual physicians. An IPA model HMO compensates an IPA on a capitated basis, and the IPA compensates the physicians in a variety of compensation arrangements. A direct model HMO that contracts directly with the physicians compensates the physicians on either a capitation or a fee-for-service basis. If the IPA cannot provide all the services required by a member, the member is referred to a specialist. The HMO must then provide for payment to the specialist for medical services separately from the primary care physician's or IPA's capitation payments. Consequently, an HMO that capitates some physicians generally compensates others on a fee-for-service basis.

The mixed model HMO is a combination of the previous categories and is a response to employers' needs for broad geographic coverage by providers. For example, large and midsized employers have employees who may reside in multiple areas, cities, and/or states. As a result, HMOs have expanded into different geographic areas, where they often acquire or affiliate with other HMOs that have different delivery structures.

Full descriptions of these types of HMOs, as well as other types of health plans, are found in Chapter 3.

Tax Exempt HMOs

Before the 1986 Tax Act

Before the 1986 Tax Act, in determining whether an HMO qualified for exempt status under Section 501(c)(3) of the Internal Revenue Code, the Internal Revenue Service (IRS) generally followed the tax court's decision in *Sound Health Association v. Commissioner*.[1] In holding that Sound Health qualified for Section 501(c)(3) status, the court made an analogy between the HMO and the tax exempt hospital described in Revenue Ruling 69-545.[2] GCM 39057 stated, however, that an HMO affiliated with an IPA did not qualify under Section 501(c)(3) because it was organized and operated primarily for the benefit of the IPA physician members. Also, *Geisinger Health Plan v. Commissioner* held that arrangements for the provision of health care to members through contracts with other entities does not qualify an HMO for exempt status under Section 501(c)(3).[3]

HMOs not resembling Sound Health may be able to qualify for exemption under Section 501(c)(4) as a social welfare organization even though there are no published revenue rulings concerning this issue. Although Revenue Ruling 86-98 held that IPAs do not qualify for tax exempt status under Section 501(c)(4) or (6), the IRS did not adopt a blanket prohibition against exempt status for IPA model HMOs.[4] Over the years, several IPA model HMOs have received favorable determination letters under Section 501(c)(4).

After the 1986 Tax Act

Effective for taxable years beginning after 31 December, 1986, Section 501(m) provides that an organization described in Section 501(c)(3) or (4) shall be exempt only if no substantial part of its activities consists of providing commercial type insurance.[5] A Section 501(c)(3) or (4) organization with insubstantial commercial insurance activities is exempt from tax, but the activity of providing commercial type insurance is an unrelated business activity. The organization is treated as an insurance company for purposes of Subchapter L with respect to this commercial insurance activity in lieu of the tax on unrelated business income of tax exempt organizations imposed by Section 511.

Although the statutory language of Section 501(m) relating to HMOs is ambiguous, the committee reports are not. The conference report to the 1986 Tax Act states that Section 501(m) is not intended to affect the exemption of any HMOs:

> The conference agreement does not alter the tax-exempt status of [HMOs]. HMOs provide physician services in a variety of practice settings, primarily through physicians who are either employees or partners of the HMO or through contracts with individual physicians or one or more groups of physicians (organized on a group practice basis or individual practice basis).[6]

Congress again explained the application of Section 501(m) to HMOs in the Technical and Miscellaneous Revenue Act of 1988 (TAMRA)[7]:

> Under the 1986 Act, the provision relating to organizations engaged in commercial-type insurance activities did not alter the tax-exempt status of [HMOs]. HMOs provide physician services in a variety of practice settings, primarily through physicians who are either employees or partners of the HMO or through contracts with individual physicians or one or more groups of physicians (organized on a group practice or individual practice basis). The conference agreement

clarifies that, in addition to the general exemption for [HMOs], organizations that provide supplemental [HMO]-type services (such as dental or vision services) are not treated as providing commercial-type insurance if they operate in the same manner as [an HMO].[8]

Despite the express congressional language in the 1986 Tax Act and TAMRA, the IRS concluded in two general counsel memoranda that the intended meaning of the HMO exception to Section 501(m) is unclear. In GCMs 39828 and 39829, the IRS stated that it does not read the legislative history to Section 501(m) as indicating that HMOs should be recognized as not providing commercial type insurance within the meaning of the section. Instead, whether an HMO is providing Section 501(m) commercial type insurance is based upon the particular facts and circumstances involved, not solely on whether an HMO operates as a staff, group, or IPA model.

Section 501(m) will not affect the tax exempt status of any of the common, existing HMOs that compensate primary care physicians exclusively on a salary, capitation, or other fixed-fee basis, even though the HMO may pay other providers on a fee-for-service basis.[9] The term *common, existing HMOs* refers to HMOs as they were commonly structured at the time of the 1986 Tax Act.[10] The IRS maintains that, although called HMOs, many of the new hybrid organizations, such as point-of-service plans or open-ended HMOs, closely resemble indemnity insurers in operation and that these hybrid HMOs are precluded from exempt status if a substantial part of their activities consists of providing out-of-plan benefits on a fee-for-service basis. Furthermore, if the activities are not substantial, the income from those activities is treated as unrelated business income.

Regardless of Section 501(m), an HMO must still qualify for tax exempt status on its merits. In GCM 39828, the IRS listed several factors that are relevant in determining whether an HMO qualifies as a tax exempt charitable organization under Section 501(c)(3). These factors are not all inclusive, nor is any one factor determinative. They include the following:

- actually providing health care services and maintaining facilities and staff
- offering services to nonmembers on a fee-for-service basis
- providing care and extending reduced rates to indigent persons
- caring for persons covered by Medicare, Medicaid, and similar programs
- making emergency department facilities available to the community regardless of an ability to pay (and informing the community about the services)
- operating a meaningful subsidized membership program
- forming a board of directors that is broadly representative of the community
- offering health education programs that are open to the community
- conducting health research programs
- having health care providers who are paid on a fixed-fee basis
- using surplus funds to improve facilities, equipment, patient care, or any of the programs described in the list

GCM 39828 lists other factors to determine whether an HMO meets the Section 501(c)(3) requirement that no meaningful restrictions be placed on membership that would preclude the HMO from serving the community as a whole. An HMO meets these requirements if:

- individuals compose a substantial portion of membership
- an active program exists to attract individual members
- uniform rates for prepaid care are provided by a community rating system
- individual and group members have similar rates

- no substantive age or health barriers exist for determining eligibility for individuals or groups

Both HMOs considered in GCM 39828 failed to qualify, in the IRS's view, for exempt status under Section 501(c)(3). The IRS ruled that the HMOs lacked sufficient community benefit and that their membership was not open to the community. The IRS also concluded that both HMOs were providing community type insurance under 501(m).

In GCM 39829, the IRS considered whether a particular HMO qualified as a tax exempt social welfare organization under Section 501(c)(4), taking Section 501(m) into consideration. The HMO had received a letter in 1978 from the IRS determining that it was exempt under Section 501(c)(4). Exemption standards under Section 501(c)(4) are similar to those outlined for Section 501(c)(3) organizations, only less restrictive. Standards under Section 501(c)(4) focus on whether membership is open to individuals and groups; whether the HMO serves low-income, high-risk, medically underserved, or elderly persons; and whether premiums are established on a community-rated basis. Provided that the HMO had not materially changed its operations from the previous determination letter, the IRS stated that the HMO could rely on its 1978 letter granting exempt status under Section 501(c)(4), at least until Section 501(m) became effective.

In determining whether commercial type insurance under Section 501(m) is being provided, GCM 39829 lists the following factors that must be analyzed:

- whether an insurance risk is being transferred and distributed
- whether, and to what extent, the entity is operated in a manner similar to that of for-profit insurers or Blue Cross/Blue Shield organizations
- whether, and to what extent, the entity is marketing a product similar to that of for-profit insurers or Blue Cross/Blue Shield organizations

- whether, and to what extent, the entity provides health care services directly

- whether, and to what extent, the entity has shifted any risk of loss to the service providers through salary or fixed-fee compensation arrangements

The IRS concluded that the IPA model HMO retained its exempt status under Section 501(c)(4) even after Section 501(m) became effective. The HMO capitated its contracted physicians, and the capitation represented about 50 percent of the HMO's total payments for medical benefits.

In GCM 39829, the IRS made the following observations about the applicability of Section 501(m) to HMOs:

- The term *insurance company* in Treasury Regulation 1.801-3(a) is not the same as *commercial type insurance* under Section 501(m). This suggests that the IRS may not agree that an HMO that is barred from tax exempt status under Section 501(m) necessarily qualifies as an insurance company for federal tax purposes.

- The only practical way to distinguish an HMO from commercial insurers or Blue Cross/Blue Shield organizations is the fact that an HMO employs its own staff, operates its own facilities, or otherwise fixes its costs by shifting a substantial portion of the risk to providers.

- Nonstaff, nongroup HMOs that pay providers on a fee-for-service basis, even when the providers are subject to a percentage withhold or reduction for overutilization, are much harder to distinguish from commercial insurance companies and Blue Cross/Blue Shield organizations. No opinion was expressed as to whether these types of HMOs primarily provide services or an insurance type benefit, or whether they fit within Section 501(m)(3)(B).

- In determining whether an HMO's insurance aspects are incidental, salary or capitation agreements with primary care physicians ordinarily should be accorded greater weight than agreements with specialists or hospitals.

The IRS has stated that it intends to issue guidance to address those issues left unresolved by GCM 39829. In particular, it will discuss whether HMOs that pay providers on a fee-for-service basis can qualify for Section 501(m)(3)(B) exception, which provides that incidental health insurance provided by an HMO shall be exempt from tax. Also, a GCM guidance is anticipated on how insubstantial open-ended benefits should be measured. GCM 39829 states that providing substantial open-ended benefits disqualifies an HMO for exemption and that insubstantial open-ended benefits are subject to tax as unrelated business income.

Taxable HMOs

Status as an Insurance Company

Regulation Section 1.801-3(a) defines an insurance company as a company whose primary and predominant activity is the business of issuing insurance contracts. This is a subjective test, one that is generally met if a company can demonstrate that more than 50 percent of its business relates to the issuance of insurance contracts.

Generally, an insurance contract exists if the contract shifts and distributes risk. These concepts were first applied by the Supreme Court in *LeGierse* and have further developed over the years.[11,12] Generally, the courts have held that an insurable risk of economic loss must be shifted from an insured to an insurer for an insurance relationship to exist. That risk must also be distributed among several unrelated insureds. Applied to an HMO, risk is shifted from the member to the HMO when the HMO contractually assumes an obligation to provide a service for the member upon illness or injury for a premium payment representing a fraction of the possible loss. The risk is distributed among the number of members.

The application of the *LeGierse* risk shifting and distributing concepts to an HMO is complicated by the fact that many HMOs assume an obligation to satisfy a member's loss by providing physician services rather than providing financial indemnification to the member. The IRS has focused on services provided by physicians rather than the HMO's payment for these services. In Revenue Ruling 68-27, the IRS determined that an organization that provided medical service contracts was not an insurance company because its primary business was not issuing insurance contracts.[13] The IRS concluded that there was no hazard or peril insured with respect to the preventive care portion of the medical service contracts. Although there was a risk with respect to the sick or disabled phase of the medical service contracts, it was a business risk of an organization furnishing medical services on a fixed-price basis, not an insurance risk. Because the essential element of an insurance contract, the transfer of an insurance risk, was lacking, the medical service contracts were not insurance contracts.

Similarly, in *Group Life & Health Insurance Co. v. Royal Drug*, the Supreme Court examined an arrangement between an HMO and a provider of health care services.[14] The court stated that, if an insurance company were to acquire a chain of drugstores to control the cost of satisfying its obligations, the acquisition would not be the business of insurance. The court reasoned that insurance is a relationship between the insurer and the insured, not between the insurer and a third party.

The IRS distinguished the principles of Revenue Ruling 68-27 in Technical Advice Memorandum 9412002 and concluded that two IPA model HMOs were insurance companies for federal income tax purposes. The HMOs were not licensed to provide medical services and contracted with physicians to provide care on a fee-for-service basis. The HMOs were not liable for any malpractice claims against affiliated physicians. Other than deductibles, copayments, and coinsurance, the HMOs had full responsibility for payments to the affiliated physicians. The

HMOs were subject to the control of the state Department of Insurance in their state of domestication. The department maintained control and approval of premiums and required the filing of an annual statement and state income taxes under the rules applicable to domestic accident and health insurance companies. The HMOs were subject to examination by the insurance department, including a review of the unearned premiums and incurred claims reserves; were required to furnish solvency deposits; and were subject to assessments to subsidize health insurance for high-risk subscribers. More than 90 percent of the HMOs' revenues were from actuarially determined member premiums.

The IRS analyzed whether the predominant business activity of the HMOs was the issuance of insurance contracts. It found that the contracts issued by the HMOs provided for risk shifting and risk distribution and were therefore insurance contracts. Because the premiums from the insurance contracts constituted more than 90 percent of the revenues, the IRS concluded that the primary and predominant business activity of the HMOs was the issuance of insurance contracts and that they should be treated as insurance companies for tax purposes. The IRS distinguished the facts from the organization in Revenue Ruling 68-27, in which the taxpayer had hired physicians, nurses, and technicians to provide care to its members.

The IRS reached a similar conclusion in Technical Advice Memorandum (TAM) 9416001. Although the taxpayer in TAM 9416001 was not an HMO, the analysis of the federal income tax treatment of the company was quite similar to that of a health care plan. The taxpayer was a provider of home warranty contracts, under which it agreed to repair or replace certain systems and appliances that broke down during the contract period. The IRS held that, unlike the taxpayer in Revenue Ruling 68-27, the taxpayer in question did not provide any services through salaried staff but rather contracted with independent contractors and technicians to provide services. Thus the home warranty contracts were insurance contracts, and, because the predominant activity of the taxpayer was issuing such contracts, it was an insurance company.

If an HMO is considered an insurance company for federal tax purposes, it is taxed as a corporation. Its taxable income is determined under rules applicable to insurance companies, including the unique treatment provided for unearned premiums, discounting of unpaid losses, proration adjustments, and salvage and subrogation.

An HMO that is considered an insurance company is faced with a unique issue. The U.S. Code and regulations presume that an insurance company annually files a uniform annual statement, the National Association of Insurance Commissioners' NAIC's yellow book, with the applicable state insurance department. Many accounting methods and tax calculations are based on the NAIC statement. HMOs do not file a yellow book, however, and may not file any statement with a regulatory authority. These companies will, therefore, experience a problem in that their information or financial statements are not in conformity with the yellow book. In some instances, this may be a mere mechanical problem, but in other instances the issue may be more troublesome.

Accrued Claim Liability

At year end, many HMOs accrue liabilities for outstanding claims (see Chapter 40). If the HMO is an insurance company, it is allowed to include in its unpaid losses a reasonable estimate of its incurred losses (see Chapter 7). If the HMO is not an insurance company, however, the liability must meet the all events test and the economic performance requirements of Section 461(h). The all events test requires that all of the events have occurred which determine the fact of the liability, and the amount of the liability must be determined with reasonable accuracy.[15] In addition, the all events test generally cannot be satisfied sooner than when economic performance occurs. If the liability of the taxpayer arises out of the providing of services to the taxpayer by another person, economic performance occurs as the person performs the services.[16]

In interpreting the all events test, the Supreme Court in *General Dynamics* held that the last event necessary to fix the taxpayer's liability was not the receipt of medical care by members but rather the filing of medical reimbursement claims.[17] Furthermore, the court continued, if the all events test permitted the deduction of incurred but not reported claims, there would have been no need for Congress to enact Sections 832(b)(5) and 832(c)(4), which explicitly allow insurance companies to deduct these reserves.

General Dynamics, however, involved self-insurance of the company's employees. The court recognized that the employees had certain motivations relating to job security to prevent or dissuade them from actually making a claim even though the medical expense was incurred. This fact is not present in a prepaid health plan such as an HMO. The physicians are motivated to file claims. Furthermore, an HMO contractually assumes an obligation to cover a member's medical loss and contracts separately with physicians. This may factually distinguish an HMO from *General Dynamics*.

In a technical advice memorandum, the IRS allowed the deduction for accrued claims in the year the services were provided to the member for a firm operating much like a staff model HMO.[18] The firm offered mental health and substance abuse counseling services through its own clinics. It entered into contracts with certain third party vendors to provide special services beyond the skills of the firm's clinic staff. Under the contracts, after the firm preauthorized the patient care to be provided by the outside vendor, the vendor was required to offer the service, and the firm was required to pay for it.

Under the firm's accrual method of accounting, the firm recorded a liability at the time of preauthorization based on the number of authorized days or visits and the specific contract or average historical rate. The firm also recorded a liability for preauthorized services to be performed in the next taxable year, relying on the recurring item exception to the economic performance rules. The firm adjusted the recorded liability if actual invoice amounts differed from the accrual, which occurred when the treatment varied from that originally authorized.

The IRS held that preauthorization of services does not constitute economic performance because all events that determine the fact of the liability will not occur until the preauthorized services are performed. In addition, the IRS stated that, because the company had failed properly to adopt the recurring item exception method of accounting, the company could not accrue amounts for services to be performed in the next taxable year. The firm had to accrue the expenses in the year the services were performed.

The recurring item exception to the economic performance rules is provided in Section 461(h)(3)(A). Under this exception, a deduction is permitted if:

1. the all events test, without regard to economic performance, is satisfied during such taxable year

2. economic performance occurs within the shorter of 8.5 months or a reasonable time after the close of such taxable year

3. the item is recurring in nature, and the taxpayer consistently treats similar items as incurred in the taxable year in which the all events test is met

4. the item is not material, or the accrual of the item in the year that the all events test is met results in a better matching of income and expense

Requirements 2 and 3 are not usually troublesome because HMOs normally pay claims within 8.5 months, and the claims are recurring in nature. Accrued claims may not be an immaterial item, however, so that an HMO must prove that the accrual of such liability in the taxable year results in more proper matching of income and deductions to satisfy requirement 4. Because a taxpayer's financial treatment of an item is considered evidence of the proper period for matching of income and deductions, HMOs that deduct accrued claims should expense these li-

abilities in the same period on their financial statements. Such a financial statement presentation normally is permissible under generally accepted accounting principles.

Withhold Arrangements

Some plans provide an incentive to providers to meet certain objectives through a withhold mechanism. Under these arrangements, a portion of the fee paid to the provider is withheld and not paid to the provider unless the provider meets certain economic criteria. Typically, the withhold is not paid until after the year end of the plan. The tax treatment of this arrangement item is receiving scrutiny from the IRS.

ADDITIONAL TYPES OF MANAGED CARE ORGANIZATIONS

In addition to the traditional model HMOs, managed care organizations (MCOs) have taken on new legal forms and business operations and new names in reaction to the rapid and dramatic changes occurring in the health care industry. Examples include integrated delivery systems (IDSs), physician–hospital organizations (PHOs), and management services organizations (MSOs), all of which are described in Chapter 4. Because some of these new types of organizations also assume insurance type risk, these new forms are herein referred to collectively as MCOs.

Tax Exempt MCOs

IDSs

The IRS has issued several rulings recognizing the tax exempt status under Section 501(c)(3) of IDSs.[19] To obtain recognition of exemption, an IDS generally must demonstrate that it is benefiting the community through some combination of charity care, treatment of Medicare and Medicaid patients, research and education activities, and the like. Also, the IRS generally insists that a majority of the voting members of a tax-exempt health care organization's board of trustees be composed of "independent community members." The IRS does not consider practicing physicians affiliated with the organization, officers, department heads, or other employees of the organization to be independent community members. In a multi-entity system, this requirement applies only to the board of trustees of the parent organization. An additional requirement is that all tax-exempt members of the system adopt a conflicts-of-interest policy. This policy applies to all "interested persons." The IRS treats a trustee, principal officer, or member of any committee with board-delegated powers who has a direct or indirect "financial interest" as an interested person. The IRS defines "financial interest" broadly as a current or potential ownership or investment interest in, or compensation arrangement with, any entity or individual with which the exempt entity has or is negotiating a transaction or arrangement.[20]

In addition, in situations where an IDS is buying a physician practice, the IRS closely reviews the methodology used in valuing the practice to ensure that no more than fair market value is paid for the practice.[21] Finally, the IRS reviews incentive compensation arrangements between the IDS and physicians to guard against the possibility of private benefit or private inurement.[22]

PHOs

The IRS's position is that PHOs generally will not qualify for tax exempt status on the basis that their activities further the private interests of the physician members of the PHO.[23] A PHO affiliated with the University of Kansas Hospital, however, received an IRS determination letter recognizing its tax exempt status under Section 501(c)(3) based on a rather narrow fact pattern.[24] Participants in the PHO were limited to the University of Kansas Hospital, 14 faculty group clinical practices were associated with the hospital, all of which were tax exempt under Section 501(c)(3), and physicians who are employees of the faculty practices and on the faculty at the University of Kansas Medical Center. The hospital had veto power over any activities of the PHO. Furthermore, the PHO's contracts for

medical services were with the affiliated hospital and the faculty practices.

MSOs

As with PHOs, the IRS's position generally is that MSOs do not qualify for tax exempt status because they are not engaged in charitable activities.[25] Conceivably, an MSO formed along the lines of the PHO affiliated with the University of Kansas Hospital discussed above could qualify for tax exempt status, but so far the IRS has not published any rulings to that effect.

Taxable MCOs

*Federal Income Tax (Including
    Unrelated Business Income Tax)*

The rules discussed above with respect to taxable HMOs apply generally to MCOs. If an MCO is determined to be an insurance company for federal income tax purposes, it is taxed as a corporation regardless of its legal form and is subject to special accounting rules. Generally, these special rules result in favorable tax treatment for an insurance company relative to a noninsurance company. In certain situations, however, these rules may result in the acceleration of income tax for many MCOs.

In addition, a tax exempt not-for-profit MCO may jeopardize its exempt status if it engages in substantial insurance activities. Insubstantial insurance activities will not threaten an MCO's exemption but may be taxed as unrelated trade or business under Section 501(m). The IRS has held that the provision of administrative and management services does not constitute an insurance activity under section 501(m).[26] The IRS has also held that income derived by a tax exempt hospital under a contract with an IPA-model HMO was not unrelated business income.[27] The contract obligated the hospital to provide hospital services and arrange for medical care for HMO members who selected primary care physicians under contract with the hospital. The HMO compensated the hospital on a capitated basis. The hospital in turn compensated the primary care physicians on a capitated basis, with an incentive component. Specialists and out-of-area providers were paid by the HMO on a fee-for-service basis. The IRS concluded that the hospital's agreement to provide medical and hospital service to HMO members was substantially related to its exempt purpose of promoting health, and therefore not an unrelated trade or business. Also, the IRS determined that the hospital was providing medical services on a prepaid basis rather than insurance under section 501(m), citing Revenue Ruling 68-27.

For federal income tax purposes, an insurance company is a company whose primary and predominant business activity during the taxable year is the issuing or reinsuring of contracts that have the elements of risk shifting and risk distribution. Although its name, charter powers, and subjection to state insurance laws are significant in determining the business that a company is authorized to conduct, it is the character of the business actually conducted in the taxable year that determines whether a company is taxable as an insurance company under the Internal Revenue Code.

Generally, health care providers will meet the risk distribution test because, to gain efficiencies and provide cost-effective services, the health care provider must provide services to a significant number of lives. Thus the essential issue is whether the contract contains risk shifting or the provision of health services. Factors that may affect the determination of whether a contract involves risk shifting or the provision of health services include the state regulatory treatment of the contract and the issuing entity, the malpractice liability retained by the entity, and the payment mechanism to the entity and to the entity's providers (i.e., salaried employees, contracted providers on a capitation basis, or contracted providers on a fee-for-service basis). Each of these, on its own, may not determine insurance company status. Taken together, however, these factors are relevant in determining whether a contract involves risk shifting or the provision of health services.

The IRS has said that it will provide guidance on its position regarding the definition of an insurance company in the health care provider context. This guidance is anticipated to be in the form of an administrative announcement (revenue ruling or revenue procedure). Although the technical analysis and eventual position of the IRS are unclear, as discussed above the IRS held in a recent private ruling that an IPA model HMO was taxed as an insurance company.

State Premium Tax

Generally, states subject premiums received by regulated insurance companies to a premium tax. Depending on the state (and type of business), premium tax rates can range from 0.5 percent to 3 percent. Many states exempt an insurance company that is subject to a premium tax from the state's corporate income tax. Several states subject insurance companies to both an income tax and the premium tax. Also, several states subject regulated HMOs to the state's corporate income tax and exclude them from the state's premium tax.

Most state tax statutes and regulations do not specifically provide for the taxation of certain types of MCOs, such as IDSs and PHOs. A position that is likely to be adopted by many states, however, is that an MCO regulated by a state as an insurance company will be subject to taxation by that state as an insurance company. Thus the regulation of an MCO as an insurance company will probably subject the MCO in many states to a premium tax.[28]

PARTICIPATION OF TAX EXEMPT HOSPITALS IN TAXABLE MCOs

Tax exempt hospitals participating in a taxable MCO arrangement with physicians should structure the arrangement in accordance with IRS guidelines so as not to jeopardize their exempt status. For example, private benefit or inurement may result if the physicians are being paid more than reasonable compensation for their services or if the hospital receives less than a fair portion of the MCO's income. Taxable MCOs are not required to have a board of directors representative of the community, however, and are not required to comply with the community board and conflict of interest requirements applicable to tax-exempt health care organizations. Furthermore, the hospital may make commercially reasonable loans or reasonable nonvoting stock investments in the MCO.[29]

CONCLUSION

The tax treatment of managed health care plans is currently in a state of change. Tax exemption requirements vary depending on the type of plan involved and are frequently revised and updated by the IRS. Also, careful analysis of the plan's activities is required to determine whether the plan qualifies as an insurance company for tax purposes. Finally, legislative and regulatory developments should be monitored to determine their impact on the tax status of the plan.

REFERENCES AND NOTES

1. 71 T.C. 158 (1978), *acq.*, 1981-2 C.B. 2.

2. 1969-2 C.B. 117. To qualify for tax exemption under Section 501(c)(3), a not-for-profit hospital must be organized and operated exclusively in furtherance of some purpose that is considered charitable (e.g., the promotion of health), and the hospital may not be operated, directly or indirectly, for the benefit of private interests. A hospital will be considered tax exempt if it is operated to serve a public rather than a private interest even though the class of beneficiaries eligible to receive a direct benefit from its activities does not include all members of the community.

3. *Geisinger Health Plan v. Commissioner*, 93-1 U.S.T.C. Paragraph 50,123 (3d Cir. 1993). In a subsequent decision, the court held that the HMO did not qualify for Section 501(c)(3) status on the basis that it was an integral part of the Geisinger system [*Geisinger Health Plan v. Commissioner*, 94-2 U.S.T.C. Paragraph 50,398 (3d Cir. 1994)].

4. 1986-2 C.B. 74.

5. The General Explanation to the Tax Reform Act of 1986 at 585 refers to *Haswell v. United States*, 74-2 U.S.T.C. 9591 (Ct. Cl. 1974), *Seasongood v. Commissioner*, 56-1 U.S.T.C. 9135 (6th Cir. 1955), and Section 501(h) for a definition of substantial.

6. H.R. Rep. 841, 99th Cong., 2d Sess., Vol. II at 346 (1986).

7. P.L. 100-647, 102 Stat. 3342.

8. H.R. Rep. 1104, 100th Cong., 2d Sess., Vol. II at 9 (1988).

9. G.C.M. 39829.

10. P.G. Royalty, IRS Toughens Its Guidelines on Tax Ex-

emption for HMOs, *Healthcare Financial Management* (1991).

11. 312 U.S. 531 (1941).

12. The courts have recognized the similarities between HMOs and insurance companies and have held that HMOs are insurance companies. See for example, *United States Fidelity & Guaranty Co. v. Group Health Plan of Southeast Michigan*, 131 Mich. App. 268, 345 N.W. 2d 683 (1983), and *West Michigan Health Care Network v. Transamerica Insurance Corp. of America*, 167 Mich. App. 218, 421 N.W. 2d 638, 642 (1988).

13. 1968-1 C.B. 315.

14. 440 U.S. 205 (1978).

15. Reg. Section 1.461-1(a)(2).

16. I.R.C. Section 461(h)(2)(A)(i).

17. 107 S. Ct. 1732, 87-1 U.S.T.C. 9280 (April 27, 1987).

18. Ltr. Ruls. 9203002 and 9203003.

19. See, for example, I.R.C. Section 501(c)(3) ruling letters (unnumbered) issued to Harriman Jones Medical Foundation (letter dated 3 February 1994), and to Friendly Hills Healthcare Network (letter dated 29 January 1993). Also see *IRS Exempt Organizations Continuing Professional Education Technical Instruction Program for FY 1996*, at page 384.

20. Draft article, "Tax-Exempt Health Care Organizations Community Board and Conflict of Interest Policy," for Internal Revenue Service's *1997 Continuing Professional Education Text, Obtained by BNA*, Daily Tax Report (BNA) No. 129, at L-1 (July 5, 1996).

21. *IRS Exempt Organizations Continuing Professional Education Technical Instruction Program for FY 1996*, at page 404.

22. G.C.M. 38283, 38905, and 39674.

23. *IRS Exempt Organizations Continuing Professional Education Technical Instruction Program for FY 1996*, at page 401.

24. I.R.C. Section 501(c)(3) determination letter (unnumbered) issued to University Affiliated Health Care, Inc. (letter dated 17 February 1995).

25. *IRS Exempt Organizations Continuing Professional Education Technical Instruction Program for FY 1996*, at page 157.

26. Technical Advice Memorandum (TAM) 9541003.

27. TAM 9246004.

28. National Association of Insurance Commissioners (NAIC), *Suggested Bulletin Regarding Certain Types of Compensation and Reimbursement Arrangements between Health Care Providers and Individuals, Employers, and Other Groups* (Kansas City, Mo.: NAIC, 1995). In this bulletin, the NAIC clarified its position that any organization assuming all or part of the risk for health care expenses is in the business of insurance.

29. *IRS Exempt Organization Continuing Professional Education Technical Instruction Program for FY 1996*, at page 403.

Chapter 42

Actuarial Services in an Integrated Delivery System

Stephen M. Cigich

The integrated delivery system (IDS), whether it is a global system of providers accepting the risk to provide all health care services under a health maintenance organization (HMO) contract or a subset of providers accepting the risk for a limited scope of services, creates new uses for the tools of actuarial science. These tools can help the IDS achieve success in many areas critical to the design and operation of the IDS.

The major goal of an IDS is to make its providers attractive to the customers of its services; customers are the members whom the providers treat and the payers who provide these members. This goal is achieved by the IDS providing value by focusing on improving efficiency and demonstrating quality in the delivery of medical services. Improved efficiency will benefit customers by keeping IDS costs low; demonstrating quality will provide customer satisfaction.

Actuarial tools can help provide financial focus in many areas:

- actuarial cost models to set budgetary targets in total, for smaller risk pools, or for

Stephen M. Cigich, F.S.A., is an actuary with the Milwaukee office of Milliman & Robertson, Inc., His area of expertise is in managed health care programs. He has assisted clients in the areas of medical delivery systems design and evaluation, product and rate manual development, experience analysis, and actuarial projections.

capitation of services performed by various providers

- fee structure analysis to determine equitable payment structures

- hospital diagnosis-related group (DRG) models to determine levels of clinical efficiencies within a hospital and among various hospitals in a community

- claim probability distributions to assess specific or aggregate stop-loss reinsurance risks

- risk pool disbursement mechanisms to allow operational (i.e., at the time of service or monthly) payments for medical services during the year and bonus distributions at year end

- incentive structure designs to make regular, budgeted payments or periodic bonus payments from IDS gains

- structures for reporting and monitoring

The use of these tools in conjunction with accepted clinical practice guidelines, education forums, feedback reporting, and incentives for efficiency and quality improvement can create an IDS with both perceived and real value to its owners, its providers, and the customers it serves.

This chapter discusses IDS actuarial tools in the broader categories of identifying opportunities, creating incentive structures, and measuring results.

IDENTIFYING OPPORTUNITIES

Actuarial Cost Models

Opportunities for efficiency in an IDS are best quantified using the actuarial cost model described in Chapter 43. Actuarial cost models reflect the interaction of all the important expense generating variables in an IDS and can be designed to focus on logical groupings of medical services to quantify utilization and cost levels.

A basic use of cost models is to identify and prioritize high-cost services to determine whether clinical opportunities exist for improvement. Cost models can also be used to compare actual results or budgets with those of a well-managed cost model. The well-managed model can be based on a best observed practices model or constructed using published data from other low-cost plans. Either review will allow the IDS to prioritize its resources in the areas with the most opportunity. Other uses of cost models include the following:

- evaluation of capitation proposals
- establishment of clinical/financial targets
- allocation of revenue among providers
- establishment of benchmarks for measurement
- quantification of medical management policy

Fee Schedule Analysis

Equitable reimbursement structures create fairness among providers. Within an IDS, a provider risk pool may be structured to be funded by a health plan on a capitated basis for all services, but payments to individual providers may be on a fee-for-service basis. These structures typically require a fee-for-service payment schedule that is the same for each service provided, regardless of the type of provider performing the service.

Creating an equitable reimbursement structure can be a difficult process that may involve merging many different payment levels currently in use by providers and payers in the IDS's service area. The Health Care Financing Administration's (HCFA's) Medicare resource-based relative value scale (RBRVS), based on relative value units (RVUs), is perhaps the best recognized relative value scale designed to create an equitable reimbursement schedule.

Each RVU reflects the physician work content of each procedure and includes physician practice and malpractice costs by area of the country. Medicare reimbursement under the RBRVS system uses the local RVUs multiplied by one of three conversion factors set by the HCFA: surgical, primary care, and non–primary care.

Few IDSs appear to be willing to adopt an RBRVS RVU schedule that is a simple multiplier of the RBRVS schedule (e.g., payment of all services using a $50.00 conversion factor). Many newly forming IDSs, in an effort to attract all specialties, will adopt a hybrid fee schedule based on Medicare's RVUs with different conversion factors for broad CPT code ranges. The conversion factors are typically chosen to accomplish the integration goal of the physicians. Examples of goals may include selection of conversion factors in such a way as to replicate most closely the fee levels currently accepted by the various physician specialties or to target, along with actuarial cost model service utilization, a reduced cost level by lowering the more highly compensated physicians (as measured by the RBRVS) relatively more than other physicians. Either approach can be implemented to allow transition to a common multiplier for all procedures in, say, a 2- to 4-year period. The development of such a hybrid fee schedule requires four general steps:

1. Create a physician database containing CPT code utilization data by physician specialty.

2. Design a fee survey from information in the database to sample the most relevant CPT codes for each physician specialty

(i.e., a unique sampling is designed for each physician specialty).

3. Survey the prospective IDS physicians and determine currently accepted market reimbursement levels.

4. Select the conversion factors required by broad CPT code ranges that most closely replicate the payment levels determined in step 3.

Given the fees set in this fashion and the relationship of the conversion factors to Medicare levels, the IDS can begin to rationalize differences in the levels of fee and, if desired, move closer to a constant percentage of Medicare payment levels over time.

Table 42–1 illustrates a portion of the output of such an evaluative tool used for an IDS wishing to create a single physician payment schedule that most closely reproduced current payments in the local service area. A stated goal of the new schedule was to not have the reimbursement for any one specialty to vary by more than 10 percent of the current average of local payer levels.

Table 42–1 conversion factors are calculated from payments made by local payers using a unique fee sample for each physician specialty. Current payment levels are expressed as both a range of payments and the average. Recommended conversion factors are shown that result from calculating conversion factors based on the recommended fee schedule using the same fee sample for each physician specialty. A fairly good database is required to perform this level of analysis. Individual physician services must be available by both type of service and physician specialty. This level of information will typically exist only in large HMOs, insurance companies, or consulting firms.

Another example for fee schedule analysis is the comparison of two different fee schedules. An HMO or employer group may propose to use its own payment schedule by procedure code to fund a risk pool for physicians. A fee comparison analysis can be made to determine whether the proposed schedule will produce enough revenue to allow the IDS to reimburse physicians from this risk pool using the IDS's fee schedule.

Fee structure analyses can also be performed for evaluating different hospitals for their inpatient hospital services. Per diems or case rates from each hospital are input into DRG form, grouped into the DRG groupings used in the cost model categories (medical, surgical, maternity, etc.), and composited into average per diem rates by cost model category using either days or admissions per 1,000 members, as appropriate. Again, this type of analysis requires a fairly extensive database to construct a reasonably credible evaluative tool.

Hospital DRG Models

Simple hospital length of stay efficiency studies can also be performed using DRG models and data that are readily available. These studies can be performed within a hospital or among hospitals in a community to help determine the hospital departments or hospitals that have had the most success in managing patient care.

Hospital length of stay efficiency analyses can be performed as follows:

1. Determine the population to be studied (e.g., HMO, preferred provider organization, commercial, Medicare, or Medicaid).

2. Obtain data from hospital discharge data (from the hospital directly, a state agency, or the HCFA).

3. Adjust the raw data to remove the effect of less frequent but more severe outlier cases.

4. Calculate the average length of stay for each DRG and group into hospital department or cost model categories (e.g., medical, surgical, etc.).

5. Compare the result with similarly grouped lengths of stay developed from best observed practices or some other well-managed standard.

Table 42–1 Physician Fee Schedule Analysis Using 199x RBRVS Conversion Factors: Specific Geographic Area Cost Indices

| | | Conversion Factors | | | |
| | | Current Payment Levels ($) | | Resulting from | Ratio of |
Physician Specialty	Payers Surveyed	Range of Surveys	Average of Surveys	Recommended Payment Schedule ($)	Recommended to Current Average
Allergy and immunology	3	25.98–33.10	30.00	29.99	1.00
Cardiovascular diseases	3	44.78–56.13	50.06	45.84	0.92
Cardiovascular and thoracic surgery	2	56.67–82.58	69.63	63.23	0.91
Colon and rectal surgery	3	46.77–74.24	58.33	58.68	1.01
Rheumatology	3	42.62–59.19	51.71	49.98	0.97
Urological surgery	3	55.15–73.87	65.87	59.11	0.90
Composite of all			49.89	49.26	0.99

Again, special data or expertise is required to perform steps 4 and 5 that will only exist in the larger HMOs, insurance companies, or consulting firms. An efficiency index for each hospital can be established by comparing the ratio of the actual length of stay to the best observed practice's length of stay using each hospital's mix of cases. Comparing each hospital or hospital department against a best observed practices standard allows benchmarking to identify, quantify and prioritize clinical opportunities. Table 42–2 presents sample output from a hospital length of stay efficiency study. Efficiency levels are stated as a percentage above or below well-managed targets on a DRG case mix–adjusted basis.

Actual inpatient clinical efficiency cannot be measured precisely using this methodology because the method does not address the appropriateness of admissions or the severity level of any given admission within a DRG. For example, Table 42–2 shows lower efficiency levels (i.e., a higher efficiency ratio) for maternity admissions than for medical or surgical admissions. This result may be due to inappropriate medical or surgical admissions of one or two days duration. Average length of stay analyses can be effectively performed across a hospital system, how-

ever, and are a reasonable indicator of the general opportunities available. In most situations, this fairly simple study is quite informative.

The hospital length of stay efficiency analysis may lead to more complex clinical studies to pinpoint specific causes of inefficient results. Clinical studies will identify appropriateness of admissions and care as well as systematic reasons for inefficient or delayed care.

Claim Probability Distributions

Actuarial cost models, by their design, represent the average, or expected, utilization and cost levels within an IDS. These models do not reflect the randomness of medical cost for an individual or the probable variation in expected medical costs for a grouping of individuals.

The risks associated with large claims for an individual or unusually large fluctuations for a grouping of individuals are analyzed using claim probability distributions (CPDs). Table 42–3 presents a typical CPD for all medical services for an individual. CPDs can be designed for any grouping of services within an IDS to assess these risks.

IDSs, using the analysis from CPDs, can establish reserve pools within their structure to im-

Table 42–2 Hospital Efficiency Analysis, Commercial Group Patients, Fiscal Year 199x

| | | Length of Stay (Days) | |
| | | Case Mix–Adjusted | Efficiency |
DRG Category	Reported	Well-Managed Model	Index Ratio
Medical			
Hospital A	2.94	2.66	110.5%
Hospital B	2.78	2.76	100.7
Surgical			
Hospital A	3.87	3.56	108.7%
Hospital B	4.30	3.41	126.1
Maternity: Cesarean section			
Hospital A	3.67	2.62	140.1%
Hospital B	3.49	2.66	131.2
Maternity: Vaginal delivery			
Hospital A	1.90	1.46	130.1%
Hospital B	2.24	1.51	148.3
Total all groups			
Hospital A	2.94	2.59	113.5%
Hospital B	3.12	2.74	113.9

Table 42–3 Sample CPD: All Members, All Medical Services, Claims Centered on 1 July 199x

Claim Distribution					Claim Cost Summary				
			Probability That Claims Are Greater	Annual Cost of Claims Greater Than or	Calendar				Value
	Total	Annual	Than or	Equal to	Year	Annual	% of $0	Monthly	of
Annual	Annual	Cost of	Equal to	Column 2	Deduct-	Claim	Deduct-	Claim	Deduct-
Frequency	Claim ($)	Claim ($)	Column 2	($)	ible ($)	Cost ($)	ible Cost	Cost ($)	ible ($)
0.193	0.00	0.00	1.000	2,634.12	0	2,634.12	100.0%	219.51	0.00
0.070	59.23	4.15	0.807	2,634.12	50	2,593.76	98.5	216.15	3.36
0.082	132.40	10.92	0.737	2,629.97	100	2,556.26	97.0	213.02	6.49
0.006	29,006.74	160.76	0.017	962.73	40,000	370.65	14.1	30.89	188.62
0.003	37,643.08	116.03	0.011	801.97	45,000	331.24	12.6	27.60	191.91
0.002	46,108.81	87.01	0.008	685.94	50,000	299.17	11.4	24.93	194.58
0.002	58,356.12	130.31	0.006	598.93	60,000	242.89	9.2	20.24	199.27

Source: Courtesy of Milliman & Robertson, Inc., Brookfield, Wisconsin.

munize their operational payments from large, randomly occurring claims. For example, global capitation payments may be made to a hospital within an IDS to provide all medical services to a certain population up to $50,000 in yearly medical expenses for any one individual. To fund individual claims above $50,000, the IDS can withhold a percentage of total expected medical costs and disburse amounts for these expenses when they occur. Thus individual hospitals within the IDS take the risk for all expenses up to $50,000 on individuals assigned to them, but the risk on claims above this amount is held at the IDS level. The IDS may then retain this risk or seek reinsurance protection from an outside source.

Individual CPDs may also be used to model the variation in total claims expected for a population of individuals. The actuarial cost model produces a point estimate for expected costs under a certain set of assumptions. This point estimate is expected to exceed actual costs approximately 50 percent of the time and to be less than actual costs about 50 percent of the time. As the number of members covered by an IDS increases, the variation about the point estimate becomes smaller. This expected variation in costs by membership size can be measured by mathematically combining several individual CPDs. This is useful in assessing and quantifying the need for aggregate reinsurance protection.

Other actuarial tools can be developed to assess other opportunities within an IDS, such as provider staffing, resource models, and compensation planning models. These are beyond the scope of this chapter but are discussed elsewhere.

CREATING INCENTIVE STRUCTURES

Incentive structures provide either financial or other reinforcement to focus providers within the IDS on attaining commonly determined goals. With proper design and monitoring, incentive structures can help achieve operating efficiency and quality.

Incentive structures are created by identifying logical groupings (or pools) of providers to share the risk/reward of managing a clinical segment of the IDS. Equally important in identifying these groupings is the operational disbursement, the method of settling up periodically, and the monitoring of each pool to ensure solvency. Ac-

tuarial tools and analyses can aid this process at each step. Some examples follow; these are not meant to be all inclusive or exhaustive.

Operational disbursements are made from each risk pool as routine payments for IDS services, on either a fee-for-service or a capitated basis. Amounts are typically withheld from these payments to protect each risk pool against excessive utilization and to ensure IDS solvency. Quarterly monitoring of each risk pool should be performed to ensure that withholds are adequate.

Annual accounting is typically performed to measure and distribute individual risk pool gains. Risk pool surpluses, before withholds are paid back, are typically used to offset any risk pool deficits of the other risk pools. After deficits are fully funded, providers receive their withhold amounts. Any remaining funds are then available to pay bonuses to the various stakeholders in each risk pool. For example, an IDS's inpatient hospital risk pool may be divided among primary care physicians, specialty care physicians, and the hospital, all of whom are stakeholders in ensuring that quality care is delivered efficiently.

Provider- or service-based risk pools can be constructed by reallocating the IDS's actuarial cost model targets. Common groupings may include hospital facility services, primary care physician capitated services, fee-for-service physician costs, other capitated expenses, and all other services. Here, data underlying the cost model may need to be reviewed and adjusted to allocate certain service categories to more than one risk pool (e.g., physician office visits would need to be allocated to both the primary care physician capitated pool and the fee-for-service physician pool to pay specialty care physicians).

Risk pools may also be established based on managing events that take place in the IDS. An event may focus solely on high-cost items handled by mainly one type of physician specialty (e.g., pregnancies handled by obstetricians) or by multiple specialties (e.g., laminectomies, which may be handled by neurosurgeons or orthopedic surgeons). A fair amount of latitude exists in defining the responsibilities of each of these event pools, which may be limited to specific physician procedure costs or may include the handling of all costs (including facility and prescription drugs) associated with treatment. Again, actuarial analysis can be used with clinical input to determine fair cost allocations into these risk pools. Risk pools may also be established based on managing diseases. For example, the costs associated with hemophiliacs may be gathered and classified into disease severity categories to assess the cost for treatment in the various categories and to prioritize areas where cost efficiency can be achieved without sacrificing quality of care.

Although the allocation of premium revenue will vary based on the many factors identified in Chapters 43 and 44, the funding of risk pools will typically be done as a fixed percentage of the medical cost component of premiums for each different office copay plan level. Table 42–4 provides an illustrative example of fixed funding percentages based on a $5 and $15 office copay plan. Base actuarial cost models are constructed for each of these broad plan options that identify each pool and PMPM costs allocated based on specific assumed utilization and provider reimbursement levels. These percentages will vary among IDSs as a result of the anticipated level of medical management, reimbursement expectations among the risk pools, and other plan design features (e.g., hospital member cost sharing will affect these percentages).

A provider and procedure code database can be used to evaluate and set provider-specific capitation rates. Capitations may be on a per member basis (which transfers the risk of occurrence to the provider) or on a case basis (which only transfers the risk of patient care to the provider). Care must be exercised to ensure that the specific services captured by the analysis reflect the services to be capitated. Adjustments may need to be made if the specific capitation is to cover all such services within the IDS. For example, if obstetrician/gynecologists are to ac-

Table 42–4 Illustrative Pool Funding Percentages by Office Copay

Risk Pool	Office Copay Level (%)	
	$5	$15
Hospital	38.4	39.8
Primary care physician	8.2	7.0
Specialty care physician	41.2	40.6
Other	12.2	12.6
Total	100.0	100.0

cept a case capitation rate for all deliveries, the utilization of family practitioners must be allocated to obstetrician/gynecologists in the database.

MEASURING RESULTS

The actuarial cost models and other models described in this chapter provide insight into identifying the important cost generating variables in the delivery of IDS services. These models are constructed using historical data and assumptions developed from many sources. They allow the IDS to identify, prioritize, and act on opportunities.

Report monitoring systems designed to capture IDS data in a format similar to these models can be used to perform actual-to-expected analyses. Such analyses allow the IDS to substitute historical data and assumptions based on outside sources with its own experience. These analyses are useful in setting future pricing levels and refining risk pool allocations and medical management policy. Actual-to-expected analyses are also used to identify, quantify, and prioritize a new set of IDS opportunities.

CONCLUSION

An IDS has many financial and clinical needs in its formation and operation. The tools of actuarial science allow focused analyses to help identify, quantify, and prioritize risk and opportunities within the IDS. Careful implementation and consideration of these tools in conjunction with accepted clinical practice guidelines, education forums, feedback reporting, and incentives for efficiency and quality improvement can help the IDS enjoy long-term success.

SUGGESTED READING

Sutton, H.L. and Sorbo, A.J. 1993. *Actuarial Issues in the Fee-For-Service/Prepaid Medical Group* (2nd ed.). Englewood, Colo.: Center for Research in Ambulatory Health Care Administration/MGMA.

Chapter 43

Rating and Underwriting

Stephen M. Cigich

Successful rating and underwriting create a balance among adequacy, competitiveness, and equity of rates in every case-specific rating situation. It can be a difficult and delicate balance to achieve. Moving too far in any direction could spell disaster for a health plan.

Rates are adequate when they are high enough to generate sufficient revenue to cover all plan expenses and yield an acceptable return on equity or contribution to reserves. Competitive rates are low enough to sell enough cases or enroll enough members to meet health plan growth goals. Rates are equitable when all factors that affect case-specific costs are appropriately reflected in the rating and underwriting process.

It is important for a health plan to assess continually its success in each of these areas. This is particularly true for a newly established plan or product offering. Until such a review, the plan cannot be certain whether a high volume of sales or successful renewals is good news or bad. After all, competitive, and perhaps equitable, rates are not necessarily adequate.

Each market segment contains different case-specific risk aspects that require different approaches to rating and underwriting. Major market segments include individual, commercial group, Medicare, and Medicaid. Each major segment has several components with unique risk characteristics that require rating and underwriting modifications. Without these modifications, the balance in rating and underwriting is not likely to be achieved.

This chapter addresses the commercial group market segment. Although the other market segments are important, most health plans offer products in the commercial market. Applying the ideas discussed here to tailor rating and underwriting tools to achieve rate adequacy, competitiveness, and equity in the other market segments will result in successful health plan operation.

Employer size, measured by number of employees, further segments the commercial group market. Small employers possess different risk characteristics than large employers. The rating and underwriting process must recognize that small employers can choose not to provide coverage for their employees. This voluntary nature of coverage presents an opportunity for the small employer to select adversely against a health plan that does not rate and underwrite this risk prudently.

Adverse selection is not unique to the small employer market segment. Employees of large employers will typically get to choose among competing health plans through an open enrollment process. Adverse selection may also occur, for example, within a plan with a poorly designed preferred provider organization plan design. Again, the design, rating, and underwriting

---
Stephen M. Cigich, F.S.A., is an actuary with the Milwaukee office of Milliman & Robertson, Inc. His area of expertise is in managed health care programs. He has assisted clients in the areas of medical delivery system design and evaluation, product and rate manual development, experience analysis, and actuarial projections.

process employed by the health plan must recognize the adverse selection risk and treat it in a way that will result in rates that are adequate, competitive, and equitable.

RATING VERSUS UNDERWRITING

Rating is the formula that solves for the expected case-specific price for a medical service product. The case-specific price will depend on the unique values that an employer group has for each cost generating variable recognized by the rating formula. This formula is sometimes called the book rate formula or manual rating structure. Underwriting will use the result of this formula alone or with case experience to produce the final rates. The underwriting process may modify the book rates and/or provide certain conditions to be satisfied by the employer or members before risk is accepted.

The rating structure must recognize all costs associated with the health plan, calculate premium rates, and be flexible to allow easy application in most situations. Health plan costs include medical services, sales/marketing, administrative, and return on equity. The rating formula will represent each cost by a specific, measurable cost generating variable. The results of the rating structure, which is typically expressed as a per member per month (PMPM) cost, must be transformed into premium rates for each employer using the employer's preferred billing basis (i.e., employee only, employee with one dependent, and employee plus two or more dependents).

The rating structure itself, or reports used to support the rating structure, will have other important applications in managing a health plan. These include establishing budgets by medical service category or department, establishing funding for provider-based risk pools, and identifying, quantifying, and ranking medical management opportunities within the health plan. Timely analysis of these data will allow the health plan to establish the proper provider-based education and incentives necessary to realize opportunities within the health plan.

Underwriting is the process used to arrive at the final rate and conditions or contingencies for accepting the employer group or individual members of the group. It modifies the results from the rating structure based on other quantitative or qualitative considerations. For small employer groups, it may consider the result of medical underwriting, the application of preexisting conditions limitations, or minimum participation requirements. For large employer groups, it may include evaluating prior claims experience or minimum penetration requirements in dual-choice offerings to employees.

RATE STRUCTURE DEVELOPMENT

The use of a rate structure will decide its construction. PMPM medical cost and revenue targets are established on a basis that allows recognition of several cost generating variables. Case-specific premium rates, the final output of the rate structure, are the translation of the PMPM targets into an employee billing basis. The most common approaches in use to establish case-specific PMPM revenue targets and premium rates are community rating, community rating by class (CRC), and adjusted community rating (ACR).

Community-rated PMPM revenue targets are the same for every group. The PMPM revenue requirements are set using communitywide data only. CRC rating uses case-specific data and the rate structure cost relativity factors to create unique revenue targets for each case situation. ACR is an extension of CRC but will also consider the employer's projected claims experience to modify the CRC rate structure result. ACR is normally reserved for large groups.

The process to translate PMPM revenue targets into premium rates is separate from the process to calculate PMPM targets, and much variation is possible. Premium rates for groups typically reflect only differences in employee billing bases using communitywide demographics. The small employer market may use a further modification by establishing billed premium rates that vary by the age and/or gender of the enrolled employees. Large cases may modify this result to reflect case-specific demographics yet still may vary final premium rates by employee billing basis only.

Medical Cost and Revenue Targets PMPM

The construction of a rating structure to develop PMPM revenue targets begins by choosing the rate structure variables and their interaction. The variables must consider all important determinants of costs yet be easy to measure and use. Given the design of the rate structure, the task turns to obtaining the necessary data to support the selected variables. Historical data will require adjustment to reflect future conditions.

Table 43–1 illustrates typical output for an actuarial cost model that details medical costs and revenue targets on a PMPM basis. A unique set of procedure codes defines each benefit service category (e.g., hospital inpatient services contain diagnosis-related group (DRG) groupings while current procedural terminology (CPT) code groupings define physician services). Further groupings may be done of the benefit service categories by existing or planned risk allocation pools. For example, Table 43–1 presents the cost for a core of narrowly defined primary care physician services in a separate section to support the capitation of those services.

The bottom of Table 43–1 presents administrative costs, coordination of benefits, and the net cost of reinsurance. Administrative revenue requirements must be sufficient to cover all functions, which may be all inclusive for a full service health maintenance organization (HMO) or just a subset of functions if the targets are for a physician–hospital organization or other provider-based group. Coordination of benefits (see Chapter 32) results in revenues back to the health plan for providing services to members who have their primary insurance elsewhere. The net cost of reinsurance is the actual cost to the health plan for providing protection against catastrophic loss and equals reinsurance premium net of reinsurance claims. Reinsurance

cost may appear elsewhere in Table 43–1 if its cost is the responsibility of a specific risk pool.

Columns 1, 2, and 4 in Table 43–1 are the cost driving variables that measure the cost to deliver medical services. Annual utilization per 1,000 members is the measure of service usage. Average cost per service is based on the fee level expectation required by the health plan and is the result of analyzing billed charges, maximum discount from billed (i.e., a fee floor acceptable by the health plan), and/or provider fee schedules. The impact of copays depends on the benefit plan design and the health plan policy for their collection.

The cost driving variables are dependent upon the values of other explanatory variables measured using formulas that are not shown in Table 43–1. Explanatory variables are either explicit (i.e., they are readily measured and reflected in the rating structure) or implicit (i.e., either their measurement or their impact is less well defined). Table 43–2 provides examples of the types of rate structure variables.

Explicit explanatory variables quantitatively measure different attributes of the rated risk and provide a measure of their impact on the cost of medical services. The member's distribution by age and gender is perhaps the best example of an explanatory variable. The rate structure will reflect the impact on various benefit groupings of the member's demographics. For example, a young, female population will have high maternity costs yet low prescription drug costs, and each benefit grouping will be adjusted using different factors.

Implicit explanatory variables are equally important in the rate structure, although by their nature they are more qualitative. The level of medical management in a health plan is a good example of an implicit explanatory variable. It is important to understand and measure the level of medical management in the data used to develop the rate structure and to make adjustments to reflect the impact of specific health plan initiatives. The overall level of health of the population modeled by the rate structure is also an important consideration. For example, the use of

Table 43–1 Actuarial Cost Model: Required Revenue for Calendar Year 19xx

Benefit	(1) Utilization per 1,000	(2) Allowed Average Charge	(3) Per Capita Monthly Claim Cost	(4) Frequency of Copay	(5) Copay	(6) Per Capita Monthly Cost Sharing Value	(7) Per Capita Monthly Net Claim Costs
Hospital inpatient							
Medical–surgical	247 Days	$1,276.76	$26.28				$26.28
Psychiatric/substance abuse	67 Days	657.31	3.67				3.67
Extended care	5 Days	250.00	0.10				0.10
Total hospital inpatient	319 Days	$1,130.56	$30.05				$30.05
Hospital outpatient							
Emergency department	261 Visits	$159.99	$3.48	196	$25.00	$0.41	$3.07
Surgery	85 Visits	1,172.46	8.30				8.30
Other outpatient services	512 Services	149.53	6.38				6.38
Total hospital outpatient			$18.16			$0.41	$17.75
Physician							
Primary care capitated							
Office and inpatient visits	2,152 Visits	$42.77	$7.67	2,035	$10.00	$1.70	5.97
Immunizations and injections	154 Procedures	17.14	0.22				0.22
Total primary care capitated			$7.89			$1.70	$6.19
Fee for service							
Surgery	374 Procedures	$266.63	$8.31				$8.31
Anesthesia	78 Procedures	575.38	3.74				3.74
Office and inpatient visits	1,025 Visits	45.78	3.91	944	$10.00	$0.78	3.13
Total fee for service			$36.44			$0.78	$35.66
Total physician			$44.33			$2.48	$41.85
Other							
Prescription drugs	5,209 Scripts	$36.00	$15.63	5,209	$5.00	$2.17	$13.46
Home health care	29 Visits	228.21	0.55				0.55
Ambulance	15 Runs	322.43	0.40				0.40
Durable medical equipment/ prosthetics	32 Units	269.54	0.72				0.72
Total other			$17.30			$2.17	$15.13
Total medical costs			$109.84			$5.06	$104.78
Administration							18.00
Coordination of benefits							(4.19)
Net cost of reinsurance							1.41
PMPM revenue required							$120.00

Table 43–2 Explanatory Rate Structure Variables

Explicit	Implicit
Member age	Medical management impact on
Member gender	• Utilization of services
Industry	• Average charge of services
Time period trend	Population overall health level
Benefit level	
Geographic service area	

health care costs in a loosely managed care environment will be different for a Medicare population than for a commercial group population. Such measurements require careful consideration, and special expertise is required to make prudent adjustments.

A premium rating structure will typically support many different benefit plan design options. It should also include adjustments necessary to reflect risk selection in dual-choice situations. Different plan designs, such as benefit rider selections, will probably be handled through adjustments to the base table costs. Selection adjustments are normally handled as multiplicative adjustments to the overall PMPM cost.

Many data sources are available to establish rate structure tables. Typically, no one data source can be used exclusively. Combining results from different data sources must be done with care. Health plan data are the best long-term source as a result of their relevance to the health plan, but newly established plans lack a credible amount of data. As a result, many health plans look to published sources or actuarial consulting firms to provide initial targets based on outside data in a structured form to allow substitution, over time, of their own health plan data.

When health plan data are used, they are summarized in 12-month segments to provide a more stable base and to avoid any seasonal conditions from influencing the results. Encounter and claim payment data (including any capitation payments to providers) are matched with health plan exposure measured in member months. Characteristics of the exposure must also be analyzed, such as member age, gender, benefit design, service area, and time period exposed. Calculations are performed to ensure that the claim data are on an incurred basis and are well matched with the exposure data.

Summarizing the results depends on both data quality and form as well as the health plan's financial organization. The definition of provider payment pools, capitated services, and any case rate arrangements must all be considered. As an example, Table 43–1 could be for a health plan where four risk pools are operating: hospital, primary care capitated services, physician fee for service, and ancillary. The hospital pool has a budget of $47.80 PMPM for both inpatient and outpatient services. Primary care physicians are paid a capitation of $6.19 PMPM for a limited grouping of CPT codes and fee for service from the physician fee-for-service pool for their remaining services. Noncapitated physician services are budgeted $35.66 PMPM. The ancillary pool has a budget of $15.13 PMPM. PMPM funding and operational fee-for-service and capitation payments can be made from these pools, and at the end of the year an accounting can be performed to decide individual pool gains or losses. These gains or losses are typically shared between the provider risk pools and the health plan in a predetermined fashion. Bonus payments to individual providers are then made from any pool gains, again on a predetermined basis.

As another alternative, the health plan might capitate mental health and substance abuse benefits. In this scenario, inpatient and outpatient mental health and substance abuse services would be removed from the various payment pools and placed in the ancillary pool as a special capitation.

Further data summaries will quantify adjustments for the explanatory variables. Details of the utilization and cost data can be allocated into the procedure code groupings. For example, physician inpatient surgery costs can be allocated by member status and age to develop relative cost relationships. Table 43–3 illustrates

Table 43–3 Physician Inpatient Surgery Cost Relativities by Age and Gender[*]

Member Age (Years)	Member Status			
	Employee		Spouse: All	Child: All
	Male	Female		
< 30	0.42	0.75		
30–39	0.53	1.30		
40–49	0.97	1.75		
50–59	2.30	2.15		
≥ 60	4.35	3.00		
Composite	1.19	1.49	1.50	0.32

[*] Overall composite of factors = 1.00.

physician inpatient surgery costs by employee age and gender, all spouses, and all children categories compared with costs for an average member. Note that the composite adjustment across all categories is equal to 1.0 when the standard rate structure demographics are used. Thus physician inpatient surgery costs assumed in the rate structure are replicated when standard demographics are used.

After historical data have been analyzed and placed into the structure required to model health plan operations, they must then be adjusted from their historical period to the pricing period for which they will be used. This adjustment is called trending. Exhibit 43–1 presents elements to consider that may change between these time periods. The elements of trend may be offsetting; for example, the underlying demand to use more health care services may be offset by anticipated improvements in the efficiencies achieved by specific medical management programs. Care must be exercised in reflecting lower projected cost in the future because this may lead to revenue shortfalls to the plan or in the unintended use of provider withhold funds (see Chapter 9) to eliminate any short fall.

The rate structure may be used in its Table 43–1 summary form for community rating, or the details behind Table 43–1 may be used for CRC. CRC will set group-specific rates using the total HMO's revenue targets adjusted using rate structure relationships for the group's unique risk characteristics. Examples of these unique risk characteristics include the following:

- employer industry classification

- age of member or subscriber

- gender of member or subscriber

- average number of members per contract type

- health status (e.g., smoker or nonsmoker, life style habits, etc.)

The purpose of CRC is to set rates closer to the rates expected given the risk characteristics of the group without using prior experience. Illustrative age and gender factors by employee contract type are shown in Table 43–4. These factors reflect the expected revenue requirements for an employee of a particular age, gender, and contract status compared with the HMO's total PMPM revenue target. For example, the expected revenue for a single male employee younger than 30 years is 50 percent

Exhibit 43–1 Components of Trend

> *Utilization*—Actual or anticipated changes in:
> - underlying demand for medical services
> - contractual benefit levels or member cost sharing
> - underwriting guidelines
> - utilization management program
> - delivery system or provider risk-sharing arrangements
>
> *Charges*—Actual or anticipated changes in:
> - fee schedules or billing practices
> - intensity of services
> - structure of provider contracts (e.g., per diem contracts may be expected to have different trend components than those with discount arrangements)

(i.e., 0.5 from Table 43–4) of the HMO's average PMPM revenue target. Note that the composite of all factors from Table 43–4 is equal to 2.32, the average number of members per employee contract. This ensures that the overall PMPM revenue is obtained when these factors are applied to the number of employee contracts.

Premium Rate Development

Several options are available for transforming the PMPM revenue targets into premium rates. The option selected will depend on the billing basis required by the employer and the level in which employer data are used to develop the premium rates. This section assumes that the case-specific PMPM revenue targets are already established.

The billing basis for employers is some form of employee contract. The contract holder (i.e., subscriber) is the employee, and the premium rates reflect all the members associated with that particular employee. Rates are sometimes expressed on a per employee basis only but are usually expressed with finer breakouts of employees by their dependent status. Table 43–5 presents common billing bases.

Community-rated premium rates are developed using community or plan assumptions regarding average number of members per employee contract type. Modified community rating will use employer membership characteristics by contract or perhaps competitive contract relativity information. Either method can develop premium rates to be charged to the group on a contract basis (e.g., all employees with spouses have the same rate) or on an age and/or gender basis by contract type (e.g., male employees age 30 have a different rate than female employees age 45). The contract basis is more common, but many small group plans will bill on an age/gender basis where allowed by law.

Despite the method employed, premium rates depend on the PMPM revenue requirements, demographic assumptions underlying their development, and targeted premium relationships. The demographic assumptions include the distribution of contracts (e.g., single employee, employee plus spouse, etc.) and the average number of members per contract. As noted above, the demographic assumptions may be expected HMO demographics (community rating) or employer demographics (modified community rating or CRC). Targeted premium relationships relate to the cost relativity among the various contract types and usually reflect competitive requirements.

Table 43–6 shows the development of a four-tier [i.e., single, employee and spouse, employee and child(ren), and family] community rating billing basis. In this example, the plan demographics assume 2.32 members per employee contract. Additionally, the average members within each contract type is also shown. Column 1 presents the distribution of employees by contract type. Column 2 presents the members for each contract type and illustrates that the weighted average of members per contract equals the total average members per contract of 2.32. Column 3 presents the premium load necessary to rate each contract type adequately and illustrates that the weighted average equals total average members per contract. Column 4 presents the HMO PMPM revenue required, and column 5, the target premium rate by contract, is

Table 43–4 Illustrative Age/Gender Factors[*]

Employee Age (Years)	Employee		Employee with Family	
	Male	Female	Male	Female
< 30	0.5	1.2	2.9	2.8
30–39	0.7	1.3	2.8	2.6
40–49	1.0	1.4	2.7	2.5
50–59	1.4	1.5	2.9	3.1
> 60	1.9	1.8	3.4	3.5

[*] Overall composite of factors = 2.32.

Table 43–5 Common Employer Billing Bases

Type*	Separate Premium Rates Calculated for
One tier	Employee
Two tiers	Employee
	Employee with family
Three tiers	Employee
	Employee with one dependent
	Employee with two or more dependents
Four tiers	Employee
	Employee with spouse
	Employee with child(ren)
	Employee with spouse and child(ren)

* These structures may also be list billed in the small case market, with premium rates being calculated by employee age and/or gender.

the multiplication of the premium load and the PMPM revenue.

The premium load in column 3 relates to a member cost relativity of 1.00 and is based on an analysis of claims costs among the various contract types. Alternatively, the premium load may reflect competitive considerations. The single premium load in Table 43–6, the ratio of the single premium to the PMPM revenue, is estimated to be 1.19. The single premium is an adult (actually an employee) only rate, whereas the PMPM revenue reflects HMO average member costs when adults and children are combined.

Because child costs are expected to be much lower than adult costs, the employee contract premium is set higher than the PMPM revenue.

In competitive situations, an HMO wishing to enter a large employer account may modify the premium load to reflect the rating relativity used by the employer's current insurance plan. For example, the employer may insist that family rates equal 3.0 times the single rate (i.e., $142.80 \times 3 = $428.40). Table 43–7 illustrates how the HMO can accomplish this and still collect the community PMPM revenue requirement of $120.00. Note the change in the relativity of all premium loading factors from Table 43–6. This is necessary to ensure that the required PMPM revenue ($278.40 divided by 2.32) is obtained.

An example of modified (or CRC) premium rating is provided in Table 43–8 using the age/gender factors from Table 43–4. The example is for an employee only contract, and the process is similar to that for other contract types. The resulting premium rate in this example is 15 percent above the PMPM revenue target (premium loading factor equals 1.15) and 3 percent below the community-rated employee premium (1.15 divided by 1.19). CRC will, of course, result in more rate variability than community rating. Table 43–8 could be modified to illustrate the type of calculation used to determine the premium required of individuals of a small employer group. For example, the premium rate to charge all male employees younger than 30 years would be $60.00 (i.e., $120 \times 0.5 = $60).

Table 43–6 Four-Tier Premium Rate Development

Contract Type	(1) Contract Distribution (%)	(2) Members Per Contract	(3) Premium Loading Factor	(4) PMPM Target Revenue Requirement	(5) Target Premium Rate ($)
Employee	41	1.0	1.19	120.00	142.80
Employee with spouse	15	2.0	3.08	120.00	369.60
Employee with child(ren)	10	2.5	2.04	120.00	244.80
Employee with spouse and child(ren)	34	4.0	3.42	120.00	410.40
Composite	100	2.32	2.32	120.00	278.40

Table 43–7 Competitively Adjusted Premium Loading Factors

Contract Type	Contract Distribution (%)	Standard Premium Loading Factor	Competitive Premium Loading Factor[*]	Resulting Competitive Premium Rate ($)
Employee	41	1.19	1.19	142.80
Employee with spouse	15	3.08	2.86	343.20
Employee with child(ren)	10	2.04	1.89	226.80
Employee with spouse and child(ren)	34	3.42	3.57	428.40
Composite	100	2.32	2.32	278.40

[*] Employee with spouse and child(ren) is set equal to 3.0 times the employee rate. Other contract factors are adjusted to maintain their standard relationship to each other.

UNDERWRITING

Underwriting is the pragmatic side of rating. Underwriting can occur at various points in an employer group's life cycle:

- at quotation, through rating adjustments
- at issue, through participation (based on work or time employed requirements)
- at time of claim, through applying preexisting contract coverage or coordination of benefits interpretations
- at renewal, through new participation requirements

This section will only discuss underwriting adjustments made at the time of quotation.

Rating adjustments made through the quotation process are made using data and judgments regarding the risk associated with enrolling a specific employer group or, in dual-choice situations, a subset of employees. The rating structure is the basis for these adjustments.

The underwriting process begins with data collected to allow premium rate calculation using the rating structure. The development of rate structure premium rates assumes that all aspects of a particular employer group have the same characteristics as the rate structure. The underwriting process will correct this assumption, as necessary and allowed by regulation, and make adjustments using qualitative and quantitative analyses. Perhaps the most notable

Table 43–8 Community Rating by Class Example (Health Plan PMPM Revenue Target, $120.00)

Employee Age (Years)	Employee	
	Male	Female
< 30	5	6
30–39	4	5
40–49	3	4
50–59	2	3
> 60	1	2
	15	20

Employee
  only premium = $120.00 × [(5)(0.5)+(4)(0.7)+
                (3)(1.0)+(2)(1.4)+(1)(1.9)+(6)(1.2)+
                (5)(1.3)+(4)(1.4)+(3)(1.5)+
                (2)(1.8)]÷(15+20)
             = $120.00 × (40.4 ÷ 35)
             = $138.51

of the adjustments made is through the experience-rating process, which uses past employer data.

Experience rating develops claims costs, revenue targets, and premium rates based entirely or partially on a group's experience. Experience rating methods may rely on actual claim costs, utilization statistics, loss ratios, or some combination of these approaches. If less than full credibility is given to the group based on too few members or other considerations, then the results of using the group's experience will be weighted with results from the rate structure to yield final results.

Experience rating is generally done on larger groups, where the experience is judged to be credible enough to justify the effort involved. The purpose is to achieve the goals introduced at the beginning of this chapter: to produce rates that are adequate, competitive, and equitable in every case-specific rating situation.

Careful judgment must be used when case-specific information is used. The data reviewed must be scrutinized carefully for inconsistencies. Similar questions must be asked of the data as when the health plan's total revenue targets

were established because the process of experience rating is similar.

Many methods are available to rate an employer group based on prior claims experience. The method chosen should be based on the quality and type of information available. A simplified example of claims-based experience rating is shown in Exhibit 43–2. Two years of claims information is used in this example to illustrate the weighing of more than 1 year of data. Multiple years are often used to reduce the impact of fluctuation that may occur in a group's year-to-year claims experience. Large claims are pooled to reduce the impact of fluctuation in the group's experience due to an unexpected number of such claims. The pooling adjustment replaces actual claims above the pooling point with the health plan's expected amount.

No explicit adjustments are made between the time periods for trend, benefit design, or demographics. Any differences are accounted for in steps 6 and 7, with the actual-to-expected ratio being calculated using the plan's expected claims based on the group's characteristics in each of the experience periods. The group's data are ratioed to the expected claims calculated using a manual rate structure for each experience year (step 7). Generally, different credibility adjustments will be applied to each year of experience, with more weight being given to the most current year. The plan's expected PMPM revenue target (step B) is calculated from the manual rate structure given the plan's current benefit design, demographics, and other rating factors reflected by the manual rate structure. Step C is the calculation that combines the employer's experience ratio for each year with the expected cost calculated from the manual rate structure. In this example, 60 percent, 20 percent, and 20 percent weight is given to the employer's most recent, the employer's second most recent, and the manual rate structure result, respectively.

Exhibit 43–3 is a simplified example of another experience rating method based on case-specific utilization statistics. Experience rating in this situation uses utilization statistics to de-

Exhibit 43–2 Claim Cost Experience Rating Example

Step A: Group-Specific Experience

Category	Year*	
	t	*t–1*
1. Paid claims	$68.00	50.00
2. Incurred claims	82.00	65.00
3. Pooling charge	8.00	7.00
4. Pooled claims	(10.00)	(2.00)
5. Claims charged (2+3+4)	$80.00	$70.00
6. Employer expected claims	$75.00	$60.00
7. Experience ratio (5 ÷ 6)	1.07	1.17
8. Credibility	60%	20%

* *t*, most recent year; *t–1*, next most recent year.

Step B: Plan Expected PMPM Revenue Target = $120

Step C: Group Experience Rating Development

PMPM Revenue Target = $120 × [(1.07)(60%)+
(1.17)(20%)+
(1.00)(20%)]

= $129.12

Exhibit 43–3 Utilization Experience Rating Example

Step A: Group Specific Utilization

Category	Year*	
	t	*t–1*
Inpatient days per 1,000		
Group (*G*)	300	350
Health plan (*H*)	280	300
Ratio (*G* ÷ *H*)	1.07	1.17
Weight	40%	40%
Office visits per 1,000		
Group	3,100	3,300
Health plan	2,900	3,000
Ratio	1.07	1.10
Weight	50%	50%
Scripts per 1,000		
Group	4,900	5,000
Health plan	4,600	4,800
Ratio	1.07	1.04
Weight	10%	10%
Average ratio	1.07	1.12†
Credibility	60%	20%

* *t*, most recent year; *t–1*, next most recent year.

† 1.12 = (1.17)(40%)+(1.10)(50%)+(1.04)(10%)

Step B: Plan Expected PMPM Revenue Target = $120

Step C: Group Experience Rating Development

PMPM Revenue Target = $120.00 × [(1.07)
(60%)+(1.12)(20%)+
(1.00)(20%)]

= $127.92

---

velop an actual-to-expected utilization (as opposed to cost) ratio for the group that is multiplied by the expected revenue target. Again, the expected revenue target is adjusted to reflect the group's benefit plan and demographics for the pricing period.

These are but two examples of experience rating methods. Others can be used, but care should always be exercised to ensure that the results are consistent with expectations and reflect the nature of the rated risk. The reader is referred to Chapter 42 for a discussion of actuarial services in managed care organizations and integrated delivery systems. The reader is also referred to Chapter 44 for an in-depth discussion of operational underwriting issues.

CONCLUSION

The success of rating and underwriting methods is measured in the ability of the health plan to meet growth and profitability goals. As shown in this chapter, there are many methods to employ for establishing revenue and premium targets. The right combinations must be selected and the resulting experience closely monitored to guarantee better the chances of success. Successful plans will employ systems that achieve the appropriate balance in rates that are adequate, competitive, and equitable on a group-specific basis.

SUGGESTED READING

Chollet, D.J. and Paul, R.R. 1994. *Community Rating: Issues and Experience*. Washington, D.C.: Alpha Center.

Dowd, B. and Feldman, R. 1995. Premium Elasticities of Health Plan Choice. *Inquiry* 31 (4): 438–444.

Chapter 44

Operational Underwriting in Managed Care Organizations

Gregory J. Lippe

Reviewing critical success factors in a managed care organization (MCO) prompts discussion of medical management, marketing, provider relations, and finance. Even experienced managed care personnel, however, often underestimate the importance of underwriting. This chapter reviews underwriting from an operations perspective to supplement the actuarial perspective provided in the previous chapter. Knowledge of risk factors and underwriting principles can benefit the MCO, its customers, and those organizations contracting with the MCO on a risk basis.

HISTORICAL OVERVIEW

Underwriting within an MCO can be defined as processes to attract, maintain, and manage the cross-section of risk reflected in the actuarial and financial assumptions of the organization's business plan. Successful underwriting yields the membership, the revenue per member per month (PMPM), and utilization levels anticipated in the MCO business plan.

Many MCOs did not historically develop strong underwriting processes. Federally qualified health maintenance organizations (HMOs) were limited in their underwriting practices by

Gregory J. Lippe is Senior Manager in the Milwaukee office of the national health care consulting practice of Ernst & Young LLP. He assists payers and providers with managed care strategy, operational assessments, mergers, acquisitions, and business development. Previously, Mr. Lippe was employed by United HealthCare Corporation, EQUICOR, and Time Insurance in a variety of executive positions.

federal regulation and related interpretations. Where not constrained by federal or state regulation, underwriting was an infrequent MCO priority. This often reflected the competencies of existing MCO management and their limited knowledge of and appreciation for underwriting. Today, some managed care personnel continue to view sales and underwriting activities as a roll of the dice rather than as integrated processes that should be managed to the benefit of the MCO.

Despite limited appreciation for and use of underwriting techniques, many MCOs were successful in the 1980s with their pricing and risk selection approaches. Previously, the dominant indemnity carrier or Blue Cross/Blue Shield (BCBS) plan serving a large employer group generally ignored the upstart MCO. The dominant carrier's arrangement with the employer often limited or eliminated health insurance risk. In many instances, the dominant carrier functioned as a third party administrator (TPA) of the employer benefit program. As a TPA, the carrier may have been paid based on the number or level of claim payments processed by the carrier. The higher the utilization of services, the more the administrative fee paid to the TPA.

Focus on larger cases tended to mitigate the MCO risk of ignoring or utilizing limited underwriting practices. Many large employers, particularly in the 1980s, offered multiple benefit plans of several different MCOs and/or insurance companies. In this dual or multiple choice environment, MCOs with relatively closed delivery systems often attracted a favorable risk selection. The closed panel delivery system (see Chapter 3) of many MCOs was a concern to potential members with an established physician relationship and whose physician did not participate in the MCO. MCO benefit program emphasis on preventive or routine services also tended to appeal to younger families. These and other factors tended to protect MCOs despite their limited use of underwriting techniques.

Most MCOs possessed the ability to increase premium to levels to fund the projected risk or claim costs during the last 25 years. These periods were marked by the willingness of employers and their employees to accept significant premium increases, especially when indemnity insurance premium increases were even higher. When an MCO suffered poor claim experience, it could increase its premium to offset the higher than anticipated utilization or cost experience. This ability to raise premium when necessary or desired reduced MCO interest in underwriting. Underwriting was often viewed as merely an improved pricing methodology.

SALES AND UNDERWRITING COLLABORATION

To encourage effective underwriting, personnel from finance/accounting and marketing/sales should share underwriting *and* sales responsibilities. Collaboration by sales and underwriting personnel within MCOs:

- encourages rational risk taking and innovative customer solutions

- improves management of factors influencing sales and underwriting results

- includes an underwriting perspective in overall MCO decision making

- influences the marketing approach and sales plan of the MCO

- balances membership growth and financial results

- utilizes underwriting information to manage new member risk

Personnel who price the MCO product follow methodologies that theoretically yield an actuarially sound outcome that is consistent with the business plan. In MCOs with only a pricing as opposed to an underwriting perspective, responsibility for overall risk selection is assumed or shared by senior personnel, including the chief financial officer. When responsibility is assumed at this senior level, there often is little accountability for day-to-day or group-specific underwriting decisions. The pricing approach prepares quotations on a timely basis but fails to manage planwide risk effectively and ignores or underestimates the importance of risk management on a product line and/or group level basis.

To support collaboration between sales/marketing and finance/accounting personnel, several MCOs have aligned compensation and bonus arrangements to balance sales growth and MCO profits. Proper alignment encourages the underwriter to build market share at a profitable premium level. Similarly, sales personnel are encouraged and rewarded for profitable business, not just membership growth.

MANAGEMENT INFORMATION SYSTEM

To operate an effective underwriting function, the MCO must possess an effective management information system (MIS). Underwriting is dependent on access to, analysis of, and interpretation of administrative, claim, and encounter data. These data must reflect all MCO health services.

Many MCOs contract out or capitate certain health services or risks, such as mental health/substance abuse (see Chapter 22), laboratory (see Chapter 21), and prescription services (see Chapter 23). Regardless of short-term contract arrangements, the MCO must capture, analyze, and routinely track services and/or risks managed by outside vendors. Access to and analysis of all health care data are essential for effective underwriting as well as for MCO initiatives involving outcomes research and disease management.

The MCO MIS must also track and monitor selected administrative services. Managing risk and improving product design can benefit from an understanding of feedback from member services and provider relations. Consistent questions or complaints related to a benefit may suggest that in the next product design cycle new wording should be added or substituted. Benefit redesign may also be considered given the frequency and risk associated with the questions or complaints. Similarly, feedback from provider relations should help identify concerns that may be causing administrative problems for the provider. Some of these concerns may affect the utilization and/or cost of the benefits provided. Consequently, if the MCO relies on an outside vendor or affiliated entity to provide member services or a 24-hour nurse referral line, the MIS must still capture and analyze the activities of these services.

Fundamentally, data must be available at the group level to assist in new case and renewal underwriting decisions. The MCO must be able to roll up data by industry, by product type, by market segment, and by age and gender. Properly managed data can also contribute to measuring the effectiveness of a sales representative, independent agent, and/or an MCO distribution channel. It is essential to measure both the level of activity and the actuarial/financial results of all MCO distribution channels, products, and market segments. The need for all these data elements and their analysis emphasizes the importance of an effective MIS to an MCO and its management challenges, including underwriting.

The underwriting function must understand and comply with regulations from several sources. If the MCO is a federally qualified HMO (see Chapter 54), it is subject to limited product and pricing requirements. If the MCO is a state-licensed HMO or a BCBS plan, it could be subject to special enabling legislation and/or state regulation (see Chapter 53). When enacted, insurance reform at the state level has produced regulation affecting MCO product design, pricing, and in some instances MCO compensation

paid to independent agents or the sales force. Serving the Federal Employees Health Benefit Program (see Chapter 45), Medicaid (see Chapter 48), and/or Medicare (see Chapters 46 and 47) under risk contracts lends additional underwriting requirements. Although this discussion encourages a proactive approach to underwriting, it views regulatory compliance as an absolute necessity and ultimately the most effective approach.

To comply with much of this regulation, the MCO must possess an MIS that is capable of tracking and modeling certain activities and outcomes. As an example, state regulation may require MCO pricing to return a minimum specified percentage of premium to members or covered persons in the form of health care benefits provided. In other cases, states may require the MCO to share a percentage of savings with the state if the percentage of benefits falls below a specified percentage of premium. Similarly, the MIS needs to monitor key benefit and premium relationships when products are offered to the Medicare market.

MAJOR RISK FACTORS

Although some suggest that underwriting is more an art than a science, experienced underwriters generally emphasize the importance of first understanding the science. Much of the science is described from an actuarial perspective in the preceding chapters. This chapter supplements the actuarial material by identifying and discussing the key elements of risk to an MCO. These same risk factors are indirectly assumed and should be understood by vendors that contract with the MCO under a fixed-price, percentage of premium, or capitated arrangement. The major risk factors include the following:

- *Demographic factors*—The age and gender of members of the group to be covered are key predictors of future utilization. Predicting utilization, even when all health care costs are fixed under capitation arrangements, is necessary to ensure that adequate resources are available to deliver high-quality and effective services. Even when the demographic factor is not specifically adjusted for on a group basis, it should be tracked by the MCO. Similarly, vendors contracting with the MCO are encouraged to analyze and track demographic factors to understand their utilization experience and assist with subsequent contract negotiations with the MCO.

- *Economic factors*—The actual costs of services and applicable rates of inflation influence reimbursement paid to providers regardless of the payment methodology because long-term, even capitated contracts get renewed. Incorporating these economic factors into the pricing methodology is essential for employer group renewals at premium levels projecting the future cost for the MCO.

- *Enrollment factors*—The size of a group is crucial. Certain services, such as billing and collection, are largely fixed costs that are more effectively spread over a larger group of covered persons. Apart from administrative efficiencies, the larger the group of covered persons, the more likely it is that a consistent claim pattern, level of health care cost, or utilization of services will emerge and be planned for accordingly. Larger groups of 1,000 employees and dependents or more are generally viewed as credible; that is, the group's previous claim experience or utilization of services should be a good predictor of future health care service requirements assuming that no major changes in the group's composition occur.

- *Industry factors*—Populations employed within a specific industry have historical claim patterns or health service requirements defined by claim experience over many years. Certain industries have been shown by actuarial studies consistently to use less than average, average, or above average levels of health care services. Even when the industry factor is not priced for on a group-specific level, it should be tracked by the MCO and considered in various analyses. Vendors contracting with the MCO under a risk arrangement would be prudent to assess and track the composite industry factor of the MCO's block of business.

- *Probability*—Variations from expected or typical utilization rates even for large groups occur over time. For the claim patterns of groups smaller than 100 covered lives, there is increased likelihood of variance and a greater range of variance from the average or MCO norm compared with a group of 1,000 covered lives. Even with several years of experience, groups with less than 100 covered lives are not credible and therefore difficult to predict as to claim experience or utilization of required services.

- *Provider practices*—The practice orientation of providers in both owned health centers and contracted physician networks significantly influences the utilization of health services. These practices can vary even within an MCO's service area. Understanding the impact of provider practices contributes to more effective pricing and improved projection of health services. Provider practices are critical to the MCO and to health care vendors contracting with the MCO on a risk basis.

- *Selection factors*—Individuals joining an MCO act in their own best interests. In a dual-choice environment where the employee has at least two benefit options to choose from, the type of enrollment appeal, including product design or delivery system, can influence member selection of a health plan and hence MCO risk selection. When the MCO is the only or dominant health care option, selection factors are obviously less important.

The more an MCO identifies, analyzes, and reacts to these variables in its operations, the greater the likelihood of improved financial performance. Underwriting should be a responsibility shared by personnel throughout the MCO. Similarly, if a vendor contracting with an MCO understands these variables, there is a greater likelihood that the vendor will sustain a financially sound relationship with the MCO over the long term.

UNDERWRITING AS AN INTERNAL CONTROL

Understanding the variables of risk enables MCO leadership to pursue prudent approaches to selecting and managing risk. These approaches reflect the art of underwriting. One fundamental process involves routinely evaluating and tracking changes and trends in the entire block of business. The MCO should also monitor performance and trends at the industry, product line, and market segment levels. Variations and potential concerns should be identified, explained, and corrected. Effective group-specific underwriting is fundamental to consistent MCO enrollment and financial success.

An effective underwriting function acts as an important internal control for the MCO. The underwriting function, through analysis of claim data, should identify emerging trends and/or abuses at the employer, employee, and/or provider level. Examples of trends or issues that have been previously identified and/or clarified by experienced underwriting personnel using standard analyses include the following:

- the need for benefit plan changes (e.g., increase the office visit copay, amend the approach to prescription drug benefits and/or mental health/substance abuse services, address utilization concerns involving the use of rehabilitation services or coverage of nondurable medical equipment)
- the need for updated review of the pricing basis as the competitive position of the MCO significantly deteriorates (or improves) as noted by the level of underwriting/sales activity and/or the ratio of closed or successful new business sales to completed quotations
- opportunities for cost reductions for health services (e.g., channeling certain services, such as mental health, laboratory, or specified radiology procedures, to an alternative or single vendor)
- the need for review of sales procedures and enrollment appeals based on monitoring of risk selection of new members joining the MCO for the first 6 months after joining the MCO (e.g., a common MCO procedure is to review the level of hospital inpatient usage of new members during their first 6 months of coverage. These analyses should be done on an ongoing new member basis as well as for new groups)

The underwriting function should contribute to the enrollment and revenue PMPM assumptions included in the annual MCO business plan. Underwriting should also help determine the demographic and industry factors of the MCO's enrollment to project future resource or health service requirements. Demographic and industry factors are explained later in the overview of MCO pricing methodologies.

EMPLOYER GROUP UNDERWRITING

Some MCOs confuse a simple pricing approach with the concepts of underwriting. These MCOs merely reply to employer group requests for quotations on specific benefit packages. Although a simple pricing approach quickly fills the request for rate quotes, it is not as productive, innovative, or proactive as group-specific and/or market segment underwriting.

Underwriting should be much more than filling orders and determining price. As previously defined, underwriting is a set of integrated processes that attract, maintain, and manage the cross-section of risk reflected in the MCO's business plan. Effective MCO underwriting is most easily demonstrated at the employer group level.

The sales and underwriting process to identify and close a new employer group includes the integrated steps shown in Exhibit 44–1. While reviewing these steps, note the desirability of strong collaboration between sales and underwriting. The new employer sales efforts are directed and include the input and/or influence of underwriting. Similarly, the final proposal developed by underwriting reflects the input of the sales team.

Renewal of an existing account should follow a pattern similar to that shown in Exhibit 44–1 to ensure that the MCO understands the current employer group environment. Making an assumption that nothing has changed at the employer group can lead to significant and unplanned variances in enrollment, risk selection, and ultimately financial performance.

Group level analysis and decisions contribute to the overall formation and management of the MCO business block. Underwriting success at a group level should be measured in several ways. Increased enrollment, improvement or maintenance of risk profiles, and improvements in premium adequacy are three key indicators. The old adage among hospitals, "No margin, no mission," also applies to MCOs today, regardless of their tax status.

Group underwriting is dependent upon employer group information. Most data on new potential employer groups are supplied to underwriting by the marketing/sales force. Many long-time and established MCOs still quote premiums and benefit plans lacking fundamental employer group information. MCO management often concludes that it has no apparent choice but to quote without all or any of the desired information. This conclusion ignores at least three alternatives. First, the MCO does not need, and only rarely may be required, to quote on a particular case. Second, the quotation prepared with limited information could reflect conservative assumptions that will encourage enhanced information gathering efforts by sales personnel in the future. Third, a quotation could

Exhibit 44–1 Steps in the Sales and Underwriting Process

Step 1: Sales and underwriting personnel collaborate on identifying and targeting key employers, industries, and/or employer characteristics for use by the sales force.

Step 2: Sales personnel contact targeted groups and collect data, prequalifying the employer group using checklist or criteria supplied by underwriting.

Step 3: Sales personnel prepare and submit a request for a quotation to underwriting.

Step 4: Underwriting reviews the request, qualifies the employer group, and identifies any additional questions that sales is requested to pursue.

Step 5: A clerk prepares an analysis of basic group characteristics and runs the initial pricing of the requested benefit plan(s) and contract effective date(s).

Step 6: An underwriter reviews the case materials, including updated data from sales, and determines whether the case should be declined or quoted.

Step 7: Through an iterative process, the underwriter develops the benefit plans, pricing, conditions, and/or options that the MCO will tentatively offer to the employer group.

Step 8: Sales reviews the underwriting proposal, and any questions or differences between sales and underwriting are resolved.

Step 9: Sales presents the MCO proposal to the targeted group, closes the sale, and assists the employer group throughout the enrollment process.

Step 10: Underwriting reviews the actual group enrollment and identifies any major variations from the assumptions made during the sales/underwriting process.

be prepared with some contingencies or requirements that serve to protect the MCO when quoting a case without basic information.

One such contingency might be a minimum level of enrollment to avoid attracting a single contract or limited enrollment at an employer group that causes administrative difficulties to both the employer and the MCO. This contingency also indirectly considers the potential adverse risk selection that could occur in a limited employer enrollment. Other contingencies could relate to changes in carriers offered, the employer's contribution strategy, and/or the benefit design by the self-funded employer group base benefit plan. Admittedly, selling proposals with contingencies is more difficult. Such contingencies will often encourage the marketing/sales personnel to eliminate the need for the contingency through securing and supplying more information.

Collection and interpretation of employer group information produce understandable tension between underwriting and sales/marketing personnel. In difficult situations with emotions running high, all MCO personnel should recall three concepts. First, even the best medical management system cannot completely offset poor or deteriorating risk selection. Second, the MCO needs more members than patients. Third, employer group decisions affect the group under review and contribute to the results for the entire block of business. These three concepts are particularly important for the MCO with a limited enrollment and capital base.

KEY EMPLOYER GROUP DATA

Employer group–specific data usually required by a proactive underwriting department include the following:

- address of business and number of years in operation

- industry of the proposed employer group and activities performed in the service area

- number and location of employees by 5-digit ZIP code within the MCO's service area

- number of contract tiers or required premiums (e.g., single, couple, family, etc.)

- mix of contracts and average number of persons covered per contract

- age and gender characteristics of at least the employee workforce

- prior year premiums of at least the dominant carrier in the group

- benefit plan options available to employees and the number of employees choosing each option

- employer contribution policy

- employee out-of-pocket cost for health care options

- requested benefit plan and tier structure of the employer or its consultant

Marketing/sales representatives who have not previously collected employer group–specific information will have understandable concerns about its availability and the ease and value of collecting it. The proactive underwriting function addresses these concerns by ensuring that the sales representative understands the need for collection and use of group-specific information. Underwriting and rate setting need not be a "black box" to marketing/sales personnel.

By utilizing group-specific and market segment information, the MCO substantially increases its chances to attract a cross-section of risk and reasonably project the size, characteristics, and health care needs of new MCO membership. The availability and use of group-specific information helps the MCO maintain and better serve employer groups during their annual renewal period. Increasingly, much of the information tracked and analyzed by the underwriting function is being requested by the employer group to improve its assessment of MCO performance and that of its benefits program. The MCO underwriting function can play an important role in responding to the data requests of employer groups. Underwriting personnel can assist sales/marketing in responding to employer requests for data. Through a collaborative approach, the MCO can offer the employer group data, and more important, analysis that turns the data into information of use to the employer group.

MARKET FACTORS AND TRENDS

The marketplace evolution in the last several years has underscored the need for proactive underwriting competencies in MCOs. Trends or factors present and projected in most markets that encourage MCO interest in underwriting include the following:

- declining ability to increase premiums
- deteriorating or poor MCO financial results
- competitors apparently buying market share
- stagnation or even loss of market share by the MCO
- complexity in renewing large employer groups
- groups requiring more data, more options, and lower health care costs
- MCO risk as the dominant carrier or insurance option at the employer group
- increased focus on midsize (100 to 500) and medium-size (25 to 99) groups
- MCO initiatives to serve small groups of less than 25 employees
- consolidation of carriers/health options within larger groups
- complexity of point-of-service and/or triple-option programs
- entry into the Medicaid market on a risk basis
- entry into the Medicare market on a risk basis
- responding to state reform initiatives

These trends or factors have prompted MCOs to review their underwriting and marketing/sales processes. Through review and analysis, many MCOs have significantly evolved their pricing and underwriting methodologies.

COMMUNITY RATING METHODOLOGIES

The pricing methodology chosen by the MCO affects and is affected by ongoing marketing, sales, and underwriting processes. Many MCOs have adopted some derivation of community rating. Under community rating, the MCO charges a similar premium to employer groups and/or individuals with like benefits and the same contract renewal date.

There are three related but distinct standard community rating methodologies: simplified community rating, adjusted community rating (ACR), and community rating by class (CRC). To explain and demonstrate each of these pricing methodologies, this section generates rates for Dream Group, Inc., a hypothetical employer. After discussing common MCO pricing methodologies, the section focuses on underwriting concepts.

Summarized in Exhibit 44–2 is the assumed group-specific information provided primarily by the sales force to the underwriting function. The importance and use of the factors are examined through review of the three rating methodologies. Note that some of the employer information is not directly used by the less sophisticated rating methodologies. Also, an MCO might have used or is now using a hybrid of the rating methodologies discussed. Addition-

---

Exhibit 44–2 Key Assumptions and Factors for Dream Group, Inc.

The group includes 500 employees all located in the same MCO service area.

The chosen benefit plan and effective date require $125 revenue PMPM.

The group has a three-tier premium scheme with single, couple, and family contracts.

The couple rate is 1.95 times the single rate; the family is 2.85 times the single rate.

The percentage mix of contracts within the group is 30/20/50 for single/couple/family.

The company reports that its average family size is 3.8 just for family contracts.

The age and gender factors of the group equal a 0.98 demographic factor.

The industry factor of the group according to an actuarial table is 0.95.

ally, some MCOs use multiple pricing methodologies, selecting a pricing methodology that responds effectively to a particular market segment. MCOs started during the last decade probably began with a more sophisticated approach to pricing and underwriting than many HMOs started before 1980. Regardless of the commencement of operations, the evolution of pricing methodologies within an MCO varies significantly among organizations.

Simplified Community Rating

Simplified community rating uses planwide assumptions as to levels of utilization, cost per unit, administrative costs, membership composition (i.e., age and gender), contract mix, and charging ratio or ratio of the rates. The charging ratio refers to the desired relationship of various premium tiers to the single premium quoted. For example, a charging ratio of 1.95 for the couple premium tier means that the MCO and/or employer group desires the couple premium to be 1.95 times the single premium quoted by the MCO. Most MCOs using simplified community rating will not make group-specific adjustments for the charging ratios. Instead, the MCO will use a standard set of charging ratios in preparing premium quotations. By using so many standard rating assumptions, an MCO needs only to know the contract effective date, the plan of benefits, and the desired tier structure of the group to quote premiums using a simplified community rating methodology.

Simplified community rating does not use the actual group-specific contract mix; in this case the 30/20/50 percentage mix for single/couple/family contracts. A standard mix assumption would probably be applied based on actuarial recommendation. This pricing methodology also does not adjust for the group-specific average family size. Average family size refers to the average number of covered persons included in a family tier contract. The demographic factor and the industry factor are adjustments typically utilized only by the CRC methodology. These factors are discussed further later.

In all three pricing methodologies, the underwriter calculates a conversion factor. The conversion factor is a statistic that, when multiplied by the required revenue PMPM produces the MCO's desired single premium. The conversion factor is dependent upon assumptions as to contract mix, contract size for each tier, and charging ratios or the ratio of the rates. Exhibit 44–3 summarizes the three steps to calculate the conversion factor, the subsequent steps to calculate premiums using simplified community rating, and the pricing methodology and mathematical result and/or calculated premium related to each of the steps.

To verify that these premiums will yield the required revenue of $125.00 PMPM as stated in the Dream Group assumptions, review the check of the computations shown in Table 44–1, which calculates the projected average premium per contract and divides this revenue per contract into the average contract size or number of covered persons per contract. This calculation yields the average projected revenue PMPM.

As shown in Table 44–1, the projected weighted average premium is $287.57. Dividing this average premium by the projected average contract size (2.30 as determined in Exhibit 44–3) yields the projected average revenue PMPM. If the rating is performed correctly, it yields the required premium PMPM, in this case $125.00 PMPM, except for a potential (and immaterial) rounding error. Dividing $287.57 (the average contract revenue PMPM) by the average contract size of 2.30 members per contract yields a projected revenue of $125.03 PMPM, reflecting rounding error and verifying the mathematical accuracy of the proposed premium rates prepared using simplified community rating.

If the group-specific characteristics varied from the standard MCO assumptions, the MCO would recognize a revenue excess or shortfall PMPM. For example, if a group with more than the assumed number or mix of large families was quoted, the MCO would experience a premium deficiency PMPM when dividing actual premiums collected by the higher than antici-

Exhibit 44–3 Calculation To Develop Simplified Community Rates for Dream Group, Inc.

Step 1: $(0.40 \times 1.00) + (0.20 \times 2.00) + (0.40 \times 3.75) = 2.30$
Average weighted contract size = Mix (column A) times contract size (column B)

Step 2: $(0.40 \times 1.00) + (0.20 \times 1.95) + (0.40 \times 2.85) = 1.93$
Average weighted charging ratio (CR) = Mix (column A) times CR (column C)

Step 3: $2.30 / 1.93 = 1.192$
Single conversion factor = Step 1 result divided by step 2 result

Step 4: 125.00 PMPM $\times 1.192 = \$149.00$
Single conversion factor times required premium PMPM equals single premium

Step 5: $\$149.00 \times 1.95 = \$290.55$
Single premium times couple CR equals couple premium

Step 6: $\$149.00 \times 2.85 = \$424.65$
Single premium times family CR equals family premium

Contract Type	(A) Contract Mix (%)	(B) Contract Size	(C) Charging Ratios	Computed Conversion Factor	Required or Estimated Premiums ($)
Single	40	1.00	1.00	1.192 (3)	149.00 (4)
Couple	20	2.00	1.95		290.55 (5)
Family	40	3.75	2.85		424.65 (6)
TOTAL	100	2.30 (1)	1.93 (2)		

pated actual number of covered persons per contract.

ACR

The financial risks assumed by the MCO in using so many standard assumptions have caused many management teams to seek improvement in the pricing methodology. Competitive pressures also have encouraged many MCOs to differentiate their premiums further on a group-specific basis while still retaining a community rating methodology. The limitations of simplified community rating and increasing competitive pressures helped encourage the development and use of ACR by many MCOs.

Table 44–1 Premium Proof of PMPM

(A) Contract Tier Mix	(B) Calculated Premium ($)	(A × B) Weighted Average Premium ($)
Single, 40%	149.00	59.60
Couple, 20%	290.55	58.11
Family, 40%	424.65	169.86
Total weighted premium		287.57
Projected weighted premium per contract*		125.03

* Total weighted premium divided by average contract size (2.30).

The use of ACR often reflects an MCO's recognition of the need for a pricing methodology that will allow it to be more price competitive while reducing the risk inherent in applying so many standard assumptions. Many MCOs found that premiums developed using simplified community rating were most price competitive in the highest-risk groups. Furthermore, groups that had significant variations from MCO standard assumptions as to contract mix, size, and charging ratios were often quoted rates that yielded unfavorable financial results.

In some MCOs, the marketing program encourages the sales force to sell the standard community rate to any interested group. This approach reflects the belief that in the long run the underlying actuarial assumptions will be achieved. In some cases, the underlying actuarial assumptions were not understood or even considered by the MCO. Therefore, although the MCO added new membership, it often attracted risk that required above average use of health services, or it experienced a degree of adverse risk selection.

Increasingly, many MCOs saw the need to make at least some group-specific adjustments to their pricing methodology. The changes were intended to improve competitive position, avoid adverse risk selection, and appropriately charge an adjusted community rate to groups with unique contract mixes, average contract sizes, or charging ratios. In making these adjustments, MCOs were also responding to increasing employer group requests for data and rationale behind the rates charged to a particular group.

ACR provides the MCO a better opportunity to attract a cross-section of risk and to quote premiums that are more likely to fund the membership risk. These improvements allow the MCO to be more proactive rather than merely hope that the actuaries will be right in the long run.

One way to understand the ACR pricing methodology is to compare it with simplified community rating. The ACR methodology uses group-specific assumptions rather than standard planwide assumptions for contract mix, contract size, and charging ratios. This pricing methodol-

ogy does not consider the demographic factor or the industry factor.

Using Dream Group, Inc. as a basis for quotation, Exhibit 44–4 calculates premiums determined by the ACR methodology using the same revenue requirement of $125.00 PMPM. Note that ACR uses the same steps as simplified community rating shown in Exhibit 44–3. Instead of planwide assumptions, ACR uses group-specific assumptions to calculate the conversion factor and proposed premiums.

Notice how different the community rates are for the same group using the ACR methodology versus the simplified approach. Compare, for example, the single rate of $149.00 under simplified community rating to $153.63 as determined by ACR. There is a family rate difference of approximately $13.00 per month. In fact, if the group-specific assumptions in Dream Group, Inc. are accurate and the membership achieved by the MCO during enrollment reflects those characteristics, the simplified approach would leave the MCO with a estimated monthly premium deficiency of $3.80 PMPM. The actual group premium, reflecting the simplified community rates but divided by the actual group contract size of 2.6 produces a premium yield of $121.20 PMPM instead of the targeted revenue of $125.00 PMPM. If the MCO enrolled 1,000 members (employees and dependents) in the group, the monthly shortfall to the MCO for this single group would be $3,800. This shortfall would need to be made up, assuming that the MCO targeted or required premium PMPM is accurate.

Clearly, ACR allows the MCO to quote group-specific community rates more accurately that yield the same revenue PMPM targeted by simplified community rating. The adjustments improve the matching of revenue and expense. ACR also helps the MCO manage its block of business and price both new and renewing groups.

Still, using ACR often creates questions. Members under the same benefit plan and contract effective date, but in separate employer groups with different characteristics, pay differ-

Exhibit 44–4 Calculation To Develop ACR for Dream Group, Inc.

Step 1: $(0.30 \times 1.00) + (0.20 \times 2.00) + (0.50 \times 3.80) = 2.60$
           Average weighted contract size = Mix (column A) times contract size (column B)
Step 2: $(0.30 \times 1.00) + (0.20 \times 1.95) + (0.50 \times 2.85) = 2.115$
           Average weighted charging ratio (CR) = Mix (column A) times CR (column C)
Step 3: $2.60 \div 2.115 = 1.229$
           Single conversion factor = Step 1 result divided by step 2 result
Step 4: $\$125.00 \text{ PMPM} \times 1.229 = \$153.63$
           Single conversion factor times required premium PMPM equals single premium
Step 5: $\$153.63 \times 1.95 = \$299.58$
           Single premium times couple CR equals couple premium
Step 6: $\$153.63 \times 2.85 = \$437.85$
           Single premium times family CR equals family premium

Contract Type	(A) Contract Mix (%)	(B) Contract Size	(C) Charging Ratios	Computed Conversion Factor	Required or Estimated Premiums ($)
Single	30	1.00	1.00	1.229 (3)	153.63 (4)
Couple	20	2.00	1.95		299.58 (5)
Family	50	3.80	2.85		437.85 (6)
TOTAL	100	2.60 (1)	2.115 (2)		

ent monthly premiums amounts. The increase in rate variation through use of ACR places greater demands on the sales force to respond to employer group questions concerning pricing. In many MCOs, the evolution from simplified community rating to ACR is where confusion arose as to pricing methodology. The arithmetic of ACR is straightforward. Inadequate communication by those in charge of pricing and/or overestimation of the complexity of determining premiums by marketing/sales personnel help create and perpetuate the "black box" of premium determination. If an individual can multiply and divide, he or she can develop premiums that reflect the ACR methodology. Given the simplicity of the arithmetic, MCOs developed computer spreadsheets to ensure that the routine calculations were properly and consistently completed. With spreadsheet software, a clerk could quickly develop premiums that reflected the group-specific assumptions.

Although ACR represents a significant advancement in pricing compared with simplified community rating, it does not address all the issues that many MCOs identified and verified as pricing difficulties. Management of MCOs recognized that the age and gender of members affect usage of health services. Moreover, MCO claim experience and/or encounter data often showed a correlation between the utilization of health services and the industry of the employer group. These observations were consistent with the advice and studies of consulting actuaries serving the health insurance industry. Recognition of the importance of age, gender, and industry factor, as well as a competitive marketplace, contributed to the development of a more sophisticated pricing methodology.

CRC

Conditions in the marketplace, specifically the use of experience rating by insurance companies, encouraged more sophistication in the MCO pricing methodology. MCOs were competing in groups whose premiums for alternative health options to the MCO reflected prior claim experience. Without additional adjustments,

MCOs found themselves being competitive on groups with above average risk and/or higher than average claim experience. Conversely, MCOs found it more difficult to price competitively in groups with favorable claim experience. Accordingly, the CRC pricing methodology arose and was applied by MCOs.

Just as the ACR methodology builds on simplified community rating, the CRC approach builds upon the ACR approach. The CRC methodology merely adds to the ACR methodology adjustments for classes that have an actuarial basis for predicting future levels of utilization.

There are two common classes defined and used by MCOs in their pricing methodology. The first class reflects the composite age and gender characteristics of the employer group. The second class considers the industry factor associated with the employer group. These two classes are independent of each other. The class factors can offset one another or be either favorable or unfavorable. In groups with favorable demographic and industry factors, the MCO charges a lesser premium for the selected benefit plan. In groups with unfavorable factors, the MCO charges a higher premium for the selected benefit plan.

The CRC methodology adjusts the ACR premiums for class adjustments tied to the demographic and industry factors. These adjustments are made to the underlying revenue requirement PMPM for the specific benefit plan under review. For example, if a group had a relatively older membership, it would possess a group-specific demographic factor over 1.00, with 1.00 representing the MCO average age and gender profile. Groups with a demographic factor over 1.00 are projected to use more than average health services over the long term. To adjust for this class, the MCO would increase the revenue requirement PMPM and apply the standard ACR methodology.

Demographic Factors

Hypothetical utilization factors by age and sex are listed in Table 44–2; *these factors are supplied only for demonstration purposes.* A mature MCO with a significant claim history can develop its own utilization factors that, when multiplied by group membership, derive the group-specific weighted demographic factor. Utilization factors also can be obtained from consulting actuarial firms for a nominal fee. Normally, the factors are summarized in quinquennial tables (5-year ranges) broken down by gender.

Note that genders of the same age generally have the same utilization factor except for the impact of maternity during the childbearing years of women. Multiplying the stated utilization factors by the number of members in each age/gender cell produces the weighted average demographic factor for the group. For example, a group with ten potential enrollees in the 26- to 45-year-old male cell and ten potential enrollees in the 46- to 65-year-old female cell would have a demographic factor of 1.125. Adjustment for the group-specific demographic factor is shown in Exhibit 44–5. Most MCOs determine the demographic factor for a new employer group based on the overall employee and (if available) dependent pool. For renewing groups, the starting point for estimating the demographic factor is the previous enrollment into the MCO program.

Industry Factors

Industry factors primarily reflect the actuarial study of years of indemnity claim experience. The historical utilization patterns of particular industries are accepted as an actuarially sound class for use in CRC. Like the age and gender demographic factors, industry factor lists are

Table 44–2 Hypothetical Utilization Factors by Age and Gender

Age Range (Years)	Male	Female
0–10	0.50	0.50
11–25	0.80	1.15
26–45	1.00	1.25
46–65	1.25	1.25

Exhibit 44–5 Calculation to Derive CRC Rates for Dream Group, Inc.

Step 1: $(0.30 \times 1.00) + (0.20 \times 2.00) + (0.50 \times 3.80) = 2.60$
        Average weighted contract size = Mix (column A) times contract size (column B)
Step 2: $(0.30 \times 1.00) + (0.20 \times 1.95) + (0.50 \times 2.85) = 2.115$
        Average weighted charging ratio (CR) = Mix (column A) times CR (column C)
Step 3: $2.60 \div 2.115 = 1.229$
        Single conversion factor = Step 1 result divided by step 2 result
Step 4: $\$116.25$ PMPM $\times 1.229 = \$142.87$
        Single conversion factor times required premium PMPM equals single premium
Step 5: $\$142.87 \times 1.95 = \$278.60$
        Single premium times couple CR equals couple premium
Step 6: $\$142.87 \times 2.85 = \$407.18$
        Single premium times family CR equals family premium

Contract Type	*(A)* Contract Mix (%)	*(B)* Contract Size	*(C)* Charging Ratios	Computed Conversion Factor	Required or Estimated Premiums ($)
Single	30	1.00	1.00	1.229 (3)	142.87 (4)
Couple	20	2.00	1.95		278.60 (5)
Family	50	3.80	2.85		407.18 (6)
TOTAL	100	2.60 (1)	2.115 (2)		

available from actuarial firms serving the health care sector.

A standard industry factor list is a necessary resource for CRC methodology to adjust premiums on a group-specific and actuarially sound basis for the class defined as industry. A typical list would include a description of the industry, a definition of the standard industry classification range, and an industry or medical factor that can be used to predict future utilization of services. Hypothetical examples of industry factors are illustrated in Table 44–3.

An employer group assigned an industry factor greater than 1.00 would be expected to use more than an average level of health services over the term of the contract. Therefore, the MCO would adjust the revenue requirement to price the product so that the group would yield revenue PMPM that reflected its actuarially sound industry factor. Those industries assigned a factor less than 1.00 would receive a reduction or discount from standard or average MCO premium requirements. Those industries with a 1.00 factor would receive the standard MCO amount; that is, no adjustment to the revenue requirement would be made.

Other Aspects of CRC

Adjusting the revenue requirement for actuarially sound classes such as industry and demographic factors causes the range of community rates to expand significantly. It is common for small groups to have appropriately assigned industry factors and/or demographic factors that increase or decrease the standard revenue requirement PMPM by 10 percent or more from the standard MCO norm. This increasing flexibility in pricing requires strong oversight of the pricing activities. Left unattended, MCO pricing functions have fallen into common pitfalls, such as pricing to the market or assuming unrealistic demographic factors to justify a lower price, especially for a first-time offering.

If the MCO uses the CRC methodology to reduce rates but fails to sell groups with net industry and demographic factors above 1.00 the required higher rate, the pricing approach is merely a discounting technique. Such an ap-

Table 44–3 Hypothetical Industry Factors

Industry Type	Industry Factor
Agriculture	1.05
Mining and quarrying (excluding metals and fuels)	1.15
Air transportation	1.00
Banking 0.95	
Hospitals 1.20	
Insurance companies	1.00
Public administration	1.10
Services for engineering, accounting, research	0.95
Retail (apparel, furniture)	1.00

proach does not comply with the spirit of community rating. In some cases, inappropriate discounting from the standard community rating requirements fails to comply with the direction of regulatory agencies, historical requirements of a federally qualified HMO, and/or requirements of such groups as the Federal Employees Health Benefit Program (see Chapter 45).

Using CRC to calculate premiums for Dream Group, Inc. reflects the ACR methodology with a simple adjustment of required revenue PMPM. In the case of this group, both the demographic factor (0.98) and the industry factor (0.95) were less than 1.00. Accordingly, Dream Group would receive a discounted rate based on the actuarially sound class adjustments. A simple discount of 7 percent could be used by the MCO to reflect the net favorable demographic (2 percent) and industry (5 percent) factors. Instead of a revenue requirement of $125.00 PMPM, the premiums quoted Dream Group will yield a revenue of $116.25 PMPM, or 7 percent less than $125.00.

In Exhibit 44–5, note that steps 1 through 3 to derive the conversion factor of 1.229 are identical between ACR and CRC. Both methodologies use group-specific assumptions. Steps 4 through 6 are also identical to those in ACR, the only change being a discounted revenue requirement PMPM of $116.25 instead of $125.00.

Summary of Community Rating Methodologies

Table 44–4 offers an actuarially sound community rate for Dream Group, Inc. as prepared by each of the three community rating methodologies reviewed. Without full understanding of the CRC pricing methodology, managed care competitors, employers, and even the MCO sales force were prone to question how community rates could vary so much, particularly when they were above the norm. Given the adjustments for mix, contract size, charging ratio, and demographic and industry factors, significant rate variation among groups with the same benefit plan and contract effective date are probable.

Given the transition to more sophisticated pricing methodologies, many employers and regulators increasingly view MCO pricing practices as similar to those used by insurance companies. Instead of charging everyone the same community rate, the MCO has adapted its community rating approach to the competitive and experience-rated marketplace. Considering the marketplace and the limited capitalization of many MCOs, these pricing adaptations were desirable and in some cases necessary for survival.

When demographic and industry factors directly affect product pricing, their impact is often limited or moderated. The MCO could consider both demographic and industry factors in choosing to cover (or decline) the group but would establish a limit for price adjustments. The MCO might limit the impact of favorable group-specific demographics to a revenue PMPM reduction of no more than 10 percent. Unfavorable demographic characteristics could be capped at 20 percent above standard.

Similar moderation could be applied to the industry factor. With proper actuarial support, all industries could be condensed within a limited range of industry factors. The majority of industries would probably be assigned a neutral factor of 1.00. The industries with significant outlier claim histories could be assigned reasonable factors while still maintaining a fairly tight range.

Table 44–4 Community Rating Summary for Dream Group, Inc.

| | Premiums Reflecting Community Rating | | |
Contract Tier	Simplified Community Rating	ACR	CRC
Single	149.00	153.63	142.87
Couple	290.55	299.58	278.60
Family	424.65	437.85	407.18

In these manners, the rate variation caused by demographic and industry factor impact is limited to a tighter range. This approach produces rates that reflect more closely the historic community rating philosophy. At the same time, the moderation of these factors complies with increasing regulation of pricing at the state level.

Even MCOs that choose not to adjust rates for such classes as age, gender, and industry often apply these concepts in developing their operational plan. MCOs utilize demographic and industry information to focus new business sales and plan renewal activities at existing clients. Analysis of demographic and industry factors is also useful in predicting the utilization levels of a particular large group or the entire MCO membership. Similarly, in assessing merger candidates or blocks of business, demographic and industry factors are components of a comprehensive analysis.

UNDERWRITING PRINCIPLES

Given this lengthy discussion of the rating methodology for a community-rated MCO, one might mistakenly conclude "So that's how managed care underwriting is done." It is critical to understand the relationship between a pricing methodology and underwriting. The pricing methodology is an important element of underwriting. Conversely, underwriting is much more than understanding and operating a pricing methodology.

In MCOs that operate "pricing mills," rate quotes are often prepared by clerks using a spreadsheet program on a personal computer. In these environments, underwriting is sometimes confused with the mere preparation of a rate quote. The rate quote reflects, where possible, exactly what the potential customer and/or sales representative requested. No additional analysis is performed. Other, more creative options are not generally identified or presented to the customer.

Today, many MCOs view the pricing process as an integral part of a successful underwriting function. Increasingly, MCOs recognize the importance of attracting a cross section of risk and properly managing millions of premium dollars. Accordingly, the compensation paid has moved the underwriting position from a clerk to an important role filled by an experienced person with important skills and broad operational understanding of the MCO and the marketplace. Clerks still work within the pricing and underwriting function, but their output is often the starting point for underwriting rather than the end point of a client proposal.

Regardless of the pricing methodology applied, there are several underwriting principles that most MCOs consider and apply. The most common underwriting principles or criteria that an employer group must satisfy include the following.

Employer Stability

Companies lacking 1 year of operations experience and/or those that have not previously offered an employee health insurance program generally are considered high risks. Some MCOs choose to decline to offer coverage in this situation. Similarly, if a company consistently changes carriers or MCOs, it suggests that a long-term relationship with the employer may be difficult to achieve. Without employer stability and a chance for a long-term relationship, it is more difficult for the MCO to fund the insurance risk of the group. Industries subject to large-scale layoffs pose an additional risk: mass individual conversions and/or extension of health benefits to former employees on a voluntary basis. Conversely, stable employer groups with rapidly expanding workforces are attractive groups for the MCO.

Employee–Employer Relationship

Entities assuming insurance risk want to attract a cross-section of risk. When the normal employee–employer relationship does not exist, the ability to attract a cross-section of risk comes into question. Historically, part-time or seasonal workers have generally demonstrated much higher risk or have required much higher levels of health services.

Employee Participation

At least 75 percent of employees who are eligible for coverage should select some form of health care coverage. In a group with lower than 75 percent participation, employees who participate are generally those who intend to utilize their coverage. Those who believe that they need not participate are assumed to be the better risk.

Employee Eligibility

An eligible employee is often defined in terms of a minimum number of hours worked per week (say, 30 hours per week). Under this definition, ineligible employees could include seasonal workers, part-time employees, and/or officers and directors of the company who are not full-time employees. By covering otherwise ineligible employees, the MCO increases its chance of adverse selection. Normally, all MCOs and

insurance options accept the same eligibility definition in large employer groups. In small employer groups of fewer than 50 lives, the definition of an employee is critical. When possible, the MCO may also include an "actively at work" clause in its contract with the small employer group. When allowed and properly constructed, this clause requires an employee to be discharged from a hospital and/or to return to work and be capable of carrying on normal tasks associated with employment before coverage commences under the MCO contract. In some cases, the "actively at work" clause also applies to dependents of the eligible employee. Once the employee returns to work and is eligible for coverage, the "actively at work" clause no longer applies. Hospitalization and/or disability of a covered person subsequent to his or her initial eligibility would be covered by the MCO. The "actively at work" clause provides some protection to the MCO against enrolling, without its knowledge or approval, disabled individuals and/or individuals confined to a hospital or home who are unable to return to work on the date of their otherwise initial eligibility date for the MCO program.

High-Risk Groups

Certain types of businesses have historically been avoided because of their perceived high risk (e.g., bars, massage parlors, and escort services). Many MCOs have lists of groups that would at least not be aggressively pursued. In some cases, some MCOs will choose not to quote a business that they believe is properly described as high risk. High-risk groups often violate several of the underwriting principles being discussed, such as low employee participation and the prevalence of part-time employees or personnel under contract who lack the typical employer–employee relationship.

Premium Differential

To attract a cross-section of risk, the MCO's premium generally must be competitive. If too expensive, the MCO would attract only a small enrollment of employees and dependents who choose to pay more to gain coverage afforded by the MCO. If substantially cheaper than other options, the MCO may have misunderstood the risk and underpriced the coverage. The MCO could be efficient and therefore much cheaper, but most underwriters are somewhat skeptical rather than perpetual optimists. The concept of premium differential must also be reviewed from an employee perspective.

Employee Out-of-Pocket Cost

Most employees pay less than 50 percent of the total cost of their health care benefits. Cost to the employee is what he or she is required to pay for a particular health care option, typically expressed on a monthly basis. Although most employers generally treat all health care options similarly, the employee out-of-pocket cost for each health care option should be considered. Historically, it was thought that an employee would pay an additional monthly amount up front in lieu of a deductible. Still, in some groups that historically did not require the employee to pay for his or her health insurance, even a small added monthly out-of-pocket cost could significantly curtail chances for a reasonable enrollment in terms of numbers and cross-section of risk.

Minimum Contract Size

Some MCOs establish administrative requirements as to the minimum size of the group. In some cases, the group minimum reflects in part the added cost of billing and premium collection in a small group. From a risk perspective, the minimum group size also serves to protect the MCO from coverage of groups that would substantially increase the risk to the MCO. Thus by stating a minimum group size, the MCO is trying to prevent potential abuse, decrease risk, and encourage the sales force to focus on groups offering a better chance of sizable enrollment in the MCO.

Employer Contribution

An eligible employer must contribute at least 50 percent and preferably more, to the single cost of the MCO premium. The employer contribution encourages a wider number of employees to participate, making it easier to spread out and manage the risk of health insurance. A low employer contribution will affect the overall level of employee participation and reflect in part the strength and stability of the employer group.

Demographic Factor Norms

The community rating approach presumes that all groups will use generally the same level of services. Groups with significantly different characteristics are often carefully reviewed before a proposal is prepared. Some MCOs will choose not to quote a business group on a risk basis whose demographic factor is substantially above the norm—say, 1.25—regardless of the ability to charge a loaded premium.

Benefit Plan Compatibility

The level of benefits offered to a group is often determined solely by the group; the employer group states what coverages it desires the MCO to offer. Blindly filling this request is not proactive underwriting as envisioned in this discussion. The MCO should ensure that the benefit plan and related premium will be compatible and competitive with the other options offered. No MCO would routinely want to be the richest benefit plan offered with a comparatively high employee out-of-pocket cost because of the probability of adverse selection. Similarly, the MCO may not wish to offer its most economical benefit plan with high copays if other options have low deductibles and/or small copays. Product design and compatibility are often difficult and controversial issues, particularly in a multiple choice environment. This refers to where the aggregate employer risk pool is split among competing carriers, each of which assumes risk for its enrollees. Where possible, the MCO should maintain control over the benefit plan offered. This is a more critical issue in the MCO with open provider access and fee-for-service reimbursement.

Summary

These principles and criteria offer a good foundation for understanding the underwriting mind set. Do not conclude that that's all there is. Moreover, do not fall prey to the fairly common error that underwriting is essentially the same for each employer group or product line. It is not!

Many MCOs have learned that their expertise and success with certain size groups or market segments did not prepare them for successful efforts in a different market segment. Large insurance carriers, expert in serving large, multisite employer groups, have encountered major challenges in successfully serving medium and small group employers. The small to medium group (50 to 500 employees) and very small group (fewer than 50 employees) markets each possess unique underwriting and distribution issues. Even within these market segments, there are subsegments that require understanding and properly designed products and underwriting.

Many groups of more than 100 employees want to share risk or attempt to self-fund their employee health insurance program. These variable funding arrangements further complicate the underwriting challenges. Therefore, the approach to underwrite a group of 7 employees is different from that for a group of 47 employees, and that underwriting process is different from that for a group of 470 or 4,700 employees. This recognition is particularly important today as many untested and inexperienced MCOs, such as the local physician–hospital organization or provider-sponsored independent practice association, begin to contract directly with employer groups, agree to serve associations of employer groups, or participate in programs that target small businesses and the uninsured. In many instances, the potential risk being assumed by these inexperienced MCOs is poorly understood

in terms of both composition and amount. Similarly, experienced MCOs entering new markets are encouraged to assess critically the underwriting requirements of the market, necessary products, and possibly alternative distribution channels.

EFFECTIVE UNDERWRITING: LESSONS LEARNED

MCOs with consistently successful underwriting have adapted their processes to the changing environment. These organizations have responded to the emerging regulation of underwriting, particularly in the small employer group market. Rather than viewing underwriting as merely a pricing methodology, these MCOs have recognized the importance of underwriting and have treated it accordingly in terms of staff, salaries, scope of responsibilities, and range of influence. It is appropriate at this point to reflect upon several of the basic lessons learned by MCOs with successful underwriting activities:

- The underwriting function requires a mix of personnel with defined careers. Mathematical, spreadsheet, and database skills are core competencies of an underwriting function.

- Underwriting assistants are necessary to perform various analyses, determine the demographic characteristics of the group, and run the initial pricing model.

- Underwriters are key MCO personnel who share management of a revenue stream in the millions of dollars. The underwriter compensation and performance requirements should reflect this scope of responsibilities.

- Underwriting must identify the impact of catastrophic or shock claims in the preparation of various analyses. Failure properly to consider shock claims (claims greater than $75,000 per person per year) could lead to faulty decision-making.

- Underwriting analyses should help focus the efforts of the sales force and support renewal activities. Some MCOs have used the list of industry factors to direct sales activities to certain industries or businesses. Internal MCO analysis of loss ratio by industry type is also beneficial to direct future sales efforts in terms of new groups and/or product designs for a particular industry or market segment.

- The actual pricing/underwriting activity is an iterative process. The underwriter infrequently accepts the initial output of the pricing spreadsheet model. Instead, the proposed premiums and benefit design are evaluated for the specific employer group environment. Several factors, such as projected employee out-of-pocket cost, benefit differences, and network issues, are reviewed for each of the projected health care options to be offered by the MCO and its competitors.

- For large, complex groups, the entire underwriting process generally takes several days of work after all the necessary data are collected. Various scenarios should be modeled with corresponding estimates as to the impact on enrollment, risk selection, revenue PMPM, and other factors. Given the slim historical margins within the health care industry, the MCO needs always to be "in the ballpark" for large groups.

- The MCO will be prudent if it aligns incentives for marketing/sales and underwriting personnel. Ideally, underwriters should share marketing/sales goals, and sales personnel should share accountability for financial results along with underwriting.

- Generally, the MCO should be leery about competing on the basis of offering the richest benefits and/or the most choice relative to certain services, such as mental health, substance abuse, prescription services, and transplants. This approach to competition is a particular concern when the MCO is at risk for the financial results.

- Increasingly, underwriters need to understand funding arrangements in which the employer group shares at least a portion of the risk with the MCO. The MCO should be cautious in approaching these arrangements because much of the MCO's profitability is tied to the assumption and management of risk. If the MCO transfers both risk and profitability to employer groups that are producing sound financial results, it will make funding the less attractive groups with more variable outcomes a greater challenge.

- Experienced underwriting personnel can contribute to a myriad of MCO decisions that influence sales and risk selection. What are the themes of the upcoming advertising campaign? Will all contracted specialist physicians be listed in the provider directory, and if so, how will they be listed? Should the MCO contract with the academic medical center, and under what terms? Should the MCO change its copay for office visits or prescriptions? All these questions (and many more) can benefit from an experienced underwriting perspective.

- As the MCO expands its product portfolio and means of distribution, reassessment of the underwriting function to support these changes would be a prudent step.

- The data gathered by underwriting, often at the individual employee or dependent level, should be used by the MCO to meet member needs and/or manage health care services more effectively. Underwriting identification of members with special needs should be routinely provided to the MCO medical management function.

- For market opportunities such as Medicaid and Medicare risk contracting, the underwriting department should assist in the assessment of the opportunity and creation of a comprehensive implementation program.

- As the MCO MIS provides increasing access to and analysis of data, the MCO must be cautious to preserve patient/member confidentiality while providing meaningful information to employer groups and other interested parties.

These lessons can be used to implement or enhance an effective underwriting function. An existing MCO may use these lessons to assess its current underwriting structure, incentives, and processes.

CONCLUSION

This chapter has provided a historical overview of MCO pricing and underwriting. It identified and discussed marketplace trends, risk factors, adaptations of pricing methodologies, and underwriting principles. Collaboration between marketing/sales and the underwriting function within the MCO was strongly encouraged.

This discussion underscores the importance of underwriting to an MCO's success even as insurance reform and government regulation increasingly limit individual- and/or group-specific underwriting. Organizations providing health services and contracting on a risk basis with an MCO are encouraged to understand basic underwriting principles and techniques used by many MCOs.

During the next decade, MCO underwriting will continue to evolve. Increasingly, underwriting will focus on attracting and managing a cross-section of health risk. Underwriting will probably be relabeled as health risk appraisal or health risk management (not to be confused with risk management, as discussed in Chapter 38). Regardless of its label or description, effective underwriting will continue to make major contributions to successful MCOs.

SUGGESTED READING

Chollet, D.J., and Paul, R.R. 1994. *Community Rating: Issues and Experience*. Washington, D.C.: Alpha Center.

Dowd, B., and Feldman, R. 1995. Premium Elasticities of Health Plan Choice. *Inquiry* 31 (4): 438–444.

Special Market Segments

"We're one
But we're not the same."

Bono, 1991

Part VI

Special Market Segments

Chapter 45

The Federal Employees Health Benefit Program and Managed Care

Joel L. Michaels and Christine C. Rinn

The Federal Employees Health Benefits Program (FEHBP), with its coverage of approximately 10 million federal employees and annuitants and their dependents, represents the largest employer-sponsored health benefits program in the United States today. The FEHBP is established pursuant to the Federal Employees Health Benefits Act, 5 U.S. Code Section 8901 *et seq.*, and is administered by the federal Office of Personnel Management (OPM). Under the FEHBP, OPM is authorized to offer certain choices of health benefits plans to federal employees. These choices include governmentwide plans and employee organization plans (which are experience rated) as well as comprehensive health plans (which are predominantly community rated). Most of the comprehensive health plans are health maintenance organizations (HMOs) and represent a significance presence by OPM as a purchaser of managed care services. Governmentwide and employee organization plans are experience rated, and HMOs are predominantly community rated.

The focus of this chapter is the FEHBP's relationship to HMOs, with particular emphasis on the continuing controversy over HMO rating practices under the FEHBP. Also discussed are issues related to benefit design, federal employee–HMO relationships, and federal preemption of state laws.

One of the key reasons why rating issues are particularly significant is that FEHBP contracting is not a competitive bidding process. Moreover, until recently, OPM did not exercise its purchasing power (at least on the front end of the rate proposal process) to achieve a better rate. More recently, however, OPM has adopted rating requirements for the FEHBP that, in effect, achieve the benefits of competitive bidding for the FEHBP with respect to the plan's two employer groups that are most similar in size to the FEHBP.

As of 1995, OPM contracts with approximately 400 comprehensive health plans, almost all of which are community-rated plans. Comprehensive plans may be group practice, individual practice, or mixed model plans depending upon the configuration of the HMO's provider delivery system. Community rating, in its most simplistic terms, means that the costs charged to an employer group represent costs spread across the community and not just the experience of a particular account. HMOs that are federally qualified under federal HMO law are required to be community rated by that statute, and OPM, under the Federal Employees Health Benefits Act, has an affirmative obligation to offer federally qualified HMOs that meet the requirements of the FEHBP.[1,2] See Chapter 55 for a discussion of federal qualification.

The concept of what constitutes community rating has changed significantly over the years under amendments to federal HMO law, thereby adding to the complexity of determining whether a community rate is truly being offered

Joel L. Michaels and Christine C. Rinn are principals in the law firm of Michaels, Wishner & Bonner P.C. in Washington, D.C.

by the HMO to the FEHBP. In some cases, this complexity has led to a concern by OPM as to certain HMO contractors that may be engaged in a pattern of selective discounting of certain nonfederal employer groups. In an effort to curb these abuses and simplify program administration, OPM has moved away from community rating requirements and has focused more on how the rates charged to the FEHBP compare with those charged to the two groups of the HMO that are most similar to the FEHBP. How similarity is defined varies with the contract year at issue and is discussed later.

THE APPLICATION PROCESS

Plans interested in participating in the FEHBP must submit an application letter to OPM by 31 January of the year preceding the year in which their contract will be effective.[3] To be approved for the FEHBP, a carrier must demonstrate substantial compliance with standards adopted by OPM, including stable management with experience pertinent to the prepaid health care provider industry and sufficient operating experience to enable OPM to evaluate realistically the plan's past and expected future performance, a rate of enrollment that ensures equalization of income and expenses within projected time frames and sufficient subscriber income to operate within budget thereafter, a health care delivery system providing reasonable access to and choice of quality primary care and specialty care throughout the service area, and establishment of firm budget projections and demonstrated success in meeting or exceeding those projections on a regular basis.[4] Once a contract is entered into, the carrier has an ongoing obligation to notify OPM of the occurrence of certain significant events that could affect the carrier's ability to satisfy the foregoing standards on an ongoing basis or could impair the carrier's ability to perform its contractual obligations.[5]

Participation in the FEHBP is open to any carrier that satisfies OPM's requirements. In addition, as noted earlier, OPM is statutorily obligated to contract with federally qualified HMOs.[6] Nevertheless, OPM has recently sought to restrict applications from community-rated plans. In 1994, OPM indicated its intention to stabilize the FEHBP by not permitting any new plans for contract year 1996 and limiting the entry of new plans thereafter. The agency's intention was formally communicated in interim regulations published in the *Federal Register* on 5 December 1994.[7] The interim regulations provided that "The Director of OPM shall consider applications to participate in the [FEHBP] from comprehensive medical plans (CMPs) at his or her discretion. If the Director of OPM determines that it is beneficial to enrollees and the [FEHBP] to invite new plans to join the program, OPM will publish a notice in the *Federal Register*."[8]

Faced with opposition from HMOs and potential legal challenges to its actions, OPM informed the HMO industry that it would not proceed with implementing the interim final regulations. Nevertheless, it is clear that OPM still intends to restrict the number of new community-rated contractors as evidenced by its reissuing the interim final regulations as a proposed rule.[9]

PREMIUM CONTRIBUTION AND BENEFIT DESIGN

Under 5 U.S. Code Section 8906, OPM pays a portion of the premium, and the employee or annuitant is responsible for the remainder. The government contribution has historically been set at 60 percent of the average premium of the Big 6 (the two high-option governmentwide plans, the two largest employee organizations, and the two largest comprehensive medical plans).[10] Since Aetna's withdrawal from the FEHBP as a governmentwide plan in 1990, OPM uses a modified formula to develop the contribution. The government's contribution, however, would be further limited by the requirement that it be no more than 75 percent of the plan's premium.[11] In such a case, if OPM's contribution would be more than 75 percent of an HMO's premium, the HMO receives a contribution from OPM equal to 75 percent of its premium.

As for benefit design, OPM is authorized to establish reasonable minimum standards. These minimum benefits include hospital benefits, surgical benefits, in-hospital surgical benefits, ambulatory patient benefits, supplemental benefits, and obstetrical benefits.[12] Although federally qualified HMOs are required to contract with OPM for the basic benefits mandated by federal HMO law, there are typically no established minimum standards by OPM for the benefits, deductibles, or copayments, with the exception of certain mandated coverages for mental health and substance abuse. Moreover, HMOs are usually not allowed to provide additional benefits unless the change is part of the HMO's community benefits package and is offered to all groups and not just the federal account. OPM's benefit instructions to plans specifically state that it is OPM's intention to purchase the benefit package purchased by the majority of the carrier's nonfederal subscribers. If, upon audit, OPM determines that a carrier failed to offer the FEHBP its most prevalent benefit package, the carrier may be subject to a premium rate adjustment.[13] Moreover, depending on the representations made by the carrier to OPM during the benefit proposal stage, OPM could claim that the contractor induced OPM into purchasing a benefit package that was not the carrier's community benefit package. The adjustment would presumably reduce the FEHBP's rate to the rate charged for the carrier's true community benefits package.

PREMIUM RATING UNDER THE FEHBP

There are two rating options under the FEHBP. One option, as mentioned earlier, is community rating. The other option is experience rating.[14] Both are discussed below. In addition, the reader is referred to Chapters 43 and 44 for detailed discussions of rating and underwriting.

Experience Rating

Under the experience rating option, carriers charge the FEHBP a rate that is based on the utilization of health care services by the federal account. This rate is retrospectively determined and should not be confused with adjusted community rating (ACR), where the experience of an account is prospectively factored into the rate charged the group. The FEHBP Acquisition Regulations (FEHBAR),[15] which govern the FEHBP, define an experience rate as follows:

> [a] rate for a given group that is the result of that group's actual paid claims, administrative expenses, retentions, and estimated claims incurred but not reported, adjusted for benefit modification, utilization trends, and economic trends. Actual paid claims include any actual or negotiated benefits payments made to providers of medical services for the provision of health care such as capitation not adjusted for specific groups, per diems, and [diagnosis-related group] (DRG) payments.[16]

The definition of experience rate did not specifically recognize provider capitation payments, which are a typical provider compensation payment arrangement utilized by HMOs, as paid claims until 1990.[17] Ironically, this amendment has particular significance for comprehensive medical plans even though they are predominantly community rated. As discussed below, the expanded definition of experience rate removed some of the barriers faced by community-rated plans in calculating a retroactive experience rate for the FEHBP in response to audit findings of defective community rating.

Community Rating

Traditional Community Rating

Before the 1991 contract year, the premium rate development of community-rated carriers participating in the FEHBP was severely restricted by OPM's rating requirements. Among these requirements was the definition of a community rate as a "rate of payment that is equivalent to that charged on the effective date to *all subscriber groups of the carrier* for the same contract period for the same level of benefits" (emphasis added).[18]

Based on this definition, any rating discrepancies between the rate charged the FEHBP and that charged any other group by the carrier that were discovered upon audit were subject to challenge as unlawful discounts. Because HMOs are permitted to use not only traditional community rating under federal HMO law but also community rating by class and ACR, the analysis of whether a discount is present is more complex. This is so because the experience and demographic characteristics of the employer group became relevant considerations.

Other Forms of Community Rating

Community rating by class. Community rating by class permits the introduction of classes, such as age and sex, in determining the HMO's revenue requirement for the community, and the amount charged an employer is then based upon the composition of the employer's workforce and dependents. In light of the development of this and other acceptable forms of community rating, OPM modified its rating requirements for community-rated plans. The FEHBAR definition of a community rate is now "a rate of payment based on a per member per month capitation rate or its equivalent that applies to a combination of the subscriber groups for a comprehensive medical plan. . . ."[19]

Thus, under this definition, OPM no longer requires that a single community rate be applicable to all a carrier's groups, including the FEHBP. The revised definition substantially relaxes the rating restrictions imposed by OPM on its community-rated carriers. In fact, one of the stated purposes of the revised definition was to "recognize the increasing diversity in community rating in the insurance industry and, specifically, within the [FEHBP]."[20]

One class used by many contractors in community rating by class is an industry adjustment factor (IAF). Before 1992, OPM recognized that its contractors used IAFs, but it prohibited their use in the premium rate development of the FEHBP. As a result, if a contractor used industry adjustment factors, OPM's rate instructions directed the contractor to use an IAF of 1.00 for the FEHBP, which would neither increase nor decrease the FEHBP's rates.

With the advent of the similarly sized subscriber group (SSSG) regulations, however (discussed below), OPM changed its view regarding IAFs. Although the 1991 rate instructions continued to require contractors to use an IAF of 1.00 for the FEHBP, contractors discovered when they submitted their rate reconciliations that if either of the SSSGs received an IAF of less than 1.00, which would decrease that group's rates, OPM demanded the same IAF for the FEHBP. Moreover, if both SSSGs were rated with IAFs, OPM demanded the lower of the two. OPM's decision regarding IAFs reflected its position that IAFs are not legitimate predictors of health care utilization. Rather, IAFs are viewed by OPM as a means by which contractors can give discounts to their commercial accounts.

With the SSSG regulations and the relaxing of OPM's community-rating requirements, OPM adopted a new policy with respect to IAFs: The IAF used in a contractor's proposed rate for the FEHBP may not exceed 1.00. OPM will examine the IAFs used to rate the SSSGs during the rate reconciliation process. Upon reconciliation, OPM will require that the IAF used for the FEHBP be no greater than 1.00 and no larger than the lowest IAF used in the premium rate development of an SSSG.

ACR. OPM also recognizes ACR as an acceptable methodology for FEHBP carriers. An adjusted community rate is a "community rate which has been adjusted for expected use of medical resources of the FEHBP group. An [ACR] is a prospective rate and cannot be retroactively revised to reflect actual experience, utilization, or costs of the FEHBP group."[21] OPM currently accepts two methods of ACR: a method based on utilization data, and a prospective method based on FEHBP claims data. OPM's requirements for ACR are set forth in its annual rate instructions to contractors.

Before the adoption of the SSSG concept by OPM (described below), a contractor using ACR for the FEHBP was required to have the methodology as well as the criteria for deciding which groups would be rated using ACR approved by OPM in advance. The purpose of this prior approval requirement was to ensure that the FEHBP was being treated in the same manner as the carrier's commercial groups of like size.

SSSGs

One of the most significant changes for the FEHBP in the area of rating requirements is the concept of SSSGs. Under the FEHBAR provisions that were in effect before 1991, a contractor had to certify that the rate charged the FEHBP was charged to all its subscriber groups that had the same contract period and benefit package as the FEHBP. Under the new provisions of the FEHBAR, contractors must certify that the FEHBP rates were developed in a manner consistent with the rating methodology used to rate the carrier's SSSGs and approved by OPM.[22]

Identifying the SSSGs

At the time the original SSSG regulations were proposed in 1989, OPM stated that the regulations reflected OPM's new policy "to obtain the market price, including applicable discounts, accorded to the two subscriber groups arithmetically closest in size to the FEHBP group for the same basic benefit package and the same contract year."[23] Thus the SSSGs were the contractor's two employer groups[24] that best met all the following conditions: "(a) Have total number of contracts at the time of the rate proposal arithmetically closest in size to the previous September's FEHBP subscriber enrollment, as determined by OPM; (b) Purchase substan-

tially the same basic benefit package proposed for the Federal group; and (c) Are renewed during the plan's fiscal year."[25]

With respect to the benefit similarity requirement referenced in (b) above, OPM never published guidelines or other instructions about the meaning of "substantially the same basic benefit package." As a result, contractors were left to select groups based on their own interpretation of the regulation. The lack of OPM guidance on this issue has resulted in adverse audit findings against community-rated contractors that selected their SSSGs based on benefit package similarities when, in practice, OPM focused principally on the size of the group in determining whether it was or was not an SSSG.

With respect to (c) above, the contract renewal date, plans interpreted this criterion to mean that groups that had a multiyear term were ineligible for SSSG purposes if these groups did not renew during the plan's fiscal year that included the FEHBP contract year. Again, contractors have learned upon audit that the renewal date requirement can be problematic.

Despite the fact that its regulations defined the SSSGs based on the three requirements discussed above, OPM began in 1993 to instruct contractors that subscriber size was the only criterion that should be used in selecting their SSSGs. In 1994, OPM adopted final regulations that reflected this.[26] The final regulations, which were effective for the 1995 contract year, define SSSGs as the HMO's two employer groups that, as of the date specified by OPM in the rate instructions, have a subscriber enrollment closest to the FEHBP subscriber enrollment, use any rating method other than retrospective experience rating, and meet the criteria specified in OPM's rate instructions. The new regulations reflect OPM's position that every group is a potential SSSG except for retrospectively experience-rated groups. Medicare and Medicaid groups are also excluded. Thus prospectively experience-rated groups, government accounts, point-of-service groups, and separate lines of business groups are all potential SSSGs. The new regulations also make clear that OPM is entitled to lowest rates using the methodology used for the SSSGs.

Other SSSG Issues

Multiyear contracts. OPM has clarified its position on multiyear contracts and whether and how groups with a multiyear contract term can be the basis for a premium rate adjustment for the FEHBP. Under OPM's policy, which to date has not been formally made a part of its instructions to carriers, groups that are rated using a multiyear contract are eligible to be considered as SSSGs. For such groups, OPM's position is as follows:

1. If such a rate group (one that has a multiyear contract) has the option of not renewing the contract in any year, OPM will determine whether the group is an SSSG in any given year. If the group was an SSSG for a specific year, OPM would then compare the group's rate with the rates given to the FEHBP and give any discounts accordingly.

2. If such a group is locked in for the duration of the multiyear period, the rules for comparing the FEHBP's rates with that group's rates are more complex. If the group was an SSSG for any year, OPM would compare the FEHBP's rates with that group's rate over all years of the multiyear contract period.

3. OPM will monitor all plans that have such a group and keep track of the ease of administration. OPM will make sure this method is not causing any inequities in the rating process. OPM may have to change this policy in the future if the need arises.

Multiple rating regions. Identifying the SSSGs can be complicated by the fact that some contractors may have distinct rating regions within a particular state and have established different community rates for those regions. In these cases, it has been unclear how contractors should select their SSSGs. For plans with multiple rating regions, OPM's policy as reflected in the 1996 rate instructions is that groups in different rating areas than the FEHBP are also eligible for SSSG purposes. Any group that is enrolled in the same legal entity that contracts with OPM is potentially an SSSG even if it is in a different rating region.

OPM AUDITS AND APPEALS

As government contractors, HMOs participating in the FEHBP are subject to periodic audit by OPM. For community-rated carriers, this means that auditors from OPM's Office of Inspector General (OIG) will seek to verify that the rate charged the FEHBP was a community rate as defined by the FEHBAR and that any benefit and other loadings to the FEHBP rate were reasonable and appropriate. To assist OPM in the conduct of audits, contractors are required to maintain their records relating to a contract year for 5 years after the expiration of that contract year.[27] The language of the record retention requirement fails to state specifically what records contractors are required to maintain. Upon audit, however, OIG auditors review state and federal rate filings, actual billings to commercial accounts, and rate worksheets used in the premium development of the audited groups.

Audits of many community-rated plans often result in findings of defective community rating and recommendations that the FEHBP is entitled to a premium adjustment as a result of the contractor's defective community-rating practices. These rating practices may range from selective discounting for certain key employer groups to the absence of a consistent rate-setting methodology from which discounting of rates can be inferred. The methodology used by the OIG auditors in determining the amount of the recommended refund for the FEHBP depends on the contract year under audit. As discussed below, OPM's remedial authority has changed over the last 6 years. With these changes, the size of the OPM claims against HMOs has increased dramatically.

OPM's OIG conducts the audit and develops the audit findings and recommendations. OPM's Office of Insurance Programs, however, is responsible for resolving the audit findings either by direct settlement negotiations with the contractor or by accepting OIG's findings and issuing a final decision, from which the contractor can pursue an administrative appeal or seek judicial review if it disagrees with the audit's findings and recommendations.[28]

Audits of Pre-1990 Contract Years

It is not too surprising that the pre-1990 definition of a community rate, a rate charged to all the contractor's groups, led to audit findings of defective community rating. Any rating discrepancies between the FEHBP's rate and the audited groups' rates that could not be attributed to benefit differences were often determined to be discounts in violation of the contractor's certificate of community rating.[29] The sources of these discrepancies could be several: using a different demographic source for the FEHBP than for commercial groups, quoting commercial groups a premium rate before state approval of the carrier's community rate, or offering a direct discount. Whatever the source of the discrepancy, the result was typically the same: a finding by OPM auditors that the contractor engaged in defective community rating and a recommendation that the contractor refund the overcharges to the FEHBP. The amount of the recommended recovery for the FEHBP depends upon the remedy used by the auditors.

Before the adoption of the FEHBAR, OPM had two options in cases of defective community. First, it could require the contractor to establish a true community rate. Alternatively, the contractor could retrospectively experience rate the FEHBP for the contract year(s) in question. Any differences between the new rate and the rate charged were required to be returned to the FEHBP. Contractors who sought to employ either remedy found that OPM had interpreted

these remedies in such a way as to make them illusory. For example, for a contractor to establish a true community rate, the auditors took the position that the contractor had to rerate all its groups, give refunds to those groups that it overcharged, and bill those that it had undercharged. A retroactive experience-rate analysis of the FEHBP was similarly impractical to many plans that lacked FEHBP-specific claims information or could otherwise not satisfy the agency's requirements.*

With the promulgation of the FEHBAR in 1987, OPM's remedies were substantially strengthened with a third remedy: the so-called most favored customer remedy.[30] The most favored customer remedy, which became effective for the 1988 contract year, gives the FEHBP the benefit of the largest discount afforded another group by an audited contractor and can result in large claims against the contractor. The most favored customer remedy became the auditors' remedy of choice in initiating a claim against a contractor, although the OPM Office of Insurance Programs did not always share this view.

Audits of Contract Year 1990 and On

The SSSG regulations replaced OPM's three remedies for defective community rating. Under the new regulations:

> If any rate established in connection with this contract was increased because (1) the Carrier furnished cost or pricing data that were not complete, accurate, or current . . . (3) the Carrier

---

* These include the following: The experience analysis must include coordination of benefits and subrogation recoveries and exclude marketing costs and interest expense; the HMO's administrative load cannot exceed a specific percentage of premium, which tends to range from 5 percent to 10 percent; and those administrative expenses that cannot be allocated to the FEHBP on a direct basis must be allocated on an indirect basis, typically by number of claims or member months.

developed FEHBP rates with a rating methodology and structure inconsistent with that used to used to develop rates for [SSSGs] . . . or (4) the Carrier furnished data or information of and description that were not complete, accurate, and current—*then the rate shall be reduced in the amount by which the price was increased because of the defective data or information.* (emphasis added)[31]

Although it was clear under the SSSG regulations that any premium adjustment due the FEHBP would be based on the rates charged the SSSGs, it was not clear how that adjustment would be determined. The regulation simply states that the FEHBP's rate shall be reduced in the amount by which the price was increased because of the defective data or information. The regulation fails to address the situation where only one of the SSSGs is defectively rated. Similarly, it was not clear what adjustment the FEHBP should receive if both SSSGs receive discounts but one discount exceeds the other. In the final regulations published in March 1994, OPM made clear that any adjustments due the FEHBP shall be based on the "lowest rates determined for the Federal group using the methodology (including discounts) for the two SSSGs."[32]

Lost Investment Income or Interest Claims

In 1993, OPM began to include with audit findings a claim for lost investment income or interest on the overpayments made by the government as a result of the contractor's defective rating practices. Because the government would calculate interest from the date the overpayment was made as opposed to when the audit findings were finalized, these interest claims often represented substantial sums. Based on applicable federal law, OPM's interest claim for 1988 and 1989 may have a legal basis. OPM admits that it

has no authority for interest claim for 1990. Finally, as a result of a change in OPM's regulations, there are compelling legal arguments that suggest that OPM has no interest authority for contract years 1991 to the present. In fact, OPM's interest authority is currently the subject of several appeals by contractors.

Defending and Settling Adverse Audit Findings

FEHBP contractors that are charged with defective community rating or pricing typically have two formal opportunities to defend themselves at the agency level. The first opportunity is in response to the findings contained in the draft audit report. The second opportunity is after receipt of the final audit report, which is issued after OPM has received the contractor's comments to the draft audit report. It is critical that both responses be comprehensive submissions that defend the contractor's rating practices, where possible, and put forth alternative analyses for the calculation of the FEHBP's damages. In this regard, there are many analyses available to a contractor. The goal, however, is to find the one that best illustrates the unreasonableness of the amount recommended by the auditors by showing that the government's actual damages as a result of the contractor's community-rating practices are much lower. The contractors' analyses can have a second purpose as well: They can serve as the basis of settlement negotiations between OPM and the contractors.

If OPM and the contractor are unable to settle their dispute, the contracting officer will issue a final decision. Although settlement negotiations may continue after a final decision has been issued, once the final decision is issued the time period for appealing the government's decision starts to run. In addition, interest on the claimed amount begins to accrue 30 days after the decision is issued.

Contract appeals are subject to the Contract Disputes Act of 1978, 41 U.S. Code Section 601 *et seq.* In appealing the contracting officer's decision, the contractor can appeal to the Armed Services Board of Contract Appeals. Alternatively, an appeal can be made by the contractor to the U.S. Court of Federal Claims. To date, few contractors have appealed a final decision, and most OPM claims have been settled at the agency level.

FEHBP AND FALSE CLAIMS LIABILITY

One of the more serious developments in the FEHBP contracting area is the potential for a community-rated plan to be held liable for filing a false certification with OPM. Before the adoption of the SSSG rules, plans were required at the time of the rate proposal and at the time of the reconciliation to certify that the rate charged the FEHBP was a community rate. Given the vagaries as to how a community rate is defined and the variety of ways in which community-rating principles can be applied to different employer groups, however, questions may arise as to whether the rate certifications provided to OPM at the time of rate reconciliation were true and accurate.

The application of SSSG principles to the FEHBP rates as described above further narrows the scope of the analysis as to whether certifications provided to OPM by the plan were true and accurate. One of the certifications that the plan is required to make at the time of the rate reconciliation is that the methodology used to determine the FEHBP rates is consistent with the methodology used to determine the rates for the plan's SSSGs. With the more recent amended definition of SSSGs, the universe of comparable groups is arguably more precise, and as a result the exposure for false claims liability may be even greater for plans that file these certifications in the SSSG years.

In the process of auditing certain HMOs, OIG has referred certain matters over to the U.S. Attorney for the District of Columbia to evaluate whether a certification filed by a plan resulted in the filing of a false claim with the federal

government as prohibited by 31 U.S. Code Section 3729 *et seq.* Section 3729(a) provides in part that any person who knowingly presents, or causes to be presented, to an officer or employee of the U.S. government a false or fraudulent claim for payment or approval is liable to the government for a civil penalty of not less than $5,000 and not more than $10,000, plus three times the amount of damages that the government sustains because of the act of that person. *Knowingly,* as defined under Section 3729(b), means that a person with respect to information has actual knowledge of the information, acts in deliberate ignorance of the truth or falsity of the information, or acts in reckless disregard of the truth or falsity of the information. No proof of specific intent to defraud is required under the statute.

In view of the exposure to treble damage liability as well as the adverse publicity associated with the filing of a false claim, the issue of whether a contractor engaged in filing a false certification either as to its community rate or as to the methodology employed in rating its SSSGs has yet to be litigated. Nevertheless, OIG has been able to recover substantial amounts of money as part of the settlements of these claims between the plans and the U.S. Attorney, the results of which are reported to Congress by OIG.

Careful review of the plan's rates and files before the execution of these certifications can diminish the potential for false claim liability. The issue of false claims and audit liability exposure, however, is particularly problematic in cases involving the acquisition of one health plan by another. The scope and extent of FEHBP audit and false claim liability is often not known at the time of the acquisition, yet the successor to the government contract is fully liable for all prior acts of the selling party under the contract. Indemnification commitments that are received by the purchaser from the selling party need to be sufficiently well defined and secured to deal with an exposure that often is not identified for many years after the acquisition occurs.

MISCELLANEOUS CONTRACTING ISSUES

Enrollment Reconciliations with Local Payroll Offices

A common problem faced by FEHBP contractors is the inability to obtain timely enrollment and disenrollment information from OPM and the local payroll offices. As a result, many contractors find that they are carrying FEHBP enrollees on their membership lists and paying capitations payments to providers for federal enrollees long after these individuals have been terminated from the FEHBP.

Under its contract with FEHBP carriers, OPM is obligated to maintain or cause to be maintained adequate enrollment information to allow contractors to maintain an accurate record of their FEHBP enrollees. Moreover, contractors are entitled to rely on this information. Despite these contractual obligations, however, OPM's position is that it is the responsibility of the contractors and the individual payroll offices to reconcile enrollment records to ensure that the contractor's records are accurate. Unfortunately, the majority of payroll offices are unwilling or unable to work with the contractors to reconcile their enrollment records. Thus the contractors are left without any definitive source in seeking to maintain accurate records.

The inability to obtain accurate and timely enrollment information has been the subject of three contractor lawsuits against OPM.[33] In all three cases, the government conceded liability, but the amount of money due the contractors was left to be determined through an audit of the contractors' databases. Two of the three lawsuits have been concluded, and OPM has been required to pay these plans millions of dollars.

Apparently in light of these lawsuits and the fact that other contractors may pursue similar lawsuits, OPM sought to amend its standard contract with community-rated plans to relieve the agency of responsibility for maintaining accurate enrollment information and providing it to plans in a timely manner.[34] Questions remain as to whether OPM's attempts to relieve it from this responsibility are lawful in light of the agency's statutory responsibility to administer the FEHBP and whether such substantive changes can only be implemented in accordance with the procedural requirements of the Administrative Procedures Act.

Federal Preemption of State Laws

FEHBP contractors can sometimes be faced with conflicting requirements as federal government contractors and as state-licensed HMOs. These conflicts can relate to benefits, rates, and terms of the federal subscriber documents. In this regard, the Federal Employees Health Benefits Act contains a preemption provision that can eliminate the need of contractors to comply with some state laws that affect the contractors' FEHBP operations. The Federal Employees Health Benefits Act states: "The provisions of any contract . . . which relate to the nature or extent of coverage or benefits (including payments with respect to benefits) shall supersede and preempt any State or local law, or any regulation issued thereunder, which relates to health insurance or plans to the extent that such law or regulation is inconsistent with such contractual provisions."[35] Thus Section 8902(m)(1) can preempt state-mandated benefit requirements to the extent that the state benefits are inconsistent with those offered by the contractor to the FEHBP. In addition, it is possible that the preemption clause may be used to preempt state laws that may not appear, on their face, to affect the nature of coverage or extent of benefits. For example, Section 8902(m)(1) could be used to preempt state prohibitions on such practices as subrogation.

The FEHBP is also exempt from the provisions of the Employee Retirement Income Security Act (ERISA; see Chapter 59).[36] As a result, ERISA preemption of state law claims does not extend to claims against FEHBP contractors.[37] The FEHBP brochure given to enrollees, however, limits recoveries to the benefits under the contract. This has been construed to limit the ability of a claimant to recover punitive damages for bad faith denials.[38] Arguably, FEHBP procedures and remedies are the sole procedures and remedies for claim denials in the FEHBP, and state actions for claims are therefore preempted by Section 8902(m)(1). Although the true scope of federal preemption of state laws under Section 8902(m)(1) has not been definitively established, the case law seems to suggest that the scope of federal preemption is broad, similar to that under ERISA.

CONCLUSION

The FEHBP will continue to be the largest employer-sponsored health benefits program. OPM's ability to administer successfully this ever-growing program and to retain desirable contractors will depend on its ability to demand accountability from its contractors while maintaining consistency in the application of its rules on rates and benefits. In this regard, one of the most important developments to date has been the move away from traditional community-rating requirements toward a focus on the FEHBP's comparability to other SSSGs. This approach appears to be preferred from the perspective of both OPM and the contractors because the latest SSSG rules define with more precision the standards by which FEHBP contractors' rates will be evaluated. It also prevents the application by OPM of remedies that are punitive in nature, such as the most favored customer rule, which disregarded the comparability of discounted employer groups to the federal account.

REFERENCES AND NOTES

1. 42 U.S.C. Sections 300 *et seq.*

2. *See* 5 U.S.C. Section 8902(1).

3. 5 C.F.R. Section 890.203(a)(1) (1993).

4. 5 C.F.R. Section 890.203(a)(3) (1993).

5. 48 C.F.R. Section 1652.222-70.

6. 5 U.S.C. Section 8902(1).

7. 59 Fed. Reg. 62,283.

8. 59 Fed. Reg. 62,284 (to be codified at 5 C.F.R. Section 890.203).

9. *See* 60 Fed. Reg. 15,074 (22 March 1995).

10. *See* 5 U.S.C. Section 890(a).

11. *See* 5 U.S.C. Section 890(b)(2).

12. *See* 5 U.S.C. Section 8904.

13. *See,* for example, FEHBP Letter No. 95-7 (13 March 1995).

14. Pursuant to 42 U.S.C. Section 300e-1, with limited exceptions, the premium rates charged by federally qualified HMOs must be based on a community-rating system. *See also* 42 C.F.R. Section 417.104.

15. 48 C.F.R. Sections 1601.101–1653.000.

16. 48 C.F.R. Section 1602.170-6 (1993).

17. *See* 55 Fed. Reg. 27406–27419 (2 July 1990).

18. 48 C.F.R. Section 1602.170-2 (1989).

19. 48 C.F.R. Section 1602.170-2(a) (1993).

20. 54 Fed. Reg. 43089 (20 October 1989).

21. 48 C.F.R. Section 1602.170-2(b) (1993).

22. 48 C.F.R. Section 1615.804-70 (1993).

23. 54 Fed. Reg. 43089 (20 October 1989).

24. Under the draft version of the SSSG regulations, a government account could not be used as an SSSG. OPM reversed its position, however, when the final regulations were published. Thus government accounts may be used provided that they are community rated.

25. 48 C.F.R. Section 1602.170-11 (1990).

26. *See* 59 Fed. Reg. 14,761–14,768 (30 March 1994).

27. *See* 48 C.F.R. Section 1652.204-70 (1993).

28. Contractor appeals of adverse audit findings are governed by the Contract Dispute Act, 41 U.S.C. Sections 601 *et seq.*

29. *See* 48 C.F.R. Section 1615.804.70 (1989).

30. 48 C.F.R. Section 1652.215-70 (1987).

31. 48 C.F.R. Section 1652.215-70 (1990) (emphasis added). The SSSG regulations, as a remedy for defective rating, was effective for the 1990 contract year. *See* 55 Fed. Reg. 27406 (2 July 1990).

32. 48 C.F.R. Section 1615.802(b)(3) (1995).

33. *See e.g., MD–Individual Practice Association, Inc. v. United States of America,* No. 93-460C (Ct. Fed. Cl. filed 23 July 1993) and *Kaiser Foundation Health Plan of the Mid-Atlantic States, Inc. v. United States of America,* No. 92-855C (Ct. Fed. Cl. filed 18 December 1992).

34. *See* FEHBP Letter No. 95-27c (10 August 1995).

35. 5 U.S.C. Section 8902(m)(1).

36. 29 U.S.C. Section 1003(b).

37. *See Pilot Life Insurance Company v. Dedeaux*, 481 U.S. 41 (1987), wherein the U.S. Supreme Court held that the civil enforcement provisions of ERISA are preemptive and provide a federal remedy for state law claims such as tortious breach of contract or bad faith conduct. Suits by enrollees challenging the denial of benefits under an employee health benefit plan may therefore be removed to federal court, where only ERISA remedies are available.

38. *See Hartenstine v. Superior Court of San Bernardino County*, 196 Cal. App. 3d 206 (1987), *cert. denied*, 488 U.S. 899 (1988).

SUGGESTED READING

Wrightson, C.W. 1990. *HMO Rate Setting & Financial Strategy*. Ann Arbor, Mich.: Health Administration Press.

Chapter 46

Medicare and Managed Care

Carlos Zarabozo and Jean D. LeMasurier

TGIF (THE GOVERNMENT IS FRIGHTENING) UNLESS YOU KNOW YOUR ACRONYMS

Although you do not need to know too many acronyms for some dealings with the government, such as buying a postage stamp or paying taxes, it helps to know an acronym or two in dealing with Medicare. On the subject of health maintenance organizations (HMOs) and Medicare, some of the acronyms that you can use at cocktail parties to sound knowledgeable (and no doubt boring) are HCFA, TEFRA, CMP, ACR, APR, and, especially, AAPCC. These acronyms are all addressed in this chapter.

Carlos Zarabozo is a social science research analyst in the Special Analysis Staff, Office of the Associate Administrator for Policy. He previously held a number of positions in the managed care office of the Health Care Financing Administration (HCFA), including Director of the Operational Analysis Staff and Special Assistant to the Director.

Jean D. LeMasurier is Director of the Division of Policy and Program Improvement of the HCFA's Office of Managed Care. She has developed policy, legislation, and regulations for Medicare contracts with health maintenance organization (HMOs) and federally qualified HMOs and other coordinated care initiatives in the HCFA's Office of Research and Demonstrations, Office of Legislation and Policy, and Office of Prepaid Health Care. In addition, she developed legislation for Medicare HMOs while serving on the U.S. Senate Finance Committee.

The views expressed in this chapter are the authors' and not those of the HCFA. All addresses and telephone numbers listed were accurate at the time of publication, but such numbers and addresses occasionally change, so that the authors make no warranty as to their currency.

All acronyms aside, what the government is attempting to do through its emphasis on managed care options, one of which is HMO* contracting, is bring down health care costs while improving the quality of care. Traditional Medicare was at one time a strictly fee-for-service system with reimbursement based on cost or charges. In the past few years the government has radically changed its reimbursement for Medicare services through such means as the well-publicized prospective payment system of inpatient reimbursement based on diagnosis-related groups (DRGs) rather than reasonable cost reimbursement. In the case of HMOs, the government looked at what was happening in the private sector and found that HMOs (which in their early history had been promoted, in a sense, by the federal government) had the potential for decreasing health care costs while bringing about possible improvements in the quality of care through managed care.

---

* Throughout this chapter, the term *HMO* is generally meant to refer to both federally qualified HMOs and organizations that are determined to be competitive medical plans (CMPs) as defined in the Tax Equity and Fiscal Responsibility Act legislation introducing the concept of CMPs. The initial discussion deals exclusively with risk-sharing HMOs and CMPs. It is also possible for an HMO or CMP to contract with the Health Care Financing Administration under a cost-reimbursement arrangement that limits the risk exposure of the HMO or CMP, as discussed in the latter part of the chapter.

UNDERSTANDING THE ADJUSTED AVERAGE PER CAPITA COST

If acronyms are not your favorite subject of discussion, we can get down to business and talk instead about money. As one would expect, money usually determines whether an HMO or competitive medical plan (CMP) will want to contract with the government. Under the risk payment methodology established in the law, a contract is expected to be financially advantageous to both the HMO/CMP and the government. HMOs with a Medicare risk contract are paid 95 percent of what the government's actuaries estimate to be the cost of medical services if the services had been obtained in traditional fee-for-service Medicare. The government should save, actuarially speaking, at least 5 percent compared with what would have been the fee-for-service costs for those Medicare beneficiaries who choose to enroll in an HMO, and the health plan is paid at 95 percent of the fee-for-service rate with the expectation that because HMOs, as organized health care delivery systems, are able to provide services more efficiently than fee for service, their cost of providing care will be at or below the 95 percent level.

The government pays risk-based HMOs a prospective monthly capitation payment for each Medicare member that is akin to the premium paid to an HMO by an employer for coverage of its employees. In exchange for this capitation payment, the HMO is required to provide the full range of health care services covered under the federal Medicare program. The adjusted average per capita cost (AAPCC) is the basis of payment to HMOs and CMPs under contract to the Health Care Financing Administration (HCFA). For each county of the United States, for each Medicare member, an HMO or CMP is paid 1 of 142 possible monthly capitation amounts (which can vary significantly by county).

You can think of these 142 rate cells as 142 amoebalike creatures floating around aimlessly in space, or you can think in the less daunting terms of the 6 (yes, a mere 6) variables used to create 140 rate cells: the demographic factors of age, sex, Medicaid eligibility, institutional status; and the entitlement factors of working aged status (i.e., aged Medicare beneficiaries with other insurance coverage that is primary in relation to Medicare), and whether a person has both parts of Medicare (part A being inpatient hospital, inpatient skilled nursing services, and home health services and part B being all other services, such as physician and outpatient services). A separate computation is made for individuals entitled to Medicare on the basis of disability, but this category is redundant with the age category, because all such individuals are under age 65. This is illustrated in Exhibit 46–1.

To restate the illustration in Exhibit 46–1, once the age and sex are established, the part A and part B rates are different for institutionalized and noninstitutionalized individuals. The noninstitutionalized are reimbursed at different rates depending on whether they have other insurance coverage and whether they are eligible for Medicaid, factors that do not affect the level of payment for the institutionalized. There are also two rate cells for each state for individuals with end-stage renal disease, making a total of 142 possible rate cells.

The AAPCC represents an actuarial projection of what Medicare expenses would have been for a given category of Medicare beneficiary had the person remained in traditional fee-for-service Medicare. The AAPCC rates change every calendar year.

Under the law, the HCFA's actuary is required to publish each calendar year's AAPCC rates by 7 September of the preceding year. Each July, the HCFA's Office of the Actuary is also required to publish information about the methodology and assumptions related to the AAPCC announcement for the following year. The announcement of rates is required to contain sufficient information for any HMO to reconstruct the manner in which AAPCC rates for the counties served by the HMO were derived. The HCFA's actuary also determines the actuarial equivalent of Medicare beneficiary liability amounts, expressed as a monthly average

Exhibit 46–1 The 140 Rate Cells That Make Up Medicare Capitation

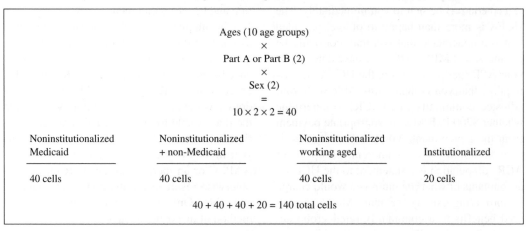

Ages (10 age groups)
×
Part A or Part B (2)
×
Sex (2)
=
$10 \times 2 \times 2 = 40$

Noninstitutionalized Medicaid	Noninstitutionalized + non-Medicaid	Noninstitutionalized working aged	Institutionalized
40 cells	40 cells	40 cells	20 cells

$40 + 40 + 40 + 20 = 140$ total cells

amount that Medicare beneficiaries have to pay for out-of-pocket expenses in fee-for-service Medicare (such as the coinsurance for physician services or the deductible a person pays on entering a hospital). When a Medicare beneficiary joins an HMO, the beneficiary deductible and coinsurance requirements are satisfied by having the beneficiary pay a monthly premium to the HMO and/or copayments for services. This actuarial equivalent is the maximum total of premiums and copayments that an HMO may charge its Medicare members to cover Medicare beneficiary liability amounts for covered services (other than under a point-of-service [POS] option).

The format of the published AAPCC rates consists of a listing, for all U.S. counties, of Medicare part A and part B base rates for the aged and the disabled (beneficiaries younger than 65 years entitled to Medicare because of their disability) together with a table of nationally used demographic factors, by which the county rates are multiplied to determine payment for a given rate cell. The published AAPCC rates are not the total projected fee-for-service rates. As published, they are 95 percent of the projected rates. As noted above, the upper limit of payment to a risk-based HMO/CMP contracting with the HCFA is the 95 percent rate.

To determine how much an HMO will be paid for its Medicare members, an HMO that is considering entering into a contract with the HCFA needs to be able to project the make-up of its Medicare population. The HMO will project how many members it will have in each rate cell of each county of its service area to determine the total payment rate and the average payment rate (APR) from the HCFA. The HCFA is able to provide a report of the demographic make-up of each U.S. county by rate cell. The same report states how many Medicare beneficiaries are currently HMO members. This type of report can be obtained through the HCFA's Office of the Actuary.

THE ADJUSTED COMMUNITY RATE/APR COMPARISON

Let us assume that you are the chief financial officer of an HMO and that, having nothing better to do one morning while reading the latest *Federal Register*, you decide to figure out how much money the government will pay you under a Medicare contract. After a little bit of effort, you have figured out that the HCFA is willing to pay you an average of, let us say, $200 per member per month (PMPM), more than any employer group ever considered paying you. You cannot wait to phone the HCFA and ask that a signed contract be sent to you immediately. The HCFA is more than happy to oblige, provided that you understand that you may not really be getting $200 PMPM. After you have determined your APR (per person) from the HCFA, the law requires that you compare this APR with your adjusted community rate (ACR) to determine whether $200 PMPM is an appropriate payment from the government. Your community rate is your premium for a commercial group. Your ACR computation is a statement to the HCFA's accountants of what premium you would charge for providing exactly the same Medicare-covered benefits to a community-rated group account, adjusted to allow for the greater intensity and frequency of utilization by Medicare recipients (because most Medicare beneficiaries are elderly). The ACR includes the normal profit of a for-profit HMO or CMP.

If your projected premium (your ACR) equals or exceeds your projected payment (your APR)—that is, if you expect your Medicare revenue to be less than or equal to your cost of providing care—then you will receive the $200 PMPM, or whatever the exact 95 percent AAPCC payment happens to be, and no more. If, however, your ACR is lower than your projected APR—if you project, for example, that you can deliver the Medicare-covered services to the population you expect to enroll at $175 PMPM—then you are required to return the surplus to the government or to your Medicare beneficiaries by accepting a reduced payment rate averaging $175 PMPM, or by returning the difference between the ACR and the APR to Medicare beneficiaries in the form of a reduced premium that would otherwise be collectible from the Medicare members, or by enriching the benefit package offered by the dollar equivalent of the surplus. That is, in the last case, if your ACR is $175 PMPM and your APR is $200, you would return $25 PMPM to the Medicare members of your HMO by providing $25 worth of additional benefits not covered by Medicare (such as drugs and routine eye care and glasses), by reducing the premium by $25 per month, or

by offering any combination of premium reduction and benefit enrichment.

A health plan may also use what is referred to as a benefit stabilization fund, through which the government withholds a portion of the difference between the ACR and the APR if the APR exceeds the ACR. The withholds can be withdrawn by the health plan in a future year so that the plan is able to offer its Medicare beneficiaries the same benefit package as in the previous year in the event that there is a reduction in the AAPCC or an increase in the ACR that would otherwise result in a reduction in the benefits available. Only a few plans have used this method of disposing of savings.

WHAT IF YOU MAKE A MISTAKE IN COMPUTING THE ACR/APR?

An HMO must sign a contract lasting at least 1 year. All HMOs with Medicare contracts currently operate on a calendar year cycle to match the AAPCC cycle because the AAPCC payment rates change each year beginning on 1 January. Contracts are automatically renewable at the end of each contract period. During the contract term, there can be no increase in the premium an HMO charges its Medicare members, nor can there be any reduction in the enriched benefits offered to Medicare members.

As a newly contracting HMO, you can either overestimate or underestimate the ACR and APR. As noted above, the HCFA will not pay you more than the 95 percent AAPCC rate, but if you have overestimated an element of the ACR computation—let us say, for example, that you have overestimated the degree to which Medicare members will require more frequent visits to their primary care physicians—you pocket the difference. If you underestimate, you lose money.

Of course, the HCFA requires that you submit a new ACR computation for each year. During the first year of contracting, you are permitted to use utilization data from other HMOs to come up with a Medicare ACR. After the first year you must use internal data, however, and in the case of pocketing the difference your internal data should show that the ACR of the first year had overestimated figures, leading to a windfall that will not be repeated in the coming year. If your ACR calculation had underestimated your cost, your recalculation would yield a higher ACR.

A LITTLE BIT OF HISTORY

Because you have now mastered the accounting aspects of Medicare contracting, we will take up the subject of history. The current body of law treating Medicare HMOs was passed in September 1982 as part of the Tax Equity and Fiscal Responsibility Act of 1982 (TEFRA). There were to be no TEFRA Medicare contractors until publication of final HCFA regulations on TEFRA contracting, however, which appeared in the 10 January 1985 *Federal Register*. The regulations became effective 1 February 1985.

There did exist pre-TEFRA risk contractors (as well as cost-reimbursed contractors) under rules in existence before TEFRA. From the beginning of the Medicare program in 1965, Medicare has recognized the unique nature of HMOs and HMO-like entities and has provided for alternative payment methodologies appropriate for such organizations. The original Medicare amendments to the Social Security Act included the authority for prepaid plans to receive payment for physician services on a basis other than individual charges (through the cost reimbursement mechanism used by what are now referred to as health care prepayment plans, HCPPs). Even before the enactment of the federal HMO Act in 1973, the 1972 amendments to the Social Security Act provided authority to contract with HMOs (as defined in the amendments) on a risk-sharing basis and on a cost basis.

The largest of the pre-TEFRA risk contractors was the Group Health Cooperative of Puget Sound. There were never more than a few health plans that chose to contract with the HCFA under the pre-TEFRA rules, although as of mid-1995 there were nearly 200 HMOs or CMPs with TEFRA risk contracts. Why the difference?

TEFRA simplified the contracting requirements and brought them more in line with the way in which HMOs normally operate. Under pre-TEFRA rules, an HMO was reimbursed at 100 percent of the AAPCC, but it was required to file cost reports with the government to establish whether there was a loss or whether there were excess government payments at the 100 percent rate. If the cost of providing services was below the 100 percent rate, the HMO could keep only a portion of the profit or savings. If the cost of providing services (as determined through submission of a cost report by the HMO) was below the 100 percent level, the HMO and the government split the savings unless savings exceeded 20 percent. If savings exceeded 20 percent, the HMO retained 10 percent of the savings, and the government kept the remainder. Losses, however, could be carried over into future years to offset the amount of savings that had to be shared with the government.

In 1982, the HCFA awarded demonstration contracts to try out the concepts of TEFRA type risk HMOs through what were referred to as Medicare competition demonstration projects. These demonstration projects, some of which were operating under a variety of waivers of parts of Section 1876 of the Social Security Act (the section entirely reworked by TEFRA), were all required to convert to TEFRA status. By the time TEFRA implementing regulations were published in January 1985, there were about 300,000 members (out of a total of about 30 million Medicare beneficiaries then) of these types of organizations. In mid-1995, Medicare membership in TEFRA risk HMOs was nearly 3 million.

What TEFRA Did

On the payment side, TEFRA introduced the concept of sharing the wealth, to use Huey Long's phrase, whereby savings are returned to Medicare beneficiaries rather than to the government, as explained in the section above on the AAPCC. The computation of savings would be done on a prospective basis, and there would be no retrospective adjustment and thus no cost reports filed by an HMO. As far as changes in contracting provisions, before TEFRA only plans that were federally qualified HMOs could have Medicare contracts. TEFRA modified HMO contracting rules to permit the HCFA to contract with a new type of entity, the CMP. A CMP is defined as an entity that:

- is state licensed (organized under the laws of any state, to use the terminology of the regulations)
- provides health care on a prepaid, capitated basis
- provides care primarily through physicians who are employees or partners of the entity (or the services are provided through groups of physicians or individuals under contract to the CMP), primarily being defined under HCFA policy to be at least 51 percent of the services provided through the CMP (thus allowing preferred provider organizations (PPOs) to be CMPs)
- assumes full financial risk on a prospective basis, with provisions for stop loss, reinsurance, and risk sharing with providers
- meets the Public Health Service Act requirements of protection against insolvency

As of mid-1995 there were 50 CMPs with Medicare contracts. As a result of the 1988 amendments to the HMO Act (the 1973 law authorizing federally qualified HMOs, Title XIII of the Public Health Service Act), the major differences that existed between federally qualified HMOs and CMPs at the time TEFRA was passed no longer exist: Federally qualified HMOs are no longer required to be separate legal entities, and they may set premium levels based on the utilization experience of groups (as opposed to the pre-1988 community-rating requirement). The major remaining differences that continue to make the CMP option more feasible for certain organizations are the level at which services may be provided through

noncontracting providers; the limitations that a CMP, but not an HMO, may impose on the scope of services; and the fact that employers may prefer to deal with non–federally qualified HMOs because of the requirement that employer contributions toward HMO coverage be nondiscriminatory (i.e., at levels similar to those for other health plan options). The 1988 HMO Act amendments introduced a provision allowing a federally qualified HMO to provide up to 10 percent of physician services outside the HMO (i.e., a self-referral option for members not wishing to use an HMO physician), whereas the requirement for the provision of medical services in a CMP is that the services be provided primarily through the CMP.

Although under a Medicare contract a CMP and an HMO would both be required to provide all Medicare-covered services, the commercial members of a CMP need not be offered certain benefits that the law requires an HMO to offer, such as home health care, mental health services, and substance abuse treatment. A CMP may also limit the scope of some of the services it is required to offer (the required services being physician services; inpatient hospital services; laboratory, radiology, emergency, and preventive services; and out-of-area coverage) and is permitted to require deductibles and copayments. A federally qualified HMO may only charge nominal copayments, a deductible for the 10 percent of physician services that the HMO is permitted to cover as out-of-plan services. A federally qualified HMO may not limit the scope of coverage except as specifically allowed in regulations (20 outpatient mental health visits per year being an example of a reduced scope of service permitted in HMO regulations).

What Congress Did after TEFRA

Over the brief history of Medicare risk contracting, a number of new provisions of the law and regulations have been added. For example, the 25 May 1984 publication of the proposed TEFRA risk contracting regulations contained a provision that required all marketing material to be reviewed and approved by the HCFA before an HMO could use the material. This requirement was dropped in the 10 January 1985, publication of the final rules, only to be added later by Congress through the Consolidated Omnibus Budget Reconciliation Act (COBRA) of 1986. COBRA also required that HMOs immediately disenroll Medicare beneficiaries who requested disenrollment as of the first day of the month after the beneficiary's request; previously an HMO could retain a Medicare member for up to 60 days before disenrollment was effective.

The Omnibus Budget Reconciliation Act of 1985 (OBRA-85) introduced more requirements and restrictions on HMOs. The importance of the 50/50 requirement was reemphasized because Congress limited the availability of waivers to government entities or to HMOs serving areas in which the Medicare/Medicaid population exceeds 50 percent of the total area population. Sanctions are to be imposed if an HMO fails to meet the 50/50 requirement: New enrollment can be prohibited, or the HCFA can permit new enrollment but the HMO will not be paid for the new enrollees.

OBRA-85 requires HMOs to inform Medicare members of their rights when the beneficiaries join the HMO and annually thereafter. It was also OBRA-85 that brought about the option of disenrollment at Social Security offices for Medicare HMO members.

OBRA-85 expanded the role of peer review organizations (PROs) in monitoring the quality of care at HMOs by requiring PRO review of HMO inpatient care and ambulatory care. PROs are charged with the responsibility of investigating any complaint submitted to a PRO by a beneficiary regarding the quality of care rendered by an HMO. OBRA provides for fines against an HMO if it is found that the HMO substantially failed to provide adequate care.

OBRA-85 also mandates that there be a study of the physician incentive arrangements in hospitals reimbursed through the Medicare prospective payment system (DRGs) as well as incentive arrangements in HMOs with a view toward imposing restrictions on the types of incentive arrangements that have an adverse effect on patient care. After several years of pondering the issue, Congress, in OBRA-90, imposed added restrictions on Medicare-contracting HMOs that prevent them from having incentive arrangements that put physicians at substantial financial risk for services that the physicians did not directly provide. If an HMO has incentive arrangements that the HCFA finds to involve such substantial financial risk, the HMO is required to have stop-loss provisions for its physicians, and the HMO must conduct beneficiary surveys to determine whether the risk arrangements affect the services members receive.

OBRA-87 required that HMOs that were terminating or not renewing a contract or were reducing their Medicare service area arrange for supplemental (Medigap) coverage to replace HMO coverage for Medicare beneficiaries affected by the HMO's decision. If an insurer imposes a waiting period for coverage of preexisting conditions, the HMO must arrange to have the waiting period waived or must otherwise provide for coverage, for up to 6 months, of services related to the preexisting condition.

OBRA-90 required Medicare-contracting HMOs to comply with Medicare requirements imposed on hospitals and other providers to make Medicare beneficiaries aware of the right to have their medical care subject to advance directives (living wills) and to have the beneficiary's instructions made part of the HMO medical record. OBRA-90 also permitted retroactive enrollment of Medicare beneficiaries who enroll in a Medicare-contracting risk HMO as retirees through an employer-sponsored health plan; individual Medicare beneficiaries may only be enrolled prospectively. The same law afforded risk HMOs hold-harmless protection limiting their liability for the coverage of services that Medicare might add during a calendar year but were not considered in determining AAPCC rates for the year. Another added provision requires risk HMOs to make prompt payment (under the same time frames as Medicare carriers and intermediaries) on claims for services provided by nonnetwork providers.

THE REQUIREMENTS TO OBTAIN A TEFRA CONTRACT

To obtain a TEFRA Medicare contract, a plan must be either a federally qualified HMO or designated by the HCFA as a CMP. For an entity that wishes to become eligible as a CMP, the only type of application that may be submitted is a combined application to be found eligible as a CMP and to be granted a Medicare contract. An HMO or CMP must meet the following TEFRA requirements to obtain a risk contract.

Membership

A nonrural plan must have at least 5,000 prepaid capitated members for which the organization is at risk for the provision of comprehensive services (although risk may be shared by providers); enrollment must be 1,500 members for a rural plan. The 5,000 rule may be satisfied by a parent organization that assumes responsibility for the financial risk and adequate management and supervision of health care services furnished by its subdivision or subsidiary, to cite the regulations. Even though the 5,000 rule may be met by a parent organization, there is a further requirement that there be a minimum membership of 1,000 at the subsidiary location before the plan may enter into a Medicare contract to establish that the subsidiary is viable and to have a valid basis for determining a Medicare ACR for the subsidiary.

An organization must have a membership that at all times during the contract does not exceed 50 percent combined Medicare and Medicaid enrollees. This provision (referred to as the 50/50 rule) can be waived only for government entities or if the HMO serves an area in which the population exceeds 50 percent Medicare/Medicaid.

Medical Services

The organization must be able to render, directly or through arrangements, all the Medicare services available in its service area. It must use Medicare-certified providers, that is, hospitals, skilled nursing facilities, and home health agencies. Physicians and suppliers used by the HMO may not include persons who have been barred from participation in either Medicare or Medicaid because of program abuse or fraud.

The HMO must be able to provide 24-hour emergency services and must have provisions for the payment of claims for emergency services within the service area and for out-of-area emergency or urgently needed services. All services that the HMO is required to render must be accessible with reasonable promptness, and there must be a recordkeeping system that ensures continuity of care.

Range of Services

The HMO must provide all the Medicare part A and B services available in the service area through staff providers or providers under contract with the HMO. Additional, non–Medicare-covered services may also be provided in several ways: as additional benefits, which are the enriched benefits provided when a risk HMO's ACR is less than its APR; as optional supplemental benefits, which any Medicare beneficiary may choose to purchase from the HMO; as mandatory supplemental benefits, which are benefits a Medicare beneficiary must purchase as a condition of enrollment (e.g., because Medicare does not cover preventive care, a standard HMO benefit, the benefit for Medicare beneficiaries is financed by mandatory premiums); as premium waivers by HMOs that choose not to charge for non–Medicare-covered benefits even though their ACR/APR computation would permit charging such a premium; and as benefits offered only to employer group retirees.

Open Enrollment

The law requires that a Medicare HMO have a 30-day open enrollment every year. An HMO must also open its enrollment to Medicare enrollees who were disenrolled from another Medicare HMO in the area as a result of a contract nonrenewal or termination. Aside from these required open enrollment periods, the HMO may have any other open enrollment period, including continuous open enrollment. During an open enrollment period, the organization must enroll any Medicare beneficiary with Part B coverage who is eligible to enroll and lives in the organization's service area. Medicare beneficiaries who are also Medicaid recipients may also enroll. Medicare beneficiaries who have end-stage renal disease (whether aged, disabled, or entitled to Medicare solely because of their disease), however, must be denied enrollment unless they are already an enrollee of the HMO. Medicare beneficiaries who have elected to be cared for in a Medicare-certified hospice are also prohibited from enrolling. If a person acquires end-stage renal disease after enrollment or elects hospice after enrollment, the HMO may not disenroll the individual.

The open enrollment requirement may be waived in one of three circumstances: The organization will exceed 50 percent Medicare/Medicaid enrollment; the organization will enroll a disproportionate share of enrollees in a particular AAPCC category, in which case the HCFA will permit the organization to discontinue enrollments in that AAPCC category; or the organization does not have the capacity to render services to any more enrollees, either commercial or Medicare. If an organization is going to limit enrollment under the third option, the HCFA must be informed 90 days before the open enrollment period so that HCFA approval can be given. In determining capacity for Medicare enrollees, the organization may set aside vacancies for expected commercial enrollees during each Medicare contract period.

Marketing Rules

An HMO must market its Medicare plan throughout the entire service area specified in the Medicare contract. All marketing materials, including membership and enrollment materials, must be approved by the HCFA before use. Prospective enrollees must be given descriptive ma-

terial sufficient for them to make an informed choice in enrolling in an HMO. Prohibited marketing activities include door-to-door solicitation, discriminatory marketing (avoiding low-income areas, for example), and misleading marketing or misrepresentation. These activities are subject to sanctions, including suspension of enrollment, suspension of payment for new enrollees, or civil monetary penalties (the government's euphemism for fines). The HCFA has 45 days to review marketing materials. If 45 days pass without HCFA comments on the material, it is deemed approved.

Ability To Bear Risk

An HMO or CMP must be able to bear the potential financial risk under a Medicare contract. The statute authorizes the HCFA to determine that an otherwise qualified HMO or CMP may not have the ability to bear the risk inherent in a Medicare risk contract; such an organization would only be permitted to contract on a cost reimbursement basis.

Administrative Ability

An organization must have sufficient administrative ability to carry out the terms of a Medicare contract. The same section of the regulations dealing with this provision mentions that an organization may not have any management, agent, or owner who has been convicted of criminal offenses involving Medicare, Medicaid, or Title XX (the regulations are silent about what the HCFA thinks of other types of felons).

Quality Assurance

HMOs are required under the Public Health Service Act to have quality assurance programs that are evaluated as part of the HMO qualification process. CMPs are required to have quality assurance programs to be granted a Medicare contract. The quality assurance program of a CMP must stress health outcomes to the extent consistent with the state of the art, must provide for peer review, must collect and interpret data systematically to make necessary changes in the provision of health services, and must include written procedures for remedial action to correct problems.

The Right To Inspect and Evaluate Records

The government has the right to inspect financial records as well as records pertaining to services performed under the contract and pertaining to enrollment and disenrollment of individuals. The right to inspect extends to entities related to the HMO, a right that was expanded in scope in OBRA-86.

Confidentiality of Records

The organization must adhere to relevant provisions of the Privacy Act and is required to maintain the confidentiality of the medical and nonmedical records of its Medicare members.

Limitations on Physician Risk

In 1996, the Office of the Inspector General of the Department of Health and Human Services issued final regulations placing limitations on the amount of risk a health plan may put a physician at in a Medicare or Medicaid program. These new regulations effectively limit the amount of risk to 25 percent, and place additional requirements on the health plan regarding stop-loss insurance and member surveys. The reader is referred to Chapter 9 for a discussion of these new regulations.

FLEXIBILITY IN CONTRACTING

The HCFA's view of the requirements for Medicare contracting has evolved since the early days of the risk-contracting program. Certain changes in policy have permitted expansion of Medicare risk contracting or have ensured the continuing participation of contractors. At the beginning of the TEFRA program, the HCFA maintained that there should be no difference between Medicare contracting and contracting with commercial groups with regard to the providers available to each type of member and the service area in which the HMO was being offered. In 1987, however, two changes were made that gave HMOs more flexibility in their Medicare-contracting options. One change was to allow HMOs to contract initially for less than their commercial service area as well as to drop counties from their service area at the end of any contract year. Because the HCFA's AAPCC payment rates vary from county to county, one consequence of this change was that, in Minnesota, for example, HMOs that included rural counties in their service area were able to discontinue their Medicare contracts in the rural counties in which AAPCC payment rates were relatively low.

Another change has permitted HMOs to have differential premiums for different groups of Medicare enrollees. Under one Medicare HMO contract, premiums may vary by county. In any case in which there are differential premiums among Medicare enrollees in an HMO, however, every Medicare beneficiary must receive the level of benefits and be charged no more than the maximum premium computed through the HMO-wide Medicare ACR process. That is, an HMO must treat all its Medicare members equally in computing its ACR to be submitted for HCFA approval. If the ACR requires that the HMO charge no more than $20 as a monthly Medicare premium, then all Medicare enrollees must be charged $20 or less. As long as all members are charged no more than $20, members who reside in certain counties, may be charged less than $20. The HMO would waive all or a portion of the otherwise collectible premium if the competitive situation in a particular county dictated such a practice.

Employer group retirees represent a special case for which differential premiums are permitted. Often, employers or unions include, in their retiree benefit packages, additional services not covered by Medicare, and the union or employer contributes toward the individual's premium. Medicare beneficiaries who wish to enroll in a Medicare-contracting HMO offered through their employer or union may pay a higher or lower premium than individual Medicare enrollees. As of 1995, group retirees could also have different copayment structures, as long as the copayment structure offered to a group was also available to any individual Medicare beneficiary. For example, if a group asked a Medicare HMO that was charging all Medicare enrollees a $5 copay for physician office visits to increase the charge to $10 for the group's retirees, the HMO could do so (and necessarily would have to reduce the Medicare premium amount in recognition of the increased revenue) as long as a $10 copay option was offered to any Medicare enrollee of the plan.

The most recent change, dating from October 1995, is the clarification of the HCFA's policy regarding a POS option for Medicare risk HMO enrollees. This option, increasingly popular in the commercial marketplace, is permitted under the TEFRA statute. HMOs may offer a POS benefit (coverage of care obtained out of network) to their Medicare enrollees as an additional benefit, a mandatory supplemental benefit, an optional supplement, or a benefit solely for employer group retirees. HMOs offering a POS option are subject to additional monitoring by the HCFA to ensure continued compliance with standards pertaining to financial solvency, availability and accessibility of care, quality assurance, member appeals, and marketing.

WHICH OFFICE DOES WHAT, WHERE TO WRITE, AND WHOM TO CALL

To obtain a contract, you must submit an application to the HCFA. You can obtain an application by writing to:

HCFA Office of Managed Care
(OMC)
Operations and Oversight
Room 3-02-01, South Building
7500 Security Boulevard
Baltimore, Maryland 21244-1850
(410) 786-1147

Write to the same office to obtain information about and an application for federally qualified HMO status or to obtain Medicare contract eligibility as a CMP.

For information about the ACR process, you should contact:

Medicare Payment and Audit Team
OMC
Room 3-02-01, South Building
7500 Security Boulevard
Baltimore, Maryland 21244-1850
(410) 786-7634

The Medicare Payment and Audit Team reviews and approves ACR submissions and is also responsible for payment activities and systems activities, such as enrollment and disenrollment from HMOs.

There are ten regional offices of the HCFA. An applicant would initially send an application for a Medicare contract (HMO or CMP) to the HCFA's regional offices, which have primary responsibility for processing Medicare contract applications and are the principal point of contact for HMOs after they have a Medicare contract. The regional offices and the HCFA central office together monitor the performance of contracting HMOs through on-site visits that occur at least biannually (and more frequently if fortune shines on your HMO). Any marketing material that an HMO prepares that is not submitted with the original application has to be reviewed by the servicing HCFA regional office. The regional offices answer most beneficiary inquiries and investigate complaints about an HMO. They perform valuable technical assistance functions in the day-to-day Medicare operations of an HMO, including resolving problems that an HMO may be having with membership data being submitted to the HCFA, Medicare coverage issues, and liaison with Social Security offices and Medicare fiscal intermediaries. In other words, the regional office contact person is a good person to get to know, although you will also have HCFA central office contact people for systems and financial functions, and each

HMO will have a central office overall plan manager.

THE STEPS OF THE CONTRACTING PROCESS

Before submitting a request for a Medicare contract as a part of a federal qualification or CMP eligibility determination, the applicant usually contacts the HCFA, if for no other reason than to obtain the most current application forms and accompanying explanatory material. The purpose of an application for a Medicare contract is to allow the HCFA to determine whether you meet all the requirements for the granting of a contract, as listed above, and whether you have a sufficient understanding of how the requirements are to be implemented. The following are some of the questions included in the application:

- types and numbers of providers the plan will use
- listing of benefits
- description of the Medicare marketing strategy
- copies of marketing material to be used
- evidence of coverage or subscriber agreement listing membership rules, enrollee rights, and plan benefits:
  1. how to use the plan to obtain services
  2. information about obtaining services after hours or in an emergency in or out of the service area
  3. how to file claims from nonplan providers
  4. the lock-in requirement
- quality assurance plan
  1. enrollment and disenrollment procedures, including a description of how the plan will meet the open enrollment requirement
  2. the plan's grievance and Medicare appeals procedures
  3. other information as necessary

If the organization wishes to apply as a CMP, you submit a combined application to the OMC. The Medicare sections of the application are reviewed by the HCFA regional office staff, and the financial and legal aspects (i.e., the structural and contractual requirements imposed by the law) are reviewed by the OMC central office staff. There will also be a site visit to decide whether you meet the criteria for designation as a CMP. If you wish to become a federally qualified HMO, you may also submit a combined application for HMO qualification and the granting of a Medicare contract; there will be a site visit to qualify you as an HMO (the qualification process is discussed in detail in Chapter 54). If you are already a federally qualified HMO, you submit a freestanding application for a Medicare contract. The evaluation of the Medicare contract application will also involve a site visit in many cases. For any of these situations, an ACR proposal must be submitted to the Medicare Payment and Audit Team. Then you wait.

The Medicare application, or the Medicare portion of your combined application, is reviewed by the regional office, and comments are sent back to you. Then they wait.

You submit a reply to the comments, fix up your marketing material, promise to obey every law in the books and whatever new laws Congress passes, and so forth. Then you wait.

In the meantime, your able accountants have submitted a beautifully done ACR proposal to Baltimore. You insisted that it be beautifully done because you know that, until the ACR proposal is accepted, the HCFA will not sign a contract. Also in the meantime, you have had your management information systems staff talking with the OMC systems staff to make sure that, when you have members to accrete to your Medicare plan, your data submission will be compatible with the HCFA's requirements. Alternatively, you may choose to submit your accretions and deletions through Litton or CompuServe, each of which has a contract with the HCFA for the processing of health plan accretions and deletions. One advantage to using CompuServe or Litton is that you can have immediate verification of Medicare eligibility and identifying data, so that your submission of an accretion will be accepted by the HCFA on the first try, and you will be paid immediately for the new member. As far as how the government pays the plan, once you have a contract you will be paid through electronic funds transfer from the Treasury Department on the first day of each month.

Assuming that you have qualified your HMO or have been deemed eligible as a CMP, the HCFA finally tells you that, yes, you can have a contract. It mails you three copies of a contract to sign and return. You are done waiting. You now mobilize your Medicare marketing forces, deluge the HCFA regional office with brand new innovative marketing material on a daily basis, and (alas) wait again for the hordes of new Medicare enrollees.

BENEFICIARY RIGHTS AND RESPONSIBILITIES

If you are a commercial member of an HMO, you know that you cannot go to any physician anywhere and expect your HMO to cover the cost of the care (other than in a POS case). If you are a Medicare beneficiary, you may not know this, even if you enrolled in a Medicare-contracting HMO. Explaining to Medicare beneficiaries how lock-in HMOs work has been a major problem. This is true partly because Medicare beneficiaries are accustomed to fee-for-service Medicare, in which a beneficiary may use almost any provider and can be assured that Medicare will pay some, if not all, of the costs of the services. It is also the case that some HMOs have enrolled Medicare beneficiaries in ways that do not adequately explain lock-in provisions (e.g., mail-in applications). The HCFA strongly recommends that there be a face-to-face discussion of the requirements of HMO membership with prospective Medicare members. To ensure that the lock-in provision is understood, and to confirm enrollment, the HCFA sends every Medicare beneficiary a notice of HMO enrollment when the HCFA computer records are

changed to annotate the individual's new HMO status.

Among the beneficiary rights is the right to remain enrolled in the health plan for the duration of the contract with the government. Involuntary disenrollment is permitted only if the person loses entitlement to part B of Medicare, commits fraud in connection with the enrollment process or permits abuse of his or her membership card, permanently leaves the HMO's service area, fails to pay premiums or copayments, or (people who write regulations like to mention the obvious) dies. There is a provision allowing disenrollment for cause or for disruptive behavior that prevents the health plan from rendering services to the member or other members; such disenrollments have to have the prior approval of the HCFA.

Beneficiaries are guaranteed certain appeal rights for decisions made by an HMO regarding liability for Medicare services or coverage of Medicare services. The appeal rights include a provision that requires HCFA review of any decision that is adverse or partly adverse to a Medicare member. The HCFA review (which is actually done by a private entity under contract to the HCFA) can be followed by appeal to an administrative law judge (if the amount is $100 or more) and, for cases involving amounts of $1,000 or more, appeal for review at the federal court level.

Beneficiaries may voluntarily disenroll from an HMO whenever they wish. COBRA-85 requires the disenrollment to be effective the first day of the month after the month of the request. As of July 1987, beneficiaries may also disenroll from an HMO through any Social Security office.

WHAT IS DIFFERENT ABOUT HAVING A MEDICARE MEMBER?

Evaluating whether the payment an HMO will receive from the government is adequate is a necessary step in determining whether an organization will contract with the HCFA to enroll Medicare members. Another factor to be considered, which may be looked at as a cost, is that enrolling Medicare members and providing services to them are not identical to enrolling and serving a commercial population. In the commercial market, an HMO signs up a group and enrolls members through the group; in Medicare, the HMO must sign up individuals one by one (i.e., retail selling). Thus the marketing strategy is different: The product is different, the means of making potential enrollees aware of the product is different, and the target of marketing is no longer a group and its representative but instead is an individual potential enrollee. These differences require an HMO to expand its marketing staff, and most HMOs with risk contracts have established a completely separate marketing department for Medicare.

There will also have to be a significant increase in the member relations staff of an HMO, again perhaps by establishing a totally separate department to deal with the Medicare membership. For a variety of reasons, Medicare beneficiaries require more hand-holding than commercial members. For example, either the member relations staff or the marketing staff will be responsible for ensuring that Medicare members understand the concept of lock-in or exclusive use of HMO providers, which is an especially difficult concept to convey to Medicare beneficiaries. The member relations staff will also be responsible for dealing with Medicare member grievances, and, along with the claims staff and medical or legal staff in the HMO, the member relations staff will probably be involved in the processing of Medicare appeals cases, which under the law must be reviewed by the HCFA when the HMO wishes to deny payment for claims or when the HMO denies a requested service.

Medicare enrollment records are not solely internal to the HMO. To be paid by the HCFA, an HMO must send its enrollment and disenrollment information to the HCFA on a monthly basis via magnetic tape or by using a commercial firm (CompuServe or Litton, currently) under contract with the HCFA to process membership data. Medicare members may disenroll at any time and may do so not only at the HMO or by writing to the HMO but also at any Social Security office. For both enrollment and disenrollment processes, there are specific regulatory requirements regarding written notice to the member and provisions regarding the timeliness of an HMO's actions.

The claims department of an HMO will be affected by a Medicare contract in that claims volume will increase for nonplan claims. For one thing, given that Medicare beneficiaries are higher utilizers of medical services, there will be a greater number of out-of-plan claims for emergency and urgently needed services. When a Medicare member uses an out-of-plan provider, a claim may be submitted to a Medicare carrier or intermediary as though the person were a fee-for-service Medicare beneficiary, but the claim will be transferred to the HMO from the Medicare carrier or intermediary (the Medicare fiscal agent for processing claims). Regulations require that an HMO process each claim received for its Medicare members and determine whether payment is appropriate. In its coordination of benefits activities, the claims department will have to become aware of Medicare coordination rules because, under a risk contract, the HMO is in a sense acting as a Medicare fiscal agent in making payment decisions.

The services that are covered under the federal Medicare program are broader than the services that a federally qualified HMO is required to provide to serve a commercial population. For example, durable medical equipment and skilled nursing facility services are not benefits usually available in a commercial group package. In addition to having to arrange such services, the HMO has to ensure that its utilization review staff are aware of what is and is not covered under Medicare.

All the above differences require the HMO either to expand its staff or to increase the responsibilities of its existing staff, which in either case usually means increased costs.

Another significant difference that will have to be considered when one is thinking about the consequences of obtaining a Medicare contract is the difference in the method of payment for Medicare members. The government does not pay an HMO in the same way that an employer group does, as explained above in the section on AAPCC payment. Consequently, an HMO may need to revise reimbursement arrangements with its existing providers and develop reimbursement arrangements with new providers (additional providers to expand capacity as well as new provider types, such as skilled nursing facilities and suppliers of durable medical equipment).

In establishing its guidelines for the ACR/APR computation explained above, the HCFA recognized that utilization by Medicare members is more frequent and more intensive than that of commercial enrollees. For example, if a physician is paid a capitation by the HMO to treat HMO commercial members, the same capitation would not be a reasonable payment to the physician for a Medicare member. If hospitals are paid a per diem rate for commercial HMO members, that same per diem may not be appropriate for Medicare members. The new reimbursement arrangements to take into account Medicare member utilization patterns need not result in a decrease in revenue on a per member basis, but it is important to know that there is more to Medicare contracting than just signing a contract and watching the AAPCC rates go up every year.

WHATEVER HAPPENED TO BIG BROTHER?

As of now, payments to HMOs are a minuscule part of the HCFA's budget. Of course, one person's minuscule is another person's majuscule: Payments to HMOs are minuscule in the context of a budget for Medicare health care expenditures that totals more than $175 billion. In a program that involves government payments of more than $1 billion each month, there is bound to be at least a slight amount of interest in having some government oversight.

Once any HMO, whether Medicare contracting or not, is qualified, or once a CMP is granted

eligibility for a Medicare contract, the HCFA maintains ongoing monitoring of the plan. The monitoring is accomplished through self-reporting of financial and other information by the HMOs and CMPs on a quarterly basis, although if certain criteria are met, this information may be reported on a yearly basis. The information is reported to the OMC on a special reporting form known as the National Data Reporting Requirements form.

Specific to Medicare is a monitoring process that is performed by the OMC and, principally, by the ten regional offices of the HCFA. By the end of the first year of contracting, each plan will have a monitoring visit conducted jointly by the OMC and the regional offices, during which the reviewers will determine whether the health plan is complying with regulatory requirements in such areas as insolvency arrangements, legal and financial requirements for the entity as a whole, quality of care issues, marketing practices, enrollment/disenrollment, claims payment, and grievance and appeals procedures. The reviewers follow a specific written protocol in conducting the review.

After such a monitoring visit, a report is prepared, and if necessary the HMO is required to submit a corrective action plan. Close monitoring of the plan continues until the HCFA is satisfied that the problems have been resolved. If the initial review goes well, there may not necessarily be a review of the same HMO for another 2 years.

As previously noted, Medicare risk-contracting HMOs are subject to external review of the quality of care they render. PROs, which also review the quality of care of hospitals in fee-for-service Medicare, review a risk HMO's inpatient and ambulatory care. This review requirement has been the subject of a great deal of controversy among HMOs. The HMOs maintain that the review procedures are overly burdensome for the results they produce and that the methodology should be more tailored to the care rendered in a managed care system. As a result, the HCFA has revised the methodology, in part on the basis of comments from the HMO industry and other outside groups such as hospital groups and the American Association of Retired Persons. The revised methodology moves away from review of individual cases and toward a collaborative approach focusing on patterns of care. This approach should be more successful in improving the care provided to Medicare beneficiaries in HMOs. [An entire issue of the *Health Care Financing Review* (volume 16, number 4, Summer 1995) is devoted to advances in quality measurement.]

ALTERNATIVES TO RISK CONTRACTING FOR THE RISK AVERSE

HMOs that are risk averse may decide to contract with the HCFA on a cost basis. Cost contracts provide that the HMO is reimbursed by the HCFA for the reasonable cost of all services actually provided to Medicare enrollees, with the only significant cost that is not reimbursed being the profit of a for-profit contractor. Medicare enrollees of a cost reimbursed organization are not locked into the plan. If a beneficiary chooses to use a nonplan provider, Medicare fee-for-service carriers and intermediaries will pay any claims without regard to the person's Medicare cost HMO status.

An HMO may obtain a cost contract under two different statutory provisions: the Social Security Act provision that also authorizes risk contracting (Section 1876), and a provision that constitutes a fragment of a sentence in Section 1833 of the Medicare law. The latter arrangement, an HCPP agreement, has minimal regulatory requirements and, beginning in 1996, will also be subject to state Medigap (Medicare supplemental insurance) regulation requirements. A Section 1876 contractor must be a federally qualified HMO or a CMP and must adhere to all the requirements that risk contractors follow other than PRO review of services (because there is no lock-in and no risk on the part of the cost HMO) and the requirement of holding an open enrollment to enroll beneficiaries leaving a risk HMO that is terminating its contract. An

HCPP, on the other hand, may health screen, need not have an open enrollment, need not provide the full range of Medicare-covered services (only certain physician and supplier services are required), and is not financially responsible for emergency care. Any organization that provides services to enrolled members through staff or contracted physicians may become an HCPP. Many of the HCPPs contracting with the HCFA are in fact labor or employer organizations that arrange for the provision of services exclusively to their members. As of August 1995, there were 30 HMO/CMP cost contractors with 181,000 enrollees and 56 HCPP contractors with 541,000 Medicare enrollees.

MEDICARE'S DUAL OPTION STRATEGY SHIFTS TO MEDICARE CHOICES

Overview

In 1985, Medicare policymakers positioned Medicare as a dual-option program: fee for service and the risk HMO option (where the plan is at full financial risk and beneficiaries are locked into the plan's network for all services except emergency or urgently needed care). The expectation was that large numbers of Medicare beneficiaries would be enrolled in HMOs by the end of the decade. By 1991, however, only 3 percent of Medicare beneficiaries were enrolled in a risk contract HMO, and only 6 percent were enrolled in any type of managed care plan.

In contrast, by 1991, according the Health Insurance Association of America, 49 percent of employees younger than 65 years who received their health benefits from an employer-sponsored health plan were enrolled in a managed care plan. Managed care plans offered by employers included a broader array of options than were available to Medicare beneficiaries, such as PPOs and POS options in addition to HMOs.

Medicare policymakers noted the divergent trends between private sector managed care enrollment and Medicare enrollment in managed care. Three perspectives were considered: the beneficiary, the HMO, and the Medicare program (discussed below). The result of this analysis was a revised managed care strategy for Medicare. The strategy incorporates three prongs based on lessons learned from the private sector: improving the Medicare risk HMO program, making the choice of managed care more widely known to Medicare beneficiaries, and adopting an incremental approach to managed care that includes offering a wider choice of hybrid managed care products.

By 1995, this strategy (together with the effects of health care reform at the federal and state levels and evolution of the market) had a substantial impact on increasing the number of HMO contracts and applicants. In addition, the percentage of Medicare beneficiaries enrolled in any type of managed care plan rose to 10 percent. Between 1993 and 1994, Medicare enrollment in risk contracts alone increased by 25 percent.

Several initiatives in 1995 also resulted in the availability of more flexible managed care models to Medicare beneficiaries: Congress extended the Medicare Select program to all 50 states (P.L. 104-18), the HCFA issued guidelines on how Medicare risk contracts could offer a POS option (a limited out-of-plan option); and the HCFA announced a new Medicare Choices demonstration program to test new managed care models (such as PPOs and provider-sponsored integrated delivery systems) and to test partial risk reimbursement methods. In addition, the HCFA supported legislation for Medicare PPOs and initiated several new research and demonstration projects to improve the payment method.

Projecting current trends forward, the HCFA estimates that the number of HMO contracts will increase from 221 to 357 by fiscal year 1998 and that the number of enrollees will increase from 3.1 to 7.4 million. In late 1995, however, Congress was considering legislation to reform Medicare. If this legislation is adopted, there may be additional incentives for beneficiaries to choose managed care plans. Congressional proposals also include provisions to expand the number and type of choices available.

MEDICARE MANAGED CARE (THE HMO MODEL)—1985–1995

The Beneficiary Experience

Although 74 percent of beneficiaries live in areas served by at least one Medicare managed care plan, by 1995 less than 3 million beneficiaries (almost 8 percent of the total Medicare population) were enrolled in a risk HMO, and an additional 2 percent were enrolled in cost plans. These statistics suggest that the demand from Medicare beneficiaries for enrollment in HMOs is low. More careful analysis, however, reveals that demand was high in some markets. Fifty percent of all Medicare beneficiaries are enrolled in an HMO in Portland, Oregon. Fifty-seven counties had Medicare enrollment of at least 40 percent. More than one third of Medicare beneficiaries were enrolled in HMOs in southern California, and 27 percent were enrolled in HMOs in south Florida. These penetration rates were similar to the rates for the nonelderly in these market areas and in some cases were higher. Tables 46–1 and 46–2 illustrate Medicare enrollment trends for both risk contract and cost contract HMOs.

Why do beneficiaries choose a lock-in HMO? Most beneficiaries are attracted by the lower out-of-pocket costs. For example, half of all risk plans waive the plan premium (which covers Medicare coinsurance and deductible payments), and most plans offer additional benefits not available in Medicare fee for service, such as prescription drugs, prevention services, eyeglasses, and hearing aids. As of 1993, 55 percent of all Medicare risk HMO enrollees were enrolled in a zero-premium plan, and 65 percent of beneficiaries were enrolled in plans offering prescription drugs (of which 69 percent charged no premium for the drugs).

Why is beneficiary enrollment low in most areas? First of all, the HMO option is not available in many areas. By 1995, only 35 percent of

Table 46–1 Medicare Managed Care Contracts, 1985 to 1995 (Cost Includes HCPPs)

Month	Number of Risk Contracts	Number of Cost Contracts
April 1985	32	109
December 1985	87	87
December 1986	149	78
December 1990	96	66
December 1994	148	86
October 1995	179	87

Source: Health Care Financing Administration.

HMOs had Medicare risk or cost contracts. In addition, Medicare did not offer beneficiaries a choice when they became entitled to Medicare. Marketing was left to the HMO. Information from focus groups suggests that beneficiaries do not necessarily understand that the HMO may offer higher coverage at lower costs. In addition, older and sicker persons are committed to their current physician. Unless this physician retires or they move, Medicare beneficiaries are reluctant to change their known source of health care. The concept of managed care, where one is locked into a health care delivery system, is not familiar to the senior population.

A recent trend that is already influencing the growth of Medicare HMO enrollment is the increasing number of beneficiaries who age in to a Medicare risk contract from an employer group contract. More employers are offering risk products to their retirees when a contract is available. In some cases, employers are leveraging their commercial HMO contracts to require Medicare risk contracts. For example, in 1994 CalPERS (the California Public Employees Retirement System, which purchases health care for state and local employees in California) required that all its contracting HMOs offer a risk contract. In some cases, employers are offering a zero-premium risk contract as the only retiree option as a method of reducing health care liability.

The HMO Experience

HMO interest in Medicare managed care can be described as a roller coaster. In 1987, 152 of more than 500 HMOs in the country had Medicare risk contracts. By 1992, the number of risk contracts declined to 87. By 1995, the number had increased to 171 with an additional 40 new applications pending. Although four HMOs continue to enroll the majority of Medicare HMO members, new plans in new areas of the country are entering the business in record numbers.

HMOs are interested in Medicare contracts for several reasons. A primary reason is that HMOs want a way to keep enrollees in their plan after they become eligible for Medicare. During the last decade, many HMOs have been successful in managing the risky Medicare population, especially through enrolling large numbers of beneficiaries (more than 25,000 to spread the risk), reducing hospital and other unnecessary service utilization, and making a corporate commitment to the Medicare line of business. These successful HMOs also learned how to manage the care of an older and sicker population (e.g., by developing special services and programs to manage or coordinate the care of the elderly). A number of these organizations are now expanding their Medicare risk contracts to new markets. As market competition increases, new plans are applying to be risk contractors.

Experience with the significant drop in risk contracts during the 1980s identified a number of issues. In many plans, the number of enrollees was insufficient to spread the risk. Others found marketing the Medicare product on an individual rather than a group basis to be expensive. A number of the contracts were victims of the merger and acquisition trend in the late 1980s. Many plans could not manage the special needs of the elderly population.

The key reason cited by plans for dropping a risk contract is that Medicare payment levels are too low. Analysis of 1994 payment rates revealed, however, that the level of Medicare HMO penetration does not necessarily vary by

Table 46–2 Medicare Managed Care Enrollment, 1985 to 1995 (Cost Includes HCPPs)

Month	Number of Risk Enrollees	Number of Cost Enrollees	Total Enrollment
April 1985	300,000	916,215	1,216,215
December 1985	440,923	731,191	1,172,114
December 1986	813,712	767,982	1,581,694
December 1990	1,263,547	731,918	1,995,465
December 1994	2,268,364	756,936	3,025,300
October 1995	2,968,791	716,036	3,684,827

Source: Health Care Financing Administration.

the level of HMO payment. Among the top 15 AAPCC counties, only southern California and south Florida counties have high HMO enrollment (Los Angeles and Orange counties in California ranked 10th and 13th in AAPCC levels, and Dade County in Florida ranked 7th). Detroit, New York (with the three highest AAPCC rates), and Philadelphia (ranking 6th) had negligible Medicare risk enrollment. In addition, two areas with low AAPCC rates—Portland, Oregon and Minneapolis, Minnesota—have high Medicare enrollment.

Medicare's Experience

Medicare's interest in managed care started with two objectives. The first was to allow Medicare beneficiaries the opportunity to choose an HMO option (the predominant managed care model in 1982 when the legislation was passed), and the second was to ensure that the Medicare payment formula realized the efficiencies of managed care. The issue of savings must be viewed from several perspectives, including the savings to the Medicare Trust Fund and the savings to the enrollee.

By law, the Medicare risk program is designed to return most of the savings to the beneficiary through additional benefits or reduced costs. In 1995, beneficiaries enrolled in risk HMOs received up to $245 per month in additional benefits or reduced premiums, with a weighted plan average of $66 per month per beneficiary.

By law the only savings that the Medicare Trust Fund can realize is a 5 percent discount from fee-for-service expenditures (i.e., the HMOs are paid 95 percent of the fee-for-service rate). Studies based on the early years of the risk program showed a net cost increase (almost 6 percent) to the Medicare program because the payment rates did not properly adjust for the health status of the beneficiaries. HMOs tend to enroll younger and healthier beneficiaries, especially plans that focus on beneficiaries who age in from employer groups or who retire to Sun Belt areas. A number of studies are currently underway to update the analysis of the savings to Medicare to reflect an older and sicker enrolled population and the maturity of many markets (i.e., a number of competing HMOs and a relative large beneficiary enrollment).

Improvements to the Medicare Risk Contract Option and Risk Payment Method

Medicare has worked aggressively to be a better business partner with HMOs that choose to enter risk contracts. These changes address both the supply side (i.e., the number of HMOs that choose to enter risk contracts) and the demand side (i.e., the number of Medicare beneficiaries who are interested in choosing a risk plan).

Medicare has forged partnerships with the industry to resolve a variety of problems in the business relationship between the purchaser and supplier, from reforming payment to improving administrative systems.

Payment Reform

Since the beginning of the TEFRA risk program, the AAPCC payment method has been considered flawed. Over time the problems have increased to the point that a number of serious options for reform are under review. If Congress does not act, the HCFA currently has statutory authority to make changes in the AAPCC to include risk adjusters and to use alternative geographic areas.

The HCFA's research and demonstration program has been the focus for testing refinements to the current AAPCC formula as a short-term strategy and for testing new payment methods as a long-term strategy. As managed care penetration increases, the preferred strategy is to separate Medicare's managed care payment from the fee-for-service base.

Health Status Adjusters

Mathematica Policy Research, in its evaluation of the Medicare risk program, found that, because of the absence of a health status adjuster, Medicare pays on average 5.7 percent more for enrollees of risk HMOs compared with what those enrollees would have cost had they remained in fee-for-service Medicare. The General Accounting Office attributed the relatively better health status of Medicare HMO enrollees to self-selection by healthier Medicare beneficiaries into HMOs. To address this issue, and to provide fairer payment to HMOs (properly compensating HMOs with adverse selection and ensuring that HMOs in competitive areas have payments adjusted to reflect the relative health status of enrollees), the HCFA has sponsored research and demonstrations over the past several years aimed at developing usable health status adjusters for Medicare HMO enrollees.

Ambulatory care groups and diagnostic cost groups are two diagnosis-based risk adjustment methodologies for which the HCFA has funded research and that may be tested in demonstrations in 1996; these methods are discussed briefly in Chapter 27. Another approach is to base health status payment adjustments on an individual's history of illness. Mathematica has recommended the use of the history of stroke, cancer, and heart disease as a simple and reliable risk adjuster. The HCFA has funded research to study this approach using those illnesses, their severity, the length of time since the last hospital stay, and comorbidities. Other research will examine the feasibility of self-reported health status as a risk adjustment mechanism.

A demonstration of an individual high-cost outlier pool is underway in Seattle, Washington and is expected to be completed in 1997. Risk HMOs in Seattle will be paid 97 percent of the AAPCC, with the additional 2 percent being used to fund a reinsurance pool for the payment of high-cost cases. Although reinsurance is common, the demonstration is expected to provide the HCFA with utilization and cost data and information about mechanisms that may be applicable to partial capitation models (favored by Joseph Newhouse and others), in which HMOs are paid partly on a prepaid capitated basis and partly on a retrospectively determined cost basis.

Alternative Geographic Areas

Although HCFA-sponsored research has shown that using a geographic unit other than the county is not necessarily a clearly superior basis for payment to HMOs, there have been proposals to change from a county-based payment to payments based on metropolitan statistical areas. Such larger areas, or market areas, are especially appropriate if payment rates are to be set through a competitive pricing mechanism in which all health plans are expected to operate throughout a wide geographic area.

Competitive Pricing

The AAPCC is often criticized as an administered pricing mechanism that does not take advantage of competition in the marketplace to set the optimum premium for HMO coverage. In September 1995, the HCFA awarded a contract to begin development of a competitive pricing demonstration for Medicare HMO contracting. This would be a managed competition model in which the government payment to HMOs would be based on a bidding process involving all HMOs in a given geographic area. The government payment would be set at the lowest bid or some average amount. All HMOs in an area willing to submit bids would be allowed to accept Medicare enrollees (i.e., it is not a winner-take-all situation). Beneficiaries could choose any participating health plan, but the government contribution toward the premium would be limited to the competitively determined rate. The government contribution toward the HMO premium would be divorced from the AAPCC (although the AAPCC might be an upper limit on payment). A competitive pricing demonstration might include standardization of benefit packages, coordinated enrollment periods, and third party (e.g., broker) enrollment and information dissemination.

Earmarked Medicare Payments

The AAPCC payment includes all Medicare program expenditures. Among those expenditures are payments to hospitals for graduate medical education (GME), indirect medical education, and disproportionate share payments. The argument has been made that, to the extent that such earmarked payments do not represent actual costs incurred by HMOs (e.g., disproportionate share payments) or are payments intended for a particular purpose but not employed for that purpose (e.g., GME payments to HMOs that do not use teaching hospitals), the AAPCC should not include those amounts or, if they are included, they should be paid only to HMOs with GME programs, for example.

Reducing Geographic Variation

There is nearly a fourfold difference between the highest and lowest AAPCCs in the United States. The AAPCCs reflect the differences among counties in Medicare's historical fee-for-service costs. The county-to-county variation reflects variation in input prices as well as other factors, such as the supply of physicians (primary care versus specialists), hospital beds, and practice styles. Some payment reform proposals call for the narrowing of this regional variation to bring counties closer to a national average.

Beneficiary Demand

On the demand side, Medicare is implementing a number of activities to ensure that Medicare beneficiaries understand that their choices for Medicare include not only fee for service but also managed care. For example, all Medicare publications have been revised to emphasize the theme of choice, and materials were provided to Social Security offices and beneficiary groups to ensure that information about beneficiary options is available. Medicare is conducting a number of focus groups and is supporting a demonstration project to understand better how to present information about Medicare choices.

Medicare is contacting employers to ensure that they understand the advantages of offering managed care options for retirees. In addition, Medicare is working with other payers, such as state Medicaid agencies, the Office of Personnel Management of the federal government, and the Department of Defense, to streamline policies for dual eligibles.

An Incremental Strategy

In 1995, 34 million Medicare beneficiaries remained in fee for service. Fee for service will continue to be an option under Medicare. Ultimately, Medicare would like all Medicare beneficiaries to have a choice between fee for service and several managed care plans (PPOs, POS, and full-risk HMOs).

The realities in 1995 (when this chapter was written), however, are that many organizations are not ready to provide services on a full-risk basis to Medicare beneficiaries throughout the nation. In addition, many beneficiaries are not ready to enroll with a comprehensive care organization that provides services through a specified network and will not pay anything when routine services are received out of plan. Thus the Medicare program, following the lead of successful efforts initiated in the private sector, has adopted an incremental managed care strategy that offers a range of managed care products. Figure 46–1 displays the continuum currently envisioned by Medicare. This continuum of complementary managed care choices will allow beneficiaries to choose the arrangement that best suits them, from fee for service to PPO models to opt-out models to risk HMO models.

Medicare Select

Medicare Select permits Medicare supplemental insurance companies to offer a PPO network type product in conjunction with their Medicare supplemental insurance (Medigap). Medigap is private insurance that covers medical costs that Medicare does not pay, such as deductibles and coinsurance. In exchange for a reduced premium, Medicare Select policies provide a financial incentive for Medicare beneficiaries to use their network of providers. For example, if a network physician is used, the Medicare Select policy will pay 20 percent coinsurance; if a nonnetwork physician is used for nonemergency services, however, the Medicare Select policy may pay no coinsurance or a reduced amount.

Medicare Select policies are considered an incremental managed care product because the financial penalty to the Medicare enrollee for using out-of-network services is minimal. Medicare will continue to pay its share (e.g., the 80

percent of the physician bill in the example cited above).

Originally approved as a pilot project in 15 states, Medicare Select was extended to June 1998 and expanded to all 50 states. The pilot program demonstrated that beneficiary premiums averaged 15 percent to 25 percent less than the premium for a comparable non-Select Medigap policy; Select insurers rarely establish aggressive case management or utilization management programs and tend to rely on discounts (waiver of the hospital deductible) to reduce costs. The final evaluation is not yet complete, but early results suggest that in some plans hospital utilization was higher for Select enrollees than for beneficiaries with non-Select policies. Many companies indicated that they did not offer a Select product because it only offered the insurer the opportunity to manage a small amount of the premium.

PPO

Medicare supports legislation that will authorize a PPO option for Medicare beneficiaries. Under a PPO, a Medicare beneficiary will pay a small amount (not more than 20 percent coinsurance) to use a provider outside the network on a self-referral basis. The PPO could choose to be paid under a partial risk basis (i.e., Medicare and the PPO will share risk over and under a specific target). The plan would be paid on a fee-for-service basis. The PPO model that Medicare prefers is a third-generation model, where the plan uses sophisticated managed care techniques such as case management, quality assessment, and utilization management to increase effi-

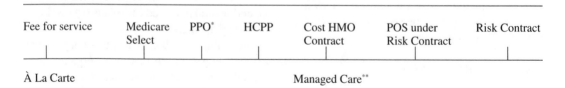

Fee for service	Medicare Select	PPO*	HCPP	Cost HMO Contract	POS under Risk Contract	Risk Contract

À La Carte   Managed Care**

Figure 46–1 Range of Medicare options. *Proposed law; **continuum reflects the range of services under managed care. *Source:* Health Care Financing Administration.

ciency and lower costs. PPOs have been successful in the private sector in providing lower premium costs and larger provider choice for persons younger than 65 years.

Improved Cost Contracting Models

Cost contracts are Medicare's outmoded hybrid managed care models. As currently designed, these options often result in higher costs than those for fee-for-service Medicare (i.e., through duplicate payment), lack of beneficiary protections, and lack of incentives for cost contractors to manage the full continuum of the patient's care. Under the incremental strategy, Medicare is proposing to replace cost contracts with an improved PPO model and to redesign the HCPP to serve union and employer retirees.

POS Option

POS models are frequently offered by employers because they provide the savings of full-risk managed care while offering the employee the flexibility to use a nonnetwork provider on a service-by-service basis. Employers use two types of POS models. The first model is a POS option offered in conjunction with an HMO product. The other model is a replacement for fee-for-service care. Experience shows that under both models most employees continue to use the plan's network, where care is coordinated and unnecessary or inappropriate care is minimized. POS provides peace of mind for the employee and allows the employer to offer a mandatory managed care product.

In 1995, Medicare issued guidelines for a POS model in conjunction with a Medicare risk contract. The Medicare POS option will be available to beneficiaries under a variety of options, depending upon the plan choice and local market conditions. For example, the Medicare POS could be offered to all enrollees or just employer groups. The POS can also be marketed as an additional benefit, a mandatory supplemental benefit, or an optional supplemental benefit. The HMOs will have flexibility to structure their POS product in a variety of ways, for example by limiting the types of benefits that may be

available through POS or by placing a financial cap on the amount of services that may be received out of plan.

Medicare Choices Program

In 1995, Medicare announced a Medicare Choices program to offer Medicare beneficiaries a broad range of health plan options similar to those available in the private sector. The demonstration program will test a variety of innovative delivery systems and risk-sharing arrangements, primarily in target markets where commercial enrollment is high and Medicare managed care enrollment is low, and in rural areas. Some of the models include integrated delivery systems, provider-sponsored networks, managed care models targeted to rural areas, PPOs, and triple-option models. The health care system is changing rapidly, and Medicare wants to be able to contract with all types of high-quality organizations that can serve beneficiaries.

CONCLUSION

As a purchaser as well as a regulator, Medicare is committed to ensuring that managed care plans offered to Medicare beneficiaries provide only the highest quality and value. Beneficiaries will have an increased choice of options to receive their health care services, ranging from fee for service to hybrid plans to full-risk lock-in HMOs. Beneficiaries will be given information that will allow them to compare their choices and make a selection based on individual preference and market conditions. Managed care plans will also have a wider array of contract options to serve the senior population. These contract options will offer partial as well as full risk payment. Medicare fee for service and the wider array of managed care plans are expected to compete on price, benefits, and, most important of all, quality. Medicare will hold all plans accountable to high standards: Each plan must be fiscally solvent, ensure appropriate access and availability of services, select quality providers and have programs in place to improve quality over time, ensure that beneficiaries have appropriate grievance and appeals processes, and ensure that beneficiaries have sufficient information to make an informed plan choice.

SUGGESTED READING

Law and Regulations

The law governing Medicare risk and cost contracts with HMOs and CMPs is found at Section 1876 of the Social Security Act or Section 1395(mm) of the U.S. Code. The fragment of a sentence that authorizes health care prepayment plans is found at Section 1833(a)(1)(A) of the Social Security Act. Title XIII of the Public Health Service Act (42 U.S.C. 300e) is the law that deals with federally qualified HMOs.

Regulations for all these entities are found in Title 42 of the Code of Federal Regulations, Sections 417.100 through 417.180 (federally qualified HMOs), Sections 417.400 through 417.694 (cost and risk HMOs and CMPs), and Sections 417.800 through 417.810 (HCPPs). Current editions of the Code of Federal Regulations also contain Sections 417.200 through 417.292, which are obsolete in that they contain only pre-TEFRA contract provisions.

For the voracious reader, the *Federal Register* of 25 May 1984, and of 10 January 1985, contains, respectively, the proposed and final versions of the TEFRA contracting regulations, which are relevant to those interested in seeing the changes between the proposed and final versions of the regulations and in knowing the types of public comments received on the regulations. Also published in the *Federal Register* was a 6 January 1986, notice (pp. 506–510) outlining the HCFA's AAPCC payment methodology. Explaining the AAPCC (and studying it) is a cottage industry of its own, as is evident from the list of additional reading materials below.

The law and regulations are available at any federal depository library, at law libraries, and through compendiums such as the Commerce Clearing House *Medicare and Medicaid Guide*. CD-ROM versions of the HCFA's regulations and manuals are also now becoming available.

Manuals

The *Medicare HMO/CMP Manual* (HCFA Publication 75) generally explains (in layperson's language), or expands on, the requirements contained in the law and regulations. All Medicare-contracting HMOs/CMPs/HCPPs receive the Manual and any updates. The Manual may be purchased through:

National Technical Information Service
Department of Commerce
5825 Port Royal Road
Springfield, Virginia 22161
(703) 487-4630
Publication PB 85-953899

Some information, including AAPCC rates, is available on the Internet at HCFA's address: http://wwwhcfa.gov.

Reports of the General Accounting Office Related to Medicare HMOs

The first two digits indicate the year in which the report was issued.

- **96-63** *Medicare HMOs: Rapid Enrollment Growth Concentrated in Selected States*
- **95-155** *Increased HMO Oversight Could Improve Quality and Access to Care*
- **95-81** *Medicare: Opportunities Are Available To Apply Managed Care Strategies*
- **94-119** *Medicare: Changes to HMO Rate Setting Method Are Needed To Reduce Program Costs*
- **92-11** *HCFA Needs To Take Stronger Actions against HMOs Violating Federal Standards*
- **91-48** *PRO Review Does Not Assure Quality of Care Provided by Risk HMOs*
- **89-46** *Medicare: Health Maintenance Organization Rate Setting Issues*
- **89-03** *Reasonableness of HMO Payments Not Assured*
- **88-12** *Physician Incentive Payments by Prepaid Health Plans Could Lower Quality of Care*
- **88-08** *Experience Shows Ways To Improve Oversight of HMOs*
- **88-07** *Issues Concerning the HealthChoice Demonstration Project*
- **88-05** *Improving Quality of Care Assessment and Assurance*
- **87-11** *Uncertainties Surround Proposal To Expand Prepaid Health Plan Contracting*
- **87-07** *Preliminary Strategies for Assessing Quality of Care*

General Accounting Office reports can be obtained from:

General Accounting Office
PO Box 6015
Gaithersburg, Maryland 20877
(202) 512-6000

The Office of the Inspector General of the Department of Health and Human Services has also issued reports on

Medicare HMOs, including the following, which can be obtained by calling the Office of Public Affairs at (202) 619-1343:

- **OEI-06-91-00730** *Beneficiary Perspectives of Medicare Risk HMOs* (March 1995)
- **OEI-06-91-00731** *Medicare Risk HMOs: Beneficiary Enrollment and Service Access Problems* (April 1995)

Books and Journal Articles

The following monographs, all by Susan Jelley Palsbo, formerly of Group Health Association of America (now with Coopers and Lybrand), are the most lucid and thorough explanation of the AAPCC:

- *The USPCC Explained* (June 1988)
- *The AAPCC Explained* (February 1989)
- *The Demographic Factors Explained* (February 1990)
- *Medicare Capitation Explained* (March 1990)

The monographs, which are all AAHP (formerly GHAA/AMCRA) publications, are available from:

American Association of Health Plans
1129 20th Street, N.W.
Suite 600
Washington, D.C. 20036
(202) 778-3200, fax (202) 331-7487

As noted in the chapter, the Summer 1995 issue of the *Health Care Financing Review* deals entirely with the issue of new initiatives and approaches in health care quality, including several articles on Medicare and Medicaid managed care.

Adamache, K., and Rossiter, L. 1987. The Entry of HMOs into the Medicare Market: Implications for TEFRA's Mandate. *Inquiry* 23:1314–1418.

Anderson, G.F., et al. 1990. Setting Payment Rates for Capitated Systems: A Comparison of Various Alternatives. *Inquiry* 27:225–233.

Ash, A., et al. 1989. Adjusting Medicare Capitation Payments Using Prior Hospitalization Data. *Health Care Financing Review* 10:17–29.

Ash, A., et al. 1990. *Clinical Refinements to the Diagnostic Cost Group Model.* Boston, Mass.: Health Policy Research Consortium, Cooperative Research Center.

Barnett, B. 1989. How To Take the Risk out of Medicare HMO Management: Opportunities and Challenges in the 1990s. *Group Pract Journal.* 38:29–30, 32–33, 36.

Bergeron, J., and Brown, R. 1992. *Why Do the Medicare Risk Plans of HMOs Lose Money?* Princeton, N.J.: Mathematica Policy Research, Inc.

Brown, B. 1989. The Structure of Quality Assurance Programs in Risk-Based HMOs/CMPs Enrolling Medicare Beneficiaries. *GHAA Journal* 10:68–82.

Brown, R., et al. 1993. Do Health Maintenance Organizations Work for Medicare? *Health Care Financing Review* 15:7–24.

Dowd, B., et al. Issues Regarding Health Plan Payments under Medicare and Recommendations for Reform. *Milbank Memorial Fund Quarterly* 70:423–449.

Health Care Financing Administration (HCFA). 1991. *Expanding Medicare Coordinated Care Choices for Employer Group Retirees.* Baltimore, Md.: HCFA Office of Coordinated Care Policy and Planning.

Hill, J.W., and Brown, R.S. 1992. *Health Status, Financial Barriers and the Decision to Enroll in Medicare Risk Plans.* Princeton, N.J.: Mathematica Policy Research, Inc.

Hill, J.W., and Brown, R.S. 1990. *Biased Selection in the TEFRA HMO/CMP Program: Final Report.* Baltimore, Md.: Health Care Financing Administration.

Hill, J.W. et al. 1992. *The Impact of the Medicare Risk Program on the Use of Services and Costs to Medicare.* Princeton, N.J.: Mathematica Policy Research, Inc.

Langwell, K. 1990. Structure and Performance of Health Maintenance Organizations: A Review. *Health Care Financing Review* 12:71–79.

Langwell, K.M., and Hadley, J.P. 1990. Insights from the Medicare HMO Demonstrations. *Health Affairs* 9:74–89.

Langwell, K.P., and Hadley, J.P. 1989. *National Evaluation of the Medicare Competition Demonstrations: Summary Report.* Baltimore, Md.: Health Care Financing Administration.

Langwell, K., et al. 1987. Early Experience of Health Maintenance Organizations under Medicare Competition Demonstrations. *Health Care Financing Review* 8:37–56.

Lichtenstein, R., et al. 1992. HMO Marketing and Selection Bias: Are TEFRA HMOs Skimming? *Medical Care* 30:329–346.

Lichtenstein, R., et al. 1991. Selection Bias in TEFRA At-Risk HMOs. *Medical Care* 29:318–331.

Lubitz, J. 1987. Health Status Adjustments for Medicare Capitation. *Inquiry* 24:362–375.

Luft, H., ed. 1994. *HMOs and the Elderly.* Ann Arbor, Mich.: AHSR Health Administration Press.

Manton, K.G., and Stallard, E. 1992. Analysis of Underwriting Factors for AAPCC. *Health Care Financing Review* 14:117–132.

McCombs, J.S., et al. 1990. Do HMOs Reduce Health Care Costs? A Multivariate Analysis of Two Medicare HMO Demonstration Projects. *Health Services Research* 25:593–613.

McGee, J., and Brown, R. 1992. *What Makes HMOs Drop Their Medicare Risk Contracts?* Princeton, N.J.: Mathematica Policy Research, Inc.

McMillan, A. 1993. Trends in Medicare Health Maintenance Organization Enrollment: 1986–1993. *Health Care Financing Review* 15:135–146.

McMillan, A., and Lubitz, J. 1987. Medicare Enrollment in Health Maintenance Organizations. *Health Care Financing Review* 8:87–94.

Morrison, E.M., and Luft, H.S. 1990. Health Maintenance Organization Environments in the 1980s and Beyond. *Health Care Financing Review* 12:81–90.

Nelson, L., and Brown, R. 1989. *The Impact of the Medicare Competition Demonstrations on the Use and Cost of Services: Final Report.* Baltimore, Md.: Health Care Financing Administration.

Newhouse, J.P. 1994. Patients At Risk: Health Reform and Risk Adjustment, *Health Affairs* 13:132–146.

Palmer, R.H. 1995. Securing Health Care Quality for Medicine. *Health Affairs* 14:89–100.

Porell, F.W., and Turner, W.M. 1990. Biased Selection under an Experimental Enrollment and Marketing Medicare HMO Broker. *Medical Care* 28:604–615.

Porell, F.W., and Wallack, S.S. 1990. Medicare Risk Contracting: Determinants of Market Entry. *Health Care Financing Review* 12:75–85.

Porell, F.W., et al. 1990. Alternative Geographic Configurations for Medicare Payments to Health Maintenance Organizations. *Health Care Financing Review* 11:17–30.

Riley, G., et al. 1991. Enrollee Health Status under Medicare Risk Contracts: An Analysis of Mortality Rates. *Health Services Research* 26:137–164.

Rossiter, L.F., and Adamache, K.W. 1990. Payment to Health Maintenance Organizations and the Geographic Factor. *Health Care Financing Review* 12:19–30.

Rossiter, L.F., et al. 1989. Patient Satisfaction Among Elderly Enrollees and Disenrollees in Medicare Health Maintenance Organizations. *Journal of the American Medical Association* 262:57–63.

Siddharthan, K. 1990. HMO Enrollment by Medicare Beneficiaries in Heterogeneous Communities. *Medical Care* 29:918–927.

Welch, W.P. 1992. Alternative Geographic Adjustments in Medicare Payment to Health Maintenance Organizations. *Health Care Financing Review* 13:97–110.

Welch, W.P. 1991. Defining Geographic Areas To Adjust Payments to Physicians, Hospitals and HMOs. *Inquiry* 28:151–160.

Welch, W.P. 1989. Improving Medicare Payments to HMOs: Urban Core versus Suburban Ring. *Inquiry* 26:62–71.

Welch, W.P., and Welch, H.G. 1995. Fee-for Data: A Strategy to Open the HMO Black Box. *Health Affairs* 14:104–116.

Wilensky, G.R., and Rossiter, L.F. 1991. Coordinated Care and Public Programs. *Health Affairs* 10:62–77.

Chapter 47

Medicare Risk Plans: The Health Plan's View

Roger S. Taylor and Craig Schub

This chapter briefly explains the history and growth of Medicare risk programs and discusses the potential for Medicare risk health maintenance organizations (HMOs) to make significant inroads into the senior market, a market niche that is expected to double in size within the next 30 years. It takes a look at how plans can become Medicare risk contractors and at some of the marketing, administrative, clinical, and customer service challenges posed by this population. The chapter also deals with ways to prepare the delivery system for the special needs of the elderly and discusses the relationship with the government as both a payer for and a partner. The reader is also strongly urged to review Chapter 46 for additional discussion of Medicare managed care.

THE ACTIVE ELDERLY

Today's seniors expect to enjoy good health during their second adulthood, a term that author

Roger S. Taylor, M.D., M.P.A., is President and Chief Executive Officer of Connecticut Health Enterprises, Monroe, Connecticut. He also serves as a Commissioner on the Physician Payment Review Commission in Washington, D.C. and has held a number of senior-level health care management and policy roles over the past 20 years.

Craig Schub is Senior Vice President of Government Programs for PacifiCare Health Systems, Inc., and President of Secure Horizons, USA, a PacifiCare subsidiary. Since 1985, he has supported the development of, and now leads, PacifiCare's Medicare risk program. That program, Secure Horizons, is the largest and fastest growing plan if its kind in the United States.

Gail Sheehy has coined to describe postretirement years that are richer in challenge and variety than ever before in our history. Indeed, only 10 percent of Americans older than 65 experience any significant limitations on their physical activities because of illness or disease. On the contrary, many are taking up new interests and hobbies. Approximately 12 percent are eschewing retirement, preferring instead to continue to work at least on a part-time basis.[1]

Seniors want to stay healthy as long as possible, but they are also realists. They have begun to feel the aches and pains of aging. Although they want to stave off the inevitable for as long as possible, the issue of how they will pay for the health care they know they will need over the years remains a key concern. As a result of government budget limitations and a growing population of seniors, there are estimates that Medicare part A will run out of funds by the year 2002.[2] Seniors are also much less financially secure than the working population.

To make matters worse, Medicare was designed 30 years ago to cover acute episodes of illness rather than to provide coordinated care for chronic or debilitating conditions that often plague today's longer-living seniors. Furthermore, despite the common agreement about the importance of preventive care, the program does not cover such basic services as regular physicals or influenza immunizations. Other valuable adjuncts to healthy aging, such as general fitness and nutrition classes or group sessions on coping with aging, are not linked closely enough with an acute illness to be considered part of coverage. Meanwhile, the percentage of seniors' total health care costs that Medicare pays for is decreasing.

HEALTH CARE OPTIONS FOR SENIORS

At the time of this writing, more than 90 percent of seniors have availed themselves of an additional benefit option to help bridge the gap between what Medicare will cover and what they perceive they may need. More than 69 percent have some form of Medigap insurance policy to supplement Medicare coverage, paid for either by seniors themselves or by previous employers.[3] A small percentage have joined Medicare Select plans, a relatively new option that provides Medigap coverage through a preferred provider network.

Others choose to belong to HMOs. Several alternatives among HMOs include cost HMOs and health care prepayment plans (HCPPs), which contract with the Health Care Financing Administration (HCFA) to provide health care services to seniors on a cost basis. Approximately 2 percent of the senior population have chosen this latter option. Eleven percent are covered by Medicaid as well as Medicare, and 2 percent receive coverage from other sources.

A growing number of seniors, 9 percent at the time of this writing and growing, have opted to join HMOs with Medicare risk contracts. In these Medicare risk HMOs, they enjoy an increased level of benefits, usually including preventive care and some prescription drug coverage. This additional level of coverage is generally provided with no deductible or coinsurance and low copayments for low or no additional monthly premiums. Members of Medicare risk programs do not need to fill out claim forms, but they must agree to get all their care through the HMO provider system except for care needed for emergencies or while traveling outside the HMO's covered service area.

For each senior who joins the Medicare risk plan, the government pays the HMO 95 percent of the average adjusted per capita cost (AAPCC), a statistic that represents the estimated cost of providing medical care through traditional fee-for-service (FFS) methods (adjusted for age, sex, county of residence, and other factors). The net result is that the plans can save the government money both from the direct discount off projected costs and by helping lower the rate of inflation in health care expenditures generally. The growth of the Medicare risk program can provide the federal government with budgetable and predictable Medicare expenses over the long term.

THE DEMOGRAPHIC IMPERATIVE

Seniors currently represent just 13 percent of the U.S. population, yet they account for more than 36 percent of total health care expenditures. By 2030, seniors, defined as those 65 years of age and older, will represent more than 21 percent of Americans, posing a significant threat to future federal budgets and the generation that will have to help pay for their care.

The growth of this segment of the population will be partly due to the aging of the Baby Boomers. People are also living longer as a result of better nutrition, preventive care (especially early cancer detection), and advances in medical technology. In 1935, the average life expectancy was 62 years. Today, Americans can expect to live until at least 75 years, with women who are free of heart disease and cancer at age 50 predicted to reach an average age of 92 years. Ten million Baby Boomers will reach the age of 90. One million will become centenarians.

These demographic changes are putting unprecedented pressures on our nation's health care resources. Medicare spending is expected to increase from $146 billion in 1993 to $259 billion in 1998, an increase of 77 percent in 5 years. Seniors already account for more than one third of the pharmaceutical industry's budget and the same proportion of our health care dollars. Both Medicare and Medicaid programs are feeling the strain, and a variety of policy proposals for fundamental change are being considered, and in some cases implemented, to address this crisis. Yet the free market system in the United States is already providing at least part of the answer in the form of HMOs, which in various important ways have had an undisputed impact in lowering the cost of health care for Americans under 65 while offering comprehensive care.

Brief History of the Medicare Risk Program

Medicare was introduced approximately 30 years ago to provide a baseline of health care services to the elderly. Authorized under Title XVIII of the Social Security Act in 1965, the government insurance program is divided in two parts: hospital insurance (part A) and supplementary medical insurance (part B). Individuals entitled to Social Security are automatically entitled to benefits when they reach age 65, as are persons with end-stage renal disease (ESRD) and individuals under 65 who are eligible for Social Security disability and have been disabled for at least 2 years. Part A covers some inpatient, skilled nursing facility, home health, and hospice care. Medicare part B is voluntary, and enrollment is open to those 65 and older or those entitled to part A benefits. Part B covers physician and other outpatient medical services.

Medicare, however, was set up to cover episodes of illness and injury rather than to preserve the long-term health of beneficiaries. In the 1960s, that approach made plenty of sense in a fragmented FFS environment, and Medicare was an instant success in the eyes of beneficiaries. Even today, as seniors battle with Medicare's increased cost sharing, claim forms hassles, and the extra cost of Medigap insurance, the majority remain firmly supportive of Medicare and are quick to come to the beleaguered program's defense.

The drain that Medicare is placing on the nation's Gross National Product, however, has not gone unnoticed by taxpayers or legislators. Since 1980, HCFA has made major changes in the way the program pays hospitals, physicians, and other health care providers in an effort to save money. Medicare introduced the prospective payment system for inpatient hospital care in 1983 to limit Medicare's liability for hospital costs. In 1992, Medicare implemented the Medicare fee schedule for physician payment, which combined aggregate volume controls with price constraints in an effort to control expenses for physician services.

To reduce Medicare expenses and to provide Medicare beneficiaries with an option similar to managed care products available in the private market, Medicare managed care was authorized by the Tax Equity and Fiscal Responsibility Act of 1982. Medicare HMOs began operation in 1985.

HMOs have three Medicare managed care contract options: risk, cost, and HCPP contracts. Risk contracts, which offer payment on a per capita basis, are the most popular contract option and account for about 75 percent of Medicare managed care enrollees. Cost contracts reimburse HMOs for the costs of all Medicare services and account for about 6 percent of Medicare managed care enrollment. HCPP contracts reimburse for the costs of Medicare part B services only and account for the remaining 18 percent of managed care enrollees. For part A services provided to enrollees, HCPPs receive FFS payment.

In addition, a number of Medicare demonstration projects have been implemented to manage cost and quality more effectively. Medicare Select plans, based on the preferred provider model, were approved for 15 states and now have been expanded nationwide. HCFA is constantly exploring ways to provide added benefits, such as prescription drug and long-term care coverage, through a range of demonstration projects such as social HMOs, studies on long-term care insurance, and projects designed to coordinate better the benefits of seniors covered by both Medicare and Medicaid. Medigap policy options have also been standardized to provide a clearer range of choices to seniors. HCFA has also approached large employer groups to gauge their interest in assuming risk for Medicare's portion of their retiree medical benefits. Most recently, HCFA has expanded its demonstration projects to include preferred provider organization and point-of-service plan options, and many in Congress want to make all the options standard. In fact, a bill that authorized a wide range of managed care and insurance options for Medicare eligibles passed both houses of congress in early 1996, but was vetoed by the President.

HCFA and other oversight agencies have closely followed the effectiveness of each initiative. For Medicare risk HMOs, HCFA concluded in 1989 that HMO members' satisfaction was equal to or greater than that of Medicare beneficiaries in the old-style FFS system.[4] These findings continue to be reinforced through privately and publicly funded research.

In 1995, HCFA reported that nearly 10 percent of payments to risk HMOs are used to provide additional benefits and that the average amount of savings passed on to Medicare enrollees was $39.36 per month, a number that many risk contractors feel significantly understates HMO savings for seniors.[5]

In short, Medicare risk HMOs, which emphasize continuity of care, health maintenance, and total patient management, are a much-appreciated option for today's longer-living, more active, and more value-conscious seniors. Medicare risk HMOs can provide equal or better care, frequently better service, definitely fewer claims hassles, and certainly more benefits than FFS Medicare and at lower cost.

Participation and Range of Experience

In 1985, 87 Medicare risk plans were on the market. By 1987, this figure had climbed to 161. During the next few years, those plans that were not successful either went under or left the market, and by 1990 the number of HMOs with risk contracts sank to 96. Since then, however, the industry has learned from the experience of successful plans that the senior market differs from the commercial market in significant ways. Senior HMOs began adjusting their delivery systems, benefits, and marketing approaches to take these differences into account. In 1995 the number of Medicare risk plans reached 154 and a growing backlog of applications are pending.

Enrollment has grown steadily from 441,000 in 1987 to 3.1 million as of January 1996 with Medicare risk membership increasing each year despite the decreasing number of plans offered in the late 1980s and early 1990s. For instance, 1995 enrollment was more than double the 1.2 million enrollees in September 1990, and between 1995 and 1996, Medicare risk program enrollment grew by a phenomenal 35 percent.

As of this writing, Medicare risk enrollment has been concentrated in five states: California (with nearly 1 million enrollees or 28 percent of the state's senior population in 1995), Florida (nearly 400,000), Arizona (more than 150,000), New York (nearly 105,000), and Oregon (more than 100,000). In fact, 64 percent of seniors in Portland, Oregon are members of Medicare risk HMOs. These clusters of membership tell their own story: If seniors are satisfied with their care, they will tell friends and peers about their experiences. Word of mouth is still the most effective marketing tool among this generation. Seniors are quick to challenge poor performance, so that a reputation for quality care and service is proving to be an invaluable asset for some HMOs.

Public Policy Challenges

Although Medicare risk programs are growing rapidly, membership is mostly concentrated in a few states where these programs are highly successful. Medicare from a national perspective, unlike the private market, which has experienced a significant shift toward managed care, remains overwhelmingly a discounted FFS system. Although 9 percent of Medicare beneficiaries are enrolled in an HMO, about 67 percent of individuals with employer health care coverage enroll in an HMO, a preferred provider organization, or a point-of-service option. Any changes in the system, especially the expansion of Medicare risk programs, threaten to rock the FFS boat as well as the livelihood of those health care providers who are unwilling to adapt to an HMO environment for their Medicare patients. These more traditional heath care interests represent a powerful group.

As a result, legislative initiatives arise from time to time designed to slow the growth of HMOs or to regulate the freedom of HMOs to manage covered services. These proposals range from alternative methods of payment, including a one-sided market bidding system (not including FFS Medicare) or caps on administrative overhead, to proposals that would affect the balance of power among plans, providers, and members, usually to the advantage of the medical profession.

Examples of such proposed legislation include the any willing provider and so-called patient protection proposals, self-referral policies, and mandatory inclusion of selected providers. For many in the industry, there seems to be almost a direct correlation between the growth of Medicare risk HMOs and the call for protectionist legislation from some traditional health care providers. These providers recognize that, once Medicare follows the private sector into managed care, the delivery of care in this country will be irreversibly changed.

Some existing legislation that may have been appropriate when first enacted also now serves to limit HMO growth. For example, the federal 50/50 rule, originally designed as a proxy for quality, requires of health plans that the number of Medicare risk members be equal to or less than the number of commercial members within a contiguous geography. This policy places severe limits on the geographical expansion of Medicare risk plans. Such controls seem redundant for established, accredited Medicare risk HMOs that have already demonstrated their credibility, longevity, and financial stability in states with more mature managed care markets. It is anticipated that many of the regulatory hindrances to the expansion of managed care into Medicare will disappear or be modified under federal reform initiatives being debated in Congress as this chapter is being written.

Despite these challenges, the success of HMOs in offering a variety of benefit plan options to seniors and delivering satisfactory, affordable care is speaking volumes to legislators about the importance of allowing free market principles to drive down costs among this population.

BECOMING A MEDICARE RISK CONTRACTOR

In 1994, HCFA established the Office of Managed Care (OMC), merging policy, operational, and planning functions for several Medicaid and Medicare programs. The OMC, with three teams covering the ten regions of the country, has lead responsibility for approving applications to operate Medicare risk plans. HCFA's main office (the OMC) also researches and recommends changes in the payment structure. HCFA's dual responsibility for stimulating innovation and competition in managed health care for the elderly while also operating a huge FFS insurance system creates unique conflicts and pressures for the agency, the administration, and Congress. HCFA's regional offices are responsible for monitoring plan quality, access, provider networks, marketing and member materials, continuous improvement programs, and outcomes data. As managed care continues to expand within the Medicare program, HCFA will be challenged to reengineer its organizational structure and regulatory capacity.

Medicare risk programs must meet federal regulatory requirements in four major areas:

1. Organizational and contractual: Does the plan have state authority to operate? Are provider contracts adequate? Do they contain the National Association of Insurance Commissioners' hold-harmless clause (see Chapter 55) and indicate provider willingness to serve Medicare recipients? Are provider compensation and incentives adequately detailed?

2. Financial: What is the plan's fiscal soundness, net operating surplus, and member protection against insolvency?

3. Medicare: Are all Medicare regulations adhered to in all regards?

4. Health care delivery: Is there adequate availability, access, and quality monitoring?

Once applications are received, it takes approximately 24 weeks to gain approval if all the facts in the application are complete and accurate. Site visits are performed at HCFA's discretion. If the application is for a new start-up, an expansion into a new region, or a large multicounty expansion, HCFA will usually conduct a site visit. If the application is a one-county expansion in an area where the HMO is already doing business or is immediately adjacent to a county that HCFA has recently reviewed, a site visit may not be conducted. The purpose of the site visit is to conduct interviews with HMO staff and contracting providers to evaluate their knowledge and skills required for the successful implementation of a Medicare risk contract. During the site review, HCFA regulators verify information included in the application and obtain additional detail and understanding of the HMO's operations. The site visit is also an opportunity for HCFA staff to validate information relating to trends in the HMO industry by obtaining feedback from multiple health plans.

The single most common problem preventing speedy approval is the failure of the plan to have a provider network in place or contracts with appropriate language signed with providers before implementation. Other frequent mistakes include the failure of the plan to develop adequate informational material, including a member handbook or evidence of coverage. In developing marketing materials, HMOs must consider HCFA's extreme sensitivity to language that is at all exaggerated and should review materials that HCFA has previously approved. In developing their applications, plans would also be wise to read the *HCFA Contractor Performance Monitoring System Reviewer's Work Guide* (HCFA, 1995 Revised Edition).

The final decision regarding approval is made by the OMC and the director of the Office of Operations. Once plans are approved, sales and marketing techniques and materials are likely to come under continuing close scrutiny by HCFA to make sure that they are not misleading to the public. Plans would be wise to err on the side of caution in explaining their benefit packages.

Once a Medicare risk contract has been implemented, HCFA performs monitoring site reviews once a year, usually lasting between 2 to 5 weeks. Plans should be prepared to establish long-term relationships with HCFA and be sensitive to the demands, both time and resource related, made on this government organization. Respect and perseverance will pay off in the long run.

The Market

Seniors present an interesting marketing challenge. They are not, as some believe, a homogenous group; rather, they are individuals with different needs and ideas about the way health care should be delivered. Their health care options today are much broader than ever before, and as discriminating buyers they are likely to take their time in making decisions. Furthermore, the senior health care market is extremely competitive.

Medicare HMOs compete for customers with Medigap insurance policies and employer-sponsored coverage. Retirees age 65 and older whose previous employers provide Medigap policies may have no price incentive to choose HMO coverage. Employers paying Medicare supplemental premiums, however, have significant incentives to reduce their direct costs and future liabilities, especially because the Federal Accounting Standards Board requires employers, as of 1993, to account for their total liability based on projected future costs of paying for retiree care.

Before a plan offers a Medicare risk product, it is important to evaluate the market and determine opportunities for growth within that market. Market research should be done to find out the number of Medicare eligibles, the monthly AAPCC payment, and the multiyear trend in that area because the payment, especially within small populations, may fluctuate widely. In addition, it is important to assess the community's provider mix and familiarity with managed care and the penetration and performance of Medicare and commercial HMOs in the area. Seniors living in areas with low HMO penetration may be less familiar with managed care and require more information about managed care concepts.

In 1995, 75 percent of eligibles lived within reach of a Medicare risk HMO. Yet only 9 percent of beneficiaries belonged to Medicare risk plans, mostly because of a lack of awareness about the benefits that managed care can offer seniors and sometimes because of the lack of a compelling value proposition due to an inefficient delivery system and relatively high premiums. Plans entering new markets must therefore be prepared to undertake comprehensive reengineering of the health delivery system and invest in education and public relations programs to improve understanding of HMOs as a category. In addition, they need to invest in advertising that clearly communicates the real advantages of their particular products.

In addition, to manage risk and maintain an adequate return on investment, Medicare risk HMOs must constantly grow and replenish their base of younger, healthier members between 65 and 74 years of age, or adverse selection of an aging membership base may become a problem. As the market becomes more and more competitive, HMOs must reinvest in the product by lowering the premium (if it is not already at zero), adding benefits and services, and becoming more creative and efficient managers of medical costs.

Distribution

As noted earlier, at the time of this writing, Medicare membership is disproportionately high in five states: California, Oregon, New York, Florida, and Arizona. This distribution has resulted from several factors. First, the presence of organized medical groups that could effectively manage care for the senior population created a platform for early success and growth.

Second, word of mouth has proved a powerful marketing tool, resulting in exponential growth where plans have most members. Third, several of these areas enjoy reasonably high AAPCC rates. These rates vary tremendously; in 1995, the monthly AAPCC varied from $574.65 in Dade County, Florida to $278.05 in Alpine, California to $74.65 in Maricao, Puerto Rico. The areas with higher AAPCCs are usually the most attractive to plans seeking a reasonable return on investment. Fourth, managed care is familiar to individuals younger than 65 in these states, leading to greater acceptance of Medicare risk HMOs and the existence of a provider network already familiar with capitated arrangements. Finally, some of these states, particularly Florida, have a disproportionate number of the elderly living within their borders.

These factors are all important in assessing the relative value of beginning operations in a given market, particularly the presence of providers educated in the delivery of care in a capitated environment. As managed care within the employed population spreads throughout the country, and as Congress considers ways to increase the AAPCC in rural or underserved areas, Medicare risk HMOs are likely to continue to expand geographic coverage, as demonstrated by HCFA's receipt of more than 100 applications in 1995 for new risk contracts or service area expansions.

Pricing and Benefit Design

Each year, participating HMOs must calculate their expected revenue requirement, known as the adjusted community rate (ACR) per member per month for providing coverage of Medicare-covered services. The ACR is based on the rates they charge to their non-Medicare members for comparable coverage, adjusted for differences in the utilization rates of Medicare and non-Medicare members. By comparing the ACR with their expected average AAPCC payment, HMOs can determine the potential viability of the program in a given county. The HMO must use any surplus to reduce the premium charged to beneficiaries or provide additional benefits at no extra charge. Any deficit must be absorbed by the HMO. This arrangement provides Medicare risk plans an opportunity for a great deal of creativity and innovation in designing benefit plans because, in a free market system, they must strive to make their services and benefits more attractive than those of competitors.

Added benefits typically include 100 percent hospitalization coverage, low office visit copayments, preventive care, wellness programs, limited prescription drug coverage, vision care, worldwide emergency care, hearing examinations, and in some cases even hearing aids as well as additional chiropractic and podiatry services. If most plans in a market offer comprehensive benefits for little or no extra monthly premiums, seniors must rely more on the perception of added value than on pricing differences in making decisions regarding which Medicare risk plan to buy.

Less obvious but often attractive features of Medicare risk plans include the lack of claims forms and related paperwork as well as free nutrition and fitness classes, which serve the dual purpose of keeping members healthy and satisfied with what they perceive as extra perks. Health plans can use their imagination in adding features that increase the value of the plan to seniors, from memberships in local health clubs to free counseling sessions addressing aging, bereavement, and loss.

Marketing and Sales

Before enrolling members, plans must prepare their staff for handling the particular needs and sensitivities of the senior market. Bear in mind that seniors' good health holds the key to their happiness and quality of life. Changing health plans is not a decision that should or can be made lightly. In making the sale, your plan is beginning a long-term relationship with the senior. Nurturing this relationship should be the primary goal of plan providers and customer service representatives, and all plan exclusions and limitations should be disclosed fully from the start. Because of the high degree of education required, Medicare HMOs have predominantly been marketed through a direct sales organization as opposed to using brokers or any other third party arrangement.

High-pressure sales techniques are a guarantee of failure. If the market does not turn on you, HCFA will. There are several key ways to generate interest in the program:

- direct mail
- print, television, and radio advertising
- media or public relations programs
- educational seminars
- special events, such as sponsorships of Senior Olympics or wellness fairs

These methods all help raise awareness of and generate interest in the plan. Sales can be gained through group and one-on-one meetings or over the telephone.

It is of great importance to make sure, after the sale, that the senior has fully understood the implications of joining your health plan. Some plans have member service representatives call new enrollees several days after the sale; others hold follow-up educational meetings to explain in greater detail how members access care and can best utilize their benefits. Some do both.

Customer Service

Member service representatives are particularly important links to senior members, especially because member retention and reputation are both keys to profitability. Some estimates put the cost of acquiring a new member at between $500 to well over $1,000. A minimally sized plan (usually estimated at 10,000 members) with even a 5 percent annual voluntary disenrollment could experience a significant shortfall in premium revenues. Seniors are smart shoppers, and with the number of Medicare risk plans now on the market they have more choices than ever before.

Customer service representatives should be well trained and polite and regard it as a requirement of their job to treat senior customers with the utmost respect. Plans that encourage member services staff to spend time on the phone with members, solve their problems promptly, and always call back with either a solution or a promise to look further into the problem at hand will find themselves winners in a competitive marketplace. Quality of care complaints should trigger quality audits, so that consistently good care is delivered. After all, the ideal scenario is for members to stay with the plan for the balance of their lifetimes, so that risk can be managed and health care resources allocated appropriately. Keeping members happy is therefore of great importance. This requires all staff, from claims processors to contracted providers, to be honest, straightforward, respectful, and patient in all their dealings with members.

Education

Educational and informational needs of seniors are often served by sending regular newsletters and magazines that emphasize the importance of staying healthy and may include feature articles about seniors pursuing active and healthy life styles. Newsletters also serve an important role in educating seniors about the philosophy of HMOs, the role of the primary care physician, and the value of the nurse case manager or triage nurse. Stories about members' experiences can reinforce the educational message. HMOs can also use these communications to remind members of services such as toll-free member service phone numbers and health care information lines. For all printed materials, use a ten-point or larger typeface and contrasting colors rather than shades or pastels, and avoid glossy paper, which can contribute to glare.

Limitations on Physician Risk

In 1996, the Office of the Inspector General of the Department of Health and Human Services issued final regulations placing limitations on the amount of risk a health plan may put a physi-

cian at in a Medicare or Medicaid program. These new regulations effectively limit the amount of risk to 25 percent, and place additional requirements on the health plan regarding stop-loss insurance and member surveys. The reader is referred to Chapter 9 for a discussion of these regulations.

PREPARING THE DELIVERY SYSTEM

Physicians who are already accustomed to working in a capitated environment are ideal recruits for Medicare risk HMO contracts. These physicians understand the need to approach health care in a much more inclusive manner, managing the overall care of the member and establishing an ongoing relationship rather than providing episodic treatment for disparate illnesses or injuries followed by piecemeal referrals to specialists. They understand that managed care saves money and improves quality by rewarding teamwork, efficiency, and the delivery of the appropriate acuity of care in a clinically appropriate setting.

They also understand the value of preventive care and the creative use of resources to achieve the desired result. The majority follow up complex consultations with regular phone calls to encourage compliance in taking prescription drugs, such as blood pressure medication. Many others conduct health risk assessments followed, where indicated, by consultation or inspection of the senior's home environment in an effort to prevent the kinds of injuries or complications that result in extended hospital stays. One medical group in California even provides its frail Medicare risk members with a free shower chair, immediately cutting down on the number of falls that are likely to result in expensive hospital stays and hip replacements. These and other creative approaches, stimulated by capitated arrangements, have a significant impact on the life of senior members, keeping them healthy, improving the quality of their lives, and at the same time ensuring a return on the investment made by the provider group in this new approach to care.

Providers with existing contracts with managed care companies appreciate the consistent cash flow and upfront capital that accompanies capitated arrangements. They have in many cases adjusted their practices accordingly, reengineering their administrative infrastructure to focus on prevention, service, and outcomes data rather than simply the payment of physicians' claims.

Challenges of the Elderly and Disabled

The elderly usually require longer appointments than patients under 65 for several reasons: They may have more questions to ask or more health problems to discuss, and they are often less rushed for time than their Baby Boomer children. That must be taken into account in scheduling time with the physician. Consulting rooms may need to be a little larger to accommodate spouses or family who accompany the elderly patient to a consultation. Bathrooms should be fitted with handrails, and more handicapped parking should be available. Even more than these alterations to the physical space, providers of care to the elderly must be patient, respectful, and willing to listen.

This does not mean that physicians need to throw their productivity standards out the window. Most successful medical groups in Medicare risk contracts have learned to utilize teams of professionals and paraprofessionals to address their HMO members' needs, resulting in both better care and increased overall efficiency.

Impact on Network Design and Staffing

More than any other factor, the design and management of the delivery system determine the success or failure of a senior HMO, and the control of hospitalization is the single most likely contributor to financial success. There are generally four main formats of provider groups, that when properly designed and managed, currently seem best suited to managing health care for seniors within a capitated environment:

1. integrated multispecialty groups with good primary care capacity
2. primary care medical groups with a limited network of contracted specialists
3. independent practice associations (IPAs) with a selective network of providers and with policy driven by primary care providers
4. other vertically aligned organizations, a category that could include such models as physician–hospital organizations (PHOs), management service organizations (MSOs), or medical foundations, assuming that they are well run, selective in network participation, and market driven and have redistributed the dollars and incentives to support growth and service

Each medical delivery system model has different advantages and disadvantages, but all will experience significant patient care demand from senior members. Medicare members utilize more services, including office visits, than commercial members. As reported in Chapter 7, commercial enrollees younger than 65 have an average of 3.6 to 3.8 physician encounters per year, of which 2.5 are primary care visits. Medicare members average 7.0 encounters per year for Medicare risk enrollees, and 6.4 encounters per year for Medicare cost enrollees[6]; these data refer to total physician encounters, not necessarily those for primary care only, and do not include encounters with nonphysicians. Nevertheless, the implications for staffing are clear: Staffing needs are greatly increased when a substantial Medicare population is served. As pointed out in Chapter 7, the majority of closed panel HMOs increased their staffing ratios for Medicare members to a mean of 1.6 per 1,000 Medicare enrollees.[7]

Although components of any of these accountable delivery systems may be paid via some form of per diem, case rate, or other FFS basis, the value of capitation is emphasized because of its power in aligning the delivery system's incentives with those of the patient and plan. With capitation, the delivery system is incented to prevent health problems, treat them well and efficiently when they occur, and keep members happy, all of which are critical variables in this market niche.

Administrative and leadership requirements are also significant and include:

- the ability to add physician capacity when membership grows
- the ability to influence practice patterns and change physician behavior to avoid unnecessary hospitalizations or referrals
- the ability to process coverage authorizations and medical claims payments within the bounds of government policy, which is generally stricter than that of the average commercial population
- the ability to manage complex cases involving a number of different specialists, hospitalizations, and prescription drugs within a variety of clinical settings
- the ability to interface with and utilize the many community agencies and support services that add value to the total care of this population

These demands have different implications for different medical group models. IPAs can generally be more flexible because they can extend their physician capacity quickly by contracting with physicians in the community at large. IPAs also often have well-established links with the community. The IPA's weaker commitment to a centralized administrative management and governance, however, may diminish the consistency and therefore the effectiveness of the group's referral and authorization policies. In addition, the lack of any centralized governance over IPAs' provider system resources prevents them from driving efficiencies through office consolidation or capitalizing either expansion sites or alternative treatment centers.

The primary medical group (PMG) can provide a closer level of coordination between the clinical and business sides of the operation and simplify the implementation of coordinated patient care management through a tighter governance structure concentrated among primary group owners. A PMG without distributed medical offices, however, may be less marketable than a contracted primary care physician network. In addition, PMGs must be particularly sensitive, as must primary care–driven IPAs, to the more complicated medical conditions found in their senior population. For example, as noted in Chapter 20, an internist or medical subspecialist may be a more effective care manager than a general practitioner in some cases.

Integrated multispecialty groups have the greatest potential to control inpatient and outpatient specialist costs and the ability to implement effective and efficient disease management programs for chronic conditions such as diabetes or cardiopulmonary disease. These groups, however, may also be more departmentally structured and traditional in their approach to the delivery of care, less likely to work as a team, and more resistant to accepting the central role of primary care as it relates to policy and income redistribution. Foundations vary; they may exhibit some of the strengths and weaknesses of multiple models.

PHOs and MSOs are the newest of the above models and, depending on their organizational structure, could exhibit all the best or all the worst of the above traits. In general, most PHOs are limiting their potential for success by failing to support the necessary redistribution of policy and income away from hospital and specialty care toward primary care. They have also typically failed to build the experienced management infrastructure and have resisted the need to push strong financial incentives down to the individual physician level. Nevertheless, if they could overcome this understandable resistance, PHOs and MSOs have better potential access to capital and organizational support than many IPAs, primary group structures, or not-for-profit foundations. Strong leadership and a willingness to accept new ways of approaching health care for seniors will go a long way toward improving the likelihood of success with every delivery model.

No matter how a plan's provider relationships are structured, there are some critical areas to examine to assess how compatible the groups are with the philosophy of capitation and its financial impact on their practices:

* governance
* commonality of purpose
* sharing of financial risk
* control of primary care physician activities, training, and reporting
* control over hospital admissions and lengths of stay
* control of specialist and ancillary expenses
* ability to finance growth
* ability and willingness to recruit new primary care physicians
* marketability
* sensitivity to the special needs of the senior population
* willingness to work as a partner with the health plan in total patient care management

Integrated delivery systems are discussed in greater detail in Chapter 4; joint ventures, mergers, and acquisitions between payers and providers are discussed in Chapter 5.

Role of Care Coordinators, Ancillary Providers, and Guidelines

Managed care has been defined as the delivery of the appropriate care at the appropriate time in the appropriate setting by the appropriate provider. The provider may be a primary care physician or specialist, but in many cases an ancillary provider, such as a nurse practitioner, physician assistant, or home health nurse, may be more appropriate.

Older members of the population, in particular, may benefit from extended conversations with nurse practitioners, who can help allay fears and discuss symptoms in some detail before giving a summary to the physician. It is important, however, to let the elderly patient know that the nurse is an added value and not a substitute for physician care. Neither should the nurse or physician assistant treat the senior in a patronizing manner; instead, all caregivers should provide an opportunity for the patient to provide full details of his or her physical problems. This level of detail can be extremely helpful in arriving at accurate diagnoses and ultimately can save time for the busy practitioner.

It is not unusual for successful medical groups to have developed extensive clinical care guidelines and active patient care committees to help their physicians decide how to provide quality care in the most cost-efficient way. Such guidelines, coupled with aggressive development of alternative care sites, have allowed medical groups to decrease significantly their number of hospital days. This reduction in expensive hospital days is achieved through using more appropriate and less expensive settings such as surgicenters, diagnostic clinics, skilled nursing or subacute care facilities, and home-based therapies. Plans and medical groups should also contract with home health agencies and hospice care to provide clinical services as appropriate.

Most large and successful capitated groups have gone beyond simple clinical care guidelines and have developed whole multidisciplinary programs to manage chronic diseases or problematic conditions. For example, one medical group serving more than 25,000 capitated senior lives has developed a program called Options to help manage the last few months of life for terminal patients. The purpose is twofold: to prevent unnecessary hospital readmissions and, more important, to improve the quality of life for the dying patient. A multifunctional team including specialists, the primary care physician, pharmacy representatives, medical technologists, home health nurses, and family members all take part in the decision-making process. Twenty-four-hour emergency care is made available as well as a 24-hour help line and re-spite or home health care to support family members and the patient during difficult times. As a result of this approach, hospital admissions have fallen dramatically, and family members report greater satisfaction with the care and quality of life of their loved ones during their final days. Not incidentally, the medical group in question also reduced expenses per member per month.

A customer service and quality focus, combined with creativity and resourcefulness, is the best indicator that a medical group is likely to be successful in a capitated, risk-sharing arrangement.

Quality Issues

As previously discussed in this chapter as well as in Chapter 25, the power of managed care to improve coordination and appropriateness of care is proving an added bonus for seniors, some of whom have been overmedicated in the past or undergone surgeries of doubtful value in a system where incentives were skewed toward an oversupply of services and procedures. Competition among senior HMOs, unheard of among the general Medicare population, has resulted in plans offering an unparalleled level of benefits.

A 1995 HCFA survey showed that, of approximately 140 plans surveyed, 131 covered routine physicals, 121 covered eye examinations, 116 covered immunizations, 100 covered ear examinations, 65 covered outpatient drugs, 48 covered dental costs, 47 covered foot care, 34 offered health education, 7 covered lenses, and 5 covered hearing aids. In addition, many plans offered fitness and nutrition classes as well as educational newsletters with information about health maintenance.

In addition to improvement in the quality of care through added benefits, plans set up quality assurance programs that monitor the amount and kind of care delivered by providers and flag inappropriate care. Members also have access to grievance procedures should they have any con-cerns about their benefits or care (see Chapter 30).

Because of the competitive nature of the market in the most highly penetrated areas, a reputation for quality becomes a valuable marketing asset as well as a moral imperative. Furthermore, the reality that Medicare risk plans are providing quality care is shown through a number of studies conducted over the past few years. According to an HCFA study, elderly HMO members with cancer were more likely to be diagnosed at an early stage than elderly people in old-style FFS plans. In that study, breast, cervical, and colon cancer, along with melanomas, were diagnosed significantly earlier in HMOs than FFS plans.[8] Another study comparing treatments and outcomes in myocardial infarction found that HMO patients received hospital care that was generally better in terms of process than that reviewed by patients in a national FFS sample.[9] In addition, a study comparing treatment decisions among 140,000 Californians with clogged coronary arteries found that HMOs offered the best way to avoid unnecessary treatment without sacrificing needed care. HMO patients underwent less surgery, yet there was no difference in death rates for HMO and FFS patients.[10] These are just a few of an expanding list of studies that suggest that innovation and quality are increasingly the accepted hallmarks of successful Medicare risk plans.

WORKING WITH SPECIAL POPULATIONS

In addition to the wide range of health care needs found within the senior population, there are a number of populations that present particular opportunities and challenges. These special populations include retirees, those with ESRD, the hospice population, the disabled, beneficiaries covered by both Medicare and Medicaid, and the frail elderly. Plans should consider carefully whether their organizational structure, physician mix, and incentive systems are set up to provide adequate care to these groups while maintaining plan viability as a business.

Each special population has different financing sources, payment methodologies, and levels. Because legislation has designated funding for programs that address specific needs, older persons with complex needs for both acute and chronic services must often rely on a number of funding sources and programs. Funding can include federal, state, and private sources. For instance, employer-sponsored retiree health care coverage is a major source of private funding. The federal Medicare program was designed to cover primarily hospital costs and some physician expenses. The Medicaid program, through both federal and state funding, covers primarily long-term care and a number of other costs for the impoverished elderly.

With some populations, the integration of state programs with the federal Medicare program through contracts or other methods will be necessary to resolve issues in fragmentation and to merge the acute and long-term care funding streams. HCFA has initiated a number of demonstration projects to finance the care of special populations through capitation and to test various payment rates, benefit designs, risk adjustment methods, and combined funding sources. Some plans use disease management programs (see Chapter 20) to monitor proactively the situations of at-risk enrollees. Case managers (see Chapter 18) assess need, develop care plans, make arrangements for care with appropriate providers, and provide follow-up and monitoring to ensure that the care selected continues to be appropriate.

Retirees

Employer-sponsored retiree health benefits cover roughly 30 percent of Medicare eligibles, representing a significant market segment with unique needs, particularly as companies recognize the impact of their generous retiree plans on their bottom line. Seniors also share their previous employers' concerns about the rising costs of health care, especially as they see other companies cut back on commitments that retirees thought were a lifetime entitlement.

Medicare risk plans are making more and more sense, especially as corporations all over America have become accustomed to the savings that commercial HMOs have brought to their health care expenditures. The retiree market therefore is likely to grow as companies seek to escape the high costs of postretirement medical coverage, especially because this liability is often unfunded and creates a negative drain on net worth.

At the time of this writing, however, most Medicare plans have had difficulty penetrating the retiree market. The mobility of recent retirees, coupled with incompatibility of locally driven HMO benefit structures with nationally standardized retiree benefits, creates special problems. As employers convert to a defined contribution approach to retiree benefits, however, the beneficiary begins to have more flexibility in the choice of plans available within each community. Likewise, many HMOs have become more flexible in providing customized plans to match the defined benefit plans of larger employers. Finally, a few plans have begun to arrange for member reciprocity with plans in other states, helping solve the service problems that go with member mobility. Point-of-service options for seniors will help in this regard as well.

The Disabled

According to HCFA's 1995 Medicare program chart book, the disabled represented an estimated 10 percent of Medicare beneficiaries in 1995. In providing services for this group, it is important for plans to develop strategic and contractual arrangements with ancillary providers such as physiatrists, physical therapists, podiatrists, chiropractors, and other specialized therapists who serve this population as well as with rehabilitation facilities, skilled nursing facilities, and long-term care facilities.

Strategies that are used to manage chronic medical conditions in the general Medicare population must be applied even more vigorously to the disabled, including close coordination with community resources and programs. Upfront risk assessment and health status profiling are key. Resources must be allocated efficiently, and strategies must be applied that enhance the best possible health status for these individuals by preventing the exacerbation of existing problems. Consistent outreach is important; so is education of members and their families regarding nutrition and how best to handle their physical challenges and maintain relative health.

Medicare-Medicaid Eligibles

A small percentage of the population is eligible for both Medicare and Medicaid benefits. Generally, the reimbursement for this group is greater than that for the average Medicare recipient. The status of these beneficiaries may change quite quickly, however, which can create problems for health plans. For example, a few years ago the government realized that its list of eligibles had not been accurate and retroactively demanded back the 3 years of surplus funding that had been inadvertently passed on to health plans, regardless of the fact that health plans had used the payment to increase benefits and/or provider payments. The unilateral ability of the government to set payment policy retroactively and regulate its subcontractors suggests that plans should use caution in this area. Further, state medicaid program requirements and oversight can add significantly to a plan's overhead and political exposure.

Despite these difficulties, however, there is a real opportunity to improve patient care and increase efficiency in this population. By combining state and federal funding into one capitation payment to an HMO, the government can be assured that there is an accountable delivery system bringing discipline to the market and access to the patient. An accountable delivery system also brings cost control and quality health care, including preventive care, to this needy and often neglected population. Success

with this group often requires additional outreach efforts, transportation support, and active coordination with community resources and support groups.

The Frail Elderly

Nursing home expenditures are consuming increasing levels of our nation's resources; predictions are that the cost to Medicaid alone will rise to $9 billion by 2010. Overall, about 70 percent of all public and private long-term health care dollars are currently spent for institutional care. Also, the number of those over 65 who are severely impaired is expected to increase by 30 percent between 1990 and 2000. The General Accounting Office estimates that in 1994 there were approximately 1.64 million seniors living in institutions. Given these statistics and demographic trends suggesting that the over-85 population is likely to increase substantially in the next 10 years, the frail elderly population (those who have a physical, cognitive, or medical condition that affects their ability to perform the activities of daily living) presents risk plans with significant opportunities and challenges.

For Medicare risk enrollees who have been a resident of a skilled nursing facility or other long-term care institution for a minimum of 30 consecutive days, HCFA will pay the Medicare risk HMO a higher capitation based on institutional status. For instance, a Medicare risk plan in Los Angeles County, California would receive $1,205.35 per member per month for male enrollees ages 70 to 74 who are institutionalized. For male enrollees within the same age range (70 to 74) who are not residents of a nursing home, the risk plan would receive $516.26 per member per month.

Plans that develop programs specifically designed to manage the particular problems associated with the frail elderly are likely to be the most successful. The successful plans will also be those that combine home care services and community-based resources in the most efficient manner, usually through a dedicated care manager. In addition, advocacy on the part of the member should become an overriding responsibility of the care manager, particularly when he or she is working with impaired members who cannot negotiate the system for themselves.

ESRD

The number of Medicare beneficiaries with ESRD grew at an average annual rate of about 10 percent from 1982 to 1992. This population, which is also likely to grow substantially in the coming years, has been the subject of much research and is part of a recent HCFA demonstration project. There are more than 186,000 ESRD beneficiaries nationwide, and more than 6,000 of these are currently enrolled in managed care organizations. Medicare risk plans cannot actively recruit members with ESRD, although this group may provide an opportunity to apply managed care principles to the benefit of both the patient and the plan.

If enrollees develop ESRD after they are already enrolled, Medicare risk contractors cannot automatically disenroll them. For ESRD enrollees, Medicare pays a capitation rate that is based on 95 percent of the average annual ESRD FFS costs statewide. Compared with the payment rate for non-ESRD enrollees, the ESRD capitation rate is based on a statewide rate rather than a county rate and does not include adjustments for age, gender, or disability status. The high FFS costs of caring for beneficiaries with ESRD is reflected in the ESRD payment, and Medicare risk members who become ESRD beneficiaries are funded at a much higher rate than non-ESRD enrollees. For example, in California the payment rate for ESRD members is about ten times the amount typically received by Medicare risk contractors for non-ESRD enrollees, and in Massachusetts the ESRD payment rate is more than eight times the non-ESRD rate. Plans must monitor the chronic care needs of ESRD enrollees and take proactive measures to improve their functioning and avoid acute care crises.

To address better the escalating costs and the unique needs of the ESRD population, Congress has mandated an ESRD demonstration project. Under the demonstration, HCFA would provide an inclusive capitation payment for all Medicare-covered part A and part B acute and chronic services. The ESRD capitation amount will be adjusted to reflect treatment status. For several years, there has been an interest in refining or adjusting the capitation rate for ESRD enrollees, particularly to cover the large cost outlays for transplant surgery and to reflect cost differences related to whether the enrollee is receiving maintenance dialysis or has successfully received a transplant.

Hospice Care

In 1995, Medicare fiscal year expenditures on hospice care were estimated at close to $1.4 billion, compared with $90 million in 1988.[11] Part of the reason for this dramatic shift was the decrease in the use of hospitals to take care of the elderly in the last month of life, when the majority of expenditures occur. The net effect of this market shift is financially positive; Medicare beneficiaries with cancer who were enrolled in a hospice cost Medicare on average $2,737 less than nonusers in the last year of life.[12]

Briefly, hospice care helps terminally ill patients spend their last months of life in the most comfortable setting possible, providing palliative care rather than making unwanted and unnecessary heroic efforts that will provide little benefit. Most managed care payers provide coverage similar to Medicare coverage for hospice services. HMOs offer these benefits in the belief that it is more cost effective to provide a person with less expensive (though prolonged) hospice care than to encourage fruitless attempts to halt the progress of a terminal disease. Expanded use of hospice benefits could represent significant potential savings to the country, given that Medicare beneficiaries in their last year of life account for approximately 27 percent of Medicare expenditures.

Managed care plans offering hospice benefits may find this feature an attractive added value to potential members as well as a cost-saving technique for the plan in the long term. This niche market, however, is also fraught with the danger of possible litigation. The attempt to persuade a patient to enter hospice care may be regarded as a sign of the plan's attempt to lower cost rather than an action taken in the interest of the patient. This is, understandably, a difficult and emotional time for the family. In fact, the most successful medical groups and risk contractors often educate their members about wills, advance directives, and powers of attorney, preparing both the family and the patient to deal better with these tough issues before the need for difficult decisions arises.

THE GOVERNMENT AS A PAYER AND A PARTNER

Medicare FFS reimbursement is a cost-based and productivity-based program. Over time, this structure has grown to become extremely costly for both Medicare enrollees and the federal government, which pays for more than a third of medical costs in the country. Medicare risk has demonstrated the ability to assume risk for the government, making costs more predictable, reducing unnecessary utilization, and at the same time increasing benefits to Medicare eligibles with equal or greater quality and satisfaction.

The increasing popularity of Medicare risk programs has presented the government with an interesting dilemma: whether to support Medicare risk HMOs and by inference agree that managed care can do a much better job of reducing costs than old-style Medicare while still delivering quality care, or whether to enact new regulations to stifle the growth of Medicare risk programs as some special interest groups would prefer. If trends in the private sector are any indication, managed care—total patient care management rather than episodic urgent or emergency care—will prove the better option for a growing senior population.

For the most part, HCFA has been a supportive and responsive partner in introducing man-

aged care to the Medicare market. First set up as a regulatory body to oversee the Medicare program, however, HCFA is currently undergoing an identity crisis of sorts. Indeed, HCFA has arguably become the largest self-insured health organization in the world. It is hardly surprising, therefore, that HCFA is reluctant to preside over its own demise. Instead, the organization from time to time attempts to bring in new regulations to improve the financing and delivery of health care in the FFS model, and it continues to fund research and pilot programs that do not address the fundamental need to change the financial incentives in the current system. Unfortunately, many of these activities simply perpetuate the problems inherent in old-style FFS. Until it is clear that HCFA, supported by Congress, sees the long-term viability of the managed care industry as an important policy goal, it will limit the industry's willingness to capitalize fully on the development of efficient, accountable delivery systems across America.

Payment Methodology

Understanding HCFA's payment methodology is one of the keys to success in Medicare risk programs. This highly important topic is also discussed in detail in Chapter 46. As previously discussed in this chapter, at the time of this writing HMOs with a risk contract are paid 95 percent of what the government's actuaries estimate to be the cost of medical services if the services had been obtained in traditional FFS Medicare. This estimate is called the AAPCC.

There are a number of questions regarding the future of this payment method. First, because the AAPCC can vary significantly from county to county simply as a result of sample size difficulties, future payment calculations may be based on larger geographic areas, such as metropolitan statistical areas. Additionally, because some areas are historically underfunded compared with others, future increases may selectively favor lower-paid areas, particularly rural areas. If this selectivity in increases occurs, it will probably be balanced by lower-than-projected increases in other, currently higher-paid areas.

Finally, the current inability of the government to provide some level of predictability in regard to reimbursement makes it difficult for HMOs to capitalize Medicare risk expansion, especially in lower reimbursement or less populated areas. Such predictability could come from a new payment system that better reflects risk or a multiyear funding plan that defines the per capita government contribution rate for all seniors living in the same geographic area. This rate would probably vary by age, sex, and other key risk selection categories.

Another area of concern for risk HMOs is that, as Medicare risk penetration increases in an area, the overall rate of health inflation is decreased. Although that is good news for HCFA, which pays only 95 percent of the resulting lower AAPCC, it means that the HMO gets punished each following year as AAPCCs decrease. This has created some defections from risk contracts into cost contracts in some areas, especially Minneapolis–St. Paul. HCFA is considering alternative ways to set payment rates in areas with high Medicare risk penetration. At the same time, the HCFA has made it harder for HMOs to discontinue risk contracts and has recommended against allowing other HMOs to convert from risk to cost contracts.

This much is certain: The expansion of senior HMOs to all markets will not occur unless the payment methodology from HCFA is viewed as both fair and predictable. Managed health care plans cannot be expected to tie their economic futures to pilot projects floated during election cycles or to arbitrary changes in revenue per member during budget cycles.

Competitive Bidding

Competitive bidding among health plan options is one avenue being discussed as a means of achieving savings. It is viewed by some as a mechanism to set the federal government's contribution through market dynamics rather than relying on AAPCC calculations. Competitive

bidding could significantly reduce the incentives for health plans to offer Medicare risk plans, however, especially if the traditional Medicare program is not held to the same government contribution maximum established through local competition.

Even if the federal government moved, as some in Congress have proposed in the past, to a defined contribution strategy, where Medicare recipients were required to pay the difference between option costs, many feel that it is premature to set the market rate through competitive bidding. With more than 90 percent of beneficiaries still in traditional Medicare and with an expected 10 percent annual increase in health care expenditures, it would seem logical to encourage the growth of Medicare risk programs rather than have them compete with each other for their current market share. When the infrastructure is in place nationally to deliver cost-effective coordinated care, and when the majority of seniors are enrolled in or comfortable with these plans, the time may be ripe for considering competitive bidding for government contracts.

Competition is already intense in markets where numerous risk contractors provide service. That competition is reflected in increased benefits and lower premiums for seniors. There is some discussion in Washington as to whether risk plans should be allowed to return (or pay) all or a part of a recipient's part B premium in lieu of increased benefits. This approach is seen by some as competitive pricing but with a floor, avoiding the potential excesses of underpricing and underserving this vulnerable population.

Interestingly enough, in this time of budget cuts in government, one of the major concerns with setting the government's contribution through competitive bidding where the delivery system is dominated by FFS providers is that the resulting premium may cost more than the current AAPCC methodology. Although capping the bid premium at AAPCC could solve this problem, it introduces an artificial pricing element that will leave many markets unattractive for development.

Other Regulatory Issues

As discussed earlier in this chapter, the growth of Medicare risk plans has also been slowed by the 50/50 rule, which requires that at least 50 percent of a plans' members come from the private sector. Now that Medicare risk plans are entering their second decade, it would seem that those that have proved their competitive mettle and are financially stable should be exempt from this rule. Also, the government would certainly stimulate the growth of managed care if it were to provide federal exemption from state anti–managed care legislation, such as any willing provider and so-called patient protection acts. Both changes are being considered by Congress at the time of this writing. The reader is referred to Chapter 2 for a discussion of the reform process at the federal level.

The role of state HMO licensure and oversight has, however, proved valuable in assessing whether adequate financial reserves, management capabilities, and delivery system controls are in place to protect the public interest (see Chapter 53). Any changes in policy at the federal level will need to take care to preserve these oversight functions. The current HCFA review process currently serves some, but not all, of the functions.

FUTURE TRENDS

Congressional interest in the power of managed care to reduce Medicare costs is spurring new demonstration projects as well as heated debate over future reimbursement issues. As the discussion broadens, there are also likely to be many new challenges and opportunities for managed care companies. Medicare point-of-service plans will make it easier for some seniors to move into managed care. These plans represent a natural evolution for HMOs, as reflected in the private sector. As HCFA demonstration projects with risk preferred provider organizations and other models evolve, we will probably see even more product choices for seniors, eventually changing the role of HCFA itself. During this period of transition, it will be important to keep a dialog going among seniors, providers, plans, and legislators to prevent the passage of well-meaning but misguided laws that could have an adverse effect on the senior market.

In truth, these are fascinating times. The opening up of the senior market presents some interesting and exciting opportunities for health plans and providers to find resourceful new ways to improve quality and efficiency. The longer-living, more active, healthier seniors of the future will be able to select plans that are best suited to their physical needs, financial situation, and delivery system preferences, all of which will become important as the discriminating Baby Boomers reach their mid-60s with higher expectations of the health system than ever before. The managed care industry will need to continue to evolve to keep up with this highly dynamic market.

REFERENCES AND NOTES

1. 1995 Retirement Guide, *U.S. News & World Report* (June 12, 1995), p. 62–69. Excerpt from *New Passages: Mapping Your Life Across Time* (New York, N.Y.: Random House, 1995).
2. If You Build It, They Will Come, *IBC's Capitation Alert!* 1(6).
3. B.C. Vladeck, *Medicare: A Profile* (Medicare Program Chart Book, U.S. Department of Health and Human Services, 1995).
4. Operations and Oversight Team of the Office of Managed Care, Health Care Financing Administration, *Medicare Managed Care Program Update* (U.S. Department of Health and Human Services, 1995) p. 134.
5. Operations and Oversight Team, *Medicare Managed Care Program Update*, p. 124.
6. Group Health Association of America, *HMO Industry Profile* (Washington, D.C.: Group Health Association of America, 1994).
7. T.H. Dial, et al., *Clinical Staffing in Staff- and Group-Model HMOs, Health Affairs* (Summer 1995): 168–180.
8. G. Riley, et al., Stage of Cancer at Diagnosis for Medicare HMO and Fee-For-Service Enrollees, *American Journal of Public Health* 84(10) (1994): 1598–1604.
9. D. Faze, et al., HMO Bests Fee-For-Service Care of Older Persons with Acute Myocardial Infarction, *American Journal of Public Health* 82 (12) (1992): 1626–1630.

10. Group Health Association of America, *HMO Fact Sheet* (Washington, D.C.: GHAA, 1995).

11. S. Becker and R.J. Pristave, Managed Care and the Provision of Hospital Care, *Managed Care Quarterly* 3(1) (1995): 39–43.

12. An Analysis of the Cost-Savings of the Medicare Hospice Benefit: Lewin-VHI Inc., Study prepared for the National Hospital Association, May 21, 1995.

SUGGESTED READING

Broude, M. 1994. Member Education: Communicating to Diverse Membership Populations; Communicating to the Older Adult; Public Relations in Managed Care: Communicating in an Era of Health Care Consumerism. Section 14, 5 pp. San Francisco, Calif., March 17-18, 1994. Washington, D.C.: American Association of Health Plans.

Eyler, A.A., Wallace, K., and Trevino, R. 1994. A New Audience: Health Promotion and Senior Care. *HMO Practice* 8(3): 139–140.

Luft, H.S. (ed.). 1994. *HMOs and the Elderly*. Ann Arbor, Mich.: Health Administration Press.

Warshawsky, M.J. 1992. *The Uncertain Promise of Retiree Health Benefits: An Evaluation of Corporate Obligations*. Washington, D.C.: AEI Press/American Enterprise Institute.

Chapter 48

Medicaid Managed Care

Robert E. Hurley, Leonard Kirschner, and Thomas W. Bone

The number of Medicaid beneficiaries enrolled in managed care arrangements increased more than fivefold from 1990 to 1995, from 2.1 million to nearly 12 million.[1] In 6 years the joint federal–state program for low-income and disabled individuals grew from less than 10 percent managed care penetration to more than 35 percent. Virtually every state in the country has implemented some type of managed care arrangement for at least some of its eligible populations. Every indicator suggests that this growth will accelerate as states move into an era in which they are granted more program flexibility in return for a substantially reduced growth rate in federal financial support.

The rapid expansion reflects the convergence of several trends. Medicaid eligibility growth and overall cost inflation have contributed to state financial distress. Widening acceptance and availability of managed care options in the commercial sector have made public policymakers eager to avail themselves of the cost savings opportunities being reported by private buyers. There has been a dramatic upsurge in interest among commercial managed care

plans to build their membership by entering the Medicaid market, a market viewed with considerable hesitancy and trepidation in the past.

In this chapter, relevant background and history that have led up to these important recent developments are examined. Some distinctive characteristics of the Medicaid program and its beneficiaries are discussed to identify how challenging crafting models to serve them has been. The principal models in use are introduced, and some experience from them is reviewed. Operational issues associated with designing and managing the Medicaid product line are examined in some depth, and the chapter concludes with an assessment of the major trends that are likely to be evident in a block grant environment.

BACKGROUND AND HISTORY

Enrollment in managed care arrangements has been permitted in Medicaid almost from the beginning of the program in 1966.[2] As a result of lack of enthusiasm among health maintenance organizations (HMOs), disinterest and/or caution among state officials, and hesitancy among beneficiaries, the numbers grew slowly. By 1981, there were only about a quarter of a million enrollees out of the roughly 20 million persons with Medicaid coverage.[3]

There had also been a notable failure of a major managed care initiative in the California Medicaid (MediCal) program in the early 1970s that had had a chilling effect on efforts to extend managed care to low-income persons.[4] Hasty,

Robert E. Hurley, Ph.D., is an Associate Professor in the Department of Health Administration at the Medical College of Virginia.

Leonard Kirschner, M.P.H., M.D., is with Electronic Data Systems and is the former Director of the Arizona Health Care Cost Containment System.

Thomas W. Bone, M.C.H.A., is with Electronic Data Systems and is the former Director of Managed Care for the Virginia Medicaid program.

ill-considered arrangements by state officials led to shabby and fraudulent behavior by prepaid health plans, many of which were formed solely to exploit this opportunity. Marketing and network abuses resulted in beneficiaries going unserved and providers unpaid. Although this was a unique situation in many respects, the experience raised many concerns about the feasibility and desirability of promoting enrollment, especially rapid and unregulated enrollment, of low-income persons in managed care arrangements.[5]

The Waiver and Demonstration Era

A major change occurred in 1981 when, in the face of rising Medicaid expenditures and growing interest in giving states more flexibility, Congress expanded the waiver-granting authority of the Health Care Financing Administration (HCFA) to allow states to experiment with many new approaches to using alternative financing and delivery arrangements.[6] Many new approaches were introduced, including the most notable: the Arizona Health Care Cost Containment System (AHCCCS), built statewide entirely on prepaid health plans. The AHCCCS program is described below.

Many other states pursued waivers for substate pilot and demonstration programs using varying levels of risk and contracting with different provider configurations.[7] This activity continued through the 1980s, and enrollment grew to about 2 million by the end of the decade, with nearly half the states introducing some form of managed care. The growth provided for much of the knowledge base and experience on which the most recent dramatic surge in managed care has drawn.

Arizona: The First of the Next Generation

The state of Arizona initiated its version of the Medicaid program in July 1982, 17 years after passage of federal Medicaid legislation. State policymakers were intent on developing a new model for health care for the poor using an inno-

vative, alternative health care system that facilitated cost containment, improved patient access, and delivered quality health care in a managed care setting. This approach rejected traditional fee-for-service arrangements in favor of private sector capitation-based contracts and was called the AHCCCS rather than the state Medicaid program. It was implemented using the Section 1115 waiver authority that the federal government issues for the purpose of conducting research and demonstration projects. For the past 14 years the program has continued as a waivered demonstration program, and the current approval allows it to continue to 1997.

Program Structure

As the first Medicaid program to implement a mandatory statewide program based solely on prepaid health plan enrollment, the AHCCCS had four key objectives:

1. competitive bidding for prepaid capitated contracts
2. development of a primary care physician gatekeeper network
3. copayments to control inappropriate utilization of medical services
4. restriction on freedom of choice after selection of a health plan

The state initially engaged a private contractor to run the day-to-day operations. After serious difficulties with this arrangement, however, the AHCCCS was established as a separate state agency with regulatory authority and operational oversight given to the agency director. During its first 13 years, the AHCCCS evolved into a national model providing capitated care to all categories of Medicaid beneficiaries as well as state-funded medically indigent and medically needy individuals.

The current program waiver permits the AHCCCS to require mandatory enrollment of all individuals in prepaid health plans with a 1-year lock-in and a 1-month open enrollment period each year. First-time enrollees get a 6-month guarantee of eligibility. Flexibility in financing allows the state to establish actuarial ranges for competitive bidding rather than having to set a rate as a percentage of fee-for-service experience. The state does not have to require plans to meet federal mandates of the "75/25 rule," meaning that a plan's AHCCCS enrollment could exceed 75 percent of total membership.

Competitive Bidding and Plan Participation

Arizona has used competitive bidding strategies to award acute care medical services contracts since the inception of the AHCCCS. Using encounter data reported by the health plans, actuarially valid rate ranges are established for various demographic groups. These include Aid to Families with Dependent Children (AFDC), Supplemental Security Income (SSI) with and without Medicare, children covered by federally mandated expansion, and state-funded medically needy and medically indigent residents. Health plans develop responses to the request for proposal and compete to serve the Medicaid population. During the 1994 competitive bidding cycle, 95 proposals were submitted to serve the state's 15 counties, and 42 contracts were awarded. The bidding resulted in a decline of 11 percent in capitation payment rates across the state. A recent federal General Accounting Office (GAO) report noted that health plans contracting with the AHCCCS accumulated substantial profits and that the state and federal governments were experiencing substantial costs savings compared with an aggregate of several other states with predominantly fee-for-service Medicaid programs.[8]

As of 1995, 14 health plans were contracting with the AHCCCS program, with the most common model being an independent practice association (IPA); staff and mixed model HMOs also were present. Plans owners included eight for-profit companies, three not-for-profit companies, two county governments, and one state agency. Plan enrollment ranged from 2,000 members in a small rural plan to more than 100,000 in a large IPA that covers multiple counties. A strong commitment to primary care

gatekeeping can be found in most of the plans, and this is viewed as effective in promoting high-quality, cost-effective care to this population. The state medical and hospital associations have been and continue to be strong supporters of Arizona's unique model.

Impacts and Implications

The AHCCCS was established as and has continued to be a research and demonstration model and as such has had thorough, continuous assessments performed by outside evaluators commissioned by the HCFA. These evaluations have chronicled nearly every aspect of the successes, problems, and lessons learned from the experience and has systematically studied cost, utilization, quality, access, and client and provider satisfaction. The overall impact on cost has been well documented and is quite positive. Total cost savings averaged 7 percent per year over the first 11 years of the program, with annual savings growing to approximately $72 million in fiscal year 1993.[9] Of particular note is the finding that aged, blind, and disabled SSI beneficiaries showed the greatest cost savings compared with the benchmark states used to derive the cost savings estimates. The GAO reported that, although "the amounts that Arizona spends to administer its program are higher than what other states spend, these additional expenditures more than pay for themselves in net program savings."[10(p.5)]

The GAO also notes "though each state's Medicaid program is different, other states that are considering implementing or are currently operating a managed care program can benefit from Arizona's experience."[11(p.3)] It appears that the innovative model implemented in Arizona in 1982 can be a road map for many other states to follow as they gain greater flexibility to redesign their Medicaid programs in the future. There are many important lessons that can be gleaned from what Arizona has accomplished. Perhaps most important, a successful program requires substantial initial investment in developing data collection and information systems and sufficient start-up time to ensure a smooth transition from a retrospective vendor payment system to a new model of health care delivery and financing.

Rapid Recent Enrollment Growth

The past 5 years have seen enrollment grow exponentially (Figure 48–1). As Medicaid expenditures reached nearly 20 percent of the typical state budget, pursuit of cost control through managed care expansion has become nearly a frenzy for states.[12] States with established programs have rapidly expanded enrollment by making it mandatory and by attempting to cover more and more categories of eligibility. They are also moving beneficiaries toward tighter models of managed care, such as fully capitated HMOs, and away from looser models. Other states with little managed care penetration have initiated low-intensity primary care case management (PCCM) programs to begin the evolution toward more extensive models as the commercial managed care market begins to mature. Even predominantly rural areas have seen a surge of interest in managed care. An example of such an approach is described below.

Most recently, states have exploited the opportunity to obtain Section 1115 waivers from the HCFA to introduce major and multiple changes in their Medicaid programs, including expanding coverage to previously uninsured individuals.[13] Some of the states with 1115 waivers, such as Oregon and Tennessee, have achieved both notability and notoriety for their ambitious designs and implementation schedules. By the end of 1995, more than 15 states had received permission to make massive overhauls in their Medicaid programs, and every one of them proposed to use managed care models as the basic delivery system reform.

Virginia: An Incremental Approach

States without substantial commercial managed care plan penetration have usually had to adapt their program design and implementation plans to a pace where Medicaid advances along with the broader market rather than trying to lead it. The experience of Virginia illustrates this approach and contrasts sharply with the Arizona approach of nearly a decade earlier and the more recent Tennessee initiative. State legislation passed in 1990 required the establishment of a managed care program for AFDC beneficiaries. Because the legislation did not specify a model, the state Medicaid agency conducted a feasibility study and concluded that an incremental

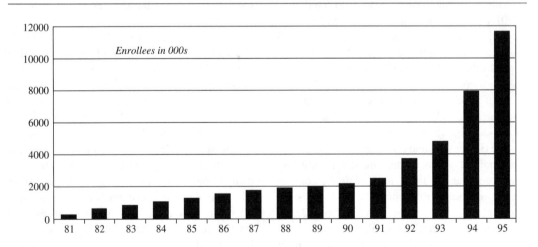

Figure 48–1 Medicaid/managed care enrollment, 1981–1995. *Source:* Health Care Financing Administration.

strategy was needed because commercial managed care penetration was low (less than 10 percent) and only present in urban areas, the state has a large nonurban population, and influential interested parties, including the state professional associations, were averse to managed care in general and HMOs in particular. The Medicaid agency established a small managed care unit to direct the program efforts and introduced the following implementation strategy.

Phase 1

In 1991, the state obtained a federal waiver to restrict freedom of choice and implemented a mandatory fee-for-service PCCM program called Medallion for AFDC beneficiaries in four diverse pilot sites with approximately 40,000 targeted enrollees. The program provided a platform for developing various operating systems and conducting extensive educational efforts for beneficiaries and providers who had limited familiarity with managed care. Once the pilot programs demonstrated program feasibility, the agency was directed to begin statewide implementation of the program on a staged, regional basis.

Program enrollment reached 350,000 by mid-1995. At that same time, the program was extended, on a mandatory basis, to nearly all noninstitutionalized Medicaid beneficiaries.

Phase 2

As HMO penetration in the commercial sector grew larger within the state, the Medicaid agency implemented in 1994 a program called Options, a voluntary HMO choice for persons wishing to opt out of Medallion. The intention of this program was to introduce mainstream managed care models to the Medicaid population and to provide the state with experience in contracting and rate setting. A master contract for HMOs was developed, and a regionalized rate structure based on the fee-for-service equivalent was set. Plans were invited to apply to qualify and were required to accept, rather than negotiate, the rates set by the state. Substantial interest was shown in the three major metropolitan areas

in the state, and by late 1995 Medicaid HMO enrollment reached nearly 80,000 members in six plans.

Phase 3

The voluntary program laid the foundation for the next phase of incremental implementation, called Medallion II, which is to be a mandatory HMO enrollment program for virtually all beneficiaries.

The state plans to sequence the implementation of this program in the urban markets with multiple competing HMOs in early 1996 and within a year to have mandatory enrollment in the major metropolitan areas. Future extension of the program will depend on how fast nonurban areas progress in terms of HMO penetration or in the emergence of provider-sponsored integrated delivery systems that can accept full risk.

Impacts and Implications

The Virginia experience demonstrates how the evolution from solely fee-for-service care toward fully capitated managed care could be accomplished on an essentially statewide basis in 4 years in a state with limited commercial managed care penetration when the process was started. The Medicaid agency worked hard to preserve beneficiary–primary care physician relationships, first through aggressive recruitment of physicians into the PCCM program and then through phasing to voluntary and finally mandatory HMO enrollment as the physicians themselves began to migrate into managed care plans. The HMO industry itself has grown over this period, with eight plans participating by late 1995 and another dozen plans in some stage of discussion with state Medicaid officials.

MEDICAID AND ITS BENEFICIARIES

Understanding the opportunities and challenges for managed care in Medicaid requires an appreciation for Medicaid itself and, in particular, for the populations covered and the distribution of expenditures. The program covered 33 million persons in 1994 with costs exceeding $150 billion and more than half the support coming from the federal government. Approximately 70 percent of the persons eligible are women and children receiving assistance from the AFDC and related assistance programs. The remainder are aged, blind, and disabled individuals whose eligibility is a function of a combination of their income, their disabilities, and their medical expenses.

Variation in Expenditures

The 70/30 percent relationship in numbers of eligibles is almost completely reversed when one looks at program expenditures by eligibility category (Figure 48–2). The reason for this discrepancy can be found in the costs of eligible groups. AFDC beneficiaries in 1993 averaged approximately $950 per year for children and $1,700 for adults, and non-AFDC beneficiary costs reached nearly $8,000. Even this high average masks enormous differences within subgroups of this high-need population. Some of these individuals are nursing home residents for whom annual costs may exceed $30,000; others are in institutions for the profoundly retarded and disabled.

Cost variability for aged, blind, and disabled beneficiaries residing in the community can also be extraordinary. Kronick et al. demonstrated in 1995 that in one state the average cost of approximately $5,000 for noninstitutionalized, non-AFDC beneficiaries included large numbers of persons with no expenses and others, such as quadriplegics or people with advanced acquired immunodeficiency syndrome (AIDS) with costs in excess of $20,000.[14] Most experience, and nearly all research, on the impacts of Medicaid managed care have focused on the AFDC population. For AFDC beneficiaries, rate development and medical management have been more similar to those for commercial HMO members and more generally acceptable to health plans. Extending managed care to Medicaid populations with special needs remains the next frontier to be addressed by states, plans, and beneficiaries.

Problems in Traditional Medicaid

Meeting the needs of AFDC beneficiaries in traditional Medicaid has itself been a major challenge. This population, comprising mainly adult women and children under the age of 18, has, by definition, limited resources and a relatively narrow spectrum of medical needs, including ob-

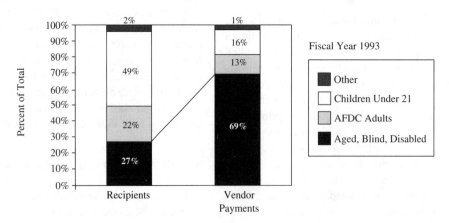

Figure 48–2 Percentage distribution of Medicaid and vendor payments by basis of eligibility. *Source:* Health Care Financing Administration.

stetrical and perinatal services and well-child care. These individuals also have other social and sociomedical challenges that influence their ability to access care (such as transportation), and they are particularly vulnerable to impoverished, urban-based life style hazards such as violence, substance abuse, inferior housing, and related concerns. Also, intermittent eligibility for cash assistance and medical benefits leads to discontinuity in coverage and service use.

The traditionally low payment rates of the Medicaid program have long discouraged many providers from participating. This compromises access and, in effect, channels beneficiaries to a limited set of providers that would not or could not refuse to serve them. Among these providers are inner city hospitals, especially emergency departments, community health centers, public health programs, and a declining number of indigenous private practitioners who have remained in areas with major Medicaid population concentrations. Reliance on the emergency department as a major source of primary care has typified the interlocking nature of this "Medicaid syndrome" because it is both clinically and economically unsuitable for the provision of routine, continuing, first-contact medical care.[15] Because the emergency department has always been available and accessible, however, its use has led to higher than necessary program expenditures for both ambulatory and inpatient services.

The Appeal of Managed Care

Managed care models have been seen as a natural antidote to this syndrome of reliance on inappropriate and excessively costly sites for uncoordinated, episodic care. Most initiatives have targeted reductions in such care and promotion of the availability of an appropriate "medical home" to improve access to primary care through either primary care gatekeeper models or fully capitated HMO enrollment.

Two persistent challenges for applying managed care principles and experience to Medicaid, however, have been lack of cost participation by beneficiaries who qualify for eligibility because of their limited income and assets, and episodic, income-based eligibility, which makes it difficult to effect sustained changes in use and outcomes of services. Altering undesirable patterns of use and promoting more desirable ones are problematic because of the minimal economic leverage providers and plans have with members. They must rely more on education and exhortation than on financial incentives and penalties. Intermittent eligibility dilutes or may undermine altogether the benefits of preventive care and early intervention, which are key parts of managed care.

MODELS AND APPROACHES TO MANAGED CARE

Early experience with managed care for Medicaid beneficiaries was exclusively with voluntary HMO enrollment in a number of well-established plans that limited enrollment to small fractions of their total membership.[16] Beginning with the waivered programs of the early 1980s, the models and types of programs showed considerable innovation and variation, offering arrangements that were not easily compared to HMOs and the emerging form of managed care called preferred provider organizations. This variation grew until the 1990s, when Medicaid arrangements began to blend more with commercial, mainstream managed care arrangements once again.

PCCM Models

Probably the most notable form of managed care, largely pioneered in Medicaid, was the PCCM model, which enrolled beneficiaries on a mandatory basis with a provider who became the exclusive portal of entry for all nonemergency services. Patterned after a private insurance company primary care gatekeeper initiative, this model was initially adopted in Medicaid programs in Michigan and Utah, which obtained waivers to allow them to restrict beneficiary choice of provider.[17,18] Primary care physicians were paid fee for service plus a case management fee (commonly $2 to $3 per member per month) to compensate them to be available 24 hours per day, 7 days per week and to deliver or authorize all nonemergency care. These programs demonstrated the ability to guarantee access and to control excessive emergency department use and "doctor-shopping" without forcing providers or beneficiaries to join organized delivery systems such as HMOs, and there were modest cost savings associated with them. The PCCM model spread rapidly to many other states.[19] Some states, such as Maryland and Massachusetts, have augmented primary care fees in lieu of paying an explicit case management fee. Other states, such as Texas, have delegated much of the program design and implementation to their fiscal intermediary.

In some states, the lack of risk sharing in PCCM models led developers to promote enhanced models that placed physicians at risk for primary care services by paying a partial capitation rate for primary care and/or allowing the physicians to share in savings in reduced referral care. Other models created pooling mechanisms to group physicians or physicians and hospitals to permit them to bear risk and for the state to pay more inclusive capitation rates.[20] Like the more modest fee-for-service PCCM model, the basic instrument of care management was the physician gatekeeper, who offered access assurance and improved care coordination. Nevertheless, these models still did not represent bona fide integrated delivery systems, nor did they permit states to shift full financial risk through a capitation payment for the full scope of Medicaid services.

Fully Capitated Managed Care Plan Model

Arizona's AHCCCS program represented the first large-scale effort to enroll beneficiaries on a mandatory basis in prepaid health plans. Other substate programs were also attempted in California, Missouri, Minnesota, and New York and later in Wisconsin and Ohio. Beneficiaries were permitted choice among plans, but traditional Medicaid was not an option for the covered eligibility groups. Despite much concern about restricting choice only to prepaid plans, the experience of most beneficiaries did not repeat the California scandals. This was due in part to federal requirements that Medicaid members could not exceed more than 75 percent of total plan membership, although waivers were granted to permit some plans to transition to this level.[21,22] Expanded oversight and better selection of contracting plans, however, also played a role in improved experience.

States reported savings and utilization experience consistent with expectations in most mandatory HMO programs, and the feasibility of executing the marketing and enrollment functions of a multiple choice program was demonstrated. In addition to these mandatory programs, a number of states began to offer HMO enrollment on a voluntary basis as an opportunity to opt out of either traditional Medicaid or a baseline PCCM program. Despite concerns about marketing abuses in some states, these programs have also proven that the choice-making process for low-income persons can be successful and that plans can adequately meet the service needs of their enrollees, nearly all of whom are AFDC adults and children. Voluntary programs are susceptible to biased selection dynamics, however, which indicate that the plans may be enrolling low-cost beneficiaries as high-cost persons remain in traditional Medicaid or PCCM programs.[23]

There are some new carve-out programs that are being developed for selected non-AFDC subpopulations or for selected services for all populations. These models are likely to be prototypes for the next generation of Medicaid managed care as we see interest in enrolling those beneficiaries who are major consumers of Medicaid expenditures.[24,25] A discussion of these programs is beyond the scope of this general presentation, but they suggest that generic managed care models may be increasingly adapted to extend coverage to persons with special needs, including chronic mental illness, physical and developmental disabilities, and other chronic, debilitating conditions such as AIDS.

IMPACTS OF MANAGED CARE

Like findings from most managed care research, the available evidence from Medicaid is relatively uneven and somewhat out of date. As public sector initiatives, however, the evaluation results are readily available, and some efforts have been made to collate the accumulated findings from the Medicaid experience.[26,27]

Cost Savings

The evidence of cost savings comes mostly from federal and state financed evaluations, which are required on waiver renewal. One problem with the reliability of these studies is that states often have had a strong interest in demonstrating savings to ensure that their waiver renewal is granted. The findings suggest savings ranging from 5 percent to 15 percent per enrolled beneficiary, which means in nearly every case AFDC beneficiaries. It is notable that savings can be guaranteed in mandatory HMO enrollment models by virtue of setting rates below expected fee-for-service expenditures, but they must be earned in PCCM programs by reducing service volumes because fee-for-service payments remain in play. Voluntary HMO enrollment programs have rarely been studied in depth because states do not need to obtain a waiver or to commission an external assessment for waiver renewal. Because selection bias is likely to occur in voluntary programs, unless this is adequately adjusted for it is difficult to ascertain whether a state achieved savings, even if plans are paid less than the expected fee-for-service–equivalent rate.

It should be emphasized again that the AFDC population incurs only about 30 percent of Medicaid costs. The only large-scale evaluation of non-AFDC beneficiaries comes from Arizona, where savings well in excess of those for AFDC enrollees have been reported, although making comparative analyses is complicated there by virtue of the fact that there was no prior Medicaid program and no in-state comparison group.[28] A recent study of Massachusetts' carved-out, single-vendor mental health program is another illustration of promising savings for such models, but more study is needed to assess the durability of reported savings.[29]

Utilization, Satisfaction, and Quality

Utilization effects indicate that both HMO and PCCM programs are reducing emergency department use and inpatient services by substantial amounts, as would be expected, although most findings indicate that further reductions in emergency department use are attainable. The effects on physician service use are more mixed, depending on the incentives in place, with some evidence showing that primary care is being substituted for specialty care and that beneficiaries see primary physicians as their medical home more frequently and receive a higher proportion of their care from them.[30] A persistent problem in measuring effects on utilization changes associated with managed care is that data availability is very uneven because PCCM programs and health plans that make capitation payments may not get reliable encounter or claims data.

Implications for satisfaction and quality effects are limited and inconclusive. Although satisfaction remains relatively high for Medicaid beneficiaries in managed care, just as in commercial managed care, there is evidence to suggest that dislocation and disruption of established provider relations in mandatory enrollment programs engender some dissatisfaction.[31,32] It should be noted, however, that there are relatively few studies of satisfaction in fee-for-service Medicaid to provide a reliable benchmark. Studies of quality of care in Medicaid managed care programs suffer from the same problem: little baseline evidence from traditional Medicaid. The limited amount of work in this area suggests neither quality gains nor losses.[33] This may be because the models of managed care in Medicaid are disparate and some have little quality improvement built into them. In addition, episodic eligibility for benefi-ciaries may undermine even the most diligent efforts to improve outcomes.

Administrative Costs and Efforts

The final areas of importance in assessing the Medicaid managed care experience from a state perspective are the level of administrative effort and the ability to get budget predictability in fu-ture cost expenditures.[34] In both instances, the PCCM programs have serious limitations. In the PCCM model, many of the administrative func-tions associated with provider recruitment and selection, enrollment, provider payment, performance monitoring, and customer service remain within the purview of the Medicaid agency because it is contracting with individual physicians rather than with a managed care en-tity. A few states, such as Massachusetts, con-tract out for management of the PCCM network, but most attempt to perform this with limited staff and other resources. Others, such as Texas use their fiscal intermediary to handle PCCM selection and ongoing provider relations activi-ties.

HMO enrollment programs afford the oppor-tunity to shift many of the administrative func-tions and their accompanying costs from the state agency to the contracting plan. Likewise, contracting with a plan for a fixed, prepaid capi-tation payment for the full scope of Medicaid benefits facilitates risk shifting and greatly im-proved budget predictability in future costs for state agencies. Future increases become subject to negotiation rather than driven by inflation and volume trends. It is for these reasons that interest in contracting with prepaid health plans has grown enormously in recent years. Coupled with the eagerness of many established plans to grow their membership from all payer sources, there has been a dramatic shift toward HMO enroll-ment as the major form of Medicaid managed care in recent years.

OPERATIONAL ISSUES FOR THE MEDICAID PRODUCT LINE

The key operational matters in Medicaid man-aged care programs vary greatly depending on the model or models that states adopt and imple-ment. The PCCM models typically are launched off the same administrative systems and infra-structure as conventional Medicaid. Fee for service is normally maintained, with reliance on the existing set of participating providers and limited efforts to foster a true network-based de-livery system. Some additional quality monitor-ing or beneficiary education programs may be overlaid on the PCCM program, but this is lim-ited. Contracting with prepaid health plans rep-resents a different approach to most operational issues, with perhaps the most crucial challenge being determination of rate structure and con-tracting strategies.

Rate Setting and Contracting

State Medicaid programs have operated under a federal requirement that their payments to capitated health plans may not exceed the ex-pected fee-for-service–equivalent costs. To comply with this requirement, rates are com-monly developed with actuarial assistance based on the fee-for-service equivalency, and then a factor of 95 percent or less is applied to deter-mine what plans will receive on a per member per month basis. Various adjustments for se-lected service carve-outs or stop-loss contribu-tions may be made, and then, depending on the complexity of the rate book developed by the state, eligibility category, demographic, and re-gional adjusters are applied to arrive at a final payment rate. This may be the rate paid, or it may represent an upper bound against which bids might be evaluated.

Who qualifies to receive capitation payments is determined by the contracting strategy of the states.[35] Some states develop a master contract and allow all plans that meet qualifications to participate; others set a limit on the number of plans with which they wish to contract and make a selection based on a variety of criteria. Voluntary enrollment programs typically have taken this latter approach because the plans are given the opportunity to entice as many of the eligible population to leave either the traditional Medicaid program or a PCCM program. Mandatory programs are more likely to limit the number of plans that can be offered and to select them based on a competitive process. A good illustration of this approach is the use of competitive bidding by plans to qualify as noted in the discussion of the AHCCS. Other states are likely to use this approach in the future to enable them to exercise leverage with a limited number of plans, to follow downward trends in the managed care market, and to manage better the choice-making environment for beneficiaries. Medicaid buying will parallel the strategies of private employers that winnow down choices for their employees for the same reasons. As noted in the description of the AHCCCS, however, many years may pass before a program is mature and stable enough to experience bona fide competitive bidding.

Eligibility, Marketing, and Enrollment

Managed care enrollment with plans or primary care physicians is significantly affected by the intermittent nature of eligibility for Medicaid beneficiaries. Income fluctuations may disrupt eligibility and thereby sever members' connection with a prepaid plan or make it necessary for them to seek care from other providers if Medicaid coverage is lost. On the front end, the enrollment process is affected by how well an individual understands the options offered at the time of gaining eligibility and how a Medicaid agency has organized the choice-making process. A growing number of states have selected independent enrollment broker or benefits counselor contractors to manage this process on behalf of the state. Brokers may disseminate information and respond to inquiries from new eligibles as well as screen the marketing and other promotional material made available to beneficiaries to promote an informed choice.

Efforts to regulate the marketing behavior of managed care plans have been controversial in the Medicaid program ever since the MediCal scandals of the early 1970s, and they continue up to the present time. As an individual choice situation, plans invest substantial resources in member acquisition activities. Some plans estimate that it may cost the equivalent of 1 month's capitation to acquire a new member.

In light of intermittent eligibility, the turnover among members is high, and aggressive marketing is used to replenish membership by many plans. Many concerns and complaints have arisen in states where enrollment grows rapidly. Critics suggest that new members are poorly informed or purposely misinformed to get them to sign up or that frivolous gimmickry is employed to cause beneficiaries to switch from one plan to another. State oversight roles vary dramatically, and it appears that some states have done a better job than others in devising prudent marketing policies and vigorous regulation and enforcement of them. Again, it is useful to look upon the role of Medicaid as the equivalent of the employee benefit manager in a private company, who negotiates with plans, makes available a limited set of choices, and then orchestrates the actual choice-making process.

A distinct challenge in enrollment in mandatory programs (and an increasing proportion of programs are becoming mandatory for many eligibles) is that a large percentage of Medicaid beneficiaries may fail to exercise a choice of plan or PCCM when offered an opportunity. Assignment techniques are used to complete this connection of a beneficiary with a source of care. Some approaches may be purely random assignment rotated across participating providers, or the process may be more systematically guided by using information about prior contact with providers by claims review, geographic proximity, specialty suitability, and other approaches. Distribution of assignees is significant, especially in prepaid arrangements, because these persons appear to be low-cost users and thus are attractive members for plans to gain.[36] Some states use this distribution process to reward plans for being low bidders or agreeing to additional service concessions, such as covering a broader territory. Other target assignees for certain types of plans may include, for example, "safety net" providers that the state may be interested in supporting or protecting.

Provider Network Issues

Most efforts to extend managed care to Medicaid beneficiaries have involved a concerted attempt to incorporate traditional providers of services to these populations into provider networks. The reasons for this are obvious because the preponderance of beneficiaries reside in areas with limited numbers of provider options. Major sources of care, such as community health centers, urban hospital outpatient programs, and indigenous community-based physicians, have provided the bulk of care both for Medicaid beneficiaries and for persons without insurance coverage, who are often the same individuals who move from periods of eligibility to ineligibility. PCCM programs typically recruit these providers to play major roles, and many prepaid health plans have incorporated them into their networks because of their location and established relationships. Inclusion of providers with strong ties to beneficiaries is an effective way to grow enrollment rapidly.

Some of these traditional providers have in fact sponsored their own health plans, although they often struggle to gain sufficient non-Medicaid members to meet the 75/25 federal mandate on maximum Medicaid membership. As more well-established commercial plans enter into the Medicaid market, new controversies have arisen about the inclusion of traditional, "safety net," or essential community providers in networks and the terms and payment rates they will receive. Past public policies have given special consideration to selected providers, such as health centers and hospitals with disproportionately high levels of uncompensated care. New contracting with private health plans may no longer perpetu-

ate such considerations, however, and this clearly places these providers in jeopardy. Policymakers will be drawn into these issues because the demise of many of these providers could create serious access problems for persons without any coverage.

A final issue that is sure to grow in importance as managed care is extended to non-AFDC populations, such as persons with chronic mental illness and developmental or physical disabilities, is how well conventional prepaid health plans or PCCM models can serve these beneficiaries. Some states permit specialists to qualify as PCCM providers for people with disabilities. Others make enrollment by special need beneficiaries voluntary rather than mandatory. In others, PCCM appears to avoid confrontations by liberally authorizing contacts with specialty providers. Special carve-out programs have been commonly used for the mentally ill in many instances; sometimes these are carved out by the state or, in other instances, by the health plans that subcontract for managed behavioral and mental health care. Plans have had limited experience with people with chronic illness or substantial disabilities, so that their existing networks and other systems may be inadequate to serve them.[37] Whether plans can and will augment their operations to expand their capacity or whether special subplans built around traditional specialty providers will arise remains to be seen.

Limitations on Physician Risk

In 1996, the Office of the Inspector General of the Department of Health and Human Services issued final regulations placing limitations on the amount of risk a health plan may put a physician at in a Medicare or Medicaid program. These new regulations effectively limit the amount of risk to 25 percent, and place additional requirements on the health plan regarding stop-loss insurance and member surveys. The reader is referred to Chapter 9 for a discussion of these new regulations.

Delivery and Utilization Management Systems

Designing delivery and utilization management systems for the Medicaid product line is challenging for plans whose membership has come from employed individuals and their dependents. Medicaid beneficiaries typically require supportive services to enable them to overcome access barriers to care, including transportation and community-based outreach and other social service efforts. Financial, safety/security, and other impediments to obtaining services on a timely basis require plans to adopt active interventions to deliver care in nontraditional locations, sometimes with diversely skilled personnel. High rates of teen pregnancy and other preventable conditions among eligible members place additional demands on HMOs that believe early intervention, health promotion, and preventive services are crucial elements of successful managed care plans.

Promoting more discreet and appropriate use of high-cost services such as emergency departments is a major goal of most plans and PCCM programs. Because hospitals are reluctant to deny care and because beneficiaries do not have cost-sharing responsibilities, hospitals frequently feel that plans and PCCM models do not do enough to reduce unneeded use despite the widespread evidence of reduced emergency department use in these programs.[38] Some plans have developed nurse call systems for off-hour coverage; others may penalize physician compensation for inappropriately authorized care. Many observers believe, however, that the availability of a bona fide primary care provider, in time, should wean most beneficiaries off the emergency department toward a legitimate medical home.

Member Education and Satisfaction

The emergency department issue also illustrates another area in which Medicaid-serving plans report added challenges: member educa-

tion. For persons without prior managed care experience, the structure and operations of organized delivery systems can be confusing and distressing. Obtaining care on a planned, regimented basis may be new for those low-income persons who have sought care on an episodic basis from as-available providers. Also, they may have lingual or educational disadvantages to overcome to access care. Orientation programs for new members are seen as crucial, as is ready access to culturally sensitive customer relations and provider personnel. Well-established commercial plans frequently find the need to hire additional multicultural and multilingual staff and to develop targeted programs to adapt their operations to serve this new customer base.

Relatively little is known about the enrollment and disenrollment patterns of Medicaid beneficiaries in managed care arrangements, especially in mandatory enrollment programs. Few states have systematically collected data on this, and many plans do not separate information about Medicaid from other enrollment/disenrollment data. The high level of involuntary disenrollment due to loss of eligibility makes it important to isolate and explore the reasons for voluntary disenrollment among Medicaid health plan members. Studies of satisfaction have typically found that Medicaid members are generally satisfied, but an important question for plans to examine in the future will be how Medicaid and commercial plan members may be similar and/or different in their levels of satisfaction. As plans are asked to enroll beneficiaries with higher or multiple needs, tracking satisfaction among such subgroups will be a focus for state purchaser and advocacy groups.

Quality Assurance/Improvement

As with other buyers of managed care, Medicaid has struggled with how to promote accountability and continuous improvement among its managed care contractors. Ironically, quality in the PCCM models has received little attention, in part because of the minimal changes these models make in the traditional fee-for-service delivery systems despite the potential barrier to care that the gatekeeper represents. Most quality concerns have focused on contracting with prepaid health plans because of the concern that the incentives may produce underserving and that the lack of financial resources of Medicaid beneficiaries impedes their ability to go out of network to get care, as is assumed to be possible among HMO members in the employed sector.

The HCFA has promoted the Quality Assurance Reform Initiative as a set of standards and policies for states to adopt and follow in their contracting with health plans. These standards require plans to have established quality improvement programs that systematically address problems that are particularly endemic to Medicaid eligibles and state Medicaid agencies to conduct oversight of these programs. In addition, states are required to have an external quality review organization conduct periodic audits of quality improvement efforts at the plan level. Some states are now exploring regional quality review organizations using the model established by Tennessee, where the organization is a contractor of the state that oversees the quality of care in HMOs. A regional quality review organization concept would establish an entity capable of conducting clinical assessments with proven methodologies to make sound comparisons of care between fee-for-service providers and HMOs and among HMOs. The regional feature would allow states to share costs and to make state-to-state managed care program comparisons using identical assessment methodologies.

A related development has been the addition of several new performance indicators in the Health Plan Employer Data Information Set (see Chapter 28) that are intended to produce uniform measures that are particularly pertinent to Medicaid beneficiaries, including stage of pregnancy at time of enrollment, cultural diversity of membership, and children's access to primary care providers. The previously discussed concerns with intermittent eligibility are particularly problematic in computing meaningful perform-

ance rates for plans serving Medicaid enrollees. In addition, discontinuity in enrollment makes it difficult to attribute accountability to a plan for effects on the health outcomes of Medicaid members.

Clearly, however, a number of states acting as aggressive purchasers are pushing plans both to report more detailed data and to demonstrate more convincingly the effects that they have on the well-being of Medicaid members. Some states are now demanding that plans submit detailed encounter level data to permit the state to compare HMO enrollee experience with non-HMO beneficiary fee-for-service experience.[39] Once again, this parallels the same types of pressures that health plans are facing from private purchasers seeking demonstrated value for their money.

Information System Sophistication and Infrastructure

Undergirding the performance of virtually all these operational functions is the presumption that states will have the data and data management capacity to make informed programmatic decisions. Rate setting and refinement, contract monitoring, eligibility and enrollment tracking, service cost and use information, member experience assessment, and evaluation of evidence of quality performance and improvement all require a systematic and sustained investment in flexible information systems. The dramatic shift from passive payer to active purchaser and sponsor has compelled state agencies and their contractors to make a major investment in these systems, without which states will fail to exploit the opportunities available to them in a buyer's market.

Some states have already made major investments in this area and are ably transitioning to this new-found status as megabuyer. Others are likely to struggle through the process of assembling the components of a bona fide managed care initiative but will fail to invest adequately in the crucial "control panel" that a sophisticated information system represents. Still other states will probably conclude that subcontracting many of these functions will be a sensible approach, one that can permit them to maintain control but not have to devote limited staff and other resources to carrying out these functions directly. The experience from Arizona suggests that an aggressive purchasing strategy may contribute to higher administrative costs, but these costs can be more than offset by greater reductions in service expenditures.[40]

FUTURE TRENDS

Major changes in Medicaid will come with the shifting of far greater administrative flexibility in return for a slowing in the rate of growth in federal support for the program. These changes will profoundly affect the extent to which states will rely on managed care models for their beneficiary groups.

Greater Variability among and within States

Approaches to adopting managed care in Medicaid programs have varied significantly among states subject to the general requirements imposed by the HCFA through the waiver granting process. The demise of much of the federal oversight role will permit states to exercise greater flexibility, resulting in less uniformity from state to state and even within states. Contracting strategies may become more focused, possibly using only a sole source in some locales, and beneficiaries may no longer have a choice of plans. The selection of risk-bearing contractors may not be limited only to established managed care organizations. Plans may also serve only Medicaid beneficiaries because the 75/25 rule will no longer exist. Relaxing these and other traditional requirements may make it possible for states to promote innovation and experimentation, but it will also make it challenging for existing plans to anticipate and respond to state strategies. For beneficiaries, it is not clear how strong state commitment to consumer protection will be.

Prepaid Managed Care Everywhere

An unprecedented cap on growth of federal financial support for Medicaid would send states a powerful and unequivocal message: Reduce the growth rate of Medicaid spending to the capped rate, or contribute more state dollars to finance the program. For many states this will mean a fierce commitment to fixing the growth rate for as much of the program as possible. One way to achieve this, in principle, is to enroll beneficiaries in prepaid managed care arrangements where future rates of growth in capitation payments are negotiated and thus fully predictable. Traditional fee-for-service PCCM models cannot provide this guarantee. As a result, it is likely that prepaid arrangements will be pursued nearly across the board for all beneficiary groups and in all locations within a state. This pressure will push managed care initiatives faster and further than they have previously gone in most states, with the exception of Arizona.

Mainstreaming versus Special Plans and Models

The frenzied pursuit of risk-bearing contractors with which to enroll beneficiaries will raise several challenges. Chief among them will be the extent to which state agencies attempt to achieve enrollment of beneficiaries in established, commercial HMOs that have a broad base of membership. Such arrangements offer the opportunity to mainstream beneficiaries in plans that serve a broad spectrum of members and have recruited into their networks those providers that have traditionally served persons covered by Medicaid. Other states may choose to contract with plans with limited or no commercial membership either because the managed care market is underdeveloped, such as in Tennessee, or because they may wish to give special opportunities to traditional "safety net" providers to develop targeted managed care programs for low-income persons, such as in California. This same issue will be played out for persons with special needs, with whom conventional

HMOs have had little experience, and for the specialty providers serving these groups, which have had limited exposure to managed care. Moving into uncharted territory will be trying for all parties concerned.

Vulnerable Populations and Endangered Providers

As managed care moves from an alternative to a mainstream delivery system status in Medicaid, its fitness for Medicaid's distinct beneficiary and provider constituencies will be tested. As noted above, some of these concerns relate to whether states aspire to and can achieve mainstreaming of beneficiaries in conventional plans. It also relates to whether the distinct character of a public "safety net" program such as Medicaid that serves populations with complex, chronic needs for multiple social and sociomedical services is compatible with the traditional medical model of plans serving mostly healthy persons.

It is also instructive to recognize that Medicaid's methods of payments to its core providers of care have become a means to cross-subsidize care for persons without coverage who rely on these same providers. Managed care contracting for Medicaid beneficiaries profoundly threatens this arrangement because it privatizes the decisions about network inclusion and methods of provider payments. Providers that serve large numbers of uninsured may not be incorporated into networks, or, if they are, payment arrangements negotiated with plans may not provide sufficient resources to support the delivery of uncompensated care. Consequently, many "safety net" providers will become genuinely endangered species as states rush into managed care arrangements. The topic of community health centers and managed care is discussed further in Chapter 16.

Public–Private Purchaser Convergence

Aligning Medicaid's purchasing posture toward managed care with what is occurring in the private sector and elsewhere in the public sector has considerable appeal, despite the caveats raised above. Some states, such as Massachusetts and Minnesota, participate actively in cross-sector purchaser alliances and initiatives, thereby adding their lives as additional leverage in health plan–buyer negotiations. Areas such as quality improvement and consumer information are especially well served when reporting requirements can be conformed across several major purchasers. Plans can develop uniform reporting mechanisms, and buyers can obtain comparable data across plans and across buyers to assess performance and promote improvement. Greater flexibility in a block grant environment should further contribute to these developments because some states will align purchasing efforts across all public programs for which they are responsible, and the step to conform their actions with those of private buyers becomes a natural one. Nevertheless, it will be important to track how private purchasers respond to what is likely to be growing pressure on plans to cross-subsidize their Medicaid product from the private customers or even from state employee contracts.

Sustainable Profitability of the Medicaid Product Line

The new era of state flexibility and reduced federal roles does present an area of considerable uncertainty and concern for managed care plans that contrasts with the otherwise bright prospects. It is not clear whether rates paid by states to enroll Medicaid beneficiaries will be sufficient, especially in future years, when the rate of program expenditure increases will flatten dramatically. Plans are legitimately anxious about this, in part because of the history of low payments in the fee-for-service Medicaid program and declining political support for public programs.

Plans are currently prepared to accept Medicaid rates apparently because they believe they can reduce utilization to outperform capitation payments; or because the additional lives that

Medicaid enrollment brings them produce additional leverage that they can use in provider negotiations, or because states have made enrolling Medicaid beneficiaries a precondition to serving other publicly sponsored groups, such as state employees. Plans also have realized, however, that states may refuse to grant increases or even may demand rollbacks in rates, and plans will have to live within budget constraints in future years. This strategy is even more likely to arise if states attempt to expand or maintain the number of persons eligible for Medicaid while they face declining federal support. There will be a level below which credible plans cannot agree to go if they are to serve enrolled populations. What this actual threshold level is cannot be predicted but will have to be discovered mutually by plans and states.

CONCLUSION

Medicaid has witnessed the same kind of transformation in its financing and delivery systems as the private sector has witnessed, despite a somewhat slower pace of transition. The pace has been modulated in part because of distinct features of a public program, its core providers, and its beneficiary populations. In addition, because Medicaid is a national program, the rate of change has varied dramatically as a result of local market conditions and developments. Current activity has taken on a accelerated pace as both purchasers and health plans are successfully overcoming many obstacles to and compunctions about contracting with one another to meet beneficiary needs.

Far greater change looms on the horizon, however, given the fundamental restructuring of the federal–state partnership on which Medicaid has been based. This restructuring will impel states to move to managed care more quickly and more inclusively, bringing managed care arrangements to many subpopulations that have not previously been exposed to managed care. The uncertainty is likely to intensify in future years as financial support for the program becomes more stressed and states face hard choices about populations and services to cover. Expanded managed care has considerable promise for state Medicaid agencies and for the beneficiaries for whom they provide coverage. For managed care plans, these developments represent both great opportunities and large risks.

REFERENCES AND NOTES

1. Health Care Financing Administration (HCFA), *Medicaid Managed Care Enrollment Report* (Baltimore, Md.: HCFA, 1995).

2. R. Stevens and R. Stevens, *Welfare Medicine in America* (New York, N.Y.: Free Press, 1974).

3. D. Freund and R. Hurley, Medicaid Managed Care: Lessons for Health Reform, *Annual Review of Public Health* 16 (1995): 473–496.

4. D. Chavin and A. Treseder, California's Prepaid Health Plans, *Hastings Law Journal* 28 (1977): 685–760.

5. H. Luft, *Health Maintenance Organizations: Dimensions of Performance* (New York, N.Y.: Basic Books, 1981).

6. D. Freund and R. Hurley, Medicaid Managed Care: Selected Issues in Program Origins, Design, and Research, *Annual Review of Public Health* 8 (1987): 137–164.

7. Freund and Hurley, Medicaid Managed Care: Lessons for Health Reform.

8. General Accounting Office (GAO), *Arizona Medicaid: Competition among Managed Care Plans Lowers Program Costs* (Washington, D.C.: GAO, 1995).

9. N. McCall, et al., Medicaid Managed Care Cost Savings: The Arizona Experience, *Health Affairs* 2 (1994): 234–245.

10. General Accounting Office, *Arizona Medicaid.*

11. General Accounting Office, *Arizona Medicaid.*

12. Kaiser Commission on the Future of Medicaid, *The Medicaid Cost Explosion* (Washington, D.C.: Kaiser Commission, 1993).

13. S. Rosenbaum and J. Darnell, *Medicaid Statewide Demonstrations: Overview of Approved and Proposed Section 1115 Proposals, Policy Brief* (Washington, D.C.: Kaiser Commission on the Future of Medicaid, 1994).

14. R. Kronick, et al., Making Risk Adjustment Work for Everyone, *Inquiry* 32 (1995): 41–55.

15. R. Hurley, et al., *Medicaid Managed Care: Lessons for Policy and Program Design* (Ann Arbor, Mich.: Health Administration Press, 1993).

16. Freund and Hurley, Medicaid Managed Care: Selected Issues.

17. S. Moore, Cost Containment through Risk-Sharing by Primary Care Physicians, *New England Journal of Medicine* 300 (1979): 1359–1362.

18. D. Freund, *Medicaid Reform: Four Studies of Case Management* (Washington, D.C.: American Enterprise Institute, 1984).

19. Hurley, et al., *Medicaid Managed Care.*

20. Hurley, et al., *Medicaid Managed Care.*

21. Kaiser Commission on the Future of Medicaid, *Medicaid Managed Care: Lessons from the Literature* (Washington, D.C.: Kaiser Commission, 1995).

22. National Academy for State Health Policy, *Medicaid Managed Care: Guide for the State*, 2d ed. (Portland, Me.: National Academy for State Health Policy, 1995).

23. Freund and Hurley, Medicaid Managed Care: Lessons for Health Reform.

24. J. Christianson, et al., Utah's Prepaid Mental Health Plan: The First Year, *Health Affairs* 14 (1995): 160–172.

25. J. Callahan, et al., Mental Health/Substance Abuse Treatment in Managed Care: The Massachusetts Medicaid Experience, *Health Affairs* 14 (1995): 173–184.

26. Hurley, et al., *Medicaid Managed Care.*

27. Kaiser Commission, *Medicaid Managed Care.*

28. McCall, et al., Medicaid Managed Care Cost Savings.

29. Callahan, et al., Mental Health/Substance Abuse Treatment.

30. Hurley, et al., *Medicaid Managed Care.*

31. R. Hurley, et al., Rollover Effects in Gatekeeper Programs: Cushioning the Impact of Restricted Choice, *Inquiry* 28 (1991): 375–384.

32. M. Gold, et al., *Managed Care and Low-Income Populations: A Case Study in Tennessee* (Washington, D.C.: Mathematica Policy Research, 1995).

33. Kaiser Commission, *Medicaid Managed Care.*

34. National Academy for State Health Policy, *Medicaid Managed Care.*

35. National Academy for State Health Policy, *Medicaid Managed Care.*

36. R. Hurley and D. Freund, Determinants of Provider Selection or Assignment in a Mandatory Case Management Program and Their Implications for Utilization, *Inquiry* 25 (1988): 402–410.

37. S. Tanenbaum and R. Hurley, The Disabled and the Managed Care Frenzy: A Cautionary Note, *Health Affairs* 14 (1996): 213–219.

38. Hurley, et al., *Medicaid Managed Care.*

39. K. Piper and P. Bartels, Medicaid Primary Care: HMOs or Fee-ForService?, *Public Welfare* (Spring 1995): 18–21.

40. General Accounting Office, *Arizona Medicaid.*

SUGGESTED READINGS

Crandal, P. and Troutman, J. 1994. Member Education: Communicating to Diverse Membership Populations–Reaching into the Medicaid Population. Public Relations in Managed Care: Communicating in an Era of Health Care Consumerism, Section 13, 9 pp. San Francisco, Calif., 17–18 March. Washington, D.C.: American Association of Health Plans (formerly GHAA).

Freund, D. 1984. *Medicaid Reform: Four Studies of Case Management.* Washington, D.C. American Enterprise Institute.

Hurley, R., D. Freund, and J. Paul, 1993. *Medicaid Managed Care: Lessons for Policy and Program Design.* Ann Arbor, MI: Health Administration Press.

Health Care Financing Administration, Medicaid Bureau. 1992. *A Health Care Quality Improvement System for Medicaid Coordinated Care: A Product of the National Quality Assurance Reform Initiative.* McLean, Va.: U.S. Department of Health and Human Services National Clearinghouse of Primary Care Information.

Health Care Financing Administration. 1995. *Medicaid Managed Care Enrollment Report.* Baltimore: HCFA.

Kaiser Commission on the Future of Medicaid. 1995. *Medicaid Managed Care: Lessons from the Literature.* Washington, D.C.

McCall, Nelda, et al. 1994. Medicaid Managed Care Cost Savings: The Arizona Experience, *Health Affairs*, 2: 234–245.

Monfiletto, E. 1994. Assimiliating the Medicaid Population. *Medical Interface* 7(7): 59–62.

National Academy for State Health Policy. 1995. *Medicaid Managed Care: Guide for the States*, 2nd ed. Portland, ME: National Academy.

Chapter 49

CHAMPUS and the Department of Defense Managed Care Programs

John F. Boyer and Larry Sobel

The military health services system (MHSS) is a large and complex health care system designed to provide, and to maintain readiness to provide, medical services and support to the armed forces during military operations and to provide medical services and support to members of the armed forces, their dependents, and others entitled to Department of Defense (DOD) medical care. To accomplish these missions, the Army, Navy, and Air Force operate more than

John F. Boyer is a retired Navy Nurse Corps officer formerly assigned as Acting Principal Director of Health Services Financing in the Office of the Assistant Secretary of Defense (Health Affairs). In this capacity, he served as the principal adviser to the Deputy Assistant Secretary of Defense for Health Services Financing in both policy and operational matters related to the delivery and financing of health care. He is currently Vice President for Strategic Planning and Contract Administration at MAXIMUS, Inc., a major health and human services corporation headquartered in McLean, Virginia. He holds master's degrees in both nursing and management as well as a doctoral degree in public administration and policy analysis.

Larry Sobel is currently Deputy Director of Managed Care Operations and a senior health care program analyst for the Deputy Assistant Secretary of Defense for Health Services Financing in matters related to managed care operations. He has more than 18 years of experience in managed health care. He holds a bachelor's degree from Harvard College and a doctoral degree in jurisprudence from Harvard Law School.

The views expressed within the chapter are those of the authors and not necessarily those of the Department of Defense.

A portion of the chapter was adapted from J. Boyer, et al., An Overview of Managed Health Care in the Department of Defense, *Medical Interface* 4 (1991): pp. 15–22. Copyright © 1991 Medicom International, Inc.

500 medical and dental treatment facilities, including 127 hospitals, located throughout the world. To augment this direct health care system, the DOD also offers care indirectly to certain beneficiaries via the Civilian Health and Medical Program of the Uniformed Services (CHAMPUS). This chapter focuses on a discussion of CHAMPUS, both the traditional medical benefits program and its managed care demonstration programs, and on TRICARE, the DOD's recently implemented, systemwide managed care initiative.

CHAMPUS is a program of medical benefits provided by the U.S. government under public law.[1] Specified categories of individuals qualify for these benefits by virtue of their relationship to one of the seven uniformed services (Army, Navy, Air Force, Marine Corps, Coast Guard, Commissioned Corps of the U.S. Public Health Service, and Commissioned Corps of the National Oceanic and Atmospheric Administration). In general, persons eligible for CHAMPUS benefits include families of active duty service members; retired service members, their spouses, and their unmarried children; survivors of active duty or retired service members; and certain former spouses of members of the military. Active duty members of the services are not covered by CHAMPUS, nor, in general, are retirees, survivors, or family members of a retiree if they are eligible for Medicare. As of 1995, there were approximately 6 million CHAMPUS-eligible beneficiaries, and the annual program budget was approximately $3.5 billion.[2,3]

LEGAL AUTHORITY AND RESPONSIBILITIES

Title X, Chapter 55 of the U.S. Code authorizes the Secretary of Defense, the Secretary of Health and Human Services, and the Secretary of Transportation jointly to prescribe regulations for the administration of CHAMPUS. Title X, Chapter 55 also authorizes the Secretary of Defense to administer CHAMPUS for the Army, Navy, Air Force, and Marine Corps under DOD jurisdiction; the Secretary of Transportation to administer CHAMPUS for the Coast Guard (when the Coast Guard is not operating as a service in the Navy); and the Secretary of Health and Human Services to administer CHAMPUS for the Commissioned Corps of the U.S. Public Health Service and the National Oceanic and Atmospheric Administration.

The Secretary of Defense has delegated authority to the Assistant Secretary of Defense for health affairs [ASD(HA)] to provide policy guidance, management control, and coordination for CHAMPUS.[4] The Secretary of Health and Human Services has delegated authority to the Assistant Secretary for Health, Department of Health and Human Services (DHHS) to consult with the Secretary of Defense or a designee and to approve and issue joint regulations implementing Title X, Chapter 55.[5] The Secretary of Transportation has delegated authority to the Commandant of the U.S. Coast Guard, to consult with the Secretary of Defense or a designee and to approve and issue joint regulations implementing 10 U.S. Code, Chapter 55.[6]

In 1974, the Office of CHAMPUS (OCHAMPUS) was established as a field activity under the policy guidance and direction of the ASD(HA) to supervise and administer the program.[7] Today, within the Office of the ASD(HA), OCHAMPUS falls under the purview of the Deputy Assistant Secretary of Defense (health services financing). In carrying out one of the most important responsibilities of the agency, the director of OCHAMPUS develops for issuance (subject to approval by the administering secretaries) such policies or regulations as required to administer and manage CHAMPUS effectively.

MEDICAL BENEFITS PROGRAM

Although similar in structure to an insurance program in many respects, CHAMPUS is not an insurance program. That is, CHAMPUS does not involve a contract guaranteeing the indemnification of an insured party against a specified loss in return for a paid premium. Furthermore, CHAMPUS is not subject to state regulatory bodies or agencies that control the insurance industry generally. Instead, CHAMPUS is a program whereby the federal government pays for certain medically or psychologically necessary services provided by an authorized health care professional to eligible beneficiaries. Specifics about program eligibility, basic program benefits, provider authorization, claims processing, and other program features are detailed in a DOD regulation.[8]

PROGRAM FUNDS

The funds used by CHAMPUS are furnished by Congress through the annual appropriations acts to the DOD and the DHHS. These funds are further disbursed by agents of the government under contracts negotiated in accordance with provisions of the Federal Acquisition Regulation by the director of OCHAMPUS.[9] These agents, commonly referred to as fiscal intermediaries (FIs), receive claims against CHAMPUS and adjudicate the claims in accordance with administrative procedures and instructions prescribed in their contracts. The funds expended for CHAMPUS benefits are federal funds provided to CHAMPUS FIs solely to pay CHAMPUS claims and are not a part of, or obtained from, the CHAMPUS FIs' funds related to other programs or insurance coverage. CHAMPUS FIs are reimbursed for the adjudication and payment of CHAMPUS claims at a rate (generally a fixed price) prescribed in their contracts.

CHAMPUS BENEFIT COVERAGE

Benefits covered under CHAMPUS roughly parallel those of high-option programs available under other public and major private health care plans. CHAMPUS coverage includes most inpatient and outpatient health services, a substantial portion of physician and hospital charges, medical supplies and equipment, and mental health services. Because CHAMPUS beneficiaries pay no premiums, and because in recent years other health benefit programs have instituted increasingly greater limits on benefits, CHAMPUS has become one of the most generous health benefit plans available in the United States today. Not surprising, then, during the late 1980s CHAMPUS experienced substantial growth in program costs and utilization. Indeed, between 1985 and 1990, both CHAMPUS expenditures and CHAMPUS claims more than doubled.[10]

CHAMPUS MANAGED CARE DEMONSTRATIONS

Faced with such statistics, the DOD implemented a number of demonstration programs to test the feasibility of employing certain managed care mechanisms and to explore their impact on the delivery of health care services under CHAMPUS. The demonstrations, which varied in design and scope, tested cost and utilization management controls in a variety of health care settings. The projects ranged in size from small-scale demonstrations at a single site for a given population to systemwide implementation of managed care mechanisms. Among the principal demonstration programs were the following:

- the CHAMPUS reform initiative (CRI)
- the New Orleans managed care demonstration
- several catchment area management (CAM) projects
- the Southeast region preferred provider organization (PPO) demonstration
- the contracted provider arrangement (CPA) in Norfolk

The CRI

The CRI was a demonstration program designed to improve CHAMPUS through competitive selection of a financially at-risk contractor to underwrite delivery of CHAMPUS health care services. The primary goal of the CRI was to improve the program's quality and cost effectiveness through the application of proven managed health care techniques. In February 1988, in accordance with requirements of the Federal Acquisition Regulation, the DOD awarded a contract to Foundation Health Corporation to conduct the demonstration in California and Hawaii. At the beginning of the demonstration, approximately 800,000 CHAMPUS-eligible beneficiaries lived within the demonstration area, or about 14 percent of the total number of program eligibles. Foundation Health began delivery of health care services in August 1988, subcontracting with three health plans and offering two alternatives to the standard CHAMPUS program: CHAMPUS Prime and CHAMPUS Extra.

In CHAMPUS Prime, which was similar to a health maintenance organization (HMO), beneficiaries enrolled, selected a primary care provider, and were required to obtain all their care through that provider. The designated provider was on staff in one of the military treatment facilities (MTFs) located in the demonstration area or was a participating civilian provider. Enrollees were also referred to participating specialists as needed. Beneficiaries paid only a small cost for each office visit or hospital day, and little paperwork was involved.

CHAMPUS Extra was essentially a PPO plan. Beneficiaries sought care from either a network provider or a nonnetwork provider; if they used the former, however, their portion of the allowable fee for the service was reduced by 5 percent on an already discounted provider fee. The beneficiaries' out-of-pocket costs, therefore, were reduced, although they paid somewhat more than CHAMPUS Prime enrollees.

From numerous surveys conducted by independent, objective investigators, satisfaction with CRI in general, as well as with the medical care received therein, was high among all beneficiary categories. The most popular features of CHAMPUS Prime among beneficiaries included the small copayments, reduced paperwork, and reasonable visit fees. From the providers' perspective, the patient referral system and the professionalism shown in the program's utilization and quality management functions were most commonly cited.

In addition to features common to many managed care plans, the CRI also included several innovative features that contributed to its successes. CHAMPUS service centers, established in all military hospitals and clinics in the demonstration area, employed registered nurses as "health care finders" to coordinate all patient referrals. These personnel managed more than 10,000 referrals per month.

Another successful feature of CRI was called resource sharing, which involved the establishment of agreements between the CRI contractor and MTFs. Under these agreements, the contractor provided personnel, supplies, or equipment to an MTF to enhance patient care capability. By 1992, more than 200 resource-sharing agreements had been executed. Enhancing the capacity of MTFs by selectively increasing staff and material resources, resource sharing enabled facilities to operate more productively and therefore proved to be a valuable component of the CRI demonstration.

The CRI demonstration ended in February 1994 when a follow-on managed care contract for California and Hawaii began operations.

New Orleans Managed Care Demonstration

Congressionally directed, the New Orleans demonstration project was designed to test the application of managed care techniques in an area without an inpatient MTF. After a competitive procurement, a contract was awarded in June 1991 to Foundation Health Federal Services, a wholly owned subsidiary of Foundation Health Corporation. Health services delivery under the demonstration began on 1 December 1991. The design features of the project were similar to those of the CRI: a risk-based contract with a triple option (i.e., HMO, PPO, and standard CHAMPUS), provider networks, and comprehensive utilization management and quality assurance programs.

CAM Demonstration Projects

CAM projects were initiated to pursue alternative management techniques within CHAMPUS in an effort to contain costs at the local level. Under CAM, a military hospital commander had responsibility for managing the delivery and financing of health care services for the entire beneficiary population residing in the hospital's catchment area (an area surrounding the facility, specified by ZIP codes, with a radius of roughly 40 miles).

In these projects, CHAMPUS funds were allocated to the hospital commander, who was then responsible for distributing the combined CHAMPUS and direct care system funds appropriately for all services within the catchment area. Although funding was limited to that which would have been spent in the absence of a demonstration, commanders were given authority to pursue alternative health care delivery methods that were not generally possible outside the demonstration area.

Within the guidelines of demonstration authority and the overall design approach established by the DOD, the Army, Navy, and Air Force implemented separate demonstration projects. The first CAM site became operational in June 1989, and ultimately the program became operational at five demonstration sites. At each site, attempts were made to maximize the opportunities for innovation available through CAM to take advantage of local geographic and health care environments. Therefore, although there was a central CAM design, significant operational differences, both interservice and intraservice, existed among CAM sites.

Among the design features common to all CAM projects were a health care finder service, enhanced claims management, enrollment, and modifications to the standard CHAMPUS benefit package. All demonstrations required enrollment for a minimum of 1 year as a condition of CAM participation. Enrollment was limited to CHAMPUS-eligible beneficiaries within the catchment area, with the family being the unit of enrollment. All CAM demonstrations entailed reduced or eliminated deductibles and/or copayments, and for some inpatient and outpatient services charges were discounted.

All the CAM designs also included both utilization management and quality assurance features. Preadmission review of inpatient care and retrospective case review were the common mechanisms applied. Some sites also conducted case management of either all patients or those with selected high-cost diagnoses. All contracted civilian providers were subject to the same utilization and quality management procedures as military providers.

Claims processing functions under CAM were simplified to relieve beneficiaries of the paperwork of claims preparation and submission. Although all the claims processing functions were similar in concept, implementation of simplified claims processing functions was site specific, depending on demonstration design and FI requirements and capabilities.

The Southeast Region PPO

The Southeast region demonstration was undertaken as a response to congressional direction to modify a regional CHAMPUS FI contract to implement managed care techniques. The primary goals were to reduce CHAMPUS cost growth and to improve beneficiary satisfaction by organizing an accessible, cost-efficient network of health care providers.

In July 1990, an FI contract was awarded to Wisconsin Physicians Service. Under the contract, a PPO was established in a five-state Southeast region of the United States to offer beneficiaries a low-cost alternative to standard CHAMPUS. To develop PPO networks and to perform utilization management, Wisconsin Physicians Services subcontracted with a national firm having expertise in those areas. In the

design of the demonstration, participants retained freedom of choice and did not enroll, but they had several incentives to use preferred providers. In particular, there were fee discounts, a 5 percent reduction in coinsurance rates, and direct claims filing by providers. The program, which covered nearly 900,000 beneficiaries in 20 military hospital catchment areas, was viewed as a support contract for individual hospital commanders in establishing relationships with civilian providers.

Additional features of the demonstration included a quality assessment program and contractor personnel on site in the military hospitals. A key component, as in the CRI and CAM demonstration projects, was that the military hospital was considered the most preferred provider. Furthermore, civilian networks were seen as complementing, rather than competing with, the MTFs.

Throughout the demonstration, where PPOs were operational, management reports were provided to military hospital commanders on all aspects of the networks, including percentage of network use by beneficiaries, type and cost of services delivered, utilization review activity, savings from provider discounts, and estimates of savings from utilization review.

CPA-Norfolk

During the 1980s, CHAMPUS costs for mental health care represented a substantial portion of the CHAMPUS budget. Before 1986, the Tidewater area of Virginia presented a particular concern because per capita costs for mental health care were found to be twice the national average. As a result of this finding, the CPA-Norfolk demonstration project was initiated to test the effects of cost and utilization controls on the delivery of mental health services in this area. The design of the demonstration included an at-risk, fixed-price contract for all necessary mental health services; case management as a prerequisite for payment; a contracted provider network with negotiated rates; claims processing and administrative functions performed by the contractor; a partial hospitalization benefit; and independent quality monitoring.

After a competitive procurement process, the DOD contracted with Sentara First Step for delivery of services, and operations commenced on 1 October 1986. Sentara First Step implemented all features of the design, including intake and case management processes, a network of preferred providers with significantly reduced rates, and an internal quality assurance program. For government monitoring purposes, an external quality monitoring effort was undertaken through a separate contract with SysteMetrics/McGraw-Hill. Delivery of services by Sentara First Step under the demonstration ceased on 31 March 1989, and after another procurement effort a follow-on contract was awarded to First Hospital Corporation–Options (FHC-Options).

In the follow-on contract, FHC-Options was responsible for all mental health care provided to CHAMPUS beneficiaries in the geographic region of the demonstration. Utilization management of all inpatient care as well as all outpatient care beyond the 23rd visit was required. The contractor was allowed to reduce or eliminate cost-sharing requirements as an inducement for beneficiaries to use those providers who joined the preferred provider network. All contracted providers were required to accept assignment on all claims and were not allowed to bill CHAMPUS beneficiaries for charges above the allowable amount. Additionally, all noncontracted providers were required to comply with utilization management activities at least 95 percent of the time or risk losing certification as CHAMPUS-authorized providers for a period of 1 year.

THE TRICARE PROGRAM

In general, the demonstrations discussed above were successful in providing evidence that innovations in the delivery and financing of health care services can help in containing the rising costs of health care, at least in the short term. The demonstrations also showed that such approaches can have a positive effect on pro-

vider and beneficiary behavior and on maintaining or improving the quality of care delivered. Therefore, many features of the DOD demonstration projects have been incorporated into TRICARE, the DOD's recently implemented, systemwide managed care initiative.

The goal of TRICARE is to bring together the health care delivery systems of each of the military departments and CHAMPUS to use most efficiently the resources available to military medicine and to serve best its beneficiaries. Under TRICARE, the military service medical departments and MTF commanders will have the tools, authority, and flexibility needed to perform the health care/medical mission more effectively, and the DOD, in general, will be better able to accomplish its mission by improving beneficiary access to health care services, controlling health care costs, and ensuring quality care to all MHSS beneficiaries.

Like several of the demonstration projects, the TRICARE program includes a triple-option benefit structure:

1. TRICARE Prime, an enrolled, HMO-like option that offers the scope of coverage available under CHAMPUS plus additional preventive services, with no deductibles or claims filing requirements for beneficiaries and lower cost sharing

2. TRICARE Extra, a PPO option that does not require enrollment and offers low out-of-pocket costs for those beneficiaries who choose to obtain care from network providers

3. TRICARE Standard, which is the same as the current CHAMPUS benefit and cost-sharing structure

To implement TRICARE, the DOD has established 12 health service regions and a new administrative structure to oversee the delivery of health care. The regions are designated on a geographic basis, and each encompasses medical facilities from all three of the military services. Within each region, the commanding officer of a component tertiary medical center is designated as the region's lead agent. Lead agents are responsible for planning, coordinating, and monitoring all health care delivered throughout their region.

The linchpin of the delivery system will be a primary care manager: a specific primary care clinic, site, provider, or group of providers with which or with whom each enrolled beneficiary will establish and maintain a medical affiliation. Some differences in the delivery of care will occur geographically because of differences in the relative capacity of MTFs. That is, in some areas MTFs have the ability to deliver extensive primary and specialty care. In other locations, MTF commanders must rely upon civilian providers to deliver care not available within the facility. In still other areas, beneficiaries rely completely on civilian providers.

Because the TRICARE program is based largely on regionally decentralized execution, certain features of the program vary among locations. Many program features, however, will be uniform. When the program is fully operational, some of the features that will be the same or similar across all regions of the country include the following:

- *Incentives based upon enrollment status and network provider use*—Beneficiaries will have financial incentives to enroll in managed care plans and to use network providers. Such differentials are designed as incentives to use the system that better ensures high-quality care and low costs.
- *Primary care managers*—MTF commanders will have the flexibility to assign each enrolled beneficiary to, or to allow each beneficiary to choose, a primary care manager who will have overall responsibility for managing the care provided to the beneficiary and family.
- *Greater uniformity in scope of covered services*—To minimize beneficiary confusion, the services covered under TRICARE will be as uniform as possible.

- *Utilization management and quality assurance programs*—Refinement and expansion of existing utilization management and quality assurance policies throughout the MHSS will permit the DOD and the military service medical departments to ensure quality improvement and cost effectiveness of TRICARE within and among geographic regions.
- *Marketing strategies*—A critical responsibility of managers at all levels is to communicate all changes in the way health care is delivered and received in the TRICARE program to all those affected. An extensive education program for both beneficiaries and health care providers is being developed to inform participants of the phased transition from the traditional framework for health care delivery to TRICARE. Education will focus on informing beneficiaries of the options available in seeking health care and ensuring that beneficiaries understand how they can maintain and improve their own health status through family risk management, diet, exercise, and appropriate use of health services.

Although traditionally MTF commanders have managed only the service operation and maintenance funds for MTFs, under TRICARE commanders also will be responsible for managing the funds that pay CHAMPUS claims. Controlling both CHAMPUS and MTF operation and management funds will provide commanders the financial flexibility and authority to ensure that beneficiaries in their service areas receive the care they need.

Managed Care Support Contracts

In addition to providing new options for health care and a new regional structure, TRICARE expands upon the DOD's experience in using contracted providers in demonstration programs to the entire MHSS. Under TRICARE, seven managed care support contracts will be procured competitively for the 12 TRICARE regions (that is, every region will be supported by a contract, but some contracts will cover more than one region). Each contract will be awarded to a private sector firm to augment the care available within the direct care system in the region and to provide administrative support to the lead agent. The contracts, in general, will be for 5 years (1 base year plus 4 option years), and all are expected to be awarded by October 1996.

The TRICARE managed care support contracts are procured centrally by OCHAMPUS, within the Office of the ASD(HA). A standard request for proposals is employed in the procurements, augmented by any unique or region-specific requirements identified by the lead agent that go beyond the standard specifications. The contracts are bid on a competitive basis and are considered fixed-price, at-risk contracts. Only the administrative portion of the contract has a fixed price, however, the health care price is subject to adjustments on the basis of risk-sharing provisions in which the contractor and the government share losses or gains beyond certain levels. Adjustments can be based on factors such as inflation, MTF workload shifts, and beneficiary population changes. The risk-sharing and bid price adjustment features are intended to protect both the contractor and the government from large risks associated with these complex contracts.

Modified Capitation Approach

TRICARE, like other managed care programs, uses a capitation method to allocate health care funds. In the past, DOD medical facilities were funded on the basis of historical workload. Thus high levels of resource utilization were, in effect, rewarded with high budget allocations. In 1994, however, as part of the transition to TRICARE, the DOD adopted a modified capitation approach in which the ASD(HA) allocates some resources to the Services' medical departments on a per capita basis. Funding for medical support functions not related to the

size of the military force (e.g., air evacuation system) are not capitated.

Funding for operating and maintaining the direct care system and CHAMPUS is capitated using a fixed dollar amount for each beneficiary that the DOD estimates is using the MHSS. The military services' medical departments, in turn, pass the funds on to the individual MTFs using their own service-unique capitation methodologies. Each MTF commander is then held accountable for providing health services to a defined population for a fixed dollar amount per beneficiary. This approach is intended to remove incentives to prolong hospital stays, inappropriately increase the number of services provided, or otherwise provide more costly care than is medically appropriate.

Summary of the TRICARE Program

In sum, TRICARE represents a major reengineering of the way health care is managed in the MHSS. Significant components include an enrollment system, modified capitation, costsharing incentives, a system of primary care managers and health care networks, and comprehensive utilization management and quality assurance programs. Lead agents and MTF commanders will be aided by changes in how the delivery of care is organized and financed and by incentives that optimize MTF utilization. Because of the scope, magnitude, and complexity of the MHSS and the extensive nature of the reforms, TRICARE will be phased in over a 3-year period, with full implementation expected by May 1997.

COMPARISON WITH MEDICARE

Finally, it may be useful to compare the development of managed care under the Medicare and CHAMPUS programs. A significant difference in this development is that, after a brief demonstration period, the Medicare HMO risk program was implemented through permanent statutory and regulatory authorities (see Chapters 46 and 47 for a detailed discussion of Medicare managed care). In contrast, all the major CHAMPUS managed care programs were originally implemented under demonstration authority and, usually, through competitive procurements.[11] The CHAMPUS managed care demonstrations were quite varied, including a multibillion dollar, triple-option, risk-based program; a much smaller triple-option, risk-based program in an area without a military hospital; a five-state, dual-option, cost plus incentives reimbursement project; and five similar Service-designed managed care projects that are managed by MTF commanders at the local level. Only recently, with the implementation of TRICARE, has a permanent regulatory basis been developed for the DOD managed care programs.[12]

A second significant difference between the Medicare HMO risk program and the major DOD risk-based contracts is the reimbursement mechanism. Whereas Medicare HMOs are totally at risk for cost overruns in the enrolled program, there are adjustments in TRICARE in the fixed price paid to the managed care support contractor for circumstances outside contractor control (e.g., the workload in the MTF). Also, there is risk sharing (and sharing in savings) between the contractor and the DOD for cost overruns (and underruns) in the contract price. Additionally, each DOD managed care support contractor is currently at risk for the entire CHAMPUS population residing in the relevant health service region, not just those beneficiaries in the enrolled option. As a result, there are no issues of adverse selection or skimming with which to contend. In fact, it is in the contractor's best financial interest to have the individuals with the more severe health problems enroll in the more closely managed HMO option.

CONCLUSION

In addition to the usual and important functions of a primary care manager coordinating different types and levels of care, managed care in the MHSS includes the essential function of coordination between the military direct care system and the civilian health care system. Along with quality, cost, and access, integrating the CHAMPUS and direct care systems has been a focal point of CHAMPUS managed care demonstrations and will continue to be a major challenge as the DOD's TRICARE program is implemented nationwide.

REFERENCES AND NOTES

1. The Dependents Medical Care Act of 1956, P.L. 84-569, 70 Stat. 250, as amended by the Military Medical Benefits Amendments of 1966, P.L. 89-614, 80 Stat. 862, P.L. 98-94, 97 Stat. 614, codified as amended in 10 U.S.C., Chapter 55, Sections 1071–1106.

2. Defense Eligibility and Enrollment Reporting System, *Enrollment Statistics (Stat. 2) Report* (Monterey, Calif.: Defense Manpower Data Center, September 1995).

3. Department of Defense Fiscal Year 1996 Defense Health Program, amended President's budget, January 1995.

4. Department of Defense Directive 5136.1, Assistant Secretary of Defense (Health Affairs), 15 April 1991.

5. The Dependents Medical Care Act of 1956.

6. The Dependents Medical Care Act of 1956.

7. Department of Defense Directive 5105.46, Civilian Health and Medical Program of the Uniformed Services, 4 December 1976.

8. Department of Defense Regulation 6010.8-R, Civilian Health and Medical Program of the Uniformed Services (CHAMPUS), July 1991 (32 C.F.R., Part 199). Department of Defense components and other uniformed services may obtain copies of this regulation through their own publication channels. Other federal agencies and the general public may obtain copies from the U.S. Department of Commerce, National Technical Information Service, 5285 Port Royal Road, Springfield, VA 22161.

9. Federal Acquisition Regulation, 1 April 1984.

10. Department of Defense, Office of the Civilian Health and Medical Program of the Uniformed Services, *CHAMPUS Chartbook of Statistics* (Aurora, Colo.: Department of Defense; December 1985 and August 1990).

11. See, in general, 10 U.S.C., Chapter 55, Section 1092.

12. See the TRICARE Final Rule amending the CHAMPUS Regulation (Department of Defense 6010.8-R), *Federal Register* 60 (5 October 1995): 52078–52103.

Chapter 50

Health Maintenance Organizations in Rural Markets

Tracey Thompson Turner, Norman C. Payson, and Richard B. Salmon

The recent local and national focus on the ability of managed care to address the issue of rising health care costs in the United States has elevated the discussion beyond mere theory to the practicality of operating managed care plans in the numerous and diverse markets of our country.[1] The diversity of these markets is notable because it has been well established that a uniform national health care plan may not be practical as a result of the local nature of health care.[2] Research as well as anecdotal evidence

Tracey Thompson Turner is Director of Communications and Corporate Investor Relations for Healthsource, Inc., a national managed care company founded in 1985, with HMOs serving New England, the Midwest, and the Southeast. In this capacity she communicates the company's growth, development, and financial strategies to the company's many clients. Turner was responsible for developing the company's external communications functions including public and customer relations.

Norman C. Payson, M.D., is President and Chief Executive Officer of Healthsource, Inc. Dr. Payson has been involved in the HMO field since 1975, first as a practicing physician, then as senior executive of a large medical group. Dr. Payson's areas of expertise include HMO development and health care financing as well as quality assurance and utilization review. Payson is an adjunct professor of Medicine at the Dartmouth Medical School and is a frequent lecturer in employee benefits and managed care at Dartmouth's Amos Tuck School of Business Administration.

Richard B. Salmon, M.D., Ph.D., is Corporate Medical Director for Healthsource, Inc. In this capacity he is responsible for developing and implementing medical management policy for Healthsource. Dr. Salmon also serves as an adjunct assistant professor of Community and Family Medicine at the Dartmouth Medical School.

bear out this assertion. Studies have documented that physician practice patterns differ from one locale to another, that financing mechanisms may vary widely from place to place, and that the needs of populations can also differ depending upon where patients are located.[3] These differences have played a significant role in the development of health maintenance organizations (HMOs) in rural areas. Managed care plans have historically been absent in rural markets, in large part because of the different operational issues that these markets present compared with larger metropolitan areas.

Although it has been demonstrated and described in other chapters of this book how managed care is successful at reducing the unit cost of health care using a variety of methodologies, it has also been noted by some industry observers that the ultimate success of managed care depends on competition. The question of whether managed care and HMO development are viable in rural markets has been a growing source of debate. As managed competition gains ground as a solution to the health care crisis, whether HMOs can effectively reduce the unit cost of products and services to consumers becomes an important consideration. The debate centers on the demographics of rural areas, which tend to have fewer health care providers than metropolitan areas and, consequently, less competition. To address this debate, it is necessary to look at the factors that differentiate rural markets and to determine whether they create sufficient barriers to the development of successful managed care operations capable of reducing the cost of health care and adding value to rural health care systems.

HISTORIC, DEMOGRAPHIC, AND GEOGRAPHIC BARRIERS

It is necessary to begin the discussion of the feasibility of HMO development in rural areas with a definition of the term *rural*. The U.S. Census Bureau defines rural as a nonurbanized area or any area with fewer than 50,000 persons, and generally fewer than 1,000 persons, per square mile.[4] An article published in 1993 in the *New England Journal of Medicine* defines rural as a "sparsely populated area of the United States where providers have a natural monopoly."[5(p.148)] For the purpose of this discussion, we focus on the latter definition because it provides the greatest challenge to the theory that HMOs can be successfully developed in the less populated parts of our country.

One of the factors that has slowed the development of the rural HMO is geography. Rural markets tend to cover large geographic areas with the population broadly covering those areas. This phenomenon has two effects. First, HMO physician recruitment is more difficult. Rural areas tend to be less attractive markets for physicians, who are generally seeking large pools of patients from which to draw. This reduces the supply of physicians in rural markets, particularly for primary care.

Geographic expansiveness also adds to the hurdles that an HMO developer must address in building a comprehensive network of providers to market to employers and consumers. Thus, although employers in rural markets may be centrally located, their employee population rarely is (it is not uncommon for a rural employer to employ workers within a 50-mile or more radius of the worksite), creating the need for a rural HMO to build equally expansive networks of providers to attract members. Because successful rural HMO development is dependent upon an adequate critical mass to deliver the cost/benefit ratios needed to run an HMO enterprise

profitably, the most remote areas of our country have gone largely untouched by HMO development.

Some exceptions to this model can be seen in two unique areas that have successfully developed HMOs built around large regional physician group practices. These are the Geisinger health plan in western Pennsylvania and the Marshfield clinic in Wisconsin. The large size of these group model HMOs has enabled them to draw a critical mass of members from the surrounding communities to their centrally located facilities. This phenomenon is exceptional, however, as evidenced by the fact that in 1991 fully half the states had less than 10 percent of their populations enrolled in HMOs.[6] The majority of those members were located in metropolitan areas. July 1994 figures showed little change in this status, with 23 states below the 10 percent mark.[7] These statistics seem to demonstrate that sparsely populated areas do present a challenge to HMO development.

Another important characteristic of rural markets is the predominance of small employers making up the workforce. According to the U.S. Department of Commerce, in 1987 98 percent of employers had fewer than 100 employees.[8] This statistic has historically created additional hurdles for rural HMO developers. Most HMOs rely on one or more large, centrally located employers to act as unofficial sponsors for the plan by providing a significant source of initial enrollment. Therefore, in the absence of critical mass in one or two large accounts, aggressive marketing is needed to replace this classic entrance strategy.

The insurance regulatory environment has also provided inadvertent obstacles to rural HMO growth. The HMO Act of 1973, the seminal HMO enabling legislation, required HMOs to community rate companies when setting premium rates. It prevented HMOs from denying coverage based on the health status of prospective members, as is the practice of traditional insurance companies. Although the effect of this was generally positive for HMO members, who could now more effectively budget family health care expenses for the full year, it did have the chilling effect of placing HMOs in a poor competitive position against indemnity insurers. In this environment, most HMOs avoided smaller groups because of their tendency to have higher claims experience and a lower membership base over which to spread that risk. Instead, HMOs favored large employer groups with much larger employee populations and more claims predictability.

It is this chain of events that has created another problem in the country today, not just in rural areas but nationwide. That is the growing problem of the uninsured. The large number of small employers in rural areas makes the uninsured problem more stark because the health care options for this population are even more limited. The scarcity of managed care options in rural areas has reduced managed care access for participants in government-subsidized programs as well. The majority of Medicare and Medicaid recipients in this country who are enrolled in managed care plans reside in urban areas. With government regulators looking to managed care to help reduce the cost of delivering health care for government-subsidized programs, it will be necessary to expand access to managed care plans in rural areas in a manner that is comparable with that available in metropolitan areas.

Before the national health care debates, an additional task for HMO developers was educating providers and consumers, who were accustomed to traditional insurance, about the mechanics of managed care plans. Although no concrete plan for a health care system resulted from these discussions, they succeeded in significantly raising the country's awareness of managed care and the role it could play in the U.S. health care delivery system in the future.

COMPETITION, PHYSICIAN SUPPLY, AND HOSPITAL CAPACITY

The theory that competition is needed to support an effective managed care system is based on the assumption that the only added value of a managed care plan is to create an auction among providers for health care services to direct patient volume to the lowest bidder. The relative lack of competition for health care dollars in rural markets suggests that it is not possible to reduce price using an auction methodology. In fact, some experts maintain that, if rural hospitals decide to increase their scope of services or prices substantially, threatening to build a competing hospital is a poor option, and transporting patients to another city may be unacceptable. Similarly, if most physicians are members of a single multispeciality group practice, purchasers have little recourse if the physicians use more, rather than fewer, resources.[9]

It is true that in many rural markets the population does not support more than one hospital. The same is often true of specialty services. For example, a rural town with a population of approximately 5,300 might support 11 primary care physicians, including pediatricians. It would not be uncommon for that town to have one obstetrics and gynecology practice, the next closest practice being 20 miles away. The same is generally true of specialty services such as neurology, dermatology, cardiology, and so forth. Using the commonly held assumption that HMOs must auction services to secure the best price and alter physician practice patterns to control cost, it would be difficult to conceive that they could have any impact in this scenario because the providers can be reasonably certain that their services will be required by the HMO's members. It has been suggested that the only recourse an HMO could find would be to develop a duplicate competing network or to redirect the patients outside the community. The first solution is unrealistic in a rural market as a result of cost and demographics, which would not support a duplicate network; the latter solution is not only disruptive but difficult to accomplish from a marketing perspective.

The ability to negotiate effectively with hospital providers could prove problematic if the hospital is operating at full bed capacity and does not view the HMO as a significant source or guarantee of future revenues. Typically, hospital costs represent approximately 40 percent of an HMO's health care costs, making the need for favored hospital pricing a critical component of an HMO's medical loss ratio and overall success.[10,11]

Geographic and competitive barriers merge when one considers the task of managing a network of providers that is geographically spread out and practicing without the influence of direct peer comparisons. Physicians practicing in more remote areas without HMOs do not have the same direct exposure to technological advances or practice innovations as physicians practicing in metropolitan areas or areas with teaching hospitals and identified centers of excellence moving toward a best-practices approach to health care delivery. Access to medical technology is the lesser of the two problems because patients can gain access to these technologies by referral. Altering physician practice patterns, especially in this era of reduced hospital lengths of stay and increasing use of in-home treatment, often runs counter to historical norms and patient expectations. Thus, although patient care could be enhanced and outcomes improved by altering practice patterns and adopting new approaches to treatment, in the absence of any outside influence rural area physicians face greater social barriers to change and therefore may be less inclined to adopt treatment pattern shifts recommended by an HMO.

REGULATORY FACTORS

It is difficult to discuss the regulatory environment surrounding health care with any certainty because it is fluid and changing rapidly nationwide. From Maine to California, legislatures are becoming more involved in the expansion of access to health care and health care coverage for their citizens. Where there were once great distinctions in the regulatory environment between a state with low managed care penetration and one with a much larger percentage of the population enrolled in HMOs, those distinctions are becoming more obscure. With health care reform now holding a prominent place on the national agenda, the increased attention has re-

sulted in less predictability in health care and insurance regulation for HMOs.

Today, many states are incorporating HMOs into expanded insurance legislation, whereas others are creating entirely new rules and regulations to govern this growing segment of the health care coverage market. Traditionally, the regulatory environment in predominantly rural states (in distinction to states such as California, Florida, or New York, which have both rural markets and large metropolitan markets) has been conservative and generally reluctant to legislate business conduct or mandate specific health care coverages. In addition, legislatures in those states with low HMO penetration have been understandably less familiar with the concepts of managed care.

This environment presents both challenges and advantages to HMO developers. Developers must undertake the time and expense of educating the regulatory community in rural states, yet they continue to enjoy the advantage of a less restrictive business climate with far less regulatory oversight. Even in rural states, however, there is an increasing focus on managed care practices. State governing bodies are beginning to consider and pass legislation that challenges some of the most basic HMO concepts. An example of this trend is the any willing provider legislation that has surfaced in a number of states. This and other legislative issues critical to HMO development (discussed at length in Chapters 2 and 53) add to the HMO development challenges in rural markets and, therefore, must be addressed by rural HMO managers.

CONQUERING THE BARRIERS TO RURAL HMO DEVELOPMENT

Several formidable barriers to successful HMO development in the rural parts of our country have been identified. Are these barriers great enough to make HMO development in rural areas a fruitless quest, or can they be sufficiently overcome to allow HMOs to take advantage of the opportunities that exist in rural America?

Earlier in our discussion, we noted that as of July 1994 half the states in our country had less than 10 percent HMO penetration. These states have populations totaling 10 million people, or 4 percent of the total population of the United States.[12] These figures exclude states with greater than 10 percent HMO penetration concentrated in the metropolitan parts of the state, leaving additional untapped potential in the rural and suburban portions of those states. The majority of employed residents have continued to be served by traditional indemnity financing systems. With the indemnity industry showing signs of deterioration, the case for entering these markets with HMO options becomes compelling. In 1987 there were 1,295 indemnity insurers serving 173.6 million individuals; by 1992 these figures dropped to 1,127 insurers providing coverage to 142.5 million people.[13] Similarly, the number of HMOs dropped from 650 in 1987 to 546 in 1992. This contraction is due to the consolidation of the industry as the HMO market has matured. Contrary to traditional insurance enrollment trends, HMO enrollment has continued to grow. In 1987, HMOs had a total of 29.3 million members enrolled in managed care plans. By 1992 those numbers had increased to 41.4 million. As of 1995, more than 51 million people had joined HMOs.[14] This growth trend shows no sign of abatement.

Because rural markets are served primarily by indemnity providers that provide retrospective coverage, there is a great deal of added value that an HMO can bring to employers and consumers in these markets simply by reducing the unit cost of health care and through prospective management of health care utilization. This added value and other HMO innovations create substantial opportunities for dramatic growth for HMO plans willing to overcome the barriers in these vastly underserved markets.

SELECTING THE RIGHT HMO MODEL FOR RURAL MARKETS

The first successful HMOs in the United States were closed panel (i.e., group and staff model) HMOs. Closed panel HMOs thrived in highly populated regions and continue to do so today because of the one-stop convenience they offer to those who live within a reasonable traveling radius of their clinics. Given the earlier discussion of the geographically dispersed nature of rural populations, closed panel HMOs that rely on the sole use of centrally located facilities are not the ideal model choice for the most rural areas. In these areas, the central facility becomes an inconvenience when greater traveling distances are involved. Therefore, it is necessary to use a model type that is more appropriate for the geographic characteristics of the rural market. The open panel (i.e., utilizing private practice physicians) HMO has been identified as the model type that is best suited for rural HMO development. Open panel HMOs have the advantage of being able to provide members with convenient health care over a broad geographic area through established community-based providers. With an open panel network, it becomes more possible to organize an HMO using existing local resources. This potential exists even in small towns with limited populations and health care resources. A skilled HMO developer can create the networks and the critical mass of members required for a successful HMO by creating a central operating hub from which it can effectively link many small communities into what amounts to a network of mini-HMOs in outlying areas serving large and widely dispersed rural populations.

DEVELOPING RURAL PROVIDER NETWORKS

One of the most critical elements in an HMO's success is the effectiveness of its provider network. Perhaps the most basic tool in HMO health care cost containment is the negotiating of favorable fee arrangements with providers in exchange for patient volume directed by the HMO. The general assumption of this strategy is that not all physicians in a given area will be participants in that network and that the participating HMO physicians therefore will benefit by making up in patient volume what they concede in discounted fees.

Unlike metropolitan areas, most rural communities do not have an oversupply of physicians, hospitals, and specialists, making it likely that a provider will get an HMO's business whether or not price concessions are made. Under these circumstances, what leverage does the HMO have in contracting with providers? The nature of rural markets dictates the use of more creative approaches to provider contracting than the pure auction model used in competitive provider markets. Several strategies exist for successful contracting with the three major provider groups necessary for building an HMO network: primary care physicians, hospitals, and specialists.

Primary Care Physicians

The key to success in building a rural HMO network is found in the need to go beyond fee schedule discounts. HMOs must focus on improving the level of care that physicians can offer patients beyond what they could achieve without the support of the HMO.

To accomplish the goal of adding value to the existing health care system in rural markets, it is first important to understand what the physician wants from the health care system. Although economic success is important to any practicing professional, rural physicians are generally also concerned about their communities and about maintaining the quality of care they provide to their patients. In the early stages of HMO development, some physicians were reluctant to participate in HMOs because they feared that the quality of the care they provided would be compromised. Therefore, it is imperative that rural HMO developers, with a limited supply of physicians, be sensitive to this concern and work in the early stages to build close working relationships with the providers in the community and to assure them that the goals of the HMO are aligned with those of the physicians.

Perhaps most important to building strong provider relationships is gaining the support of the most prominent providers in a community and involving these key physicians in the highest levels of the HMO's governance structure. This can bring the HMO rapid credibility among providers and is often instrumental in recruiting additional physicians to a fledgling network. Other methods include establishing peer review committees and standards of treatment committees charged with overseeing the quality of care delivered and developing practice pattern standards that are in keeping with the way medicine is practiced locally. In this way, the physicians are able to view the HMO as "their plan," one in which the local community standards are reflected and in which they have a voice in plan governance. Once the physician community has reached a level of comfort with the HMO and believes that patients will benefit from its presence in the community, they are more inclined to join as participating providers and to cooperate with the HMO's managed care goals.

To serve the dispersed employer and patient population adequately, it is necessary to duplicate this recruitment strategy throughout the area under development. Many HMOs have chosen to limit their networks to small groups of providers, upon which they shower all their patient volume. A limited provider network strategy would not work in a rural area because it would be difficult, if not impossible, to provide close and convenient care to the geographically spread out patient population. A successful rural HMO network is geographically dispersed and should ideally include as many of the physicians in a town or area as possible to achieve maximum marketing appeal for consumers. Management of a broad network does require more operational resources for the HMO, but the advantages of this strategy generally outweigh the additional expenditures.

Establishing fair and consistent compensation methodologies for primary care physicians is important to the long-term stability of the HMO network. Yet in rural networks it is necessary to go beyond mere compensation incentives by providing additional support services to network physicians that augment the level of patient care they are able to provide as solo or small group practices. For example, the HMO can, by integrating its resources into the traditional health care process, provide participating physicians with tools and infrastructure that improve health care quality by employing a global care management approach. Arranging for mammograms and cancer screenings, monitoring the care of asthmatics and diabetics, reducing the incidence of low-birthweight infants and establishing local centers of excellence for high-cost procedures are some examples of initiatives that an HMO can employ. Rural HMOs in the role of health care integrator add significant value through their ability to provide data, use of HMO nurse managers as practice extenders, and use of extensive financial resources. In most rural areas, these are services that an independent physician could not afford on his or her own.

Hospital Providers

Contracting with rural hospitals offers similar challenges to HMO developers. As discussed earlier, many rural towns are sufficiently small to support only one acute care hospital. In many cases the next closest facility could be 25 miles away or more. As with primary care physicians, this virtually eliminates the use of the auction for securing favorable prices. Alternative approaches to hospital contracting must be devised. Under these circumstances, an HMO should always attempt to enlist the assistance of participating primary care and other key specialty physicians to help secure favorable pricing arrangements from the hospital. This tactic can be effective in some markets but may not be practical in every circumstance. To succeed, the rural HMO developer must strive for a cooperative approach in single hospital situations. Understanding the hospital's goals and assisting in the achievement of those goals represent the HMO's single best approach.

The expansion of managed care and the movement away from inpatient hospital stays toward outpatient treatment, less costly surgical centers, and the unbundling of other traditionally hospital-based services have caused many hospitals to downsize their operations. They are increasingly concerned about their long-term survival as complete resources of health care for their communities. By eliminating the auction environment and not attempting to reduce hospital revenues through unbundling, the HMO developer can forge a positive working relationship with the hospital that allows it to retain revenue-generating outpatient services in exchange for favorable pricing arrangements.

HMOs can further enhance this relationship through capitated arrangements with hospitals, which serve to guarantee hospital revenues and allow the HMO to budget its hospital costs effectively. Capitation can prove extremely profitable for the hospital provider if it includes not only traditional commercial business but also a number of other market segments under contract with the HMO, including Medicare, Medicaid, and small employer groups, segments for which many rural hospitals typically receive little or, in the case of the large uninsured population, no reimbursement. Moreover, through the HMO's managed care referral activities, fewer hospital dollars will be "leaked" unnecessarily to referral hospitals in other areas. Therefore, even with a zero-sum scenario, where the HMO may spend a lower total amount on inpatient care for a population than its indemnity counterpart, the amount received by the local community hospital can be greater because of its ability to capture outpatient revenue, for example revenue from high-technology imaging technologies or, most important, from sending far fewer hospital procedures outside the community.

If a capitated hospital arrangement is negotiated, it is incumbent upon the rural HMO entering into that arrangement to assist hospital personnel with the task of managing costs using its managed care expertise. In this way, the HMO can ensure the hospital's financial success in the capitated system and build a strong foundation for a long-term cooperative relationship with this critical provider.

Specialists

Rural HMO strategies for contracting with specialty providers can vary greatly depending upon the supply of specialists in the area. Even in many rural areas there exists an oversupply of certain specialties. Additionally, patients are more willing to travel for specialty services, making patient redirection to more cost-effective outlets feasible. In more competitive areas, the classic auction approach can be employed. In less competitive areas, other methods must be devised.

The primary issue that an HMO must confront in managing specialty care is the frequency of utilization of those services. Where specialty services are scarce the cost of services cannot be effectively addressed with discounted fee schedules. Therefore, the HMO must focus first on effective control of utilization, which is best done through the primary care physicians who serve as gatekeepers to high-cost and high-intensity specialty services. Critical to the success of primary care physicians as effective gatekeepers is the use of reliable health claims data to support the need to alter established referral patterns. Access to data that support the use or reduction of use of particular specialists provides the primary care physician with logical explanations for altering practice patterns. Data also enable the HMO to establish community-specific standards for treatment of certain diagnoses. These data greatly assist the primary care physician in making future decisions about specialty referrals. Although a specialist in a rural area may face far less competition than an urban colleague, the specialist still relies on the primary care physician as a referral source. Once the primary care physician is fully educated through data supplied by the HMO on cost and quality parameters of specialty referrals, the specialist's performance can be measured and becomes a key indicator for future referrals. In the indemnity model, a primary care physician is not knowledgeable about the cost of a specialty referral and therefore does not have the tools needed to be discerning. In a well-run rural HMO, once a primary physician learns, for example, that the average cost per referral of orthopedic cases is $600 whereas the industry norm for a similar population is $400, then that primary physician becomes the HMO's ally in bringing the local specialist in line with the norm. In this way, a rural HMO can manage the cost and utilization of specialists within its network in the absence of greater competitive forces.

INTEGRATED HEALTH CARE DELIVERY SYSTEMS

Recent entrants into the contracting fray have been physician–hospital organizations (PHOs), management services organizations (MSOs), and other forms of integrated delivery systems, all of which are described in Chapter 4. PHOs and MSOs are alliances of hospitals and physicians whose purpose is to create an integrated delivery system to improve their contracting leverage with third party payers and, in some cases, to enable them to contract directly with employers. PHOs and MSOs are relatively new phenomena in the rural parts of our country. They are more likely to be found in states with more than 15 percent managed care penetration.[15] Yet these hospital-based networks are in their infancy, and as the sector matures it is likely that they will become a more significant factor for rural HMO developers.

As discussed earlier in the chapter, it is critical for rural HMOs to add value to the existing health care infrastructure to be successful. The stated goal of the PHO/MSO is much the same, creating a potential conflict with the HMO if the PHO/MSO perceives itself as an HMO replacement. Given their stage of development, rural markets are more likely to experience, in the near term, PHOs and MSOs organized for the purpose of contracting as a single entity with HMOs and other third party payers.

The advantage to the rural HMO developer in contracting with a PHO or MSO is the ability to organize a provider network quickly to offer to employers when entering a new market. In addition, the efficiency of contracting with one entity instead of hundreds of individual physicians can be appealing. PHOs and MSOs are often willing to enter into capitated arrangements with HMOs, allowing the HMO to transfer significant health care cost risk. Use of these strategies may be advised in markets where PHOs or MSOs are the only contracting options. Although these advantages are attractive on the surface, the negatives of PHO/MSO contracting may also be important to consider for the HMO in rural or less populated regions.

In rural markets with limited populations, it is important for the HMO trying to attract a critical mass of members to have a product that can be easily distinguished in the market. Contracting with large organized networks that are likely also to contract with competing HMOs removes the rural HMO's most important differentiating factor: the provider network. In markets where all competing health plans have the same or similar networks, the HMO has added little value.

HMOs focused on achieving the best cost containment results must also remain immersed in the health care delivery process and therefore may be reluctant to contract out a significant portion of this responsibility to a PHO. The reason for this reluctance is that currently PHOs and MSOs do not have the same motivation to achieve cost savings for employers as HMOs. Even with the proper motivation, the political relationships among the PHO's constituents (e.g., hospital, specialists, and primary care physicians) might preclude it from using the discipline demonstrated by an HMO working closely with primary care physicians to be sure, for example, that orthopedic referrals are not inappropriately expensive. Moreover, frequently they do not possess data tracking systems comparable with those used by most HMOs to assert such discipline.[16] This lack of technological sophistication would probably result in less favorable cost and health care outcomes than the HMO could achieve on its own.

Therefore, HMOs operating in the financially challenging markets that rural areas present must conduct a careful evaluation of the capabilities of a PHO or MSO to determine whether it has the political wherewithal and technical expertise to deliver the cost/benefit ratios to support the HMO's decision to entrust utilization review and cost containment, the mainstays of the HMO's value-added services, to an outside entity that may have a limited managed care track record. Thus, although some markets will support this approach, other markets will dictate that the HMO's purposes are better served by contracting directly with physicians to achieve the best cost containment results.

MARKETING STRATEGIES FOR RURAL HMOS

In tandem with developing a comprehensive network of providers, the rural HMO developer must create appropriate marketing strategies for rural areas. To sell an HMO product effectively, it is necessary for the prospective purchasers to have a working understanding of the basic tenets and concepts of managed care. Before the national health care debates and the resulting increased public awareness of managed care, rural HMO developers were faced with the need first to educate and then sell employers and their employees on the concepts of managed care. Although our nation has had its consciousness raised about HMOs, it is likely that in the most remote or frontier regions of our country the need to educate rural populations still exists.

The most practical and effective method for accomplishing this dual goal of educating and selling, particularly in medium to large employer accounts, is with a dedicated direct marketing force. Unlike insurance brokers, which sell the products of several companies, a direct marketing force that is employed by the HMO has allegiance only to the HMO and is well versed in the HMO's products. In addition, the need for a two-tiered sell (first to the employer and then to the employee) requires multiple site visits. This is most economically and efficiently performed by a direct marketing representative, who is generally not paid on a commission-only basis and whose selling efforts can be easily coordinated with the HMO's advertising activities. Marketing representatives can also serve an important public relations function as ambassadors for the HMO in the rural communities they serve through involvement in Chamber of Commerce groups, local charities, and other community-based activities.

In many developing HMOs, the marketing department also plays a role in regulatory and legislative relations. As stated earlier, states are increasingly regulating HMO operations in the form of benefit mandates and provider network legislation. Whether through the efforts of the HMO's marketing staff or the use of professional lobbyists, it is imperative that rural HMO developers work closely with state insurance regulators and legislators. These efforts not only should focus on lobbying on specific pieces of legislation but also should attempt to provide state officials with a clear understanding of HMO concepts and goals. Failure to invest in this area could result in a highly regulated and restrictive environment.

As rural Americans move out of traditional indemnity products into managed care, it is essential that HMOs in these areas have a broad array of managed care products, and some traditional insurance lines as well, to meet the varied needs of health care consumers and to guarantee a sufficient critical mass to support a successful HMO operation. An HMO with the flexibility to sell several product options can successfully eliminate the need for employers to seek the services of competitive vendors when designing their corporate benefits plans. This gives the HMO a distinct advantage with employers and can greatly assist the plan in expanding market share.

Also important to the rural HMO marketing effort is the inclusion of as many market segments as possible into the mix of business. Therefore, rural HMO developers should aggressively seek out opportunities to enter new areas, such as the small group market, Medicare, and Medicaid, the latter two of which have now been made more accessible to HMOs by state and federal health care reform.

BALANCING THE ECONOMIC EQUATION

HMOs are trying harder than ever to squeeze the waste out of the health care system and pass savings on to consumers in the form of lower premiums. This industry factor, coupled with the generally higher costs associated with HMO development for a widely dispersed population with the attendant customization required to attract broad membership, could cause a rural HMO developer to fail. The combination of lower enrollment opportunities and higher administrative costs can lead new HMO entrants in rural markets to experience a much longer time period to break even and achieve a return on invested capital. With the stakes so high, even a well-capitalized HMO would not wish to mount an unprofitable development campaign in a rural market for very long. Therefore, when an HMO developer is entering a rural market, it is crucial to achieve a financial balance quickly between development costs and revenue generation.

The need for rapid break-even, particularly in rural markets with smaller and less concentrated populations, has had a significant influence on the type of HMO developer that has attempted the challenge of entering the least penetrated markets of our country. The need for significant up-front capital for staffing (especially to attract top-flight management), information systems, marketing, and provider recruitment has made it difficult for a small enterprise to start a local HMO from scratch. Consequently, two primary methods for successful rural HMO start-up have evolved. First is the independent provider–sponsored HMO. Provider-sponsored HMOs have usually grown in response to the development or growth of closed panel HMOs in the region. Closed panel HMOs threaten the independent physician's practice by luring patients away with attractive benefits at lower cost. In response to this threat, physicians have, either on their own or in partnership with an outside HMO developer, raised the capital to start competitive open panel HMOs. Without skilled HMO managers to negotiate favorable pricing and monitor utilization—in essence, to instill discipline among the sponsors—many of these provider-backed initiatives have been unprofitable or have failed. Today, many of these plans are being acquired by large regional and national HMO firms seeking to expand their market share.

The second, and more common, development strategy, the one that is proving the most successful in today's competitive market, is for a large, regional, entrepreneurial managed care company to enter a new market, often in alliance with a prominent local health care provider or employer. The advantage of this model is that the regional managed care company has the cost containment expertise and market experience needed to succeed. An entrepreneurial rather than a bureaucratic culture will afford the managed care company the nimbleness needed to respond to the specific provider and marketplace conditions. The local sponsor helps the HMO shorten its time to break-even by rapidly delivering a provider network, in the case of a health care provider sponsor, or, if the sponsor is a large employer group, by delivering the critical mass of members that allows the HMO to generate revenues rapidly to offset development expenses.

Given the austere premium pricing environment in which all HMOs must operate today and the added challenges that rural markets present, it is essential to manage costs carefully to move with (but not faster than) premium pricing. An HMO developer must be adept at negotiating fees with providers and making sure that provider compensation is structured to give physicians incentives to use health care services appropriately. In addition, the HMO must have skilled managers capable of working with the provider community to lower utilization using practice pattern modification, preventive care, disease management, and other tools of managed care.

Of equal importance to achieving financial success in rural markets is managing administrative costs. Most of the administrative costs associated with the early stages of HMO development are dedicated to salaries and advertising. Hiring strong, capable representatives for the plan is critical to initial success in the marketplace, making it a mistake to hire low-cost, unskilled workers. Advertising, however, is an area where modifications can be made. Because rural markets are so geographically spread out, the cost/benefit ratio of mounting a large advertising campaign is questionable. An HMO starting in a rural area would be well advised to engage in a targeted advertising campaign focused around key enrollment periods. Beyond that, extending the advertising dollar through less costly but equally effective public and community relations efforts can have the same desired effect of gaining marketplace credibility and name recognition.

Successful transitioning of our nation's large and diverse population into the era of managed care carries the weighty responsibility of ensuring a high level of quality associated with the care provided. Employers and their employees will pay a premium for an HMO plan that offers a quality network, improves their access to quality care, and has the mechanisms in place to measure this added value. Additionally, HMOs offering a superior product that not only will attract new members but, more important, will retain them once they join (studies show that, the longer a member is with a plan, the more profitable he or she becomes for the plan[17]) continue to expand their revenue base without having continually to replace disenrolled members. Able customer service staff who can educate members on how best to access the system and can help manage patient expectations are critical to improving member satisfaction and retention. These factors can be financially significant in rural markets, where demographics dictate that HMOs have smaller populations from which to draw than HMOs located in metropolitan areas. Developing early discipline in the areas of medical and administrative costs, quality improvement, and member retention will increase the HMO's chances of achieving rapid return on capital and long-term bottom line success.

MAINECARE: A CASE STUDY OF THE UNINSURED MARKET[18]

The problem of the uninsured has long plagued rural America. With the majority of rural populations employed by small businesses, high health care costs have resulted in small employers that are unable or unwilling to provide health care coverage for their workers. The large number of working uninsured in rural areas and an improving regulatory environment for small group coverage provide rural HMO developers with a unique opportunity as our nation moves toward its goal of universal health care coverage.

One recent example of a successful managed care solution to the uninsured problem is MaineCare, a pilot program cosponsored by the state of Maine, the Robert Wood Johnson Foundation, and Healthsource Maine, Inc., a for-profit HMO based in Freeport, Maine. Maine is dominated by small employers: Six of every ten businesses in the state employ fewer than five workers. According to research by the Edmund S. Muskie Institute for Public Affairs at the University of Southern Maine, a group dedicated to reversing the uninsured trend in Maine, fewer than half the state's small businesses (those with fewer than 20 employees) offered group health coverage to their workers. In the Bath–Brunswick area, one of two MaineCare pilot sites, the situation was even more serious: Some 54 percent of the businesses were uninsured before the MaineCare program was established.

In an effort to attack the problem, the state Department of Health Services contracted with Healthsource, a managed care developer specializing in rural HMO development, to provide coverage to businesses or self-employed individuals who had been without insurance for at least 6 months. The state then subsidized premiums for employees on a sliding scale based on household income. Employers were required to pay at least half the unsubsidized premium amount for each employee, and partial subsidies were available for low-income self-employed persons, including part-time employees.

To reduce premiums further, three area hospitals agreed to 30 percent discounts on charges for MaineCare patients. The incentive for agreeing to the discounts was that the hospitals would recover 70 percent of the charges incurred by patients who would otherwise be uninsured. According to the hospital's figures, only about 47 percent of the cost of care to uninsured patients was typically recovered before MaineCare was established. Through its relationships with the physician and hospital communities in Maine, Healthsource was able to negotiate favorable prices for MaineCare.

Although MaineCare was targeted at low-income individuals, the members shared in the cost of the program. Private funding from employees and employers accounted for more than 53 percent of the premiums. The majority of this additional money was spent on preventive and routine care, effectively reducing the use of emergency departments for postponed primary care.

Throughout the duration of the project, which ended in 1993 as a result of the elimination of funding subsidies from the state, MaineCare's utilization results, as measured by annual hospital discharges and annual inpatient days per 1,000 members, were the lowest of all but 1 of the 11 demonstration projects supported by the Robert Wood Johnson Foundation Health Care for the Uninsured Program and were well below nationwide HMO averages.[19]

CONCLUSION

It is evident from our discussion that the difficulties associated with the development of HMOs in rural areas are numerous and not to be underestimated. Yet it is our conclusion that skilled HMO managers can overcome these hurdles and achieve success in underpenetrated markets if they can add significant value to the existing rural health care infrastructure. This can be accomplished by using the financial and human resources available to the HMO to fill the voids that currently exist in the underserved areas of our country.

Furthermore, it has been demonstrated that a traditional competitive model is not required for an HMO to succeed in its task of reducing the unit price and utilization of health care services. Critical in the equation for success, however, is the need for close working relationships with physicians and credible data to support the need for changing long-held practice patterns and medical traditions.

Market responsiveness and flexibility are also key ingredients for rural HMO success. Developing HMOs must create products with broad appeal, products that take into account the diversity of employer groups and the geographically dispersed nature of the rural market. In these relatively less populated areas, a broad array of managed care products is needed to attract employer groups at different stages of migration from traditional insurance into the realm of managed care. Although this flexibility may raise administrative costs above those of HMOs with fewer options, reading the market in this way helps the rural HMO achieve critical mass and shorten its time to break-even.

With the national consciousness raised and our country moving rapidly toward managed care solutions in every segment of the health care industry, the time has never been more opportune than it is today for HMO development nationwide. With a keen focus on cost management and a true understanding of the unique features of rural markets, the savvy HMO developer can successfully debunk the myths surrounding rural HMO development and add significant value to the existing health care infrastructure by improving the level of care and affordability of health care available to the residents of America's rural areas.

REFERENCES AND NOTES

1. R. Kronick, et. al., Special Report—The Market Place in Health Care Reform: The Demographic Limitations of Managed Competition, *New England Journal of Medicine* 328 (1993): 148–152.

2. Kronick, et al., Special Report, 148.

3. L.L. Hicks and J.K. Glenn, Too Many Physicians in the Wrong Places and Specialties? Populations and Physicians from a Market Perspective, *Journal of Health Care Marketing* 9 (1989): 18–26.

4. Bureau of the Census, *1990 Census of Population and Housing: Summary Population and Housing Characteristics—California*. Bureau of the Census Report CPH-1-6 (Washington, D.C.: Government Printing Office, 1991).

5. Kronick, et al., Special Report, 148.

6. InterStudy, *Quarterly Report of the HMO-Managed Care Industry*, Vol. 1, No. 1 (Excelsior, Minn.: InterStudy, 1991), 23–25.

7. InterStudy, *Research and Reports for Market-Driven Health Care* (St. Paul, Minn.: InterStudy, 1995), 30–32.

8. Bureau of the Census, *1987 Enterprise Statistics: Company Summary*. Bureau of the Census Report ES87-3-7 (Washington, D.C.: Government Printing Office, 1991).

9. Kronick, et al., Special Report, 148.

10. N. Payson, Innovations in Medical Cost Control (Presentation at the Lehman Brothers Health Conference, Washington, D.C., June 1994).

11. The medical loss ratio is the cost ratio of health benefits used compared with revenue received. It is calculated as total medical expenses divided by total revenue.

12. InterStudy, *Research and Reports*, 30–32.

13. Health Insurance Association of America (HIAA), *Source Book of Health Insurance Data* (Washington, D.C.: HIAA, 1995), 37–38.

14. Group Health Association of America (GHAA), *1995 National Directory of HMOs* (Washington, D.C.: GHAA, 1995), 21.

15. F. Abbey and M. Treash, Jr., Reasons Providers Form PHOs, *Health Care Financial Management* 49 (1995): 38.

16. Abbey and Treash, Reasons Providers Form PHOs.

17. B.J. Tyrrell, *Member Satisfaction and Retention Research Report* (Concord, N.H.: Healthsource New Hampshire, Inc., 1993), 1.

18. Healthsource, Inc., *1992 Annual Report* (Hooksett, N.H.: Healthsource, 1992), 9–24.

19. D. Campion, et al., *Meeting the Health Insurance Needs of Uninsured Small Businesses: Market Research and*

New Products (Washington, D.C.: Alpha Center, 1992) 1–34.

SUGEGSTED READING

Samuels, M.E. and Shi, L. 1993. *Physician Recruitment and Retention: A Guide for Rural Medical Group Practice*. Englewood, Colo.: Center for Research in Ambulatory Health Care Administration/MGMA.

Savitch, L.A. and Brown, H.W. 1994. Will Managed Care Succeed in Rural Areas? *Hospitals & Health Networks* 68 (1): 13.

Weaver, D.L., Hinman, E., and Davis, D. 1994. Recruitment and Retention of Physicians in Rural and Urban Areas. Delivering Managed Care to the Underserved in Rural and Urban America, Section 14, p. 45. Orlando, Fla., April 20-21. Washington, D.C.: American Association of Health Plans.

Chapter 51

Managed Care Dental Benefits

Fred L. Horowitz

To begin, we must agree on a definition of the term *managed care* as used in the dental care delivery field. This term has come to represent any plan offered by a carrier or organization that offers some type of benefit plan that is different from traditional fee for service (indemnity). This includes dental health maintenance organizations (HMOs or prepaid plans), preferred provider organizations (PPOs), referral plans, and discount or access plans.

A dental HMO is an organization that provides dental services to enrollees (members) for some form of prepayment. Those services are provided through a group practice or network of dentists, and payment for dental services rendered is through per member per month payments (capitation) to the practitioners. Differing significantly from the indemnity world, in dental HMOs claims are a minor or nonexistent part of prepaid plans. A gatekeeper approach to specialty care and some form of quality assessment program are hallmarks of these programs. As marketed today, they are really the only widespread type of truly managed dental care on the

market because they have management components in addition to direct cost regulation.

Dental HMOs are currently found in 47 states and three countries outside the United States (Canada, Mexico, and Great Britain). Since 1990, the growth of dental HMOs has been phenomenal, from approximately 7.8 million members in 1990 to 18.4 million in 1994 in the United States alone (Figure 51–1).[1] As would be expected, the location of this participating population is concentrated in the most populous states and regions. California has the most enrollment, with approximately 4.5 million residents participating in dental HMOs. California, Michigan, Florida, Texas, and Minnesota combined account for more than 60 percent of the total enrollment (Figure 51–2). The top ten states account for more than 75 percent of the enrollment, concentrated in the metropolitan areas. According to the National Association of Dental Plans (NADP), in 1995 the industry was projected to grow an additional 19.5 percent.

Concomitantly, the location and numbers of participating practitioners follow a similar pattern. More than 17,000 general dentists and 9,000 specialists report participating in one or more dental HMOs.[2] This represents more than 18 percent of all dentists in private practice.

The majority of dental HMO benefit plans are sold to employer groups. Of those, approximately 56 percent are paid for in whole or in part by the employer.[3] Another 26 percent are sold on a voluntary basis through employers with no employer contribution. The remaining 18 per-

Fred L. Horowitz, D.M.D., is currently Executive Vice President of Business and Market Development for Dental Health Providers, Bethesda, Md. Formerly, he was Vice President, Dental Products for Employers Health Insurance Co., a wholly owned subsidiary of Humana, Inc. He has been involved with the dental managed care industry for the past 15 years as both provider and administrator. He currently serves on the Board of Directors of the National Association of Dental Plans and its nonprofit foundation for research in the dental benefits industry.

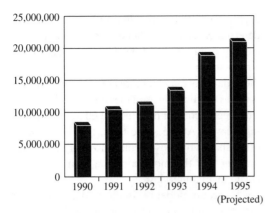

Figure 51–1 Dental HMO membership. *Source:* Data from National Association of Dental Plans Statistical Profile, p. 5, 1995.

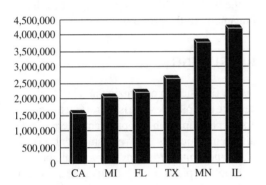

Figure 51–2 State dental enrollment. *Source:* Data from National Association of Dental Plans Statistical Profile, p. 19, 1995.

cent are individual plans and those plans serving the public sector.

A dental PPO provides services to its members through a contracted network of dentists. By utilizing one of those participating dentists the member will usually reduce his or her out-of-pocket expense, and the carrier will pay a discounted reimbursement to the practitioner. Like traditional indemnity plans, PPOs provide compensation to their practitioners through claims processing on a fee-for-service basis. Although a gatekeeper approach to specialty care and quality assessment programs could be utilized in this delivery system, they have not been generally

applied. The most widely marketed dental PPOs today are the enhanced PPOs, in which seeking care from a participating practitioner will result in higher benefit levels than standard. The second form is the punitive PPO, in which going out of network results in a greatly diminished benefit from standard.

Point-of-service plans are a form of either a PPO or a prepaid plan combined with an indemnity product. They allow members to choose either the managed care plan or the indemnity plan at the time that they make their appointment rather than the time of enrollment. If the member goes out of network, the dentist is paid on a fee-for-service basis, but the level of reimbursement is usually reduced. If the member seeks care on an in-network basis, out-of-pocket cost is reduced. In this case the dentist is paid on some form of capitation, reduced fee for service, or a combination of the two. This type of plan is popular for medical insurance, but it is not widespread in the dental market, although it will probably be a high-growth product. Thus its ability to control costs has not been demonstrated on a large enough population to date.

Access plans and referral plans are not managed care. Rather, they are a form of marketing large networks of providers to the public for a small fee. They offer a benefit in the form of access to a provider network where reduced fees are offered to subscribers.

For the remainder of this chapter, the term *managed care* will be limited to dental HMOs (prepaid plans) because they are the only form of true dental managed care on the market today. Like medical HMOs and insurance carriers, these entities are regulated at the state level under one of the following enabling statutes (as of June 1995):

- limited health service organization (8 states)

- single service HMOs (9 states)

- prepaid dental plans (10 states)

- dental service corporation or plan (15 states)

- dental-only health corporation (1 state)
- no regulation (4 states and the District of Columbia)

In addition some states allow life and health indemnity carriers to offer prepaid products. Unlike medical HMOs, dental HMOs cannot be licensed at the federal level. Thus the homogeneous elements of medical HMOs (e.g., financial requirements, grievance procedures, etc.) are often absent in the prepaid dental plan.

The NADP, the industry trade group, was originally established to propose a standard licensing statute. The limited health service organization model was promulgated by the National Association of Insurance Commissioners with input from the NADP. To date, this enabling act has been adopted in ten states, with minor variances. As the industry matures and more national companies become involved, regulations should become more constant from state to state.

THE DENTAL DELIVERY SYSTEM

Dental HMOs offer benefits through a network of practicing dentists. This network can consist of the following types of practices, either alone or in combination. Many dental HMOs are now using a combination of these models to offer their members more variety and stable rates from year to year.

The staff practice model is similar to the earliest forms of medical HMOs. In this model, the carrier or plan owns the facilities and utilizes employee dentists and ancillary personnel to provide care. This is usually the most restrictive network in that choice is limited to those sites that the plan operates. Although no conclusive research has been done, anecdotal surveys indicate that this is the most profitable type of arrangement for the plans and has the most predictable costs.

The independent practice association (IPA) is a network made up of independently practicing dentists, usually at many sites, who contract individually with the plan to provide care at a predetermined rate. The benefit to the member is usually a larger selection of practitioners from which to choose. The payment mechanism to those dentists may be more complex and usually is not as predictable as in the staff model because a degree of control is relinquished to the practicing dentist. At the same time, the risk is more often shared by those dentists to a larger degree, making this the most common form of dental HMO available today.

The group model is similar to the IPA model except that the dentists are organized into one or more groups, which in turn contract with the carrier or plan. This may give the groups a better negotiating edge with the carrier, but the needs of the individual dentists may be lost to the homogeneity of the group's contract.

RECRUITING

The first step in organizing an HMO, after licensure and plan design, is recruiting the providers to participate in the program. Here a major difference occurs between medical prepaid plans and dental programs. In medical plans, one or more hospitals are the focus of the program, and the networks of practicing physicians are recruited to complement those care centers. In contrast, the dental delivery system is focused on the individual dental office, so that there is no central organization around which to recruit. Most dental plans start by recruiting a core group of dentists and then extending the network, by referral, from that core group. The recruitment process can be tedious and slow because there are no central bodies, such as hospitals, to endorse one plan or another or to aid in recruitment through its membership. This difference becomes a bit less apparent if the network is a staff or group model.

CREDENTIALING

Because of the lack of federal regulation, the credentialing process varies greatly from state to state and from company to company. Some states, such as California, prescribe specific quality assessment standards that affect the credentialing process. Others have no standards at all and may even not require a credentialing process. The industry as a whole is moving toward the requirement for credentialing. At a minimum, licensing, liability insurance protection, and compliance with Occupational Safety and Health Administration guidelines and the standard of care in the specific geographic area of practice are verified. Some companies require the practicing dentist and his or her office to undergo a multiple site visit procedure, which will include the above plus chart review, emergency protocols, access to care standards, and compliance with more rigorous practice guidelines. This area is of keen interest to most plans today, to the benefit of all involved.

COMPENSATION

Because dental plans are less complex than their medical counterparts, so too are their compensation mechanisms. There are no hospitals involved in the delivery system, so that the dental HMO contracts directly with its participating providers or a group representing those providers (an IPA). Most dental HMOs compensate their participating general dentists on a per member per month or per subscriber per month basis (a subscriber is the "paying unit"; members are subscribers and their dependents).

There are two commonly used methods for determining the amount of capitation as well as any member copayment. The first involves calculating the anticipated number and type of procedures that will be performed in a specified time period for a specific population and assigning a fee-for-service equivalent to those procedures. After member copayments are determined (for the most part a market-driven event), the per member per month amount can be derived from the anticipated fee-for-service equivalent. The amount is usually discounted based upon factors such as reduced billing costs,

marketing and collection activities, and increased volume. The second, and probably more accurate, method is to assign relative time units to each anticipated procedure. These time units can then be assigned a dollar value depending upon geographic, population, and practice style factors. From this a per member per month amount can be determined.

Specialty practitioners can also be compensated based upon a similar capitation process. To be successful, however, a large volume of prospective patients is required. Many dental HMOs do not have adequate membership to make this a viable alternative, so that compensation is usually made on a negotiated fee-for-service basis, similar to a PPO. As the industry matures, more plans will turn to capitating their participating specialists. In parts of the country where dental HMOs have not reached a level of sophistication comparable with that of their medical counterparts, specialty services may be offered on a discounted fee-for-service basis to the member with no compensation (no risk) from the dental HMO.

UTILIZATION REVIEW

To ascertain whether a particular dental plan is meeting its goals to its members, clients, and providers, a form of utilization review must take place. This includes comparing the total number of procedures performed in a time period with that of the model that was used to determine compensation to the dentists. In addition, individual practices need to be evaluated periodically to verify that the population assumptions as well as the specific compensation compared with that of the group were correct. For the client, this evaluation process determines whether the premiums being paid are in line with the amount and type of services being performed. This, coupled with a comprehensive quality assessment program, would allow everyone participating in the dental HMO to determine its value. The quality assessment program must include processes to evaluate standards of care, access to care, compliance with policies and procedures, and, although subjective, a general understanding of the practice style. This information is critical to the long-term success of any dental HMO.

SPECIALTY CARE

Provision for specialty care providers is key to obtaining and maintaining the dental health of an insured population. In addition to recruiting networks of primary care providers, maturing dental HMOs and PPOs must recruit, credential, and maintain networks of specialty care dentists, including oral and maxillofacial surgeons, endodontists, periodontists, pedodontists, and prosthodontists. Access to these specialists is usually provided through some form of gatekeeper approach. The primary care provider and the dental HMO/PPO, working in combination, control the referral process. When the need for a specialist to provide care is determined by the general dentist, a referral is made to a previously credentialed member of the specialty network following the procedures and protocols of the specific carrier or plan. For a routine procedure, this usually involves the general dentist submitting a written request to the carrier, along with a narrative and supporting radiographic documentation, requesting that certain benefits be approved at the specialist's office. After review, the carrier then notifies the referring dentist, the patient, or (in the best of circumstances) both of the approved procedures and benefit levels. The member is then able to make an appropriate appointment with the specialist. In some programs, the carrier or the primary provider actually makes the appointment for the member. Also, many programs allow the primary dentist and the patient a choice of specialists, so that a referral can be made taking into account convenience of location, hours of service, and specific skill sets required.

With the evolution of electronic data interchange, some carriers are streamlining this process for routine referrals, allowing on-line, real-time approval of specialty care referrals. As the technology improves and becomes more widespread, it is anticipated that this will become the standard for referrals.

ACCREDITATION

Unlike the case for medical HMOs, there does not exist an accepted standard to measure outcomes or processes of dental HMOs or PPOs. The National Committee on Quality Assurance (see Chapter 37) currently has voluntary advisory protocols for medical HMOs that contract with dentists for certain services. These protocols are based on medical practice, are process oriented, and thus are probably not appropriate for application to dental HMOs or PPOs, at least in their current form. In addition, other groups in the dental care delivery industry are attempting to devise various standards to apply to the dental managed care format. None to date has been widely accepted, and most are more involved with process measures than outcome measures. Within the next 2 to 3 years, we should see a growing interest in this area with some form of standards eventually produced.

CONCLUSION

By far the largest growing segment in the dental benefits industry, as in the medical benefits industry, are various forms of managed care delivery. Statistics from various sources indicate the strong growth of the dental HMO and PPO markets at the expense of the traditional indemnity plan. The specific plan type varies from geographic area to geographic area, with dental HMOs being strongest in large metropolitan centers and dental PPOs being strongest in smaller cities and more rural environs.

As these plans mature, their success will be dependent upon the cooperative working relationship of dentists, carriers, and employers to ensure that proper plan designs, access, delivery of care, and compensation are provided. As in the medical managed care industry, this maturation process seems to occur in large population centers first and then migrates to smaller communities over time. If successful, these types of plans will become the dominant form of dental insurance within the next few years because they provide cost predictability, comprehensive coverage, and access to care for the largest population at the most appropriate cost.

The dental HMOs are represented by the NADP, which is located in Dallas, Texas. This trade organization was established in 1989 to act as a forum and voice for the industry. Further information about this growing industry may be obtained by contacting the NADP at 5001 LBJ Freeway, Suite 375, Dallas, Texas 75244 or calling (214) 458-6998.

REFERENCES AND NOTES

1. InterStudy, *1995 National Dental HMO Statistical Profile* (Dallas, Texas: InterStudy Publications and National Association of Dental Plans, 1995).
2. InterStudy, *1995 National Dental HMO Statistical Profile*.
3. InterStudy, *1995 National Dental HMO Statistical Profile*.

SUGGESTED READING

Dental Benefits–A Survey. 1995. New York, N.Y.: William M. Mercer, Inc.

Quattlebaum, B. 1995. *Managed Care in Dentistry*. Tulsa, Okla.: PennWell Books.

Chapter 52

Workers' Compensation: Toward Comprehensive Medical Event Management

Gregory L. Johnson and Edward H. Lipson

Until recently, an employer's prime health care cost concern has been to control the escalating cost of traditional group health plans. The upward spiraling of medical costs, coupled with the intense competitive pressures employers face, has fueled an explosive growth in managed care. Although the use of health maintenance organizations (HMOs), preferred provider organizations (PPOs), and point-of-service plans has been successful in holding down costs in group plans, many employers have not taken similar steps in their workers' compensation programs. With disability-related costs rising to more than $140 billion a year, however, many employers are beginning to demand tighter and more comprehensive cost controls.

This chapter identifies the key trends in workers' compensation managed care and suggests some future solutions. The most important long-term trend is the convergence of the health care, workers' compensation, and group disability industries. Although complete integration is sev-

Gregory L. Johnson, Ph.D., is the National Director of Workers' Compensation Consulting Services for the Human Resource Consulting Group of Ernst & Young LLP. Dr. Johnson specializes in program development for HMOs, insurance carriers, and employers.

Edward H. Lipson, M.D., is the National Director of Time Loss Management for the Human Resource Consulting Group of Ernst & Young LLP. A partner based in the consulting firm's New York office, Dr. Lipson specializes in planning, implementing, and evaluating integrated health care management programs, including managed care, for health benefits, workers' compensation, and managed disability.

eral years away, the impact of the larger health care industry is already having a dramatic effect on workers' compensation.

THE LANGUAGE OF CHANGE

It is important in any discussion of new concepts that all the participants share common definitions of terms and phrases that may be in a constant state of evolution. The term *24-hour coverage*, for example, has often been used to describe a seamless health care delivery system that is blind to the origin of the illness or injury. The difficulty with that term, however, is that it only addresses issues of insurance coverage rather than total management of medical events. The search for a more accurate description of the concept of total managed care has given rise to some of the following terms:

- *Integrated benefits* is another term used to signify the integration of workers' compensation, employee medical benefits, and perhaps disability benefits. As noted below, workers' compensation is not so much a benefit as it is an entitlement mandated as an issue of social policy.

- *Total managed care* refers to the application of traditional medical management tools and care delivery through specified provider networks under employee health benefit, workers' compensation, and disability programs. The problem with this term is that it highlights managing care.

Where does this leave the management of employee downtime and return to work?

- *Comprehensive medical event management*, although cumbersome, does cover the important bases. *Comprehensive* bridges occupational and nonoccupational settings. *Medical event* subsumes both the need for medical services and recovery, rehabilitation, and return to work.

WORKERS' COMPENSATION: THE ORIGIN OF THE SOCIAL CONTRACT

Workers' compensation was the first widely developed form of social insurance in the United States. It is designed to provide prompt and effective medical care to workers injured on the job and to provide replacement of a portion of wages lost while the worker is recovering from injury. In exchange for these benefits, the injured worker relinquishes his or her right to sue the employer for negligence. Thus the social contract that underlies workers' compensation is a form of mutual protection of the employer and employee. It is this mutual protection that is the fundamental difference between providing health care under a workers' compensation system and an employer's traditional group health plan. Although it has traditionally been the last refuge of an unfettered fee-for-service system, the workers' compensation system has begun to undergo changes. Exhibit 52–1 illustrates the cost of workers' compensation to employers.

Workers' compensation is essentially a state system with variations in benefit levels, medical reimbursement schedules, and the degree to which an employer can control the medical choices made by the employee. The existence of state regulations governing workers' compensation, however, does not prohibit the employer from exercising a degree of control over medical costs. In fact, most states allow employers to direct how employees are cared for after a work-related injury, although the degree of control allowed varies greatly. These state variations must be understood before appropriate managed care

Exhibit 52–1 Employer Costs for Workers' Compensation (as a Percentage of Total Compensation)

By occupational category, March 1995
- Blue collar: 4.3%
- Service: 3.4%
- White collar: 1.2%

By region
- Northeast: 2.0%
- South: 2.5%
- Midwest: 2.3%
- West: 2.4%

By bargaining status
- Union: 3.2%
- Nonunion: 2.1%

By establishment size (number of workers)
- 1–99:   2.8%
- 100–499:   2.4%
- 500 or more: 1.5%

For all workers in private industry, 1990–1995
- March 1990:   2.1%
- March 1991:   2.1%
- March 1992:   2.2%
- March 1993:   2.3%
- March 1994:   2.3%
- March 1995:   2.4%

Source: Reprinted from Comp Costs Edged Down to 1993 Levels, *BNA's Workers' Compensation Report*, Vol. 6, pp. 423–424, 1995, Bureau of National Affairs.

products can be designed for employers across the country. Although state regulations differ, the trend is clearly toward integrating workers' compensation into a truly managed, single-source health care delivery system.

As one of the last fee-for-service systems, workers' compensation has often been the victim of cost shifting from more managed payment systems or upcoding of conditions by physicians, who know that workers' compensation will pay more. These differences in medical practice patterns were documented in a study by the Minnesota Department of Labor and Industry, which indicated that workers' compensation charges for back injuries were 250 percent more expensive when handled as a workers' compensation claim compared with the average Blue Cross Blue Shield charge for identical back injuries.[1] A similar finding was made in a study by the Workers' Compensation Research Institute, which found that workers' compensation medical costs have grown more rapidly than non–workers' compensation medical costs, particularly since 1980.[2]

INITIAL EFFORTS AT COST CONTAINMENT

The trend toward integrating workers' compensation with traditional health care delivery systems has been driven in part by the changing role that insurers have played in the market. Nearly two thirds of all American employers are currently covered for their workers' compensation costs through property/casualty insurance on a guaranteed-cost, fully insured basis. This trend is the converse of traditional group health, where 60 percent of companies are self-insured and only 40 percent are in fully insured plans. Insurance carriers generally have viewed workers' compensation medical and indemnity costs as a pass through to the insured employers, to be recouped the following year in higher premiums.

Worsening losses, however, coupled with price competition during the 1980s led many workers' compensation carriers to seek solutions to control their costs more effectively, especially medical costs. This cost crisis led to the first generation of medical cost containment: hospital and medical bill audits and PPO discounts. These first-generation techniques have produced varying results, depending on the effectiveness of their execution. The highest-yield programs audit all hospital and medical bills and drive more than 30 percent of all provider billings into PPO networks, with discounts averaging 25 percent. Most payers continue to rely on these first-generation controls.

The second generation of cost control rests on a cardinal principle of managed care: To be effective, both unit price and volume of services must be controlled. Many workers' compensation payers that adopted first-generation controls experienced continued escalation of medical costs in the face of reports purporting to show substantial savings. This contradiction exposed the weak link in first-generation cost containment: inadequate controls on utilization. Many medical providers offered discounts on each unit of service while compensating for revenue shortfalls by increasing utilization.

Second-generation techniques apply utilization controls, including hospital, surgical, and diagnostic test preauthorization, as well as focused management of high-volume, specialized providers (chiropractors and physical therapists). To be optimally effective, utilization management must be closely integrated with the claims function as well as with first-generation techniques. For example, the claims adjuster must be aware of the utilization review findings because the adjuster can override any decision. Claims adjusters control millions of dollars in medical reserves and are key members of the carrier's team. Although they do not have any clinical training, they can be roadblocks to effective managed care. Second, the utilization review decision must be part of the bill audit process because some unauthorized services may be paid without timely input from utilization review.

Recently, employers and carriers have begun to address the indemnity (disability) portion of workers' compensation. Disability costs represent 55 percent of all workers' compensation expenditures. No payer would approve a plan that drives up disability costs while controlling medical costs. Like hospital utilization review, disability management uses diagnosis-specific templates of expected lengths of disability. The most effective disability management programs adjust these templates for variations in sex, age, and occupation. In addition to disability duration guidelines, advanced disability management programs utilize clinical personnel to verify impairment, establish disability, determine functional capacity, and promote early return to work.

HMOs have demonstrated the ability to manage and control group health costs. Employers and policymakers have encouraged HMOs to deliver workers' compensation services, and now more than 100 HMOs have workers' compensation departments. HMO products range from enhanced delivery of workers' compensation medical care to complete equity ownership of a workers' compensation carrier.

A study of workers' compensation in Florida found that even the most modest managed care strategies can have a dramatic impact on costs. This study showed that, compared with a control group, workers covered by an HMO had total direct claims costs that were 60 percent lower than those of the controls. These employees also had a duration of disability averaging 44 percent shorter and indemnity claims 52 percent lower than those receiving traditional care.[3] Although these results are not representative of many other settings because of the minimal managed care activities of the baseline control group, they did make policymakers and industry leaders take notice.

KEY SUCCESS FACTORS FOR HMOs IN WORKERS' COMPENSATION

Matching Physician Skills to Needs

To succeed in the workers' compensation market, HMOs must retool their group health provider networks to provide comprehensive workers' compensation services. Less than 10 percent of group health medical providers understand workers' compensation medical treatment and reporting protocols. Knowledgeable providers must be identified, and specialists should be linked to primary care providers through specific referral procedures.

In identifying physicians, organized health plans must be attentive to the difference between primary and occupational care. Many primary care physicians do not understand occupational medicine beyond the most rudimentary treatments. These primary physicians must understand when the appropriate time is to refer a patient to an occupational medicine specialist. Such specialists understand the difference between functional capacity and disability. Rather than simply labeling the worker disabled, it is essential to understand whether the person can actually do the specific job at which he or she is working. Technology now exists to identify selectively and profile physicians on a case-matched basis based upon their degree of efficiency in delivering occupational medical care.

Physician Reimbursement Methods

Fee-for-service medicine in workers' compensation has generally rewarded the inefficient providers that drive up employer costs. To succeed in workers' compensation, managed care plans must develop pricing and provider reimbursement methods that depart from the usual fee-for-service workers' compensation billing methods. Typically, these methods include shared risk arrangements with financial incentives that encourage physicians to manage utilization better and limit excessive referrals to specialists. As with employee health benefits, the key in a workers' compensation environment is to control both the volume and the intensity of medical services provided. Innovative methods of reimbursement include case rates, capitation, and modified bonus systems.

Capitated Arrangements

This strategy involves the health plan absorbing the workers' compensation risk on a prepaid basis. This risk can include the medical portion of workers' compensation losses (about 45 percent of the loss cost) or the disability lost-time portion of the risk (about 55 percent of the cost). This strategy requires careful actuarial analysis because many injured workers may seek care outside the contracted provider network, the long period of treatment for some claims requires multiyear estimates of loss development, and many injured workers have prior medical conditions that increase risk at the time of policy inception.

Case Rate Arrangements

Via this reimbursement method, organized providers receive one fixed payment for all medical treatment for a particular diagnosis (backs, knees, carpal tunnel, etc.). This method requires a larger number of claims to spread risk and audit controls to ensure that upcoding to higher-valued diagnoses (e.g., Medicare diagnosis-related groups) does not occur.

Modified Fee for Service

Under this method, providers would be paid a discount from the state fee schedule. That discount would be held in a fund that would later be paid back with a bonus above the fee schedule if medical and disability cost reduction goals were met.

Addressing Worker Expectations

When treating and counseling injured workers, the managed care professional must understand the concepts of entitlement and secondary gain. The injured worker, protected by law from copayments and deductibles, generally feels entitled to benefits. This perspective can inflate workers' compensation medical costs when workers demand excessive medical services and delay their return to work as long as possible. Although most workers (85 percent) do not respond to an injury this way, the 15 percent who do account for a disproportionate share of cost to the employer.[4]

Moreover, the majority of workers' compensation costs (55 percent) are not for medical benefits, but for disability benefits, primarily wage replacement. These benefits create, especially for low-wage workers, a secondary gain from the injury, whereby the worker benefits from a more exaggerated injury and higher medical expenses, which create a greater disability award.

These two simple concepts help us understand the opportunities and limitations in applying the precepts of managed care to workers' compensation. The most effective techniques to control workers' expectations involve clarity of clinical directions, treatment, and return to work date.

Developing Protocols for Case Management

The most effective managed care plans will carefully incorporate medical and disability protocols into utilization management. Disability protocols will be based not simply on duration guidelines (specific target disability days by diagnosis) but rather on a complex understanding of the injury, the age and occupation of the injured worker, and the match of the functional capacity of the worker with specific job skills.

Medical protocols will be attentive to the requirement of some workers' compensation claims for intensive medical treatment early in the claim, including physical therapy and diagnostic testing. This type of treatment, which sometimes facilitates return to work, differs significantly from group health managed care protocols. Moreover, the most successful plans will incorporate methods for educating, monitoring, and reeducating providers regarding adherence to both types of protocols.

Establishing Managed Care Alliances

HMOs have been involved in several alliances with workers' compensation carriers. Several types of alliances exist, depending upon the degree of integration occurring.

Equity-based alliances involve the purchase of a workers' compensation carrier by a health plan. This type of alliance generally involves flexible bundled pricing, unified underwriting templates, single enrollment and early intervention, integrated case and claims management, and unified reporting. From a financial standpoint, the health carrier, whose losses are generally confined to a calendar year, must plan for the multiyear claims of its workers' compensation subsidiary.

Administrative-based alliances involve a front-end composite of the administrative features of group health, disability, and workers' compensation without equity ownership. This approach may involve a pooled joint venture into a separate entity funded by each party. Additionally, it usually involves early intervention, triage across benefits, identification of duplicate coverage, and composite pricing.

Marketing alliances involve the side-by-side marketing of policies between a health plan and a workers' compensation insurance carrier via the sharing of customer and prospect lists. Additionally, the preferred use of the health plan's provider network for workers' compensation care is an important ingredient. This type of alliance may be a pilot predecessor to one of the two types of more integrated alliances described above.

Within all these types of alliances, it is likely that the workers' compensation insurance industry will gradually be eclipsed by the health care industry, which is significantly larger. For that reason, the workers' compensation insurance carriers are attempting to assert their distinctive capabilities (underwriting of long-tail risk, administration of claims, and safety and return to work procedures). These capabilities have not been strong in the health care industry, which is relying on its expertise in managed care for hegemony in workers' compensation. This perspective is not likely to succeed unless health plans address several of the key issues described above.

THE EMPLOYER PERSPECTIVE: CHANGING THE CORPORATE CULTURE

Managed workers' compensation has been a vendor-driven phenomenon. Employers are starting to realize its importance as a way of integrating benefits. Savvy employers now recognize two major areas where change must occur. First, employee health benefits, workers' compensation (both medical care and disability), group disability, wellness, and employee assistance programs have been administered largely as separate undertakings. The risk management

department, on the finance side of the organization, traditionally administers workers' compensation as part of its property and casualty responsibilities. Human resources and employee benefits, a separate corporate silo, take responsibility for health benefits. Long-term disability may not be on anyone's radar screen because it is often insured rather than offered as a benefit by a self-funded plan under the Employee Retirement Income Security Act (ERISA; see Chapter 59). Thus the transition operation will probably include the removal of organizational silos and the fusion of a time-loss management program.

In addition to these internal barriers, purchasers have been faced with a proliferation of specialty vendors that promise to manage certain elements of the employer's exposure more effectively. On the health benefits side, these carve-outs include behavioral health, various drug programs, wellness, and, more recently, disease-specific management. In workers' compensation, employers can choose third party administrators, medical and hospital bill review organizations, case management, specialty providers for back or repetitive motion injuries, and a host of others. The cost of administering a multitude of carve-out vendors has led some employers to conclude that they are giving back the medical management savings in administrative friction and expense. For these employers, the prospect of carving in, or consolidating the management of all benefits, is attractive.

THE NEXT STEP FOR EMPLOYERS: COMPREHENSIVE MEDICAL EVENTS MANAGEMENT

The goal of comprehensive medical event management is to minimize administrative expenses by creating centralized management of the entire range of health care services provided to employees, both occupational and nonoccupational. Although the concept may appear simple and straightforward, major changes in corporate culture and organizational structure must occur, and territorial issues between human resource departments and risk managers must be settled. Not to be underestimated, demands and expectations of workers must be addressed.

After a vision is developed of how medical events and overall employee downtime will be managed in the future, the challenge is how to get there from the current state of normal operations. Designers of a corporate benefits network must look at all the components of employee downtime, whether it be a workers' compensation injury, other illness, or even a family crisis, with an eye on integration of those benefits so that workers do not migrate from a restricted managed care medical benefit into an unlimited workers' compensation and disability program.

For many employers seeking to control both occupational (workers' compensation) and nonoccupational medical and disability costs and to maximize productivity, comprehensive medical event management will be the foundation of future health care savings. The core function in such a management system will be a single point of entry for notification and tracking of all medical events. This front end will be a robust triage system for tracking calls from employees and supervisors. There are three key benefits to establishing a single point of entry: early capture of lost-time events so that they can be managed optimally, construction of a data file for tracking multiple calls concerning a single event, and creation of a foundation for developing an enterprisewide database on lost time.

An essential capability of the single point of entry function will be integrated partnerships with managed care organizations. These organizations will have the ability to manage occupational or nonoccupational acute medical events efficiently and appropriately. In addition, future delivery models will have a mechanism for placing individual providers at partial risk for return to work.

The totally managed model will incorporate process maps for the optimal claims administration of each of the benefit systems that flow from the single entry point. For disability and work-

ers' compensation, these claims processing maps will include claims notification, case management, reserve setting, diagnosis-specific treatment protocols, return to work protocols, medical direction systems, and payment systems. For medical benefits, the administrative flow will be directed toward utilizing credentialed and contracted medical providers proficient in disability management. Finally, future savings strategies will include various programs such as comprehensive demand management, including self-care and life style management, health promotion and disease prevention, safety, and ergonomics.

CONCLUSION

Given the fact that $42 billion was paid to workers' compensation beneficiaries in 1991, up from $38 billion in 1990, and that no long-term abatement in that trend is likely, it seems inevitable that managed care techniques will be applied increasingly to the workers' compensation market.[5] The signs are already apparent. Direct, first-dollar, guaranteed-cost insurance for workers' compensation is declining in significance, and more and more managed care providers are developing products to meet the needs of comprehensive medical event management.

The workers' compensation insurance marketplace will probably become increasingly usurped by HMOs and other managed health plans. Insurers will play an increasingly administrative role, and employees will receive a seamless benefit package regardless of the place of injury.

To succeed in a state-regulated workers' compensation world, designers of the new integrated, single-source health plans must emphasize the appropriate and efficient management of medical events. The recent health care reform debate exposed the pitfalls in attempting to weave ERISA plans for employer-sponsored health benefits into the patchwork quilt of statutory workers' compensation programs. Farsighted managed care organizations and carriers will deemphasize the issues of funding and risk financing in favor of high-quality, efficient medical event management. Furthermore, employer interest in reducing employee downtime and the focus on return to work offer opportunities for organizations to integrate the management of both workers' compensation and group short- and long-term disability.

REFERENCES AND NOTES

1. B. Zaidman, *Industrial Strength Medicine: A Comparison of Workers' Compensation and Blue Cross Health Care in Minnesota* (Minneapolis, Minn.: Minnesota Department of Labor and Industry, 1990), 83.

2. L.L. Boden and C.A. Fleischman, *Medical Costs in Workers' Compensation: Trends and Interstate Comparisons* (Cambridge, Mass.: Workers' Compensation Research Institute, 1989).

3. Final Florida Pilot Shows Big Gains from HMO, PPO, *Workers' Compensation Managed Care* (September 1994): 7.

4. J.R. Douglas, *Managing Workers' Compensation* (New York, N.Y.: Wiley Law Publications, 1994), 11.

5. Employee Benefits Research Institute, *EBRI Databook on Employee Benefits*, 3d ed. (Washington, D.C., 1995), 594.

SUGGESTED READING

Doyle, R.L. *Healthcare Management Guidelines: Return-to-Work Planning*. Milliman & Robertson. Updated periodically.

Part VII

Regulatory and Legal Issues

"A wise government knows how to enforce
with temper or to conciliate
with dignity."

George Grenville
(1712–1770)
Speech against expulsion of John Wilkes, in Parliament (1769)

Chapter 53

State Regulation of Managed Care

Garry Carneal

Integration and innovation by managed care organizations (MCOs) are rapidly changing the health care marketplace. These changes pose significant challenges for state and federal regulators charged with protecting consumer interests and maintaining a level regulatory playing field. A central goal of licensure requirements is to ensure that consumers receive the medical coverage that they have been promised.

Regulators, through appropriate statutory authority, must issue and update regulations continually and revitalize efforts to oversee health plan operations to provide strong consumer protections for all health plan enrollees. These efforts are necessary to ensure a fair and level competitive environment. The organizational structure of managed care plans, however, usually determines how they are regulated by government officials, especially in the states. In addition to enabling statutes and regulations, other sources of authority govern MCO operations. Regulators supplement their regulations with written policy statements, and internal office policies help them address specific issues. Federal oversight also may play an important role, depending on the managed care product offering.

Garry Carneal is Vice President of the American Association of Health Plans (recently formed through the merger of the Group Health Association of America, Inc. and the American Managed Care Review Association, Inc.).

In most cases, the key to state regulation is the fact that the MCO has assumed insurance risk for the provision of medical services [e.g., health maintenance organizations (HMOs) and physician–hospital organizations (PHOs)], or the MCO provides one or more services pursuant to a fully insured arrangement [e.g., preferred provider organizations (PPOs) and utilization review organizations (UROs)].

This chapter highlights the role of state regulation and MCO operations. In particular, it describes governance of HMO operations. HMOs serve as the best case study of state-based managed care regulation because they have been regulated the most extensively by the states. Many of the regulatory concerns detailed below are based on the HMO Model Act and the *HMO Examination Handbook*, both of which were adopted by the National Association of Insurance Commissioners (NAIC).[1] The NAIC represents insurance departments in the 50 states and U.S. territories. In 1972, the NAIC adopted the HMO Model Act. The NAIC wanted to create a model bill that clearly authorized the establishment of HMOs and provided for an ongoing regulatory monitoring system. The HMO Model Act, or substantial portions thereof, has now been enacted by 28 states. The NAIC, along with the National Association of Managed Care Regulators, continues to develop new regulatory guidelines for the MCO and insurance industries.

STATE OVERSIGHT: THE REGULATORY PROCESS

HMOs

On the state level, HMOs usually are regulated by more than one agency. Typically, regulatory supervision is shared by the departments of insurance and health. Insurance regulators assume principal responsibility for the financial aspects of HMO operations. Health regulators focus on quality of care issues, utilization patterns, and the ability of participating providers to provide adequate care. In a few instances, other state subdivisions may be charged with some supervisory duties. For example, whereas California's Department of Insurance is charged with overseeing PPOs, the state's Department of Corporations regulates HMOs, which are organized under the California Knox Keene Act. In a few states, only one agency oversees all MCO questions. For example, the North Carolina Department of Insurance regulates HMOs, PPOs, and indemnity plans.

Licensure

HMOs obtain licensure by applying for a certificate of authority (COA). An organization may be incorporated for the sole purpose of becoming licensed as an HMO, or an existing company may sponsor an HMO product line through a subsidiary or affiliated organization. Applications usually are processed by the insurance department and, among other items, include the following documents: corporate bylaws, sample provider and group contract forms, evidence of coverage forms, financial statements, financial feasibility plan, description of service area, internal grievance procedures, and the proposed quality assurance program. Payment of licensing fees is usually required, and about one third of the states assess premium taxes against HMOs.[2]

The licensure and recertification process provides state officials with a mechanism to ensure that the HMO is operating properly and is in compliance with all the applicable laws and regulations. If an HMO or other health plan fails to submit to this oversight, it probably will be considered by regulators as engaging in the unauthorized practice of insurance and may be subject to criminal and civil penalties.

Certificate of Need

In addition to obtaining a COA, HMOs may be subject to a state's certificate of need (CON) law. Thirty-four states and the District of Columbia have CON statutory provisions that regulate the construction, alteration, or licensing of a health care facility. About 25 state CON laws can apply to HMOs.[3] CON approval also may be required for the acquisition of equipment and changes in the level of services or beds. Insofar as HMOs operate and run health care facilities, regulatory permission may be required to carry out these types of activities.

Enrollee Information

The HMO Model Act sets forth requirements for communicating health plan information to HMO enrollees. Enrollees are entitled to receive a copy of individual and group contracts. Misleading, confusing, and unjust provisions are prohibited. Each contract must contain basic information describing eligibility requirements, covered benefits, out-of-pocket expenses, limitations and exclusions, termination or cancellation of policies, claims processing, grievance procedures, continuation of benefits, conversion rights, subrogation rights, term of coverage, and grace period after nonpayment of premiums. Regulators require these documents to be filed with and approved by the regulatory body in charge of reviewing contracts.

In addition to individual and group contacts, the HMO Model Act requires HMOs to make other disclosures. Every enrollee is entitled to receive a document referred to as the evidence of coverage, which describes essential features and services of the HMO. Plans also must provide details about how services can be obtained through the HMO network and a telephone number at the plan for answers to additional questions. Upon enrollment or reenrollment, members must receive a list of all health plan providers. Within 30 days after a material change in the plan, HMOs must notify enrollees of the change if it has a direct impact on them.

Access to Medical Services

HMOs must ensure the availability and accessibility of medical services. HMO patients should have access to medical care during reasonable hours; emergency care should be provided 24 hours a day, 7 days a week. Regulators limit an HMO's COA to designated service areas (usually established by ZIP code regions or counties) where a determination has been made that the HMO has a sufficient provider network. Regulators also establish protocols governing HMO specialty referrals to ensure appropriate accessibility. In addition, most states require HMOs to offer an annual open enrollment period to prospective enrollees or in the event of another health plan's insolvency.[4]

Provider Issues

HMOs are required to execute written contracts with providers that join the HMO's network, commonly referred to as participating providers. Upon initial application for a COA, and periodically thereafter, regulators review sample contracts for primary care, specialty care, and ancillary services. Contracts must contain a number of provisions, including a list of covered services, details about how physicians will be paid, hold-harmless language, the contract term, termination procedures, and an obligation to adhere to HMO quality assurance and utilization management programs.

Regulators also are concerned about provider risk-sharing arrangements. Most HMOs share the risk for the cost of health care with their providers (principally primary care physicians) through performance-based reimbursement, including capitated payment mechanisms, and periodically through withholds and pooling arrangements. Under capitation, a provider usually is compensated on a fixed, prepaid basis (e.g., per member per month). In addition, providers may participate in a withhold arrangement under which the HMO withholds a portion of the provider's payment (e.g., 5 percent) during a 12-month period to cover excess medical expenses; providers receive any funds that remain in the pool at the end of the contract period. Regulators carefully scrutinize these types of reimbursement formulas to ensure that quality of care is not compromised and that provider solvency is not jeopardized.

Reports and Rate Filings

State regulators employ a number of methods to ensure that licensed HMOs remain in compliance with the law. Typically, HMOs must file an annual report with the insurance department. This report must include audited financial statements, a list of participating providers, an update and summary of enrollee grievances handled during the year, and any additional information that regulators deem necessary to make a proper review of the organization.

The HMO Model Act also requires HMOs to file a schedule of premium rates or a methodology for determining premium rates with the insurance department. Regulators normally will approve the schedule or methodology if premiums are not excessive, inadequate, or unfairly discriminatory.

In addition, states require HMOs to update regulators automatically if there are changes in documents that were part of the initial COA application filing (or part of the annual filings). Regulators keep permanent records, including primary care physician agreements, specialist provider contracts, group and individual contracts, certificate of coverage, and other pertinent information.

Quality Assurance and Utilization Review

The NAIC's model requires HMOs to file a description of their proposed quality assurance program before obtaining state licensure. HMOs must also establish procedures to ensure that the health care services provided to their enrollees are "rendered under reasonable standards of quality of care consistent with prevailing professionally recognized standards of medical practice."[5] In most states, statutory and regulatory quality assurance requirements are supplemented with internal departmental guidelines, as exemplified in the NAIC's *HMO Examination Handbook.*

Examination of an HMO's quality assurance program begins with a review of relevant documents, including a comprehensive description of the program. Regulators then assess how well the HMO is carrying out its quality assurance responsibilities. Preventive care activities, program administration, provider credentialing, utilization review (UR) procedures, risk management, provider payment mechanisms, access to HMO services, medical records, claims payment procedures, and management information services are reviewed carefully in the quality assurance evaluation. Some states, notably Kansas and Pennsylvania, require an HMO to obtain an independent external review of its quality assurance program from approved review agencies, such as the National Committee for Quality Assurance (NCQA; see Chapter 37).

HMOs often are subject to a higher level of regulatory oversight for quality assurance activities than other MCOs and indemnity health plans, in part because HMOs were the first plans to link prepaid health care delivery systems and financial insurance. Furthermore, HMOs are subject to multiple quality assurance regulations. Sources of quality assurance oversight include a state's HMO enabling law, the federal HMO Act (see Chapter 54), the Medicare risk-contracting program (see Chapters 46 and 47), Medicaid managed care laws (see Chapter 48), and private accrediting organizations such as the NCQA.

Grievance Procedures

The HMO Model Act requires establishment of a grievance procedure to help resolve enrollee complaints (see Chapter 30 for an example). States often specify how these grievances should be handled. Typically, regulators require each HMO to form a grievance committee to hear complaints. Enrollees must be informed of their right to a hearing, usually in writing, when they join the HMO. Decisions by the committee may be appealed within the HMO, and if necessary the state may step in to hear the complaint. The number of grievances filed and processed by an HMO also must be reported on a regular basis to the appropriate regulatory body.

Solvency Protection

The HMO Model Act establishes specific capital, reserve, and deposit requirements for HMOs to protect consumers and other interested parties against insolvency. Before a COA is issued, an initial net worth requirement of $1.5 million is required. After issuance, a minimum net worth must be maintained by the HMO equal to the greater of $1 million, the sum of 2 percent of annual premiums on the first $150 million of premiums and 1 percent on the excess, the sum of 3 months' uncovered health care costs, or the sum of 8 percent of annual health expenditures (except those paid on a capitated basis or a managed hospital payment basis) and 4 percent of annual hospital expenses paid on a managed payment basis.

The HMO Model Act also requires a minimum deposit of $300,000 with the insurance department. The deposit is considered an admitted asset of the HMO in the determination of its net worth, but it is used to protect the interests of HMO enrollees or to cover administrative costs if the HMO goes into receivership or liquidation. As mentioned above, most states also require HMOs to include hold-harmless clauses in their provider contracts. In situations where the HMO fails to pay for covered medical care, such clauses prohibit providers from seeking collection from the enrollees. California and New York have statutory hold-harmless requirements protecting enrollees even in the absence of a contractual provision. Many states also require that HMOs enter into reinsurance arrangements to cover liabilities in the event of an insolvency.

A few states (Alabama, Florida, Illinois, Vermont, Virginia, and Wisconsin) also require HMOs to participate in guaranty fund programs.[6] These state programs provide funding to cover an HMO's potential liabilities for health care services if it becomes insolvent. Regulators may use this money to reimburse nonparticipating providers, to pay for the continuation of benefits, and to cover conversion costs. Guaranty funds have been implemented almost universally for life, health, and accident insurance policies. Only one or two states, however, require HMO participation in their life and health guaranty associations. In four states, HMOs reinsure each other through a standalone HMO guaranty association or insolvency assessment fund. The NAIC HMO Model Act also includes a provision to establish an insolvency assessment fund based on a law in the Commonwealth of Virginia. The NAIC drafting notes accompanying this section in the HMO Model Act, however, specifically state that this mechanism is not recommended for all states because there may be inadequate premium volume or too few HMOs to make an assessment feasible.

States often require HMOs to establish contingency plans for insolvency that allow for the continuation of benefits to enrollees during the contract period for which premiums have been paid. If necessary, insurance departments require HMOs to take further precautions to safeguard enrollee benefits. These additional measures might include purchasing additional insurance, entering into contracts obligating providers to continue delivering care if the HMO ceases operation, setting aside additional solvency reserves, or securing letters of credit.

If a regulator determines that an HMO's financial condition threatens enrollees, creditors, or the general public, the regulator usually has broad discretion to order the HMO to take specific corrective actions. Such actions may include reducing potential liabilities through reinsurance, suspending the volume of new business for a period of time, or increasing the HMO's capital and surplus contributions.

Financial Examinations and Site Visits

Regulators also can conduct specialized inquiries, which often examine HMO finances, marketing activities, and quality assurance programs. In part, the objective of these regulatory reviews is to determine the HMO's financial solvency and statutory compliance and whether any trends can be identified that may cause problems in the future. For example, the HMO Model Act requires the insurance department to complete a detailed examination of the HMO's financial affairs at least once every 3 years. The NAIC's *HMO Examination Handbook* sets forth specific procedures for examining HMO balance sheet assets and liabilities. The goals are to verify ownership and stated asset amounts and to ensure the adequacy of the HMO's net worth to meet current and future liabilities. Examiners may review an HMO's existing cash resources; investments; premium receivables; interest receivables; prepaid expenses; restricted assets; leasehold arrangements; accounts payable; unpaid claims; unearned premiums; outstanding loans; statutory liability; building, land, equipment, and inventory lists; and other company assets and costs.

If the HMO is undercapitalized or otherwise short of funds, regulators usually provide an opportunity for the HMO to take corrective action. Regulators take financial shortfalls seriously, however, and will suspend or revoke an HMO's license if necessary to protect consumer interests.

As part of the examination process, regulators may conduct a site visit to see the HMO's operations first hand, to review health plan documents, and to assess the efficiency and soundness of plan operations. The site visit may be relatively brief, or it can take place over a period of days or weeks. Occasionally, regulators contact participating providers and enrollees directly to determine how the HMO is operating.

Point-of-Service Offerings

Interest in coverage that includes a point-of-service option has grown in recent years; more than 10 million HMO enrollees now participate in such a plan.[7] This interest has been fueled by employers, which are seeking better control over their health care expenditures while trying to provide their employees the freedom to choose whether to seek health care within or outside the HMO provider network. HMOs prefer to market point-of-service products on their own by underwriting out-of-plan benefits, referred to as a standalone product. Most state laws, however, prohibit HMOs from offering a point-of-service product without entering into an agreement with an insurance company to cover the out-of-plan usage, referred to as a wraparound product.

In 1993, Group Health Association of America (GHAA) examined the ability of HMOs to offer point-of-service products at the state level.[8] Eleven states (Alabama, Iowa, Maine, Michigan, Minnesota, North Carolina, Oklahoma, Pennsylvania, Utah, Virginia, and Wisconsin) have adopted laws, regulations, or published other guidelines allowing HMOs to market standalone point-of-service products, where the HMO underwrites out-of-plan usage. Five states (Indiana, Kentucky, Louisiana, Maryland, and New Jersey) permit a standalone HMO point-of-service offering if approved by the appropriate state agency. The remaining 34 states and the District of Columbia either do not expressly regulate or prohibit HMOs from offering point-of-service products on a standalone basis.

Thirty-seven states, however, may allow HMO-sponsored point-of-service products on a wraparound basis through statute, regulation, or rule or after an agency review. Thirteen states and the District of Columbia either do not expressly regulate or prohibit HMOs from offering a point-of-service product on a wraparound basis. GHAA's 1993 survey identified the following corporate relationships underpinning wraparound offerings:

- *HMO-controlled offerings*, where the HMO contracts with an indemnity carrier directly (the employer signs one contract with the HMO and pays one premium)

- *shared venture offerings*, where the HMO and the indemnity carrier contract separately with the employer (the employer signs two contracts and pays two premiums)

- *multiple licensed parent company offerings*, where the HMO and the indemnity carrier are affiliates or subsidiaries of the same parent company, which offers both plans to the employer

- *insurance company offerings*, where the HMO must be a licensed insurance company

- *indemnity trust agreements*, where the indemnity carrier issues the indemnity portion to a trust, which then contracts with employer groups

In the states that regulate HMO-sponsored point-of-service products, the following provisions are typical: a limit on the percentage (5 percent to 20 percent) of total health care expenditures for enrollees who obtain services outside the plan; an increased net worth requirement; a tracking system to measure in-network and out-of-network utilization separately; authority and encouragement to use increased copayments, deductibles, and limits on covered out-of-plan benefits as disincentives to the use of out-of-plan services; and a mechanism for processing and paying for all out-of-plan service claims.

In 1995, three states adopted laws mandating that HMOs offer point-of-service products in certain situations. Oregon's SB 979 and Maryland's SB 449 require HMOs to offer point-of-service options to employer groups if the HMO offers a traditional closed panel option, and New York passed SB 5469A requiring all HMOs to offer individuals (i.e., nongroup coverage) a point-of-service option. Previously, New York also adopted a law mandating that HMOs offer a closed panel product to individuals under the state's 1992 community rating/open enrollment law. Ironically, these new laws fail to provide the same consumer protections as those in states that have adopted voluntary point-of-service provisions, as described in the preceding paragraph. This situation is a byproduct of recent Provider Protection Act (PPA) initiatives, which are discussed later.

Multistate Operations

With many HMOs now operating in more than one state, HMOs must comply with the regulations of each jurisdiction. Other multistate MCOs can face the same regulatory challenge when complying with the rules in more than one state as well. Most states mandate that foreign HMOs meet the same requirements applicable to domestic HMOs. States also may require that out-of-state HMOs register to do business under the appropriate foreign corporation law and appoint an agent in the state for receipt of legal notifications.

Multistate operations can become expensive if plans are subject to numerous financial examinations and other regulatory requirements. To alleviate this concern, some states permit regulators who are considering the application of a foreign HMO to accept financial reports and other information from the HMO's state of origin. The NAIC also has established guidelines for coordinating examinations of HMOs licensed in more than one state. The coordinated examination is called for by the lead state, where the HMO is domiciled; other states where the HMO operates are encouraged to participate. Occasionally, regulations in one state may adversely affect or hinder the operations of an HMO licensed in another state.

Historically, group insurance policies generally have been subject to the law of the state of issuance. A policy issued in state A would be subject to that state's insurance laws and regulations, including mandated benefits. This general rule has been eroded by extraterritorial application of state insurance law. The laws of state B may require that any state B resident covered under a group health policy, even if issued in state A, receive the same coverage that would be required had the group policy been issued in state B.

PPOs

PPOs are created when a health insurer contracts with a group of providers to provide medical care. PPOs are open panel or point-of-service arrangements where consumers can choose between participating providers and nonparticipating providers outside the network. By staying in the PPO network, the consumer's out-of-pocket costs are lower and benefit levels higher.

PPOs are regulated on the state level, usually by the state insurance department. In 29 states, PPO enabling legislation has been adopted.[9] In the remaining states and the District of Columbia, PPO activities are regulated by insurance laws governing indemnity plans and managed care functions. PPO regulatory supervision is not as intense as HMO oversight. For example, the NAIC's HMO Model Act has 34 sections covered in 31 pages, whereas the NAIC's PPO Model Act has nine sections covered in four pages. Many regulators believe that fewer regulations are needed to govern PPO operations because PPOs already are regulated through other insurance laws and regulations. Furthermore, PPOs often are less structured than HMOs. For example, a PPO could be just a contractual arrangement without being formally incorporated.

Of the states that have enacted specific PPO laws, the most common areas of regulatory oversight include provider participation requirements (21 states), UR (19 states), restrictions on provider incentives (18 states), access to providers (16 states), and benefit level differentials (15 states). Other areas include manner of provider payments (12 states), emergency care (12 states), quality assurance and improvement (12 states), grievance procedures (10 states), enrollee contracts (8 states), solvency requirements (6 states), and unlicensed insurers (5 states).[10]

Some experts have expressed concerns about the inequities between PPO and HMO regulation. For example, noticeably absent from the NAIC's PPO Model Act is oversight of quality assurance, including credentialing requirements for PPOs. This may explain why most states do not regulate the quality assurance activities of PPOs and why, in the 12 states that do, such regulations are less stringent than those applied to HMOs.

Inequities between PPO and HMO regulations may begin to diminish in the near future, however. For example, the NAIC is currently drafting eight new regulatory standards dealing with quality assurance, credentialing, UR, grievance procedures, provider contracting, data reporting, confidentiality, and accessibility. If adopted, these standards would serve as a baseline for HMOs, PPOs, and other MCOs.

PHOs

PHOs are joint ventures between physicians and hospitals that contract with employers and health plans to provide medical services and other functions. The PHO may be organized for a single purpose, such as acting as a single agent for managed care contracting, or it may be organized for multiple purposes. A PHO may perform the same functions as an HMO, including the promise to provide comprehensive coverage on a prepaid capitated basis. A PHO also could function in a fashion similar to a PPO or other MCO arrangements. There are also other forms of integrated delivery systems as described in Chapter 4, but the issues that pertain to all of them will be discussed here in the context of PHOs.

The NAIC has called attention to the rising number of unregulated, risk-bearing PHOs and recently issued a model bulletin for use by state insurance commissioners calling for the licensure of such plans. In circumstances where PHOs assume full or limited insurance risk directly from the employer, most state regulators believe that they have the statutory authority to require the licensure of a PHO as a health plan to safeguard consumer interests. Simply put, regulators use the "duck test": If a PHO looks, waddles, and quacks like an HMO, it should be licensed as a HMO.

A 1995 survey, however, revealed that some gaps in state oversight exist, particularly when PHOs assume full or partial insurance risk directly from employers.[11] Regulators in 25 states in 1995 responded that they have no affirmative policy to require licensure of a PHO when the transfer of risk to a PHO from an employer is limited (e.g., up to 110 percent of an annual predetermined budget). Regulators in nine states reported that they have no affirmative policy to require PHOs to become licensed as an HMO or to meet similar requirements if the PHO assumes full financial risk (i.e., the PHO contracts directly with the employer on a prepaid capitated basis for all medical services). In addition, most regulators replied that no state licensure is necessary for PHOs if they accept downstream transfers of insurance risk or if they assume no risk because the employer self-funds in accordance with the Employee Retirement Income Security Act (ERISA; see Chapter 59) of 1974.

Even in states where regulators said that PHO licensure would be required under one or more of the proposed scenarios, regulators often did not know how many risk-bearing PHOs were in operation within their respective states. In many states, actual enforcement of regulatory standards for PHOs is often passive or nonexistent. Enforcement patterns have begun to improve in some states, however, as regulators become more aware of the existence of risk-bearing entities (PHOs and similar unregulated entities) and strive to maintain a level regulatory playing field. As a result, active regulatory oversight should increase the level of consumer protections, including solvency and quality of care safeguards.

Prepaid Limited Health Service Organizations

A prepaid limited health service organization is a corporate venture that contracts on a prepaid basis to provide or arrange for provision of one or more limited health services to enrollees. Health services are usually limited to mental health, substance abuse, dental services, pharmaceutical services, podiatric care, and vision care. According to the NAIC, only seven states have enacted legislation authorizing these limited managed care businesses.[12] General regulatory requirements for prepaid limited health service organizations are similar to, but not as comprehensive as, those in the HMO Model Act. Requirements include licensure and issuance of a COA, filing requirements, review of payment methodologies, development of a complaint system, periodic examinations, financial and investment guidelines, insolvency protections, oversight of agents, confidentiality rules, issuance of a fidelity bond for officers and employees, and provider contracting standards.

UROs

With the growing demand by employers to manage utilization of health care services and to control costs, independent UROs have proliferated quickly. At least 28 states have enacted comprehensive UR laws that require specific protocols and mandate licensure of individuals or corporate entities that conduct UR.[13,14] At least 16 of the states include full or partial exemptions for HMOs that conduct their own UR activity because HMOs' UR activity is regulated through state HMO laws.

One example of a comprehensive UR law is Connecticut's statute that requires UROs to be licensed and meet strict minimum standards. Licensed UROs in Connecticut must do the following:

* maintain and make available procedures for providing notification of admissions or coverage determinations to the provider or plan enrollee

* maintain and make available a written description of the appeal procedure by which either the enrollee or the provider may seek review of determinations not to certify an admission, service, procedure, or extension of stay

* provide for an expedited appeals process for emergency or life-threatening situations

* use established, written clinical criteria and review procedures that are to be periodically evaluated and updated with provider input

* ensure that nurses, practitioners, and other licensed health professionals making UR decisions have current licenses

* ensure that, in cases where an appeal to reverse a determination not to certify is unsuccessful, a practitioner in a specialty related to the condition is reasonably available to review the case

* make review staff available by a toll-free telephone number at least 40 hours per week during normal business hours

* comply with all federal and state laws to protect the confidentiality of individual medical records

* allow a minimum of 24 hours after an emergency admission, service, or procedure for an enrollee or his or her representative to notify the URO and request certification or continuing treatment for that condition

If a URO contracts on an exclusive basis with self-funded employers, its operations are regulated by ERISA, and state law does not apply. Currently, however, ERISA does not regulate UR activities. Many state regulators argue that, if a URO has even one commercial contract where a health plan is assuming the insurance risk (not the employer), all the URO's operations are subject to state laws.

Unfortunately, the combination of standalone UR laws and UR requirements in HMO laws (i.e., in states where HMOs are not exempted from the comprehensive UR law) can create confusion and be unnecessarily duplicative. For example, single-state HMOs can become subject to interstate UR regulations, thereby creating numerous problems. Several states require that all UR agents who inquire about a patient's treatment be licensed in that particular state to gain access to medical records and other pertinent information.[15] Occasionally, a HMO primary care physician cannot obtain his or her enrollee's medical information because the enrollee is injured in another state, and the physician is not a licensed UR agent where the patient is hospitalized. Such interpretations would require single-state HMOs to apply for UR licensure in dozens of states simply to gain access to HMO members' files should individuals need out-of-area emergency treatment.

Third Party Administrators

A third party administrator (TPA) is an organization that administers group benefits and claims for a self-funded company or group. A TPA normally does not assume any insurance risk. Thirty-six states require licensure of TPAs if they do business in a state.[16] Almost half these states require licensure even if there only is one plan participant residing in the state. Approximately five states require licensing if a certain percentage or number of plan participants reside in the state. About one third of all states provide for an exemption for state licensure if the TPA administers only single-employer self-funded plans. State TPA laws typically govern the following[17]:

- the TPA's written agreement with insurers, including a statement of duties
- payment methodology
- maintenance and disclosure of records
- insurer responsibilities, such as determination of benefit levels
- fiduciary obligations when the TPA collects charges and premiums
- issuance of TPA licenses and grounds for suspension or revocation
- filing of annual reports and payment of fees

Self-Funded Plans

Under self-funded arrangements, where the employer assumes the financial risk of its employees' health care costs, state regulators can do little to supervise employer efforts to manage its health plan. Self-funded arrangements usually are defined as employee benefit plans under

ERISA and thus are exempt from state regulation. In essence, these plans are not considered in the business of insurance for the purpose of any state law governing insurance activities. With the growing trend by employers to self-fund, state regulators have expressed concern over the lack of authority to protect consumers under these arrangements. It is now common for large employers to use managed care in a self-funded arrangement, thereby avoiding state regulations such as mandated benefits and premium taxes.

MCOs that otherwise have state-licensed products usually can offer limited services under self-funded arrangements in at least two ways:

1. *Administrative services only*—Regulated entities such as insurance companies and HMOs can offer a nonregulated managed care product under an administrative services only arrangement with an employer that assumes the financial risk of the benefits plan. The MCO handles administrative functions for the employer group.

2. *Exclusive provider organizations*—By definition, exclusive provider organizations are not regulated because they coordinate health services in self-funded plans and administrative services only arrangements. Under these circumstances, an HMO or PPO could rent out its provider panel to a self-funded employer. The employer would pay the MCO on a fee-for-service basis for medical services rendered to avoid any transfer of insurance risk from the employer to the MCO or providers.

ANTI–MANAGED CARE LEGISLATION

According to operators of HMOs and other MCO delivery systems, these organizations cannot operate successfully—that is, provide high-quality, cost-effective care—in the absence of certain features, including quality assurance procedures, prepayment for services, and selective contracting. Recently, however, many states have moved toward redefining the ground rules and interfering with the basic underpinnings of MCO operations.

PPA Proposals

In 1995, the American Medical Association and state medical societies aggressively promoted provider protection initiatives, the socalled PPA, in most states and in Congress. Under the guise of consumer protection, these bills call for regulatory controls over HMOs and other MCOs. Much of this regulation, however, already exists at both state and federal levels. When these duplicate requirements are stripped away from most PPA proposals, the remaining provisions are primarily special preferences that physicians are seeking for themselves, not consumers. Specific PPA components include the following[18]:

- mandatory point-of-service offerings
- burdensome due process protocols for aggrieved physicians as well as restrictions on a health plan's ability to remove physicians from their network
- any willing credentialing requirements (mandating health plans to credential all providers who apply to become a "participating provider" even if the health plan is not expanding its network) and disclosure of credentialing standards
- prohibition of certain generally accepted financial incentives as well as disclosure of all financial incentives
- establishment of duplicate health plan standards and state certification requirements

Generally, PPA regulations would damage the ability of HMOs and other MCOs to select the physicians who are best suited to the needs of their members by providing physicians with unprecedented rights to affiliate with managed care plans. PPA bills were introduced in more than 25 states during 1995. At the time of this writing, PPA bills were defeated in 20 states, and two scaled-back versions were adopted in Oregon and Maryland.

Any Willing Provider Initiatives

The creation of selective provider panels is a cornerstone of MCO operations. Many states, however, have enacted laws, commonly referred to as any willing provider (AWP) laws, that prevent MCOs from selectively contracting with a limited group of providers. The classic AWP law requires an MCO to accept into its network any nonparticipating provider willing to meet the terms and conditions of the MCO. The Federal Trade Commission concurs with MCO professionals' opinion that such legislation threatens the viability of MCOs. Thus in nine states (California, Illinois, Massachusetts, Montana, Nevada, New Hampshire, Pennsylvania, South Carolina, and Texas) that have considered AWP legislation, the Federal Trade Commission has written opinion letters indicating that AWP bills pose a serious anticompetitive threat. The NAIC and the National Governors Association also have issued statements opposing AWP laws.[19]

Furthermore, several studies have documented the potential costs of implementing AWP laws. In June 1994, Atkinson & Company, an actuarial firm retained by GHAA, published a study of AWP laws. Among other findings, the study reported that the combined increases in administrative and health care costs resulting from AWP provisions would force HMOs to increase premiums by 9.1 percent to 28.7 percent. This would translate into premium increases of up to $458 per individual and $1,284 per family, thus totaling more than $45 billion per year.[20]

Another 1994 study published by Arthur Anderson & Company, an actuarial firm commissioned by the state of Florida House of Representatives Committee on Appropriations, assessed the potential cost effects of several health reform proposals, including an AWP mandate in Florida. Among its findings, the study indicated that HMO premiums in Florida were 25 to 30 percent less than premiums of indemnity plans. If the AWP law were implemented, most savings attributable to provider discounts and reduced utilization would probably be lost. As a result, the study predicted that per member per month costs for private sector managed care plans would increase by approximately 15 percent.[21]

Approximately 33 AWP laws affecting MCOs have been adopted in 27 states.[22,23] Fifteen states have full or partial exemptions for HMOs. AWP laws often apply to certain designated providers, such as chiropractors, optometrists, pharmacists, nurse practitioners, nurse-midwives, podiatrists, psychologists, and other allied health professionals. The most popular type, adopted in 14 states, requires health plans to accept into the plan's network nonparticipating pharmacists willing to meet the terms and conditions of the MCO. In seven states, HMOs receive full or partial exemptions from such open pharmacy requirements.

It is important to note that ten states (Arkansas, Georgia, Idaho, Illinois, Indiana, Kentucky, Texas, Utah, Virginia, and Wyoming) have adopted AWP laws that include physicians as possible beneficiaries. Most states traditionally have exempted HMOs from such requirements. This can be explained in part because such a law would violate the federal HMO Act, which prohibits state laws designating the number or percentage of physicians who must participate in an HMO network.[24] Four states (Arkansas, Idaho, Kentucky, and Wyoming), however, recently failed to exempt federally qualified HMOs. This lack of exemption represents a disturbing new trend by state legislatures.

State AWP laws may be subject to challenge on the basis of federal preemption under at least two theories. First, as noted, an attempt to implement an AWP provision with respect to physicians is in violation of federal law (as applied to physician services).[25] Second, federal courts have found that HMOs are not in the business of insurance for the purpose of ERISA's savings clause.[26] In either case, a state's AWP law as applied to HMOs may be ruled unenforceable because federal law supersedes state law.

Two AWP legal challenges currently underway are testing these and other legal theories. The state of Louisiana is appealing a federal district court decision holding that the state's AWP law is preempted under ERISA.[27] The district court found that the law affects employers' and sponsors' discretion as to the structuring of health benefits under employee benefit plans because it explicitly directs plan administrators not to structure their plans so as to exclude any provider willing and qualified to participate in the network. In July 1995, the Prudential Insurance Company filed a federal lawsuit seeking to prevent the state of Arkansas from enforcing its AWP law.[28] The lawsuit contends that the state AWP law is preempted by several federal statues, including ERISA, the federal HMO Act, and the Federal Employee Health Benefits Act. The suit further alleges that the AWP law would interfere with the private relationship between health plans and employers, thereby impeding health plans' ability to offer high-quality, affordable health care to Arkansas consumers.

Direct Access Legislation

With growing frequency during the 1990s, states have considered direct access legislation (sometimes referred to as freedom of choice initiatives), which would give MCO enrollees unbridled authority to seek care outside MCO participating provider networks. Like AWP laws, these laws can be inconsistent with managed care principles and thus may threaten the viability of HMOs. Direct access initiatives can take several forms: "requiring insurers to offer an indemnity plan if they offer a network plan; preventing the designation of a single source provider (e.g., a pharmacy or medical equipment supply chain); or requiring MCOs to cover services rendered by non-participating providers."[29]

Fourteen states have enacted direct access laws that apply to many types of health plans, including traditional indemnity insurance, Blue Cross/Blue Shield plans, PPOs, and HMOs.[30] Three states have implemented provisions that apply only to HMO operations; Louisiana, Mississippi, and New Jersey limit the ability of HMOs to designate pharmacies or pharmacy mail order houses.[31]

Mandated Benefits Requirements

State laws governing HMOs require that their enrollees be offered comprehensive health care services. In fact, the industry's ability to provide broad coverage has been one of its distinctive trademarks. Nevertheless, many states now require coverage of specialty and nonessential services, too. States now require more than 1,000 specific benefits to be offered by health plans; at least 200 of these apply to HMOs.[32-34] Recently, bills setting minimum requirements for coverage of postpartum hospital length of stay and bills requiring payment for emergency department services even in nonurgent circumstances have gained popularity during the 1995 legislative session. As of 1 October 1995, mandatory length-of-stay laws were enacted in Maryland, New Jersey, and North Carolina. During 1995, three states (Arkansas, Louisiana, and Virginia) enacted legislation governing how plans cover emergency services. These laws typically seek either to redefine emergency services or to limit HMOs and other managed care plans authorizing procedures to approve payment for emergency services.

Where state legislatures mandate coverage of expensive services or mandate medical protocols that may not always be necessary, a point of diminishing returns is quickly reached. Many fear that less money will be spent on basic health care as funds are rerouted to cover the nonessential mandates. Mandated benefits also reduce HMOs' flexibility in structuring benefit packages to suit the needs of a particular group.

INSURANCE REFORM INITIATIVES

While the congressional health reform debate ebbs and flows, states are actively considering a variety of health care measures. During the last 4 years alone, more than 2,000 health care proposals were introduced in state legislatures that would have expanded coverage to the uninsured and underinsured.[35] This section examines small group and individual market reforms and their impact on HMO operations.

Since 1990, 46 states have adopted small group reform measures, many based on the model laws adopted by the NAIC (the NAIC first adopted the Premium Rate and Renewability Model Act in 1991; the Small Employer Health Insurance Model Act in 1991, which was revised in 1994; and the Model Regulations To Implement the Small Employer Health Insurance Availability Model Act in 1993). Typical changes in the NAIC's latest small group model (specifically, the Small Employer Health Insurance Availability Model Act, for prospective reinsurance with or without an opt out) to increase the availability of health insurance coverage to small employers include the following: an open enrollment period and a guarantee issue requirement for all products that a small group carrier offers to the small group market (i.e., businesses with up to 50 employees); a community-rating requirement that adjusts for geographic location, age, and family composition; limits on waiting periods for preexisting conditions; and choice of at least two standardized benefit packages.

HMO participation in the small group market has increased dramatically in recent years. For example, from 1992 to 1993 alone, the percentage of HMOs offering small group coverage rose from 52.7 percent to 71.4 percent. The aggregate percentage of HMO business comprising of small groups also increased from 10.0 percent to 13.1 percent during the same period.[36]

Although the HMO industry supports small group reforms, several problems can arise after a state adopts such a measure. For example, federally qualified HMOs "shall provide, without limitations as to time or cost . . . basic and supplemental health services to its members."[37] Many HMO experts interpret this provision as a prohibition on the use of waiting periods for preexisting medical conditions for HMO coverage. Moreover, the way HMOs do business does not lend itself to excluding an HMO enrollee from coverage because of a preexisting medical condition. As a result, 12- or 6-month waiting periods commonly are used by indemnity carriers but not by federally qualified HMOs. This can place HMOs at a competitive disadvantage because federally qualified HMOs must offer full coverage to new enrollees of a small group immediately. The NAIC recently recognized this dilemma by adding to its model the option of imposing a postenrollment or affiliation waiting period for health plans that do not use waiting periods for preexisting conditions. Few states explicitly recognize this option, however.

Another concern relates to rating methodologies used by small group carriers. In compliance with both federal and state requirements, HMOs use community rating more than 80 percent of the time.[38] Most states that have adopted small group reforms, however, still permit health plans to use a modified form of experience rating that limits variation in premiums charged to different small groups.[39] As a result, HMOs sometimes are placed at a competitive disadvantage because they often must make community-rated policies available to small groups, whereas other health plans can sell experience-rated policies (see Chapter 44).

It also can be difficult for HMOs to satisfy a state's requirement for standardized benefit packages for small businesses. Typically, a state adopts a requirement that two standardized policies must be available. Usually, one is a "bare bones" option. Many HMOs cannot offer such a benefit package, however, because HMOs must offer comprehensive policies pursuant to state and federal HMO laws. For example, federally qualified HMOs must offer comprehensive health services as defined by the federal HMO Act and regulations.

Similar issues may arise as the states, and possibly the federal government, attempt to provide better access and more affordable coverage to individuals who are not employed or who choose not to purchase coverage through a group policy. Since 1992, about a dozen states have adopted individual reforms, and the NAIC may propose a model act to address this issue in 1995.[40] Interestingly, the percentage of HMOs selling individual coverage increased from 24.6 percent in 1992 to 41.9 percent in 1993, although individual policies still represent only a small portion of HMO business.[41]

REGULATION BY MARKET SEGMENTS

It is important to note that, because regulation is driven by market segments, a typical MCO is regulated by several entities, depending on the combination of product lines it offers. The primary regulatory bodies responsible for protecting consumers are the following:

- *state insurance and health departments* for health care coverage purchased by individuals, offered to state employees, and provided to employees of a business where the health plan retains the insurance risk
- *U.S. Department of Labor* for coverage offered to employees when employers retain the insurance risk, either on a standalone basis or through a multiple employer welfare arrangement (i.e., self-funding pursuant to ERISA)
- *the Health Care Financing Administration* for Medicare and Medicaid coverage and all policies sold by federally qualified HMOs
- *state welfare departments*, which share responsibility with the Health Care Financing Administration for Medicaid coverage
- *U.S. Office of Personnel Management* for coverage sold to federal employees (i.e., the Federal Employees Health Benefits Program)
- *U.S. Department of Defense* for coverage offered to active and retired military personnel

Because so many regulatory agencies have statutory authority to oversee managed care and other health plan operations, the percentage of the entire marketplace that states regulate exclusively is estimated at between 15 percent and 20 percent of the U.S. population. In contrast, most health care policies now issued are regulated by the federal government. For example, about 45 percent of the U.S. population is regulated through ERISA. When one adds other federal programs, such as the Federal Employees Health Benefit Program and the Civilian Health and Medical Program of the Uniformed Services, the total exceeds 50 percent. In some cases, the state and federal governments share responsibility. For instance, under the Medicare and Medicaid programs, state and federal regulators share jurisdiction. In any circumstance where there is a conflict between federal and state oversight under these joint oversight programs, however, federal law preempts state law.

THE STATE EXPERIENCE

Throughout the years, states have retained the lion's share of regulatory authority over commercially insured products. The McCarran-Ferguson Act of 1945 reaffirmed the states' primary role. As a result of the recent expansion of managed care and the increasing complexity of state and federal oversight of all health plan operations, however, traditional notions and boundaries of how managed care and other insurance products should be regulated by government officials are being challenged.

Although different regulatory standards may be applied to different managed care offerings depending on the various market segments, many of the core health care services and functions are the same (e.g., the emphasis on primary care services). Therefore, why have so many different regulatory agencies overseeing similar, if not identical, product lines? This is a question that is not easily answered and may be more a result of the U.S. political system than anything else. In any event, regulatory inconsistency is a problem that needs further evaluation to safeguard consumers and to ensure fair competition among managed care plans.

A central goal of future health reform initiatives should be to achieve a seamless regulatory system, wherever possible, that focuses on the activities of each managed care plan rather than on how a health care entity is licensed through the state or federal government. Additional objectives should include establishing the proper equilibrium between federal and state oversight and between regulatory centralization and regional oversight.

REFERENCES AND NOTES

1. National Association of Insurance Commissioners (NAIC), *HMO Examination Handbook* (NAIC, 1990). In addition to the HMO Model Act and *HMO Examination Handbook*, the NAIC has adopted other model regulations for HMOs, including the Model Regulation To Implement Rules Regarding Contract and Services of HMOs, the HMO Producer Model Regulation, and the *HMO Investment Guidelines*.

2. National Association of Insurance Commissioners (NAIC), *Compilation of State Laws: Premium Taxation of HMOs* (Kansas City, Mo.: NAIC, 1993).

3. Aspen Systems Corporation, *A Report to the Governor on State Regulation of Health Maintenance Organizations* (Rockville, Md.: Aspen Systems Corp., 1993).

4. National Association of Insurance Commissioners (NAIC), *Open Enrollment Periods for HMOs* (Kansas City, Mo.: NAIC, 1993).

5. National Association of Insurance Commissioners HMO Act, Section 7(A).

6. National Association of Insurance Commissioners (NAIC), *Health Maintenance Organization: Coverage by Guaranty Fund* (Kansas City, Mo.: NAIC, 1994). Florida's HMO Consumer Assistance Plan, Virginia's Insolvency Assessment Fund, and Wisconsin's Insurance Security Fund for all insurers are specific examples of guaranty fund programs in which HMOs are required to participate.

7. Group Health Association of America (GHAA), *Patterns in HMO Enrollment* (Washington, D.C.: GHAA, 1995), 36, American Association of Health Plans (AAHP), 1996 database.

8. Group Health Association of America (GHAA), *Stateside Report* (Washington, D.C.: GHAA, 28 January 1993), 2, 16–42.

9. D. Marsan and R. Quigley, *Guide to State PPO Laws and Regulations* (Washington, D.C.: Group Health Association of America/AMCRA, 1995).

10. Marsan and Quigley, *Guide to State PPO Laws and Regulations*.

11. Group Health Association of America (GHAA), *PHOs and the Assumption of Insurance Risk: A 50-State Survey of Regulators' Attitudes toward PHO Licensure* (Washington, D.C.: GHAA, 1995).

12. National Association of Insurance Commissioners Prepaid Limited Health Service Organization Model Act, Appendix.

13. Group Health Association of America (GHAA), *Stateside Report* (Washington, D.C.: 8 September 1993), 6, 46–68.

14. National Association of Insurance Commissioners (NAIC), *State Laws Regarding Utilization Review Agents/Standards* (Kansas City, Mo.: NAIC, 1994).

15. G. Carneal and D. Marsan, The Need for UR Standardization, *HMO Magazine* (November/December 1993): 13–17.

16. National Association of Insurance Commissioners (NAIC), *Society of Professional Benefit Administrators Survey and Third Party Administrator Licensure and Bond Requirements* (Kansas City, Mo.: NAIC, 1994).

17. National Association of Insurance Commissioners Model Third Party Administrator Statute (1977, revised 1991). This model (or similar legislation) has been adopted in 22 states.

18. Group Health Association of America (GHAA), *In the States* (Washington, D.C.: GHAA, 28 February 1995).

19. National Association of Insurance Commissioners, letter to congressional leadership, 10 August 1994; NGA Policy Statement, 21 July, 1994.

20. Atkinson & Company, *The Cost Impact of Any Willing Provider Legislation* (Silver Spring, Md.: Atkinson & Company, 1995).

21. Arthur Anderson & Co., *Florida Health Security Program: Actuarial Report* (Tampa, Fla.: Arthur Anderson & Co., 1994).

22. Group Health Association of America (GHAA), (Washington, D.C.: GHAA, 1994).

23. Blue Cross/Blue Shield Association, *State Legislative Health Care and Insurance Issues: 1994 Surveys of Plans* (Washington, D.C.: Blue Cross/Blue Shield Association, 1994).

24. 42 U.S.C. 300e-10 (1994).

25. 42 U.S.C. 300e-10 (1994).

26. *Pomeroy v. Johns Hopkins Medical Services*, Lexis 16418 (U.S. Dist. Ct. Md., 1994); *O'Reilly v. Ceuleers*, 912 F.2d 1383 (11th Cir. 1990); *McGee v. Equitable HCA Corp.*, 953 F.2d 1192 (10th Cir. 1992); *Dearmas v. Av-Med, Inc.*, 814 F. Supp. 1103 (S.D. Fla. 1993); and *In re International Medical Centers, Inc.*, 604 So. 2d 505 (Fla. App., 1st Dist. 1992). See also *Hollis v. Cigna Health Care of Connecticut, Inc.*, no. 705357 (Sup. Ct.,

Hartford–New Britain Judicial District, Ct. 5 December 1994).

27. *Cigna Healthplan of Louisiana, Inc. v. State of Louisiana*, No. 94-885 (M.D. La., 17 April 1995).

28. *Prudential Insurance Company v. State of Arkansas*, No. LR-C-95-514 (W.D. Ark., 21 July 1995).

29. Blue Cross/Blue Shield Association, *State Barriers to Managed Care: Results of a National Survey of Blue Cross and Blue Shield Association Plans* (Washington, D.C.: Blue Cross/Blue Shield Association, 1991), 13.

30. Blue Cross/Blue Shield Association, *State Barriers to Managed Care*, 13.

31. Blue Cross/Blue Shield Association, *State Barriers to Managed Care*, 13.

32. *Mandated Benefits Manual* (Alexandria, Va.: Scandlen, 1992).

33. Health Care Financing Administration, *Annual Report to the Governor on State Regulation of Health Maintenance Organizations* (Rockville, Md.: Aspen Systems Corp., 1993).

34. Group Health Association of America (GHAA), *Stateside Report* (Washington, D.C.: GHAA, 17 November 1993), 3–5.

35. Data based on Commerce Clearing House's and StateNet's state legislative tracking computer system, 1991–1994.

36. Group Health Association of America (GHAA), *Annual HMO Industry Survey* (Washington, D.C.: GHAA, 1994).

37. 42 U.S.C. 300e(b) (1994).

38. Group Health Association of America (GHAA), *HMO Industry Profile* (Washington, D.C.: GHAA, 1994), 101. Of all HMOs, 28.5 percent use standard community rating, 26.9 percent use community rating by class, 26.1 percent use adjusted community rating, 12.6 percent use prospective experience rating, and 5.9 percent use retrospective experience rating.

39. Blue Cross/Blue Shield Association, *State Small Group Insurance Reform Legislation* (Washington, D.C.: Blue Cross/Blue Shield Association, 1994).

40. Blue Cross/Blue Shield Association, *State Individual Insurance Reform Legislation* (Washington, D.C.: Blue Cross/Blue Shield Association, 1994).

41. Group Health Association of America, *Annual HMO Industry Survey*.

SUGGESTED READING

Carneal, G., and Marsan, D. 1993. State Oversight of HMO-Sponsored Point-of-Service Products. *Medical Interface* (August): 105–106, 108.

In the States, a periodical published by the American Association of Health Plans, Washington, D.C.

Chapter 54

Federal Qualification: A Foundation for the Future

Christine C. Boesz

Enactment of the federal Health Maintenance Organization (HMO) Act in 1973 set the stage for the development of today's managed care industry and introduced the notion of federal qualification. Although *federal qualification* is not a defined term in the statute, it is commonly used to describe HMOs and the health benefit plans that they offer when both the benefits and the HMOs meet federal requirements. The status of federal qualification pertains to the HMO as a legal entity or line of business, its administrative and management systems, its health delivery system, its fiscal soundness, and its health benefit packages. Federal qualification also requires that consumer interests be protected by full and fair disclosure in marketing, adequate protection in the event of insolvency, community rating of

Christine C. Boesz is Vice-President of Government Programs at NYLCare. She provides corporate leadership in NYLCare's Medicare and Medicaid managed care programs. Her responsibilities include developing new markets and opportunities for these special populations, assuring NYLCare's continuing compliance with government requirements, and supporting government relation activities to advance managed care options. Prior to joining NYLCare, Ms. Boesz was Director, Office of Operations and Oversight, for the Office of Managed Care. In this position she directed the Medicare managed care and the HMO federal qualification programs for the Health Care Financing Administration.

Ms. Boesz is a doctoral candidate at the University of Michigan as a PEW Fellow. She holds a masters degree from Rutgers University in Mathematical Statistics and a bachelors degree from Douglass College in Mathematics.

Ms. Sylvia Hendel and Ms. Lisa Ferdon provided valuable assistance to the author. Their contribution is gratefully acknowledged.

premiums, available and accessible health services, grievance procedures, and quality assurance programs that will identify issues and take remedial action.

Federal qualification status is important to HMOs for two reasons. First, it signifies to employers and other consumers of health care that an HMO meets the standards as defined by the federal HMO Act and its implementing regulations.[1] Second, it establishes the eligibility of an HMO to contract with the federal government to serve Medicare beneficiaries.[2] From 1973 through 1981, federally qualified HMOs were eligible for federal financial assistance through developmental grants and direct loans or loan guarantees to cover initial operating deficits. Such financial assistance is no longer available.

FEDERAL QUALIFICATION

Federally qualified HMOs must provide or arrange for the delivery of comprehensive health benefits, including all medically necessary care and preventive health services, without limits as to time or cost. In general, federally qualified HMOs must hold and manage the financial risk for the provision of health services, operate quality assurance programs and other consumer protection activities, provide comprehensive benefits to enrollees, and use community rating in pricing benefit plans. Federal qualification status differs from state licensure. It is voluntary and is not required for market entry.

The status of federal qualification for an HMO and its health benefit plans is determined by the U.S. Department of Health and Human Services. Specifically, the Office of Managed Care (OMC) within the Health Care Financing Administration (HCFA) is responsible for administering the process of ascertaining whether an individual HMO meets the standards. The OMC is also responsible for overseeing continuing compliance activities.

This chapter presents an overview of the requirements and process of seeking, receiving, and maintaining federal qualification. Because many HMOs seeking federal qualification are also simultaneously applying for a Medicare contract, some details about Medicare-specific requirements are included. The reader is advised to consult Chapters 46 and 47 for more detailed information about specific Medicare contracting standards.

MEDICARE CONTRACTING

Applicants for federal qualification may apply concurrently for a Medicare contract (a Medicare contract is also known as a Section 1876 risk or cost contract). If a Medicare contract is desired, the applicant needs to demonstrate operational experience by meeting minimal enrollment levels. At the time of this writing, to be eligible for a Medicare risk-based contract the HMO must have a minimum of 5,000 prepaid enrollees (1,500 if its operations are in a rural area[3]). If the minimum enrollment cannot be met, a contract is still possible if the HMO is a subdivision or subsidiary of an organization that meets the minimum membership requirements. In such instances, the organization that meets the membership requirement must assume responsibility for the financial risk, management, and supervision of the health care services. If the HMO is applying for a cost-based Medicare contract, the minimum enrollment is 1,500 members.

The OMC recognizes that newly developing organizations may not be able to meet the minimal requirements at the time that the application is filed but will be able to do so by the time approval is expected. Therefore, applicants may file an application with 1,000 enrollees (500 in a rural area). The enrollment count cannot include Medicaid members. Before a contract is approved, however, an enrollment of 5,000 or 1,500 must be met.

In addition, the membership in each geographic area must comply with the requirement that the number of Medicare and Medicaid enrollees may not exceed 50 percent of the enrollment in the geographic area. This requirement is commonly called the 50/50 rule.[4] Two waivers of this enrollment standard are possible: when the HMO is owned or operated by a government entity for a maximum period of 3 years, and when the geographic area has more than 50 percent of its population as Medicare beneficiaries and Medicaid recipients.

The organization that is applying for a risk-based contract must have its adjusted community rate (ACR) approved by the HCFA. As part of the ACR approval, the OMC approves the premiums and benefit packages for basic and high-option plans. If the organization is applying for a cost-based contract, a cost budget must be submitted for approval.

A risk-based contract may not be approved for an organization that terminated or did not renew a risk-based Medicare contract in the preceding 5 years unless the OMC determines that circumstances warrant special consideration. If your organization is in this situation, you should contact the OMC before preparing the Medicare portion of the application to ascertain whether contracting will be feasible.

THE APPLICATION: OVERVIEW

The purpose of the application is to provide federal reviewers with information about how the managed health care organization is complying with requirements as a federally qualified HMO. The application format may be obtained from the OMC. The application may be prepared either manually or through a computer-assisted format.

All sections of the application must be complete before federal reviewers will begin their evaluation of the information. It is the responsibility of the applicant to ensure that all necessary information is submitted. Incomplete applications will not be processed and will be returned to the applicant, causing delays in the review process. For many parts of the application, you may be able to use materials that were used in applying for your state license. Be sure that this material is current and accurately describes the organization and its operations.

The OMC provides general assistance with the process and regulatory requirements to all applicants. Figure 54–1 shows the organization of the OMC and provides information about how to access the OMC. The HCFA's regional office personnel provide assistance on issues related to Medicare contracting, including health service delivery arrangements, quality assurance programs, and contract administration requirements. The HCFA has ten regional offices. Refer to Exhibit 54–1 to see which regional office serves your local operations.

Application fees for federal qualification as of 1995 are assessed as follows:

- $18,400 for an HMO.
- $18,400 for each regional component of an HMO. A regional component is geographically distinct from any other regional component and provides substantially the full range of basic health services to members without extensive referral among components.[5] The advantage to an HMO of establishing regional components is that separate community rates may be determined for separate regional components.
- $6,900 for a service area expansion. This fee is for the service area expansion of either the HMO or a regional component of an HMO. There is a separate fee for each component being expanded.
- $3,100 for a Medicare contractor that received the contract as a competitive medical plan.[6]

The logistics of assembling and submitting the application are contained in the application form. The application form also contains important technical instructions on how to use the computer-assisted format. The computer format is organized around the master document feature of *WordPerfect 5.1* and *WordPerfect 6.1* for Windows. This feature assembles the application by automatically pulling together the subdocuments that the applicant prepares as separate files. This feature is also useful for preparing applications for service area expansions. A reasonable expectation for approval is 6 months from the time the application is determined to be complete by federal reviewers.

Waivers

There are four requirements for federal qualification that may be waived or approved under certain conditions:

1. *Time-phased plan for transitional HMOs*[7]—The HMO has up to 3 years to bring its current health benefit plans into conformance with federal requirements. Enrollees after federal qualification must receive a fully qualified benefit plan. Since the 1988 amendments to the federal HMO Act, transitional status is less onerous because the HMO as a legal entity may offer benefit plans that do not meet federal standards. The HMO, however, cannot represent that these benefits are federally qualified.

2. *Community rating*[8]—If an HMO is providing comprehensive health services on a prepaid basis before it becomes a federally qualified HMO, community rating requirements may be waived up to 4 years.

3. *Separate community rating by regional component*[9]—An HMO may establish separate community rates for separate regional components. The community rate for each regional component must be based on the different costs of providing health care in each region.

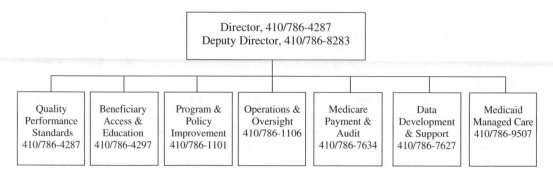

Figure 54–1 OMC organizational chart as of 1995.

4. *Exclusion from coverage of unusual and infrequently provided services not necessary for the protection of an individual's health*[10]—To date, the following procedures have been approved as excluded benefits: in vitro fertilization, reversal of voluntary vasectomy, transsexual surgery, gamete intrafallopian transfer, and zygote intrafallopian transfer. Any other services must be specifically approved by the OMC before the HMO can exclude them as federally qualified benefits.

Service Area

The notion of a service area is an important aspect of federal qualification. Each federally qualified HMO has a geographically defined service area in which health care services must be available and accessible. Service areas may be described in terms of geographic subdivisions such as counties, cities, and townships. If service areas are less than a full county, ZIP codes are used to describe the area. An HMO may have service areas that are noncontiguous.

You must provide evidence of arrangements for basic health services in the requested service area. Physicians, hospitals, and other health care providers must be specifically identified by name and location. If the application is also for a Medicare contract, explicit information about how Medicare beneficiaries will receive serv-

ices must be provided. The health delivery system for serving Medicare beneficiaries must be substantially the same as the delivery system for commercial enrollees.

The general criterion for assessing whether providers of care are appropriately located throughout the service area is the rule of 30. Enrolled members must be able to reach all primary care medical services, and most specialty services, within 30 miles from their homes or within a 30-minute driving time. Rural areas may have special circumstances (e.g., no physicians or inpatient facilities may exist within the rule of 30). Reviewers will be assessing the HMO's health delivery system in comparison with the normal pattern for primary and specialty care within a specific area. If the application is also for a Medicare contract, any difference in service area for the Medicare beneficiaries must be described. Full counties must be used for Medicare contracting unless the HMO is federally qualified in less than the full county; exceptions are possible if they are justified to the OMC.

Applications must contain detailed maps of each service area. These maps should show the location of primary care physicians, referral specialty physicians, and inpatient providers. The boundaries of the service area should be clearly marked. Main travel routes and physical barriers, such as rivers and mountains, should be indicated. Mean travel times from six points on the boundary line to the nearest ambulatory and in-

Exhibit 54–1 HCFA Regional Office Medicare HMO Coordinators

For Connecticut, Maine, Massachusetts, New Hamp-
shire, Rhode Island, and Vermont:
John F. Kennedy Federal Building
Room 2375
Boston, MA 02203
(617) 565-1234

For New Jersey, New York, Puerto Rico, and the
Virgin Islands:
26 Federal Plaza
Room 3800
New York, NY 10278
(212) 264-8522

For Delaware, the District of Columbia, Maryland,
Pennsylvania, Virginia, and West Virginia:
3535 Market Street
Room 3100
Philadelphia, PA 19101
(215) 596-1332

For Alabama, Florida, Georgia, Kentucky, Mississippi,
North Carolina, South Carolina, and Tennessee:
101 Marietta Tower
Suite 702
Atlanta, GA 30323
(404) 730-3782

For Illinois, Indiana, Michigan, Minnesota, Ohio, and
Wisconsin:
105 West Adams Street
15th Floor
Chicago, IL 60603
(312) 353-5737

For Arkansas, Louisiana, Oklahoma, New Mexico, and
Texas:
1200 Main Tower Building
Dallas, TX 75202
(214) 767-4467

For Iowa, Kansas, Missouri, and Nebraska:
New Federal Office Building
601 East 12th Street
Room 220
Kansas City, MO 64106
(816) 426-2866

For Colorado, Montana, North Dakota, South Dakota,
Wyoming, and Utah:
Federal Office Building
1961 Stout Street
Room 522
Denver, CO 80294
(303) 844-6136

For Arizona, California, Guam, Hawaii, Nevada, and
Samoa:
75 Hawthorne Street
4th Floor
San Francisco, CA 94105
(415) 744-3621

For Alaska, Idaho, Oregon, and Washington:
Mail Stop 44
2201 6th Avenue
Seattle, WA 98121
(206) 615-2352

Note: HCFA is in the process of transferring more operational responsibilities to its regional offices. Contact the OMC for the latest
information about which office has responsibility for application processing.

---

patient facility must be listed. Accuracy in estimating travel time is important. These distances
will be verified by the on-site review team.

**Organizational and Contractual
Requirements**

This section of the application establishes the
HMO's legal ability to do business and describes
its corporate persona. Information about the legal entity will include such items as the official
name of the HMO, "doing business as," product
names, legal history (including the existence of
predecessor organizations), reorganizations, and
changes in ownership (the "doing business as"
and product names are important so that the federally qualified and Medicare product lines can
be identified easily). If the federally qualified
HMO functions as a line of business, other lines
of business of the legal entity must be described

briefly. This information is used to gain insight into the relative importance of the qualified business to the legal entity. Also, enrolled members must be able to distinguish between federally approved products and other lines of business. This distinction is usually accomplished by using different product names.

Included in the application are state licenses or certificates. If the state approval process is running concurrently with the federal process, describe the state approval process and anticipated time frames. The federal reviewers coordinate approvals with state regulatory officials (see Chapter 53). Because of past problems in Medicare marketing, the oversight of marketing representatives, producers, or agents is of special interest to the HCFA. Be prepared to describe the state's oversight in considerable detail. You should be able to demonstrate that the HMO's oversight of marketing personnel dovetails with federal and state expectations.

An understanding of how the HMO is organized is important in assessing whether the HMO has appropriate administrative and managerial arrangements. The application form asks that two organizational charts be provided. The first will show lines of authority, including the relationships among the policymaking body, the chief operating officials, and the medical/health services delivery components. The second will show any contractual relationships between the HMO and contractors for health services, marketing, and management.

Risk management is a critical area for successful HMO operations. Federal regulations require that HMOs retain responsibility for full financial risk.[11] Risk sharing with providers, however, is permissible. Descriptions of these arrangements must be presented in detail with cross-references to applicable sections of provider contracts.

Reinsurance is not required for federal qualification. To the extent that reinsurance is used, however, it must be described. Other insurance or protection arrangements for loss and liability must be disclosed. Insurance coverage for out-of-area emergencies, medical malpractice, casu-

alty, fire, and theft are common. A fidelity bond is required. For each type of insurance, you will need to provide the name of the carrier, premiums, period of coverage, deductibles, coinsurance, and other features. The policies may be reviewed by the on-site reviewers. A federally qualified HMO must have administrative and managerial arrangements that are acceptable to the HCFA. Federal reviewers are interested in how the oversight body reviews and evaluates management. All key managers must be identified. Contracts for management services must be included in the application. Management services include marketing, claims processing, data processing, and general administration. If there are, or have been, legal actions against the HMO, a brief description of the complaints and their status must be included.

As previously mentioned, the health service delivery system must be described in great detail. At the time the application is submitted, documentation of the arrangements for basic health services must be presented. Acceptable documentation consists of the names of each independent practice association (IPA) and medical group that is or will be providing services. If you are applying for a Medicare contract, explicit arrangements for Medicare members must be detailed. Provider contracts must specifically reference compensation arrangements for services that they provide to Medicare members. Although the application process provides an opportunity to describe provider arrangements that are not yet executed, you should not submit the application without a substantial portion of your delivery system in place. You will need to submit a copy of each executed contract between the HMO and the medical groups and IPAs. If there are multiple groups or IPAs and the contract or agreement forms are the same, a specimen copy is sufficient, with copies of signature pages for executed contracts. Specimen copies of contracts used by IPAs and medical groups with health professionals must also be included. If you have more than 15 signature pages in any category, you may list the providers who have signed contracts and the dates of execution. The providers documented in this section must be the same as the providers located on the map of the service area.

The subscriber contracts and agreements, or evidence of coverage, must be included in the application as they will be issued in the marketplace. Group, nongroup, and conversion contracts are the three general categories for commercial enrollment. All marketing literature, including member handbooks, must be submitted to demonstrate that full and fair disclosure requirements are being met.[12]

Although consumer grievance procedures are required by regulation, the HMO should consider complaints and grievances important sources of information in evaluating how well the enrollee is being served. The grievance procedure must be detailed in the application. It must also be disclosed to members.

Management

The policymaking body of the HMO is responsible for setting policy and overseeing operations. The federal reviewers will be interested in learning about the composition of this body and how it functions. Names, positions held, occupations, and terms address composition. The application asks questions about the ways in which the policymaking body carries out its responsibilities. Questions include frequency of meetings, how many meetings have been held in the year preceding the filing of the application, quorum requirements, and whether management decisions are ratified by the full body. Because the chief executive officer (CEO) is a key person in the HMO, there are questions about the policymaking body's authority to appoint, evaluate, and remove the CEO. On-site reviewers will review the minutes of the policymaking body and major committees. They will also inspect administrative and procedure manuals. The purpose of this review is to verify that the HMO is operating in accordance with its own bylaws and procedures as well as regulations.[13] This review focuses on the consistency between the written documents and actual performance.

In addition to the CEO, the reviewers are interested in key staff in the functional areas: medical care, utilization review, finance, marketing, and management information systems. If the application is also for Medicare, the Medicare coordinator must be identified. Brief position descriptions and resumes for the incumbents must be provided in the application.

Health Services Delivery

The application will ask you to describe the health care delivery system and how physician services are provided. Full-time equivalents of physicians, by specialty area of medical practice, are requested. The following information about each physician is required: name, specialty, board status, practice location, hospital privileges, and availability for commercial or Medicare (or both). If ambulatory centers are used, their names, locations, hours of service, and types of services must be described. Detailed information must be provided also about hospitals and other contracting providers, such as skilled nursing facilities, psychiatric hospitals, home health agencies, surgical centers, and laboratories.

The providers for Medicare required services must be identified by name. It is important to remember that providers that are excluded from participation in Medicare and Medicare cannot be a part of the HMO. If the HMO offers benefits in addition to those in Medicare parts A and B, the providers of these services must also be identified. Such optional benefits include services such as vision care, dental care, hearing care, outpatient prescription drugs, long-term care, and inpatient mental health.

Financial

The fiscal soundness of the HMO is a fundamental requirement for federal qualification, just as it is for state licensure. The HMO's total assets must exceed its total unsubordinated liabilities. The HMO must have sufficient cash flow and adequate liquidity to meet its obligations as they become due.[14] These conditions are assessed by independent evaluation of certified audited financial statements. All applicants must provide audited statements for the three most recent fiscal years (or less if the HMO has been operational for a shorter period of time). If the HMO is a line of business, the audited statements of the legal entity must be provided. Updated financial statements must be available for the federal reviewer during the on-site visit.

Federal qualification standards for fiscal soundness are based on generally accepted accounting principles (GAAP), which are different in some respects from statutory accounting principles used by state regulators (see Chapter 40). An important aspect of GAAP is the method of accounting for incurred but not reported (IBNR) claims. Failure to estimate IBNR claims accurately has caused serious financial impairment in HMOs. With capitation of physicians and other providers, the importance of IBNR shifts. Nevertheless, the HMO is expected to have an IBNR estimation method for all direct provider payments.

Applicants are required to submit financial projections to demonstrate that fiscal soundness can be achieved and maintained. Applicants that meet the following five conditions can be exempt from providing projections:

1. has operated as a prepaid health plan for at least 3 years
2. has a positive net worth as established by GAAP
3. has earned a net operating surplus or profit (after taxes) during the HMO's most recent fiscal year
4. has sustained a cumulative net operating surplus at the end of the three most recent fiscal years
5. has demonstrated the above with audited financial statements

All five of these conditions must be met for the exemption to apply. When a federally qualified HMO meets all five of these conditions, it is called a type B HMO; otherwise, it is a type A HMO.

The financial projections should be prepared using accrual accounting. Operational HMOs should provide actual data from the date of the latest annual audit. Preoperational HMOs should provide projections from the date of expected start of operations. Projections should be provided through 1 year beyond break-even. If break-even has been reached, then projections are required for 1 year beyond the expected date of qualification.

The formats for the projections are included in the application form. The basic requirements are quarterly balance sheets, quarterly revenue and expense statements, and quarterly statements of cash flow. The assumptions used in preparing the projections should be presented in sufficient detail that a knowledgeable reviewer can find them convincing. Operating and capital budget details must be included. Medical cost and volume assumptions should be supported by actual operations or reliable data sources. Enrollment projections for Medicare, Medicaid, and commercial members should be identified and justified separately.

The enrollment projections will be assessed for their reasonableness. If the HMO is a line of business, the financial assumptions need only support the projections of the line. During the site visit, reviewers will ask to see the analysis prepared by independent actuaries in developing the financial assumptions. If actuaries are not used, the HMO must provide other justification of the assumptions.

If the financial plan projects a deficit, the HMO must submit evidence in the application of financing arrangements to handle the deficits. Such arrangements may include loans, contributed capital, and lines of credit. There are specific criteria for the acceptability of these arrangements. You should contact the HCFA early in the application preparation process for guidance.

When HMOs fail, regulators are obligated to protect enrollees. Federal requirements focus on three provisions for such protection in the event of insolvency:

1. payment for services for the duration of the contract period for which payment has been made

2. payment for continuation of services until the time of discharge for members confined in an inpatient facility

3. protection of members from incurring liability for services provided before the HMO's insolvency

The notions of hold-harmless provisions in provider contracts and uncovered expenditures are used to help HMOs meet these requirements. Hold-harmless provisions state that the provider will look only to the HMO for payment of services, even in the event of insolvency. If an IPA or medical group is involved as an intermediary organization between the HMO and the individual providers, it is not sufficient for the IPA and medical group contracts to have this provision; the subcontracting physician contract must also contain the appropriate provision. The OMC accepts the model language that was adopted by the National Association of Insurance Commissioners and the National Association of Managed Care Regulators as described in Chapter 55. If an HMO wishes to use other than the model language, there are guidelines that specify what provisions must be included. If you decide to use other than the model provision, you should have it approved by the OMC before you include it in your provider contracts. Federal reviewers are interested in knowing whether providers understand the hold-harmless provisions and assess the provider's understanding through interviews with participating physicians.

The purpose of insolvency protection is to protect the enrollees. Uncovered expenditures are the medical, hospital, and other health care costs that would be the responsibility of the HMO in the event of insolvency. Expenses are covered by hold-harmless provisions, insolvency insurance, letters of credit, state-restricted reserves, guarantees, and state laws that prohibit providers from billing the HMO's enrollees.

Net worth may be considered in satisfying insolvency requirements if the HMO has operated for 3 years, has a positive net worth, has a net operating surplus during the most recent fiscal year, and has a cumulative net operating surplus for the three most recent fiscal years. The HMO must have a minimum net worth of $1 million excluding land, buildings, and equipment or $5 million with land, buildings, and equipment. The portion of the net worth that may be used toward covered expenses is determined by a formula. If the HMO's net worth is more than $35 million, then no additional insolvency protection requirements are necessary. If the net worth is less than $35 million, the actual net worth is divided by $250,000 and then multiplied by $100,000 to calculate the HMO's adjusted net worth that may be applied toward covered expenses.

To determine whether your HMO has met the insolvency protection standard, use the uncovered expenditures calculation worksheet that is provided as part of the application. The basis for estimating the HMO's liabilities at the time of insolvency is 2 months' worth of medical and hospital expenses (1 month before insolvency and 1 month after). The calculation assumes that the HMO ceases operations at the end of the first month. The second month is an estimate of expenses that are to be paid as continuation of benefits. The 2-month calculation is only a formula. It is merely an estimate that balances the interests of an HMO's enrollees with the HMO's need to access its assets without stringent regulator constraints. The specific requirements are that insolvency protection must provide benefits "for all enrollees, for the duration of the contract period for which payment has been made" and "for enrollees who are in an inpatient facility on the date of insolvency, until they are discharged from the facility."[15] Hold-harmless provisions only apply to 1 month, namely the first month while the HMO is still operating. If your HMO wishes to use provisions in provider contracts to cover continuation of benefit requirements, those contracts must include specific language that addresses the provision of services after insolvency without recourse to the enrollee. Such provisions in contracts are not typical because the provider has no way to recover costs after the event of insolvency. Usually, HMOs use other arrangements, such as guarantees or insolvency insurance.

Attention to the details of developing a plan for the protection of members in the event of insolvency will expedite the application process. For example, if you are relying on hold-harmless provisions in physician contracts, then the appropriate language must be in the executed contracts. If such language is not present, then physician services will not be considered covered expenses. Because of the time required to modify contracts, you may need to make other arrangements for these expenses to have an acceptable insolvency plan. There is no magic to developing an acceptable plan; just use logic and acceptable provisions. Shortcuts will not pay off. An inadequate insolvency plan is one of the common reasons for long delays in the application process.

Community Rating

Although community rating has always been one fundamental principle of federal qualification, the specific requirements have changed over the years. Today, the requirements are quite flexible but retain the concept of prospective rating. Rating by class and for specific groups is permissible. You will need to describe in detail the method used by your HMO, including the projected mix of contracts, average contract size, family size, and required revenue yield.

If you intend to use community rating by class, you must receive prior approval from the HCFA for the factors that you will use. This approval is routine for the factors of age, sex, family size, marital status, industry type, and health behavior, specifically smoking. If you wish to use other factors, you must request approval by letter to the OMC. Your request for approval must include the rationale as to why the factor, and thus classes, will reasonably predict differences in the use of HMO services by the indi-

viduals and families in the class. Statistical data from primary or secondary sources are necessary to defend your rationale.

If you expect to set separate community rates for specific groups, you will need to describe the method and formula you plan to use. For groups of 100 or less, rates may not be set higher than 110 percent of the community rate. In no case is rating by individual health status permissible. Age-banded ratings are not allowed. All these rating methodologies are described in Chapters 43 and 44.

Management information systems are essential for the day-to-day management of key operational functions. A brief description of key reports must be included in the application, along with an indication of which personnel use the reports. The reviewers will evaluate the reports and their use during the site visit. The use of management information systems for long-term planning and for completion of the national data reporting requirements (NDRRs) is important.

Federal qualification requires that the HMO provide or arrange for the provision of comprehensive health benefits. Deductibles are not permissible. Copayments, however, are common. If a copayment is required for any basic health service, limitations apply. No more than 50 percent of the HMO's cost of a single service type may be charged as a copayment. Also, a 20 percent limit exists for the total cost of services to an individual enrollee in any one year. If your benefits include copayments, the HMO is responsible for notifying subscribers at least annually of the specific annual maximum copayment amounts to which they are subject. The HMO must also have a process to assist a member when the maximum is reached.

Marketing

If you are not requesting a Medicare contract as part of your application for federal qualification and the HMO is exempt from submitting financial projections, marketing information is not required. If you are requesting a Medicare contract, information about Medicare marketing is necessary. If a financial plan is necessary, then information about commercial marketing must be provided.

Enrollment projections are critical elements of an application because they indicate the potential success of the HMO in its market. The information related to marketing strategy should give reviewers confidence that the projections are obtainable. An enrollment history of the HMO must be described briefly. The purpose of this narrative is to provide a sense of how successful past marketing strategies have been. Comparisons of actual enrollment with projected enrollment are requested and are useful in demonstrating the effectiveness of marketing.

To assess the competitive position of the HMO, descriptions of existing benefit coverage in the service area must be provided. The application asks for major competitors by name, current benefit and premium levels, and respective market shares. Because this type of information is needed to assess and develop marketing strategies by the HMO, the request for this material does not excessively burden the HMO.

Enrollment projection assumptions are necessary. Your application must include information about the number of eligibles residing within the service area, actual and projected penetration rates, and rationales for initial enrollments and reenrollments. The assumptions should reflect a good understanding of the local market.

A viable marketing strategy is essential for success in the market. The application asks that the HMO's strategy be described in detail. The strategy should address the criteria for selecting primary and secondary targets, use of underwriting guidelines, account development, sales approaches, and advertising and promotion strategies.

Up until October 1995, the federal HMO Act required that employers that had 25 or more employees residing in the service area of the HMO offer an HMO if the HMO was federally qualified and mandated the employer. This requirement is known as the dual-choice provision or federal mandate. Although this provision no longer applies, employers that offer federally qualified HMO benefits are now required to provide a fair contribution toward the HMO benefits.[16]

A detailed marketing budget in support of the marketing strategy is requested. The budget must link to the overall financial plan items such as compensation, travel, equipment, printing, public relations, and advertising. If a Medicare contract is requested, separate marketing projections, strategies, and budgets must be submitted.

During the site visit, reviewers will inspect underwriting guidelines and account files for groups included in enrollment projections. The account files should include contact persons, telephone numbers, comparisons of benefits and premiums, and other anniversary dates. The application contains an enrollment projection worksheet. You will find this worksheet to be convenient in developing the group-specific quarterly enrollment information.

Medicare marketing is a vital function for the successful Medicare contractor. Your assessment of your competition is important to federal reviewers and is requested in the application. In general, your Medicare marketing strategy must include information about advertising and promotions, community education, and public relations. The staffing and budget must support the strategy. The quarterly Medicare projections will be included in the application through the enrollment projection worksheet.

Commission-only is not a desirable method of compensation for Medicare sales personnel. Salary is the preferred method, but a combination of salary and bonus based on retention is acceptable. Compensation arrangements that provide economic incentives to reward long-term enrollment are encouraged. Because Medicare beneficiaries are only locked into an HMO for 30 days at a time, incentives that favor and support responsible sales practices will be less confusing to the beneficiaries and will benefit the HMO.

Because Medicare marketing differs significantly from commercial approaches, you will need to describe your plans for conducting sales and enrollment. If your HMO currently offers a

Medicare supplemental policy, you will need to address how you will ensure that no health screening of members will occur for members transferring from the supplement to a risk contract. Procedures to handle enrollments, disenrollments, and appeals are also important functions of Medicare contracting. They must be prepared carefully in accordance with specific HCFA guidelines.

THE FEDERAL REVIEW: WHAT TO EXPECT

When your application arrives, it will be checked for completeness. This review is not trivial. The federal reviewer will determine whether your application contains sufficient information to continue with an in-depth review. Two frequent problem areas are inadequate documentation of fiscal soundness and an insufficient number of executed physician contracts to demonstrate existence of a health delivery system. An incomplete application causes unnecessary delay and added expense. You will be given 60 days to provide additional information.

Once your application is determined to be complete, you will be notified in writing of when to expect a site visit. If you are expanding an existing service area, a site visit may not be necessary. The federal reviewers will make this determination based on the complexity of your request and how long it has been since your last site visit.

Once your application is complete, a federal review team will begin an in-depth analysis. From time to time, the federal review team will include consultants who work for the OMC as specialty reviewers. You will be given the names of all reviewers. Do not hesitate to notify your federal contact if you believe that any reviewer has a conflict of interest or special situation with respect to your HMO.

Each reviewer will prepare a report of initial findings. These findings, called a desk report, identify additional documentation that is necessary to justify assumptions or ascertainments made in the application, to identify specific functional areas that will be addressed during the site visit, and to indicate the individuals who will be interviewed during the visit. You will receive a copy of the desk report along with specific information concerning a site visit as necessary.

The purpose of the site visit is to verify the information that was provided in the application and to assess whether the HMO is operating in accordance with its written procedures. Do not underestimate the importance of matching written procedures to actual operations. Many an approval is delayed while an HMO writes and implements accurate and appropriate procedures.

A site visit normally lasts 2 to 4 days. After an opening session that will provide an overview of the process, interviews with individual executives, managers, physicians, and others will be conducted. Reviewers will focus on functional areas of financial, health service delivery, quality assurance, and Medicare (if applicable) systems. They will also examine legal documents, including (but not limited to) insurance policies, state license(s), board minutes, and administrative policy manuals. At the end of the visit, you may receive a request for additional information. Normally, you have 2 weeks to provide this material.

The review team then prepares final reports, which represent a recommendation to the federal official who is responsible for determining approval (at the time of this writing, the director of operations and oversight in the OMC makes the decision about whether to approve federal qualification and to initiate a Medicare contract; HCFA may reorganize this function at any time, however). If your HMO meets all requirements, you will receive a letter of approval. If you have deficiencies that, in the opinion of federal reviewers, can be corrected in 60 days, you will receive an intent to deny. If you have serious issues that will require longer than 60 days for correction, your application will be disapproved. Also, if you do not satisfactorily respond to the intent to deny within 60 days, you will be disapproved. You may request a conference with the federal reviewers to review any issue that is cited as the basis for an intent to deny or a denial. The process of evaluating an application is designed to provide the HMO with feedback at several times during the review. Few HMOs are denied, but denials do happen. The primary reasons are deficient financial plans and inadequate health delivery systems. Usually, both problems are present at the time the application is filed. You should avoid filing an application if serious deficiencies exist in these or other areas.

AFTER QUALIFICATION

After an HMO is qualified, it must continue to comply with federal requirements. Federally qualified HMOs are monitored through the NDRRs. The NDRRs are submitted on a quarterly (type A) or annual (type B) basis. Because the states and the federal government all use the same financial reporting forms, the burden of filing financial reports is minimal.

Any time a complaint is received, the HMO will be contacted by a federal official. Although a site visit is rare for a single complaint, the OMC may use the procedures outlined in the federal HMO Act to conduct an investigation of the facts. These procedures are designed to provide the HMO with appropriate due process. If your HMO finds itself under investigation, you are advised to consider the matter seriously and to cooperate fully. The OMC is interested in protecting HMO members, but it also respects the interests of the HMO. The compliance process is well documented in regulations.[17] If an HMO does not correct its problems and return to compliance, the federal qualification will be revoked. As a point of interest, an HMO may voluntarily relinquish federal qualification at any time. Whether the loss of federal qualification is voluntary or involuntary, the HMO has an obligation to notify employers and members of this change in status.

Medicare contracting has routine on-site reviews. In 1996, annual on-site monitoring reviews will begin. In previous years, biannual visits were the norm. As the Medicare managed care program continues to grow, more frequent oversight will permit HMOs and competitive medical plans to correct any problems before they are long standing. The HCFA hopes that the increased frequency will provide better service to both beneficiaries and the managed care contractors.

CONCLUSION

When applying for federal qualification, an HMO is engaging in a process. This process asks for documentation of all aspects of an HMO's corporate body and operations. The effort required by the process is substantial for both the applicant and the federal reviewers. Although there are no short cuts to success, a thorough, accurate application will greatly facilitate the process. Incomplete or inaccurate applications consume time and human resources and result in delays.

Your federal contact will provide you with technical assistance on the process and specific requirements. The application itself contains numerous helpful hints and supporting documents. If you are applying for a Medicare contract, you should consult other chapters in this book. This chapter does not attempt to provide you with all that you need to know.

Once your HMO is federally qualified, service area expansion applications are frequently simplified. You are advised to consult with your federal contact to find out what specific information is needed. Remember that federal reviewers coordinate with state regulator officials. If you are having any difficulties with state officials, you should disclose this information as soon as possible. If your HMO is investigated for noncompliance with any requirements, take it seriously. The process of receiving federal qualification is demanding. Keeping this status is a responsibility. A focus on customer service, continuous quality improvement, and management decisions based on data will give your HMO a good basis for success in meeting the demands of federal qualification.

REFERENCES AND NOTES

1. The federal HMO Act is Title XIII of the Public Health Service Act, as amended (42 U.S.C. 300-e *et seq.*). The implementing regulations are found in 42 C.F.R. Part 417.

2. Section 1876 of Title XVIII of the Social Security Act, as amended by the Tax Equity and Fiscal Responsibility Act of 1982, establishes the criteria for prepaid Medicare contracting. Federal qualification establishes eligibility.

3. *Rural* is defined in 42 C.F.R. 417.413.

4. The 50/50 rule is a statutory requirement. Refer to 42 C.F.R. 417.413(d) for the implementing regulations. At the time of this writing, there are several proposals being considered that will relax this requirement. The reader should be aware that such a change is possible.

5. *Regional component* is defined in 42 C.F.R. 417.104(b)(4).

6. *Competitive medical plan* is the statutory term used for an organization that meets eligibility requirements for Medicare contracting under Section 1876 of the Social Security Act, as amended, but is not federally qualified in the contract service area.

7. 42 C.F.R. 417.142(d).

8. 42 C.F.R. 417.104(c).

9. 24 C.F.R. 417.104(b)(4).

10. 42 C.F.R. 417.101(d)(16).

11. 42 C.F.R. 417.120(b).

12. 42 C.F.R. 417.124(b).

13. 42 C.F.R. 417.124(a).

14. 42 C.F.R. 417.120(a). Although a current ratio of 1:1 is not required, reviewers will expect to see how the HMO manages to pay providers and other creditors on a reasonable schedule.

15. 42 C.F.R. 417.122(b).

16. The 1988 amendments to the HMO Act specifically state that employer contributions on behalf of employees who enroll in an HMO may not "financially discriminate" against these employees. This requirement will be met if the method of determining the contribution on behalf of all employees is reasonable and is designed to ensure employees a fair choice among health benefit plans.

17. 42 C.F.R. 417.160–163.

Chapter 55

Legal Issues in Provider Contracting

Mark S. Joffe

The business of a managed health care plan is to provide or arrange for the provision of health care services. Most managed health care plans, such as health maintenance organizations (HMOs) and preferred provider organizations, provide their services through arrangements with individual physicians, independent practice associations (IPAs), medical groups, hospitals, and other types of health care professionals and facilities. The provider contract formalizes the managed health care plan–provider relationship. A carefully drafted contract accomplishes more than mere memorializing of the arrangement between the parties. A well-written contract can foster a positive relationship between the provider and the managed health care plan. More-

over, a good contract can provide important and needed protections to both parties if the relationship sours.

This chapter is intended to offer to the managed health care plan and the provider a practical guide to reviewing and drafting a provider contract. Appendixes 55–A and 55–B are a sample HMO–primary care physician agreement and a sample HMO–hospital agreement, respectively. These contracts, which have been provided solely for illustrative purposes, have been annotated by the author. Although these agreements are used by an HMO, most provisions have equal applicability to other managed care plans.

Contracts need not be complex or lengthy to be legally binding and enforceable. A single-sentence letter agreement between a hospital and a managed health care plan that says that the hospital agrees to provide access to its facility to enrollees of the managed health care plan in exchange for payment of billed charges is a valid contract. If a single-paragraph agreement is legally binding, why is it necessary for managed health care plan–provider contracts to be so lengthy? The answer is twofold. First, many terms of the contract, although not required, perform useful functions by articulating the rights and responsibilities of the parties. As managed care becomes an increasingly important revenue source to providers, a clear understanding of these rights and responsibilities becomes increasingly important. Second, a growing number of contractual provisions are required by state licensure regulations (e.g., a hold-harmless

Mark S. Joffe is an attorney in private practice in Washington, D.C., and specializes in legal and business issues affecting managed health care delivery systems, including HMOs and PPOs.

Mr. Joffe was previously the Associate Counsel, Group Health Association of America, the HMO trade association. Prior to that position, he was a Senior Attorney with the Office of the General Counsel, Department of Health and Human Services.

Mr. Joffe has a Masters of Arts degree in Health Services Administration at The George Washington University. He is Assistant Professorial Lecturer in Health Services Administration at The George Washington University and a guest lecturer at the Center for Managed Health Care, University of Missouri-Kansas City. Mr. Joffe also publishes *Federal Health Bulletin*, a weekly newsletter summarizing current Federal legislative and regulatory developments affecting health care.

clause) or by government payer programs (e.g., Medicare and Medicaid).

An ideal contract or contract form does not exist. Appropriate contract terms vary depending on the issues of concern and the objectives of the parties, each party's relative negotiating strength, and the desired degree of formality. Although the focus of this chapter is explaining key substantive provisions in a contract, the importance of clarity cannot be overstated. A poorly written contract confuses and misleads the parties. Lack of clarity increases substantially the likelihood of disagreements over the meaning of contract language. A contract not only should be written in simple, commonly understood language but also should be well organized so that either party is able to find and review provisions as quickly and easily as possible.

The need for clarity has become more important as contracts have become increasingly complex. Many managed health care plans may act as an HMO, a preferred provider organization, and a third party administrator. Those health care plans will frequently enter into a single contract with a provider to provide services in all three capacities. In addition, this single contract may obligate the provider to furnish services not only to the managed health care plans enrollees but to enrollees of a number of affiliates of the managed health care plan.

The following discussion is designed to provide a workable guide for managed health care plans and providers to draft, amend, or review contracts. Much of the discussion is cast from the perspective of the managed health care plan, but the points are equally valid from the provider's perspective. Most of the discussion relates to contracts directly between the managed health care plan and the provider of services. When the contract is between the managed health care plan and an IPA or medical group, the managed health care plan needs to ensure that the areas discussed below are appropriately addressed in both the managed health care plan's contract and the contract between the IPA or medical group and the provider.

GENERAL ISSUES IN CONTRACTING

Key Objectives

The managed health care plan should divide key objectives into two categories: those that are essential and those that, although not essential, are highly desirable. Throughout the negotiation process, a managed health care plan needs to keep in mind both the musts and the highly desirables. Not infrequently, a managed health care plan or a provider will suddenly realize at the end of the negotiation process that it has not achieved all its basic goals. The managed health care plan's key objectives will vary. If the managed health care plan is in a community with a single provider of a particular specialty service, merely entering into a contract on any terms with the provider may be its objective. On the other hand, the managed health care plan's objectives might be quite complex, and it may demand carefully planned negotiations to achieve them.

"Must" objectives may derive from state and federal regulations, which may require or prohibit particular clauses in contracts. Managed health care plans need to be aware of these requirements and make sure that their contracting providers understand that these provisions are required by law.

Beyond the essential objectives are the highly desirable ones. Before commencing the drafting or the negotiation of the contract, the managed health care plan should list these objectives and have a good understanding of their relative importance. This preliminary thought process assists the managed health care plan in developing its negotiating strategy.

Annual Calendar

Key provider contracts may take months to negotiate. If the contemplated arrangement with the provider is important to the managed health care plan's delivery system, the managed health care plan will want to avoid the diminution of its bargaining strength as the desired effective date approaches.

The managed health care plan should have a master schedule identifying the contracts that need to be entered into and renewed. This schedule should include time lines that identify dates by which progress on key contract negotiations should take place. Although such an orderly system may be difficult to maintain, it may protect the managed health care plan from potential problems that may arise if it is forced to operate without a contract or negotiate from a weakened position.

Letter of Intent Compared with a Contract

The purpose of a letter of intent is to define the basic elements of a contemplated arrangement or transaction between two parties. A letter of intent is used most often when the negotiation process between two parties is expected to be lengthy and expensive (e.g., a major acquisition). A letter of intent is a preliminary, nonbinding agreement that allows the parties to ascertain whether they are able to agree on key terms. If the parties agree on a letter of intent, the terms of that letter serve as the blueprint for the contract. Some people confuse a letter of intent with a letter of agreement. Because a letter of intent is not a legally binding agreement, regulators will not consider them in evaluating whether a managed care organization meets availability and accessibility requirements. Therefore, the use of a letter of intent should be limited to identifying the general parameters of a future contract.

Negotiating Strategy

Negotiating strategy is determined by objectives and relative negotiating strength. Depending on the locale or market dynamics, either the managed health care plan or the provider may have greater negotiating strength. Except in circumstances in which the relative negotiating strength is so one-sided that one party can dictate the terms to the other party, each party should identify for itself before beginning nego-

tiations the negotiable issues, the party's initial position on each issue, and the extent to which it will compromise. Because a managed health care plan may use the same contract form as the contract for many providers, the managed health care plan needs to keep in mind the implications of amending one contract for the other contracts that use the same form.

A recurring theme presented at conference sessions discussing provider contracting and provider relations is the need to foster a win–win relationship, where both parties perceive that they gain from the relationship. The managed health care plan's objective should be fostering long-term, mutually satisfactory relationships with providers. When managed health care plans have enough negotiating strength to dictate the contract terms, they should exercise that strength cautiously to ensure that their short-term actions do not jeopardize their long-term goals.

CONTRACT STRUCTURE

As mentioned above, clarity is an important objective in drafting a provider contract. A key factor affecting the degree of clarity of a contract is the manner in which the agreement is organized. In fact, many managed health care plan contracts follow fairly similar formats. The contract begins with a title describing the instrument (e.g., "Primary Care Physician Agreement"). After this is the caption, which identifies the names of the parties and the legal action taken, along with the transition, which contains words signifying that the parties have entered into an agreement. Then, the contract includes the recitals, which are best explained as the "whereas" clauses. These clauses are not intended to have legal significance but may become relevant to resolve inconsistencies in the body of the contract or if the drafter inappropriately includes substantive provisions in them. The use of the word *whereas* is merely tradition and has no legal significance.

The next section of the contract is the definitions section, which includes definitions of all key contract terms. The definitions section precedes the operative language, including the substantive health-related provisions that define the responsibilities and obligations of each of the parties, representations and warranties, and declarations. The last section of the contract, the closing or testimonium, reflects the assent of the parties through their signatures. Sometimes, the drafters of a provider contract decide to have the signature page on the first page for administrative simplicity.

Contracts frequently incorporate by reference other documents, some of which will be appended to the agreement as attachments or exhibits. As discussed further below, managed health care plans frequently reserve the right to amend some of these referenced documents unilaterally.

The contract's form or structure is intended to accomplish three purposes: to simplify a reader's use and understanding of the agreement, to facilitate amendment or revision of the contract where the contract form has been used for many providers, and to streamline the administrative process necessary to submit and obtain regulatory approvals. Clarity and efficiency can be attained by using commonly understood terms, avoiding legal or technical jargon, using definitions to explain key and frequently used terms, and using well-organized headings and a numbering system. The ultimate objective is that any representative of the managed health care plan or the provider who has an interest in an issue will be able to find the pertinent contract provision easily and understand its meaning.

Exhibits and appendixes are frequently used by managed health care plans to promote efficiency in administering many provider contracts. The managed health care plan, to the extent possible, could design many of its provider contracts or groups of provider contracts around a core set of common requirements. Exhibits may be used to identify the terms that may vary, such as payment rates and provider responsibilities. This approach has several advantages. First, it eases the administrative burden in drafting and revising contracts. Second, if an appendix or exhibit is the only part of the contract that is being

amended and has a separate state insurance department provider number, the managed health care plan need only submit the amendment for state review. Third, when a contract is under consideration for renewal and the key issue is the payment rate, having the payment rate listed separately in the appendix lessens the likelihood that the provider will review and suggest amending other provisions of the contract.

COMMON CLAUSES, PROVISIONS, AND KEY FACTORS

Names

The initial paragraph of the contract will identify the names of the parties entering into the agreement. It is always a good idea to ensure that the parties named in the opening paragraph are the parties that are signing the agreement. If a managed health care organization is signing the agreement on behalf of affiliates, the provider may want to have the signing party represent and warrant that it is authorized to sign on behalf of the nonsigning party. If the nonsigning party is much stronger financially than the signing party, it would be worthwhile to have a representation directly from the nonsigning party that the signing party may enter into the agreement on its behalf. In reviewing a contract, providers should be particularly sensitive to the responsibilities of nonparties to the agreement and the ability of the provider to enforce these responsibilities. For example, if a managed care organization is offering services to self-insured employers, is the self-insured employer a party to the agreement? If not, what assurances does the provider have that the self-insured employer will fulfill its responsibilities?

Recitals

A contract will typically contain, in rather legalistic prose, a series of statements describing who the parties are and what they are trying to accomplish. These recitals should be general statements. Periodically, however, contract drafters insert substantive requirements in the recitals section. Contract reviewers should be sensitive to this possibility.

Table of Contents

Although a table of contents has no legal significance, the reader will be greatly assisted in finding pertinent sections in a long contract by referring to the table of contents. One common failing in contract renegotiations is neglecting to update the table of contents after the contract has been amended.

Definitions

The definitions section of a contract plays an essential role in simplifying the structure, and the reader's understanding, of a contract. The body of the contract often contains complicated terms that merit amplification and explanation. The use of a definition, although requiring the reader to refer back to an earlier section for a meaning, simplifies greatly the discussion in the body of the agreement. A poorly drafted contract will define unnecessary terms or define terms in a manner that is inconsistent with their use in the body of the agreement.

Defined terms are frequently capitalized in a contract to alert the reader that the word is defined. Definitions are almost essential in many contracts, but their use may complicate the understanding of the agreement. Someone who reads a contract will first read a definition without knowing its significance. Later, when he or she reads the body of the contract, he or she may no longer recall a term's meaning. For this reason, someone reviewing a contract for the first time should read the definitions twice: initially and then in the context of each term's use. Definitions sections tend to err on the side of containing too many definitions. A term that is used only once in a contract need not be defined. On the other hand, a critical reader of a contract will identify instances in which the contract could be improved by the use of additional definitions.

In reviewing a contract, managed health care organizations and providers should not underestimate the importance of definitions of the parties' responsibilities.

An occasional defect in some contracts is that the drafter includes substantive contract provisions in the definitions. A definition is merely an explanation of a meaning of a term and should not contain substantive provisions. This does not mean that a definition that imposes a substantive obligation on a party is invalid. In reviewing a contract, if a party identifies a substantive provision in a definition, the party should ensure that its usage is consistent with the corresponding provision in the body of the contract.

Terms that are commonly defined in a managed care context are *member, subscriber, medical director, provider, payer, physician, primary care physician, emergency, medically necessary,* and *utilization review program.* Some of these terms, such as *medically necessary,* are crucial to a party's understanding of its responsibilities and should be considered carefully in the review of a contract. In many managed care agreements, payers and not the managed health care organization are responsible for payment under the contract. In this case, who is a payer and how a payer is selected and removed become important to the provider. The definition of *member* or *enrollee* is also important. The contract should convey clearly who is covered under the agreement, but it should be clear as to whom the managed health care organization can add in the future. The managed health care plan and provider should ensure that these terms are consistent, if appropriate, with those in other contracts (e.g., the group enrollment agreement).

Provider Obligations

Provider Services

Because the purpose of the agreement is to contract for the provision of health services, the description of those services in the contract is important. As mentioned above, the recitation of services to be furnished by the provider could be set out either in the contract or in an exhibit or attachment. An exhibit format frequently allows the party more flexibility and administrative simplicity when it amends the exhibited portion of the agreement, particularly when the change requires regulatory approval.

Contracts may use the term *provider services* to denote the range of services that is to be provided under the contract. Managed health care organizations frequently adapt physician contracts to apply to ancillary providers. In so doing, the managed health care organization may not revise language that is applicable only to physicians and apply it to an ancillary provider. Nonphysician providers should consider this issue in reviewing a contract.

The contract needs to specify to whom the provider is obligated to furnish services. Although the answer is that the provider furnishes services to covered enrollees, the contract needs to define what is meant by *covered enrollee*, explain how the provider will learn who is covered, and assign the responsibility for payment if services are furnished to a noncovered person. Managed health care organizations and providers frequently disagree on this issue. The providers' view is frequently that if the managed care organization represented that the individual was covered, the managed care organization should be responsible for payment. In contrast, the managed care organization frequently asserts that it should not be responsible for the costs of services provided to noncovered enrollees and that the provider should seek payment directly from the individual. This issue is oftentimes resolved based on relative negotiating strength.

Provider contracts should also cover adequately a number of other provider responsibilities, including the provider's responsibilities to refer or to accept referrals of enrollees, the days and times of days the provider agrees to be available to provide services, and substitute on-call arrangements, if appropriate. Provider contracts may also specify the qualifications necessary for the provider of back-up services when the provider is not available. Some of these func-

tions may be prescribed as conditions of participation in public programs, such as the Medicare risk-contracting program.

If the provider is a hospital, the contract will include language identifying the circumstances in which the managed health care plan agrees to be responsible or not responsible for services provided to nonemergency patients. A fairly common provision in hospital contracts states that the hospital, except in emergencies, must as a prerequisite to admit have the order of the participating physician or other preadmission authorization. The hospital contract also should have an explicit provision requiring that the managed health care plan be notified within a specified period after an emergency admission. A related policy and contracting issue is whether the hospital should be entitled to reimbursement for performing the initial screen that is required when a patient goes to the emergency department.

A good provider contract must be supplemented by a competent provider relations program to ensure that problems that arise are resolved and that the providers have a means to answer questions about their contract responsibilities. Providers will frequently be given the opportunity to appeal internally claim denials and decisions of non–medical necessity by the managed care organization.

Nondiscriminatory Requirements

Provider agreements frequently contain clauses obligating the provider to furnish services to the health care plan's patients in the same manner as the provider furnishes services to non–managed health care patients (i.e., not to discriminate on the basis of payment source). In addition, a clause is used to prohibit other types of discrimination on the basis of race, color, sex, age, disability, religion, and national origin. Government contracts may require the use of specific contract language, including a reference to compliance with the Americans with Disabilities Act. As an alternative, the managed care organization and provider may want to add a second contract clause that requires compliance with all nondiscrimination requirements under federal, state, and local law. These obligations may also apply to subcontractors of the provider.

Compliance with Utilization Review Standards and Protocols and the Quality Assurance Program

The success of the managed care organization is dependent on its providers being able and willing to control unnecessary utilization. To do so, the providers need to follow the utilization review guidelines of the managed health care plan. The contract needs to set out the provider's responsibilities in carrying out the managed health care plan's utilization review program. The managed health care plan's dilemma is how to articulate this obligation in the contract when the utilization review program may be quite detailed and frequently is updated over time. One option used by some managed care organizations is to append the utilization review program to the contract as an exhibit. A second option is merely to incorporate the program by reference. In either case, it is important for the managed health care plan to ensure that the contract allows it to amend the utilization review standards in the future without the consent of the provider. If the managed health care plan does not append a cross-referenced standard, the managed health care plan should give each provider a copy of the guidelines and any amendments. Without this documentation, the provider might argue that it did not agree to the guidelines or subsequent amendments.

The contract needs to inform providers of their responsibilities to cooperate in efforts by the managed health care plan to ensure compliance and the implications of the provider not meeting the guidelines. Contracts differ on whether the managed health care plan is seeking the provider's cooperation or compliance. The current Health Care Financing Administration (HCFA) guidelines for provider contracts require that the provider cooperate with and participate in the managed health care plan's quality assurance program, member grievance system, and utilization review program. Providers gener-

ally favor an obligation to cooperate with these programs rather than one to comply because a requirement to comply with the programs decisions seems to preclude the right to disagree.

The same basic concepts and principles apply to the provider's acceptance of the managed health care plan's quality assurance program. Some managed health care plans tend to equate their utilization review and their quality assurance programs. This attitude not only reflects a misunderstanding of the objectives of the two programs but is likely to engender the concern or criticism of government regulators, which view the two programs as being separate. In the last several years, as managed health care plans have placed greater emphasis on their quality assurance/quality improvement programs, provider compliance responsibilities have increased correspondingly. To provide some guidance on the nature of these responsibilities, some managed health care organizations have appended summaries of these quality programs to the contracts to give providers a better idea of their responsibilities.

The contract should include a provision requiring the provider to cooperate both in furnishing information to the managed health care plan and in taking corrective actions, if appropriate.

Acceptance of Enrollee Patients

A provider contract, particularly with a physician or physician group, will need a clause to ensure that the provider will accept enrollees regardless of their health status. This provision is more important when the risk-sharing responsibilities with the providers are such that the physician has an incentive to dissuade high utilizers from becoming part of his or her panel. Most provider contracts with primary care physicians also include a minimum number of members that the physician will accept into his or her panel (e.g., 250 members). The contract should also include fair and reasonable procedures for allowing the provider to limit or stop new members from being added to his or her panel (at a point after the provider has accepted at least the minimum number of members) and a mechanism to notify the managed health care plan when these changes take place. The managed health care plan needs to have data regarding which providers are limiting their panel size to comply with regulatory requirements.

The contract should also specify the circumstances in which the provider, principally a primary care physician, can cease being an enrollee's physician. Examples may be an enrollee's abusive behavior or refusal to follow a recommended course of treatment. This contract language would need to be consistent with language in the member subscriber agreement and in compliance with licensure requirements, which frequently identify the grounds on which a physician may end the physician–enrollee relationship.

Enrollee Complaints

The contract should require the provider to cooperate in resolving enrollee complaints and to notify the managed health care plan within a specified period of time when any complaints are conveyed to the provider. The provider should also be obligated to advise the managed health care plan of any coverage denials so that the managed health care plan can anticipate future enrollee complaints. To the extent that governmental payer programs require special enrollee grievance procedures, the language in the contract should be written sufficiently broadly to ensure provider cooperation with those procedures.

Maintenance and Retention of Records and Confidentiality

Provider contracts should require the provider to maintain both medical and business records for specified periods of time. For example, these agreements could provide that the records must be maintained in accordance with federal and state laws and consistent with generally accepted business and professional standards as well as whatever other standards are established by the managed health care plan. If the managed health care plan participates in any public or private payer program that establishes certain specific records retention requirements, those requirements should be conveyed to the providers. The contract should state that these obligations survive the termination of the contract.

The managed health care plan also needs a legal right to have access to books and records. The contract will want to state that the managed health care plan, its representatives, and government agencies have the right to inspect, review, and make or obtain copies of medical, financial, and administrative records. The provider would want the availability of this information to be limited to services rendered to enrollees, after reasonable notice, and during normal business hours. The cost of performing these services is often an issue of controversy. If there are no fees for copying these records, the contract should so state. When the managed health care organization is acting on behalf of other payers, it is desirable to have language acknowledging that the other payers have agreed to comply with applicable confidentiality laws.

In addition to the availability of books or records, the managed health care plan might also want the right to require the provider to prepare reports identifying statistical and descriptive medical and patient data and other identifying information as specified by the managed health care plan. If such a provision is included in the contract, the managed health care plan should inform the provider of the types of reports it might request to minimize any future problems. Finally, the provider should be obligated to provide information that is necessary for compliance with state or federal law.

An often neglected legal issue is how the managed health care plan obtains the authority to have access to medical records. Provider agreements periodically contain an acknowledgment by the provider that the managed health care plan is authorized to receive medical records. The problem with this approach is that the managed health care plan might not have the right to have access to this information, and, if it does not, an acknowledgment of that right in the contract has no legal effect. Some state laws give insurers and HMOs, as payers, a limited right of access to medical records. This right may arise if the managed health care organization is performing utilization review on behalf of an enrollee. Managed health care plans should review their state law provisions on this issue and their procedures for obtaining the appropriate consents of their members to have access to this information. Many managed health care plans obtain this information through signatures that are part of the initial enrollment materials. These consents could also be obtained at the time health services are rendered.

Managed health care organizations frequently include provisions in contracts in which the provider acknowledges that the managed health care organization has the right of access to enrollee records. The provider should be reluctant to agree to this provision without consulting state law. Although the clause acknowledging the right of access may make it easier to persuade a reluctant provider to release an enrollee's medical records, the managed health care plan needs to remember that that statement, or for that matter similar statements in the group enrollment agreement, do not confer that right. Finally, the contract should state explicitly that the provisions concerning access to records survive the termination of the agreement.

A related provision almost always included in provider contracts is a requirement that the provider maintain the confidentiality of medical records. A common clause is a provision that the provider will only release the records in accordance with the terms of the contract, in accordance with applicable law, or upon appropriate consent. State law will frequently allow disclosure of information without patient identifiers for purposes of research or education. Managed health care plans and providers need to be sensitive to confidentiality concerns with regard to minors, incompetents, and persons with communicable diseases for which there are specific state confidentiality statutes governing disclosure of information.

A medical record issue may arise when a managed health care plan wants the right to perform certain medical tests outside the hospital before an enrollee's admission. The contract between the managed health care plan and the hospital may allow for such tests and the inclusion of the test results into the hospital's medical record. The hospital may insist that the results of the tests be in a format acceptable to the hospital's medical record committee, that the laboratory results be properly certified, and that the duties performed shall be consistent with the proper practice of medicine.

Payment

The payment terms of the agreement often represent the most important provision for both the provider and the managed health care plan. As mentioned earlier, the payment terms are frequently set forth in an exhibit appended to the contract and are cross-referenced in the body of the agreement. A number of payment issues should be covered in the contract. For example, who will collect the copayments? If the managed health care plan pays the provider on a fee-for-service basis, a provision needs to state that unauthorized or uncovered services are not the responsibility of the managed health care plan. To avoid members' receiving unexpected bills from providers for noncovered services, contracts may say that the provider must inform the member that a service will not be covered by the health plan before providing the service. In addition, the contract may preclude the provider from ever billing an enrollee when the managed health care organization has determined that the service is not medically necessary.

From the provider's perspective, he or she needs a clear understanding of what is necessary for a service to be authorized. If the provider submits claims to the managed health care plan, the contract should set out the manner in which the claim is to be made and either identify the information to be provided in the claim or give the managed health care plan the right to designate or revise that information in the future. If the contract specifies the information to be included in a claim, the managed health care plan should also have the unilateral right to make changes in the future.

The agreement should also obligate the provider to submit claims within a specified period and obligate the managed health care plan to pay claims within a certain number of days. The latter requirement should not apply to contested claims. Also, special provisions will apply to claims for which another carrier may be the primary payer. A common way to address this issue in a balanced manner is to allow a 2-month period for collection from the purported primary carrier. If unsuccessful, the managed health care plan would pay while awaiting resolution of the dispute.

At issue is the time in which the managed health care organization is required to pay on claims. Contracts frequently identify a specific time period (e.g., 30 to 60 days) during which payment on clean claims is to be made. Provider contracts rarely impose an interest penalty for late payment, reflecting the greater bargaining strength of the managed health care organization. Some contracts require the managed health care organization to make a good faith effort to pay within a specified period. From the provider's perspective, the weakness of this provision is that a good faith standard is probably too ambiguous to be enforceable. Some states have laws requiring insurers and HMOs to pay interest on late claims.

The contract needs also to address reconciliations to account for overpayments or underpayments. To avoid these issues from lingering for an inordinately long period of time, some managed health care plans limit the adjustment period to a specified period (e.g., 6 months). Also, some managed health care plans use contract provisions that do not allow for a reconciliation if the amount in controversy falls below a specified amount.

The most complex aspects of provider contracts are often the risk-sharing arrangements (see Chapters 9, 12, and 14). Risk can be shared with providers in significantly varying degrees depending on the initial amount of risk transferred, the services for which the provider is at risk, and whether the managed health care organization offers stop-loss protection. Risk pools with complicated formulas determining distributions are frequently used both when services are capitated and when payments are based on a fee schedule. Although the primary objective of these arrangements is to create incentives to discourage unnecessary utilization, the complexity of many of these arrangements has confused providers and engendered their distrust when their distribution falls below expectations. Some managed health care plans that had complex risk-sharing arrangements are now realizing that simpler, more understandable arrangements are preferable. If the arrangement designed by the managed health care plan is somewhat complex, the provider's understanding will be greatly enhanced by the use of examples that illustrate for providers the total payments they will receive in different factual scenarios.

The most significant trend in provider payment arrangements has been the growth of arrangements where physician–hospital organizations (PHOs) or other integrated delivery systems are willing to accept a percentage of the managed health care plan premium as compensation for the services they provide (see Chapter 4 and 5). An important, related issue is the extent to which state regulators will want to oversee these arrangements directly or indirectly through licensure requirements applicable to the licensed entities to which the PHOs contract (see Chapter 53). The PHO assumes the role of a super-IPA as it becomes responsible for providing, or arranging for the provisions of, all or almost all the managed health care plan's services for enrollees assigned to it. In fact, the PHO does not typically provide services itself; the PHO arranges for the health services through affiliated hospitals, physician groups, and other health care providers. In developing its relationships with a managed health care plan, the PHO must be mindful of how it is transferring the obligations to provide services to its subcontractors.

The compensation arrangements typically provide that the PHO will receive a specified percentage of the amount that the managed health care plan or other payer receives. To reduce the risk of inappropriate adverse or favorable selection, the payment amounts may be adjusted to account for expected utilization based on demographic factors, such as age, sex, and other predictors of health care utilization. Also, the amount of risk assumed by the PHO might be limited until the number of enrollees assigned to the PHO reaches a critical size. The amount of compensation received by the PHO would be reduced to reflect the cost of services that the PHO does not assume responsibility for or stop-loss coverage that is provided by the managed health care plan.

Another issue to consider is whether the managed health care plan will have the right to have the services performed by other providers if it is not satisfied with the contracted provider's performance. Because the PHO is assuming virtually all the risk for the defined population, the PHO needs to consider carefully the assumptions that have been made regarding the demographics and health needs of the covered population.

In recent years, as providers gain more experience with managed health care plans, they are becoming more sophisticated in analyzing and evaluating payment arrangements and are more aware of the ability or inability of managed health care plans to produce the volume promised. A growing number of contracts are being renegotiated in light of the actual volume of patients that a managed health care plan is able to deliver to the provider. Contracts are also now beginning to allow volume as a factor affecting payment amount.

Some of the payment-related issues that should be addressed in a contract are as follows: What if services are provided to a person who is no longer eligible for enrollment? What if services are provided to a nonenrollee who obtained services by using an enrollee's membership card? Who has the responsibility to pursue third party recoveries? What are the notice requirements when the nonresponsible party finds out about a potential third party recovery? Some

managed health care plans allow their providers to collect and keep third party recoveries, whereas others will require that the information be reported and the recovered amount deducted (see Chapter 32). One sensitive issue is the potential liability of a managed health care plan if a provider collects from Medicare inappropriately when another carrier under the Medicare secondary payer rules had primary responsibility. Under the regulations of the HCFA, the managed health care plan is legally responsible and may be forced to pay back the HCFA even if the payment was received by the provider without the knowledge of the managed health care plan. Managed health care plans should include a contract provision transferring the liability to the provider in this circumstance.

Another issue that should be addressed in the contract is the responsibility of the managed health care plan as a secondary carrier if the provider bills the primary carrier an amount greater than the amount the provider would have received from the managed health care plan. From the managed health care plan's perspective, it will want a contract provision relieving the managed health care plan of any payment responsibility if the provider has received at least the amount that he or she would have been entitled to under the managed health care plan–provider contract.

Hold-Harmless and No Balance Billing Clauses

Virtually all provider contracts contain a hold-harmless clause, under which the provider agrees not to sue or assert any claims against the enrollee for services covered under the contract, even if the managed health care plan becomes insolvent or fails to meet its obligations. A no balance billing clause is similar (and may be used synonymously) and states that a provider may not balance bill a member for any payment owed by the plan, regardless of the reason for nonpayment; the provider may bill the member for any amount that the member is required to pay, such as copayment or coinsurance, or for services not covered under the schedule of benefits (e.g., cosmetic surgery). Many state insurance departments (or other agencies having regulatory oversight in this area) will not approve the provider forms without inclusion of a hold-harmless clause containing specific language. HCFA also has adopted recommended model hold-harmless language applicable to federally qualified HMOs that was approved by the National Association of Insurance Commissioners.

Relationship of the Parties

Provider contracts usually contain a provision stating that the managed health care plan and the provider have an independent contractual arrangement. The purpose of this provision is to refute an assertion that the provider serves as an employee of the managed health care plan. The reason is that, under the legal theory of respondeat superior, the managed health care plan would automatically be liable for the negligent acts of its employees. Although managed health care plans frequently include a provision such as this in their provider contracts, it has limited value. In a lawsuit against the managed health care plan by an enrollee alleging malpractice, the court is likely to disregard such language and to focus on the relationship between the managed health care plan and the provider and the manner in which the managed health care plan represented the provider in evaluating whether the managed health care plan should be vicariously liable.

A related clause frequently used in provider contracts states that nothing contained in the agreement shall be construed to require physicians to recommend any procedure or course of treatment that physicians deem professionally inappropriate. This clause is intended, in part, to affirm that the managed health care plan is not engaged in the practice of medicine, an activity that the managed health care plan may not be permitted to perform. Another reason for this clause is to protect the managed health care plan from liability arising from a provider's negligence.

Use of Name

Many provider contracts limit the ability of either party to use the name of the other. This is done by identifying the circumstances in which the party's name may or may not be used. Contract clauses may allow the managed health care plan the right to use the name of the provider for the health benefits accounts, the enrollees, and the patients of the participating providers. Otherwise, the party needs the written approval of the other party. The use applies not only to the name but also to any symbol, trademark, and service mark of the entity. The managed health care plan and the provider will want to ensure that proprietary information is protected. The contract should require that the provider keep all information about the managed health care plan confidential and prohibit the use of the information for any competitive purpose after the contract is terminated. With medical groups frequently switching managed care affiliations, this protection is important to the managed health care plan.

Notification

The managed health care plan needs to ensure that it is advised of a number of important changes that affect the ability of the provider to meet his or her contractual obligations. The contract should identify the information that needs to be conveyed to the managed health care plan and the time frames for providing that information. For example, a physician might be required to notify a managed health care plan within 5 days upon loss or suspension of his or her license or certification, loss or restriction of full active admitting privileges at any hospital, or issuance of any formal charges brought by a government agency. Although specific events should be identified in the contract, a broad catch-all category should also be included, such as an event that, if sustained, would materially impair the provider's ability to perform the duties under the contract. The contract should require immediate notification if the provider is sanctioned under the Medicare or Medicaid programs. If the managed care organization is contracting with a provider who has been sanctioned, the organization may no longer be eligible to receive Medicare and Medicaid funds.

In a hospital contract, the corresponding provisions would be when the hospital suffers from a change that materially impairs its ability to provide services or if action is taken against it regarding certifications, licenses, or federal agencies or private accrediting bodies.

Insurance and Indemnification

Insurance provisions in contracts are fairly straightforward. The obligations in the contract may be for both professional liability coverage and general liability coverage. The managed health care plan wants to ensure that the provider has resources to pay for any eventuality. The contract will state particular insurance limits, provide that the limits will be set forth in a separate attachment, or leave it up to the managed health care plan to specify. A hospital agreement may require only that the limits be commensurate with limits contained in policies of similar hospitals in the state. From the managed health care organization's perspective, it will probably want a specific requirement to ensure adequate levels of insurance. There also should be a provision requiring the provider to notify the managed health care plan of any notification of cancellations of the policy. Another needed notification in a physician context is notification of any malpractice claims.

Cross-indemnification provisions, in which each party indemnifies the other for damages caused by the other party, are common in contracts. One weakness of the clause is that some professional liability carriers will not pay for claims arising from these clauses because of general exclusions in their policies for contractual claims. Although these clauses are frequently used, this limitation and the fact that a provider should still be liable for his or her negli-

gent acts suggest that these indemnification clauses are not essential.

Term, Suspension, and Termination

One section of most contracts identifies the term of the contract and the term of any subsequent contract renewals. Many contracts have automatic renewal provisions if no party exercises its right to terminate. Both managed health care plans and providers should give careful thought to the length of the contract and the renewal periods.

Some contracts give a right of suspension to the managed health care plan. In suspension, the contract continues, but the provider loses specific rights. For example, if a provider fails to follow utilization review protocols a specified number of times, the provider will not be assigned new HMO members or perhaps will receive a reduction in the amount of payment. The advantage of a suspension provision is that total termination of a contract might be counterproductive for the managed health care plan, but a suspension might be sufficiently punitive to persuade the provider to improve.

Termination provisions fall into two categories: termination without cause, and termination with cause. The value of having a provision that allows the managed health care plan to terminate without cause is that the managed health care plan need not defend a challenge by the provider on the substantive issue of whether the grounds were met. A 90-day period is fairly common. If the managed health care plan has the right to terminate without cause, frequently the provider will also be given that right. A regulatory issue to be aware of is that some state laws require providers to continue to provide services for a specified period of time after their contract has terminated. These requirements relate to the state's requirements for the managed health care plan to have protections against insolvency and have to be reflected in the contract.

Terminations with cause allow the health plan to terminate faster and should be used in situations where the managed health care plan needs to act quickly. The contract might establish two different categories: one for immediate termination and another for termination within a 30-day period. Many contracts give either party a period of time to cure any contract violations. This time period, although useful to the managed health care plan if it has allegedly violated the agreement, extends the period of time in which it can terminate the contract. Grounds for termination for cause may be suspension or revocation of a license, loss of hospital privileges, failure to meet accreditation and credentialing requirements, failure to provide services to enrollees in a professionally acceptable manner, and refusal to accept an amendment to the contract agreement. A general clause also allows for termination if the provider takes any actions or makes any communications that undermine or could undermine the confidence of enrollees in the quality of care provided by the managed health care plan. This last clause has been variably interpreted by health plans and has been the subject of some state regulation. The clause should make clear that a physician is free to make medical recommendations, but is not free to disparage the plan.

The contract should be clear that a provider, upon termination, is required to cooperate in the orderly transfer of enrollee care, including records, to other providers. The provider also should cooperate in resolving any disputes. Finally, the provider should continue to furnish services until the services being rendered to enrollees are complete or the managed health care plan has made appropriate provisions for another provider to assume the responsibility. The contract should also be clear that the provider is entitled to compensation for performing these services.

In general, too little consideration has been given to preparing for contract terminations. When the provider and the managed health care plan enter into a contract, little thought is given to what will occur when the contract ends. Often, relationships end acrimoniously, and it is in both parties' best interest to consider how their interests will be protected in the event that the contract is terminated.

Declarations

In declarations, the parties provide answers to a number of "what if" questions. These clauses are common to all contracts.

A *force majeure* clause relieves a party of responsibility if an event occurs beyond its control. In a provider contract, this instance is more likely to arise if the provider is no longer able to provide services. In considering *force majeure* clauses, the parties need to distinguish between events that are beyond a party's control and those that disadvantage a party but for which the party should still be obligated to perform the contract's responsibilities.

A choice of law provision identifies the law that will apply in the event of a dispute. Absent a violation of public policy in the state in question, a court will apply the agreed-upon law. Frequently, lawyers draft contracts using the state in which their client is located without consideration of the advantages and disadvantages of the underlying law. In provider contracts where the managed health care plan and the provider are located in the same state, this clause has little relevance.

A merger clause specifies that only the language in the agreement shall constitute the contract. Such a clause prevents a party from arguing that oral conversations or other documents not included in the contract modify the contract's terms.

A provision allowing or not allowing parties to assign their rights is frequently included in contracts. Provider contracts usually prohibit a provider from assigning its rights under a contract. Some contracts are silent on the right of the managed health care plan to assign the contract. Silence would allow the managed health care plan to assign the contract. An option is to allow the managed health care plan to assign the contract only to an affiliate or a successor without the written consent of the provider.

A clause identifying how the contract will be amended is almost always included in a provider contract. A contract will frequently give the managed health care plan the unilateral right to amend the contract absent an objection by the provider. This procedure is necessary when the managed health care plan has a large provider panel and it is administratively difficult to obtain the signatures of all the providers.

A severability clause allows the contract to continue if a court invalidates a portion of the contract. This is a common provision in a contract, but it is unlikely that the problem will arise.

Contracts also set forth a notice requirement identifying how notices are provided to parties and to whom. The manner in which notice is provided is important. If a notice requires that the communication be conveyed by certified mail with return receipt requested, an alternative form of delivery is not valid. Parties should consider what is administratively feasible before agreeing on how notice will be given.

Closing

Both parties need to confirm that the parties identified at the beginning of the contract are the parties that sign the contract. Also, if a corporation is one of the parties, the signatory needs to be authorized on behalf of the corporation to sign the agreement.

CONCLUSION

The provider contract establishes the foundation for the working relationship between the managed health care plan and the provider. A good contract is well organized and clearly written and accurately reflects the full intentions of the parties. In drafting and reviewing provider contracts, the managed health care plan and the provider need to keep in mind their objectives in entering the relationship, the relationship of this contract to other provider contracts and agreements, and applicable regulatory requirements.

Sample Physician Agreement

AGREEMENT BETWEEN

_____

AND

PRIMARY CARE PHYSICIAN

THIS AGREEMENT, made and entered into the date set forth on the signature page hereto, by and between _____, Inc., a _____ corporation (hereinafter referred to as "HMO"), which is organized and operated as a health maintenance organization under the laws of the State of _____ and the individual physician or group practice identified on the signature page hereto (hereinafter referred to as "Primary Care Physician").

WHEREAS, HMO desires to operate a health maintenance organization pursuant to the laws of the State of _____; and

WHEREAS, Primary Care Physician is a duly licensed physician (or if Primary Care Physician is a legal entity, the members of such entity are duly licensed physicians) in the State of _____, whose license(s) is (are) without limitation or restriction[1]; and

WHEREAS, HMO has as an objective the development and expansion of cost-effective means of delivering quality health services to Members, as defined herein, particularly through prepaid health care plans, and Primary Care Physician concurs in, actively supports, and will contribute to the achievement of this objective; and

WHEREAS, HMO and Primary Care Physician mutually desire to enter into an Agreement whereby the Primary Care Physician shall provide and coordinate the health care services to Members of HMO.

NOW, THEREFORE, in consideration of the premises and mutual covenants herein contained and other good and valuable consideration, it is mutually covenanted and agreed by and between the parties hereto as follows:

---

[1] Although there is nothing wrong with having a statement here that the primary care physician's license is not restricted, the body of the contract, as is the case in this contract in Part IV (H), needs to contain this requirement and provide that the failure to maintain the license is grounds for termination.

PART I. DEFINITIONS

A. *Covered Services* means those health services and benefits to which Members are entitled under the terms of an applicable Health Maintenance Certificate which may be amended by HMO from time to time.[2]

B. *Emergency Services* means those Medically Necessary services provided in connection with an "Emergency," defined as a sudden or unexpected onset of a condition requiring medical or surgical care which the Member secures after the onset of such condition (or as soon thereafter as care can be made available but which in any case is not later than twenty-four (24) hours after onset) and in the absence of such care the Member could reasonably be expected to suffer serious physical impairment or death. Heart attacks, severe chest pain, cardiovascular accidents, hemorrhaging, poisonings, major burns, loss of consciousness, serious breathing difficulties, spinal injuries, shock, and other acute conditions as HMO shall determine are Emergencies.[3]

C. *Encounter Form* means a record of services provided by Physician to Members in a format acceptable to the HMO.[4]

D. *Health Maintenance Certificate* means a contract issued by HMO to a Member or an employer of Members specifying the services and benefits available under the HMO's prepaid health benefits program.

E. *Health Professionals* means doctors of medicine, doctors of osteopathy, dentists, nurses, chiropractors, podiatrists, optometrists, physician assistants, clinical psychologists, social workers, pharmacists, occupational therapists, physical therapists, and other professionals engaged in the delivery of health services who are licensed, practice under an institutional license, and are certified or practice under other authority consistent with the laws of the State of _____.

F. *Medical Director* means a Physician designated by HMO to monitor and review the provision of Covered Services to Members.

G. *Medically Necessary* services and/or supplies means the use of services or supplies as provided by a hospital, skilled nursing facility, Physician, or other provider required to identify or treat a Member's illness or injury and which, as determined by HMO's Medical Director or its utilization review committee, are: (1) consistent with the symptoms or diagnosis and treatment of the Member's condition, disease, ailment, or injury; (2) appropriate with regard to standards of good medical practice; (3) not solely for the convenience of the Member, his or her physician, hospital, or other health care provider; and (4) the most appropriate supply or level of service which can be safely provided to the Member.[5] When specifically applied to an inpatient Mem-

---

[2] This definition notes the HMO's right to revise the covered services that the primary care physician is required to provide. If the physicians were capitated for those services, a mechanism would need to be available to revise the capitation rate accordingly. If the services were not limited to HMO enrollees (e.g., covered persons under an administrative services only arrangement with a self-insured employer), this definition would have to be written more broadly.

[3] The definition for emergency services would be coordinated with the definition used in the HMO's group enrollment agreement. The examples are a useful method of illustrating the types of conditions that are considered emergencies. Some contracts will exclude deliveries during the last month of pregnancy while the mother is traveling outside the service area.

[4] By stating that the encounter form must be acceptable to the HMO, the contract allows the HMO to change its requirements in the future.

[5] This clause gives the HMO the authority to deny coverage for a medically appropriate procedure where another procedure is also appropriate. Although this clause does not explicitly address the subject, it is intended to give the HMO the right to cover the most cost-effective, medically appropriate procedure. An alternative way of addressing the issue is to state explicitly as one of the criteria that the procedure performed is the "least costly setting or manner appropriate to treat the Enrollee's medical condition."

ber, it further means that the Member's medical symptoms or condition requires that the diagnosis or treatment cannot be safely provided to the Member as an outpatient.[6]

H. *Member* means both a Subscriber and his or her eligible family members for whom premium payment has been made.[7]

I. *Participating Physician* means a Physician who, at the time of providing or authorizing services to a Member, has contracted with or on whose behalf a contract has been entered into with HMO to provide professional services to Members.

J. *Participating Provider* means a Physician, hospital, skilled nursing facility, home health agency, or any other duly licensed institution or Health Professional under contract with HMO to provide professional and hospital services to Members.

K. *Physician* means a duly licensed doctor of medicine or osteopathy.

L. *Primary Care Physician* means a Participating Physician who provides primary care services to Members (e.g., general or family practitioner, internist, pediatrician, or such other physician specialty as may be designated by HMO) and is responsible for referrals of Members to Referral Physicians, other Participating Providers, and, if necessary, non-Participating Providers. Each Member shall select or have selected on his or her behalf a Primary Care Physician.

M. *Referral Physician* means a Participating Physician who is responsible for providing certain medical referral physician services upon referral by a Primary Care Physician.

N. *Service Area* means those counties in _____ set forth in Attachment A and such other areas as may be designated by HMO from time to time.

O. *Subscriber* means an individual who has contracted, or on whose behalf a contract has been entered into, with HMO for health care services.

PART II. OBLIGATIONS OF HMO

A. *Administrative Procedures.* HMO shall make available to Primary Care Physician a manual of administrative procedures (including any changes thereto) in the areas of recordkeeping, reporting, and other administrative duties of the Primary Care Physician under this Agreement. Primary Care Physician agrees to abide by such administrative procedures including, but not limited to, the submission HMO Encounter Forms documenting all Covered Services provided to Members by Primary Care Physician.[8]

B. *Compensation.* For all Medically Necessary Covered Services provided to Members by Primary Care Physician, HMO shall pay to Primary Care Physician the compensation set forth in Attachment B.[9] Itemized statements on HMO Encounter Forms, or approved equivalent, for all Covered Services rendered by Primary Care Physician must be submitted to HMO within ninety (90) days of the date the service was rendered in order to be compensated by HMO. The purpose of the risk sharing/incentive compensation arrangement set forth in Attachment B is to monitor utilization, to control costs of health services, including hospitalization, and to achieve utilization goals while maintaining quality of care.

---

[6] This last sentence is a good addition to the definition. It makes clear the preference of outpatient care over inpatient care.

[7] *Member* is usually regarded as synonymous with *enrollee*. The definition of *member* would be consistent with the definition used in the group enrollment agreement.

[8] This paragraph allows the HMO to designate and amend the information, including the claims form, that the primary care physician provides the HMO without obtaining the prior approval of the primary care physician.

[9] This contract reimburses primary care physicians on a fee-for-service basis. Attachment B also sets forth alternative language if an HMO pays its primary care physicians on a capitated basis.

C. *Processing of Claims.* HMO agrees to process Primary Care Physician claims for Covered Services rendered to Members. HMO will make payment within thirty (30) days from the date the claim is received with sufficient documentation. Where a claim requires additional documentation, HMO will make payment within thirty (30) days from date of receipt of sufficient documentation to approve the claim.[10]

D. *Eligibility Report.* HMO shall provide Primary Care Physician with a monthly listing of eligible Members who have selected or have been assigned to Primary Care Physician.

E. *Reports.* HMO will provide Primary Care Physician with periodic statements with respect to the compensation set forth in Attachment B and with utilization reports in accordance with HMO's administrative procedures. Primary Care Physician agrees to maintain the confidentiality of the information presented in such reports.

PART III. OBLIGATIONS OF PRIMARY CARE PHYSICIAN

A. *Health Services.* Primary Care Physician shall have the primary responsibility for arranging and coordinating the overall health care of Members, including appropriate referral to Participating Physicians and Participating Providers, and for managing and coordinating the performance of administrative functions relating to the delivery of health services to Members in accordance with this Agreement. In the event that Primary Care Physician shall provide Member non-Covered Services, Primary Care Physician shall, prior to the provision of such non-Covered Services, inform the Member:

1. of the service(s) to be provided,
2. that HMO will not pay for or be liable for said services, and
3. that Member will be financially liable for such services.[11]

For any health care services rendered to or authorized for Members by Primary Care Physician for which HMO's prior approval is required and such prior approval was not obtained, Primary Care Physician agrees that in no event will HMO assume financial responsibility for charges arising from such services, and payments made by HMO for such services may be deducted by HMO from payments otherwise due Primary Care Physician.[12]

B. *Referrals.* Except in Emergencies or when authorized by HMO, Primary Care Physician agrees to make referrals of Members only to Participating Providers, and only in accordance with HMO policies. Primary Care Physician will furnish such Physicians and providers complete information about treatment procedures and diagnostic tests performed prior to such referral. Upon referral, Primary Care Physician agrees to notify HMO of referral. In the event that services required by a Member are not available from Participating Providers, non-Participating Physicians or Providers may be utilized with the prior approval of HMO. HMO will periodically furnish Primary Care Physician with a current listing of HMO's Participating Referral Physicians and Participating Providers.

C. *Hospital Admissions.* In cases where a Member requires a non-Emergency hospital admission, Primary Care Physician agrees to secure authorization for such admission in accordance with

---

[10] This paragraph allows the HMO to delay payment to the physician while waiting for sufficient documentation.

[11] This prior notification requirement is an important requirement and often is required by state law.

[12] It is important for the HMO to make sure that the physicians know the circumstances or conditions in which prior HMO approval is required.

HMO's procedures prior to the admission. In addition, the Primary Care Physician agrees to abide by HMO hospital discharge policies and procedures for Members.[13]

D. *Primary Care Physician's Members.* The Primary Care Physician shall not refuse to accept a Member as a patient on the basis of health status or medical condition of such Member, except with the approval of the Medical Director. Primary Care Physician may request that he/she does not wish to accept additional Members (excluding persons already in Primary Care Physician's practice who enroll in HMO as Members) by giving HMO written notice of such intent thirty (30) days in advance of the effective date of such closure. Primary Care Physician agrees to accept any HMO Members seeking his/her services during the thirty (30) day notice period. Primary Care Physician agrees to initiate closure of his/her practice to additional Members only if his/her practice, as a whole, is to be closed to additional patients or if authorized by HMO. A request for such authorization shall not be unreasonably denied. HMO may suspend, upon thirty (30) days prior written notice to Primary Care Physician, any further selection of Primary Care Physician by Members who have not already sought Primary Care Physician's services at the time of such suspension.

In addition, a physician who is a Participating Provider may request, in writing to HMO, that coverage for a Member be transferred to another Participating Physician. Participating Physician shall not seek without authorization by HMO to have a Member transferred because of the amount of services required by the Member or because of the health status of the Member.

E. *Charges to Members.* Primary Care Physician shall accept as payment in full, for services which he/she provides, the compensation specified in Attachment B. Primary Care Physician agrees that in no event, including, but not limited to, nonpayment, HMO insolvency, or breach of this Agreement, shall Physician bill, charge, collect a deposit from, seek compensation, remuneration, or reimbursement from, or have any recourse against Subscriber, Member, or persons other than the HMO acting on a Member's behalf for services provided pursuant to this Agreement. This provision shall not prohibit collection of copayments on HMO's behalf made in accordance with the terms of the Health Maintenance Certificate between HMO and Subscriber/Member. Primary Care Physician further agrees that:

1. this provision shall survive the termination of this Agreement regardless of the cause giving rise to termination and shall be construed to be for the benefit of the HMO Member, and that

2. this provision supersedes any oral or written contrary agreement now existing or hereafter entered into between Primary Care Physician and Member, or persons acting on their behalf.[14]

F. *Records and Reports.*

1. Primary Care Physician shall submit to HMO for each Member encounter an HMO Encounter Form which shall contain such statistical and descriptive medical and patient data as specified by HMO. Primary Care Physician shall maintain such records and provide such medical, financial, and administrative information to HMO as the HMO determines may be necessary for compliance by HMO with state and federal law, as well as for pro-

---

[13] Here, again, it is important for the HMO to ensure that the primary care physicians have full notice of all the requirements for prior authorization and discharges.

[14] State regulatory agencies often dictate the precise language of this clause.

gram management purposes. Primary Care Physician will further provide to HMO and, if required, to authorized state and federal agencies, such access to medical records of HMO Members as is needed to ensure the quality of care rendered to such Members. HMO shall have access at reasonable times, upon request, to the billing and medical records of the Primary Care Physician relating to the health care services provided Members, and to information about the cost of such services, and about copayments received by the Primary Care Physician from Members for Covered Services. Utilization and cost data relating to a Participating Physician may be distributed by HMO to other Participating Physicians for HMO program management purposes.

2. HMO shall also have the right to inspect, at reasonable times, Primary Care Physician's facilities pursuant to HMO's credentialing, peer review, and quality assurance program.

3. Primary Care Physician shall maintain a complete medical record for each Member in accordance with the requirements established by HMO. Medical records of Members will include the recording of services provided by the Primary Care Physician, specialists, and hospitals and other reports from referral providers, discharge summaries, records of Emergency care received by the Member, and such other information as HMO requires.[15] Medical records of Members shall be treated as confidential so as to comply with all federal and state laws and regulations regarding the confidentiality of patient records.[16]

G. *Provision of Services and Professional Requirements.*

1. Primary Care Physician shall make necessary and appropriate arrangements to ensure the availability of physician services to his/her Member patients on a twenty-four (24) hours per day, seven (7) days per week basis, including arrangements to ensure coverage of his/her Member patients after hours or when Primary Care Physician is otherwise absent, consistent with HMO's administrative requirements. Primary Care Physician agrees that scheduling of appointments for Members shall be done in a timely manner. The Primary Care Physician will maintain weekly appointment hours which are sufficient and convenient to serve Members and will maintain at all times Emergency and on-call services. Covering arrangements shall be with another Physician who is also a Participating Provider or who has otherwise been approved in advance by HMO. For services rendered by any covering Physician on behalf of Primary Care Physician, including Emergency Services, it shall be Primary Care Physician's sole responsibility to make suitable arrangements with the covering Physician regarding the manner in which said Physician will be reimbursed or otherwise compensated, provided, however, that Primary Care Physician shall ensure that the covering Physician will not, under any circumstances, bill HMO or bill Member for Covered Services (except copayments), and Primary Care Physician hereby agrees to indemnify and hold harmless Members and HMO against charges for Covered Services rendered by physicians who are covering on behalf of Primary Care Physician.

---

[15] This paragraph contains an important requirement. The primary care physician serves as a gatekeeper and the coordinator of care for this HMO. To serve this function, the primary care physician needs information from referral providers. Of course, there needs to be a requirement in the contracts with referral physicians that this information shall be provided to the applicable primary care physician.

[16] For this sentence to be effective, the HMO needs to ensure that its staff and the primary care physician understand state and federal confidentiality laws. Special requirements often arise in some areas, such as acquired immunodeficiency syndrome and mental health and substance abuse services.

2. Primary Care Physician agrees:

(a) not to discriminate in the treatment of his/her patients or in the quality of services delivered to HMO's Members on the basis of race, sex, age, religion, place of residence, health status, disability, or source of payment, and

(b) to observe, protect, and promote the rights of Members as patients. Primary Care Physician shall not seek to transfer a Member from his/her practice based on the Member's health status, without authorization by HMO.

3. Primary Care Physician agrees that all duties performed hereunder shall be consistent with the proper practice of medicine, and that such duties shall be performed in accordance with the customary rules of ethics and conduct of the applicable state and professional licensure boards and agencies.

4. Primary Care Physician agrees that, to the extent he/she utilizes allied Health Professionals and other personnel for delivery of health care, he/she will inform HMO of the functions performed by such personnel.

5. Primary Care Physician shall be duly licensed to practice medicine in _____ and shall maintain good professional standing at all times. Evidence of such licensing shall be submitted to HMO upon request. In addition, Primary Care Physician must meet all qualifications and standards for membership on the medical staff of at least one of the hospitals, if any, which have contracted with HMO and shall be required to maintain staff membership and full admission privileges in accordance with the rules and regulations of such hospital and be otherwise acceptable to such hospital. Finally, Primary Care Physician shall be a duly qualified provider under the Medicare program. Physician agrees to give immediate notice to HMO in the case of suspension or revocation, or initiation of any proceeding that could result in suspension or revocation, of his/her licensure, hospital privileges, or Medicare qualification status or the filing of a malpractice action against the Primary Care Physician.

H. *Insurance.* Primary Care Physician, including individual Physicians providing services to Members under this Agreement if Primary Care Physician is a legal entity, shall provide and maintain such policies of general and professional liability (malpractice) insurance as shall be necessary to insure the Primary Care Physician and his/her employees against any claim or claims for damages arising by reason of personal injuries or death occasioned, directly or indirectly, in connection with the performance of any service by Primary Care Physician. The amounts and extent of such insurance coverage shall be subject to the approval of HMO. Primary Care Physician shall provide memorandum copies of such insurance coverage to HMO upon request.[17]

I. *Administration.*

1. Primary Care Physician agrees to cooperate and participate in such review and service programs as may be established by HMO, including utilization and quality assurance pro-

---

[17] The HMO should have this insurance information on file. Thus the HMO, as a matter of course, should request this information and require notification of changes in the insurance coverage.

grams, credentialing, sanctioning, external audit systems, administrative procedures, and Member and Physician grievance procedures. Primary Care Physician shall comply with all determinations rendered through the above programs.

2. Primary Care Physician agrees that HMO may use his/her name, address, phone number, picture, type of practice, applicable practice restrictions, and an indication of Primary Care Physician's willingness to accept additional Members, in HMO's roster of physician participants and other HMO materials. Primary Care Physician shall not reference HMO in any publicity, advertisements, notices, or promotional material or in any announcement to the Members without prior review and written approval of HMO.

3. Primary Care Physician agrees to provide to HMO information for the collection and coordination of benefits when a Member holds other coverage that is deemed primary for the provision of services to said Member and to abide by HMO coordination of benefits and duplicate coverage policies. This shall include, but not be limited to, permitting HMO to bill and process forms for any third party payer on the Primary Care Physician's behalf for Covered Services and to retain any sums received. In addition, Primary Care Physician shall cooperate in and abide by HMO subrogation policies and procedures.

4. Primary Care Physician agrees to maintain the confidentiality of all information related to fees, charges, expenses, and utilization derived from, through, or provided by HMO.

5. In the event of:

    (a) termination of this Agreement,
    (b) the selection by a Member of another Primary Care Physician in accordance with HMO procedures, or
    (c) the approval by HMO of Primary Care Physician's request to transfer a Member from his/her practice,

    Primary Care Physician agrees to transfer copies of the Member's medical records, radiographs, or other data to HMO when requested to do so in writing by HMO, at the reasonable, customary, and usual fee for such copies.

6. In the event that this Agreement is terminated by either HMO or Primary Care Physician, Primary Care Physician shall return to HMO any and all materials used by Primary Care Physician in the provision of services to HMO Members. Upon termination of the Agreement, the Primary Care Physician shall not use any information obtained during the course of the Agreement in furtherance of any competitors of the HMO.

7. Primary Care Physician warrants and represents that all information and statements given to HMO in applying for or maintaining his/her HMO Primary Care Physician Agreement are true, accurate, and complete. The HMO Physician application shall be incorporated by reference into this Agreement. Any inaccurate or incomplete information or misrepresentation of information provided by Primary Care Physician may result in the immediate termination of this Agreement by HMO.

8. Primary Care Physician shall cooperate with HMO in complying with applicable laws relating to HMO.

PART IV. MISCELLANEOUS

A. *Modification of this Agreement.* This Agreement may be amended or modified in writing as mutually agreed upon by the parties. In addition, HMO may modify any provision of this Agreement upon thirty (30) days' prior written notice to Primary Care Physician. Primary Care Physician shall be deemed to have accepted HMO's modification if Primary Care Physician fails to object to such modification, in writing, within the thirty (30) day notice period.[18]

B. *Interpretation.* This Agreement shall be governed in all respects by the laws of the State of _____. The invalidity or unenforceability of any terms or conditions hereof shall in no way affect the validity or enforceability of any other terms or provisions. The waiver by either party of a breach or violation of any provision of this Agreement shall not operate as or be construed to be a waiver of any subsequent breach thereof.

C. *Assignment.* This Agreement, being intended to secure the services of and be personal to the Primary Care Physician, shall not be assigned, sublet, delegated, or transferred by Primary Care Physician without the prior written consent of HMO.

D. *Notice.* Any notice required to be given pursuant to the terms and provisions hereof shall be sent by certified mail, return receipt requested, postage prepaid, to HMO or to the Primary Care Physician at the respective addresses indicated herein. Notice shall be deemed to be effective when mailed, but notice of change of address shall be effective upon receipt.[19]

E. *Relationship of Parties.* None of the provisions of this Agreement is intended to create nor shall be deemed or construed to create any relationship between the parties hereto other than that of independent entities contracting with each other hereunder solely for the purpose of effecting the provisions of this Agreement. Neither of the parties hereto, nor any of their respective employees, shall be construed to be the agent, employer, employee, or representative of the other, nor will either party have an express or implied right of authority to assume or create any obligation or responsibility on behalf of or in the name of the other party. Neither Primary Care Physician nor HMO shall be liable to any other party for any act, or any failure to act, of the other party to this Agreement.

F. *Gender.* The use of any gender herein shall be deemed to include the other gender where applicable.

G. *Legal Entity.* If Primary Care Physician is a legal entity, an application for each Physician who is a member of such entity must be submitted to and accepted by HMO before such Physician may serve as a Primary Care Physician under this Agreement.

H. *Term and Termination.* The term of this Agreement shall be for three (3) years from the "effective date" set forth on the signature page. This Agreement may be terminated by either party at any time without cause by prior written notice given at least sixty (60) days in advance of the effective date of such termination. This Agreement may also be terminated by HMO effective immediately upon written notice if Primary Care Physician's (or, if a legal entity, any of the entity's physicians') medical license, Medicare qualification, or hospital privileges are suspended, limited, restricted, or revoked, or if Primary Care Physician violates Part III(E), (G)(3), (G)(5), (H), (I)(1), or (I)(4) herein. Upon termination, the rights of each party hereunder shall terminate, provided, however, that such action shall not release the Primary Care Physician or HMO from their obligations with respect to:

(1) payments accrued to the Primary Care Physician prior to termination;

---

[18] This is a common provision and useful in simplifying the administrative work associated with amending the agreement. Needless to say, it is important for the HMO to explain clearly the nature of the amendment to the primary care physician.

[19] Before adopting this paragraph, an HMO should consider whether it is necessary to require that all notifications be sent by certified mail, return receipt requested. If the HMO has a large provider panel, it might prefer the right to send information by regular mail.

(2) the Primary Care Physician's agreement not to seek compensation from Members for Covered Services provided prior to termination; and

(3) completion of treatment of Members then receiving care until continuation of the Member's care can be arranged by HMO.

In the event of termination, no distribution of any money accruing to Primary Care Physician under the provisions of Attachment B shall be made until the regularly scheduled date for such distributions. Upon termination, HMO is empowered and authorized to notify Members and prospective Members, other Primary Care Physicians, and other persons or entities whom it deems to have an interest herein of such termination, through such means as it may choose.

In the event of notice of termination, HMO may notify Members of such fact and assign Members or require Members to select another Primary Care Physician prior to the effective date of termination. In any event, HMO shall continue to compensate Primary Care Physician until the effective date of termination as provided herein for those Members who, because of health reasons, cannot be assigned or make such selection during the notice of termination period and as provided by HMO's Medical Director.

IN WITNESS WHEREOF, the foregoing Agreement between _____ and Primary Care Physician, is entered into by and between the undersigned parties, to be effective this ____ day of _____, 19___.

PRIMARY CARE PHYSICIAN

_____   By:_____

(Name of Individual Physician
or of Group Practice—Please
Print)

_____   _____

(Mailing Address)   (Date)

_____

(City, State, ZIP)

_____

(Telephone Number)

_____

(Taxpayer Identification Number)

_____

(DEA #)

_____

(Signature)

_____

(Name and Title if signing as
authorized representative of
Group Practice)

_____

(Date)

ATTACHMENT B
COMPENSATION SCHEDULE

PRIMARY CARE PHYSICIAN AGREEMENT

I. *Services Rendered by Physicians*

For Covered Services provided by Primary Care Physician in accordance with the terms of this Agreement, HMO shall pay Primary Care Physician his/her Reimbursement Allowance, less any applicable copayment for which the Member is responsible under the applicable Health Maintenance Certificate, and less the Withhold Amount, as described below. "Reimbursement Allowance" shall mean the lower of (i) the usual and customary fee charged by Primary Care Physician for the Covered Service, or (ii) the maximum amount allowed under the fee limits established by HMO.

II. *Withholds from Reimbursement Allowance*

HMO shall withhold from each payment to Primary Care Physician a percentage of the Reimbursement Allowance ("Withhold Amount") and shall allocate an amount equal to such withhold to an HMO Risk Fund. HMO shall have the right, at its sole discretion, to modify the percentage withheld from Primary Care Physician if, in its judgment, the financial condition, operations, or commitments of the HMO or its expenses for particular health services or for services by any particular Participating Providers warrant such modification.

III. *Withhold Amount Distributions*

HMO may, at its sole discretion, from time to time distribute to Primary Care Physician Withhold Amounts retained by HMO from payments to Primary Care Physician, plus such additional amounts, if any, that HMO may deem appropriate as a financial incentive to the provision of cost-effective health care services. HMO may, from time to time, commit or expend Withhold Amounts, in whole or in part, to ensure the financial stability of or commitments of the HMO or health care plans or payers with or for which the HMO has an agreement to arrange for the provision of health care services, or to satisfy budgetary or financial objectives established by HMO.

Subject to HMO's peer review procedures and policies, a Primary Care Physician may be excluded from any distribution if he/she does not qualify for such distribution, for example, if he/she has exceeded HMO utilization standards or criteria. No Primary Care Physician shall have any entitlement to any funds in the HMO Risk Fund.

IV. *Accounting*

Primary Care Physician shall be entitled to an accounting of Withhold Amounts from payments to him/her upon written request to HMO.

ATTACHMENT B (ALTERNATIVE)
CAPITATION PAYMENT

PRIMARY CARE PHYSICIAN AGREEMENT

Compensation

I. *Capitation Allocation*

The total monthly amounts paid to Primary Care Physician will be determined as follows:
For each Member selecting Primary Care Physician ("selecting" also includes Members assigned to a Primary Care Physician), 90 percent of the monthly Primary Care Service capitation set forth below for Primary Care Services shall be paid by HMO to Primary Care Physician by the 5th day of the following month. The capitation shall be set according to the particular benefit plan in which each Member is enrolled. Where the capitation is not currently adjusted for age and/or sex, HMO reserves the right to make such age and/or sex adjustment to the capitation rates upon thirty (30) days' notice. In consideration of such payments, Primary Care Physician agrees to provide to Members the Primary Care Services set forth in Attachment C hereto.
Health Plan shall allocate the remaining 10 percent of the monthly capitation payments to a Risk Reserve Fund, which fund is subject to the further provisions of this Attachment. The capitation payments to Primary Care Physician for Primary Care Services, subject to the above withhold, are as follows:

Coverage Plans

Age/Sex	Commercial Plan __ Capitation Payment	Commercial Plan __ Capitation Payment	Commercial Plan __ Capitation Payment
0-24 Months/M/F	$ _____	$ _____	$ _____
2-4 Years/M/F	$ _____	$ _____	$ _____
5-19 Years/M/F	$ _____	$ _____	$ _____
20-39 Years/F	$ _____	$ _____	$ _____
20-39 Years/M	$ _____	$ _____	$ _____
40-49 Years/F	$ _____	$ _____	$ _____
40-49 Years/M	$ _____	$ _____	$ _____
50-59 Years/F	$ _____	$ _____	$ _____
50-59 Years/M	$ _____	$ _____	$ _____
>60 Years/F	$ _____	$ _____	$ _____
>60 Years/M	$ _____	$ _____	$ _____

Primary Care Physician is financially liable for all Primary Care Services rendered to Members under the above capitation. If Primary Care Physician fails to do so, HMO may pay for such services on behalf of Primary Care Physician and deduct such payments from any sums otherwise due Primary Care Physician by HMO.

Sample Hospital Agreement

HEALTH MAINTENANCE ORGANIZATION

PARTICIPATING HOSPITAL AGREEMENT[1]

THIS AGREEMENT, made and entered into on the date set forth on the signature page hereto, by and between (the "Hospital"), a facility duly licensed under the laws of the State of _____ and located at _____, and _____ ("HMO"), a corporation organized under the _____ law, and located at _____.

WHEREAS, HMO provides a plan of health care benefits (the "Plan") to individuals and their eligible family members and dependents who contract with HMO or who are the beneficiaries of a contract with HMO for such benefits ("Members"), and in connection with such Plan, arranges for the provision of health care services, including Hospital Services, to such Members; and

WHEREAS, the Hospital desires to provide Hospital Services to Members in accordance with the terms and conditions of this Agreement as hereinafter set forth; and

WHEREAS, HMO desires to arrange for the services of the Hospital for the benefit of the Members of the Plan.

NOW, THEREFORE, in consideration of the foregoing recitals and the mutual covenants and promises herein contained and other good and valuable consideration, receipt and sufficiency of which are hereby acknowledged, the parties hereto agree and covenant as follows:

PART I. DEFINITIONS

A. *Covered Services* means those health services and benefits to which Members are entitled under the terms of the applicable Health Maintenance Certificate, which may be amended by HMO from time to time.

B. *Emergency Services* means those Medically Necessary services provided in connection with an "Emergency," defined as a sudden or unexpected onset of a condition requiring medical or surgical care which the Member receives after the onset of such condition (or as soon thereafter

---

[1] For consistency, the HMO has used the same definitions for this agreement and the primary care physician agreement shown in Appendix 55–A. This agreement also uses some of the same provisions as in the primary care physician agreement. Comments made to those provisions in the primary care physician agreement are not repeated here.

as care can be made available but not more than twenty-four (24) hours after onset) and in the absence of such care the Member could reasonably be expected to suffer serious physical impairment or death. Heart attacks, severe chest pain, cardiovascular accidents, hemorrhaging, poisonings, major burns, loss of consciousness, serious breathing difficulties, spinal injuries, shock, and other acute conditions as HMO shall determine are Emergencies.

C. *Health Maintenance Certificate* means a contract issued by HMO to a Member or an employer of Members specifying the services and benefits available under the HMO's prepaid health benefits program.

D. *Hospital Services* means all inpatient services, emergency department, and outpatient hospital services that are Covered Services.

E. *Medical Director* means a Physician designated by HMO to monitor and review the provision of Covered Services to Members.

F. *Medically Necessary* services and/or supplies means the use of services or supplies as provided by a hospital, skilled nursing facility, Physician, or other provider required to identify or treat a Member's illness or injury and which, as determined by HMO's Medical Director or its utilization management committee, are: (1) consistent with the symptoms or diagnosis and treatment of the Member's condition, disease, ailment, or injury; (2) appropriate with regard to standards of good medical practice; (3) not solely for the convenience of the Member, his or her Physician, hospital, or other health care provider; and (4) the most appropriate supply or level of service which can be safely provided to the Member. When specifically applied to an inpatient Member, it further means that the Member's medical symptoms or condition requires that the diagnosis or treatment cannot be safely provided to the Member as an outpatient.

G. *Member* means both an HMO subscriber and his/her enrolled family members for whom premium payment has been made.

H. *Participating Physician* means a Physician who, at the time of providing or authorizing services to a Member, has contracted with or on whose behalf a contract has been entered into with HMO to provide professional services to Members.

I. *Participating Provider* means a Physician, hospital, skilled nursing facility, home health agency, or any other duly licensed institution or health professional under contract with HMO to provide health care services to Members. A list of Participating Providers and their locations is available to each Member upon enrollment. Such list shall be revised from time to time as HMO deems necessary.

J. *Physician* means a duly licensed doctor of medicine or osteopathy.

K. *Primary Care Physician* means a Participating Physician who provides primary care services to Members (e.g., general or family practitioner, internist, pediatrician, or such other physician specialty as may be designated by HMO) and is responsible for referrals of Members to referral Physicians, other Participating Providers, and if necessary, non-Participating Providers.

PART II. HOSPITAL OBLIGATIONS

A. Hospital shall provide to Members those Hospital Services which Hospital has the capacity to provide. Such services shall be provided by Hospital in accordance with the provisions of its Articles of Incorporation and bylaws and medical staff bylaws and the appropriate terms of this Agreement.

B. Hospital shall render Hospital Services to Members in an economical and efficient manner consistent with professional standards of medical care generally accepted in the medical community. Hospital shall not discriminate in the treatment of members and, except as otherwise required by this Agreement, shall make its services available to Members in the same manner as to its other patients.[2] In the event that an admission of a Member cannot be accommodated by Hospital, Hospital shall make the same efforts to arrange for the provision of services at another facility approved by HMO that it would make for other patients in similar circumstances. In the event that Hospital shall provide Member non-Covered Services, Hospital shall, prior to the provision of such non-Covered Services, inform the Member:

    (i)   of the service(s) to be provided,

    (ii) that HMO will not pay for or be liable for said services, and

    (iii) that Member will be financially liable for such services.

C. Except in an Emergency, Hospital shall provide Hospital Inpatient Services to a Member only when Hospital has received certification from HMO in advance of admission of such Member. Services which have not been so approved or authorized shall be the sole financial responsibility of Hospital.[3]

D. If, and to the extent that, the Hospital is not authorized to perform preadmission testing, the Hospital agrees to accept the results of qualified and timely laboratory, radiological, and other tests and procedures which may be performed on a Member prior to admission. The Hospital will not require that duplicate tests or procedures be performed after the Enrollee is admitted, unless such tests and procedures are Medically Necessary.

E. In an Emergency, Hospital shall immediately proceed to render Medically Necessary services to the Member. Hospital shall also contact HMO within twenty-four (24) hours of the Emergency treatment visit or emergency admission. HMO has 24-hour on-call nurse coverage for notification of emergency services or admits.

If Hospital fails to notify HMO within the required time period, neither HMO nor the Member shall be liable for charges for Hospital Services rendered subsequent to the required notification period that are deemed by HMO not to be Medically Necessary.[4]

F. Hospital shall cooperate with and abide by HMO's programs that monitor and evaluate whether Hospital Services provided to Members in accordance with this Agreement are Medically Necessary and consistent with professional standards of medical care generally accepted in the medical community. Such programs include, but are not limited to, utilization management, quality assurance review, and grievance procedures. In connection with HMO's programs, Hospital shall permit HMO's utilization management personnel to visit Members in the Hospital and, to the extent permitted by applicable laws, to inspect and copy health records (including medical records) of Members maintained by Hospital for the purposes of concurrent and retrospective utilization management, discharge planning, and other program management purposes.

G. Hospital shall cooperate with HMO in complying with applicable laws relating to HMO.

PART III. LICENSURE AND ACCREDITATION

Hospital represents that it is duly licensed by the Department of Health of the State of _____ to operate a hospital, is a qualified provider under the Medicare program, and is

---

[2] This requirement serves the same purpose as its counterpart in the primary care physician agreement of requiring the hospital to treat HMO members in the same manner as fee-for-service patients.

[3] A growing issue, not addressed in this provision, is the HMO's responsibility for hospital charges incurred to provide a medical screening examination, as required by Section 1867 of the Social Security Act, to enrollees seeking care from the hospital's emergency department. The hospital may want to seek an explicit statement requiring the HMO to cover the cost of that examination.

[4] To avoid disputes, the hospital and HMO need a common understanding of the meaning of the term *medically necessary*. The definition of that term used in this contract favors the HMO by allowing for its interpretation.

accredited by the Joint Commission on the Accreditation of Healthcare Organizations ("Joint Commission"). Hospital shall maintain in good standing such license and accreditation and shall notify HMO immediately should any action of any kind be initiated against Hospital which could result in:

(i)   the suspension or loss of such license;

(ii)   the suspension or loss of such accreditation; or

(iii)   the imposition of any sanctions against Hospital under the Medicare or Medicaid programs.

Hospital shall furnish to HMO such evidence of licensure, Medicare qualification, and accreditation as HMO may request.

PART IV. RECORDS

A. Hospital shall maintain with respect to each Member receiving Hospital Services pursuant to this Agreement a standard hospital medical record in such form, containing such information, and preserved for such time period(s) as are required by the rules and regulations of the _____ Department of Health, the Medicare program, and the Joint Commission. The original hospital medical records shall be and remain the property of Hospital and shall not be removed or transferred from Hospital except in accordance with applicable laws and general Hospital policies, rules, and regulations relating thereto; provided, however, that HMO shall have the right, in accordance with paragraph (B) below, to inspect, review, and make copies of such records upon request.

B. Upon consent of the Member and a request for such records or information, Hospital shall provide copies of information contained in the medical records of Members to other authorized providers of health care services and to HMO for the purpose of facilitating the delivery of appropriate health care services to Members and carrying out the purposes and provisions of this Agreement, and shall facilitate the sharing of such records among health care providers involved in a Member's care. HMO, and if required, authorized state and federal agencies, shall have the right upon request to inspect at reasonable times and to obtain copies of all records that are maintained by Hospital relating to the care of Members pursuant to this Agreement.

PART V. INSURANCE AND INDEMNIFICATION

A. Hospital shall secure and maintain at its expense throughout the term of this Agreement such policy or policies of general liability and professional liability insurance as shall be necessary to insure Hospital, its agents, and its employees against any claim or claims for damages arising by reason of injury or death, occasioned directly or indirectly by the performance or nonperformance of any service by Hospital, its agents, or its employees. Upon request, Hospital shall provide HMO with a copy of the policy (or policies) or certificate(s) of insurance which evidence compliance with the foregoing insurance requirements. It is specifically agreed that coverage amounts in general conformity with other similar type and size hospitals within the State of _____ shall be acceptable to HMO and be considered satisfactory and in compliance with this requirement.[5]

---

[5] This paragraph reflects the difference in relative bargaining strength that the HMO has with hospitals and physicians. Although the HMO–primary care physician agreement gives the HMO the right to approve malpractice coverage, no such right is contained in the HMO–participating hospital agreement. Another factor may be that the concern for inadequate coverage may be greater for a physician than a hospital.

B. Hospital and HMO each shall indemnify and hold the other harmless from any and all liability, loss, damage, claim, or expense of any kind, including costs and attorney's fees, arising out of the performance of this Agreement and for which the other is solely responsible.

PART VI. MEDICAL STAFF MEMBERSHIP

Notwithstanding any other provision of this Agreement, a Participating Physician may not admit or treat a Member in the Hospital unless he/she is a member in good standing of Hospital's organized medical staff with appropriate clinical privileges to admit and treat such Member.[6]

PART VII. HMO OBLIGATIONS

A. HMO shall provide to or for the benefit of each Member an identification card which shall be presented for purposes of assisting Hospital in verifying Member eligibility. In addition, HMO shall maintain other verification procedures by which Hospital may confirm the eligibility of any Member.
B. HMO shall provide thirty (30) days' advance notice to Hospital of any changes in Covered Services or in the copayments or conditions of coverage applicable thereto.
C. HMO will, whenever an individual, admitted or referred, is not a Member, advise Hospital within thirty (30) days from the date of receipt of an invoice from Hospital for services to such an individual. In such cases, Hospital shall directly bill the individual or another third party payer for services rendered to such individual.
D. In the event that continued stay or services are denied after a patient has been admitted, HMO or its representative shall inform the patient that services have been denied.

PART VIII. USE OF NAME

Except as provided in this paragraph, neither HMO nor Hospital shall use the other's name, symbols, trademarks, or service marks in advertising or promotional material or otherwise. HMO shall have the right to use the name of Hospital for purposes of marketing, informing Members of the identity of Hospital, and otherwise to carry out the terms of this Agreement. Hospital shall have the right to use HMO's name in its informational or promotional materials with HMO's prior approval, which approval shall not be unreasonably withheld.

PART IX. COMPENSATION

Hospital will be compensated by HMO for all Medically Necessary Covered Services provided to Members in accordance with the provisions of Attachment A annexed hereto and incorporated herein.[7]

PART X. PAYMENT TO HOSPITAL BY HMO

For Hospital Services rendered to Members, Hospital shall invoice HMO at Hospital's current charges. [Alternative: For Hospital Services rendered to Members, Hospital shall invoice HMO.[8]] Except for Hospital Services which HMO determines require further review under

---

[6] Requiring the HMO's physicians to comply with the hospital's medical staff requirements is important and reasonable.

[7] Attachment A provides for payment as a percentage of charges. By structuring the agreement in this manner, the HMO is able to negotiate different payment arrangements with hospitals without revising the body of the agreement.

[8] This broader alternative language, along with the cross-reference to Attachment A in the preceding paragraph, allows the body of the contract to be used for any type of payment arrangement. An alternative Attachment A is offered that establishes per diem rates for inpatient stays and a percentage of charges for outpatient services.

HMO's utilization management procedures, or when there are circumstances which are beyond the control of HMO, including submission of incomplete claims, HMO shall make payment of invoices for Hospital Services within thirty (30) calendar days after the HMO's receipt thereof. HMO authorized copayments shall be collected by the Hospital from the Member and the Member shall be solely responsible for the payment of such copayments. All billings by Hospital shall be considered final unless adjustments are requested in writing by Hospital within sixty (60) days after receipt of original billing by HMO, except for circumstances which are beyond the control of Hospital.[9] No payment shall be made unless the invoice for services is received within sixty (60) days after the date of discharge of the Member or date of service, whichever occurs later. Hospital shall interim bill HMO every thirty (30) days for patients whose length of stay is greater than thirty (30) days.

PART XI. PROHIBITIONS ON MEMBER BILLING

Hospital hereby agrees that in no event, including, but not limited to, nonpayment by HMO, HMO's insolvency, or breach of this Agreement, shall Hospital bill, charge, collect a deposit from, seek compensation, remuneration, or reimbursement from, or have any recourse against a Member or persons other than HMO acting on a Member's behalf for services provided pursuant to this Agreement. This provision shall not prohibit collection of copayment on HMO's behalf in accordance with the terms of the Health Maintenance Certificate between HMO and Member. Hospital further agrees that:

(i)   this provision shall survive the termination of this Agreement regardless of the cause giving rise to termination and shall be construed to be for the benefit of the Member; and

(ii)   this provision supersedes any oral or written contrary agreement now existing or hereafter entered into between Hospital and Member, or persons acting on their behalf.

PART XII. INSPECTION OF RECORDS

Upon request, and at reasonable times, HMO and Hospital shall make available to the other for review such books, records, utilization information, and other documents or information relating directly to any determination required by this Agreement. All such information shall be held by the receiving party in confidence and shall only be used in connection with the administration of this Agreement.

PART XIII. COORDINATION OF BENEFITS

Hospital agrees to cooperate with HMO toward effective implementation of any provisions of HMO's Health Maintenance Certificates relating to coordination of benefits and claims by third parties. Hospital shall forward to HMO any payments received from a third party payer for authorized Hospital Services where HMO has made payment to Hospital covering such Hospital Services and such third party payer is determined to be primarily obligated for such Hospital Services under applicable Coordination of Benefits rules. Such payment shall not exceed the amount paid to Hospital by HMO. Except as otherwise required by law, Hospital agrees to permit HMO to bill and process forms for any third party payer on Hospital's behalf, or to bill such third party directly, as determined by HMO. Hospital further agrees to waive, when requested, any claims against third party payers for its provision of Hospital Services to Members and to execute any further documents that reasonably may be required or appropriate for this

---

[9] To avoid potential disputes, the hospital and the HMO should have some general understanding of the meaning of the term *beyond the control of Hospital.*

purpose. Any such waiver shall be contingent upon HMO's payment to Hospital of its (HMO's) obligations for charges incurred by Member.

PART XIV. TERM AND TERMINATION

A. This Agreement shall take effect on the "effective date" set forth on the signature page and shall continue for a period of one (1) year or until terminated as provided herein.

    1. Either party may terminate this Agreement without cause upon at least ninety (90) days' written notice prior to the term of this Agreement.

    2. Either party may terminate this Agreement with cause upon at least thirty (30) days' prior written notice.

B. HMO shall have the right to terminate this Agreement immediately by notice to Hospital upon the occurrence of any of the following events:

    (i)   the suspension or revocation of Hospital's license;

    (ii)   the suspension, revocation, or loss of the Hospital's Joint Commission accreditation or Medicare qualification; or

    (iii) breach of Part II(E) or Part XI of this Agreement.

C. HMO shall continue to pay Hospital in accordance with the provisions of Attachment A for Hospital Services provided by Hospital to Members hospitalized at the time of termination of this Agreement, pending clinically appropriate discharge or transfer to an HMO-designated hospital when medically appropriate as determined by HMO. In continuing to provide such Hospital Services, Hospital shall abide by the applicable terms and conditions of this Agreement.

PART XV. ADMINISTRATION

Hospital agrees to abide by and cooperate with HMO administrative policies including, but not limited to, claims procedures, copayment collections, and duplicate coverage/subrogation recoveries. Nothing in this Agreement shall be construed to require Hospital to violate, breach, or modify its written policies and procedures unless specifically agreed to herein.

PART XVI. MEMBER GRIEVANCES

Hospital agrees to cooperate in and abide by HMO grievance procedures in resolving Member's grievances related to the provision of Hospital Services. In this regard, HMO shall bring to the attention of appropriate Hospital officials all Member complaints involving Hospital, and Hospital shall, in accordance with its regular procedure, investigate such complaints and use its best efforts to resolve them in a fair and equitable manner. Hospital agrees to notify HMO promptly of any action taken or proposed with respect to the resolution of such complaints and the avoidance of similar complaints in the future. The Hospital shall notify the HMO after it has received a complaint from an HMO Member.

PART XVII. MISCELLANEOUS

A. If any term, provision, covenant, or condition of this Agreement is invalid, void, or unenforceable, the rest of the Agreement shall remain in full force and effect. The invalidity or unenforceability of any term or provision hereof shall in no way affect the validity or enforceability of any other term or provision.

B. This Agreement contains the complete understanding and agreement between Hospital and HMO and supersedes all representations, understandings, or agreements prior to the execution hereof.

C. HMO and Hospital agree that, to the extent compatible with the separate and independent management of each, they shall at all times maintain an effective liaison and close cooperation with each other to provide maximum benefits to Members at the most reasonable cost consistent with quality standards of hospital care.

D. No waiver, alteration, amendment, or modification of this Agreement shall be valid unless in each instance a written memorandum specifically expressing such waiver, alteration, amendment, or modification is made and subscribed by a duly authorized officer of Hospital and a duly authorized officer of HMO.

E. Hospital shall not assign its rights, duties, or obligations under this Agreement without the express, written permission of HMO.

F. None of the provisions of this Agreement is intended to create nor shall be deemed to create any relationship between HMO and Hospital other than that of independent entities contracting with each other hereunder solely for the purpose of effecting the provisions of this Agreement. Neither of the parties hereto, nor any of their respective employees, shall be construed to be the agent, employer, employee, or representative of the other.

G. This Agreement shall be construed in accordance with the laws of the State of _____.

H. The headings and numbers of sections and paragraphs contained in this Agreement are for reference purposes only and shall not affect an any way the meaning or interpretation of this Agreement.

I. Any notice required or permitted to be given pursuant to the terms and provisions of this Agreement shall be sent by registered mail or certified mail, return receipt requested, postage prepaid, to:

_____

_____

_____

_____

and to Hospital at:

_____

_____

_____

_____

IN WITNESS WHEREOF, the foregoing Agreement between _____ and Hospital is entered into by and between the undersigned parties, to be effective the _____ day of _____, 19_____.

By:_____

Title:_____

Date:_____

HOSPITAL

By:_____

Title: Administrator_____

Date:_____

ATTACHMENT A
PARTICIPATING HOSPITAL COMPENSATION

Subject to the terms and conditions set forth in this Agreement, HMO shall pay Hospital (____ %) of Hospital's schedule of charges effective _____ as submitted and approved by HMO, for Medically Necessary Covered Services provided to Members.

ATTACHMENT A [ALTERNATIVE]
PARTICIPATING HOSPITAL COMPENSATION

Subject to the terms and conditions set forth in this Agreement, HMO shall pay Hospital as follows:

Service	Type of Reimbursement	Total Reimbursement
Inpatient care		
Nonmaternity–Secondary	Per Diem	$_____
Nonmaternity–Tertiary	Per Diem	$_____
Maternity	Per Diem	$_____
Psychiatric	Per Diem	$_____
Well newborn children	Per Diem	$_____
Outpatient care		
Other than outpatient surgery	Percentage Discount	_____%

Outpatient Surgery — Hospital will be reimbursed (1) the percentage discount stated above, (2) any guaranteed maximum "global" rate program adopted by the Hospital for ambulatory surgical procedures,[10] or (3) 125 percent[11] of the per diem payment amount had the Enrollee been admitted to the Hospital, whichever is least.

---

[10] If Medicare adopts a global fee for reimbursement of outpatient hospital costs, an increasing number of HMO–hospital contracts are likely to adopt a similar approach.

[11] This percentage commonly varies from 100 percent to 125 percent.

Chapter 56

Legal Issues in Integrated Delivery Systems

Jerry R. Peters

DEFINITIONS

An integrated delivery system (IDS; see also Chapter 4) is an organization or group of legally affiliated organizations in which hospitals and physicians combine their assets, activities, risks, and rewards to deliver comprehensive health care services. This classic definition of an IDS is often confused in two ways.

First, there are numerous terms that are used in place of *IDS*, including *integrated health care organization, integrated health care system, integrated health care network, integrated service network,* and *organized delivery system.* The particular label one gives to the IDS is unimportant, the fundamental question is whether there is a legally affiliated system that controls the delivery of hospital and physician services.

The second, and more recent, area of confusion arises from the use of the term *IDS* to describe arrangements that are actually physician–hospital organizations (PHOs) or management service organizations (MSOs). From a legal perspective, the PHO and MSO are both arrangements in which a hospital is not legally affiliated

Jerry R. Peters, Esq., is a partner practicing in the San Francisco office of Latham & Watkins' health care practice group. He has spoken extensively and published several books and numerous articles on physician–hospital business arrangements, including integrated delivery systems. He was an adjunct professor in health care law, and graduated Phi Beta Kappa in economics from the University of California, Berkeley. He received his law degree from Hastings College of the Law.

with the physician practice but enters into a joint venture (the PHO) or contractual arrangement (the MSO) with the legally separate physician organization.

To get a better understanding of the differences among an IDS, PHO, and MSO, one must first identify the two types of integration: structural integration and operational integration. Structural integration occurs when previously separate businesses combine into either a single organization or a group of affiliated organizations that are under common ownership and control. This may occur when a hospital and physician practice merge into a single organization or when a hospital or physician practice places itself under the common control of a single parent holding company.

Operational integration is the merger and consolidation of previously separate business operations into a single business operation. Typically, it is evidenced by factors such as the common development of operational systems, the consolidation of management into a single management team, the joint planning and implementation of services by the hospital and physician practice, and the general consolidation of staff and other functions. There is no clear standard to determine when an operational integration has occurred. Instead, there are degrees or levels of operational integration. A hospital and physician practice achieve more operational integration when they operate under a consolidated budget, consolidated management and governance, a consolidated strategic plan, a unified marketing program, a single payer contracting process, and a coordinated operating system.

Structural integration is often the first focus of developing an IDS. As difficult as the merger of a hospital business into a physician practice may be, such structural integration is often more simple than operational integration. In fact, many current IDS efforts are foundering in the waters of operational integration, and there is a growing backlash developing against IDSs because of the costs, time, and lost opportunities associated with operational integration.

Given this distinction between operational integration and structural integration, the difference among an IDS, PHO, and MSO is that the IDS includes both structural and operational integration between a hospital and a physician practice. Both the PHO and the MSO do not undergo structural integration; instead, the hospital and the physician practice maintain separate businesses from each other. This lack of structural integration in a PHO and MSO means that such arrangements have additional legal risks (compared with an IDS), and there is less economic incentive to implement operational integration between the parties (a hospital may not be willing to invest significant capital in a medical practice that is free to leave the hospital's sphere of influence or otherwise use the capital to the detriment of the hospital).

It should be noted that, in the current environment, the terms *IDS*, *PHO*, and *MSO* are often used interchangeably. To differentiate among these terms, it is important to determine whether the parties intend to integrate structurally (i.e., merge their businesses into a single economic enterprise—IDS) or whether each party will remain a separate business (i.e., each retains the right to its own revenue stream and controls its own means of production—PHO and MSO). In addition, one should determine what level of operational integration the parties intend to implement, recognizing that it is possible (even if not always economically preferable) to implement a significant degree of operational integration regardless of the level of structural integration between the parties.

IDS MODELS

There are several variables that combine to create numerous IDS models (e.g., nonprofit model, for-profit model, foundation model, integrated health care organization model, etc.). Important variables include the number of organizations in the IDS, whether the organizations are nonprofit or for profit, whether the organizations are taxable or tax exempt, the degree to which the organizations are operationally integrated, the relationship between the IDS and the physicians (i.e., employees or independent contractors), who controls the IDS (physicians, shareholder-investors, or nonprofit community directors), and how physicians are compensated. In developing an IDS, an advisor should examine each of these issues with his or her clients to determine what structure best meets the clients' goals. A few examples are illustrative of how one might structure an IDS.

The California foundation model typically involves a parent holding company, which is a nonprofit corporation that obtains tax exempt status. This parent holding company has two subsidiaries: one that operates the hospital and another that operates a medical practice (the medical practice corporation is typically called the foundation). The California foundation model is inherently a nonprofit, tax exempt model because California's corporate practice of medicine doctrine/licensure laws require that the physician practice organization (i.e., the foundation) be tax exempt. In the Friendly Hills determination letter, the Internal Revenue Service (IRS) imposed certain requirements (see below) upon the foundation, including restrictions on the number of physicians who may serve on the board of directors of the foundation. California's corporate practice of medicine doctrine also requires that the physicians be independent contractors to the foundation (thus the physicians are not employees of the foundation but instead organize their own professional corporation, which enters into a professional services agreement with the foundation under an independent contractor arrangement). Under this model, the

IDS is ultimately controlled by nonprofit community directors (who typically control the parent holding company and the subsidiaries). Although this model has been copied in other states, there is no legal requirement that the structure be adopted in states that either do not have a corporate practice of medicine doctrine or have a more lenient doctrine than California.

In some states (other than California), the parties might establish a single for-profit IDS organization that is exclusively or predominantly owned by physicians (often called an integrated health care organization). This organization may acquire a hospital and then enter into contracts with payers to provide comprehensive hospital and physician services. This model is a for-profit organization whereby physicians own and are employed by the organization.

Another alternative is for physicians to own their medical practice and to establish a separate organization that owns the means of production (i.e., space, equipment, staff, etc.) for the physicians to operate their practice. This separate organization is often referred to as an MSO. The MSO may acquire a hospital and its assets. In addition, the MSO may have investors (in addition to the physician owners, who typically control a majority of the MSO). The MSO leases its assets to the physician practice, and the physician practice pays a fee to the MSO that must, at a minimum, equal the cost of operating the MSO.

This alternative illustrates the blurry distinction between an IDS and an MSO. In this example, the physician practice effectively functions as an IDS (it controls the revenues of both the physician and hospital practice and controls the operations of the hospital through the MSO lease arrangement), even though the hospital is technically owned by a separate organization. The common control by the physicians over both organizations, however, combined with the unification of economic incentives between the hospital and physicians, arguably makes this arrangement an IDS.

Given the various options for structuring an IDS, there are numerous models that can be de-veloped. It is important for the parties to begin their integration process by identifying their goals and structuring the IDS to meet those goals. If the parties encounter significant differences in their goals or are unable to agree on the fundamental structural issues (nonprofit or for profit, physician controlled or community director controlled, etc.), the parties should not be afraid to postpone or discontinue their integration discussions. It is most often better to use these warnings signs to avoid a bad marriage than to embark upon integration efforts with an incompatible partner.

GOVERNANCE

If the IDS is organized as a professional corporation (or some other type of professional organization under state law), the state's corporate practice of medicine doctrine or other licensing laws may restrict who may serve on the board of directors of the organization (typically, only physicians or other licensed persons may serve on the board). If the IDS is formed as a nonprofit corporation under state law, state corporate law may again restrict the number or types of persons who may serve on the board (e.g., some laws require that no more than 49 percent of the board members be interested directors, as that term is defined in the state corporate law). Finally, if the IDS applies for federal tax exempt status under Internal Revenue Code Section 501(c)(3), it will most likely need to address the safe harbor requirements regarding governance that are imposed by the IRS. The IRS has set forth its safe harbors in its 1994, 1995, and 1996 Continuing Professional Education Exempt Organizations Technical Instruction Program (CPE guidelines), copies of which may be obtained from the IRS.

To meet the safe harbor requirements, no more than 20 percent of an IDS board should consist of physicians who are financially related, directly or indirectly, to the IDS (the IRS has allowed physician representation to exceed 20 percent where the physicians at issue have no past or present financial interest in the IDS organization). The 20 percent rule includes physicians who have retired from a medical group and, until recently, also included anyone else who is financially related to the IDS. Although in certain cases the IRS applied the safe harbor to include salaried managers or administrators of the hospital participants, it now applies the safe harbor only to physicians selling assets to or providing professional services in conjunction with the IDS organization. In the IRS's view, any physician who sells assets to, is employed by, or receives significant referrals from an IDS is "tainted" and can never serve as a disinterested physician on the board of directors.

Historically, the 20 percent limitation applied to the chief executive officer and other key employees of the IDS. Recently, however, the IRS has begun to exclude IDS employees and is only focusing its 20 percent limitation on physicians who contract with the IDS. In the 1996 CPE guidelines, the IRS clarified its current position:

> The Service has, under certain circumstances, allowed physician representation on the board of directors of an IDS organization to exceed 20 percent where the physicians at issue have no past or present financial interest in the IDS. Also, while in one or two IDS cases the Service may have applied the 20 percent safe harbor to include salaried managers or administrators of hospital participants, the Service now applies the 20 percent safe harbor only to physicians selling assets to or providing professional services in conjunction with the IDS organization.

> For example, in a particular case involving a 10 person board of directors, the Service approved the inclusion of three physicians as members. Two physicians were allowed to have a direct or indirect financial interest in the IDS organization. The third physician did not and could not have any direct or indirect financial interest in the IDS

organization. In this situation, the third physician member was an employee of the hospital, the sole corporate member of the IDS organization. Another situation where the safe harbor was allowed to be exceeded was when the third physician on a 10 person board was retired and had no past or present direct or indirect financial interest in the IDS organization or any acquired physician practice.

> In general, any physician selling assets to, employed by, or providing professional services to or on behalf of an IDS organization is "tainted" and can never serve as a "disinterested" physician on an IDS organization's board of directors. Also, any physician receiving significant referrals from an IDS organization may be considered financially interested and precluded from being considered a disinterested physician member.[1]

The 20 percent limitation applies to an IDS regardless of whether it seeks tax exempt financing. Until recently, only an organization that sought tax exempt financing was restricted by bond counsel to the 20 percent physician director rule set forth in the safe harbor of Revenue Procedure 82-15 (as replaced by Revenue Procedure 93-19). Now, this 20 percent rule applies to all IDSs and possibly to all exempt organizations. IRS officials have informally indicated their willingness to examine the application of the safe harbor on a case-by-case basis. Although the 1996 CPE guidelines admit to a limited exception allowed by the IRS, counselors should prepare their clients to expect strict imposition of this 20 percent safe harbor by the IRS in granting a determination letter.

IDS participants should also note that the 20 percent limitation applies to quorum and voting requirements on the board. Thus an IDS may not require a supermajority vote that effectively gives the physicians the power to block an activity. The overall principle is that the community members of the board must have control over the activities of the IDS.

If physician participation on the board is an important issue in consummating a transaction, legal counsel should carefully consider exceeding the 20 percent limitation pursuant to the following legal analysis:

- *Legal authority*—Neither the CPE guidelines nor Revenue Ruling 69-545 cited any legal authority that limits physician participation to 20 percent.
- *Influence*—IRS analysis appears to confuse the concept of influence with that of control. The IRS has conceded that physicians may have influence on the board (by allowing 20 percent physician board members). Physician control of the board would not begin until physicians had 50 percent or more of the board positions. Arguably, physicians should be allowed up to 49 percent of the board seats with increasing legal risk to the IDS (because the physicians would still only have influence, not control, over the IDS). Once physicians have 50 percent or more of the board seats, the physicians arguably control the organization, and the legal arguments favoring revocation of tax exempt status are more significant. The IRS has given no rationale explaining the difference between influence and control or any explanation as to why 20 percent physician participation is safer for the IDS than 49 percent or less participation.
- *Private benefit*—The IRS's best argument supporting the 20 percent safe harbor is that physicians benefit more than incidentally if they sell their practices, enter into a professional services agreement with the IDS, and receive influence over the organization in an amount exceeding 20 percent. There are two problems with this argument:

  1. The IRS has opined numerous times that the benefit of forming an IDS outweighs the incidental private benefit to physicians when their practices are sold, a professional services agreement is entered into, and 20 percent of the board comprises physicians. The issue is whether giving the physicians an additional 29 percent of the board seats is the "straw that breaks the camel's back." The IRS may have a difficult time convincing a court that the additional 29 percent of board seats suddenly creates incidental private benefit, especially because the physicians still would not have control over the organization.

  2. The IRS has already granted tax exempt status to many physician organizations that have more than 50 percent physician board composition. The IRS has shown no inclination to revoke those exemptions or require modifications. One must question whether the IRS would now litigate a case in which less than 50 percent of the board comprised physicians.

- *Proposed legislation*—It should be noted that congressional committees have proposed that legislation be enacted limiting the board of directors of tax exempt organizations to 20 percent or less of financially interested persons (which would include physicians in an IDS setting). It also should be noted that such legislation has not become law as of the time this chapter was written. Nonetheless, strict adherence to the IRS's safe harbor would have the effect of making this 20 percent guideline into a law (even though Congress has thus far not found it appropriate to enact such a law). One must question the significance of Congress' failure to enact a 20 percent limitation into the actual law of the land.

- *Unenforceability*—After an IDS obtains tax exempt status by acquiescing to the 20 percent safe harbor rule, it could reconstitute its board so that physicians have 49 percent or less of the board seats (the IDS should report this change in its subsequent Form 990 report or in a separate notice to the IRS). If the organization has a conflict of interest policy that excludes physician board members from all votes in which they have a conflicting financial interest and no actual act of inurement occurs, one must wonder whether a court would uphold the IRS's attempt to revoke exemption.

- *Physician expertise*—The purpose of establishing an IDS is to merge the interests of hospitals and physicians into a single organization that motivates providers to deliver high-quality, cost-efficient health care services. Physicians control the delivery (i.e., the quality and efficiency) of most services. By restricting physician participation in the IDS governance structure, the IRS is mandating that physicians be alienated from decisions that affect the delivery process. This limits the IDS's use of physician expertise in certain areas and imparts a message to physicians that they are no longer responsible for organizational performance. This alienation of physicians from the IDS can result in reduced efficiency and quality of care. Physicians are not a single person; the diversity of their opinions often requires more than 20 percent representation on the board.

- *Acquisition costs*—Finally, removing physicians from governance raises the costs of developing an IDS. Physicians typically require a greater purchase price in exchange for their assets if they have little control in the resulting IDS.

One alternative to the IRS's 20 percent limitation is to structure the IDS as follows:

- A majority of the IDS board must comprise persons who do not have a material financial interest in the IDS. Thus a chief executive officer director and any physicians who provide services for the IDS must make up a minority of the board. A quorum for voting must consist of a majority of noninterested directors.

- A financially interested director may not participate in discussions, or vote, regarding any matter in which the director has a financial interest. The director may answer questions from the board before leaving the room.

- Physician directors should be allowed to vote on the IDS's budget, but physician compensation should be separately voted upon by nonphysician directors only.

These safeguards ensure that the IDS will not make decisions that excessively benefit private individuals. At the same time, these safeguards allow physicians to participate in the overall governance of the IDS and allow the IDS to benefit from the physicians' expertise in areas where no conflict of interest exists. See also Chapter 6 for additional governance-related discussion.

COMMITTEES

Any committee or subcommittee created to consider the business or charitable operations of the IDS must be independent and broadly representative of the community. Although the meaning of the phrase *independent and broadly representative of the community* was previously unclear, the IRS now requests that IDS committees, with a few exceptions, comply with the 20 percent safe harbor.[2]

Again, the IRS and/or legal counsel should carefully consider the strength of the IRS's position before enforcing it against an IDS (for the same reasons as those set forth above with respect to the 20 percent safe harbor limit for directors). This is particularly true when the committees are advisory to the board (but see below). Nonetheless, the IRS's rationale for limiting committee participation should be reviewed and understood by the client before the client decides to assume the risk of noncompliance (IRS rationale is addressed in the 1996 CPE guidelines).

There are two committees that the IRS has made particular statements regarding: the compensation committee and the fee committee. The IRS insists that physicians who have (or have had) a financial relationship with the IDS (or the predecessor physician group) may not serve on any committee that recommends or determines physician compensation. The problem with this limitation is that it prevents the IDS from utilizing physician expertise regarding compensation and physician incentives. As long as the compensation committee is advisory to the board and the board has the full power to accept, reject, and/or modify the committee's recommendations, some physician representation on this committee might be beneficial. In general, the physicians are likely to know more about physician compensation than the average person. This expertise should not be lost to the IDS.

At the same time, the IDS board cannot simply accept the committee's recommendation without scrutiny. The board should have outside expertise to verify the committee's report. The board should also examine regional or national compensation surveys. If the committee's report is unreasonable, the board must appoint nonphysicians to negotiate physician compensation with the physicians and reject the committee's recommendation.

This issue may be a red herring in that physicians might not serve on the committee directly but will participate via their negotiations with the committee. Practically speaking, physicians will participate in compensation deliberations however the organization is structured. Nonetheless, if the parties intend to go outside the safe harbors with respect to other issues (e.g., 49 percent of the directors will be physicians), they might carefully consider complying with this particular safe harbor to reduce the probability of an IRS challenge (and to increase the probability of a court victory if a challenge does occur). Legal counsel should weigh the risks of going outside too many safe harbors and should

advise clients to be moderate and establish safeguards that protect the organization's charitable assets against excessive private benefit.

The IRS safe harbor also requires that physician participation in the committee that determines IDS fees be limited to a minority of the total committee members. Physician participation on the committee may not be equal to nonphysician participation. Because the IRS is allowing significant physician participation on the fee committee, its position is more palatable to physicians and most likely would be defensible in court. Therefore, IDS participants should consider compliance with this particular safe harbor requirement.

Finally, the 1996 CPE guidelines specifically differentiate between the board-delegated authority committees and advisory committees:

> Most IDS organizations have provisions in their bylaws for the creation and operation of various committees. Normally, an IDS organization will have an executive committee, finance and planning committee, and provisions for various other committees or subcommittees. Often these committees have substantial authority to study, create, implement, and review charitable and business activities as well as the clinical aspects of the organization's operations. Generally, a committee has either advisory authority or specific powers delegated to it by the board of directors.[3]

DELEGATED BOARD AUTHORITY

In situations where an organization's bylaws grant board of directors powers to a committee or subcommittee, the IRS requests that the organization's bylaws state that no more than 20 percent of its committee members may be physicians who are financially interested or related, directly or indirectly, to any owner, partner, shareholder, or employee of the medical group or other physicians providing services in conjunction with the IDS organization. It should be noted that the IRS's position allows unlimited physician representation on any committees or subcommittees that have authority over the clinical aspects of the organization's activities.[4]

ADVISORY COMMITTEES

Committees that do not have board of directors powers but are merely advisory in nature may also create concerns for the IRS. To elucidate these issues, some background information may be useful. The tax exempt status of the IDS presents several difficult issues. Generally speaking, IDS organizations are created through the purchase of one or more existing private medical practices, and the individual physicians become employees or contractors of the IDS organization. These are factually intensive cases with important issues that the IRS must address. The benefit to the community from the formation of the IDS must be carefully weighed against the benefit to the physicians from the sale of their practices and subsequent professional services agreements. Unless there is a significant community benefit, these transactions may benefit the physicians more than unsubstantially.

Integration also raises serious concerns for physicians. After integration, physicians face a totally different employment or service environment; they may be hesitant to relinquish control of their former medical practice. The IRS, on the other hand, is concerned that the community receive a substantial benefit because of the large amount of charitable assets involved in the purchase of physicians' medical practice assets. In contrast, the physicians may believe that, as the former owners of a valuable business, they should continue to exert considerable control. The IRS acknowledges this expertise but seeks to ensure that there is a significant community benefit, which in certain situations may conflict directly with the interests of the physicians.

Because of the perceived loss of control, physicians often seek to become designated members of committees having substantial day-to-

day operational powers as well as considerable influence over business and charitable programs. In many cases, these committees are the important bodies that weigh all the facts and circumstances in a complicated proposed action. These committees often make recommendations based upon complex fact patterns to the board of directors. Typically, the full board of directors meets infrequently. Because of workload demands, the limited expertise of board members, and the complexity of issues, the board often is unable to give detailed attention to every item that comes before it for a vote. Under certain circumstances, the IRS is concerned that the board will routinely accept the recommendations of committees that have significant control by financially interested parties. Because the IRS has no accurate tool to measure the actual control exercised by physicians or other financially interested individuals who are members of committees, it will, under appropriate circumstances, apply the 20 percent safe harbor to committees.

CONFLICT OF INTEREST POLICY

The IDS should be careful to comply with state law regarding the development of a conflict of interest policy and its operations. This is particularly important if the IDS is a nonprofit organization because most states regulate conflicts of interest with respect to nonprofit directors and officers. In addition, if the IDS seeks tax exempt status, the IRS has set forth guidelines as to how it prefers to see the conflict of interest policy developed for the IDS. In the 1996 CPE Guidelines, the IRS states:

> The Service has expressed concerns about interested party control of IDS organizations through its 80 percent community board safe harbor. The Service is also concerned about private benefit and inurement issues that may arise because of the relationship between an exempt organization providing IDS services and its physician employees/contractors, officers, di-

rectors and key employees. In most situations, the best protection for a charitable trust is well-defined, written policy governing conflicts of interest. This serves to educate effected individuals and limit their activities under appropriate circumstances. Because most IDS organizations include some financially interested individuals on their governing boards, they may wish to adopt a clear conflicts of interest policy.[5]

Although not required, the IRS favorably views organizations having policy statements in their bylaws that clearly identify situations where a conflict might arise. The IRS believes that directors of tax exempt IDS organizations must exercise their powers in good faith and in a manner that they believe to be in the organization's best interests. Furthermore, organizations that educate their new directors, employees, and officers regarding conflicts of interest and concerns about private benefit and inurement help eliminate problems arising from lack of knowledge.

An example of a conflict of interest policy that is viewed favorably by the IRS is one that requires that, in the event that the board of directors considers entering into any transaction or arrangement with a corporation, entity, or individual in which a director has an interest:

- the interested director must disclose the potential conflict of interest to the board
- the board may ask the interested director to leave the meeting during the discussion of the matter that gives rise to the potential conflict
- the interested director will not vote on the matter that gives rise to the potential conflict
- the board must approve the transaction or arrangement by a majority vote of the directors present at a meeting that has a quorum, not including the vote of the interested director

- the board meeting minutes must state which directors were present for the discussion and vote, the content of the discussion, and any roll call of the vote

In addition, if a director has any interest in a transaction or arrangement that might involve personal financial gain or loss for the director, the policy should contain the following provisions:

- If appropriate, the board may appoint a noninterested person or committee to investigate alternatives to the proposed transaction or arrangement.
- To approve the transaction, the board must first find, by a majority vote of the directors then in office without counting the vote of the interested director, that the proposed transaction or arrangement is in the IDS organization's best interest and for its own benefit, that the proposed transaction is fair and reasonable to the IDS organization, and, after reasonable investigation, that the board had determined that the IDS organization cannot obtain a more advantageous transaction or arrangement with reasonable efforts under the circumstances.
- The interested director will not be present for the discussion or vote regarding the transaction or arrangement.
- The transaction or arrangement must be approved by a majority vote of the directors, not including interested directors.

TAX EXEMPTION AND CHARITABLE BENEFIT

In addition to the restrictions mentioned above, the IRS will impose additional requirements on an IDS that seeks federal tax exempt status under Internal Revenue Code Section 501 (c)(3). For this reason, many parties should consider carefully whether tax exemption is in their best interest. Some of the advantages of tax exemption are that net income is not subject to federal income taxes (except unrelated business income tax); that the organization may qualify for exemption from state, sales, and/or property tax; that the organization may qualify for tax exempt bond financing; and that contributions to the organization are tax deductible (thereby increasing the probability of the organization receiving grants). The disadvantages include the restrictions placed by the IRS on the organization, the requirement to disclose the tax exemption application and Form 990 to the public (thereby disclosing the salaries of key employees and officers), limitations on the organization's ability to dissolve, and limitations on the use of facilities that were financed by tax exempt bond proceeds.

If the IDS decides to seek exemption from federal taxation under Internal Revenue Code Section 501(c)(3), it must demonstrate that it serves a charitable purpose more than incidentally. This is a facts and circumstances test in which the IRS (or the court) considers all the activities of the IDS to determine whether its primary function is charitable.

The IRS has set forth several requirements, based on Revenue Ruling 69-545 [which sets forth guidelines for a hospital to qualify for Section 501(c)(3)], for an IDS to qualify for tax exempt status under Section 501(c)(3). Although no single factor is determinative, certain factors are more important (and the probability of obtaining tax exempt status is low if such factors are not present):

- *Open medical staff*—Any hospital operated by an IDS must have an open medical staff. Although clinic facilities (in which physicians practice medicine) are not required to have an open medical staff, this policy has created some controversy because of the need for an IDS to control hospital utilization (which is best done by the IDS physicians, not independent physicians who have no economic incentive to control hospital utilization).
- *Medicare/Medicaid patients*—The IDS must be receptive to providing services to

all Medicare and Medicaid patients in a nondiscriminatory manner at IDS sites. This has been generally interpreted to mean that the IDS may not open specific Medicaid clinical facilities and refer all Medicaid patients to those facilities. If the IDS is in a state that has a Medicaid contracting program, the IDS must negotiate in good faith to enter into such a contract with the government. Although this is a financially difficult requirement for an IDS to meet, it is a significant factor that the IRS is likely to treat as mandatory.

- *Emergency services*—All IDS facilities must treat emergency or urgent care patients regardless of their ability to pay. This applies to both the hospital facilities and the physician clinical facilities. Exceptions might be available where emergency services are not offered, but this requirement is relatively important to the IRS.
- *Charity care*—Although the IRS does not always require that an IDS provide a specific amount of charity care, in those situations where the IRS determines that the organization is unlikely to provide charity care, the IRS may require the IDS to budget a specific amount of charity care to be provided each year. If the IDS can show that it benefits the community in significant other ways (see the other requirements), there is a chance that the IRS will not require charity care by the IDS.
- *Miscellaneous*—The 1995 CPE guidelines listed the following factors as indicators of community benefit:
  1. All medical functions and records are integrated for each individual patient.
  2. Anyone in need of care is treated at any clinic location without regard to ability to pay.
  3. The IDS treats patients seeking urgent care at its urgent care centers without regard to ability to pay.
  4. The clinic participates in, or has made good faith efforts to participate in, the

Medicaid program in a nondiscriminatory manner.

5. Contract physicians do not discriminate against patients based on ability to pay and will see Medicaid patients on a nondiscriminatory basis.

6. A specified minimum amount is spent each year for charity care.

7. The IDS conducts health education programs.

8. A substantial number of the physicians provide coverage in the hospital emergency department and render care in those emergency departments without regard to the patients' ability to pay.

PHYSICIAN COMPENSATION

An IDS must be careful that it distributes its income to physicians in a manner that complies with the Ethics and Patient Referrals Act of 1989 (the Stark law) as amended (Stark II; currently, proposed legislation will significantly reduce the scope of Stark II and make it much easier for an IDS to operate outside the scope of this law). In addition, any state anti-referral laws should be examined before a physician compensation arrangement is finalized.

Generally, the IRS is concerned that a tax exempt IDS does not share its net profits with physicians or otherwise use the IDS organization as a joint venture with physicians. This leaves significant leeway for a tax exempt organization to develop a physician compensation plan based on production, quality of care delivered to patients, and other quantifiable measures (other than the net profits of the organization).

The IRS has made clear that it will closely scrutinize situations where an IDS pays significant amounts for the intangible value of the acquired practice and, at the same time, pays significant annual compensation to the physicians. In the 1996 CPE guidelines, the IRS discusses its concerns regarding compensation and sets forth a list of the data that it will examine to determine whether compensation paid to the physicians is reasonable under all of the circumstances. The 1996 CPE guidelines state "Compensation issues often arise in IDS organizations, faculty group practice plans, clinics, hospitals converting from for-profit to nonprofit status, and joint ventures and partnerships involving exempt organizations, as well as ruling requests regarding these entities. Compensation arrangements often provide for base salaries, fringe benefits, deferred payments, income guarantees, contingencies to compensation, and incentive bonuses."[6]

In most situations, the IRS wants to review certain basic information involving compensation arrangements. Although the compensation arrangements and the accompanying professional services agreement may be included in the file, they are complex, and often it is difficult ultimately to determine actual compensation. Thus the IRS often requests more specific information, adding additional time to the rulings process. The following is a reproduction of the typical compensation questions that the IRS asks (it expedites matters if this information is included in the original submission to the IRS):

- How many physicians do you employ, and how many do you contract with for professional services?

- Please submit a compensation contract for each physician employee. You may black out the physician's name and assign a letter or number to each contract if you are concerned about privacy issues.

- For each compensation arrangement, please provide the following:

1. A realistic estimate of *total* projected physician's compensation (including base, bonus, benefits, and managed care risk pool withholds or other risk pool participation) for a *3-year period* (the estimate could be for 1 year of actual operation and 2 years of projections, depending upon how long you have been operational). The estimate must be

based on the terms contained in the compensation agreement.

2. A realistic estimate of 3 years' projected gross receipts (the estimate could be for 1 year of actual operation and 2 years of projections, depending upon how long you have been operational). The estimate must be supported by data used in preparing actual or future financial reports or projections.

3. A statement establishing that the physician's total compensation is reasonable based on the geographic locale and the physician's specialty. You can establish reasonableness by the use of compensation data for the physician specialty based upon compensation studies produced by local, regional, or national medical associations; the American Hospital Association, the Medical Group Management Association, the Hay Group, or other knowledgeable consultants.

4. Are there any caps (ceilings) on total compensation?

5. Before total compensation of all physicians (base and benefits minus bonus and risk pool withholds) is determined, how much surplus remains for the exempt organization? After *total* compensation is determined, how much surplus remains? What percentage of surplus do the physicians receive? What percentage does your organization receive?

Physician compensation is also discussed in Chapter 10.

PRACTICE ACQUISITIONS/ VALUATION

If the IDS will acquire assets from an existing physician practice, the parties must structure the transaction (i.e., sales, lease, etc.). A tax specialist should be consulted as to the tax conse-

quences of the transaction to any for-profit organization (either the IDS or the physicians). Tax issues for managed care organizations and IDSs are discussed in Chapter 41.

If the IDS is a tax exempt organization, the parties should consult the guidelines set forth in the 1996 CPE guidelines with respect to physician practice acquisitions. These guidelines include a discussion of how the IRS would prefer to see valuations performed. Nonetheless, they indicate a variety of methods recognized by the IRS as to how valuations may be performed. Instead of insisting on the discounted cash flow valuation method, the IRS is recognizing (and is evidencing its own sophistication in this area) that various valuation methods are appropriate in different situations.

One particularly difficult situation occurs when an IDS acquires a small practice or solo practice (especially in a rural area, where the intangible value of the practice is low). In these situations, the IDS does not wish to pay for a valuation fee (often, the valuation fee is higher than the intangible value to be paid to the physician). In these situations, the IDS should obtain an independent valuation for this first practice acquisition. Thereafter, someone employed by the IDS should use the same procedures used by the independent valuation association (and should pay careful attention to the 1996 CPE guidelines) and document the value of the practice. As long as the IDS has carefully demonstrated the reason why it has paid fair market value to the physician, the IRS is unlikely to challenge the arrangement in court.

MEDICARE/MEDICAID PROVIDER NUMBERS

Medicare/Medicaid part B payment rules only allow for payment to the patient or to the patient's physician. In addition, the physician is not allowed to assign his or her right to such income to another party. There are two relevant exceptions to this assignment prohibition: Payment may be made to the employer of the provider of services if the employee is required, as a condition of employment, to pay over such amounts to the employer; and if the services are provided in a hospital, rural primary care hospital, or other facility, payment may be made to the facility in which the service was provided if the facility has a contractual agreement with the provider of services and that agreement requires the facility to submit the bill for such service.

If an IDS acquires a physician practice (including accounts receivable), the assignment of Medicare and Medicaid accounts receivable by the physician to the IDS might constitute a violation of the assignment prohibition. In addition, if physicians are contractually established as independent contractors of the IDS, the IDS may have difficulty receiving the Medicare or Medicaid receivables for the performance of services. Practically speaking, most physicians are employed by the IDS, and this problem does not arise. If the problem exists, however, the IDS may contract with the physician for everything except Medicaid services, and the physician's Medicaid provider number might be used to bill and collect all revenues for Medicaid patients. The total amount paid by the IDS to the physician would be net of any Medicaid receipts received by the physician.

ANTITRUST LAW

There are two types of risks that potentially arise from the development of an IDS: the risk from developing the IDS (i.e., monopoly and other risks associated with consolidating a hospital and a physician practice), and the risk arising from the ongoing operations of the IDS (i.e., tying arrangements and other illegal activities conducted by the IDS).

With respect to the development of an IDS, the parties should carefully examine Section 7 of the Clayton Act, which prohibits mergers and acquisitions that have the potential to restrain competition in the market unreasonably. If the development of an IDS creates a monopoly power or even market dominance with respect to any particular service (e.g., outpatient surgery or other services), the IDS arrangement might be

challenged. Nonetheless, the parties should review the most recent developments in the Marshfield Clinic case and assess whether the facts of that case are applicable to their own particular IDS.[7] In addition, the parties should review the enforcement policy statements issued by the Department of Justice and the Federal Trade Commission on 27 September 1994 to assess the risk of government action against the proposed IDS.[8]

In assessing whether the development of an IDS presents risk, the parties should first determine whether the formation creates too much market power for the IDS and its participants. Critical to this analysis is the definition of the market, which can be summarized as the area in which consumers will freely move to receive similar services. This is a highly factual determination. If physicians who join the IDS previously competed with each other and, through the merger of their practices into the IDS, effectively eliminated competition among themselves, the risk of an antitrust challenge increases as the percentage of physicians who otherwise would have competed with each other (absent the IDS) increases.

If the IDS has an exclusive relationship with a significant number of physicians so that no other hospital can contract with a sufficient number of physicians to develop a competing IDS product, the monopolist IDS may be subject to a successful challenge. Presently, exclusive dealing arrangements can tie up to 35 percent of total physicians in a particular specialty in the market without raising significant antitrust concerns.

Another issue is that the IDS may not participate in an agreement among competitors by which it refuses to deal with other competitors (or causes others not to deal with those competitors). Such group boycotts generally are illegal if they foreclose excluded competitors from something that those competitors need to compete effectively in the market. A fourth issue is that the IDS should not condition its sale of a service (such as hospital services) in which the IDS enjoys market power upon the payer's agreeing to purchase another service offered by the IDS (such as physician services). Finally, the parties should be careful not to engage in any price-fixing activities before they form the IDS and should not engage in any price-fixing activities with independent physicians after they form the IDS.

Although it is not common in the IDS setting, the parties should determine whether they need to file a Hart-Scott-Rodino notification. This premerger notification must be filed if the parties merge, if one party acquires the assets or stock of the other parties, or if new legal entities are established to operate the IDS and if all three of the following conditions are met:

1. The IDS or at least one participant is engaged in or affects commerce.
2. The transaction (merger of the parties or acquisition) involves the acquisition of assets or voting securities, the acquired firm has total assets of $10 million or more, and the acquiring firm has annual net sales or total assets of $100 million or more; or the acquired firm has total assets or annual net sales of $100 million or more; and the acquiring firm has total assets or annual net sales of $10 million or more.
3. If the transaction results in the acquiring party obtaining 15 percent or more of the voting securities or assets of the acquired party, or the acquiring party obtains voting securities or assets of the acquired party that in aggregate exceed $15 million, the third condition is met.

At the time of this writing, the filing fee is $45,000 for the premerger notification.

The reader is also referred to Chapter 57 for additional discussion of antitrust issues and network selection.

INDEPENDENT CONTRACTOR STATUS

The IDS must decide whether it will employ its physicians or contract with them as independent contractors. This decision will have several ramifications, including the IDS's liability for the actions of the physicians and the inclusion of physicians in the employee benefits plans of the IDS. In addition, this decision will determine whether the IDS issues a W-2 or 1099 form to the physicians.

Most often, this issue is resolved by law, not by the business decision of the parties. Even if the IDS enters into a contract with a physician as an independent contractor, the law may reclassify the physician as an employee of the IDS (and assess back taxes and penalties against the IDS). Thus it is important for a tax specialist to determine whether the physician should be treated as an employee or independent contractor for the purposes of tax reporting and for an employee benefits specialist to determine whether the physician must be offered employee benefits.

An employer must withhold payroll taxes from the wages that the employer pays to its employees.[9] These payroll taxes include federal income tax withholding, Federal Insurance Contribution Act (FICA) taxes, and Federal Unemployment Tax Act taxes. If a physician is not an employee (but is an independent contractor) of the employer, the employer is not fully responsible for these taxes. Thus employers prefer to classify workers as independent contractors, but the IRS prefers that workers be classified as employees (thereby ensuring collection of the taxes).

Recently, the IRS has given increased attention to the classification of individual service providers as independent contractors. The Comprehensive Audit Program conducted by the IRS has specifically targeted this issue as an area of focus (because the IRS might be able to collect revenues from the exempt organization if it finds that a worker has been misclassified as an independent contractor). Typically, the structure and documentation of the worker's arrangement will determine proper classification.

An employer–employee relationship generally exists if the employer has common law control over the worker. The IRS has established a list of 20 factors that are used to determine whether sufficient control exists to constitute an employer–employee relationship.[10] The 20 factors are weighed as part of a subjective balancing test. The Internal Revenue Manual states "Any single fact or small group of facts is not conclusive evidence of the presence or absence of control."[11] The 20 factors are listed in Exhibit 56–1. Taken together, the 20 factors are balanced on a case-by-case basis to determine whether a worker (or a class of workers) is an employee. When the 20 factors determine that an employer–employee relationship exists, it is immaterial to the IRS which label the parties attach to the relationship.[12]

The IRS has established audit guidelines that focus on specific factors for assessing whether physicians should be classified as independent contractors, including the following[13]:

- whether the physician has a private practice
- whether the hospital pays wages to the physician
- whether the hospital provides supplies and support staff to the physician
- whether the hospital bills and collects revenues for the physician
- whether the physician and hospital divide the physician's professional fees on a percentage basis
- whether the hospital regulates or otherwise has the right to control the physician
- whether the physician has specific hours to be on duty at the hospital
- whether the physician's uniform has the hospital's logo or name
- whether the hospital pays the physician's malpractice insurance premiums

The audit guidelines instruct IRS agents to pay particular attention to hospital-based specialists, such as radiologists, pathologists, and anesthesiologists. The IRS particularly believes that such physicians should be employees of the hospital for purposes of federal employment taxes (regardless of the state's corporate medicine doctrine).

The IRS has instituted a health care industry specialization program, pursuant to which it conducts coordinated audits of tax exempt health organizations. As part of this program, the IRS has developed a physician issue paper that sets forth the IRS's proposed position regarding the independent contractor/employee classification of hospital-based physicians. This paper still relies on the 20-factor test identified in Exhibit 56–1 but attempts to assign emphasis to certain of the 20 common law factors for the analysis of relationships with physicians. Its approach is to give less emphasis to factors that are common to all hospital–physician relationships, thereby making it easier to isolate the factors that are strong indicators of employee versus independent contractor status. The paper identifies several factors as important in classifying a physician as an employee of a hospital, including whether the hospital reserves the right to specify the physician's hours, whether the hospital is entitled to the physician's professional fees, and whether the hospital bears the risk and expenses associated with the physician's delivery of services (e.g., operating costs).

The paper also provides examples of when a hospital-based physician would be classified as an independent contractor, when a physician should be characterized as an employee of his or her own professional corporation, and when the physician must be recognized as having dual status (i.e., the physician is both an employee and an independent contractor of the same organization when he or she is acting in more than one capacity for that organization). It also states categorically that residents and interns are almost always common law employees of the hospital at which they are being trained.

Internal Revenue Code Section 530 precludes the IRS from challenging an employer for failure to withhold federal employment taxes with respect to certain independent contractor arrangements. An employer can avoid retroactive assessments of federal employment taxes caused by reclassification of workers from independent

Exhibit 56–1 IRS's 20 Factors Used in Determining Employer–Employee Relationship

1. *Instructions.* An employer may require an employee to follow instructions. An independent contractor may only be required to follow overall project specifications.

2. *Training.* An employer generally trains an employee as to its methodologies and practices. An independent contractor generally has his or her own style and does not require training.

3. *Integration.* When a person is so integrated into a business that the success or failure of the business depends a good deal on such person's performance, the worker is under the employer's control. An independent contractor is generally not necessary for the longevity of the employer.

4. *Services rendered personally.* Employees provide services personally. An independent contractor can generally assign a task; qualified people are fungible.

5. *Hiring, supervising, and paying assistants.* An employee generally works with other people who are also employees of the employer; an employee does not hire, fire, supervise, or pay assistants. Independent contractor, however, hire, supervise, and pay their own assistants.

6. *Continuing relationship.* The longer a relationship continues between an employer and a worker, the more likely it is that relationship is an employer–employee relationship. This may include services that recur frequently, even if at irregular intervals (e.g., either on call by the employer or whenever the work is available).

7. *Set hours of work.* The more formal and rigid a worker's hours, the more control the employer has over the worker. An independent contractor generally works on his or her own schedule and only has specified overall project or task deadlines.

8. *Full time required.* When a worker works substantially full time for an employer and does not work for any other employers, the employer has control over the worker's time. An independent contractor usually works for several employers at the same time. An employee may also have more than one employer, however.

9. *Doing work on employer's premises.* Evidence of control over an employee exists when an employer can designate the place where work is to be done and has control over that environment.

10. *Order or sequence set.* If an employer retains the right to control the order or sequence of the work that is to be performed and the type of work does not naturally dictate the order or sequence, evidence of control over the worker exists.

11. *Oral or written reports.* The more often a worker reports to an employer, the more likely it is that the employer controls the worker. It is acceptable for an independent contractor to issue progress reports as phases of a project are completed, however.

12. *Payment by hour, week, or month.* An employee generally receives a set wage based upon a time period. On the other hand, an independent contractor receives payment based upon a project or straight commission. A contract may specify when payments are due. The independent contractor should invoice the employer for amounts due, however. The payments should not be made automatically.

13. *Payment of business and/or traveling expenses.* When an employer controls expenses, the employer also controls the worker's activities. Generally, independent contractors take care of their own incidental expenses.

14. *Furnishing of tools and materials.* The more tools and materials supplied by the employer, the more likely it is that the worker is an employee. The weight of this factor will depend on the occupation of the worker and the type of tools and materials supplied.

15. *Significant investment.* If a worker makes an investment in facilities or tools that are not normally invested in by employees, this factor will show a lack of control by the employer. Use of an employer's facilities generally indicates control by the employer. Facilities include premises and equipment, such as office furniture and machinery.

16. *Realization of profit or loss.* Employees have no opportunity to realize a gain or loss. Independent contractors, however, are business people who take risks expecting either to enhance their return or to suffer a loss.

17. *Working for more than one firm at a time.* When an individual works for more than one firm and performs de minimis services for each, it is likely that none of the firms will have control over the individual. Even if a person works for more than one employer, however, if enough control exists, the person could be considered to be an employee of more than one employer.

18. *Making services available to the general public.* The more a person offers services to the general public, the less likely it is that control will be found to exist. Indicia of making services available to the general public are advertising, business cards, stationery, telephone listings, holding a license, and the like.

(continues)

Exhibit 56–1 continued

19. *Right to discharge.* If a person can be discharged at will, then the person is an employee. The person who possesses the right to discharge is an employer. Independent contractors cannot be fired so long as they are in compliance with the contract.

20. *Right to terminate.* Independent contractors cannot quit; employees can terminate at will. Therefore, to be an independent contractor there must be a legal obligation to complete the contract.

contractors to employees if each of the following three requirements is met:

1. The employer must have a reasonable basis for treating the worker as an independent contractor (it is not clear whether this reasonable basis must have existed before 31 December 1978). There are four safe harbors for meeting this requirement: reliance on a published IRS ruling or judicial precedent; reliance on the outcome of a prior audit by the IRS if the IRS reviewed workers who held similar positions as the position that is at issue; reliance on the long-standing recognized practice of a significant segment of the industry, even if the practice of treating the worker as an independent contractor is not uniform throughout the entire industry; or any other reasonable basis for not classifying a worker as an employee.[14]

2. The employer must not have treated the worker as an employee anytime after 1977. In particular, the employer should not have withheld federal income tax or FICA taxes from the worker's wages, must not have filed certain employment tax returns for the worker, and must not have treated any worker holding a similar position as an employee for any period after 31 December 1977.

3. The employer must have filed all appropriate federal tax returns in a manner that is timely and consistent with the worker not being treated as an employee (e.g.,

1099 forms must have been filed properly.)

The IRS has published form SS-8, which may be used by a taxpayer to request that the IRS determine whether a person is an employee or an independent contractor. This form may be submitted either by an employer or an employee. It may not always be advisable to submit this form, however, because once an answer is received, the employer has no basis for treating a worker contrary to the IRS's determination.

If a worker is misclassified as an independent contractor and is later determined to be an employee, the employer is then liable for the employment taxes not previously paid plus interest and any penalties that may be imposed by the IRS. If an independent contractor is reclassified as an employee, the employer must review the tax-qualified pension and employee benefit plans for the years at issue. In situations where qualification was marginal, the reclassification of independent contractors may disqualify pension or benefit plans.

Failure to classify a worker properly as an employee and then having a nonfavorable redetermination can cause severe financial hardship to an enterprise and to the enterprise participants. Past payroll taxes and the associated penalties and interest can bankrupt many small enterprises. If the enterprise cannot pay the IRS's payroll tax assessment, the participants in the enterprise may be personally liable for the assessment, depending on the enterprise participant's role in the enterprise and/or the type of entity chosen for the enterprise. Last, if payroll taxes are assessed personally against an enterprise participant, the taxes may not be discharged in bankruptcy proceedings.

COVENANTS NOT TO COMPETE

In its first determination letters (e.g., the Friendly Hills determination letter), the IRS put certain restrictions on the covenants not to compete that an IDS may enforce against physicians. This created a controversy because it restricted the IDS from realizing the full benefit of its covenant not to compete and thereby prevented the IDS from realizing the full benefits of the amounts paid to physicians in exchange for the covenants not to compete (the IRS would counter that the IDS should have simply paid less for the covenant not to compete). In the 1996 guidelines and in recent determination letters, there appears to be a loosening of this attitude by the IRS. Presently, it is not clear whether the IRS has any restrictions upon covenants not to compete. Parties should negotiate a significant covenant not to compete between themselves and should wait for the IRS to make any modifications (and then argue with the IRS regarding those modifications before conceding the point).

CONCLUSION

The development of an IDS also involves an examination of numerous business issues (which are beyond the scope of this chapter but are addressed in part in Chapters 4 and 5). Most important, the parties should be careful that their cultural differences (e.g., physicians are independent and hospital administrators are committee oriented) are identified and addressed. Numerous miscellaneous legal issues (e.g., employee benefits law, labor law, tax identification numbers, certificate of need law, corporate/partnership law, financing law, state licensuring and corporate practice of medicine law, malpractice liability law, rate and review law, real property laws, recordkeeping laws, state antireferral laws, securities law, tax law and tax exemption law, insurance issues, intellectual property law, medical staff issues, and possibly environmental law) must be considered.

One should not expect an IDS to be developed overnight, but one also should not languish into the 18- to 24-month backwater of merger negotiations. Most important, the parties must recognize that, after the merger is done, the real work begins. They must decide how well they work together, and they should not try to integrate themselves operationally more than they are culturally capable of tolerating. Often, an IDS will simply allow the physician organization to operate separately from the hospital organization and will look for common areas where capital allocations improve the overall delivery of health care services to the community. The parties must commit themselves to some level of operational integration (including capital planning, strategic planning, payer contracting, etc.), or else they should question why they developed the IDS in the first place. Nonetheless, they should be careful not to integrate their operations excessively if such integration will cause undue burden or strains upon the parties.

Finally, the parties should be careful to address any political issues that arise from the formation of the IDS. Most importantly, reaction of independent physicians who are not part of the IDS can be a fatal factor if IDS leadership does not properly address those physicians' concerns. An IDS is not for everyone, and the parties should be careful before expending the time and money in developing an IDS to determine that the effort will generate appropriate benefits for themselves and their constituents.

REFERENCES AND NOTES

1. 1996 CPE at pp. 390–391.
2. See 1996 CPE at p. 389 and 1995 CPE at p. 227. Some IRS officials have defended their 20 percent restriction based on the fact that physicians do not represent more than 20 percent of a community. Thus no more than 20 percent of a board or committee can comprise physicians if it is to be broadly representative of the community. This logic has not yet been extended to race, sex, or age (or other occupations), but one might wonder why

not. Also, it should be noted that the IDS may create committees to consider the clinical or professional service aspects of the health care to be provided by the IDS and that these committees may contain unlimited physician representation.

3. 1996 CPE at p. 388.

4. See 1994 CPE at p. 227 for more information about the 20 percent safe harbor.

5. 1996 CPE at pp. 386–387.

6. 1996 CPE at p. 391.

7. *Blue Cross & Blue Shield United of Wisc. & Compcure Health Services Insur Corp. v. The Marshfield Clinic & Security Health Plan of Wisc., Inc.*, 881 F. Supp. 1309 (W.D. Wisc. 1994).

8. *Statements of Enforcement Policy and Analytical Principles Relating to Health Care and Antitrust.* U.S. Department of Justice and Federal Trade Commission (September 27, 1994).

9. I.R.C. Section 3402.

10. Rev. Rul. 87-41, 1987-1 C.B. 296.

11. *2 Internal Revenue Manual* (CCH) 8465 (1988).

12. Treas. Reg. Sections 31.3306(i)–1(d), 31.3121(d)–1(a)(3), and 31.3401(b)–1(e).

13. *IRS Audit Guidelines for Hospitals*, Manual Transmittal 7 (10) 69–38; *Exempt Organizations Guidelines Handbook* Section 331(1) (27 March 1992).

14. See Priv. Ltr. Rul. 8733004.

SUGGESTED READING

Peters, G.R. 1995. *Healthcare Integration: A Legal Manual for Constructing Integrated Organizations.* Washington, D.C. National Health Lawyers Association.

National Health Lawyers Association. 1994. *Health Law Practice Guide.*

Health Law Center. 1995. *Managed Care Law Manual.* Gaithersburg, Md.: Aspen.

Chapter 57

Antitrust Implications of Provider Exclusion

William G. Kopit and Alexandre B. Bouton

Managed care organizations (MCOs) must be able to limit their provider networks. Thus an understanding the antitrust principles underlying provider exclusion is of great importance because claims by providers excluded from MCOs and other entities represent the largest number of antitrust challenges brought in the health care field.[1]

Typically, provider exclusion issues can arise where MCOs seek to limit the size and composition of their provider networks or where they enter into exclusive contracts with provider groups and agree not to contract with competing groups. This chapter surveys and provides a framework for the analysis of the antitrust issues raised by provider exclusion by MCOs. In addition, the chapter discusses the impact of state any willing provider (AWP) laws on the ability of MCOs to limit physician participation.

It is important to recognize that exclusionary conduct by single entities not controlled by providers should present little antitrust risk in most cases.[2] This holds true even where the MCO has a dominant market position.[3] In such circumstances, a claim under Section 1 of the Sherman Act cannot be maintained unless the excluded provider can show a conspiracy between the MCO and providers in competition with the excluded provider.[4] Similarly, a claim under Section 2 of the Sherman Act is not viable unless the MCO is a current or potential monopolist *and* is engaged in unjustifiable exclusionary or predatory conduct.[5]

In contrast, significant antitrust concerns may arise when the excluding entity is provider controlled or where it agrees to the exclusion with other providers. In either case, an unlawful group boycott, constituting a violation of Section 1, may be found.

Still, any arrangement that promotes efficiencies should be encouraged, at least so long as the potential to harm consumers remains remote. In each case, the task is first to identify the relevant market, which may vary depending on the nature of the claim, and then to determine whether the arrangement under scrutiny has market power within that market. When market power does not exist, that should conclude the analysis. If market power does exist, however, the analysis should next turn to the nature and extent of the efficiencies claimed and the potential anticompetitive effects, if any.

THE IMPORTANCE OF MARKET POWER

Firms without market power, by definition, cannot harm consumers. Market power is simply

William G. Kopit is a partner with the Washington, D.C. office of Epstein Becker & Green, P.C., where he represents a variety of managed care payers and health care providers.

Alexandre B. Bouton is an associate in the Washington, D.C. office of Epstein Becker & Green, P.C., where he specializes in health care antitrust law. His practice involves both counseling and litigation relating to the development of managed care organizations and other collaborative activities among health care entities.

Epstein Becker & Green has, since 1974, counseled hundreds of HMOs, PPOs, and insurers. The firm has also been involved in several landmark health care antitrust cases.

the ability "to force a purchaser to do something that he would not do in a competitive market."[6] Where market choices are sufficient to prevent an arrangement from developing market power, the development and/or operation of the arrangement should remain free from antitrust scrutiny.

Market power is the power to maintain prices profitably above competitive levels. Without market power, a defendant, by definition, lacks the ability to injure consumers by charging supracompetitive prices. Thus the legitimacy of particular business practices depends on the market power of the actor as well as on the character of the conduct.[7]

As Judge Easterbrook has succinctly explained, liability "in antitrust law almost always requires proof of market power. This is because market power is an essential ingredient of injury to consumers. Market power means the ability to injure consumers by curtailing output and raising price; no possible injury, no market power; no market power, no violation; injury to consumers is therefore an essential ingredient of liability."[8]

Furthermore, "As an economic matter, market power exists whenever prices can be raised above the levels that would be charged in a competitive market."[9]

Where an excluded provider cannot establish that the defendant MCO has market power in any health care financing market or submarket, a provider exclusion claim is virtually impossible to maintain. Without market power, there can be no harm to competition or injury to consumers, even if the conduct is unfair or egregious. As stated by Judge Easterbrook, "[w]ho says that competition is supposed to be fair, that we judge the behavior of the market-place by the ethics of the courtroom? Real competition is bruising rivalry, in which people go out of business under intense pressure. . . . [C]ompetition is a 'gale of creative destruction.' "[10]

Market power must be determined in terms of a relevant product or service market and a corresponding geographic market.[11] A product or service market is composed of products or services that consumers view as reasonably interchangeable.[12] Market definition must be undertaken from the prospective of consumers, the intended beneficiaries of the antitrust laws. The consumers' perspective determines the market.[13] "For antitrust purposes, defining the product market involves identification of the field of competition: the group or groups of sellers or producers who have actual or potential ability to deprive each other of significant levels of business."[14]

Thus, even though competitors may be harmed by the operation of networks, the antitrust laws provide no remedy for such harm unless the conduct causes consumers to suffer higher prices or lower quality or output.[15] To be able to cause such effects on consumers, the parties whose conduct is being challenged must have significant market power in the properly defined relevant market.[16]

In most cases, a party's market share of the relevant market is used as a surrogate for market power.[17] Market share is simply a party's percentage of the total input or output in the relevant market. Other factors may also be considered in determining a party's market power, however, including "the strength of the party's competition, probable development of the industry, the barriers to entry, the nature of the challenged conduct, and elasticity of consumer demand."[18]

The case law establishes that MCOs are unlikely to be viewed as having market power (defined as the power to restrict output in the market or to raise price significantly above competitive level) when they cover less than 30 percent of the relevant health financing market.[19] Without market power, the MCO cannot maintain premiums (prices) above competitive levels.[20] In addition, where no significant barriers to entry are present, there can be no market power, regardless of the market share represented by the defendant MCO.[21] Indeed, a defendant can successfully argue "that proof of its 100% market share does not demonstrate that it had the power to control prices or exclude competition in the absence of any evidence that it could prevent entry of other market participants. . . . A high market share, though it may ordinarily raise an inference of monopoly power, will not do so in a market with low entry barriers or other evidence of a defendant's inability to control prices or exclude competitors."[22]

"The focus [of a rule of reason analysis] is on the actual effects that the challenged restraint has had on competition in a relevant market."[23] A Section 1 claim can be maintained only where there is an adverse impact on the price, quality, and quantity of goods and services offered to consumers; activities that leave that process intact should not be restricted.[24] Mere competitive advantage, or unfair conduct by itself, is insufficient to show anticompetitive effects and to create a violation.[25]

THE RELEVANT MARKET

The relevant market comprises two components: a relevant product or products, and a corresponding geographic market.[26] The relevant geographic market is dependent upon the "area of effective competition . . . where buyers can turn for alternative sources of supply."[27] Generally, health care markets are relatively small, narrow geographic areas because consumers typically will not travel great distances to seek medical services (especially primary care services).[28] In establishing the relevant geographic market, it is necessary to determine the percentage of consumers in the area who receive medical services from the providers within the area as well as the percentage of consumers from outside the area who seek services within the area, the so-called Elzinga-Hogarty test. The geographic area should include the locations of all sources of supply to which consumers could turn if market participants exercised market power by increasing prices or by lowering quality or output.

It is often a difficult task to identify the relevant product market for the purpose of determining whether a restraint related to a managed care arrangement is permissible under the antitrust laws. Ultimately, restraints created by any managed care arrangement must affect the health financing market or a subset of that market.[29] The initial focus of the restraint, however, is likely to be in the market for some, or all, provider services.[30]

EXCLUSIVE DEALING ARRANGEMENTS

Generally

With the exception of per se cases, where harm to competition may be presumed, the antitrust laws require plaintiff to establish that the defendant has actually harmed competition by increasing prices above competitive levels or by decreasing output or quality below competitive levels. Excluded providers may be able to demonstrate a loss of patients as a result of the challenged arrangement, but a supplier's "loss is no concern of the antitrust laws, which protect consumers from suppliers rather than suppliers from each other."[31] As stated by the Seventh Circuit Court, "Competition is ruthless, unprincipled, uncharitable, unforgiving—and a boon to society, Adam Smith reminds us, precisely because of these qualities that make it a bane to other producers."[32]

Although a competitor of a health plan or provider group may be harmed by exclusive dealing arrangements, the antitrust laws are designed to protect competition, not competitors[33]: "Even an act of pure malice by one business competitor against another does not, without more, state a claim under the federal antitrust laws; those laws do not create a federal law of unfair competition or 'purport to afford remedies for all torts committed by or against persons engaged in interstate commerce.' "[34] Thus the "mere existence of an exclusive dealing clause in a contract does not establish an antitrust violation."[35]

Exclusive dealing arrangements almost always are analyzed under the rule of reason. Indeed, such arrangements "may be substantially procompetitive by ensuring stable markets and encouraging long-term, mutually advantageous business relationships."[36] Efficiencies that may result from exclusive contracting between a health plan and providers include enhancing price or quality competition between networks and plans, lowering administrative costs, maintaining quality of care, and providing a stable source of supply for medical services to plan subscribers.

Conclusory allegations that an exclusive contract injures competition by depriving consumers of provider choice or by eliminating or curtailing competition between providers, without more, are insufficient to maintain an antitrust claim. Such allegations do not adequately establish injury to competition. "There is a sense in which eliminating even a single competitor reduces competition. But it is not the sense that is relevant in deciding whether the antitrust laws have been violated. Competition means that some may be forced out of business. The antitrust laws are not designed to guarantee every competitor tenure in the marketplace."[37] As the court in *Rutman Wine Co. v. E. & J. Gallo Winery* plainly stated, an "agreement between a manufacturer and a distributor to establish an exclusive distributorship is not, standing alone, a violation of antitrust laws, and in most circumstances does not adversely affect competition in the market."[38]

MCOs are free to exclude providers from participation in their networks without risk of antitrust liability. Indeed, such exclusions are a normal consequence of any contract between a purchaser and its suppliers.[39] The courts have made it clear that the exclusion of a single supplier of services due to defendant's contract with another supplier is not enough to demonstrate actual detrimental effects on competition.[40]

Unless consumers are harmed by higher prices or lower-quality services, exclusions of competing suppliers are irrelevant in antitrust cases.[41] Claims by excluded providers often "have confused an agreement to boycott with an agreement to buy and sell services."[42] As the Tenth Circuit Court recently concluded, the replacement of one health services provider by another is only a reshuffling of competitors. This reshuffling has no detrimental effect on competition.[43]

The mere exclusion of a provider is not in any way a reduction in output in the relevant market. From the perspective of consumers, the only effect is that one provider has been substituted by another. Indeed, consumers necessarily limit their choice of health service providers by selecting to participate in any type of managed care plan. If consumers are dissatisfied with a plan, they may simply select another. When consumers are dissatisfied for whatever reason, including price or quality, they can, and do, switch to other health plans or other types of health care financing. It is the availability of that choice—selecting from among competing health plans—that the antitrust laws are designed to protect. Conduct that affects only the party challenging the conduct is not unreasonable under Section 1 of the Sherman Act. As the Supreme Court has recently stated, "The purpose of the [Sherman] Act is not to protect businesses from the working of the market; it is to protect the public from the failure of the market."[44]

Foreclosure

The threshold issue in analyzing exclusive dealing arrangements is the foreclosure effects of such arrangements. There is "one common danger for competition: an exclusive arrangement may 'foreclose' so much of the available supply or outlet capacity that existing competitors or new entrants may be limited or excluded and, under certain circumstances, this may reinforce market power and raise prices for consumers."[45]

In *Tampa Electric Co. v. Nashville Coal Co.*,[46] however, the Supreme Court, considering the effects of exclusive dealing arrangements, held not only that the percentage of the market foreclosed by the arrangement should be determined but that the court should also "weigh the probable effect of the contract on the relevant area of effective competition, taking into account the relative strength of the parties, the proportionate volume of commerce involved in relation to the total volume of commerce in the relevant market area, and the probable immediate and future effects which pre-emption of that share of the market might have on effective competition therein."[47] This qualitative analysis regarding effects of exclusive dealing arrangements has been consistently applied by the courts and the federal enforcement agencies.

The Federal Trade Commission (FTC), in *In re Beltone Electronics Corp.*, discussed the analysis to be applied in determining whether an exclusive dealing arrangement violates the antitrust laws.[48] "If . . . the degree of foreclosure caused by the exclusivity indicates without serious doubt that the party imposing exclusive contracts possesses substantial market power, then that foreclosure will be a more significant factor of the case against the restraint. Where the degree of foreclosure is less substantial, other measures of market performance are more likely to determine the overall effect of the restraint on competition."[49]

In *Beltone*, although the foreclosure levels were not clearly insignificant, the FTC dismissed the complaint after taking a closer look at the dynamics of the affected market.[50] Courts have also embraced the qualitative analysis of *Tampa Electric*: "Where the degree of foreclosure caused by the exclusivity provisions is so great that it invariably indicates that the supplier imposing the provisions has substantial market power, we may rely on the foreclosure rate alone to establish the violation. However, where, as here, the foreclosure rate is neither substantial nor even apparent, the plaintiff must demonstrate that other factors in the market exacerbate the detrimental effect of the challenged restraint."[51]

These other factors include the willingness of consumers to comparison shop and their loyalty to existing distributors, the existence of entry barriers to new distributors, the availability of alternative methods of distribution, and any trend toward growth (or decline) in the level of competition at the supplier level.[52] Nevertheless, it is clear that the initial point in the analysis of

an exclusive dealing arrangement is the foreclosure effects of the restraint. Such effects are measurable from the market power of the participants in the arrangement.

THE IMPORTANCE OF EFFICIENCIES

Even where an arrangement may create or enhance market power, the existence and/or operation of the network may be permissible if there is a legitimate efficiency basis for the challenged conduct, unless there are also demonstrable anticompetitive effects that outweigh the benefits of the efficiencies claimed. Mere increases in market share or decreases in the number of competitors or independent pricing options available should not be a sufficient basis to challenge the formation or operation of a managed care arrangement.

ANTITRUST STANDING

An antitrust plaintiff must allege injury of the type the antitrust laws were designed to prevent.[53] More specifically, an antitrust plaintiff must demonstrate an integral relationship between its particular injury and injury to competition.[54] In this regard, it is insufficient merely to assert that a managed care plan has selected certain hospitals to the exclusion of others, even through the use of unfair means.[55] In addition, courts require a causal connection between the challenged conduct and the alleged injury (i.e., proximate cause).[56]

The Supreme Court has recognized the importance of requiring antitrust plaintiffs to demonstrate standing under the Sherman and Clayton Acts: "Congress did not intend the antitrust laws to provide a remedy in damages for all injuries that might conceivably be traced to an antitrust violation."[57] The analysis used to approach a standing issue is to evaluate the plaintiff's harm, the alleged wrongdoing by the defendant, and the relationship between them.[58]

As the Supreme Court stated in *Brunswick Corp. v. Pueblo Bowl-O-Mat, Inc.*, plaintiffs "must prove *antitrust injury*, which is to say injury of the type the antitrust laws were intended to prevent and that flows from that which makes defendants' acts unlawful."[59] The Supreme Court reaffirmed the antitrust injury requirement in *Atlantic Richfield Co. v. USA Petroleum Co.*[60]: "Antitrust injury does not arise . . . until a private party is adversely affected by an *anticompetitive* aspect of the defendant's conduct."[61]

It is clear that the antitrust injury requirement only allows parties standing to bring a private antitrust action if that party's injury is the result of acts that also cause "higher prices or lower output, the principal vices proscribed by the antitrust laws."[62] The antitrust injury doctrine of *Atlantic Richfield* "requires every plaintiff to show that its loss comes from acts that reduce output or raise prices to consumers."[63]

In most instances, excluded providers' allegations of injury simply do not amount to antitrust injury. In *Capital Imaging v. Mohawk Valley Medical Associates*, the court, considering the injury allegations of an excluded provider, stated "it is clear that the bulk of plaintiff's claim—that *plaintiff* is or will be harmed by defendants' agreement with [plaintiff's competitor]—is not 'antitrust injury.' Plaintiff is not entitled to relief for losing out to another competitor . . . in the agreement to provide [health care] services for defendants."[64]

Invariably, excluded providers' objection is not that an MCO contracts selectively with providers but rather that they have not been selected. In essence, excluded providers object to being excluded from the "conspiracy": "That kind of injury hardly makes [the excluded provider] a proper party to enforce the law against conspiracies in restraint of trade."[65] To ensure that only proper plaintiffs are permitted to enforce the antitrust laws, the courts have required that the plaintiff be a consumer or competitor of the defendant.[66] Failing this, excluded providers lack standing to bring suit under the antitrust laws.[67]

Significantly, the interests of an antitrust plaintiff must be aligned with the interests of

consumers to establish the requisite antitrust injury. "Whenever the plaintiff and consumers have divergent rather than congruent interests, there is a potential problem in finding 'antitrust injury.' "[68] In this connection, meritless antitrust actions by competitors have a singular potential for mischief.[69] Such actions are time consuming and expensive to defend and carry great risks to defendants because of the treble damages and attorney fees provisions of the antitrust laws.[70] When competitors, rather than consumers, bring antitrust claims, courts examine those claims with a particularly skeptical eye: "competitors' theories of injury . . . deserve particularly intense scrutiny."[71] Baseless suits must be addressed at the summary judgment stage.[72]

There can be no doubt that such baseless competitor suits are all too frequent. Indeed, an empirical examination by two noted antitrust scholars found relatively few meritorious antitrust actions brought by competitors.[73] Thus, as Judge Easterbrook has written, when "a business rival brings suit, it is often safe to infer that the [challenged] arrangement is beneficial to consumers."[74]

A recent case decided by a Florida federal district court illustrates the standard applied to bar antitrust suits by excluded providers that lack standing.[75] The plaintiff physician, in that case, brought federal antitrust claims and pendent state law claims against several Orlando hospitals, a health maintenance organization (HMO), and a physician advocacy group made up of HMO physicians. The federal antitrust claims against the defendant hospitals alleged a conspiracy in violation of Section 1 of the Sherman Act. The court held that the plaintiff physician's suspension from the hospitals did not constitute antitrust injury and that plaintiff thereby lacked standing to bring a claim under Section 1 of the Sherman Act.

The plaintiff physician claimed that the defendant HMO had refused to include him as a member of its affiliated physician advocacy group. Based on this occurrence, the plaintiff alleged that the advocacy group, the HMO, the Orlando Regional Medical Center, and Sand Lake Hospital had monopolized, attempted to monopolize, and conspired to monopolize the provision of medical services by physicians and hospitals to patient members of the HMO in the Orlando area, in violation of Section 2 of the Sherman Act. In addition, plaintiff also claimed that the advocacy group and its member physicians as well as the HMO had conspired to restrict unreasonably the availability of and competition among health care providers for the consumers of the HMO, in violation of Section 1 of the Sherman Act.

In granting summary judgment for the defendants, the court applied a two-pronged approach to determine whether the plaintiff had antitrust standing: A plaintiff must have suffered an antitrust injury and must be an efficient enforcer of the antitrust laws. The court held that, if the physician had brought the suit to force defendants to accept him as a member of the HMO's closed panel preferred provider organization (PPO), he lacked standing because he could not claim to have suffered antitrust injury. In the alternative, the court found that, if the plaintiff brought the action to force the HMO into operating as an open panel PPO, the plaintiff lacked standing because he was not an efficient enforcer of the antitrust laws. In holding that plaintiff was not an efficient enforcer, the court found that any damage plaintiff might claim was entirely speculative. The court reasoned that, if the HMO were to operate as an open panel PPO, there would be no way to predict the number of physicians who would participate and hence no way to calculate the possible effect on plaintiff's practice. The court thus granted summary judgment to the defendants, holding that the plaintiff lacked standing.[76]

GROUP BOYCOTTS: EXCLUSION OF PROVIDERS

Generally

Exclusionary conduct by single entities not controlled by providers may present little anti-trust risk in many circumstances.[77] Nevertheless, concerns more often arise when the excluding entity is provider controlled or where it agrees to the exclusion with providers.

In most cases the per se rule is inappropriate, and courts apply the rule of reason. Under the rule of reason, group boycott claims have generally been unsuccessful because of the failure of plaintiffs to establish anticompetitive effects (i.e., adverse effects on price, quality, or output resulting from the exclusion).[78] Except in situations in which the network has an exclusive arrangement with a dominant health plan in the relevant product market, this burden should prove impossible.

An MCO should not be required to demonstrate any procompetitive justifications for its conduct unless the existence of market power is established. Even where market power is established, however, the exclusion should be permissible if there is a legitimate quality or economic justification for the conduct.

Managed care plans have been widely viewed as procompetitive entities with the capacity substantially to reduce health care costs. The Department of Justice and the FTC have acknowledged this potential as well as the procompetitive justifications and market efficiencies of provider networks.[79] Yet, limiting the size of provider panels is an important aspect of managed care plans. Indeed, one of the essential features of an HMO or other managed care plan is that "it selects preferred physicians [suppliers] and excludes others thereby creating competition among the providers of health care services."[80] Thus, by contracting with only a limited number of physicians and hospitals, managed care plans may actually encourage competition.

Antitrust enforcement agencies also consider exclusions of providers (suppliers) from HMOs and other managed care delivery systems as procompetitive.[81] For example, the FTC has determined that "exclusive arrangements between HMOs and their participating [providers] . . . are likely to benefit consumers by stimulating competition among medical prepayment plans and physicians."[82]

If a managed care plan were required to contract with every available hospital and physician, there would be no cost benefit to the plan. In effect, the managed care plan would become an indemnity product by another name. It is only by limiting its hospital and physician panel that a managed care plan differentiates itself from indemnity insurance plans. This differentiation typically benefits consumers by offering them a greater choice of health plans.

The Case Law

The development of the courts' approach to the exclusion of providers by MCOs can be traced through a series of cases starting with *Northwest Wholesale Stationers, Inc. v. Pacific Stationery & Printing Co.*[83] In *Northwest Wholesale*, the court held that market power was a sine qua non for establishing a group boycott claim under both the per se rule and the rule of reason. The court went on to identify the three essential characteristics of per se illegal group boycotts as follows: The boycott cuts off access to a supply, facility, or market necessary for the firm that is subject to the boycott to be able to compete; the defendant possesses a dominant market position; and the conduct or practices of the defendant are not justified by plausible arguments that they enhance overall efficiency or competition. Since *Northwest Wholesale*, courts have applied this basic analytical framework in determining whether various exclusionary practices constitute illegal group boycotts in violation of the antitrust laws.

In *Hassan*, the independent practice association (IPA), in the context of a cost-containment effort, terminated and refused to readmit two allergists because they did not provide cost-effective care to subscribers.[84] The court held that this did not constitute an illegal group boycott under the rule of reason. The court, citing *Northwest Wholesale*, granted defendants' motion for summary judgment, holding that the IPA did not have the market power in the health care financing market—the relevant product market—necessary to find a violation of the Sherman Act and

that the conduct did not result in any anticompetitive market effects.[85]

In *Northwest Medical Laboratories v. Blue Cross & Blue Shield*, the exclusion of providers of radiology and laboratory services from a closed panel HMO—found to be a legitimate joint venture—was analyzed under the rule of reason.[86] The conduct was held not to constitute an illegal group boycott because the defendant did not possess market power and had demonstrated legitimate procompetitive justifications for the exclusion, including utilization control, economies of scale, and cost and quality control. Nevertheless, the court noted that these procompetitive justifications might not have saved defendants had they been found to possess market power.

Two recent cases support the view that the federal antitrust laws typically do not prevent HMOs from excluding physicians even where the HMO is controlled by competitors of the excluded physician.[87] The first case, *Capital*, involved a joint venture between an IPA ("MVMA") and a health plan ("MVP") operating as an IPA-HMO ("HMO").[88] A private practice radiology group ("Capital") was denied membership in MVMA because its offices were located outside the HMO's service area. MVMA's policy was to waive the service area requirement only if there was a need for the type of providers seeking membership, and such was not the case.

Capital sued the HMO for violations of Sections 1 and 2 of the Sherman Act. The district court easily disposed of the Section 2 claim based on the absence of market power. As held by the court, "[n]ot only is there no *dangerous probability* that defendants will succeed in monopolizing the markets identified by plaintiff . . . there is no present *possibility* defendants will do so.[89] Capital did not press this claim on appeal.

Under Section 1, Capital alleged that the HMO and a competing radiology group ("Two Rivers") conspired to exclude Capital from providing services to the HMO. In spite of extensive discovery, Capital remained unable to show that the HMO's conduct constituted an unreasonable restraint of trade. Specifically, the court held that there was no agreement between MVMA and Two Rivers. The court also held that Capital failed to show either actual injury to competition or that the HMO had market power sufficient to create an inference of injury to competition. The court stated that one of the essential features of an HMO is that "it selects preferred physicians and excludes others thereby creating competition among the providers of health care services."[90]

Appealing the Section 1 claim, Capital for the first time argued that MVMA, an organization of physicians, was a "walking conspiracy." Although it determined that sufficient evidence existed to support this new theory, the court of appeals affirmed the district court's grant of summary judgment. Specifically, the court held that Capital failed to establish that the challenged conduct would adversely affect competition and consumers. The court stated "Capital's position is simply that it has been harmed as an individual competitor. It has not shown that defendants' activities have had any adverse impact on price, quality, or output of medical services offered to consumers in the relevant market."[91]

The court elaborated on Capital's failure to meet its burden of showing any adverse impact on competition:

> Capital concedes in its brief that whether or not it is admitted into the physicians' association, the fee for radiological services would remain the same. In addition, Capital failed to adduce significant evidence that its exclusion has, in fact, resulted in any decrease in the quality of radiology services to the HMO's patients. Therefore, Capital has not made an adequate showing of detrimental effects to obviate the need to show that appellees possess market power sufficient to stifle competition.[92]

The court of appeals affirmed the district court's judgment because neither MVMA nor MVP possessed market power. MVMA and MVP, the appeals court found, had a de minimis market share in the relevant market defined by the plaintiffs. Attempts by the plaintiff to redefine the relevant market to avoid the fatal consequences of its initial (and revised) definitions were summarily rejected by the court.

The court of appeals' conclusion that the HMO lacked the power to injure competition or force consumers to accept higher premiums or lower-quality medical care was based upon evidence that revealed that, within the geographic market defined by Capital, the HMO's enrollees represented 2.3 percent of all HMO enrollees and 1.15 percent of the total patient population and that the HMO contracted with only 6.75 percent of the physicians.

In *Williamson v. Sacred Heart Hospital*, the plaintiff, Angel Williamson, a radiologist located in Pensacola, Florida with a specialty in radiology services related to comprehensive breast care, provided services almost exclusively on an outpatient basis.[93] The plaintiff requested staff privileges at defendant Sacred Heart Hospital and defendant Baptist Hospital. Both hospitals had exclusive radiology contracts with other radiology groups, however, and rejected the plaintiff's request for staff privileges. Sacred Heart and Baptist, along with Blue Cross of Florida, were also joint venturers in an HMO, and the HMO's IPA established a policy requiring physicians to have staff privileges at either Baptist or Sacred Heart as a precondition for participation in the HMO. Because Williamson did not have privileges at either hospital, the IPA rejected her application to participate in the HMO.

Williamson brought suit against both hospitals, their medical groups, and the IPA, claiming a series of conspiracies in restraint of trade in violation of Section 1 of the Sherman Act. After the close of discovery, all defendants moved for summary judgment. Initially these motions were denied, and the defendants requested reconsideration. Upon reconsideration, the court granted summary judgment as to all defendants holding that the plaintiff had not introduced sufficient evidence of the conspiracy or of market power sufficient to establish an unreasonable restraint of trade. Although the court did not spend much time discussing the cost-saving features of HMOs, it did note that HMOs do, indeed, have such cost-savings potential.[94]

The court of appeals affirmed the district court's decision on all counts. Specifically, the court held that Williamson lacked standing. As the court stated, "[b]ecause there has been no harm to competition [i.e., lower output or higher prices], there has been no antitrust injury, and consequently appellant lacks standing."[95] In any event, the court found that Williamson's claims were untenable because she could not present evidence of a conspiracy.[96] The challenged conduct was insufficient to create an inference of antitrust conspiracy because it either was unilateral on the part of the various defendants or was taken to further legitimate and procompetitive ends.[97] Antitrust conspiracy cannot be inferred from economically rational conduct.[98] As stressed by the court, nothing in the antitrust laws imposes an obligation on competitors to help one another.[99]

Thus it is clear that HMOs must have the right to exclude providers to offer additional patients to those providers that it selects in return for those providers' willingness to accept lower per patient payments. Other cases have reached similar results. Thus, in *Blue Cross v. Kitsap Physicians Service*, a Blue Cross HMO agreed with a clinic that the clinic would be the sole provider to HMO subscribers.[100] In holding that this arrangement did not constitute an illegal group boycott, the court stressed the HMO's freedom to contract with providers of its choice.

In *Nacouzi v. IPA of the Redwoods*, a California state court action under the California antitrust laws upheld an IPA's right to exclude physicians, holding that the IPA's practice of limiting membership to board-eligible or board-certified physicians did not constitute an unreasonable restraint of trade under California antitrust laws.[101] The plaintiff failed to show that the membership requirement was an activity of the type that restrains trade. Nor could the plaintiff demonstrate that the defendant possessed market power or that the restraint was likely to have a significant anticompetitive impact. The court noted that the defendant "competes with other care providers in Sonoma County and makes up only 17% of the market."[102] Consequently, the plaintiff in this case had "access to all patients in Sonoma County except for approximately 17% of the [defendant's] patients. Such a limitation does not constitute a substantial restraint of trade in the relevant market. . . ."[103]

By contrast, in *Reazin v. Blue Cross & Blue Shield*, Blue Cross terminated a provider contract with a hospital because of the hospital's affiliation with an HMO that competed with Blue Cross.[104] The court held that the exclusion of the hospital by Blue Cross, in concert with two other hospitals, constituted an illegal conspiracy in restraint of trade in violation of Section 1 of the Sherman Act, based on its finding that the defendants possessed market power and that there was evidence of conspiratorial conduct and of actual anticompetitive effects.

Nevertheless, in *Doctor's Hospital v. Southeast Medical Alliance, Inc.*, a Louisiana district court upheld a provider-controlled PPO's right under the antitrust laws to terminate the contract of a previously participating hospital to contract with a competing hospital.[105] The excluded hospital alleged that the new exclusive arrangement constituted an unlawful group boycott in violation of Section 1 of the Sherman Act. The court, however, granted summary judgment for the defendant, relying heavily on the precedent set in *U.S. Healthcare, Inc. v. Healthsource*.[106] In the court's view, the PPO was a legitimate joint venture, and the arrangement was no different from any contractual arrangement under which a firm elects to do business with a second firm instead of with a competitor of the second firm and therefore was properly dealt with under the rule of reason.[107] The court found that the exclusive arrangement for hospital services was not a per se violation of the antitrust laws because it was purely vertical in nature. In this connection, the court found no evidence that the providers controlling the PPO had conspired, and the arrangement thus could not be transformed from a vertical into a horizontal one. The exclusive hospital provider was not represented on the PPO's board, and no evidence indicated that the board had acted in any way contrary to the PPO's legitimate business interests.

Under the rule of reason, the plaintiff's claims failed because it could not establish that the PPO had market power. Indeed, the PPO represented only 6 percent of plaintiff's revenue at the time the contract was terminated. In addition, the court noted that there was insufficient evidence of anticompetitive effects; that is, the plaintiff could not show that prices to consumers had actually increased (a mere likelihood of price increase, without more, is insufficient to establish antitrust injury).

In another case, *Eastmoreland General Hospital, Inc. v. PACC*, that involved an excluded hospital provider, the plaintiff, Eastmoreland General Hospital (EGH), asserted that the defendant, PACC, had engaged in a conspiracy in violation of Section 1 of the Sherman Act.[108] PACC is a nonprofit corporation providing prepaid health insurance through a variety of HMO, PPO, and Medicare products. The essence of the claim was that PACC excluded EGH by selecting other hospitals to participate in PACC's provider network. In addition, EGH contended that PACC deprived it of a major source of patients by requiring PACC participating physicians to refer all health plan patients only to participating hospitals.

Clearly, the rule of reason was the appropriate framework of analysis in *PACC* because the arrangement, involving the purchase of hospital services by PACC from another hospital to the exclusion of EGH, was a classic example of a vertical, nonprice restraint.[109] In this connection, courts have unambiguously recognized that "restraints imposed by agreement between competitors have traditionally been denominated as horizontal restraints, and those imposed by agreement between firms at different levels of distribution as vertical restraints."[110]

Moreover, the rule of reason would seem to be appropriate even if the alleged agreement in *PACC* were to be characterized as horizontal.

The Supreme Court has made it clear that even horizontal boycotts or refusals to deal must be treated under the rule of reason, unless the participants in the alleged conspiracy have a dominant market position and are able to cut off access to a supply, facility, or market necessary to enable the boycotted party to compete[111]:

> A plaintiff seeking application of the *per se* rule must present a threshold case that the challenged activity falls into a category likely to have predominantly anticompetitive effects. The mere allegation of a concerted refusal to deal does not suffice because not all concerted refusals to deal are predominantly anticompetitive. . . . [S]ome showing must be made that the [defendant] possesses market power or unique access to a business element necessary for effective competition.[112]

Clearly, the existence of a conspiracy under Section 1 of the Sherman Act is a critical issue in antitrust cases involving the exclusion of a provider or class of providers from the network or panel of a health plan or a hospital. It is unusual for a plaintiff to be able to show such a conspiracy with direct evidence. Therefore, plaintiffs must rely upon inferences drawn from the circumstances alleged to establish a tacit agreement or conspiracy. The courts have devised specific guidelines regarding evidentiary inferences for such conspiracies at the summary judgment stage of litigation. These standards are important because a defendant can have a case dismissed without trial if the plaintiff cannot meet the summary judgment standards.

The Third Circuit Court of Appeals discussed the inferences necessary to withstand summary judgment and the limitations of their applications.[113] First, the focus of determining whether a conspiracy exists must necessarily be directed at the evidence offered by the plaintiff and whether that evidence tends to exclude the possibility that the defendant(s) acted independently. Second, the plaintiff's conspiracy theory must be economically plausible. Third, the alleged conspiracy must not have the effect of deterring significant procompetitive conduct. Fourth, mere parallel behavior by the defendants will not establish an antitrust conspiracy.

In a case with some significance with respect to the ability of excluded providers to establish a conspiracy for purposes of Section 1 of the Sherman Act, a New York federal district court ruled that, under certain circumstances, medical staffs can conspire with hospitals.[114] The court noted that the federal courts of appeal are spilt on the issue of whether a hospital and members of its medical staff are a single entity for the purpose of allegations claiming a conspiracy under the antitrust laws. Specifically, the Third, Fourth, and Sixth Circuits have determined that a hospital and its staff cannot conspire for the purposes of the Sherman Act.[115] The Ninth and Eleventh Circuits, however, have determined that a hospital and its medical staff can conspire.[116] For the most part, the circuits that say there can be no conspiracy analogize the medical staff physicians to employees of the hospital or health plan, pointing out that there can be no conspiracy between a company and its employees. On the other hand, the circuits that permit the inference of conspiracy point out that physicians making the recommendations can be competitors of the excluded physicians. Courts in other jurisdictions that have not as yet adopted a categorical position, as did the court in *Balaklaw*, often analyze the specific structure and the conduct of the hospital and its medical staff to determine whether they could have conspired within the meaning of the antitrust laws. They look at whether the physicians and the hospitals are competitors of the excluded physicians. Where they are, the courts determine whether the hospital would have a legitimate reason in excluding the physicians aside from any competitive advantage it would provide.

It is not difficult to draw an analogy between the relationship of a hospital and its medical staff and that of a health plan and its provider network for the purposes of determining their ability to conspire under the Sherman Act.

Where the provider network is critical to the exclusion of the physician, the courts may permit the inference of a conspiracy, as was the case in *Capital Imaging*. There can be little doubt that the issue is important and that it will continue to be raised, both in the context of health plans and in the context of the relationships between hospitals and their medical staffs. Ultimately, the Supreme Court will probably have to resolve the conflict.

Sherman Act Section 2 Claims

Excluded providers may also challenge the MCO's action under Section 2 of the Sherman Act. Section 2 prohibits a party with monopoly power or a dangerous probability of attaining monopoly power from engaging in exclusionary or predatory conduct.[117] Section 2 "makes the conduct of a single firm unlawful only when it actually monopolizes or dangerously threatens to do so."[118] As a consequence, any finding of liability under Section 2 is dependent on a showing that the defendant has market (or monopoly) power in the relevant market.[119] Networks can possess monopoly power, and the mere fact that conduct may exclude competitors is not determinative. "Liability turns, then, on whether 'valid business reasons' can explain [defendant's] actions."[120]

MCOs should be able to establish procompetitive business justifications and economic efficiencies for many of their exclusive arrangements. Thus MCOs offering risk-based products exclusively through a network could argue that, without the exclusive arrangements, the product would not be available at all. In contrast, MCOs with economic power will have a difficult time arguing that fee-for-service products must be sold exclusively through the network.

Some courts have ruled that a defendant may establish a prima facie case of *lawful* conduct by asserting valid business justifications for its challenged conduct.[121] Other courts have determined that a business justification must be accepted unless the plaintiff can establish that the proposed justification has no legitimate basis.[122] Indeed, the Supreme Court has recognized that a monopolist may establish procompetitive justifications or market efficiencies to outweigh any anticompetitive effects.[123]

As stated earlier, market power is the power "to force a purchaser to do something that he would not do in a competitive market."[124] "Monopoly power under Section 2 requires, of course, something greater than market power. . . ."[125] Monopoly power has most often been defined as the "power of controlling prices or unreasonably restricting competition."[126]

The existence of monopoly power typically can be inferred from the elimination of all market competition through the defendant's conduct.[127] Similarly, monopoly power can be inferred from the defendant's ability to raise prices profitably above competitive levels and to restrict output.[128]

Often, courts also permit an inference of market power, or monopoly power, to be drawn from the existence of a predominant or overwhelming market share, as long as there are no readily available substitutes.[129] Even an overwhelming market share, however, will not establish monopoly power when barriers to entry are low.[130] To be actionable, a predatory or exclusionary scheme must enable the monopolist to maintain its monopoly power long enough to achieve a monopoly return.[131] *Brook Group*, which reaffirms the holding of *Spectrum Sports*, also makes clear that monopoly pricing cannot be shown without commensurate proof of output reduction and reiterates that expert economic testimony that does not reflect market realities must be rejected on summary judgment.[132]

STATE AWP LEGISLATION

Generally

Insurance statutes and nonprofit health service plan laws sometimes include AWP or mandated provider type requirements (also see Chapter 53). As of 1995, approximately 20 states had adopted such laws.[133] It is essential to understand the functioning of these laws be-

cause they can become a major impediment to the effective development and operation of MCOs.

AWP legislation is favored by provider groups that perceive themselves as losing access to segments of their client base. On the other hand, the requirements are bitterly opposed by payers that claim they need flexibility to control utilization by the selection of cost-effective providers. AWP laws may hamper or completely foil an MCO's credentialing and utilization management plans by requiring the system to include all applicant providers in managed care panels and/or subjecting health plans to litigation when they seek to limit the size of their panels.[134] Although these statutes can be interpreted narrowly by regulators, where they are not, they arguably chill the operation of some forms of MCOs.[135]

MCOs are also hampered by legislation requiring that certain classes of providers be included in a preferred provider network.[136] Such requirements limit the ability to create a cost-effective managed care product and have prompted calls for federal preemption of such state anti–managed care statutes.

Avenues of Challenge to AWP Laws

Several avenues exist to challenge state AWP laws. The possible causes of action identified and discussed herein include preemption under the Employee Retirement Income Security Act of 1974 (ERISA; see Chapter 59), preemption under the Federal Employees Health Benefit Act (FEHBA; see Chapter 45), preemption under the Federal HMO Act (see Chapter 54), and invalidation under the Contract Clause to the United States Constitution. Because of the paucity of case law in this area, the likely success of these possible avenues of challenge cannot be ascertained. Each has merit, however, and can be argued on the basis of existing law.

ERISA Preemption

AWP statutes arguably are preempted by ERISA. AWP statutes relate to employee benefit plans and therefore are preempted by ERISA. Moreover, AWP statutes do not regulate the business of insurance, and therefore are not saved from preemption pursuant to ERISA's savings clause.

Whether AWP laws relate to employee benefit plans. The first issue in the ERISA preemption analysis is whether the AWP statute relates to employee benefit plans and consequently is superseded by ERISA. In the course of reviewing and developing the law in this area, the Supreme Court has stressed that the phrase *relates to* is to be given a broad, common sense meaning.[137] In *Shaw*, the Court stated that a law relates to an employee benefit plan where "it has a connection with or reference to such a plan."[138] The Court also noted, however, that some state actions "may affect employee benefit plans in too tenuous, remote, or peripheral a manner to warrant a finding that the law 'relates to' the plan."[139]

Typically, courts consider several factors in analyzing a state statute's impact on an ERISA plan. The Eighth Circuit, for instance, considers whether the state law negates an ERISA plan provision, the state law affects the relations among primary ERISA entities, the state law affects the structure of ERISA plans, the state law affects the administration of ERISA plans, the state law has an economic impact on ERISA plans, preemption of the state law is consistent with other ERISA provisions, and the state law is an exercise of traditional state power.[140] Nevertheless, courts generally have construed ERISA's "relates to" language broadly.

Typically, AWP laws dictate which providers will supply plan benefits and thereby will have a direct effect on a plan's cost, structure, and administration. Commentators, insurers, and employee groups have historically opposed AWP and other mandated-provider laws because they interfere with attempts to lower health care costs through the formation of provider networks.[141] Thus, as applied to employee benefit plans, AWP laws are arguably preempted by ERISA.[142]

Whether AWP laws regulate the business of insurance. A determination that a statute relates to employee health plans, however, is only the first step in an ERISA preemption analysis. Consistent with the federal policy embodied in the McCarran-Ferguson Act of leaving the regulation of insurance to the states, Congress saved from ERISA preemption any state law that regulates insurance.[143] Consequently, the second step in the ERISA preemption analysis is whether the AWP law regulates insurance. In determining whether a state law regulates insurance, courts have generally applied a common sense analysis of the issue followed by an interpretation of the business of insurance as such term has been interpreted under the McCarran-Ferguson Act.[144]

It can be argued that AWP laws do not constitute the business of insurance and therefore are not within the scope of the ERISA insurance savings clause. First, AWP laws do not regulate the transfer or spreading of risk. The risk of loss is transferred in the insurance contracts with the insureds, and the transfer of risk is complete at the time the contract is formed.[145] AWP and other mandated-provider laws operate after this risk is transferred to require insurers to reimburse particular providers if those providers supply goods or services that the insured is already obligated to pay for under its policies. At least arguably, AWP laws do not regulate the transfer or spreading of risk but merely regulate an insurer's subsequent arrangements with providers for the purchase of goods and services. Such laws act only after the insurer is already obligated to provide the benefits under the policies.[146] Second, AWP laws are not an integral part of the relationship between insurer and policyholder. Rather, they regulate the relationship between the insurer and providers. Third, AWP and other mandated-provider laws involve entities that are outside the insurance industry. By regulating the relationship with providers, these laws have a direct and intended impact on providers.

Nevertheless, in *Stuart Circle Hospital Corp. v. Aetna Health Management*, the Fourth Circuit Court of Appeals applied the criteria set forth in *Metropolitan Life* and found a Virginia statute that prohibited discrimination in establishing

PPOs to constitute the business of insurance. In its ruling, the court first found that the mandated-provider law did operate to transfer or spread risk. By preventing the unreasonable restriction of provider choice, the "statute spreads the cost component of the policyholder's risk among all the insureds, instead of requiring the policyholder to shoulder all or part of this cost when seeking care or treatment from an excluded [provider]. . . ."[147]

Second, the court found the statute to be an integral part of the insurer–insured relationship because it regulated both the treatment and the cost components under the insurance relationship.[148] Thus, in a sense, the decision views provider selection as integral to the bargained-for coverage.

Finally, the court found the statute to be limited to entities within the insurance industry. Although the statute regulates the insurer–insured relationship indirectly through the formation of PPOs, it was found nonetheless to be a law that regulates the business of insurance and one that merely regulates the implementation of the policy terms by the insurer.[149]

Notwithstanding the Fourth Circuit's decision in *Stuart Circle*, it can very well be argued that the case was wrongly decided. Indeed, it can be argued that the holding in *Stuart Circle* was contrary to the Supreme Court's finding in *Metropolitan Life*, which required the consistent interpretation of the ERISA savings clause and the McCarran-Ferguson Act. Moreover, the criteria enunciated to determine what constitutes the business of insurance under the McCarran-Ferguson Act clearly indicate that a state law does not regulate the business of insurance merely because it purports to regulate an insurance company. As the Supreme Court noted in *Royal Drug*, it is the business of insurance that is exempted, not the business of insurance companies.[150]

Consequently, it is not surprising that, despite the ruling of the Fourth Circuit in *Stuart Circle*, a court outside the Fourth Circuit recently issued an order granting a motion for declaratory judgment on the grounds of ERISA preemption. Spe-cifically, in *Cigna Healthplan v. Louisiana*, the federal district court for the Middle District of Louisiana (which is in the Fifth Circuit) granted the plaintiffs' motion for a declaratory judgment on the grounds that Louisiana's AWP statute, to the extent that it applied to health care service plans that serve participants and beneficiaries of employee welfare benefit plans regulated by ERISA, was preempted by ERISA and therefore violated the Supremacy Clause of the United States Constitution.[151,152] In applying the Fifth Circuit's multifactor test for the applicability of ERISA's insurance savings clause, the court found that the statute met neither a common sense test that it was specifically directed toward regulating insurance nor the third of the McCarran-Ferguson factors (i.e., that it was limited to entities within the insurance industry).[153]

A key factor for the court in its ruling was the applicability of the statute to noninsurance entities. "The Court finds that the [AWP] Statute . . . is not specifically directed towards the insurance industry, but, rather, it expressly applies to entities outside the insurance industry, such as employers and Taft-Hartley trusts."[154] Thus the ERISA preemption argument may be more compelling to the extent that AWP laws apply broadly.

FEHBA Preemption

AWP statutes also may be challenged on the basis of FEHBA preemption. Although such a cause of action utilizes many of the same principles as ERISA preemption, the FEHBA preemption argument is especially powerful because FEHBA, unlike ERISA, does not include an insurance savings clause.[155]

Little case law discusses the scope of FEHBA's preemptive power. With respect to the requirement that the state law must relate to the FEHBA plan, however, the court in *Hayes v. Prudential Insurance Co. of America*, interpreted the language in a manner analogous to its broad treatment under ERISA.[156,157]

In *MedCenters Health Care, Inc. v. Ochs*, the court addressed whether state subrogation laws were inconsistent with the contractual provisions set forth in a FEHBA plan.[158] Although the court opined that section 8902(m)(1) does not entirely displace state law, it ultimately held that a state common law that denies the effect of a contractual provision is inconsistent with that provision.[159] Specifically, the court noted that the congressional purpose in enacting FEHBA was to "protect federal employees against high and unpredictable costs of medical care and to assure that federal employee health benefits are equivalent to those in the private sector. . . ."[160] In addition, the court drew the distinction between plans covered by ERISA and those covered by FEHBA, stating that, unlike ERISA, under FEHBA "the mechanisms for achieving uniformity of treatment are in place at the formation phase of the contracts when the oversight of the [Office of Personnel Management] is taken into consideration."[161]

A strong argument could be fashioned that, as a matter of public policy, AWP laws unfairly restrict the ability of a plan to comply with the legislative intent of FEHBA. As procompetitive organizations, health care insurers that are attempting to manage care rely on their ability to select preferred providers as a vehicle to create competition and thereby reduce costs. By mandating that any willing provider be afforded the opportunity to contract with a plan, a plan's costs are likely to increase as plan administration and quality control become ever more difficult to regulate.

This rationale was set forth in *Nesseim v. Mail Handlers Benefit Plan*.[162] In *Nesseim*, a federal employee was denied coverage under a federally qualified FEHBA plan. After losing an administrative appeal, the U.S. District Court for the District of South Dakota held that the agency decision was arbitrary, capricious, and contrary to law.[163] On appeal, the Eighth Circuit reversed the lower court ruling, noting that FEHBA empowers the agency with the authority to determine the scope of benefits that will be included in each contact.[164]

As applied to challenges to AWP laws, it is clear that provider selection is central to plan design and plays an integral role in establishing contractual obligations with the government employer. By regulating provider participation, the AWP laws impede controlling costs, extending benefits, and administrating the terms of coverage. As such, mandated provider restrictions are arguably inconsistent with existing contractual arrangements and thereby are preempted under FEHBA.

Still, although the preemptive power of FEHBA is quite broad, FEHBA preemption, compared with ERISA preemption, is more narrowly targeted because it is likely to preempt state law only with respect to contracts with FEHBA plans. Consequently, the limited provider panels that would otherwise violate an AWP statute could only be offered to FEHBA plans. This would place health care insurers that were attempting to manage health care in the difficult position of having to maintain separate provider panels for FEHBA and non-FEHBA plans. Although one could argue that FEHBA preemption consequently should, operate to exempt insurers from the Arkansas AWP Act altogether, it is unclear, although probably unlikely, that the courts would be sympathetic to such a result.

Federal HMO Act Preemption

To the extent that AWP laws relate to the operation of federally qualified HMOs, they may run afoul of the Supremacy Clause of the United States Constitution because they may be incompatible with the Federal HMO Act.[165] The courts have held that state law provisions that do not expressly conflict with the HMO Act are not generally preempted.[166]

Specifically, by requiring HMOs to allow providers willing to meet an HMO's conditions to join the HMO's panel of providers, AWP laws arguably conflict with the explicit preemption language of the HMO Act, which provides that state laws that interfere with the operation of HMOs by setting provider participation levels shall not apply to HMOs.[167] What a plaintiff must show, however, is that the AWP law prevents the HMO from operating. The best argument in this connection is that provider selection and the ability to limit the number of physicians on a panel are vital for the ability of HMOs to contain costs. Indeed, AWP laws, by dictating which providers will supply plan benefits, are likely to increase the costs of plan administration, affect plan structure, force the inclusion of less efficient providers (thereby increasing the costs of providing services), and create disuniformities in multistate plans.

Research of the case law has revealed no cases that have construed Section 300e-10(a)(1)(C), and only three cases have dealt with other aspects of Section 300e-10: *Selcke*, *Physician's Health Plan*, and *Schweiker*. Moreover, none of these cases found state law to be preempted under Section 300e-10.[168] The court in *Schweiker*, however, did note that the five types of regulations preempted by the HMO Act were known and had typically been applied to prevent the development of HMOs and other types of group practice at the time the HMO Act was passed. Consequently, the court went on to reason, when evaluating regulatory schemes unknown at that time (such as the diagnosis-related group plan at issue in the case), "the court's inquiry cannot end with [Section] 300e-10."[169] The court, however, concluded that the diagnosis-related group plan did not conflict with the intent of the HMO Act and refused to preempt the plan, stating that "Congressional intent to preempt laws is not to be lightly inferred. . . ."[170] Nevertheless, this type of inquiry is not likely to be relevant to a challenge of AWP laws because such laws, at least arguably, fall within the scope of Section 300e-10(a)(1)(C).

Of course, a private party would not have standing to file an action under this section unless the existence of a private right of action may be inferred. In this regard, cases addressing preemption appear to assume, without discussion, that there is a private right of action. Indeed, it would appear that the provision would be rendered meaningless without such a right because the HMO Act does not specify a role for the federal government in enforcing the provision, except for collecting information and providing technical assistance to the states.[171]

Contract Clause

Although this strategy for challenging an AWP statute has little authority directly on point, an argument can be made that AWP laws violate Article I, Section 10 of the United States Constitution (the Contract Clause). The language of the Contract Clause is unambiguous and absolute: "No State shall . . . pass any . . . Law impairing the Obligation of Contracts." If read literally, it would seem that AWP laws that impose on insurers obligations that did not exist at the time the contracts were made would violate the Contract Clause.

The Contract Clause is not read literally, however. As the Supreme Court has noted, "literalism in the construction of the contract clause . . . would make it destructive of the public interest by depriving the State of its prerogative of self-protection."[172] In *Allied Structural Steel v. Spannaus*, the Court struck down a retroactive statute that changed the terms of private companies' pension plans.[173] In so doing, the Supreme Court stated "[n]ot only did the state law thus retroactively modify the compensation that the company had agreed to pay its employees from 1963 to 1974, but also it did so by changing the company's obligations in an area where the element of reliance was vital—the funding of a pension plan."[174]

In addition to enumerating several factors that may be weighed to determine whether a state action violates the Contract Clause, the Supreme Court followed the reasoning set forth in *W.B. Worthen Co.*, which held that an Arkansas law that exempted the proceeds of a life insurance policy from collection by a beneficiary's judgment creditor was improper in that its retroactive effect was not precisely and reasonably designed to address a temporary emergency in the public's interest.[175,176] Emphasizing the hardship that retroactivity would impose on existing contracts, the Court stated further that, even when public welfare is invoked as an excuse, the law must be reasonable.[177]

The Eighth Circuit has followed the principles set forth in *Allied Structural Steel Co.* through a three-prong test: whether the state regulation substantially impairs a contractual obligation, whether the state had a legitimate public purpose behind the regulation, and whether the adjustment of the rights of the contracting parties is based on reasonable conditions that justified adoption of the legislation and is of a character appropriate to the public purpose.[178]

Recent cases following this analysis have shed light on the significance of substantial impairment under the first prong of the test. In *In re Workers Compensation Refund*, for example, the court held that, where an agreement specified the terms of distributing an insurance fund, a subsequently enacted state law violated the Contract Clause by mandating terms of dispersement contrary to those in the agreement.[179] The court held that this was true even though the contract itself included language providing for statutory changes in the law.[180]

In determining whether the state law substantially impaired the contractual agreement in question, the court asserted that it must consider the extent to which the parties' reasonable contractual expectations are disrupted.[181] A related consideration is the level of government regulation of the industry in which the parties are engaged.[182] Finally, the court asserted that heightened levels of contractual impairment increase the level of scrutiny to which the legislation is subject.[183] Although the parties were engaged in the highly regulated insurance practice of workers' compensation, the court nonetheless held that the state law substantially impaired the terms of the contract, noting that there are limitations even in regulated industries.

Similarly, in *Minnesota Association of Health Care v. Minnesota Departments of Public Welfare*, the Eighth Circuit considered the constitutionality of a Minnesota statute that limited the differential rates that nursing homes (seeking to participate in the state Medicaid program) could charge between those residents who did and those who did not receive state medical assistance benefits.[184] The court held that, although

prospective application of the statute passed constitutional muster, the retroactive application of the statute to obtain restitution of charges in excess of the differential was a substantial impairment of contracts that was not based upon reasonable conditions or otherwise appropriate to the statute's purpose. As the court stated, "This statute goes too far because it disrupts settled and completed financial arrangements under contracts made in reliance on existing law."[185]

Arguably, AWP laws violate the Contract Clause under the requirements set forth in *Allied Structural Steel Co.* and its progeny. By mandating that any willing provider be entitled to participate in a plan, AWP laws arguably impair the ability of the health care insurer to compete in a cost-efficient manner without sacrificing the quality of care rendered to its subscribers. Furthermore, it is questionable whether AWP laws truly cater to a public purpose; rather, such laws are arguably skewed in favor of providers at the expense of the health care plans and arguably the public at large because they will probably increase operational expenses while diminishing quality control and administrative uniformity. Finally, to the extent that the AWP laws are applied retroactively, it can be argued that there was a reasonable reliance on the existing standards in establishing a network.

CONCLUSION

Both the specific application of the antitrust laws and the enactment of state AWP laws can create challenges for MCOs looking to restrict providers. In many cases, however, MCOs will have a sound basis to resist legal challenge by providers seeking to force entry. Similarly, there are sound legal bases upon which to challenge state enactment of AWP laws. The foregoing analysis attempts to provide a useful framework setting forth the legal bases upon which both judicial and statutory attempts to restrict the ability of MCOs to limit their provider networks can be resisted.

REFERENCES AND NOTES

1. Such claims may be brought under Sections 1 and 2 of the Sherman Act. *See, e.g., Capital Imaging Assocs., P.C. v. Mohawk Valley Medical Assocs., Inc.*, 791 F. Supp. 956 (N.D.N.Y. 1992) ("*Capital II*"), *aff'd*, 996 F.2d 537 (2d Cir.), *cert. denied*, 114 S. Ct. 388 (1993).

2. *See, e.g., EGH, Inc. v. Blue Cross & Blue Shield*, Civ. No. 90-1210-FR, 1991-2 Trade Cas. (CCH) ¶ 69,642 (D. Or. Sept. 26, 1991); *Wildenauer v. Blue Cross & Blue Shield*, 737 F. Supp. 64 (D. Minn. 1989); *Michigan State Podiatry Ass'n v. Blue Cross & Blue Shield*, 671 F. Supp. 1139 (E.D. Mich. 1987).

3. *See Ball Memorial Hosp. v. Mutual Hosp. Ins., Inc.*, 784 F.2d 1325 (7th Cir. 1986).

4. Section 1 of the Sherman Act prohibits concerted (joint) action (i.e., contracts, combinations, and conspiracies) that restrains trade unreasonably. 15 U.S.C. § 1.

5. Section 2 prohibits monopolization, attempted monopolization, and conspiracies to monopolize. 15 U.S.C. § 2.

6. *Eastman Kodak Co. v. Image Technical Servs., Inc.*, 112 S. Ct. 2072, 2080 (1992) (citing *Jefferson Parish Hosp. v. Hyde*, 466 U.S. 2, 14 (1984)).

7. *Ocean State Physicians Health Plan, Inc. v. Blue Cross & Blue Shield*, 883 F.2d 1101, 1111–12 (1st Cir. 1989), *cert. denied*, 494 U.S. 1027 (1990).

8. *Doctors Steuer & Latham, P.A. v. National Medical Enters., Inc.*, 672 F. Supp. 1489, 1504 (D.S.C. 1987) (citing *Fishman v. Estate of Wirtz*, 807 F.2d 520, 568 (7th Cir. 1986) (Easterbrook, J., dissenting in part)), *aff'd*, 846 F.2d 70 (4th Cir. 1988); *Flip Side Prods., Inc. v. Jam Prods., Ltd.*, 843 F.2d 1024, 1032 (7th Cir.), *cert. denied*, 488 U.S. 909 (1988).

9. *Jefferson Parish Hosp. v. Hyde*, 466 U.S. 2, 7 n.46. *See also NCAA v. Board of Regents*, 468 U.S. 85, 109 n.38 (1984); *International Distribution Ctrs., Inc. v. Walsh Trucking Co.*, 812 F.2d 786, 791 n.3 (2d Cir.), *cert. denied*, 482 U.S. 915 (1987); *Ball Memorial*, 784 F.2d at 1330–31.

10. *Fishman v. Estate of Wirtz*, 807 F.2d 520, 577 (7th Cir. 1986) (Easterbrook, J., dissenting).

11. *Tampa Elec. Co. v. Nashville Coal Co.*, 365 U.S. 320, 327 (1961); *Morgan, Strand, Wheeler & Biggs v. Radiology, Ltd.*, 924 F.2d 1484, 1489 (9th Cir. 1991).

12. *Id.*

13. *See NCAA*, 468 U.S. at 112–113.

14. *Morgan, Strand*, 924 F.2d at 1489 (citations omitted).

15. *NCAA*, 468 U.S. at 106–08; *Jefferson Parish*, 466 U.S. at 31 n.52.

16. *NCAA*, 468 U.S. at 110; *see also Capital II*, 996 F.2d 537.

17. *Eastman Kodak*, 504 U.S. at 2081.

18. *Barr Lab., Inc., v. Abott Lab.*, 978 F.2d 98, 112 (3d Cir. 1992) (citations omitted).

19. *Ball Memorial*, 784 F.2d at 1330–31; *Forro Precision, Inc. v. IBM*, 673 F.2d 1045, 1058–59 (9th Cir. 1982), *cert. denied*, 471 U.S. 1130 (1985) (35 percent market share does not support a claim for market power).

20. *Hassan v. Independent Practice Assocs.*, 698 F. Supp. 679, 694–95 (E.D. Mich. 1988); *Northwest Medical Labs. v. Blue Cross & Blue Shield*, 794 P.2d 428 (Or. 1990).

21. *United States v. Syufy Enters.*, 903 F.2d 659, 671 (9th Cir. 1990); *Morgan, Strand*, 924 F.2d at 1484, 1940; *Ball Memorial*, 784 F.2d at 1330–33; *Hassan*, 698 F. Supp. at 694–95.

22. *Los Angeles Land Co. v. Brunswick*, 6 F.3d 1422, 1425–26 (9th Cir. 1993), *cert. denied*, 114 S. Ct. 1307 (1994) (citations omitted).

23. *Bhan v. NME Hospitals, Inc.*, 929 F.2d 1404, 1410 (9th Cir.), *cert. denied*, 502 U.S. 994 (1991).

24. *Cayman Exploration Corp. v. United Gas Pipe Line Co.*, 873 F.2d 1357, 1360 (10th Cir. 1989); *Smith Mach. Co. v. Hesston Corp.*, 878 F.2d 1290, 1295–96 (10th Cir. 1989), *cert. denied*, 493 U.S. 1073 (1990); *Westman Comm'n Co. v. Hobart Int'l, Inc.*, 796 F.2d 1216, 1220 (10th Cir. 1986), *cert. denied*, 486 U.S. 1005 (1988); *Sewell Plastics, Inc. v. Coca-Cola Co.*, 720 F. Supp. 1196, 1218 (W.D.N.C. 1989), *aff'd*, 912 F.2d 463 (4th Cir. 1990), *cert. denied*, 498 U.S. 1110 (1991); *Interface Group, Inc. v. Massachusetts Port Auth.*, 816 F.2d 9, 10 (1st Cir. 1987).

25. *Seagood Trading Corp. v. Jerrico, Inc.*, 924 F.2d 1555, 1573 (11th Cir. 1991); *L.A. Draper & Son v. Wheelabrator-Frye, Inc.*, 735 F. 2d 414, 421 (11th Cir. 1984); *Indiana Grocery, Inc. v. Super Valu Stores, Inc.*, 864 F.2d 1409, 1413 (7th Cir. 1989); *Harron v. United Hosp. Ctr., Inc.*, 522 F.2d 1133 (4th Cir. 1975), *cert. denied*, 424 U.S. 916 (1976); *International Logistics Group, Ltd. v. Chrysler Corp.*, 884 F.2d 904, 909 (6th Cir. 1989), *cert. denied*, 494 U.S. 1066 (1990).

26. *Tampa Electric*, 365 U.S. at 327. *See 1992 Joint DOJ/ FTC Merger Guidelines* § 1, 4 Trade Reg. Rep. (CCH) ¶ 13, 104, at 20,571.

27. *Morgan, Strand*, 924 F.2d at 1490.

28. *Robinson v. Magovern*, 521 F. Supp. 842, 884–85 (W.D. Pa. 1981), *aff'd*, 688 F.2d 824, *cert. denied*, 459 U.S. 971 (1982).

29. *See U.S. Healthcare, Inc. v. Healthsource, Inc.*, 986 F.2d 589, 598–99 (1st Cir. 1993); *Blue Cross & Blue Shield v. Marshfield Clinic*, 65 F.3d 1406, 1409–10 (7th Cir. 1995).

30. *Marshfield Clinic*, 65 F.3d at 1409–10.

31. *Stamatakis Indus., Inc. v. King*, 965 F.2d 469, 471 (7th Cir. 1992).

32. *Id.*

33. *Brook Group, Ltd. v. Brown & Williamson Tobacco Corp.*, 113 S. Ct. 2578, 2588–89 (1993); *Reiter v. Sonotone Corp.*, 442 U.S. 330, 342 (1979).

34. *Brook Group*, 113 S. Ct. at 2589 (quoting *Hunt v. Crumboch*, 325 U.S. 821, 826 (1945)).

35. *Bob Maxfield, Inc. v. American Motors Corp.*, 637 F.2d 1033, 1036 (5th Cir.), *cert. denied*, 454 U.S. 860 (1981).

36. *Jefferson Parish*, 466 U.S. at 45 (J. O'Connor, concurring opinion).

37. *Rutman Wine Co. v. E. & J. Gallo Winery*, 829 F.2d 729, 735 (9th Cir. 1987) (citing *Great Escape, Inc. v. Union City Body Co.* 791 F.2d 532, 540 (7th Cir. 1986)).

38. *Id.*

39. *See Barry v. Blue Cross*, 805 F.2d 866, 871 (9th Cir. 1986); *Konik v. Champlain Valley Physicians Hosp. Medical Ctr.*, 733 F.2d 1007, 1014 (2d Cir. 1984).

40. *Hassan*, 698 F. Supp. at 696; *Bhan*, 929 F.2d at 1414; *L.A. Draper*, 735 F.2d at 421; *Harron*, 522 F.2d 1133; *Crane & Shovel Sales Corp. v. Bucyrus-Erie Co.*, 854 F.2d at 810; *Copy-Data Sys., Inc. v. Toshiba Am., Inc.*, 663 F.2d 405, 410 (2d Cir. 1981).

41. *Barry*, 805 F.2d at 871 (citations omitted); *Drs. Steuer & Latham*, 672 F.2d at 1504 (citing *Fishman*, 807 F.2d at 568 (Easterbrook, J., dissenting in part)); *Flip-Side*, 843 F.2d at 1032.

42. *Barry*, 805 F.2d at 871.

43. *Coffey v. Healthtrust, Inc.*, 955 F.2d 1388, 1393 (1992), *aff'd*, 1 F.3d 1101 (10th Cir. 1993); *see also Bhan*, 929 F.2d at 1414; *L.A. Draper*, 735 F.2d at 421; *Harron*, 522 F.2d 1133; *Hassan* 698 F. Supp. at 696.

44. *Spectrum Sports, Inc. v. McQuillan*, 113 S. Ct. 884, 891–92 (1993).

45. *U.S. Healthcare*, 986 F.2d at 595.

46. 365 U.S. 623.

47. *Id.* at 628–29.

48. 100 F.T.C. 68 (1982).

49. *Id.* at 209.

50. *Id.* at 209–210.

51. *Ryko Mfg. Co. v. Eden Servs.*, 823 F.2d 1215, 1233 (8th Cir. 1987), *cert. denied*, 484 U.S. 1026 (1988).

52. *Ryko*, 823 F.2d at 1234; *Beltone*, 100 F.T.C. at 210.

53. *Associated Gen. Contractors, Inc. v. California State Council of Carpenters*, 459 U.S. 519 (1983); *Military Serv. Realty, Inc. v. Realty Consultants, Ltd.*, 823 F.2d 829, 831–32 (4th Cir. 1987). *See also Brandenburg v. Seidel*, 859 F.2d 1179, 1189 n.11 (4th Cir. 1988) (con-

trasting antitrust injury to Racketeer Influences Corrupt Organizations Act (RICO) injury).

54. *Brunswick Corp. v. Pueblo Bowl-O-Mat, Inc.*, 429 U.S. 477, 489 (1977); *Stearns v. Genrad, Inc.*, 752 F.2d 942, 945–46 (4th Cir. 1984); *Windham v. American Brands, Inc.*, 565 F.2d 59, 65 (4th Cir. 1977), *cert. denied*, 435 U.S. 968 (1978).

55. *L.A. Draper*, 735 F.2d at 421: *See also Smith Machinery*, 878 F.2d 1290; *Harron*, 522 F.2d 1133.

56. *See, e.g., City of Chanute v. Williams Natural Gas Co.*, 955 F.2d 641, 652 (10th Cir. 1992). *See also Sharp v. United Airline, Inc.*, 967 F.2d 404, 406–407 (10th Cir. 1992); *Todorov v. DCH Healthcare Auth.*, 921 F.2d 1438, 1451–55 (11th Cir. 1991).

57. *Associated General*, 459 U.S. at 534.

58. *Id.* at 535.

59. 429 U.S. 477, 489 (1977) (emphasis in original).

60. 495 U.S. 328 (1990).

61. *Id.* at 339 (emphasis in original).

62. *Ball Memorial*, 784 F.2d at 1334.

63. *Stamatakis*, 965 F.2d at 471 (citing *Chicago Professional Sports Limited Partnership v. National Basketball Ass'n.*, 961 F.2d 667, 670 (7th Cir. 1992)).

64. *Capital Imaging Assocs., P.C. v. Mohawk Valley Medical Assocs., Inc.*, 725 F. Supp 669, 677 (N.D.N.Y. 1989) ("*Capital I*") (emphasis in original).

65. *Exhibitors' Service, Inc. v. American Multi-Cinema, Inc.*, 788 F.2d 574, 580 (9th Cir. 1986).

66. *Id.* at 579.

67. *Id.* at 578–580.

68. *Tennessean Truckstop, Inc. v. NTS, Inc.*, 875 F.2d 86, 90 (6th Cir. 1989) (citing *Ball Memorial*, 784 F.2d at 1334).

69. *See* Frank H. Easterbrook, *The Limits of Antitrust*, 63 Tex. L. Rev. 1 (1984); *Syufy Enterprises*, 903 F.2d at 663, 673.

70. *Indiana Grocery*, 864 F.2d at 1419.

71. *Id.*; *Alberta Gas Chem., Ltd. v. E.I. du Pont de Nemours & Co.*, 826 F.2d 1235, 1239 (3d Cir. 1987), *cert. denied*, 486 U.S. 1059 (1988).

72. *See, e.g.*, W.H. Page and R.D. Blair, *Controlling the Competitor Plaintiff In Antitrust Litigation*, 91 Mich. L. Rev. 111, 119 (1992).

73. E.A. Snyder and T.E. Kauper, *Misuse of the Antitrust Laws: The Competitor Plaintiff*, 90 Mich. L. Rev. 551, 575–76 (1991).

74. F.H. Easterbrook, *The Limits of Antitrust*, 63 Texas L. Rev. 1, 11 (1984). *See also* Snyder and Kauper, *Misuse of the Antitrust Laws: The Competitor Plaintiff*, 90 Mich. L. Rev. 551 (1991) (concluding that antitrust suits by competitor plaintiffs are not successful, and for good reason).

75. *Levine v. Central Florida Medical Affiliates, Inc.*, 864 F. Supp. 1175 (M.D. Fla. 1994).

76. Although the court disposed of the claims based on plaintiff's lack of standing, it nevertheless paused to note that the plaintiff could not have prevailed because of the untenable nature of plaintiff's market definition and market power argument.

77. *See, e.g., EGH*, 1991–2 Trade Cas. (CCH) ¶ 69, 642; *Wildenauer*, 737 F. Supp. 64; *Michigan State Podiatry*, 671 F. Supp. 1139.

78. *See supra* section I.A. at pp. 2–5. *See also Hassan*, 698 F. Supp. 679; *Williamson v. Sacred Heart Hosp.*, No. 89-30084-RV, 1993 WL 543002 (N.D. Fla. May 28, 1993), *aff'd without opinion*, 41 F.3d 667 (11th Cir. 1994), *cert. denied*, 115 S. Ct. 2556 (1995); *but see Hahn v. Oregon Physicians' Service*, 868 F.2d 1022 (9th Cir. 1988), *cert. denied*, 493 U.S. 846 (1989).

79. Department of Justice and Federal Trade Commission, *Statements of Antitrust Enforcement Policy in the Health Care Area* 33 (Sept. 15, 1993).

80. *See Capital I*, 725 F. Supp. at 673; *Northwest Medical*, 794 P.2d 428 (discussing the role of the HMO concept in fostering competition in health care financing markets).

81. *Capital I*, 725 F. Supp. at 673.

82. Letter from Jeffrey Zuckerman, Director, Federal Trade Commission Bureau of Competition, Consumer Protection, and Economics, to David Gates, Insurance Commissioner, State of Nevada (Nov. 5, 1986), at 1.

83. 472 U.S. 284 (1985).

84. 698 F. Supp. 679.

85. *Id.* at 694–97.

86. 775 P.2d 863 (Or. Ct. App. 1989), *aff'd*, 794 P.2d 428 (Or. 1990).

87. *Capital Imaging Assocs., P.C. v. Mohawk Valley Medical Assocs., Inc.*, 725 F. Supp. 669 (N.D.N.Y. 1989) ("*Capital I*"); *Capital Imaging Assocs., P.C. v. Mohawk Valley Medical Assocs., Inc.*, 791 F. Supp. 956 (N.D.N.Y. 1992) ("*Capital II*"), *aff'd*, 996 F.2d 537 (2d Cir.), *cert. denied*, 114 S. Ct. 388 (1993); *Williamson v. Sacred Heart Hosp.*, No. 89-30084-RV, 1993 WL 543002 (N.D. Fla. May 28, 1993), *aff'd without opinion*, 41 F.3d 667 (11th Cir. 1994), *cert. denied*, 115 S. Ct. 2556 (1995).

88. *See supra* note 87.

89. *Capital I*, 725 F. Supp. at 678 (emphasis in original).

90. *Id.* at 673.

91. *Capital II*, 996 F.2d at 547.

92. *Id.* at 546.

93. *See supra* note 87.

94. *See also U.S. Healthcare*, 986 F.2d at 591.

95. *Williamson*, No. 93-2796, Slip op. at 4 (11th Cir. Nov. 18, 1994).

96. *Id.* at 4–11.

97. *Id.*

98. *Id.* at 10–11.

99. *Id.* at 5, 7, 9.

100. No. C81-918V, 1982-1 Trade Cas. (CCH) ¶ 64,589 (W.D. Wash. 1981).

101. Case No. 204453 (Cal. Super. Ct. June 24, 1994).

102. *Id.*, slip op. at 3.

103. *Id.*

104. 663 F. Supp. 1360 (D. Kan. 1987), *aff'd*, 899 F.2d 951 (10th Cir.), *cert. denied*, 497 U.S. 1005 (1990).

105. 889 F. Supp. 879 (D. La. 1995), *amended & modified in part*, 897 F. Supp. 290 (D. La. 1995).

106. 986 F.2d 589.

107. It is noteworthy that the court conferred joint venture status on the PPO. The federal antitrust enforcement agencies—the FTC and the Department of Justice— have not as yet addressed this issue and typically have focused on risk-sharing devices, such as capitation, as the touchstone of joint venture status for provider-controlled entities. Although they have not as yet stated that without such risk sharing a provider-controlled entity can not be a legitimate joint venture, they have not stated that it could be.

108. No. CV-91-1334-JO (D. Or. filed Dec. 24, 1991).

109. *Capital I*, 725 F. Supp. at 677; *Northwest Medical*, 794 P.2d at 433.

110. *Business Elecs. Corp. v. Sharp Elecs. Corp.*, 485 U.S. 717, 728 (1988).

111. *Northwest Wholesale*, 472 U.S. at 294.

112. *Id.* at 298.

113. *Petruzzi's IGA Supermarkets, Inc. v. Darling-Delaware Co.*, 998 F.2d 1224 (3d Cir. 1993), *cert. denied*, 114 S. Ct. 554 (1993).

114. *Balaklaw v. Lovell*, 822 F. Supp. 892 (N.D.N.Y. 1993), *aff'd*, 14 F.3d 793 (2d Cir. 1994).

115. *See Weiss v. York Hosp.*, 745 F.2d 786 (3d Cir. 1984), *cert. denied*, 470 U.S. 1060 (1985); *Nurse Midwifery Assoc. v. Hibbett*, 918 F.2d 605 (6th Cir.), *modified on rehearing*, 927 F.2d 904 (6th Cir.), *cert. denied*, 502 U.S. 952 (1991); *Oksanen v. Page Memorial Hosp.*, 945 F.2d 696 (4th Cir.) (en banc), *cert. denied*, 502 U.S. 1074 (1992).

116. *See Oltz v. St. Peter's Community Hosp.*, 861 F.2d 1440 (9th Cir. 1988); *Bolt v. Halifax Hosp. Medical Center*, 891 F.2d 810, 819 (11th Cir. 1988), *cert. denied*, 495 U.S. 924 (1990).

117. *Trans Sport, Inc. v. Starter Sportswear, Inc.*, 964 F.2d 186, 189 (2d Cir. 1992); *see also Spectrum Sports*, 113 S. Ct. at 890; *Eastman Kodak*, 112 S. Ct. at 2090–91.

118. *Spectrum Sports*, 113 S. Ct. at 890, 892.

119. *Id.* at 890.

120. *Eastman Kodak*, 112 S. Ct. at 2091 (citing *Aspen Skiing Co. v. Aspen Highlands Skiing Corp.*, 472 U.S. 585, 605 (1985)); *United States v. Aluminum Co. of America*, 148 F.2d 416, 432 (2d Cir. 1945).

121. *Trans Sport*, 964 F.2d at 191.

122. *Oksanen*, 945 F.2d at 710.

123. *Eastman Kodak*, 112 S. Ct. at 2092.

124. *Eastman Kodak*, 112 S. Ct. at 2080 (citing *Jefferson Parish*, 466 U.S. at 14).

125. *Eastman Kodak*, 112 S. Ct. at 209 (citation omitted).

126. *United States v. E.I. du Pont de Nemours & Co.*, 351 U.S. 377, 391 (1956).

127. *See Los Angeles Land*, 6 F.3d at 1426–27.

128. *Eastman Kodak*, 112 S. Ct. at 2081; *see also Brook Group*, 113 S. Ct. at 2578, 2593.

129. *Eastman Kodak*, 112 S. Ct. at 2081, 2090. Generally, the greater the market share, the more likely a court will be to permit an inference that the defendant possesses market power or even meets the more stringent monopoly power standard of Section 2. *Id.*

130. *Los Angeles Land*, 6 F.3d at 1425–26; *see also United States v. Waste Management, Inc.*, 743 F.2d 976, 981–84 (2d Cir. 1984); *International Distribution Centers*, 812 F.2d at 793; *Lektro-Vend Corp. v. Vendo Co.*, 660 F.2d 255, 270–71 (7th Cir. 1981), *cert. denied*, 455 U.S. 921 (1982).

131. *See Brook Group*, 113 S. Ct. at 2592 (citing *Matsushita Elec. Indus. Co. v. Zenith Radio Corp.*, 475 U.S. 574, 589 (1986)).

132. *Brook Group*, 113 S. Ct. at 2589, 2593, 2598.

133. *See* Gary A. Francesconi, *ERISA Preemption of "Any Willing Provider" Laws—An Essential Step Toward National Health Care Reform* 73 Wash. Univ. L.Q. 227 (1995).

134. It should be noted that numerous states have expressly exempted HMOs from the application of their AWP laws. Some statutes exempt all HMOs or all federally qualified HMOs, whereas others exempt HMOs that meet certain operational criteria or participate in particular state health programs. Other states, however, do not exempt HMOs, and some, such as Arkansas, expressly include HMOs.

135. Georgia regulators, for instance, interpret their code to require that all providers have an opportunity to apply to participate but not to require that the insurer sign an unlimited number of contracts and not to preclude the application of utilization standards in determining whether a contract will be offered. *See* GA. Code Ann. § 33-30-24 (Supp. 1989).

136. *See, e.g.*, Cal Ins. Code § 10180(b)(1) (Deering Supp. 1989) (an insurer may not exclude providers from a preferred network because of their category of license); Fla. Stat. Ann. § 627.4191 (1990) (interpreted as requiring contracts with dentists, optometrists, podiatrists, and chiropractors).

137. *See Ingersoll-Rand Co. v. McClendon*, 498 U.S. 133, 138–42 (1990); *Metropolitan Life Ins. Co. v. Massachusetts*, 471 U.S. 724, 739 (1985); *Shaw v. Delta Air Lines*, 463 U.S. 85, 96–97 (1983).

138. *Shaw*, 463 U.S. at 96–97 (footnote omitted).

139. *Id.* at 100 n.21. *See New York State Conference of Blue Cross & Blue Shield Plans v. Travelers Ins. Co.*, 115 S. Ct. 1671 (1995). In *New York State Conference*, the Court held that ERISA did not preempt a state surcharge on the hospital patients of commercial insurers where such surcharge resulted in an indirect economic influence on ERISA plans that was not substantial. This decision should not diminish the prospects of a challenge to an, AWP statute, however, to the extent that such statute has a direct impact upon employee benefit plans.

140. *Arkansas Blue Cross & Blue Shield v. St. Mary's Hospital Inc.*, 947 F.2d 1341, 1344–45 (8th Cir. 1991), *cert. denied*, 112 S. Ct. 2305 (1992).

141. *See* Robert S. McDonough, *ERISA Preemption of State Mandated Provider Laws*, 1985 Duke L.J. 1194 (1985).

142. *See Taylor v. Blue Cross & Blue Shield*, 684 F. Supp. 1352, 1360–63 (E.D. La. 1988).

143. 29 U.S.C. § 1144(b)(2)(A).

144. *See Pilot Life Ins. Co. v. Dedeaux*, 481 U.S. 41, 48 (1987).

145. *See Union Labor Life Ins. Co. v. Pireno*, 458 U.S. 119, 130–31 (1982).

146. *See Group Life & Health Ins. Co. v. Royal Drug*, 440 U.S. 205, 213–15 (1979).

147. *Stuart Circle Hospital Corp. v. Aetna Health Management*, 995 F.2d 500, 503 (4th Cir. 1993), *cert. denied*, 114 S. Ct. 579 (1993).

148. *Id.*

149. *Id.* The Fourth Circuit adopted the same reasoning and reached the same conclusion as did the Tenth Circuit in *Blue Cross & Blue Shield v. Bell*, 798 F.2d 1331, 1334–36 (10th Cir. 1986).

150. 440 U.S. at 216–17.

151. 883 F. Supp. 94 (M.D. La. 1995).

152. The statute provides, inter alia, that no licensed provider, other than a hospital, that agrees to the terms and conditions of a preferred provider contract can be denied the right to become a preferred provider. La. Rev. Stat. Ann. § 2202(5)(c) (West 1995). A PPO is defined as "a contractual agreement . . . between a provider . . . and a group purchaser . . . to provide for alternatives

rates of payment specified in advance for a defined period of time. . . ." *Id.* § 2202(5)(a). A group purchaser includes "[e]ntities which contract for the benefit of their insured, employees, or members such as insurers, self-funded organizations, Taft-Hartley trusts, or employers who establish or participate in self-funded trusts or programs." *Id.* § 2202(3).

153. The plaintiffs had raised an alternative claim that the AWP statute violated the Due Process Clause of the Fourteenth Amendment. *CIGNA*, 883 F. Supp. at 99–100. This claim was premised upon the alleged interference with their liberty interest in contracting with providers of their choice to establish an economically viable PPO. *Id.* Specifically, the plaintiffs argued that the statute, which would purportedly spread a limited number of patients over an unlimited number of providers, would increase costs for both managed care entities and patients, a direct contravention of the statute's purposes. The court concluded, however, without determining whether the plaintiffs had a protected liberty or property right, that the statute was rationally related to the state's legitimate and asserted purpose of ensuring patient access to quality care without restricting provider selection. *Id.*

154. *Id.* at 104. The court did note, however, the Fourth Circuit's determination in *Stuart Circle* that the Virginia statute was expressly limited to insurance industry entities. *Id.*

155. 5 U.S.C. § 8902(m)(1).

156. 819 F.2d 921, 926 (9th Cir. 1987), *cert. denied*, 484 U.S. 1060 (1988).

157. *See also Blue Cross & Blue Shield v. Department of Banking & Finance*, 791 F.2d 1501, 1505 (11th Cir. 1986) (FEHBA designed to preempt the application of state laws that specify types and providers of medical care); *Myers v. United States*, 767 F.2d 1072, 1074 (4th Cir. 1985) (a state law that purports to allow recovery of additional benefits that are not contemplated by a federal insurance contract is to be deemed inconsistent with FEHBA); *Barr v. Arkansas Blue Cross & Blue Shield, Inc.*, 761 S.W.2d 174, 176 (Ark. 1988) (asserting that Congress' intent and purpose in enacting ERISA are equally applicable to FEHBA, the court adopted the rationale set forth in *Hayes* giving the phrase *relates to* its broad, common sense meaning).

158. 854 F. Supp. 589 (D. Minn. 1993), *aff'd*, 26 F.3d 865 (8th Cir. 1994).

159. *Id.* at 593.

160. *Id.* at 594.

161. *Id.*

162. 995 F.2d 804 (8th Cir. 1993).

163. *Id.* at 806.

164. *Id.*

165. 42 U.S.C. § 300e-10(a)(1)(C).

166. *Selcke v. MedCare HMO*, 147 B.R. 895 (N.D. Ill. 1992), *aff'd sub nom. Matter of Estate of MedCare HMO*, 998 F.2d 436 (7th Cir. 1993); *Physicians Health Plan, Inc. v. Citizens Ins. Co. of Am.*, 673 F. Supp. 903 (W.D. Mich. 1987); *Health Care Plan, Inc. v. Schweiker*, 553 F. Supp. 440 (D.N.J. 1982), *aff'd*, 707 F.2d 1391 (3d Cir.), *cert. denied sub nom. Health Care Plan, Inc. v. Heckler*, 464 U.S. 815 (1983).

167. 42 U.S.C. § 300e-10(a)(1)(C).

168. The cases also note that an express conflict with the HMO Act is required to preempt a challenged state law.

169. *Schweiker*, 553 F. Supp. at 445.

170. *Id.* at 446.

171. It must be noted that, in the analogous situation of the private enforcement of the HMO employer mandate (42 U.S.C. § 300e-9(a)(1)(B)), the courts have not been sympathetic to HMOs' attempts at private actions. *See Travelers Health Network v. Orleans Parish School Bd.*, 842 F. Supp. 236 (E.D. La. 1994). Unlike the HMO employer mandate, however, it seems clear that the preemption section must have been designed to benefit HMOs.

172. *W.B. Worthen Co. v. Thomas*, 292 U.S. 426, 433 (1934).

173. 438 U.S. 234 (1978).

174. *Id.* at 246 (footnote omitted).

175. In reaching its conclusion, the Supreme Court cited *Home Building & Loan Assn. v. Blaisdell*, 290 U.S. 398 (1934), which set forth the following factors: whether a state legislature declared in the act itself that there is an emergency need for the protection of the kind provided in the statute, whether the state law is enacted to protect the basic societal interest rather than the interest of a favored group, whether the relief included in this statute is appropriately tailored to the emergency that it was designed to meet, whether the imposed conditions are reasonable, and whether the legislation is limited to the duration of the emergency.

176. *Id.* at 243.

177. *Id.*

178. *Burlington Northern R.R. Co. v. Nebraska*, 802 F.2d 994 (8th Cir. 1986).

179. 842 F. Supp. 1211 (D. Minn. 1994).

180. *Id.* at 1216. The legislation mandated that a workers' compensation fund distribute its surplus funds in a manner that would divest the group of close to $.5 billion. *Id.*

181. *Id.* at 1215.

182. *Id.*

183. *Id.*

184. 742 F.2d 442 (8th Cir. 1984), *cert. denied*, 469 U.S. 1215 (1985).

185. *Id.* at 451. *See also Whirlpool Corp. v. Ritter*, 929 F.2d 1318, 1322–23 (8th Cir. 1991) (holding that an Oklahoma statute that prohibited a decendent's former spouse from being the beneficiary of a life insurance policy, if the policy was formed before the divorce, effected a fundamental change in such contracts and was unconstitutional as to contracts entered into before the statute's effective date).

SUGGESTED READING

Managed Care Law Manual. 1995. Gaithersburg, Md.: Aspen Publishers.

Chapter 58

Medical Management and Legal Obligations to Members

James L. Touse

Managed care organizations (plans) are subject to a variety of legal and regulatory obligations related to the development and operation of their medical management programs. This chapter briefly discusses those obligations and plans' legal liability exposure if they fail to satisfy those obligations. The chapter also suggests what can be done to minimize that liability exposure while still accomplishing the organization's medical management objectives. The reader is referred to Chapter 38 for additional discussion of related issues.

The terms *medical management program* and *medical management activities* are used to refer to the types of activities that plans utilize to control the cost and quality of health care services provided to their members. Those activities can be broadly categorized as utilization management, quality assurance, and dispute resolution programs. Utilization management activities may include referral management programs; preadmission, concurrent, and retrospective review programs; utilization reporting and evaluation programs; case management programs; and

James L. Touse is the Vice President and General Counsel of Blue Cross Blue Shield of Tennessee (BCBSTN). Mr. Touse has previously served as legal counsel to other insurance companies, health maintenance organizations, and the Ohio Department of Insurance.

The views presented in this chapter are intended to stimulate consideration and discussion concerning an evolving area of the law and should not be interpreted to constitute legal advice or to describe standards applicable to BCBSTN or any other managed care organizations for the conduct of medical management activities.

provider incentive arrangements. Quality assurance activities may include provider selection, credentialing, or privileging programs; quality assurance and assessment programs; peer review activities; and the implementation of medical policies, protocols, and practice guidelines. Although member and provider grievance programs have not traditionally been considered medical management activities, they are discussed in this chapter because they may permit management to identify and resolve disputes related to other medical management activities before those disputes escalate into costly and time-consuming legal or regulatory actions against the plan.

The statutory and common (i.e., case) law related to plans' medical management obligations is evolving rapidly. If there is any generally accepted rule concerning what plans should do to avoid liability related to their medical management activities, it is that they must understand their obligations and act in a reasonable manner when making medical management determinations. If an organization acts reasonably, it should be able to avoid any catastrophic legal liability exposure while still conducting effective medical management activities.

OBLIGATIONS TO CONDUCT MEDICAL MANAGEMENT ACTIVITIES

Plans must implement and operate medical management programs pursuant to applicable laws, accreditation standards, and their agreements with customer groups. Failure to comply with those obligations may, at best, expose a plan to increased oversight or, at worst, result in the plan being ordered to cease doing business if its noncompliance jeopardizes its members' health.

It is clearly beyond the scope of this chapter to evaluate all the state and federal statutes, rules, and regulations (laws) that are applicable to plans' medical management activities. The term *plan* is used throughout this chapter, but there are many different types of managed care organizations. Those distinctions are most relevant when one is determining what laws are applicable to plans' medical management activities.

Health maintenance organizations (HMOs) are generally required to establish medical management programs pursuant to state HMO laws. As an example, the National Association of Insurance Commissioners Model HMO Act (see Chapters 53 and 55), which served as a model for most states' HMO statutes, requires HMOs to ensure "that the health care services provided to enrollees shall be rendered under reasonable standards of quality of care consistent with prevailing professionally recognized standards of medical practice."[1] HMOs are also required to establish grievance procedures to address and attempt to resolve member grievances, including grievances related to such organizations' medical management activities, as discussed in greater detail in Chapter 30.[2]

If an HMO is federally qualified (see Chapter 54), it will also have to comply with the requirements of the federal HMO statute. That statute requires federally qualified HMOs to have an ongoing quality assurance program that stresses health outcomes and provides for peer review of the services provided to members. It also requires qualified HMOs to have an effective procedure for collecting, evaluating, and then reporting information concerning the utilization of services to the Secretary of the Department of Health and Human Services (DHHS).[3]

Regulatory oversight of an HMO's medical management activities varies, depending on the jurisdiction where the HMO is licensed and whether it is federally qualified. The Model

HMO Act empowers the state regulatory agency to fine an HMO or to suspend or revoke its license if it fails to comply with its statutory obligations.[4] The Secretary of DHHS may also revoke the qualification of any HMO that fails to comply with the assurances given to DHHS concerning its medical management activities.[5]

The potential consequences of failing to comply with applicable statutory obligations are illustrated by actions taken against plans in Florida and California. In March 1995, the Florida Agency for Health Care Administration, which regulates that state's managed Medicaid plans, fined 21 plans a total of $520,000, in addition to restricting the growth of 19 plans and freezing the enrollment of 2 of those plans, for violating patient quality standards. The reported violations included failing to perform required medical screenings, not requiring providers to maintain acceptable medical records, and not checking the credentials of participating physicians.[6]

In 1994, the California Department of Corporations fined TakeCare Health Plan $500,000 based upon the failure of a contracting provider group, to which the plan had delegated utilization management responsibilities, to pay for the removal of a member's life-threatening tumor. The provider group denied coverage because neither the pediatric surgeon who performed that operation nor the hospital where it was performed were participating providers. The Department of Corporations determined that that was actionable because no participating provider had the expertise necessary to perform the required operation, so that the refusal to pay for those services denied the member access to covered services.[7]

There are generally fewer regulatory requirements applicable to the medical management activities of other types of managed care organizations. Only 29 states have enacted preferred provider organization (PPO) statutes. Such statutes require PPOs to have grievance procedures in 10 states, a quality assurance program in 12 states, and a utilization review program in 19 states.[8] Only 27 states regulate utilization review organizations, 8 regulate some utilization review activities, and 15 do not regulate such organizations or activities.[9] There is little uniformity among those statutes, but they frequently regulate such matters as hours of operation, staffing, review criteria, and reconsideration procedures of utilization review organizations operating in that state.

Most plans can comply fairly easily with such regulatory medical management obligations. It may be more difficult to comply with those requirements in the future, however. As an example, Florida has enacted a statute requiring HMOs to be accredited by an accreditation organization approved by the department, as a condition of doing business in the state.[10] Other states may follow Florida's lead by requiring plans to be accredited to provide external verification that they are monitoring the quality of services provided to their members.

There are a number of private accreditation organizations, but the most widely accepted HMO accreditation agency is the National Committee for Quality Assurance (NCQA; see Chapter 37). The NCQA accreditation process evaluates an applicant's compliance with specific quality management and improvement, utilization management, credentialing, member rights and responsibilities, preventive health service, and medical records standards.

An increasing number of customer groups are also contractually requiring that plans be accredited as a condition of being offered to the groups' employees. Those groups are requiring plans to be accredited because of their concern that they will be held liable for breaching their fiduciary duties pursuant to the Employee Retirement Income Security Act (ERISA) of 1974, as amended (see Chapter 59)[11], or for negligence if they fail to exercise reasonable care when selecting and supervising the activities of contracting plans.[12]

Other groups do not require accreditation but require contracting plans to satisfy specified medical management standards as a condition of being offered to the groups' members. As an example, the Federal Employees Health Benefit Program (FEHBP; see Chapter 45) requires contracting plans to develop and implement a quality assurance program that assesses the utilization of services, credentialing of providers, risk arrangements with providers, and member satisfaction with the plan. Article IV(B) of the Medicare HMO contract goes even further, requiring plans to contract with a peer review organization (PRO) to review the services provided to Medicare enrollees. That agreement permits the PRO to review inpatient and outpatient services provided by the plan, to determine whether they meet professionally recognized standards of care, and to evaluate any written complaints from beneficiaries concerning the quality of services provided by a contracting plan.

CONTRACTUAL ACTIONS RELATED TO MEDICAL MANAGEMENT ACTIVITIES

Most medical management issues have, to date, related to the denial of claims or authorization to provide services to members (referred to as adverse determinations) when such services allegedly should have been covered pursuant to a plan's certificate of coverage. Those cases have generally considered whether an adverse determination was reasonable based upon the terms of the certificate and factual circumstances of that case.

There have been significant developments related to plans' contractual obligations to their members during the past several years. During that period, the bad faith theory of liability has been accepted by certain state courts, most notably California.[13] That theory has, in turn, been preempted by ERISA in many cases.

ERISA provides that it preempts "any and all State laws insofar as they now or hereafter relate to any employee benefit plan."[14] The Supreme Court has stated that the preemption provision should be liberally construed as follows: "a law 'relates to' an employee benefit plan, in the normal sense of the phrase, if it has a connection with or reference to such a plan."[15] ERISA also includes what is referred to as the savings clause, however, which states that "nothing in this sub-chapter shall be construed to exempt or relieve any person from any law of any State which regulates insurance, banking, or securities."[16] The apparent conflict between the broad pre-emption of any law related to an ERISA plan and the savings clause was addressed in *Pilot Life Insurance Co. v. Dedeaux*.[17] In that case, the Supreme Court decided that ERISA preempted a bad faith judgment against an insurance company because Mississippi's bad faith law was not specifically directed at regulating the insurer's activities. *Pilot Life* held that ERISA only permits a plan participant or beneficiary "to recover benefits due to him under the terms of his plan, to enforce his rights under the terms of the plan, or to clarify his rights to future benefits under the terms of the plan."[18]

Although *Pilot Life* held that ERISA preempts bad faith actions, plans must not ignore their potential bad faith liability exposure when conducting medical management activities. ERISA is not applicable to government, church, or nongroup benefit plans.[19] FEHBP imposes limitations similar to those of ERISA, but actions by other government employees will probably not be preempted by ERISA.

The basis for a bad faith action is an allegation that a plan breached its implied duty of good faith and fair dealing when conducting medical management activities. The consequences of violating that implied duty can be catastrophic. In *Fox v. HealthNet*, a jury in Riverside, California, awarded the family of a school teacher, Nelene Fox, $89.3 million based upon the plan's failure to authorize coverage for a bone marrow transplant to treat her metastatic breast cancer.[20] That award included $212,000 plus interest to pay for the cost of the transplant, $12.1 million for breach of the duty of good faith and infliction of emotional distress, and the remainder as punitive damages.

Mrs. Fox was diagnosed with breast cancer in June 1991; the tumor had metastasized to her bone marrow by December. Her treating oncologist requested that HealthNet's contracting medical group approve a referral to the University of Southern California (USC) for further evaluation, which was denied by the medical group. Mrs. Fox was evaluated despite that decision, and USC agreed to perform the bone marrow transplant. HealthNet subsequently received a request to authorize the transplant on 5 June 1992, received requested medical records on 10 June, and denied the transplant as investigational on 12 June. The Foxes conducted extensive fundraising activities and paid for the transplant after the plan's denial of coverage. The transplant was performed at USC in late August, but Mrs. Fox's cancer did not go into remission. She died in April 1993.

At trial, the plaintiff's attorney, who was Mrs. Fox's brother, alleged that HealthNet had breached the covenant of good faith and fair dealing by refusing to cover the transplant procedure. His trial brief alleged that Mrs. Fox's certificate specifically provided coverage for bone marrow transplants under the following provision: "The member must satisfy the medical criteria developed by HealthNet Participating Medical Group and by the referral facility performing the transplant."[21] He maintained that Mrs. Fox had satisfied those conditions because her treating oncologist had recommended the bone marrow transplant and referred her to USC, which agreed to perform that procedure. The oncologist allegedly changed his mind about the need for the transplant only after a discussion with the plan's associate medical director, during which "financial issues" were discussed. The brief further argued that the experimental and investigative procedure exclusion of the certificate was ambiguous, as evidenced by the fact that the plan subsequently expanded that exclusion from one sentence to an entire page; the plan's independent technology assessment in 1990 concluded that the procedure had gained widespread acceptance; and the plan had paid for bone marrow transplants for two other members in similar circumstances. Finally, the brief alleged that the bonus of the medical director, who made the decision to deny coverage, was based on the plan's medical loss ratio, providing an incentive to deny the transplant.

The lesson of the *Fox* case is that a plan must consider how a jury will view its conduct when it decides to deny coverage for a procedure recommended by a participating provider. In that case, the plaintiff was able to persuade the jury that the plan had acted in bad faith by its interpretation of the coverage and exclusion provisions of the certificate (as evidenced by the revision of the exclusion language), its efforts to get the oncologist to change his mind (as evidenced by the discussion of financial issues after he had written letters supporting the transplant), differentiating in the treatment of members with similar conditions, and paying a reported $5.5 million in bonuses to key executives of the plan at the same time that it was denying coverage for Mrs. Fox's transplant.

It must be emphasized that the most critical issue in the *Fox* case was the ambiguity of the certificate concerning whether transplants were covered services. Other cases have upheld denials of coverage in similar circumstances when the plan specifically excluded autologous bone marrow transplants for breast cancer or excluded coverage for transplants that were not specifically listed as being covered or when the certificate referenced the Medicare coverage manual to determine whether a procedure was experimental.[22–24]

Even if a plan has a clear exclusion in its certificate, the *Warne v. Lincoln National Administrative Services Corp.* case illustrates the importance of making certain that the plan's promotional materials are consistent with the terms of that certificate.[25] In that case, a jury awarded the plaintiffs, who were also covered by a school district plan, $26.8 million for the plan's failure to cover Mr. Warne's liver transplant, which was clearly excluded by Mr. Warne's certificate. Unfortunately, the plan's benefit brochure stated that the cost of organ transplants was a covered benefit. The jury found that the denial of coverage in such circumstances constituted bad faith and awarded the plaintiffs $320,000 for breach of contract, $1.5 million for pain and suffering, and $25 million in punitive damages.

The decision in another bad faith case, *Hughes v. Blue Cross of Northern California,* provides a good example of what a plan should not do when making a medical management decision.[26] In that case, the California Court of Appeals upheld an award of $150,000 in compensatory damages and $700,000 in punitive damages against Blue Cross based upon its denial of claims totaling $17,000 for psychiatric inpatient services. The Court stated:

> . . . there was evidence that the denial of respondent's claim was not simply the unfortunate result of poor judgment but the product of the fragmentary medical records, a cursory review of the records, the consultant's disclaimer of any obligation to investigate, the use of a standard of medical necessity at variance with community standards, and the uninformative follow-up letters sent to the treating physician. The jury could reasonably infer that these practices, particularly the reliance on a restrictive standard of medical necessity and the unhelpful letter to the treating physician, were all rooted in established company practice. The evidence hence was sufficient to support a finding that *the review process operated in conscious disregard of the insured's rights* (emphasis added).[27]

In short, the plan acted in bad faith because it did not conduct a reasonable evaluation, give the treating physician the opportunity to provide additional information, or, most important, balance the member's interests in having services covered against the plan's interests in containing costs when making medical management decisions. Other bad faith cases have held plans liable for failing to contact the member's attending physician concerning the member's condition before denying coverage on the basis of a preexisting condition, failing to obtain pertinent sections of a patient's medical record and not requiring medical review of a claim before determining that services were not medically necessary, or failing to inform members of their right to appeal an adverse determination.[28–30]

The *Hughes* case also illustrates the scope of ERISA, however, because it was subsequently overturned by the Supreme Court of California, which concluded that California's bad faith common law was preempted by ERISA based on the *Pilot Life* decision.[31] ERISA has, therefore, significantly lowered the stakes in contract actions against plans if members are covered by an ERISA plan. Those members cannot recover damages for breach of contract, pain and suffering, emotional distress, or punitive damages, in contrast to the plaintiffs in *Hughes*, *Fox*, and *Warne* cases.

ERISA may limit the damages that may be awarded, but it does not relieve a plan of its responsibility to act in a reasonable manner when making medical management determinations. Plan administrators are prohibited from acting in an arbitrary and capricious manner when making such determinations.

A number of cases have addressed the question of what constitutes arbitrary and capricious behavior. If the plan has been granted discretionary authority to make benefit determinations by the ERISA plan sponsor, the courts generally defer to the administrator's determination unless it is clearly unreasonable. In *Jett v. Blue Cross and Blue Shield of Alabama*, the court stated "the function of the court is to determine whether there was a reasonable basis for the decision based on the facts known to the administrator at the time that the decision was made."[32]

A subsequent decision by the Eleventh Circuit Court in *Brown v. Blue Cross and Blue Shield of Alabama* indicated that a plan does not have unlimited discretion when making such determinations.[33] In that case, the court noted that the plan had an inherent conflict of interest because it offered insured coverage to the plaintiff's employer, so that any benefits were paid from the plan's funds. The court stated "When a plan beneficiary demonstrates a substantial conflict of interest . . . the burden shifts to the fiduciary to prove that its interpretation of plan provisions committed to its discretion was not tainted by self-interest. That is, a wrong but apparently reasonable interpretation is arbitrary and capricious if it advances the conflicting interest of the fiduciary at the expense of the affected beneficiary."[34]

Those cases demonstrate that the arbitrary and capricious standard requires a plan to act in a reasonable manner when making medical management determinations. The following has been held to be arbitrary and capricious conduct: relying on undisclosed medical criteria that are more restrictive than the policies utilized by other insurers, basing an adverse determination on an ambiguous provision of the member's benefit agreement, and failing to comply with the notification and reconsideration procedures mandated by ERISA when that precludes the member from requesting reconsideration of an adverse determination.[35–37]

The fact that a plan will not be subject to a bad faith action does not mean that it can afford to be cavalier when making adverse determinations. If a plan acts in an arbitrary and capricious manner, ERISA permits courts to require the plan to pay the member's attorney's fees and legal costs, which can be a significant penalty. As an example, in *Egert v. Connecticut General Life Insurance Co.*, the insurer utilized inconsistent and undisclosed medical coverage policies to deny coverage for Ms. Egert's infertility treatments.[38] The court ordered the insurer to pay for treatments that had already been rendered and to cover Ms. Egert's future infertility treatments. It also awarded her $160,000 in legal fees and costs to "deter plan administrators from developing unreasonable interpretations of ERISA plans as a means of wrongly denying coverage to plan participants."[39]

NEGLIGENCE ACTIONS RELATED TO MEDICAL MANAGEMENT ACTIVITIES

The actions discussed in the preceding section alleged that a plan breached its contractual obligations to members. There have also been an increasing number of actions alleging that plans have acted in a negligent manner when performing medical management activities. Other cases have also sought to hold plans liable for the negligence of their participating providers. Those lawsuits seek to recover damages for a member's injuries, which may amount to millions of dollars in certain cases. In negligence actions, juries may award damages for lost wages, pain and suffering, medical expenses, and any other losses directly caused by that negligent conduct. Such damages may also include punitive damages if the plan acts in a wanton, willful, or intentional manner.

Negligent conduct is defined as "conduct which falls below the standard established by law for the protection of others against unreasonable risk of harm."[40] In other words, plans are required to exercise the level of care that would be exercised by a reasonably prudent managed care organization in similar circumstances to avoid causing foreseeable injuries to their members.

Like so many other medical management issues, there have been relatively few cases specifically addressing the duty of care that plans must exercise when conducting medical management activities. One of the most significant unanswered questions is whether such negligence actions are preempted by ERISA, if the member is covered by an ERISA plan.

Negligent Medical Management Activities

The courts have consistently held that actions alleging that plans have acted negligently when conducting utilization management activities are preempted by ERISA because those decisions relate to the benefit plan. As an example, in *Tolton v. American Brodyne*, the family of a man who committed suicide after being denied authorization for inpatient psychiatric care brought a wrongful death action against the plan.[41] The court decided that the claim was preempted because it related to the administration of an ERISA plan.

The Supreme Court has refused to review lower court decisions holding that ERISA preempts negligence actions against plans for failing to authorize the hospitalization of a mother during a high-risk pregnancy, allegedly resulting in the death of her unborn child, in *Corcoran v. United Healthcare, Inc.* and for failing to authorize heart surgery for a member in *Kuhl v. Lincoln National Health Plan of Kansas City.*[42,43] That does not mean that plans should not exercise reasonable care when making medical management decisions. They may be required to pay for services that should have been covered, plus the legal fees and costs incurred by a member in recovering those benefits, if its decision is determined to be arbitrary and capricious pursuant to ERISA. Plans may also be sued for negligence by members who are not covered by ERISA plans.

Wickline v. State of California was the first widely reported case that suggested that a plan might be held liable for the negligent design of its utilization review program.[44] The court stated, in dicta (a statement of opinion that did not support the ultimate decision in that case), that the failure to offer a physician the right to appeal a nonauthorization decision might be negligent. The court decided, however, that the failure to offer such an appeal procedure did not cause Ms. Wickline's injuries, despite the refusal to authorize continued hospitalization, because her attending physician had discharged her without any effort to appeal that decision. The court concluded that the attending physician was solely responsible for the consequences of his decision to discharge Ms. Wickline, consistent with the generally accepted rule that an attending physician is ultimately responsible for making treatment decisions concerning the care of his or her patients.[45]

In *Wilson v. Blue Cross of Southern California*, however, the court stated that Blue Cross might be held liable for negligence even though the attending physician had not appealed the denial of authorization to continue Mr. Wilson's hospitalization.[46] The court noted that the plan only had an informal reconsideration process and concluded that it would not have reversed its initial decision even if the attending physician had attempted to appeal that decision. It returned the case to the trial court, which decided that Blue Cross' failure to authorize continued hospitalization did not directly contribute to Mr. Wilson's death.

Despite the trial court's decision, the *Wilson* case has been interpreted to erode the traditional distinction between a physician's obligation to make treatment decisions and a plan's obligation to make benefit determinations. In the future, courts may decide that plans have a duty to exercise reasonable care, even if the attending physician does not appeal an adverse determination, if it is reasonably foreseeable that a denial of authorization will preclude members from receiving necessary covered services.

In another negligent design case, *Bush v. Dake*, the court indicated that a plan might also be liable for negligence if it implements an incentive compensation arrangement that encourages participating providers to withhold necessary treatment from members.[47] That case conflicts with the decision in *Pulvers v. Kaiser Foundation Health Plan*, however, which held that "the use of such incentive plans is not only recommended by professional organizations . . . but that they are specifically required by Section 1301 of the Health Maintenance Act."[48]

Plans clearly must be concerned about their potential liability if their failure to exercise reasonable care when designing their medical management programs or making utilization decisions contributes to a reasonably foreseeable injury to a member. Plans can avoid such liability, however, if they demonstrate that they have exercised reasonable care when making medical management decisions, implemented formal appeal procedures to permit physicians to challenge adverse decisions, and established effective quality management programs to ensure that providers are not withholding necessary services from members.

Negligence Related to the Selection and Supervision of Participating Providers

There have been a number of cases in which hospitals have been held to be liable for failing to exercise reasonable care when selecting or supervising their staff physicians. The landmark case holding hospitals liable in such circumstances is *Darling v. Charleston Community Memorial Hospital*.[49] In that case, the court concluded that the hospital had an independent duty to oversee the care provided to patients in accordance with applicable licensing regulations, accreditation standards, and the hospital's own bylaws. The court rejected the hospital's argument that it should not be held liable for a physician's negligence, noting "the state licensing regulations and the defendant's bylaws demonstrate the medical profession and other responsible authorities regard it as both desirable and feasible that a hospital assume certain responsibilities for the care of the patient."[50]

Similar issues can be raised concerning a plan's obligation to exercise reasonable care in selecting and supervising its participating providers. The most widely reported case addressing a plan's potential liability for such negligence is *Harrell v. Total Health Care*.[51] In that case, the member's negligence action against the HMO was dismissed based on a unique Missouri statute that immunizes nonprofit HMOs against liability in such circumstances. The Missouri Court of Appeals stated, however, that the HMO might have been held liable, absent such immunity, because it failed to exercise reasonable care when credentialing the participating specialist who caused Ms. Harrell's injuries. The court noted that the HMO had solicited applications from specialists by mail and had limited its evaluation of such applications to determining whether the applicant was licensed, could dispense narcotics, and had hospital admitting privileges. It had not conducted personal interviews, checked references, or otherwise investigated the applicant's credentials before accepting that physician as a participant. The court concluded that the failure to conduct a reasonable investigation created a foreseeable risk of harm to members who were required to utilize that specialist.

Again, there is a question of whether ERISA preempts a negligent credentialing action against a plan. In *Altieri v. Cigna Dental Health, Inc.*, the court dismissed a member's claim that the plan was negligent when evaluating a participating dentist's competence during its credentialing process. The court concluded that such claims have a substantial enough effect on a benefit plan to trigger preemption because "plaintiff's negligence, misrepresentation . . . and breach of contract claims have one central feature: the circumstances of [the plaintiff's] medical treatment under his employer's [dental] services plan."[52]

The *Harrell* and *Darling* decisions raise the possibility that a plan might be held liable for negligence if it fails to exercise reasonable care when selecting and supervising its participating providers, if such actions are not preempted by ERISA. The plan should be able to avoid such liability, however, if it fully investigates an applicant's credentials, submits applications for peer review before accepting a physician as a participating provider, and conducts quality management programs in accordance with generally accepted managed care medical management policies and procedures.

Liability for the Negligence of Participating Providers

Although the courts have held that actions against plans based upon their alleged negligence when administering benefits plans are preempted by ERISA, they are split as to whether ERISA preempts a negligence claim against a plan based upon the alleged malpractice of its participating providers. In fact, the trend appears to hold that such actions are not preempted by ERISA.

An employer may be held liable for the conduct of its employees based on the theory referred to as respondeat superior. The basis of

that theory is that the employer is able to control its employees' conduct and should, therefore, be held responsible if they injure someone when acting within the scope of their duties. Another legal theory, referred to as the ostensible agent theory, permits a plan also to be held liable for negligence of an independent contractor if a member reasonably believes that the contractor is acting as a representative of the plan. Such actions are referred to as vicarious liability actions because, unlike cases seeking to hold a plan liable for its own negligence, vicarious liability actions seek to hold the plan liable solely because of its relationship with the negligent provider.

In *Dukes v. Healthcare, Inc.*, the plaintiffs claimed that the plan should be held vicariously liable for the negligence of its contracting providers, who allegedly failed to order blood tests that would have prevented Mr. Duke's death.[53] The court held that the malpractice action should not be removed to the federal courts because it was not a claim for benefits or to clarify the member's right to benefits under an ERISA plan. The court returned the case to the state court to determine whether the plan should be held vicariously liable for the malpractice of its contracting providers. The Supreme Court refused to reconsider an appeal of that decision.

Another federal circuit court has gone even further, in *Pacificare of Oklahoma, Inc. v Burrage,* holding that a vicarious liability claim against a plan based upon the alleged malpractice of its contracting primary care physician was not preempted by ERISA.[54] The court reasoned that the claim did not involve the administration of the benefit plan and was, therefore, "too tenuous, remote or peripheral . . . to warrant a funding that the law 'relates to' the plan."

In *Nealy v. U.S. Healthcare,* however, the plaintiffs alleged that the plan should be held liable for the failure of a contracting primary care physician to refer Mr. Nealy to a cardiologist before his death due to a heart attack.[55] The court concluded that the negligence action was preempted by ERISA. It reasoned that the ERISA plan created the relationship between the plan and Mr. Nealy and that the malpractice action related to the administration of the plan because the plaintiffs claimed that the plan failed to provide timely and adequate treatment to Mr. Nealy. In response to an allegation that the plaintiffs would be left without an adequate remedy, the court noted that the preemption of the action against the plan did not affect the plaintiff's state law malpractice action against the involved providers.

Even if such vicarious liability actions are not preempted by ERISA, the generally accepted common law rule holds that plans should not be held vicariously liable for the negligence of an independent contractor.[56] In *Williams v. Good Health Plus, Inc.,* the court not only refused to hold the plan liable for the actions of its contracting provider but also emphasized that an HMO could not practice medicine pursuant to the Texas Medical Practice Act.[57] It stated that the plan could not, therefore, be held liable for negligence related to the provision of medical services to members.

Other courts are beginning to challenge that rule, however, particularly when members are required to be treated by a designated participating provider. As an example, in *Schleier v. Kaiser Foundation Health Plan*, the court held Kaiser liable for the malpractice of a contracting cardiologist.[58] It based that decision on the facts that the plan restricted members' access to a limited number of physicians, paid those physicians to provide services that it was obligated to provide to members pursuant to its certificate, and had some right to control the physicians' behavior. The court concluded that those were all attributes of an employer–employee relationship, so that the plan could be held vicariously liable for the contracting specialist's negligence.

In *Boyd v. Albert Einstein Medical Center*, the court reversed a summary judgment against the plaintiffs because it concluded that there was a question of fact concerning whether the contracting provider was acting as the plan's ostensible agent when he negligently treated Ms. Boyd.[59] The court noted that the plan advertised that its participating providers were competent,

required members to utilize network physicians, required primary care physicians to refer members to participating specialists, made capitation payments to primary care physicians, and exercised some control over the physicians' conduct pursuant to the terms of its participation agreement. On that basis, the court concluded that Ms. Boyd could reasonably have believed that her primary care physician was acting as an agent of the plan when he instructed her to have diagnostic tests performed at his office instead of at the hospital emergency department. Ms. Boyd died of a heart attack after leaving the emergency department, so the court concluded that the trial court might find that the physician was acting as the plan's ostensible agent when he failed to authorize the diagnostic tests that would have disclosed Ms. Boyd's heart condition.

Those cases illustrate the danger that courts will increasingly hold plans vicariously liable for the conduct of contracting providers in the future. That liability exposure may increase as plans implement medical management programs that include practice guidelines, financial incentives to practice cost effectively, and limitations on which providers can treat members. The possibility that plans may be held vicariously liable for the negligence of contracting providers may be one of the most significant medical management liability issues confronting plans in the future. The very actions that they take to control the cost and improve the quality of services provided to members may lead to the conclusion that they either control such providers' conduct or are permitting them to act as representatives of the plan.

RECOMMENDATIONS

It is recommended that plans take the following actions to comply with their medical management obligations and to minimize their liability exposure related to their medical management activities:

- Monitor significant court decisions and proposed legislation through trade publications, seminars, and discussions with legal counsel to understand how those developments may affect the plan's medical management obligations.

- Periodically update the plan's certificates to ensure that they clearly express the intended contractual obligations to members. As examples, plans should incorporate specific definitions (e.g., of medical necessity, emergency services, experimental or investigational procedures, and custodial care) and specifically explain any exclusions or limitations (e.g., of dental, cosmetic, rehabilitation, mental health, and other services) to avoid any ambiguity concerning what services are covered by their certificates.

- Ensure that marketing brochures accurately describe the benefits, exclusions, and limitations of the certificate to avoid conflicts between those documents.

- Make a reasonable effort to ensure that any medical management issues are thoroughly investigated before the organization makes an adverse benefit determination. As an example, it may be advisable to develop a checklist of the type of information that should be obtained to document that the plan has fully and fairly evaluated the circumstances of each case before an adverse determination is made. That checklist might ask reviewers to review applicable provisions of a member's certificate, to review relevant medical policies, to contact the member's attending physician(s), to obtain pertinent medical information, to refer issues requiring specialized knowledge or training to a qualified specialist, and generally to follow established policies or procedures before making an adverse determination.

- Ensure that the plan's medical policies are consistent with generally accepted standards of medical practice. As an example, it may be advisable to submit proposed policies and review criteria to a panel of physicians to ensure that they are not overly restrictive or at variance with community standards. After those policies have been approved, they should be distributed to participating providers. Distributing those policies to providers should limit the plan's liability exposure. The plan will not need to make adverse determinations assuming participating providers do not order services that they know will not be covered by the plan.

- Implement a provider appeal procedure similar to that used to resolve member grievances. That procedure should permit providers to request a hearing before an impartial and appropriately qualified physician hearing officer to present and explain their arguments concerning a disputed medical management determination. That procedure should also provide for an expedited review if the attending physician reasonably believes that an adverse determination may preclude a member from receiving urgently needed services. The ability to identify and resolve disputes quickly, or at least to demonstrate that the plan fully and fairly considered relevant information before making an adverse determination, should significantly reduce the plan's liability exposure, particularly in bad faith or negligence actions.

- Obtain current technology assessments concerning the status of new, experimental, or investigational procedures. Such assessments should help demonstrate that the plan acted in good faith and exercised reasonable care when making decisions concerning the coverage of those procedures.

- State that the plan has discretionary authority to make eligibility and coverage determinations in its agreements with contracting groups. Reserving such discretionary authority should encourage the courts to defer to the plan's determinations in ERISA cases.

- Comply with ERISA's notice and reconsideration requirements. Failure to provide the specific information required by ERISA might be deemed to be arbitrary and capricious, bad faith, or negligent conduct if it deprives members of their right to request reconsideration of an adverse determination.

- Bonuses payable to plan employees who are responsible for making medical management decisions should not be based primarily upon the plan's utilization experience.

- Provider bonuses should consider performance measures, such as member satisfaction, compliance with applicable administrative standards, and satisfying quality of care requirements, in addition to the provider's utilization experience. That will limit any incentive to deny necessary care to members. The plan should also ensure that members have the right to appeal any provider's decision to deny or limit access to covered services directly to the plan.

- Refer questions concerning the interpretation of members' certificates to the plan's legal counsel. Acting upon the advice of counsel may establish that the determination was reasonable and made in good faith. It may also provide protection against the disclosure of privileged attorney–client or attorney work product information if the plan is sued based on its determination.

- If the plan makes exceptions to the exclusions or limitations of the certificate, those extracontractual benefits should be described in a separate written agreement with the member. That agreement should explain the reason for that exception, state that it is not intended to create a precedent in future cases, and prohibit the member from disclosing any information about that agreement, including its existence, to third parties.

- Clearly explain the independent contractor relationship between the organization and its participating providers in certificates, brochures, and provider participation agreements. Such provisions should emphasize that providers are solely responsible for all treatment decisions and also explain how providers or members can appeal adverse determinations.

- Implement quality assurance programs to evaluate members' access to services, any apparent underutilization of services, and patient complaints to prove that the plan has exercised reasonable care in reviewing the quality of services provided to members.

- Adopt credentialing criteria, including verification of an applicants' professional references, malpractice history, insurance coverages, hospital privileges, and licensure. Incomplete applications, unsolicited applications, or applications indicating that a provider does not meet the plan's participation requirements (e.g., no staff privileges at a participating hospital) should not be accepted for further review. If applicants satisfy the plan's screening criteria, their application should be submitted to a peer review committee for evaluation of their professional reputation, qualifications, and experience.

- Thoroughly investigate any questions concerning a participating provider's conduct or competence. The plan should terminate the participation of any providers who are unable or unwilling to comply with the organization's medical management requirements. The plan's sanction procedure should also permit immediate termination if a provider's incompetence, misconduct, or reputation creates a risk of harm to the organization or its members (see Chapter 26).

- Do not delegate medical management responsibilities to another entity (e.g., an independent practice association) unless that entity's medical management programs are comparable with the plan's programs. The plan should retain the right to audit that entity's activities to ensure that it exercises reasonable care when performing delegated management activities. The provider entity should also be required to refer all complaints to the plan so that it can promptly address any problems related to that entity's performance of its delegated duties.

- Consider purchasing professional liability coverage, if it is available at reasonable cost, to protect against the possibility that the plan will be held vicariously liable for providers' negligence. As an alternative, the plan may require providers to indemnify (i.e., hold it harmless) if the plan is held vicariously liable for the provider's negligence by either including an indemnification provision in provider contracts or enforcing the plan's common law right to indemnification in such circumstances.

CONCLUSION

Plans have a variety of regulatory, contractual, and duty of care obligations related to the organization and operation of their medical management programs. Although the laws concerning plans' liability for failing to satisfy those obligations are rapidly changing and evolving, the fundamental issue in all the cases discussed in this chapter has been whether an organization acted reasonably when conducting its medical management activities.

The ability to make benefit determinations to control the cost of providing covered services to members is one of the fundamental purposes of a medical management program. A plan will not be competitive if it is unable to deny claims for services that are specifically excluded by its certificate or for services that are not medically necessary or appropriately authorized by participating providers. Plans should not permit their potential liability exposure to deter them from making appropriate benefit determinations, provided that they can prove that such determina-

tions are reasonable and give the member's interest in obtaining covered services equal weight to the plan's interest in containing costs. If a plan conducts medical management activities in such a fair, reasonable, and well-documented manner, it should be able to achieve its essential medical management objectives without having to be overly concerned about the regulatory or legal liability consequences of those activities.

REFERENCES AND NOTES

1. Section 7 of the Model HMO Act.
2. Section 11 of the Model HMO Act.
3. 42 U.S.C. 300e(c)(6) and (8).
4. Section 25 of the Model HMO Act.
5. 42 U.S.C. 300e-11.
6. "Florida fines a dozen HMOs . . .," *State Health Watch*, April, 1995, p. 3.
7. "California Fines TakeCare $500,000 . . .," *BNA's Health Law Reporter*, December 1, 1994, p. 1709.
8. "GHAA Survey: Utilization Review Laws and Proposals," October 1991.
9. "AMCRA Releases Model State Law for Regulation of UR Activities," *BNA's Health Law Reporter*, May 11, 1995, pp. 726–727.
10. Fl. Code Section 641 12.
11. 29 U.S.C. 1001 *et seq.*
12. Scogland, "Fiduciary Duty: What Does It Mean?" 24 *Tort & Ins L J* 803 (1989).
13. See Kornblum, "Bad Faith and Punitive Damages Litigation in the US," 23 *Tort & Ins L J* 812 (1989).
14. 29 U.S.C. 1144(a).
15. 463 U.S. 95, 96-7, 103 S. Ct. 2890 (1983).
16. 29 U.S.C. 1144(b)(2)(A).
17. 481 U.S. 41, 107 S. Ct. 1549 (1987).
18. 29 U.S.C. 1132(a)(1)(b).
19. 29 U.S.C. 1003(b).
20. 21692 (Sup. Ct. Riverside Co., Ca.) (1994).
21. "Trial Brief," *Fox v. HealthNet*, Superior Court of the State of California, Case No. 219692, November 1, 1993, p. 8, FN. 2.
22. *Roger v. Espy*, 836 F. Supp. 869 (N.D. Ga. 1993).
23. *Caudill v. Blue Cross and Blue Shield of N.C.*, 999 F.2d 74 (4th Cir. 1993).
24. *Beechtold v. Physicians Health Plan of Northern Indiana, Inc.*, 19 F.3d (7th Cir. 1994).

25. Idaho D. Ct. July 20, 1994. Reported in *Health Law Perspectives*, November 30, 1994, p. 1.

26. 245 Cal. Rptr. 273 (1988).

27. *Hughes v. Blue Cross of California*, 255 Cal. Rptr. at 858–9 (1989).

28. *Linthiacum v. Nationwide Life Insurance Company*, 723 P.2d 675 (Az.) (1986).

29. *Aetna Life Insurance Company v. Lavio*, 505 So. 2d 1050 (Al. 1986).

30. *Sarchett v. Blue Cross of California*, 43 Cal. 3d 1 (1987).

31. *Hughes* at 813.

32. 890 F.2d 1137, 1139 (11th Cir.) (1989).

33. 898 F.2d 1556 (11th Cir.) (1990).

34. *Brown* at pp. 1566–67.

35. *Bucci v. Blue Cross and Blue Shield of Connecticut, Inc.*, 764 F. Supp. 728 (D. Ct.) (1991).

36. *Kunin v. Benefit Trust Life Insurance Company*, 910 F.2d 534 (9th Cir.), *cert. denied*, 111 S. Ct. 581 (1991).

37. *DePina v. General Dynamics Corp.*, 674 F. Supp. 46 (E.D. Mass.) (1987).

38. 768 F. Supp. 216 (N.D. 111) (1991).

39. *Egert*, at p. 218.

40. Restatement (Second) of Torts, Section 282.

41. 25 F.3d 937 (6th Cir. 1995).

42. 965 F.2d 1321 (5th Cir.), *cert. denied*, 113 S.Ct. 812 (1992).

43. 999 F.2d 298 (8th Cir. 1993), *cert. denied*, 114 S.Ct. 694 (1994).

44. 183 Cal. App. 3d 1064, 228 Cal. Rptr. 661 (1986).

45. See Boyd, "Cost Containment and the Physician's Fiduciary Duty to the Patient," 39 *DePaul L Rev.*

46. 271 Cal. Rptr. 876, 222 Cal. App. 3d 660 (1990).

47. No. 86-25767-NM (Mich. Cir. Ct., Saginaw City, April 27, 1989).

48. 99 Cal. App. 3d 560, 565 (1980).

49. 211 N.E. 2d 253 (1965), *cert. denied*, 383 U.S. 946 (1966).

50. *Darling*, at p. 257.

51. 1989 W.L. 153066 (Mo. Ct. App.) (1989), *aff'd on other grounds*, 782 S.W.2d 58 (Mo. 1989).

52. 753 F. Supp. 61, 64 (D. Comm. 1990), citing *Rollo v. Maxicare of Louisiana, Inc.*, 695 F. Supp. 245, 248 (E.D. La.) (1988).

53. 57 F.3d 350 (3rd Cir. 1995) U.S. Sup. Ct., No. 95-442, *review denied* 12/4/95.

54. 59 F.3d 151 (10th Cir. 1995).

55. 844 F. Supp. 966 (S.D.N.Y. 1994).

56. 478 N.Y.S. 2d 911 (App. Div. 1984).

57. 743 S.W. 2d 373 (Tex. App. 1987).

58. 876 F.2d 174 (1989).

59. 547 A.2d 1229 (Pa. Super, 1988).

SUGGESTED READING

BNA's Health Law Reporter. Washington, D.C.: The Bureau of National Affairs.

Hastings, D.A., Krasner, W.L., Michaels, J.L., and Rosenberg, N.D. 1990. *The Insider's Guide to Managed Care: A Legal and Operational Roadmap*. Washington, D.C.: National Health Lawyer's Association.

Health Law Digest. Washington, D.C.: National Health Lawyers' Association.

Government Affairs Bulletin. Washington, D.C.:AAHP.

In the States. Washington, D.C.: AAHP.

Managed Care Law Manual. 1995. Gaithersburg, Md.: Aspen Publishers.

Managed Care Law Outlook. Alexandria, Va.: Capitol Publications, Inc.

Chapter 59

ERISA and Managed Care

Jacqueline M. Saue and Gregg H. Dooge

Few federal laws have a greater impact on the operations of managed care organizations (MCOs) than the Employee Retirement Income Security Act (ERISA) of 1974, as amended.[1] Although ERISA does not directly regulate MCOs, it does regulate most employer-sponsored employee benefit plans to which MCOs market their products. ERISA will affect the nature, design, and administration of such products by MCOs. Moreover, ERISA will determine what state laws can be applied to such products as well as what legal challenges can be made to the administration of such products.

This chapter is designed to provide MCOs with a working knowledge of the provisions of ERISA that are likely to affect their operations. Topics addressed include ERISA's documentation, reporting, and disclosure requirements;

benefit plan design considerations; the amendment of benefit plans; the duties of ERISA fiduciaries, which may include MCOs; challenges to benefit denials; ERISA's civil enforcement scheme and remedies; and the effect of ERISA preemption of state laws and causes of actions on MCOs' operations.

DOCUMENTATION, REPORTING, AND DISCLOSURE REQUIREMENTS

A plan maintained by a nongovernment employer that provides health care or health care benefits to employees (including plans providing coverage or benefits through a managed care arrangement) generally constitutes an employee benefit plan subject to ERISA.[2] Such plans must meet the documentation, reporting, and disclosure requirements set forth in ERISA.

Plan Document

Every employee benefit plan governed by ERISA is required to be set forth in a written plan document (or documents) that detail the operative provisions governing benefits under the plan.[3] In the case of health care benefits that are provided through an insurance contract or a contract with an MCO, the sponsoring employer might maintain a simple plan document that describes certain of the plan's rules, such as a description of the plan's eligibility and amendment provisions, but that otherwise refers to the insurance or managed care contract for the description of plan benefits.

Jacqueline M. Saue is a partner with the firm of Foley & Lardner in Washington, D.C., having received her law degree from Georgetown University Law Center in 1975 and her bachelor's degree magna cum laude from Mount Holyoke College in 1972. She is a member of the District of Columbia Bar and the State Bar Association of Maryland. Ms. Saue concentrates her practice in the area of health law and has written and spoken frequently on health law issues, including managed care, ERISA, and health antitrust.

Gregg H. Dooge is a partner in the Milwaukee, Wisconsin office of Foley & Lardner, practicing in the area of employee benefits. He is a 1981 graduate of the University of Wisconsin-Madison and a 1984 graduate of Stanford University Law School. In addition to his private practice, he is an Adjunct Professor at Marquette University School of Law, and is a member of Wisconsin Retirement Plan Professionals, Ltd. and the Greater Milwaukee Employee Benefits Council.

Summary Plan Description

A summary plan description is a booklet that describes the operative provisions of a plan in lay language. The Department of Labor has prescribed the types of information that are required to be included in the summary plan description.[4] For insured or managed care plans, employers often use the booklet published by the insurance company or MCO as the basis for the summary plan description, although the employer generally will have to add certain administrative information to comply with the Department of Labor requirements concerning summary plan descriptions. In some cases, a health care plan contains detailed benefit schedules that are difficult to summarize. In lieu of repeating the benefit schedules, the summary plan description may provide a general description of the types of benefits provided if the summary informs participants that the complete schedules are available for their review.[5]

The summary plan description must be distributed to participants within 120 days after the date on which the plan is adopted or made effective (or, in the case of an employee who becomes a participant after the adoption or effective date of the plan, within 90 days after the date on which the employee becomes a participant).[6] In general, a new summary plan description must be issued every 5 years, although if there have been no amendments to the plan, distribution of a new summary plan description can be made every 10 years.[7]

Summary of Material Modifications

If there are changes in the plan that affect the information provided in the summary plan description at a time when the plan sponsor is not required to publish a new summary plan description, the employer must publish a summary of material modifications.[8] The summary of material modifications explains the plan changes and acts as a supplement to the summary plan description until a revised summary plan description is distributed. The summary of material modifications must be distributed to plan participants within 210 days after the close of the plan year in which the plan amendment is adopted.[9] Alternatively, the plan sponsor may at any time publish an updated summary plan description in lieu of the summary of material modifications.

Discrepancies in Plan Documentation

Although the summary plan description and summary of material modifications are intended, as their names suggest, as summaries of the actual plan document, some courts have held that the summaries override the terms of the plan where the plan and the summaries conflict.[10] Thus, where the summary plan description provides for benefits in a situation not covered under the formal plan document, the summary plan description might govern, particularly if the participant or beneficiary is able to demonstrate reliance on the faulty summary plan description.

Government Reporting Requirements

The plan administrator of an ERISA welfare benefit plan (including plans that provide benefits pursuant to a managed care contract) must file a variety of documents with either the Department of Labor or the Internal Revenue Service. Each year, the plan administrator must file an annual return unless the plan is exempt from filing.[11] Generally, an annual return (filed on Form 5500) is required for plans that have more than 100 participants as of the first day of the plan year. Plans with fewer than 100 participants as of the first day of the plan year generally are exempt from filing if benefits are provided through insurance contracts, the premiums for which are paid from the plan sponsor's general corporate assets, directly by the plan sponsor out of general corporate assets, or a combination of the two.[12] A plan in which benefits or insurance premiums are payable through a trust does not qualify for the exception, and an annual return is required to be filed even though the plan might have fewer than 100 participants.[13]

Some health plans are operated in conjunction with a "flexible spending arrangement" or "cafeteria plan" under Section 125 of the Internal Revenue Code. A simple example would be a health plan in which the employer requires its employees to pay a portion of the premium. The employer then establishes a plan under Section 125 that enables a plan participant to make so-called salary reduction contributions; that is, the participant reduces his or her salary in exchange for the employer's payment of the employee premium contribution. Even if the arrangement covers fewer than 100 participants, an annual report is required with respect to the Section 125 arrangement.[14]

The annual return is due on or before the last day of the seventh month after the close of the plan year, although certain extensions are possible.[15] The return is filed with the Internal Revenue Service and is provided by the Service to the Department of Labor. The annual return is not distributed to plan participants as a general matter, although a plan participant must be allowed to review and make copies of the annual return.[16]

PLAN DESIGN CONSIDERATIONS

Substantive Regulation under ERISA

ERISA provides little regulation of the content of employee welfare benefit plans (a category that includes health benefit plans). In stark contrast to the regulation of pension plans, where ERISA provides detailed requirements, the only areas in which ERISA substantively regulates the terms and conditions of employer-sponsored health benefit plans are as follows:

- An employer-sponsored health plan is required to comply with the terms of a qualified medical child support order. A qualified medical child support order is a court order or court-approved property settlement agreement that is entered pursuant to state domestic relations law or certain state Medicaid laws and that provides for health insurance coverage for a child of an employee.[17]

- A group health plan, if it otherwise provides coverage for dependent natural children, is required to provide identical coverage for children who are placed for adoption with the covered employee.[18]

- A group health plan may not reduce its coverage of pediatric vaccines below the level of coverage that it provided as of 1 May, 1993.[19]

- A plan of an employer with 20 or more employees is required to provide employees and their covered dependents whose coverage under the plan would otherwise cease as a result of termination of employment or certain other "qualifying events" the opportunity to purchase continued coverage under the plan for a limited period of time.[20]

Despite the limited regulation of the content of employee welfare benefit plans, ERISA's impact is considerable.

ERISA Preemption of State Insurance Laws Affecting Plan Design

Generally

As is explained in more detail in the section of this chapter devoted to ERISA preemption, ERISA broadly preempts all state law (and state law causes of action) that relate to ERISA plans.[21] Although limited exceptions exist for state laws that regulate insurance, banking, or securities as well as for certain generally applicable laws, ERISA's preemptive scope provides plan sponsors with great flexibility with respect to the design of their benefit programs, because ERISA generally will preempt state law attempts to regulate the terms and conditions of ERISA plans.

Distinction between Insured and Self-Insured Plans

The exception for state laws that regulate the "business of insurance" creates an interesting distinction between health benefit plans that purchase insurance and those for which the plan sponsor self-insures (or self-funds) the benefits. So-called mandated benefits laws—that is, state laws that mandate that health insurance contracts subject to the state's jurisdiction provide coverage or benefits for certain conditions or illnesses—constitute laws that regulate the business of insurance, and are saved from preemption.[22] A self-insured (or self-funded) plan does not purchase insurance, however, and a provision of ERISA known as the "deemer clause" prevents a state from directly applying its insurance regulation to the employee benefit plan.[23] The result is a significant distinction between insured and self-insured plans. Although a state may not directly regulate an employee benefit plan, the state may indirectly regulate the content of an insured plan by regulating the terms and conditions of the insurance contract that the plan purchases. A state may not, however, directly or indirectly regulate the terms and conditions of a self-insured plan.

When Is a Plan Self-Insured?

Historically, most managed care programs were insured arrangements, although today a growing number of plan sponsors have adopted self-insured arrangements that incorporate a preferred provider organization (PPO), point-of-service product, or other feature generally associated within the rubric of managed care. Because of the significance of the distinction between insured and self-insured plans, courts and state regulators have been called upon to determine whether certain plans are insured or self-insured.

This issue typically arises when the plan claims to be self-insured, but the plan or the plan sponsor then purchases stop-loss or excess loss insurance to protect the plan or plan sponsor from large losses. Stop-loss or excess loss insurance provides reimbursement to the plan or plan sponsor in the event that benefits paid by the plan to or on behalf of a plan participant or all plan participants as a group exceed thresholds established in the insurance policy. Stop-loss coverage is written with either or both a specific

or individual attachment point and an aggregate attachment point. Above the specific or individual attachment point, the plan or plan sponsor is entitled to reimbursement for claims paid during the policy year with respect to a single plan participant. Above the aggregate attachment point, the plan or the plan sponsor is entitled to reimbursement for claims paid during the policy year with respect to all plan participants.

Plans that purchase stop-loss or excess loss insurance coverage generally have been considered self-insured for the purposes of the preemption rules described above, so that a state is not allowed to regulate the plan indirectly through application of its mandated benefit or other health insurance laws to the terms and conditions of the insurance contract.[24] Rather, the stop-loss or excess loss contract typically is viewed as property and casualty insurance that is subject to the state's rules and regulations for such insurance. This characterization is subject to two caveats. First, the plan participant should have no rights to claim benefits directly against the stop-loss or excess loss insurer. Stop-loss or excess loss insurance is intended to provide reimbursement to the plan or the plan sponsor for losses incurred beyond certain thresholds. If the plan participant has a direct claim against the insurer, however, the stop-loss or excess loss contract arguably constitutes a direct health insurance contract that the state could regulate as such.

Second, the thresholds at which the insurance company reimburses the plan or the plan sponsor should be sufficient so that the plan or the plan sponsor bears substantial risk for the provision of benefits under the plan (other than the risk of the insurance carrier's bankruptcy). A number of courts have suggested that, if the thresholds are set so low that they constitute a disguised deductible, the insurance contract, even though treated by the parties as providing stop-loss or excess loss coverage, might be treated as direct health insurance.[25] Similarly, several states have promulgated regulations to the effect that stop-loss or excess loss policies with threshold points below certain amounts would be regulated as direct health insurance contracts, allowing the state to assert the applicability of its mandated benefit laws to the contract.[26] More recently in 1995, the National Association of Insurance Commissioners adopted a Stop-Loss Insurance Model Act, under which a self-insured plan would be treated as having purchased health insurance, which would be subject to all state insurance mandates, if the specific attachment point is less than $20,000. Similar rules would apply with respect to the aggregate attachment point. For groups of 50 or more, the plan will be treated as fully insured if the aggregate attachment point is less than 110 percent of expected claims. For groups of 50 or less, the aggregate attachment point must be at least equal to the greater of $4,000 times the number of employees, 120 percent of expected claims, or $20,000.[27]

Limits on ERISA Preemption

ERISA's preemptive reach is extremely broad, although not all encompassing. For example, a New York law that imposed surcharges on hospital bills was not preempted by ERISA.[28] Although the surcharges undoubtedly had an impact on a self-insured plan by increasing the cost of the benefits provided by the plan, the New York surcharge system did not relate to ERISA plans and therefore was not preempted. Although this type of indirect impact law may survive preemption, a state law that attempts to regulate the benefits provided by the plan will be preempted unless saved, in the case of an insured plan, as a law regulating the business of insurance. Thus plan sponsors have significant flexibility with respect to the design of health benefit plans.

Other Federal Laws Affecting Plan Design

Although ERISA grants plan sponsors considerable flexibility with respect to the design of their health care plans, other federal laws may restrict a plan sponsor's discretion to some extent. For example, a plan may not discriminate on the basis of age or other protected classifica-

tion.[29] Moreover, a plan may not discriminate on the basis of disability in a manner than violates the Americans with Disabilities Act (ADA).[30]

The ADA contains several rules that, apparently, were designed to protect employee benefit plans. For example, the ADA does not prohibit an insurer, health maintenance organization (HMO), hospital, or medical service company from underwriting risks, classifying risks, or administering risks in a manner that is not based on or not inconsistent with state law.[31] Similarly, the ADA does not prohibit a person or organization from establishing, sponsoring, observing, or administering the terms of a bona fide benefit plan that is not subject to state laws that regulate insurance (i.e., a self-insured plan).[32] In all cases, however, the protection provided under these provisions of the ADA is not available if the practice or plan provision is used as a subterfuge to evade the purposes of the ADA.[33]

The degree to which the ADA regulates employer-sponsored health plans is as yet uncertain. The Equal Employment Opportunity Commission has indicated that the ADA does not prohibit broad limitations on the nature and scope of services covered under the plan, such as a general exclusion on preexisting conditions or a separate annual or lifetime maximum on the amount of benefits payable for nervous and mental disorders.[34] These broad limitations affect plan participants generally whether or not the plan participant is disabled within the meaning of the ADA. Where a plan excludes or provides limited coverage for a specific disabling condition or illness (such as human immunodeficiency virus infection), however, the provision violates the ADA.[35]

Although the case law on this subject is only beginning to appear, early indications are that courts will overturn provisions in employer-sponsored group health plans that discriminate on the basis of disability. For example, in *Henderson v. Bodine Aluminum, Inc.*, the U.S. Court of Appeals for the Eighth Circuit issued an injunction preventing the defendant company from denying coverage for expenses incurred by a cancer patient in connection with high-dose chemotherapy treatments.[36] The health plan in question excluded coverage of high-dose chemotherapy for certain types of cancer, an exclusion that the Eighth Circuit Court concluded might violate the ADA. The decision is potentially important because ERISA itself has provided little opportunity for participants to challenge plan provisions that exclude coverage for particular illnesses or treatment programs.

AMENDMENT OF PLANS

Generally

ERISA requires that every employee benefit plan provide a procedure for amending the plan and for identifying the persons who have authority to amend the plan.[37] Generally, a plan sponsor reserves to itself the power and authority to amend (or even terminate) a plan. The employer's reserved amendment authority and the process by which the employer exercises that authority have been the subject of considerable debate.

Benefit Reductions

Many employers provide health plan coverage to former employees who retired after attaining a certain age and after completing a minimum period of service specified in the plan (e.g., age 55 and 10 years of service). Traditionally, the employer had few retirees relative to active employees, and health care costs were reasonable. As health care costs escalated, however, and as the employer's population shifted to include a greater number of retirees relative to active employees, employers began to modify (and in some cases terminate) the coverage provided to retirees.

Predictably, retirees whose coverage was modified or eliminated challenged many of the benefit cut-backs. Although early cases were far from uniform—some favoring the employer, some applying a rebuttable presumption in favor of the retiree—more recent cases, although still not entirely uniform, have become more homogenous in their approach. In particular, the cases have rejected a per se rule and have instead viewed the issue as a question of plan interpretation. Where the employer (plan sponsor) has reserved to itself the authority to amend, modify, or terminate the plan, the employer's exercise of that right has been upheld.[38] Where the employer has not reserved to itself the authority to amend, modify, or terminate the plan, however, or if the plan language is ambiguous, the courts will seek to ascertain the parties' intent when creating the plan (i.e., did the employer or, in the case of a collectively bargained arrangement, the parties to the contract intend to create vested benefit rights that cannot thereafter be modified by the employer?).[39] The starting point, however, is the plan language concerning the employer's right to amend the plan.

A developing theme in the case law is that, even where the plan documents reserve to the employer the right to amend, modify, or terminate the plan, the employer might be estopped from implementing the change as a result of prior assurances provided to plan participants. For example, in *Sprague v. General Motors Corp.*, the court determined that General Motors had agreed to provide lifetime benefits as part of an early retirement program, a commitment that in the court's opinion overrode the employer's rights under the plan document.[40] Similarly, in a recent case involving Unisys Corporation retirees, the U.S. Court of Appeals for the Third Circuit permitted a retiree challenge to proceed based on a breach of fiduciary duty theory despite the fact that the plan document had at all times reserved to the employer the right to amend, modify, or terminate benefits.[41] The retirees alleged that plan fiduciaries had violated their fiduciary duties by consistently misrepresenting to plan participants over a period of years that retiree benefits were lifetime benefits.

Amendment Procedure

Even where a plan document reserves to the employer the right to amend the plan, employees and retirees have challenged the process by which amendments have been adopted. In *Schoonejongen v. Curtiss-Wright Corp.*, the employer terminated a retiree health insurance program.[42] The plan reserved to the employer the right to amend or terminate the plan but did not specify the process by which amendments could be adopted or the persons or person with the authority to amend the plan. The U.S. Court of Appeals for the Third Circuit held that the plan amendment procedure, and thus the amendment terminating the plan, was invalid under ERISA.

The Third Circuit position was short-lived. The U.S. Supreme Court reversed, holding that the plan amendment procedure was valid even though it did not specifically identify the person or persons with the authority to amend the plan.[43] Also, the U.S. Court of Appeals for the Seventh Circuit refused to set aside an amendment terminating a retiree welfare plan even though the plan did not contain an adequate amendment procedure under ERISA.[44] It would thus appear that the courts will not easily set aside plan changes communicated by the employer to plan participants. Nevertheless, a plan sponsor would be well advised to avoid the issue altogether by specifying the amendment procedure in the plan document and, having done so, to follow that procedure.

FIDUCIARY DUTIES

ERISA imposes special duties on plan fiduciaries. ERISA's definition of *fiduciary* is functional, that is, a person, regardless of formal title or position, is a fiduciary to the extent that he or she exercises discretionary authority and control over the operation or administration of the plan, exercises any control over plan assets, or renders investment advice for a fee.[45]

ERISA prescribes the minimum standard of conduct applicable to fiduciaries, the so-called fiduciary duties. A fiduciary with respect to a plan must discharge his or her obligations with respect to a plan solely in the interests of the plan participants and beneficiaries and for the exclusive purpose of providing benefits to plan participants and their beneficiaries and defraying reasonable expenses of administering the plan.[46] Furthermore, the fiduciary must act in accordance with the plan documents (except to the extent that the documents are themselves inconsistent with ERISA) and with the care, skill, and diligence that a prudent person familiar with such matters would use in a similar enterprise.[47] Finally, if the plan is funded, plan investment must be diversified to minimize the risk of large losses.[48]

Often, a plan fiduciary is also an officer of the sponsoring employer, raising the question of when such a person is wearing his or her "fiduciary hat," and thus is required to act in the sole interest of plan participants and their beneficiaries, and when the fiduciary is wearing his or her "corporate hat," and thus is able to act in the best interests of the plan sponsor. Although the distinction is not always clear, the authority to amend or even terminate the plan is a "settlor function," that is, an employer is not acting in a fiduciary capacity when deciding to amend or terminate a plan.[49] Thus an employer might prospectively amend its group health plan to eliminate certain coverages (assuming that such elimination does not violate the ADA), and this action, although detrimental to plan participants, does not implicate the fiduciary's obligations under ERISA. Similarly, the decision to terminate a plan is a "settlor" or business decision of the plan sponsor. Although certain aspects of the termination process might constitute fiduciary functions, the decision to terminate does not.

In addition to ERISA's general fiduciary responsibility rules, ERISA also prohibits a plan fiduciary from engaging in a number of transactions known as prohibited transactions.[50] There are two sets of prohibited transactions. The first set prohibits a plan fiduciary from causing a plan in engage in certain transactions (such as sale or lease of property or extension of credit) between a plan and a party in interest. A party in interest includes a fiduciary with respect to the plan, persons who perform services for a plan, and other persons or entities related to such fiduciaries or service providers.[51] Unless advance approval is obtained from the Department of Labor, this type of related party transaction is prohibited without regard to the economic benefits of the transaction to the plan.

A second branch of the prohibited transaction rules proscribes a fiduciary from acting in certain conflict of interest situations or from receiving compensation from a third party in connection with a transaction involving the assets of the plan. For example, a fiduciary with respect to the plan may not cause the plan to retain the fiduciary (or a related party) to perform additional services for a fee. Where a fiduciary uses the authority, discretion, and control that makes him or her a fiduciary to cause the plan to pay an additional fee to the fiduciary, the fiduciary has engaged in a prohibited act of self-dealing.[52]

CHALLENGES TO BENEFIT DENIALS

Claims Procedure

Every employee benefit plan under ERISA is required to establish a procedure whereby a plan participant or beneficiary may challenge a denial of his or her claim for benefits.[53] A claims procedure will be deemed reasonable if a plan participant's or beneficiary's claim is answered in writing, with explanation of the reasons for the decision and references to pertinent plan provisions, within 90 days. If the claim is denied and the plan participant or beneficiary wishes to purse the matter further, an appeal may be filed with the appropriate fiduciary designated by the plan. The appeal must be answered in writing, again with explanation of the reasons for the decision and references to pertinent plan provisions, within 60 days after the date on which the appeal is filed. In certain cases, the 90 day- and 60-day periods can be extended if the plan participant or beneficiary is notified of the need for additional time before expiration of the initial period.[54]

Standard of Review in Court Action

If the plan participant is not satisfied with the disposition of his or her claim at the plan level,

he or she can file suit in state or federal court. An important threshold question involves the standard of review that the court will apply in reviewing the plan administrator's denial of the plan participant's claim.

In *Firestone Tire & Rubber Co. v. Bruch*, the U.S. Supreme Court determined that, in accordance with established principles of trust law, a plan participant's or beneficiary's challenge to a denial of benefits is to be reviewed under a de novo standard—that is, the court independently reviews and weighs the evidence and makes its decision accordingly, with deference to the decision made by the plan administrator—unless the plan document grants to the plan administrator or other appropriate fiduciary the discretionary authority and control to determine eligibility for benefits or to construe the terms of the plan.[55] Where the plan grants the administrator such discretionary authority and control, the court is to review the benefit denial under the more deferential arbitrary and capricious standard of review. Under this standard, the court reviews the evidence but overturns the plan administrator's decision only if it represents a clearly unreasonable interpretation or construction of the plan.

The Supreme Court's decision, although based upon principles of trust law, is a puzzlement to many. Although the general rule is de novo review, the Supreme Court's decision creates an exception that potentially eliminates the general rule. By including appropriate language in the plan document, a plan sponsor changes the standard of review that a court will apply in the event that a plan participant challenges a benefit denial. More generally, why should a plan sponsor be allowed to select the standard of review through its decision to include or not include certain language in the plan document?

In the years after the Supreme Court's *Bruch* decision, the lower federal courts have struggled with the implications of the decision. In a number of decisions, courts have applied the de novo standard even though the document contained evidence that the plan administrator (or other fiduciary) was intended to have considerable authority and control with respect to the plan. For example, in *Michael Reese Hospital & Medical Center v. Solo Cup Employee Health Benefit Plan*, even though the plan document gave the administrator the authority to control and manage the operation and administration of the plan, it was held that the plan demonstrated insufficient intent to grant to the administrator discretionary authority to determine eligibility or to construe the terms of the plan.[56] Similarly, in *Nelson v. EG&G Energy Measurements Group*, the plan document granted to the administrator the authority to "control and manage the operation and administration of the plan" and to promulgate rules and regulations as deemed necessary and proper to interpret or administrator the plan," yet the court applied the de novo standard.[57] Although it is not necessary that the plan document contain "magic words" to demonstrate an appropriate grant of discretion, the arbitrary and capricious standard will apply only if there is evidence to show that the administrator has the power to construe uncertain terms or that eligibility and benefit determinations are to be given deference.[58]

In other cases, particularly those involving self-funded arrangements for which benefits are payable from the plan sponsor's general corporate assets, courts have focused on the conflict of interest under which a plan fiduciary may operate because a denial of benefits is directly beneficial to the plan sponsor's treasury.[59] If a plan fiduciary with the discretion to construe plan terms and make eligibility and benefit determinations also has a conflict of interest, courts will apply a less deferential standard of review than the arbitrary and capricious standard that would normally be applicable.[60]

Right to Jury Trial

Most courts have held that ERISA does not provide a right to a jury trial, reasoning that benefit claims under ERISA are equitable in nature.[61] The decisions are not uniform, however, and a minority of courts have found a right to jury trial.[62]

ERISA'S CIVIL ENFORCEMENT SCHEME AND REMEDIES

In addition to suits for benefits brought by a plan participant or beneficiary, ERISA authorizes a plan participant, beneficiary, fiduciary, or the secretary of the Department of Labor to bring a variety of civil actions. Among the more important suits are those that involve the right of a plan participant, beneficiary, fiduciary, or the secretary to bring an action for breach of fiduciary duty under Section 502(a)(2) of ERISA.[63] Also, a plan participant, beneficiary, or fiduciary may bring an action under Section 502(a)(3) of ERISA to enjoin any act or practice that violates (or to enforce the provisions of) Title I of ERISA or the terms of the plan or to obtain other appropriate equitable relief.[64]

Although ERISA authorizes a variety of civil actions, the remedies that are available to a successful plaintiff have been quite limited. An action for breach of fiduciary duty under Section 502(a)(2) of ERISA is an action brought on behalf of the plan and all recovery runs in favor of the plan. Accordingly, the U.S. Supreme Court in *Massachusetts Mutual Life Insurance Co. v. Russell*, held that a plan participant or beneficiary could not recover extracontractual or punitive damages.[65] Later, the Supreme Court in *Mertens v. Hewitt Associates* held that Section 502(a)(3) authorizes only traditional forms of equitable relief, not monetary damages.[66]

The Supreme Court's restrictive interpretation of Sections 502(a)(2) and 502(a)(3) takes on added significance in light of ERISA's preemption of state laws and state law causes of action that relate to ERISA-governed employee benefit plans. Because of ERISA's preemptive reach, plaintiffs may not forego ERISA's civil enforcement scheme in favor of state law remedies, which might, if not preempted, include punitive or extracontractual damages.[67]

After the Supreme Court's holding in *Russell* and *Mertens*, the lower federal courts have struggled to attempt to provide meaningful remedies to plan participants and beneficiaries in actions brought under Section 502(a)(3) of

ERISA. For example, in *Watkins v. Westinghouse Hanford Co.*, the U.S. Court of Appeals for the Ninth Circuit ruled that a plan participant could not recover under Section 502(a)(3) benefits allegedly due the plan participant as a result of a misrepresentation.[68] In other cases, such as *Howe v. Varity Corp.*, successful plaintiffs have recovered what are, in effect, monetary damages by framing the action for benefits as a claim for restitution, an equitable remedy.[69] As a result, recovery under Section 502(a)(3) remains an open issue.

ERISA PREEMPTION

Arguably, no provision of ERISA has more of an effect on the operations of MCOs than ERISA's preemption clause. This section explains the general principles of preemption and discusses the impact of preemption on the following activities of MCOs: utilization review determinations; the establishment of provider networks; the provision of health care services, either directly or by contract; representations of eligibility and coverage to health care providers; and the provision of administrative and other noninsurance services to ERISA plans.

General Principles of Preemption

When Congress enacted ERISA, it intended to make the regulation of employee benefit plans an exclusively federal concern. Congress, however, also did not want to divest the states of their traditional power to regulate insurance. Pursuant to this scheme, Congress enacted three clauses relating to the preemptive effect of ERISA:

1. *The preemption clause*—This clause provides that ERISA supersedes any and all state laws insofar as they may relate to any employee benefit plan subject to ERISA, except to the extent that such laws may be "saved" from preemption by the savings clause.[70]

2. *The savings clause*—This clause preserves from preemption any law of any state that regulates insurance, banking, or securities except as provided in the deemer clause.[71]

3. *The deemer clause*—This clause provides that an employee benefit plan shall not be deemed to be an insurance company or other insurer, bank, trust company, or investment company or to be engaged in the business of insurance or banking for the purposes of any law of any state purporting to regulate insurance companies, insurance contracts, banks, trust companies, or investment companies.[72]

The Preemption Clause

As noted above, Section 514(a) of ERISA preempts "any and all State laws insofar as they may now or hereafter relate to any employee benefit plan." A law relates to an employee benefit plan if it has "a connection with or reference to such a plan."[73] The preemption clause is "conspicuous for its breadth," however, preempting not only state laws that are specifically designed to affect employee benefit plans but also those that may only indirectly affect such plans.[74,75] Those state laws that courts have found not to be preempted under Section 514(a) are generally limited to laws of general applicability that only tangentially affect ERISA plans.[76]

The Savings Clause

A state law that relates to an ERISA plan may be saved from preemption if it falls within Section 514(b)(2)(A), which excepts from preemption those state laws that regulate the "business of insurance." In *Pilot Life Insurance Co. v. Dedeaux*, the U.S. Supreme Court used a two-part analysis to determine whether a state law regulates the business of insurance.[77,78] First, the Supreme Court took a common sense approach, determining that, in order to regulate insurance, a law must be specifically directed toward the insurance industry. Second, the Supreme Court applied the three-part test for determining whether a practice constituted the business of insurance formulated for the McCarran-Ferguson Act, namely, whether the practice had the effect of transferring or spreading a policyholder's risk, whether the practice was an integral part of the policy relationship between the insured and the insurer, and whether the practice was limited to entities within the insurance industry.[79] Since *Pilot Life*, courts have recognized the necessity of a state law meeting both parts of the test to fall within the protection of the savings clause.[80]

The Deemer Clause

The deemer clause exempts from any direct or indirect state regulation self-funded employee benefit plans.[81] All power to regulate insurance reserved to the states under the savings clause is taken away with respect to self-insured plans under the deemer clause. The language of the deemer clause, according to the U.S. Supreme Court, is either coextensive with or broader, not narrower, than that of the savings clause.[82] Thus state laws that relate to employee benefit plans but that are saved from preemption under Section 514(b)(2)(A) are still preempted as applied to self-funded ERISA plans. Although, as discussed above in regard to the benefit design of ERISA plans, this interpretation establishes a disparity between the regulation of insured and uninsured plans, the U.S. Supreme Court has determined that such a dichotomy was the intent of Congress when it enacted the statute.[83]

Utilization Review Decisions

The consensus among courts seems to be that utilization review decisions by MCOs, even when they involve medical decisions, are an integral part of the administration of ERISA plans. Consequently, they relate to such plans and are preempted by ERISA.

The U.S. Court of Appeals for the Sixth Circuit recently had occasion to reaffirm this conclusion. In *Tolton v. American Biodyne, Inc.*, the coadministrators of the estate of a mental patient who had committed suicide sued, among others, the patient's ERISA plan administrator, the plan's mental health utilization review company, and the psychologists performing utilization review on behalf of the utilization review company, alleging that the plan administrator wrongfully denied benefits for inpatient psychiatric care based upon the utilization review company's refusal to authorize such care.[84] Plaintiffs' state law claims based on such utilization review decision included wrongful death, improper refusal to authorize benefits, medical malpractice, and insurance bad faith. The court held that such claims clearly related to the ERISA plan and were preempted by ERISA.

In reaching its decision, the *Tolton* court relied on an earlier opinion of the U.S. Court of Appeals for the Fifth Circuit, *Corcoran v. United Healthcare, Inc.*[85] In *Corcoran*, the utilization review decision at issue was the refusal by the defendant utilization review company to precertify hospitalization for a high-risk pregnancy despite the recommendation of the patient's physician. Instead, the defendant authorized 10 hours per day of home nursing care. The patient, who had already been admitted to the hospital, returned home when she learned that the expenses for her hospitalization would not be covered. At a time when no nurse was on duty, her fetus went into distress and died. The patient and her husband then sued the defendant, alleging wrongful death and medical malpractice.

The Fifth Circuit Court acknowledged that utilization reviewers make medical decisions despite any disclaimers to the contrary in policy manuals or promotional materials. The court found, however, that the medical decisions made by the defendant were inseparable from its determinations regarding what benefits were available under the plan. The court found that the wrongful death claim related to a denial of benefits under the plan and so was preempted by ERISA. Other courts have followed the reasoning of the *Corcoran* case and have preempted claims arising out of utilization review decisions.[86]

Credentialing Decisions

Like the analogous duty imposed on hospitals to exercise reasonable care in the selection and granting of privileges to its medical staff, an MCO has a duty to conduct a reasonable investigation of the qualifications and competence of the health care providers to whom they refer patients.[87,88] Courts have declined to describe what will constitute a reasonable investigation of a provider's credentials, stating that its scope will vary from case to case.[89] Recent cases have focused not on the nature or extent of the investigation of a provider's qualifications, but on whether a claim that an MCO did not conduct the requisite investigation is preempted by ERISA. Most courts that have considered the issue have ruled in favor of ERISA preemption.

A representative case is *Kearney v. U.S. Healthcare, Inc.*[90] In *Kearney*, plaintiff filed wrongful death and survival claims against an HMO, alleging that decedent's primary care physician failed to diagnose properly decedent's condition or to refer decedent to a hospital for specialized treatment. Plaintiff claimed that the HMO breached its contract to provide needed specialized care by limiting or discouraging the use of specialists, hospitalization, and state-of-the-art diagnostic procedures; misrepresented the primary care physician's competence; and was negligent in selecting and supervising the primary care physician. Plaintiff also claimed that the HMO was vicariously liable for the malpractice of the primary care physician. The court held that a "claim that an operator or administrator of a plan failed to use due care in selecting those with whom it contracted to perform services relates to the manner in which benefits are administered or provided and is preempted."[91] The court dismissed not only plaintiff's claims of negligent selection but also the claim for misrepresentation and breach of contract. As discussed further below, however, the court held that plaintiff's claim that the HMO was vicariously liable for the malpractice of the primary care physician on ostensible agency grounds was not preempted.

Although the list of courts in agreement with the preemption of negligent selection claims is impressive, there is some authority to the contrary.[92] For example, in *Jackson v. Roseman*, plaintiff brought a medical malpractice case against his physicians and the HMO with which they contracted.[93] Plaintiff alleged that the HMO was vicariously liable for the negligence of his physicians in allowing the growth and ultimate metastasis of a malignant cancer in his mouth. The court noted that the complaint could also be read as asserting a claim of direct negligence on the part of the HMO for negligent hiring and supervision of its contracting physicians.[94] Although the court declined to address the merits of whether a negligent hiring and/or supervision claim went to the heart of the benefit plan's administration, the court indicated that it agreed with the reasoning of the U.S. Court of Appeals for the Second Circuit in a case involving claims of negligent hiring and/or supervision of a psychologist.[95] In that case, the Second Circuit rejected defendant's argument that claims of negligent hiring and supervision of health care providers so resembled a denial of benefits or a denial of some other plan-created right as to support the removal of such claims from state court to federal court.[96]

Despite the cases to the contrary, an MCO can take some comfort from the likelihood that a court will find that claims that an MCO has negligently selected or retained a participating provider who committed malpractice are preempted. The same court, however, may not preempt a claim against the MCO based on vicarious liability for the malpractice of a provider, as discussed below.

Vicarious Liability for Medical Malpractice

Of the various tort theories used to impose liability on MCOs for the medical malpractice of health care providers to whom they refer patients, none has generated more recent litigation than that of apparent or ostensible agency. Although the elements of apparent or ostensible agency vary from jurisdiction to jurisdiction, a common allegation is that the patient reasonably relied upon actions or representations of the MCO, which "held out" the negligent provider as its employee or agent, the degree of reliance required of the patient being subject to judicial debate.[97]

As in the area of negligent credentialing, ERISA plays a crucial role in determining whether an MCO will be vicariously liable for the malpractice of health care providers. The courts have been sharply divided as to whether ERISA preempts such claims, however.

Courts holding that medical malpractice claims against MCOs are not preempted have found that such claims do not sufficiently relate to the employee plan to warrant preemption.[98] Such courts point out that such claims do not involve the administration of benefits or the level or quality of benefits provided under plan; they merely allege negligence by a physician and an agency relationship between the physician and the MCO. Courts reaching the opposite conclusion have reasoned that a vicarious liability malpractice claim concerns the delivery of benefits under the ERISA plan and that the claim requires the examination of the terms of the ERISA plan to determine the quality and quantity of services required of physicians and the relationship between the ERISA plan and the physicians.[99]

Although the lower courts have been almost evenly split as to whether ERISA preempts medical malpractice claims against MCOs based on vicarious liability theories, two recent Circuit Court decisions indicate that the trend may be against preemption. The U.S. Court of Appeals for the Tenth Circuit in the case of *Pacificare of Oklahoma, Inc. v. Burrage* identified four categories of laws that related to an employee benefit plan: laws that regulated the type of benefits or terms of ERISA plans; laws that created reporting, disclosure, funding, or vesting requirements for ERISA plans; laws that provided rules for the calculation of the amount of benefits to be paid under ERISA plans; and laws and common law rules that provided remedies for misconduct growing out of the administration of ERISA plans.[100] The Tenth Circuit held that a claim that an HMO was vicariously liable for the malpractice of one of its primary care physicians did not involve the administration of benefits or the level or quality of benefits promised by the plan; it merely alleged negligent care by the physician and an agency relationship between the physician and the HMO. The court pointed out that ERISA would not preempt the malpractice claim against the physician and concluded that ERISA should similarly not preempt the vicarious liability claim against the HMO if the HMO held the physician out as its agent. Reference to the ERISA plan to resolve the agency issue did not "implicate the concerns of ERISA preemption."[101]

In *Dukes v. U.S. Healthcare, Inc.*, the U.S. Court of Appeals for the Third Circuit addressed the issue of whether vicarious liability malpractice claims against the defendant HMO could be removed from the state court to federal court.[102] The lower federal courts had allowed such a removal and then had dismissed the claims, holding that they were preempted by ERISA. The Third Circuit reversed, noting that not all claims preempted by ERISA were subject to removal. The court held that removal was improper where plaintiffs were merely attacking the quality of the benefits received and were not claiming that the ERISA plans had erroneously withheld benefits that were due or were not seeking to enforce rights under the terms of their respective plans or to clarify rights to future benefits. The court expressly distinguished the situation where the HMO denied benefits in its utilization review role.[103,104]

It should be noted that the Third Circuit's decision in *Dukes* was limited to the issue of whether a defendant MCO can remove a medical malpractice claim from state court to federal court.[105] That court's discussion of the distinction between the quantity of benefits due under an ERISA plan and the quality of the benefits provided under such plan, however, will probably be cited by other courts as authority for a refusal to preempt malpractice claims challenging the quality of services provided to plan participants and beneficiaries.

Negligent Representations by MCOs to Providers

Whether claims by a provider that an MCO misrepresented the existence or extent of coverage is preempted by ERISA may hinge on whether the provider is suing in its own capacity or as assignee of the MCO's insured or member. A majority of courts have held that state law causes of action brought by a provider suing in its own capacity are not preempted by ERISA, even though such causes of action would be preempted if the provider was suing in a derivative capacity as assignee for the insured or member.

For example, in the influential case of *Memorial Hospital System v. Northbrook Life Insurance Company*, the plaintiff hospital had treated a patient after the hospital had called the employer of the patient's husband and verified that the patient had coverage for the hospital care under a group insurance policy issued and administered by defendant.[106] Subsequently, the patient and her husband assigned their benefits to the hospital. Upon the hospital's request for payment, however, defendant informed the hospital that the patient had not been eligible for benefits on the date of her hospitalization and denied benefits. The hospital subsequently sued, alleging that the employer acted as defendant's agent in verifying coverage and asserting state law causes of deceptive and unfair trade practices under the Texas insurance code, breach of contract, negligent misrepresentation, and equitable estoppel.

The lower court dismissed the hospital's claims for breach of contract and deceptive and unfair trade practices, finding that those claims were brought by the hospital in a derivative capacity, were related to a claim for benefits under an ERISA plan, and were consequently preempted. The lower court reached the opposite conclusion with respect to the claims of misrep-

resentation and estoppel, however, finding that those claims were based on the hospital's independent position as a third party health care provider, were not related to the ERISA plan, and thus "were not caught in the broad net of ERISA preemption."[107]

The hospital appealed the dismissal of the deceptive and unfair trade practices claim, alleging that the lower court had mischaracterized it as a derivative claim for benefits. The U.S. Court of Appeals for the Fifth Circuit agreed, holding that it was merely a Texas codification of the common law doctrine of negligent misrepresentation. Nevertheless, the Fifth Circuit felt "compelled to enter the preemption thicket" and determine whether such cause of action was sufficiently related to the employee benefit plan at issue so as to be preempted.[108] The court ultimately held that it was not sufficiently related to be preempted. It is worthwhile, however, to examine in some detail the court's analysis of the policy issues involved in determining whether to preempt a provider's claims based on an erroneous verification of a patient's eligibility and coverage because the same reasoning has been adopted by courts in subsequent cases.

Before determining the legal issue of preemption, the court found it necessary to examine the "commercial realities" of the hospital's position as a health law provider.

> The scenario depicted in Memorial's appeal is one that is reenacted each day across the country. A patient in need of medical care requests admission to a hospital (or seeks treatment from a physician). The costs of medical care are high, and many providers have only limited budget allocations for indigent care and for losses from patient nonpayment. Naturally, the provider wants to know if payment reasonably can be expected. Thus one of the first steps in accepting a patient for treatment is to determine a financial source for the cost of care to be provided.[109]

The court recognized that it was customary practice for a provider to communicate with plan agents to verify eligibility and coverage and viewed the issue of a mistaken verification of eligibility and coverage by such plan agents as solely one of allocation of risks, namely, whether the risk of nonpayment of the provider's costs "should remain with the provider or be shifted to the insurance company, which through its agents misrepresented to the provider the patient's coverage under the plan," noting that enforcing "the allocation of risks between commercial entities that conduct business in a state is a classically important state interest."[110]

The court remained unconvinced that "either the commercial scenario described above, or its state law vindication, raises any issue concerning the matters that Congress intended to be regulated exclusively by ERISA."[111] Moreover, the court was unpersuaded that "insulating plan fiduciaries from the consequences of their commercial dealings with third-party providers would further any of ERISA's goals."[112] According to the court, a one-time recovery by the hospital against the insurer or its putative agent, the employer, would not affect the ongoing administration or obligations of an ERISA plan. In addition, the court found that, if providers were held to have no recourse under either ERISA or state law in situations where there was no coverage under the express terms of the plan but providers had relied on assurances that there was such coverage, providers would be understandably reluctant to accept the risk of nonpayment and might require upfront payment by beneficiaries or impose other inconveniences before treatment would be rendered: "This does not serve, but rather directly defeats, the purpose of Congress in enacting ERISA."[113]

Finally, noting that a health care provider did not have independent standing to seek redress under ERISA, the Fifth Circuit found that, although employees had received protection under ERISA in exchange for certain rights to sue under previous federal and state law, the plaintiff and "the countless other health care providers were not a party to this bargain."[114] The court

stated that it could not believe that "Congress intended the preemptive scope of ERISA to shield welfare plan fiduciaries from the consequences of their acts toward non-ERISA health care providers when a cause of action based on such conduct would not relate to the terms or conditions of a welfare plan, nor affect—or affect only tangentially—the ongoing administration of the plan."[115] The court concluded that ERISA's "preemption provision designed to prevent state interference with federal control of ERISA plans does not require the creation of a fully insulated legal world that excludes these plans from regulation of any purely local transaction."[116] Other courts have adopted the reasoning of the *Memorial Hospital System* case and refused to insulate ERISA plans, their sponsors, or their administrators from liability when they mistakenly verify eligibility or coverage to a health care provider.[117]

Preemption of State Insurance Regulation

State insurance laws and regulations often expressly exempt ERISA employee benefit plans from their application.[118] In the absence of such express exemption, however, it has been increasingly common for state insurance authorities to attempt to apply insurance laws and regulations directly to noninsurance products of MCOs as well as to integrated delivery systems and other entities that have contracted to provide services to ERISA plans. Whether state insurance laws and regulations are preempted by ERISA depends on a combination of the nature of the state law or regulation at issue and the nature of the services being provided to the ERISA plan.

Under the traditional preemption analysis, the first issue to be addressed is whether the state law or regulation relates to the ERISA plan. If so, the law or regulation will be preempted unless it is "saved" from preemption because it regulates the "business of insurance." The nature of the services being provided to the ERISA plan and that the state is seeking to regulate, however, must constitute the "business of insurance"; it is not sufficient that the services are being provided by an insurance company or other entity subject to insurance regulation or that the state law or regulation is part of the insurance code.

The U.S. Supreme Court has held that the underwriting or spreading of risk is an "indispensable characteristic of insurance."[119] According to the Supreme Court, the spreading of risk means that the entity engaged in the business of insurance accepts a number of risks, some of which involve losses, and spreads such losses over all the risks to enable the entity to accept each risk at a slight fraction of the possible liability upon it.[120] Courts also have held, however, that an incidental element of insurance in a contract does not bring the contract within the regulatory power of the insurance laws.[121] Because some element of risk is inherent in any business transaction, the primary effect of the contract at issue must be assumption and spreading of risk.

ADMINISTRATIVE SERVICES ONLY CONTRACTS

In the situation where the entity contracting with the ERISA plan merely provided administrative services to such plan, courts have determined that such services did not constitute the business of insurance, and therefore ERISA preempted the application of state insurance laws and regulations to such services. For example, the U.S. Court of Appeals for the Fifth Circuit held that a third party administrator of an ERISA plan was not engaged in the business of insurance where it performed no risk-bearing function.[122] Consequently, ERISA preempted a Texas statute imposing regulations, fees, and taxes to the extent that the statute applied to such third party administrator.

Similarly, the U.S. Court of Appeals for the Fourth Circuit held that, where an insurer acted as a third party administrator, providing purely claims processing functions for an ERISA plan pursuant to an administrative services agreement with the employer, the insurer was not engaged in the business of insurance.[123] According

to the court, the ERISA savings clause covered the same category of state insurance regulation as the McCarran-Ferguson Act,[124] which preserves to the states the right to regulate insurance, and the McCarran-Ferguson Act did not "purport to make the States supreme in regulating all the activities of insurance *companies*; . . . only when they are engaged in the 'business of insurance' does the statute apply."[125]

Finally, the U.S. Court of Appeals for the Third Circuit, in the often cited case *Insurance Board of Bethlehem Steel Corp. v. Muir*, found that the Pennsylvania Blue Cross and Blue Shield (BCBS) plans were not engaged in the business of insurance where they performed no underwriting function and received only an administrative fee based on the number and type of plan participants, regardless of the fact that plan participants and beneficiaries used BCBS claim forms, BCBS staff processed the claims, BCBS made initial determinations regarding coverage, and BCBS paid plan participants and beneficiaries directly and was reimbursed by the employer.[126] According to the court, because "ERISA creates a scheme in which any entity engaged in the business of insurance, except an ERISA employee benefit plan, is subject to state insurance regulation," the controlling question was whether BCBS was engaging in the business of insurance when it sold administrative services to the ERISA plan.[127] The court held that it was not because it did not assume any financial risk of a valid claim, it did not provide a service that was an essential part of the insurance relationship but instead merely provided administrative services, and other entities outside the insurance industry provided the same administrative services provided by BCBS.

In summary, so long as the services being provided by contract to the ERISA plan do not constitute the assumption and spreading of risk (i.e., the "business of insurance"), any attempted state regulation of those services, including regulation under the insurance code, will be preempted by ERISA.[128] As the discussion below of the preemption of state any willing provider (AWP) laws demonstrates, however, the dividing line between the "business of insurance" and the provision of professional services is not always clear.

AWP LAWS

One of the hottest legal battles in the managed care arena is the fight between states and MCOs over the applicability of AWP laws to networks that contract with ERISA plans. Although the terms of AWP statutes differ from state to state, in general AWP statutes require that MCOs and other entities establishing provider networks not discriminate against a provider so long as the provider meets the network's general qualifications and is willing to be compensated at the network's reduced payment rate. Under some state statutes, patients also cannot be penalized through reduced benefits if they seek treatment from providers outside their designated network.

The problem with AWP statutes from the managed care industry's viewpoint is that they eliminate the means by which MCOs persuade providers to accept lower rates of compensation for their services. The attraction of MCOs for health care providers, despite the reduced compensation, is the increased volume of patients that can be generated through limiting the network of participating providers. By preventing MCOs from differentiating between participating and nonparticipating providers, a certain number of patients cannot be ensured to providers, thereby eliminating the leverage with which MCOs bargain for lower rates of payment.

Proponents of AWP statutes argue that AWP laws protect patient choice and that the identity of the treating provider is a part of the overall package of benefits. According to such proponents, consumers should not be forced to accept providers chosen by an MCO by a threat of reduced levels of benefits.

The current debate over AWP statutes centers on ERISA and whether MCOs that service ERISA plans are subject to state AWP statutes. As explained above, under ERISA, any state law that relates to an ERISA employee benefits plan is preempted. ERISA makes an exception to its broad preemption provision, however, for any state law that regulates the "business of insurance." Courts have interpreted that phrase to require a two-part analysis. First, courts look to whether common sense dictates that the state statute regulates insurance. Then they decide whether a state statute affects a practice that has the effect of transferring or spreading a policyholder's risk, is an integral part of the relationship between the insurer and the insured, and is limited to entities within the insurance industry. If it does, then the statute is not preempted by ERISA as applied to a fully insured ERISA plan. As applied to a self-funded ERISA plan, however, the statute is still preempted.

The difference of opinion regarding the scope of ERISA with respect to AWP statutes arises from the uncertainty as to whether regulating the identities of a network's participating providers is a regulation of the business of insurance or a regulation of noninsurance business. Defenders of AWP statutes argue that AWP statutes regulate the business of insurance because they define the type of policy that can be issued. HMOs and other MCOs that maintain closed provider networks increase the costs of patients who use nonparticipating providers by reducing or eliminating benefits for services received from those providers. An AWP statute allows a patient to obtain care from a provider who might otherwise be excluded from a network without a reduction of benefits. This prohibition on closed networks, it is argued, spreads the policyholders' risk insofar as it shifts to MCOs and physician groups the costs to patients of seeking treatment from providers who otherwise would be excluded from a network.

In addition to spreading policyholder risk, defenders of AWP statutes argue that such statutes affect an integral part of the relationship between the insurer and the insured: treatment and cost. AWP statutes help define the nature of the available services, who can provide them, and how those providers will be paid. In this respect, AWP statutes have been analogized to mandated benefits laws, which require insurers to include certain types of benefits in their insurance policies. Mandated benefits laws were found to be saved from ERISA preemption because they regulate the scope of the insurance coverage and the availability of services. In the same manner, it is argued, AWP statutes affect the type of benefits that an insured receives by determining who can provide covered services and how those providers are selected. Opponents of preemption assert that such regulation touches upon a vital part of the insurer–insured relationship.

On the other hand, proponents of ERISA preemption contend that such statutes do not regulate the business of insurance, although they may regulate the business of insurance companies. They argue that AWP statutes do not spread policyholder risk. Instead, such statutes are merely cost-saving mechanisms. According to this argument, contracts between MCOs and providers, whereby the provider receives a reduced rate of compensation in exchange for a certain volume of patients, are merely contracts for the purchase of goods and services. The transfer of risk occurs when an HMO insures an ERISA plan, not when it or another MCO attempts to minimize costs through its contracts with providers. The contracts are seen as identical to many other arrangements whereby MCOs try to reduce costs.

Finally, proponents of preemption argue that the practice of establishing a closed network does not affect an integral part of the relationship between an insurer and the insured. The agreements at issue are between the insurer and the providers. They do not affect the amount or the type of benefit that a patient receives, only the vehicle through which such services are rendered.

Because of the runaway costs of health care and the concerted effort to find means by which to curb health care expenses, there are also strong policy reasons for finding ERISA preemption of AWP statutes. As discussed above, if MCOs are prohibited from closing their networks, they can no longer ensure a certain volume of business. In this manner, AWP statutes eliminate any leverage MCOs may have had to bargain with providers for reduced rates of com-

pensation, effectively eliminating the benefits of establishing a provider network.

Thus far, courts have reached different conclusions as to whether particular AWP statutes regulate "the business of insurance." One of the first AWP statutes to be challenged by the managed care industry was in Virginia.[129] Virginia's AWP statute allowed insurers to form PPOs and establish terms and conditions that physicians, hospitals, or other providers had to meet to qualify as a preferred provider. The statute, however, prohibited insurers from both unreasonably discriminating against and among such providers and from excluding providers willing to meet the terms and conditions for participation in the PPO. The challenge to the Virginia statute arose after a PPO established by Aetna, which provided services exclusively to employee benefit plans, refused to allow a hospital to participate in its network. Instead, the PPO only contracted with hospitals that were already participants in Aetna's HMO. The hospital sued Aetna for failing to comply with the AWP statute and excluding it from the PPO network for the sole reason that it was not a member of Aetna's HMO. Aetna defended on the ground that the statute was preempted by ERISA.

In the Virginia case, the court first found that the AWP statute related to ERISA plans. The statute not only expressly provided that it applied to health benefit programs offered or administered by insurers but also restricted the ability of an insurer to limit the choice of providers that would otherwise confine the plan participants of an ERISA plan to those preferred by the insurer.

Next, the court held that the statute was rescued from preemption because it regulated the business of insurance and consequently fell under the ERISA savings clause. According to the court, the statute spread policyholder risk because insurers whose benefits otherwise would be reduced or denied if they sought treatment from nonparticipating providers would receive full benefits under the statute. In addition, the court asserted, the statute affected an integral part of the relationship between the insured and the insurer because the statute affected the provision for treatment and cost. Finally, the Virginia statute was explicitly limited to entities within the insurance industry, thus satisfying the third McCarran-Ferguson criterion. Consequently, the court held that Virginia AWP statute was not preempted by ERISA.[130]

A federal court in Louisiana reached the opposite conclusion in a recent challenge to Louisiana's AWP statute.[131] Like the Virginia court, it held that the Louisiana statute related to ERISA plans. Indeed, the statute explicitly mentioned employee benefit plans. In addition, the court found that application of the statute affected the employer's or plan sponsor's discretion as to how health benefits could be structured under its employee benefit plans, pointing out that the statute explicitly directed that it could not structure its programs to exclude any provider willing and able to participate. The court then found, however, that the Louisiana statute did not regulate the business of insurance. The statute was not specifically addressed to the insurance industry but applied to entities such as employers and Taft-Hartley trusts. Consequently, the court held that it did not meet the common definition of insurance test or the third prong of the McCarran-Ferguson test. The legal challenges to the application of state AWP statutes to networks established by MCOs and provided to ERISA plans are certain to increase.

CAPITATED ADMINISTRATIVE SERVICES ONLY CONTRACTS

Another legal battle is brewing over the extent to which providers who have contracted to provide health care services to either MCOs or self-funded employers on a capitated basis is subject to the insurance laws. The answer depends on whether such capitated contracts are construed as insurance contracts.

In an opinion dated 19 June, 1990, the Maryland Attorney General addressed whether a third party administrator that had established a provider network and offered that network to self-funded ERISA plans was engaged in the business of insurance and, thus, needed an insurance license.[132] The Attorney General opined that it was not. The Attorney General warned, however, that the providers might need an insurance license if they agreed to be paid on a capitated basis. The rationale for the Attorney General's opinion was that, by agreeing to be paid on a capitated basis, the providers had assumed risk and, therefore, were engaged in the business of insurance. The Attorney General concluded that an employer's creation of a self-funded employee benefit plan, protected from state regulation by ERISA, did not also exempt the providers of services to that plan from state insurance regulation.

On 18 May 1995, the Office of the Georgia Commissioner of Insurance notified a physician– hospital organization that offered its services on a capitated basis that the Georgia insurance statutes "do not permit a hospital or medical group or combination of both to provide health care services or benefits directly to patients for a monthly capitation fee unless fully licensed as an insurer by this department."[133] The commissioner ordered the immediate discontinuance of the physician–hospital organization's health care program unless it was being underwritten by a licensed insurer. With respect to the issue of ERISA preemption, the commissioner took the position that the health care program at issue was being offered to multiple employers but did not meet ERISA's definition of an employee benefit plan.

Similarly, the Virginia Bureau of Insurance recently notified the managed care industry that health care providers and other entities that provide health care services to self-funded employers on a capitated basis either would have to obtain insurance licenses or would have to provide such services through licensed entities, such as HMOs.[134] If the health care services were provided on a capitated basis by means of a contract with an MCO that in turn contracted with a self-funded employer for administrative services only (a so-called capitated administrative services only contract), then the capitated administrative services only contract would be considered an at-risk contract by the Bureau of Insurance and would be subject to the full panoply of the insurance code, including reserves requirements and assessments. The Bureau of Insurance took the position that capitated administrative services only contracts were insurance contracts and, therefore, were saved from ERISA preemption by the savings clause.

The managed care industry would disagree. It seems likely that MCOs and integrated delivery systems will seek both legislative and judicial relief from insurance commissioners' efforts to regulate capitated arrangements and that ERISA will continue to play a prominent role.

CONCLUSION

ERISA can affect many of the core functions of an MCO, from product design to administration to issues of legal liability. Accordingly, MCOs would be well advised to acquire a proficiency with respect to the requirements of this far-reaching statute and the rapidly developing body of case law interpreting it.

REFERENCES AND NOTES

1. 29 U.S.C. § 1001 *et seq.*
2. 29 U.S.C. §§ 1002(2), 1002(3), 1003.
3. 29 U.S.C. § 1102.
4. 29 U.S.C. § 1022; 29 C.F.R. § 2520.104b-2.
5. 29 C.F.R. § 2520.102-3(j).
6. 29 U.S.C. § 1024.
7. *Id.*
8. *Id.*
9. *Id.*
10. *See, e.g., Aiken v. Policy Management Sys. Corp.*, 13 F.3d 138 (4th. Cir. 1993) and *Edwards v. State Farm Mut. Auto. Ins. Co.*, 851 F.2d 134 (6th Cir. 1988).
11. 29 U.S.C. § 1024.
12. 29 C.F.R. § 2520.104-20.
13. Dep't Labor Adv. Op. 92-24A (Nov. 6, 1992).
14. 26 U.S.C. § 6039D.
15. 29 U.S.C. § 1024.
16. *Id.*
17. 29 U.S.C. § 1169.
18. *Id.*
19. *Id.*
20. 29 U.S.C. §§ 1161–1168.
21. 29 U.S.C. § 1144.
22. *Metropolitan Life Ins. Co. v. Mass.*, 471 U.S. 724 (1985).
23. *FMC Corp. v. Holliday*, 498 U.S. 52 (1990).
24. *Drexelbrook Eng'g Co. v. Travelers Ins. Co.*, 891 F.2d 280 (3d Cir. 1989) and *United Food & Commercial Workers v. Pacyga*, 801 F.2d 1157 (9th Cir. 1986).
25. *Brown v. Granatelli*, 897 F.2d 1351 (5th. Cir.), *cert. denied*, 498 U.S. 848 (1990).
26. *See, e.g.*, Mo. Code Regs. tit. 20, § 400-2.150 (1993).
27. NAIC Stop Loss Insurance Model Act (1995).
28. *N.Y. State Conference of Blue Cross & Blue Shield Plans v. Travelers Ins. Co.*, ____ U.S. ____, 115 S. Ct. 1671 (1995).
29. *See, e.g.*, Age Discrimination in Employment Act of 1967, as amended, 29 U.S.C. § 621 *et seq.*
30. 42 U.S.C. § 12101 *et seq.*
31. 42 U.S.C. § 12202.
32. *Id.*
33. *Id.*
34. 29 C.F.R. Part 1630, EEOC Interpretative Guidance on Title I of the Americans with Disabilities Act.
35. *Id.*
36. No. 95-2469, 1995 W.L. 506941 (8th Cir. July 21, 1995).
37. 29 U.S.C. § 1102.
38. *See, e.g., Boyer v. Douglas Components Corp.*, 986 F.2d 999 (6th Cir. 1993).
39. *Id.*
40. 857 F. Supp. 1182 (E.D. Mich. 1994).
41. *In re Unisys Corp. Retiree Medical Benefit "ERISA" Litigation*, 57 F.3d 1255 (3d Cir. 1995).
42. 18 F.3d 1034 (3d Cir. 1994).
43. *Curtiss-Wright Corp. v. Schoonejongen*, ____ U.S. ____, 115 S. Ct. 1223 (1995).
44. *Murphy v. Keystone Steel & Wire Co.*, 61 F.3d 560 (7th Cir. 1995).
45. 29 U.S.C. § 1002(21).
46. 29 U.S.C. § 1104.
47. *Id.*
48. *Id.*
49. *Curtiss-Wright Corp. v. Schoonejongen*, ____ U.S. ____, 115 S. Ct. 1223 (1995).
50. 29 U.S.C. § 1106.
51. 29 U.S.C. § 1002(14).
52. 29 C.F.R. § 2550.408b-2.

53. 29 U.S.C. § 1133.

54. 29 C.F.R. § 2560.503-1.

55. 489 U.S. 101 (1989).

56. 899 F.2d 639 (7th Cir. 1990).

57. 37 F.3d 1384 (9th Cir. 1994).

58. *Fuller v. CBT Corp.*, 905 F.2d 1055 (7th Cir. 1990).

59. *See Brown v. Blue Cross & Blue Shield of Ala., Inc.*, 898 F.2d 1556 (11th Cir. 1990), *cert. denied sub nom. Blue Cross & Blue Shield v. Brown*, 498 U.S. 1040 (1991).

60. *Id.*

61. *See, e.g., Cox v. Keystone Carbon Co.*, 894 F.2d 647 (3d Cir.), *cert. denied*, 498 U.S. 811 (1990) and *Chilton v. Savannah Foods & Indus., Inc.*, 814 F.2d 620 (11th Cir. 1987).

62. *Blue Cross & Blue Shield v. Lewis*, 753 F. Supp. 345 (D. Ala. 1990).

63. 29 U.S.C. § 1132(a)(2).

64. 29 U.S.C. § 1132(a)(3).

65. 473 U.S. 134 (1985).

66. 113 S. Ct. 2063 (1993).

67. *See, e.g., Pilot Life Insurance Co. v. Dedeaux*, 481 U.S. 41 (1987).

68. 12 F.3d 1517 (9th Cir. 1993).

69. 36 F.3d 746 (8th Cir. 1994), *opinion clarified*, 41 F.3D 1263 (8th Cir. 1994), *cert. granted*, ____U.S.____, 115 S. Ct. 1792 (1995).

70. Section 514(a) of ERISA; 29 U.S.C. § 1144(a).

71. Section 514(b)(2)(A) of ERISA; 29 U.S.C. § 1144(b)(2)(A).

72. Section 514(b)(2)(B) of ERISA; 29 U.S.C. § 1144(b)(2)(B).

73. *Shaw v. Delta Air Lines, Inc.*, 463 U.S. 85, 96–97 (1983).

74. *FMC Corp. v. Holliday*, 498 U.S. 52, 58 (1990).

75. *Ingersoll-Rand Co. v. McClendon*, 498 U.S. 133 (1990); *United Wire, Metal & Mach. Health & Welfare Fund v. Morristown Memorial Hosp.*, 995 F.2d 1179 (3d Cir.), *cert. denied*, ____ U.S. ____, 114 S. Ct. 382–83 (1993) (a state law may be preempted even though it has no direct nexus with ERISA plans if its effect is to dictate or restrict the choices of ERISA plans with regard to their benefits, structure, reporting, and administration).

76. *See FMC Corp. v. Holliday*, 498 U.S. 52, 58 (1990); *Shaw v. Delta Air Lines, Inc.*, 463 U.S. 85, 100 n. 21 (1983) (some state actions may affect employee benefit plans in "too tenuous, remote, or peripheral a manner to warrant a finding that the law 'relates to' the plan"); *Mackey v. Lanier Collection Agency & Serv., Inc.*, 486 U.S. 825 (1988).

77. 481 U.S. 41 (1987).

78. *Id.* at 48–49 (citing *Metropolitan Life Ins. Co. v. Mass.*, 471 U.S. 724 (1985)).

79. *Id.* (quoting *Union Labor Life Ins. Co. v. Pireno*, 458 U.S. 119 (1982)).

80. *See, e.g., NGS American, Inc. v. Barnes*, 998 F.2d 296, 299 (5th Cir. 1993).

81. *FMC Corp. v. Holliday*, 498 U.S. 52, 64–65 (1990).

82. *Id.*

83. *Id.* ("Our interpretation of the deemer clause makes clear that if a plan is insured, a State may regulate it indirectly through regulation of its insurer and its insurer's insurance contracts; if the plan is uninsured, the State *may not regulate it*") (emphasis added).

84. 48 F.3d 937 (6th Cir. 1995).

85. 965 F.2d 1321 (5th Cir.), *cert. denied*, 506 U.S. 1033 (1992).

86. *See also Kuhl v. Lincoln Nat'l Health Plan*, 999 F.2d 298 (8th Cir. 1993), *cert. denied*, ____ U.S. ____, 114 S. Ct. 694 (1994) (ERISA preempted a wrongful death claim based on a delay in precertification of surgery because the precertification decision related to the administration of benefits); *Rodriguez v. Pacificare of Tex., Inc.*, 980 F.2d 1014 (5th Cir.), *cert. denied*, ____ U.S. ____, 113 S. Ct. 2456 (1993).

87. *See Johnson v. Misericordia Community Hosp.*, 99 Wis.2d 708, 301 N.W.2d 156 (1981).

88. *See Harrell v. Total Health Care, Inc.*, No. W.D. 39809, 1989 W.L. 153066 (Mo. Ct. App. Apr. 25, 1989), *aff'd on other grounds*, 781 S.W.2d 58 (Mo. 1989); *McClellan v. Health Maintenance Org.*, 413 Pa. Super. 128, 604 A.2d 1053, *appeal denied sub nom. Health Maintenance Org. v. McClellan*, 532 Pa. 664, 616 A.2d 985 (1992).

89. *See Harrell v. Total Health Care, Inc.*, No. W.D. 39809, 1989 W.L. 153066 (Mo. Ct. App. Apr. 25, 1989), *aff'd on other grounds*, 781 S.W.2d 58 (Mo. 1989).

90. 859 F.Supp. 182 (E.D. Pa. 1994).

91. *Id.* at 187.

92. *See, e.g., Butler v. Wu*, 853 F.Supp. 125 (D.N.J. 1994); *Elsesser v. Hosp. of the Philadelphia College of Osteopathic Medicine*, 802 F.Supp. 1286 (E.D. Pa. 1992); *Altieri v. CIGNA Dental Health, Inc.*, 753 F.Supp. 61 (D. Conn. 1990).

93. 878 F.Supp. 820 (D. Md. 1995).

94. *Id.* at 824 n. 6.

95. *Lupo v. Human Affairs Int'l, Inc.*, 28 F.3d 269 (2d Cir. 1994).

96. *See also Stratton v. Bryant*, No. 92-CV-3873, 1994 W.L. 837450 (E.D. Pa. Nov. 18, 1992) (ERISA did not preempt the claim against the HMO based on its negli-

gent selection, supervision, and monitoring of the treating physician who negligently delivered plaintiffs' son); *McClellan v. Health Maintenance Org.*, 413 Pa. Super. 128, 604 A.2d 1053, *appeal denied sub nom. Health Maintenance Org. v. McClellan*, 532 Pa. 664, 616 A.2d 985 (1992).

97. *See Raglin v. HMO Illinois, Inc.*, 230 Ill. App. 3d 642, 595 N.E.2d 153 (1992); *McClellan v. Health Maintenance Org.*, 413 Pa. Super. 128, 604 A.2d 1053, *appeal denied sub nom. Health Maintenance Org. v. McClellan*, 532 Pa. 664, 616 A.2d 985 (1992); *Boyd v. Albert Einstein Medical Center*, 377 Pa. Super. 609, 547 A.2d 1229 (1988); *Decker v. Saini*, No. 88361768 N.H., 1991 W.L. 277590 (Mich. Cir. Ct. Sept. 17, 1991).

98. *See Jackson v. Roseman*, 878 F.Supp. 820 (D. Md. 1995); *Kearney v. U.S. Healthcare, Inc.*, 859 F.Supp. 182 (E.D. Pa. 1994); *Haas v. Group Health Plan, Inc.*, 875 F.Supp. 544 (S.D. Ill. 1994); *Dearmas v. Av-Med, Inc.*, 865 F.Supp. 816 (S.D. Fla. 1994); *Paterno v. Albuerne*, 855 F.Supp. 1263 (S.D. Fla. 1994); *Elsesser v. Hosp. of the Philadelphia College of Osteopathic Medicine*, 802 F.Supp. 1286 (E.D. Pa. 1992); *Independence HMO, Inc. v. Smith*, 733 F.Supp. 983 (E.D. Pa. 1990); *Pickett v. CIGNA Healthplan of Texas, Inc.*, 742 F.Supp. 946 (S.D. Tex. 1990); *McClellan v. Health Maintenance Org.*, 413 Pa. Super. 128, 604 A.2d 1053, *appeal denied sub nom. Health Maintenance Org. v. McClellan*, 532 Pa. 664, 616 A.2d 985 (1992).

99. *See Pomeroy v. John Hopkins Medical Servs., Inc.*, 868 F.Supp. 110 (D. Md. 1994); *Nealy v. U.S. Healthcare HMO*, 844 F.Supp. 966 (S.D.N.Y. 1994); *Butler v. Wu*, 853 F.Supp. 125 (D.N.J. 1994); *Ricci v. Gooberman*, 840 F.Supp. 316 (D.N.J. 1993); *Altieri v. CIGNA Dental Health, Inc.*, 753 F.Supp. 61 (D. Conn. 1990).

100. 59 F.3d 151 (10th Cir. 1995).

101. *Id.* at 155.

102. 57 F.3d 350 (3d Cir. 1995), *cert. denied sub nom. Healthcare Inc. v. Dukes*, ____U.S.____, 116 S. Ct. 546 (1995).

103. The Third Circuit acknowledged that the distinction between the quantity of benefits due under an ERISA plan and the quality of those benefits would not always be clear. The court recognized that there could be cases where the quality of care rendered was so low as to constitute a denial of benefits or the ERISA plan had described a benefit in terms related to the quality of services and the plan participant was claiming damages resulting from a failure to provide services of the promised quality. The court also noted that an employer and an HMO could agree that a quality of care standard articulated in their contract could replace standards that would otherwise be supplied by applicable state tort law but declined to express an opinion as to whether

such an agreement would be enforceable. 57 F.3d at 358-359.

104. *Id.* at 360–361.

105. The Seventh and Second Circuit Courts also have held that a vicarious liability professional malpractice claim was not removable to state court. *Rice v. Panchal*, 65 F.3d 637 (7th Cir. 1995); *Lupo v. Human Affairs Int'l, Inc.*, 28 F.3d 269 (2d Cir. 1994); *see also Muller v. Maron*, No. 94-5052, 1995 W.L. 605483 (E.D. Pa. Oct. 13, 1995).

106. 904 F.2d 236 (5th Cir. 1990), *reh'g denied*, No. 89-2513, 1990 U.S. App. LEXIS 13227 (5th Cir. July 16, 1990).

107. *Id.* at 239.

108. *Id.* at 244.

109. *Id.* at 246.

110. *Id.*

111. *Id.* at 247.

112. *Id.*

113. *Id.* at 247–48.

114. *Id.* at 249.

115. *Id.* at 250.

116. *Id.*

117. *See The Meadows v. Employers Health Ins.*, 47 F.3d 1006 (9th Cir. 1995); *Lordmann Enters., Inc. v. Equicor, Inc.*, 32 F.3d 1529 (11th Cir. 1994), *cert. denied sub nom. Equicor, Inc. v. Lordmann Enters.*, ____ U.S. ____, 116 S. Ct. 335 (1995); *Hospice of Metro Denver, Inc. v. Group Health Ins. of Okla., Inc.*, 944 F.2d 752 (10th Cir. 1991); *Rehabilitation Inst. v. Group Adm'rs, Ltd.*, 844 F.Supp. 1275 (N.D. Ill. 1994); *Hoag Memorial Hosp. v. Managed Care Adm'rs*, 820 F.Supp. 1232 (C.D. Cal. 1993); *Gaston Memorial Hosp. Home Health Servs., Inc. v. Bridgestone/Firestone, Inc.*, 830 F.Supp. 287 (W.D.N.C. 1993); *Suburban Hosp., Inc. v. Sampson*, 807 F.Supp. 31 (D. Md. 1992).

118. *See, e.g.*, Md. Ann. Code Art. 48A, § 681 (1994), regulating third party administrators, which states, in relevant part, that the term *administrator* does not include a person who administers only plans that are subject to ERISA and do not provide benefits through insurance, unless any of the plans administered is a multiple employer welfare arrangement (MEWA).

119. *Group Life & Health Ins. Co. v. Royal Drug Co.*, 440 U.S. 205, 212 (1979); *Anglin v. Blue Shield*, 693 F.2d 315 (4th Cir. 1982); *GAF Corp. v. County Sch. Bd.*, 629 F.2d 981 (4th Cir. 1980) (transferring and distribution of risks are two elements of insurance).

120. *Royal Drug*, 440 U.S. at 211.

121. *See GAF Corp. v. County Sch. Bd.*, 629 F.2d 981 (4th Cir. 1980); *Jordan v. Group Health Ass'n*, 71 App.

D.C. 38, 107 F.2d 239 (1939) (where the primary purpose of a corporation was to arrange for the delivery of health services to its members and not to protect against financial loss caused by unusual occurrences, the corporation was not in the business of insurance regardless of any incidental element of risk distribution or assumption that was present in its contracts).

122. *NGS American, Inc. v. Barnes*, 998 F.2d 296 (5th Cir. 1993).

123. *Powell v. Chesapeake & Potomac Tel. Co.*, 780 F.2d 419, 423 (4th Cir. 1985), *cert. denied*, 476 U.S. 1170 (1980).

124. 15 U.S.C. § 1011 *et seq.*

125. *Powell v. Chesapeake & Potomac Tel. Co.*, 780 F.2d at 423 (quoting *SEC v. Nat'l Sec., Inc.*, 393 U.S. 453, 460 (1969)).

126. 819 F.2d 408 (3d Cir. 1987).

127. *Id.* at 411.

128. *See also O'Reilly v. Ceuleers*, 912 F.2d 1383, 1389 (11th Cir. 1990) (the court held that, when an HMO merely acted as a third party administrator, it was not engaged in the business of insurance and was, consequently, not within the insurance exception savings clause); *Aetna Life Ins. Co. v. State Bd. of Equalization*, 11 Cal. App. 4th 1207, 15 Cal. Rptr. 2d 26 (1992) (the court held that a California premiums tax was inapplicable to fees collected by an insurance company when the company was acting in the capacity of an administrator and not an insurer); *but see Benefax Corp. v. Wright*, 757 F.Supp. 800 (W.D. Ky. 1990) (third party administrators were subject to Kentucky administrator licensing statutes).

129. *Stuart Circle Hosp. Corp. v. Aetna Health Management*, 995 F.2d 500 (4th Cir.), *cert. denied*, ____ U.S. ____, 114 S. Ct. 579 (1993).

130. *See also Blue Cross & Blue Shield v. Bell*, 798 F.2d 1331 (10th Cir. 1986); *Blue Cross & Blue Shield v. St. Mary's Hosp. of Richmond, Inc.*, 245 Va. 24, 426 S.E.2d 117 (1993); *Blue Cross Hosp. Serv., Inc. v. Frappier*, 698 S.W.2d 326 (Mo. 1985).

131. *Cigna Healthplan of La., Inc. v. State ex rel. Ieyoub*, 883 F.Supp. 94 (M.D. La. 1995).

132. 75 Op. Att'y Gen. (1990) (Opinion No. 90-030 (September 1, 1990)).

133. Letter of William C. Lorick, Deputy Insurance Commissioner, to Northwest Georgia Physician Hospital Organization dated 18 May 1995.

134. Admin. Letter 1995-10 dated 11 September 1995.

SUGGESTED READING

American Bar Association Section of Labor and Employment Law, Employee Benefits Law (1991).

Chapter 60

Effective Utilization of Legal Services

James L. Touse

The managed care industry has grown and prospered during the past several decades based upon its proven ability to manage effectively the utilization of expensive medical services. It is surprising that so little attention has been devoted to managing the utilization of expensive legal services, particularly when managed care organizations are so profoundly affected by legal and regulatory issues. In fact, many plans do not employ legal counsel or even maintain an ongoing relationship with outside legal counsel. They only retain counsel on an episodic basis when absolutely necessary to respond to a legal or regulatory crisis.

Experience has shown that waiting to respond to a medical crisis is not an effective way to manage the utilization of limited medical resources. The same is true for the utilization of legal resources. The purpose of this chapter is to suggest how to manage effectively the utilization of legal resources to ensure that a plan complies with its legal obligations, avoids foreseeable risks, and takes advantage of opportunities created by applicable laws and regulations.

THE ROLE OF LEGAL COUNSEL

Someone must be accountable for ensuring that the plan has access to high quality legal services in a timely and cost-effective manner as

necessary to achieve its business objectives. That person may be a member of the plan's management staff, but it is generally more appropriate to hire or retain an experienced managed care attorney to perform those duties. There is an analogy between the role of the plan's counsel and that of a primary care physician. As the plan's "primary care attorney," counsel should be responsible for providing primary legal services and managing the utilization of outside legal counsel to provide needed specialty services to the plan's management staff and employees.

Primary legal services are needed on a continuing basis to comply with applicable laws, to avoid foreseeable legal risks, and to operate the plan. Such services include litigation and risk management services; coordinating regulatory compliance activities; negotiating, drafting, and/ or reviewing contracts; participating in marketing and product development initiatives; addressing employment law issues; performing corporate governance activities (e.g., conducting board meetings); directing lobbying, trade association, and other policy development initiatives; and responding to the plethora of legal or regulatory issues that arise in connection with a plan's day-to-day operations.

Legal specialty services are distinguishable from primary services in that they either are needed on an episodic basis or require the services of an attorney who devotes substantially his or her full time to practicing in a particular field of the law. Examples of specialty services include litigation, antitrust, trademark, and securities law services.

James L. Touse is the Vice President and General Counsel of Blue Cross Blue Shield of Tennessee (BCBSTN). Mr. Touse has previously served as legal counsel to other insurance companies, health maintenance organizations, and the Ohio Department of Insurance.

Like a primary care physician, the plan's counsel must maintain continuing and collaborative relationships with clients to understand their business activities, objectives, and potential sources of legal liability exposure. Such relationships should permit counsel to anticipate clients' legal needs, provide risk management services to limit the plan's liability exposure, and appropriately allocate available legal resources to achieve the plan's business objectives.

DETERMINING THE LIKELY DEMAND FOR LEGAL SERVICES

The demand for legal services is affected by the external legal environment and the plan's internal organization, operations, and objectives. The first step in the legal management process is to assess the external and internal environment to determine what legal services will probably be required to satisfy the plan's legal obligations and achieve its business objectives.

Managed care organizations are among the most regulated entities operating in this country. They must be organized and operated in accordance with a variety of federal, state, and local laws or regulations. It is beyond the scope of this chapter to list all of the laws affecting a plan's operations, but they include corporate laws governing the formation and operation of the plan, licensure or qualification laws, tax laws, employment laws, securities laws, property laws, contract laws (e.g., contracting with government entities), and criminal laws. If a plan fails to comply with those laws, it may be subject to some type of disciplinary action, including, in extreme cases, being forced out of business.

The enactment of new laws or the reinterpretation of existing laws may create significant challenges and opportunities for managed care organizations. The spectacular growth of the managed care industry after enactment of federal and state health maintenance organization laws illustrates how changes in applicable laws can create new opportunities for managed care organizations. The pace of change is likely to accelerate in the future, driven by the demand for creative new managed care arrangements.

Counsel must also provide those legal services required to avoid foreseeable risks and respond to legal actions against the plan. Such legal risks or actions may be based on either the statutes listed above or what are referred to as the plan's common law obligations (i.e., obligations not arising from statutes or regulations). Examples of a plan's common law obligations include its contractual duties (to customer groups, members, participating providers, employees, vendors, or others) and what are referred to as tort law obligations, which provide legal remedies if someone is injured by the plan's negligent or intentional misconduct. If the plan fails to comply with those obligations, it may be exposed to potentially catastrophic legal liability, as has been demonstrated by several well-publicized multimillion dollar judgments against managed care organizations. Even if the plan is not held liable, it may be forced to incur significant defense costs and to devote a significant amount of management time and attention to defending against such actions. Obviously, it is more cost effective to devote resources to risk management activities than to respond to actions against the plan. Unfortunately, it is not always possible to avoid such actions despite an effective risk management program (see Chapter 38). Counsel must, therefore, be prepared to provide both risk and litigation management services to clients.

The plan's internal organization, operations, and objectives will also affect the demand for legal services. Such organizational or operational considerations include the following: Does the plan operate on a national, regional, or local basis? Is it a staff, group, independent practice association, or mixed model plan? What products does it offer or plan to offer in the future? What are the types, size, number, and distribution of the plan's customer groups and members? Is the plan a nonprofit or a for-profit company? Is it a corporation, partnership, or other type of entity? Does an outside vendor perform administrative services on behalf of the plan? The need for legal services will presumably be much greater if counsel represents a large, multistate, mixed model, public corporation offering a variety of products to diverse customers than for a small independent practice association that offers a limited number of products to local customer groups within a single state service area.

Finally, the demand for legal services will be affected by the plan's objectives. As an example, a small local plan may require more support services than a large multistate plan if it decides to initiate an aggressive expansion of its product offerings, delivery system, capitalization, and/or service area. Because the plan's objectives can have such a significant impact on the demand for legal services, it is essential that counsel participate in clients' planning activities on an ongoing basis. Such participation will permit counsel to alert clients to potential legal issues, help them identify opportunities created by applicable laws, and anticipate what legal services will be needed to help them achieve their objectives.

ASSESSING AVAILABLE RESOURCES

After projecting the likely demand for legal services, counsel must assess what resources are and/or will be needed to satisfy those demands. There would be no need to manage the utilization of legal services if counsel had an unlimited budget and could simply hire additional staff or refer matters to outside counsel as necessary to provide services to clients in a timely manner. Unfortunately, counsel is more often confronted with the challenge of having limited resources to satisfy what, at times, seems like an unlimited demand for legal services. Counsel must be creative in allocating those limited resources to meet clients' demands without sacrificing the quality or timeliness of the services provided or restricting clients' access to needed legal services.

The first step in the resource allocation process is to compare prior years' legal budgets against actual expenditures during those years. If actual expenditures have consistently exceeded the legal department's budget, either in total or for specific budget categories, counsel should determine whether that was caused by unforeseeable crises, overly optimistic estimates, an inefficient use of available resources, or a combination of those factors. If actual expenditures have been below the budgeted amounts, counsel should determine whether that was the result of good luck, good planning, or not providing needed services to clients.

Evaluating the plan's past legal expenditures may reveal opportunities to provide services more cost effectively in the future. As an example, counsel may discover that outside counsel has been providing primary legal services to clients. It is generally more cost effective to hire attorneys, paralegals, or legal assistants than to retain outside counsel to perform such services. Hiring staff may also improve the quality and continuity of services provided to clients because staff members will be able to devote their full time to understanding the plan's organization, operations, and objectives; developing the expertise necessary to address managed care issues; and maintaining close working relationships with clients.

That does not mean that counsel should simply hire staff to perform all needed legal services. It is usually more cost effective to retain outside counsel to provide specialty services on an as-needed basis. Utilizing outside counsel to perform specialty services permits counsel to respond to variations in the demand for such services and to select the outside counsel who has the expertise necessary to perform a specific specialty legal service.

After deciding what services should be performed by the plan's staff versus outside counsel, counsel should determine what staffing arrangement will permit the legal department to provide services to clients most efficiently and effectively. If the plan has an existing legal staff, counsel should consider whether clients are satisfied with the services being provided by that staff; whether the legal department has an appropriate mix of attorneys, paralegals, and legal assistants; whether those staff members have the skills and expertise necessary to perform their assigned duties; and whether duties are being delegated appropriately among staff members and to clients. Counsel can obtain such performance information by evaluating client satisfaction surveys, staff time records or activity reports, and information concerning the types of assistance being requested by clients and how long it takes to respond to those requests. This is discussed in greater detail in a later section.

If counsel concludes that the plan needs to hire additional staff members or to reorganize the legal department, he or she must decide what staffing arrangement will best permit the department to satisfy the projected demand for legal services. Counsel must decide whether it is better to recruit a small number of experienced, and presumably more expensive, staff members or a large number of less experienced and less expensive individuals to provide services to clients. He or she will also have to decide whether it is more cost effective to hire attorneys, who are licensed to perform legal services independently, or paralegals and legal assistants, who can only perform services under the supervision of an attorney. The answers to those staffing questions will be affected by the types of services being requested by clients, the ability to recruit qualified applicants, and counsel's attitudes concerning the role of paralegals and legal assistants in providing services to clients.

Assuming that counsel has both a limited budget and a limited amount of time to train and supervise inexperienced staff members, it may be most productive to hire one or more experienced attorneys to supervise a small staff of paralegals and/or legal assistants. Using qualified paralegals or legal assistants to triage requests for assistance, conduct investigations, prepare documents, and address routine matters should permit each experienced attorney to take full advantage of his or her legal expertise. That staffing arrangement may also be less expensive than hiring inexperienced attorneys to perform those triage functions.

The final matter that should be considered is to determine whether the plan can minimize the use of outside counsel or the need to hire staff by delegating certain duties to clients. Although counsel clearly should be accessible and willing to help clients respond to legal issues, he or she must also ensure that the plan is not utilizing expensive legal resources to perform services that could be performed by less expensive administrative staff members. A later section of this chapter discusses how counsel can appropriately delegate duties to clients.

BUDGETING FOR THE COST OF PROVIDING SERVICES TO CLIENTS

Counsel should involve clients in the legal department's planning and budgeting process to encourage them to accept responsibility for utilizing legal services in a cost-effective manner. Some plans create such accountability by requiring clients to budget and pay for all legal services, including the cost of services provided by the legal staff. The advantages of that arrangement are that clients are directly accountable for their use of legal services and can compare the costs and results of the services provided by the legal department with those provided by outside counsel. The disadvantages are that such arrangements may encourage clients to attempt to save money by not utilizing counsel to provide preventive legal services and the potential for conflicts related to the cost of services provided by the legal department or outside counsel.

An alternative budgeting arrangement is to require counsel to budget and pay for all legal services. The advantages of that arrangement are that it encourages clients to utilize preventive legal services, increases counsel's ability to manage how services are provided, and minimizes conflicts with clients. The principal disadvantage is that it may create an incentive for clients to refer matters inappropriately to the legal department so that they can devote their resources to other, more pressing matters.

A hybrid budgeting arrangement may be the most appropriate way to encourage clients to utilize legal services effectively. That arrangement requires counsel to budget and pay for all services requested by clients in accordance with agreed-upon guidelines. Those guidelines should include mutually acceptable standards concerning when clients should request assistance from the legal department, what duties they are responsible for performing (e.g., negotiating the business terms of form contracts), and how much lead time will be required to respond to various types of requests for assistance. Clients should be responsible for the cost of retaining outside counsel if they fail to comply with those guidelines. That budgeting arrangement encourages a collaborative counsel–client relationship because clients can avoid incurring legal costs if they comply with these guidelines.

MANAGING THE PROVISION OF SERVICES TO CLIENTS

All the planning and budgeting activities discussed above will not result in the efficient utilization of legal resources unless counsel implements those plans and continually looks for ways to improve the quality, responsiveness, and cost effectiveness of the services provided to clients. The remainder of this chapter suggests how counsel can manage the provision of services to clients to achieve those objectives.

Managing the Legal Staff

This section assumes that counsel is managing a legal staff, although the same principles are applicable if counsel is the only member of the plan's legal staff or if outside counsel is acting as the plan's counsel. To manage effectively the provision of services to clients, counsel must delegate duties to those individuals who can most appropriately provide needed services, evaluate whether they are performing those duties as efficiently as possible, and ensure that clients are satisfied with the services that they receive from the legal department.

The issue of who should perform services will be governed by the size, structure, and duties of the legal department. There are a number of alternative methods of organizing the legal department, including assigning staff members to support specific clients, to respond to all requests for certain types of services (e.g., regulatory compliance services), or to perform all types of primary legal services. If the department has several staff members, it will generally be most efficient to have them specialize in assigned areas of responsibility. Such internal specialization will permit counsel to recruit staff members who have the expertise in a specific area of the law and to permit those individuals to build relationships with those clients who most frequently utilize those services. Counsel should also involve staff members in cross-functional projects or assignments, however, to avoid creating a "stovepipe" organizational structure. A cross-functional structure encourages staff members to consider all the legal issues that may be involved in addressing a specific matter, permits them to back each other up and respond to variations in the demand for certain types of legal services, and provides them with professional development opportunities.

After deciding how to organize the department, counsel needs to ensure that each staff member is performing his or her assigned duties as efficiently as possible. The most accurate way to monitor staff members' performance is to require them to maintain time records showing what they are working on, for what client, and how much time they devoted to that task. The advantage of such time records is that they provide detailed information about what services are being performed by each staff member. The disadvantage is that it takes time and discipline to complete and evaluate such reports. Requiring staff members to complete time reports may be counterproductive, if counsel is not prepared to devote the time necessary to evaluate and make management decisions based upon those reports.

An alternative may be to require staff members to complete periodic activity reports. Such activity reports can be structured to provide needed information about each staff member's accomplishments, the status of pending projects, and his or her planned activities during the next reporting period. Although activity reports may not provide as detailed information as time reporting systems, they are less burdensome to complete and may provide sufficient information to monitor and manage the provision of services by the plan's legal staff.

Time or activity reports will help measure the quantity of work produced, but counsel also needs to have some method of evaluating the responsiveness and quality of services provided to clients. One method of measuring staff responsiveness is to record what types of assistance are being requested by clients and how long it takes to respond to such requests. Tracking and trending such information should help determine whether staff members are responding to client requests for assistance in a timely manner. They may also help identify the need to adjust staffing levels, increase the use of outside counsel, or adopt more reasonable response guidelines if the legal department is unable to respond to requests for assistance within the agreed-upon response periods.

Finally, counsel should determine whether clients are satisfied with the services being provided by the legal department. Although staff members may be productive and responsive, it does not do much good if clients are not satisfied with the services being provided. Counsel should periodically survey clients to ascertain whether they are satisfied with the quality, relevance, responsiveness, and results of the services being provided by the legal department. Those surveys are not a substitute to maintaining regular contact with clients and responding promptly to any concerns related to the services being provided, but clients may be more willing to evaluate objectively the quality of services in a written survey rather than in a conversation with counsel. Conducting periodic surveys also provides the basis for implementing continuous quality improvement programs to enhance clients' satisfaction with the services provided by the legal department.

Delegating Duties to Clients

Counsel's evaluation of staff performance information may identify duties that can be delegated to clients with appropriate assistance and oversight from the legal staff. Such assistance includes providing clients with the training, tools, and legal advice that they need to perform their day-to-day activities in a legally appropriate manner.

In general, clients are in the best position to identify and respond to most day-to-day legal issues. It is also generally less costly to have administrative staff members perform quasi-legal activities, such as investigating complaints, conducting negotiations concerning business issues, and performing routine regulatory compliance activities, than to require the plan's legal staff or outside counsel to perform such activities.

If counsel does not have sufficient resources to respond expeditiously to clients' requests for assistance, requiring clients to refer everything to the legal department for review and approval is likely to create a bottleneck. Clients will either have to wait an unreasonable period of time to receive needed services or be forced to circumvent the legal department so that they can achieve their objectives in a timely manner. That will create an adversarial relationship and impair counsel's ability to manage the provision of services to clients.

Effectively delegating responsibilities requires that counsel train clients to identify and appropriately respond to potential legal issues. Such training activities may include distributing manuals, memos, and other information explaining how to address legal issues affecting the plan's operations. As an example, counsel might distribute a manual that describes the plan's regulatory compliance obligations. Although it takes time to draft such a manual, that will be an effective use of resources if it helps clients understand applicable laws and advises them when they should request assistance in addressing compliance-related issues.

The guidelines mentioned earlier in this chapter should explain when and how clients should request assistance from the legal department. Those guidelines should request that each department designate one or more senior managers to act as liaisons with the legal department. The reason for designating such liaisons is not to restrict access to needed legal services. The liaison's role is to ensure that different individuals from the same department are not making redundant requests for assistance, that management is aware of the types of assistance being requested by their staff, that someone is accountable for providing any information needed to respond to such requests, and that the liaisons know how to respond to similar legal issues in the future, all of which will improve the legal department's ability to provide high-quality services to clients in a timely and cost-effective manner.

Tracking requests for assistance will permit counsel to identify the most common types of legal services being requested by clients. That may reveal opportunities to develop policies, procedures, or form documents to address common legal problems. As an example, counsel should work with clients to draft form contracts that they can use to contract with providers, customers, and vendors. Those agreements should include any provisions necessary to protect the plan against foreseeable legal risks. Once those agreements are finalized, the legal department will only need to become involved in contract negotiations if the other party refuses to accept the approved form contract. In fact, empowering clients to negotiate contracts within approved parameters may discourage third parties from requesting modifications of those form contracts because modifications will need to be submitted to the legal department and/or regulatory agencies for approval.

Counsel should also develop and implement procedures to enable clients promptly to identify and resolve disputes with members, providers, and other parties. Such dispute resolution procedures should empower the plan's administrative staff to investigate and resolve routine disputes, if possible, within established guidelines. Implementing such procedures will minimize the need to involve legal staff members in routine disputes. If a dispute cannot be resolved, following established procedures will limit the plan's liability exposure by demonstrating that the plan acted in a consistent, appropriate, and good faith manner in attempting to resolve that dispute. Tracking and trending disputes may also permit counsel to identify and address systemic problems that are creating dissatisfaction with the plan, further reducing the plan's liability exposure and the need to devote legal resources to resolve disputes concerning those matters.

Effectively delegating duties to clients requires that counsel monitor the performance of those duties. Such oversight may include periodically auditing clients' activities or requiring clients to submit specified reports or documents to the legal department for review. The purpose of such oversight activities should be to ensure that counsel has provided sufficient training, tools, and advice to permit clients to perform delegated duties in an appropriate manner. The failure to provide such oversight and assistance may mean that counsel will ultimately need to devote more resources to addressing problems caused by the inappropriate delegation of duties to clients than would have been necessary had those duties been performed by the legal staff or outside counsel.

Managing Outside Counsel

Effectively managing outside counsel requires selecting the right attorney to provide needed services, prospectively agreeing upon the scope and cost of the services to be performed, and evaluating the attorney's performance from both a cost and an outcome perspective. Such evaluation should also consider whether the plan could achieve the same or better results at less cost by having staff or clients perform certain services, using different outside counsel, or changing how the plan pays for outside counsel's services.

Selecting the right outside counsel requires an assessment of which attorneys have the professional expertise to provide needed specialty services. Although those attorneys will probably work for a law firm, counsel should select the most qualified attorney, not the law firm, to perform such services. Counsel should require that the selected attorney be designated as the managing attorney accountable for both the quality and the cost of the services provided to the plan as a condition of referring a matter to the selected attorney's law firm.

If there are several equally qualified attorneys who can provide needed specialty services, counsel should consider requesting proposals from those attorneys or their law firms. Although it is generally not cost effective to request proposals for isolated referrals, requesting proposals to handle major transactions or a significant volume of the plan's specialty services may result in significant cost savings to the plan. Counsel should not agree to use a firm on an exclusive basis, however, because utilizing several firms promotes healthy competition, permits counsel to compare the quality of services rendered by each firm, and ensures that a conflict of interest does not leave the plan without legal representation when it is most needed.

Counsel should establish and maintain a collaborative working relationship with outside counsel. Although there are firms that specialize in reviewing and challenging law firms' fees after they have performed services, that creates an adversarial relationship between the plan and its outside counsel. Assuming that counsel wants to establish a long-term relationship with selected attorneys and firms, the parties should agree upon the scope of services that will be rendered and the charges for those services before outside counsel begins to work on a matter.

The foundation of such a collaborative relationship is to require that the managing attorney submit a written plan and budget for each matter referred to that attorney. The detail provided in that plan and budget will be dictated by the scope of the matter being referred to outside counsel. Counsel and the managing attorney should then discuss that plan and budget to ensure that there is agreement concerning what services will be rendered, the projected costs of those services, and when that plan or budget can be modified (e.g., if unanticipated issues arise while working on that matter). The managing attorney should then be required to keep counsel advised of the status of a referred matter either on a periodic basis or upon the completion of a significant milestone listed in the plan. Such ongoing consultation will provide a continuing opportunity for counsel to participate in the management of that matter.

Counsel should request that outside counsel propose alternative or incentive billing arrangements when preparing budgets. Such arrangements might include fixed fee arrangements, which are most appropriate for projects or transactions; blended fee arrangements, where the firm charges the same fee for each attorney who works on that matter; outcome-based incentive arrangements, where the fee is increased or decreased based upon some performance measure, such as the total cost to resolve a lawsuit; or "rent-an-attorney" arrangements, where the plan agrees to pay part of an attorney's or paralegal's salary based upon the amount of time he or she devotes to providing services to the plan. Such alternative billing arrangements are growing in popularity because they provide law firms with an incentive to help manage the quality and cost of services provided to the plan. Those arrangements are preferable to discounted hourly fee arrangements, which may encourage the provision of unnecessary services to maximize the firm's reimbursement from the plan.

Counsel should require firms to submit all bills for services in an agreed-upon billing format. Traditionally, it has been difficult to compare and evaluate attorneys' bills because each firm has used its own billing forms and codes. Fortunately, representatives of the American Bar Association, the American Corporate Counsel Association, and a group of major corporate law departments issued the Uniform Task-Based Management System: Litigation Code Set in May of 1995. That group has also drafted uniform task-based code sets for transactional services and general legal counseling services. The implementation of those task-based billing codes will permit counsel to require all outside counsel to utilize the same codes to bill for services on behalf of the plan. Such uniformity should provide a powerful management tool because it will permit counsel to compare and contrast the charges for defined tasks performed by a firm in different cases or by different firms when performing similar tasks. That information should permit counsel to negotiate budgets more effectively with outside counsel, suggest alternative billing arrangements, and decide what services should be performed by staff, clients, and outside counsel than has been possible when firms have used incompatible billing and coding systems.

CONCLUSION

Effective legal management is fundamentally no different from any other management activity. Counsel must understand how the plan's legal obligations and business objectives will affect the demand for legal services, determine what resources will be needed to meet those demands, and creatively allocate available resources to provide needed legal services in a timely and cost-effective manner. The need to manage effectively the availability, quality, and cost of legal services will increase in importance in the future. The demand for legal services will likely increase as a plans need to respond to current and developing theories of legal liability, to comply with applicable laws, and to take advantage of novel business opportunities at the same time that competitive pressures force plans to limit their administrative expenditures. This chapter has suggested how plans can effectively manage the utilization of legal services to achieve the plan's objectives in such a dynamic legal, regulatory, and competitive environment.

SUGGESTED READING

ACCA Docket. Washington, D.C.: American Corporate Counsel Association.

Block, D.J., and Epstein, M.A. 1994. *The Corporate Counsellor's Deskbook*, 4th ed. Englewood Cliffs, N.J.: Aspen Law & Business, A Division of Aspen Publishers, Inc.

Chayes, A. 1985. *Managing The Corporate Legal Function: The Law Department, Outside Counsel and Legal Costs.* New York, N.Y.: Matthew Bender & Company, Inc.

"Managing a Corporation's Law Department 1988." 1988. *Commercial Law and Practice Course Handbook Services*, Number 481. New York, N.Y.: Practicing Law Institute.

Managed Care Law Manual. 1995. Gaithersburg, Md.: Aspen Publishers, Inc.

Afterword

What Might the Future Hold?

*Frederick B. Abbey, Garry Carneal, Peter D. Fox, Robert E. Hurley,
Peter R. Kongstvedt, Jerry R. Peters, Jacqueline M. Saue, Craig Schub,
Roger S. Taylor, and Carlos Zarabozo*

As noted in the introduction to this book, the world of managed health care is highly volatile and ever-changing. These changes apply equally to managed care organizations (MCOs), providers, and the legislative and regulatory environment. Therefore, it is very likely that certain issues discussed in this book will have changed by the time of publication. That cannot be helped, but this afterword is our effort at discussing some of the possible changes to come. This afterword builds upon the relevant chapters that precede it in the book, and presents the opinions of the authors as of the Spring of 1996.

THE FEDERAL SECTOR

The federal sector continues to undergo significant pressures, both political and economic. While the federal sector encompasses many areas, this afterword will examine only two: Medicaid and Medicare.

Medicaid

The Medicaid program, while administered by the states, has significant federal involvement and has become a focal point in the budget reconciliation impasse between Congress and the President for both fiscal and ideological reasons. Congressional Republicans have targeted Medicaid for a dramatically reduced rate of growth in federal support to achieve their balanced budget goal. In addition, they have advocated—with the strong support of many governors—converting the structure of the program to a block grant to states, thereby repealing Title XIX and eliminating federally-guaranteed individual entitlement to Medicaid eligibility. The Clinton Administration has counter-proposed a more modest reduction in the growth rate along with somewhat greater flexibility for states, while retaining eligibility guarantees. Efforts have been made by the National Governors Association to narrow or close the gap, but these have yet to succeed at the time of this writing.

Despite the lack of agreement on the ultimate shape of Medicaid, there are two key areas of certainty in the reform of the Medicaid program being crafted by Congress, the Clinton Administration, and the state governors. One of these is that the future cost growth rates in Medicaid will be substantially below recent historical experience and possibly even below general inflation rates. The other area in which the direction of change is certain is that states will get expended flexibility in designing and managing their Medicaid programs, including determination of who is eligible, which services will be covered, and how providers will be paid. Whether the flexibility comes in the form of full block grants, narrowed and reduced federal requirements, or liberalized waiver-granting policy, the net effect is likely to be the same—variation among states will grow as will their reliance on managed care.

Rapid and pervasive conversion of Medicaid's delivery system to a managed care model seems assured. Shifting greater risk for financing Medicaid cost growth to states will intensify their desires to transmit this risk to prepaid managed care plans. While primary care case management models will be preferred in some states with low health maintenance organization (HMO) penetration, these are likely to be interim arrangements until organized delivery systems evolve. Reduced federal financial participation will also lead states to try to reduce their own administrative costs; contracting with prepaid health plans allows them to offload many administrative functions, such as provider payment, to the plans. Elimination of payment mandates and relaxation of benefit requirements will allow states to exercise more discretion and flexibility in contracting, and in how and how much they will pay for services. Likewise, federal structures on marketing, enrollment, plan qualification, and selection (such as the 75/25 rule) will disappear or be liberalized to enable states to maneuver more freely in the managed care marketplace. Until such liberalization is forthcoming, states will move ahead as they have in the past, by maneuvering and negotiating through the existing 1915b and 1115 waiver processes.

Perhaps the most critical area of uncertainty hanging over Medicaid reform is whether states will be mandated to continue to cover all or some of the currently eligible beneficiaries in an expanded flexibility environment where the entitlement to benefits may be altered or eliminated. There seems to be general consensus that women and children (at least up to a specified maximum age) will get some sort of guarantee, as will people with disabilities. Both of these groups will be getting their services predominantly through prepaid managed care arrangements. Other current beneficiaries may continue to get some or all of their existing coverage, again through a growing transition to managed care models, including persons in long term care.

Also uncertain is whether states will avail themselves of opportunities to expand coverage for currently enrolled populations by perhaps providing them access to a reduced benefit package. Certainly, many of the current crop of 1115 waivers—which have been a kind of de facto block grant in some cases—initially were committed to this goal. Recent experience, however, suggests this goal is proving elusive with several states with waivers in hand, unable to finance expansions or openly skeptical about the sustainability of these efforts in the face of reduced rates of financial support. A more plausible, and ominous, scenario is that states may be forced to reduce coverage for even traditionally eligible populations in the future, particularly if savings associated with the embrace of managed care are more modest than expected.

Medicare

It is highly likely that significant Medicare reform will occur during the life span of this book. Below is a brief description of some directions that reform could take.

Reduction in Budgeted Inflation Rate for Medicare

As currently funded and administered, the Medicare program will run out of money, even before the baby boom generation reaches 65 years of age. To preserve Medicare, the choices for Congress and the President are limited. They must either increase funding (taxes or the deficit), reduce benefits (including increasing cost sharing, reducing coverage, or modifying eligibility by, for example, raising eligibility age), and/or restructure the method of delivery.

Raising taxes or decreasing coverage for services are the least popular options, leaving restructuring of the delivery system and some manipulation of eligibility and cost sharing as the politically viable options for future savings. Indeed, it is to these options that both the President and Congress have turned.

In regard to the level of budgeted reduction in inflation, there is general agreement in Washington that one cannot balance the budget and avoid raising taxes without significantly reducing Medicare's 10% inflation rate. The congressional Republicans, through the Medicare Preservation Act of 1995, would reduce inflation by $200 billion over the next seven years. The conservative Democrats proposed a $125 billion reduction. The President has tacitly supported the smaller reduction but would use different methods to get there. But everyone agrees the issue needs to be addressed.

Medicare Managed Care Payment Reform

Payment reform proposals include the establishment of a "floor" for average area per capita cost (AAPCC) payments in the range of $300 or more, with the intent of making current low-payment areas attractive to managed care organizations. The AAPCC would exclude medical education and disproportionate share payments to hospitals, but the Health Care Financing Administration (HCFA) would make medical education payments directly to teaching hospitals rendering services to Medicare risk HMO enrollees. Although a voucher or defined contribution approach to Medicare managed care payments appears unlikely, yearly payment changes for risk HMOs after a given base year will be at a specified rate (7% in one proposal), with a minimum increase incorporated into law (2%). The Republican Congress proposal sets an administrative cap on annual inflation over a seven-year period, whereas the administration has suggested a number of separate mechanisms to gain its savings targets. The AAPCC might also become a blend of national and local area costs, with the share of each being split so that the local costs are the larger share (70/30, for example). These payment changes may be phased in over a certain period of time.

Current proposals would redistribute payments from areas of high managed care penetration to areas of low penetration. The proposal's objectives are to encourage MCOs to enter new markets and to encourage new types of MCOs. The estimated result of these proposals, according to the Congressional Budget Office, would be to increase national managed care penetration to about 22%. These are conservative estimates that do not take into account any behavioral changes due to changes in the enrollment process.

Expansion in Product Offerings to Medicare Eligibles

The success of private sector employees in controlling the rate of health care inflation has not gone unnoticed in Washington, D.C. The Medicare Preservation Act of 1995 borrows heavily from large employers' experience, offering Medicare recipients a choice of HMOs, point of service (POS) plans, preferred provider organizations (PPOs) and fee-for-service plans. As in the private sector, Medicare recipients would be responsible for choosing the plan that best meets their needs. If the plan they choose is more expensive, they would pay the difference. Figure A–1 presents these choices schematically, and they are discussed below.

Both parties support this expansion of choice as a method to allow the market to restructure the delivery system, but the President and Congress have some key differences on what the options are and how they are paid. For example, the President has opposed the idea of allowing any plan to offer less than a full Medicare benefit. This has put him at odds with congressional Republicans who support the idea of a catastrophic coverage option (e.g., $6,000 deductible plan) combined with a Medicare savings account (MSA) in which the beneficiary deposits any savings in Medicare premium experienced by the government. The principal concern expressed by the Administration and others, is that favorable risk selection will result in the government contributing an inappropriately high sum to the MSA, thereby costing the government more.

Another choice not explicitly developed in the President's plan is provider-sponsored organizations (PSOs), sometimes called provider-sponsored networks (PSNs). While this is not technically another benefit plan option because PSOs must be an HMO, PPO, POS, or a fee-for-service plan, it is certainly a hot political issue. By approving some relaxation of licensure and other restrictions on PSO sponsors of Medicare Plus Plans, the congressional Republicans created support within the medical and hospital in-

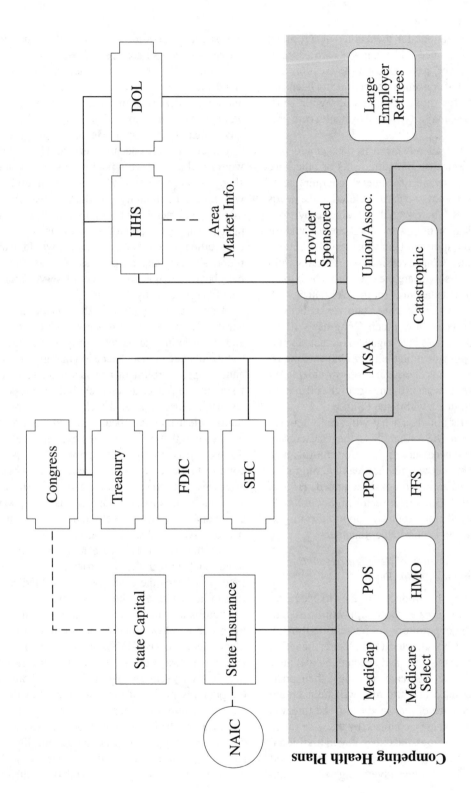

Figure A–1 Medicare's Future: Oversight and Choices. *Source:* Courtesy of Analysis of Medicare Preservation Act, Ernst & Young LLP, 1995, Washington, D.C.

dustry associations for their bill. The President and the insurance and managed care associations, however, have opposed the creation of a lower level of consumer protection and licensure standards for those organizations which just happen to be majority-owned by health care providers.

The proposals advanced to date would preempt State licensure requirements or otherwise enable PSOs to meet the licensure requirements through solvency standards tailored to the needs of the PSOs. There would be waiver provisions or modification of how members are counted for meeting the minimum enrollment and 50/50 requirements. Controversial issues that would have to be resolved are the extent to which there will be variant standards for these organizations, their status with respect to State versus Federal regulation (i.e., how much Congress will be willing to reduce states' rights to regulate the insurance options within their borders), and the issue of what kinds of organizations would qualify as PSOs (e.g., what is the nature of the affiliation among providers within the PSO).

While it's not clear what will finally happen as it relates to MSAs and PSOs, the restructuring of Medicare necessary for inflation control and a balanced budget will require massive migration of beneficiaries into prepaid (capitated) HMOs, PPOs, and POS plans. It seems highly probable that the legislation needed to support this migration will occur sooner rather than later.

Increased Education of Beneficiaries and Coordination of Enrollment

Expanding the product offerings to Medicare beneficiaries creates both opportunities and threats. The opportunity of course, is that many seniors will be attracted to the better benefits, preventive care focus, and accountable delivery systems in managed care offerings; their positive experience and training will help create wide acceptance of managed care. The threat is that seniors might be confused by the wide range of product offerings and either stay in traditional Medicare out of fear or confusion, or be swayed by slick and misleading advertising to join a plan that spends its entire budget on marketing and provides very poor service and benefits.

To ensure that Medicare beneficiaries understand the range of options and have a realistic and unbiased view of the advantages and disadvantages of each option, all parties agree that the government must support Medicare reform with a regular (annual) education effort. That effort would include a government-published spreadsheet of the Medicare Plus options available within each community. In addition, marketing material and member information must, in most plans, be approved by HCFA, and must conform to specified standards. Further, there would in all proposals be an appeals process to ensure members have the right to receive all services and benefits promised by the plan.

In an attempt to simplify the education and enrollment management process, both Congress and the Administration have proposed concentrating all education and decision making into an annual open enrollment period for all seniors. Using the employer group model, these proposals also require an annual lock-in; that is, once seniors elect a certain health plan option, they must stay in that plan until the next annual election period (with some exceptions). This is in contrast to the current system which allows beneficiaries to change plans on a monthly basis. The goal of this lock-in approach is to support the annual enrollment cycle and to reduce the risk of adverse selection; that is, to reduce the chance that sicker Medicare recipients would move back into the less restrictive traditional Medicare during the year, leaving the Medicare Plus options with a healthier risk mix.

There is a growing camp, however, that feel the group employer model doesn't apply to seniors. Medicare Risk HMOs and Medigap insurance have always been an individual insurance decision, with seniors able to elect in and out of the plan any month of the year. With less than 10% of seniors in managed care, and with seniors valuing the freedom of choice the way they do, this camp argues that an annual enrollment and lock-in will frighten seniors unfamiliar with managed care and retard the growth of Medicare

Plus. Additionally, the annual lock-in limits the individual's ability to select the most qualified plan and protect themselves from being locked into a substandard system.

This camp proposes an annual education effort, and possibly even a single month when all plans are open for enrollment, but they would permit plans to continue monthly enrollment if they so choose. Likewise, this camp would allow seniors to change plans (possibly with some frequency limit) when they choose, although they have acknowledged that some form of lock-in may be less problematic in highly penetrated markets where seniors are more familiar with managed care options and delivery systems have developed adequate capacity and flexibility to manage the large annual shift in membership.

Whatever the actual model finally adopted, it's likely that marketing and general communication with Medicare beneficiaries will be more managed, as will the enrollment and disenrollment process.

Modification of the Rules for Operation and Expansion

For the budgeting goals of Medicare reform to occur, a large percentage of beneficiaries must shift into the premium-controlled Medicare Plus plans. As a result, most proposals make it easier for existing Medicare Plus participants (including Medicare Risk HMO) to expand to new markets. One common method is the elimination of the 50/50 requirement for experienced plans, so they no longer need at least 50% commercial enrollment in each new market, although at the time of this writing, there was some interest on the part of some members of Congress to retain it. Also common to most proposals is a decrease in administrative oversight of materials and processes already approved for other markets, and a time limit on how long HCFA can take to disapprove or approve submissions.

Finally, there is a large grab bag of proposals designed to ensure members' rights are preserved, quality of care is delivered, proper data is captured and reported, appeal and grievances are processed appropriately, and plans are operated in compliance with all established rules and regulations. As those supporting free market controls debate these details with those who only trust that which is tightly regulated and audited, it's too early to predict the level of new regulation that will ultimately control Medicare Plus operations. At a minimum, there will be requirements that protect patients' rights and general plan compliance with federal policy.

Many proponents of managed care see this last areas as the most subtly dangerous of the five areas of reform. While they feel they can debate and win on many elements of budgeting, product expansion, and beneficiary education, it is in the operating rules that they fear opponents of managed care could seed trouble. Under the popular banner of "patient protection" and "fairness to providers," legislation could pass that might threaten the very core of how HMOs work. In the future, under the banner of "administrative and quality oversight," managed care could be burdened with extensive and expensive processes and reporting requirements not expected from their less managed competitors. Fortunately, many in the Administration and Congress have educated themselves on these issues and are anxious not to overly restrict the marketplace. The level of anti-managed care sentiment in the media today, however, could increase the calls for regulatory control. As with all other elements of reform being debated, only time will tell.

SAFE HARBORS

The area of "safe harbors" from fraud and abuse regulations has been a murky one regarding managed care. On January 26, 1996, the Health and Human Services Inspector General issued a final rule clarifying and revising an interim rule it had published on November 5, 1992. The rule affects interactions between providers, health plans, and beneficiaries. The first safe harbor allows health plans to offer enrollees certain incentives such as waivers of deductible and coinsurance amounts. Two standards must be met for incentives offered to enrollees: the same incentive must be offered to all enrollees for all covered services, and a health plan may not claim the cost of the incentive as bad debt or shift the cost to Medicare or state health care programs.

The second safe harbor protects price reduction agreements between participating providers and health plans. These agreements must meet certain criteria in regard to length of contract (at least one year), the scope of covered services, reports to HCFA which state the amount a provider has been paid, and an understanding that the provider could not claim payment of the discounted amount from HCFA or state health care programs without specific authorization.

In addition to these new safe harbors, the existing safe harbor addressing waiver of beneficiary coinsurance and deductible amounts was amended to protect certain agreements entered into between hospitals and Medicare SELECT hospitals. The final rule reflects industry comments by expanding the definition of a health plan and narrowing the prohibition against cost shifting which had appeared in an interim rule. The definition of a health plan now includes physician hospital organizations, ERISA plans, and organizations that act as intermediaries (such as PPOs) between participating health care providers and employers, union welfare funds, or insurance companies. An entity also must furnish or arrange for the provision of items or services in exchange for either a premium or fee to be considered a health plan. Cost shifting is now prohibited against the Medicare and state health care programs only, instead of all payers as had been the case in the interim rule.

FEDERAL INSURANCE REFORM

In the Spring of 1996, the Senate passed the Kassebaum-Kennedy health insurance reform bill (S.1028). Differences between the legislation the House passed in March and the Senate bill will be reconciled in conference. The obstacles to final passage (or signature by the President) are the inclusion of MSAs (opposed by the Democrats and the President) and the Mental Health Parity clause (requiring equal levels of coverage for behavioral health services compared to medical-surgical services; this is opposed by many conservatives and businesses). Other contentious provisions include caps on malpractice awards and some relaxation of restrictions on multiple employer welfare associations (MEWAs) that allow smaller employers to band together to become technically self-funded under ERISA. If these contentious provisions are eliminated, there is a high liklihood that the bill will become law.

The significance of this bill is multifaceted. Congressional efforts to reform health care could either decrease the amount of uncompensated care delivered by providers or increase the price of insurance—with a corresponding surge in the ranks of the uninsured. Why such different outcome scenarios for a bill described as an incremental attempt to improve access the health insurance for individuals who lose their jobs or are moving between jobs? The bill's impact is highly dependent on characteristics of local health care markets. Also, some states wouldn't be affected by the bill because they already have portability laws that exceed the requirements in Kassebaum-Kennedy. As many as 32 states may receive exemptions from the bill's rules since the bill has safe harbor provisions that apply to states with guaranteed issue regulations or medical high-risk pools.

The impact of health insurance laws on providers is inextricably tied to their effect on premiums. Although Kassebaum-Kennedy would likely increase premiums if every other aspect of the health care market were held constant, the bill's effect may be masked by the overall trend of stable or slightly decreasing costs in the health care industry. Kassebaum-Kennedy also contains a long-term care provision that may assist providers who generate significant amounts of revenue from long-term care services. The provision provides tax deductibility for long-term care expenses including insurance premiums.

The following are market conditions that may increase the impact of the Kassebaum-Kennedy bill:

- large number of small employers
- highly mobile population
- low degree of portability of coverage allowed in existing state insurance laws
- local market cost of health insurance higher than the national average
- high percentage of self-pay patients
- high percentage of revenues from mental health services
- high percentage of revenues from long-term care services

ERISA

The year 1993 may have represented the high water mark for defendants in cases involving the Employee Retirement Income Security Act of 1974, as amended (ERISA). ERISA preempted most state law claims; causes of action not specifically recognized under ERISA were held not to be available to plaintiffs. Remedies available to a successful plaintiff were for the most part limited to recovery of benefits due under the terms of the plan and traditional forms of equitable relief. Over the past three years, the unmistakable trend has been to provide plaintiffs and state governments with additional powers or remedies. Although ERISA preemption is and will continue to be far-reaching, there are an increasing number of cases that hold that particular state laws, actions, or remedies are exempt from ERISA's preemptive reach. Moreover, the lower federal courts have been increasingly receptive to claims of breaches of fiduciary duty, without necessarily defining the fiduciary duty that has been breached, and to characterizing awards of money damages as being equitable in nature. This trend is likely to continue unless and until the United States Supreme Court—which generally has interpreted the ERISA preemption

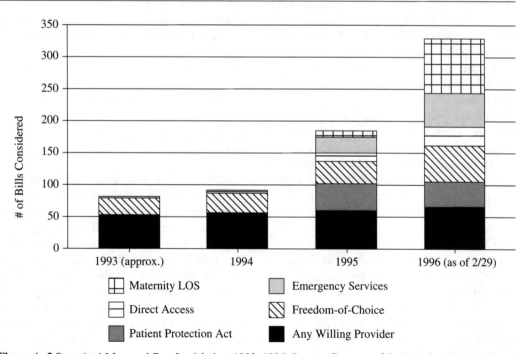

Figure A–2 State Anti-Managed Care Legislation, 1993–1996. *Source:* Courtesy of the American Association of Health Plans, Washington, D.C.

provision broadly and its remedies narrowly—
intervenes.

STATE REGULATORY ISSUES

In the state arena, it is likely that several issues will continue to have a high level of activity
in the next several years.

Regarding general licensing and regulatory
issues, states will lobby Congress for more regulatory responsibility including Medicare and
Medicaid programs. They will also continue actively licensing provider-sponsored managed
care organizations (e.g., PSOs or PSNs) through
existing enabling laws that currently apply to
managed care organizations such as HMOs or
preferred provider organizations.

State regulators will also be more active in
authorizing and regulating HMO-sponsored
POS products where the out-of-plan coverage is
underwritten by the HMO (HMO enrollees in
POS products should jump from 2.6 million in
1993 to an estimated 15 million in 1997). States
will further regulate stop-loss coverage for
health services; and update and expand their
managed care laws through the adoption of risk-
based capital standards for health plans, additional grievance procedures, and perhaps experimental treatment protocols—among other
initiatives.

Anti-managed care legislation will continue
to be introduced in record numbers. Figure A–2
demonstrates the rise in a representative sample
of anti-managed care bills introduced during the
past four years—from approximately 100 proposals in 1993 to a projected 500 proposals in
1996. However, only a small percentage of
proposed anti-managed care bills will be enacted
in the states. For example in 1995, 63 any willing provider bills were introduced in 28 states,
but only three bills in Texas and Arkansas were
enacted. Moreover, 41 provider protection
initiatives (so-called patient protection acts)
were introduced in over 20 states, but only two
limited bills in Maryland and Oregon were
adopted. This trend should continue in 1996 and
1997.

Anti-managed care and other burdensome
proposals that should receive a fair amount of
state attention during the next several years include mandated benefits, direct access and freedom of choice requirements, any willing provider proposals, disclosure provisions,
emergency room coverage mandates for nonemergency services, unitary drug pricing, and
limits on physician compensation arrangements
(e.g., capitation, withholds). Although maternity
length-of-stay requirements will be enacted by
at least a dozen states in 1996, legislative activity in this area in 1997 may begin to dwindle.

Heading out a few years, the most popular private market reforms will be directed at the individual insurance coverage and the refinement of
previously enacted market reforms, especially
for small group coverage. Any federal action,
however, could change this scenario. Reform
proposals that were popular in the states in 1990
to 1994—such as community rating/guaranteed
issue requirements for small businesses, purchasing alliances, employer mandates, play or
pay proposals, single payer systems, and universal access requirements—will continue to drop
in frequency. Medical savings account proposals
will remain popular through 1996 but should begin to drop in 1997 because at least half of the
states will have adopted MSA enabling legislation (i.e., MSA deductibility from state taxes).

LEGAL ISSUES AFFECTING
INTEGRATED DELIVERY SYSTEMS

Although the Federal Budget Bill has not been
enacted at the time of this writing, it includes
several changes that may affect organizers of an
integrated delivery system (IDS).

First, it is anticipated that the Stark law will be
significantly revised to exclude compensation as
a "financial interest." If this occurs, it will be
simpler to establish compensation arrangements
within an IDS, as well as compensation relationships with subcontracting physicians. An analysis would still need to be made of any such arrangement, however, under anti-kickback laws
and tax-exempt status rules (if applicable).

The proposed legislation reportedly seeks to make it easier for the Office of Inspector General (OIG) to prosecute anti-kickback law violations. The primary legal change is for the word "willful" to be removed from the statute, thereby effectively overruling *Hanlester*.[1] It is not clear what practical effect this statutory revision will have on the development of an integrated delivery system, but the OIG may use it to challenge systems that it believes are disguised payments to lock in patient referrals to a hospital. A particular concern would be situations in which a hospital develops an IDS with a physician group using a competing hospital. If the physician group shifts all or most of its patients to the purchasing hospital after receiving a large acquisition payment from the hospital, the OIG may decide to challenge the arrangement.

The Internal Revenue Service may be given new authority to impose intermediate sanctions against individuals in a tax-exempt organization who develop or approve arrangements that result in excessive private benefit or inurement. Under this proposed legislation, the IRS could hold responsible persons personally liable for allowing an improper transaction or arrangement with "insiders" to occur. This potentially significant language has been significantly emasculated, however, by a narrow definition of who constitutes an insider. Reportedly, only transactions with persons who are actually on the organization's board of directors (or officers of the organization) would constitute insiders. Thus, this proposed legislation would only affect a narrow group of IDSs which are being developed.

THE PROVIDER WORLD

The world of providers is continuing to consolidate. On the hospital side, hospitals are actively seeking partners or merger candidates. The number of not-for-profit hospitals being acquired by for-profit hospital companies continues to rise at a very rapid rate, especially in urban or highly competitive areas. Some even think that it is possible that in the next 10 years,

there will be between 40 and 1,000 integrated delivery systems (IDSs) in the country, with each major statistical metropolitan area supporting between 3 and 7 such systems, and many of these systems will be part of larger national or regional chains.[2]

With the consolidation of institutional providers and the increase in enrollment in managed care among the Medicare population, Medicare payments to hospitals would be reduced to about 40% of expenditures by the year 2002, from about 50% today.

Physicians will likewise be compelled to organize into larger systems. These may be vertical alignments (e.g., becoming employed by hospitals) or they may be horizontal alignments (e.g., large single- or multi-specialty group practices). Physician practice management companies will also play a role in the continued aggregation of physicians into larger organizations. It is not clear how many of these new organizations will be stable. With a number of large, vertically aligned HMOs spinning off their medical groups and hospitals, it is possible that many of the vertically integrated health systems will ultimately spin off their physician practices as well, implying that many current integration activities are transitional in nature.

The era of solo physicians or small groups will slowly come to a close. Existing practices of successful physicians will most probably be able to weather the changes until retirement, but physicians new to practice, burdened with debt and needing to meet target incomes, will find that joining groups or large organizations will be their most attractive options, while new solo physicians will find it increasingly hard to access revenue.

With the ascendancy of primary care as the focal point of many managed care systems, specialty physicians will continue to feel the pressures, at least in highly competitive markets. This may lead to more specialists migrating to less competitive markets, thereby creating a medical marketplace that in turn becomes more competitive. Specialists will also continue to form new types of organizations in hopes of being able to exert economically greater control and benefit. It is possible that specialty physicians will divide up into those who, through either large groups or by being part of organized systems, will prosper but work very hard, and those who will be economically squeezed.

One issue that is not at all clear is the degree that individual physicians will be reimbursed through capitation. In some mature markets such as Minneapolis, the degree of capitation is actually quite low, with salary and fee-for-service being strong forms of payment. Given the degree of margin inherent in capitation, it is possible that some HMOs as well as large employers, will be unwilling to cede that margin.

THE PAYOR WORLD

Consolidation in MCOs will also continue. Although there are more newly licensed HMOs in 1995 than in previous years, the market concentration of the largest MCO companies remains formidable. Many of these new starts are reactive on the part of IDSs wanting to gain more control, while others are entrepreneurial in nature and have as their goal selling out to a larger firm. This market concentration will continue, especially in urban areas. It is also likely that large MCOs will be compelled to vigorously enter the public sector market in order to sustain growth.

The number of MCOs willing to contract with IDSs on a percent of premium basis will increase, barring a regulatory challenge to the practice (i.e., global capitation on a percent of premium basis may be considered too much risk transfer by some insurance departments). The number of joint ventures between payors and providers will also increase, but many will flounder. Those MCOs that rely primarily on driving ever lower unit prices from providers (e.g., ever lower fees or per diems) may provoke a backlash by IDSs to try to access the market through other channels (e.g., by obtaining their own license), an action that would become necessary if the MCO does not even pay the direct cost of care provided.

MEDICAL MANAGEMENT

Medical management continues to advance as well. Utilization levels found in certain parts of California are now being found in other parts of the nation as well. New techniques in medical management, described in this book and elsewhere, are slowly becoming more mainstream, replacing older models of utilization and quality management. Many mature MCOs desire to get out of the business of micromanaging medical care, and would prefer to delegate those activities to providers. As providers organize into systems of care and adopt advanced medical management techniques, this becomes ever more possible.

CONCLUSION

The pace of change in health care today can only accelerate in the near term. Whatever a MCO or IDS looks like today, it will not look that way in the years to come. Those legislative events occuring today will be modified in years to come. We will enter the millennium in a state of continual change. Some of that change will be painful and not necessarily positive; for example, if monetary resources become desperately low, then no amount of management will be able to create value from nothing. But most change will ultimately be beneficial, providing more efficient, higher quality medical care for less cost. As American medicine moves from a cottage industry to an organized system, we stand able to leverage new resources to continue forward progress.

REFERENCE AND NOTE

1. *Hanlester Network v. Shalala*, 95 Daily Journal D.A.R. 4286, 4290 (April 6, 1995). It should be noted that the *Hanlester* case is only binding in the Ninth Circuit. The government has decided not to appeal *Hanlester*, but will fight the issues anew in other circuits.

2. K.C. Nolan, 1995. Unpublished data, Ernst & Young, LLP, Washington, D.C.

Glossary of Terms and Acronyms

"Words are not as satisfactory as we should like them to be,
but, like our neighbours, we have got to live with
them and must make the best and
not the worst of them."

Samuel Butler
(1835–1902)
Samuel Butler's Notebooks (1951)

AAHP—American Association of Health Plans. The trade organization that represents all forms of MCOs. Created in 1996 by the merger of GHAA and AMCRA. Based in Washington, D.C., the AAHP has a heavy focus on lobbying, educational activities, and service to member plans.

AAPCC—Adjusted average per capita cost. The HCFA's best estimate of the amount of money it costs to care for Medicare recipients under fee-for-service Medicare in a given area. The AAPCC is made up of 142 different rate cells; 140 of them are factored for age, sex, Medicaid eligibility, institutional status, working aged, and whether a person has both part A and part B Medicare. The 2 remaining cells are for individuals with end-stage renal disease.

AAPPO—American Association of Preferred Provider Organizations. A trade organization for PPOs.

Accrete—The term used by the HCFA for the process of adding new Medicare enrollees to a plan. See also *delete*.

Accrual—The amount of money that is set aside to cover expenses. The accrual is the plan's best estimate of what those expenses are and (for medical expenses) is based on a combination of data from the authorization system, the claims system, the lag studies, and the plan's history.

ACG—Ambulatory care group. ACGs are a method of categorizing outpatient episodes. There are 51 mutually exclusive ACGs, which are based on resource use over time and are modified by principal diagnosis, age, and sex. See also *ADG* and *APG*.

ACR—Adjusted community rate. Used by HMOs and CMPs with Medicare risk contracts. A calculation of what premium the plan would charge for providing exactly the Medicare-covered benefits to a group account adjusted to allow for the greater intensity and frequency of utilization by Medicare recipients. The ACR includes the normal profit of a for-profit HMO or CMP. The ACR may be equal to or lower than the APR but can never exceed it. See also *APR*.

Actuarial assumptions—The assumptions that an actuary uses in calculating the expected costs and revenues of the plan. Examples include utilization rates, age and sex mix of enrollees, and cost of medical services.

ADG—Ambulatory diagnostic group. ADGs are a method of categorizing outpatient episodes. There are 34 possible ADGs. See *ACG* and *APG*.

Adverse selection—The problem of attracting members who are sicker than the general population (specifically, members who are sicker than was anticipated when the budget for medical costs was developed).

ALOS—See *LOS*.

AMCRA—American Managed Care and Review Association. A trade association that represented managed indemnity plans, PPOs, MCOs, and HMOs. Merged with GHAA in 1995 to become the AAHP in 1996. See also *AAHP*.

APG—Ambulatory patient group. A reimbursement methodology developed by 3M Health Information Systems for the HCFA. APGs are to outpatient procedures what DRGs are to inpatient days. APGs provide for a fixed reimbursement to an institution for outpatient procedures or visits and incorporate data regarding the reason for the visit and patient data. APGs prevent unbundling of ancillary services. See also *ACG* and *ADG*.

APR—Average payment rate. The amount of money that the HCFA could conceivably pay an HMO or CMP for services to Medicare recipients under a risk contract. The figure is derived from the AAPCC for the service area adjusted for the enrollment characteristics that the plan would expect to have. The payment to the plan, the ACR, can never be higher than the APR, but it may be less.

ASO—Administrative services only (sometimes referred to as an administrative services contract [ASC]). A contract between an insurance company and a self-funded plan where the insurance company performs administrative services only and does not assume any risk. Services usually include claims processing but may include other services, such as actuarial analysis, utilization review, and so forth. See also *ERISA*.

Assignment of benefits—The payment of medical benefits directly to a provider of care rather than to a member. Generally requires either a contract between the health plan and the provider or a written release from the subscriber to the provider allowing the provider to bill the health plan.

AWP (any willing provider)—This is a form of state law that requires an MCO to accept any provider willing to meet the terms and conditions in the MCO's contract, whether the MCO wants or needs that provider or not. Considered to be an expensive form of anti-managed care legislation.

AWP (average wholesale price)—Commonly used in pharmacy contracting, the AWP is generally determined through reference to a common source of information.

Balance billing—The practice of a provider billing a patient for all charges not paid for by the insurance plan, even if those charges are above the plan's UCR or are considered medically unnecessary. Managed care plans and service plans generally prohibit providers from balance billing except for allowed copays, coinsurance, and deductibles. Such prohibition against balance billing may even extend to the plan's failure to pay at all (e.g., because of bankruptcy).

Capitation—A set amount of money received or paid out; it is based on membership rather than on services delivered and usually is expressed in units of PMPM. May be varied by such factors as age and sex of the enrolled member.

Carve-out—Refers to a set of medical services that are carved out of the basic arrangement. In terms of plan benefits, may refer to a set of benefits that are carved out and contracted for separately; for example, mental health/substance abuse services may be separated from basic medical–surgical services. May also refer to carving out a set of services from a basic capitation rate with a provider (e.g., capitating for cardiac care but carving out cardiac surgery and paying case rates for that).

Case management—A method of managing the provision of health care to members with high-cost medical conditions. The goal is to coordinate the care to improve both continuity and quality of care and to lower costs. This generally is a dedicated function in the utilization management department. The official definition, according to the Certification of Insurance Rehabilitation Specialists Commission, is as follows: "Case management is a collaborative process which assesses, plans, implements, coordinates, monitors, and evaluates the options and services required to meet an individual's health needs, using communication and available resources to promote quality, cost-effective outcomes" and "occurs across a continuum of care, addressing ongoing individual needs" rather than being restricted to a single practice setting. When focused solely on high-cost inpatient cases, may be referred to as large case management or catastrophic case management.

Case mix—Refers to the mix of illness and severity of cases for a provider.

Certificate of coverage—Refers to the document that a plan must provide to a member to show evidence that the member has coverage and to give basic information about that coverage. Required under state regulations.

CHAMPUS—Civilian Health and Medical Program of the Uniformed Services. The federal program providing health care coverage to families of military personnel, military retirees, certain spouses and dependents of such personnel, and certain others.

Churning—The practice of a provider seeing a patient more often than is medically necessary, primarily to increase revenue through an increased number of services. Churning may also apply to any performance-based reimbursement system where there is a heavy emphasis on productivity (in other words, rewarding a provider for seeing a high volume of patients, whether through fee for service or through an appraisal system that pays a bonus for productivity).

CLM—Career-limiting move. A boneheaded mistake by a manager. What this book is designed to try to prevent.

Closed panel—A managed care plan that contracts with physicians on an exclusive basis for services and does not allow those physicians to see patients for another managed care organization. Examples include staff and group model HMOs. Could apply to a large private medical group that contracts with an HMO.

CMP—Competitive medical plan. A federal designation that allows a health plan to obtain eligibility to receive a Medicare risk contract without having to obtain qualification as an HMO. Requirements for eligibility are somewhat less restrictive than for an HMO.

COA—Certificate of authority. The state-issued operating license for an HMO.

COB—Coordination of benefits. An agreement that uses language developed by the National Association of Insurance Commissioners and prevents double payment for services when a subscriber has coverage from two or more sources. For example, a husband may have Blue Cross/Blue Shield through work, and the wife may have elected an HMO through her place of employment. The agreement gives the order for what organization has primary responsibility for payment and what organization has secondary responsibility for payment.

COBRA—Consolidated Omnibus Budget Reconciliation Act. A portion of this act requires employers to offer the opportunity for terminated employees to purchase continuation of health care coverage under the group's medical plan. Another portion eases a Medicare recipient's ability to disenroll from an HMO or CMP with a Medicare risk contract. See also *conversion*.

Coinsurance—A provision in a member's coverage that limits the amount of coverage by the plan to a certain percentage, commonly 80 percent. Any additional costs are paid by the member out of pocket.

Cold claim—A claim for medical services received by the plan for which no authorization has been received; i.e., it arrives "cold."

Commission—The money paid to a sales representative, broker, or other type of sales agent for selling the health plan. May be a flat amount of money or a percentage of the premium.

Community rating—The rating methodology required of federally qualified HMOs, HMOs under the laws of many states, and occasionally indemnity plans under certain circumstances. The HMO must obtain the same amount of money per member for all members in the plan. Community rating does allow for variability by allowing the HMO to factor in differences for age, sex, mix (average contract size), and industry factors; not all factors are necessarily allowed under state laws, however. Such techniques are referred to as community rating by class and adjusted community rating. See also *experience rating*.

CON—Certificate of need. The requirement that a health care organization obtain permission from an oversight agency before making changes. Generally applies only to facilities or facility-based services.

Concurrent review—Refers to utilization management that takes place during the provision of services. Almost exclusively applied to inpatient hospital stays.

Contract year—The 12-month period for which a contract for services is in force. Not necessarily tied to a calendar year.

Contributory plan—A group health plan in which the employees must contribute a certain amount toward the premium cost, with the employer paying the rest.

Conversion—The conversion of a member covered under a group master contract to coverage under an individual contract. This is offered to subscribers who lose their group coverage (e.g., through job loss, death of a working spouse, and so forth) and who are ineligible for coverage under another group contract. See also *COBRA*.

Copayment—That portion of a claim or medical expense that a member must pay out of pocket. Usually a fixed amount, such as $5 in many HMOs.

Corporate practice of medicine acts or statutes—State laws that prohibit a physician from working for a corporation; in other words, a physician can only work for himself or herself or another physician. Put another way, a corporation cannot practice medicine. Often created through the effort on the part of certain members of the medical community to prevent physicians from working directly for managed care plans or hospitals.

Cost sharing—Any form of coverage in which the member pays some portion of the cost of providing services. Usual forms of cost sharing include deductibles, coinsurance, and copayments.

Cost shifting—When a provider cannot cover the cost of providing services under the reimbursement received, the provider raises the prices to other payers to cover that portion of the cost.

CPT-4—*Current Procedural Terminology*, 4th edition. A set of five-digit codes that apply to medical services delivered. Frequently used for billing by professionals. See also *HCPCS*.

Credentialing—The most common use of the term refers to obtaining and reviewing the documentation of professional providers. Such documentation includes licensure, certifications, insurance, evidence of malpractice insurance, malpractice history, and so forth. Generally includes both reviewing information provided by the provider and verification that the information is correct and complete. A much less frequent use of the term applies to closed panels and medical groups and refers to obtaining hospital privileges and other privileges to practice medicine.

Custodial care—Care provided to an individual that is primarily the basic activities of living. May be medical or nonmedical, but the care is not meant to be curative or as a form of medical treatment, and it is often life long. Rarely covered by any form of group health insurance or HMO.

CVO—Credentialing verification organization. This is an independent organization that performs primary verification of a professional provider's credentials. The managed care organization may then rely on that verification rather than requiring the provider to provide credentials independently. This lowers the cost and

"hassle" for credentialing. The NCQA has issued certification standards for CVOs. See also *NCQA*.

CWW—Clinic without walls. See *GPWW*.

Date of service—Refers to the date that medical services were rendered. Usually different from the date a claim is submitted.

DAW—Dispense as written. The instruction from a physician to a pharmacist to dispense a brand-name pharmaceutical rather than a generic substitution.

Days per thousand—A standard unit of measurement of utilization. Refers to an annualized use of the hospital or other institutional care. It is the number of hospital days that are used in a year for each thousand covered lives.

DCI—Duplicate coverage inquiry. A document used in COB when one plan contacts another to inquire about dual coverage of medical benefits.

Death spiral—An insurance term that refers to a vicious spiral of high premium rates and adverse selection, generally in a free-choice environment (typically, an insurance company or health plan in an account with multiple other plans, or a plan offering coverage to potential members who have alternative choices, such as through an association). One plan, often the indemnity plan competing with managed care plans, ends up having continually higher premium rates such that the only members who stay with the plan are those whose medical costs are so high (and who cannot change because of provider loyalty or benefits restrictions, such as preexisting conditions) that they far exceed any possible premium revenue. Called the death spiral because the losses from underwriting mount faster than the premiums can ever recover, and the account eventually terminates coverage, leaving the carrier in a permanent loss position.

Deductible—That portion of a subscriber's (or member's) health care expenses that must be paid out of pocket before any insurance coverage applies, commonly $100 to $300. Common in insurance plans and PPOs, uncommon in

HMOs. May apply only to the out-of-network portion of a point-of-service plan. May also apply only to one portion of the plan coverage (e.g., there may be a deductible for pharmacy services but not for anything else).

Delete—The term used by the HCFA for the process of removing Medicare enrollees from a plan. See also *accrete*.

Dependent—A member who is covered by virtue of a family relationship with the member who has the health plan coverage. For example, one person has health insurance or an HMO through work, and that individual's spouse and children, the dependents, also have coverage under that contract.

DHMO—Dental health maintenance organization. An HMO organized strictly to provide dental benefits.

Direct contracting—A term describing a provider or integrated health care delivery system contracting directly with employers rather than through an insurance company or managed care organization. A superficially attractive option that occasionally works when the employer is large enough. Not to be confused with direct contract model.

Direct contract model—A managed care health plan that contracts directly with private practice physicians in the community rather than through an intermediary, such as an IPA or a medical group. A common type of model in open panel HMOs.

Discharge planning—That part of utilization management that is concerned with arranging for care or medical needs to facilitate discharge from the hospital.

Disease management—The process of intensively managing a particular disease. This differs from large case management in that it goes well beyond a given case in the hospital or an acute exacerbation of a condition. Disease management encompasses all settings of care and places a heavy emphasis on prevention and maintenance. Similar to case management, but more focused on a defined set of diseases.

Disenrollment—The process of termination of coverage. Voluntary termination would in-clude a member quitting because he or she simply wants out. Involuntary termination would include a member leaving the plan because of changing jobs. A rare and serious form of involuntary disenrollment is when the plan terminates a member's coverage against the member's will. This is usually only allowed (under state and federal laws) for gross offenses such as fraud, abuse, nonpayment of premium or copayments, or a demonstrated inability to comply with recommended treatment plans.

DME—Durable medical equipment. Medical equipment that is not disposable (i.e., is used repeatedly) and is only related to care for a medical condition. Examples include wheelchairs, home hospital beds, and so forth. An area of increasing expense, particularly in conjunction with case management.

Dread disease policy—A peculiar type of health insurance that only covers a specific and frightening type of illness, such as cancer. Uncommon.

DRG—Diagnosis-related group. A statistical system of classifying any inpatient stay into groups for the purposes of payment. DRGs may be primary or secondary; an outlier classification also exists. This is the form of reimbursement that the HCFA uses to pay hospitals for Medicare recipients. Also used by a few states for all payers and by many private health plans (usually non-HMO) for contracting purposes.

DSM-IV—*Diagnostic and Statistical Manual of Mental Disorders*, 4th edition. The manual used to provide a diagnostic coding system for mental and substance abuse disorders. Far different from ICD-9-CM. See also ICD-9-CM.

Dual choice—Sometimes referred to as Section 1310 or mandating. That portion of the federal HMO regulations that required any employer with 25 or more employees that resided in an HMO's service area, paid minimum wage, and offers health coverage to offered a federally qualified HMO as well. The HMO had to request it. This provision was "sunsetted" in 1995. Another definition, unrelated to the previous one, pertains to point of service. See also *POS*.

Dual option—The offering of both an HMO and a traditional insurance plan by one carrier.

Duplicate claims—When the same claim is submitted more than once, usually because payment has not been received quickly. Can lead to duplicate payments and incorrect data in the claims file.

DUR—Drug utilization review.

EAP—Employee assistance program. A program that a company puts into effect for its employees to provide them with help in dealing with personal problems, such as alcohol or drug abuse, mental health or stress issues, and so forth.

Effective date—The day that health plan coverage goes into effect or is modified.

Eligibility—When an individual is eligible for coverage under a plan. Also used to determine when an individual is no longer eligible for coverage (e.g., a dependent child reaches a certain age and is no longer eligible for coverage under his or her parent's health plan).

ELOS—See *LOS*.

Encounter—An outpatient or ambulatory visit by a member to a provider. Applies primarily to physician office visits but may encompass other types of encounters as well. In fee-for-service plans, an encounter also generates a claim. In capitated plans, the encounter is still the visit, but no claim is generated. See also *statistical claim*.

Enrollee—An individual enrolled in a managed health care plan. Usually applies to the subscriber or person who has the coverage in the first place rather than to their dependents, but the term is not always used that precisely.

EOB—Explanation of benefits (statement). A statement mailed to a member or covered insured explaining how and why a claim was or was not paid; the Medicare version is called an explanation of Medicare benefits, or EOMB. See also *ERISA*.

EPO—Exclusive provider organization. An EPO is similar to an HMO in that it often uses primary physicians as gatekeepers, often capitates providers, has a limited provider panel, and uses an authorization system. It is referred to as exclusive because the member must remain within the network to receive benefits. The main difference is that EPOs are generally regulated under insurance statutes rather than HMO regulations. Not allowed in many states that maintain that EPOs are really HMOs.

Equity model—A term applied to a form of for-profit vertically integrated health care delivery system in which the physicians are owners.

ERISA—Employee Retirement Income Security Act. One provision of this act allows self-funded plans to avoid paying premium taxes, complying with state-mandated benefits, or otherwise complying with state laws and regulations regarding insurance, even when insurance companies and managed care plans that stand risk for medical costs must do so. Another provision requires that plans and insurance companies provide an explanation of benefits statement to a member or covered insured in the event of a denial of a claim, explaining why the claim was denied and informing the individual of his or her rights of appeal. Numerous other provisions in ERISA are important for a managed care organization to know.

Evidence of insurability—The form that documents whether an individual is eligible for health plan coverage when the individual does not enroll through an open enrollment period. For example, if an employee wants to change health plans in the middle of a contract year, the new health plan may require evidence of insurability (often both a questionnaire and a medical examination) to ensure that it will not be accepting adverse risk.

Experience rating—The method of setting premium rates based on the actual health care costs of a group or groups.

Extracontractual benefits—Health care benefits beyond what the member's actual policy covers. These benefits are provided by a plan to reduce utilization. For example, a plan may not provide coverage for a hospital bed at home, but it is more cost effective for the plan to provide such a bed than to keep admitting a member to the hospital.

FAR—Federal acquisition regulations. The regulations applied to the federal government's acquisition of services, including health care services. See also *FEHBARS*.

Favored nations discount—A contractual agreement between a provider and a payer stating that the provider will automatically provide the payer the best discount it provides anyone else.

Federal qualification—Applies to HMOs and CMPs. It means that the HMO/CMP meets federal standards regarding benefits, financial solvency, rating methods, marketing, member services, health care delivery systems, and other standards. An HMO/CMP must apply for federal qualification and be examined by the OMC, including an on-site review. Federal qualification does place some restrictions on how a plan operates but also allows it to enter the Medicare and FEHBP markets in an expedited way. Federal qualification is voluntary and not required to enter the market.

Fee schedule—May also be referred to as fee maximums or a fee allowance schedule. A listing of the maximum fee that a health plan will pay for a certain service based on CPT billing codes.

FEHBARS—Federal Employee Health Benefit Acquisition Regulations. The regulations applied to OPM's purchase of health care benefits programs for federal employees.

FEHBP—Federal Employee Health Benefits Program. The program that provides health benefits to federal employees. See also *OPM*.

FFS—Fee for service. A patient sees a provider, and the provider bills the health plan or patient and gets paid based on that bill.

Flexible benefit plan—When an employer allows employees to choose a variety of options in benefits up to a certain total amount. The employee then can tailor his or her benefits package among health coverage, life insurance, child care, and so forth to optimize benefits for his or her particular needs.

Formulary—A listing of drugs that a physician may prescribe. The physician is requested or required to use only formulary drugs unless there is a valid medical reason to use a nonformulary drug.

Foundation—A not-for-profit form of integrated health care delivery system. The foundation model is usually formed in response to tax laws that affect not-for-profit hospitals or in response to state laws prohibiting the corporate practice of medicine. The foundation purchases both the tangible and intangible assets of a physician's practice, and the physicians then form a medical group that contracts with the foundation on an exclusive basis for services to patients seen through the foundation. See also *corporate practice of medicine acts or statutes*.

Foundation model—Refers to an integrated health care delivery system in which a not-for-profit foundation is responsible for providing the income to a medical group that is exclusive with the foundation. The foundation is usually, but not necessarily, associated with a not-for-profit hospital and is often found in states with corporate practice of medicine acts.

FPP—Faculty practice plan. A form of group practice organized around a teaching program. It may be a single group encompassing all the physicians providing services to patients at the teaching hospital and clinics, or it may be multiple groups drawn along specialty lines (e.g., psychiatry, cardiology, or surgery).

FTE—Full-time equivalent. The equivalent of one full-time employee. For example, two part-time employees are 0.5 FTE each, for a total of 1 FTE.

Full capitation—A loose term used to refer to a physician group or organization receiving capitation for all professional expenses, not just for the services it provides itself; does not include capitation for institutional services. The group is then responsible for subcapitating or otherwise reimbursing other physicians for services to its members. See *global capitation*.

Gatekeeper—An informal, although widely used, term that refers to a primary care case management model health plan. In this model, all care from providers other than the primary care physician, except for true emergencies, must be authorized by the primary care physician before rendered. This is a predominant feature of almost all HMOs.

Generic drug—A drug that is equivalent to a brand-name drug but usually less expensive. Most managed care organizations that provide drug benefits cover generic drugs but may require a member to pay the difference in cost between a generic drug and a brand-name drug or pay a higher copay, unless there is no generic equivalent.

GHAA—Group Health Association of America, now AAHP. A trade association that represented managed care with a focus on HMOs, both open and closed panel. Merged with AMCRA in 1995. See also *AAHP*.

Global capitation—A capitation payment that covers all medical expenses, including professional and institutional expenses. May not necessarily cover optional benefits (e.g., pharmacy). Sometimes called total capitation.

GPWW—Group practice without walls. A group practice in which the members of the group come together legally but continue to practice in private offices scattered throughout the service area. Sometimes called a clinic without walls (CWW).

Group—The members who are covered by virtue of receiving health plan coverage at a single company.

Group model HMO—An HMO that contracts with a medical group for the provision of health care services. The relationship between the HMO and the medical group is generally close, although there are wide variations in the relative independence of the group from the HMO. A form of closed panel health plan.

Group practice—The American Medical Association defines group practice as three or more physicians who deliver patient care, make joint use of equipment and personnel, and divide income by a prearranged formula.

HCFA—Health Care Financing Administration. The federal agency that oversees all aspects of health financing for Medicare and also oversees the Office of Managed Care.

HCFA-1500—A claims form used by professionals to bill for services. Required by Medi-

care and generally used by private insurance companies and managed care plans.

HCPCS—HCFA Common Procedural Coding System. A set of codes used by Medicare that describes services and procedures. HCPCS includes CPT codes but also has codes for services not included in CPT, such as DME and ambulance. Although HCPCS is nationally defined, there is provision for local use of certain codes.

HCPP—Health care prepayment plan. A form of cost contract between the HCFA and a medical group to provide professional services but does not cover Medicare Part A institutional services.

HEDIS—Healthplan Employer Data Information Set. Developed by the NCQA with considerable input from the employer community and the managed care community, HEDIS is an ever-evolving set of data reporting standards. HEDIS is designed to provide some standardization in performance reporting for financial, utilization, membership, and clinical data so that employers and others can compare performance among plans.

HMO—Health maintenance organization. The definition of an HMO has changed substantially. Originally, an HMO was defined as a prepaid organization that provided health care to voluntarily enrolled members in return for a preset amount of money on a PMPM basis. With the increase in self-insured businesses, or with financial arrangements that do not rely on prepayment, that definition is no longer accurate. Now the definition needs to encompass two possibilities: a licensed health plan (licensed as an HMO, that is) that places at least some of the providers at risk for medical expenses, and a health plan that utilizes designated (usually primary care) physicians as gatekeepers (although there are some HMOs that do not). Many in the field have given up and now use the looser term *MCO* because it avoids having to make difficult definitions such as this one.

IBNR—Incurred but not reported. The amount of money that the plan had better accrue for medical expenses that it knows nothing about yet. These are medical expenses that the authorization system has not captured and for which claims have not yet hit the door. Unexpected IBNRs have torpedoed more managed care plans than any other cause.

ICD-9-CM—*International Classification of Diseases*, 9th revision, clinical modification. The classification of disease by diagnosis codified into six-digit numbers. The ICD-10 will use alphanumeric codes and is scheduled for publication soon.

IDFN—See *IDS*.

IDFS—See *IDS*.

IDN—See *IDS*.

IDS—Integrated delivery system; also referred to as an integrated health care delivery system. Other acronyms that mean the same thing include IDN (integrated delivery network), IDFS (integrated delivery and financing system), and IDFN (integrated delivery and financing network). An IDS is a system of health care providers organized to span a broad range of health care services. Although there is no clear definition of an IDS, in its full flower an IDS should be able to access the market on a broad basis, optimize cost and clinical outcomes, accept and manage a full range of financial arrangements to provide a set of defined benefits to a defined population, align financial incentives of the participants (including physicians), and operate under a cohesive management structure. See also *IHO, IPA, PHO, MSO, equity model, staff model, foundation model*.

IHO—Integrated health care organization. An IDS that is predominantly owned by physicians. Not a common term at the time this edition was written.

IPA—Independent practice association. An organization that has a contract with a managed care plan to deliver services in return for a single capitation rate. The IPA in turn contracts with individual providers to provide the services either on a capitation basis or on a fee-for-service basis. The typical IPA encompasses all specialties, but an IPA can be solely for primary care, or it may be a single specialty. An IPA may also be the "PO" part of a PHO.

Joint Commission (formerly JCAHO)— Joint Commission for the Accreditation of Healthcare Organizations. A not-for-profit organization that performs accreditation reviews primarily on hospitals, other institutional facilities, and outpatient facilities. Most managed care plans require any hospital under contract to be accredited by the Joint Commission.

Lag study—A report that tells managers how old the claims are that are being processed and how much is paid out each month (both for that month and for any earlier months, by month) and compares these with the amount of money that was accrued for expenses each month. A powerful tool used to determine whether the plan's reserves are adequate to meet all expenses. Plans that fail to perform lag studies properly may find themselves staring into the abyss.

Line of business—A health plan (e.g., an HMO, EPO, or PPO) that is set up as a line of business within another, larger organization, usually an insurance company. This legally differentiates it from a freestanding company or a company set up as a subsidiary. It may also refer to a unique product type (e.g., Medicaid) within a health plan.

LOS/ELOS/ALOS—Length of stay/estimated length of stay/average length of stay.

Loss ratio—See *medical loss ratio*.

MAC—Maximum allowable charge (or cost). The maximum, although not the minimum, that a vendor may charge for something. This term is often used in pharmacy contracting; a related term, used in conjunction with professional fees, is *fee maximum*.

Managed health care—A regrettably nebulous term. At the very least, a system of health care delivery that tries to manage the cost of health care, the quality of that health care, and access to that care. Common denominators include a panel of contracted providers that is less than the entire universe of available providers, some type of limitations on benefits to subscribers who use noncontracted providers (unless authorized to do so), and some type of authorization system. Managed health care is actually a spectrum of systems, ranging from so-called managed indemnity through PPOs, POS plans, open panel HMOs, and closed panel HMOs. For a better definition, the reader is urged to read this book and formulate his or her own.

Mandated benefits—Benefits that a health plan is required to provide by law. This is generally used to refer to benefits above and beyond routine insurance type benefits, and it generally applies at the state level (where there is high variability from state to state). Common examples include in-vitro fertilization, defined days of inpatient mental health or substance abuse treatment, and other special condition treatments. Self-funded plans are exempt from mandated benefits under ERISA.

Master group contract—The actual contract between a health plan and a group that purchases coverage. The master group contract provides specific terms of coverage, rights, and responsibilities of both parties.

Maximum out-of-pocket cost—The largest amount of money a member will ever need to pay for covered services during a contract year. The maximum out-of-pocket cost includes deductibles and coinsurance. Once this limit is reached, the health plan pays for all services up to the maximum level of coverage. Applies mostly to non-HMO plans such as indemnity plans, PPOs, and POS plans.

MCE—Medical care evaluation. A component of a quality assurance program that looks at the process of medical care.

MCO—Managed care organization. A generic term applied to a managed care plan. Some people prefer it to the term *HMO* because it encompasses plans that do not conform exactly to the strict definition of an HMO (although that definition has itself loosened considerably). May also apply to a PPO, EPO, IDS, or OWA.

Medical loss ratio—The ratio between the cost to deliver medical care and the amount of money that was taken in by a plan. Insurance companies often have a medical loss ratio of 92 percent or more; tightly managed HMOs may have medical loss ratios of 75 percent to 85 percent, although the overhead (or administrative cost ratio) is concomitantly higher. The medical loss ratio is dependent on the amount of money brought in as well as on the cost of delivering care; thus, if the rates are too low, the ratio may be high even though the actual cost of delivering care is not really out of line.

Medical policy—Refers to the policies of a health plan regarding what will be paid for as medical benefits. Routine medical policy is linked to routine claims processing and may even be automated in the claims system; for example, the plan may only pay 50 percent of the fee of a second surgeon or may not pay for two surgical procedures done during one episode of anesthesia. This also refers to how a plan approaches payment policies for experimental or investigational care and payment for noncovered services in lieu of more expensive covered services.

Member—An individual covered under a managed care plan. May be either the subscriber or a dependent.

Member months—The total of all months for which each member was covered. For example, if a plan had 10,000 members in January and 12,000 members in February, the total member months for the year to date as of 1 March would be 22,000.

MeSH—Medical staff–hospital organization. An archaic term. See *PHO*.

MET—Multiple employer trust. See *MEWA*.

MEWA—Multiple employer welfare association. A group of employers who band together for purposes of purchasing group health insurance, often through a self-funded approach to avoid state mandates and insurance regulation. By virtue of ERISA, such entities are regulated little, if at all. Many MEWAs have enabled small employers to obtain cost-effective health coverage, but some MEWAs have not had the financial resources to withstand the risk of medical costs and have failed, leaving the members without insurance or recourse. In some states, MEWAs and METs are no longer legal.

MIS—Management information system (or service). The common term for the computer hardware and software that provides the support for managing the plan, or a department or group that administers and maintains such computer hardware and software.

Mixed model—A managed care plan that mixes two or more types of delivery systems. This has traditionally been used to describe an HMO that has both closed panel and open panel delivery systems.

MLP—Midlevel practitioner. Physician's assistants, clinical nurse practitioners, nurse midwives, and the like. Nonphysicians who deliver medical care, generally under the supervision of a physician but for less cost.

MSO—Management service organization. A form of integrated health delivery system. Sometimes similar to a service bureau, the MSO often actually purchases certain hard assets of a physician's practice and then provides services to that physician at fair market rates. MSOs are usually formed as a means to contract more effectively with managed care organizations, although their simple creation does not guarantee success. See also *service bureau.*

Multispecialty group—Just what it sounds like: a medical group made up of different specialty physicians. May or may not include primary care.

NAHMOR—National Association of HMO Regulators.

NAIC—National Association of Insurance Commissioners.

NCQA—National Committee on Quality Assurance. A not-for-profit organization that performs quality-oriented accreditation reviews of HMOs and similar types of managed care plans. The NCQA also accredits CVOs and develops HEDIS standards.

NDC—National drug code. The national classification system for identifying prescription drugs.

Network model HMO—A health plan that contracts with multiple physician groups to deliver health care to members. Generally limited to large single-specialty or multispecialty groups. Distinguished from group model plans that contract with a single medical group, IPAs

that contract through an intermediary, and direct contract model plans that contract with individual physicians in the community.

Nonpar—Short for nonparticipating. Refers to a provider that does not have a contract with the health plan.

OBRA—Omnibus Budget Reconciliation Act. What Congress calls the many annual tax and budget reconciliation acts. Most of these acts contain language important to managed care, generally in the Medicare market segment.

OMC—Office of Managed Care. The latest name for the federal agency that oversees federal qualification and compliance for HMOs and eligibility for CMPs. Old names were HMOS (Health Maintenance Organization Service), OHMO (Office of Health Maintenance Organizations), OPHC (Office of Prepaid Health Care), and OPHCOO (Office of Prepaid Health Care Operations and Oversight). Once part of the Public Health Service, the OMC and most of its predecessors are now part of the HCFA. This agency could be reorganized yet again as this book is being written, so heaven only knows what its new acronym will be.

Open enrollment period—The period when an employee may change health plans; usually occurs once per year. A general rule is that most managed care plans will have around half their membership up for open enrollment in the fall for an effective date of 1 January. A special form of open enrollment is still law in some states. This yearly open enrollment requires an HMO to accept any individual applicant (i.e., one not coming in through an employer group) for coverage, regardless of health status. Such special open enrollments usually occur for 1 month each year. Many Blue Cross/Blue Shield plans have similar open enrollments for indemnity products.

Open panel HMO—A managed care plan that contracts (either directly or indirectly) with private physicians to deliver care in their own offices. Examples include direct contract HMOs and IPAs.

OPL—Other party liability. See *COB.*

OPM—Office of Personnel Management. The federal agency that administers FEHBP. This is the agency with which a managed care plan contracts to provide coverage for federal employees.

Outlier—Something that is well outside an expected range. May refer to a provider who is using medical resources at a much higher rate than his or her peers, or to a case in a hospital that is far more expensive than anticipated, or in fact to anything at all that is significantly more or less than expected.

OWA—Other weird arrangement. A general acronym that applies to any new and bizarre managed care plan that has thought up a new twist.

Package pricing—Also referred to as bundled pricing. An MCO pays an organization a single fee for all inpatient, outpatient, and professional expenses associated with a procedure, including preadmission and postdischarge care. Common procedures that use this form of pricing include cardiac bypass surgery and transplants.

Par provider—Shorthand term for participating provider (i.e., one who has signed an agreement with a plan to provide services). May apply to professional or institutional providers.

PAS norms—The common term for Professional Activity Study results of the Commission on Professional and Hospital Activities. Broken out by region; the western region has the lowest average LOS, so that it tends to be used most often to set an estimated LOS. Available as *LOS: Length of Stay by Diagnosis*, published by CPHA Publications, Ann Arbor, Michigan.

Pay and pursue—A term in OPL that refers to a plan paying for a benefit first, then pursuing another source of payment (e.g., from another plan). Also referred to as "pay and chase." See also *Pursue and pay*.

PCCM—Primary care case manager. This acronym is used in Medicaid managed care programs and refers to the state designating PCPs as case managers to function as gatekeepers, but reimbursing those PCPs using traditional Medic-

aid fee for service as well as paying them a nominal management fee, such as $2 to $5 PMPM.

PCP—Primary care physician. Generally applies to internists, pediatricians, family physicians, and general practitioners and occasionally to obstetrician/gynecologists.

Per diem reimbursement—Reimbursement of an institution, usually a hospital, based on a set rate per day rather than on charges. Per diem reimbursement can be varied by service (e.g., medical–surgical, obstetrics, mental health, and intensive care) or can be uniform regardless of intensity of services.

PHO—Physician–hospital organization. These are legal (or perhaps informal) organizations that bond hospitals and their attending medical staff. Frequently developed for the purpose of contracting with managed care plans. A PHO may be open to any member of the staff who applies, or it may be closed to staff members who fail to qualify (or who are part of an already overrepresented specialty).

PMG—Primary medical group. A group practice made up of primary care physicians, although some may have obstetrician/gynecologists as well.

PMPM—Per member per month. Specifically applies to a revenue or cost for each enrolled member each month.

PMPY—Per member per year. The same as PMPM, but based on a year.

POD—Pool of doctors. This refers to the plan grouping physicians into units smaller than the entire panel but larger than individual practices. Typical PODs have between 10 and 30 physicians. Often used for performance measurement and compensation. The POD is often not a real legal entity but rather a grouping. Not to be confused with the pod people from *Invasion of the Body Snatchers*.

POS—Point of service. A plan where members do not have to choose how to receive services until they need them. The most common use of the term applies to a plan that enrolls each member in both an HMO (or HMO-like) system and an indemnity plan. Occasionally referred to as an HMO swingout plan, an out-of-plan benefits rider to an HMO, or a primary care PPO. These plans provide a difference in benefits (e.g., 100 percent coverage rather than 70 percent) depending on whether the member chooses to use the plan (including its providers and in compliance with the authorization system) or to go outside the plan for services. Dual choice refers to an HMO-like plan with an indemnity plan, and triple choice refers to the addition of a PPO to the dual choice. An archaic but still valid definition applies to a simple PPO where members receive coverage at a greater level if they use preferred providers (albeit without a gatekeeper system) than if they choose not to do so.

PPA—Preferred provider arrangement. Same as a PPO but sometimes used to refer to a somewhat looser type of plan in which the payer (i.e., the employer) makes the arrangement rather than the providers. Archaic term.

PPM—Physician practice management company. An organization that manages physicians' practices and in most cases either owns the practices outright or has rights to purchase them in the future. PPMs concentrate only on physicians, not on hospitals, although some PPMs have also branched into joint ventures with hospitals and insurers. Many PPMs are publicly traded.

PPO—Preferred provider organization. A plan that contracts with independent providers at a discount for services. The panel is limited in size and usually has some type of utilization review system associated with it. A PPO may be risk bearing, like an insurance company, or non-risk bearing, like a physician-sponsored PPO that markets itself to insurance companies or self-insured companies via an access fee.

PPS—Prospective payment system. A generic term applied to a reimbursement system that pays prospectively rather than on the basis of charges. Generally it is used only to refer to hospital reimbursement and is applied only to DRGs, but it may encompass other methodologies as well.

Precertification—Also known as preadmission certification, preadmission review, and precert. The process of obtaining certification or authorization from the health plan for routine hospital admissions (inpatient or outpatient). Often involves appropriateness review against criteria and assignment of length of stay. Failure to obtain precertification often results in a financial penalty to either the provider or the subscriber.

Preexisting condition—A medical condition for which a member has received treatment during a specified period of time before becoming covered under a health plan. May have an effect on whether treatments for that condition will be covered under certain types of health plans.

Private inurement—What happens when a not-for-profit business operates in such a way as to provide more than incidental financial gain to a private individual; for example, if a not-for-profit hospital pays too much money for a physician's practice or fails to charge fair market rates for services provided to a physician. The IRS frowns heavily on this.

PRO—Peer review organization. An organization charged with reviewing quality and cost for Medicare. Established under TEFRA. Generally operates at the state level.

Prospective review—Reviewing the need for medical care before the care is rendered. See also *precertification*.

PSA—Professional services agreement. A contract between a physician or medical group and an IDS or MCO for the provision of medical services.

PSN—Provider-sponsored network; occasionally the acronym stands for provider–service network. Also referred to as a PSO (provider-sponsored organization). A network developed by providers, whether as a vertically integrated IDS with both physicians and hospitals or as a physician-only network. Formed for the purpose of direct contracting with employers and government agencies. A PSN may even end up being an HMO, but its origins are with sponsoring providers rather than nonproviders.

PSO—See *PSN*.

PTMPY—Per thousand members per year. A common way of reporting utilization. The most common example is hospital utilization, expressed as days per thousand members per year.

Pursue and pay—A term used in OPL that refers to a plan not paying for a benefit until alternate sources of payment (e.g., another plan) have been pursued. Also referred to as "chase and pay." See also *Pay and pursue.*

QA or QM—Quality assurance (older term) or quality management (newer term).

Rate—The amount of money that a group or individual must pay to the health plan for coverage. Usually a monthly fee. Rating refers to the health plan developing those rates.

RBRVS—Resource-based relative value scale. This is a relative value scale developed for the HCFA for use by Medicare. The RBRVS assigns relative values to each CPT code for services on the basis of the resources related to the procedure rather than simply on the basis of historical trends. The practical effect has been to lower reimbursement for procedural services (e.g., cardiac surgery) and to raise reimbursement for cognitive services (e.g., office visits).

Reinsurance—Insurance purchased by a health plan to protect it against extremely high-cost cases. See also *stop loss.*

Reserves—The amount of money that a health plan puts aside to cover health care costs. May apply to anticipated costs, such as IBNRs, or to money that the plan does not expect to have to use to pay for current medical claims but keeps as a cushion against future adverse health care costs.

Retrospective review—Reviewing health care costs after the care has been rendered. There are several forms of retrospective review. One form looks at individual claims for medical necessity, billing errors, or fraud. Another form looks at patterns of costs rather than individual cases.

Risk contract—Also known as a Medicare risk contract. A contract between an HMO or CMP and the HCFA to provide services to Medicare beneficiaries under which the health plan receives a fixed monthly payment for enrolled Medicare members and then must provide all services on an at-risk basis.

Risk management—Management activities aimed at lowering an organization's legal and financial exposures, especially to lawsuits.

SCP—Specialty care physician. A physician who is not a PCP.

Second opinion—An opinion obtained from another physician regarding the necessity for a treatment that has been recommended by another physician. May be required by some health plans for certain high-costs cases, such as cardiac surgery.

Self-insured or self-funded plan—A health plan where the risk for medical cost is assumed by the company rather than an insurance company or managed care plan. Under ERISA, self-funded plans are exempt from state laws and regulations, such as premium taxes and mandatory benefits. Self-funded plans often contract with insurance companies or third party administrators to administer the benefits. See also *ASO.*

Sentinel effect—The phenomenon that, when it is known that behavior is being observed, that behavior changes, often in the direction the observer is looking for. Applies to the fact that utilization management systems and profiling systems often lead to reductions in utilization before much intervention even takes place simply because the providers know that someone is watching.

Service area—The geographic area in which an HMO provides access to primary care. The service area is usually specifically designated by the regulators (state or federal), and the HMO is prohibited from marketing outside the service area. May be defined by county or by ZIP code. It is possible for an HMO to have more than one service area and for the service areas to be either contiguous (i.e., they actually border each other) or noncontiguous (i.e., there is a geographic gap between the service areas).

Service bureau—A weak form of integrated delivery system in which a hospital (or other organization) provides services to a physician's practice in return for a fair market price. May also try to negotiate with managed care plans, but generally is not considered an effective negotiating mechanism.

Service plan—A health insurance plan that has direct contracts with providers but is not necessarily a managed care plan. The archetypal service plans are Blue Cross/Blue Shield plans. The contract applies to direct billing of the plan by providers (rather than billing of the member), a provision for direct payment of the provider (rather than reimbursement of the member), a requirement that the provider accept the plan's determination of UCR and not balance bill the member in excess of that amount, and a range of other terms. May or may not address issues of utilization and quality.

Shadow pricing—The practice of setting premium rates at a level just below the competition's rates whether or not those rates can be justified. In other words, the premium rates could actually be lower, but to maximize profit the rates are raised to a level that will remain attractive but result in greater revenue. This practice is generally considered unethical and, in the case of community rating, possibly illegal.

SHMO—Social health maintenance organization. An HMO that goes beyond the medical care needs of its membership to include their social needs as well. A relatively rare form of HMO.

Shoe box effect—When an indemnity type benefits plan has a deductible, there may be beneficiaries who save up their receipts to file for reimbursement at a later time (i.e., they save them in a shoe box). Those receipts then get lost, or the beneficiary never sends them in, so that the insurance company never has to pay.

Single point of entry—A relatively new term that means that an individual uses the same system to access both group health medical benefits and benefits for work-related medical conditions.

SMG—Specialty medical group. A medical group made up predominantly of specialty physicians. May be a single-specialty group or a multispecialty group.

Specialty network manager—A term used to describe a single specialist (or perhaps a specialist organization) that accepts capitation to manage a single specialty. Specialty services are supplied by many different specialty physicians, but the network manager has the responsibility for managing access and cost and is at economic risk. A relatively uncommon model as this book is being written.

Staff model HMO—An HMO that employs providers directly, and those providers see members in the HMO's own facilities. A form of closed panel HMO. A different use of this term is sometimes applied to vertically integrated health care delivery systems that employ physicians but in which the system is not licensed as an HMO.

Statistical claim—Another term for an encounter when the data is entered by an MCO's claims department but no FFS payment is made. Occurs in a capitated environment.

Stop loss—A form of reinsurance that provides protection for medical expenses above a certain limit, generally on a year-by-year basis. This may apply to an entire health plan or to any single component. For example, the health plan may have stop-loss reinsurance for cases that exceed $100,000. After a case hits $100,000, the plan receives 80 percent of expenses in excess of $100,000 back from the reinsurance company for the rest of the year. Another example would be the plan providing a stop loss to participating physicians for referral expenses greater than $2,500. When a case exceeds that amount in a single year, the plan no longer deducts those costs from the physician's referral pool for the remainder of the year.

Subacute care facility—A health facility that is a step down from an acute care hospital. May be a nursing home or a facility that provides medical care but not surgical or emergency care.

Subrogation—The contractual right of a health plan to recover payments made to a member for health care costs after that member has received such payment for damages in a legal action.

Subscriber—The individual or member who has health plan coverage by virtue of being eligible on his or her own behalf rather than as a dependent.

Sutton's law—"Go where the money is!" Attributed to the Depression era bank robber Willy Sutton, who, when asked why he robbed banks, replied "That's where the money is." Sutton apparently denies ever having made that statement. In any event, it is a good law to use when determining what needs attention in a managed care plan.

TAT—Turnaround time. The amount of time it takes a health plan to process and pay a claim from the time it arrives.

TEFRA—Tax Equity and Fiscal Responsibility Act. One key provision of this act prohibits employers and health plans from requiring full-time employees between the ages of 65 and 69 to use Medicare rather than the group health plan. Another key provision codifies Medicare risk contracts for HMOs and CMPs.

Termination date—The day that health plan coverage is no longer in effect.

Time loss management—The application of managed care techniques to workers' compensation treatments for injuries or illnesses to reduce the amount of time lost on the job by the affected employee.

Total capitation—The term used when an organization receives capitation for all medical services, including institutional and professional. The more common term is global capitation.

TPA—Third party administrator. A firm that performs administrative functions (e.g., claims processing, membership, and the like) for a self-funded plan or a start-up managed care plan. See also *ASO*.

TPL—Third party liability. Also called OPL. See *COB*.

Triage—The origins of this term are grizzly: the process of sorting out wounded soldiers into those who need treatment immediately, those who can wait, and those who are too severely injured to try to save. In health plans, this refers to the process of sorting out requests for services by members into those who need to be seen right away, those who can wait a little while, and those whose problems can be handled with advice over the phone.

Triple option—The offering of an HMO, a PPO, and a traditional insurance plan by one carrier.

Twenty-four-hour care—An ill-defined term that essentially means that health care is provided 24 hours per day regardless of the financing mechanism. Applies primarily to the convergence of group health, workers' compensation, and industrial health all under managed care.

UB-92—The common claim form used by hospitals to bill for services. Some managed care plans demand greater detail than is available on the UB-92, requiring hospitals to send additional itemized bills.

UCR—Usual, customary, or reasonable. A method of profiling prevailing fees in an area and reimbursing providers on the basis of that profile. One common technology is to average all fees and choose the 80th or 90th percentile, although a plan may use other technologies to determine what is reasonable. Sometimes this term is used synonymously with a fee allowance schedule when that schedule is set relatively high.

Unbundling—The practice of a provider billing for multiple components of service that were previously included in a single fee. For example, if dressings and instruments were included in a fee for a minor procedure, the fee for the procedure remains the same, but there are now additional charges for the dressings and instruments.

Underwriting—In one definition, this refers to bearing the risk for something (e.g., a policy is underwritten by an insurance company). In another definition, this refers to the analysis of a group that is done to determine rates and benefits or to determine whether the group should be offered coverage at all. A related definition refers to health screening each individual applicant for insurance and refusing to provide coverage for preexisting conditions.

Upcoding—The practice of a provider billing for a procedure that pays better than the service actually performed. For example, an office visit that would normally be reimbursed at $45 is coded as one that is reimbursed at $53.

URAC—Utilization Review Accreditation Commission. A not-for-profit organization that performs reviews of external utilization review agencies (freestanding companies, utilization management departments of insurance companies, or utilization management departments of managed care plans). Its sole focus is managed indemnity plans and PPOs, not HMOs or similar types of plans. States often require certification by URAC for a utilization management organization to operate.

URO—Utilization review organization. A freestanding organization that does nothing but utilization review, usually on a remote basis using the telephone and paper correspondence. It may be independent or part of another company, such as an insurance company that sells utilization review services on a standalone basis.

Wholesale HMO—A term occasionally used when a licensed HMO does not market itself directly, but rather contracts with another licensed HMO and accepts capitation in return. This most commonly occurs when an IDS wants to accept global capitation from an HMO, and in turn capitate other providers, since many states will only allow an HMO to capitate providers. There-fore, the IDS obtains an HMO license, but does not go directly to market to the public, and thus does not disrupt existing relationships with other MCOs.

Workers' compensation—A form of social insurance provided through property–casualty insurers. Workers' compensation provides medical benefits and replacement of lost wages that result from injuries or illnesses that arise from the workplace; in turn, the employee cannot normally sue the employer unless true negligence exists. Workers' compensation has undergone dramatic increases in cost as group health has shifted into managed care, resulting in workers' compensation carriers adopting managed care approaches. Workers' compensation is often heavily regulated under state laws that are significantly different from those used for group health insurance and is often the subject of intense negotiation between management and organized labor. See also *time loss management and twenty-four-hour care*.

Wraparound plan—Commonly used to refer to insurance or health plan coverage for copays and deductibles that are not covered under a member's base plan. This is often used for Medicare.

Zero down—The practice of a medical group or provider system distributing all the capital surplus in a health plan or group to the members of the group rather than retaining any capital or reinvesting it in the group or plan.

Index

B

U

About the Editor

Peter R. Kongstvedt, M.D., F.A.C.P., is a partner in the Washington, D.C., office of Ernst & Young LLP. He is responsible for both leading and assisting consulting engagements in managed care strategy and operations as well as numerous other projects for the firm. He is a frequent lecturer and writer in managed health care and functions in a thought leadership role.

Dr. Kongstvedt has extensive experience in managed care, particularly in the health maintenance organization industry. He has served as chief executive officer of several large health maintenance organizations, as chief operating officer of a large insurer and managed care company, as a regional officer of a large insurer, and in many other operating positions in the managed health care industry.

Dr. Kongstvedt has served on a number of state and national level health care policy and strategy committees. In 1991 he was appointed by the Air Force Surgeon General as a consultant on managed care for the Air Force. Prior appointments include serving on the Governor's Pennsylvania Health Care Cost Containment Council, serving as a Medical Services Reviewer for the Department of Health and Human Services, and serving on the Nebraska State Board of Health and as a liaison to the Governor's Health Promotion Coordination Council in Nebraska. He also serves on the editorial board of many publications in the field.

Dr. Kongstvedt is a board-certified internist, currently licensed in five states. He received his undergraduate and medical degrees from the University of Wisconsin. He is a fellow of the American College of Physicians and a member of a number of professional societies. He is the editor and principal author of previous editions of *The Managed Health Care Handbook* and its academic version, *The Essentials of Managed Health Care.*